The Oxford Handbook of Social Cognition

OXFORD LIBRARY OF PSYCHOLOGY

EDITOR-IN-CHIEF:

Peter E. Nathan

AREA EDITORS:

Clinical Psychology
David H. Barlow

Cognitive Neuroscience
Kevin N. Ochsner and Stephen M. Kosslyn

Cognitive Psychology
Daniel Reisberg

Counseling Psychology
Elizabeth M. Altmaier and Jo-Ida C. Hansen

Developmental Psychology
Philip David Zelazo

Health Psychology
Howard S. Friedman

History of Psychology
David B. Baker

Methods and Measurement
Todd D. Little

Neuropsychology
Kenneth M. Adams

Organizational Psychology
Steve W. J. Kozlowski

Personality and Social Psychology
Kay Deaux and Mark Snyder

OXFORD LIBRARY OF PSYCHOLOGY

Editor in Chief PETER E. NATHAN

The Oxford Handbook of Social Cognition

Edited by

Donal E. Carlston

 OXFORD
UNIVERSITY PRESS

OXFORD
UNIVERSITY PRESS

Oxford University Press is a department of the University of Oxford.
It furthers the University's objective of excellence in research, scholarship,
and education by publishing worldwide.

Oxford   New York
Auckland   Cape Town   Dar es Salaam   Hong Kong   Karachi
Kuala Lumpur   Madrid   Melbourne   Mexico City   Nairobi
New Delhi   Shanghai   Taipei   Toronto

With offices in
Argentina   Austria   Brazil   Chile   Czech Republic   France   Greece
Guatemala   Hungary   Italy   Japan   Poland   Portugal   Singapore
South Korea   Switzerland   Thailand   Turkey   Ukraine   Vietnam

Oxford is a registered trademark of Oxford University Press in the UK and certain other
countries.

Published in the United States of America by
Oxford University Press
198 Madison Avenue, New York, NY 10016

Library of Congress Cataloging-in-Publication Data
The Oxford handbook of social cognition / edited by Donal E. Carlston.
   pages cm
ISBN-13: 978–0–19–973001–8 (alk. paper)
ISBN-10: 0–19–973001–6 (alk. paper)
1. Social perception,   2. Social psychology.   3. Cognitive psychology.   I. Carlston, Donal E.
BF323.S63O94 2013
153.7—dc23
2012045390

SHORT CONTENTS

OXFORD LIBRARY OF PSYCHOLOGY

The Oxford Library of Psychology, a landmark series of handbooks, is published by Oxford University Press, one of the world's oldest and most highly respected publishers, with a tradition of publishing significant books in psychology. The ambitious goal of the Oxford Library of Psychology is nothing less than to span a vibrant, wide-ranging field and, in so doing, to fill a clear market need.

Encompassing a comprehensive set of handbooks, organized hierarchically, the Library incorporates volumes at different levels, each designed to meet a distinct need. At one level is a set of handbooks designed broadly to survey the major subfields of psychology; at another are numerous handbooks that cover important current focal research and scholarly areas of psychology in depth and detail. Planned as a reflection of the dynamism of psychology, the Library will grow and expand as psychology itself develops, thereby highlighting significant new research that will have an impact on the field. Adding to its accessibility and ease of use, the Library will be published in print and, later on, electronically.

The Library surveys psychology's principal subfields with a set of handbooks that capture the current status and future prospects of those major subdisciplines. This initial set includes handbooks of social and personality psychology, clinical psychology, counseling psychology, school psychology, educational psychology, industrial and organizational psychology, cognitive psychology, cognitive neuroscience, methods and measurements, history, neuropsychology, personality assessment, developmental psychology, and more. Each handbook undertakes to review one of psychology's major subdisciplines with breadth, comprehensiveness, and exemplary scholarship. In addition to these broadly conceived volumes, the Library also includes a large number of handbooks designed to explore in depth more specialized areas of scholarship and research, such as stress, health and coping, anxiety and related disorders, cognitive development, and child and adolescent assessment. In contrast to the broad coverage of the subfield handbooks, each of these latter volumes focuses on an especially productive, more highly focused line of scholarship and research. Whether at the broadest or most specific level, however, all of the Library handbooks offer synthetic coverage that reviews and evaluates the relevant past and present research and anticipates research in the future. Each handbook in the Library includes introductory and concluding chapters written by its editor to provide a roadmap to the handbook's table of contents and to offer informed anticipations of significant future developments in that field.

An undertaking of this scope calls for handbook editors and chapter authors who are established scholars in the areas about which they write. Many of the nation's and the world's most productive and most highly respected psychologists have agreed to edit Library handbooks or write authoritative chapters in their areas of expertise.

For whom has the Oxford Library of Psychology been written? Because of its breadth, depth, and accessibility, the Library serves a diverse audience, including graduate students in psychology and their faculty mentors as well as scholars, researchers, and practitioners in psychology and related fields. Each will find in the Library information on the subfield or focal area of psychology in which they work or are interested.

Befitting its commitment to accessibility, each handbook includes a comprehensive index as well as extensive references to help guide research. And because the Library was designed from its inception as an online as well as a print resource, its structure and contents will be readily and rationally searchable online. Further, once the Library is released online, the handbooks will be regularly and thoroughly updated.

In summary, the Oxford Library of Psychology will grow organically to provide a thoroughly informed perspective on the field of psychology, one that reflects both psychology's dynamism and its increasing interdisciplinarity. Once published electronically, the Library is also destined to become a uniquely valuable interactive tool, with extended search and browsing capabilities. As you begin to consult this handbook, we sincerely hope you will share our enthusiasm for the more than 500-year tradition of Oxford University Press for excellence, innovation, and quality, as exemplified by the Oxford Library of Psychology.

Peter E. Nathan
Editor-in-Chief
Oxford Library of Psychology

ABOUT THE EDITOR

Donal E. Carlston

Dr. Donal E. Carlston won the Society of Experimental Social Psychology Dissertation Award in 1978 for his early work in social cognition and subsequently coauthored two of the first books in the field in 1979 and 1980. He was editor of the journal, *Social Cognition*, from 1993 to 2005 and has been organizer of the prestigious Duck Conference on Social Cognition since 1994. In 2009 he received the Ostrom Award for Lifetime Contributions to Social Cognition.

CONTRIBUTORS

David M. Amodio
Department of Psychology
New York University
New York, NY

Joanna Anderson
Department of Psychology
University of Waterloo
Waterloo, Ontario, Canada

Jamie Arndt
Department of Psychological Sciences
University of Missouri
Columbia, MO

Evelyn W.-M. Au
School of Social Sciences
Singapore Management University
Singapore

Emily Balcetis
Department of Psychology
New York University
New York, NY

D. Vaughn Becker
Psychonomic Evolutionary Science
Arizona State University
Tempe, AZ

Denise R. Beike
Department of Psychology
University of Arkansas
Fayetteville, AR

Christina M. Brown
Department of Psychology
Saint Louis University
St. Louis, MO

C. Daryl Cameron
Department of Psychology
University of North Carolina at Chapel Hill
Chapel Hill, NC

Donal E. Carlston
Department of Psychological Sciences
Purdue University
West Lafayette, IN

Chi-yue Chiu
Division of Strategy, Management, and
    Organization
Nanyang Business School
Nanyang Technological University
Singapore

Shana Cole
Trope Lab
New York University
New York, NY

Jeremy Cone
Department of Psychology
Cornell University
Ithaca, NY

Laura A. Creighton
Department of Psychology
The University of Western Ontario
London, Ontario, Canada

Ap Dijksterhuis
Department of Behavioural Change
Radboud University Nijmegen
Nijmegen, The Netherlands

Elizabeth A. Dyczewski
Department of Psychology
Ohio University
Athens, OH

Richard P. Eibach
Psychology Department
University of Waterloo
Waterloo, Ontario, Canada

Baruch Eitam
Psychology Department
University of Haifa
Haifa, Israel

Melissa Ferguson
Department of Psychology
Cornell University
Ithaca, NY

Gráinne M. Fitzsimons
The Fuqua School of Business
Duke University
Durham, NC

Alexandra Frischen
University of Waterloo
Waterloo, Ontario, Canada

Margarida V. Garrido
Utrecht University
Utrecht, The Netherlands
CIS/ISCTE, University Institute of Lisbon
Lisbon, Portugal

Bertram Gawronski
Department of Psychology
The University of Western Ontario
London, Ontario, Canada

Jeff Greenberg
Department of Psychology
University of Arizona
Tucson, AZ

Ana Guinote
Division of Psychology and Language Science
University College London
London, UK

David L. Hamilton
Department of Psychology
University of California, Santa Barbara
Santa Barbara, CA

Erin P. Hennes
Department of Psychology
University of California at Los Angeles
Los Angeles, CA

Gail D. Heyman
Department of Psychology
University of California, San Diego
La Jolla, CA

E. Tory Higgins
Psychology Department
Columbia University
New York, NY

Kurt Hugenberg
Department of Psychology
Miami University
Oxford, OH

Linda M. Isbell
Department of Psychology
University of Massachusetts at Amherst
Amherst, MA

John T. Jost
Department of Psychology
New York University
New York, NY

Frank R. Kardes
Carl H. Linder College of Business
University of Cincinnati
Cincinnati, OH

Yoshihisa Kashima
School of Psychological Sciences
The University of Melbourne
Melbourne, Australia

Douglas T. Kenrick
Department of Psychology
Arizona State University
Tempe, AZ

John F. Kihlstrom
Department of Psychology
University of California, Berkeley
Berkeley, CA

Laura M. Kressel
Department of Psychology
New York University
New York, NY

Elicia C. Lair
Department of Psychology
University of Massachusetts at Amherst
Amherst, MA

Alan J. Lambert
Department of Psychology
Washington University
St. Louis, MO

Ying Lan
School of Psychological Sciences
The University of Melbourne
Parkville, Australia

Mark J. Landau
Department of Psychology
University of Kansas
Lawrence, KS

Howard Lavine
Department of Political Science
University of Minnesota
Minneapolis, MN

Mark R. Leary
Department of Psychology and Neuroscience
Duke University
Durham, NC

Cristine H. Legare
Department of Psychology
University of Texas, Austin
Austin, TX

John M. Levine
Department of Psychology
University of Pittsburgh
Pittsburgh, PA

Lisa K. Libby
Department of Psychology
The Ohio State University
Columbus, OH

Nira Liberman
Department of Psychology
Tel-Aviv University
Tel-Aviv, Israel

Jill E. Gulker
Department of Psychology
Purdue University
West Lafayette, IN

Keith D. Markman
Department of Psychology
Ohio University
Athens, OH

Randy J. McCarthy
Department of Psychology
Northern Illinois University
DeKalb, IL

Gary McClelland
Department of Psychology and Neuroscience
University of Colorado Boulder
Boulder, CO

Allen R. McConnell
Department of Psychology
Miami University
Oxford, OH

David B. Miele
Department of Human Development
University of Maryland
College Park, MD

Margo J. Monteith
Department of Psychology
Purdue University
West Lafayette, IN

Sadia Najmi
Department of Psychology
San Diego State University
San Diego, CA

Steven L. Neuberg
Department of Psychology
Arizona State University
Tempe, AZ

Sharon S.-L. Ng
Nanyang Technological University
Singapore

Tomás Palma
Utrecht University
Utrecht, The Netherlands
CIS/ISCTE, University Institute of Lisbon
Lisbon, Portugal

B. Keith Payne
Department of Psychology
University of North Carolina at Chapel Hill
Chapel Hill, NC

Elise J. Percy
Department of Psychological and Brain
  Sciences
Indiana University
Bloomington, IN

Richard E. Petty
Department of Psychology
Ohio State University
Columbus, OH

Kyle G. Ratner
Department of Psychology
New York University
New York, NY

Glenn D. Reeder
Department of Psychology
Illinois State University
Normal, IL

SoYon Rim
Department of Psychology
New York University
New York, NY

Laura Scherer
Department of Psychological Sciences
University of Missouri
Columbia, MO

Frederick Schauer
School of Law
University of Virginia
Charlottesville, VA

Erica D. Schneid
Purdue University
West Lafayette, IN

Gün R. Semin
Utrecht University
Koç University
İstanbul, Turkey

Oren Shapira
Tel-Aviv University
Tel-Aviv, Israel

Hao Shen
Department of Marketing
Chinese University of Hong Kong
Hong Kong SAR, China

Jeffrey W. Sherman
Department of Psychology
University of California, Davis
Davis, CA

Steven J. Sherman
Department of Psychological
and Brain Sciences
Indiana University
Bloomington, IN

Tonya M. Shoda
Department of Psychology
Miami University
Oxford, OH

John J. Skowronski
Department of Psychology
Northern Illinois University
DeKalb, IL

Daniel Smilek
Department of Psychology
University of Waterloo
Waterloo, Ontario, Canada

Eliot R. Smith
Department of Psychological and Brain
Sciences
Indiana University
Bloomington, IN

Courtney K. Soderberg
University of California, Davis
Davis, CA

Barbara A. Spellman
Department of Psychology and School of Law
University of Virginia
Charlottesville, VA

Shelley E. Taylor
Department of Psychology
University of California, Los Angeles
Los Angeles, CA

Meredith L. Terry
Department of Psychology and Neuroscience
Duke University
Durham, NC

Mark Travers
Department of Psychology and Neuroscience
University of Colorado Boulder
Boulder, CO

Yaacov Trope
Department of Psychology
New York University
New York, NY

James S. Uleman
Department of Psychology
New York University
New York, NY

Leaf Van Boven
Department of Psychology and Neuroscience
University of Colorado Boulder
Boulder, CO

Duane T. Wegener
Department of Psychology
Ohio State University
Columbus, OH

Brett M. Wells
Department of Psychology
Northern Illinois University
DeKalb, IL

Jacob Westfall
Department of Psychology
University of Colorado Boulder
Boulder, CO

John Paul Wilson
Department of Psychology
Miami University
Oxford, OH

Anna Woodcock
Department of Psychological Sciences
Purdue University
West Lafayette, IN

Robert S. Wyer Jr.
Department of Marketing
Chinese University of Hong Kong
Hong Kong SAR, China

Alison Jing Xu
Rotman School of Management
University of Toronto
Toronto, Ontario, Canada

CONTENTS

History and Foundations of Social Cognition

CHAPTER

1

On the Nature of Social Cognition:
My Defining Moment

Donal E. Carlston

Abstract

Social cognition is often defined as an approach rather than as a content subfield of social psychology. This chapter defines each, argues that social cognition is both, and describes how the various chapters in this *Handbook* reflect these two facets. The first two parts, together, represent the core content of social cognition. Part One of the *Handbook* provides a historical perspective, with special emphasis on various content areas that contributed to its early development, including the core fields of impression formation and person perception. Part Two includes chapters on cognitive representation and process, and on various stages of information processing. The remainder of the *Handbook* represents social cognition as an approach. Part Three chapters describe how social cognition has contributed to other areas of social psychology, especially those involving motivation and the self. Then, Part Four illustrates synergies between social cognition and more distant fields such as evolutionary psychology, law and health.

Key Words: social cognition, impression formation, person perception

A visitor to Purdue University recently asked me to define social cognition, and I reflexively responded that it is "a subfield of social psychology focused on the role of cognition in human social behavior." He responded with a puzzled look that told me that my previously acceptable response was inadequate. I'm sure I've puzzled people before (and not always with my definitions), but this particular occasion left me silently parsing my language in an attempt to determine exactly where I had gone wrong. What in my wording failed to pass muster?

The visitor then posed an equally perplexing follow-up question, which I shall return to later in this chapter. But for the moment, indulge me as I take this embarrassingly public opportunity to refine my answer to his initial query. I believe that properly defining social cognition is a challenging but important exercise for the editor of a *Handbook* on the subject—and perhaps also for many others

in the field. And I doubt that I am unique in having provided a glib, superficial, and ultimately unsatisfactory response when asked to define this complex, evolving discipline.

In retrospect, I think that my answer fell short primarily in two respects (not to mention being somewhat circular, which is generally tolerated in psychological definitions). First, I referred to social cognition as a *subfield*—that is, as a content area within social psychology. Many no longer view it this way, referring instead to social cognition as an approach, orientation, viewpoint, or perspective. And second, my definition described a focus ("the role of cognition") that today might be construed as too generic to be meaningful. In the modern era, *cognition* embraces a larger range of processes and phenomena than it once did, so describing this as the field's cynosure barely narrows the definition at all. I will address these issues in turn.

Social Cognition: Content Area or Approach?

Once upon a time, social cognition was thought of as an emerging research area—a field or subfield, if you will—joining other content areas of social psychology such as attitudes, group processes, social influence, aggression, and altruism. It was characterized as a field in the first *Handbook of Social Cognition,* by editors Robert Wyer and Thomas Srull (p. vii) and by contributor Tom Ostrom in his classic chapter, "The Sovereignty of Social Cognition" (1994, pp. 1–2). Although the field was not always explicitly defined, it was clearly characterized by a core set of topics and issues that were being addressed by small groups of like-minded researchers in their labs and at conferences (see, e.g., Hastie, Ostrom, Ebbeson, Wyer, Hamilton, & Carlston, 1980; Wyer & Srull, preface, 1984). Those core topics and issues basically reflected a concern with people's perceptions and impressions of others, and I shall argue shortly that such content was, and is, at the heart of social cognition.

But even then there was a kind of ideological fervor among social cognitionists that translated readily into a general orientation or approach.[1] The construal of social cognition as an approach grew as it became a much broader enterprise, embracing seemingly divergent fields, unified more by a common point of view than overlapping research interests. In 1989, Sherman, Judd, and Park stated in their annual review article that, "In our view, social cognition is not a substantive domain within social psychology but an approach that guides research and thinking in a variety of domains" (p. 315). Ostrom's preface to the Wyer and Srull (1994) *Handbook* describes social cognition as an approach, perspective, and orientation (p. ix). A similar opinion was expressed by Devine, Hamilton, and Ostrom (1994, p. 4), who argued that social cognition could not really be considered a content area because that implied a "limited range of applicability," which was belied by the "broad range of topics" already being addressed by the "approach." Wyer and Srull (1994) expanded on this point, noting in the second *Handbook of Social Cognition* that social cognition's influence had extended beyond its own borders "to many other subareas (health psychology, clinical psychology, personality, etc.)," as well as to some "totally different disciplines (political science, marketing and consumer behavior, organizational behavior, etc.)" (p. xiii).[2] This trend continues, as documented particularly in Parts Three and Four of the present volume.

Currently, the home page of the International Social Cognition Network boldly states, much as Sherman et al. did in 1989, that, "Social cognition is not a content area, but rather is an approach to understanding social psychology." This claim is made unabashedly, without reservation or explanation, as though it reflects a universally accepted truth. Certainly, the claim that social cognition has provided a useful perspective for researchers in a variety of disciplines is incontrovertible. But does construing it as an approach necessarily preclude it from also being a content area? Does the field's breadth inherently imply a lack of focus? I would argue that if one bypasses the satellite disciplines that orbit social cognition and penetrates the philosophical aura surrounding it, there is still a substantive core of research and content that represents the central focus of the field.

The Core of Social Cognition

Early in its existence, Wegner and Vallacher (1977) defined social cognition as "how people think about people" (p. viii). The prototypic social cognitive event arguably involved a perceiver who encounters or learns about another person, forms or refines an impression, and then departs, taking away various thoughts and memories. This was a simple and tractable caricature of human social cognition, and it governed (at least implicitly) a great deal of work in the field. Harry meets Sally. Harry forms an impression of Sally. Harry departs and retains memories of Sally.[3]

This prototypical event is, of course, a stereotype—an oversimplified representation that is readily communicated and understood, but that captures little of the richness of the thing that it describes. Still, like most stereotypes, it is simple, social, and cognitive. And by focusing on Harry and a minimal construal of his mental activities, it served to distinguish the social cognitive character of these events from other social psychological processes that provide the focus for other, related fields of inquiry. This, then, I would argue, was the original core focus of social cognition.

However, a number of events conspired to make that core focus more diffuse than it once was. First, there was an increased recognition that impression formation is a more complex social process than described above. Second, the information processing model (which, as we shall see, is a key component of the social cognition approach) expanded our understanding of many different aspects of impression formation. Third, that model in particular, and the field more generally, stretched to accommodate a variety of different concepts from mainstream social psychology, such as motivation and affect, that were not always given their due in early social cognition. And finally, as already noted, the definition of *cognition* itself has expanded over the years.

These kinds of cognitive complexities are well illustrated in the chapters in Part Two of this *Handbook*, as well as in some chapters that come later. Harry's memories of Sally no longer consist only of semantic trait impressions that are retrieved at will. Today, they include visual images, affective material, and relationship schemas that are not only explicitly stored and retrieved but also represented implicitly in the recesses of perceivers' minds. Today, impression formation is no longer a single process, but rather is subdivided into various stages of information processing, some newly posited (e.g., thought suppression), and most affected by contextual factors, motivational states, goals, and affect. And today, mental processes are guided not just by accessibility, effort, and capacity but also by construal level, regulatory focus, and even thoughts of mortality and the vestiges of evolution. So, when I describe the core of the field as impression formation, I refer to more than just the simple "Harry meets Sally" prototype described above. I refer to today's new, expanded, and improved understanding of impression formation, along with various other related processes and phenomena.

SOCIALIZING IMPRESSION FORMATION

It is important to recognize that this new understanding is fairly fluid and can readily spread into adjacent fields that are less centrally "social cognitionish" than described above. A thorough articulation of Harry's meeting with Sally opens the floodgates, diluting the definition of social cognition and washing away any distinction between this subfield and others in social psychology. For example, while Harry is forming an impression of Sally, she is likewise sizing him up. And he knows it, as does she, with such knowledge affecting the thoughts, self-presentations, behaviors, and interactions of each party. In fact, without this knowledge and interplay, the social cognitive situation we have described is barely social; it has all the resonance of one hand clapping.

Taking into account the other hand (that would be Sally) only begins to deal with the unarticulated complexities of our scenario. In addition to Harry and Sally, their meeting involves a situational context, which may among other things include other people, either in person or in the mental representations of the participants. Moreover, except for chance first encounters, most interactions eventuate because of various aspects of the participants' histories, personalities, relationships, motivations, goals, intentions, and plans. These factors then converge, along with numerous aspects of the social environment, to shape the communication and interaction between the participants, which in turn has the potential to feed back and influence the things that brought the participants together or contributed to their impressions of each other. Finally, all of these processes and their outcomes affect whether those involved will meet and interact again, under what circumstances and for what purposes; whether they will influence or affect each other in other ways, even in absentia; or whether the whole interaction will only reverberate in their respective memories, and perhaps in enduring changes in their attitudes, personalities, intentions, expectancies, and the like.

When thoroughly elaborated, the social cognitive event described in the opening paragraph of this section is thus actually quite complex and multifaceted—and it seemingly touches almost every aspect of human social behavior. When the various pieces are colored in, the emerging portrait looks less like a thumbnail of one small corner of human cognition and more like a representation of the greater part of social psychology. This *Handbook* fleshes out this portrait with chapters covering everything from goal pursuit to personal relationships, and from emotions to group processes. In fact, most of the book relates in one way or another to social psychology, broadly defined, and many chapters could (with minor alterations in title and emphasis) appear in a book on that subject. Have we reached the point, then, where social cognition, the subfield, is equivalent to social psychology, the field? Where, as Tom Ostrom (1994, p. xii) famously forecast, the *Handbook of Social Cognition* can serve as the *Handbook of Social Psychology*?

If we seem to have reached that point, it might help to explain our Purdue visitor's befuddlement at my definition of social cognition as a "subfield." Subfields, after all, should be subordinate to the fields they are part of, and not redundant with them (or "sovereign" over them, as Ostrom suggested in 1984). But the fact that a broad construal of social cognition implicates many other aspects of social psychology does not necessarily imply that social cognition and social psychology are synonymous. Some of the complexities involved when Harry meets Sally are not fundamentally socially cognitive; for example, many aspects of their inter-action might be better understood in terms of what we know about self-presentation or personal rela-tionships than in terms of impressions, perceptions, and memories. Other aspects bridge the boundar-ies (such as they are) between social cognition and other subfields of social psychology. And still others, while located solidly in the body of social cognition work, are fairly distant from its heart.

Perhaps my definition confused our visitor fur-ther because I cavalierly implied that the core of social cognition pertained to "the role of cognition" in human social behavior. When social cognition was first conceived, cognition was often interpreted as referring to deliberate and conscious thought, and sometimes even misinterpreted as rational-ity. This latter characterization may have been fit-ting given the kinds of logical thinking presumed by early attribution theories (e.g., Jones & Davis, 1965, Kelley, 1967), though social cognitivists gen-erally argued that even conscious thought could be brief, sloppy, or misguided. But in any case, *cogni-tion* typically implied a form of thought that would today be characterized as "controlled," meaning voluntary, directed, conscious, and effortful (utiliz-ing limited mental resources). Moreover, it often implied a form of thought that was verbal or seman-tic, though other forms (e.g., episodic memories) were also sometimes posited.

But today, *cognition* encompasses subconscious goals, automatic processes, and implicit memories. It is now understood to comprise many processes that once would have been excluded. Habits are cognitive, and so are simple associations, including those once subsumed by classical and even operant conditioning. Moods, emotions, and motivation are cognitive. The effects of undetected stimuli are cognitive, as are the preconscious mechanisms by which these influence behavior and memory. In fact, almost anything that implicates the mind is considered cognitive today. And since virtually all human activity implicates the mind, virtually every-thing is cognitive.

So, when I stated in my insouciant definition that social cognition focuses "on the role of cogni-tion in human social behavior," I might as well have just said that it focuses on "human social behavior." This sounds, once again, too much like basic social psychology. Whether due to the expansion of social cognition in particular, or to the expansion of cog-nitive psychology more generally, it is understand-able that my questioner wondered where the edges of the field might be. This confusion was reflected in his follow-up question, "Can you name a topic in social psychology that you would *not* consider to be social cognition?" An awkward but understandable silence followed. Given my original definition, I was essentially being asked to name a form of human social behavior that *does not in any way* implicate the mind.[4]

On reflection, I appreciate more than ever that social psychology is not a discipline for which bor-ders can be clearly drawn on the research landscape. Instead, the boundaries of social psychological subfields are fuzzy and overlapping, only vaguely delineating one discipline from another. This is probably even truer for social cognition than for most because, as discussed later, this particular sub-field is not just a field with one, broad, core focus but also an approach that contributes to other sub-fields with entirely different foci. The solution to this state of affairs is not to throw up one's hands and declare that social cognition is no longer a subfield, but rather to recognize its dual nature. As a subfield with fuzzy boundaries, it may best be defined by a prototype, even if this does leave its more distant perimeters in question. The prototype that I per-ceive as representing the core of social cognition involves Harry's formation of an impression of Sally and other closely related processes and representa-tions. As an approach, it may instead be defined by a philosophy or set of principles, such as I outline later in this chapter.

Organization of the Handbook

Overall, the organization of this *Handbook* reflects the view of social cognition I have just tried to articulate. More specifically, it reflects a progres-sion from history and the content core of the field through related topics in social psychology, gen-eral psychology, and then other fields of social sci-ence to which the approach has contributed. The first two parts thus serve to define social cognition as a subfield, and the latter ones to define it as an approach. At a very general level, this mimics the organization of Wyer and Srull's (1994) *Handbook*, which was divided into two volumes, *Basic Processes* and *Applications*. But the gradations among chap-ters here are finer, and my characterization of those gradations is different. Of course, one needn't agree with my organizational scheme to appreciate the richness of the material provided in these chapters, each of which stands on its own.

Some difficult decisions had to be made in terms of where individual chapters were placed within this organizational scheme. Should Skowronski,

McCarthy, and Wells' chapter on person memory, with its historical bent, be placed among other historical accounts, or where it is, in the middle of chapters on information processing? Should Isbell and Lair's chapter, "Moods, Emotions, and Evaluations as Information," go in the information processing section, or perhaps even earlier, among the chapters on mental representation? Should Beike's chapter on autobiographical memory sit alongside Skowronski et al.'s on person memory? Should later chapters on socially situated cognition, evolutionary psychology, and neuroscience be treated as synergies between social cognition and other, external fields or as altogether new scientific foundations for the field of social cognition? I hope that the organization of the volume I settled on is useful, but I acknowledge that other schemes were possible and that these might support alternative conceptions of the field.

Social Cognition as a Content Subfield
Part One: History and Foundations of Social Cognition

This first section of this *Handbook* provides a history of the field (Carlston & Hamilton, Chapter 2) along with a chapter on social cognition methodology, which is also historically inclined (Lambert & Scherer, Chapter 3). What follows, then, are four chapters on important areas of social psychology that originated before the social cognition era, laid the foundation for this field, and, to varying extents, were ultimately subsumed by it. These four areas—impression formation, stereotyping, attribution, and attitudes—all focus to some extent on how people think about people (i.e., on impression formation). They thus help to define the central focus of the field of social cognition, at least historically.[5]

IMPRESSION FORMATION

The most obvious antecedent for social cognition is the area termed *impression formation* or *person perception*. This research area existed long before the social cognition era, though it was approached somewhat differently in those early days (see Uleman & Kressel, Chapter 4, this volume). Much of the original interest in impression formation centered either on perceivers' accuracy (especially as an individual difference variable) or on the cues that perceivers use in sizing up other people. After Cronbach (1955) effectively discouraged research on the former issue, such research lay dormant for more than 30 years, until resurrected more recently (see, e.g., Kenny & Albright, 1987). Instead, for a time, the field devoted most

of its energy to the latter issue, cataloging the influence of physical attractiveness, race, gender, stigma, clothing, and the like on perceptions of others (see Carlston & Mae, 2000, for a brief review). In such work, perceivers were commonly instructed to form impressions, and these were then assessed using transparent trait rating scales, with the implicit assumption that these procedures reflected both the formation and the underlying representation of person impressions. Person perception in this era was simple, but like the prototypic "Harry meets Sally" situation described earlier, not really that social (or that cognitive, for that matter, by current standards; Carlston, 2010a).

In their seminal volume, *Social Cognition, Inference and Attribution*, Wyer and Carlston (1979) argued that "additional emphasis needs to be placed on the cognitive representations of social information *that people actually and spontaneously use*" (p. 364, emphasis added). In the impression formation area, this was accomplished by Winter and Uleman (1984), who eschewed giving subjects instructions to form impressions and employed a cognitive measure of impression formation (based on the encoding specificity principle) that was not dependent on overt trait rating scales. Their conclusion that perceivers form impressions spontaneously spurred lengthy programs of research involving both Uleman and his students, and later, me and my students.[6] This and subsequent work in impression formation (see Uleman & Kressel, Chapter 4, this volume) differ from most early work in the area by emphasizing issues of spontaneity and automaticity, examining implicit as well as explicit representations, exploring associative and inferential processes, and adopting cognitive methods that sidestep the need to directly ask people what their impressions are. As we shall see later, such characteristics are hallmarks of the modern social cognition approach.

STEREOTYPING

Another historically important antecedent research area focused on prejudice and stereotyping, as reflected in Allport's classic volume, *The Nature of Prejudice* (1954). Stereotypes (of people) are a kind of impression based on race, gender, or other overgeneralized attributes and were construed as both a facet and cause of prejudice against others. Stereotypes and their development remain a central concern today (see, e.g., Sherman, Sherman, Percy, & Soderberg, Chapter 27, this volume), though the manner in which the topic is addressed has changed considerably. As with impression formation, the shift has been away from intentional processes, transparent measures, and explicit representations toward more implicit versions of all three (Montieth, Woodcock, & Lybarger, Chapter 5, this volume). With these adjustments, the study of prejudice and stereotyping has continued to be one of the most active and influential areas of social psychology.

ATTRIBUTION

A third important research area that preceded and fed into social cognition was attribution theory, which dominated social psychology journals in the 1970s (see Reeder, Chapter 6, this volume), but may be less central today. The stated concern of work on attribution was the naïve perception of causation, but much of the theory and research centered more specifically on people's perceptions of the causes of others' behaviors. Because these causes were often thought to be personality traits, "perceiving causes" generally meant "inferring traits"—making the overlap with impression formation theory and research obvious. Consequently, the field of attribution lay much of the groundwork for the eventual emergence of social cognition.

But for the most part, causes and attributions were measured using instructions and measures that were transparent, explicit, and ill suited to assess how people actually think about such matters. Moreover, attribution work rarely took into account the impact of such processes as attention, perception, and memory. The theories were cognitive in a loose sense, but also parochial, having little in common with other cognitive theories, such as those derived from the field of cognitive psychology. Consequently, such work clashed somewhat with the social cognition perspective, which ultimately reinterpreted and transformed the subfield of attribution and then absorbed what was left of it.

ATTITUDES

Finally, it is probably evident that impressions of others can be construed (at least partly) as attitudes toward them, so that the massive literature in the latter area is integral to any discussion of the former. Indeed, attitudes and evaluations are so central to impression formation that the combination was once a subfield of its own (*interpersonal attraction*). Harry's impression of Sally may consist largely of traits and memories, but both of these are colored by, and combined with, the extent to which Harry likes Sally. Given the extent to which attitudes and impressions are intertwined, it is probably not surprising that many researchers and developments in

the attitudes area helped to shape social cognition (and vice versa), and that these disciplines developed convergently. In fact, Wegener and Petty (Chapter 7, this volume) view them as so closely related that they refer to attitudes and social cognition as "siblings."

OVERLAP

I would suggest that these four research areas—impression formation, stereotyping, attribution, and attitudes—have a great deal of overlap and that their centroid can be properly characterized as a concern with how people form impressions or, more generally, with "how people think about people." (It should probably be acknowledged that, excepting impression formation, each of these arguably also covers territory that falls outside of the regions where they overlap). What these areas lacked, to some extent, was integration; each laid claim to its own insular theories without much regard for what was transpiring on the mainland of cognitive psychology.

Of course, social cognition does not represent simply the convergence of earlier fields; to some extent, it also represents an elaboration and transformation of them. This elaboration and transformation partly reflects the aforementioned concern for what perceivers actually, spontaneously do, how they do it, and how the results of these processes are represented cognitively. From a contemporary perspective, Harry will form an impression of Sally whether he tries to or not. That impression is likely to comprise many elements beyond simple trait ascriptions (see Carlston, 1992, 1994), and whether intentionally recalled or not, those elements are likely to have myriad effects. Concerns such as these led early social cognitionists (e.g., Hamilton, 1981; Hastie et al., 1980; Higgins, Herman, & Zanna, 1981; Wyer & Carlston, 1979), to embrace theories and methods from cognitive psychology, a phenomenon I will address more thoroughly when I turn to social cognition as an approach. But even without delving into such detail, it is evident that the concern with cognitive representations and processes imbues social cognition approaches to impression formation with many flavors that make it distinct from the fields that preceded it. Readers are given a taste of these in Part Two of the *Handbook*.

Part Two: Mental Representation and Information Processing

The first four chapters of this section reflect the just-mentioned concern with cognitive representation, a subject of long-standing interest in the field

(Carlston, 2010b; Carlston & Smith, 1996; Wyer & Carlston, 1994).[7] Libby and Eibach (Chapter 8) review the role of visual imagery in social cognition and suggest that imagery may play an important role in abstract, as well as concrete, thinking. Hugenberg and Wilson (Chapter 9) focus more specifically on one form of image, the human face, in impression formation and stereotyping, arguing that "Faces Are Central to Social Cognition." Rim, Trope, Liberman, and Shapira (Chapter 10) next delve into Trope's important distinction between concrete and abstract representations, delineating the many ways in which psychological, physical, and temporal distance affect these representations. Chapter 11 by Payne and Cameron on implicit mental representation then provides a segue from issues of representation to issues of processing. In this chapter and the three that follow (Chapters 12–14 by Dijksterhuis; Wyer, Shen, & Xu; and Gawronski & Creighton), we see the increased emphasis on unintentional, automatic, and unconscious processing that is so representative of modern social cognition. These chapters thus help to define, in important ways, how modern social cognition differs from its earlier forms.

INFORMATION PROCESSING

Part Two of the *Handbook* then concludes with a series of chapters that reflect central components of an elaborated information processing model. The information processing model was embraced by social cognitionists (e.g., Hamilton, 1981; Ostrom, 1994; Wyer & Carlston, 1979) partly because it resonated with their interest in how perceivers process information about others, but also because it fit with their infatuation with cognitive psychology. These undercurrents will be described further below, when social cognition is discussed as an approach.

Following cognitive psychology, social cognition commonly subdivided mental processing into such stages as attention, perception, memory, and judgment (see, e.g., Hastie & Carlston, 1980). In this *Handbook*, contemporary reviews are provided of these traditional stages by Smilek and Frischen (Chapter 15 on attention), Balcetis and Cole (Chapter 16 on perception), Skowronski, McCarthy, and Wells (Chapter 17 on memory), and van Boven, Travers, Westfall, and McClelland (Chapter 18 on judgment). To these have been added less traditional stages of mental simulation (Markman & Dyczewski, Chapter 19) and thought suppression (Najmi, Chapter 20).

Among other things, these chapters serve to elaborate the social-cognitive scenario described earlier in this chapter. Harry has to first notice and attend to Sally, and doing so brings into play a variety of factors, including distraction, emotion, and motivation. His perceptions or interpretations of Sally are similarly affected by a host of factors, including mental shortcuts, prior knowledge, and personal goals. And ultimately issues arise concerning what Harry will remember about Sally, what memories will be suppressed, and how information that Harry retrieves contributes to his judgments and mental simulations. From one perspective, then, these chapters arguably continue the historical focus on aspects of impression formation and person perception, but now informed by the information processing account.[8]

The central stage in this more complex information processing account is seemingly memory. Memory is central to information processing because it ties together the stimulus world that is attended and perceived and the mental world that later contributes to judgments, behavior, and all other residual effects of stimuli once they are no longer present. Early social cognitionists (e.g., Wyer & Carlston, 1979) criticized the foundational subfields (such as attribution) for paying insufficient attention to processes and issues of memory. As a consequence of such neglect, early social cognition research was emphatically devoted to such issues (see Chapter 3 by Lambert & Scherer on social cognition methodologies). In fact, memory was so much a focus of early research that the nascent field was even referred to by some as "person memory," a term that appropriately conveys its kinship with, and complement to, the earlier field of person perception. The *Person Memory* label was affixed to one of the earliest books on the subject (Hastie et al., 1980) and to an associated conference that continues to this day (PMIG: the annual meetings of the Person Memory Interest Group).

The information processing account pervades social cognition, both as a framework for examining impression formation and as a philosophical tenet of the approach (see below). But this is not your father's information processing model. Our understanding of both "information" and "processing" are considerably broader today than they were in earlier eras. The former now includes moods, emotions, and motivation, both explicit and implicit, and the latter includes both willful and automatic processes. Moreover, the simple linear and sequential parade of information processing stages seemingly implied by the earliest models has almost universally been recognized as a convenient shorthand rather than an inviolate sequence. Every stage actually feeds back and affects the stages before it, and each may have unmediated influences on stages that follow later in the chain of information processing. We next consider why the information processing approach is so central to social cognition, in relation to defining social cognition as an approach.

Social Cognition as an Approach

Wyer and Carlston (1979) characterized their early social cognition approach as reflecting dissatisfaction with the fragmented, unintegrated nature of earlier work on social inference, a concern with people's phenomenology, the perception of potential symbiosis between social and cognitive psychologies, an emphasis on actual, spontaneous, mental representations, and faith in the information processing model. Devine et al. (1994) emphasized the investigation of cognitive structures and processes underlying social phenomena, adoption of the information processing model, and assumptions of commonality across different domains of psychology. Fiske and Taylor (1991) described social cognition research as involving "unabashed mentalism, orientation toward process, cross-fertilization between cognitive and social psychologies, and at least some concern with real world social issues" (p. 14). And in a previous chapter (Carlston, 2010a), I characterized the approach as a set of beliefs: that cognitive processes are a major determinant of human judgments and behavior, that it is more useful to employ general concepts and theories than idiosyncratic micro-theories, that the information processing model provides a universally useful structure for examining cognition, that mediating processes should be measured (generally using methods borrowed from cognitive psychology) rather than just assumed, and (based on the preceding beliefs) that "there should be one universal set of concepts, principles, and practices underlying most, if not all, psychological theorizing and research" (pp. 64–65).

Despite their differences, these various descriptions have a great deal in common. Most often mentioned are the importance of mental processes, the synergies between social and cognitive psychology, devotion to the information processing model, and the desire for a broad, perhaps universal, integration of disparate fields of psychology. Although noted only by Fiske and Taylor (1991), a concern with real-world issues is also an important characteristic of social cognition, which, though occasionally

neglected, affirms the "social" nature of the social cognition approach. This aspect of social cognition is amply demonstrated by the final chapters in this volume.

Allow me now to attempt a systematic restructuring of this "list" of attributes into a coherent philosophical approach. My view is that social cognition represents a focus on how people actually think about social things (especially other people) and how this thinking ultimately affects judgment and behavior (especially that with important societal consequences). This focus elevates mentalistic models above purely descriptive ones and emphasizes the role of cognitive processes in human behavior. Historically, this has led to the adoption of the information processing model as a general framework and to the employment of methods and theories borrowed from cognitive psychology. More generally, it discourages reliance on insular theories and approaches and encourages integration with other fields of social psychology, psychology, and social science in general. As a consequence, the approach is ideally suited for investigating the kinds of real-world social issues that have long been of interest to social psychologists and that are central to many other disciplines.

Parts Three and Four of this *Handbook* illustrate these principles, but especially underscore the integrative and "social issue" emphases described above. Thus, for example, chapters address the integration of the social cognition approach with evolutionary psychology (Neuberg, Becker, & Kenrick, Chapter 32), neuroscience (Amodio & Ratner, Chapter 34), communication (Kashima & Lan, Chapter 35), and social development (Heyman & Legare, Chapter 36), among many others. In terms of social issues, various chapters highlight the implications of social cognition for such realms as personal relationships (Fitzsimons & Anderson, Chapter 29), prejudice (Montieth et al., Chapter 5), consumer behavior (Kardes & Wyer, Chapter 39), health (Taylor, Chapter 42), law (Spellman & Schauer, Chapter 40), and politics (Jost, Hennes, & Lavine, Chapter 41), again among many others. We turn now to a more detailed description of these chapters.

Part Three: Social Cognition and Social Psychology

As noted earlier, affect and motivation were largely disregarded by the early information processing approach (see, e.g., Forgas, 1983; Zajonc, 1980) but were central to social psychology, where robust literatures developed on these topics. Social cognition generally, and information processing more particularly, quickly expanded to incorporate such work. In fact, by 1981, Kossylyn and Kagan defined social cognition in terms of two kinds of cognition, one of which was "that colored by feelings, motives, attitudes and emotional states" (p. 82). Recent thinking and research about such "hot" forms of cognition are reviewed in Chapter 21 on "Moods, Emotions, and Evaluations" by Isbell and Lair, and in the chapters on motivated memory (Eitam, Miele, & Higgins, Chapter 22) and goal pursuit (Ferguson and Cone, Chapter 23). Additional examples elsewhere in the volume include Chapter 15 on "The 'Cold' and 'Hot' Sides of Attention" by Smilek and Frischen and Chapter 41on "'Hot' Political Cognition" by Jost et al.

Research on the self also has a lengthy history in social psychology (e.g., James, 1893), and the area could have been included in Part One as one of the foundations of modern social cognition. Instead, it is covered here in the social psychology section of the *Handbook* because it has somewhat different concerns and consequences than work focusing directly on impressions of others. Relevant chapters are a general review by McConnell, Brown, and Shoda (Chapter 24), along with chapters focused specifically on autobiographical memory (Beike, Chapter 25) and self-evaluation (Leary & Terry, Chapter 26), respectively. In essence, Harry meets himself instead of Sally, forms an impression, and then for the remainder of the movie, thinks about and remembers himself instead of her.

Part Three concludes with four chapters tying the social cognition approach to different domains of social psychology: stereotype formation (Sherman et al., Chapter 27), social power (Guinote, Chapter 28), personal relationships (Fitzsimons & Anderson, Chapter 29), and group processes (Levine & Smith, Chapter 30). Of course, the final four chapters of Part One would fit here as well because impression formation, stereotyping, attribution, and attitudes were also domains of social psychology and are all extant today, at least in some form. But the chapters in Part One address topics close to the center of social cognition, whereas those included here wander a little further afield.

Part Four: Synergies with Other Realms of Social Science

I spent a fair amount of time trying to decide what to call this final section of the *Handbook*. On the one hand, many of the chapters in this section deal with what are often called *applications* of social cognition. But such a heading fails on at least three counts. First, it isn't always clear that the chapters deal with applications of social cognition to other realms; in some cases, instead, the chapters seem to deal with applications of other realms to social cognition. Second, the term *application* trivializes the symbiotic relationship between social cognition and the other realms to which the approach has been "applied." This material does not simply reflect one field reinterpreting or extending another; more often two different fields influence, strengthen, and enhance each other. And finally, some of the realms with which social cognition interacts are not so much "subfields" as they are approaches in their own right. What results, then, is not so much an "application" of one to the other, but rather a new hybrid approach that differs from both of its constituents. Hence I prefer to use the term *synergies*, rather than *applications*. The *American Heritage Dictionary* (1996) defines *synergy* as "The interaction of two or more agents or forces so that their combined effect is greater than the sum of their individual effects." Such synergies are evident in virtually every chapter in this final section of the *Handbook*.

The earlier chapters in this section represent social science "realms" that are really perspectives, orientations, or approaches in much the way that social cognition is said to be. Examples include the chapters on socially situated cognition (Semin, Garrido, & Palma, Chapter 31), evolutionary social cognition (Neuberg, Becker, & Kenrick, Chapter 32), mortality salience (Greenberg, Landau, & Arndt, Chapter 33), and social cognitive neuroscience (Amodio & Ratner, Chapter 34). Each of these involves new theories, new issues, and new ways of doing research. And in every instance, the chapters make clear that the combination of approaches is greater than just the sum of their individual contributions.

The next four chapters in the section deal with the symbiosis between social cognition and areas of mainstream psychology, including communication (Kashima & Lan, Chapter 35), social development (Heyman & Legare, Chapter 36), culture (Chiu, Ng, & Au, Chapter 37), and personality (Kihlstrom, Chapter 38). These are representative of the spread of social cognition beyond core social psychology to a diversity of affiliated fields. The chapters provide a mixture of application, review, synthesis, and philosophy (as do many of the other chapters in the book as well) and expand the scope of social cognition considerably.

Finally, the last four chapters constitute outer reaches of the spiraling spread of social cognition, involving domains most distant from the center of the field. These chapters cover consumer psychology (Kardes & Wyer, Chapter 39), law (Spellman & Schauer, Chapter 40), politics (Jost et al., Chapter 41), and health (Taylor, Chapter 42). Each provides a unique perspective on the "application" of the social cognition approach. Kardes and Wyer (Chapter 39), for example, describe a great deal of consumer-related research stimulated and shaped by social cognition. Spellman and Schauer (Chapter 4) describe how social cognition has addressed past legal issues, but more importantly, how it can also shed light on unaddressed aspects of the law that are more central to our system than the prototypical, but rare, jury trial. Jost et al. (Chapter 41) describe the connections between motivated cognition and ideology and discuss how social cognition and political science can advance each other. And Taylor (Chapter 42) reviews several decades of research on social cognition and health psychology, emphasizing the many advances in the latter field stimulated by the former. As a set, then, these final chapters provide several different kinds of synergistic commingling of social cognition with other realms of social science.

The chapters in Parts Three and Four, as a group, confirm the widespread influence of social cognition and the principles it represents. Social science today focuses more than previously on how people actually think about things, from law to politics, and from culture to health, and also on how such thoughts affect socially and societally important behaviors. Arguably, psychological theories today are less insular and more integrative, less descriptive, and more mentalistic. Cognitive theories are widely used, as are cognitive methods, though both have been supplemented with tools borrowed from a wider variety of fields. And as much as social cognition has influenced the rest of academia, the rest of academia has also influenced social cognition.

Definition Redux

Before turning back to the definitional issue with which this chapter began, let me first get all my ducks in a row by addressing several aspects of the content-versus-approach debate that I have glossed over to this point. These are: (1) whether content and approach are actually distinguishable; and if they are, (2) whether it really matters whether social cognition is framed as a content area, as well as an approach, rather than simply as the latter; and if it does, (3) whether reflecting both a content subfield

and a philosophical approach makes social cognition unique.

Are Content and Approach Distinguishable?

Astute readers may have noticed that in discussing the "content" chapters of Parts One and Two, I referred to the field's emphasis on the information processing model, its infatuation with all things cognitive, its fuzzy boundaries, and its rejection of insular theories. In other words, I spent a fair amount of time referencing the social cognition approach, even though I was arguing for social cognition as a subfield.

It is also probably true that the vast majority of the chapters in these first two parts—and perhaps all of them—are consistent with at least some of the principles of the social cognition approach. They assume the centrality of mentalistic processes, include extensive discussions of cognitive concepts, theories, and methods, conform to the information processing model, and so on. Consequently, though I characterized these chapters as representative of the central content of social cognition, they could just as easily have been characterized as representative of the approach instead.

It is hardly surprising that contemporary work on the core content issues of social cognition is predominantly conducted using a social cognition approach. The two are intimately intertwined in ways that have already been described. They really diverge only when the approach is applied to issues and areas distant from those at the heart of the field. This is true, for example, in many chapters later in this *Handbook*, which tend to travel progressively further away from impression formation through other areas of social psychology, general psychology, and then social science more generally. By Part Four, many chapters have little direct bearing on Harry's impression of Sally, though they nonetheless embody social cognition principles that should be familiar by now. In such chapters, the approach achieves some separation from the content of social cognition, though with only a little imagination, the material covered still comes into play whenever two people (like Harry and Sally, for example) meet and interact.

Does Content Matter?

If social cognition is incontestably an approach and only debatably a content area, why not just concede the definitional ground to advocates of the former position, rather than making a ruckus? First, I don't believe it is historically accurate to describe the field as simply an approach. Social cognition once occupied considerably less territory than it does today, and though I have no desire to erect exclusionary fences around its historical boundaries, some recognition of its traditional focus seems appropriate. To me, one way to do this is to recognize that the subfield of social cognition centers on impression formation or, more generally, on how people think about people.

Second, the central principles of the social cognition approach are so widely accepted today that defining *social cognition* solely in terms of such principles may ultimately dilute the meaning of the term. If everyone agrees that it is desirable to have one unified psychology of human behavior, and that this psychology will to some extent incorporate elements of both social and cognitive psychologies, then is everyone a social cognitionist? A discipline without boundaries can hardly be characterized as a discipline at all.

Third, the principles that compose the social cognition approach cohere largely because they derive from empirical attempts to better understand how people actually and spontaneously think about other people. I attempted to describe this coherence in my introduction to the "Social Cognition as an Approach" section of this chapter. Take away the core concern with the representations and processes underlying Harry's impressions and memories of Sally, and one is arguably left with some disembodied platitudes like, "Isn't cognitive psychology wonderful?" and "Wouldn't it be nice if different areas of psychology didn't contradict each other?" I believe the social cognition approach to be more profound than that, and it is so to some extent because it is not just an approach, but rather an approach defined in part by the prototypic issues on which it has historically been turned.

Fourth, and finally, recognizing that there is a core content area in social cognition allows us to talk meaningfully about the degree to which particular research or theory falls within that area, overlaps with it, falls near (or far) from its boundaries, or occupies neighboring turf, but with a similar perspective or approach. I consider all of the chapters in this *Handbook* to represent social cognition, or I wouldn't have included them! But they represent social cognition in different ways. The chapters in Parts One and Two represent the core content areas of interest in the field, focusing on how people think about people. And I suspect that most of the authors who contributed these chapters think of themselves as social cognitionists.[9]

The chapters in Parts Three and Four represent exciting synergies that occur when psychologists combine other content areas or perspectives with the social cognition approach. In doing so, these chapters at least occasionally deal with content similar to that in the core area of social cognition. But their primary focus is elsewhere: on groups, personal relationships, law or health, for example. And I suspect that most of the authors who contributed chapters to these sections self-identify primarily with areas other than social cognition.

Is Social Cognition Unique?

If one accepts the premise that social cognition can best be defined as both a content subfield and an approach, does this make it unique within social psychology? Or are there other realms of social psychological endeavor that might be characterized similarly? The answer, I think, is that social cognition exemplifies this kind of dual role, but that other disciplines are beginning to follow suit. Two examples come readily to mind, though I suspect there are others as well. One is social cognitive neuroscience. Social cognitive neuroscience has for some time been a content subfield of psychology with its own focal issues, theories, and methods. But neuroscience today also provides an approach that is increasingly being applied to other areas of social psychology (see Amodio & Ratner, Chapter 34, and discussions in many other chapters). I suspect that, as with social cognition, some of those who use the approach focus on the core facets of that field and identify principally as social cognitive neuroscientists. But as the theoretical and methodological tools of that trade (especially modern neuroimaging technology) become more widely available, more and more social psychologists with other principal interests are adopting social neuroscience as an approach.

A second example is evolutionary psychology. Here, again, we have a dedicated cadre of researchers who have had their own theories and methods and who have historically pursued their research within the boundaries of their own subfield. But as the tenets of the evolutionary approach have gained broader acceptance, the evolutionary hypotheses and methods have spilled over into many other areas of psychology (see Neuberg, Becker, & Kenrick, Chapter 32, as well as many other chapters).

The dual roles played by social cognitive neuroscience and evolutionary theory are illustrated by their representation both in separate chapters on these subjects and, frequently, in chapters by other authors focused principally on other subjects. Like social cognition itself, these two subfields (and probably others not mentioned here) are growing from constrained content areas to widely accepted orientations. From a social cognition standpoint, this development is welcome. It represents further progress toward the "broad, perhaps universal, integration of disparate fields of psychology" called for in the social cognition philosophy.

The Definitive Definition

Whether or not the authors of various chapters in this *Handbook* self-identify as social cognitionists, all contribute enormously to our understanding of what social cognition is today. It is their collective understanding and commentary that truly define the field, and the approach, of social cognition. This is an impressive group of authors, including a few rising stars, a number of mid-career leaders in social cognition, and a rare assemblage of seven winners of the Ostrom Award for Lifetime Contributions to Social Cognition. In the long run, it matters much more how they construe social cognition than how I might conceive of it. Consequently, it is this book, rather than this chapter, that I believe will ultimately stand as my "defining moment."

Maybe I shouldn't even try to define the field (particularly given my fumbling attempts to do so when queried by the Purdue visitor mentioned above). When asked to define social cognition, perhaps I should just reply that, "I know it when I see it" (Stewart, 1964). And I see it principally in two ways: first, as a subarea of social psychology that examines all of the countless cognitive complexities, mental representations, and processes implicated when Harry meets or thinks about Sally; and second, as an approach to studying Harry, Sally, the pair of them, or the groups, cultures, and societies to which they belong, in a manner consistent with the principles of the approach described earlier. Together, these two facets of social cognition create one of the most exciting, fascinating, influential, and important social sciences to come along in some time. The chapters of this *Handbook* convey that excitement and fascination in describing the content and approach that constitute the field today.

Acknowledgment

Special thanks to Lynda Mae and Erica Schneid for their helpful comments and suggestions on earlier drafts of this chapter.

Notes

1. I'll defer describing the details of that approach until later.
2. At least Wyer and Srull implied that social cognition had borders, which might be an implicit acknowledgment of its status as an independent field.

3. To be honest, in most social cognition research, Harry (the subject) rarely actually met Sally (the stimulus), but he did learn about her, form an impression, and report it to the experimenter.
4. My knee-jerk reaction is that reflexes may be the only behaviors that don't implicate the mind in any way.
5. I absolve the authors of any responsibility for my claims regarding centrality because none were aware in advance of the spin that I am now putting on their work.
6. I acknowledge that my involvement in this line of research may impugn my assertion that this topic is central to the field of social cognition. But bear with me.
7. It may appear from these citations that this interest was principally mine, but in actuality, I think these simply reflect the self-perpetuating nature of chapter writing.
8. Of course, these chapters focus on other issues as well, reflecting the expansive nature of the current field of social cognition.
9. Or, for those who find this term annoying, as "researchers in the field of social cognition."

References

Allport, G. W. (1954). *The nature of prejudice*. New York: Addison-Wesley.

American heritage dictionary of the English language (3rd ed.). (1996). Boston: Houghton Mifflin.

Carlston, D. E. (1992). Impression formation and the modular mind: The associated systems theory. In L. Martin & A. Tesser (Eds.), *Construction of social judgment* (pp. 301–341). Hillsdale, NJ: Erlbaum.

Carlston, D. E. (1994). Associated systems theory: A systematic approach to the cognitive representation of persons and events. In R. S. Wyer (Eds.), *Advances in social cognition: Vol. 7. Associated systems theory* (pp. 1–78). Hillsdale, NJ: Erlbaum.

Carlston, D. E. (2010a). Social cognition. In R. Baumeister & E. Finkel (Eds.), *Advanced social psychology* (pp. 63–99). New York: Oxford University Press.

Carlston, D. E. (2010b). Models of implicit and explicit mental representation. In B. Gawronski & B. K. Payne (Eds.), *The handbook of implicit social cognition: Measurement, theory and applications* (pp. 38–61). New York: Guilford Press.

Carlston, D. E., & Mae, L. (2000). Impression formation. In A. E. Kazdin (Ed.), *Encyclopedia of psychology*. Washington, DC: American Psychological Association.

Carlston, D. E., & Smith, E. R. (1996). Principles of mental representation. In E. T. Higgins & A. W. Kruglanski (Eds.), *Social psychology: Handbook of basic principles* (pp. 194–210). New York: Guilford Press.

Cronbach, L. (1955). Processes affecting scores on "understanding of others" and "assumed similarity." *Psychological Bulletin, 52,* 177–193.

Devine, P. G., Hamilton, D. L., & Ostrom, T. M. (1994). *Social cognition: Impact on social psychology*. San Diego: Academic Press.

Fiske, S. T., & Taylor, S. E. (1991). *Social cognition* (2nd ed.). New York: McGraw-Hill.

Forgas, J. P. (1983). What is social about social cognition? *British Journal of Social Psychology, 22*(2), 129–144.

Hamilton, D. L. (1981). *Cognitive processes in stereotyping and intergroup behavior*. Hillsdale, NJ: Erlbaum.

Hastie, R., & Carlston, D. E. (1980). Theoretical issues in person memory. In Hastie et al. (Eds.). *Person memory: The cognitive bases of social perception* (pp. 1–53). Hillsdale, NJ: Lawrence Erlbaum & Associates, Inc.

Hastie, R., Ostrom, T., Ebbeson, E., Wyer, R., Hamilton, D., & Carlston, D. E. (1980). *Person memory: The cognitive bases of social perception*. Hillsdale, NJ: Erlbaum.

Higgins, E. T., Herman, C. P., & Zanna, M. P. (1981). *Social cognition: The Ontario symposium* (Vol. 1*)*. Hillsdale, NJ: Erlbaum.

James, W. (1893). *The principles of psychology*. Cambridge, MA: Harvard University Press. (Originally published in 1890).

Jones, E. E., & Davis, K. E. (1965). From acts to dispositions: The attribution process in person perception. In L. Berkowitz (Ed.), *Advances in experimental social psychology* (Vol. 2, pp. 219–266). New York: Academic Press.

Kelley, H. H. (1967). Attribution theory in social psychology. In D. Levine (Ed.), *Nebraska symposium on motivation* (Vol. 15, pp. 192–240). Lincoln, NE: University of Nebraska Press.

Kenny, D. A., & Albright, L. (1987). Accuracy in interpersonal perception: A social-relations analysis. *Psychological Bulletin*, *102*(3), 390–402.

Ostrom, T. M. (1984). The sovereignty of social cognition. In R. S. Wyer & T. K. Srull (Eds.), *Handbook of social cognition* (1st ed., Vol. 1, pp. 1–38.) Hillsdale, NJ: Erlbaum.

Ostrom, T. M. (1994). Forward. In R. S. Wyer & T. K. Srull (Eds.), *Handbook of social cognition* (2nd ed., Vol. 1, pp. vii–xii). Hillsdale, NJ: Erlbaum.

Sherman, S. J., Judd, C. M., & Park, B. (1989). Social cognition. In M. R. Rosenzweig & L. W. Porter (Eds.), *Annual review of psychology* (Vol. 40, pp. 281–326). Palo Alto, CA: Annual Reviews.

Stewart, P. (1964). In Jacobellis v. Ohio, 378. U.S. 184.

Wegner, D. M., & Vallacher, R. R. (1977). *Implicit psychology: An introduction to social cognition*. New York: Oxford University Press.

Winter, L., & Uleman, J. S. (1984). When are social judgments made? Evidence for the spontaneousness of trait inferences. *Journal of Personality and Social Psychology, 47*, 237–252.

Wyer, R. S., Jr., & Carlston, D. E. (1979). *Social cognition, inference, and attribution*. Hillsdale, NJ: Erlbaum.

Wyer, R. S., & Carlston, D. E. (1994). The cognitive representation of persons and events. In R. S. Wyer & T. K. Srull (Eds.), *Handbook of social cognition: Vol. 1. Basic processes* (2nd ed., pp. 41–98). Hillsdale, NJ: Erlbaum.

Wyer, R. S., & Srull T. K. (1984). *Handbook of social cognition* (1st ed., Vol. 1). Hillsdale, NJ: Erlbaum.

Wyer, R. S., & Srull T. K. (1994). *Handbook of social cognition* (2nd ed., Vol. 1). Hillsdale, NJ: Erlbaum.

Zajonc, R. B. (1980). Feelings and thinking: Preferences need no inferences. *American Psychologist*, *35*(2), 151–175.

The Emergence of Social Cognition

David L. Hamilton *and* Donal E. Carlston

Abstract

This chapter focuses on the ideas, publications, and events that contributed to the emergence of social cognition. It traces early developments in the history of psychology, as well as in cognitive and social psychologies, that served as a foundation for the field and describes some of the initial empirical work in social cognition that suddenly blossomed in the latter half of the 1970s. It is argued that the social cognition approach represents a merging of a number of important ideas and trends, including the historical cognitivist orientation of social psychology, Gestalt theory principles, and the inception of modern cognitive psychology.

Key Words: social cognition, history of psychology, Gestalt theory

Social psychology has always had a somewhat unique position within the broader discipline of psychology. Psychology is a young science, and although one can trace its origins in philosophical thinking back through the centuries, it was during the 20th century that psychology developed into a scientific discipline. It was during this period that psychology became an empirical science in which knowledge was based on findings from experimental research rather than on armchair theorizing or clinical insights. These developments evolved in both the United States and in Europe, but in quite different ways.

The two approaches that dominated early empirical psychology were behaviorism in the United States and Gestalt psychology in Europe. Both were arguably reactions against the failures of the earlier structuralist approach, which sought to decompose people's thoughts into constituent elements, relying heavily on carefully structured ("trained") introspectionism. Behaviorism rejected the idea of studying thought entirely, preferring to focus on "more scientific" observables such as stimuli and behavioral responses. Gestalt psychology represented a less radical rebellion, rejecting the structuralist focus on presumed constituent elements, but still acknowledging the importance of people's thoughts and phenomenological experiences.

In this brief review of the "prehistory" of social cognition, we trace some of the developments in psychology in general and social psychology in particular that ultimately culminated in social cognition. This is not intended as a complete history of social cognition, as such histories exist elsewhere (e.g., North & Fiske, 2011; see also Carlston, 2010), and are more thoroughly articulated not only in the other chapters of this section but also in other chapters in this volume. Instead, our goal is to provide a summary of ideas and publications central to the emergence of social cognition.

Roots of Social Cognition
Behaviorism

During much of the 20th century, American experimental psychology focused heavily on learning and motivation processes, guided by the behaviorist perspective. This theoretical approach studied the formation of stimulus–response (S-R) associations and the laws that govern their formation, use, and change. Several theorists (Hull, Spence, Skinner, and others) were enormously influential and productive, and the research they and their students generated dominated American psychology for two thirds of the century (roughly from World War I through World War II, and in some contexts, all the way to the Vietnam War!). One of the important features of this approach was a hesitancy to consider the mental processes going on in organisms when learning and motivation occurred. For this reason, it was a strict S-R psychology, seeking to establish laws between properties of manipulated stimuli and consequent overt responses. Skinner was most insistent that psychology could not look into the "black box" and speculate about mental processes that could not be directly observed. This was perhaps a tenable position during this era, when experimental research testing behaviorist ideas and hypotheses was conducted using white rats, whose mental processes were difficult to observe and measure. It became more problematic as researchers began to explore the mental processes of humans.

The behaviorist movement played an important role in establishing psychology as a rigorous, empirical science. Its influence ultimately waned, however, owing to its failure to adequately recognize and investigate the mental processes mediating between the external stimulus and the observed response. This shortcoming was even evident in the behaviorist approach to learning and memory. The "verbal learning" tradition in behaviorist psychology actually had its roots in earlier work by Hermann Ebbinghaus (1885), who rejected the introspective methods of the structuralists and set out to show that cognitive processes could be scientifically examined from an associationistic perspective. Although Ebbinghaus's emphasis on cognitive processes conflicted with a central tenet of the later behaviorist approach, his reliance on simple, meaningless stimulus materials and associationistic principles was congenial to the behaviorists. More specifically, Ebbinghaus examined the role of repetition and rehearsal on the memorization and recall of three-letter nonsense syllables, known as *CVCs* because each consisted of a consonant-vowel-consonant letter string. Although he used only himself as a subject and was denied promotion because of his low level of publication, Ebbinghaus made major contributions, discovering both the learning and forgetting curves, the primacy and recency effects in list learning, and the facilitating effects of previously learned and forgotten material on its relearning (savings effects).

In the verbal learning tradition that later derived from Ebbinghaus's work, researchers presented participants with pairs of CVC nonsense syllables (e.g., DAX—FEP; LIS—PUZ) that they were to learn and commit to memory over a series of trials. Participants were later given the first CVC in each pair and asked to report the second member of that pair. This, of course, is simple associationism, akin to classical conditioning, which may explain why verbal learning persisted as one of the few cognitive foci during the behaviorist era. However, the task reflects some interesting characteristics of memory research during this era. First, the materials were entirely devoid of meaning. In fact, CVCs were pretested to guarantee that they didn't generate any meaningful associates, and any CVCs that were words (BUG, RIP) or resembled meaningful words or concepts (DUM) were excluded. Thus, research on human memory typically presented extremely simplistic and entirely meaningless stimuli. Second, because the stimuli were meaningless, the participant could not draw on prior knowledge to facilitate learning of the associations, eliminating any influence of existing knowledge on the learning of new information.

Researchers adopted such a strategy because their primary interest was in identifying basic laws of association, and therefore their goal was to understand those laws in the absence of other factors (e.g., prior knowledge) that might affect learning. One might legitimately wonder, though, how often people are confronted with the task of learning materials that are totally lacking in meaning and how often they are unable to draw on prior knowledge and experience to comprehend new information. In fact, even researchers within this tradition began to wonder those very things and to study the mnemonics people generated in their efforts to learn the CVC pairs. That is, they came to realize that participants "made up" new (meaningful!) terms that would tie together concepts that were suggested by the CVC nonsense syllables.

The importance of mental processes in constructing "meaning" from stimuli was more congruent with the Gestalt approach, to which we turn in the next section. But behaviorism's failure to explore such processes was only one among many factors that ultimately led to its downfall. Chomsky (1959) wrote a highly influential review of Skinner's 1957 book, *Verbal Behavior,* that convincingly attacked behaviorism as a whole, as well as its specific applications to language. Moreover, the invention of the computer provided a metaphor for the operations of the mind (the "information processing model") that made research into the mind's processes more tractable, and behaviorism's rejection of such processes more arbitrary. As described in the next section, the Second World War led to a new emphasis on the complexities of human behavior for which simple S-R associationistic principles were not adequate. And ultimately, it was probably the emergence of modern cognitive psychology in the 1960s and 1970s that swept behaviorism (and the verbal learning approach) aside and allowed more complex approaches to human cognition to flourish. We briefly consider some of these transitions.

Gestalt Psychology

In contrast to the predominance of behaviorism in America, the development of psychology in Europe was heavily influenced by Gestalt psychology. Whereas the behaviorist movement emphasized learning processes, an important focus of Gestalt psychology was on perception, and particularly on the frequent discrepancy between the percept actually registered by the retina and the perceptual experience of the observer. For example, when looking down railroad tracks, the eye literally sees two converging lines, and yet the mind knows and perceives those tracks to be parallel. Similarly, fragments of a picture can be perceived as the object it represents because the mind "fills in gaps" to make the picture whole. Thus, the whole (the stimulus as perceived) can be greater than the sum of its parts (the fragmentary pieces literally seen). Finally, Gestalt researchers identified a number of illusions in which the identical stimulus can be perceived differently depending on aspects of the context in which it is perceived. For example, in the Müller-Lyer illusion, two lines of identical length are seen as being different lengths owing to the placement of shorter, angled lines at each end. When those lines project inward (toward the center of the line), they resemble arrowheads at each end of the line. When they face outward (away from the center of the line), they look like tails at each end of the line. The original "shaft" is the same length in both cases, but the perceiver "sees" the line with arrowheads as being shorter than the line with tails. This effect demonstrates an important, more general point that the perception of an object (the shaft) can be influenced by elements in the context (e.g., arrowheads) in which that stimulus is seen. This principle permeates the Gestalt approach and, as we shall see, becomes a fundamental principle of social cognition as well.

This Gestalt tradition was most prominently developing during the 1920s and 1930s in Germany. By the mid-1930s, the political climate in Germany had become a serious concern for Jews, and consequently a number of leading Gestalt scholars who were Jewish migrated from Germany to the United States. They brought with them a way of thinking about psychological phenomena that was quite different from the prevailing behaviorist orientation in America.

Development of Cognitive Psychology

Modern cognitive psychology is sometimes dated with the publication of Ulric Neisser's *Cognitive Psychology* textbook in 1967. Certainly, the text helped give form and substance to a discipline that had been emerging over the preceding decade or so, through various publications described below. Early cognitive psychology focused largely on "front-end" (or "lower level") cognitive processes, especially attention and perception, rather than higher order processes such as memory and judgment, which are amply represented in the field today. And much early work in the area continued the behaviorist and verbal learning traditions of using tightly controlled, if not always nonsensical, stimuli and learning conditions. In fact, Neisser (1978) himself urged his cognitive colleagues to get out of their research labs and study memory for more meaningful materials in more meaningful settings.

THE SCHEMA CONCEPT

Contrary to the implications of behaviorism, people seek meaning in the information they encounter and process. In addition, in doing so, they make use of the accumulated knowledge and experience they have had in processing similar information in the past. Though embedded in Gestalt approaches in Europe and in occasional writings in social psychology, this perspective was a minority view until modern cognitive psychology emerged in the 1960s and 1970s. One early proponent of this view was British psychologist Frederick Bartlett, who is generally credited with introducing the concept of "schema," a cognitive structure representing past knowledge that influences the cognitive processing of new information.

In Bartlett's (1932) best-known study, research participants read a story titled "The War of the Ghosts," which was based on native American folklore and thus contained ideas and constructs quite foreign to Bartlett's British students. In attempting to reproduce this story later, these participants introduced many errors and distortions, which led Bartlett to conclude, among other things, that memory for unfamiliar material is poor. More importantly, he suggested that people use their existing knowledge structures ("schemas") to reconstruct recalled material in a way that makes it sensible to them, reproducing elements that are consistent with their schemas, distorting material that can be made to fit, and omitting material that cannot. He believed that these distortions are introduced at recall, though his methods were not suitable for demonstrating such a claim, and subsequent theorists have generally held that schematic biases can also influence processing when information is first encountered and comprehended.

As interest in cognitive analyses grew, schema-like effects were documented in the nascent cognitive literature. For example, Bransford and Johnson (1973) showed that seemingly nonsensical sentences like, "The notes were sour because the seam was split" could be better recalled when a relevant schema ("bagpipes") was activated than when it was not. Similarly, Anderson (1976) demonstrated that an ambiguous paragraph that might be describing either a card game or a woodwind rehearsal was remembered quite differently by physical education students and music majors. In essence, the existence of preexisting knowledge structures guided the interpretation of, and memory for, schema-related information, just as Bartlett had suggested. More generally, the idea that past knowledge shapes the acquisition and use of new knowledge became a basic tenet of the field.

DUAL-PROCESSING MODELS

In 1977, Schneider and Shiffrin published two important *Psychological Review* articles (Schneider & Shiffrin, 1977; Shiffrin & Schneider, 1977) distinguishing between two kinds of information processing, automatic detection and controlled search. These articles applied this distinction principally to attention, a process that had fascinated psychologists back to William James (1890). The challenging issue for psychologists was what mechanisms allowed people to deal with the vast amount of information in the environment by selectively attending to some while ignoring others. Miller (1956) put a number on people's capacity limitations, suggesting that they can really only deal with about seven separate things in short-term memory at any time. And Broadbent (1958) suggested that the selective attention to these "things" was accomplished by some kind of filtering mechanism that operated on physical properties of stimuli. This view prevailed for a while, though ultimately theorists acknowledged that filtering was incomplete and that it was based on semantic knowledge as well as physical properties of environmental stimuli.

The central contribution of the Schneider and Shiffrin (1977) dual processing model was that it suggested that capacity limitations were really only relevant to one kind of processing—that is, controlled processing. They argued that an additional kind of processing—automatic processing—also occurs and that it is independent of capacity limitations and reinforced by repeated practice on a task. In some respects, Miller (1956) anticipated aspects of this argument, noting that past experience and practice could cause pieces of information to be formed into larger chunks (like letters forming a known word), with only the aggregate chunk counting toward the capacity limitations of short-term memory. But Schneider and Shiffrin posited the existence of two entirely distinct processes that could contribute to the recognition of stimuli, and they reported a series of experiments to support their distinction. Later refinements in the theory acknowledged that the characteristics distinguishing these two processes were not perfectly correlated, so tasks might vary on some but not all dimensions, making them relatively, rather than absolutely, automatic or controlled.

JUDGMENT HEURISTICS

People are continually faced with an overwhelming amount of information as they cope with and adapt to a complex stimulus world. Yet accurate judgments and optimal decision making require that people attend to and make use of that information. In the early 1970s, the landmark work of Tversky and Kahneman (1973, 1974; Kahneman & Tversky, 1972, 1973) proposed that people do not logically analyze the implications of all relevant information in making decisions, but rather rely on heuristics or simplifying strategies. These heuristics, though employing nonoptimal procedures, save time and mental effort and also provide reasonably accurate judgments (if they didn't, they wouldn't be useful). However, because they are shortcuts, they can also result in biases and erroneous judgments.

Tversky and Kahneman (1974) generated many ingenious studies documenting people's use of and reliance on heuristics in making everyday judgments. The representativeness heuristic (Kahneman & Tversky, 1972) estimates the likelihood that a particular exemplar is a member of a category by evaluating its resemblance or "goodness of fit" to a prototype or other members of the category. The availability heuristic assesses the frequency of some class of stimuli by relying on the ease with which instances of that category can be retrieved from memory. A third heuristic, anchoring and adjustment, begins the search for an answer with any convenient reference point and then adjusts away from that in keeping with other available information. However, people often do not adjust enough, and therefore their judgments are biased by their initial anchor.

These heuristics provide quick-and-easy ways of making judgments that, rationally, could be quite complex. If it looks, walks, and sounds like a duck, it's probably a duck (representativeness). If it's easy to retrieve some instances of a category, there must be a lot of them (availability). The problem is that these heuristics, though useful, have fallacies built into them that can lead to faulty judgments and decisions.

Tversky and Kahneman's argument that people rely on simplifying heuristics in making judgments, both mundane and important, challenged many more formal models of judgment and decision making that prevailed in the literature and represented a dramatic departure from previous thinking about how judgments are made. Their work also contradicted prevailing economic models of decision making and ultimately led to Kahneman being awarded the 2002 Nobel Prize in Economics.

Social Psychological Antecedents of Social Cognition

To fully understand the antecedents of social cognition, we need to understand some aspects of the development of social psychology as an academic discipline. Although there had been isolated instances (including some very important ones) of social psychological research in the early part of the 20th century, it was in the late 1940s that social psychology became a viable and active enterprise. Why?

In writing about the development of social psychology, Cartwright (1979) made the following observation.

> There can be little doubt that the most important single influence on the development of social psychology...came from outside the system itself. I am referring, of course, to the Second World War and the political upheaval in Europe that preceded it. If I were required to name one person who has had the greatest impact on the field, it would have to be Adolph Hitler. (p. 84)

There are (at least) two reasons for Cartwright's bold statement (both of which he noted). One concerns a consequence of the political climate in Germany, and the other concerns the experiences of American psychologists in the military.

New Arrivals

As already noted, many Jewish scholars in Germany (in all fields of study) left Germany and came to the United States during the 1930s, as the thrust of Hitler's ideology and intentions became clear. Several leaders in early social psychology are in this category. One in particular was influential in the formation of social psychology.

Kurt Lewin was a German psychologist who gained prominence in the 1920s and 1930s for his innovative research and ideas exploring social behavior and strategies for social change. He was also Jewish, and in the face of increased anti-Semitism in Germany, he felt compelled to leave his academic position in Berlin and move to the United States in the 1930s. Lewin's conceptual approach stressed the importance of understanding social behavior in terms of the individual's perceptions of forces within his own "life space," as mentally represented. The idea of "mentally represented forces" operating in one's "mentally represented life space" was, of course, anathema to the behavioristic tradition Lewin encountered when he arrived in America. Lewin's fundamental premise—that it is important to understand how the individual "sees" the social world and the factors that exert influence within it—represents one long-lasting aspect of his contribution to social psychology.

Lewin is consensually acknowledged to be one of the "founding fathers" of experimental social psychology, for several reasons: (1) Beginning in the 1930s, he conducted (and inspired in his students) some of the early, groundbreaking experimental studies that effectively demonstrated that complex aspects of social life could be studied using experimental methods that permit testing theoretical hypotheses. Among them, for example, were studies comparing the effectiveness of different leadership styles, as well as strategies for influencing people to eat less palatable foods in response to war-time shortages. (2) He and his students essentially created an entire new subfield focused on studying group processes, again applying experimental methods to complex and previously uncharted problems. After World War II, Lewin established a Center for Group Dynamics at MIT (which later, after his death, moved to the University of Michigan, where it still exists). (3) He attracted bright and energetic young students (e.g., Leon Festinger, Harold Kelley, Morton Deutsch) who, along with their students, went on to establish some of the premier social psychology programs at major universities in the United States. These researchers also pioneered new domains of research and created new theoretical perspectives that guided this new approach.

Returnees

In addition to the important contributions of newly arrived scholars from Germany, the end of World War II saw many psychologists return from the war effort to their former roles as professors and researchers. During the war, many American psychologists served in the military as experts addressing important practical national war needs, for example, conducting research on what makes propaganda most effective and on increasing the effectiveness of leadership and performance in military units. After the war, these psychologists returned to their academic positions with new interest in studying such topics as attitude change and group dynamics. The specific questions that had to be addressed while trying to solve immediate, practical problems in the war context then led these psychologists, when they returned to their universities, to think about the same questions in more general theoretical terms.

Perhaps the most important example of this effect had an enormous influence on the study of attitudes and attitude change. Carl Hovland, initially trained in learning theory (his Ph.D. advisor at Yale in the 1930s was the prominent learning theorist Clark Hull), spent three years during World War II leading a team of researchers investigating the impact of the Army's morale films and the factors that influenced their effectiveness. After the war Hovland continued this work by establishing the Yale Attitude Change Program at Yale University, bringing together a group of researchers (e.g., Irving Janis, Harold Kelley, William McGuire, Robert Abelson), some of whom had been a part of his research program in the Army. The research conducted by this group (and a series of influential volumes they produced) laid the groundwork for future attitude research (Hovland, 1957; Hovland & Janis, 1959; Hovland, Janis, & Kelley, 1953; Hovland, Lumsdaine, & Sheffield, 1949).

Initially guided by Hovland's behaviorist/learning theory roots, the approach of the Yale group conceptualized attitude change as a process by which the recipient of persuasive communication "learns" that message and, as a function of numerous factors,

is or is not persuaded to accept that communication. Several stages in the process were identified, including attention to the message, comprehension of the message argument, acceptance of or yielding to the message, and retention of the argument, all of which were said to precede behavior change. Research investigated the effects of numerous independent variables – source credibility, order of presentation of arguments, one-sided vs. two-sided arguments, fear appeals, personality characteristics (e.g., persuasibility) of the recipient – on both initial and long-term change in attitudes and behavior (see McGuire, 1969, 2003).

Although its conceptual roots were in the learning theory tradition, over time this approach increasingly focused on cognitive variables that are important in the attitude change process (McGuire, 2003). In fact, this work represents an early example of an information processing approach that ultimately became central to social cognition and that also anticipated later developments in the attitudes literature, such as dual process theories of attitude change (the Heuristic-Systematic Model, Chaiken, 1980; Chaiken, Liberman, & Eagly, 1989; the Elaboration Likelihood Model, Petty & Cacioppo, 1986; the MODE Model, Fazio, 1990).

Other post-war researchers developed new ways of thinking that were more amenable to analyzing and studying their research questions than were behavioristic principles. In this way an emphasis on perceptual and cognitive processes became an important underlying theme in social psychology almost from its beginnings. For these reasons, Lewin's thinking, emphasizing mental representations and their influence on perception and cognition, became an inherent part of the then-emerging discipline of social psychology. It is in this sense that some commentators (e.g., Zajonc, 1980, p. 186) have observed that "social psychology has been cognitive for a very long time." This emphasis was manifested in several theoretical developments that became prominent as social psychology evolved during the 1950s and 1960s. Here, we briefly mention three of these theoretical approaches that further defined and established social psychology for a significant period. Each of them gave a crucial role to cognitive processes in their analyses.

Cognitive Social Psychology
BALANCE THEORY

Fritz Heider, an Austrian contemporary of Lewin, who was also his good friend, similarly emigrated from Europe to the United States. He introduced his "naïve psychology" in the 1940s (Heider, 1944) and later developed it further in an important book, *The Psychology of Interpersonal Relations* (Heider, 1958). Heider's analysis focused on the individual's efforts to understand the regularities ("invariances") in the behaviors, traits, and motives of others, as a means of anticipating future behaviors. Balance theory extended this analysis to interpersonal relations. His P-O-X model considered the relations among three elements: a person (P), another person (O), and some third element (X), which could be another person, some issue, some object, and so forth. Importantly, these relations were defined in terms of how they are perceived by P. For example, P might like O, might like foreign films, and might perceive O as also liking foreign films. The driving principle in this model is that these relations must be in balance, as in the above example. In contrast, if P likes O and foreign films but perceives O as not liking foreign films, then the system is out of balance. According to the theory, P is motivated to maintain balance in these relations, so when they are out of balance, P seeks to change one of the relations and thereby restore balance. In this example, P might decide he doesn't actually like foreign films or perhaps doesn't care so much for O after all.

COGNITIVE DISSONANCE THEORY

Leon Festinger (a student of Kurt Lewin) introduced cognitive dissonance theory in an important volume in 1957 (Festinger, 1957). Like balance theory, dissonance theory examines the relations between cognitive elements, which may be in consonant or dissonant relations. Two elements, *X* ("It is important to eat healthy foods") and *Y* ("I gorge on fast foods"), are dissonant if *Y* follows from *Not-X* ("Fast foods are unhealthy"). Given a dissonant state, the individual will be motivated to reduce dissonance and restore consonance, again by changing one of the elements ("I'll stop eating French fries"). The goal is to maintain consistency among cognitions.

Both balance theory and dissonance theory are, at their core, motivational theories. One's goal is to maintain balance and consonance, and when that fails, one is motivated to take (cognitive or actual) action to restore balance and reduce dissonance. In both cases, however, the motivation derives from the relations between cognitive elements, and successful resolution of this motivated state requires change in at least one of those cognitions. Consequently, a central element of both theories was a focus on the organization of concepts in the individual's mind.

This emphasis later was further developed in social cognitive analyses of cognitive structures. Thus, in the 1950s, we can see the emergence of a clear focus on cognition and its importance in achieving desired end states.

ATTRIBUTION THEORY

In the late 1960s, social psychological theorizing moved another step in the cognitive direction (and away from the motivation for consistency) with the introduction of attribution theories. These theories were derived from Heider's (1944, 1958) writings on "phenomenal causality." As noted earlier, Heider emphasized the perceiver's search for invariances in people's behaviors as a means of anticipating future behaviors and, hopefully, thereby increasing the effectiveness of interpersonal interactions. Heider's analysis, therefore, saw the individual as oriented toward understanding the causes of people's behaviors. He made an important distinction concerning the perceived locus of causation, differentiating *internal* causes (originating within the actor, such as traits, motives, attitudes) and *external* causes (originating outside the actor, representing situational forces that guide or constrain behavior).

Harold Kelley (another of Lewin's students) developed a theory (Kelley, 1967) specifically concerned with the question of when and on what basis perceivers make internal versus external attributions. He reasoned that, for example, if Abe criticized Brad at a poker game, three kinds of information would be extremely useful in making an attribution about why that occurred: consistency (does Abe always criticize Brad at poker games?), distinctiveness (does Abe also criticize others, or just Brad, at poker games?), and consensus (do others also criticize Brad at poker games?). Answers to these three questions should, according to Kelley's theory, help the perceiver decide whether Abe's behavior was due to (caused by) something about Abe (internal) or the social context, of which Brad is part (external). This theory generated many studies testing the attributional implications of these ideas. Later, Kelley (1972) expanded on his theory by stipulating that people hold "causal schemas" that provide generalized representations of how certain types of causes and outcomes are related to each other, enabling the perceiver to make causal judgments even in the absence of some of the information necessary to answer the earlier questions.

Jones and Davis' (1965) correspondent inference theory was also based on Heider's writings but was specifically focused on the question of when people make correspondent inferences, moving "from acts to dispositions." A correspondent inference involves inferring, from a person's behavior, that the person possesses a trait that corresponds to the manifest properties of the behavior. For example, observing that "Jennifer forcefully interjected her opinion into the group discussion" generates the inference that Jennifer is "assertive." Jones and Davis' theory was concerned with the conditions under which such inferences are or are not likely to be made. They postulated that correspondent inferences would be made unless certain constraining conditions were present, such as the behavior being highly normative (virtually everyone is quiet in a library), socially desirable (behaviors governed by social approval are usually positive in value), or lack of choice (he had to do it or he'd be in trouble with his boss.)

These attribution theories were extremely influential and generated enormous amounts of research through the 1970s. It seemed that every issue of *JPSP* contained several articles testing new implications of these theories. There is, though, one characteristic that they share that turns out to be very important. As theories, they are prescriptive and rational. That is, the theories delineated conditions under which one logically *should* make a person or a situation attribution, or when a correspondent inference *should* (or should not) be made. However, as research on attribution progressed, experiments revealed a number of ways in which human perceivers are not as systematic, nor as rational, as these theories described. Study after study uncovered biases by which the perceiver deviated from optimal use of information in processing it and using it for making judgments. Some of these biases reflected the perceiver's selective attention to subsets of information; some involved the use of shortcuts rather than thorough consideration of the available information; and some reflected differentially weighing the implications of various aspects of that information. In other cases, judgments and decisions were influenced by self-serving biases or by ingroup-favoring motives. Thus, the theories were describing *what could be*, but not necessarily *what is*. It became clear that human judgment is often seriously biased and that those biases may have cognitive or motivational origins (Nisbett & Ross, 1980; Ross, 1977).

Comment on the Antecedents

The theories discussed in this section—balance, dissonance, and attribution—were enormously important in helping social psychology emerge from its roots into a full-blown experimental science.

Moreover, in all three cases, the theories were focused in one way or another on cognitions. Balance theory was concerned with the relations among cognitive representations of P, O, and X and especially with the implications of that balance or imbalance for interpersonal relations. Dissonance theory focused on the relation between two cognitive elements, a belief ("I know that smoking causes cancer") and a represented behavior ("I smoke"), and on how the individual resolves the dissonance between the two. Attribution theory sought to understand people's cognitions about the causes of a person's behavior, seeking to answer the question "Why?" in explaining the causal forces driving people's behaviors. If social psychology had a cognitive flavor from its origins, that cognitive aspect clearly developed further during this period.

Despite the important role of cognitions in these theories, it was typically the case that the nature of the relevant cognitive processes was more assumed than investigated. That is, the theories specified various antecedent conditions (independent variables) that would influence processing, and the effect of those presumed processes were assessed on various outcomes (dependent measures). However, it became apparent that, although the theories predicted certain *outcomes* under certain conditions, they did not adequately articulate the *processes* by which those outcomes (e.g., judgments, changes in attitude, decisions) come about. Understanding (and studying) those underlying processes would become a major objective of social cognition.

Emergence of Social Cognition

The history we have briefly summarized established social psychology as a vibrant, exciting area of psychology that was generating fresh new ideas and perspectives on many fronts. By the mid-1970s, however, some new developments began to emerge. The "revolution" in cognitive psychology produced several new theoretical perspectives for thinking about cognitive functioning. Also, cognitive psychologists had developed new methodologies for directly measuring and investigating those processes. Some social psychologists came to realize that these theoretical ideas provided new frameworks for thinking about questions that had long been prominent in social psychology (including the cognitive processes that seemed central to the theories we have just summarized). Moreover, the new methodological techniques developed in that cognitive work provided useful strategies for empirically testing them.

The consequence was that social psychologists began to conduct research drawing on and expanding these conceptual frameworks and methodological tools in order to understand, in new ways, topics that had been studied and discussed for a long time. Consider the following examples, all of which were published *within a five-year period.*

Priming

Higgins, Rholes, and Jones (1977) showed that introducing certain trait concepts in one task can influence people's interpretation of ambiguous trait-relevant information in a completely independent subsequent task. In the first task, participants were exposed to either positive or negative terms for the same trait concept (e.g., adventurous or reckless). Then, in a seemingly independent study, they read about a person who engaged in behaviors related to that trait dimension (e.g., hang gliding, river rafting), and that could be interpreted either positively (e.g., "adventurous") or negatively (e.g., "reckless"). Those who had been primed with positive traits in the first task rated the target person who engaged in related behaviors in the later experiment more favorably. Thus, the activation of a construct in memory persisted and influenced the interpretation of information presented later. Soon thereafter, Srull and Wyer (1979) extended this work and showed that the strength and duration of such priming effects on subsequent processing are a function of both the frequency and the recency of trait activation.

Both the concept of semantic priming and the models used to explain it were imported from cognitive psychology (Collins & Loftus, 1975; Collins & Quillian, 1969; Quillian, 1967). There were, of course, meaningful differences introduced in these extensions of the cognitive work. Typically, social cognitive priming studies focused on effects occurring longer after priming than did the cognitive studies, and typically, the social cognitive studies assessed priming effects using more complex target stimuli (e.g., behavioral descriptions), whereas cognitive studies examined effects on simple semantic concepts. Nonetheless, similar associative mechanisms were used to model and explain priming in both domains, with the social cognitive models deriving partly from earlier cognitive ones.

Cognitive Structures

Concepts (such as the traits used by Higgins et al., 1977) are mental representations or cognitive structures that pertain to some domain of content. Other structures refer to categories or types and are similarly represented in memory and can similarly influence processing. Cantor and Mischel (1977) demonstrated that personality trait information is represented in memory in an organized fashion, with prototypic representations of trait domains. Participants read personality trait items describing an extraverted and an introverted person. Some traits were prototypic of the target type, whereas others were not. Participants recognized traits prototypic of extraversion—both traits that had described the person and nonpresented traits similar in meaning to the prototype—as having been presented earlier. These results show that personality information is organized in memory in terms of trait prototypes and that activation of the prototype can lead to "apparent" recognition of prototypic information, whether or not it was actually presented.

In cognitive research on object categorization, Rosch and her colleagues (e.g., Rosch, Mervis, Gray, Johnson, & Boyes-Braem, 1976) showed that categories have a hierarchical structure, with broad, superordinate categories (e.g., furniture) having subtypes (e.g., chairs, tables), which in turn can themselves have subtypes (easy chair, dining room chair). Rosch's argument was that categorization often occurs at an intermediate level (chair), which is sufficiently broad to be inclusive of numerous instances and yet specific enough to afford meaningful distinctions from other types of instances (table). Any level in the hierarchy can be used in categorizing, but there is an intermediate or "basic" level that is most useful.

Drawing on Rosch et al.'s (1976) work, Cantor and Mischel (1979) argued that prototypic representations are often stored in hierarchies, with each lower level in a hierarchy being subsumed within progressively higher level representations. For example, priests, rabbis, and ministers are all religious leaders, so they all are subgroups under the more general prototype of religious leaders. In turn, religious leaders are a subtype of a more general category of committed persons, which would include other subtypes (e.g., politically committed individuals). At each level, the category is represented by a prototype, and those prototypes can then influence processing and retention, as Cantor and Mischel (1979) showed.

Brewer, Dull, and Lui (1981) documented parallel effects in a very different domain. They proposed that stereotypes are hierarchical structures in memory that can contain different levels of generality. For example, the stereotype of "old people" has subtypes of grandmother types, elder statesmen, and senior citizens. Moreover, different sets of attributes are stereotypically associated with each subtype. Thus, these studies (Brewer et al., 1981; Cantor & Mischel, 1977, 1979) introduced a new way of conceptualizing cognitive structures and demonstrated similar effects in two different content domains. They showed that the same cognitive models can be applied to different areas of content.

Self Structures

Writings about the nature of the self extend back in time to well before psychology became a discipline. Throughout the 20th century, innumerable articles have reported a variety of means by which one's self-concept and self-esteem can be measured, and several theories about the nature and functioning of the self have been proposed. In 1977, Markus introduced a new approach. She proposed that self-knowledge is organized in terms of schematic structures (self-schemas), based on and developed from our past experiences. A self-schema is the cognitive representation of what we know and believe to be true and characteristic of our selves. Self-schematic information is highly accessible in memory, and these schematic structures are used to organize and guide the processing of self-relevant information.

To test her ideas, Markus (1977) identified (through pretesting) groups of participants who differed in traits for which they were schematic (e.g., dependent/independent) and then presented a list of trait terms reflecting the poles of such traits. Participants' task was to indicate whether each trait described them or not. Participants responded more quickly to traits for which they were schematic than those for which they were not. Thus, Markus showed that knowledge of self is organized and stored in self-schemas, that those schemas (and hence self-schematic information) are highly accessible, and that they can therefore influence subsequent processing. Of course, different people are schematic for different traits. Therefore, this concept of self-schema provided a cognitive basis for understanding individual differences in domains of self-understanding.

Stereotypes and Stereotyping

Social psychological research on stereotypes has a long history, extending back at least 80 years (Katz & Braly, 1933). For several decades, the primary focus of this research was on assessing the content of stereotypes, using an adjective checklist (Brigham, 1971). Although useful in tracking the content of various racial, national, gender, and other stereotypes and their changes over time, that body of work (and its methodology) could provide very little information about the mechanisms involved in the formation of stereotypes, how they are represented in our minds, and how they influence our perceptions of and behaviors toward members of targeted groups. In the 1970s, that began to change.

As discussed earlier, schemas are cognitive structures that can guide the interpretation of new information and reconstruction of stored material in a schema-consistent manner (Bartlett, 1932). Stereotypes are cognitive structures that contain one's knowledge and beliefs about a group, and research sought to determine whether they function in the same way.

Cohen (1981), for example, informed participants that a stimulus person was either a waitress or a librarian and then showed them a videotape of this person coming home, having dinner, and so on. The tape contained cues that were consistent with each stereotype. Participants who thought that the target was a waitress better remembered cues consistent with that stereotype (e.g., that she drank beer, watched TV), whereas those who thought that she was a librarian better remembered cues consistent with that stereotype (e.g., that she drank wine, listened to classical music).

Similarly, participants in another study (Rothbart, Evans, & Fulero, 1979) were led to believe that a group was either intelligent or friendly and then read statements describing behaviors performed by individual group members. Each behavior was intelligent, friendly, unintelligent, or unfriendly. Participants later recalled those behaviors. Like Cohen's (1981) recognition findings, Rothbart et al. (1979) found that memory was better for behaviors consistent with the trait expectancy. These authors also manipulated when the trait expectancy induction was induced, either before or after behavior presentation. The better recall of expectancy-consistent items occurred when participants had the group expectancy before presentation of the items, but not when it was induced afterward. This difference showed that the recall effects were due to biased processing during encoding and not during retrieval.

If stereotypes are cognitive structures, they may also influence how information about groups is represented in memory, as shown by Rothbart, Fulero, Jensen, Howard, and Birrell, (1978). Imagine that, in learning about a group, you learn one fact (behavior, trait) about each of many members of the group. Further, imagine that 60% of those facts are of negative valence (e.g., lazy). Alternatively, imagine that you learn the same facts (again, 60% negative), but some group members are presented multiple times, always described by the same fact, and other members occur only once. The people presented multiple times all do negative acts, whereas the people presented once do positive acts, and each subgroup is the same size. Thus, 60% of the facts about group members are negative, suggesting an overall negative impression of the group, but exactly half of the group members do negative things and half do positive things, suggesting a more balanced view. What does all of this mean?

As Rothbart et al. (1978) pointed out, if your memories of and judgments about the group are based on the overall facts learned about group members (60% negative), then the overall valence of your group impression would be negative. If, in contrast, your representation of the group was organized according to the individual group members, half of whom were described only by positive facts and the other half by negative facts, then your memories about and impression of the group would be neutral. Thus, the same information about a group can be represented in memory in different ways. Rothbart et al. (1978) showed that these differences can generate different memories for, and judgments of, the group as a whole. Moreover, this research also showed that the way information gets represented in memory can differ depending on the amount of information being processed. Specifically, heavy task demands can generate different representations (and hence different outcomes) than a light memory load.

Hamilton and Gifford (1976) demonstrated a different role of cognitive processes in stereotype formation. They showed that a cognitive bias in the way people process information that co-occurs with differing frequencies can result in an illusory correlation, such that two groups are perceived differently despite having been described by evaluatively equivalent information. Participants read statements describing behaviors performed by members of two groups, identified only as Groups A and B. There were more statements about Group A members than about Group B members, and a majority of those behaviors were desirable, but the percentage of desirable and undesirable statements describing each group was the same. Information that was distinctive or salient owing to its infrequency (instances of Group B performing undesirable behaviors) had greater impact on subsequent judgments (frequency estimates and group evaluations)

than did less distinctive information. Thus, people perceived an association between group membership and behavior desirability that was not present in the information they read, producing a difference in the evaluative perceptions of the groups that was unwarranted.

Taylor, Fiske, Etcoff, and Ruderman (1978) showed another consequence of distinctive or salient information in a group context. In a small group, one person (a solo) who is of different race or gender than other group members is salient and therefore draws a perceiver's attention. As a consequence, that salient person is seen as having had greater influence on and greater participation in that group's discussion, even though all group members (confederates) participated equally.

The important role of categorization in intergroup perception has been known since Allport's (1954) classic analysis of prejudice. Taylor et al. (1978) introduced what became known as the "who said what" paradigm to demonstrate that categorization occurs spontaneously as group-relevant information is encoded. Participants who had witnessed a discussion among six people (e.g., three white and three black men) were later shown pictures of the men along with a listing of comments made during the discussion. Participants' task was to indicate which person had made each comment. The finding was that people could accurately indicate the race of the person who made each comment, but made more errors in identifying which person within each race had done so. Thus, information was encoded and represented in memory in terms of racial categories of the group members, rather than in terms of individual persons.

Impression Formation and Person Memory

The study of person impressions began with Asch (1946) and has been an active topic of inquiry ever since. Over this time period, numerous theories were proposed about how impressions are formed and how they affect perceptions, but their implications were typically tested by looking at the effects of various manipulations on trait inferences or liking judgments. Hastie and Kumar (1979) introduced a cognitive processing perspective by investigating how information is processed, stored in memory, and retrieved during the impression formation process. They found the counterintuitive result that behaviors that are incongruent with a first impression are recalled better than impression-consistent behaviors. They introduced an associative network-based process model to account for this outcome, adopting principles originally described in the cognitive literature (e.g., J. R. Anderson & Bower, 1973; Collins & Loftus, 1975; Collins & Quillian, 1969; Smith, Shoben, & Rips, 1974). The model described differences in the processing of congruent and incongruent items both during encoding and at retrieval. The specificity of their theoretical account (identifying what happens during encoding and during retrieval to produce an effect) was clearly a new, more focused level of conceptual analysis than had been presented in earlier theorizing on impression formation. Because of that specificity, new (and sometimes nonobvious) hypotheses could be developed to test the model. As a consequence, their model not only stimulated a great deal of research during the next decade but also, and perhaps more importantly, reoriented the nature of impression research to focusing on underlying cognitive processes.

In his classic paper, Asch (1946) had proposed that impressions are organized around trait themes that define the person's personality. Although several studies had reported (and debated) results supporting (or questioning) this proposal, Hamilton, Katz, and Leirer (1980a, 1980b) were able to provide new support for this hypothesis. Participants were first given either impression formation or memory task instructions, and then read a series of items describing behaviors. The behaviors reflected four different trait constructs, several items for each trait, presented randomly. Later, participants were asked to recall those behaviors. Participants given impression formation instructions recalled more items than did memory instruction participants. In addition, participants in the impression condition (but not in the memory condition) recalled the items in a way that was organized (clustered) by traits. Apparently, then, compared with a memory task, the goal of forming an impression induced people to use the trait themes as an organizing framework in processing the items, and that organization facilitated recall of those items. This outcome is reminiscent of Miller's (1956) demonstration that chunking stimulus items into larger units can aid retention. Hamilton et al.'s (1980b) research provided direct evidence that people impose organization on information as they process it during the impression formation process.

These memory findings are only part of the information processing that goes on during impression formation. Carlston (1980) showed that, in addition to what is encoded and stored in memory, inferences drawn from that encoded information can be a basis for later judgments about a person.

Participants read either positively or negatively valenced descriptions of a person and then were induced to make a favorable or unfavorable inference about the person. Their later judgments of the person were influenced not only by the valence of the information they read but also by the valence of the trait inference that had been induced. Thus, inference processes engaged after stimulus information was encoded influenced later evaluative judgments. These findings indicate that different cognitive processes can interact during processing in their influence on dependent measures.

Nonconscious Processing

In much of the work in social psychology before the mid-1970s, an implicit assumption was that people generally know what they're doing and why they're doing it. That is, they have some general cognizance of the mental processes underlying their judgments, preferences, decisions, and behaviors. Beginning in the mid-1970s, some social psychologists began to question that assumption.

Langer (1978; Langer, Blank, & Chanowitz, 1978) argued that behavior often occurs mindlessly, that is, without conscious thought and attention. People have mental representations, called *scripts* (Abelson, 1976), of well-learned routines—for example, about the kinds of behavior sequences that typically occur in various situations. Activation of such a representation can guide behavior in that situation without a person consciously attending to either the stimulus that triggered the representation or the reasons for enacting the behaviors. Such behaviors are, then, "mindless."

Langer et al. (1978) had an assistant approach a copy machine where someone was already making copies and ask to use the machine. Such a request would seemingly require some reason to justify the imposition. In one condition the assistant said, "I have five pages. May I use the Xerox machine because I'm in a rush?," which provided a rationale for the interruption. Most people granted the request. In contrast, in another condition, the person said, "I have five pages. May I use the Xerox machine because I have to make some copies?" This person's request has the general *form* of a justification, but it actually doesn't provide any reason. Yet most people let the assistant use the copy machine (at least when the request wasn't large enough for them to begin processing more carefully). These people acted mindlessly, agreeing to the request without thinking about the actual information provided by the assistant. Although particulars of the study attracted some criticism, Langer's general premise about mindlessness nonetheless raised the possibility that we are not fully cognizant of why we do what we do.

To understand why we do what we do, we would need to be aware of the mental processes that govern our choices, decisions, preferences, and the like. An important article by Nisbett and Wilson (1977) challenged the extent to which people actually have access to the nature of those mental processes. They argued that people often cannot accurately report the effects of stimuli on their inferences, evaluations, and choices, so that when they do describe those processes, they are frequently wrong. Nisbett and Wilson documented numerous ways in which people's verbal reports about how or why they did something were at variance with known causes of their actions (e.g., those manipulated in an experiment).

The papers by Langer and by Nisbett and Wilson were important antecedents to work that soon followed by Bargh (1982, 1984). This work, based in part on Schneider and Shiffrin's (1977) dual processing model, contrasted automatic processes that were unintentional, uncontrollable, outside of awareness, and capacity independent with controlled processes that required conscious intentions, monitoring, and capacity. Bargh (1982, 1984) brought this distinction into social psychology, and the task of understanding that distinction and its ramifications for numerous aspects of social psychological functioning became an important focal point of research for the next two decades.

A New Way of Thinking

The studies cited in this section represent a sampling of a new kind of research that differed from traditional social psychology research in important ways. A new language and, to many social psychologists, some strange terminology were introduced to refer to aspects of mental functioning (cognitive structures, schemas, priming, encoding versus retrieval, associative networks, nonconscious processes). These new ways of conceptualizing reflected a rather dramatic departure from traditional theorizing in social psychology. In addition, these studies included a variety of measures that were quite atypical in traditional social psychology experiments (free recall, clustering in recall, recognition memory, frequency estimation, response times). These research efforts no longer relied on previously popular measures such as Likert rating scales and checklists.

Several points about this work are noteworthy. First, the topics cited above refer to widely varying areas of social psychology—impression formation, the self, stereotypes, judgment and decision making, nonconscious processes—that have separate histories in our literature. By and large (and certainly historically), people working in one area were not also working in the other areas. The studies we have described were conducted independently, yet nearly simultaneously, and in most cases without the researchers being aware of other ongoing research described in this section. Thus, the work we have described is *not* the product of a small group of people interacting with each other and together launching a new enterprise. Instead, it is a reflection of a convergence of several factors simultaneously influencing the ideas and experiments of a number of independent researchers.

Second, all of the research described above introduced new perspectives, new conceptual analyses, and new methodologies in investigating long-standing topics in social psychology. Yet all of these studies were published *within a five-year period*. Something fundamental was happening, something that was bringing about innovative changes in the conceptual and methodological underpinnings of research on several distinct topics. And in every case, the innovations focused on understanding the cognitive processes underlying important social psychological phenomena. We believe these innovations reflect the confluence of several things we have discussed in this chapter—beginning with the perceptual/cognitive tradition of social psychology, combined with the conceptual and methodological fruits of the revolution in cognitive psychology, along with growing frustrations with the limitations of some traditional approaches in social psychology. These developments converged and led to the dramatic changes we have described. In our view, what happened can be referred to as the *emergence of social cognition*.

Social Cognition: An Approach

The emergence of social cognition represents a variety of new research strategies bringing new insights to old topics, spanning several substantive areas. These advances in the late 1970s were soon followed by extension of social cognition into other content areas. The 1980s saw this orientation applied to several new topics, including attitude formation and change, judgment processes, decision making, categorization and intergroup relations, and attribution, among others (see Devine, Hamilton, & Ostrom, 1994).

Given the breadth of topics to which this perspective can be usefully applied, one can easily view social cognition as a general approach that is independent of specific content, rather than as a content area within the spectrum of social psychology. The content view is frequently reflected in numerous social psychological texts that include social cognition as a chapter among others on attitudes, group processes, interpersonal relations, the self, prejudice, personal relationships, aggression, and so forth. But social cognition can be viewed more generally as a conceptual framework and methodological approach for understanding the cognitive underpinnings of any of these topic areas.

What are the basic elements of this approach? There are several common elements in the research examples (described in previous section) that were formative in the emergence of social cognition. Simply stated, we might say that social cognition represents a focus on cognitive structures and cognitive processes. Let us briefly expand on each of these elements.

Structure

The individual does not come to any social perception, social interaction, or intergroup situation in a vacuum. Rather, the individual has a lifetime of experiences that have generated numerous mental representations that can be used in processing new information. Cognitive structure is a generic term that represents any mental representation constructed from past experiences, essentially encompassing concepts of all kinds: traits, attitudes, beliefs, values, memories, scripts, stereotypes, self concepts, and expectancies, among others. These structures contain the person's knowledge, beliefs, and expectancies about some stimulus domain. A social cognition analysis seeks to understand the nature of those generalized representations—how they are represented in memory, the relations among them, the preconditions for their activation, and the nature and consequences of their use in processing information. These preexisting structures can influence all aspects of information processing.

Process

Similarly, *cognitive process* is an umbrella term that represents the variety of mental activities that are engaged in comprehending and elaborating encountered information. A social cognition analysis differentiates several more specific processes and attempts to locate their effects, for example, attention, interpretation, evaluation, inference, attribution, representation in memory, retrieval from memory, and judgment. An important element in a social cognition approach is the effort to measure, rather than assume, their operation. In addition, there is a concern with the *interrelations* among those processes, seeking to understand how each one can influence others in the overall process of taking in and using information.

Interplay Between Structure and Process

The recognition that people have cognitive structures that provide expectancies for various stimulus domains, and that they employ a variety of processes in processing information, leads naturally to another important element in a social cognition analysis: the *interplay* between structure and process. The inherent assumption is that cognitive structures can influence all of the processes that might be, and are, used in processing information. So, for example, stereotype-based expectancies about a target group will influence what aspects of the stimulus information a person attends to, how that information is interpreted, how it is evaluated, the inferences drawn from it, and how (and in what aspects) it is represented in, and then later retrieved from, memory. Similarly, an impression that a person is untrustworthy may guide one's attention to certain aspects of her behavior, color the interpretation of ambiguous behavior that may suggest dishonesty, generate inferences about her that are consistent with this impression, color one's evaluation, and bias retention of and memory for instances that seemingly confirm this impression. Thus, the information originally encountered is transformed by the influence of cognitive structures, such that the mental representation of that information can differ as a consequence of various processes that have operated on it.

Automatic-Controlled Continuum

Finally, any of the processes referred to here may function rather automatically (without the person's intention or awareness) or may execute in a very conscious, deliberate fashion. Whereas the automatic-controlled distinction was originally conceived as dichotomous, we now know that most processing is neither "purely automatic" nor "purely controlled." Thus, we refer to an *automatic-controlled continuum*. The important point here is that any information processing can occur at any point along that continuum. In a social cognition analysis, it is important to determine the mix of automatic and controlled processes that are operative at any given moment.

All of these points are common aspects of a social cognition analysis of any given subject matter, and they are reflected (in varying degrees) in the research examples that we described earlier. Importantly, these points are consistent with the view that social cognition is an *approach* that can be used in analyzing and investigating virtually any topic in social psychology.

A Comment from the Authors

The astute reader of Chapters 1 and 2 may have noticed a bit of a paradox. In this section, we have just argued that social cognition is an *approach* that can be (and has been) beneficially used to guide research on any social psychological topic. One of the current authors feels this is the best, and really the only, way to characterize social cognition, because it is not really a social psychological *content area* (like attitude change, decision making, the self, group processes, personal relationships, etc.). On the other hand, the other author argued in Chapter 1 that social cognition *is* a content area, as well as a useful conceptual and methodological approach to a broad range of topics. He strongly holds that view. The difference, of course, concerns whether social cognition does in fact have a core area of content or whether it is best construed only as an approach to conceptual and methodological analysis.

Well, what can we say? Good friends can disagree—and undoubtedly will discuss the question at length with a bottle of wine on several occasions (and remain good friends). We won't bother you with details of that debate here (but would gladly share the wine with you). We hope that the two viewpoints are clearly developed in these two chapters so that you can form your own informed opinion.

In Perspective

This chapter traces the ideas that contributed to the emergence of modern social cognition, including those both outside and inside the field of social psychology. Arguably, social psychology has always had a cognitive bent, and with the importation of Gestalt theorists and their ideas after the Second World War, this cognitive orientation became more pronounced. But it was really the development of cognitive psychology as a discipline that seemed to stimulate the new form of cognitive social psychology that ultimately became known as social cognition. We outlined three aspects of cognitive psychology that seemed to have had particular influence on social cognition—schema theories, dual processing models, and heuristic reasoning—though we could easily

have emphasized others as well (e.g., depth of processing, associative network models of memory). Stimulated by such ideas, a number of new and important lines of research blossomed during the late 1970s that propelled social cognition into the forefront of social psychology. During a five-year interval, work was published advancing "social cognitionish" approaches to trait priming, the structure of social cognitions, the self, stereotyping, impression formation, and nonconscious priming.

Within a short time, social cognition grew and further expanded its reach. It wasn't long before social cognition had its first edited volumes (Hamilton, 1981; Hastie, Ostrom, Ebbesen, Wyer, Hamilton, & Carlston, 1980; Higgins, Herman, & Zanna, 1981; Wyer & Carlston, 1979), its own journal (*Social Cognition*, begun in 1982), its first textbook (Fiske & Taylor, 1984), and its first handbook (Wyer & Srull, 1984). With these developments, then, social cognition moved from an emerging innovation into an active and dynamic force in social psychology.

Acknowledgment

Special thanks to Anthony Greenwald for his helpful comments and suggestions on earlier drafts of this chapter.

References

Abelson, R. P. (1976). Script processing in attitude formation and decision making. In J. S. Carroll & J. W. Payne (Eds.), *Cognition and social behavior* (pp. 33–46). Hillsdale, NJ: Erlbaum.

Allport, G. W. (1954). *The nature of prejudice.* Cambridge, MA: Addison-Wesley.

Anderson, J. R., & Bower, G. H. (1973). *Human associative memory.* Washington, DC: V. H. Winston.

Anderson, R. C., Reynolds, R. E., Schallert, D. L., & Goetz, E. T. (1976). *Frameworks for comprehending discourse* (Tech Rep. #12). Urbana, IL: Laboratory for Cognitive Studies in Education, University of Illinois at Urbana-Champaign.

Asch, S. E. (1946). Forming impressions of personality. *Journal of Abnormal and Social Psychology, 41*(3), 258–290.

Bargh, J. A. (1982). Attention and automaticity in the processing of self-relevant information. *Journal of Personality and Social Psychology, 43*(3), 425–436.

Bargh, J. A. (1984). Automatic and conscious processing of social information. In Wyer, R. S., Jr., & Srull, T. K. (Eds.) *Handbook of social cognition* (Vol. 3, pp. 1–43). Hillsdale, NJ: Erlbaum.

Bartlett, F. C. (1932). *Remembering: A study in experimental and social psychology.* Cambridge, UK: Cambridge University Press.

Bransford, J. D., & Johnson, M. K. (1973). Consideration of some problems of comprehension. In W. G. Chase (Ed.), *Visual information processing* (pp. 383–438). New York: Academic Press.

Brewer, M. B., Dull, V., & Lui, L. (1981). Perceptions of the elderly: Stereotypes as prototypes. *Journal of Personality and Social Psychology, 41*(4), 656–670.

Brigham, J. C. (1971). Ethnic stereotypes. *Psychological Bulletin*, *76*(1), 15–38.

Broadbent, D. (1958). *Perception and communication*. London: Pergamon.

Cantor, N., & Mischel, W. (1977). Traits as prototypes: Effects on recognition memory. *Journal of Personality and Social Psychology*, *35*(1), 38–48.

Cantor, N., & Mischel, W. (1979). Prototypicality and personality: Effects on free recall and personality impressions. *Journal of Research in Personality*, *13*(2), 187–205.

Carlston, D. E. (1980). The recall and use of traits and events in social inference processes. *Journal of Experimental Social Psychology*, *16*(4), 303–328.

Carlston, D. E. (2010). Social cognition. In R. Baumeister & E. Finkel (Eds.), *Advanced social psychology* (pp. 63–99). New York: Oxford University Press.

Cartwright, D. (1979). Contemporary social psychology in historical perspective. *Social Psychology Quarterly*, *42*(1), 82–93.

Chaiken, S. (1980). Heuristic versus systematic information processing and the use of source versus message cues in persuasion. *Journal of Personality and Social Psychology*, *39*, 752–766.

Chaiken, S., Liberman, A., & Eagly, A. H. (1989). Heuristic and systematic processing within and beyond the persuasion context. In J. S. Uleman & J. A. Bargh (Eds.), *Unintended thought* (pp. 212–252). New York: Guilford Press.

Chomsky, N. (1959). A review of B. F. Skinner's Verbal Behavior. *Language*, *38*(1), 26–59.

Cohen, C. E. (1981). Person categories and social perception: Testing some boundaries of the processing effects of prior knowledge. *Journal of Personality and Social Psychology*, *40*, 441–452.

Collins, A. M., & Loftus, E. F. (1975). A spreading activation theory of semantic processing. *Psychological Review*, *82*(6), 407–428.

Collins, A. M., & Quillian, M. R. (1969). Retrieval time from semantic memory. *Journal of Verbal Learning and Verbal Behavior*, *8*, 240–248.

Devine, P. G., Hamilton, D. L., & Ostrom, T. M. (Eds.), (1994). *Social cognition: Impact on social psychology*. San Diego, CA: Academic Press.

Ebbinghaus, H. (1885). *Über das Gedchtnis. Untersuchungen zur experimentellen Psychologie. Leipzig*: Duncker & Humblot; English ed.: Ebbinghaus, H. (1913). *Memory. A contribution to experimental psychology*. New York: Teachers College, Columbia University (Reprinted Bristol: Thoemmes Press, 1999).

Fazio, R. H. (1990). Multiple processes by which attitudes guide behavior: The MODE model as an integrative framework. In M. P. Zanna (Ed.), *Advances in experimental social psychology* (Vol. 23, pp. 75–109). New York: Academic Press.

Festinger, L. (1957). *A theory of cognitive dissonance*. Evanston, IL: Row, Peterson.

Fiske, S. T., & Taylor, S. E. (1984). *Social cognition*. New York: Random House.

Hamilton, D. L. (1981). *Cognitive processes in stereotyping and intergroup behavior*. Hillsdale, NJ: Erlbaum.

Hamilton, D. L., & Gifford, R. K. (1976). Illusory correlation in interpersonal perception: A cognitive basis of stereotypic judgments. *Journal of Experimental Social Psychology*, *12*(4), 392–407.

Hamilton, D. L., Katz, L. B., & Leirer, V. O. (1980a). Cognitive representation of personality impressions: Organizational processes in first impression formation. *Journal of Personality and Social Psychology*, *39*(6), 1050–1063.

Hamilton, D. L., Katz, L. B., & Leirer, V. O. (1980b). Organizational processes in impression formation. In R. Hastie, T. M. Ostrom, E. B. Ebbesen, R. S. Wyer, Jr., D. L. Hamilton, & D. E. Carlston (Eds.), *Person memory* (pp. 121–153). Hillsdale, NJ: Erlbaum.

Hastie, R., & Kumar, P. A. (1979). Person memory: Personality traits as organizing principles in memory for behaviors. *Journal of Personality and Social Psychology*, *37*(1), 25–38.

Hastie, R., Ostrom, T. M., Ebbesen, E. B., Wyer, R. S., Jr., Hamilton, D. L., & Carlston, D. E. (Eds.). (1980). *Person memory*. Hillsdale, NJ: Erlbaum.

Heider, F. (1944). Social perception and phenomenal causality. *Psychological Review*, *51*, 358–374.

Heider, F. (1958). *The psychology of interpersonal relations*, New York: Wiley.

Higgins, E. T., Herman, C. P., & Zanna, M. P. (Eds.). (1981). *Social cognition: The Ontario Symposium* (Vol. 1). Hillsdale, NJ: Erlbaum.

Higgins, E. T., Rholes, W. S., & Jones, C. R. (1977). Category accessibility and impression formation. *Journal of Experimental Social Psychology*, *13*(2), 141–154.

Hovland, C. I. (1957). *Order of presentation in persuasion*. New Haven: Yale University Press.

Hovland, C. I., & Janis, I. L. (1959). *Personality and persuasibility*. New Haven: Yale University Press.

Hovland, C. I., Janis, I. L., & Kelley, H. H. (1953). *Communication and persuasion*. New Haven: Yale University Press.

Hovland, C. I., Lumsdaine, A. A., & Sheffield, F. D. (1949). *Experiments on mass communication*. Princeton: Princeton University Press.

James, W., (1890). *The principles of psychology*. New York: Holt.

Jones, E. E., & Davis, K. E. (1965). From acts to dispositions: The attribution process in social perception. In L. Berkowitz (Ed.), *Advances in experimental social psychology* (Vol. 2, pp. 219–266). New York: Academic Press

Kahneman, D., & Tversky, A. (1972). Subjective probability: A judgment of representativeness. *Cognitive Psychology*, *3*(3), 430–454.

Kahneman, D., & Tversky, A. (1973). On the psychology of prediction. *Psychological Review*, *80*(4), 237–251.

Katz, D., & Braly, K. (1933). Racial stereotypes of one hundred college students. *Journal of Abnormal and Social Psychology*, *28*, 280–290.

Kelley, H. H. (1967). Attribution theory in social psychology. In D. Levine (Ed.), *Nebraska symposium on motivation*. Lincoln, NE: University of Nebraska Press.

Kelley, H. H. (1972). Causal schemata and the attribution process. In E. E. Jones, D. E. Kanouse, H. H. Kelley, R. E. Nisbett, S. Valins, & B. Weiner (Eds.), *Attribution: Perceiving the causes of behavior*. Morristown, NJ: General Learning Press.

Langer, E. J. (1978). Rethinking the role of thought in social interaction. In J. H. Harvey, W. I. Ickes, & R. F. Kidd (Eds.), *New directions in attribution research* (Vol. 2, pp. 35–58). Hillsdale, NJ: Erlbaum.

Langer, E. J., Blank, A., & Chanowitz, B. (1978). The mindlessness of ostensibly thoughtful action: The role of "placebic" information in interpersonal interaction. *Journal of Personality and Social Psychology*, *36*(6), 635–642.

Markus, H. (1977). Self-schemata and processing information about the self. *Journal of Personality and Social Psychology*, *35*(2), 63–78.

McGuire, W. J. (1969). Attitude and attitude change. In G. Lindzey & E. Aronson (Eds.), *Handbook of social psychology* (Vol. 3, pp. 136–314). Reading, MA: Addison-Wesley.

McGuire, W. J. (2003). The morphing of attitude change into social cognition research. In G. V. Bodenhausen & A. J. Lambert, *Foundations of social cognition: A Festschrift in honor of Robert S. Wyer, Jr.* (pp. 7–24). Mahwah, NJ: Erlbaum.

Miller, G. A. (1956). The magical number seven, plus or minus two: Some limits on our capacity for processing information. *Psychological Review, 63*(2), 81–97.

Neisser, U. (1967). *Cognitive psychology.* New York: Meredith.

Neisser, U. (1978). Memory: What are the important questions? In M. M. Gruneberg, P. E. Morris, & R. N. Sykes (Eds), *Practical aspects of memory.* London: Academic Press.

Nisbett, R. E., & Ross, L. D. (1980). *Human inference: Strategies and shortcomings of social judgment.* Englewood Cliffs, NJ: Prentice-Hall.

Nisbett, R. E., & Wilson, T. D. (1977). Telling more than we can know: Verbal reports on mental processes. *Psychological Review, 84*(3), 231–259.

North, M. S., & Fiske, S. T. (2011). The history of social cognition. In A. W. Kruglanski & W. Stroebe (Eds.), *Handbook of the history of social psychology* (pp. 81–100). New York: Psychology Press.

Petty, R.E., & Cacioppo, J.T. (1986). The elaboration likelihood model of persuasion. In L. Berkowitz (Ed.), *Advances in experimental social psychology* (Vol. 19, pp. 123–205). New York: Academic Press.

Quillian, M. R. (1967). Word concepts: A theory and simulation of some basic semantic capabilities. *Behavioral Science, 12,* 410–430.

Rosch, E. M., Mervis, C. B., Gray, W. D., Johnson, D. M., & Boyes-Braem, P. (1976). Basic objects as natural categories. *Cognitive Psychology, 8*(3), 382–439.

Ross, L. (1977). The intuitive psychologist and his shortcomings: Distortions in the attribution process. In L. Berkowitz (Ed.), *Advances in experimental social psychology* (Vol. 10, pp. 173–240). Orlando, FL: Academic Press.

Rothbart, M., Evans, M., & Fulero, S. (1979). Recall for confirming events: Memory processes and the maintenance of social stereotypes. *Journal of Experimental Social Psychology, 15*(4), 345–355.

Rothbart, M., Fulero, S., Jensen, C., Howard, J., & Birrell, P. (1978). From individual to group impressions: Availability heuristics in stereotype formation. *Journal of Experimental Social Psychology, 14,* 237–255.

Schneider, W., & Shiffrin, R. M. (1977). Controlled and automatic human information processing: I. Detection, search, and attention. *Psychological Review, 84*(1), 1–66.

Shiffrin, R. M., & Schneider, W. (1977). Controlled and automatic human information processing: II. Perceptual learning, automatic attending and a general theory. *Psychological Review, 84*(2), 127–190.

Skinner, B. F. (1957). *Verbal behavior.* Acton, MA: Copley Publishing Group.

Smith, E. E., Shoben, E. J., & Rips, L. J. (1974). Structure and process in semantic memory: A featural model for semantic decisions. *Psychological Review, 81,* 214–241.

Srull, T. K., & Wyer, R. S. (1979). The role of category accessibility in the interpretation of information about persons: Some determinants and implications. *Journal of Personality and Social Psychology, 37,* 1660–1672.

Taylor, S. E., Fiske, S. T., Etcoff, N. L., & Ruderman, A. J. (1978). Categorical and contextual bases of person memory and stereotyping. *Journal of Personality and Social Psychology, 36*(7), 778–793.

Tversky, A., & Kahneman, D. (1973). Availability: A heuristic for judging frequency and probability. *Cognitive Psychology, 5*(2), 207–232.

Tversky, A., & Kahneman, D. (1974). Judgment under uncertainty: Heuristics and biases. *Science, 185,* 1124–1131.

Wyer, R., & Carlston, D. E. (1979). *Social cognition, inference and attribution.* Hillsdale, NJ: Erlbaum.

Wyer, R. S., Jr., & Srull, T. K. (Eds.) (1984). *Handbook of social cognition.* Hillsdale, NJ: Erlbaum.

Zajonc, R. B. (1980). Cognition and social cognition: A historical perspective. In L. Festinger (Ed.), *Retrospectives on social psychology* (pp. 180–204). New York: Oxford University Press.

Measurement and Methodology in Social Cognition: A Historical Perspective

Alan J. Lambert *and* Laura Scherer

Abstract

This chapter offers a historical perspective on the methodological trajectory of social cognition. It begins by considering a number of preliminary issues as they bear on the various definitions of *social cognition,* with special consideration of how methodological issues figure prominently in those definitions. The chapter next considers the various desiderata in methodology, highlighting cases in which these issues are particularly germane to social cognition. This is followed by discussion of the circumstances surrounding the rise and fall in popularity of some prominent methodological paradigms in the field, including a number of important methodological issues surrounding the emergence of dual-process models. The final section considers some recent critiques of the "social cognition approach," placing them in a larger historical context and discussing how they overlap with a long-running debate about the value of experimental paradigms in social psychology.

Key Words: social cognition, methodology, historical perspective

Introduction

Let's face it: chapters on measurement and methodology aren't sexy. Or, at least they're not supposed to be. This state of affairs may be attributable to a general perception about the science of method, often regarded as less enticing than the world of theory. As Diener (2009) has noted, "many people, even researchers themselves, think of measurement as a technical affair to be performed by the slower and less creative scientists, while the geniuses are busy formulating grand theories" (p. 1). However, methodology isn't the Rodney Dangerfield of science it might appear to be: It's actually gotten a lot of respect over the years. For example, many people are surprised to learn that the majority of Nobel prizes in science have been awarded for developments in method and measurement, not theory (Greenwald, 2012).

In actuality, of course, method and theory cannot be separated. These elements are intertwined in any empirical science (Cronbach & Meehl, 1955), producing a bidirectional dynamic such that method can influence, as well as be influenced by, the process in which researchers develop, test, and refine their theoretical formulations. These are the considerations that led Greenwald (2012) to suggest, "there is nothing so theoretical as a good method," an obvious allusion to Kurt Lewin's (1951) famous dictum ("there is nothing so practical as a good theory"). Like Greenwald, we believe that methodology and theory are interconnected. Much of this chapter was written with this principle in mind.

In this chapter, we offer a historical perspective to the methodological trajectory of social cognition. We begin by considering a number of preliminary issues as they bear on the various definitions of *social cognition,* with special consideration of how methodological issues figure prominently in those definitions. We next consider the various desiderata in methodology, highlighting cases in which these issues are particularly germane to social cognition. This is followed by discussion of the circumstances surrounding the rise and fall in popularity of some prominent methodological paradigms in the field. We then consider a number of important methodological issues surrounding the emergence of dual-process models. In the last section of our chapter, we consider some recent critiques of the "social cognition approach." We place these critiques in a larger historical context, discussing how they overlap with a long-running debate about the value of experimental paradigms in social psychology.

Why Methodology Is Especially Relevant to Social Cognition

One of the overall goals of our chapter was to take a "historical approach" to the methodological trajectory of social cognition. In other words, we wished to understand where the field has been, and how and why it got there. However, such discussion begs the question: What, exactly, is *social cognition?* Several writers have attempted to answer this question, each arriving at a somewhat different conclusion (e.g., Devine, Hamilton, & Ostrom, 1994; Hamilton, 2005; Wyer & Srull, 1989; see also Chapter 2 of the present volume). In most cases, however, writers emphasize the importance of method, even to the point of making methodology, quite literally, a defining feature of the field.

For example, according to one view, "social cognition is not defined by any particular content or substantive issue, but rather by an *approach* to one's content or issues" (Devine et al., 1994; p. 5, emphasis in original). By "approach," Devine et al. refer not only to foundational theoretical assumptions (say, about the importance of underlying process) but also to the methodological tools used to understand the phenomenon. A similar perspective is offered by Hamilton (2005), as well as by Wyer and Srull (1989). As such, social cognition can be regarded as a subdiscipline of psychology in which researchers rely on the theory, method, and perspective of cognitive psychology to study matters of long-standing interest to social psychology.

This does not mean that it is useful or meaningful to identify someone as "doing social cognition research" simply because (for example) he or she likes to use priming measures. The key is how those methodological techniques are being *used* on a theoretical level. In other words, social cognition researchers tend to use methodological techniques from the cognitive domain precisely because those techniques are able to provide leverage about issues

(say, prejudice) that social psychologists tend to care about. However, one must be careful not to overstate the influence of cognitive psychology, either. For one thing, even if some of the more frequently used methodologies were originally developed by cognitive psychologists, social cognition researchers often *use* these methodologies in different ways.

To choose just one example, priming methodologies (defined broadly) have been used in a wide variety of substantive and methodological contexts (cf. Bargh & Chartrand, 2000). In the cognitive literature, these tasks were originally developed, at least in part, to understand the automatic and controlled processes involved in semantic activation or other aspects of lexical processing (cf. Meyer & Schvaneveldt, 1971; Neely, 1977; West & Stanovich, 1982). However, priming tasks have been employed by social cognition researchers (with countless variations) in the service of studying all sorts of phenomena that fall well outside of the typical range of issues in cognitive psychology, such as research on mood and emotion (Beall & Herbert, 2008; De Houwer & Hermans, 1994), stereotyping and prejudice (Devine, 1989; Fazio, Jackson, Dunton, & Williams, 1995; Jones & Fazio, 2010), and research on the self (Kraus & Chen, 2009).

What Makes for a Good Method?

Earlier in this chapter, we suggested that there is nothing so theoretical as a good method. However, this begs the question: What determines whether any given method is, in fact, "good?" One easy answer is that good methods satisfy all of the usual criteria one would find in any standard discussion of research design, including various aspects of construct validity and statistical reliability (Campbell & Fiske, 1959; Shadish, Cook, & Campbell, 2002).

Concern with psychometric issues tends to become important whenever a subdiscipline is grappling with a rapid influx of new measurement techniques. The recent surge in popularity of indirect attitude measures (Gawronski & Payne 2010) provides a case in point. On the one hand, many of these measures employ priming-based techniques quite different from traditional, pencil-and-paper approaches (DeHouwer, 2006). Although this *methodological approach* to measuring attitudes is relatively new, the *questions being asked* about these measures are not.

For example, one of the critical questions to be raised about these new measures is the extent to which they are tapping sentiments different from those tapped by traditional attitude techniques (Klauer & Musch, 2003) and whether behaviors predicted by indirect measures tend to be similar to, or different from, the actions predicted by more traditional assessment techniques (Greenwald, Poehlman, Uhlmann, & Banaji, 2009; Lambert, Payne, Ramsey, & Shaffer, 2005; McConnell & Liebold, 2001). This is, essentially, a question about validity. As such, these issues are relevant to important principles (e.g., the well-known "nomological net") laid out by Cronbach and Meehl (1955) more than 50 years ago. Historical concern with reliability (internal, test-retest; cf. Cronbach, 1951) have recently been raised in this area as well. For example, researchers have probed whether such techniques are more prone to measurement error than other measures, as well as whether measurements taken at any given session are likely to be reasonably stable over time (Cunningham, Preacher, & Banaji, 2001).

The aforementioned research nicely illustrates the interrelation between methodology and theory. For example, one provocative aspect of the implicit attitude literature has been the strikingly low correlations sometimes observed between direct and indirect measures. Such dissociations are sometimes used to justify and defend the view that these measures are tapping distinct and largely independent processing systems (cf. Roediger, 1990). However, the lack of correlation between these measures can be partially attributed to the relatively low reliability of indirect measures compared with direct measures. Although this state of affairs is not optimum, there are ways of correcting for such differences in measurement error (e.g., through the use of structural equation modeling techniques). Use of such techniques has revealed that the actual correspondence between direct and indirect measures may be substantially greater than is commonly thought. As Cunningham et al. (2001) note, such results have important theoretical implications, to the extent that they may "contradict the idea of a complete dissociation between implicit and explicit attitudes" (p. 17; see also Greenwald & Nosek, 2008).

Our purpose here was not to provide an extensive cataloguing of the numerous questions that have been raised about indirect measures (see Gawronski & Payne, 2010, for an excellent overview). Rather, our intent was to drive home a larger point: Concerns about the psychometric properties of such measures ("methodology") are inextricably connected to questions about the underlying nature of the attitudes that are supposedly tapped by them ("theory"). At the same time, good methods are not *only* about satisfying well-known criteria of validity and reliability. Below we consider some additional issues that, in our view, are equally important.

Good Methods Offer Strong Theoretical Leverage

Methodological paradigms can also be evaluated in terms of their ability to provide good *theoretical leverage*. In other words, methods can be appraised in terms of their ability to provide insight into, and the opportunity to test, one or more conceptual frameworks of interest. However, measures that have long been considered to be useful (i.e., "good") may turn out to be less useful in the wake of important shifts in theoretical assumptions. We are certainly not the first to make this point. However, its implications are worth exploring in the specific context of research and theory in social cognition.

As one example, research and theory on impression formation was, for many years, dominated by the Asch/Anderson methodological paradigms in which participants were given a list of trait adjectives that ostensibly described a single individual (Anderson, 1971; Asch, 1946). However, the limitations of this approach started to become apparent by the early or mid-1970s, with the "cognitive revolution" within psychology (Baars, 1986). This was especially true with respect to the lack of insight these older methodologies provided about the various stages of information processing (Hastie et al., 1980). As a result, new methodological paradigms, about which we will have more to say later, developed within the field of social cognition to provide better leverage on these matters (Wyer & Srull, 1989).

There is a related sense in which methodologies can offer theoretical leverage: so-called *critical tests*, in which researchers attempt to resolve a controversy between two or more theoretical models. One important issue is whether the method or measure at hand is one for which the competing theories offer distinctly different predictions. If not, this obviously limits opportunity to distinguish between the theories in the first place. In the face of such limited leverage, researchers may of course wish to devise a methodology that can provide better leverage. However, the competing theoretical models, *themselves*, may not be amenable to a critical test in the first place. This can occur for several reasons, but one determining factor is that one or more both models may not be sufficiently well specified on a theoretical level to offer predictions that are empirically distinct from the other model. Unfortunately, such scenarios occur more often than one might think. Indeed, despite the intrinsic appeal of critical tests designed to end theoretical debates, these tests rarely result in a satisfactory resolution to the controversy in question (Greenwald, 1975; 2012; see also Barsalou, 1990).

We have gone into some depth on this issue because it provides some key insights into the trajectory and growth of social cognition. The early years of our field were dominated by experimental paradigms designed to test the ways that people represent information about individuals and groups in long-term memory (Hastie & Kumar, 1979; Wyer & Gordon, 1984). As we shall discuss in more detail later, researchers ultimately discovered that it is relatively difficult to develop methodological paradigms that can provide clear-cut evidence for one type of mental representation over another (Barsalou, 1990). This lack of methodological traction may have been partially responsible for a shift in the theoretical and methodological approach of social cognition research, away from a central concern with mental representation, and more toward what has variously been called *co-acting subsystems* (Abelson, 1994) or *dual processing models* (Chaiken & Trope, 1999; see also Chapter 14 of the present volume).

Good Methods Are Flexible

Good methodologies are *flexible*, in the sense that they can be safely modified (i.e., without jeopardizing the integrity of their original design) to yield new insight into one or more theoretical issues. Here again, this is relevant to the growth and expansion of social cognition. For example, one strength of sequential priming tasks (Neely, 1977) is that the stimulus onset asynchrony (SOA; the length of time between the presentation of the prime and the subsequent target) can be easily modified. This flexibility allows insight into the role of controlled processes because such processes are more likely to occur if SOA is large than if it is small. This flexibility has, in turn, allowed researchers to gain valuable insight into the interplay between automatic and controlled processes (Fazio, 1990; see also Payne, Jacoby, & Lambert, 2005). Our point is not simply that SOA is related to the study of controlled processes because this is already widely known. Rather, the important issue, from our perspective, is that sequential priming procedures are unusually adaptable and that this methodological flexibility, *in and of itself,* has facilitated a great deal of research and theory on the nature of dual processing theories.

As another and fairly recent example, researchers have proposed and implemented modifications of the implicit attitude task (implicit measures; cf. Greenwald, McGhee, & Schwarz, 1998), such as whether participants are instructed to categorize the target stimuli in terms of global "good versus bad" categories or, alternatively, in terms of categories that are more relevant to people's personal attitudes (Olson & Fazio, 2004). The recognition that the implicit measures could be systematically modified has turned out to be valuable in its own right, providing insight into a number of broad theoretical issues in ways that would not have been possible if researchers had simply continued to use the task in a format identical to the way that it was originally proposed.

The "Catchiness" Factor

It is easy to find examples of sound methods that meet any and all criteria for methodological goodness, including but not limited to those noted above (validity, reliability, theoretical leverage, modifiability). However, some methods are more impactful—"catchier"—than others. Here, we refer not only to sheer popularity of a measure (i.e., the number of labs using methodology X), although to be sure, it is remarkable how certain methodologies are adopted more readily than others. Rather, the most impactful methodological paradigms are those that ultimately influence how researchers *think about* one or more substantive issues. What factors make any given method impactful? Or, to borrow terminology from the best-selling book, *Made to Stick* (Heath & Heath, 2007), what determines whether any given method seems to have that inherent "stickiness" of all good ideas?

As Fiske (2003) has noted, one way of predicting the impact of social psychological research is determining the extent to which it surprises us or even makes us uncomfortable, in the sense of challenging our comforting beliefs and intuitions about human nature:

> Having to rearrange how one understands a corner of human nature is very annoying—and a significant sign of a classic in the making. The old classics all had that property of being obnoxious. Who wanted to know that human beings would shock each other to death, simply because a nondescript experimenter told them to do so (Milgram, 1965)? Too disturbing. Who wanted to know that people would believe their own falsehoods, simply because they had been underpaid to lie (Festinger & Carlsmith, 1959)? Very disruptive. Who wanted to know that people would fail to help someone dying, simply because they were ready to let someone else do it (Darley & Latané, 1968)? Quite disillusioning. Yet these are the counterintuitive studies that attracted many of us to social psychology. (p. 203)

Here, Fiske (2003) was primarily focused on the reasons why certain theoretical paradigms seem to "catch on" in the field of social psychology (and, perhaps, other fields as well). However, her point is relevant, too, to method. Without question, the most popular methodologies within social cognition are those that have been used to *demonstrate* these surprising and/or disturbing insights into human nature. As we discuss later, two of the more influential methodological paradigms in our field—priming and memory—were stimulated by some classic studies whose counterintuitive findings strongly challenged conventional assumptions. One could argue that it was the *theoretical implications* of these findings that were most important, not the methodological operations that produced them. We agree. However, such important theoretical findings would have never seen the light of day if the researchers had not been able to formulate methods capable of reliably generating such findings over a wide variety of different experimental settings.

A Tale of Two Paradigms: Priming and Memory

There is no single "defining" method of social cognition. Nevertheless, if one were forced to choose the types of methodological paradigms that are most *representative* of the "social cognition approach" (i.e. the methodologies that most clearly articulate what is distinctive about our field), we believe that these would probably be priming and memory (see Chapters 11 and 17 of the present volume). This point should be self-evident to anyone with even a passing familiarity with the field. However, in case anyone needs some concrete documentation, consider a list of key readings in social cognition recently presented by Hamilton (2005). Of the 32 empirical articles included in that volume, nearly all used some sort of priming or memory method. We consider these two paradigms in turn below.

Priming Paradigms

We use the term *priming paradigm* in a broad way, to include procedures designed to gain insight into the antecedents and/or consequences of mental accessibility (for an excellent review, see Bargh & Chartrand, 2000). In other words, our focus is on a complex *class* of methodological operations, as opposed to any specific type of priming task per se. Priming paradigms have always played an important role in social cognition, beginning with the now familiar "Donald paradigm" used in a series of well-known articles that appeared in the late

1970s and early 1980s (Higgins, Rholes, & Jones, 1977; Srull & Wyer, 1979). In this paradigm, the cognitive accessibility of a given trait was shown to systematically influence the interpretation of an ambiguously described target person (see also Wyer & Srull, 1981).

The actual priming procedures used in these studies were, arguably, not particularly novel. In particular, they often represented relatively modest modifications of methodological techniques that have been used by cognitive psychologists for decades. Hence, the value and impact of these paradigms was not so much that they literally represented brand new methodological innovations. Rather, their impact was driven, at least in part, by the fact that they brilliantly synthesized theory and method, insofar as they showed how the use of well-established priming paradigm could be creatively *applied* to the study of impression formation and other matters of historical interest to social psychologists.

THREE FUNCTIONAL APPLICATIONS
OF PRIMING METHODOLOGIES

Although this delineation is somewhat artificial, priming paradigms (at least as they have been used in social cognition) can be clustered into three broad, somewhat overlapping categories. Beginning in the mid-1970s, priming paradigms were used in the capacity as an *independent* variable, manipulating (often with between-subjects manipulations) the relative accessibility of a given set of targeted constructs. The main thrust of this work was to show how manipulation of cognitive accessibility could have an effect on a variety of different stages of processing, including attention, encoding, and retrieval of social information. Early on, a major focus was on how manipulation of accessibility could affect how people process information about others (Bargh & Pietromonaco, 1982; Higgins et al., 1977; Srull & Wyer, 1979), but later on, this research was extended to show the consequences of such manipulations for the behavior of the self (e.g., Bargh, Chen, & Burrows, 1996; Dijksterhuis & van Knippenberg, 1998).

A second "individual difference" orientation also used priming paradigms. However, the primary focus here was on the use of such methodologies as a psychological *measure* of accessibility, rather than as a manipulation. The main assumption of this work, rooted in early theoretical work by George Kelly (1955), was that certain types of personality constructs are likely to be habitually (chronically) accessible, owing to the centrality of those traits to the self and/or their frequent activation over time (Bargh, Bond, Lombardi, & Tota, 1986; Markus, 1977). For example, "independent self-schematics" are people for whom the trait *independent* is likely to be chronically accessible, as a basis for processing information not only about the self but about others as well.

Priming paradigms also became popular in a third way, when used in the service of assessing attitudes, including but not limited to people's evaluation of stereotyped groups. This paradigm can be seen as a hybrid of the two approaches described above. On the one hand, this approach was concerned with the measurement of individual differences in automatic processing, in the sense that the attitudes being assessed were assumed, at least at the outset of this research, to be based on relatively stable, preexisting associations (Fazio et al., 1995; Greenwald et al., 1998; but see also Scherer & Lambert, 2009a, for a challenge to some of these assumptions). On the other hand, this paradigm also involves manipulation of prime type, although such manipulations are made on a trial-by-trial basis (i.e., within subjects) rather than between subjects. The nature of the target, too, is typically manipulated within subjects, so as to yield all possible combinations of prime and target for each participant. For example, a typical sequential priming task might manipulate the nature of the prime (e.g., black vs. white vs. control) along with target words (e.g., *hostile, kind, wonderful, evil*) that vary in their evaluative consistency and/or denotative relatedness to the primed category.

Hence, one can readily see that the term *priming paradigm* can mean several different things. Nonetheless, most priming paradigms are bound together by a common theme, namely that many aspects of social life are driven by automatized processes over which we have limited control and which often occur largely outside of conscious awareness. Here again, the "discomfort" factor, highlighted by Fiske (2003), becomes relevant. The large role of automaticity in human thought and action is now generally accepted by most researchers. However, the rapid growth and popularity of these priming paradigms can be attributed to the then-radical (and still unsettling) idea that many aspects of our social life are governed by processes over which we have relatively little control. This challenge to our "comfort zone" was perhaps most obvious in the field of prejudice. Here, priming methodologies showed that people's automatized sentiments toward minority groups are often more negative than their own

personal beliefs. Such implications were first demonstrated in a classic and highly impactful study by Devine (1989), about which we will have more to say in a later section.

Explicit Memory Paradigms

As in the previous section, it is important to define our terms at the outset. By "explicit memory paradigms," we refer to studies that used measures of memory (free recall and, to a lesser extent, recognition) in which overt queries are used to probe memories about a previous event (Richardson-Klavehn & Bjork, 1988). As with priming procedures, such measures were originally developed by cognitive psychologists. Further paralleling the trajectory of priming research, the surge of interest in these measures among *social* psychologists was driven by a set of influential articles that appeared in the late 1970s and early 1980s. Just two years after the appearance of the seminal priming article by Higgins et al. (1977), another highly influential article appeared, that by Hastie and Kumar (1979), which employed a widely used measure of memory from cognitive psychology—free recall—as its primary dependent variable. A large part of the excitement over the Hastie and Kumar (1979) article can be attributed to what was, at the time, regarded as a rather counterintuitive finding. In particular, their findings showed that people displayed better recall of information that was *inconsistent* with their overall expectations about another person. Such results were seemingly at odds with the kinds of predictions that a motivational account (say, dissonance theory) might offer, which would often predict better recall of information that was consistent, not inconsistent, with one's prior expectations.

The Hastie and Kumar (1979) article was no less influential than that of Higgins et al. (1977). Indeed, Hastie and Kumar are widely acknowledged as helping to stimulate the emergence of what is generally known as the *person memory paradigm*. This paradigm (which, again, is best regarded as a class of methodologies, rather than any specific technique) most often involved giving participants an initial expectancy about a target person (e.g., as being a warm, kind person), followed by descriptions of behaviors (e.g., *helped an old woman cross the street; set a cat's tail on fire; cheated on a chemistry exam*) that varied in their evaluative consistency with, and descriptive relevance to, that expectancy. The primary dependent variable in such paradigms typically included a surprise free recall task. Importance was placed not only on the types of information that participants recalled about the target person but also on the order in which the information was recalled, the latter typically analyzed through clustering analyses (Roenker, Thompson, & Brown, 1971).

Much of the early momentum driving the emergence of the person memory paradigm reflected underlying interest in explaining why, exactly, one might find superior recall for expectation-inconsistent information and to identify the conditions under which one might find the opposite effect (i.e., a recall advantage for expectancy-consistent information). This goal led to the development of theoretical models that stipulated how overall expectations about a particular person might lead to the formation of different kinds of associative links with specific behaviors or traits, depending on their descriptive and/or evaluative consistency with those expectations (Wyer & Srull, 1989).

However, researchers working in this area eventually developed a much broader set of theoretical aspirations that went far beyond merely trying to explain why people might have better memory for information that violated their expectations. For example, this approach was employed to gain insight into the way that people represent information about various elements of their social environment (people, social categories, events) in long-term memory (e.g., Carlston, 1980; Dreben, Fiske, & Hastie, 1979; Hamilton, Katz, & Leirer, 1980; Lingle & Ostrom, 1979; Srull, Lichtenstein, & Rothbart, 1985; Wyer & Martin, 1986). Such research led, in turn, to further use of traditional memory paradigms in the service of gaining insight into other issues, such as the degree to which people make spontaneous trait attributions about others (e.g., Carlston & Skowronski, 2005; Skowronski, Carlston, Mae, & Crawford, 1998).

A CAVEAT

We do not wish to give the impression that social cognition has been literally restricted to the use of two methodological paradigms, one using priming and one using memory. Indeed, entire subdisciplines within the field, such as attribution research (e.g., Gilbert & Hixon, 1991) and research and theory on emotion (Schwarz & Clore, 2007), do not fall neatly into either of these two classes. Nevertheless, even if those areas did not literally employ priming or memory operations, the *theoretical models* relevant to those areas was heavily influenced by research that did. For example, most of what we now know about the difference between automatic and controlled processing has been afforded by the use of priming methodologies. These insights led, in turn, to an understanding of the differences between heuristic and systematic processes in attitude change and persuasion (Chen & Chaiken, 1999; Petty & Wegener, 1999). This is true even though persuasion paradigms, themselves, rarely use priming methods.

To summarize, a large part of the birth and development of social cognition has been driven—directly or indirectly—by the use of two general classes of methodological paradigms, memory and priming. Without question, these paradigms heavily dominated social cognition for at least 15 years. The more interesting question, however, is why one of these paradigms has continued to thrive and grow, whereas the other has not. We address this issue below.

On the Use of Priming Versus Explicit Memory Paradigms Across Four Decades of Social Psychological Research

During the preparation of this chapter, we wondered if there might be a way of empirically documenting the rapid rise of interest in priming and memory methodologies in the field of social psychology as a whole. As we shall show, although this endeavor confirmed some of our hunches, other aspects of this analysis produced some rather surprising results.

Such an analysis could be done in any number of ways, each with its own respective advantages and disadvantages. For our purposes, we took a fairly straightforward approach, in which we simply tracked the frequency of representative terms appearing in the abstract of articles published in all three sections of the *Journal of Personality and Social Psychology* (hereinafter, *JPSP*). This analysis was done for four separate decades (1970–1979, 1980–1989, 1990–1999, and 2000–2009). As for our focus on *JPSP*, this choice was driven by the fact that this journal is widely acknowledged as the premier outlet in social psychology as a whole and is not specifically oriented toward social cognition research. This provided us with an opportunity to show, albeit in a broad way, historical trends in the use of priming and memory paradigms in a major journal that does *not* explicitly cater to more cognitively oriented research programs. (A parallel set of comparisons was made with other top-tier journals, including *Personality and Social Psychological Bulletin* and the *Journal of Experimental Social Psychology,* and these yielded implications very similar to those reported below.)

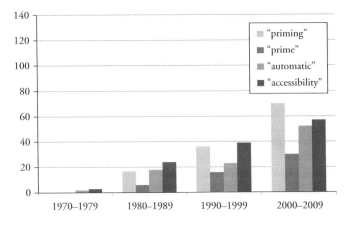

Figure 3.1 Frequency count of priming studies published in JPSP: 1970–2009

In the case of priming, we conducted separate frequency counts for two terms obviously associated with this methodology (*priming, prime*) along with two terms (*automatic, accessibility*) that lie at the heart of the processes tapped by these operations. As seen in the top part of Figure 3.1, these trends suggest a clear and consistent increase in the use of priming methodologies since 1970. Most impressive is the fact that priming methodologies (along with the relevant processes tapped by these measures) were, at least in the pages of *JPSP*, almost unheard of before 1980.

Now consider the explicit memory paradigms. In this case, we conducted an analogous frequency analysis of the general term *memory* along with two specific classes of memory measures (*recall* and *recognition*) and the obviously related term *retrieval*. The results of this analysis are shown in Figure 3.2. On the one hand, one aspect of this analysis parallels that seen with priming paradigms: Beginning in the 1980s, there was a dramatic increase in the number

of *JPSP* publications that employed traditional measures of memory. This trend is almost certainly attributable to the emergence of the aforementioned literature on person memory. It is worth noting that the person memory paradigm relied on free recall far more than recognition. If the popularity of memory studies in *JPSP* was attributable to the rise of person memory studies, then one ought to find the most dramatic increase in studies that used the former (recall) as opposed to the latter (recognition). As seen in Figure 3.2, this is in fact the case.

However, these analyses also reveal something else: a dramatic *drop* in the number of memory studies published after 2000. This decrease is particularly evident in the case of free recall. Indeed, between 2000 and 2009, the number of studies using free recall (N = 22) was about one fifth the number (N = 110) published between 1980 and 1989. Even more surprising, the number of such studies published in the past 10 years is less than half of the number of studies published in the

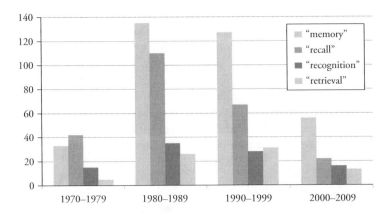

Figure 3.2 Frequency count of traditional memory studies published in JPSP: 1970–2009

10 years *before* the emergence of social cognition (1970–1979).

A Tale of Two Paradigms, Redux

What would have caused a rapid decline in research employing traditional memory paradigms while, at the same time, research relying on priming methodologies continued to thrive and grow? It initially occurred to us that this change might have reflected a *general* disenchantment with explicit memory measures not only among social psychologists but also among cognitive psychologists. This explanation is appealing in that it could also explain the simultaneous rise and sustained growth of priming paradigms that, as noted earlier, can be used as a way to gain insight into implicit memory processes.[1]

As compelling as this explanation might seem, it does not appear to be true. If our analyses reflected a general loss of interest in explicit (vs. implicit) memory processes, one would expect to see a parallel decline in cognitive psychology. To investigate this possibility, we conducted an additional search for the frequency of studies using traditional memory measures (using the same search terms as noted above), but this time focusing on the *Journal of Experimental Psychology/Learning, Memory, and Cognition (JEP/LMC),* a major outlet for the experimental study of memory in cognitive psychology. As before, we conducted these analyses across four decades (1970–1979; 1980–1989; 1990–1999; 2000–2009). These analyses revealed no evidence, whatsoever, of any decline of interest in explicit memory processes, as the frequency with which studies published in *JEP/LMC* remained virtually unchanged during this period. Hence, whatever the reason for the decline in interest in traditional memory paradigms, this decline appears to be specific to social psychology.

In our view, the key to understanding these changes is to consider how these measures were being *used* (i.e., the theoretical issues that were being probed by employing them). In the case of cognitive psychology, such measures have long been used to understand something basic about memory processes per se, such as those factors that can determine one's ability to remember a list of previously presented information. In other words, the memory measure was being used to understanding something about *memory*. Arguably, this was less true of social cognition research. In other words, the original reason for the explosion of interest in memory paradigms, dating back to the late 1970s, arguably had little to do with an interest in social memory per se. Rather, the primary use of such measures was often as a vehicle to gain insight into the kinds of cognitive representations that people might form of single individuals as well as social categories.

This approach was extremely impressive in terms of the level of specificity it attempted to provide about the representations that people might form about their social environment, including the various levels (and sublevels) of the representations that people might form about a single individual. At the same time, researchers were well aware that any given set of "objective" information could be cognitively organized in a variety of different ways. This being the case, researchers naturally started to consider ways of formulating studies that could provide diagnostic tests for whether representational model X versus. representational model Y provided the best fit to the observed data.

Around the late 1980s and early 1990s, researchers began to realize that it was difficult to test between rival (i.e., competing) models of memory representation. As Barsalou (1990) has noted, for example, there is no easy way to test the viability of prototype-based versus exemplar-based models of categorization. This is because any given model can, with only the most modest modifications, handle almost any pattern of results. A similar problem arose for the aforementioned research in social cognition, which relied heavily on memory measures to postulate the existence of rather complex representations of individual targets and/or social categories. Any given pattern of data was, more often than not, consistent with a wide range of representational models. Hence, it became difficult to test whether any given hypothesized representation was superior to other, alternative representational models. This, of course, calls into question the utility of such measures, at least in the context in which they were being used.

A second problem concerned the kinds of theoretical assumptions being made about the tests themselves. Although this was rarely stated explicitly, the prevailing assumption seemed to be that recall and recognition measures were largely free of the influence of controlled processes. This assumption turned out to be unrealistic because any given measure of memory often reflects the operation of controlled as well as automatic processes (cf. Jacoby, 1991). This realization, in turn, arguably began to erode and undercut the usefulness of these measures (again, at least in the context in which they were being employed).

A General Shift in Focus from Mental Representation to Co-acting Subsystems

The differences in trajectory for priming versus traditional memory paradigms can be seen as reflecting a more general shift in focus away from cognitive representation, in the direction of gaining insight into different types of cognitive processes. This includes but is not limited to the distinction between automatic and controlled processes. Although cognitive psychologists had been aware of the importance of this distinction for some time (cf. Schneider & Shiffrin, 1977), it was not until the mid to late 1990s that social cognition researchers really began to probe this distinction (and its potential implications) in any systematic way. One of the earliest signposts of this change appeared in 1994, when Robert Abelson suggested that "the understanding of independent, often antagonistic mental subsystems is, I believe, of great potential importance for social psychology" (Abelson, 1994, p. 27). Abelson's prediction turned out to be prescient, as he correctly anticipated an explosion of interest in a variety of such process dualities (cf. Chaiken & Trope, 1999; Smith & Decoster, 2000).

Theoretical assumptions about process (say, about the nature of automatic vs. controlled processes) are nearly always related to assumptions about cognitive representation. Hence, we do not mean to suggest social cognition has completely lost all interest in mental representation. To choose just one example, one of the current issues to arise from this literature is whether "automatic stereotype activation" is best understood in terms of the activation of exemplars, as opposed to abstracted information about the category as a whole (De Houwer, 2001; Mitchell, Nosek, & Banaji, 2003). Such questions are relevant to a variety of choices that researchers make about the design of their studies, such as whether the task, itself, uses specific exemplars (e.g., individual pictures of black or white faces) as opposed to abstract category labels (e.g., *black, white*). Nevertheless, it would be fair to say that the *primary* interest in these measures is in terms of the information that they yield about process, rather than mental representation.

Earlier in this chapter we suggested (following Fiske, 2003) that such "waves of interest" often occur when research paradigms are able to generate results that not only are counterintuitive but also have the potential to make us feel uncomfortable. This is certainly true in this case as well. Indeed, Abelson (1994) proposes that part of the appeal

of research on these co-acting subsystems is that they suggest some rather disturbing disparities that could exist within any given individual, especially with respect to socially sensitive beliefs and attitudes. One of the first demonstrations of this point was made by Devine (1989), in what is generally regarded to be one of the most influential papers to appear in all of experimental social psychology during the past 50 years.

Through the use of a priming task, Devine (1989) was able to demonstrate the existence of negative, automatized associations with the category of blacks, even among participants whose own personal beliefs about this group were apparently quite positive. Although some of the specific implications of the Devine (1989) article have been modified or qualified over the years (e.g. Lepore & Brown, 1997; see also Gawronksi & Payne, 2010), its impact on the field as a whole cannot be overestimated, especially in terms of effectively calling attention to the importance of considering the role of automatic versus controlled processes in driving social behavior and judgment (see also Chapter 5 of the present volume).

A Closer Look at the Methodologies Used to Test Dual Processing Models

Most researchers now accept the basic premise that mental life involves the operation of dual processes (or, to use Abelson's phraseology, co-acting subsystems), of which the most well known is the distinction between automatic and controlled processes. But how, exactly, did psychologists come to believe that these subsystems exist? What measures and methodologies were used to demonstrate evidence for them?

Here again, there has been a heavy "borrowing" from cognitive psychology and, in particular, theory and research on observed dissociations between different types of memory measures. On historical grounds, one of the earliest discussions of such dissociations comes from a well-known case involving the Swiss neurologist Claparède (1911), who concealed a sharp pin in his fingers while shaking the hand of one of his amnesic patients. As described by Feinstein, Duff, and Tranel (2010),

> The sharp pin surprised the patient and elicited a small amount of pain that quickly dissipated. Within minutes, the patient had forgotten the encounter. Yet, when Claparède tried to reintroduce himself shortly thereafter, the amnesic patient adamantly refused to shake his hand. When pressed to explain her reaction,

the patient retorted, "Is there perhaps a pin hidden in your hand?" Claparède claims, however, that even with repeated questioning the patient could never explicitly remember that she, herself, had been stuck in the hand with a pin. (p. 7674)

Hence, even though the patient displayed no conscious recollection of the traumatic incident when specifically asked, that patient's *actions* (in the form of avoidance behavior) seemed to reflect retention of some sort of memory of the doctor. In essence, then, even though the patient knew that she felt uncomfortable around the doctor, she did not appear to be able to remember the specific episode that gave rise to that discomfort.

As we can see, then, cognitive psychologists have long been aware of the potential for such memory dissociations. However, the current explosion of interest in memory dissociations can be traced, in large part, to the emergence of now-classic series of studies that appeared in the cognitive literature in the early to mid-1980s (Graf & Mandler, 1984; Graf & Schacter, 1985; Jacoby & Dallas, 1981; Schacter, 1987; see also Warrington & Weiskrantz, 1968). Without question, the impact of this research was due to the enormous impact that such studies had on the kinds of theoretical models that researchers developed in a number of different areas, including but not limited to memory. Here again, though, methodology is also important. In particular, researchers were able to develop elegant procedures that could reliably *demonstrate* such dissociations with relatively straightforward laboratory tasks. For example, participants who show poor performance in their ability to remember a previously presented word from an earlier study list (e.g., *dinosaur*) nonetheless showed significantly better than chance performance on a word stem/fragment completion (e.g., *d_n_sa__*) compared with participants who had never been exposed to that word in the first place (Graf, Squire, & Mandler, 1984).

There are at least two ways of interpreting such findings (Roediger, 1990). One, the *separate systems* view, assumes that these different types of memory tasks are thought to tap different and largely independent memory systems, which are assumed to involve the activation of neurologically distinct areas in the brain. In this case, one should expect dissociations between direct and indirect tasks because they are under the influence of largely independent memory systems. The idea of mapping task onto process has proved to be popular in the social cognition literature, especially when explaining dissociations

between traditional (e.g., pencil-and-paper) measures of attitudes and priming-based methodologies. In other words, the dissociations between these measures are often taken as evidence that the two types of tasks are tapping fundamentally different processing systems.

As intuitive as this "different tasks for different systems" view is, it is almost certainly false, at least in its strong form. In other words, it is unlikely that all measures must, necessarily, fall into one of two contrast categories that tap one or the other of two fundamentally different types of memory systems. As Roediger (1990) notes,

> An alternative proposal is that many dissociations between standard explicit and implicit memory tests may reflect the operation of different cognitive procedures required by the tests. Rather than assume that implicit and explicit tests tap separate memory systems, the guiding assumption of processing theories is that memory tests are composed of various component processes and dissociations between tests reflect the operation of different processes. Because it is well-known that many variables can create dissociations between different types of explicit memory tests (such as recall and recognition) the same explanatory principles used in understanding these dissociations can be brought to bear in explaining dissociations between explicit and implicit tests. (p. 1048)

This position (often called the *processing* or *procedural view*) has generally received good support. One of the most significant implications of this work is that it is important to *identify the specific type of cognitive operation being measured or manipulated by any given task*. This is important because two tasks can often tap distinctly different processes, even though they might each "belong" to the same category of task type (i.e., are both considered to be explicit, or are both considered to be implicit).

A concrete example may be useful at this point. Among the many types of implicit memory tasks developed in the literature, some tend to focus on so-called lower level perceptual processes, whereas others are more relevant to higher order conceptual meaning (Cabeza, 1994). Research has shown that performance on one type of implicit task can overlap with (i.e., correlate with, or influence) another type of implicit task, provided that the tasks are sufficiently similar in terms of the kinds of processes they recruit. Conversely, dissociation effects are likely to occur, even between two seemingly similar implicit tasks, if there is a "mismatch" in the type of processes to which they are relevant. Such dissociation might arise, for example, if one measure taps perceptual processes and the other taps conceptual mechanisms. Explicit tasks, too, can vary in terms of whether they tap perceptual or conceptual processes, and replicable dissociations can arise even between two seemingly similar explicit tasks if they are tapping different processes.

Mapping Process onto Measures, and Vice Versa: Challenges to the Process-Pure Assumption

The processing view, noted above, is sometimes misunderstood to imply that there must be a simple one-to-one correspondence between any given task and a single type of cognitive operation, in the sense that any given task recruits one and only one type of cognitive process. However, any given task can, in fact, tap more than one process. As a convenient example from the prejudice literature, consider so-called old-fashioned measures of racism (cf. McConahay, 1986), in which participants are asked to indicate their attitudinal reactions (along a Likert-type scale) toward a series of blatant racial statements (e.g., *blacks are inferior to whites*). Such measures seem worlds apart from a priming-based indirect measure of racial attitude. In other words, such tasks make no attempt, whatsoever, to disguise the fact that they are concerned with racial prejudice. Moreover, the response itself (circling a number) entails an overt, highly controllable action.

Nevertheless, several different kinds of automatic processes are likely to play an important role in guiding responses in such blatant measures of racism, despite their manifest dissimilarity with indirect measures. For one thing, the process of reading and comprehending the question, itself, involves largely automatic processes. This might seem to be a trivial point, but it is not. This is because the racial referents—*blacks* versus *whites*—are quite ambiguous, in the sense that participants could spontaneously interpret the term *blacks* to refer to a particular subgroup, such as poor, young, urban black males, without consciously realizing that they are doing so. For example, the term *blacks* could, depending on the context in which it is encountered, lead to the spontaneous activation of certain types of exemplars over others, and this could obviously affect how people answer the question. The upshot of these considerations is that even the most explicit attitude task is likely to involve a combination of automatic and controlled processes.

An analogous set of considerations applies to many IATs. As just one example, consider the well-known weapon identification task initially developed by Payne (2001). On the one hand, the task satisfies all of the important criteria that are usually associated with implicit measures: Even though the task is designed to measure racial attitudes and beliefs, this is done in a way that avoids overtly asking participants to reveal such information. Moreover, the task itself contains several elements designed to severely restrict the capacity of participants to exert cognitive control over their responses, such as the use of extremely short SOAs. This task also employs the use of a short response window, which forces participants to respond extremely quickly.

These features allow researchers to assess the presence of automatized associations by tracking the impact of white and black primes on the frequency of errors that participants make on the target task. (Most participants are significantly more likely to misidentify a tool as a weapon when it is immediately preceded by a black as opposed to a white prime.) Even with all of these elements in place, controlled processes, too, ultimately play an important role in this type of task (Payne, 2005). Stated differently, even though the task is designed to minimize opportunity for control, it is unlikely that there is a task that literally reduces the role of cognitive control to zero. Hence, just as explicit tasks are likely to involve important roles of automatic as well as controlled processes, the same is true of implicit tasks.

Process Dissociation

The upshot of these considerations is that there is no such thing as a process-pure measure (Jacoby & Dallas, 1981). Or, at the very least, psychologists have yet to find one. Appreciation of this principle has been aided by the process dissociation procedure, as proposed by Jacoby (1991). Originally developed in the cognitive domain (largely in the context of memory research), this procedure has, in recent years, been extended and expanded to the realm of social psychology in a variety of different ways. (Readers seeking more detailed discussion of the process dissociation procedure and its potential applicability to the study of automaticity and control in social cognition may wish to consult more detailed analyses offered by Payne and Bishara (2009; see also Payne, Jacoby, & Lambert, 2005; Sherman, 2008). However, it is useful to offer some general comments on this procedure in the larger historical context of how social cognition researchers have attempted to study automaticity and control.

The process dissociation procedure (hereinafter, PDP) cannot neatly be categorized as a methodological procedure, or as an analytic technique, or as a theory of automaticity versus control. In fact, it is all of these things. The PDP is derived from the theoretical logic of creating two different kinds of within-subjects conditions in which the automatic and controlled processes either do or do not work in opposition to each other. This theoretical logic applies to all implementations of the PDP, including memory, but articulation of this logic in the context of the guns and tools task, noted above, provides a convenient example. In that task, some trials are designed so that automatic processes would foster one kind of response, whereas controlled processes would favor another. This would include, for example, trials in which a tool is paired with a black prime. Here, because the target is actually a tool, the ability of participants to attend to the properties of the target and to maintain accurate control at the response stage (i.e., respond in line with one's conscious intentions) is under the dominion of controlled processes. However, the automatized associations of weapons with blacks is what drives participants to mistakenly press the "gun" key, despite the fact that the target is, in fact, a tool. Other trials are designed so that reliance on either automatic or controlled processes would lead to the identical response. This would include, for example, trials in which black primes were paired with guns; note here that the correct response, "gun," would be made regardless of whether automatic or controlled processes were being used as a basis for responding.

Including both types of conditions in a single study affords the opportunity to derive estimates of the degree to which automatic as well as controlled processes are playing a role in a particular task. As with all statistical or analytic procedures, derivation of these estimates are based on some important assumptions, perhaps the most important of which is that automatic and controlled processes are independent (Jacoby, 1991). Although this assumption has elicited some debate over the years (Curran & Hintzman, 1995; Jacoby, Begg, & Toth, 1997), such independence is, in fact, empirically verifiable. For example, a critical aspect of the guns and tools paradigm is that manipulations influencing opportunity to exert cognitive control, such as varying SOAs, should affect values of the controlled, but not the automatic, parameter. Conversely, manipulations relevant to the accessibility of mental constructs, such as the nature of the prime being presented, should affect the automatic, but not the controlled, parameter.

The PDP provides a compelling illustration of how theoretical a good method can be. Indeed, in recent years, PDP has, in one form or another, been used to address several long-standing issues of theoretical interest to social psychologists (Conrey, Sherman, Gawronski, Hugenberg, & Groom, 2005; Ferreira, Garcia-Marques, Sherman, & Sherman, 2006; Sherman, 2008). To choose just one example from our own research, this approach allowed us to gain leverage on a long-standing ambiguity in what is one of the oldest research paradigms in social psychology: social facilitation (cf. Triplett, 1898). Briefly, the social facilitation paradigm has been concerned with the interesting consequence of public (or quasi-public) settings, namely, that they tend to increase the probability that people rely on well-learned, dominant responses. Two different explanations have been offered for such findings (cf. Baron, 1986). According to the automaticity-based explanation, public settings strengthen or augment the activation of the well-learned associations underlying the production of the dominant response in question. A different, control-based explanation assumes, instead, that the public settings erode people's ability to exert cognitive control over their responses, making it more likely that people will rely on well-learned basis for responses. In other words, the same finding—increased likelihood of dominant responses in public settings—can be explained in terms of changes in automaticity, changes in control, or changes in both kinds of processes.

Lambert, Payne, Jacoby, Shaffer, Chasteen, and Khan (2003) investigated these matters in the context of a series of studies on stereotyping and prejudice. We were drawn to this domain because social facilitation theory offers a rather counterintuitive prediction with respect to the effects of private versus public settings on the propensity of people to act in stereotypical or prejudicial ways. To the extent that stereotypes or prejudicial feelings represent a kind of dominant (i.e., well-learned) response, certain types of public settings should have the potential to increase, not decrease, the probability that people will rely on these stereotypical beliefs as a basis for judgment. This is opposite to what one might intuitively guess to be the impact of public settings, in which normative pressures to avoid the appearance of bias is presumably stronger than in private settings. Across a series of studies, Lambert et al. (2003) were able to show that public settings did in fact produce this kind of counterintuitive result. But, more importantly, use of the PDP permitted heretofore unavailable leverage in showing that these effects were due to decreases in control rather than to changes in automaticity (see also Conrey et al., 2005).

Critiques of the Social Cognition Approach

The social cognition approach has not been without its critics (Baumeister, Vohs, & Funder, 2007; Patterson, 2008) lamenting, among other things, the proliferation of "finger movement" methodologies. We suspect that many of the readers of this handbook take it for granted that studying social psychological phenomena using cognitive methods is a legitimate endeavor. However, this view is not shared by all. Although methodological tools from cognitive psychology *can* be applied to the study of social psychological issues, the question of whether social psychologists *should* be doing so represents a lively area of debate. As one might expect, our own position on this debate is hardly unbiased. Nevertheless, dogmatic defense of any scientific discipline is rarely a good thing, and the growth and maturity of a discipline can often be facilitated by careful and thoughtful consideration of such critiques.

Given the theme of this chapter, it is perhaps fitting that we consider these critiques in a larger historical context. To begin, there is a long history of controversy with respect to the methodologies used within social psychology, with lively and often contentious debate between those who have voiced opposition to laboratory-based methodologies in social psychology (e.g., Babbie, 1975; Bannister, 1966; Gilmour & Duck, 1980; Harre & Secord, 1972; Strickland, Aboud, & Gergen, 1976) and those who have offered vigorous defense of such approaches (Anderson, Lindsay, & Bushman, 1999; Berkowitz & Donnerstein, 1982; Mook, 1983). This debate, which began to emerge in the 1960s, has surrounded several well-known experimental paradigms, including the Milgram obedience studies (Milgram, 1965), the bogus stranger attraction paradigm (Byrne, 1969), and the minimal group paradigm (Billig & Tajfel, 1973).

At least three themes emerge from this debate, including (1) laments about the general artificiality of laboratory settings; (2) concern about the use of self-reports or other pseudobehaviors, such as button pushing, that have no recognizable connection to real-life behavior; and (3) paucity of research on actual behavior between and among two or more individuals. Three viewpoints, below, provide a representative sampling of this perspective. The first was directed specifically at the bogus stranger paradigm

developed by Byrne (1969), whereas the second and third provide critiques of laboratory research more generally:

> What is glaringly wrong here is the contrast between the laboratory situation, in which the action of the participants is confined to a series of dispassionate judgments based upon written descriptions, and the face-to-face situation where a person reacts to another person with warmth and friendliness and a feeling of spontaneous liking…the dissimilarity between the life situation and the laboratory situation is so marked that the laboratory experiment really tells us *nothing* about the genesis of liking and friendship among real people. (Harre & Secord, 1972; pp. 51–52, italics in original)

> The greatest weakness of laboratory experiments lies in their artificiality. Social processes observed to occur within a laboratory setting might not necessarily occur within more natural social settings. (Babbie, 1975, p. 254)

> In order to behave like scientists we must construct situations in which our subjects…can behave as little like human beings as possible and we do this in order to allow ourselves to make statements about the nature of their humanity. (Bannister, 1966, p. 24)

Toward a Greater Understanding of the Meaning of "Artificiality"

As a number of theorists have noted (cf. Mook, 1983), such critiques were likely to have elicited some head scratching among many practicing researchers, who take it for granted that many aspects of their methodologies are, in fact, artificial. What seemed to be missing in these critiques is the recognition that studying human behavior in the laboratory is rarely an end in and of itself. Rather, such observation is made in the service of gaining greater insight into *psychological process*. Clearly, methodologists needed a new vocabulary to make this distinction more clear.

This need was met, elegantly, by Aronson and Carlsmith (1968) through their introduction of the terms *mundane realism* and *psychological realism*. Mundane realism refers to the extent to which the actual methodological procedures in the study correspond to the kinds of experiences we have in everyday life. Many—although certainly not all—laboratory paradigms tend to be low in mundane realism, insofar as several aspects of their methods have no obvious counterpart in real life. On the other hand, *psychological realism* refers to the extent to which the study captures underlying psychological *processes* that are occurring outside of the laboratory. Most important for our purposes, a study can be low in mundane realism but high in psychological realism. For example, the Milgram paradigm is obviously artificial. However, it has been quite successful in showing how certain elements of obedience processes can play an important role outside of the laboratory (e.g., as a way of explaining the actions of prison guards during the Holocaust).

Analogous considerations apply to many methodological paradigms in social cognition. For example, many priming methods are undeniably low in mundane realism (i.e., are "artificial"). However, these studies are designed to yield insight into aspects of automatic and controlled processes that may play an important role in driving behavior outside of the laboratory. For example, there are many real-life domains in which people's ability—or lack thereof—to suppress unwanted impulses is extremely important, such as those pertaining to depressive rumination or to people's efforts to suppress cravings of various sorts (cf. Wegner, 1989). Much of what we now know about suppression in these and many other domains have been derived from laboratory-based priming studies. Again, these methods are often artificial. However, when such priming studies are successful, they are successful precisely *because* they are able to offer insight into relevant processes of automaticity driving behavior in many real-life contexts.

There is another advantage to the distinction between psychological and mundane realism. In particular, it sidesteps the potential confusion arising from the use of the older term *external validity*, which had multiple meanings depending on the context in which it was used. In some contexts, external validity was used more or less synonymously with what Aronson and Carlsmith (1968) would call mundane realism: the extent to which the methodological operations resemble situations and events one sees outside of the laboratory. In other cases, external validity referred to the "generalizability" of the findings, that is, whether their implications extended beyond the specific context in which the study was conducted (e.g., whether a study conducted with adults would be replicated with children; cf. Shadish et al., 2002). Generalizability is an important issue, but it is distinct from the issue of mundane vs. psychological realism.

To summarize, there are three distinct issues at hand here, all of which speak to different aspects of method. One issue is whether any given method does or does not resemble real-life scenarios. This is mundane realism. Another issue is whether the method is able to yield insight into processes that operate outside of the laboratory. This is psychological realism. Entirely distinct from these two types of realism, however, is a third issue, that of generalizability, which raises question as to whether the findings obtained in any given study are likely to be observed for other samples or in other contexts, not part of the original study.

A SENSE OF DÉJÀ VU?

The recent critiques of social cognition are certainly worth attending to, in the spirit of fair and open debate. Nonetheless, it is also fair to ask whether these critiques are specific to social cognition per se or whether they seem to reflect the same concern over laboratory-based artificiality seen in the aforementioned articles, published nearly 40 years ago. In our view, at least, the latter is more likely. For example, these newer critiques offer (among other things) concern about the "science of self reports and finger movements" (Baumeister, Vohs, & Funder, 2007), along with laments about the artificiality of laboratory studies and the lack of attention to actual social behavior (e.g., Furr & Funder, 2007; Hebl & Dovidio, 2005; Patterson, 2008; see also Ickes, Robertson, Tooke, & Teng, 1986; Neisser, 1980).

These authors raise a number of good points. Nevertheless, many (although perhaps not all) of the concerns being voiced by these writers seem very similar to the aforementioned critiques that emerged in the 1960s and 1970s. Curiously, though, these newer critiques make no mention of this earlier debate. This disconnect is unfortunate. Most important is that the distinction between mundane and psychological realism (Aronson & Carlsmith, 1968) helped diffuse some key misunderstandings in a similar debate 30 years ago, and it seems (to us, anyway) that these distinctions would be useful in the current debate as well. The point is not whether finger movements are any "less real" than a handshake. Human behavior comes in all shapes and sizes. The key point, to our mind, is how much we can *learn* by observing any behavior in a variety of different sorts of contexts.

It is also important to realize that various aspects of *mental* life—our thoughts, cognitions, hopes, dreams, fantasies, speculations, wishes, memories, emotions—are an important part of human psychology. In some cases, such mental activity is directly tied to behavior. In other cases, however, the connection is less apparent. Alternatively, there may be no connection at all. We mention this point because there is a temptation to conclude that the *ultimate purpose* of social psychological studies is to understand and predict overt behavior.

To be sure, explaining and understanding behavior is very important. However, understanding behavior is not the *sole* purpose of social psychology. Here, we draw from Gordon Allport's famous (and widely accepted) definition of social psychology: an attempt to understand and explain how the *thought, feeling, and behavior* of individuals are influenced by the actual, imagined, or implied presence of others (Allport, 1985, p. 5; emphasis added). Suppose that Allport had left out "thought" and "feeling" from the foregoing passage and focused only on "behavior." If so, then one could use that perspective as justification for insisting that the validity of any study depends, ultimately, on what it tells us about behavior. However, we suspect that Allport chose his words carefully, highlighting the fact that mental life can be worthy of study in its own right, regardless of whether it is connected to "overt behavior" or not.

Looking Forward

In writing this chapter, our main goal was to provide a historical perspective of social cognition, focusing on its origins and how it has developed and grown over the years. What, then, of the future? We are mindful of the fact that people are not particularly good at predicting their own behavior (Epley & Dunning, 2000; Vallone, Griffin, Lin, & Ross, 1990). What kind of success, then, could we ever have in predicting the behavior of a whole generation of researchers? Nevertheless, it may be useful to offer a few tentative assessments about the future.

One question concerns what the future might hold with respect to research and theory on implicit attitudes and, in particular, the proliferation of different methodological techniques used to measure them. The number of such tasks has now grown to the point that, in a recent volume by Gawronski and Payne (2010), *three separate chapters* were required to address the proliferation of IATs: one for the IAT (Teige-Mocigemba, Klauer, & Sherman, 2010), a second for sequential priming tasks (Wentura & Degner, 2010), and a third for more traditional, pencil-and-paper techniques (Sekaquaptewa, Vargas, & von Hippel, 2010).

On the one hand, the proliferation of these tasks can be seen as a good thing. In other words, the development of new measurement techniques certainly has the potential to generate new insights into the nature

of implicit attitudes. On the other hand, the rapidly growing number of measures raises the risk of theoretical fragmentation and isolation because individual researchers develop preferences for using one particular task to the exclusion of others. In theory, much leverage can be gained by comparing, in a single study, the results obtained by two or more types of implicit measures. There are some theoretical and methodological challenges to the multimethod approach in this literature (involving, e.g., complications arising from the administration of multiple priming tasks to the same participant). However, when such an approach *is* used, it can be very effective.

At least two areas of new growth already seem to be in full stride in social cognition, with each responsible for the introduction of a new set of methodological techniques. One is the rapid growth and expansion of social neuroscience, which, as the term implies, uses methodological techniques from neuroscience (e.g., functional magnetic resonance imaging and electroencephalography) in the service of shedding further light on many of the same basic issues that have long been of interest to social cognition researchers, such as attention, categorization processes, and emotion (Amodio, 2010; Lieberman, 2010; see also Chapter 34 of the present volume).

A second area of research already showing sure signs of growth is developmental social cognition, that is, the application and extension of existing theoretical models within social cognition to the study of judgment and behavior among young children and even infants (Baron & Banaji, 2006; Dunham, Baron, & Banaji, 2007; Olson & Dunham, 2010; see also Chapter 36 of the present volume). This latter point is worth emphasizing, insofar as this extension is clearly relevant to the aforementioned issue of generalizability. In other words, setting aside debates about the supposed artificiality of laboratory settings, an important goal of social cognition research is, indeed, to investigate whether extant theoretical models can be extended to samples and methodological settings not yet considered by previous research.

A Final Word

It has been more than 25 years since the publication of the first handbook of social cognition (Wyer & Srull, 1984). That three-volume set, adorned in a bright green cover, consisted of 17 chapters, nearly all of which were concerned with the already rapid growth in substantive areas of research within the field (e.g., person memory, categorization, automatic vs. controlled processes). Within that volume was a provocative and brilliantly integrative methodology chapter written by Thomas Srull (1984). Looking back at that chapter, it is striking to see how much has changed. These changes pertain to differences not only in the methodological tools being used by researchers but also in the kinds of questions being asked. As social cognition continues to grow and expand, we have little doubt that this will lead to the emergence of new questions along with new tools that are designed to answer them.

Author Notes

This chapter is dedicated to the spirit and creative enthusiasm of Robert S. Wyer, whose general perspective on social cognition pervades much of what we have written here. Special appreciation is expressed to Tony Greenwald and Roddy Roediger for their valuable comments on earlier drafts of this chapter. The authors also wish to gratefully acknowledge the input of several additional colleagues who offered valuable "early perspective" regarding the historical trajectory of social cognition, well before we began writing this chapter, including comments by Mahzarin Banaji, Tory Higgins, Larry Jacoby, Norbert Schwarz, Jim Sherman, and Eliot Smith.

Notes

1. The distinction between "priming tasks" and "memory tasks" is meaningful and reflects a basic distinction made in a number of different disciplines. Nevertheless, this distinction is, in one sense, artificial. In particular, one could make the case that many priming tasks are, de facto, measures of memory. For example, most if not all instances of facilitation in priming paradigms depend on some sort of retrieval of a representation stored in long-term memory. In the absence of this memorial activation, there is no priming. Also, methods that are called "memory tasks" in the cognitive literature are often referred to as "priming tasks" in the social cognition literature. However, these complications pertain mostly to the overlap between priming and *implicit* (as opposed to explicit) memory tasks. The authors wish to thank Mahzarin Banaji for her valuable perspective on this particular point.

References

Abelson, R. P. (1994). A personal perspective on social cognition. In P. G. Devine, D. L. Hamilton, & T. M. Ostrom (Eds.), *Social cognition: Impact on social psychology* (pp. 15–37). San Diego, CA: Academic Press.

Allport, G. W (1985). The historical background of social psychology. In Lindzey, G; Aronson, E. *Handbook of social psychology*. New York: McGraw-Hill.

Amodio, D. M. (2010). Can neuroscience advance social psychological theory? Social neuroscience for the behavioral social psychologist. *Social Cognition, 28*, 695–716.

Anderson, C. A., Lindsay, J. J., & Bushman, B. J. (1999). Research in the psychological laboratory: Truth or triviality? *Current Directions in Psychological Science, 8*, 3–9.

Anderson, N. H. (1971). Integration theory and attitude change. *Psychological Review, 78*, 171–206.

Aronson, E., & Carlsmith, J. M. (1968). Experimentation in social psychology. In G. Lindzey and E. Aronson (Eds.), *Handbook of social psychology* (2nd ed., Vol. 2). Cambridge, MA: Addison Wesley.

Asch, S. E. (1946) Forming impressions of personality. *Journal of Abnormal and Social Psychology, 41*, 258–290.

Baars, B. J. (1986) *The cognitive revolution in psychology.* New York: Guilford Press.

Babbie, E. R. (1975). *The practice of social research*. Belmont, CA: Wadsworth.

Bannister, D. (1966). Psychology as an exercise in paradox. *Bulletin of the British Psychological Society, 19*, 21–26.

Bargh, J. A., Bond, R. N., Lombardi, W. J., & Tota, M. E. (1986). The additive nature of chronic and temporary sources of construct accessibility. *Journal of Personality and Social Psychology, 50*, 869–878.

Bargh, J. A., & Chartrand, T. L. (2000). The mind in the middle: A practical guide to priming and automaticity research. In H. T. Reis & C. M. Judd (Eds.), *Handbook of research methods in social and personality psychology* (pp. 253–285). New York: Cambridge University Press.

Bargh, J. A., Chen, M., & Burrows, L. (1996). Automaticity of social behavior: Direct effects of trait construct and stereotype activation on action. *Journal of Personality and Social Psychology, 71*, 230–244.

Bargh, J. A., & Pietromonaco, P. (1982). Automatic information processing and social perception: The influence of trait information presented outside of conscious awareness on impression formation. *Journal of Personality and Social Psychology, 43*, 437–449.

Baron, A., & Banaji, M. (2006). The development of implicit attitudes: Evidence of race evaluations from ages 6, 10, and adulthood. *Psychological Science, 17*, 53–58.

Baron, R. S. (1986). Distraction-conflict theory: Progress and problems. In L. Berkowitz (Ed.), *Advances in experimental social psychology* (Vol. 19, pp. 1–40). New York: Academic Press.

Barsalou, L. W. (1990). On the indistinguishability of exemplar memory and abstraction in category representation. In T.K. Srull & R.S. Wyer (Eds.), *Advances in social cognition, Vol. III: Content and process specificity in the effects of prior experiences* (pp. 61–88). Hillsdale, NJ: Erlbaum.

Baumeister, R. F., Vohs, K. D., & Funder, D. C. (2007). Psychology as the science of self-reports and finger movements: Or whatever happened to actual behavior? *Perspectives on Psychological Science, 4*, 396–403.

Beall, P. M., & Herbert, A. M. (2008). The face wins: Stronger automatic processing of affect in facial expressions than words in a modified Stroop task. *Cognition and Emotion, 22*(8), 1613–1642.

Berkowitz, L., & Donnerstein, E. (1982), External validity is more than skin deep: Some answers to criticisms of laboratory experiments. *American Psychologist, 37*, 245–257.

Billig, M., & Tajfel, H. (1973), Social categorization and similarity in intergroup behavior. *European Journal of Social Psychology, 3*, 27–51.

Byrne, D. (1969). Attitudes and attraction. In L. Berkowitz (Ed.), *Advances in experimental social psychology* (Vol. 4). New York: Academic Press.

Cabeza, R. (1994). A dissociation between two implicit conceptual tests supports the distinction between types of conceptual processing. *Psychonomic Bulletin & Review, 1*, 505–508.

Campbell, D. T., & Fiske, D. W. (1959). Convergent and discriminant validation by the multitrait-multimethod matrix. *Psychological Bulletin, 56*, 81–105.

Carlston, D. E. (1980). The recall and use of traits and events in social inference processes. *Journal of Experimental Social Psychology, 16,* 303–328.

Carlston, D. E., & Skowronski, J. J. (2005). Linking versus thinking: Evidence for the different associative and attributional bases of spontaneous trait transference and spontaneous trait inference. *Journal of Personality and Social Psychology, 89,* 884–898.

Chaiken, S., & Trope, Y. (1999). *Dual-process theories in social psychology.* New York: Guilford Press.

Chen, S., & Chaiken, S. (1999). The heuristic-systematic model in its broader context. In S. Chaiken & Y. Trope (Eds.), *Dual-process theories in social and cognitive psychology* (pp. 73–96). New York: Guilford Press.

Claparède, E. (1911/1951): Recognition and me-ness. In: D. Rapaport (Ed.), *Organization and pathology of thought: Selected sources* (pp. 58–75). New York: Columbia University Press.

Conrey, F. R., Sherman, J. W., Gawronski, B., Hugenberg, K., & Groom, C. J. (2005). Separating multiple processes in implicit social cognition: The Quad Model of Implicit Task Performance. *Journal of Personality and Social Psychology, 89*(4), 469–487.

Cronbach, L. J. (1951). Coefficient alpha and the internal structure of tests. *Psychometrika, 16,* 297–334.

Cronbach, L. J., & Meehl, P. E. (1955). Construct validity in psychological tests. *Psychological Bulletin, 52,* 281–302.

Cunningham, W. A., Preacher, K. J., & Banaji, M. R. (2001). Implicit attitude measures: Consistency, stability, and convergent validity. *Psychological Science, 12,* 163–170.

Curran, T., & Hintzman, D. L. (1995). Violations of the independence assumption in process dissociation. *Journal of Experimental Psychology: Learning, Memory, and Cognition, 21,* 531–547.

De Houwer, J. (2001). A structural and process analysis of the Implicit Association Test. *Journal of Experimental Social Psychology, 37,* 443–451.

De Houwer, J. (2006). What are implicit measures and why are we using them. In R. W. Wiers & A. W. Stacy (Eds.), *The handbook of implicit cognition and addiction* (pp. 11–28). Thousand Oaks, CA: Sage.

De Houwer, J., & Hermans, D. (1994). Differences in the affective processing of words and pictures. *Cognition and Emotion, 8,* 1–20.

Devine, P. G. (1989). Stereotypes and prejudice: Their automatic and controlled components. *Journal of Personality and Social Psychology, 56,* 5–18.

Devine, P. G., Hamilton, D. L., & Ostrom, T. M. (Eds.) (1994). *Social cognition: Impact on social psychology.* San Diego, CA: Academic Press.

Diener, E. (2009). *The science of well-being: The collected works of Ed Diener. Social Indicators Research Series (*Vol. 37*).* The Netherlands: Springer.

Dijksterhuis, A., & van Knippenberg, A. (1998). The relation between perception and behavior or how to win a game of Trivial Pursuit. *Journal of Personality and Social Psychology, 74,* 865–877.

Dreben, E. K., Fiske, S. T., & Hastie, R. (1979). The independence of item and evaluation information: Impression and recall order effects in behavior-based impression formation. *Journal of Personality and Social Psychology, 37,* 1758–1768.

Dunham, Y., Baron, A., & Banaji, M. R. (2007). Children and social groups: A developmental analysis of implicit consistency in Hispanic Americans. *Self and Identity, 6*(2–3), 238–255.

Epley, N., & Dunning, D. (2000). Feeling "holier than thou": Are self-serving assessments produced by errors in self or social psychology? *Journal of Personality and Social Psychology, 79,* 861–875.

Fazio, R. H. (1990). Multiple processes by which attitudes guide behavior: The MODE model as an integrative framework. In M. P. Zanna (Ed.), *Advances in experimental social psychology* (Vol. 23, pp. 75–110). New York: Academic Press.

Fazio, R. H., Jackson, J. R., Dunton, B. C., & Williams, C. J. (1995). Variability in automatic activation as an unobtrusive measure of racial attitudes: A bona fide pipeline? *Journal of Personality and Social Psychology, 69,* 1013–1027.

Feinstein, J. S., Duff, M. C., & Tranel, D. (2010). The sustained experience of emotion after loss of memory in patients with amnesia. *Proceedings of the National Academy of Sciences, 107,* 7674–7679.

Ferreira, M. B., Garcia-Marques, L., Sherman, S. J., & Sherman, J. W. (2006). Automatic and controlled components of judgment and decision making. *Journal of Personality and Social Psychology, 91*(5), 797–813.

Fiske, S. T. (2003). The discomfort index: How to spot a really good idea whose time has come. *Psychological Inquiry, 14,* 201–206.

Furr, R. M., & Funder, D. C. (2007). Behavioral observation. In R. Robins, C. Fraley, & R. Krueger (Eds.), *Handbook of research methods in personality psychology* (pp. 273–291). New York: Guilford Press

Gawronski, B., & Payne, B. (Eds.) (2010). *Handbook of implicit social cognition: Measurement, theory, and applications.* New York: Guilford Press.

Gilbert, D. T., & Hixon, J. G. (1991). The trouble of thinking: Activation and application of stereotypic beliefs. *Journal of Personality and Social Psychology, 60,* 509–517.

Gilmour, R., & Duck, S. (1980). *The development of social psychology.* London: Academic Press

Graf, E., Squire, L. R., & Mandler, G. (1984). The information that amnesic patients do not forget. *Journal of Experimental Psychology: Learning, Memory, and Cognition, 10,* 164–178.

Graf, P., & Mandler, G. (1984). Activation makes words more accessible, but not necessarily more retrievable. *Journal of Verbal Learning and Verbal Behavior, 23,* 553–568.

Graf, P., & Schacter, D. L. (1985). Implicit and explicit memory for new associations in normal and amnesic subjects. *Journal of Experimental Psychology: Learning, Memory, and Cognition, 11,* 501–551.

Greenwald, A. G. (1975). On the inconclusiveness of "crucial" cognitive tests of dissonance versus self-perception theories. *Journal of Experimental Social Psychology, 11,* 490–499.

Greenwald, A. G. (2012). There is nothing so theoretical as a good method. *Perspectives on Psychological Science, 77,* 99–108.

Greenwald, A. G., McGhee, D. E. & Schwartz, J. L. (1998). Measuring individual differences in implicit cognition: The implicit association test. *Journal of Personality and Social Psychology, 74,* 1464–1480.

Greenwald, A. G., & Nosek, B. A. (2008). Attitudinal dissociation: What does it mean? In R. E. Petty, R. H. Fazio, & P. Briñol (Eds.), *Attitudes: Insights from the new implicit measures* (pp. 65–82). Hillsdale, NJ: Erlbaum.

Greenwald, A. G., Poehlman, T. A., Uhlmann, E. L., & Banaji, M. R. (2009). Understanding and using the Implicit Association Test: III. Meta-analysis of predictive validity. *Journal of Personality and Social Psychology, 97,* 17–41.

Hamilton, D. (Ed.). (2005). *Social cognition: Key readings*. New York: Psychology Press.

Hamilton, D. L., Katz, L. B., & Leirer, V. O. (1980). Organizational processes in impression formation. In R. Hastie, T. M. Ostrom, E. B.Ebbesen, R. S. Wyer, D. L. Hamilton, & D. E. Carlston (Eds.), *Person memory: The cognitive basis of social perception* (pp. 121–153). Hillsdale, NJ: Erlbaum.

Harre, R., & Secord, P. F. (1972). *The explanation of social behaviour*. Oxford, UK: Blackwell.

Hastie, R., & Kumar, P. A. (1979). Person memory: Personality traits as organizing principles in memory for behaviors. *Journal of Personality and Social Psychology, 37*, 25–38.

Hastie, R., Ostrom, T. M., Ebbesen, E. B., Wyer, R. S., Hamilton. D. L., & Carlston, D. E. (Eds.) (1980). *Person memory: The cognitive basis of social perception*. Hillsdale, NJ: Erlbaum.

Hebl, M., & Dovidio, J. F. (2005). Promoting the "social" in the examination of social stigmas. *Personality and Social Psychological Review, 9*, 156–182.

Heath, C., & Heath, D. (2007). *Made to Stick: Why Some Ideas Survive and Others Die*. Random House.

Higgins, E. T, Rholes, W. S., & Jones, C. R. (1977). Category accessibility and impression formation. *Journal of Experimental Social Psychology, 13*, 141–154.

Ickes, W., Robertson, E., Tooke, W., & Teng, G. (1986). Naturalistic social cognition: Methodology, assessment, and validation. *Journal of Personality and Social Psychology, 51*, 66–82.

Jacoby, L. L. (1991). A process dissociation framework: Separating automatic from intentional uses of memory. *Journal of Memory and Language, 30*, 513–541.

Jacoby, L. L., Begg, I. M., & Toth, J. P. (1997). In defense of functional independence: Violations of assumptions underlying the process–dissociation procedure? *Journal of Experimental Psychology: Learning, Memory, and Cognition, 23*, 484–495.

Jacoby, L. L., & Dallas, M. (1981). On the relationship between autobiographical and perceptual learning. *Journal of Experimental Psychology: General, 110*, 306–334.

Jones, C. R., & Fazio, R. H. (2010). Person categorization and automatic racial stereotyping effects on weapon identification. *Personality and Social Psychology Bulletin, 36*, 1073–1085.

Kelly, G. (1955). *The psychology of personal constructs* (Vols. I, II). New York: W. W. Norton.

Klauer, K. C. & Musch, J. (2003). Affective priming: Findings and theories. In J. Musch & K. C. Klauer (Eds.), *The psychology of evaluation: Affective processes in cognition and emotion* (pp. 7–50). Mahwah, NJ: Erlbaum.

Kraus, M. W., & Chen, S. (2009). Striving to be known by significant others: Automatic activation of self-verification goals in relationship contexts. *Journal of Personality and Social Psychology, 97*, 58–73.

Lambert, A. J., Payne, B. K., Jacoby, L. L. Shaffer, L. M., Chasteen, A. L., & Khan, S. K. (2003). Stereotypes as dominant responses: On the "social facilitation" of prejudice in anticipated public contexts. *Journal of Personality and Social Psychology, 84*, 277–295.

Lambert, A. J., Payne, B. K., Ramsey, S., & Shaffer, L. M. (2005). On the predictive validity of implicit attitude measures: The moderating effect of perceived group variability *Journal of Experimental Social Psychology, 41*, 114–128.

Lepore, L., & Brown R. (1997). Category and stereotype activation: Is prejudice inevitable? *Journal of Personality and Social Psychology, 72*(2), 275–287.

Lewin, K. (1951) *Field theory in social science: Selected theoretical papers*. In: D. Cartwright (Ed.). New York: Harper & Row.

Lieberman, M. D. (2010). Social cognitive neuroscience. In : S. T. Fiske, D. T. Gilbert, & G. Lindzey (Eds.), *Handbook of social psychology* (5th ed., pp. 143–193). New York: McGraw-Hill.

Lingle, J. H., & Ostrom, T. M. (1979). Retrieval selectivity in memory based impression judgments. *Journal of Personality and Social Psychology,37*, 180–194.

Markus, H. (1977). Self-schemata and processing information about the self. *Journal of Personality and Social Psychology, 35*, 63–78.

McConnell, A. R., & Liebold, J. M. (2001). Relations between the implicit association test, explicit racial attitudes, and discriminatory behavior. *Journal of Experimental Social Psychology, 37*,435–442.

McConahay, J. B. (1986). Modern racism, ambivalence, and the Modern Racism Scale. In J. Dovidio & S. Gaertner (Eds.), *Prejudice, discrimination, and racism* (pp. 91–125). Orlando, FL: Academic Press.

Meyer, D. E., & Schvaneveldt, R. W. (1971). Facilitation in recognizing pairs of words: Evidence of a dependence between retrieval operations. *Journal of Experimental Psychology: General, 90*, 227–234.

Milgram, S. (1965). Some conditions of obedience and disobedience to authority. *Human Relations, 18*(1), 57–76.

Mitchell, J. P., Nosek, B. A., & Banaji, M. R. (2003). Contextual variations in implicit evaluation. *Journal of Experimental Psychology: General, 132*, 455–469.

Mook, D. G. (1983). In defense of external invalidity. *American Psychologist, 38*, 379–387.

Neely, J. H. (1977). Semantic priming and retrieval from lexical memory: Roles of inhibitionless spreading activation and limited-capacity attention. *Journal of Experimental Psychology: General, 106*, 226–254.

Neisser, U. (1980). On "social knowing." *Personality and Social Psychology Bulletin, 6*, 601–605.

Olson, K. R., & Dunham, Y. (2010). The development of implicit social cognition. In B. Gawronski and B. Payne (Eds.), *Handbook of implicit social cognition: Measurement, theory, and applications* (pp. 241–254). New York, NY: Guilford Press.

Olson, M. A., & Fazio, R. H. (2004). Reducing the influence of extra-personal associations on the Implicit Association Test: Personalizing the implicit measures. *Journal of Personality and Social Psychology, 86*, 653–667.

Patterson, M. L. (2008). Back to social behavior: Mining the mundane. *Basic and Applied Social Psychology, 30*, 93–101.

Payne, B. K. (2001). Prejudice and perception: The role of automatic and controlled processes in misperceiving a weapon. *Journal of Personality and Social Psychology, 81*, 181–192.

Payne, B. K. (2005). Conceptualizing control in social cognition: How executive control modulates the expression of automatic stereotyping. *Journal of Personality and Social Psychology, 89*, 488–503.

Payne, B., & Bishara, A. J. (2009). An integrative review of process dissociation and related models in social cognition. *European Review of Social Psychology, 20*, 272–314.

Payne, B. K., Jacoby, L. L., & Lambert, A. J. (2005). Attitudes as accessibility bias: Dissociating automatic and controlled components. In R. Hassin, J. Bargh, J. & Uleman, (Eds.), *The New Unconscious*. New York: Oxford University Press.

Petty, R. E., & Wegener, D. T. (1999). The Elaboration Likelihood Model: Current status and controversies. In

S. Chaiken & Y. Trope (Eds.), *Dual process theories in social psychology* (pp. 41–72). New York: Guilford Press.

Richardson-Klavehn, A., Bjork, R. A. (1988): Measures of memory. *Annual Review of Psychology, 36,* 475–543.

Roediger, H. L. (1990). Implicit memory: Retention without remembering. *American Psychologist, 45,* 1043–1056.

Roenker, D. L., Thompson, C. P., & Brown, S. C. (1971). Comparison of measures for the estimation of clustering in free recall. *Psychological Bulletin, 76,* 45–48.

Schacter, D. L. (1987). Implicit memory: History and current status. *Journal of Experimental Psychology: Learning, Memory, and Cognition, 13,* 501–518.

Scherer, L. D., & Lambert, A. J. (2009a). Contrast effects in priming paradigms: Implications for theory and research on implicit attitudes. *Journal of Personality and Social Psychology, 97,* 383–403.

Scherer, L. D., & Lambert, A. J. (2009b). Counterstereotypic exemplars in context: Evidence for intracategory differentiation using implicit measures. *Social Cognition, 27,* 523–550.

Schneider, W., & Shiffrin, R. M., (1977). Controlled and automatic human information processing: Detection, search, and attention. *Psychological Bulletin, 84,* 1–66.

Schwarz, N., & Clore, G. L. (2007). Feelings and phenomenal experiences. In E. T. Higgins & A. Kruglanski (Eds.), *Social psychology: Handbook of basic principles* (2nd ed., pp. 385–407). New York: Guilford Press.

Sekaquaptewa, D., Vargas, P., & von Hippel, W. (2010). A practical guide to paper and pencil implicit measures of attitudes. In B. Gawronski & B. K. Payne (Eds.), *Handbook of implicit social cognition: Measurement, theory and applications.* New York: Guilford Press.

Shadish, W. R., Cook, T. D., & Campbell, D. T. (2002). *Experimental and quasi-experimental designs for generalized causal inference.* Boston: Houghton-Mifflin.

Sherman, J. W. (2008). Controlled influences on implicit measures: Confronting the myth of process-purity and taming the cognitive monster. In R. E. Petty, R. H. Fazio, P. Briñol, R. E. Petty, R. H. Fazio, & P. Briñol (Eds.), *Attitudes: Insights from the new implicit measures* (pp. 391–426). New York: Psychology Press.

Skowronski, J. J., Carlston, D. E., Mae, L., & Crawford, M. T. (1998). Spontaneous trait transference: Communicators take on the qualities they describe in others. *Journal of Personality and Social Psychology, 74,* 837–848.

Smith, E. R., & DeCoster, J. (2000). Dual-process models in social and cognitive psychology: Conceptual integration and links to underlying memory systems. *Personality and Social Psychology Review, 4,* 108–131.

Srull, T. K. (1984). Methodological techniques for the study of person memory and social cognition. In R. S. Wyer, Jr., & T. K. Srull (Eds.), *Handbook of social cognition* (Vol. 2, pp. 1–72). Hillsdale, NJ: Erlbaum.

Srull, T. K., Lichtenstein, M., & Rothbart, M. (1985). Associative storage and retrieval processes in person memory. *Journal of Experimental Psychology: Learning, Memory, and Cognition, 11,* 316–345.

Srull, T. K., & Wyer, R. S. (1979). The role of category accessibility in the interpretation of information about persons: Some determinants and implications. *Journal of Personality and Social Psychology, 37,* 1660–1672.

Strickland, L. J., Aboud, F. E., & Gergen, K. J. (1976). (Eds.), *Social psychology in transition.* New York: Plenum Press.

Teige-Mocigemba, S., Klauer, K. C., & Sherman, J. W. (2010). Practical guide to Implicit Association Task and related tasks. In B. Gawronski & B. K. Payne (Eds.), *Handbook of implicit social cognition: Measurement, theory, and applications* (pp. 117–139). New York: Guilford Press.

Triplett, N. (1898). The dynamogenic factors in pacemaking and competition. *American Journal of Psychology, 9,* 507–533.

Vallone, R. P., Griffin, D. W., Lin, S., & Ross, L. (1990). Overconfident prediction of future actions and outcomes by self and others. *Journal of Personality and Social Psychology, 58,* 582–592.

Warrington, E. K., & Weiskrantz, L. (1968). New method of testing long-term retention with special reference to amnesic patients. *Nature, 217,* 972–974.

Wegner, D. M. (1989). *White bears and other unwanted thoughts: Suppression, obsession, and the psychology of mental control.* New York: Viking/Penguin.

Wentura, D., & Degner, J. (2010). A practical guide to sequential priming and related tasks. In B. Gawronski, & B. K. Payne (Eds.), *Handbook of implicit social cognition: Measurement, theory, and applications* (pp. 95–116). New York: Guilford Press.

West, R. F. & Stanovich, K. E. (1982). The source of inhibition in experiments on the effects of sentence context on word recognition. *Journal of Experimental Psychology: Learning, Memory, and Cognition, 8,* 385–399.

Wyer, R. S., & Gordon, S. E. (1984). The cognitive representation of social information. In R. S. Wyer & T. K. Srull (Eds.), *Handbook of social cognition* (pp. 73–150). Hillsdale, NJ: Erlbaum.

Wyer, R. S., & Martin, L. L. (1986). Person memory: The role of traits, group stereotypes and specific behaviors in the cognitive representation of persons. *Journal of Personality and Social Psychology, 50,* 611–675.

Wyer, R. S., & Srull, T. K. (1981). Category accessibility: Some theoretical and empirical issues concerning the processing of social stimulus information. In E. T. Higgins, C. P. Herman, & M. P. Zanna (Eds.), *Social cognition: The Ontario symposium* (Vol. 1, pp. 161–197). Hillsdale, NJ: Erlbaum.

Wyer, R. S., & Srull, T. K. (Eds.) (1984). *Handbook of social cognition* (Vols. 1–3). Hillsdale, NJ: Erlbaum.

Wyer, R. S., & Srull, T. K. (1989). Memory and cognition in its social context. Hillsdale, NJ: Erlbaum.

A Brief History of Theory and Research on Impression Formation

James S. Uleman *and* Laura M. Kressel

Abstract

Why do we view people as we do? What is scientifically tractable, in that view? How did subjective concepts such as traits become legitimate "objects of perception"? Thorndike, Asch, and Cronbach were critical. This chapter traces Asch's legacy to the present and describes the strange independence of research on accuracy from social cognition. Impressions' internal organization (not accuracy) became the foundation of research on the Big Two (warmth and competence), facial trait dimensions, and morality's unique status. Associative memory structures and schemata provided the language. The unique impact of negative information is reviewed, along with behaviors' diagnosticity and how the morality and competence domains differ. The chapter highlights the importance of goals in shaping impressions, of forming impressions without goals (spontaneously), and of stages in forming spontaneous trait inferences. It also notes the importance of social cognitive transference, perceptions of persons and groups, and conceptions of persons as moral agents and objects.

Key Words: accuracy, competence, diagnosticity, goal, impression, morality, spontaneous, subjective, unconscious, warmth

Hindsight is 20/20, they say derisively. It cannot isolate causes or predict the future. There are no control groups, and who's to say it could not have been otherwise. We are experimental social psychologists, plagued by counterfactuals and mistrustful of post hoc explanations. So take this brief selective history with a large grain of salt.

Also note that any history of impression formation is, in part, a history of how we have viewed ourselves. More than most topics in this handbook, it has been affected by widespread practices in how we (the broad culture and/or the scientific community) describe people. We take the long view and focus broadly on early history, rather than exclusively on the most recent developments. We sketch how the research community came to believe in the things we study as "impression formation," and provide a few interesting stories and ideas along the way.

Understanding impression formation has probably been a human concern ever since our ancestors had the metacognitive realization that impressions do form and are not simply reflections of some reality out there—ever since, putting aside naïve realism and assumed similarity, one person gestured or grunted to another, "How could you possibly believe that about them?" Rossano (2007) argued that as long ago as the Upper Paleolithic (late Stone Age; 45,000 to 10,000 B.C.E.), our species showed unusual levels of cooperation and social organization, and that the development of religion (ancestor worship, shamanism, and belief in animal and natural spirits) supported this by providing "permanent social scrutiny." Inherent in this were theories (stories) about what these spirits were like, and how they could be pleased, appeased, or offended. Such theories must have existed about people as well.

Disagreements about impressions, in these egalitarian societies, would have raised questions about the processes of impression formation—the topic of this chapter.

Diversity of Conceptions of Persons

People's descriptions of others are remarkably diverse and have changed over time. This diversity arose because, unlike the perception of objectively measurable physical properties (e.g., how visible light's wavelengths relate to perception of color), person "perception" is not about physically objective reality. Modern psychology regards the properties we "see" in others as largely inferred, assumed, felt, and/or enacted (e.g., Uleman, Saribay, & Gonzalez, 2008). What we "see" has been wondrously diverse across time, culture, and subculture.

Lillard (1998) provides an overview and numerous examples, focused on theories of mind. The Quechua people in the Andes believe each person consists of two selves: the everyday self and the self of altered states of consciousness as when dreaming or drunk (Carpenter, 1992). Despite the contentious history of the Sapir-Whorf hypothesis, it is now clear that language affects multiple cognitive processes (e.g., Hardin & Banaji, 1993). Thus, the absence in English of an equivalent to the Hindu emotion of *lajya* (shyness + shame + embarassment) or the Japanese behavior of *amae* (to depend and presume upon another's benevolence) affects these language communities' impressions of other people. Instead of speaking of the mind, the Philippines' Illongot speak of *rinawa*, which "unites concerns for thought and feeling, inner life and social context, violent anger, and such desirable consequences as fertility and health" (Rosaldo, 1980, p. 26, quoted in Lillard, 1998). One's *rinawa* can depart during sleep, and it gradually leaves one over a lifetime. Other living things (e.g., plants) also have *rinawa*, so it resembles the *force vitale* or *vitalisme* of 18th-century Western thought. *Rinawa* also resembles the ancient Greeks' concept of *psuche* (soul), but the ancient Greeks also spoke of *thymos* (which produced action) and *noos* (which produced ideas and images) as additional parts of the "mind" (from Snell, 1953, in Lillard, 1998). In Japanese, there is no clear separation between mind and body, and a variety of terms (*kokoro, hara, seishim*, and *mi*) refer to various aspects of the mind-body (Lebra, 1993).

Lillard (1998) describes many peoples who "view the mind as unknowable and unimportant." The "Gusii prefer to discuss overt behavior, and they avoid talking about intentions and other aspects of mind…the Baining of Papua New Guinea…rarely comment on reasons for actions, even their own… Bimin-Kuskusmin…and the Ommura…—both of Papau New Guinea—and the Kaqchikel Maya…are other cultures that are said to view the mind as unknowable and unimportant" (p. 13). Lillard guesses that members of these cultures have concepts about mental states, but regard them as so private or unknowable that they are absent from conversations, including discussions of fault and justice.

We usually assume that mental events (desires, intentions, beliefs) cause actions, but this view is not universal. Cultural differences associated with individualism and collectivism (including the latter's greater sensitivity to situations) are well known (Kitayama, Duffy, & Uchida, 2007). Many peoples credit gods, spirits, dead ancestors, witches, and ghosts with causing people's actions. The Salem witch trials in North America were only 320 years ago (see also LeVine, 2007).

Natural History of Human Nature

How did we arrive at the conceptions of persons that we now "see"—from our prehistoric past through the time of Homer's gods and heroes (800–900 B.C.E.), through Galen's (about 150 A.D.) four temperaments (sanguine, choleric, melancholic, and phlegmatic) based on bodily humors, and ancient Roman and Judeo-Christian conceptions of persons as codified in their contrasting laws and codes of conduct, through the Middle Ages (fifth–15th centuries) dominated by Roman Catholic beliefs about God and salvation, to the European Renaissance (14th–17th centuries) with its renewed emphasis on observation, nature, and the individual? This is largely a Western history because modern science only arose in the West. A detailed description is beyond the scope of this chapter. But Robinson (1995) provides an account of the history of thought about human nature in the West, based on ideas from philosophy, art, religion, literature, politics, and science, with particular emphasis on discrepancies between humanistic and scientific conceptions. Political thought based on various conceptions of human nature can be traced from Plato (about 400 B.C.E.) through Machiavelli (1469–1527 A.D). And Baumeister (1987) presents an interesting overview of how conceptions of the self have changed from the late Middle Ages to the present, with the rise of self-consciousness, the Victorian imposition of repression and resulting hypocrisy, and the consequent modern emphasis on unconscious processes.

Even today there is little consensus on the nature of human nature. Anyone who has taught Milgram's (1974) work on obedience is confronted with the question of whether people are basically morally good or evil. Pinker (2002) organizes his book on human nature around three still-controversial themes: whether innate traits exist, whether essentially good human nature is corrupted by society, and whether we have souls that allow choice unconstrained by biology. Behavioral economics has challenged classical economics' acceptance of *homo economicus*, the view that people are naturally rational and narrowly self-interested (e.g., Henrich et al., 2004). There is disagreement about whether or not people have free will, with Wegner (2005) among others contending that they do not, and Nahmias (2005) disputing this. Much depends on how "free will" is defined (see Baer, Kaufman, & Baumeister, 2008; Dennett, 2011).

Given this diversity of viewpoints on human nature, it is remarkable that a science of impression formation emerged at all.

Early Research on Impression Formation

Social psychology arose within both psychology and sociology, each tradition producing their first textbooks in 1908 (McDougall and Ross, respectively). F. H. Allport's textbook, *Social Psychology* (1924), focused more on empirical studies than had earlier texts, and included a section on "reactions to persons as stimuli." Empirical studies in social psychology had begun appearing in sufficient number that the following year, the *Journal of Abnormal Psychology* changed its title to *Journal of Abnormal and Social Psychology*. The most interesting report that year was from the $5,000 Award Committee, offering this sum "to any person claiming to produce supernormal material phenomena…under rigid laboratory conditions and by recognized scientific methods, in full light…" (Shapley et al., 1925). No award was made, and Mr. Houdini's unusual abilities were apparently never required. What is remarkable is that less than 100 years ago, American psychologists gave any credence at all to such supernormal conceptions of persons. If impression formation was to be studied, there was still little stable consensus on what these impressions were about.

Meanwhile, real progress was being made in the measurement of subjective phenomena such as personality characteristics and attitudes. Likert (1932) scaling was introduced, and Thurstone (1928) developed the method of paired comparisons for measuring attitudes. "The revolutionary aspect of

Thurstone's study was that he borrowed methods from psychophysics without simultaneously assuming the existence of a physical attribute to which to relate psychological judgments" (Dawes & Smith, 1985, p. 513). These and related developments (such as factor analysis) freed empirical psychologists from the "brass instruments" approach that so dominated the early part of the century, and put the study of subjective phenomena on a sound scientific footing. If you can measure it with rigorous quantitative methods, then it must be real. The widespread use of these methods—in government, education, and industry—increased acceptance of the reality that they measured, and helped separate it in most people's minds from supernormal phenomena. With the help of logical positivism, what was not measured faded into ephemera, or migrated to other scholarly fields.

It is no accident that conceiving of personality in measurable terms preceded research on impression formation. In fact, just as social psychology arose at the intersection of sociology and psychology, sustained research on impression formation depended on developments in both social and personality psychology. Uleman and Saribay (2012) argue that the study of initial impressions "bring together personality and social psychology like no other field of study—'personality' because (1) impressions are about personalities, and (2) perceivers' personalities affect these impressions; and 'social' because (3) social cognitive processes of impression formation, and (4) sociocultural contexts have major effects on impressions" (p. 337). Thus, the study of impression formation depends on developments in many areas, some of them surprising at first glance, such as scaling and factor analysis, and the widespread acceptance of measures that make concrete the unobservable.

Social psychology was becoming more experimental. Murphy and Murphy published their *Experimental Social Psychology* text in 1931, and Newcomb was added as an author in 1937, contributing sections on measuring both personality and attitudes. It was also becoming more applied, with the deepening worldwide Great Depression of the 1930s; military adventurism in the Far East, Spain, and Ethiopia; and World War II in the early 1940s. American social psychology benefited from an influx of European immigrants (e.g., Fritz Heider in 1930, and Kurt Lewin in 1932) who were influenced less by American behaviorism and more by German gestalt psychology. Work on impression formation gained practical importance as government and industry programs expanded in the war effort, and better ways were sought to place the right workers in the right jobs. Clinical and actuarial assessment of skills and personality were among the urgent problems of the day. And impression formation was central to this.

There are several good histories of social psychology, including those by Jones (1985), Zajonc (1999), and Ross, Lepper, and Ward (2009). Jones (1985, pp. 71–72) has an interesting discussion of the incompatibility of S-R psychology with social psychology, particularly social as practiced by Lewin and Festinger. Jones frequently mentions impression formation as a moderator or mediator, if not the focus of investigation. This characterized his own research as well (e.g., Jones, 1990) and reminds us that the study of impression formation, isolated from the urgencies of particular social situations and goals, can become a pallid and lifeless affair. Jones (1985) also discusses "the rise of subjectivism in the 1930s and 1940s," particularly its importance in legitimizing Lewin's approach. "W. K. Estes [a student of Skinner's and pioneer in mathematical learning theory]...found Lewinian field theory incapable of a priori prediction and lacking in functional relationship statements that could be anchored in measureable stimuli and observable responses" (p. 84). And so it is. Nevertheless, the enterprise prospered.

Research on Impression Formation Before Social Cognition

To take advantage of the hindsight that PsycINFO (now ProQuest) citation counts afford, we examined them for publications through 1980 that are retrieved by the key words *impression formation, person perception, social cognition,* or *social perception.* There were only three articles with more than 50 citations before 1950, and they reflect the diversity of traditions that contributed to research on impression formation. The earliest, by Thorndike and Stein (1937), is in the burgeoning psychometric tradition noted above. Some 17 years earlier, Thorndike had suggested that there are three types of intelligence: abstract, mechanical, and social ("the ability to understand and manage people"). Thorndike and Stein (1937) reviewed the most widely used measures of the day. They found that their social intelligence measure correlated poorly with other such measures and was hardly distinct from abstract intelligence. This raised the questions of whether such a trait can be measured solely with paper-and-pencil tests and of whether it even exists. This existence question contradicts the recurring

strong belief that people (judges) differ in their ability to perceive others accurately. Although subsequent research largely concluded that it does not exist in any strong form, the intuition persists and supports contemporary efforts to isolate the characteristics of socially sensitive judges (e.g., Mayer, Roberts, & Barsade, 2008).

The other two articles with more than 50 citations sidestep the accuracy conundrum by focusing almost entirely on the judge. Heider's (1944) paper is characteristically theoretical and lacks data. Under headings such as "persons as origins" and "the relations between causal units and the properties of their parts," he uses gestalt principles of perceptual organization to develop some of the central ideas that became attribution theory. The other article was the classic paper by Asch (1946), to which we return below.

Two lines of research with more than 50 citations surfaced in the 1950s. Tajfel's (1959) paper became important for research on social categorization and social identity, which remained a distinctly European line of research for several decades. Even though social identity and ingroup/outgroup status have important effects on impression formation (see Tajfel, 1969, 1970), Tajfel does not appear in the name index of Schneider, Hastorf, and Ellsworth's (1979) text on person perception. He makes only two minor appearances in the first edition of Fiske and Taylor's (1984) text on social cognition, in discussions of schemata. These were lean years for European social psychology. To aid its recovery, the European Association for Social Psychology was founded in 1966 with American support, and Henri Tajfel (née Hersz Mordche, 1919–1982) was central in this effort.

The other papers concerned accuracy in person perception. Bieri (1955) investigated the role of judges' cognitive complexity. Taft (1955) reviewed research on five prominent ways to identify good judges, discussed several factors that led to inconsistent research results, and counted "motivation (to make accurate judgments)" as probably the most important of these. The number of combinations of tasks and criteria and judges' cognitive and motivational characteristics was daunting and precluded any clear conclusions. Two other papers—by Cronbach (1955) and Gage and Cronbach (1955)—presented trenchant criticisms of accuracy research. This diverted research away from accuracy for decades, encouraged research on attributions because they usually sidestepped accuracy, and laid the foundation for modern accuracy research. We pick up this thread below.

During the 1960s, four trends can be seen. First, accuracy disappeared as a prominent research topic. Although occasional studies concerned real people, research increasingly employed artificial stimuli for which traditional "accuracy" had no meaning. Second, attribution theory and other cognitive approaches developed rapidly. The cognitive revolution came to social psychology and merged with its gestalt tradition. Attributions developed as a separate research tradition. Motivational and functional approaches receded in importance and were often at odds with cognitive ones (e.g., Bem, 1967). "Information" (colloquially, rather than in the sense of Shannon & Weaver, 1949) became the coin of the realm (e.g., Jones, Davis, & Gergen, 1961). Interest surged in schemata (or schemas) of all kinds, including stereotypes. Kuethe (1962) recast gestalt unit formation ideas in terms of social schema and response sets and biases, and demonstrated again the strong effects of perceivers' schemata on "perception." Crowne and Marlowe (1960) developed their measure of social desirability response bias, to make measures of self-perceptions more accurate. And De Soto, London, and Handel (1965) examined the use of spatial schemata in solving linear syllogisms, as when *better* and *worse* are placed on a vertical axis. They made the very gestalt-like suggestion "that the linear ordering is a preeminent cognitive good figure" (p. 513).

Third, the field confronted the problem of proliferating dependent variables. The terms in which one conceives of others are innumerable. Rosenberg, Nelson, and Vivekananthan (1968) tackled this problem in the most widely cited paper of the decade. They used multidimensional scaling to analyze the co-occurrence of trait terms in participants' descriptions of 10 acquaintances, and then multiple regression to interpret the resulting dimensions. (Twenty years earlier, without computers to do the calculations, this research would have been prohibitively laborious.) They identified two dimensions: good–bad intellectual (e.g., *scientific* vs. *foolish*) and good–bad social (e.g., *honest* vs. *unhappy*), both evaluative but in distinct ways. Evaluation emerged as the preferred dependent variable in other work. Parducci (1968) found context effects for evaluative ratings of misdeeds, from "not particular bad" to "very evil." Byrne, London, and Reeves (1968) found that a stranger's attractiveness was more affected by attitudinal similarity than physical attractiveness, supporting his similarity theory of attraction. Although evaluations miss much of the meaning of traits and other descriptive terms (see especially Peabody,

1970), they have the virtues of ubiquity and of naturally linking to the literature on attitudes.

Fourth, Norman Anderson's work (1965, 1971, 1974, 1981) on predicting evaluative impressions from linear combinations of traits' valences, and on order effects, achieved considerable prominence. Linear functions certainly provide good first approximations for many things, and are clear and tractable. But Anderson's models assumed that the evaluative meanings of individual traits are invariant and unaffected by context—an assumption already contradicted by considerable research. His work was challenged; a spirited controversy ensued (e.g., Anderson, 1971; Hamilton & Zanna, 1974); and the field lost interest in his models. But the controversy nicely illustrates the difference between models that predict outcomes with some precision and models that also represent the processes involved. In resolving this controversy in favor of meaning change, the field moved deeper into analyzing processes, setting the stage for the sovereignty of social cognition (Ostrom, 1984).

Updating Enduring Research Traditions from Pre-1970

The papers discussed above are widely cited because they continue to inspire research and generate new insights. We briefly trace their influence, and its evolution into the social cognition of impression formation, by picking up three major threads.

Asch and the Focus on Traits

Asch's (1946) classic paper, although in the gestalt tradition, cut through the many theoretical complexities of impression formation by offering a simple experimental paradigm and focusing on traits. Asch presented participants with fictional target people described in lists of traits and asked them to form impressions, sometimes in brief sketches and sometimes on bipolar scale ratings. Results enabled him to identify some traits (*warm, cold*) as central (vs. peripheral) in that they had more effect on the overall impression and on the meanings of other traits. He also discussed order effects ("primacy," in which the first items in the list affect impressions more; and "recency," in which the last items affect impressions more) and halo effects (in which the evaluation associated with some traits spreads to others). He argued that impressions have structure and that the meanings of their elements (traits) depend on which other elements are present. Anticipating future research, he wondered whether similar principles govern impressions of groups (e.g., entitativity) or relationships. As important as Asch's ideas were, the paradigm pioneered in his paper is just as important. It initiated the experimental study of impression formation, focused on traits and their combinations, and still inspires research.

Luchins (1948) soon offered many criticisms, perhaps best summed up this way: "To begin with discrete traits, to take the processes involved in the formation and growth of impressions of people out of their natural milieu, and to neglect personal and social influences may achieve experimental neatness, but at the expense of understanding of everyday judgments of people" (p. 325). Others took these criticisms as empirical challenges and began building on the paradigm, enriching the stimuli and focusing on differences among perceivers. For example, Jones (1954) had navy recruits listen to mock interviews with a platoon leader, form written impressions, and then rate him on 30 traits. The interviews portrayed either a forceful or passive leader. Among other findings, "authoritarians seem to be more insensitive...to the psychological and personality characteristics of others" (p. 126). In another dissertation study, Gollin (1954) found "that the formation of an impression of the personality of another is a function not only of the characteristics of the person being observed, but also...of the underlying perceptual-cognitive organizing process in the observer" (p. 76). Students watched film clips of a woman behaving promiscuously in two clips and kindly in three clips, so they had to resolve inconsistencies. Those who "simplified" rather than "aggregated" or "related" impressions from the clips made more extreme evaluative ratings.

Decades later, Asch (and Zukier, 1984) returned to trait stimuli to explore the many ways in which inconsistencies are resolved. They characterized targets with pairs of inconsistent traits and asked participants to describe the targets and explain the traits' interrelations. Participants did this easily and exhibited seven "modes of resolution," including enabling, means–ends, cause–effect, and inner–outer relations. Asch and Zukier noted that more "elementaristic" approaches to impression formation (e.g., Anderson, 1981) cannot accommodate these findings. Formally describing and predicting the many ways that inconsistent elements can be combined to form impressions still remains a challenge.

TRAIT CENTRALITY

What makes warm–cold central? Wishner (1960) found that central traits are those that correlate highly with the other traits that are assessed. Thus, a pair such as *polite–blunt* that is not ordinarily central can be made central by tapping impressions on scales that correlate highly with it. This correlational approach to the organization of traits was extended by Rosenberg et al. (1968). Zanna and Hamilton (1972) showed that trait descriptions could change impression ratings on one dimension without affecting the other. *Industrious* vs. *lazy* affected ratings on only the intellectual dimension, whereas *warm* vs. *cold* affected the social dimension.

Orehek, Dechesne, Fishbach, Kruglanski, and Chun (2010) obtained evidence that this structure depends on perceivers' beliefs about traits' unidirectional implications for other traits. They showed that implications between traits are unidirectional rather than bidirectional as correlational or co-occurrence analyses assume; that individual differences in these beliefs mediate such effects; that manipulating these beliefs changes these effects; and that they are reduced under cognitive load when the stimuli are blurry. These results are inconsistent with the bidirectional links in most current associative models of impression formation.

RECENT EXTENSIONS OF ASCH

Recently the Asch paradigm was employed in two research programs that Asch (1908–1996) would have enjoyed. Williams and Bargh (2008) added to the growing evidence that bodily experience can unconsciously affect behaviors and cognitions. They had participants form impressions of a target person described by the same list of traits that Asch (1946) used, but without the traits *warm* or *cold*. Participants incidentally held either a warm or a cold cup of coffee before making their ratings. The warm or cold cup had the same effect on impressions as Asch demonstrated with traits 62 years earlier. Participants were completely unaware of these effects, suggesting that awareness of some stimuli's relevance (or irrelevance) for the task at hand is not required for trait centrality effects.

The second research program concerns Trope and Liberman's (2010) construal level theory (CLT) of the effects of psychological distance. CLT holds that more distant stimuli are processed more abstractly. Based on the ideas that schema-driven processing is more abstract than piecemeal processing and that the primacy effect is schema based, Eyal, Hoover, Fujita, and Nussbaum (2011) found primacy effects for temporally distant targets and among participants primed to think abstractly. When targets were temporally near or participants were primed to think concretely, recency effects occurred. McCarthy and

Skowronski (2011b) examined the effect of psychological distance on the impact of *warm–cold* on impressions. Because Asch (1946) argued that this impact depends on abstract configurational thinking, they manipulated spatial distance in Study 1a and temporal distance in Study 1b. In both studies, the effect of *warm–cold* was greater the more distant the target was. Thus, "looking at old paradigms through the lens of new theories and knowledge will continue to produce fruitful results" (p. 1306).

Cronbach and the Question of Accuracy

Cronbach published his classic paper in 1955 on accuracy in impression formation and how it should be measured, using an elegant ANOVA-like analysis of the multiple processes that contribute to accuracy. For example, it was well known by then that people usually assume that others are similar to themselves. So if they actually are, their impressions will be accurate; otherwise, not. The paper decomposed both accuracy and assumed similarity scores. It showed how accuracy can be decomposed into independent contributions from judges' assumptions or knowledge about (1) the general level of traits among targets, (2) the differences among trait levels across targets, (3) the differences among targets across traits, and (4) the unique standing of particular targets on particular traits. Apparently, "assumed similarity" can be similarly decomposed.

Cronbach's analysis might have led to further studies on accuracy, but it did not. Instead, it seemed to discourage further research on the problem because of its complexity. Thus, the question of accuracy in person perception essentially disappeared from the research agenda until Kenny and Albright (1987) revived it 30 years later. It is beyond the scope of this chapter to describe what followed, except to say that Kenny, his models, his colleagues, and the desk-top computer have put the study of accuracy in person perception back on solid theoretical and methodological ground. Kenny (1994) presented his basic social relations model, which disentangles "three fundamentally different types of perceptions: other-perception, self-perception, and meta-perception" (p. 15). This requires a research design in which many participants act as both perceivers and targets so that perceiver, target, and interaction effects can be distinguished. He pointed out that person perception differs from object perception. "First, person perception is two-sided: Each person is both perceiver and target. Second, ... perceivers attempt to read the minds of targets and engage in what is called 'meta-perception.' Third, ... there is

a close linkage between self- and other-perception. Fourth, ... people, unlike objects, change when they are with different interaction partners" (p. 14).

There is more. Kenny's (2004) PERSON "model can explain the low level of consensus in person perception, the fact that consensus does not increase with greater acquaintance, the strong stability of interpersonal judgment, the overconfidence effect, and the fact that short-term judgments are sometimes as accurate as long-term judgments" (p. 265), among other things. Kenny, West, Malloy, and Albright (2006) discussed the general advantages and disadvantages of componential analyses of interpersonal perception. Kenny and West (2010) presented "new measures of assumed similarity and self-other agreement using the Social Relations Model [which, based on a meta-analysis,] seem to be relatively independent of [several potential] moderators" (p. 196). And West and Kenny (2011) described a general model for measuring truth (accuracy) and bias ("any systematic factor that judgments are being attracted toward, besides the truth," p. 360). Meanwhile, the intuition persists that there exist both good judges (Christiansen, Wolcott-Burnam, Janovics, Quirk, & Burns, 2005; Mayer et al., 2008) and social intelligence (Weis & Süß, 2007) that somehow trump the statistical interactions among perceiver, target, and task and provide simpler answers to this complex problem of accuracy in person perception.

Models that take accuracy criteria into account *are* relevant to process questions. Simulation theory (Perner & Kühberger, 2005; Saxe, 2005) holds that perceivers infer characteristics of others by imagining themselves in the same situation, interrogating their knowledge of themselves in that situation, and adjusting for known self–other differences to derive characterizations of others. Errors in the first step of imagining oneself in another situation arise from "the empathy gap" (Van Boven & Lowenstein, 2003), and errors occur in perceiving self–other differences (e.g., Pronin, Gilovich, & Ross, 2004).

Oddly, such accuracy research does not fall within traditional "social cognition," which is typically unconcerned with accuracy or interactions between real people (see also Funder, 1995; Gill & Swann, 2004; and Ickes, 2009). The research designs, stimuli, dependent variables, and statistical analyses are too different, even though both traditions rely heavily on trait concepts and ratings, and both examine processes (cognitive and interpersonal, respectively). Although the divergence in these lines of research made advances in each possible, they will have to be reunited in the future.

Rosenberg and the Organization of Impressions

Rosenberg et al. (1968) identified two relatively independent evaluative dimensions underlying trait impressions. Do these dimensions reflect the underlying structure of personality and behavior (realism), or merely perceivers' theories about what things go together (idealism)? Such theories are known as implicit personality theories (Rosenberg & Sedlak, 1972; Schneider, 1973). Passini and Norman (1966) had shown that trait ratings of complete strangers yield the same structure (the "Big Five") as rating of well-known others, suggesting that semantic structure, rather than actual co-occurrences, is responsible. Sorting this out has not been easy because it depends on distinguishing sources of biases from accuracy, the very issues that Cronbach (1955) and Kenny (1994) grappled with and that West and Kenny (2011) address directly in their truth and bias model. There is no general answer because in each specific circumstance, the influences of truth and bias depend on relations between behavioral or self-report criteria and perceivers' prior theories, goals, attention and memory, communications among perceivers in acquiring new information, and so forth. For example, Anderson and Shirako (2008) had people negotiate with each other over several weeks to discover how much actual behavior predicted negotiating reputation. "Individuals' reputations were only mildly related to their history of behavior. However, the link between reputation and behavior was stronger for…individuals who were more well-known and received more social attention in the community. In contrast, for less well-known individuals, their behavior had little impact on their reputation. The findings have implications for psychologists' understanding of reputations, person perceptions in larger groups, and the costs and benefits of social visibility" (p. 320)

Ignoring issues of accuracy, however, as most impression formation research has done, there are surprising regularities in the underlying structure of people's judgments of others. We note three of them here. The first follows directly from the thinking behind Rosenberg et al. (1968) and is based on correlations or co-occurrences among rating scales. The second builds on the generic gestalt concept of "schemata," organized structures that affect how knowledge is interpreted and remembered (e.g., Bartlett, 1932). The third derives from British associationism and conceives of impression structures in terms of interconnected nodes in associative memory networks and the connections between them.

It was inspired by developments in cognitive psychology at about this time (e.g., Anderson & Bower, 1973; Collins & Quillian, 1969).

FUNDAMENTAL DIMENSIONS OF SOCIAL JUDGMENT

Judd, James-Hawkins, Yzerbyt, and Kashima (2005) have dubbed the warmth and competence dimensions of Rosenberg et al. (1968) as fundamental (or the "Big Two," in homage to the Big Five personality dimensions) because they keep reappearing in impressions of both individuals and groups. They form the basis for the stereotype content model (SCM; Fiske, Cuddy, Glick, & Xu, 2002) and its more recent elaboration, the Behaviors from Intergroup Affect and Stereotypes (BIAS) map (Cuddy, Fiske, & Glick, 2007). In these models, impressions of group members vary along the two dimensions of competence, predicted by social status, and warmth, predicted by low social competition with perceivers. The low-low quadrant contains such groups as the homeless and poor, toward whom people feel contempt and resentment; and the high-high quadrant contains professionals and ingroup members, toward whom people feel pride and admiration. The low-competence, high-warmth quadrant describes the elderly, who elicit pity and sympathy, whereas the other ambivalent quadrant (high-low) contains the wealthy, the "top 1%," who elicit envy and jealousy. The BIAS map (Cuddy et al., 2007) relates all this to behaviors toward stereotyped groups, with characteristic emotions mediating relations between stereotypes and behaviors. Talaska, Fiske, and Chaiken's (2008) meta-analysis showed that emotions predict discrimination twice as well as stereotypes. Groups in the low-low quadrant are less likely to elicit the medial prefrontal cortex activity that is characteristic of "mentalizing" about others, suggesting that dehumanization and becoming the target of atrocities is more likely for such groups (Harris & Fiske, 2009).

In comparative judgments of social groups, these two dimensions have a compensatory relationship so that, for example, learning that a group is high on competence lowers estimates of warmth (Yzerbyt, Provost, & Corneille, 2005). There is a "tendency to differentiate two social targets in a comparative context on the two fundamental dimensions by contrasting them in a compensatory direction" (Kervyn, Yzerbyt, Judd, & Nunes, 2009, p. 829). Aaker, Vohs, and Mogilner (2010) have extended this to impressions of companies. They showed that firms with Internet addresses ending in dot-com are seen as more competent but less warm than dot-org firms, and that perceptions of competence drive purchasing decisions. In contrast, Abele and Bruckmueller (2011) found that for person perception, warmth information is preferentially processed.

Two similar dimensions turn up in inferences of personality from faces. Todorov, Said, Engel, and Oosterhof (2008) asked for personality trait impressions from a wide range of computer-generated faces with neutral expressions. They found that "trait inferences can be represented within a 2D space defined by valence/trustworthiness and power/dominance evaluation of faces.... based on similarity to expressions signaling approach or avoidance behavior and features signaling physical strength, respectively" (p. 455). Stewart et al. (2012) found that participants took longer to consciously see untrustworthy and dominant faces and that this delay was longer for trusting perceivers, pointing to unconscious evaluation of faces on these social dimensions.

How ubiquitous is this two-dimensional organization of person information? Is it specialized for and used only for social perception, or is it less conditional? Garcia-Marques et al. (2010) used the Deese-Roediger-McDermott (DRM) false recognition paradigm to study this. Participants heard lists of 10 traits from one of the four quadrants, mixed with six nontraits, and were asked to either form an impression of the person or memorize the list. After a 10-minute distracter, they performed a recognition test of 43 items, including 20 critical lures that had not been heard, five from each quadrant. The DRM paradigm typically finds high false recognition for words conceptually related to study words. This effect was higher for those under impression instructions than under memory instructions, suggesting "that different encoding goals can lead to the activation of somewhat different semantic structures" (pp. 565–566).

Two dimensions may be too few because "morality" is especially important for ingroup perception. Leach, Ellemers, & Barreto (2007) pointed out that warmth includes both sociability and morality and found morality is more important than competence or sociability in affecting ingroup evaluations and group-related self-concept. Furthermore, "identification with experimentally created...and preexisting...in-groups predicted the ascription of morality, but not competence or sociability, to the in-group" (p. 234). These two aspects of warmth—morality and sociability—seem to play different roles in the perception of both individuals and groups. Brambilla, Rusconi, Sacchi, and Cherubini

(2011) found that when forming global impressions, participants preferred morality information to both sociability and competence information about other people, and this preference changed for other goals. Perceivers were also most likely to use a disconfirming strategy in verifying morality traits.

Therefore, these two (or three) fundamental dimensions provide one way to describe the relatively stable (and conditionally invoked; Garcia-Marques et al., 2010) semantic space within which impressions of persons and groups can be located. But this kind of structure is relatively static and unrelated to the dynamics of information processing. This is not true of the next two approaches.

ASSOCIATIVE MEMORY NETWORKS

Social psychologists appropriated this idea from cognitive psychologists (e.g., Anderson & Bower, 1973; Collins & Quillian, 1969), for whom performance on various memory tasks is an essential tool for uncovering the structures and processing of mental representations. (You cannot really talk about processes separate from structure because they depend on each.) These networks describe mental structures as nodes (concepts) connected by links that transmit activation (and sometimes inhibition) among nodes. Nodes become linked to each other when they are activated together (contiguity), thereby building up a structure of associated concepts. Memory performance (errors, reaction times, etc.) is a function of such structures and how they are used. Unlike the Big Two, these structures are dynamic and built to change. Smith (1998) provides an excellent overview of ways of thinking about mental representations and memory, including associative memory networks; and see Chapters 10 and 11 of this volume for others.

The notion that concepts activated in semantic memory play a role in person perception has been around at least since Bruner (1957) outlined how activation increases a concept's accessibility (i.e., its likelihood of being used to process incoming information.) Higgins, Rholes, and Jones (1977) demonstrated this in their classic study of the fictional Donald. Participants for whom "reckless" (versus "adventurous") was unobtrusively activated, and who then read an ambiguous description of Donald's actions to which either concept was applicable, were more likely to characterize him in terms of the primed trait. Both frequent and recent concept use (activation) increases accessibility for subsequent information processing, with effects of recent activation decaying more quickly than those of frequent activation (Higgins, Bargh, & Lombardi, 1985).

Concept nodes are linked in associative networks, and activation (and inhibition) spreads from one node to others. Such structures have been used to describe many aspects of semantic memory (e.g., Anderson & Bower, 1973). Hastie and Kumar (1979) used such a model to describe how people organize information about others in memory. Their participants formed impressions and remembered information about a small number of targets. Each target was described first by eight synonyms of a trait, setting up an expectation, and then by many behaviors. Most were consistent with the trait, but some were inconsistent, and some were neutral. Contrary to what simple schema (e.g., Bartlett, 1932) and prototype theories (Cantor & Mischel, 1977) would predict, the proportion of free recall was better for inconsistent than consistent behaviors, and this effect was greater for shorter inconsistent lists.

To account for these results, Hastie and Kumar (1979) proposed that participants constructed hierarchical network structures with the person node (e.g., James Bartlett) at the top, linked to several "organizing principles" such as traits (honest, deceitful) below that, each of which is linked in turn to the several behaviors (returned a lost wallet, cheated at poker) below that. Then recall occurs by starting at the top target node, traversing descending links with probabilities equal to the inverse of the number of links from that node, and reading out behaviors that have not yet been recalled. This alone cannot account for the superior recall of inconsistent behaviors because there are fewer inconsistent trait–behavior links. But they also proposed that inter-item links among behaviors occur whenever the items are surprising or novel and require elaboration or explanation. This produces more links to inconsistent items, increasing their likelihood of recall (see Figure 5.6 in Hastie, 1980).

This general cognitive structure was invoked by Hamilton, Leirer, and Katz (1980) to explain their finding that people recall more behavioral information about target persons if they acquire it under an impression formation than under a memory goal. The information about each target could be organized around a few traits, and because forming an impression requires organizing information, this is what impression formation (as opposed to memory) participants did by creating inter-item links. This affected not only the amount of free recall but also the degree to which the recalled items were clustered by trait.

Klein and Loftus (1990) provided evidence that superior recall under impression formation may be due, not to more inter-item links, but rather to more semantic elaboration of the items themselves. And of course other organizational structures are possible, depending on the perceiver's goals and the information itself. Sedikides and Ostrom (1988) did a meta-analysis of studies that asked participants to form impressions of multiple unfamiliar targets accompanied by other information (hobbies, hometowns, etc.) that might be used to organize this information in memory. Based on clustering in free recall, they concluded that "person categories are no more preferred than nonperson categories... [and] seem not to hold a privileged position in the organization of social information" (p. 263).

Associative network models are powerful because they can make many precise predictions, including serial-position effects (how the order of studied items affects likelihood of recall), recall and recognition times, and clustering in free recall. Even though the full power of associative network models has seldom been exploited by social psychologists, such general frameworks—with traits connected to targets, behaviors connected to traits, and spreading activation among them—remain common in social cognitive theories of impression formation. Hastie and Kumar's (1979) model was among the first to exemplify the ideal of a fully explicit cognitive structure with mechanical (non-anthropomorphic) procedures for employing it. However, its precise and explicit nature limited applications because it only applies to a circumscribed set of conditions. Furthermore, social (vs. cognitive) psychologists are relatively disinterested in detailed modeling of particular cognitive processes and in testing them with parametric studies. Many social psychologists needed a way to talk about knowledge structures and their operation at a more general level, while avoiding such "premature" precision. Schemata fill the bill.

SCHEMATA

Schemata are organized knowledge structures that summarize experience and/or information about particular objects (the self-schema, stereotypes) or events (the restaurant and birthday party scripts). They are typically richer, more complex, and more vaguely specified than associative networks built up node by link by node. They're often referred to as "top-down" rather than "bottom-up" because they influence processing of current information rather than describe how these structures are built up. They usually operate outside of consciousness and affect the direction of attention at encoding, the interpretation of ambiguous events, inferences about things not directly observed including causality, and retrieval cues and processing strategy. They vary in accessibility, depending on their frequency and recency of use (Higgins, 1996). Schemata may be primed, provided, directly assessed, or simply assumed. Much social cognition research on impression formation is conceptualized in terms of schemata.

For example, in a study designed to show that traits function as prototypes, Cantor and Mischel (1977) developed four stimulus targets based on pretesting trait adjectives for their perceived likelihood of describing an introvert or extravert (prototypes). Then participants read descriptions of an introvert, an extravert, and two unrelated targets under memory instructions, each containing about 40 traits. Their recognition memory for traits was tested, and their confidence in recognizing each item was rated. Even though participants showed considerable accurate recognition memory, their confidence in "recognizing" introvert- or extravert-related but nonpresented trait foils was elevated when the trait list suggested (or explicitly mentioned) introversion or extraversion. That is, the lists primed introvert, extravert, or neither, and these schemata guided subsequent recognition performance, leading to schema-consistent errors. Andersen and Klatzky (1987) examined whether introverted and extraverted "social stereotypes" (i.e., types, such as *brain, politician,* and *comedian*) are associatively richer and more distinctive than trait prototypes. They found support for this idea in cluster analyses of trait sorting data, number of features generated to traits versus types, and the structure of their associations.

Some Major Topics in Social Cognitive Studies of Impression Formation

By 1980, social cognition had emerged as a distinctive approach to issues in social psychology, and impression formation was at its center. Some of this was presaged by Wegner and Vallacher's (1977) *Implicit Psychology,* but neither of them had the position or the students at the time to power a movement. In 1980, *Person Memory* (Hastie, Ostrom, Ebbesen, Wyer, Hamilton, & Carlston, 1980) was published by the group of scholars who were central in shaping the social cognition approach. It was the year after Wyer and Carlston's (1979) groundbreaking book and theory, focused largely on impression formation. The following year, the first Ontario Symposium (Higgins, Herman, & Zanna, 1981) appeared, devoted to social cognition and with

contributions by Ostrom, Pryor, and Simpson; Hastie; Taylor, and Crocker; Hamilton; Wyer, and Srull; McArthur (née Zebrowitz); Ebbesen; M. Snyder; M. Ross; R. M. Krauss; and Higgins, Kuiper, and Olsen. The first issue of *Social Cognition* hit the stands in 1982, under Dave Schneider's editorship. So 1980 was a watershed year. The distinctive social cognition emphases on understanding processes rather than merely outcomes, and on the use of memory and response time measures to do so, had been established.

It is beyond the scope of this chapter to trace all the important lines of research addressing impression formation; and some have already been sketched. Furthermore, many of other the chapters of this handbook address topics that include sections on impression formation, including at least Chapters 6 (on, attribution theory), 7 (on attitudes, for implicit and explicit evaluations of others), 9 (on facial processing, for how faces provide information on traits, group membership, and affect), 10 (on mental representation, for the variety of ways in which person information can be represented), 11 (on implicit representation), and 13 (on behavior productions, for interpreting others' behaviors, as well as Chapters 5 and 27 (on prejudice and stereotyping, for an aspect of impression formation that has burgeoned into its own extensive literature). In fact, we often contend that impression formation is "about everything" in social psychology, so also see Chapters 29 (on relational cognition), 34 (on social cognitive neuroscience), 36 (on social cognitive development), 37 (on cross-cultural psychology), 38 (on personality), 39 (on behavioral economics), and 41 (on political psychology).

Instead of trying to be encyclopedic, we sketch major developments since 1980 on several topics not likely to be treated elsewhere in this volume: the dominance of negative information in impression formation; effects of goals on forming impressions, including forming impressions without impression formation goals (spontaneous trait inferences); and then briefly, effects of significant others on perceiving strangers (social cognitive transference); forming impressions of people and groups; and the perception of people as moral agents and as human beings.

Negativity Effects

NEGATIVE ITEMS HAVE MORE WEIGHT

In early work on Anderson's (1965, 1974) information integration, weighted averaging model, the meanings of traits on some (usually evaluative) dimension that described a target were averaged to predict the overall impression. One finding was that negative (and extreme) traits were given greater weight in the average, so that a −5 (dishonest) and a +1 (polite) produced a −3 rather than a −2. Several models attempted to explain this, in terms of stimulus values. Skowronski and Carlston (1989) outline all these models clearly, along with their failings. Expectancy-contrast theories assume that stimuli for impressions are evaluated relative to a standard that is moderate and positive, and that this produces contrast effects (more extreme evaluations) for the stimuli. Such standards (e.g., adaptation levels) do exist, but they should already be incorporated into the original evaluations of the individual stimulus items (traits). Frequency-weight theories assume that more costly (Jones & McGillis, 1976) or more novel (Fiske, 1980) behaviors are more informative and hence weighted more heavily. Although there is some support for these theories, there is also research indicating that cost and novelty do not completely account for the greater weight of negative (and extreme) behaviors. Finally, range theories (e.g., Wyer, 1973) predict impressions from the overlap in the range of (usually evaluative) implications of the behaviors or traits. Unfortunately, these theories break down when there are three or more cues.

Skowronski and Carlston (1989) offered their own "category diagnosticity approach," which states that cues (traits, behaviors, etc.) have more weight if they are more diagnostic of the dimension or category of judgment. Diagnosticity is defined in terms of reducing uncertainty in choosing among responses or categories, consistent with Shannon and Weaver (1949) definition of information. This definition, coupled with the observation that negative (and extreme) behaviors are generally more diagnostic, produces negativity effects. Note that diagnosticity reflects perceivers' implicit theories of relations between cues and judgments, which may or may not be captured by cue properties alone, such as how novel or ambiguous or counternormative the cues are. Critically, the diagnosticity of cues depends on their meaning in the context of particular judgment tasks and is not inherent in any invariant property of the cues in isolation. Skowronski and Carlston (1989) cite considerable evidence supporting this formulation, including Reeder and Brewer's (1979) work on how schemata for judging ability and morality differ, with a positivity bias more common for ability and a negativity bias more common for morality. Superior performance (which is positive) is more diagnostic of high ability

than poor performance (which is negative) is of low ability because anyone can have a bad day, whereas immoral behavior (negative) is more diagnostic of morality than is moral behavior (positive) because even evil people can act good. Thus, behavior diagnosticity is not independent of domain or valence.

PERSONALITY DOMAIN EFFECTS

Wojciszke, Brycz, and Borkenau (1993) documented differences between positivity and negativity biases in the ability and morality domains, by varying behavioral extremity. Participants read about targets who performed four behaviors, all either in the ability or morality domain, and all either moderate or extreme. They found that in terms of trait inferences and global evaluations, "extremely evaluative information results in negativity effects whereas moderately evaluative information results in positivity effects" (p. 332). There were two main effects and no interaction. And ratings were positive for ability but negative for morality. Their findings link to Skowronski and Carlston (1989) in that more extreme behaviors were more prototypical for relevant traits. But their larger claim is that these two main effects "reflect the goals and interests of perceivers....If they [others] are not competent...they [perceivers] can usually turn to someone else....In contrast, perceivers are more affected by the immoral than moral behavior of other persons because immoral behavior may threaten perceivers' well-being..." (p. 333). Therefore, domain and perceivers' potential outcomes are crucial. Immorality in others is more harmful than competence is beneficial, so the result is a bias toward negativity. This focus on the consequences of behaviors for perceivers, as a determinant of target ratings, is supported and elaborated by Vonk (1996, 1998).

PROCESSING DIFFERENCES

There are also important valence differences in early stages of information processing. Pratto and John (1991) found that negative information automatically attracts attention more than positive information and leads to higher incidental memory (free recall). They measured the capture of attention by asking subjects to name the colors in which trait words were printed. Subjects were significantly slower to name colors for negative traits (23 milliseconds across three studies) because negative traits captured more of their attention. This was unrelated to traits' extremity or base rates. Although not tested here, these automatic effects might well contribute to negativity effects in impression formation, especially when subjects do not have an impression formation goal and when impressions are memory based. Such effects differ from those based on diagnosticity because they are insensitive to extremity, which usually correlates with diagnosticity.

Processing differences were also found by Abele and Bruckmueller (2011), but based on domain rather than valence. After Wojciszke et al.'s (1993) emphasis on perceivers' outcomes, they posited that of the Big Two domains noted above— agency (competence) and communion (including morality)—communal traits would be processed more readily. They used a pool of 112 traits rated on valence, agency, and communion, and balanced for frequency in German. Communal traits were recognized faster than agency traits in a lexical decision task, and were categorized faster by valence than agency words, independent of valence. Forty behaviors implying helpful and friendly (for communal) and competent and determined (for agency) were probed for their trait implications; responses were faster for communal behaviors, and this was also unaffected by counterbalanced valence. Finally, participants freely described a fellow student. Communal traits were used more frequently than agency traits and occurred earlier in the descriptions. This "preferential processing" of communal information is functional because communal traits have greater potential to help or harm perceivers and to signal approach or avoidance. It is also consistent with De Bruin and Van Lange's (2000) demonstration that people select communal over agency information to find out about a future interaction partner, and spend more time reading the communal information.

GENERALITY OF NEGATIVITY

Negativity effects are quite general. Klein (1996) showed that negative personality traits were more predictive of overall evaluations and voting behavior than positive traits. And negativity effects go beyond impression formation. Baumeister, Bratslavsky, Finkenauer, and Vohs (2001) and Rozin and Royzman (2001) offered wide-ranging surveys of the ways in which negative information dominates positive. Baumeister et al. (2001) reviewed research on relationships, emotions, learning and memory, neuroscience, the self, health, and so forth. Rozin et al. (2001) were even broader, drawing on literary, historical, religious, and cultural material. They note four ways in which negative events have more weight. Negative events are more potent than equally positive events; they have steeper gradients,

in that negativity increases more rapidly with approach in space or time; they dominate equally positive events when information is integrated (seen clearly in impression formation); and they are more differentiated and complex. This last feature is seen in the 20 languages Rozin, Berman, and Royzman (2010) surveyed, in that negative events are more likely to be lexicalized and are described by marked rather than unmarked adjectives.

Compelling as this generality is, it is unclear how much these negativity effects are based on the same processes. After all—as with assimilation and contrast effects—dividing phenomena into dichotomous categories such as positive and negative is almost guaranteed to combine outcomes with diverse origins. Yet negativity in all its varieties is widespread. The search for unifying processes, more specific than general appeals to evolutionary survival, will continue.

Goals: Conscious and Nonconscious, Present and Absent

Goals have top-down effects on a wide variety of psychological processes (see Chapter 23) and impression formation is no exception. They create expectancies, make relevant concepts selectively active or inactive, shape interpretations and memories, entail standards of comparison, and so forth. In an early symposium at Harvard University on person perception, Jones and Thibaut (1958) emphasized the importance of situations, roles, and goals for impression formation. They described value maintenance, causal-genetic, and situation-matching goals as each producing its unique "inferential set." Cohen (1961) looked at goals' effects on the resolution of inconsistent trait information. Those presented with trait lists and given the goal of conveying their impressions to others were more likely to ignore inconsistent information and form extreme impressions. Hoffman and colleagues examined effects of goals on how others are construed from behaviors. Hoffman, Mischel, and Mazze (1981) showed that memory and empathy goals favored construal in goal terms, whereas impression formation and prediction goals favored trait terms. Hoffman, Mischel, and Baer (1984) showed that verbal (vs. nonverbal) communication goals make perceivers more likely to use trait constructs.

Hilton and Darley (1991) summarized the effects of a variety of interpersonal goals on impression formation. They distinguish between action and assessment "sets," and within assessment, they distinguish between effects of global and circumscribed sets. Not surprisingly, different sets have different effects. One influential example concerns power, defined and manipulated in various ways. Fiske initially looked at effects of powerlessness, that is, being dependent on others for desirable outcomes (Erber & Fiske, 1984; Neuberg & Fiske, 1987), and followed up with studies of effects of power and dominance in producing biased perception and inequality (Goodwin, Operario, & Fiske, 1998). Since then, studies of effects of power, powerlessness, and differential status on impression formation have multiplied, adding to a still-developing and complex picture (e.g., Overbeck & Park, 2006; Vescio & Guinote, 2010; see also Chapter 28).

NONCONSCIOUS GOALS

Much of the early work manipulated goals explicitly, or put participants into situations in which they were presumed to have various goals. But the number of possible goals is innumerable, and simply describing effects of various classes of goals—from Jones and Thibaut's (1958) through Hilton and Darley's (1991) to Fiske's (2004) classifications, to say nothing of McDougall's (1908) teleological instincts—can be tedious and arbitrary, unless one is interested in particular goals. However, the study of goals' effects on impression formation took a whole new turn with the advent of modern approaches to unconscious goals (see Chapter 23; see also Dijksterhuis & Aarts, 2010).

Using priming methods, Bargh (1990) and his colleagues showed how to activate specific goals without participants' awareness, thereby avoiding effects of demand characteristics and participants' theories of goals' effects. In contrast to primed semantic concepts, primed goal effects persist over time unless and until the goal is satisfied, and also differ in other ways. In a now-classic demonstration, Chartrand and Bargh (1996) showed that impression formation and memorization goals could be primed unconsciously and that these unconscious goals had the same effects on memory for person information—in both amount and clustering in free recall—that Hamilton et al. (1980) showed for conscious goals.

Moskowitz, Gollwitzer, Wasel, and Schaal (1999) were interested in the ways that chronic egalitarian goals may inhibit the activation of stereotypes. They first established that those with and without chronic egalitarian goals had the same knowledge of stereotypes. Then they showed that priming these stereotypes reduced response times to stereotype features among those without chronic egalitarian goals, but not among those with such goals. Thus, chronic egalitarian "goals are activated and used preconsciously to prevent stereotype activation, demonstrating both the controllability of stereotype activation and the implicit role of goals in cognitive control" (p. 167). Moskowitz, Li, and Kirk (2004) demonstrated how nonchronic goals that one temporarily adopts, but then from which one consciously disengages, can continue to operate preconsciously. They call this "implicit volition," and it represents another instance of nonconscious goals. Although most of the work on conscious and nonconscious control of the effects of beliefs and expectancies on impression formation has occurred in the context of stereotyping (because controlling stereotypes is both desirable and problematic), the nonconscious activation and control processes it delineates are more broadly applicable to impression formation. (For much more on inhibiting or counteracting the effects of beliefs and expectations, especially stereotypes, on impression formation; see Chapter 5).

IMPRESSIONS WITHOUT GOALS; SPONTANEOUS TRAIT INFERENCES

Srull and Wyer (1979) were interested in the conditions under which traits are inferred from behaviors. They posited that such inferences required, among other things, the goal of forming an impression. Winter and Uleman (1984) doubted this. They presented a set of trait-implying sentences to participants who were merely asked to memorize them. Cued recall results indicated that trait inferences did occur, and other tests showed that participants were unaware of inferring them. These unintended and unconscious inferences were dubbed spontaneous trait inferences (STIs). Subsequent studies showed that they occur under other goal instructions, such as identifying the gender of each pronoun in the sentences, or judging whether you would do the behaviors described. These and other goals affect the likelihood of STIs, even as they remain unintended and unconscious (Uleman & Moskowitz, 1994). Although most STI research has used verbal descriptions of behavior, visual presentations also support them (Fiedler, Schenck, Watling, & Menges, 2005). And not surprisingly, individual differences play a role. Participants who differ in authoritarianism also differ in their inferences (Uleman, Winborne, Winter, & Shechter, 1986), and those high on the personal need for cognition are more likely to make STIs (Moskowitz, 1993).

Other inferences occur spontaneously, including causes, goals, beliefs, counterfactuals, and values (see

Uleman, Saribay, & Gonzalez, 2008, pp. 335–336, for a review), all with clear implications for impression formation. Furthermore, Ham and Vonk (2003) have shown that traits and situations can be inferred simultaneously, as when "John gets an A on the test" implies both *smart* and *easy*. These inferences are likely inputs to conscious attributional and impression formation processes. Trait inferences from behaviors can also become erroneously associated with informants rather than actors (Skowronski, Carlston, Mae, & Crawford, 1998), in which case they are called spontaneous trait transferences (STTs). That is, if I tell you that John is smart, I am more likely to be judged as smart later. An interesting research literature explores the processing differences between STIs and STTs (Carlston & Skowronski, 2005).

Are STIs about actors or merely their behaviors? Some of the paradigms used to detect STIs (e.g., lexical decision, and probe reaction time) merely detect concept activation, and results from the cued recall paradigm were ambiguous with regard to reference. These paradigms were not developed to detect relations between actors and trait concepts. This changed with Carlston and Skowronski's savings-in-relearning paradigm (Carlston & Skowronski, 1994). In it, participants "familiarized themselves" with photo–behavior pairs. Then after some intervening tasks, they studied pairs of photos and traits, some of which reflected the STIs presumably made earlier and some of which were novel. When tested on these paired associates, learning was better for the pairs reflecting initial STIs than for the other pairs. This "savings" shows that STIs are about actors because the savings is specific to trait–actor pairs. Todorov and Uleman (2002) used a false recognition paradigm to make the same point. They had participants study photo–behavior pairs for a subsequent memory test, and after some delay, presented photo–trait pairs and asked whether the traits had appeared in the sentences with the photos. (Some of the sentences contained traits, and others did not.) False recognition rates were higher when implied traits were presented with the photos about whom the traits were implied than with other familiar photos.

Recently, researchers have recognized that paradigms tapping trait activation and trait binding to actors tap separable stages of the impression formation process. First, trait concepts are activated by behaviors, and then they are bound to the actor. Finally, explicit trait inferences may (or may not) occur. This is illustrated in two lines of research. Saribay, Rim, and Uleman (2012) primed either independent or interdependent self-concepts. Using stimulus material affording both trait and situation inferences, they found that priming had no effect on spontaneous activation or binding of traits or situations. But it did affect explicit inferences. Priming independence increased explicit trait relative to situation inferences, whereas priming interdependence did not.

In a series of studies of the effects of unconscious goals on STI, Rim, Min, Uleman, Chartrand, and Carlston (2012) primed an affiliation goal, without participants being aware of the prime's effects. Using a lexical decision STI task, they found that primed participants took longer to recognize non-trait concepts, relative to participants not so primed. This "goal shielding" thereby focused attention on affiliation relevant concepts, namely traits, and left other concepts relatively inaccessible. In a second study, they used the false recognition STI task and found that affiliation priming bound positive traits to actors more than negative traits. Thus, the unconscious affiliation goal produced goal shielding (which was insensitive to trait valence) at the activation stage, and trait binding that was sensitive to trait valence at the binding stage. This suggests that the well-known positivity bias in affiliation is due to selective binding of positive inferences to actors and not to selective activation of positive traits.

The "stages" approach to STI and impression formation in general can become quite complex. In the Rim et al. (2012) work referred to above, there are three stages: unconscious goal activation, selective focusing on traits (vs. nontraits), and selective binding of positive traits. If these feed into subsequent explicit inferences, a fourth stage is added. Recent work by Ferreira et al. (2012) throws light on the transition to this last stage by identifying an "inference monitoring process" that is engaged by conscious impression formation goals. This process produces "awareness and monitoring of otherwise unconscious inferences "…so they can be "used toward attaining conscious goals" (p. 2). Evidence for this process came to light in a series of studies that addressed the following paradox. Hamilton et al. (1980) found clustering in free recall when target behaviors were learned under impression formation but not memory instructions, suggesting that trait-based clusters only formed under impression formation. But Winter and Uleman (1984) found that people infer traits even under memory instructions. So why was there no such clustering by traits in Hamilton et al. (1980) under memory instructions? The inference monitoring process provides a tentative answer.

Finally, consider automatic processes, their role in STI, and their definition. Much of the initial work on STI in the mid-1980s sought to examine whether or not it is automatic, according to the criteria delineated by Bargh (1994) 10 years later: awareness, intention, efficiency, and control. STI is clearly unconscious, unintended, and relatively (but not completely) efficient. But it is subject to at least indirect control, as noted above (e.g., Rim et al., 2012; Uleman & Moskowitz, 1994). Part of the problem is that Bargh's four criteria do not always covary; thus, "automatic" in this sense in not a unitary concept (see Chapter 12). It also has the disadvantage that any task shown to be automatic, even in part, becomes viewed as beyond conscious control. This has been particularly true of research on stereotyping (e.g., Bargh, 1999), but it occurs elsewhere too. The solution is to abandon the dichotomous and mutually exclusive definitions of automatic and controlled processes and to adopt a model and procedures that recognize that both automatic and controlled processes operate in almost any task of sufficient complexity to be of interest to social psychologists. Jacoby's (1991) process dissociation procedure (PDP) does this. It was used to examine STI first by Uleman, Blader, and Todorov (2005), and most recently by McCarthy and Skowronski (2011a). These results show that STI involves both automatic and controlled processes, operating together. Thinking of automatic and controlled as a dichotomy is less useful than conceiving of them as independent processes that both contribute to social cognition.

There is much more to STIs (as well as the other topics we have touched on). A more complete version of the STI story was recently published by Uleman, Rim, Saribay, and Kressel (2012).

Other Topics

These are only a few topics illustrating the social cognitive approach to impression formation. Here are three others that we might have covered more fully, had there been more space.

SOCIAL COGNITIVE TRANSFERENCE

Rather than conceiving of impressions as formed from observations of behavior and inferences of traits, this work takes existing conceptions of significant others as the starting point for forming impressions of strangers. If a stranger shares some features with a significant other, additional features of the significant other are assumed or extrapolated onto the stranger. This holds for traits, evaluations, and the other usual features of impressions, but also for a wide range of the perceivers' other responses to strangers, including emotions, aspects of the perceivers' self-concepts (relational selves) when with the significant other, and perceivers' behaviors. Thus, social cognitive transference engages a wider range of dependent variables and extends the usual definition of an "impression" (see Andersen, Reznik, & Glassman, 2005).

IMPRESSIONS OF PERSONS AND GROUPS

How is impression formation of persons similar to and different from impressions of groups, and how are these related? This is an old set of questions related to stereotyping (e.g., Rothbart, 1978) that has acquired new life in research by Hamilton, Sherman, and colleagues on group entitativity, that is, group cohesion, longevity, impermeability of boundaries, and so forth (e.g., Lickel, Hamilton, & Sherman, 2001). In an interesting connection with STIs, Crawford, Sherman, and Hamilton (2002) showed that spontaneously inferred traits about one member of a group are generalized to other group members if the group is high in entitativity, but not otherwise.

PEOPLE AS MORAL AGENTS AND OBJECTS

Judging people on a moral dimension has long been recognized as a high priority of perceivers. What is less clear is how targets' morality is judged, that is, what constitutes morally good and bad behavior, and when judgments based on behaviors (or group membership, etc.) affect perceptions of targets' temporary states of mind or enduring traits. To what degree are these judgments cognitive versus affective or emotional? To what extent are the inference processes conscious or nonconscious, deliberate or spontaneous, automatic and controlled, or post hoc justifications? And who is accorded the status of a moral agent, rather than being dehumanized? The social cognitive approach to impression formation (along with, e.g., experimental philosophy, social neuroscience, and developmental psychology) are contributing much to addressing and refining such questions. A quick overview of some recent viewpoints in this area is provided by Gray, Young, and Waytz's (2012) target article and reactions to it.

The Future of Social Cognition and Impression Formation

Social cognition is an experimental approach to understanding our thoughts (conscious and not) about social events. Historically, it has focused on measures such as memory performance and response times, and on concepts such as automaticity and implicit cognitive organization (e.g., Uleman, Saribay, & Gonzalez, 2008). These methods and concepts continue to be adopted more and more widely, and newer methods (e.g., social neuroscience) that give us better tools to investigate processes are becoming part of the social cognitive approach. At the same time, conceptions of what "impression formation" is about have broadened well beyond traits and social preoccupations of the Western college sophomore. The legacy of social cognitive research on impression formation is secure, and the future is wide open.

References

Aaker, J., Vohs, K. D., & Mogilner, C. (2010). Nonprofits are seen as warm and for-profits as competent: Firm stereotypes matter. *Journal of Consumer Research,37*, 224–237.

Abele, A. E., & Bruckmueller, S. (2011). The bigger one of the "Big Two"? Preferential processing of communal information. *Journal of Experimental Social Psychology, 47*, 935–948.

Allport, F. H. (1924). *Social psychology*. Boston: Houghton Mifflin.

Andersen, S. M., & Klatzky, R. L. (1987). Traits and social stereotypes: Levels of categorization in person perception. *Journal of Personality and Social Psychology, 53*, 235–246.

Andersen, S. M., Reznik, I., & Glassman, N. S. (2005). The unconscious relational self. In R. R. Hassin, J. S. Uleman, & J. A. Bargh (Eds.), *The new unconscious* (pp. 421–481). New York: Oxford University Press.

Anderson, C., & Shirako, A. (2008). Are individuals' reputations related to their history of behavior? *Journal of Personality and Social Psychology,94*, 320–333.

Anderson, J. R., & Bower, G. H. (1973). *Human associative memory*. Washington, D.C.: Winston & Sons.

Anderson, N. H. (1965). Averaging versus adding as a stimulus-combination rule in impression formation. *Journal of Experimental Psychology, 70*, 394–400.

Anderson, N. H. (1971). Two more tests against change of meaning in adjective combinations. *Journal of Verbal Learning and Verbal Behavior, 10*, 75–85.

Anderson, N. H. (1974). Cognitive algebra. In L. Berkowitz (Ed.), *Advances in Experimental Social Psychology* (Vol. 7, pp. 1–101). New York: Academic Press.

Anderson, N. H. (1981). *Foundations of information integration theory*. New York: Academic Press.

Asch, S. E. (1946). Forming impressions of personality. *Journal of Abnormal and Social Psychology, 41*, 258–290.

Asch, S. E., & Zukier, H. (1984). Thinking about persons. *Journal of Personality and Social Psychology, 46*, 1230–1240.

Baer, J., Kaufman, J. C., & Baumeister, R. F. (Eds.) (2008). *Are we free? Psychology and free will*. New York: Oxford University Press.

Bargh, J. A. (1990). Auto-motives: Preconscious determinants of social interaction. In E. T. Higgins & R. M. Sorrentino. (Eds.), *Handbook of motivation and cognition: Foundations of social behavior* (Vol. 2, pp. 93–130). New York: Guilford Press.

Bargh, J. A. (1994). The four horsemen of automaticity: Awareness, intention, efficiency, and control in social cognition. In R. S. Wyer, Jr., & T. K. Srull (Eds.), *Handbook of social cognition: Vol. 1, Basic processes* (2nd ed., pp. 1–40). Hillsdale, NJ: Erlbaum.

Bargh, J. A. (1999). The cognitive monster: The case against the controllability of automatic stereotype effects. In S. Chaiken & Y. Trope (Eds.), *Dual-process theories in social psychology* (pp. 361–382). New York: Guilford Press.

Bartlett, F. C. (1932). *Remembering: A study in experimental and social psychology*. New York: Cambridge University Press.

Baumeister, R. F. (1987). How the self became a problem: A psychological review of historical research. *Journal of Personality and Social Psychology, 52*, 163–176.

Baumeister, R. F., Bratslavsky, E., Finkenauer, C., & Vohs, K. D. (2001). Bad is stronger than good. *Review of General Psychology, 5*, 323–370.

Bem, D. J. (1967). Self-perception: An alternative interpretation of cognitive dissonance phenomena. *Psychological Review, 74*, 183–200.

Bieri, J. (1955). Cognitive complexity-simplicity and predictive behavior. *Journal of Abnormal and Social Psychology, 51*, 263–268.

Brambilla, M., Rusconi, P., Sacchi, S., & Cherubini, P. (2011). Looking for honesty: The primary role of morality (vs. sociability and competence) in information gathering. *European Journal of Social Psychology, 41*, 135–143.

Bruner, J. S. (1957). On perceptual readiness. *Psychological Review, 64*, 123–152.

Byrne, D., London, O., & Reeves, K (1968). The effects of physical attractiveness, sex, and attitude similarity on interpersonal attraction. *Journal of Personality, 36*, 259–271.

Cantor, N., & Mischel, W. (1977). Traits as prototypes: Effects on recognition memory. *Journal of Personality and Social Psychology, 35*, 38–48.

Carlston, D. E., & Skowronski, J. J. (1994). Savings in the relearning of trait information as evidence for spontaneous inference generation. *Journal of Personality and Social Psychology, 66*, 840–856.

Carlston, D. E., & Skowronski, J. J. (2005). Linking vs. thinking: Evidence for the different associative and attributional bases of spontaneous trait transference and spontaneous trait inference. *Journal of Personality and Social Psychology, 89*, 884–898.

Carpenter, K. K. (1992). Inside/outside, which side counts? In R. V. H. Dover, K. E. Seibold, &. J H. McDowell (Eds.), *Andean cosmologies through time* (pp. 115–136). Bloomington, IN: Indiana University Press.

Chartrand, T. L., & Bargh, J. A. (1996). Automatic activation of impression formation and memorization goals: Nonconscious goal priming reproduces effects of explicit task instructions. *Journal of Personality and Social Psychology, 71*, 464–478.

Christiansen, N. D., Wolcott-Burnam, S. B., Janovics, J. E., Quirk, S. W., & Burns, G. N. (2005). The good judge revisited: Individual differences in the accuracy of personality judgments. *Human Performance, 18*, 123–149.

Cohen, A. R. (1961). Cognitive tuning as a factor affecting impression formation. *Journal of Personality, 29*, 235–245.

Collins, A. M., & Quillian, M. R. (1969). Experiments on semantic memory and language comprehension. In L. W. Gregg (Ed.), *Cognition and learning*. New York: Wiley.

Crawford, M. T., Sherman, S. J., & Hamilton, D. L. (2002). Perceived entiativity, stereotype formation, and the interchangeability of group members. *Journal of Personality and Social Psychology, 83,* 1076–1094.

Cronbach, L. (1955). Processes affecting scores on "understanding of others" and "assumed similarity." *Psychological Bulletin, 52,* 177–193.

Crowne, D. P., & Marlowe, D. (1960). A new scale of social desirability independent of psychopathology. *Journal of Consulting Psychology, 24,* 349–354.

Cuddy, A. J. C., Fiske, S. T., & Glick, P. (2007). The BIAS map: Behaviors from intergroup affect and stereotypes. *Journal of Personality and Social Psychology, 92,* 631–648.

Dawes, R. M., & Smith, T. (1985). Attitude and opinion measurement. In G. Lindzey & E. Aronson (Eds.), *Handbook of social psychology* (3rd ed., Vol. 1., pp. 509–566). New York: Random House.

De Bruin, Ellen N. M., & Van Lange, Paul A. M. (2000). What people look for in others: Influences of the perceiver and the perceived on information selection. *Personality and Social Psychology Bulletin, 26,* 206–219.

Dennett, D. C. (2011). *"My brain made me do it" (when neuroscientists think they can do philosophy).* Max Weber Programme, European University Institute, Florence, Italy.

De Soto, C. B., London, M., & Handel, S. (1965). Social reasoning and spatial paralogic. *Journal of Personality and Social Psychology, 2,* 513–521.

Dijksterhuis, A., & Aarts, H. (2010). Goals, attention, and (un)consciousness. *Annual Review of Psychology, 61,* 467–490.

Erber, R., & Fiske, S. T. (1984). Outcome dependency and attention to inconsistent information. *Journal of Personality and Social Psychology, 47,* 709–726.

Eyal, T., Hoover, G. M., Fujita, K., & Nussbaum, S. (2011). The effect of distance-dependent construals on schema-driven impression formation. *Journal of Experimental Social Psychology, 47,* 278–281.

Ferreira, M. B., Garcia-Marques, L., Hamilton, D., Ramos, T., Uleman, J. S., & Jerónimo, R. (2012). On the relation between spontaneous trait inferences and intentional inferences: An inference monitoring hypothesis. *Journal of Experimental Social Psychology, 48,* 1–12.

Fiedler, K., Schenck, W., Watling, M., & Menges, J. I. (2005). Priming trait inferences through pictures and moving pictures: The impact of open and closed mindsets. *Journal of Personality and Social Psychology, 88,* 229–244.

Fiske, S. T. (1980). Attention and weight in person perception: The impact of negative and extreme behavior. *Journal of Personality and Social Psychology, 38,* 889–906.

Fiske, S. T. (2004). *Social beings: A core motives approach to social psychology.* Hoboken, NJ: John Wiley & Co.

Fiske, S. T., Cuddy, A. J. C., Glick, P., & Xu, J. (2002). A model of (often mixed) stereotype content: Competence and warmth respectively follow from perceived status and competition. *Journal of Personality and Social Psychology, 82,* 878–902.

Fiske, S. T., & Taylor, S. E. (1984). *Social cognition.* Reading, MA: Addison-Wesley.

Funder, D. C. (1995). On the accuracy of personality judgment: A realistic approach. *Psychological Review, 102,* 652–670.

Gage, N. L., & Cronbach, L. (1955). Conceptual and methodological problems in interpersonal perception. *Psychological Review, 62,* 411–422.

Garcia-Marques, L., Ferreira, M. B., Nunes, L. D., Garrido, M. V., & Garcia-Marques, T. (2010). False memories and impressions of personality. *Social Cognition, 28,* 556–568.

Gill, M. J., & Swann, W. B. (2004). On what it means to know someone: A matter of pragmatics. *Journal of Personality and Social Psychology, 86,* 405–418.

Gollin, E. S. (1954). Forming impressions of personality. *Journal of Personality, 23,* 65–76.

Goodwin, S. A., Operario, D., & Fiske, S. T. (1998). Situational power and interpersonal dominance facilitate bias and inequality. *Journal of Social Issues, 54,* 677–698.

Gray, K., Young, L., & Waytz, A. (2012). Mind perception is the essence of morality. *Psychological Inquiry, 23,* 101–124. See also commentaries and reply, pp. 125–215.

Ham, J., & Vonk, R. (2003). Smart and easy: Co-occurring activation of spontaneous trait inferences and spontaneous situation inferences. *Journal of Experimental Social Psychology, 39,* 434–447.

Hamilton, D. L., Leirer, V., & Katz, L. B. (1980). Cognitive representation of personality impressions: Organizational processes in 1st impression-formation. *Journal of Personality and Social Psychology, 39,* 150–163.

Hamilton, D. L., & Zanna, M. P. (1974). Context effects in impression formation: Changes in connotative meaning. *Journal of Personality and Social Psychology, 29,* 649–654.

Hardin, C., & Banaji, M. R. (1993). The influence of language on thought. *Social Cognition, 11,* 277–308.

Harris, L., & Fiske, S. T. (2009). Social neuroscience evidence for dehumanized perception. *European Review of Social Psychology, 20,* 192–231.

Hastie, R. (1980). Memory for behavioral information that confirms or contradicts a personality impression. In R. Hastie, T. M. Ostrom, E. B. Ebbesen, R. S. Wyer Jr., D. L. Hamilton, & D. E. Carlston (Eds.). (1980). *Person memory: The cognitive basis of social perception* (pp. 155–177). Hillsdale, NJ: Erlbaum.

Hastie, R., & Kumar, P. A. (1979). Person memory: Personality traits as organizing principles in memory for behaviors. *Journal of Personality and Social Psychology, 37,* 25–38.

Hastie, R., Ostrom, T. M., Ebbesen, E. B., Wyer, R. S. Jr., Hamilton, D. L., & Carlston, D. E. (1980). *Person memory: The cognitive basis of social perception.* Hillsdale, NJ: Erlbaum.

Heider, F. (1944). Social perception and phenomenal causality. *Psychological Review, 51,* 358–374.

Henrich, J., Boyd, R., Bowles, S., Camerer, C., Fehr, E., & Gintis, H. (Eds.) (2004). *Foundations of human sociality: Economic experiments and ethnographic evidence from fifteen small-scale societies.* New York: Oxford University Press.

Higgins, E. T. (1996). Knowledge activation: Accessibility, applicability, and salience. In E. T. Higgins & A. W. Kruglanski (Eds.), *Social psychology: Handbook of basic principles* (pp. 133–168). New York: Guilford Press.

Higgins, E. T., Bargh, J. A., & Lombardi, W. J. (1985). Nature of priming effects on categorization. *Journal of Experimental Psychology: Learning, Memory, and Cognition, 11,* 59–69.

Higgins, E. T., Herman, C. P., & Zanna, M. P. (1981). *Social cognition: The Ontario Symposium* (Vol. 1). Hillsdale, NJ: Erlbaum.

Higgins, E. T., Rholes, W. S., & Jones, C. R. (1977). Category accessibility and impression formation. *Journal of Experimental Social Psychology, 13,* 141–154.

Hilton, J. L., & Darley, J. M. (1991). The effects of interaction goals on person perception. In M. P. Zanna (Ed.), *Advances in Experimental Social Psychology* (Vol. 24, pp. 235–267). San Diego, CA: Academic Press.

Hoffman, C., Mischel, W., & Baer, J. S. (1981). Language and person cognition: Effects of communicative set on trait attribution. *Journal of Personality and Social Psychology, 46*, 1029–1043.

Hoffman, C., Mischel, W., & Mazze, K. (1984). The role of purpose in the organization of information about behavior: Trait-based versus goal-based categories in person cognition. *Journal of Personality and Social Psychology, 40*, 211–225.

Ickes, W. (2009). *Strangers in a strange lab: How personality shapes our initial encounters with others.* New York: Oxford University Press.

Jacoby, L. L. (1991). A process dissociation framework: Separating automatic from intentional uses of memory. *Journal of Memory and Language, 30*, 513–541.

Jones, E. E. (1954). Authoritarianism as a determinant of first-impression formation. *Journal of Personality, 23*, 107–127.

Jones, E. E. (1985). Major developments in five decades of social psychology. In G. Lindzey & E. Aronson (Eds.), *The handbook of social psychology* (3rd ed., Vol. 1, pp. 47–108). New York: Random House.

Jones, E. E. (1990). *Interpersonal perception.* New York: W. H. Freeman.

Jones, E. E., Davis, K. E., & Gergen, K. J. (1961). Role playing variations and their informational value for person perception. *Journal of Abnormal and Social Psychology, 63*, 302–310.

Jones, E. E., & McGillis, D. (1976). Correspondent inferences and the attribution cube: A comparative reappraisal. In J. Harvey, W. Ickes, & R. Kidd (Eds.), *New directions in attribution research* (Vol. 1, pp. 390–420). Hillsdale, NJ: Erlbaum.

Jones, E. E., & Thibaut, J. W. (1958). Interaction goals as bases of inference in interpersonal perception. In R. Tagiuri & L. Petrullo (Eds.), *Person perception and interpersonal behavior* (pp. 151–178). Stanford, CA: Stanford University Press.

Judd, C. M., James-Hawkins, L., Yzerbyt, V., & Kashima, Y. (2005). Fundamental dimensions of social judgment: Understanding the relations between judgments of competence and warmth. *Journal of Personality and Social Psychology, 89*, 899–913.

Kenny, D. A. (1994). *Interpersonal perception: A social relations analysis.* New York: Guilford.

Kenny, D. A. (2004). PERSON: A general model of interpersonal perception. *Personality and Social Psychology Review, 8*, 265–280.

Kenny, D. A., & Albright, L. (1987). Accuracy in interpersonal perception: A social relations analysis. *Psychological Bulletin, 102*, 390–402.

Kenny, D. A., & West, T. V. (2010). Similarity and agreement in self- and other perception: A meta-analysis. *Personality and Social Psychology Review, 14*, 196–213

Kenny, D. A., West, T., V., Malloy, T. E., & Albright, L. (2006). Componential analysis of interpersonal perception data. *Personality and Social Psychology Review, 10*, 282–294.

Kervyn, N., Yzerbyt, V. Y., Judd, C. M., & Nunes, A. (2009). A question of compensation: The social life of the fundamental dimensions of social perception. *Journal of Personality and Social Psychology, 96*, 828–842.

Kitayama, S., Duffy, S., & Uchida, Y. (2007). Self as cultural mode of being. In S. Kitayama & D. Cohen, *Handbook of cultural psychology* (pp. 136–174). New York: Guilford Press.

Klein, J. (1996). Negativity in impression of political candidates revisited: The 1992 election. *Personality and Social Psychology Bulletin, 22*, 288–295

Klein, S. B., & Loftus, J. (1990). Rethinking the role of organization in person memory: An independent trace storage model. *Journal of Personality and Social Psychology, 59*, 400–410.

Kuethe, J. L. (1962). Social schemas. *Journal of Abnormal and Social Psychology, 64*, 31–38.

Leach, C. W., Ellemers, N., Barreto. (2007). Group virtue: The importance of morality (vs. competence and sociability) in the positive evaluation of in-groups. *Journal of Personality and Social Psychology,93*, 234–249.

Lebra, T. S. (1993). Culture, self, and communication in Japan and the United States. In W. B. Gudykunst (Ed.), *Communication in Japan and the United States* (pp. 51–87). Albany, NY: State University of New York Press.

LeVine, R. A. (2007). Anthropological foundations of cultural psychology. In S. Kitayama & D. Cohen, *Handbook of cultural psychology* (pp. 40–58). New York: Guilford Press.

Lickel, B., Hamilton, D. L., & Sherman, S. J. (2001). Elements of a lay theory of groups: Types of groups, relationship styles, and the perception of group entitativity. *Personality and Social Psychology Review, 5*, 129–140.

Likert, R. (1932). A technique for the measurement of attitudes. *Archives of Psychology, 140*, 1–55.

Lillard, A. (1998). Ethnopsychologies: Cultural variations in theories of mind. *Psychological Bulletin, 123*, 3–32.

Luchins, A. S. (1948). Forming impressions of personality: A critique. *Journal of Abnormal and Social Psychology, 43*, 318–325.

Mayer, J.D., Roberts, R.D., & Barsade, S. (2008). Human abilities: Emotional intelligence. *Annual Review of Psychology, 59*, 507–536.

McCarthy, R. J., & Skowronski, J. J. (2011a). The interplay of automatic and controlled processing in the expression of spontaneously inferred traits: A PDP analysis. *Journal of Personality and Social Psychology, 100*, 229–240.

McCarthy, R. J., & Skowronski, J. J. (2011b). You're getting warmer: Level of construal affect the impact of central traits on impression formation. *Journal of Experimental Social Psychology, 47*, 1304–1307

McDougall, W. (1908). *Introduction to social psychology.* London: Methuen & Co.

Milgram, S. (1974). *Obedience to authority: An experimental view.* New York: Harper & Row.

Moskowitz, G. B. (1993). Individual differences in social categorization: The effects of personal need for structure on spontaneous trait inferences. *Journal of Personality and Social Psychology, 65*, 132–142.

Moskowitz, G. B., Gollwitzer, P. M., Wasel, W., & Schaal, B. (1999). *Journal of Personality and Social Psychology, 77*, 167–184.

Moskowitz, G. B., Li, P., & Kirk, E. R. (2004). The Implicit Volition Model: On the preconscious regulation of temporarily adopted goals. In M. P. Zanna (Ed.), *Advances in experimental social psychology* (Vol. 36, pp. 317–413). San Diego, CA: Elsevier Academic Press.

Murphy, G., & Murphy, L. B. (1931). *Experimental social psychology.* New York: Harper.

Murphy, G., Murphy, L. B., & Newcomb, T. M. (1937). *Experimental social psychology* (rev. ed.). New York: Harper.

Nahmias, E. (2005). Agency, authorship, and illusion. *Consciousness and Cognition: An International Journal. Special Issue: The Brain and Its Self. 14*, 771–785.

Neuberg, S., & Fiske, S. T. (1987). Motivational influences on impression formation: Outcome dependency, accuracy-driven attention, and individuating processes. *Journal of Personality and Social Psychology, 53*, 431–44.

Orehek, E., Dechesne, M., Fishbach, A., Kruglanski, A. W., & Chun, W. Y. (2010). On the inferential epistemics of trait centrality in impression formation. *European Journal of Social Psychology, 40,* 1120–1135.

Ostrom, T. M. (1984). The sovereignty of social cognition. In R. S. Wyer, Jr., & T. K. Srull (Eds.), *Handbook of social cognition* (Vol. 1, pp. 1–38). Hillsdale, NJ: Erlbaum.

Overbeck, J. R., & Park, B. (2006). Powerful perceivers, powerless objects: Flexibility of powerholders' social attention. *Organizational Behavior and Human Decision Processes, 99,* 227–243.

Parducci, A. (1968). The relativism of absolute judgments. *Scientific American, 219,* 84–90.

Passini, F. T., & Norman, W. T. (1966). A universal conception of personality structure. *Journal of Personality and Social Psychology, 4,* 44–49.

Peabody, D. (1970). Evaluative and descriptive aspects in personality perception: A reappraisal. *Journal of Personality and Social Psychology, 16,* 639–646.

Perner, J., & Kühberger, A. (2005). Mental simulation: Royal road to other minds? In B. F. Malle & S. D. Hodges (Eds.), *Other minds: How humans bridge the divide between self and others* (pp. 174–189). New York: Guilford Publications.

Pinker, S. (2002). *The blank slate: The modern denial of human nature.* New York: Viking.

Pratto, F., & John, O. P. (1991). Automatic vigilance: The attention-grabbing power of negative social information. *Journal of Personality and Social Psychology, 61,* 380–391.

Pronin, E., Gilovich, T., & Ross, L. (2004). Objectivity in the eye of the beholder: Divergent perceptions of bias in self versus others. *Psychological Review, 111,* 781–799.

Reeder, G. D., & Brewer, M. B. (1979). A schematic model of dispositional attribution in interpersonal perception. *Psychological Review, 86,* 61–79.

Rim, S., Min, K. E., Uleman, J. S., Chartrand, T. L., & Carlston, D. E. (2012, under review). A functional approach to the stages of spontaneous impression formation: How an affiliation goal affects spontaneous trait activation and binding. *Journal Experimental Social Psychology,*

Robinson, D. N. (1995). *An intellectual history of psychology* (3rd ed.). Madison, WI: University of Wisconsin Press.

Rosaldo, M. Z. (1980). *Knowledge and passion: Illongot notions of self and social life.* Cambridge, UK: Cambridge University Press.

Rosenberg, S., Nelson, C., & Vivekananthan, P. (1968). A multidimensional approach to the structure of personality impressions. *Journal of Personality and Social Psychology, 9,* 283–294.

Rosenberg, S., & Sedlak, A. (1972). Structural representations of implicit personality theory. In L. Berkowitz (Ed.), *Advances in experimental social psychology* (Vol. 6, pp. 235–297). New York: Academic Press.

Ross, E. A. (1908). *Social psychology: An outline and source book.* New York: Macmillan.

Ross, L., Lepper, M., & Ward, A. (2009). History of social psychology: Insights, challenges, and contributions to theory and application. In D. T. Gilbert, S. T. Fiske, & G. Lindzey (Eds.), *The handbook of social psychology* (5th ed., Vol. 1, pp. 3–50). Hoboken, NJ: John Wiley & Sons.

Rossano, M. J. (2007). Supernaturalizing social life: Religion and the evolution of human cooperation. *Human Nature, 18,* 272–294.

Rothbart, M. (1978). From individual to group impressions: Availability heuristics in stereotype formation. *Journal of Experimental Social Psychology, 14,* 237–255.

Rozin, P., Berman, L., & Royzman, E. B. (2010). Biases in the use of positive and negative words across twenty natural languages. *Cognition and Emotion, 24,* 536–248.

Rozin, P., & Rozyman, E. B. (2001). Negativity bias, negativity dominance, and contagion. *Personality and Social Psychology Review, 5,* 296–320.

Saribay, S. A., Rim, S., & Uleman, J. S. (2012, in press). Primed self-construal, culture, and stages of impression formation. *Social Psychology, 43,* 196–204.

Saxe, R. (2005). Against simulation: The argument from error. *Trends in Cognitive Science, 9,* 174–179.

Schneider, D. J. (1973). Implicit personality theory: A review. *Psychological Bulletin, 79,* 294–309.

Schneider, D. J., Hastorf, A. H., & Ellsworth, P. C. (1979). *Person perception* (2nd ed.). Reading, MA: Addison-Wesley.

Sedikides, C., & Ostrom, T. M. (1988). Are person categories used when organizing information about unfamiliar sets of persons? *Social Cognition, 6,* 252–267.

Shannon, C. E., & Weaver, W. (1949). *The mathematical theory of communication.* Champaign-Urbana, IL: University of Illinois Press.

Shapley, H., Lyman, T., Cannon, W. B., Pratt, C. C., Houdini, H., & Wolbach, S. B. (1925). Report of the $5000 Award Committee appointed by the Journal of Abnormal and Social Psychology. *Journal of Abnormal and Social Psychology, 20,* 359–361.

Skowronski, J. J., & Carlston, D. E. (1989). Negativity and extremity biases in impression formation: A review of explanations. *Psychological Bulletin, 105,* 131–142.

Skowronski, J. J., Carlston, D. E., Mae, L., & Crawford, M. T. (1998). Spontaneous trait transference: Communicators take on the qualities they describe in others. *Journal of Personality and Social Psychology, 74,* 837–848.

Smith, E. R. (1998). Mental representation and memory. In D. T. Gilbert, S. T. Fiske, & G. Lindzey (Eds.), *The handbook of social psychology* (4th ed., Vol. 1, pp. 391–445). Boston: McGraw-Hill.

Snell, B. (1953). *The discovery of the mind: The Greek origins of European thought.* Cambridge, MA: Harvard University Press.

Srull, T. K., & Wyer, R. S., Jr. (1979). The role of category accessibility in the interpretation of information about persons: Some determinants and implications. *Journal of Personality and Social Psychology, 37,* 1660–1672.

Stewart, L. H., Ajina, S., Getov, S., Bahrami, B., Todorov, A., & Rees, G. (2012). Unconscious evaluation of faces on social dimensions. *Journal of Experimental Psychology: General, 141,* 715–727.

Taft, R. (1955). The ability to judge people. *Psychological Bulletin, 52,* 1–23

Tajfel, H. (1959). The anchoring effects of value in a scale of judgments. *British Journal of Psychology, 50,* 294–304.

Tajfel, H. (1969). Social and cultural factors in perception. In G. Lindzey & E. Aronson (Eds.), *Handbook of social psychology,* 2nd ed (Vol. 3, pp. 315–394). Cambridge, MA: Addison-Wesley.

Tajfel, H. (1970). Experiments in intergroup discrimination. *Scientific American, 223,* 96–102.

Talaska, C. A., Fiske, S. T., & Chaiken, S. (2008). Legitimating racial discrimination: Emotions, not beliefs, best predict discrimination in a meta-analysis. *Social Justice Research, 21,* 263–296.

Thorndike, R. L., & Stein, S. (1937). An evaluation of the attempts to measure social intelligence. *Psychological Bulletin, 34,* 275–285.

Thurstone, L. L. (1928). Attitudes can be measured. *American Journal of Sociology, 33,* 529–554.

Todorov, A., Said, C. P., Engel, A. D., & Oosterhof, N. N. (2008). Understanding evaluation of faces on social dimensions. *Trends in Cognitive Sciences,12*, 455–460.

Todorov, A., & Uleman, J. S. (2002). Spontaneous trait inferences are bound to actors: Evidence from false recognition. *Journal of Personality and Social Psychology, 83*, 1051–1065.

Trope, Y., & Liberman, N. (2010). Construal-Level Theory of psychological distance. *Psychological Review, 117*, 440–463.

Uleman, J. S., Blader, S. L., & Todorov, A. (2005). Implicit impressions. In R. R. Hassin, J. S. Uleman, & J. A. Bargh (Eds.), *The new unconscious* (pp. 362–392). New York: Oxford University Press.

Uleman, J. S., & Moskowitz, G. B. (1994). Unintended effects of goals on unintended inferences. *Journal of Personality and Social Psychology, 66*, 490–501.

Uleman, J. S., Rim, S., Saribay, S. A., & Kressel, L. M. (2012). Controversies, questions, and prospects for spontaneous social inferences. *Personality and Social Psychology Compass, 6*, 657–673.

Uleman, J. S., & Saribay, S. A. (2012). Initial impressions of others. In K. Deaux & M. Snyder (Eds.), *The Oxford handbook of personality and social psychology* (pp. 337–366). New York: Oxford University Press.

Uleman, J. S., Saribay, S. A., & Gonzalez, C. (2008). Spontaneous inferences, implicit impressions, and implicit theories. *Annual Review of Psychology, 59*, 329–360.

Uleman, J. S., Winborne, W. C., Winter, L., & Shechter, D. (1986). Personality differences in spontaneous personality inferences at encoding. *Journal of Personality and Social Psychology, 51*, 396–403.

Van Boven, L., & Loewenstein, G. (2003). Social projection of transient drive states. *Personality and Social Psychology Bulletin, 29*, 1159–1168.

Vescio, T. K., & Guinote, A. (Eds.). (2010). *The social psychology of power*. New York: Guilford Press.

Vonk, R. (1996). Negativity and potency effects in impression formation. *European Journal of Social Psychology, 26*, 851–865.

Vonk, R. (1998). Effects of behavioral causes and consequences on person judgments. *Personality and Social Psychology Bulletin, 24*, 1065–1074

Wegner, D. M. (2005). Who is the controller of controlled processes? In R. R. Hassin, J. S. Uleman, & J. A. Bargh (Eds.), *The new unconscious* (pp. 19–36). New York: Oxford University Press.

Wegner, D. M., & Vallacher, R. R. (1977). *Implicit psychology: An introduction to social cognition*. New York: Oxford University Press.

Weis, S., & Süß, H. M. (2007). Reviving the search for social intelligence: A multitrait-multimethod study of its structure and construct validity. *Personality and Individual Differences, 42*, 3–14.

West, T. V., & Kenny, D. A. (2011). The truth and bias model of judgment. *Psychological Review, 118*, 357–378.

Williams, L. E., & Bargh, J. A. (2008). Experiencing physical warmth promotes interpersonal warmth. *Science, 322*, 606–607.

Winter, L., & Uleman, J. S. (1984). When are social judgments made? Evidence for the spontaneousness of trait inferences. *Journal of Personality and Social Psychology, 47*, 237–252.

Wishner, J. (1960). Reanalysis of "impressions of personality." *Psychological Review, 67*, 96–112.

Wojciszke, B., Brycz, H., & Borkenau, P. (1993). Effects of information content and evaluative extremity on positivity and negativity biases. *Journal of Personality and Social Psychology, 64*, 327–335.

Wyer, R. S., Jr. (1973). Category ratings for "subjective expected values": Implications for attitude formation and change. *Psychological Review, 80*, 446–467.

Wyer, R. S., Jr., & Carlston, D. E. (1979). *Social cognition, inference, and attribution*. Hillsdale, NJ: Erlbaum.

Yzerbyt, V., Provost, V., & Corneille, O. (2005). Not competent but warm…really? Compensatory stereotypes in the French-speaking world. *Group Processes & Intergroup Relations, 8*, 291–308.

Zajonc, R. B. (1999). One hundred years of rationality assumptions in social psychology. In A. Rodrigues & R. V. Levine (1999). *Reflections on 100 years of experimental social psychology* (pp. 200–214). New York: Basic Books.

Zanna, M. P., & Hamilton, D. L. (1972). Attribute dimensions and patterns of trait inferences. *Psychonomic Science, 27*, 353–354.

Automaticity and Control in Stereotyping and Prejudice: The Revolutionary Role of Social Cognition Across Three Decades of Research

Margo J. Monteith, Anna Woodcock, *and* Jill E. Gulker

Abstract

This chapter provides a historical overview of research on stereotyping and prejudice inspired by social cognition. Before the 1980s, social cognition stimulated understandings of stereotype development, organization, and use. Social cognition research burgeoned in the 1980s and thereafter, emphasizing most notably the roles of automaticity (or implicit processes) and control. The focus on automatic processes came at a crucial juncture in the 1980s, when consciously held attitudes alone could not explain racial biases. The 1990s saw the development of sophisticated procedures for assessing individual differences in automaticity and increased understanding of self-regulation and control. These emphases continued in the 2000s, along with advances in process parsing, neuroscientific approaches, and investigations of malleability. Altogether, the chapter makes clear the revolutionary role of the social cognition approach.

Key Words: stereotyping, prejudice, social cognition, automaticity, control, implicit processes, self-regulation, malleability

Most researchers who study stereotyping and prejudice rely on the social cognition approach in at least some aspect, if not in most aspects, of their work. Indeed, we would go so far as to argue that social cognition is part and parcel of contemporary research in this area. The approach has been revolutionary, shaping not only *how* we study phenomena related to stereotyping and prejudice but also our recognition of *what* phenomena call for scientific investigation. In other words, social cognition has not just contributed to progress in stereotyping and prejudice, it has also played a critical, generative role.

Our goal in this chapter is to trace the building of an "edifice" of knowledge concerning stereotyping and prejudice across three decades. Our first goal in the chapter is to provide a brief historical overview of the ways in which stereotyping and prejudice were studied before the advent of the

social cognition approach, which can be contrasted with later years. Next, we highlight the transformative effect of the social cognition approach on the research questions and methods used in the study of stereotyping and prejudice. In the interest of providing a thorough but not overwhelmingly dense account, we limit our focus in the next three (and main) sections of the chapter. Specifically, our main goal of the chapter, as reflected in these sections, is to trace how social cognition has contributed to our understanding of the role of automatic and controlled processes in stereotyping and prejudice. As will be seen, the foundations were laid for studying automaticity and control in stereotyping and prejudice in the 1980s, and considerable research built on these foundations in the 1990s. The first decade of the new millennium was a ripe time for taking stock. Researchers challenged the existing knowledge base and in so doing made renovations, did fine-tuning, and created additions. These challenges and changes, we would argue, have made our knowledge structure even stronger, and we expect even greater things in the future through application of the social cognition approach.

Historical Overview
Early Approaches to Stereotyping and Prejudice

Until the 1920s, researchers approached matters related to group membership (particularly racial group membership) by identifying and seeking explanations for the supposed mental superiority of whites compared with "backward" races (see Duckitt, 1992). However, historical and societal changes prompted an evolution in thinking that resulted in a radical shift in the way race matters were conceptualized. For example, World War I, the Civil Rights Movement in the United States in the 1920s, and immigration patterns all contributed to the view that negative racial attitudes were actually a social problem (see Duckitt, 1992). Also around this time, journalist Walter Lippmann published his book, *Public Opinion* (1922). In this book, he coined the term "stereotype" as it is used by social scientists today, borrowing the word from the printing industry, which used it to refer to a metal plate used for duplicating pages. Lippmann described stereotypes as "pictures in our heads," arguing that stereotypic preconceptions greatly simplify our processing of complex social reality.

As the study of stereotyping and prejudice started to take shape, early discourse was aimed at addressing definitional issues (e.g., are stereotypes incorrect and therefore based on faulty reasoning? Does prejudice involve only negative attitudes, or can there also be positive prejudice?). Researchers also focused on measurement issues. Various means of assessing prejudiced attitudes were developed (see Harding, Proshansky, Kutner, & Chein, 1969), such as Bogardus's (1925) social distance measure. In contrast, a more singular focus was evident for stereotype measurement. Specifically, the well-known Katz-Braly (1933) method involved providing participants with an adjective checklist, asking them to check the adjectives that described a particular group, and then defining the stereotype content based on the adjectives that were most frequently checked. This became the standard method of stereotype assessment for several decades. Katz and Braly's (1933) original study was replicated on two later occasions (Gilbert, 1951; Karlins, Coffman,

& Walters, 1969), forming the "Princeton trilogy." Despite its popularity, the method had some serious drawbacks. For example, it required that stereotypes be consensually rather than individually defined, and only content that the researchers chose to include on the trait adjective checklist could be considered part of the stereotype.

In addition to definition and measurement issues, three distinct orientations for explaining stereotyping and prejudice gained prominence (see Ashmore & Del Boca, 1981). First, during the 1930s to 1950s, there was a strong motivational emphasis derived from the psychodynamic perspective and illustrated by work on the "authoritarian personality" (Adorno, Frenkel-Brunswik, Levinson, & Sanford, 1950). Second, researchers pursued a sociocultural approach, especially in the 1960s and 1970s, which emphasized the role of family, peers, the media, and "cultural-bound traditions" (Allport, 1954, p. 202) in the acquisition and maintenance of biased beliefs and attitudes (e.g., Pettigrew, 1958; Proshansky, 1966). In the latter part of this period, researchers linked intergroup bias to competition (Sherif, 1966) and to social structural conditions (e.g., Blauner, 1972).

The third distinct orientation for understanding stereotyping and prejudice was the cognitive perspective. As illustrated in the following quotes, this orientation had an early beginning in the writings of Lippmann (1922) and Allport (1954):

> Modern life is hurried and multifarious.... There is neither time nor opportunity for intimate acquaintance. Instead we notice a trait which marks a well known type, and fill in the rest of the picture by means of the stereotypes we carry about in our heads.... The subtlest and most pervasive of all influences are those which create and maintain the repertory of stereotypes. We are told about the world before we see it. We imagine most things before we experience them. And those preconceptions...govern deeply the whole process of perception.... They are aroused by small signs.... Aroused, they flood fresh vision with older images, and project into the world what has resurrected in memory. (Lippmann, 1922, pp. 89–90)

> The human mind must think with the aid of categories.... Once formed, categories are the basis for normal prejudgment. We cannot possibly avoid this process. Orderly living depends on it.... Our experience in life tends to form itself into clusters (concepts, categories), and while we may call on the right cluster at the wrong time, or the wrong

cluster at the right time, still the process in question dominates our entire mental life. A million events befall us every day. We cannot handle so many events. If we think of them at all, we type them. (Allport, 1954, p. 20)

Lippmann's (1922) quote underscores his keen awareness of the many ways in which stereotypes bias social perception. The quote from Allport (1954) draws attention to the need for humans to categorize and the idea that this is an inevitable process from which stereotyping naturally follows. The prescient thinking of Lippmann and Allport continues to inspire present-day social scientists. However, the tools and methods to investigate their ideas empirically did not become available until the development of the social cognition approach.

The Transformative Years: Stereotyping and Prejudice from a Social Cognitive Perspective

Social cognition gained momentum in social psychology and in the study of stereotyping and prejudice following the cognitive revolution and the development of the field of cognitive psychology. This approach placed stereotyping and prejudice squarely in the realm of basic, normal cognitive processing. Stereotypes and prejudice were no longer seen necessarily as the result of affective and motivational distortions or based on a history of intergroup conflict, but rather as resulting from normal information processing. By the 1980s, this approach had begun to transform not only how stereotyping and prejudice researchers did their research but also the nature of the questions they asked. In other words, social cognition introduced a whole new way of thinking about and investigating stereotypes and prejudice (cf., Hamilton, Stroessner, & Driscoll, 1994). This new way of thinking resulted in much exploration into the formation, organization, and application of stereotypes and prejudices.

For example, great progress was made toward understanding the processes that give rise to stereotype formation, a topic covered in depth in Chapter 27 of this volume. Also, researchers began to conceptualize stereotypes as a cognitive structure. This work went beyond the mere notion that certain traits define stereotypes to investigate issues like how groups were represented and organized and how representational features might affect judgments, behaviors, and chances of stereotype change. For example, are stereotypes prototypes within a hierarchical categorization system (Rosch, 1978), are they instead judgmental generalizations based on stored exemplar information (Smith & Zarate, 1992), or is their structure best represented by a combination of prototypic and exemplar information (see Hamilton & Sherman, 1994)?

Researchers also focused on how stereotypes affect information processing and related outcomes. This emphasis included questions related to attention, such as whether participants attend more or less to stereotype-consistent or stereotype-inconsistent information (Bodenhausen, 1988; Sherman & Hamilton, 1994). It also spurred the now classic work showing that people's interpretation of targets' behavior can be biased by hypothesis (stereotype)-confirming information processing (e.g., Darley & Gross, 1983; Sagar & Schofield, 1980). Further, research found that perceivers' stereotypes can lead to targets behaving in expectancy-confirming ways, or to self-fulfilling prophecies (Snyder, Tanke, & Berscheid, 1977; Word, Zanna, & Cooper, 1974). Throughout this work, there seemed to be an implicit assumption that many of the studied processes operated and produced their effects without people's awareness. For example, stereotyped targets were assumed to adopt behavior that was consistent with perceiver's expectancies without necessarily having the knowledge that they were doing so. Thus, the idea of *unconscious influences* was taking form—a perspective that would become critical to most social cognition research on stereotyping and prejudice in the future.

In sum, whereas early stereotyping research inspired by the Katz-Braly (1933) approach produced a nearly exclusive focus on stereotype content, the social cognition approach stimulated new understandings of stereotype development, organization, and use. In addition to these research developments, the social cognition approach opened up the study of automatic and controlled processes as they relate to the operation and use of stereotypes and prejudiced attitudes. Indeed, between 1980 and present, the literature on stereotyping and prejudice has been steadily flooded with research addressing issues of automaticity and control. This has easily been the reigning emphasis, and our plan for the remainder of this chapter is to focus on this topic. Specifically, we will trace major theoretical, methodological, and empirical developments resulting from the focus on automaticity and control. We divide our review of this literature into three sections corresponding to the 1980s, 1990s, and the first decade of the 21st century (hereafter 2000s) to more clearly highlight the primary questions of interest and research progress made since the social cognition approach took root.

Automaticity and Control in Stereotyping and Prejudice
The 1980s: Laying Foundations

When social cognition took hold in social psychology, societal prejudice in the United States appeared to be changing from an "old-fashioned" variety that involved blatantly negative attitudes that people expressed in brazen and unapologetic ways to a more modern form. Researchers became aware of this change as they observed inconsistencies between self-report measures of prejudice and continuing evidence of behavioral racial bias. For example, Crosby, Bromley, and Saxe's (1980) influential review pointed to anti-black biases in experiments on helping behavior, aggression, and nonverbal communication, despite survey evidence suggesting that anti-black prejudice had declined. How could such discrepancies be explained? Perhaps events such as the Civil Rights Movement and accompanying legislative changes had prompted a cultural transformation that encouraged people to hide their prejudiced attitudes, even though bias continued to seep out in subtle ways to affect behavior. Crosby et al. (1980) favored this impression management explanation, concluding that "...our own position has been to question the assumption that verbal reports reflect actual sentiments, and we inferred from the literature that whites today are, in fact, more prejudiced than they are wont to admit" (p. 557).

However, advances brought by the social cognition approach made it possible to view the stark inconsistency between self-reported attitudes and persisting prejudiced responses in a different light. During the 1980s, these advances took the form of both measurement and theory development, which laid the essential foundations for decades of subsequent research examining automaticity and control in stereotyping and prejudice.

MEASURING STEREOTYPIC AND PREJUDICED ASSOCIATIONS

Researchers in the 1980s borrowed heavily from associative network models describing representations of information in long-term memory. Specifically, researchers argued that pieces of information were held in an associative network and that each piece of information was linked to multiple knowledge representations (e.g., see Carlston, 1994). Thus, predictive patterns of activation would occur from repeatedly connecting certain objects in the environment (Srull & Wyer, 1979). For example, the presentation of bread results in easier and faster activation of "butter" than of "tree." Stereotypically associated constructs were assumed to be arranged in the same way, such that the presentation of a black person may result in easier and faster activation of "dangerous" than "intelligent." Whereas the former example has the adaptive consequence of facilitating information processing and innocuous social consequences, the latter may well have substantial negative social consequences and discriminatory outcomes.

Consistent with trends in cognitive psychology (Neely, 1977; Shiffrin & Schneider, 1977), social psychologists posited that the retrieval of information from associative networks was driven by two processes: automatic and controlled. At this time, social psychologists thought of these processes as distinct and mutually exclusive. Automatic processes were believed to be uncontrollable, unintentional, and efficient and to occur without awareness. These criteria became known as the *four horsemen of automaticity* (Bargh, 1984), and meeting all four criteria was considered the hallmark of automaticity. In contrast, controlled cognitive processes were believed to be under the individual's conscious control and to require intention, effort, and time to operate. During the 1980s, automatic and controlled processes were seen as both mutually exclusive and exhaustive modes of processing. This "either/or" view of automaticity and control dominated research and theorizing during this decade.

Measuring the outcome of automatic cognitive processing in the form of the automatic activation of stereotypic and evaluative associations posed a challenge to researchers. Social psychologists had a long tradition of measuring explicit attitudes, the product of controlled processing, but few tools for the detection of automatic cognitive processes. Priming procedures borrowed from cognitive psychologists offered one such potential tool (e.g., Neely, 1977; Posner & Snyder, 1975).

For example, Dovidio, Evans, and Tyler (1986) used a priming paradigm in which racial category primes (black, white) were paired with positive and negative stereotypic traits of blacks and whites. Each pairing was projected onto a screen in turn, and participants judged whether the trait could "ever be true" or was "always false" of the category shown. Dovidio and colleagues found faster respond times when black primes preceded negatively valenced traits and when white primes preceded positively valenced traits (i.e., evaluative bias). Also, the black primes elicited faster responses to stereotypically black traits, and white primes elicited faster responses to stereotypically white traits (i.e., stereotypic bias).

Gaertner and McLaughlin (1983) were the first researchers to use a modified lexical decision task (Meyer & Schvaneveldt, 1976) to assess race-related associations. Participants were presented with two words simultaneously on a series of slides shown with a carousel projector, and indicated on each trial whether both strings of letters were words (YES response) or one was a nonword (NO response). Reaction times in milliseconds (ms) were recorded for each trial with a digital clock. Gaertner and McLaughlin found that participants responded faster when the category word WHITES was paired with positive words (e.g., AMBITIOUS) than when the category word BLACKS was paired with positive words, but reaction times did not differ as a function of category word when negative words were presented. This pattern was interpreted as an ingroup favoritism.

These priming paradigms, although useful for detecting associations, presented stimuli long enough so that they could be consciously processed and other influences (e.g., social desirability) could influence responses if participants were so inclined. A method for precluding conscious awareness was needed. In addition, a theoretical framework was needed for understanding how people with biased associations could simultaneously profess low-prejudice attitudes. Fortunately, a groundbreaking manuscript published by Patricia Devine in 1989 met both of these needs.

DEVINE'S LANDMARK CONTRIBUTION

Devine (1989) argued that people who consciously hold low-prejudice attitudes as well as people who endorse high-prejudice attitudes are knowledgeable of cultural evaluations and stereotypes of groups such as blacks. Knowledge of these evaluations and stereotypes are naturally acquired, Devine pointed out, through social learning experiences. This argument was convincingly supported in the first of her studies, which showed that participants were equally adept at listing the cultural stereotypes of blacks regardless of whether they self-reported low- or high-prejudice attitudes toward blacks.

Devine further argued that stereotypic knowledge can be automatically activated and result in stereotype-consistent responses among both low- and high-prejudice individuals. This idea was tested (Study 2) by priming participants with category labels of blacks (e.g., blacks, negroes) and stereotypes of blacks (e.g., poor, lazy) for 80 ms (i.e., below conscious awareness) using a tachistoscope. In a subsequent task, participants rated the level of hostility in a vignette describing ambiguously hostile behavior. Devine was interested in whether the subliminal activation of blacks and stereotypically black traits would facilitate the subsequent application of the construct of hostility (which is stereotypically associated with blacks). Indeed, regardless of their reported level of prejudice against blacks on a traditional scale, participants who were subliminally primed with black stereotypes applied the stereotypically black trait of hostility to the judgment of ambiguous behavior.

Finally, Devine's third study showed that, when given the opportunity to consider their personal beliefs about blacks consciously, low-prejudice participants listed beliefs that were indeed much less negative than participants classified as high prejudice (based on a self-report measure of attitudes toward blacks). Based on this series of results, Devine argued that culturally prevalent stereotypic associations provided the default, automatic response regardless of people's consciously held beliefs. However, when given the opportunity to bring their conscious beliefs to mind, low-prejudice individuals can replace automatically activated bias with more egalitarian responses through controlled processing.

Devine's (1989) perspective was especially well suited to emerging findings in the prejudice literature that were perplexing at best and very disheartening at worst. Were individuals who espoused low-prejudice attitudes but sometimes responded in prejudiced ways merely masking their true prejudices (Crosby et al., 1980; see also Gaertner & Dovidio, 1986)? Devine's (1989) analysis offered the alternative interpretation that people's conscious reports were honest and sincere and that low-prejudice individuals were in the process of "breaking the prejudice habit," or learning how to respond in egalitarian ways through controlled processing.

Other theories related to stereotyping and prejudice emerged in the 1980s that also distinguished between automatic and controlled processing. Among these "dual processing" theories was Fiske and Neuberg's continuum model of impression formation (Fiske & Neuberg, 1990; Fiske, Neuberg, Beattie, & Milberg, 1987). This model posits that people automatically and initially form impressions based on stored category information, but when motivated for accuracy, they engage in more controlled and effortful processing that involves seeking out and processing individuating information. Similarly, Brewer's dual processing model of information processing (Brewer & Feinstein, 1999) distinguishes between top-down and bottom-up processing of information. Top-down (schema-to-person) or category-based impression formation is constrained by preexisting categories and schemas and represents automatic processing. Conversely, controlled processing is represented by bottom-up (person-to-representation) or person-based impression formation that utilizes individuated information about the person to form an impression.

In sum, during the 1980s, researchers embraced the theorizing and methodology of the "cognitive revolution" and in so doing started to explore the automatic and controlled components of stereotyping and prejudice. Although the dual-category theories delineated roles for both automatic and controlled processing, each model begins with automatic processing as the default and controlled processing overriding automatic processing only when there is sufficient motivation and ability to do so.

The 1990s: Building on the Foundations

Researchers were positioned to move in a number of new and exciting directions after the distinction between automatic and controlled processes in stereotyping and prejudice was introduced in the 1980s. And researchers took full advantage of this position, making tremendous advances across the next decade. Facilitating this progress were the ready availability of computers and sophisticated programming tools for designing studies that had much more precision and flexibility for investigating automatic processes. Indeed, as will be seen, the decade of the 1990s was ripe for a variety of groundbreaking methodological advances, and with them came theoretical progress.

WIDESPREAD EVIDENCE OF AUTOMATIC PROCESSES IN INTERGROUP BIAS

Researchers assessed "automatic stereotyping" in the 1990s using a variety of methods. For example, Banaji, Hardin, and Rothman (1993) used a semantic priming procedure with conscious presentation of the primes. Participants unscrambled sentences describing neutral behaviors or behaviors stereotypically related to dependence or aggression. The neutral priming did not affect subsequent ratings of male and female targets. In contrast, priming *dependence* led participants to perceive a female target as more dependent than a male target, and priming *aggression* resulted in higher aggression ratings for a male than a female target. Because there was no relationship between explicit memory for the primes and participants' target ratings, Banaji et al. (1993) argued that evidence of automatic gender stereotyping was obtained.

Rather than inferring evidence of automaticity from measures like memory, an increasingly common approach for assessing automaticity in stereotyping involved computer-controlled priming with very brief (<300 ms) stimulus onset asynchronies (SOAs), which are too fast to achieve conscious awareness. For instance, a prime might be presented for 200 ms, followed by a mask presented for 100 ms, and then the target would appear on the computer screen until the participant responded. Banaji and Hardin (1996) used this procedure to examine gender stereotyping. The primes were gender-related words (e.g., NURSE, MRS., and DOCTOR, MR.), the targets were male and female pronouns (e.g., HER and HIM), and participants' task was to judge the target words as either female or male. Results showed faster reaction times to pronouns preceded by consistent rather than inconsistent gender primes, suggesting that gender information conveyed through words can influence gender-related judgments through automatic processes.

The use of nonconscious priming procedures also allowed researchers to go beyond demonstrations of automaticity to test whether important stereotyping effects observed in previous research emerged under conditions that precluded conscious processing. For example, Chen and Bargh (1997) revisited the topic of self-fulfilling prophecies. They showed that presenting photographs of black males below conscious awareness led white perceiver participants to behave in stereotype-consistent ways toward white target participants (i.e., with greater hostility). This behavior then caused the white target participants to adopt stereotype-consistent (i.e., hostile) behavior. Fein and Spencer's (1997) research supporting the self-image maintenance function of prejudice was also extended. The original findings indicated that suffering a blow to one's self-esteem causes one to degrade and evaluate members of stereotyped groups more negatively, and this in turn helps to restore one's self-esteem. In subsequent research, these researchers found that the activation of stereotypes following an experience that reduced one's self-esteem even occurs under conditions of resource depletion (Spencer, Fein, Wolfe, Fong, & Dunn, 1998). Another seminal paper appeared in 1994, which tested the Lippmann's (1922) assertion that stereotypes serve the essential function of freeing up cognitive resources. Macrae, Milne, and Bodenhausen (1994) examined stereotypes as "energy-saving devices" using a dual-task paradigm in which participants formed target impressions based on presented information while they simultaneously performed a secondary task (e.g., monitoring prose). The critical manipulation was whether participants were primed (subliminally in Studies 2 and 3) with stereotype labels that could facilitate the impression-formation task. Results showed that participants did indeed perform better on the secondary task when their ability to form impressions was facilitated by the priming. Sherman, Lee, Bessenoff, and Frost (1998) extended these findings by showing that the efficiency gained by stereotype activation even extends to the processing of stereotype-inconsistent information.

In sum, a good deal of research in the 1990s was focused on demonstrating that stereotypes and evaluative biases could be activated effortlessly and influence subsequent judgments without the perceiver's awareness. However, researchers also discovered limitations to the idea that stereotype activation is unconditionally automatic. For instance, cognitive busyness could decrease rather than increase the likelihood of stereotype activation (Gilbert & Hixon, 1991; Spencer et al., 1998), and stereotype activation occurred only if targets were processed in socially meaningful ways (Macrae, Bodenhausen, Milne, Thorn, & Castelli, 1997). Automaticity versus control began to be conceptualized as running along a continuum rather than as distinct either/or processing options, and researchers tended to refer to processes as automatic if they at satisfied at least some aspects of the four horsemen of automaticity (Bargh, 1994).

IMPLICIT (VERSUS EXPLICIT) MEASURES OF INTERGROUP BIAS

Whereas the early 1990s included a focus on demonstrating that stereotypes and intergroup biases *could* be activated in a relatively automatic manner, the latter 1990s saw a shift to focusing on the *extent* to which these biases were activated. Researchers reasoned that one ought to be able to measure individual differences in automatic activation of intergroup bias, whether what is activated is conceptualized as stereotypic knowledge (Devine, 1989), as a personal attitude (Fazio, 1990), or as a mediator of favorable or unfavorable reactions to social objects (Greenwald & Banaji, 1995). Researchers began to refer to such assessment tools

as *implicit* measures, which aim to assess bias even if people are either unwilling or unable to report it. Furthermore, researchers reasoned that performance on implicit versus explicit measures should be distinguishable, and each type of measure should uniquely predict evaluative, judgmental, and behavioral responses.

Various individual difference measures of implicit bias based on response latencies (and errors) were developed. The most widely known and used is Greenwald, McGhee, and Schwartz's (1998) Implicit Association Test (IAT). This computer-based task can be used to assess either evaluative or stereotypic group-based associations. In the case of evaluative (prejudiced) associations, this dual-categorization task measures the ease with which participants can associate the categories white and black (with exemplars being faces of each ethnicity) with pleasant and unpleasant words (e.g., rainbow and diamond; vomit and filth). Participants receive practice blocks of trials to familiarize them with the various categorizations involved in the task, and then there are two test blocks of interest. One test block assesses the ease with which participants can categorize white + pleasant (using the same response key for either a white face or a pleasant word appearing on each trial) and black + unpleasant (using an alternate response key for either a black face or an unpleasant word appearing on each trial). The other test block assesses the ease of categorizing white + unpleasant and black + pleasant. The reasoning is that, to the extent that participants' evaluative associations favor whites over blacks, they will have faster reaction times on trial blocks when white is paired with pleasant and black is paired with unpleasant than when these pairings are reversed. To assess stereotypic associations with the IAT, the pleasant/unpleasant portion of the task is replaced by categories (e.g., motivated versus lazy) and exemplars (e.g., achiever and deadbeat) related to group stereotypes. Although the measure created some controversy, many researchers across the world began using the IAT because of its ease of administration, large effect sizes, adequate test-retest reliability, and predictive validity (see Greenwald, Poehlman, Uhlmann, & Banaji, 2009; Nosek, Greenwald, & Banaji, 2007).

Fazio, Jackson, Dunton, and Williams (1995) developed a method for assessing individual differences in automatically activated racial attitudes based on evaluative priming. A prime and a target are presented in short succession on a computer screen, and the participant's task is to categorize the target as "good" or "bad" as quickly as possible based on its evaluative connotation. For example, racial attitudes can be assessed by presenting white or black faces as primes and words like "pleasant" and "awful" as targets. Relatively greater facilitation for negative than positive adjectives when those adjectives are preceded by black than by white faces indicates a more negative attitude toward blacks.

Semantic priming paired with a lexical decision task provided another useful way to assess automatically activated biases. Building on earlier work (e.g., Dovidio et al., 1986), Wittenbrink, Judd, and Park (1997) restricted the presentation of racial category labels (WHITE or BLACK) as primes to just 15 ms, which was immediately followed by a mask and then the lexical decision trial. That is, participants saw a string of letters that they were to identify either as a word or nonword. Of key interest were trials in which negative or positive words stereotypic of either blacks or whites were presented. For example, greater facilitation of the word/nonword judgment on trials in which the prime BLACK was followed by stereotypes of blacks, relative to trials with neutral primes (XXXXX), would be indicative of stronger stereotypic associations.

Although other types of implicit bias measures surfaced in the 1990s and after (for a recent review, see Correll, Judd, Park, & Wittenbrink, 2010), computer-based latency paradigms stimulated the most research on distinguishing implicit from explicit bias measures and examining their differential relations to various outcome variables (e.g., behavioral discrimination). In several landmark studies, the extent of bias shown on implicit measures was at best moderately correlated with explicit measures (Dovidio, Kawakami, Johnson, Johnson, & Howard, 1997; Fazio et al., 1995; Greenwald et al., 1998; Kawakami, Dion, & Dovidio, 1998; Wittenbrink et al., 1997). Furthermore, performance on implicit measures appeared to be more related to behavioral measures that afforded little conscious control (e.g., subtle indicators of friendliness in interracial interactions), and performance on explicit measures was more related to deliberative behaviors (e.g., juridical decisions).

Such findings led to an emerging understanding that intergroup bias activated through automatic processes did not necessarily reflect consensually shared knowledge, as Devine (1989) had suggested (see also Lepore & Brown, 1997). Exactly how this variability was interpreted varied depending on researchers' theoretical orientation. For example, Fazio et al. (1995) maintained that people's "true" attitude was reflected in performance on the evaluative priming measure, but it could be masked and distorted based on motivations to control outward indicators of prejudice (Dunton & Fazio, 1997). Others' interpretations were more consistent with a view that implicit and explicit measures tap into different underlying mental representations (or connections) that are governed by different processes (e.g., Greenwald & Banaji, 1995). Based on this interpretation, people could be internally motivated to control their prejudice but at the same time be prone to responding in biased ways because of their automatically activated biases (e.g., Devine, Monteith, Zuwerink, & Elliot, 1991; Monteith & Voils, 1998).

Regardless of which interpretation of performance on implicit measures was favored, the strong propensity for biases to be automatically activated and influence people's responses made researchers keenly aware of the need to understand whether and how control over such biases could be achieved. We now summarize what was learned about issues of control during this decade.

EXERCISING CONTROL

The dual processing models prevalent in the 1990s (see Chaiken & Trope, 1999) emphasized that automatically activated constructs need not provide the default response, particularly if people have the motivation and ability (cognitive resources) to engage in more deliberate thought. This focus on control led to a shift in the person perception literature from portraying people as "cognitive misers" (a view of people as lazy thinkers prevalent in the 1980s) to the "motivated tactician" metaphor: People use stereotypes as the default but can also follow more effortful paths to generating responses that are not based on stereotypes. The leading models of person perception during the 1990s (Brewer & Feinstein, 1999; Fiske, Lin, & Neuberg, 1999) described how the motivated perceiver goes beyond the immediately available category-based and stereotypic information to gather additional information about a target. A fitting example of this information-gathering process is provided in a study reported by Sherman, Stroessner, Conrey, and Azam (2005). They found that low-prejudice participants' (deliberative) judgments of a target closely mirrored presented individuating information, whereas high-prejudice participants' judgments were aligned with stereotypes.

Another strategy for controlling the application of activated bias involves replacement. Consistent with Devine's (1989) analysis, people who are personally committed to egalitarian ideals can use their consciously activated attitudes as replacements for automatically activated constructs when they have the time and cognitive resources available. Likewise, being externally motivated (e.g., to conform to "politically correct" standards) can prompt replacement. Evidence of replacement resulting in relatively egalitarian responses has been garnered across a variety of outcome measures, including stereotype endorsement (Devine, 1989; Plant & Devine, 1998), self-reported racial attitudes (Dunton & Fazio, 1997; Fazio et al., 1995), evaluations of racially charged events (Fazio et al., 1995), racial humor (Monteith, 1993), juridical judgments (Dovidio et al., 1997), and evaluations following interracial interactions (Dovidio et al., 1997).

Another means to achieving control involves direct attempts at suppressing stereotypic thoughts. Macrae, Bodenhausen, and Milne (1994) conducted the first series of studies to investigate this strategy. Participants were asked to write a passage about a target shown in a picture that had all of the visual markers of a skinhead. Half of the participants were instructed not to rely on stereotypes when writing their passage, and the other participants were given no special instructions. Although the suppression instructions caused participants to write less stereotypic passages, these participants later showed greater evidence of stereotype use and accessibility than participants who had not suppressed in the first place. This stereotype rebound effect was explained in terms of Wegner's (e.g., 1994) mental control model, which posits that suppression results in the simultaneous engagement of a controlled operating system and an automatic monitoring system. Whereas the monitoring system continuously monitors for evidence of the to-be-suppressed material, the operating system engages in effortful processes to generate "distracter" thoughts. The operating system will successfully keep stereotypic thoughts at bay when fueled by sufficient motivation and cognitive resources. However, the monitoring system continually serves to prime the unwanted thoughts so that, once motivations are relaxed or cognitive resources are taxed, the stereotypic thoughts can "return with a vengeance." This explains why stereotypic thoughts can become hyperaccessible during, and more likely to be applied following, suppression than would be the case if suppression were never attempted (see also Macrae, Bodenhausen, Milne, and Wheeler, 1996).

In sum, stereotype suppression can actually have ironic, counterproductive effects. However, some people and situations are less likely to be associated with rebound effects (see Monteith, Sherman, & Devine, 1998). For example, suppression is more likely to be effective to the extent that participants are internally motivated to control their prejudice (Gordijn, Hindriks, Koomen, Kijksterhuis, & Van Knippenberg, 2004; Monteith, Spicer, & Tooman, 1998).

How much optimism did these top-down control strategies inspire for the elimination of discriminatory outcomes? The obvious problems are that people often are not sufficiently motivated to avoid a reliance on automatically activated biases and/or they lack the time, focused attention, or cognitive resources to engage the strategies. Furthermore, the fact that stereotypic and evaluative biases can be activated and applied without any conscious awareness raised the additional questions of whether people can even accept the possibility of such unconscious influences or realize ways in which they may be influenced (Bargh, 1999). It seemed necessary to examine other avenues of possible control that involved inhibitory processes acting on bias activation itself. That is, rather than focusing on stopping the influence of activated stereotypes, could activation itself be controlled?

Moskowitz, Gollwitzer, Wasel, & Schaal (1999) built on Bargh's (1990) auto-motive model to argue that chronically accessible egalitarian goals can be used preconsciously to prevent stereotype activation. Of course, this requires that people actively and consciously pursue their egalitarian goals enough so that they become chronically accessible and can serve as rivals to automatically activated biases. Blair and Banaji (1996) provided participants with counter-stereotypic expectancies (e.g., expect to see a male name following a female-related prime) and found that this interfered with automatic stereotype activation. These lines of research raised some criticisms (see Bargh, 1999) and a good number of questions about precise mechanisms and underlying processes. Nonetheless, they stimulated a transition toward exploring conditions under which automatically activated bias could be controlled in a more bottom-up manner.

Monteith's (1993) self-regulation of prejudice (SRP) model represents another effort in this direction by detailing how motivational and learning processes operate to help people learn how to inhibit and control prejudiced responses. Leading to the development of the SRP were findings across many studies showing that participants reported catching themselves having prejudiced responses toward members of stereotyped groups that violated their personal egalitarian attitudes, and that awareness of these prejudice-related discrepancies resulted in feelings of guilt and self-disappointment (for a review, see Monteith & Mark, 2006). According to the SRP model, such prejudice-related discrepancies activate the behavioral inhibition system (BIS; Gray, 1982, 1987), thereby increasing vigilance, attention, and arousal. This activity results in associations being built between one's prejudiced response, the negative affect resulting from the failure to live up to one's standards, and stimuli surrounding one's prejudiced response. These associations, or *cues for control,* can serve as signals in future situations in which prejudiced responses may occur. Specifically, the cues instigate BIS activity once again to encourage more careful processing and the recruitment of resources for controlling and replacing potentially biased responses. Monteith's (1993; see also Monteith, Ashburn-Nardo, Voils, & Czopp, 2002) empirical findings supported this model and opened up the possibility that the consistent self-regulation of prejudiced responses may result in the automatization of the regulation process.

In sum, research during the 1990s extended the basic methodological and theoretical foundations from the 1980s in colossal ways. There was rapid growth in the development and use of methods for assessing automaticity in stereotyping and prejudice, and also in the development of procedures to assess individual differences in the extent to which intergroup biases operate automatically. In addition, concerted efforts were made to understand various pathways for controlling the potential influence of biases resulting from automatically activated constructs, so that nonprejudiced responses could be provided instead. Much of this research on control focused on top-down regulation, whereby people were motivated and able to engage in effortful rather than more automatic processing. However, some research involved elements of bottom-up regulation, whereby control could be exerted on the automatic processes themselves (for further discussion, see Monteith, Lybarger, & Woodcock, 2009). This trend would be followed into the 2000s, when the interplay between and simultaneous operation of automatic and controlled processes became much more evident.

The 2000s: Renovations, Fine-Tuning, and Additions

Researchers on the cusp of the new millennium were prepared with technologically sophisticated measurement tools and deeper insight into the nature of automaticity in stereotyping and prejudice and into the interplay between automaticity and controlled processes. With these tools and the plethora of generated research came the need to fine-tune measures and definitions (e.g., what is really meant by "implicit attitude" or "implicit measure?") and to gain a more complete understanding of how the mind works to produce responses on implicit and explicit measures. In addition, empirical work in the 2000s began to test an assumption that seemed to be held by many researchers—that implicit biases were fixed and unamenable to change.

NEW IMPLICIT MEASURES OF INTERGROUP BIAS

Two new implicit measures were introduced in the 2000s, joining the ranks of the IAT and various priming measures developed in the 1990s. One was the Affect-Misattribution Procedure (AMP; Payne, Cheng, Govorun, & Stewart 2005). The AMP was designed to capture attitudes through the combination of projective testing and priming. Participants rate whether they perceive various abstract patterns (i.e., Chinese characters) as pleasant or unpleasant. Before the presentation of the abstract pattern, a black or white face prime is shown (i.e., when racial attitudes are the attitude object of interest), which participants are instructed to disregard. Payne et al. (2005, Study 6) found that both black and white participants rated the Chinese characters more favorably when they were preceded by ingroup primes relative to outgroup primes, and this effect was moderated by motivation to control prejudice for white participants.

Second, weapon paradigms were developed for measuring the influence of a target's race on the decision to shoot (shooter bias task; Correll, Park, Judd, & Wittenbrink, 2002) and on the identification of weapons (weapons identification task, WIT; Payne, 2001). These tasks were developed with real-world events in mind, such as in 1999 when Amadou Diallo (a West African immigrant) was caught in a hail of police bullets when he reached for his wallet for identification and police thought he was reaching for a gun. In the shooter bias paradigm, armed and unarmed blacks and whites appear one at a time in a video game simulation, and participants' task is to "shoot" (by pressing a shoot button) each target who is holding a gun but to press the "don't shoot" button when a target holds a neutral object (such as a wallet or cell phone). With the WIT, black or white faces briefly precede pictures of either guns or tools across trials, and participants' task is to respond as quickly as possible by pressing a specified key to correctly identify each object as a gun or a tool. Race bias has been revealed repeatedly with these weapons paradigms. For example, on the shooter bias task, white participants erroneously shoot black targets holding neutral objects more than white targets holding neutral objects. With the WIT, white participants are more likely to misidentify neutral objects as guns when they are preceded by black rather than white faces.

CHALLENGES, CONTROVERSIES, AND LESSONS LEARNED

Researchers started to take a more critical view of implicit measures of intergroup bias during the 2000s. One troubling problem was the often low correspondence between different types of implicit measures (e.g., Fazio & Olson, 2003), leading researchers to question whether different implicit measures were tapping into different underlying processes or constructs. Cunningham, Preacher, and Banaji (2001) showed that the correspondence between evaluative priming and an evaluative IAT increased when corrections were made for measurement error. Also, correcting for measurement error increased the stability of each implicit measure across time. Nonetheless, it is imperative that researchers consider precisely what constructs and processes their implicit measures are designed to tap into (De Houwer & Moors, 2010; Fazio & Olson, 2003). Along similar lines, controversies grew about how these measures were used, particularly the IAT. Critics argued that the psychometric properties and arbitrary metrics of the IAT make it impossible to use for making diagnostic inferences about individuals (Blanton, Jaccard, Gonzales, & Christie, 2006; Fiedler, Messner, & Bluemke, 2006).

Lively debates also developed in which researchers questioned whether what the field sometimes casually called "implicit measures" were truly implicit, and further muddying the waters was the fact that different researchers have defined "implicit" differently (for an excellent review, see Payne & Gawronski, 2010). Although the details of this debate are beyond the scope of this chapter, suffice it to say that we have now gone well beyond Bargh's (1994) four horsemen of automaticity to recognizing the need for considerably more precision in defining what we are measuring. Also important is the consideration of precisely what types of associations are assessed given the parameters of our measures. For example, the IAT variant known as the *personalized IAT* (using "I like" and "I dislike" category labels in

place of "pleasant and unpleasant" labels; Olson & Fazio, 2004) may tap into personal attitudes more than extrapersonal associations (e.g., knowledge of cultural stereotypes). However, another possibility is that the personalized IAT triggers more controlled processing (cf. Rydell & McConnell, 2010).

Aiding in precision has been the recognition that no measure is process pure (Sherman, 2008) and the development of methods for parsing performance on implicit tasks into different underlying processes. Two such methods have been developed for tasks based on processes of response compatibility (e.g., the IAT and the WIT): the process dissociation procedure (PDP; Jacoby, 1991) and the quadruple process model (QUAD; Conrey, Sherman, Gawronski, Hugenberg, & Groom, 2005). The PDP is based on Jacoby's (1991) memory research, and it allows researchers to determine the extent to which task responses involve automatic versus controlled processes. For example, in the first application of this task in the domain of stereotyping and prejudice, Payne (2001) demonstrated that automatic rather than controlled processing was associated with race bias on the WIT. Interesting extensions have provided a variety of novel insights. For example, Stewart, von Hippel, and Radvanski (2009) found that older adults' greater expression of prejudice on the IAT (compared with younger adults) is due to having less control rather than to stronger automatically activated associations. Stewart and Payne (2008) found that having participants employ a conscious intention to think in nonstereotypic ways during the WIT and the IAT decreased evidence of race bias, and that this was due to decreased automatic processing, rather than increased control.

The QUAD (Conrey et al., 2005; see also Chapter 3, this volume) model parses performance into four distinct processes: automatic activation of associations (AC), the ability to detect an appropriate response (D), the success at overcoming automatically activated associations (OB), and guessing (G). The AC parameter measures associations that are automatically activated; thus, the stronger the association, the greater the likelihood of it influencing behavior. The D parameter measures a relatively controlled process that detects appropriate and inappropriate responses. The OB parameter measures the ability to regulate and overcome automatic associations when those associations are detected and conflict with the correct response. The G parameter measures guessing (Conrey, et al., 2005).

The QUAD model has been used in a variety of studies measuring implicit bias (see Sherman, 2006;

Sherman, Gawronski, Gonsalkorale, Hugenberg, Allen, & Groom, 2008). For example, Gonsalkorale, von Hippel, Sherman, and Klauer (2009) examined the interplay between automatic activation of associations (AC) and the ability to overcome bias (OB) on impressions made by white participants when interacting with a Muslim confederate. They found that when AC was strong, the confederate's rating of liking for the participant increased to the extent that participants also scored higher on the OB parameter. Note that this type of control is different from the deliberate activation of, for instance, nonprejudiced racial attitudes. As Gonsalkorale et al. (2009) concluded, these findings suggest that "'upstream' self-regulatory processes that directly oppose activated associations may impact the quality of intergroup interactions" (p. 165). This finding, as well as PDP findings, underscores the potential for these new process-parsing methods to provide novel theoretical insights into the role of automaticity and control in stereotyping and prejudice.

The use of social neuroscientific methods during the 2000s has presented another inroad for learning about the complex network of neural systems involved in automatic and controlled processes in stereotyping and prejudice. Substantial research now suggests that the amygdala is triggered by the presentation of outgroup members' faces (Amodio, Harmon-Jones, & Devine, 2003; Hart, Whalen, Shine, McInerney, Fischer, & Rauch, 2000; Phelps, O'Connor, Cunningham, Funayama, Gatenby, Gore, & Banaji, 2000), which is sensible given the amygdala's presumed fast, unconscious assessment of potential threats (e.g., Phan, Wager, Taylor, & Liberzon, 2002). In addition, the extent of amygdala activity is correlated with implicit evaluations of racial groups (Cunningham et al., 2001; Phelps et al., 2000). However, recent findings suggest that a perceiver's goals at the time of processing can modulate both amygdala and implicit stereotype activation. Such results point to the malleability of brain activity and concomitant implicit bias based on conscious processing goals (Wheeler & Fiske, 2005).

Researchers have also focused on the role of the anterior cingulate cortex (ACC) in prejudice control. The ACC monitors for the presence of conflicts among cognitions and action tendencies and recruits resources for exerting control (Botvinick, Braver, Barch, Carter, & Cohen, 2001). Activity of the ACC appears to play a critical role in detecting the need for cognitive control in relation to one's prejudiced responses (Amodio, Devine, & Harmon-Jones, 2008;

Amodio, Kubota, Harmon-Jones, & Devine, 2006; Cunningham et al., 2001; Richeson et al., 2003). For example, Amodio et al. (2008) found greater ACC activity on trials of the WIT that required stereotype inhibition. Such findings are consistent with the possibility of preconscious regulation. As Stanley, Phelps, and Banaji (2008) summarized, "Evidence now suggests that the detection of conflict between implicit and explicit beliefs, as well as some aspects of their regulation, is an automatic process that is not dependent on the allocation of cognitive resources and may be outside the perceiver's conscious goals in the immediate moment" (pp. 168–169).

Complimenting the possibility of upstream regulation at the behavioral level were Monteith, Ashburn-Nardo, Voils, and Czopp's (2002) series of experiments examining the establishment and operation of cues for control in relation to one's prejudiced responses. Recall that Monteith (1993) suggested that these cues were critical to triggering conflict monitoring and inhibition activity so that prejudiced responses could be averted. In Monteith et al. (2002), established cues for control were shown to trigger inhibition (brief slowing of responses) and to facilitate nonprejudiced responses in an evaluative categorization task. In other words, regulatory activity and ultimately nonbiased responses were triggered by the presence of cues for control.

Another challenge embraced during the 2000s was to gain a better theoretical understanding of why implicit and explicit measures of intergroup attitudes are so often unrelated and are associated with different types of behaviors (e.g., Dovidio, Kawakami, & Gaertner, 2002; McConnell & Liebold, 2001). Dual processing theories of the 1990s certainly provided relevant working frameworks (e.g., Nosek, 2007), but researchers in the 2000s retooled existing theories and generated new ones for a deeper understanding. This work was generated by attitude theorists to apply broadly across attitude domains, opening up avenues for application to stereotyping and prejudice.

For example, the associative-propositional evaluation (APE) model (Gawronski & Bodenhausen, 2006) assumes two different types of evaluative processes. Associative processes determine affective reactions that are automatically activated to an attitude object and are related to factors such as learning history, context, and motivational states. Propositional processes underlie explicit attitude expression and result from "syllogistic inferences derived from any kind of propositional information that is considered for a given judgment" (Gawronksi & Bodenhausen,

2006, p. 694). The systems of evaluation model (SEM; Rydell & McConnell, 2006; Rydell, McConnell, Mackie, & Strain, 2006) describes an associative system and a rule-based system and conceptualizes the two as at least partially independent aspects of the mind. Whereas similarity and association dictate implicit attitude formation and change, conscious deliberation and syllogistic reasoning dictate explicit attitude formation and change.

In contrast to both of these models is the constructivist perspective (e.g., Schwarz, 2007), which maintains that attitudes are epiphenomena constructed in the moment based on what information is currently accessible, which can include what information attitude measures ask participants to consider. Still different is Fazio's (2007) motivation and opportunity as determinants (MODE) model, which posits a single attitudinal evaluation that can be automatically activated if the association between the evaluation and the attitude object is strong. However, the expression of one's attitude can be moderated (e.g., based on social desirability concerns) if one has the motivation and ability to alter their expression.

Critical tests that pit these theories against each other are needed, and as has traditionally been the case, focusing on stereotyping and prejudice is likely to provide fertile grounds for conducting this research. Certainly, these theories aid in understanding not only our potential for regulating and inhibiting prejudices and stereotypes but also our ability to modify and change automatically activated biases. This question of precisely how automatically activated biases can be changed is a question of great importance at present, given a huge literature accumulated primarily during the 2000s indicating that automatic biases are malleable. We turn now to a brief review of this literature.

Malleability of Automatic Biases

A growing body of research (more than 200 published studies at the time of writing) cites evidence that a variety of techniques and conditions can shift implicit biases—both stereotyping and prejudice—at least in the short term. In 2002, Blair's review led her to conclude that automatic associations are not as fixed as once assumed. Mechanisms such as self-motives and social motives, strategies, focus of attention, and the configuration of stimulus cues can all affect performance on implicit bias measures (Blair, 2002). Lenton and her colleagues (2009) conducted a meta-analysis on the efficacy of different strategies on the reduction of implicit gender bias. Like Blair, they found that strategies such as

attentional distraction, counter-stereotypic exemplars, and *stereotype negation* were effective at reducing implicit bias. The techniques and conditions shown to reduce implicit bias can be broadly summarized as: the context and attributes of the target, the state and situation of the perceiver, and specialized intervention strategies carried out by the perceiver. The sheer number and breadth of experiences shown to have an impact on measures of implicit bias suggest that implicit intergroup bias is not as unyielding as once believed. However, to what extent does short-term malleability point to lasting change? What processes in the underlying associative structure are associated with this change? In this final section, we will summarize empirical evidence of implicit bias malleability. A short caveat is in order. For the purpose of clarity, we will forgo some definitional precision and use the terms *implicit stereotyping* and *implicit evaluation* to refer to stereotypic and evaluative intergroup bias activated through automatic processes.

In addition to summarizing the types of experiences shown to reduce implicit intergroup bias, we will draw on empirical evidence pointing to possible processes associated with such reductions. Plausible processes for change include a situational increase in control over automatically activated associations, the activation of alternative nonbiased associations, or a more permanent change in the relative strengths of the associative paths.

CONTEXT AND ATTRIBUTES OF THE TARGET

Both the valence (positive vs. negative) and the stereotypicality of the context in which one encounters a stigmatized target or outgroup member can influence performance on measures of implicit bias. Specifically, encounters with blacks in positive contexts, such as in church compared with in prison (Allen, Sherman, & Klauer, 2010), at a family barbeque compared with involvement in gang activity, and in church compared with at a graffiti-emblazoned street corner (Wittenbrink, Judd, & Park, 2001), engender significantly less implicit pro-white racial bias. Similarly, the positivity of the roles occupied by targets can influence measures of implicit bias. For example, negative implicit evaluation is reduced in response to exposure to blacks who are presented in relatively positive roles, such as a factory worker or lawyer versus a prisoner (Barden, Maddux, Petty, & Brewer, 2004). Similarly, the stereotypicality of positive contexts also engenders less implicit prejudice. For example, Asians are implicitly evaluated more positively in a stereotype-congruent class-room setting and blacks more positively in a stereotype-congruent basketball court than in the reverse, stereotype-incongruent contexts where Asians are encountered on a basketball court and blacks in a classroom (Barden et al., 2004).

People often occupy multiple roles or categories, and the relative salience of one over another can also influence implicit bias. For example, increasing the relative salience of blacks' gender or occupation over ethnicity reduced negative implicit evaluations by whites (Mitchell, Nosek, & Banaji, 2003). Similarly, focusing on the age rather than the ethnicity of blacks eliminated whites' implicit stereotyping as measured by the WIT (Jones & Fazio, 2010). The physical attributes of individual stigmatized group members can also be important. For example, blacks with more prototypical features (i.e., Afrocentric facial features, hair texture, and skin color) elicit greater negative implicit evaluation than do those who are less prototypical (Livingston & Brewer, 2002).

Evidence of the influence of contextual variables on implicit intergroup bias comes from single-shot laboratory experiments. Although lacking the scope to speak to long-term reduction in bias, analysis of the controlled and automatic processes captured by implicit bias measures provides clues to the nature of this situational change. For example, using process dissociation, Payne, Lambert, and Jacoby (2002) found that race bias on the WIT could be accounted for by automatic processes rather than by (reduced) cognitive control.

STATE AND SITUATION OF THE PERCEIVER

In addition to contextual factors, many variables specific to the perceiver (both transient and more stable factors) also influence implicit bias. For example, perceivers in a positive rather than negative mood have a greater proneness to both implicit stereotyping and prejudice (Huntsinger, Sinclair, & Clore, 2009; Huntsinger, Sinclair, Dunn, & Clore, 2010). Negative emotions such as anger and disgust increase implicit bias, but only when the specific emotion is stereotypically related to the target (e.g., disgust increases implicit anti-gay bias, and anger increases anti-Muslim bias; Dasgupta, DeSteno, Williams, & Hunsinger, 2009). Although being in a positive mood increases implicit bias, the act of smiling upon encountering a member of a stigmatized group reduces implicit negative evaluations (Ito, Chiao, Devine, Lorig, & Cacioppo, 2006).

The perceivers' power relative to the target also moderates implicit bias. Being in a subordinate position to a woman increases men's implicit negative gender evaluation, but not stereotyping (Richeson & Ambady, 2001). Increased social power reduces women's implicit gender stereotypes (Haines & Kray, 2005). However, with regard to race, expecting to interact with a black in a superior position reduced whites' implicit negative evaluation (Richeson & Ambady, 2003), which has many positive implications for intergroup relations.

Research indicates that automatic processing may also be sensitive to the immediate situation of the perceiver. The risk of one's biases being made known to others reduces negative racial implicit evaluations about blacks and gay men (Barnes-Holmes, Hayden, Barnes-Holmes, & Stewart, 2008; Boysen, Vogel, & Madon, 2006). The mere presence of others (Castelli & Tomelleri, 2008) and the implied anti-biased attitudes of others in the situation (Lowery, Hardin, & Sinclair, 2001; Sinclair, Lowery, Hardin, & Colangelo, 2005) also reduce implicit racial evaluations. Finally, research suggests that physical and psychological proximity between the perceiver and a target group member may influence implicit bias. Imagined positive contact or interaction with a target outgroup member (Turner & Crisp, 2010), having a black roommate (Shook & Fazio, 2008), and blurring racial boundaries by emphasizing what blacks and whites have in common (Hall, Crisp, & Suen, 2009) all reduce implicit racial prejudice. Sharing and reinforcing membership of a common ingroup with blacks also significantly reduces whites' implicit racial prejudice (Woodcock & Monteith, 2010). Process dissociation analyses revealed that this effect of common ingroup membership corresponded with a reduction in the automatic activation of biased associations and not with an increase in control.

More stable individual differences between perceivers also affect implicit bias. For example, individuals who are highly motivated by internalized egalitarian values to control prejudice are less prone to implicit stereotyping and prejudice. QUAD modeling suggests that this corresponds with a decrease in the activation of biased associations and an increase in response monitoring (Gonsalkorale, Sherman, Allen, Klauer, & Amodio, 2011). As we noted earlier, Stewart et al. (2009) found that older adults were more prone to implicit racial prejudice than younger adults, which could be accounted for in PDP analyses by less ability for controlled processing.

TARGETED INTERVENTIONS

A variety of interventions have shown promise for reducing implicit intergroup bias. The use of counter-stereotypes forms the basis of many such strategies. Employing vivid counter-stereotypical mental imagery, such as imagining "strong women" (Blair, Ma, & Lenton, 2001), reduces implicit gender prejudice. Exposure to counter-stereotypic exemplars such as famous female leaders (Dasgupta & Asgari, 2004), famous admired blacks and older adults (Dasgupta & Greenwald, 2001), admired famous Asians (McGrane & White, 2007), and admired members of the gay community (Dasgupta & Rivera, 2008) significantly reduces implicit prejudice toward these groups. More intensive techniques utilizing conditioning have been developed whereby individuals repeatedly affirm specific counter-stereotypes (such as blacks and intelligence) and/or negate stereotypes (such as blacks and lazy and unsuccessful) across hundreds of computer trials. Extensive counter-stereotype affirmation and stereotype negation conditioning significantly reduce implicit stereotyping in both the immediate and longer term—lasting for at least 24 hours (Kawakami, Dovidio, Moll, Hermsen, & Russin, 2000). The affirmation of positive counter-stereotypes, rather than the negation of negative stereotypes, has been shown to drive this effect (Gawronski, Bertram, Deutsch, Mbirkou, Seibt, & Strack, 2008). PDP analyses revealed that these counter-stereotype conditioning effects corresponded with a reduction in the automatic activation of biased associations and not with an increase in control (Woodcock & Monteith, 2010).

A number of deliberative strategies that task perceivers to invoke specific implementation intentions have also proved effective in the reduction of implicit bias. Although the active suppression of stereotypes actually increases implicit stereotyping (Galinsky & Moskowitz, 2000; Wyer, Mazzoni, Perfect, Calvini, & Neilens, 2010), implementation intentions such as "think safe" (Stewart & Payne, 2008) or "If a see a person I will ignore his race"(Mendoza, Gollwitzer, & Amodio, 2010) when encountering blacks reduces related implicit stereotypes (i.e., blacks and danger and violence). Practicing the self-regulation of prejudice (Monteith, 1993) in daily life, by consciously replacing prejudiced responses toward blacks with nonprejudiced responses, significantly reduces implicit racial prejudice (Woodcock & Monteith, 2009). Implicit racial prejudice was found to decrease over the course of 3 weeks with daily self-regulation practice, and QUAD analysis

indicated that this effect was associated with a reduction in the activation of "black–bad" associations.

Situational goals and the perceivers' ideology regarding race relations can also influence implicit biases. Research suggests that subscription to multiculturalism rather than colorblindness ideology (Correll, Park, & Allegra Smith, 2008), undergoing diversity training with a cooperation rather than a tolerance perspective (Blincoe & Harris, 2009), enrollment in a prejudice seminar (Rudman, Ashmore, & Gary, 2001), and the inclusion of an Equal Opportunity statement on employment materials (Malinen & Johnston, 2007) all reduce implicit biases. Similarly, implicit bias reduction is also achieved by activating certain goals, such as equality (Zogmaister, Arcuri, Castelli, & Smith, 2008) or creativity and creative thinking (Sassenberg & Moskowitz, 2005).

Collectively, these studies have shown that intergroup bias activated through automatic processes can be influenced, certainly in the short term, by a variety of experiences and contexts. Because the vast majority of evidence comes from single-session experiments, we cannot draw conclusions about whether any sort of permanent change to underlying associations has occurred. What lies ahead will be the investigation of longer term change in implicit bias, an examination of the relative effectiveness of different strategies, and an understanding of how different strategies may affect different underlying processes in the production of lasting change.

In sum, the 2000s were a critical time when renovations and fine-tuning took place in connection with our thinking about implicit measures and their underlying (more or less) automatic and unconscious processes. Strides were made theoretically and empirically as researchers sought greater precision and understanding, and these advances most often resulted from the use of new methods (e.g., the QUAD model, social neuroscience research). Finally, a massive literature mushroomed showing that the extent of intergroup implicit bias fluctuates depending on the context and attributes of the target, the state and situation of the perceiver, and targeted interventions. However, future research will need to address whether this malleability constitutes transient fluctuation or can take the form of sustained bias reduction.

Conclusion

Social cognition has had a profound and indelible impact on stereotyping and prejudice research. It paved the way for the study of automatic processes in stereotyping and prejudice at a crucial juncture when consciously held attitudes alone did not seem to account for the nature of racial attitudes in the United States. Three decades of research have solidified the place of automaticity as a central construct in research on stereotyping and prejudice, revealing much about the influence and operation of controlled processes as well. Using techniques borrowed from cognitive psychology, research conducted in the 1980s confirmed that stereotypically and evaluatively biased associations can be automatically activated, and this led to the characterization of bias as a default outcome to be overcome only by motivated and able perceivers. As the cognitive and technological revolutions converged in the 1990s, many sophisticated measures were developed, and the ubiquity of automatic stereotypic and evaluative processing was highlighted and measured as an individual difference variable. Researchers also discovered new ways of exerting control over responses resulting from automatic processes and entertained the possibility that control efforts might actually change the operation of automatic processes. In other words, rather than solely being an alternative to prejudiced responses resulting from automatic processing, controlled processes might act to interrupt automatic processes. During the first decade of the 21st century, researchers took a critical look at the vast literature and identified important challenges. More importantly, they addressed these challenges with informative studies, the use of new methods, and additional theoretical development. A very large literature also grew demonstrating that implicit intergroup bias is malleable.

Our review was intended to provide a historical overview of the progression and progress of social cognition research on issues related to automaticity and control in stereotyping and prejudice. The essential foundations were laid in the 1980s, and a tremendous amount of work went into building from the foundations during the 1990s. Researchers stepped back in the 2000s to renovate, fine-tune, and add new knowledge. Social cognition has revolutionized research on stereotyping and prejudice, and we have little doubt that it will be equally prominent and generative in the decades to come.

Author Notes

Writing of this chapter was facilitated by a National Science Foundation grant (BCS 0921516) to the first author.

References

Adorno, T. W., Frenkel-Brunswik, E., Levinson, D. J., & Sanford, R. N. (1950). *The authoritarian personality*. New York: Harper & Row.

Allen, T. J., Sherman, J. W., & Klauer, K. C. (2010). Social context and the self-regulation of implicit bias. *Group Processes and Intergroup Relations, 13,* 137–149.

Allport, G.W. (1954). *The nature of prejudice.* Reading. MA: Addison-Wesley.

Amodio, D. M., Kubota, J. T., Harmon-Jones, E., & Devine, P. G. (2006). Alternative mechanisms for regulating racial responses according to internal and external cues. *Social Cognitive and Affective Neuroscience, 1,* 26–36.

Amodio, D. M., Master, S. L., Yee, C. M., & Taylor, S. E. (2008). Neurocognitive components of the behavioral inhibition and activation systems: Implications for theories of self-regulation. *Psychophysiology, 45,* 11–19.

Amodio, D. M., Harmon-Jones, E., & Devine, P. G. (2003). Individual differences in the activation and control of affective race bias as assessed by startle eyeblink responses and self-report. *Journal of Personality and Social Psychology, 84,* 738–753.

Ashmore, R. D., & Del Boca, F. K. (1981). Conceptual approaches to stereotypes and stereotyping. *Cognitive Processes in Stereotyping and Intergroup Behavior, x,* 1–35.

Banaji, M. R., Hardin, C., & Rothman, A. J. (1993). Implicit stereotyping in person judgment. *Journal of Personality and Social Psychology, 65,* 272–281.

Banaji, M. R., & Hardin, C. D. (1996). Automatic stereotyping. *Psychological Science, 7,* 136–141.

Barden, J., Maddux, W. W., Petty, R. E., & Brewer, M. B. (2004). Contextual moderation of racial bias: The impact of social roles on controlled and automatically activated attitudes. *Journal of Personality and Social Psychology, 87,* 5–22.

Bargh, J. A. (1984). Automatic and conscious processing of social information. In R. S. Wyer, Jr., & T. K. Srull (Eds.), *Handbook of social cognition* (Vol. 3, pp. 1–43). Hillsdale, NJ: Erlbaum.

Bargh, J. A. (1990). Auto-motives: Preconscious determinants of social interaction. In E. T. Higgins & R. M. Sorrentino (Eds.), *Handbook of motivation and cognition* (Vol. 2, pp. 93–130). New York: Guilford.

Bargh, J. A. (1994). The Four Horsemen of automaticity: Awareness, efficiency, intention, and control in social cognition. In R. S. Wyer, Jr., & T. K. Srull (Eds.), *Handbook of social cognition* (2nd ed., pp. 1–40). Hillsdale, NJ: Erlbaum.

Bargh, J. A. (1999). The cognitive monster: The case against controllability of automatic stereotype effects. In S. Chaiken & Y. Trope (Eds.), *Dual process theories in social psychology* (pp. 361–382). New York: Guilford.

Barnes-Holmes, D., Hayden, E., Barnes-Holmes, Y., & Stewart, I. (2008). The Implicit Relational Assessment Procedure (IRAP) as a response-time and event-related-potentials methodology for testing natural verbal relations: A preliminary study. *Psychological Record, 58,* 497–516.

Blair, I. V. (2002). The malleability of automatic stereotypes and prejudice. *Personality and Social Psychology Review, 6,* 242–261.

Blair, I. V., & Banaji, M. R. (1996). Automatic and controlled processes in stereotype priming. *Journal of Personality and Social Psychology, 70,* 1142–1163.

Blair, I. V., Ma, J. E., & Lenton, A. P. (2001). Imagining stereotypes away: The moderation of implicit stereotypes through mental imagery. *Journal of Personality and Social Psychology*, *81*, 828–841.

Blincoe, S., & Harris, M. J. (2009). Prejudice reduction in White students: Comparing three conceptual approaches. *Journal of Diversity in Higher Education, 2*, 232–242.

Blanton, H., & Jaccard, J., Gonzales, P., & Christie, C. (2006). Decoding the Implicit Association Test: Implications for criterion prediction. *Journal of Experimental Social Psychology, 42*, 192–212.

Blauner, R. (1972). *Racial oppression in America*. New York: Harper & Row.

Bodenhausen, G. V. (1988). Stereotypic biases in social decision making and memory: Testing process models of stereotype use. *Journal of Personality and Social Psychology, 55*, 726–737.

Bogardus, E. S. (1925). Social distance and its origins. *Journal of Applied Sociology. 9*, 299–308.

Botvinick, M. M., Braver, T. S., Carter, C. S., Barch, D. M., & Cohen, J. D. (2001). Conflict monitoring and cognitive control. *Psychological Review. 108*, 624–652.

Boysen, G. A., Vogel, D. L., & Madon, S. (2006). A public versus private administration of the Implicit Association Test. *European Journal of Social Psychology, 36*, 845–856.

Brewer, M. B., & Feinstein, A. S. H. (1999). Dual processes in the cognitive representation of persons and social categories. In S. Chaiken & Y. Trope (Eds.), *Dual-process theories in social psychology* (pp. 255–270). New York: Guilford Press.

Carlston, D. E. (1994). Associated Systems Theory: A systematic approach to the cognitive representation of persons and events. In R. S. Wyer (Ed.), *Advances in social cognition, Vol. 7: Associated systems theory* (pp. 1–78). Hillsdale, NJ: Erlbaum.

Castelli, L., & Tomelleri, S. (2008). Contextual effects on prejudiced attitudes: When the presence of others leads to more egalitarian responses. *Journal of Experimental Social Psychology, 44*, 679–686.

Chaiken, S., & Trope, Y. (Eds.). (1999). *Dual process theories in social psychology*. New York: Guilford.

Chen, M., & Bargh, J. A. (1997). Nonconscious behavioral confirmation processes: The self-fulfilling nature of automatically-activated stereotypes. *Journal of Experimental Social Psychology, 33*, 541–560.

Conrey, F. R., Sherman, J. W., Gawronski, B., Hugenberg, K., & Groom, C. (2005). Separating multiple processes in implicit social cognition: The Quad-Model of implicit task performance. *Journal of Personality and Social Psychology, 89*, 469–487.

Correll, J., Judd, C. M., Park, B., & Wittenbrink, B. (2010). Measuring prejudice, stereotypes, and discrimination. In J. F. Dovidio, M. Hewstone, Glick, P., & V. M. Esses (Eds.), *Sage handbook of prejudice, stereotyping, and discrimination* (pp. 45–62). Thousand Oaks, CA: Sage.

Correll, J., Park, B., & Allegra Smith, J. (2008). Colorblind and multicultural prejudice reduction strategies in high-conflict situations. *Group Processes and Intergroup Relations, 11*, 471–491.

Correll, J., Park, B., Judd, C. M., & Wittenbrink, B. (2002). The police officer's dilemma: Using ethnicity to disambiguate potentially threatening individuals. *Journal of Personality and Social Psychology, 83*, 1314–1329.

Crosby, F., Bromley, S., & Saxe, L. (1980). Recent unobtrusive studies of Black and White discrimination and prejudice: A literature review. *Psychological Bulletin, 87*, 546–563.

Cunningham, W. A., Preacher, K. J., & Banaji, M. R. (2001). Implicit attitude measures: Consistency, stability, and convergent validity. *Psychological Science, 12*, 163–170.

Dasgupta, N., & Asgari, S. (2004). Seeing is believing: Exposure to counterstereotypic women leaders and its effect on the malleability of automatic gender stereotyping. *Journal of Experimental Social Psychology, 40*, 642–658.

Dasgupta, N., DeSteno, D., Williams, L. A., & Hunsinger, M. (2009). Fanning the flames of prejudice: The influence of specific incidental emotions on implicit prejudice. *Emotion, 9*, 585–591.

Dasgupta, N., & Greenwald, A. G. (2001). On the malleability of automatic attitudes: Combating automatic prejudice with images of admired and disliked individuals. *Journal of Personality and Social Psychology, 81*, 800–814.

Dasgupta, N., & Rivera, L. M. (2008). When social context matters: The influence of long-term contact and short-term exposure to admired outgroup members on implicit attitudes and behavioral intentions. *Social Cognition, 26*, 112–123.

Darley, J. M., & Gross, P. H. (1983). A hypothesis-confirming bias in labeling effects. *Journal of Personality and Social Psychology, 44*, 20–33.

De Houwer, J., & Moors, A. (2010). Implicit measures: Similarities and differences. In B. Gawronski, & B. K. Payne (Eds.), *Handbook of implicit social cognition: Measurement, theory, and applications*. New York, NY: Guilford Press.

Devine, P. G. (1989). Stereotypes and prejudice: Their automatic and controlled components. *Journal of Personality and Social Psychology, 56*, 5–18.

Devine, P. G., Monteith, M., Zuwerink, J. R., & Elliot, A. J. (1991). Prejudice with and without compunction. *Journal of Personality and Social Psychology, 60*, 817–830.

Dovidio, J. F., Evans, N., & Tyler, R. B. (1986). Racial stereotypes: The contents of their cognitive representations. *Journal of Experimental Social Psychology, 22*, 22–37.

Dovidio, J. F., Kawakami, K., & Gaertner, S. L. (2002). Implicit and explicit prejudice and interracial interaction. *Journal of Personality and Social Psychology, 82*, 62–28.

Dovidio, J. F., Kawakami, K., Johnson, C., Johnson, B., & Howard, A. (1997). On the nature of prejudice: Automatic and controlled processes. *Journal of Experimental Social Psychology: Special Issue on Unconscious Processes in Stereotyping and Prejudice, 33*, 510–540.

Duckitt, J., (1992). Psychology and prejudice: A historical analysis and integrative framework. *American Psychologist, 10*, 1182–1193.

Dunton, B. C., & Fazio, R. H. (1997). An individual difference measure of motivation to control prejudiced reactions. *Personality and Social Psychology Bulletin, 23*, 316–326.

Fazio, R. H. (1990). Multiple processes by which attitudes guide behavior: The MODE model as an integrative framework. In: M. P. Zanna (Ed.), *Advances in experimental social psychology* (Vol. 23, pp. 75–109). San Diego, CA: Academic Press.

Fazio, R. H. (2007). Attitudes as object-evaluation associations of varying strength. *Social Cognition, 25*, 603–637.

Fazio, R. H., Jackson, J. R., Dunton, B. C., & Williams, C. J. (1995). Variability in automatic activation as an unobtrusive measure of racial attitudes: A bona fide pipeline? *Journal of Personality and Social Psychology, 69*, 1013–1027.

Fazio, R. H., & Olson, M. A. (2003). Implicit measures in social cognition research: Their meaning and use. *Annual Review of Psychology, 54*, 297–327.

Fein, S., & Spencer, S. J. (1997). Prejudice as self-image maintenance: Affirming the self through negative evaluations of others. *Journal of Personality and Social Psychology, 73*, 31–44.

Fiedler, K., Messner, C., & Bluemke, M. (2006). Unresolved problems with the "I", the "A", and the "T": A logical and psychometric critique of the Implicit Association Test (IAT). *European Review of Social Psychology, 17*, 74–174.

Fiske, S. T., Lin, M. H., & Neuberg, S. L. (1999). The Continuum Model: Ten years later. In S. Chaiken, S. & Y. Trope (Eds.), *Dual process theories in social psychology* (pp. 231–254). New York: Guilford.

Fiske, S. T., & Neuberg, S. L. (1990). A continuum of impression formation, from category-based to individuating processes: Influences of information and motivation on attention and interpretation. *Advances in Experimental Social Psychology, 23*, 1–74.

Fiske, S. T., Neuberg, S. L., Beattie, A. E., & Milberg, S. J. (1987). Category-based and attribute-based reactions to others: Some informational conditions of stereotyping and individuating processes. *Journal of Experimental Social Psychology, 23*, 399–427.

Gaertner, S. L., & Dovidio, J. F. (1986). The aversive form of racism. In J. F. Dovidio & S. L. Gaertner (Eds.), *Prejudice, discrimination, and racism*. Orlando, FL: Academic Press.

Gaertner, S. L., & McLaughlin, J. P. (1983). Racial stereotypes: Associations and ascriptions of positive and negative characteristics. *Social Psychology Quarterly, 46*, 23–30.

Galinsky, A. D., & Moskowitz, G. B. (2000). Perspective-taking: Decreasing stereotype expression, stereotype accessibility, and in-group favoritism. *Journal of Personality and Social Psychology, 78*, 708–724.

Gawronski, B., & Bodenhausen, G. V. (2006). Associative and propositional processes in evaluation: An integrative review of implicit and explicit attitude change. *Psychological Bulletin, 132*, 692–731.

Gawronski, B., Deutsch, R., Mbirkou, S., Seibt, B., & Strack, F. (2008). When "just say no" is not enough: Affirmation versus negation training and the reduction of automatic stereotype activation. *Journal of Experimental Social Psychology, 44*, 370–377.

Gilbert, G. M. (1951). Stereotypic persistence and change among college students. *Journal of Personality and Social Psychology, 46*, 245–254.

Gilbert, D. T., & Hixon, J. G. (1991). The trouble of thinking: Activation and application of stereotypic beliefs. *Journal of Personality and Social Psychology, 60*, 509–517.

Gonsalkorale, K., Sherman, J. W., Allen, T. J., Klauer, K. C., & Amodio, D. M. (2011). Accounting for successful control of implicit racial bias: The roles of association activation, response monitoring, and overcoming bias. *Personality and Social Psychology Bulletin, 37*, 1534–1545.

Gonsalkorale, K., von Hippel, W., Sherman, J. W., & Klauer, K. C. (2009). Bias and regulation of bias in intergroup interactions: Implicit attitudes toward Muslims and interaction quality. *Journal of Experimental Social Psychology, 45*, 161–166.

Gordijn, E.H., Hindriks, I., Koomen, W., Dijksterhuis, A., & van Knippenberg, A. (2004). Consequences of stereotype suppression and internal suppression motivation: A self-regulation approach. *Personality and Social Psychology Bulletin, 30*, 212–224.

Gray, J. A. (1982). *The neuropsychology of anxiety: An enquiry into the functions of the septo-hippocampal system*. Oxford, UK: Oxford University Press.

Gray, J. A. (1987). *The psychology of fear and stress*. Cambridge, UK: Cambridge University Press.

Greenwald, A. G., & Banaji, M. R. (1995). Implicit social cognition: Attitudes, self-esteem, and stereotypes. *Psychological Review, 102*, 4–27.

Greenwald, A. G., McGhee, D. E., & Schwartz, J. K. L. (1998). Measuring individual differences in implicit cognition: The Implicit Association Test. *Journal of Personality and Social Psychology, 74*, 1464–1480.

Greenwald, A. G., Poehlman, T. A., Uhlmann, E. L., & Banaji, M. R. (2009). Understanding and using the Implicit Association Test: III. Meta-analysis of predictive validity. *Journal of Personality and Social Psychology, 97*, 17–41.

Hart, A. J., Whalen, P. J., Shine, L. M., McInerney, S. C., Fischer, H., & Rauch, S. L. (2000). Differential response in the human amygdala to racial outgroup vs ingroup face stimuli. *NeuroReport, 11*, 2351–2355.

Haines, E. L., & Kray, L. J. (2005). Self-power associations: The possession of power impacts women's self-concepts. *European Journal of Social Psychology, 35*, 643–662.

Hall, N. R., Crisp, R. J., & Suen, M. (2009). Reducing implicit prejudice by blurring intergroup boundaries. *Basic and Applied Social Psychology, 31*, 244–254.

Hamilton, D. L., & Sherman, J. W. (1994). Stereotypes. In R. S. Wyer, Jr., & T. K. Srull (Eds.), *Handbook of social cognition* (2nd ed.). Hillsdale, NJ: Erlbaum.

Hamilton, D. L., Stroessner, S. J., & Driscoll, D. M. (1994). Social cognition and the study of stereotyping. In P. G. Devine, D. L. Hamilton, & T. M. Ostrom (Eds.), *Social cognition: Impact on social psychology* (pp. 292–323). San Diego, CA: Academic Press.

Harding, J., Proshansky, H., Kutner, B., & Chein, I. (1969). Prejudice and ethnic relations. In G. Lindzey & E. Aronson (Eds.), *The handbook of social psychology* (2nd ed., Vol. 5). Reading, MA: Addison-Wesley.

Huntsinger, J. R., Sinclair, S., & Clore, G. L. (2009). Affective regulation of implicitly measured stereotypes and attitudes: Automatic and controlled processes. *Journal of Experimental Social Psychology, 45*, 560–566.

Huntsinger, J. R., Sinclair, S., Dunn, E., & Clore, G. L. (2010). Affective regulation of stereotype activation: It's the (accessible) thought that counts. *Personality and Social Psychology Bulletin, 36*, 564–577.

Ito, T. A., Chiao, K. W., Devine, P. G., Lorig, T. S., & Cacioppo, T. (2006). The influence of facial feedback on race bias. *Psychological Science, 17*, 256–261.

Jacoby, L. L. (1991). A process dissociation framework: Separating automatic from intentional uses of memory. *Journal of Memory and Language, 30*, 513–541.

Jones, C. R., & Fazio, R. H. (2010). Person categorization and automatic racial stereotyping effects on weapon identification. *Personality and Social Psychology Bulletin, 36*, 1073–1085.

Katz, D., & Braly, K. (1933). Racial stereotypes of one hundred college students. *Journal of Abnormal and Social Psychology, 28*, 280–290.

Karlins, M., Coffman, T. L., & Walters, G. (1969). On the fading of social stereotypes: Studies in three generations of college students. *Journal of Personality and Social Psychology, 13*(1), 1–16.

Kawakami, K., Dion, K. L., & Dovidio, J. F. (1998) Racial prejudice and stereotype activation. *Personality and Social Psychology Bulletin, 24*, 407–416.

Kawakami, K., Dovidio, J. F., Moll, J., Hermsen, S., & Russin, A. (2000). Just say no (to stereotyping): Effects of training in the negation of stereotypic associations on stereotype activation. *Journal of Personality and Social Psychology, 78*, 871–888.

Lenton, A. P., Bruder, M., & Sedikides, C. (2009). A meta-analysis on the malleability of automatic gender stereotypes. *Psychology of Women Quarterly, 33*, 183–196.

Lepore, L., & Brown, R. (1997). Category and stereotype activation: Is prejudice inevitable? *Journal of Personality and Social Psychology, 72*(2), 275–287.

Lippmann, W. (1922). *Public opinion.* New York: Macmillan.

Livingston, R. W., & Brewer, M. B. (2002). What are we really priming? Cue-based versus category-based processing of facial stimuli. *Journal of Personality and Social Psychology, 82*, 5–18.

Lowery, B. S., Hardin, C. D., & Sinclair, S. (2001). Social influence effects on automatic racial prejudice. *Journal of Personality and Social Psychology, 81*, 842–855.

Macrae, C. N., Bodenhausen, G. V., & Milne, A. B., & Jetten, J. (1994). Out of mind but back in sight: Stereotypes on the rebound. *Journal of Personality and Social Psychology, 67*, 808–817.

Macrae, C. N., Bodenhausen, G. V., Milne, A. B., Thorn, T. M. J., & Castelli, L. (1997). On the activation of social stereotypes: The moderating role of processing objectives. *Journal of Experimental Social Psychology, 33*, 471–489.

Macrae, C. N., Bodenhausen, G. V., Milne, A. B., & Wheeler, V. (1996). On resisting the temptation for simplification: Counterintentional effects of stereotype suppression on social memory. *Social Cognition, 14*, 1–20.

Macrae, C. N., Milne, A. B., & Bodenhausen, G. V. (1994). Stereotypes as energy-saving devices: A peek inside the cognitive toolbox. *Journal of Personality and Social Psychology, 66*, 37–47.

Malinen, S., & Johnston, L. (2007). The influence of an equity statement on perceivers' implicit and explicit associations between males and science. *New Zealand Journal of Psychology, 36*, 18–24.

McConnell, A. R., & Liebold, J. M. (2001). Relations among the Implicit Association Test, discriminatory behavior, and explicit measures of racial attitudes. *Journal of Experimental Social Psychology, 37*, 435–442.

McGrane, J. A., & White, F. A. (2007). Differences in Anglo and Asian Australians' explicit and implicit prejudice and the attenuation of their implicit in-group bias. *Asian Journal of Social Psychology, 10*, 204–210.

Mendoza, S. A., Gollwitzer, P. M., & Amodio, D. M. (2010). Reducing the expression of implicit stereotypes: Reflexive control through implementation intentions. *Personality and Social Psychology Bulletin, 36*, 512–523.

Mitchell, J. P., Nosek, B. A., & Banaji, M. R. (2003). Contextual variations in implicit evaluation. *Journal of Experimental Psychology-General, 132*, 455–469.

Monteith, M. J. (1993). Self-regulation of prejudiced responses: Implications for progress in prejudice-reduction efforts. *Journal of Personality and Social Psychology, 65*, 469–485.

Monteith, M. J., Ashburn-Nardo, L., Voils, C. I., & Czopp, A. M. (2002). Putting the brakes on prejudice: On the development and operation of cues for control. *Journal of Personality and Social Psychology, 83*, 1029–1050.

Monteith, M. J., Lybarger, J. E., & Woodcock, A. (2009). Schooling the cognitive monster: The role of motivation in the regulation and control of prejudice. *Social and Personality Compass, 3*, 211–226.

Monteith, M. J., & Mark, A. Y. (2006). Changing one's prejudice ways: Awareness, affect, and self-regulation. *European Review of Social Psychology, 16*, 113–154.

Monteith, M. J., Sherman, J., & Devine, P. G. (1998). Suppression as a stereotype control strategy. *Personality and Social Psychology Review, 2*, 63–82.

Monteith, M. J., & Spicer, C. V., & Tooman, G. (1998). Consequences of stereotype suppression: Stereotypes on AND not on the rebound. *Journal of Experimental Social Psychology, 34*, 355–377.

Monteith, M. J., & Voils, C. I. (1998). Proneness to prejudiced responses: Toward understanding the authenticity of self-reported discrepancies. *Journal of Personality and Social Psychology, 75*, 901–916.

Moskowitz, G. B., Gollwitzer, P. M., Wasel, W., & Schaal, B. (1999). Preconscious control of stereotype activation through chronic egalitarian goals. *Journal of Personality and Social Psychology, 77*, 167–184.

Meyer, D. E., & Schvaneveldt, R. W. (1976). Meaning, memory structure, and mental processes. *Science, 192*, 27–33.

Neely, J. H. (1977). Semantic priming and retrieval from lexical memory: Roles of inhibitionless spreading activation and limited-capacity attention. *Journal of Experimental Psychology: General, 106*, 226–254.

Nosek, B.A. (2007). Implicit-explicit relations. *Current Directions in Psychological Science, 16*, 65–69.

Nosek, B. A., Greenwald, A. G., & Banaji, M. R. (2007). The Implicit Association Test at age 7: A methodological and conceptual review (pp. 265–292). In J. A. Bargh (Ed.), *Automotive processes in social thinking and behavior.* New York: Psychology Press.

Olson, M. A., & Fazio, R. H. (2004). Reducing the influence of extra-personal associations on the Implicit Association Test: Personalizing the IAT. *Journal of Personality and Social Psychology, 86*, 653–667.

Olson, M. A., & Fazio, R. (2009). Implicit and explicit measures of attitudes: The perspective of the MODE model. In R. E. Petty, R. H. Fazio & P. Brinol (Eds.), *Attitudes: Insights from the new implicit measures.* New York: Taylor & Francis.

Payne, B. K. (2001). Prejudice and perception: The role of automatic and controlled processes in misperceiving a weapon. *Journal of Personality and Social Psychology, 81*, 181–192.

Payne, B. K., Cheng, C. M., Govorun, O., & Stewart, B. (2005). An inkblot for attitudes: Affect misattribution as implicit measurement. *Journal of Personality and Social Psychology, 89*, 277–293.

Payne, B. K., Lambert, A. J., & Jacoby, L. L. (2002). Best laid plans: Effects of goals on accessibility bias and cognitive control in race-based misperceptions of weapons. *Journal of Experimental Social Psychology, 38*, 384–396.

Payne, B. K., & Gawronski, B. (2010). A history of implicit social cognition: Where is it coming from? Where is it now? Where is it going? In B. Gawronski & B. K. Payne (Eds.), *Handbook of implicit social cognition: Measurement, theory, and applications.* New York: Guilford Press.

Pettigrew, T. F. (1958). Personality and sociocultural factors in intergroup attitudes: A cross-national comparison. *Journal of Conflict Resolution, 2*, 29–42.

Phan, K. L., Wager, T., Taylor, S. F., Liberzon, I. (2002). Functional neuroanatomy of emotion: A meta-analysis of emotion activation studies in PET and fMRI. *NeuroImage, 16*, 331–348

Phelps, E. A., O'Connor, K. J., Cunningham, W. A., Funayama, E. S., Gatenby, J. C., Gore, J. C., & Banaji, M. R. (2000). Performance on indirect measures of race evaluation predicts amygdala activation. *Journal of Cognitive Neuroscience, 12,* 729–738.

Plant, E. A., & Devine, P. G. (1998). Internal and external motivation to respond without prejudice. *Journal of Personality and Social Psychology, 75,* 811–832.

Posner, M. I., & Snyder, C. R. R. (1975). Facilitation and inhibition in the processing of signals. In P. M. Rabbitt. & S. Dornic (Eds.), *Attention and performance* (Vol. 5, pp. 669–682). San Diego, CA: Academic Press.

Proshansky, H. M. (1966). The development of intergroup attitudes. In L. W. Hoffman & M. L. Hoffman (Eds.), *Review of child development research* (Vol. 2, pp. 311–371). New York: Russell Sage Foundation.

Richeson, J. A., & Ambady, N. (2001). Who's in charge? Effects of situational roles on automatic gender bias. *Sex Roles, 44,* 493–512.

Richeson, J. A., Baird, A. A., Gordon, H. L., Heatherton, T. F, Wyland, C. L., Trawalter, S., & Shelton, J. N. (2003). An fMRI examination of the impact of interracial contact on executive function. *Nature Neuroscience, 6,* 1323–1328.

Richeson, J. A., & Ambady, N. (2003). Effects of situational power on automatic racial

Rosch, E. (1978). *Principles of categorization.* In E. Rosch & B. B. Lloyd (Eds.), *Cognition and categorization.* Hillsdale, NJ: Erlbaum.

Rudman, L. A., Ashmore, R. D., & Gary, M. L. (2001). "Unlearning" automatic biases: The malleability of implicit prejudice and stereotypes. *Journal of Personality and Social Psychology, 81,* 856–868.

Rydell, R. J., & McConnell, A. R. (2006). Understanding implicit and explicit attitude change: A systems of reasoning analysis. *Journal of Personality and Social Psychology, 91,* 995–1008.

Rydell, R. J., & McConnell, A. R. (2010). Consistency and inconsistency in implicit social cognition: The case of implicit and explicit measures of attitudes. In B. Gawronski & B. K. Payne (Eds.), *Handbook of implicit social cognition* (pp. 295–310). New York: Guilford Press.

Rydell, R. J., McConnell, A. R., Mackie, D. M., & Strain, L. M. (2006). Of two minds: Forming and changing valence-inconsistent implicit and explicit attitudes. *Psychological Science, 17,* 954–258.

Sagar, H. A., & Schofield, J. W. (1980). Racial and behavioral cues in black and white children's perceptions of ambiguously aggressive acts. *Journal of Personality and Social Psychology, 19,* 590–598.

Sassenberg, K., & Moskowitz, G. B. (2005). Don't stereotype, think different! Overcoming automatic stereotype activation by mindset priming. *Journal of Experimental Social Psychology, 41,* 506–514.

Schwarz, N. (2007). Attitude construction: Evaluation in context. *Social Cognition, 25,* 638–656.

Sherif, M. (1966*) In common predicament: Social psychology of intergroup conflict and cooperation.* Boston: Houghton-Mifflin.

Sherman, J. W., Gawronski, B., Gonsalkorale, K., Hugenberg, K., Allen, T. J., & Groom, C. J. (2008). The self-regulation of automatic associations and behavioral impulses. *Psychological Review, 115,* 314–335.

Sherman, J. W., & Hamilton, D. L. (1994). On the formation and interitem associative links in person memory. *Journal of Experimental Social Psychology, 30,* 203–217.

Sherman, J. W., Lee, A. Y., Bessenoff, G. R., & Frost, L. A. (1998). Stereotype efficiency reconsidered: encoding flexibility under cognitive load. *Journal of Personality and Social Psychology, 75,* 589–606.

Sherman, J. W., Stroessner, S. J., Conrey, F. R., & Azam, O. A. (2005). Prejudice and stereotype maintenance processes: Attention, attribution, and individuation. *Journal of Personality and Social Psychology, 89,* 607–622.

Sherman, J. W. (2006). Clearing up some misconceptions about the Quad Model. *Psychological Inquiry, 17,* 269–276.

Sherman, W. (2008). Controlled influences on implicit measures: Confronting the myth of process-purity and the cognitive monster. In R. E. Petty, R. H. Fazio, and P. Brinol (Ed.), *Attitudes: Insights from the new implicit measures* (pp. 391–426). New York: Psychology Press.

Shiffrin, R. M., & Schneider, W. (1977). Controlled and automatic human information processing: II. Perceptual learning, automatic attending and a general theory. *Psychological Review, 84,* 127–190.

Shook, N. J., & Fazio, R. H. (2008). Interracial roommate relationships. *Psychological Science, 19,* 717–723.

Sinclair, S., Lowery, B. S., Hardin, C. D., & Colangelo, A. (2005). Social tuning of automatic racial attitudes: The role of affiliative motivation. *Journal of Personality and Social Psychology, 89,* 583–592.

Smith, E. R., & Zarate, M. A. (1992). Exemplar-based model of social judgment. *Psychological Review, 99,* 3–21.

Snyder, M., Tanke, E. D., & Berscheid, E. (1977). Social perception and interpersonal behavior: On the self-fulfilling nature of social stereotypes. *Journal of Personality and Social Psychology, 35,* 656–666.

Spencer, S. J., Fein, S., Wolfe, C. T., Fong, C., & Dunn, M. A. (1998). Automatic activation of stereotypes: The role of self-image threat. *Personality and Social Psychology Bulletin, 24,* 1139–1152.

Srull, T. K., & Wyer, R. S. (1979). The role of category accessibility in the interpretation of information about persons: Some determinants and implications. *Journal of Personality and Social Psychology, 37,* 1660–1672.

Stanley, D., Phelps, E. A., & Banaji, M. R. (2008). The neural basis of implicit attitudes. *Current Directions in Psychological Science, 17,* 164–170.

Stewart, B. D., & Payne, B. (2008). Bringing automatic stereotyping under control: Implementation intentions as efficient means of thought control. *Personality and Social Psychology Bulletin, 34,* 1332–1345.

Stewart, B. D., von Hippel, W., & Radvansky, G. A. (2009). Age, race, and implicit prejudice: Using process dissociation to separate the underlying components. *Psychological Science, 20,* 164–168.

Turner, R. N., & Crisp, R. J. (2010). Imagining intergroup contact reduces implicit prejudice. *British Journal of Social Psychology, 49,* 129–142.

Wegner, D. M. (1994). Ironic processes of mental control. *Psychological Review, 101,* 34–52.

Wheeler, M. E., & Fiske, S. T. (2005). Controlling racial prejudice and stereotyping: Social cognitive goals affect amygdala and stereotype activation. *Psychological Science, 16,* 56–63.

Wittenbrink, B., Judd, C. M., & Park, B. (1997). Evidence for racial prejudice at the implicit level and its relationship with questionnaire measures. *Journal of Personality and Social Psychology, 72,* 262–274.

Wittenbrink, B., Judd, C. M., & Park, B. (2001). Spontaneous prejudice in context: Variability in automatically activated attitudes. *Journal of Personality and Social Psychology, 81*, 815–827.

Woodcock, A., & Monteith, M. J. (2009). Reducing implicit bias through the self-regulation of prejudiced responses. Paper presented at the Midwestern Psychological Association.

Woodcock, A., & Monteith, M. J. (2010). Creating a common ingroup to combat implicit bias. Paper presented at the Midwestern Psychological Association.

Word, C. O., Zanna, M. P., & Cooper, J. (1974). The nonverbal mediation of self-fulfilling prophecies in interracial interaction. *Journal of Experimental Social Psychology, 10*, 109–120.

Wyer, N. A., Mazzoni, G., Perfect, T. J., Calvini, G., & Neilens, H. L. (2010). When not thinking leads to being and doing: Stereotype suppression and the self. *Social Psychological and Personality Science, 1*, 152–159.

Zogmaister, C., Arcuri, L., Castelli, L., & Smith, E. R. (2008). The impact of loyalty and equality on implicit ingroup favoritism. *Group Processes and Intergroup Relations, 11*, 493–512.

Attribution as a Gateway to Social Cognition

Glenn D. Reeder

Abstract

Attribution is concerned with how we make sense of our world. We often wonder why people say and do the things they do. This chapter summarizes the main contributions of attribution research, particularly as it helped to shape the development of social cognition. Beginning with the person perception insights of Fritz Heider (1944, 1958), classic attribution theories were proposed (Bem, 1967; Jones & Davis, 1965; Kelley, 1967) and applied to almost every area of social psychology. Around 1980, cross-fertilization began between attribution and social cognition models of dispositional inference which incorporated automaticity (Gilbert, Pelham, & Krull, 1988; Trope, 1986). The chapter also covers biases in the attribution process such as naïve realism and recent advances in mindreading (which concerns inferences about mental states such as beliefs, intentions, and motives) as well as the application of neuroscience to attribution.

Key Words: attribution, social cognition, person perception, dispositional inference, automaticity, naïve realism, intention, mindreading, neuroscience

Attribution as a Gateway to Social Cognition

A new idea can be exciting. In 1971, for many graduate students in social psychology, the new ideas came fast and furious from the attribution perspective. Like underground music, a series of preprinted chapters on this topic were making their way into graduate seminars. The authors of these chapters included well-known figures such as Ned Jones and Harold Kelley, but also newcomers such as Bernard Weiner and Richard Nisbett. A year later, these chapters were bound together in an orange book entitled, *Attribution: Perceiving the Causes of Behavior* (Jones, Kanouse, Kelley, Nisbett, Valins, & Weiner (1972). As of March 2013, Google Scholar listed 2,786 citations of the Jones and Nisbett (1972) chapter, which proposed actor versus observer differences in attribution. Two additional chapters by Kelley (1972a, 1972b) and another by Weiner, Frieze, Kukla, Reed, Rest, and Rosenbaum (1972)

were each cited more than 1100 times. What can account for the immediate splash and undeniably lasting impact of this work (Weiner, 2008)?

Attribution is concerned with how we make sense of our world (Kelley, 1967). It addresses questions of subjective validity: How do we know what is true and what is not? What causes people to do the things they do? These questions were implicit in much of what social psychologists did before the 1960s, but dimly realized. Asch's (1946) studies of impression formation provided participants with lists of traits to be integrated, but his procedure did not include information about the situational context, or even the behaviors upon which the traits were based. In fact, Asch's (1956) studies of conformity raised issues that are more in tune with the attribution perspective. Participants in these studies were faced with the dilemma of trusting their own perceptions regarding the length of lines or trusting "social reality," in the form of erroneous judgments provided by others (who were confederates of the experimenter). In part, our fascination with these studies involves wanting to know how Asch's participants decided what was real. How did they account for the behavior of the other participants? An underlying assumption of these questions is that social behavior is guided by people's perceptions, understanding, and construal of social events (Heider, 1958; Ross, & Nisbett, 1991). The attribution perspective offered a tool to address these issues.

This chapter summarizes some of the main contributions of attribution research, particularly as it helped to shape the development of social cognition. As shown in Figure 6.1, the organization is chronological to some extent. The first section describes the inspiration and pioneering ideas—primarily from Fritz Heider (1944, 1958)—that laid the groundwork for what I will call "classic attribution" research. The classic attribution period began around 1960 and peaked before 1980. As described in this second section, the early insights of attribution led to landmark empirical advances (e.g., Bem, 1967; Jones & Harris, 1967), systematic theories of person perception (e.g., Jones & Davis, 1965; Kelley, 1967), and applications to almost every area of social psychology (Harvey, Ickes, & Kidd, 1976, 1978, 1981). Around 1980, cross-fertilization began between attribution and early social cognition. Accordingly, the third section describes stage

models of dispositional inference (Gilbert, Pelham, & Krull, 1988; Trope, 1986). These models linked the information-processing approach of cognitive psychology (Neisser, 1967) and the nascent literature on automaticity (e.g., Bargh & Pietromonaco, 1982; Schneider & Shiffrin, 1977) with more traditional attribution concepts such as causal discounting (Kelley, 1972a). The final section of the chapter focuses on attribution of mind, which concerns inferences about mental states such as beliefs, goals, and motives (Epley & Waytz, 2010; Malle & Hodges, 2005). Recent contributions of neuroscience to attribution are also noted (Lieberman, 2010; Mason & Morris, 2010). The developments in these areas once again illustrate the interconnections between attribution and social cognition as they co-evolve.

The focus of the chapter is necessarily selective, emphasizing cognitive process, especially as it relates to later developments in social cognition. Where appropriate, I attempt to link classic ideas and findings with references to more current work on the same issues. Readers interested in more in-depth coverage of causal attribution, per se, and the application of attribution concepts to a variety of social psychological topics are referred to other sources (Cheng, 1997; Forsterling, 2001; Gilbert, 1998; Harvey et al., 1976, 1978, 1981; Hewstone, 1989; Kelley & Michaela, 1980; Ross & Fletcher, 1985; Weiner, 1995).

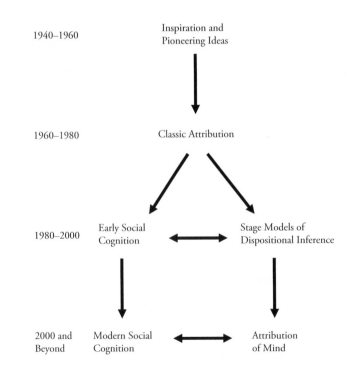

Figure 6.1 Timeline of evolution for attribution and social cognition.

At the beginning of this chapter, I posed the question of why attribution held such wide appeal to social psychologists in the 1970s. The sudden surge of interest in attribution can be traced to several factors (Aronson, 1997). First, although social psychology was always cognitive (Asch, 1946; Heider, 1944, 1958; Fiske & Taylor, 1991), systematic theoretical advances in the 1960s demonstrated the breadth and persuasiveness of an attributional analysis (Jones & Davis, 1965; Kelley, 1967). For instance, a topic such as source credibility in persuasion took on new significance when viewed through the attributional lens: Did a communicator advocate position A because of a personal bias or because of the soundness of that position? Second, the popularity of cognitive psychology contributed to a zeitgeist whereby motivational explanations (e.g., cognitive dissonance) were considered passé. Methodological issues played a role as well. In the wake of Milgram's (1974) controversial studies of obedience and the sometimes elaborate laboratory hoaxes needed to investigate cognitive dissonance, many social psychologists became wary of deceiving research participants. Attribution studies could be done simply, without deception. Most important, the new approach quickly yielded a plethora of important new findings (Harvey et al., 1976; Jones et al., 1972; Jones, 1979; Kelley & Michela, 1980; Nisbett & Ross, 1980; Weiner, 1979).

Inspiration and Pioneering Ideas from Heider

Where attribution is concerned, it is no exaggeration to say that it all began with Fritz Heider (1944, 1958). Although others such as Gustav Ichheiser (1970) and Albert Michotte (1963) also made lasting contributions, Heider (1958) summarized the most important of these in his magnum opus, *The Psychology of Interpersonal Relations*. Heider's insight was deep and penetrating. More than 50 years after his book appeared, it is possible to trace most of the important advances in attribution to elements in that book. It is well known that many of the early theoretical statements of attribution drew heavily from Heider (Jones & Davis, 1965; Jones & McGillis, 1976; Kelley, 1967, 1973; Reeder & Brewer, 1979; Weiner, 1979). Perhaps less acknowledged is that Heider hinted about additional topics that later appeared as empirical findings in the literature. A partial list of these topics would include covariation and discounting of causes (Kelley, 1967; 1973), correspondence bias (Gilbert & Malone, 1995; Jones, 1979), attribution of achievement (Weiner, 1979),

the actor versus observer bias (Jones & Nisbett, 1972; Malle, 2006), false consensus (Ross, Greene, & House, 1977), attribution of responsibility (Fincham & Jaspers, 1980), and self-serving attribution biases (Taylor & Brown, 1988). Heider's contributions follow four themes: (1) naïve psychology matters, (2) perceivers draw causal inferences, (3) gestalt principles organize impressions, and (4) attributions are biased by perceiver motivations.

Naïve Psychology Matters

All of us are amateur or naïve psychologists, gathering information about the people around us—and often struggling to understand it. From a distance, we wonder why political figures act as they do, while closer to home we try to figure out the nature of our spouse or lover. Heider's great insight was to take these perceptions seriously. He assumed not only that social perceptions were of interest in their own right but also that such perceptions underlie and determine all our social interactions with other people. Our unique (and sometimes biased) construal of events is what matters (Ross & Nisbett, 1991). For instance, if we think a candidate for political office is dishonest, we are unlikely to vote for or provide financial support for that candidate. Likewise, if we come to view a spouse or lover as cruel and heartless, we are more likely to end the relationship. Because of its central role, Heider believed that the study of naïve psychology (or social cognition, as we now know it), should take precedence over other areas of social psychology (Ostrom, 1984).

But what are the rules of naïve psychology? Heider noted that these rules are implicit, rather than explicit: We act in accord with these principles without necessarily being consciously aware of them (Nisbett & Wilson, 1977). Modern research on implicit social cognition and the automatic influence of attitudes certainly validates Heider's position (Fazio & Olson, 2003; Greenwald & Banaji, 1995). Heider also believed that language and communication styles need to be explicated so that we may understand their subtle influences (Hilton, 1995; Semin & Fiedler, 1988). For example, concepts such as desire, ought, and revenge were analyzed in detail (Heider, 1958).

Perceivers Draw Causal Inferences

People see events in both the physical and social world as causally connected. Just as a dam or levee may break because of heavy storm waters, a person's angry outburst may be seen as caused by a stressful day at the office. Heider suggested that perceivers put the various causes of human behavior into two categories: causes within the person (e.g., dispositional characteristics such as having a "quick temper") and causes within the environment or surrounding situation (e.g., looming deadlines in the workplace). Three noteworthy themes emerge in the discussion of these causal forces. First, perceivers expect causes to interact in systematic ways. Second, perceivers prefer certain stable, invariant causes (e.g., traits) over other types of explanations. Finally, Heider noted some differences between personal causality (i.e., intentional acts) and impersonal causality (i.e., unintentional acts).

EXPECTATIONS ABOUT CAUSAL INTERACTION

Heider's (1958) rather simplistic distinction between dispositional and situational causality became the bedrock assumption of early attribution theories. If behavior was seen as due to the actor, perceivers could feel free to attribute corresponding traits and dispositions to the target person, whereas if the behavior was seen as caused by situational forces, little could be learned about the target person (Bem, 1967; Jones & Davis, 1965; Kelley, 1967). In other words, dispositional and situational causality were placed at odds with one another—in a hydraulic relationship—where strength in one implied weakness in the other. Although the hydraulic idea may be intuitively appealing, recent findings suggest that perceivers often see *both* dispositional and situational factors as necessary to produce behavior (Gawronski, 2004; McClure, 1998; Reeder, Vonk, Ronk, Ham, & Lawrence, 2004). For instance, situational forces (such as an incentive to steal) tend to be seen as drawing out (or motivating) a person to express a given trait (such as dishonesty). Thus, rather than discounting the role of a disposition, sometimes the situation can explain *why* the disposition came to be expressed.

Heider (1958) provided a more elaborate description of causal interaction in his "naïve analysis of action." For instance, imagine a person who attempted to row a boat across a lake. Progress toward the goal will be seen as a joint function of forces within the person (such as effort and ability) and situational forces (such as a wind that either hinders or facilitates the boat's progress). Heider described the relation between effort and ability as multiplicative: When a person with high ability exerts high effort on a task, the resulting effect should be much more dramatic than when a person of low ability exerts the same effort (Anderson & Butzin, 1974; Reeder, Hesson-McInnis, Kroshse, &

Scialabba, 2001). For instance, if a person is weak and uncoordinated, the person's efforts to concentrate on rowing will have minimal impact.

PERCEIVERS PREFER INVARIANT CAUSES

When looking for an explanation, perceivers want to know the underlying cause. Heider (1958) provided an example in which he found sand on his desk, traced it to a crack on the ceiling and, ultimately, to a weakness in the walls. So too, in Heider's view of social perception, perceivers are less interested in the changing circumstances surrounding behavior than in stable factors that may reliably determine actions in the future. If perceivers are searching for such invariance, they often find it in a target person's traits and dispositions. In making such dispositional attributions, Heider (1958) implied that perceivers are prone to underestimating situational forces. At least two tendencies may account for such a bias. First, target persons are seen as "action centers," sufficient causes of their behavior. Second, a target's behavior stands out (relative to the situation) and tends to capture our attention: "…behavior in particular has such salient properties it tends to engulf the total field…" (p. 54). The general notion that perception of causality follows causal salience proved influential (Pryor & Kriss, 1977; Taylor & Fiske, 1978). Nevertheless, Heider's observations about "behavior engulfing the field" led to controversy. On the one hand, his emphasis of dispositional attribution set the stage for later research on the correspondence bias (Gilbert & Malone, 1995; Jones, 1979) and the so-called fundamental attribution error (Ross, 1977). On the other hand, much research indicates that perceivers can be highly attentive to situational information (Gawronski, 2004; Malle, Knobe, & Nelson, 2007), even when their goal is to form trait judgments (Gosling, Ko, Mannarelli, & Morris, 2002; Reeder, Monroe, & Pryor, 2008).

PERSONAL CAUSALITY VERSUS
IMPERSONAL CAUSALITY

Most researchers in attribution took their cue from Heider's distinction between dispositional and situational causes, a distinction concerned with the locus of causality. Researchers gave less attention to a related distinction Heider (1958) drew between personal and impersonal causality (see also Malle, 2004, 2008). Personal causality refers to instances in which action is produced intentionally—with a purpose behind it. In contrast, impersonal causality can refer to environmentally produced events (as when rocks fall from a mountain) or a person's unintentional actions. The reader may rightly ask how the personal causality distinction (personal vs. impersonal) differs from the locus of causality distinction (dispositional vs. situational). The difference can be clarified in the case of unintended behavior. Suppose a person is seen to fall on an icy sidewalk. The behavior is clearly unintentional, an instance of impersonal causality. But locus of causality is still at issue: Was the fall due to something about the person (e.g., a lack of coordination) or due to the icy conditions? In more recent discussions of this issue, researchers suggest that intentional actions (such as donating to a charity) are typically explained in terms of a person's goals, motives, or reasons (Malle, 1999; Reeder, 2009a; White, 1991). Such reason explanations often recognize the role of situational factors (e.g., the recipients of the donation were very needy). In contrast to intentional behavior, unintentional acts are explained in terms of causal locus: Was the act caused by something in the person or something in the situation?

Given the goal directed nature of intentional actions, Heider (1958) noted at least two implications. First, perceivers assume that intentional actions are characterized by *equifinality*. By this, Heider meant that when a person has a goal in mind, we expect that a variety of strategies or means may be employed to achieve that goal, depending on the circumstances. For instance, a graduate student who has the goal of becoming a college professor may find herself switching research topics or changing faculty mentors if new job opportunities require a different research emphasis. In other words, given a constant goal, the means to achieve the goal may show much variability.

A second implication is that perceivers tend to hold people more responsible for their intentional actions than their unintentional actions (Alicke, 2000; Hart, 1968; Malle, 2004; Shaver, 1985; Weiner, 1995). For instance, if a person threw a stone with the intention of hitting someone, we would judge the person more harshly than if the stone had gone off course and produced accidental harm.

But Heider (1958) acknowledged that matters of responsibility can be more complicated. He hinted at a model of responsibility with five levels (Shaw & Sulzer, 1964). First, based on mere associations, people may be held at least partly responsible for outcomes not of their own doing (Collins & Loftus, 1975; Gawronski & Bodenhausen, 2006; Skowronski, Carlston, Mae, & Crawford, 1998). For instance, a tourist visiting in a foreign country may be condemned for outcomes of a war (involving the tourist's home country) that took place centuries ago. At the second level, people may be held responsible for outcomes they caused unintentionally. Thus, a person who was driving within the speed limit may be held partly responsible for hitting a child who suddenly darted out between two parked cars. The third level of responsibility involves cases in which the outcome could have been foreseen, but was not intended. Thus, a person may be held more responsible for an auto accident when speeding was involved. Presumably, the driver should have realized the increased dangers that come with speed. In making such a judgment, the perceiver may consider alternative scenarios in which a more thoughtful or moral person would not have behaved in this way (Hilton & Slugoski, 1986; Roese, 1997). The fourth level concerns cases in which a person's actions appear at least partly justified by the situation. For instance, if a supervisor lost her temper in response to the dishonest behavior of a subordinate, we might say she was "provoked." Responsibility, in this case, would be discounted relative to a situation that involved lesser provocation (Kelley, 1972a; McClure, 1998). Finally, at the fifth level, people are held fully responsible for their intentional acts. Thus, a wealthy person who swindled small investors might be seen in a particularly negative light.

Gestalt Principles Organize Impressions

Like other pioneers of social cognition (Asch, 1946; Festinger, 1957), Heider stressed consistency and organization in social perception (Koffka, 1935). First, perceivers search for the meaning behind action. In an early demonstration, Heider and Simmel (1944) created a film with black geometric figures moving against a white background. Perceivers who viewed the film engaged in a bit of anthropomorphism (Epley, Waytz, & Cacioppo, 2007), endowing the figures with motives in order to make sense of what they saw. Thus, when a large triangle moved toward a circle, perceivers saw the triangle as a "bully" who was chasing the circle. Similarly, when we read a book or watch a movie, our attribution of motives to the characters allows us to comprehend the meaning of events and better understand how the different aspects of an individual's personality fit together (Read & Miller, 1993, 2005; Reeder & Trafimow, 2005).

A second indicator of the search for consistency is that persons and their acts tend to be seen as one (Heider, 1944). Although Heider believed that actual behavior reflected an interaction between both the environment and the person, he suggested that naïve perceivers stress the role of personal causes in this equation (Jones, 1979; Ross, 1977). Heider (1944, 1958) also stressed certain types of content in the impression, particularly competence (or ability, as indicated by success) and morality (or warmth), which may organize our overall reaction to the person (Fiske, Cuddy, & Glick, 2006; Reeder & Brewer, 1979; Skowronski & Carlston, 1989; Wojciszke, 2005).

Third, consistency can lead perceivers to try to "match" a cause with its effect. The linking of cause with effect is sometimes as simple as assuming that a bad act must have been caused by a bad person. But Heider (1958, p. 51) also described more complex matching strategies that promote economy in the impression. For instance, when perceivers are confronted with a series of acts from a target person, they try to identify a cause or motive that integrates or reconciles the different behaviors. Suppose a young worker, who appeared to worship a company executive, was promoted by that executive to a position of authority. But once entrusted with the trade secrets of the company, the worker quit the job and took a lucrative position with a competing company. In order to account for the full pattern of behavior, perceivers may cite a single motive—ambition or perhaps avarice—that links the different actions together.

Attribution Can Be Biased

Finally, Heider's (1944) perceiver also engaged in a good deal of wishful thinking: "The tendency to keep the ego level high is a good example" (p. 368). When seeking an explanation for an outcome, perceivers are likely to choose a cause or reason that (1) fits their own wishes and (2) fits with the available data. Two manifestations of such bias relate to the self-serving bias in attribution (Bradley, 1978; Taylor & Brown, 1988) and the tendency to perceive events egocentrically (Inhelder & Piaget, 1958; L. Ross & Ward, 1996; M. Ross & Sicoly, 1979). In line with a self-serving bias, Heider suggested that people can be quick to deny personal responsibility for a failure or frustrating event, while eager to place the blame on a scapegoat (Fein & Spencer, 1997; Haslam, 2006).

In discussing egocentrism, Heider's view of the perceiver was quite similar to what we now call the *naïve realist* (Ross & Ward, 1996)—one who believes that he or she sees objects and events in the world objectively (as they really are). Being unaware of subjectivity has several consequences. First, a person may not realize the influence that he or she has on other persons (Heider, 1958, p. 55; Gilbert & Jones, 1986). For instance, a professor with a hilarious sense of humor may create a humorous classroom atmosphere, leading the professor to mistakenly conclude that students typically joke-around in the classroom. Second, perceivers may not realize that the situation they see is not the one that others see. When Marie Antoinette was informed that the people of France were hungry because they had no bread, she is reputed to have asked why they did not eat cake instead. Finally, perceivers tend to engage in social projection, believing that others hold similar attitudes to their own (Robbins & Krueger, 2005; Ross, Greene, & House, 1977).

Despite the multitude of topics covered here, this review barely scratches the surface of what Heider (1944, 1958) offered to social cognition. The difficulty in summarizing his work relates, in part, to the countless insights he offered. Many of his writings also lack the systematic organization that one expects from scientific theory. Nevertheless, future researchers are likely to continue to mine his writings for inspiration and new ideas to study. Forty years ago, when graduate students were looking for an interesting thesis topic, they were advised to "read Heider!" For the serious student of social cognition, the advice remains as true today as it was then.

Classic Attribution: Systematic Theory, Findings, and Applications

Two theoretical papers in the 1960s are largely responsible for the rapid growth of attribution in the decade to follow. In 1965, Jones and Davis proposed the first systematic model of dispositional inference. Two years later, Kelley (1967) published a more general theory of causal thinking in social situations. Kelley's analysis applied not only to attributions about persons but also to attributions about situational forces. These two papers, along with the volume by Jones et al. (1972), had immediate impact. A number of important empirical findings followed quickly, and the attribution approach was applied widely in social psychology and elsewhere.

The Jones and Davis (1965) Theory of Correspondent Inferences

We see other people behave in contexts in which a variety of behavioral choices are available to them. Job candidates decide how to present themselves in an interview, depending on the nature of the job. High school seniors select a college to attend among those schools to which they were accepted. When we witness these choices being made, how do we come to infer the stable characteristics (i.e., traits and attitudes) of the actors involved? Jones and Davis (1965) addressed this question in their theory of correspondent inferences.

Following Heider (1958), Jones and Davis began with the assumption that perceivers seek to understand the social interactions they witness and to attribute stable characteristics to those involved. Any behavior could potentially be analyzed in terms of an endless causal regress, whereby immediate action (e.g., U.S. President Obama criticized oil company executives) can be traced to a prior event (an oil rig exploded), which in turn is explainable by earlier causes (lax safety regulations). Yet perceivers mainly seek a sufficient cause, rather than a complete explanation. According to Jones and Davis, the sufficient cause typically comes in the form of an *intention*. By intention, Jones and Davis meant the reason or motive underlying the behavior (Malle, 2004; Reeder, 2009a). Knowing a person's intention, then, allows the perceiver to make a trait inference.

It is important to note that Jones and Davis limited their attributional analysis to intentional action, apparently in the belief that a target person's unintentional acts carry less relevant information about the target. Assumptions about the target person's knowledge and ability were seen as playing a crucial role in determining intentionality (Malle & Knobe, 1997). If a person is assumed to have lacked foreknowledge of the consequences of his or her behavior, or lacked the ability to bring about those consequences, those consequences cannot be seen as the reasons for the behavior. For example, imagine that a small child tripped while carrying a 45-caliber pistol, leading the gun to discharge and kill someone. We would be unlikely to think the child intended harm if (1) the child thought the gun was unloaded and (2) the child lacked the strength to willfully pull the trigger.

INFERRING INTENTIONS

When the assumptions of knowledge and ability are satisfied, how do perceivers infer a person's specific intention? In considering this question, Jones and Davis focused on cases in which target persons made choices between available alternatives. The unique effects associated with the chosen alternative are then viewed as revealing of the target's intention. For instance, imagine that a talented high school senior named Emma has been admitted to two prestigious universities, State U and Private U. Both offer quality programs, but State U has lower tuition,

and is closer to home, and some of Emma's friends will enroll there. The main attraction of Private U, on the other hand, is its location in a city with many cultural opportunities. But Emma is aware that the city also has a high crime rate. Some of the effects of attending each university are shared or *common*. For instance, both schools are prestigious and have quality programs. According to Jones and Davis, these common effects are relatively uninformative: If Emma selected State U over Private U, we would be unlikely to say the quality of the school was the main reason for her selection.

In contrast, effects that are unique to the chosen alternative are more revealing of a target person's intentions. In the example above, if Emma chose to attend State U, we would explain her choice as due to some combination of its low cost, its proximity to home, and the fact that her friends are going there. On the other hand, if Emma selected Private U, the uniqueness of its cultural opportunities would likely be cited as the reason for her choice. Jones and Davis acknowledged additional complexities in that unique effects that are *socially desirable* are more likely to be seen as reasons for the choice (e.g., Because the cultural opportunities of Private U are socially desirable, whereas its crime rate is not so desirable, perceivers should see cultural opportunities as motivating Emma's choice). In addition, the *number of unique effects* is important as well. Perceivers should be more certain of the target's intention when the chosen alternative has only one such socially desirable effect, as opposed to when there are many such effects (Jones, Davis, & Gergen, 1961; Newtson, 1974). Therefore, perceivers should be more certain of Emma's intention if she selects Private U over State U (because State U is associated with many socially desirable effects).

In summary, only effects that the target person knew about and had the ability to produce are informative about a person's intentions. The perceiver considers the different alternatives from which the target chose and notes the effects that are unique to each alternative. If the chosen alternative has only one socially desirable and unique effect, the perceiver will be confident that the target had the intention of bringing about that effect.

THE DETERMINANTS OF CORRESPONDENT INFERENCES ABOUT DISPOSITIONAL CHARACTERISTICS

Once an intention is isolated, perceivers are in a position to infer the dispositional characteristics of the target person. Jones and Davis introduced the term *correspondence* in this context. Correspondence refers to the extent to which a target person's behavior—and the intention on which it is based—are similar to the underlying characteristics that are attributed to the target. Consider the example in which Emma chose to attend Private U because she desired cultural opportunities. A correspondent dispositional inference would occur to the extent the perceiver views Emma as a cultured, sophisticated person. In other words, high correspondence is present if the perceiver infers a disposition that is congruent with (or corresponds to) the observed behavior.

Yet perceivers may not always attach much significance to knowing that a person acted with a given intention or wanted a particular outcome. What, then, are the determinants of correspondent inferences? Jones and Davis (1965) suggest that correspondence is high for an act that is (1) socially undesirable, (2) freely chosen, and (3) done for a clear reason (i.e., there is only one unique effect). The role of these three factors can be illustrated by the unflattering dispositional characteristics we would attribute to a bank teller who stole $10,000. Our negative reaction reflects our beliefs that the act of stealing was socially undesirable, unforced, and clearly done for the purpose of obtaining ill-gotten gain.

THE ROLE OF PERCEIVER MOTIVATIONS

Jones and Davis (1965) also followed Heider by assuming that attributions can be biased. The main biasing factors are *hedonic relevance* and the related concept of *personalism*—both of which increase the extent of correspondence between actions and attributed dispositional inferences. Hedonic relevance is present to the extent that a target person's actions produce consequences that either "…promote or undermine the perceiver's values…" (p. 237). For instance, if the owner of a company made bad business decisions that put the company workers' pensions in jeopardy, company workers would likely make harsh judgments about the owner (Jones & deCharms, 1957). As the social cognition perspective developed, the presence of such "outcome dependency" was found to also influence attentional processes related to seeking accuracy and greater individuation in the impression (Fiske & Neuberg, 1990; Neuberg & Fiske, 1987).

In the example above in which the company owner made bad decisions, there is no reason for the workers to assume negative intent on the owner's part. In contrast, personalism represents a special case of hedonic relevance in which the perceiver

believes the actor *intended* to alter the outcomes of the perceiver. For instance, if the company owner was seen as deliberately slashing worker pension benefits in order to increase his or her own wealth, the example would qualify as an instance of personalism: Not only were benefits decreased, but pensioners could also assume that the owner was well aware of this effect. Thus, personalism represents an extreme case of hedonic relevance that is revealing of the actor's motives and can lead to especially extreme reactions to the target person (Dodge & Crick, 1990).

In summary, Jones and Davis (1965) proposed the first systematic model of dispositional inference, and many of their ideas were incorporated into the social cognition literature, including intentionality (Malle & Knobe, 1997), mental states such as motives (Ames, 2004; Dodge & Crick, 1990; Read & Miller, 1993; Kammrath, Mendoza-Denton, & Mischel, 2005; Reeder, 2009a), chosen and non-chosen alternatives (Roese, 1997), and motivational bias (Fiske & Neuberg, 1990).

Kelley's Covariation Approach to Causal Attribution

More so than Jones and Davis (1965), Harold Kelley's work (1967, 1973) addressed the central question of *causal attribution*: How do perceivers decide if a given effect (e.g., a target person's behavior) was caused by something about the person or by environmental factors surrounding the target's behavior? In addition, whereas Jones and Davis focused on intentions and dispositions internal to the target person (attempting to rule out situational determinants), Kelley aimed to illuminate external attributions about the situation or environment. Following Heider's (1958) reliance on J. S. Mills' method of difference, Kelley proposed *covariation* logic as the crucial tool of attribution: "The effect is attributed to that condition which is present when the effect is present and which is absent when the effect is absent." For instance, if a child typically misbehaves only after ingesting large quantities of sugar, the misbehavior will be viewed as caused by the sugar. In this example, causality will be assigned externally (to the sugar), rather than internally (to the child).

Kelley (1967) further elaborated his model by identifying three important sources of information that are used in the covariation analysis: (1) The *distinctiveness* of the behavior across similar stimuli, (2) the agreement or *consensus* between the target person's reaction to the stimulus and the reactions of other people, and (3) the *consistency* of the target person's behavior across time and modality (i.e., ways of being exposed to the stimulus). To apply the model, consider the example of the child who misbehaved after eating sugar. The perceiver will be highly confident of an external attribution under the following pattern of information: Distinctiveness is high (the child misbehaves only after eating sugary foods), consensus is high (other children also tend to misbehave after eating sweets), and the child's misbehavior after eating sweets is relatively constant across time and modality (at school, home, and on the ball field). On the other hand, the perceiver would be more confident of an internal attribution given a pattern of this sort: Distinctiveness is low (the child misbehaves after eating a wide variety of foods), consensus is low (other children typically do not misbehave after eating sugar), and the child's (negative) reaction to sweets is relatively consistent (McArthur, 1972).

Notice that the covariation model (Kelley, 1967) assumes the perceiver was able to accumulate quite a bit of information about the target person's behavior over time, all the while keeping track of the behavior's covariation with other types of stimuli (distinctiveness), the reactions of others (consensus), and different locales (modality). Perhaps Kelley overestimated the capabilities of the perceiver. For instance, subsequent social cognition research on illusory correlation suggested that perceivers have considerable difficulty assessing covariation between social groups and the positive versus negative behaviors of the group members (Hamilton & Gifford, 1976; see also Alloy & Tabachnik, 1984).

In later papers, Kelley (1972b, 1973) simplified matters by acknowledging that perceivers often make attributions after only a single observation of behavior. With restricted information, perceivers can still react to the configuration of causes, based on their expectations or *schemata* about how causes typically interact. According to Kelley's *discounting principle*, the role of a given cause will be discounted if other possible causes are also present. Thus, if an interviewee claimed to be an extravert while applying for a lucrative job that required an outgoing person, perceivers should attribute the behavior to (external) job demands, rather than to (internal) dispositional characteristics (Jones et al., 1961). There is a second, related principle, called the *augmentation effect*, whereby the presence of an inhibitory (external) cause heightens the perceived causal importance of an alternative (internal) cause. For example, suppose the interviewee above claimed to be an extravert while applying for a job that required a person who could work long hours in solitude. In this situation, the interviewee should be seen as especially extraverted.

The discounting and augmentation principles make essentially the same predictions as the more elaborate Jones and Davis (1965) analysis of unique effects. Consequently, over the next 20 years, Kelley's more parsimonious account tended to be incorporated into models of dispositional inference (Gilbert et al., 1988; Reeder & Brewer, 1979; Trope, 1986). For the time being, at least, Jones and Davis' (1965) analysis of intentionality, and its concern with perceived intentions, fell by the wayside.

SELF-ATTRIBUTION

Kelley (1967) viewed his covariation model as applying to judgments about the self as well as to judgments about others. Consider the strength with which a person holds a given attitude toward an object (Petty & Krosnick, 1995). Kelley suggested that a person would be more committed to the attitude to the extent that he or she typically feels the same way about that object (consistency) and notices that other people feel the same (consensus).

Kelley (1973) also applied the discounting principle to self-attribution (Bem, 1972; Lepper, Greene, & Nisbett, 1973; Miller & Ross, 1975; Nisbett & Wilson, 1977; Taylor & Brown, 1988). When Bem (1967) proposed his theory of self-perception as an alternative to cognitive dissonance theory (Festinger, 1957), he drew a parallel between attributions to self and attributions to others. When making either type of attribution, the perceiver compares the relative strength of internal and external forces operating on the actor's behavior. For example, consider the forced-compliance studies of attitude change first popularized by cognitive dissonance theorists. In the most famous of these studies (Festinger & Carlsmith, 1959), an experimenter offered participants either $1 or $20 to tell another person that a tedious peg-turning task was "interesting." Those who complied for the low incentive typically came to believe in the attitudinal position they advocated more so than those who complied for a higher incentive. Bem (1967) demonstrated the exact same pattern of inference among "outside" observers, who were merely told that the subject complied for either the low or high incentive. Kelley (1973) interpreted this evidence as support for his discounting principle: Both the original actors and their observers apparently concluded that compliance in the face of a large, external incentive ($20) was relatively unrevealing about the (internal) attitudes of the actor.

BIAS IN ATTRIBUTION

Kelley (1967) pointed to some important sources of bias in attribution, including a tendency toward *pluralistic ignorance* (Prentice & Miller, 1996), whereby people assume that they, unlike other people, are immune to social influence and conformity pressures [see also Pronin's (2007) concept of the *bias blind spot*]. Kelley (1967) also gave insightful descriptions of situations that can mislead people into making biased attributions. For example, recall that in forced-compliance studies (Bem, 1967; Festinger & Carlsmith, 1959), both the original actors and their observers attributed stronger attitudes (in line with the actor's behavior) when the incentive for complying was small (e.g., $1), as opposed to large ($20). This pattern implies that perceivers assumed different degrees of consensus for compliance in the two incentive conditions, such that almost everyone was thought to comply with the experimenter's request in the $20 condition, but not in the $1 condition. Given this assumption, perceivers could feel justified in attributing an extreme attitude for "low consensus" behavior in the $1 condition. But the assumption of differential compliance is mistaken—compliance rates in both conditions are near 95%. The error represents an *illusion of freedom,* whereby perceivers overlook the fact that the actor in the low incentive condition complied because of subtle social pressure applied by the experimenter.

In summary, Kelley (1967, 1973) extended Heider's (1958) theorizing by focusing squarely on causal attribution as an instance of seeking subjective validity. The covariation principle and causal schemata that he proposed could be applied to both self and other perception. Although both Jones and Davis (1965) and Kelley (1967, 1973) anticipated bias in attribution, their basic models implied a highly logical attributional calculus—a rational baseline (Jones & McGillis, 1976). This idealized view of the perceiver proved to be somewhat unrealistic. As empirical findings and applications accumulated in the attribution literature, perceivers came to be portrayed in less flattering fashion—as falling prey to correspondence bias, self-enhancement bias, and naïve realism/social projection. The emerging research also demonstrated the importance of considering the dimensions of causality (e.g., locus, stability, and controllability) and cultural differences in attribution.

Important Findings and Applications
CORRESPONDENCE BIAS

The correspondence bias refers to a tendency for dispositional inferences to be based on observed behavior and insufficiently adjusted for situational factors. In an influential study by Jones and Harris (1967), perceivers read about a target person who wrote an essay either defending Fidel Castro's record in Cuba or criticizing that record. In the "free choice" condition, the target could write on either side of the issue. In the "no choice" condition, however, the target was assigned to support one side of the issue, and the resulting essay complied with the assignment. In line with what Kelley (1973) later called the "discounting principle," perceivers inferred less extreme, essay-correspondent attitudes in the no choice than free choice condition. Nevertheless, discounting in the no choice condition was "incomplete." That is, perceivers still tended to infer attitudes that corresponded to the direction of the essay the target composed. The correspondence bias proved to be remarkably robust, although it could be diminished somewhat if situational constraints on the target were emphasized (Jones, 1979).

A variety of theoretical factors are apparently involved in correspondence bias (Gawronski, 2004; Gilbert & Malone, 1995; Ross, 1977). First, perceivers may fail to notice or give *inadequate attention* to situational forces surrounding behavior (Heider, 1958; Ross Amabile, & Steinmetz, 1977; Taylor & Fiske, 1978). Second, situational expectations (e.g., expecting sad behavior at a funeral) can lead perceivers to make an *inflated behavior categorization* (e.g., identifying a neutral expression as "sad"), leading to a relatively extreme dispositional inference about the person (e.g., this woman really is depressed), as described by Trope's (1986) model of dispositional inference. Third, adjusting a dispositional inference for situational factors may require *cognitive resources*, which may be in short supply for perceivers involved in a social interaction (Gilbert et al., 1988; Gilbert, Krull, & Pelham, 1988). Fourth, when perceivers are suspicious of a target person's ulterior motives, they may engage in more extensive processing, thereby increasing the use of situational information—which can decrease correspondence bias (Fein, 1996; Reeder et al., 2004).

Finally, perceivers may have *unrealistic expectations* concerning how situations affect behavior. Reeder and Brewer (1979) elaborated on Kelley's (1973) causal schemata by describing perceivers' expectations about how traits and attitudes are related to the expression of corresponding behaviors. For instance, perceivers expect that writers will compose essays reflecting their personal opinions and think that an experimenter's instructions are insufficient to lead writers to express alternative opinions. Consequently, regardless of the situational constraints surrounding the creation of an essay, perceivers may see the essay as highly diagnostic of the writer's true opinion (Gawronski, 2003: Reeder, Fletcher, & Furman, 1989). Trait-behavior expectations can also explain the tendency for behaviors demonstrating either high ability or low morality to produce highly correspondent trait inferences (Reeder, 1993; Skowronski & Carlston, 1989; Trafimow & Schneider, 1994; Trafimow & Trafimow, 1999; Vonk, 1998; Vonk & Van Knippenberg, 1994). In the case of ability, perceivers expect that a person with high ability (e.g., a professional tennis player) can perform at either a high level or a low level, depending on motivation. But perceivers expect that a person with low ability can only perform at a low level. In the case of morality, however, immoral persons are expected to emit both moral and immoral behaviors, whereas highly moral persons are expected to always behave in a moral fashion. The upshot of these asymmetrical trait-behavior expectations is that behavioral demonstrations of either high ability or immoral behavior lead to especially correspondent inferences (i.e., that the target person has high ability or is immoral, respectively). These patterns occur because persons without the corresponding disposition are assumed unlikely to have behaved in that fashion.

SELF-ENHANCEMENT BIAS

The pioneers of attribution (Heider, 1958; Jones & Davis, 1965; Kelley, 1967) proposed a self-enhancement bias in the perceiver, and subsequent research clearly validated that assumption (Bradley, 1978; Taylor & Brown, 1988). For example, perceivers are more likely to credit themselves for a successful outcome than a failure. At least in part, this self-serving bias reflects motivational factors related to maintaining high self-esteem and protecting the self from threats (Miller, 1976; Sedikides, Gaertner, & Vevea, 2005; Taylor & Brown, 1988). Still, a tendency to take relatively greater credit for success can also reflect seemingly rational tendencies—such as intending to succeed, rather than fail (Miller & Ross, 1975))—and self-enhancement biases can also be subject to cultural differences (Kitayama, Markus, Matsumoto, & Norasakkunkit, 1997).

ACTOR VERSUS OBSERVER DIFFERENCES

In an influential paper mentioned at the beginning of this chapter, Jones and Nisbett (1972) made a simple, yet provocative, suggestion: They proposed that actors tend to attribute their behavior to situational forces, whereas observers tend to attribute the actor's behavior to dispositions within the actor. Notice that the observers' tendency to draw dispositional inferences is reminiscent of the correspondence bias mentioned earlier. Jones and Nisbett (1972) suggested that actor versus observer differences could arise because actors typically have more background *information* about the situation surrounding their actions (e.g., the actor knows that her angry outburst was provoked by an earlier insult). In addition, actors tend to focus their *attention* on the situation at hand, whereas for the observer, the actor's behavior draws attention because it is dynamic and appears figural against the background of the situation.

Although the Jones and Nisbett (1972) actor versus observer hypothesis seemed highly plausible to many social psychologists, subsequent empirical work was more equivocal. An early review of the literature found, for instance, that actors and observers did not differ in terms of their tendency to draw dispositional inferences for the actor's behavior (Watson, 1982). A recent meta-analysis of 173 published studies reported further limitations (Malle, 2006). The average effect size for the traditional actor versus observer bias was quite small ($d < .10$), and moderator analysis indicated that the bias emerged under a restricted range of circumstances. For example, the traditional bias is strong for attributions about negative events (e.g., relative to observers, actors downplay their personal role in failures), but not for attributions about positive events (for which actors readily take credit). This latter pattern, of course, describes a self-serving bias (Taylor & Brown, 1988). Malle et al. (2007) suggest that there are indeed actor versus observer differences, but the real differences are not those of the traditional actor versus observer hypothesis. For instance, relative to observers, actors are more likely to explain their own behavior in terms of *reasons* (e.g., a situation that influenced their motivation). This difference may arise because actors are relatively more (1) *aware* of their own motives and (2) *motivated* to portray themselves as rational (which can be accomplished by citing good reasons for their actions).

NAÏVE REALISM AND SOCIAL PROJECTION

Naïve realism is the assumption that one perceives events "objectively," as they actually are in the external world (Heider, 1958; Jones & Nisbett, 1972; Kelley, 1967; Ross & Ward, 1996). Social projection is one important manifestation of realism: Perceivers tend to think that other people see the world as they do. Thus, a person who believes in the existence of extraterrestrial beings and alien abduction is likely to think that others believe similarly (Gunther & Christen, 2002). Although this *false consensus* bias (Ross, Greene, & House, 1977) is remarkably robust, it is stronger for attributions about the ingroup than outgroup (Robbins & Krueger, 2005) and may be influenced by a variety of processes, including selective exposure to information, focus of attention, and both logical and motivational factors (Marks & Miller, 1987).

Another important manifestation of realism involves the perception of unfairness or bias in other people (Ross & Ward, 1996). For instance, fans of opposing teams tend to see more rule infractions on the side of the other team (Hastorf & Cantril, 1954), and political partisans are especially alert to a *hostile media bias*, whereby supporters of each side of a controversial issue think the media has been unfair to their side (Vallone, Ross, & Lepper, 1985). Moreover, political partisans tend to see people on the other side of the issue as ignorant of the facts and biased by both ideology and self-serving motives (Reeder, Pryor, Wohl, & Griswell, 2005; Robinson, Keltner, Ward, & Ross, 1995). In contrast, perceivers tend to see themselves—and others who agree with their opinions—as relatively free from bias (Pronin, 2007).

DIMENSIONS OF CAUSALITY

Perceivers can conceptualize the causes of a behavior in terms of a variety of dimensions (e.g., locus of the cause and its stability), with each dimension having a unique effect on cognitive, affective, and behavioral reactions to the behavior (Abramson, Seligman, & Teasdale, 1978; Weiner, 1985). Consider the case of a young scholar who took great pride in composing a manuscript, yet received a rejection letter after submitting it to a journal. According to Abramson et al. (1978), the scholar is likely to experience feelings of hopelessness, lowered self-esteem, and depression to the extent that he or she attributes the rejection to causes that are *internal* ("I am not very creative"), *stable* ("This is the third time this article has been rejected"), and *global* ("Even my love life is in the dumps"). On the

other hand, by attributing to external, unstable, and specific causes, the scholar may maintain a more optimistic outlook (Seligman, 1990).

Bernard Weiner (1979, 1985; 1995) offered what is, perhaps, the most comprehensive analysis of the dimensions of causality. Weiner suggested that the stability of an outcome influences the expectancy of future success (e.g., a stable cause should lead to the reoccurrence of the outcome), whereas the locus of the cause affects self-esteem and pride (e.g., an internal attribution for success increases pride). In addition to locus and stability, Weiner stressed the *controllability* of outcomes. The controllability dimension influences a variety of social emotions as well as judgments of responsibility. In the case of social emotions, perceivers tend to feel anger when a target person fails because of a controllable cause (e.g., lack of effort), but pity when the cause is less controllable (e.g., lack of ability). In addition, targets are held more responsible for producing negative outcomes that were relatively more controllable (Weiner, 1995).

CULTURAL DIFFERENCES

As we are socialized in a given culture, we come to acquire implicit assumptions about causality. Individualist cultures such as Western Europe and the United States tend to emphasize personal causality for social behavior, whereas collectivist cultures such as China tend to emphasize more situational and holistic thinking about causality (Mason & Morris, 2010; Morris & Peng, 1994; Nisbett, Peng, Choi, & Norenzayan, 2001). For instance, when describing a crime such as murder, English-language newspapers tend to stress the dispositional characteristics of the perpetrator, whereas Chinese-language newspapers tend to stress situational explanations (Morris & Peng, 1994).

Social Cognition Meets Attribution: Stage Models of Dispositional Inference

The social cognition perspective emerged full-force with the nearly simultaneous publication of three volumes circa 1980 (Hastie, Ostrom, Ebbesen, Wyer, Hamilton, & Carlston, 1980; Higgins, Herman, & Zanna, 1981; Wyer, & Carlston, 1979). The impetus for these volumes appears to be two-fold. First, person perception researchers grew disenchanted with the then current algebraic (Anderson, 1974) and structural (Rosenberg & Sedlak, 1972) approaches in the field. Although Heider (1958) had hinted about a hierarchy of processing stages (p. 80–81), research before the 1980s typically shed little light on underlying cognitive processes—the events that intervene between stimulus and response (Hastie & Carlston, 1980). Second, rapid advances in theory and method in cognitive psychology held the promise of better elucidating these processes. For instance, by employing measures such as response time and recall, researchers believed they could better understand the information processing sequence of (1) acquisition and encoding of information, (2) representation and retention, and (3) retrieval and decision making.

The shift toward social cognition soon began to transform models of person perception (see Figure 6.1). Dispositional inference now became a matter of anchoring/adjustment because dispositional inferences were viewed as being "adjusted" in response to perceived situational forces (Jones, 1979; Quattrone, 1982). Accordingly, initial dispositional inferences were made spontaneously, a finding called *spontaneous trait inference* (Winter & Uleman, 1984). On this foundation, stage models of dispositional inference could then be proposed, with the early stages of inference being relatively automatic and the later stages being of a more controlled nature (Gilbert et al., 1988; Trope, 1986).

Anchoring/Adjustment

The *anchoring/adjustment heuristic* describes a decision-making tendency whereby an initial estimate is adjusted (often insufficiently) for additional factors that may be relevant (Tversky & Kahneman, 1974). For instance, after watching a TV commercial that portrayed product X as superior to its competitors, a viewer might initially be very impressed, then realize the biased nature of the information source, yet still maintain a relatively positive view of product X (Gilbert, 1991). Quattrone (1982) proposed an explanation of the correspondence bias (Jones & Harris, 1967) based on this anchoring/adjustment idea. The innovation—straight from the playbook of social cognition—was that dispositional inferences often undergo a *change* as the attribution process unfolds. For instance, consider a perceiver who learned that a target person wrote a pro-marijuana essay after being assigned to write in favor of marijuana. The perceiver would begin be inferring a correspondent attitude in the target ("This writer must really *love* marijuana!"), but subsequently consider the situational constraints ("On the other hand, the experimenter did pressure the writer to praise marijuana"), and then make an adjustment ("Well, maybe the writer only *likes* marijuana").

This view suggests that perceivers in the attitude attribution paradigm typically anchor on a correspondent attitudinal inference and then make insufficient adjustment for situational factors. In short, dispositional inference initially comes easy to the perceiver. Quattrone (1982) provided evidence for a general anchoring/adjustment explanation by demonstrating that, under special circumstances, perceivers could be led to anchor on situational factors and, ultimately, overemphasize those situational factors. Perceivers were told that a target person had either a pro or anti attitude toward marijuana legalization and were then shown an essay that the target wrote which expressed that very attitude. Perceivers also received information about the subtle ways that experimenters can influence their subjects. Notice that, despite the possibility of this situational influence, the target's own attitude is a sufficient explanation for the direction taken in the essay. Nevertheless, in line with the anchoring/adjustment tendency, perceivers who read the pro-marijuana (rather than anti-marijuana) essay saw the situation as applying relatively more pressure to write in favor of legalizing marijuana. In other words, perceivers apparently anchored on an extreme situational attribution, and then made insufficient adjustment for the writer's personal attitude as a cause of the behavior.

Spontaneous Trait Inference

The notion that dispositional inference comes easy to the perceiver received further support from research on spontaneous trait inference (STI). Winter and Uleman (1984) adapted the encoding specificity paradigm (Tulving & Thomson, 1973) by having research participants read behavioral descriptions (e.g., The secretary solves the mystery halfway through the book) that implied traits (i.e., clever). The participants were simply instructed to memorize the sentences, and traits words were never explicitly presented at study time. Nevertheless, when participants attempted to recall the sentences, the implied trait words served as powerful recall cues—even though participants were unaware of having made trait inferences at encoding. The overall pattern suggests that trait inference occurs as part of the normal comprehension process (Asch, 1946; Gilbert, 1991).

Although STI is now recognized as a robust phenomenon (Uleman, Saribay, & Gonzalez, 2008), the original Winter and Uleman (1984) method was limited because it was unclear whether the effect was due to an encoding process or a retrieval process (Carlston & Skowronski, 1994). For instance, it is possible that participants used the trait cue provided at recall (e.g., clever) to think of associated behaviors (e.g., correctly guessed the direction of the stock market) that could then cue recall of the sentence stimuli. Stronger evidence in favor of STI emerged when cognitive load at encoding was shown to decrease the effectiveness of traits as recall cues, implying that the locus of the effect was indeed at encoding (Uleman, Newman, & Winter, 1992). In addition, when encoding goals were manipulated, recall was similarly affected (Uleman & Moskowitz, 1994). Finally, Carlston and Skowronski employed a *relearning paradigm* in which participants first learned trait-implying behavioral descriptions that were accompanied by a photo of the actor (Carlston & Skowronski, 1994; Carlston, Skowronski, and Sparks, 1995). In a second task, participants were asked to learn pairings of photos and traits, such that some of the traits had been implied by the earlier behavioral descriptions. Recall for a trait was better when the trait had been implied by the (earlier presented) behavioral descriptions. This finding strongly suggests that traits were inferred as the behavioral descriptions were originally encoded, and this "learning" made it easier to relearn the association between the photo and the trait.

Stage Models of Dispositional Inference

As researchers began to suspect that some types of information could be processed with special ease (Quattrone, 1982; Winter & Uleman, 1984), it was just a matter of time before models of dispositional inference incorporated ideas about automaticity (Bargh & Pietromonaco 1982; Schneider & Shiffrin, 1977). Stage models of dispositional inference proposed by Trope (1986) and Gilbert (1989; Gilbert et al., 1988) were particularly influential. Each model suggested that the initial stages of processing were relatively automatic, followed by more controlled processing. These models and an important theoretical extension are described next.

TROPE'S TWO-STAGE MODEL

Heider (1958) noted that we often experience our perceptions as a given—they just occur to us—without consciously realizing the underlying mediating mechanisms. Trope (1986; Trope & Liberman, 1993) contributed by clarifying the perceptual mechanisms by which perceivers initially interpret and identify attribution-relevant information. At the initial *identification stage* of the model, perceivers notice three types of information: (1) behavioral cues (e.g., the target person appears slightly anxious), (2) situational cues (e.g., an interviewer asked the target about some embarrassing experiences in her past), and (3) prior cues about the target (e.g., from past experience, the perceiver believes the target is a calm person). Information is often ambiguous, however, and its interpretation is context dependent (Asch, 1946; Higgins & Bargh, 1987). For instance, consider the example of a woman who appears vaguely anxious while answering questions posed by an interviewer. Given that the target's behavior is ambiguous (e.g., is she anxious or just pleasantly excited?), the perceiver's identification of her behavior will be affected by other cues that are less ambiguous (e.g., if the interview situation involves the target answering anxiety-inducing questions, her behavior may appear more anxious). At the initial stage of processing, then, the identification of any given informational cue tends to be assimilated in the direction of other cues that are clearer, or less ambiguous. This "disambiguation" occurs more of less unconsciously and automatically (Bargh & Chartrand, 1999).

At the second stage of the model—*dispositional inference*—the identifications of behavior, situation, and prior information are combined by more controlled processing to produce a dispositional inference. Of greatest relevance, behavior cues contribute additively to the dispositional inference. Thus, if the target is identified as behaving in a very anxious manner, the target will tend to be seen as having a very anxious disposition. In contrast, situational information at this stage is *subtracted* from the dispositional inference. In the example above, the target person in the interview will be attributed a less anxious disposition to the extent the anxiety-inducing situation appears to account for her display of anxiety. Trope (1986) suggested that the perceiver's reasoning at this stage reflects the application of causal schemata associated with the discounting principle (Kelley, 1973; Reeder & Brewer, 1979; Reeder, 1997).

By clarifying the relatively automatic processes by which informational cues are identified, Trope (1986) was able to reconcile apparently conflicting findings in the literature. Some studies reported evidence supportive of the discounting principle, whereby situational factors "subtract" from dispositional inferences (e.g., Jones et al., 1961). Nevertheless, many others reported weak or "insufficient discounting," in line with the correspondence bias (Jones, 1979; Jones & Harris, 1967), and other studies found an opposite effect whereby situational forces apparently "added" to a dispositional inference (e.g., Snyder & Frankel, 1976). Trope's (1986) model was able to account for such additive effects of the situation by focusing on the identification stage. For instance, if a target person displayed vague signs of anxiety during an interview, that same behavior might be identified as strong anxiety by a perceiver who believed the target was answering anxiety-inducing questions. At the dispositional inference stage, when the situation is subtracted from the trait inference, that subtraction may not overcome the effect of the earlier, extreme behavior identification. Consequently, the target in this example could ultimately be seen as *more* dispositionally anxious precisely because she was asked anxiety-inducing questions.

GILBERT'S THREE-STAGE MODEL

In contrast to Trope (1986), who focused on early perceptual processing, Gilbert (1989; Gilbert, Pelham, & Krull, 1988) investigated the more controlled, downstream stage of dispositional inference. His model contains three stages: (1) *categorization* of behavior, which resembles Trope's (1986) identification stage; (2) *characterization*, which involves an automatic, correspondent dispositional inference; and (3) *correction*, whereby the dispositional inference is adjusted for the influence of situations forces. The latter two stages of characterization and correction represent an "unpacking" of dispositional inference as the endpoint of the process.

Recall that Quattrone (1982) and research within the STI paradigm (Winter & Uleman, 1984) suggested that trait inference, or characterization as Gilbert called it, could be relatively automatic. A series of clever experiments by Gilbert (1989) supported this notion and—more importantly— demonstrated that the correction stage required cognitive resources. In one of these studies, participants watched a woman who behaved anxiously while being interviewed about topics that were either anxiety inducing (e.g., sexual fantasies) or relaxation inducing (e.g., world travel). In addition, half of those in each condition were simultaneously given a memory task that consumed additional cognitive resources. These cognitively busy perceivers were predicted to be unable to use the situational information (about the interview topics) to correct their dispositional inferences about the target person. In line with this prediction, nonbusy perceivers demonstrated attributional discounting by attributing relatively less dispositional anxiety to the target when the interview topics were anxiety inducing, rather than relaxation inducing. In contrast,

cognitively busy perceivers made dispositional inferences of anxiety that were little affected by the interview topics. Additional studies demonstrated that a variety of cognitive demands in everyday life, such as trying to make a positive impression during a social interaction, can disrupt the correction stage of dispositional inference (Gilbert, 1989; Gilbert & Malone, 1995).

EXTENSION OF THREE-STAGE MODEL

The three-stage process described above assumes that perceivers begin with the goal of dispositional inference. Krull (1993) extended the model by suggesting that the process could be more flexible and dependent on the perceiver's goals. In this *mixed model*, perceivers can begin with the goal of assessing the potency of situational factors (e.g., Is Bob's success due to his taking a simple test?), automatically infer situational causality at the second stage of characterization (The test must be easy), and then adjust that inference to reflect the influence of the actor's disposition (...then again, Bob might be a competent guy).

In summary, although attribution research provided one of the foundations for the development of social cognition, the social cognition perspective also transformed the way attribution questions were studied. Concepts from cognitive psychology such as anchoring/adjustment (Tversky & Kahneman, 1974) and encoding specificity (Tulving & Thomson, 1973) were instrumental in establishing that aspects of trait inference could occur relatively automatically (Quattrone, 1982; Winter & Uleman, 1984). Building on these findings, stage models of dispositional inference were proposed that integrated the automatic and controlled stages of processing. The confluence of attribution and social cognition was now complete, setting the stage for an exciting new topic, called *attribution of mind*, and a new method of inquiry, called *social neuroscience*.

Current Directions: Attribution of Mind and Social Neuroscience

The common thread of attribution research is social construal—the processes by which people come to understand social reality. Perceivers strive to make sense of human action by wondering about its causes (e.g., What is the President really like, and how much of what he says and does is shaped by outside forces such as current politics, long-range goals, and even family obligations?). In seeking to address these questions, attribution researchers have traditionally collected data on two types of content and employed two types of methods. In terms of content, the preponderance of research examined either causal attributions (including judgments of control, responsibility, and blame) or trait inferences. The methodology either relied on simple paper-and-pencil surveys or (more recently) borrowed from cognitive psychology by using computers to precisely time and manipulate the presentation of stimuli and collection of responses. Exciting new research in the field is extending both the contents and methods of attributional inquiry. As described below, attribution of mind (Epley & Wayatz, 2010) examines the beliefs, desires, intentions, and experiential capacities (e.g., feelings and emotions) we attribute to others. In addition, social neuroscience (Lieberman, 2010; Van Overwalle, 2009) examines the brain to advance our understanding of both traditional topics like trait attribution and newer topics related to mind attribution.

Attribution of Mind

Research on mindreading represents the newest extension of the attribution perspective (Epley & Waytz, 2010; Malle & Hodges, 2005). On the one hand, work in this area can be seen as extending attribution's long-standing concerns with perceived mental states such as beliefs and intentions (Jones & Davis, 1965; Heider, 1958). On the other hand, the study of mindreading appears somewhat revolutionary owing to the multidisciplinary contributions from developmentalists (e.g., Apperly & Butterfill, 2009), neuroscientists (e.g., Iacoboni, 2009; Mitchell, 2009), and philosophers (e.g., Goldman, 2006). New questions are being raised about the attribution of psychological capacities (Epley, Waytz, & Cacioppo, 2007; Gray & Wegner, 2009), folk psychology and perceived intentionality (Lillard,1998; Malle, 2004), and the attribution of mental states such as goals and motives (Ames, 2004; Read & Miller, 2005; Reeder, 2009a). As in the case of stage models of dispositional inference, most of these new research areas can be viewed as branches of social cognition.

ATTRIBUTION OF PSYCHOLOGICAL CAPACITIES

What qualities of mind separate an infant, a woman, a man in a persistent vegetative state, a frog, a chimpanzee, a dead woman, God, and a robot? When asked this question, people's answers tend to fall along the two dimensions of conscious experience and intentional agency (Gray & Wegner, 2009). Conscious experience involves the capacity to feel emotions such as fear and experience states such as hunger. Intentional agency, in contrast, involves self-control, planning, and morality. Normal adults tend to be perceived as high on both of these dimensions, whereas robots and God are perceived as having agency, but little capacity for experience. Additional research examined the tendency to view physical objects (e.g., a computer) as human (Epley et al., 2007). Perceivers are prone to anthropomorphize when human-related knowledge is accessible and there are strong needs to be effective or make a social connection. The other side of the coin is dehumanization (Haslam, 2006; Leyens, Cortes, Demoulin, Dovidio, Fiske, & Gaunt et al., 2003), such that outgroup members and enemies are seen as animalistic (e.g., coarse, lacking moral sensibility) and machine-like (e.g., lacking emotional responsiveness).

FOLK PSYCHOLOGY AND PERCEPTION OF INTENTIONALITY

Folk psychology refers to the set of commonsense principles that laypersons employ to explain human behavior (Lillard, 1998; Malle, 1999). In line with Heider's (1958) distinction between personal and impersonal causality, Malle (1999, 2004) suggested that intentional behavior tends to be described primarily in terms of the actor's goals and motives (i.e., reasons). In contrast, unintentional behavior tends be explained in terms of causes (e.g., by the relatively mechanistic, internal vs. external causality distinction). Of course, the criteria that perceivers use to distinguish between intentional and unintentional behavior are crucial (Guglielmo & Malle, 2010; Malle & Knobe, 1997; Monroe & Reeder, 2011). When discussing intentionality, Aristotle (1941) described a beleaguered ship captain who threw cargo overboard during a storm in order to save the ship. According to the five criteria offered by Malle and Knobe (1997), the sea captain's act will be judged intentional to the extent the following five criteria are met: The captain *desired* to save the ship, *believed* that throwing cargo overboard would accomplish that outcome, *planned* his actions, had the requisite *skill* or ability, and was *aware* of what he did. Notice, however, that employing these five criteria could involve a great deal of analytic thought. Perceivers may also infer intentionality in a more intuitive fashion, relying on simple heuristics (Morris & Mason, 2009; Reeder, 2009b). For example, jerky movements or verbal expressions of "Oops!" tend to imply unintentional behavior. Most inferences of intentionality are probably implicit (and possibly below awareness) in the sense that perceivers simply assume, by default, that action is usually intentional (Rosset, 2008).

PERCEPTION OF MENTAL STATES SUCH AS GOALS AND MOTIVES

If intentional actions are explained by the actor's goals and motives, how are such mental states inferred? Building on earlier insights (Jones & Davis, 1965; Heider, 1958), recent approaches to motive attribution fall into two categories: simulation and reliance on implicit theory (Ames, 2004; Epley & Waytz, 2010; Goldman, 2006; Reeder & Trafimow, 2005). When using *simulation*, people use themselves as a point of departure for judging others, essentially asking themselves, "What would my motives be if I were in the actor's situation?" Immediate, intuitive reactions often follow this projection tendency, which may then be followed by a more controlled "adjustment" for additional information (Epley, Keysar, Van Boven, & Gilovich, 2004). When using *implicit theory* to predict motives, perceivers may rely on group stereotypes (e.g., People from the X political party have self-serving motives" or other types of abstract knowledge. But what determines which strategy is employed? It appears that when perceivers feel similar to the actor, they gravitate toward the simulation strategy (Ames, 2004; Mitchell, 2009).

Finally, perceived motives play an important role in recent models of dispositional inference (Kammrath et al., 2005; Read & Miller, 2005; Reeder, 2009a). According to the multiple inference model (MIM), perceivers process intentional behavior in the context of situational forces that give it meaning, allowing perceivers to infer one or more underlying motives (Reeder, 2009a, 2009b). In contrast to the view of the perceiver as a naïve dispositionist (Ross & Nisbett, 1991), MIM holds that situational information can be of great interest to the perceiver because it helps to identify the motives or reasons behind behavior. Perceivers then use information about motives to infer where the target stands on one or more trait dimensions.

In an early test of MIM, perceivers read about a soccer player who deliberately injured another player in response to different forms of situational encouragement (Reeder, Kumar, Hesson-McInnis, & Trafimow, 2002). When the aggression followed an earlier provocation (e.g., an insult from a member of the opposing team), perceivers inferred a revenge motive. But when the aggression was due to the exceptionally skillful play of the opposing player, perceivers inferred a selfish motive (i.e., wanting to win

the game). In each case, the situation (provocation vs. skillful play by the opposing player) encouraged the aggression, yet the different situations suggested unique motives. In turn, these motives led to different sorts of trait inferences about morality. Perceivers saw the aggressor as higher in dispositional morality if he was motivated by revenge, rather than by selfishness. According to this model, perceivers can integrate a variety of types of information simultaneously—including motives and traits—to create a coherent impression (Asch, 1946; Kammrath et al., 2005; Read & Miller, 1993, 2005; Roese & Morris, 1999; Todd, Molden, Ham, & Vonk, 2011).

Application of Social Neuroscience to Attribution

Neuroscience represents what is, perhaps, the newest and most controversial tool available to attribution research—and social cognition more generally. Although recognizing its limitations, advocates of this new approach point to its unique strengths relative to traditional behavioral observation (Lieberman, 2010). For instance, multiple systems can be investigated simultaneously, without the potentially contaminating influence of instructional sets or manipulations of attentional focus. A skeptical reader might ask sarcastically, "How so, by pointing to brain regions where an attribution happens? If the anterior cingulate *lights up*, how does that explain the correspondence bias?!" But there is, in fact, a good case to be made for brain mapping (Iacoboni, 2009; Lieberman, 2010; Mitchell, 2009; Van Overwalle, 2009). Neuroscientists have made vast strides in isolating brain regions that perform particular mental tasks and computations. Some areas of the brain like the amygdala seem to be involved in emotional reactions, whereas areas of the prefrontal cortex are involved in complex problem solving. Armed with information about the typical cognitive tasks accomplished by a given brain area, attributions researchers can begin to test hypotheses of particular relevance to their own field. For example, if an attribution theory implies that a particular social inference task is cognitively taxing (rather than relatively automatic), the brain of perceivers who engage in that task should actually light up precisely in neural territory where other types of serious computation occur. In other words, brain outcomes can serve as another form of evidence to test a hypothesis (Amodio, 2008; Lieberman, 2010; Spunt, Satpute, & Lieberman, 2011). The discussion below will consider how neurological findings can address the question of whether automatic processing and controlled processing rely on separate systems.

For more than 25 years, stage models of attribution have assumed there is a crucial distinction to be drawn between automatic (associative, intuitive) processing and controlled (deliberate, rule-based) processing (Gilbert et al., 1988; Trope, 1986). Yet others have challenged this assumption as unwarranted, suggesting instead that all processing is rule based, such that the same rules can underlie both types of processing (Kruglanski & Gigerenzer, 2011). So is it really necessary to think in terms of two different systems of information processing? Although a variety of perspectives should be considered, evidence from neuroscience can help answer this question.

In an important paper, Lieberman, Gaunt, Gilbert, and Trope (2002) described the neural substrates of an X-system and a C-system. The X-system uses pattern recognition to allow perceivers to form quick and easy impressions of an actor's behavior and traits. This system is responsible for automatic social cognition and appears to involve a variety of brain areas, including the *lateral temporal cortex* and *superior temporal sulcus*. The system progressively analyzes visual information, identifying both *what* the stimulus is and *where* it is (Mason & Morris, 2010). Thus, it provides the basis for general semantic categorization and for what attribution researchers specifically refer to as *behavior identification* (Gilbert et al., 1988; Krull, 1993; Reeder, 1993; Trope, 1986). The neural perspective suggests that layers of analysis occur within (automatic) visual processing, implying that there are important differences in the ways visual and verbal information are handled (Morris & Mason, 2009).

In contrast, the C-system relies on symbolic logic and reflective awareness (Lieberman et al., 2002). It reacts to the output of the X-system, particularly when there is a "lack of fit" between elements of information. For instance, the X-system might see evil and immorality at work when a participant in a psychological experiment is observed pressing a shock key to deliver a 450-volt shock to an innocent person (Milgram, 1974). But the C-system can "correct" that initial impression by recognizing that the participant was motivated to obey an experimenter who ordered the delivery of the shock (Reeder et al., 2008). The deliberate processing involved when dispositional inferences are adjusted to take account of situational factors appears localized in areas of the *prefrontal cortex* (Lieberman et al., 2002; Mason & Morris, 2010). This area of the brain is known to be involved in propositional reasoning and hypothesis formation. In short, separate areas of the brain produce the different computations attributed to automatic and controlled processing. These different neural substrates offer one more line of supporting evidence for stage models of attribution.

Final Thoughts

Attribution questions about social reality served as an important launching pad for social cognition in the late 1970s and early 1980s. The voluminous literature on attribution firmly established a tradition within social psychology of taking cognition seriously, allowing the field to more easily embrace a social cognition approach. Also, attributional questions, such as those concerning the automaticity of trait inferences (Winter & Uleman, 1984), inspired some of the earliest social cognition studies. In turn, the social cognition approach, with its emphasis on stages of processing, broadened the analysis of attribution—so much so, that it is now difficult to separate attribution research from social cognition. New attribution questions are likely to emerge in the future, continually expanding the borders of social cognition. It is equally clear, however, that the theory and methodology of social cognition will continue to shape the nature of such attribution research.

References

Abramson, L., Seligman, M., & Teasdale, J. (1978). Learned helplessness in humans: Critique and reformulation. *Journal of Abnormal Psychology, 87*, 49–74.

Alicke, M. D. (2000). Culpable control and the psychology of blame. *Psychological Bulletin, 126*, 556–574.

Alloy, L. B., & Tabachnik, N. (1984). Assessment of covariation by humans and animals: The joint influence of prior expectations and current situational information. *Psychological Review, 91*, 112–149.

Ames, D. R. (2004). Mental state inference in person perception: Everyday solutions to the problem of other minds. *Journal of Personality and Social Psychology, 87*, 340–353.

Amodio, D. M. (2008). The social neuroscience of intergroup relations. *European Review of Social Psychology, 19*, 1–54.

Anderson, N. H. (1974). Cognitive algebra: Integration theory applied to social attribution. In L. Berkowitz (Ed.,), *Advances in experimental social psychology* (Vol. 7, pp. 1-101). New York: Academic Press.

Anderson, N. H., & Butzin, C. A. (1974). Performance = motivation x ability: An integration-theoretical analysis. *Journal of Personality and Social Psychology, 85*, 598–604.

Apperly, I. A., & Butterfill, S. A. (2009). Do humans have two systems to track beliefs and belief-like states? *Psychological Review, 116*, 953–970.

Aristotle (1941). Nicomachean ethics. In R. McKeon (Ed.), *The basic works of Aristotle* (pp. 964–984). New York: Random House.

Aronson, E. (1997). Back to the future: Retrospective review of Leon Festinger's "A theory of cognitive dissonance." *American Journal of Psychology, 110*, 127–137.

Asch, S. E. (1946). Forming impressions of personality. *Journal of Abnormal and Social Psychology, 41*, 258–290.

Asch, S. E. (1956). Studies of independence and conformity: A minority of one against a unanimous majority. *Psychological Monographs, 70*(9, Whole No. 416).

Bargh, J. A., & Chartrand, T. L. (1999). The unbearable automaticity of being. *American Psychologist, 54*, 462–479.

Bargh, J. A., & Pietromonaco, P. (1982). Automatic information processing and social perception: The influence of trait information presented outside of conscious awareness on impression formation. *Journal of Personality and Social Psychology, 43*, 437–449.

Bem, D. J. (1967). Self-perception: An alternative interpretation of cognitive dissonance phenomena. *Psychological Review, 74*,183–200.

Bem, D. J. (1972). Self-perception theory. In L. Berkowitz (Ed.), *Advances in experimental social psychology* (Vol. 6, pp. 1–62). San Diego, CA: Academic Press.

Bradley, G. W. (1978). Self-serving biases in the attribution process: A reexamination of the fact or fiction question. *Journal of Personality and Social Psychology, 36*, 56–71.

Carlston D. E., & Skowronski, J. J. (1994). Savings in the relearning of trait information as evidence for spontaneous inference generation. *Journal of Personality and Social Psychology, 66*, 840–856.

Carlston, D. E., Skowronski, J. J., & Sparks, C. (1995). Savings in relearning: II. On the formation of behavior-based trait associations and inferences. *Journal of Personality and Social Psychology, 69*, 420–436.

Cheng, P. W. (1997). From covariation to causation: A causal power theory. *Psychological Review, 104*, 367–405.

Collins, A., & Loftus, E. (1975). A spreading-activation theory of semantic processing. *Psychological Review, 82*, 407–428.

Dodge, K. A., & Crick, N. R. (1990). Social information-processing bases of aggressive behavior in children. *Personality and Social Psychology Bulletin, 16*, 8–22.

Epley, N., Keysar, B., Van Boven, L., & Gilovich, T. (2004). Perspective taking as egocentric anchoring and adjustment. *Journal of Personality and Social Psychology, 87*, 327–339.

Epley, N., & Waytz, A. (2010). Mind perception. In S. T. Fiske, D. T. Gilbert, & G. Lindzey (Eds.), *The handbook of social psychology* (5th ed., pp. 498–541). New York: Wiley.

Epley, N., Waytz, A., & Cacioppo, J. T. (2007). On seeing human: A three-factor theory of anthropomorphism. *Psychological Review, 114*, 864–886.

Fazio, R. H., & Olson, M. A. (2003). Implicit measures in social cognition research: Their meaning and uses. *Annual Review of Psychology, 54*, 297–327.

Fein, S. (1996). Effects of suspicion on attributional thinking and the correspondence bias. *Journal of Personality and Social Psychology, 70*, 1164–1184.

Fein, S., & Spencer, S. J. (1997). Prejudice as self-image maintenance: Affirming the self through derogating others. *Journal of Personality and Social Psychology, 73*, 31–44.

Festinger, L. (1957). *A theory of cognitive dissonance.* Stanford, CA: Stanford University Press.

Festinger, L., & Carlsmith, J. M. (1959). Cognitive consequences of forced compliance. *Journal of Abnormal and Social Psychology 58*, 203–210.

Fincham, F. D., & Jaspars, J. M. (1980). Attribution of responsibility: From man the scientist to man as lawyer. In L. Berkowitz (Ed.), *Advances in experimental social psychology* (Vol. 13, pp. 8l–138). New York: Academic Press.

Fiske, S. T., Cuddy, A., & Glick, P. (2006). Universal dimensions of social cognition: Warmth and competence. *Trends in Cognitive Sciences, 11*, 77–83.

Fiske, S. T., & Neuberg, S. L. (1990). A continuum of impression formation, from category-based to individuating processes: Influences of information and motivation on attention and interpretation. In M. P. Zanna (Ed.), *Advances in experimental social psychology* (Vol. 23, pp. 1–74). San Diego, CA: Academic Press.

Fiske, S. T., & Taylor, S. E. (1991). *Social cognition.* New York: McGraw-Hill.

Forsterling, F. (2001). *Attribution: An introduction to theories, research, and applications.* Philadelphia: Taylor & Francis

Gawronski, B. (2003). Implicational schemata and the correspondence bias: On the diagnostic value of situationally constrained behavior. *Journal of Personality and Social Psychology, 84*, 1154–1171.

Gawronski, B. (2004). Theory-based bias correction in dispositional inference: The fundamental attribution error is dead, long live the correspondence bias. *European Review of Social Psychology, 15*, 183–217.

Gawronski, B., & Bodenhausen, G. V. (2006). Associative and propositional processes in evaluation: An integrative review of implicit and explicit attitude change. *Psychological Bulletin, 132*, 692–731.

Gilbert, D. T. (1989). Thinking lightly about others: Automatic components of the social inference process. In J. Uleman & J. A. Bargh (Eds.). *Unintended thought* (pp. 189–211). New York: Guilford.

Gilbert, D. T. (1991). How mental systems believe. *American Psychologist, 46*, 107–119.

Gilbert, D. T. (1998). Ordinary personology. In D. T. Gilbert, S. T. Fiske, & G. Lindzey (Eds.), *The handbook of social psychology* (4th ed., Vol. 2, pp. 89–150). Boston: McGraw-Hill.

Gilbert, D. T., & Jones, E. E. (1986). Perceiver-induced constraint: Interpretations of self-generated reality. *Journal of Personality and Social Psychology, 50*, 269–280.

Gilbert, D. T., Krull, D. S., & Pelham, B. W. (1988). Of thoughts unspoken: Social inference and the self-regulation of behavior. *Journal of Personality and Social Psychology, 55*, 685–694.

Gilbert, D. T., & Malone, P. S. (1995). The correspondence bias. *Psychological Bulletin, 117*, 21–38.

Gilbert, D. T., Pelham, B. W., & Krull, D. S. (1988). On cognitive busyness: When person perceivers meet persons perceived. *Journal of Personality and Social Psychology, 54*, 733–740.

Goldman, A. I. (2006*). Simulating minds: The philosophy, psychology and neuroscience of mindreading.* New York: Oxford University Press.

Gosling, S. D., Ko, S. J., Mannarelli, T., & Morris, M. E. (2002). A room with a cue: Personality judgments based on offices and bedrooms. *Journal of Personality and Social Psychology, 82*, 379–398.

Gray, K., & Wegner, D. M. (2009). Moral typecasting: Divergent perceptions of moral agents and moral patients. *Journal of Personality and Social Psychology, 96*, 505–520.

Greenwald, A. G., & Banaji, M. R. (1995). Implicit social cognition. *Psychological Review, 102*, 4–27.

Guglielmo, S., & Malle, B. F. (2010). Can unintended side effects be intentional? Resolving a controversy over intentionality and morality. *Personality and Social Psychology Bulletin, 36,* 1635–1647.

Gunther, A. C., & Christen, C. T. (2002). Projection or persuasive press? Contrary effects of personal opinion and perceived news coverage on estimates of public opinion. *Journal of Communication, 52,* 177–195.

Hamilton, D. L., & Gifford, R. K. (1976). Illusory correlation in intergroup perception: A cognitive bias of stereotypic judgments. *Journal of Experimental Social Psychology, 12,* 392–407.

Hart, H. L. A. (1968). *Punishment and responsibility.* New York: Oxford University Press.

Harvey, J. H., Ickes, W. J., & Kidd, R. F. (1976). *New directions in attribution research* (Vol. 1). Hillsdale, NJ: Erlbaum.

Harvey, J. H., Ickes, W. J., & Kidd, R. F. (1978). *New directions in attribution research* (Vol. 2). Hillsdale, NJ: Erlbaum.

Harvey, J. H., Ickes, W. J., & Kidd, R. F. (1981). *New directions in attribution research* (Vol. 3). Hillsdale, NJ: Erlbaum.

Haslam, N. (2006). Dehumanization: An integrative review. *Personality and Social Psychology Review, 10,* 252–264.

Hastie, R., & Carlston, D. (1980). Theoretical issues in person memory. In R. Hastie, T. M. Ostrom, E. B. Ebbesen, R. S. Wyer, D. L. Hamilton, & D. Carlston (Eds.), *Person memory: The cognitive basis of social perception.* Hillsdale, NJ: Erlbaum.

Hastie, R., Ostrom, T. M., Ebbesen, E. B., Wyer, R. S., Hamilton, D. L., & Carlston, D. E. (1980). *Person memory: The cognitive basis of social perception.* Hillsdale, NJ: Erlbaum.

Hastorf, A., & Cantril, H. (1954). They saw a game: A case study. *Journal of Abnormal and Social Psychology, 49,* 129–134.

Heider, F. (1944). Social perception and phenomenal casuality. *Psychological Review, 51,* 358–374.

Heider, F. (1958). *The psychology of interpersonal relations.* New York: Wiley.

Heider, F., & Simmel, M. (1944). An experimental study of apparent behavior. *American Journal of Psychology, 57,* 243–259.

Hewstone, M. (1989). *Causal attribution: From cognitive processes to collective beliefs.* Cambridge, MA: Basil Blackwell.

Higgins, E. T., & Bargh, J. A. (1987). Social cognition and social perception. *Annual Review of Psychology, 38,* 369–425.

Higgins, E. T., Herman, C. P., Zanna, M. P. (1981). *Social cognition: The Ontario symposium.* Hillsdale, NJ: Erlbaum.

Hilton, D. J. (1995). The social context of reasoning: Conversational inference and rational judgment. *Psychological Bulletin, 118,* 248–271.

Hilton, D. J., & Slugoski, B. R. (1986). Knowledge-based causal attribution: The abnormal conditions focus model. *Psychological Review, 93,* 75–88.

Iacoboni, M. (2009). Imitation, empathy and mirror neurons. *Annual Review of Psychology, 60,* 653–670.

Ichheiser, G. (1970). *Appearances and realities.* San Francisco: Jossey-Bass.

Inhelder, B., & Piaget, J. (1958). *The growth of logical thinking from childhood to adolescence.* New York: Basic Books.

Jones, E. E. (1979). The rocky road from acts to dispositions. *American Psychologist, 34,* 107–117.

Jones, E. E., & Davis, K. E. (1965). From acts to dispositions: The attribution process in person perception. In L. Berkowitz (Ed.), *Advances in experimental social psychology* (Vol. 2, pp. 219–266). New York: Academic Press.

Jones, E. E., Davis, K. E., & Gergen, K. J. (1961). Role playing variations and their informational value for person

perception. *Journal of Abnormal and Social Psychology, 63,* 302–310.

Jones, E. E., & deCharms, R. (1957). Changes in social perception as a function of the personal relevance of behavior. *Sociometry, 20,* 175–185.

Jones, E. E., & Harris, V. A. (1967). The attribution of attitudes. *Journal of Experimental Social Psychology, 3,* 1–24.

Jones, E. E., Kanouse, D. E., Kelley, H. H., Nisbett, R. E., Valins, S., & Weiner, B. (1972). *Attribution: Perceiving the causes of behavior.* Morristown, NJ: General Learning Press.

Jones, E. E., & McGillis, D. (1976). Correspondent inference and the attribution cube: A comparative reappraisal. In J. H. Harvey, W. J. Ickes, & R. F. Kidds (Eds.), *New directions in attribution research* (Vol. 1, pp. 389–420). Hillsdale, NJ: Erlbaum.

Jones, E. E., & Nisbett, R. E. (1972). The actor and the observer: Divergent perceptions of the causes of behavior. In E. E. Jones, D. E. Kanouse, H. H. Kelley, R. E. Nisbett, S. Valins, & B. Weiner (Eds.), *Attribution: Perceiving the causes of behavior* (pp. 79–94). Morristown, NJ: General Learning Press.

Kammrath, L. K., Mendoza-Denton, R., & Mischel, W. (2005). Incorporating *if…then…* personality signatures in person perception: Beyond the person-situation dichotomy. *Journal of Personality and Social Psychology, 88,* 605–618.

Kelley, H. H. (1967). Attribution theory in social psychology. In D. Levine (Ed.), *Nebraska symposium on motivation* (Vol. 15, pp. 192–241). Lincoln, NE: University of Nebraska Press.

Kelley, H. H. (1972a). Attribution in social interaction. In E. E. Jones, D. E. Kanouse, H. H. Kelley, R. E. Nisbett, S. Valins, & B. Weiner (Eds.), *Attribution: Perceiving the causes of behavior* (pp. 1–26). Morristown, NJ: General Learning Press.

Kelley, H. H. (1972b). Causal schemata and the attribution process. In E. E. Jones, D. E. Kanouse, H. H. Kelley, R. E. Nisbett, S. Valins, & B. Weiner (Eds.), *Attribution: Perceiving the causes of behavior* (pp. 151–174). Morristown, NJ: General Learning Press.

Kelley, H. H. (1973). The process of causal attribution. *American Psychologist, 28,* 107–128.

Kelley, H. H., & Michaela, J. L. (1980). Attribution theory and research. *Annual Review of Psychology, 31,* 457–501.

Kitayama, S., Markus, H. R., Matsumoto, H., & Norasakkunkit, V. (1997). Individual and collective processes in the construction of the self: Self-enhancement in the United States and self-criticism in Japan. *Journal of Personality and Social Psychology, 72,* 1245–1267.

Koffka, K. (1935). *Principles of gestalt psychology.* New York: Harcourt, Brace, & World.

Kruglanski, A. W., & Gigerenzer, G. (2011). Intuitive and deliberate judgments are based on common principles. *Psychological Review, 118,* 97–109.

Krull, D. S. (1993). Does the grist change the mill? The effect of the perceiver's inferential goal on the process of social inference. *Personality and Social Psychology Bulletin, 19,* 340–348.

Lepper, M. R., Greene, D., & Nisbett, R. E. (1973). Undermining children's intrinsic interest with extrinsic rewards: A test of the "overjustification" hypothesis. *Journal of Personality and Social Psychology, 28,* 129–137.

Leyens, J. P., Cortes, B. P., Demoulin, S., Dovidio, J. F., Fiske, S. T., Gaunt, R., et al. (2003). Emotional prejudice, essentialism, and nationalism. *European Journal of Social Psychology, 33,* 704–717.

Lieberman, M. D. (2010). Social cognitive neuroscience. In S. T. Fiske, D. T. Gilbert, & G. Lindzey (Eds.), *The handbook of social psychology* (5th ed., pp. 143–193). New York: McGraw-Hill.

Lieberman, M. D., Gaunt, R., Gilbert, D. T., & Trope, Y. (2002). Reflection and reflexion: A social cognitive neuroscience approach to attributional inference. In M. Zanna (Ed.), *Advances in experimental social psychology* (Vol. 34, pp. 199–249). New York: Academic Press.

Lillard, A. (1998). Ethnopsychologies: Cultural variations in theories of mind. *Psychological Bulletin, 123*, 3–32.

Malle, B. F. (1999). How people explain behavior: A new theoretical framework. *Personality and Social Psychology Review, 3*, 23–48.

Malle, B. F. (2004). *How the mind explains behavior: Folk explanations, meaning, and social interaction.* Cambridge, MA: MIT Press.

Malle, B. F. (2006). The actor-observer asymmetry in attribution: A (surprising) meta-analysis. *Psychological Bulletin, 132*, 895–919.

Malle, B. F. (2008). Fritz Heider's legacy: Celebrated insights, many of them misunderstood. *Social Psychology, 39*, 163–173.

Malle, B. F., & Hodges, S. D. (2005). *Other minds: How humans bridge the divide between self and others.* New York: The Guilford Press.

Malle, B. F., & Knobe, J. (1997). The folk concept of intentionality. *Journal of Experimental Social Psychology, 33*, 101–121.

Malle, B. F., Knobe, J. M., & Nelson, S. E. (2007). Actor–observer asymmetries in explanations of behavior: New answers to an old question. *Journal of Personality and Social Psychology, 93*, 491–514.

Marks, G., & Miller, N. (1987). Ten years of research on the false consensus effect: An empirical and theoretical review. *Psychological Bulletin, 102*, 72–90.

Mason, M. F., & Morris, M. W. (2010). Culture, attribution and automaticity: A social cognitive neuroscience view. *Social Cognitive and Affective Neuroscience, 5*, 292–306.

McArthur, L. Z. (1972). The how and what of why: Some determinants and consequences of causal attribution. *Journal of Personality and Social Psychology, 13*, 733–742.

McClure, J. (1998). Discounting causes of behavior: Are two reasons better than one? *Journal of Personality and Social Psychology, 74*, 7–20.

Michotte, A. (1963). *The perception of causality.* London: Methuen.

Milgram, S. (1974). *Obedience to authority: An experimental view.* New York: Harper & Row.

Miller, D. T. (1976). Ego involvement and attributions for success and failure. *Journal of Personality and Social Psychology, 34*, 901–906.

Miller, D. T., & Ross, M. (1975). Self-serving bias in the attribution of causality: Fact or fiction? *Psychological Bulletin, 82*, 213–225.

Mitchell, J. P. (2009). *Inferences about mental states. Philosophical Transactions of the Royal Society of London, 364*, 1309–1316.

Monroe, A. E., & Reeder, G. D. (2011). Motive-matching: Perceptions of intentionality for coerced action. *Journal of Experimental Social Psychology, 47*, 1255–1261.

Morris, M. W., & Mason, M. F. (2009). Intentionality in intuitive versus analytic processing: Insights from social cognitive neuroscience. *Psychological Inquiry, 20*, 58–65.

Morris, M. W. & Peng, K. (1994). Culture and cause: American and Chinese attributions for physical and social events. *Journal of Personality and Social Psychology, 67*, 949–971.

Neuberg, S., & Fiske, S. T. (1987). Motivational influences on impression formation: Outcome dependency, accuracy-driven attention, and individuating processes. *Journal of Personality and Social Psychology, 53*, 431–444.

Neisser, U. (1967). *Cognitive psychology,* New York: Appleton-Century-Crofts.

Newtson, D. (1974). Dispositional inference from effects of actions: Effects chosen and effects forgone. *Journal of Experimental Social Psychology, 5*, 489–496.

Nisbett, R. E., Peng, K., Choi, I., & Norenzayan, A. (2001). Culture and systems of thought: Holistic versus analytic cognition. *Psychological Review, 108*, 291–310.

Nisbett, R. E., & Ross, L. (1980). *Human inference: Strategies and shortcomings of social judgment.* Englewood Cliffs, NJ: Prentice Hall.

Nisbett, R. E., & Wilson, T. D. (1977). Telling more than we can know: Verbal reports on mental processes. *Psychological Review, 84*, 231–259.

Ostrom, T. M. (1984). The sovereignty of social cognition. In R. S. Wyer and T. K. Srull (Eds.), *Handbook of social cognition* (Vol. 1, pp. 1–38). Hillsdale, NJ: Erlbaum.

Petty, R. E., & Krosnick, J. A. (1995). *Attitude strength: Antecedents and consequences.* Mahwah, NJ: Erlbaum.

Prentice, D. A., & Miller, D. T. (1996). Pluralistic ignorance and the perpetuation of social norms by unwitting actors. In M. P. Zanna (Ed.), *Advances in experimental social psychology* (Vol. 28, pp. 161–209). New York: Academic Press.

Pronin, E. (2007). Perception and misperception of bias in human judgment. *Trends in Cognitive Sciences, 11*, 37–43.

Pryor J. B., & Kriss, M. (1977). The cognitive dynamics of salience in the attribution process. *Journal of Personality and Social Psychology, 35*, 49–55.

Quattrone, G. A. (1982). Overattribution and unit formation: When behavior engulfs the person. *Journal of Personality and Social Psychology, 42*, 593–607.

Read, S. J., & Miller, L. C. (1993). Rapist or "regular guy": Explanatory coherence in the construction of mental models about others. *Personality and Social Psychology Bulletin, 19*, 526–541.

Read, S. J., & Miller, L. C. (2005). Explanatory coherence and goal-based knowledge structures in making dispositional inferences. In B. F. Malle and S. D. Hodges (Eds.), *Other minds: How humans bridge the divide between self and others* (pp. 124–139). New York: Guilford.

Reeder, G. D. (1993). Trait-behavior relations in dispositional inference. *Personality and Social Psychology Bulletin, 19*, 586–593.

Reeder, G. D. (1997). Dispositional inferences of ability: Content and process. *Journal of Experimental Social Psychology, 33*, 171–189.

Reeder, G. D. (2009a). Mindreading: Judgments about intentionality and motives in dispositional inference. *Psychological Inquiry, 20*, 1–18.

Reeder, G. D. (2009b). Mindreading and dispositional inference: MIM revised and extended. *Psychological Inquiry, 20*, 73–83.

Reeder, G. D., & Brewer, M. B. (1979). A schematic model of dispositional attribution in interpersonal perception. *Psychological Review, 86*, 61–79.

Reeder, G. D., Fletcher, G. J. O., & Furman, K. (1989). The role of observers' expectations in attitude attribution. *Journal of Experimental Social Psychology, 25*, 168–188.

Reeder, G. D., Hesson-McInnis, M., Krohse, J. O., & Scialabba, E. A. (2001). Inferences about effort and ability. *Personality and Social Psychology Bulletin, 27*, 1225–1235.

Reeder, G. D., Kumar, S., Hesson-McInnis, M. S., & Trafimow, D. (2002). Inferences about the morality of an aggressor: The role of perceived motive. *Journal of Personality and Social Psychology, 83*, 789–803.

Reeder, G. D., Monroe, A. E., & Pryor, J. B. (2008). Impressions of Milgram's obedient teachers. Situational cues inform inferences about motives and traits. *Journal of Personality and Social Psychology, 95*, 1–17.

Reeder, G. D., Pryor, J. B., Wohl, M. J. A., & Griswell, M. J. (2005). On attributing negative motives to others who disagree with our opinions. *Personality and Social Psychology Bulletin, 31*, 1498–1510.

Reeder, G. D., & Trafimow, D. (2005). Attributing motives to other people. In B. F. Malle and S. D. Hodges (Eds.), *Other minds: How humans bridge the divide between self and others* (pp. 106–123). New York: The Guilford Press.

Reeder, G. D., Vonk, R., Ronk, M. J., Ham, J. & Lawrence, M. (2004). Dispositional attribution: Multiple inferences about motive-related traits. *Journal of Personality and Social Psychology, 86*, 530–544.

Robbins, J. M., & Krueger, J. (2005). Social projection to ingroups and outgroups: A review and meta-analysis. *Personality and Social Psychology Review, 9*, 32–47.

Robinson R. J., Keltner, D., Ward, A., & Ross, L. (1995). Actual versus assumed differences in construal: "Naïve realism" in intergroup perception and conflict. *Journal of Personality and Social Psychology, 68*, 404–417.

Roese, N. J. (1997). Counterfactual thinking. *Psychological Bulletin, 121*, 133–148.

Roese, N. J., & Morris, M. W. (1999). Impression valence constrains social explanations: The case of discounting versus conjunction effects. *Journal of Personality and Social Psychology, 77*, 437–448.

Rosenberg, S., & Sedlak, A. (1972). Structural representations of implicit personality theory. In L. Berkowitz (Ed.), *Advances in experimental social psychology* (Vol. 6, pp. 235–297). New York: Academic Press.

Ross, L. (1977). The intuitive psychologist and his shortcomings: Distortions in the attribution process. In L. Berkowitz (Ed.), *Advances in experimental social psychology* (Vol. 10, pp. 173–220). New York: Academic Press.

Ross, L., Amabile, T. M., & Steinmetz, J. L. (1977). Social roles, social control, and biases in social-perception processes. *Journal of Personality and Social Psychology, 35*, 485–494.

Ross, L., Greene, D., & House, P. (1977). The false consensus effect: An egocentric bias in social perception and attributional processes. *Journal of Experimental Social Psychology, 13*, 279–301.

Ross, L., & Nisbett, R. E. (1991). *The person and the situation: Perspectives of social psychology*. New York: McGraw-Hill.

Ross, L., & Ward, A. (1996). Naïve realism in everyday life: Implications for social conflict and misunderstanding. In E. S. Reed, E. Turiel, & T. Brown. (Eds.), *Values and knowledge* (pp. 103–135). Mahwah, NJ: Erlbaum.

Ross, M., & Fletcher, G. J. O. (1985). Attribution and social perception. In G. Lindzey & E. Aronson (Eds.), *Handbook of social psychology* (3rd ed., Vol. 2, pp. 73–122). New York: Random House.

Ross, M., & Sicoly, F. (1979). Egocentric biases in availability and attribution. *Journal of Personality and Social Psychology, 37*, 322–336.

Rosset, E. (2008). It's no accident: Our bias for intentional explanations. *Cognition, 108*, 771–780.

Schneider, W., & Shiffrin, R. M. (1977). Controlled and automatic human information processing: 1. Detection, search, and attention. *Psychological Review, 84*, 1–66.

Sedikides, C., Gaertner, L., & Vevea, J. L. (2005). Pancultural self-enhancement reloaded: A meta-analytic reply to Heine (2005). *Journal of Personality and Social Psychology, 89*, 539–551.

Seligman, M. E. P. (1990). *Learned optimism: How to change your mind and your life*. New York: Knopf.

Semin G. R., & Fiedler, K. (1988). The cognitive functions of linguistic categories in describing persons: Social cognition and language. *Journal of Personality and Social Psychology, 54*, 558–568.

Shaver, K. G. (1985). *The attribution of blame: Causality, responsibility, and blameworthiness*. New York: Springer-Verlag.

Shaw, M. E., & Sulzer, J. L. (1964). An empirical test of Heider's levels in attribution of responsibility. *Journal of Abnormal and Social Psychology, 69*, 39–46.

Skowronski, J. J., & Carlston, D. E. (1989). Negativity and extremity biases in impression formation: A review of explanations. *Psychological Bulletin, 105*, 131–142.

Skowronski, J. J., Carlston, D. E., Mae, L., & Crawford, M. T. (1998). Spontaneous trait transference: Communicators take on the qualities they describe in others. *Journal of Personality and Social Psychology, 74*, 837–848.

Snyder, M. L. & Frankel, A. (1976). Observer bias: A stringent test of behavior engulfing the field. *Journal of Personality and Social Psychology, 34*, 857–864.

Spunt, R. P., Satpute, A. B., & Lieberman, M. D. (2011). Identifying the what, why, and how of an observed action: An FMRI study of mentalizing and mechanizing during action observation. *Journal of Cognitive Neuroscience, 23*, 63–74.

Taylor, S. E., & Brown, J. D. (1988). Illusion and well-being: A social psychological perspective on mental health. *Psychological Bulletin, 103*, 193–210.

Taylor, S. E., & Fiske, S. T. (1978). Salience, attention, and attribution: Top of the head phenomena. In L. Berkowitz (Ed.), *Advances in experimental social psychology* (Vol. 11, pp. 249–288). New York: Academic Press.

Todd, A. R., Molden, D. C., Ham, J., & Vonk, R. (2011). The automatic and co-occurring activation of multiple social inferences. *Journal of Experimental Social Psychology, 47*, 37–49.

Trafimow, D., & Schneider, D. J. (1994). The effects of behavioral, situational, and person information on different attribution judgments. *Journal of Experimental Social Psychology, 30*, 351–369.

Trafimow, D., & Trafimow, S. (1999). Mapping perfect and imperfect duties onto hierarchically and partially restrictive trait dimensions. *Personality and Social Psychology Bulletin, 25*, 686–695.

Trope, Y. (1986). Identification and inferential processes in dispositional attribution. *Psychological Review, 93*, 239–257.

Trope, Y., & Liberman, A. (1993). The use of trait conceptions to identify other people's behavior and to draw inferences about their personalities. *Personality and Social Psychology Bulletin, 19*, 553–562.

Tulving, E., & Thomson, D. M. (1973). Encoding specificity and retrieval processes in episodic memory. *Psychological Review, 80*, 352–373.

Tversky, A., & Kahneman, D. (1974). Judgment under uncertainty: Heuristics and biases. *Science, 185*, 1124–1131.

Uleman, J. S., & Moskowitz, G. B. (1994). Unintended effects of goals on unintended inferences. *Journal of Personality and Social Psychology, 66*, 490–501.

Uleman, J. S., Newman, L. S., & Winter, L. (1992). Can personality traits be inferred automatically? Spontaneous inferences require cognitive capacity at encoding. *Consciousness and Cognition: An International Journal, 1*, 77–90.

Uleman, J. S., Saribay, S. A., & Gonzalez, C. (2008) Spontaneous inferences, implicit impressions, and implicit theories. *Annual Review of Psychology, 59*, 329–360.

Vallone, R. P., Ross, L., & Lepper, M. R. (1985). The hostile media phenomenon: Biased perception of perceptions of media bias in coverage of the Beirut massacre. *Journal of Personality and Social Psychology 49*, 577–585.

Van Overwalle, F. (2009). Social cognition and the brain: A meta-analysis. *Human Brain Mapping, 30*, 829–858.

Vonk, R. (1998). Effects of behavioral causes and consequences on person judgments. *Personality and Social Psychology Bulletin, 24*, 1065–1074.

Vonk, R., & van Knippenberg, A. (1994). The sovereignty of negative inferences: Suspicion of ulterior motive does not reduce the negativity effect. *Social Cognition, 12*, 169–186.

Watson, D. (1982). The actor and the observer: How are their perceptions of causality different? *Psychological Bulletin, 92*, 682–700.

Weiner, B. (1979). A theory of motivation for some classroom experiences. *Journal of Educational Psychology, 71*, 3–25.

Weiner, B. (1985). An attributional theory of achievement motivation and emotion. *Psychological Review, 92*, 548–573.

Weiner, B. (1995). *Judgments of responsibility*. New York: Guilford Press.

Weiner, B. (2008). Reflections on the history of attribution theory and research. *Social Psychology, 39*, 151–156.

Weiner, B., Frieze, I., Kukla, A., Reed, L., Rest, S., & Rosenbaum, R. M. (1972). Perceiving the causes of success and failure. In E. E. Jones, D. E. Kanouse, H. H. Kelley, R. E. Nisbett, S. Valins, & B. Weiner (Eds.), *Attribution: Perceiving the causes of behavior* (pp. 95–120). Morristown, NJ: General Learning Press.

White, P. A. (1991). Ambiguity in the internal/external distinction in causal attribution. *Journal of Experimental Social Psychology, 27*, 259–270.

Winter, L., & Uleman, J. S. (1984). When are social judgments made? Evidence for the spontaneousness of trait inferences. *Journal of Personality and Social Psychology, 47*, 237–252.

Wojciszke, B. (2005). Morality and competence in person and self perception. *European Review of Social Psychology, 16*, 155–188.

Wyer, R. S., & Carlston, D. E. (1979). *Social cognition, inference, and attribution*. Hillsdale, NJ: Erlbaum.

CHAPTER 7

Attitudes and Social Cognition as Social Psychological Siblings

Duane T. Wegener *and* Richard E. Petty

Abstract

Attitudes and social cognition have many common conceptual roots. This chapter reviews the interwoven history of the attitudes and social cognition areas. It discusses the separation of the approaches in the early days of the social cognition movement when social cognition borrowed heavily from models of cold cognition in cognitive psychology. The chapter compares the development of research on attitudes, attitude change, and persuasion with that in social cognition during the past 30 to 40 years. In that time, attitudes and social cognition researchers have created prominent dual and multiple process theories, and common themes have resonated with attitudes and social cognition researchers. Finally, the chapter discusses the broadening of the social cognition area into a general approach to social psychological research. There are a number of ways in which the maturation of the social cognition perspective has brought it closer to the attitudinal roots that were at least partially rejected in the early days of social cognition.

Key Words: attitudes, attitude change, persuasion, social cognition

Since the late 1970s, Attitudes and Social Cognition have shared a section of the *Journal of Personality and Social Psychology*. There are good reasons to house these research areas under the same roof. At the same time, like siblings in the same house, there have also been certain tensions between the areas, perhaps especially as the burgeoning area of social cognition grew and sought conceptual and methodological independence in the late 1970s and early 1980s.

Both of the current authors took courses (one of us in "person perception" and the other in "social cognition") from one of the founders of contemporary social cognition, Thomas Marshall Ostrom. Tom helped to found the social psychology program at Ohio State in the mid-1960s with Timothy Brock and Anthony Greenwald (and, soon thereafter, Bibb Latané). Greenwald was not as exclusively identified with the "social cognition" moniker as Ostrom.

However, Greenwald was instrumental in bringing cognitive approaches to social psychology in his early work on the self (Greenwald, 1980) and subliminal persuasion (Greenwald, Spangenberg, Pratkanis, & Eskenazi, 1991), and as we note shortly, especially in his more recent work on implicit measures of attitudes (Greenwald, McGhee, & Schwartz, 1998).

Ostrom conducted attitudes research into the 1970s, edited attitudes books in the Ohio State series in the late 1960s and early 1980s (i.e., Greenwald, Brock, & Ostrom, 1968; Petty, Ostrom, & Brock, 1981), and taught attitude measurement into the mid-1990s. Thus, Tom's direct involvement in attitudes research came before the development of contemporary dual and multiple process models, such as the elaboration likelihood model (ELM; Petty & Cacioppo, 1986a, 1986b) and the heuristic/systematic model (HSM; Chaiken, Liberman, & Eagly, 1989). Yet, he had conducted a healthy amount of attitudes research, especially dealing with issues of attitude structure (Ostrom, 1969; Ostrom & Brock, 1969), measurement (Ostrom, 1973; Ostrom & Upshaw, 1968), and change (Ostrom, 1970; Steele & Ostrom, 1974). Tom also founded the Social Cognition Research Group at Ohio State and was active in developing the international Person Memory Interest Group (PMIG)—one of the original venues for discussions of social cognition research, and now a popular preconference held each year before the Society of Experimental Social Psychology meeting. In this chapter, we present an Ostromian view of early social cognition. Like the field more generally, if Tom were still with us, he would likely hold different views today about what does or does not qualify as social cognition. We wish he were still with us, but we will try to construct as accurate a set of recollections as we can (with apologies to those who knew some of these details more intimately than we do).

We begin our chapter by providing a historical backdrop for the development of social cognition, including traditional research on attitudes/persuasion and impression formation as well as responses to crises in these fields in the 1970s. We then discuss the early days of the social cognition movement when cold cognition initially ruled and social cognition borrowed heavily from models in cognitive psychology. We continue to compare the development of attitudes and social cognition research during the past 30 to 40 years. We focus our comparison on prominent dual and multiple process theories of attitude change and of impression formation. The next part of the chapter identifies a number of themes that have resonated with both attitudes and social cognition researchers, though these common themes have sometimes been studied under different names. Finally, we discuss the maturation and broadening of the social cognition area into a general approach to social psychological research and theorizing. In so doing, we point out some ways in which this maturation of the social cognition perspective has brought it closer to some of the attitudinal roots that were at least partially rejected in the early days of social cognition.

Backdrop of Traditional Research on Attitudes and Attitude Change

The study of attitudes and attitude change can be thought of as a series of (partially overlapping) eras in which particular questions or developments took center stage (see Briñol & Petty, 2012, for a history of attitudes research). In the early days, tracing back

to Thurstone's declaration that "Attitudes Can Be Measured" (Thurstone, 1928), the focus of much attitudes research was on assessing attitudes (e.g., Guttman, 1944; Likert, 1932; Thurstone & Chave, 1929). Following World War II, Carl Hovland assembled a group of researchers at Yale University focused on attitude change. Hovland and colleagues relied on the cognitive/learning theories of the time to understand persuasion using a broad set of assumptions referred to as the Message Learning Approach (Hovland, Janis, & Kelley, 1953). Throughout the 1950s, 1960s, and early 1970s, attitudes work could be characterized as driven by a variety of individual theories postulating a central process that would produce attitude effects. These theories, some of which were cognitive, but others of which were motivational, included classical conditioning (Staats & Staats, 1958), cognitive dissonance (Festinger, 1957, 1964), balance (Heider, 1958), congruity (Osgood & Tannenbaum, 1955), social judgment (Sherif, Sherif, & Nebergall 1965), cognitive response (Greenwald, 1968), information integration (Anderson, 1971), and expectancy-value (Fishbein & Ajzen, 1975) approaches. Late in the 1960s and into the 1970s, dissonance (Festinger, 1964) and self-perception (Bem, 1967) theories vied with one another as competing explanations for effects of behavior on attitudes. Some researchers lamented the ability of each theory to account for results predicted by the other and suggested that empirical attempts to differentiate the theories would fail (Greenwald, 1975).

In the same era (i.e., the late 1960s and early 1970s), the accumulated attitudes literature was coming under attack. In particular, research dealing with attitude–behavior relations was criticized by Wicker (1969, 1971) and others as indicating woefully low predictive ability for attitudes. Soon thereafter, Sherif (1977) and others bemoaned the lack of generalizable principles in the literature on attitude change. Many findings from the Hovland era, such as source credibility effects on persuasion, for example, occurred in some studies but not in others. In fact, other researchers at the time questioned whether influences on attitudes were real or epiphenomenal (a product of asking people questions in the lab), observing that many attitude changes in the lab were no longer present when research participants took up their daily lives (Cook & Flay, 1978). Of course, some research on attitudes had identified lasting persuasion (e.g., Freedman, 1965; Mann & Janis, 1968), though many effects were, in fact, short-lived. Yet, as of the mid-1970s, no theoretical framework had been developed to account for (or predict) such variation, either in persuasive effects or persistence of the observed changes. In many respects, this time of crisis ushered in the modern dual/multiple process era, not only in attitude theorizing (e.g., Petty & Cacioppo, 1986b) but also, for some similar reasons, in the development of social cognition.

An Impression Formation Context for the Development of Social Cognition

Ostrom's background was thoroughly rooted in attitudes research. He was the intellectual grandson of Louis Thurstone—through Harry Upshaw, Ostrom's graduate school advisor. Ostrom also had direct connections to research on impression formation. Indeed, work on context effects in impression formation had direct connections to psychophysical judgment (and Thurstone's work on psychophysical judgment laid the foundation for his research on attitude measurement; Thurstone, 1928). Many early social cognition researchers initially identified with research on impression formation, and many still do (see Chapter 2). Similar to the attitudes domain, by the mid-1970s, there was growing frustration with existing theories of impression formation. Like the dissonance/self-perception competition in the attitudes domain, the general approaches of meaning change (Asch, 1946) and information integration (Anderson, 1966, 1970) had been viewed as competing theories that provided different explanations for context effects in impression formation. In the meaning change approach, the connotations of specific traits differed depending on the constellation of other traits or information available about the target person. In contrast, the information integration approach suggested that perceptions of component traits could be constant, but that different overall impressions would result from differential weighting of the component traits in forming the overall impression. Ostrom (1977) suggested that neither the change of meaning approach nor the information integration approach was sufficiently specified to make clear predictions that could be differentiated from one another. That is, Ostrom (1977) suggested that each approach was sufficiently ambiguous that the approaches could be adjusted to account for virtually any result after the fact, but that each position made precious few a priori predictions (for similar criticisms of the information integration approach to attitude change, see Petty & Cacioppo, 1981).

Impression formation studies of the 1960s and 1970s presented traits as the input to impression processes. This research approach paralleled stimulus–response approaches from the learning tradition (that also formed the foundation for early attitudes research; Hovland et al., 1953) and was viewed by early social cognition researchers as providing relatively little leverage on the cognitive processes at work. Furthermore, because traits or other information were typically presented to research participants who were then directly asked for a judgment, concerns arose that responses to such questions might not reflect what people do when they learn about similar information in the real world (e.g., by observing behaviors and spontaneously inferring traits; Winter & Uleman, 1984; cf., Cook & Flay, 1978). Ostrom (1977) argued that it would be beneficial if impression formation theories began to rely on advances in cognitive psychology to make more specific predictions about the mechanisms underlying change of meaning effects (including more direct study of the content, structure, and processing of cognitions about the target person). To this end, Ostrom suggested supplementing the traditional trait-rating paradigms to include techniques such as reaction times (Anderson & Hastie, 1974), recall (Lingle & Ostrom, 1981), and free association (Deese, 1965). Furthermore, presaging later theoretical developments, Ostrom (1977) suggested that a more fruitful theoretical stance to the dueling-theories approach of the previous decade would be to suggest that each basic type of process (i.e., integration of components and meaning shifts) contributes to impression formation, but with specific circumstances determining the relative importance of each type of process.

Responses to Crisis

The attitudes and social cognition areas developed in remarkable ways following the crises of the 1970s. On the attitude side, the puzzle of attitude–behavior relations was addressed on the measurement front (e.g., Fishbein & Ajzen, 1974) and by theoretical approaches that emphasized mediation of attitude effects (by behavioral intentions; Fishbein & Ajzen, 1975) or moderation of attitude effects (by features of the attitude, such as direct experience, Fazio & Zanna, 1981, knowledge, Davidson et al., 1985, and other attitude strength properties; see Petty & Krosnick, 1995). The theories of dissonance and self-perception were successfully distinguished by focusing on the hypothesized discomfort associated with dissonance but absent from self-perception (Fazio, Zanna, & Cooper, 1977; Zanna & Cooper, 1974; see Wegener & Carlston, 2005, for discussion). Moreover, theoretical models were developed that specified when relatively thoughtful versus nonthoughtful processes would influence attitudes. These models used the moderators of motivation and ability to think carefully about attitude-relevant information (e.g., Chaiken, 1980; Chaiken, Liberman, & Eagly, 1989; Petty, 1977; Petty & Cacioppo, 1979, 1986a, 1986b), and various processes initially studied in the 1950s, 1960s, and early 1970s—including dissonance and self-perception—could be placed at different points along the elaboration continuum (Petty & Cacioppo, 1981; Petty & Wegener, 1998). The multiple process approach quickly became dominant in the attitudes field. In addition to organizing past attitude processes and persuasion effects, the multiple process approach postulated that the amount of thought about the attitude object moderated the extent to which the attitude persisted over time and had lasting impact (e.g., Petty & Cacioppo, 1986a).

Alongside the criticisms of attitude–behavior and attitude change research, researchers (including Ostrom) who had been examining person impressions using Anderson's information integration approach were also becoming disenchanted with that approach. Indeed, at one point (if our memories for Tom's stories serve us well), a number of researchers, including Ostrom, made a pact to never again conduct an information integration study. Against this backdrop, the modern era of social cognition research commenced. In the new-style social cognition research, participants often encountered descriptions of behaviors rather than traits (also present in the attribution research that might be viewed as a bridge between early impression formation studies and social cognition; see Chapter 6). In addition, judgmental outcomes were often accompanied by measurements of reaction times or recall/recognition of traits or behaviors. These measures were intended to tap into the cognitive processes that linked perception of behaviors to trait inferences, judgments, or behaviors toward the target. Emphasis was placed on the use of models and methods from cognitive psychology as tools to help researchers understand how social information (especially information about people) came to be processed, remembered, and integrated into judgments.

From an attitude researcher's point of view, it is easy to understand why early social cognition researchers had become disenchanted with the information integration approach. This approach had not taken a central position within the attitude change literature, in part, because information integration was more of a description than a theory. That is, whereas the information integration equations could potentially identify the differential weights associated with the impact of particular information on impressions or attitudes, information integration per se did not predict what these weights should be, leaving many researchers unsatisfied (including Ostrom, 1977). With this search in cognitive psychology for tools to study impression formation, the sibling discipline of social cognition was born. (At least that is one version of the story.)

The Early Days of Social Cognition

Like a younger sibling attempting to escape the shadow of the older sibling, many topics that had been common constructs in the attitudes domain, such as the role of emotions or motivation in evaluation, became almost taboo in social cognition. Whether this was intentional or simply a consequence of the focus on cognitive mechanisms per se is unclear. Our guess is that the vision of mental processes of the day within cognitive psychology was simply a vision of "cold" cognition that eschewed the more messy "hot" cognition constructs (Abelson, 1963). If motivation and emotion were discussed at all in the early days of social cognition, they were described in cold cognitive terms.

Lots of interesting and influential work captured the imagination of the first generation of social cognition researchers. Much of that work addressed the canonical cognitive categories of activation (accessibility), automaticity, and mental representation (for reviews, see Bargh, 1994; Carlston & Smith, 1996; Higgins, 1996). Indeed, we recall a student of Ostrom's quipping that, "If you are not dealing with encoding, storage, and retrieval, you are not dealing with social cognition." Methodologically, some researchers we knew complained that editors like Ostrom (then editing the *Journal of Experimental Social Psychology*) didn't view work as being social cognition unless the dependent measure was reaction time or ARC scores (a measure of clustering in free recall). Indeed, these were two of Ostrom's favorite outcome measures, whether or not they formed an operational definition of which research qualified as social cognition. At any rate, the early days of social cognition were heady days full of much enthusiasm—enthusiasm that snowballed into a thriving new approach to social psychology (see Chapter 2).

Without a doubt, this enthusiasm was also fueled by small research meetings of social cognition researchers, perhaps the most prominent being the PMIG meetings prior to the Society of Experimental Social Psychology meetings in the fall and the summer meetings in Nags Head, North Carolina (and later, the Duck Conference on Social Cognition). Like the area of social cognition more generally, the PMIG and Duck meetings have continued to become broader over time. In their early days, however, these separate meetings (perhaps especially the PMIG meeting) contributed to views of social cognition researchers as somewhat exclusive and, perhaps, arrogant. Ostrom surely contributed to perceptions of social cognition research as arrogant and rather imperialistic with his lead chapter in the 1984 *Handbook of Social Cognition* volume titled, "The Sovereignty of Social Cognition" (Ostrom, 1984). This was one of the great paradoxes of Tom Ostrom. He was extremely inclusive and friendly, especially in gathering and connecting those he viewed as kindred spirits. Yet, he could also lead the charge to claim the superiority of his preferred view of the world (and, in the process, at least to some readers, the inferiority of all other approaches). At times, some have questioned whether Ostrom was simply trying to be provocative with his chapter title or whether he even believed what he was saying at the time (or just being extreme to try to make a point). But 10 years later, in his preface to the 1994 *Handbook of Social Cognition* (and, unfortunately, the year of Tom's passing), he headed a section of the preface with "Is Social Cognition Sovereign?" and began the paragraph with "Of course it is."

It is difficult to say whether any of this "separatist" sentiment in the early days of social cognition paralleled the common motivations of younger siblings to demonstrate to their parents, older siblings, and the world at large that they are autonomous and fully functioning individuals. Many areas of social psychology might be characterized as having less cognitive roots than the attitudes domain, so this attempt to differentiate social cognition from other areas of inquiry was likely viewed as much broader than simply differentiating from research on attitudes. However, the early choices to focus social cognition on cold cognition (ushered in by the computer analog of the brain that came with the development of cognitive psychology more generally) marked a clear departure from attitudes research. The tradition and ongoing character of attitudes research included the study of cognitive processes but certainly also considered emotional and motivational processes.

Similarities and Dissimilarities in How Attitudes and Social Cognition Developed since the Mid-1970s

As noted previously, social cognition research responded to dissatisfaction with stimulus–response types of theorizing by orienting themselves toward methods and models in cognitive psychology. The intent, of course, was to more directly address the cognitive mechanisms underlying the resulting impressions or behaviors. Therefore, in some respects, one might think of the social cognition response to the concerns of the day as focusing on cognitive *mediation*. Some social cognition research also focused directly on the issue of what social perceivers do naturally (such as spontaneously form trait inferences, Winter & Uleman, 1984; see also Carlston & Skowronski, 1994). In comparison, although some research in the attitudes domain focused on straight mediation (e.g., theory of reasoned action, Fishbein & Ajzen, 1975; cognitive responses, Greenwald, 1968), most of the attitudes response to the crises of the 1970s focused on identification of *moderators*. Over time, these moderators coalesced into overall models of attitude change (e.g., Chaiken, 1980; Chaiken et al., 1989; Petty, 1977; Petty & Cacioppo, 1986a) and attitude–behavior relations (Fazio, 1986, 1990). These models proposed factors that determined when various influences on attitudes would have their greatest impact, how long resulting attitudes would persist over time (if unchallenged), how easily they could be changed (when challenged), and which attitudes would be most likely to influence behaviors. As described in more detail shortly, a core idea in these models was that sometimes people engage in little thought prior to making judgments, in which case simple and quick inferences and cues determine evaluations, whereas at other times people engage in much thought, in which case deliberative processes and careful analysis of information determine judgments. These dual and multiple process frameworks presaged later development of dual systems models of judgment within social cognition (e.g., Deutsch & Strack, 2006; Smith & DeCoster, 2000; see Petty & Briñol, 2006b).

To be sure, characterizing 1970s and 1980s social cognition as emphasizing mediation and attitudes work as emphasizing moderation is a simplification. Emphases on cognitive mediators naturally implied certain moderators of the proposed cognitive mechanisms. Likewise, moderators of influences on attitudes were hypothesized to result from moderation of the cognitive processes (mediators) at work. Thus, although people did not use the term in those days, each literature included elements of moderated mediation (Muller, Judd, & Yzerbyt, 2005; Wegener & Fabrigar, 2000; see Chaiken & Maheswaran, 1994, and Petty, Schumann, Richman, & Strathman, 1993, for persuasion examples). Still, the relative focus on mediating cognitive mechanisms versus moderators to organize existent effects did serve to carve out distinct paths for social cognition and attitudes researchers. These paths also fit with certain distinctive features of how the areas came to define themselves. That is, by emphasizing evaluation as the core defining feature of what constituted attitudes research, no particular emphasis on any one type of process became emblematic of an "attitudinal" approach. In a sense, all mechanisms were fair game. In contrast, although social cognition has significantly broadened since its inception (see Wegener & Carlston, 2005), its early emphasis on cold cognitive processes did make the type of process emblematic of a "social cognition" approach (regardless of whether one was studying evaluative or nonevaluative outcome judgments or behaviors).

Thus, one way in which the attitudes and social cognition paths diverged in the late 1970s and early 1980s was in terms of the breadth of potential mediators and independent variables addressed. As we have already noted, early social cognition researchers focused intently on cognitive mediators, often to the exclusion of motivational or emotional constructs. In traditional attitudes work, many different mechanisms and independent variables were considered. A partial list of processes includes learning (e.g., conditioning, Staats & Staats, 1958; effectance motivation, Byrne & Clore, 1967) and cognitive consistency processes (e.g., dissonance, Festinger, 1957; congruity, Osgood & Tannenbaum, 1955; tripartite attitude structure, Rosenberg & Hovland, 1960) as well as other motivational (e.g., attitude functions, Katz, 1960, Smith, Bruner, & White, 1956; ego-involvement, Sherif & Hovland, 1961; reactance, Brehm, 1966) and perceptual (e.g., adaptation level, Helson, 1964; assimilation-contrast, Sherif et al., 1965; variable perspective, Ostrom & Upshaw, 1968; for reviews, see Briñol & Petty, 2012, Ostrom, 1968) processes. Attitude researchers did not discard the variables or mechanisms involved in these domains or recast them in purely cognitive terms. Rather, attitude researchers sought to integrate those processes into overarching theories that provided a context for when each of the proposed mechanisms might have the strongest effects (see Petty & Cacioppo, 1986a, 1986b). Therefore, in a sense, the attitudes literature progressed by embracing the variety of past findings and attempting to account for them. In contrast, early social cognition research rejected previous means of studying the questions of interest (clearing the decks, so to speak) and started from scratch with a new emphasis on cognitive process (often defined as specifically dealing with encoding, representation in memory, or retrieval—in the process also rejecting alternative "cognitive" measures).

Whether intended or not, these different points of departure have had important consequences for the two literatures ever since. For example, in the 35 years since the development of the ELM (Petty, 1977) and HSM (Chaiken, 1978), the various overarching theories in the attitude change domain have provided central shared structures that have guided much of the research. When the research has not tested particular tenets of those core theories, the accumulated literature surrounding those theories has provided a rich context for identifying the conditions in which particular variables are likely to have certain effects. Because so much research has either directly concerned these core theories or used them as a salient backdrop for the research, we believe that this could lead to the false impression that research is not developing as quickly or changing as much in the attitudes domain as in other areas (like social cognition) that have not developed the same kinds of core, overarching theories.

Although many specific cognitive principles have been identified over the years, a large proportion of the social cognition research has seemed to fall outside of broad overarching theories. This is not to suggest that broad social cognition theories have been absent. Perhaps most salient in this regard are overarching theories of impression formation (e.g., Brewer, 1988; Fiske & Neuberg, 1990) and some broad but straightforward notions, such as schemas (Hastie, 1981) and associative networks (Anderson, 1980; Rumelhart, Lindsay, & Norman, 1972), developed early on and were used to explain a wide variety of phenomena. Yet, in many areas of social cognition, significant work proceeded to address questions lying somewhat outside the confines of the overarching theories (such as spontaneous trait transference in the impression formation domain; Skowronski, Carlston, Mae, & Crawford, 1998). Perhaps, in part, because of the weaker role that overarching theories played in (especially early) social cognition research, interested readers may have perceived each new piece of evidence as another separate log that brightened the blaze of social cognition. In contrast, research building on existing overarching theories can be viewed as less groundbreaking. It is an interesting philosophy of science question to ask how the presence of broad organizing theories influences perceptions of progress in developing areas of science.

Dual and Multiple Process Theories of Attitude Formation and Change

Broad theories of attitude formation and change were based on the notion that people are not always willing and able to think carefully about attitude-relevant information (Chaiken, 1980; Chaiken et al., 1989; Petty & Cacioppo, 1979, 1986a). Therefore, these theories were oriented around the level of motivation and ability people possessed in a given evaluative setting as determinants of the level of *elaboration* or *systematic processing* in which people engage. These theories addressed the varied effects of source, message, recipient, and context/channel factors (Lasswell, 1948) by suggesting that low levels of information processing allowed peripheral cues (Petty & Cacioppo, 1986b; or aspects of a persuasive appeal associated with available cognitive heuristics, Chaiken, 1987) to have the dominant effect on resulting attitudes. In contrast, higher levels of processing led to greater effects of the effortfully assessed merits of the persuasive appeal.

Under the rubric of "multiple roles," the ELM also proposed that a given variable can influence attitudes for different reasons at different levels of elaboration. That is, a variable can act as a cue and have a relatively direct effect on attitudes when motivation or ability to think is low (i.e., when elaboration likelihood is low). However, when people are motivated and able to elaborate, the same variable can influence attitudes through more elaborative processes, such as serving as an argument, biasing processing of available information, or validating thoughts about the attitude object. Finally, the same variable may often influence the extent of elaboration if neither motivation nor ability is constrained to be high or low (for reviews see Petty & Cacioppo, 1986a; Petty & Briñol, 2012; Petty & Wegener, 1999). The ELM addressed not only 1970s criticisms concerning unexplained variation in persuasion effects (Sherif, 1977) but also concerns that attitude effects were fleeting (e.g., Cook & Flay, 1978) by noting that the amount of elaboration moderated the extent to which attitudes endured over time, resisted change, and predicted behavior (Petty et al., 1995; Wegener, Petty, Smoak, & Fabrigar, 2004).

To test effects of elaboration (or other attitude-strength-related variables) on persistence, resistance, or behavior prediction, researchers have to equate the extremity of attitudes across the crucial high versus low thinking conditions. By doing this, attitude extremity is not confounded with the level of elaboration (or other dimension of attitude strength that is being tested). Therefore, much work comparing relatively nonthoughtful and thoughtful processes in attitude change has identified settings in which more and less elaborative processes result in the same judgmental impact (i.e., in the same attitudinal judgments). For example, Petty et al. (1993) tested the effects of happy versus neutral mood on attitudes when processing of information was relatively high or low. Happy mood led to more favorable attitudes than neutral mood and did so to the same degree across high and low levels of processing (equating the level of extremity across conditions). More importantly, when processing was high, the valence of generated thoughts about the persuasive appeal was significantly affected by mood, and the difference in the favorability of thoughts across conditions mediated the impact of mood on attitudes (i.e., mood-biased processing; see also DeSteno, Petty, Rucker, Wegener, & Braverman, 2004; Wegener, Petty, & Klein, 1994). However, at low levels of processing, mood had no effect on the thoughts produced (i.e., mood did not bias thoughts, but rather was used as a cue or heuristic).

Conceptually similar effects—showing equal effects on attitudes across levels of processing—have been demonstrated for variables such as the expertise of a message source (Chaiken & Maheswaran, 1994) and also on nonevaluative dependent measures, such as stereotypes influencing trait ratings (Wegener, Clark, & Petty, 2006) or numerical anchors influencing numerical estimates (Blankenship, Wegener, Petty, Detweiler-Bedell, & Macy, 2008). Because the attitudes or nonevaluative judgments in these studies have been equally extreme across levels of elaboration, the studies have appropriately set the stage for examination of elaboration effects on the consequences of those judgments (such as persistence over time, resistance to change, and the like). Consistent with the ELM notion that elaboration will lead to enhanced impact of the judgments over time, more thoughtful stereotyping and more thoughtful versions of numerical anchoring have been shown to resist attempts at social influence better than nonthoughtful versions of each effect (Blankenship et al., 2008; Wegener et al., 2006). Similarly, thoughtful anchoring persists longer over time than nonthoughtful anchoring (despite the initial anchored judgments looking the same—being equally extreme across elaboration conditions—Blankenship et al., 2008). Also, other ELM-inspired studies have created equal initial attitudes through more versus less elaborative means (e.g., through thoughtful influences of message arguments in one condition and nonthoughtful influences of message sources or the sheer number of arguments in another condition) and produced differences in consequences of the resulting attitudes across levels of elaboration (see Petty et al., 1995; Wegener et al., 2004).

In the current context, it is interesting to note that the term *elaboration* was chosen for reasons that seem quite compatible with the social cognition rumblings that were beginning when the ELM was developed (Petty, 1977). In contrast with the Message Learning approach of the 1950s, elaboration reflects the idea that scrutiny of an attitude object goes beyond passive receipt or memorization of presented information. Rather, elaboration includes attention to any presented information, attempts to access relevant information from both external (message) and internal (knowledge) sources (including one's previous evaluations), attempts to scrutinize and make inferences about attitude-relevant information in light of other available knowledge and standards, drawing conclusions about merits of the attitude object or recommendation, and derivation of an overall evaluation that combines the outputs of these efforts (see Petty & Cacioppo, 1986a). Thus, as discussed by Petty and Cacioppo (1986a), the concept of elaboration was an extension of the concepts of depth of processing and elaboration from cognitive psychology (Craik & Lockhart, 1972; Craik & Tulving, 1975; where depth of processing and elaboration each involved connecting to-be-remembered material to other knowledge structures). In common parlance, though terms such as *scrutiny*, *effortful processing*, and *careful thinking* can be used as synonyms, ELM researchers considered *elaboration* as best capturing the range of cognitive activities involved.

The amount of elaboration is correlated with, but not synonymous with, distinctions such as automatic versus controlled processing used in both cognitive (Schneider & Shiffrin, 1977) and social psychology (Devine, 1989), or spontaneous versus intentional impression formation (Uleman, 1999). For example, processes that lie toward the low end of an amount-of-thinking continuum could involve many settings in which people have no intention to form an impression. However, in many low-thought

settings, there may be some level of intention to form an impression, but there is a lack of motivation to put effort into forming that impression. Similarly, although an automatically activated attitude might be perfectly capable of influencing judgments or behaviors in low-thought settings, the automatically activated attitude could also be used in elaborative processes of assessing the merits of the object.

If persuasion researchers had endeavored to index the amount of elaboration through the accessibility of resulting attitudes (one of a number of cognitive outcomes of high levels of elaboration; Petty et al., 1995), perhaps ELM and HSM research would have been more likely to be considered as social cognition research. We suspect that Ostrom would have been more likely to view it as such. Indeed, research on attitude accessibility (e.g., Fazio, Powell, & Herr, 1983), which used the language of associative network models, was regarded as falling more clearly into the social cognition category. However, ELM researchers identified other ways to assess the extent of elaboration in processing of persuasive communications. The most popular procedure has been to manipulate the quality of the arguments contained in a message and to gauge the extent of elaboration by the relative size of the argument quality effect on postmessage attitudes (e.g., Petty et al., 1976; Petty, Cacioppo, & Goldman, 1981). Research has supported the idea of high elaboration being associated with greater attitude accessibility (Bizer, Tormala, Rucker, & Petty, 2006; Kokkinaki & Lunt, 1999; Rennier, 1988; Priester & Petty, 2003). However, little research to date has examined accessibility as a mediator of elaboration effects on consequences, such as persistence over time, resistance to change, or impact on behavior (though some research has related attitude accessibility to an attitude's persistence over time, Zanna, Fazio, & Ross, 1994; or resistance to change, Bassili & Fletcher, 1991, without directly addressing the level of elaboration involved).

Dual Process Approaches to Impression Formation

Similar to the concept of elaboration, the core distinction between automatic and controlled processes was evident from early social cognitive studies of stereotyping (e.g., Devine, 1989) and also in prominent models of impression formation (e.g., Brewer 1988; Fiske & Neuberg, 1990). For example, the continuum model (Fiske & Neuberg, 1990) differentiated between less effortful category-based assessments of people and more effortful assessments based on piecemeal processing (i.e., attribute-by-attribute analysis) of individuating information. When a target is first encountered, one starts by categorizing the person based on salient features (e.g., skin color, body shape). If the target is of little interest or importance, then the social perceiver has little motivation to engage in more effortful (piecemeal) processing and relies on the initial categorization. However, given sufficient motivation or lack of categorical fit, one is likely to assess the target on a more effortful attribute-by attribute (piecemeal) basis. In general, these models predict that stereotyping will be less likely when piecemeal processing occurs, either because the category is set aside for attribute-by-attribute processing or because the category ends up being treated simply as one attribute among many that contribute to the overall impression (Fiske, Lin, & Neuberg, 1999). Consistent with such theoretical frameworks, the majority of research on the judgmental effects of stereotypes has emphasized the possible use of stereotypes as heuristics or shortcuts to judgment (e.g., Bodenhausen, 1990; Bodenhausen, Sheppard, & Kramer, 1994; Macrae, Milne, & Bodenhausen, 1994).

Comparing the Models

It is difficult to say whether the earlier dual or multiple process models of attitude change had any direct impact on the subsequent dual process models of impression formation (though there was clearly a developing zeitgeist of the time; compare Brewer, 1988; Chaiken et al., 1989; Fiske & Neuberg, 1990; Petty & Cacioppo, 1986a, 1986b; see Chaiken & Trope, 1999; Smith & DeCoster, 2000, for reviews). There are many similarities across these models. Perhaps the most notable is the idea that target evaluation can sometimes be relatively thoughtful, but, at other times, can be significantly less cognitively demanding. Despite these similarities, the focus on consequences of attitudes (i.e., lasting over time, resisting change, and predicting behavior) has led to more ELM-based research on the multiple ways that the same judgments can occur and on the differences in persistence, resistance, or impact on other thinking or behavior that is associated with different levels of elaboration contributing to those judgments (see Petty et al., 1995; Wegener et al., 2006). This is not to say that theories of impression formation cannot allow for thoughtful effects of categories. However, the emphasis on different sizes of the category effects across levels of thinking might have made such studies less likely. It remains to be seen whether recent work applying a more ELM-inspired approach to stereotyping and person perception (Wegener et al., 2006) will or will not motivate more impression formation research aimed at examining lasting impact of the resulting impressions.

When the ELM addresses biases in processing, such biases can be either motivational or ability based. That is, biases can be based in biased perceptions or interpretations of information that follow from motives to end up with particular views of oneself or the issue (e.g., the motivational "reactance" bias can lead people to counterargue a message; Petty & Cacioppo, 1979). Alternatively, the bias can follow from existing knowledge. For example, the person could have more knowledge consistent rather than inconsistent with his or her current attitude, and that knowledge could produce attitude-consistent biases in related judgments—an ability-based bias (e.g., Lord, Ross, & Lepper, 1979; Wood, 1982; cf., Kunda, 1990, on motivational biases).[1]

Research on outcome dependency (i.e., situations in which one's outcomes depend on the actions of another person) forms much of the research that underlies the continuum model of impression formation. However, research on outcome dependency has been variously characterized as suggesting that outcome dependency creates motivational biases (i.e., motivations for one's own outcomes to be positive, e.g., Klein & Kunda, 1992; Kunda, 1990) or simply creates differences in amount of processing (with outcome dependency increasing extent of processing, Devine, Sedikides, & Fuhrman, 1989; Neuberg & Fiske, 1987; much like increases in personal relevance increase processing of persuasive messages, Petty & Cacioppo, 1979).

Clark and Wegener (2008) used impression formation materials fashioned after persuasive message argument quality manipulations to argue that outcome dependency can both increase processing and positively bias processing, depending on the setting. That is, when people expected to meet a person and have a conversation with him or her (in a study presumably examining the factors that lead to a pleasant interaction), they processed information about the target person more than when they did not expect to meet the person. This increase in mere amount of processing led to more favorable thoughts about the person and to more favorable judgments of the person's qualities if the provided information was positive, but led to less favorable thoughts about the person and to less favorable judgments of the person's qualities if the provided information was less positive. However, expecting to interact with a person in a setting where substantial awards could be received for a smooth interaction led to positive biases in processing. That is, thoughts and judgments of the person's qualities showed the same differences across the target quality manipulation (consistent with equally high levels of processing when expecting to meet the person and when expecting to meet the person with the opportunity for substantial rewards for smooth interaction). In addition, thoughts and judgments were more positive when substantial awards for a later smooth interaction were available than when the research participant simply expected to interact with the person or do so with minimal reward for a smooth interaction.

More Recent Theoretical Developments

Both the attitudes and social cognition areas have seen development of new theories in recent years. In the attitudes domain, some have suggested taking an approach that harkens back to the syllogistic and probabilistic theories of the 1960s and 1970s (e.g., McGuire, 1960; Wyer, 1974), treating all attitude-relevant information as evidence and all persuasion as due to inferential reasoning about that evidence (e.g., Kruglanski & Thompson, 1999; for application of this idea to impression formation, see Erb et al., 2003). Even in this suggestion, however, motivation and ability to think carefully about the evidence at hand are said to result in assessment of the relevance of the evidence to the evaluation (with greater weighting given to relevant over irrelevant information when motivation and ability to think are high; Pierro, Mannetti, Kruglanski, & Sleeth-Keppler, 2004). This proviso makes the theory highly compatible with the ELM notion that high levels of motivation and ability result in scrutiny of the merits of all available attitude-relevant information (Petty & Cacioppo, 1986a; see Wegener & Carlston, 2005). Other theories have more directly spoken to issues of attitude representation (e.g., Lord & Lepper, 1999; Petty, Briñol, & DeMarree, 2007) and discrepancies between implicit and explicit indices of attitudes (e.g., Gawronski & Bodenhausen, 2006; Petty, Briñol, & DeMarree, 2007; Rydell & McConnell, 2006).

In the social cognition area, new theories have addressed mechanisms that drive responses to reaction time tasks (Conrey, Sherman, Gawronski, Hugenberg, & Groom, 2005), the role of the active self concept in priming effects on judgments and behaviors (Wheeler, DeMarree, & Petty, 2007), the various forms in which impressions might be represented in memory (Carlston, 1994), different memory/reasoning systems involved in social judgment and decision making (Rydell & McConnell, 2006; Strack & Deutsch, 2004), and many others discussed throughout this volume.

As interest in implicit measures and implicit/explicit discrepancies have grown in both the attitudes and social cognition areas (e.g., see Petty, Briñol, & Johnson, 2012), theories to address those phenomena can scarcely be categorized as attitude theories or social cognition theories, and that is perhaps as it should be. From the very beginnings of the social cognition movement, the attitudes and social cognition domains have shared various interests and research questions. Yet, those interests and questions have often been addressed in rather distinct ways.

Common Themes

Despite the different approaches that attitudes and social cognition researchers took in the late 1970s and 1980s, there continued to be a number of questions and themes that appeared and reappeared across both of these areas. In the following sections, we will note some of these shared research questions, and in many cases, related answers to those research questions.

Distinctions between Content and Rating of Perceptions

When asking research participants to provide judgments (of evaluations, traits, or other perceptions), both attitude researchers and social cognition researchers have acknowledged that the judgments might not always directly reflect the person's perceptions. In their variable perspective theory, Ostrom and Upshaw (1968) suggested that ratings of the perceptions of social perceivers reflect not only the content of their views but also their translation of that content onto the rating scale. Key to this translation was the perspective used to define the meaning of the scale anchors. In other words, when rating a subjective scale, such as "good" to "bad" (Osgood, Suci, & Tannenbaum, 1957) or "light" to "heavy" (Sherif, Taub, & Hovland, 1958), respondents call to mind examples of objects that could represent the scale anchors, and this perspective on the anchors then forms the context for their translation of the content of their views to be reported on the scale. Thus, if something in the research setting expands a person's perspective by calling to mind more extreme exemplars for the anchor (such as a heavier weight to anchor the "heavy" scale anchor, Sherif et al., 1958, or a more favorable behavior or instance of the object category to anchor the "good" scale anchor), this could lead to a change in rating without any necessary change in content of the perception. Ostrom (1970; Steele & Ostrom, 1974) used variable perspective theory to examine belief and attitude change (see Petty & Cacioppo, 1981). However, as the weight example suggests, this point of view is directly applicable to a variety of non-evaluative judgments.

For example, a person could view a 5'10" man and a 5'10" woman as equally tall in a perceptual sense and rate them the same on a "content" inches scale, but rate the man as average in height and the woman as quite tall on the same "short" to "tall" subjective "rating" scale. From the point of view of variable perspective theory, this could be because different content perspectives come to mind to anchor the rating scales for men and women. This difference in perspective bears close resemblance to the use of shifting standards across stereotyped groups (e.g., Biernat, Manis, & Nelson, 1991; Biernat, Vescio, & Manis, 1998) but with some differences in emphasis. For instance, Biernat and colleagues have suggested that objective measures might often result in an assimilation of judgments toward the stereotypes of the groups. Assimilation to the stereotypes of men and women would result in judgments of taller men than women, even when the exemplars in the study are equated for height (Biernat et al., 1991). However, subjective judgments (such as a "tallness" scale, rather than judgments of feet and inches) make use of different standards (different perspectives) for the different groups. These different standards or perspectives can eliminate or sometimes reverse the differences in judgments (e.g., judging the women to be "taller" than the men, similar to the perspective theory example).

The variable perspective distinction between content and rating has also influenced discussions of survey responding and attitude measurement (e.g., Tourangeau & Rasinski, 1988), and the scale anchoring component of variable perspective theory has played a role in theories of assimilation and contrast (especially in the inclusion/exclusion model of Schwarz & Bless, 1992, 2007).

Indirect (Implicit) Measures

Not too long after it was clear that attitudes could be measured, attitude researchers developed concerns that respondents to direct (explicit) measures might screen their judgments or be unwilling to accurately report their evaluations (Doob, 1948; Hovland et al., 1953). Because of concerns about social desirability and other motives for people to hide their true attitudes, indirect measures were developed in an attempt to index people's attitudes. Indirect measures typically took advantage of attitudinal processes, such as activation and use of knowledge that is directionally consistent with the attitude (e.g., Hammond, 1948), the tendency to like others more when they held similar rather than dissimilar attitudes (e.g., Hendrick & Seyfried, 1974), or the tendency to behave more positively toward people, objects, or causes one likes rather than dislikes (e.g., Byrne, Ervin, & Lamberth, 1970; Milgram, Mann, & Harter, 1965). More recently, with the influence of social cognition, indirect measures have more often been referred to as implicit measures (loosely following the concept in cognitive psychology of implicit memory—whereby the person cannot explicitly remember a piece of information, but performance on other tasks shows that the information is still in memory; see Roediger, 2003).[2] This new generation of indirect (implicit) measures also makes use of attitudinal processes—especially of spreading activation of the evaluation, such that, after activation of the attitude, respondents are better prepared to identify like-valenced stimuli rather than stimuli that mismatch the valence of the attitude (e.g., Fazio, Jackson, Dunton, & Williams, 1995; Wittenbrink, Judd, & Park, 1997).

Generally, the critical difference between "explicit" (direct) and "implicit" (indirect) measures is that the latter assess the activation of an attitude without asking the respondents to report their attitude. Because of this, on implicit measures, respondents are relatively unaware that their attitude is being assessed (or, in some cases, respondents might become aware of the measurement attempt, but have some difficulty controlling the impact of the attitude on responses, as in the Implicit Association Test, or IAT; Greenwald et al., 1998). Whether a given implicit measure primarily taps one's attitude per se is another matter, however, and, when controversial attitude objects are addressed, one cannot simply use the direct measure as a comparison for construct validity purposes. However, in many instances, various indirect (implicit) measures fail to relate closely to one another or to direct (explicit) measures, even when addressing less controversial issues. Thus, it is not surprising that criticisms that the indirect measures might measure something other than the attitude (e.g., Kidder & Campbell, 1970) seem to resurface with each new generation of indirect measures (see Fazio & Olson, 2003).

In the case of contemporary indirect (implicit) measures, there have been debates about the relative contributions of "personal" and "extrapersonal" (normative) associations to popular measures, such as the IAT (Greenwald & Nosek, 2009; Karpinski & Hilton, 2001; Olson & Fazio, 2004). Even beyond these debates, it seems worth highlighting one additional issue related to the constructs being addressed. Because contemporary indirect measures often rely on spreading activation, they primarily tap the influences of relatively strong (accessible) attitudes (Fazio, 1995). Thus, at least part of the lack of relation between direct and indirect measures (even with noncontroversial topics) is likely that indirect measures tap into both the evaluation and its accessibility, whereas direct measures tap into the evaluation (relatively) separately from its accessibility. Furthermore, direct measures might also tap into the perceived validity of any evaluation that automatically comes to mind (Petty, Briñol, & DeMarree, 2007). Consistent with these observations, tapping stronger (especially more accessible) attitudes (e.g., LeBel, 2010; Nosek, 2005) and encouraging people to view their automatic or gut reactions as valid (e.g., Jordan, Whitfield, & Zeigler-Hill, 2007; Loersch, McCaslin, & Petty, 2011) increase the relation between implicit and explicit measures.

Implicit/Automatic versus Explicit/Controlled Processes

Closely related to the work on implicit measures is the more general attention given to unconscious or automatic processes versus explicit (conscious) or controlled processes. On some level, attention to automatic/implicit processes has become a hallmark of social cognition research (even though many processes may possess only some features of automaticity; Bargh, 1994). That is, if one has any question about whether a given research question is social cognitive in nature, one can confidently answer in the affirmative if the question addresses unconscious or automatic processes (especially if indexed by reaction time measures). Although certain tools for examining such questions have developed along with the blossoming of social cognition, similar research questions had been present in the attitudes arena for some time. Indeed, Hovland et al. (1953) conceptually distinguished among *attitudes* (that were implicit tendencies to approach or avoid a given attitude object), *opinions* (that were verbalizable anticipations, expectations, and evaluations), and overt *responses* (that were often consistent with

opinions, but could result from dissimulation, distortion, or lying). Thus, the attitude construct was connected very early on with implicit processes and potential for lack of awareness of its effects on other thinking and behavior.

Consistent with this observation, it is interesting to note that many of the examples provided in the landmark Greenwald and Banaji (1995) paper on implicit social cognition addressed evaluative processes. The research on mere exposure is a good example. That is, when novel objects are encountered repeatedly, people often evaluate the objects more favorably (Zajonc, 1968), even if the people cannot say whether or not they have previously seen the object (Kunst-Wilson & Zajonc, 1980). Bornstein (1989; Bornstein & D'Agostino, 1994) explained such exposure effects as due to increases in perceptual fluency, which perceivers might attribute to liking for the object, but which they might also attribute to other stimulus dimensions (Mandler, Nakamura, & Shebo Van Zandt, 1987), perhaps including disliking if the stimulus is negatively valenced (Klinger & Greenwald, 1994). Similar to other demonstrations of misattribution, when familiarity can be attributed to previous presentations rather than liking, mere exposure effects are diminished. Thus, mere exposure effects are reduced when exposure lasts for longer periods of time (Bornstein & D'Agostino, 1992) or when people are told that the stimuli have been presented previously (Bornstein & D'Agostino, 1994).

The interplay of implicit (automatic) and explicit (deliberative) processes in the formation of attitudes is a very active current area of research in models such as the associative–propositional evaluation (APE) model (Gawronski & Bodenhausen, 2006) and the metacognitive model (MCM) of attitude structure (Petty, Briñol, & DeMarree, 2007). One could certainly draw parallels between associative processes and the heuristic or cue-based processes of the HSM or ELM and between propositional processes and the systematic processing or elaboration in the HSM or ELM. However, associative processes could be involved in both relatively thoughtful (biased processing) and nonthoughtful (cue-based) mechanisms. Similarly, propositional processes could be applied in relatively thoughtful or nonthoughtful ways. The APE couches the associative and propositional processes in thoroughly social cognitive terms and has inspired a variety of studies that address differences in evaluative outcomes when indexed through implicit (associative) versus explicit (propositional) means. In our reading, the available evidence indicates that change on both implicit and explicit attitude measures can be mediated by both implicit and explicit processes (Petty, & Briñol, 2010; Whitfield & Jordan, 2009).

Perhaps one of the earliest and best single examples of attitudes research making use of tools and concepts from contemporary cognitive and social cognitive psychology is the research on attitude accessibility (i.e., the speed and ease with which attitudes come to mind upon encountering the attitude object). Following up on early research on direct experience and attitude confidence as factors that increase attitude–behavior consistency (e.g., Fazio & Zanna, 1978; Regan & Fazio, 1977), Russ Fazio and his colleagues turned their attention to attitude accessibility for a more process-oriented explanation of why particular attitudes have greater influence on behaviors. Early research in this program identified attitudes formed through direct experience as coming to mind more quickly upon encountering the attitude object and also showed that more accessible attitudes lead to higher attitude–behavior consistency (Fazio, Chen, McDonel, & Sherman, 1982). Soon thereafter, Fazio adapted the work on concept priming (e.g., Higgins, Rholes, & Jones, 1977) to examine evaluative priming. That is, spontaneous activation of one's attitude upon encountering the attitude object (even if one was not asked to evaluate the object) influenced judgments of the motives underlying a target person's behaviors, and this evaluative priming was more likely when the person already possessed an accessible attitude toward the object (Fazio et al., 1983).

Although this research suggested that strong object-evaluation associations facilitate spontaneous activation of attitudes, it did not directly address whether the spontaneous activation of attitudes qualifies as being automatic rather than controlled (Shiffrin & Schneider, 1977). To address this question more directly, Fazio and his colleagues adapted sequential priming techniques from cognitive psychology in which presentation of a category label facilitates identifying a target word as a word when that target is semantically related to the category (e.g., Neely, 1977). The automaticity of the attitude activation was addressed by setting the stimulus onset asynchrony (SOA; i.e., the delay between presentation of the attitude object and the target adjective) to be too short (i.e., 300 milliseconds) for controlled processing of the attitude object. Automatic activation of the attitude was evidenced by speeded identification of the valence of like-valenced adjectives compared with opposite-valenced adjectives in

these short-SOA conditions. Automatic activation of attitudes was present when attitude objects were identified as associated with relatively strong object-evaluation associations (by measuring reaction times to dichotomous evaluative reports) or were manipulated to have strong object-evaluation associations (through repeated expression of the attitude; Fazio, Sanbonmatsu, Powell, & Kardes, 1986).

This research might also constitute the best example of a program of research that served to advance both the attitudes and social cognition areas. It served as one of the earliest adaptations of sequential priming techniques to social stimuli. More generally, the evaluative priming outcomes, moderated by attitude accessibility, also illustrated that abstract socially relevant concepts can be spontaneously activated when related objects are encountered (which is a key factor in various types of situated cognition; Robbins & Aydede, 2009). In addition, research from this program suggested that objects toward which people hold accessible attitudes receive more immediate visual attention (Roskos-Ewoldsen & Fazio, 1992) and that multiply categorizable targets are more readily identified as members of categories toward which people have accessible attitudes (Smith, Fazio, & Cejka, 1996). The research on attitude accessibility also led to development of a prominent model of attitude–behavior relations (i.e., the Motivation and Opportunity as DEterminants of attitude–behavior processes, or MODE; Fazio, 1990). In addition to attitude–behavior relations, the MODE model also forms a prominent approach to conceptualizing sources of discrepancy between implicit and explicit attitude measures (see Olson & Fazio, 2009), and a version of the sequential priming technique has served as a prominent implicit measure of racial attitudes (Fazio et al., 1995).

Role of Memory in Evaluations and Impressions

An early question presaging later social cognitive emphases on memory addressed the possible links between memory and evaluations. This question formed a key component of the message learning approach to attitude change (Hovland et al., 1953) and was addressed in a number of ways. Although some studies identified parallel effects on retention of information from a persuasive message and resulting attitudes (e.g., Eagly, 1974; McGuire, 1957), other studies failed to find relations between memory for message arguments and resulting attitudes (e.g., Hovland & Weiss, 1951; Insko, 1964; Miller

& Campbell, 1959; Osterhouse & Brock, 1970) or found that changes in attitudes were often not accompanied by changes in memory for related information (or vice versa; e.g., Watts & McGuire, 1964). By the 1960s, attitude researchers were no longer emphasizing memory for the verbatim information in a persuasive message. Instead, researchers treated message recipients' idiosyncratic interpretations of the information or their cognitive responses to the information as more important determinants of the extent of persuasion or resistance (e.g., Festinger & Maccoby, 1964; Greenwald, 1968). Alternatively, some researchers weighted memory for persuasive information by message recipients' propensity to yield to that information, rather than assuming that memory of the information alone would predict resulting attitudes (e.g., McGuire, 1968).

This approach to attitude change has many parallels with the postulated independence of impressions and memory for impression-relevant information (Lingle & Ostrom, 1979, 1981). A number of social cognition theorists suggested that this independence is especially likely when social perceivers form impressions online (as social information is received) but is less likely when perceivers cannot or do not form impressions until later (and use what they remember to create memory-based impressions; e.g., Hastie & Park, 1986; Tormala & Petty, 2001). In the attitudes domain, the key variables from the ELM and HSM (i.e., motivation and ability to process attitude-relevant information) were found to moderate the extent to which evaluations correlated with memory for message arguments (with larger memory-attitude correlations following low motivation or low ability when receiving the persuasive message; e.g., Haugtvedt & Petty, 1992; Mackie & Asuncion, 1990). Interestingly, these differences also helped to account for ELM-based predictions regarding the likelihood of primacy effects versus recency effects in persuasion (e.g., Petty, Tormala, Hawkins, & Wegener, 2001), a previously unsolved puzzle from early attitudes research (e.g., Hovland, 1957; Miller & Campbell, 1959; see Haugtvedt & Wegener, 1994, for discussion).

Subtyping

When people receive information that does not fit with existing beliefs or attitudes, what do they do? Early cognitive consistency theories suggested that there can be a number of different types of reactions. For example, if a person learns that a friend disagrees with him or her about some attitude object, Heider (1958) suggested that the person could either change the attitude (belief) to fit the friend's opinion, deny the disagreement (by viewing the friend as actually holding an agreeable point of view), or cognitively differentiate between the part of the person responsible for the disagreement (and dislike that part of the person) and the part of the person that one likes overall. Abelson (1959) more directly addressed the microprocesses potentially involved and suggested that mechanisms such as denial of the disagreement, bolstering of one's own opinion, and differentiation of the other varied in the extent to which the perceiver had to exert effort in that mode of inconsistency resolution. Relatively little research in attitudes directly addressed the various modes of inconsistency resolution and often fixed the conditions to make attitude change the most likely mode (but see Rosenberg & Abelson, 1960; Simon, Greenberg, & Brehm, 1995). However, the cognitive differentiation mode of inconsistency resolution bears a good deal of resemblance to subtyping research in stereotyping, where people split out a subtype (e.g., working women) from a larger category (e.g., women) as a means to diminish the inconsistency within the category and avoid pressures to change beliefs about the category as a whole (Johnston & Hewstone, 1992; Weber & Crocker, 1983). Similar subtyping effects have been observed on both implicit and explicit measures of attitudes (Barden, Maddux, Petty, & Brewer, 2004).

Assimilation and Contrast

Early research on attitude change incorporated the idea that people's views of attitude-related stimuli can be distorted by comparisons of the stimuli with their own attitudes (e.g., in social judgment theory; Sherif & Hovland, 1961). These judgmental distortions could be assimilation (i.e., viewing the evaluative stimuli as more similar to one's own attitude) or contrast (i.e., viewing the evaluative stimuli as less similar to one's own attitude; Hovland, Harvey, & Sherif, 1957). In social judgment research, evaluative stimuli that fell relatively close to the person's own attitude (i.e., within one's latitude of acceptance) were assimilated toward one's attitude, whereas evaluative stimuli that fell relatively far away from the person's own attitude (i.e., in one's latitude of rejection) were contrasted even farther away from one's attitude. In the early 1980s, similar principles were applied to nonevaluative judgments (e.g., size), such that more extreme contexts (i.e., farther from the target) created contrast, but less extreme contexts (i.e., closer to the target) created assimilation (Herr, Sherman, & Fazio, 1983).

Over the years, in addition to the variable perspective approach mentioned earlier, a number of social cognitive accounts of assimilation and contrast developed. The majority of early social cognitive research on assimilation and contrast dealt with assimilation toward or contrast away from concept primes (e.g., Lombardi, Higgins, & Bargh, 1987). Prominent theories in this area initially treated assimilation of judgments toward the primes (i.e., typical priming effects) as the default, and contrast away from the primes as efforts to exclude or partial out reactions to the target that were attributed to the primes (e.g., the set/reset approach, Martin, 1986; Martin, Seta, & Crelia, 1990; and the inclusion/exclusion approach, Schwarz & Bless, 1992). Later research on theory-based correction suggested that either assimilation or contrast could be the default bias (consistent with Herr et al., 1983), but that corrections could then proceed in either direction and in amounts guided by the extent to which judgments were perceived as influenced by the context (e.g., Petty & Wegener, 1993; Wegener & Petty, 1995; see Wegener & Petty, 1997, for a review). This theoretical approach was also broadly applicable to many potentially biasing stimuli, including source characteristics in persuasive messages (Kang & Herr, 2006; Petty, Wegener, & White, 1998).

Priming-based work on assimilation and contrast also began to address different types of priming effects (such as exemplar primes leading to contrast, Herr, 1986, but trait primes leading to assimilation, Srull & Wyer, 1979). Eventually, research also addressed mindsets that could determine the extent to which the same stimuli led to assimilation or contrast effects (e.g., local vs. global processing, Förster, Liberman, & Kuschel, 2008; similarity vs. dissimilarity testing, Mussweiler, 2003; reflection vs. evaluation, Markman & McMullen, 2003). Coming somewhat full circle is recent work on determinants of when people might be likely to test similarities or differences. One approach is to focus on the potential dimensional overlap between the contextual and target stimuli, such that assimilation occurs when the ranges of potential values for the context and target overlap, but contrast occurs when the ranges of potential values for the context and target do not overlap (Chien, Wegener, Hsiao, & Petty, 2010). That is, whereas social judgment theory addressed contexts (existing attitudes) as representing ranges of potential values (i.e., latitudes of acceptance; Sherif & Sherif, 1967) and feature-matching views incorporated ambiguity of the target (i.e., different sizes of potential ranges of target qualities, Herr

et al., 1983), recent research suggests that overlap or lack thereof in both context and target ranges should influence the direction of context effects.

Metacognition

One growing topic in both the attitudes and social cognition areas is metacognition (i.e., thinking about thinking). Work on metacognition emerged in cognitive psychology with a focus on perceptions of people's own memories (e.g., feeling of knowing; Costermans, Lories, & Ansay, 1992) and was brought into prominence within social cognition in the late 1990s (see Jost, Kruglanski, & Nelson, 1998; Yzerbyt, Lories, & Dardenne, 1998). Petty, Briñol, Tormala, and Wegener (2007) listed a number of types of thoughts one can have about one's own thoughts, including the *target* of the thought (what the thought is about), the *origin* (source) of the thought, the *valence* of the thought (regarding whether the thought conveys positive or negative qualities of the target), perceived *amount* of thinking, *evaluation* of the thought (whether the thought is desirable or not, appropriate or not, etc.), and *confidence* in the thought.

In the attitudes domain, metacognition, though not initially labeled as such, was of widespread interest as a factor related to the strength of attitudes. That is, a number of traditional strength-related properties of attitudes can be considered metacognitions (i.e., perceptions of one's attitudes). These properties include the confidence (Allport, 1924) or subjective ambivalence (Tourangeau, Rasinski, Bradburn, & D'Andrade, 1989) with which the attitude is held and the amount of perceived knowledge underlying the attitude (Davidson et al., 1985; see Wegener, Downing, Krosnick, & Petty, 1995, for a review). These strength-related properties of attitudes have been associated with many outcomes, including increased persistence of the attitudes over time, resistance to change, and guiding of future thinking and behavior. Also, when people possessing these attitudes encounter additional persuasive information, the properties of the attitude also influence the amount of processing of that new information (e.g., see Clark & Wegener, 2013). Unfortunately, a full review of these effects could fill the current volume, so we are unable to provide a complete review of metacognition and attitudes (see Briñol & DeMarree, 2012; Petty & Krosnick, 1995; Petty et al., 2007, for reviews). Recently, people's perceptions of their own degree of elaboration (Barden & Petty, 2008) have been added to the traditional measures. Perceptions of amount of elaboration have accounted for links between traditional measures of amount of elaboration (e.g., number of thoughts listed) and the confidence with which the attitude is held.

Research on thought confidence (i.e., self-validation; Petty, Briñol, & Tormala, 2002) has demonstrated that many factors, including message recipient emotion, source credibility, and power of the message recipient can influence confidence in thoughts that people have previously generated when processing a persuasive message under high-elaboration conditions (see Briñol & Petty, 2009, for a review). In each of these cases, the validating factor increases confidence in thoughts regardless of whether the thought is relatively favorable or unfavorable (i.e., regardless of whether the message consists of relatively strong or weak arguments).

Interestingly, when people form impressions of others, it appears that another form of self-validation can occur. When people generate initial reactions to a target person under conditions conducive to relatively thoughtful processing of impression-relevant information, confidence in these initial reactions is higher after later learning that the person is a member of a group stereotyped as consistent with the initial impression. This increase in confidence leads to stronger influences of the initial (stereotype-consistent) impressions on related judgments and recommendations regarding the target (Clark, Wegener, Briñol, & Petty, 2009). This type of "matching-based" validation creates an instance in which high levels of processing produce another high-thought form of stereotyping that is influential and potentially difficult to overcome (because of the associated high level of elaboration; cf., Wegener et al., 2006).

Much of the earliest metacognitive research in social cognition addressed the ease with which information comes to mind (similar to the research on perceptual fluency – see earlier discussion of mere exposure research and Alter & Oppenheimer, 2009, Claypool, Mackie, & Garcia-Marques, in press, for reviews). In particular, ease of generation has been shown to influence the impact of information on judgments of self and others. For example, when people can easily generate a few instances of when they have been assertive in the past, they judge themselves as being more assertive than when they must generate many instances of being assertive (and have a difficult time doing so; Schwarz et al., 1991). Many effects of ease have influenced evaluations. For example, the easier it seems for people to generate positive thoughts about an object or issue,

the more people like that object or issue (Haddock, Rothman, & Schwarz, 1996; Tormala, Petty, & Briñol, 2002; Wänke, Bless, & Biller, 1996), and ease of generation also makes people more confident in their attitudes (Haddock, Rothman, Reber, & Schwarz, 1999) and their thoughts (Tormala et al., 2007). Ease of retrieval can also influence other judgments, such as likelihood estimates (e.g., Hirt, Kardes, & Markman, 2004; Wänke, Schwarz, & Bless, 1995) and risk assessments (Grayson & Schwarz, 1999). Some of this research also suggests that ease effects can be mediated by confidence (perceptions of validity) associated with the easily generated thoughts (e.g., Tormala et al., 2002; see also Wänke & Bless, 2000).

The earlier discussion of bias correction also relates to metacognition because assessments of thought content (valence and source of the thought), evaluation, and validity likely all come into play (see Petty et al., 2007). Before closing this section, it is important to note that metacognition has also recently taken a role in the mental representation of attitudes. Specifically, in the MCM of attitudes, perceptions of the attitude's validity are a part of the structure of the attitude (Petty & Briñol, 2006a; Petty, Briñol, & DeMarree, 2007). The MCM represents attitudes as including associations between the attitude object and both positive and negative evaluations. Along with these associations, however, the MCM includes validity tags for these evaluative associations. When evaluative responses are relatively nondeliberative (even automatic), such responses may be guided by activated evaluative associations. However, when they are more deliberative (i.e., when people think about them more carefully), these responses may be influenced in important ways by the perceptions of validity of the positive versus negative evaluations.

Embodied Cognition

A final area in which the domains of attitudes and social cognition have had separate histories but have come together more recently is with respect to the use of one's own body in influencing thoughts and judgments, an area known as *embodied cognition* (see Briñol & Petty, 2008; Semin & Smith, 2008). It is obvious that the mind and mental states influence the body in many ways (e.g., happiness leading to smiling), but a core notion of embodied (Lakoff & Johnson, 1999) or grounded (Barsalou, 2008) cognition is that the movement and placement of one's body can influence the mind and mental states as well. Within cognitive psychology, numerous embodiment effects have been shown, including people remembering more of a story when they physically act it out (Scott, Harris, & Rothe, 2001).

Within attitudes and social cognition, interest in embodied cognition stems from two distinct sources. The first is Darwin's theory of evolution. Indeed, the link between the attitude concept and bodily responses has a long history going back to the use of the term *attitude* to refer to the posture of one's body (Galton, 1884) and to expressive motor behaviors (e.g., a scowling face was said to indicate a hostile attitude; Darwin, 1965/1872). Although much early attitudes research focused on how the body or bodily movements could reflect one's attitudes (e.g., Hess & Polt, 1960; Solarz, 1960), more contemporary studies have examined how the body can affect one's evaluations. For example, researchers have shown that (1) nodding one's head in a vertical rather than a horizontal manner during presentation of a strong persuasive message can increase the persuasiveness of that message (Wells & Petty, 1980), (2) holding a pen between one's teeth (which facilitates a facial expression similar to smiling) versus holding a pen between one's lips (which inhibits smiling) can enhance the perceived humor in cartoons (Strack, Martin, & Stepper, 1988), and (3) information presented while performing an approach behavior (e.g., using one's hands to pull up from underneath a table) is evaluated more positively than information presented during an avoidance behavior (e.g., pushing down on a table top surface; Cacioppo, Priester, & Berntson, 1993; cf. Seibt, Neumann, Nussinson, & Strack, 2008).

A second important influence on contemporary studies of embodiment comes from work in cognitive psychology and linguistics on metaphors (Lakoff & Johnson, 1980). Embodied metaphors would include examples such as people verbalizing that someone is "above" them or has control "over" them. These metaphors likely stem from early experiences in childhood when adults were taller than children. Another example would be associating warm temperatures with caring. This metaphor might stem from a childhood of snuggling close to a nurturing parent. These early experiences can then lead adults to feel less powerful when other people are literally placed higher in physical location than they are (Briñol, Petty, Valle, Rucker, & Becerra, 2007) and to view another person as more caring after simply touching a hot coffee mug (Williams & Bargh, 2008).

Although much work on embodiment in social psychology has focused on linking behaviors directly to judgments, more recent work has attempted to understand the mechanisms by which evaluations stem from the body. Perhaps not surprisingly, work within the ELM framework has shown that a person's bodily movements or responses, like other variables, can influence attitudes by affecting one or more of the core influence processes noted earlier. For example, simple cue effects of the body (e.g., based on arm flexion) are more likely to have a direct impact on judgments when thinking is low (Priester, Cacioppo, & Petty, 1996). When thinking is high, bodily movements such as head nodding (Briñol & Petty, 2003) or sitting in an erect rather than slumped posture (Briñol, Petty, & Wagner, 2009) can validate one's thoughts. And, if elaboration is not already constrained to be high or low by other variables, body-relevant factors can affect the extent of information processing. For example, people are less likely to think carefully about a message when they are placed in a powerful or confident (standing) rather than a powerless and vulnerable (reclining) posture (Petty, Wells, Heesacker, Brock, & Cacioppo, 1983), and they are more likely to think about a message extensively when it is presented on a heavy (signifying weighty or important) rather than a light clipboard (Jostmann, Lakens, & Schubert, 2009). In addition to examining the basic mechanisms by which embodiment works, research in both attitudes and social cognition is likely to focus in the future on whether embodiment effects are the same as or different from other forms of conceptual priming.

Maturation and Broadening of Social Cognition

As noted earlier, especially in the 1970s and early 1980s, the emphasis in social cognition was on cold cognition (i.e., cognition without extra-cognitive motives or emotion). This emphasis might have partially come from developments in the 1960s and early 1970s in areas such as causal attribution (e.g., Jones & Davis, 1965; Kelley, 1967; see Chapter 6) and aided by the computer analogy and mathematical/computational models of cognitive (often evaluative) systems and processes (e.g., Fishbein, 1963; McGuire, 1960; Wyer, 1974). In comparison, it is certainly true that social cognition of the 1990s and 2000s became considerably more diverse. The traditional attitudinal topics of motivation and emotion have been rediscovered (though couched in terms of cognitive antecedents, processes, and, in many cases, consequences). This does not mean, however, that social cognition researchers have embraced traditional attitudes research as part of the social cognition enterprise. In some ways, this seems unfortunate because the development of contemporary attitude theories and the development of the social cognition movement were, in certain respects, responses to similar concerns. It is also unfortunate because, at least in our "attitudinal" view, it stems in part from the original rather narrow (often unstated) view of what qualified as social cognition. This view has changed to some extent as social cognition has become more of an approach than an area of research (originally almost synonymous with impression formation or person memory, hence the development of the PMIG meeting). Still, there is a bit of an "I know it when I see it" quality to identifying when one uses a social cognition approach, and some of the telltale signs of the approach continue to involve use of a reaction time or memory measure to talk about concept activation, representation in memory, or automatic processes. To be sure, the number and type of measures that both attitudes and social cognition researchers use has expanded over time. However, addressing activation or automatic processes (still most typically identified through use of reaction time measures) remains a nearly sufficient criterion for judging research to be social cognition.

As noted by Wegener and Carlston (2005), the current operational definition of "cognitive process" in social psychology has become quite broad and applicable to research across many domains and using many methods. Indeed, in contemporary social psychology, one could often drop the "cognitive" from the term "cognitive process" with little change in meaning. The term *cognitive* is used very broadly, virtually as a synonym for "psychological" or "mental." If the human brain is involved, a process is cognitive. Because the brain is almost always involved, few activities fall outside the cognitive umbrella (including habits, directly primed behaviors, and other phenomena that once would have been viewed as not particularly cognitive). Moreover, traditional alternatives to cognition such as motivation and emotion are treated as having cognitive antecedents, as operating on knowledge structures stored in memory, and as having cognitive consequences (Wegener & Carlston, 2005; see also Markus & Zajonc, 1985).

During this transformation in social cognition, definitions of what people consider to be a "cognitive approach" have shifted. As discussed earlier, attitudes research has included many sorts of cognitive processes and constructs, such as comprehension, retention, balance, cognitive dissonance, and cognitive response. Yet, many of the original treatments of these processes were not identified as "social cognition" in the early days of that approach because the original attitude theories did not directly address the core cognitive processes of encoding, storage (representation in memory), or retrieval. We can't help but wonder if many such questions and methods might have been embraced by early social cognition researchers if the questions and methods had not predated the beginnings of the earnest social cognition movement. That is, if the attitudinal questions and measures had developed alongside or after, rather than prior to, the pact to abandon information integration research, perhaps contemporary attitudes and social cognition domains would have developed more like twins (with potentially different interests, but the same basic genetics), instead of older and younger siblings attempting to carve out their own independent identities.

Notes

1. Kunda (1990) described some research originally formulated as an ability-based bias (e.g., attitudinal schemas biasing assimilation of new information; Lord et al., 1979) in more motivational terms, consistent with her focus on making the case for motivational bias. Regarding that focus, it is interesting to note that Kunda (1990) characterized the most extensive literature on directional motives biasing processing as coming from work on cognitive dissonance (Festinger, 1957, 1964). Indeed, this research might also constitute some of the strongest evidence of such biases. At least in our reading, many of the other oft-cited studies (e.g., examining judgments of self vs. others) seemed more vulnerable than dissonance experiments to cognitive (ability-based) alternative explanations (because of knowledge content differences when dealing with oneself rather than another person).

2. It is interesting to note that Roediger (2003), among others, has come to prefer the terms "direct" and "indirect" measures over "explicit" and "implicit" measures because, clearly, implicit measures can be influenced by explicit processes, and explicit measures can be influenced by implicit processes. Thus, at least some cognitive psychologists have come back around to the terminology that was common in earlier research on attitude measurement.

References

Abelson, R. P. (1959). Modes of resolution of belief dilemmas. *Journal of Conflict Resolution, 3,* 343–352.

Abelson, R. P. (1963). Computer simulation of "hot cognitions." In S. S. Tomkins & S. Mesick (Eds.), *Computer simulation of personality.* New York: Wiley.

Allport, F. H. (1924). *Social psychology.* Boston: Houghton Mifflin.

Alter, A. L., & Oppenheimer, D. M. (2009). Uniting the tribes of fluency to form a metacognitive nation. *Personality and Social Psychology Review, 13,* 219–235.

Anderson, J. R. (1980). *Cognitive psychology and its implications*. San Francisco: Freeman.

Anderson, J. R., & Hastie, R. (1974). Individuation and reference in memory: Proper names and definite descriptions. *Cognitive Psychology, 6,* 495–514.

Anderson, N. H. (1966). Component ratings in impression formation. *Psychonomic Science, 6,* 179–180.

Anderson, N. H. (1970). Functional measurement and psychophysical judgment. *Psychological Review, 77,* 153–170.

Anderson, N. H. (1971). Integration theory and attitude change. *Psychological Review, 78,* 171–206.

Asch, S. E. (1946). Forming impressions of personality. *Journal of Abnormal and Social Psychology, 41,* 258–290.

Barden, J., Maddux, W. W., Petty, R. E., & Brewer, M. B. (2004). Contextual moderation of racial bias: The impact of social roles on controlled and automatically activated attitudes. *Journal of Personality and Social Psychology, 87,* 5–22.

Barden, J., & Petty, R. E. (2008). The mere perception of elaboration creates attitude certainty: Exploring the thoughtfulness heuristic. *Journal of Personality and Social Psychology, 95,* 489–509.

Bargh, J. A. (1994). The four horsemen of automaticity: Awareness, intention, efficiency, and control in social cognition. In R. S. Wyer, Jr., & T. K. Srull (Eds.), *Handbook of social cognition* (2nd ed., Vol. 1, pp. 1–40). Hillsdale, NJ: Erlbaum.

Barsalou, L. W. (2008). Grounded cognition. *Annual Review of Psychology, 59,* 617–645.

Bassili, J. N., & Fletcher, J. F. (1991). Response-time measurement in survey research. *Public Opinion Quarterly, 55,* 331–346.

Bem, D. J. (1967). Self-perception: An alternative interpretation of cognitive dissonance phenomena. *Psychological Review, 74,* 183–200.

Biernat, M., Manis, M., & Nelson, T. E. (1991). Stereotypes and standards of judgment. *Journal of Personality and Social Psychology, 60,* 485–499.

Biernat, M., Vescio, T. K., & Manis, M. (1998). Judging and behaving toward members of stereotyped groups: A shifting standards perspective. In C. Sedikides, J. Schopler, & C. A. Insko (Eds.), *Intergroup cognition and intergroup behavior* (pp. 151–175). Mahwah, NJ: Erlbaum.

Bizer, G. Y., Tormala, Z. L., Rucker, D. D., & Petty, R. E. (2006). Memory-based versus on-line processing: Implications for attitude strength. *Journal of Experimental Social Psychology, 42,* 646–653.

Blankenship, K. L., Wegener, D. T., Petty, R. E., Detweiler-Bedell, B., & Macy, C. L. (2008). Elaboration and consequences of anchored estimates: An attitudinal perspective on numerical anchoring. *Journal of Experimental Social Psychology, 44,* 1465–1476.

Bodenhausen, G. V. (1990). Stereotypes as judgmental heuristics: Evidence of circadian variations in discrimination. *Psychological Science, 1,* 319–322.

Bodenhausen, G. V., Sheppard, L. A., & Kramer, G. P. (1994). Negative affect and social judgment: The differential impact of anger and sadness. *European Journal of Social Psychology, 24,* 45–62.

Bornstein, R. F. (1989). Exposure and affect: Overview and meta-analysis of research, 1968–1987. *Psychological Bulletin, 106,* 265–289.

Bornstein, R. F., & D'Agostino, P. R. (1992). Stimulus recognition and the mere exposure effect. *Journal of Personality and Social Psychology, 63,* 545–552.

Bornstein, R. F., & D'Agostino, P. R. (1994). The attribution and discounting of perceptual fluency: Preliminary tests of a perceptual fluency/attributional model of the mere exposure effect. *Social Cognition, 12,* 103–128.

Brehm, J. W. (1966). *A theory of psychological reactance*. San Diego, CA: Academic Press.

Brewer, M. B. (1988). A dual process model of impression formation. In T. K. Srull & R. S. Wyer (Eds.), *Advances in social cognition* (Vol. 1, pp. 1–36). Hillsdale, NJ: Erlbaum.

Briñol, P., & DeMarree, K. (Eds.) (2012). *Social metacognition*. New York: Psychology Press.

Briñol, P., & Petty, R. E (2003). Overt head movements and persuasion: A self-validation analysis. *Journal of Personality and Social Psychology, 84,* 1123–1139.

Briñol, P., & Petty, R. E. (2008). Embodied persuasion: Fundamental processes by which bodily responses can impact attitudes. In G. R. Semin & E. R. Smith (Eds.), *Embodiment grounding: Social, cognitive, affective, and neuroscientific approaches* (pp. 184–207). Cambridge, UK: Cambridge University Press.

Briñol, P., & Petty, R. E. (2009). Persuasion: Insights from the self-validation hypothesis. In M. P. Zanna (Ed.), *Advances in experimental social psychology*. New York: Academic Press.

Briñol, P., & Petty, R. E. (2012). The history of attitudes and persuasion research. In A. Kruglanski & W. Stroebe (Eds.), *Handbook of the history of social psychology*. New York: Psychology Press.

Briñol, P., Petty, R. E., Valle, C., Rucker, D. D., & Becerra, A. (2007). The effects of message recipients' power before and after persuasion: A self-validation analysis. *Journal of Personality and Social Psychology, 93,* 1040–1053.

Briñol, P., Petty, R. E., & Wagner, B. (2009). Body posture effects on self-evaluation: A self-validation approach. *European Journal of Social Psychology, 39,* 1053–1064.

Byrne, D., & Clore, G. L. (1967). Effectance arousal and attraction. *Journal of Personality and Social Psychology, 6,* 1–18.

Byrne, D., Ervin, C. R., & Lamberth, J. (1970). Continuity between the experimental study of attraction and "real life" computer dating. *Journal of Personality and Social Psychology, 16,* 157–165.

Cacioppo, J. T., Priester, J. R., & Berntson, G. G. (1993). Rudimentary determinants of attitudes II: Arm flexion and extension have differential effects on attitudes. *Journal of Personality and Social Psychology, 65,* 5–17.

Carlston, D. E. (1994). Associated Systems Theory: A systematic approach to the cognitive representation of persons and events. In R. S. Wyer (Ed.) *Advances in Social Cognition: Vol. 7. Associated Systems Theory* (pp. 1–78). Hillsdale, NJ: Erlbaum.

Carlston, D. E., & Skowronski, J. J. (1994). Savings in the relearning of trait information as evidence for spontaneous inference generation. *Journal of Personality and Social Psychology, 66,* 840–856.

Carlston, D. E., & Smith, E. R. (1996). Principles of mental representation. In E. T. Higgins & A. W. Kruglanski (Eds.), *Social psychology: Handbook of basic principles* (pp. 194–210). New York: Guilford Press.

Chaiken, S. (1978). *The use of source versus message cues in persuasion: An information processing analysis*. Unpublished doctoral dissertation, University of Massachusetts, Amherst, MA.

Chaiken, S. (1980). Heuristic versus systematic information processing in the use of source versus message cues in persuasion. *Journal of Personality and Social Psychology, 39,* 752–766.

Chaiken, S. (1987). The heuristic model of persuasion. In M. P. Zanna, J. M. Olson, & C. P. Herman (Ed.), *Social influence: The Ontario symposium* (Vol. 5, pp. 3–39). Hillsdale, NJ: Erlbaum.

Chaiken, S., Liberman, A., & Eagly, A. H. (1989). Heuristic and systematic information processing within and beyond the persuasion context. In J. S. Uleman & J. A. Bargh (Eds.), *Unintended thought* (pp. 212–252). New York: Guilford.

Chaiken, S., & Maheswaran, D. (1994). Heuristic processing can bias systematic processing: Effects of source credibility, argument ambiguity, and task importance on attitude judgment. *Journal of Personality and Social Psychology, 66*, 460–473.

Chaiken, S., & Trope, Y. (Eds.) (1999). *Dual process theories in social psychology.* New York: Guilford Press.

Chien, Y.-W., Wegener, D. T., Hsiao, C.-C., & Petty, R. E. (2010). Dimensional range overlap and context effects in consumer judgments. *Journal of Consumer Research, 37*, 530–542.

Clark, J. K., & Wegener, D. T. (2008). Unpacking outcome dependency: Differentiating effects of dependency and outcome desirability on the processing of goal-relevant information. *Journal of Experimental Social Psychology, 44*, 586–599.

Clark, J. K., & Wegener, D. T. (2013). Message position, information processing, and persuasion: The Discrepancy Motives Model. In P. Devine & A. Plant (Eds.), *Advances in Experimental Social Psychology* (Vol. 47, pp. 189–231). San Diego, CA: Academic Press.

Clark, J. K., Wegener, D. T., Briñol, P., & Petty, R. E. (2009). Discovering that the shoe fits: The self-validating role of stereotypes. *Psychological Science, 20*, 846–852.

Claypool, H. M., Mackie, D. M., & Garcia-Marques, T. (in press). Fluency and attitudes: Effects on evaluation and processing. *Social and Personality Psychology Compass.*

Conrey, F. R., Sherman, J. W., Gawronski, B., Hugenberg, K., & Groom, C. J. (2005). Separating multiple processes in implicit social cognition: The Quad Model of implicit task performance. *Journal of Personality and Social Psychology, 89*, 469–487.

Cook, T. D., & Flay, B. R. (1978). The persistence of experimentally induced attitude change. In L. Berkowitz (Ed.), *Advances in experimental social psychology* (Vol. 11, pp. 1–57). New York: Academic Press.

Costermans, J., Lories, G., & Ansay, C. (1992). Confidence level and feeling of knowing in question answering: The weight of inferential processes. *Journal of Experimental Psychology: Learning, Memory, & Cognition, 18*, 142–150.

Craik, F. I., & Lockhart, R. S. (1972). Levels of processing: A framework for memory research. *Journal of Verbal Learning and Verbal Behavior, 11*, 671–684.

Craik, F. I., & Tulving, E. (1975). Depth of processing and the retention of words in episodic memory. *Journal of Experimental Psychology: General, 104*, 268–294.

Darwin, C. (1965). *The expression of emotions in man and animals.* Chicago: The University of Chicago Press. (Original work published 1872.)

Davidson, A. R., Yantis, S., Norwood, M., & Montano, D. E. (1985). Amount of information about the attitude object and attitude-behavior consistency. *Journal of Personality and Social Psychology, 49*, 1184–1198.

Deese, J. (1965). *The structure of associations in language and thought.* Baltimore: Johns Hopkins Press.

DeSteno, D., Petty, R. E., Rucker, D. D., Wegener, D. T., & Braverman, J. (2004). Discrete emotions and persuasion: The role of emotion-induced expectancies. *Journal of Personality and Social Psychology, 86*, 43–56.

Deutsch, R., & Strack, F. (2006). Duality-models in social psychology: From opposing processes to interacting systems. *Psychological Inquiry, 17*, 166–172.

Devine, P. G. (1989). Stereotypes and prejudice: Their automatic and controlled components. *Journal of Personality and Social Psychology, 56*, 5–18.

Devine, P. G., Sedikides, C., & Fuhrman, R. W. (1989). Goals in social information processing: The case of anticipated interaction. *Journal of Personality and Social Psychology, 56*, 680–690.

Doob, L. W. (1948). *Public opinion and propaganda.* New York: Holt.

Eagly, A. H. (1974). Comprehensibility of persuasive arguments as a determinant of opinion change. *Journal of Personality and Social Psychology, 29*, 758–773.

Erb, H.-P., Kruglanski, A. W., Chun, W. Y., Pierro, A., Mannetti, L., & Spiegel, S. (2003). Searching for commonalities in human judgment: The parametric unimodel and its dual mode alternatives. *European Review of Social Psychology, 14*, 1–49.

Fazio, R. H. (1986). How do attitudes guide behavior? In R. M. Sorrentino & E. T. Higgins (Ed.), *Handbook of motivation and cognition: Foundations of social behavior* (pp. 204–243). New York: Guilford Press.

Fazio, R. H. (1990). Multiple processes by which attitudes guide behavior: The MODE model as an integrative framework. In M. P. Zanna (Ed.), *Advances in experimental social psychology* (Vol. 23, pp. 75–109). San Diego, CA: Academic Press.

Fazio, R. H. (1995). Attitudes as object-evaluation associations: Determinants, consequences, and correlates of attitude accessibility. In R. E. Petty & J. A. Krosnick (Eds.), *Attitude strength: Antecedents and consequences* (pp. 247–282). Mahwah, NJ: Erlbaum.

Fazio, R. H., Chen, J., McDonel, E. C., & Sherman, S. J. (1982). Attitude accessibility, attitude-behavior consistency, and the strength of the object-evaluation association. *Journal of Experimental Social Psychology, 18*, 339–357.

Fazio, R. H., Jackson, J. R., Dunton, B. C., & Williams, C. J. (1995). Variability in automatic activation as an unobtrusive measure of racial attitudes: A bona fide pipeline? *Journal of Personality and Social Psychology, 69*, 1013–1027.

Fazio, R. H., & Olson, M. A. (2003). Implicit measures in social cognition research: Their meaning and use. *Annual Review of Psychology, 54*, 297–327.

Fazio, R. H., Powell, M. C., & Herr, P. M. (1983). Toward a process model of the attitude-behavior relation: Accessing one's attitude upon mere observation of the attitude object. *Journal of Personality and Social Psychology, 44*, 723–735.

Fazio, R. H., Sanbonmatsu, D. M., Powell, M. C., & Kardes, F. R. (1986). On the automatic activation of attitudes. *Journal of Personality and Social Psychology, 50*, 229–238.

Fazio, R. H., & Zanna, M. P. (1978). On the predictive validity of attitudes: The roles of direct experience and confidence. *Journal of Personality, 46*, 228–243.

Fazio, R. H., & Zanna, M. P. (1981). Direct experience and attitude behavior consistency. In L. Berkowitz (Ed.), *Advances in experimental social psychology* (Vol. 14, pp. 161–202). New York: Academic Press.

Fazio, R. H., Zanna, M. P., & Cooper, J. (1977). Dissonance and self-perception: An integrative view of each theory's proper domain of application. *Journal of Experimental Social Psychology, 13*, 464–479.

Festinger, L. (1957). *A theory of cognitive dissonance*. Evanston, IL: Row, Peterson.

Festinger, L. (1964). *Conflict, decision, and dissonance*. Stanford, CA: Stanford University Press.

Festinger, L., & Maccoby, N. (1964). On resistance to persuasive communications. *Journal of Abnormal and Social Psychology, 68*, 359–366.

Fishbein, M. (1963). An investigation of the relationship between beliefs about an object and the attitude toward that object. *Human Relations, 16*, 233–240.

Fishbein, M., & Ajzen, I. (1974). Attitudes toward objects as predictors of single and multiple behavioral criteria, *Psychological Review, 81*, 59–74.

Fishbein, M., & Ajzen, I. (1975). *Belief, attitude, intention, and behavior: An introduction to theory and research*. Reading, MA: Addison-Wesley.

Fiske, S. T., Lin, M., & Neuberg, S. L. (1999). The continuum model: Ten years later. In S. Chaiken & Y. Trope (Eds.), *Dual-process theories in social psychology* (pp. 231–245). New York: Guilford Press.

Fiske, S. T., & Neuberg, S. L. (1990). A continuum of impression formation, from category-based to individuating processes: Influences of information and motivation on attention and interpretation. In M. P. Zanna (Ed.), *Advances in experimental social psychology* (Vol. 23, pp. 1–74). New York: Academic Press.

Förster, J., Liberman, N., & Kuschel, S. (2008). The effect of global versus local processing styles on assimilation versus contrast in social judgment. *Journal of Personality and Social Psychology, 94*, 579–99.

Freedman, J. L. (1965). Long-term behavioral effects of cognitive dissonance. *Journal of Experimental Social Psychology, 1*, 145–155.

Galton, F. (1884). Measurement of character. *Fortnightly Review, 42*, 179–185.

Gawronski, B., & Bodenhausen, G. V. (2006). Associative and propositional processes in evaluation: An integrative review of implicit and explicit attitude change. *Psychological Bulletin, 132*, 692–731.

Grayson, C. E., & Schwarz, N. (1999). Beliefs influence information processing strategies: Declarative and experiential information in risk assessment. *Social Cognition, 17*, 1–18.

Greenwald, A. G. (1968). Cognitive learning, cognitive response to persuasion, and attitude change. In A. G. Greenwald, T. C. Brock, & T. M. Ostrom (Ed.), *Psychological foundations of attitudes* (pp. 147–170). New York: Academic Press.

Greenwald, A. G. (1975). On the inconclusiveness of "crucial" cognitive tests of dissonance versus self-perception theories. *Journal of Experimental Social Psychology, 11*, 490–499.

Greenwald, A. G. (1980). The totalitarian ego: Fabrication and revision of personal history. *American Psychologist, 35*, 603–618.

Greenwald, A. G., & Banaji, M. R. (1995). Implicit social cognition: Attitudes, self-esteem, and stereotypes. *Psychological Review, 102*, 4–27.

Greenwald, A. G., Brock, T. C., & Ostrom, T. M. (Eds.), (1968). *Psychological foundations of attitudes*. New York: Academic Press.

Greenwald, A. G., McGhee, D. E., & Schwartz, J. L. K. (1998). Measuring individual differences in implicit cognition: The implicit association test. *Journal of Personality and Social Psychology, 74*, 1464–1480.

Greenwald, A. G., & Nosek, B. A. (2009). Attitudinal dissociation: What does it mean? In R. E. Petty, R. H. Fazio, & P.

Briñol (Eds.), *Attitudes: Insights from the new implicit measures* (pp. 65–82). New York: Psychology Press.

Greenwald, A. G., Spangenberg, E. R., Pratkanis, A. R., & Eskenazi, J. (1991). Double-blind tests of subliminal self-help audiotapes. *Psychological Science, 2*, 119–122.

Guttman, L. (1944). A basis for scaling qualitative data. *American Sociological Review, 9*, 139–150.

Haddock, G., Rothman, A. J., Reber, R., & Schwarz, N. (1999). Forming judgments of attitude certainty, intensity, and importance: The role of subjective experiences. *Personality and Social Psychology Bulletin, 25*, 771–782.

Haddock, G., Rothman, A. J., & Schwarz, N. (1996). Are (some) reports of attitude strength context dependent? *Canadian Journal of Behavioral Science, 24*, 313–317.

Hammond, K. R. (1948). Measuring attitudes by error choice: An indirect method. *Journal of Abnormal and Social Psychology, 43*, 38–48.

Hastie, R. (1981). Schematic principles in human memory. In E. T. Higgins, C. P. Herman, & M. P. Zanna (Eds.), *Social cognition: The Ontario symposium* (Vol. 1, pp. 39–88). Hillsdale, NJ: Erlbaum.

Hastie, R., & Park, B. (1986). The relationship between memory and judgment depends on whether the judgment task is memory-based or on-line. *Psychological Review, 93*, 258–268.

Haugtvedt, C. P., & Petty, R. E. (1992). Personality and persuasion: Need for cognition moderates the persistence and resistance of attitude changes. *Journal of Personality and Social Psychology, 63*, 308–319.

Haugtvedt, C. P., & Wegener, D. T. (1994). Message order effects in persuasion: An attitude strength perspective. *Journal of Consumer Research, 21*, 205–218.

Heider, F. (1958). *The psychology of interpersonal relations*. New York: Wiley.

Helson, H. (1964). *Adaptation-level theory: An experimental and systematic approach to behavior*. New York: Harper & Row.

Hendrick, C., & Seyfried, B. A. (1974). Assessing the validity of laboratory-produced attitude change. *Journal of Personality and Social Psychology, 29*, 865–870.

Hess, E. H., & Polt, J. M. (1960). Pupil size as related to interest value of visual stimuli. *Science, 132*, 349–350.

Herr, P. M. (1986). Consequences of priming: Judgment and behavior. *Journal of Personality and Social Psychology, 51*, 1106–15.

Herr, P. M., Sherman, S. J., & Fazio, R. H. (1983). On the consequences of priming: Assimilation and contrast effects. *Journal of Experimental Social Psychology, 19*, 323–340.

Higgins, E. T. (1996). Knowledge activation: Accessibility, applicability, and salience. In E. T. Higgins & A. W. Kruglanski (Eds.), *Social psychology: Handbook of basic principles* (pp. 133–168). New York: Guilford.

Higgins, E. T., Rholes, W. S., & Jones, C. R. (1977). Category accessibility and impression formation. *Journal of Experimental Social Psychology, 13*, 141–154.

Hirt, E. R., Kardes, F. R., & Markman, K. D. (2004). Activating a mental simulation mind-set through generation of alternatives: Implications for debiasing in related and unrelated domains. *Journal of Experimental Social Psychology, 40*, 374–383.

Hovland, C. I. (1957). Summary and explications. In C. I. Hovland (Ed.), *The order of presentation in persuasion* (pp. 129–157). New Haven, CT: Yale University Press.

Hovland, C. I., Harvey, O. J., & Sherif, M. (1957). Assimilation and contrast effects in reactions to communications and attitude change. *Journal of Abnormal and Social Psychology,* 55, 244–252.

Hovland, C. I., Janis, I. L., & Kelley, H. H. (1953). *Communication and persuasion: Psychological studies of opinion change.* New Haven, CT: Yale University Press.

Hovland, C. I., & Weiss, W. (1951). The influence of source credibility on communication effectiveness. *Public Opinion Quarterly,* 15, 635–650.

Insko, C. A. (1964). Primacy versus recency in persuasion as a function of the timing of arguments and measures. *Journal of Abnormal and Social Psychology,* 69, 381–391.

Johnston, L., & Hewstone, M. (1992). Cognitive models of stereotype change: 3. Subtyping and the perceived typicality of disconfirming group members. *Journal of Experimental Social Psychology,* 28, 360–386.

Jones, E. E., & Davis, K. E. (1965). From acts to dispositions: The attribution process in person perception. In L. Berkowitz (Ed.), *Advances in experimental social psychology* (Vol. 2, pp. 219–266). New York: Academic Press.

Jordan, C. H., Whitfield, M., & Zeigler-Hill, V. (2007). Intuition and the correspondence between implicit and explicit self-esteem. *Journal of Personality and Social Psychology,* 93, 1067–1079.

Jost, J. T., Kruglanski, A. W., & Nelson, T. O. (1998). Social meta-cognition: An expansionist review. *Personality and Social Psychology Review,* 2, 137–154.

Jostmann, N. B., Lakens, D., & Schubert, T. W. (2009). Weight as an embodiment of importance. *Psychological Science,* 20, 1169–1174.

Kang, Y. S., & Herr, P. M. (2006). Beauty and the beholder: Toward an integrative model of communication source effects. *Journal of Consumer Research,* 33, 123–130.

Karpinski, A., & Hilton, J. L. (2001). Attitudes and the implicit association test. *Journal of Personality and Social Psychology,* 81, 774–788.

Katz, D. (1960). The functional approach to the study of attitudes. *Public Opinion Quarterly,* 24, 163–204.

Kelley, H. H. (1967). Attribution theory in social psychology. In D. Levine (Ed.), *Nebraska symposium on motivation* (Vol. 15, pp. 192–238). Lincoln, NE: University of Nebraska Press.

Kidder, L. H., & Campbell, D. T. (1970). The indirect testing of social attitudes. In G. F. Summers (Ed.), *Attitude measurement* (pp. 333–385). Chicago: Rand McNally.

Klein, W. M., & Kunda, Z. (1992). Motivated person perception: Constructing justifications for desired beliefs. *Journal of Experimental Social Psychology,* 28, 145–168.

Klinger, M. R., & Greenwald, A. G. (1994). Preferences need no inferences? The cognitive basis of unconscious mere exposure effects. In P. M. Niedenthal & S. Kitayama (Eds.), *The heart's eye: Emotional influences in perception and attention* (pp. 67–85). San Diego: Academic Press.

Kokkinaki, F., & Lunt, P. (1999). The effect of advertising message involvement on brand attitude accessibility. *Journal of Economic Psychology,* 20, 41–51.

Kruglanski, A. W., & Thompson, E. P. (1999). Persuasion by a single route: A view from the unimodel. *Psychological Inquiry,* 10, 83–109.

Kunda, Z. (1990). The case for motivated reasoning. *Psychological Bulletin,* 108, 480–498.

Kunst-Wilson, W. R., & Zajonc, R. B. (1980). Affective discrimination of stimuli that cannot be recognized. *Science,* 207, 557–558.

Lakoff, G., & Johnson, M. (1980). *Metaphors we live by.* Chicago, IL: University of Chicago Press.

Lakoff, G., & Johnson, M. (1999). *Philosophy in the flesh: The embodied mind and its challenge to Western thought.* New York: Basic Books.

Lasswell, H. D. (1948). The structure and function of communication in society. In L. Bryson (Ed.), *The communication of ideas: Religion and civilization series* (pp. 37–51). New York: Harper & Row.

LeBel, E. P. (2010). Attitude accessibility as a moderator of implicit and explicit self-esteem correspondence. *Self and Identity,* 9, 195–208.

Likert, R. (1932). A technique for the measurement of attitudes. *Archives of Psychology,* 140, 44–53.

Lingle, J. H., & Ostrom, T. M. (1979). Retrieval selectivity in memory-based impression judgments. *Journal of Personality and Social Psychology,* 37, 180–194.

Lingle, J. C., & Ostrom, T. M. (1981). Principles of memory and cognition in attitude formation. In R. E. Petty, T. M. Ostrom, & T. C. Brock (Eds.), *Cognitive responses in persuasion* (pp. 399–420). Hillsdale, NJ: Erlbaum.

Loersch, C., McCaslin, M. J., & Petty, R. E. (2011). Exploring the impact of social judgeability concerns on the interplay of associative and deliberative attitude processes. *Journal of Experimental Social Psychology,* 47, 1029–1032.

Lombardi, W. J., Higgins, E. T., & Bargh, J. A. (1987). The role of consciousness in priming effects on categorization: Assimilation versus contrast as a function of awareness of the priming task. *Personality and Social Psychology Bulletin,* 13, 411–429.

Lord, C. G., & Lepper, M. R. (1999). Attitude representation theory. In M. P. Zanna (Ed.), *Advances in experimental social psychology* (Vol. 31, pp. 265–343). Mahwah, NJ: Erlbaum.

Lord, C. G., Ross, L., & Lepper, M. R. (1979). Biased assimilation and attitude polarization: The effects of prior theories on subsequently considered evidence. *Journal of Personality and Social Psychology,* 37, 2098–2109.

Mackie, D. M., & Asuncion, A. G. (1990). On-line and memory-based modification of attitudes: Determinants of message recall-attitude change correspondence. *Journal of Personality and Social Psychology,* 59, 5–16.

Macrae, C. N., Milne, A. B., & Bodenhausen, G. V. (1994). Stereotypes as energy-saving devices: A peek inside the cognitive toolbox. *Journal of Personality and Social Psychology,* 66, 37–47.

Mann, L., & Janis, I. L. (1968). A follow-up study on the long-term effects of emotional role playing. *Journal of Personality and Social Psychology,* 8, 339–342.

Mandler, G., Nakamura, Y., & Shebo Van Zandt, B. J. (1987). Nonspecific effects of exposure on stimuli that cannot be recognized. *Journal of Experimental Psychology: Learning, Memory, and Cognition,* 13, 646–648.

Markman, K. D., & McMullen, M. N. (2003). A reflection and evaluation model of comparative thinking. *Personality and Social Psychology Review,* 7, 244–267.

Markus, H., & Zajonc, R. B. (1985). The cognitive perspective in social psychology. In G. Lindzey & E. Aronson (Eds.), *The handbook of social psychology* (3rd ed., Vol. 1, pp. 137–230). New York: Random House.

Martin, L. L. (1986). Set/reset: Use and disuse of concepts in impression formation. *Journal of Personality and Social Psychology,* 51, 493–504.

Martin, L. L., Seta, J. J., & Crelia, R. A. (1990). Assimilation and contrast as a function of people's willingness and ability to expend effort in forming an impression. *Journal of Personality and Social Psychology,* 59, 27–37.

McGuire, W. J. (1957). Order of presentation as a factor in "conditioning" persuasiveness. In C. I. Hovland (Ed.), *The order of presentation in persuasion* (pp. 98–114). New Haven, CT: Yale University Press.

McGuire, W. J. (1960). A syllogistic analysis of cognitive relationships. In C. I. Hovland, & M. J. Rosenberg (Ed.), *Attitude organization and change: An analysis of consistency among attitude components* (pp. 65–111). New Haven, CT: Yale University Press.

McGuire, W. J. (1968). Personality and attitude change: An information-processing theory. In A. G. Greenwald, T. C. Brock, & T. M. Ostrom (Ed.), *Psychological foundations of attitudes* (pp. 171–196). New York: Academic.

Milgram, S. L., Mann, L., & Harter, S. (1965). The lost-letter technique: A tool of social science research. *Public Opinion Quarterly, 29*, 437–438.

Miller, N., & Campbell, D. T. (1959). Recency and primacy in persuasion as a function of the timing of speeches and measurements. *Journal of Abnormal and Social Psychology, 59*, 1–9.

Muller, D., Judd, C. M., & Yzerbyt, V. Y. (2005). When moderation is mediated and mediation is moderated. *Journal of Personality and Social Psychology, 89*, 852–863.

Mussweiler, T. (2003). Comparison processes in social judgment: Mechanisms and consequences. *Psychological Review, 110*, 472–489.

Neely, J. H. (1977). Semantic priming and retrieval from lexical memory: Roles of inhibitionless spreading activation and limited-capacity attention. *Journal of Experimental Psychology: General, 106*, 225–254.

Neuberg, S. L., & Fiske, S. T. (1987). Motivational influences on impression formation: Outcome dependency, accuracy-driven attention, and individuating processes. *Journal of Personality and Social Psychology, 53*, 431–444.

Nosek, B. A. (2005). Moderators of the relationship between implicit and explicit evaluation. *Journal of Experimental Psychology: General, 134*, 565–584.

Olson, M. A., & Fazio, R. H. (2004). Reducing the influence of extrapersonal associations on the implicit association test: Personalizing the IAT. *Journal of Personality and Social Psychology, 86*, 653–667.

Olson, M. A., & Fazio, R. H. (2009). Implicit and explicit measures of attitudes: The perspective of the MODE model. In R. E. Petty, R. H. Fazio, & P. Briñol (Eds.), *Attitudes: Insights from the new implicit measures* (pp. 19–63). New York: Psychology Press.

Osgood, C. E., Suci, G. J., & Tannenbaum, P. H. (1957). *The measurement of meaning*. Urbana, IL: University of Illinois Press.

Osgood, C. E., & Tannenbaum, P. H. (1955). The principle of congruity in the prediction of attitude change. *Psychological Review, 62*, 42–55.

Osterhouse, R. A., & Brock, T. C. (1970). Distraction increases yielding to propaganda by inhibiting counterarguing. *Journal of Personality and Social Psychology, 15*, 344–358.

Ostrom, T. M. (1968). The emergence of attitude theory: 1930–1950. In A. G. Greenwald, T. C. Brock, & T. M. Ostrom (Eds.), *Psychological foundations of attitudes* (pp. 1–32). New York: Academic Press.

Ostrom, T. M. (1969). The relationship between the affective, behavioral, and cognitive components of attitude. *Journal of Experimental Social Psychology, 5*, 12–30.

Ostrom, T. M., (1970). Perspective as a determinant of attitude change. *Journal of Experimental Social Psychology, 6*, 280–292.

Ostrom, T. M. (1973). The bogus pipeline: A new ignis fatuus? *Psychological Bulletin, 79*, 252–259.

Ostrom, T. M. (1977). Between-theory and within-theory conflict in explaining context effects in impression formation. *Journal of Experimental Social Psychology, 13*, 492–503.

Ostrom, T. M. (1984). The sovereignty of social cognition. In R. S. Wyer, Jr. & T. Srull (Eds.), *Handbook of social cognition* (Vol. 1, pp. 1–38). Hillsdale, NJ: Erlbaum.

Ostrom, T. M., & Brock, T. C. (1969). Cognitive bonding to central values and resistance to a communication advocating change in policy orientation. *Journal of Experimental Research in Personality, 4*, 42–50.

Ostrom, T. M. & Upshaw, H. S. (1968). Psychological perspective and attitude change. In A. G. Greenwald, T. C. Brock, & T. M. Ostrom (Eds.), *Psychological foundations of attitudes* (pp. 217–242). San Diego, CA: Academic Press.

Petty, R. E. (1977). *A cognitive response analysis of the temporal persistence of attitude changes induced by persuasive communications*. Unpublished doctoral dissertation, Ohio State University, Columbus, OH.

Petty, R. E., & Briñol, P. (2006a). A meta-cognitive approach to "implicit" and "explicit" evaluations: Comment on Gawronski and Bodenhausen (2006). *Psychological Bulletin, 132*, 740–744.

Petty, R. E. & Briñol, P. (2006b). Understanding social judgment: Multiple systems and processes. *Psychological Inquiry, 17*, 217–223.

Petty, R. E., & Briñol, P. (2010). Attitude structure and change: Implications for implicit measures. In B. Gawronski & B. K. Payne (Eds.), *Handbook of implicit social cognition: Measurement, theory, and applications* (pp. 335–352). New York: Guilford Press.

Petty, R. E., & Briñol, P. (2012). The Elaboration Likelihood Model. In P. A. M. Van Lange, A. Kruglanski, & E. T. Higgins (Eds.), *Handbook of theories of social psychology* (Vol. 1, pp. 224–245). London, UK: Sage.

Petty, R. E., Briñol, P., & DeMarree, K. G. (2007). The meta-cognitive model (MCM) of attitudes: Implications for attitude measurement, change, and strength. *Social Cognition, 25*, 657–686.

Petty, R. E., Briñol, P., & Johnson, I. (2012). Implicit ambivalence. In B. Gawronski, & F. Strack (Eds.), *Cognitive consistency: A fundamental principle in social cognition* (pp. 178–201). New York: Guilford Press.

Petty, R. E., Briñol, P. & Tormala, Z. L. (2002). Thought confidence as a determinant of persuasion: The self-validation hypothesis. *Journal of Personality and Social Psychology, 82*, 722–741.

Petty, R. E., Briñol, P., Tormala, Z. L., & Wegener, D.T. (2007). The role of metacognition in social judgment. In A. W. Kruglanski & E. T. Higgins (Eds.), *Social psychology: Handbook of basic principles* (2nd ed., pp. 254–284). New York: Guilford.

Petty, R. E., & Cacioppo, J. T. (1979). Issue involvement can increase or decrease persuasion by enhancing message-relevant cognitive responses. *Journal of Personality and Social Psychology, 37*, 1915–1926.

Petty, R. E., & Cacioppo, J. T. (1981). *Attitudes and persuasion: Classic and contemporary approaches*. Dubuque, IA: Wm. C. Brown.

Petty, R. E., & Cacioppo, J. T. (1986a). *Communication and persuasion: Central and peripheral routes to persuasion*. New York: Springer-Verlag.

Petty, R. E., & Cacioppo, J. T. (1986b). The Elaboration Likelihood Model of persuasion. In L. Berkowitz (Ed.), *Advances in experimental social psychology* (Vol. 19, pp. 123–205). New York: Academic Press.

Petty, R. E., Cacioppo, J. T., & Goldman, R. (1981). Personal involvement as a determinant of argument-based persuasion. *Journal of Personality and Social Psychology, 41*, 847–855.

Petty, R. E., Haugtvedt, C. P., & Smith, S. M. (1995). Elaboration as a determinant of attitude strength: Creating attitudes that are persistent, resistant, and predictive of behavior. In R. E. Petty & J. A. Krosnick (Eds.), *Attitude strength: Antecedents and consequences* (pp. 93–130). Mahwah, NJ: Erlbaum.

Petty, R. E., & Krosnick, J. A. (Eds.) (1995). *Attitude strength: Antecedents and consequences.* Mahwah, NJ: Erlbaum.

Petty, R. E., Ostrom, T. M., & Brock, T. D. (Eds.) (1981). *Cognitive responses in persuasion.* Hillsdale, NJ: Erlbaum.

Petty, R. E., Schumann, D. W., Richman, S. A., & Strathman, A. J. (1993). Positive mood and persuasion: Different roles for affect under high- and low-elaboration conditions. *Journal of Personality and Social Psychology, 64*, 5–20.

Petty, R. E., Tormala, Z., Hawkins, C., & Wegener, D. T. (2001). Motivation to think and order effects in persuasion: The moderating role of chunking. *Personality and Social Psychology Bulletin, 27*, 332–344.

Petty, R. E., & Wegener, D. T. (1993). Flexible correction processes in social judgment: Correcting for context-induced contrast. *Journal of Experimental Social Psychology, 29*, 137–165.

Petty, R. E., & Wegener, D. T. (1998). Attitude change: Multiple roles for persuasion variables. In D. Gilbert, S. Fiske, & G. Lindzey (Eds.), *The handbook of social psychology* (4th ed., pp. 323–390). New York: McGraw-Hill.

Petty, R. E., & Wegener, D. T. (1999). The Elaboration Likelihood Model: Current status and controversies. In S. Chaiken & Y. Trope (Eds.), *Dual process theories in social psychology* (pp. 41–72). New York: Guilford Press.

Petty, R. E., Wegener, D. T., & White, P. (1998). Flexible correction processes in social judgment: Implications for persuasion. *Social Cognition, 16*, 93–113.

Petty, R. E., Wells, G. L., & Brock, T. C. (1976). Distraction can enhance or reduce yielding to propaganda: Thought disruption versus effort justification. *Journal of Personality and Social Psychology, 34*, 874–884.

Petty, R. E., Wells, G. L., Heesacker, M., Brock, T. C., & Cacioppo, J. T. (1983). The effects of recipient posture on persuasion: A cognitive response analysis. *Personality and Social Psychology Bulletin, 9*, 209–222.

Pierro, A., Mannetti, L., Kruglanski, A. W., & Sleeth-Keppler, D. (2004). Relevance override: On the reduced impact of "cues" under high-motivation conditions of persuasion studies. *Journal of Personality and Social Psychology, 86*, 251–264.

Priester, J. R., Cacioppo, J. T., & Petty, R. E. (1996). The influence of motor processes on attitudes toward novel versus familiar semantic stimuli. *Personality and Social Psychology Bulletin, 22*, 442–447.

Priester, J. R., & Petty, R. E. (2003). The influence of spokesperson trustworthiness on message elaboration, attitude strength, and advertising effectiveness. *Journal of Consumer Psychology, 13*, 408–421.

Regan, D. T., & Fazio, R. H. (1977). On the consistency between attitudes and behavior: Look to the method of attitude formation. *Journal of Experimental Social Psychology, 13*, 28–45.

Rennier, G. A. (1988). *The strength of the object-evaluation association, the attitude-behavior relationship, and the Elaboration Likelihood Model of persuasion.* Unpublished doctoral dissertation, University of Missouri, Columbia, MO.

Robbins, P., & Aydede, M., (2009) (Eds.). *The Cambridge handbook of situated cognition.* Cambridge, UK: Cambridge University Press.

Roediger, H. L. (2003). Reconsidering implicit memory. In J. S. Bowers & C. J. Marsolek (Eds.),, *Rethinking implicit memory* (pp. 3–18). New York: Oxford University Press.

Rosenberg, M. J., & Abelson, R. P. (1960). An analysis of cognitive balancing. In C. I. Hovland, & M. J. Rosenberg (Eds.), *Attitude organization and change: An analysis of consistency among components* (pp. 112–163). New Haven, CT: Yale University Press.

Rosenberg, M. J., & Hovland, C. I. (1960). Cognitive, affective, and behavioral components of attitudes. In M. Rosenberg, C. Hovland, W. McGuire, R. Abelson, & J. Brehm (Eds.), *Attitude organization and change* (pp. 1–14). New Haven, CT: Yale University Press.

Roskos-Ewoldsen, D. R., & Fazio, R. H. (1992). On the orienting value of attitudes: Attitude accessibility as a determinant of an object's attraction of visual attention. *Journal of Personality and Social Psychology, 63*, 198–211.

Rumelhart, D. E., Lindsay, P. H., & Norman, D. A. (1972). A process model for long-term memory. In E. Tulving & W. Donaldson (Eds.), *Organization of memory* (pp. 197–246). New York: Academic Press.

Rydell, R. J., & McConnell, A. R. (2006). Understanding implicit and explicit attitude change: A systems of reasoning analysis. *Journal of Personality and Social Psychology, 91*, 995–1008.

Schneider, W., & Shiffrin, R. M. (1977). Controlled and automatic human information processing: 1. Detection, search, and attention. *Psychological Review, 84*, 1–66.

Schwarz, N., & Bless, H. (1992). Constructing reality and its alternatives: An inclusion/exclusion model of assimilation and contrast effects in social judgment. In L. L. Martin & A. Tesser (Eds.), *The construction of social judgments* (pp. 217–245). Hillsdale, NJ: Erlbaum.

Schwarz, N., & Bless, H. (2007). Mental construal processes: The inclusion/exclusion model. In D. A. Stapel & J. M. Suls (Eds.), *Assimilation and contrast in social psychology* (pp. 119–141). New York: Psychology Press.

Schwarz, N., Bless, H., Strack, F., Klumpp, G., Rittenauer-Schatka, H., & Simons, A. (1991). Ease of retrieval as information: Another look at the availability heuristic. *Journal of Personality and Social Psychology, 61*, 195–202.

Scott, C. L., Harris, R. J., & Rothe, A. R. (2001). Embodied cognition through improvisation improves memory for a dramatic monologue. *Discourse Processes, 31*, 293–305.

Seibt, B., Neumann, R., Nussinson, R., & Strack, F. (2008). Movement direction or change in distance? Self- and object-related approach-avoidance motions. *Journal of Experimental Social Psychology, 44*, 713–720.

Semin, G. R., & Smith, E. R. (Eds.) (2008). *Embodiment grounding: Social, cognitive, affective, and neuroscientific approaches.* Cambridge, UK: Cambridge University Press.

Sherif, C. W., Sherif, M., & Nebergall, R. E. (1965). *Attitude and attitude change: The social judgment-involvement approach.* Philadelphia: Saunders.

Sherif, M. (1977). Crisis in social psychology: Some remarks towards breaking through the crisis. *Personality and Social Psychology Bulletin, 3*, 368–382.

Sherif, M., & Hovland, C. I. (1961). *Social judgment: Assimilation and contrast effects in communication and attitude change.* New Haven, CT: Yale University Press.

Sherif, M., & Sherif, C. W. (1967). Attitude as the individual's own categories: The social judgment-involvement approach to attitude and attitude change. In C. W. Sherif & M. Sherif (Eds.), *Attitude, ego-involvement, and change* (pp. 105–139). New York: Wiley.

Sherif, M., Taub, D., & Hovland, C. I. (1958). Assimilation and contrast effects of anchoring stimuli on judgments. *Journal of Experimental Psychology, 55,* 150–155.

Shiffrin, R. M., & Schneider, W. (1977). Controlled and automatic human information processing: II. Perceptual learning, automatic attending, and a general theory. *Psychological Review, 84,* 127–190.

Simon, L., Greenberg, J., & Brehm, J. (1995). Trivialization: The forgotten mode of dissonance reduction. *Journal of Personality and Social Psychology, 68,* 247–260.

Skowronski, J. J, Carlston, D. E., Mae, L., & Crawford, M. T. (1998). Spontaneous trait transference: Communicators take on the qualities they describe in others. *Journal of Personality and Social Psychology, 74,* 837–848.

Smith, E. R., & DeCoster, J. (2000). Dual-process models in social and cognitive psychology: Conceptual integration and links to underlying memory systems. *Personality and Social Psychology Review, 4,* 108–131.

Smith, E. R., Fazio, R. H., & Cejka, M. A. (1996). Accessible attitudes influence categorization of multiply categorizable objects. *Journal of Personality and Social Psychology, 71,* 888–898.

Smith, M. B., Bruner, J. S., & White, R. W. (1956). *Opinions and personality.* New York: Wiley.

Solarz, A. K. (1960). Latency of instrumental responses as a function of compatibility with the meaning eliciting verbal signs. *Journal of Experimental Psychology, 59,* 239–245.

Srull, T. K., & Wyer, R. S., Jr. (1979). The role of category accessibility in the interpretation of information about persons: Some determinants and implications. *Journal of Personality and Social Psychology, 37,* 1660–1672.

Staats, A. W., & Staats, C. K. (1958). Attitudes established by classical conditioning. *Journal of Abnormal and Social Psychology, 57,* 37–40.

Steele, C. M., & Ostrom, T. M. (1974). Perspective-mediated attitude change: When is indirect persuasion more effective than direct persuasion? *Journal of Personality and Social Psychology, 29,* 737–741.

Strack, F., & Deutsch, R. (2004). Reflective and impulsive determinants of social behavior. *Personality and Social Psychology Review, 8,* 220–247.

Strack, F., Martin, L., & Stepper, S. (1988). Inhibiting and facilitating conditions of the human smile: A nonobtrusive test of the facial feedback hypothesis. *Journal of Personality and Social Psychology, 54,* 768–777.

Thurstone, L. L. (1928). Attitudes can be measured. *American Journal of Sociology, 33,* 529–544.

Thurstone, L. L., & Chave, E. J. (1929). *The measurement of attitude.* Chicago: University of Chicago Press.

Tormala, Z. L., Falces, C., Briñol, P., & Petty, R. E. (2007). Ease of retrieval effects in social judgment: The role of unrequested cognitions. *Journal of Personality and Social Psychology, 93,* 143–157.

Tormala, Z. L., & Petty, R. E. (2001). On-line versus memory based processing: The role of "need to evaluate" in person perception. *Personality and Social Psychology Bulletin, 12,* 1599–1612.

Tormala, Z., Petty, R. E., & Briñol, P. (2002). Ease of retrieval effects in persuasion: The roles of elaboration and thought confidence. *Personality and Social Psychology Bulletin, 28,* 1700–1712.

Tourangeau, R., & Rasinski, K. A. (1988). Cognitive processes underlying context effects in attitude measurement. *Psychological Bulletin, 103,* 299–314.

Tourangeau, R., Rasinski, K. A., Bradburn, N., & D'Andrade, R. (1989). Belief accessibility and context effects in attitude measurement. *Journal of Experimental Social Psychology, 25,* 401–421.

Uleman, J. S. (1999). Spontaneous versus intentional inferences in impression formation. In S. Chaiken & Y. Trope (Eds.), *Dual-process theories in social psychology* (pp. 141–160). New York: Guilford.

Wänke, M., & Bless, H. (2000). The effects of subjective ease of retrieval on attitudinal judgments: The moderating role of processing motivation. In H. Bless & J. P. Forgas (Eds.), *The message within: The role of subjective experience in social cognition and behavior* (pp. 143–161). Philadelphia: Taylor & Francis.

Wänke, M., Bless, H., & Biller, B. (1996). Subjective experience versus content of information in the construction of attitude judgments. *Personality and Social Psychology Bulletin, 22,* 1105–1113.

Wänke, M., Schwarz, N., & Bless, H. (1995). The availability heuristic revisited: Experienced ease of retrieval in mundane frequency estimates. *Acta Psychologica, 89,* 83–90.

Watts, W. A., & McGuire, W. J. (1964). Persistence of induced opinion change and retention of the inducing message contents. *Journal of Abnormal and Social Psychology, 68,* 233–241.

Weber, R., & Crocker, J. (1983). Cognitive processes in the revision of stereotypic beliefs. *Journal of Personality and Social Psychology, 45,* 961–977.

Wegener, D. T., & Carlston, D. E. (2005). Cognitive processes in attitude formation and change. In D. Albarracin, B. Johnson, & M. Zanna (Eds.), *The handbook of attitudes* (pp. 493–542). Mahwah, NJ: Erlbaum.

Wegener, D. T., Clark, J. K., & Petty, R. E. (2006). Not all stereotyping is created equal: Differential consequences of thoughtful versus nonthoughtful stereotyping. *Journal of Personality and Social Psychology, 90,* 42–59.

Wegener, D. T., Downing, J., Krosnick, J. A., & Petty, R. E. (1995). Measures and manipulations of strength-related properties of attitudes: Current practice and future directions. In R. E. Petty & J. A. Krosnick (Eds.), *Attitude strength: Antecedants and consequences* (pp. 455–487). Mahwah, NJ: Erlbaum.

Wegener, D. T. & Fabrigar, L. R. (2000). Analysis and design for nonexperimental data: Addressing causal and noncausal hypotheses. In H. T. Reis & C. M. Judd (Eds.), *Handbook of research methods in social and personality psychology* (pp. 412–450). New York: Cambridge University Press.

Wegener, D. T., & Petty, R. E. (1995). Flexible correction processes in social judgment: The role of naive theories in corrections for perceived bias. *Journal of Personality and Social Psychology, 68,* 36–51.

Wegener, D. T., & Petty, R. E. (1997). The flexible correction model: The role of naive theories of bias in bias correction. In M. P. Zanna (Ed.), *Advances in experimental social psychology* (Vol. 29, pp. 141–208). New York: Academic Press.

Wegener, D. T., Petty, R. E., & Klein, D. J. (1994). Effects of mood on high elaboration attitude change: The mediating role of likelihood judgments. *European Journal of Social Psychology, 24*, 25–43.

Wegener, D. T., Petty, R. E., Smoak, N. D., & Fabrigar, L. R. (2004). Multiple routes to resisting attitude change. In E. S. Knowles & J. A. Linn (Eds.), *Resistance and persuasion* (pp. 13–38). Mahwah, NJ: Erlbaum.

Wells, G. L., & Petty, R. E. (1980). The effects of overt head movements on persuasion: Compatibility and incompatibility of responses. *Basic and Applied Social Psychology, 1*, 219–230.

Wheeler, S. C., DeMarree, K. G., & Petty, R. E. (2007). Understanding the role of the self in prime-to-behavior effects: The active self account. *Personality and Social Psychology Review, 11*, 234–261.

Whitfield, M., & Jordan, C. H. (2009). Mutual influences of explicit and implicit attitudes. *Journal of Experimental Social Psychology, 45*, 748–759.

Wicker, A. W. (1969). Attitudes versus actions: The Relationship of verbal and overt behavioral responses to attitude objects. *Journal of Social Issues, 25*, 41–78.

Wicker, A. W. (1971). An examination of the "other-variables" explanation of attitude-behavior inconsistency. *Journal of Personality and Social Psychology, 19*, 18–30.

Williams, L. E., & Bargh, J. A. (2008). Experiencing physical warmth promotes interpersonal warmth. *Science, 322*(5901), 606–607.

Winter, L., & Uleman, J. S. (1984). When are social judgments made? Evidence for the spontaneousness of trait inferences. *Journal of Personality and Social Psychology, 47*, 237–252.

Wittenbrink, B., Judd, C. M., & Park, B. (1997). Evidence for racial prejudice at the implicit level and its relationship with questionnaire measures. *Journal of Personality and Social Psychology, 72*, 262–274.

Wood, W. (1982). Retrieval of attitude-relevant information from memory: Effects on susceptibility to persuasion and on intrinsic motivation. *Journal of Personality and Social Psychology, 42*, 798–810.

Wyer, R. S., Jr. (1974). *Cognitive organization and change: An information-processing approach.* Hillsdale, NJ: Erlbaum.

Yzerbyt, V. Y., Lories, G., & Dardenne, B. (1998). *Metacognition: Cognitive and social dimensions.* Thousand Oaks, CA: Sage.

Zajonc, R. B. (1968). Attitudinal effects of mere exposure. *Journal of Personality and Social Psychology Monograph Supplements, 9*, 1–27.

Zanna, M. P., & Cooper, J. (1974). Dissonance and the pill: An attribution approach to studying the arousal properties of dissonance. *Journal of Personality and Social Psychology, 29*, 703–709.

Zanna, M. P., Fazio, R. H., & Ross, M. (1994). The persistence of persuasion. In R. C. Schank & E. Langer (Eds.), *Beliefs, reasoning, and decision making: Psychologic in honor of Bob Abelson* (pp. 347–362). Hillsdale, NJ: Erlbaum.

PART 2

Mental Representation and Information Processing

The Role of Visual Imagery in Social Cognition

Lisa K. Libby *and* Richard P. Eibach

Abstract

This chapter outlines the history of theoretical beliefs about mental imagery's status as a representational tool and reviews evidence supporting the current predominant view, focusing on visual imagery's relevance to social cognition. According to the current predominant view, visual imagery is a legitimate form of mental representation that functions specifically in representing concrete, perceptual information. However, emerging evidence suggests imagery may also have the capacity to represent abstract information. The authors propose potential revisions to the current predominant view, incorporating a function of imagery in the process of abstraction. The chapter explores how variation in imagery ability and use, as well as perceptual qualities of images (e.g., vividness, visual perspective), correspond with variation in social information processing. Evidence illuminates the function of visual imagery in a wide range of social cognitive processes including attribution, impression formation, memory, emotion, mental simulation, persuasion, communication, and judgment and decision making. And, findings demonstrate implications for understanding social phenomena such as addiction, false memories, supernatural belief, and cultural differences.

Key Words: visual imagery, mental simulation, mental representation, social cognition, vividness, visual perspective, abstraction

"The soul never thinks without an image."—Aristotle

The idea that mental imagery serves a representational function can be traced back at least as far as the ancient Greeks. People can experience mental imagery in all sensory modalities. In this chapter, we focus on mental imagery in the visual modality, the most common modality in which people report experiencing mental imagery in their everyday lives (Kosslyn, Seger, Pani, & Hillger, 1990). Psychologists' views on the role of imagery in cognition have varied widely over the years, ranging from positions like Aristotle's—that imagery is the basis for all thought—to the other extreme—that images are irrelevant to cognition—and occupying various points in between. We begin with a brief overview of the history of views on imagery in psychology. We then elaborate on the

current predominant view, focusing on the evidence as it relates to social cognition. We end by presenting recent findings that pose a potential challenge to this view and speculate about possible revisions.

What Is Imagery?

Before starting out, it will be important to clarify exactly what we mean when we use the term *imagery* in this chapter. Informally, the term can be understood to refer to "pictures in the mind." For a more technical definition, we turn to Stephen Kosslyn and his colleagues, who have conducted some of the most influential psychological research on visual imagery. In the words of these experts:

A mental image occurs when a representation of the type created during the initial phases of perception is present but the stimulus is not actually being perceived; such representations preserve the perceptible properties of the stimulus and ultimately give rise to the subjective experience of perception. (Kosslyn, Thompson, & Ganis, 2006, p. 4)

This definition highlights two features of mental imagery that are essential to understanding and evaluating its role in cognition. First, imagery is fundamentally tied to sensory modalities. In the case of visual imagery, this means that the brain recruits the visual system to form and maintain mental images. Second, images are characterized by a perceptual correspondence with objects and events they represent. These features of imagery distinguish it from other forms of representation that are proposed to be amodal—not tied to any particular sensory system—and do not bear any necessary resemblance to the objects or events they represent. For example, an image that represents the concept of "dog" has the visual properties one would perceive if encountering an actual dog (i.e., the image looks like a dog), whereas this is not true of a set of propositional statements or semantic associations that represent the concept of "dog" amodally.

A central question when it comes to evaluating the role of imagery[1] in cognition is whether imagery is functional, in the sense that it is involved in carrying out cognitive processes, or whether it is epiphenomenal, in the sense that it is a by-product that serves no purpose in and of itself. The field has gone back and forth on this question over time, and the details of this history are an interesting topic in their own right (e.g., see Kosslyn, 1980; Kosslyn et al., 2006; Tye, 2000). For the purposes of this chapter, it is most important just to hit the highlights, and it is these that we outline next.

A Brief History of Imagery

Imagery was a central topic of study in the early days of psychology. This was the time when introspection was the dominant tool for investigation, and upon introspection, images can be quite prominent in mind. Wilhelm Wundt found them so prominent, in fact, that he came to a conclusion that echoed Aristotle's: Images were the basis for all thought (Wundt, 1894). William James also deemed imagery to be a legitimate cognitive tool, although his introspections suggested a more circumscribed function: Images represent concrete objects, but words represent abstract concepts (James, 1890/1950). James was not the only one who failed to experience imagery associated with all thought,

and Wundt's position was challenged (e.g., Mayer & Orth, 1901; Marbe, 1901, as cited in Humphrey, 1951). Wundt countered this "imageless thought" critique with further introspective evidence, thus proving the futility of using this methodological tool as a basis for settling the debate.

The problems with introspectionism were not limited to the study of imagery, and behaviorism was a response to these problems. From the perspective of behaviorism, imagery was by definition irrelevant to understanding human psychology. According to John Watson, images were "sheer bunk" (1928, p. 76) and could be accounted for by subvocalizations that contained the information allegedly depicted in imagery. B. F. Skinner (1953) allowed that images might actually exist but argued that they were epiphenomenal and could be explained as conditioned behaviors. Although behaviorism avoided the difficulties of studying mental contents, such as imagery, it also was unable to account for aspects of human functioning that depended on them. Thus, the cognitive revolution was born, bringing new tools for studying internal representations, including imagery.

Using these tools, Allan Paivio (1969) found that words differed in the extent to which they evoked imagery and that those that evoked imagery were better recalled. Roger Shepard and Jaqueline Metzler (1971) showed that the time it took to determine whether two rotated geometric figures were the same or different corresponded linearly to the angle they needed to be rotated to make the comparison. Stephen Kosslyn and colleagues demonstrated that the time it took to shift attention from one part of an imaged object to another corresponded to the physical distance between those two points on the physical object itself (Kosslyn, 1973; Kosslyn, Ball, & Reiser, 1978). Although such findings provided compelling support for the status of imagery as a functional form of representation, it was possible to come up with explanations that accounted for them without relying on imagery, and Zenon Pylyshyn did just that (e.g., 1973). Known as "the imagery debate," the disagreement persisted for quite some time (see Tye, 2000). However, once again, methodological advances and theoretical shifts helped move the understanding of imagery forward. Neuroimaging techniques provided converging evidence that helped resolve the debate for many (Kosslyn et al., 2006; Reed, 2010). Currently, there seems to be a good amount of agreement across areas of psychology about the legitimacy of imagery and also about its limitations. We outline this current predominant view next, focusing on the implications for social cognition.

The Current Predominant View

It is now generally agreed that imagery is a legitimate representational tool. Images exist as representations that are generated within the visual system and are perceptually isomorphic with the objects and events they represent. In addition, it is now widely believed that images play a functional role in cognition. However, it is also widely believed that as a representational tool, imagery has limitations. The predominant view holds that imagery is not the only form of representation, and it works better for some kinds of information and tasks than for others. We believe that emerging evidence presents potential challenges to the predominant view about the limitations of imagery. However, before discussing potential revisions to the predominant view, we devote this section to reviewing the evidence that supports it, first outlining evidence to support claims about the legitimacy of imagery and then outlining evidence to support claims about the limitations of imagery.

Imagery Is Legitimate

One of the challenges in studying imagery is that images cannot be directly observed by anyone but the person having them. Luckily, we have many more methodological tools at our disposal than the introspectionists did. Although we still can't look into people's minds and see the images they report, we can look into their brains and see the patterns that are activated. Given the topographical nature of coding in areas of primary visual cortex, this can come pretty close to directly observing mental images. For example, in one experiment, participants visualized a geometric figure either in a vertical or a horizontal orientation. Corresponding differences in activation were observed in an area of primary visual cortex that codes the vertical or horizontal orientation of externally observed objects. In fact, the patterns of activation in this area when participants visualized the figure were nearly identical to those that appeared when participants viewed external images of the visualized figure (Klein, Dubois, Mangin, Kherif, Flandin, Polin, et al., 2004). Other investigations have used more complex social objects and have found analogous effects. For example, there are areas of the brain that differentially activate in response to viewing faces versus places. These same areas are also differentially activated when people visually imagine faces versus places (O'Craven & Kanwisher, 2000). Whether or not these areas are necessarily unique to faces versus places (cf. Gauthier, Skudlarski, Gore, & Anderson, 2000), the result does support the idea that the same areas involved in visual perception are involved in visual mental imagery.

Some elegantly simple reaction-time experiments provide converging evidence that these images are perceptually similar to actual objects they represent. Participants were presented with sentences describing events (e.g., *The ranger saw an eagle in the sky.*); after each sentence, an outline of an object appeared, and participants had to indicate whether or not the object was part of the event in the sentence. On trials in which the object had appeared, the outline either matched the shape implied by the sentence (e.g., eagle with wings outstretched) or mismatched that shape (e.g., eagle with wings folded). Participants were quicker to respond when the outline matched, suggesting not only that had they formed images of the events while reading the sentences but also that the perceptual features of the images matched the perceptual features of the events described (Zwaan, Stanfield, & Yaxley, 2002). Similar results were obtained in experiments in which participants read sentences involving objects that would have appeared at varying levels of resolution (e.g., seeing a moose through foggy vs. clear goggles) and then responded to photographs of those objects that varied in their resolution. Participants were quicker to respond when the resolution of the photograph matched the implied resolution in the sentence than when it did not (Yaxley & Zwaan, 2007).

Together, neuroimaging and behavioral data provide compelling evidence that imagery is "real": images perceptually resemble the objects they represent, and these images are based in the same brain system as visual perception. However, this sort of evidence does not itself establish the status of imagery as a representational tool. It could be that the visual system is indeed used to create pictures in the mind, but that these pictures are purely epiphenomenal. Indeed, people report that the majority of their everyday experiences of imagery occur spontaneously and seem to serve no identifiable purpose (Kosslyn et al., 1990). On the other hand, people also report sometimes using imagery deliberately to solve problems and to regulate emotion and motivation (Kosslyn et al., 1990). Although individuals do have privileged access to the subjective qualities of their own mental images, self-reports about the processes by which cognition occurs are unreliable (e.g., Nisbett & Wilson, 1977). Thus, to establish the status of imagery as a functional tool, it is crucial to review evidence from experiments that objectively assess its role in cognitive processes.

The Functional Role of Imagery Is Legitimate

One approach to studying the functional role of imagery is to test the effect of impairments of the visual system. If images created by the visual system play a functional role in cognition, then impairments of the visual system should impair performance on tasks proposed to rely on imagery. Another approach to studying the functional role of imagery is to test the effect of variation in the perceptual qualities of images. If images serve a representational function, then variation in the perceptual qualities of those images should correspond with variation in information represented, and this should have consequences for responses made on the basis of those images. We will review evidence from each approach in turn. Taken together, the evidence provides strong support for the claim that not only are visual images "real" but also that they are used to carry out cognitive processes, thus establishing imagery as a legitimate representational tool.

VARIATION IN ABILITY TO USE THE VISUAL SYSTEM

Impairments to the visual system produce corresponding impairments on tasks proposed to rely on visual imagery. Some evidence for this comes from studies of individuals with physical impairments to the visual system. For example, one case study followed a patient who underwent a medically necessary procedure to remove one side of her occipital lobe, thus reducing by half the width of the brain area used to topographically represent objects in visual space. Comparison of the horizontal and vertical span of the patient's mental images before and after the procedure revealed that the horizontal span in particular was reduced by roughly half, corresponding to the brain area removed (Farah, Soso, & Dasheiff, 1992). Other research has investigated congenitally blind individuals. It is possible to represent spatial relations without visual imagery, but fundamentally visual aspects of imagery should not be possible without the visual system and thus should not be observed in blind individuals. Indeed, although blind individuals can accurately perform tasks such as reporting on which letters of the alphabet have any curved lines (e.g., by simulating the motion of writing), blind individuals show impaired performance on tasks that require an

understanding of a fundamentally visual property of the way objects appear in space—specifically, that objects appear smaller at greater physical distances (Arditi, Holtzman, & Kosslyn, 1988). Use of the visual system can also be manipulated temporarily by means of transcranial magnetic stimulation. Introducing a magnetic field over the area of the head where visual cortex is located causes impairments in visual perception and corresponding impairments on performance in tasks proposed to rely on imagery (Kosslyn, Pascual-Leone, Felician, Camposano, Keenan, Thompson, et al., 1999).

Another way to interfere with the use of the visual system for creating imagery is by introducing a competing visual task. If visual processing resources are tied up in processing externally generated information, they should be less available to form mental images, and thus performance that relies on them should be compromised. The implications for social cognition are demonstrated in an experiment on impression formation (Claypool & Carlston, 2002). Participants formed impressions about individuals on the basis of a photograph and verbal description. The photographs were either attractive or unattractive, and the descriptions were either positive or negative. After forming an impression, participants engaged in a distractor task that either involved the use of the visual system or did not. Then, they were asked to rate the attractiveness of the individuals from the photographs. The visual distractor task, but not the control distractor task, reduced the effect of the photographs on judgments, suggesting that the visual system was needed to incorporate the visual information into the evaluation of the individual. Thus, regardless of whether the visual system is physically or behaviorally impaired, permanently or temporarily, corresponding impairments emerge in performance on tasks proposed to rely on imagery. This supports the idea that images created by the visual system play a functional role in cognition.

VARIATION IN THE PERCEPTUAL QUALITIES OF IMAGES

Further evidence for the functional value of imagery comes from experiments that investigate variation in perceptual qualities of images. If images serve a representational function, variation in their perceptual qualities should correspond with variation in responses made on the basis of those images. Specifically, there should be evidence both that variation in the perceptual qualities of images causes corresponding variation in responses and that people employ variation in perceptual qualities of images in the service of achieving corresponding effects on their responses. We review both sorts of evidence with regard to two sorts of variation in perceptual qualities: vividness and visual perspective.

Vividness

Images can vary in how vividly they depict the perceptual properties of objects and events. If this depictive aspect of imagery is functional, then the more clearly the image depicts the object or event, the better that image should function as a cognitive tool. In support of this logic, research from clinical psychology suggests that reduced image vividness is at least partly responsible for effects like the one we described earlier in which a competing visual task reduces the effectiveness of imagery. For example, engaging in a competing visual task reduces the vividness of traumatic images in individuals with post-traumatic stress disorder, and with this reduction in vividness comes a reduction in emotive response (Andrade, Kavanagh, & Baddeley, 1997).

Other research has applied a similar methodology to explore the implications for understanding and treating addiction. It has been proposed that when people crave addictive substances, they form images of those substances that further intensify the craving, and thereby promote the addictive behavior (Kavanagh, Andrade, & May, 2005). Support for this hypothesis comes from research that tested the effect of image vividness on food cravings, which contribute to compulsive eating and binging. Engaging in a competing visual task reduces vividness of food imagery and thereby reduces cravings (Kemps, Tiggemann, & Hart, 2005; Kemps, Tiggemann, Woods, and Soekov, 2004; McClelland, Kemps, & Tiggemann, 2006). Notably, the same reduction in vividness and cravings does not occur when the competing task uses verbal processing (Kemps et al., 2005). Thus, reducing the vividness of imagery influences emotion regulation in the case of trauma, and self-regulation in the case of food cravings.

Converging evidence that variation in the vividness of images produces changes in responses based on those images comes from research that investigates the effect of individual differences in the ability to create vivid images. This research uses a self-report questionnaire (e.g., Marks, 1973) that asks respondents to form a variety of different visual images and report how vivid those images are. On the basis of these responses, individuals can be classified as more or less vivid imagers, and this classification is then compared with performance on tasks proposed to rely on imagery. One line of work used this approach to demonstrate consequences of image vividness for memory of social information. If images serve to represent information in memory, then when people form images, vivid imagers should remember more information. Indeed, when participants were instructed to recall information from a video interview, vivid imagers correctly recalled more information than did nonvivid imagers. This result was not due to vivid imagers just being better at memory in general; the memory advantage for vivid imagers emerged only when participants were asked to recall information from a video interview, not from an audio interview (Swann & Miller, 1982). In other words, when there was something to form a visual image of, vivid imagers performed better because they could form clearer images, and these images functioned to aid their memory.

Not only does variation in the vividness of imagery have demonstrable psychological effects, but also people attempt to deliberately cultivate more vivid imagery to achieve certain effects. For example, in one well-publicized case, a man who was accused of ritual satanic abuse of his children tried to vividly visualize the crimes he was accused of in an attempt to retrieve possibly repressed memories of these events (Wright, 1994). Through this process, he came to believe in and confess to crimes that he initially denied. However, evidence suggests that his memories of these crimes may have been the result of his vividly visualizing them rather than his actually committing them. An investigator who was suspicious of the man's confessions made deliberately false accusations against him to test the effect on the man's later confessions. The investigator's suspicions were confirmed when the man came to confess to these fictitious crimes.

Further evidence consistent with the idea that these false confessions were a result of the man's vivid visualizations comes from empirical research documenting that vividly visualizing fictitious autobiographical events can lead to the formation of false memories (Hyman & Pentland, 1996). These results are troubling because guided imagery is a technique that many therapists report using to recover repressed memories of childhood abuse (Poole, Lindsay, Memon, & Bull, 1995). Vivid mental imagery is also deliberately cultivated in the religious rituals of many cultures. For example, novice shaman are trained in techniques to increase the vividness of their visual imagery of the supernatural, and this appears to have the intended effect of heightening their feelings of spiritual awareness

(Noll, 1985). Recently, Luhrmann and Morgain (2012) studied cultural training in imagery techniques using an experimental design and found that participants who were randomly assigned to undergo intensive training in an imagery-based prayer technique commonly practiced within Evangelical Christian communities subsequently reported experiencing stronger sensory experiences of contact and dialogue with God compared to a control group who were trained in a non-imagery based prayer technique.

Visual Perspective

When it comes to social cognition, actions and events are an important source of information, and people often picture actions and events in their mind's eye when they think about them (Moulton & Kosslyn, 2009). Social events can be pictured from various vantage points. To the extent that images play a functional role in representing and processing information about social events, variation in visual perspective should correspond with variation in the information that is represented and have corresponding consequences for responses made on the basis of that information. Here we focus on the use of visual perspective in imagery to represent two aspects of events—motion and content—and we highlight implications for comprehension, memory, emotion, judgment, and culture.

Representing Direction of Motion

Motion is a central aspect of many events, ranging in significance from crossing the road to walking down the aisle. When motion occurs, it is possible to witness that motion as movement away from a vantage point or as movement towards a vantage point. There are subtle variations in language that implicitly code which reference point is intended (Fillmore, 1966). For example, when describing a wedding, the officiant would say that the bride "came" down the aisle (i.e., motion toward the self), whereas the tardy guest who made it into the back of the church just as the wedding march began would say that the bride "went" down the aisle (i.e., motion away from the self). Research on event comprehension suggests that people also use imagery—specifically, the visual perspective of that imagery—to represent this aspect of motion, and, further, that this has consequences for emotion.

An early suggestion that people use visual perspective in imagery to represent direction of motion in social events came from experiments that measured comprehension time for pairs of sentences in which the first sentence specified a reference location (e.g., "Mary was reading a book in her room," implies a reference point inside Mary's room) and the second sentence described motion relative to that location (e.g., a person walking into Mary's room) (Black, Turner, & Bower, 1979). The key manipulation involved the verb used to describe the motion in the second sentence—it either implied the same reference point as was specified in the initial sentence (e.g., "John came in," implies that the action is perceived from a reference point inside Mary's room, as motion toward that point) or implied a shift in reference point (e.g., "John went in," implies that the action is perceived from a reference point located somewhere outside Mary's room, as movement away from that point going into the room). Participants took longer to comprehend the information when the verb implied a shift in reference point location than when it did not. This result is consistent with the idea that people had been forming images of the event as a mode of comprehension: creating a new image from a different reference point perspective should have taken longer than maintaining an image from the reference point perspective already established.

Although reference point perspectives from which an event is perceived can be specified in event descriptions, people also vary in the reference points they habitually tend to adopt, as a function of their tendency to understand events from others' perspectives. Those from Eastern cultures tend to understand events from others' perspectives more than those from Western cultures do, and evidence is consistent with the idea that imagery plays a role in supporting this cultural difference (Cohen, Hoshino-Browne, & Leung, 2007). For example, Asian American participants were quicker to comprehend sentences in a story about a friend when the language implied the friend's perspective as the reference point from which action was perceived (e.g., the teacher "came" toward the friend) than when it did not (e.g., the teacher "went" towards the friend), whereas European American participants showed no such facilitation (Cohen et al., 2007).

These differences in comprehension time as a function of reference point shifts are consistent with the idea that people use imagery to code the direction of motion in social events. Of course, it is also possible that processing was disrupted by a nonconventional use of language, rather than use of images. Further evidence for the imagery interpretation comes from research documenting differences in speed of comprehension based on past experience with seeing actions from the implied perspective (Jiang & Wyer, 2009). For example, men have more experience seeing someone walk into a men's restroom than women do; women have more experience seeing someone walk into a women's restroom than men do. People should be quicker to construct an image of a scene when it has been more frequently observed, so if people use imagery as a representational tool, people should be quicker to comprehend actions described with reference points that match their experience than with reference points that don't. Indeed, this is the case. Further, the effect is not limited to experiences that vary by gender—for example, college students of both genders were quicker to comprehend "Frank went into the prison" than "Frank came into the prison," consistent with their lack of experience viewing events from inside a prison—and the effect is not dependent on familiarity with the events (apart from the perspective from which they are most often observed). However, the effect is moderated by individual differences in chronic tendencies to use imagery. Some people tend to think with images more than others do (Childers, Houston, & Heckler, 1985), and it was only among those who tended to think in images that the past experience with seeing actions from specified reference points influenced comprehension (Jiang & Wyer, 2009). This is exactly what should happen if the effect depends on the use of imagery as a functional tool.

Converging evidence that this variation in imagery is serving a functional purpose in the processing of information, rather than simply being an epiphenomenon, comes from a follow-up study that measured emotional responses to events depending on the implied direction of motion in language. The emotion-evoking potential of some events varies depending on the physical location with which one witnesses them. For example, being inside a bank that is being robbed is more frightening than being outside of it. If images have a functional impact on the meaning that is represented, then emotional responses to events should vary depending on the implied reference point of motion, and this should be true only to the extent that people use imagery to represent the event. Indeed, "the robber came into the bank" produces a greater emotional response than "the robber went into the bank," but only among people who tend to think in terms of images (Jiang & Wyer, 2009). Thus, implied perspective in language influenced the emotional impact of events as a result of variation in a feature of images—their perspective. Together with the results of the comprehension studies, these findings show that people

shift perspective in imagery according to the direction of motion implied and that this variation is not epiphenomenal; it has consequences for event comprehension and emotional response.

Representing the Visual and Psychological Content of Events

In addition to occupying different positions relative to motion in a scene, different viewpoints also afford access to different visual details in a scene. For example, in a game of poker, each player's viewpoint affords information about the cards in her own hands, but not the cards in the other players' hands (if everyone is playing fairly!). Different viewpoints also tend to be associated with access to different types of information. For example, in that game of poker, each player's viewpoint is associated with direct access to her own thoughts, feelings, and bodily sensations but not those of the other players, and each player's viewpoint affords her access to others' external appearance but not her own. To the extent that imagery plays a functional role in cognition, the perspective people use to picture a scene should influence the details incorporated into their representation of it, and conversely people should shift perspective according to the details they intend to incorporate. We review evidence for such effects and highlight consequences for memory, emotion, judgment, and culture.

In an early investigation (Abelson, 1975), participants listened to a story about a character walking down a street lined with buildings. Participants had been told to visualize the events from the perspective of the character or from the perspective of an observer on a hotel balcony, or they were given no visualization instructions at all. Afterward, they completed a surprise memory test for details in the story. On the cued-recall portion of the test, balcony-observer participants had better memory than did actor participants for "far visual details," features that were better viewed from the balcony vantage point (e.g., a sign above a bank building). Actor participants had better memory than did balcony-observer participants for details about the physical sensations the character experienced (e.g., sore arm, drinking hot coffee). In each of these categories, no-visualization participants tended to score similarly to participants in the "wrong" perspective condition—that is, relatively poorly. Supporting the idea that these effects were the result of visual images, the differences between the perspective conditions were more pronounced among those with better visualization skills. Further, when asked to reproduce as much of the story as they could from memory, no-visualization participants recalled less overall than did participants in either of the visualization conditions, who did not differ in the amount recalled, although the content was again biased by perspective (Abelson, 1975). Other research replicated such effects of perspective-taking on memory when participants were instructed to visualize a scene from a character's perspective, but not when they were instructed to empathize with that character (Fiske, Taylor, Etcoff, & Laufer, 1979). This result provides converging evidence that the effects of visual perspective manipulations on memory for the content of events depend on visual imagery per se.

Just as people can form images of events they hear described in language, they can also form images of events they experienced in their own lives. And, given the reconstructive nature of memory, life events can be pictured from different perspectives as well: the *first-person* visual perspective that one occupied while the event was occurring or a *third-person* visual perspective that an observer would have had (Nigro & Neisser, 1983). The effect of visual perspective on the types of information recalled from one's own life events mirrors those observed in the experiments on memory for events described in stories. For example, in one experiment, participants completed a series of manual tasks (e.g., folding paper with gloved hands to match an abstract model, throwing a basketball through a hoop, molding clay) and then were taken to a different room where they were asked to recall as much as they could of what they had just done. All participants were instructed to visualize the events, but some were instructed to use a first-person perspective, and others were instructed to use a third-person perspective. First-person participants recalled more about their bodily sensations, affective reactions, and psychological states than third-person participants did. Third-person participants recalled more about their physical appearance and the spatial layout of the room than first-person participants did (McIsaac & Eich, 2002).

Investigations of memory for life events occurring spontaneously outside the lab, and at longer intervals, suggest a similar effect of imagery perspective on recall of emotions experienced during the event: people reported recalling more of their original emotion when using the first-person than the third-person perspective (although accuracy of these reports was not measured) (McIsaac & Eich, 2004; Robinson & Swanson, 1993). Experimental manipulations provide converging evidence that this effect reflects the representational function of imagery perspective. For example, people are especially likely to spontaneously adopt the first-person perspective to picture real life events when they are told to describe the feelings they experienced at the time, compared with when they are asked to describe the "concrete, objective circumstances" (Nigro & Neisser, 1983). This work provides evidence for the function of first-person imagery in representing details about one's own internal experiences; other work provides converging evidence for the function of third-person imagery in representing details about how one appears from an external vantage point.

One line of research investigates the attributional consequences of variations in perspective. The well-known tendency for observers to attribute greater responsibility to actors than actors themselves do may be in part because actors are more salient objects of attention from observers' point of view than from actors' (Jones & Nisbett, 1972). Consistent with this idea, research that uses video to manipulate actual visual perspective shows that people attribute more causal responsibility to the actor who was most visually salient from their experimentally assigned point of view (Storms, 1973; Taylor & Fiske, 1975). It turns out that visual perspective in mental imagery can have the same effect on attributions. For example, people were more likely to attribute their behavior in a social interaction to their personality traits when they visualized the interaction from the third-person perspective than when they visualized it from the first-person perspective (Frank & Gilovich, 1989).

Not only does the third-person perspective provide individuals access to information about how they appear from an external vantage point, but evidence also suggests that people may actively adopt the third-person perspective in imagery of past events when seeking out that very information. For example, people from Eastern cultural backgrounds are more likely than those from Western cultural backgrounds to adopt the third-person perspective when recalling situations in which they were the center of attention (Cohen & Gunz, 2002). This may be because Eastern cultures emphasize an interdependent self and thus encourage people to monitor how their behavior might be perceived by others in their social group. The third-person perspective could provide just this sort of information. Also, within Western culture women are more motivated than men are to monitor how they appear to others in mixed-sex recreational situations, and women are also more likely than men are to adopt the third-person perspective when recalling past events of that type (Huebner & Fredrickson, 1999).

The evidence reviewed thus far supports the conclusion that imagery is "real": the pictures that people report experiencing in their minds share many of the properties and are represented using much of the same machinery as is visual perception of external objects. Further, evidence supports the conclusion that imagery is not merely epiphenomenal: variation in use of the visual system corresponds with variation in the effect of visual information on judgment, and variation in the images people form corresponds to variation in what and how much people recall about events, how well they comprehend events, how they respond emotionally, and how they explain the causes of behavior. Cumulatively, these findings explain why it is widely believed that the functional role of imagery is legitimate. We also noted that it is widely believed that the functional role of imagery is limited. We turn to the evidence consistent with this conclusion next.

The Functional Role of Imagery Is Limited: Images Specialize in Representing Concrete, Perceptual Information

> No image could ever be adequate to the concept of a triangle in general. It would never attain that universality of the concept which renders it valid of all triangles, whether right-angled, obtuse-angled, or acute angled; it would always be limited to a part only of this sphere. (Kant, 1781/1965, p. 182)

Kant argued that the representational value of images is limited to the depiction of perceptual information. Because abstract ideas generalize beyond perceptual features, images should not be adequate to represent abstract ideas. Because perceptual features tend to be what define concrete, specific instances as such, imagery should be well suited for representing concrete ideas and specific events. James (1890/1950) came to a similar conclusion, and classic work in cognitive psychology suggests empirical support: Concrete nouns are better remembered than are abstract nouns because only concrete nouns evoke imagery, and this facilitates memory (Paivio, 1969). On the basis of his work, Paivio (1971; 1986) proposed the dual-coding hypothesis: that information can be represented in two separate modes—one based on imagery and the other based on abstract meaning. The currently predominant view of imagery in cognitive psychology and social cognition

reflects a similar assumption—that the brain uses amodal forms of representation, in addition to imagery. The current predominant view also holds that the functional value of imagery has to do with the representation of concrete information. There is a good deal of evidence that appears consistent with these conclusions, both from cognitive psychology and social cognition, as we will review next. However, to foreshadow where we will go after that, we believe that these tenets of the predominant view are the ones most likely to change in light of emerging evidence, and we will conclude the chapter with a discussion of potential revisions.

EVIDENCE FROM COGNITIVE PSYCHOLOGY

As did Paivio's model, currently dominant models of imagery in cognitive psychology make the assumption that the brain uses dual or multiple systems of representation: sensory forms (e.g., visual imagery) and amodal forms (Kosslyn et al., 2006; Reed, 2010). By these accounts, the function of imagery stems from the fact that it makes perceptual information about objects and events immediately apparent, and thus the function of imagery should be analogous to the function of vision (Kosslyn, 1995).

One function of vision is to track moving objects (e.g., for the purpose of navigation and action control). Correspondingly, evidence mentioned earlier shows that imagery is also used to track motion, as when comprehending action in events (Black et al., 1979; Cohen et al., 2007; Jiang & Wyer, 2009). Imagery ability has also been shown to predict performance at sports that rely on precise planning of motion through space (e.g., MacIntyre, Moran, & Jennings, 2002).

A second function of vision is to identify the features and orientation of objects. Correspondingly, evidence mentioned earlier shows that imagery is used to represent the features and orientation of objects (Klein et al., 2004; Yaxley & Zwaan, 2007; Zwaan et al., 2002). Kosslyn (1995) argues that people are especially likely to use imagery to access information about perceptual features of objects when those features have not previously been explicitly considered or labeled and thus cannot be inferred based on semantic knowledge (e.g., People tend to report using imagery to respond to the question, "Which is darker green, a Christmas tree or a pea?"). When people do have semantic knowledge, they report relying on that instead.

Results from research on eyewitness identification are consistent with Kosslyn's claim (Schooler & Engstler-Schooler, 1990). Face perception typically operates on the basis of perceptual gestalt, which is not well captured in language (Fallshore & Schooler, 1995). And, instructing people to verbally rehearse the features of faces reduces eyewitness identification accuracy relative to instructing them to rehearse mental images or providing no instructions at all, which produce equivalent levels of accuracy (Schooler & Engstler-Schooler, 1990). Thus, in a domain where people do not typically have semantic knowledge because perception relies on a perceptual gestalt, they tend to use a form of representation—imagery—that captures the appearance of the gestalt directly. However, inducing people to "translate" the perceptual information into semantic knowledge leads them to rely on that instead, reducing their accuracy because perceptual gestalt is not well captured in language. This result, along with the fact that accuracy is equivalent in the imagery and no-instruction conditions, supports the idea that imagery functions to provide direct access to perceptual information.

Other research suggests that, as a result of highlighting perceptual features, imagery promotes a concrete understanding of objects and ideas. Participants received instructions to study a list of animal names either by picturing each animal or by repeating the names verbally. Later, participants were asked to provide associations to each animal name. Those who had used visual imagery to study the animals were more likely to provide associations that related to physical features of the animals (e.g., dog → brown), whereas those who had used verbal processing were more likely to provide associations based on category membership (e.g., dog → animal) (Aylwin, 1977). Picturing the object leads people to understand its verbal label in terms of the specific instance that was visually represented, whereas thinking about the verbal label itself leads people to understand it in terms of its abstract meaning in relation to conceptual structures. Thus, changing the format of the representation appeared to change the stimulus itself, defining it either as a specific instance or as representative of a category.

Support for the idea that it is the visual component of imagery that is responsible for promoting a concrete construal of the stimulus comes from research that manipulated whether stimulus objects were presented using verbal labels or line drawings. Concrete construals of stimuli are linked to psychological closeness (e.g., temporally, socially; Trope & Liberman, 2010), and a series of experiments showed that people interpret information as closer on a variety of dimensions (e.g., temporal, cultural)

when it is conveyed in pictures than in words (Amit, Algom, Trope, & Liberman, 2009).

EVIDENCE FROM SOCIAL COGNITION

To the extent that models of social cognition explicitly consider the role of imagery, they tend to adopt the same basic assumptions as the cognitive models do. First, these models assume that the brain uses amodal forms of representation in addition to imagery. And, second, these models assume that as a result of depicting perceptual features of objects and events, imagery functions in representing and reasoning about specific, concrete instances rather than representing and reasoning about abstract concepts or semantic knowledge (Carlston, 1994; Wyer, 2004; Wyer & Radvansky, 1999). For example, according to Wyer and Radvansky (1999), when comprehending a statement, people first represent it in terms of its semantic meaning and then only if the information pertains to a temporally and situationally constrained instance do they construct a mental simulation involving imagery. Thus, people would use imagery to represent the statement, "the man bought a car" but not to represent "the man owns a car." Earlier, we described experiments in which participants used imagery in the process of representing and comprehending social information presented in language (Black et al., 1979; Jiang & Wyer, 2009; Zwaan et al., 2002). The information tended to pertain to specific events (e.g., "The ranger saw the eagle in the sky" or "John went into Mary's room"), and this may have been crucial in producing the effects that were observed.

Evidence from a variety of domains is consistent with the idea that imagery specializes in the processing of information about specific instances rather than abstract facts. We describe findings that illustrate implications for persuasion, emotion, and judgment and decision making.

Persuasion

Research on persuasion is consistent with the idea that people are more likely to experience imagery when processing information about specific instances than about abstract facts. And, as should be the case if this selective use of imagery is functional, imagery appears to contribute to the persuasive power of appeals that rely on narratives about specific instances, but not appeals that rely on abstract facts. According to the transportation-imagery model of narrative persuasion, visual imagery evoked by narratives of specific events promotes transportation—a state in which the reader becomes absorbed in the story and leaves the real world behind (Green & Brock, 2002). And, when people are more transported into a narrative, they are more likely to change their attitudes to fit the themes of the narrative (Green & Brock, 2000). For example, after reading a story about a young child who was brutally stabbed to death in a mall parking lot by a psychiatric patient, participants who reported high levels of transportation into the story, imaging it vividly, later estimated that violence was more common and the world was less just compared with participants who reported low levels of transportation.

Further evidence that imagery enhances the persuasiveness of narratives of specific events comes from a study in which researchers measured individual differences in the vividness of visual imagery and then assigned participants to view one of two videotapes of a media story about a UFO sighting (Sparks, Sparks, & Gray, 1995). One version was the original news story containing images of the alleged UFO. The other version was the same news story with the UFO images edited out. When participants saw the version containing images, high- and low-vivid imagers did not differ in their ratings of the believability of the story or their belief in UFOs. However, when participants saw the version with the images edited out, high-vivid imagers rated the story as more believable and reported more belief in UFOs than did low-vivid imagers. These results suggest that when no images of the UFO were shown to participants, the high-vivid imagers generated their own mental imagery of UFOs and thereby found the story more persuasive. Thus, vivid imagery evoked by narratives of specific events appears to enhance the effectiveness of those narratives in shaping people's attitudes.

Other evidence suggests that whereas imagery contributes to the persuasion process as it occurs in response to narratives of specific events, imagery does not contribute to the persuasion process as it occurs in response to abstract facts (Adaval & Wyer 1998; Petrova & Cialdini, 2005). For example, imagery instructions and the presentation of supporting photographs strengthened the persuasive power of a travel advertisement that followed a narrative format, leading to a significant increase in persuasion when both were included. This did not occur when the advertisement was structured in a factual format (Adaval & Wyer 1998). Conversely, whereas attitude change in response to appeals based on abstract facts is reliably correlated with individual differences in need for cognition, attitude change in response to imagery evoked by narratives of specific events is not (Green & Brock, 2000).

Converging evidence that narrative persuasion reflects the use of visual imagery per se comes from an experiment that manipulated participants' ability to use the visual system in processing information from radio advertisements (Bolls & Muehling, 2007). These advertisements were either high or low in imageability, as determined by pilot test ratings. Inspecting the content of the advertisements reveals that highly imageable ads tended to use a narrative format (e.g., a story in which a woman's business presentation was saved by AT&T fax service), whereas low-imageable ads consisted of appeals based on factual information (e.g., dexterity is needed to button the fly of Levi's jeans). While listening to the advertisements, some participants were assigned to engage in a competing visual task, and others were not. Later evaluation of the products in the advertisements revealed that the visual task reduced effectiveness of high-imagery radio advertisements but had no effect on the effectiveness of low-imagery advertisements. These results are consistent with the idea that the effectiveness of the narrative advertisements depended on the visual system to produce imagery, whereas the effectiveness of the factual advertisements did not. Narratives depict a specific, concrete instance, whereas abstract facts do not. Thus, the evidence that people use imagery when processing narratives in particular, along with the evidence that imagery contributes to the persuasive impact of narrative appeals in particular, is consistent with the idea that imagery specializes in representing concrete information.

Emotion

Other research has investigated the effect of imagery on emotion, suggesting that imagery enhances emotions in part because it focuses people on the concrete features of an emotionally charged event. In a series of experiments, participants listened to emotional scenarios and were instructed either to visualize them or to focus on the verbal meaning. Imagery increased the emotional impact of the scenarios, increasing negative feelings in response to negative scenarios (Holmes & Mathews, 2005) and increasing positive feelings in response to positive scenarios (Holmes, Mathews, Dalgleish, & Mackintosh, 2006). Analysis of the subjective interpretations of scenarios when they were imaged versus processed verbally supports the idea that imagery produced a greater emotional response by leading people to think about the scenarios in more concrete and specific terms. Participants who were instructed to visualize the scenarios were more likely to think of the scenarios as involving the self, specific events, and specific emotions and sensations, whereas participants who were instructed to verbally process the scenarios were more likely to call on generic semantic knowledge with less personal and emotional impact (Holmes, Mathews, Mackintosh, & Dalgleish, 2008).

Judgment and Decision Making

Research in judgment and decision making is also consistent with the idea that people process information more concretely when they use images rather than words. According to some dual-process models, judgments are the product of an intuitive system that is automatic, fast, capable of parallel processing, associative, holistic, and affective; and of a rational system that is intentional, slow, reliant on serial processing, rule based, analytic, and relatively cold (Epstein, 1994; Kahneman & Frederick, 2002). These models propose that the intuitive system operates primarily on concrete, imagistic representations (Epstein & Pacini, 2000–2001; Kahneman & Frederick, 2002; Slovic, 2007). If images function to create such representations, then people should be more likely to engage in intuitive processing when information is represented using imagery than without using imagery.

One experiment that supports this hypothesis investigated the effects of imagery on the ratio bias. This bias is the preference to play a gambling game in which one selects items from a large bowl containing 10 winning items and 90 losing items over playing the same game with a small bowl containing 1 winning item and 9 losing items (Kirkpatrick & Epstein, 1992). People feel that they have a stronger chance of winning with the large bowl because the concrete number of winning items in the larger bowl is much larger than in the smaller bowl, even though the abstract ratio is the same. The ratio bias is believed to result from intuitive processing because most people acknowledge that the preference for the large bowl is illogical even as they feel intuitively compelled to prefer it (Kirkpatrick & Epstein, 1992). People exhibit the ratio bias when they are asked to choose between two real bowls, but not in a hypothetical version of the game in which the bowls and their contents are described in words (Kirkpatrick & Epstein, 1992). However, if in the hypothetical version participants are instructed to form visual images of the two bowls before expressing a preference between them, they exhibit the ratio bias about as much as participants who play the real version of the game (Epstein & Pacini, 2000–2001). Furthermore, in the hypothetical version with visualization instructions, participants who report poor visual imagery do not exhibit the ratio bias. Thus, the power of the visualization instructions to induce the bias appeared to rely on the formation of images.

Other findings are also consistent with the idea that representing information by means of imagery promotes intuitive processing. Implicit measures provide a window on intuitive processing by capturing responses in the relative absence of rational elaboration. If images evoke intuitive processing, then implicit measures should predict individuals' responses better when they represent information using images than without using images. Evidence supporting this logic comes from an experiment in which participants were led to believe that they would be interacting with another student in a situation that would offer the opportunity to express power and affiliation motives (Schultheiss & Brunstein, 1999). First, all participants completed implicit measures of their power and affiliation motives. Next, some participants were instructed to visualize the upcoming social situation, whereas others received no such visualization instructions. Then, all participants completed measures of their affective state and their commitment to success in the interaction. Participants' implicit motive scores were significant predictors of their affective responses and goal commitment in the imagery condition, but not in the control no-imagery condition. This suggests that mental imagery facilitates the engagement of intuitive processes (Schultheiss & Brunstein, 1999).

The idea that intuitive processing depends on imagery could explain some of the limitations and shortcomings of intuitive processes. For example, people's affective responses to a situation are remarkably insensitive to information about the scope of a problem (Hsee & Rottenstreich, 2004; Slovic, 2007) or the probability of various outcomes (Rottenstreich & Hsee, 2001). Scope and probability tend to be abstract features of events, and if the function of imagery is limited to representing concrete information, then imagery should not be an effective medium for encoding information about scope and probability. To the extent that people's intuitive emotional responses to events depend on the images those events evoke, these affective responses should be insensitive to information about scope and probability. So, people may be willing to pay approximately the same amount to save 2,000 migratory birds from an oil spill as they are to save 200,000 birds because the mental image that they form of an oil-drenched bird, and thus the feelings of outrage they experience, are likely to be the same regardless of the number of birds at risk (Kahneman & Frederick, 2002).

Although as devices for representing concrete, perceptual information images may tend not to include information about scope and probability, Slovic (2007) suggests that it is possible to use creative techniques to incorporate scope information into visual imagery and thereby enhance emotional responsiveness to scope information. To illustrate this point, Fetherstonhaugh, Slovic, Johnson, and Friedrich (1997) reviewed examples of activists who attempted to make the scope of social problems imageable through techniques like imagining the 170 million people executed in state-sanctioned killings during the 20th century as "a chain of bodies laid head to toe reaching from Honolulu, across the Pacific and the continental U.S., to Washington D.C. and then back again more than 16 times" (p. 284). Thus, by making abstract information about the scope of a problem more concrete and imageable, it may be possible to influence people to be more emotionally responsive to scope.

Considering the evidence we have reviewed in this section, it makes sense that there is widespread agreement that the function of imagery is limited to representing concrete, perceptual information. Results appear consistent with the idea that imagery specializes in processing the details of specific instances as opposed to general, abstract facts. And, results also appear consistent with the idea that this use of imagery has corresponding functional consequences, shaping processing to rely on specific, concrete instances. Further, these effects have been observed in a wide range of contexts: narrative persuasion, emotion, motivation, and intuitive judgment. If it sounds like we are hedging our bets in summarizing this evidence, it is because we are. Although we do not doubt the quality of the evidence, we do think that there is reason to hold off on using it to draw definitive conclusions about the representational limits of imagery. If the history of study on this topic has taught us anything, it's that another change in understanding could be right around the corner. In the next, and final, section of this chapter we review some findings that suggest it may be reasonable to reconsider the conclusion that the functional value of imagery is limited to representing concrete, perceptual information, and we speculate on various ways this conclusion might be modified.

Does the Current Predominant View Need Revision?

Although, as the previous section demonstrates, there is widespread agreement that the function of imagery is limited to representing concrete, perceptual information, there is some evidence that suggests the possibility that imagery could be a more flexible form of representation. We already mentioned speculation about creative ways that abstract information could be made concrete in order to incorporate it into imagery (Slovic, 2007). However, it may be possible not only to incorporate abstract information into concrete images but also to manipulate imagery to influence whether people process the same set of information concretely or abstractly. We begin this section by reviewing some of this evidence (for a more complete review, see Libby & Eibach, 2011a). The findings challenge the idea that the representational value of imagery is limited to its ability to depict concrete, perceptual information. The evidence suggests that simply varying a qualitative feature of event imagery—specifically, the visual perspective from which it is constructed—allows images to function either to represent the concrete features of an event or to represent its abstract meaning.

For example, in a series of experiments (Libby, Shaeffer, & Eibach, 2009), participants pictured themselves engaging in a variety of actions (e.g., locking a door, painting a room, voting). They either received instructions to form the images from their own first-person perspective or from an observer's third-person perspective. After they had formed the image of each action (e.g., voting), they were given two potential descriptions of it: both were accurate, but one was concrete, describing the specific, observable motions involved in the action (e.g., pulling a lever), and the other was abstract, framed in terms of traits, goals, or identities (e.g., influencing the election). Results revealed an increased preference for abstract descriptions when participants used the third-person as opposed to first-person perspective to picture themselves doing the actions. In another experiment, participants also pictured themselves engaging in the actions, but this time the actions were introduced either in concrete or abstract terms (e.g., pulling a lever while voting vs. influencing the election while voting), and participants were simply instructed to picture themselves doing the actions from whichever perspective they chose. Results revealed an increased tendency for participants to use the third-person perspective when the actions were described in abstract as opposed to concrete terms (Libby et al., 2009).

Other experiments replicated these findings using the same designs but manipulating and measuring visual perspective with photographs rather than mental imagery, thus supporting the idea that the findings are indeed a product of visual images. Earlier, we noted that different visual perspectives often afford access to different information in a scene; however, the relationship between perspective and abstraction does not depend on such differences. Evidence shows that the link between perspective and abstraction only became stronger when visual perspective was manipulated with photographs that varied visual perspective independent of the objects that were visible in the scene and the physical distance to the action (Figure 8.1; Libby et al., 2009, Shaeffer, Libby, & Eibach, 2013). Thus, the effect of perspective on action construal appears to be a function of the point of view on the action and not variation in which objects are depicted in the scene, nor the physical distance to the action. Together, these findings suggest the possibility that the representational value of imagery may not be limited to depicting concrete, perceptual details. Imagery—in this case, third-person imagery—seems to have the potential to represent more abstract interpretations.

Further evidence provides additional support for this idea and demonstrates the implications for social cognition. One set of studies shows that when people recall and imagine real-life events, thinking about those events in terms of the meaning in their lives more broadly, as opposed to thinking about the concrete details of what happened, makes people more likely to picture the events from the third-person perspective (Libby & Eibach, 2011b). Other research demonstrates that manipulating perspective influences the extent to which people think about actual life events abstractly in terms of the meaning in relation to their general self-knowledge, and this has consequences for self-judgment, emotion, motivation, and behavior (Libby, Eibach, & Gilovich, 2005; Libby, Valenti, Pfent, & Eibach, 2011; Libby, Shaeffer, Eibach, & Slemmer, 2007; Valenti, Libby, & Eibach, 2011; Vasquez & Buehler, 2007).

For example, using the third-person as opposed to first-person perspective to picture working on an upcoming assignment caused students to construe that assignment in terms of its relevance to their academic goals more broadly, and this caused them to be more motivated to complete the project (Vasquez & Buehler, 2007). A similar effect was observed on actual behavior in an experiment that manipulated the perspective that citizens used to picture themselves voting in an upcoming election. Using the third-person perspective caused citizens to be more likely to actually turn out to the polls (Libby et al., 2007).

Other work shows that the accessibility of self-knowledge is more biased by abstract self-beliefs when people picture events from the third-person as opposed to first-person perspective, and emotional responses to those events show the same pattern (Libby et al., 2011; Valenti et al., 2011). For example, picturing a past personal failure from the third-person as opposed to first-person perspective caused the accessibility of positive versus negative self-knowledge to be more biased in the direction of participants' trait self-esteem. Accordingly, using the third-person perspective to picture failure decreased feelings of shame among those with high self-esteem but increased feelings of shame among those with low self-esteem (Libby et al., 2011).

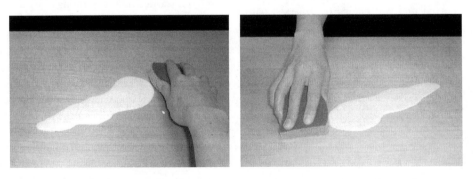

Figure 8.1 An example of the distance-controlled action photograph pairs used to measure and manipulate visual perspective in studies testing the link between perspective and abstraction (Libby et al., 2009; Shaeffer et al., 2013). These photographs depict the action of wiping up a spill. **Left:** First-person perspective. **Right:** Third-person perspective. From Libby et al. (2009), p. 511, published by American Psychological Association.

Earlier, we described research suggesting that people report reliving emotions more from the first-person perspective, and this effect is often interpreted to mean that first-person imagery is necessarily more emotional (e.g. McIsaac & Eich, 2004). However, the greater reliving reported with first-person imagery may be limited to emotions that reflect an immediate response to the concrete situation—for example, fear in response to being approached by an assailant. Other types of emotional responses—for example, shame in response to failure—reflect the event's abstract meaning when considered in the broader context of one's life. When this level of construal increases the emotional impact of an event—for example, in the case of low self-esteem individuals recalling failure—third-person imagery increases rather than decreases such emotional responses (Libby et al., 2011). This result supports the idea that third-person imagery represents events in terms of their meaning in relation to abstract self-knowledge structures.

Thus, evidence from experiments that measure the visual perspective that people spontaneously adopt in their imagery reveals that an effort to frame an event abstractly in terms of general self-knowledge, as opposed to concretely in terms of its specific details, causes people to use the third-person perspective. And, research that manipulates the perspective that participants adopt in their imagery reveals that using third-person, rather than first-person, imagery to picture an event causes people to understand that event abstractly in terms of their general self-knowledge rather than specific details. Together, these findings are consistent with the idea that imagery can function to represent abstract ideas, in addition to functioning to represent concrete information. Our purpose in presenting this evidence is not to provide definitive proof of this hypothesis, but rather to suggest that it is reasonable to consider the possibility. Next, we speculate on ways the currently predominant view of imagery's limitations could be revised to incorporate a functional role of images in representing abstract ideas, and we identify open questions that these speculations highlight.

Alterative Accounts of How Imagery May Be Used to Represent Abstract Information

THE NUCLEAR OPTION

One possible interpretation of the emerging evidence that imagery can function to represent abstract ideas is to conclude that Aristotle was right: images are fundamentally involved in representing all thought, including abstract thought. Thus, rather than there being two modes or systems of representation, as the currently dominant view suggests, there is only one, and it is based in imagery. This may seem at odds with findings we reviewed that distinguished effects of imagery from nonimagistic thought. And, wasn't it the failure to account for "imageless thought" that sunk Wundt's image-based theory so long ago? However, emerging theoretical frameworks and new evidence about how cognition works suggests that the experience of "imageless thought" need not be at odds with the idea that imagery is involved in representing all knowledge.

Embodied theories of cognition propose that all knowledge is grounded in modality-specific representations that employ sensorimotor systems (Barsalou, 1999; Niedenthal, Barsalou, Winkielman, Krauth-Gruber, & Ric, 2005). This claim directly contradicts a fundamental assumption of the predominant view on imagery that we have outlined here. That view assumes that images function as part of a representational system separate from (although interacting with) amodal forms of representation. But, in embodied accounts, there are no amodal representations; people use sensorimotor systems even to represent abstract information. There is compelling evidence to support this theory. For example, people systematically attribute specific spatial relations to abstract concepts such as hope and respect (Richardson, Spivey, Edelman, & Naples, 2001), and processing these abstract words activates the associated spatial dimension (Richardson, Spivey, Barsalou, & McRae, 2003). Other work demonstrates that the abstract concepts of personal warmth and importance are associated with and activated by concrete sensations of physical warmth (Williams & Bargh, 2008) and physical heaviness (Jostmanns, Lakens, & Schubert 2009), respectively. One reason that such findings are so intriguing is that introspection provides no evidence of the involvement of sensory and motor systems that the results suggest is occurring. This speaks to a fundamental idea in embodied theories, which is that much of the perceptual representation on which thought is based occurs outside of conscious awareness.

Thus, perhaps "imageless thought" is not imageless after all, but rather involves nonconscious imagery. At first, the idea of nonconscious imagery seems like an oxymoron: imagery is typically thought of as fundamentally defined by subjective experience. In fact, we ourselves defined visual imagery that way in the introduction to this chapter. However, other phenomena that people typically think of as defined by subjective experience have been shown to operate nonconsciously—for example, emotion (Winkielman & Berridge, 2004). Further evidence supporting the idea of nonconscious imagery comes from the phenomenon of "blindsight" (Weiskrantz, Warrington, Sanders, & Marshall, 1974). Individuals with this condition report not to be able to see anything in a particular region of their visual field, yet reliably can respond appropriately to information presented there. This suggests that the visual system can represent and process information without conscious awareness, implying that nonconscious imagery could be possible.

The idea that images can be nonconscious invites a reframing of results we presented earlier suggesting that responses to information differ depending on manipulations that instruct people to use image-based processing or alternate forms. Instead, these results may reflect a difference in response depending on whether images are conscious and intentional as opposed to nonconscious and unintentional. This possibility maps onto the broader question about the role of consciousness in cognition more generally (Winkielman & Schooler, 2008). This question has yet to be definitively answered; however, there are other examples in which making a process conscious changes the outcome (e.g., Wilson, Dunn, Kraft, & Lisle, 1989) and even evidence consistent with the argument that consciousness serves a functional purpose (Hoffmann & Wilson, 2010). Thus, the idea that conscious imagery could be functionally different from nonconscious imagery would not be unprecedented. It would be a radical overhaul, though, of predominant views on imagery to claim that images are the representational form for all thought.

THE GOLDILOCKS OPTION

A potentially less radical revision would maintain the notion that images are not the only form of representation. However, analogous to the idea that words can be used to represent both concrete and abstract ideas, it could be the case that images can also be used to represent both concrete and abstract ideas. If we retain the idea that there are multiple modes of representation, then an important question is how they interact. Paivio's (1969) classic work suggests that concrete words create a link from amodal (verbal) to sensory (visual) forms of representation: concrete words activate images of their referents. It could be the case that certain forms of

imagery, for example, third-person imagery, create a link from visual representation to amodal representation. If this were true, results suggesting that third-person imagery promotes abstract representations could reflect third-person images activating relevant amodal representations such as semantic knowledge. This would be complementary to Paivio's finding that concrete words activate visual representations.

In addition to considering how imagery and amodal varieties of representation interact, it would also be important to resolve whether the two modes have equal capacities to represent information along the dimension of abstraction or whether images are still generally better for representing concrete information and amodal forms for representing abstract information, even though there may be overlap in the ranges the two modes can represent. To distinguish between these possibilities with regard to the function of perspective, in particular, it would be informative to know how first- and third-person imagery compare with nonvisual processing of events (assuming amodal representation exists). None of the experiments we referenced linking perspective to abstraction included nonimagery conditions.

It is possible that there are a variety of dimensions on which images can vary, allowing them to represent abstract ideas. The evidence that we are aware of, and that we presented in this chapter, focused on variation in the perspective of images depicting experiences, actions, and events involving social agents. To the extent that the ability of images to represent abstract information is limited to variation in imagery perspective, it is possible that the abstract functions of imagery are limited to representing information about social events (see Kosslyn & Kagan, 1981, for a relevant discussion of the potential role of imagery in social cognitive development).

Concepts from the study of memory suggest one way to conceptualize the role of imagery perspective in representing social event information at different levels of abstraction. Episodic memory involves representing the experience of a specific event, whereas semantic memory involves representing abstract knowledge, apart from the experience of the event in which it was acquired (Tulving, 1972). Given that much of the same mental machinery is used in recalling the past as in thinking about the future, it has been proposed that episodic and semantic memory are also relevant for understanding how people represent information about the future (Atance & ONeill, 2001; Schacter, Addis, & Buckner, 2007). In the research we reviewed implicating third-person imagery in abstract representation, picturing specific actions and events from the third-person perspective led people to define those actions and events in terms of abstract knowledge about traits, goals, and identities. Thus, third-person imagery could function by creating a link from episodic representations to semantic knowledge.

Evidence consistent with this interpretation comes from a series of experiments that involved participants' memory for events that occurred in their childhoods (Libby, 2003). In one experiment, participants were first asked to indicate which incidents on a list had actually occurred, but the wording of the questionnaire was manipulated. Participants were either asked to indicate which items on the list they "remember doing" or were asked to indicate which items on the list "happened to you." In both conditions, participants were asked to recall the events they endorsed and to report the visual perspective they used. Participants were more likely to use the third-person perspective when the events were identified as ones that had "happened to" them as opposed to ones they "remembered doing." "Remember doing" references a specific instance, whereas "happened to you" can rely on semantic knowledge. Thus, the results are consistent with the idea that first-person imagery is used to represent episodic information and third-person imagery is used to represent semantic information.

Follow-up experiments suggested not only that perspective varies according to the type of representation people are referencing but also that the perspective of images serves as a cue to identify event information as episodic or semantic. Participants either were instructed to use the first-person or third-person perspective to imagine events having occurred in their childhood that had in fact not. Later, participants were asked to complete the same inventory of childhood events that was used in the initial experiment, and the wording was manipulated in the same way. The false childhood events appeared on the list, and participants' tendency to endorse those events as having occurred depended on the match between the perspective they had used to imagine them and the wording of the questionnaire. The pattern of results suggested that when participants were asked to indicate events that they "remembered doing," they evaluated their memories for evidence of episodic knowledge, and first-person images they had generated of the false events were more likely to be mistaken as that sort of evidence than were third-person images. When participants were asked to indicate events that "happened to

them," they evaluated their memories for evidence of semantic knowledge, and third-person images were more likely to be mistaken for that sort of evidence than were first-person images. Thus, together with the earlier experiment, these findings are consistent with the possibility that imagery plays a functional role in representing both episodic and semantic knowledge about the self, with perspective serving to define the representation one way or the other.

To summarize, the evidence showing that imagery is implicated in at least some abstract representations suggests that it may be necessary to revise the consensus view that imagery only supports concrete thought. Future research will determine how extensive the revision to the existing consensus will need to be. One possibility is the radical revision suggested by embodied cognition, which proposes that all thought, including highly abstract concepts, may be dependent on sensory imagery. Another possibility is a more modest revision that maintains the consensus opinion that imagery primarily specializes in representing concrete information but proposes that certain types of imagery—for example, third-person imagery—may be functionally implicated in abstract representations in a limited set of contexts—for example, those involving social agents.

Conclusion
The field's understanding of imagery is still evolving. At this stage, it seems safe to conclude that images are "real" in the sense that they are visual representations created within the visual system that are perceptually isomorphic with the objects they represent. In addition, it seems safe to conclude that images play a functional role in cognition. When it comes to the boundary conditions of this function, the picture is not quite as clear. Although there is a good deal of evidence that appears consistent with the idea that images function specifically for representing concrete, perceptual information, other evidence supports the exciting possibility that images also have the capacity to represent more abstract information. We look forward to the next methodological and theoretical advances that will bring us closer to knowing whether or not Aristotle was right all along.

Notes
1. Henceforth, our use of the term *imagery* in this chapter is intended to refer to visual mental imagery in particular, unless otherwise noted.

References

Abelson, R. P. (1975). Does a story understander need a point of view? In B. Nash-Webber & R. Shcank (Eds.), *Theoretical issues in natural language processing* (pp. 140–143). Cambridge, MA: Bolt, Beranek, & Newman.

Adaval, R., & Wyer, S. (1998). The role of narratives in consumer information processing. *Journal of Consumer Psychology, 7*, 207–245.

Amit, E., Algom, D., Trope, Y., Liberman, N. (2009). "Thou shalt not make unto thee any graven image": The distance dependence of representation. In K. D. Markman, W. M. P. Klein, & J. A. Suhr (Eds.), *Handbook of imagination and mental simulation* (pp. 53–68). New York: Psychology Press.

Andrade, J., Kavanagh, D., & Baddeley, A. (1997). Eye-movements and visual imagery: A working memory approach to the treatment of post-traumatic stress disorder. *British Journal of Clinical Psychology, 36*, 209–223.

Arditi, A., Holtzman, J. D., & Kosslyn, S. M. (1988). Mental imagery and sensory experience in congenital blindness. *Neuropsychologia, 26*, 1–12.

Atance, C. M., & O'Neill, D. K. (2001). Episodic future thinking. *Trends in Cognitive Sciences, 5*, 533–539.

Aylwin, S. (1977). The structure of visual and kinaesthetic imagery: A free association study. *British Journal of Psychology, 68*, 353–360.

Barsalou, L. W. (1999). Perceptual symbol systems. *Behavioral and Brain Sciences, 22*, 577–660.

Black, J. B., Turner, T. J., & Bower, G. H. (1979). Point of view in narrative comprehension, memory, and production. *Journal of Verbal Learning & Verbal Behavior, 18*, 187–198.

Bolls, P. D., & Muehling, D. (2007). The effects of dual-task processing on consumers' responses to high- and low-imagery radio advertisements. *Journal of Advertising, 36*, 35–47.

Carlston, D. E. (1994). Associated Systems Theory: A systematic approach to cognitive representations of persons. In R. S. Wyer (Ed.), *Associated Systems Theory: A systematic approach to cognitive representations of persons* (pp. 1–78). Hillsdale, NJ: Erlbaum.

Childers, T. L., Houston, M. J., & Heckler, S. E. (1985). Measurement of individual differences in visual versus verbal information processing. *Journal of Consumer Research, 12*, 125–134.

Claypool, H. M., & Carlston, E. (2002). The effects of verbal and visual interference on impressions: An associated-systems approach. *Journal of Experimental Social Psychology, 38*, 425–433.

Cohen, D., & Gunz, A. (2002). As seen by the other...perspectives on the self in the memories and emotional perceptions of Easterners and Westerners. *Psychological Science, 13*, 55–59.

Cohen, D., Hoshino-Browne, E., & Leung, A. K. Y. (2007). Culture and the structure of personal experience. In M. P. Zanna (Ed.), *Advances in experimental social psychology* (Vol. 39, pp. 1–67). San Diego, CA: Academic Press.

Epstein, S. (1994). Integration of the cognitive and the psychodynamic unconscious. *American Psychologist, 49*, 709–724.

Epstein, S., & Pacini, R. (2000–2001). The influence of visualization on intuitive and analytical information processing. *Imagination, Cognition and Personality, 20*, 195–216.

Fallshore, M., & Schooler, W. (1995). Verbal vulnerability of perceptual expertise. *Journal of Experimental Psychology: Learning, Memory, and Cognition, 21*, 1608–1623.

Farah, M. J., Soso, M. J., & Dasheiff, R. M. (1992). Visual angle of the mind's eye before and after unilateral occipital lobectomy. *Journal of Experimental Psychology: Human Perception and Performance, 18*, 241–246.

Fetherstonhaugh, D., Slovic, P., Johnson, S. M., & Friedrich, J. (1997). Insensitivity to the value of human life: A study of psychophysical numbing. In H. J. Langholtz (Ed.), *The psychology of peacekeeping* (pp. 75–88). Westport, CT: Praeger Publishers/Greenwood Publishing Group.

Fillmore, C. (1966). Deictic categories in the semantics of come. *Foundations of Language, 2*, 219–227.

Fiske, S. T., Taylor, S. E., Etcoff, N. L., & Laufer, J. K. (1979). Imaging, empathy, and causal attribution. *Journal of Experimental Social Psychology, 15*, 356–377.

Frank, M. G., & Gilovich, T. (1989). Effect of memory perspective on retrospective causal attributions. *Journal of Personality and Social Psychology, 57*, 399–403.

Gauthier, I., Skudlarski, P., Gore, J. C., & Anderson, A. W. (2000). Expertise for cars and birds recruits brain areas involved in face recognition. *Nature Neuroscience, 3*, 191–197.

Green, M. C., & Brock, C. (2000). The role of transportation in the persuasiveness of public narratives. *Journal of Personality and Social Psychology, 79*, 701–721.

Hoffmann, W., & Wilson, T. D. (2010). Consciousness, introspection, and the adaptive unconscious. In B. Gawronski & B. K. Payne (Eds.), *Handbook of implicit social cognition: Measurement, theory and applications,* (pp. 197–215). New York: Guilford.

Holmes, E. A., & Mathews, A. (2005). Mental imagery and emotion: A special relationship? *Emotion, 5*, 489–497.

Holmes, E. A., Mathews, A., Dalgleish, T., & Mackintosh, B. (2006). Positive interpretation training: Effects of mental imagery versus verbal training on positive mood. *Behavior Therapy, 37*, 237–247.

Holmes, E. A., Mathews, A., Mackintosh, B., & Dalgleish, T. (2008). The causal effect of mental imagery on emotion assessed using picture-word cues. *Emotion, 8*, 395–409.

Hsee, C. K., & Rottenstreich, Y. (2004). Music, pandas, and muggers: On the affective psychology of value. *Journal of Experimental Psychology: General, 133*, 23–30.

Huebner, D. M., & Fredrickson, L. (1999). Gender differences in memory perspectives: Evidence for self-objectification in women. *Sex Roles, 41*, 459–467.

Humphrey, G. (1951). *Thinking: An introduction to its experimental psychology*. London: Methuen.

Hyman, I. E., & Pentland, J. (1996). The role of mental imagery in the creation of false childhood memories. *Journal of Memory and Language, 35*, 101–117.

James, W. (1890/1950). *The principles of psychology* (Vol. 1). New York: Dover.

Jiang, Y., & Wyer, R. S. (2009). The role of visual perspective in information processing. *Journal of Experimental Social Psychology, 45*, 486–495.

Jones, E. E., & Nisbett, R. E. (1972). The actor and the observer: Divergent perceptions of the causes of the behavior. In E. E. Jones, D. E. Kanouse, H. H. Kelley, R. E. Nisbett, S. Valins, & B. Weiner (Eds.), *Attribution: Perceiving the causes of behavior* (pp. 79–94). Morristown, NJ: General Learning Press.

Jostmanns, N. B., Lakens, D., & Schubert, T. W. (2009). Weight as an embodiment of importance. *Psychological Science, 20*, 1169–1174.

Kahneman, D., & Frederick, S. (2002). Representativeness revisited: Attribute substitution in intuitive judgment. In

T. Gilovich, D. Griffin, D. Kahneman (Eds.), *Heuristics and biases: The psychology of intuitive judgment.* (pp. 49–81). New York: Cambridge University Press.

Kant, I. (1781/1965). *Critique of pure reason.* New York: St. Martin's Press.

Kavanagh, D. J., Andrade, J., & May, J. (2005). Imaginary relish and exquisite torture: The elaborated intrusion theory of desire. *Psychological Review, 112,* 446–467.

Kemps, E., Tiggemann, M., & Hart, G. (2005). Chocolate cravings are susceptible to visuo-spatial interference. *Eating Behaviors, 6,* 101–107.

Kemps, E., Tiggemann, M., Woods, D., & Soekov, B. (2004). Reduction of food cravings through concurrent visuospatial processing. *International Journal of Eating Disorders, 36,* 31–40.

Kirkpatrick, L. A., & Epstein, S. (1992). Cognitive-experiential self-theory and subjective probability: Further evidence for two conceptual systems. *Journal of Personality and Social Psychology, 63,* 534–544.

Klein, I., Dubois, J., Mangin, J. M., Kherif, F., Flandin, G., Polin, J. B., et al. (2004). Retinotopic organization of visual mental images as revealed by functional magnetic resonance imaging. *Cognitive Brain Research, 22,* 26–31.

Kosslyn, S. M. (1973). Scanning visual images: Some structural implications. *Perception & Psychophysics, 14,* 90–94.

Kosslyn, S. M. (1980). *Image and mind.* Cambridge, MA: Harvard University Press.

Kosslyn, S. M. (1995). Mental imagery. In S. M. Kosslyn and D. N. Osherson (Eds.), *An Invitation to Cognitive Science: Visual Cognition* (Vol 2, 2nd Edn.). Cambridge, MA: MIT Press.

Kosslyn, S. M., Ball, T. M., & Reiser, B. J. (1978). Visual images preserve metric spatial information: Evidence from studies of image scanning. *Journal of Experimental Psychology: Human Perception and Performance, 4,* 47–60.

Kosslyn S. M., & Kagan, J. (1981). "Concrete thinking" and the development of social cognition. In J. H. Flavell & L. Ross (Eds.), *Social cognitive development: Frontiers and possible futures* (pp. 82–96). New York: Cambridge University Press.

Kosslyn, S. M., Pascual-Leone, A., Felician, O., Camposano, S., Keenan, J. P., Thompson, W. L., et al. (1999). The role of Area 17 in visual imagery: Convergent evidence from PET and rTMS. *Science, 284,* 167–170.

Kosslyn, S. M., Seger, C., Pani, J. R., & Hillger, L. A. (1990). When is imagery used in everyday life? A diary study. *Journal of Mental Imagery, 14,* 131–152.

Kosslyn, S. M., Thompson, W. L., & Ganis, G. (2006). *The case for mental imagery.* New York: Oxford University Press.

Libby, L. K. (2003). Imagery perspective and source monitoring in the imagination inflation paradigm. *Memory & Cognition, 31,* 1072–1081.

Libby, L. K., & Eibach, R. P. (2011a). Visual perspective in mental imagery: A representational tool that functions in judgment, emotion, and self-insight. In M. P. Zanna and J. M. Olson (Eds.), *Advances in experimental social psychology* (Vol. 44, pp. 185–245). San Diego, CA: Academic Press.

Libby, L. K., & Eibach, R. P. (2011b). Self-enhancement or self-coherence? Why people shift visual perspective in mental images of the personal past and future. *Personality and Social Psychology Bulletin, 37,* 714–726.

Libby, L. K., Eibach, R. P., & Gilovich, T. (2005). Here's looking at me: The effect of memory perspective on assessments of personal change. *Journal of Personality and Social Psychology, 88,* 50–62.

Libby, L. K., Shaeffer, E. M., & Eibach, R. P. (2009). Seeing meaning in action: A bidirectional link between visual imagery perspective and action identification level. *Journal of Experimental Psychology: General, 138,* 503–516.

Libby, L. K., Shaeffer, E. M., Eibach, R. P., & Slemmer, J. A. (2007). Picture yourself at the polls: Visual perspective in mental imagery affects self-perception and behavior. *Psychological Science, 18,* 199–203.

Libby, L. K., Valenti, G., Pfent, A., & Eibach, R. P. (2011). Seeing failure in your life: Imagery perspective determines whether self-esteem shapes reactions to recalled and imagined failure. *Journal of Personality and Social Psychology, 110,* 1157–1173.

Luhrmann, T. M., & Morgain, R. (2012). Prayer as inner sense cultivation: An attentional learning theory of spiritual experience. *Ethos, 40,* 359–389.

MacIntyre, T., Moran, A., & Jennings, D. J. (2002). Is controllability of imagery related to canoe-slalom performance? *Perceptual and Motor Skills, 94,* 1245–1250.

Marbe, K. (1901). *Experimentell-psychologische Untersuchungen über das Urteil: Eine Einleitung in die Logik.* Leipzig: Engelmann.

Marks, D. F. (1973). Visual imagery differences in the recall of pictures. *British Journal of Psychology, 64,* 17–24.

Mayer, A., & Orth, J. (1901). Zur qualitativen Untersuchung der Association. *Zeitschrift für Psychologie und Physiologie der Sinnesorgane, 26,* 1–13.

McClelland, A., Kemps, E., & Tiggemann, M. (2006). Reduction of vividness and associated craving in personalized food imagery. *Journal of Clinical Psychology, 62,* 355–365.

McIsaac, H. K., & Eich, E. (2002). Vantage point in episodic memory. *Psychonomic Bulletin & Review, 9,* 146–150.

McIssac, H. K., & Eich, E. (2004). Vantage point in traumatic memory. *Psychological Science, 15,* 248–253.

Moulton, S. T. & Kosslyn, S. M. (2009). Imagining predictions: Mental imagery as mental emulation. *Philosophical Transactions of the Royal Society B, 364,* 1273–1280.

Niedenthal, P. M., Barsalou, L. W., Winkielman, P., Krauth-Gruber, S., & Ric, F. (2005). Embodiment in attitudes, social perception, and emotion. *Personality and Social Psychology Review, 9,* 184–211.

Nigro G., & Neisser, U. (1983). Point of view in personal memories. *Cognitive Psychology, 15,* 467–482.

Nisbett, R. E., & Wilson, T. D. (1977). Telling more than we can know: Verbal reports on mental processes. *Psychological Review, 84,* 231–259.

Noll, R. (1985). Mental imagery cultivation as a cultural phenomenon: The role of visions in Shaminism. *Current Anthropology, 26,* 443–451.

O'Craven, K. M., & Kanwisher, N. (2000). Mental imagery of faces and places activates corresponding stimulus-specific brain regions. *Journal of Cognitive Neuroscience, 12,* 1013–1023.

Paivio, A. (1969). Mental imagery in associative learning and memory. *Psychological Review, 76,* 241–263.

Paivio, A. (1971). *Imagery and Verbal Processes.* New York: Holt, Rinehart and Winston.

Paivio, A. (1986). *Mental Representations: A Dual Coding Approach.* New York: Oxford University Press.

Petrova, P. K., & Cialdini, B. (2005). Fluency of consumption imagery and the backfire effects of imagery appeals. *Journal of Consumer Research, 32,* 442–452.

Poole, D. A., Lindsay, D. S., Memon, A., & Bull, R. (1995). Psychotherapy and the recovery of memories of childhood sexual abuse: U.S. and British practitioners' opinions, practices, and experiences. *Journal of Consulting and Clinical Psychology, 63*(3), 426–437.

Pylyshyn, Z. W. (1973). What the mind's eye tells the mind's brain: A critique of mental imagery. *Psychological Bulletin, 80*, 1–24.

Reed, S. K. (2010). *Thinking visually*. New York: Psychology Press.

Richardson, D. C., Spivey, M. J., Barsalou, L. W., & McRae, K. (2003). Spatial representations activated during real-time comprehension of verbs. *Cognitive Science, 27*, 767–780.

Richardson, D. C., Spivey, M. J., Edelman, S., & Naples, A. D. (2001). "Language is spatial": Experimental evidence for image schemas of concrete and abstract verbs. In *Proceedings of the 23rd annual meeting of the cognitive science society* (pp. 873–878). Mawhah, NJ: Erlbaum.

Robinson, J. A., & Swanson, K. L. (1993). Field and observer modes of remembering. *Memory, 1*, 169–184.

Rottenstreich, Y., & Hsee, K. (2001). Money, kisses, and electric shocks: On the affective psychology of risk. *Psychological Science, 12*, 185–190.

Schacter, D. L., Addis, D. R., & Buckner, R. L. (2007). Remembering the past to imagine the future: The prospective brain. *Nature Reviews Neuroscience, 8*, 657–661.

Schooler, J. W., & Engstler-Schooler, T. Y. (1990). Verbal overshadowing of visual memories: Some things are better left unsaid. *Cognitive Psychology, 22*, 36–71.

Schultheiss, O. C., & Brunstein, C. (1999). Goal imagery: Bridging the gap between implicit motives and explicit goals. *Journal of Personality, 67*, 1–38.

Shaeffer, E. M., Libby, L. K., & Eibach, R. P. (2013). *Perspective primes processing style*. Manuscript in preparation.

Shepard, R. N., & Metzler, J. (1971). Mental rotation of three-dimensional objects. *Science, 171*(3972), 701–703.

Skinner, B. F. (1953). *Science and Human Behavior*. New York: The Free Press.

Slovic, P. (2007). "If I look at the mass I will never act": Psychic numbing and genocide. *Judgment and Decision Making, 2*, 79–95.

Sparks, G. G., Sparks, C. W., & Gray, K. (1995). Media impact on fright reactions and belief in UFOs: The potential role of mental imagery. *Communication Research, 22*, 3–23.

Storms, M. D. (1973). Videotape and the attribution process: Reversing actors' and observers' points of view. *Journal of Personality and Social Psychology, 27*, 165–175.

Swann, W. B., & Miller, C. (1982). Why never forgetting a face matters: Visual imagery and social memory. *Journal of Personality and Social Psychology, 43*, 475–480.

Taylor, S. E., & Fiske, T. (1975). Point of view and perceptions of causality. *Journal of Personality and Social Psychology, 32*, 439–445.

Trope, Y., & Liberman, N. (2010). Construal-level theory of psychological distance. *Psychological Review, 117*, 440–463.

Tulving, E. (1972). Episodic and semantic memory. In E. Tulving & W. Donaldson (Eds.), *Organization of memory* (pp. 381–403). New York: Academic Press.

Tye, M. (2000). *The imagery debate*. Cambridge, MA: The MIT Press.

Valenti, G., Libby, L. K., Eibach, R. P. (2011). Looking back with regret: Visual perspective in memory images differentially affects regret for actions and inactions. *Journal of Experimental Social Psychology, 47*, 730–737.

Vasquez, N. A., & Buehler, R. (2007). Seeing future success: Does imagery perspective influence achievement motivation? *Personality and Social Psychology Bulletin, 33*, 1392–1405.

Watson, J. B. (1928). *The ways of behaviorism*. New York: Harper & Brothers.

Weiskrantz, L., Warrington, E., Sanders, M., & Marshall, J. (1974). Visual capacity in hemianopic field following a restricted occipital ablation. *Brain, 97*, 709–728.

Williams, L. E., & Bargh, J. A. (2008). Experiencing physical warmth promotes interpersonal warmth. *Science, 322*, 606–607.

Wilson, T. D., Dunn, D. S., Kraft, D., & Lisle, D. J. (1989). Introspection, attitude change, and attitude-behavior consistency: The disruptive effects of explaining why we feel the way we do. In L. Berkowitz (Ed.), *Advances in experimental social psychology* (Vol. 22, pp. 287–343). Orlando, FL: Academic Press.

Winkielman, P., & Berridge, K. C. (2004). Unconscious emotion. *Current Directions in Psychological Science, 13*, 120–123.

Winkielman, P., & Schooler, J. (2008). Unconscious, conscious, and metaconscious in social cognition. Strack, F. & Foerster, J. (Eds.), *Social cognition: The basis of human interaction* (pp 49–69). Philadelphia: Psychology Press.

Wright, L. (1994). *Remembering Satan: A tragic case of recovered memory*. New York: Vintage.

Wundt, W. (1894). *Lectures on human and animal psychology*. New York: Macmillan.

Wyer, R. S., & Radvansky, A. (1999). The comprehension and validation of social information. *Psychological Review, 106*, 89–118.

Wyer, R. S. (2004). *Social comprehension and judgment: The role of situation models, narratives, and implicit theories*. Mahwah, NJ: Erlbaum.

Yaxley, R. H., & Zwaan, A. (2007). Simulating visibility during language comprehension. *Cognition, 105*, 229–236.

Zwaan, R. A., Stanfield, R. A., & Yaxley, R. H. (2002). Language comprehenders mentally represent the shape of objects. *Psychological Science, 13*, 168–171.

Faces are Central to Social Cognition

Kurt Hugenberg *and* John Paul Wilson

Abstract

The human face provides a wealth of information about others, including both situationally invariant information such as facial identity and social categories and situationally variable information such as others' emotions and intentions. This informational richness makes the face central to our social interactions and cognitions. This chapter first reviews the current literature on the cognitive processes that underlie face perception and then turns to a review of both bottom-up effects (e.g., how facial structure influences attention and social inferences) and top-down effects (e.g., how beliefs, expectations, and values influence how faces are perceived, remembered, and interpreted) in face perception. In summary, not only do faces yield extensive information about others, but also how (and whether) that information is extracted, encoded, and processed is subject to perceivers' motives and expectations about others.

Key Words: social cognition, face perception, stereotyping, facial expressions of emotion, face recognition

Faces are central to social cognition. A wealth of critical information can be extracted from the faces of those around us. From structurally invariant information, such as facial identities and social categories (e.g., sex, race, age), to more situationally variable information, such as physical health, evaluations, emotions, and intentions, faces can communicate a vast body of information quickly and efficiently.

It is this informational richness of faces that makes them so valuable. Indeed, simple social interactions are substantially facilitated by facial cues. For example, successful coalition building rests in part on the ability to extract and recall the identities of others. Remembering one's allies and enemies is a key skill in group living (Pokorny & de Wall, 2009). Similarly, facial cues are highly valuable in regulating social interactions (Argyle & Cook, 1976; Frischen, Bayliss, & Tipper, 2007). For example,

gazing toward a speaker can indicate interest and desire for interaction (e.g., Richmond, McCroskey, & Hickson, 2008), whereas gazing away can signal social rejection (Wirth, Sacco, Hugenberg, & Williams, 2010). Similarly, extracting others' emotional states and intentions can yield powerful predictions about their future behaviors (Fridlund, 1994). Knowing this information even before an interaction begins can help us select interaction partners, establish social control and affiliation (see Kleinke, 1986), and otherwise help interactions go smoothly (e.g., Nummenmaa, Hyönä, & Hietanen, 2009). Conversely, individuals who do not preferentially attend to faces or have difficulty understanding facial cues (e.g., eye gaze) commonly experience social (Yardley, McDermott, Pisarski, Duchaine, & Nakayama, 2008) and developmental (e.g., autism; see Baron-Cohen, Wheelwright, & Jolliffe, 1997) deficits.

Despite the centrality of faces to social cognition, most social cognitive psychologists have not consistently treated face perception as a central topic of study (see Macrae & Quadflieg, 2010; Zebrowitz, 2006). Although many of our classic experimental paradigms employ faces as stimuli (e.g., the "who-said-what" paradigm; Taylor, Fiske, Etcoff, Ruderman, 1978), until recently social cognition has generally ignored how face perception can influence social behavior. There have been some notable exceptions to this. For example, research on physical attractiveness (e.g., Dion, Berscheid, & Walster, 1972), on babyfacedness (e.g., Zebrowitz, Olson, & Hoffman, 1993), and on facial expressions (e.g., Ekman & Friesen, 1971) have all been well represented in social psychological journals. More recently, however, social cognitive psychologists have begun to take the face seriously as a stimulus in its own right. For example, recent evidence has shown that facial structures have powerful influences on discrimination (e.g., Blair, Judd, & Chapleau, 2004), evaluations, and social judgments (e.g., Oosterhof & Todorov, 2008), all topics central to social cognition. Similarly, social cognitive processes such as categorization, motivation, and goal activation have been recently implicated in even low-level face perception processes, "feeding down" into visual attention (e.g., DeWall & Maner, 2008), perceptual feature integration (e.g., Hugenberg & Corneille, 2009; Michel, Corneille, & Rossion, 2007; Ratner & Amodio, 2013), and face memory (e.g., Ackerman et al., 2006; Hugenberg, Miller, & Claypool, 2007; see Hugenberg & Sacco, 2008, for a review).

We believe it is important for social cognitive psychologists to treat seriously the topic of face perception, and in this vein we offer a review of research at the interface of social cognition and face perception. In the current chapter, we focus first on the "building blocks" of face perception, delving into the literature on the cognitive processes underlying face perception. We then provide a brief overview of the burgeoning research on the interplay of social cognition and face perception. To do this, we focus first on "bottom-up" effects of faces on social cognition, with a particular focus on how facial structures and facial expressions can lead to powerful influences on visual attention, trait inferences, social judgments, and social interactions. We then focus on "top-down" effects of beliefs, social categories, and stereotypes on key processes in face perception, such as attention, evaluation, and the recognition of faces and facial expressions.

Building Blocks of Face Perception: Cognitive Processes, Neural Structures, and Attentional Preference

"If I look at a photograph of myself, I don't know it's me. I don't recognize my wife or seven children, either, even when I'm looking right at them."

—Barry Wainwright, *The Guardian*

In his 2008 autobiographical article in *The Guardian*, Barry Wainwright describes his experiences, both comedic and heartbreaking, with prosopagnosia. Described most simply as "face blindness," prosopagnosia is a neurologic disorder leaving individuals unable to extract identities from faces. What is remarkable about Mr. Wainwright is that his agnosia appears specific to faces. Mr. Wainwright has no clear cognitive deficits across other dimensions. And he can identify others by their physical mannerisms (e.g., their gait), their clothing (e.g., his friend Steve's brown shoes), or the context (e.g., the person tromping down the stairs in the morning is his wife). However, as one might imagine, this cognitive deficit has led to real difficulty in social settings. By his own report, his face blindness meant the childhood playground was a daunting place, leading him to avoid social settings where misidentifications were likely to occur.

Because of either developmental disability or injury, true prosopagnosics have lost the ability to recognize faces, but without other cognitive deficits. This face-specific agnosia indicates that faces may be a special type of stimulus (Riddoch, Johnston, Bracewell, Boutsen, & Humphreys, 2008). Contentious debates about the domain specificity of face processing aside (see Gauthier & Bukach, 2007; McKone, Kanwisher, & Duchaine, 2006; Robbins & McKone, 2007), it does seem clear that faces are unlike most other stimuli across a number of dimensions. First, faces are processed in a manner (i.e., configural processing) seen with few other stimuli. Second, face processing appears to be supported by neural structures that are uniquely sensitive to faces. Finally, humans appear hard-wired to attend to faces more quickly and powerfully than other non-face stimuli.

The fact that prosopagnosia can dissociate face processing deficits from other deficits is one clear indication that faces are processed in a special manner. Prosopagnosics, it seems, lack the ability to process faces *configurally* (e.g., Barton, Press, Keenan, & O'Connor, 2002; Riddoch et al., 2008). Whereas prosopagnosics can typically process the individual features of faces (and even recognize faces by distinct features, such as a prominent nose), they cannot see how the features "fit together" into a meaningful gestalt. This ability to process the configuration of facial features and to integrate them into a meaningful whole is one hallmark of face processing (De Gelder & Rouw, 2000; Farah, Klein, & Levinson, 1995; see Maurer, LeGrand, & Mondloch, 2002, for a review). Although with a great deal of expertise, individuals can learn to process non-face stimuli configurally (e.g., dog experts can process dog faces configurally; Gauthier, Curran, Curby, & Collins, 2003; Tanaka & Curran, 2001; but see Robbins & McKone, 2007), one thing that sets faces apart from other stimuli is that everyone (excepting prosopagnosics) appears to integrate facial features into a gestalt configuration. Importantly, configural processing has been implicated in the extraction of facial information of all types, from facial identity (Yin, 1969) to facial expressions (Calder, Young, Keane, & Dean, 2000; Young & Hugenberg, 2010). Taken together, this indicates that the ability to process the *configuration* of facial features appears to be key in face processing and part of what makes faces relatively unique stimuli (Maurer et al., 2002).

Also supporting the argument that humans are biologically prepared for face perception is the localized nature of face perception in the brain (see Macrae & Quadflieg, 2010, for a recent review). Specifically, the fusiform face area (FFA) and the occipital face area (OFA) both appear to play pivotal roles in face perception. FFA activation is correlated with the integration of features into a single, gestalt representation. The FFA appears sensitive to multiple different means of disrupting the typical organization of the face (e.g., face inversion, face composite effects), indicating that the FFA supports configural processing (see Kanwisher & Yovel, 2006). The OFA, however, which is insensitive to such disruptions in configural processing (Yovel & Kanwisher, 2005), appears to support the processing of facial features, but not their configurations. As with most cognitive processes, face perception certainly ramifies throughout the brain (Haxby, Hoffman, & Gobbini, 2000); however, that perception and integration of facial structures appear localized in the brain does support the claim that humans are biologically prepared for face perception.

Beyond being processed in a unique manner, faces are unique stimuli in other ways as well. For example, faces also draw attention in ways that few other stimuli do. Remarkably, infants as young as 30 minutes post-birth orient to and visually track faces and face-like stimuli (eyes-over-mouth organization)

better than they do nonface stimuli, including even "jumbled" or inverted faces (e.g., Farroni, Johnson, Menon, Zulian, Faraguna, & Csibra, 2005; Goren, Sarty, & Wu, 1975; Johnson, Dziurawiec, Ellis, & Morton, 1991). Moreover, face learning in infants occurs quite swiftly after birth, with infants making distinctions between their mother's faces and strangers faces within a few days of birth (e.g., Bushnell, Sai, & Mullin, 1989; Field, Cohen, Garcia, & Greenberg, 1984). Although there is some debate about whether the ability to learn faces is due to a domain-general or a domain-specific processing system (see Liu & Chaudhuri, 2003, for a review), the evidence clearly indicates that face detection (i.e., attention) in infants is an innate ability (see De Gelder & Rouw, 2001; Morton & Johnson, 1991). It seems that humans are born to attend to faces.

Among adults, faces continue to be "special" stimuli, likely in part because they remain so informationally rich and so central to social interactions. Faces, and especially emotional or hedonically charged faces, appear to grab and hold visual attention, relative to non-face stimuli (see Palermo & Rhodes, 2007, for a review). For example, in a change detection paradigm, Ro, Russel, and Lavie (2001) found that changes to faces are easier to detect than changes to non-face objects, which is indicative of attentional allocation. Moreover, extensive evidence indicates that expressive faces attract attention even above non-expressive faces. For example, threat-relevant facial expressions (e.g., fear, anger; Öhman, Lundqvist, & Esteves, 2001; Vuilleumier, 2005) and happy facial expressions (e.g., Brosch, Sander, Pourtois, & Scherer, 2008) elicit rapid spatial orientation. In fact, detecting a face and interpreting it as a face may be an obligatory process in normally functioning perceivers (see Palermo & Rhodes, 2007). Whether this attentional preference for faces, and obligatory processing of faces, in adult perceivers is due more to learning or to biology is a matter of some debate (e.g., Frank, Vul, & Johnson, 2009); however, it does seem clear that faces tend to attract attention throughout the developmental trajectory.

Bottom-Up Effects in Face Perception

One critical consequence of the primacy of the face in cognitive processing is its ability to influence person perception in a bottom-up fashion, with targets' facial characteristics (e.g., facial structures, skin tone) influencing social cognition. Recent evidence indicates that such bottom-up effects on social cognition can even occur without mediation of higher-order cognitive processes, such as beliefs or stereotypes. As we will see, these bottom-up effects also appear to occur quite quickly and can occur outside of awareness, making them difficult to control or correct. In the current section, we review how both stable facial characteristics (e.g., facial structure) and labile facial characteristics (e.g., facial expression; eye gaze) can influence a large variety of social cognitive processes, such as evaluation, stereotyping, and social interaction.

Role of Facial Structure in Inferences and Attention

ATTRACTIVENESS

One of the most apparent ways in which facial information influences the person perception process is through facial attractiveness. The adage that "what is beautiful is good" certainly plays out in person perception. Attractive people have been found to enjoy advantages across many types of judgments and contexts. Relative to unattractive people, attractive people are judged to be kinder, warmer, more sociable, more interesting, and more successful (Dion et al., 1972). Although attractive individuals may be seen as more materialistic, vain (Dermer & Thiel, 1975), and less helpful (Sacco, Hugenberg, & Kiel, 2013) than their less attractive counterparts, positive impressions resulting from attractiveness tend to far outweigh the negative (see Zebrowitz, 1997). So-called halo effects of attractiveness on trait judgments are generally consistent across cultures, though the specific trait judgments that are influenced by attractiveness do vary somewhat (Bond, 1991; Langlois & Stephan, 1977; Wheeler & Kim, 1997; Zebrowitz, Montepare, & Lee, 1993).

In addition to trait judgments, attractiveness effects have been observed in multiple consequential domains. Not surprisingly, attractiveness has been shown to predict romantic interest in dating scenarios, even to the exclusion of other plausible predictors such as social skills and intelligence (Feingold, 1990; Lunn & Shurgot, 1984; Walster, Aronson, Abrahams, & Rottman, 1966). The importance of attractiveness in selecting mating partners has been found to be highly consistent across cultures (Buss et al., 1990). Attractive people also tend to enjoy more influence over others (Chaiken, 1986) and more occupational success (Bull & Rumsey, 1988; Collins & Zebrowitz, 1995). These realities are in line with perceivers' judgments of attractive people—attractive people enjoy benefits that others do not. For example, attractive people receive more

help than do their unattractive peers (e.g., Martin, Friedmeyer, & Moore, 1977; Patzer, 1985) and are punished less for their transgressions (e.g., Stewart, 1980). In sum, facial attractiveness holds powerful influence over social judgments.

BABYFACEDNESS

Attractiveness is not the only means by which facial configuration can influence social perception. Another well-researched example is babyfacedness. A substantial body of work has established that babies' faces elicit both automatic attention (e.g., Brosch, Sander, & Scherer, 2007) and spontaneous warm and protective responses from adults, likely for adaptive reasons (Zebrowitz, 1997). Moreover, even adult faces with relatively babyish facial characteristics (e.g., large eyes, high eyebrows) tend to elicit spontaneously warm and protective responses as well. Thus, the biologically adaptive response to succor babies is overgeneralized even to adults with relatively babyish facial features (Zebrowitz, 1997). In other words, it is adaptive to be protective of young and vulnerable members of one's species, and the facial cues that elicit such protective behavior are so powerful that they generalize to adults possessing baby-like features.

Thus, even adult targets with babyish faces are believed to have more baby-like traits than targets with more mature facial features (Zebrowitz, & Montepare, 1992). For instance, large-eyed targets elicit elevated ratings of honesty, naïveté, warmth, and compliance relative to small-eyed targets (McArthur & Apatow, 1983). Conversely, targets with non-babyish (low) eyebrows are rated as more respected and less submissive than those with babyish eyebrows (Keating, Mazur, & Segall, 1977). Similar results have been observed for faces that vary along other babyfacedness-relevant dimensions (i.e., rounder faces, larger and rounder eyes, high eyebrows, smaller noses); individuals who are higher in overall babyfacedness have been rated as submissive, weak, and naïve to a greater extent than those who differ on just single features (McArthur & Apatow, 1983). In sum, independent of the influence of behavioral information or social categories, perceivers tend to see people with babyish faces as less dominant and less intelligent but warmer than those with less babyish faces (Montepare & Zebrowitz, 1998).

Babyfacedness has been found to predict differences in important social judgments as well. Data from mock hiring decisions have shown that babyfaced individuals are more likely to be recommended for jobs calling for submissiveness and warmth, whereas non-babyfaced individuals tend to be chosen for jobs calling for dominance, coldness, and shrewdness (Copley & Brownlow, 1995; Zebrowitz, Tenenbaum, & Goldstein, 1991). Subsequent research has found that these mock decisions are mirrored by reality. In a separate study that involved rating faces and job characteristics, Collins and Zebrowitz (1995) found that babyfaced women tended to hold jobs characterized by traits typically ascribed to babyfaced people, such as teaching and nursing. Facial maturity has also been found to be positively correlated with important outcomes such as professional promotions (Mazur, Mazur, & Keating, 1984; Mueller & Mazur, 1996). Finally, even the results of small claims court cases reflect babyfacedness stereotypes—babyfaced individuals are less likely than mature-faced individuals to be found at fault for intentional actions, but not for unintentional or negligent actions (Zebrowitz & McDonald, 1991).

FACIAL TRUSTWORTHINESS AND DOMINANCE

Just as the effects of babyfacedness are likely the result of babyfaced overgeneralizations, face evaluation also reflects an overgeneralization of cues resembling emotional expressions (Oosterhof & Todorov, 2009; Todorov, 2011). Even neutral faces are often perceived as conveying dominance and valence information owing to structural variations that resemble facial expressions. Neutral expression faces that structurally resemble happiness engender inferences of trustworthiness, whereas neutral expression faces that resemble anger engender inferences of dominance (Oosterhof & Todorov, 2009).

Importantly, perceivers appear to automatically appraise faces along two primary, orthogonal dimensions: valence and dominance. Oosterhof and Todorov (2008) found that the dimensions of valence (or trustworthiness) and dominance account for the majority of the variance in trait judgments of neutral expression faces. Furthermore, perceivers extract this trustworthiness and dominance information from neutral expression faces rapidly and efficiently. People can make trustworthiness judgments of faces that have been presented for as little as 33 milliseconds (ms; just at the threshold for even consciously realizing that they have seen a face), and trustworthy and untrustworthy faces presented as primes for just 20 ms (too fast to realize a face has been presented) have been shown to influence evaluations of subsequent supraliminally presented faces (Todorov, Pakrashi, & Oosterhof, 2009). Todorov and colleagues flashed participants images of computer-generated trustworthy and

untrustworthy faces for 20 ms, followed immediately by a completely neutral face for 50 ms. Binary trustworthiness judgments of the neutral target showed a priming effect, such that flashing a trustworthy face before presenting a neutral face made the neutral face appear more trustworthy, and vice versa with untrustworthy faces.

Judgments and trait inferences based on structural qualities of faces are often consequential, even if they usually lack accuracy (Hassin & Trope, 2000; Todorov, 2008). In fact, perceivers are usually better off ignoring facial structures and relying on base rates (i.e., average levels of a trait in the population) to make their predictions (Olivola & Todorov, 2010). However, facial trustworthiness and dominance do influence our decisions in a number of important domains. For example, facial dominance has been found to predict the extent to which members of the military advance in rank (Mazur, Mazur, & Keating, 1984; Mueller & Mazur, 1996). Furthermore, judgments of competence based solely on rapid exposures to faces accurately predicted political candidates' electoral success (Ballew & Todorov, 2007; Todorov, Mandisodza, Goren, & Hall, 2005). Competence judgments of candidates made when seeing the candidate's face for only 100-ms exposures were just as predictive as the same judgments made with unlimited exposure. Such judgments are made so automatically, in fact, that deliberation by participants who were told to think carefully about their judgments actually interfered with accuracy (Ballew & Todorov, 2007).

FEATURE BASED STEREOTYPING

The previous sections have summarized work on social judgments that are based on structural qualities of faces, posited to be due to overgeneralizations of baby-like characteristics and overgeneralizations to faces with structures that appear happy and angry. However, there is also a literature on bottom-up person perceptual biases that are more directly related to existing social categories. Multiple papers over the past decade have investigated the role of features that are prototypic of African American faces in stereotyping and evaluation. Generally speaking, Black targets who have more "Afrocentric" features (e.g., darker skin; fuller lips; see Blair, Judd, Sadler, & Jenkins, 2002) tend to elicit more negative evaluations and judgments than do targets with less Afrocentric features (e.g., lighter skinned Black targets). These recent findings mesh well with the historical observation of "colorism," with darker skinned African Americans experiencing worse outcomes (Neal & Wilson, 1989; Russell, Wilson, & Hall, 1992). Similar effects occur across ethnic groups in a number of countries, with darker skin tone eliciting more negative evaluations, even within a racial or ethnic group (Goldberg, 1973). Afrocentric facial structures can elicit stereotyping effects through two mechanisms. First, Afrocentric Black targets are highly race prototypic and can thus elicit stronger category activation. More interesting, however, is that there also appear to be bottom-up effects of the facial structures themselves, even outside of the activation of social categories (see Livingston & Brewer, 2002).

Evidence suggests that White perceivers' cognitive representations of Blacks differ based on facial skin tone. Maddox and Gray (2002) investigated this possibility using a who-said-what paradigm, in which they found that participants made as many within-skin-tone errors as they did within-race errors. In other words, skin tone was used to organize memory for others. Further investigation showed that people may organize stereotype knowledge about Blacks according to skin tone. Maddox and Gray found evidence that people categorize based on skin tone, suggesting a possibility of top-down tone-related influences. However, these effects can also occur without being mediated by categorization. Across five studies using several different methodologies, Livingston and Brewer (2002) found that automatic evaluations of faces were driven by perceptual characteristics of the faces. Highly racially prototypic Black targets were consistently evaluated more negatively than Black targets low in prototypicality. Moreover, Blair, Judd, Sadler, and Jenkins (2002) found that more racially prototypic Black targets were judged more likely to have traits stereotypic of African Americans. Remarkably, this effect was maintained even when the strength of category activation was statistically controlled. Although category activation did affect judgment independent of facial characteristics, it appears that Afrocentric facial characteristics have a direct effect on stereotypic trait inferences that is separate from activation of the social category.

One particularly pernicious aspect of evaluations and stereotypes based on race-related features rather than social category activation is the apparent uncontrollability of the bias. In a set of studies adapted from Blair and colleagues' (2002) methodology, Blair, Judd, and Fallman (2004) found that participants are generally aware of race-based stereotypes and can exert some degree of control over them; however, participants were unable to control the influence of feature-based stereotyping, even when explicitly instructed to do so. Such biases were shown to operate efficiently and automatically. These results are consistent with other research demonstrating that people corrected for biasing effects of target sex when judging leadership capabilities; however, when targets' faces were manipulated to appear more masculine or feminine, participants failed to correct for prototypicality of physical appearance (Sczesny & Kuhnen, 2004).

Further research shows that such feature-based biases can have far-reaching consequences. One troubling example of the powerful influence of these biases is criminal sentencing. Some researchers have found that race itself may not currently bias the harshness of sentences once other variables are controlled for (Spohn, 2000; Tonry, 1995). However, given that feature-based biases appear to operate outside of awareness and may be difficult to control, such biases may be particularly influential in determining criminal sentences. In an archival analysis of a database maintained by the State of Florida Department of Corrections, Blair, Judd, and Chapleau (2004) found this to be the case. They randomly selected images of Black and White inmates sentenced during a four-year period and coded facial features and criminal histories. Unsurprisingly, the seriousness of the offense committed accounted for most of the variance in sentence length. Race did not account for additional variance over and above the effects of seriousness and number of offenses. However, the level of Afrocentricity displayed by a face was a significant predictor of sentence length. For both White and Black defendants, length of sentence increased as faces became more Afrocentric. The relationship between Afrocentricity and sentence length did not differ based on defendant race. In similar work, Eberhardt, Davies, Purdie-Vaughns, and Johnson (2006) found that, in cases involving a White victim, Black defendants were more likely to be sentenced to death if they had a facial structure that was more prototypically Black (i.e., more Afrocentric). Such feature-based biases influence behavior as well. In an extension of work showing that target race moderates shoot/don't shoot decisions in a task designed to approximate real-life crime situations (see Correll, Park, Judd, & Wittenbrink, 2002), Ma and Correll (2011) found that target prototypicality influences these shooting decisions. In particular, White faces that are low in prototypicality (i.e., do not look like a "typical" White person) elicit a heightened tendency for incorrect "shoot" decisions (i.e., when those individuals are actually unarmed).

In conclusion, judgments based on facial structural information tend to occur quickly and efficiently, with even less than 100 ms of exposure to a face (Willis & Todorov, 2006; Todorov et al., 2009). Put simply, feature-based first impressions occur with remarkable speed. Moreover, feature-based impressions appear quite difficult to control. Even though people are commonly unaware of the influence of such bottom-up processes on social judgment, explicit attempts at control appear ineffective (Blair et al., 2004).

Facial Expressions of Emotion

Although facial structures certainly signal characteristics about others, facial expressions of emotions are perhaps the most commonly discussed facial signals that can be seen in a face. The study of facial expressions has been deeply influenced by functionalist or evolutionary perspectives, dating back to the seminal work of Darwin (1965/1872), which argued that both the signals and morphology of expressions are evolved systems. Indeed, multiple lines of work are converging on the conclusion that certain facial structures may have evolved to mimic facial expressions (Oosterof & Todorov, 2009; Said, Sebe, & Todorov, 2009) and vice versa (Marsh, Adams, & Kleck, 2005; Sacco & Hugenberg, 2009). A full review of the literature on facial expressions is far beyond the scope of the current work. We instead focus on two domains of research that are of continued interest to social cognitive psychologists: the functions of facial expressions and the origins of these expressive signals.

FUNCTIONS OF EXPRESSIONS: COMMUNICATION AND ACTION

There is strong consensus among theorists that facial expressions of the six "basic" emotions (i.e., happiness, sadness, anger, disgust, fear, and surprise) have evolved as a means of social communication (e.g., Ekman et al., 1989; Fridlund, 1994; Frijda & Tcherkassof, 1997). It seems clear that facial expressions do indeed effectively and efficiently communicate information about affective states, motives, traits, and future behaviors (see Parkinson, 2005, for a review). For example, a happy expression sends a signal of affiliation, an angry expression sends a signal of dominance, and fearful and sad expressions signal submissiveness (e.g., Knutson, 1996). By understanding the motives and traits of others, this can afford one the ability to navigate complex social interactions more effectively.

Moreover, these "basic" facial expressions appear to be universal expressive signals of underlying states. Perhaps best known among demonstrations of this phenomenon is Ekman and Friesen's (1971; see also Ekman, Sorenson, & Friesen, 1969) cross-cultural work. In this work, they presented photos of facial expressions made by White North Americans (i.e., encoders) to perceivers in the Fore linguistic-cultural group of the South East Highlands of New Guinea (i.e., decoders), a hunter-gatherer society extremely isolated from the broader worldwide material or popular culture. In other words, they found participants who had the least possible experience with Western culture, and then showed them expressions made by individuals steeped in Western culture. Ekman and Friesen told participants brief stories (e.g., "Her friends have come and she is happy") and had them select which of three pictures displayed the accurate expression. Remarkably, expression recognition was well above chance, indicating that facial expressions of emotions show universality in communicating underlying states. Moreover, when mistakes were made, they were made most commonly between related emotions. Whereas a happy story rarely elicited errors where participants selected anger or disgust, fearful stories commonly elicited the selection of surprise. Thus, emotions that share a great deal of phenomenological experience (e.g., fear and surprise) also share more expressive signal than do experiences that are quite distinct (e.g., fear and happiness; see also Smith, Cottrell, Gosselin, & Schyns, 2005). Although different cultures display expressions in different situations (e.g., Ekman, 1972; Matsumoto, 1989) and display the basic expressions somewhat differently (e.g., Elfenbein & Ambady, 2003), there appears to be universality in the underlying affect program (Ekman, 1972).

Beyond communication, facial expressions can have a powerful influence on both the sender (encoder) and the receiver (decoder) of an expression. For the encoder of an expression, expressions themselves can create or enhance the experience of an emotion. Comics seem funnier to readers posing a happy expression and lose their comedic value for readers posing sad expressions (Strack, Martin, & Stepper, 1988). Similarly, pronouncing syllables that lead individuals to mimic happy expressions (e.g., ah and e) improve mood, whereas pronouncing syllables that mimic frowning have the opposite effect (e.g., u; see Zajonc, Murphy, & Inglehart, 1989).

For the decoder of expressions, others' emotional displays can prepare decoders for action. Simply perceiving a facial expression of emotion can potentiate approach or avoidance motor responses. For example, angry expressions can flexibly potentiate behavioral approach- or avoidance-related responses. Marsh, Ambady, and Kleck (2005) found that viewing angry facial expressions facilitates arm extension (i.e., pushing away) responses, a known associate of avoidance-related responses (Cacioppo, Priester, & Berntson, 1993). Wilkowski and Meier (2010), however, found that perceivers are particularly adept at approaching angry expressions, a phenomenon that is especially true when such approach facilitates overcoming the social challenge posed by the angry expressions. Although still an open question, whether angry expressions facilitate avoidance or approach likely depends on perceiver motives to submit to an angry expression or overcome the challenge posed by an angry expression. Conversely, perceiving fearful expressions appears to potentiate approach-related behaviors (Marsh et al., 2005). Although fearful expressions are negative stimuli, fear is a signal of submission that appears to elicit reaffiliative or conciliatory behavior.

WHY EXPRESSIONS APPEAR THE WAY THEY DO

Although a great deal of evidence speaks to the communicative function of facial expressions, it does not address the question of why the emotions take on their specific universal expressions. In other words, why does the fear expression appear as it does, with a mouth agape and eyes widened? Is this constellation of features arbitrary, or has it evolved because the specific arrangement of features itself is functional? Many theorists agree that the specific expressions themselves are functional, but there are two broad theoretical positions on the functional origins of facial expression configurations. The first might be referred to as a *communicative* argument (e.g., expressions appear as they do because that configuration most efficiently communicates the underlying motive or emotion), whereas the second might be referred to as an *egocentric function* argument, with each expression configuration serving a function for the sender outside of communication (e.g., wide-eyed fear facilitates visual attention). In actuality, both theoretical positions have garnered support, and they are likely not truly mutually exclusive explanations.

Communicative Configurations

The first position argues that facial expressions evolved their current configuration because these configurations are maximally informative of the underlying emotion or motivation. That is, the

configuration itself is a highly efficient vehicle for communicating the underlying state. There are two ways to understand this proposition. First, to be maximally communicative, expressions should be maximally *distinct*, with different expressions having different configurations that are difficult to confuse with one another. Second, expressions may have evolved to co-opt facial structural signals that our ancestors were already well suited to decode and respond to (e.g., babyfacedness).

In fact, there is evidence that both of these are true. As previously noted, dissimilar psychological states (e.g., anger and happiness) rarely elicit facial expression confusions (e.g., Ekman & Friesen, 1971). Smith, Cottrell, Gosselin, and Schyns (2005) report both behavioral and computational evidence that most "basic" facial expressions have little overlap in the information communicated by the face. In this work, they showed participants a series of basic expressions that were visually degraded, with some areas of the face (i.e., pixels in the picture) being more visible than others. Over thousands of trials, this allowed the authors to compute which pixels, and thus which areas of the face, were most useful in accurately categorizing the degraded expressions. The locations of expression-diagnostic information show low overlap between expressions. In other words, the specific parts of the face useful for categorizing anger are uncorrelated with those useful for categorizing happiness. The only strong overlap between signals was again between surprise and fear. This suggests that one selection pressure for facial expressions is the efficiency of communication. Expressions, it seems, have evolved to be orthogonal signals.

A good expressive signal, however, is one that is both distinct and *strong*. A number of theorists have recently argued that many facial expression configurations co-evolved with other facial-structural signals, enhancing the strength of the expressive signal. For example, consider fear. Our fearful expressions are at their most successful when they effectively communicate submission to those who seek to aggress against us. Successfully sending the signal of submission may allow everyone to avoid a potentially dangerous confrontation. Marsh, Adams, and Kleck (2005; see also Le Gal & Bruce, 2002) argue that by co-opting the facial structural signal of babyfacedness, fearful expressions become more efficient signals of submission. In fact, the fearful expression *does* have structural characteristics similar to a babyish face (Berry & McArthur, 1985), with enlarged eyes and higher, arched brows. Conversely, angry expressions with their narrowed eyes and lower brows do adopt characteristics typical of more mature faces. Consistent with this hypothesis, Marsh and colleagues found that targets expressing fear are rated as having traits characteristic of babyfaced individuals (e.g., dependence, weakness, submissiveness) to a greater degree than targets expressing anger, who were judged to have more mature traits (e.g., strength, dominance). Further supporting this hypothesis, Sacco and Hugenberg (2008) found that faces with more babyish facial structures (e.g., faces with large eyes or round faces) sent stronger signals of fear, whereas faces with mature facial structures (e.g., small eyes, narrow faces) send stronger signals of anger.

Very similar arguments have been made regarding signals of facial-structural masculinity and femininity and expressions of anger and happiness. For example, a number of studies have consistently found that decisions about the sex and the emotional expressions on faces are not made independently (e.g., Becker, Kenrick, Neuberg, Blackwell, & Smith, 2007; Hess, Adams, Grammer, & Kleck, 2009; Hugenberg & Sczesny, 2006; Le Gal & Bruce, 2002). One argument for this lack of independence is that the characteristics that signal facial masculinity overlap with the characteristics that signal anger (e.g., lower brows, flared nostrils), whereas the facial characteristics that signal femininity overlap with those characteristics that signal happiness (e.g., higher brows, large eyes, round face). In fact, manipulating faces to appear more masculine does make them appear more dominant or angry (e.g., Becker et al., 2007), whereas happy expressions are extracted more efficiently from female faces (e.g., Hugenberg & Sczesny, 2006). Thus, the configurations of expressions that signal dominance (anger) and affiliation (happiness) may have their origins in sexually dimorphic facial structures.

Egocentric Functions of Emotional Expressions

The hypothesis that the morphologies of facial expressions have specific, egocentric functions other than mere communication can be traced back to Darwin (1965/1872). For example, Darwin observed that the disgust expression in response to bitter flavors (even as observed in newborns, Rosenstein & Oster, 1988) involves an opened mouth, commonly with down-turned corners, "as if to let an offensive morsel drop out." Conversely, Darwin argued that emotional expressions of surprise and fear involve elevated eyebrows "in order that the eyes should be opened quickly and widely" to best survey the environment.

Although the hypothesis that expressions serve such egocentric functions is long-standing, Susskind and colleagues (2008) have recently provided evidence that both disgust and fear expressions function in preparation for situationally relevant action. For example, disgusted expressions attenuate the exposure of facial sensory organs to the environment. In their work, Susskind and colleagues (2008) had participants pose disgusted expressions and found that disgusted expressions limited the eye aperture (i.e., less of the eye was exposed to the environment), with a concomitant reduction in the visual field. Similarly, nasal inspiratory capacity and volume are reduced by facial expressions of disgust. Thus, both the velocity and amount of air intake is reduced by disgusted expressions. Put simply, disgusted expressions appear to protect one's delicate eyes and nasal mucous membranes from potentially noxious stimuli, while also allowing disgusting material to exit the mouth. Similarly, Susskind and colleagues (2008) found that fearful expressions enhance exposure of the eyes, thereby enhancing the size of the visual field. In a related vein, fearful expressions also increase the velocity of saccadic eye movements, indicating that fearful expressions potentiate the scanning of the environment. Finally, arguably in preparation for aerobic activity (i.e., fighting or fleeing), fearful expressions also increase both inspiratory nasal air velocity and volume.

Eye Gaze

When considering bottom-up processes in face perception, the importance of eye gaze cannot be ignored. The direction of others' eye gaze is a primary characteristic in "mind reading" their intentions and future actions. To the extent that we need to detect what social targets are thinking and doing, we need to be able to rapidly and automatically decode where others are looking. In fact, gaze detection is so important and occurs so spontaneously that some theorists argue that humans have likely evolved a module specifically for it (Baron-Cohen, 1995; Batki, Baron-Cohen, Wheelwright, Connellan, & Ahluwalia, 2000). Developmental research supports this idea. Very early after birth, infants show more interest in the eyes than in other parts of the face (Farroni, Csibra, Simion, & Johnson, 2002; Morton & Johnson, 1991), and neonates preferentially gaze at a photo of a woman with eyes open relative to eyes closed (Batki et al., 2000). Children as young as 9 to 18 months look to targets' eyes as potential signals of intention (Phillips, Baron-Cohen, & Rutter, 1992).

DIRECTING ATTENTION AND SIGNALING FUTURE BEHAVIOR

One way that others' eyes provide social information is in their ability to direct our attention. Here, others' eye gaze direction is crucial because perceivers use it to infer the location and importance of objects in the environment. Once again, evidence suggests that children are sensitive to gaze direction early in development. By the age of 4 months, children show the ability to discriminate direct from averted eye gaze (Vecera & Johnson, 1995). Moreover, people make use of others' eye direction to attribute mental states to them (Smith et al., 2005) and to predict their future behaviors (Nummenmaa et al., 2009); and without the ability to detect eye gaze, it would be extremely difficult to predict or interpret others' actions (Baron-Cohen, 1995).

Important here is joint attention: the phenomenon by which perceivers follow a target's averted gaze to the object of attention. It has been shown that perceivers reflexively shift their gaze to follow the gaze of a target person, particularly in paradigms in which the location of a target object is correctly predicted by gaze direction (Driver et al., 1999). Joint attention is an important building block of social cohesiveness and trust, such that faces whose gaze correctly predicts the location of a target are judged to be more trustworthy than those that do not (Bayliss & Tipper, 2006). Not only do people attend automatically to eye gaze (e.g., Friesen & Kingstone, 1998), but also joint attention deficits are associated with autism (Baron-Cohen et al., 1997), a syndrome characterized by theory of mind deficits (i.e., difficulty in mindreading or attributing mental states to others).

Part of why others' eye gaze is so valuable a signal (and is part of mind reading others) is that it provides a valid cue to their approach or avoidance behaviors. Avoidance emotions such as embarrassment and sorrow are typically communicated with averted gaze, whereas approach emotions such as happiness and anger are more associated with direct gaze (Argyle & Cook, 1976). In the same vein, showing emotion-congruent gaze has been found to facilitate the processing of facial expressions, such that perceivers are faster to see anger and joy on faces showing direct gaze, whereas averted gaze facilitates the recognition of fear and sadness (Adams & Kleck, 2003, 2005). Similar patterns of results have been observed for head orientation, and participants' emotional reactions to seeing emotional faces are dependent on a match between expression and head orientation (Hess, Adams, & Kleck, 2007). These and other results from eye-gaze studies suggest an important role of gaze detection in modulating our interpretations of the relevance, emotions, and intentions of social stimuli.

EYE GAZE AND EVALUATION

Consistent with the idea that eye gaze is crucial for social action, eye gaze has powerful evaluative consequences. People rate social targets more positively under conditions of increased eye contact (Cook & Smith, 1975; Scherer, 1974). Further, perceivers make inferences based on eye gaze even when they are not personally involved in an interaction. Target persons in photographs (Lim, 1972) and videos (Kleinke, Meeker, & La Fong, 1974) are estimated to like each other more when they are sharing gaze, and target persons are rated more positively when they approach others with moderate, rather than low, levels of gaze (Cary, 1978). Supporting this, eye gaze has been established as an important signal of liking and social connection. People tend to prefer social partners who initiate moderate amounts of shared eye gaze, rather than no gaze or constant gaze (Argyle, Lefebvre, & Cook, 1974; Exline, 1971). Conversely, a lack of eye gaze is sufficient to signal social exclusion, engendering feelings of ostracism (Wirth et al., 2010). Furthermore, when one is initiating social interaction, eye gaze is used as an important cue in the decision whether or not to pursue conversations (Kendon & Ferber, 1973).

In addition to research finding affiliative effects of mutual gaze, recent research has provided evidence that objects that are perceived to be the target of attention acquire positive valence. In two studies, participants reported more explicit liking for objects that had been previously associated with eyes gazing at them, an effect that did not occur when the eyes were replaced by arrows (Bayliss, Paul, Cannon, & Tipper, 2006) or when the faces had disgusted expressions (Bayliss, Frischen, Fenske, & Tipper, 2007). In one creative display, Corneille, Mauduit, Holland, and Strick (2009) found that objects perceived to be the target of a dog's gaze gained positive valence in an affective priming task. Although this study made use of non-human faces, it does add to the growing body of evidence linking eye gaze and object evaluation.

ENGAGING SOCIAL COGNITION

Eye gaze is so important to social interaction that it can actually modulate basic social cognitive phenomena, such as person categorization and stereotyping (Macrae, Hood, Milne, Rowe, & Mason, 2002).

In a speeded categorization task, Macrae et al. found that faces showing direct (straight ahead toward the perceiver) eye gaze were more quickly categorized according to gender, relative to faces showing averted eye gaze. They further found that direct eye gaze facilitated the classification of stereotype-relevant words. In other words, perceivers were quicker to access important information about targets when they displayed direct gaze, perhaps because these targets are construed as more relevant social targets. Put differently, we may only process people as relevant social targets if we can engage them through eye contact. To the extent that targets are displaying averted gaze, we may simply not consider them to be worth processing, and we are less likely to activate the categories to which they belong.

Bottom-Up Effects in Summary

The literature on bottom-up effects in face perception is a large one, spanning multiple disciplines throughout psychology and the cognitive sciences. However, a number of themes emerge. First, it seems clear that we extract information from the faces of others quite quickly and efficiently, and this information can have a powerful (if sometimes unacknowledged) influence on our inferences and behaviors. For example, the ability to extract others' facial expressions and eye gaze quickly and accurately is of major benefit in social interactions. With a flick of the eyes, we can signal interest, or with a brief roll of the eyes signal social rejection. Similarly, with a slight curl of the lip or arch of the brow, we can signal disagreement or pique. Further, joint attention (or joint emotions) can afford the experience of social connectedness, and the ability to experience such joint attention appears to underlie theory of mind and other cornerstones of social cognition.

Remarkably, this ability to so accurately and efficiently extract the facial cues of others has an interesting side effect: the *overgeneralization* of facial cues. Indeed, some of the effects of facial structure on social cognition are due to this tendency to overgeneralize cues of babyfacedness or cues of emotional expressions. Related to this issue, as a second major theme, it seems clear that the structure of targets' faces can matter a great deal in our social cognitions. When someone has a facial structure that appears attractive (or unattractive), babyish (or mature), trustworthy (or untrustworthy), dominant (or submissive), or even prototypic of a racial category (their own racial category or another), these facial structural cues can play a potent role in the inferences we draw about them.

Finally, a third major theme of this literature is that the processing of these bottom-up facial cues—be they facial expressions or facial structures—can occur so quickly and efficiently that we don't even realize that we've done it. We can extract and integrate information from faces about their attractiveness, their trustworthiness, their dominance, their gaze, and their expressions at time scales that approximate an eyeblink. These spontaneous inferences that we draw about faces from their facial structures can have powerful implications for how we treat them—from simple social interactions to criminal sentencing—even without our awareness.

Top-Down Effects in Face Perception

One central theme running through a vast body of research in social psychology is the ability of beliefs, desires, contexts, and motives to shape perception. Social psychologists know well that perceivers commonly go "beyond the information given" (Bruner, 1957), using contexts and beliefs to interpret ambiguous situations, and using our motives and desires to direct attention and processing (Fiske, 2004). Such top-down effects are rife in the domain of face perception as well, with top-down effects playing out in attention to and evaluation of faces, biasing the interpretation of facial expressions, and even influencing which faces are remembered and which are forgotten. Notably, many of the well-documented top-down effects on face and emotion perception have their basis in the stereotyping and prejudice literature, a literature with a particular focus on racial attitudes and categorization. This means that the preponderance of these phenomena have been documented primarily with race; however, as we will see, recent research has begun to extend these effects to various other social categories and group distinctions as well.

Categories Bias Attention to and Early Evaluation of Faces

The influence of top-down processes becomes apparent early in the perceptual stream. For example, social categories have been found by a number of researchers to influence how perceivers attend to and process faces at very early stages in perception. In one influential example, Ito and Urland (2003) found electrocortical evidence that perceivers covertly attend to race and gender within a few hundred milliseconds of seeing a target image. White perceivers who viewed White and Black targets showed differential event-related potential (ERP) responses to targets according to race as early as

122 ms after stimulus onset and to gender at about 176 ms, long before conscious, deliberate decisions about stimuli are made. This occurred regardless of whether or not the categories were relevant to participants' task. Race effects emerge early even when perceivers are told to categorize targets by gender, and gender effects emerge even when perceivers are told to categorize targets by race. Modulation of these early components has previously been associated with attentional orienting to stimuli that are attention grabbing (Luck & Hillyard, 1994). Interestingly, responses to Black faces were of larger magnitude in the earlier components, but this was reversed for the later component, suggesting that attention may be initially directed toward outgroup members, but that ingroup faces may be processed more deeply over time.

These effects have been echoed in studies that more directly investigate visual attention. For example, as part of a larger investigation into the effects of racial stereotypes on visual processing, Eberhardt, Goff, Purdie, and Davies (2004) observed that White participants preferentially direct their gaze toward White faces relative to Black faces, unless black stereotypic concepts like crime or basketball are primed. These attentional preferences for ingroup faces are observed at a stimulus onset asynchrony (SOA; i.e., the amount of time between stimulus presentation and the presentation of a visual mask) of 450 ms and seem to be consistent with the deeper ingroup processing that occurs later in the cognitive stream, as posited by Ito and Urland (2003). More recent research has further contributed to the view that White perceivers may have their attention drawn to Black targets at extremely early SOAs (i.e., very fast stimulus presentation times). Richeson and Trawalter (2008) found that participants high in external motivation to respond without prejudice (Plant & Devine, 1998) were quicker to orient attention to black faces presented for 30 ms, but away from Black faces presented for 450 ms. Similarly, Donders, Correll, and Wittenbrink (2008) showed that the extent to which participants oriented early attention to Black faces presented for 40 ms was predicted by their Black-danger stereotype associations. Participants who associate Black with danger were faster to orient attention to Black faces than White faces. Together, this research suggests that social categorization influences how we attend to faces and that categorical influences on attention are dynamic over time.

Thus, social categorization influences visual attention to faces. Even more surprisingly, category information seems to moderate the basic process by which faces are processed as faces. As we discussed previously, faces seem to be processed in a unique manner by the FFA (Kanwisher & Yovel, 2006). However, even this basic process has been found to be moderated by social categorization. For example, Golby, Gabrieli, Chaio, and Eberhardt (2001) presented Black and White participants with a series of Black and White faces as well as non-face objects. Viewing of faces, of course, was associated with greater FFA activation than viewing of objects. More interestingly, participants of both races showed greater activation in response to faces of their own race, relative to outgroup faces. More recent research has demonstrated that this ingroup-outgroup effect generalizes beyond race. Van Bavel, Packer, and Cunningham (2011) arbitrarily assigned participants to membership on one of two teams—Leopards or Tigers. They then viewed a series of White and Black faces purported to belong to one of the two groups, or to neither group. Participants then engaged in a neuroimaging task in which they viewed the faces again. Interestingly, participants showed heightened FFA activation in response to ingroup faces, and this effect was not moderated by target race. As we will see later, this mere ingroup membership also influences the extent to which faces are processed configurally (Hugenberg & Corneille, 2009)—a hallmark of face processing. Thus, even novel and seemingly arbitrary group distinctions can influence the extent to which faces are processed as faces.

Social categories influence not only attention to and encoding of faces but also automatic evaluations of faces. Research in neuroimaging has been vital to our knowledge in this area to date. For example, in a study utilizing both White and Black participants, Hart et al. (2000) discovered that people exhibit differential patterns of amygdala activation to neutral racial ingroup and outgroup faces. This research was based on findings suggesting that the amygdala not only is involved in fear and emotional responses (e.g., Öhman, 2005) but also is generally responsive to faces and important to social communication (Adolphs, Tranel, & Damasio, 1998; Kling & Brothers, 1992). Presenting pictures of White and Black targets for 1 second each, Adolphs et al. observed that participants exhibited no differences in amygdala activation when faces were first presented. However, when the same faces were presented again, participants now showed reduced amygdala activity in response to ingroup faces. In other words, amygdala responses habituated more quickly to ingroup faces than to outgroup faces. These results may best be interpreted in light of previous research showing that the amygdala is most responsive to new objects in the environment (DuBois et al., 1999). Participants in this research, then, seem to have been slower to exhibit familiarity-related responses to outgroup faces. Such race-modulated amygdala activity is also predictive of automatic evaluative responses on behavioral measures. Phelps et al. (2000) discovered that increased amygdala activity in White participants was positively correlated with pro-White, anti-Black bias on the Implicit Association Test (IAT), a response time index of implicit race bias, as well as a measure of eyeblink startle response to black faces. Amygdala activity was not, however, correlated with more explicit, controlled measures of racial prejudice. These effects did not occur for Black faces that were familiar and generally well liked, suggesting a role for individuation in modulating race-based evaluations.

Although it seems curious that amygdala activity was not elevated for outgroup faces in general in these studies, the results are actually consistent with a dynamic conceptualization of category-based face processing. Cunningham and colleagues (2004) revisited the issue in an attempt to disentangle the times at which we may see more or less amygdala activation in response to ingroup and outgroup faces. Based on a body of research demonstrating both automatic and controlled components of social evaluation (Bargh, 1996; Devine, 1989; Greenwald & Banaji, 1995), they posited that amygdala activity would be elevated for outgroup faces presented for an extremely short duration, while controlled processes might override this amygdala activity at longer SOAs (longer stimulus presentations allow for controlled rather than only spontaneous processes to occur). They presented White and Black faces to White participants for either 30 ms (at the threshold of awareness, eliminating the ability to use controlled processing) or 525 ms (fast, but allowing sufficient time for controlled processing to occur). Participants also completed an IAT and a measure of explicit prejudice. They found that, on short-SOA trials, Black faces elicited elevated amygdala activity, whereas White faces elicited reduced amygdala activity, relative to non-face trials. However, on long-SOA trials, this difference was reduced. Importantly, on long trials, participants exhibited elevated activity in the right ventrolateral prefrontal cortex and the anterior

cingulate in response to Black faces. These areas have been associated with regulation and executive function (Beauregard, Levesque, & Bourgouin, 2001; Ochsner, Bunge, Gross, & Gabrieli, 2002). Cunningham and colleagues (2004) argued that these results suggest that processes arising from automatic activity can be overridden by more controlled responses to racial outgroup faces.

Finally, the work of Richeson, Trawalter, and colleagues bears directly on this issue of amygdala activation for ingroups and outgroups. As was discussed earlier in this chapter, eye gaze is a critical component of social interaction, and we may see people who are looking away from us as somewhat socially irrelevant. Richeson, Todd, Trawalter, and Baird (2008) found that averted gaze exerts an influence even on neural activity indicative of evaluation. They observed that White participants showed greater amygdala activation in response to Black faces than to White faces, but that this difference was eliminated when the targets displayed averted eye gaze. Although Black faces elicit threat responses when looking directly at participants, this threat response does not occur when the target is looking away. In related research, Trawalter, Todd, Baird, and Richeson (2008) found that averted eye gaze also eliminated an attentional bias toward Black faces relative to White faces. We see in this research that social categorization plays an important and related role in processes underlying attention and evaluation.

Top-Down Effects in Face Memory

Attention and evaluation are not the only areas in which top-down influences affect processing. Memory for faces, too, falls under the influence of similar top-down effects. As discussed previously, accurate memory for and identification of previously seen faces is crucial to meaningful social interaction and group living. The failure to properly recognize people with whom you have interacted can cause confusion, embarrassment, and social difficulty. Perhaps more concerning is the possibility for mistaken identity, manifested as eyewitness misidentifications, influencing legal decisions. A rapidly growing body of evidence suggests that categorical person perception processes often underlie biases in face memory. In some cases, these effects can be considered "cold," in that they rely purely on well-known phenomena arising from categorization. In other cases, however, the effects are more a product of "hot" perceiver motives to individuate (or not to individuate) faces.

CATEGORICAL ASSIMILATION EFFECTS IN FACE PERCEPTION AND RECOGNITION

Research on category-based perceptual assimilation effects in face perception has its roots in the classic research of Tajfel and Wilkes (1963). In this work, Tajfel and Wilkes showed participants a series of six lines that increased monotonically in length. Remarkably, they found that when the shorter three lines were given one label (e.g., labeled as As) and the longer three lines were given a different label (e.g., labeled as Bs), these categories warped perceptions of line lengths. The mere fact of categorization led perceivers to minimize perceived within-category differences and to accentuate between-category differences. Faces, too, are subject to such perceptual assimilation effects; faces believed to belong to a social category are perceived as and remembered as being more prototypic than they actually are.

For example, the race of a face biases perception of its facial characteristics in a racially prototypic direction. In one well-known series of studies, MacLin and Malpass (2001, 2003) showed Hispanic participants images of ethnically ambiguous faces (Hispanic/Black). In order to induce racial categorization of the faces, they added hairstyles to each face that were typical of either Hispanic or Black people. Race categorization was found to influence perceptions of facial features. Faces categorized as Black (by having a Black-typical hairstyle) were judged to have darker skin tone than were faces categorized as Hispanic. In a more recent extension, Levin and Banaji (2006) investigated how targets' race influenced perceivers' ability to match a color palate to targets' skin tone. Levin and Banaji found that the category of the target (White vs. Black) influenced perceivers' judgments of the targets' skin tone. Even racially ambiguous faces that were labeled as Black led perceivers to judge the skin tone of the target as darker than when that same target was labeled as White. Such work strongly suggests that race categorizations can feed down into perceptions of facial characteristics.

Analogous perceptual assimilation effects in the domain of face memory have recently been demonstrated by Corneille, Huart, Becquart, and Brédart (2004). Using faces morphed along continua from Caucasian to North African (or Caucasian to Asian), Corneille and colleagues found that memory for previously seen faces was distorted toward the ethnic prototype. In other words, participants first encoded a face that was morphed to be 70% North African and 30% Caucasian (or vice versa). In the recognition phase, they had to select the face they had seen from a set of similar morphs, ranging from 50% to 90% North African. At recognition, participants showed a reliable shift toward more prototypical faces, such that participants who initially saw a face that was 70% North African remembered the face as being more prototypically (80% or 90%) North African. Such distortions did not occur for highly ambiguous faces (50%) because they were not easily categorized as belonging to one or the other ethnicity. It seems that categorizing faces based on ethnic features led to within-category perceptual assimilation. Once a face was perceived to belong to one ethnicity, it was remembered as being more prototypically ethnic than it actually was. Similar work utilized a more typical face recognition paradigm to investigate the extent to which ingroup faces may be perceptually assimilated to the category under certain conditions. In research by Young, Hugenberg, Bernstein, and Sacco (2009), participants exhibited the classic other race effect (ORE) in a face memory task, such that they more accurately recognized previously seen same-race faces than other-race faces. However, simply priming an intergroup context elicited significantly worse same-race recognition sensitivity. In short, when White participants were made to consider themselves as White, they became less able to recognize fellow White faces. In fact, even exposure to a single other-race face before encoding same-race faces led to worse same-race recognition. The presence of other-race faces induced participants to process faces more categorically than they otherwise would, and we once again observe an exacerbation of within-category errors when categories are salient.

MOTIVATED FACE ENCODING AND MEMORY

Whereas categorical assimilation effects occur through mere categorization (a "cold" cognitive effect; Tajfel & Wilkes, 1963), another body of work shows that categorical influences on face perception and face memory occur through more motivated (i.e., "hot") processes. Indeed, perceiver motives appear to play a potent role in recruiting perceivers' attention to, processing of, and memory for faces. In most situations, perceivers do not necessarily need to process the individuating characteristics of faces (Rodin, 1987). Instead, simply knowing the category-relevant features of faces (e.g., sex, race, age) can be sufficient to successfully navigate the situation. This tendency for perceivers to attend to the category-diagnostic information occurs in all manner of situations in which others' identity is not relevant to the task at hand (e.g., others in line at the bank) but is particularly acute with members of outgroups (Hugenberg et al., 2010; Levin, 1996), leading in part to the well-known Other Race Effect (ORE). The ORE, or the tendency to have worse recognition for other-race than for same-race faces, has served as a particularly fruitful focus of recent research on how perceiver motivations can act in a top-down manner to bias face perception (Meissner & Brigham, 2001). Critically, recent research has indicated that perceivers' motives, whether engaged by target categories or behaviors, or by effects exogenous to the targets (e.g., task instructions) can affect face encoding and face memory, creating, reducing, or even eliminating this bias in face memory.

Motivated Processes in Face Encoding

Recent evidence indicates that social categories influence the processes by which facial features are integrated during face encoding. Indeed, top-down categorical processes can influence the extent to which faces are processed *configurally*. As noted earlier, such processing is thought to underlie the ability to accurately remember faces (Farah, Wilson, Drain, & Tanaka, 1998) and thus is extremely important in face perception (Maurer et al., 2002). For example, Michel, Rossion, Han, Chung, and Caldara (2006) found that same-race faces (i.e., racial ingroup members) are processed more configurally than are other-race faces, an effect that occurs even when ambiguous-race faces are merely categorized as same-race or other-race, even holding the face itself constant (Michel, Corneille, & Rossion, 2007). Thus, the perceptual process that is the hallmark of efficacious face processing appears to be modulated by how a perceiver categorizes a target.

In fact, Hugenberg and colleagues (2010) have recently argued that people selectively deploy configural processing resources for targets who are subjectively important to process. Thus, the most efficacious face processing techniques are reserved for the most subjectively important targets. Indeed, recent research indicates that faces that perceivers believe to be more subjectively important to process elicit more configural processing. For example, Hugenberg and Corneille (2009) found that merely categorizing a target as an ingroup or an outgroup member affects configural processing. Targets who were categorized as ingroup members (a shared university affiliation) were processed more configurally than were targets categorized as outgroup members (students at a different university), an effect that was true even when target race was held constant. Ratcliff, Shriver, Hugenberg, and Bernstein (2010)

utilized a very different manipulation to achieve a similar result. In this work, they manipulated the perceived social status of targets, with some faces ascribed relatively high-status social positions (e.g., CEOs, doctors) and others lower status positions (e.g., plumbers, mechanics). Ratcliff and colleagues found that the high-status targets were processed more configurally than lower status targets. Taken together, this represents an important manifestation of higher order cognitive processes such as social categorization and perceiver motives feeding down to influence the perceptual processes by which faces are encoded.

Further, these motivated processes also influence how we deploy attention to and remember faces—it goes without saying that we must visually attend to faces in order to remember them. In fact, there is some evidence that people will preferentially allocate visual attention to target faces based on social categories, in tasks allowing for deliberate gazing. For example, He, Ebner, and Johnson (2011) have recently demonstrated that both young and old perceivers spent more time looking at faces from members of their own age group. All faces were presented for passive viewing for 4 seconds, and participants were instructed to "look naturally at whatever is interesting you in the images." Eye-tracking data showed that participants looked more at own-age than other-age faces. Importantly, gaze time predicted recognition memory, such that more gaze time was associated with better recognition. It remains to be seen whether such group-based differences in attention allocation influence recognition for other social categories. Notably, however, the relationship between looking time and accurate recognition is not absolute, and some research actually shows a dissociation between attention and memory. Ackerman et al. (2009) studied attention to and recognition of disfigured faces. Although disfigured faces were likely to hold attention relative to normal faces in a dot-probe task, they were remembered poorly. Thus, characteristics of faces that draw attention may not always be associated with better recognition, and they may at times even interfere with accurate recognition.

Categories Motivate Face Individuation

A growing body of literature provides evidence that social categories motivate individuation, enhancing face memory. Insofar as perceivers are generally more motivated to individuate racial ingroup members, this can translate into a deficit in other-race face memory. A spate of recent research, however, has sought to investigate similar biases in face memory, while clarifying the motivating nature of category distinctions. In one of the first demonstrations that perceivers individuated ingroup faces more than outgroup faces, MacLin and Malpass (2001, 2003) used racially ambiguous Black/Hispanic faces and manipulated the race of the targets using race-typical hairstyles. Remarkably, Hispanic participants recognized the same face better when it wore a Hispanic-typical hairstyle. Even when the facial structure itself was held constant, categorizing the target as an ingroup member elicited better face recognition. More recently, Pauker and colleagues (2009) found similar effects, with racially ambiguous faces categorized as racial ingroup members being better recognized than when the same faces were categorized as racial outgroup members.

Further supporting the case that ingroups and outgroups differentially motivate face encoding, recent evidence also indicates that Other Race-like effects have been observed for categories outside of race, for example, other-sex and same-sex relative to other-sex targets (e.g., Cross, Cross, & Daly, 1971; Wright & Sladden 2003). Similarly, other-age effects have also been observed (e.g., Anastasi & Rhodes, 2005; Rodin 1987; Wright & Stroud 2002). More recently, Rule, Ambady, Adams, and Macrae (2007) have shown an other-sexual orientation effect, such that targets of one's own sexual orientation were better recognized than were targets in the outgroup. Not only were perceivers able to categorize target faces' sexual orientation accurately more than 60% of the time, but also correct categorizations were associated with better ingroup memory. Correctly categorized gay targets were better recognized by gay perceivers, and heterosexual targets by heterosexual perceivers. This research shows that categorization is an important antecedent to group-based face memory biases. More recent research shows similar results for religion (faces of Mormons and non-Mormons), powerfully demonstrating the breadth of influence that social categories can exert on face memory (Rule, Garrett, & Ambady, 2010).

Indeed, even relatively arbitrary, experimentally constructed social categories can lead to an ingroup advantage in face memory. In one such demonstration, Bernstein, Young, and Hugenberg (2007) report a "Cross Category Effect" wherein the faces of mere ingroup members were better recognized than the faces of mere outgroup members. In this research, participants better recognized faces categorized as sharing a university affiliation, or even the same personality type, better than faces

labeled as attending a different university or having a different personality type. Moreover, this was true even holding the faces constant using counterbalancing, ensuring that the results were not due to different facial structures of or practice with ingroup and outgroup members. More recently, Hehman, Mania, and Gaertner (2010) have experimentally crossed university affiliation with race to create cross-cutting categories. Drawing from the Common Ingroup Identity Model (Gaertner & Dovidio, 2000), the authors argue that outgroup members who are redefined as ingroup members will be individuated as ingroup members. White and Black faces were presented in clusters, either defined by racial group or university affiliation. When White and Black faces appeared together under a university label, perceivers showed a university ingroup recognition advantage, regardless of target race. However, when the cluster was defined by race, other-race university ingroup members were remembered no better than outgroup members. These results suggest that it is possible to redefine other-race faces as ingroup members (see also Van Bavel et al., 2011, for a recent replication), though race is such a powerful category that this recategorization may not be easily achieved in all contexts (Brewer, 1988; see also Shriver et al., 2008). Taken together, these data indicate that ingroup members, whether defined by ascribed categories such as race, sex, or sexual orientation or by acquired categories such as university affiliation or religion, appear to create motivated biases in face memory. In short, perceivers better recognize ingroup members than outgroup members.

Non-category Target Characteristics also Motivate Individuation

Despite the strong influence of categories on face memory, there are also instances in which noncategory target characteristics can motivate individuation. The crux of the issue is that, for individuation to occur, the target must be important or relevant in some way to the perceiver. In many cases, mere ingroup status is enough to induce individuation; however, there are multiple cues outside of ingroup status that can motivate perceivers to individuate others. For example, attractive targets (and especially attractive female targets) can motivate strong face encoding. According to Maner and colleagues (2003), attractive women both received more visual attention and are better remembered than are less attractive female faces, an effect that occurs for both male and female perceivers. Further research demonstrates that such biases also play out in a paradigm requiring participants to remember both facial identity and target location (Becker, Kenrick, Guerin, & Maner, 2005).

Target power is another cue to individuate faces. High-power faces are recognized better than are low-power faces (Ratcliff et al., 2010). Remarkably, target power is such a potent cue of individuation that it can overcome outgroup status as a cue for disregard. Indeed, powerful members of outgroups are recognized just as well as are ingroup members. Thus, power can elicit individuation of even the typically poorly encoded outgroup targets. In one example, Ackerman et al. (2006) showed White participants images of neutral-expression and angry black and White target faces. Recognition scores for neutral-expression faces replicated past work; the ORE was observed. However, the ORE was eliminated for angry faces, by an improvement in recognition for Black (i.e., outgroup) faces. To the extent that black faces are more associated with threat than White faces (Hugenberg & Bodenhausen, 2003, 2004; Maner et al., 2005), signals of anger from Black targets may be a potent display of potential force and thus worthy of individuation. Other research manipulated power more explicitly. Shriver and Hugenberg (2010) showed White participants images of Black and White targets paired with behaviors that implied the targets were high or low in power. Regardless of whether power stemmed from physical threat (e.g., gang violence) or from economic power (e.g., vast wealth), powerful Black targets were remembered just as well as White targets. From the perspective that people individuate targets who appear situationally relevant, it is perfectly sensible that socially powerful targets (i.e., potential bosses, attackers) would be better individuated than powerless targets.

This functional account of the ORE is strengthened by recent work by Adams, Pauker, and Weisbuch (2010), in which targets' eye gaze modulates the ORE. Adams and colleagues (2010) found that same-race targets were better remembered than other-race targets, but only if they were displaying direct gaze. Targets displaying averted gaze elicited low levels of recognition sensitivity regardless of race. Thus, the advantage that ingroup members typically enjoy in face memory does not occur when their eyes gaze away from perceivers, rather than toward them. Indeed, the lack of direct eye gaze appears to undermine the subjective importance of ingroup members, which is an important demonstration that well understood, bottom-up

motivators of processing can influence individuation and face memory.

Situationally Induced Motives to Individuate

In addition to target characteristics influencing face memory, situational characteristics can also create or eliminate motivated biases in face recognition. In fact, this can be achieved simply by instructing participants to individuate other-race targets. Hugenberg, Miller, and Claypool (2007) found that White perceivers who were informed of the existence of the ORE and given a brief strategy to overcome it were able to do so. Merely instructing participants to attend to the individuating characteristics of outgroup faces was sufficient to increase other-race recognition to same-race levels. The efficacy of these instructions has been established multiple times (e.g., Young, Bernstein, & Hugenberg, 2010; Rhodes, Locke, Ewing, & Evangelista, 2009). In each case, participants were able to individuate other-race faces without having received any extra experience doing so.

Additional research involving recognition of ambiguous-race faces is exemplary of the influence of situational characteristics. For example, Pauker and colleagues (2009) instructed participants to include biracial targets in the ingroup, to avoid the appearance of prejudice. Remarkably, perceivers who were given motivation to include biracial targets in their own group exhibited improved recognition for racially ambiguous targets (i.e., "biracial" targets), but not for unambiguously other-race targets. By inducing participants to include biracial targets in the ingroup, with instructions exogenous to the faces themselves, Pauker and colleagues were able to substantially improve recognition for those faces.

Perceiver Motives Can Lead to Ingroup Homogeneity

Despite a strong default tendency for perceivers to individuate ingroup members, the motive to individuate ingroup members is not universal across all situations. Perceiving high variability only for ingroup members, but not for outgroup members, is likely only motivationally appealing in situations in which perceivers are motivated to perceive the ingroup as more heterogeneous than the outgroup. Indeed, Wilson and Hugenberg (2010) have found that motivating perceivers to desire ingroup *homogeneity* can lead to a motivated reduction in ingroup recognition. Drawing on Social Identity Theory (Tajfel & Turner, 1986), Wilson and Hugenberg found that threatening participants' ingroup distinctiveness can motivate ingroup homogeneity.

White American participants read a fabricated news articles noting that Hispanic immigration to the United States was growing rapidly and that existing cultural boundaries between Whites and Hispanics could blur permanently. Not only did participants who experienced this cultural distinctiveness threat experience the situation as aversive, but also their desire for ingroup homogeneity manifested as a reduction in same-race recognition (i.e., a more *perceptually* homogeneous ingroup), relative to participants who did not experience the distinctiveness threat.

Taken together, the role of individuation motives in face processing is clear. Categories can signal that a face is important to individuate; however, other target cues (e.g., target attractiveness, target power) and situational cues (e.g., instructions) can also powerfully induce face individuation. These cues to individuation can act in concert or in opposition to influence face memory in complex ways across different contexts; however, it is clear that perceivers' motives act in a top-down way to influence face recognition.

Contexts, Categories and the Biased Perception of Facial Expressions

BIASES IN INTERPRETATION

Just as evaluation and processing of facial identity can be influenced in a top-down manner, so too can the perception of facial expressions be influenced by perceivers' motives, targets' social categories, and the contexts in which targets are perceived. Indeed, when it comes to interpreting expressions, context matters. In one well-known empirical demonstration of this, Carroll and Russell (1996) paired unambiguous facial expressions with vignettes describing the elicitation of the emotion. Importantly, the facial expressions differed from the emotion that is typically elicited by the event. For example, a normatively angry expression was shown to participants, but participants were led to believe that the expression was displayed by a failed skydiver who balked at jumping from the airplane. Participants overwhelmingly interpreted that angry expression as fear. Similarly, a fearful expression shown toward a maître d' who refused to honor a table reservation was commonly interpreted as anger. Thus, the social context can play a potent role in how expressions are interpreted. The emotional state of a perceiver can also serve as a context for interpreting facial expressions. For example, Niedenthal, Halberstadt, Margolin, and Innes-Ker (2000) induced participants to experience a happy

or a sad mood by watching a video clip. Participants then viewed a series of "morph movies," watching faces change expression from happiness and sadness to neutrality. Participants were asked to indicate at what point the original expression (i.e., happy, sad) dissipated. Notably, Niedenthal and colleagues found that perceivers' experienced emotion influenced their experience of the targets' facial expressions. Happy perceivers saw happiness lingering longer on the happy-to-neutral movies, whereas sad perceivers saw happiness offsetting more quickly. Thus, both the social context and perceiver moods can serve as lenses through which faces and facial expressions can be interpreted.

Perceiver goals and motives can also act to bias how facial expressions are interpreted. For example, Maner and colleagues (2005) found that sexual arousal (i.e., a mate-search motive) leads men to interpret ambiguous-expression attractive female faces to be displaying sexual interest (see also Haselton & Buss, 2000). Similarly, both male and female perceivers who prefer more low-attachment sexual partners, rather than fewer high-attachment partners (i.e., "sociosexually unrestricted" individuals), perceived higher levels of sexual arousal in opposite-sex faces. Maner and colleagues (2005) also found that self-protective motives play a similar biasing role in the interpretation of facial expressions as well. For example, White participants with an activated self-protection motive interpreted neutral expressions on Black male and Arab male faces as angrier than did participants without an activated self-protection motive. Notably, however, self-protective motives did not lead all targets to seem angry, but only targets who were members of stereotypically threatening groups (e.g., Black males, Arab males). Thus, it seems that motives can act hand in hand with social categories to influence the interpretation of others' facial expressions.

Related work has found that prejudice can also act in concert with social categories to bias the interpretation of facial expressions in a stereotypic direction. For example, Hugenberg and Bodenhausen (2003, 2004; see also Bijlstra, Holland, & Wigboldus, 2010; Kang & Chasteen, 2009, for similar results) provide evidence of a Black-anger link, an effect congruent with the stereotype of Blacks as hostile or aggressive. In one set of studies, White participants viewed morph videos (see Niedenthal et al., 2000) of computer-generated Black and White targets' facial expressions changing from anger to happiness and were tasked with reporting when the original angry expression dissipated. The Black and White targets were matched perfectly for facial structure, so that at each point in the angry-to-happy movies, the only difference between the Black and White targets was the skin tone and hairstyle. The results indicated that anger was seen as lingering for longer on Black compared with White faces, an effect that was at its strongest for perceivers highest in implicit anti-Black prejudice. Analogous effects were observed for anger onset, with neutral-to-angry movies eliciting perceptions of anger earlier on Black relative to White faces, an effect that was again strongest for perceivers high in implicit, anti-Black prejudice. In related work, Hugenberg and Bodenhausen (2004) found the Black-anger link to be bidirectional, with expressions influencing the racial categorization of targets. Across two experiments, White participants were more likely to categorize a racially ambiguous Black/White face as Black when it displayed anger, relative to when the same face displayed happiness. As in the previous studies, the magnitude of this effect increased as perceivers' implicit anti-Black prejudice increased. In this case, the expression on the face appears to have been used to disambiguate the race of otherwise ambiguous social targets. More recently, Inzlicht, Kaiser, and Major (2008) found related prejudice-expression links with sex. Specifically, Inzlicht and colleagues had male and female participants watch morph movies of (White) male and female faces changing in expression from contempt to happiness (or anger to happiness). Women who believed that they were chronically subject to sexism (i.e., stigma-conscious women) saw contempt lingering on male, relative to female, faces. Inzlicht and colleagues argue that because male sexism is commonly observed as a contemptuous prejudice, the stigma-conscious women were sensitized to displays of male contempt, leading to the perception that contempt was lingering on male faces. Taken together, these data indicate that perceivers' social beliefs (prejudice, stigma consciousness) can interact with targets' categories (race, sex) to influence the perception of facial expressions. Moreover, this also serves as an example of how social cognitive processes such as evaluations and beliefs can play out in the domain of face perception.

Broader category-expression links can be observed for sex stereotypes as well. For example, a female-positivity link appears to reliably play out in facial expression perception. Hess and colleagues (1997) found that ambiguously happy faces female faces are rated as happier than ambiguously happy male faces. Thus, the interpretation of the expression is assimilated to the evaluative associations typical of the sex category (see Plant et al., 2004, for a related finding). In a similar vein, happiness is recognized more quickly and more accurately on female compared with male faces (Hugenberg & Sczesny, 2006), whereas anger is detected more quickly on male compared with female faces (Becker et al., 2007). Notably, whereas Hugenberg and Bodenhausen (2003, 2004) held facial structure constant, isolating these effects to the role of social categories, this has not been done with the work on the female-happiness and male-anger links. In fact, these links are due at least in part to bottom-up effects of the facial structural differences between female and male faces. On average, male and female faces differ on their babyfacedness; female faces, relative to male faces, have more babyfaced characteristics (e.g., small chin, large eyes). Because female faces have more babyfaced characteristics (e.g., large eyes) and male faces have more mature characteristics (e.g., small eyes), this facial structural difference facilitates the recognition of happy expressions on female and angry expressions on male faces, respectively (Becker et al., 2007; Marsh et al., 2005). Thus, at least some of the "category-based" biases in interpreting facial expressions likely operate in both a top-down and a bottom-up manner.

PERCEPTUAL ATTUNEMENT

Although categories and motives can serve to bias the perception of facial expressions, they can also *attune* perceivers to facial expressions. Thus, motives and categories can both bias perceivers and make them more sensitive to social signals. First, social category membership can moderate the accuracy with which facial expressions are recognized. Recognition of basic emotional expressions is universally substantially above chance, and this is even true when the expression encoder and decoder are of very different cultural backgrounds (e.g., Ekman et al., 1969; Ekman & Friesen, 1971). However, recent evidence has revealed an ingroup emotion recognition advantage, indicating that cultural "accents" exist and influence recognition. For example, even among faces of one's own race, facial expressions displayed by members of one's own *culture* (e.g., White American for White American perceivers) are more accurately decoded than are expressions displayed by members of another closely related culture (e.g., White Australian; see Elfenbein & Ambady, 2003). Elfenbein and Ambady (2003) propose Dialect Theory to explain these findings, positing that there are subtle but distinct differences in how discrete emotions are expressed across cultures. These local variations in facial expressions of emotions—analogous to dialects of a spoken language—are overlaid on a universally shared non-verbal affect program. Importantly, Dialect Theory proposes that perceivers become perceptually attuned to the non-verbal accents of ingroup members. Just as with language, our visual system becomes attuned through extensive training to the non-verbal "accent" used by the ingroup.

More recently, however, Young and Hugenberg (2010) have found that even quite minimal ingroup/outgroup differences can elicit analogous results, even when holding the non-verbal dialect constant. Across three studies, White American participants were randomly assigned to an ingroup based on the results of a bogus personality inventory. Participants were assigned to "red" and "green" personality types and were then shown a series of faces displaying unambiguous facial expressions (e.g., anger, fear, happiness), displayed on red and green backgrounds (which were ostensibly indicative of the personality type of the faces). Across all of the studies, participants more accurately recognized the expressions on faces they believed were fellow ingroup members (i.e., shared "personality types") compared with outgroup members, even though all participants and all of the expression encoders were from the same larger cultural ingroup. Notably, Young and Hugenberg (2010) found that perceivers' motivation was an important part of this ingroup advantage. When the ability of perceivers to deploy motivated processing was attenuated (e.g., by truncating the amount of time perceivers had to process the faces), the ingroup advantage was attenuated as well. Thus, the perceptual attunements that result for ingroup members' expressions appear to be the result of both perceiver expertise (e.g., Marsh, Elfenbein, & Ambady, 2003) and perceiver motivation.

Beyond these broad ingroup advantages in expression recognition, it seems clear that specific motives and life experiences can attune perceivers to functionally important facial expressions and facial signals. Motives can serve a preparatory function and can mobilize perceivers' cognitive and perceptual resources in preparation for action. Thus, certain motives appear capable of attuning perceivers to motivationally relevant facial expressions. For example, although past research has shown that mating goals can lead perceivers to read more sexual arousal into potential sexual partners than actually exists (e.g., Maner et al., 2005), the ability to discriminate between the receptivity of potential partners is also of key importance. In fact, Sacco,

Hugenberg, and Sefcek (2009) found that participants who are sociosexually unrestricted (i.e., preferring many short-term partners) are particularly adept at discriminating among the magnitude of women's smiles. Such sensitivity may help determine mating opportunities.

We see similar motivationally based perceptual attunements occurring in very different settings as well. For example, Sacco and Hugenberg (2012) found that perceivers experiencing interdependent motives (i.e., motives to cooperate with others or compete with others) also become better able to discriminate among facial signals of cooperation and competition (happiness and anger). Chronically activated self-protective motives also appear to act in a similar manner, creating perceptual attunements for angry facial expressions. For example, physically abused children not only attend to angry expressions more strongly than do non-abused children (e.g., Pollak & Tolley-Schell, 2003) but also become quite sensitive to the signals of anger in faces. Thus, in morph-movie-style tasks, abused children see the onset of anger very early in expressions blends (e.g., Pollak & Kistler, 2002; Pollak, Messner, Kistler, & Cohn, 2009; Pollak & Sinha, 2002), indicating that the chronic threat experienced in their environment attunes them to even slight signals of anger in the faces of adults. Although this likely has some dysfunctional consequences (e.g., hostile attribution bias), being very sensitive to the anger of others may serve to provide early warning of adults' anger.

Thus, it appears clear that contexts, motives, and social categories can all serve to both bias the interpretation of facial expressions and enhance perceivers' sensitivity to facial expressions. Although these two bodies of findings may initially seem discrepant, in actuality they need not be. In signal-detection terms, sensitivity and bias are separable effects. Thus, in the case of mating goals, one can simultaneously read more sexual interest into the faces of many potential partners, while still becoming attuned to the difference between those who are more and less interested. In the former case, this may ensure that few chances to mate are missed (i.e., an "error management" perspective; Haselton & Buss, 2000), while still affording the ability to discriminate between more likely and less likely partners.

Top-Down Effects in Summary

The literature on top-down effects in face perception—as with bottom-up effects—spans multiple scientific literatures in the social and cognitive sciences. However, here too there are some clear consistencies among the findings. First, categories are extracted quickly and easily from faces. The perceptual differentiation among facial structural signals of race or sex (for example) occurs quite early in the perceptual stream, and these effects then ramify throughout subsequent processing, and as with bottom-up effects, these top-down effects of categories and expectations can occur quickly and without our awareness.

A second major theme that shines through this literature is that what we see in a face is due, in part, to what we *expect* to see—our expectations, beliefs, and stereotypes can warp how we see faces. For example, whether an expression seems angry or happy depends in part on top-down influences such as the context (e.g., is the expresser Black or White; is the expression shown at a birthday party or a funeral?).

Finally, an emerging theme from these top-down effects is that face perception is a *motivated* phenomenon. Indeed, the now classic "motivated tactician" perspective applies broadly across domains of person perception, face perception included. In this vein, not all faces are equal to us—we work harder to extract information from some faces than others. For example, we are better at encoding and remembering the faces and facial expressions of those who we believe are important to us (ingroup members, powerful or threatening individuals), relative to others. Similarly, when appropriately motivated, we attune our perception to faces or facial expressions that are motivationally relevant—we attend to faces and discriminate among expressions that are of use in meeting our currently activated goals.

Conclusion

Faces are central to social cognition. They are informationally rich and are processed with remarkable efficiency. Across multiple lines of converging evidence, it seems quite clear that face perception and our social cognitions about others are intimately linked. The facial structures and characteristics of others can spontaneously influence our judgments about others' traits and intentions. Moreover, our beliefs about others' categories and intentions can bias our perceptions of faces. Many of these biasing effects can occur with remarkable speed and without intent or awareness, spontaneously influencing our social perceptions. The fact that both such processes can occur has already had a powerful influence on the field and will likely continue to do so. For example, the knowledge that facial characteristics (e.g., skin tone, facial structure)

can independently influence social cognition (e.g., prejudice, trait inferences) in a bottom-up manner offers new insight into well-researched domains. Conversely, the fact that perceivers' motives can drive perceptual and memorial effects, such as motivated biases in face recognition, can provide a new top-down look at domains previously believed to be driven primarily by bottom-up processes (e.g., the ORE). We see such recent advances at the interface of social cognition and face perception to be an exciting development, with social cognitive psychologists increasingly treating the face as a serious topic of study. Given the centrality of faces to social cognition, we believe this new direction is an important one. Finally, this new work promises to bring a meaningful integration of social cognition and other cognitive sciences focusing on face perception, yielding a more complete perspective on this most social of stimuli: the human face.

Author Note

Correspondence can be addressed to Kurt Hugenberg or John Paul Wilson, Department of Psychology, Miami University, Oxford, OH 45056, USA, email: hugenbk@muohio.edu. Preparation of this manuscript was supported by National Science Foundation grant BCS-0951463, awarded to the first author.

References

Ackerman, J. M., Becker, D. V., Mortensen, C. R., Sasaki, T., Neuberg, S. L., & Kenrick, S. L. (2009). A pox on the mind: Disjunction of attention and memory in the processing of physical disfigurement. *Journal of Experimental Social Psychology, 45,* 478–485.

Ackerman, J. M., Shapiro, J. R., Neuberg, S. L., Kenrick, D. T., Becker, D. V., Griskevicius, V., Maner, J. K., & Schaller, M. (2006). They all look the same to me (unless they're angry): From out-group homogeneity to out-group heterogeneity. *Psychological Science, 17,* 836–840.

Adams, R. B., & Kleck, R. E. (2003). Perceived gaze direction and the processing of facial displays of emotion. *Psychological Science, 14,* 644–647.

Adams, R. B., & Kleck, R. E. (2005). The effects of direct and averted gaze on the perception of facially communicated emotion. *Emotion, 5,* 3–11.

Adams, R. B., Pauker, K., & Weisbuch, M. (2010). Looking the other way: The role of gaze direction in the cross-race memory effect. *Journal of Experimental Social Psychology, 46,* 478–481.

Adolphs, R., Tranel, D., & Damasio, A. R. (1998). The human amygdala in social judgment. *Nature, 393,* 470–474.

Anastasi, J. S., & Rhodes, M. G. (2005). An own-age bias in face recog- nition for children and older adults. *Psychonomic Bulletin & Review, 12,* 1043–1047.

Argyle, M., & Cook, M. (1976). *Gaze and mutual gaze.* Cambridge, UK: Cambridge University Press.

Ballew, C. C., & Todorov, A. (2007). Predicting political elections from rapid and unreflective face judgments. *Proceedings of the National Academy of Sciences of the USA, 104*, 17948–17953.

Bargh, J. A. (1996). Automaticity in social psychology. In E. T. Higgins & A. W. Kruglanski, (Eds.), *Social psychology: Handbook of basic principles* (pp. 169–183). New York: Guilford Press.

Baron-Cohen, S. (1995). *Mindblindness: An essay on autism and theory of mind.* Cambridge, MA: MIT Press.

Baron-Cohen, S., Wheelwright, S., & Jolliffe, T. (1997). Is there a "language of the eyes"? Evidence from normal adults, and adults with autism or Asperger syndrome. *Visual Cognition, 4*, 311–331.

Barton, J. J. S., Press, D. Z., Keenan, J. P., & O'Connor, M. (2002). Lesions of the fusiform area impair perception of facial configuration in prosopagnosia. *Neurology, 58*, 71–78.

Batki, A., Baron-Cohen, S., Wheelwright, S., Connellan, J., & Ahluwalia, J. (2000). Is there an innate gaze module? Evidence from human neonates. *Infant Behavior & Development, 23*, 223–229.

Bayliss, A. P., Frischen, A., Fenske, M. J., & Tipper, S. P. (2007). Affective evaluations of objects are influenced by observed gaze direction and emotional expression. *Cognition, 104*, 644–653.

Bayliss, A. P., Paul, M. A., Cannon, P. R., & Tipper, S. P. (2006). Gaze cuing and affective judgments of objects: I like what you look at. *Psychonomic Bulletin & Review, 13*, 1061–1066.

Bayliss, A. P., & Tipper, P. (2006). Predictive gaze cues and personality judgments: Should eye trust you? *Psychological Science, 17*, 514–520.

Beauregard, M., Lvesque, J., & Bourgouin, P. (2001). Neural correlates of conscious self-regulation of emotion. *Journal of Neuroscience, 21*, 6993–7000.

Becker, D. V., Kenrick, D. T., Guerin, S., & Maner, J. M. (2005). Concentrating on beauty: Sexual selection and sociospatial memory. *Personality and Social Psychology Bulletin, 12*, 1643–1652.

Becker, D. V., Kenrick, D. T., Neuberg, S. L., Blackwell, K. C., & Smith, D. M. (2007). The confounded nature of angry men and happy women. *Journal of Personality and Social Psychology, 92*, 179–190.

Bernstein, M., Young, S. G., & Hugenberg, K. (2007). The Cross-Category Effect: Mere social categorization is sufficient to elicit an Own-Group Bias in face recognition. *Psychological Science, 18*, 706–712.

Berry, D. S., & McArthur, L. (1985). Some components and consequences of a babyface. *Journal of Personality and Social Psychology, 48*, 312–323.

Bijlstra, G., Holland R. W., & Wigboldus, D. H. J. (2010). The social face of emotion recognition: Evaluations versus stereotypes. *Journal of Experimental Social Psychology, 46*, 657–663.

Blair, I. V., Judd, C. M., & Chapleau, K. M. (2004). The influence of Afrocentric facial features in criminal sentencing. *Psychological Science, 15*, 674–679.

Blair, I. V., Judd, C. M., & Fallman, J. L. (2004). The automaticity of race and Afrocentric facial features in social judgments. *Journal of Personality and Social Psychology, 87*, 763–778.

Blair, I. V., Judd, C. M., Sadler, M. S., & Jenkins, C. (2002). The role of Afrocentric features in person perception: Judging by features and categories. *Journal of Personality and Social Psychology, 83*, 5–25.

Bond, M. H., (1991). *Beyond the Chinese face: Insights from psychology.* Hong Kong: Oxford University Press.

Brewer, M. B. (1988). A dual-process model of impression formation. In T. Srull & R. Wyer (Eds.), *Advances in social cognition* (Vol. 1, pp. 1–36). Hillsdale, NJ: Erlbaum.

Brosch, T., Sander, D., Pourtois, G., & Scherer, K. R. (2008). Beyond fear: Rapid spatial orienting toward positive emotional stimuli. *Psychological Science, 19*, 362–370.

Brosch, T., Sander, D., & Scherer, K. R. (2007). That baby caught my eye…Attention capture by infant faces. *Emotion, 7*, 685–689.

Bruner, J. S. (1957). Going beyond the information given. In J. S. Bruner, E, Brunswik, L. Festinger, F. Heider, K. F. Muenzinger, C. E. Osgood, & D. Rapaport, (Eds.), *Contemporary approaches to cognition* (pp. 41–69). Cambridge, MA: Harvard University Press.

Bull, R., & Rumsey, N. (1988). *The social psychology of facial appearance.* New York: Springer-Verlag.

Bushnell, I., Sai, F., & Mullin, J. (1989). Neonatal recognition of the mother's face. *British Journal of Developmental Psychology, 7*, 3–15.

Buss, D. M., Abbott, M., Angleitner, A., Asherian, A., et al. (1990). International preferences in selecting mates: A study of 37 cultures. *Journal of Cross-Cultural Psychology, 21*, 5–47.

Cacioppo, J. T., Priester, J. R., & Berntson, G. G. (1993). Rudimentary determinants of attitudes: II. Arm flexion and extension have different effects on attitudes. *Journal of Personality and Social Psychology, 65*, 5–17.

Calder, A. J., Young, A. W., Keane, J., & Dean, M. (2000) Configural information in facial expression perception. *Journal of Experimental Psychology: Human Perception and Performance, 26*, 527–555.

Carroll, J. M., & Russell, J. A. (1996). Do facial expressions signal specific emotions? Judging emotion from the face in context. *Journal of Personality and Social Psychology, 70*, 205–218.

Cary, M. S. (1978). Does civil inattention exist in pedestrian passing? *Journal of Personality and Social Psychology, 36*, 1185–1193.

Chaiken, S. (1986). Physical appearance and social influence. In C. P. Herman, M. P. Zanna, & E. T. Higgins (Eds.), *Physical appearance, stigma, and social behavior: The Ontario Symposium* (Vol. 3, pp. 143–177). Hillsdale, NJ: Erlbaum.

Collins, M. A., & Zebrowitz, A. (1995). The contributions of appearance to occupational outcomes in civilian and military settings. *Journal of Applied Social Psychology, 25*, 129–163.

Cook, M., & Smith. M. C. (1975). The role of gaze in impression formation. *British Journal of Social and Clinical Psychology, 14*, 19–25.

Copley, J. E., & Brownlow, S. (1995). The interactive effects of facial maturity and name warmth on perceptions of job candidates. *Basic and Applied Social Psychology, 16*, 251–265.

Corneille, O., Huart, J., Becquart, E., & Brédart, S. (2004). When memory shifts towards more typical category exemplars: Accentuation effects in the recollection of ethnically ambiguous faces. *Journal of Personality and Social Psychology, 86*, 236–250.

Corneille, O., Mauduit, S., Holland, R. W., & Strick, M. (2009). Liking products by the head of a dog: Perceived orientation of attention induces valence acquisition. *Journal of Experimental Social Psychology, 45*, 234–237.

Correll, J., Park, B., Judd, C. M., & Wittenbrink, B. (2002). The police officer's dilemma: Using ethnicity to disambiguate potentially threatening individuals. *Journal of Personality and Social Psychology, 83*, 1314–1329.

Cross, J. F., Cross, J., & Daly, J. (1971). Sex, race, age, and beauty as factors in recognition of faces. *Perception & Psychophysics, 10*, 393–396.

Cunningham, W. A., Johnson, M. K., Raye, C. L., Gatenby, J. C., Gore, J. C., & Banaji, M. R. (2004). Separable neural components in the processing of black and white faces. *Psychological Science, 15*, 806–813.

Darwin, C. (1965/1872). *The expression of the emotions in man and animals* (Rev. ed.). Chicago: University of Chicago Press. (Original work published 1872.)

De Gelder, B., & Rouw, R. (2000). Paradoxical configuration effects for faces and objects in prosopagnosia. *Neuropsychologia, 38*, 1271–1279.

De Gelder, B., & Rouw, R. (2001). Beyond localisation: A dynamical dual route account of face recognition. *Acta Psychologica, 107*, 183–207.

Dermer, M., & Thiel, L. (1975). When beauty may fail. *Journal of Personality and Social Psychology, 31*, 1168–1176.

Devine, P. G. (1989). Stereotypes and prejudice: Their automatic and controlled components. *Journal of Personality and Social Psychology, 56*, 5–18.

DeWall, C. N., & Maner, J. K. (2008). High status men (but not women) capture the eye of the beholder. *Evolutionary Psychology, 6*, 328–341.

Dion, K. K., Berscheid, E., & Walster, E. (1972). What is beautiful is good. *Journal of Personality and Social Psychology, 24*, 285–290.

Donders, N. C., Correll, J., & Wittenbrink, B. (2008). Danger stereotypes predict racially biased attentional allocation. *Journal of Experimental Social Psychology, 44*, 1328–1333.

Driver, J., Davis, G., Ricciardelli, P., Kidd, P., Maxwell, E., & Baron-Cohen, S. (1999). Gaze perception triggers reflexive visuospatial orienting. *Visual Cognition, 6*, 509–540.

Dubois, S., Rossion, B., Schiltz, C., Bodart, J. M., Michel, C., Bruyer, R., & Crommelinck, M. (1999). Effect of familiarity on the processing of human faces. *Neuroimage, 9*, 278–289.

Eberhardt, J. L., Davies, P. G., Purdie-Vaughns, V. J., & Johnson, S. L. (2006). Looking deathworthy: Perceived stereotypicality of black defendants predicts capital-sentencing outcomes. *Psychological Science, 17*, 383–386.

Eberhardt, J. L., Goff, P. A., Purdie, V. J., & Davies, P. G. (2004). Seeing black: Race, crime, and visual processing. *Journal of Personality and Social Psychology, 87*, 876–893.

Ekman, P. (1972). Universals and cultural differences in facial expressions of emotion. In J. Cole (Ed.), *Nebraska Symposium on Motivation 1971* (Vol. 19, pp. 207–283). Lincoln, NE: University of Nebraska Press.

Ekman, P., & Friesen, V. (1971). Constants across cultures in the face and emotion. *Journal of Personality and Social Psychology, 17*, 124–129.

Ekman, P., Friesen, W. V., O'Sullivan, M., Chan, A., Diacoyanni-Tarlatzis, I, Heider, K., et al. (1989). Universals and cultural differences in the judgments of facial expressions of emotion. *Journal of Personality and Social Psychology, 53*, 712–717.

Ekman, P., Sorenson, E. R., & Friesen, W. V. (1969). Pan-cultural elements in facial display of emotions. *Science, 164*, 86–88.

Elfenbein, H. A., & Ambady, N. (2003). When familiarity breeds accuracy: Cultural exposure and facial emotion recognition. *Journal of Personality and Social Psychology, 85*, 276–290.

Exline, R. V. (1971). Visual interaction: The glances of power and preference. *Nebraska Symposium on Motivation, 19*, 163–206.

Farah, M. J., Klein, K. L., & Levinson, K. L. (1995). Face perception and within-category discrimination in prosopagnosia. *Neuropsychologia, 33*, 661–674.

Farah, M. J., Wilson, K. D., Drain, M., & Tanaka, J. N. (1998). What is "special" about face perception? *Psychological Review, 105*, 482–498.

Farroni, T., Csibra, G., Simion, F., & Johnson, M. H. (2002). Eye contact detection in humans from birth. *Proceedings of the National Academies of Sciences of the United States of America, 99*, 9602–9605.

Farroni, T., Johnson, M. H., Menon, E. Zulian, L., Faraguna, D., & Csibra, G. (2005). Newborns' preference for face-relevant stimuli: Effects of contrast polarity. *Proceedings of the National Academy of Sciences USA, 102*, 17245–17250.

Feingold, A. (1990). Gender differences in effects of physical attractiveness on romantic attraction: A comparison across five research paradigms. *Journal of Personality and Social Psychology, 59*, 981–993.

Field, T. M., Cohen, D., Garcia, R., & Greenberg, R. (1984). Mother-stranger face discrimination by the newborn. *Infant Behavior and Development, 7*, 19–25.

Fiske, S. T. (2004). *Social beings: A core motives approach to social psychology.* New York: Wiley.

Frank, M. C., Vul, E., & Johnson, S. P. (2009). Development of infants' face preference during the first year. *Cognition, 110*, 160–170.

Fridlund, A. J. (1994). *Human facial expression: An evolutionary view.* San Diego, CA: Academic Press.

Friesen, C. K., & Kingstone, A. (1998). The eyes have it! Reflexive orienting is triggered by nonpredictive gaze. *Psychonomic Bulletin & Review, 5*, 490–495.

Frijda, N. H., & Tcherkassof, A. (1997). Facial expressions as modes of action readiness. In J. A. Russel & J. M. Fernandez-Dols (Eds.), *The psychology of facial expression* (pp. 78–102). New York: Cambridge University Press.

Frischen, A., Bayliss, A. P., & Tipper, S. P. (2007). Gaze cueing of attention: Visual attention, social cognition, and individual differences. *Psychological Bulletin, 133*, 694–724.

Gaertner, S. L., & Dovidio, J. F. (2000). *Reducing intergroup bias: The common ingroup identity model.* Philadelphia: Psychology Press.

Gauthier, I., & Bukach, C. (2007). Should we reject the expertise hypothesis? *Cognition, 103*, 322–330.

Gauthier, I., Curran, T., Curby, K. M., & Collins, D. (2003). Perceptual interference supports a non-modular account of face processing. *Nature Neuroscience, 6*, 428–432.

Golby, A. J., Gabrieli, J. D. E., Chaio, J. Y., & Eberhardt, J. L. (2001). Differential fusiform responses to same- and other-race faces. *Nature Neuroscience, 4*, 845–850.

Goldberg, F. J. (1973). The question on skin color and its relation to Japan. *Psychologia: An International Journal of Psychology in the Orient, 16*, 132–146.

Goren, C. C., Sarty, M., & Wu, P. Y. K. (1975). Visual following and pattern discrimination of face-like stimuli by newborn infants. *Pediatrics, 56*, 544–549.

Greenwald, A. G., & Banaji, M. R. (1995). Implicit social cognition: Attitudes, self-esteem, and stereotypes. *Psychological Review, 102*, 4–27.

Hart, A. J., Whalen, P. J., Shin, L. M., McInerney, S. C., Fischer, H., & Rauch, S. L. (2000). Differential response in the human amygdala to racial outgroup vs ingroup face stimuli. *Neuroreport, 11,* 2351–2355.

Haselton, M. G., & Buss, D. M. (2000). Error management theory: A new perspective on biases in cross-sex mind reading. *Journal of Personality and Social Psychology, 78,* 81–91.

Hassin, R., & Trope, Y. (2000). Facing faces: Studies on the cognitive aspects of physiognomy. *Journal of Personality and Social Psychology, 78,* 837–852.

Haxby, J., Hoffman, E., Gobbini, M. (2000). The distributed human neural system for face perception. *Trends in Cognitive Sciences, 4,* 223–233.

He, Y., Ebner, N. C., & Johnson, M. K. (2011). What predicts the own-age bias in face recognition memory? *Social Cognition, 29,* 97–109.

Hehman, E., Mania, E. W., & Gaertner, S. L. (2010). Where the division lies: Common ingroup identity moderates the cross-race facial-recognition effect. *Journal of Experimental Social Psychology, 46,* 445–448.

Hess, U., Adams Jr., R. B., Grammer, K., & Kleck, R. E. (2009). Face gender and emotion expression: Are angry women more like men? *Journal of Vision, 9,* 1–8.

Hess, U., Adams, R. B., & Kleck, R. E. (2007). Looking at you or looking elsewhere: The influence of head orientation on the signal value of emotional facial expressions. *Motivation and Emotion, 31,* 137–144.

Hess, U., Blairy, S., & Kleck, R. E. (1997). The intensity of emotional facial expressions and decoding accuracy. *Journal of Nonverbal Behavior, 21,* 241–257.

Hugenberg, K., & Bodenhausen, G. V. (2003). Facing prejudice: Implicit prejudice and the perception of facial threat. *Psychological Science, 14,* 640–643.

Hugenberg, K., & Bodenhausen, G. V. (2004). Ambiguity in social categorization: The role of prejudice and facial affect in face categorization. *Psychological Science, 15,* 342–345.

Hugenberg, K., & Corneille, O. (2009). Holistic processing is tuned for in-group faces. *Cognitive Science, 33,* 1173–1181.

Hugenberg, K., Miller, J., & Claypool, H. M. (2007). Categorization and individuation in the cross-race recognition deficit: Toward a solution to an insidious problem. *Journal of Experimental Social Psychology, 43,* 334–340.

Hugenberg, K., & Sacco, D. F. (2008). Social categorization and stereotyping: How social categorization biases persona perception and face memory. *Compass in Social Psychology, 2,* 1052–1072.

Hugenberg, K., & Sczesny, S. (2006). On wonderful women and seeing smiles: Social categorization moderates the happy face response latency advantage. *Social Cognition, 24,* 516–539.

Inzlicht, M., Kaiser, C. R., & Major, B. (2008). The face of chauvinism: How prejudice expectations shape perceptions of facial affect. *Journal of Experimental Social Psychology, 44,* 758–766.

Ito, T. A., & Urland, R. (2003). Race and gender on the brain: Electrocortical measures of attention to the race and gender of multiply categorizable individuals. *Journal of Personality and Social Psychology, 85,* 616–626.

Johnson, M. H., Dziurawiec, S., Ellis, H. D., & Morton, J. (1991). Newborns' preferential tracking of faces and its subsequent decline. *Cognition, 40,* 1–19.

Kang, S. K., & Chasteen, A. L. (2009). Beyond the double-jeopardy hypothesis: Assessing emotion on the faces of multiply-categorizable targets. *Journal of Experimental Social Psychology, 45,* 1281–1285.

Kanwisher, N., & Yovel, G. (2006). The fusiform face area: A cortical region specialized for the perception of faces. *Philosophical Transactions of the Royal Society B, 361,* 2109–2128.

Keating, C. F., Mazur, A., & Segall, M. H. (1977). Facial gestures which influence the perception of status. *Social Psychology Quarterly, 40,* 374–378.

Kendon, A., & Ferber, A. (1973). A description of some human greetings. In P. M. Michael & J. H. Cook (Eds.), *Comparative ecology and behavior of primates.* London: Academic Press.

Kleinke, C. L. (1986). Gaze and eye contact: A research review. *Psychological Bulletin, 100,* 78–100.

Kleinke, C. L., Meeker, E B., & La Fong, C. (1974). Effects of gaze, touch, and use of name on evaluation of "engaged" couples. *Journal of Research in Personality, 7,* 368–373.

Kling, A. S., & Brothers, L. A. (1992). The amygdala and social behavior. In J. P. Aggleton (Ed.), *The amygdala: Neurobiological aspects of emotion, memory, and mental dysfunction* (pp. 353–377). New York: Wiley-Liss.

Knutson, B. (1996). Facial expressions of emotion influence interpersonal trait inferences. *Journal of Nonverbal Behavior, 20,* 165–182.

Langlois, J. H., & Stephan, C. (1977). The effects of physical attractiveness and ethnicity on children's behavioral attributions and peer preferences. *Child Development, 48,* 1694–1698.

Le Gal, P. M., & Bruce, V. (2002). Evaluating the independence of sex and expression in judgments of faces. *Perception & Psychophysics, 64,* 230–243.

Levin, D. T. (1996). Classifying faces by race: The structure of face categories. *Journal of Experimental Psychology: Learning, Memory, and Cognition, 22,* 1364–1382.

Levin, D. T., & Banaji, R. (2006). Distortions in the perceived lightness of faces: The role of race categories. *Journal of Experimental Psychology: General, 135,* 501–512.

Lim, B. (1972). Interpretations from pictures: The effects on judgments of intimacy of varying social context and eye contact. *Journalism Abstracts, 10,* 152–153.

Liu, C. H., & Chaudhuri, A. (2003). What determines whether faces are special? *Visual Cognition, 10,* 385–408.

Livingston, R. W., & Brewer, B. (2002). What are we really priming? Cue-based versus category-based processing of facial stimuli. *Journal of Personality and Social Psychology, 82,* 5–18.

Luck, S. J., & Hillyard, A. (1994). Spatial filtering during visual search: Evidence from human electrophysiology. *Journal of Experimental Psychology: Human Perception and Performance, 20,* 1000–1014.

Ma, D. S., & Correll, J. (2011). Target prototypicality moderates racial bias in the decision to shoot. *Journal of Experimental Social Psychology, 47,* 391–396.

MacLin, O. H., & Malpass, S. (2001). Racial categorization of faces: The ambiguous race face effect. *Psychology, Public Policy, and Law, 7,* 98–118.

MacLin, O. H., & Malpass, S. (2003). The ambiguous-race face illusion. *Perception, 32,* 249–252.

Macrae, C. N., Hood, B. M., Milne, A. B., Rowe, A. C., & Mason, M. F. (2002). Are you looking at me? Eye gaze and person perception. *Psychological Science, 13,* 460–464.

Macrae, C. N., & Quadflieg, S. (2010). Perceiving people. In D. T. Gilbert & S. T. Fiske (Eds.), *The handbook of social psychology* (5th ed.). New York: McGraw-Hill.

Maddox, K. B., & Gray, A. (2002). Cognitive representations of Black Americans: Reexploring the role of skin tone. *Personality and Social Psychology Bulletin, 28,* 250–259.

Maner, J. K., Kenrick, D. T., Becker, D. V., Delton, A. W., Hofer, B., Wilbur, C. J., et al. (2003). Sexually selective cognition: Beauty captures the mind of the beholder. *Journal of Personality and Social Psychology, 85*, 1107–1120.

Maner, J. K., Kenrick, D. T., Becker, D. V., Robertson, T. E., Hofer, B., Neuberg, S. L., et al. (2005). Functional projection: How fundamental social motives can bias interpersonal perception. *Journal of Personality and Social Psychology, 88*, 63–78.

Maner, J. K., Kenrick, D. T., Neuberg, S. L., Becker, D. V., Robertson, T., Hofer, B., Delton, A., Butner, J., & Schaller, M. (2005). Functional projection: How fundamental social motives can bias interpersonal perception. *Journal of Personality and Social Psychology, 88*, 63–78.

Marsh, A. A., Adams Jr., R. B., & Kleck, R. E. (2005). Why do fear and anger look the way they do? Form and social function in facial expressions. *Personality and Social Psychology Bulletin, 31*, 73–86.

Marsh, A. A., Elfenbein, H. A., & Ambady, N. (2003). Nonverbal "accents": Cultural differences in facial expressions of emotion. *Psychological Science, 14*, 373–376.

Martin, P. J., Friedmeyer, M. H., & Moore, J. E. (1977). Pretty patient-healthy patient? A study of physical attractiveness and psychopathology. *Journal of Clinical Psychology, 33*, 990–994.

Matsumoto, D. (1989). Cultural influences on the perception of emotion. *Journal of Cross-Cultural Psychology, 20*, 92–105.

Maurer, D., Le Grand, R., & Mondloch, C. (2002). The many faces of configural processing. *Trends in Cognitive Science, 6*, 255–260.

Mazur, A., Mazur, J., & Keating, C. (1984). Military rank attainment of a West Point class: Effects of cadets' physical features. *American Journal of Sociology, 90*, 125–150.

McArthur, L. Z., & Apatow, K. (1983). Impressions of baby-faced adults. *Social Cognition, 2*, 315–342.

McKone, E., Kanwisher, N., & Duchaine, B. C. (2006). Can generic expertise explain special processing for faces? *Trends in Cognitive Science, 11*, 8–15.

Meissner, C. A., & Brigham, C. (2001). Thirty years of investigating the own-race bias in memory for faces: A meta-analytic review. *Psychology, Public Policy, and Law, 7*, 3–35.

Michel, C., Corneille, O., & Rossion, B. (2007). Race categorization modulates holistic face encoding. *Cognitive Science, 31*, 911–924.

Michel, C., Rossion, B., Han, J., Chung, C., & Caldara, R. (2006). Holistic processing is finely tuned for faces of our own race. *Psychological Science, 17*, 608–615.

Montepare, J. M., & Zebrowitz, L. A. (1998). Person perception comes of age: The salience and significance of age in social judgments. In M. P. Zanna (Ed.), *Advances in Experimental Social Psychology* (Vol. 30). San Diego, CA: Academic Press.

Morton, J., & Johnson, M. H. (1991). CONSPEC and CONLERN: A two-process theory of infant face recognition. *Psychological Review, 98*, 164–181.

Mueller, U., & Mazur, A. (1996). Facial dominance in West Point cadets as a predictor of later military rank. *Social Forces, 74*, 823–850.

Neal, A. M., & Wilson, L. (1989). The role of skin color and features in the Black community: Implications for Black women and therapy. *Clinical Psychology Review, 9*(3), 323–333.

Niedenthal, P. M., Halberstadt, J. B., Margolin, J., & Innes-Ker, A. H. (2000). Emotional state and the detection of change in facial expression of emotion. *European Journal of Social Psychology, 30*, 211–222.

Nummenmaa, L., Hyönä, J., & Hietanen, J. K. (2009). I'll walk this way: Eyes reveal the direction of locomotion and make passersby look and go the other way. *Psychological Science, 20*, 1454–1458.

Ochsner, K. N., Bunge, S. A., Gross, J. J., & Gabrieli, J. D. E. (2002). Rethinking feelings: An fMRI study of the cognitive regulation of emotion. *Journal of Cognitive Neuroscience, 14*, 1215–1229.

Öhman, A. (2005). The role of the amygdala in human fear: Automatic detection of threat. *Psychoneuroendocrinology, 30*, 953–958.

Öhman, A., Lundqvist, D., & Esteves, F. (2001). The face in the crowd revisited: A threat advantage with schematic stimuli. *Journal of Personality and Social Psychology, 80*, 381–396.

Olivola, C. Y., & Todorov, A. (2010). Fooled by first impressions? Re-examining the diagnostic value of appearance-based inferences. *Journal of Experimental Social Psychology, 46*, 315–324.

Oosterhof, N. N., & Todorov, A. (2008). The functional basis of face evaluation. *Proceedings of the National Academy of Sciences USA, 105*, 11087–11092.

Oosterhof, N. N., & Todorov, A. (2009). Structural resemblance to emotional expressions predicts evaluation of emotionally neutral faces. *Emotion, 9*, 128–133.

Palermo, R., & Rhodes, G. (2007). Are you always on my mind? A review of how face perception and attention interact. *Neuropsychologia, 45*, 75–92.

Parkinson, B. (2005). Do facial movements express emotions or communicate motives? *Personality and Social Psychology Review, 9*, 278–311.

Patzer, G. L. (1985). *The attractiveness phenomenon*. New York: Plenum Press.

Pauker, K., Weisbuch, M., Ambady, N., Sommers, S. R., Adams, R. B., & Ivcevic, Z. (2009). Not so black and white: Memory for ambiguous group members. *Journal of Personality and Social Psychology, 96*, 795–810.

Phelps, E. A., O'Connor, K. J., Cunningham, W. A., Funayama, E. S., Gatenby, J. C., Gore, J. C., et al. (2000). Performance on indirect measures of race evaluation predicts amygdala activation. *Journal of Cognitive Neuroscience, 12*, 729–738.

Phillips, W., Baron-Cohen, S., & Rutter, M. (1992). The role of eye contact in goal detection: Evidence from normal infants and children with autism or mental handicap. *Development and Psychopathology, 4*, 375–383.

Plant, E. A., & Devine, G. (1998). Internal and external motivation to respond without prejudice. *Journal of Personality and Social Psychology, 75*, 811–832.

Plant, E. A., Kling, K. C., & Smith, G. L. (2004). The influence of gender and social role on the interpretation of facial expressions. *Sex Roles, 51*, 187–196.

Pokorny, J. J., & de Wall, F. B. M. (2009). Monkeys recognize the faces of group mates in photographs. *Proceedings of the National Academy of Sciences USA, 106*, 21539–21543.

Pollak, S. D., & Kistler, D. J. (2002). Early experience is associated with the development of categorical representations for facial expressions of emotion. *Proceedings of the National Academy of Sciences USA, 99*, 9072–9076.

Pollak, S. D., Messner, M., Kistler, D. J., & Cohn, J. F. (2009). Development of perceptual expertise in emotion recognition. *Cognition, 110*, 242–247.

Pollak, S. D., & Sinha, P. (2002). Effects of early experience on children's recognition of facial displays of emotion. *Developmental Psychology, 38*, 784–791.

Pollak, S. D., & Tolley-Schell, S. A. (2003) Selective attention to facial emotion in physically abused children. *Journal of Abnormal Psychology, 112,* 323–338.

Ratcliff, N., Shriver, E. R., Hugenberg, K., & Bernstein, M. J. (2010). The allure of status: High-status targets are privileged in face processing and memory. Manuscript under review.

Ratner, K. G., & Amodio, D. M. (2013). Seeing "us vs. them": Minimal group effects on the neural encoding of faces. *Journal of Experimental Social Psychology, 49,* 298–301.

Rhodes, G., Locke, V., Ewing, L., & Evangelista, E. (2009). Race coding and the other-race effect in face recognition. *Perception, 38,* 232–241.

Richeson, J. A., Todd, A. R., Trawalter, S., & Baird, A. A. (2008). Eye-gaze direction modulates race-related amygdala activity. *Group Processes & Intergroup Relations, 11,* 233–246.

Richeson, J. A., & Trawalter, S. (2008). The threat of appearing prejudiced and race-based attentional biases. *Psychological Science, 19,* 98–102.

Richmond, V. P., McCroskey, J. C., & Hickson, M. L., III (2008). Eye behavior. In *Nonverbal behavior in interpersonal relations* (pp. 85–96). Boston: Pearson.

Riddoch, M. J., Johnston, R. A., Bracewell, R. M., Boutsen, L., & Humphreys, G. W. (2008). Are faces special? A case of pure prosopagnosia. *Cognitive Neuropsychology, 25,* 3–26.

Ro, T., Russell, C., & Lavie, N. (2001). Changing faces: A detection advantage in the flicker paradigm. *Psychological Science, 12,* 94–99.

Robbins, R., & McKone, E. (2007). No face-like processing for objects-of-expertise in three behavioral tasks. *Cognition, 103,* 34–79.

Rodin, M. J. (1987). Who is memorable to whom? A study of cognitive disregard. *Social Cognition, 5,* 144–165.

Rosenstein, D., & Oster, H. (1988). Differential facial responses to four basic tastes in newborns. *Child Development, 59,* 1555–1568.

Rule, N. O., Ambady, N., Adams, R. B., & Macrae, C. N. (2007). Us and them: Memory advantages in perceptually ambiguous groups. *Psychonomic Bulletin & Review, 14,* 687–692.

Rule, N. O., Garrett, J. V., & Ambady, N. (2010). Places and faces: Geographic environment influences the ingroup memory advantage. *Journal of Personality and Social Psychology, 98,* 343–355.

Russell, K. Y., Wilson, M., & Hall, R. E., (1992). *The color complex: The politics of skin color among African Americans.* Chicago: Harcourt Brace Jovanovich.

Sacco, D. F., & Hugenberg, K. (2009). The look of fear and anger: Facial maturity modulates the recognition of fearful and angry expressions. *Emotion, 9,* 39–49.

Sacco, D. F., & Hugenberg, K. (2012). Cooperative and competitive motives enhance perceptual sensitivity to angry and happy facial expressions. *Motivation & Emotion, 36,* 382–395.

Sacco, D. F., Hugenberg, K., & Kiel, E. J. (2013). Facial attractiveness and helping behavior: Both attractive and unattractive targets are believed to be unhelpful relative to neutrally attractive targets. Manuscript under review.

Sacco, D. F., Hugenberg, K., & Sefcek, J. A. (2009). Sociosexuality and social perception: Unrestricted sexual orientation facilitates sensitivity to female facial cues. *Personality and Individual Differences, 47,* 777–782.

Said, C. P., Sebe, N., & Todorov, A. (2009). Structural resemblance to emotional expressions predicts evaluation of emotionally neutral faces. *Emotion, 9,* 260–264.

Scherer, S. E. (1974). Influence of proximity and eye contact on impression formation. *Perceptual and Motor Skills, 38,* 538.

Sczesny, S., & Kuhnen, U. (2004). Meta-cognition about biological sex and gender-stereotypic physical appearance: Consequences for the assessment of leadership competence. *Personality and Social Psychology Bulletin, 30,* 13–21.

Shriver, E. R., & Hugenberg, K. (2010). Power, individuation, and the cross-race recognition deficit. *Journal of Experimental Social Psychology, 46,* 767–774.

Shriver, E. R., Young, S. G., Hugenberg, K., Bernstein, M. J., & Lanter, J. R. (2008). Class, race, and the face: Social context modulates the cross-race effect in face recognition. *Personality and Social Psychology Bulletin, 34,* 260–274.

Smith, M. L., Cottrell, G. W., Gosselin, F., & Schyns, P. G. (2005). Transmitting and decoding facial expressions. *Psychological Science, 16,* 184–189.

Spohn, C. C. (2000). Thirty years of sentencing reform: The quest for a racially neutral sentencing process. In J. Horney (Ed.), *Criminal justice 2000: Vol. 3. Policies, processes, and decisions of the criminal justice system* (pp. 427–501). Washington, DC: U.S. Department of Justice, National Institute of Justice.

Stewart, J. E. (1980). Defendant's attractiveness as a factor in the outcome of criminal trials: An observational study. *Journal of Applied Social Psychology, 10,* 348–361.

Strack, F., Martin, L., & Stepper, S. (1988). Inhibiting and facilitating conditions of the human smile: A nonobtrusive test of the facial feedback hypothesis. *Journal of Personality and Social Psychology, 54,* 768–777.

Susskind, J. M., Lee, D. H., Cusi, A., Feiman, R., Grabski, W., & Anderson, A. K. (2008). Expressing fear enhances sensory acquisition. *Nature Neuroscience, 11,* 843–850.

Tajfel, H., & Turner, J. C. (1986). The social identity theory of inter-group behavior. In S. Worchel & L. W. Austin (Eds.), *Psychology of intergroup relations.* Chicago: Nelson-Hall.

Tajfel, H., & Wilkes, L. (1963). Classification and quantitative judgement. *British Journal of Psychology, 54,* 101–114.

Tanaka, J. W., & Curran, T. (2001). A neural basis for expert object recognition. *Psychological Science, 12,* 43–47.

Taylor, S. E., Fiske, S. T., Etcoff, N. L., & Ruderman, A. J. (1978). Categorization and contextual bases of person memory and stereotyping. *Journal of Personality and Social Psychology, 36,* 778–793.

Todorov, A. (2008). Evaluating faces on trustworthiness: An extension of systems for recognition of emotions signaling approach/ avoidance behaviors. In A. Kingstone & M. Miller (Eds.), *The Year in Cognitive Neuroscience 2008, Annals of the New York Academy of Sciences, 1124,* 208–224.

Todorov, A. (2011). Evaluating faces on social dimensions. In A. Todorov, S. T. Fiske, & D. Prentice (Eds.), *Social neuroscience: Toward understanding the underpinnings of the social mind* (pp. 54–76). Oxford, UK: Oxford University Press.

Todorov, A., Mandisodza, A. N., Goren, A., & Hall, C. C. (2005). Inferences of competence from faces predict election outcomes. *Science, 308,* 1623–1626.

Todorov, A., Pakrashi, M., & Oosterhof, N. N. (2009). Evaluating faces on trustworthiness after minimal time exposure. *Social Cognition, 27,* 813–833.

Tonry, M. (1995). *Malign neglect: Race, crime, and punishment in America.* New York: Oxford University Press.

Trawalter, S., Todd, A. R., Baird, A. A., & Richeson, J. A. (2008). Attending to threat: Race-based patterns of selective attention. *Journal of Experimental Social Psychology, 44,* 1322–1327.

Van Bavel, J. J., Packer, D. J., & Cunningham, W. A. (2011). Modulation of the Fusiform Face Area following minimal exposure to motivationally relevant faces: Evidence of in-group enhancement (not out-group disregard). *Journal of Cognitive Neuroscience, 23,* 3343–3354.

Vecera, S. P., & Johnson, M. H. (1995). Gaze detection and the cortical processing of faces: Evidence from infants and adults. *Visual Cognition, 2,* 59–87.

Vuilleumier, P. (2005). Staring fear in the face. *Nature, 433,* 22–23.

Wainwright, B. (2008, November 22). I don't recognize my own face. *The Guardian.* Retrieved from http://www.guardian.co.uk.

Walster, E., Aronson, V., Abrahams, D., & Rottman, L. (1966). Importance of physical attractiveness in dating behavior. *Journal of Personality and Social Psychology, 4,* 508–516.

Wheeler, L., & Kim, Y. (1997). What is beautiful is culturally good: The physical attractiveness stereotype has different content in collectivistic cultures. *Personality and Social Psychology Bulletin, 23*(8), 795–800.

Wilkowski, B. M., & Meier, B. P. (2010). Bring it on: Angry facial expressions potentiate approach-motivated motor behavior. *Journal of Personality and Social Psychology, 98,* 201–210.

Willis, J., & Todorov, A. (2006). First impressions: Making up your mind after a 100-ms exposure to a face. *Psychological Science, 17,* 592–598.

Wilson, J. P., & Hugenberg, K. (2010). When under threat, we all look the same: Distinctiveness threat induces ingroup homogeneity in face recognition. *Journal of Experimental Social Psychology, 46,* 1004–1010.

Wirth, J. H., Sacco, D. F., Hugenberg, K., & Williams, K. D. (2010). Eye gaze as relational evaluation: Averted eye gaze leads to feelings of ostracism and relational devaluation. *Personality and Social Psychology Bulletin, 36,* 869–882.

Wright, D. B., & Sladden, B. (2003). An own gender bias and the importance of hair in face recognition. *Acta Psychologica, 114,* 101–114.

Wright, D. B., & Stroud, J. N. (2002). Age differences in lineup identification accuracy: People are better with their own age. *Law & Human Behavior, 26,* 641–654.

Yardley, L., McDermott, L., Pisarski, S., Duchaine, B., & Nakayama, K. (2008). Psychosocial consequences of developmental prosopagnosia: A problem of recognition. *Journal of Psychosomatic Research, 65,* 445–451.

Yin, R. K. (1969). Looking at upside-down faces. *Journal of Experimental Psychology, 81,* 141–145.

Young, S. G., Bernstein, M. J., & Hugenberg, K. (2010). When do own-group biases in face recognition occur? Encoding versus post-encoding. *Social Cognition, 28,* 240–250.

Young, S. G., & Hugenberg, K. (2010). Mere social categorization modulates identification of facial expressions of emotion. *Journal of Personality and Social Psychology, 99,* 964–977.

Young, S. G., Hugenberg, K., Bernstein, M. J., & Sacco, D. F. (2009). Interracial contexts debilitate same-race face recognition. *Journal of Experimental Social Psychology, 45,* 1123–1126.

Yovel, G., & Kanwisher, N. (2005). The neural basis of the behavioral face-inversion effect. *Current Biology, 15,* 2256–2262.

Zajonc, R. B., Murphy, S. T., & Inglehart, M. (1989). Feeling and facial efference: Implications for the vascular theory of emotion. *Psychological Review, 96,* 395–416.

Zebrowitz, L. A. (1997). *Reading faces: Window to the soul?* Boulder, CO: Westview Press.

Zebrowitz, L. A. (2006). Finally, faces find favor. *Social Cognition, 24,* 657–701.

Zebrowitz, L. A., & McDonald, M. (1991). The impact of litigants' baby-facedness and attractiveness on adjudications in small claims courts. *Law and Human Behavior, 15,* 603–623.

Zebrowitz, L. A., & Montepare, M. (1992). Impressions of babyfaced individuals across the life span. *Developmental Psychology, 28,* 1143–1152.

Zebrowitz, L. A., Montepare, J. M., & Lee, H. K. (1993). They don't all look alike: Individual impressions of other racial groups. *Journal of Personality and Social Psychology, 65,* 85–101.

Zebrowitz, L. A., Olson, K., & Hoffman, K. (1993). Stability of babyfaceness and attractiveness across the life span. *Journal of Personality and Social Psychology, 64,* 453–466.

Zebrowitz, L. A., Tenenbaum, D. R., & Goldstein, L. H. (1991). The impact of job applicants' facial maturity, gender, and academic achievement on hiring recommendations. *Journal of Applied Social Psychology, 21,* 525–548.

The Highs and Lows of Mental Representation: A Construal Level Perspective on the Structure of Knowledge

So Yon Rim, Yaacov Trope, Nira Liberman, *and* Oren Shapira,

Abstract

This chapter presents a perspective on the mental representation of persons, groups, and the self that parsimoniously unifies existing distinctions, such as abstract versus concrete, schematic versus aschematic, and prototype versus exemplar, within the umbrella of high- versus low-level construal. This perspective is derived from construal level theory (CLT; see Trope & Liberman, 2010, for a review), which offers one perspective on when high-level construal will be favored over relatively more low-level construal. Specifically, CLT is a theory that explains the relationship between psychological distance and level of construal. The chapter reviews past work on the structure of mental representations and describes relevant research within CLT, as well as other aspects of high- and low-level construal that go beyond traditional distinctions. Finally, research is presented on the associations among different construal level dimensions that supports the argument for a common underlying function: namely, that high-level construals, by preserving essential features, support "mental travel," whereas low-level construals are bound to "me here and now."

Key Words: mental representation, level of construal, psychological distance

Mental representations are constructions of the world that people form, store in memory, and use in various ways. Thus, one's idea of what a "telephone" looks like and sounds like and how it functions is a mental representation. Similarly, a mental construction of one's mother, including her appearance, mannerism, personality, goals, and one's feelings when with her, is a mental representation. As we navigate the social environment, we not only form mental representations online, which are affected by the immediate context, but we also access existing representations that help us interpret the incoming stream of information.

Representations exist both in terms of abstract schemas, or structured units of knowledge, and in terms of more specific information that is rich in details. In representing objects, people have knowledge of prototypes (a typical dog), an abstraction that captures the commonalities among all category exemplars, and also knowledge regarding individual exemplars (Dorie, my gray and white Lhasa Apso). In representing people, schematic knowledge exists in the form of traits or stereotypes (women are nurturing), which provide generalizations regarding social categories such as gender as well as more specific trait or behavioral information about particular individuals (Sophie bakes her friends cookies). Lastly, in representing events, we have scripts that inform us about how to behave in certain situations (how to order food at a restaurant), but we also have more specific knowledge about how to behave in very particular situations (at Dojo's, one must pay at the counter).

When do people form more abstract, schema-based versus more concrete, individuated representations? Described in more detail in subsequent sections of this chapter, past research has typically implicated accuracy motivation, outcome dependency, accountability, and cognitive capacity as some of the potential moderators. For example, when people are held accountable for the impressions they form about a target actor, they base their impressions less on stereotypes and more on individuating information. Alternatively, when overloaded by a concurrent cognitive task, perceivers are more likely to rely on heuristics, like stereotypes, in forming impressions (for reviews, see Bodenhausen, Macrae, & Sherman, 1999; Fiske, Lin, & Neuberg, 1999).

Construal level theory (CLT; see Liberman & Trope, 2008; Trope & Liberman, 2010, for reviews) is a theory of mental representation that offers one perspective on *when* more abstract, schematic, and prototype-based representations will be favored over more concrete, aschematic, and exemplar-based representations. CLT distinguishes between what are termed high-level and low-level construals. The commonality underlying various dimensions of high-level construal (e.g., traits, stereotypes, prototypes) is their relative abstractness and their quality of preserving the central "essence" of the referent object; low-level construals (e.g., behaviors, other idiosyncrasies, exemplars), in comparison, are more concrete and include peripheral details that are not central to the representation. Thus, this distinction subsumes the schematic versus aschematic and prototype versus exemplar dichotomies that have been the focus of traditional research on the structure of mental representation and includes other aspects of representations (e.g., analog versus symbolic; global versus local; means versus ends) that have not been addressed in previous research.

A core tenet of CLT is that high-level construals are more functional for representing entities that are psychologically distant (e.g., in space, time, and social distance) from the self, whereas low-level construals are more functional for representing proximal entities. The rationale is that high-level construals "travel well" across distances because they preserve the essential features of the representation, are not context bound, and in that sense, are stable. They serve to anticipate events that are not present—events that occur in other places, at other times, to other people, and in hypothetical situations. On the other hand, low-level construals include concrete details that are usually peripheral to the core representation and are context specific. Thus, high-level representations enable "mental travel," whereas low-level representations are bound to "me here and now."

In this chapter, our focus is to describe distinctions that have been made in past literatures on the structure of mental representations as they pertain to persons, groups, and the self, and to lend a unique perspective derived from CLT: that these distinctions parsimoniously fall under the umbrella of high- and low-level construals. We begin by describing CLT in more detail and summarizing its basic assumptions. We then discuss past work on the structure of mental representations and describe pertinent research within CLT. Next, we cover other aspects of high- and low-level construals that go beyond traditional distinctions derived from schema and exemplar models of representation. Finally, we describe research on the association among different construal level dimensions that supports the argument for a common function underlying dimensions of mental construal, and we end with concluding remarks.

Levels of Construal and Psychological Distance

Building on past literatures that distinguish between different levels of representation (Rosch, 1975; Vallacher & Wegner, 1987), high-level construals are defined as relatively more abstract, schematic, and decontextualized than low-level construals. According to CLT, moving from a concrete, low-level representation to an abstract, high-level representation involves omitting incidental details that are irrelevant to the core essence of the representation. For example, imagine observing a man running 10 laps around the park without losing speed or breaking a sweat. You might represent this person in terms of his concrete behavior (e.g., easily runs 10 laps around the park) or more abstract personality trait (e.g., is athletic). Traits are high level compared with behaviors in the sense that they are relatively more abstract and decontextualized. In addition, traits are more central in that changing a person's trait has a greater impact on the representation of that individual than changing a specific behavior. Furthermore, insofar as traits are considered to be internal causes of behaviors, they are superordinate in that the presence of a behavior depends on (i.e., is caused by) the presence of the corresponding trait, but not vice versa. Shifting from a low-level representation based on behaviors, "easily runs 10 laps around the park," to a high-level representation, "is athletic," involves shedding incidental details such as "the park" and the particular act of running and retaining the essential, core aspect of the person representation.

It is important to mention that high-level construals are not necessarily more impoverished compared with low-level construals. While omitting certain concrete details, abstract representations often include additional information regarding the structure of the representation and its relation to other related representations. For example, "is athletic" includes assumptions about the person's other behaviors ("might play soccer well too") and places the single behavioral instance within the context of other potential behaviors.

The central claim of CLT is the functional link between psychological distance and high-level construal and psychological proximity and low-level construal. Psychological distance is egocentric; objects that are distant from the self in time (past and future), space, social distance, and hypotheticality are conceptualized as being psychologically distant. High-level construals, by virtue of capturing the essential features of objects, are more stable and retain their applicability as psychological distance expands. For instance, representing one's action as "gaining knowledge" rather than "studying for an organic chemistry exam" is more functional for imagining the distant future where the particular class might not be organic chemistry and the action might not necessarily involve studying for a class. Likewise, "gaining knowledge" is more useful for representing hypothetical alternatives, such as, "what if I were not studying organic chemistry but American literature?" Thus, high-level mental construals facilitate mental travel in time and space, across social perspective, and across counterfactual alternatives to reality. CLT contends that this association between distance and high-level construal and proximity and low-level construal is then overgeneralized and applied to situations in which variability is no longer an issue. For the example stated earlier, one may have knowledge that one will repeat the exact same organic chemistry class one year from now. Still, because of this overgeneralized association between distance and level of construal, one will represent the distant future event at a high level as "gaining knowledge" and the near future event at a low level as "studying for an organic chemistry exam."

High-level and low-level construals serve a social communicative function in interacting with distal and proximal entities, respectively. As stated earlier, abstract, high-level construals capture the gist of the referent object, event, or person and are relatively invariant across specific contexts compared with concrete, low-level construals. This quality of high-level representations makes them better suited for communicating with psychologically distal others who may not have the same access to incidental details of a particular situation and thus for whom low-level representations may not be understandable. For example, imagine that one wants to communicate to a relative living in a rural, European town that one has just seen an amazing concert at Madison Square Garden. A high-level representation of Madison Square Garden as an *arena* would enable communication and facilitate understanding, whereas *Madison Square Garden* is a relatively low-level representation that is meaningless to someone who has never heard of it. In this way, high-level construals enable shared reality between the self and distant others, creating common ground for meaningful social interactions.

Traditional Distinctions Map onto Construal Levels
Construal of People

The representation of persons is one of the oldest and most central topics in social cognition research (Asch, 1946; Funder, 1999; Tagiuri & Petrullo, 1958; Wyer & Lambert, 1994). In forming an impression of another person, perceivers rely on both high-level, schematic knowledge, such as information about the person's traits or category membership, or on more low-level, concrete information about the person's specific behaviors, the context surrounding the behavior, or other idiosyncrasies. In this section, we discuss traditional dichotomies within the literature on person representation and propose that these distinctions are subsumed under the common umbrella of high-level versus low-level construals.

TRAIT VERSUS BEHAVIORAL REPRESENTATIONS

The fact that individuals readily think of others in terms of their dispositional traits and that traits are important in impression formation is not a point of debate (Asch, 1946; Heider, 1958; Jones & Davis, 1965). Research on spontaneous trait inference (STI; Winter & Uleman, 1984) demonstrates that people make trait inferences from behaviors without explicitly having the intention to form impressions (i.e., through task instructions) and without being explicitly aware of having made any inferences. Going beyond basic representation, we also know from classic research on attribution that people have an overwhelming tendency to focus on traits as internal causes of behavior, even behaviors that are clearly constrained by the situation (Jones, 1979). The question is not *whether* traits are important in impression formation but rather *when* are they more likely to be influential in behavioral encoding. Also, what factors affect the extent to which traits play a role in attribution?

Spontaneous Trait Inferences

Trait inferences are often made from observing other people's behaviors. Asch (1946) theorized that impressions form "immediately" upon encountering a person and that the impression formation process ensues with "remarkable rapidity and great ease" (p. 258). However, the first definitive empirical evidence that such impressions can form spontaneously (i.e., without conscious awareness or explicit intention to form any inference) was provided by Winter and Uleman (1984) with their research on the phenomenon of STI. Using the encoding specificity principle (Tulving & Thomson, 1973), which states that encoded information serves as an efficient retrieval cue for other information presented at the time of encoding, Winter and Uleman reasoned that traits spontaneously inferred during behavioral encoding should be good retrieval cues for those behaviors. Participants were initially presented with behaviors that implied traits (e.g., *The secretary solved the mystery halfway through the book,* implies *clever*) under memory instructions and subsequently completed a cued recall test. As expected, trait cues led to greater recall of behaviors compared with no cue and were as effective as strong semantic cues. Subsequent work demonstrated the robustness of this effect even under various manipulations, such as concurrent cognitive load (Todorov & Uleman, 2003; Winter, Uleman, & Cunniff, 1985) and extremely short, two-second exposure to a large set of behavioral stimuli (Todorov & Uleman, 2003). These manipulations should have interfered with the trait-encoding process if it were not highly automatic. STI formation has been covertly assessed by the use of various procedures, such as cued recall, recognition probe, the savings-in-relearning paradigm, and the false recognition paradigm, adapted from memory research (see Chapter 17 for more on person memory).

Are STIs mental representations of people or merely abstract representations of behaviors? To address this question, Carlston and Skowronski (1994) developed an adaptation of the savings-in-relearning paradigm (Ebbinghaus, 1964; MacLeod, 1988) and showed that inferred traits are linked to specific actors and are not just associates of the behaviors. In this paradigm, participants see a series of photos of individuals paired with trait-implying sentences about them in an initial learning phase. After some filler tasks, participants are exposed to photos seen during the learning phase, either correctly paired with the traits implied about them earlier or mismatched. If traits were encoded during initial learning, the correctly matched photo–trait pairs should be "relearned" and therefore easier to learn than mismatched pairs. Indeed, they found this to be the case, indicating that STIs are meaningfully linked to actors in memory. Todorov and Uleman (2002) developed an adaptation of the false recognition paradigm that provided further support for the notion that STIs are meaningfully bound to actor representations.

STIs represent relatively abstract, high-level construals of others compared with behaviors. Traits are high level in that they are relatively (1) more abstract and stable, (2) more central to the person representation (i.e., changing a person's personality trait changes the person more fundamentally than changing a specific behavior), and (3) superordinate to behaviors in that traits as internal causes bring about specific behaviors (i.e., being *clever* causes one to *solve the mystery halfway through the book*). Thus, a CLT analysis of STIs suggests that STI formation will be enhanced for psychologically distal versus proximal actors, and research supports this idea. Rim, Uleman, and Trope (2009) found that perceivers formed more STIs from behaviors of others who were described as being in a spatially remote versus proximal location (Study 1) and from behaviors believed to have occurred in the distant versus recent past (Study 2); amount and content of actor information were held constant across distances. These effects were not attributable to differences in perceived similarity with the actors (Studies 1 and 2) or to differences in level of familiarity with the distal and proximal locations (Study 1). Rim et al. (2009) speculated that STIs are more functional for representing distant others because the specifics of the immediate situation (e.g., exact behaviors) may not always hold for those individuals. Abstract traits are more invariant across psychological distance and hence are more useful in representing distal people. This set of studies on STIs provides the most direct evidence that increasing psychological distance increases the tendency to mentally represent others using abstract, high-level construals. And downstream effects of psychological distance on attribution (discussed next), evaluation, or explicit judgment may be built on this initial inference.

Traits as Causes of Behavior: Attribution

The correspondence bias describes the tendency for people to be biased toward attributing the behaviors of others to internal, dispositional causes even when they are aware that the behaviors are situationally constrained (see Gilbert & Malone, 1995; Jones, 1979). In our terms, the correspondence bias means that people are biased toward high-level representation of others in terms of abstract, decontextualized traits and that this leads to correspondent inferences in attribution of behaviors.

The actor–observer effects describes the tendency for people to attribute others' behaviors (failing an exam) to dispositional causes (because he is stupid) while attributing one's own behaviors to situational causes (because the exam was unfair). Classic theories of attribution are reviewed elsewhere in this handbook (see Chapter 6), so we will not go into detail here. The actor–observer effect is consistent with the CLT prediction, at least with respect to social distance, that increasing psychological distance increases the tendency to use high-level construals. Others are, by definition, more distant from the self than the self is from the self. Therefore, the fact that others' behaviors are thought of in terms of traits more than the same behaviors by the self is consistent with CLT. However, differences in amount of information and differences in informational salience could account for these effects as well. Thus, an important question is whether psychological distance affects the tendency to give a dispositional attribution for an actor's situationally constrained behavior, controlling for the nature and amount of information given. Nussbaum, Trope, and Liberman (2003) found the answer to be affirmative. Participants were students at an Israeli university, and they read an essay purportedly written by another student arguing in favor of Israel's withdrawal from Southern Lebanon, which was then still occupied by Israel. In the constrained condition, participants were told that the writer was instructed to write the pro-withdrawal essay, and in the unconstrained condition, they were told that the writer was free to express his or her own opinion. Correspondent attitude inferences in the constrained condition were greater after participants had made judgments regarding the writers' distant versus near future behaviors. Henderson, Fujita, Trope, and Liberman (2006) replicated this effect manipulating spatial distance. That is, perceivers were more likely to ignore situational information and draw correspondent inferences when the actor was believed to be spatially remote versus proximal.

This research demonstrated that increasing temporal or spatial distance of the actor's behavior increases the tendency for perceivers to draw correspondent inferences even when amount and type of information given is held constant.

If high-level mental construal functions to enable mental travel, as CLT contends, the reverse direction of influence may also be true. Thinking about a person in terms of their traits may lead to perceptions of that person as more psychologically distant than when thinking about a person in terms of their behaviors. Making dispositional, rather than situational, attributions for actors' behaviors may also facilitate thinking about those actors as being temporally, spatially, or socially remote. There is some evidence for this idea. Semin and Smith (1999; Study 2) found that linguistic abstractness affects time estimation. Specifically, they asked participants to recall either a time when they "helped someone" (concrete action) or a time when they displayed "helpfulness" (abstract trait). Abstract trait cues led to retrieval of more distant past memories than concrete action cues. Stephan, Liberman, and Trope (2010a) used politeness of addressing a person as an indicator of felt social distance to that person and showed that describing a person in terms of traits (versus behaviors) increased perceived social distance from that person (see also Stephan, Liberman, & Trope, 2010b, for resource allocation as another indication of social distance).

STEREOTYPING VERSUS INDIVIDUATION

Perceivers use generic prior knowledge, or schemas, as organizational frameworks in interpreting new information (Bruner, 1957; Minsky, 1975; Neisser, 1976). In person perception, social categories provide schematic knowledge about a target's characteristics that perceivers then use to construct coherent impressions. Stereotypes free up cognitive resources (Macrae, Milne, & Bodenhausen, 1994) and act as heuristics in making quick and efficient, albeit sometimes inaccurate, judgments (Bodenhausen, 1988, 1990). If one is walking along a dark street and sees a young Black man with a shiny object in his hand, one might weigh all of the pieces of information at hand (e.g., that this is a safe, college neighborhood and that the man is probably a student holding a cell phone) or one might make a quick, heuristic judgment based on one's stereotype of young Black men as violent and aggressive and cross the street to the other side. Categorization occurs rapidly (for reviews, see Dovidio & Gaertner, 1993; Fiske, 1998) and comprises top-down processing. This is contrasted from more systematic, bottom-up processing, whereby attributes of a person are encoded in a more piecemeal fashion building up to a final impression (Anderson, 1981; Fiske & Neuberg, 1990).

In addition to acting as heuristics, stereotypes serve other informational purposes. For one, stereotypes disambiguate information in a stereotype-consistent manner (Darley & Gross, 1983; Duncan, 1976; Sagar & Schofield, 1980; Kunda, 1990; Trope, 1989). If a target is categorized as a Southerner, a mildly aggressive behavior (e.g., bumping into someone in the street) is more likely to be interpreted as violent. Moreover, stereotypes can be used to draw inferences about a person that are not necessarily warranted by the available information (e.g., Fiske & Neuberg, 1990), such as when one infers that a black coworker is musical without direct knowledge regarding this person's musical abilities. Stereotypes can also affect memory processes such that stereotype-consistent information is falsely reconstructed and remembered at a later time (e.g., Fyock & Stangor, 1994), although others have found that stereotype-inconsistent information is remembered better because of deeper, more elaborate processing of that information (e.g., Hastie & Kumar, 1979; for a review, see Stangor & McMillan, 1992).

Fiske and Neuberg's (1990) and Brewer's (1988) dual process models account for how and when category-based versus attribute-based processing occurs in impression formation (for a review, see Fiske et al., 1999). Importantly, both models are serial in that categorization is thought to occur first and dominates over individuation unless (1) there is a poor fit between the target and the stereotype or (2) the perceiver possesses sufficient motivation and cognitive capacity to override the categorization process, which is more of the default (Brewer, 1988; Bodenhausen et al., 1999; Fiske & Neuberg; 1990). For example, if one finds out that the garbage man does crossword puzzles and visits art museums in his free time, one is unlikely to use one's stereotypic knowledge of garbage men (e.g., unintelligent, uncultured) in forming an impression of him. More likely, this person will be individuated based on known information (Fiske, Neuberg, Beattie, & Milberg, 1987).

Motivation and cognitive capacity are also important determinants of whether categorization or individuation processes will ensue. Social categorization has been shown to occur more readily when cognitive capacity is low (Gilbert & Hixon, 1991; Macrae, Hewstone, & Griffiths, 1993; Macrae et al., 1994) and when attentional resources are depleted, such as in the face of time pressure (Heaton & Kruglanski, 1991; Jamieson & Zanna, 1989; Kaplan, Wanshula, & Zanna; Kruglanski & Webster, 1993; Pratto & Bargh, 1991), excessive arousal (Kim & Baron, 1988; Wilder & Simon, 2004), or anxiety (Wilder & Shapiro, 1989a; 1989b). Furthermore, research indicated that complex judgments, such as judgments of criminal guilt, recruit more stereotypic knowledge than simple judgments, such as those about a person's traits (Bodenhausen & Lichtenstein, 1987). Competition also leads to greater individuation of one's opponent (Ruscher & Fiske, 1990).

In CLT terms, social category information, such as age, gender, or race, is relatively more high level than individuating information, such as a person's actions and intentions. Compared with individuating information, a person's social category membership is relatively (1) more broad and inclusive in that social categories are associated with multiple goal and trait characterizations and (2) superordinate in that social categories are often essentialized and thought to cause the manifestation of certain goals and traits (e.g., thinking that being Black causes one to be unintelligent, athletic, and musical). Based on CLT then, social category information should have greater weight in representing psychologically distal versus proximal others, and stereotyping will be more likely with increasing psychological distance. Indeed, research has shown that individuals are more likely to stereotype outgroup members who, in CLT terms, are socially distal, compared with ingroup members who are socially proximal (for reviews, see Hewstone, Rubin, & Willis, 2002; Hilton & von Hippel, 1996). However, this effect could be attributed to a difference in amount of information; one generally has more information and more concrete information about ingroup than outgroup members, so the former are individuated while the latter are stereotyped. Future studies could examine the influence of social distance (e.g., ingroup versus outgroup) on the extent to which general stereotypes versus more specific goals, intentions, or behaviors are used to form impressions of individuals when amount of information is held constant. Extensions to other dimensions of psychological distance (e.g., spatial or temporal) would be interesting as well. Relatedly, people may apply stereotypes relevant to a person's broader social category membership, such as race, to psychologically distant others and those relevant to a person's more narrow and specific category membership, such as occupation, to proximal others.

PROTOTYPES VERSUS EXEMPLARS

Prototypes are another form of schematic knowledge that people use in basic categorization and identification as well as in forming judgments and evaluations. According to prototype theory (Medin & Smith, 1981, 1984), categorization occurs through comparison of novel objects to an abstracted prototype representation. Prototypes are summary representations of categories that contain characteristic features usually present in members of the category. Based on this conceptualization, people can classify a tree they have never seen before as a tree based on a prototypical representation of trees. In a seminal study, Posner and Keele (1968) demonstrated that prototypes are abstracted and used to classify novel entities (see also, Reed, 1972). Other research found that people falsely recognize, on a recognition memory test, new stimuli with resemblance to an abstracted prototype (Franks & Bransford, 1971; Posner & Keele, 1970; Reitman & Bower, 1973). Prototypes are conceptually similar to schemas in that they serve as organizing frameworks by which subsequent information is processed.

In the social domain, certain traits can be conceptualized as prototypes. For example, "extravert" is an organizing prototype for the following traits: boisterous, spirited, outgoing, lively, and exuberant (Cantor & Mischel, 1977). In an experiment by Cantor and Mischel (1977), participants were given four trait lists that described a prototypical extravert, a prototypical introvert, and two control characters who were neither extraverted nor introverted. For half of the participants, the prototype was only implied, and for the other half, it was explicitly given. On a subsequent recognition test, participants were more confident that nonpresented, prototype-related traits had been seen earlier during the acquisition stage than nonpresented, prototype-unrelated traits for the prototypical extravert and introvert, regardless of whether the prototype was given implicitly or explicitly. This false recognition bias was not observed for nonprototypical control characters. Cantor and Mischel (1979) also found that increasing a representation's prototypicality increased memory for the representation's features (see also Brewer, Dull, & Lui, 1981). This memory advantage demonstrates the efficiency of prototypes in structuring and organizing knowledge.

Exemplar-Based Person Judgments

Exemplar theories argue not only that people store information in terms of prototypes but also that they encode specific exemplars. In cognitive psychology, exemplar theorists rejected the notion of abstract summary representation altogether and instead argued for the idea that a category is represented by all of the individual exemplars of that category. According to exemplar theory, classification of novel objects occurs based on the objects' similarity to all known category exemplars (Medin & Schaffer; 1978; Nosofsky, 1987). Similarity is not fixed but modulated by context-dependent attention to particular stimulus dimensions.

In the social domain, Smith and Zárate (1992) presented a similar model and extended the role of exemplars in identification and categorization to social judgments and evaluations. According to this exemplar-based model, people not only store abstract, schematic knowledge in memory but also store exemplar representations (i.e., representations of specific people), which they retrieve and use in making judgments about other people. Exemplars need not be individuals one has actually met but can be mental constructions, such as hippie or political activist, formed based on acquired knowledge. Evidence suggests that exemplars influence inferences and judgments. For instance, fictitious college football players were rated as having higher potential for future success when superficially linked versus not linked to a famous football player (Gilovich, 1981). Apparently, similarity led to activation of the representation of that famous football player, which then influenced judgment of the college players. Past research also found that exemplars influence affective reactions to novel people. In a study by Lewicki (1986), participants who were initially insulted by an experimenter later avoided interacting with another experimenter who had the same hairstyle as the offending one.

Social Cognitive Transference

The representations that people store in memory of various significant others (i.e., influential people in their lives) are a special class of exemplars that are brought to bear when a new person is encountered. Representations of significant others are set apart from other exemplars in that they are highly accessible (Andersen & Cole, 1990; Andersen, Glassman, Chen, & Cole, 1995) and are used to understand new persons even when those representations have no apparent applicability (Andersen et al., 1995; Chen, Andersen & Hinkley, 1999). In this sense, then, representations of significant others are chronically and automatically activated. According to Andersen and colleagues, however, such representations are activated most strongly when a new person resembles one's significant other in some way (for reviews, see Andersen & Chen, 2002; Andersen & Saribay, 2005; Chen & Andersen, 2008). Features of the significant other that are present in a new person act as cues that set into motion an inference process whereby perceivers "go beyond the information given" and assume that other, unobserved features of the significant other are present in the new person as well. This phenomenon of *transference* has been widely demonstrated and proved to be quite robust, occurring for both positive and negative significant others (e.g., Andersen & Baum, 1994; Andersen, Reznik, & Manzella, 1996), across gender (because most studies include both male and female participants) and other individual differences, such as history of abuse within the relationship (e.g., Berenson & Andersen, 2006).

In a typical study, participants imagine a significant other and freely generate a list of his or her features, such as habits, attitudes, physical characteristics, and traits, in a preliminary experimental session. In a second, presumably unrelated, session two weeks later, participants are exposed to information about an "interaction partner" whom they will supposedly meet. This information contains some of the features of the significant other listed by the participant during the earlier session and also other new features. On a subsequent recognition test, participants falsely remember features of the significant other, not presented in the information about the new person, as having been learned, thereby demonstrating transference. Not only does the representation of one's significant other influence inference and memory processes, but this representation also activates a *relational self* or "the self when with the significant other" (for recent reviews, see Andersen & Saribay, 2005; Chen & Andersen, 2008). This notion of the relational self is discussed in more detail in a later section. The point to be made here is that the body of research on social cognitive transference provides strong support for the notion of exemplars as mental representation that are stored and used in making judgments about new people.

Determinants of Prototype Versus Exemplar Retrieval

A prototype is an abstracted summary representation containing features that are most central to a category. On the other hand, exemplars are specific instantiations that include not only essential information but also peripheral and irrelevant details. For example, one's prototype of an extravert contains abstract information about what a typical extravert is like: boisterous, outgoing, sociable. On the other hand, an exemplar of an extravert is a particular person one knows whose representation contains information regarding that person's hair color, eye color, height, and so forth that are irrelevant to the representation of an extravert. In this sense, prototypes are high level in that they convey the essence, and exemplars are low level in that they also contain irrelevancies. As such, prototypes should play a larger role in forming judgments regarding psychologically distal others, whereas exemplars should play a larger role in forming judgments regarding proximal others. For instance, in evaluating an outgroup member (i.e., a socially distal person) on intellectual ability, one might try to decide whether this person fits with one's idea of what a prototypical smart person is like. In contrast, in evaluating an ingroup member (i.e., a socially proximal person), one might compare this person to specific smart people (exemplars) one has encountered in the past.

There may be within-prototype and within-exemplar effects of distance. For instance, prototypes can be relatively abstract (an extravert) or concrete (a typical fraternity member). CLT would predict that as psychological distance increases, so does the tendency to use increasingly abstract prototypes as a basis for social judgment. Similarly, exemplars vary in level: Some exemplars are fairly abstract (socially constructed representation of a president based on media exposure), and others are concrete (President Barack Obama). Psychological distance should be associated with the use of more abstract versus concrete exemplars. Furthermore, exemplars that are similar to the target on relatively low-level versus high-level dimensions may be retrieved for making judgments about psychologically proximal others, and vice versa for psychologically distal others. With respect to research on social cognitive transference, it would be interesting to see whether distance moderates what features of a significant other are transferred from the representation of that significant other to a new person. Based on CLT, a new person who is psychologically distal might lead to greater transfer of high-level features, such as one's significant other's traits (e.g., honest), whereas a psychologically proximal new person might lead to greater transfer of low-level features, such as the significant other's behaviors (e.g., hogs the remote).

Construal of Groups

People store representations of individual persons as well as groups of individuals, and research on group perception is critical for understanding topics that have had central importance in social psychological research, such as the formation and use of stereotypes (Crawford, Sherman, & Hamilton, 2002; Fiske, 1998; Gilbert & Hixon, 1991; Hilton & von Hippel, 1996; Kunda & Spencer, 2003; Levy, Stroessner, & Dweck, 1998; Macrae & Bodenhausen, 2000) and social categorization of ingroups and outgroups in social identity theory (Allport, 1954; Tajfel, 1978; Turner, Brown, & Tajfel, 1979). So, what determines whether a collection of people is seen as a meaningful group? How do group versus individual perceptions differ? What factors have been shown to influence whether a group is perceived as a structured, coherent, and unified entity or as a disparate collection of individuals? These are the questions we address in this section. Lastly, we discuss the implications of CLT for the study of group perception.

GROUP VERSUS INDIVIDUAL REPRESENTATIONS

Past research has shown that information about groups is processed differently than information about individuals, which leads to differences in memory and judgment (McConnell, Sherman, & Hamilton, 1994b; Lichtenstein & Srull; 1987; Srull, 1981; Srull, Lichtenstein, & Rothbart, 1985). For example, judgments of individuals tend to be based on inferences formed online, whereas judgments of groups are more memory based (Hamilton & Sherman, 1989; McConnell, Sherman, & Hamilton, 1994; Sanbonmatsu, Sherman, & Hamilton, 1987). Sanbonmatsu et al. (1987) found that perceivers presented with the same information about a group versus an individual overestimated the frequency of distinctive, negative information and gave more negative evaluations when the behaviors were said to describe a group as opposed to an individual. This was consistent with the literature on memory-based processes, which are characterized by efficient encoding of distinctive information and superior memory for the information during judgment (for a review, see Hastie & Park, 1986). Furthermore, Susskind, Maurer, Thakkar, Hamilton, and Sherman (1999) found that individuals made faster and more extreme trait judgments from behavioral information about individuals compared with groups. In sum, representations of individuals tend to be formed online (e.g., STIs; Uleman, Saribay, & Gonzalez, 2008), whereas representations of groups are relatively more memory based.

Moreover, recency effects are observed for group information, whereas primacy effects are observed for individual information due to the memory-based versus online nature of the two types of representations, respectively (Hilton & von Hippel, 1990; Manis & Paskewitz, 1987). In a study by Manis and Paskewitz (1987), participants saw a series of items that purportedly described one individual or several individuals in a group and were subsequently asked to make an overall judgment about the individual or the group based on the given information. When participants thought that the information described a single individual, their judgments were based more on information presented early in the series (i.e., a primacy effect). On the other hand, judgments about a group were influenced more by later information (i.e., a recency effect). This study demonstrated that impressions of individuals are formed online, during encoding of information, whereas impressions of groups are constructed at the time of judgment, based on the most easily retrieved information, which is usually the last information encountered.

Expectations for internal consistency also differ for individuals and groups, leading to differences in judgment and memory. For instance, perceivers generally tend to remember expectancy-incongruent information better than expectancy-congruent information about individual actors (Hastie & Kumar, 1979; for a meta-analysis, see Stangor & McMillan, 1992). However, research has found that when learning about groups, this incongruency effect does not occur (Srull, 1981; Srull et al., 1985; Stern, Marrs, Millar, & Cole, 1984; Wyer, Bodenhausen, & Srull, 1984). Furthermore, perceivers construct causal explanations for individuals' incongruent behaviors (Crocker, Hannah, & Weber, 1983; Hastie, 1984), presumably as a way to reconcile inconsistent information with one's expectations, but do so far less when processing information about a group (Susskind et al., 1999). Thus, perceivers process expectancy-incongruent information differently for groups and individuals.

Entitativity and Mental Construal of Groups

Hamilton and Sherman's (1996) model explains the difference in group versus person representations in terms of a difference in perceptions of "entitativity" (see also Brewer & Harasty, 1996). This term was first introduced by Campbell (1958) and refers to the perception of a group as having "the nature of an entity, of having a real existence" (p. 17). Groups can vary in the extent to which they are entitative depending on the degree of similarity among, and proximity between, the members of the group (Campbell, 1958) and also other factors such as the extent to which members are interdependent and expected to display behavioral consistency (Hamilton & Sherman, 1996). Individuals and groups can both vary in their level of entitativity. For example, a person with frequent mood swings is less entitative than a person with a relatively stable disposition, and similarly, a group standing in line to buy tickets to a movie is less entitative than members of a chess club. In general, perceivers tend to perceive individuals as being higher in entitativity than groups, which results in the processing and memory differences described above. Hamilton and Sherman (1996) surmised that the variability in processing of individuals versus groups may be eliminated if perceived entitativity is equated for both types of targets. Indeed, McConnell, Sherman, and Hamilton (1997) found that when expectations of entitativity, in terms of similarity and behavioral consistency, were held constant, participants engaged in integrative, online, rather than nonintegrative, memory-based, processing of behavioral information regardless of whether the target was an individual or a group. An earlier set of studies manipulated processing instructions directly and found that instructions that encouraged integrative over nonintegrative processing led to more online versus memory-based judgments, irrespective of the type of target (group versus individual; McConnell, Sherman, & Hamilton, 1994b).

The structure of mental representations of high- and low-entitativity groups have been shown to differ. Johnson and Queller (2003) examined whether representations of low-entitativity groups are stored more in terms of specific behavioral exemplars than representations of high-entitativity groups. Using a modified version of Klein and Loftus's (1993a) task facilitation paradigm, participants were asked to learn a series of behaviors performed by either a high- or low-entitativity group. Subsequently, they completed one of two tasks. In the Describe + Recall Task, participants saw a trait word (e.g., adventurous) exemplified by some of the behaviors learned earlier and were asked to decide whether that word described the group or not. Immediately following that judgment, they were asked to recall a specific behavior that was consistent with the presented trait. In the Define + Recall Task, the initial task was to think about the definition of the presented trait

word followed by the same Recall Task. Perceivers were faster to recall a trait-consistent behavior followed by a Describe (versus Define) Task only when the group was perceived to be low in entitativity; when perceived to be a high-entitativity group, the Describe Task did not facilitate recall of behaviors compared with the Define Task. These findings demonstrate that representations of low- and high-entitativity groups are structured differently, with the former being composed more of specific behavioral exemplars than the latter, which are presumably more likely to be abstracted summaries.

Perceptions of entitativity not only affect basic processing and memory but also have wide-ranging downstream effects on stereotyping, attribution, and judgments of blame and collective responsibility. For instance, Spencer-Rodgers, Hamilton, and Sherman (2007) found that entitativity predicts stereotyping of groups, with higher perceptions of entitativity leading to greater facilitation of stereotyping. Along a similar vein, Crawford et al. (2002) found that perceivers formed STIs about members of both high- and low-entitativity groups, but only transferred inferred traits to other group members of the former group. Presumably, members of high-entitativity groups are more likely to be perceived as interchangeable and are more easily stereotyped. In addition, entitativity affects judgments of collective responsibility, with increasing perceptions of entitativity leading to a greater tendency to see group members as sharing the blame for the wrongdoings of a single member (Denson, Lickel, Curtis, Stenstrom, & Ames, 2006; Lickel, Schmader, & Hamilton, 2003). With respect to attribution, Yzerbyt, Roger, and Fiske (1998) found that perceivers attributed behaviors of high-entitativity group members to internal dispositions more than low-entitativity group members. Entitativity has also been shown to affect the persuasiveness of messages; messages presented by high-entitativity groups are processed more deeply than those of low-entitativity groups and are thus more persuasive when strong versus weak (Rydell & McConnell, 2005).

Factors that Affect Perceptions of Entitativity

Perceptions of entitativity fundamentally affect the structure of mental representations of groups, the processing of information about groups, and downstream judgments and evaluations with respect to stereotyping and assignment of blame. Thus, it is important to consider the factors that affect whether a group is perceived as being high or low in entitativity. For one, certain inherent properties of groups make them more entitative than others. For example, intimacy groups are perceived as highest in entitativity, followed by task groups and then social categories as lowest in entitativity (Lewis, Sherman, & Uhles, 2000; Lickel, Hamilton, & Sherman, 2001). Furthermore, there are individual differences in the level of entitativity perceived in groups. Implicit person theories regarding the stability versus mutability of skills and abilities (entity versus incremental theories, respectively) affect stereotyping such that entity theorists engage in more stereotyping than incremental theorists. Interestingly, this relationship was found to be mediated by perceptions of entitativity: Entity theorists perceived groups to be more entitative than incremental theorists, and this led to increased stereotyping (Rydell, Hugenburg, Ray, & Mackie, 2007). Moreover, there are cultural differences in the extent to which groups are perceived to be entitative. Spencer-Rodgers, Williams, Hamilton, Peng, and Wang (2007) found that Chinese participants perceived greater entitativity in groups and stereotyped group members more than American participants.

Much research has shown that people's perceptions of groups that are socially distant (e.g., outgroups) are distinct from their perceptions of groups that are socially proximal to the self (e.g., ingroups; Judd, Park, Yzerbyt, Gordijn, & Muller, 2005; Mackie & Hamilton, 1993; Park & Rothbart, 1982; Tajfel & Turner, 1986; Yzerbyt, Judd, & Corneille, 2004). The outgroup homogeneity effect describes the tendency for perceivers to have biased perceptions of outgroup members as being more homogenous, or similar, than members of their own ingroup, who are more distinct from one another (Park & Rothbart, 1982; for a review, see Simon, 1992). Insofar as different dimensions of psychological distance are interrelated (Bar-Anan, Liberman, Trope, & Algom, 2007; Stephan, Liberman, & Trope, 2010b), it is possible that distances other than social distance similarly affect perceptions of homogeneity. For instance, groups that are located far away may be seen as more homogenous (and therefore more entitative; Campbell, 1958; Lickel, Hamilton, Wieczorkowska, Lewis, Sherman, & Uhles, 2000; Rothbart & Park, 2004)[1] than similar groups located nearby. Along a similar vein, thinking about a group in the distant future as opposed to the near future may lead to perceptions of greater homogeneity among its members and, in turn, a greater tendency to conceptualize the group as a unified entity.

In addition to evidence from past research with respect to social distance, psychological distance, more generally, affects whether information is processed as an integrated, unified whole or as discrete parts of the whole. Discussed in more detail in a later section, research has shown that increasing psychological distance is associated with more global versus local processing of stimuli (Förster, Friedman, & Liberman, 2004; Liberman & Förster, 2009a, 2009b; Smith & Trope, 2006; Wakslak, Trope, Liberman, & Alony, 2006). In other words, when perceiving distal entities, the focus is on the gestalt, or the forest, rather than the trees. This type of global processing facilitates perceptions of greater entitativity, which by definition refers to perceptions of a group as a meaningful unit or unified whole. Following this reasoning, groups that are distanced from the self (e.g., in space, time, or social distance) should be processed more globally and thus be perceived as more entitative than similar groups that are proximal to the self. Supporting this notion, Henderson (2009) found that physical distance from task groups led to an increased tendency to perceive group members' behaviors as being geared toward common group goals, which is one perceived characteristic of highly entitative groups (Lickel et al., 2000).

Psychological distance also affects breadth of categorization (Liberman, Sagristano, & Trope, 2002; Wakslak et al., 2006). For instance, participants grouped the same objects (e.g., items to take on a camping trip) into fewer, broader categories when the objects were related to a distant versus proximal future event (Liberman et al., 2002; Study 1). In other words, inclusiveness of categorization increased with psychological distance. Similarly, given the same group of individuals, increasing psychological distance may lead to broader categorization of the individuals into a single group rather than multiple discrete groups. The tendency to categorize distal entities more broadly may support perceptions of greater group entitativity. And distance-dependent differences in mental construal may then lead to differences in more downstream judgments, such as stereotyping, evaluation, and attribution. For example, psychologically distal groups are more likely to be stereotyped than proximal groups.

It would be interesting to explore whether greater entitativity of groups promotes thinking about those groups in more distant situations. For example, groups that are high on entitativity may be perceived as having a longer history and may be afforded a greater sense of fixedness; they may be assumed to have existed in the distant past and to continue to exist in the distant future. High-entitativity groups might also be expected to be located in more remote places and to be more different from the perceiver than a low-entitativity group. This reverse direction of influence speaks to the function of high- and low-level representations in enabling mental travel.

PERCEPTIONS OF GROUP STRUCTURE AND BALANCE

Systems of social relations can be in a state of balance or imbalance, according to Heider's theory of structural balance (Heider, 1946, 1958). A balanced system is one in which the constituent relations map onto a schema of reciprocity and transitivity. For example, in a group consisting of three individuals, Persons A, B, and C, if Person A likes Person B, then Person B is expected to like Person A (reciprocity). Furthermore, if Person A dislikes Person C, then Person B is expected to dislike Person C as well (transitivity). Imbalanced systems, on the other hand, do not conform to these rules. For instance, in the network described above, imbalance would result if Person A and B like each other, and Person A likes Person C, but Person B dislikes Person C. Supporting Heider's (1958) propositions, past research has shown that people tend to regard balanced systems as more pleasant than imbalanced systems (e.g., Jordan, 1953; Morrissette, 1958; Price, Harburg, & Newcomb, 1966) and remember balanced networks better than imbalanced ones (e.g., Picek, Sherman, & Shiffrin, 1975; Zajonc & Burnstein, 1965a, 1965b; Zajonc & Sherman, 1967). Other work found that people impose a balance schema on incomplete networks and tend to misremember relations in a way that creates balance in the system (e.g., De Soto & Kuethe, 1959; Morrissette, 1958).

Research to be discussed in the following section found that representations of distant future selves are more abstract and structured and less complex compared with near future selves (Wakslak, Nussbaum, Liberman, & Trope, 2008). Furthermore, research on perceptual focus has shown that psychological distance increases the tendency to focus on the global forest rather than the local trees (Liberman & Förster, 2009b). Thus, if distance facilitates the top-down use of schemas in representations and a focus on the global structure rather than the constituent parts, the well-known tendency to better remember balanced versus imbalanced networks might be exacerbated as psychological distance between the self and a given network increases.

Moreover, greater psychological distance may result in a greater tendency to impose a balance schema on incomplete networks, resulting in more false memory for nonpresented relations that achieve balance.

Construal of the Self

People simultaneously conceptualize themselves as stable entities who display consistent and enduring qualities across the span of time and space and as fluid and dynamic entities who change depending on the particular context and through the course of the life span. What kinds of mental representations support these apparently disparate views of the self? How do people form and maintain relatively stable versus situationally flexible representations of the self? In this section, we review the literature on self-schemas that act as organizing frameworks for processing and interpreting information about the self. We also describe the abstraction versus exemplar model of self-representation. Along the way, we discuss findings from CLT that shed light on when representations will be more trait-based or more schematic and also make suggestions for future research.

SCHEMATIC VERSUS ASCHEMATIC REPRESENTATIONS

There is a considerable amount of evidence that supports the notion of schematic self-representations, especially in content domains that are important to a person's self-concept. In a highly influential paper, Markus (1977) defined self-schemas as "cognitive generalizations about the self, derived from past experience, that organize and guide the processing of self-related information contained in the individual's social experiences" (p. 64). Markus (1977) explored the idea that individuals who are schematic for a certain trait process relevant information in a fundamentally different way than those who are aschematic for that trait. Indeed, participants schematic for the trait domain of independence–dependence (i.e., they rated themselves as highly independent or highly dependent on a separate pretest) made "me/not me" judgments for traits in a schema-consistent way. For example, participants schematic for independence made faster "me" judgments for independence-related (versus dependence-related) traits, and the opposite occurred for those schematic for dependence. Importantly, aschematic participants showed no processing advantage for independence- or dependence-related words. Furthermore, participants schematic for independence–dependence recalled behavioral examples for schema-consistent traits more than schema-inconsistent ones; aschematics showed no difference in recalling behaviors corresponding to independence or dependence. Having a self-schema also led to confidence in making future predictions about schema-related behaviors and to an unwillingness to accept schema-inconsistent information about themselves. Similar results were obtained for gender schemas (Crane & Markus, 1982; Markus, Crane, Bernstein, & Siladi, 1982; Markus, Smith, & Moreland, 1985) and the trait domain of extraversion–introversion (Fong & Markus, 1982). Since this research was first conducted, much work has been done to demonstrate that self-schemas guide not only basic information processing but also behaviors, affective responses, and motivations in a schema-consistent manner (for a review, see Markus & Wurf, 1987). Although this is beyond the scope of this chapter, self-schemas even influence perceptions of other people (for a review, see Markus & Sentis, 1982; Markus & Smith, 1981).

What factors affect the extent to which the self will be represented schematically versus aschematically? Pronin and Ross (2006) found that people are more likely to represent their distant past and distant future selves in terms of personality traits. Along a similar vein, Wakslak et al. (2008) found that individuals' representations of their distant (versus near) future selves were more abstract, simple, and structured, as reflected using numerous different measures. In a series of studies, Wakslak et al. (2008) found that participants' representations of distant future selves were characterized by broader categorizations of the self (e.g., a woman versus a woman in her early 20s) and less complexity and differentiation as measured using an adaptation of Linville's (1985) self-complexity sorting task and Donahue and colleagues' (1993) measure of self-concept differentiation (SCD). Furthermore, distant future self-representations were more trait-based, as evidenced by shorter latencies in making me/not me trait judgments, and distant future selves were expected to be more cross-situationally consistent. Participants also rated distant future behaviors as more representative of themselves and were less likely to rate behaviors incongruent with their self-concept as expressing their "real" self. These results indicate that temporally distant selves are represented more schematically, in terms of general, decontextualized traits, and are less structurally complex than temporally proximal selves. It would be interesting to explore whether other dimensions of psychological distance also affect the structure of self-representations. For example, would imagining a hypothetical self (i.e., a possible self), or the self in a remote location lead to more abstract, schematic representations? According to this view, construal of the self is more likely to be more high-level, abstract, and schematic when the self is viewed from a distanced perspective—from the perspective of other people, in hypothetical situations, and in remote places.

Types of Self-Schemas

A person might possess multiple self-schemas that pertain to different aspects of the self or specific situational contexts. For instance, people have schemas pertaining to possible selves, both desired and undesired, and these schemas shape behavior by acting as incentives and also guide perceptions and evaluations of the current self (Markus & Nurius, 1986). Higgins and colleagues have researched three aspects of self-representation identified as the actual self, the ideal self (i.e., the self one would ideally like to be), and the ought self (i.e., the self one feels one should be based on one's own and others' expectations; Higgins, Bond, Klein, & Strauman, 1986). Discrepancies between the actual self and the ideal self and between the actual self and the ought self lead to specific emotional and behavioral consequences (Higgins, 1996, 1998), and there are individual differences in the amount and type of discrepancy people perceive. One's actual self can be thought of as anchored in the here and now while other "desired selves" (i.e., ought and ideal) are psychologically distal. Thus, a person's actual self-schema might be recruited in making self-relevant judgments in a proximal perspective while ought and ideal self-schemas may be more influential for judgments that are more psychologically removed (e.g., for imagining oneself in the distant future, in a remote location, in a hypothetical situation). It is not surprising that this would be the case for making judgments about the self in hypothetical situations because desired selves are, by definition, aspired and therefore not real. However, CLT predicts the same will occur when thinking about the self in the distant future or distant past, or in remote locations.

Individuals also possess representations of themselves when with various significant others in their lives, or relational selves (for a review, see Andersen & Saribay, 2005). When a new person is encountered who resembles one's significant other, this triggers one's affective reaction (positive versus negative), motivational orientation (approach versus avoidance), expectation of acceptance or rejection, and evaluation of oneself when with the significant other (Andersen et al., 1996; Berk & Andersen, 2000; Hinkley & Andersen, 1996). And the consequence of this transference process can be behavioral confirmation (Berk & Andersen, 2000). Relational selves contain aspects that are relatively high level versus low level. For example, a high-level aspect may be a goal that is activated by one's significant other, whereas a relatively low-level aspect might be an idiosyncratic behavior or gesture one displays when with that significant other. Increasing psychological distance between the self and a new person who resembles one's significant other may lead to greater activation of high-level (versus low-level) aspects of the relational self.

ABSTRACTION OF TRAITS VERSUS BEHAVIORAL EXEMPLARS

Klein and colleagues (for a review, see Klein & Loftus, 1993b) found evidence that summary representations of individuals' traits are stored separately in memory from specific behaviors that exemplify those traits. Thus, self-information is represented both in terms of one's traits abstracted from multiple trait-consistent behaviors and in terms of the specific behaviors themselves, supporting the dual exemplar plus summary representation view endorsed by many researchers (e.g., Bower & Gilligan, 1979; Cantor & Kihlstrom, 1986; Kihlstrom & Cantor, 1984; Kihlstrom, Cantor, Albright, Chew, Klein, & Niedenthal, 1988; Mancuso & Ceely, 1980). In a typical study using the task facilitation paradigm, participants complete three tasks in counterbalanced order: (1) a descriptive task in which they should judge whether a presented trait (e.g., honest) describes the self, (2) an autobiographical task in which they should think of a specific behavioral episode exemplifying this trait, and (3) a semantic (control) task in which participants generate a definition for the trait and response latencies are measured. The logic was that if traits do not exist in the form of abstract summaries, trait judgments (i.e., Am I honest?) must be made by retrieval of specific behaviors. In this case, the descriptive task should facilitate responses to the autobiographical task, which would support the pure exemplar view of self-representation. On the contrary, Klein and Loftus (1993b) found that there was no facilitation on the self-descriptive task following the autobiographical task, or vice versa, thereby supporting the idea that trait summaries do exist and are stored independently of behavioral representations. This was true regardless of trait centrality in representation, contrary to speculation that summary representations might only exist for central traits (Kihlstrom & Cantor, 1984; Kihlstrom et al., 1988). However, one moderator was people's amount of experience in a particular context. For instance, first-year college students were asked to complete the above-described task regarding a highly experienced context (home) versus a less experienced context (college). In the high-experience condition, there was evidence for abstracted trait knowledge independent of specific behaviors, whereas in the low-experience context condition, responses on the descriptive task were facilitated by the autobiographical task, thereby showing that in contexts in which one has less experience, one is less likely to have abstracted trait summary representations and is more likely to refer to specific behavioral exemplars in making trait judgments.

From the perspective of CLT, psychologically distant selves should be represented more in terms of abstracted trait summaries than psychologically proximal selves, holding amount of information or experience constant. It would be interesting to examine this idea using the task facilitation paradigm. Although Wakslak et al. (2008) found that participants were faster to make me/not me trait judgments for their distant (versus near) future selves, it is not clear whether these trait judgments were based on trait representations formed online and existing in memory or on behavioral exemplars retrieved at the time of judgment.

Construal of Causal Relationships

A large body of literature in social psychology has been devoted to understanding the ways in which people explain their own and others' actions and the circumstances under which they engage in this kind of causal thinking (Gilbert & Malone, 1995; Hastie, 1984; Heider, 1958; Kelley, 1957; Kelley & Michela, 1980; Ross, 1977; Schank, 1986; Trope, 1986). Classic research on the correspondence bias demonstrated that people are biased toward attributing the behaviors of others to internal, dispositional causes even when they are aware that the behaviors are situationally constrained (see Gilbert & Malone, 1995; Jones, 1979). Relatedly, actor–observer effects describe the tendency for people to attribute others' behaviors (failing an exam) to dispositional causes (because he is stupid) while attributing one's own behaviors to situational causes (because the exam was unfair). These theories are built on the premise that causal thinking occurs. And research has shown that, indeed, causal inferences are made spontaneously.

INFERENCES ABOUT CAUSES AND CONSEQUENCES

Weiner (1985) examined coding of written material (e.g., newspaper articles, business reports, and letters) to demonstrate the prominence of causal explanations (e.g., Lau, 1984; Lau & Russell, 1980). These observations were made across a wide range of written text: newspaper articles on sporting events and political events, advice columns, letters, children's journal entries, and corporate annual reports. For instance, across 107 newspaper articles, Lau and Russell (1980) found a total of 594 attributional statements, which averages to about 5.5 causal explanations per article. In another study, participants read hypothetical scenarios in which they experienced various events (e.g., failed a midterm test; Wong & Weiner, 1981). Then they were asked to report what questions, if any, came to mind. Three types of questions were asked by a majority of participants—attribution, action oriented, and reevaluation—but attribution questions predominated. The prominence of causal statements in written text and spontaneous responses speaks to the notion that causal thinking is naturally occurring and important in everyday life.

Hassin, Bargh, and Uleman (2002) found evidence for the formation of spontaneous causal inferences from events using a stricter criterion for spontaneity. For an inference to be spontaneous, it must not be suggested in the task instructions, participants should not have an explicit intention to form the inference, and they should not be aware of having made the inference. Participants initially read a series of short scenarios about various events, some of which implied particular causes (e.g., *After spending a day exploring beautiful sights in the crowded streets of New York, Jane discovered that her wallet was missing*, implies *pickpocketed*). Their task was to rate the scenarios on how interesting they were. After completing a five-minute filler task to clear working memory, participants were given a surprise recall test in which they were prompted to recall the previously read scenarios. Implied causes were presented as cues that participants were told they could use to remember the sentences. Cause cues led to better memory for cause-implying sentences than control sentences that did not imply causes, thus showing spontaneous causal inference formation.

People infer not only the causes of events but also the consequences. McKoon and Ratcliff (1986) demonstrated that implied consequences (*dead*) serve as effective retrieval cues for sentences (*The director and cameraman were ready to shoot close-ups when suddenly the actress fell from the 14th story*), suggesting that predictive inferences had been made during initial encoding. The series of studies by Hassin et al. (2002) described previously served as a complement to this work by McKoon and Ratcliff (1986). Hassin et al. (2002) concluded that "the mind not only spontaneously attaches a 'cause tag'—it also attaches an 'effect tag,' hence, spontaneously covering the whole range of causal relations" (p. 520). However, unlike inferences about causes, the consensus in the literature is that predictive inferences are made during reading but only when certain conditions are met. For example, predictive inferences are made when the surrounding context strongly supports the inference (Cook, Limber, & O'Brien, 2001; Murray, Klin, & Myers, 1993) and when the implying context is encountered immediately before inference formation is assessed (e.g., Keefe & McDaniel, 1993; McKoon Ratcliff, 1986; Murray et al., 1993). This contrasts with causal inferences, which are considered necessary for text comprehension. Relatedly, research in language production has shown that people infer consequences of events (Arnold, 2001; Majid, Sanford, & Pickering, 2007; Stevenson, Crawley, & Kleinman, 1994). When presented with short scenarios (e.g., John sent a telegram to Mary), participants were found to spontaneously form more continuations that elaborated on the consequence than on the antecedent (Arnold, 2001).

DETERMINANTS OF ANTECEDENT VERSUS CONSEQUENTIAL THINKING

Several factors have been identified in the literature as affecting the extent to which causal inferences are formed. For one, causal attribution is especially likely for negative outcomes (e.g., Wong & Weiner, 1981; for a review, see Weiner, 1983) or for outcomes that are unexpected (e.g., Hastie, 1984; Lau & Russell, 1980; Pyszczynski & Greenberg, 1983; Wong & Weiner, 1981; for a review, see Weiner, 1985). Hastie (1984) presented participants with lists of behaviors describing hypothetical persons. Each list was associated with a particular trait (e.g., intelligent); two thirds of the behaviors in each list were congruent with that trait (e.g., won the chess tournament) and one third were incongruent (e.g., failed organic chemistry). Causal attribution was assessed by participants' sentence completions of the behaviors (e.g., won the chess tournament... *because he had studied the game for five years*). Participants generated more causal explanations for unexpected or incongruent behaviors of actors and had better memory for those behaviors on a surprise free recall test. Outcome dependency also affects causal processing of information (Berscheid, Graziano, Monson, & Dermer, 1976; Monson, Keel, Stephens, & Genung, 1982). Berscheid et al. (1976) found that people are more likely to engage in causal thinking about a person they expect to date versus not date. In the work described earlier in language production, Majid et al. (2007) identified the type of verb used in the sentence as a determinant of whether antecedent or consequence continuations are spontaneously preferred. They found that interpersonal verbs (e.g., John *hugged* Mary) invite cause continuations, whereas transfer verbs (e.g., John *threw* the ball to Mary) lead to predominantly consequence continuations.

Causes and consequences share some of the features of high- and low-level construals, respectively. Most importantly, consequences are subordinate to causes in that a change in the cause brings about a change in the consequence, but not vice versa. Relatedly, causes constrain the meaning of consequences and shape people's interpretation of a given situation more than the other way around (Proctor & Ahn, 2007). For example, one's impression of a student who aced an exam will differ depending on whether the good grade was a result of an overly easy test, the student having cheated, or the student having studied particularly hard to prepare for it. And in the cognitive literature on concept representation and categorization, a concept's causal features are considered to be more central than its effect features because causes are more immutable and afford greater inductive power (Ahn, 1998; Ahn, Kim, Lassaline, & Dennis, 2000; Kim & Ahn, 2002). Thus, causal features have been shown to have greater weight than effect features in feature induction (Proctor & Ahn, 2007). Similarly, in the text comprehension literature, causal antecedent inferences are considered more central to basic comprehension than inferences about causal consequences (Guéraud, Tapiero, & O'Brien, 2008).

Based on the association between distance and level of construal postulated by CLT, a psychologically distal perspective may facilitate representation of events more in terms of their underlying causes than consequences, whereas a psychologically proximal perspective facilitates representation of events more in terms of their consequences than causes. Supporting this prediction, Rim, Hansen, and Trope (2013) found that priming a high-level low-level mindset led to greater rated ease of generating causes versus effects of various events (e.g.,

getting a tooth cavity) compared with priming a low-level mindset. In a second study, they examined the effect of temporal distance and found that participants generated more causes than consequences for events that they imagined to be temporally distant (occurring one year from now) versus temporally proximal (occurring tomorrow) participants generated. A third study extended this effect to social distance and showed that people spontaneously think about what caused certain events to occur when those events involve other people and think about the consequences of those same events when they involve the self.

There is also evidence for the reverse direction of causality. Participants who generated causes (versus effects) of events were more likely to think about a given action (e.g., read a book) in terms of high-level, abstract, and central ends (e.g., gaining knowledge) versus low-level, concrete, and peripheral means (e.g., following lines of print). Furthermore, thinking about causes (versus effects) of events led participants to estimate that they would take place in the more distant future and in more distant geographic locations (Rim et al., 2013).

This link between psychological distance and causal focus has important downstream consequences. For example, Rim et al. (2013) found that when participants imagined a self-regulatory issue (e.g., stress causing low-energy) one year from now (versus tomorrow), they preferred to engage in a behavior that would regulate the underlying cause (the stress) versus the consequence (low-energy). Presumably this preference is a result of a greater tendency to focus on causes versus consequences as distance increases. The implication is that a distal perspective may promote more long-term change via regulation of the root cause of a problem, whereas a proximal perspective would lead to more short-term change. Another study examined the weighting of causes and effects in distant versus near prospective judgments. Participants were given information about people with two causally related mental illness symptoms (e.g., *S. S. recurrent suspicions about her husband's fidelity caused her to require excessive attention*). Subsequently, participants were asked to make predictive judgments about two symptoms, one cause-related and the other effect-related for the distant (one year from now) or near (tomorrow) future. Specifically, participants were asked to rate on a scale of 1 (very unlikely) to 9 (very likely), "How likely do you think it is that S. S. will have doubts about the loyalty of her friends one year from now (or tomorrow)?" which is related to the existing causal symptom, and "How likely is it that S. S. will fish for compliments about her appearance one year from now (or tomorrow)?" which is related to the existing effect symptom. Cause-related symptoms were rated as more likely in the distant future while effect-related symptoms were rated as more likely in the near future. Other downstream consequences of cause-versus-effect mental representations are currently being explored.

Generalized Construals: Further Distinctions

The aim of the preceding sections has been to describe the primary distinctions that have been drawn in representing persons, groups, and the self. It is evident that much of the traditional focus, at least with respect to the *structure* of mental representations, has been on distinguishing schematic versus aschematic, prototype versus exemplar, and trait versus behavioral representations (Smith, 1998; Wyer, 2007; Wyer & Carlston, 1994). In the present section, we introduce additional distinctions that have been made, albeit to a lesser degree, and discuss them in connection with research within CLT.

Global Versus Local Visual Processing

Objects and scenes can be processed by the visual system globally, according to the overall gestalt, or locally, according to their constituent details. In other words, one can represent "the forest" or "the trees" as the proverbial distinction goes. Global processing is consistent with high-level construal, which is characterized by the ability to extract the essence and see the gestalt, whereas local processing is consistent with low-level construal, which is associated with a focus on the incidental and concrete details. Thus, based on the link between level of construal and psychological distance, a distal perspective should facilitate global processing, whereas a proximal perspective engages local processing of the same stimulus object.

Liberman and Förster (2009b) examined this idea in a series of studies in which participants were primed with psychological distance and then completed the Navon Task (Navon, 1977). In this well-known task, participants see a series of letters made up of smaller letters and are asked to indicate as quickly as possible whether a target letter (e.g., *H*) appeared on the screen. When primed to think about the distant future (Study 1), a distant spatial location (Study 2), and distant social relations (Study 3), participants were faster to indicate that a target letter (*H*) had appeared on the screen

when it was the global (*H* made up of *L*s) versus the local (*L* made up of *H*s) letter. When primed with proximity, in time, space, and social relations, participants were faster when the target letter was the local (versus global) letter.

Other research found converging evidence using different measures of global and local processing: the Gestalt Completion Task (GCT: Street, 1931; see also Ekstrom, French, Harman, & Dermen, 1976) and the Wechsler Intelligence Scale for Children (WISC; Wechsler, 1991), respectively. In the GCT, participants see fragmented pictures and have to identify what those pictures depict. Performance on this task depends on the ability to detect the global pattern and abstract visual coherence from the fragmented visual input. Participants who completed the GCT under the pretense that it was a practice version for the actual task performed better when they imagined doing the actual task in the distant future (Förster et al., 2004) and when they thought the actual task was unlikely to be completed (Wakslak et al., 2006). Furthermore, Smith and Trope (2006) used a variant of the GCT and found converging effects with the social distance dimension of power. Participants primed with high power were better able to see the structure in random fragmented pictures than those primed with low power. On the contrary, performance on the WISC reflects the ability to see the parts within the whole. The task involves detecting missing items from a series of pictures (e.g., the labels missing from a row of cans at a grocery store where a woman is shopping). Wakslak et al. (2006) found that participants performed better on this (practice) task when they thought it was highly likely to be the main task versus less likely.

Analogue Versus Symbolic Representations

Theories of mental simulation (Schacter & Addis, 2007) and embodied cognition (Barsalou, 1999; Winkielman, Niedenthal, & Oberman, 2008) suggest that memory enables prospection through a constructive process of mentally simulating future episodes. Such simulations are analogical and multimodal and serve to guide choice and action with respect to the future (Barsalou, 2008). CLT adds to this view in several respects. First, it is possible that simulations vary in level of construal, ranging from multimodal simulations that are rich in contextual detail and resemble the kind of analogical representation identified by embodied cognition researchers to general simulations that retain common elements and omit incidental detail. CLT predicts that the latter, higher level simulations are more likely to be used with increasing distance of the past episodes from which simulations are constructed and of the future target situation to which the simulation is applied. For example, a simulation of a future meeting with a friend is likely to be more abstract (i.e., contain less detail on the tone of her voice and the look of the room in which the meeting would take place) to the extent that the meeting with the friend is expected in the relatively distant future or location. Second, it is possible that as distance increases, prospection is increasingly more likely to be based on amodal symbolic representations. For example, a representation of a more distant future meeting with a friend who works in a high-tech company may refer more to semantic knowledge about layoffs in the high-tech industry and include less detail related to perceptual properties, such as the tone of her voice. Third, symbolic representations might also differ in abstraction, ranging from broad abstractions (she is a woman) to more narrowly applied knowledge (she is a single mother of four and a high-tech manager who is afraid to lose her job). Thus, according to CLT, both analogical simulations and symbolic representations can vary in level of construal. Distance may determine whether an analogical or symbolic representation is constructed and the level of abstractness at which it will be constructed.

Recent research on pictorial and linguistic representations is consistent with this analysis (Amit, Algom, & Trope; 2009; Amit, Algom, Trope, & Liberman, 2009). Pictures are icons, analogue representations of objects, whereas words are symbolic representations of objects. A pictorial representation of an object bears concrete resemblance to it and contains incidental details, whereas a word to describe the same object is abstract and captures its essence. Even a line drawing of an object is more concrete than a word representing the same object. Also, a word (e.g., *chair*) represents many possible exemplars (e.g., *office chair, kitchen stool, armchair, rocking chair*), whereas a picture is an "*n* of 1" exemplar. Therefore, verbal representations are relatively more high level than pictorial representations. Consistent with CLT, participants were faster to identify spatially, temporally, and socially proximal (versus distal) pictures and faster to identify spatially, temporally, and socially distal (versus proximal) words on a speeded identification task (Amit et al., 2009). Furthermore, distance affected memory for pictures versus words. Using various dimensions of psychological distance (spatial, temporal, and social), Amit, Rim, Halbeisen, Algom, and Trope (2013) found that proximal pictures were remembered better than distal pictures and that distal words were remembered better than proximal words. Thus, words and pictures behave like other dimensions of high- and low-level construals and are associated with distance versus proximity, respectively.

Moreover, as evidenced by a host of findings in the traditions of grounded cognition and embodiment, sensorimotor experience can exert a powerful influence on what and how people think (Barsalou, 2008; Niedenthal, Barsalou, Winkielman, Krauth-Gruber, & Ric, 2005). CLT suggests conditions that temper or enable this influence, proposing that level of mental construal may moderate the role of temporary physical state in judgment. Specifically, insofar as the sensorimotor information responsible for grounding cognition constitutes an incidental and thus low-level feature of a situation, it should exert less influence from an abstract or high-level (versus concrete or low-level) frame of mind. Recent research by Maglio and Trope (2012) provides initial support for this prediction: Contextual bodily information affected visual length estimates (Study 1) and importance ratings (Study 2) for people led to think concretely but not for those thinking abstractly.

Breadth of Categorization

The same object or event can be represented using different levels of categorization. For instance, *dog* represents the basic level of categorization, whereas *mammal* represents a superordinate category and *cockapoo* represents a subordinate category of the same family pet. Broader categories (e.g., *mammal*) represent higher levels of construal than narrow categories (e.g., *cockapoo*). Liberman et al. (2002) found that objects imagined to be used in the distant future (e.g., things to take on a camping trip one year from now) were grouped into fewer, broader categories than those expected to be used in the near future (e.g., tomorrow). Furthermore, participants primed with high power (social distance) were more inclusive in categorizing atypical exemplars (e.g., *sled* for the category *vehicle*) than those primed with low power (Smith & Trope, 2006).

Distance effects were also found with respect to chunking or segmentation of events. When ongoing events were described as psychologically distal, they were chunked into broader and fewer segments than when they were described as psychologically proximal (Henderson et al., 2006). Participants watched an animated film clip depicting two triangles and a circle (Heider & Simmel, 1944) and segmented the clip into as many meaningful sections as they thought appropriate. Participants in New York were told that the film portrayed the actions of three teenagers at a summer camp either on the East Coast (spatially proximal condition) or the West Coast (spatially distal condition). As predicted based on the association between distance and level of construal, participants segmented the video into fewer, broader sections when they believed it portrayed a spatially distal (versus proximal) event. Converging evidence was found using subjective probability as a manipulation of psychological distance; unlikely, therefore distal, events were chunked into broader units than were likely events (Wakslak et al., 2006).

Evidence has also been found for the opposite direction of causality. Priming people to think of narrow, specific categories leads to perceptions of greater psychological distance with respect to probability (Wakslak et al., 2006). In one study, participants compared two objects (cameras) using information on alignable (same) versus nonalignable (different) attributes. The idea was that participants who compared the objects on nonalignable attributes would engage in greater abstraction to make the objects comparable. Again consistent with prediction, individuals induced to think more abstractly (by comparing objects on nonalignable features) thought events involving those objects were less likely to occur than those induced to think more concretely (by comparing objects on alignable features).

Ends Versus Means

Actions can be represented in terms of the reasons *why* one performs an action, the ends, or in terms of *how* the action is performed, the means. Ends are relatively more superordinate and abstract and therefore represent higher level construals than means, which are more subordinate and concrete (Vallacher & Wegner, 1989). For instance, the action *studying* can be represented in terms of the high-level goal of studying, *doing well in school*, or the low-level means, *reading a textbook*. Vallacher and Wegner (1989) demonstrated that individuals differ in the extent to which they tend to represent actions in terms of higher level ends or lower level means.

Research found that when given a choice, people choose to represent psychologically distal actions more in terms of high-level ends rather than low-level means, and vice versa for psychologically proximal actions (Liberman & Trope, 2008; Liviatan, Trope, & Liberman, 2008; Wakslak et al., 2006). For instance, using interpersonal similarity as a manipulation of social distance, Liviatan et al.

(2008, Study 1) found that actions of dissimilar others were represented more in terms of high-level ends than the same actions of similar others.

Associations Among Construal Level Dimensions

We have speculated that traditional distinctions in mental representation fall under the common rubric of high versus low level and that they are associated with psychological distance. The commonality among high-level construal dimensions is that they are abstract, are stable, and convey the central essence or gist compared with low-level construal dimensions, which include more concrete and peripheral details and are context bound. The nature of high-level construals makes them especially well suited for mental travel. When imagining the distant future, events occurring in a remote location or to a dissimilar other, or hypothetical alternatives to reality, high-level construal are useful in that they are not bound to a particular context and are relatively stable. Without claiming that different ways to characterize high and low (e.g., trait versus behaviors, global versus local, words versus pictures) are the same, we propose that they have this underlying similarity or shared aspect that makes them useful for representing distal versus proximal entities, respectively. In the present section, we shed light on this issue of commonality among construal dimensions and present evidence from various studies that show the hypothesized association.

Empirical Evidence

Thinking in terms of categories rather than specific exemplars leads to a greater tendency to form STIs from other people's behaviors (Rim et al., 2009; Study 3). Participants completed one of two tasks: (1) a category generation task in which participants generated superordinate categories (e.g., beverage) for a list of 40 items (e.g., soda) or (2) an exemplar generation task in which they generated subordinate exemplars (e.g., Sprite) for the same list of items. Results showed that generating categories, and thus engaging in abstract, high-level construal, led participants to spontaneously infer traits from behaviors to a greater extent than when they generated exemplars, which are more low level. Another study found that global (versus local) processing leads to greater inclusion of atypical exemplars in a category (Rim, Amit, & Trope, 2011). For instance, participants rated *piano* as fitting into the category of *furniture* more highly when in a global (versus local) perceptual focus. Furthermore, thinking about high-level ends (*why* do you maintain good health?) versus low-level means (*how* do you maintain good health?) led to more global versus local processing.

A recent series of studies looked specifically at the relationship between medium (words and pictures) and other dimensions of construal level (Rim, Amit, Trope, Halbeisen, & Fujita, 2013). Because words represent a higher level of construal than pictures, they should be associated with other high-level construal dimensions (e.g., global processing, broader categorization), whereas pictures should be associated with the corresponding low-level construals (e.g., local processing, narrower categorization). Providing support for this idea, participants reported thinking about high-level ends (e.g., *why* do you maintain good health?) rather than low-level means (e.g., *how* do you maintain good health?) more in terms of words than pictures, and they grouped objects into fewer, broader categories when the items were presented in verbal (versus pictorial) form. In addition, participants primed with a series of words (e.g., the word *apple*) versus a series of pictures (e.g., a picture of an apple) showed enhanced global processing on an adaptation of the Navon Task (Gasper & Clore, 2002; Kimchi & Palmer, 1982).

Concluding Remarks

In summary, traditional distinctions that have been made regarding the structure of mental representations of persons, groups, and the self may fall under a common rubric of high-level versus low-level construal. Schematic representations (e.g., traits, stereotypes, and prototypes) are more abstract and central, reflecting the core essence of the referent entity, compared with their counterparts (e.g., behaviors, individuating information, and exemplars). That classifies the former as high level and the latter as low level in the language of CLT. Along with other high- and low-level construal dimensions (e.g., global–local, superordinate–subordinate, words–pictures), these various representations are associated with psychological distance. High-level construals are more likely to be used in representing psychologically distal entities, whereas low-level construals are used to represent proximal entities. Low-level concrete construals spell out in detail the specifics of social objects, including their peripheral and incidental aspects. Thereby, they support immersion in the here and now. In contrast, high-level, abstract construals, by extracting the central features of a social object, go beyond a particular instantiation of an object, implying what

the object can be and the different ways in which it might manifest. High-level construals thus afford transcending the here and now, enabling people to expand their mental and social horizons.

Adaptive functioning requires both the ability to navigate the immediate situation and the ability to broaden one's horizons to include more remote entities. At times, effective behavior involves adapting to the local demands and affordances of the current context. At other times, individuals need to expand their mental horizon to consider objects, events, and people outside of their immediate situation. Switching between levels of construals to more abstract or more concrete modes of representation enables people to flexibly expand and contract their social horizon. High-level construals, which incorporate centrality and generality, should allow people to transcend the particularities of the here and now and therefore to self-regulate effectively in pursuit of distant ends. In contrast, because the peripheral and specific aspects of an experience tend to contain unique details of the current context, low-level construals that focus on peripherals and specifics should help people immerse themselves in the here and now and effectively self-regulate toward proximal ends.

The different levels of construal are particularly relevant to functioning in the social world. The invariances composing high-level construals enable us to predict and relate to people who are unlike ourselves—people who are temporally, spatially, socially, and probabilistically remote. In contrast, the contextualized details composing low-level construals allow us to predict and relate to people who are like ourselves. The different levels of construal thus support communication, learning, and exchange among relatively small and homogeneous groups as well as increasingly large, complex, and diverse groups of individuals.

Notes

1. It is beyond the scope of this chapter to discuss the relationship between these concepts in much detail, so we refer to entitativity and homogeneity in a loosely interchangeable way in this section (for a thorough discussion of various concepts relevant to group perception, see Hamilton, 2007; Yzerbyt et al., 2004). Past research has shown that these concepts are highly related, with some studies reporting significant correlations between them (Lickel et al., 2000; Spencer-Rodgers et al., 2007).

Author Note

This research was supported by BSF Grant #2007247 to Nira Liberman and Yaacov Trope. SoYon Rim is now a postdoctoral research fellow at

Harvard University at the Harvard Kennedy School of Government. Address correspondence to SoYon Rim, 79 JFK Street, Mailbox 126, Cambridge, MA, 02138. E-mail: Soyon_Rim@hk;s.harvard.edu.

References

Ahn, W. (1998). Why are different features central for natural kinds and artifacts? The role of causal status in determining feature centrality. *Cognition*, *69*(2), 135–178.

Ahn, W., Kim, N. S., Lassaline, M. E., & Dennis, M. J. (2000). Causal status as a determinant of feature centrality. *Cognitive Psychology*, *41*(4), 361–416.

Allport, G. W. (1954). *The nature of prejudice*. Oxford, UK: Addison-Wesley.

Amit, E., Algom, D., & Trope, Y. (2009). Distance-dependent processing of pictures and words. *Journal of Experimental Psychology: General*, *138*(3), 400–415.

Amit, E., Algom, D., Trope, Y., & Liberman, N. (2009). "Thou shalt not make unto thee any graven image": The distance dependence of representation. In K. D. Markman, W. M. P. Klein & J. A. Suhr (Eds.), *Handbook of imagination and mental simulation* (pp. 53–68). New York: Psychology Press.

Amit, E., Rim, S., Halbeisen, G., Algom, D., & Trope, Y. Distance-dependent memory for pictures and words. Manuscript submitted for publication.

Andersen, S. M., & Baum, A. (1994). Transference in interpersonal relations: Inferences and affect based on significant-other representations. *Journal of Personality, Special Issue: Psychodynamics and Social Cognition: Perspectives on the Representation and Processing of Emotionally Significant Information*, *62*(4), 459–497.

Andersen, S. M., & Chen, S. (2002). The relational self: An interpersonal social-cognitive theory. *Psychological Review*, *109*(4), 619–645.

Andersen, S. M., & Cole, S. W. (1990). "Do I know you?": The role of significant others in general social perception. *Journal of Personality and Social Psychology*, *59*(3), 384–399.

Andersen, S. M., Glassman, N. S., Chen, S., & Cole, S. W. (1995). Transference in social perception: The role of chronic accessibility in significant-other representations. *Journal of Personality and Social Psychology*, *69*(1), 41–57.

Andersen, S. M., Reznik, I., & Manzella, L. M. (1996). Eliciting facial affect, motivation, and expectancies in transference: Significant-other representations in social relations. *Journal of Personality and Social Psychology*, *71*(6), 1108–1129.

Andersen, S. M., & Saribay, S. A. (2005). The relational self and transference: Evoking motives, self-regulation, and emotions through activation of mental representations of significant others. In M. W. Baldwin (Ed.), *Interpersonal cognition* (pp. 1–32). New York: Guilford Press.

Anderson, N. H. (1981). *Foundations of information integration theory*. New York: Academic Press.

Arnold, J. E. (2001). The effect of thematic roles on pronoun use and frequency of reference continuation. *Discourse Processes*, *31*(2), 137–162.

Asch, S. E. (1946). Forming impressions of personality. *Journal of Abnormal and Social Psychology*, *41*(3), 258–290.

Bar-Anan, Y., Liberman, N., Trope, Y., & Algom, D. (2007). Automatic processing of psychological distance: Evidence from a Stroop Task. *Journal of Experimental Psychology: General*, *136*(4), 610–622.

Barsalou, L. W. (1999). Perceptual symbol systems. *Behavioral and Brain Sciences*, *22*(4), 577–660.

Barsalou, L. W. (2008). Grounded cognition. *Annual Review of Psychology*, *59*, 617–645.

Berenson, K., & Andersen, S. M. (2006). *Childhood physical abuse by a parent: Transference effects in adult interpersonal relations*. Personality and Social Psychology Bulletin, *32*, 1509–1522.

Berk, M. S., & Andersen, S. M. (2000). The impact of past relationships on interpersonal behavior: Behavioral confirmation in the social–cognitive process of transference. *Journal of Personality and Social Psychology*, *79*(4), 546–562.

Berscheid, E., Graziano, W., Monson, T., & Dermer, M. (1976). Outcome dependency: Attention, attribution, and attraction. *Journal of Personality and Social Psychology*, *34*(5), 978–989.

Bodenhausen, G. V. (1988). Stereotypic biases in social decision making and memory: Testing process models of stereotype use. *Journal of Personality and Social Psychology*, *55*(5), 726–737.

Bodenhausen, G. V. (1990). Stereotypes as judgmental heuristics: Evidence of circadian variations in discrimination. *Psychological Science*, *1*(5), 319–322.

Bodenhausen, G. V., & Lichtenstein, M. (1987). Social stereotypes and information-processing strategies: The impact of task complexity. *Journal of Personality and Social Psychology*, *52*(5), 871–880.

Bodenhausen, G. V., Macrae, C. N., & Sherman, J. S. (1999). On the dialectics of discrimination: Dual processes in social stereotyping. In S. Chaiken, & Y. Trope (Eds.), *Dual-process theories in social psychology* (pp. 271–290). New York: Guilford Press.

Bower, G. H., & Gilligan, S. G. (1979). Remembering information related to one's self. *Journal of Research in Personality*, *13*(4), 420–432.

Brewer, M. B. (1988). A dual process model of impression formation. In T. K. Srull, & R. S. Wyer Jr. (Eds.), *A dual process model of impression formation* (pp. 1–36). Hillsdale, NJ: Erlbaum.

Brewer, M. B., Dull, V., & Lui, L. (1981). Perceptions of the elderly: Stereotypes as prototypes. *Journal of Personality and Social Psychology*, *41*(4), 656–670.

Bruner, J. S. (1957). On perceptual readiness. *Psychological Review*, *64*(2), 123–152.

Campbell, D. T. (1958). Common fate, similarity, and other indices of the status of aggregates of persons as social entities. *Behavioral Science*, *3*, 14–25.

Cantor, N., & Kihlstrom, J. F. (1986). *Personality and social intelligence*. Englewood Cliffs, NJ: Prentice-Hall.

Cantor, N., & Mischel, W. (1977). Traits as prototypes: Effects on recognition memory. *Journal of Personality and Social Psychology*, *35*(1), 38–48.

Cantor, N., & Mischel, W. (1979). Prototypicality and personality: Effects on free recall and personality impressions. *Journal of Research in Personality*, *13*(2), 187–205.

Carlston, D. E., & Skowronski, J. J. (1994). Savings in the relearning of trait information as evidence for spontaneous inference generation. *Journal of Personality and Social Psychology*, *66*(5), 840–856.

Chen, S., & Andersen, S. M. (2008). The relational self in transference: Intrapersonal and interpersonal consequences in everyday social life. In J. V. Wood, A. Tesser & J. G. Holmes (Eds.), *The self and social relationships* (pp. 231–253). New York: Psychology Press.

Chen, S., Andersen, S. M., & Hinkley, K. (1999). Triggering transference: Examining the role of applicability in the activation and use of significant-other representations in social perception. *Social Cognition, 17*(3), 332–365.

Cook, A. E., Limber, J. E., & O'Brien, E. J. (2001). Situation-based context and the availability of predictive inferences. *Journal of Memory and Language, 44*(2), 220–234.

Crane, M., & Markus, H. (1982). Gender identity: The benefits of a self-schema approach. *Journal of Personality and Social Psychology, 43*(6), 1195–1197.

Crawford, M. T., Sherman, S. J., & Hamilton, D. L. (2002). Perceived entitativity, stereotype formation, and the interchangeability of group members. *Journal of Personality and Social Psychology, 83*(5), 1076–1094.

Crawford, M. T., Skowronski, J. J., Stiff, C., & Scherer, C. R. (2007). Interfering with inferential, but not associative, processes underlying spontaneous trait inference. *Personality and Social Psychology Bulletin, 33*(5), 677–690.

Crocker, J., Hannah, D. B., & Weber, R. (1983). Person memory and causal attributions. *Journal of Personality and Social Psychology, 44*(1), 55–66.

Darley, J. M., & Gross, P. H. (1983). A hypothesis-confirming bias in labeling effects. *Journal of Personality and Social Psychology, 44*(1), 20–33.

Denson, T. F., Lickel, B., Curtis, M., Stenstrom, D. M., & Ames, D. R. (2006). The roles of entitativity and essentiality in judgments of collective responsibility. *Group Processes & Intergroup Relations, 9*(1), 43–61.

De Soto, C. B., & Kuethe, J. L. (1959). Subjective probabilities of interpersonal relationships. *Journal of Abnormal and Social Psychology, 59*(2), 290–294.

Donahue, E. M., Robins, R. W., Roberts, B. W., & John, O. P. (1993). The divided self: Concurrent and longitudinal effects of psychological adjustment and social roles on self-concept differentiation. *Journal of Personality and Social Psychology, 64*(5), 834–846.

Dovidio, J. F., & Gaertner, S. L. (1993). Stereotypes and evaluative intergroup bias. In D. M. Mackie, & D. L. Hamilton (Eds.), *Affect, cognition, and stereotyping: Interactive processes in group perception* (pp. 167–193). San Diego, CA: Academic Press.

Duncan, B. L. (1976). Differential social perception and attribution of intergroup violence: Testing the lower limits of stereotyping of blacks. *Journal of Personality and Social Psychology, 34*(4), 590–598.

Ebbinghaus, H. (1964). *Memory: A contribution to experimental psychology*. Oxford, UK: Dover.

Ekstrom, R. B., French, J. W., Harman, H. H., & Dermen, D. (1976). *Manual for kit of factor-referenced cognitive tests*. Princeton, NJ: Educational Testing Service.

Fiske, S. T. (1998). Stereotyping, prejudice, and discrimination. In D. T. Gilbert, S. T. Fiske & G. Lindzey (Eds.), *The handbook of social psychology* (4th ed., Vols. 1 and 2, pp. 357–411). New York: McGraw-Hill.

Fiske, S. T., Lin, M., & Neuberg, S. L. (1999). *The continuum model: Ten years later*. In S. Chaiken, & Y. Trope (Eds.), *Dual-process theories in social psychology* (pp. 231–254). New York: Guilford Press.

Fiske, S. T, & Neuberg, S. L. (1990). A continuum of impression formation, from category-based to individuating processes: Influences of information and motivation on attention and interpretation. In M. P. Zanna (Ed.), *Advances in experimental social psychology* (Vol. 23, pp. 1–74). New York: Academic Press.

Fiske, S. T., Neuberg, S. L., Beattie, A. E., & Milberg, S. J. (1987). Category-based and attribute-based reactions to others: Some informational conditions of stereotyping and individuating processes. *Journal of Experimental Social Psychology, 23*(5), 399–427.

Fong, G. T., & Markus, H. (1982). Self-schemas and judgments about others. *Social Cognition, 1*(3), 191–204.

Förster, J., Friedman, R. S., & Liberman, N. (2004). Temporal construal effects on abstract and concrete thinking: Consequences for insight and creative cognition. *Journal of Personality and Social Psychology, 87*(2), 177–189.

Franks, J. J., & Bransford, J. D. (1971). Abstraction of visual patterns. *Journal of Experimental Psychology, 90*(1), 65–74.

Funder, D. C. (1999). *Personality judgment: A realistic approach to person perception*. San Diego, CA: Academic Press.

Fyock, J., & Stangor, C. (1994). The role of memory biases in stereotype maintenance. *British Journal of Social Psychology, 33*(3), 331–343.

Gasper, K., & Clore, G. L. (2002). Attending to the big picture: Mood and global versus local processing of visual information. *Psychological Science, 13*(1), 34–40.

Gilbert, D. T., & Hixon, J. G. (1991). The trouble of thinking: Activation and application of stereotypic beliefs. *Journal of Personality and Social Psychology, 60*(4), 509–517.

Gilbert, D. T., & Malone, P. S. (1995). The correspondence bias. *Psychological Bulletin, 117*(1), 21–38.

Gilovich, T. (1981). Seeing the past in the present: The effect of associations to familiar events on judgments and decisions. *Journal of Personality and Social Psychology, 40*(5), 797–808.

Guéraud, S., Tapiero, I., & O'Brien, E. J. (2008). Context and the activation of predictive inference. *Psychonomic Bulletin & Review, 15*(2), 351–356.

Hamilton, D. L. (2007). Understanding the complexities of group perception: Broadening the domain. *European Journal of Social Psychology, 37*(6), 1077–1101.

Hamilton, D. L., & Sherman, S. J. (1989). Illusory correlations: Implications for stereotype theory and research. In D. Bar-Tal, C. F. Graumann, A. W. Kruglanski, & W. Stroebe (Eds.), *Stereotyping and prejudice: Changing conceptions* (pp. 59–82). New York: Springer-Verlag.

Hamilton, D. L., & Sherman, S. J. (1996). Perceiving persons and groups. *Psychological Review, 103*(2), 336–355.

Hassin, R. R., Bargh, J. A., & Uleman, J. S. (2002). Spontaneous causal inferences. *Journal of Experimental Social Psychology, 38*(5), 515–522.

Hastie, R. (1984). Causes and effects of causal attribution. *Journal of Personality and Social Psychology, 46*(1), 44–56.

Hastie, R., & Kumar, P. A. (1979). Person memory: Personality traits as organizing principles in memory for behaviors. *Journal of Personality and Social Psychology, 37*(1), 25–38.

Hastie, R., & Park, B. (1986). The relationship between memory and judgment depends on whether the judgment task is memory-based or on-line. *Psychological Review, 93*(3), 258–268.

Heaton, A. W., & Kruglanski, A. W. (1991). Person perception by introverts and extraverts under time pressure: Effects of need for closure. *Personality and Social Psychology Bulletin, 17*(2), 161–165.

Heider, F. (1946). Attitudes and cognitive organization. *Journal of Psychology: Interdisciplinary and Applied, 21*, 107–112.

Heider, F. (1958). *The psychology of interpersonal relations*. Hoboken, NJ: John Wiley & Sons Inc.

Heider, F., & Simmel, M. (1944). An experimental study of apparent behavior. *American Journal of Psychology*, *57*, 243–259.

Henderson, M. D. (2009). Psychological distance and group judgments: The effect of physical distance on beliefs about common goals. *Personality and Social Psychology Bulletin*, *35*, 1330–1341.

Henderson, M. D., Fujita, K., Trope, Y., & Liberman, N. (2006). Transcending the "here": The effect of spatial distance on social judgment. *Journal of Personality and Social Psychology*, *91*(5), 845–856.

Hewstone, M., Rubin, M., & Willis, H. (2002). Intergroup bias. *Annual Review of Psychology*, *53*(1), 575–604.

Higgins, E. T. (1996). The "self digest": Self-knowledge serving self-regulatory functions. *Journal of Personality and Social Psychology*, *71*(6), 1062–1083.

Higgins, E. T. (1998). The aboutness principle: A pervasive influence on human inference. *Social Cognition, Special Issue: Naive Theories and Social Judgment*, *16*(1), 173–198.

Higgins, E. T., Bond, R. N., Klein, R., & Strauman, T. (1986). Self-discrepancies and emotional vulnerability: How magnitude, accessibility, and type of discrepancy influence affect. *Journal of Personality and Social Psychology*, *51*(1), 5–15.

Hilton, J. L., & von Hippel, W. (1990). The role of consistency in the judgment of stereotype-relevant behaviors. *Personality and Social Psychology Bulletin*, *16*(3), 430–448.

Hilton, J. L., & von Hippel, W. (1996). Stereotypes. *Annual Review of Psychology*, *47*, 237–271.

Hinkley, K., & Andersen, S. M. (1996). The working self-concept in transference: Significant-other activation and self change. *Journal of Personality and Social Psychology*, *71*(6), 1279–1295.

Jamieson, D. W., & Zanna, M. P. (1989). Need for structure in attitude formation and expression. In A. R. Pratkanis, S. J. Breckler & A. G. Greenwald (Eds.), *Attitude structure and function* (pp. 383–406). Hillsdale, NJ: Erlbaum.

Johnson, A. L., & Queller, S. (2003). The mental representations of high and low entitativity groups. *Social Cognition*, *21*(2), 101–119.

Jones, E. E. (1979). The rocky road from acts to dispositions. *American Psychologist*, *34*(2), 107–117.

Jones, E. E., & Davis, K. E. (1965). From acts to dispositions: The attribution process in person perception. In L. Berkowitz (Ed.), *Advances in experimental social psychology* (Vol. 2, pp. 219–266). San Diego, CA: Academic Press.

Jordan, N. (1953). Behavioral forces that are a function of attitudes and of cognitive organization. *Human Relations*, *6*, 273–287.

Judd, C. M., Park, B., Yzerbyt, V., Gordijn, E. H., & Muller, D. (2005). Attributions of intergroup bias and outgroup homogeneity to ingroup and outgroup others. *European Journal of Social Psychology*, *35*(6), 677–704.

Kaplan, M. F., Wanshula, L. T., & Zanna, M. P. (1993). Time pressure and information integration in social judgment: The effect of need for structure. In O. Svenson, & A. J. Maule (Eds.), *Time pressure and stress in human judgment and decision making* (pp. 255–267). New York: Plenum Press.

Keefe, D. E., & McDaniel, M. A. (1993). The time course and durability of predictive inferences. *Journal of Memory and Language*, *32*(4), 446–463.

Kelley, H. H. (1967). Attribution theory in social psychology. *Nebraska Symposium on Motivation*, *15*, 192–238.

Kelley, H. H., & Michela, J. L. (1980). Attribution theory and research. *Annual Review of Psychology*, *31*, 457–501.

Kihlstrom, J. F., & Cantor, N. (1984). Mental representations of the self. In L. Berkowitz (Ed.), *Advances in experimental social psychology* (Vol. 17, pp. 1–47). New York: Academic Press.

Kihlstrom, J. F., Cantor, N., Albright, J. S., Chew, B. R., Klein, S. B., & Niedenthal, P. M. (1988). Information processing and the study of the self. In L. Berkowitz (Ed.), *Annual meeting of the American Psychological Association, 93rd, Aug 1985, Los Angeles, CA, US* (pp. 145–178). San Diego, CA: Academic Press.

Kim, H., & Baron, R. S. (1988). Exercise and the illusory correlation: Does arousal heighten stereotypic processing? *Journal of Experimental Social Psychology*, *24*(4), 366–380.

Kim, N. S., & Ahn, W. (2002). Clinical psychologists' theory-based representations of mental disorders predict their diagnostic reasoning and memory. *Journal of Experimental Psychology: General*, *131*(4), 451–476.

Kimchi, R., & Palmer, S. E. (1982). Form and texture in hierarchically constructed patterns. *Journal of Experimental Psychology: Human Perception and Performance*, *8*(4), 521–535.

Klein, S. B., & Loftus, J. (1993a). Behavioral experience and trait judgments about the self. *Personality and Social Psychology Bulletin*, *19*(6), 740–745.

Klein, S. B., & Loftus, J. (1993b). The mental representation of trait and autobiographical knowledge about the self. In T. K. Srull, & R. S. Wyer Jr. (Eds.), *The mental representation of trait and autobiographical knowledge about the self* (pp. 1–49). Hillsdale, NJ: Erlbaum.

Kunda, Z. (1990). The case for motivated reasoning. *Psychological Bulletin*, *108*(3), 480–498.

Kunda, Z., & Spencer, S. J. (2003). When do stereotypes come to mind and when do they color judgment? A goal-based theoretical framework for stereotype activation and application. *Psychological Bulletin*, *129*(4), 522–544.

Lau, R. R. (1984). Dynamics of the attribution process. *Journal of Personality and Social Psychology*, *46*(5), 1017–1028.

Lau, R. R., & Russell, D. (1980). Attributions in the sports pages. *Journal of Personality and Social Psychology*, *39*(1), 29–38.

Levy, S. R., Stroessner, S. J., & Dweck, C. S. (1998). Stereotype formation and endorsement: The role of implicit theories. *Journal of Personality and Social Psychology*, *74*(6), 1421–1436.

Lewicki, P. (1986). Processing information about covariations that cannot be articulated. *Journal of Experimental Psychology: Learning, Memory, and Cognition*, *12*(1), 135–146.

Liberman, N., & Förster, J. (2009a). Distancing from experienced self: How global-versus-local perception affects estimation of psychological distance. *Journal of Personality and Social Psychology*, *97*(2), 203–216.

Liberman, N., & Förster, J. (2009b). The effect of psychological distance on perceptual level of construal. *Cognitive Science: A Multidisciplinary Journal*, *33*(7), 1330–1341.

Liberman, N., Sagristano, M. D., & Trope, Y. (2002). The effect of temporal distance on level of mental construal. *Journal of Experimental Social Psychology*, *38*(6), 523–534.

Liberman, N., & Trope, Y. (2008). The psychology of transcending the here and now. *Science*, *322*(5905), 1201–1205.

Lichtenstein, M., & Srull, T. K. (1987). Processing objectives as a determinant of the relationship between recall and judgment. *Journal of Experimental Social Psychology*, *23*(2), 93–118.

Lickel, B., Hamilton, D. L., & Sherman, S. J. (2001). Elements of a lay theory of groups: Types of groups, relationship styles, and the perception of group entitativity. *Personality and Social Psychology Review, 5*(2), 129–140.

Lickel, B., Hamilton, D. L., Wieczorkowska, G., Lewis, A., Sherman, S. J., & Uhles, A. N. (2000). Varieties of groups and the perception of group entitativity. *Journal of Personality and Social Psychology, 78*(2), 223–246.

Lickel, B., Schmader, T., & Hamilton, D. L. (2003). A case of collective responsibility: Who else was to blame for the columbine high school shootings? *Personality and Social Psychology Bulletin, 29*(2), 194–204.

Linville, P. W. (1985). Self-complexity and affective extremity: Don't put all of your eggs in one cognitive basket. *Social Cognition, Special Issue: Depression, 3*(1), 94–120.

Liviatan, I., Trope, Y., & Liberman, N. (2008). Interpersonal similarity as a social distance dimension: Implications for perception of others' actions. *Journal of Experimental Social Psychology, 44*(5), 1256–1269.

MacLeod, C. M. (1988). Forgotten but not gone: Savings for pictures and words in long-term memory. *Journal of Experimental Psychology: Learning, Memory, and Cognition, 14*(2), 195–212.

Macrae, C. N., & Bodenhausen, G. V. (2000). Social cognition: Thinking categorically about others. *Annual Review of Psychology, 51*, 93–120.

Macrae, C. N., Hewstone, M., & Griffiths, R. J. (1993). Processing load and memory for stereotype-based information. *European Journal of Social Psychology, 23*(1), 77–87.

Macrae, C. N., Milne, A. B., & Bodenhausen, G. V. (1994). Stereotypes as energy-saving devices: A peek inside the cognitive toolbox. *Journal of Personality and Social Psychology, 66*(1), 37–47.

Maglio, S. J., & Trope, Y. (2012). Disembodiment: Abstract construal attenuates the influence of contextual bodily state in judgment. *Journal of Experimental Psychology: General, 141*, 211–216.

Majid, A., Sanford, A. J., & Pickering, M. J. (2007). The linguistic description of minimal social scenarios affects the extent of causal inference making. *Journal of Experimental Social Psychology, 43*(6), 918–932.

Mancuso, J. C., & Ceely, S. G. (1980). The self as memory processing. *Cognitive Therapy and Research, 4*(1), 1–25.

Manis, M., & Paskewitz, J. R. (1987). Assessing psychopathology in individuals and groups: Aggregating behavior samples to form overall impressions. *Personality and Social Psychology Bulletin, 13*(1), 83–94.

Markus, H. (1977). Self-schemata and processing information about the self. *Journal of Personality and Social Psychology, 35*(2), 63–78.

Markus, H., Crane, M., Bernstein, S., & Siladi, M. (1982). Self-schemas and gender. *Journal of Personality and Social Psychology, 42*(1), 38–50.

Markus, H., & Nurius, P. (1986). Possible selves. *American Psychologist, 41*(9), 954–969.

Markus, H. J., & Sentis, K. (1982). The self in social information processing. In J. Suls (Ed.), *Psychological perspectives on the self* (Vol. *1*, pp. 41–70). Hillsdale, NJ: Erlbaum.

Markus, H., & Smith, J. (1981). The influence of self-schema on the perception of others. In N. Cantor & J. F. Kihlstrom (Eds.), *Personality, cognition and social interaction* (pp. 233–262). Hillsdale, NJ: Erlbaum.

Markus, H., Smith, J., & Moreland, R. L. (1985). Role of the self-concept in the perception of others. *Journal of Personality and Social Psychology, 49*(6), 1494–1512.

Markus, H., & Wurf, E. (1987). The dynamic self-concept: A social psychological perspective. *Annual Review of Psychology, 38*, 299–337.

McConnell, A. R., Sherman, S. J., & Hamilton, D. L. (1994). Illusory correlation in the perception of groups: An extension of the distinctiveness-based account. *Journal of Personality and Social Psychology, 67*(3), 414–429.

McConnell, A. R., Sherman, S. J., & Hamilton, D. L. (1997). Target entitativity: Implications for information processing about individual and group targets. *Journal of Personality and Social Psychology, 72*(4), 750–762.

McKoon, G., & Ratcliff, R. (1986). Inferences about predictable events. *Journal of Experimental Psychology: Learning, Memory, and Cognition, 12*, 82–91.

Medin, D. L., & Schaffer, M. M. (1978). Context theory of classification learning. *Psychological Review, 85*(3), 207–238.

Medin, D. L., & Smith, E. E. (1981). Strategies and classification learning. *Journal of Experimental Psychology: Human Learning and Memory, 7*(4), 241–253.

Medin, D. L., & Smith, E. E. (1984). Concepts and concept formation. *Annual Review of Psychology, 35*, 113–138.

Minsky, H. P. (1975). A framework for representing knowledge. In P. H. Winston (Ed.), *The psychology of computer vision.* New York: McGraw-Hill.

Monson, T. C., Keel, R., Stephens, D., & Genung, V. (1982). Trait attributions: Relative validity, covariation with behavior, and prospect of future interaction. *Journal of Personality and Social Psychology, 42*(6), 1014–1024.

Morrissette, J. O. (1958). Experiments on the theory of balance. *Dissertation Abstracts, 18*, 1519–1520.

Murray, J. D., Klin, C. M., & Myers, J. L. (1993). Forward inferences in narrative text. *Journal of Memory and Language, 32*(4), 464–473.

Navon, D. (1977). Forest before trees: The precedence of global features in visual perception. *Cognitive Psychology, 9*(3), 353–383.

Neisser, U. (1976). *Cognition and reality: Principles and implications of cognitive psychology.* New York: W H Freeman/Times Books/ Henry Holt & Co.

Nosofsky, R. M. (1987). Attention and learning processes in the identification and categorization of integral stimuli. *Journal of Experimental Psychology: Learning, Memory, and Cognition, 13*(1), 87–108.

Nussbaum, S., Trope, Y., & Liberman, N. (2003). Creeping dispositionism: The temporal dynamics of behavior prediction. *Journal of Personality and Social Psychology, 84*(3), 485–497.

Park, B., & Rothbart, M. (1982). Perception of out-group homogeneity and levels of social categorization: Memory for the subordinate attributes of in-group and out-group members. *Journal of Personality and Social Psychology, 42*(6), 1051–1068.

Picek, J. S., Sherman, S. J., & Shiffrin, R. M. (1975). Cognitive organization and coding of social structures. *Journal of Personality and Social Psychology, 31*(4), 758–768.

Posner, M. I., & Keele, S. W. (1968). On the genesis of abstract ideas. *Journal of Experimental Psychology, 77*(3), 353–363.

Posner, M. I., & Keele, S. W. (1970). Retention of abstract ideas. *Journal of Experimental Psychology, 83*(2), 304–308.

Pratto, F., & Bargh, J. A. (1991). Stereotyping based on apparently individuating information: Trait and global components of sex stereotypes under attention overload. *Journal of Experimental Social Psychology, 27*(1), 26–47.

Price, K. O., Harburg, E., & Newcomb, T. M. (1966). Psychological balance in situations of negative interpersonal attitudes. *Journal of Personality and Social Psychology, 3*(3), 265–270.

Proctor, C., & Ahn, W. (2007). The effect of causal knowledge on judgments of the likelihood of unknown features. *Psychonomic Bulletin & Review, 14*, 635–639.

Pronin, E., & Ross, L. (2006). Temporal differences in trait self-ascription: When the self is seen as an other. *Journal of Personality and Social Psychology, 90*(2), 197–209.

Pyszczynski, T., & Greenberg, J. (1983). Determinants of reduction in intended effort as a strategy for coping with anticipated failure. *Journal of Research in Personality, 17*(4), 412–422.

Reed, S. K. (1972). Pattern recognition and categorization. *Cognitive Psychology, 3*(3), 382–407.

Reitman, J. S., & Bower, G. H. (1973). Storage and later recognition of exemplars of concepts. *Cognitive Psychology, 4*(2), 194–206.

Rim, S., Amit, E., & Trope, Y. (2011). [*Association among high-level and low-level representations in construal level theory*]. Unpublished raw data.

Rim, S., Amit, E., Trope, Y., Halbeisen, G., & Fujita, K. *Verbalizing the high and visualizing the low: The relationship between medium and level of construal.* Unpublished manuscript, New York University.

Rim, S., Hansen, J., & Trope, Y. (2013). *What happens why? Psychological distance and focusing on causes versus consequences of events, Journal of Personality and Social Psychology, 104*, 457–472.

Rim, S., Uleman, J. S., & Trope, Y. (2009). Spontaneous trait inference and construal level theory: Psychological distance increases nonconscious trait thinking. *Journal of Experimental Social Psychology, 45*(5), 1088–1097.

Rosch, E. (1975). The nature of mental codes for color categories. *Journal of Experimental Psychology: Human Perception and Performance, 1*(4), 303–322.

Ross, L. (1977). The intuitive psychologist and his shortcomings: Distortions in the attribution process. In L. Berkowitz (Ed.), *Advances in experimental social psychology* (Vol. 10, pp. 174–221). Orlando, FL: Academic Press.

Rothbart, M., & Park, B. (2004). The mental representation of social categories: Category boundaries, entitativity, and stereotype change. In V. Yzerbyt, C. M. Judd & O. Corneille (Eds.), *The psychology of group perception: Perceived variability, entitativity, and essentialism* (pp. 79–100). New York: Psychology Press.

Ruscher, J. B., & Fiske, S. T. (1990). Interpersonal competition can cause individuating processes. *Journal of Personality and Social Psychology, 58*(5), 832–843.

Rydell, R. J., Hugenberg, K., Ray, D., & Mackie, D. M. (2007). Implicit theories about groups and stereotyping: The role of group entitativity. *Personality and Social Psychology Bulletin, 33*(4), 549–558.

Rydell, R. J., & McConnell, A. R. (2005). Perceptions of entitativity and attitude change. *Personality and Social Psychology Bulletin, 31*(1), 99–110.

Sagar, H. A., & Schofield, J. W. (1980). Racial and behavioral cues in black and white children's perceptions of ambiguously aggressive acts. *Journal of Personality and Social Psychology, 39*(4), 590–598.

Sanbonmatsu, D. M., Sherman, S. J., & Hamilton, D. L. (1987). Illusory correlation in the perception of individuals and groups. *Social Cognition, 5*(1), 1–25.

Schank, R. C. (1986). *Explanation patterns: Understanding mechanically and creatively.* Hillsdale, NJ: Erlbaum.

Semin, G. R., & Smith, E. R. (1999). Revisiting the past and back to the future: Memory systems and the linguistic representation of social events. *Journal of Personality and Social Psychology, 76*(6), 877–892.

Simon, B. (1992). Intragroup differentiation in terms of ingroup and outgroup attributes. *European Journal of Social Psychology, 22*(4), 407–413.

Smith, E. R. (1998). Mental representation and memory. In D. T. Gilbert, S. T. Fiske & G. Lindzey (Eds.), *The handbook of social psychology (4th ed., Vols. 1 and 2*, pp. 391–445). New York: McGraw-Hill.

Smith, E. R., & Zárate, M. A. (1992). Exemplar-based model of social judgment. *Psychological Review, 99*(1), 3–21.

Smith, P. K., & Trope, Y. (2006). You focus on the forest when you're in charge of the trees: Power priming and abstract information processing. *Journal of Personality and Social Psychology, 90*(4), 578–596.

Spencer-Rodgers, J., Hamilton, D. L., & Sherman, S. J. (2007). The central role of entitativity in stereotypes of social categories and task groups. *Journal of Personality and Social Psychology, 92*(3), 369–388.

Spencer-Rodgers, J., Williams, M. J., Hamilton, D. L., Peng, K., & Wang, L. (2007). Culture and group perception: Dispositional and stereotypic inferences about novel and national groups. *Journal of Personality and Social Psychology, 93*(4), 525–543.

Srull, T. K. (1981). Person memory: Some tests of associative storage and retrieval models. *Journal of Experimental Psychology: Human Learning and Memory, 7*(6), 440–463.

Srull, T. K., Lichtenstein, M., & Rothbart, M. (1985). Associative storage and retrieval processes in person memory. *Journal of Experimental Psychology: Learning, Memory, and Cognition, 11*(2), 316–345.

Stangor, C., & McMillan, D. (1992). Memory for expectancy-congruent and expectancy-incongruent information: A review of the social and social developmental literatures. *Psychological Bulletin, 111*(1), 42–61.

Stephan, E., Liberman, N., & Trope, Y. (2010a). Politeness and psychological distance: A construal level perspective. *Journal of Personality and Social Psychology, 98*(2), 268–280.

Stephan, E., Liberman, N., & Trope, Y. (2010b). The effects of time perspective and level of construal on social distance. *Journal of Experimental Social Psychology, 47, 397–402.*

Stern, L. D., Marrs, S., Millar, M. G., & Cole, E. (1984). Processing time and the recall of inconsistent and consistent behaviors of individuals and groups. *Journal of Personality and Social Psychology, 47*(2), 253–262.

Stevenson, R. J., Crawley, R. A., & Kleinman, D. (1994). Thematic roles, focus and the representation of events. *Language and Cognitive Processes, 9*(4), 519–548.

Street, R. F. (1931). *A Gestalt completion test.* PhD Thesis, Teachers College at Columbia University, New York.

Susskind, J., Maurer, K., Thakkar, V., Hamilton, D. L., & Sherman, J. W. (1999). Perceiving individuals and groups: Expectancies, dispositional inferences, and causal attributions. *Journal of Personality and Social Psychology, 76*, 181–191.

Tagiuri, R., & Petrullo, L. (1958). *Person perception and interpersonal behavior.* Stanford, CA: Stanford University Press.

Tajfel, H. (1978). *Differentiation between social groups: Studies in the social psychology of intergroup relations.* Oxford, UK: Academic Press.

Tajfel, H., & Turner, J. C. (1986). The social identity theory of intergroup behavior. In S. Worchel & W. G. Austin (Eds.), *Psychology of intergroup relations* (pp. 7–24). Chicago: Nelson-Hall.

Todorov, A., & Uleman, J. S. (2002). Spontaneous trait inferences are bound to actors' faces: Evidence from a false recognition paradigm. *Journal of Personality and Social Psychology, 83*(5), 1051–1065.

Todorov, A., & Uleman, J. S. (2003). The efficiency of binding spontaneous trait inferences to actors' faces. *Journal of Experimental Social Psychology, 39*(6), 549–562.

Trope, Y. (1986). Identification and inferential processes in dispositional attribution. *Psychological Review, 93*(3), 239–257.

Trope, Y. (1989). Levels of inference in dispositional judgment. *Social Cognition, 7*(3), 296–314.

Trope, Y., & Liberman, N. (2010). Construal-level theory of psychological distance. *Psychological Review, 117*(2), 440–463.

Tulving, E., & Thomson, D. M. (1973). Encoding specificity and retrieval processes in episodic memory. *Psychological Review, 80*(5), 352–373.

Turner, J. C., Brown, R. J., & Tajfel, H. (1979). Social comparison and group interest in ingroup favouritism. *European Journal of Social Psychology, 9*(2), 187–204.

Uleman, J. S., Saribay, S. A., & Gonzalez, C. (2008). Spontaneous inferences, implicit impressions, and implicit theories. *Annual Review of Psychology, 59*, 329–360.

Vallacher, R. R., & Wegner, D. M. (1987). What do people think they're doing? Action identification and human behavior. *Psychological Review, 94*(1), 3–15.

Vallacher, R. R., & Wegner, D. M. (1989). Levels of personal agency: Individual variation in action identification. *Journal of Personality and Social Psychology, 57*(4), 660–671.

Wakslak, C. J., Nussbaum, S., Liberman, N., & Trope, Y. (2008). Representations of the self in the near and distant future. *Journal of Personality and Social Psychology, 95*(4), 757–773.

Wakslak, C. J., Trope, Y., Liberman, N., & Alony, R. (2006). Seeing the forest when entry is unlikely: Probability and the mental representation of events. *Journal of Experimental Psychology: General, 135*(4), 641–653.

Wechsler, D. (1991). *Wechsler Intelligence Scale for Children* (3rd ed.). San Antonio, TX: Psychological Corporation

Weiner, B. (1983). Some methodological pitfalls in attributional research. *Journal of Educational Psychology, 75*(4), 530–543.

Weiner, B. (1985). "Spontaneous" causal thinking. *Psychological Bulletin, 97*(1), 74–84.

Wilder, D. A., & Shapiro, P. (1989a). Effects of anxiety on impression formation in a group context: An anxiety-assimilation hypothesis. *Journal of Experimental Social Psychology, 25*(6), 481–499.

Wilder, D. A., & Shapiro, P. N. (1989b). Role of competition-induced anxiety in limiting the beneficial

impact of positive behavior by an out-group member. *Journal of Personality and Social Psychology, 56*(1), 60–69.

Wilder, D., & Simon, A. F. (2004). Affect as a cause of intergroup bias. In M. B. Brewer, & M. Hewstone (Eds.), *Emotion and motivation* (pp. 113–131). Malden, MA: Blackwell.

Winkielman, P., Niedenthal, P. M., & Oberman, L. (2008). The embodied emotional mind. In G. R. Semin, & E. R. Smith (Eds.), *Embodied grounding: Social, cognitive, affective, and neuroscientific approaches* (pp. 263–288). New York: Cambridge University Press.

Winter, L., & Uleman, J. S. (1984). When are social judgments made? Evidence for the spontaneousness of trait inferences. *Journal of Personality and Social Psychology, 47*(2), 237–252.

Winter, L., Uleman, J. S., & Cunniff, C. (1985). How automatic are social judgments? *Journal of Personality and Social Psychology, 49*(4), 904–917.

Wong, P. T., & Weiner, B. (1981). When people ask "why" questions, and the heuristics of attributional search. *Journal of Personality and Social Psychology, 40*(4), 650–663.

Wyer, R. S., Jr. (2007). Principles of mental representation. In A. W. Kruglanski, & E. T. Higgins (Eds.), *Social psychology: Handbook of basic principles (2nd ed.,* pp. 285–307). New York: Guilford Press.

Wyer, R. S., Jr., & Carlston, D. E. (1994). The cognitive representation of persons and events. In R. S. Wyer Jr., & T. K. Srull (Eds.), *Handbook of social cognition, Vol. 1: Basic processes; Vol. 2: Applications* (2nd ed., pp. 41–98). Hillsdale, NJ: Erlbaum.

Wyer, R. S., Jr., & Lambert, A. J. (1994). The role of trait constructs in person perception: An historical perspective. In P. G. Devine, D. L. Hamilton & T. M. Ostrom (Eds.), *Social cognition: Impact on social psychology* (pp. 109–142). San Diego, CA: Academic Press.

Wyer, R. S., Bodenhausen, G. V., & Srull, T. K. (1984). The cognitive representation of persons and groups and its effect on recall and recognition memory. *Journal of Experimental Social Psychology, 20*(5), 445–469.

Yzerbyt, V., Judd, C. M., & Corneille, O. (Eds.). (2004). *The psychology of group perception. Perceived variability, entitativity, and essentialism.* London: Psychology Press.

Yzerbyt, V. Y., Rogier, A., & Fiske, S. T. (1998). Group entitativity and social attribution: On translating situational constraints into stereotypes. *Personality and Social Psychology Bulletin, 24*(10), 1089–1103.

Zajonc, R. B., & Burnstein, E. (1965a). The learning of balanced and unbalanced social structures. *Journal of Personality, 33*(2), 153–163.

Zajonc, R. B., & Burnstein, E. (1965b). Structural balance, reciprocity, and positivity as sources of cognitive bias. *Journal of Personality, 33*(4), 570–583.

Zajonc, R., & Sherman, S. (1967). Structural balance and the induction of relations. *Journal of Personality, 35*(4), 635–650.

Implicit Social Cognition and Mental Representation

B. Keith Payne *and* C. Daryl Cameron

Abstract

This chapter reviews theoretical approaches to mental representation and how these relate to implicit social cognition. The focus is on associative network, schema, and connectionist models, which have received a lot of attention in social cognition, as well as on embodied cognition, situated cognition, and multiple format models, which are areas of active growth. Each theory is scrutinized in relation to posing three questions. First, in what sense are representations implicit or explicit? Second, are the representations themselves implicit, or is the use of representations implicit? Third, are representations implicit permanently or only temporarily, depending on factors such as attention? The chapter discusses common themes and points of divergence across models and concludes with a discussion of attributional models, which suggest that important aspects of implicitness (such as consciousness, intent, and effort) may depend on inferences or construals people make about their own representations.

Key Words: mental representation, implicit social cognition, implicit representation, consciousness, unconscious cognition, implicit cognition

Theories of mental representation are always metaphors (Wyer, 2007). We talk of bins, of nodes, and of traces as ways to transform abstract information into solid topics of study. In some ways, this abstractness can be dangerous, leading to debates about semantic ideas that might be difficult or impossible to verify. We believe that such models are nonetheless important because metaphors matter. Metaphors matter because they can radically change the way scientists understand the operation of a system. The history of science is full of examples in which changing metaphors changed everything.

Gustave le Bon changed the way social scientists saw groups when he argued that society was like an organism, a whole that functioned differently than any of its individual parts. And Virchow advanced cell theory by arguing that organisms were like societies, for the same reasons (Mazzarello, 1999). For decades, the computer metaphor has been the

dominant metaphor for the human mind. This is mainly because computers are easier to understand than minds. It is interesting that with recent advances in understanding neural networks, computers are becoming much more like brains. More importantly, models of brains are becoming more like brains. Abstract or not, as knowledge about a field grows, the metaphors inevitably change, with some metaphors working better than others. When William Harvey discovered the circulation of the blood, the heart became a pump, rather than the heater it was previously understood to be. Suddenly, its mysterious sounds made a lot more sense.

Can models of mental representation help make sense of findings in social cognition? Our aim in this chapter is to overview theories of mental representation from the perspective of implicit social cognition. We do not evaluate whether the theories are true or false, but we consider which ones are most helpful for thinking about implicit social cognition. Before doing that, we need to say more about what we mean by representations, and what we mean by implicit cognition.

What Is a Mental Representation?

Defining mental representations is not simple because the term is used promiscuously across all areas of psychology. A PsycINFO search using the key words "mental representation" returned 1,254 articles. Browsing the abstracts, we noted that the term was used to refer to categories, exemplars, symbols, mental images, memories, grammar, syntax, narratives, truth values, probabilities, and number lines. And that was only the first 25 papers. Clearly, a mental representation can be virtually anything that a person can perceive, think, remember, or know. We therefore adopt a deliberately broad definition of mental representations as any mental content or operation that stands for something else in the world. Theorists sometimes make more fine-grained distinctions, such as whether a representation should be thought of as a state versus a thing (Smith, 1998), or whether it is an abstract symbol versus a physical, bodily state (Barsalou, 2008). We do not incorporate these features into our definition because the theories of mental representation that we review differ on these important points. Rather than defining any of these features in or out at the start, we will address the specific features associated with each theory in the course of our discussion.

What Is Implicit?

We begin by adopting a conventional definition of implicitness, summarized in Bargh's (1994) "four horsemen" of automaticity. Implicit representations lack awareness, are efficient, do not require intent, and escape control. Notice that how well these criteria make sense when applied to mental representations may differ depending on your theory of representation. If we think of a representation as a symbol resting inertly in memory, then it makes sense to say that a person is unaware of the representation. For instance, a person might hold an unconscious racial stereotype about a specific ethnic group, transmitted through exposure to popular culture. But thinking of representations as inert thing-like symbols causes problems for the other criteria. How can a symbol be efficient or inefficient? Intended or unintended? Controlled or uncontrolled? The use of the thing, rather than the thing itself, might be said to have these characteristics.

This brings us to another distinction that is important to consider when defining implicitness. Some theories consider implicitness or explicitness to be features of the representation itself. By such theories, a person might have two representations of the same thing—one that is implicit and one that is explicit—and the two might be quite different (e.g., Wilson, Lindsey, & Schooler, 2000). A person might have an implicit representation that a specific racial group is unfriendly, but also an explicit representation that this same group is perfectly sociable. The representation that is active at a particular time would determine how a person perceives, interprets, and responds in situations involving that group. Others emphasize that a given representation can be *used* either explicitly or implicitly (Jacoby & Kelley, 1987; Jacoby, Kelley, Brown, & Jasechko, 1989). So a person might access a stereotype about a specific racial group, and whether that stereotype translates into judgment or behavior will depend on how much awareness and intentional control the person has over its application (Devine, 1989). Our review will consider how each representational model addresses implicit representations versus implicit use of representations.

A related issue is whether a representation is always implicit, as opposed to momentarily implicit. Your representation of your breathing rate was probably outside of awareness until you read this sentence. In this example, the representation was momentarily implicit, but a shift in attention can make it explicit. In contrast, no shift of attention or anything else can make explicit the processes by which your brainstem is controlling your breathing. Some representations might be inaccessible under any circumstances. Where possible, we consider what is implicit about implicit representations from both the momentary and permanent perspectives.

Why does the distinction between implicit and explicit mental representations matter? We believe that exploring this distinction matters because it informs how we think about the control of behavior. Placing mental representations as implicit or explicit helps us to figure out if we have desires or beliefs—such as racial stereotypes—that are unconscious or counter to our considered goals and values. If implicit representations are implicit in themselves—that is, unconscious or unintentional—then that suggests specific techniques for raising mental representations into conscious awareness. If implicit representations are implicit in how they are *used*, on the other hand, then that suggests we need to cultivate awareness of how these representations influence our behavior in everyday life (Hall & Payne, 2010). And the success of these efforts will depend on whether representations are temporarily or permanently implicit. If they are permanently implicit, then there might be no hope for cultivating awareness of representational influences on behaviors. But if representations are implicit only temporarily, then we might successfully learn to guide behavior in deliberative, goal-directed ways. Understanding the systematic operating conditions for implicit and explicit mental representations can help us to guide our behavior in ways that we want.

Organization of the Chapter

We consider several models in terms of three questions: (1) By what criteria can representations be said to be implicit or explicit? (2) Is implicitness a feature of the representation itself, or how it is used? (3) Are implicit representations necessarily implicit, or available to be made implicit or explicit, depending on factors such as attention? Table 11.1 organizes the different models and how they answer these three questions about implicitness. With these goals in mind, the review that follows is necessarily selective. It omits many theories of mental representation in favor of focusing specifically on those theories that have direct implications for implicit processes (see Chapter 10 for a more general treatment of mental representation). We also omit several important dual process or dual systems models whose focus is on dynamics of automatic and controlled processes, rather than mental representations per se (see Chapter 14 for a review of dual process and dual systems models). We therefore focus on theories of mental representation that have been influential and on those that we believe may become influential in implicit social cognition.

Table 11.1 How Different Models of Mental Representation Address Key Questions About Implicit and Explicit Mental Representation

	In what sense are representations implicit or explicit?	Are the representations implicit, or is representation *use* implicit?	Are representations implicit temporarily or permanently?
Associative network models	Nodes and spreading activation are unconscious; representations are implicit until they pass the threshold of conscious awareness	Representations and their use are implicit until they pass the threshold of conscious awareness	Representations can become explicit when they cross threshold of conscious activation or after serial search through network
Schema models	Schemas are not necessarily unconscious but can influence behavior and judgments unconsciously	Schema representations are not implicit in themselves but are used implicitly	Schemas and their influence are only temporarily implicit based on direction of attention
Connectionist models	Distributed representations are conscious, but not the workings of the connectionist network	Active representational patterns are conscious but network is not; use is generally implicit	Representational patterns can be made conscious, but workings of network are inaccessible
Multiple format models	Different representational systems can be more or less accessible to conscious awareness	For some representational systems, both representations and use are implicit; for other systems, only use is implicit	Some representational systems are permanently implicit; others are only temporarily implicit
Embodied cognition models	Sensory representations can be conscious, but this might vary by sensory modality	Bodily representations and their use can be either explicit or implicit	Representations are only temporarily implicit, but this might vary by sensory modality
Situated cognition models	Situated representations can be more or less conscious depending on contextual salience	Situated representations and use might be more or less conscious, but distinction collapses if representations involve action	Situated representations are only temporarily implicit, but this might vary contextually

Models of Mental Representation
Associative Network Models

Associative network models are probably the most commonly used models of mental representation in social cognition research. These models posit that mental representations are built from discrete, interconnected nodes. The nodes stand for concepts (e.g., CAT), and the links between the nodes stand for relationships between these concepts. Figure 11.1 displays a schematic of an associative network. These links are formed through experience, based on which concepts tend to be thought about in conjunction. The nodes have varying levels of activation based on prior experience and current conditions, and the links between the nodes are of varying strength. There is some controversy about the level of abstraction at which nodes should be interpreted (e.g., CAT vs. SIAMESE CAT), and whether the links or relationships between concepts carry any propositional meaning (i.e., does the link between the nodes "CAT" and "MISCHIEVOUS" imply the proposition "cats are mischievous"?; Fiske & Taylor, 1991; Wyer & Carlston, 1994). But, in general, associative network models agree that meaning is constructed dynamically and bottom-up from the linked combinations of related nodes. For instance, Fazio's (1990) MODE model posits that an attitude is the association between a node representing an attitude object (e.g., a person) and a node representing an evaluation of that attitude object (e.g., good or bad).

Associative network models have been especially influential for understanding accessibility and priming effects. The strength of links is thought to be determined by the frequency and recency of activation (Higgins, 1996; Higgins, Bargh, & Lombardi, 1985). This provides a natural explanation for chronic accessibility effects because the most frequently activated sets of associations maintain a high level of activation (or, strengthened links) and therefore are easily activated for use in processing new information. It also provides a natural explanation for priming effects because activating a concept with a prime leaves it momentarily higher in activation and ready to be engaged in subsequent processing.

Most applications of associative networks in social cognition have invoked "parallel search" models, in which activation spreads automatically among connected nodes, like electricity through a circuit or water finding its way through the contours in a rock face (Anderson, 1983; Collins & Loftus, 1975; Wyer & Carlston, 1979). This spreading activation is typically treated as unconscious. But when activation crosses a high enough threshold, the concept is said to come to mind, meaning that it is consciously thought about. In what sense, then, are representations implicit or explicit? Parallel search models suggest that people are not aware of the nodes themselves or of the spreading of activation along the links. However, they become aware of the concept that results from nodes that have reached the threshold of consciousness. Parallel search models also imply that the process of spreading activation is efficient, in that people do not need to expend cognitive effort; activation automatically spreads along interconnected linkages. Spreading activation needs neither intention to begin, nor can people control the spreading once it has started. Thus, parallel search versions of associative network theories suggest that representations (i.e., nodes and the links among them) are thoroughly implicit (according to all four criteria of

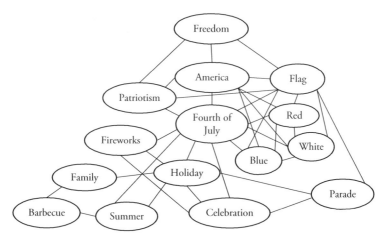

Figure 11.1 Schematic illustration of an associative network model.

awareness, efficiency, intent, and control) until activation reaches threshold level. After that point, the conscious manipulation of that thought lies outside the scope of associative network theories.

The distinction between subthreshold activation and suprathreshold activation also addresses the questions of permanent versus temporarily implicit representations, and implicit representations versus implicit use. The process of spreading activation is always unconscious, efficient, and immune to intent and control. But the representation that results from activation spreading among nodes can become conscious, and therefore can be manipulated and used explicitly.

In contrast to parallel search theories, some researchers have invoked "serial search" versions of associative network theories. The nodes and linkages are the same as in parallel search theories. But rather than automatically spreading activation, there is an intentional search following linked nodes until a concept is retrieved (Anderson & Bower, 1973; Carlston & Skowronski, 1986). For instance, if you are trying to consciously remember something about a person, you might consider specific cues that you associate with that person, following the links between the nodes to reach the information that you want (see Srull, 1981, for an application to person memory). According to serial search models, the nodes and pathways are themselves unconscious, except for the node that is the present focus of the serial search. The search process itself, however, is thought to be conscious, effortful, intentional, and under voluntary control. Thus, representations in serial search models are only momentarily implicit or explicit, and it is the direction of attention (i.e., the focus of the search) that determines what is implicit and what is explicit.

Parallel and serial search models share the basic architecture of nodes and links. They differ dramatically in how activation spreads, and in what this means for the implicitness of representations. The two types of models are not necessarily exclusive, however. Because they work on the same basic architecture, people might be said to make use of that structure both implicitly (via parallel search) and explicitly (via serial search). Construing associative networks in this way essentially builds a dual process model of representation, grounded in the metaphor of a network of nodes and links. If we consider this as a unified dual process model, then there are two distinct ways that implicit representations can become explicit. One is by spreading activation that crosses a threshold; this is a quantitative distinction that depends only on the level of excitation. The second is by intentionally performing a serial search; this is a qualitative distinction that rests on different ways of searching the cognitive system. Many studies in social cognition tacitly assume dual processes of explicit and implicit memory searches, and they often use the language of associative network theory (e.g., spreading activation, links, and nodes). Formulating such a dual process associative model more explicitly might help make clear the assumptions underlying these ideas and the theoretical commitments that result.

Schema Models

Schema models of mental representation have also been extremely popular in social cognition research, dating back in principle to the gestalt psychologists and Bruner's (1957) famous notion that perceivers "go beyond the information given" in making social judgments. Unlike the bottom-up dynamics posited by associative network models, schema models take a top-down approach: schemas are broad representations that structure and make sense of psychological experience. These large chunks of general knowledge might be thought of as different lenses with which to view the world. Like lenses, schemas are activated and used one at a time, although the other schemas can have varying levels of accessibility that bring them closer to or farther from being activated. Once activated, a schema brings online all of its general knowledge and, as a consequence, it directs attention, memory, and judgment.

Consider some classic examples of schemas in action. In a famous experiment, Chen and Bargh (1997) subliminally primed participants with either black or white faces as they were completing a visualization task. Priming was meant to activate the stereotype schema for black individuals as hostile. Participants then interacted with another person in a taped interaction. Compared with participants who were subliminally primed with white faces, participants who were subliminally primed with black faces were rated by their interaction partners as displaying more hostility. Moreover, participants who had been primed with black faces also reported that their *partners* were more hostile. Thus, activation of the black–hostility schema made people act more hostile in line with the schema, and then interpret retaliatory hostility as due to the inherent hostility of the interaction partner.

Although schema theories have not been formally developed to address the implicit–explicit distinction, the ways that they are used in research provides some idea of researchers' commonly held assumptions. Schema theories suggest that knowledge structures are used implicitly in the processing of new information, but not that the content of the schemas themselves are unconscious. In fact, researchers often measure the contents of schemas using self-reports (e.g., Bem, 1974; Markus, Crane, Bernstein, & Siladi, 1982). Therefore, the content of schemas might be said to be implicit or explicit only temporarily, as attention is directed toward or away from any given aspect of the knowledge base.

A good deal of research has been conducted on the implicitness of schemas in the form of person memory and stereotyping research. In research on person memory, traits are commonly considered to be schemas summarizing a person's behaviors (Srull & Wyer, 1979). Stereotypes are considered schemas summarizing the traits of groups of people (Hilton & von Hippel, 1996). Studies of how people use traits suggests that inferences about traits can be made spontaneously (i.e., without intent) and effortlessly (i.e., efficiently) upon learning about a person's behaviors (Carlston & Skowronski, 1994; Todorov & Uleman, 2003; Uleman, 1987). In related research on dispositional attributions, people are more likely to ascribe behaviors to an actor's traits (as opposed to constraints of the situation) when cognitive capacity is low (Gilbert & Osborne, 1989). Finally, many studies have shown that stereotypes can be activated automatically (e.g., Blair & Banaji, 1996; Devine, 1989; Gaertner & McLaughlin, 1983; Payne, 2001; for reviews, see Banaji, 2001; Bargh, 1999) and that people are more likely to use stereotypes when cognitive capacity is low (Bodenhausen, 1990; Govorun & Payne, 2006; Macrae, Milne, & Bodenhausen, 1994). Together, these studies suggest that schemas can be used efficiently, without intent, and without deliberate control. Although the content of the traits, stereotypes, and other schemas may be available to consciousness, their activation and application in thinking and judging is presumably unconscious (Kunda & Spencer, 2003).

It is difficult to characterize the implicitness of schemas more precisely because, as a number of authors have argued, these models are more vaguely specified than many models of representation (Fiske & Linville, 1980; Smith, 1996). Schemas are sometimes invoked simply as a way to describe a person's general knowledge. When used in this way, schema theory does not specify how one schema is linked to other schemas, or how knowledge within a schema is organized (Carlston, 2010; Smith, 1998). Some authors have suggested that schemas might be incorporated into associative network models, as "local networks" of nodes which are so tightly connected that activating any one node activates all the rest (Carlston & Smith, 1996; Carlston, 2010; Smith, 1996). Taking this approach makes schema theories more precise, but it does so at the expense of turning them into associative network theories. Some recent approaches have tried to revitalize Bruner's (1957) original theorizing by integrating schema theory with neurobiology, revealing how schemas exert top-down influence on early forms of visual and attentional processing in animals and humans (Rauss, Schwartz, & Pourtois, 2011). Although these approaches might add much greater predictive specificity to schema theories, they remain to be incorporated more systematically into social psychological research.

Connectionist Models

Connectionist models have been widespread in cognitive psychology for the past two decades, but have only slowly been brought into social cognition research. They are intended to mimic the network structure of human neurons. Like associative networks, connectionist networks contain multiple processing nodes at varying levels of activation, which are connected by weighted links allowing for the transmission of this activation (Rumelhart, McClelland, & the PDP Research Group, 1987). However, there are fundamental differences between the two types of models. Unlike associative network models, most connectionist models do not assume that specific nodes have semantic meaning. Rather, representations are distributed as emergent patterns across the entire set of connected nodes. When given a set of inputs, the network eventually settles into a pattern that satisfies the parallel constraints of the activated nodes and the weighted connections between them. Importantly, distributed representations are not discrete because there are not distinct representations "stored" anywhere in the connectionist network (Smith, 1996). Different representations are only different recombinations of the same set of nodes and connection weights. Moreover, representations are not static. Each time the network instantiates a distributed pattern (or representation), it will be slightly different because of contextual factors and slowly learned changes in connection weights (Smith, 1996). Figure 11.2 displays a connectionist network model.

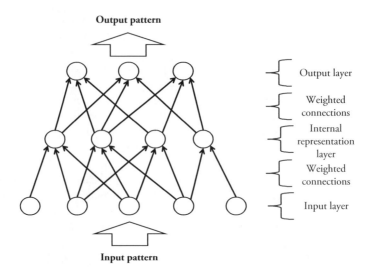

Output pattern

Output layer

Weighted connections

Internal representation layer

Weighted connections

Input layer

Input pattern

Figure 11.2 Schematic illustration of a connectionist model.

Consider how a connectionist network might settle into a pattern for the representation of "CAT." The first step toward connectionist representation is a set of inputs to the network, which could involve cues such as "claws," "meow," and "purr." Over lengthy experience, such cues will have come together via a set of connection weights to instantiate the distributed representational pattern of "CAT." Thus, the system learns to more quickly settle into this pattern in the future based on prior learning. However, there is no *single* distributed representation for "CAT." Rather, each time, the nodes and weighted connections will reach a slightly different approximation based on the combination of prior experiences, the specific features fed into the network, and other contextual influences.

Whereas most treatments of connectionism suggest that single nodes only have meaning in the context of the larger distributed pattern, others have argued that single nodes can have semantic meaning, as in associative networks (Bowers, 2009; Page, 2000; Read, Vanman, & Miller, 1997). Such localist connectionist models retain the parallel constraint satisfaction logic described above, but allow for discrete, static representations. For instance, some have argued for "grandmother cells"—single neurons that represent specific things, places, or persons, such as your grandmother. Drawing on a variety of single-cell electrophysiological studies, Bowers (2009) argues that localist connectionist networks better account for the data than do some kinds of distributed connectionist networks. However, many researchers argue that localist connectionist

networks are more similar to associative network models than to connectionist models because these models abandon the assumption of distributed pattern completion (Smith, 1996). Table 11.2 lists some key features and operating conditions distinguishing associative networks, distributed connectionist networks, and localist connectionist networks (cf. Smith, 1996). Localist connectionist models are similar to associative network models in many ways, but they are distinguished by the operating principle of parallel constraint satisfaction (Read, Vanman, & Miller, 1997). Although the localist versus distributed debate is controversial, it suggests that the distributed representation assumption may not be necessary within connectionist models.

Research applying connectionist models has not typically been concerned with questions of consciousness or automaticity. Instead, most studies have used connectionist networks to model the learning and use of patterns. However, the operating characteristics of such networks are suggestive. Connectionist networks are thought to always be active, constantly changing and settling into new patterns (Conrey & Smith, 2007). And because these patterns are either recombinations or re-creations of the same set of nodes and connection weights, they will always include some uninvited bits of stored information (Carlston & Smith, 1996). The distributed representations of connectionist networks might therefore be described as efficient and unintentional. People tend to become aware of the final emergent pattern, but not the workings of the connectionist network itself, and it is not clear

Table 11.2 Comparing Associative Network, Distributed Connectionist, and Localist Connectionist Models

	Associative Network Models	Distributed Connectionist Models	Localist Connectionist Models
Are these models of representational process, structure, or both?	Only structure; additional explanation needed for process of information retrieval	Process and structure are the same; pattern completion is the representation and the process	Only structure; additional explanation needed for process of information retrieval
Are representations localist or distributed?	Localist; individual nodes have semantic meaning	Distributed; individual nodes have semantic meaning only relative to pattern across nodes	Localist; individual nodes have semantic meaning
How quickly do network structures change?	Nodes and links change very quickly	Connection weights change very slowly	Nodes and links change very quickly
Nature of spreading activation between linked nodes	Spreading activation	Spreading activation with parallel constraint satisfaction	Spreading activation with parallel constraint satisfaction
Direction of spreading activation between linked nodes	Both ways	One way	Both ways
Role of context in influencing representations	Meaning of nodes does not change depending on context, so another mechanism is needed to account for contextual influences	Meaning of nodes changes depending on context, resulting in new distributed pattern	Meaning of nodes does not change depending on context, so another mechanism is needed to account for contextual influences

that this machinery could be made fully conscious. Finally, in some cases, control does seem possible: people are capable of inputting new cues into the connectionist network to modulate the pattern that eventually emerges (Conrey & Smith, 2007).

At least some of the time, these new cues might be qualitatively unique. Some theorists have posited an additional explicit processor overlaid on top of an implicit connectionist processor (Sloman, 1996; Smith, 1996; Smith & DeCoster, 2000; Smolensky, 1988). In such cases, the explicit processor is said to operate via conscious manipulation of linguistic or propositional representations. By contrast, the connectionist processor governs the unconscious, implicit, or intuitive processing of associations. The similarities between connectionist and associative network models suggest the possibility that activation of a pattern above some threshold could be used to model explicitly represented concepts. However, we are not aware of any research that has taken this approach. In short, the currently available research seems to assume that connectionist models are primarily models of implicit representation.

Connectionist models are able to account for many of the same effects as associative network and schema models. Instead of appealing to spreading activation to explain evaluative and semantic priming effects, connectionist models can utilize the notion of pattern completion and overlapping patterns (Carlston, 2010; Smith, 1996). Triggering one pattern may make it easier to complete similar patterns representing other concepts. This can also account for recency effects because recently instantiated patterns make the connectionist network more likely to fall into similar patterns for a certain period of time. Chronic accessibility effects can be accounted for by appeal to slowly learned changes in weights between nodes, making some patterns more likely to emerge on the network's outputs than others. Finally, connectionist models can account for schematic processing: triggering one portion of a given representational pattern makes it easier for the rest of the pattern to complete. Connectionist networks do not make a distinction between process and content. The pattern of connection weights between nodes acts both as the process of representing and the content of the representation (Carlston, 2010; Smith, 1996). Because of this, the question of the implicitness of the representation versus the implicit use of the representation does not apply. The representation and its use are the same.

Although connectionist models are becoming increasingly popular in social cognition, there are some drawbacks. First, distributed connectionist models can be complex to implement and interpret (Read, Vanman, & Miller, 1996), although models have been successfully developed for attitude learning (Eiser, Fazio, Stafford, & Prescott, 2003) and attitude change (Cunningham, Zelazo, Packer, & Bavel, 2007). Second, there is still heated debate about whether distributed or localist connectionist networks are more appropriate for modeling social psychological effects, which might obscure the advantages that could otherwise accrue from this general perspective. And finally, it is still unclear how connectionist models are supposed to account for differences between implicit and explicit representations—whereas some models posit a separate "explicit processor" (Smith & DeCoster, 2000; Smolensky, 1988), others account for explicit representations by appealing to control of inputs to the system that alter pattern completion (Conrey & Smith, 2007; Gawronski & Bodenhausen, 2006).

Multiple Format Models

The aims of the foregoing models are broad: they intend to account for how information is represented in general. However, some recent models suggest that there are multiple *kinds* of representation that are processed in qualitatively distinct ways.

Carlston's associated systems theory (AST; Carlston, 1994) posits four distinct processing systems: verbal, visual, behavioral, and affective. Critically, representations in each of the four systems are qualitatively distinct. The individual systems are arranged hierarchically, from lower level representations that correspond to neural and physiological processes to higher level representations that are more complex, consciously accessible, and amenable to verbal description. These higher level representations consist of propositions in the verbal system, images in the visual system, goals in the behavioral system, and verbal representations of emotion in the affective system. Higher level representations can reinstantiate lower level representations within their respective systems. They can also intermingle in a shared associative structure across systems, leading to hybrid representations between systems. For instance, evaluations combine affective and verbal representations; orientations combine affective and action representations; categorizations combine verbal and visual representations; and behavioral observations combine action and visual representations.

Qualitative differences between the systems have important implications for whether representations are implicit or explicit. Different kinds of representations might be implicit to differing degrees. AST posits that all lower level representations are permanently inaccessible to conscious awareness. Higher level representations can all be made temporarily conscious, but the ease with which this happens varies from system to system. For instance, affect and action representations are more self-focused and less world focused than verbal and visual representations. It might therefore be more difficult to construct and utilize higher level affect and action representations without unintentionally drawing on irrelevant information (Carlston, 2010). Indeed, source-monitoring errors are commonly seen in attributions of affect (Payne, Hall, Cameron, & Bishara, 2010) and agency (Wegner, 2002). For these reasons, affect and action representations may be more difficult to make conscious, and may be somewhat more unintentional and uncontrollable, than visual and verbal representations.

Like AST, the memory systems model (MSM; Amodio, 2008; Amodio & Ratner, 2011) is pluralist. The MSM is critical of traditional associative network, schema, and connectionist models, which tend to assume that all representations are cut from the same cloth and operate in the same way. Whereas such models might effectively capture certain kinds of semantic processes, they might fail to do justice to affective processes and behavioral outcomes (Amodio & Ratner, 2011). To address these concerns, the MSM appeals to distinct memory systems with unique operating characteristics and neural underpinnings (Squire & Zola, 1996). The model distinguishes between a semantic associative system, an affective memory system, and a procedural memory system. The affective memory system learns through mechanisms, including fear conditioning, that are implemented by subcortical pathways in which the amygdala is central. The semantic memory system learns through more conceptual means that are implemented by neocortical regions. And the procedural memory system learns through a network connecting the striatum and basal ganglia to prefrontal cortex and motor regions.

In some cases, the kinds of tasks used in social cognition may be used to dissociate the effects of the distinct systems. For instance, Amodio and colleagues (2003) found that people exhibited greater startle eyeblink responses to black compared with white and Asian faces. The startle response is believed to specifically reflect activity in the central nucleus of the amygdala, which is responsible for fear conditioning. This result suggested an affective form of implicit racial bias based on learned fear.

In other cases, the distinctions between memory systems may not map on well to the implicit–explicit distinction as used in social cognition. For all three systems, processing is presumed to be unconscious, though the outcome (e.g., a semantic idea, an affective reaction, or a habitual response) may become temporarily conscious. This model is new, and we are not aware of any research that has evaluated the model in terms of awareness, efficiency, intention, and control. A strength of this model is that it highlights the functional links between specific kinds of learning and specific classes of behavior. These links are based, not on conceptual similarities, but on neurological pathways. Cases in which these pathways do—and do not—map on to the implicit–explicit distinction will provide valuable new evidence for the kinds of metaphors that are most useful in understanding social behavior.

Embodied Cognition Models

Within social cognition research, associative network models and schema models have been the two classic, complementary perspectives on mental representation. Because they work from a computer metaphor of the mind, they are often called "symbolic" models of mental representation (Smith, 1996). Connectionist models challenged this metaphor by positing distributed representations and moving past the idea that ideas are like static, individuated files in a cabinet. The multiple format models posed another challenge, suggesting that there might be different modes of representation that the previous models had not accounted for. Now, we move to a set of models that raise an even more fundamental challenge: Do mental representations extend outside the mind, both to the body and to the external environment? And does changing how we think about the nature of mental representation fundamentally change how we think about implicit and explicit cognition?

Embodied social cognition models posit a fundamental distinction between "amodal" and "modal" forms of mental representation. Amodal representations are abstract and disembodied symbols of objects or events that do not retain the sensory components from the original experiences of those objects or events. For instance, I might think about coffee as warm, tasty, and arousing, but in an abstract and conceptual way, that does not actually call upon sensory information or details. By contrast, modal representations draw upon and are constituted by those sensory experiences: the heat of the coffee, the flavor of the beans, the caffeinated alertness. The critical issue is whether or not those sensory details are retained in the stored mental representation, to call back up for future use.

Embodied models of mental representation criticize associative network, schema, and connectionist models for overlooking modal mental representations (Niedenthal et al., 2005). The two sets of models agree that when faced with a given object (e.g., a cup of coffee), a variety of modal states arise in different sensory systems (e.g., visual, auditory, motor, somatosensory). For amodal models, the specific details of this embodiment do not matter because they assume that the modality-specific information is translated into an abstract, disembodied format for further use (e.g., Fodor & Pylyshyn, 1988). But in embodied models, details of body matter for details of mind. Embodied information is not translated into some kind of abstract currency, but rather is itself the basis of mental representation. The smell, sight, and taste of the coffee are stored, in their original sensory format, as part of the representation of a cup of coffee.

One of the most prominent examples of an embodiment model of mental representation is Barsalou's perceptual symbol systems (PSS) theory (for more details, see Barsalou, 2008; Niedenthal et al., 2005). When viewing an object, multiple types of information are registered across different sensory modalities, before being integrated to create a higher order, multimodal representation. Over repeated encounters with similar objects, typical features across modalities are used to update this representation. This slow-learned, distributed, multimodal representation of a category is called a *simulator*. After a long history with cups of coffee, I will tend to have a simulator for "cup of coffee" that includes typical sights, smells, touches, and tastes. The critical contribution of PSS theory is that these simulators can then be used to run "offline" simulations that call up the original embodied information. Even if I am not currently presented with a cup of coffee, I can draw upon the simulator and re-enact some of the original sensory information. As with connectionist models, this re-enactment of the stored representation will be imperfect and contextually situated. But in a very real sense, I can smell a cup of coffee without having one in front of me, owing to the embodied content stored in the corresponding mental representation.

Embodied cognition models are not limited to a person's past perceptual experience. Other models allow for embodied simulation of the emotions, intentions, and goals of other people in our environment. Recent work on "mirror neurons" suggests that when we perceive the action of another person, motor neurons are activated that simulate the action in our own minds (Gallese, 2001). Put another way, we catch the motor and action representations of the other person, creating a "shared manifold" across agents (Gallese, 2001). Moreover, it has been speculated that mirror neurons might be responsible for basic forms of empathy and representing the intentions, goals, and mental states of others (Gallese, 2007).

How do embodied cognition models handle the implicit–explicit distinction? It seems that this distinction may be orthogonal to the modal versus amodal format of representations. Representations from different embodied modalities might be more or less conscious, intentional, controllable, or efficient, as in our discussion of multiple format models. The multimodal representations used in simulations seem to be only temporarily implicit, inasmuch as conscious attention can shift focus to information resulting from specific modalities. And implicitness resides as much in embodied representations themselves as in how they are used.

However, there has been more debate over the implicit use of embodied representations. The embodied simulations underwritten by mirror neurons are hypothesized to be efficient, uncontrollable, and unintentional, although their results are amenable to conscious awareness with proper attentional direction (Gallese, 2007). On the other hand, PSS theory suggests that simulation using embodied information is an effortful process, contingent on cognitive capacity and motivation. A person can intentionally draw upon embodied, modality-specific information, for instance by trying to use his or her taste palate (and its history) to understand the ingredients of a dish. Under less ideal circumstances, people are thought to use "shallow conceptual" processing, or simple rules that do not re-enact modality-specific states (Niedenthal et al., 2005). This perspective suggests that embodied information is *less* implicit in its use than amodal information. As new embodiment models are further developed, it is our hope that the implicit and explicit uses of embodied information will be more clearly defined.

In addition to the question of whether embodied representations are implicit, many researchers have also examined how embodiment influences implicit processes. For example, in one study people were subliminally primed with words related to the black hostility stereotype, before completing an implicit aggression measure (DeMarree, Brinol, & Petty, unpublished; cf. Briñol & Petty, 2008). After the subliminal priming induction, people were asked to either shake their heads from side to side (an embodied cue for disagreement) or nod their heads up and down (an embodied cue for validation). Only people in the head-nodding condition showed priming of the hostility stereotype on implicit aggression, suggesting that embodiment can moderate classic prime-to-behavior effects.

In another intriguing study, Witt and colleagues (2010) examined how embodied cues for tool use influence automatic recognition of tools. People squeezed a ball in one hand while quickly identifying whether objects were tools or animals. They were faster to accurately identify tools whose handles were facing away from the hand grasping the ball. By grasping a ball, people appear to have blocked the automatic motor simulations that would otherwise have been activated when seeing images of tools whose handles faced the grasping hand.

Finally, embodied social cognition models can help us better understand implicit attitude measurement. For instance, embodiment perspectives can illustrate how different implicit measures might rely on different types (i.e., modal vs. amodal) of mental representations. In one study, people were asked to hold a pen in their mouth—thus blocking the use of the zygomatic facial muscle—while they completed an evaluative priming task and an Implicit Association Test (IAT; Foroni & Semin, 2011). Whereas this manipulation had no influence on IAT performance, it disrupted affective priming, presumably because it blocked the facial muscle movements that occur after affect-inducing primes and that would facilitate speeded responding to affectively congruent targets. Findings such as these suggest that embodied social cognition perspectives might help to resolve long-standing debates about the mental representations assessed by different implicit measures.

In summary, embodied social cognition models offer much promise in revising how we think about implicit and explicit mental representations and how they are measured. Perhaps the biggest drawback at this point is lack of theoretical integration across the fast-growing number of studies showing embodiment effects. With the exception of PSS theory (Barsalou, 2008), there is little guidance for how to integrate embodied social cognition with long-standing questions in implicit social cognition. However, we believe that the two fields can offer each other quite a bit. Much as embodied cues are being shown to moderate priming effects, perhaps thinking about how to distinguish implicit and explicit representations from an embodied perspective can help reveal the operating conditions for embodied phenomena more generally.

Situated Cognition Models

Just as details of body matter, so do details of environment. Drawing upon James' (1890) famous dictum that thinking is for doing, the situated cognition movement argues that mental representations result from dynamic interactions between the brain, body, and environment (Chemero, 2009; Clark, 1997; Robbins & Aydede, 2009). Although there is overlap between situated and embodied perspectives—indeed, situated cognition theorists often cite embodiment as a core premise (Smith & Semin, 2004)—there are key ontological assumptions distinguishing the two. Although embodiment perspectives allow that sensory details can comprise mental representations, they usually maintain that these representations are still fundamentally internal to the individual. Situated cognition theorists, on the other hand, often put forward more liberal definitions of mental representation that do not require representations to be internal at all. As we have progressed through this chapter, we have moved further away from file-drawer and computer metaphors. With situated cognition, we take this progression to its logical extreme: mental representations might not be files in a cabinet or on a computer, but instead might be the entire dynamic interaction that takes place between worker, cabinet, and computer on a daily basis.

Situated cognition perspectives challenge the traditional design assumption that brains must house tons of information in order to function adaptively. Rather than store full-fledged representations of the world internally, the brain might only house information on a need-to-know basis. By relying on less internal information, the brain can delegate much of the support work for adaptive behavior to features of the environment that "scaffold" and simplify decision making (Clark, 2007). Think about the absent-minded person who covers his or her desk with reminders on Post-It notes; inasmuch as these external media are aiding

memory, they might be seen as constituting mental representations (Clark, 1997). Or think about how we outsource our memory to Internet search engines such as Google (Sparrow, Liu, & Wegner, 2011). Even the term *smart phone* implies that we recognize how external devices can supplement, and even partially constitute, the mind. These ecological considerations can be melded with more traditional models: for instance, Post-It notes or Google might simplify a cognitive problem, aiding in the pattern completion process of a connectionist network (Clark, 1997). From a situated cognition perspective, mental representations emerge out of a loose but adaptive assemblage of neurological, bodily, and environmental conditions, which is distributed across this dynamic union.

This, in turn, suggests fundamental shifts in how we describe a mental representation. Some have argued that the term "representation" be dispensed with altogether because it does not track any concrete aspect of the interaction between a person and the environment, referring neither to the environmental conditions nor to brain or body responses (Chemero, 2009; Keijzer, 2002; Varela, Thompson, & Rosch, 1992). For example, Schwarz (2007) has argued that the term "attitude" (as a specific kind of representation) is only a reification, which glosses over the ways that evaluations change with context. Others have been more cautious, arguing that there is still a place for the notion of representation in cognitive science (Bechtel, 1998; Clark, 1997). But regardless of the resolution of this debate, all sides agree that any internal "representations" will be limited in scope and heavily guided toward action. Just as embodied cognition researchers argue against amodal representations that ignore body state, situated cognition researchers argue against the existence of mental representations that ignore the pragmatics of acting in situated contexts.

What do situated cognition perspectives imply for the implicit–explicit distinction? As with embodied cognition, this distinction might be orthogonal to any fundamental changes in the nature or definition of "mental representation." Even if mental representations are distributed across mind and environment, and emerge from a dynamic interplay therein, this does not necessitate strong conclusions about consciousness, intentionality, controllability, or efficiency. Much as people delegate skilled behaviors out of conscious awareness, they might delegate important informational tasks out of conscious awareness—and out of the brain—to environmental scaffolds or other agents. However, a person could still consciously use these external supports to supplement decision making, so that any implicitness of representation or representation use is temporary and not permanent. For example, people often intentionally manipulate the environment to facilitate problem solving (e.g., rearranging Scrabble tiles to think up new words; Kirsh, 2009). Similarly, people can intentionally distribute memory across a network of individuals and consult those members when needed (Wegner, Erber, & Raymond, 1991). Intriguingly, situated cognition models resemble connectionist models in collapsing the distinction between implicit representation and implicit use. Instead of representations being in the head and representation use being in the world, representations now just *are* the process of navigating and interacting with the world.

To illustrate this point, consider Semin and Cacioppo's (2009) social cognition model of adaptive interpersonal behavior. When a person sees someone else's action, two concurrent synchronization processes are activated. One is an efficient, unintentional, uncontrollable, and nonconscious monitoring process that mirrors and continually simulates the action of the other person. The other is a conscious, controllable, and intentionally goal-directed process that allows for adaptive, complementary action simulations. These two synchronization processes mutually constrain each other during an interaction and result in a motor representation that drives behavior. This representation, a product of embodied simulation, is not merely in the head of the actor; rather, it is an emergent product distributed over the dyadic encounter. These representations can have varying degrees of conscious awareness, efficiency, intentionality, and controllability, depending on the relative contributions of the two synchronization processes; the implicitness here is only temporary and, because of the connection with situated action, is fundamentally tied up with both representation structure and representation use.

Besides specific situated cognition models, the general principles avowed by the movement are starting to be felt in implicit social cognition research more generally. One such principle is the notion of situational "affordances" (Gibson, 1977). As defined by Gibson (1977), affordances refer to implied possibilities for action that are present in the environment. For example, a guitar sitting in the corner might afford me the possibility of playing a song. These possibilities for action can be measured objectively (i.e., the guitar is playable) and are independent of my ability to perceive that possibility (i.e., even if I forget the guitar is there, it is still playable). On the other hand, the afforded action will only come about if I have the ability to make it happen—if I know nothing about using a guitar, I might not be able to play a song. Recently, social psychologists have begun to consider how different physical and interpersonal environments afford different questions or concerns that might capture attention and shape implicit social cognition.

Implicit social cognition researchers have long recognized that situations can automatically cue certain kinds of behavior. However, this has often been taken to mean that situations cue the activation of representations, which then have invariant relationships to behavior (e.g., the stereotype representation for black people cues aggressive behavior; Bargh, Chen, & Burrows, 1996). More recent models have challenged this assumption, positing that different situations also afford different interpretive possibilities. For example, Cesario and colleagues (2010) showed that primed black faces (vs. white faces) had different influences on behavior, depending on what kinds of action possibilities were afforded by the experiment location. When primed by black faces in a small room, which did not afford an opportunity to escape, "fight" words became more accessible for people with black–danger associations. When primed by black faces in an open field, which did afford the opportunity to escape, "flight" words became more accessible for people with black–danger associations.

Similarly, the situated inference model (Loersch & Payne, 2011) suggests that when primed representations are misattributed to one's own response to a situation, they alter judgments, goals, or behaviors based on what kind of tacit question the situation affords (e.g., "Who/what is that?" "What will I do?" "What do I want?"). For instance, if the goal of cooperation is made accessible in my mind, it will influence me in different ways depending on my focus. If I am focused on evaluating someone else, I might judge that person to be more trustworthy. If I am focusing on what to do next, I might act agreeably. And if I am focusing on what I want, the prime might instill the goal to be cooperative with others. Thus, not only do situations cue certain representations, they also cue different kinds of use of those representations. As situated cognition models become more prominent, both on their own and as their principles are applied to implicit social cognition research, it seems likely that there will be an increasing focus on the implicit and explicit *use* of mental representations by people acting in situated contexts. Although some have criticized situated perspectives for taking the extreme position that attitudes and mental states are wholly constructed by context (for debate on this point, see Fazio, 2007; Schwarz, 2007), we believe that situated cognition approaches are more likely to add theoretically useful nuance to our understanding of how implicit social cognition works in the real world.

Emerging Themes and New Perspectives on the Implicitness of Representations

We have reviewed many metaphors for mental representation, both classic and modern. As seen in Table 11.1, these models have found different ways to address the three questions about implicitness: (1) By what criterion is a representation implicit or explicit? (2) Is implicitness a feature of the representation or how it is used? (3) Is implicitness permanent or temporary? The models differed on whether the building blocks of representations (e.g., nodes, links, knowledge structures) are themselves conscious. They agreed, however, that the concept, idea, or thought that results from an activated representation can become conscious under the right circumstances. This idea of temporary explicitness is a theme that unifies the various models we have discussed. Whether a particular representation becomes conscious depends on certain critical factors, such as the focus of attention and environmental cues.

The models also disagreed on whether the representation itself can be considered primarily implicit or explicit. But they generally agreed that the use of a representation might be either implicit or explicit, under different conditions. This distinction is important, first, because the implicit use of information is often more easily verified empirically than the implicitness of an abstract representation. Gawronski, Hofmann, and Wilbur (2006) reached a similar conclusion about the nature of implicit attitude measures. They reviewed studies of implicit attitudes to evaluate the evidence for three types of unconscious processing: unawareness of the attitude itself, unawareness of the source of the attitude, and unawareness of the impact (i.e., use) of attitudes in judgments, decisions, and behavior. They concluded that there was little evidence for unawareness of the attitude itself. The main source of evidence consisted of null correlations between implicit attitude scores and self-reported attitudes. Null correlations, however, have been found to result from a number of psychological processes like social desirability and measurement issues like low reliability

(Cunningham, Preacher, & Banaji, 2001; Payne, Burkley, & Stokes, 2008). There is evidence that people are often unaware of the source of their attitudes, but this is the case both for explicit attitudes and implicit attitudes (do you remember where you learned your explicit attitudes toward broccoli or Republicans?).

On the other hand, it is the use, or influence, of attitudes that seems to best distinguish implicit and explicit attitudes (see Hall & Payne, 2010; Uhlmann, Pizarro, & Bloom, 2008, for similar arguments). For example, some implicit tests, such as the IAT or evaluative priming, rely on the mechanism of response interference. In these tasks, there are some trials in which prime–target combinations are affectively congruent or stereotypically consistent, and other trials in which they are not. On these tasks, people are often aware of making mistaken judgments on incongruent trials because they can feel that some kinds of trials are more difficult than others. And yet, they cannot control that influence on their performance. Other implicit tests, such as the affect misattribution procedure (Payne, Cheng, Govorun, & Stewart, 2005), have different operating conditions (Deutsch & Gawronski, 2009). In this task, people have to judge ambiguous Chinese pictographs as positive or negative after being primed with attitude objects. People tend to misattribute their affective reactions from the attitude objects to the pictographs, unaware of this priming influence (Payne, Cheng, Govorun, & Stewart, 2005). And just as attitudes can influence performance on implicit tests without awareness, intention, or control, they may also influence other decisions and behaviors implicitly.

Because the themes of *temporary explicitness* and *implicit use* run through many models of representation, we end our chapter by discussing two theories that highlight these themes most directly. These theories focus less on representations themselves than on the use of representations. They are concerned specifically with how the use of information may become implicit or explicit as a function of the circumstances.

The Self-Inference Model

In their classic review, Nisbett and Wilson (1977) argued that people come to know (or fail to know) the causes of their own behavior by using lay theories. Rather than having privileged introspective access, people make inferences about the causes of their behavior the same way that they infer the causes of other people's behavior (see also Bem, 1972).

Hofmann and Wilson's (2010) self-inference model elaborates this idea in the context of modern implicit social cognition research. Hofmann and Wilson assume that people cannot perceive their representations directly. In other words, representations are not themselves conscious. But representations cause a variety of consequences that are consciously perceptible. Specifically, representations can give rise to feelings (e.g., affective feelings, fluency, familiarity, and confidence), and they can give rise to behaviors. People can monitor those feelings and behaviors to make inferences about their underlying representations. For example, if you feel sick when you look at oysters, then you can easily infer that you have a negative attitude toward oysters. And if you physically recoil from them, you can also draw a similar inference from your behavior. According to this theory, you are not aware of the attitude representation, but by observing the co-occurrence of the oysters and your feelings or behavior you can infer what kind of attitude you have.

The model posits two factors that influence how likely people are to draw an inference about their representations. First is the strength of the representation. The stronger the link between oysters and negative affect, the more likely it is to initiate the inference process. Second is the focus of attention. The more closely you are paying attention to the co-occurrence of the oysters and your reaction, the more likely you are to infer an attitude. In many cases, the reaction may be too subtle, or attention may be elsewhere, leading to no inference being made. In such cases, the attitude can be described as implicit.

The self-inference model draws connections between the problem of consciousness and Brunswik's (1956) ecological approach to perception. The main idea is that when people don't have direct access to the underlying truth, they draw inferences from available cues. The accuracy of the inference depends on how valid the cues are and how effectively people utilize the cues. When the cues are misleading or people use them poorly, their inferences will be mistaken. When applied to introspection, mistaken inferences amount to a version of implicitness because what people are "aware" of is not the real representation that caused their reactions.

The self-inference model advances thinking about the implicitness of representation by clarifying the necessary conditions for becoming aware of a representation (even if indirectly). There must be perceptible feelings or behaviors that accompany a stimulus, and people must use these cues

effectively. It also clarifies factors that promote good versus poor inferences (e.g., strong representations, focused attention). Although this model does not focus much on the nature of representations themselves, it goes a long way toward integrating several of the key themes that emerged across many of the representation models reviewed above. How we use our representations in making self-inferences might be as, if not more, important than the implicitness of the representations themselves.

Jacoby's Attributional Model of Memory

Much of the research in implicit social cognition has roots in implicit memory research. Jacoby and colleagues developed an attributional framework for understanding the role of subjective experience in memory, with relevance for implicit representation in general (Jacoby, Kelley, & Dywan, 1989; Kelley & Jacoby, 1990). Like the self-inference model, this theory draws on Brunswik's ecological model of perception, along with von Helmholtz's (1967/2000) work on visual experience and Marcel's (1983) work on subliminal perception. The main idea is that the subjective experiences of remembering cannot be explained by the properties of a memory trace. Instead, traces of past experience can influence current processing, resulting in certain perceptible cues. For example, prior experience can make people process information more fluently when it is encountered again. People often interpret this fluent processing as remembering. Events we have experienced are more likely to be recalled with vivid sensory detail than events we only thought about. Thus, when people recall experiences with vivid details, they often interpret that they are remembering these experiences.

If the subjective experience of memory relies on the interpretation of cues, then this model predicts specific kinds of memory illusions. For example, experiments that make an item come easily to mind should lead people to believe they experienced that item before. Jacoby and colleagues have conducted a number of studies demonstrating just such effects (Jacoby & Whitehouse, 1989; Jacoby, Kelley, Brown, & Jasechko, 1989). For example, Jacoby and Whitehouse (1989) manipulated how fluently words on a recognition memory test were read. They subliminally primed each word on the recognition test with either itself (a match) or a different word (a nonmatch). Priming with a matching word caused subjects to "recognize" the word as previously studied, regardless of whether it had actually been studied or not.

This attributional model links consciousness and intention because it treats intentions as an inference, just like conscious experience. Once a memory comes to mind, people may infer that they are trying to remember; once an action begins, they perceive a variety of cues related to bodily movement and infer that they intended to move (see also Wegner, 2002). Intentions are not, however, treated as purely passive observations. Instead, intentions can both result from and inform actions. Once an intention has been formed, it can guide further actions.

This model loosely links representations to conscious experience and intention. Because memory traces are one possible source of changes in processing and actions, they can serve as cues for inferring conscious memory or intention. But these cues are not always reliable, and they can occur in the absence of a memory trace, such as when lay theories or tricky experimenters cause certain thoughts to come easily to mind. If a person fails to make an inference, or makes an incorrect inference based on available but inappropriate cues, the underlying representation is considered to be implicit, in the sense that it remains unconscious or its effects are perceived as unintended.

Although this model was developed to explain subjective experiences of memory, it has also been applied in social cognition research (Payne, 2001; Payne, Jacoby, & Lambert, 2004). The affect misattribution procedure (Payne et al., 2005) relies on attribution principles to implicitly measure attitudes. In this task, subjects misattribute their reactions to primes for their reactions to Chinese symbols, despite being explicitly warned against such effects. Subjects appear to infer that their evaluations reflect properties of the symbols, when they are in fact driven by reactions to the primes. Cases of misattribution, by definition, imply unawareness of a response's true cause. Some theories of implicit attitudes suggest that implicit and explicit tests reflect distinct attitude representations (e.g., Wilson, Lindsey, & Schooler, 2000). In an attributional model, however, direct expressions of explicit evaluations of an object and implicitly measured reactions need not imply distinct representations. Rather, the difference lies in the interpretation of cues that result from those representations.

If a person feels uneasy looking at a picture of the President, she might infer that she dislikes the President. However, if she infers that her uneasiness is caused instead by the Chinese symbol presented just after the president's photo, then she may not make any inference about her attitude toward the President at all. These different inferences about responses to the same item form the basis for a distinction between implicit and explicit attitudes that has little to do with underlying representations, at least initially. After forming these inferences, however, a person might remember her earlier conclusions, altering future interpretations of her own attitudes. Memory representations may thus be one basis among many for distinguishing between implicit and explicit cognition.

Conclusion

We have reviewed several different approaches to mental representation and how these relate to the implicit–explicit distinction (see Table 11.1). Although these theories approach the implicit–explicit distinction very differently, some key themes emerge. First, most theories suggest that when a representation is implicit, it is only temporarily implicit. Schemas, embodiment cues, and situated representations can all be made explicit by directing attention to them, although more research is needed on the implicit–explicit distinction from embodied and situated cognition perspectives. Whereas some parts of the underlying representational system—like spreading activation in associative networks or connection weights in connectionist networks—and some *types* of representational systems (according to multiple format models) are permanently inaccessible, their outputs often become conscious. Second, most theories agree that it is the use of representations that can best be described as implicit or explicit, rather than the representation itself. Because most types of representation can be made consciously accessible, the real action lies in knowing how to use these representations in an explicit, goal-directed manner. And this knowledge of how to use representations is often provided or prompted by the situated contexts we find ourselves in. In our view, attributional theories offer a natural way to explain these functional, flexible aspects of implicitness. We began this chapter by discussing the ways that metaphors can change the scientific understanding of abstract ideas. Attributional theories of consciousness suggest that this is just as true of how people understand their own minds. When a person's lay theory or a tricky experiment shifts how we interpret the effects of a representation, it shifts what the representation means. From this perspective, awareness, efficiency, intent, and control are not qualities that a representation has; they describe activities that people do.

References

Amodio, D. M. (2008). The social neuroscience of intergroup relations. *European Review of Social Psychology, 19,* 1–54.

Amodio, D. M., Harmon-Jones, E., & Devine, P. G. (2003). Individual differences in the activation and control of affective race bias as assessed by startle eyeblink responses and self-report. *Journal of Personality and Social Psychology, 84,* 738–753.

Amodio, D. M., & Ratner, K. G. (2011). A memory systems model of implicit social cognition. *Current Directions in Psychological Science, 20,* 143–148.

Anderson, J. R. (1983). *The architecture of cognition.* Cambridge, MA: Harvard University Press.

Anderson, J. R., & Bower, G. H. (1973). *Human associative memory.* Washington, DC: Winston.

Banaji, M. R. (2001). Implicit attitudes can be measured. In H. L. Roediger, III & J. S. Nairne (Eds.), *The nature of remembering: Essays in honor of Robert G. Crowder* (pp. 117–150). Washington, DC: American Psychological Association.

Bargh, J. A. (1994). The four horsemen of automaticity: Awareness, intention, efficiency, and control in social cognition. In R. S. Wyer & T. K. Srull (Eds.), *Handbook of social cognition* (2nd ed., pp. 1–40). Hillsdale, NJ: Erlbaum.

Bargh, J. A. (1999). The cognitive monster: The case against the controllability of automatic stereotype effects. In S. Chaiken & Y. Trope (Eds.), *Dual process theories in social psychology* (pp. 361–382). New York: Guilford.

Bargh, J. A., Chen, M., & Burrows, L. (1996). Automaticity of social behavior: Direct effects of trait construct and stereotype-activation on action. *Journal of Personality and Social Psychology, 71,* 230–244.

Barsalou, L. (2008). Grounding symbolic operations in the brain's modal systems. In G. R. Semin & E. R. Smith (Eds.), *Embodied grounding: Social, cognitive, affective, and neuroscientific approaches* (pp. 9–42). New York: Cambridge University Press.

Bechtel, W. (1998). Representations and cognitive explanations: Assessing the dynamicist's challenge in cognitive science. *Cognitive Science, 22,* 295–318.

Bem, D. (1972). Self-perception theory. *Advances in Experimental Social Psychology, 6,* 2–62.

Bem, S. (1974). The measurement of psychological androgyny. *Journal of Consulting and Clinical Psychology, 42,* 155–162.

Blair, I. V., and Banaji, M. R. (1996). Automatic and controlled processes in stereotype priming. *Journal of Personality and Social Psychology, 70,* 1142–1163.

Bodenhausen, G. (1990). Stereotypes as judgmental heuristics: Evidence of circadian variations in discrimination. *Psychological Science, 1,* 319–322.

Bowers, J. S. (2009). On the biological plausibility of grandmother cells: Implications for neural network theories in psychology and neuroscience. *Psychological Review, 116,* 220–251.

Briñol, P., & Petty, R. E. (2008). Embodied persuasion: Fundamental processes by which bodily responses can impact attitudes. In G. R. Semin & E. R. Smith (Eds.), *Embodiment grounding: Social, cognitive, affective, and neuroscientific approaches* (pp. 184–207). Cambridge, UK: Cambridge University Press.

Bruner, J. (1957). On perceptual readiness. *Psychological Review, 64,* 123–152.

Brunswik, E. (1956). *Perception and the representative design of psychological experiments* (2nd ed.). Berkeley, CA: University of California Press.

Carlston, D. E. (1994). Associated systems theory: A systematic approach to the cognitive representation of persons and events. In R. S. Wyer (Ed.), *Advances in social cognition: Vol 7. Associated systems theory* (pp. 1–78). Hillsdale, NJ: Erlbaum.

Carlston, D. E. (2010). Models of implicit and explicit mental representation. In B. Gawronski & B. K. Payne (Eds.), *Handbook of implicit social cognition: Measurement, theory, and applications* (pp. 38–61). New York: Guilford Press.

Carlston, D. E., & Skowronski, J. J. (1986). Trait memory and behavior memory: The effects of alternative pathways on impression judgment response times. *Journal of Personality and Social Psychology, 50,* 5–13.

Carlston, D. E., & Skowronski, J. J. (1994). Saving in the relearning of trait information as evidence for spontaneous inference generation. *Journal of Personality and Social Psychology, 66,* 840–856.

Carlston, D.E., & Smith, E.R. (1996). Principles of mental representation. In E. T. Higgins & A. W. Kruglanski (Eds.), *Social psychology: Handbook of basic principles* (1st ed., pp. 184–210). New York: Guilford Press.

Cesario, J., Plaks, J. E., Hagiwara, N., Navarette, C. D., & Higgins, E. T. (2010). The ecology of automaticity: How situational contingencies shape action semantics and social behavior. *Psychological Science, 21,* 1311–1317.

Chemero, A. (2009). *Radical embodied cognitive science.* Cambridge, MA: MIT Press.

Chen, M., & Bargh, J. A. (1997). Nonconscious behavioral confirmation processes: The self-fulfilling consequences of automatic stereotype activation. *Journal of Experimental Social Psychology, 33,* 541–560.

Clark, A. (1997). *Being there: Putting brain, body, and world together again.* Cambridge, MA: MIT Press.

Clark, A. (2007). Soft selves and ecological control. In D. Ross, D. Spurrett, H. Kincaid, & G. L. Stephens (Eds.), *Distributed cognition and the will: Individual volition and social context* (pp. 101–122). Cambridge, MA: MIT Press.

Collins, A., & Loftus, E. (1975). A spreading-activation theory of semantic processing. *Psychological Review, 82,* 407–428.

Conrey, F. R., & Smith, E. R. (2007). Attitude representation: Attitudes as patterns in a distributed, connectionist representational system. *Social Cognition, 25,* 718–735.

Cunningham, W. A., Preacher, K. J., & Banaji, M. R. (2001). Implicit attitude measures: Consistency, stability, and convergent validity. *Psychological Science, 12,* 163–170.

Cunningham, W. A., Zelazo, P. D., Packer, D. J., & Van Bavel, J. J. (2007). The iterative reprocessing model: A multilevel framework for attitudes and evaluation. *Social Cognition, 25,* 736–760.

Deutsch, R., & Gawronski, B. (2009). When the method makes a difference: Antagonistic effects on "automatic evaluations" as a function of task characteristics of the measure. *Journal of Experimental Social Psychology, 45,* 101–114.

Devine, P. G. (1989). Stereotypes and prejudice: Their automatic and controlled components. *Journal of Personality and Social Psychology, 56,* 5–18.

Eiser, J. R., Fazio, R. H., Stafford, T., & Prescott, T. J. (2003). Connectionist simulation of attitude learning: Asymmetries in the acquisition of positive and negative evaluations. *Personality and Social Psychology Bulletin, 29,* 1221–1235.

Fazio, R. H. (1990). Multiple processes by which attitudes guide behavior: The MODE model as an integrative framework. *Advances in Experimental Social Psychology, 23,* 75–109.

Fazio, R. H. (2007). Attitudes as object-evaluation associations of varying strength. *Social Cognition, 25*, 603.

Fiske, S., & Linville, P. W. (1980). What does the concept of schema buy us? *Personality and Social Psychology Bulletin, 6*, 543–557.

Fiske, S., & Taylor, S. E. (1991). *Social cognition* (2nd ed.). New York: McGraw-Hill.

Fodor, J. A., & Pylyshyn, Z. (1988). Connectionism and cognitive architecture: A critical analysis. *Cognition, 28*, 3–71.

Foroni, F., & Semin, G. (2011). Not all implicit measures of attitudes are created equal: Evidence from an embodiment perspective. *Journal of Experimental Social Psychology.*

Gaertner, S. L., & McLaughlin, J. P. (1983). Racial stereotypes: Associations and ascriptions of positive and negative characteristics. *Social Psychology Quarterly, 46*, 23–30.

Gallese, V. (2001). The 'shared manifold' hypothesis: From mirror neurons to empathy. *Journal of Consciousness Studies, 8*, 33–50.

Gallese, V. (2007). Before and below 'theory of mind': Embodied simulation and the neural correlates of social cognition. *Philosophical Transactions of the Royal Society, 362*, 659–669.

Gawronski, B., & Bodenhausen, G. V. (2006). Associative and propositional processes in evaluation: an integrative review of implicit and explicit attitude change. *Psychological Bulletin, 132*, 692.

Gawronski, B., Hofmann, W., & Wilbur, C. J. (2006). Are "implicit" attitudes unconscious? *Consciousness and Cognition, 15*, 485–499.

Gibson, J. J. (1977). The theory of affordances. In R. Shaw & J. Bransford (Eds.), *Perceiving, acting, and knowing: toward an ecological psychology* (pp. 67–82). Hillsdale, NJ: Lawrence Erlbaum.

Gilbert, D. T., & Osborne, R. E. (1989). Thinking backward: Some curable and incurable consequences of cognitive busyness. *Journal of Personality and Social Psychology, 57*, 940–949.

Govorun, O., & Payne, B. (2006). Ego-depletion and prejudice: Separating automatic and controlled components. *Social Cognition, 24*, 111–136.

Hall, D., & Payne, B. K. (2010). Unconscious attitudes, unconscious influence, and challenges to self-control. In Y. Trope, K. Ochsner, & R. Hassin (Eds.), *Social, cognitive, and neuroscientific approaches to self-control*. New York: Oxford University Press.

Higgins, E. T. (1996). Knowledge activation: Accessibility, applicability, and salience. In E. T. Higgins & A. W. Kruglanski (Eds.), *Social psychology: Handbook of basic principles* (pp. 184–210). New York: Guilford Press.

Higgins, E., Bargh, J., & Lombardi, W. (1985). Nature of priming effects on categorization. *Journal of Experimental Psychology: Learning, Memory, and Cognition, 11*, 59–69.

Hilton, J., & von Hippel, W. (1996). Stereotypes. *Annual Review of Psychology, 47*, 237–271.

Hofmann, W. & Wilson, T. D. (2010). Consciousness, introspection, and the adaptive unconscious. In: B. Gawronski, & B. K. Payne (Eds.), *Handbook of implicit social cognition: Measurement, theory, and applications* (pp. 197–215). New York: Guilford Press.

Jacoby, L. L., & Kelley, C. M. (1987). Unconscious influences of memory for a prior event. *Personality and Social Psychology Bulletin, 13*, 314–336.

Jacoby, L. L., Kelley, C. M., Brown, J., & Jasechko, J. (1989). Becoming famous overnight: Limits on the ability to avoid unconscious influences of the past. *Journal of Personality and Social Psychology, 56*, 326–338.

Jacoby, L., Kelley, C., & Dywan, J. (1989). Memory attributions. *Varieties of memory and consciousness: Essays in honour of Endel Tulving* (pp. 391–422). Hillsdale, NJ: Erlbaum.

Jacoby, L., & Whitehouse, K. (1989). An illusion of memory: False recognition influenced by unconscious perception. *Journal of Experimental Psychology: General, 118*, 126–135.

James, W. (1890). *The principles of psychology*. New York: Holt.

Keijzer, F. (2002). Representation in dynamic and embedded cognition. *Cognitive Systems Research, 3*, 275–288.

Kelley, C. M., & Jacoby, L. L. (1990). The construction of subjective experience: Memory attributions. *Mind & Language, 5*, 49–68.

Kirsh, D. (2009). Problem solving and situated cognition. In P. Robbins & M. Aydede (Eds.), *The Cambridge handbook of situated cognition* (pp. 236–263). New York: Cambridge University Press.

Kunda, Z., & Spencer, S. (2003). When do stereotypes come to mind and when do they color judgment? A goal-based theoretical framework for stereotype activation and application. *Psychological Bulletin, 129*, 522–544.

Loersch, C., & Payne, B. K. (2011). The situated inference model: An integrative account of the effects of primes on perception, behavior, and motivation. *Perspectives on Psychological Science, 6*, 234–252.

Macrae, C., Milne, A., & Bodenhausen, G. (1994). Stereotypes as energy-saving devices: A peek inside the cognitive toolbox. *Journal of Personality and Social Psychology, 66*, 37–47.

Marcel, A. (1983). Conscious and unconscious perception: An approach to the relations between phenomenal experience and perceptual processes. *Cognitive Psychology, 15*, 238–300.

Markus, H., Crane, M., Bernstein, S., & Siladi, M. (1982). Self-schemas and gender. *Journal of Personality and Social Psychology, 42*, 38–50.

Mazzarello, P. (1999). A unifying concept: The history of cell theory. *Nature Cell Biology, 1*, E13–E15.

Niedenthal, P. M., Barsalou, L. W., Winkielman, P., Krauth-Gruber, S., & Ric, F. (2005). Embodiment in attitudes, social perception, and emotion. *Personality and Social Psychology Review, 9*, 184–211.

Nisbett, R., & Wilson, T. D. (1977). Telling more than we can know: Verbal reports on mental processes. *Psychological Review, 84*, 231–259.

Page, M. (2000). Connectionist modeling in psychology: A localist manifesto. *Behavioral and Brain Sciences, 23*, 443–467.

Payne, B. K. (2001). Prejudice and perception: The role of automatic and controlled processes in misperceiving a weapon. *Journal of Personality and Social Psychology, 81*, 181–192.

Payne, B. K., Burkley, M., & Stokes, M. B. (2008). Why do implicit and explicit attitude tests diverge? The role of structural fit. *Journal of Personality and Social Psychology, 94*, 16–31.

Payne, B. K., Cheng, C. M., Govorun, O., & Stewart, B. (2005). An inkblot for attitudes: Affect misattribution as implicit measurement. *Journal of Personality and Social Psychology, 89*, 277–293.

Payne, B. K., Hall, D., Cameron, C. D., & Bishara, A. (2010). A process model of affect misattribution. *Personality and Social Psychology Bulletin, 36*, 1397–1408.

Payne, B. K., Jacoby, L. L., & Lambert, A. J. (2004). Memory monitoring and the control of stereotype distortion. *Journal of Experimental Social Psychology, 40*, 52–64.

Rauss, K., Schwartz, S., & Pourtois, G. (2011). Top-down effects on early visual processing in humans: A predictive coding framework. *Neuroscience and Biobehavioral Reviews, 35*, 1237–1253.

Read, S. J., Vanman, E. J., & Miller, L. (1997). Connectionism, parallel constraint satisfaction processes, and Gestalt principles: (Re)introducing cognitive dynamics to social psychology. *Personality and Social Psychology Review, 1*, 26–53.

Robbins, P., & Aydede, M. (2009) *The Cambridge handbook of situated cognition*. New York: Cambridge University Press.

Rumelhart, D. E., McClelland, J. L., & the PDP Research Group. (1987). *Parallel distributed processing* (Vol. 1). Cambridge, MA: MIT Press.

Schwarz, N. (2007). Attitude construction: Evaluation in context. *Social Cognition, 25*, 638–656.

Semin, G. R., & Cacioppo, J. T. (2009). From embodied representation to co-regulation. In J. A. Pineda (Ed.), *Mirror neuron systems: Role of mirroring processes in social cognition* (pp. 107–120). Totowa, NJ: The Humana Press.

Sloman, S. A. (1996). The empirical case for two systems of reasoning. *Psychological Bulletin, 119*, 3–22.

Smith, E. R. (1996). What do connectionism and social psychology offer each other? *Journal of Personality and Social Psychology, 70*, 893–912.

Smith, E. R. (1998). Mental representation and memory. In D. T. Gilbert, S. T. Fiske, & G. Lindsey (Eds.), *Handbook of social psychology* (4th ed., Vol. 2, pp. 391–445). New York: McGraw-Hill.

Smith, E. R., & DeCoster, J. (2000). Dual-process models in social and cognitive psychology: Conceptual integration and links to underlying memory systems. *Personality and Social Psychology Review, 4*, 108–131.

Smith, E. R., & Semin, G. R. (2004). Socially situated cognition: Cognition in its social context. *Advances in Experimental Social Psychology, 36*, 53–117.

Smolensky, P. (1988). On the proper treatment of connectionism. *Behavioral and Brain Sciences, 11*, 1–74.

Sparrow, B., Liu, J., & Wegner, D. M. (2011). Google effects on memory: Cognitive consequences of having information at our fingertips. *Science, 333*, 776–778.

Squire, L. R., & Zola, S. M. (1996). Structure and function of declarative and nondeclarative memory systems. *Proceedings of the National Academy of Sciences, 93*, 13515–13522.

Srull, T. K. (1981). Person memory: Some tests of associative storage and retrieval models. *Journal of Experimental Psychology: Human Learning and Memory, 7*, 440–463.

Srull, T. K., & Wyer, R. S. (1979). The role of category accessibility in the interpretation of information about persons: Some determinants and implications. *Journal of Personality and Social Psychology, 37*, 1660–1672.

Todorov, A., & Uleman, J. (2003). The efficiency of binding spontaneous trait inferences to actors' faces. *Journal of Experimental Social Psychology, 39*, 549–562.

Uhlmann, E. L., Pizarro, D. A., & Bloom, P. (2008). Varieties of unconscious social cognition. *Journal for the Theory of Social Behaviour, 38*, 293–322.

Uleman, J. (1987). Consciousness and control: The case of spontaneous trait inferences. *Personality and Social Psychology Bulletin, 13*, 337–354.

Varela, F. J., Thompson, E., & Rosch, E. (1992). *The embodied mind: Cognitive science and human experience*. Cambridge, MA: MIT Press.

von Helmholtz, H. (2000). Concerning the perceptions in general. *Visual perception: Essential readings* (pp. 24–44). New York: Psychology Press.

Wegner, D. M. (2002). *The illusion of conscious will*. Cambridge, MA: MIT Press.

Wegner, D., Erber, R., & Raymond, P. (1991). Transactive memory in close relationships. *Journal of Personality and Social Psychology, 61*, 923–929.

Wilson, T. D., Lindsey, S., & Schooler, T. Y. (2000). A model of dual attitudes. *Psychological Review, 107*, 101–126.

Witt, J. K., Kemmerer, D., Linkenauger, S. A., & Culham, J. (2010). A functional role for motor simulation in identifying tools. *Psychological Science, 21*, 1215–1219.

Wyer, R. S., Jr. (2007). Principles of mental representation. In A. W. Kruglanski & E. T. Higgins (Eds.), *Social psychology: Handbook of basic principles* (2nd ed., pp. 285–307). New York: Guilford Press.

Wyer, R. S., Jr., & Carlston, D. E. (1979). *Social cognition, inference, and attribution*. Hillsdale, NJ: Erlbaum.

Wyer, R. S., Jr., & Carlston, D. E. (1994). The cognitive representation of persons and events. In R. S. Wyer, Jr., & T. K. Srull (Eds.), *Handbook of social cognition* (2nd ed., Vol. 1, pp. 41–98). Hillsdale, NJ: Erlbaum

Automaticity

Ap Dijksterhuis

Abstract

This chapter on automaticity centers around two distinctions that are vital for understanding human behavior: The first is that some behavior is voluntary, whereas other behavior is involuntary. The second is that some behavior is conscious, whereas other behavior is unconscious. In the first part of this chapter, classic lines of research on automaticity—research on incubation, on introspection, on skill acquisition, on preconscious processing, and on imitation and priming—are briefly reviewed. The second part of the chapter deals with our current understanding of the relation between goals, attention, and consciousness. Attention and consciousness are clearly distinguished, and it is argued that goals guide attention, but not consciousness. The chapter ends with a contemporary perspective on control and on the relation between consciousness, goals, and flexibility in behavior.

Key Words: Automaticity, unconscious, consciousness, goals, attention, control, flexibility

"It wasn't me, it was my head!"

Four-year old Julius Strick (cousin of the author) after his father asked why he had changed his mind yet again.

The origins of our own actions can sometimes seem mysterious. We do things, we feel things, we think things, and we far from always know—or at least think we know—why. We often do things that are clearly against our better judgment ("Why am I eating this chocolate bar?"), and we may even find ourselves doing things without any apparent cause at all ("So why am I in the secretary's office? Was there something I was going to do here"?). Because it sometimes feels as if the forces driving our actions are coming from nowhere (or, just as confusing, from everywhere), we can become aware of the fact that our thoughts and actions are inconsistent and that we seem to accommodate multiple agents that "we" lack control over. We can choose between chocolate and bubblegum; we first think we prefer chocolate, but at the very last second we pick bubblegum. This sensation of lack of control was already documented by Socrates and Plato (380 B.C.)—though not in the domain of a choice between chocolate and bubblegum—and it can be vividly experienced by an intelligent four-year old boy.

The feeling of being a human ping-pong ball, whose movements are determined by various unidentified forces, points at the two most important reasons that the topic of *automaticity* is both intriguing and important. The first is the notion that some behavior is clearly *involuntary*. Again, we do things while it is not clear that we actually want to do them, and we even do things that we (or at least "part of us") do not want to do. ("Why did I order the pastrami sandwich when I reminded myself this morning to order the salad for lunch?"). The second is that we are *unaware* of many things. We routinely do things without being conscious of the reasons, or even without being conscious of the action itself.

In this chapter on automaticity, the starring roles will be played by these two important psychological distinctions: the extent to which our behavior is involuntary (versus voluntary), and the extent to which our behavior is unconscious (versus conscious).

This chapter continues with a brief discussion of various lines of thought and research that form the foundations of contemporary automaticity research. In the next section, various definitional issues are discussed. The second major part of the chapter deals with the relation between the two psychological distinctions alluded to above. Intuitively, most people think that there is a strong (cor)relation between voluntariness and consciousness, in that people are usually aware of voluntary behavior and often unaware of involuntary behavior. In addition, people think that voluntary control of behavior is the consequence of, or at least strongly related to, consciousness (Wegner, 2002). This position is at least partly rooted in theorizing from the 19th century. In those days, the term *unconscious* was often used to refer to processes that we now call *unintentional* (or indeed, *involuntary*) processes. For example, Darwin talked about "unconscious selection" processes in nature and contrasted such processes with the intentional selection processes used by animal breeders and farmers (Bargh & Morsella, 2008). However, as will be discussed later, the equation of unconscious with unintentional is not supported by recent neuroscientific and psychological research.

Foundations of Research on Automaticity

Contemporary research on automaticity is rooted in a number of older ideas and research traditions. Most of these speak to both the questions of which actions are voluntary or involuntary and which actions are conscious or unconscious (see also Dijksterhuis, 2010, for a more elaborate discussion). The term *automaticity* will be defined more precisely later, but for now it suffices to conceive as automatic psychological processes those processes that are involuntary, unconscious, or both.

Incubation and Unconscious Thought

The possibility that thought processes serving creativity and problem solving can ensue unconsciously has been observed by many great thinkers through history. St. Thomas Aquinas, Shakespeare, Dante, Goethe, Leonardo da Vinci, and Schopenhauer all marvelled about the unconscious. It is not a coincidence that these particular observers recognized

the wonders of the unconscious because they were not only more intelligent and inquisitive than most people but also, most of all, very creative. Creative people have long emphasized the importance of the unconscious. Mozart, when asked to explain his extraordinary creativity, said he just "heard" his compositions: "...the whole, though it be long, stand almost complete and finished in my mind, so that I can survey it, like a fine picture or a beautiful statue, at a glance. Nor do I hear in my imagination successively, but I hear them, as it were, all at once. What a delight this is I cannot tell!" (Andreasen, 2005, p. 40). Mozart's compositions were the result of unconscious processes that caused music to simply pop up in consciousness. Scientists have given similar accounts. Einstein did, often suddenly and unexpectedly, simply "see" solutions to scientific problems. Poincaré's (1913) detailed introspective account of his most important mathematical discovery is justifiably famous. At first, he could not solve a mathematical problem and went to the countryside with the goal to relax and to not think about it for a few days. Completely unexpectedly, the solution to the problem came like a flash at the exact moment he boarded a train. Researchers in the creativity domain have named this process—whereby thought continues in the absence of conscious guidance—incubation (Wallas, 1926). Others have called it unconscious thought (Andreasen, 2005; Dijksterhuis, 2004; see also Schopenhauer, 1851).

Various empirical demonstrations of incubation effects—including effects of sleep—were recently published by Stickgold and colleagues (e.g., Stickgold & Walker, 2004). In one of their experiments on insight, participants were asked to perform a somewhat boring task in which they had to do some simple arithmetic. Unknown to the participants, the task could be done much faster after one had discovered a specific rule. This rule, however, was not obvious. All participants had a go at the task for some time, after which they engaged in other activities for a while. Some participants were actually allowed to sleep. As it turned out, 59% of the participants who slept discovered the hidden rule (and became faster), whereas only 25% of the participants who did not sleep discovered the rule.

Dijksterhuis and colleagues (Dijksterhuis, Bos, Nordgren, & van Baaren, 2006; Dijksterhuis & Nordgren, 2006) have applied the idea of incubation to decision making. In many of their experiments, they gave participants information on several choice alternatives (e.g., houses, cars, roommates). Participants then either made their choices immediately after reading the decision information, after some period of conscious thought, or after a period during which they were distracted but during which it is assumed they thought unconsciously. Not only are unconscious thinkers often quite capable of making a decision, but their decisions are often better than decisions made after conscious thought or those made without thought (i.e., immediately after information acquisition).

Poor Introspective Abilities

A second important notion is that we often show poor introspective abilities (Wilson, 2002). Just as we are not able to look through a computer screen to see what exactly happens inside, we are usually unaware of the inner workings of the mind. Our conscious knowledge about ourselves is limited, and many thoughts, feelings, and actions come from behind a veil that we can often barely peer beneath.

Long ago, the German researcher Watt (1905) showed that we do not have conscious access to how we think. In his delightful experiment, participants were presented with nouns (e.g., trout) and were asked to come up with an association as quickly as they could. Sometimes participants were requested to name a superordinate word (trout–fish), whereas on other occasions they were asked to come up with a part (trout–fin). This way, thinking could be divided into four stages: the instructions (e.g., superordinate or part), the presentation of the noun (e.g., trout), the search for an appropriate association, and the verbalization of the reply (e.g., fish). Participants were asked to introspect on all four stages separately, to assess the contribution of consciousness during each stage. Watt first asked people what they thought the stage was where the real thinking takes place, and there was general agreement that this was the third stage. The third stage—the search for an association—represented actual thought and was therefore seen as the most interesting stage. However, unlike the other stages, this stage was introspectively blank: Participants could not report anything. The instruction in combination with the presentation of the noun automatically started the thinking process. The thinking itself was unconscious, at least until the answer surfaced.

People are often also unaware of the reasons for their actions, even when these actions are quite important. A well-known social psychological example is the bystander effect: The more people witness an accident, the less likely it is that someone will intervene (Latane & Darley, 1970). However, when witnesses are asked why they did not intervene, they tend to come up with other reasons. Such effects, whereby people do something because of reason x but claim they do it because of y, have been extensively documented by Nisbett and Wilson (1977).

A strong example of poor introspection on the causes of people's behavior comes from recent research by Nordgren, van der Pligt, and van Harreveld (2006), in their research on the hot/cold empathy gap (Loewenstein, 1996). These researchers had some participants take a challenging memory test while they were experiencing mild pain (they kept their nondominant arm in a bucket of ice water). Indeed, compared with control participants, who had kept their hand in room-temperature water, the participants in pain underperformed on the memory test. Only 10 minutes after the memory test, some of the participants who had experienced pain before were again asked to keep their hand in ice water, whereas others were not—they placed their hand in room temperature water. Participants were then asked to explain their earlier poor performance on the memory test. The participants who experienced pain while they explained the cause correctly attributed their performance to the earlier pain. However, participants who made their attributions pain free did so to a much lesser extent, despite the fact that they were in pain only 10 minutes ago.

Skill Acquisition

William James wrote extensively about the importance of habits. He advised young people to develop useful social and mental habits: "We must make automatic and habitual, as early as possible, as many useful actions as we can" (1890, p. 122). In his various writings, he stressed two good reasons for developing habits. The first is that strong habits invariably lead to appropriate behavior (which is also why he warned against developing bad habits). The second is that conscious thought is a scarce resource, so the more one can do without it, the better it is. We can consciously think about important matters—such as an upcoming meeting with the dean—during many routine daily activities, because these routines do not need conscious guidance. Important goals would be much more difficult to fulfill if things such as driving, taking a shower, or brushing one's teeth required conscious guidance (see also Aarts & Dijksterhuis, 2000).

Shiffrin and Schneider (1977) performed an important set of experiments on skill acquisition. In their experiments, participants looked at an array of stimuli with the goal of searching for a particular target stimulus (e.g., the letter *G*) as quickly as possible. Participants practiced, and as one would expect, the more distracter stimuli depicted in an array, the longer it took to find the target stimulus. However, this effect disappeared over time. After a period of practice, finding the target became an automatic process, so that the number of distracter stimuli (4, 9, or 16) no longer influenced the speed with which the target was detected. The key in the Shiffrin and Schneider (1977) experiments was attention. At first, participants searched for the targets by devoting attention to each stimulus separately. After practice, attention became parallel, in that multiple stimuli could be attended to simultaneously. Such processes can often be witnessed in real life, such as when people try to master driving a car.

Preconscious Processing

Another vital line of research can be traced back to the general theoretical work (not the psychoanalytic work) of Sigmund Freud. The logic behind the notion of preconscious processing is that before something reaches consciousness, some kind of constructive perceptual or conceptual analysis has to take place. For example, we do not "see" a door. We see a blue, rectangular shape, a little bigger than a person, surrounded by something large and white. Only after some preconscious construction processes are we consciously aware of the fact that it is a door.

The literature on *selective attention* (Broadbent, 1958; Moray, 1959; Treisman, 1960) provided further evidence for preconscious processing. Various researchers demonstrated that we perceive much more than what reaches consciousness and that information that we do not attend to is "filtered out." For example, Treisman (1960) found that a story presented to an unattended ear was sometimes attended when it became relevant for the story presented to the attended ear. Another vivid example is the cocktail-party effect (Moray, 1959). At a party where people are chatting in various small groups, an individual generally only attends to the conversation in his or her own group. However, when someone else in an adjacent group mentions that individual's first name, he or she hears this immediately.

Recent research on *inattentional* blindness and *change* blindness also fits this tradition. In a spectacular demonstration, Simon and Chabris (1999) showed that when people watch a group of people playing basketball with the goal of counting the number of passes, they can be completely oblivious to a gorilla (a person dressed as a gorilla, that is) walking through the group. Perceived stimuli that are normally extremely salient can fail to reach consciousness when attention is directed elsewhere. This experiment—a movie demo of which is now probably used by the majority of Introductory Psychology teachers—demonstrates in a remarkable way just how important attention is. This will be discussed more extensively later in this chapter.

Imitation and Priming

Human behavior is to some extent governed by subtle (social) cues in the environment. People are rarely consciously aware of such subtle effects of stimuli on behavior. William James (1980) recognized that merely thinking about an action can be enough to evoke the action itself. When we see a bowl with peanuts, while having a conversation in a bar, we absentmindedly reach for it. Central to this process of ideomotor action is that the mere activation of the mental representation (by either thought or perception) is enough to elicit overt behavior. This process has consequences for our understanding of imitation and for priming effects.

The more that researchers investigate imitation, the more they realize it is ubiquitous. Research has shown that people mimic postures, gestures, facial expression, and a multitude of speech-related phenomena (Chartrand & van Baaren, 2008; Dijksterhuis, Chartrand & Aarts, 2007). Chartrand and Bargh (1999) investigated whether people might even automatically mimic completely mundane and inconsequential actions such as foot shaking or nose rubbing. In their first experiment, a confederate worked on a task with participants, and this confederate was instructed to either rub her nose or shake her foot while working on this task. During the few minutes during which the confederate and participants worked together, the behavior of the participants was surreptitiously videotaped. Their hypothesis, that participants would indeed mimic the behavior of the confederate, was confirmed. Under conditions in which the confederate rubbed her nose, participants engaged in more nose rubbing than foot shaking, whereas the opposite was true when participants interacted with the confederate who shook her foot. As one may have expected, participants were completely unaware of their imitative behavior. Chartrand and Bargh (1999) replicated and extended their findings in further experiments.

Bargh, Chen, and Burrows (1996, Experiment 2) were the first to report effects of priming on motor behavior. In their experiment, half of the participants were primed with the category of "elderly," whereas others were not. The participants were primed by exposing them to words related to the elderly (e.g., *gray, bingo, walking stick, Florida*). Participants in the control condition completed the same task without exposure to the critical, elderly-related, words. After participants finished the priming task, they were told that the experiment had finished. However, the time it took participants to walk from the experimental room to the nearest elevator was surreptitiously recorded. The data showed that participants primed with the elderly category walked significantly slower than control participants. Participants displayed behavior in line with the activated stereotype of elderly people. Elderly people are associated with slowness, and activating this stereotype led to slowness among the participants. Later, Dijksterhuis, Spears, and Lepinasse (2001) and Kawakami, Young, and Dovidio (2002) published conceptual replications in which they demonstrated that priming participants with "elderly" similarly reduced speed on a reaction-time task.

Priming effects on behavior are not confined to effects on motor behavior. Dijksterhuis and van Knippenberg (1998) improved people's intellectual performance by priming them with a corresponding stereotype. They requested some of their participants to think about college professors and to write down everything that came to mind regarding the typical attributes of professors, whereas others were not given this task. In an ostensibly unrelated second phase, participants were asked to answer 42 general knowledge questions that were taken from the game "Trivial Pursuit" (such as "What is the capital of Bangladesh?" a. Dhaka, b. Bangkok, c. Hanoi, d. Delhi). In line with the prevailing stereotype of professors as intelligent, primed participants answered more questions correctly than did no-prime control participants. In other experiments, it was shown that participants could also be led to perform worse on a general knowledge task by having them first think about soccer hooligans, a social group that is associated with stupidity.

What these effects show is that when people strongly associate two concepts, such as professors and intelligence, priming one concept can lead to behavioral effects corresponding to the second concept. Zhong and Liljenquist (2006) recently published a spectacular example of another such effect. They hypothesized that people tend to associate a physical sense of personal hygiene with a moral sense of being virtuous because this association is promoted by many of the world's religions. The term *clean* is, in many languages, associated with a clean body as well as with a clean mind. The researchers' experiments indeed showed effects of this association. People who were reminded of one of their own morally dubious acts in the past experienced a stronger desire to clean themselves. In one experiment, some participants had to recall a morally compromising act they had performed in the past, whereas others did not do this. Afterward, all participants could choose between two small gifts, a pencil and an antiseptic wipe. Most participants who recalled their own morally questionable behavior chose the wipe, whereas this was not true for control participants.

It should be noted that such priming effects do not affect behavior per se, in the sense that they do not evoke new actions. People do not walk the hallway or complete a general knowledge questionnaire because they are primed; rather, they do so because an experimenter asks them to. However, they do it slower or faster or better or worse, etcetera, because they are primed. Rather than eliciting new behavior, such priming effects change the parameters of ongoing behavior.

Definitional Issues

The research areas discussed above are quite different, and combined they show that automaticity is a multidimensional concept. Effects of incubation demonstrate that important mental activity takes place *unconsciously*, that is, outside of conscious awareness. In addition, such effects feel as if they do not require *effort or attention*. The work on people's lack of introspective abilities again points at the importance of the *unconscious*, but also at the fact that human behavior does not necessarily follow conscious choice or conscious *volition*. The experiments on skill acquisition are primarily concerned with *effort*: Practice can lead to automatized behavior that does not require any effort. The literature on preconscious processing again emphasizes the importance of *unconscious* processes, but also of *volition*. What we perceive is not simply a matter of conscious choice. Finally, priming effects show essentially that behavior is not always *voluntary* nor the consequence of a *conscious* choice.

For some time, the prevailing view on the concepts of automaticity and its counterpart, control, was that they created a dichotomy based on various dimensions (e.g., Posner and Snyder, 1975; but see Kahneman, 1972). Automatic action was *unintentional*, it did not need *attention*, it occurred outside of *conscious awareness*, and once started, it was *uncontrollable*. Conversely, controlled action was intentional, effortful, controllable, and dependent on conscious guidance. The problem with such a multidimensional dichotomy was that it did not capture the full range of human behaviors very well. In fact, behavior is rarely controlled on all dimensions, and although behaviors that are fully automatic do exist, such behaviors (e.g., reflexes) are not the ones psychologists are interested in.

Later, the dominant view became that these four different dimensions (or "the four horsemen"; see Bargh, 1994) should be treated as being at least partly independent. Most behavior is automatic on some dimensions and controlled on others. Driving a car is intentional and controllable, but also largely effortless (at least for a skilled driver), and many of the subactions required do not need any conscious guidance. This taxonomy has been extremely helpful in understanding various social psychological phenomena, including key social psychological processes such as attitudinal processes and prejudice.

It should be noted that not all areas of psychology define the key concepts in the same way. For example, some researchers—mainly cognitive psychologists—chose to define unconscious processes in an extremely narrow fashion (e.g., Loftus & Klinger, 1992). Basically, unconscious was defined as subliminal, and some cognitive psychologists still maintain that unconscious psychological processes are dumb and only capable of performing routine actions. As Bargh and Morsella (2008) remarked, unconscious processes—like conscious processes—have been evolved to deal with naturally occurring stimuli and not with very subtle, subliminal stimuli. Assessing the unconscious "in terms of processing subliminal stimuli is analogous to evaluating the intelligence of a fish based on its behavior out of water" (Bargh & Morsella, 2008, p. 74). Social psychologists, however, have defined the term *unconscious* with reference to psychological processes rather than to the perception of stimuli. This not only does better justice to the historical use of the term but also makes for a much more insightful analysis.

Recently, various researchers proposed that a more simple decomposition of automaticity is possible by incorporating the concept of goals (e.g., Moors & De Houwer, 2006; see also Bargh Gollwitzer, Lee-Chai, Barndollar, & Trotschel, 2001; Dijksterhuis, 2010). A key psychological distinction, as argued above, is whether behavior is voluntary or not. In light of current knowledge,

one could make a more precise distinction among actions that are goal directed, goal dependent, or not goal dependent. Behavior that is goal directed, that is, behavior that serves a proximal goal, can be said to be intentional (Moors & De Houwer, 2006). Behavior that is goal dependent is only evoked when a specific goal is active. It is important to realize that in such a framework (see also Moors & De Houwer, 2006), there is no need for a separate place for control. Control is always defined as the capacity to stop or change ongoing behavior. However, this is a goal. That is, control is simply a specific goal—namely to stop or change what one is currently doing. The role of attention (or effort) in this framework is that it is a consequence of goals. The extent to which psychological processes are aimed at completing goals is the main determinant of the amount of attention such psychological processes require (Aarts, 2007; Badgaiyan, 2000; Dijksterhuis & Aarts, 2010; Hassin, Bargh, Engell, & McCulloch, 2009).

Hence, the four horsemen of automaticity can be brought back to two: The first question one can ask is whether behavior requires conscious guidance or not. The second question is whether behavior relies on active goals, and if so, whether behavior is goal directed or merely goal dependent (see also Dijksterhuis, 2010). The answer to the latter question also speaks to the role of (or need for) attention or effort because attention is largely driven by goals (see Dijksterhuis & Aarts, 2010, for a more elaborate treatment). In addition, the latter feature also includes the role of control. Control is, according to this framework, a special goal. In this chapter, the focus will be on consciousness and on goals, whereas the distinction between goal directedness and goal dependency will not be dealt with (see Chapter 23).

Relation Between Goals and Consciousness

As mentioned before, many people implicitly assume that volition and consciousness are intimately linked. It is tempting to think that volitional behavior is accompanied by conscious awareness or even caused by conscious decisions. Likewise, people often assume that involuntary behavior is caused by unconscious forces. However, research—especially research done in the last 30 years—shows that this link is not nearly as strong as often suggested. In fact, one could say that the aim of automaticity research is to investigate the link (or better, the absence thereof) between volition and consciousness. As a consequence, advocates of automaticity research often find themselves trying to convince others of the weakness of that link.

The idea that consciousness is necessary to evoke volitional behavior was severely shaken by a famous experiment by Libet and colleagues (Libet, Gleason, Wright, & Pearl, 1983). They asked participants to freely choose when to move their index fingers. Participants were asked to report when exactly they decided to start the movement, while the experimenters measured the movement itself and the onset of the brain's readiness potentials preparing the movement. As expected, the conscious decision preceded the act itself (roughly by one fourth of one second). However, readiness potentials could be identified up to a full second before the actual movement, clearly demonstrating that the brain started to prepare the movement long before the conscious "decision" to make the movement was made.

Libet's work is controversial. Arguably the most important problem in interpreting Libet's findings is that one can argue that the movement still starts with a conscious decision (van de Grind, 2002). After all, the chain of events starts with an experimenter instructing participants to move their finger and, obviously, participants are consciously aware of this instruction. One could conclude that participants unconsciously decided *when* to make the actual movement, but not *whether* to make the movement in the first place.

Recently, Soon and colleagues (Soon, Brass, Heinze, & Haynes, 2008) extended the findings by Libet and colleagues. They changed the paradigm in such a way that participants chose not only chose when to engage in a specific act but also which one of two possible acts to engage in. They replicated Libet's work and found readiness potentials (in supplementary motor area) some time before participants reported making a conscious decision about which act to engage in. More importantly, they found activity predictive of the specific act in the frontal and parietal cortex up to 10 seconds before the actual act. In other words, we unconsciously "choose" which behavior to engage in long before we are consciously aware of it.

The assumption that the role of consciousness in volitional behavior is much more modest than long assumed was also emphasized by recent research showing that goals and higher cognitive processes that rely on cortical brain areas can be modulated by unconscious stimuli. In a recent experiment, for instance, Lau and Passingham (2007) instructed participants to prepare either a phonological judgment or a semantic judgment on an upcoming word. In some trials, however, they were subliminally primed to do the opposite. On these trials, it was found that

brain activity in areas relevant to the instructed task was reduced, whereas activity related to the primed task was enhanced. The cognitive control system, in other words, can be activated by subliminal stimuli. In addition, Pessiglione and colleagues (Pessiglione et al., 2007) showed that strength of motivation can be subliminally primed. Participants in their experiment did a task whereby they could win money on successive trials by squeezing a handgrip. The amount of money at stake (one pound versus one penny) was subliminally primed during each trial, and it indeed affected force of handgrip, along with skin conductance and activation in the ventral palladium, an area devoted to emotional and motivational output of the limbic system. In an extension of this research, Bijleveld, Custers, and Aarts (2009) recently showed that people recruit more resources in response to high (compared with low) subliminal reward cues, but only when the reward requires considerable mental effort to obtain. This research demonstrates that people use reward information in a strategic manner to recruit resources, without this information ever reaching conscious awareness.

These findings concur with a growing body of literature from the social cognition domain showing that goals can affect higher cognitive processes and overt behavior without conscious awareness of the goal. For example, Bargh and colleagues (Bargh et al., 2001) unobtrusively exposed participants to words such as "strive" and "succeed" to prime an achievement goal and then gave them the opportunity to perform well by giving them anagrams. Participants primed with an achievement goal outperformed those who were not primed with the goal. Bargh et al. (2001) also demonstrated that such goal priming leads to qualities associated with motivational states or goal directedness, such as persistence and increased effort (for other such demonstrations, see e.g., Aarts, Custers, & Marien, 2008; Fitzsimons & Bargh, 2003; Shah, Friedman, & Kruglanski, 2002).

In sum, people become consciously aware of an act only after they unconsciously start to prepare for it. In addition, factors that affect people's strength of motivation can exert their influence unconsciously. Finally, goals can be primed and affect behavior while bypassing conscious awareness. Goals, in other words, do not rely on consciousness to guide behavior.

Relation Between Goals and Attention

Although consciousness may not be nearly as important for goal-directed action as once was thought, attention is. Attention is the vehicle with which goals affect overt behavior (Monsell & Driver, 2000). Attention is a functional process that selects and biases the incoming flow of information and internal representations in the service of effective goal achievement. Thus, the content of attention represents the goals that are active at a specific moment in time. If a goal could always be executed directly in the very same environment, attention would merely reflect the translation of a perceived relevant stimulus into a response in real time. However, because goals cannot always be acted on directly in the same situation, we often have to take temporal and spatial aspects into account. Moreover, the (social) environment often poses conflicts among our goals such that interfering information needs to be ignored or inhibited for effective goal performance to proceed. In short, attention does not only orient and alert the person to goal-relevant information, it also plays a supervisory role in translating goals into behavior (Posner & Fan, 2004).

Indeed, recent research has started to model goal-directed behavior in terms of executive control processes (Funahashi, 2001; Miller & Cohen, 2001; Baddeley & Logie, 1999). An important aim of this research is to understand how people maintain and manipulate information in the service of goal pursuit and to provide a neurocognitive account for the ability to guide attention and action in accord with goals. A common framework proposed in this research is that the prefrontal cortex (PFC), anterior cingulate cortex (ACC) and posterior parietal cortex (PPC) are the main areas taking care of attentional and control processes, consistent with theories of PFC function and the involvement of these areas in the distributed working memory system. Importantly, these cortical areas are believed to be part of a network for conscious processes and hence are implicated in volitional behavior (Baars & Franklin, 2003; Baddeley, 1993; Haggard, 2008; Smith & Jonides, 1999). Thus, the functionality and structure of executive control and working memory are examined by presenting participants *explicitly* with materials that they *explicitly* have to work on. That is, participants are explicitly instructed to keep goal information active over time or to ignore irrelevant information in order to keep focused on the goal, thereby assuming (at least implicitly) that these processes also occur during self-motivated performance. However, under this working assumption, it is difficult to understand how goal pursuit is supported by attention and higher cognitive processes that make use of executive control structures without the person being aware of it. That is, how

can goal-directed attention to, and transformation of, relevant information occur outside of conscious awareness?

One way to approach this issue is to propose that, in principle, the operation of higher cognitive processes does not depend much on the conscious state of the individual. In other words, conscious and unconscious goals (partly) rely on the same functional architecture of attention. Moreover, the same cognitive functions and hardware are recruited and shared to translate goals into behavior (Aarts, 2007; Badgaiyan, 2000; Hassin, Bargh, Engell, & McCulloch, 2009). Thus, goals modulate attention processes, irrespective of the (conscious or unconscious) source of the activation of the goal.

From work on working memory we know that the activation of semantic items decays in short-term memory over very short periods of time, usually within a couple of seconds, unless some intervention or goal holds the items active (Baddeley & Logie, 1999; McKone, 1995). Exploiting this notion, research has demonstrated that goals that are activated unconsciously can keep relevant information active as well. For instance, Aarts, Custers, and Holland (2007) examined how the accessibility of a desired goal after a short interval changes as a function of subliminally priming the goal. In one of their studies, participants were either primed with the goal to socialize or not, and after a delay of two minutes, the accessibility of the goal was assessed in a lexical decision task by measuring the recognition speed of words related to the goal. Results showed that the representation of the goal remained accessible when participants were primed to attain the goal, but that the sustained activation faded away quickly as soon as the desire to attain that goal was gone. Comparable persistent activation effects of unconsciously activated desired goal states have been obtained in other studies (Aarts, Gollwitzer, & Hassin, 2004; Bargh et al., 2001), suggesting that some kind of focus or rehearsal process keeps goal-relevant information active unconsciously.

Furthermore, recent work has started to explore whether humans can keep their eyes on their ongoing goal pursuit in an unconscious manner when competing goals or temptations conflict with these pursuits. For instance, if one wants to lose weight, one has to be able to resist the temptation to eat a late-night snack. People usually engage in this type of attentional process when they have to deal with interference that stems from other goals or temptations. An instance in which goals or temptations compete is commonly conceived of as requiring conscious and intentional control (see, e.g., work on delay of gratification; Mischel, Shoda & Rodriguez, 1989). However, there are studies that tell a somewhat different story. For instance, Shah and colleagues (2002) demonstrated that when participants are given an unconscious goal (by subliminal exposure to words representing the goal, e.g., of studying) they inhibit competing accessible goals (e.g., going out). This process of inhibition, in turn, facilitates achievement of the unconsciously activated goal. These findings provide support for the existence of an unconscious attention–inhibition mechanism that shields goals from distracting thoughts (see also Aarts et al., 2007; Fishbach, Friedman, & Kruglanski, 2003; Papies, Stroebe, & Aarts, 2008).

In sum, several lines of research suggest that goals can be translated into overt behavior outside the person's awareness of the activation and operation of the goal. Furthermore, unconscious goal pursuit is supported by attention that operates on higher cognitive processes according to principles of executive control and working memory. And these processes (and the information on which they operate) seem to run below the threshold of consciousness.

Relation Between Attention and Consciousness

Given that attention plays a key role in guiding goal-directed action, some wonder why consciousness is more or less irrelevant for launching goal-directed behavior. Isn't attention strongly linked to consciousness? The answer, based on recent insights from neuroscience, is that it is not. Researchers who advocate the importance of unconscious processes by demonstrating that important psychological processes do not need any conscious guidance (e.g., Bargh, Chen, & Burrows, 1996; Bargh et al., 2001; Dijksterhuis & Nordgren, 2006; Libet et al., 1983; Reber, 1967) often meet with resistance because it feels as if consciousness simply *must* be involved in these important processes. However, attention is the guiding force here, not conscious awareness. Part of the confusion arises because attention (especially top-down attention) and consciousness are correlated in real-life experiences. When one pays more attention to an incoming stimulus, the probability that one becomes consciously aware of it increases.

Attention and consciousness, however, are distinct. Increasingly, recent research and theorizing are aimed at understanding the distinction, and there is now some agreement that psychological processes

can best be understood as falling into one of the cells of a two-by-two taxonomy based on whether stimuli are attended to or not and whether they are reportable or not (i.e., whether one is consciously aware of them or not; Baars, 1997; Damasio, 1999; Dehaene, Changeux, Naccache, Sackur, & Sergent, 2006; Koch & Tsuchiya, 2006; Lamme, 2003; Wegner & Smart, 1997). An abundance of priming research shows that stimuli that do not reach conscious awareness can still influence various psychological processes, including overt behavior (see, e.g., Dijksterhuis & Bargh, 2001, for a review), but some degree of attention to these stimuli is necessary for these effects to occur. Likewise, recent research shows that people can engage in rather complicated activities in the absence of conscious awareness (Bargh et al., 2001; Dijksterhuis, Bos, Nordgren, & van Baaren, 2006); however, these processes are goal dependent and most likely do require a certain degree of attention (Bos, Dijksterhuis, & van Baaren, 2008). Conversely, people can be consciously—often fleetingly—aware of stimuli without paying (much) attention to them.

Whereas recent theorizing is mostly based on findings on visual perception, Wegner and Smart (1997) applied the above taxonomy to a broader domain. They distinguished between activation level and consciousness. Specifically, in addition to states of no activation (no attention, no consciousness) and full activation (both attention and consciousness), they also distinguished states of deep activation (stimuli that are attended but are unconscious) and surface activation (stimuli that are not attended but are conscious). An example of deep activation based on Wegner's own work (e.g., Wegner, 1994) is thoughts that are temporarily suppressed. Such thoughts are highly active, but do not appear in consciousness, at least not while suppression is successful. Good examples of surface activation are the sort of fleeting thoughts we may have when we daydream or associate freely. We do not pay attention to them, but they can briefly appear in consciousness.

To recapitulate, goals do not necessarily need consciousness, and it is certainly not the case that goals are only activated after people make a "conscious decision." Goal striving does require attention, though, and the main determinants of where people's attention is focused are most likely goals. The importance of attention may lead people to think that goals require consciousness because attention and consciousness are most likely correlated in real life: The more attention we pay to something, the more likely it is that it appears in consciousness. However, theoretically, attention and consciousness are orthogonal.

Control

In a chapter on automaticity, it is customary to also extensively discuss its counterpart: control. As alluded to earlier, at first automaticity and control were seen as opposites. This made sense because control was seen as something requiring conscious awareness. However, strictly speaking, control means nothing more or less than willfully being able to change or stop an ongoing psychological process (Dijksterhuis, 2010; Moors & De Houwer, 2006). Control, in other words, is simply a special goal: The goal to stop or change current behavior. As we have seen in the previous section, goals do usually not need conscious guidance, and therefore, control should not necessarily need consciousness either. If we, as we have always done, classify unconscious actions as automatic, the irony is complete: Control is automatic! Who would have thought so in the 1970s?

This change of perspective is the consequence of experiments showing that actions that we have always associated with control—such as preventing stereotypes from biasing our social judgments—can be executed without conscious guidance. Most of the early relevant work was done by researchers interested in prejudice, and this has always been a highly useful topic for investigating the interplay between automatic and controlled processes. Simply stated: Stereotype activation is largely automatic (Bargh, Chen, & Burrows, 1996; Devine, 1989), but also undesirable, so how we can control it?

Moskowitz, Gollwitzer, Wasel, and Schaal (1999) performed an interesting experiment demonstrating unconscious control. They recruited male participants who had chronic egalitarian goals toward women as well as participants who had no such goals. In the experiment, participants had to pronounce trait words as quickly as possible. Some of these traits were stereotypical for women and some were stereotypical for men. These trait words were preceded by a photograph of either a man or woman. Under normal circumstances, participants should show evidence of stereotype activation: Female traits should be pronounced more quickly when they follow a photograph of a woman than when they follow a photograph of a man. This was indeed found for people who had no goal to be egalitarian. However, for individuals who had the chronic goal to be egalitarian, no stereotype activation was apparent. In fact, they seemed to inhibit

stereotype activation, thereby successfully engaging in preconscious control. In other studies (Galinsky & Moskowitz, 2000), it was also found that preconscious control of stereotype activation was possible with temporary goals (such as perspective taking) rather than chronic goals (for more early examples, see Moskowitz, Li, & Kirk, 2004).

Such automatic control processes, however, are not confined to the domain of prejudice. Fishbach and colleagues (Fishbach et al., 2003; Trope & Fishbach, 2000; Myrseth, Fishbach, 2009) proved that people can unconsciously resist the effects of temptations. In a series of studies, Fishbach, Friedman, and Kruglanski (2003) divided people into two groups: people for whom a particular goal, such as staying slim or getting high grades, was important, and people for whom these goals were less important. They found, in a sequential lexical decision task, that goals may activate temptations for people for whom the goal is not all that important. For instance, studying may automatically lead to activation of tempting alternative courses of action such as watching TV. More importantly, people with strong goals demonstrated the opposite. For them, temptations activated the goal. That is, people with the goal of staying slim automatically activated this goal when confronted with a piece of chocolate, thereby increasing the chance of regulatory success. People do not need to be aware of the temptations for this powerful regulatory mechanism to be launched.

In summary, control, defined as stopping or changing the course of current (unwanted) action, can be achieved without conscious awareness of the unwanted behavior. In fact, control can take place on the mere perception of a stimulus that may lead to unwanted action.

Flexibility Without Consciousness

The fact that goals—even goals to control other actions—guide our actions largely without conscious guidance may lead to the question of whether unconscious mechanisms have enough flexibility. People have to be able to respond appropriately to changing circumstances, and important long-term goals often require the completion of very different stages. In other words, goal completion requires a certain degree of flexibility.

Recent research on unconscious goal pursuit indeed shows that people pursuing certain goals show remarkable flexibility in the face of changing circumstances. Moreover, this flexibility is very often achieved without conscious guidance. The research discussed above by Fishbach and colleagues (Fishbach et al., 2003) on temptation and the research by Strick and colleagues (2010) provide nice examples of the flexibility that people achieve without conscious awareness, but there are many others.

First, although people evaluate incoming stimuli automatically (Bargh, Chaiken, Govender, & Pratto, 1992; Fazio, Sanbonmatsu, Powell, & Kardes, 1986), the way in which stimuli are evaluated depends on goals. Water may under most circumstances be a rather neutral stimulus, but when one is extremely thirsty—and the goal to quench this thirst is highly active—water becomes a positive stimulus. Indeed, Ferguson and Bargh (2004) demonstrated that things that are normally evaluated as neutral can be automatically evaluated as positive when detecting these things serves a current goal. Similarly, smokers automatically evaluate a cigarette as positive when they truly crave one, but they may evaluate a cigarette as negative after they have just had one (Sherman, Presson, Chassin, Rose, & Koch, 2003). The process of automatic evaluation is another example of goal-independent automaticity. The process is automatic and does not require any conscious intervention, but it is flexible in that it is moderated by active goals.

The strength of a goal or the intensity with which we pursue goals can also be flexibly regulated without any conscious guidance. The research by Bijleveld and colleagues (2009) discussed earlier provides an example of such a process, but recent research has come up with other examples. In a series of experiments, Ferguson (2008) demonstrated that the evaluation of stimuli depends not only on activated goals but also on goal strength. In one of her experiments, some participants were unconsciously primed with the goal to eat. Participants who were primed with this goal evaluated food-related stimuli more positively than participants who were not primed. However, this effect was fully moderated by the time that had passed since participants had their last meal. Only primed participants who hadn't eaten for hours (and who were most likely hungry) evaluated food-related stimuli more positively. If anything, participants who had just eaten showed the reverse effect. Interestingly, the evaluations were not affected by how hungry participants thought they were, but only by the time since their last meal. So, not only were the evaluations influenced by variations in goal strength, but also the relevant variations were inaccessible to consciousness.

Foerster, Liberman, and Higgins (2005) obtained similar effects. In their experiments, participants searched for target stimuli among other stimuli. A variety of measures indicated that the target stimuli were highly accessible before participants found the target. However, the targets were inhibited after participants found them, that is, after goal fulfillment. Interestingly, the strength of these effects was proportional to the strength of the motivation.

Perhaps the most impressive evidence for the flexibility of unconscious goal-driven processes comes from the work by Hassin and colleagues (Hassin, Bargh, Engell, & McCulloch, 2009; Hassin, Bargh, & Zimerman, 2009). Goal pursuit requires various forms of flexibility, but one important aspect of goal pursuit is that it entails the "recognition of new opportunities and the realization of blocked ones" (Hassin, Bargh, & Zimerman, 2009, p. 20). Hassin and colleagues investigated the extent to which people pursuing a goal can deal with new rules and new procedures without being aware of the goal in the first place. In one of their experiments, some participants were unconsciously primed with the goal to achieve, whereas others were not. Participants then performed the Wisconsin Card Sorting Test (WCST). The WCST is a frequently administered neuropsychological test used to assess flexible adaptation. The test consists of four response cards and 128 stimulus cards that depict figures of varying colors (red, blue, yellow, or green), forms (stars, triangles, circles, or crosses), and numbers (one, two, three, or four). Participants are presented with individual cards and are asked to match these cards with one of the response cards. The sorting rules can be either based on color, on form, or on number. While participants do this task, they receive feedback in terms of whether a match is right or wrong; hence, they can discover the sorting rule. However, after 10 correct sortings, the rule changes. Participants have to learn the new rule again on the basis of the feedback.

On the WCST, people can make various kinds of errors, but the most important ones are *perseverance* errors. Perseverance errors are indicative of the speed with which people can adopt a new procedure and are thus indicative of flexibility. The fewer errors one makes, the more flexible one is. Hassin and colleagues showed that unconsciously priming people with achievement decreased the number of perseverance errors. These results are illuminating because they demonstrate that people can become more flexible if this serves a goal—in this case achievement or performance—without being consciously aware of the goal in the first place.

We also know from other research that the WCST is sensitive to damage in the dorsolateral prefrontal cortex, a region that is also associated with working memory. Working memory allows people "to comprehend and mentally represent their immediate environment, to retain information about their immediate past experience, to support the acquisition of new knowledge, to solve problems, and to formulate, relate and act on current goals" (Baddeley & Logie, p. 28; see also Hassin, Bargh & Zimerman, 2009). Working memory was traditionally associated with consciousness; in fact, for some time, it seemed fashionable to think that working memory basically *is* consciousness (LeDoux, 1996).

Hassin and colleagues (Hassin, Bargh, Engell, & McCulloch, 2009) questioned this strong relation between working memory and consciousness, based on abundant social psychological research showing that processes that are attributed to working memory—for example, problem solving and goal pursuit—do not need consciousness (e.g., Bargh et al., 2001; Dijksterhuis & Nordgren, 2006). They devised a new working memory task in which participants had to extract and apply various patterns online and showed repeatedly that participants achieved this without being consciously aware of the patterns. On the basis of their results, they called for a theoretical broadening of the working memory literature so that it can encompass implicit working memory.

Scott and Dienes (2010) recently published other evidence for the unconscious operation of a flexible psychological process traditionally associated with consciousness. In their experiment, participants learned a form of artificial grammar (e.g., Reber, 1967). Although it is known that people can learn to apply rules without being consciously aware of them (e.g., Reber, 1989), the role of consciousness in applying these rules to new domains is still subject to debate. Scott and Dienes showed that people can indeed apply rules learned in one modality (letters) to another modality (musical notes) without becoming aware of these rules. In fact, this unconscious transfer of knowledge seemed to be more efficient than conscious transfer. That is, conscious deliberation actually hampered successful transfer.

To recapitulate, there are many ways in which people pursuing goals need to be flexible, but recent research shows that many of these forms of flexibility can be achieved without conscious guidance. However, in the final section, we will review findings on an emerging idea that does relate consciousness to flexibility, but in a different way. It may well be that the function of consciousness is not flexibility

per se, but rather changing the balance between focus and flexibility.

Consciousness, Focus, and Flexibility

Once people start to pursue a goal, they repeatedly compare their desired state with their actual state. When discrepancies are detected, adjustments have to be made (Powers, 1973). In addition, new goals may enter the scene that lead to a changed course of action. Given the potential interference of distracting information on the one hand, and the dynamic nature of our world on the other, people face the challenge to remain focused on pursuing their goals and, at the same time, to be flexible and to adjust behavior to deal with changing circumstances. Although operating in an antagonistic way, both aspects of attention are needed for goal pursuit. That is, adaptive volitional behavior requires a context-dependent balance between focus and flexibility.

Although recent research recognizes the importance of a balance between focus and flexibility for effective goal pursuit, little is known about the mechanisms involved in establishing and maintaining this balance. Research among patients with frontal-lobe damage shows that they display rigid behaviors and less flexibility in tasks that require switching between cognitive rules (Luria, 1973; Shallice, 1988; Stuss & Levine, 1992). Moreover, these patients seem to be unable to suppress impulses and well-practiced habits in response to objects and tools, also known as *utilization behavior* (Lhermitte, 1983).

Given that frontal cortical areas are involved in the dynamic balance between focus and flexibility, one may raise the possibility that consciousness plays a prominent role in this process. However, this suggestion is empirically questionable. For instance, studies using a set-switching task or selective visual attention task have shown that the balance between focus and flexibility is modulated by the incidental activation of positive affect or reward cues (Della Libera, & Chelazzi, 2006; Dreisbach & Goschke, 2004). According to Cohen and colleagues (Cohen, Aston-Jones, & Gilzenrat, 2004; Aston-Jones & Cohen, 2005), the regulation of the balance is "hard-wired" in the brains. Although the neurological basis is not yet fully delineated, it appears that flexible action is driven by subcortical output that releases dopamine in the PFC. This release is elicited by rewards or other positive cues that signal the incentive value of a goal (Berridge, 2007). Furthermore, enhanced focus is more likely to ensue when action is required to keep the goal active and to shield it from distraction. Such goal-related monitoring processes are controlled by the ACC, which triggers the release of norepinephrine in the locus coeruleus, thereby enhancing focused attention processes in the PFC.

The balance between focus and flexibility is guided by rewards and requirements associated with the goals. Given the finding that reward-priming effects on decision making and resource recruitment can be brought about unconsciously (e.g., Bijleveld et al., 2009; Pessiglione et al., 2007), and given the human capacity to monitor goal-directed behavior unconsciously (e.g., Custers & Aarts, 2007; Fourneret & Jeannerod, 1998), it appears that the dynamic balance between focus and stability can occur in the absence of conscious awareness. This line of reasoning is consistent with research in social cognition that considers the motivation and attentional operation of goals to emerge from unconscious interactions of representations of goals and positive affect that can act as an incentive or effort mobilizer (Aarts et al., 2008; Custers & Aarts, 2005).

When unconscious goals interact with the environment in a proper way, goals remain unconscious. However, this does not imply that consciousness plays no role in goal-directed volitional behavior. Sometimes, the balance between focus and flexibility is imperfect or severely disturbed, and people become aware of their unconscious goals. Indeed, research shows that the probability that unconsciously activated goals will reach conscious awareness increases when goal progress is obstructed (Bongers, Dijksterhuis, & Spears, 2010), and it is this event that is said to typify a shift from unconscious, automated behavior to conscious, willful behavior (e.g., James, 1890; Norman & Shallice, 1986). However, how this state of conscious awareness unfolds and whether it serves a causal role in guiding volitional behavior is an essential problem in its own right and remains a topic of intriguing theorizing and empirical scrutiny (Aarts et al., 2007; Blackmore, 2003; Dijksterhuis & Aarts, 2010).

Assuming that conscious awareness of goals directs attention in a manner similar to unconscious goals, effects on behavior may depend on whether conscious attention co-occurs with, and is directed at, the imperfect balance between focus and flexibility during the process of goal pursuit. When conscious attention coincides with, and is directed at, restoring an imperfect balance, it may improve performance and adaptive behavior. However, when conscious awareness of goals emerges while the balance between focus and flexibility operates adequately—that is, when keeping one's eye on the goal and tuning behavior to changing circumstances act in close harmony—performance may not benefit from conscious awareness. In fact, it may even be jeopardized by conscious awareness. Such impairments may arise when people are explicitly forced to focus conscious attention on their behavior, thereby disturbing rather than promoting a good balance. A few examples of both beneficial and harmful effects of conscious awareness will be given below.

Positive effects may occur when an imperfect balance during unconscious goal pursuit is encountered that requires a mode of information processing that cannot be relied on outside of conscious awareness. Specifically, we may encounter a deadlock, such as when goal-directed behavior is obstructed in such a way that neither focus nor flexibility is adaptive to deal with the problem. Often, this implies the planning of a course of action that is totally new or that has never been executed before in a given situation. According to global workspace theory (e.g., Baars, 1997; 2002), conscious awareness then helps to mobilize and integrate brain functions that otherwise operate independently in the process of building up an action that is not available in the person's repertoire. It offers a "facility for accessing, disseminating, and exchanging information, and for exercising global coordination and control" (Baars, 1997, p. 7).

In research on the cognitive underpinnings of action planning, it has been suggested that planning integrates sensorimotor information regarding one's future behavior into a novel action representation that should be capable of bridging the gap between goals and behavior (Hommel, Müsseler, Aschersleben, & Prinz, 2001). Furthermore, various studies have shown that conscious planning can lead to more successful goal achievement when such plans establish links between representations of relevant actions and cues (Gollwitzer & Sheeran, 2006). That is, forming implementation intentions as to when, where, and how one will act to attain one's goal helps the progress of goal pursuit. Importantly, once the plan is formed, subsequent action initiation and performance display features of automaticity, in the sense that the action can be directly triggered by and executed in the anticipated environment without much conscious intervention. Thus, it seems that the obstruction of unconscious goal pursuit can benefit from the conscious awareness it evokes by rendering plans that specify how one needs to proceed. As soon as goal pursuit is reinitiated, the imbalance between focus and flexibility is restored, and unconscious goals can continue to do their work.

It is clear that conscious awareness can help goal pursuit. However, there are also detrimental effects of externally forced conscious awareness on goals. The attentional blink phenomenon provides an interesting example (e.g., Chun & Potter, 1995; Marois & Ivanoff, 2005; Raymond, Shapiro, & Arnell, 1992). When participants are asked to detect two briefly presented target stimuli within a stream of distracter stimuli, they show an impaired ability to identify the second of the two targets, when these are presented in close succession. Whereas this attentional blink effect is generally thought to reflect a fundamental cognitive limitation, recent research indicates that an overinvestment of conscious attention to the stream of stimuli may drive the effect (Colzato, Slagter, Spapé, & Hommel, 2008; Olivers & Nieuwenhuis, 2005, 2006). This research has demonstrated that a reduction in conscious attention limits the number of items in the stream that are fully processed and, as a consequence, reduces the attentional blink effect. Also, incidental activation of positive affect or higher central dopaminergic function during the task decreases the attentional blink effect, a finding that is in line with the idea that positive affect modulates the balance between rigidly focusing on a task and a more flexible mode of processing. In short, conscious attention to goals can cause people to concentrate too hard, and this promotes rather than prevents the occurrence of a rigid mode of information processing, as reflected in the attentional blink effect.

Another recent line of research that demonstrates detrimental effects of conscious awareness comes from studies on decision making. Although conscious thought about a decision problem sometimes helps one reach more rationale decisions (see, e.g., Newell, Lagnado, & Shanks, 2007), an abundance of research shows that conscious thought can also interfere with proper decision making (Dijksterhuis & Nordgren, 2006; Schooler, Ohlsson, & Brooks, 1993; Reyna & Brainerd, 1995; Wilson & Schooler, 1991). When people make goal-directed decisions they can readily deal with unconsciously (i.e., when there is a good balance between focus and flexibility), conscious thought can interfere with decision making. One major problem is that people can often weight the relative importance of attributes quite well unconsciously (Dijksterhuis & Nordgren, 2006; Wilson & Schooler, 1991), but conscious thought leads to biases in this weighting process.

One important reason is that conscious thought tends to cause verbalizable information to receive too much weight and nonverbalizable information to receive too little weight (Reyna & Brainerd, 1995; Schooler, Ohlsson, & Brooks, 1993; Wilson & Schooler, 1991). This jeopardizes the decision process.

A third example concerns skills. Skillful behavior can usually ensue without conscious awareness, and skills are often stored as abstract high-level patterns that serve a goal. When thirsty, for instance, grasping a glass and bringing it to one's mouth usually leads to taking a sip. When goals guide attention in good balance between focus and flexibility, the person can unconsciously execute individual action sequences that capture the essential structure of the skill (e.g., when and how much a hand should be opened to reach for the glass), and adjust to changes in circumstances (e.g., different distance to or weight of the glass). It has been shown that consciously focusing on the execution of specific components of a complex motor skill can impair performance (e.g., Baumeister, 1984; Beilock & Carr, 2001; Lewis & Linder, 1997). For instance, experienced soccer players handle the ball better with their dominant foot when they are distracted from executing a skill (e.g., dribbling) than when they are asked to consciously focus on specific action components. An explanation for this "choking under pressure" effect is that the conscious attention to separate components overrules the more efficient organizational structure of the skill. In other words, it disturbs the balance between focus and flexibility. This causes the building blocks of the skill to function as separate components, in a manner similar to before the skill was acquired. Once the structure breaks down, each component is executed separately, which takes more time and leaves more room for error.

In summary, conscious awareness can make us more but also less flexible—in case more focus is needed. One could say that consciousness is not related to flexibility per se, but rather to "meta-flexibility."

The Unconscious Will

The chapter opened with the observation that people have long thought about two different distinctions pertaining to human action: To what extent is behavior willful and goal driven, and to what extent is behavior guided by consciousness? Not surprisingly—because it is intuitively compelling (see Custers & Aarts, 2010; Wegner, 2002)—people have also always assumed that these two distinctions are strongly related. Willful behavior is conscious, and involuntary behavior is mostly unconscious.

Recent research from psychology and neuroscience indicates that the relation between volition and consciousness is much weaker than previously assumed. Whether actions are caused by goals, and whether actions are guided by consciousness, are two different things. A lot of our behavior is driven by goals, but the most important "tool" these goals use is attention, not conscious awareness. Even control, a capacity that we have always associated with consciousness, can be unconscious.

We do have a will, but it seems to be an unconscious one.

Author Note

This chapter was supported by a VICI grant from NWO (453–05–004). Correspondence can be directed to: Ap Dijksterhuis, Behavioral Science Institute, Radboud University Nijmegen, P.O. Box 9104, 6500 HE Nijmegen, The Netherlands; e-mail: a.dijksterhuis@psych.ru.nl.

References

Aarts, H. (2007). Unconscious authorship ascription: The effects of success and effect-specific information priming on experienced authorship. *Journal of Experimental Social Psychology, 43*, 119–126.

Aarts, H., Custers, R., & Holland, R. W. (2007). The nonconscious cessation of goal pursuit: When goals and negative affect are coactivated. *Journal of Personality and Social Psychology, 92*, 165.

Aarts, H., Custers, R., & Marien, H. (2008). Preparing and motivating behavior outside of awareness. *Science, 319*, 1639.

Aarts, H., & Dijksterhuis, A. (2000). Habits as knowledge structures: Automaticity in goal-directed behavior. *Journal of Personality and Social Psychology, 78*, 53–63.

Aarts, H., Gollwitzer, P. M., & Hassin, R. R. (2004). Goal contagion: Perceiving is for pursuing. *Journal of Personality and Social Psychology, 87*, 23–37.

Andreasen, N. C. (2005). *The creative brain*. New York: Plume.

Aston-Jones, G., & Cohen, J. D. (2005). An integrative theory of locus coeruleus-norepinephrine function: Adaptive gain and optimal performance. *Annual Review of Neuroscience, 28*, 403–450.

Baars, B. J. (1997). *In the theatre of consciousness: The workspace of the mind*. New York: Oxford University Press.

Baars, B. J. (2002). The conscious access hypothesis: Origins and recent evidence. *Trends in Cognitive Sciences, 6*, 47–52.

Baars, B. J., & Franklin, S. (2003). How conscious experience and working memory interact. *Trends in Cognitive Sciences, 7*, 166–172.

Baddeley, A. D. (1993). Working memory and conscious awareness. In A. Collins & S. Gathercole (Eds.), *Theories of memory* (pp. 11–28). Hillsdale, NJ: Erlbaum.

Baddeley, A. D., & Logie, R. H. (1999). The multiple-component model. In A. Miyake & P. Shah (Eds.), *Models of working memory: Mechanisms of active maintenance and executive control* (pp. 28–61). Cambridge, UK: Cambridge University Press.

Badgaiyan, R. D. (2000). Executive control, willed actions, and nonconscious processing. *Human Brain Mapping, 9*, 38–41.

Bargh, J. A. (1994). The four horsemen of automaticity: Awareness, intention, efficiency and control in social cognition. In R. S. Wyer Jr. & T. K. Srull (Eds.), *The handbook of social cognition* (Vol. 2, pp. 1–40). Hillsdale, NJ: Erlbaum.

Bargh, J. A., Chaiken, S., Govender, R., & Pratto, F. (1992). The generality of the automatic evaluation effect. *Journal of Personality and Social Psychology, 62*, 893–912.

Bargh, J. A., & Chartrand, T. L. (1999). The unbearable automaticity of being. *American Psychologist, 54*, 462–479.

Bargh, J. A., Chen, M., & Burrows, L. (1996). Automaticity of social behavior: Direct effects of trait construct and stereotype activation on action. *Journal of Personality and Social Psychology, 71*, 230–244.

Bargh, J. A., & Gollwitzer, P. M. (1994). Environmental control of goal-directed action: Automatic and strategic contingencies between situations and behavior. In W. D. Spaulding (Ed.), *Integrative views of motivation, cognition, and emotion. Nebraska symposium on motivation* (Vol. 41, pp. 71–124). Lincoln, NE: University of Nebraska Press.

Bargh, J. A., Gollwitzer, P. M., Lee-Chai, A., Barndollar, K., & Trotschel, R. (2001). The automated will: Nonconscious activation and pursuit of behavioral goals. *Journal of Personality and Social Psychology, 81*, 1014–1027.

Bargh, J. A., & Morsella, E. (2008). The unconscious mind. *Perspectives on Psychological Science, 3*, 73–79.

Baumeister, R. F. (1984). Choking under pressure: Self-consciousness and paradoxical effects on incentives on skillful performance. *Journal of Personality and Social Psychology, 46*, 610–620.

Beilock, S. L., & Carr, T. H. (2001). On the fragility of skilled performance: What governs choking under pressure? *Journal of Experimental Psychology: General, 130*, 701–725.

Berridge, K. C. (2007). The debate over dopamine's role in reward: The case for incentive salience. *Psychopharmacology, 191*, 391–431.

Bijleveld, E., Custers, R., & Aarts, H. (2009). The unconscious eye opener: Pupil dilation reveals strategic recruitment of mental resources upon subliminal reward cues. *Psychological Science, 20*, 1313–1315.

Blackmore, S. (2003). *Consciousness: An introduction*. New York: Oxford University Press.

Bongers, K. C. A., Dijksterhuis, A., & Spears, R. (2010). On the roile of conscious in goal pursuit. *Social Cognition, 28*, 262–272.

Bos, M. W., Dijksterhuis, A., & Baaren, R. B. (2008). On the goal-dependency of unconscious thought. *Journal of Experimental Social Psychology, 44*, 1114–1120.

Broadbent, D.E. (1958). *Perception and communication*. New York: Pergamon Press.

Chartrand, T. L., & Bargh, J. A. (1999). The chameleon effect: The perception-behavior link and social interaction. *Journal of Personality and Social Psychology, 76*, 893–910.

Chartrand, T. L., & Van Baaren, R. B. (2008). Human mimicry. *Advances in Experimental Social Psychology, 41*, 219–274.

Chun, M. M., & Potter, M. C. (1995). A two-stage model for multiple target detection in rapid serial visual presentation. *Journal of Experimental Psychology, 21*, 109–127.

Cohen, J. D., Aston-Jones, G., & Gilzenrat, M. S. (2004). A systems-level theory on attention and cognitive control: Guided activation, adaptive gating, conflict monitoring, and exploitation versus exploration. In M. Posner (Ed.), *Cognitive neuroscience of attention* (pp. 71–90). New York: Guilford Press.

Colzato, L. S., Slagter, H. A., Spapé, M. M. A., & Hommel, B. (2008). Blinks of the eye predict blinks of the mind. *Neuropsychologia, 46*, 3179–3183.

Custers, R., & Aarts, H. (2005). Positive affect as implicit motivator: On the nonconscious operation of behavioral goals. *Journal of Personality and Social Psychology, 89*, 129–142.

Custers, R., & Aarts, H. (2007). In search of the unconscious sources of goal pursuit: Accessibility and positive affective valence of the goal state. *Journal of Experimental Social Psychology, 43*, 312–318.

Custers, R., & Aarts, H. (2010). The unconscious will: How the pursuit of goals operates outside of conscious awareness. *Science, 329*, 47–50.

Custers, R., Maas, M., Wildenbeest, M., & Aarts, H. (2008). Nonconscious goal pursuit and the surmounting of physical and social obstacles. *European Journal of Social Psychology, 38*, 1013–1022.

Damasio, A. R. (1999). *The feeling of what happens: Body and emotion in the making of consciousness.* New York: Harcourt.

Dehaene, S., Changeux, J. P., Naccache, L., Sackur, J., & Sergent, C. (2006). Conscious, preconscious, and subliminal processing: A testable taxonomy. *Trends in Cognitive Sciences, 10*, 204–211.

Della Libera, C., & Chelazzi, L. (2006). Visual selective attention and the effects of monetary rewards. *Psychological Science, 17*, 222–227.

Devine, P. G. (1989). Stereotypes and prejudice: Their automatic and controlled components. *Journal of Personality and Social Psychology, 56*, 5–18.

Dijksterhuis, A. (2004). Think different: The merits of unconscious thought in preference development and decision making. *Journal of Personality and Social Psychology, 87*, 586–598.

Dijksterhuis, A. (2010). Automaticity and the unconscious. In S.T. Fiske, D. T. Gilbert, & G. Lindzey (Eds.). *The handbook of social psychology* (5th ed., pp. 228–267). Boston, MA: McGraw-Hill.

Dijksterhuis, A., & Aarts, H. (2010). Goals, attention, and (un)consciousness. *Annual Review of Psychology, 61*, 467–490.

Dijksterhuis, A., & Bargh, J. A. (2001). The perception-behavior expressway: Automatic effects of social perception on social behavior. *Advances in Experimental Social Psychology, 33*, 1–40.

Dijksterhuis, A., Bos, M. W., Nordgren, L. F., & Van Baaren, R. B. (2006). On making the right choice: The deliberation-without-attention effect. *Science, 311*, 1005–1007.

Dijksterhuis, A., Chartrand, T. L., & Aarts, H. (2007). Effects of priming and perception on social behavior and goal pursuit. In J.A. Bargh (Ed.), *Social psychology and the unconscious: The automaticity of higher mental processes*, p. 51–132. Philadelphia: Psychology Press.

Dijksterhuis, A., & Nordgren, L. F. (2006). A theory of unconscious thought. *Perspectives on Psychological Science, 1*, 95–109.

Dijksterhuis, A., Spears, R., & Lepinasse, V. (2001). Reflecting and deflecting stereotypes: Assimilation and contrast in impression formation and automatic behavior. *Journal of Experimental Social Psychology, 37*, 286–299.

Dijksterhuis, A., & van Knippenberg, A. (1998). The relation between perception and behavior or how to win a game of Trivial Pursuit. *Journal of Personality and Social Psychology, 74*, 865–877.

Dreisbach, G., & Goschke, T. (2004). How positive affect modulates cognitive control: Reduced perseveration at the cost of increased distractibility. *Journal of Experimental Psychology Learning Memory and Cognition, 30*, 343–353.

Fazio, R. H., Sanbonmatsu, D. M., Powell, M. C., & Kardes, F. R. (1986). On the automatic activation of attitudes. *Journal of Personality and Social Psychology, 50*, 229–238.

Ferguson, M. J. (2008). On becoming ready to pursue a goal you don't know you have: Effects of nonconscious goals on evaluative readiness. *Journal of Personality and Social Psychology, 95*, 1268–1294.

Ferguson, M. J., & Bargh, J. A. (2004). Liking is for doing: The effects of goal pursuit on automatic evaluation. *Journal of Personality and Social Psychology, 87*, 557–572.

Fishbach, A., Friedman, R. S., & Kruglanski, A. W. (2003). Leading us not unto temptation: Momentary allurements elicit overriding goal activation. *Journal of Personality and Social Psychology, 84*, 296–309.

Fitzsimons, G. M., & Bargh, J. A. (2003). Thinking of you: Nonconscious pursuit of interpersonal goals associated with relationship partners. *Journal of Personality and Social Psychology, 84*, 148–164.

Foerster, J., Liberman, N., & Higgins, E. T. (2005). Accessibility from active and fulfilled goals. *Journal of Experimental Social Psychology, 41*, 220–239.

Fourneret, P., & Jeannerod, M. (1998). Limited conscious monitoring of motor performance in normal subjects. *Neuropsychologia, 36*, 1133–1140.

Funahashi, S. (2001). Neuronal mechanisms of executive control by the prefrontal cortex. *Neuroscience Research, 39*, 147–165.

Galinsky, A. D., & Moskowitz, G. B. (2000). Perspective taking: Decreasing stereotype expression, stereotype accessibility and in-group favouritism. *Journal of Personality and Social Psychology, 78*, 708–724.

Gollwitzer, P. M., & Sheeran, P. (2006). Implementation intentions and goal achievement: A meta-analysis of effects and processes. *Advances in Experimental Social Psychology, 38*, 69–120.

Haggard, P. (2008). Human volition: Towards a neuroscience of will. *Nature Reviews: Neuroscience, 9*, 934–946.

Hassin, R. R., Bargh, J. A., Engell, A. D., & McCulloch, K. C. M. (2009). Implicit working memory. *Consciousness and Cognition, 18*, 665–678.

Hassin, R. R., Bargh, J. A., & Zimerman, S. (2009). Automatic and flexible: The case of nonconscious goal pursuit. *Social Cognition, 27*, 20–36.

Hommel, B., Müsseler, J., Aschersleben, G., & Prinz, W. (2001). The theory of event coding (TEC): A framework for perception and action planning. *Behavioral and Brain Sciences, 24*, 849–878.

James, W. (1890). *The principles of psychology.* New York: Henry Holt.

Kahneman, D. (1972). *Attention and effort.* Englewood Cliffs, NJ: Prentice-Hall.

Kawakami, K., Young, H., & Dovidio, J. F. (2002). Automatic stereotyping: Category, trait, and behavioral activations. *Personality and Social Psychology Bulletin, 28*, 3–15.

Koch, C., & Tsuchiya, N. (2006). Attention and consciousness: Two distinct brain processes. *Trends in Cognitive Sciences, 11,* 16–22.

Lamme, V. A. F. (2003). Why visual attention and awareness are different. *Trends in Cognitive Sciences, 7,* 12–18.

Latane, B., & Darley, J. M. (1970). *The unresponsive bystander: Why doesn't he help?* New York: Appleton-Century-Crofts.

Lau, H. C., & Passingham, R. E. (2007). Unconscious activation of the cognitive control system in the human prefrontal cortex. *Journal of Neuroscience, 27,* 5805.

Lewis, B. P., & Linder, D. E. (1997). Thinking about choking? Attentional processes and paradoxical performance. *Personality and Social Psychology Bulletin, 23,* 937–944.

Lhermitte, F. (1983). "Utilization behavior" and its relation to lesions of the frontal lobes. *Brain, 106,* 237–255.

Libet, B., Gleason, C. A., Wright, E. W., & Pearl, D. K. (1983). Time of conscious intention to act in relation to onset of cerebral activity (readiness-potential): The unconscious initiation of a freely voluntary act. *Brain, 106,* 623.

Loewenstein, G. (1996). Out of control: Visceral influences on behavior. *Organizational Behavior and Human Decision Processes, 65,* 272–292.

Loftus, E. F., & Klinger, M. R. (1992). In the unconscious smart or dumb? *American Psychologist, 47,* 761–765.

Luria, A. R. (1973). *The working brain.* New York: Basic Books.

Marois, R., & Ivanoff, J. (2005). Capacity limits of information processing in the brain. *Trends in Cognitive Sciences, 9,* 296–305.

McKone, E. (1995). Short-term implicit memory for words and nonwords. *Journal of Experimental Psychology: Learning, Memory, and Cognition, 21,* 1108–1126.

Miller, E. K., & Cohen, J. D. (2001). An integrative theory of prefrontal cortex function. *Annual Review of Neuroscience, 24,* 167–202.

Mischel, W., Shoda, Y., & Rodriguez, M. I. (1989). Delay of gratification in children. *Science, 244,* 933–938.

Monsell, S., & Driver, J. (2000). *Control of cognitive processes: Attention and performance* (Vol. xviii). Cambridge, MA: MIT Press.

Moors, A., & De Houwer, J. (2006). Automaticity: A theoretical and conceptual analysis. *Psychological Bulletin, 132,* 297–326.

Moray, N. (1959). Attention in dichotic listening: Affective cues and the influence of instructions. *Quarterly Journal of Experimental Psychology, 11,* 56–60.

Moskowitz, G. B., Gollwitzer, P. M., Wasel, W., & Schaal, B. (1999). Preconscious control of stereotype activation through chronic egalitarian goals. *Journal of Personality and Social Psychology, 77,* 167–184.

Moskowitz, G. B., Li, P., & Kirk, E. R. (2004). The implicit volition model: On the preconscious regulation of temporarily adopted goals. *Advances in Experimental Social Psychology, 36,* 317–414.

Myrseth, K. O. R., & Fishbach, A. (2009). Self-control. *Current Directions in Psychological Science, 18,* 247–252.

Newell, B. R., Lagnado, D. A., & Shanks, D. R. (2007). *Straight choices: The psychology of decision making.* New York: Routledge.

Nisbett, R. E., & en Wilson, T. D. (1977). Telling more than we can know: Verbal reports on mental processes. *Psychological Review, 84,* 231–253.

Nordgren, L.F., van der Pligt, J., & van Harreveld, F. (2006). Visceral drives in retrospect: Explanations about the inaccessible past. *Psychological Science, 17,* 635–640.

Norman, D. A., & Shallice, T. (1986). Attention to action: Willed and automatic control of behaviour. In G. E. Schwartz & D. Shapiro (Eds.), *Consciousness and self-regulation* (Vol. 4). New York: Plenum Press.

Olivers, C. N. L., & Nieuwenhuis, S. (2005). The beneficial effect of concurrent task-irrelevant mental activity on temporal attention. *Psychological Science, 16,* 265–269.

Olivers, C. N. L., & Nieuwenhuis, S. (2006). The beneficial effects of additional task load, positive affect, and instruction on the attentional blink. *Journal of Experimental Psychology: Human Perception and Performance, 32,* 364–379.

Papies, E. K., Stroebe, W., & Aarts, H. (2008). The allure of forbidden food: On the role of attention in self-regulation. *Journal of Experimental Social Psychology, 44,* 1283–1292.

Pessiglione, M., Schmidt, L., Draganski, B., Kalisch, R., Lau, H., Dolan, R. J., & Frith, C. D. (2007). How the brain translates money into force: A neuroimaging study of subliminal motivation. *Science, 316,* 904–906.

Poincaré, H. (1913). *The foundations of science.* Lancaster, PA: Science Press.

Posner, M. I., & Fan, J. (2004). Attention as an organ system. In J. Pomerantz (Ed.), *Neurobiology of perception and communication: From synapse to society. The IVth de Lange conference.* Cambridge, UK: Cambridge University Press.

Posner, M. I., & Snyder, C. R. R. (1975). Attention and cognitive control. In R. L. Solso (Ed.), *Information processing and cognition: The Loyola symposium* (pp. 55–85). Hillsdale, NJ: Erlbaum.

Powers, W. T. (1973). *Behavior: The control of perception.* Chicago: Aldine.

Raymond, J. E., Shapiro, K. L., & Arnell, K. M. (1992). Temporary suppression of visual processing in an RSVP task: An attentional blink. *Journal of Experimental Psychology: Human Perception and Performance, 18,* 849–860.

Reber, A. S. (1967). Implicit learning of artificial grammars. *Journal of Verbal Learning & Verbal Behavior, 6,* 855–863.

Reber, A. S. (1989). Implicit learning and tacit knowledge. *Journal of Experimental Psychology: General, 118,* 219–235.

Reyna, V. F., & Brainerd, C. J. (1995). Fuzzy-trace theory: An interim synthesis. *Learning and Individual Differences, 7,* 1–75.

Schooler, J. W., Ohlsson, S., & Brooks, K. (1993). Thoughts beyond words: When language overshadows insight. *Journal of Experimental Psychology General, 122,* 166–183.

Schopenhauer, A. (1851/1970). *Essays and aphorisms.* London: Penguin.

Scott, R. B., & Dienes, Z. (2010). Knowledge applied to new domains: The unconscious succeeds where the conscious fails. *Consciousness and Cognition, 19,* 391–398.

Shah, J. Y., Friedman, R., & Kruglanski, A. W. (2002). Forgetting all else: On the antecedents and consequences of goal shielding. *Journal of Personality and Social Psychology, 83,* 1261–1280.

Shallice, T. (1988). *From neuropsychology to mental structure.* Cambridge, UK: Cambridge University Press.

Sherman, S. J., Rose, J. S., Koch, K., Presson, C. C., & Chassin, L. (2003). Implicit and explicit attitudes toward cigarette smoking: The effects of context and motivation. *Journal of Social and Clinical Psychology, 22,* 13–39.

Shiffrin, R. M., & Schneider, W. (1977). Controlled and automatic human information processing. II: Perceptual learning, automatic attending, and a general theory. *Psychological Review, 84,* 127–190.

Simon, D. J., & Chabris, C. F. (1999). Gorillas in our midst: Sustained inattentional blindness for dynamic events. *Perception, 28,* 1059–1074.

Smith, E. E., & Jonides, J. (1999). Storage and executive processes in the frontal lobes. *Science, 283,* 1657–1661.

Soon, C. S., Brass, M., Heinze, H. J., & Haynes, J. D. (2008). Unconscious determinants of free decisions in the human brain. *Nature Neuroscience, 11,* 543–545.

Stickgold, R., & Walker, M. (2004). To sleep, perchance to gain creative insight? *Trends in Cognitive Science, 8,* 191–192.

Stuss, D. T., & Levine, B. (1992). Adult clinical neuropsychology: lessons from studies of the frontal lobe. *Annual Review of Psychology, 33,* 401–433.

Treisman, A. (1960). Contextual cues in selective listening. *Quarterly Journal of Experimental Psychology, 52,* 347–353.

Trope, Y., & Fishbach, A. (2000). Counteractive self control in overcoming temptation. *Journal of Personality and Social Psychology, 79,* 493–506.

Van de Grind, W. (2002). Physical, neural, and mental timing. *Consciousness and Cognition, 11,* 241–264.

Wallas, G. (1926). *The art of thought.* London: Cape.

Watt, H. J. (1905). Experimentelle Beitrage zur einer Theorie des Denkens. *Archiv für die Geschichte der Psychologie, 4,* 289–436.

Wegner, D. M. (1994). Ironic processes of mental control. *Psychological Review, 101,* 34–52.

Wegner, D. M. (2002). *The illusion of conscious will.* Cambridge, MA: The MIT Press.

Wegner, D. M., & Smart, L. (1997). Deep cognitive activation: A new approach to the unconscious. *Journal of Consulting and Clinical Psychology, 65,* 984–995.

Wilson, T. D. (2002). *Strangers to ourselves.* Cambridge: Belknap.

Wilson, T. D., & Schooler, J. W. (1991). Thinking too much: Introspection can reduce the quality of preferences and decisions. *Journal of Personality and Social Psychology, 60,* 181–192.

Zhong, C. B., Liljenquist, K. (2006). Washing away your sins: Threatened morality and physical cleansing. *Science, 313,* 1451–1452.

The Role of Procedural Knowledge in the Generalizability of Social Behavior

Robert S. Wyer Jr., Hao Shen, *and* Alison Jing Xu

Abstract

Cognitive and motor behavior either can be mediated by conscious decisions about how to attain an objective to which it is relevant or can occur automatically without awareness of either the goal to which the behavior is relevant or even the behavior itself. These effects may be governed by different cognitive systems. A conceptualization of these systems and how they interface is used as a framework for reviewing the role of procedural knowledge at several stages of information processing, including attention, comprehension, evaluation, response generation, and decision making. Particular emphasis is given to the effects of goal-directed behavior at one point of time on behavior that is later performed in a quite different situation in pursuit of a goal that is unrelated to the first. In this context, a distinction is made between *mindsets*, which govern sequences of behavioral decisions without consciousness of the reason for making these decisions, and cognitive *productions*, which elicit behavior automatically and often without awareness of the behavior itself.

Key Words: procedural knowledge, mindsets, productions, behavior, decisions, information processing

Behavior normally comprises a sequence of cognitive or motor actions. In some cases, it is guided by a series of decisions that we consciously make in the course of pursuing a particular goal, based on a procedure that we retrieve from memory and consult in much the same way we might consult a recipe for baking a cake. At other times, however, we behave with little if any cognitive deliberation and often without conscious awareness of the goals to which our behavior is relevant.

These sequences of cognitive and motor operations constitute *procedures*. This chapter is concerned with the structure of these procedures, the factors that give rise to their application and the generality of their effects. An understanding of procedures draws on research and theory in a number of areas of social cognition, including knowledge accessibility, the representation of knowledge in memory, goal-directed cognitive processing,

automaticity, and dual processing models of cognitive functioning. However, many of the phenomena we consider are not normally discussed in reviews of this research.

To understand the role of procedures in cognitive and motor behavior, it is necessary to distinguish their effects from the effects of the goals to which they are directed. When a goal is strongly associated with the procedure that is used to attain it, this distinction can be difficult. In many instances, however, a similar procedure is involved in the attainment of more than one goal. In such cases, individuals' use of the procedure to attain one goal can influence the behavior they perform in pursuit of a quite different objective in a later, unrelated situation. By examining the conditions in which this occurs, the effect of the procedure per se can be isolated.

The present chapter employs this strategy. We first describe two different ways that procedures are represented in memory and their different roles in information processing. One type of procedure comes into play in deliberative, goal-directed activity, and the other occurs automatically, without any objective in mind. After discussing the general nature of these procedures, we review research that exemplifies the conditions in which they come into play and discuss the factors that give rise to their activation.

Representation of Procedures in Memory

A specification of how procedures influence cognitive and social behavior requires assumptions about the manner in which these procedures are represented in memory. Conceptualizations of goal-directed processing (Anderson, 1983; Kruglanski et al., 2002; Markman & Brendl, 2000; Schank & Abelson, 1977) make implicit or explicit assumptions about the nature of these representations. These conceptualizations all recognize that procedures can be activated by both external and internally generated stimulation. However, they differ in the emphasis they place on (1) the conditions under which procedures are chosen and performed consciously and (2) the conditions under which they are applied automatically, with little cognitive effort and little if any awareness.

The procedures that guide deliberative goal-directed activity are typically assumed to be represented in memory as part of declarative knowledge. These procedures are each associated with a goal to which it is relevant and can be viewed as a *plan* for attaining this goal.

Such plan–goal representations are often located within a hierarchical system of concepts pertaining to the goals and the means of attaining them (Kruglanski et al., 2002; Markman & Brendl, 2000; Wyer & Srull, 1989). Other procedures, which govern automatic processing, have the character of learned stimulus–response associations and have alternatively been characterized as habits (Wood & Neal, 2007), perception–behavior links (Bargh, 1997; Dijksterhuis & Bargh, 2001; Goldstone & Barsalou, 1998), or *productions* (Anderson, 1982, 1983; Smith, 1990, 1994). As we conceptualize them in this chapter, productions can often be activated by stimuli of which individuals may or may not be aware. In either case, however, they are applied with little conscious monitoring and often without consciousness of the actions themselves.

The role of both deliberative and automatic goal-directed activity is widely recognized (Chaiken & Trope, 1999). Nevertheless, few formulations specify precisely how they interface. Strack and Deutsch (2004), for example, propose that automatic and deliberative processes are governed by separate systems, with the automatic ("impulsive") system serving as a default when the deliberative ("reflective") system is dormant. In Wyer and Srull's (1986, 1989) metaphorical model of information processing, deliberative cognitive activity is governed by goal schemas that are drawn from long-term memory and are consciously consulted in determining the sequence of cognitive steps that are necessary to attain the goal in question. In contrast, automatic processing is typically governed by routines that are called on by an executive unit to perform more specific functions without awareness of the cognitive operations that are involved. Thus, individuals are conscious of the input and output of these latter routines but not of the cognitive procedures that are involved in their implementation.

Wyer and Srull's (1989) conceptualization has the potential for integrating specific theories of goal-directed processing within a common framework for addressing many of the phenomena to which dual processing models pertain (Wyer, 2006, 2011). However, it focuses largely on more general cognitive processes that occur en route to a goal (e.g., comprehension, storage and retrieval, inference) and does not address the manner in which the two different types of procedural knowledge combine to influence behavior in specific situations.

In this chapter, we provide a general description of plans and productions and the factors that give rise to their activation and use. We then review representative research on the way that goal-directed behavior activates these different types of procedures and their consequent impact on behavior and decisions in later, quite unrelated situations.

Plans: Representation of Procedures in Declarative Knowledge
STRUCTURAL ASSUMPTIONS

A plan can be represented in memory in a manner similar to that proposed by Kruglanski et al. (2002; see also Srull & Wyer, 1986), and its structure may resemble that of an event prototype (Wyer, 2004) or script (Graesser, 1981; Schank & Abelson, 1977). That is, it may consist of a series of temporally related event concepts (frames) that, in combination, specify the steps to be taken to attain the goal to which it is associated. Thus, a plan for "seeing a movie" might include concepts pertaining to "getting tickets," "arranging for a babysitter," "driving to the theater," and so forth, the terminal event of which is the goal being sought.

In effect, the concepts that compose a plan denote *subgoals*, each of which can itself potentially be attained by invoking a plan at a higher level of situational specificity, and the subgoals that compose this plan may each be attained through a plan at a still more specific level. Thus, a plan for getting tickets could include finding the telephone number, calling the box office, and so forth, and the plan for finding the telephone number might include looking in the yellow pages, and so forth. The relation of goals and subgoals might be described metaphorically as a goal–plan hierarchy of the sort shown in Figure 13.1.

Goal and subgoal concepts, and consequently the plans for attaining them, can vary in abstractness or generality. The concept of "buying potatoes," for example, is an exemplar of "buying groceries" or, at a still more abstract level, "making a purchase." Two other features of a plan–goal hierarchy are characterized by Kruglanski et al. (2002) as *equifinality* and *multifinality*. First, more than one plan can be associated with the same goal concept (equifinality). For example, deciding which of two products one prefers might be accomplished either (1) by computing the overall favorableness of each alternative separately and choosing the one with the higher overall value, or (2) by performing a dimension-by-dimension comparison and choosing the alternative that is superior to the other along the greater number of dimensions. Second, the subgoal concepts contained in one plan can be part of other plans as well (multifinality). To continue our example, deciding which of two products to buy might entail a procedure that is also involved in determining which of two countries to visit or deciding which of two students to hire as a research assistant.

PROCESSING ASSUMPTIONS

The goal and subgoal concepts that compose a plan do not have direct behavioral implications. Rather, they describe end states that individuals consciously decide to pursue in order to attain their primary objective. Thus, external or internal stimulation to attain a particular goal might activate a concept pertaining to this goal, and this concept might activate a plan for attaining it. If individuals identify such a plan, they are likely to assess the feasibility of attaining the subgoals that compose it, and if a subgoal can be attained immediately, they may decide to pursue it. This decision, in turn, might stimulate the identification of a plan for attaining the subgoal, and a consequent decision to attain the subgoals that compose this plan. In each case, the attainment of a subgoal might stimulate a decision to attain the next subgoal in the plan that contains it, and so on.

The conscious identification of a plan for use in attaining a goal is presumably governed by principles of declarative knowledge accessibility. Several theories specify these principles, each of which is based on assumptions about the organization of concepts and knowledge in memory (for a review of these theories, see Carlston & Smith, 1996). The hierarchical set of concepts shown in Figure 13.1 might suggest the use of an associative network metaphor

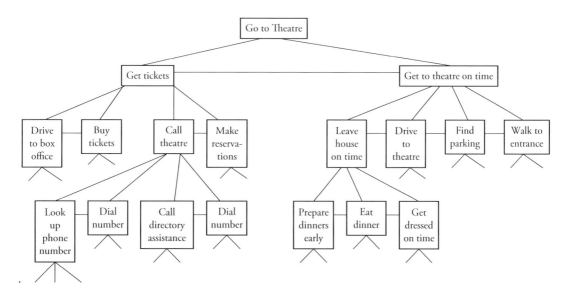

Figure 13.1 Simplified hierarchy of goal and subgoal concepts associated with going to the theatre.

(Collins & Loftus, 1975; Wyer & Carlston, 1979). As the equifinality and multifinality principles make salient, however, a complete description of the interconnectedness of goals and plans in these terms would be quite complex. A "tuning fork" metaphor similar to that proposed by Ratcliff (1978; see also Wyer, 2004) might ultimately be more useful. According to this latter conceptualization, representations are stored independently. However, the activation of one representation resonates with others to more or less extent, depending on the features they have in common, thereby affecting the likelihood that these representations are activated as well.

Despite differences in their underlying assumptions, theories of declarative knowledge accessibility converge on two general propositions:

Proposition 1. Thinking about a goal or subgoal can activate a plan for attaining it. When more than one plan or subgoal is applicable, the one that comes to mind most quickly is likely to be identified and pursued. This, in turn, is likely to be one that has been used frequently or recently in the past (Higgins et al., 1985; Srull & Wyer, 1979).

Proposition 2. The use of a plan to attain a situation-specific objective can activate goal or subgoal concepts at a higher level of generality, thereby increasing the accessibility of these concepts in memory. As a result, other plans whose components exemplify these concepts are more likely to be activated and applied in a later situation in pursuit of a quite different goal. Thus, performing goal-directed behavior in one situation can influence the way a goal is pursued in a later situation even when the goals pursued in the two situations differ considerably.

The components of a plan refer to the outcomes of goal-directed activity and specify the decisions that must be made in order to achieve these outcomes. Consequently, individuals are normally conscious of selecting a particular plan for attaining a goal and of the decisions they make in implementing it. However, they might not be aware of why they have selected this plan rather than another plan that might be equally or more effective (cf. Bargh, 1997; Bargh & Pietromonaco, 1982; Dijksterhuis & Bargh, 2001). To this extent, Principle 2 implies that if individuals have engaged in goal-directed behavior in one situation, the concepts that are activated in the course of performing this behavior can influence the procedure they use to attain an unrelated goal in a different situation. Several examples of this influence are provided in later sections of this chapter.

Automatic Behavior Activation

The plans that are stored as part of declarative knowledge are intentionally consulted in the course of making decisions about how to attain a particular objective. However, the components of these plans are not themselves behaviors. The way in which the concepts that compose a plan are transformed into actual cognitive or motor actions remains to be specified. Two conceptualizations that address this transformation are worth mention: Anderson's (1982, 1983, 1996) conception of cognitive productions (see also Smith, 1984, 1990, for applications to social cognition) and Wood and Neal's (2007) analysis of the role of habits in social behavior.

PRODUCTIONS

Anderson (1983, 1996) assumes that as a result of repetition, individuals acquire cognition–behavior associations in the form of "*if* [X], *then* [Y]" (or [X]→[Y]) *productions,* where [X] is a configuration of external or internally generated stimulus features and [Y] is a sequence of cognitive or motor behaviors that are activated and performed automatically when the conditions specified in [X] exist. To this extent, [Y] is analogous to a complex conditioned response that is elicited with little if any conscious cognitive monitoring.

The sequence of actions that compose a production may originally have been conscious and deliberate, based on instructions or the consultation of a procedure that is stored as part of declarative knowledge. With repetition, however, the sequence of actions becomes so well learned that it can be performed with little cognitive mediation (Schneider & Shiffrin, 1977). Many of the steps involved in driving a car or using a word processor, for example, initially require cognitive deliberation, but after considerable practice, they are ultimately performed with little thought.

Although production-based activity may ultimately predominate over the use of declarative knowledge, this knowledge is not erased from memory. Thus, the concepts (plans) that initially guided production-related activity can be retrieved and consulted if circumstances change and the production is no longer effective (e.g., if one transfers from a desktop computer to a laptop, or if one buys a new model car in which the dashboard displays are located in different places). However, the declarative knowledge that was employed in deliberative processing can become "buried" with disuse and therefore can be difficult to retrieve. Thus, for example, an experienced typist might find it more difficult to report the position of letters on the keyboard than a beginner might.

An understanding of the situations that stimulate the use of a production requires a specification of the features that compose its precondition [X]. These features can include both a processing objective (e.g., eating at Miko's restaurant) and characteristics of the immediate situation at hand. Thus, a driver with the goal of eating at Miko's, in combination with a particular street sign, might activate a production of the form:

[Miko's; "Prospect Street"]→[turn left ...]

and may elicit an automatic "left turning" procedure. However, neither the street sign itself nor the goal of going to Miko's alone would have this effect if encountered in isolation.

The configuration of features that compose a precondition can be fairly complex. However, people presumably respond to the configuration as a whole rather than to its individual features. Consequently, the precondition can often include features of which they are not consciously aware. To this extent, features that happen to be accessible in memory for reasons that have nothing to do with the objective that individuals are consciously pursuing could fortuitously be included in the configuration that defines a precondition and, therefore, could determine which of several productions is activated and applied. Furthermore, this production might not always be appropriate. Thus, to continue our earlier example, an individual's repertoire might include not only the production noted earlier but also the production:

[office; "Prospect Street"]→[turn right ...]

Therefore, if the individual is on his way to Miko's but happens to be thinking about a paper he has to write at the time he gets to Prospect Street, he might unexpectedly find himself in front of his office instead of the restaurant.

On the other hand, not all of the features that compose a production's precondition are required in order to activate it. It may only be necessary for the similarity of situational features to the features of a production's precondition to be above some minimal threshold. This implies that although a production is normally acquired in the course of goal-directed activity, it may later be elicited by a subset of features that do not include a specification of the goal. To this extent, the behavior that is governed by a production can occur independently of the goal to which it was originally relevant. For that matter, it might occur without any goal in mind at all.

HABITS

Although we will typically use the construct of a production in conceptualizing the research to be reported in this chapter, an alternative conceptualization was proposed by Wood and Neal (2007) in resurrecting the construct of a "habit" (for a somewhat different conceptualization, see Verplanken, 2006.) Wood and Neal conceptualize a habit as a well-learned sequence of behaviors that can be performed without any goal in mind whatsoever. The behavior might have been consciously goal directed at the time it was learned. Over time and repetition, however, it has become autonomous of its original objective and can be elicited by features of a situation independently of the purpose for which it was first acquired.

These assumptions are generally compatible with the construct of a production, which might also be viewed as a complex "conditioned response" ([Y]) to a configuration of stimulus features ([X]). Furthermore, the non–goal directedness of a habit is compatible with the assumption that not all of the features that enter into the initial learning of a production need to be present in order to elicit it. A possible difference between the habit construct and the production construct nevertheless arises in conceptualizing the specificity of the behavior to which the constructs pertain. Ji and Wood (2007), for example, give several instances in which individuals' actual behavior is inconsistent with their reported intentions to engage in this behavior. However, the behaviors they consider (e.g., taking the bus, eating fast foods, brushing their teeth in the morning) are conceptualized at a more general level than the behaviors that are theoretically governed by a production. Moreover, the actions are likely to be mediated by conscious decisions to engage in the behavior.

In contrast, a production governs more concrete situation-specific sequences of behavior that are often performed without awareness of the specific actions involved. From this perspective, a more general habit (e.g., taking the bus) is likely to reflect the inclusion of situational features in the precondition of a production that elicits a situation-specific sequence of motor behavior. The recurrence of this behavior simply reflects the fact that the features of the situation in which the behaviors are elicited are themselves likely to recur. On the other hand, discrepancies between individuals' reported intentions and their actual behavior (Ji & Wood, 2007) could be attributable to the fact that different subsets of concepts are activated in the situations in which intentions are reported and in the situations in which actual behaviors occur.

Wood and Neal's conceptualization is not intended to reflect the more traditional conceptions of the "habit" construct developed in early theories of learning (Hull, 1934; Spence, 1956). A consideration of the construct in terms of these earlier formulations is nonetheless of interest because the formulations could have implications for productions as well.

1. The strength of a habit theoretically increases with the number of times the response has been made and "reinforced." In many cases, the reinforcement is simply the attainment of the goal toward which the response is directed. In some cases, however, a behavior might be reinforced by a positive event that occurs for reasons that are quite unforeseen. At the same time, performing the behavior in the absence of any reinforcement at all theoretically decreases habit strength, ultimately leading it to be extinguished. Thus, although a representation of the goal is not a necessary precondition for the activation of a habit, the behavior will not persist indefinitely in the absence of reinforcement. And, although a habit can be activated without any goal in mind, goal satisfaction is nonetheless a contingency in its persistence over time.

2. The strength and persistence of a habit presumably depends on the nature of the reinforcement schedule. For example, intermittent reinforcement leads to slower learning but greater resistance to extinction than continuous reinforcement. To the extent these learning processes also govern the acquisition of a production, they suggest that a sequence of actions will become more strongly associated with a precondition and will be more likely to persist, if it has not always been successful in attaining the objective that stimulated its development.

3. According to learning theory, behavior is a function of not only habit but also motivation. That is, Response = Habit * Drive. This suggests that the invocation of a production is a function of not only the strength of its association with the precondition but also the level of arousal that one is experiencing at the time. This arousal could sometimes be a function of the importance of the goal that individuals are consciously pursuing. However, it could also occur for other, extraneous reasons.

Thus, the habit construct and the production construct are fairly congenial, and a complete conceptualization of automatic behavior activation is likely to incorporate the implications of both. Considered in isolation, however, it is unclear how the habit construct could account for the fact that a sequence of behavior that is activated in the pursuit of one objective can increase the likelihood of performing a similar behavior in pursuit of a different goal in a totally unrelated situation. Thus, it might have difficulty in explaining much of the research to be reviewed in this chapter. For this reason, we will use the production construct in conceptualizing this research.

Deliberative–Automatic Interface

Virtually all information processing involves a continual interplay of deliberative goal-directed cognitive activity and automatic behavior that is not consciously monitored. Driving to a restaurant, for example, requires conscious awareness of the situational cues that determine when to stop or turn right (e.g., a red light, or a street sign) and of other unexpected events that occur en route (e.g., a pedestrian crossing the street). However, although these cues are conscious, the motor reactions they elicit, which are guided by productions, are automatic.

Few conceptualizations provide a clear statement of how deliberative and automatic processes interface. The aforementioned formulation by Strack and Deutsch (2004), for example, distinguishes between impulsive and reflective memory systems, the first of which operates automatically and is driven by associative processes and the latter of which comes into play in conscious goal-directed activity. However, this conceptualization does not explain how the two systems interact in a particular situation.

The production construct may be more useful in conceptualizing how automatic processes interface with conscious goal-directed activity. For example, suppose an individual with the goal of seeing a movie decides to get the entertainment section of the newspaper and read the movie reviews. This sequence of decisions composes a plan that is constructed on the basis of concepts stored as part of declarative knowledge. However, attaining the subgoals that compose this plan (e.g., finding the entertainment section, reading the review) requires specific cognitive and motor activities. These activities are likely to be guided by productions that are elicited by a cluster of cognitions that include a goal specification (read the review), the external stimulus (the review), and in some cases, other goal-irrelevant cognitions that happen fortuitously to be accessible in memory at the time and determine the particular production to be applied (e.g., reading quickly or reading slowly). The semantic and perceptual features that activate a production can often include concepts that were activated by recent experiences for reasons that are irrelevant to the situation at hand. In fact, subliminally primed features, in combination with other, situational features, can determine the production that governs behavior.

However, although individuals may not be aware of all of the features that activate a production, they may nevertheless be aware that they have engaged in the activity that the production elicits. In fact, the activity can sometimes elicit subjective reactions. For example, individuals who read a review might experience difficulty in doing so. As Schwarz (1998, 2004) points out, the ease of processing information can often influence evaluations of the information's referent independently of the implications of the information itself.

The primary focus of this chapter is on the effects of past behavior on future cognitive and motor activity. However, the production construct is generally useful in conceptualizing the impact of activating semantic concepts on behavior. Several studies by John Bargh and his colleagues provide examples. Although this research is discussed in more detail elsewhere (see Chapter 12), it is worth noting briefly in the present context as well.

UNCONSCIOUS GOAL ACTIVATION

People are often unaware of the goals to which their behavior is relevant. In a study by Chartrand and Bargh (1996), for example, participants were unobtrusively exposed to concepts associated with either memory or impression formation. Later, they were given a series of behaviors with instructions to comprehend them. Their subsequent recall of the behaviors showed a pattern similar to that of participants who are explicitly asked either to remember the behaviors or to form an impression of a person they described (Hamilton, Katz, & Leirer, 1980; Srull & Wyer, 1979). In interpreting this finding, however, it is important to note that participants obviously had *some* objective in mind when they processed the behaviors (e.g., to comprehend the information). However, concepts activated by the priming task, along with those of the immediate situation (the stimulus behaviors), presumably activated a production that determined the particular strategy they employed in attaining this objectives. This occurred with little if any awareness of the cognitive operations they performed and without consciousness of *other* goals to which their actions were also relevant.

PERCEPTION–BEHAVIOR LINK

The unconscious influence of semantic concepts on behavior has sometimes been attributed to the existence of a perception–behavior link, that is, a direct association between the perception of a stimulus and overt behavior that is not mediated by cognitions about the perceived stimulus or its behavioral implications (Bargh, 1997; Dijksterhuis & Bargh, 2001). In a well-known study by Bargh, Chen, and Burrows (1996), for example, exposing participants to concepts associated with elderly people led them to walk more slowly to the elevator upon leaving the experiment. In a second study, unobtrusively priming concepts associated with rudeness or politeness affected participants' likelihood of interrupting an experimenter's conversation with a graduate student in order to turn in a questionnaire. In each study, goal-related situational features (getting on the elevator, or turning in a questionnaire) may have combined with the primed concepts that happened to be accessible in memory to activate a production that spontaneously elicited behavior without awareness of the conditions that gave rise to its activation.

The utility of the production construct conceptualizing these effects is further evidenced by studies in which African American faces were primed subliminally, activating a stereotype of African Americans. Features of the stereotype typically include both "aggressive" and "unmotivated to perform well in academic achievement" situations. In a third experiment by Bargh et al. (1996), this priming led European American participants to display greater nonverbal indications of irritation upon being asked to repeat a boring task. In a quite different study (Colcombe & Wyer, 2001; see Wyer, 2004), however, the same priming decreased European Americans' performance on a test of mathematical ability and increased their performance on tests of rhythm memory and basketball shooting. Although the same stereotype-based concepts were activated in all cases, different subsets of these concepts were relevant in the situations constructed in these different experiments. Consequently, different situation-specific productions were apparently activated, depending on the nature of these situations.

MIMICRY

As we noted earlier, a subset of the features that compose the precondition of a production may be sufficient to elicit it, and this subset does not necessarily include a goal concept. Imitative behavior provides an example (for reviews, see Chartrand, this volume; Chartrand & Bargh, 2002). As Bandura (1986) demonstrated many years ago, people may acquire a learned disposition to imitate others' behavior at a very early age, owing in part to its utility in attaining desired goals (e.g., social approval). Once acquired, however, a disposition to imitate may be activated independently of any particular goal to which it is relevant. For example, Chartrand and Bargh (1999) found that individuals who interacted with someone in the course of an informal conversation imitated their partner's incidental behavior (e.g., face rubbing) without awareness of doing so. More recent studies (Lakin & Chartrand, 2003) have shown that this imitation depends in part on persons' liking for the individual with whom they interact. This does not mean that their imitation was conscious, however. Rather, it suggests that the precondition that elicits imitative behavior can include affective features as well as descriptive ones.

EMBODIED COGNITION

An increasing number of studies demonstrate that individuals' judgments and decisions can be influenced by the proprioceptive feedback produced by bodily states or movements. In an early series of studies, Strack and his colleagues demonstrated that unobtrusive manipulations of individuals facial expressions influenced the amusement they reported experiencing in response to cartoons (Strack, Martin, & Stepper, 1988) and that their posture while completing a questionnaire (upright or slumped) influenced their self-judgments of pride (Stepper & Strack, 1993). In a later study, extending the middle finger while reading a target's ambiguously aggressive behavior increased judgments of the target as hostile, whereas extending the thumb upward increased the favorableness of a target's evaluations (Chandler & Schwarz, 2009). Flexing the arms can activate concepts associated with approach and extending the arms can activate concepts associated with avoidance, leading individuals to drink more of a pleasant-tasting beverage in the former condition than in the second (Förster, 2003). Head movements (nodding or shaking) can influence individuals' reactions to persuasive communications (Brinol & Petty, 2003) and their memory for stimuli whose valence is consistent with implications of these movements (Förster & Strack, 1996). Although other explanations of these effects are possible, it seems reasonable to suppose that proprioceptive feedback, or concepts associated with it, might be contained in the precondition of a production that elicits a processing strategy underlying the judgments or decisions at hand without consciousness of its influence.

OVERVIEW

In the remaining sections of this chapter, we consider the effect of procedural knowledge on both goal-directed and non–goal-directed behavior. As we noted earlier, goals and means are often strongly associated in memory. It is therefore sometimes difficult to distinguish between the factors that influence the selection of a goal and the factors that influence the selection of a procedure for attaining it. When alternative procedures for attaining a goal are potentially available, however, the effect of procedural knowledge can be inferred from the effects of goal-directed activity in one situation on the behavior that is performed in a second, ostensibly unrelated situation in the pursuit of a quite different objective. This strategy is applied in the research we review in the remainder of this chapter.

It is also hard to distinguish empirically between (1) the effect of plans that are stored as part of declarative knowledge and used as a basis for conscious behavioral decisions and (2) the effect of productions that are applied automatically without cognitive deliberation and often without awareness. We nevertheless organize our discussion in terms of research in which one or the other effect is likely to predominate. The next section reviews evidence of the effects of productions of which individuals are unaware. We then consider conditions in which people are aware of the outcome of applying a production but are unaware of both the reason the production was activated and the steps involved in its implementation. Finally, we consider the effects of plans that people store in memory as part of declarative knowledge and deliberately consult in the course of making an evaluation or behavioral decision.

In our review, we take into account the fact that the accessibility of knowledge is a function of its frequency of prior use as well as its recency of use (Higgins, Bargh, & Lombardi, 1985; Srull & Wyer, 1979). This implies that if a procedure has been used frequently over a period of time, it becomes *chronically* accessible and, therefore, might be used as a default when the use of this particular procedure is arbitrary. Bargh, Bond, Lombardi, and Tota (1986) found that chronically accessible trait concepts affect the interpretation of behavioral information and that these effects are independent of situational factors that influence their accessibility. This could be true of procedures as well. That is, both (1) plans that are stored as part of declarative knowledge and (2) productions that are elicited by this knowledge can be chronically accessible and have much the same influence as procedures that are primed by situational factors. Examples of this possibility are provided in the discussion to follow.

Unconscious Influences of Productions on Behavior

To reiterate, productions govern concrete, situation-specific behavior. This behavior can be elicited by stimulus features of which individuals are unaware. Moreover, the behavior itself can occur without awareness. These conditions can arise at several stages of processing ranging from the input stage (when individuals first encounter stimulus information) to the output stage (when people generate an overt cognitive or motor response). These possibilities are exemplified by research in quite diverse areas, including anchoring effects, automatic evaluation processes, verbal overshadowing, and the effect of a goal's desirability on the performance of goal-related behavior.

ANCHORING PROCESSES
Effects on Response Generation

When individuals are asked to make a judgment along a scale and do not have a clear a priori conception of the value they should use, they may select an extreme end of the scale as an "anchor" and then adjust either upward or downward along the scale until they reach a value they consider to be plausible (Tversky & Kahneman, 1974). A range of values are plausible, however, and people typically stop searching when they encounter a value they consider to be reasonable. Consequently, they are likely to make higher estimates when they have used the high end of the scale as an anchor than when they have used the low end.

The selection of an anchor is often arbitrary and occurs with little cognitive deliberation. Consequently, its use in one situation may activate a production that is later applied in a quite different situation. For example, asking participants to rank-order stimuli from high to low with respect to a given attribute could activate a disposition to consider high values before low ones, and this disposition might generalize to a rating task that the participants perform subsequently. Ranking stimuli from low to high could of course have the opposite effect.

Schwarz and Wyer (1985) found this to be true. Moreover, the effects they identified were evident regardless of the nature of the ratings. That is, ranking social issues from high to low in importance (relative to ranking from low to high) led participants to rate these issues as not only higher in importance along

a scale of importance but also higher in triviality along a scale of triviality. Furthermore, importance ratings of social issues were affected in a similar way by ranking the qualities of a marriage partner.

Effects on Selective Attention

The concepts activated by a past behavior can be contained in the precondition of productions at several different stages of processing. The concepts involved in rank-ordering provide an example. Participants in one study (Shen & Wyer, 2008) were asked to rank-order attributes of a commercial product either from most to least favorable or from least to most. This procedure presumably activated a disposition to process favorable information before unfavorable information in the first case, but to process unfavorable information before favorable information in the second. Participants were then given descriptions of a computer containing five favorable and five unfavorable attributes and were allowed either 15 seconds or as much time as they wanted to evaluate it.

The ranking procedure that participants employed at the outset influenced the order in which the information was considered. When participants did not have enough time to process all of the information they received, they evaluated the computer more favorably when the search strategy they had applied in the initial task had disposed them to consider favorable pieces of information before unfavorable pieces. When participants had time to think about all of the information provided, however, they gave greater weight to attributes they had considered most recently and thus were most easily accessible in memory. Consequently, they evaluated the product more favorably when the production activated by the rank-ordering task disposed them to consider favorable attributes last.

The preceding studies exemplify the possibility that concepts elicited by the same past behavior (rank-ordering) can elicit different productions, depending on the task-related features of the situation at hand. By the same token, the pursuit of different objectives can sometimes activate the same production. Shafir (1993), for example, found that people typically focus on favorable attributes if they are asked whether they would choose the product, but they focus on unfavorable attributes if they are asked whether they would reject it. To this extent, making these different types of judgments could activate concepts very similar to those activated by rank-ordering. Shen and Wyer (2008) confirmed this hypothesis as well. That is, participants who were under time pressure made relatively more favorable ratings of the products described by an array of attributes if they had decided whether to choose stimuli in an earlier situation than if they had decided whether to reject these stimuli. When participants had an unlimited time to process the product information, the reverse was true.

Other studies indicated that participants had no insight into the effects of their past behavior on their later estimates. For example, they reported that they considered the first stimuli *presented* before later ones independently of their value and independently of the type of rank-ordering they had performed. Moreover, the effects of rank-ordering generalized over content domains. For example, ranking sets of course grades in an initial task affected participants' later evaluations of a product on the basis of a list of consumer ratings. This finding reinforces the assumption that the effects of past behavior were mediated by a production that participants applied to the task they performed later without making a conscious decision to do so.

AUTOMATIC EVALUATION EFFECTS

The studies by Schwarz and Wyer (1985) and Shen and Wyer (2008) demonstrate the effects of a production at both the output stage of processing and the input stage. However, products can influence behavior at other stages as well. One of the most provocative examples of the effect of a production on inference and evaluation processes is provided by John Bargh's research on automatic evaluation effects (Bargh, Chaiken, Govender, & Pratto, 1992; Bargh, Chaiken, Raymond, & Hymes, 1996). This research demonstrates not only that individuals have a chronic disposition to categorize information as either favorable or unfavorable but also that these processes occur without conscious awareness. In this research paradigm, participants are typically asked to respond to a favorable or unfavorable word following a context word that is either evaluatively similar or evaluatively dissimilar to it. The first word is normally presented subliminally. Participants respond more quickly to the second word when it is evaluatively similar to the subliminally primed word than when it is evaluatively different.

In interpreting these results, three additional findings are noteworthy. First, the effect is equally strong regardless of the evaluative extremity of the words presented. Second, the effects occur even when participants are simply asked to pronounce the second word rather than to evaluate it (Bargh et al., 1996). Third, the effects are evident even when the

first, priming word is novel (Duckworth, Bargh, Garcia, & Chaiken, 2002). Note that this latter finding argues against an alternative interpretation of the findings. That is, the first word might simply elicit a previously conditioned affective reaction that either facilitates or interferes with participants' affective response to the second. However, the fact that novel context stimuli have similar effects argues against this possibility. As Wyer (2004) suggested, the results seem most easily interpretable as evidence of a spontaneous *categorization* process. That is, categorizing the first word as favorable or unfavorable may activate a production that is applied without awareness to the second word and either facilitates or interferes with the process of categorizing it. (It is interesting to speculate that this production reflects a wired-in tendency to evaluate stimulus objects as either potentially harmful or benign that has evolutionary roots.)

VERBAL OVERSHADOWING

The interference effects of simultaneously activated productions are also suggested by research on verbal overshadowing (Dodson, Johnson, & Schooler, 1997; Schooler & Engstler-Schooler, 1990). In a particularly interesting study (Dodson et al., 1997), participants were first exposed to a series of faces and then asked to describe one of the faces verbally. Generating this description increased participants' difficulty in recognizing not only this face but also other faces they had seen but had not described verbally. Dodson et al. concluded that verbally encoding a face in the course of describing it activated a verbal processing strategy that interfered with the visual processing that was necessary for accurate recognition of the faces that participants encountered subsequently. Furthermore, this interference generalized to stimuli other than the one to which the verbal encoding strategy had initially been applied.

EFFECT OF DESIRABILITY ON
PRODUCTION-MEDIATED BEHAVIOR

The behavior that is governed by a production can often be activated and applied without awareness. Moreover, although the behavior may be relevant to the goal that individuals are pursuing, it can later be elicited by features of a production that do not include a goal representation. In conceptualizing this possibility, Shen, Wyer, and Cai (2012) distinguish between a *goal* concept that is activated in the course of conscious goal-directed activity and a *behavior* concept that is applied to behavior independently of its goal relevance. The same action could exemplify either. For example, "speaking quickly" could be a goal that is deliberately pursued in order to attain a higher order objective. Or, it could refer to a behavior that is purely descriptive in nature. The effect of activating a goal concept on the motivation to engage in goal-relevant behavior (e.g., on the effort expended to attain this goal) is likely to depend on the goal's desirability. In contrast, the behavior concept (or a more general concept that it exemplifies) could be part of the precondition of a production that elicits behavior independently of any goal to which it is relevant.

Shen et al. (2012) provided evidence of this distinction. Participants first shadowed a speech that was delivered at either a rapid or slow rate, thus requiring them to speak either quickly or slowly. Then, as part of an ostensibly different experiment, they completed a marketing survey. Participants completed the survey more quickly when they had spoken quickly during the shadowing task than when they had spoken slowly.

In further studies, however, participants' speed of performing the shadowing task was associated with either positive or negative affect, leading the goal of speaking quickly (and consequently the more general goal of doing things quickly) to be seen as more or less desirable. Then, before beginning work on the marketing survey, participants in some conditions were told that the time available for completing it was limited (thus calling attention to the goal of completing it quickly). These participants completed the survey more quickly when speaking quickly during the speech-shadowing task was desirable, and completed it less quickly when speaking quickly during this task was undesirable. When the time to complete the survey was not mentioned, however, the speed with which participants completed the survey was guided by a production that was independent of the desirability of the goal to which it was relevant.

Role of Productions in Comprehension

The examples provided in the preceding section exemplify conditions in which individuals' past goal-relevant behavior influenced their behavior in a later situation with little if any awareness of the behavior itself. In other cases, individuals may be aware of the consequences of applying a production but are not conscious of either the reason for selecting it or of the specific steps involved in implementing it.

These conditions most obviously come into play in the comprehension of information.

Comprehension can often be automatic. It is hard *not* to comprehend statements such as, "the boy kicked the ball." By the same token, we immediately recognize that "the ball kicked the boy" is anomalous. When information is conveyed in a social context, the process of comprehending it may be guided in part by Gricean principles of communication (Grice, 1975). That is, individuals may spontaneously construe the literal meaning of the information and might engage in more deliberative attempts to construe its implications only if its literal meaning violates these principles (Wyer & Radvansky, 1999; for discussions of the role of these processes in both humor elicitation and communication and persuasion, see Wyer & Collins, 1992; Wyer & Gruenfeld, 1995).

Comprehension can vary along several dimensions. For example, individuals could apply either concrete concepts or more abstract ones; they could interpret individual pieces of information either independently or in relation to one another and their context; they could either encode information verbally or construct visual images of the objects and events described. These comprehension strategies could sometimes be employed deliberately to attain a goal that requires them. They could also reflect a chronic disposition to employ a procedure that has been used frequently in the past. In still other cases, however, the strategies might reflect the use of a production that is activated by concepts made accessible by performing behavior in an earlier situation and that is applied spontaneously without a conscious decision to do so.

It is not always clear a priori whether comprehension strategies are applied without awareness or deliberately. That is, the decision to employ a given comprehension strategy might be conscious. Nevertheless, the influence of past behavior on this decision and the specific activities involved in its implementation could occur without awareness. This possibility is exemplified by research in three areas that concerns (1) the abstractness of concepts used to comprehend information, (2) the interpretation of individual items of information in relation to one another, and (3) the consequences of dispositions to form visual images on the basis of information.

LEVEL OF ABSTRACTNESS

The concepts that are used to interpret information can vary in abstractness. A pet, for example, might be encoded as either "Rover," a "collie," a "dog," or an "animal." Similarly, an event could be interpreted as both "buying meat and eggs" and "shopping," or as both "rereading class notes" and "studying." There may be basic levels of abstractness at which objects and events are typically encoded (Rosch et al., 1976). However, situational factors can also play a role. For example, a pet is more likely to be called a "collie" if its picture is accompanied by pictures of a dachshund and a Labrador retriever than if it is accompanied by pictures of a chimpanzee and George W. Bush. It seems likely that the use of abstract (vs. concrete) concepts to interpret information in one situation can induce a disposition to encode information conveyed at a similar level in a later situation as well. This disposition could affect both memory for the information and the implications that are drawn from it.

Effects of Temporal Construal

Situational differences in the abstractness of the concepts used to interpret information are suggested by construal level theory (Trope & Liberman; 2003, 2010; see also Liberman, Trope, & Stephan, 2007; Trope, Liberman, & Wakslak, 2007). For example, individuals categorize objects and events more broadly if they anticipate encountering them in the future than if they expect to do so immediately (Liberman, Sagristano, & Trope, 2002; Trope et al., 2007). Moreover, this disposition, once activated, may generalize to situations in which psychological distance is not itself involved. In a series of experiments by Wakslak, Trope, Liberman, and Alony (2006), some participants were led to believe that the experimental task they were performing would not be completed until some time in the future, thereby creating a disposition to process information in terms of abstract concepts. These participants later performed better on a task that required the abstraction of stimuli from a complex background, but performed less well on tasks that required attention to details, than individuals who believed that the first task would be completed within the same experimental session.

A more compelling demonstration of the effects of time perspective on the abstractness of concepts used to interpret information was reported by Förster, Liberman, and Kuschel (2008, Experiment 3). Participants first compared their athletic ability to that of either a moderately athletic standard (Michael Schumacher, a racecar driver) or a moderately unathletic one (Bill Clinton). After doing so, they imagined themselves participating in an athletic competition either the next day or a year later and estimated their performance and their general athletic ability. Individuals who had considered participating in the future used broader concepts in comparing themselves to the standard and judged their athletic skills to be relatively similar this person. However, individuals who contemplated participating immediately used narrower concepts and distinguished between themselves and the standard. Consequently, the standard had contrast effects on their self-judgments.

Global Versus Local Processing

More direct evidence of the effect of past behavior on the abstractness of concepts applied in responding to information is provided by Jens Förster's research on global versus local processing (Förster & Dannenberg, 2010; Förster, 2011). In this research, individuals are exposed to a set of stimuli, each consisting of a large figure made up of small figures of a different type (e.g., a large H composed of smaller Ts, or a square formed of an array of triangles) and are asked over a series of trials to identify either the large figure or the small one. Thus, they are primed to respond either "globally" or "locally." Individuals who have responded to the whole, relative to those who have focused on stimulus components, generate more unusual uses for a brick (a reflection of their use of broader concepts for categorizing the stimulus being judged; Förster & Friedman, 2010). Moreover, they make longer estimates of psychological (e.g., geographical or temporal) distance between themselves and other stimuli (Liberman & Förster, 2009) and generate relatively more similarities than differences between television shows (Förster, 2009).

A particularly provocative series of studies (Förster, in press) show that the effects of activating global and local processing generalize over sensory stimulus domains. For example, participants who had been primed to respond to the whole rather than to the components of a visual stimulus generated more global (vs. detailed) descriptions of a poem that was delivered orally, spent more time touching global than detailed features of a stimulus object in a blindfolded object-recognition task, and reported fewer distinct taste sensations after tasting a complex mixture of food ingredients. Moreover, a different series of studies showed that the direction of causality could be reversed.

Many other factors can influence the abstractness of the concepts that individuals use (Förster et al., 2008). In a study by Stapel and Semin (2007), for example, participants watched a short film in which chess pieces moved in ways that were conducive to an anthropomorphic interpretation of what went on. Some participants then described the pieces' "behavior," whereas others described the pieces' "personalities." Participants typically used concrete verbs in their behavioral descriptions but used abstract trait adjectives in their personality descriptions. Then, in a later task, participants were asked to indicate which of two geometric figures—a large square that was formed from a number of smaller triangles or a large triangle that was formed from a number of smaller squares—was more similar to a target figure (a triangle or a square). Participants were more likely to base their judgment on the target's similarity to the large figure if they had generated abstract personality descriptions in the first task than if they had generated more concrete behavior descriptions.

RELATIONAL THINKING

Situationally Activated Productions

Individuals who receive a number of pieces of information could potentially encode each piece of information independently. Alternatively, they could consider the information items in relation to one another or to the context in which they occur. (People who encounter a male and female couple, for example, could describe them either individually, as a "man" and a "woman," or in terms of their marital or social relationship.) The use of these thinking styles in one situation could activate a production that is used to comprehend the information encountered in a later situation.

Several studies confirm this speculation. In an experiment by Kim and Meyers-Levy (2007), some participants were first given a series of stimuli with instructions to form a mental representation of the features of each stimulus individually. Others were told to organize the stimuli into groups that were similar to one another, and still others were told to group them "in such a way that stimuli in one category were different from those in the other categories." After performing this task, participants read an ad for a vacation resort that contained features related to both price and quality. Later, they recalled the features in the ad. Participants' recall protocols indicated that the strategy they had used to process information in the first task generalized to the second. That is, the recalled items were clustered to a greater extent in terms of the general category to which they belonged when participants had been primed to think relationally than when they had been primed to consider stimuli individually, and this was true regardless of whether the primed relationship pertained to similarity or dissimilarity. Although judgment data were more complicated, the authors

concluded that relational thinking played a role in evaluations of the target stimulus as well.

Of particular interest is the possibility that inducing individuals to think about *themselves* either independently or in relation to others can activate a disposition that influences their later responses to stimuli to which their self-perceptions are quite irrelevant. Participants in a study by Kühnen and Oyserman (2002) initially performed a task that required them to circle either first-person singular pronouns ("I," "me," etc.) or first person plural pronouns ("we," "us," etc.) in a passage they were reading. Using "we" presumably activates a tendency to think about oneself in relation to other persons, whereas using "I" activates a disposition to think about oneself as independent of others. These dispositions may give rise to productions that affect self-irrelevant processing in subsequent situations. Then, as part of an ostensibly unrelated study, participants were shown an array of 28 objects (a house, a moon, etc.), after which they were given a blank sheet of paper and asked to write the names of the objects in the positions they were shown. Priming had little influence on the actual number of objects recalled. However, participants were relatively more accurate in positioning the objects in relation to one another when they had been primed with "we" than when they had been primed with "I." These findings provide strong evidence that stimulating participants to think about themselves as part of a group activates a production that induces them to think about stimuli in general in relation to one another, whereas stimulating them to think about themselves as individuals activates a production that leads them to think about stimuli independently of one another. These productions, once activated, are reapplied in quite different situations that have nothing to do with oneself whatsoever.

Chronically Accessible Productions

We noted earlier that if a cognitive or motor procedure has been applied repeatedly over a period of time, it can become chronically accessible and, therefore, might be applied spontaneously in situations in which it is applicable. The disposition to think about stimuli individually or relationally provides an example. Cultural differences in the disposition to think of oneself either independently or in relation to others are well recognized (Markus & Kitayama, 1991; Triandis, 1989). Specifically, East Asians have a tendency to think of themselves in relation to other members of the society in which they live, whereas North Americans are disposed to think of themselves as independent. These chronic dispositions may be spontaneously applied in comprehending stimuli in a number of quite different domains.

Studies by Nisbett and colleagues (for reviews, see Nisbett, 2003; Norenzayan, Choi, & Peng, 2007) confirm this speculation. For example, Asians spend more time than European Americans looking at background features of a visual display (Chua, Boland, & Nisbett, 2005) and are relatively more sensitive to changes in these contextual features (Masuda & Nisbett, 2001). At the same time, they are relatively less likely to ignore irrelevant contextual cues in performing a perceptual task. In a particularly interesting experiment, Park, Nisbett, and Hedden (1999) asked Asian and American participants to learn a series of words. Each word was presented on a separate card. In some conditions, the word was shown in isolation. In other conditions, the word was surrounded by pictures of people and objects that were irrelevant to the word's meaning. Participants were later asked to recall the words they had read. One might intuitively expect the irrelevant context stimuli to be distracting and to decrease participants' attention to the words. In fact, however, Asians' recall of the words was actually *greater* when the contextual stimuli were presented. This was not true of the Americans.

VISUAL VERSUS VERBAL COMPREHENSION STRATEGIES

As noted earlier, individuals might interpret "the boy kicked the ball" on the basis of the semantic knowledge they have acquired about the meaning of the words (kick, ball, etc.). On the other hand, they might form a visual image of the event described that involves a specification of the type of ball and the situational context in which the event occurs. These different comprehension strategies can often depend on the type of information presented (Colcombe & Wyer, 2002) and on specific instructions to employ one strategy or another (Kosslyn, 1975, 1976; Petrova & Cialdini, 2005). However, they can also reflect the use of a production that, if activated in one situation, may generalize to other, unrelated situations.

Furthermore, the productions employed, like those that underlie relational thinking, could either be situationally induced or result from an accumulation of experiences that have occurred frequently in the past and have become chronically accessible. A series of studies by Jiang and his colleagues (Jiang, Steinhart & Wyer, 2010; Jiang & Wyer, 2009) suggest both possibilities.

Chronic Productions

To distinguish between the effects of verbal processing and the effects of visual processing, Jiang capitalized on a characteristic of visual images that does not come into play when information is processed verbally. That is, visual images are formed from a particular perspective, or visual point of view, and this perspective can be influenced by the way an event is described. For example, entering a room could be described from the perspective of someone outside the room ("He went into the room") or someone inside ("He came into the room"). Although the semantic meaning of the statements is the same, the images that are formed of the events are likely to differ.

In one series of studies (Jiang & Wyer, 2009), participants reported their reactions to positively and negatively valenced events that were described verbally from the perspective of either someone at the location in which the events occurred ("the actress came into the room and sang a beautiful song," "the drunk came into the kitchen and threw up on the floor") or someone outside ("the actress went...," "the drunk went..."). Participants with a chronic disposition to form visual images were identified on the basis of their responses to Childers, Houston, and Heckler's (1985) style-of-processing scale. These participants reported more extreme emotional reactions to events if they were described from the perspective of someone at the location in which the event occurred than if the events were described from an external perspective. In contrast, individuals with a predisposition to process information semantically without forming visual images reported similar reactions regardless of the perspective from which the events were described.

Considered in isolation, these results might be attributed to differences in the *ability* to construct visual images rather than the disposition to do so. In a second set of conditions, however, participants were explicitly instructed to form visual images of the events. In this case, participants reported more extreme reactions to events that were described from an inside perspective regardless of their chronic disposition to form images. This indicates that visual processing strategies are under conscious control.

Verbal and visual processing strategies can influence the ease with which information can be comprehended as well as the reactions that result from this comprehension. In a second set of studies, Jiang and Wyer (2009) asked participants to comprehend a series of statements, four of which referred to a person (1) going into the men's room, (2) going into the ladies' room, (3) coming into the men's room, or (4) coming into the ladies' room. Persons with a disposition to form visual images were expected to have difficulty imagining an event from an unfamiliar perspective. Differences in comprehension time confirmed this conjecture. Males and females with a disposition to form visual images did not differ in the time they took to comprehend statements that described someone *going* into a restroom regardless of the type of room described because both events were familiar. However, male visualizers took significantly longer to comprehend a statement that described someone *coming* into the ladies' room than a statement that described someone coming into the men's room, whereas female imagers took significantly less time to comprehend the first statement than the second. In contrast, individuals with a disposition to process information verbally did not differ in the ease of comprehending the two types of statements.

Situational Versus Chronic Differences in Production Accessibility

A different series of studies (Jiang, Steinhart, & Wyer, 2009; see Wyer, Hung, & Jiang, 2008) provided evidence that the visual and verbal comprehension processes can be situationally activated as well as chronic and that they have similar effects on comprehension in each case. In one study, verbal and visual processing strategies were induced by asking participants to perform either a hidden-word task (which required the identification of words that were embedded in an array of letters) or a hidden-figures task (which required the identification of geometrical shapes that were embedded in a picture). Then, in an ostensibly different experiment, participants

evaluated a computer mouse on the basis of verbal descriptions of its attributes. The attribute descriptions were the same in all cases. In some conditions, however, they allegedly pertained to a standard optical mouse of the sort that most college students use on a daily basis. In other conditions, they ostensibly pertained to a "trackball" mouse that is typically used only by graphic designers and with which participants were unfamiliar.

The visual processing required by the hidden figures task, in combination with features of the judgment task that participants performed subsequently, presumably disposed participants to construct a visual representation of the mouse to use as a basis for evaluating it. However, they found this difficult to accomplish when the object was unfamiliar and a previously formed visual representation of it did not exist in memory. Consequently, as shown in the left half of Table 13.1, they evaluated the trackball mouse less favorably than the standard one. (For evidence that difficulty in processing information about an object decreases evaluations of it, see Schwarz, 1998, 2004; Winkielman & Cacioppo, 2001; Winkielman, Schwarz, Fazendeiro, & Reber, 2003). In contrast, performing the hidden-word task activated a disposition to employ a verbal processing strategy in comprehending the information of the stimuli. Consequently, these participants did not form visual images of the stimuli and evaluated them similarly regardless of how familiar they were.

Note that if a picture of the unfamiliar product is presented, it should increase visual information processors' ability to form a representation of the product and should increase their evaluations of it. However, a picture should have relatively little impact on individuals who are disposed to process

Table 13.1 **Mean product evaluations as a function of product familiarity, the presence of a picture, and production activation**

	No picture		Picture	
	Visual Mindset	**Verbal Mindset**	**Visual Mindset**	**Verbal Mindset**
Situationally induced production				
Familiar mouse	5.02	5.00	5.33	5.82
Unfamiliar mouse	3.63	5.02	5.21	4.08
Chronic production				
Familiar mouse	4.52	4.57	5.22	5.45
Unfamiliar mouse	2.97	4.78	4.17	3.74

Based on data from Jiang et al., 2008.

information verbally. Data presented in the right half of Table 13.1 confirmed this possibility as well. That is, a picture had an appreciable influence on visual information processors' evaluations of an unfamiliar product but had little effect on their evaluations of a familiar one. In contrast, the presence of a picture *decreased* verbal processors' evaluations of the unfamiliar product, suggesting that if anything, it interfered with their processing of the verbal descriptions.

Finally, a parallel study was conducted in which chronic differences in processing were assessed using the Childers et al. (1985) scale mentioned earlier. This study yielded virtually identical results, as shown in the bottom half of Table 13.1. Thus, the effects of visual and verbal processing strategies were similar regardless of whether they were activated in an ostensibly unrelated recent situation or were chronically accessible.

Information-Elicited Productions

Although the application of a production to information can be influenced by chronic or situational factors that exist before exposure to this information, it can often be stimulated by the information itself. Carlston's (1994) associated systems theory assumes that verbal processing and visual processing are governed by different cognitive systems. Thus, when information about a target is conveyed in different modalities, it may spontaneously elicit two productions, each of which is applied to the information conveyed in a different modality. The results of processing in each modality could often have different, perhaps conflicting implications for judgments and decisions. If this is so, however, factors that interfere with the use of results of processing in one modality may lead the results of processing in the other modality to have more impact.

A study by Claypool and Carlston (2002) suggests this possibility. Participants were given both a picture of a target person and a verbal description of his personality attributes and then were asked to evaluate either (1) his general personality or (2) his physical attractiveness. Thus, the information stimulated both verbal and visual processing. However, the results of visual processing were largely irrelevant to judgments of the target's personality, whereas the results of verbal processing were irrelevant to judgments of his physical attractiveness. Consequently, the simultaneous consideration of both sets of results in combination was likely to create confusion and to have an adverse effect on both judgments.

In some conditions, however, participants before making judgments were asked to remember verbal information about a *different* person, thus creating interference with the verbal processing of the target information. Although this cognitive activity decreased the effect of the original information on personality judgments of the target, it *increased* its impact on judgments of his attractiveness. Correspondingly, asking participants to remember the picture of a different person before making judgments decreased their judgments of the target's attractiveness but increased their evaluations of his personality. In short, factors that decreased the likelihood of using the results of processing in one modality had adverse effects on judgments to which this processing was relevant but increased the effect of information on judgments in a domain to which the processing was irrelevant.

SUMMARY

In the situations described earlier in this chapter, performing goal-directed activity in one situation activated a production that influenced behavior in a later situation without awareness of the behavior itself. In contrast, individuals in the situations reviewed in this section were likely to be aware of the consequences of the production-elicited behavior they performed (e.g., the abstractness of the concepts they applied, the construction of a visual image). Nevertheless, the behavior itself was likely to be performed automatically without a conscious decision to engage in it and without awareness of the cognitive and motor actions that led to these outcomes. Thus, the effects are distinguished from those to be discussed in the next section of this chapter, which concerns the influence of past behavior on the goal-directed strategies that individuals consciously decide to apply in goal-directed activity, albeit without awareness of why they selected these strategies rather than equally viable alternatives.

Generalization of Plans in Deliberative Goal-Directed Processing

As we have noted, conscious goal-directed behavior often requires a deliberate consultation of a plan that is retrieved from declarative knowledge and used as a guide in deciding the sequence of steps to be performed in attaining the objective at hand. In these instances, individuals' behavior in a past situation can influence the plan they consult. As Wyer and Xu (2010) suggest, these effects can be characterized as *behavioral mindsets* that operate primarily at the evaluation and decision stages of processing.

The effects have been identified in several areas of research, including communication and persuasion, promotion and prevention motivation, uncertainty avoidance, variety seeking, and decision making.

Impact of Behavioral Mindsets

RESPONSES TO PERSUASIVE MESSAGES: BOLSTERING AND COUNTERARGUING MINDSETS

Individuals who receive a communication and are motivated to evaluate its implications might marshal support for the validity of the assertions contained in the message. Alternatively, they might attempt to refute the validity of these assertions by counterarguing. These different cognitive responses can depend on numerous factors, including individuals' a priori attitudes toward the situation or event to which the message pertains, the strength of the arguments conveyed in the message, and the recipients' ability or motivation to think carefully about the implications of these arguments (Chaiken, 1987; Petty & Cacioppo, 1986). When individuals do not have a strong attitude toward the topic of the message they receive, however, their decision to engage in these alternative processes could be influenced by recent experiences they had before the information is encountered.

A recent series of studies by Jing Xu (2010; Xu & Wyer, 2012) provides a compelling demonstration that inducing a disposition to elaborate or counterargue in one situation can induce a mindset that influences responses to communications encountered in a later, quite unrelated situation. Participants in one study were asked to list their thoughts about each of three propositions. In some cases, the wording of the propositions (e.g., "Reading enriches the mind," "The University of Illinois should not increase tuition fees") led participants to agree with them. In other cases, the wording ("Reading is bad for the mind," "The University should increase tuition fees") led participants to disagree. Thus, the thoughts that participants listed were similar regardless of how the propositions were worded. However, the procedure of generating the thoughts was stimulated by an attempt to support the propositions in the first case (i.e., to "bolster") but to counterargue the propositions in the second. A third, control group of participants generated thoughts about evaluatively neutral propositions.

After completing their thought listings, participants as part of an unrelated study read an advertisement for a vacation spot and evaluated its desirability. The descriptions of the vacation were attractive in one condition but relatively unattractive in the other. Regardless of the vacation's a priori attractiveness, however, participants evaluated it more favorably when they had listed supportive thoughts in the priming task, and less favorably when they had listed counterarguments, than they did in control conditions.

Two qualifications on the generality of these findings are important. First, inducing a bolstering or counterarguing mindset is likely to have an appreciable effect only if participants are unlikely to generate these cognitive responses spontaneously. Participants in the aforementioned experiment expected the vacation spots being advertised to be relatively desirable and may have spontaneously elaborated the ad's implications. Consequently, the effect of inducing a bolstering mindset was small and nonsignificant. In a second study, the ad extolled the virtues of exotic Chinese cuisine (including scorpions and sea horses) that participants were likely to consider undesirable on a priori grounds. In this case, inducing a bolstering mindset had a significant positive effect, whereas inducing a counterarguing mindset had little effect.

Second, a counterarguing mindset is likely to have a negative impact on responses to a communication only if the implications of the message are easy to refute. If these implications are difficult to refute, inducing participants to counterargue may increase their perception that the implications are credible and thus may increase the impact of the message rather than decreasing it. In a third study, participants received a donation appeal from UNICEF whose implications were difficult to discredit. In this case, inducing a counterarguing mindset had a boomerang effect, increasing the impact of the appeal on both participants' reported urge to help and the amount of money they were willing to donate.

Mindsets can be activated by covert cognitive activity as well as overt behavior. In another study by Xu and Wyer (2012), Democrats and Republicans who had listened to a political speech by their preferred Presidential candidate (Barack Obama or John McCain) were subsequently more influenced by a speech promoting Toyota than control participants were, whereas those who had listened to a speech by the opposing candidate (and thus spontaneously counterargued) were less influenced by the Toyota speech.

COUNTERFACTUAL MINDSETS

When individuals' behavior has negative consequences, they are likely to think about what they might have done to avoid those consequences.

The consideration of alternative possibilities could induce a "counterfactual" mindset that leads them to consider alternative possibilities in a later situation as well.

Although we know of no evidence bearing directly on this possibility, more general evidence of a counterfactual mindset has been obtained in several studies. Hirt, Kardes, and Markman (2004), for example, found that participants who had generated alternative hypotheses concerning which TV sitcom would win a "best program" award made less extreme estimates than control participants of the likelihood that a favored basketball team would win the NBA championship.

To the extent that inducing a counterfactual mindset is characterized by a general disposition to consider alternatives, it could facilitate performance on tasks that require cognitive flexibility. Galinsky and Moskowitz (2000) confirmed this possibility in research on creative problem solving. Participants read a series of scenarios that stimulated them to imagine what might have occurred if a course of action had not been taken. This activity increased their likelihood of solving a creativity task that required recognition of the fact that an object can serve multiple purposes (e.g., that a box of tacks can be used as a base for mounting a candle as well as a container).

PREVENTION AND PROMOTION MINDSETS

Higgins (1997, 1998) distinguished between the disposition to focus on positive consequences of a behavior decision (i.e., a *promotion* focus) and the tendency to emphasize its negative consequences (a *prevention* focus). Thus, when stimuli have both positive and negative features, these dispositions can influence the evaluation of the stimulus and, in some cases, the preference for one stimulus over another. For example, suppose alternative A has the values +3 and −3 along two attribute dimensions and alternative B has values of +1 and −1, respectively. Someone who focuses on positive outcomes is likely to prefer A, but someone who focuses on negative outcomes is more likely to choose B. These dispositions can be either situationally induced or chronic. In either case, their activation may give rise to a processing strategy that generalizes over diverse judgment and decision situations.

Evidence of this generalization is largely indirect. For example, when people consider how they would ideally like to be, they may think about attributes they would like to acquire and behavior that would facilitate their acquisition. In contrast, people who think about how *others* would like them to be may focus their attention on avoiding actions that might have negative consequences or be considered undesirable (Higgins, 1997, 1998). The latter (prevention) focus can also be induced by stimulating persons to think of themselves as part of a group, thus making salient their responsibility to others. Thus, for example, it can result from performing a task with others rather than individually (Briley & Wyer, 2002), from constructing sentences that refer to "we" rather than "I" (Gardner, Gabriel, & Lee, 1999; Kühnen & Oyserman, 2002), and from consciousness of one's cultural group identity (Briley & Wyer, 2002). These activities activate a disposition to avoid negative outcomes, and this disposition can generalize to other goal-directed behavior that participants perform subsequently.

In support of this conjecture, Briley and Wyer (2002) showed that when participants had performed behavior that increased their consciousness of belonging to a group, they were more likely to choose "B" in a decision task similar to that described earlier in this section, more likely to use equality as a decision criterion in a reward allocation task (thus minimizing the negative affect experienced by both self and other), and more likely to choose different types of candies as a gift upon leaving an experiment (minimizing the negative consequences of making an incorrect decision). These studies do not provide direct evidence of the effect of past behavior on future behavior. Nevertheless, they suggest that behavior that increases people's consciousness of their group membership activates a disposition to avoid negative outcomes in group-related activity and that this disposition, in turn, induces a "prevention" mindset that affects decisions in unrelated situations.

Chronic Dispositions

The disposition to give different weight to positive and negative criteria in making evaluations and decisions may be chronic. This disposition could be partly the consequence of socialization practices. Based on observations of parent–child interactions in different cultures, Miller and her colleagues (Miller, Fung, & Mintz,1996; Miller, Wiley, Fung, & Liang, 1997) concluded that American parents typically minimize the negative implications of their child's misbehavior for his or her value as a person. In contrast, Asian parents are inclined to treat negative behavior as a personality deficit that reflects on their child's character and needs to be corrected. These different socialization practices could dispose Americans to focus on positive consequences of their behavior but could lead Asians to be more concerned about avoiding negative behavioral consequences. Once activated, these dispositions could generalize to situations of little if any social relevance.

Consistent with this possibility, Briley, Morris, and Simonson (2000) found that in a product choice situation similar to that described earlier in this section, East Asians were more likely than North Americans to choose the option that minimized the negative consequences of their decision. This was only true, however, if participants were asked to give a reason for their choice. In later series of studies (Briley et al., 2005), bicultural Chinese participants were likely to make choices that minimized negative consequences when the experiment was conducted in Chinese but not when it was conducted in English. In both studies, therefore, the application of the decision criteria was not spontaneous. Rather, calling participants' attention to culture-related norms and values was necessary in order to activate a norm-based decision strategy that influenced the choices they made.

UNCERTAINTY AVOIDANCE MINDSETS

Briley and Wyer's (2002) studies suggest that a disposition to avoid the risk of negative behavioral consequences generalizes over diverse choice situations. A closely related disposition may be the avoidance of uncertainty. Suppose individuals are confronted with a choice of either (1) receiving $150 with .5 probability or (2) receiving $150 with an unstated probability that could vary between 0 and 1. The expected likelihood of winning is the same in both cases. Nevertheless, individuals with a disposition to avoid uncertainty are inclined to prefer option 1 over option 2.

A series of studies by Muthukrishnan, Wathieu, and Xu (2009) demonstrate the effects of both chronic and situationally induced differences in the disposition to avoid uncertainty. In two initial studies, individuals' chronic dispositions to avoid uncertainty were inferred from their responses to items of the sort noted in the previous paragraph. Then, in a product choice task, these individuals were asked their preference for either an established brand with inferior attributes or an unknown brand with superior attributes. Participants with a chronic disposition to avoid uncertainty were more inclined to choose the established brand than other participants were. This was particularly true when the product was high tech and thus uncertainty was more acute.

However, the effects of these individual differences in uncertainty avoidance decreased over time. This indicates that chronic differences in uncertainty avoidance are only evident when the concepts activated by the procedures used to assess them are accessible in memory.

In an additional study, however, uncertainty avoidance was situationally manipulated by exposing participants to a series of gambles in which either the payoff probabilities of both choice options were unambiguous or, alternatively, one payoff probability was uncertain. Making choices in the second condition was expected to induce a disposition to avoid uncertainty. Participants' later behavior in a product choice task similar to that used in other studies confirmed this expectation. That is, only 49% of participants in the first condition opted for the established brand with inferior attributes. However, 64% of the participants in the second condition did so. Thus, both chronic and situationally induced dispositions to avoid uncertainty in one situation appear to generalize to other, unrelated situations that participants encounter subsequently.

VARIETY-SEEKING MINDSETS

A quite different type of decision situation in which the procedural knowledge activated by past behavior influences future decisions was identified by Hao Shen (Shen & Wyer, 2010). Individuals often have occasion to choose several articles of a given type for use over a period of time. Grocery shoppers, for example, may stock up on items for use over several days in order to avoid numerous trips to the store. When packing for a vacation trip, people might take a number of books to read or a number of DVDs to play. In such situations, individuals might sometimes be inclined to select several items of the same type (e.g., the type they prefer most) for use on each occasion. At other times, they might choose a variety of items.

These different decision strategies can depend in part on the type of item being considered. For example, people are likely to choose the same brand of beer or bottled water for use on each occasion, but to choose different kinds of vegetables to eat for dinner each evening. When individuals do not have a clear a priori preference for diversity, however, their choice strategy may depend in part on factors that have induced them to make the same or different responses repeatedly in a previous situation.

Participants in the experiments by Shen (Shen & Wyer, 2010) were asked to answer questions about four animals: a dog, a tiger, a chicken, and a pig.

In *different-choice* priming conditions, the answer to each question differed ("Which animal is largest?", "Which animal is most loyal?"). In *same-choice* priming conditions, the answer to each question was the same ("Which animal is largest?" " Which animal is most ferocious?"). Then, as part of an ostensibly different experiment, participants were told to assume that they were shopping for herbal tea and to indicate which of four brands they would choose to drink on each of the next four days. Participants chose a greater variety of teas when they had made different responses to the animal questions than when they had made the same response repeatedly.

The generalization of these effects over quite different stimulus domains confirms the assumption that the behavior performed in one situation activated a behavioral mindset that influenced that strategy that individuals applied in a later situation without consciousness of why they selected this strategy. In fact, making them aware of the reason this strategy came to mind appears to eliminate the effects we observed. In other conditions of Shen's study, participants were asked before performing the product choice task to indicate the number of different answers they had given in the animal judgment task, thus calling their attention to their behavior in this task. In this condition, the effect of the strategy employed in the first task was eliminated.

Sequential Decision Making

As noted earlier, goal-directed processing can involve a sequence of decisions, each pertaining to a different subgoal. People who contemplate an evening's entertainment, for example, might first decide *whether* to see a movie. Then, if they decide affirmatively, they may decide *which* movie to see. Finally, they might decide *how* to implement this choice. In these situations, an additional implication of the conceptualization outlined at the beginning of this chapter becomes relevant. If a subgoal of a plan to attain a particular objective has been pursued in an earlier situation, it is likely to increase the accessibility of a more general concept that the subgoal exemplifies. Consequently, if a second exemplar of this concept is relevant to the attainment of a goal that individuals pursue in a later task, it might be activated and applied. Moreover, this could sometimes occur without engaging in the behavior relevant to subgoals that precede it in the goal-relevant plan that has been activated. Thus, in our example, people might perform the actions involved in deciding how to implement the attainment of an object or activity without ever having consciously decided

whether they actually *want* to attain it. Similarly, they might decide which of two alternatives they want without ever having considered the possibility of choosing nothing at all. Two bodies of research bear on this possibility.

IMPLEMENTAL VERSUS DELIBERATIVE MINDSETS

Gollwitzer and his colleagues (Gollwitzer & Bayer, 1999; Gollwitzer, Heckhausen, & Stoller, 1990) speculated that whereas processing at the deliberative stage entails a consideration of the pros and cons of pursuing a goal, processing at the implemental stage entails an evaluation of alternative means of accomplishing the goal once a decision to pursue it has already been made. Gollwitzer et al. speculated that if individuals are stimulated to think about how to attain a goal without first considering whether they actually want to attain it, they acquire an implemental "mindset" that, once activated, might generalize to situations they encounter later.

Henderson, de Liver, and Gollwitzer (2008) obtained indirect evidence that this is the case. Participants were first asked either to consider *whether* they might pursue a particular objective or, alternatively, to plan *how* they would do so. The process of deciding whether to engage in an action typically involves an evaluation of both positive and negative consequences of the action. Therefore, it is likely to result in some ambivalence about whether to take the action or not. However, considering how to engage in the activity presupposes that the action is desirable and that a decision to pursue it has already been made. In this case, ambivalence should be less. In short, participants' consideration of whether to engage in an activity should stimulate a deliberative mindset, whereas a consideration of how to engage in it should activate an implemental mindset. If these mindsets generalize to situations the individuals encounter later, their effects may be reflected in the ambivalence associated with judgments made in these situations.

This appears to be the case. After performing the initial priming task, participants in Henderson et al.'s (2008) study were asked to consider a series of objects and report how ambivalent they felt about each. As expected, participants reported feeling generally more ambivalent when they had previously considered whether to pursue an unrelated objective than if they had considered how to do so. Analogous results occurred when participants were asked to report their attitude toward a social issue.

The generalizability of implemental mindsets has been observed in other studies as well (Gollwitzer & Bayer, 1999; Taylor & Gollwitzer, 1995). For example, the adoption of an implemental mindset in one situation, which diverts individuals' attention from a consideration of whether to attain a goal, decreases their sensitivity to the risk associated with choices in an unrelated domain (Taylor & Gollwitzer, 1995). The effect of "shopping momentum" provides a further example. In a study by Dhar, Huber, and Kahn (2007), participants were given an opportunity to purchase a pen for a low price in some conditions and for a high price in other conditions. They typically decided to buy the pen in the first condition but to reject it in the second. Later in the experimental session, they were given an opportunity to buy a moderately expensive key chain. Participants were more likely to buy the key chain if they had previously decided to make a purchase than if they had refused. Although other interpretations of this effect are possible, it is consistent with the possibility that a positive purchase decision induced an implemental mindset that was reapplied at the later, decision stage without deliberative processing having occurred at all.

WHICH-TO-CHOOSE MINDSETS

If individuals have been induced to state a preference for two alternatives, this activity may activate a "which-to-choose" subgoal that, once activated, leads individuals to make a choice in a later situation without considering the possibility of not choosing anything. In a study by Jing Xu, for example (Xu & Wyer, 2007), some participants were given descriptions of five pairs of options (restaurants, elective courses, etc.) and, in each case, indicated their preference for one of the alternatives. After the experiment was ostensibly over, both these participants and those who had not performed the preference task were given an opportunity to buy one of two types of candies that had ostensibly been used as incentives in a previous study and were being sold at half price. Twenty-eight percent of the participants who had performed the preference task purchased candy, whereas only 6% of the control participants did so.

A second series of studies (Xu & Wyer, 2008) provides further support for the generality of a which-to-choose mindset over content domains. In one study, participants in *preference judgment* conditions were exposed to 10 pairs of wild animals (an elephant vs. a hippopotamus, a kangaroo vs. a zebra, etc.) and asked which type of animal they preferred. In a second, *attribute judgment* condition, they were

Table 13.2 Effects of reporting preferences for animals and comparing their physical attributes on purchase decisions and dating partner choices

	Preference Judgmen	Attribute Judgment	Control
Likelihood of choosing Product	.64	.68	.40
Likelihood of choosing dating partner	.75	.70	.47
Likelihood of making an actual purchase	.51	.52	.37

Simplified hierarchy of goal and subgoal concepts associated with going to the theatre.
Based on data from Xu & Wyer, 2008.

asked to compare the animals with respect to a particular attribute (i.e., "Which is heavier, an elephant or a hippopotamus?" "Which can run faster, a kangaroo or a zebra?"). These participants, along with control participants who were not exposed to either task, received descriptions of two computers (A and B) and were asked whether they would be willing to purchase A, B, or neither. A second study was similar, except the alternatives pertained to dating partners. Finally, participants in a third study were given an opportunity to purchase one of a number of products (candy, chips, etc.) that had ostensibly been used as incentives in other experiments and were on sale at half price.

The effects of making initial comparative judgments, shown in Table 13.2, were similar in all cases. That is, participants were more likely to choose one of the alternatives described in the target task (rather than choosing neither) if they had either reported their preferences for animals or had compared them with respect to a physical attribute than they were under control conditions. This was true regardless of whether the alternatives pertained to products or dating partners, and regardless of whether the choice was hypothetical or real.

Conclusion

In this chapter, we have distinguished between two types of procedures. One type, plans, consists of sequences of goal-directed actions that are stored in memory as part of declarative knowledge and provide the basis for decisions about how to attain the goal being sought. The second type, productions, are similar to those proposed by Anderson (1982, 1983) and stimulate sequences of behavior with little cognitive effort and often without awareness. Goal-directed behavior often requires both types of procedures. Both types can be activated by either external or internally generated stimulation. However, we have focused our review primarily on a form of internal stimulation, namely, the concepts activated by past behavior and their consequent influence on behavior and decisions in later situations that are quite unrelated to those in which the initial behavior occurred.

As our review attests, this influence can occur at many stages of processing, including attention, comprehension, evaluation, and decision making. Furthermore, it is evident in research conducted within a variety of theoretical frameworks. Thus, the conceptualization of social phenomena from the perspective we have outlined has both heuristic and integrative value. We hope that this chapter succeeds in conveying this value.

Author Note

This preparation of this article and some of the research described herein was supported in part by grants GRF 453110 and GRF 640011 from the Research Grants Council, Hong Kong and grant no. 491127 from the Social Sciences Research Council, Canada. The authors are greatly indebted to Donal Carlston for exceptionally perceptive and constructive suggestions concerning both the substance and presentation of the material.

References

Anderson, J. R. (1982). Acquisition of cognitive skill. *Psychological Review, 89*, 369–406.

Anderson, J. R. (1983). *The architecture of cognition*. Cambridge, MA: Harvard University Press.

Anderson, J. R. (1996). ACT: A simple theory of complex cognition. *American Psychologist, 51*, 355–365.

Bandura, A. (1986). *Social foundations of thought and action: A social cognitive theory*. Englewood Cliffs, NJ: Prentice Hall.

Bargh, J. A. (1997). *The automaticity of everyday life*. In R. S. Wyer (Ed.), *Advances in social cognition* (Vol. 10, pp. 1–62). Mahwah, NJ: Erlbaum.

Bargh, J. A., Bond, R. N., Lombardi, W. J., & Tota, M. E. (1986), The additive nature of chronic and temporary sources of construct accessibility, *Journal of Personality and Social Psychology, 50*, 869–878.

Bargh, J. A., Chaiken, S., Govender, R., & Pratto, F. (1992). The generality of the automatic attitude activation effect. *Journal of Personality and Social Psychology, 62*, 893–912.

Bargh, J. A., Chaiken, S., Raymond, P., & Hymes, C. (1996). The automatic evaluation effect: Unconditionally automatic attitude activation in a pronunciation task. *Journal of Experimental Social Psychology, 32*, 104–120.

Bargh, J. A., Chen, M., & Burrows, L. (1996). Automaticity of social behavior: Direct effects of trait construct and stereotype activation on action. *Journal of Personality and Social Psychology, 71*, 230–244.

Bargh, J. A., & Pietromonaco, P. (1982). Automatic information processing and social perception: The influence of trait information presented outside of conscious awareness on impression formation. *Journal of Personality and Social Psychology, 43*, 437–449.

Briley, D. A., Morris, M., & Simonson, I. (2000). Reasons as carriers of culture: Dynamic versus dispositional models of cultural influence on decision making. *Journal of Consumer Research, 27*, 157–178.

Briley, D. A., Morris, M., & Simonson, I. (2005). Language triggers cultural frames: In bicultural Hong Kong consumers, English versus Chinese communication evokes divergent cultural patterns of decision making. *Journal of Consumer Psychology, 27*, 157–178.

Briley, D. A., & Wyer, R. S. (2002). The effect of group membership salience on the avoidance of negative outcomes: Implications for social and consumer decisions. *Journal of Consumer Research, 29*, 400–415.

Brinol, P., & Petty, R. E. (2003). Overt head movements and persuasion: A self-validation analysis. *Journal of Personality and Social Psychology, 84*, 1123–1139.

Carlston, D. E. (1994). Associated systems theory: A systematic approach to the cognitive representation of persons. In R. S. Wyer (Ed.), *Advances in social cognition* (Vol. 7, pp. 1–78). Hillsdale, NJ: Erlbaum.

Carlston, D. E., & Smith, E. R. (1996). Principles of mental representation. In E. T. Higgins & A. W. Kruglanski (Eds.), *Social psychology: Handbook of basic principles* (pp. 184–210). New York: Guilford Press.

Chaiken, S. (1987). The heuristic model of persuasion. In M. P. Zanna, J. M. Olson, & C. P. Herman (Eds.): *Social influence: The Ontario Symposium* (Vol. 5, pp. 3–39). Hillsdale, NJ: Erlbaum.

Chaiken, S., & Trope, Y. (1999). *Dual-process theories in social psychology*. New York: Guilford Press.

Chandler, J., & Schwarz, N. (2009). How extending your middle finger affects your perception of others: Learned movements influence cognitive accessibility. *Journal of Experimental Social Psychology, 45*, 123–128.

Chartrand, T. L., & Bargh, J. A. (1996). Automatic activation of impression formation and memorization goals: Nonconscious goal priming reproduces effects of explicit task instructions. *Journal of Personality and Social Psychology, 71*, 464–478.

Chartrand, T. L., & Bargh, J. A. (1999). The chameleon effect: The perception-behavior link and social interaction. *Journal of Personality and Social Psychology, 76*, 893–910.

Chartrand, T. L., & Bargh, J. A. (2002). Nonconscious motivations: their activation, operation and consequences. In A. Tesser & D. Stapel (Eds.), *Self and motivation: Emerging psychological perspectives* (pp. 13–41). Washington DC: American Psychological Association.

Childers, T. L., Houston, M. J., & Heckler, S. E. (1985). Measurement of individual differences in visual versus verbal information processing. *Journal of Consumer Research, 12*, 125–134.

Chua, H. F., Boland, J. E., & Nisbett, R. E. (2005). Cultural variation in eye movements during scene perception. *Proceedings of the National Academy of Sciences USA, 102*, 12629–12633.

Claypool, H. M., & Carlston, D. E. (2002). The effects of verbal and visual interference on impressions: A associated-systems approach. *Journal of Experimental Social Psychology*, 38, 425–433.

Colcombe, S. J., & Wyer, R. S. (2001). *The effects of image-based priming on lexical access, conceptual activation, and behavior*. Unpublished manuscript, University of Illinois at Urbana-Champaign.

Colcombe, S. J., & Wyer, R. S. (2002). The role of prototypes in the mental representation of temporally-related events. *Cognitive Psychology*, 44, 67–103.

Collins, A. M., & Loftus, E. F. (1975). A spreading activation theory of semantic processing. *Psychological Review*, 82, 407–428.

Dhar, R., Huber, J., & Khan, U. (2007), The shopping momentum effect. *Journal of Marketing Research*, 44, 370–378.

Dijksterhuis, A., & Bargh, J. A. (2001). The perception-behavior expressway: Automatic effects of social perception on social behavior. In M. P. Zanna (Ed.), *Advances in experimental social psychology* (Vol. 33, pp.1–40), San Diego, CA: Academic Press.

Dodson, C. S., Johnson, M. K., & Schooler, J. W. (1997). The verbal overshadowing effect: Why descriptions impair face recognition. *Memory & Cognition*, 25, 129–139.

Duckworth, K. L., Bargh, J. A., Garcia, M., & Chaiken, S. (2002). The automatic evaluation of novel stimuli. *Psychological Science*, 13, 514–520.

Förster, J. (2003). The influence of approach and avoidance motor actions on food intake. *European Journal of Social Psychology*, 33, 339–350.

Förster, J. (2009). Relations between perceptual and conceptual scope: How global versus local processing fits a focus on similarity versus dissimilarity. *Journal of Experimental Psychology: General*, 138, 98–111.

Förster, J. (2011). Local and global cross-modal influences between vision and hearing, tasting, smelling or touching. *Journal of Experimental Psychology: General*, 140, 364–389.

Förster, J., & Dannenberg, L. (2010). GLOMO: A systems account of global versus local processing. *Psychological Inquiry*, 21, 175–197.

Förster, J., Liberman, N., & Kuschel, S. (2008). The effect of global versus local processing styles on assimilation versus contrast in social judgment. *Journal of Personality and Social Psychology*, 94, 579–599.

Förster, J., & Strack, F. (1996), The influence of overt head movements on memory for valenced words: A case of conceptual-motor compatibility. *Journal of Personality ad Social Psychology*, 71, 421–430.

Gardner, W. L., Gabriel, S., & Lee, A. Y. (1999). "I" values freedom, but "we" value relationships: Self-construal priming mirrors cultural differences in judgment. *Psychological Science*, 10, 321–326.

Gollwitzer, P. M., & Bayer, U. (1999), Deliberative versus implemental mindsets in the control of action. In S. Chaiken & Y. Trope (Eds.), *Dual-process theories in social psychology* (pp. 403–422). New York: Guilford Press.

Goldstone, R. L., & Barsalou, L. W. (1998). Reuniting perception and conception. *Cognition*, 65, 231–262.

Gollwitzer, P. M., Heckhausen, H., & Steller, B. (1990). Deliberative and implemental mind-sets: Cognitive tuning toward congruous thoughts and information. *Journal of Personality and Social Psychology*, 59, 1119–1127.

Graesser, A. C. (1981). *Prose comprehension beyond the word*. New York: Springer-Verlag.

Grice, H. P. (1975). Logic and conversation. In P. Cole & J. L. Morgan (Eds.), *Syntax and semantics: Speech acts* (pp. 41–58). New York: Academic Press.

Hamilton, D. H., Katz, L. B., & Leirer, V. O. (1980). Organizational processes in impression formation. In R. Hastie, T. Ostrom, E. Ebbesen, R. Wyer, D. Hamilton, & D. Carlston (Eds.), *Person memory: The cognitive basis of social perception* (pp. 121–153). Hillsdale, NJ: Erlbaum.

Henderson, M. D., de Liver, Y., & Gollwitzer, P. M. (2008). The effects of implemental mindset on attitude strength. *Journal of Personality and Social Psychology*, 94, 96–411.

Higgins, E. T. (1997). Beyond pleasure and pain. *American Psychologist*, 55, 1217–1233.

Higgins, E. T. (1998). Promotion and prevention: Regulatory focus as a motivational principle. In M. P. Zanna (Ed.), *Advances in experimental social psychology* (Vol. 30, pp. 1–46). San Diego, CA: Academic Press.

Higgins, E. T., Bargh, J. A., & Lombardi, W. (1985). The nature of priming effects on categorization. *Journal of Experimental Psychology: Learning, Memory, and Cognition*, 11, 59–69.

Hirt, E. R., Kardes, F. R., & Markman, K. D. (2004). Activating a mental simulation mind-set through generation of alternatives; Implications for debiasing in related and unrelated domains. *Journal of Experimental Social Psychology*, 40, 374–383.

Hull, C. L. (1934). The concept of the habit-family hierarchy and maze learning: Part I. *Psychological Review*, 41, 33–54.

Ji, M. F., & Wood, W. (2007). Procedures and consumption habits: Not necessarily what you intend. Journal of Consumer Psychology, 17, 261–276.

Jiang, Y., Steinhart, Y., & Wyer, R. S. (2009). *The role of visual and semantic processing strategies in consumer information processing*. Unpublished manuscript, Hong Kong University of Science and Technology.

Jiang, Y., & Wyer, R. S. (2009). The role of visual perspective in information processing. *Journal of Experimental Psychology*, 45, 486–495.

Kim, K., & Meyers-Levy, J. (2007). Context effects in diverse-category brand environments: The influence of target product positioning and consumers' processing mindset. *Journal of Consumer Research*, 34(2):174–186.

Kosslyn, S. M. (1975). On retrieving information from visual images. In R. Schank & B. L. Nash-Webber (Eds.), *Theoretical issues in natural language processing*. Proceedings of conference at Massachusetts Institute of Technology, Cambridge, MA, June 10–13.

Kosslyn, S. M. (1976). Can imagery be distinguished from other forms of internal representation? Evidence from studies of information retrieval time. *Memory & Cognition*, 4, 291–297.

Kruglanski, A. W., Shah, J. Y., Fishbach, A., Friedman, R., Chun, W. Y., & Sleeth-Keppler, D. (2002). A theory of goal systems. In M. P. Zanna (Ed.), *Advances in experimental social psychology* (Vol. 34, pp. 331–378). San Diego, CA: Academic Press.

Kühnen, U., & Oyserman, D. (2002). Thinking about the self influences thinking in general: Cognitive consequences of salient self-concept. *Journal of Experimental Social Psychology*, 38, 492–499.

Lakin, J., & Chartrand, T. L. (2003). Using nonconscious behavioral mimicry to create affiliation and rapport. *Psychological Science*, 14, 334–339.

Liberman, N., & Förster, J. (2009). Distancing from experienced self: How global-versus-local perception affects estimation of psychological distance. *Journal of Personality and Social Psychology, 97,* 203–216.

Liberman, N., Sagristano, M., & Trope, Y. (2002). The effect of temporal distance on level of mental construal. *Journal of Experimental Social Psychology, 38,* 523–534.

Liberman, N., Trope, Y., & Stephan, E. (2007), Psychological distance, In A. W. Kruglanski & E. T. Higgins (Eds.), *Social psychology: Handbook of basic principles* (2nd ed., pp. 353–383). New York: Guilford Press.

Markman, A. B., & Brendl, C. M. (2000). The influence of goals on value and choice. *Psychology of Learning and Motivation, 39,* 97–128.

Markus, H. R., & Kitayama, S. (1991). Culture and the self: Implications for cognition, emotion and motivation. *Psychological Review, 98,* 224–253.

Masuda, T., & Nisbett, R. E. (2001). Attending holistically versus analytically: Comparing the context sensitivity of Japanese and Americans. *Journal of Personality and Social Psychology, 81,* 922–934.

Miller, P. J., Fung, H., & Mintz, J. (1996). Self-construction through narrative practices: A Chinese and American comparison of early socialization. *Ethos, 24,* 237–280.

Miller, P. J., Wiley, A. R., Fung, H., & Liang, C. H. (1997). Personal storytelling as a medium of socialization in Chinese and American families. *Child Development, 68,* 557–568.

Muthukrishnan, A. V., Wathieu, L., & Xu, A. J. (2009). *Ambiguity aversion and preference for established brands.* Unpublished manuscript, Hong Kong University of Science and Technology.

Nisbett, R. E. (2003). *The geography of thought: How Asians and Westerners think differently.* New York: Free Press.

Norenzayan, A., Choi, I., & Peng, K. (2007). Perception and cognition. In S. Kitayama & D. Cohen (Eds.), *Handbook of cultural psychology* (pp. 569–594). New York: Guilford Press.

Park, D. C., Nisbett, R. E., & Hedden, T. (1999). Culture, cognition, and aging. *Journal of Gerontology, 54B,* 75–84.

Petrova, P. K., & Cialdini, R. B. (2005). Fluency of consumption imagery and the backfire effects of imagery appeals. *Journal of Consumer Research, 32,* 442–452.

Petty, R. E., & Cacioppo, J. T. (1986) *Communication and persuasion: Central and peripheral routes to attitude change.* New York: Springer-Verlag.

Ratcliff, R. (1978). A theory of memory retrieval. *Psychological Review, 85,* 59–108.

Rosch, E., Mervis, C. B., Gray, W., Johnson, D., & Boyes-Braem, P. (1976). Basic objects in natural categories.*Cognitive Psychology, 8,* 382–439.

Schank, R. C., & Abelson, R. P. (1977). *Scripts, plans, goals and understanding.* Hillsdale, NJ: Erlbaum.

Schneider, W., & Shiffrin, R. M. (1977), Controlled and automatic human information processing: I. Detection, search, and attention." *Psychological Review, 84,* 1–66.

Schooler, J. W., & Engstler-Schooler, T. Y. (1990). Verbal overshadowing of visual memories: Some things are better left unsaid. *Cognitive Psychology, 22,* 36–71.

Schwarz, N. (1998). Accessible content and accessibility experiences: The interplay of declarative and experiential information in judgment. *Personality and Social Psychology Review, 2,* 87–99.

Schwarz, N. (2004). Metacognitive experiences in consumer judgment and decision making. *Journal of Consumer Psychology, 14,* 332–348.

Schwarz, N., & Wyer, R. S. (1985) Effects of rank ordering stimuli on magnitude ratings of these and other stimuli, *Journal of Experimental Social Psychology, 21,* 30–46.

Shafir, E. (1993). Choosing vs. rejecting: Why some options are both better and worse than others. *Memory & Cognition, 21,* 546–556.

Shen, H., & Wyer, R. S. (2008). Procedural priming and consumer judgments: Effects on the impact of positively and negatively valenced information. *Journal of Consumer Research, 34,* 727–737.

Shen, H., Wyer, R. S., & Cai, F. (2012). The generalization of deliberative and automatic behavior: The role of procedural knowledge and affective reactions. *Journal of Experimental Social Psychology, 48,* 819–828.

Smith, E. R. (1984). Model of social inference processes. *Psychological Review, 91,* 392–413.

Smith, E. R. (1990). Content and process specificity in the effects of prior Experiences. In T. K. Srull & R. S. Wyer (Eds.), *Advances in Social Cognition,* (Vol. 3, pp. 1–59). Hillsdale, NJ: Erlbaum.

Smith, E. R. (1994), Procedural knowledge and processing strategies in social cognition. In R. S. Wyer & T. K. Srull (Eds.), *Handbook of social cognition* (2nd ed., Vol. 1, pp. 101–151.). Hillsdale, NJ: Erlbaum.

Spence, K. (1956). *Behavior theory and conditioning.* New Haven, CT: Yale University Press.

Srull, T. K., & Wyer, R. S. (1979). The role of category accessibility in the interpretation of information about persons: Some determinants and implications. *Journal of Personality and Social Psychology, 37,* 1660–1672.

Srull, T. K., & Wyer, R. S. (1986). The role of chronic and temporary goals in social information processing. In E. T. Higgins & R. Sorrentino (Eds.), *Handbook of cognition and motivation.* New York: Guilford Press.

Stapel, D. A., & Semin, G. R. (2007). The magic spell of language: Linguistic categories and their perceptual consequences. *Journal of Personality and Social Psychology, 93,* 23–33.

Stepper, S., & Strack, F. (1993). Proprioceptive determinants of emotional and nonemotional feelings. *Journal of Personality and Social Psychology, 64,* 211–220.

Strack, F., & Deutsch, R. (2004). Reflective and impulsive determinants of social behavior. *Personality and Social Psychology Review, 8,* 220–247.

Strack, F., Martin, L., & Stepper, S. (1988). Inhibiting and facilitating conditions of the human smile: A non-intuitive test of the facial feedback hypothesis. *Journal of Personality and Social Psychology, 54,* 768–777.

Taylor, S. E., & Gollwitzer, P. M. (1995). Effects of mindset on positive illusions. *Journal of Personality and Social Psychology, 69,* 213–226.

Triandis, H. C. (1989). The self and social behavior in differing cultural contexts. *Psychological Review, 96,* 506–520.

Trope, Y., & Liberman, N. (2003), Temporal construal. *Psychological Review, 110,* 403–421.

Trope, Y., & Liberman, N. (2010). Construal-level theory of psychological distance. *Psychological Review, 117,* 440–463.

Trope, Y., Liberman, N., & Wakslak, C. (2007), Construal levels and psychological distance: Effects on representation, prediction, evaluation, and behavior. *Journal of Consumer Psychology, 17*(2), 83–95.

Tversky, A., & Kahneman, D. (1974). Judgment under uncertainty: Heuristics and biases, *Science, 185*, 1124–1130.

Verplanken, B. (2006). Beyond frequency: Habit as mental construct. *British Journal of Social Psychology, 45*, 639–656.

Wakslak, C. J., Trope, Y., Liberman, N., & Alony, R. (2006). Seeing the forest when entry is unlikely: Probability and the mental representation of events. *Journal of Experimental Psychology: General, 135*, 641–653.

Winkielman, P., & Cacioppo, J. T. (2001). Mind at ease puts a smile on the face: Psychophysiological evidence that processing facilitation elicits positive affect. *Journal of Personality and Social Psychology, 81*, 989–1000.

Winkielman, P., Schwarz, N., Fazendeiro, T. A., & Reber, R. (2003). The hedonic marking of processing fluency: Implications for evaluative judgment. In J.Musch & K. C. Klauer (Eds.), *The psychology of evaluation: Affective processes in cognition and emotion* (pp. 189–217). Mahwah, NJ: Erlbaum.

Wood, W., & Neal, D. T. (2007). A new look at habits and the habit-goal interface. *Psychological Review, 114*, 843–863.

Wyer, R. S. (2004). *Social comprehension and judgment: The role of situation models, narratives, and implicit theories.* Mahwah, NJ: Erlbaum.

Wyer, R. S. (2006). Three models of information processing: An evaluation and conceptual integration. *Psychological Inquiry, 17*, 185–194.

Wyer, R. S. (2011). A theory of social information processing. In P. van Lange, A. W. Kruglanski, & E. T. Higgins (Eds.), *Handbook of theories of social psychology* (Vol. 1, pp. 158–177). Thousand Oaks, CA: Sage.

Wyer, R. S., & Carlston, D. E. (1979). *Social cognition, inference and attribution.* Hillsdale, NJ: Erlbaum.

Wyer, R. S., & Collins, J. E. (1992). A theory of humor elicitation. *Psychological Review, 99*, 663–688.

Wyer, R. S., & Gruenfeld, D. H. (1995) Pragmatic information processing in social contexts: Implications for social memory and judgment. In M. Zanna (Ed.), *Advances in experimental social psychology* (Vol. 27, pp. 49–92) San Diego, CA: Academic Press.

Wyer, R. S., Hung, I. W., & Jiang, Y. (2008). Visual and verbal processing strategies in comprehension and judgment. *Journal of Consumer Psychology, 18*, 244–257.

Wyer, R. S., & Radvansky, G. A. (1999). The comprehension and validation of social information. *Psychological Review, 106*, 89–118.

Wyer, R. S., & Srull, T. K. (1986). Human cognition in its social context. *Psychological Review, 93*, 322–359.

Wyer, R. S. & Srull, T. K. (1989). *Memory and cognition in its social context.* Hillsdale, NJ: Erlbaum.

Wyer, R. S., & Xu, A. J. (2010). The role of behavioral mindsets in goal-directed activity: Conceptual underpinnings and empirical evidence. *Journal of Consumer Psychology, 20*, 107–125.

Xu, A. J. & Wyer, R. S. (2007). The effect of mindsets on consumer decision strategies. *Journal of Consumer Research, 34*, 556–566.

Xu, A. J., & Wyer, R. S. (2008). The comparative mindset: From animal comparisons to increased purchase intentions. *Psychological Science, 19*, 859–864.

Xu, A. J., & Wyer, R. S. (2012) The role of bolstering and counterarguing mindsets in persuasion. *Journal of Consumer Research, 38,* 920–932.

Dual Process Theories

Bertram Gawronski *and* Laura A. Creighton

Abstract

Dual process theories divide the realm of mental processes into two general categories depending on whether they operate automatically or in a controlled fashion. This chapter provides an overview of dual process theories in social psychology, focusing on their historical and conceptual developments. Identifying three general categories of dual process theories, the chapter distinguishes between domain-specific theories that focus on particular phenomena, generalized dual process theories that identify domain-independent principles underlying various kinds of phenomena, and formalized dual process theories that quantify the joint contributions of automatic and controlled processes to responses within a single task. The chapter also discusses critical arguments against each type of dual process theorizing, which are integrated in a general outlook on future directions.

Key Words: attitudes, attribution, automaticity, control, dual process theories, impression formation, persuasion, prejudice, stereotyping

Introduction

For the past three decades, a large body of research in social cognition has been shaped and guided by a class of theories that are generically described as *dual process theories* (Chaiken & Trope, 1999). The defining characteristic of these theories is that they divide the mental processes underlying social judgments and behavior into two general categories depending on whether they operate automatically or in a controlled fashion. Because the distinction between automatic and controlled processes has become a central component in virtually all areas of social psychology (see Chapter 12), it is difficult to imagine what contemporary social psychology would look like without the theoretical guidance of dual process theories.

Whereas early dual process theories focused primarily on domain-specific phenomena, such as persuasion (e.g., Chaiken, 1987; Petty & Cacioppo, 1986), attitude–behavior relations (e.g., Fazio, 1990;

Wilson, Lindsey, & Schooler, 2000), prejudice and stereotyping (e.g., Devine, 1989), impression formation (e.g., Brewer, 1988; Fiske & Neuberg, 1990), and dispositional attribution (e.g., Gilbert, 1989; Trope, 1986), dual process theorizing in the past decade shifted toward integrative models that aim at identifying general principles assumed to be domain independent. These integrative models can be further divided into generalized dual process theories that describe mental processing by means of two domain-independent operating principles (e.g., Epstein, 1994; Kahneman, 2003; Lieberman, 2003; Smith & DeCoster, 2000; Strack & Deutsch, 2004) and formalized dual process theories that quantify the contributions of distinct mental processes to behavioral responses by means of mathematical modeling techniques (e.g., Payne, 2008; Sherman et al., 2008).

The aim of the current chapter is to provide a general overview of dual process theories in social cognition with the goal of identifying both historical and conceptual developments since their emergence in the mid-1980s. For this purpose, we first provide a brief discussion of the distinction between automatic and controlled processes, which serves as a basis for our overview of dual process theories. We then review the most influential phenomenon-specific theories that have set the foundation for the ubiquitous dual process paradigm within social psychology. Expanding on this review, the following two sections discuss the tenets of generalized and formalized dual process theories that have gained considerable impact within and beyond social psychology during the past decade. At the end of each section, we also discuss critical arguments that have been raised against phenomenon-specific, generalized, and formalized dual process theories, which are integrated in our outlook in the final part of this chapter.

Automaticity and Control

Dual process theories have their roots in the assumption that the universe of mental processes can be divided into two general classes: those that operate automatically and those that operate in a controlled fashion (Posner & Snyder, 1975; Shiffrin & Schneider, 1977). In social cognition, automatic processes are typically characterized in terms of four operating conditions: (1) they are elicited unintentionally; (2) they require little amounts of cognitive resources; (3) they cannot be stopped voluntarily; and (4) they occur outside of conscious awareness (Bargh, 1994). Conversely, controlled processes are characterized as those that (1) are initiated intentionally; (2) require considerable amounts of cognitive resources; (3) can be stopped voluntarily; and (4) operate within conscious awareness (for a more fine-grained analysis of these features and their interrelations, see Moors & De Houwer, 2006).

Initially, automatic and controlled processes were conceptualized in an all-or-none fashion, implying that a given process can be characterized either by the four features of automatic processing or by the four features of controlled processing. According to this dual mode view, the "four horsemen" of automaticity (i.e., intentionality, efficiency, controllability, awareness) constitute a fixed set of characteristics that are perfectly correlated (see Moors & De Houwer, 2006). However, challenging the usefulness of this all-or-none conceptualization, it soon turned out that there is virtually no process that meets all four operating criteria (Bargh, 1992). Instead, most processes studied within social

psychology involve combinations of the proposed features, which classify them as "automatic" in one sense and "controlled" in another (Bargh, 1994). This insight has inspired a disjunctive conceptualization of automaticity, according to which a process can be characterized as automatic if it meets at least one of the four criteria of automaticity. That is, a process can be described as automatic if it is either (1) unintentional, (2) efficient, (3) uncontrollable, or (4) unconscious.

Even though the disjunctive treatment of automaticity is rather common in social psychology, it involves several problems. First, if the presence of a single feature is sufficient to call a process automatic or controlled, it is possible that a given process will have to be described as automatic and controlled at the same time. Needless to say, such a description can be rather confusing if it is not specified in which particular sense the process is described as automatic and in which sense it is described as controlled. Second, the generic use of the term *automatic* to describe any of the four operating conditions can lead to confusion about conceptually distinct findings that are described with the same term. For example, a given Process A may be described as automatic because it does not require a large amount of cognitive resources, whereas another Process B may be described as automatic because it is elicited unintentionally. Yet, the two processes may still differ in their operating conditions, if, for example, Process A, but not Process B, can be stopped voluntarily. Based on these considerations, several theorists have recommended that researchers should be more precise in their use of terminology by describing each feature of automaticity with its proper label, that is, unintentional, efficient, uncontrollable, or unconscious (Bargh, 1994; Moors & De Houwer, 2006). As we will outline in the following sections, different kinds of dual process theories emphasize different features of automaticity, which makes terminological precision particularly important to avoid conceptual confusion.

Phenomenon-Specific Dual Process Theories

As noted in the introductory section of this chapter, early dual process theories tended to be domain specific in that they focused on particular phenomena. In the current section, we first review the core assumptions of the most influential theories of this kind and then discuss criticism that has been raised against phenomenon-specific dual process theories.

Persuasion

Two of the most prominent dual process theories are the elaboration likelihood model (ELM; Petty & Cacioppo, 1986) and the heuristic systematic model (HSM; Chaiken, 1987) of persuasion. The central question of these models concerns the conditions under which different aspects of a persuasive message (e.g., strength of arguments, attractiveness of the source) influence the effectiveness of persuasive appeals.

ELABORATION LIKELIHOOD MODEL

The central notion of Petty and Cacioppo's (1986) ELM is that attitude change occurs along an elaboration continuum whereby persuasion is determined by how motivated and able an individual is to engage in effortful information processing (Figure 14.1). The basic assumption is that the higher an individual's cognitive elaboration, the more likely he or she is to process all object-relevant information. At the high end of the elaboration continuum, people

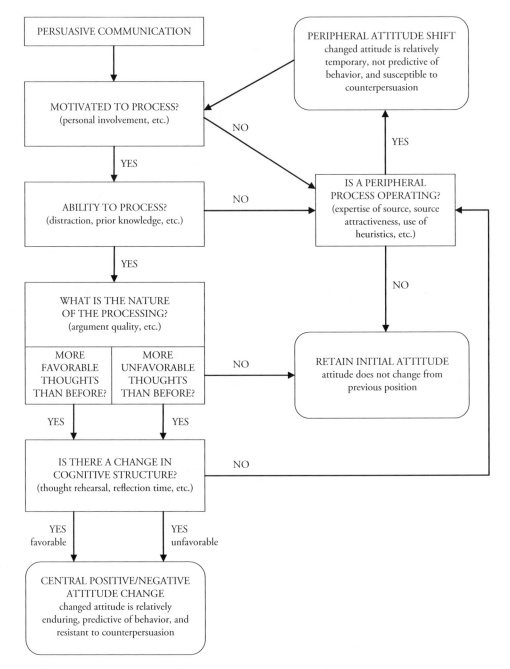

Figure 14.1 The elaboration likelihood model of persuasion. (Adapted from Petty & Cacioppo, 1986. Reprinted with permission.)

assess all of the available object-relevant information (e.g., strength of the presented arguments) and integrate this information with their stored knowledge in order to obtain a carefully considered (although not necessarily unbiased) evaluation (*central route*). Conversely, at the low end of the elaboration continuum, people engage in considerably less scrutiny of object-relevant information (*peripheral route*). When elaboration is low, attitude change can be effected from a cursory examination of the available information (e.g., by examining only a subset of the available information) or by the use of heuristics and other types of information processing shortcuts (e.g., *I agree with people I like*). Compared with attitudes that are changed through the central route, attitudes changed through the peripheral route tend to be relatively weak, susceptible to counterpersuasion, and less predictive of behavior (e.g., Petty, Cacioppo, & Schumann, 1983).

Addressing a common misconception about the ELM, Petty and Wegener (1999) pointed out that the influence of a particular persuasion variable will not necessarily increase or decrease as one moves along the elaboration continuum. For example, a common interpretation of the ELM is that high elaboration increases the impact of primary features of the persuasive message (e.g., argument quality), whereas low elaboration increases the impact of secondary cues (e.g., source attractiveness). This interpretation is qualified by the ELM's *multiple-roles hypothesis,* which specifies that a given variable can influence attitudes by different processes at different points along the elaboration continuum. To illustrate this assumption, consider a commercial ad in which a physically attractive source endorses either a beauty product (relevant source attractiveness) or the services of a roofing company (irrelevant source attractiveness; see Petty & Cacioppo, 1984). Under conditions of low elaboration, source attractiveness may have a positive effect on evaluations of both the beauty product and the roofing company by virtue of mere association. Under conditions of high elaboration, however, source attractiveness may influence evaluations through a different process with different outcomes for the two products. Whereas evaluations of the beauty product may be influenced by source attractiveness because of its perceived relevance for evaluating the product, the persuasive effect on evaluations of the roofing company may be attenuated because of the perceived irrelevance of source attractiveness. Overall, the multiple-roles hypothesis states that any persuasion variable can influence attitudes in four different ways: (1) by serving as an argument,

(2) by serving as a cue, (3) by determining the extent of cognitive elaboration, and (4) by producing a bias in the processing of the available information (Petty & Wegener, 1999). These assumptions make the model very flexible in accounting for a variety of effects in the persuasion literature. At the same time, the multiple-roles hypothesis makes it difficult to predict the outcome for a given persuasion situation, if the conditions under which a particular variable will take on any of the proposed roles are not specified.

HEURISTIC SYSTEMATIC MODEL

Similar to Petty and Cacioppo's (1986) ELM, Chaiken's (1987) HSM describes two basic persuasion processes that may guide an individual's judgments of an attitude object (see also Chen & Chaiken, 1999; Chaiken, Liberman, & Eagly, 1989). *Systematic processing* involves comprehensive consideration of object-relevant information, which requires high levels of motivation and ability to engage in effortful processing. *Heuristic processing*, in contrast, relies on the activation, accessibility, and applicability of learned heuristics that require relatively few cognitive resources (e.g., *I agree with people I like*). According to the HSM, the likelihood that an individual engages in systematic processing is guided by the *sufficiency principle*, which states that the motivation to engage in systematic processing increases to the extent that an individual's desired level of confidence falls below his or her actual level of confidence. That is, individuals are more likely to engage in systematic processing when the difference between their desired and their actual levels of confidence is high. Conversely, people are more likely to engage in heuristic processing when the difference between their desired and actual levels of confidence is low. Importantly, systematic processing may not necessarily lead to unbiased judgments because systematic processing can be influenced by *defense motivation* and *impression management*. Defense motivation refers to the desire to defend preexisting attitudes, whereas impression management refers to the desire to hold attitudes that satisfy specific social goals.

Another central assumption of the HSM is that heuristic and systematic processing may co-occur and interact with each other to exert either independent or interactive effects on evaluations. First, according to the model's *attenuation hypothesis*, systematic processing can completely override the effects of heuristic processing (e.g., Maheswaran & Chaiken, 1991). Such attenuation effects are likely to occur when systematic processing yields information that contradicts the validity of simple persuasion heuristics. Second, the information generated by heuristic and systematic processing may jointly influence evaluations in an additive manner (e.g., Maheswaran, Mackie, & Chaiken, 1992). According to the model's *additivity hypothesis,* such effects are likely to occur when the two processing modes do not yield conflicting reactions. Finally, when the message content is ambiguous, heuristic cues may bias the effects of systematic processing, as described by the model's *bias hypothesis.* For example, if the strength of a persuasive argument is ambiguous, the argument may be perceived as more convincing if it is presented by an expert than if it is presented by a layperson (e.g., Chaiken & Maheswaran, 1994).

In terms of its core assumptions, the HSM shows considerable resemblance to the ELM (Petty & Cacioppo, 1986). For example, both models maintain that attitude change can occur through either (1) systematic/central processing that requires some degree of motivation and capacity or (2) heuristic/peripheral processing that is assumed to require little motivation or capacity. However, the two models differ in their treatment of heuristic and peripheral processes (Chen & Chaiken, 1999). Whereas the ELM assumes an inverse relationship between central and peripheral processing along the elaboration continuum, the HSM assumes that systematic and heuristic processing may occur simultaneously with either independent or interactive effects. Hence, the ELM holds that there is a trade-off between peripheral and central processing, such that the importance of one processing mode decreases as the importance of the other processing mode increases. In contrast, under the HLM's conceptualization, individuals can engage in systematic and heuristic processing simultaneously.

Attitude–Behavior Relations

Expanding on the question of how attitudes are formed and changed, another class of dual process theories describes the mechanisms by which attitudes guide behavior. These models have been inspired by recurring debates about whether and to what extent attitudes influence behavior (e.g., Wicker, 1969). By shifting the focus from asking *"Do attitudes guide behavior?"* to the question, *"How do attitudes guide behavior?"* dual process theorizing provided important insights into the conditions under which attitudes do or do not influence behavior.

MODE MODEL

One such dual process theory is Fazio's (1990) *Motivation and Opportunity as DEterminants* (MODE) model, which specifies two distinct processes by which attitudes can guide behavior depending on the person's motivation and opportunity to engage in deliberate processing (for recent reviews, see Fazio, 2007; Olson & Fazio, 2009). A central component of the MODE model is the definition of *attitude* as the mental association between an object and a person's summary evaluation of that object (Fazio, 1995, 2007). To the extent that this association is sufficiently strong, the evaluation associated with the object may be activated automatically upon encountering that object (i.e., without intention to evaluate the object; see Fazio, Sanbonmatsu, Powell, & Kardes, 1986). Such automatically activated attitudes are assumed to influence an individual's spontaneous interpretation of the current situation, which in turn will guide the individual's behavior without him or her necessarily being aware of the attitude's influence (*spontaneous attitude–behavior process*). Alternatively, individuals may scrutinize specific attributes of the object and the current situation (*deliberate attitude–behavior process*). However, such deliberate analyses require that an individual has both the motivation and the opportunity (i.e., adequate time and cognitive resources) to engage in effortful information processing. Thus, to the extent that either the motivation or the opportunity to engage in effortful processing is low, automatically activated attitudes may guide behavior through their effect on the spontaneous construal of the current situation. However, if both the motivation and the opportunity to engage in effortful processing are high, the impact of automatically activated attitudes on behavior will depend on particular aspects of the current situation, including specific attributes of the attitude object or salient norms (Fazio, 1990; see also Ajzen & Fishbein, 1980).

An important application of the MODE model concerns the relation between explicit and implicit measures of attitudes (see Fazio & Olson, 2003, Olson & Fazio, 2009). According to the MODE model, implicit measures of attitudes—such as evaluative priming (Fazio, Jackson, Dunton, & Williams, 1995) or the implicit association test (Greenwald, McGhee, & Schwartz, 1998)—reduce participants' opportunity to engage in effortful processing. Consequently, participants' responses on these measures will directly reflect their automatically activated attitudes (but see Olson & Fazio, 2004). In contrast, verbally reported evaluations assessed by explicit measures are relatively easy to control. Thus, to the extent that participants lack either the motivation or the opportunity to engage in effortful processing, explicit measures should reveal the same automatically activated attitudes that are reflected in implicit measures. If, however, participants have both the motivation and the opportunity to engage in a deliberate analysis of the current situation, explicit measures may reflect whatever evaluation is implied by these inferences. Within the domain of racial prejudice, for example, the influence of an automatically activated prejudicial attitude on verbally reported evaluations may be mitigated if an individual is motivated to control his or her prejudiced reactions. Consequently, automatic prejudicial attitudes assessed by implicit measures should be directly reflected in explicit evaluative judgments when the motivation to control prejudiced reactions is low, but not when it is high (e.g., Dunton & Fazio, 1997). More generally, these assumptions imply that implicit attitude measures should be better predictors of spontaneous behaviors that are relatively difficult to control (e.g., nonverbal behavior), whereas explicit attitude measures should be better predictors of deliberate behaviors that are relatively easy to control (e.g., content of verbal responses).

DUAL ATTITUDE MODEL

Similar predictions are implied by Wilson and colleagues' (2000) dual attitude model, even though its underlying assumptions about attitude representation are quite different from the core assumptions of the MODE model. According to the dual attitude model, people may simultaneously hold two attitudes toward the same object, which are described as *implicit attitude* and *explicit attitude* (see also Greenwald & Banaji, 1995). Such dual representations are assumed to emerge when a previously acquired attitude is challenged by counterattitudinal information, and the newly formed, explicit attitude does not erase the previously acquired, implicit attitude from memory. To the extent that the old, implicit attitude is highly overlearned, it may be activated automatically. In contrast, retrieving the newly formed, explicit attitude from memory is assumed to require cognitive effort. As a result, earlier acquired, implicit attitudes should guide judgments and behavior when either the motivation or the capacity to engage in effortful processing is low. However, judgments and behavior should be influenced by more recently acquired, explicit attitudes when both the motivation and the capacity to engage in effortful processing are high.

Another important implication of the dual attitude model is that implicit attitudes should be more difficult to change than explicit attitudes. Even though this prediction has been confirmed in several studies that used implicit measures to assess implicit attitudes and self-report measures to assess explicit attitudes (e.g., Gawronski & Strack, 2004; Gregg, Seibt, & Banaji, 2006), there is accumulating evidence that attitudes assessed with implicit measures can sometimes change rather quickly, with little counterattitudinal information (e.g., Gawronski & LeBel, 2008; Olson & Fazio, 2006). In addition, attitudes assessed with implicit measures have been shown to be highly context sensitive, such that the same object may elicit different evaluative responses as a function of the context in which it is encountered (for a review, see Gawronski & Sritharan, 2010). These findings have inspired the development of alternative models that were especially designed to explain different patterns of implicit and explicit attitude change (e.g., Gawronski & Bodenhausen, 2006a, 2011; Petty, Briñol, & DeMarree, 2007).

Prejudice and Stereotyping

One of the most striking findings in research on prejudice and stereotyping is that public opinion polls in North America showed a steady decline in negative evaluations of racial minority groups after World War II, whereas racial conflicts showed only a moderate reduction (e.g., Greeley & Sheatsley, 1971; Taylor, Sheatsley, & Greeley, 1978). This discrepancy inspired social psychologists to postulate more subtle forms of racial prejudice, such as modern (McConahay, 1986), aversive (Gaertner & Dovidio, 1986), or symbolic (Sears, 1988) racism. The general notion underlying these constructs is that racial prejudice has simply changed its face, rather than been abandoned. A very similar idea provided the inspiration for Devine's (1989) dissociation model, which was seminal in introducing the distinction between automatic and controlled processes to research on prejudice and stereotyping.

DISSOCIATION MODEL

A central aspect of Devine's (1989) dissociation model is the distinction between the *knowledge* of a social stereotype and the *belief* in the accuracy of that stereotype. According to Devine, both low-prejudice and high-prejudice individuals tend to be familiar with the contents of prevailing cultural stereotypes. However, the two groups differ with respect to their personal beliefs about the accuracy of these stereotypes. To the extent that stereotypic knowledge is acquired during early childhood and highly overlearned as a result of socialization processes, stereotypic knowledge is assumed to be activated automatically upon encountering members of stereotyped groups, and this occurs for both low-prejudice and high-prejudice individuals. In contrast, the rejection of stereotypic knowledge is assumed to be the result of egalitarian, nonprejudicial beliefs, which tend to be acquired later in the socialization process (e.g., Banse, Gawronski, Rebetez, Gutt, & Morton, 2010). Because these beliefs are less overlearned than earlier acquired stereotypic knowledge, replacing automatically activated stereotypes with egalitarian, nonprejudicial beliefs requires the operation of controlled processing. In other words, while the model assumes that automatic stereotype activation is equally strong and inescapable for both high-prejudice and low-prejudice individuals, the two groups differ at the level of controlled processing, such that low-prejudice but not high-prejudice individuals replace automatically activated stereotypes with egalitarian, nonprejudicial beliefs. In terms of the four characteristics of automaticity, these assumptions imply that the activation of social stereotypes occurs unintentionally, even though their impact on overt behavior can be controlled through effortful processes.

A notable aspect of Devine's (1989) dissociation model is that it implies a rather different view on the roles of personal beliefs and social contexts than the MODE model. Whereas the MODE model assumes that personal attitudes tend to be activated automatically and that the overt expression of these attitudes is sometimes suppressed when they conflict with social norms (Fazio et al., 1995), the dissociation model proposes that socially transmitted stereotypes are activated automatically and that the overt expression of these stereotypes is suppressed when they conflict with personal beliefs (Devine, 1989). In other words, whereas the MODE model locates an individual's authentic self at the level of automatic processes and extrinsic, social influences at the level of controlled processes, the dissociation model locates extrinsic, social influences at the level of automatic processes and the individual's authentic self at the level of controlled processes. Even though questions about what should be considered the "authentic self" are philosophical rather than empirical, these diverging views have important implications for the interpretation of automatic stereotypic biases (Gawronski, Peters, & LeBel, 2008). One example is the automatic tendency to misidentify harmless objects as weapons when they are held by a black person rather than a white person (for a review, see Payne, 2006). According to the MODE model, such unintentional errors reveal an individual's personal attitudes when the individual does not have the opportunity to adjust his or her automatic responses to egalitarian norms. In contrast, from the perspective of Devine's (1989) model, unintentional errors in weapon identification reveal the ubiquitous influence of cultural stereotypes that are independent of the individual's personal beliefs.

Impression Formation

Similar to Devine's (1989) dissociation model of prejudice and stereotyping, dual process theories of impression formation emphasize the role of social category information in early processing stages. However, whereas Devine's model focuses particularly on the unintentional activation versus controlled suppression of stereotypes, dual process theories of impression formation specify the conditions under which personal impressions of an individual are dominated by category-related or person-specific information.

CONTINUUM MODEL

Fiske and Neuberg's (1990) continuum model of impression formation proposes that the processes by which people form opinions of other individuals operate along a continuum that reflects the degree to which perceivers utilize category-related versus person-specific information (Figure 14.2). The basic assumption of the model is that category information enjoys general priority because the processing of such information does not require substantial amounts of cognitive resources. Specifically, perceivers are assumed to categorize individuals on the basis of salient category cues (e.g., gender, age, ethnicity), and this categorization is assumed to occur unintentionally upon encountering a target individual. Contingent on the relevance of the target for the perceiver's momentary goals, perceivers will direct their attention to individual attributes of the target, thereby moving toward the more thoughtful end of the processing continuum. If the target is judged to be irrelevant to the perceiver's momentary goals, the final impression of the target will be based exclusively on the initial categorization. If, however, the target is judged to be relevant to the perceiver's momentary goals, the perceiver will attempt to integrate person-specific attributes into a coherent impression of the target.

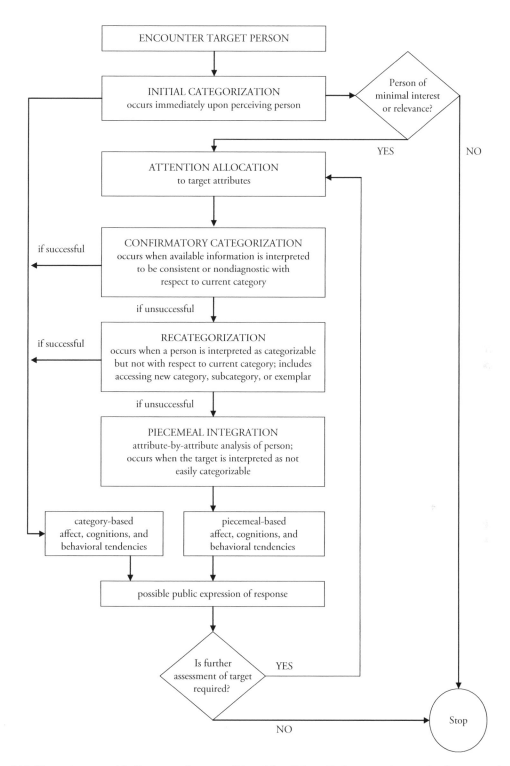

Figure 14.2 The continuum model of impression formation. (Adapted from Fiske & Neuberg, 1990. Reprinted with permission.)

Overall, the continuum model assumes that perceivers attempt to maintain the impression implied by their initial categorization while processing individual attributes of the target. To the extent that the additional information is interpreted to be consistent with the initially identified category, the final impression of the target will be based on the initial categorization. If, however, the additional information is inconsistent with the initial categorization, perceivers will attempt to recategorize the target in an attempt to find a more suitable category than the initial one. For example, if person-specific attributes of a target individual seem inconsistent with the impression implied by his or her category membership, perceivers may use subtypes to assign the target to a more appropriate category than the initial, general category (Richards & Hewstone, 2001). If this recategorization process successfully integrates the available information about the target, the final impression will be based on this newly applied category. However, if the attempt to recategorize the target fails, perceivers are assumed to move on to a process of piecemeal integration, in which they engage in an attribute-by-attribute assessment of individual characteristics of the target. Yet, according to Fiske, Lin, and Neuberg (1999), such piecemeal integration occurs quite rarely, given that perceivers tend to construct ad hoc theories to account for contradictory information in the initial stages of the impression formation continuum (e.g., Asch & Zuckier, 1984; Kunda, Miller, & Claire, 1990; Leyens & Yzerbyt, 1992).

DUAL PROCESS MODEL

Whereas Fiske and Neuberg's (1990) continuum model attributes a dominant role to category-based processing, Brewer's (1988) dual process model argues that impression formation may take either a top-down or a bottom-up route (see also Brewer & Harasty-Feinstein, 1999). Both routes are assumed to start with an automatic identification of salient features of the stimulus person (Figure 14.3). This processing step can be described as the mere recognition of feature configurations (e.g., male, dark skin color, business suit). To the extent that the target is irrelevant to the perceiver, the processing sequence is assumed to remain at this level without further processing of category-related or person-related implications of the identified features. If, however, the target is relevant to the perceiver, further processing of the identified features can take either a top-down or a bottom-up route depending on the relative involvement of the perceiver.

Bottom-up processing is assumed to occur under conditions of high involvement, in which perceivers are assumed to adopt an interpersonal orientation. In this person-based processing mode,

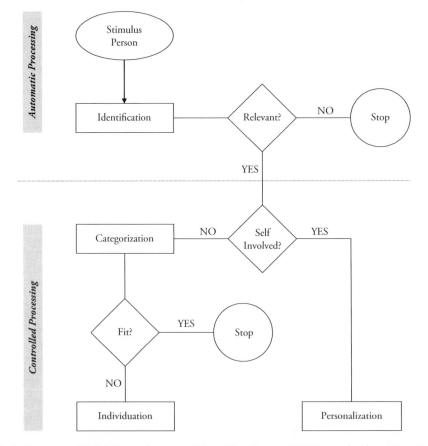

Figure 14.3 The dual-process model of impression formation. (Adapted from Brewer, 1988. Reprinted with permission.)

perceivers are assumed to draw inferences directly from the identified features, which are integrated into a coherent impression of the target (*personalization*). Depending on the motivation and ability to engage in effortful processing, this person-based impression may be more or less complex. In other words, personalization is not an effortful process per se. Rather, the degree of cognitive elaboration is assumed to influence the complexity of the final impression, such that low elaboration will lead to relatively simple person-based impressions, whereas high elaboration will lead to relatively complex person-based impressions.

Top-down processing is assumed to occur under conditions of low involvement, in which perceivers are assumed to adopt an intergroup orientation. In this category-based processing mode, the target is initially categorized on the basis of salient features (e.g., black businessman). This categorization process, in turn, may activate stereotypic contents associated with the applied category, which serve as a filter for the integration of other target-specific information. Whereas target-specific information that is related to the stereotypic content of the category will be integrated into a coherent impression, target-specific information that is unrelated to the category stereotype will be ignored. To the extent that the category-related target information is consistent with the category stereotype, the process is assumed to stop at this point, leading to a target impression in line with the category stereotype (*stereotyping*). If, however, the category-related target information is inconsistent with the category stereotype, the inconsistency has to be resolved in order to achieve a coherent impression of the target. The result of the latter process is an individuated impression of the target, which is based on a systematic integration of target-specific information (*individuation*). However, this integration is still regarded as a category-based process, given that the initial categorization of the target serves as a filter for the processing of category-related versus category-unrelated target information. Thus, like person-based processing, category-based processing can be more or less effortful, such that stereotyping is the likely outcome of low elaboration, whereas individuation usually requires high elaboration.

Dispositional Attribution

Another important question in the context of impression formation is how perceivers make sense of other people's behavior. To describe the processes that underlie inferences from observed behavior,

social psychologists in the 1960s proposed various theories of causal (e.g., Kelley, 1967) and dispositional (e.g., Jones & Davis, 1965) attribution (see Chapter 6). However, deviating from the predictions of these models, empirical research soon demonstrated that perceivers tend to give more weight to dispositional compared with situational factors (e.g., Jones & Harris, 1967; Ross, Amabile, & Steinmetz, 1977). This tendency to overestimate the role of dispositional compared with situational factors has become known as the *fundamental attribution error* (Ross, 1977). A particular instantiation of the fundamental attribution error is the *correspondence bias* (Gilbert & Malone, 1995; Jones, 1990), which is defined as the tendency to draw correspondent dispositional inferences from observed behavior even if the behavior is constrained by situational factors (for a discussion of conceptual differences between the fundamental attribution error and the correspondence bias, see Gawronski, 2004). In the 1970s, the discrepancy between theoretically derived predictions and empirical results led to the odd situation that the models that had originally been designed to describe and explain perceivers' inferences acquired a normative status, such that empirically observed deviations were depicted as judgmental biases or errors (see Kruglanski & Ajzen, 1983) instead of counterevidence against the proposed models. This situation did not change until the emergence of dual process theories in the mid-1980s. These theories turned attention back to describing the processes that underlie perceivers' inferences, with a particular focus on explaining when and why the correspondence bias occurs.

THREE-STAGE MODEL

One such dual process theory is Gilbert's (1989) three-stage model of dispositional inference. According to this model, dispositional inferences involve three sequential processes that are claimed to require different amounts of cognitive resources: (1) *behavioral categorization* (i.e., what is the actor doing?), (2) *dispositional characterization* (i.e., what disposition does the behavior imply?), and (3) *situational correction* (i.e., what situational determinants might have caused the behavior?). Whereas behavioral categorization and dispositional characterization are assumed to occur unintentionally without requiring large amounts of cognitive resources, situational correction is assumed to be an intentional, relatively effortful process. Applied to the correspondence bias, these assumptions imply that the tendency to draw correspondent dispositional inferences from situationally constrained behavior should be lower when perceivers have both the motivation and the cognitive capacity to engage in the effortful process of situational correction. However, the tendency to commit the correspondence bias should be enhanced if either the motivation or the cognitive capacity to engage in effortful processing is low. These predictions have been confirmed in several studies that investigated effects of processing motivation (e.g., D'Agostino & Ficher-Kiefer, 1992; Vonk, 1999; Webster, 1993) and cognitive capacity (e.g., Gilbert, Pelham, & Krull, 1988) on dispositional inferences from situationally constrained behavior.

An important extension of Gilbert's (1989) three-stage model was proposed by Krull (1993), who merged Gilbert's (1989) assumptions about the effortfulness of situational correction with previous research on judgmental anchoring in dispositional inference (Quattrone, 1982). Deviating from Gilbert's (1989) assumption that social inferences follow a fixed sequence, Krull (1993) argued that the particular sequence of processes depends on the inferential goal of the perceiver. According to Krull, perceivers interested in inferring an actor's disposition will (1) categorize the behavior, (2) characterize a corresponding disposition, and then (3) correct these characterizations for situational constraints. If, however, perceivers are interested in the causal impact of situational factors, they will (1) categorize behavior, (2) characterize the situation, and then (3) correct these characterizations for dispositional factors. In other words, the contents of both the characterization and the correction stage are assumed

to depend on the inferential goal of the perceiver. Because correction processes are assumed to require more capacity compared with characterization processes, motivation and cognitive capacity to engage in effortful processing should have different effects on social inferences as a function of perceivers' inferential goals. Specifically, reduced cognitive elaboration should increase the tendency to commit the correspondence bias when perceivers have the goal of inferring dispositional characteristics of the actor. In contrast, reduced cognitive elaboration should have the opposite effect when perceivers are interested in characteristics of the situation (e.g., Krull, 1993; Krull & Dill, 1996; Krull & Erickson, 1995).

TWO-STAGE MODEL

Another influential model that aims to describe the processes underlying dispositional attributions is Trope's (1986) two-stage model. According to this model, trait judgments are the product of two sequential processes, which are described as *identification* and *inference* (Figure 14.4). At the identification stage, perceivers categorize momentarily available cues in trait-relevant terms. These cues may be related to the actor's behavior (*behavioral cues*), the situational context of the behavior (*situational cues*), or the actor's personal characteristics or group membership (*prior cues*). For example, a person's behavior might be categorized as friendly or hostile, the situational context as facilitating friendly or hostile reactions, and the actor as belonging to a stereotypically friendly or hostile group. To the extent that the relevant cues within each of the three dimensions are unambiguous, they fully constrain

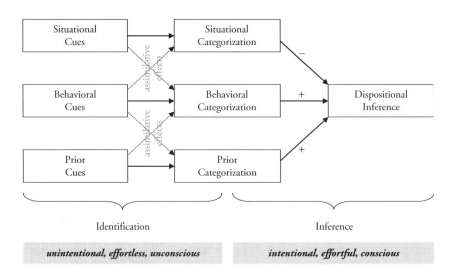

Figure 14.4 The two-stage model of dispositional inference. (Adapted from Trope, 1986. Reprinted with permission.)

their corresponding categorizations. That is, behavioral cues fully determine the categorization of the behavior, situational cues fully determine the categorization of the situation, and prior cues fully determine the categorization of the actor. If, however, a particular cue is ambiguous, its categorization may be biased by contextual cues in an assimilative manner. For example, if an actor's behavior is ambiguously hostile, it may be perceived as more hostile when the situational context is known to facilitate hostile rather than friendly behavior (e.g., Snyder & Frankel, 1976; Trope, Cohen, & Alfieri, 1991; Trope, Cohen, & Maoz, 1988) or when the actor belongs to a stereotypically hostile rather than a stereotypically friendly group (e.g., Duncan, 1976; Gawronski, Geschke, & Banse, 2003; Hugenberg & Bodenhausen, 2003; Kunda & Sherman-Williams, 1993; Sagar & Schofield, 1980). Similar effects may occur for the categorization of ambiguous situational cues (e.g., Trope & Cohen, 1989) and the categorization of ambiguous prior cues (e.g., Hugenberg & Bodenhausen, 2004), both of which may be biased by unambiguous behavioral cues. Because perceivers tend to consider their subjective categorizations "as perceptual givens rather than as context-derived" (Trope & Gaunt, 1999, p. 170), deliberate correction of such biased perceptions is rather unlikely, even when the validity of the biasing contextual information is discredited afterward (e.g., Trope & Alfieri, 1997). In combination with studies showing biasing effects of contextual cues under conditions of depleted cognitive resources (e.g., Trope & Alfieri, 1997; Trope & Gaunt, 2000), these findings suggest that the processes involved at the identification stage operate unintentionally, efficiently, and outside of conscious awareness (for a review, see Trope & Gaunt, 1999).

Once behavioral, situational, and prior cues have been categorized, the outputs of the identification stage serve as inputs for more or less deliberate dispositional inferences (see Figure 14.4). At this stage, perceivers' categorizations of the behavior, the situation, and the actor are integrated into a unified judgment of the actor's disposition. However, in contrast to the generally assimilative nature of contextual influences at the identification stage, dispositional judgments at the inferential stage are influenced by the three kinds of information in different ways. Whereas both behavioral and prior information influence trait judgments in a positive direction, situational information has a subtractive effect. For example, behavior that is categorized as hostile will facilitate correspondent inferences of dispositional

hostility. Similarly, categorization of the actor as a member of a stereotypically hostile group will also promote inferences of dispositional hostility. Situational cues identified to provoke hostile reactions, however, should have an inhibitory effect on inferences of dispositional hostility. Such information should discount the informational value of the other two dimensions, and hence reduce correspondent inferences of dispositional hostility (see Kelley, 1972). Importantly, whereas contextual influences at the identification stage are assumed to operate efficiently, unintentionally, and outside of conscious awareness, the integration of the different kinds of information at the inference stage is assumed to be a conscious, intentional process that requires varying amounts of cognitive resources depending on the salience of the three kinds of information (Trope & Gaunt, 2000).

Like Gilbert's (1989) three-stage model, Trope's (1986) two-stage model implies that the tendency to draw correspondent dispositional inferences from situationally constrained behavior should be more pronounced when cognitive elaboration is low than when it is high (but see Trope & Gaunt, 2000, for a qualification of this prediction). However, Trope's model also implies that perceivers may sometimes draw strong correspondent inferences from situationally constrained behavior even when perceivers consider the importance of situational factors at the inference stage. To illustrate this case, consider a study by Snyder and Frankel (1976) in which participants were presented with a videotaped interview of a target behaving somewhat anxiously. The sound of the interview was muted, so that participants focused only on the target's behavior. Half of the participants were told that that the target person was interviewed about an anxiety-provoking topic (e.g., sexual fantasies), whereas the remaining half were told that the topic was not anxiety provoking (e.g., favorite books). Results showed that participants in both conditions inferred equal levels of dispositional anxiety from the observed behavior. At first glance, this result may suggest that participants in the anxious topic condition ignored the anxiety-provoking topic as a situational factor for the observed behavior when they made their attributions of dispositional anxiety. However, Snyder and Frankel's (1976) data also showed that participants perceived the target's behavior as more anxious when they believed that she was interviewed about sexual fantasies than when they believed that she was interviewed about favorite books. Given that higher levels of perceived *behavioral* anxiety should promote corresponding attributions of *dispositional* anxiety, the biasing effect of situational information on the identification of the target's behavior may have concealed the subtractive influence of situational information at the inference stage. In other words, participants perceived the target's behavior as more anxious when the interview topic was anxiety provoking, but then they considered the anxiety-provoking nature of the interview topic as a situational explanation for this behavior when they drew correspondent dispositional inferences. These considerations imply that the presumed interview topic may influence dispositional attributions in Snyder and Frankel's (1976) paradigm in two different ways. First, the interview topic may have an *indirect positive effect* on attributions of dispositional anxiety that is mediated by the biased identification of the target's behavior. Second, the interview topic may have a *direct negative effect* if it is considered a situational explanation for the observed behavior (e.g., Trope & Alfieri, 1997). Because the proposed indirect effect of situational information is opposite to the proposed direct effect, the two effects may sometimes cancel each other out on measures of trait attribution unless the proposed indirect effect is statistically controlled (e.g., Gawronski et al., 2002). Importantly, this pattern of simultaneous, yet antagonistic, direct and indirect effects implies that perceivers may draw strong correspondent inferences from situationally constrained behavior, even if they consider situational factors to have a strong impact on the target's behavior. In other words, they commit the correspondence bias, even though they do not commit the fundamental attribution error (Gawronski, 2004).

Criticism of Phenomenon-Specific Dual Process Theories

Overall, the reviewed phenomenon-specific dual process theories have gained strong empirical support, and many of them have been seminal in shaping the field of social psychology over the past decades. Nevertheless, these theories have also been the target of criticism. One of the most important arguments raised against these models is that they equate distinct contents with distinct processes (e.g., Kruglanski, Pierro, Mannetti, Erb, & Chun, 2007). For example, Kruglanski and Thompson (1999) argued that dual process theories of persuasion tend to conflate different types of evidence (e.g., message arguments, characteristics of the source) with different types of processes (e.g., peripheral vs. central; heuristic vs. systematic), even though the processes

by which the two kinds of information are integrated into attitudinal judgments may be the same (e.g., Erb, Pierro, Mannetti, Spiegel, & Kruglanski, 2007). According to this criticism, the two kinds of information may simply differ in their levels of complexity, thereby requiring different amounts of processing resources. Thus, if the complexity of the two kinds of information is controlled or independently manipulated, message arguments may influence attitudes even under conditions of low elaboration (e.g., when their complexity is low), or source characteristics may influence attitudes only when cognitive elaboration is high (e.g., when their complexity is high).

Similar arguments have been raised against dual process theories of dispositional attribution (e.g., Chun, Spiegel, & Kruglanski, 2002) and dual process theories of impression formation (e.g., Chun & Kruglanski, 2006). For example, challenging Trope's (1986) assumption that the biasing influence of contextual cues in the categorization of ambiguous behavior is an efficient process, Chun and colleagues (2002) have shown that the effects of assimilative behavior identification are attenuated by cognitive load when the categorization of ambiguous behavior is relatively difficult. Along the same lines, Chun and Kruglanski (2006) showed that individuating information has a stronger impact compared with category information under conditions of resource depletion if the complexity of the individuating information is lower compared with the complexity of the category information. This finding challenges a central assumption of Fiske and Neuberg's (1990) continuum model, which implies that category information enjoys general priority. As an alternative to phenomenon-specific dual process theories, Kruglanski and colleagues (2007) proposed a unimodel of human judgment, which proposes that different kinds of evidence (e.g., message arguments vs. source characteristics; category vs. individuating information) are integrated in a single inferential process whose outcome depends on several judgmental parameters, including information relevance, processing difficulty, processing motivation, processing capacity, and processing order.

A related concern about phenomenon-specific dual process theories is that they all seem to address very similar issues. Yet, it remains unclear how the different models are related to each other and what general principles of information processing underlie the studied phenomena. This concern echoes criticism by Kruglanski and colleagues'

(2007) unimodel, according to which different kinds of information are integrated in a single epistemic process that is influenced by several processing parameters. An alternative response is implied by generalized dual process theories, which identify two general processing principles that are assumed to provide the foundation for the reviewed domain-specific phenomena.

Generalized Dual Process Theories

Generalized dual process theories aim at identifying domain-independent principles of social information processing that underlie various kinds of phenomena. Most of these theories fall into the category of dual system theories, in that they propose two processing systems that operate on the basis of qualitatively distinct principles. In the following sections, we first review the core assumptions of the most prominent examples, and then discuss criticism that has been raised against generalized dual process theories.

Cognitive-Experiential Self-Theory

The groundwork for generalized dual process theories was put in place by Epstein's (1994) cognitive-experiential self-theory (CEST), which is based on his foundational work on the nature of the self-concept as a global theory of personality (Epstein, 1973). In general terms, CEST proposes two interacting systems that are characterized by different processing principles. The first is described as the *experiential system*; the second is described as the *rational system* (for an overview, see Epstein & Pacini, 1999).

The experiential system is assumed to operate in an automatic, effortless manner on the basis of associative connections that are closely linked to affective principles of pleasure and pain (i.e., what feels good or bad). Encoding of reality in the experiential system is claimed to occur in concrete images, metaphors, and narratives, involving holistic responses that are oriented toward immediate action. As such, responses driven by the experiential system are characterized by broad, schematic generalizations that tend to be incoherent, crudely integrated, and context specific. Changes in the experiential system are assumed to occur slowly, requiring repetitive or relatively intense experiences. These processing principles are assumed to be rooted in brain structures that developed early in evolution and that have not been replaced by more recently evolved structures that build the foundation for the second, rational system.

The rational system is characterized by intentional, effortful processing that is based on logical relations between elements (i.e., what is rational). Encoding of reality in the rational system is claimed to occur in abstract symbols, words, and numbers, involving analytic responses that are oriented toward delayed action. Thus, responses driven by the rational system are characterized by differentiated, highly integrated representations that tend to be abstract, logically coherent, and context independent. Changes in the rational system are assumed to occur more quickly compared with the experiential system, with changes depending on argument strength and availability of new evidence.

According to Epstein (1994), the two systems operate in parallel, such that each system can independently produce its own response tendency. In cases in which these response tendencies are incongruent, people tend to experience a "conflict between the head and the heart" (p. 710), such that the experiential system may produce an intuitive, affective response tendency that conflicts with a rational, logical response tendency produced by the rational system. At the same time, the two systems may interact with each other, such that preconscious processes in the experiential system may continuously influence conscious processing in the rational system. However, the proposed interaction between the two systems is assumed to be asymmetrical because influences from the experiential system usually remain outside of conscious awareness. As a result, these influences often remain uncontrolled by the rational system because there is no awareness that there is anything to control to begin with. Still, there can be individual and situational variations in the relative dominance of the two systems. For example, Epstein, Pacini, Denes-Raj, and Heier (1996) developed the Rational-Experiential Inventory (REI), which includes two individual difference measures that are specifically designed to identify stable individual differences in the dominance of intuitive-experiential and analytical-rational thinking styles. Other moderating factors include situational circumstances and emotional arousal. Whereas circumstances that require a formal analysis of the current situation are assumed to give priority to the rational system, emotional arousal is assumed to shift the balance toward the experiential system.

Although the role of CEST in empirical research has mostly taken the form of a conceptual framework for the interpretation of results rather than a source for the deduction of testable predictions, it clearly deserves the credit of setting the groundwork for generalized dual process theorizing. In fact, many of its core assumptions can be found in its successors, some of which have been more successful in generating novel predictions through the specification of earlier claims and the inclusion of new propositions. During the past few years, these theories have gained more impact compared with CEST. Yet, as the first theory of this kind, CEST still enjoys the status of being the most frequently cited generalized dual process theory.

Associative Versus Ruled-Based Processing

Another milestone in the development of generalized dual process theories is Smith and DeCoster's (2000) conceptual integration of various domain-specific dual process theories. Drawing on Sloman's (1996) distinction between associative and rule-based processing and McClelland and colleagues' work on fast-learning versus slow-learning memory systems (McClelland, McNaughton, & O'Reilly, 1995), Smith and DeCoster (2000) argued that the phenomena identified and studied by domain-specific dual process theories reflect the operation of two distinct memory systems that are guided by different processing principles: a slow-learning system that is characterized by associative processing and a fast-learning system that is characterized by rule-based processing. Associative processing is further specified as being structured by similarity and contiguity, drawing on simple associations between objects and events that are learned slowly over many experiences. Associative processing is assumed to occur automatically in a parallel fashion without awareness of the involved processing steps, even though their output may be accessible to conscious awareness. Rule-based processing, in contrast, is characterized as being structured by language and logic, drawing on symbolically represented rules that can be learned quickly with very few experiences. Attributing a dominant role to associative processing, rule-based processing is further assumed to occur optionally in a sequential fashion if both the motivation and the capacity to engage in effortful processing are present. Its processing steps are often accessible to conscious awareness, such that the applied rules of inference can be verbalized. Similar to Epstein's (1994) CEST, Smith and DeCoster (2000) propose an asymmetrical interaction between the two memory systems, such that rule-based processing may draw on inputs from both memory systems, whereas associative processing is exclusively based on the slow-learning system.

Using the distinction between associative and rule-based processing in the two memory systems, Smith and DeCoster (2000) integrated the phenomena identified and studied by various domain-specific dual process theories within a single generalized framework. For example, peripheral/heuristic processing in dual process theories of persuasion (Chaiken, 1987; Petty & Cacioppo, 1986) is characterized as the use of well-learned associations of salient cues (e.g., source attractiveness) with positive or negative evaluations. Central/systematic processing, in contrast, is described as the effortful search for relevant information that is evaluated using rule-based processes on the basis of logical principles. Along the same lines, automatic attitude activation in Fazio's (1990) MODE model is described as automatic access to evaluations that are associated with an attitude object through repeated pairings. Deliberate analysis of an object's attributes, in contrast, is characterized as the search for and appraisal of relevant information on the basis of logical rules of inference. Correspondent dispositional inferences in Gilbert's (1989) three-stage model are described as the use of traits that are semantically associated with a person's observed behavior, whereas inferences about alternative causes (e.g., situational factors) are assumed to involve rule-based processes that are guided by principles of logical inference. Similar considerations apply to Devine's (1989) dissociation model of prejudice and stereotyping, such that automatic stereotype activation is assumed to be the result of highly overlearned associations between social groups and stereotypic information, whereas suppression of these automatically activated stereotypes involves effortful access to personal beliefs in order to override the impact of stereotypic information. Finally, automatic categorization in dual process theories of impression formation (Brewer, 1988, Fiske & Neuberg, 1990) is described as the use of information that is associated with a person's salient category (e.g., gender, race, age), whereas individuation involves the processing and appraisal of multiple individual characteristics to form a personal impression.

System 1 and System 2 Processing

Working toward a theoretical integration of earlier research on heuristics and biases (for reviews, see Gilovich, Griffin, & Kahneman, 2002; Kahneman, Slovic, & Tversky, 1982), Kahneman (2003) presented a generalized dual process theory that shares many features with Smith and DeCoster's (2000) and Epstein's (1994) models. To this end,

Kahneman (2003) distinguished between two systems, generically described as *System 1* and *System 2* (cf. Stanovich & West, 2000), that are assumed to underlie intuition versus reasoning. Sharing characteristics of basic perceptual processes, intuitive processing in System 1 is described as fast, parallel, automatic, effortless, associative, slow learning, and emotional. In contrast, reasoning processes in System 2 are described as slow, serial, controlled, effortful, rule governed, fast learning, and emotionally neutral. At the same time, information processing in the two systems is assumed to differ from basic perceptual processes, in that both intuition and reasoning can be evoked by verbal information, involving conceptual representations of the past, the present, and the future. These features differ from basic perceptual processes, which involve stimulus-bound percepts that are driven by current stimulation. Thus, whereas the outputs of System 1 may be described as intuitive *impressions*, the outputs of System 2 are *judgments* that can be based on impressions or on deliberate reasoning. In that sense, an important function of System 2 is to monitor the activities and inputs of System 1. If no intuitive response is generated by System 1, judgments and behavior are exclusively computed by System 2. If, however, System 1 provides an intuitive response as input for System 2, System 2 may either (1) endorse this response, (2) adjust the response for other features that are recognized to be relevant, (3) correct the response for a recognized bias, or (4) block the response from overt expression if it is identified to violate a valid rule of inference.

Whereas the intuitive responses generated by System 1 are determined by the accessibility of mental contents (Higgins, 1996), processing in System 2 is guided by the application of logical rules of inference. In the case of heuristic judgments, highly accessible contents in System 1 will often pass the monitoring activities of System 2 through a process of attribute substitution. In general terms, attribute substitution occurs when an "individual assesses a specified target attribute of a judgment object by substituting a related heuristic attribute that comes more readily to mind" (Kahneman, 2003, p. 707). This process can be illustrated with the well-known Linda problem that has been used to demonstrate the conjunction fallacy (Tversky & Kahneman, 1983, p. 297): "*Linda is 31 years old, single, outspoken and very bright. She majored in philosophy. As a student, she was deeply concerned with issues of discrimination and social justice, and also participated in anti-nuclear demonstrations.*" According

to Tversky and Kahneman (1983), people commit the conjunction fallacy when they judge Linda as more likely to be (1) a bank teller and active in the feminist movement than (2) a bank teller. Because the conjunction of two distinct events can never be more likely than one of the two events by itself, such a judgment violates basic principles of statistical probability. Drawing on Kahneman's (2003) theoretical conceptualization, this judgmental tendency can be explained by accessibility-driven attribute substitution, in that individuals substitute a relevant judgmental attribute (i.e., statistical probability) with an irrelevant, yet highly accessible attribute (i.e., feature similarity). Other examples of accessibility-driven attribute substitution include framing effects, in which people tend to show a preference for positively over negatively framed objects, events, and decisions (e.g., a sausage that is described as 80% lean vs. 20% fat), even if the two descriptions are semantically equivalent.

Although Kahneman (2003) adopted the System 1/System 2 distinction from Stanovich and West's (2000) influential work on rationality in human reasoning, his reanalysis of key findings of the heuristics and biases research program contributed significantly to the current dominance of this distinction in the literature on judgment and decision making. This impact went even beyond the traditional boundaries of psychology, in that philosophers have started to use it as a basis for speculations about the general architecture of the human mind (e.g., Carruthers, 2009; Samuels, 2009). Yet, similar to Epstein's (1994) CEST, the theory has been criticized for providing no more than a conceptual framework that can be applied to empirical data in a post hoc fashion without generating novel predictions that could be empirically confirmed or disconfirmed (Keren & Schul, 2009). We will return to this concern in our overarching discussion of criticism against generalized dual process theories.

Reflection–Reflexion Model

The reflection–reflexion model proposed by Lieberman (2003; see also Lieberman, Gaunt, Gilbert, & Trope, 2002) combines the basic idea of the dual system approach with recent advances in social cognitive neuroscience (see Chapter 34). Deviating from conceptualizations that describe automatic processes as more efficient variants of insufficiently practiced controlled processes (e.g., Bargh, 1997), the reflection–reflexion model argues that automatic and controlled processes use qualitatively distinct representations that have their basis in distinct neural structures. According to Lieberman (2003), the automatic–controlled distinction is insufficient, if not misleading, because it simply describes the *operating conditions* of a given process (i.e., when does the process operate?) without specifying the underlying *computational properties* (i.e., what is the process doing?). Because the reflection–reflexion model assumes distinct representational underpinnings, it also allows for complex interactions between automatic and controlled processes. Such interactions are difficult to reconcile with the view that automatic and controlled processes draw on the same underlying mental representations, the only difference being that automatic processes operate more efficiently as a result of practice.

The first system, called the *X-system* with reference to the term *reflexive*, is proposed to involve the amygdala, basal ganglia, and lateral temporal cortex. Reflexive processes in the X-system link affect and meaning to currently represented stimuli by means of simple stimulus-stimulus associations (semantic meaning) or stimulus-outcome associations (affective meaning). These associations build the foundation for a person's implicit theories and generalized expectations about the world, which are assumed to develop slowly over time and over extended periods of learning. The neurons in the X-system are highly interdependent, in that they are mutually influenced by the neurons they are influencing. As a result, the activation of associations in the X-system operates in a parallel fashion on the basis of similarity and pattern matching, such that observed relations of the format "if p, then q" will create a reflexive tendency to draw the logically incorrect inference "if q, then p."

The second system, called the *C-system* with reference to the term *reflective*, is proposed to involve the anterior cingulate cortex, prefrontal cortex, and medial temporal lobe. The operation of the C-system is assumed to be conditional on the failure of the X-system to achieve a momentary goal, such that reflective processes are initiated only if (1) the implicit theories or generalized expectancies in the X-system are violated, or (2) there are no implicit theories or generalized expectancies in the X-system that are applicable to guide behavior in a novel situation. As such, the primary function of the C-system is to handle context-specific "exceptions to the rule" for which the generalizations in the X-system are not prepared. Reflective inferences in the C-system are assumed to operate in a sequential manner on the basis of causal and logical relations, which allows the C-system to block logically

incorrect inferences of p in the presence of q from observed relations of the format "if p, then q."

Arguably, the most significant contribution of the reflection–reflexion model is the identification of distinct neural underpinnings of automatic and controlled processes. Thus, it does not seem surprising that the theory has enjoyed its strongest influence in the area of social cognitive neuroscience (for a review, see Lieberman, 2007). Yet, in traditional social psychology, its impact has mostly taken the form of citations in sample lists of generalized dual process theories, with few examples of studies that have tested novel predictions derived from the theory.

Reflective–Impulsive Model

One the most influential dual system theories to date is Strack and Deutsch's (2004) reflective–impulsive model (RIM) of social behavior. The RIM argues that social behavior is guided by two simultaneously operating systems of information processing, which are described as the *reflective system* (RS) and the *impulsive system* (IS), respectively. Even though both systems are assumed to operate in parallel, the IS enjoys priority over the RS because the RS operates only under conditions of sufficient cognitive capacity, whereas information processing in the IS is assumed to be resource independent. Similar to other dual system theories, the RIM states that the IS operates on the basis of simple associative links between elements that are formed and activated according to the principles of similarity and contiguity. Information processing in the RS, in contrast, is assumed to involve propositionally represented relations between elements, which are tagged with truth values (i.e., true vs. false). These operating characteristics make the RS capable of various operations that cannot be performed by the IS, the most important of which are the processing of negations and representations of the future. Thus, even though accessible associations in the IS provide the basis for propositional representations in the RS, their functionally distinct operating principles can have different behavioral implications if processing in the RS involves the negation of activated associations in the IS (see Deutsch, Gawronski, & Strack, 2006; Gilbert, 1991) or the delay of gratification (see Metcalfe & Mischel, 1999).

Another central assumption of the RIM concerns the translation of mental representations into behavior. The RIM assumes that the RS and the IS influence behavior through a common pathway that includes the activation of behavioral schemata of varying abstractness (Norman & Shallice, 1986). These behavioral schemata can be activated directly through the spread of activation from momentarily accessible associations in the IS, which may elicit an impulsive tendency to either approach or avoid a given object. Alternatively, behavioral schemata may be activated indirectly through behavioral intentions generated in the RS, which are guided by (1) the subjective hedonic quality of future states that may result from a given behavior (i.e., value) and (2) the subjective probability with which the behavior may produce the focal outcome (i.e., expectancy).

Going beyond other dual process models that focus primarily on cognitive and affective processes, the RIM attributes an important role to motivational processes, which may operate in the IS in at least two different ways. First, the RIM assumes that motivational orientations to approach or avoid an object may be elicited by mere processing of positive or negative information, mere perception of approach or avoidance movements, the experience of positive or negative affect, or the execution of approach or avoidance motor actions. Conversely, motivational orientations of approach or avoidance are assumed to facilitate the processing of information, the experience of affective states, and the execution of behavior that are compatible with the current motivational state (see Neumann, Förster, & Strack, 2003). Second, the RIM integrates basic principles of homoeostatic dysregulation, such that deprivation of basic needs is assumed to activate behavioral schemata that are linked to successful satisfaction of those needs through a history of past experiences.

To date, the RIM enjoys the status of being the most influential dual system theory in the generation of empirical research. This research includes a wide range of topics within and beyond social psychology, such as the roles of impulse and control in self-regulation (e.g., Hofmann, Rauch, & Gawronski, 2007), limits in the processing of negations (e.g., Deutsch et al., 2006), the relation between personality traits and behavior (e.g., Back, Schmukle, & Egloff, 2009), and emotional effects of food deprivation (e.g., Hoefling et al., 2009).

Associative-Propositional Evaluation Model

Even though Gawronski and Bodenhausen's (2006a, 2006b, 2007, 2011) associative–propositional evaluation (APE) model was originally designed to resolve various inconsistencies in the literature on implicit and explicit attitude change, its emphasis on general principles of information processing make it more similar to generalized dual process theories than phenomenon-specific dual process theories of persuasion. The theoretical core of the APE model is the distinction between associative and propositional processes. Associative processes are defined as the *activation* of associations in memory, which is driven by principles of similarity and contiguity. Propositional processes are defined as the *validation* of the information implied by activated associations, which is assumed to be guided by principles of logical consistency. To the extent that the propositional information implied by activated associations is consistent, it will be used for judgments and behavioral decisions. If, however, the information implied by activated associations is inconsistent, aversive feelings of dissonance will induce a tendency to resolve the dissonance-provoking inconsistency before a judgment or behavioral decision is made (see Festinger, 1957). In general terms, inconsistency may be resolved either by rejecting one of the propositions that are involved in inconsistent belief systems or by searching for an additional proposition that resolves the inconsistency (Gawronski & Strack, 2004). To the extent that the inconsistency is resolved by rejecting one of the involved propositions, activated associations and endorsed propositional beliefs will show a dissociation because mere negation of a proposition (e.g., "it is not true that old people are bad drivers") does not necessarily deactivate the mental associations that underlie that proposition (i.e., the association between the concepts *old people* and *bad drivers*). The prototypical example of such cases are dissociations between explicit and implicit measures, given that explicit self-report measures assess the outcome of propositional validation processes (e.g., survey questions asking participants to report their agreement or disagreement with a particular statement), whereas implicit measures (e.g., implicit association test, sequential priming tasks) provide a proxy for the activation of associations in memory. Even though the original formulation of the APE model was primarily concerned with the role of associative and propositional processes in evaluation (Gawronski & Bodenhausen, 2006a, 2006b), its basic principles are equally applicable to nonevaluative, semantic information (Gawronski, LeBel, & Peters, 2007; for an example, see Peters & Gawronski, 2011).

By emphasizing the ubiquitous roles of associative and propositional processes in social information processing, the APE model has a strong resemblance to other generalized dual process theories. However, the APE model also includes a number of assumptions that distinguish it from these models. First, whereas most generalized dual process theories propose the existence of two systems with distinct operating characteristics (e.g., Epstein, 1994; Kahneman, 2003; Lieberman, 2003; Smith & DeCoster, 2000; Strack & Deutsch, 2004), the APE model does not make any assumptions about inherent links between processes and systems (Gawronski & Bodenhausen, 2011). In that sense, the APE model can be described as a *dual process theory* in the original sense of the term, whereas most other generalized dual process theories represent examples of *dual system theories*. Second, the APE model does not make any claims implying that one process is fast learning whereas the other is slow learning. To the contrary, the APE model argues that either the outcome of associative processes or the outcome of propositional processes can be more or less robust against external influences depending on (1) the nature of the external influence, and (2) mutual interactions between the two processes (Gawronski & Bodenhausen, 2006a, 2007, 2011). Third, the APE model makes specific assumptions about how associative and propositional processes interact with each other. These assumptions imply a number of novel predictions about the conditions under which a given factor should produce (1) changes in explicit but not implicit evaluations (e.g., Gawronski & Strack, 2004; Gregg, Seibt, & Banaji, 2006); (2) changes in implicit but not explicit evaluations (e.g., Gawronski & LeBel, 2008; Grumm, Nestler, & von Collani, 2009); (3) corresponding changes in explicit and implicit evaluations, with changes in implicit evaluations being mediated by changes in explicit evaluations (e.g., Peters & Gawronski, 2011; Whitfield & Jordan, 2009); and (4) corresponding changes in explicit and implicit evaluations, with changes in explicit evaluations being mediated by changes in implicit evaluations (e.g., Gawronski & LeBel, 2008; Whitfield & Jordan, 2009). Finally, the APE model draws a sharp line between operating principles (i.e., associative vs. propositional) and operating conditions (i.e., automatic vs. controlled) of mental processes, in that operating principles represent definitions of what a given process is doing, whereas operating conditions represent empirical assumptions about the conditions under which the process is operating. Importantly, the model assumes that there is no perfect overlap between operating principles and operating conditions, such that both associative and propositional processes can have features of automatic or controlled

processes (Gawronski & Bodenhausen, 2007, 2009, 2011). For example, even though the activation of associations may occur unintentionally, associations may also be activated intentionally. In a similar vein, complex propositional inferences may require cognitive effort, but propositional inferences may occur quickly and effortlessly if the complexity of these inferences is low (see Gawronski & Bodenhausen, 2007, 2011).

Criticism of Generalized Dual Process Theories

During the past decade, generalized dual process theories have been extremely influential in guiding interpretations of empirical data far beyond the boundaries of social psychology. In fact, their steadily increasing impact seems to be associated with a decreasing influence of their phenomenon-specific precursors, some of which have already acquired the status of "historical milestones" that have ceased to inspire novel research. However, despite their overwhelming influence, generalized dual process theories have also been the target of criticism.

One argument that has been raised against the distinction between associative and rule-based processes is that information processing can be parsimoniously described in terms of general *if–then* rules (e.g., Kruglanski & Dechesne, 2006; Kruglanski, Erb, Pierro, Mannetti, & Chun, 2006). Because this description can be applied to both associative and rule-based processes, the proposed distinctions between qualitatively distinct processes is claimed to be misleading. In an abstract sense, all inference processes could be described as rule-based in terms of general *if–then* rules. According to Kruglanski and colleagues, such rule-based inferences may be influenced by various judgmental parameters, such as subjective relevance, task demands, cognitive capacity, accessibility, and different kinds of motivations. Thus, data patterns that have been interpreted as reflecting the operation of qualitatively distinct processes may in fact reflect the operation of a single rule-based process that is modulated by the proposed processing parameters.

In response to this criticism, however, one could object that the proposed interpretation in terms of general *if–then* rules seems too abstract to specify how exactly rule-based processes are operating. In fact, claiming that all psychological processes follow general *if–then* rules does not go far beyond stating that all psychological processes follow identifiable regularities instead of being completely random. Because all of the reviewed models agree that both associative and rule-based processes follow identifiable regularities and that neither of them is random, one could argue that the single-process criticism misconstrues the basic distinctions of generalized dual process theories. According to these theories, associative processes are guided by similarity and contiguity, whereas rule-based processes are guided by syllogistic relations and logical consistency. Moreover, by introducing several parameters that presumably modulate a single rule-based process, the proposed alternative implicitly assumes that the operation of these parameters does not require further specification—an assumption that is rejected by generalized dual process theories. For example, stating that rule-based inferences are influenced by subjective relevance does not clarify how relevance is determined in the first place. Similarly, stating that accessibility influences what information is considered in rule-based inferences does not clarify why some information tends to be more accessible than other information. From a dual process perspective, one could argue that the process of determining the subjective relevance of accessible information is functionally equivalent to the process of propositional validation, whereas accessibility is determined by the similarity matching principles of associative processes.

Another, more fundamental criticism is that generalized dual process theories have a tendency to create lists of process characteristics that may not necessarily overlap (Keren & Schul, 2009). This criticism has been raised in particular against dual system theories, which describe the proposed systems by means of several features that may not covary. For example, describing one system as affective, automatic, holistic, and associative and the other one as cognitive, controlled, analytic, and logical (e.g., Epstein & Pacini, 1999) raises questions about whether cognitive processes cannot be automatic, holistic, or associative. This criticism resembles earlier concerns about the conflation of different features of automaticity, stating that a given process rarely meets all of the four criteria (i.e., unintentional, efficient, uncontrollable, unconscious; see Bargh, 1994).

Related to this argument, generalized dual process theories have been criticized for lacking conceptual precision, which makes it difficult to identify empirical evidence that could disprove them. In fact, it has been argued that these theories provide no more than nominal lists of definitions instead of empirically testable predictions. For example, Keren and Schul (2009) raised concerns that dual system theories in particular can accommodate virtually every empirical finding in a post hoc fashion. At the same time, they do not provide precise predictions that could disconfirm them, nor do they include specific claims that could empirically distinguish them from other dual system theories. Even though these concerns seem applicable to several of the reviewed models, it is important to note that they also apply to the single process models that have been proposed as superior alternatives. Of course, this does not invalidate the criticism of imprecision and lack of testable predictions. To the contrary, the fact that theories with a high degree of *generality* often lack the level of *specificity* that is required for the derivation of testable predictions (Quine & Ullian, 1978) has important implications for theory construction in social psychology. We will return to this issue in the final section of this chapter.

Formalized Dual Process Theories

Simultaneous to the emergence of generalized dual process theories, social cognition researchers realized that many behaviors that had been presumed to reflect automatic processes are not process pure, but instead conflate the joint contributions of automatic and controlled processes. In addition, many researchers became concerned about method-related confounds between processes and tasks, for example, when automatic processes are assessed with one type of task (e.g., implicit measures) and controlled processes with another (e.g., explicit measures). These concerns have led researchers to adopt mathematical modeling procedures from cognitive psychology to quantify the joint contributions of automatic and controlled processes to behavioral responses within a single task.

Control-Dominating Process Dissociation Model

The most prominent of these modeling techniques is Jacoby's (1991) process dissociation (PD) model. The basic idea of PD models is that automatic and controlled processes sometimes work in concert to produce a behavioral response, while at other times automatic and controlled processes work in opposition to each other (for reviews, see Payne, 2008; Payne & Bishara, 2009). For example, many implicit measures—such as the implicit association test (Greenwald et al., 1998) or evaluative priming (Fazio et al., 1995)—involve one class of trials that is described as *compatible* and another class of trials that is described as *incompatible* (see Gawronski, Deutsch, LeBel, & Peters, 2008). The basic idea is that both automatic and controlled processes will lead to the correct response on compatible trials (thereby facilitating fast and accurate responses). On incompatible trials, however, only controlled processes will lead to the correct response, whereas automatic processes will lead to the incorrect response (thereby inhibiting fast and accurate responses). For example, in an implicit association test designed to measure automatic racial bias (Greenwald et al., 1998), controlled identification of a black or white face will produce an accurate key response in both the compatible and the incompatible block. In contrast, automatic racial bias will produce an accurate key response in the compatible

block, but an incorrect response in the incompatible block.

These influences can be depicted graphically as processing trees that describe how automatic and controlled processes may interactively determine correct versus incorrect responses on a given task. In Jacoby's (1991) PD model, controlled processes are assumed to dominate, in that automatic processes influence the behavioral outcome only if controlled processes fail (Figure 14.5a). If controlled processes succeed (depicted as *C* in Figure 14.5a), participants will show the correct response on both compatible and incompatible trials. If,

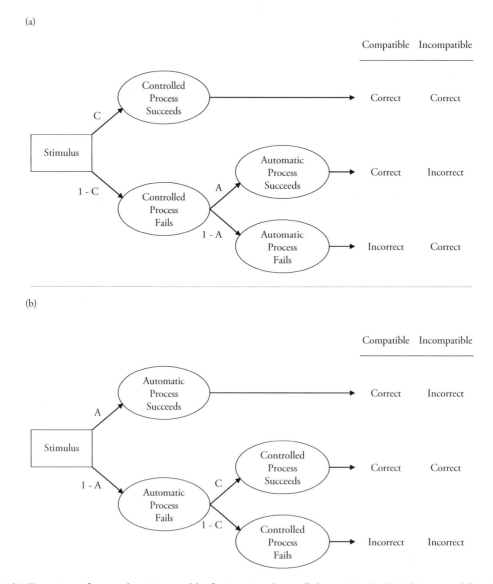

Figure 14.5 Two variants of process dissociation models of automatic and controlled processing. Panel (a) depicts a model in which controlled processes are assumed to dominate; panel (b) depicts a model in which automatic processes are assumed to dominate. (Adapted from Conrey, Sherman, Gawronski, Hugenberg, & Groom, 2005. Reprinted with permission.)

however, controlled processes fail (depicted as *1 − C* in Figure 14.5a), the behavioral outcome depends on the operation of automatic processes. If automatic processes drive the response (depicted as *A* in Figure 14.5a), participants will show the correct response on compatible trials but the incorrect response on incompatible trials. Yet, if automatic processes fail (depicted as *1 − A* in Figure 14.5a), the model assumes a bias in the opposite direction, such that participants will show the incorrect response on compatible trials but the correct response on incompatible trials.

The advantage of formalized dual process models is that they provide mathematical equations that can be used to quantify the relative contributions of distinct processes to performance on tasks in which automatic and controlled processes can work in concert or in opposition. The basic idea is to derive two equations from the proposed structure in the processing tree, one for the probability of correct responses on compatible trials and one for the probability of correct responses on incompatible trials. In Jacoby's (1991) PD model, these equations include two parameters as unknowns: *C,* which is supposed to capture the impact of controlled processes; and *A,* which is supposed to capture the impact of automatic processes. Using the empirically observed probabilities of correct responses on compatible and incompatible trials in a given data set, the particular values of these unknowns can be calculated through simple algebra.

For example, using the graphical depiction of Jacoby's (1991) model in Figure 14.5a, the probability of a correct response on compatible trials should be equal to all processing paths from left to right that lead to a correct response in the "compatible" column. The two paths that produce such a response are *Controlled Process Succeeds,* which can be depicted as *C,* and *Controlled Process Fails* in conjunction with *Automatic Process Succeeds,* which can be depicted as *(1 − C) × A.* Thus, in statistical terms, the probability of a correct response on compatible trials can be described as:

$$p(\text{correct} \mid \text{compatible}) = C + (1 − C) \times A$$

The same logic can be applied to the probability of a correct response on incompatible trials. The two paths that produce such a response are *Controlled Process Succeeds,* which is again depicted as *C,* and *Controlled Process Fails* in conjunction with *Automatic Process Fails,* which is depicted as *(1 − C) × (1 − A).* On the basis of these processing paths, the probability of a correct response on incompatible trials can be described as:

$$p(\text{correct} \mid \text{incompatible}) = C + (1 − C) \times (1 − A)$$

Through the use of linear algebra, these equations can be solved for *C* and *A,* which allows researchers to quantify the relative impact of automatic and controlled processes. Without going into the details of the mathematical conversion, the controlled process can be quantified algebraically as:

$$C = p(\text{correct} \mid \text{compatible}) − p(\text{incorrect} \mid \text{incompatible})$$

Using the specific number that has been computed for *C,* the automatic process can then be calculated as:

$$A = p(\text{incorrect} \mid \text{incompatible})/(1 − C)$$

For example, if the empirically observed probability of correct responses on compatible trials is .74 and the probability of correct responses on incompatible trials is .46, the resulting estimate for *C* is .20 and the estimate for *A* is .675.[1] Such estimates can be calculated for each participant in a given sample, allowing the use of these estimates as dependent variables in experimental designs or as independent variables in individual difference designs.

Automaticity-Dominating Process Dissociation Model

Even though Jacoby's (1991) PD model has been successfully applied to various tasks in the social-cognitive literature (for a review, see Payne & Bishara, 2009), the model's premise that automatic processes operate only when controlled processes fail does not seem applicable to tasks in which automatic processes play a dominant role despite the potential operation of controlled processes. For example, in the Stroop task, automatic word reading may elicit a tendency to respond on the basis of the semantic meaning of a colored word, which has to be overcome by controlled processes if the word meaning does not match the ink color in which the word is presented. To address this problem, Lindsay and Jacoby (1994) presented a modified variant of Jacoby's (1991) PD model, in which automatic processes are assumed to dominate, such that controlled processes drive responses only if automatic processes fail. This model can again be depicted as a processing tree (see Figure 14.5b). Even though the positions of automatic and controlled processes are reversed in Lindsay and Jacoby's (1994) model, the underlying logic remains the same. If automatic processes drive the response (depicted as *A* in Figure 14.5b), participants will show the correct response on compatible trials but the incorrect response on incompatible trials. If, however, automatic processes fail (depicted as *1 − A* in Figure 14.5b), the final response depends on the operation of controlled processes. If controlled processes succeed (depicted as *C* in Figure 14.5b), participants will show the correct response on both compatible and incompatible trials. However, if controlled processes fail (depicted as *1 − C* in Figure 14.5b), the model assumes incorrect responses on both compatible and incompatible trials. Using the algebraic logic outlined for Jacoby's (1991) PD model, the probability of a correct response on compatible trials can be formalized as follows:

$$p(\text{correct} \mid \text{compatible}) = A + (1 - A) \times C$$

Conversely, the probability of a correct response on incompatible trials can be formalized as follows:

$$p(\text{correct} \mid \text{incompatible}) = (1 - A) \times C$$

On the basis of these equations, the automatic process can be quantified algebraically as follows:

$$A = p(\text{correct} \mid \text{compatible}) - p(\text{correct} \mid \text{incompatible})$$

Using the quantitative estimates for *A*, the controlled process can then be calculated as follows:

$$C = p(\text{correct} \mid \text{incompatible})/(1 - A)$$

Although applications of PD have mostly used Jacoby's (1991) original formulation instead of Lindsay and Jacoby's (1994) modified version, the data analytic strategy of PD has been successfully applied to a wide range of questions in social psychology (for a review, see Payne & Bishara, 2009). Examples of such applications include racial bias in weapon identification (e.g., Payne, 2001), stereotypic biases in memory (e.g., Sherman, Groom, Ehrenberg, & Klauer, 2003), the use of heuristics in social judgment (e.g., Ferreira, Garcia-Marques, Sherman, & Sherman, 2006), and mood effects on automatic evaluations (e.g., Huntsinger, Sinclair, & Clore, 2009).

Quadruple-Process Model

A shared assumption of the two PD models is that one of the two processes operates only to the extent that the other one fails. For example, in Jacoby's (1991) model, automatic processes are assumed to operate only if controlled processes fail (see Figure 14.5a). Conversely, in Lindsay and Jacoby's (1994) model, controlled processes are assumed to operate only if automatic processes fail (see Figure 14.5b). Conrey, Sherman, Gawronski, Hugenberg, and Groom (2005) argued that these assumptions make the two PD models less suitable to capture situations in which automatic and controlled processes operate simultaneously, as is the case when one process overrides the impact of another process (see also Sherman et al., 2008). To address this limitation, Conrey et al. proposed their quadruple process model (quad model), which includes statistical parameters for four (instead of two) qualitatively distinct processes: (1) the likelihood that an automatic association is activated (described as *association activation* or *AC*); (2) the likelihood that the correct response to the stimulus can be determined (described as *discriminability* or *D*); (3) the likelihood that an automatic association is successfully overcome in favor of the correct response (described as *overcoming bias* or *OB*); and (4) the likelihood that a general response bias (e.g., right-hand bias) drives the response (described as *guessing* or *G*).

The proposed interplay of these processes in the quad model can again be depicted as a processing tree that specifies how their joint operation can lead to correct or incorrect responses on compatible and incompatible trials (Figure 14.6). The most significant component of the model is the assumption that activated associations (reflected in the *AC* parameter) and identification of the correct response (reflected in the *D* parameter) can produce two response tendencies that may be congruent or incongruent with each other. If they are incongruent, inhibitory control has to be engaged to suppress the response tendency elicited by activated associations in favor of the correct response (reflected in the *OB* parameter). For example, in an Implicit Association Test designed to measure automatic preferences for whites over blacks, automatic stereotypic associations may elicit a tendency to press the "negative" key in response to a black face. In the so-called incongruent block, this tendency has to be inhibited in favor of the correct "black" response. In this case, the quad model's *AC* parameter reflects the strength of automatic stereotypic associations; the *D* parameter reflects participants' ability to identify

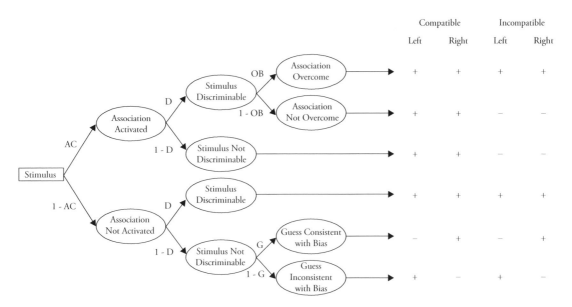

Figure 14.6 The quadruple process model of automatic and controlled processing. (Adapted from Conrey, Sherman, Gawronski, Hugenberg, & Groom, 2005. Reprinted with permission.)

the correct response; and the *OB* parameter reflects participants' success in inhibiting automatic stereotypic associations in favor of the correct response. In addition, the quad model's *G* parameter reflects the strength of general response tendencies, such as the tendency to show a right-hand response.

Although the higher number of processes increases the complexity of the mathematical equations in the quad model, the derivation of these equations is equivalent to the two PD models. For example, if the correct response for incompatible trials in a given task is defined as the right key, the three paths that lead to a correct response in the quad model's processing tree (see Figure 14.6) produce the following equation:

$$p \text{ (correct | incompatible-right)} = [AC \times D \times OB] + [(1 - AC) \times D] + [(1 - AC) \times (1 - D) \times G]$$

The same logic applies to the derivation of the equations for the observed probabilities of correct responses on the other types of trials. Yet, an important difference between the quad model and PD models is that the latter produce two equations with two unknowns that can be solved through linear algebra, whereas the quad model entails more equations than unknowns. Consequently, parameter values cannot be calculated directly through linear algebra, but have to be estimated through alternative procedures. The procedure employed by the quad model is multinomial modeling (for a review, see Batchelder & Riefer, 1999), which uses maximum

likelihood statistics to identify parameter estimates that minimize the discrepancy between the empirically observed probabilities of correct and incorrect responses and the corresponding probabilities that are predicted through the equations of the model (for more details regarding the statistics underlying the quad model, see Conrey et al., 2005).

Even though the conceptual relation between the quad model's parameters to the parameters of the two PD models is still under debate (Payne & Bishara, 2009; Sherman, Klauer, & Allen, 2010), the quad model's integration of multiple distinct processes provides a more fine-grained analysis compared with traditional dual process theories (Sherman, 2006). In a technical sense, the quad model is thus better described as a *multiple process model* rather than a *dual process model*, although it retains the emphasis on automatic and controlled processes. So far, the quad model has demonstrated its potential mostly in the analysis of data obtained with implicit measures, which often remain ambiguous as to whether a given effect is driven by differences in automatic associations or by any of the other three processes proposed by the model. Whereas in some cases, previous interpretations turned out to be accurate, interpretations of other findings had to be revised, such that effects that have been attributed to differences in automatic associations turned out to be driven by other processes, such as differences in overcoming the biasing influence of automatic associations (for a review, see Sherman et al., 2008).

Criticism of Formalized Dual Process Theories

Compared with phenomenon-specific and generalized dual process theories, formalized models have a unique advantage, in that they provide mathematical implementations that allow researchers to quantify the relative contributions of the proposed processes to a given task. At the same time, there have been controversies surrounding the proper interpretation of the obtained parameter estimates (Payne & Bishara, 2009; Sherman et al., 2010). An important issue—which applies equally to the two PD models as well as the quad model—is that formalized models are often assumed to provide direct access to automatic and controlled processes through the nature of their algebraic logic. For example, researchers using Jacoby's (1991) PD model often assume that the two processes captured by the model are *defined* as automatic or controlled through the basic logic of the model. In part, this assumption has its roots in misleading depictions of the parameter estimates as *automatic* (using the acronym A) and *controlled* (using the acronym C). Such depictions are problematic for at least two reasons. First, as outlined in the initial sections of this chapter, the different features of automaticity and control do not necessarily covary (Bargh, 1994; Moors & De Houwer, 2006), which makes generic descriptions of parameters as automatic or controlled misleading, as long as it is not specified in which particular sense the captured process is supposed to be automatic or controlled. Second, and more seriously, generic descriptions of parameters as automatic and controlled conflate the nature of a given process (i.e., what is the process doing?) with its operating conditions (i.e., under which conditions does the process operate?). After all, any claims about the conditions under which a process is operating represent empirical assumptions that have to be tested as such, and this empirical work cannot be delegated to the application of a mathematical procedure.

To illustrate this issue, consider Payne's (2001) application of Jacoby's (1991) PD model to a sequential priming task designed to investigate stereotypic biases in weapon identification. On each trial of the task, participants are briefly presented with either a black or a white face prime, which is immediately followed by a target picture showing either a gun or a harmless object. The target picture is quickly replaced by a black-and-white pattern mask, and participants' task is to indicate whether the target picture showed a gun or a harmless object.

The common result is that harmless objects were more frequently misidentified as guns when the face prime was black than when it was white, whereas guns were more frequently misidentified as harmless objects when the face prime was white than when it was black (for a review, see Payne, 2006). Using Jacoby's (1991) PD model, Payne (2001) calculated separate estimates reflecting participants' ability to identify guns and harmless objects (reflected in the model's C parameter) and stereotypic biases in guessing the nature of the target stimulus if participants were unable to identify the stimulus (reflected in the model's A parameter). Importantly, whether or not the two processes—identification of the target object and stereotypic bias in guessing the nature of the target—operate unintentionally, efficiently, unconsciously, and uncontrollably is an empirical question about the conditions under which the two processes operate; it is not an inherent feature of the two processes per se.

Addressing this concern, Payne and Bishara (2009) have argued that applications of PD models to particular tasks usually involve one feature of automaticity by definition, whereas claims about other features represent empirical hypotheses that have to be tested as such. With regard to weapon identification, for example, Payne and Bishara have argued that C depicts an intentional process and A an unintentional process, with their (un)intentionality being defined a priori through the basic structure of the task. However, this conceptualization stands in contrast to research showing that estimated values of A increased when participants were instructed to intentionally use race as a cue in identifying the target object (Payne, Lambert, & Jacoby, 2002). Applied to Payne and Bishara's argument, this result leads to the paradoxical conclusion that a process that is *defined* as unintentional can be intentional. Describing the process captured by the A parameter as stereotypic bias without reference to intentionality (or other features of automaticity) avoids this problem because stereotypic biases can operate either intentionally or unintentionally. Similar considerations apply to the interpretation of the C parameter. In the weapon identification task, this parameter reflects the identification of the target object, which may or may not be intentional, conscious, resource dependent, and controllable. The bottom line is that formalized dual process (and multiple process) theories are very well suited to quantifying the contribution of qualitatively distinct processes (e.g., identification of target object, stereotypic bias). However, any claims about the *operating conditions* of these processes are empirical assumptions that have to be tested as such. The mere application of mathematical procedures cannot replace this empirical work.

Outlook

Dual process theories play a central role in social psychology, and the amount of research that has been stimulated by these theories is simply enormous. In addition to reviewing the core assumptions of the most prominent theories, we have tried to provide a historical perspective by describing the development of dual process theorizing from the emergence of phenomenon-specific theories in the 1980s to the recent advances made by generalized and formalized dual process theories. An interesting question is where dual process theorizing will go from here. In the final sections of this chapter, we offer some conceptual considerations regarding the current state of theorizing and discuss how some limitations of current theories could possibly be overcome.

Models Versus Theories

In line with the common usage of terminology in social psychology, we have used the terms *theory* and *model* interchangeably. Yet, many philosophers of science consider theories and models as conceptually distinct. Whereas theories are usually regarded as sets of well-specified *if–then* conditionals that link two or more concepts in a particular manner, models are regarded as nominal descriptions that provide a conceptual frame of reference. Even though the boundaries between theories and models may become somewhat blurry when the distinction is applied to theorizing in social psychology, it seems useful to keep the distinction in mind when comparing different types of dual process theories. For example, phenomenon-specific dual process theories seem closer to the notion of *theory*, in that they include specific *if–then* conditionals about links between psychological concepts. In contrast, many (though not all) of the reviewed generalized dual process theories seem closer to the notion of *model*, in that they primarily include nominal descriptions. To the extent that these models lack clearly specified *if–then* conditionals, their descriptive classifications do not imply any predictions that could be confirmed or disconfirmed. Instead, their functional value lies in their integrative capacity as frames of reference to describe observed phenomena. Similar considerations can be applied to formalized dual process theories, which also seem closer to the notion of *model*. To be sure, formalized models are extremely valuable in providing quantifications of qualitatively distinct processes. However, these models usually do not include any *if–then* conditionals about these processes that could be tested empirically. Of course, it is entirely possible to use formalized models to conduct more stringent tests of predictions made by other theories that include *if–then* conditionals. Yet, any such predictions are extrinsic to these models, in that they are not logically derived from their core assumptions.

These considerations have important implications for dual process theorizing. During the past decade, generalized dual process *models* have clearly proved their usefulness as integrative frameworks by providing conceptual links between phenomena and research findings that have not been related before. Similarly, formalized dual process *models* provide a powerful tool, not only to disentangle, but also to quantify the contributions of qualitatively distinct processes to overt behavioral responses. Yet, what is still missing in both kinds of models is a conceptual integration of the empirically confirmed *if–then* conditionals that have contributed to the rise of phenomenon-specific dual process *theories* in 1980s and 1990s. In addition, it seems desirable to formulate new *if–then* conditionals that allow researchers to derive novel predictions. Thus, an important task for future theorizing is to combine the unique characteristics of the three dual process approaches: (1) the predictive power of phenomenon-specific dual process theories, (2) the integrative capacity of generalized dual process models, and (3) the methodological advantages of formalized dual process models.

How Many Processes Are There?

A final question that deserves attention in a chapter on dual process theories is: How many processes are there? During the past decade, this question has sparked controversial debates, with some theorists arguing for the classic dual process distinction (e.g., Deutsch & Strack, 2006) and others endorsing either single process (e.g., Kruglanski et al., 2006) or multiple process alternatives (e.g., Sherman, 2006). In evaluating the arguments that have been raised in these debates, it is important to note that existence claims—such as claims about the existence of one, two, or multiple processes—are ontological in nature. In the philosophy of science, ontological claims fall into the realm of metaphysics, which means that they cannot be tested empirically (e.g., Popper, 1934; Quine, 1960). In other words, we cannot test empirically if there are one, two, or multiple processes. Still, researchers can make decisions about the usefulness of ontological claims by empirically testing assumptions *about* the proposed processes. To the extent that the predictions implied by a particular class of theories are confirmed, their underlying ontological claims are typically regarded as justified. Yet, if these predictions are continuously disconfirmed, it seems likely that researchers will at some point reject the underlying ontological claims. Note, however, that in these cases it is not the existence claim itself that is confirmed or disconfirmed, but the assumptions that are made about the proposed entities.

Evaluated from this point of view, dual process theories have fared very well, which explains their dominant role in social psychology. At the same time, it is essential to reiterate the quest for novel predictions, which still represent the hallmark of theory evaluation. As noted in our earlier discussion of generality–specificity trade-offs, theories with a high degree of generality are certainly functional in their capacity to explain a wide range of phenomena with a parsimonious set of basic principles. At the same time, highly integrative theories often come at the cost of specificity, which is essential for the derivation of novel predictions (Quine & Ullian, 1978). Even though this concern has been raised in particular against generalized dual process theories (e.g., Keren & Schul, 2009), it is important to note that it equally applies to their single process alternatives, whose high levels of generality make them capable of explaining almost any observable outcome in a post hoc fashion. Yet, their capacity for making predictions often seems rather weak, in that it is difficult to specify in an a priori fashion what outcome one would expect for a particular set of conditions. Thus, what seems essential to evaluate any type of ontological premise—be it in single process, dual process, or multiple process theorizing—is the formulation of precise *if–then* conditionals that generate novel predictions. Ideally, such *if–then* conditionals should be formulated in a manner that specifies not only which events are implied by the theory but also which events should not happen according to the theory. After all, the informative value of a scientific theory increases with the number of observations that are "prohibited" by the theory, not with the number of observations that are "allowed" (Popper, 1934). Thus, an important task for the refinement of dual process theorizing is the simultaneous consideration of generality and specificity to maximize both their explanatory and their predictive power.

Conclusion

During the past three decades, dual process theorizing has exerted an overwhelming impact on research in social psychology. Despite the reviewed criticism of dual process theorizing, it seems highly unlikely that this influence will dissipate in the near future. After all, the enormous body of research that has been inspired by dual process theories speaks for itself, and it is difficult to imagine how a posteriori explanations of alternative accounts could lead to a full replacement of the dual process idea. Yet, many of the concerns that have been raised against dual process theories seem justified on conceptual grounds. To the extent that dual process theorists take these concerns seriously, theorizing in social psychology can only become stronger.

Author Note

Preparation of this chapter has been supported by the Canada Research Chairs Program and the Social Sciences and Humanities Research Council of Canada. We are grateful to Jeff Sherman for valuable comments on an earlier version of this chapter. Please address correspondence to Bertram Gawronski, Ph.D., Department of Psychology, The University of Western Ontario, Social Science Centre, London, Ontario N6A 5C2 Canada; e-mail: bgawrons@uwo.ca.

Notes

1. Note that p(correct | compatible) = 1 − p(incorrect | compatible). Correspondingly, p(correct | incompatible) = 1 − p(incorrect | incompatible).

References

Ajzen, I., & Fishbein, M. (1980). *Understanding attitudes and predicting social behavior*. Englewood Cliffs, NJ: Prentice-Hall.

Asch, S. E., & Zuckier, H. (1984). Thinking about persons. *Journal of Personality and Social Psychology*. 46, 1230–1240.

Back, M. D., Schmukle, S. C., & Egloff, B. (2009). Predicting actual behavior from the explicit and implicit self-concept of personality. *Journal of Personality and Social Psychology*, 97, 533–548.

Banse, R., Gawronski, B., Rebetez, C., Gutt, H., & Morton, J. B. (2010). The development of spontaneous gender stereotyping in childhood: Relations to stereotype knowledge and stereotype flexibility. *Developmental Science*, 13, 298–306.

Bargh, J. A. (1992). The ecology of automaticity: Toward establishing the conditions needed to produce automatic processing effects. *American Journal of Psychology*, 105, 181–199.

Bargh, J. A. (1994). The four horsemen of automaticity: Awareness, intention, efficiency, and control in social cognition. In R. S. Wyer & T. K. Srull (Eds.), *Handbook of social cognition* (pp. 1–40). Hillsdale, NJ: Erlbaum.

Bargh, J. A. (1997). The automaticity of everyday life. In R. S. Wyer, Jr. (Ed.), *Advances in social cognition* (Vol. 10, pp. 1–61). Mahwah, NJ: Erlbaum.

Batchelder, W. H., & Riefer, D. M. (1999). Theoretical and empirical review of multinomial process tree modeling. *Psychonomic Bulletin and Review, 6*, 57–86.

Brewer, M. B. (1988). A dual process model of impression formation. In T. K. Srull & R. S. Wyer (Eds.), *Advances in social cognition* (Vol. 1, pp. 1–36). Hillsdale, NJ: Erlbaum.

Brewer, M. B., & Harasty-Feinstein, A. S. (1999). Dual processes in the representation of persons and social categories. In S. Chaiken & Y. Trope (Eds.), *Dual-process theories in social psychology* (pp. 255–270). New York: Guilford Press.

Carruthers, P. (2009). An architecture for dual reasoning. In J. St. B. T. Evans & K. Frankish (Eds.), *In two minds: Dual processes and beyond* (pp. 109–127). New York: Oxford University Press.

Chaiken, S. (1987). The heuristic model of persuasion. In M. P. Zanna, J. M. Olson, & C. P. Herman (Eds.), *Social influence: The Ontario Symposium* (Vol. 5, pp. 3–39). Hillsdale, NJ: Erlbaum.

Chaiken, S., Liberman, A., & Eagly, A. H. (1989). Heuristic and systematic processing within and beyond the persuasion context. In J. S. Uleman & J. A. Bargh (Eds.), *Unintended thought* (pp. 212–252). New York: Guilford Press.

Chaiken, S., & Maheswaran, D. (1994). Heuristic processing can bias systematic processing: Effects of source credibility, argument ambiguity, and task importance on attitude judgment. *Journal of Personality and Social Psychology, 66*, 460–473.

Chaiken, S., & Trope, Y. (Eds.). (1999). *Dual-process theories in social psychology*. New York: Guilford Press.

Chen, S., & Chaiken, S. (1999). The Heuristic-Systematic Model in its broader context. In S. Chaiken, & Y. Trope (Eds.), *Dual-process theories in social psychology* (pp. 73–96). New York: Guilford Press.

Chun, W. Y., & Kruglanski, A. W. (2006). The role of task demands and processing resources in the use of base-rate and individuating information. *Journal of Personality and Social Psychology, 91*, 205–217.

Chun, W. Y., Spiegel, S., & Kruglanski, A. W. (2002). Assimilative behavior identification can also be resource dependent: A unimodel perspective on personal-attribution phases. *Journal of Personality and Social Psychology, 83*, 542–555.

Conrey, F. R., Sherman, J. W., Gawronski, B., Hugenberg, K., & Groom, C. (2005). Separating multiple processes in implicit social cognition: The Quad-Model of implicit task performance. *Journal of Personality and Social Psychology, 89*, 469–487.

D'Agostino, P. R., & Fincher-Kiefer, R. (1992). Need for cognition and the correspondence bias. *Social Cognition, 10*, 151–163.

Deutsch, R., Gawronski, B., & Strack, F. (2006). At the boundaries of automaticity: Negation as reflective operation. *Journal of Personality and Social Psychology, 91*, 385–405.

Deutsch, R., & Strack, F. (2006). Duality models in social psychology: From dual processes to interacting systems. *Psychological Inquiry, 17*, 166–172.

Devine, P. G. (1989). Stereotypes and prejudice: Their automatic and controlled components. *Journal of Personality and Social Psychology, 56*, 5–18.

Duncan, B. L. (1976). Differential perception and attribution of intergroup violence: Testing the lower limits of stereotyping of Blacks. *Journal of Personality and Social Psychology, 34*, 590–598.

Dunton, B. C., & Fazio, R. H. (1997). An individual difference measure of motivation to control prejudiced reactions. *Personality and Social Psychology Bulletin, 23*, 316–326.

Epstein, S. (1973). The self-concept revisited. Or a theory of a theory. *American Psychologist, 28*, 404–416.

Epstein, S. (1994). Integration of the cognitive and the psychodynamic unconscious. *American Psychologist, 49*, 709–724.

Epstein, S., & Pacini, R. (1999). Some basic issues regarding dual-process theories from the perspective of Cognitive-Experiential Self-Theory. In S. Chaiken, & Y. Trope (Eds.), *Dual-process theories in social psychology* (pp. 462–482). New York: Guilford Press.

Epstein, S., Pacini, R., Denes-Raj, V., & Heier, H. (1996). Individual differences in intuitive-experiential and analytical-rational thinking styles. *Journal of Personality and Social Psychology, 71*, 390–405.

Erb, H. P., Pierro, A., Mannetti, L., Spiegel, S., & Kruglanski, A. W. (2007). Biased processing of persuasive evidence: On the functional equivalence of cues and message arguments. *European Journal of Social Psychology, 37*, 1057–1075.

Fazio, R. H. (1990). Multiple processes by which attitudes guide behavior: The MODE model as an integrative framework. *Advances in Experimental Social Psychology, 23*, 75–109.

Fazio, R. H. (1995). Attitudes as object-evaluation associations: Determinants, consequences, and correlates of attitude accessibility. In R. E. Petty & J. A. Krosnick (Eds.), *Attitude strength* (pp. 247–282). Mahwah, NJ: Erlbaum.

Fazio, R. H. (2007). Attitudes as object-evaluation associations of varying strength. *Social Cognition, 25*, 603–637.

Fazio, R. H., Jackson, J. R., Dunton, B. C., & Williams, C. J. (1995). Variability in automatic activation as an unobtrusive measure of racial attitudes: A bona fide pipeline? *Journal of Personality and Social Psychology, 69*, 1013–1027.

Fazio, R. H., & Olson, M. A. (2003). Implicit measures in social cognition research: Their meaning and use. *Annual Review of Psychology, 54*, 297–327.

Fazio, R. H., Sanbonmatsu, D. M., Powell, M. C., & Kardes, F. R. (1986). On the automatic activation of attitudes. *Journal of Personality and Social Psychology, 50*, 229–238.

Ferreira, M. B., Garcia-Marques, L., Sherman, S. J., & Sherman, J. W. (2006). A dual-process approach to judgment under uncertainty. *Journal of Personality and Social Psychology, 91*, 797–813.

Festinger, L. (1957). *A theory of cognitive dissonance*. Evanston, IL: Row Peterson.

Fiske, S. T., Lin, M., & Neuberg, S. L. (1999). The continuum model: Ten years later. In S. Chaiken & Y. Trope (Eds.), *Dual-process theories in social psychology* (pp. 231–254). New York: Guilford Press.

Fiske, S. T., & Neuberg, S. L. (1990). A continuum of impression formation, from category-based to individuating processes: Influences of information and motivation on attention and interpretation. *Advances in Experimental Social Psychology, 23*, 1–74.

Gaertner, S. L., & Dovidio, J. F. (1986). The aversive form of racism. In J. F. Dovidio, & S. L. Gaertner (Eds.), *Prejudice, discrimination, and racism* (pp. 61–89). Orlando, FL: Academic Press.

Gawronski, B. (2004). Theory-based bias correction in dispositional inference: The fundamental attribution error is dead, long live the correspondence bias. *European Review of Social Psychology, 15*, 183–217.

Gawronski, B., Alshut, E., Grafe, J., Nespethal, J., Ruhmland, A., & Schulz, L. (2002). Prozesse der Urteilsbildung über bekannte und unbekannte Personen: Wie der erste Eindruck die Verarbeitung neuer Informationen beeinflusst [Processes of judging known and unknown persons: How the first impression influences the processing of new information]. *Zeitschrift für Sozialpsychologie, 33*, 25–34.

Gawronski, B., & Bodenhausen, G. V. (2006a). Associative and propositional processes in evaluation: An integrative review of implicit and explicit attitude change. *Psychological Bulletin, 132*, 692–731.

Gawronski, B., & Bodenhausen, G. V. (2006b). Associative and propositional processes in evaluation: Conceptual, empirical, and meta-theoretical issues. Reply to Albarracín, Hart, and McCulloch (2006), Kruglanski and Dechesne (2006), and Petty and Briñol (2006). *Psychological Bulletin, 132*, 745–750.

Gawronski, B., & Bodenhausen, G. V. (2007). Unraveling the processes underlying evaluation: Attitudes from the perspective of the APE Model. *Social Cognition, 25*, 687–717.

Gawronski, B., & Bodenhausen, G. V. (2009). Operating principles versus operating conditions in the distinction between associative and propositional processes. *Behavioral and Brain Sciences, 32*, 207–208.

Gawronski, B., & Bodenhausen, G. V. (2011). The associative-propositional evaluation model: Theory, evidence, and open questions. *Advances in Experimental Social Psychology, 44*, 59–127.

Gawronski, B., Deutsch, R., LeBel, E. P., & Peters, K. R. (2008). Response interference as a mechanism underlying implicit measures: Some traps and gaps in the assessment of mental associations with experimental paradigms. *European Journal of Psychological Assessment, 24*, 218–225.

Gawronski, B., Geschke, D., & Banse, R. (2003). Implicit bias in impression formation: Associations influence the construal of individuating information. *European Journal of Social Psychology, 33*, 573–589.

Gawronski, B., & LeBel, E. P. (2008). Understanding patterns of attitude change: When implicit measures show change, but explicit measures do not. *Journal of Experimental Social Psychology, 44*, 1355–1361.

Gawronski, B., LeBel, E. P., & Peters, K. R. (2007). What do implicit measures tell us? Scrutinizing the validity of three common assumptions. *Perspectives on Psychological Science, 2*, 181–193.

Gawronski, B., Peters, K. R., & LeBel, E. P. (2008). What makes mental associations personal or extra-personal? Conceptual issues in the methodological debate about implicit attitude measures. *Social and Personality Psychology Compass, 2*, 1002–1023.

Gawronski, B., & Sritharan, R. (2010). Formation, change, and contextualization of mental associations: Determinants and principles of variations in implicit measures. In B. Gawronski, & B. K. Payne (Eds.), *Handbook of implicit social cognition: Measurement, theory, and applications* (pp. 216–240). New York: Guilford Press.

Gawronski, B., & Strack, F. (2004). On the propositional nature of cognitive consistency: Dissonance changes explicit, but not implicit attitudes. *Journal of Experimental Social Psychology, 40*, 535–542.

Gilbert, D. T. (1989). Thinking lightly about others: Automatic components of the social inference process. In J. S. Uleman & J. A. Bargh (Eds.), *Unintended thought* (pp. 189–211). New York: Guilford Press.

Gilbert, D. T. (1991). How mental systems believe. *American Psychologist, 46,* 107–119.

Gilbert, D. T., & Malone, P. S. (1995). The correspondence bias. *Psychological Bulletin, 117*, 21–38.

Gilbert, D. T., Pelham, B. W., & Krull, D. S. (1988). On cognitive busyness: When person perceivers meet persons perceived. *Journal of Personality and Social Psychology, 54*, 733–740.

Gilovich, T., Griffin, D., & Kahneman, D. (Eds.). (2002). *Heuristics and biases: The psychology of intuitive judgment.* Cambridge, UK: Cambridge University Press.

Greeley, A. M., & Sheatsley, P. B. (1971). Attitudes toward racial integration. *Scientific American, 225*, 13–19.

Greenwald, A. G., & Banaji, M. R. (1995). Implicit social cognition: Attitudes, self-esteem, and stereotypes. *Psychological Review, 102*, 4–27.

Greenwald, A. G., McGhee, D. E., & Schwartz, J. K. L. (1998). Measuring individual differences in implicit cognition: The Implicit Association Test. *Journal of Personality and Social Psychology, 74*, 1464–1480.

Gregg, A. P., Seibt, B., & Banaji, M. R. (2006). Easier done than undone: Asymmetry in the malleability of implicit preferences. *Journal of Personality and Social Psychology, 90*, 1–20.

Grumm, M., Nestler, S., & von Collani, G. (2009). Changing explicit and implicit attitudes: The case of self-esteem. *Journal of Experimental Social Psychology, 45*, 327–335.

Higgins, E. T. (1996). Knowledge activation: Accessibility, applicability, and salience. In E. T. Higgins & A. W. Kruglanski (Eds.), *Social psychology: Handbook of basic principles* (pp. 133–168). New York: Guilford Press.

Hoefling, A., Likowski, K. U., Deutsch, R., Häfner, M., Seibt, B., Mühlberger, A., Weyers, P., & Strack, F. (2009). When hunger finds no fault with moldy corn: Food deprivation reduces food-related disgust. *Emotion, 9*, 50–58.

Hofmann, W., Rauch, W., & Gawronski, B. (2007). And deplete us not into temptation: Automatic attitudes, dietary restraint, and self-regulatory resources as determinants of eating behavior. *Journal of Experimental Social Psychology, 43*, 497–504.

Hugenberg, K., & Bodenhausen, G. V. (2003). Facing prejudice: Implicit prejudice and the perception of facial threat. *Psychological Science, 14*, 640–643.

Hugenberg, K., & Bodenhausen, G. V. (2004). Ambiguity in social categorization: The role of prejudice and facial affect in racial categorization. *Psychological Science, 15*, 342–345.

Huntsinger, J. R., Sinclair, S., & Clore, G. L. (2009). Affective regulation of implicitly measures stereotypes and attitudes: Automatic and controlled processes. *Journal of Experimental Social Psychology, 45*, 560–566.

Jacoby, L. L. (1991). A process-dissociation framework: Separating automatic from intentional uses of memory. *Journal of Memory & Language, 30*, 513–541.

Jones, E. E. (1990). *Interpersonal perception.* New York: Freeman.

Jones, E. E., & Davis, K. E. (1965). From acts to dispositions: The attribution process in person perception. *Advances in Experimental Social Psychology, 2*, 219–266.

Jones, E. E., & Harris, V. A. (1967). The attribution of attitudes. *Journal of Experimental Social Psychology, 3*, 1–24.

Kahneman, D. (2003). A perspective on judgment and choice: Mapping bounded rationality. *American Psychologist, 58*, 697–720.

Kahneman, D., Slovic, P., & Tversky, A. (1982). *Judgment under uncertainty: Heuristics and biases.* Cambridge, UK: Cambridge University Press.

Kelley, H. H. (1967). Attribution theory in social psychology. In D. Levine (Ed.), *Nebraska symposium on motivation* (pp. 192–240). Lincoln, NE: University of Nebraska Press.

Kelley, H. H. (1972). Causal schemata and the attribution process. In E. E. Jones, D. E. Kanouse, H. H. Kelley, R. E. Nisbett, S. Valins, & B. Weiner (Eds.), *Attribution: Perceiving the causes of behavior* (pp. 151–174). Morristown, NJ: General Learning Press.

Keren, G., & Schul, Y. (2009). Two is not always better than one: A critical evaluation of two-systems theories. *Perspectives on Psychological Science, 4*, 533–550.

Kruglanski, A. W., & Ajzen, I. (1983). Bias and error in human judgment. *European Journal of Social Psychology, 13*, 1–44.

Kruglanski, A. W., & Dechesne, M. (2006). Are associative and propositional processes qualitatively distinct? Comment on Gawronski and Bodenhausen (2006). *Psychological Bulletin, 132*, 736–739.

Kruglanski, A. W., Erb, H. P., Pierro, A., Mannetti, L., & Chun, W. Y. (2006). On parametric continuities in the world of binary either ors. *Psychological Inquiry, 17*, 153–165.

Kruglanski, A. W., Pierro, A., Mannetti, L., Erb, H. P., & Chun, W. Y. (2007). On the parameters of human judgment. *Advances in Experimental Social Psychology, 39*, 255–303.

Kruglanski, A. W., & Thompson, E. P. (1999). Persuasion by a single route: A view from the unimodel. *Psychological Inquiry, 10*, 83–109.

Krull, D. S. (1993). Does the grist change the mill? The effect of the perceiver's inferential goal on the process of social inference. *Personality and Social Psychology Bulletin, 19*, 340–348.

Krull, D. S., & Dill, J. C. (1996). On thinking first and responding fast: Flexibility in the social inference process. *Personality and Social Psychology Bulletin, 22*, 949–959.

Krull, D. S., & Erickson, D. J. (1995). Judging situations: On the effortful process of taking dispositional information into account. *Social Cognition, 13*, 417–438.

Kunda, Z., Miller, D. T., & Claire, T. (1990). Combining social concepts: The role of causal reasoning. *Cognitive Science, 14*, 551–577.

Kunda, Z., & Sherman-Williams, B. (1993). Stereotypes and the construal of individuating information. *Personality and Social Psychology Bulletin, 19*, 90–99.

Leyens, J. P., & Yzerbyt, V. Y. (1992). The ingroup overexclusion effect: The impact of valence and confirmation on information search. *European Journal of Social Psychology, 22*, 549–569.

Lieberman, M. D. (2003). Reflective and reflexive judgment processes: A social cognitive neuroscience approach. In J. P. Forgas, K. R. Williams, & W. von Hippel (Eds.), *Social judgments: Implicit and explicit processes* (pp. 44–67). New York: Cambridge University Press.

Lieberman, M. D. (2007). Social cognitive neuroscience: A review of core processes. *Annual Review of Psychology, 58*, 259–289.

Lieberman, M. D., Gaunt, R., Gilbert, D. T., & Trope, Y. (2002). Reflection and reflexion: A social cognitive neuroscience approach to attributional inference. *Advances in Experimental Social Psychology, 34*, 199–249.

Lindsay, D. S., & Jacoby, L. L. (1994). Stroop process-dissociations: The relationship between facilitation and interference. *Journal of Experimental Psychology: Human Perception & Performance, 20*, 219–234.

Maheswaran, D., & Chaiken, S. (1991). Promoting systematic processing in low-motivation settings: Effects of incongruent information on processing and judgment. *Journal of Personality and Social Psychology, 61*, 13–25.

Maheswaran, D., Mackie, D. M., & Chaiken, S. (1992). Brand name as an heuristic cue: The effects of task importance and expectancy confirmation on consumer judgments. *Journal of Consumer Psychology, 1*, 317–336.

McClelland, J. L., McNaughton, B. L., & O'Reilly, R. C. (1995). Why there are complementary learning systems in the hippocampus and neocortex? Insights from the successes and failures of connectionist models of learning and memory. *Psychological Review, 102*, 419–457.

McConahay, J. B. (1986). Modern racism, ambivalence, and the modern racism scale. In J. D. Dovidio, & S. L. Gaertner (Eds.), *Prejudice, discrimination, and racism* (pp. 91–125). Orlando, FL: Academic Press.

Metcalfe, J., & Mischel, W. (1999). A hot/cool-system analysis of delay of gratification. Dynamics of willpower. *Psychological Review, 106*, 3–19.

Moors, A., & De Houwer, J. (2006). Automaticity: A conceptual and theoretical analysis. *Psychological Bulletin, 132*, 297–326.

Neumann, R., Förster, J., & Strack, F. (2003). Motor compatibility: The bidirectional link between behavior and emotion. In J. Musch & K. C. Klauer (Eds.), *The psychology of evaluation: Affective processes in cognition and emotion* (pp. 371–391). Mahwah, NJ: Erlbaum.

Norman, D. A., & Shallice, T. (1986). Attention to action: Willed and automatic control of behavior. In R. J. Davidson, G. E. Schwartz, & D. Shapiro (Eds.), *Consciousness and self-regulation: Advances in research* (pp. 1–18). New York: Plenum.

Olson, M. A., & Fazio, R. H. (2004). Reducing the influence of extra-personal associations on the Implicit Association Test: Personalizing the IAT. *Journal of Personality and Social Psychology, 86*, 653–667.

Olson, M. A., & Fazio, R. H. (2006). Reducing automatically activated racial prejudice through implicit evaluative conditioning. *Personality and Social Psychology Bulletin, 32*, 421–433.

Olson, M. A., & Fazio, R. H. (2009). Implicit and explicit measures of attitudes: The perspective of the MODE model. In R. E. Petty, R. H. Fazio, & P. Briñol (Eds.), *Attitudes: Insights from the new implicit measures* (pp. 19–63). New York: Psychology Press.

Payne, B. K. (2001). Prejudice and perception: The role of automatic and controlled processes in misperceiving a weapon. *Journal of Personality and Social Psychology, 81*, 181–192.

Payne, B. K. (2006). Weapon bias: Split second decisions and unintended stereotyping. *Current Directions in Psychological Science, 15*, 287–291.

Payne, B. K. (2008). What mistakes disclose: A process dissociation approach to automatic and controlled processes in social psychology. *Social and Personality Psychology Compass, 2*, 1073–1092.

Payne, B. K., & Bishara, A. J. (2009). An integrative review of process dissociation and related models in social cognition. *European Review of Social Psychology, 20*, 272–314.

Payne, B. K., Lambert, A. J., & Jacoby, L. L. (2002). Best laid plans: Effects of goals on accessibility bias and cognitive control in race-based misperceptions of weapons. *Journal of Experimental Social Psychology, 38*, 384–396.

Peters, K. R., & Gawronski, B. (2011). Mutual influences between the implicit and explicit self-concepts: The role of memory activation and motivated reasoning. *Journal of Experimental Social Psychology, 47*, 436–442.

Petty, R. E., Briñol, P., & DeMarree, K. G. (2007). The meta-cognitive model (MCM) of attitudes: Implications for attitude measurement, change, and strength. *Social Cognition, 25*, 657–686.

Petty, R. E., & Cacioppo, J. T. (1984). Source factors and the elaboration likelihood model of persuasion. *Advances in Consumer Research, 11,* 668–672.

Petty, R. E., & Cacioppo, J. T. (1986). The Elaboration Likelihood Model of persuasion. *Advances in Experimental Social Psychology, 19,* 123–205.

Petty, R. E., Cacioppo, J. T., & Schumann, D. W. (1983). Central and peripheral routes to advertising effectiveness: The moderating role of involvement. *Journal of Consumer Research, 10,* 135–146.

Petty, R. E., & Wegener, D. T. (1999). The Elaboration Likelihood Model: Current status and controversies. In S. Chaiken & Y. Trope (Eds.), *Dual process theories in social psychology* (pp. 41–72). New York: Guilford Press.

Popper, K. R. (1934). *Logic of scientific discovery.* New York: Basic Books.

Posner, M. I., & Snyder, C. R. R. (1975). Attention and cognitive control. In R. L. Solso (Ed.), *Information processing and cognition: The Loyola Symposium.* Hillsdale, NJ: Lawrence Erlbaum Associates Inc.

Quattrone, G. A. (1982). Overattribution and unit formation: When behavior engulfs the person. *Journal of Personality and Social Psychology, 42,* 593–607.

Quine, W. V. O. (1960). *Word and object.* Cambridge MA: MIT Press.

Quine, W. V. O., & Ullian, J. S. (1978). *The web of belief* (2nd ed.). New York: McGraw-Hill.

Richards, Z., & Hewstone, M. (2001). Subtyping and subgrouping: Processes for the prevention and promotion of stereotype change. *Personality and Social Psychology Review, 5,* 52–73.

Ross, L. D. (1977). The intuitive psychologist and his shortcomings: Distortions in the attribution process. *Advances in Experimental Social Psychology, 10,* 173–220.

Ross, L. D., Amabile, T. M., & Steinmetz, J. L. (1977). Social roles, social control, and biases in social-perception processes. *Journal of Personality and Social Psychology, 35,* 485–494.

Sagar, H. A., & Schofield, J. W. (1980). Racial and behavioral cues in black and white children's perceptions of ambiguously aggressive acts. *Journal of Personality and Social Psychology, 39,* 590–598.

Samuels, R. (2009). The magical number two, plus or minus: Dual-process theory as a theory of cognitive kinds. In J. St. B. T. Evans & K. Frankish (Eds.), *In two minds: Dual processes and beyond* (pp. 129–146). New York: Oxford University Press.

Sears, D. O. (1988). Symbolic racism. In P. A. Katz, & D. A. Taylor (Eds.), *Eliminating racism: Profiles in controversy* (pp. 53–84). New York: Plenum.

Sherman, J. W. (2006). On building a better process model: It's not only how many, but which ones and by which means. *Psychological Inquiry, 17,* 173–184.

Sherman, J. W., Gawronski, B., Gonsalkorale, K., Hugenberg, K., Allen, T. J., & Groom, C. J. (2008). The self-regulation of automatic associations and behavioral impulses. *Psychological Review, 115,* 314–335.

Sherman, J. W., Groom, C., Ehrenberg, K., & Klauer, K. C. (2003). Bearing false witness under pressure: Implicit and explicit components of stereotype-driven memory bias. *Social Cognition, 21,* 213–246.

Sherman, J. W., Klauer, K. C., & Allen, T. J. (2010). Mathematical modeling of implicit social cognition: The machine in the ghost. In B. Gawronski & B. K. Payne (Eds.), *Handbook of implicit social cognition: Measurement, theory, and applications* (pp. 156–175). New York: Guilford Press.

Shiffrin, R., & Schneider, W. (1977). Controlled and automatic human information processing: II. Perceptual learning, automatic attending and a general theory. *Psychological Review, 84,* 127–190.

Sloman, S. A. (1996). The empirical case for two systems of reasoning. *Psychological Bulletin, 119,* 3–22.

Smith, E. R., & DeCoster, J. (2000). Dual-process models in social and cognitive psychology: Conceptual integration and links to underlying memory systems. *Personality and Social Psychology Review, 4,* 108–131.

Snyder, M. L., & Frankel, A. (1976). Observer bias: A stringent test of behavior engulfing the field. *Journal of Personality and Social Psychology, 34,* 857–864.

Stanovich, K. E., & West, R. F. (2000). Individual differences in reasoning: Implications for the rationality debate? *Behavioral and Brain Sciences, 23,* 645–726.

Strack, F., & Deutsch, R. (2004). Reflective and impulsive determinants of social behavior. *Personality and Social Psychology Review, 8,* 220–247.

Taylor, D. G., Sheatsley, P. B., & Greeley, A. M. (1978). Attitudes toward racial integration. *Scientific American, 238,* 42–49.

Trope, Y. (1986). Identification and inferential processes in dispositional attribution. *Psychological Review, 93,* 239–257.

Trope, Y., & Alfieri, T. (1997). Effortfulness and flexibility of dispositional judgment processes. *Journal of Personality and Social Psychology, 73,* 662–674.

Trope, Y., & Cohen, O. (1989). Perceptual and inferential determinants of behavior-correspondent attributions. *Journal of Experimental Social Psychology, 25,* 142–158.

Trope, Y., Cohen, O., & Alfieri, T. (1991). Behavior identification as a mediator of dispositional inference. *Journal of Personality and Social Psychology, 61,* 873–883.

Trope, Y., Cohen, O., & Maoz, Y. (1988). The perceptual and inferential effects of situational inducements on dispositional attribution. *Journal of Personality and Social Psychology, 55,* 165–177.

Trope, Y., & Gaunt, R. (1999). A dual-process model of overconfident attributional inferences. In S. Chaiken & Y. Trope (Eds.), *Dual-process theories in social psychology* (pp. 161–178). New York: Guilford Press.

Trope, Y., & Gaunt, R. (2000). Processing alternative explanations of behavior: Correction or integration? *Journal of Personality and Social Psychology, 79,* 344–354.

Tversky, A., & Kahneman, D. (1983). Extensional vs. intuitive reasoning: The conjunction fallacy in probability judgment. *Psychological Review, 90,* 293–315.

Vonk, R. (1999). Effects of outcome dependency on correspondence bias. *Personality and Social Psychology Bulletin, 25,* 382–389.

Webster, D. M. (1993). Motivated augmentation and reduction of the overattribution bias. *Journal of Personality and Social Psychology, 65,* 261–271.

Whitfield, M., & Jordan, C. H. (2009). Mutual influences of explicit and implicit attitudes. *Journal of Experimental Social Psychology, 45,* 748–759.

Wicker, A. W. (1969). Attitudes versus actions: The relationship of verbal and overt behavioral responses to attitude objects. *Journal of Social Issues, 25,* 41–78.

Wilson, T. D., Lindsey, S. & Schooler, T. Y. (2000). A model of dual attitudes. *Psychological Review, 107,* 101–126.

The "Cold" and "Hot" Sides of Attention

Daniel Smilek *and* Alexandra Frischen

Abstract

Attention biases information processing and, as such, is critically involved in almost everything we do, ensuring adaptive interaction with our environment. In recent years, the study of attention has immensely benefited from the conceptual and methodological convergence with social cognition. Thus, it has become apparent that the way in which attention is allocated and sustained is not merely subject to sensory influences such as perceptual salience but also is greatly influenced by social relevance, such as where someone else is directing their attention, and other complex factors such as emotion. Furthermore, translating lab-based studies of attention into real-world settings and supplementing traditional reaction time–based attention measures with social cognition tools such as self-report measures provide novel insights into how attention operates in everyday life. We discuss this issue in the context of research on sustained attention, attention lapses and mind wandering. Taken together, research on attention shows that attention is tightly linked with mood and emotion and that it is not an isolated process that is encapsulated within the individual, but rather comprises highly dynamic and flexible mechanisms that can be distributed across individuals, affecting the way in which people encode their surroundings and interact with each other.

Key Words: attention, sustained attention, social interaction, emotion, mood, attention lapses, mind wandering

Introduction

It is Friday evening. You are at the office, about to leave to meet your friends at the pub. You spend a moment or two scanning the content of your desk until you find your keys, then you pick them up, and off you go. The pub is packed, but after a while you spot one of your friends at the other side of the room. You wave until you catch her eye, and motion toward a table that has just become available in the far corner to invite her to join you. Every one of this diverse range of tasks—finding your keys, picking them up, spotting your friend, making eye contact, and wordlessly communicating to move to the table—may seem trivial, but in fact, each involves a highly complex interplay of dynamic cognitive processes, ranging from rudimentary visual perception,

to object recognition, to action. One mechanism that is critically involved in each of these processes is attention.

Traditionally, attention studies have been highly constrained and focused on "cold" cognition, such as sensory perception. Increasingly, however, attention researchers are studying "hot" cognitions, such as emotion or social relevance, as well as individual differences. The purpose of this chapter is to provide a brief overview of these new developments. We begin by briefly outlining the complex phenomenon that is attention. We then focus on two broad aspects of attention: spatial allocation of attention and sustained attention. These are perhaps the most well-researched facets of attention with regard to sensory processes and, more recently, with regard to processing social information. They are therefore prime examples to illustrate the way in which these formerly disparate but now increasingly overlapping fields have benefited from conceptual and methodological convergence and to highlight how attention researchers are beginning to extend their work from controlled laboratory tasks to everyday life.

What Is Attention?

At every moment, our senses are bombarded with an abundance of information: As soon as you open your eyes, you likely find yourself surrounded by hundreds of individual objects, and you hear traffic noise, birds chirping, people talking, and so on. Imagine that your brain was processing all of this information to an equal degree at every single moment—you would not be able to make sense of anything. The overload would be particularly evident at the level of response: if you want to pick up your keys from your desk, you certainly don't want to (nor could you) pick up the entire contents of the desk at the same time. Even though our brains are capable of processing vast amounts of information, the capacity for simultaneous processing of multiple stimuli at high levels of representation, for example, in working memory, is limited (Luck & Vogel, 1997). The plethora of external (e.g., sounds and sights) and internal (e.g., thoughts and feelings) inputs and sensations therefore compete with one another for access to high-level processing and conscious awareness; at some level, there will invariably be a bottleneck.

Attention is an umbrella term for a range of neural operations that selectively enhance processing of information, allowing it to pass through this bottleneck. This way, the processing of pertinent information can be prioritized, which substantially increases the chance that you will indeed lock your office with your keys and not the cup of cold coffee that was sitting next to them on the desk. Attention affects spatial (e.g., Posner, 1980) and temporal (e.g., Coull & Nobre, 1998; Loach & Marí-Beffa, 2003) processing of information for every sensory modality (e.g., touch: Burton et al, 1999; smell: Zelano et al., 2005; hearing: Spence & Driver, 1994; although visual attention has perhaps been studied most extensively). And it does so at every level, from early perception (e.g., Motter, 1993) to planning and execution of overt responses (e.g., Loach, Frischen, Bruce, & Tsotsos, 2008). In other words, attention is at the heart of virtually everything we do.

Despite this diversity, attentional biasing is commonly assumed to rely on two basic mechanisms: *facilitation* and *inhibition*. Facilitation enhances

neural responses to salient or goal-relevant information while inhibition simultaneously reduces interference from irrelevant and distracting information (Desimone & Duncan, 1995; Houghton & Tipper, 1994; Kastner & Ungerleider, 2000; Neumann & DeSchepper, 1991; Tsotsos et al., 1995). This is not to say that inhibited information is not processed at all; on the contrary, objects that are outside the primary focus of attention may provide critical contextual information about the target item. In fact, distractor stimuli can be processed in parallel with target information to very sophisticated levels, with inhibition affecting the level of processing at which the competition between target and distractor takes place. This level changes with the nature of the task and depends on the behavioral goal. For example, if the aim is to locate a target, inhibition acts on the cognitive representation of the location of distractors that compete for this response (Milliken, Tipper, & Weaver, 1994); if a task requires identification of a target, inhibition acts on higher-level semantic representations (Tipper & Driver, 1988). Similarly, the degree of attentional biasing that is required for successful conflict resolution depends on the relative perceptual and behavioral salience of targets and distractors: the more salient a distractor is, the more strongly it competes for response, and the more the strength of the applied inhibition correspondingly increases (Grison & Strayer, 2001; Tipper, Meegan, & Howard, 2002). Thus, attentional biasing is highly flexible and dynamically adjusts to current cognitive and behavioral demands.

Because attention is involved in so many different cognitive operations, it is not surprising that researchers have created an abundance of experimental paradigms to study particular aspects of attention and their relation to other variables. Here, we focus our discussion on spatial allocation of attention and sustained attention. These facets of attention have been thoroughly researched in the cold cognitive domain, and more recently have been utilized to study hot social cognition processes. Furthermore, research into these aspects of attention has been invigorated with methodological transitions outside the lab and into the real world.

Spatial Allocation of Attention

As noted, not all information available to our eyes can be processed to the same level at the same time. For adaptive encoding of, and interaction with, objects and persons in one's environment, attention needs to be selectively deployed to areas or objects of potential interest. For the present chapter, we focus our discussion of spatial allocation of attention primarily on two commonly used experimental paradigms that expose the cognitive mechanisms that support or influence such deployment of attention. The *spatial cueing paradigm* (Posner, 1980) examines the precise cognitive mechanics involved in orienting attention to locations of interest, usually in response to isolated events. The *visual search paradigm* (Treisman & Gelade, 1980) is used to assess deployment of focused attention in the face of cluttered environments and provides insight into factors that influence or "guide" the allocation of attention. It should be noted that the underlying attentional processes are not mutually exclusive; instead, they represent different facets of spatial allocation of attention that dynamically complement each other. For example, basic mechanisms of attentional orienting (see "Orienting of Attention," below) are involved in serial visual search (see "Visual Search," below), whereas parallel visual search processes (see "Visual Search," below) may provide the signals that trigger targeted spatial shifts of attention. In this section, we briefly outline each of these aspects of spatial allocation of attention and introduce the two aforementioned experimental paradigms as they are traditionally used to study cold sensory processing operations before turning our attention to their application to hot information processing in social cognition.

Orienting of Attention

Selective deployment of attention to objects or locations of potential interest is achieved by aligning or *engaging* the focus of attention with hitherto unattended locations, while *disengaging* attention from the currently attended location. This *orienting* of attention allows for rapid allocation of attention to salient events in one's environment, facilitating their subsequent encoding and high-level processing (Posner, 1980). Traditionally, attention research has distinguished between *exogenous* (stimulus-driven) orienting and *endogenous* (goal-driven) orienting. A classic example of exogenous orienting is illustrated in Figure 15.1A: The participant fixates on the cross that is displayed at the center of the computer display flanked by empty placeholders. The outline of one of the placeholders flashes abruptly. This abrupt perceptual event triggers a rapid shift of attention to this cued location. Thus, targets that subsequently appear in this location at brief cue-target stimulus onset asynchronies (SOAs) are responded to faster than targets appearing in uncued locations. At longer intervals between cue and target onset, this pattern reverses so that paradoxically, reaction times (RTs) on cued trials are slower than on uncued trials (Posner & Cohen, 1984; see Figure 15.1C). This inhibition of return (IOR) effect shows that facilitatory and inhibitory attention mechanisms

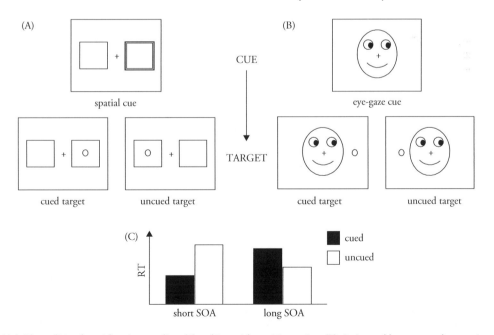

Figure 15.1 The traditional spatial cueing paradigm (**A**) and its social cognition variant (**B**). In **A,** a sudden perceptual event triggers a shift of attention to the location that has been cued in this manner. In **B,** a centrally presented face averts its gaze, triggering a shift of attention toward the gazed-at location. A reaction time (RT) target (o) subsequently appears in the previously cued or gazed-at location, or in the uncued location. At short stimulus onset asynchronies (SOAs), RTs to cued targets are faster than RTs to uncued targets (**C**); at long SOAs, this pattern typically reverses, although with gaze cues, this is only observed under certain conditions.

operate in tandem. Facilitation dominates immediately after attention has shifted to the cued location, and inhibition effects emerge after some time has elapsed, to promote the perception of novel stimuli in other locations by keeping attention from becoming trapped at the already examined location (Klein, 1988; Klein & MacInnes, 1999).

These RT patterns consistently emerge when sudden perceptual events are used as cues, despite the fact that the cues do not predict where the target will appear, even if the cue is counterpredictive (i.e., if the target is more often presented in the uncued location; e.g., Remington, Johnston, & Yantis, 1992). This pattern of results is considered to be a hallmark of reflexive orienting of attention, whereby attention automatically shifts to the location of a perceptually salient event, even if it is not strategically advantageous to do so. This is in contrast to endogenous orienting that is, at least partly, under voluntary control. For example, when a symbolic cue such as an arrow pointing to the left or right is presented at the center of the display, attention also orients rapidly toward the direction indicated by the arrow, but this is not strictly automatic because it can be overridden by conflicting goals. If participants know that the target stimulus will be presented more often in the opposite (not pointed-at) location, they can ignore the cue and shift their attention to the expected location instead (Friesen, Ristic, & Kingstone, 2004; Pratt & Hommel, 2003; Ristic, Friesen & Kingstone, 2002;

Tipples, 2002). Thus, attention research has rested for a long time on the assumption that reflexive and automatic attention shifts occur only in response to low-level perceptually salient events; attention shifts in response to semantically meaningful symbolic cues were considered not reflexive because they require interpretation and do not directly mark a spatial location.

Visual Search

In daily life, salient events are rarely encountered in isolation. Instead, one is usually confronted with a number of target and distractor items (e.g., your keys among the clutter on the desk). During *visual search*, attention is first distributed diffusely to provide a coarse analysis of the visual field, whereby many items are processed in parallel without the benefit of attentional biasing. Perceptually salient targets (e.g., those characterized by unique features; see Figure 15.2A) quickly guide focused attention to their location where optimized higher-level processing can take place, culminating in the confirmation that the target has been found. This pop-out search is expressed in RTs that are not much influenced by the number of distracting items in the display (the "set size"), thus producing a relatively flat search function. Parallel processing may not suffice if the target shares defining features with the distractors (see Figure 15.2B); in this case, successful search depends more strongly on focused attention being allocated to each search item in turn to

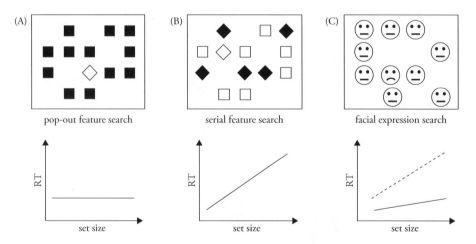

Figure 15.2 The traditional visual search paradigm (**A** and **B**) and its social cognition variant (**C**). In **A**, the unique target (the *white diamond*) does not share any defining features (its color or shape) with the distractors. It is therefore detected quickly, and the number of distractors (set size) does not influence reaction times (RTs), resulting in a flat search slope. In **B**, the same target shares critical features with all of the distractors. Search performance in this case is much more effortful, with RTs increasing linearly as the set size increases. In **C**, the target is a face that bears a different emotional expression from the distractor faces. The efficiency of search performance differs depending on the emotional expression of the target; typically, faces with negative expressions such as anger or sadness are found more efficiently, leading to shallower search slopes (*solid line*) compared with target faces with other expressions (*dashed line*).

facilitate identification and matching of the item to a template of the search target held in working memory, until the target is located. During such serial search, RTs increase linearly with growing set size, producing a steep slope (Treisman & Gelade, 1980; see Wolfe, 2003, for a review). By comparing the search slopes for different types of target that are embedded in the same distractor context, one can assess the relative effectiveness with which a given target preattentively guides focused attention to its location (this concept of examining the relative rather than absolute steepness of search slopes is illustrated in Figure 15.2C; Eastwood, Smilek, & Merikle, 2001).

Traditionally, only low-level perceptually salient events, such as sudden changes in luminance or motion, were thought to trigger exogenous shifts of attention (e.g., Egeth & Yantis, 1997). Likewise, only basic perceptual features such as color and orientation were thought to guide focused attention during visual search (Wolfe & Horowitz, 2004). These mechanisms presumably evolved because they enable rapid prioritized encoding of potentially life-threatening events like the presence of a predator, which would be signaled by such elementary sensory information. However, humans have evolved into highly social beings; one would therefore expect that hot high-level social factors might also have influences on fundamental cold cognitive processes such as orienting of attention or visual search. The following sections review recent research on social influences on attention processes. First, we focus on orienting of attention in response to social signals before examining the influence of social factors on visual search.

Social Orienting of Attention: Other People's Actions Influence Selective Deployment of Attention

At the heart of social interactions is the ability to discern other people's intentions and mental states so that one may interpret their behavior and react accordingly. Let's return to our pub example. In order to communicate to your friend across the noisy room that you want her to join you at the table in the corner, you will first establish eye contact and then look or gesture toward the table. Given that people typically look at the item they are currently attending, someone's direction of eye gaze is an observable sign of where that person is currently focusing attention. Thus, by shifting one's own attention in the same direction, one will come to focus on the same location, which provides

information about the other's likely object of reference or imminent action.

This *joint attention* is a fundamental skill. Even newborn infants are able to tell the difference between averted gaze and direct gaze, and then shift their attention in the direction of observed gaze, suggesting that the capacity for this skill might be innate (Farroni, Csibra, Simion, & Johnson, 2002; Farroni, Massaccesi, Pividori, & Johnson, 2004; Hood, Willen, & Driver, 1998). Indeed, some degree of gaze following can also be observed in animals. In particular, animals that rely on social cooperation, such as birds, dogs, dolphins, and some species of primates, have been shown to possess the capacity to interpret human and conspecifics' referential gestures, supporting the notion that joint attention is useful for organisms that rely on social cooperation and communication (for reviews, see Emery, 2000; Shepherd, 2010).

Joint attention is commonly seen as a precursor for higher-level cognitive skills and the development of *theory of mind* abilities, that is, the capacity to discern cognitive and emotional states in other people, allowing one to empathize and understand others' intentions and behavior. Normally developing young children learn to use other's gaze direction to make attributions about the other person's cognitive states, such as desire, and to detect deception (Baron-Cohen, Campbell, Karmiloff-Smith, Grant, & Walker, 1995; Freire, Eskritt, & Lee, 2004). Conversely, children with autism, a developmental disorder characterized by poor social cognition skills and theory of mind deficits, show either poor or atypical joint attention behavior, being less susceptible to contextual factors such as target expectancy or clues for intention (Baron-Cohen et al., 1996; Leekam, López, & Moore, 2000; Pierno, Mari, Glover, Georgiou, & Castiello, 2006; Senju, Tojo, Dairoku, & Hasegawa, 2004).

During the past decade, cognitive psychologists have begun to study the attentional mechanisms underlying joint attention (see Frischen, Bayliss, & Tipper, 2007, for a review). These studies use modifications of the spatial cueing paradigm in which a centrally presented face stimulus (which may be a cartoon drawing or a naturalistic photograph) averts its gaze before the RT target appears (see Figure 15.1B). As with peripheral sudden-onset cues, participants are quicker to notice targets in the cued (here: looked-at) location immediately after the onset of the cue (Driver, Ricciardelli, Kidd, Maxwell & Baron-Cohen, 1999; Friesen & Kingstone, 1998; Langton & Bruce, 1999). After long delays following the cue onset,

RTs on cued trials tend to be slower if attention is shifted away from the gazed-at location (the IOR effect; Frischen, Smilek, Eastwood, & Tipper, 2007; Frischen & Tipper, 2004). Furthermore, attention is oriented toward the gazed-at location even if the gaze cue is counterpredictive (Driver et al., 1999; Friesen, Ristic, & Kingstone, 2004).

These results show that another person's gaze direction can serve as a strong attentional cue; its effects bear the hallmarks of exogenous, or reflexive, orienting of attention. This occurs despite the fact that in contrast to peripheral sudden-onset cues, eye gaze does not directly indicate the location of a potential event, but rather requires interpretation. For example, an ambiguous stimulus has to be perceived as a face in order for gaze cueing to occur (Ristic & Kingstone, 2005). Furthermore, if the face stimulus is rotated so that it is no longer upright (e.g., it "lies" on its side), attention shifts in the direction that the face physically looks toward in its current orientation (e.g., downward) but also in the direction that the face would be looking at if it were encountered in its normal upright orientation (e.g., to the left; Bayliss, di Pellegrino, & Tipper, 2004; Bayliss & Tipper, 2006a). These findings impressively demonstrate that reflexive orienting of attention is not merely subject to low-level perceptual influences but also is triggered and modified by higher order social factors.

Indeed, although gaze cueing itself is a very robust effect, it is not immune to further social influences such as affective and interpersonal inferences. For example, personally familiar or famous faces can lead to more robust gaze cueing effects than unfamiliar faces (Deaner, Shepherd, & Platt, 2007; Frischen & Tipper, 2006). Gaze cueing is sensitive to the experienced interaction between the observer and the person doing the gazing: When the behavior of the person who is gazing is experienced as not being related to the observer, or the observer's attention is not engaged with the face stimulus in the first place, the gaze cue has less signal value (Farroni, Mansfield, Lai, & Johnson, 2003; Hietanen, 1999). Neural activity that is associated with observing gaze involves brain areas that are also recruited by theory of mind tasks such as attribution of intentions and beliefs (Calder et al., 2002). Accordingly, neural activity elicited by gaze cues is influenced by the perceived intention of the gazing person and by its goal-related context (e.g., whether the face is gazing into empty space or toward an object; see Hoehl, Reid, Mooney, & Striano, 2008; Pelphrey, Singerman, Allison, & McCarthy, 2003).

Interestingly, observing gaze direction also triggers tendencies to overtly imitate the observed behavior: When viewing paintings or photographs of natural scenes, people exhibit an increased likelihood of fixating on objects at which a person in the scene is looking, especially when the task requires interpretation of the social context of the scene (Castelhano, Wieth, & Henderson, 2007; Dukewich, Klein, & Christie, 2008; Zwickel & Vö, 2010). Variants of the spatial cueing paradigm in which participants' eye movements are recorded show that spontaneous and involuntary saccades in the corresponding direction occur even if participants are told to keep their gaze fixated in the middle of the display, and even if overt gaze following is detrimental to the task at hand (Itier, Villate, & Ryan, 2007; Kuhn & Kingstone, 2009; Mansfield, Farroni, & Johnson, 2003; Ricciardelli, Bricolo, Aglioti, & Chelazzi, 2002). Automatic tendencies to imitate observed actions are based on neural activity in a specialized class of neurons in the premotor cortex, which is responsible for planning of complex actions. These *mirror neurons* activate when performing a particular intentional action (e.g., grasping) as well as when merely watching somebody else perform such an action (di Pellegrino, Fadiga, Fogassi, Gallese, & Rizzolatti, 1992; Grafton, Arbib, Fadiga, & Rizzolatti, 1996; Grosbras, Laird, & Paus, 2005; Shepherd, Klein, Deaner, & Platt, 2009).

It has recently been shown that selective allocation of attention is influenced not only by others' gaze behavior but also by other observed actions that elicit imitation tendencies. Frischen, Loach, and Tipper (2009) demonstrated that observing another person selectively reach for targets among distractors that vary in their level of behavioral salience leads the observer to inhibit the same distractors that compete for the other person's response, rather than those distractors that are most salient from the observer's own perspective. This study did not use the spatial cueing paradigm, but instead required participants to reach out and touch a red target while ignoring a green distractor. Stimulus locations were either close to them or far away. The closer a distracting stimulus, the more strongly it competes for response and the more strongly it has to be inhibited to avoid interference; distractors that are far away do not provide much interference and do not require strong inhibition. Indeed, when the participants performed the task on their own, they inhibited distractors that were located close to them. However, when they watched another person who was seated opposite them perform the same reaching task, participants inhibited distractors that were far away and therefore not salient from their own perspective but that were close to the observed person and therefore salient from the other person's point of view. Thus, mirroring other people's attention processes allows the observer to literally adopt the other person's point of view, by encoding their own environment in the same way that the other person does as he or she is interacting with it. This suggests that social influences on attention may be the basis for perspective taking, a key element of empathy and interpersonal interactions.

Visual Search of Social Information: Emotional Signals Guide Attention

Emotional expressions are important social signals that convey a wealth of information regarding the other person's state of mind and their intentions. Indeed, emotional expressions are processed very rapidly, even if they are not within the focus of attention or even consciously perceived (see Palermo & Rhodes, 2007, for a review). Although guidance of focused attention is commonly assumed to be under control of low-level perceptual salience, one might expect that semantically meaningful stimuli such as emotional expressions are salient enough to bias allocation of attention. For example, gaze cueing can be affected by the emotional expression of a face, so that attention shifts to gazed-at locations are stronger with fearful emotional expressions, particularly if the observer has elevated anxiety levels (Fox, Mathews, Calder, & Yiend, 2007; Holmes, Richards, & Green, 2006; Mathews, Fox, Yiend, & Calder, 2003; Tipples, 2006). Furthermore, emotional expressions bias allocation of attention to their location when emotional faces are used as sudden-onset cues in spatial orienting paradigms (Fox, Russo, Bowles, & Dutton, 2001; Mogg & Bradley, 1999).

Results from visual search studies suggest that emotional expressions are able to guide attention to their location preattentively, that is, before they are within the selective focus of attention. For example, Eastwood et al. (2001; see Figure 15.2C) showed that when a schematic face with an emotional expression (the target) was embedded among varying numbers of neutral faces (the distractors), search efficiency differed depending on the emotional expression of the target. Compared with searching for positive target faces, the average time to locate a target face with a negative expression was relatively less influenced by the number of distractors in the display. This was expressed in a shallower search slope for negative faces compared with the search slope for positive faces (this

is illustrated in Figure 15.2C; see also Hahn, Carlson, Singer, & Gronlund, 2006; Suslow, Junghanns, & Arolt, 2001). Of course, positive and negative expressions differ not only in terms of their emotional valence but also in terms of perceptual facial features, raising the possibility that mere perceptual salience (such as the conspicuous "V" shape of furrowed eye brows in an angry face) rather than emotion per se is guiding the spatial allocation of focused attention. Gerritsen, Frischen, Blake, Smilek, and Eastwood (2008) sought to avoid perceptual confounds by pairing neutral faces with positive or negative meaning through an associative learning procedure. Although perceptually identical and bearing neutral expressions, faces were again found to direct attention more efficiently when they had acquired a negative connotation than when they had positive associations. Taken together, these findings strongly suggest that the emotional meaning, rather than (or in addition to) mere physical salience, is capable of guiding the spatial allocation of focused attention (see also Fox & Damjanovic, 2006; Tipples, Atkinson, & Young, 2002). Thus, it appears that preattentive search processes are sensitive to the emotional signal value of faces and not merely controlled by low-level perceptual salience.

Further support for the notion that emotional faces are capable of guiding attention to their location preattentively comes from findings that the visual search for faces is no longer influenced by their emotion when such guidance is prevented. Smilek, Frischen, Reynolds, Gerritsen, and Eastwood (2007) eliminated the usually observed difference in search efficiency for emotional faces by hiding unattended items from view. In this study, search items were hidden from view by square placeholders. When a mouse pointer was moved over a placeholder, it disappeared, revealing the search item (a face) hidden underneath it. After the mouse pointer moved off the search item, the placeholder was replaced, hiding the search item from view. This ensured that search items were visible only when they were within the focus of attention and that unattended faces could not guide attention. As noted, the results showed that under these conditions, the normally observed difference in search slopes between positive and negative faces was eliminated. This finding rules out the possibility that the previously observed differences in search performances for emotional faces were due to processing operations taking place *after* the focus of attention had already been allocated to the face stimulus (e.g., emotion may have affected the speed of response selection processes). The emotional expression of the target face also influences eye movements occurring before the target is fixated for the first time rather than afterward, corroborating the notion that emotional expressions affect search before the emotional face is fixated (i.e., preattentively; see Reynolds, Eastwood, Partanen, Frischen, & Smilek, 2009).

Eye movements provide an indicator of exactly where attention is allocated overtly, in real time. Stimuli that are fixated project onto the fovea where visual input receives optimal processing. When viewing natural scenes, the eyes preferentially fixate on regions of high contrast, high spatial frequency, and high edge density, rather than on vast stretches of uniform "empty" space (Bruce & Tsotsos, 2009). In other words, overt attention is guided exogenously by cold perceptual salience. However, eye movements are also guided to areas that are semantically informative (see Henderson, 2007, for a review). Viewers take into account the semantic context of the scene and orient their eyes to locations where they expect to find a certain object, even when that area is in fact empty (Richardson & Spivey, 2000). This effectively streamlines the allocation of fixations and distribution of attention across the scene to areas that are relevant to the current goal or that are likely to be informative within a given semantic context. For example, when searching the kitchen for a saucepan, you are more likely to be successful if you direct your eyes toward the stovetop than the trashcan, even if the white stove happens to be less perceptually salient than the bright orange trashcan.

When a natural scene contains people, observers fixate preferentially on the socially significant parts of the scene, that is, the faces and especially the eye regions of the faces (Birmingham, Bischof, & Kingstone, 2008a). Birmingham et al. (2008a) showed that this bias emerges early (during the first second of viewing) and that the eye regions are revisited frequently during extended viewing. Interestingly, this fixation pattern is affected by the social context of the scene: Observers look at the eyes longer and more frequently when there are several people compared with just one person. Furthermore, fixations to faces and eyes occur more frequently when the observer's goal is to infer the direction of attention of the depicted individuals (Birmingham, Bischof, & Kingstone, 2008b; Smilek, Birmingham, Cameron, Bischof, & Kingstone, 2006).

Subjective reports confirm this impression and even provide additional insights. In addition to measuring eye movements, Smilek et al. (2006) asked their participants to verbally describe the viewed scene. Observers who were asked to infer where the depicted persons were attending were more likely to refer to the direction of gaze and body posture and, interestingly, to use contextual knowledge (e.g., "the basketball player is looking toward the net," even if the net was off-screen and therefore not a visible part of the scene), compared with observers who were simply asked to describe what they saw. These findings show that people's faces and eyes are used as the primary sources of information when making inferences about others' mental states, and that observers' attention is biased toward these socially significant regions rather than toward merely perceptually salient areas of natural scenes. These studies also suggest that observing naturally occurring behavior in settings that are less constrained than typical lab-based cognitive psychology studies, supplemented with subjective verbal descriptions, provides new and important insights into how people allocate their attention in the real world (Kingstone, Smilek, & Eastwood, 2008).

Summary

Studies of spatial attention have immensely benefited from the conceptual and methodological convergence with social cognition. These studies demonstrate that attention is not merely subject to cold sensory influences, such as perceptual salience, but is greatly influenced by social relevance, such as where someone else is directing their attention, and by other hot cognitions such as emotion. Importantly, these findings show that attention is not an isolated process that is encapsulated within the individual, but instead comprises highly dynamic and flexible mechanisms that can be distributed across individuals, affecting the way in which people encode their surroundings and interact with each other. In addition, the previous section has demonstrated how the study of attention benefits from being applied to social variables and sources of information. In the next section, we focus on sustained attention to illustrate how methodological advances and techniques borrowed from social psychology can inform our understanding of attention and related cognitive processes in real-life situations.

Sustained Attention in the Lab and in Life

In everyday life, attention is noticed most often when it fails. In some cases, attention failures are manifested as slips of action (see Reason, 1979; 1984; Reason & Lucas, 1984; Norman, 1981). For instance, a person might find himself putting a plastic lid on his porcelain coffee mug at the coffee shop or trying to unlock his office door with the fob that unlocks his car. Cases such as these were extensively documented by Reason (1979) in several diary studies. Following a detailed analysis and categorization of the reported slips of action, Reason (1979, p. 83) concluded that, "A large proportion of these slips appear to have resulted from the misdirection of focal attention." Reason also noted that the slips often occurred when the task at hand was easy and well learned and so the errors were not the result of cognitive overload or confusion when trying to complete complex novel tasks. Instead, the failures were likely due to peoples' inability to sustain their attention on a simple task over an extended period of time.

Of course, failures of sustained attention do not only lead to minor slips of action; they can also lead to serious accidents (see Reason 1979, 1988, for numerous examples). For instance, one of the worst mistakes a railroad engineer can make is to fail to stop at a red signal. A red signal often means that a train, sharing the same track, is coming from the opposite direction. Failing to stop sets the stage for a possible fatal collision. Obviously, no engineer wants to run a red signal. Yet each year there are cases in which engineers notice it too late and come screeching to a stop beyond the safe area, just barely avoiding a major accident. And this occurs despite the engineer seeing and calling into a radio a prior yellow signal indicating that a red signal is likely ahead. Analysis of some of these events reveals that the engineers had a lapse of attention, which led them to commit an attention-related memory error, namely forgetting they had just seen a yellow signal and that they were approaching a red signal (Jamieson & Smilek, 2010).

Although research on sustained attention has had a long history (see Broadbent, 1953), recently there has been a renewed interest in this aspect of attention. We have chosen to focus on recent developments in this area of attention research for three primary reasons. The first reason is that recent studies of sustained attention have successfully integrated many different methods, including (1) self-report diary studies (e.g., Reason, 1979), (2) analysis of accidents (e.g., Reason, 1988), (3) behavioral tasks in the laboratory (e.g., Robertson, Manly, Andrade, Baddeley, & Yiend, 1997), (4) self-report scales of everyday attention failures (e.g., Brown & Ryan, 2003; Cheyne, Carriere, & Smilek, 2006), (5) structural equation modeling (e.g., Carriere, Cheyne, & Smilek, 2007), (6) thought probe techniques (e.g., Giambra, 1995; Smallwood, Obonsawin, & Heim, 2003), (7) neuroimaging methods such as functional magnetic resonance imaging (e.g., Mason, Norton, Van Horn, Wegner, Grafton, & Macrae, 2007) and measuring event-related potentials (Smallwood, Beach, Schooler, & Handy, 2008), and (8) eye-monitoring techniques (e.g., Reichle, Reineberg, & Schooler, in press; Smilek, Carriere, & Cheyne, 2010). In doing so, these studies have made a concerted effort to bridge the existing gap between studies of attention in the laboratory using simple controlled tasks and studies of how sustained attention operates in everyday life. Second, we chose to focus on sustained attention because it is another area of attention research that is beginning to show strong links between attention and emotion. We begin by outlining how sustained attention is studied in the laboratory using computer-based tasks. We then review how self-report measures, which are perhaps not usually part of the core repertoire of attention researchers, can provide important insights about the relationship between cold attention processes and hot cognitions, including mood. Finally, we review studies on sustained attention and mind wandering that have benefited from directly converging these methodologies with neuroimaging techniques.

Behavioral Measures of Sustained Attention

One task that is increasingly being used to index sustained attention mechanisms is the Sustained Attention to Response Task (often referred to as the SART) developed by Robertson et al. (1997). In the SART, participants are shown a random sequence of digits (e.g., 1–9) on the computer screen. Each digit is shown on a computer monitor for roughly 250 milliseconds (ms), and then a visual mask is shown for about 900 ms. A sequence of several trials of the SART is shown in Figure 15.3. The participant's task is to press a response key on the keyboard every time a digit (e.g., a 2) appears, except for when a specified target digit (e.g., the digit 3) is shown; when the target appears, the participant is to withhold responding on that trial.

Sustained attention is indexed in this task by the frequency of commission errors on NOGO trials (when the target digit is presented), commonly referred to as *SART Errors.* Surprisingly, even though the task is very easy to perform, participants make a substantial number of SART Errors, in some cases incorrectly responding on roughly 40% to 50% of SART NOGO trials. In fact, people make many SART Errors precisely because the task is so easy to perform. Indeed, one of the key characteristics of the SART is that the repetition in responding places

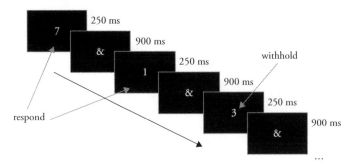

Figure 15.3 An example of a sequence of trials in the Sustained Attention to Response Task (SART; Robertson et al., 1997). Participants are required to respond by pressing a response key to each stimulus (i.e., each digit), except for a predetermined target stimulus (in this case the digit 3).

the participant into a relatively automatic mode of behavior (Robertson et al., 1997). As this happens, attention disengages, and participants have difficulty sustaining attention to the task at hand. Because controlled processing is required to withhold responding on the critical target item, and controlled processing requires focused attention, a commission error (SART Error) is likely to occur when attention is not available.

Based on a detailed assessment of performance on the SART, Cheyne, Solman, Carriere, and Smilek (2009) proposed that as sustained attention fails, an individual progresses through three states of inattention. In the first state, attention is mostly focused on the details of the task at hand but disengages from the immediate aspects of the task for brief moments. In the SART, this state is indexed by increased variability in the response times when pressing the key to nontarget items. In the second state of disengagement, attention is no longer on the detailed moment-to-moment aspects of the task at hand (e.g., the identity of the digit) but remains engaged with the general or global components of the task (e.g., pressing a key in rhythm to the rate of presentation of the digits). In the SART, the second state can be indexed by observing whether participants produce anticipatory responses to the digits (i.e., responses less than 100 ms following the onset of the presentation of the digit). The speed of these anticipatory responses suggests that the responses are not driven by the identity of the digits, but rather by the general cadence of the task. Finally, in the third state of disengagement, participants completely disconnect from even the general aspects of the task and might even cease to respond. In SART, this would be observed as a failure to respond to nontargets, which are essentially errors of omission. Importantly, Cheyne et al. (2009) found that the specific SART indices of the

three states (State 1: response time variability; State 2: frequency of anticipatory responses; and State 3: frequency of omissions) correlate with the frequency of SART Errors and account for unique variance in SART Error scores.

The SART has been employed quite widely as an index of sustained attention in various special groups of individuals. For example, individuals who have had a brain injury commit significantly more SART errors than matched control participants (Dockree, Kelly, Roche, Hogan, Reilly & Robertson, 2004; Robertson et al., 1997; see also Whyte, Grieb-Neff, Gantz, & Polansky, 2007). And, individuals with attention-deficit/hyperactivity disorder (ADHD) also commit more SART Errors and show greater variability in their response times on nontarget trials (*SART RT*) than control participants, suggesting that children with ADHD have problems with sustaining attention over successive trials and that their attention to the task waxes and wanes quite rapidly (Johnson, Kelly, Bellgrove, Cox, Gill, & Robertson, 2007; Johnson, Robertson, Kelly, Silk, Barry, Daibhis, et al., 2007).

Self-Report Measures of Sustained Attention

A critical assumption underlying the preceding studies of sustained attention is that the SART measures the likelihood that an individual will experience sustained attention failures in everyday life. To validate the SART, Robertson and colleagues (1997; see also Manly, Robertson, Galloway, & Hawkins, 1997) evaluated the association between SART performance and people's reports of cognitive failures in their everyday lives as measured by the Cognitive Failure Questionnaire (CFQ; Broadbent, Cooper, FitzGerald & Parks, 1982). The CFQ is a general measure of everyday slips of attention and action with items such as, "Do you read something and find you haven't been thinking about it and must read it again?" In several samples, Robertson and colleagues (1997; Manly, et al., 1999) showed a positive association between frequency of SART Errors and the CFQ scores. This relationship has been confirmed in a recent meta-analysis (see Smilek, Carriere, & Cheyne, 2010) of available studies assessing the association between SART Errors and CFQ scores, and a novel large sample, supporting the idea that the SART indexes, at least to some extent, everyday attention failures. However, Smilek et al. (2010) pointed out that the CFQ does not solely measure everyday sustained attention, but that it also measures a wide variety of cognitive failures (such as memory failure), which limits its utility as a tool for validating highly specific behavioral measures of sustained attention failure such as the SART.

To address the lack of a subjective report scale of attention failures, Cheyne et al. (2006) developed the Attention-Related Cognitive Errors Scale (ARCES). This scale was inspired by items included in the CFQ that assess attention failures, by the variety of attention failures reported by Reason (1979; 1984), and by the authors' own experiences. In addition to the ARCES, Cheyne et al. also included a scale used to assess absentmindedness or attention lapses developed by Brown and Ryan (2003) known as the Mindful Attention Awareness Scale (MAAS). In addition to these subjective report scales, Cheyne et al. had participants complete the SART assessing both SART Errors and SART RTs. Structural equation modeling supported the idea that the ARCES and SART Errors are related indices of attention-related *errors* and that the MAAS and SART RT are specific and related indices of attention *lapses*. The specificity shown by the measures is striking and goes a long way toward validating both the subjective report scales and SART measures. Taken together, the available evidence validates the SART as a measure of one's ability to sustain attention and, more importantly, reveals a close relationship between sustained attention failure and people's propensity to commit cognitive errors and behavioral lapses in everyday life. In addition, the findings show how subjective report measures can be used to buttress conclusions drawn from behavioral tasks conducted in the laboratory.

Sustained Attention and Mood

Further studies using the measures just discussed have revealed interesting links between attention lapses and affective dysfunction such as negative mood states (e.g., Smallwood, Obonsawin, Baracaia,

Reid, O'Connor, & Heim, 2003; Smallwood, Davies, Heim, Finnigan, Sudberry, et al., 2004), depression (Carriere, Cheyne & Smilek, 2008; Smallwood, O'Connor, Sudberry, & Obonsawin, 2007), and boredom (Carriere et al., 2008). For example, Carriere et al. (2008) evaluated the relationship between attention, memory, and the negative affective states of boredom and depression. The measures of attention included the MAAS (attention lapses) and the ARCES (attention-related errors). Memory failures were measured by the Memory Failures Scale (MFS). Finally, depression was measured using the Beck Depression Inventory (BDI–II—a registered trademark of Pearson Inc.), and boredom was measured using the Boredom Proneness Scale (BPS, Farmer & Sundberg, 1986). The relation among the measures was modeled using structural equation modeling. An assessment of several models revealed that the best fit of the data was a model in which attention and memory failures ultimately led to depression and boredom rather than the reverse. Thus, it appears that in the long run, one of the consequences of increased everyday attention lapses is affective dysfunction. This is likely because an individual with a propensity toward attention lapses fails to successfully connect with her environment, and this failure of engagement leads to prolonged experiences of negative mood.

Recent evidence also suggests that when people are in a negative mood, they are more likely to experience attention lapses (Smallwood, Fitzgerald, Miles, & Phillips, 2009). Taken together, studies of sustained attention and mood/emotion suggest that the relation between mood and attention is bidirectional. One way to combine the available findings is to suggest that in a given moment a person's mood state can influence his ability to sustain attention, yet over the long term, a person's trait tendency to experience failures of sustained attention can lead to prolonged negative moods.

Sustained Attention and Mind Wandering: Combining Behavioral, Self-Report, and Neuroimaging Methods

One of the reasons that people often fail to sustain their attention on a primary task is that their attention has shifted away from the primary task and has been applied to internal thoughts. Indeed, in his analysis of action slips, Reason (1979) alluded to the possibility that attention might shift to internal thoughts when individuals are performing automatic (open-loop) tasks. In recent investigations, moments when attention is shifted to internal thoughts have been referred to as episodes of *mind wandering* (see Smallwood & Schooler, 2006, for a review). In their thorough review of studies on mind wandering, Smallwood and Schooler (2006) highlight the fact that internal thoughts require attentional engagement, which affects the ability to keep attention focused on external tasks (see also Giambra, 1995). Thus, when a person's mind wanders, the person essentially enters into a dual task situation wherein her attention is divided between the task at hand and her internal thoughts (see Smallwood, Obonsawin, & Heim, 2003).

One line of research on mind wandering has been chiefly interested in the conditions that influence how often attention is shifted from an immediate task to internal thoughts (see Smallwood & Schooler, 2006, for a review). Giambra (1995) introduced the *probe method* for assessing frequency of task-unrelated thoughts (TUTs) during various sustained attention tasks. For instance, in one experiment, participants were required to detect targets (three red squares) in a sequence of distractor items (green circles). Giambra varied the attentional demands of the attention task by varying the speed with which items were presented and the probability with which a target was presented. At various intervals in the task, a tone (i.e., the probe) was presented signaling the participant to report whether they experienced any TUTs in the interval before the tone. The results showed that participants experienced more TUTs when the sustained attention task was less demanding.

Studies of mind wandering have also evaluated the immediate *consequences* of shifting attention from the task being performed and onto internal thoughts. Smallwood and colleagues (2004) showed that participants who experienced a lot of TUTs made more SART errors (responding to targets they were not supposed to respond to) when they were experiencing TUTs compared with when they were not experiencing TUTs. Thus, mind wandering has a direct effect on performance in sustained attention tasks. The results also showed that some of the internal thoughts were completely unrelated to the task at hand, whereas other internal thoughts concerned global aspects of the task, such as thoughts about how to improve performance. The fact that participants sometimes think about how they are performing the task might explain Cheyne et al.'s (2009) observation that in the SART, people are more likely to commit a SART error for targets that immediately follow a target on which they have just made an error. Committing an error likely leads to ruminations about task performance, which take

attention away from the immediate task, leading to a subsequent error.

These findings support the general idea that switching attention to internal thoughts leads to a reduction in the processing of external visual environment (see also Smallwood & Schooler, 2006). This general conclusion is also supported by studies measuring brain activity by monitoring event-related potentials (ERPs). Smallwood et al. (2008) have shown that when the mind wanders, brain areas responsible for processing stimuli viewed by the eyes are less active. In addition, studies using magnetic resonance imaging have shown that mind wandering leads to greater activity in a specific network known as the *default network*. This network is typically recruited when the brain is not directly focused on the primary task at hand (see Christoff, Gordon, Smallwood, Smith, & Schooler, 2009; Mason et al., 2007).

The foregoing conclusions dovetail nicely with prior research showing that awareness of an external stimulus is reduced when attention is directed away and not focused directly on the stimulus. Indeed, Merikle and Joordens (1997; see also Merikle, Smilek, & Eastwood, 2001) have suggested that diverting attention away from a stimulus has an impact on awareness similar to reducing the perceptual quality of the stimulus (e.g., reducing its luminance). Support for this view comes from studies reported by Mack and Rock (1998) showing that when attention is diverted away from an object, the object will go unnoticed even though it is presented in a location where the person is looking. Mack and Rock (1998) refer to this phenomenon as *inattentional blindness*. Inattentional blindness has also been demonstrated in a fascinating study reported by Simons and Charbis (1999). In this study, participants watched videos of people passing a basketball back and forth. The participants' task was to keep track of the number of times the ball was passed. In a critical condition, a harry gorilla (a person in a gorilla suit and not a real gorilla) passed through the scene, moving between the players. Strikingly, very few participants ever noticed that a gorilla had passed through the scene—a very salient example of inattentional blindness. Participants were attending to the ball and completely missed the gorilla. The close relation between attention and awareness has also been observed in studies of *change blindness*, which refers to the demonstration that individuals fail to become aware of a change across successive presentations of a photograph even though at times the change can be quite large (see Rensink, O'Regan, & Clark, 1997).

Summary

The rapidly growing area of sustained attention research has gone a long way toward making links between attention failures as measured in the lab and as they are reported to occur in everyday life. The research in this area also provides a good example of how a variety of methods are being used together to mutually buttress interpretations of findings and conclusions about attention. And, as with studies of spatial attention described above, research on sustained attention is revealing a strong link between attention and emotion (in this case, mood).

Future Directions

As the field of attention moves forward, we suggest several issues that could benefit from further research. First, studies of spatial attention imply that both simple stimulus features and socially meaningful aspects of objects influence the deployment of attention. However, there are some discrepancies in the emphasis of the role of features versus meaning between studies using the visual search paradigm and studies assessing eye movements during scene viewing. Whereas studies of visual search emphasize the primary role of low-level features (Wolfe & Horowitz, 2004), studies of scene viewing highlight the importance of observer knowledge and stimulus meaning (see Henderson, 2007). Future studies should focus on resolving this discrepancy.

Second, we note that, to date, attention has typically been thought of as a process that occurs in an individual's mind/brain. Future research should focus on what aspects of attention might be better conceptualized as a distributed process that is the property of the individual and the environment or that is distributed among two or more individuals (see Frischen et al., 2009; Hutchins, 1996).

Finally, although considerable progress has been made in the field of attention when it comes to bridging the gap between the laboratory and real life, there is still a long way to go before a satisfactory integration is achieved. We suggest that studies of attention should be concerned with not only controlling variables in the laboratory but also *observing* naturally occurring variability in the real world (see Kingstone, Smilek, & Eastwood, 2008).

Conclusion

Attention biases information processing in the brain and is involved in virtually every cognitive process. Not surprisingly, it comprises a vast array of mechanisms and phenomena that have been primarily the focus of cognitive psychology and related disciplines. However, conceptual and methodological aspects of social cognition are increasingly being incorporated into traditional cognitive psychology theories and experimental paradigms. These studies show that, in contrast to traditional views that have focused on cold cognitions such as sensory salience, attention is strongly and reciprocally influenced by social interactions and hot cognitions such as emotion. Furthermore, this new approach to studying attention reveals important insights into how attention operates in everyday life, which will ultimately help to prevent failures of attention and their often disastrous consequences. This strong and ever-expanding knowledge base provides a solid basis for future research with mutual benefits for the merging fields of cognitive neuroscience and social neuroscience.

References

Baron-Cohen, S., Campbell, R., Karmiloff-Smith, R., Grant, J., & Walker, J. (1995). Are children with autism blind to the mentalistic significance of the eyes? *British Journal of Developmental Psychology, 13*, 379–398.

Baron-Cohen, S., Cox, A., Baird, G., Swettenham, J., Nightingale, N., Morgan, K., Drew, A. & Charman, T. (1996). Psychological markers in the detection of autism in infancy in a large population. *British Journal of Psychiatry, 168*, 158–163.

Bayliss, A. P., di Pellegrino, G., & Tipper, S. P. (2004). Orienting of attention via observed eye gaze is head-centred. *Cognition, 94*, B1–B10.

Bayliss, A. P., & Tipper, S. P. (2006a). Gaze cues evoke both spatial and object-centred shifts of attention. *Perception & Psychophysics, 68*, 310–318.

Birmingham, E., Bischof, W. F., & Kingstone, A. (2008a). Social attention and real world scenes: The roles of action, competition, and social content. *Quarterly Journal of Experimental Psychology, 61*, 986–998.

Birmingham, E., Bischof, W. F., & Kingstone, A. (2008b). Gaze selection in complex social scenes. *Visual Cognition, 16*, 341–355.

Broadbent, D. E. (1953). Noise, paced performance and vigilance tasks. *British Journal of Psychology, 44*, 295–303.

Broadbent, D. E., Cooper, P. F., FitzGerald, P., & Parkes, K. R. (1982). The cognitive failures questionnaire (CFQ) and its correlates. *British Journal of Clinical Psychology, 21*, 1–16.

Bruce, N. D. B., & Tsotsos, J. K. (2009). Saliency, attention, and visual search: An information theoretic approach. *Journal of Vision, 9*, 1–24.

Burton, H., Abend, N. S., MacLeod, A. M. K., Sinclair, R. J., Snyder, A. Z., & Raichle, M. E. (1999). Tactile attention tasks enhance activation in somatorsensory regions of parietal cortex: A positron emission tomography study. *Cerebral Cortex, 9*, 662–674.

Calder, A. J., Lawrence, A. D., Keane, J., Scott, S. K., Owen, A. M., Christoffels, I., et al. (2002). Reading the mind from eye gaze. *Neuropsychologia, 40*, 1129–1138.

Carriere, J. S. A., Cheyne, J. A., & Smilek, D. (2008). Everyday attention lapses and memory failures: The affective consequences of mindlessness. *Consciousness and Cognition, 17*, 835–847.

Castelhano, M. S., Wieth, M. S., & Henderson, J. M. (2007). I see what you see: Eye movements in real-world scenes are affected by perceived direction of gaze. In L. Paletta & E. Rome (Eds.), *Attention in cognitive systems* (pp. 252–262). Berlin: Springer.

Cheyne, J. A., Carriere, J. S. A., & Smilek, D. (2006). Absent-mindedness: Lapses of conscious awareness and everyday cognitive failures. *Consciousness and Cognition, 15,* 578–592.

Cheyne, J. A., Solman, G. J. F., Carriere, J. S. A., & Smilek, D. (2009). Anatomy of an error: A bidirectional state model of task engagement/disengagement and attention-related errors. *Cognition, 111,* 98–113.

Christoff, K., Gordon, A. M., Smallwood, J., Smith, R., & Schooler, J. W. (2009) Experience sampling during fMRI reveals default network and executive system contributions to mind wandering. *Proceedings of the National Academy of Sciences USA, 106,* 8719–8724.

Coull, J. T., & Nobre, A. C. (1998). Where and when to pay attention: The neural systems for directing attention to spatial locations and to time intervals as revealed by both PET and fMRI. *Journal of Neuroscience, 15,* 7426–7435.

Deaner, R. O., Shepherd, S. V., & Platt, M. L. (2007). Familiarity accentuates gaze cueing in women but not men. *Biology Letters, 3,* 64–67.

Desimone, R., & Duncan, J. (1995). Neural mechanisms of selective visual attention. *Annual Review of Neuroscience, 18,* 193–222.

Di Pellegrino, G., Fadiga, L., Fogassi, L., Gallese, L., & Rizzolatti, G. (1992). Understanding motor events: A neurophysiological study. *Experimental Brain Research, 91,* 176–180.

Dockree, P. M., Kelly, S. P., Roche, R. A., Hogan, M. J., Reilly, R. B., & Robertson, I. H. (2004). Behavioral and physiological impairments of sustained attention after traumatic brain injury. *Brain Research Cognitive Brain Research, 20,* 403–414.

Dukewich, K., Klein, R. M., & Christie, J. (2008). The effect of gaze on gaze direction while looking at art. *Psychonomic Bulletin & Review, 15,* 1141–1147.

Eastwood, J. D., Smilek, D., & Merikle, P. M. (2001). Differential attentional guidance by unattended faces expressing positive and negative emotion. *Perception & Psychophysics, 63,* 1004–1013.

Egeth, H. E., & Yantis, S. (1997). Visual attention: Control, representation, and time course. *Annual Review of Psychology, 48,* 269–297.

Farmer, R., & Sundberg, N. D. (1986). Boredom proneness: The development and correlates of a new scale. *Journal of Personality Assessment, 50,* 4–17.

Farroni, T., Csibra, G., Simion, F., & Johnson, M. H. (2002). Eye contact detection in humans from birth. *Proceedings of the National Academy of Sciences, 99,* 9602–9605.

Farroni, T., Mansfield, E. M., Lai, C., & Johnson, M. H. (2003). Infants perceiving and acting on the eyes: Tests of an evolutionary hypothesis. *Journal of Experimental Child Psychology, 85,* 199–212.

Farroni, T., Massaccesi, S., Pividori, D., & Johnson, M. H. (2004). Gaze following in newborns. *Infancy, 5,* 39–60.

Fox, E., & Damjanovic, L. (2006). The eyes are sufficient to produce a threat-superiority effect. *Emotion, 6,* 534–539.

Fox, E., Mathews, A., Calder, A. J., & Yiend, J. (2007). Anxiety and sensitivity to gaze direction in emotionally expressive faces. *Emotion, 7,* 478–486.

Freire, A., Eskritt, M., & Lee, K. (2004). Are eyes windows to a deceiver's soul? Children's use of another's eye gaze cues in a deceptive situation. *Developmental Psychology, 40,* 1093–1104.

Friesen, C. K., & Kingstone, A. (1998). The eyes have it! Reflexive orienting is triggered by nonpredictive gaze. *Psychonomic Bulletin & Review, 5,* 490–495.

Friesen, C. K., Ristic, J., & Kingstone, A. (2004). Attentional effects of counterpredictive gaze and arrow cues. *Journal of Experimental Psychology: Human Perception & Performance, 30,* 319–329.

Frischen, A., Bayliss, A. P., & Tipper, S. P. (2007). Gaze cueing of attention: Visual attention, social cognition and individual differences. *Psychological Bulletin, 133,* 694–724.

Frischen, A., Loach, D., & Tipper, S. P. (2009). Seeing the world through another person's eyes: Simulating selective attention via action observation. *Cognition, 111,* 212–218.

Frischen, A., Smilek, D., Eastwood, J. D., & Tipper, S. P. (2007). Inhibition of return in response to gaze cues: Evaluating the roles of time course and fixation cue. *Visual Cognition, 15,* 881–895.

Frischen, A., & Tipper, S. P. (2004). Orienting attention via observed gaze shift evokes longer term inhibitory effects: Implications for social interactions, attention, and memory. *Journal of Experimental Psychology: General, 133,* 516–533.

Gerritsen, C., Frischen, A., Blake, A., Smilek, D., & Eastwood, J. D. (2008). Visual search is not blind to emotion. *Perception & Psychophysics, 70,* 1047–1059.

Giambra, L. M. (1995). A laboratory method for investigating influences on switching attention to task-unrelated imagery and thought. *Consciousness and Cognition, 4,* 1–21.

Grafton, S. T., Arbib, M. A., Fadiga, L., & Rizzolatti, G. (1996). Localisation of grasp representations in humans by positron emission tomography: 2. Observation compared with imagination. *Experimental Brain Research, 112,* 103–111.

Grison, S., & Strayer, D. L. (2001). Negative priming and perceptual fluency: More than what meets the eye. *Perception & Psychophysics, 63,* 1063–1071.

Grosbras, M. H., Laird, A. R., & Paus, T. (2005). Cortical regions involved in eye movements, shifts of attention and gaze perception. *Human Brain Mapping, 25,* 140–154.

Hahn, S., Carlson, C., Singer, S., & Gronlund, S. D. (2006). Aging and visual search: Automatic and controlled attentional bias to threat faces. *Acta Psychologica, 123,* 312–336.

Henderson, J. M. (2007). Regarding scenes. *Current Directions in Psychological Science, 16,* 219–222.

Hietanen, J. K. (1999). Does your gaze direction and head orientation shift my visual attention? *NeuroReport, 10,* 3443–3447.

Hoehl, S., Reid, V., Mooney, J., & Striano, T. (2008). What are you looking at? Infants' neural processing of adult's object-directed gaze. *Developmental Science, 11,* 10–16.

Holmes, A., Richards, A., & Green, S. (2006). Anxiety and sensitivity to eye gaze in emotional faces. *Brain & Cognition, 60,* 282–294.

Hood, B. M., Willen, J. D., & Driver, J. (1998). Adult's eyes trigger shifts of visual attention in human infants. *Psychological Science, 9,* 131–134.

Houghton, G., & Tipper, S. P. (1994). A model of inhibitory mechanisms in selective attention. In D. Dagenbach & T. H. Carr (Eds.), *Inhibitory processes in attention, memory, and language.* San Diego, CA: Academic Press.

Hutchins, E. (1996). *Cognition in the wild*. Cambridge, MA: MIT Press.

Jamieson, R., & Smilek, D. (2010). Root cause analysis investigation of major rule violations: Metrolink Commuter rail operations 2005–2010. Technical Report for Veolia Transportation Inc.

Johnson, K. A., Kelly, S. P., Bellgrove, M. A., Barry, E., Cox, M., Gill, M., et al. (2007). Response variability in attention deficit hyperactivity disorder: Evidence for neuropsychological heterogeneity. *Neuropsychologia, 45*, 630–638.

Johnson, K. A., Robertson, I. H., Kelly, S. P., Silk, T. J., Barry, E., Dáibhis, A., et al (2007). Dissociation of performance of children with ADHD and high-functioning autism on a task of sustained attention. *Neuropsychologia, 45*, 2234–2245.

Kastner, S., & Ungerleider, L. G. (2000). Mechanisms of visual attention in the human cortex. *Annual Review of Neuroscience, 23*, 315–341.

Kingstone, A., Smilek, D., & Eastwood, J. D. (2008). Cognitive ethology: A new approach for studying human cognition. *British Journal of Psychology, 99*, 317–340.

Klein, R. (1988). Inhibitory tagging system facilitates visual search. *Nature, 334*, 430–431.

Klein, R. M., & MacInnes, W. J. (1999). Inhibition of return is a foraging facilitator in visual search. *Psychological Science, 10*, 346–352.

Kuhn, G., & Kingstone, A. (2009). Look away! Eyes and arrows engage oculomotor responses automatically. *Attention, Perception, & Psychophysics, 71*, 314–327.

Leekam, S. R., López, B., & Moore, C. (2000). Attention and joint attention in preschool children with autism. *Developmental Psychology, 36*, 261–273.

Loach, D., Frischen, A., Bruce, N., & Tsotsos, J. K. (2008). An attentional mechanism for selecting appropriate actions afforded by graspable objects. *Psychological Science, 19*, 1253–1257.

Loach, D., & Marí-Beffa, P. (2003). Post-target inhibition: A temporal binding mechanism. *Visual Cognition, 10*, 513–526.

Luck, S. J., & Vogel, E. K. (1997). The capacity of visual working memory for features and conjunctions. *Nature, 390*, 279–81.

Mack, A., & Rock, I. (1998). *Inattentional blindness*. Cambridge, MA: MIT Press.

Manly, T., Robertson, I. H., Galloway, M., & Hawkins, K. (1999). The absent mind: Further investigations of sustained attention to response. *Neuropsychologia, 37*, 661–670.

Mansfield, E. M., Farroni, T., & Johnson, M. H. (2003). Does gaze perception facilitate overt orienting? *Visual Cognition, 10*, 7–14.

Mason, M. F., Norton, M. I., Van Horn, J. D., Wegner, D. M., Grafton, S. T., & Macrae, C. N. (2007). Wandering minds: The default network and stimulus-independent thought. *Science, 315*, 393–395.

Mathews, A., Fox, E., Yiend, J., & Calder, A. (2003). The face of fear: Effects of eye gaze and emotion on visual attention. *Visual Cognition, 10*, 823–835.

Merikle, P. M., & Joordens, S. (1997). Parallels between perception without attention and perception without awareness. *Consciousness and Cognition, 6*, 219–236.

Merikle, P. M., Smilek, D., & Eastwood, J. D. (2001). Perception without awareness: Perspectives from cognitive psychology. *Cognition, 79*, 115–134.

Milliken, B., Tipper, S. P., & Weaver, B. (1994). Negative priming in a spatial localization task: Feature mismatching and distractor inhibition. *Journal of Experimental Psychology: Human Perception & Performance, 20*, 624–646.

Motter, B. C. (1993). Focal attention produces spatially selective processing in visual cortical areas V1, V2, and V4 in the presence of competing stimuli. *Journal of Neurophysiology, 70*, 909–919.

Neumann, E., & DeSchepper, B. G. (1991). Costs and benefits of target activation and distractor inhibition in selective attention. *Journal of Experimental Psychology: Learning, Memory, and Cognition, 17*, 1136–1145.

Norman, D. A. (1981). Categorization of action slips. *Psychological Review, 88*, 1–15.

Palermo, R., & Rhodes, G. (2007). Are you always on my mind? A review of how face perception and attention interact. *Neuropsychologia, 45*, 75–92.

Pelphrey, K. A., Singerman, J. D., Allison, T., & McCarthy, G. (2003). Brain activation evoked by perception of gaze shifts: The influence of context. *Neuropsychologia, 41*, 156–170.

Pierno, A. C., Mari, M., Glover, S., Georgiou, I., & Castiello, U. (2006). Failure to read motor intentions from gaze in children with autism. *Neuropsychologia, 44*, 1483–1488.

Posner, M. I. (1980). Orienting of attention. *Quarterly Journal of Experimental Psychology, 32*, 3–25.

Posner, M. I., & Cohen, Y. A. (1984). Components of visual orienting. In H. Bouma & D. G. Bouwhuis (Eds.), *Attention and performance X* (pp. 531–556). Hillsdale, NJ: Erlbaum.

Pratt, J., & Hommel, B. (2003). Symbolic control of visual attention: The role of working memory and attentional control settings. *Journal of Experimental Psychology: Human Perception & Performance, 29*, 835–845.

Reason, J. T. (1979). Actions not as planned: The price of automatization. In G. Underwood & R. Stevens (Eds.), *Aspects of consciousness* (pp. 67–89). London: Academic Press.

Reason, J. T. (1984). Lapses of attention in everyday life. In R. Parasuraman & D. R. Davies (Eds.), *Varieties of attention*. New York: Academic Press.

Reason, J. T. (1988). Modelling the basic error tendencies of human operators. *Reliability Engineering & System Safety, 22*, 137–153.

Reason, J. T., & Lucas, D. (1984). Absent-mindedness in shops: Its incidence, correlates and consequences. *British Journal of Clinical Psychology, 23*, 121–131.

Reichle, E. D., Reineberg, A. E., & Schooler, J. W. (2010). Eye movements during mindless reading. *Psychological Science, 21*(9), 1300–1310.

Remington, R. W., Johnston, J. C., & Yantis, S. (1992). Involuntary attentional capture by abrupt onsets. *Perception & Psychophysics, 51*, 279–290.

Rensink, R. A., O'Regan, J. K., & Clark, J. J. (1997). To see or not to see: The need for attention to perceive changes in scenes. *Psychological Science, 8*, 368–373.

Reynolds, M. G., Eastwood, J. D., Partanen, M., Frischen, A., & Smilek, D. (2009). Monitoring eye movements while searching for affective faces. *Visual Cognition, 17*, 318–333.

Ricciardelli, P., Bricolo, E., Aglioti, S. M., & Chelazzi, L. (2002). My eyes want to look where your eyes are looking: Exploring the tendency to imitate another individual's gaze. *NeuroReport, 13*, 2259–2264.

Richardson, D. C., & Spivey, M. J. (2000). Representation, space and Hollywood Squares: Looking at things that aren't there anymore. *Cognition, 76*, 269–295.

Ristic, J., Friesen, C. K., & Kingstone, A. (2002). Are eyes special? It depends on how you look at it. *Psychonomic Bulletin & Review, 9*, 507–513.

Ristic, J., & Kingstone, A. (2005). Taking control of reflexive social attention. *Cognition, 94,* B55–B65.

Robertson, I. H., Manly, T., Andrade, J., Baddeley, B. T., & Yiend, J. (1997). 'Oops!': Performance correlates of everyday attentional failures in traumatic brain injured and normal subjects. *Neuropsychologia, 35,* 747–758.

Senju, A., Tojo, Y., Dairoku, H., & Hasegawa, T. (2004). Reflexive orienting in response to eye gaze and an arrow in children with and without autism. *Journal of Child Psychology and Psychiatry, 45,* 445–458.

Shepherd, S. V. (2010). Following gaze: Gaze-following behavior as a window into social cognition. *Frontiers in Integrative Neuroscience, 4.* Published online 19 March 2010. doi: 10.3389/fnint.2010.00005.

Shepherd, S. V., Klein, J. T., Deaner, R. O., & Platt, M. L. (2009). Mirroring of attention by neurons in macaque parietal cortex. *Proceedings of the National Academy of Sciences USA, 106,* 9489–9494.

Simons, D. J., & Charbis, C. F. (1999). Gorillas in our midst: Sustained inattentional blindness for dynamic events. *Perception, 28,* 1059–1074.

Smallwood, J., Beach, E., Schooler, J. W., & Handy, T. C. (2008). Going AWOL in the brain: Mind wandering reduces cortical analysis of external events. *Journal of Cognitive Neuroscience, 20,* 458–469.

Smallwood, J., Davies, J. B., Heim, D., Finnigan, F., Sudberry, M., O'Connor, R., & Obonsawin, M. (2004). Subjective experience and the attentional lapse: Task engagement and disengagement during sustained attention. *Consciousness and Cognition, 13,* 657–690.

Smallwood, J., Fitzgerald, A., Miles, L. K., Phillips, L. H. (2009). Shifting moods, wandering minds: Negative moods lead the mind to wander. *Emotion, 9,* 271–276.

Smallwood, J., Obonsawin, M. C., Baracaia, S. F., Reid, H., O'Connor, R., & Heim, D. (2003). The relationship between rumination, dysphoria, and self-referent thinking: Some preliminary findings. *Imagination, Cognition, and Personality, 22,* 317–342.

Smallwood, J., Obonsawin, M. C., & Heim, S. D. (2003). Task-unrelated thought: The role of distributed processing. *Consciousness and Cognition, 12,* 169–189.

Smallwood, J. M., O'Connor, R. C., Sudberry, M. V., & Obosawin, M. (2007). Mind-wandering and dysphoria. *Cognition and Emotion, 21,* 816–842.

Smallwood, J. M., & Schooler, J. W. (2006). The restless mind. *Psychological Bulletin, 132,* 946–958.

Smilek, D., Birmingham, E., Cameron, D., Bischof, W. F., & Kingstone, A. (2006). Cognitive ethology and exploring attention in real world scenes. *Brain Research, 1080,* 101–119.

Smilek, D., Carriere, J. S. A., & Cheyne, J. A. (2010). Failures of sustained attention in life, lab, and brain: Ecological validity of the SART. *Neuropsychologia, 48,* 2564–2570.

Smilek, D., Frischen, A., Reynolds, M. G., Gerritsen, C., & Eastwood, J. D. (2007). What influences visual search efficiency? Disentangling contributions of preattentive and post-attentive processes. *Perception & Psychophysics, 69,* 1105–1116.

Spence, C. J., & Driver, J. (1994). Covert spatial orienting in audition: Exogenous and endogenous mechanisms. *Journal of Experimental Psychology: Human Perception & Performance, 20,* 555–574.

Suslow, T., Junghanns, K., & Arolt, V. (2001). Detection of facial expressions of emotions in depression. *Perceptual and Motor Skills, 92,* 857–868.

Tipper, S. P., & Driver, J. (1988). Negative priming between pictures and words in a selective attention task: Evidence for semantic processing of ignored stimuli. *Memory and Cognition, 16,* 64–70.

Tipper, S. P., Meegan, D., & Howard, L. A. (2002). Action-centred negative priming: Evidence for reactive inhibition. *Visual Cognition, 9,* 591–684.

Tipples, J. (2006). Fear and fearfulness potentiate automatic orienting to eye gaze. *Cognition & Emotion, 20,* 309–320.

Tipples, J., Atkinson, A. P., & Young, A. W. (2002). The eyebrow frown: A salient social signal. *Emotion, 2,* 288–296.

Treisman, A., & Gelade, G. (1980). A feature integration theory of attention. *Cognitive Psychology, 12,* 97–136.

Tsotsos, J. K., Culhane, S., Wai, W., Lai, Y., Davis, N., & Nuflo, F. (1995). Modeling visual attention via selective tuning. *Artificial Intelligence, 78,* 507–545.

Whyte, J., Grieb-Neff, P., Gantz, C., & Polansky, M. (2007). Measuring sustained attention after brain injury: Differences in key findings from the sustained attention to response task (SART). *Neuropsychologia, 44,* 2007–2014.

Wolfe, J. M. (2003). Moving towards solutions to some enduring controversies in visual search. *Trends in Cognitive Sciences, 7,* 70–76.

Wolfe, J. M., & Horowitz, T. S. (2004). What attributes guide the deployment of visual attention and how do they do it? *Nature Reviews Neuroscience, 5,* 1–7.

Zelano, C., Bensafi, M., Porter, J., Mainland, J., Johnson, B., Bremner, E., Telles, C., Khan, R., & Sobel, N. (2005). Attentional modulation in human primary olfactory cortex. *Nature Neuroscience, 8,* 114–120.

Zwickel, J., & Vö, M. L.-H. (2010). How the presence of persons biases eye movements. *Psychonomic Bulletin & Review, 17,* 257–262.

On Misers, Managers, and Monsters: The Social Cognition of Visual Perception

Emily Balcetis *and* Shana Cole

Abstract

Perceptual experience is not simply the product of qualities of actual objects, the environment, or information present. It is also the product of perceivers' characteristics. This chapter uses two classic metaphors originally proposed within models of cognitive information processing and proposes a new one to describe ways that people process visual information. The authors suggest that people act as *perceptual misers*, using perceptual shortcuts to reduce the amount of visual information to be processed. People act as *perceptual monsters*, allowing chronic knowledge structures to bias visual perception in ways that may have deleterious outcomes for themselves and others. And people act as *perceptual managers*, perceiving the world in ways that assist in the pursuit of active goals. The chapter synthesizes an emerging body of research and suggests that the miser, monster, and manager shape not only the ways people think about the world but also what they literally see in the world.

Key Words: visual perception, information processing, goals

During the 2010 FIFA World Cup, the United States' soccer team battled Slovenia's to advance in the tournament. The game was tied at 2–2 in the 85th minute. Then, an American player, Maurice Edu, took a shot on goal. It went in. However, the referee did not award the point. Instead, he called a foul that he claimed to have seen just before the shot. Of course, what the referee saw was contested. Some commentators saw what the referee saw; they claimed that shoving in the box, an offense that could have stopped the game before the shot occurred, came from both teams. Other commentators saw something different; they claimed the video footage actually depicted only Slovenian aggression and thus did not warrant the stoppage of play. The goal was disallowed, and the United States was forced to settle for a draw against Slovenia. In the end, the referee's call decided the game and started a controversy. How could so many people watching the exact same footage see such different behaviors and come to such very different conclusions?

This example illustrates a common occurrence. The way someone sees and understands an event can be discrepant from the way another person sees the same event. People's perceptual experiences of the same instance, object, or information can be quite different. Situations like these may be puzzling because discrepancies in perceptual experience contradict people's lay conception of how the mind works. People believe that they experience the world in a way that maps precisely and accurately onto reality. However, anecdotes, research, and situations like the one that opens this chapter undermine the assumption that what people see is an exact replica of the world around them.

There may be two primary reasons why perceptual representations fail to accurately and completely correspond to reality. First, perceptual processing resources are limited. In the above example, the referee and Slovenian fans saw a foul when American soccer fans did not. The environment presents the visual system with a wealth of ambiguous information that must be quickly and efficiently managed, but the resources available to do so are limited. Indeed, the referee experienced a rich visual scene—players in brightly colored jerseys whizzing by, entangled arms and legs fighting for the upper hand, the checkered ball bouncing along the green grass, and thousands of fans cheering and jeering from the stands. Although people might benefit from accurate perceptual experiences, rarely does this or can this occur.

The outside world is complex, and the capabilities of perceptual systems are relatively limited. In fact, foveal view, where visual experiences are most precise, comprises only 1 or 2 degrees of the field of view—roughly twice the width of the thumbnail on an outstretched arm (Rock, 1975). Because focused attention must be directed, some information may never be perceived. Evidence confirms this. In a flight simulator, seasoned pilots certified to fly Boeing model 727 aircrafts made decisions about whether to land a plane. When attention was divided, two out of four pilots failed to notice an obstruction—a large jet sitting diagonally across the simulated runway—and decided to land the simulated plane. When asked about his incorrect choice, one pilot proclaimed, "I honestly did not see anything on that runway" (Fischer, Haines, & Price, 1980).

Likewise, even when attention is fixed on a single scene under optimal viewing conditions, some perceivers fail to register information that might seem plainly obvious to others. For example, when engaged in a face-to-face discussion, approximately 50% of people did not notice that the person with whom they were speaking was replaced by another person midway through the conversation (Levin, Simons, Angelone, & Chabris, 2002). The limited resources of the visual system impair processing when perceivers attend to and manage the barrage of visual information that environments offer.

A second problem that the visual system faces is that much of the information to which it is exposed can be interpreted in multiple ways. As a result, what perceivers "see," or the percept they come to consciously experience, is subjective. Perceptual experience is a product not simply of the qualities of the actual object present but also of characteristics of the perceiver that shape interpretations of the ambiguity. Although they were exposed to the same visual information, the referee and Slovenian supporters saw the pushing and shoving in the box

as a foul, whereas American supporters did not. Perceivers' processing styles, current cognitions, motivations, moods, and expectations influence interpretation of visual ambiguity.

When the visual system is exposed to a complex and ambiguous visual scene, it selects and interprets visual information in line with internal states of the perceiver. In this chapter, we expand on the perceptual dilemma. We explore how characteristics of perceivers influence visual processing in light of and in the service of addressing the complications faced by perceptual systems. We suggest that at different times and under varying situations, the ways people process, extract, and manipulate perceptual information can take on several qualities.

The qualities or processing styles that emerge as people engage with their environment can be described with metaphors—metaphors that find their origins within classic models of cognitive information processing. Specifically, the varied ways in which people make judgments have been described using the labels of the *cognitive miser* (Fiske & Taylor, 1984), *cognitive monster* (Bargh, 1999), and *cognitive manager* (see Bargh & Morsella, 2010, for related theory of the unconscious behavioral guidance system). These processing styles have been systematically and extensively documented within judgment and decision making, person perception, and other cognitive tasks. We have adopted these metaphors in the service of explaining how people solve the perceptual dilemma. Specifically, when people engage with their environment, they might assume processing styles that can be labeled as the *perceptual* miser, *perceptual* monster, and *perceptual* manager, and these provide a framework for understanding how and why visual perception is biased.

First, people cope with the barrage of complex information presented to their senses by processing information in ways similar to *perceptual misers*. People use perceptual shortcuts, like filtered perceiving, to reduce the amount of visual information that needs to be processed. Because capacity limitations are universal, the processing style of the perceptual miser is common among all human beings.

Second, perceivers process visual information as *perceptual monsters*. Perceivers' stable, chronic, and global knowledge structures bias visual perception. Consequently, biases caused by the perceptual monster should be more characteristic of some individuals than others. This style of processing disproportionately weights the activation of negative compared to positive knowledge structures. As a result, this phenomenon is documented most often when the outcomes are negative, when people perceive their worlds in ways that may be damaging to themselves and to others. We refer to the style of processing whereby chronic aspects of perceivers bias perception, the outcomes of which tend to be disproportionately negative, as the perceptual monster.

Finally, perceivers process visual information as *perceptual managers*. People perceive the world in ways that help them accomplish their temporarily accessible and short-term goals. That is, active motivations guide and shape visual experiences. Reciprocally, perception can actually be a tool used in the service of goal pursuit. By perceiving the world in systematically biased ways, people may be more likely to meet their goals. Therefore, we refer to the processing style whereby individuals' frequently changing needs, motives, and goals bias perception as the perceptual manager.

Because the perceptual miser, monster, and manager describe processing styles, or ways in which the visual system manipulates perceptual information, they need not be considered mutually exclusive. That is, qualities of these processing styles can occur simultaneously, or they may occur sequentially. Aspects of the situation, the person, or the information at hand may lead to one style of processing. However, the processing style can flexibly shift as the demands of the situation or qualities of the perceiver change.

We build these metaphorical *perceptual misers, monsters,* and *managers* in reference to their cognitive counterparts, which have been well documented in the social cognition and information processing literature. We synthesize an emerging body of research and suggest that the miser, monster, and manager shape not only the way people think about the world in which they live but also what people literally see in that world.

What Is Perception?

Before we describe how perception is biased, we must first define what perception is. Perception is a construct separate from sensation. Sensation reflects the stimulation that falls upon sensory organs that then absorb and convert the signal. But it is difficult to capture and measure a moment of pure sensation. In fact, William James (1890) argued that sensation "is an abstraction never realized" (p. 76). The difficulty, if not impossibility, of isolating and measuring a raw sensation occurs because nearly simultaneously as sensory systems register incoming information, the process of perception begins. Sensations quickly, but not quite immediately, arouse related thoughts, feelings, and previous experiences. This activated information helps to transpose sensations into perceptual experience, to go beyond the literal information extracted from the environment. Wittgenstein noted that, "what [perceivers] really see must surely be what is produced in [them] by the influence of the object" (p. 199). Whereas sensation is a process of gathering visual stimulation from the environment, perception is the process of combining sensations and concurrently activated cognitions. As a result, "what is said to be perceived is in fact inferred" (Bartlett, 1932, p. 33).

Because perception is the product of both sensory input and activated cognitions, perception is subjective. Qualities of the perceiver determine attention and perceptual experience. As a result, it is fair to say that perception is not the study of objective reality (Rock, 1975). Perception is a constructed process composed of the phenomenological experiences that perceivers come to have, ones that are influenced by the perceivers themselves.

This chapter documents how a perceiver influences the perceived. Just as theories of social cognition have detailed ways that the social perceiver processes information and have explored how the perceiver comes to "see" (or rather judge) others, we document in this chapter three different styles used flexibly by the visual perceiver when attending to and perceiving the surrounding world. We document how these visual processing styles lead to very different understandings of the outside world.

In so doing, this chapter discusses the influence of perceivers' qualities on multiple tasks that are involved in forming perceptual representations. Perceptual tasks can be plotted on a continuum demarcating efficiency, automaticity, and depth of processing. One end of the continuum might be the very first tasks the visual system must take on—the earliest responses to the perceptual details to which people are exposed and that visual systems process. The other end might be effortful perceptual conclusions regarding this input; although still not quite conscious cognitive judgments, they do require a great deal of processing. Plotted on this continuum between these endpoints are other tasks like directed attention, meaning extraction, and object identification. These tasks implicate early perceptual processes, but they may not avoid all possible contributions of conscious judgment. Thus, although we discuss the effects of processing styles on visual perception and the ways in which people come to extract input from their surroundings, we also discuss other tasks the perceptual system must take on that, to some, may appear to conflate perceptual and cognitive processes.

One task that seems to combine aspects of early automatic perceptual processes and later more deliberate processes is directed attention. Perceivers must extract perceptual input from environments, and one way this occurs is through directed attention. Attention is the process of discriminating between what is important and what is irrelevant. William James noted that attention, "is the taking possession of the mind, in clear and vivid form, of one out of what seem several simultaneously possible objects " (1890, p. 403). This process of determining importance and directing attention may happen very early in the perceptual process without perceivers' awareness, or may occur later in the process in a more effortful way. Although attention is a phenomenon that is conceptually distinct from perception, attention does play an important role because it often underlies perceptual experience. In other words, perceptions may ultimately come to be biased because attention is biased or is oriented in a specific manner. Thus, in this chapter, we discuss effects on perception but also include examples of effects on attention, given the important role attention plays in the perceptual process.

A New Look at the New Look

Asking how and why perception is biased is reminiscent of the New Look perspective (Bruner & Minturn, 1955). The New Look, which peaked in the late 1950s, is among the most dedicated historical eras of psychology that examined these issues. New Look researchers proposed a constructivist approach to perception whereby characteristics of the perceiver and complex yet unconscious processes interact with visual input. They denounced what seemed to be an overemphasis on the objective stimulus and the passive perceiver in the predominantly behaviorist psychological climate at the time. Bruner and Goodman (1947) wrote, "Throughout the history of modern psychology, until very recent times, perception has been treated as though the perceiver were a passive recording instrument of rather complex design....One might, in most experiments, describe him in much the same graphical terms as one uses to describe the latest piece of recording apparatus" (p. 33). They argued instead for the importance of studying how perceivers actively construct and interpret the world around them and not just how they respond to stimuli in their environment. The New Look resolved to demonstrate that perceptual experience was subject to other concurrent processes. Their goal was "to rid psychology of the *pure percept*" (Bruner, 1992).

Although the New Look perspective was met with much enthusiasm, inspiring nearly 300 experiments in the decade after its inception, withering critiques quickly followed (Eriksen, 1958; Eriksen & Browne, 1956; Goldiamond, 1958; Prentice, 1958; Wohlwill, 1966). Reactionaries argued that the effects described as perceptual in nature were actually the result of poor methodological techniques that were not able to rule out effects of judgment. For example, the phenomena of perceptual vigilance and defense were difficult to disentangle from biased response selection and conscious reporting issues (Erdelyi, 1974, 1985). That is, original paradigms could not distinguish between whether participants failed to actually see words like "sex" as quickly as less taboo words, or whether participants simply were reticent to report what they saw when presented with salacious words. Additionally, aspects of the stimuli themselves were confounded with motivational strength (Adkins, 1956; Howes & Solomon, 1950; McCurdy, 1956). For instance, original paradigms could not disentangle motivationally relevant words from those that were simply more familiar or more positive.

These critiques, confounds, and problems certainly corroborated the view of a historical counter-perspective that did not agree that perception could be influenced by aspects of the perceiver. Indeed, some theorists and researchers assert that perception is entirely objective. They refuse to consider mediating, internal constructs and processes in explaining perception and human behavior more generally (Skinner, 1938, 1953, 1971). Such objectivists do not believe that perception can be influenced by sources of input external to the stimuli. They instead argue that perceptual processing is encapsulated. Central to their argument is the belief that higher order constraints influence, not basic perception, or early vision as they call it, but rather later stages of the perceptual process (see Fodor, 1983; Pylyshyn, 1999).

To support this dual stage model of visual perception, objectivists reference certain phenomena that seem immune to external influence. Some visual phenomena are particularly tricky to influence with situational features or aspects of the perceiver. For example, under most circumstances, people have difficulty realizing that the parallel lines marked by different end caps, depicted in the Müller-Lyer illusion, are actually identical in length (Delboeuf, 1893). Even after explicitly being told that they are identical, people still have the perceptual experience that they are not. Theorists who argue for the encapsulated nature of perception refer to the rigidity and persistence of this illusion as evidence for the fact that external influences only affect judgment but not actual perception (but see McCauley & Henrich, 2006, for a full discussion of this issue and illusion).

Although disciples of the New Look and objectivists disagree about whether perception itself can be influenced by states of the perceiver, much of what the original New Look theorists proposed continues to inform contemporary cognitive and perceptual psychology in fundamental ways. For example, contemporary psychologists uniformly agree with the New Look tenet that much of cognition happens outside of a person's awareness, monitoring, or control (Greenwald, 1992; Wegner & Bargh, 1998). It is now accepted that identification, recognition, and categorization are directed by perceivers' current and previous visual experiences (Biederman, Mezzanotte, & Rabinowitz, 1982; Boyce & Pollatsek, 1992; Li & Warren, 2004; Long & Toppino, 2004). The conscious representation people form of the world omits a good deal of information that the environment actually contains (Allport, 1989). The research described in this chapter is a testament to the lasting influence and interest in the New Look perspective.

The Perceptual Miser

Reportedly, former Broncos quarterback John Elway used to travel incognito around Denver by wearing his own jersey. He claims, "I go to the mall that way. They know it's not me because they say there's no way Elway would be wearing his own jersey in the mall. So it actually is the safest thing to do" (Patrick, 2010).

Given prevailing social norms for dress and customs for some semblance of modesty, few people would assume that the person walking past them would be wearing a shirt that clearly announces his celebrity. It is a safe and generally accurate heuristic, or mental shortcut, to assume that people wearing sports-like attire on which are emblazoned names are actually not the characters associated with those names. People use cognitive shortcuts like these to make judgments about people and information around them. These shortcuts, or heuristics, help balance the wealth of information that cognitive systems must process against the limited resources that are available to do so. When information processing needs are high but processing resources are limited, the "cognitive miser" calls on simple shortcuts to increase efficiency in information processing (Fiske & Taylor, 1984). People use categories based on prior information—including schemas, scripts, and other knowledge structures—to expedite processing. In so doing, people tend to produce judgments about new information that do not stray far from established beliefs (Fiske & Taylor, 1984). This style of processing has historically been described as the cognitive miser.

People tend to handle visual information like a miser as well. When temporary processing demands are high and resources relatively low, perceivers expedite visual information processing by using shortcuts and heuristics. When processing input as a perceptual miser, people expend the minimum amount of resources required to arrive at a perceptual conclusion. When processing needs are high, people use activated categories to assist in forming perceptual conclusions quickly and efficiently.

To summarize, cognitive information processing uses activated categories to make the process of reaching discrete social judgments more efficient (Allport, 1954; Bodenhausen & Macrae, 1998; Brewer, 1988; Bruner, 1957; Fiske, 1998; Fiske, Lin, & Neuberg, 1999). We reference this information processing style in analogically suggesting that people process visual information like a perceptual miser. Activated categories help increase the efficiency with which a perceiver reaches discrete conclusions. In this section, we discuss phenomena that suggest people at times and under certain circumstances process visual information in ways akin to a perceptual miser.

Perceptual and Conceptual Filters

When processing information like a perceptual miser, people use heuristics or perceptual shortcuts. In this section, we focus on one particularly prominent perceptual shortcut that allows perceivers to cope with the multitude of information the system receives: filters. Filters act as categories, which sort visual input in order to expedite the process of reaching perceptual conclusions. Filters come in two varieties: perceptual and conceptual. Perceptual filters activate categories related to the details, aspects, or qualities of the stimuli themselves like luminance, color, or shape. Perceptual filters sift visual input in accordance with these low-level perceptual details. Conceptual filters activate categories related to the semantic overlap, categorical similarity, or meaning related to the input, including superordinate group membership or class. Conceptual filters sift visual input in accordance with high-level conceptual, cognitive information. Although their activated categories differ in content, both perceptual and conceptual filters reduce the ambiguity of the visual stimulus so that the perceiver experiences seeing one discrete, categorical percept, by eliminating information that suggests another percept.

PERCEPTUAL FILTERS

Previously seen images or objects can activate perceptual filters that bias visual experience in general, and object identification in particular (for a discussion, see Balcetis & Dale, 2007). For example, previous exposure to category exemplars, like specific animals, activates a number of physical local features associated with each category. Previous visual exposure can increase the salience of these low-level features, thereby activating a filter based on these stimulus features. The contents of these activated perceptual filters subsequently bias identification of ambiguous input. For example, participants in experiments who just viewed pictures of animals were more likely to categorize an ambiguous drawing that can be interpreted in multiple ways as a rat rather than the alternative, a man's face. However, those who previously viewed pictures of human faces categorized it as the face of a man (Bugelski & Alampay, 1961; Crandall & de Lissovoy, 1977).

Expectations that are established through co-occurrence can also establish perceptual filters that bias object identification. For example, visual information that co-occurs in a visual scene can establish expectations that serve as filters (Bar, 2004; Biederman, Mezzanotte, & Rabinowitz, 1982; Boyce & Pollatsek, 1992). Because perceivers learn the relative co-occurrence of objects in contexts or situations, perceiving the context activates expectations for corresponding visual information. These expectations help the visual system to identify components of the scene more easily and more efficiently (Bar, 2004). For example, hairstyles can establish expectations for what the rest of a face should look like. Participants in one experiment saw stereotypically black or white hairstyles atop racially ambiguous faces. Faces with black hairstyles were rated as having more black facial features than the same faces paired with white hairstyles (MacLin & Malpass, 2001). Perceptual features and their relative co-occurrence can establish perceptual filters that shape identification of subsequently or concurrently presented ambiguous visual information.

CONCEPTUAL FILTERS

The second type of filter is a *conceptual filter*. Unlike perceptual filters, conceptual filters do not contain information that is physically descriptive or perceptually predictive of an upcoming visual experience at the feature level. Instead, conceptual filters suggest a visual experience without directly describing it. For example, Brugger and Brugger (1993) asked people as they entered a zoo in either October or at Easter to describe an ambiguous line drawing that could be seen, at any one time, as either a bird or as a rabbit. The drawing, though categorized as a bird by the majority in October, was more often categorized as a rabbit when participants were asked at Easter. Likewise, children drew the image of Santa Claus larger at Christmas time relative to the size of their drawing a few weeks earlier or later (Sechrest & Wallace, 1964). Presumably, around these holidays, thoughts of Easter baskets and presents delivered in the night occupied the minds of the participants and led to perceptual interpretations and size distortions consistent with conceptual filters activated by the time of year.

Temporarily accessible thoughts can similarly activate conceptual filters that subsequently affect object identification. For example, some participants read a story about music file sharing while others read about the history of pornography. Participants then reported what they saw when briefly exposed to the *Sara Nader* ambiguous line drawing (Shepard, 1990) that simultaneously depicted a saxophone player and the outline of a face. Of those participants who read a story about music file sharing, 23% categorized the ambiguous drawing as a saxophone player, whereas no one who read about pornography did; instead, these participants categorized the line drawing as a face (Balcetis & Dale, 2007). Similarly, participants saw an ambiguous line drawing that depicted the outline of a face and the word liar. Of those who had just thought about deception, 75% subsequently categorized the figure as the word "liar," whereas only 13% who had thought about flirting interpreted it as such (Balcetis & Dale, 2003). Thus, the cognitive contents of perceivers' minds can serve as conceptual filters through which visual information is processed and subsequently categorized.

Categorical Perception of Other People

Both perceptual and conceptual filters sift visual information simultaneously as people look around the world. We describe some evidence that suggests that low-level perceptual information can be quickly extracted from information in the environment. These building blocks of perception then activate other global categories, which subsequently bias object identification. Perceptual and conceptual filters can and do interact to influence perception.

Perceivers rapidly detect low-level perceptual features present in people at whom they are looking. These cues activate social categories and influence subsequent perceptual processing. In other words, only minimal visual information is needed to influence perception. For example, it takes relatively little input or time to identify whether someone is angry or happy, male or female, or healthy or of low fitness (see Montepare, 2010, for a review). Perceivers' attentional gaze tends to orient toward categorically relevant aspects of the target individual quickly. When perceivers saw full body images of people, attentional eye gaze tended to focus on the waist and hips. Focusing on these cues activated related sex categories (i.e., male or female). The activation of these conceptual filters subsequently influenced categorization of the sex of the target individual (Johnson & Tassinary, 2005).

Likewise, people extract category information from much less salient perceptual cues, including facial features to which perceivers are exposed for short periods of time. For example, people accurately categorized photographs of men as gay or straight at above chance levels when exposed to the photographs for as little as 50 milliseconds (ms; Rule & Ambady, 2008; Rule, Macrae, & Ambady, 2009). Similarly, perceivers correctly categorized photographs of political candidates as Republican or Democrat at better than chance levels when exposed to the target faces for a short, although variable, amount of time (Rule & Ambady, 2010). Interestingly, the researchers demonstrated statistically that political category membership judgments were made on the basis of perceptions of traits stereotypically associated with the political parties. Participants extracted perceptual cues from the photographs. Candidates whose photographs depicted power were categorized as Republican, whereas candidates whose photographs depicted warmth were categorized as Democrat. Categorizing the photographs based on the perceptual cues associated with these personality traits led to increased accuracy in categorization.

Body motion is another perceptual cue that is efficiently extracted. For example, body motion can affect identification of target individuals (Loula, Prasad, Harber, & Shiffrar, 2005) and their emotional state, deceptive intent, motor effort, vulnerability,

and gender (Brownlow, Dixon, Egbert, & Radcliffe, 1997; Dittrich, Troscianko, Lea, & Morgan, 1996; Runeson & Frykholm, 1981, 1983). In addition, body motion can serve as a diagnostic cue to sexual orientation. Observers viewed point-light displays of people walking. Researchers created the point-light displays by affixing four infrared markers to men and women's hips and shoulders. Digital recordings of the targets walking on a treadmill captured the relative movement of the four markers. This yielded dynamic images of the outline of the individuals but obscured the details (e.g., color of clothing, skin, hair). Observers viewed these degraded videos and judged the sexual orientation of the walking targets. Gender-atypical motion, such as hip sway exhibited by men and shoulder swagger exhibited by women, activated social categories and compelled more accurate perceptions of homosexuality (Johnson, Gill, Reichman, & Tassinary, 2007).

To summarize, basic perceptual cues like body motion and facial features that differentiate gender and sexual orientation categories are easily extracted. Such perceptual cues filter visual information and activate conceptual filters. These co-occurring processes bias the identification of target individuals along other categorical dimensions. Thus, low-level perceptual information and high-level category information interact to allow for efficient processing of visual information.

Automaticity of Perceptual Miserliness

As Allport (1954) noted, "the human mind must think with the aid of categories.... We cannot possibly avoid this process" (p. 20). Indeed, a decade of empirical debate suggests that the cognitive miser's use of categorical thinking to expedite information processing occurs uncontrollably and automatically (e.g., Bargh, 1999; but see also Macrae & Bodenhausen, 2001; Monteith, Lybarger, & Woodcock, 2009).

Similarly, emerging evidence suggests that people *see* with the aid of categories. The perceptual miser, like its cognitive counterpart, engages in filtered, categorical perceptual processing quickly, easily, and automatically. For example, attention is directed to diagnostic perceptual cues in the environment for purposes of categorization. Importantly, directed attention occurs immediately upon stimulus presentation and often outside of participants' conscious control. One way that this can be assessed is by measuring event-related potential (ERP) responses. ERP responses reflect fluctuations in the electrical activity of the brain, which occur in response to specific stimuli. Specifically, the P200 and N200 are ERP components that occur less than 300 ms after stimulus onset and that mark attentional orienting to threat cues (Carretie, Martin-Loeches, Hinojosa, & Mercado, 2001; Eimer, Holmes, & McGlone, 2003). The P200 and N200 ERP responses indicate that people distinguish between black and white faces quickly and automatically; these attentional differences emerge even when participants are instructed to focus on tasks unrelated to race (Ito & Urland, 2003). Thus, even with minimal visual input and when the task is unrelated, the system discretely categorizes faces according to racial categories. Perceptual processes are filtered through attentional mechanisms very early in processing and without participants' intention, knowledge, or control. In these ways, the perceptual miser seems less like a consciously chosen strategy and more like an automatic process.

Summary

When current visual input demands outweigh resources available, people adopt a style of processing we refer to as the perceptual miser. Like the cognitive miser, the visual system uses heuristics and shortcuts that assist processing. When acting like a perceptual miser, perceivers use low-level perceptual cues and conceptual information to create filters, which influence perception. Visual input is quickly and efficiently categorized according to the activated filters. This strategy helps perceivers respond to the complex and demanding processing needs asked of the visual system when attempting to represent the complex outside world.

The Perceptual Monster

In October 1995, an African American man named Johnny Gammage drove a Jaguar sedan through a predominately white Pittsburgh suburb. He was pulled over by three white police officers for allegedly driving erratically. During what the police later reported was a scuffle, Gammage was suffocated on the pavement. The officers testified that they saw Gammage emerge from his vehicle carrying a gun—an item that later was confirmed to be a cellular phone. Eventually, all officers were acquitted (Jenkins, 1995).

The dramatic course of action that led to the death of Johnny Gammage prompted researchers to ask why the police officers saw only one interpretation—the wrong interpretation—of the object. (This, of course, assumes that the police officers actually did see the object as a gun, as they report.) Although the factors contributing to this horrible event are multiple to be sure, the story of Johnny Gammage serves to exemplify another important phenomenon within vision. Specifically, perception, and behavioral responses to perceptual experiences, can be influenced by characteristics of perceivers themselves. Although we will never know for sure whether the police officers actually misperceived the phone as a gun, it is indeed possible that they categorized the ambiguous shape as such. It is also possible that individual differences in implicit and explicit stereotypic beliefs, societal values, expectations, and community relations led the police to this misperception and subsequent response.

Some forms of perceptual bias occur as a result of these chronic, enduring, and stable characteristics of the perceiver. Such biases can produce harmful and deleterious consequences. This phenomenon we refer to as the perceptual monster. The perceptual monster can create exceptionally unfortunate consequences for the perceiver and the perceived.

Again, we define qualities of the perceptual monster by making an analogy to a phenomenon well established in the cognitive, information processing literature. The perceptual monster can be likened to the "cognitive monster" (Bargh, 1999). The cognitive monster refers to a style of information processing that calls on stable aspects of social perceivers or of the objects that are perceived. These stable, chronic, and enduring qualities exert influences on judgment outside of conscious control (Bargh, 1999). For example, perception of easily discernible group features (e.g., skin color, gender, and age-related characteristics) automatically activates stereotypes, which affect trait attributions (e.g., Gilbert, 1989; Winter & Uleman, 1984), self-judgments (Bargh & Tota, 1988), and behavioral inference (Bargh & Thein, 1985). Thus, stable aspects of the social perceiver and the perceived automatically influence judgment and occur outside of conscious awareness and control.

Visual perception can also be likened to a monster. Stable, chronic, and enduring aspects of both the perceiver and the perceived affect visual experience. People process aspects of their surroundings in ways shaped by preexisting beliefs, ideas, knowledge structures, and stereotypes. This can happen automatically, without awareness, and can be difficult to override. In the sections that follow, we outline research suggesting that information residing within the perceiver biases visual perception like a perceptual monster.

First, an important caveat must be made. The automatic influence of stable aspects of the perceiver on perception or judgment is not necessarily, by default, a helpful or harmful phenomenon. However, most lines of inquiry, to date, have explored those instances when the consequences are negative, given the relative gravity of their impact. Negative information packs a bigger downstream punch than does positive information (Baumeister, Bratslavsky, Finkenhauer, & Vohs, 2001). For example, the effects of stereotype threat on subsequent performance are greater in magnitude than the effects of stereotype lift (Walton & Cohen, 2003). That is, negative stereotypes impair performance more than positive stereotypes enhance performance. Likewise, negative information a perceiver holds about others affects person perception more than does positive information (Skowronski & Carlston, 1989). Researchers traditionally test the effect of stable qualities of the social perceiver in domains where the outcomes are harmful to the perceiver or the perceived given the disproportionate impact of negative information. Similarly, researchers investigate the effect of chronic, stable qualities of the perceiver. Because the influence of stable qualities of the perceiver often leads to misperception, misjudgment, and potentially destructive outcomes, research tends to gravitate toward studying the negative side of this effect. As a result, we chose to apply the label of "monster" to this style of processing. We will detail times in which the consequences of such biased perceptual representations can be exceptionally detrimental.

Stereotypes

Long-standing stereotypes and well-established belief structures shape multiple aspects of perceptual processing. For example, when environments include members of racial minorities, stereotypic beliefs influence identification of other elements of the environment. Participants are more likely to misidentify a tool as a gun when held by a black target rather than a white target (Correll, Park, Judd, & Wittenbrink, 2002). After subliminal exposure to black faces, participants subsequently identified degraded images of guns and knives more quickly than participants subliminally exposed to white faces (Eberhardt, Goff, Purdie, & Davies, 2004). Stereotypic beliefs can lead to perceptual interpretations consistent with those beliefs.

The consequences of rapid identification of dangerous objects, and the misidentification of harmless ones, can be deleterious. Participants who read a news story about a black criminal were more likely to shoot black targets in a video game even when the black target was holding an innocuous object such as a wrench (Correll, Park, Judd, & Wittenbrink, 2007). Thus, stereotypic beliefs and the ambiguity of degraded visual input interact to influence object identification and behavioral outcomes.

Personality Traits and Psychological Disorders

Stable aspects of perceivers' personality traits and chronic life orientations shape perception. For example, people with high fear of spiders reported more rapid forward motion when watching a video of a spider compared with people with low fear (Riskind, Moore, & Bowlby 1995). Similarly, snake-phobic individuals verbally reported more flickering snake tongue movements and spider-phobic individuals reported more spider jumping movements relative to their nonphobic peers (Rachman, & Cuk, 1992).

Stable personality qualities also influence attentional orienting. For example, participants' eyes were tracked as they viewed images of skin cancer or control images. Chronically pessimistic young adults fixated more on the skin cancer images than did their optimistic peers (Isaacowitz, 2005). When primed with ideas of infidelity, people high in chronic levels of romantic jealousy attended more vigilantly to physically attractive same-sex targets who could presumably act as a romantic threat (Maner, Miller, Rouby, & Gailliot, 2009). In addition, women who chronically expected to be the target of prejudice or outgroup rejection from men perceived contempt as lingering longer on the faces of men depicted in videos (Inzlicht, Kaiser, & Major, 2008). These forms of anxiety direct visual attention to material consistent with the content of the anxious thoughts.

The relationship between chronic personality traits and perceptual and attentional biases is mutually sustaining. For instance, anxiety shapes perception and directs attention, and the resulting perceptual experiences serve to confirm, maintain, or exacerbate the anxiety. Patients with generalized anxiety disorder (Mogg, Bradley, Williams, & Mathews, 1993), post-traumatic stress disorder (Kaspi, McNally, & Amir, 1995), and obsessive-compulsive disorder (Foa & McNally, 1986) attended to threatening visual information more than did control participants, perhaps further reinforcing their anxieties (see also Mogg, Millar, & Bradley, 2000; Williams, Watts, MacLeod, & Mathews, 1997; Yovel & Mineka,

2005). Social phobics, compared with healthy peers, demonstrated an attentional bias to angry relative to neutral faces (Gamble & Rapee, 2010). They also demonstrated an attentional bias toward heart-rate information, which is an internal cue for feelings of threat (Pineles & Mineka, 2005). Individuals with high attachment-related anxiety were hypervigilant to emotional expressions on the faces of others, but were not necessarily accurate in identifying the true expression (Fraley, Niedenthal, Marks, Brumbaugh, & Vicary, 2006). In addition, patients coping with psoriasis demonstrated an attentional bias in a modified Stroop task for disease-specific words (Fortune, Richards, Corrin, Taylor, Griffiths, & Main, 2003). The perceptual input that these anxious patients receive depicts a more threatening world than less anxious patients experience. People prone to anxiety often think about the ways in which they could experience threat, which produces perceptual and attentional biases that confirm these cognitions.

Body Image

People with body image disorders perceive themselves differently than do people without disorders (Williamson, 1990). When people look at their reflection in the mirror, individuals who are preoccupied with body size and shape generally see themselves as larger than they really are and do so automatically and without awareness (Williamson, 1996). Emotion and stress exacerbate discrepancies between perceived and actual body size (Baker, Williamson, & Sylve, 1995; McKenzie, Williamson, & Cubic, 1993; Slade, 1985). People who ruminate over body image attend to and remember body-related stimuli more than people who are not ruminators, thus perpetuating dissatisfaction with body size (Sebastian, Williamson, & Blouin, 1996; Watkins, Martin, Muller, & Day, 1995). The reciprocal relationship between chronic cognition and stable misperceptions of oneself serves as one factor that maintains and exacerbates body image disorders.

Visual Ecology

Another stable individual difference that shapes perceptual experience is the visual ecology in which people of different communities live. That is, the physical space that chronically surrounds perceivers exerts a fundamental influence on how they perceive the world. Primarily by directing attention, visual ecologies, in a sense, train people to have the conscious experience of perceiving some elements of the environment and remaining blind to others. Although the study of visual ecology does not

directly document instances in which biased perceptual experiences lead to negative outcomes for the perceiver or the perceived, there is the possibility for this to occur given the sort of "blindness" that ecologies create.

The visual ecologies of Asia and North American are very different. For example, Miyamoto, Nisbett, and Masuda (2006) quantified the difference in the visual ecology of Japanese and North American street scenes. They randomly photographed a large number of scenes in the United States and Japan, from which they created a set of images that served as representations of the two visual ecologies. Analysis of the images showed that the Japanese ecologies contained more objects than American ecologies. Also, Japanese ecologies contained more objects with ambiguous boundaries than American ecologies.

Because of these differences, the researchers conjectured that these distinct visual ecologies engender different attentional processing styles. Implied in this growing body of research is the idea that although visual ecologies might tune people to certain elements of the environment and ways of processing information to which they are exposed, there are also elements that are overlooked, ignored, or go unregistered. In a sense, visual ecologies could lead to a sort of perceptual or attentional blindness. It is possible that cultural influences may make it difficult for people to accurately assess the full extent of what their environments afford.

In fact, some researchers have suggested that culture can affect patterns of attention that lead to a sort of blindness. Members of some cultures attend to focal elements at the expense of information contained in the more global context. For example, researchers presented participants with images that flickered (Masuda & Nisbett, 2006). That is, two photographs that were very similar but not identical were each presented for 560 ms, separated by a blank screen for 80 ms. Between the two photographs, the researchers altered either the focal object or the context slightly. They presented the photographs in alternation repeatedly until participants indicated that they detected a change and could report what it was. Although both Americans and East Asians were able to detect that a focal object changed relatively quickly, Americans took considerably longer than East Asians to accurately detect that the surrounding context changed. These data suggest that members of different cultures tend to allocate their attention differently. Members of Eastern cultures focus attention on context, whereas members of Western cultures focus primarily on the target object or individual.

Furthermore, differences in patterns of attention were found using eye-tracking measures. Chua, Boland, and Nisbett (2005) found that Americans looked at central objects sooner and longer than Asian participants. In addition, Asian participants made more eye movements to the background, in addition to more total eye movements, compared with American participants. It appears that East Asians tend to physically allocate their attention to the context, whereas North Americans tend to allocate attention to the focal elements at the expense of the context.

Summary

As a wealth of research evidence suggests, chronic, stable qualities of perceivers and their surroundings shape perception and attention. The effects of chronic personality and situational variables occur quickly, at times automatically, and nonconsciously. Because these effects tend to be more prominent and pervasive when the personality variables and outcomes are harmful or maladaptive to the perceiver or the perceived, we liken these phenomena to a perceptual monster.

The Perceptual Manager

In August 2010, conservative talk-radio host and Fox News commentator, Glenn Beck, held what he called a "rally to restore honor" in Washington, DC. Beck and former Alaska Governor, Sarah Palin, spoke in front of the Lincoln Memorial to a large crowd. But how large was it? Sky News, a sister to Fox News, reported that more than 500,000 people attended (Cole, 2010). Even more striking was Republican Congresswoman Michele Bachmann's statement, "We're not going to let anyone get away with saying there were less than a million here today—because we were witnesses." After the rally, CBS commissioned the company AirPhotosLive. com, a nonpartisan organization that specializes in computing attendance. Based on aerial pictures it took of the rally, AirPhotosLive.com estimated the crowd at a mere 87,000, with a 9,000-person margin of error (Sundy, 2010). How could perceptions of the number of people attending the rally differ so drastically?

Although explanations for the discrepancy are abundant, it is quite possible that goals and motivations influenced the way in which politicos saw the size of the crowd. Republicans held the goal of trumping up support for a burgeoning cause. They

had a perceptual experience that differed from that of, say, Democrats who were less motivated to see the rally as suggesting support. In seeing the crowds as ridiculously large or unfairly small, people may have actually satisfied active political goals. For instance, biased perceptions of crowd size may have helped quell their anxiety about a movement slow to get off the ground, their concern that a new political party was on the rise, or any other politically relevant motivations. In this section, we detail some ways in which active goals influence visual perception. We also suggest ways in which biased visual perception actually helps people to accomplish these goals. In so doing, we suggest that the visual system processes information in a manner that can be described as a perceptual manager.

The phenomenon has not yet received the term "manager" explicitly in the literature; however, much relevant literature documents the ways in which goals influence cognition. People evaluate objects, make decisions, and consider information in ways that align with their current goal states. For example, goals influence object evaluation; active goals lead people to evaluate goal-relevant objects more favorably when those objects are capable of satisfying goals (Ferguson & Bargh, 2004). People also evaluate objects more negatively when those objects get in the way of satisfying goals (Fishbach, Zhang, & Trope, 2010). In addition to goals influencing cognition, cognition influences goal pursuit. Consider that automatic attitudes, which are difficult to monitor or control and which people do not even explicitly know they hold, are strong predictors of successful self-regulatory behaviors (Ferguson, 2007). Although these are just a few examples, much literature documents how goals shape cognition and, reciprocally, how cognition shapes goals. We rely on this literature to suggest that the perceptual manager influences visual information processing.

One characteristic consistent with the perceptual manager phenomenon is that goals shape perception. For example, a puzzle book appears bigger to perceivers who have the goal to do puzzles, and a rake appears bigger to people with a gardening goal (Aarts, Custers, & Veltkamp, 2008). A second characteristic of this processing style is that biased visual perception can shape goal progress. This may occur in two ways (Bargh, 1990; Bargh & Chartrand, 1999; Bargh & Ferguson, 2000; Berkowitz 1984, 1997). First, perception can hinder goal pursuit. For instance, when preschool children visually attended to a delectable marshmallow in their field of view, they could only wait 6 minutes, on average, before failing at the goal of delaying consumption (Mischel & Ebbesen, 1970). However, children who could not see the delicious marshmallow, because it was obstructed from view, were able to wait 11 minutes, on average, before succumbing to the temptation. Visual attention to the tempting treat led to increased difficulties maintaining the already challenging goal.

Second, perception can aid in goal pursuit. For instance, successful dieters perceived an apple as larger, after a food prime, compared with unsuccessful dieters (van Koningsbruggen, Stroebe, & Aarts, 2011). Because size distortions relate to subjective changes in evaluation of goal-relevant objects, biased size perception predicts behavioral choices that assist in goal pursuit. In addition, directed attention predicts goal pursuit. For example, people with goals to regulate negative emotions attended less to negative than to positive images (Xing & Isaacowitz, 2006). Thus, goals can change perception and attention and, reciprocally, help goal pursuit.

In this section, we argue that the visual system processes information in ways that can be described with a metaphor of a perceptual manager. Perception responds to and is influenced by active goals. In addition, perception is systematically biased in ways that aid effective self-regulation. We give brief overviews of the myriad ways that the visual system is biased by goals and promotes biological and psychological goal-relevant action.

Visual Perception Serves Biological Self-Regulation

VISCERAL NEEDS

Visceral need states affect perception. Once temporary need states are activated, ambiguous information is interpreted in a way that is related to, or actually will assist in, satisfying that need. For example, Changizi & Hall (2001) demonstrated that thirsty participants identified more transparency, a common property of water, in ambiguous visual stimuli than did participants who were not thirsty. Thirst can also drive attention and memory. Thirsty people remembered seeing more objects in a room that were related to quenching thirst than did those who were not thirsty (Aarts, Dijksterhuis, & DeVries, 2001). These results suggest that thirst systematically directed attention to goal-relevant objects in the environment.

When experiencing physical deprivation, like nicotine craving, people misperceive the size of objects capable of satisfying the need. For example, participants indicated the true length of a cigarette by selecting one of 14 pictures that varied in the length of the cigarette depicted (Brendl, Markman, & Messner, 2003; Study 1). High-deprived nicotine-addicted participants picked a longer cigarette than low-deprived participants. Likewise, participants indicated that glasses of water were taller in direct proportion to their level of deprivation; the thirstier participants were, the larger the glasses of water appeared (Veltkamp, Aarts, & Custers, 2008). Thus, active visceral need states bias perceptions of objects capable of satisfying those needs.

Reciprocally, biased perceptions aid acquisition of these objects. When experiencing visceral states, people are motivated to engage in actions that assist in alleviating the need. These action tendencies seem to be strongest when people, and other animals, perceive goal-relevant objects to be in close physical proximity. For example, rats are energized to take on approach behaviors to the extent that they are in close proximity to desirable objects; thirsty rats run faster the closer they are to drinkable water (Hull, 1932; Dollard & Miller, 1950). Thus, perceptions of proximity relate to action tendencies that assist in actions necessary for goal satisfaction.

Just as actual proximity energizes approach behaviors that help acquire an object, research suggests that visual systems bias distance perception in order to encourage approach behaviors that would assist in fulfilling active goals. In other words, perceivers see desirable objects as closer than less desirable objects, in order to incite approach. For example, participants who felt thirsty after consuming a portion of dry salty pretzels perceived a full bottle of water as 9% closer to themselves than participants whose thirst had been quenched (Balcetis & Dunning, 2010). These data demonstrate that active needs and goals produced misperceptions of distance. Based on existing literature, this research suggests that illusory perceptions of proximity occur in order to help the perceiver regulate behaviors that serve active goals.

ENERGY EXPENDITURE AND CONSERVATION

Another important aspect of goal pursuit is expending energy when it is abundant and conserving it when it is in short supply. Visual perception assists in this aspect of self-regulation (Bhalla & Proffitt, 1999). For example, when energy is low, as is the case when one is fatigued, elderly, or carrying a heavy backpack, people perceive hills as steeper and distances as farther compared with when energy is abundant (Bhalla & Proffitt, 1999; Proffitt, Stefanucci, Banton, & Epstein, 2003). When physical resources are in short supply, environments appear more extreme than when physical resources are plentiful. Thus, perceptions are biased when goals to conserve energy are active.

New research suggests why such perceptual biases arise. This work argues that biased estimates of distance efficiently guide the actions of the perceiver. People perceive environments as more extreme (e.g., distances as farther, hills as steeper) in order to dissuade themselves from expending energy in that environment. For example, exaggerated estimates of distance might lead perceivers to evaluate a task as physiologically costly and to conserve energy by avoiding such physical challenges. Patients diagnosed with chronic pain perceived target distances to be farther away compared with a control group not experiencing the same pain (Witt, Linkenauger, Bakdash, Augustyn, Cook, & Proffitt, 2009). The physical, and emotional, costs of chronic pain may affect spatial perceptions in order to discourage the patient from engaging in costly actions. Distance perception and regulation of physiological energy reserves interact to promote optimal functioning in one's environment (Esteve-Lanao, Lucia, deKoning, & Foster, 2008).

REPRODUCTION

Survival may literally depend on an individual's ability to identify other individuals who can assist in accomplishing reproductive goals. Accordingly, perceivers should be attuned to perceptual information that will enhance the chances of reproductive success (see Miller & Todd, 1998). Such information includes cues that specify sex and sexual orientation. In addition, perceptual attunement should be greater at certain time points than others—like when women are capable of becoming pregnant rather than times when they are not. Research supports this hypothesis. Women were faster to categorize photographs of men as male during periods of high rather than low conception probability, but showed no difference in speed to categorize faces of women as female. Pregnant women, who were in a (temporary) state of zero conception likelihood, showed no facilitation effects to either sex (Johnston, Arden, Macrae, & Grace, 2003). This suggests that women display enhanced perceptual sensitivity for reproductively relevant stimuli, like sexually mature male faces, when their own conception probability is high (Macrae, Alnwick, Milne, & Schloerscheidt, 2002).

Men, too, are perceptually attuned to visual information that is relevant to reproduction. Researchers tested men's sensitivity to cyclical changes in female fertility, using the same sex-categorization task (Johnston, Miles, Carter, & Macrae, 2005). Photographs were taken of women who were either taking or not taking birth control pills. The women were also photographed at two different time points during their cycle: once at midcycle and once during menstruation. Among women not taking the pill, midcycle reflects a time of high fertility, whereas menstruation is a time of low fertility. Among women taking the pill, midcycle and menstruation reflect the same time points, and fertility is actually low. Male perceivers were faster to correctly categorize the photographed women as female when the pictures depicted a woman photographed at menstruation rather than at midcycle, regardless of whether the women who appeared in the photographs were taking or not taking birth control pills at the time they were photographed. They also showed no bias to categorize ovulating women faster when they were in states of high rather than low fertility. This suggests that males were sensitive not to markers of current high fertility (ovulation) but rather to markers of longer term fertility or reproductive viability (menstruation).

Visual Perception Serves Psychological Self-Regulation

SEXUAL DESIRE

Although biological factors associated with reproductive likelihood influence the efficiency of sex-based categorization (Macrae et al., 2002; Johnston et al., 2003), perceptual sensitivity for perceiving the sex of another person appears to be driven also by psychological motives (Brinsmead-Stockham, Johnston, Miles, & Macrae, 2008). Sexual interest, desire, and activity are greatest for women, both homosexual and heterosexual, around ovulation (Baker & Bellis, 1995; Harvey, 1987; Hill, 1988; Matteo & Rissman, 1984). Women should be especially attuned to elements of their environment—namely people—they find sexually desirable at this time. To test this idea, lesbian participants who maintained a regular menstrual cycle and were not using birth control categorized photographs by gender. They showed facilitated categorization when they themselves were experiencing high fertility. However, unlike heterosexual women, homosexual women were faster to identify faces of women during periods of high rather than low fertility. These results support the idea that conception likelihood is not the sole predictor of perceptual sensitivity. Instead, sexual interest and desire also predict enhanced sensitivity to targets capable of satisfying the desire.

SELF-ENHANCING MOTIVATIONS

People harbor a strong desire and tendency to think well of themselves. The majority of people believe themselves to be more moral, kind, civic minded, and generous than their peers (Baumhart, 1968; Epley & Dunning, 2000, 2006). This drive to think in self-enhancing ways is a pervasive phenomenon, particularly in Western cultures. Recent research argues that such enhancing cognitions are also evident in visual perception.

One domain in which people are particularly motivated to self-enhance is physical appearance. People want to think of themselves as being more physically attractive than they actually are. Such desires extend to the literal ways in which people perceive their own image. In a series of studies (Epley & Whitchurch, 2008), photographs of participants' faces were made more or less attractive using a morphing program. Participants' task was to choose their own true photograph from a lineup of the morphed images. Participants selected and more rapidly identified an attractively enhanced version of their face as their own—a tendency that was also related to implicit measures of self-worth. This suggests that people maintain a perceptual representation of themselves as more attractive than they actually are.

People also want to consider themselves lucky, with positive prospects for the future, and such motivations infiltrate object identification. In one study, participants tended to interpret an ambiguous figure in a manner that fit with their desires to be lucky people (Balcetis & Dunning, 2006). Participants knew they would soon be asked to drink either freshly squeezed orange juice or a gelatinous green slime labeled "organic veggie smoothie." They also knew that the computer would assign the beverage by presenting either a number or a letter on the screen. Half the participants knew that if they saw a letter they would drink the desirable beverage. For the other half, a number meant they would drink the desirable beverage. When the computer flashed an ambiguous line drawing that could be interpreted as either a B or 13, 82% of participants reported the desired interpretation (Study 1). This and other studies demonstrated that desires influenced object identification, allowing participants to sustain the belief that their futures were more

likely to bring them positive rather than unpleasant experiences.

Within this work, the researchers demonstrated that people's desires influenced object identification before conscious awareness. This fact was established through experimental manipulation (Balcetis & Dunning, 2006; Study 5). After first establishing a reward structure and presenting the ambiguous stimulus, but before participants reported their interpretation, the experimenter feigned a computer crash. The experimenter told participants this occurred because the reward structure was miscommunicated to them. At that point, the experimenter switched the reward structure. The experimenter then asked participants, coyly, if anything had appeared on their screen before the crash. If participants had any awareness of the ambiguity or could reconstruct the ambiguous figure in their minds, they should have reported what ultimately aligned with their desires after the switch of the reward structure. They could not. In fact, in one condition 100% of participants reported seeing an interpretation of the ambiguous figure that ultimately turned out to be aligned with an undesired outcome. These data suggest that participants' desires at the time when they first received the visual information quickly led to favorable interpretations of the ambiguous object.

Importantly, by changing the reward structure and asking participants to self-report their perceptual experience, this study addressed one pervasive concern that plagued the original New Look research in the 1950s. People criticized New Look research for its inability to eliminate the possibility that participants were strategically responding and consciously choosing what they would report seeing (Erdelyi, 1974, 1985). These self-report issues are of less concern in Balcetis and Dunning's (2006, Study 5) experiment. If participants were consciously introducing bias in their self-report of their perceptual experience, then they should have reported what ultimately was associated with the desirable outcome, after the reward structure shifted. This experiment provided an opportunity for response selection and self-reporting biases to emerge, but the evidence suggests that they did not.

SPORTS PERFORMANCE

Emerging evidence suggests a relationship between visual perception and improved performance on athletic motor performance goals. Although this line of research is still new, some evidence suggests that certain perceptual biases might predict improved performance. For instance, field goal kickers who made more successful kicks perceived the goalposts to be farther apart and perceived the crossbar to be closer to the ground compared with participants who made fewer kicks (Witt & Dorsch, 2009). Golfers who sank more putts judged the hole to be bigger than did golfers who did not play as well (Witt, Linkenauger, Bakdash, & Proffitt, 2008). It is yet to be determined whether the perceptual bias itself causes improved sports performance, but the relationship exists between size distortion and the attainment of athletic performance goals.

DISSONANCE REDUCTION

Visual perception can serve another goal—namely the desire to reduce the unpleasant experience of cognitive dissonance. Cognitive dissonance arises when attitudes and actions contradict one another. The need to reduce dissonance can shift perception in ways that relieve discomfort. Balcetis and Dunning (2007) had participants perform an aversive task, such as wearing a costume reminiscent of Carmen Miranda, the Brazilian performer usually clad in a coconut bra and large fruit-basket headdress, while walking across a crowded park. Before completing the task, participants' subjective feelings of choice were manipulated to be either high or low. Under high choice, people experienced dissonance caused by their voluntary agreement to perform the aversive task. Under low choice, dissonance was less prominent because participants could attribute their agreement to lack of choice (Linder, Cooper, & Jones, 1967). When experiencing dissonance aroused by choosing to perform an aversive task, perceptions of the natural environment shifted. Under conditions of dissonance, distances to be walked while wearing the costume were perceived as 40% shorter and hills to be traversed were perceived as 23% less steep. This work suggests that environments were perceived in less extreme ways in order to reduce the negative affect associated with the experience of dissonance.

AGE AND TIME PERSPECTIVE

Age and, more broadly, one's stage in life influence the types of goals that individual pursue. Life goals bias visual perception in ways that help serve these goals. With increasing age, goal hierarchies are reorganized, such that goals to obtain emotional satisfaction are prioritized over goals that maximize long-term payoffs (Carstensen, Isaacowitz, & Charles, 1999). When time is construed as open ended, as is often the case for younger, healthy adults,

goals of expanding one's knowledge base and experiencing novelty weigh heavily. However, as people approach the end of life because of age or terminal illness, goals associated with emotional meaning and well-being increase in salience, whereas goals associated with acquiring knowledge for future use decrease (Carstensen & Fredrickson, 1998).

People differentially prioritize emotional and informational goals, which exert varying influences on visual perception. Young adults' attention is initially directed toward fearful faces rather than happy faces (Isaacowitz, Wadlinger, Grolen, & Wilson, 2006). However, older adults' attention is directed initially towards happy rather than neutral faces, and toward neutral rather than negative faces (Mather & Carstensen, 2003). Interestingly, older adults in bad moods demonstrate an attentional bias toward happy faces and away from negatives faces. However, older adults in good moods demonstrate no attentional biases (Isaacowitz, Toner, Goven, & Wilson, 2008). The focus on emotional goals among older adults leads them to favor positive information and avoid attending to and processing negative information, particularly when this visual attention bias can serve an emotion regulation goal.

Culture

Cultures prioritize different self-relevant motivations, which lead to different ways of attending to the surrounding world. For example, individuals from independent, Western cultures prioritize the individual self and produce a focused attentional strategy; attention is focused on individual objects, people, or events. Alternatively, individuals from interdependent, Eastern cultures prioritize communal relationships, which lead attention to be dispersed among different objects (Duffy & Kitayama, 2010; Kitayama, Duffy, Kawamura, & Larsen, 2003).

Research in fact corroborates the idea that members of cultures that specify divergent goals and motivations attend to information in systematically different ways. For example, researchers manipulated either features of a face (e.g., different eye color) or configurations of these features (e.g., different distance between the nose and mouth). Japanese participants were more likely to detect *configural* changes in a cartoon depiction of face. However, American participants were more likely to detect *featural* changes in the cartoon face. This suggests that Japanese participants perceived the face more holistically, whereas Americans were more likely to attend to individual features (Masuda et al.,

2008). Moreover, Japanese participants considered the emotional expressions of other individuals in the picture when identifying the emotional expressions of a target. Americans' judgments, however, were not influenced by the facial expressions of the individuals in the background (Masuda et al., 2008). This evidence suggests that culture shifts aspects of perceptual processing and attentional style. People from independent cultures tend to have a more feature-based, focused attentional strategy, whereas individuals from interdependent cultures tend to have a more holistic, dispersed attentional strategy.

Summary

People's thoughts, decisions, and judgments are often directed by their active goals. Thinking, feeling, and evaluating are often in the service of "doing" (Ferguson & Bargh, 2004; Fiske, 1992). Recent evidence lends support to Gibson's (1979) assertion—perceiving is also for doing. Perceptual managers literally see the world in accordance with their goals and needs. As an abundant amount of research across a wide variety of domains suggests, the visual system processes information in biased ways to aid effective goal pursuit.

Moderators of Visual Biases

When processing perceptual information as a miser, monster, or manager, people tend to see the world in ways that differ dramatically from reality, from how other people see the world, or from the experience they would have in other circumstances. That said, perceptual experiences do maintain a degree of external validity. There is a correspondence between perceivers' perceptual representations and what reality actually offers to perceptual systems. Cleveland basketball fans, no matter how much they would like to see him, rarely open their doors to find the once star player of the Cavaliers, Lebron James, standing outside—particularly given that he left (or abandoned, if you will) the team. Reality does have a way of constraining perceivers' visual experiences. The actual features and properties of natural environments do influence visual perception. Thus, there must exist limits to the influence of the perceptual miser, monster, and manager on visual perception. Indeed, we can think of three such boundaries.

Ambiguity in the Environment

Perceptual biases might be reduced, or even eliminated, when objects and the environments surrounding them are less ambiguous. It would be difficult, if not impossible, to peer into a stroller and see a full-grown adult man rather than a tiny infant. The ambiguity or clarity of a stimulus can come from two different sources. First, the stimulus itself might be readily perceived and easily identifiable. If the thing is shiny, pointy, has a handle, and easily cuts through a tomato, the visual system may aptly report that the object is knife. Second, the context surrounding the stimulus might constrain interpretations of what the stimulus is. If one is watching Anthony Bourdain in a back room at the restaurant *Les Halles*, there is further evidence that that shiny object is a knife. Just as reality can constrain judgment (Kunda, 1990), so, too, can reality constrain the products of visual perception.

Accountability

Personal accountability to others might also constrain the degree to which the visual system can process information in a manner akin to a miser, monster, and manager. Given that accountability reduces tendencies to exaggerate judgments (for an extensive review, see Lerner & Tetlock, 1999), accountability may also reduce bias in perceptual experiences. Accountability might lead perceivers to see their world in ways that more closely align with reality.

In fact, data informally suggest that personal accountability reduces the impact of motivational biases in visual perception. In one study, participants explicitly reported interpretations of ambiguous visual information (Balcetis & Dunning, 2006, Study 3). In that same study, nonconscious, eye-tracking measures corroborated their self-reports. Specifically, participants' initial eye movement and subsequent fixation on a category label were measured. This categorization measure was not one that could be consciously directed because initial saccades are difficult to control. Also, participants did not know their eye movements were monitored. The lack of controllability and lack of participant awareness reduce the possibility that explicit, conscious response selection pressures were at play. Arguably, because the explicit measure required perceivers to report their perceptual experience to others, the explicit measure may have cued greater accountability than did the nonconscious measure. Data confirm this. The statistical size of the perceptual bias varied greatly depending on whether the bias was measured through explicit or nonconscious measures. The effect size when measuring the perceptual bias using an explicit measure—the one with greater accountability—was a 0.6 standard deviation difference. However, the size of the effect nearly doubled when the perceptual bias was assessed through the nonconscious measure where accountability was lower. With this measure, the size of the effect rose to 1.2 standard deviations. This suggests that personal accountability may lead participants to offer more conservative and less biased reports of their perceptual experience than the one initially offered by the visual system.

Immediacy of Required Action

To pursue goals, one must accurately perceive cues that suggest which actions are most appropriate and required in the situation. For example, a freshly collected sample of dog feces sitting on the other side of the room rarely requires an immediate response, whereas an angry automobile driver barreling down the road when one is in the middle of the pedestrian crosswalk surely does. Discriminating the qualities inherent in a threatening object from those of a disgusting object is necessary for basic goal pursuit in order to engage the right behavioral response. Indeed, perception of disgusting and threatening objects is related to different action tendencies. Perceiving a threatening object will increase blood pressure and cortisol, which prepares the body for action, whereas perceiving a disgusting object will decrease blood pressure and cortisol, which leads to withdrawal and inaction (Lerner, Gonzalez, Dahl, Hariri, & Taylor, 2005). Accurately detecting the perceptual cues that suggest threat or disgust is necessary to produce the neuroendocrine responses that lead to appropriate action in that environment. Thus, objects that evoke different emotions and behavioral reactions might differentially affect goal pursuit.

Perceptual Misers, Monsters, and Managers Operating in Parallel

In this chapter, we suggest that the metaphors of the perceptual miser, monster, and manager can be used to understand how people come to reach perceptual conclusions about information in their environments. However, in the examples we presented, we have focused primarily on the *products* of visual perception. Equally important is an investigation of the *processes* by which percepts are formed, the processes by which the perceptual miser, monster, and manager exert their influences. These three styles of processing do not operate in isolation, to the exclusion of the others. Instead, it seems more likely that these processes occur simultaneously, in parallel. Perceptual filters might be activated upon the quick perception of low-level perceptual features, as a result of the efficiency of the perceptual miser. Simultaneously, the qualities of the perceptual monster may activate categories that shape perception while active goals of the perceptual manager further direct how the object will be perceived. For example, a perceiver might find himself in a neighborhood known for high crime rates and notice an object marked by a relative lack of luminance and relatively great height. This person might use these low-level perceptual features, in addition to the contextual environment, and subsequently identify the figure as a black man. This information may activate the race category of African American and all relevant stereotypes. When this information is coupled with the perceivers' active goal to be vigilant for threat in the high-crime neighborhood, the perceiver may identify an ambiguous object in the man's hand as a gun. This may explain, in part, how three police officers came to shoot Amidou Diallo, a Guinean man living in a poverty-stricken south central neighborhood in the Bronx, who was holding a wallet rather than a gun the officers claimed they saw.

Thus, these three styles of perceptual processing can simultaneously interact to predict conscious perceptual experience. Although the products of perceptual processes are discrete (i.e., categorizing a visual stimulus as a gun), the process of perceptual organization unfolds over time. Evidence suggests this is the case. Freeman, Ambady, Rule, and Johnson (2008) measured the *process* of social categorization in addition to the *product* of social categorization. Participants categorized faces by gender. They moved their mouse from a central starting point to either end of the computer screen, where they clicked a category label. The targets included a sex-specifying perceptual cue that was either typical for their sex (long hair for women) or atypical (short hair for women). These researchers measured the streaming x, y coordinates of hand movements as participants categorized typical and atypical faces by sex. Specifically, participants moved the mouse from a central location to one of two sex category labels located on opposite sides of the computer screen. When a target included an atypical perceptual cue, mouse movements seemed slightly "pulled" toward the opposite-sex category label. Although the perceptual product was largely accurate, the "pulled" motor movement suggested that the percept unfolded over time. This kind of motor movement attraction indicated dynamic competition between multiple social categories, until the decision was made. This evidence suggests that perceptual features that partially activate competing category representations gradually cascade into a discrete social categorical percept over the course of a second or so. Importantly, the process by which the discrete percept is formed reflects the interaction between multiple perceptual strategies. Although perception may appear to be filtered, investigations of the process suggest that perception does not function as an all-or-nothing process (Locke, Macrea, & Eaton, 2005, p. 418). It instead reflects the composite of multiple sources of information that unfold over time.

The parallel manner in which multiple systems interact to inform perception solves a problem faced by the original New Look researchers. Critics argued that perceptual defense is a misnamed effect; they claimed it an illogical notion that perception of a threatening object could be inhibited or defended. Because perception was then considered a linear series of stages, an object must first be perceived before a perceiver could know, at some level, that it must defend against it. Thus, critics argued that perceptual defense must not have been perceptual at all. The New Look movement was flummoxed.

Although this seemed a logical paradox at the time, the advent of theories detailing how multiple processes to operate in parallel solves the conundrum. If low-level information is extracted, categorical information activated, and self-regulatory systems engaged to simultaneously shape perceptual experience, it is possible to perceptually defend against something without becoming consciously aware of the threat. That is, if the visual system can process input like a miser, monster, and manager simultaneously, then perceptual defense mechanisms, as posited by the original New Look researchers, can indeed be perceptual phenomena rather than cognitive, reporting biases. Thus, these influences on perception work together in parallel to mutually constrain, shape, and predict representation.

Conclusion

Major League Baseball's "perfect game" is illusive to say the least. In order for a pitcher to pitch a perfect game, no opposing player can reach a base throughout the entire game for any reason. The extraordinary feat has only been achieved 20 times in the 135-year history of Major League Baseball. In June of 2010, Armando Galarraga of the Detroit Tigers was poised to make history. In the bottom of the ninth inning and with two outs, Galarraga was just one out away from becoming the 21st pitcher to pitch a perfect game. Fans were on the edge of their seats. Galarraga wound up, pitched, and heard the unmistakable crack of the bat as the Indians player hit a ground ball toward first base. As the first baseman left the bag to make the play, Galarraga rushed from the mound to cover the base. The first baseman fielded the ball and tossed it to Galarraga, who caught it and tagged the base just as the runner arrived. In the split second after the play, Tigers players and fans immediately began to celebrate. The third baseman jumped for joy, the outfielders began running in from the field, and the Tigers dugout was poised to rush out and mob Galarraga in exuberant celebration. Before they had the chance, the first base umpire signaled that the runner was safe, killing Galarraga's otherwise perfect game. Tigers players and fans were stunned and angry; the boos from the 17,000 fans were deafening. After the game, the umpire, a 22-year veteran, watched the replays. In slow motion, removed from the emotionally charged atmosphere of the game, the umpire saw a quite different scene. Indeed, he was near tears during a post-game press conference as he admitted he blew the call, saying that he went with what he saw at the time. "I was convinced he beat the throw…until I saw the replay."

Perceivers face a daunting task from the moment they open their eyes in the morning to the moment they close them at night. They must navigate their environment and interact with the objects and people in it, despite incomplete and sometimes erroneous representations of the world around them. Because at any moment it is virtually impossible for the visual system to take in all of the information the environment offers, perceivers must adopt a strategy to efficiently categorize the world. People quickly pick up on diagnostic cues, then take perceptual shortcuts like making categorical perceptual decisions in the service of expediting visual information processing. This style of processing we refer to as the perceptual miser.

Because perception is a subjective process, influenced by factors external to the stimulus and internal to the perceiver, the visual system does not simply mirror the outside world. Instead, dispositional qualities of perceivers themselves often affect the way they see their environment. Chronic, stable, and enduring qualities of people, culture, and environments influence perception and attention. In so doing, these stable qualities are capable of perpetuating harmful beliefs, traits, and disorders and can cause potentially harmful behavioral consequences. This phenomenon we refer to as the perceptual monster.

Perceivers' goals, needs, and desires also influence perception, and systematically biased perceptual experiences feed back to shape and serve motivations. People perceive the world in biased ways and attend to aspects of their environment that their temporarily active goals ready them to experience. Reciprocally, biased visual perception can assist active goal pursuit, helping the perceiver regulate behavior meant to achieve goals. Through these processes, the perceiver comes to influence the perceived. This phenomenon we refer to as the perceptual manager.

Final Thoughts

Perception is the product of qualities of the perceiver. Certainly, the view people have of the world will depend on the window through which they see it. This chapter described different aspects of people that have been shown to systematically bias cognition. That is, much evidence suggests that people are efficient and miserly in their cognitive processing, at times leading to outcomes that are exceptionally negative (and perhaps even monsterly). At the same time, their judgments are the product of active goals they are attempting to regulate. This chapter asked whether these same qualities in perceivers similarly influence visual perception as well. A growing body of literature suggests this is the case. Perhaps by studying the perceptual miser, monster, and manager, it is possible to offer insight into the architecture of the window through which people see the world.

References

Aarts, H., Custers, R., & Veltkamp, M. (2008). Goal priming and the affective-motivational route to nonconscious goal pursuit. *Social Cognition, 26,* 555–577.

Aarts, H., Dijksterhuis, A., & De Vries, P. (2001). On the psychology of drinking: Being thirsty and perceptually ready. *British Journal of Psychology, 92,* 631.

Adkins, L. J. (1956). Critical comment on the measurement of familiarity in personality perception experiments. *Perceptual and Motor Skills, 6,* 147–151.

Allport, A. (1989). Visual attention. In M. I. Posner (Ed.), *Visual attention* (pp. 631–682). Cambridge, MA: MIT Press.

Allport, G. W. (1954). *The nature of prejudice.* Oxford, UK: Addison-Wesley.

Baker, J. D., Williamson, D. A., &, Sylve, C. (1995). Body image disturbance, memory bias, and body dysphoria: Effects of negative mood induction. *Behavior Therapy, 4,* 747–759.

Baker, R. R., & Bellis, M. A. (1995). *Human sperm competition: Copulation, masturbation and infidelity.* London: Chapman and Hall.

Balcetis, E., & Dale, R. (2003). The eye is not naked: Context clothes visual perception. In *Proceedings of the 25th Cognitive Science Society* (pp. 109–114). Mahwah, NJ: Erlbaum.

Balcetis, E., & Dale, R. (2007). Conceptual set as a top-down constraint on visual object identification. *Perception, 36,* 581–595.

Balcetis, E., & Dunning, D. (2006). See what you want to see: Motivational influences on visual perception. *Journal of Personality and Social Psychology, 91,* 612–625.

Balcetis, E., & Dunning, D. (2007). Cognitive dissonance and the perception of natural environments. *Psychological Science, 18,* 917–921.

Balcetis, E., & Dunning, D (2010). Wishful seeing: Desired objects are seen as closer. *Psychological Science, 21,* 147–152.

Bar, M. (2004). Visual objects in context. *Nature Reviews of Neuroscience, 5,* 617–629.

Bargh, J. A. (1990). Goal ≠ intent: Goal-directed thought and behavior are often unintentional. *Psychological Inquiry, 1,* 248–251.

Bargh, J. A. (1999). The cognitive monster: The case against the controllability of automatic stereotype effects. In S. Chaiken, & Y. Trope (Eds.), *Dual-process theories in social psychology* (pp. 361–382). New York: Guilford Press.

Bargh, J. A., & Chartrand, T. L. (1999). The unbearable automaticity of being. *American Psychologist, 54,* 462–479.

Bargh, J. A., & Ferguson, M. J. (2000). Beyond behaviorism: On the automaticity of higher mental processes. *Psychological Review, 126,* 925–945.

Bargh, J. A., & Morsella, E. (2010). Unconscious behavioral guidance systems. In C. R. gnew, D. E. Carlston, W. G. Graziano, & J. R. Kelly (Eds.), *Then a miracle occurs: Focusing on behavior in social psychological theory and research* (pp. 89–118). New York: Oxford University Press.

Bargh, J. A., & Thein, R. D. (1985). Individual construct accessibility, person memory, and the recall-judgment link: The case of information overload. *Journal of Personality and Social Psychology, 49,* 1129–1146.

Bargh, J. A., & Tota, M. E. (1988). Context-dependent automatic processing in depression: Accessibility of negative constructs with regard to self but not others. *Journal of Personality and Social Psychology, 54,* 925–939.

Bartlett, F. C. (1932). *Remembering.* Oxford, UK: University Press.

Baumeister, R. F., Bratslavsky, E., Finkenauer, C., & Vohs, K. D. (2001). Bad is stronger than good. *Review of General Psychology, 5,* 323–370.

Baumhart, R. (1968). *An honest profit: What businessmen say about ethics in business,* New York: Holt, Rinehart and Winston.

Berkowitz, L. (1984). Some effects of thoughts on anti- and prosocial influences of media events: A cognitive-neoassociation analysis. *Psychological Bulletin, 95,* 410–427.

Berkowitz, L. (1997). Some thoughts extending Bargh's argument. In R. S. Wyer (Ed.), *Advances in social cognition* (Vol. 10, pp. 83–94). Mahwah, NJ: Erlbaum.

Bhalla, M., & Proffitt, D. R. (1999). Visual-motor recalibration in geographical slant perception. *Journal of Experimental Psychology: Human Perception and Performance, 25,* 1–21.

Biederman, I., Mezzanotte, R. J., & Rabinowitz, J. C. (1982). Scene perception: Detecting and judging objects undergoing relational violations. *Cognitive Psychology, 14,* 143–177.

Bodenhausen, G. V., & Macrae, C. N. (1998). Stereotype activation and inhibition. In R. S. Wyer, (Ed.), *Stereotype activation and inhibition. Advances in social cognition* (Vol. 11, (pp. 1–52). Mahwah, NJ: Erlbaum.

Boyce, S. J., & Pollatsek, A. (1992). Identification of objects in scenes: The role of scene background in object naming.

Journal of Experimental Psychology: Learning, Memory, and Cognition, 18, 531–543.

Brendl, C. M., Markman, A. B., & Messner, C. (2003). The devaluation effect: Activating a need devaluates unrelated objects. *Journal of Consumer Research, 29,* 463–473.

Brewer, M. B. (1988). A dual process model of impression formation. In T. K. Srull & R. S. Wyer (Eds.), *A dual process model of impression formation: Advances in social cognition* (Vol. 1, pp. 1–36). Hillsdale, NJ: Erlbaum.

Brinsmead-Stockham, K., Johnston, L., Miles, L., & Macrae, C. N. (2008). Female sexual orientation and menstrual influences on person perception. *Journal of Experimental Social Psychology, 44,* 729–734.

Brownlow, S., Dixon, A. R., Egbert, C. A., & Radcliffe, R. D. (1997). Perception of movement and dancer characteristics from point-light displays of dance. *Psychological Record, 47,* 411–421.

Brugger, P., & Brugger, S. (1993). The Easter bunny in October: Is it disguised as a duck? *Perceptual and Motor Skills, 76,* 577–578.

Bruner, J. S. (1957). On perceptual readiness. *Psychological Review, 64,* 123–152.

Bruner, J. (1992). Another look at New Look. *American Psychologist, 47,* 780–783.

Bruner, J. S., & Goodman, C. C. (1947). Value and need as organizing factors in perception. *Journal of Abnormal and Social Psychology, 42,* 33–44.

Bruner, J. S., & Minturn, A. L. (1955). Perceptual identification and perceptual organization. *Journal of General Psychology, 53,* 21–28.

Bugelski, B. R., & Alampay, D. A. (1961). The role of frequency in developing perceptual sets. *Canadian Journal of Psychology, 15,* 205–211.

Carretie, L., Martin-Loeches, M., Hinojosa, J. A., & Mercado, F. (2001). Emotion and attention interaction studied through event-related potentials. *Journal of Cognitive Neuroscience, 13,* 1109–1128.

Carstensen, L. L., & Fredrickson, B. L. (1998). Influence of HIV status and age on cognitive representations of others. *Health Psychology, 17,* 494–503.

Carstensen, L. L., Isaacowitz, D. M., & Charles, S. T. (1999). Taking time seriously: A theory of socioemotional selectivity. *American Psychologist, 54,* 165–181.

Changizi, M. A., & Hall, W. G. (2001). Thirst modulates a perception. *Perception, 30,* 1489–1497.

Chua, H. F., Boland, J. E., & Nisbett, R. E. (2005). Cultural variation in eye movements during scene perception. *Proceedings of the National Academy of Sciences, 102,* 12629–12633.

Cole, R. (2010, August 29). Right wing rally to restore US Honour. News.sky.com. Retrieved March 14, 2013, from http://news.sky.com/story/802073/right-wing-rally-to-restore-us-honour.

Correll, J., Park, B., Judd, C. M., & Wittenbrink, B. (2002). The police officer's dilemma: Using ethnicity to disambiguate potentially threatening individuals. *Journal of Personality and Social Psychology, 83,* 1314–1329.

Correll, J., Park, B., Judd, C. M., & Wittenbrink, B. (2007). The influence of stereotypes on decisions to shoot. *European Journal of Social Psychology, 67,* 1102–1117.

Crandall, S. J., & de Lissovoy, V. (1977). Perceptual set in preschool children. *Journal of Genetic Psychology, 131,* 327–328.

Delboeuf, J. L. R. (1893). Sur une novelle illusion d'optique [On a new optical illusion]. *Bulletin de l'Academie Royale Belgique, 24,* 545–558.

Dittrich, W. H., Troscianko, T., Lea, S. & Morgan, D. (1996). Perception of emotion from dynamic point-light displays represented in dance. *Perception, 25,* 727–738.

Dollard, J., & Miller, N. E. (1950). *Personality and psychotherapy.* New York: McGraw-Hill.

Duffy, S., & Kitayama, S. (2010). Cultural modes of seeing through cultural modes of being: Cultural influences on visual attention. In E. Balcetis & G. D. Lassiter (Eds.) *Social psychology of visual perception* (pp. 51–75). New York: Psychology Press.

Eberhardt, J. L., Goff, P. A., Purdie, V. J., & Davies, P. G. (2004). Seeing Black: Race, crime, and visual processing. *Journal of Personality and Social Psychology, 87,* 876–893.

Eimer, M., Holmes, A., & McGlone, F. P. (2003). The role of spatial attention in the processing of facial expression: An ERP study of rapid brain responses to six basic emotions. *Cognitive, Affective & Behavioral Neuroscience, 3,* 97–110.

Epley, N., & Dunning, D. (2000). Feeling "holier than thou": Are self-serving assessments produced by errors in self- or social prediction? *Journal of Personality & Social Psychology, 79,* 861–875.

Epley, N., & Dunning, D. (2006). The mixed blessings of self-knowledge for behavioral prediction: Enhanced discrimination but exacerbated bias. *Personality and Social Psychology Bulletin, 32,* 641–655.

Epley, N., & Whitchurch, E. (2008). Mirror, mirror on the wall: Enhancement in self-recognition. *Personality and Social Psychology Bulletin, 34,* 1159–1170.

Erdelyi, M. H. (1974). A new look at the new look: Perceptual defense and vigilance. *Psychological Review, 81,* 1–25.

Erdelyi, M. H. (1985). *Psychoanalysis: Freud's cognitive psychology.* New York: W. H. Freeman.

Eriksen, C. W. (1958). Effects of practice with or without correction on discrimination learning. *American Journal of Psychology, 71,* 350–358.

Eriksen, C. W., & Browne, T. (1956). An experimental and theoretical analysis of perceptual defense. *Journal of Abnormal and Social Psychology, 52,* 224–230.

Esteve-Lanao J., Lucia A., de Koning J. J., & Foster C. (2008) How do humans control physiological strain during strenuous endurance exercise? *PLoS ONE, 3,* e2983.

Ferguson, M. J. (2007). On the automatic evaluation of end-states. *Journal of Personality and Social Psychology, 92,* 596–611.

Ferguson, M. J., & Bargh, J. A. (2004). Liking is for doing: The effects of goal pursuit on automatic evaluation. *Journal of Personality and Social Psychology, 87,* 557–572.

Fischer, E., Haines, R. F., & Price, T. A. (1980). Cognitive issues in head-up displays. *NASA Technical Paper 1711.* Moffett Field, CA: NASA Ames Research Center.

Fishbach, A., Zhang, Y., & Trope, Y. (2010). Counteractive evaluation: Asymmetric shifts in the implicit value of conflicting motivations. *Journal of Experimental Social Psychology, 46,* 29–38.

Fiske, S. T. (1992). Thinking is for doing: Portraits of social cognition from daguerreotype to laserphoto. *Journal of Personality & Social Psychology, 63,* 877–889.

Fiske, S. T. (1998). Stereotyping, prejudice, and discrimination. In D. T. Gilbert, S. T. Fiske, &G. Lindzey (Eds.), *The handbook of social psychology* (4th ed., pp. 357–411). New York: Oxford University Press.

Fiske, S. T., Lin, M., & Neuberg, S. L. (1999). The continuum model: Ten years later. In S. Chaiken & Y. Trope (Eds.), *Dual-process theories in social psychology* (pp. 231–254). New York: Guilford.

Fiske, S. T., & Taylor, S. E. (1984). *Social cognition.* New York: Random House.

Foa, E. B., & McNally, R. J. (1986). Sensitivity to feared stimuli in obsessive-compulsives: A dichotic listening analysis. *Cognitive Therapy & Research, 10*, 477–485.

Fodor, J. A. (1983). *The modularity of mind: An essay on faculty psychology.* Cambridge, MA: MIT Press.

Fortune, D. G., Richards, H. L., Corrin, A., Taylor, R. J., Griffiths, C. E. M., & Main, C. J. (2003). Attention bias for psoriasis-specific and psychosocial threat in patients with psoriasis. *Journal of Behavioral Medicine, 26*, 211–224.

Fraley, R. C., Niedenthal, P. M., Marks, M., Brumbaugh, C., & Vicary, A. (2006). Adult attachment and the perception of emotional expressions: Probing the hyperactivating strategies underlying anxious attachment. *Journal of Personality, 74*, 1163–1190.

Freeman, J. B., Ambady, N., Rule, N. O., & Johnson, K. L. (2008). Will a category cue attract you? Motor output reveals dynamic competition across person construal. *Journal of Experimental Psychology: General, 137*, 673–690.

Gamble, A. L., & Rapee, R. M. (2010). The time-course of attention to emotional faces in social phobia. *Journal of Behavior Therapy and Experimental Psychiatry, 41*, 39–44.

Gibson, J. J. (1979). *The ecological approach to visual perception.* London: Erlbaum.

Gilbert, D. T. (1989). Thinking lightly about others: Automatic components of the social inference process. In J. S. Uleman & J. A. Bargh (Eds.), *Unintended thought* (pp. 189–211). New York: Guilford.

Goldiamond, I. (1958). Indicators of perception: I. Subliminal perception, subception, unconscious perception: An analysis in terms of psychophysical indicator methodology. *Psychological Bulletin, 55*, 373–411.

Greenwald, A. G. (1992). New Look 3: Unconscious cognition reclaimed. *American Psychologist, 47*, 766–779.

Harvey, S. M. (1987). Female sexual behavior: Fluctuations during the menstrual cycle. *Journal of Psychosomatic Research, 31*,101–110.

Hill, E. M. (1988). The menstrual cycle and components of human sexual behavior. *Journal of Social Biological Structures, 11*, 443–455.

Howes, D. H., & Solomon, R. L. (1950). A note on McGinnies' "Emotionality and perceptual defense." *Psychological Review, 57*, 229–234.

Hull, C. L. (1932). The goal gradient hypothesis and maze learning. *Psychological Review, 39*, 25–43.

Inzlicht, M., Kaiser, C. R., & Major, B. (2008). The face of chauvinism: How prejudice expectations shape perceptions of facial affect. *Journal of Experimental Social Psychology, 44*, 758–766.

Isaacowitz, D. M. (2005). The gaze of the optimist. *Personality and Social Psychology Bulletin, 31*, 407–415.

Isaacowitz, D. M., Toner, K., Goren, D., & Wilson, H. R. (2008). Looking while unhappy: Mood congruent gaze in young adults, positive gaze in older adults. *Psychological Science, 19*, 848–853.

Isaacowitz, D. M., Wadlinger, H. A., Goren, D., & Wilson, H. R. (2006). Selective preference in visual fixation away from negative images in old age? An eye-tracking study. *Psychology and Aging, 21*, 40–48.

Ito, T. A., & Urland, G. R. (2003). Race and gender on the brain: Electrocortical measures of attention to race and gender of multiply categorizable individuals. *Journal of Personality and Social Psychology, 85*, 616–626.

James, W. (1890). *The principles of psychology.* New York: Holt.

Jenkins, B. (1995). *Three white police officers charged in death of black man.* CNN U.S. News.

Johnson, K. L., Gill, S., Reichman, V., & Tassinary, L. G. (2007). Swagger, sway, and sexuality: Judging sexual orientation from body motion and morphology. *Journal of Personality and Social Psychology, 93*, 321–334.

Johnson, K. L. & Tassinary, L. G. (2005). Perceiving sex directly and indirectly: Meaning in motion and morphology. *Psychological Science, 16*, 890–897.

Johnston, L., Arden, K., Macrae, C. N., & Grace, R. C. (2003). The need for speed: The menstrual cycle and person construal. *Social Cognition, 21*, 89–99.

Johnston, L., Miles, L., Carter, C., and Macrae, C. N. (2005) Menstrual influences on person perception: Male sensitivity to fluctuating female fertility. *Social Cognition, 23*, 279–290.

Kaspi, S. P., McNally, R. J., & Amir, N. (1995). Cognitive processing of emotional information in post-traumatic stress disorder. *Cognitive Therapy and Research, 19*, 433–444.

Kitayama, S., Duffy, S., Kawamura, T., & Larsen, J. T. (2003). Perceiving an object and its context in two cultures: a cultural look at New Look. *Psychological Science, 14*, 201–206.

Kunda, Z. (1990). The case for motivated reasoning. *Psychological Bulletin, 108*, 480–498.

Lerner, J. S., Gonzalez, R. M., Dahl, R. E., Hariri, A. R., & Taylor, S. E. (2005). Facial expressions of emotion reveal neuroendocrine and cardiovascular stress responses. *Biological Psychiatry, 58*, 743–750.

Lerner, J., & Tetlock, P. E. (1999). Accounting for the effects of accountability. *Psychological Bulletin, 125*, 255–275.

Levin, D. T., Simons, D. J., Angelone, B. L., & Chabris, C. F. (2002). Memory for centrally attended changing objects in an incidental real-world change detection paradigm. *British Journal of Psychology, 93*, 289–302.

Li, L., & Warren, W. H. J. (2004). Path perception during rotation: Influence of instructions, depth range, and dot density. *Vision Research, 44*, 1879–1889.

Linder, D. E., Cooper, J., & Jones, E. E. (1967). Decision freedom as a determinant of the role of incentive magnitude in attitude change. *Journal of Personality & Social Psychology, 6*, 245–254.

Locke, V., Macrae, C. N., & Eaton, J. L. (2005). Is person categorization modulated by exemplar typicality? *Social Cognition, 23*, 417–428.

Long, G. M., & Toppino, T. C. (2004). Enduring interest in perceptual ambiguity: Alternating views of reversible figures. *Psychological Bulletin, 130*, 748–768.

Loula, F., Prasad, S., Harber, K., & Shiffrar, M. (2005). Recognizing people from their movement. *Journal of Experimental Psychology: Human Perception and Performance, 31*, 210–220.

MacLin, O. H., & Malpass, R. S. (2001). Racial categorization of faces: The ambiguous race face effect. *Psychology, Public Policy, and Law, 7*, 98–118.

Macrae, C. N., Alnwick, K. A., Milne, A. B., & Schloerscheidt, A. M. (2002). Person perception across the menstrual cycle: Hormonal influences on social-cognitive functioning. *Psychological Science, 13*, 532–536.

Macrae, C. N., & Bodenhausen, G. V. (2001). Social cognition: Categorical person perception. *British Journal of Psychology, 92*, 239–255,

Maner, J. K., Miller, S. L., Rouby, D. A., & Gailliot, M. T. (2009). Intrasexual vigilance: The implicit cognition of romantic rivalry. *Journal of Personality and Social Psychology, 97*, 74–87.

Masuda, T., Ellsworth, P., Mesquita, B., Leu, J., Tanida, S., & Van de Veerdonk, E. (2008). Placing the face in context: Cultural differences in the perception of facial emotion. *Journal of Personality and Social Psychology, 94*, 365–381.

Masuda, T., & Nisbett, R. E. (2006). Culture and change blindness. *Cognitive Sciences, 30*, 381–399.

Mather, M., & Carstensen, L. L. (2003). Aging and attention biases for emotional faces. *Psychological Science, 14*, 409–415.

Matteo, S., & Rissman, E. F. (1984). Increased sexual activity during the midcycle portion of the human menstrual cycle. *Hormones and Behavior, 18*, 249–255.

McCauley, R. N., & Henrich, J. (2006). Susceptibility to the Muller-Lyer Illusion, theory-neutral observation, and the diachronic penetrability of the visual input system. *Philosophical Psychology, 19*, 79–101.

McCurdy, H. G. (1956). Coin perception studies and the concept of schemata. *Psychological Review, 63*, 160–168.

McKenzie, S. J., Williamson, D. A., & Cubic, B. A. (1993). Stable and reactive body image disturbances in bulimia nervosa. *Behavior Therapy, 24*, 195–207.

Miller, G. F., & Todd, P. M. (1998). Mate choice turns cognitive. *Trends in Cognitive Sciences, 2*, 190–198.

Mischel, W., & Ebbesen, E. B. (1970). Attention in delay of gratification. *Journal of Personality and Social Psychology, 16*, 329–337.

Miyamoto, Y., Nisbett, R. E., & Masuda, T. (2006). Culture and the physical environment: Holistic versus analytic perceptual affordances. *Psychological Science, 17*, 113–119.

Mogg, K., Bradley, B. P., Williams, R., & Mathews, A. (1993). Subliminal processing of emotional information in anxiety and depression. *Journal of Abnormal Psychology, 102*, 304–311.

Mogg, K., Millar, M., & Bradley, B. P. (2000). Biases in eye movements to threatening facial expressions in generalized anxiety disorder and depressive disorder. *Journal of Abnormal Psychology, 109*, 695–704.

Monteith, M. J., Lybarger, J. E., & Woodcock, A. (2009). Schooling the cognitive monster: The role of motivation in the regulation and control of prejudice. *Social and Personality Psychology Compass, 3*, 211–226.

Montepare, J. M. (2010). "Cue, view, action": An ecological approach to person perception. In E. Balcetis & G. D. Lassiter (Eds.), *The social psychology of visual perception* (pp. 299–324). New York: Psychology Press.

Patrick, D. (2010, October). Just my type. *Sports Illustrated SI Vault Blog*. Retrieved July 1, 2011, from: http://sportsillustrated.cnn.com/vault/article/magazine/MAG1175387/4/index.htm#ixzz13B5W9onC.

Pineles, S. L., & Mineka, S. (2005). Attention biases to internal and external sources of potential threat in social anxiety. *Journal of Abnormal Psychology, 114*, 314–318.

Prentice, W. C. H. (1958). Perception. *Annual Review of Psychology, 9*, 1–18.

Proffitt, D. R., Stefanucci, J., Banton, T., & Epstein, W. (2003). The role of effort in perceiving distance. *Psychological Science, 14*, 106–112.

Pylyshyn, Z. W. (1999). Is vision continuous with cognition? The case for cognitive impenetrability of visual perception. *Behavioral and Brain Sciences, 22*, 341–423.

Rachman, S., & Cuk, M. (1992). Fearful distortions. *Behavioral Research Therapy, 30*, 583–589.

Riskind, J., Moore, R., & Bowley, L. (1995). The looming of spiders: The fearful perceptual distortion of movement and menace. *Behaviour Research and Therapy, 33*, 171–178.

Rock, I. (1975). *An introduction to perception.* New York: Macmillan.

Rule, N. O., & Ambady, N. (2008). Brief exposures: Male sexual orientation is accurately perceived at 50 ms. *Journal of Experimental Social Psychology, 44*, 1100–1105.

Rule, N. O., & Ambady, N. (2010). Democrats and Republicans can be differentiated from their faces. *PLoS ONE, 5*, e8733.

Rule, N. O., Macrae, C. N., & Ambady, N. (2009). Ambiguous group membership is extracted automatically from faces. *Psychological Science, 20*, 441–443.

Runeson, S., & Frykholm, G. (1981). Visual perception of lifted weight. *Journal of Experimental Psychology: Human Perception and Performance, 7*, 733–740.

Runeson, S., & Frykholm, G. (1983). Kinematic specification of dynamics as an informational basis for person-and-action perception: Expectation, gender recognition, and deceptive intention. *Journal of Experimental Psychology: General, 112*, 585–615.

Sebastian, S. B., Williamson, D. A., & Blouin, D. C. (1996). Memory bias for fatness stimuli in the eating disorders. *Cognitive Therapy & Research, 20*, 275–286.

Sechrest, L., & Wallace, J. (1964). Figure drawings and naturally occurring events. *Journal of Educational Psychology, 55*, 42–44.

Shepard, R. N. (1990) *Mindsights.* New York: W. H. Freedman.

Skinner, B. F. (1938). *The behavior of organisms.* New York: Appleton-Century-Crofts.

Skinner, B. F. (1953). *Science and human behavior.* New York: Free Press.

Skinner, B. F. (1971). *Beyond freedom and dignity.* New York: Knopf.

Skowronski, J. J., & Carlston, D. E. (1989). Negativity and extremity biases in impression formation: A review of explanation. *Psychological Review, 105*, 131–142.

Slade, P. D. (1985). A review of body-image studies in anorexia nervosa and bulimia nervosa. *Journal of Psychiatric Research, 19*, 255–265.

Sundy, A. (2010, August 28). Glenn Beck rally attracts estimated 87,000. *CBS News.* Retrieved July 5, 2011, from http://www.cbsnews.com/8301-503544_162-20014993-503544.html.

van Koningsbruggen, G. M., Stroebe, W., & Aarts, H. (2011). Through the eyes of dieters: Biased size perception of food following tempting food primes. *Journal of Experimental Social Psychology, 47*, 293–299.

Veltkamp, M., Aarts, H., & Custers, R. (2008). Perception in the service of goal pursuit: Motivation to attain goals enhances the perceived size of goal-instrumental objects. *Social Cognition, 26*, 720–736.

Walton, G. M., & Cohen, G. L. (2003). Stereotype lift. *Journal of Experimental Social Psychology, 39*, 456–467.

Watkins, P. C., Martin, C., Muller, S., & Day, S. K. (1995). Cognitive biases associated with feelings of fatness: Unhealthy responses to healthy messages. *Advances in Health Care Research, 14*, 67–73.

Wegner, D. M., & Bargh, J. A. (1998). Control and automaticity in social life. In D. T. Gilbert, S. T. Fiske, & G. Lindzey.

(Eds.), *The handbook of social psychology* (pp. 446–496). New York: McGraw-Hill.

Williams, J. M., Watts, F. N., MacLeod, C., & Mathews, A. (1997). *Cognitive psychology and emotional disorders*. Chichester, UK: John Wiley & Sons.

Williamson, D. A. (1990). *Assessment of eating disorders: Obesity, bulimia, and anorexia nervosa*. New York: Pergamon.

Williamson, D. A. (1996). Body image disturbance in eating disorders: A form of cognitive bias. *Eating Disorders: The Journal of Treatment & Prevention, 4*, 47–58.

Winter, L., & Uleman, J. S. (1984). When are social judgments made? Evidence for the spontaneousness of trait inferences. *Journal of Personality and Social Psychology, 47*, 237–252.

Witt, J. K., & Dorsch, T. E. (2009). Kicking to bigger uprights: Field goal kicking performance influences perceived size. *Perception, 38*, 1328–1340.

Witt, J. K., Linkenauger, S. A., Bakdash, J. Z., Augustyn, J. A., Cook, A. S., & Proffitt, D. R. (2009). The long road of pain: Chronic pain increases perceived distance. *Experimental Brain Research, 192*, 145–148

Witt, J. K., Linkenauger, S. A., Bakdash, J. Z., & Proffitt, D. R. (2008). Putting to a bigger hole: Golf performance relates to perceived size. *Psychonomic Bulletin & Review, 15*, 581–585.

Wohlwill, J. F. (1966). The physical environment: A problem for a psychology of stimulation. *Journal of Social Issues, 22*, 29–38.

Xing, C., & Isaacowitz, D. M. (2006). Aiming at happiness: How motivation affects attention to and memory for emotional information. *Motivation and Emotion, 30*, 243–350.

Yovel, I., & Mineka, S. (2005). Emotion-congruent attention biases: The perspective of hierarchical models of emotional disorders. *Personality and Individual Differences, 38*, 785–795.

Person Memory: Past, Perspectives, and Prospects

John J. Skowronski, Randy J. McCarthy, *and* Brett M. Wells

Abstract

What information do we remember about others and why do we remember it? The answers to those questions are informed by the scholarship described in this chapter. The chapter notes that most person memory research addresses one or more of four facets: (1) the content of person memories, (2) information processing and person memories; (2) the nature of memory storage systems and person memory; and (4) the role of biology in the functioning of person memory. A selective review of research in person memory illustrates how research fits into these facets. The review is also used to illustrate possible new directions for person memory research.

Key Words: person memory, information processing, memory storage systems, role of biology

The study of *person memory* reflects those elements of an individual's memory system that reflect memory for specific people and includes an understanding of cognitive, social, and individual variables that are related to such recall. The word *social* in our definition is especially important. The study of person memory is seen by some in social psychology as a specialized offshoot of cognitive psychology that has been pursued only by those who have little interest in how people navigate the real world. Such a perception is grossly misguided, and is surely influenced by the fact that the study of person memory has often focused on individual measures of memory obtained in minimally social contexts. However, it is a mistake to confuse the individualistic contexts in which person memory research is typically pursued with the social importance of person memory. We assert that person memory is absolutely central to how people think about others, and consequently, is absolutely central to how people interact with others.

To understand this view, imagine how difficult life would be if you had no person memory. Each

person who walked thorough the door into your room would be a cipher. You would not know to seek the support of a person who was your faithful and loving spouse. You would not know to avoid the threat posed by someone who, in the past, repeatedly stole your cash. Because of your impaired person memory, you would not know what to do because you would not know who the new arrivals were. Clearly, your ability both to take advantage of the opportunities presented by the social world and to avoid its risks would be severely impaired by an absence of person memory.

This functionality has been taken for granted by person memory researchers. Hence, only a minority of studies have explored how person memories are used or what they are good for. Instead, person memory research and theory have tended to focus on the memories themselves.

Even this specific focus has led to the emergence of a vast literature. The vastness of this literature makes it hard to "get one's head around" the topic, and certainly makes the literature difficult to covey in a short chapter such as this. An example of this vastness is illustrated by the research and theory described in two hefty volumes that appeared in 2007 (Toglia, Read, Ross, & Lindsay, 2007; Lindsay, Ross, Read, & Toglia, 2007). However, even those volumes are incomplete—understandable given that their focus is on person memory in contexts relevant to crime and the legal system.

Given that presenting a comprehensive review cannot be a goal of this chapter, what are we trying to do here? We have two goals in mind. First, to help the readers of this chapter to "get their heads around" the topic; and to aid our presentation, we will first describe four facets of research and theory that have driven, and that continue to drive, the science of person memory. In this description of the facets, we attempt to provide a structure that might be useful when readers think about person memory theory and research. In subsequent sections, we describe the historical context of person memory research and specific areas of research that have pursued the science of person memory. In these descriptions, we relate the research and theory described back to the facets that we outlined. Our goals in presenting these specific areas of research and theory are both to increase the reader's knowledge about person memory and to facilitate the reader's understanding of the facets. Our review is necessarily selective (with heartfelt apologies to those who do not see their favorite areas described herein). The areas of research and theory that we present have been selected because of their historical importance, their contemporary importance, their interest value, and/or the extent to which they serve as good illustrations of some of the facets that we have outlined.

Four Facets of Person Memory
Facet 1—Recall for What?

One facet of person memory concerns content for the diverse *elements of a person*: What is it about another person that is remembered? A moment's reflection will suggest that because there is a lot about others that can be remembered, the answer to this question can get very complicated.

For example, imagine that Mona is your long-time companion, so you can remember a lot about her. Your memories of Mona can include a lot of different things. One is recognition of her identity, including her name (that's Mona!). You can recall Mona's physical characteristics, including her appearance (face, physique, gait, hair color) and vocal qualities (dusky voice). Your can recall behaviors that Mona exhibited when she was with you (she sank a 50-foot putt to beat me in our match last week), how she

interacted with you (e.g., when doing a dancing routine with her), behaviors that she exhibited elsewhere (she aced her psychology test), or events that happened to her (she was hit by a meteor). You can also recall your feelings toward her (she made me so angry), and perhaps even re-experience some of those feelings. One goal in this chapter is to illustrate this diversity by describing research that touches on a number of these different attributes.

Facet 2—Processing and Person Memory

Clearly, there's a lot to remember about Mona. Why do people remember some things and not others? This question can be partially answered by looking at a second facet of person memory: the *cognitive processes of acquisition, encoding, storage, retrieval, and reprocessing*. Because of the importance of this perspective to the area of person memory, this chapter will talk a lot about research that relates to these processes.

These processes can be illustrated by using some examples related to the hypothetical Mona. For example, assume that before you met Mona you were led to believe that she was hot-blooded. Because this expectation may have tuned your attention to trait-related behavior and affected how you thought about such behavior, you might be especially likely to now recall that on your first date, Mona berated the waiter who screwed up the dinner order. A second hypothetical example might come from the fact that you have noticed that there are a few ways in which Mona is exceptional or violates expectations (e.g., she's 6'5"); you might be especially likely to remember such features because they attract your attention and/or because you think about them a lot. A third hypothetical example is that you might be unable to recall the dress that Mona wore to the Christmas party, but you recognize it when you see it. This example illustrates the idea that what is recalled about a person often depends on the context in which information is recalled and the recall cues that are available. A fourth hypothetical example might be that you often recall the story of how Mona embarrassed her logic-driven Economics professor by repeatedly asking questions about research exploring psychological heuristics. You might remember this fact because the story often gets a laugh in social situations, so you tell it often. This example illustrates two important ideas related to processing: (1) rehearsal matters to memory, and (2) social factors can influence rehearsal tendencies. Consider a fifth hypothetical example. You might be astonished to see how a friend's long-lost video of the class session with the Econ professor differs from your recall of the situation. You might realize that the disparity has occurred because you have embellished the story with repeated retellings. This example illustrates the notions that (1) memories for others can be flawed, and (2) these flaws can be introduced by the way in which events are rehearsed or reprocessed.

Facet 3—Bins, Boxes, or Bags: Where Do Memories Get Stored?

Once you've acquired information about Mona, where do you put it? This question addresses a third facet of person memory, the *structure of memory*. One fundamental question about structure is whether memory is just one big storage area, or whether different memory subsystems tend to handle different kinds of information (e.g., one for visual memories, a second for semantic facts). If memory consists of specialized subsystems, one would like to know the answers to a lot of different questions, such as (1) how many subsystems are there? (2) what are the different properties (e.g., are there different forgetting rates?) of the different subsystems? (3) is there a hierarchy (e.g., do I recall emotions first?) among the subsystems? and (4) how does information from the various subsystems get reassembled or combined when one thinks of a person?

One implication of the presence of different subsystems is that information in the different subsystems might become disassociated; that is, one type of information about a person might be recalled while a second type is forgotten. For example, imagine that five years ago you were introduced to Mona. Also imagine that when meeting her again at a recent party, you had the embarrassing experience of knowing you had met her before (i.e., remembering that you had interacted with her), but could not recall who she was (i.e., were unable to retrieve her identity). It is thought by some that such dissociations reflect the fact that identity information about others and appearance information are stored in different memory subsystems.

The information presented in this chapter will reflect the interest of person memory researchers in the possibility that different memory storage systems exist and the attributes that such storage systems exhibit.

Facet 4—Biology: Questions of Structure, Questions of Evolution

A fourth facet of the study of person memory concerns the biology of person memory. One sub-facet of this approach concerns brain structure and brain activity: the ideas about memory structures and cognitive processes that are invoked to study person memory need to be grounded in biologically plausible theories of brain structure and brain function. In terms of our recurring hypothetical Mona example, if Smedley the psychologist postulates that your memories about Mona are present because of the action of widgets on the brain, then those widgets should at least be biologically plausible and, ideally, should be potentially detectable.

A second sub-facet considers person memory from the perspective of evolution. For example, one of the important environmental selection pressures that may have acted on early pre-human hominid species may have come from the social habit of the species. One evolutionary response to this selection pressure may have been to selectively "tune" the brain so that it could be especially facile at navigating this social world. One element of this selective tuning might involve social memory. Hence, to return to our recurring example, you might have better memory for characteristics of Mona than for characteristics of algebra because evolution has given you a brain and a processing system that have been tuned by evolution to provide especially good recall for the attributes of others.

Ideas about biology and evolution have only recently received much scrutiny in the study of person memory. Thus, although this chapter does discuss some of the research in this area, the chapter also spends some time exploring the possibilities for new research that can be spawned from this perspective.

Ascent of Person Memory in Social Psychology
Prehistorical Context of Person Memory

Before moving on to specific domains, we'd like to briefly place the area of person memory in historical context. An examination of that context suggests that memory for aspects of people has for a long time been a topic of interest in psychology. For example, one of the great practical problems of life occurs when one recognizes a person as familiar, but can't recall their name. Proposed solutions to this specific problem of person memory appeared early in the scientific psychology literature (see chapters on *Memory of Names* and *Memory of Faces* in Atkinson, 1903). The study of memory for the attributes of other people also has a strong tradition coming from the study of individual differences. For example, Gould (1917) described development of a test to assess an individual's ability to remember names and faces. Tests examining these abilities were later folded into assessments of the individual differences construct of social intelligence (e.g., Moss & Hunt, 1927; Moss, Hunt, Omwake, & Bonning, 1927; Moss, Hunt, Omwake, & Woodward, 1955). In fact, as best as can be determined, the term *person memory* appears to have originally been used by scholars working in the social intelligence tradition. A PsychInfo search conducted on January 5, 2011 identified an article published by Probst (1975) as the first to use that specific term.

Then Lightning Strikes...: Person Memory and the Ascent of Social Cognition

However, despite the broad early scientific interest in memory for attributes of people, the term *person memory* is more closely associated with the emergence of the social cognitive perspective in social psychology. Much of the emphasis of this perspective reflects Facet 2 in the scheme described in prior pages, suggesting that how a perceiver processes information about others helps to determine aspects of memory for the information that was processed. Three vanguard articles published in 1978–1980 illustrate this perspective.

The first of these articles appeared in 1978. Taylor, Fiske, Etcoff, and Ruderman reported results from research in which perceivers observed interacting small groups. The individuals in the group differed from each other in terms of their gender or ethnicity. The perceivers then tried to remember who said what. The researchers observed systematicity in source monitoring errors, finding that perceivers more often confused communicators within social categories (e.g., attributing one woman's comments to another woman) than between social categories (e.g., attributing a woman's comments to a man). The authors attributed such errors to the tendency to think about others in terms of social categories. They speculated that this tendency then played a role when trying to attribute comments to sources, with increased errors occurring when people used the social category to which an informant belonged in the process of reconstructing who said what.

The second of the two vanguard articles appeared in 1980. Hamilton, Katz, and Leirer published research that explored participant performance on a task that required recall of a series of behavior descriptions. Before encountering the list of descriptions, participants had been instructed to either recall the descriptions or to form impressions of the individuals who enacted the behaviors described. The results of the studies consistently showed that people instructed to form impressions recalled more of the behavior descriptions than those who did not.

Hamilton et al. tied this result to both the cognitive processes in which people engaged as they encountered the items and the cognitive structures that were produced by such thought. That is, Hamilton et al. postulated that the process of forming an impression prompted integration of the available information into an organized cognitive representation of the target person. Hamilton et al. suggested that this organization would facilitate later retrieval of the individual descriptive items, which is exactly the outcome that they found.

The third of the vanguard articles appeared in 1979. Hastie and Kumar published research that explored how memories for the behaviors of actors might be affected by the kinds of trait expectancies that one has about those actors. In their studies, they provided perceivers with a trait expectancy about an actor, then presented a series of actor behaviors that were either consistent with the expectancy, inconsistent with the expectancy, or irrelevant to the expectancy. They found that the expectancy affected recall such that perceivers were least likely to recall the trait-irrelevant information, moderately likely to recall the trait-consistent information, and most likely to recall the trait-inconsistent information. Hastie and Kumar explained this finding in terms of the kinds of cognitive processing that the experimental situation prompted during behavior encoding and the kinds of mental representations of the actors that resulted and that were presumed to guide recall.

As evidenced by the gush of research that followed, the vanguard articles (these and more) that appeared in the late 1970s and early 1980s stimulated a lot of research and shaped the content of that research. This kind of research came to be known by the term *person memory*, a term that was stamped indelibly into the literature by the landmark 1980 book titled *Person Memory: The Cognitive Basis of Social Perception.*

The opening chapter of the book, penned by Reid Hastie and Donal Carlston, identified this new field as growing out of an attempt to apply the theories, principles, and methods of cognitive psychology to the "formation, representation, and retrieval of first impressions of other people" (p. 1). (Note that the frequency with which Donal Carlston's first name has been mis-recalled by others as "Donald" may itself attest to the power of these principles.) The chapters in the book described theory and research reflecting such topics. One of these research topics was Hastie's incongruity research. Other chapters explored (1) whether the behaviors that an actor performed about a person might be organized in memory around various themes, including situations and traits; (2) the extent to which trait inferences might be stored in memory and used (instead of behavior recall) to make subsequent judgments about an actor; and (3) the extent to which memory reflects domain expertise that is expressed through processes of encoding that occur while viewing an ongoing sequence of behaviors. Still other chapters provided general cognitive frameworks for the study of person memory, describing how various processes and structures might be involved in person memory and detailing some methods and approaches that one might use to study such processes and structures.

The echoes of these scholarly products still reverberate in contemporary theory and research. For example, researchers are still exploring the extent to which stereotypes and traits affect memory for behaviors. They are sometimes now doing so in the context of a single paradigm that simultaneously manipulates both stereotypes and traits (Gingrich, Houston, & Lupfer, 1998; Heider, Scherer, Skowronski, Wood, Edlund, & Hartnett, 2007). Other research explores how false memories for a person's traits can sometimes come from implicit personality theories, hypothetical memory structures that link one trait to another. When people remember one trait, this implicit personality memory structure can induce a false memory for a second trait that the implicit personality theory links to the first (Garcia-Marques, Ferreira, Nunes, Garrido, & Garcia-Marques, 2010). Increasingly sophisticated analyses are being applied to the kinds of data obtained in the Taylor et al. (1978) who-said-what paradigm with the hope of disentangling the various mental processes that might contribute to the source memory errors that have been observed (e.g., Klauer & Wegener, 1998). Other studies have explored the downstream implications of kinds of representations formed when people process behaviorally incongruent information about others (Garcia-Marques, Hamilton, & Maddox, 2002). We now discuss some of this work in more detail.

Illustrative Themes and Threads in Person Memory Research and Theory
The Incongruity Paradigm in Person Memory: What Has It Wrought?
FROM THE BEGINNING: INCONGRUITY, ENCODING, AND AN EMPHASIS ON ASSOCIATIONISM

Hastie and Kumar's (1979) results, described earlier, suggested that perceivers better recall trait-inconsistent information than trait-consistent or trait-irrelevant information. This result was especially interesting because it contradicted the expectation, derived from the cognitive schema literature, that expectancy-congruent information should be preferentially remembered (e.g., see Johnson, Doll, Bransford, & Lapinski, 1974; Thorndyke & Hayes-Roth, 1979). One explanation for this unexpected effect was that people noted the discrepancies among the behaviors, prompting cognitive processing aimed at reconciling those discrepancies (see Hamilton & Garcia-Marques, 2003; Hastie & Kumar, 1979, Newman, 2001; Wyer & Srull 1989).

Alternative conceptions debated the exact nature of this reconciliation. Some (as in Srull, 1981) suggested that reconciliatory activity was prompted by behaviors that had inconsistent trait implications (e.g., an honest-implying behavior and a dishonest-implying behavior). Others (as in Wyer & Srull, 1989) thought that a focus on trait implications was too specific, believing that reconciliatory activity could be prompted by simple evaluative inconsistency among behaviors. Regardless of the exact nature of the reconciliatory processing involved, it was generally hypothesized that reconciliatory processing produced more retrieval paths to expectancy-incongruent (trait-inconsistent) items than to expectancy-congruent (trait-consistent) items. This advantage in the number of available retrieval pathways led expectancy-incongruent items to be especially likely to be recalled.

Analyses of spew orders (the orders in which people listed events as they recalled them) at recall (e.g., Srull, 1981) seemed to confirm the theory: Studies revealed a high probability of recalling an expectancy-incongruent behavior after recalling an expectancy-congruent behavior. This evidence was taken to reflect pathways formed between items during reconciliation. This idea is easily understandable: If one spends time and effort trying to figure out how a person who returns a lost wallet to its owner can also steal from the church collection box, then at a later time recalling one of these two behaviors is likely to cue recall of the other.

However, after a spurt of supportive research results, one crack in the theory emerged: The spew order data failed to support this inter-item reconciliation notion when perceivers were given multiple trait expectancies, instead of just one, about the actor (Hamilton, Driscoll, & Worth, 1989; Trafimow & Finlay, 2001).

Moreover, inter-behavior reconciliation was only one possible explanation for the incongruity effect (see Fiske & Taylor, 1991). An alternative idea, advocated by Stangor and McMillan (1992) and reiterated by Kunda (1999), suggested that expectancy-incongruent items triggered attempts to reconcile those items with the trait implied by the initial behavior encountered (e.g., "How can a kind person steal from the church collection box?"). However, this explanation did not seem to gain much traction in the literature. Although the reason is unclear, most likely this lack of traction occurred because this explanation did not readily account for the data derived from the spew orders produced at recall.

ALTERNATIVE VIEWS AND PROBLEMS FOR THE ASSOCIATIONISTIC APPROACH

Another alternative explanation was that the expectancy-incongruent item was simply unexpected (e.g., Carlston & Smith, 1996; also see Frey, 1986); it was this unexpectedness that caused perceivers to shift additional processing to that item. Such processing should *increase the distinctiveness of that item's memory trace* in the memory representation of the target person. This idea is consistent with results from recognition tasks showing that expectancy-incongruent items are more recognizable (as measured by indices such as d') than expectancy-congruent items (see Forster, Higgins, & Strack, 2000). However, as with the trait-reconciliation mechanism, this explanation seemed incomplete because it did not provide an adequate account for the spew order data.

However, the veracity of the results yielded by the spew order analyses (e.g., Srull, 1981) was called into question by Skowronski and Welbourne (1997). The spew order analyses relied on calculations of conditional probabilities derived from the spew orders (e.g., given recall of an expectancy-congruent item, how likely is recall of an expectancy-congruent item?). Skowronski and Welbourne argued that the conditional probability calculations typically used in incongruity studies were potentially contaminated by differential recall rates among item types. For example, assume that a study presented some behaviors that had kind implications and others that had unkind implications. Assume that two hypothetical participants, Jade and Bettina, each recalled five kind items. If Jade remembered 10 unkind items and Bettina remembered two, *then simply by chance*, Jade would have a greater likelihood than Bettina of recalling an unkind item after recalling a kind item.

Given the enhanced recall for expectancy-incongruent items observed in many studies, Skowronski and Welbourne suggested that disparities

in the content of the items recalled could be causing the conditional probability effects that were observed. Indeed, even though an incongruity effect was evident in their recall data, after correcting for differences in the recall rates of expectancy-congruent items and expectancy-incongruent items, Skowronski and Gannon (2000) found no evidence that expectancy-incongruent items were especially likely to be recalled after recalling an expectancy-congruent item (also see Skowronski, Betz, Sedikides, & Crawford, 1998). Such results seriously challenged the inter-item reconciliation mechanism: If the incongruity effect occurs even when there is no evidence of more memory links to incongruent items than to congruent items, then another mechanism must be responsible.

Uncertainty about the mechanism that underlies the incongruity effect was prompted by yet another finding that often emerged in the stereotyping literature: When perceivers received a stereotype-based expectancy and were later exposed to stereotype-relevant items, they often evinced especially good memory for the *stereotype-congruent* items (Bodenhausen, 1988; Crawford & Skowronski, 1998; Sherman & Frost, 2000; for a meta-analysis, see Fyock & Stangor, 1994).

One might explain these divergent effects in terms of differences in the properties of trait expectancies and stereotype expectancies (as did Stangor & McMillan, 1992), but research suggests that this does not suffice. For example, this idea cannot account for stereotyping studies that show that recall is sometimes better for stereotype-incongruent actor behaviors than for stereotype-congruent actor behaviors (e.g., Dijksterhuis & van Knippenberg, 1995, 1996; Dijksterhuis, van Knippenberg, Kruglanski, & Schaper, 1996; Heider et al., 2007; Plaks, Stroessner, Dweck, & Sherman, 2001; Scherer, Heider, Skowronski, & Edlund, 2012. More confusion comes from the fact that the stereotype-related recall pattern can change across circumstances. For example, preferential recall for stereotype-consistent or stereotype-inconsistent information depends on whether the target is an out-group member or an in-group member (Bardach & Park, 1996; Wanke & Wyer, 1996).

A MODERN SYNTHESIS: MEMORY IN THE FULL CONTEXT OF ENCODING-DRIVEN COGNITIVE ACTIVITIES

Our current view is that to understand such mixed findings, one must pull back from the original theoretical focus on inter-item reconciliatory processing.

Instead, one needs to consider the potential cascade of cognitive effects that can occur in response to inconsistency. Among these are: (1) A perceiver's attention might be drawn to inconsistent events (White & Carlston, 1983); (2) such events can be difficult to encode conceptually, so they are processed longer and produce a stronger perceptual representation (von Hippel, Jonides, Hilton, & Narayan, 1993); (3) people might attempt to construct a story to accommodate the inconsistent facts (e.g., Pennington & Hastie, 1993); (4) people might try to develop attributions for expectancy-incongruent events (Crocker, Hannah, & Weber, 1983); or (5) people can seek to explain expectancy-incongruent events (Hastie, 1984). All of these mechanisms can potentially alter memory for expectancy-relevant behaviors without involving inter-behavior reconciliatory activity. Such an approach exemplifies what we call "the modern synthesis" in the approach to the study of person memory.

Additional explanatory power might be achieved by avoiding a sole focus on the processing of expectancy-incongruent behaviors, also considering processes pertaining to the processing of expectancy-congruent behaviors. For example, as von Hippel et al. (1993) note, congruous events are processed in a more conceptual and less perceptual manner than incongruous events (for a similar point, see Ebbesen, 1980). More generally, one might posit that expectancy-congruent items may receive a recall boost (relative to both incongruent and neutral items) because of the ease with which they can be conceptually encoded and because the expectancy can serve as a retrieval cue once behaviors have been encoded in terms of that expectancy. In contrast, expectancy-incongruent items might sometimes receive a recall boost because they are scrutinized for an especially long time and especially carefully. Such processing can yield a memory trace that is especially strong and detailed, that can be easily distinguished from other memory traces, and that might be especially immune to various false memory phenomena such as the implantation of false details in the memory.

In addition, these processes might be altered as situational conditions change. For example, Sherman's (2001) encoding flexibility model posits that people have flexibility in how they allocate processing resources, and will change their allocations as circumstances require. Consistent with this idea, Sherman, Conrey, and Groom (2004) found that a cognitive load increased the attention paid to stereotype-inconsistent information, and decreased the attention paid to stereotype-consistent information.

Cognitive load also enhanced the perceptual encoding of inconsistent information while diminishing the perceptual encoding of consistent information. Allen, Sherman, Conrey, and Stroessner (2009) found similar results in two experiments that manipulated cognitive load, and showed that when participants had full cognitive capacity, greater stereotype strength was associated with increased attention toward stereotype-consistent (as opposed to inconsistent) information. However, when capacity was diminished by load, greater stereotype strength was associated with increased attention to stereotype-inconsistent information. Given these results, the authors suggested that strong stereotypes may act as self-confirming filters when processing capacity is plentiful, but as efficient information gathering devices, which maximize the acquisition of novel (disconfirming) information, when capacity is depleted.

Another example of how a nuanced view of the entire sequence of information processing can help to explain these kinds of memory effects comes from data reported by Sherman, Stroessner, Conrey, and Azam (2005). They were interested in how a perceiver's prejudice level affected their treatment of incoming information that was either consistent with a stereotype of an actor or was inconsistent with that stereotype. The results provided by the research team suggested that, as measured by a recognition-discrimination score, high levels of prejudice were associated with attending to and encoding inconsistent information more thoroughly than consistent information. Results from an additional study suggested that these effects are related to the types of attributions high-prejudice persons make for consistent behaviors and inconsistent behaviors. Stereotype-inconsistent behaviors tend to prompt external attributions, whereas stereotype-consistent behaviors tend to prompt internal attributions. The authors argue that these findings suggest that high-prejudice people set a higher threshold for accepting stereotype-inconsistent behavior than for accepting stereotype-consistent behavior and scrutinize the former much more carefully than the latter when they possess the resources to do so.

Most of the processes described in the paragraphs above focus on processes that affect event encoding and storage. However, detailed attention to the mental processes that are involved in the methods used to assess memory also can aid an understanding of memory effects. For example, Sherman, Groom, Ehrenberg, and Klauer (2003) conducted research that tried to understand why people falsely remember stereotype-consistent information when cognitive resources are depleted. A task adapted from Jacoby's (1991) process dissociation procedure assessed participants' ability to distinguish between distracter items and descriptions of behaviors performed by a stereotyped target that had actually been presented. Results from a multinomial analysis of behavior recognition data revealed that when under cognitive load, participants' recognition judgments were especially unlikely to be related to actual behavior recollection. Instead, these judgments were especially influenced by behavior familiarity. Because familiarity is in part determined by the relation of a behavior to a stereotype, under cognitive load, people were especially likely to falsely recognize the familiar stereotype-consistent behaviors.

The kind of work that is described in these studies reflects the complexity of the modern synthesis that characterizes contemporary work in person memory. Overall, we opine that the modern synthesis has clearly advanced our understanding of how the various expectancy-relevant processes occurring at event encoding can affect person memory. However, it is also clear that the problem is not yet entirely solved. For example, one of the deficiencies of this modern synthesis is that it has not left a place for the associationistic ideas (e.g., Hastie & Kumar, 1979) that originally drove research in this area. These ideas have survived, and even prospered, in other guises (e.g., Garcia-Marques, Hamilton, & Maddox, 2002). Hence, the omission of such ideas from recent theorizing is rather puzzling.

Such omissions may reflect the fact that researchers may have become bored with the view that focused on reconciliation and the associations among behaviors prompted by such reconciliatory activity and moved on to explore other processes. Alternatively, such omissions may reflect the fact that the modern synthesis does not place much credence in the validity of the reconciliation/association view. Indeed, our own view (influenced by Heider at al., 2007; Skowronski & Gannon, 2000) doubts that reconciliatory processing has much to do with the kinds of memory effects that one sees in the typical person memory paradigm.

However, that's not to say that such reconciliation/association processes may not be important to person memory, at least under some circumstances. For example, the typical person memory paradigm offers participants scant time and minimal motivation to reconcile discrepant behaviors or to reconcile discrepancies among behaviors and expectancies. However, the kinds of reconciliatory processing and mental representations postulated by the reconciliation/association view might indeed emerge under specific conditions that promote association-producing processing, or even that force such processing. Such research is important because many studies inferred such processing from other measures (recall rates, spew orders, recall times), but to our knowledge not many tried to directly assess or manipulate whether such processing actually occurs (one exception is Scherer et al., 2012). We suggest such research not because we have much fondness for the reconciliation/association view. However, we do believe that it is a viable perspective that has become a bit lost in the current cognitive synthesis, and we would like to be able to see it tested more rigorously in the context of that perspective—either to see it garner support or to see it definitively put to rest.

Event Processing Effects on Other Elements of Person Memory

As noted when we described Facet 1 of the person memory domain, there are a lot of attributes that can be remembered about others. Memory for many of these attributes can also be influenced by the kinds of processing that occur when first encountering information about a person. A recent example comes from work by Wyer, Perfect, and Pahl (2010). Participants in their study had a brief interaction with a confederate. On arrival at the laboratory, participants were told of an imaginary task that was to be performed soon (e.g., delivering a speech at 3 P.M. the next day) or in the long-term future (e.g., 5–7 months in the future). The authors hypothesized that the temporal focus (e.g., Trope & Liberman, 2010) induced by the distant task should induce global processing, which should facilitate face memory. To test this idea, participants later tried to identify the face of the confederate from a lineup (for more on face processing, see Chapter 9). Identification accuracy was best for those in the distant-term focus condition. These effects occurred across various imagined tasks (going camping, moving to a new apartment, going to a garage sale).

Results with similar implications come from studies that have explored person memory in an eyewitness context. Two of the important questions to be addressed in legal proceedings are "Who did it?" and "What did they do?" Considerable scholarship has addressed these two questions (an excellent entrée into this area of scholarship can be found in Wells, Memon, & Penrod, 2006). The results of such scholarship clearly indicate that eyewitness identifications of perpetrators can be wrong. How wrong? Consider this study reported by Buckhout (1980). Buckhout arranged for the staging of a mock crime—a mugging and purse snatch. Conditions were designed to reflect the difficulties inherent in observing actual crimes. The film was shown to 2,145 viewers (median age, 26 years) in small audiences under controlled conditions (as well as on a TV newscast). A few moments after the crime, witnesses were shown a lineup and asked to identify the culprit. Some might take comfort in the fact that viewer identification performance was significantly better than chance. However, another view of the data suggests to some that performance was spectacularly bad: only 74% of viewers attempted an identification, and only 19% of those attempts were correct.

However, eyewitness performance levels are obviously not always this poor: The viewing conditions that Buckhout (1980) established were difficult. Performance would obviously have been better under conditions more optimal for viewing. Indeed, a number of variables have been shown to moderate the accuracy of identifications. Some of these variables are straightforward applications of principles of learning and memory. For example, as the time spent processing a perpetrator's face increases, so does performance in a face identification task (Memon, Hope, & Bull, 2003). Similarly, as the lag between the event exposure and the test increases, identification performance decreases (for a review, see Shapiro & Penrod, 1986; also note that Dysart & Lindsay, 2007, say that this relation is merely "probable").

Two of the more unexpected effects that have emerged from this literature are the own-race identification bias and the weapons focus effect. The own race identification bias is straightforward: Perceivers seem to have a much better chance of correctly identifying a perpetrator who is of the same race as a perpetrator than of identifying one who is of a different race (for a review, see Meissner & Brigham, 2001; for a paradoxical reversal of this effect, see Edlund & Skowronski, 2008). This own-race bias has recently been extended, with data suggesting that there are own-age biases (see Harrison & Hole, 2009; Wright & Stroud, 2002) as well as own-gender biases (Wright & Sladden, 2003).

There is considerable debate about the theoretical origins of these effects. The most recent theorizing combines elements of the major theories and adds a new twist. This theorizing suggests that own-race bias results from a confluence of social categorization, various forms of motivation, and perceptual experience (Hugenberg, Young, Bernstein, & Sacco, 2010). Data supporting this view come from the results of studies suggesting that in the own-race bias effect, the other-ethnicity cue from a face disrupts the holistic processing that occurs when viewing own-race faces (Hills & Lewis, 2006). Obviously, such an explanation requires both the presence of the holistic processing and the presence of the socially derived race cue. Support for the motivational component included in the model comes from studies showing that motivation to include or exclude individuals in one's social group also influences race-related face recognition accuracy (Pauker, Weisbuch, Ambady, Sommers, Adams, & Ivcevic, 2009).

Other information-processing relevant findings show that perceiver attention is drawn to especially salient elements in a perceiver's environment. One of those elements can be a weapon used in the commission of a crime. Attention to the weapon can reduce attention paid to the perpetrator, which should (and does) reduce identification accuracy (for a recent overview, see Pickel, 2007): This is the weapon focus effect. The fact that attention is involved in the weapon focus effect (instead of stress or arousal) is reflected by the fact that unexpectedness moderates the effect. For example, results of a series of experiments reported by Pickel (2009) suggested that a handgun reduced the accuracy of witnesses' descriptions of a female perpetrator (gun very unexpected) more than descriptions of a male perpetrator (gun less unexpected). Additionally, memory for a female perpetrator was more severely impaired if the female carried a folding knife as opposed to a knitting needle, but the reverse was true when the perpetrator was male. Finally, the weapon focus effect was eliminated for perpetrators of both genders if witnesses saw them as dangerous individuals.

Post-Event Processing and Person Memory

The research described in the previous section suggests that the way in which information is processed during its encoding affects the way in which it is stored, and hence, its later recall. As such, it is a perfect illustration of Facet 2—processing and person memory. However, other research in the area has examined this facet in different ways. For example, one important thread of person memory research explored how person memories might be altered because of things that happen *after* the event had ended.

Post-Event Influence of Others on Person Memory

One example of the power of post-event influence on person memory came from Elizabeth Loftus' research program. For example, Loftus (1975) reported results from a series of experiments in which participants saw films of complex, fast-moving events. The participants were later asked questions about the events. The purpose of the experiments was to investigate how the wording of questions asked immediately after an event might influence participants' memory for the event when it was assessed at a later time. The results suggested that the initial questions (what was asked and the way in which it was asked) could, indeed, alter an individual's later reconstruction of the event. To put this in another way, the questions that were asked right after observing the event affected the way in which participants recalled the event at a later time. Many studies now attest to this tendency to reconstruct memories of the past so that they become altered by events that occur, and information that is encountered, after the original event is over (for reviews, see Hirt, McDonald, & Markman, 1998; Schacter, 1996).

Snyder and Uranowitz (1979) provided another example of such research. Participants in their studies read a case history of an individual (Betty K), who was later assigned the stereotypic label of "lesbian." The impact of this new information on recognition memory for factual events in Betty K's life was assessed one week after reading the case history. The results of a recognition memory test showed that subjects selectively affirmed events that supported and bolstered their post-reading interpretations of Betty K. That is, their recognition memories were biased in the direction of the lesbian label that was applied to Betty K.

The fact that such post-event labels can considerably distort memories of others is a bit disconcerting. Yet, such effects seem to occur in the real world with some degree of regularity, and with serious consequences. For example, data suggest that is not too uncommon for people to falsely recall being traumatized by another person. The false recollection can be unintentionally induced by unsuspecting individuals. For example, police questioners or clinicians who question the victim or who interact with the victim (see McNally, 2003) can introduce the false or misleading information in their interrogations or interactions.

Other research in the area has explored additional sources of post-event influence on memory reports.

One powerful source of influence is the memory reports of other people (so-called co-witnesses; for a review, see Granhag, Memon, & Roos af Hjelmsater, 2010). An example of such influence comes from a study conducted by Gabbert, Memon, and Allan (2003). In this study, participants witnessed and then discussed a criminal event. However, each member of a dyad watched a different video of the same event, and each video contained unique items that were thus seen only by one participant. Dyads in one condition were encouraged to discuss the event, and then each witness (individually) performed a recall test. A significant proportion (71%) of witnesses who had discussed the event went on to mistakenly recall items that they had not actually seen but that had been presented by others during the discussion. Thus, many people "adopted" the memories provided by others and reported them as their own.

One largely unaddressed issue in this literature is whether such effects reflect mere changes in memory reports (which are theoretically reversible) or real changes in the memory for the event (which would not be reversible). One of the few sets of studies to address this issue was reported by Betz, Skowronski, and Ostrom (1996). Participants in their studies read a story about an actor and then completed a multiple-choice recognition test assessing recall for actor-relevant facts from the story. After answering some recognition test items, participants were shown a bogus tally of the responses that other participants supposedly made to the same items. Data from a later memory test indicated that viewing this bogus tally sometimes induced participants to change memory responses that were correct on an initial recognition test to responses that were incorrect, matching the incorrect responses provided by the bogus others. This effect was more likely when apparent agreement among the bogus responses was high, and less likely when item memorability was high.

The unique contribution of the Betz et al. (1996) study, however, was that it produced evidence that these effects occurred even when participants were *unable* to accurately remember the bogus memory reports received from others. Moreover, these effects occurred even when participants were instructed to *ignore* such second-hand information. Such findings suggest that some subset of the memory responses that were changed reflected "real" changes in memory. That is, participants experienced a failure of source monitoring, and in doing so, adopted the information provided by bogus others into their private (e.g., thought to be real) memories for the event.

How an Informant's Own Post-Event Activities Can Influence Person Memory
Social Discourse and Person Memory

Although some details about people might be learned from informants, one of the more fascinating, and perhaps under-explored, potential sources of post-event distortions in person memory might emanate from an informant's tendency to relate events to others. The first author of this chapter, John Skowronski, has often wondered about such effects. One reason is that John's longtime collaborator, Don Carlston, has been fond of telling a story about when the two of them first met. The setting was on a softball diamond. Don was on second base while John was playing centerfield. Don tells the story of how he tried to score from second base on a hit by a teammate, only to have John throw him out at home plate. Don has re-told this story often, and in subsequent retellings John's throw became worthy of Willie Mays—a rope from deep centerfield that was delivered with pinpoint accuracy. John remembers the event somewhat differently: The ball was sharply hit and arrived in John's vicinity on one very congenial hop, and John was charging the ball as he received it so that he was not very far from home plate when the throw was delivered. It is possible that Don's retelling has been influenced by post-event knowledge (e.g., learning that the author was a pitcher in college). It is also possible that Don embellished the story for dramatic effect, and has come to believe the embellishments. Regardless, John has often wondered about the extent to which Don has come to believe the exaggerated details of the story that he routinely conveyed. (Note, in his review of this paragraph, Don congenially pointed out that John is egotistically assuming that it is Don's memory that is distorted. In reply, John congenially points out that Don may be overlooking his oft-professed tendency to forget.)

Existing evidence suggests that the biasing effects of storytelling are a definite possibility. Dudukovic, Marsh, and Tversky (2004) reported the results of a study in which some participants told a story with instructions to be accurate, whereas others told a story with instructions to be entertaining. Later, these participants tried to recall the original stories. The memory protocols of those with an entertainment goal were judged to be less accurate than the protocols of those with an accuracy goal. Similar conclusions came from research reported by Tversky and Marsh (2000). These researchers asked participants to read a story and then asked some to write a biased letter about one of the story characters. The

perspective that a participant was asked to adopt affected the amount of information recalled in later story memory tasks, and also influenced the direction of memory errors. Other research conducted in contexts in which informants conveyed information to audiences (Higgins & Rholes, 1978; also see Pasupathi, Stallworth, & Murdoch, 1998) suggests that informants bias descriptions to suit their own goals and come to believe those biased descriptions, thus exhibiting erroneous recall for the original events (for a more recent view, see Echteroff, Higgins, & Levine, 2009).

In our view, one relatively unexplored avenue of investigation that is suggested by such research might attempt to explicitly link the habitual, socially mandated goals that people have in conversations to the kinds of person memory effects that occur as a result of those conversations. Such an idea was suggested by Skowronski and Walker (2004) in the context of autobiographical memories, but this idea should just as easily apply in the context of memories about others. Building on the work of Pasupathi (2001), they argue that the operation of these norms can have an impact on the frequency of event conveyance and the content of such conveyance. According to Pasupathi's model, such norms create a social context that helps people select, organize, and interpret individual event memories.

We agree with the thesis that social norms can affect person memory through their influence on social disclosure. Such influence might include alterations in the recall of a given memory, the content of the memory, the accuracy of the memory, the reconstructed temporal location of the memory, and emotions accompanying the memory. Skowronski and Walker describe numerous conversational norms that might influence person memory. We will not review them all, but instead will simply provide a couple of examples.

One example comes from Skowronski and Walker's suggestion that information conveyed in conversations is to be kept relevant and interesting. This norm requires that the speaker understands the goals of the listener and provides input that meets these goals. One component of relevance is interest value. If a conversation is not relevant to a listener, then a speaker runs the risk of boring the listener. Relative brevity may help to avoid such boredom. Moreover, because the social rehearsal of event memories consumes cognitive and temporal resources, it makes sense that listeners do not want superfluous detail. Note that this does not mean that listeners do not want a richly detailed narrative (after all, such details are often essential to a good story), but they do expect that the discourse will proceed in a timely manner. When an informant adheres to this norm, the listener can both process the input without becoming bored and respond appropriately.

However, this brevity may come at a cost to the speaker. By retelling a brief version of the story, noncentral contextual details may become deleted from the informant's own private memory for the story. Thus, even though repeated discussion of an event might cause a person's behavior to remain highly accessible in memory, with repeated retelling, the behavior might tend to become increasingly semantic in nature. Translating this into the language of memory researchers, a frequently described event might be well "known" (e.g., recalled semantically) but not well "remembered" (e.g., recalled episodically; for a recent example of the use of this paradigm in a person memory context, see Barsics & Bredart, 2011). Despite the sensibility of this hypothesis, we do not believe that it has been directly tested in the context of person memory.

One other implication of the interest-value maxim is that it specifies the content of things that are to be conveyed about others. Facts about another person that are likely to be seen as interesting are often those events that are extreme, novel, or negative. It is, perhaps, no coincidence that real-world measures of memory for others often reflect these characteristics (Skowronski, Betz, Thompson, & Shannon, 1991). In this context, the negativity effect that sometimes emerges in recall for others is especially notable given that it is the opposite of the positivity effect often seen in recall for the self. Thus, as Skowronski et al. (1991) suggest, controlling for the myriad other factors that affect real-world memory, we often seem to recall the best about ourselves, but the worst about others.

One might expect that the relevance and interest norm should work against frequent retelling of a tale about others, but as we all know, this is not the case. Informants sometimes have goals (e.g., levity, conveying the "essence" of another) that prompt repetition of the same tale. In pursuit of such goals, one might repeatedly recount an anecdote from a friend's life, even though others have already heard the anecdote. This repetition is tolerated because it meets the goals of the message recipient.

For example, the laughter provoked by a story may be the main point of the communication, not the new information conveyed by the story's content. Similarly, in an attempt to be supportive of a disheartened colleague, one might frequently relate a well-known episode from another person's past (e.g., "Buck up. Look at the career of Dr. Brilliant. She was denied tenure at her first job and only recently won the mid-career award in social psychology. The lesson: Do good work and you'll be fine."). These examples suggest that those facts that describe another person that are thought to be particularly useful or illustrative can be repeatedly described when circumstances are right, and the high frequency with which such facts are repeated should substantially influence elements of those person memories.

The above example suggests that retelling information that characterizes others in order to achieve commonly encountered social goals can change the memory for that information. However, retelling one (or a small number) of stories has other implications for person memory. One of these is that people often can recall information about others (e.g., Facet 1). However, over multiple social interactions, one may restrict the recall of other-relevant information to a small subset of interesting, extreme, or exemplary memories and rarely, if ever, prompt conveyance of relatively mundane information.

Such selectivity can have important implications. For example, when reporting global impressions of others, this small subset of behaviors may be overly influential in the induction of an impression. This could be caused by such information being readily retrieved from memory or, as in the availability heuristic, the subjective ease with which the information is brought to mind can affect the reported impression.

Self-Enhancement and Person Memory

Of course, one of the main goals that an informant might have in social discourse is to present the self in a positive way. Particularly suggestive is research by the Ross and Wilson team (e.g., Wilson & Ross, 2001). Results from that research have shown that in the service of enhancing the current self, one might sometimes distort past events so that they seem even more negative than objective reality suggests.

One might extend this finding into the person memory domain, speculating that such self-enhancement might cause an informant to denigrate others. For example, when trying to convey how great one might be as an academic mentor, one might point to how lousy Joe Graduate Student's scholarship was before he came under the influence of one's tutelage. The Wilson and Ross research program suggests that in constructing such a tale, Joe's initial performance might come to be recalled as even worse than it actually was.

A similar effect might occur when one is trying to convey the extent to which one has improved at a task. For example, one might tell a personal story indicating that when one started to play chess, one was so bad that one was routinely beaten by the mentally challenged kid down the block. As a result of telling this tale, one might recall that kid as having been worse at chess than he really was. Despite the sensibility of such effects, to our knowledge, they have not been demonstrated in research.

Of course, one of the other implications of the Wilson and Ross team's research program is that sometimes one might enhance attributes of others when it serves the goal of enhancing the current self. For example, assume that one wants to convey to others that before one's knees were injured, one was a basketball stud. In doing so, one might retell the tale of the time that one scored 50 points in a game against a traveling team on which Michael Jordan (falsely) played. Again, despite the sensibility of such effects, to our knowledge they have not been demonstrated in research.

How a Person's Post-Event Activities Can Affect Person Memory: Final Issues

There is prolific evidence that things that happen after an event is perceived can influence memory for the event. However, there are lots of important questions that remain unaddressed and lots of ways to take that research in new directions. For example, one unresolved issue concerns the exact effect of post-event information on memory. When the initial information was directly obtained (e.g., by observation), does post-event activity alter the episodic experience? Are multiple memory traces for the event created, and if so, how does the cognitive system handle those multiple memory traces (e.g., Facet 3)? Can implicit measures be used to obtain evidence for the presence of the original memory trace, even when people no longer feel as if they have it?

A second major research direction involves linking the individual effects observed to the greater social and cultural contexts in which remembering exists. If person memories can be shaped or distorted by the themes of the tales that one retells, and if societies or cultures dictate differences in the kinds of tales that are told or the frequency with which they are told, then one might expect to see consistent cross-cultural differences in the kinds of shaping and distortion that occur in the event memories that people possess about others.

Speculations on Evolution and the Functionality of Person Memory
How Can Evolution Apply to Person Memory?

The material that has been discussed so far has reflected a prolific program of research that has done much to aid our understanding of person memory. Unfortunately, the scope of the research has also been a bit restricted. Those restrictions stem from the historical roots of the research. These roots lie in actor behaviors and the information processing mechanisms that people bring to bear on such behaviors. Obviously, there is more to remember about a person than the person's behavior (see Facet 1), and there are more theoretical perspectives to apply to an understanding of person memory than are found in the information processing view reflected in Facet 2.

One example lies in the evolutionary perspective (e.g., Klein, Robertson, & Delton, 2010; Nairne, 2010) that fits into Facet 4 of the organizational scheme used in this chapter. Having a good memory can be a very functional attribute. Memory for elements of the environment that present opportunities or dangers can aid an organism's ability to engage in either appropriate approach behaviors or appropriate avoidance behaviors. In the scheme of evolution, it is the ability to engage in such environmentally appropriate behaviors that helps individuals to pass their genes forward to future generations.

It has been argued that one of the important environmental contexts for the human species was other species members (Sedikides & Skowronski, 1997, 2003, 2009; Sedikides, Skowronski, & Dunbar, 2006). Humans exhibit strong social tendencies, so other people are a frequent element of an individual's environment. Given this social habit, one can make a reasonable argument that having a good person memory—memory for other people and their characteristics and behaviors—ought to be an evolutionary imperative (see Klein, Cosmides, Tooby, & Chance, 2002; for a broader view on evolution and social thought, see Dunbar, 2003; Forgas, Haselton, & von Hippel, 2007; see also Chapter 32). After all, individual species members often exhibit different characteristics and emit different behaviors, and remembering those characteristics and behaviors might enhance an individual's chances of survival. Examples might be memories of the times that individual A shared food with others, memories of the times that individual B was receptive to sexual advances, and memories of the times that individual C acted in a violent manner toward others. Functional memories can also include memory for another's general tendencies, which may include traits (they're often helpful) or evaluations (one of the good guys). Any or all of these memories could guide functional behavior when interacting with the other person.

An example of this idea, and how it might be tied into the biology of the brain (which, in part, is shaped by evolution), comes from results reported by Somerville, Wig, Whalen, and Kelley (2006). This team conducted a study in which subjects learned common first names for unfamiliar faces in the presence or absence of additional contextual information that was positive, negative, or neutral in valence (e.g., Emily helps the homeless, Bob is a deadbeat dad, Eric likes carrots). Later, while in a brain scanner, subjects performed a face recognition memory test. Brain scan results revealed a functional dissociation between the right hippocampus and right amygdala. The results showed greater hippocampal activity during recognition of faces previously presented with contextual information, and this activity was directly linked to conscious recollection of the valenced contextual material. However, there was heightened activity in the amygdala during recognition of faces that had been learned in the presence of an emotional context, and this heightened activity was *not* dependent on conscious recollection of the emotional context. Somerville et al. (2006) speculate that the amygdala may act independently of the hippocampus and in concert with other cortical regions (e.g., the insular cortex) to ensure that behaviors in social encounters are appropriate, even in the absence of conscious recollections of others. Such dissociations are consistent with conceptions, such as Carlston's (1994) associated systems theory, that postulate that people use different storage subsystems for different kinds of memory, and that these subsystems can possess at least some degree of functional independence.

The notion that one important element of thinking is that it can guide subsequent appropriate behavior is not a new one. For example, in a spirited article, Fiske (1992) cogently reminded social psychologists that, "Social thinking is for doing." This section of this chapter embraces such functional pragmatism and attempts to place it in the contexts of evolution and social memory (for a similar idea, see Klein et al., 2010).

Certainly, the possible relevance of evolution in this regard is clear. Evolution emphasizes functionality. It does so by suggesting that some traits are influenced by biology, that some traits are functional in a given context, and that functional traits are especially likely to be passed on to offspring. Accordingly, one might at least consider the possibility that the human species may have developed enhanced person memory abilities because of the possible functionality of person memory.

Evidence for an Evolution-Person Memory Link
BEHAVIORS AND TRAITS

Evidence for the functional evolutionary imperative of person memory would be especially strong if the evidence supported the presence of biological systems or mental modules that were specifically tuned to the task of remembering information about others. A research team led by Klein, Cosmides, and Tooby has recently argued that such biologically determined modules may be relevant to the distinction that has emerged between episodic memories about others and semantic memories about others (see Klein, Cosmides, Gangi, Jackson, Tooby, & Costabile, 2009). This team became interested in the classic findings from social psychology research suggesting that episodic memories about others and trait memories about others might be stored in ways that allowed them to be functionally independent (e.g., one type could be accessed without necessarily accessing the other type). More specifically, this team noted three results that were suggested by the research (also see Wyer & Carlston, 1994): (1) Long-term knowledge of a person's traits is abstracted from experiences with trait-relevant behavioral information and represented in semantic memory in summary form (for an overview, see Skowronski, Carlston, & Hartnett, 2008); (2) trait judgments about a person are made by accessing these summary representations without reference to the specific behavioral experiences from which they presumably were derived (Carlston, 1980; Carlston & Skowronski, 1986); and (3) summary trait representations are functionally independent of memories of trait-relevant behavioral experiences (e.g., Klein & Loftus, 1990; Klein, Robertson, Gangi, & Loftus, 2008).

Klein et al. (2002) argued that these two forms of memory may have been biologically selected in the social domain because they serve different but complementary functions. Retrieving a summary trait judgment that has been made about a person has the advantage of allowing new judgments to be made with rapidity and ease. That is, new judgments need not be reconstructed from recalled behaviors each time a judgment is needed; instead, under many circumstances, existing judgments can simply be rapidly and easily retrieved from memory. Such a process can allow rapid and appropriate environmental action.

Klein, et al. (2002) also point out that stored trait summaries possess a couple of potential deficiencies. First, they only give information about a person's behavior under average circumstances: They are not informative about the circumstances under which a person's behavior deviates from the person's average. This deficiency is potentially remedied by episodic memories. Memories of behavioral episodes can provide boundary conditions on the scope of trait generalizations, allowing for accurate judgments to be made about those times when behavior deviates from the norm (for evidence, see Babey, Queller, & Klein, 1998). Klein et al. also suggested that another potential benefit of episodic memory is that it allows reevaluation of the conclusions that a perceiver might draw about others (for relevant evidence, see Klein et al., 2009).

Such evidence does not exclude the possibility that memory for other people can involve elements of a "general-purpose" memory system, and many social psychologists who have thought about person memory have placed it in the context of such a system (examples come from Carlston, 1994; Hastie & Carlston, 1980, Wyer & Srull, 1980; for an overview of memory systems, see Tulving & Craik, 2000). However, if at least some elements of person memory fit into the scheme of evolution, then one might expect to see evidence that at least some types of person memory are modulated by specific biological systems or are processed in areas of the brain that seem to be specifically devoted to elements of social memory. The argument of the Klein, Cosmides, and Tooby team is that the presence of distinct episodic memory and semantic memory systems might be seen in light of evolution and might provide suggestive evidence with regard to the kinds of mental modules selected by evolution.

PERSON MEMORY, EVOLUTION, AND FACES

The problem with using episodic memory and semantic memory to make such a point, however, is that these memory systems are not specifically tuned to the processing of, and memory for, social stimuli. Stronger evidence for the evolutionary position would come from studies showing evidence of such "social-specific" tuning. One area of research—the recognition of others—may reflect the presence of such systems.

Consider a study by Chang and Sanfey (2009). Participants in their study played a bargaining game. Their results indicated that participants with low expectations about a partner's initial offer demonstrated augmented memory for the faces of proposers who made fair offers. In comparison, participants with high expectations about a partner's initial offer had increased recognition memory for the faces of proposers who made unfair offers. These effects were not simply a function of incongruity: Results from brain imaging conducted during the face memory test revealed that these memory effects were specifically related to activation of areas in the brain that are especially involved in social information processing. Activation in these social brain areas was not present when participants viewed faces of partners who offered more than the participants initially expected. Instead, social thought circuits in the brain were especially activated when participants viewed partners that offered less than the participant initially expected. The author speculated that in this latter condition, participants sometimes pondered the "why" of another's behavior. By activating brain systems involved in social thought, such pondering may have contributed to enhanced recognition of the faces of those who engaged in such behavior.

Additional evidence suggestive of the idea that elements of person memory might be "special" comes from recent studies that are in the tradition of social intelligence research. These studies try to document individual differences in memory for faces and to establish that these memory differences cannot be accounted for by other elements of the cognitive system (e.g., general memory abilities or general cognitive abilities). A historical overview (Kihlstrom & Cantor, 2000) reveals that many have tried to include social memory as a special ability that can vary across individuals, but these attempts have generally met with limited success. However, such attempts continue, and may recently have succeeded. For example, consider a recent study by Wilhelm, Herzman, Kunina, Danthiir, Schacht, and Sommer (2010). Two experiments provided performance data on a broad variety of face cognition tasks. Using responses to these tasks, three component abilities of face cognition—face perception, face memory, and the speed of face cognition—were psychometrically identified. Results suggested that these three face cognition abilities were clearly distinct from immediate memory and delayed memory, mental speed, general cognitive ability, and object cognition. The authors' data led them to conclude that their results provide a first step toward establishing face processing abilities, one of which is memory for faces, as independent abilities.

Perhaps more potent evidence about the evolutionary importance of the social tuning of the brain as reflected in the ability to recognize known others comes from the study of *prosopagnosics* (Busigny, Graf, Mayer, & Rossion, 2010)—individuals who have difficulty identifying others on seeing their faces. Certainly, from a functional perspective, it is difficult to imagine how one could function well in a social context without being able to recognize others. Such recognition is the critical cue that unlocks memory access to what others are like and what they've done. To understand the difficulty that such a deficit presents, consider this blog quote from a person afflicted with the disorder:

> The month before, I had visited our Canada office, and I was really frustrated by my inability to recognize anyone. Someone that I had a long conversation with would come up to me hours later, and I'd have no idea who they were. I found myself constantly explaining to everyone that I was face blind. I started to do this to a coworker that I didn't know up there, only to find out that he worked two offices away from mine back in our California office, and we'd talked several times. (Paradox_puree, 2009)

Some cases of prosopagnosia occur as a result of traumatic injury. It is true that many cases of prosopagnosia are accompanied by deficits that go beyond processing of the face, seemingly leaving open the possibility that the disorder might reflect damage to the general-purpose memory system. However, a recent review of the literature by Busigny et al. (2010), accompanied by a new series of studies, suggests otherwise. These authors (also see Gruter, Gruter, & Carbon, 2008; Tree & Wilkie, 2010) concluded that at least some cases of prosopagnosia reflect deficits that are specific to face processing (e.g., deficits do not appear in object processing; also see Kanwisher, 2000). Also favoring the special-mechanisms-for-face-processing hypothesis are data suggesting that object agnosia without prosopagnosia can occur (Moscovitch, Winocur, & Behrmann, 1997). Finally, some cases of prosopagnosia appear to be caused by inborn deficiencies, another piece of evidence suggesting that the brain is structured to promote recognition of identities from faces.

However, Busigny et al. (2010) are careful to note that such evidence does not necessarily imply the presence of mental modules that are specific to face memory. Instead, they note that the processes recruited to process faces may reflect needed expertise, and that such processes may also, under the correct circumstances, be recruited for object recognition. More generally, it is clear that expertise in domains can be acquired by experience. Meadows (1974) eloquently expressed this point of view: "We learn to distinguish faces to a degree not seen with other categories because facial recognition is from the very earliest age and throughout life such an essential and determining aspect of daily living" (p. 490).

Because of this ambiguity, other evidence is needed to support the possible biological specialness of face recognition memory. Another individual difference variable that may relate to the special mechanism idea is autism. Individuals with autism have deficits in areas that are relevant to social information processing and understanding the minds of others. Hence, one might expect that those with autism could also show deficits in memory for social information. Especially revealing would be evidence that memory deficits were limited to, or especially profound for, people compared with non-social stimuli.

Such evidence is not extensive, but there are some data from studies of face memory that support this idea. For example, Hauck, Fein, Maltby, Waterhouse, and Feinstein (1998) conducted a study in which 24 autistic boys aged seven to 12 years and normal controls matched for verbal age and mental age were administered parallel social and non-social matching and memory tasks. Results showed that the children with autism were impaired relative to the normal children only on the social (face recognition) memory task (for similar results, see Boucher & Lewis, 1992; Boucher, Lewis, & Collis, 1998; De Gelder, Vroomen, & van de Heide, 1991).

Such results have been widely interpreted as suggesting that individuals with autism have idiosyncratic ways of processing faces (e.g., a focus on local cues rather than holistic processing), which may account for their impairments in face memory. However, recent brain-scanning evidence suggests that these memory deficits may not reflect deficits in discerning identities from faces, but instead may reflect other deficits (Webb et al., 2010). Moreover, in a review of the literature, Jemel, Mottron, and Dawson (2006) point out that results across studies are sometimes inconsistent and suggest that caution be used when interpreting these findings in terms of social-specific processing deficits. Here again, a case for the biologically driven specialness of face recognition memory is not a slam-dunk, but rather requires additional bolstering. To do so, we turn to another area of potential interest: memory for cheaters.

Memory for Cheaters

Social contract theory (see Tooby & Cosmides, 2005) postulates that brain mechanisms have been selected during human evolution that are functionally specialized to detect cheaters. Integrated into a "cheater-detection module," these mechanisms supposedly allow a perceiver to quickly and easily draw inferences about whether someone has cheated in prior social exchanges or is about to cheat in future social interactions.

Some have argued that this theory has implications for person memory. For example, Mealey, Daood, and Krage (1996) used this theory to examine the notion that faces of cheaters should be remembered better than faces associated with other types of behavior. Indeed, consistent with this view, Mealy et al. reported that old–new discrimination of faces varied as a function of whether the depicted persons were described as cheaters, as trustworthy, or in a way that was irrelevant to the cheating–trustworthiness dimension. However, recent studies have been unable to replicate the Mealey et al. (1996) finding (Barclay, 2008; Barclay & Lalumière, 2006; Mehl & Buchner, 2008), so one must view the Mealey results with caution.

If one follows the logic of social contract theory, humans should have evolved cognitive mechanisms enabling the detection of and memory for cheaters. Enhanced recognition memory for cheaters' faces in and of itself is not a benefit in social exchange. What is beneficial is especially good memory for the knowledge that specific others are cheaters. This prediction has been confirmed; participants are especially good at remembering the source information for individuals described as cheaters (Bell & Buchner, 2010a; Buchner, Bell, Mehl, & Musch, 2009. This enhanced memory also extends to cheaters' names (Bell & Buchner, 2009). This line of research is a good example of the contributions that an evolutionary perspective can offer to our knowledge of person memory. Not only is there an evolutionarily derived hypothesis for person memory (i.e., humans should have enhanced memory for cheaters), but there is also a specific prediction of the type of memory that should be held (i.e., recall for source memory as opposed to old–new recognition).

However, in the absence of detailed evidence suggestive of specific biological mechanisms related to cheater processing, one must exercise caution in interpreting the theoretical meaning of such results.

For example, more recent evidence suggests that the enhanced memory effects observed in the studies reported above may not be cheating specific, but may instead reflect a general person negativity effect (Bell & Buchner, 2010b). Alternatively, such memory effects may simply reflect the enhanced processing given to people who are especially important (Bell, Buchner, & Musch, 2010). Despite such cautions, it is clear that the evolution-driven research on memory for the attributes of cheaters has stimulated significant amounts of research, and likely will continue to do so.

Memory for Another's Identity Is Influenced by Chemical Substances

One final set of clues suggesting that evolution may have favored humans' abilities to remember attributes of others comes from studies that have directly manipulated elements of human chemistry. These studies examined the effect that chemicals known as peptides have on social recognition memory. For example, oxytocin is a brain chemical that has been implicated in a number of human social responses, including feelings of contentment, reductions in anxiety, and feelings of calmness and security around a mate. As it turns out, oxytocin is also related to memory. More importantly for the special-mechanism hypothesis, oxytocin seems to have different effects in the domain of social memory than in the domain of non-social memory. Data suggest that some non-social learning and memory functions are impaired by administration of oxytocin (see de Oliveira, Camboim, Diehl, Consiglio, & Quillfeldt, 2007). However, in contrast, oxytocin seems to facilitate learning and memory for some social information. For example, males receiving doses of oxytocin showed improved memory for human faces, particularly happy faces (Guastella, Mitchell, & Mathews, 2008; Rimmele, Hediger, Heinrichs, & Klaver, 2009; also see Campbell, 2010). Although not established for humans, gene knockout studies in mice have established that there may be a genetic basis for these kinds of recognition effects. These effects have been established for at least two brain peptides: oxytocin and vasopressin. Additional work continues to attempt to understand the brain circuitry on which these peptides operate (Insel & Fernald, 2004; Winslow & Insel, 2004).

Some Implications of a Functional/ Evolutionary Approach: Looking Forward

In this section of the chapter, we have advocated that the cognoscenti consider how the possible evolutionarily determined functionality of person memory might inform future research. For example, consider ways in which memory for others might differ from (e.g., be better than?) memory for non-social objects. In the context of the functionality/ evolution perspective, such a view makes good sense, and this was exactly the idea underlying research reported by Mesoudi, Whiten, and Dunbar (2006). They reported the results of two experiments that found that social material was conveyed with greater accuracy and was remembered better than non-social material. In three experiments, Reysen and Adair (2008) extended this finding (also see Reysen, 2009), producing data showing that both social and non-social material were remembered better when subjects thought that the material was conveyed by another human instead of by a computer.

A second example of how this evolutionarily influenced memory idea might influence person memory comes from the domain of source monitoring. Many studies have been conducted that have examined the extent to which people can remember the source of acquired information. In the context of social interactions, such research is often in the spirit of the Taylor et al. (1978) who-said-what paradigm and involves identifying which informant provided critical information (for more recent examples, see Gordon, Franklin, & Beck, 2005; Nash, Bryer, & Schlaghecken, 2010). On the other hand, many studies have used non-social information "sources" in the context of similar paradigms (e.g., Klauer & Kellen, 2010; Kuhlmann & Touron, 2010). The functional/evolutionary approach provides a reason to look for differences in the nature of the strength of source monitoring between social sources and non-social sources. Such differences might go beyond differences in levels of performance and could reflect the different types of information that cue recall (e.g., episodic information vs. semantic information) and different brain areas that are recruited during processing and recall.

An additional approach, one that has already been the subject of empirical research, involves the relation between source monitoring and the theory of mind (TOM). The term *TOM* refers to the ability to attribute mental states to oneself and to others. There is considerable support for the idea that the ability to develop TOM is a consequence of the development of the social brain. For example, one hallmark of autism is an apparent deficit in this ability (e.g., see Chakrabarti & Baron-Cohen, 2008). A connection between source monitoring and TOM abilities was discussed by Welch-Ross (1999), who suggested that individuals who can deftly reason

about others should be less likely to make source monitoring errors than individuals who are deficient in such understanding. Accumulating data (e.g., Evans & Roberts, 2008; Welch-Ross, 1999) now support the link between TOM and the ability to correctly monitor and report the sources of acquired information, as well as supporting the notion that children with well-developed TOM have ideas about source expertise and reliability that can be reflected in their source monitoring performance (for an overview, see Roberts, 2000).

Despite such supportive results, it is quite obvious that more data are needed before one can unequivocally accept the thesis that evolution has induced humans to be especially fluent in at least some domains of person memory. However, we hope that the literature reviewed in this section suffices to suggest that the idea is not beyond reason. In reviewing this research, we suggest that the information processing perspective (described in Facet 2) that has guided much person memory research during the past 40 years, one that has been incredibly prolific in terms of the amount of research and theory that has been generated, could benefit by adopting perspectives that are grounded in evolution and the biology of the brain.

Biology, Evolution, and Person Memory: A Summary

We argued that because of the functional significance of the social context to human behavior, there may be reason to believe that evolution might have developed special mechanisms to handle memories for others. Evidence for this proposition has come from a number of domains, but may be most powerful in the domain of face and identity recognition. This is logical, given human reliance on vision. It also makes sense to those who study the architecture of the brain. Although very speculative, one might guess that the ability to recognize the identity of others from their gait or their physiognomy may be similarly privileged, as might voice recognition systems or even smell recognition systems (via pheromones).

Our second main point was to not throw the baby out with the bathwater. The information processing perspective has yielded many interesting and useful results, even in domains, such as face processing, that many suspect are evolutionarily privileged. In this regard, it is also useful to remember that ideas about evolution are not antithetical to the information processing perspective, but rather complement it. A good example of such complementarity comes from the learning literature. Some stimulus–response relations are learned with relative ease; others are learned only with difficulty (e.g., see Garcia & Koelling, 1966). So, too, it may be with evolution and social memory. It may be that evolution has designed us so that person memory, or at least some elements or person memory, are particularly easy to learn, or are retained in memory for an especially long time.

Person Memory: Coda

What information do we remember about others and why do we remember it? The answer to that question is informed by the scholarship described in this chapter. How information is processed when it is received, how people might be induced to think about information after it has been received, and biological/evolutionary considerations were identified in the chapter as three broad forces that influence person memory.

However, the issue is complex and requires approaches from multiple viewpoints. One of the best indices of the health of this area is that everyone has their fingers in the pie—research and theory both come from almost all of the subareas of psychology. Although it makes this area somewhat daunting, it also makes the area tremendously exciting. We have tried to convey this excitement by illustrating several new avenues of research that are open to person memory researchers (e.g., the self and person memory). We have been impressed by the research and theory that have already been produced in this area, and we look forward to the new research and ideas that we are sure will be produced for years to come.

Author Note

Please address correspondence to John J. Skowronski, Department of Psychology, Northern Illinois University, DeKalb, IL, 60115; e-mail: jskowron@niu.edu.

References

Allen, T. J., Sherman, J. W., Conrey, F. R., & Stroessner, S. J. (2009). Stereotype strength and attentional bias: Preference for confirming versus disconfirming information depends on processing capacity. *Journal of Experimental Social Psychology, 45*, 1081–1087.

Atkinson, W. W. (1903). *Memory culture: The science of observing, remembering and recalling* (pp. 81–85). New York: Psychic Research.

Babey, S. H., Queller, S., & Klein, S. B. (1998). The role of expectancy violating behaviors in the representation of trait knowledge: A summary-plus-exception model of social memory. *Social Cognition, 16*, 287–339.

Barclay, P. (2008). Enhanced recognition of defectors depends on their rarity. *Cognition, 107*, 817–828.

Barclay, P., & Lalumière, M. L. (2006). Do people differentially remember cheaters? *Human Nature, 17*, 98–113.

Bardach, L., & Park, B. (1996). The effect of in-group/out-group status on memory for consistent and inconsistent behavior of an individual. *Personality and Social Psychology Bulletin, 22*, 169–178.

Barsics, C., & Bredart, S. (2011). *Consciousness and Cognition: An International Journal, 20*, 303–308.

Bell, R., & Buchner, A. (2009). Enhanced source memory for names of cheaters. *Evolutionary Psychology, 7*, 317–330.

Bell, R., & Buchner, A. (2010a). Justice sensitivity and source memory for cheaters. *Journal of Research in Personality, 44*, 677–683.

Bell, R., & Buchner, A. (2010b). Valence modulates source memory for faces. *Memory & Cognition, 38*, 29–41.

Bell, R., Buchner, A., & Musch, J. (2010). Enhanced old-new recognition and source memory for faces of cooperators and defectors in a social-dilemma game. *Cognition, 117*, 261–275.

Betz, A. L., Skowronski, J. J., & Ostrom, T. M. (1996). Shared realities: Social influence and stimulus memory. *Social Cognition, 14*, 113–140.

Bodenhausen, G. V. (1988). Stereotypic biases in social decision making and memory: Testing process models of stereotype use. *Journal of Personality and Social Psychology, 55*, 726–737.

Boucher, J., & Lewis, V. (1992). Unfamiliar face recognition in relatively able autistic children. *Journal of Child Psychology and Psychiatry, 33*, 843–859.

Boucher, J., Lewis, V., & Collis, G. (1998). Familiar face and voice matching and recognition in children with autism. *Journal of Child Psychology and Psychiatry, 39*, 171–181.

Buchner, A., Bell, R., Mehl, B., & Musch, J. (2009). No enhanced recognition memory, but better source memory for faces of cheaters. *Evolution and Human Behavior, 30*, 212–224.

Buckhout, R. (1980). Nearly 2,000 witnesses can be wrong. *Bulletin of the Psychonomic Society, 16*, 307–310.

Busigny, T., Graf, M., Mayer, E., & Rossion, B. (2010). Acquired prosopagnosia as a face-specific disorder: Ruling out the general visual similarity account. *Neuropsychologia, 48*, 2051–2067.

Campbell, A. (2010). Oxytocin and human social behavior. *Personality and Social Psychology Review, 14*, 281–295.

Carlston, D. E. (1980). The recall and use of traits and events in social inference processes. *Journal of Experimental Social Psychology, 16*, 303–328.

Carlston, D. E. (1994). Associated Systems Theory: A systematic approach to the cognitive representation of persons and events. In R. S. Wyer (Ed.), *Advances in Social Cognition, Vol. 7: Associated Systems Theory* (pp. 1–78). Hillsdale, NJ: Erlbaum.

Carlston, D. E., & Skowronski, J. J. (1986). Trait memory and behavior memory: The effects of alternative pathways on impression judgment response times. *Journal of Personality and Social Psychology, 50*, 5–13.

Carlston, D. E., & Smith, E. R. (1996). Principles of mental representation. In E. T. Higgins & A. W. Kruglanski (Eds.), *Social psychology: Handbook of basic principles* (pp. 184–210). New York, NY: Guilford Press.

Chakrabarti, B., & Baron-Cohen, S. (2008). The biology of mind reading. In N. Ambady & J. J. Skowronski (Eds.), *First impressions*. New York: Guilford Press.

Chang, L. J., & Sanfey, A. G. (2009). Unforgettable ultimatums? Expectation violations promote enhanced social memory following economic bargaining. *Frontiers in Behavioral Neuroscience*, *3*, 1–12.

Crawford, M. T., & Skowronski, J. J. (1998). When motivated thought leads to heightened bias: High need for cognition can enhance the impact of stereotypes on memory. *Personality & Social Psychology Bulletin*, *24*, 1075–1088.

Crocker, J., Hannah, D. B., & Weber, R. (1983). Person memory and causal attributions. *Journal of Personality & Social Psychology*, *44*, 55–66.

De Gelder, B., Vroomen, J., & van der Heide, L. (1991). Face recognition and lip-reading in autism. *European Journal of Cognitive Psychology*, *3*, 69–86.

de Oliveira, L. F. Camboim, C., Diehl, F., Consiglio, A. R., & Quillfeldt, J. A. (2007). Glucocorticoid-mediated effects of systemic oxytocin upon memory retrieval. *Neurobiology of Learning and Memory*, *87*, 67–71.

Dijksterhuis, A., & van Knippenberg, A. (1995). Memory for stereotype-consistent and stereotype-inconsistent information as a function of processing pace. *European Journal of Social Psychology*, *25*, 689–693.

Dijksterhuis, A., & van Knippenberg, A. (1996). Trait implications as a moderator of recall of stereotype-consistent and stereotype-inconsistent behaviors. *Personality & Social Psychology Bulletin*, *22*, 425–432.

Dijksterhuis, A., van Knippenberg, A., Kruglanski, A. W., & Schaper, C. (1996). Motivated social cognition: Need for closure effects on memory and judgment. *Journal of Experimental Social Psychology*, *32*, 254–270.

Dudukovic, N. M., Marsh, E. J., & Tversky, B. (2004). Telling a story or telling it straight: The Effects of entertaining versus accurate retellings on memory. *Applied Cognitive Psychology*, *18*, 125–143.

Dunbar, R. I. M. (2003). The social brain: Mind, language, and society in evolutionary perspective. *Annual Review of Anthropology*, *32*, 163–181.

Dysart, J. E., & Lindsay, R. C. L. (2007). The effects of delay on eyewitness identification accuracy: Should we be concerned? In R. C. L. Lindsay, D. F. Ross, J. D. Read, & M. P. Toglia (Eds.), *The handbook of eyewitness psychology, Vol. II: Memory for people* (pp. 361–376). Mahwah, NJ: Erlbaum.

Ebbesen, E. B. (1980). Cognitive processes in understanding ongoing behavior. In R. Hastie, T. M. Ostrom, E. B. Ebbesen, R. S. Wyer Jr., D. L. Hamilton, & D. Carlston (Eds.), *Person memory: The cognitive basis of social perception*. Hillsdale, NJ: Erlbaum.

Edlund, J. E., & Skowronski, J. J. (2008). Eyewitness racial attitudes and perpetrator identification: The lineup method matters. *North American Journal of Psychology*, *10*, 15–36.

Echterhoff, G., Higgins, E. T., & Levine, J. M. (2009). Shared reality: Experiencing commonality with others' inner states about the world. *Perspectives on Psychological Science*, *4*, 496–521.

Evans, A. D., & Roberts, K. P. (2008). Children in an information society: The relations between source monitoring, mental-state understanding, and knowledge acquisition in young children. In M. R. Kelley (Ed.), *Applied memory* (pp. 236–252). Hauppauge, NY: Nova Science.

Fiske, S. T. (1992). Thinking is for doing: Portraits of social cognition from Daguerreotype to laserphoto. *Journal of Personality and Social Psychology*, *63*, 877–889.

Fiske, S. T., & Taylor, S. E. (1991). *Social cognition* (2nd ed.). New York: McGraw-Hill.

Forgas, J. P., Haselton, M. G., & von Hippel, W. (Eds.) (2007). *Evolution and the social mind: Evolutionary psychology and social cognition*. New York: Psychology Press.

Forster, J., Higgins, E. T., & Strack, F. (2000). When stereotype disconfirmation is a personal threat: How prejudice and prevention focus moderate incongruency effects. *Social Cognition*, *18*, 178–197.

Frey, D. (1986). Recent research on selective exposure to information. *Advances in Experimental Social Psychology*, *19*, 41–80.

Fyock, J., & Stangor, C. (1994). The role of memory biases in stereotype maintenance. *British Journal of Social Psychology*, *33*, 331–343.

Gabbert, F., Memon, A., & Allan, K. (2003). Memory conformity: Can eyewitnesses influence each other's memories for an event? *Applied Cognitive Psychology*, *17*, 533–543.

Garcia, J., & Koelling, R. A. (1966). Relation of cue to consequence in avoidance learning. *Psychonomic Science*, *4*, 123–124.

Garcia-Marques, L., Ferreira, M. B., Nunes, L. D., Garrido, M. V., & Garcia-Marques, T. (2010). False memories and impressions of personality. *Social Cognition*, *28*, 556–568.

Garcia-Marques, L., Hamilton, D. L., & Maddox, K. B. (2002). Exhaustive and heuristic retrieval processes in person cognition: Further tests of the TRAP model. *Journal of Personality and Social Psychology*, *82*, 193–207.

Gingrich, B. E., Houston, D. A., & Lupfer, M. B. (1998). Combining trait and stereotype expectancies in person memory. *Personality and Social Psychology Bulletin*, *24*, 1120–1129.

Gordon, R., Franklin, N., & Beck, J. (2005). Wishful thinking and source monitoring. *Memory & Cognition*, *33*, 418–429.

Gould, R. L. (1917). A test for memory of names and faces. *Journal of Applied Psychology*, *1*, 321–324.

Granhag, P. A., Memon, A., & Roos af Hjelmsater, E. (2010). Social influence on eyewitness memory. In P. A. Granhag (Ed.), *Forensic psychology in context: Nordic and international approaches* (pp. 139–153). Devon, UK: Willan Publishing.

Gruter, T., Gruter, M., & Carbon, C. C. (2008). Neural and genetic foundations of face recognition and prosopagnosia. *Journal of Neuropsychology*, *2*, 79–97.

Guastella, A. J., Mitchell, P. B., & Mathews, F. (2008). Oxytocin enhances the encoding of positive social memories in humans. *Biological Psychiatry*, *64*, 256–258.

Jacoby, L. L. (1991). A process dissociation framework: Separating automatic from intentional uses of memory. *Journal of Memory and Language*, *30*, 513–541.

Hamilton, D. L., Driscoll, D. M., & Worth, L. T. (1989). Cognitive organization of impressions: Effects of incongruency in complex representations. *Journal of Personality and Social Psychology*, *58*, 1–14.

Hamilton, D. L., & Garcia-Marques, L. (2003). Effects of expectancies on the representation, retrieval, and use of social information. In G. V. Bodenhausen & A. J. Lambert (Eds.), *Foundations of social cognition: A festschrift in honor of Robert S. Wyer, Jr.* (pp. 25–50). Mahwah, NJ: Erlbaum.

Harrison, V., & Hole, G. J. (2009). Evidence for a contact-based explanation of the own-age bias in face recognition. *Psychonomic Bulletin & Review*, *16*, 264–269.

Hastie, R. (1984). Causes and effects of causal attribution. *Journal of Personality and Social Psychology*, *46*, 44–56.

Hastie, R., & Carlston, D. E. (1980). Theoretical issues in person memory. In R. Hastie, E. B. Ebbesen, R. S. Wyer Jr., D. L. Hamilton, & D. E. Carlston (Eds.), *Person memory: The cognitive basis of social perception*, (pp. 1–53). Hillsdale, NJ: Erlbaum.

Hastie, R. & Kumar, P. A. (1979). Person memory: Personality traits as organizing principles in memory for behaviors. *Journal of Personality and Social Psychology, 37*, 25–38.

Hauck, M., Fein, D., Maltby, N., Waterhouse, L., & Feinstein, C. (1998). Memory for faces in children with autism. *Child Neuropsychology, 4*, 187–198.

Heider, J. D., Scherer, C. R., Skowronski, J. J., Wood, S. E., Edlund, J. E., & Hartnett, J. L. (2007). Trait expectancies and stereotype expectancies have the same effect on person memory. *Journal of Experimental Social Psychology, 43*, 265–272.

Higgins, E. T., & Rholes, W. S. (1978). "Saying is believing": Effects of message modification on memory and liking for the person described. *Journal of Experimental Social Psychology, 14*, 363–378.

Hills, P. J., & Lewis, M. B. (2006). Reducing the own-race bias in face recognition by shifting attention. *Quarterly Journal of Experimental Psychology, 59*, 996–1002.

Hirt, E. R., McDonald, H. E., & Markman, K. D. (1998). Expectancy effects in reconstructive memory: When the past is just what we expected. In S. J. Lynn & K. M. McConkey (Eds.), *Truth in memory* (pp. 62–89). New York: Guilford Press.

Hugenberg, K., Young, S. G., Bernstein, M. J., & Sacco, D. F. (2010). The categorization-individuation model: An integrative account of the other-race recognition deficit. *Psychological Review*, 1168–1187.

Insel, T. R., & Fernald, R. D. (2004). How the brain processes social information: Searching for the social brain. *Annual Review of Neuroscience, 27*, 697–722.

Jemel, B., Mottron, L., & Dawson, M. (2006). Impaired face processing in autism: Fact or Artifact? *Journal of Autism and Developmental Disorders, 36*, 91–106.

Johnson, M. K., Doll, T. J., Bransford, J. D., & Lapinski, R. H. (1974). Context effects in sentence memory. *Journal of Experimental Psychology, 103*, 358–360.

Kanwisher, N. (2000). Domain specificity in face perception. *Nature Neuroscience, 3*, 759–763.

Kihlstrom, J. F., & Cantor, N. (2000). Social intelligence. In R.J. Sternberg (Ed.), *Handbook of intelligence* (2nd ed., pp. 359–379). Cambridge, UK: Cambridge University Press.

Klauer, K. C., & Kellen, D. (2010). Toward a complete decision model of item and source recognition: A discrete-state approach. *Psychonomic Bulletin & Review, 17*, 465–478.

Klauer, K. C., & Wegener, I. (1998). Unraveling social categorization in the "Who said what?" paradigm. *Journal of Personality and Social Psychology, 75*, 1155–1178.

Klein, S. B., Cosmides, L., Gangi, C. E., Jackson, B., Tooby, J., & Costabile, K. A. (2009). Evolution and episodic memory: An analysis and demonstration of a social function of episodic recollection. *Social Cognition, 27*, 283–319.

Klein, S. B., Cosmides, L., Tooby, J., & Chance, S. (2002). Decisions and the evolution of memory: Multiple systems, multiple functions. *Psychological Review, 109*, 306–329.

Klein, S. B., & Loftus, J. (1990). Rethinking the role of organization in person memory: An independent trace storage model. *Journal of Personality and Social Psychology, 59*, 400–410.

Klein, S. B., Robertson, T. E., & Delton, A. W. (2010). Facing the future: Memory as an evolved system for planning future acts. *Memory & Cognition, 38*, 13–22.

Klein, S. B., Robertson, T. E., Gangi, C. E., & Loftus, J. (2008). The functional independence of trait self-knowledge: Commentary on Sakaki (2007). *Memory, 16*, 556–565.

Kuhlmann, B. G., & Touron, D. R. (2011). Older adults' use of metacognitive knowledge in source monitoring: Spared monitoring but impaired control. *Psychology and Aging, 26*, 143–149.

Kunda, Z. (1999). *Social cognition: Making sense of people.* Cambridge, MA: MIT Press.

Lindsay, R. C. L., Ross, D. F., Read, J. D., Toglia, M. P. (Eds.). (2007). *The handbook of eyewitness psychology, Vol. II: Memory for people*. Mahwah, NJ: Erlbaum.

Loftus, E. F. (1975) Leading questions and the eyewitness report. *Cognitive Psychology, 7*, 560–572.

McNally, R. J. (2003). *Remembering trauma.* Cambridge, MA: Belknap Press/Harvard University Press.

Meadows, J. C. (1974). The anatomical basis of prosopagnosia. *Journal of Neurology, Neurosurgery, and Psychiatry, 37*, 489–501.

Mealey, L., Daood, C., & Krage, M. (1996). Enhanced memory for faces of cheaters. *Ethology and Sociobiology, 17*, 119–128.

Mehl, B., & Buchner, A. (2008). No enhanced memory for faces of cheaters. *Evolution & Human Behavior, 29*, 35–41.

Meissner, C. A., & Brigham, J. C. (2001). Thirty years of investigating the own-race bias in memory for faces: A metaanalytic review. *Psychology, Public Policy, and Law, 7*, 3–35.

Memon, A., Hope, L., & Bull, R. (2003). Exposure duration: Effects on eyewitness accuracy and confidence. *British Journal of Psychology, 94*, 339–354.

Mesoudi, A., Whiten, A. & Dunbar, R. (2006). A bias for social information in human cultural transmission. *British Journal of Psychology, 97*, 405–423.

Moscovitch, M., Winocur, G., & Behrmann, M. (1997). What is special about face recognition? Nineteen experiments on a person with visual object agnosia and dyslexia but normal face recognition. *Journal of Cognitive Neuroscience, 9*, 555–604.

Moss, F. A., & Hunt, T. (1927). Are you socially intelligent? *Scientific American, 137*, 108–110.

Moss, F. A., Hunt, T., Omwake, K. T., & Bonning, M. M. *Social intelligence test.* (1927). Oxford, UK: Center for Psychological Service.

Moss, F. A., Hunt, T., Omwake, K. T., & Woodward, L. G. (1955). *Manual for the George Washington University Series Social Intelligence Test.* Washington, DC: Center for Psychological Service.

Nairne, J. S. (2010). Adaptive memory: Evolutionary constraints on remembering. In B. H. Ross (Ed.), *The psychology of learning and motivation: Advances in research and theory* (Vol. 53, pp. 1–32). San Diego, CA: Elsevier Academic Press.

Nash, R. A., Bryer, O. M., & Schlaghecken, F. (2010). Look who's talking! Facial appearance can bias source monitoring. *Memory, 18*, 451–457.

Newman, L. S. (2001). A cornerstone for the science of interpersonal behavior? Person perception and person memory, past, present, and future. In G. B. Moskowitz (Ed.), *Cognitive social psychology: The Princeton Symposium on the Legacy and Future of Social Cognition* (pp. 191–207). Mahwah, NJ: Erlbaum.

Paradox_puree (Thursday, July 23rd, 2009, 8:39 pm). *Coming out faceblind at work*. Retrieved January 3, 2011, from http://community.livejournal.com/faceblind/.

Pasupathi, M. (2001). The social construction of the personal past and its implications for adult development. *Psychological Bulletin, 127*, 651–672.

Pasupathi, M., Stallworth, L. M., & Murdoch, K. (1998). How what we tell becomes what we know: Listener effects on speakers' long-term memory for events. *Discourse Processes, 26*, 1–25.

Pauker, K., Weisbuch, M., Ambady, N., Sommers, S. R., Adams, R. B. Jr., & Ivcevic, Z. (2009). Not so black and white: Memory for ambiguous group members. *Journal of Personality and Social Psychology, 96*, 795–810.

Pennington, N., & Hastie, R. (1993). The story model for juror decision making. In R. Hastie (Ed.), *Inside the juror: The psychology of juror decision making. Cambridge series on judgment and decision making* (pp. 192–221). New York: Cambridge University Press.

Pickel, K. L. (2007). Remembering and identifying menacing perpetrators: Exposure to violence and the weapons focus effect. In R. C. L. Lindsay, D. F. Ross, J. D. Read, & M. P. Toglia (Eds.), *The handbook of eyewitness psychology, Vol. II: Memory for people* (pp. 339–360). Mahwah, NJ: Erlbaum.

Pickel, K. L. (2009). The weapon focus effect on memory for female versus male perpetrators. *Memory, 17*, 664–678.

Plaks, J. E., Stroessner, S. J., Dweck, C. S., & Sherman, J. W. (2001). Person theories and attention allocation: Preferences for stereotypic versus counterstereotypic information. *Journal of Personality and Social Psychology, 80*, 876–893.

Probst, P. (1975). An empirical investigation of the construct of social intelligence. *Diagnostica, 21*, 24–47.

Reysen, M. B. (2009). Remembering social information: A functional analysis. In M. R. Kelley (Ed.), *Applied memory* (pp. 185–197). Hauppauge, NY: Nova Science.

Reysen, M. B., & Adair, S. A. (2008). Social processing improves recall performance. *Psychonomic Bulletin & Review, 15*, 197–201.

Roberts, K. P. (2000). An overview of theory and research on children's source monitoring. In K. P. Roberts & M. Blades (Eds.), *Children's source monitoring* (pp. 11–57). Mahwah, NJ: Erlbaum.

Rimmele, U., Hediger, K., Heinrichs, M., & Klaver, P. (2009). Oxytocin makes a face in memory familiar. *Journal of Neuroscience, 29*, 38–42.

Schacter, D. L. (1996). *Searching for memory: The brain, the mind, and the past*. New York: Basic Books.

Scherer, C. S., Heider, J. D., Skowronski, J. J., & Edlund, J. E. (2012). *Trait expectancies and stereotype expectancies affect person memory similarly in a jury context. Journal of Social Psychology, 152*, 613–622.

Sedikides, C., & Skowronski, J. J. (1997). The symbolic self in evolutionary context. *Personality and Social Psychology Review, 1*, 80–102.

Sedikides, C., & Skowronski, J. J. (2003). Evolution of the self: Issues and prospects. In M. R. Leary, & J. P. Tangney (Eds.), *Handbook of self and identity* (pp. 594–609). New York: Guilford Press.

Sedikides, C., & Skowronski, J. J. (2009). Social cognition and self-cognition: Two sides of the same evolutionary coin? *European Journal of Social Psychology, 39*, 1245–1249.

Sedikides, C., Skowronski, J. J., & Dunbar, R. I. M. (2006). When and why did the human self evolve? In M. Schaller, J. Simpson, & D. T. Kenrick (Eds.), *Evolution and social psychology* (pp. 55–80). Madison, CT: Psychosocial Press.

Shapiro, P. N., & Penrod, S. (1986). Meta-analysis of facial identification studies. *Psychological Bulletin, 100*, 139–156.

Sherman, J. W. (2001). The dynamic relationship between stereotype efficiency and mental representation. In G. B. Moskowitz (Ed.), *Cognitive social psychology: The Princeton symposium on the legacy and future of Social Cognition* (pp. 177–190). Mahwah, NJ: Erlbaum.

Sherman, J. W., Conrey, F. R., & Groom, C. J. (2004). Encoding flexibility revisited: Evidence for enhanced encoding of stereotype-inconsistent information under cognitive load. *Social Cognition, 22*, 214–232.

Sherman, J. W., & Frost, L. A. (2000). On the encoding of stereotype-relevant information under cognitive load. *Personality & Social Psychology Bulletin, 26*, 26–34.

Sherman, J. W., Groom, C. J., Ehrenberg, K., & Klauer, K. C. (2003). Bearing false witness under pressure: Implicit and explicit components of stereotype-driven memory bias. *Social Cognition, 21*, 213–246.

Sherman, J. W., Stroessner, S. J., Conrey, F. W., & Azam, O. A. (2005). Prejudice and stereotype maintenance processes: Attention, attribution, and individuation. *Journal of Personality and Social Psychology, 89*, 607–622.

Skowronski, J. J., Betz, A. L., Sedikides, C., & Crawford, M. T. (1998). Raw conditional probabilities are a flawed index of associative strength: Evidence from a multitrait paradigm. *European Journal of Social Psychology, 28*, 437–456.

Skowronski, J. J., Betz, A. L., Thompson, C. P., & Shannon, L. (1991). Social memory in everyday life: The recall of self-events and other-events. *Journal of Personality and Social Psychology, 60*, 831–843.

Skowronski. J. J., Carlston, D. E., & Hartnett, J. L. (2008). Spontaneous impressions derived from observations of behavior: What a long, strange trip it's been (and it's not over yet). In N. Ambady & J. J. Skowronski (Eds.), *First impressions* (pp. 313–333). New York: Guilford Press.

Skowronski, J. J., & Gannon, K. (2000). Raw conditional probabilities are a flawed index of associative strength: Evidence from a single trait expectancy paradigm. *Basic & Applied Social Psychology, 22*, 9–18.

Skowronski, J. J., & Walker, R. W. (2004). How describing autobiographical events can affect autobiographical memory. *Social Cognition, 22*, 555–590.

Skowronski, J. J., & Welbourne, J. (1997). Conditional probability may be a flawed measure of associative strength. *Social Cognition, 15*, 1–12.

Snyder, M., & Uranowitz, S. W. (1979). Reconstructing the past: Some cognitive consequences of person perception. *Journal of Personality and Social Psychology, 36*, 941–950.

Somerville, L. H., Wig, G. S., Whalen, P. J., & Kelley, W. M. (2006). Dissociable medial temporal lobe contributions to social memory. *Journal of Cognitive Neuroscience, 18*, 1253–1265.

Srull, T. K. (1981). Person memory: Some tests of associative storage and retrieval models. *Journal of Experimental Psychology: Human Learning and Memory, 7*, 440–463.

Stangor, C., & McMillan, D. (1992). Memory for expectancy-congruent and expectancy-incongruent information: A review of the social and social developmental literatures. *Psychological Bulletin, 111*, 42–61.

Taylor, S. E., Fiske, S. T., Etcoff, N. L., & Ruderman, A. J. (1978). Categorical and contextual bases of person memory and stereotyping. *Journal of Personality and Social Psychology, 36*, 778–793.

Thorndyke, P. W., & Hayes-Roth, B. (1979). The use of schemata in the acquisition and transfer of knowledge. *Cognitive Psychology, 11,* 82–106.

Toglia, M. P., Read, J. D., Ross, D. F., & Lindsay, R. C. L. (Eds.). (2007). *The handbook of eyewitness psychology, Vol. I: Memory for events.* Mahwah, NJ: Erlbaum.

Tooby, J., & Cosmides, L. (2005). Conceptual foundations of evolutionary psychology. In D. M. Buss (Ed.), *The handbook of evolutionary psychology* (pp. 5–67). Hoboken, NJ: John Wiley & Sons.

Trafimow, D., & Finlay, K. A. (2001). An investigation of three models of multitrait representations. *Personality & Social Psychology Bulletin, 27,* 226–241.

Tree, J. J., & Wilkie, J. (2010). Face and object imagery in congenital prosopagnosia: A case series. *Cortex: A Journal Devoted to the Study of the Nervous System and Behavior, 46,* 1189–1198.

Trope, Y., & Liberman, N. (2010). Construal level theory of psychological distance. *Psychological Review, 117,* 440–463.

Tulving, E., & Craik, F. L. M. (2000). *The Oxford handbook of memory.* New York: Oxford University Press.

Tversky, B., & Marsh, E. J. (2000). Biased retellings of events yield biased memories. *Cognitive Psychology, 40,* 1–38.

von Hippel, W., Jonides, J., Hilton, J. L., & Narayan, S. (1993). Inhibitory effect of schematic processing on perceptual encoding. *Journal of Personality & Social Psychology, 64,* 921–935.

Wanke, M., & Wyer, R. S., Jr. (1996). Individual differences in person memory: The role of sociopolitical ideology and in-group versus outgroup membership in responses to socially relevant behavior. *Personality and Social Psychology Bulletin, 22,* 742–754.

Webb, S. J., Jones, E. J. H., Merkle, K., Murias, M., Greenson, J., Richards, T., Aylward, E., & Dawson, G. (2010). *International Journal of Psychophysiology, 77,* 106–117.

Welch-Ross, M. K. (1999). Preschoolers' understanding of mind: Implications for suggestibility. *Cognitive Development, 14,* 101–131.

Wells, G. L., Memon, A., & Penrod, S. D. (2006). Eyewitness evidence: Improving its probative value. *Psychological Science in the Public Interest, 7,* 45–75.

White, J. D., & Carlston, D. E. (1983). Consequences of schemata for attention, impressions, and recall in complex social interactions. *Journal of Personality & Social Psychology, 45,* 538–549.

Wilhelm, O., Herzmann, G., Kunina, O., Danthiir, V., Schacht, A., & Sommer, W. (2010). *Journal of Personality and Social Psychology, 99,* 530–548.

Wilson, A. E., & Ross, M. (2001). From chump to champ: People's appraisals of their earlier and present selves. *Journal of Personality and Social Psychology, 80,* 572–584.

Winslow, J. T., & Insel, T. R. (2004). Neuroendocrine basis of social recognition. *Current Opinion in Neurobiology, 14,* 248–253.

Wright, D. B., & Sladden, B. (2003). An own gender bias and the importance of hair in face recognition. *Acta Psychologica, 114,* 101–114.

Wright, D. B., & Stroud, J. N. (2002). Age differences in lineup identification accuracy: People are better with their own age. *Law and Human Behavior 26,* 641–654.

Wyer, N. A., Perfect, T. J., & Pahl, S. (2010). Temporal distance and person memory: Thinking about the future changes memory for the past. *Personality and Social Psychology Bulletin, 36,* 805–816.

Wyer, R. S. Jr., & Carlston, D. E. (1994). The cognitive representation of persons and events. In R. S. Wyer Jr. & T. K. Srull (Eds.), *Handbook of social cognition: Vol. 1. Basic processes* (2nd ed., pp. 41–98). Hillsdale, NJ: Erlbaum.

Wyer, R. S., & Srull, T. K. (1980). The processing of social stimulus information: A conceptual integration. In R. Hastie, E. B. Ebbesen, R. S. Wyer Jr., D. L. Hamilton, & D. E. Carlston (Eds.), *Person memory: Cognitive basis of social perception* (pp. 227–300). Hillsdale, NJ: Erlbaum.

Wyer, R. S., & Srull, T. K. (1989). *Memory and cognition in its social context.* Hillsdale, NJ: Erlbaum.

Judgment and Decision Making

Leaf Van Boven, Mark Travers, Jacob Westfall, *and* Gary McClelland

Abstract

This chapter reviews classic and contemporary phenomena in the field of judgment and decision making, particularly as they relate to social psychology and social cognition. The review focuses on the cluster of ideas encapsulated in the "heuristics and biases" perspective. This perspective views judgments and decisions as the product of a relatively small number of mental shortcuts, and often compares how people *actually* make judgments and decisions with how they *ought* to make judgments and decisions. Topics regarding decision making include prospect theory and reasoned-based choice. Topics regarding judgment under uncertainty include representativeness, availability, and anchoring and adjustment. Also reviewed are studies concerning confidence, the correction of judgment, and emerging ideas about the interaction of emotion, judgment, and decision making. A discussion of the two-systems view of judgment and decision making and emerging questions for future research concludes the chapter.

Key Words: judgment, decision making, choice, intuition, prospect theory, heuristics, biases

Science fiction sometimes offers unique insight into psychological reality. In *The Adjustment Bureau* (2011), the central science fiction conceit is that a handful of mysterious "adjusters" occasionally intervene, through seemingly trivial acts, to guide regular mortals' judgments and decisions so that they are kept in line with "The Plan." This conceit affords such dramatic lines as, "People call it 'chance' when their coffee spills or their Internet goes down or they misplace their keys. Sometimes it is. Sometimes it's us nudging you back on Plan" and "Her decision tree is diverging from our models!"

Setting aside the issue of whether "nudges" and "decision trees" make for high-quality cinema, psychological scientists in the audience might have noticed two things in this conceit that relate to the scientific study of judgment and decision making. First, the idea that seemingly trivial events— spilt coffee, malfunctioning Internet, and other

"nudges"—can substantially alter the path of one's thoughts and behaviors is an important assumption of judgment and decision making research, and of social psychology more generally. Slight changes in question wording or decision framing can substantially, even qualitatively, alter people's judgments and decisions.

Second, *The Adjustment Bureau* rests on an assumption that the types of everyday experiences with which social psychologists are concerned— falling in love, career ambitions, political discourse and behavior—can be represented and understood through the lens of judgment and decision making. Indeed, the film recognizes a fact that is not always adequately understood by social psychologists: people's thoughts about themselves and the social world—their self-perceptions, attitudes, and assumptions about social groups—are *judgments*. And people's behaviors—their conformity to group norms, failure to intervene in emergency situations, and romantic relations—are *decisions*. The study of judgment and decision making is therefore not a specialized subtopic of social psychology or cognitive psychology, or, for that matter, of economics or behavioral economics. Rather, the study of judgment and decision making is the study of everyday thoughts and behavior, of thinking and deciding. The assumption that judgment and decision making inform and are informed by everyday thinking and behavior is central to this chapter.

The purpose of this chapter is to review important findings and ideas from the field of judgment and decision making, particularly as those findings and ideas are relevant to people's thoughts, feelings, and behaviors in the social world. The review is necessarily limited. We aim to describe a relatively small set of research findings from judgment and decision making that has influenced social psychology generally and social cognition specifically.

Our focus is on a cluster of ideas encapsulated in the "heuristics and biases" perspective on judgment and decision making. This perspective views judgments and decisions in everyday life as shaped by a relatively small number of mental shortcuts (heuristics). These shortcuts are grounded in basic mental operations such as similarity assessments, meta-cognition, and emotion. These mental shortcuts are elicited by particular domains, the particular way that questions are worded, and the way that decisions are framed. These mental shortcuts yield judgments and decisions that are relatively easily rendered and are reasonably accurate. However, because these processes are not grounded algorithmic computation of correct responses—time-consuming, psychologically expensive processes—people's judgments can be systematically biased, and their decision patterns can be reversed.

If students of social cognition sense familiar themes in this brief characterization of heuristics and biases research, it is because they reflect many prominent ideas in social cognition. Consider causal attribution. When observing someone engaging in situationally constrained behavior (such as a student who is "cold called" by a professor to answer a challenging question), people tend to infer that the person's behavior reflects his or her underlying, stable dispositions (in this case, that the person is dispositionally anxious and lacking in verbal fluency) to an unwarranted degree. Observers tend to underestimate the influence of situational factors (that being singled out by a professor is naturally anxiety provoking and that answering with fluency

and clarity is nearly impossible). Causal attribution reflects a conceptual binding of observable behavior and personal disposition, that is naturally evoked by the context in which it occurs (observing behavior naturally invites causal attributions; Uleman, Newman, & Moskowitz, 1996). Causal attributions are often accurate because personal dispositions do shape behavior. Yet this naturally evoked process can produce systematic biases and errors (i.e., the correspondence bias, or fundamental attribution error; Jones & Davis, 1965; Ross, 1977). The correspondence bias and many other social cognitive phenomena can thus be understood through the lens of heuristics and biases research reviewed in this chapter.

In this chapter, we first review research on models of decision making, with an emphasis on prospect theory (Kahneman & Tversky, 1979b), a value based theory of choice that describes systematic departures from expected utility theory, and recent developments in reason-based choice (Shafir, Simonson, & Tversky, 1993), which describes how choices are shaped by reasons for and against choosing alternatives. Second, we summarize the heuristics and biases program of research, including the availability, representativeness, and anchoring heuristics. We describe the initial ideas behind these heuristics, along with contemporary understanding of the processes that characterize these heuristic effects. Third, we discuss how overconfidence, hindsight bias, and confirmation bias pose barriers to learning from mistaken judgments. Fourth, we discuss emerging research on the interrelations among emotion, judgment, and decision making. Finally, we describe the emerging view of judgment and decision making as the result of two mental systems: one fast, easy, and intuitive; the other slower, more effortful, and analytic. Before delving into the substance of our review, we first consider the historical context from which the heuristics, biases, values, and frames research emerged.

A Brief History of Judgment and Decision Making

The field of judgment and decision making unabashedly borrowed principles of rational behavior from mathematics, and later economics, to serve as models of human behavior. Even before there were formal "researchers," the probability theorists of the 17th century who developed the expected value principle for guiding behavior in gambling games realized that there were many instances, such as the affinity for gambling and the purchase of insurance, in which humans chose options with unfavorable expected values. One of these instances was the St. Petersburg paradox that involves the following game of chance:

> You pay a fee to play the game in which a fair coin is tossed repeatedly until a tail appears, ending the game. The pot starts at $1 and is doubled every time a head appears. You win whatever is in the pot after the game ends. Thus, you win $1 if a tail appears on the first toss, $2 if a head appears on the first toss and a tail on the second, $4 if a head appears on the first two tosses and a tail on the third, $8 if a head appears on the first three tosses and a tail on the fourth, and so on. In short, you win 2^{k-1} dollars if the coin is tossed k times until the first tail appears.

What would be a fair price to pay for entering the game? To answer this question, one should first compute the expected payout: 50% of $1, 25% of $2, 12.5% of $4, and so on. The expected value of this gamble is infinite:

$$EV = \sum_{k=1}^{\infty} \frac{1}{2} = \infty$$

A player should therefore be willing to pay almost any price offered. In real life, however, few people are willing to pay more than $10.

Bernoulli (1738/1954) resolved some of these issues by introducing the concepts of decreasing marginal utility, risk aversion, and risk premium. Bernoulli's ideas formed the foundation of modern decision theory and underlie many modern conceptualizations of human decision making. Of particular importance was Bernoulli's notion of decreasing marginal utility, which implied that changes of the absolute value of wealth are decreasingly impactful as they become more extreme. For example, the difference between $0 and $10 is much larger than the difference between $1,000 and $1,010. The utility of wealth thus followed a power function similar to other psychophysical functions that describe, for example, perceived weight or brightness. Under this formulation the expected *utility* (not expected value) of St. Petersburg gamble is less than infinity.

Formal research on decision making in risk contexts had its beginnings in the axiomatic system for subjective expected utility (SEU) theory published by von Neumann and Morgenstern (1947). Their theory was crafted in response to criticisms of earlier editions of their game theory book that there was no justifiable method for measuring either subjective probabilities or utilities, which we might consider like psychophysical transformations of objective probabilities and money, respectively. For example, a decision maker might be offered a choice between one of two lotteries: the first lottery has a 1/3 chance of winning $600 or else $0; the second lottery has a 2/3 chance of winning $300 or else $0. SEU holds that people choose an alternative as though they were maximizing a utility function of the alternatives at hand; each individual alternative is evaluated as the sum of the products of the probabilities and the monetary values for each and every outcome that might result from choosing that alternative (von Neumann & Morgenstern, 1947). In this case, SEU predicts that decision makers would be indifferent between the lotteries because they have equal expected utility of $200 = 1/3 × $600 + 2/3 × $0 = 2/3 × $300 + 1/3 × $0. SEU is normatively appealing, providing a consistent basis for decision making across contexts and problem framing. After all, if one were to play either of the gambles mentioned above (1/3 chance of $600 or 2/3 chance of $300) many times, both gambles would yield $200, on average. Because the utility of the expected value of $200 is the same in both cases, people should be indifferent between those gambles.

With methods to infer subjective probabilities and utilities from choices among gambles, the door to scientific research was opened. Preston and Barrata (1948) immediately put the measurement model to use and discovered the enduring result that low probabilities are overweighted and high probabilities are underweighted. Mosteller and Nogee (1951) used SEU to measure the nonlinear relationship between money and utility.

But then the economist Allais (1953) produced two sets of examples, later known as the *Allais paradox*, for which almost everyone makes a pair of choices that violate the SEU axioms. Consider the choice between:

A: 10% chance of winning $5,000 or else nothing
B: 11% chance of winning $1,000 or else nothing

Most people prefer A given that the expected outcome ($500 = .10 × $5,000) is substantially higher than the alternative ($110 = .11 × $1,000). Now consider a different choice, this time between:

C: 89% chance of $1,000; 10% chance of $5,000; 1% chance of nothing
D: $1,000 for sure

Given this choice, most people prefer D, even though C has higher expected value ($1,390 = .89 × $1,000 + .10 × $5,000). Not only does the choice of D over C violate expected utility theory, also the overall pattern of choices—preferring A over B and D over C—reflects inconsistent preferences. To see why, note that C is equal to A plus an 89% chance of winning $1,000 and that D is equal to B plus an 89% chance of winning $1,000. Because the 89% chance of winning $1,000 is a "sure thing" in options C and D, that is, the decision maker enjoys the 89% chance of winning $1,000 no matter which option is chosen, the overall pattern of choices is a violation of the sure-thing principle, and a violation of SEU (Savage, 1954; Slovic & Tversky, 1974).

It turns out that there are many examples of systematic patterns of human decision making that violate SEU (Allais, 1953; Ellsberg, 1961; Fishburn & Kochenberger, 1979; Slovic, Fischhoff, & Lichtenstein, 1977). Edwards (1953) showed that, inconsistent with SEU theory, people had preferences for betting on certain probabilities, e.g., probability = 0.5 gambles (50% of $30) were preferred to 0.75 gambles (such as 75% of $20) even when expected value ($15) was equated). Coombs and Komorita (1958) first noted the disturbing inconsistency that stated preferences for gambles systematically deviate from actual choices among those same gambles.

These and other violations of SEU opened Pandora's box for judgment and decision-making researchers. Many subsequent researchers tried to find the many ways in which human behavior differed from the axiomatic, rational SEU theory, whereas economists tried to provide looser models that were close enough to be characterized as SEU, yet descriptively more realistic. As we discuss later, many behavioral decision theorists consider the problem of SEU violations to be essentially "solved" by prospect theory (Kahneman & Tversky, 1979b) and by the more general rank-dependent expected utility models (Quiggin, 1993). These theories incorporate and to some extent formalize many psychological concepts foreign to SEU.

The history of the study of intuitive judgments follows a similar path. By the 1950s, there existed a well-articulated normative model of human judgment, based on Bayesian statistics. The idea was that people update their prior beliefs in the direction of observed evidence, following Bayesian principles. Ward Edwards, a student of the statistician Frederick Mosteller who was influenced by statistician Jimmy Savage's book on Bayesian inference, is often credited with establishing the study of intuitive judgment within the field of behavioral decision research (Edwards, 1954, 1961). Edwards was

an early advocate for Bayesian analysis in psychological research (1963) and put his model for the revision of probabilities to the test in his lab at the University of Michigan. He concluded that people were "conservative Bayesians," revising the probabilities in light of new information in ways qualitatively consistent with Bayes' theorem, but tending not to revise their probabilities as far from the prior probabilities as predicted.

In collaboration with Daniel Kahneman, Edward's student Amos Tversky demonstrated that human judgment was inconsistent with not only Bayes' theorem (e.g., people ignored base rate probabilities whenever they could) but also most every other formal property of probability theory. Other students of Edwards such as Paul Slovic and Sarah Lichtenstein put decision-making theories to the test in actual games in a casino and extended the field to the study of natural hazard, health, and technological risks. Together, this University of Michigan cohort—Dawes, Tversky, Kahneman, Slovic, Lichtenstein—and their collaborators and students ushered a paradigm shift in the study of human judgment and decision making, developing the heuristics, biases, values, and frames approach that has characterized the study of judgment and decision making since then.

One of us (Gary McClelland) was a student at Michigan shortly after this time, and it is instructive to reflect on the academic zeitgeist of those days. Gary recalls,

> As a group we were pretty haughty and thought we were the best and that indeed we would change the world. I was very interested in axiomatic conjoint measurement (Dave Krantz and Clyde Coombs were the leaders there) and thought it would revolutionize psychological measurement. We thought it was a paradigm shift. (But we were totally wrong about that. Norm Cliff later wrote about the revolution that never happened.) We did think the judgment and decision making models would be useful everywhere in psychology and started right away doing that. Yaacov Trope applied Bayesian models to social psychology. Frank Yates did a number of extensions. Dennis Fryback soon founded the Medical Decision Making Society. We never doubted we were good. As a group we sometimes referred to ourselves as the Michigan Mafia and had no doubt about our intentions to impose our views on the world.

Whether a result of the Michigan Mafia's aspiration for intellectual domination or the result of the inherent scientific merit of the new program of research, it is fair to say that the heuristics and biases view now dominates psychological understanding of human judgment and decision making. In what follows, we provide a selective summary of the "greatest hits" of heuristics, biases, values, and frames research.

Decision Making: Values, Frames, and Reasons

Herbert Simon's idea of satisficing (Simon, 1955, 1957) was an early breakthrough toward a theory of decision making that was more descriptive than subjective expected utility was. Simon's insight was that subjective expected utility theory made unrealistic assumptions about decision makers' psychological capacities. Even if people wanted and attempted to make decisions in adherence with subjective expected utility, the demands on psychological resources make such decision making impossible. Simon proposed, instead, that people made decisions that were "good enough" within the particular decision-making context. People pursued principles of expected utility theory insofar as their psychological resources allowed, and in accordance with the importance of the decision at hand. This satisficing idea is quite similar to the "cognitive miser" idea in social cognition, according to which people reason about the social world in a generally miserly fashion, seeking the least cognitively expensive means of rendering the best possible social cognition (Fiske & Taylor, 1984).

But some violations of subjective expected utility theory were not readily attributable to satisficing. Indeed, it is implausible that the pattern of behavior in the Allais paradox is attributable to limited processing because calculation of expected utility is trivial. Rather, people's preferences are guided by psychological principles that are qualitatively different (not merely quantitatively limited) from making decisions by maximizing subjective expected utility. In the Allais instance, people seem inordinately attracted to the certainty of winning $1,000. The intuitive importance of certainty seemed to require new psychological principles.

Prospect Theory

The predominant descriptive theory of how people make decisions is prospect theory (Kahneman & Tversky, 1979b, 2000). Like subjective expected utility theory, prospect theory models choices between different gambles, or "prospects," in which various outcomes are associated with known probabilities. Drawing on well-established principles from perceptual psychology and psychophysics, prospect theory describes the process by which people make decisions, and describes a value function that translates outcomes into psychological units of utility, along with a probability weighting function that translates probabilities (expectations) into psychological weights.

Value Function

Prospect theory's value function describes the utility associated with various potential outcomes. The utility function has three features. First, according to long established notions of utility from Bernoulli, people are assumed to exhibit diminishing marginal sensitivity to increasingly extreme outcomes. The difference in utility between $1 and $11, for example, is much larger than the difference in utility between $1,001 and $1,011.

Second, outcomes are valued as gains or losses relative to some neutral reference point rather than as absolute states of wealth. A person who values a house as a seller, for example, considers giving up the house as a loss relative to the reference point of owning the house. A person who values the same house as a buyer, in contrast, considers getting the house as a gain relative to the reference point of not owning the house. So the same object (the house) is evaluated differently (as a loss or gain) depending on the person's reference point.

Finally, the value function is steeper for losses than for gains. That is, people tend to assign greater value to objects when evaluating them as losses than when evaluating them as gains. For example, the (negative) utility experienced by losing $100 is greater than the (positive) utility experienced by winning $100. Across many studies over several decades with both hypothetical and real choices, the magnitude of this loss aversion has been estimated to be about 2:1. A loss of a given objective magnitude feels about twice as bad as a gain of the same magnitude. Losses loom larger than gains.

Weighting Function

The probability weighting function of prospect theory describes the decision weight of various probabilities, analogous to how the value function describes the utility associated with various objective outcomes. The probability weighting function has three important features. First, people weight certain probabilities (0% and 100%) more heavily than uncertain probabilities (between 0% and 100%). People are consequently more sensitive to changes in probability away from certainty, such as moving from 0% to 5% or from 100% to 95%, than they are to changes within the realm of uncertainty, such as moving from 5% to 10% or from 90% to 85%. Second, probability weighting tends to be regressive for most probabilities such that the difference in the weight of 60% and 55% is less than 5%. Finally, people tend to overweight very small probabilities and underweight very large probabilities.

Prospect theory's value function and weighting function explain previously paradoxical findings such as the Allais paradox. There, the effect of certainty in probability weighting (that makes 100% chance of winning more impactful than 99% chance of winning), combined with the regressive tendency for most probabilities (that makes 10% seem nearly identical to 11%) explains why, when faced with the decision alternatives A, B, C, and D described in the previous section, people's choices are inconsistent between A versus B, and C versus D.

Framing Effects

Prospect theory also generates novel predictions, many of which center on the way problems are framed. One well known example is the "Asian disease" problem (Tversky & Kahneman, 1981):

Imagine that the U.S. is preparing for the outbreak of an unusual Asian disease, which is expected to kill 600 people. Two alternative programs to combat the disease have been proposed. Assume that the exact scientific estimates of the consequences of the programs are as follows:

If Program A is adopted, 200 people will be saved.
If Program B is adopted, there is 1/3 probability that 600 people will be saved, and 2/3 probability that no people will be saved.
The majority of participants presented with this scenario chose Program A, the "risk averse" option. However, for a second group of participants, the options were described as:
If Program C is adopted 400 people will die.
If Program D is adopted there is 1/3 probability that nobody will die, and 2/3 probability that 600 people will die.

When the options were framed as mortality (loss) rather than survival (gain), the majority of participants chose Program D, the "risk-seeking" option. Notice, of course, that Programs A and C are identical, as are Programs B and D. The outcomes are simply framed differently.

The tendency to be risk averse when choosing between gain framed prospects but to be risk seeking when choosing between loss framed prospects has been termed the *framing effect*. By simply framing a choice problem differently, one can induce changes in the neutral reference point and thereby alter choice behavior. In this example, the first pair of options are framed such that the reference point is at 0 people being saved, so that each person saved represents a "gain" relative to the reference point. Because sensitivity to additional gains decreases with additional distance from the reference point, implying a value function that is concave (or "decelerating") in the domain of gains, the appeal of 1/3 probability of saving 400 additional lives over the sure-thing option is not great enough to justify the 2/3 probability of saving no lives, replicating the familiar phenomenon of risk aversion. The options in the second pair, on the other hand, are framed such that the reference point is at 0 people dying, so that each person who dies represents a "loss" relative to the reference point. Because decreasing marginal sensitivity to losses implies a value function that is convex (or "accelerating") in the domain of gains, under this framing, the appeal of 1/3 probability of losing 400 fewer lives than in the sure-thing option is great enough to justify the 2/3 probability of losing all 600 lives, resulting in a risk-seeking decision.

Endowment Effect

Prospect theory was developed to explain findings from the domain of risky choice in which decision makers choose between alternatives that might occur with varying probabilities. Many of prospect theory's principles also explain "riskless" choice in which people choose between outcomes with no uncertainty. The endowment effect is a prominent example. The amount that a person would be willing to accept in order to give up a good that the person happens to own is greater than the amount that the person would be willing to pay to acquire that exact same good had he or she not owned it (Birnbaum & Stegner, 1979; Kahneman, Knetsch, & Thaler, 1991; Knetsch & Sinden, 1984; Thaler, 1980).

The endowment effect is puzzling from the subjective expected utility perspective. In both the roles of owner and nonowner, the good being gained or given up is the same, so there is no reason for the good to be valued differently. Stated differently, the endowment effect implies that consumers are more sensitive to out-of-pocket costs (where one gives up money to acquire a good) than to opportunity costs (where one passes up money to keep a good), despite the economic equivalence of these costs.

The endowment effect is readily explained by prospect theory. For the "buyer" of a hypothetical good, the transaction is framed as involving the gain of the good. For the "seller," the transaction is viewed as involving the loss of the good (Carmon & Ariely, 2000). Because losses loom larger than gains, it follows that, all else being equal, the seller will often demand more to give up the good than the buyer will be willing to pay to acquire it.

Mental Accounting

An idea related to the endowment effect is mental accounting (Kahneman & Tversky, 1984; Thaler, 1980, 1985; Tversky & Kahneman, 1981). Consider the following example:

Problem A: Imagine that you have decided to see a play and paid the admission price of $10 per ticket. As you enter the theater, you discover that you have lost the ticket. The seat was not marked, and the ticket cannot be recovered. Would you pay $10 for another ticket?

Problem B: Imagine that you have decided to see a play for which admission is $10 per ticket. As you enter the theater, you discover that you have lost a $10 bill. Would you still pay $10 for a ticket for the play?

For Problem A, a slight majority of participants preferred not to buy the ticket ("I'm not paying for the same ticket twice!"). For Problem B, however, participants overwhelmingly preferred to buy the ticket ("What does losing the $10 bill have to do with the play?"). Of course, both problems are normatively equivalent: in each case, the choice is between having $10 less and missing the play or having $20 less and seeing the play. It appears that rather than regarding all of their wealth as fully fungible or interchangeable, people compartmentalize their wealth into a series of "mental accounts" that they must continually segregate or integrate. In Problem A, the cost of buying the second ticket is integrated with the cost of buying the original ticket, resulting in a loss that many apparently find unacceptable. In Problem B, on the other hand, the cost of the original ticket and the loss of the money are kept in segregated "accounts." The idea of mental accounting considerably extends prospect theory by elaborating specifically on how choice problems will tend to be framed and how gains and losses will be mentally coded.

Reason-Based Choice

Prospect theory describes how people value various outcomes and weight various probabilities. But prospect theory provides limited descriptions of the psychological processes that lead people to value outcomes and weight probabilities as they do. That is, prospect theory describes *what* people do more than it describes *how* people make decisions. Other theories concern themselves more with describing the psychological processes influencing choice. Among the most prominent and relevant to social psychologists is reason-based choice.

The reason-based choice perspective suggests that people make decisions based on the reasons they bring to mind when contemplating the decision (Shafir et al., 1993). People choose the option that is favored by the balance of reasons for and against that option. Reason-based choice is highly compatible with prospect theory. Indeed, it yields many of the same predictions as prospect theory. Reason-based choice is more descriptively realistic regarding the psychological processes people see themselves and others engage in when making decisions. When choosing which job offer to accept, for example, people often generate specific reasons to choose one job over another; they less frequently estimate probabilities of distinct outcomes and their associated utilities, which they combine to evaluate the prospect of one job over another.

Reason-based choice also provides a natural way to think about decision conflict, which occurs when the balance of reasons equally favors more than one option. In response to conflict, people are often motivated to seek out additional information that might tip the scales of reason in one direction or another. Consider the following problem in which students were asked to consider the choice of an apartment from a larger list (Shafir, et al., 1993):

E: $290 monthly rent, 25 minutes from campus
F: $350 monthly rent, 7 minutes from campus

Both have one bedroom and a kitchenette. You can choose now between the two apartments, or you can continue to search for apartments (to be selected at random from the list you reviewed). In that case, there is some risk of losing one or both of the apartments you have found.

In this problem, people experience conflict because there is no clear reason to choose E or F because the two relevant attributes, price and commute distance, are crossed. Because they experience conflict, most people choose to continue searching for apartments rather than choosing between E and F. Now consider the following choice pair:

E: $290 monthly rent, 25 minutes from campus
G: $350 monthly rent, 25 minutes from campus

Here, there is no conflict because E dominates G: There is a clear reason for choosing E. Most people consequently do not opt to continue searching for apartments. When presented with an option E that dominates the alternative G, when there is a clear reason for choosing one option, people do not feel compelled to seek out additional reasons in the form of additional apartments. When there is no clear reason for choosing one option E over an alternative F, people seek out additional options, even though most people thought that at least one of the options (E) was good enough not to seek out additional options. Reason-based choice also implies that once people choose to seek out additional options, they are more likely to choose those options than they would be if the same options had been presented as part of the initial choice set (Bastardi & Shafir, 1998; Redelmeier, Shafir, & Aujla, 2001).

The idea of reason-based choice is of particular relevance to social cognition, we believe, because it provides a bridge between social psychological and behavioral decision theory approaches to understanding decision making. Cognitive dissonance (Festinger, 1957), self-perception (Bem, 1972), and accountability (Tetlock, 1992), for example, are social cognition constructs grounded in the idea that people make decisions, make inferences about their decisions, and justify decisions based on the perceived reasons surrounding their decisions. Reason-based choice thus adopts a language familiar to social cognition researchers and provides a familiar means of understanding such phenomena as the certainty effect ("I don't like the gamble because you never know what might happen"), risk seeking in the domain of losses ("I'll take the gamble because there's a chance of not losing anything at all"), loss aversion and the endowment effect ("I know that I like what I own, so why trade it?"), and other behavioral patterns derived from prospect theory.

Summary

Prospect theory and the related ideas derived from it have been enormously influential in the social sciences (and beyond). Indeed, Daniel Kahneman was awarded the 2002 Nobel Memorial Prize in Economics based largely on prospect theory (the prize was awarded only to Kahenman because it cannot be awarded posthumously; Kahneman's longtime collaborator Amos Tversky passed away in 1996). Prospect theory is the basis for analyses of myriad social phenomena, including politics (McDermott, 2004), economic sanctions (Berejikian, 2002), goal setting (Heath, Larrick, & Wu, 1999), conflict (Deutsch, Coleman, & Marcus, 2006), and negotiation (Neale & Bazerman, 1990).

Yet it is our impression that prospect theory and its associated ideas have been less influential in social psychology. Literature searches of social psychology's premier empirical outlet, the *Journal of Personality and Social Psychology*, yield only a handful of publications with titles or key words containing prospect theory (six), loss aversion (two), or the endowment effect (one). For example, Van Boven and colleagues (2003) used the endowment effect as a context in which to examine emotional perspective taking regarding loss aversion. Eibach and Keegan (2006) used loss aversion to explain blacks' and whites' different assessments of racial progress (see also Pratto & Glasford, 2008). And Linville & Fischer (1991) tested predictions derived from prospect theory about the combination versus separation of gains versus losses. Other researchers have discussed ideas closely related to prospect theory, including the mere ownership effect (Beggan, 1992) and promotion versus prevention focus as an account of differing motivation (Higgins, 1997).

It is astounding to us that one of the most prominent psychological theories of choice, one of the foundational theories of behavioral economics, is so little referenced or examined in mainstream social psychology. This seems a major oversight. We suspect there are two reasons for social psychologists' neglect of prospect theory. One is that prospect theory is, in a sense, too well established for researchers to claim ownership of the ideas. In an era with fierce competition to propose new theoretical processes (and to give them new names), researchers may fret about simply "applying" someone else's ideas.

Another reason is that prospect theory is, by design, behavioral. It describes value and probability weighting as simple stimulus–response functions. This approach, although descriptively powerful, lacks the rich internal discourse that characterizes much of modern social psychological theories. We suspect that if prospect theory was prominently as a multistep process, dual process it might gain wider traction among social psychologists. Whatever the reason, we believe that prospect theory could provide a powerful basis for social psychological explanation and prediction.

Heuristics and Biases in Judgment Under Uncertainty

Much of the research on heuristics and biases in judgment under uncertainty arose from a simple question: How good are people as intuitive statisticians? Many of the intuitive judgments people make in everyday life can be characterized as statistical questions, such as: How do people judge the likelihood that the value of a mutual fund will increase over a five-year period (and thus decide where to invest their children's college savings)? How do people judge the likelihood that a "100-year" flood will damage their property, given that the area suffered major flooding 10 years ago (and thus decide whether and how much flood insurance to purchase)? Given knowledge that last winter's snowfall was slightly below average, how do people estimate this year's likely snowfall (and thus decide whether to invest in a season ski pass)? Normatively speaking, such questions can be answered based on simple statistical principles such as knowledge of relevant statistical base rates, or simple logical principles such as that the likelihood of events A and B both occurring cannot be more likely than event B occurring in isolation (i.e., the conjunction rule of probability).

The relevant statistical principles usually are neither conceptually nor computationally demanding. For example, knowledge that the base rate of past events (e.g., average annual snowfall) should be heavily weighed in predicting future events (next year's snowfall) is not a complicated concept and requires virtually no computation. But just as people's decision making is qualitatively (rather than merely quantitatively) different from subjective expected utility theory, the processes by which people render intuitive judgments under uncertainty is qualitatively different from simple statistical principles. The application of simple statistical principles is not natural. That is, seeing statistical principles does not come as easily to people as, for instance, assessing the similarity of two events, or as assessing how easily one can mentally simulate the event.

The foundation of the research program that became known as the "heuristics and biases" program described three heuristics people use to make probability judgments under uncertainty (Tversky & Kahneman, 1974). The heuristics include representativeness, availability, and anchoring and adjustment. The central idea behind these three heuristics is that people answer seemingly difficult questions about target attributes (what is this year's likely snowfall?) by answering with more easily substituted attributes (what was last year's snowfall?). This process of "attribute substitution" turns questions that are difficult to answer into questions that are easy and natural to answer (Kahneman & Frederick, 2002).

Representativeness

People often judge the likelihood that an object belongs to a particular class of objects by assessing how much that object resembles, or is representative of, that class of objects (Tversky & Kahneman, 1974). Representativeness is typically a reasonable means of judging probability. Instances typically *do* resemble the category of events from which they are drawn. However, the degree to which an instance is representative of a class of instances is not the same as the likelihood that an instance actually belongs to that class of instances. Judgments based on representativeness can therefore depart from normative principles of probability judgment.

An early demonstration of how reliance on representativeness can lead to biased judgments is illustrated by the study of the hypothetical Tom W. (Kahneman & Tversky, 1973). In this classic experiment, participants read the following scenario:

> Tom W. is of high intelligence, although lacking in true creativity. He has a need for order and clarity, and for neat and tidy systems in which every detail finds its appropriate place. His writing is rather dull and mechanical, occasionally enlivened by somewhat corny puns and by flashes of imagination of the sci-fi type. He has a strong drive for competence. He seems to feel little sympathy for other people and does not enjoy interacting with others. Self-centered, he nonetheless has a deep moral sense.

Participants were divided into three groups. Participants in one group estimated how similar (representative) they thought Tom W. was to the typical member of each of nine college majors. Participants in another group judged the likelihood that Tom W. was a member of each of the college majors. Participants in a third group estimated the percentage of the total student population in each of the nine majors, a measure of the perceived base rate of majors. As predicted by representativeness, the judgments of similarity were nearly perfectly correlated with the judgments of probability. Both groups judged Tom W. to be most similar to or most likely to be an engineer and least similar to or least likely to be a social science/social work student. Furthermore, likelihood judgments were not correlated at all with perceived base rates, even though perceived base rates are normatively appropriate bases for judging likelihood. Even though engineers were determined by participants in the third condition to represent one of the smallest student populations, people estimated that Tom W. was most likely to be an engineer, in contrast with the base rates.

Base rate neglect, as this phenomenon has become known, occurs when people ignore prior probabilities and instead base their judgments on other, often more salient, informational cues.

Beyond simply neglecting base rates, the estimation of likelihood or frequency by representativeness can produce violations of simple logical rules of probability (Tversky & Kahneman, 1983). Consider the study in which people read about Linda:

> Linda is 31 years old, single, outspoken, and very bright. She majored in philosophy. As a student, she was deeply concerned with issues of discrimination and social justice, and also participated in antinuclear demonstrations.

Participants read the above scenario and were asked to estimate the probability that Linda was (A) a bank teller, and (B) a bank teller who was active in the feminist movement. According to the aforementioned conjunction rule of probability, the conjunction of two events cannot be more likely than one of the constituent events: $p(A \& B) \leq p(A)$. Among the set of bank tellers in the world, some of them are undoubtedly feminist. But there cannot be *more* feminist bank tellers than there are bank tellers (regardless of their feminist status) or than there are feminists (regardless of their employment status). People nevertheless estimated the conjunction that Linda was both a bank teller and a feminist as more likely than that Linda was simply a bank teller. The reason is that the description of Linda was designed to resemble a feminist more than a bank teller. The conjunctive event of being a bank teller and a feminist is therefore more representative of Linda's description than is simply being a bank teller. Reliance on representativeness can therefore cause people to deviate from normative principles of probability judgment.

Availability

Why do people significantly overestimate the amount of people who die from tornado strikes yet underestimate the number of deaths due to asthma (Lichtenstein, Slovic, Fischhoff, Layman, & Combs, 1978)? Why do people judge the reliability and competence of a large-scale automobile manufacturer based solely on the clunker their neighbors bought 15 years ago? One explanation of such judgments is that such examples are easier to bring to mind than are the relevant base rates. The availability heuristic describes people's tendency to judge the likelihood of events based on the ease with which instances can be brought to mind (Tversky & Kahneman, 1973).

Availability is typically a reasonable means of judging probability because events that are more common or probable are usually easier to bring to mind than events that are less common or probable. The ease with which instances can be brought to mind is not the same as the likelihood those instances will occur, however, so judgments based on availability can also deviate from normative principles of probability judgment.

Many initial studies examined the availability heuristic by demonstrating systematic biases in probability judgment (Tversky & Kahneman, 1974). In one study, researchers asked a group of participants to estimate whether words in the English language were more likely to begin with the letter *r*, or to have the letter *r* in the third position. Because it is easier to think of instances when *r* is the first letter of a word (i.e., ratify, right, rhinoceros, etc.) than the third letter (perturb, car, etc.), participants estimated that more English words began with the letter *r* even though the reverse is, in fact, true (Tversky & Kahneman, 1973). Availability also provided a natural explanation of other important judgmental biases, including illusory correlation, which arises from the relative ease with which people can retrieve the co-occurrence of distinct events (e.g., a black man acting aggressively), and the overestimation of small risks such as terrorist attacks and airplane crashes, which are often vividly covered in the media and hence easier to bring to mind than more probable risks such as auto crashes.

Initial studies of availability focused on applications and extensions such as using availability to explain social attributional processes. Ross and Sicoly (1979) found that husbands and wives tend to believe that they each perform a greater share of the household chores than they actually do; when asked to estimate the percentage that they are personally responsible for, these pairs of percentages typically summed to significantly more than 100%. Invoking availability as an explanation for results, Ross and Sicoly found a significant correlation between the magnitude of overestimation by each partner and how many self-generated examples of performing a chore each spouse listed. Subsequent studies showed that overestimation bias could be attenuated by having participants focus on the other side's actions, presumably increasing the availability of other's actions and thus reducing the tendency to overestimate one's own contributions to the overall task.

As availability became more widely replicated and extended, researchers also began to scrutinize more carefully the explanations underlying availability. It became apparent, in particular, that instances of events that could be brought to mind more easily were also brought to mind more plentifully (Schwarz et al., 1991; Schwarz & Vaughn, 2002). For example, people could not only more *easily* think of words that begin with *r* than with *r* in the third position, they could also think of *more* examples of words that begin with *r*. That is, the experiential information of how easily examples were brought to mind was confounded with the declarative information of how many examples were brought to mind. This confound implied, obviously, that it was unclear whether judgment by availability reflected judgments based on experiential or declarative information.

These two explanations were disentangled by a set of experiments that pitted against each other predictions derived from experiential information versus declarative information (Schwarz, et al., 1991). In one study, participants were asked to recall instances in which they acted assertively before judging their overall assertiveness. Participants were asked to recall either six or 12 instances of their assertiveness. Six instances are much easier to retrieve than 12 instances. Judgments based on experiential information (subjective ease) thus imply that participants who recalled six instances should judge themselves as more assertive compared with participants who recalled 12 instances; judgments based on declarative information, in contrast, imply that participants who recalled six instances should judge themselves as less assertive compared with participants who recalled 12 instances. In the study, participants judged themselves as more assertive after recalling six instances of assertive behavior, supporting the role of experiential information. The "ease vs. number" paradigm has been used to disentangle experiential and declarative information in many judgments including one's susceptibility to heart disease (Rothman, Haddock, & Schwarz, 2001), the frequency with which certain letters appear in various positions of words (Wanke, Schwarz, & Bless, 1995), and students' course evaluations (Fox, 2006). Such evidence makes clear that people's subjective experience when bringing information to mind influences judgments, independent of, if not despite, the amount of information brought to mind (Schwarz & Vaughn, 2002).

The clarifying discovery that availability was grounded in experiential information jibed with cognitive psychological research on processing fluency, or the ease with which people process information (Jacoby & Dallas, 1981; Johnston,

Dark, & Jacoby, 1985). In one study, participants judged the truth of certain statements such as "Orsono is a city in Chile" (Reber & Schwarz, 1999). Experimenters manipulated whether the statement was printed in an easy to read font or a difficult to read font. Participants judged statements that were easier to read as more truthful than statements that were difficult to read. In another study, participants judged the veracity of equivalent statements that either rhymed (e.g., woes unite foes) or not (e.g., woes unite enemies; (McGlone & Tofighbakhsh, 2000). Rhyming statements were judged as truer than nonrhyming statements. Fluency effects have been shown to influence other types of judgment such as liking (Reber, Winkielman, & Schwarz, 1998) and confidence (Kelley & Lindsay, 1993).

Anchoring and Adjustment

The third of the initial judgmental heuristics identified a two-part judgmental process by which people started from a judgmental anchor and then adjusted toward the target to yield their final estimate. For instance, when researchers asked people to estimate the value of one of two equivalent equations, "$8 \times 7 \times 6 \times 5 \times 4 \times 3 \times 2 \times 1$" or "$1 \times 2 \times 3 \times 4 \times 5 \times 6 \times 7 \times 8$", under time pressure, participants gave higher responses when the expression began with the larger numbers than when the equation began with the smaller numbers (Tversky & Kahneman, 1974). People presumably answer such questions by beginning the relatively easy computation and then adjusting upward ("8 times 7 is 56 times 6 is about 300 so the answer must be a lot more than that…" or, "1 times 2 is 2 times 3 is 6 so the answer must be more than that…"). Because people's initial calculation yields a higher number when the first numbers are large, their final estimate is higher (median = 2,250) compared with when the initial numbers are low (median = 512). The true answer happens to be 40,320.

Anchoring and adjustment is something of a "meta heuristic" in that it describes the sequential operation of two mental operations. The first operation, the anchor, is an initial, easy, intuitive response; the subsequent adjustment is a more careful, systematic, effortful estimate (Tversky & Kahneman, 1974). As revealed by this description, anchoring and adjustment provided some initial evidence and theorizing for what we now understand to the be interaction of two systems of reasoning: a fast, associative, intuitive system and a slower, rule-based, reasoning system.

As with representativeness and availability, initial studies emphasized replication, extension, and application of "anchoring effects." Most anchoring studies adopted a similar paradigm, illustrated by one early and often-replicated study that asked participants to consider the percentage of African countries represented in the United Nations (U.N.). Before participants provided their estimate, a number between 0 and 100 was randomly selected by the spin of a lottery wheel. In the first, comparative phase, participants were asked to indicate whether the fraction of African countries in the U.N. was equal to that number. In the second, estimation phase, participants were then asked to estimate the true fraction of African countries in the U.N. The arbitrarily determined anchor value influenced participants' estimates. The wheel was rigged to yield a low value of 10 or a high value of 65. The median percentage estimate of African countries represented in the U.N. when the lottery spin yielded a 10 was 25%. When the lottery spin yielded a value of 65, the median estimate increased to 45%.

Many researchers have noted that evidence for an actual process of anchoring and adjustment is rather slim, and the description of that process not much more than metaphorical. It is now clear that "anchoring effects" are the result of at least three distinct processes. One process concerns the differential accessibility of anchor-consistent information. According to "selective accessibility," anchoring effects occur because of increased accessibility of anchor-consistent information (Mussweiler & Strack, 1999, 2000; Strack & Mussweiler, 1997). In the initial, comparative phase of the standard anchoring paradigm, participants first test whether the answer might actually equal the anchor, for example, whether the fraction of African countries in the U.N. is actually 65. Because people test hypotheses by seeking confirmatory information, this hypothesis testing strategy increases the accessibility of information consistent with the anchor (Crocker, 1982; Snyder & Swann, 1978; Trope & Bassok, 1982; Wason, 1960; Wason & Johnson-Laird, 1972). Then, during the second estimation phase, the anchor-consistent information biases the answer participants ultimately provide. This selective accessibility account undoubtedly explains many anchoring effects, particularly those demonstrated in the standard comparison-estimation procedure.

A second and related process is that anchors prime magnitudes that make similar magnitudes more likely to come to mind. In one study, people's arbitrary ID numbers influenced their estimates of the number of physicians listed in a phone book (Wilson, Houston, Etling, & Brekke, 1996; see also Smith & Windschitl, 2011; Wong & Kwong, 2000). In another study, the magnitude of numbers in the environment were shown to produce anchoring effects, such as when participants were shown a photograph of a football player and asked how many sacks he would record this season, numerical estimates were influenced by the number (high/low anchor) on the player's jersey (Critcher & Gilovich, 2008). In these examples, participants are not directly testing the legitimacy of anchor value, so selective accessibility is unlikely. Rather, the presence of large or small numbers seems to prime large or small numbers when generating an estimate.

A final process is the deliberate sequential adjustment away from an anchor that is "close but not quite correct," as the heuristic was initially characterized (Epley & Gilovich, 2001, 2004). Judgments often follow this sequential adjustment process when they entail self-generated anchors that are close, such as when people are asked, "When did the second European explorer, after Columbus, land in the West Indies?" (Epley & Gilovich, 2001). People naturally think of "1492" as a relevant number that is close but not quite right, and they adjust away from this number. This process was confirmed through a series of studies (Epley & Gilovich, 2001) in which participants were asked to either nod or shake their heads (under the guise of evaluating the quality of headphones they were asked to wear) while answering questions that involved adjustment away from a self-generated anchor. Previous research (Wells & Petty, 1980) showed that people are more likely to accept propositions when nodding rather than shaking their head. If serial adjustment away from a self-generated anchor were indeed occurring, then nodding one's head would result in decreased adjustment away from an anchor as well as decreased response time compared with shaking one's head. This is exactly how participants behaved, exhibiting larger anchor effects when nodding rather than shaking their heads.

The anchoring and serial adjustment process also provides evidence for insufficient adjustment. Results from a control condition (no head movement) in the study just described revealed that participants underadjusted for most responses. For instance, people estimated on average that George Washington was elected President in 1779 and that vodka freezes at 1.75 degrees Fahrenheit. Correct answers are 1787 and −20 degrees Fahrenheit, respectively.

Summary

The idea that intuitive judgment is grounded in a relatively small number of heuristics has been enormously influential in social cognition, explaining myriad social cognitive phenomena. Representativeness helps explains people's readiness to infer causal relationships between observed effects and potential explanations that resemble those effects (Downing, Sternberg, & Ross, 1985) and the widespread tendency to neglect base rates (Ajzen, 1977; Ginosar & Trope, 1980), such as when people commit the planning fallacy, being unrealistic about future task completion times and neglecting base rate information about how long it has taken to complete similar tasks in the past (Buehler, Griffin, & Ross, 1994; Kahneman & Tversky, 1979a). Availability has been used to explain illusory correlations, which, in turn, explain many instances of stereotypic social judgment (Hamilton & Gifford, 1976). And anchoring and adjustment underlies prominent theories of how people make attributions about others' behavior, anchoring on initial, automatic dispositional inferences (Uleman, et al., 1996) before effortfully adjusting that initial inference to account for situational factors (Gilbert, 2002).

Although representativeness, availability, and anchoring have had substantial influence on social cognition, one important unanswered question concerns the nature of stimuli that elicit specific heuristic responses. Previous research has demonstrated that people use particular heuristics in contexts prototypically designed to elicit those heuristics, such as when people are provided with a personality sketch (e.g., Tom W.) and asked to estimate the likelihood that the target is a student of various majors. What about more generic questions such as how students evaluate an instructor's quality after the first day of class? Do students ask themselves how much the instructor resembles the prototype of outstanding or disappointing instructors? Do students try to think of examples of how much they've learned in the first week, using the ease with which they can generate examples to estimate how much they will learn? Do students start with a relatively extreme value ("Many instructors at my school are outstanding, 10 out of 10!") and then adjust ("But this guy is new, so he may not be as good.")? Absent from our current understanding is what specifically triggers different kinds of heuristic processes. Mapping these heuristics to eliciting stimuli will be an important task for future research.

Confidence, Confirmation, and Hindsight

The heuristics underlying intuitive judgment produce systematic biases that depart from normative statistical models of judgment under uncertainty. The prevalence of such biases naturally raises the question of whether such judgmental biases are likely to persist over time, or whether the feedback people receive in the real world about their biased judgments might help them correct such judgments. In real life outside the laboratory, the argument goes, people have ample opportunities to carefully examine the accuracy of their judgments and to correct mistaken judgments, a process that is often facilitated by swift, accurate feedback from social and market forces about judgment accuracy.

In reality, however, people tend to respond to real-world information and feedback in ways that undermine the value of feedback. Specifically, people tend to be overconfident in their own judgments, which makes them hesitant to revise their judgments, leads them to "test" hypotheses primarily by seeking confirmatory information, makes it unlikely they will notice that a judgment is biased, and causes them to revise judgments in hindsight in the direction of what they now know to be true.

Overconfidence

Do we believe, with confidence, that investing five (or more) years in graduate school followed by two (or more) years of a post doc will result in a tenure-track academic offer? Do we think that our start-up company has a greater chance of success than the dismal base rate data might indicate? When considering questions of this kind, our confidence in the correctness of our judgments and decisions plays a critical role in guiding future behavior, and in critically evaluating the judgments and decisions we have already made. We may, for instance, believe that our chance of survival in academia or in an entrepreneurial venture (Camerer & Lovallo, 1999) far exceeds the stultifying base rate information, leading us to (foolhardily?) pursue these paths.

If people were perfectly calibrated in confidence, the frequency of observed outcomes based on their predictions would mirror the confidence estimates with which they assessed such predictions. But such calibration is uncommon. Research has generally found people to be overconfident in their predictions. When answering general-knowledge questions, for instance, people's estimated frequencies of correct responses typically exceed the observed frequencies of correct responses (Fischhoff, Slovic, & Lichtenstein, 1977; Koriat, Lichtenstein, &

Fischhoff, 1980; Nickerson & Mcgoldrick, 1965). Overconfidence seems to be moderated in part by the difficulty of the task: as task difficulty increases, the tendency to exhibit overconfidence is exacerbated (Gigerenzer, Hoffrage, & Kleinbolting, 1991; Lichtenstein & Fischhoff, 1977; Soll, 1996). Incidentally, one noteworthy and perhaps surprising exception to the general finding of overconfidence is judgments by meteorologists, who are actually quite well calibrated in their expressions of uncertainty in their estimates of weather patterns (Lichtenstein, Fischhoff, & Phillips, 1982).

Overconfidence has been shown to extend into the realm of self and social prediction. In one study, college students made a number of social predictions, such as predicting a roommate's future behavior, and were asked to specify confidence intervals around those social predictions (Dunning, Griffin, Milojkovic, & Ross, 1990). The confidence associated with people's predictions of others' behavior vastly exceeded their objective accuracy, which was close to chance. People are similarly overconfident when predicting their own behavior, indicating that people are overconfident even when highly familiar with the prediction target (i.e., themselves). When college students were asked to make forecasts about certain events they may experience in the future, they again exhibited overconfidence (Dunning & Story, 1991).

Overconfidence is pervasive and does not appear to be moderated by expertise: expert judgment is susceptible to the same pattern of overconfidence as novice judgment. CIA analysts, for example, are overconfident in their predictions of future world events (Cambridge & Shreckengost, 1980), and clinical psychologists are overconfident in the accuracy of their diagnoses after reviewing a patient's case record (Oskamp, 1965).

The reasons underlying overconfidence are not fully understood. One explanation is that people conflate the confidence with which they can evaluate evidence and the confidence with which they can render an estimate. People can be highly confident in their evaluation that Tom W. resembles a computer scientist major more than an English major. But the confidence they have in evaluating the resemblance should not be translated into confidence predicting that Tom actually is a computer science major. Overconfidence can thus occur when people translate their evaluation of the evidence into confidence in the quality of their prediction (Kahneman & Tversky, 1979a). The prediction-by-translation tendency is endemic to heuristic judgment because heuristic evaluations are typically made with high confidence.

A second explanation starts with the observation that the study of confidence can be broken down into two distinct factors: the strength of the evidence at hand and the relative weight that should be apportioned to that evidence (Griffin & Tversky, 1992). For example, when deciding to accept or reject a candidate for graduate school based on a letter of recommendation, people focus on the strength of the letter (i.e., exactly how glowing or prosaic the recommendation seems to be) as well as the weight of the letter (i.e., how much the source of information is valued compared with other sources). People's confidence seems to be more closely linked to the strength of the information than to the weight of information because strength is typically more salient and intuitively appealing. Overconfidence in judgment thus occurs when strength is high and weight is low—which is often the case in real-world environments—and underconfidence in judgment occurs when strength is low and weight is high. This strength/weight framework successfully explains patterns of confidence across a range of experimental evidence on judgment under uncertainty, including evaluating statistical hypotheses (i.e., base rate neglect and insensitivity to sample size) and confidence in knowledge (i.e., effects of difficulty and illusions of validity).

Confirmation Bias

Another explanation of overconfidence is the related judgmental phenomenon of confirmation bias (Rottenstreich & Tversky, 1997; Tversky & Koehler, 1994). People tend to "test" hypotheses by seeking confirming rather than disconfirming information. Confirmatory information is usually easily found, so people see ample support for their estimates and inclinations. The tendency to evaluate hypotheses by confirming them also presents a substantial barrier to the discovery that an estimate is incorrect.

Early studies of confirmation bias originated with a simple logical reasoning task (Wason, 1960, 1968). Participants were asked to consider sets of three numbers. They were informed that there existed a rule by which three numbers could be strung together, and one such string that followed the rule was 2, 4, 6. Participants were then asked to generate their own string of numbers to see whether those numbers conformed to the rule. They could do this as many times as needed, until they believed they had discovered the rule. Results showed that people attempted to discover the rule by way of positive hypothesis testing strategies. For instance, believing that the rule involved successive even numbers, participants would test confirmatory combinations such as 8, 10, 12 and 20, 22, 24. Such a strategy is often inappropriate from a normative standpoint, and it is likely to lead people to believe in their hypothesized rule simply because they do not solicit evidence that may disconfirm it (but see Klayman & Ha, 1987). The rule in question can be more effectively tested by seeking disconfirming information, for example, testing a sequence such as 3, 2, 1.

Other evidence for the confirmation bias came from the "card selection task." In one version, participants are asked to consider four cards that have a letter on one side and a number on the other. Participants only see the side that is face up and are asked to confirm the rule, "if a card has a vowel on one side, then it has an even number on the other side." They are asked to do so by turning the fewest number of cards over. Suppose that participants see cards E, G, 4, and 7. What cards must they turn over to confirm the rule? The correct answer is E and 7. A failure to find an even number opposite of E would disconfirm the rule, as would the discovery of a vowel opposite of 7. (The opposite side of G could have either an odd or even number without disconfirming the rule, as could the presence of a vowel or consonant opposite of 4.) Only about 5% of people answer correctly (Wason, 1968). Most people correctly select E, but wrongly select 4, as they follow positive hypothesis testing strategies, and fail to see that 7 must be turned over to verify that there is not a vowel on its opposite side.

The confirmation bias is itself multiply determined. Underlying processes include: restriction of attention to favored hypotheses (Beyth-Marom & Fischhoff, 1983), preferential treatment of evidence supporting existing beliefs (Baron, 1991a, 1991b), overweighting positive confirmatory evidence (Fischhoff & Beyth-Marom, 1983), and seeing what one is looking for (Nickerson, 1998). The tendency to "test" hypotheses by seeking confirmatory information may also be based in representativeness, specifically the belief that samples should resemble populations and that instances should resemble their categories. Confirmatory information increases perceived resemblance between observed information and presumed reality.

Hindsight Bias

Hindsight bias is the tendency to view events in hindsight as more likely to have occurred than when viewed in foresight (Fischhoff & Beyth, 1975). In a demonstration of hindsight bias, participants were asked to estimate the probability that uncertain future events would occur, such as President Nixon's trips to Peking and Moscow. Some time later, participants were asked to recall their earlier predictions, now knowing whether the events had occurred. Participants consistently overestimated the probabilities they had assigned to the events that did occur, and they underestimated the probabilities they had assigned to events that did not occur. In a similar experiment, participants were asked to estimate what they believed to be the probabilities associated with various outcomes of a 19th-century military conflict between the British and Gurkhas. The outcomes were defined as British victory, Gurkha victory, stalemate with a peace settlement, or stalemate with no peace settlement. Participants were then given (false) outcome knowledge. One group was told that the British had, in fact, prevailed in the conflict, whereas another group was told that stalemate with no peace settlement ensued. Results showed that, across conditions, outcome knowledge caused people to rate the outcome to which they were assigned as having been more likely in hindsight. These findings reflected what the authors referred to as "creeping determinism," whereby people view events in hindsight as being more inevitable than when they were viewed in foresight.

As with other judgmental biases, there followed many replications and extensions of the hindsight bias (Blank, Musch, & Pohl, 2007). Hindsight has been shown to affect judgmental contexts, including medical diagnoses (Arkes, Saville, Wortmann, & Harkness, 1981; Detmer, Fryback, & Gassner, 1978), election results (Leary, 1982), sporting events (Leary, 1981), legal judgments (Kamin & Rachlinski, 1995; LaBine & LaBine, 1996), and labor disputes (Christensenszalanski & Willham, 1991; Hawkins & Hastie, 1990; Mark & Mellor, 1991).

Psychologists have made considerable efforts to understand conditions under which people could be debiased of the pervasive hindsight bias. For instance, one potent remedy is to force oneself to argue against the inevitability of the outcome in question and think about ways in which it might have turned out otherwise (Fischhoff & Macgregor, 1982). Experimental data suggest that such a method can attenuate the effects of hindsight bias but does not eliminate it (Koriat, Lichtenstein, & Fischhoff, 1980; Slovic & Fischhoff, 1977). The method can sometimes backfire, however, if the search for counterarguments is subjectively difficult (Sanna & Schwarz, 2003; Sanna, Schwarz, & Small, 2002).

Like other judgmental biases, hindsight bias has multiple causes. Early explanations focused largely on the role of memory distortion, both in terms of memory impairment and biased reconstruction of pre-outcome judgments, with various cognitive process models emerging to account for the bias (Blank & Nestler, 2007; Hertwig, Fanselow, & Hoffrage, 2003; Hoffrage, Hertwig, & Gigerenzer, 2000; Pohl, Eisenhauer, & Hardt, 2003). More recent evidence has emphasized the motivational and self-regulatory underpinnings of the hindsight bias. For example, focusing on the apparent ineluctability of certain negative outcomes (e.g., rejection from a selective postgraduate program) can help people cope with the disappointment associated with negative experiences (Sanna & Chang, 2003; Wann, Grieve, Waddill, & Martin, 2008).

Summary

Biases of confidence, confirmation, and hindsight imply that people may rarely notice or correct biased judgments. Because people tend to have unrealistically high confidence in their judgments, they may be reluctant to evaluate them critically. When people do "critically" evaluate their judgments, they may do so in a confirmatory manner, reaffirming their judgmental correctness. Finally, even when people make judgments about which reality might provide relevant feedback—such as a prediction about whether stocks will increase by a certain amount, or that a favored sports team will win the pennant—their recalled judgment in hindsight tends to be biased in the direction of actual events.

Emotional Judgments and Decisions

The early examination of judgment and decision making research was guided by two prominent null hypotheses: subjective expected utility (as a model for decision making) and normative statistical analyses (as a model for judgment under uncertainty). Given these null hypotheses and the scientific milieu of the "cognitive revolution," there was little exploration of emotional influences on judgment and choice. Many studies, in fact, purposefully sought purely cognitive explanations for emotional and motivational explanations of behavior (e.g., Brehmer, 1976; Einhorn & Hogarth, 1978; Ross, 1977).

Although research in the heuristics and biases tradition provided more realistic descriptions of human judgment decision making, the approach left individuals (and critics) cold. The sometimes overwhelming importance of emotion in shaping thoughts and behavior was largely neglected. The cognitive emphasis of judgment and decision making research was, in some ways, an astounding oversight. It is now clear that emotional influences are fundamental, often primary influences on judgment and decision making.

There is currently a flurry of research seeking to understand the role of emotion in judgment and decision making. The research tends to focus on one of three types of emotion. *Anticipated emotions* refer to people's predictions about the emotional consequences of decision outcomes. Anticipated emotions guide decisions as people choose options that maximize expectations of positive emotions and minimize expectations of negative emotions. Other emotions are experienced in the moment of rendering judgments or making decisions, rather than one's expectations about the emotional consequences of outcomes. Of these immediately experienced emotions, *integral emotions* refer to those that are experienced as a direct result of thinking about or interacting with a decision alternative, such as the dread that might result from thinking about a terrorist attack (Brehmer, 1976; Einhorn & Hogarth, 1978). *Incidental emotions* refer to emotional states that are present at the time of the decision but are caused by something other than the decision alternatives that are actually at hand, such as when being angry because of a tense work situation influences one's behavior toward family and pets at home (Lerner & Tiedens, 2006).

Anticipated Emotions

One way in which decision theorists have attempted to incorporate emotion into models of decision making has been to allow the value of an alternative (its utility) to depend on the expectation that it will lead to various counterfactual emotions, including regret, rejoicing, disappointment, elation, and surprise. Decision affect theory assumes that people can accurately predict how they will feel about the outcomes of decisions, and use those predictions to guide decisions (Bell, 1982; Gul, 1991; Loomes & Sugden, 1982; Mellers, Schwartz, Ho, & Ritov, 1997; Mellers, Schwartz, & Ritov, 1999). In one series of experiments, researchers measured the counterfactual emotions participants experienced after a series of gambles with real money. Participants were presented with a series of pairs of gambles and asked to choose which gamble they would play. These gambles involved various combinations of gains and losses of up to +$32 and –$32, respectively. After learning the outcome of each choice, participants indicated their emotional response toward the outcome. There were three primary findings. First, the same magnitude of gain was seen as more pleasurable when its probability was lower, and likewise the same magnitude of loss was seen as more painful when its probability was lower. This illustrates a surprise effect: emotional reactions to events are more intense when those events are more rare. Second, the same outcome was seen as more pleasurable or less painful if the alternative outcome was a lesser gain or greater loss, respectively. This disappointment/elation effect meant that small losses were often actually seen as slightly pleasurable if the alternative was an even greater loss. Third, the same outcome was seen as less pleasurable if the unchosen gamble happened to yield a larger gain or smaller loss, or was seen as more pleasurable if the unchosen gamble yielded a smaller gain or larger loss, demonstrating a regret/rejoicing effect.

Decision affect theory assumes that people correctly anticipate the emotional consequences of decision outcomes and make decisions accordingly. But people often mispredict the impact of emotionally arousing situations on their feelings, preferences, and behaviors (Loewenstein & Schkade, 1999; Wilson & Gilbert, 2003). In one study, Andrade and Van Boven (2010) found that people who chose a riskless outcome, avoiding a gamble, underestimated the intensity of their emotional reactions to the foregone outcome, underestimating their pleasure upon finding out that they would have lost the gamble and underestimating their displeasure upon finding out that they would have won (Andrade & Van Boven, 2010). This underestimation seemed partly attributable to the fact that by choosing not to gamble, people believed they were avoiding personal responsibility for the gamble's outcome, thereby avoiding the emotional intensity typically associated with personal responsibility.

Two general tendencies characterize the ways that people tend to mispredict their reactions to emotional situations. First, people tend to overestimate the intensity and duration of emotional reactions, such as when people overestimate how upset they would be if a favored sports team lost an important match (Wilson, Wheatley, Meyers, Gilbert, & Axsom, 2000). Second, people tend to underestimate the impact of emotional situations on their behavior, such as when people underestimate the lengths they would take to escape an embarrassing situation (Van Boven, Loewenstein, & Dunning, 2005; Van Boven, Loewenstein, Welch, & Dunning, 2010). Although these tendencies—overestimating the intensity and duration of emotion

and underestimating the behavioral lengths taken to address emotional drives—may seem contradictory, both reflect a tendency to underestimate one's coping response to emotional situations. People respond to emotional situations that they cannot avoid or that have already happened by neutralizing emotional reasons through rationalization and "normalization" (Wilson & Gilbert, 2003). People also enact behavioral opportunities to satisfy emotional drives, reducing an unpleasant emotion or enhancing pleasant emotions. Whether people overestimate emotional intensity or underestimate behavioral responses thus seems to hinge on whether people are provided behavioral opportunities to act to satisfy emotional drives or must reduce emotional drives by minimizing emotional intensity. In both cases, people underestimate reactions to emotional situations, with the direction of their reaction shaped by the behavioral or normalization opportunities available to them (Van Boven, et al., 2010).

Affect Heuristic

One reason that people have difficulty accurately anticipating their emotional reactions is that immediate, integral emotions exert substantial influence over judgments and decisions. A variety of judgments are influenced by people's feelings about the target of judgment, including risk perception (Slovic, Finucane, Peters, & MacGregor, 2004), assessments of punitive damages (Kahneman, Schkade, & Sunstein, 1998), and moral judgments (Rozin, Lowery, Imada, & Haidt, 1999). Emotion's pervasive and potent influence on judgment reflects a general affect heuristic, in which people's estimation of target attributes is influenced by the affect people experience about that attribute (Finucane, Alhakami, Slovic, & Johnson, 2000; Slovic, Finucane, Peters, & MacGregor, 2002).

Because affect is aroused by factors other than the objective scope of the target that people evaluate, the affect heuristic contributes to "scope neglect," the tendency to neglect information about the objective magnitude of the target. Risk perceptions are influenced by affect more than by likelihood, which contributes to people's overweighting of small but frightening probabilities such as those associated with terrorism or environmental threats (Slovic, 1987; Sunstein, 2002, 2004). Economic values of many kinds, in fact, tend to be insensitive to scope and highly sensitive to emotion. In one study, for example, respondents indicated that they would be willing to pay $80, $78, and $88 to save 2,000, 20,000, or 200,000 migrating birds from drowning in oil ponds, showing almost complete insensitivity to the objective scope of the outcome (Desvousges et al., 1993).

One way to model the effect of emotion on decision making is by modifying prospect theory's value function and probability weighting function to reflect different reactions to highly emotional versus less emotional outcomes. Considering the value function, people are relatively less sensitive to changes in the objective magnitude of outcomes that are relatively more emotional. In one study (Hsee & Rottenstreich, 2004), participants were asked how much they would be willing to donate to save panda bears. In a between-subjects design, the researchers crossed scope (1 vs. 4 pandas saved) with presentation (dots vs. cute pictures of pandas on a map). Consistent with the hypothesis that affect-rich decisions produce scope insensitivity, when pandas were displayed as cute pictures, participants' donation amounts did not differ significantly across scope. When pandas were displayed as dots, however, participants donated more money to save four pandas than one panda.

Considering the probability weighting function, when people make decisions about emotionally rich outcomes, they become relatively less sensitive to most changes in probability value and more sensitive to changes away from or toward certainty (0% and 100%). In one study demonstrating this effect, participants were asked to consider their willingness to pay for a 1% or 99% chance of winning a $500 coupon (Rottenstreich & Hsee, 2001). Participants were told that the coupon could either be used to pay for tuition (affect-poor condition) or toward a European vacation (affect-rich condition). At a 1% chance of winning, participants were willing to pay more money for the vacation coupon. At 99%, however, participants were willing to pay more money for the tuition coupon. These results provide evidence that people are more sensitive to changes in probabilities associated with outcomes when the decision is affect-poor instead of affect-rich.

Sometimes emotions are so intense and potent that they directly influence behavior in ways that are independent and even in opposition to people's intentional better interest (Bechara, Damasio, & Damasio, 2000; Bechara, Damasio, Damasio, & Anderson, 1994; Loewenstein, 1996). For example, an individual might succumb to a cigarette craving despite his best interests and intentions, and even with full awareness that smoking is not an action he planned or wanted or "decided," in the traditional meaning of that term. It may be, in fact, that acting on strong, overwhelming cravings and other bodily drives is better characterized as instinctual behavior rather than as a decision (Buck, 1999). In any event, emotional arousal clearly exerts potent influence on judgment and decision making in ways that can reflect radical change to utility, probability weighting, and behavior.

Incidental Emotions

We have thus far reviewed two relatively simple ways that emotion influences judgment and decision making, through its influence on expectations (anticipated emotion), value function, and weighting functions. But emotions can also indirectly influence judgment and decision making. This can happen three ways: through indirect informational influences, through broader patterns of appraisal, and through influences on processing depth.

EMOTION AS INFORMATION

Incidental emotions are those that are aroused and present while making a judgment or decision, but that are incidental to the judgment or decision at hand. This might happen, for example, when one makes judgments and decisions while in a happy or sad mood (Andrade & Cohen, 2007; Loewenstein & Lerner, 2003). The feelings-as-information hypothesis (Schwarz, 2002a) implies that people will rely on feelings when making judgments and decisions, as long as those feelings are perceived as being relevant to the judgment or decision at hand—and so long as people are unaware of the true incidental source of the feelings.

In one study, respondents to a telephone survey were contacted on either sunny days or rainy days and asked about their current mood level and their overall level of life satisfaction (Schwarz & Clore, 1983). Respondents not only indicated that they were in better moods on sunny days than on rainy days but also indicated an overall greater level of life satisfaction on sunny days than on rainy days, indicating that their transient, weather-induced mood influenced their assessment of overall life quality. However, in two crucial conditions in which respondents were reminded about the current weather before being asked about their life satisfaction—either by the interviewer casually asking the respondent what the whether was like, or by directly informing them that the survey was related to the effect of the current weather on mood—the effect of weather on life satisfaction judgment was significantly reduced. According to the feelings-as-information hypothesis, when not reminded about the about the weather, respondents tended to misattribute their current weather-induced mood to their life satisfaction, but when reminded about the weather, respondents were able to correctly recognize that their happy or sad mood was probably due to the weather and was therefore not relevant to the judgment about life satisfaction.

Because the feelings-as-information hypothesis characterizes incidental emotion as influencing judgment according to the emotion's perceived informational value, it makes several interesting predictions beyond those simply concerning positive and negative moods. Under some circumstances, for example, a positive mood could lead to a more negative judgment, or vice versa. In one experiment, participants were asked to read and evaluate a story that was either intended to be happy or intended to be sad, and they did so while in either a happy mood or sad mood (Martin, Ward, Achee, & Wyer, 1993). Participants' evaluations of the stories were highest when their moods matched the moods that the stories were intended to convey, and lowest in both mismatched cases, when sad participants evaluated a happy story or when happy participants evaluated a sad story. Being in a happy mood does not always raise evaluative judgments, but instead affects judgments according to its informational value. Participants seem to be reasoning that if the story intended to make them feel sad, but they felt themselves in a happy mood, then it must not be a very good story at all.

APPRAISAL TENDENCY

Beyond their effect on feelings, emotions can also influence judgment and decision making through associated cognitive appraisals that can shape information processing (Lerner & Keltner, 2000, 2001; Lerner & Tetlock, 1999). Appraisal tendency theory suggests that the arousal of incidental emotions influences processing, specifically by arousing appraisals of confidence or uncertainty, which can moderate people's risk perception and extensiveness of information processing. These effects of confidence are independent of valence.

In one set of studies, participants were induced to feel angry or fearful—both negative emotions, but with anger more closely associated with certainty—by describing autobiographical events that aroused the target emotion (Lerner & Keltner, 2000, 2001). Although fear and anger are both characterized by negativity, fear is associated with appraisals of situational control and low certainty, whereas anger is associated with appraisals of personal control and

high certainty. Anger should therefore reduce risk judgments and risk aversion. Consistent with this analysis, angry participants judged that they would be less likely to experience negative events such as embarrassing themselves during a job interview or getting lost at night, and more likely to experience positive events such as getting a good postgraduation job or having good health at 60 years of age. The senses of uncertainty and lack of personal control arising from the incidental fearful mood led people to perceive the world around them as relatively unpredictable and uncontrollable, whereas the certainty and sense of control imparted by the anger manipulation led people to give more optimistic judgments about their susceptibility to risk.

More generally, feelings associated with a sense of certainty (such as contentment or anger) should lead to a greater reliance on heuristic cues in response persuasion attempts, whereas feelings associated with a sense of uncertainty (such as worry or surprise) should lead to more careful, systematic processing in response to persuasion attempts (Tiedens & Linton, 2001). Thus, emotions such as anger that arouse feelings of certainty seem to reduce risk perception, reduce risk aversion, and increase heuristic judgment.

VALENCE AND PROCESSING DEPTH

Feelings-as-information hypothesis and appraisal tendency both describe how the content of specific emotions can influence the content of judgment. Emotions can also influence judgment and decision making by influencing the extent or depth of information processing. Judgments and decisions that are rendered after relatively shallow processing tend to rely more on mental shortcuts such as heuristics and stereotypes compared with judgments and decisions that are rendered after relatively deeper processing. Because positive moods tend to signal that "all is well," they tend to promote less effortful, more theory-driven processing, whereas negative moods, by signaling to the decision maker that "something is amiss," tend to promote a more careful, effortful, and data-driven style of processing (Lerner & Keltner, 2001).

There is a wide variety of evidence in support of the claim that positive emotion promotes relatively heuristic judgment and decision making. For example, participants in positive moods performed worse on difficult deductive reasoning problems (Oaksford, Morris, Grainger, & Williams, 1996) and were more likely than participants in negative moods to commit the fundamental attribution error

(Forgas, 1998). Participants in negative moods, conversely, were less persuaded by weak arguments, whereas happy participants tended to be persuaded by both weak and strong arguments (Bless, Bohner, Schwarz, & Strack, 1990). And sad participants were less likely to exhibit halo effects than were happy participants (Sinclair, 1988).

This pattern of results does not imply, however, that positive emotion generally promotes careless judgment. Positive emotion is also associated with more creative, broader thinking. People in positive moods, compared with those in negative moods, perform better on problem-solving tasks that require creative thinking (Bless et al., 1996; Hirt, Melton, McDonald, & Harackiewicz, 1996; Isen, Daubman, & Nowicki, 1987; Schwarz, 2002b).

Summary

Early approaches to understanding the role of emotion in judgment and decision making yielded relatively simple, valence-based predictions such that positive moods tended to yield more positive judgments than negative moods, which tended to yield more pessimistic judgments (Johnson & Tversky, 1983). Such models were enmeshed in cognitive psychology's "mood congruency" models of the 1970s and 1980s (Bower, 1981). But modern models of emotion recognize the complexity and subtlety of emotional drives, interpretation, and appraisals. Emotion seems to shape judgment and decision making through anticipation, an affect heuristic, and indirectly through information, appraisal, and processing. We suspect that the natural evolution of studies will begin conceptual consolidation in the coming decades as researchers strive toward simpler, more theoretically powerful means of understanding the effects of emotion on judgment and decision making.

Dual Systems of Judgment and Decision Making

Among the more challenging questions for judgment and decision making research is to understand when people make biased judgments and decisions and when they make rational, optimal judgments and decisions. One candidate explanation, that some people are simply smarter than others, does not appear to explain a large fraction of the variance in judgment and decision making. People who are perfectly capable of rational analysis sometimes are perfectly biased at other times (Thaler & Sunstein, 2008). What accounts for these differences?

An approach that has gained prominence and explanatory power in judgment and decision making, in social cognition and beyond, suggests that people's thoughts and behaviors are guided by two systems of reasoning. These dual process frameworks are widespread. Research on causal attribution implies that people initially and automatically draw dispositional influences about others through a reflexive system of reasoning, before more subsequently correcting those inferences though a reflective system of reasoning (Lieberman, Gaunt, Gilbert, & Trope, 2002). Research on persuasion implies two separate routes to attitude change: one that is responsive to peripheral, heuristic cues and one that is responsive to central, substantive cues (Petty & Cacioppo, 1986a, 1986b). Elsewhere, social cognition researchers have proposed dual process frameworks to account for person perception (Brewer, 1988; Fiske & Neuberg, 1990) and stereotyping processes (Devine, 1989).

Ideas about dual systems of reasoning have made substantial explanatory progress in judgment and decision making by explaining and predicting the conditions in which people adjust, or correct, their heuristic judgments and inconsistent decisions. Dual systems explanations typically distinguish between System 1 and System 2 (Stanovich & West, 2000). System 1, so called because it is considered primary in temporal order and in prominence (and not because the label is particularly informative), is characterized by an effortless, associational, and intuitive mode of processing. System 2, so called because it is considered secondary in temporal precedence and in prominence over everyday reasoning (and, again, not because the label is particularly informative), is characterized by rational, controlled, and rule-based processing.

In this model, judgments and decisions begin with System 1, which operates in the background of psychological awareness, typically producing (sufficiently) accurate intuitive judgment and (satisfactory) decisions (Kahneman, 2003). The prevalence and characteristics of System 1 are very similar to those of perceptual processes. Just as people are seldom cognizant and directive of their perceptual processes, they are seldom cognizant and directive of their System 1 processes. But just as people sometimes note that perceptions are biased and intervene, psychologically, to arrive at a correct belief about the world, such as when witnessing an optical illusion and entertaining the belief that the illusion conveys a fiction, people sometimes note, by means of System 2, that System 1 has produced a biased or erroneous thought, impression, or behavior. In this sense, System 2 monitors System 1, intervening when the output has gone awry.

One important prediction implied by the dual systems model is that people can hold simultaneous, inconsistent beliefs—just as people exposed to an optical illusion can "see" a reality that they know is false. In reasoning tasks, people's dual systems can lead them to sense that two different conclusions are simultaneously compelling (Sloman, 1996). In these cases, people can know the correct solution (System 2), even though it doesn't "feel right" (System 1).

The conjunction fallacy, illustrated earlier by the Linda problem, illustrates these conflicting systems. In such conjunction problems, people realize and can articulate, often after the fact, that a conjunction (a woman being a bank teller and a feminist) cannot be more likely than either of its constituent elements (being a bank teller). But the fact that the conjunctive event resembles the description more strongly than the disjunctive event can lead people to answer in a way that they recognize is logically incorrect (Tversky & Kahneman, 1983).

The dual systems view also explains why people may offer incorrect responses to simple questions that most people can correctly answer with simple reflection. Consider the following puzzle: "A bat and ball cost $1.10 in total. The bat costs exactly $1 more than the ball. How much does the ball cost?" (Kahneman & Frederick, 2002). Although the intuitive response is that the ball costs $0.10, a moment's reflection reveals that answer is incorrect (because $0.10 plus $1.10 is $1.20), and that the correct answer is $0.05 (because $0.05 plus $1.05 is $1.10). In this case, the puzzle is worded such that the response "$0.10" comes to mind easily and naturally (System 1), and there is no clear signal to correct that initial response (System 2). The incorrect responses arise because of the inaction of System 2 to correct the output of System 1.

The inaction of System 2 is not an issue of intelligence. A survey of students at various schools indicated that a large fraction of students at highly selective institutions (such as Harvard and Princeton, but except for highly reflective MIT students) and at less selective institutions (such as the University of Toledo) provide incorrect but intuitive responses to such puzzles. Rather, it seems that System 1 hums along, rendering intuitive responses to problems encountered in everyday life, with System 2 only sometimes noticing and adjusting incorrect responses.

This analysis obviously raises the question of what triggers System 2 to correct System 1. One tentative, emerging answer is that System 2 carefully monitors and adjusts the output of System 1 in situations in which contextual or psychological cues signal that a judgment or decision is unusually important (such as when the financial or emotional stakes are high) or in which System 1 is unlikely to produce an accurate response (such as when the pull of self-interest may be unusually strong and unwanted; Wilson & Brekke, 1994). In support of this analysis, when the metacognitive experience associated with a decision is made difficult, people are more likely to engage in System 2 processing (Alter, Oppenheimer, Epley, & Eyre, 2007). In one experiment, researchers had participants consider the case of Tom W. (Tversky & Kahneman, 1983) while either furrowing their brow (a posture that is associated with the exertion of cognitive effort) or puffing their cheeks (a control expression). Participants were more likely to rely on System 1 representativeness operation when puffing their cheeks and were more likely to engage in System 2 correction when furrowing their brow, which signaled metacognitive difficulty.

Detrimental Deliberation

Although it has been proposed that System 2 monitors the output of System 1, this does not imply that System 2 processing is qualitatively superior to System 1 processing. System 2 may sometimes produce inferior judgments and decisions than System 1. Research on gist knowledge and complex decision making has shown that intuitive, associational processing can, in certain decision-making settings, outperform explicit rule-based processing (Reyna, 2004). For example, in naturalistic studies of on-the-job decision making by firefighters and paramedics, these experts often rely on the automatic recognition of a situation when formulating their decisions on how best to proceed (Klein, 1999). And in popular discourse, there is intuitive resonance that people's intuitive, rapid, automatic assessments are of relatively high quality (Gladwell, 2005).

Some research suggests, moreover, that conscious deliberation during complex decision making can actually be harmful, that complex decisions are sometimes best left to nonconscious processing (Dijksterhuis, Bos, Nordgren, & van Baaren, 2006; Wilson et al., 1993). In one experiment, participants were asked to compare four cars on a number of different attributes and select their favorite car (Dijksterhuis, et al., 2006). Experimenters engineered a situation in which one car was, in fact, superior to the others and manipulated participants' processing style (conscious vs. unconscious) and number of attributes corresponding to each of the cars (few vs. many). In support of the benefits of a deliberation-without-attention processing style in complex decisions, results showed that unconscious thinkers were more likely to choose the best car when the number of attributes was high than were the conscious thinkers.

Our view is that the conclusions based on these studies implying that deliberation can be detrimental are highly tentative. It is not yet clear what boundaries there are to the benefits of non-conscious processing, or to the detriments of conscious deliberation. There is obviously some important aspect involving the development of expertise. Until these issues are more fully understood, we would avoid major policy decisions (personal or political), medical decisions, or financial decisions based solely on non-conscious processing.

Summary

In light of the growing influence of dual systems models on psychological theory, it is worth reflecting on their theoretical purpose and empirical value. As some scholars wryly point out, dual process explanations are useful because they involve the least complicated method of complication—namely, extending single process models of psychological functioning to dual process models. Harsher critics of the dual processes perspective argue that such interpretations create and reify false or misleading psychological distinctions (Keren & Schul, 2009). In the case of dual process theories, however, it is difficult to ignore the gains made from interpreting psychological phenomena as broadly deriving from two sets of distinct processes. Moreover, the striking commonalities that underlie conceptualizations of dual processes across dissimilar psychological research domains strongly suggest that there is an important distinction to be made between the different modes of processing.

Conclusion

Sometimes it can be informative and clarifying to tell others about one's research interests. In such conversations, one of us recently noticed a curious discrepancy. Following queries about his area of research, the response, "I study how people make judgments and decisions" elicited somewhat different reactions by fellow psychological scientists than by laypeople. The psychologists seemed to infer that "judgment and decision making" described a relatively narrow range of psychology involving studies of gambles, naïve probability estimates, and the setting of confidence intervals. The laypeople (e.g., fellow parents at soccer games and friends on bicycle rides), in contrast, see "judgment and decision making" as describing a broad range of behavior, everything from choosing menu items at a restaurant, to guessing what someone is "really like," to deciding whom to vote for, to deciding whether to pay for an expensive procedure for one's elderly pet.

We think in this case that the layperson's impression is a more accurate description of what the study of judgment and decision making could be, and should be. A great deal of what people are interested in and concerned about in their daily life pertains to the judgments they make about themselves and the social world, about understanding and improving their own decisions, and about understanding the role of emotion in these processes. The study of judgment and decision making is thus the study of everyday thinking and behavior. That the field of judgment and decision making is sometimes narrowly construed by psychologists reflects more the historical baggage of the field's origins than its proper place in the realm of psychological science.

Author Note

NSF Grants 0552120 and 1049125 supported the writing of this chapter. Correspondence should be addressed to Leaf Van Boven, UCB 345, Department of Psychology and Neuroscience, University of Colorado Boulder, CO, 80309–0345; e-mail: vanboven@colorado.edu.

References

Ajzen, I. (1977). Intuitive theories of events and the effects of base rate information on prediction. *Journal of Personality and Social Psychology, 35*, 303–314.

Allais, M. (1953). Le comportement de l'homme rationnel devant le risque: Critique des postulats et axiomes de l'école Américaine. *Econometrica, 21*, 503–546.

Alter, A. L., Oppenheimer, D. M., Epley, N., & Eyre, R. (2007). Overcoming intuition: Metacognitive difficulty activates analytic reasoning. *Journal of Experimental Psychology: General, 136*(4), 569–576.

Andrade, E., & Cohen, J. B. (2007). Affect-based evaluation and regulation as mediators of behavior: The role of affect in risk taking, helping and eating patterns. In K. Vohs, R. F. Baumeister, & G. Loewenstein (Eds.), *Do emotions help or hurt section making?* New York: Russell Sage Foundation Press.

Andrade, E., & Van Boven, L. (2010). Feelings not forgone: underestimating affective reactions to what does not happen. *Psychological Science, 21*, 706–711.

Arkes, H. R., Saville, P. D., Wortmann, R. L., & Harkness, A. R. (1981). Hindsight bias among physicians weighing the likelihood of diagnoses. *Journal of Applied Psychology, 66*(2), 252–254.

Aronson, E., Wilson, T. D., & Akert, R. M. (2010). *Social psychology* (7th ed.). Upper Saddle River, NJ: Prentice Hall.

Baron, J. (1991a). Beliefs about thinking. In J. F. Voss, D. N. Perkins & J. W. Segal (Eds.), *Informal reasoning and education*. Hillsdale, NJ: Erlbaum.

Baron, J. (1991b). Myside bias in thinking about abortion. *Thinking and Reasoning, 1*, 221–235.

Bastardi, A., & Shafir, E. (1998). On the pursuit and misuse of useless information. *Journal of Personality and Social Psychology, 75*, 19–32.

Bechara, A., Damasio, H., & Damasio, A. R. (2000). Emotion, decision making, and the orbitofrontal cortex. *Cerebral Cortex, 10*, 295–307.

Bechara, A., Damasio, H., Damasio, A. R., & Anderson, S. W. (1994). Insensitivity to future consequences following damage to human prefrontal cortex. *Cognition, 50*, 7–15.

Beggan, J. K. (1992). On the social nature of nonsocial perception: The mere ownership effect. *Journal of Personality and Social Psychology, 62*(2), 229–237.

Bell, D. (1982). Regret in decision making under uncertatinty. *Operations Research, 30*, 961–981.

Bem, D. (1972). Self-perception theory. In L. Berkowitz (Ed.), *Advances in experimental social psychology* (Vol. 6, pp. 1–62). New York: Academic Press.

Berejikian, J. D. (2002). A cognitive theory of deterrence. *Journal of Peace Research, 39*, 165–183.

Bernoulli, D. (1738/1954). Exposition of a new theory on the measurement of risk, *Econometrica, 22*(1), 23–36.

Beyth-Marom, R., & Fischhoff, B. (1983). Diagnosticity and pseudo-diagnosticity. *Journal of Personality and Social Psychology, 45*, 1185–1195.

Birnbaum, M. H., & Stegner, S. E. (1979). Source credibility in social judgment: Bias, expertise, and the judge's point of view. *Journal of Personality and Social Psychology, 37*, 48–74.

Blank, H., Musch, J., & Pohl, R. F. (2007). Hindsight bias: On being wise after the event. *Social Cognition, 25*(1), 1–9.

Blank, H., & Nestler, S. (2007). Cognitive process models of hindsight bias. *Social Cognition, 25*(1), 132–146.

Bless, H., Bohner, G., Schwarz, N., & Strack, F. (1990). Mood and persuasion: A cognitive response analysis. *Personality and Social Psychology Bulletin, 16*, 331–345.

Bless, H., Clore, G. L., Schwarz, N., Golisano, V., Rabe, C., & Wolk, M. (1996). Mood and the use of scripts: Does a happy mood really lead to mindlessness? *Journal of Personality and Social Psychology, 71*, 665–679.

Bower, G. H. (1981). Mood and memory. *American Psychologist, 36*, 129–148.

Brehmer, B. (1976). Social judgment theory and the analysis of interpersonal conflict. *Psychological Bulletin, 83*, 985–1003.

Brewer, M. B. (1988). A dual process model of impression formation. In R. S. Wyer (Ed.), *Advances in social cognition* (Vol. 1). Hillsdale, NJ: Erlbaum.

Buck, R. (1999). The biological affects: A typology. *Psychological Review, 106*, 301–336.

Buehler, R., Griffin, D., & Ross, M. (1994). Exploring the "planning fallacy": Why people underestimate their task completion times. *Journal of Personality and Social Psychology, 67*, 366–381.

Cambridge, R. M., & Shreckengost, R. C. (1980). *Are you sure? The subjective probability assessment test*. Langley, VA: Office of Training, Central Intelligence Agency.

Camerer, C., & Lovallo, D. (1999). Overconfidence and excess entry: An experimental approach. *American Economic Review, 89*(1), 306–318.

Carmon, Z., & Ariely, D. (2000). Focusing on the forgone: How value can appear so different to buyers and sellers. *Journal of Consumer Research, 27*(December), 360–370.

Christensenszalanski, J. J. J., & Willham, C. F. (1991). The hindsight bias: A metaanalysis. *Organizational Behavior and Human Decision Processes, 48*(1), 147–168.

Coombs, C. H., & Komorita, S. S. (1958). Measuring utility of money through decisions. *The American Journal of Psychology, 71*(2), 383–389.

Critcher, C. R., & Gilovich, T. (2008). Incidental environmental anchors. *Journal of Behavioral Decision Making, 21*(3), 241–251.

Crocker, J. (1982). Biased questions in judgment of covariation studies. *Personality and Social Psychology Bulletin, 8*, 214–220.

Desvousges, W. H., Johnson, F., Dunford, R., Hudson, S., Wilson, K., & Boyle, K. (1993). Measuring resource damages with contingent valuation: Tests of validity and reliability. In J. Hausman (Ed.), *Contingent valuation: A critical assessment* (pp. 91–164). Amsterdam: North-Holland.

Detmer, D. E., Fryback, D. G., & Gassner, K. (1978). Heuristics and biases in medical decision-making. *Journal of Medical Education, 53*(8), 682–683.

Deutsch, M., Coleman, P. T., & Marcus, E. C. (2006). *The handbook of conflict resolution: Theory and practice*. San Francisco: John Wiley & Sons.

Devine, P. G. (1989). Stereotypes and prejudice: Their automatic and controlled components. *Journal of Personality and Social Psychology, 56*(1), 5–18.

Dijksterhuis, A., Bos, M. W., Nordgren, L. F., & van Baaren, R. B. (2006). Complex choices better made unconsciously? *Science, 313*, 760–761.

Downing, C. J., Sternberg, R. J., & Ross, B. H. (1985). Multicausal inference: Evaluation of evidence in causally complex situations. *Journal of Experimental Psychology: General, 114*, 239–263.

Dunning, D., Griffin, D. W., Milojkovic, J. D., & Ross, L. (1990). The overconfidence effect in social prediction. *Journal of Personality and Social Psychology, 58*, 568–581.

Dunning, D., & Story, A. L. (1991). Depression, realism, and the overconfidence effect: Are the sadder wiser when predicting future actions and events? *Journal of Personality and Social Psychology, 61*, 521–532.

Edwards, W. (1953). Probability-preferences in gambling. *The American Journal of Psychology*, 349–364.

Edwards, W. (1954). The theory of decision making. *Psychological Bulletin, 51*(4), 380.

Edwards, W. (1961). Behavioral decision theory. *Annual Review of Psychology, 12*(1), 473–498.

Eibach, R. P., & Keegan, T. (2006). Free at last? Social dominance, loss aversion, and white and black Americans' differing assessments of racial progress. *Journal of Personality and Social Psychology, 90*, 453–467.

Einhorn, H. J., & Hogarth, R. M. (1978). Confidence in judgment: Persistence of the illusion of validity. *Psychological Review, 85*, 395–416.

Ellsberg, D. (1961). Risk, ambiguity, and the Savage axioms. *Quarterly Journal of Economics, 75*, 643–669.

Epley, N., & Gilovich, T. (2001). Putting adjustment back in the anchoring and adjustment heuristic: Differential processing of self-generated and experimenter-provided anchors. *Psychological Science, 12,* 391–396.

Epley, N., & Gilovich, T. (2004). Are adjustments insufficient? *Personality and Social Psychology Bulletin, 30,* 447–460.

Festinger, L. (1957). *A theory of cognitive dissonance.* Stanford, CA: Stanford University Press.

Finucane, M. L., Alhakami, A., Slovic, P., & Johnson, S. M. (2000). The affect heuristic in judgments of risks and benefits. *Journal of Behavioral Decision Making, 13,* 1–17.

Fischhoff, B., & Beyth, R. (1975). "I knew it would happen": Remembered probabilities of once-future things. *Organizational Behavior and Human Performance, 13,* 1–16.

Fischhoff, B., & Beyth-Marom, R. (1983). Hypothesis evaluation from a Bayesian perspective. *Psychological Review, 90,* 239–260.

Fischhoff, B., & Macgregor, D. (1982). Subjective confidence in forecasts. *Journal of Forecasting, 1*(2), 155–172.

Fischhoff, B., Slovic, P., & Lichtenstein, S. (1977). Knowing with certainty: Appropriateness of extreme confidence. *Journal of Experimental Psychology-Human Perception and Performance, 3*(4), 552–564.

Fishburn, P. C., & Kochenberger, G. A. (1979). Two-piece von Neumann-Morgenstern utility functions. *Decision Sciences, 10,* 503–518.

Fiske, S. T., & Neuberg, S. L. (1990). A continuum model of impression formation from category-based to individuating processes: Influences of information and motivation on attention and interpretation. In M. P. Zanna (Ed.), *Advances in experimental social psychology* (Vol. 3, pp. 1–74). New York: Academic Press.

Fiske, S. T., & Taylor, S. E. (1984). *Social cognition.* Reading, MA: Addison-Wesley.

Forgas, J. P. (1998). On being happy and mistaken: Mood effects on the fundamental attribution error. *Journal of Personality and Social Psychology, 75,* 318–331.

Fox, C. R. (2006). The availability heuristic in the classroom: How soliciting more criticism can boost your course ratings. *Judgment and Decision Making Journal, 1*(1), 86–90.

Gigerenzer, G., Hoffrage, U., & Kleinbolting, H. (1991). Probabilistic mental models: A Brunswikian theory of confidence. *Psychological Review, 98*(4), 506–528.

Gilbert, D. T. (2002). Inferential correction. In T. Gilovich, D. Griffin, & D. Kahneman (Eds.), *Heuristics and biases: The psychology of intuitive judgment* (pp. 167–184). Cambridge, UK: Cambridge University Press.

Gilovich, T., Keltner, D., & Nisbett, R. (2010). *Social psychology* (2nd ed.). Boston: W. W. Norton.

Ginosar, Z., & Trope, Y. (1980). The effects of base rates and individuating information on judgments about another person. *Journal of Experimental Social Psychology, 16,* 228–242.

Gladwell, M. (2005). *Blink: The power of thinking without thinking.* New York: Back Bay Books.

Griffin, D., & Tversky, A. (1992). The weighing of evidence and the determinants of confidence. *Cognitive Psychology, 24,* 411–435.

Gul, F. (1991). A theory of disappointment aversion. *Econometrica, 59,* 667–686.

Hamilton, D. L., & Gifford, R. K. (1976). Illusory correlation in interpersonal perception: Cognitive basis of stereotypical judgments. *Journal of Experimental Social Psychology, 12,* 392–407.

Hawkins, S. A., & Hastie, R. (1990). Hindsight: Biased judgments of past events after the outcomes are known. *Psychological Bulletin, 107*(3), 311–327.

Heath, C., Larrick, R. P., & Wu, G. (1999). Goals and reference points. *Cognitive Psychology, 38,* 79–109.

Hertwig, R., Fanselow, C., & Hoffrage, U. (2003). Hindsight bias: How knowledge and heuristics affect our reconstruction of the past. *Memory, 11*(4–5), 357–377.

Higgins, E. T. (1997). Beyond pleasure and pain. *American Psychologist, 52,* 1280–1300.

Hirt, E. R., Melton, R. J., McDonald, H. E., & Harackiewicz, J. M. (1996). Processing goals, task interest, and the mood-performance relationship: A mediational analysis. *Journal of Personality and Social Psychology, 71,* 245–261.

Hoffrage, U., Hertwig, R., & Gigerenzer, G. (2000). Hindsight bias: A by-product of knowledge updating? *Journal of Experimental Psychology: Learning Memory and Cognition, 26*(3), 566–581.

Hsee, C. K., & Rottenstreich, Y. (2004). Music, pandas, and muggers: On the affective psychology of value. *Journal of Experimental Psychology: General, 133,* 23–30.

Isen, A. M., Daubman, K. A., & Nowicki, G. P. (1987). Positive affect facilitates creative problem solving. *Journal of Personality and Social Psychology, 52*(6), 1122–1131.

Jacoby, L. L., & Dallas, M. (1981). On the relationship between autobiographical memory and perceptual learning. *Journal of Experimental Psychology: General, 3,* 306–340.

Johnson, E. J., & Tversky, A. (1983). Affect, generalization, and the perception of risk. *Journal of Personality and Social Psychology, 45,* 20–31.

Johnston, W. A., Dark, V. J., & Jacoby, L. L. (1985). Perceptual fluency and recognition judgments. *Journal of Experimental Psychology: Learning, Memory, and Cognition, 11,* 3–11.

Jones, E. E., & Davis, K. E. (1965). From acts to dispositions: The attribution process in personal perception. In L. Berkowitz (Ed.), *Advances in experimental social psychology* (Vol. 2, pp. 219–266). New York: Academic Press.

Kahneman, D. (2003). A perspective on judgment and choice: Mapping bounded rationality. *American Psychologist, 58,* 697–720.

Kahneman, D., & Frederick, S. (2002). Representativeness revisited: Attribute substitution in intuitive judgment. In T. Gilovich, D. Griffin, & D. Kahneman (Eds.), *Heuristics and biases: The psychology of intuitive judgment.* (pp. 49–81). New York: Cambridge University Press.

Kahneman, D., Knetsch, J., & Thaler, R. (1991). The endowment effect, loss aversion, and status quo bias. *Journal of Economic Perspectives, 5,* 193–206.

Kahneman, D., Schkade, D. A., & Sunstein, C. R. (1998). Shared outrage and erratic awards: The psychology of punitive damages. *Journal of Risk and Uncertainty, 16,* 49–86.

Kahneman, D., & Tversky, A. (1973). On the psychology of prediction. *Psychological Review, 80,* 313–327.

Kahneman, D., & Tversky, A. (1979a). Intuitive prediction: Biases and corrective procedures. *TIMS Studies in Management Science, 12,* 313–327.

Kahneman, D., & Tversky, A. (1979b). Prospect theory: An analysis of decision under risk. *Econometrica, 47,* 263–291.

Kahneman, D., & Tversky, A. (1984). Choices, values and frames. *American Psychologist, 39,* 341–350.

Kahneman, D., & Tversky, A. (Eds.). (2000). *Choices, values, and frames.* New York: Cambridge University Press.

Kamin, K. A., & Rachlinski, J. J. (1995). Ex post-not-equal-ex ante: Determining liability in hindsight. *Law and Human Behavior, 19*(1), 89–104.

Kelley, C. M., & Lindsay, L. D. (1993). Remembering mistaken for knowing: Ease of retrieval as a basis for confidence in answers to general knowledge questions. *Journal of Memory and Language, 32*, 1–24.

Keren, G., & Schul, Y. (2009). Two is not always better than one: A critical evaluation of two-system theories. *Perspectives on Psychological Science, 4*, 533–550.

Klayman, J., & Ha, Y. W. (1987). Confirmation, disconfirmation, and information in hypotheses testing. *Psychological Review, 94*, 211–228.

Klein, G. (1999). *Sources of power: How people make decisions.* Cambridge, MA: MIT Press.

Knetsch, J. L., & Sinden, J. A. (1984). Willingness to pay and compensation demanded: Experimental evidence of an unexpected disparity in measures of value. *The Quarterly Journal of Economics, 99*, 507–521.

Koriat, A., Lichtenstein, S., & Fischhoff, B. (1980). Reasons for confidence. *Journal of Experimental Psychology: Human Learning and Memory, 6*, 107–118.

LaBine, S. J., & LaBine, G. (1996). Determinations of negligence and the hindsight bias. *Law and Human Behavior, 20*(5), 501–516.

Leary, M. R. (1981). The Distorted Nature of Hindsight. *Journal of Social Psychology, 115*(1), 25–29.

Leary, M. R. (1982). Hindsight Distortion and the 1980 Presidential-Election. *Personality and Social Psychology Bulletin, 8*(2), 257–263.

Lerner, J., & Keltner, D. (2000). Beyond valence: Toward a model of emotion-specific influences on judgment and choice. *Cognition and Emotion, 14*, 473–493.

Lerner, J., & Keltner, D. (2001). Fear, anger, and risk. *Journal of Personality and Social Psychology, 81*, 146–159.

Lerner, J., & Tetlock, P. E. (1999). Accounting for the effects of accountability. *Psychological Bulletin, 125*, 255–275.

Lerner, J. S., & Tiedens, L. Z. (2006). Portrait of The Angry Decision Maker: How Appraisal Tendencies Shape Anger's Influence on Cognition. *Journal of Behavioral Decision Making, 19*, 115–137.

Lichtenstein, S., & Fischhoff, B. (1977). Do Those Who Know More Also Know More About How Much They Know. *Organizational Behavior and Human Performance, 20*(2), 159–183.

Lichtenstein, S., Fischhoff, B., & Phillips, L. D. (1982). Calibration of probabilities: The state of the art to 1980. In D. Kahneman, P. Slovic & A. Tversky (Eds.), *Judgment under uncertainty: Heuristics and biases* (pp. 306–334). Cambridge, UK: Cambridge University Press.

Lichtenstein, S., Slovic, P., Fischhoff, B., Layman, M., & Combs, B. (1978). Judged frequency of lethal events. *Journal of Experimental Psychology: Human Learning and Memory, 4*(6), 551–578.

Lieberman, M. D., Gaunt, R., Gilbert, D. T., & Trope, Y. (2002). Reflexion and reflection: A social cognitive neuroscience approach to attributional inference. In M. Zanna (Ed.), *Advances in experimental social psychology* (Vol. 34, pp. 199–249). San Diego: Academic Press.

Linville, P., & Fischer, G. W. (1991). Preferences for separating or combining events. *Journal of Personality and Social Psychology, 60*, 5–23.

Loewenstein, G. (1996). Out of control: Visceral influences on behavior. *Organizational Behavior and Human Decision Processes, 65*, 272–292.

Loewenstein, G., & Lerner, J. (2003). The role of emotion in decision making. In R. J. Davidson, H. H. Goldsmith, & K. R. Scherer (Eds.), *Handbook of affective science.* Oxford, UK: Oxford University Press.

Loewenstein, G., & Schkade, D. (1999). Wouldn't it be nice? Predicting future feelings. In D. Kahneman, E. Diener, & N. Schwarz (Eds.), *Well being: The foundation of hedonic psychology* (pp. 85–108). New York: Russell Sage.

Loomes, G., & Sugden, R. (1982). Regret theory: An alternative theory of rational choice under uncertainty. *Economic Journal, 92*, 805–824.

Mark, M. M., & Mellor, S. (1991). Effect of self-relevance of an event on hindsight bias—The foreseeability of a layoff. *Journal of Applied Psychology, 76*(4), 569–577.

Martin, L. L., Ward, D. W., Achee, J. W., & Wyer, R. S. (1993). Mood as input: People have to interpret the motivational implications of their moods. *Journal of Personality and Social Psychology, 64*, 317–326.

McDermott, R. (2004). Prospect theory in political science: Gains and losses from the first decade. *Political Psychology, 25*, 289–312.

McGlone, M. S., & Tofighbakhsh, J. (2000). Birds of a feather flock conjointly (?): Rhyme as reason in aphorisms. *Psychological Science, 11*(5), 424–428.

Mellers, B., Schwartz, A., Ho, K., & Ritov, I. (1997). Decision affect theory: Emotional reactions to the outcomes of risky options. *Psychological Science, 8*(6), 423–429.

Mellers, B., Schwartz, A., & Ritov, I. (1999). Emotion-based choice. *Journal of Experimental Psychology: General, 128*(3), 332–345.

Mosteller, F., & Nogee, P. (1951). An experimental measurement of utility. *Journal of Political Economy, 59*, 371–404.

Mussweiler, T., & Strack, F. (1999). Comparing is believing: A selective accessibility model of judgmental anchoring. In W. Stroebe & M. Hewstone (Eds.), *European Review of Social Psychology* (Vol. 10). Chichester, UK: Wiley.

Mussweiler, T., & Strack, F. (2000). Numeric judgment under uncertainty: The role of knowledge in anchoring. *Journal of Experimental Social Psychology, 36*, 495–518.

Neale, M. A., & Bazerman, M. H. (1990). *Cognition and rationality in negotiation.* New York: The Free Press.

Nickerson, R. S. (1998). Confirmation bias: A ubiquitous phenomenon in many guises. *Review of General Psychology, 2*, 175–220.

Nickerson, R. S., & McGoldrick, C. C. (1965). Confidence ratings and level of performance on a judgmental task. *Perceptual and Motor Skills, 20*(1), 311–316.

Oaksford, M., Morris, F., Grainger, B., & Williams, J. M. G. (1996). Mood, reasoning, and central executive processes. *Journal of Experimental Psychology: Learning Memory and Cognition, 22*, 476–492.

Oskamp, S. (1965). Overconfidence in case-study judgments. *Journal of Consulting Psychology, 29*(3), 261–265.

Petty, R. E., & Cacioppo, J. T. (1986a). *Communication and persuasion: Central and peripheral routes to attitude change.* New York: Springer-Verlag.

Petty, R. E., & Cacioppo, J. T. (1986b). The Elaboration Likelihood Model of persuasion. In L. Berkowitz (Ed.), *Advances in experimental social psychology* (Vol. 19, pp. 123–205). New York: Academic Press.

Pohl, R. F., Eisenhauer, M., & Hardt, O. (2003). SARA: A cognitive process model to simulate the anchoring effect and hindsight bias. *Memory, 11*(4–5), 337–356.

Pratto, F., & Glasford, D. E. (2008). Ethnocentrism and the value of a human life. *Journal of Personality and Social Psychology, 95*, 1411–1428.

Preston, M. G., & Baratta, P. (1948). An experimental study of the auction-value of an uncertain outcome. *The American Journal of Psychology*, 183–193.

Quiggin, J. (1993). *Generalized expected utility theory: The rank-dependent model*. Springer .

Reber, R., & Schwarz, N. (1999). Effects of perceptual fluency on judgments of truth. *Consciousness and Cognition, 8*, 338–342.

Reber, R., Winkielman, P., & Schwarz, N. (1998). Effects of perceptual fluency on affective judgments. *Psychological Science, 9*, 45–48.

Redelmeier, D., Shafir, E., & Aujla, P. (2001). The beguiling pursuit of more information. *Medical Decision Making, 21*, 376–381.

Reyna, V. F. (2004). How people make decisions that involve risk: A dual process approach. *Current Directions in Psychological Science, 13*, 60–66.

Ross, L. (1977). The intuitive psychologist and his shortcomings: Distortions in the attribution process. In L. Berkowitz (Ed.), *Advances in Experimental Social Psychology* (Vol. 10, pp. 174–221). New York: Academic Press.

Ross, M., & Sicoly, F. (1979). Egocentric biases in availability and attribution.*Journal of Personality and Social Psychology, 37*(3), 322.

Rothman, A. J., Haddock, G., & Schwarz, N. (2001). "How many partners is too many?" Shaping perceptions of personal vulnerability. *Journal of Applied Social Psychology, 31*(10), 2195–2214.

Rottenstreich, Y., & Hsee, C. K. (2001). Money, kisses, and electric shocks: On the affective psychology of risk. *Psychological Science, 12*(3), 185–190.

Rottenstreich, Y., & Tversky, A. (1997). Unpacking, repacking, and anchoring: Advances in Support Theory. *Psychological Review, 104*, 406–415.

Rozin, P., Lowery, L., Imada, S., & Haidt, J. (1999). The CAD triad hypothesis: A mapping between three moral emotions (contempt, anger, disgust) and three moral codes (community, autonomy, divinity). *Journal of Personality and Social Psychology, 76*, 574–586.

Sanna, L. J., & Chang, E. C. (2003). The past is not what it used to be: Optimists' use of retroactive pessimism to diminish the sting of failure. *Journal of Research in Personality, 37*(5), 388–404.

Sanna, L. J., & Schwarz, N. (2003). Debiasing the hindsight bias: The role of accessibility experiences and (mis)attributions. *Journal of Experimental Social Psychology, 39*(3), 287–295.

Sanna, L. J., Schwarz, N., & Small, E. M. (2002). Accessibility experiences and the hindsight bias: I knew it all along versus it could never have happened. *Memory & Cognition, 30*(8), 1288–1296.

Savage, L. J. (1954). *The foundations of statistics*. New York: Wiley.

Schwarz, N. (2002a). Feelings as information: Moods influence judgments and processing strategies. In T. Gilovich, D. Griffin, & D. Kahneman (Eds.), *Heuristics and biases: The psychology of intuitive judgment* (pp. 534–547). New York: Cambridge University Press.

Schwarz, N. (2002b). Situated cognition and the wisdom of feelings: Cognitive tuning. In L. F. Barrett & P. Salovey (Eds.), *The wisdom in feelings: Psychological processes in emotional intelligence* (pp. 144–166). New York: Guilford.

Schwarz, N., Bless, H., Strack, F., Klumpp, G., Rittenauer-Schatka, H., & Simmons, A. (1991). Ease of retrieval as information: Another look at the availability heuristic. *Journal of Personality and Social Psychology, 61*, 195–202.

Schwarz, N., & Clore, G. L. (1983). Mood, misattribution, and judgments of well-being: Informative and directive functions of affective states. *Journal of Personality and Social Psychology, 45*, 513–523.

Schwarz, N., & Vaughn, L. A. (2002). The availability heuristic revisited: Ease of recall and content of recall as distinct sources of information. In T. Gilovich, D. Griffin, & D. Kahneman (Eds.), *Heuristics and biases: The psychology of intuitive judgment.* (pp. 103–119). New York: Cambridge University Press.

Shafir, E., Simonson, I., & Tversky, A. (1993). Reason-based choice. *Cognition, 49*, 11–36.

Simon, H. A. (1955). A behavioral model of rational choice. *Quarterly Journal of Economics, 69*, 99–118.

Simon, H. A. (1957). *Models of man: Social and rational*. New York: Wiley.

Sinclair, R. C. (1988). Mood, categorization breadth, and performance appraisal: The effects of order of information acquisition and affective state on halo, accuracy, information retrieval, and evaluations. *Organization Behavior and Human Decision Processes, 42*, 22–46.

Sloman, S. A. (1996). The empirical case for two systems of reasoning. *Psychological Bulletin, 119*, 3–22.

Slovic, P. (1987). Perception of risk. *Science, 9*, 223–224.

Slovic, P., Finucane, M., Peters, E., & MacGregor, D. (2002). The affect heuristic. In T. Gilovich, D. Griffin, & D. Kahneman (Eds.), *Heuristics and biases: The psychology of intuitive judgment* (pp. 397–420). New York: Cambridge University Press.

Slovic, P., Finucane, M. L., Peters, E., & MacGregor, D. (2004). Risk as analysis and risk as feelings: Some thoughts about affect, reason, risk, and rationality. *Risk Analysis, 24*(2), 311–322.

Slovic, P., Fischhoff, B., & Lichtenstein, S. (1977). Behavioral decision theory. *Annual Review of Psychology, 28*, 1–39.

Slovic, P., & Tversky, A. (1974). Who accepts Savage's axiom? *Behavioral Science, 19*, 363–373.

Smith, A. R., & Windschitl, P. D. (2011). Biased calculations: Numeric anchors influence answers to math equations. *Judgment and Decision Making, 6*(2), 139–146.

Snyder, M., & Swann, W. B. (1978). Hypothesis-testing processes in social interaction. *Journal of Personality and Social Psychology, 36*, 1202–1212.

Soll, J. B. (1996). Determinants of overconfidence and miscalibration: The roles of random error and ecological structure. *Organizational Behavior and Human Decision Processes, 65*(2), 117–137.

Stanovich, K. E., & West, R. F. (2000). Individual differences in reasoning: Implications for the rationality debate. *Behavioral and Brain Sciences, 23*, 645–665.

Strack, F., & Mussweiler, T. (1997). Explaining the enigmatic anchoring effect: Mechanisms of selective accessibility. *Journal of Personality and Social Psychology, 73*, 437–446.

Sunstein, C. R. (2002). *Risk and reason: Safety, law, and the environment*. New York: Cambridge University Press.

Sunstein, C. R. (2004). Terrorism and probability neglect. *Journal of Risk and Uncertainty, 26*(2–3), 121–136.

Tetlock, P. E. (1992). The impact of accountability on judgment and choice: Toward a social contingency model. In

M. P. Zanna (Ed.), *Advances in experimental social psychology* (Vol. 25, pp. 331–346). New York: Academic Press.

Thaler, R. (1980). Toward a positive theory of consumer choice. *Journal of Economic Behavior and Organization, 1*, 39–60.

Thaler, R. (1985). Mental accounting and consumer choice. *Marketing Science, 4*, 199–214.

Thaler, R. H., & Sunstein, C. R. (2008). *Nudge: Improving decisions about health, wealth, and happiness.* New Haven, CT: Yale University Press.

Tiedens, L. Z., & Linton, S. (2001). Judgment under emotional certainty and uncertainty: The effects of specific emotions on information processing. *Journal of Personality and Social Psychology, 81*, 973–988.

Trope, Y., & Bassok, M. (1982). Confirmatory and diagnosing strategies in social information gathering. *Journal of Personality and Social Psychology, 43*, 22–34.

Tversky, A., & Kahneman, D. (1973). Availability: A heuristic for judging frequency and probability. *Cognitive Psychology, 5*, 207–232.

Tversky, A., & Kahneman, D. (1974). Judgment under uncertainty: Heuristics and biases. *Science, 185*, 1124–1131.

Tversky, A., & Kahneman, D. (1981). The framing of decisions and the psychology of choice. *Science, 211*, 453–458.

Tversky, A., & Kahneman, D. (1983). Extensional versus intuitive reasoning: The conjunction fallacy in probability judgment. *Psychological Review, 90*, 293–315.

Tversky, A., & Koehler, D. J. (1994). Support theory: A nonextensional representation of subjective probability. *Psychological Review, 101*, 547–567.

Tykocinski, O. E. (2001). I never had a change: Using hindsight tactics to mitigate disappointments. *Personality and Social Psychology Bulletin, 27*(3), 376–382.

Uleman, J. S., Newman, L. S., & Moskowitz, G. B. (1996). People as flexible interpreters: Evidence and issues from spontaneous trait inference. In M. Zanna (Ed.), *Advances in experimental social psychology* (Vol. 29, pp. 211–279). San Diego: Academic Press.

Van Boven, L., Loewenstein, G., & Dunning, D. (2003). Mispredicting the endowment effect: Underestimation of owners' selling prices by buyer's agents. *Journal of Economic Behavior and Organization, 51*, 351–365.

Van Boven, L., Loewenstein, G., & Dunning, D. (2005). The illusion of courage in social predictions: Underestimating the impact of fear of embarrassment on other people. *Organizational Behavior and Human Decision Processes, 96*, 130–141.

Van Boven, L., Loewenstein, G., Welch, E., & Dunning, D. (2010). The illusion of courage in self-predictions:

Mispredicting one's own behavior in embarrassing situations. *Journal of Behavioral Decision Making, 25*, 1–12.

von Neumann, J., & Morgenstern, O. (1947). *Theory of games and economic behavior* (2nd ed.). Princeton, NJ: Princeton University Press.

Wanke, M., Schwarz, N., & Bless, H. (1995). The availability heuristic revisited: Experienced ease of retrieval in mundane frequency estimates. *Acta Psychologica, 89*, 83–90.

Wann, D. L., Grieve, F. G., Waddill, P. J., & Martin, J. (2008). Use of retroactive pessimism as a method of coping with identity threat: The impact of group identification. *Group Processes & Intergroup Relations, 11*, 439–450.

Wason, P. C. (1960). On the failure to eliminate hypotheses in a conceptual task. *Quarterly Journal of Experimental Psychology, 12*(129–140).

Wason, P. C. (1968). Reasoning about a rule. *Quarterly Journal of Experimental Psychology, 20*, 273–281.

Wason, P. C., & Johnson-Laird, P. N. (1972). *The psychology of reasoning.* Cambridge, MA: Harvard University Press.

Wells, G. L., & Petty, R. E. (1980). The effects of overt head movements on persuasion: Compatibility and incompatibility of responses. *Basic and Applied Social Psychology, 1*(3), 219–230.

Wilson, T. D., & Brekke, N. (1994). Mental contamination and mental correction: Unwanted influences on judgments and evaluations. *Psychological Bulletin, 116*, 117–142.

Wilson, T. D., & Gilbert, D. T. (2003). Affective forecasting. In L. Berkowitz (Ed.), *Advances in experimental social psychology* (Vol. 35, pp. 345–411). San Diego, CA: Academic Press.

Wilson, T. D., Houston, C., Etling, K. M., & Brekke, N. (1996). A new look at anchoring effects: Basic anchoring and its antecedents. *Journal of Experimental Psychology: General, 4*, 387–402.

Wilson, T. D., Lisle, D. J., Schooler, J. W., Hodges, S. D., Klaaren, K. J., & Lafleur, S. J. (1993). Introspecting about reasons and reduce post-choice satisfaction. *Personality and Social Psychology Bulletin, 19*(3), 331–339.

Wilson, T. D., Wheatley, T., Meyers, J. M., Gilbert, D. T., & Axsom, D. (2000). Focalism: A source of the durability bias in affective forecasting. *Journal of Personality and Social Psychology, 78*, 821–836.

Wong, K. F. E., & Kwong, J. Y. Y. (2000). Is 7300 m equal to 7.3 km? Same semantics but different anchoring effects. *Organizational Behavior & Human Decision Processes, 82*, 314–333.

CHAPTER 19

Mental Simulation: Looking Back in Order to Look Ahead

Keith D. Markman *and* Elizabeth A. Dyczewski

Abstract

Mental simulation refers to the imagination of alternative, counterfactual realities. This chapter provides an overview of research on simulations of the past—*retrospective* simulation—and simulations of the future—*prospective* simulation. Two major themes run throughout. The first is that both retrospective and prospective thinking are inextricably linked, relying on a mixture of episodic and semantic memories that share common neural substrates. The second is that retrospective and prospective simulation present trade-offs for the individual. On the one hand, they are functional, identifying causal inferences and potential obstacles that prepare us to try harder and perform better in the future. On the other hand, they sometimes produce bias—retrospective thinking can enhance hindsight bias, whereas prospective thinking can evoke biased predictions about the likelihood of certain events as well how one is going to feel about those events in the future. Fortunately, however, these biases can be diminished with debiasing techniques.

Key Words: mental simulation, counterfactual, predictions, bias, debiasing, past, future, memories, functional

"To think...what might have been!" "And now, what lies ahead?" *Mental simulations* of this kind function as the glue that binds the tapestry of our past and present lives to our thoughts about the future. This chapter will provide an overview of 30 years of research on simulations of the past— *retrospective* simulation—and simulations of the future—*prospective* simulation. Two major themes will be echoed along the way. The first is that both retrospective and prospective thinking are inextricably linked, relying on a mixture of episodic and semantic memorial representations that share common neural substrates. The second is that retrospective and prospective simulation present trade-offs for the individual. On the one hand, they are functional, identifying causal inferences and potential obstacles that prepare us to try harder and perform better in the future. On the other hand, they

sometimes produce bias—retrospective thinking can enhance the hindsight bias, whereas prospective thinking can evoke biased predictions about the likelihood of certain events as well how one is going to feel about those events in the future. Importantly, however, we will also point out how such biases can be attenuated by employing debiasing strategies such as counterexplanation and shifting attention away from focal outcomes.

Retrospection: Counterfactual Thinking and the Imagining of Alternative Paths

In 1982, Kahneman and Tversky wrote a short but provocative monograph about the *simulation heuristic*. They noted that, "There appear to be many situations in which questions about events are answered by an operation that resembles the running of a simulation model," and suggested that "we construe the output of simulation as an assessment of the ease with which the model could produce different outcomes" (p. 201). Later, within the context of a theory of coping, Taylor and Schneider (1989) defined simulation as "the cognitive construction of hypothetical scenarios or the reconstruction of real scenarios" (p. 175). Essentially all of the research that has followed the publication of these two papers is indebted to their basic conceptualization of mental simulation.

Kahneman and Tversky (1982) and Taylor and Schneider (1989) devoted significant attention in their respective papers to counterfactual thinking, a phenomenon that philosophers have been discussing for centuries. The term *counterfactual thinking* refers to the ubiquitous human tendency to imagine alternatives to the past (e.g., "If only I had studied harder in college," "If only I had proposed to her when I had the chance"). Early theorizing about counterfactual thinking suggested that exemplars from memory composed the basic substrate of counterfactual generation. In 1986, Kahneman and Miller published an important paper about counterfactuals that described norm theory. According to norm theory, counterfactuals are mental representations of alternatives to the past that are constructed from stored representations that combine traces from episodic and semantic memory. To illustrate, the counterfactual "If I only I hadn't changed my answer on the exam…" is directly linked to an episodic memory involving a past event when an individual switched from the correct answer to an incorrect answer. In turn, the counterfactual also draws on semantic memory by referring to a generalization about how one perceives the world (e.g., always stick with your first instinct).

Norm theory (Kahneman & Miller, 1986) highlights the psychological importance of discrepancies between an experienced factual outcome and a counterfactual standard. For instance, the comparison between a student's B on an exam and the A that the student would have preferred elicits disappointment, exemplifying a *contrast effect* on judgment. However, the innovation of norm theory over previous social judgment formulations [e.g., Helson's (1964) adaptation level theory; Thibaut & Kelley's (1959) comparison level theory] was the assertion that judgmental standards are constructed *on-line* in response to specific outcomes. Thus, although the basis for a norm is certainly constructed from prior beliefs and expectancies, the particular character of each norm is, as Roese and Olson (1995) described it, "a combination of a priori beliefs

reconstructed uniquely in light of a specific outcome" (p. 7). Kahneman and Miller also employed the term *mutability* to describe the relative ease with which aspects of reality (i.e., antecedent to a factual outcome) can be cognitively altered in order to construct a counterfactual (see also Hofstadter, 1985). When mutable antecedents (e.g., effort, action) precede a factual outcome, the outcome will be perceived as abnormal, and (normal) counterfactual alternatives will become more available, whereas when immutable antecedents (e.g., height, gravity) precede a factual outcome, counterfactual alternatives will become less available, and the outcome will be perceived as normal.

Contrastive Effects on Judgments

Counterfactual thinking has implications for a variety of social judgments, including expressions of sympathy and blame. With regard to sympathy, Miller and McFarland (1986) found that thinking about how a victim's misfortune could easily have been avoided rendered the outcome more poignant, thereby causing participants to feel more sympathy for the victim and to recommend a higher level of monetary compensation. In a similar vein, Branscombe and Weir (1992) found that rape victims who offered a high degree of resistance were blamed more for their misfortune than those offering more moderate resistance. These types of effects have also been observed for ascriptions of personal blame. For instance, Davis, Lehman, Silver, Wortman, and Ellard (1996) found that the degree to which respondents with spinal cord injuries believed they could have avoided their accident predicted their level of self-blame.

More generally, the role of counterfactual thinking in assessing causality has received a great deal of attention (e.g., Alicke, 2000; Cheng & Novick, 1990; Hilton & Slugoski, 1986; Lipe, 1991; Mandel, 2003; McGill, 1989). Wells and Gavanski (1989) hypothesized that a factual event will be judged as causal to the extent that its default—the alternative event that most readily comes to mind when a factual event is mentally mutated—successfully undoes the outcome. In one study, a woman was described as having died from an allergic reaction to a meal ordered by her boss. When the boss was described as having considered ordering another meal without the allergic ingredient, his causal role in the death was judged to be greater than when the alternative meal was also described as having had the allergic ingredient. However, although additional demonstrations of the role of counterfactual thinking in shaping causal assessments can be found in the literature (e.g., Branscombe, Crosby, & Weir, 1993; Branscombe & Weir, 1992; Roese & Olson, 1996), current theorizing (e.g., Mandel, 2003, 2005; Mandel & Lehman, 1996) suggests that counterfactual thinking may be more directed toward establishing perceptions of avoidability and preventability than toward assessing causality.

In addition to disappointment, regret is a negative emotion that derives from imagining how one's present situation would have or could have been better (for reviews, see Markman & Beike, 2012; Roese, 1997; Zeelenberg, 1999), and Kahneman and Miller (1986) suggested that regret is elicited by counterfactual generation (see also Landman, 1993; Lecci, Okun, & Karoly, 1994). Other types of emotions may also be evoked as a function of the types of counterfactual antecedents that are mutated. For instance, Niedenthal, Tangney, and Gavanski (1994) showed that the experience of shame relies on counterfactual inferences that mutate characterological aspects of the self (e.g., "If only I were a more honest person..."), whereas guilt is engendered by counterfactual inferences that mutate one's behavior (e.g., "If only I had listened to her more closely...").

Counterfactuals and the Hindsight Bias

A common finding regarding reactions to unexpected events is that after having learned the outcome, the event in hindsight seems to have been more predictable and inevitable than it would have been without the benefit of outcome knowledge. This phenomenon, known as the *hindsight bias,* has been described as a projection of new knowledge into the past paired with a denial of the influence of outcome information (Hawkins & Hastie, 1990). In an initial study exploring the hindsight bias (Fischhoff, 1975), participants read about an obscure historical event, the 19th-century wars between the British and the Ghurka of Nepal. Some participants read of a battle that ended with a British victory, others with a Ghurka victory, and some were provided with no outcome information. Those participants who received outcome information reported a higher a priori likelihood of that outcome occurring than did those who did not receive outcome information. The result is what Fischhoff (1975) described as "creeping determinism": a post hoc perception of outcome inevitability. Attempts to make sense of the outcome and create a coherent causal narrative lead one to selectively recall outcome-consistent antecedent information and assimilate it with outcome knowledge.

It seems intuitive that the consideration of counterfactuals would diminish the hindsight bias. Indeed, counterfactual thinking was originally thought to reduce inevitability perceptions by illustrating how alternative outcomes were in fact possible. Sherman (1991) argued that, "to the extent that counterfactuals are easily and spontaneously generated, the past seems less inevitable: other outcomes were clearly possible" (p. 182), and Fischhoff and colleagues were, in fact, able to reduce the strength of the hindsight bias by instructing participants to consider alternative outcomes (Fischhoff, 1976; Slovic & Fischhoff, 1977). Considering opposing or alternative outcomes apparently aids in shifting the focus from the focal hypothesis—that the focal outcome had to occur—to an alternative hypothesis, that a different outcome could have occurred (Hirt & Markman, 1995; Koehler, 1991). Thus, the consideration of how the same antecedent events could lead to a different outcome has been found to reduce the hindsight bias.

On the other hand, others have argued that counterfactual thinking could lead individuals to perceive events as *more* rather than less determined. Roese and colleagues proposed that counterfactual thinking enhances the hindsight bias to the extent that counterfactual thinking aids in the identification of a coherent causal narrative (Roese, 2004; Roese & Maniar, 1997; Roese & Olson, 1996). These researchers suggested that counterfactual thinking does not necessitate the consideration of an alternative outcome but, rather, can be utilized to make sense of the outcome. To illustrate, Roese and Maniar (1997) described how a sports fan could make sense of a team's loss with the counterfactual that the team would have won had it not been for an injury earlier in the game. In the absence of the injury, the team would have won, but given the injury, the loss is construed as inevitable. Utilizing both laboratory and field studies, Roese and colleagues found that counterfactual thinking directed toward an explanation leads to increases in the hindsight bias (Roese & Maniar, 1997; Roese & Olson, 1996). Similarly, Nestler and von Collani (2008) found that priming counterfactual thinking and activating a counterfactual mindset led to increases in the hindsight bias.

Functions of Retrospective Thinking
UPWARD AND DOWNWARD COUNTERFACTUALS

Early research on counterfactual thinking focused nearly exclusively on the negative emotions that accrue from contrastive counterfactual comparisons. Later, researchers (e.g., Markman,

Gavanski, Sherman, & McMullen, 1993; McMullen, Markman, & Gavanski, 1995; Roese, 1994; Sanna, 1996) found it useful to classify counterfactuals on the basis of their direction of comparison. Borrowing a theoretical distinction drawn in the social comparison literature between upward and downward comparisons (e.g., Collins, 1996; Taylor, Buunk, & Aspinwall, 1990; Wood, 1989), counterfactuals were classified into those that construct imagined alternatives that are better than reality (i.e., *upward* counterfactuals) and those that are worse than reality (i.e., *downward* counterfactuals). In an initial demonstration of contrastive emotional responses following the generation of upward and downward counterfactuals, Markman et al. (1993) employed a computer-simulated blackjack game that allowed for an examination of the spontaneous generation of counterfactuals within the context of two manipulated situational factors—outcome valence and event repeatability. Evidencing contrast, negative and repeatable outcomes evoked a greater tendency to engage in upward than downward counterfactual thinking, which in turn heightened feelings of dissatisfaction (see also McMullen, Markman, & Gavanski, 1995). In a more direct test, Roese (1994) induced participants to consider either upward or downward counterfactuals about a recent life event. Those who generated upward counterfactuals subsequently reported more negative affect than those who generated downward counterfactuals.

Medvec and her colleagues subsequently provided some particularly compelling demonstrations of counterfactual contrast. In observations of Olympic athletes, Medvec, Madey, and Gilovich (1995) found that silver medalists actually experienced less satisfaction with their achievement than did bronze medalists, presumably because the former were focused on not having won the gold medal (i.e., an upward counterfactual), whereas the latter were focused on the possibility of not having won a medal at all (i.e., a downward counterfactual). Similarly, Medvec and Savitsky (1997) found more negative affect expressed by students who nearly attained a cutoff point (i.e., a grade of 89%), than by students who just barely attained a cutoff point (i.e., a grade of 87%). According to Medvec and colleagues, proximity to category boundaries draws attention to counterfactual outcomes, thereby eliciting contrastive effects on subsequent affective responses (see also Mellers, Schwartz, Ho, & Ritov, 1997; Sanna, Turley-Ames, & Meier, 1999; Wohl & Enzle, 2003).

Affective Contrast and Affective Assimilation

The first wave of research on counterfactual thinking assumed that contrast-based reactions to counterfactual generation—by which judgments are displaced way from the counterfactual standard—were the default: Upward counterfactuals elicit negative affect, whereas downward counterfactuals elicit positive affect (e.g., Larsen, McGraw, Mellers, & Cacioppo, 2004; Markman et al., 1993; Medvec et al., 1995; Sanna, 1996; Wohl & Enzle, 2003). However, subsequent work (e.g., Boninger, Gleicher, & Strathman, 1994; Landman & Petty, 2000; Markman, McMullen, & Elizaga, 2008; Markman & Tetlock, 2000; McMullen, 1997; McMullen & Markman, 2000, 2002; McMullen et al., 1995; Sanna, 1997; Teigen, 2005; Tetlock, 1998) indicated that assimilation-based reactions to counterfactual generation—by which judgments are pulled toward the counterfactual standard—are also common, meaning that upward counterfactuals can also elicit positive affect, and downward counterfactuals can also elicit negative affect. Markman and McMullen (2003, 2005) developed a process model—reflection and evaluation model of comparative thinking—that accounts for the elicitation of assimilative and contrastive responses to upward and downward counterfactuals. At the heart of the model is the assertion that two psychologically distinct modes of mental simulation operate during comparative thinking. The first of these modes is *reflection*, an experiential ("as if") mode of thinking whereby one vividly simulates that information about the comparison standard is true of, or is part of, oneself or one's present standing, and the second of these modes is *evaluation*, whereby the outcome of a mental simulation run is used as a reference point against which to evaluate oneself or one's present standing.

To illustrate with a counterfactual thinking example, consider the student who receives a B on an exam but realizes that an A was easily attainable with some additional studying. In the case of upward evaluation, the student switches attention between the outcome (a grade of B) and the counterfactual standard (a grade of A). According to the reflection and evaluation model, such attentional switching ("I got a B; I could have gotten an A, but instead I got a B") involves using the standard as a reference point and thereby instigates evaluative processing. In the case of upward reflection, however, the student's attention is focused mainly on the counterfactual itself. Focusing on the counterfactual instigates reflective processing whereby the student considers the implications of the counterfactual and temporarily experiences the counterfactual as if it were real ("What if I had actually gotten an A?"). In a sense, the student is "transported" into the counterfactual world (Green & Brock, 2000). Likewise, consider the case of a driver who pulls away from the curb without carefully checking rear- and side-view mirrors, and subsequently slams on the brakes as a large truck whizzes by. In the case of downward evaluation, the driver switches attention between the counterfactual standard (being hit by the truck) and the outcome (not being hit by the truck), thereby instigating evaluative processing ("I was fortunate to not have been hit by that truck"). In the case of downward reflection, however, the driver's attention is mainly focused on the counterfactual itself, thereby instigating reflective processing ("I nearly got hit by that truck").

Content-Specific and Content-Neutral Pathways

More recently, Epstude and Roese (2008) drew a distinction between content-specific and content-neutral pathways that link counterfactual thinking to action (see also Gollwitzer and Moskowitz, 1996). According to Epstude and Roese, counterfactual thought is directly converted into action along the content-specific pathway by eliciting inferences (e.g., "I didn't study the right material") that are channeled into behavioral intentions that then direct the performance of corresponding behavior. Along the content-neutral pathway, by contrast, counterfactual thinking indirectly affects behavior by inducing emotional responses, motivational states, or information processing styles (e.g., mindsets) that then affect performance and induce behavior change.

There is indirect evidence that the content-specific pathway can lead to behavior change. For instance, Smallman and Roese (2009) used a sequential priming paradigm to demonstrate that counterfactual thinking (e.g., "might have eaten more carefully") facilitates behavioral intentions to perform specific content-related acts (e.g., "In the future I will eat more carefully"). More generally, an extensive program of research conducted by Gollwitzer and colleagues (e.g., Gollwitzer, 1993, 1999; Gollwitzer & Sheeran, 2006) has provided evidence for a link between the expression of implementation intentions (e.g., "I will study for the chemistry exam next Tuesday evening for 3 hours") and subsequent content-related behavior. It should be noted, however, that implementation intentions have been shown to have a stronger relationship to subsequent behavior than do behavioral intentions because the former are more specific,

more concrete, and linked to a specific moment of opportunity. Thus, in order for counterfactuals to influence actions through the content-specific pathway, specific moments of opportunity need to arise (Fazio, 1990), and the individual needs to be both willing and able to seize on the opportunity to act (Azjen & Fishbein, 1980).

According to Epstude and Roese's (2008) distinction, the thought-to-behavior pathway described by the reflection and evaluation model (Markman & McMullen, 2003) would tend to fall into the content-neutral category because of the model's emphasis on the role of affect in mediating the relationship between mental simulation and motivation. Drawing on Schwarz and Clore's (1983) feelings-as-information perspective, the reflection and evaluation model posits that counterfactuals that elicit negative affect should encourage greater task persistence than should counterfactuals that elicit positive affect. Thus, because upward evaluation is more likely than upward reflection to elicit negative affect, upward evaluation should also be more likely to heighten motivation. Conversely, the reflection and evaluation model argues that downward reflection should heighten motivation, whereas downward evaluation should engender complacency. According to the model, the negative affect elicited by downward reflection raises an individual's awareness of the possibility that a negative goal state may be attained (see also Lockwood, Jordan, & Kunda, 2002), whereas the positive affect elicited by downward evaluation suggests that a negative goal state has been successfully avoided. Providing support for these suppositions, Markman, McMullen, and Elizaga (2008) instructed participants to generate either upward or downward counterfactuals regarding their anagram performance and were further instructed to do this within a reflective mode (i.e., "Vividly imagine the counterfactual outcome you just described") or an evaluative mode (i.e., "Vividly imagine the counterfactual outcome you just described and compare that outcome to the outcome that actually happened"). Consistent with predictions, subsequent anagram performance showed the greatest improvement following upward evaluative and downward reflective counterfactuals, and the relationship between simulation type and anagram persistence was mediated by (negative) affect.

Mental Simulation Mindsets

Another process that can effect behavior change along the content-neutral pathway involves the elicitation of information processing styles. As described earlier, scenarios that contain salient mutable components tend to elicit counterfactual thoughts (Kahneman & Miller, 1986). In a separate literature, research on mindset priming has demonstrated how completing a cognitive activity in one domain can carry over to another domain (Gollwitzer, Heckhausen, & Steller, 1990; Kulpe, 1904). This idea has been imported into research on counterfactuals by demonstrating how counterfactual thinking in one context (e.g., reading a scenario about Jane, who switches her seat at a rock concert and subsequently wins a free trip to Hawaii) elicits a mindset that encourages the consideration of alternatives in a completely unrelated context (e.g., Galinsky & Kray, 2004; Galinsky & Moskowitz, 2000; Kray & Galinsky, 2003). For instance, counterfactual mindset activation was shown to improve decision accuracy by promoting synergistic coordination—the tendency of group members to build on and develop relationships between each other's ideas (Galinsky & Kray, 2004; Liljenquist, Galinsky, & Kray, 2004). In addition, counterfactual mindsets reduce the confirmation bias by encouraging skepticism about the dominant hypothesis (Galinsky & Moskowitz, 2000; Kray & Galinsky, 2003).

In earlier studies it was assumed that the activation of counterfactual mindsets elicits a general tendency to consider a wider range of alternatives. However, Kray, Galinsky, and Wong (2006) found that counterfactual mindsets actually impaired performance on tasks involving the generation of novel ideas. To clarify the effects of counterfactual mindsets, Markman, Lindberg, Kray, and Galinsky (2007) noted that previous research had manipulated them through the use of scenarios that tended to elicit subtractive counterfactuals—counterfactuals that remove an antecedent action (i.e., "If only I *had not*," see Roese & Olson, 1993). According to these researchers, subtractive counterfactuals activate a relational processing style in which people consider associations and relationships among stimuli, leading them to "think *within* the box." On the other hand, Markman et al. reasoned that additive counterfactuals—counterfactuals that add an antecedent action (i.e., "If only I *had*") should enhance creativity by activating an "expansive processing style that broadens conceptual attention" (p. 312), thereby encouraging people to generate novel ideas and to "think *outside* the box." In support, they found that additive counterfactual mindsets enhanced performance on idea generation tasks (e.g., uses for a brick, Scattergories), whereas subtractive counterfactual mindsets enhanced performance on association tasks (Remote Associates

Test, syllogisms). More recently, Kray, Galinsky, and Markman (2009) demonstrated that negotiators who generated additive counterfactuals about a past negotiation were subsequently more likely to create an integrative deal than negotiators who generated subtractive counterfactuals. Because additive counterfactuals add hypothetical elements to the past, they likely evoke an expansive processing style that aids in creative generation (cf. Guilford, 1950).

Prospection: Looking Back in Order to Look Ahead

At one point in the film *Inception* (Nolan, 2010), Dom Cobb (played by Leonardo DiCaprio), a master at extracting secret information from others' dreams, enters into a shared dream-space with young apprentice Ariadne (played by Ellen Page) in order to share his knowledge about the inner workings of dreams and the subconscious mind. As he observes her manipulating the architecture of the dream, he cautions her to, "Never recreate from your memory. Always imagine new places." This observation about the relationship between waking life and dreaming life is striking in the way it maps onto the hypothesized relationship between memory and (waking life) mental simulation. The idea is that just as individuals can vividly recollect their personal pasts, they can also travel forward in time to vividly "pre-experience" or "pre-feel" their personal futures (Atance & O'Neill, 2001; Buckner & Carroll, 2007; Gilbert & Wilson, 2007; Schacter & Addis, 2007; Suddendorf & Corballis, 1997; Tulving, 1972). When individuals simulate the future, they sample exemplars from remembered events that help generate a virtually unlimited number of potential future scenarios (Corballis, 2003; Suddendorf & Corballis, 1997). In this way, episodic memory is a constructive system that enables individuals to simulate both their personal pasts and their possible futures (Schacter & Addis, 2007).

In support, recent empirical work has shown that there is considerable overlap in the psychological and neural processes involved in remembering the past and simulating the future. For example, it has been shown that personal past and future thought can be impaired in amnesic patients (e.g., Klein, Loftus, & Kihlstrom, 2002; Tulving, 1985) and that both share common neural correlates (Addis, Wong, & Schacter, 2007; Okuda et al., 2003; Szpunar, Watson, & McDermott, 2007) traditionally associated solely with remembering the past (Maguire, 2001). To illustrate, Szpunar et al. (2007) instructed participants to remember specific past events, imagine specific future events, or imagine specific events involving Bill Clinton. These researchers found that imagining specific past and future events resulted in similar patterns of activity in the bilateral frontopolar and medial temporal lobe regions, as well as posterior cingulated cortex. The fact that these regions were *not* activated to the same magnitude when imagining events involving Bill Clinton appears to demonstrate a neural signature that is unique to the construction of events in one's personal past or future.

More generally, it appears that human beings spend a great deal of time musing about possible futures. Neuroimaging studies reveal that both the prefrontal cortex and the media temporal lobes are strongly activated by prospection (Schacter, Addis, & Buckner, 2007; Szpunar, Watson, & McDermott, 2007), and these regions appear to be part of a "default network" that is activated when individuals are not specifically engaged in other tasks (Raichle et al., 2001). The intriguing implication of this work is that when the mind is not busy perceiving the present it tends to gravitate toward simulations of the future (Buckner & Carroll, 2007).

Biasing Effects of Prospective Simulations

The term *reality monitoring* refers to one's ability to discriminate between what has been generated and what has been perceived. Thus, individuals can confuse what they imagined with what they saw (e.g., Durso & Johnson, 1980), and the more often they think about something, the more often they think they saw it (Johnson, Raye, Wang, & Taylor, 1979; Johnson, Taylor, & Raye, 1977). Related work on the phenomenon of "imagination inflation" has shown how imagination can lead to the creation of false memories (e.g., Bernstein, Godfrey, & Loftus, 2009; Goff & Roediger, 1998; Seamon, Philbin, & Harrison, 2006), and explaining how particular events might have occurred in one's life (Sharman, Manning, & Garry, 2005) can enhance confidence that these events actually occurred in adolescence.

Explanation Bias

People often mentally simulate the future in order to predict whether a particular outcome is likely to occur. There is a considerable amount of research (Johnson & Sherman, 1990; Koehler, 1991), however, demonstrating that merely specifying a particular future outcome to think about leads people to subsequently perceive that outcome as more likely. This is referred to as the *explanation bias*. Typically, study participants who are asked to imagine or explain how

a hypothetical outcome might be true show increased subjective likelihood estimates for the target outcome relative to participants who are not asked to imagine an outcome. For instance, Ross, Lepper, Strack, and Steinmetz (1977) instructed participants to read clinical case histories of psychiatric patients, after which they were asked to write explanations for why patients might have engaged in various behaviors (e.g., participating in the Peace Corps) later in their lives. Even though the behaviors to be explained were known to be hypothetical, participants who had explained behaviors believed that the patients were more likely to perform those behaviors in the future (see also Anderson, Lepper, & Ross, 1980; Carroll, 1978; Hirt & Sherman, 1985; Sherman, Zehner, Johnson, & Hirt, 1983). Research has also indicated that explanation biases can occur when one is explaining hypothetical future events involving themselves. Sherman, Skov, Hervitz, and Stock (1981) found that participants who explained hypothetical success on a future anagram task believed that success was more likely in the future. The changes in likelihood estimates that occur after explanation tasks also appear to be quite resistant to change. For instance, Anderson (1983) found that participants continued to exhibit increased confidence in the validity of explanation-induced social theories a week after they completed an explanation task.

The underlying mechanism that is assumed to account for the explanation bias is the availability heuristic (Tversky & Kahneman, 1973), whereby individuals judge the likelihood of future outcomes on the basis of the ease with which similar instances can be brought to mind. Outcomes whose instances readily come to mind are judged more likely than outcomes whose instances do not readily come to mind. Thus, bias results because causal arguments consistent with that outcome are more readily and easily retrieved at the time of judgment than are arguments consistent with alternative outcomes (Anderson et al., 1980; Anderson, New, & Speer, 1985).

Debiasing the Effects of Explanations

Although explanations can lead to bias, it is also possible to diminish, if not completely eradicate, the biasing effects of explanations. Fischhoff (1982) suggested that one of the most effective strategies for reducing judgmental biases is to prompt individuals to consider alternatives. In fact, subsequent studies have shown that a consideration of alternatives can be an effective debiasing strategy for reducing the hindsight bias (Sanna & Schwarz, 2003; Sanna, Schwarz, & Stocker, 2002), the explanation effect

(Hirt & Markman, 1995; Lord, Lepper, & Preston, 1984), and overconfidence (Hoch, 1985; Koriat, Lichtenstein, & Fischhoff, 1980).

By what mechanism does considering alternatives reduce bias? In the lab, a counterexplanation task presents participants with the task of considering one alternative outcome for the event in question: Participants must undo their prior explanation for the event and construct an explanation supporting a different outcome. Hirt and Markman (1995) posited that successful completion of a counterexplanation task should lead participants to realize that the outcome of an event is not as predictable as previously believed. This realization may then lead participants to consider additional alternatives (beyond those specified in the explanation and counterexplanation tasks) in making their likelihood judgments. To do so, participants are presumed to use the simulation heuristic and engage in multiple simulation runs of the potential outcomes of the event. According to the simulation heuristic, people judge the likelihood of an outcome on the basis of the ease with which scenarios leading to a particular outcome can be constructed (Kahneman & Tversky, 1982); outcomes that are easily simulated are judged to be relatively likely, and outcomes more difficult to imagine are judged to be relatively unlikely (Sherman, Cialdini, Schwartzman, & Reynolds, 1985). Notably, however, to the extent that scenarios consistent with an alternative outcome are found to be easy to simulate, counterexplanation participants will be spurred on to consider *additional* alternatives and engage in mental simulation runs for those alternatives. In this way, the counterexplanation task leads participants to consider a fuller, more complete set of alternatives when they judge the likely outcome of the event. Thus, debiasing results from the fact that the simulation of additional alternative outcomes for the event reveals that plausible alternatives to the initially explained outcome exist. Participants then base their likelihood judgments on the results of the simulation process, judging the most easily simulated outcome to the event to be most probable.

To provide evidence for the debiasing effects of counterexplanations, Hirt and Markman (1995, Study 2) had participants first explain a focal event (a win by a particular football team) and then explain an alternative outcome. The nature of the alternative outcome was varied such that in some cases it was opposite to the first outcome (e.g., a convincing win by team B after explaining a convincing win by team A), but in other cases, it was an alternative version of the same outcome (e.g., a convincing win by Team B after explaining a narrow victory by team B). The results indicated that in all cases, the consideration of an alternative outcome debiased likelihood judgments. Moreover, the consideration of an alternative to the focal outcome led participants to spontaneously consider and mentally simulate additional alternatives beyond those they were asked to explicitly consider. Thus, it appears that simply having individuals consider alternatives, even when the alternative does not undo the outcome, is sufficient to break the inertia that sets in after the initial explanation, resulting in a more thorough evaluation of the evidence at the time of judgment. Notably, the consideration of alternatives can be motivated as well. For example, accountability pressure can lead individuals to engage in preemptive self-criticism, whereby one anticipates the potential objections of others by considering multiple perspectives (Lerner & Tetlock, 1999; Tetlock, 1983).

Adding complexity to the story, research has also shown that the consideration of alternatives as a debiasing strategy can sometimes backfire as a function of the influence of metacognitive thoughts. That is, when the consideration of alternatives is experienced as particularly difficult, bias is amplified rather than attenuated (Hirt, Kardes, & Markman, 2004; Sanna et al., 2002). The reason appears to be that the process of generating or retrieving information from memory renders two sources of information accessible: the specific content that comes to mind (accessible content) and the subjective ease with which that content comes to mind (accessibility experiences; Schwarz, 1998; Schwarz & Vaughn, 2002). When asked to consider alternatives that are easy to generate, bias is reduced because individuals acknowledge that there are many other plausible alternatives to the focal outcome. However, when the consideration of alternatives is perceived to be difficult, individuals conclude that few if any plausible alternatives exist and become more convinced that the focal outcome is inevitable.

Sanna et al. (2002) demonstrated the implications of these accessibility experiences for hindsight bias. Participants were provided with descriptions of the British-Gurkha war (Fischhoff, 1975) and asked to generate two or 10 examples about how the war could have turned out differently. Participants asked to generate two examples found the task easy, leading them to infer that there were several plausible alternatives for this event, significantly reducing hindsight bias. By contrast, participants asked to generate 10 examples found the task difficult.

Their negative accessibility experience apparently led them to believe that there were few plausible alternatives to the focal outcome, thereby increasing hindsight bias.

Affective Forecasting

It is common for individuals to make predictions or have expectations about how they are going to feel in the future. A great deal of recent research, however, has demonstrated that individuals' mental simulations regarding their prospective feelings are often inaccurate, leading them to overestimate (e.g., Buehler & McFarland, 2001; Gilbert, Morewedge, Risen, & Wilson, 2004) and sometime underestimate (e.g., Dunn, Biesanz, Human, & Finn, 2007; Gilbert, Gill, & Wilson, 2002) the extremity of emotional responses they will experience in the future. Such miscalibrated judgments have been referred to as "affective forecasting errors." Affective forecasts necessarily rely on memory, including most notably, memories of feelings. The problem is that individuals often use unrepresentative memories as a basis for simulation (Gilbert & Wilson, 2007). To illustrate, when people experience unpleasant episodes that end in relief—such as waiting on several interminably long check-in lines in order to board multiple planes for a vacation destination—they tend to remember peak moments of the experience (e.g., swimming in crystal-clear water when they finally arrive at the beach) rather than the most typical moments. They then use these more unrepresentative memories to construct a simulation of what it will be like to repeat that event (e.g., taking another vacation to a beach locale) that leads them to underestimate how frustrating the repeat experience will be (Frederickson & Kahneman, 1993).

One mechanism that is suggested to account for affective forecasting errors is implicit in our earlier discussion of the biasing effects of explanations, namely, *focalism*. When perceivers engage in focalism, they are directing their attention solely to the focal event while failing to take into consideration the impact of other events (Wilson, Wheatley, Meyers, Gilbert, & Axsom, 2000). Consider a study in which students were asked to imagine living in California versus the Midwest (Schkade & Kahneman, 1998). Students residing in both places anticipated that living in California would lead to greater life satisfaction than living in the Midwest. However, this prediction stemmed from the fact that students focused heavily on the differences between the two regions—particularly California's superior weather—when imagining what it would be like

to live in the other region. Yet, actual satisfaction may depend on a much broader set of life conditions (e.g., job opportunities, daily hassles) that are fairly similar across regions. Indeed, students living in the Midwest reported life satisfaction levels that were equivalent to those of their counterparts in California.

Affective forecasters also commonly exhibit an *impact bias*, a tendency to overestimate the intensity and duration of their own emotional responses to events (Gilbert, Driver-Linn, & Wilson, 2002). For example Gilbert, Pinel, Wilson, Blumberg, and Wheatley (1998) asked Democrats to predict how they would feel if George W. Bush were elected governor of Texas. Although they predicted that they would be miserable, their default levels of happiness had not only returned by the time Bush was elected governor, but they had also developed a more positive view of Bush, suggesting that they were finding silver linings in the situation. Gilbert et al. (1998) suggested that forecasters succumb to the impact bias because they fail to foresee the palliative influence of the *psychological immune system*, which tends to minimize the extremity of negative and positive emotional responses (see also Taylor, 1991). Employing the language of cognitive-experiential self-theory (Epstein, 1994, 1998), immune neglect emerges because the rational system fails to appreciate the important role that the experiential system plays in shaping emotional experience (Dunn, Forrin, & Ashton-James, 2009).

In addition, affective forecasters tend to ignore the influence of visceral factors. If, as cognitive-experiential self-theory suggests, the rational system is a cold system driven by reason whereas the experiential system is a hot system driven by emotions, then individuals commonly find themselves imagining how they will feel in a hot state when they are in fact in a cold state. This creates what Loewenstein and colleagues have called a *hot/cold empathy gap* (e.g., Loewenstein, O'Donoghue, & Rabin, 2003; Loewenstein & Schkade, 1999; Van Boven & Loewenstein, 2003). The hot/cold empathy gap reflects a struggle between the cold rational system and the hot experiential system. As Gilbert and Wilson (2007) noted, "People do not imagine feeling anxious while having a colonoscopy so much as they imagine a colonoscopy, feel anxious, and then take this anxiety as an indicator of the feelings they can expect to experience during the procedure itself" (p. 1352). In one study, individuals who completed a quiz were offered, as reimbursement, either a candy bar or the answers to the quiz questions (Loewenstein, Prelec, & Shatto, 1998). Among those who made their choice before taking the quiz, only 21% chose the answers. However, a significantly higher proportion of individuals (60%) chose the answers after having taken the quiz. In their cold state, before taking the quiz, individuals apparently underestimated their subsequent curiosity and its effect on their behavior.

Debiasing Affective Forecasts

Just as there are debiasing techniques to counter the effects of focalism on explanations (e.g., Hirt & Markman, 1995; Hirt et al., 2004), there are also ways to increase the accuracy of affective forecasts. Recently, Dunn et al. (2009) made the observation that, "affective forecasting depends in part on the extent to which the rational system has access to complete and correct information about the reality of emotional experiences in everyday life" (p. 341). In support, Dunn, Brackett, Ashton-James, Schneiderman, and Salovey (2009) had participants complete a measure of emotional intelligence (Salovey & Mayer, 1990). Emotional intelligence reflects knowledge about the causes and consequences of one's own and others' experience of emotions. Participants were then asked to predict how they would feel two days after a U.S. presidential election (Study 1a), three weeks after an academic exam (Study 1b), or the morning after a college basketball game (Study 2). Next, participants were asked to report how they were actually feeling after each event. Consistent with predictions, the discrepancies between the affective forecasts and experiences of individuals high in emotional intelligence were smaller in comparison to the discrepancies reported by individuals low in emotional intelligence. Thus, when making affective forecasts, it would appear useful to teach the rational system to incorporate and utilize inputs (e.g., feelings, "vibes") that it receives from the experiential system (see also Hoerger, Quirk, Lucas, & Carr, 2009). More directly, Wilson et al. (2000) conducted a diary study and found that simply thinking about peripheral future activities decreased focalism and enhanced the accuracy of affective forecasts.

Functions of Prospective Thinking

Prospective mental simulations are a particularly powerful means by which to strengthen links between thinking, motivation, and behavior. Pham and Taylor (1999; Taylor & Pham, 1999) drew a distinction between simulations of desired goals (outcome simulations) and simulations of the steps leading to desired goals (process simulations). In one study (Pham & Taylor, 1999), for five to seven days before a midterm examination, college freshmen either mentally simulated the steps that needed to be taken in order to do well on the exam (good study habits) or simply simulated the desired outcome (getting a good grade). Results indicated that compared with outcome simulations, process simulations enhanced studying and improved grades. Thus, it is apparently not enough to merely envision a better future outcome in order to attain a desired goal. Rather, individuals also need to simulate the means by which they will pursue that goal.

The importance of thinking about routes to goal achievement and the obstacles one might encounter along the way has been formalized in an important theory developed by Oettingen and her colleagues. Fantasy realization theory (e.g., Oettingen, Pak, & Schnetter, 2001) describes three routes to goal setting that result from how individuals deal with their fantasies about desired futures. The expectancy-based route involves mentally contrasting fantasies about a desired future with aspects of present reality that stand in the way of reaching the desired future. According to the theory, mental contrasting transforms the desired future into something that is to be achieved, and reality into something that is to be changed. This induces a necessity to act that activates relevant expectations that in turn determine the strength of commitment to fantasy realization. The second route involves merely fantasizing about a positive future (indulging). Unfortunately, such indulgences only lead one to mentally enjoy the desired future in the here and now. In this case, a necessity to act is not induced, and expectations of success are not activated. Finally, the third route involves reflecting on negative realities, but such dwellings wind up being merely ruminative. Once again, a necessity to act is not induced, and expectations are not activated. Overall, the superiority of mental contrasting to indulging and dwelling with regard to increasing goal pursuit and enhancing performance has been documented in many studies and across many contexts (e.g. Oettingen, 2000; Oettingen, Hönig, & Gollwitzer, 2000; Oettingen et al., 2001, 2009; Oettingen, Mayer, Thorpe, Janetzke, & Lorenz, 2005).

In sum, it appears that human beings need to look back in order to look ahead because thoughts about the future emerge from a blend of episodic and semantic memories. Moreover, prospective thinking can become biased, as when individuals inflate their beliefs about the probability of certain outcomes and mispredict how they are going to feel about those outcomes in the future. Fortunately, however, these biases can be counteracted. The effect of explanations on biasing predictions can be attenuated by considering alternatives, and attending to input from the experiential system can minimize affective forecasting errors. More generally, human beings spend a lot of time thinking about the future, and this appears to be the case because prospective simulation is functional. As long as they are contrasted against obstacles in reality that might stand in the way, such simulations are a critical impetus for goal setting and goal commitment. Without mentally simulating the future, we could not make goals for the future.

Conclusion

Although this chapter focused on work examining prospective and retrospective mental simulations, we would be remiss in not pointing out that a great deal of research has also focused on mental simulation in the present. For instance, recent neuropsychological work on empathy (e.g., Decety & Jackson, 2004, 2006; Jeannerod, 1994; Lamm, Batson, & Decety, 2007) demonstrating that the same neurons involved in acting are also involved in *simulating* those actions provides further evidence of the powerful connection between mental simulation and action. Likewise, visual imagery has been shown to exert significant effects on behavior (for a review, see Kosslyn & Moulton, 2009). Revealing what is being simulated or imagined in the brain would seem to offer much with regard to furthering our understanding of the role that mental simulations play in creating action, and why some simulations might be more effective than others.

Even though mental simulations can become biased, they are functional in many respects. Although past research focused on the negative emotional consequences of counterfactual simulations, more recent research has demonstrated their motivational value. Mental simulations of past failures, though at times emotionally painful, allow us nevertheless to recognize our mistakes and potentially identify avenues by which we can improve on them in the future. And, in kind, mental simulations of the future allow us to set and commit to goals, enhancing goal directed persistence and performance. When contrasted against obstacles that might stand in our way, mental simulations are absolutely necessary for effective goal formation and pursuit, energizing us to try harder and perform better than we did before.

References

Addis, D. R., Wong, A. T., & Schacter, D. L. (2007). Remembering the past and imagining the future: Common and distinct neural substrates during event construction and elaboration. *Neuropsychologia, 45,* 1363–1377.

Alicke, M. (2000). Culpable control and the psychology of blame. *Psychological Bulletin, 126,* 556–574.

Anderson, C. A. (1983). Abstract and concrete data in the perseverance of social theories: When weak data lead to unshakable beliefs. *Journal of Experimental Social Psychology, 19,* 93–108.

Anderson, C. A., Lepper, M. R., & Ross, L. (1980). Perseverance of social theories: The role of explanation in the persistence of discredited information. *Journal of Personality and Social Psychology, 39,* 1037–1049.

Anderson, C. A., New, B. L., & Speer, J. R. (1985). Argument availability as a mediator of social theory perseverance. *Social Cognition, 3,* 235–249.

Atance, C. M., & O'Neill, D. K. (2001). Episodic future thinking. *Trends in Cognitive Science, 5,* 533–539.

Bernstein, D. M., Godfrey, R. D., & Loftus, E. F. (2009). False memories: The role of plausibility and autobiographical belief. In K. D. Markman, W. M. P. Klein, & J. A. Suhr (Eds.), *The handbook of imagination and mental simulation* (pp. 89–102). New York: Psychology Press.

Boninger, D. S., Gleicher, F., & Strathman, A. (1994). Counterfactual thinking: From what might have been to what might be. *Journal of Personality and Social Psychology, 67,* 297–307.

Branscombe, N., Crosby, P., & Weir, J. A. (1993). Social inferences concerning male and female homeowners who use a gun to shoot an intruder. *Aggressive Behavior, 19,* 113–124.

Branscombe, N. R., & Weir, J. A. (1992). Resistance to stereotype-inconsistency: Consequences for judgments of rape victims. *Journal of Social and Clinical Psychology, 11,* 80–102.

Buckner, R. L., & Carroll, D. C. (2007). Self-projection and the brain. *Trends in Cognitive Science, 11,* 49–57.

Buehler, R., & McFarland, C. (2001). Intensity bias in affective forecasting: The role of temporal focus. *Personality and Social Psychology Bulletin, 27,* 1480–1493.

Carroll, J. S., (1978). The effect of imagining an event on expectations for the event: An interpretation in terms of the availability heuristic. *Journal of Experimental Social Psychology, 14,* 88–96.

Chen, P. W., & Novick, L. R. (1990). Causes versus enabling conditions. *Journal of Personality and Social Psychology, 58,* 545–567.

Collins, R. L. (1996). For better or for worse: The impact of upward social comparison on self-evaluations. *Psychological Bulletin, 119,* 51–69.

Corballis, M. (2003). Recursion is the key to the human mind. In K. Sterelny & J. Finess (Eds.), *From mating to mentality: Evaluating evolutionary psychology* (pp. 155–171). New York: Psychology Press.

Davis, C. G., Lehman, D. R., Silver, R. C., Wortman, C. B., & Ellard, J. H. (1996). Self-blame following a traumatic life event: The role of perceived avoidability. *Personality and Social Psychology Bulletin, 22,* 557–567.

Decety, J., & Jackson, P. (2004). The functional architecture of human empathy. *Behavioral and Cognitive Neuroscience Reviews, 3,* 71–100.

Decety, J., & Jackson, P. (2006). A social neuroscience perspective on empathy. *Current Directions in Psychological Science, 12,* 406–411.

Dunn, E. W., Biesanz, J. C., Human, L. J., & Finn, S. (2007). Misunderstanding the affective consequences of everyday social interactions: The hidden benefits of putting one's best face forward. *Journal of Personality and Social Psychology, 92,* 990–1005.

Dunn, E. W., Brackett, M.A., Ashton-James, C., Schneiderman, E., & Salovey, P. (2009). On emotionally intelligent time travel: Individual differences in affective forecasting ability. *Personality and Social Psychology Bulletin, 33,* 85–93.

Dunn, E. W., Forrin, N. D., & Ashton-James, C. E. (2009). On the excessive rationality of the emotional imagination: A two systems account of affective forecasts and experiences. In K. D. Markman, W. M. P. Klein, & J. A. Suhr (Eds.), *The handbook of imagination and mental simulation* (pp. 331–346). New York: Psychology Press.

Durso, F. T., & Johnson, M. K. (1980). The effects of orienting tasks on recognition, recall, and modality confusion of pictures and words. *Journal of Verbal Learning and Verbal Behavior, 19,* 416–429.

Epstein, S. (1994). Integration of the cognitive and the psychodynamic unconscious. *American Psychologist, 49,* 709–724.

Epstein, S. (1998). Cognitive-experiential self-theory. In D. F. Barone, M. Hersen, & V. B. Van Hasselt (Eds.), *Advanced personality* (pp. 211–238). New York: Plenum Press.

Epstude, K., & Roese, N. J. (2008). The functional theory of counterfactual thinking. *Personality and Social Psychology Bulletin, 12,* 168–192.

Fazio, R. H. (1990). Multiple processes by which attitudes guide behavior: The MODE model as an integrative framework. In M. P. Zanna (Ed.), *Advances in experimental social psychology* (Vol. 23, pp. 75–109). New York: Academic Press.

Fischhoff, B. (1975). Hindsight does not equal foresight: The effect of outcome knowledge on judgment under uncertainty. *Journal of Experimental Psychology: Human Perception and Performance, 1,* 288–299.

Fischhoff, B. (1976). The effect of temporal setting on likelihood estimates. *Organizational Behavior and Human Decision Processes, 15,* 180–194.

Fischhoff, B. (1982). Debiasing. In D. Kahneman, P. Slovic, & A. Tversky (Eds.), *Judgment under uncertainty: Heuristics and biases* (pp. 422–444). Cambridge, UK: Cambridge University Press.

Fredrickson, B. L., & Kahneman, D. (1993). Duration neglect in retrospective evaluations of affective episodes. *Journal of Personality and Social Psychology, 65,* 45–55.

Galinsky, A. D., & Kray, L. J. (2004). From thinking about what might have been to sharing what we know: The effects of counterfactual mind-sets on information sharing in groups. *Journal of Experimental Social Psychology, 36,* 257–383.

Galinsky, A. D., & Moskowitz, G. B. (2000). Counterfactuals as behavioral primes: Priming the simulation heuristic and consideration of alternatives. *Journal of Experimental Social Psychology, 36,* 257–383.

Gilbert, D. T., Gill, M. J., & Wilson, D. T. (2002). The future is now: Temporal correction in affective forecasting. *Organizational Behavior and Human Decision Processes, 88,* 690–700.

Gilbert, D. T., Morewedge, C. K., Risen, J. L., & Wilson, T. D. (2004). Looking forward to looking backward: The misprediction of regret. *Psychological Science, 15,* 346–350.

Gilbert, D. T., Pinel, E. C., Wilson, T. D., Blumberg, S. J., & Wheatley, T. P. (1998). Immune neglect: A source of durability bias in affective forecasting. *Journal of Personality and Social Psychology, 75,* 617–638.

Gilbert, D. T., & Wilson, T. D. (2007). Prospection: Experiencing the future. *Science, 317,* 1351–1354.

Goff, L. M., & Roediger, H. L. III (1998). Imagination inflation for action events: Repeated imaginings lead to illusory recollections. *Memory & Cognition, 26,* 20–33.

Gollwitzer, P. M. (1993). Goal and achievement: The role of intentions. In W. Stroebe & M. Hewstone (Eds.), *European review of social psychology* (Vol. 4, pp. 141–185). Chichester, UK: Wiley.

Gollwitzer, P. M. (1999). Implementation intentions: Strong effects of simple plans. *American Psychologist, 54,* 493–503.

Gollwitzer, P. M., Heckhausen, H., & Steller, B. (1990). Deliberative and implemental mind-sets: Cognitive tuning toward congruous thoughts and information. *Journal of Personality and Social Psychology, 59,* 1119–1127.

Gollwitzer, P. M., & Moskowitz, G. B. (1996). Goal effects on action and cognition. In E. T. Higgins, & A. W. Kruglanski (Eds.), *Social psychology: Handbook of basic principles* (pp. 361–399). New York: Guilford Press.

Gollwitzer, P. M., & Sheeran, P. (2006). Implementation intentions and goal achievement: A meta-analysis of effects and processes. *Advances in Experimental Social Psychology, 38,* 69–119.

Green, M. C., & Brock, T. C. (2000). The role of transportation in the persuasiveness of public narratives. *Journal of Personality and Social Psychology, 79,* 701–721.

Guilford, J. P. (1950). Creativity. *American Psychologist, 5,* 444–454.

Hawkins, S. A., & Hastie, R. (1990). Hindsight: Biases judgments of past events after the outcomes are known. *Psychological Bulletin, 107,* 311–327.

Helson, H. (1964). *Adaptation-level theory.* New York: Harper.

Hilton, D. J., & Slugoski, B. R. (1986). Knowledge-based causal attribution: The abnormal conditions focus model. *Psychological Review, 93,* 75–88.

Hirt, E. R., Kardes, F. R., & Markman, K. D. (2004). Activating a mental simulation mind-set through generation of alternatives: Implications for debiasing in related and unrelated domains. *Journal of Experimental Social Psychology, 40,* 374–383.

Hirt, E. R., & Markman, K. D. (1995). Multiple explanation: A consider-an-alternative strategy for debiasing judgments. *Journal of Personality and Social Psychology, 69,* 1069–1086.

Hirt, E. R., & Sherman, S. J. (1985). The role of prior knowledge in explaining hypothetical events. *Journal of Experimental Social Psychology, 21,* 519–543.

Hoch, S. J. (1985). Counterfactual reasoning and accuracy in predicting personal events. *Journal of Experimental Psychology: Learning, Memory, and Cognition, 11,* 719–731.

Hoerger, M., Quirk, S. W., Lucas, R. E., & Carr, T. H. (2009). Immune neglect in affective forecasting. *Journal of Research in Personality, 43,* 91–94.

Hofstadter, D. R. (1985). *Metamagical themas.* New York: Basic Books.

Jeannerod, M. (1994). The representing brain: Neural correlates of motor intention and imagery. *Behavioral and Brain Sciences, 17,* 187–202.

Johnson, M. K., & Raye, C. L. (1981). Reality monitoring. *Psychological Review, 88,* 67–85.

Johnson, M. K., Raye, C. L., Wang, A. Y., & Taylor, T. H. (1979) Fact and fantasy: The roles of accuracy and variability in confusing imaginations with perceptual experiences. *Journal of Experimental Psychology: Human Learning and Memory, 5,* 229–240.

Johnson, M. K., & Sherman, S. J. (1990). Constructing and reconstructing the past and future in the present. In E. T. Higgins & R. M. Sorrentino (Eds.), *Handbook of motivation and social cognition: Foundations of social behavior* (pp. 482–526). New York: Guilford Press.

Johnson, M. K., Taylor, T. H., & Raye, C. L. (1977). Fact and fantasy: The effects of internally generated events on the apparent frequency of externally generated events. *Memory & Cognition, 5,* 116–122.

Klein, S. B., Loftus, J., & Kihlstrom, J. F. (2002). Memory and temporal experience: The effects of episodic memory loss on an amnesic patient's ability to remember the past and imagine the future. *Social Cognition, 20,* 353–379.

Kosslyn, S. M., & Moulton, S. T. (2009). Mental imagery and implicit memory. In K. D. Markman, W. M. P. Klein, & J. A. Suhr (Eds.), *The handbook of imagination and mental simulation* (pp. 35–52) New York: Psychology Press.

Kray, L. J., & Galinsky, A. D. (2003). The debiasing effect of counterfactual mind-sets: Increase the search for disconfirmatory information in group decisions. *Organizational Behavior and Human Decision Processes, 91,* 69–81.

Kulpe, O. (1904). Versuche uber Abstraktion. In, *Bericht uber den erste Kongress fur experimentelle Psychologie* (pp. 56–68). Leipzig: Barth.

Lamm, C., Batson, C. D., & Decety, J. (2007). The neural substrate of human empathy: Effects of perspective-taking and cognitive appraisal. *Journal of Cognitive Neuroscience, 19,* 42–58.

Landman, J. (1993). *Regret: The persistence of the possible.* New York: Oxford University Press.

Lecci, L., Okun, M., & Karoly, P. (1994). Life regrets and current goals as predictors of psychological adjustment. *Journal of Personality and Social Psychology, 66,* 731–741.

Lipe, M. G. (1991). Counterfactual reasoning as a framework for attribution theories. *Psychological Bulletin, 109,* 456–471.

Kahneman, D., & Miller, D. T. (1986). Norm theory: Comparing reality to its alternatives. *Psychological Review, 93,* 136–153.

Kahneman, D., & Tversky, A. (1982). The simulation heuristic. In D. Kahneman, P. Slovic & A. Tversky (Eds.), *Judgment under uncertainty: Heuristics and biases* (pp. 201–208). Cambridge, UK: Cambridge University Press.

Koehler, D. J. (1991). Explanation, imagination, and confidence in judgment. *Psychological Bulletin, 110,* 499–519.

Koriat, A., Lichtenstein, S., & Fischhoff, B. (1980). Reasons for confidence. *Journal of Experimental Psychology: Human Learning and Memory, 6,* 107–118.

Kray, L. J., & Galinsky, A. D. (2003). The debiasing effect of counterfactual mind-sets: Increasing the search for disconfirmatory information in group decisions. *Organizational and Human Decision Processes, 91,* 69–81.

Kray, L. J., & Galinsky, A. D., & Markman, K. D. (2009). Counterfactual structure and learning from experience in negotiations. *Journal of Experimental Social Psychology, 45,* 979–982.

Kray, L. J., & Galinsky, A. D., & Wong, E. M. (2006). Thinking within the box: The relational processing style elicited by counterfactual mind-sets. *Journal of Personality and Social Psychology, 91,* 33–48.

Landman, J., & Petty, R. (2000). "It could have been you": How states exploit counterfactual thought to market lotteries. *Psychology and Marketing, 17,* 299–321.

Larsen, J. T., McGraw, A. P., Mellers, B. A., & Cacioppo, J. T. (2004). The agony of victory and the thrill of defeat: Mixed emotional reactions to disappointing wins and relieving losses. *Psychological Science, 15,* 325–330.

Lerner, J. S., & Tetlock, P. E. (1999). Accounting for the effects of accountability. *Psychological Bulletin, 125,* 255–275.

Loewenstein, G. F., & Schkade, D. (1999). Wouldn't it be nice? Predicting future feelings. In D. Kahneman, E. Diener, & N. Schwarz (Eds.), *Well-being: The foundations of hedonic psychology* (pp. 85–105). New York: Russell Sage Foundation.

Loewenstein, G., O' Donoghue, T., & Rabin, M. (2003). Projection bias in predicting future utility. *Quarterly Journal of Economics, 118,* 1209–1248.

Loewenstein, G., Prelec, D., & Shatto, C. (1998). *Hot/cold intrapersonal empathy gaps and the underprediction of curiosity.* Unpublished manuscript, Carnegie Mellon University, Pittsburg, PA.

Lockwood, P., Jordan, C. H., & Kunda, Z. (2002). Motivation by positive or negative role models: Regulatory focus determines who will best inspire us. *Journal of Personality and Social Psychology, 83,* 854–864.

Lord, C. G., Lepper, M. R., & Preston, E. (1984). Considering the opposite: A corrective strategy for social judgment. *Journal of Personality and Social Psychology, 47,* 1231–1243.

Maguire, E. A. (2001). Neuroimaging studies of autobiographical event memories. *Philosophical Transactions of the Royal Society, 356,* 1441–1451.

Mandel, D. R. (2003). Judgment dissociation theory: An analysis of differences in causal, counterfactual and covariational reasoning. *Journal of Experimental Psychology: General, 137,* 419–434.

Mandel, D. R. (2005). Are risk assessments of a terrorist attack coherent? *Journal of Experimental Psychology: Applied, 11,* 277–288.

Mandel, D. R., & Lehman, D. R. (1996). Counterfactual thinking and ascriptions of cause and preventability. *Journal of Personality and Social Psychology, 71,* 450–463.

Markman, K. D., & Beike, D. R. (2012). Regret, consistency, and choice: An opportunity X mitigation framework. In B. Gawronski & F. Strack (Eds.), *Cognitive consistency: A fundamental principle in social cognition* (pp. 305–325). New York: Guilford Press.

Markman, K. D., Elizaga, R. A., Ratcliff, J. J., & McMullen, M. N. (2007). The interplay between counterfactual reasoning and feedback dynamics in producing inferences about the self. *Thinking and Reasoning, 13,* 188–206.

Markman, K. D., Gavanski, I., Sherman, S. J., & McMullen, M. N. (1993). The mental simulation of better and worse possible worlds. *Journal of Experimental Social Psychology, 29,* 87–109.

Markman, K. D., Lindberg, M. J., Kray, L. J., & Galinsky, A. D. (2007). Implications of counterfactual structure for creative generation and analytical problem solving. *Personality and Social Psychology Bulletin, 33,* 312–314.

Markman, K. D., & McMullen, M. N. (2003). A reflection and evaluation model of comparative thinking. *Personality and Social Psychology Review, 7,* 244–267.

Markman, K. D., & McMullen, M. N. (2005). Reflective and evaluative modes of mental simulation. In D. R. Mandel, D. J. Hilton, & P. Catellani (Eds.), *The psychology of counterfactual thinking* (pp. 77–93). London: Routledge.

Markman, K. D., McMullen, M. N., & Elizaga, R. (2008). Counterfactual thinking, persistence and performance:

A test of the reflection and evaluation model. *Journal of Experimental Social Psychology, 44,* 421–428.

Markman, K. D., & Tetlock, P. E. (2000). Accountability and close-call counterfactuals: The loser who nearly won and the winner who nearly lost. *Personality and Social Psychology Bulletin, 26,* 1213–1224.

McGill, A. L. (1989). Context effects in judgments of causation. *Journal of Personality and Social Psychology, 57,* 189–200.

McMullen, M. N. (1997). Affective contrast and assimilation in counterfactual thinking. *Journal of Experimental Social Psychology, 33,* 77–100.

McMullen, M. N., & Markman, K. D. (2000). Downward counterfactual and motivation: The wake-up call and the Pangloss effect. *Personality and Social Psychology Bulletin, 26,* 575–584.

McMullen, M. N., & Markman, K. D. (2002). Affect and close counterfactuals: Implications of possible futures for possible pasts. *Journal of Experimental Social Psychology, 38,* 64–70.

McMullen, M. N., Markman, K. D., & Gavanski, I. (1995). Living in neither the best nor worst of all possible worlds: Antecedents and consequences of upward and downward counterfactual thinking. In N. J. Roese & J. M. Olson (Eds.), *What might have been: The social psychology of counterfactual thinking* (pp. 133–167). Hillsdale, NJ: Erlbaum.

Medvec, V. H., Madey, S. F., & Gilovich, T. (1995). When less is more: Counterfactual thinking and satisfaction among Olympic medalists. *Journal of Personality and Social Psychology, 69,* 603–610.

Medvec, V. H., & Savitsky, K. K. (1997). When doing better means feeling worse. *Journal of Personality and Social Psychology, 72,* 1284–1296.

Mellers, B. A., Schwartz, A., Ho, K., & Ritov, I. (1997). Decision affect theory: Emotional reactions to the outcomes of risky options. *Psychological Science, 8,* 423–429.

Miller, D. T., & McFarland, C. (1986). Counterfactual thinking and victim compensation: A test of norm theory. *Personality and Social Psychology Bulletin, 12,* 513–519.

Niedenthal, P. M., Tangney, J. P., & Gavanksi, I. (1994). "If only I weren't" versus "If only I hadn't": Distinguishing shame and guilt in counterfactual thinking. *Journal of Personality and Social Psychology, 67,* 584–595.

Nestler, S., & von Collani, G. (2008). Hindsight bias and the activation of counterfactual mind-sets. *Experimental Psychology, 55,* 342–349.

Nolan, C. (Producer & Director). (2010). *Inception* [Motion Picture]. United States: Warner Bros.

Oettingen, G. (2000). Expectancy effects on behavior depend on self-regulatory thought. *Social Cognition, 18,* 101–129.

Oettingen, G., Hönig, G., & Gollwitzer, P. M. (2000). Effective self-regulation of goal attainment. *International Journal of Education Research, 33,* 705–732.

Oettingen, G., Mayer, D., Sevincer, A. T., Stephens, E. J., Pak, H., & Hagenah, M. (2009). Mental contrasting and goal commitment: The mediating role of energization. *Personality and Social Psychology Bulletin, 35,* 608–622.

Oettingen, G., Mayer, D., Thorpe, J. S., Janetzke, H., & Lorenz, S. (2005). Turning fantasies about positive and negative futures into self-improvement goals. *Motivation and Emotion, 29,* 237–267.

Oettingen, G., Pak, H., & Schnetter, K. (2001). Self-regulation of goal setting: Turning free fantasies about the future into binding goals. *Journal of Personality and Social Psychology, 80,* 736–753.

Okuda, J., Fujii, T., Ohtake, H., Tsukiura, T., Tanji, K., Suzuki, K., et al. (2003). Thinking of future and past: The roles of the frontal pole and the medial temporal lobes. *Neuroimage, 19,* 1369–1380.

Pham, L., & Taylor, S. (1999). From thought to action: Effects of process- versus outcome-based mental simulations on performance. *Personality and Social Psychology Bulletin, 25,* 250–260.

Raichle, M. E., MacLeod, A.M., Snyder, A. Z., Powers, W. J., Gusnard, D. A., & Shulman, G. L. (2001). A default mode of brain function. *Proceedings of the National Academy of Sciences USA, 98,* 676–682.

Roese, N. J. (1994). The functional basis of counterfactual thinking. *Journal of Personality and Social Psychology, 66,* 805–818.

Roese, N. J. (1997). Counterfactual thinking. *Psychological Bulletin, 121,* 133–148.

Roese, N. J. (2004). Twisted pair: Counterfactual thinking and the hindsight bias. In D. Koehler & N. Harvey (Eds.), *Blackwell handbook of judgment and decision making* (pp. 258–273). Oxford, UK: Blackwell.

Roese, N. J., & Hur, T. (1997). Affective determinants of counterfactual thinking. *Social Cognition, 15,* 274–290.

Roese, N. J., & Maniar, S. D. (1997). Perceptions of purple: Counterfactual and hindsight judgments at Northwester Wildcats football games. *Personality and Social Psychology Bulletin, 23,* 1245–1253.

Roese, N. J., & Olson, J. M. (1993). The structure of counterfactual thought. *Personality and Social Psychology Bulletin, 19,* 312–319.

Roese, N. J., & Olson, J. M. (1995). Counterfactual thinking: A critical overview. In N. J. Roese & J. M. Olson (Eds.), *What might have been: The social psychology of counterfactual thinking* (pp. 1–55). Mahwah, NJ: Erlbaum.

Roese, N. J., & Olson, J. M. (1996). Counterfactuals, causal attributions, and the hindsight bias: A conceptual integration. *Journal of Experimental Social Psychology, 32,* 197–227.

Ross, L., Lepper, M. R., Strack, F., & Steinmetz, J. (1977). Social explanation and social expectation: Effects of real and hypothetical explanations on subjective likelihood. *Journal of Personality and Social Psychology, 35,* 817–829.

Salovey, P., & Mayer, J. D. (1990). Emotional intelligence. *Imagination, Cognition, and Personality, 9,* 185–211.

Sanna, L. J. (1996). Defensive pessimism, optimism, and simulating alternatives: Some ups and downs of prefactual and counterfactual thinking. *Journal of Personality and Social Psychology, 71,* 1020–1036.

Sanna, L. J. (1997). Self-efficacy and counterfactual thinking: Up a creek with and without a paddle. *Personality and Social Psychology Bulletin, 23,* 654–666.

Sanna, L. J., & Schwarz, N. (2003). Debiasing hindsight: The role of accessibility experiences and attributions. *Journal of Experimental Social Psychology, 39,* 287–295.

Sanna, L. J., Schwarz, N., & Stocker, S. L. (2002). When debiasing backfires: Accessible content and accessibility experiences in debiasing hindsight. *Journal of Experimental Psychology: Learning, Memory, and Cognition, 28,* 497–502.

Sanna, L.J., Turley-Ames, K.J., & Meier, S. (1999). Mood, self-esteem, and simulated alternatives: Thought provoking affective influences on counterfactual direction. *Journal of Personality and Social Psychology, 76,* 543–558.

Schacter, D. L., & Addis, D. R. (2007). The cognitive neuroscience of constructive memory: Remembering the past and imagining the future. *Philosophical Transactions of the Royal Society B: Biological Sciences, 362,* 773–786.

Schacter, D. L., Addis, D. R., & Buckner, R. (2008). Episodic simulation of future events: Concepts, data and applications. *Annals of the New York Academy of Sciences, 1124,* 39–60.

Schkade, D. A., & Kahneman, D. (1998). Does living in California make people happy? A focusing illusion in judgments of life satisfaction. *Psychological Science, 9,* 340–346.

Schwarz, N. (1998). Accessible content and accessibility experiences: The interplay of declarative and experiential information in judgment. *Personality and Social Psychology Review, 2,* 87–99.

Schwarz, N., & Clore, G. L. (1983). Mood, misattribution, and judgments of well-being: Informative and directive functions of affective states. *Journal of Personality and Social Psychology, 45,* 513–523.

Schwarz, N., & Vaughn, L. A. (2002). The availability heuristic revisited: Recalled content and ease of recall as information. In T. Gilovich, D. Griffin, & D. Kahneman (Eds.), *Heuristics and biases: New perspectives on judgment under uncertainty* (pp. 103–119). Cambridge, UK: Cambridge University Press.

Seamon, J. G., Philbin, M. M., Harrison, L. G. (2006). Do you remember promising marriage to the Pepsi machine? False recollections from a campus walk. *Psychonomic Bulletin and Review, 13,* 752–756.

Sharman, S. J., Manning, C. G., & Garry, M. (2005). Explain this: Explaining childhood events inflates confidence for those events. *Applied Cognitive Psychology, 19,* 67–74.

Sherman, S. J. (1991). Thought systems for the past as well as for the future. In R. S. Wyer, Jr., & T. K. Srull (Eds.), *Advances in social cognition* (Vol. 4, pp. 173–195). Hillsdale, NJ: Erlbaum.

Sherman, S. J., Cialdini, R. B., Schwartzman, D. F., & Reynolds, K. D. (1985). Imagining can heighten or lower the perceived likelihood of contracting a disease: The mediating effect of ease of imagery. *Personality and Social Psychology Bulletin, 11,* 118–127.

Sherman, S. J., Skov, R. B., Hervits, E. F., & Stock, C. B. (1981). The effects of explaining hypothetical future events: From possibility to probability to actuality and beyond. *Journal of Experimental Social Psychology, 17,* 142–158.

Sherman, S. J., Zehner, K. S., Johnson, J., & Hirt, E. R. (1983). Social explanation: The role of timing, set, and recall on subjective likelihood estimates. *Journal of Personality and Social Psychology, 44,* 1127–1143.

Smallman, R., & Roese, N. J. (2009). Counterfactual thinking facilitates behavioral intentions. *Journal of Experimental Social Psychology, 45,* 845–852.

Suddendorf, T., & Corballis, M. C. (1997). *Mental time travel and the evolution of the human mind.* New York: Basic Books.

Szpunar, K. K., Watson, J. M., & McDermott, K. B. (2007). Neural substrates of envisioning the future. *Proceedings of the National Academy of Sciences USA, 104,* 642–647.

Taylor, S. E. (1991). Asymmetrical effects of positive and negative events: The mobilization-minimization hypothesis. *Psychological Bulletin, 110,* 67–85.

Taylor, S. E., Buunk, B. P., & Aspinwall, L. (1990). Social comparison, stress and coping. *Personality and Social Psychology Bulletin, 16,* 74–89.

Taylor, S., & Pham, L. (1999). The effect of mental simulation on goal-directed performance. In Sheikh, A. (Ed.), *Imagery and Human Development.* New York, NY: Baywood.

Taylor, S. E., & Schneider, S. K. (1989). Coping and the simulation of events. *Social Cognition, 7,* 176–196.

Teigen, K. H. (2005). When a small difference makes a big difference: Counterfactual thinking and luck. In D. R. Mandel, D. J. Hilton, & P. Catellani (Eds.), *The psychology of counterfactual thinking* (pp. 129–146). Oxon, UK: Routledge.

Tetlock, P. E. (1983). Accountability and complexity of thought. *Journal of Personality and Social Psychology, 45,* 74–83

Tetlock, P. E. (1998). Close-call counterfactual and belief-system defense: I was not almost wrong, but I was almost right. *Journal of Personality and Social Psychology, 75,* 639–652.

Thibaut, J. W., & Kelley, H. H. (1959) *The social psychology of groups.* New York: Free Press.

Tulving, E. (1972). Episodic and semantic memory. In E. Tulving & W. Donaldson (Eds.), *Organization of memory* (pp. 381–403). New York: Academic Press.

Tulving, E. (1985). How many memory systems are there? *American Psychologist, 40,* 385–398.

Tversky, A., & Kahneman, D. (1973). Availability: A heuristic for judging frequency and probability. *Cognitive Psychology, 5,* 207–232.

Van Boven, L., & Loewenstein, G. (2003). Social projection of transient drive states. *Personality and Social Psychology Bulletin, 29,* 1159–1168.

Wells, G. L., & Gavanski, I. (1989). Mental simulation of causality. *Journal of Personality and Social Psychology, 56,* 161–169.

Wohl, M. J. A., & Enzle, M. E. (2003). The effects of near wins and near losses on self-perceived personal luck and subsequent gambling behavior. *Journal of Experimental Social Psychology, 39,* 184–191.

Wilson, T. D., Wheatley, T. P., Meyers, J. M., Gilbert, D. T., & Axsom, D. (2000). Focalism: A source of the durability bias in affective forecasting. *Journal of Personality and Social Psychology, 78,* 821–836.

Wood, J. V. (1989). Theory and research concerning social comparison of personal attributes. *Psychological Bulletin, 106,* 231–248.

Zeelenberg, M. (1999). The use of crying over spilt milk: A note on the rationality and functionality of regret. *Philosophical Psychology, 12,* 325–340.

Thought Suppression

Sadia Najmi

Abstract

Thought suppression is the conscious attempt to not think about something. More than two decades of experimental investigation of this topic reveal that this mental control strategy can be successful for short periods of time. But for the most part, the strategy is not simply ineffective but rather produces the exact opposite of the intended outcome. This chapter reviews extant research on thought suppression. It describes the nature of the unintended effects of suppression and the theory underlying these effects. Next, it focuses on the suppression of particularly unacceptable thoughts, and on individual differences in ability to suppress, followed by a brief review of the vast literature on suppression and psychopathology. The chapter concludes with a summary of findings and a recommendation to turn the focus of research in this area from the failures of suppression to the conditions under which suppression might be effective in a sustainable way.

Key Words: suppression, thought suppression, ironic process theory, mental control, cognitive control

"Try to pose for yourself this task: not to think of a polar bear, and you will see that the cursed thing will come to mind every minute." This observation that Fyodor Dostoevsky (1995) made in *Winter Notes on Summer Impressions* inspired a century later what is commonly referred to as the white bear study, which in turn has spawned more than two decades of experimental investigation on the topic of thought suppression. In the original white bear study, Dan Wegner and colleagues (Wegner, Schneider, Carter, & White, 1987) asked participants to think out loud. Half of these participants formed an initial suppression group in that they were instructed to suppress the thought of a white bear for 5 minutes. Next, they were given expression instructions, that is, they were asked to think about a white bear for 5 minutes. The other half of participants received instructions in the reversed order;

that is, they first engaged in expression and then in suppression. All participants were instructed to ring a bell whenever they thought of the white bear. On average, people instructed to suppress thoughts of a white bear mentioned it about once per minute. During the expression period, it appeared that participants who had suppressed the thought earlier mentioned it almost continuously, in fact much more than did those who had been asked to think about the white bear from the start. This simple experiment made two vital points: (1) It is difficult to suppress a thought completely, and (2) suppression can lead to a postsuppression rebound of the target thought. In the sections that follow, I review what we have learned from the experimental study of thought suppression since these two points were first noted, and conclude with some thoughts on where this research might be headed in the future.

What Is Thought Suppression and What Is It Not?

According to Wegner (1994), successful suppression is achieved by increasing the accessibility of distracter thoughts. Usually, when people try to suppress thoughts, they tend to do so using an *unfocused* distraction strategy, that is, they use many different distracters iteratively instead of focusing on one distracter thought. The rebound of the suppressed thought occurs after people use this unfocused distraction strategy (Wegner, Schneider, Knutson, & McMahon, 1991). However, the use of a *focused* distracter thought can eliminate, or at least attenuate, the rebound effect. In a much less famous second study in the original white bear article, Wegner et al. (Experiment 2, 1987) found that focused distraction can indeed result in successful suppression of unwanted thoughts. For example, in their study, participants were quite effective at suppressing thoughts of a white bear if they focused instead on thoughts of a red Volkswagen. Throughout this chapter, unless otherwise stated, suppression is considered to be by means of *unfocused* distraction.

Given the abundance of seemingly related constructs in the literature (e.g., expressive suppression, Gross, 1998; repression, Freud, 1896; directed forgetting, Anderson, 2005; inhibition, Anderson and Levy, 2009), it is important to clarify at the outset what is meant by suppression in this chapter. The focus of this chapter is thought suppression, the conscious attempt to not think about something. Expressive suppression (Gross, 1998) is the conscious attempt to inhibit the outward expression of emotion. Research shows that this strategy does not alleviate the subjective experience of the emotion. Instead, suppression of emotional expression is associated with an increase in sympathetic arousal. Thus, although the outcomes of expressive suppression and thought suppression might be similar in that they (ironically) heighten the concomitant emotion, the two strategies are distinct.

Another construct seemingly related to thought suppression is the Freudian notion of repression. Although Freud initially argued that repression occurs unconsciously, he often used the terms *repression* and *suppression* interchangeably, stating that repression may be both conscious and unconscious (Erdelyi, 2006). Thought suppression, on the other hand, is defined specifically as the *conscious* attempt to not think of something. Moreover, Freud (1950) described the counter-will: "the antithetic idea gains the upper hand as a result of general exhaustion" (p. 125). This is consistent with Wegner's (1994)

findings that unwanted thoughts surface when a person is under cognitive load. Whereas Freud went on to attribute the reduction in mental capacity to repressed sexual and aggressive conflicts, evidence from suppression research reveals that mental capacity can be reduced by more mundane things (e.g., time pressures, stress, concurrent tasks).

Directed forgetting is another method related to putting material out of consciousness (e.g., Brewin & Andrews, 1998). In a directed forgetting task, participants are presented with words and are instructed either to remember or to forget these words. A surprise recall of all the words follows to assess memory for both the to-be-remembered words and the to-be-forgotten words. The typical result is that participants recall fewer of the to-be-forgotten words than of the to-be-remembered words (Bjork, Bjork & Anderson, 1998). Whereas directed forgetting tasks are aimed at forgetting several words that are usually unrelated to each other, thought suppression methods are aimed at forgetting a single piece of information. Results of these two types of studies suggest that it is easier to forget several unrelated words but a single thought is difficult to suppress.

In 2009, Anderson and Levy argued that memories can be suppressed effectively using mechanisms similar to those used to inhibit reflexive motor responses. To study how we inhibit the retrieval of memories, Anderson and Green (2001) developed the think/no-think task, modeled after the Go/N-Go Task that is used to study motor inhibition. In the think/no-think task, during the training phase, participants study unrelated cue–target word pairs and are trained to recall the second word whenever they see the first word. Next, in the think/no-think phase of the study, participants are asked think of the second word when they see the first word, but only for some of the words ("think" words); for other words ("no think" words), they are asked to not think of the second word when they see the first word. Finally, participants are shown the cue words and are asked to recall every target word that they had earlier learned. The typical result is that participants recall fewer of "no think" words than "think" words. The inclusion of a third set of control word pairs—which appear in the training phase but do not appear in the think/no-think phase—shows that there is indeed enhanced memory for "think" words and impaired memory for "no think" words, relative to the control words. The authors conclude that when we try to not be reminded of something, the reminders not only fail to boost memory but also trigger inhibitory processes that actually weaken memory.

This conclusion is the opposite of what the thought suppression research would predict. According to Levy and Anderson (2008), this difference could be explained by the different way in which the tasks are structured. For instance, in the thought suppression paradigm, the only way participants know whether or not they are on task is to remind themselves of the suppression target ("Am I thinking about the white bears right now?") but this is not so in the think/no-think task. Additionally, the authors suggest that another potential difference between the two tasks might have to do with the specificity of reminders: In the think/no-think task, the participant has to suppress a thought (i.e., the thought of a target word) related to a specific reminder (i.e., the cue specific to that target), whereas in the thought suppression task, the participant has to suppress a target thought that could be related to a host of reminders. In other words, the conflicting findings might be explained by the difference between suppressing a single thought and suppressing many thoughts at once.

Historical Context

Before we describe the details of the theory behind this phenomenon, let us discuss how we place the study of thought suppression in the larger context of other research in psychology. As Wegner and Schneider tell us in *The White Bear Story* (Wegner & Schneider, 2003), the original thought suppression study was a product of the zeitgeist in social psychology. Indeed it was part of a movement in social psychology, pioneered by John Bargh (Bargh & Pietromonaco, 1982; Uleman & Bargh, 1989), to understand the unconscious aspects not just of social behavior but also of consciousness itself. For example, it was around that time that Gilbert's (1991) research examined the automatic and controlled aspects of how we form beliefs and Devine (1989) conducted research on the automatic—versus the controlled—aspects of stereotyping. Empirical work on thought suppression crossed these two lines of research: Wegner's ironic process theory of mental control explained the mechanisms underlying thought suppression in terms of an automatic monitoring process and a controlled operating process, whereas Macrae and colleagues (Macrae, Bodenhausen, Milne, & Jetten, 1994) spawned much empirical investigation into the effects of suppressing prejudiced thoughts. A unique aspect of thought suppression research was its obvious relevance to psychopathology. Indeed, the role of thought suppression in disorders of perseverative thinking has been studied extensively

(for reviews, see Rassin, 2005; Wenzlaff & Wegner, 2000; Najmi & Wegner, 2008a). This, too, fit neatly into a larger trend within psychology. For example, around the same time that Wenzlaff spearheaded the research on the unhealthy effects of suppressing negative thoughts in clinical disorders (e.g., Wenzlaff, Wegner, & Roper, 1988), Pennebaker (1985) was investigating the beneficial health effects of the opposite phenomenon, namely disclosure of negative thoughts. Thus, the research on thought suppression started in an attempt to understand the unconscious aspects of conscious thinking and over the years found its way into numerous other lines of research within social psychology and beyond.

The Theory

Several years into the discovery of the effects of thought suppression, there was still no theory explaining why completely successful suppression is nearly impossible and why suppression leads to a rebound of the target thought. But in 1992, Wegner and Erber found that people suppressing a thought under cognitive load showed selective attention for the suppressed thought in a modified Stroop task. In the original version of the Stroop (1935) task, participants are required to name the color in which a word is printed while attempting to ignore the meaning of the word itself. Investigators have found a robust effect such that participants take less time to name colors when the word is congruent (e.g., the word GREEN printed in green ink) than when the word is incongruent (e.g., the word BLUE printed in green ink). A modified version of the Stroop task has since been used to show that people are slower to name words that are emotionally relevant to them, indicating selective attention to these words (for a review, see Williams, Mathews, and MacLeod, 1996). Wegner and Erber (1992) asked participants to complete a modified Stroop task while either suppressing thoughts of a target or concentrating on it, either under high cognitive load (i.e., simultaneously rehearsing a nine-digit number) or low cognitive load (i.e., simultaneously rehearsing a one-digit number). They found that people suppressing a thought under high cognitive load experienced interference for the suppression target (i.e., slower responses to color-naming the target). Remarkably, this interference was even greater than the interference found when people were concentrating on the thought under load. These results suggested that suppression resulted in increased accessibility (the authors coined the term "hyperaccessibility") of the suppressed thought, and that this effect was especially evident under conditions of mental load.

These findings, combined with contemporary thinking on automatic and controlled aspects of information processing, led to Wegner's (1994) proposal regarding the theoretical underpinnings of the thought suppression effect. The framework for the theory was borrowed from *control theory* in engineering, which deals with the behavior of dynamic systems. According to control theory, a sensor monitors the output of a system and sends the data to a computer, which continuously adjusts the control input as necessary to maintain the desired output. Thus, the monitor provides feedback on how the system is actually performing and allows the control process to compensate dynamically for potential errors in the system. According to Wegner's ironic process theory, mental control involves processes that usually work together to effect thought suppression, but they can fail and yield intrusions under conditions of high mental load. The theory posits (1) an effortful and conscious operating process that diverts attention away from unwanted thoughts: The person engaged in suppressing white bear thoughts, for example, might attend to other things. In other words, successfully focusing on things other than the white bear achieves the state of not thinking of a white bear. The theory also posits (2) an effortless and unconscious ironic monitoring process that both maintains vigilance for occurrences of the unwanted thought and triggers further action of the operating process if the unwanted thought appears in awareness. Thus, these two processes work hand in hand to ensure that unwanted thoughts remain outside of consciousness—the operating process bringing other thoughts into awareness and the monitoring process checking for errors (e.g., the thought of a white bear entering consciousness).

Ironically, however, by maintaining vigilance for the unwanted thought, the monitoring system helps assure that the unwanted thought never becomes dormant. The problem occurs when people relinquish efforts to suppress or when their efforts are undermined by cognitive load: This interferes with the workings of the conscious and effortful operating system but will not disturb the automatic monitoring process. In other words, conscious attempts at distracting oneself away from the unwanted thought will get interrupted while the ironic monitor will continue to sensitize us to the thought we are trying to suppress. Thus, when mental capacity is compromised by cognitive load, the control falls below a baseline level and produces the opposite of the intended

effect, such that a thought one is trying to suppress becomes more accessible under mental load. This ironic effect has been observed when people's efforts to relax (e.g., Wegner, Broome, & Blumberg, 1997), concentrate (e.g., Wegner, Erber, & Zanakos, 1993), sleep (e.g., Ansfield, Wegner, & Bowser, 1996), avoid being prejudiced (e.g., Macrae et al., 1994), or ignore pain (e.g., Cioffi & Holloway, 1993) are compromised by competing cognitive demands.

Macrae and colleagues (Macrae et al., 1994; 1998) offered a twist on the ironic process theory's explanation for the postsuppression rebound. They argued that the target of suppression becomes activated repeatedly during an active suppression attempt as the person repeatedly detects it in consciousness. This repeated activation ultimately results in priming the unwanted thought, hence leading to heightened accessibility and the ironic rebound. Macrae and colleagues argued that, in addition to the hyperaccessibility of the unwanted thought described by Wegner (1994), the rate of decay of this hyperaccessibility decreases when the thought is more frequently activated, leading to an even greater accessibility of the thought. Thus, according to Macrae et al. (1994), the primary mechanism underlying the rebound effect is a priming effect.

In recent years, some researchers (e.g., Forster & Liberman, 2001; 2004; Martin & Tesser, 1996) have contested the ironic process theory of mental control and have suggested, instead, that motivational processes are responsible for the rebound of suppressed thoughts. Their argument is based on the classic Zeigarnik effect (1927), namely, that information that relates to unfulfilled goals is maintained in a state of enhanced cognitive activation. According to this argument, people typically have intrusions of the suppressed thoughts during active attempts at suppression, and these intrusions mark the goal of suppression as being unfulfilled. As a result, the Zeigarnik effect serves to enhance the accessibility of the suppressed thought. The one study to date that has directly contrasted this motivational explanation for the postsuppression rebound with the ironic process theory found preliminary support for the motivational account (Enticott & Gold, 2002). In this study, participants first suppressed and then expressed thoughts of a white bear. In one condition, participants were required to complete a memory task simultaneously and were encouraged to attribute the difficulty of suppression to the memory task; in another condition, participants were required to complete a memory task simultaneously and were encouraged to attribute the difficulty of suppression to the requirement of the suppression task itself. They found that participants who attributed difficulty to the suppression task itself experienced a greater rebound than did those who attributed difficulty to the memory task. Additionally, in some conditions, either an intentional or an unintentional delay was introduced between the suppression and expression periods. Results revealed that participants in the intentional delay condition showed a reduction in suppression-related rebound, compared with participants in the unintentional delay condition. Although these findings are not clearly in support of either one of the suppression theories, the authors interpreted the results as supporting the motivational account of the suppression-related rebound.

Neural Correlates of Thought Suppression

Preliminary evidence in support of the dual processes comprising the ironic process theory of mental control (Wegner, 1994) comes from neuroimaging studies of instructed thought suppression. Wyland, Kelley, Macrae, Gordon, and Heatherton (2003) found that the anterior cingulate cortex was activated when participants were instructed to suppress a specific, personally relevant, thought. This region has been implicated in earlier investigations of the neural correlates of cognitive control. Given earlier evidence for the role of the anterior cingulate in conflict monitoring for response competition and interference (Botvinick, Braver, Barch, Carter, & Cohen, 2001), Wyland et al. (2003) proposed that this region likely acts as a vigilance monitor for intrusions of unwanted thoughts. More recently, Mitchell et al. (2007) conducted a neuroimaging study in which participants were instructed to suppress thoughts of a white bear. Neural models of executive control suggest that the prefrontal cortex underlies sustained control processes and that the anterior cingulate cortex underlies the temporary need for additional control. Consistent with this, Mitchell et al. (2007) found that the dorsolateral prefrontal cortex showed sustained increases in activation during suppression attempts, whereas the anterior cingulate cortex showed temporary increases associated with occurrences of the to-be-suppressed thought. These data provide initial evidence of distinct neural mechanisms underlying the components of the dual process model of Wegner's ironic process theory.

The Nature of Suppressed Thoughts

As explained above in the context of the ironic process theory, once suppression is compromised by mental load or stress, or if suppression efforts are terminated voluntarily, previously suppressed thoughts do indeed return with a vengeance. This so-called rebound effect that was first seen in the original white bear study has since been observed repeatedly (see reviews by Abramowitz, Tolin, & Street, 2001; Rassin, 2005; Wenzlaff & Wegner, 2000). A study examining suppression of thoughts over a longer duration concluded that these thoughts tend to intrude into consciousness for days (Trinder & Salkovskis, 1994). In this study, participants were first asked to identify a personally relevant, intrusive thought. Next, they were instructed to suppress this thought over a 4-day period, to think about it, or to simply record its occurrence. Results revealed that those participants who suppressed a personally relevant, negative thought over a 4-day period experienced a higher frequency of the thought and found it more uncomfortable than did those who were instructed to think about it or to simply record its occurrence.

Another characteristic of suppressed thoughts is that they tend to return in dreams. Wegner, Wenzlaff, and Kozak (2004) asked participants to spend five minutes before sleep writing their stream of consciousness report as they either suppressed thoughts of a target person or thought of the person. The person was either someone whom the participant identified as a "romantic crush" or someone whom the participant liked but not romantically. Those in the suppression condition reported increased dreaming about the person afterward. Importantly, this effect was observed regardless of emotional attraction to the person. These findings were replicated in a more recent study (Taylor & Bryant, 2007), which showed, in addition, that the dream rebound effect was stronger for those people who had a propensity to suppress in daily life.

Because suppressed thoughts intrude consciousness relentlessly, we may be tempted to attribute special psychological meaning to them, or to see them, as Freud did, as manifestations of some intrapsychic struggle. However, what research in this area has shown is that suppressed thoughts of even the most mundane things return relentlessly, for instance, when people are instructed to suppress thought of white bears (Wegner, Schneider, Carter, & White, 1987), houses (Wegner & Erber, 1992), rabbits (Clark, Ball, & Pape, 1991), and vehicles (Lavy & van den Hout, 1990).

An intriguing feature of thought suppression is that the mood we are in while suppressing can influence our ability to suppress effectively. Wyland and Forgas (2007) found that a negative mood improved people's ability to suppress thoughts of a white bear during suppression but then led to a larger postsuppression rebound. However, a positive mood impaired the ability to suppress during active suppression, but did not lead to a postsuppression rebound. Thus, it appears that negative mood facilitates and positive mood inhibits people's ability to suppress unwanted thoughts, but that, much like the ironic process theory would predict, more effective suppression in the short term is likely to be followed by an ironic rebound.

Another remarkable feature of suppressed thoughts is that there exists a certain asymmetry in the way they are linked to other thoughts in our associative networks: We find ourselves being reminded of a particular unwanted thought by many cues in the environment, but the thought itself seems to remind us of nothing more than our desire to eliminate it from consciousness. To examine this unusual asymmetry in the way unwanted thoughts are linked to other thoughts, Najmi and Wegner (2008b) asked participants to suppress a thought or to concentrate on it while completing an associative priming lexical decision task. This task assesses the influence of priming on reaction time to word/nonword judgments. Results indicated that suppression under cognitive load produced asymmetrical priming: Priming with the associate of a suppressed word facilitated response to the suppressed word, but priming with a suppressed word did not facilitate response to associated words. This suggests that suppression induces an unusual form of cognitive accessibility in which movement of activation toward the suppressed thought from associates is facilitated but movement of activation away from the suppressed thought to associates is undermined. Thus, suppression of an unwanted thought ironically increases its return while precluding other related thoughts from entering into awareness. Indeed, Kozak, Sternglanz, Viswanathan, and Wegner (2008) have shown that people experience a sensation of being mentally blocked when attempting to produce associates for words that are semantically related to a previously suppressed word. In other words, suppressed thoughts appear to be a cognitive dead-end of sorts.

How Robust Is the Suppression-Related Rebound Effect?

In the past two decades of thought suppression research, there have been some failures to replicate the postsuppression rebound effect (e.g., Muris, Merckelbach, & de Jong, 1993; Roemer & Borkovec, 1994). However, various differences in the design of the thought suppression studies have made it difficult to compare the mixed results. For instance, in some studies, during the postsuppression period, participants were asked to think of anything that comes to mind, whereas in others, they were asked to think specifically of the suppression target. In some studies, the target of suppression was a personally relevant thought, whereas in others, it was a neutral object such as a white bear. For instance, Kelly and Kahn (1994) demonstrated that people can suppress their personally relevant intrusive thoughts fairly effectively, whereas their attempts at suppressing neutral thoughts specified by the experimenter met with an ironic rebound of the thought. Differences also exist in form of the suppression target used in the study (e.g., is it a discrete concept such as a white bear, or is it more complex, such as a story or a memory of an event?), the valence of the suppression target (e.g., is it a memory of a happy event or of a traumatic event?), or the method for measuring thought frequency (e.g., are occurrences of the thought counted from the participant's verbal stream of conscious report or written diary record, or by the participant marking each intrusion with a counter, and finally, are the intrusions and the stream of consciousness recorded out loud or covertly?).

After more than a decade of research on this topic, a meta-analysis was finally conducted to address these concerns. In their meta-analysis of 44 controlled studies, Abramowitz et al. (2001) took into account the various study design parameters and provided evidence for a firm conclusion. Results of the meta-analysis indicated a moderate rebound effect of thought suppression that varied in magnitude depending on the nature of the target thought (e.g., smaller rebound effect for discrete thoughts) and the method that was used to measure thought frequency (e.g., covert methods such as pressing a counter silently yielded greater rebound effects than did more overt methods such as reporting a stream of consciousness). Moreover, the study demonstrated that suppression can indeed be achieved but only over small periods of time, and it becomes less and less effective as time progresses.

Suppression of Taboo Thoughts

Several studies have found evidence for the ironic rebound of stereotype suppression (e.g., Macrae et al., 1994; Macrae, Bodenhausen, Milne, & Ford, 1997; Sherman, Stroessner, Loftus, & Deguzman, 1997; Wyer, Sherman, & Stroessner,

1998). Stereotypes are often activated automatically, but many people are motivated to suppress them because of personal standards or for social acceptability (Devine, 1989; Monteith, Sherman, & Devine, 1998). The first study of stereotype suppression was conducted by Macrae and colleagues (1994). In this study, participants (at the University of Wales) were first presented with a photograph of a male skinhead and were instructed to write for five minutes details of the target's typical day. Half the participants were instructed to do so while avoiding thinking about the target in a stereotypic way. The authors anticipated that these instructions would encourage participants to suppress their stereotypic thoughts about skinheads (in other words, this was the suppression group). The other half of the participants were not given any additional instructions. Results showed that participants who were in the suppression group experienced enhanced postsuppression stereotyping, as reflected in their behavior: Participants in this group kept more distance from the chair in the waiting room that was ostensibly occupied by the above-mentioned skinhead, who, they were told, had just stepped out. One caveat acknowledged by the authors of this study was that no strong social norms existed against stereotyping skinheads negatively; therefore, without explicit instructions to suppress, participants in the study were unlikely to be motivated to suppress stereotyping. Wyer, Sherman, and Stroessner (2000) argued that stereotypes that the individual is motivated to suppress (e.g., racial stereotypes that the individual has rejected because of personal, egalitarian beliefs about stereotyping or pressures to be *politically correct*) are likely to produce different suppression-related outcomes. Indeed, Wyer et al. demonstrated that a rebound in stereotyping occurs only when both motivation to avoid stereotyping and cognitive capacity are undermined. Other studies show that the suppression of stereotype-congruent memories leads to enhanced recall and recognition of the material when suppression is discontinued (Macrae et al., 1997; Sherman et al., 1997). Thus, it may be the case that well-meaning people try to avoid stereotypes, but if their efforts are interrupted or if mental capacity is at all compromised by cognitive load or stress, their attempts may well result in an ironic rebound of the very thoughts they are trying to inhibit, and this rebound can have consequences for behavior (e.g., Macrae et al., 1994) and memory (e.g., (Macrae et al., 1997; Sherman et al., 1997).

It turns out that the ironic rebound of socially inappropriate thoughts in general—not just those related to stereotypes— is quite common. Consequently, if we are particularly anxious to create a positive impression, one way we might attempt this is by suppressing socially undesirable thoughts. It follows that these thoughts become vulnerable to an ironic rebound, particularly under conditions of stress. For instance, in laboratory experiments, participants instructed to not think of sex show greater arousal (as measured by skin conductance) than do those asked to not think of a neutral topic, and similar arousal to those who are asked to concentrate on these thoughts (e.g., Wegner, Shortt, Blake, & Page, 1990). In a grim extension of this research, Johnston, Hudson, and Ward (1997) found that, after instructions to suppress sexually deviant thoughts, chronic child molesters showed increased interference for child- and sex-related words on a modified Stroop task than did people who were not chronic child molesters or sexual offenders.

Similar to socially inappropriate thoughts, thoughts deemed to be secret tend to be particularly vulnerable to ironic effects. Based on a series of studies on the cognitive effects of keeping secrets, Lane and Wegner (1994, 1995) proposed the *preoccupation model of secrecy*. According to this model, attempts at secrecy activate a chain of cognitive processes, starting with suppressing thoughts of the secret, presumably because pushing the secret out of consciousness allows the person to direct attention away from the secret topic during conversations with others. The chain ends with the ironic rebound of intrusive thoughts of the secret, making it even more accessible to consciousness. In a laboratory study, Wegner and Gold (1995) found that participants asked to suppress thoughts of a still-desired crush from the past showed greater physiological arousal (again, as measured by skin conductance) than did those who were allowed to think about the crush. In a similar vein, research (e.g., Wegner, Lane, & Dimitri, 1994) suggests that suppression of thoughts of a secret romantic relationship has the potential of fueling the intensity of the relationship. If an individual is initially attracted to someone, and the person repeatedly attempts to suppress thoughts about the attraction, and if these thought rebound repeatedly, one might expect the attraction to gain steam as the preoccupation with the attraction increases. For example, in the now famous "footsie study," Wegner and colleagues (Wegner, Lane, & Dimitri, 1994) found that participants were more attracted to a stranger who played footsie with them under the table but only when they had to keep this secret from others at the table. As Oscar Wilde pointed out in *The Picture of Dorian Gray*, "The commonest thing is delightful if only one hides it." Suppression of this hidden thought might lead to a preoccupation with the thought and/or increased physiological arousal, which the individual might then interpret as "delight" or attraction. Thus, the footsie study suggests that thought suppression is a likely mechanism for imbuing secret thoughts with excitement.

A somewhat different example of unacceptable thoughts is provided by a dieter's thoughts of forbidden foods. Anyone who has ever gone on a strict diet can likely relate to the ironic rebound of suppressing food-related thoughts. The dieter is understandably motivated to avoid thoughts of ice cream and hamburgers, lest allowing them into consciousness might trigger the impulse to give in to them and violate the diet. Thus, thoughts of tasty, fatty foods are not taboo thoughts per se, but rather have been, in a sense, rendered unacceptable by the dieter. And, ironically, a common outcome of dieting is the preoccupation with these forbidden foods. Harnden, McNally, and Jimerson (1997) found that nondieters instructed to suppress thoughts of weighing themselves experienced a significant rebound of these thoughts, thus implicating suppression in the development of weight-related preoccupations. Moreover, Boon, Stroebe, Schut, and Ijntema (2002) found that, consistent with the ironic process theory of mental control, the imposition of a cognitive load led to an ironic rebound, in that dieters ate more high-calorie foods but not low-calorie foods. These results were replicated in a recent study by Erskine and Georgiou (2010), who found that dieters instructed to suppress thoughts of chocolate consumed significantly more chocolate than did dieters in control conditions, including those who were instructed specifically to think of chocolate.

Suppression of Pain

Physical pain is obviously something that people are motivated to avoid. But achieving this by suppressing thoughts of pain turns out to be counterproductive. Muris, Jongh, Merckelbach, Postema, and Vet (1998) conducted a study with participants recruited from a dentist office's waiting room. They found that participants in the suppression condition, who were instructed to suppress thoughts about pain during their impending dental procedure, later reported that they had increased anxiety and intrusive negative thoughts during the procedure. Thus,

suppression of thoughts of pain ended up intensifying the suffering in terms of anxiety and negative thoughts.

Cioffi and Holloway (1993) demonstrated that the rebound effect of suppressing thoughts of pain extended to the actual somatic experience of pain. During a cold-presser pain task, participants who were instructed to suppress thoughts of the pain experienced the slowest recovery from pain compared with those who were instructed to focus their attention on a different object and those who were instructed to pay attention to the pain. Moreover, those who had suppressed thoughts of pain earlier demonstrated lower pain tolerance in a subsequent task. Evidence for this rebound of physical pain after suppression of thoughts of pain has been replicated since (Masedo & Esteve, 2007; Sullivan, Rouse, Bishop, & Johnston, 1997).

In an interesting extension of this line of research, Burns et al. (2008) examined the effect of suppression of anger-related thoughts on pain. Extant research implicates the regulation of anger as a robust determinant of chronic pain severity (e.g., Burns, Johnson, Devine, Mahoney, & Pawl, 1998), but few studies have examined the effect of suppressing anger-related thoughts on pain. In their study, Burns et al. (2008) found that attempts to suppress anger-inducing thoughts during provocation (performing a computer maze task while being pestered by a confederate) resulted in an increase in these thoughts and in self-reported pain intensity in a sample of chronic pain patients.

Individual Differences in Ability to Suppress

The research covered so far appears to suggest that suppression attempts will necessarily meet with failure. But is there anything that can help us suppress thoughts effectively? There is some evidence to suggest that suppression under hypnosis can be successful (Bryant & Sindicich, 2008; Bryant & Wimalaweera, 2006). In the two studies conducted in this area, low-hypnotizable participants instructed to suppress personally relevant thoughts experienced a postsuppression rebound of the thought, whereas high-hypnotizable participants given the same instructions did not experience an increase in thought frequency. The authors explained their findings in terms of using hypnosis to minimize the effect of the cognitive load that undermines suppression effort.

Of course, because suggestibility is normally distributed, high hypnotizability is something that only a small percentage of the population enjoys.

For the rest of us, it turns out that greater working memory capacity or intelligence might be what we need in order to suppress more effectively. If, as proposed in the ironic process theory of mental control, the operating process that searches for distracters (i.e., thoughts that are other than the target of suppression) is an effortful process that is demanding of cognitive resources, it stands to reason that individuals with heightened cognitive capacity might be particularly good at suppressing. One aspect of cognitive capacity is working memory capacity, which reflects individual differences in the extent to which controlled attention can be used for the execution of a task. Working memory capacity is measured by tasks that require items to be remembered while simultaneously performing a different task (e.g., solving an arithmetic equation). Indeed, researchers (Brewin & Beaton, 2002; Brewin & Smart, 2005) have found that successful thought suppression is associated with higher working memory capacity, as measured by the operation span with words (OSPAN) task. Another aspect of heightened cognitive capacity is intelligence. In the same study, the authors found that successful thought suppression was predicted independently by fluid intelligence (the ability to solve new problems and adapt to new situations, as measured by Raven's Standard Progressive Matrices task; Raven, Court, & Raven, 1977), but not by crystallized intelligence (acquired knowledge and skills, as measure by the National Adult Reading Test [NART-2]; Nelson & Willison, 1991). Thus, individual differences in ability to suppress successfully are a function of working memory capacity and a particular kind of smarts.

In another approach to this question, researchers have identified a group of people who are particularly skilled at suppressing thoughts. These are people who are said to have a repressor coping style, that is, people who deny experiencing distress in their conscious reports yet show evidence of physiological manifestations of stress. More specifically, repressors are defined as people who score low on self-report measures of trait anxiety (e.g., Taylor Manifest Anxiety Scale; Taylor, 1953) and score high on a self-report measure of defensiveness (e.g., Marlowe-Crowne Social Desirability Scale; Crowne & Marlowe, 1960). In response to a laboratory stressor, participants identified as repressors deny increases in anxiety in their self-report, but show evidence of increases in physiological measures of arousal (Weinberger, Schwartz, & Davidson, 1979). The research is not clear on whether these individuals are unaware of their emotional response

or unwilling to acknowledge it, or if they are simply better than others at keeping their negative thoughts under wraps. To test the latter hypothesis, Barnier, Levin, and Maher (2004) tested whether repressors are better than controls at intentionally suppressing thoughts about a past negative event. In the suppression conditions, they instructed participants to suppress thoughts of a recent event that made them either feel proud or embarrassed. Results of this study revealed that everyone was equally skilled at suppressing thoughts of the proud event, but, compared with the nonrepressors, repressors reported the fewest intrusions of thoughts of the embarrassing event. This was true even in the condition in which they were not instructed to suppress. In addition, repressors showed no signs of the postsuppression ironic rebound of thoughts of the embarrassing event. Consistent with the Brewin and Smart (2005) study, Geraerts, Merckelbach, Jelicic, and Habets (2007) showed that the superior ability of repressors to suppress negative thoughts could be explained largely by their higher working memory capacity.

Later, Geraerts and colleagues (Geraerts, Merckelbach, Jelicic, & Smeets, 2006) replicated the finding that, in the laboratory, repressors reported fewer intrusions of their most anxious memory than did nonrepressors, but in an interesting extension of this study, they found that over a 7-day period, repressors reported the largest ironic rebound of the suppressed thought. It appears that the repressive coping style might be beneficial in the short term but counterproductive in the long run. These findings are consistent with popular conceptions of repressors as people who may experience little distress in the moment but then suffer for it later.

Thought Suppression and Psychopathology

Repetitive, unwanted, intrusive thoughts surface as symptoms across a surprising range of psychological disorders, from generalized anxiety and obsessive-compulsive disorder (OCD) to depression and beyond (Clark, 2005). How might this bombardment of intrusive thoughts in these disorders begin in the first place? One possibility proposed in the theory of *synthetic obsessions* (Wegner, 1989) is that suppression itself is the cause of subsequent intrusions and obsessive thinking. This idea that suppression failure is causally related to certain disorders has dictated much of the research on thought suppression in psychopathology. Another possibility is that suppression acts as a complication of psychopathology (Najmi & Wegner, 2008a; Najmi

& Wegner, 2009). According to the latter theory, suppression complicates all disorders: In some disorders, it does so by leading to an ironic rebound of the unwanted thoughts, but in most, the cost of an effortful strategy such as suppression is a cognitive load, which in turn compromises the ability to suppress. Finally, unrealistic expectations of suppression success and inevitable failure to achieve these unrealistic expectations set off a cycle of distress, mental load, and unwanted thoughts.

It turns out that people suffering from psychological disorders often believe in the effectiveness of suppression. They tend to score high on the Thought Control Beliefs factor of a questionnaire designed to assess beliefs about the process and outcome of thinking (Metacognitive Beliefs Questionnaire [MCBQ]; Clark, Purdon, & Wang, 2003). Typical items on the questionnaire include: "I should be able to gain complete control over my mind if I exercise enough will power."

Obsessive-Compulsive Disorder

OCD patients are high on the list of those who believe that perfect suppression of their obsessive thoughts can and should be attained. OCD is a disorder that is defined by the persistence of intrusive thoughts, and people with OCD report engaging in frequent, effortful, unsuccessful suppression of unwanted thoughts (Purdon, Rowa, & Antony, 2007). In fact, in laboratory studies, Purdon, Rowa, and Antony (2005) found that individuals with OCD exerted effort to suppress their obsessional thought even when instructed explicitly not to suppress. This highlights the sheer relentlessness of the suppression-related cognitive load experienced by these patients. Tolin, Abramowitz, Przeworski, and Foa (2002) found that OCD patients experienced a postsuppression rebound of the thought of a white bear. But, interestingly, there is no evidence to suggest that they are particularly ineffective at suppressing personally relevant thoughts (Janeck & Calamari, 1999; Najmi, Riemann, & Wegner, 2009). That said, failure of suppression is associated with worse mood, and faulty appraisals of suppression failure (e.g., "I am mentally weak because I cannot suppress thoughts perfectly") may lead to greater effort to suppress (Clark, 2004; Purdon et al., 2005). Consistent with this, Tolin, Abramowitz, Hamlin, Foa, and Synodi (2002) observed that OCD patients were more likely than anxious and nonanxious controls to attribute a failure of thought suppression to internal, negative attributions (e.g., "I am mentally weak"). These

beliefs may predispose the individual to try harder to suppress, and the increase in cognitive load may eventually lead to the counterproductive effects of mental control, thus contributing to the obsessional state.

Post-traumatic Stress Disorder

Post-traumatic stress disorder (PTSD) is characterized by unwanted intrusions of traumatic recollections and avoidance of all things associated with the trauma. In other words, individuals with PTSD are motivated to suppress trauma-related thoughts. However, recent evidence suggests that this may be particularly difficult because suppression enhances memory bias for threat-related material: Compared with a thought concentration condition, the thought suppression condition, the increases memory for threat-related information relative to memory for neutral information (Kircanski, Craske, & Bjork, 2008). Research on thought suppression in PTSD indicates that, unlike OCD, this disorder is characterized by a bias in the ability to suppress trauma-related thoughts. Several studies to date (Beck, Gudmundsdottir, Palyo, Miller, & Grant, 2006; Shipherd & Beck, 1999, 2005) suggest that the effort to suppress trauma-related thoughts serves only to exacerbate trauma-related intrusions and associated distress.

Worries

Patients suffering from generalized anxiety disorder (GAD) are plagued by the persistence of uncontrollable worries. Becker, Rinck, Roth, and Margraf (1998) tested the hypothesis that patients with GAD show a bias in ability to suppress their worries. Consistent with their hypothesis, they observed that GAD patients found it more difficult to suppress thoughts of their worries than thoughts of a neutral target. Persistent worries are the primary feature not only of GAD but also of clinical insomnia. It turns out that people with insomnia report a greater use of suppression to control their presleep worries than do controls (Harvey, 2003). Furthermore, those with insomnia instructed to suppress worries report taking longer to go to sleep and report worse sleep quality once they eventually do fall asleep than do those with insomnia in the no-suppression condition. An interesting aspect of these findings is that, although suppression exacerbated sleep disturbance, it did not lead to a rebound of worries. Thus, it may be the case that the effort exerted to suppress presleep worries ends up ironically exacerbating the disorder.

Depression

There is plenty of evidence to suggest that the suppression of depressive thoughts results in a rebound of these thoughts (Conway, Howell, & Giannopoulos, 1991; Howell & Conway, 1992; Renaud & McConnell, 2002; Wenzlaff, 2005; Wenzlaff, Wegner, & Klein, 1991; Wenzlaff, Wegner, & Roper, 1988). This may well be so because when depressed people attempt to suppress, they do so by choosing distracters that are mood congruent (Wenzlaff, Wegner, & Roper, 1988b). Because these distracters are mood congruent, they tend to be linked closely to the suppression target, thereby causing a quick return of attention to the unwanted thought. A recent study extended these findings to the domain of autobiographical memory (Dalgleish & Yiend, 2006). Results showed that in dysphoric individuals, the suppression of a negative memory resulted in increased activation of other negative information, presumably distracters used to achieve suppression.

Research suggests that depression interferes mostly with effortful processing and only minimally with automatic processing (Hartlage, Alloy, Vázquez, & Dykman, 1993). Thus, according to the ironic process theory (Wegner, 1994), suppression undertaken during a depressed mood should impair functioning of the effortful operating process (which searches for distracters—things other than the target thought) and should leave unfettered the functioning of the automatic monitoring process (which searches for occurrences in awareness of the target thought). The result is an increase in intrusions of the target thought.

An interesting line of research in this area overseen by Wenzlaff (Wenzlaff & Bates, 1998) supports the idea that thought suppression masks a cognitive vulnerability to depression (Wegner & Zanakos, 1994; Wenzlaff & Eisenberg, 2001; Wenzlaff, Meir, & Salas, 2002; Wenzlaff, Rude, Taylor, Stultz, & Sweatt, 2001). These studies are conducted with samples of remitted-depressed individuals, that is, individuals who do not exhibit depressive symptoms currently but who were depressed in the past and therefore are more likely to possess an underlying vulnerability to depression. One such study, for example, revealed that the imposition of a cognitive load caused remitted-depressed individuals to interpret recorded homophones in a more negative fashion, performing more like currently depressed than control participants. Moreover, the increase in negative thinking induced by the cognitive load was significantly correlated with Wegner and Zanakos's (1994) questionnaire measure of propensity to suppress unwanted thoughts.

Substance Abuse

Studies with individuals in the process of quitting smoking show that people experience an enhancement of smoking-related intrusions under suppression (Salkovskis & Reynolds, 1994). Palfai, Colby, Monti, and Rohsenow (1997) found that, in a sample of heavy social drinkers, suppression of urges to drink led to increased accessibility of alcohol-related information, particularly information regarding expectancies about the effects of alcohol. Klein (2007) found that alcohol-abusing participants who had tried to suppress thoughts of alcohol before performing a modified Stroop task showed increased interference for the word *alcohol* compared with those who had expressed thoughts about alcohol freely before the task.

Summary

Taken together, it appears that thought suppression clearly plays a role in a range of clinical disorders. However, in the past two decades, theories of suppression in psychological disorder have become increasingly nuanced. The earliest research in this area focused primarily on the ironic return of the unwanted thoughts. We now know that across many disorders, the hidden cost of thought suppression (Najmi & Wegner, 2009) is a persistent cognitive load, which in turn undermines the ability to suppress and sets off a relentless cycle of failed expectations and suffering.

Conclusion and Future Directions

In summary, what has the experimental study of thought suppression taught us? We now know that suppression can be effective for short periods of time (Wegner, 1994) and that some individuals are better able to suppress than are others (e.g., Barnier et al., 2004; Brewin & Beaton, 2002). Moreover, our mood can have an effect on how well we suppress (Wyland & Forgas, 2007). However, for the most part, when someone tries to suppress a single piece of information, it can return relentlessly for days (e.g., Trinder & Salkovskis, 1994) and can even appear in dreams more than it would if the person were concentrating on the thought (e.g., Wegner, Wenzlaff, & Kozak, 2004). The suppressed thought is especially likely to rebound when the person is stressed or under mental load (e.g., Wegner & Erber, 1992). Furthermore, thoughts related to the target of suppression tend to serve as reminders of the target, but the target thought itself does not remind the person of anything else, not even related thoughts (Najmi & Wegner, 2008b). Because suppressed thoughts return with relentless predictability, one might be tempted to attribute special psychological significance to them, but it appears that the postsuppression rebound occurs for even the most ordinary things. That said, the suppression of personally or socially unacceptable thoughts is particularly prone to the effects of an ironic rebound (e.g., Johnston, Hudson, & Ward, 1997). Finally, there is considerable evidence for the role of suppression in exacerbating suffering across a range of psychological disorders.

Taken together, most of the research in this area has focused on the failures of suppression. It follows that the next phase in this research must focus on its successes. Specifically, what are the conditions under which successful suppression might be achieved in a sustainable way? More importantly, if suppression is successful, is it no longer associated with negative outcomes? Empirical investigation of successful suppression might offer new insights into the phenomenology of suppression.

For example, a new line of research suggests that self-affirmation eliminates the rebound effects of thought suppression (Koole & Knippenberg, 2007). Self-affirmation theory (Steele, 1998) proposes that a self-affirming, image-restoring process is triggered by anything that threatens this image (e.g., negative evaluation by others, negative judgment of oneself, one's own behavior contradicting personal values). The image-restoring process comprises rationalizations and justifications that potentially alter attitudes and/or behavior. In their study, Koole and van Knippenberg (2007) induced participants to either suppress or use a social stereotype and then supplied them with either self-affirming (e.g., "You are very social") or nonaffirming (e.g., "You are reasonably social") personality feedback. Consistent with other work on thought suppression of stereotypes (e.g., Macrae et al., 1994), the authors found that suppressing stereotypes enhanced the accessibility of stereotypes and increased the use of stereotypes. Consistent with self-affirmation theory (Steele, 1988) and motivational models of thought suppression (e.g., Forster & Liberman, 2001), they found that self-affirmation facilitated the effectiveness of thought suppression. Although the precise mechanisms underlying these findings are unclear, these data nonetheless suggest that people may have some agency in preventing postsuppression rebound effects. These findings clearly need to be replicated across a range of content areas of the suppression target (in addition to stereotype suppression) in order for us to understand more comprehensively the role of self-affirmation in effective suppression.

Along these lines, the less known second study in the original white bear article (Wegner et al., 1987, Experiment 2) revealed that suppression by means of focusing on one other thought can be quite effective in suppressing unwanted thoughts. As described above, in this study, participants were able to suppress thoughts of a white bear successfully when asked to think instead of a red Volkswagen. The important implication of this finding is that successful suppression can be achieved by concentrating on a single focus of attention, unlike what people usually do when suppressing, that is, use many different distracters, one after the other. Studies conducted with nonclinical individuals (Salkovskis & Campbell, 1994) and with patients with OCD (Najmi et al., 2009) have demonstrated that focused distraction is more effective in reducing the frequency of the unwanted, intrusive thoughts than is suppression by means of unfocused distraction. Thus, the adverse consequences of attempts at thought suppression reflect failure of participants to use focused distraction rather than failure to control unwanted thought in general.

The idea that successful suppression of unwanted thoughts is a beneficial strategy flies in the face of conventional wisdom in the clinical world, where treatments are based on the exposure principle. According to this principle, avoidance of affectively charged, unwanted thoughts worsens unwanted emotion and hence is contraindicated. But, as discussed above, suppressing by means of focused distraction away from the unwanted thought is identical to concentration by means of focusing attention on something other than that unwanted thought. Individual differences in the efficacy of a top-down process like the strategic focus of attention on a distracter may distinguish successful from failed attempts at controlling negative thoughts. For instance, Anderson and Levy (2009) have shown that people who are better able to engage brain systems thought to underlie executive control are more successful at avoiding unwanted thoughts. Thus, when top-down cognitive control fails to keep distress in check, one intervention—a bottom-up solution—has been exposure to negative thoughts and emotions, whereas an alternative—top-down solution—may be to buttress cognitive control. It follows that future research should turn to methods for understanding what makes suppression effective and how suppression efforts may be buttressed.

References

Abramowitz, J. S., Tolin, D. F., & Street, G. P. (2001). Paradoxical effects of thought suppression: A meta-analysis of controlled studies. *Clinical Psychology Review, 21*, 683–703.

Anderson, M. C. (2005). The role of inhibitory control in forgetting unwanted memories: A consideration of three methods. In C. MacLeod & B. Uttl (Eds.), *Dynamic cognitive processes* (pp. 159–190). Tokyo: Springer-Verlag.

Anderson, M. C., & Green, C. (2001). Suppressing unwanted memories by executive control. *Nature, 410*, 366–369.

Anderson, M. C., & Levy, B. J. (2009). Suppressing unwanted memories. *Current Directions in Psychological Science, 18*, 189–194.

Ansfield, M. E., Wegner, D. M. & Bowser, R. (1996) Ironic effects of sleep urgency. *Behaviour Research and Therapy, 34*, 523–531.

Bargh, J. A., & Pietromonaco, P. (1982). Automatic information processing and social perception: The influence of trait information presented outside of conscious awareness on impression formation. *Journal of Personality and Social Psychology, 43*, 437–449.

Barnier, A. J., Levin, K., & Maher, A. (2004). Suppressing thoughts of past events: Are repressive copers good suppressors? *Cognition and Emotion, 18*, 513–531.

Beck, J. G., Gudmundsdottir, B., Palyo, S. A., Miller, L. M., & Grant, D. M. (2006). Rebound effects following deliberate thought suppression: Does PTSD make a difference? *Behavior Therapy, 37*, 170–180.

Becker, E. S., Rinck, M., Roth, W. T., & Margraf, J. (1998). Don't worry and beware of white bears: Thought suppression in anxiety patients. *Journal of Anxiety Disorders, 12*, 39–55.

Bjork, E., Bjork, R., & Anderson, M. C. (1998). Varieties of goal-directed forgetting. In J. M. Golding & C. M. MacLeod, (Eds.), *Intentional forgetting: Interdisciplinary approaches,* (pp. 103–137). Mahwah, NJ: Erlbaum.

Boon, B., Stroebe, W., Schut, H., & Ijntema, R. (2002). Ironic processes in the eating behavior of restrained eaters. *British Journal of Health Psychology, 7*, 1–10.

Botvinick, M., Braver, T., Barch, D. Carter, C. & Cohen, J. (2001). Conflict monitoring and cognitive control. *Psychological Review, 108*, 624–652.

Brewin, C. R., & Andrews, B. (1998). Recovered memories of trauma: Phenomenology and cognitive mechanisms. *Clinical Psychology Review, 18*, 949–970.

Brewin, C. R., & Beaton, A. (2002). Thought suppression, intelligence, and working memory capacity. *Behaviour Research and Therapy, 40*, 923–930.

Brewin, C. R., & Smart, L. (2005). Working memory capacity and suppression of intrusive thoughts. *Journal of Behavior Therapy and Experimental Psychiatry, 36*, 61–68.

Bryant, R. A., & Sindicich, N. (2008). Hypnosis and thought suppression—more data: A brief communication. *International Journal of Clinical and Experimental Hypnosis, 56*, 37–46.

Bryant, R. A., & Wimalaweera, S. (2006). Enhancing thought suppression with hypnosis. *International Journal of Clinical and Experimental Hypnosis, 54*, 488–499.

Burns, J. W., Johnson, B., J., Devine, J., Mahoney, N., & Pawl, R. (1998). Anger management style and the prediction of treatment outcome among male and female chronic pain patients. *Behaviour Research and Therapy, 36*, 1051–1062.

Burns, J. W., Quartana, P., Gilliam, W., Gray, E., Matsuura, J., Nappi, C., et al. (2008). Effects of anger suppression on pain severity and pain behaviors among chronic pain patients: Evaluation of an ironic process model. *Health Psychology, 27*, 645–652.

Cioffi, D., & Holloway, J. (1993) Delayed costs of suppressed pain. *Journal of Personality and Social Psychology, 64*, 274–282.

Clark, D. A. (2004). *Cognitive-behavioral therapy for OCD.* New York: Guilford Press.

Clark, D. A. (Ed.). (2005). *Intrusive thoughts in clinical disorders: Theory, research, and treatment.* New York: Guilford Press.

Clark, D. A., Purdon, C., & Wang, A. (2003). The Meta-Cognitive Beliefs Questionnaire: Development of a measure of obsessional beliefs. *Behaviour Research and Therapy, 41*, 655–669.

Clark, D. M., Ball, S. & Pape, D. (1991) An experimental investigation of thought suppression. *Behaviour Research and Therapy, 29*, 253–257.

Conway, M., Howell, A., & Giannopoulos, C. (1991). Dysphoria and thought suppression. *Cognitive Therapy and Research, 15*, 153–166.

Crowne, D. P., & Marlowe, D. A. (1960). A new scale of social desirability independent of psychopathology. *Journal of Consulting Psychology, 24*, 349–354.

Dalgleish, T., & Yiend, J. (2006). The effects of suppressing a negative autobiographical memory on concurrent intrusions and subsequent autobiographical recall in dysphoria. *Journal of Abnormal Psychology, 115*, 467–473.

Devine, P. G. (1989). Stereotypes and prejudice: Their automatic and controlled components. *Journal of Personality and Social Psychology, 56*, 5–18.

Dostoevsky, F. (1955). *Winter notes on summer impressions* (R. L. Renfield, Trans.). New York: Criterion Books.

Enticott, P. G., & Gold, R. S. (2002). Contrasting the ironic monitoring and motivational explanations of postsuppressional rebound. *Psychological Reports, 90*, 447–450.

Erdelyi, M. H. (2006). The unified theory of repression. *Behavioral and Brain Sciences, 29*, 499–511.

Erskine, J. A. K., & Georgiou, G. J. (2010). Effects of thought suppression on eating behavior in restrained and non-restrained eaters. *Appetite. 54*, 499–503..

Forster, J., & Liberman, N. (2001). The role of attribution of motivation in producing post-suppressional rebound. *Journal of Personality and Social Psychology, 81*, 377–390.

Forster, J., & Liberman, N. (2004). A motivational model of post-suppressional rebound. In W. Stroebe & M. Hewstone (Eds.), *European review of social psychology* (Vol. 15, pp. 1–32). New York: Wiley.

Freud, S. (1896). The aetiology of hysteria. In J. Strachey (Ed.), *The standard edition of the complete works of Sigmund Freud* (Vol. 3, pp. 191–221). London: Hogarth Press.

Freud, S. (1950). A case of successful treatment by hypnotism (with some remarks on the origin of hysterical symptoms through the "counter-will"). In J. Strachey (Ed.), *The standard edition of the complete psychological works of Sigmund Freud, 1*, 115–128.

Geraerts, E., Merckelbach, H., Jelicic, M., & Habets, P. (2007). Suppression of intrusive thoughts and working memory capacity in repressive coping. *American Journal of Psychology, 120*, 205–218.

Geraerts, E., Merckelbach, H., Jelicic, M., & Smeets, E. (2006). Long term consequences of suppression of intrusive thoughts and repressive coping. *Behaviour Research and Therapy, 44,* 1451–1460.

Gilbert, D. T. (1991). How mental systems believe. *American Psychologist, 46,* 107–119.

Gross, J. J. (1998). Antecedent- and response-focused emotion regulation: Divergent consequences for experience, expression, and physiology. *Journal of Personality and Social Psychology, 74,* 224–237.

Harnden, J. L., McNally, R. J., & Jimerson, D. C. (1997). Effects of suppressing thoughts about body weight: A comparison of dieters and nondieters. *International Journal of Eating Disorders, 22,* 285–290.

Hartlage, S., Alloy, L. B., Vázquez, C., & Dykman, B. (1993). Automatic and effortful processing in depression. *Psychological Bulletin, 113,* 247–278.

Harvey, A. G. (2003). The attempted suppression of presleep cognitive activity in insomnia. *Cognitive Therapy and Research, 27,* 593–602.

Howell, A., & Conway, M. (1992). Mood and the suppression of positive and negative self-referent thoughts. *Cognitive Therapy and Research, 16,* 535–555.

Janeck, A. S., & Calamari, J. E. (1999). Thought suppression in obsessive-compulsive disorder. *Cognitive Therapy and Research, 23,* 497–509.

Johnston, L., Hudson, S. M., & Ward, T. (1997). The suppression of sexual thoughts by child molesters: A preliminary investigation. *Sexual Abuse: Journal of Research and Treatment, 9,* 303–319.

Kelly, A. E., & Kahn, J. H. (1994). Effects of suppression of personal intrusive thoughts. *Journal of Personality and Social Psychology, 66,* 998–1006.

Kircanski, K., Craske, M. G., Bjork, R. A. (2008). Thought suppression enhances memory bias for threat material. *Behaviour Research and Therapy, 46,* 462–476.

Klein, A. A. (2007). Suppression-induced hyperaccessibility of thoughts in abstinent alcoholics: A preliminary investigation. *Behaviour Research and Therapy, 45,* 167–177.

Koole, S. L., & van Knippenberg, A. (2007). Controlling your mind without ironic consequences: Self-affirmation eliminates rebound effects after thought suppression. *Journal of Experimental and Social Psychology, 43,* 671–677.

Kozak, M., Sternglanz, R. W., Viswanathan, U., & Wegner, D. M. (2008). The role of thought suppression in building mental blocks. *Consciousness and Cognition, 17,* 1123–1130.

Lane, J. D., & Wegner, D. M. (1994). Secret relationships: The back alley to love. In R. Erber & R. Gilmour (Eds.), *Theoretical frameworks for personal relationships* (pp. 67–85). Hillsdale, NJ: Erlbaum.

Lane, J. D., & Wegner, D. M. (1995). The cognitive consequences of secrecy. *Journal of Personality and Social Psychology, 69,* 237–253.

Lavy, E. H., & van den Hout, M. A. (1990) Thought suppression induces intrusions. *Behavioural Psychotherapy, 18,* 251–258.

Levy, B. J., & Anderson, M. C. (2008). Individual differences in the suppression of unwanted memories: The executive deficit hypothesis. *Acta Psychologica, 127,* 623–635.

Macrae, C. N., Bodenhausen, G. V., & Milne, A. B. (1998). Saying no to unwanted thoughts: Self-focus and the regulation of mental life. *Journal of Personality and Social Psychology, 74,* 578–589.

Macrae, C. N., Bodenhausen, G. V., Milne, A. B., & Ford, R. L. (1997) On regulation of recollection: Intentional forgetting of stereotypical memories. *Journal of Personality and Social Psychology, 72,* 709–719.

Macrae, C. N., Bodenhausen, G. V., Milne, A. B., & Jetten, J. (1994) Out of mind but back in sight: Stereotypes on the rebound. *Journal of Personality and Social Psychology, 67,* 808–817.

Martin, L. L., & Tesser, A. (1996). Some ruminative thoughts. In R. S. Wyer (Ed.), *Advances in social cognition* (Vol. 9, pp. 1–47). Mahwah, NJ: Erlbaum.

Masedo, A. I., & Esteve, M. R. (2007). Effect of suppression, acceptance and spontaneous coping on pain tolerance, pain intensity and distress. *Behaviour Research and Therapy, 45,* 199–209.

Mitchell, J. P., Heatherton, T. F., Kelley, W. M., Wyland, C. L., Wegner, D. M., & Macrae, C. N. (2007). Separating sustained from transient aspects of cognitive control during thought suppression. *Psychological Science, 18,* 292–297.

Monteith, M. J., Sherman, J. W., & Devine, P. G. (1998). *Personality and Social Psychology Review, 2,* 63–82.

Muris, P., Jongh, A. D., Merckelbach, H., Postema, S., & Vet, M. (1998). Thought suppression in phobic and non-phobic dental patients. *Anxiety, Stress, & Coping, 11,* 275–287.

Muris, P., Merckelbach, H., & de Jong, P. (1993). Verbalization and environmental cuing in thought suppression. *Behaviour Research and Therapy, 35,* 769–774.

Najmi, S., Riemann, B. C., & Wegner, D. M. (2009). Managing unwanted intrusive thoughts in obsessive-compulsive disorder: Relative effectiveness of suppression, focused distraction, and acceptance. *Behaviour Research and Therapy, 47,* 494–503.

Najmi, S., & Wegner, D. M. (2008a). Thought suppression and psychopathology. In A. J. Elliott (Ed.), *Handbook of approach and avoidance motivation.* Mahwah, NJ: Erlbaum.

Najmi, S., & Wegner, D. M. (2008b). The gravity of unwanted thoughts: Asymmetric priming effects in thought suppression. *Consciousness & Cognition, 17,* 114–124.

Najmi, S., & Wegner, D. M. (2009). Hidden complications of thought suppression. *International Journal of Cognitive Therapy, 2,* 210–223.

Nelson, H. E., & Willison, J. (1991). *National Adult Reading Test: Test manual* (2nd ed.). Windsor, UK: NFER Nelson.

Palfai, T. P., Colby, S. M., Monti, P. M., & Rohsenow, D. J. (1997). Effects of suppressing the urge to drink on smoking topography: A preliminary study. *Psychology of Addictive Behaviors, 11,* 115–123.

Pennebaker, J. W. (1985). Traumatic experience and psychosomatic disease: Exploring the roles of behavioral inhibition, obsession, and confiding. *Canadian Psychology, 26,* 82–95.

Purdon, C. L., Rowa, K., & Antony, M. M. (2005). Thought suppression and its effects on thought frequency, appraisal and mood state in individuals with obsessive-compulsive disorder. *Behaviour Research and Therapy, 43,* 93–108.

Purdon, C. L., Rowa, K., & Antony, M. M. (2007). Daily records of thought suppression by individuals with obsessive-compulsive disorder. *Behavioural and Cognitive Psychotherapy, 35,* 47–59.

Rassin, E. (2005). *Thought suppression.* New York: Elsevier.

Raven, J. C., Court, J. H., & Raven, J. (1977). *Manual for Raven's progressive matrices.* London: H. K. Lewis.

Renaud, J. M., & McConnell, A. R. (2002). Organization of the self-concept and the suppression of self-relevant thoughts. *Journal of Experimental Social Psychology, 38,* 79–86.

Roemer, L., & Borkovec, T. D. (1994). Effects of suppressing thoughts about emotional material. *Journal of Abnormal Psychology, 103,* 467–474.

Salkovskis, P. M., & Campbell, P. (1994). Thought suppression induces intrusion in naturally occurring negative intrusive thoughts. *Behaviour Research and Therapy, 32,* 1–8.

Salkovskis, P. M., & Reynolds, M. (1994). Thought suppression and smoking cessation. *Behaviour Research and Therapy, 32,* 193–201.

Sherman, J. W., Stroessner, S. J., Loftus, S. T. & Deguzman, G. (1997) Stereotype suppression and recognition memory for stereotypical and nonstereotypical information. *Social Cognition, 15,* 205–215.

Shipherd, J. C., & Beck, J. G. (1999). The effects of suppressing trauma-related thoughts on women with rape-related post-traumatic stress disorder. *Behaviour Research and Therapy, 37,* 99–112.

Shipherd, J. C., & Beck, J. G. (2005). The role of thought suppression in posttraumatic stress disorder. *Behavior Therapy, 36,* 277–287.

Steele, C. M. (1988). The psychology of self-affirmation: Sustaining the integrity of the self. In L. Berkowitz (Ed.), *Advances in experimental social psychology* (Vol. 21, pp. 261–302). New York: Academic Press.

Stroop, J. R. (1935). Studies of interference in serial verbal reactions. *Journal of Experimental Psychology, 18,* 643–662.

Sullivan, M. J. L., Rouse, D., Bishop, S., & Johnston, S. (1997). Thought suppression, catastrophizing, and pain. *Cognitive Therapy and Research, 21,* 555–568.

Taylor, F., & Bryant, R. A. (2007). The tendency to suppress, inhibiting thoughts, and dream rebound. *Behaviour Research and Therapy, 45,* 163–168.

Taylor, J. A. (1953). A personality scale of manifest anxiety. *Journal of Abnormal and Social Psychology, 48,* 285–290.

Tolin, D. F., Abramowitz, J. S., Hamlin, C., Foa, E. B., & Synodi, D. S. (2002). Attributions for thought suppression failure in obsessive-compulsive disorder. *Cognitive Therapy and Research, 26,* 505–517.

Tolin, D. F., Abramowitz, J. S., Przeworski, A., & Foa, E. B. (2002). Thought suppression in obsessive-compulsive disorder. *Behaviour Research and Therapy, 40,* 1255–1274.

Trinder, H., & Salkovskis, P. M. (1994). Personally relevant intrusions outside the laboratory: Long-term suppression increases intrusion. *Behaviour Research and Therapy, 32,* 833–842.

Uleman, J. S., & Bargh, J. A. (1989). *Unintended thought.* New York: Guilford Press.

Wegner, D. M. (1989). *White bears and other unwanted thoughts: Suppression, obsession, and the psychology of mental control.* New York: Viking/Penguin.

Wegner, D. M. (1994). Ironic processes of mental control. *Psychological Review, 101,* 34–52.

Wegner, D. M., Broome, A., & Blumberg, S. J. (1997) Ironic effects of trying to relax under stress. *Behaviour Research and Therapy, 35,* 11–21.

Wegner, D. M., & Erber, R. E. (1992). The hyperaccessibility of suppressed thoughts. *Journal of Personality and Social Psychology, 63,* 903–912.

Wegner, D. M., Erber, R. E., & Zanakos, S. (1993) Ironic processes in the mental control of mood and mood-related thought. *Journal of Personality and Social Psychology, 65,* 1093–1104.

Wegner, D. M., & Gold, D. B. (1995). Fanning old flames: Emotional and cognitive effects of suppressing thoughts of a past relationship. *Journal of Personality and Social Psychology, 68,* 782–792.

Wegner, D. M., Lane, J. D., & Dimitri, S. (1994). The allure of secret relationships. *Journal of Personality and Social Psychology, 66,* 287–300.

Wegner, D. M., Schneider, D. J., Carter, S., & White, T. (1987). Paradoxical effects of thought suppression. *Journal of Personality and Social Psychology, 53,* 5–13.

Wegner, D. M., Schneider, D. J., Knutson, B., & McMahon, S. R. (1991). Polluting the stream of consciousness: The effect of thought suppression on the mind's environment. *Cognitive Therapy and Research, 15,* 141–152.

Wegner, D. M., & Schneider, D. J. (2003). The white bear story. *Psychological Inquiry, 14,* 326–329.

Wegner, D. M., Shortt, J. W., Blake, A. W., & Page, M. S. (1990). The suppression of exciting thoughts. *Journal of Personality and Social Psychology, 58,* 409–418.

Wegner, D. M., Wenzlaff, R. M., & Kozak, M. (2004). Dream rebound: The return of suppressed thoughts in dreams. *Psychological Science, 15,* 232–236.

Wegner, D. M., & Zanakos, S. (1994). Chronic thought suppression. *Journal of Personality, 62,* 615–640.

Weinberger, D. A., Schwartz, G. E., & Davidson, R. J. (1979). Low-anxious, high-anxious, and repressive coping styles: Psychometric patterns and behavioral and physiological responses to stress. *Journal of Abnormal Psychology, 88,* 369–380.

Wenzlaff, R. M. (2005). Seeking solace but finding despair: The persistence of intrusive thoughts in depression. In D. A. Clark (Ed.), *Intrusive thoughts in clinical disorders: Theory, research, and treatment* (pp. 54–85). New York: Guilford Press.

Wenzlaff, R. M., & Bates, D. E. (1998). Unmasking a cognitive vulnerability to depression: How lapses in mental control reveal depressive thinking. *Journal of Personality and Social Psychology, 75,* 1559–1571.

Wenzlaff, R. M., & Eisenberg, A. R. (2001). Mental control after dysphoria: Evidence of a suppressed, depressive bias. *Behavior Therapy, 32,* 27–45.

Wenzlaff, R. M., Meir, J., & Salas, D. M. (2002). Thought suppression and memory biases during and after depressive moods. *Cognition and Emotion, 16,* 403–422.

Wenzlaff, R. M., Rude, S. S., Taylor, C. J., Stultz, C. H., & Sweatt, R. A. (2001). Beneath the veil of thought suppression: Attentional bias and depression risk. *Cognition and Emotion, 15,* 435–452.

Wenzlaff, R. M., & Wegner, D. M. (2000). Thought suppression. In S. T. Fiske (Ed.), *Annual review of psychology* (Vol. 51, pp. 59–91). Palo Alto, CA: Annual Reviews.

Wenzlaff, R. M., Wegner, D. M., & Klein, S. B. (1991). The role of thought suppression in the bonding of thought and mood. *Journal of Personality and Social Psychology, 60,* 500–508.

Wenzlaff, R. M., Wegner, D. M., & Roper, D. W. (1988). Depression and mental control: The resurgence of unwanted negative thoughts. *Journal of Personality and Social Psychology, 55,* 882–892.

Williams, J. M. G., Mathews, A., & MacLeod, C. (1996). The emotional Stroop task and psychopathology. *Psychological Bulletin, 120,* 3–24.

Wyer, N., Sherman, J. W., & Stroessner, S. J. (1998). The spontaneous suppression of racial stereotypes. *Social Cognition, 16,* 340–352.

Wyer, N., Sherman, J. W., & Stroessner, S. J. (2000). The roles of motivation and ability in controlling the consequences of stereotype suppression. *Personality and Social Psychology Bulletin, 26,* 13–25.

Wyland, C. L., & Forgas, J. P. (2007). On bad mood and white bears: The effects of mood state on ability to suppress unwanted thoughts. *Cognition and Emotion, 21,* 1513–1524.

Wyland, C. L., Kelley, W. M., Macrae, C. N., Gordon, H. L., & Heatherton, T. F. (2003). Neural correlates of thought suppression. *Neuropsychologia, 41,* 1863–1867.

Zeigarnik, B. (1927). On the memory for completed and uncompleted actions. *Psychologische Forschung, 9,* 1–85.

PART 3

Social Cognition and Social Psychology

CHAPTER 21

Moods, Emotions, and Evaluations as Information

Linda M. Isbell *and* Elicia C. Lair

Abstract

Affect plays a pervasive role in social cognition. Research demonstrates that moods, emotions, and evaluative reactions can influence social cognitive processes in a large number of diverse ways by serving as a source of information. This chapter first discusses the direct influence of affect on judgment and on other social cognitive processes that can influence judgment, including memory processes, attention, and perception. It then reviews the impact of affect on information processing styles, focusing on the extent to which affect provides information that leads individuals to process in a global, heuristic manner versus a local, systematic one. Finally, a new development that emphasizes the highly contextualized and malleable nature of the influence of affect on information processing is presented. Throughout this chapter, the social cognitive consequences of different types of affective information are considered, including moods, emotions, and evaluations.

Key Words: affect, social cognition, emotion, mood, information processing, affect-as-information

Introduction

Questions about the relationship between feeling and thinking are certainly not of recent vintage—they date back to ancient Greek philosophers, including Plato and Aristotle, and such enlightenment philosophers as Descartes. Within modern psychology, such questions have been largely neglected until about three decades ago. Consistent with Plato's classical thinking, cognitive psychology has long believed that affect adversely alters rational cognitive processes so that any influence of affect on cognition should be eradicated. In contrast, more contemporary scholars have discovered that affect is a fundamental part of human cognition and that affective experiences convey valuable information that guides individuals' thoughts, judgments, and behaviors. Rather than antagonists, affect and cognition are necessary allies that work in tandem to produce adaptive responses to the world (e.g., Damasio, 1994; Davidson, 2003; Storbeck & Clore, 2007; Schwarz & Clore, 1983). Consistent with this view, research demonstrates that

individuals who are unable to use affective information suffer profound deficits in their judgment and decision making (Damasio, 1994).

In this chapter, we review evidence concerning the relationship between affect and cognition. We first define what is meant by affect and discuss three distinct types of affective experiences (moods, emotions, and evaluations). Then, consistent with what is traditionally done in the affect literature, we consider two major lines of research examining affective influence. First, we examine the influence of affect on judgment, as well as on various social cognitive processes (i.e., memory, attention, and perception) that can influence judgment. Second, we examine the specific ways in which affect can influence information processing, focusing on the extent to which affective experiences lead individuals to process in a global, heuristic manner versus a more local, systematic one. Within each of these two major sections, we review the ways in which moods, emotions, and evaluations can influence cognition.

What Is Affect?

It is a seemingly simple question to ask, "What is affect?" yet there has been surprisingly little consensus in the field on how best to define affect and how to identify what qualifies as an affective experience. Indeed, this definitional puzzle has perplexed affect scholars for ages, and William James' (1890) oft-cited question, "What is an emotion?" still leads to a variety of conflicting responses. Although the field has collectively struggled to come to consensus in defining what affect is and what it is not, many researchers agree that valence is a key component of an affective experience (e.g., Ortony, Clore, & Collins, 1988; Russell, 2003). That is, all affective experiences involve positive or negative responses to something.

Beyond valence, affective experiences are often categorized as moods or emotions. Moods are typically conceptualized as diffuse, long-lasting, low-intensity feeling states that are not linked to specific eliciting conditions. Compared with moods, emotions are frequently conceptualized as more differentiated affective experiences that are of shorter duration and greater intensity, and that are tied to specific eliciting conditions (Isbell & Burns, 2007; Morris, 1989; see Keltner & Lerner, 2010, for a review). For example, when it is a warm and sunny day, we may be unaware of why we are feeling a diffuse happy state, thus rendering these feelings a mood. In contrast, emotions are characterized as being "about" something specific, such as feeling hopeful about an upcoming job opportunity. Given that emotions are more contextualized than moods, moods and emotions can have different effects on social cognitive processes, yet they are often theorized to serve similar functions. That is, both moods and emotions serve to signal individuals about the nature of ongoing events in their environment and to alert individuals about whether and how to respond to such events (e.g., Frijda, 1986; Simon, 1967). In this way, these experiences motivate behavior.

Theoretically, points of divergence emerge when considering what specific components are needed to characterize an experience as an emotion (see Keltner & Lerner, 2010, for a review). Although the earliest theories of emotion were noncognitive and based largely on the presence of specific physiological responses (James, 1890/1983; Lange, 1885/1912), recent theorizing includes a more central role for cognition. Cognitive appraisal theories proposed during the past three decades posit that emotions result from cognitive appraisals of one's current situation (e.g., Ortony et al., 1988; Roseman, 1984;

Smith & Ellsworth, 1985). For example, fear results from appraisals of a situation as negative, as having an uncertain outcome, and as under situational control, whereas anger results from appraisals of a situation as negative, as having a certain outcome, and as being under the control of some other individual (Smith & Ellsworth, 1985).

The notion that cognition is a necessary component of affective experience has received considerable empirical support, but a classic debate between Zajonc (1980) and Lazarus (1982) raised significant questions about the relationship between affect and cognition. Zajonc (1980) argued that the affective and cognitive systems are independent and proposed that affective responses are automatic and primary, with cognitive processes following affective ones. Lazarus (1982) countered that emotions are the product of cognition and that cognitive appraisals are a necessary precondition for emotions. This debate is partly the result of definitional disagreements concerning what affect is. Whereas Zajonc identified automatic evaluations of liking/disliking as affect (i.e., valence-based preferences), Lazarus's theorizing was more specific to moods and emotions.

Currently, most researchers consider moods, emotions, and evaluations all as falling under the large conceptual umbrella of "affect"; however, researchers overwhelmingly view moods, emotions, and evaluations as distinct types of affect that can have different effects on social cognitive processes. For this reason, we examine each type of affective experience separately when discussing the role of affect on judgment and processing. In doing so, we extricate ourselves from lingering debates that might exist concerning the independence of affect and cognition (e.g., Zajonc, 2000) and instead take the position that affect and cognition are integrated, reciprocal, and inextricably linked (e.g., Davidson, 2003; Storbeck & Clore, 2007). Further, we take the theoretical perspective that affective experiences serve as a source of information that can have a ubiquitous influence on our judgments and processing. In this chapter, we review the evidence for this position.

Affect and Judgment

An overwhelmingly large and impressive body of literature demonstrates that positive and negative feelings lead individuals to render mood-congruent judgments in many different contexts (see Clore, Wyer, et al., 2001; Schwarz, 1990, 2012; Schwarz & Clore, 2007; Wyer, Clore, & Isbell, 1999, for reviews). For example, compared with individuals in a negative mood, those in a positive mood report more favorable judgments of life satisfaction (e.g., Schwarz & Clore, 1983), political candidates (e.g., Isbell & Wyer, 1999; Ottati & Isbell, 1996), the self (e.g., Sedikides, 1992, 1995), and consumer products (e.g., Pham, 1998). Feelings can similarly influence many significant real-world judgments, including evaluations of job applicants (e.g., Baron, 1993), medical school admission decisions (Redelmeier & Baxter, 2009), and stock market investments (Hirshleifer & Shumway, 2003). One of the most compelling theoretical explanations for the large and diverse set of findings concerning the influence of mood on judgments lies in the affect-as-information (AAI) approach (see Schwarz, 2012; Schwarz & Clore, 2007).

Moods as Information

According to the mood-as-information approach, people rely on their feelings as a direct source of information when making judgments (Schwarz & Clore, 1983; Wyer & Carlston, 1979). For example, when individuals are asked to make an evaluative judgment about a person, they may simply ask themselves how they feel about this person rather than conduct an exhaustive assessment of the person's attributes. Often, how we feel about a target is strongly related to what we know about the target. In these cases, reliance on such *integral* affect (i.e., affective responses elicited directly from a target; Bodenhausen, 1993) is highly relevant to the judgment, and thus, it is meaningful and adaptive to rely on it (Damasio, 1994). In many situations, however, individuals are unable to differentiate the influence of integral affect from the influence of *incidental* affect (i.e., feelings that one just happens to be experiencing at the moment; Bodenhausen, 1993). Consistent with the gestalt perspective (Asch, 1946; Heider, 1958), individuals tend to perceive affective experiences as an integrated whole rather than as distinct parts. Just as we do not typically experience a portrait as two eyes, two ears, a nose, and a mouth (Farah, Wilson, Drain, & Tanaka, 1998), we do not experience our affective reactions to an object as coming from distinct sources. Consequently, we typically do not parse our affective reactions. As Schwarz and Clore (2007) noted, we have only "one window on our experience" (p. 386). Thus, whatever reactions we experience while focusing on a specific target are experienced as being "about" the target (Clore et al., 2001; Higgins, 1998). This tendency to misattribute one's current feelings to whatever is in one's mind at the time happens automatically and

does not necessitate a conscious attribution process (Schwarz, 2012; Schwarz & Clore, 2007).

Although incidental affective cues have the power to color many of our evaluative judgments, a key tenant of the AAI approach is that these cues are only relied on if they are perceived to be relevant to a judgment. If the informational value of these feelings is called into question (e.g., by bringing participants' attention to judgment-irrelevant reasons for their affect), these feelings no longer influence judgments. In a now classic and highly cited paper, Schwarz and Clore (1983) provided the first evidence for this effect. In one study, participants were telephoned on either rainy or sunny days and interviewed about their life satisfaction. Some participants responded to the survey without any cueing from the interviewer about the weather, whereas others responded after a brief mention of the weather. Participants in the no-cueing condition relied on their current affect as a source of information about their life satisfaction, reporting greater life satisfaction on sunny days than on rainy ones. In contrast, participants for whom the weather was made salient showed no mood effects on their judgments. In this case, participants attributed their current moods to the weather, thereby discounting the relevance of these feelings to their judgments.

Numerous studies have subsequently reported similar findings (e.g., Gasper & Clore, 1998; Savitsky et al., 1998; Siemer & Reisenzein, 1998). The simple act of prompting individuals to label their feelings can also eliminate mood effects on judgments (e.g., Keltner, Locke, & Audrain, 1993). Mood effects are also diminished when individuals have time and other information on which to base their judgment (Siemer & Reisenzein, 1998; see Wyer, Clore, & Isbell, 1999, for a review), when making a judgment for another person rather than themselves (Raghunathan & Pham, 1999), when judging central rather than peripheral aspects of the self (Sedikides, 1995), and when forming intentions to perform a behavior driven by instrumental motives (e.g., to watch a movie in order to be eligible to earn money in a subsequent research study) rather than consummatory ones (e.g., to watch a movie for enjoyment; Pham, 1998).

ADDITIONAL MODERATORS OF THE EFFECTS OF MOOD ON JUDGMENT

Three additional lines of research conducted in the AAI tradition demonstrate that moods can meaningfully and systematically influence judgments in ways that do not result in mood-congruent judgments. This can occur when individuals attempt to correct their judgments for the influence of affect, when an individual's affective state (or information related to it) is used as a standard of comparison, and when the judgmental context is altered. We briefly review each of these here.

CORRECTION

As described earlier, discounting the informational relevance of one's affect eliminates the impact of affect on judgment; however, such a process assumes that individuals have other relevant nonaffective information to rely on when making their judgments. Often, this is not the case, and when individuals lack alternative information, they may attempt to correct their judgments for the perceived bias of affect. Given that we tend to experience our affective reactions as a unified whole, we are not particularly good at identifying, estimating, and correcting for such biases, and may often lack the motivation and ability to do so (Wegener & Petty, 1997; Wilson & Brekke, 1994). Even when correction processes do occur, we tend to overcorrect, leading to mood-incongruent effects. For example, Ottati and Isbell (1996) and Isbell and Wyer (1999) found that experienced political information processors, who possessed both the motivation and the ability to correct their judgments for the influence of irrelevant affect, judged an unknown political candidate more favorably when they were sad than when they were happy, reflecting overcorrection. Inexperienced political information processors presumably lacked the motivation and ability to correct, and therefore judged the candidate more favorably when they were happy than when they were sad. Thus, expertise can moderate the impact of mood on judgments.

STANDARD OF COMPARISON

When an affective state, or specific cognitive information that accompanies it, serves as a standard of comparison, mood-congruency effects may be eliminated or reversed (Schwarz, Strack, Kommer, & Wagner, 1987). For example, Schwarz et al. (1987) found that participants seated in a pleasant laboratory room rated their life satisfaction more favorably than those seated in an unpleasant room; however, no such effects were found in judgments of participants' overall satisfaction with their current housing. In this case, the room served as a standard of comparison by providing participants with relevant nonaffective information on which to base their judgment. People also relied on recalled affective experiences to a greater extent when judging their life satisfaction if the experiences were recalled in a vivid and emotional manner rather than a more pallid one (Strack, Schwarz, & Gschneidinger, 1985). In pallid conditions, the affective descriptions served as a standard of comparison for participants in judging their lives. In this case, individuals who wrote about a positive experience judged their life satisfaction to be lower than those who wrote about a negative one. In contrast, participants in the vivid conditions used the affect that the recalled events elicited as a source of information, resulting in a mood assimilation effect. Collectively, these results demonstrate that mood-congruency effects can be altered in systematic ways depending on the relevance of an affect-eliciting event to a specific domain of judgment.

CONTEXT EFFECTS

Although much work demonstrates that individuals rely on their feelings as a basis for answering the question, "How do I feel about it (i.e., the target of judgment)?" mood can also be used as information to respond to whatever question individuals have in mind at the time (e.g., "Do I have enough information to make a judgment?"; Martin, Ward, Achee, & Wyer, 1993; Schwarz, 2012). In this case, mood effects will vary depending on the specific question under consideration. For example, Martin and colleagues (Martin et al., 1993) instructed individuals in happy and sad moods to form an impression of an unknown target. While doing the task, half of the participants were instructed to ask themselves whether they felt like continuing the task, whereas the other half were instructed to ask themselves whether they had enough information. Participants in the first condition were more likely to continue the task if they were happy than if they were sad, whereas participants in the latter condition showed the opposite effect. These results demonstrate that mood serves as input to whatever question participants are considering at the time and that different affective states may have different implications for judgment and behavior.

Mood can also serve as input when individuals rely on their current feelings as a basis for evaluating whether a target accomplished what was expected (Martin, Abend, Sedikides, & Green, 1997). For example, if individuals expect a story to be sad, then sad feelings lead individuals to evaluate the story more positively than do happy feelings. In this case, the comparison of current feelings with expected feelings provides information about the target. Matches signal that the target successfully accomplished what it intended, whereas mismatches lead one to conclude that it did not. In these cases, happy or sad moods can lead to either positive (in matching conditions) or negative (in mismatching conditions) judgments of a target. Similar effects emerge when participants judge a vacation that is advertised as either adventurous or serene (Kim, Park, & Schwarz, 2010). When participants' current feelings matched the claim, participants evaluated the vacation more favorably than when their feelings did not match. In this case, participants used their feelings as information about whether the vacation is likely to live up to its promise.

Emotions as Information

Early research investigating the influence of affect on judgment focused extensively on moods that are either positive or negative (or happy or sad) and observed their impact on dependent variables that are largely evaluative in nature (e.g., life satisfaction judgments, liking judgments). Based on our earlier definitions of moods and emotions, it is clear that moods should be more likely than emotions to be misattributed to a target. That is, moods by definition are diffuse positive or negative feelings that are not tied to a specific eliciting object, whereas emotions are more specific reactions to a specific target. For this reason, some scholars believed that emotions are unlikely to be confused with reactions to targets that did not elicit them; however, work over the past two decades has found that discrete emotions can have profound and specific influences on judgment.

As we mentioned earlier, cognitive appraisal theories of emotion suggest that emotional experiences reflect underlying appraisal dimensions that not only inform one that an event is positive or negative, but also provide information about myriad ways in which it is so (e.g., Lerner & Keltner, 2000, 2001; Ortony et al., 1988). Recall that we previously identified anger and fear as negative emotions, but made the distinction that anger is associated with appraisals of certainty and individual control, whereas fear is associated with appraisals of uncertainty and situational control (e.g., Roseman, 1984; Smith & Ellsworth, 1985). Given that different emotions result from different cognitive appraisal patterns, emotions necessarily provide more specific information than do moods. Consequently, emotions have more constrained effects on judgment. Emotion effects on judgment are especially likely under conditions in which the emotion's underlying appraisal pattern is relevant to the

judgment at hand. In such cases, appraisal-congruent judgments typically emerge. Such effects have been found in a variety of domains, including judgments about causality and fairness, intergroup and interpersonal judgments, risk and likelihood judgments, and morality-based judgments. We review the evidence in each of these domains below.

JUDGMENTS ABOUT CAUSALITY AND FAIRNESS

In one of the first examinations of the impact of discrete affective experiences on judgment, Keltner, Ellsworth, and Edwards (1993) examined the impact of sadness and anger on attributions for why an event occurred. Consider, for example, that you are in a car crash. If you believe that the crash was the result of an intoxicated driver (other-caused), you are likely to feel angry; however, if you believe the crash was the result of icy roads (situation-caused), you are likely to feel sad (Keltner et al., 1993). Given that different appraisals give rise to different emotional experiences, multiple appraisal dimensions (i.e., valence, certainty, control) that are activated at the time of an event can carry over to influence subsequent judgments (Keltner et al., 1993; Lerner, Goldberg, & Tetlock, 1998; Lerner & Keltner, 2000). Consistent with this idea, research demonstrates that compared with neutral feelings or sadness, anger leads individuals to blame others more than situations (Keltner et al., 1993; Lerner et al., 1998) and to make more punitive attributional judgments of responsibility for harm (Lerner et al., 1998)

Anger also leads individuals to perceive the behavior of others to be less fair (Keltner et al., 1993). For example, in one study, participants played an ultimatum game (after writing about an anger-inducing life experience) and were presented with a series of offers, including both fair and unfair offers. Participants made decisions either to accept or reject each offer (Srivastava, Espinoza, & Fedorikhin, 2009). Compared with participants who were led to correctly attribute their anger to the story they wrote, those who misattributed their anger to the unfair offers were significantly more likely to reject these offers. No differences were found for the fair offers. Together, these findings demonstrate that emotions associated with appraisals of control and certainty can influence judgments of causality, fairness, and blame.

INTERGROUP AND INTERPERSONAL JUDGMENTS

The idea that emotions play a key role in intergroup judgment has a long history in social psychology dating back more than 50 years (e.g., Allport, 1954). Although the vast majority of research has broadly conceptualized prejudice as a negative evaluation of a group, recent work demonstrates that different outgroups elicit more discrete emotions (e.g., Cottrell & Neuberg, 2005; Fiske, Cuddy, Glick, & Xu, 2002). For example, research suggests that homosexuals tend to elicit disgust (Cottrell & Neuberg, 2005), whereas Arabs tend to elicit anger (Dasgupta, DeSteno, Williams, & Hunsinger, 2009). Recently, researchers have begun to investigate the impact of discrete emotional experiences on reactions to different outgroups.

Feelings of anger and disgust, but not sadness or neutrality, can create biased automatic evaluations of an unknown outgroup (Dasgupta et al., 2009; DeSteno, Dasgupta, Bartlett, & Cajdric, 2004). Such findings are consistent with the notion that both anger and disgust are aroused in response to threats to one's own group (e.g., threats to freedom or property, threats of moral or physical contamination; Cottrel & Neuberg, 2005; Fiske et al., 2002), whereas sadness is less relevant to threat. Consequently, sadness does not influence implicit (i.e., unconscious) outgroup evaluations. Dasgupta et al. (2009) found that the impact of specific emotions on implicit biases (i.e., unconscious prejudice) against outgroups is strongly related to the threats posed by the group. For example, disgust (but not anger) creates implicit biases against homosexuals, whereas anger (but not disgust) creates implicit biases against Arabs.

Much of the research examining the influence of affect in intergroup and interpersonal contexts has focused primarily on negative emotions, but some recent work has explored the impact of discrete positive emotions. For example, Williams and DeSteno (2009) found that feelings of pride led participants to take on a dominant leadership role during a group problem-solving task, which resulted in these individuals receiving more favorable evaluations from their interaction partners. Experimental inductions of gratitude likewise have positive effects in interpersonal contexts. For example, gratitude increases cooperative behavior in dilemma situations (DeSteno, Bartlett, Baumann, Williams, & Dickens, 2010), trust in others (Dunn & Schweitzer, 2005; Gino & Schweitzer, 2008), receptivity to advice (Gino & Schweitzer, 2008), and elicits costly helping behavior (Bartlett & DeSteno, 2006). The effects of gratitude on trust are unique from amusement (Bartlett & DeSteno, 2006) and are especially influenced by emotions

that result from appraisals of other-control (e.g., anger) rather than appraisals of personal (e.g., pride, guilt) or situational (e.g., sadness) control (Dunn & Schweitzer, 2005). Consistent with the AAI conceptualization, the effects of gratitude are eliminated when individuals are made aware of the source of their emotions (Bartlett & DeSteno, 2006; Dunn & Schweitzer, 2005).

Much of the research on interpersonal judgments, as discussed in this section, has concluded that positive affect often leads to positive interpersonal results. It should be noted, however, that a significant body of research on processing effects actually concludes the opposite, that positive affect encourages heuristic processing, which in turn leads to negative interpersonal effects (e.g., stereotyping; Bodenhausen, Kramer, & Susser, 1994). Such processing mediated effects will be discussed more fully in the second half of this chapter.

RISK AND LIKELIHOOD JUDGMENTS

Early work (Johnson & Tversky, 1983) demonstrated that the influence of affect on risk judgments is global and related to the valence of an affective state; however, work in recent years has been more definitive in demonstrating that this is not the case. During the past decade, a general consensus has been reached that specific emotions have more specific influences on risk and likelihood judgments, and the prevailing explanation is that appraisals of certainty and control moderate these effects (Lerner & Keltner, 2001).

Affective states that result from appraisals of events as uncertain and outside of one's control (e.g., fear, distress, anxiety) promote preferences for safer consumer products (Raghunathan, Pham, & Corfman, 2006), inflate the likelihood of sad events occurring (DeSteno, Petty, Wegener, & Rucker, 2000), heighten predictions of poor risk outcomes (Gasper & Clore, 1998), and discourage risk-seeking choices and behaviors (Druckman & McDermott, 2008; Lerner & Keltner, 2000, 2001). Conversely, affective states that result from appraisal of certainty and control (e.g., anger, happiness) encourage high-risk and high-reward decisions in gambling (Raghunathan & Pham, 1999), promote risk-seeking choices and behavior (Druckman & McDermott, 2008), and increase the prediction of positive outcomes (Mayer et al., 1992). Compared with individuals who were induced to feel angry following the 9/11 terrorist attacks, those induced to feel fear estimated the future risk of terrorism to be greater (Lerner & Keltner, 2001), reported preferences for more precautionary behaviors (Lerner, Gonzalez, Small, & Fischoff, 2003), and reported inflated judgments of past risks (Fischoff, Gonzalez, Lerner, & Small, 2005). Relative to anger, anxiety increased perceptions of risk associated with the Iraq war and decreased support for the war (Huddy, Feldman, & Cassese, 2007).

Consistent with the AAI account, emotions that do not provide relevant information about the judgment at hand do not have an influence on these judgments. For example, emotions that are not heavily influenced by control and certainty appraisals (e.g., enthusiasm) do not influence risk-associated judgments (Druckman & McDermott, 2008). Likewise, DeSteno and colleagues (DeSteno et al., 2000) found evidence for a "matching" effect between the judgment domain and the emotion being experienced. For example, anger increased individuals' likelihood estimates for future angering events (e.g., being stuck in traffic), but not for future sad events (e.g., best friend moving far away). Individuals who were sad showed the opposite pattern. A number of findings demonstrating that the influence of affect on risk and likelihood judgments is undermined when current affect is attributed to sources other than the object of judgment are also consistent with the AAI perspective (e.g., DeSteno, et al., 2000, Gasper & Clore, 1998).

MORALITY-BASED JUDGMENTS

Both psychologists and philosophers have long believed that judgments concerning morality are the result of rational cognitive processes (see Haidt, 2001; Haidt & Kesebir, 2010, for reviews); however, recent work has shifted to examine the role that intuition and emotion might play in these important decisions. This work reveals that emotions and intuitions may frequently be the driving force behind morality- and value-based judgments, with reason being a by-product of them. Although several different moral domains have been identified (e.g., harm/care, fairness/reciprocity, ingroup/loyalty, authority/respect, and purity/sanctity; see Haidt & Kesebir, 2010), the majority of research on the relationship between affect and morality-based judgments has focused on the link between judgments and purity or disgust.

Disgust, a negative emotion that results from appraisals of objects as contaminated and impure, promotes a desire to expel, reject, and avoid such objects (Rozin & Fallon, 1987) and leads individuals to decrease the value of disgust-associated objects (Lerner, Small, & Lowenstein, 2004). In the first experimental test of the impact of manipulated disgust reactions on moral judgments, participants were conditioned to respond to an arbitrary word with flashes of disgust as a result of a post-hypnotic suggestion (Wheatley & Haidt, 2005). Participants then read vignettes that either did or did not include the disgust-conditioned word. When the vignettes included the word, participants made harsher judgments of the characters in the vignettes.

In subsequent research, disgust was empirically differentiated from other negative affective experiences. In four experiments, Schnall, Haidt, Clore, and Jordan (2008) experimentally induced disgust by having participants view a disgusting video, complete the experiment in a disgusting room, recall a disgusting experience, or smell a disgusting odor. Regardless of the manipulation, participants exposed to the disgust manipulations judged morally ambiguous behaviors described in vignettes to be more immoral than those who were not exposed to these manipulations. This effect was especially pronounced among individuals who have a tendency to pay attention to their bodily experiences. Feelings of disgust also result in increased rejections of unfair offers in an ultimatum game (Moretti & di Pellegrino, 2010) and increased implicit prejudice against homosexuals (Dasgupta et al., 2009). The effects of disgust on purity-related moral judgments are reliably different from those produced by sadness and anger and may be domain specific (Horberg, Oveis, Keltner, & Cohen, 2009). For example, in a study by Horberg and his colleagues (2009), disgust influenced judgments related to purity, but not those related to harm/care and justice.

Interestingly, research demonstrates that morality judgments can also be influenced by manipulations of purity. For example, Schnall, Benton, and Harvey (2008) found that participants who were instructed to wash their hands after watching a video that induced disgust made more favorable morality judgments than those who did not have this cleansing opportunity. Fluent processing (a positive experience; Winkielman, Schwarz, Reber, & Fazendeiro, 2003) also results in lower judgments of moral wrongness than does disfluent processing (a negative experience; Laham, Alter, & Goodwin, 2009). Together, these recent studies suggest that morality-based judgments and behaviors can be affected by inductions of disgust and purity, as well as more general positive affect that may be experienced in response to fluent processing. Future research is needed to identify more clearly the impact of disgust and other affective states on judgments in different domains of morality.

Evaluations as Information

In addition to events that clearly elicit consciously experienced affect (i.e., moods, emotions), there are many conditions in which judgments may be influenced by evaluative reactions without necessarily being mediated by consciously experienced affect. That is, many different types of information provide evaluative cues that may be used as inputs to judgment. Not all of this evaluative information may be relevant to the judgment at hand, and in many cases, this information may be confused with or misattributed to an unrelated object of judgment. Typically, the valence-based congruency effects that we described for mood hold under these conditions. That is, the influence of evaluative information on judgments often parallels other known affective influences (Clore & Colcombe, 2003). This is true for a variety of types of information that provide evaluative information, including facial expressions and other embodied experiences, evaluative primes, and the metacognitive experience of perceptual fluency.

FACIAL EXPRESSIONS AND OTHER EMBODIED EXPERIENCES

The idea that an emotion is the reflection of our facial expressions dates back to both Darwin (1872/1965) and James (1890). Indeed, James (1890) believed that an emotion is the conscious perception of bodily activity that occurs in response to encountering affective stimuli. Although most contemporary researchers believe that emotions are composed of more than facial expressions and bodily reactions (see Keltner & Lerner, 2010, for a review), such experiences alone can certainly influence emotional responses and judgments (see Ping, Dhillon, Beilock, 2009, for a review). In a classic and highly cited article, Strack, Martin, and Stepper (1988) demonstrated that individuals judged comics to be more humorous when they held a pen in their mouths in a way that promoted rather than inhibited smiling. Such positive facial feedback can also serve to reduce implicit racial biases against blacks (Ito, Chiao, Devine, Lorig, & Cacioppo, 2006). Larsen, Kasimatis, and Frey (1992) found that judgments can be similarly enhanced by negative facial feedback. For example, participants who were instructed to furrow their brows as they judged sad photos, judged the photos to be sadder than participants who did not engage in this behavior.

Additional evidence for the profound influence of facial expressions on affective experiences comes from a recent study in which participants were injected with either Botox (which paralyzes facial muscles) or a cosmetic filler (that has no impact on facial muscles; Davis, Senghas, Brandt, & Ochsner, 2010). Compared with the no-Botox control group, the Botox group reported reduced emotional experiences in response to affect-eliciting videos, suggesting that the absence of facial feedback can alter affective experiences. The presence of facial expressions is not always used as feedback, however. For example, among individuals who have difficulties with emotional processing (i.e., those with autistic spectrum disorders), facial feedback is not informative (Stel, van den Heuvel, & Smeets, 2008).

Similar affective influences also emerge for other types of embodied experiences (see Niedenthal, Barsalou, Winkielman, Krauth-Gruber, & Ric, 2005, for a review). For example, compared with being slumped in a chair, sitting up straight leads participants to experience more pride in response to success feedback (Stepper & Strack, 1993). Approach and avoidance motor behaviors correspondingly influence our judgments of objects. For example, arm flexion, which involves drawing objects near to oneself, is associated with approach motivation; in contrast, arm extension, which involves pushing objects away from oneself, is associated with avoidance motivation. Research demonstrates that arm flexion leads individuals to rate novel stimuli (i.e., Chinese ideographs) more favorably than arm extension (Cacioppo, Priester, & Berntson, 1993). Likewise, arm flexion leads to greater preferences for neutral nonwords than does arm extension (Priester, Cacioppo, & Petty, 1996).

More recently, Centerbar and Clore (2006) found that the relationship between approach/avoidance behavior and evaluation of stimuli depends on the valence of the stimuli being judged. Evaluations of negatively valenced stimuli were more heavily influenced by arm extension than arm flexion, whereas evaluations of positively valenced stimuli were more heavily influenced by arm flexion. Lench (2009) similarly found that positive affective primes increased likelihood judgments for future events (e.g., planting a garden) when coupled with arm flexion, whereas negative affective primes decreased likelihood judgments when coupled with arm extension. In mismatched condition (e.g., negative primes with arm flexion; positive primes with arm extension), however, this effect was reduced. In a related vein, research demonstrates that the meaning and implications of nonconsciously experienced affective cues (e.g., subliminally presented smiling or frowning faces) depends on the context in which the cues are experienced (Tamir, Robinson, Clore, Martin, & Whitaker, 2004). For example, smiling faces presented after one's own performance increase evaluations of one's performance, but smiling faces presented after an opponent's performance decrease evaluations of one's own performance. Thus, contrary to earlier research that suggests that affective cues tend to lead to congruent judgments (e.g., Murphy & Zajonc, 1993), this body of work suggests that the influence of these cues is context dependent—a finding that is consistent with the context-dependent effects of moods and emotions discussed earlier.

EVALUATIVE PRIMES

Although Zajonc's (1980) assertion that affective reactions can be elicited automatically and without conscious mediation was contentious three decades ago when it was introduced (e.g., Lazarus, 1982), it is now widely accepted that exposure to a valenced stimulus (e.g., an attitude object) can automatically activate an associated evaluation (e.g., Russell, 2003). This evaluation may facilitate the speed with which individuals respond to subsequently encountered affectively congruent stimuli (e.g., Bargh, Chaiken, Govender, & Pratto, 1992; Fazio, Sanbonmatsu, Powell, & Kardes, 1986; but see Storbeck & Robinson, 2004, for boundary conditions) as well as individuals' evaluations of subsequently encountered stimuli (Murphy & Zajonc, 1993; Winkielman, Zajonc, & Schwarz, 1997). Interest in this later effect has recently been revitalized in social psychology (e.g., Jones, Fazio, & Olson, 2009).

The process by which individuals' evaluations of an object are formed or altered as a result of being paired with positively or negatively valenced stimuli is referred to as evaluative conditioning (Jones et al., 2009). Typically, targets paired with positive stimuli are evaluated more favorably than those paired with negative stimuli. For example, exposure to emotionally expressive faces influences evaluations of subsequently presented neutral objects (i.e., Chinese ideographs) in an affect-congruent manner without eliciting consciously experienced affect (Murphy & Zajonc, 1993; Winkielman et al., 1997). Likewise, novel objects are evaluated more favorably on both implicit and explicit measures when the objects are paired with positive rather than negative stimuli (Olson & Fazio, 2001).

Recent work demonstrates that such evaluative conditioning effects can emerge even for objects about which one has preexisting attitudes. For example, Olson and Fazio (2006) found that pairing positive stimuli with photos of blacks decreased white participants' automatically activated racial attitudes toward blacks both immediately after conditioning and after a two-day delay. This effect is not limited to evaluations of others, but emerges for the self as well. For example, Dijksterhuis (2004) found that pairing "I" with positive traits in an evaluative conditioning task increased participants' implicit self-esteem and made them insensitive to negative feedback about their intelligence. A recent meta-analysis suggests that effects of evaluative conditioning may be smaller for attitude objects for which individuals already have a valenced response (e.g., blacks, the self) than for those that do not (e.g., Chinese ideographs; Hofman, De Houwer, Perugini, Baeyens, & Crombez, 2010).

The AAI model can account for evaluative conditioning and other affect-priming effects by invoking a misattribution explanation in which an evaluation elicited from one object is confused with or misattributed to another object. Consistent with this theoretical approach, Jones and his colleagues (Jones et al., 2009) found that variables that increase confusion concerning the source of one's affective reaction served to increase the magnitude of the evaluative conditioning effect. For example, in Jones and colleagues' studies, source confusion and the corresponding evaluative conditioning effect increased under conditions in which eye gaze shifted frequently between valenced and neutral stimuli, when valenced and neutral stimuli were in close spatial proximity, and when the neutral stimuli were larger (i.e., more salient) than the valenced stimuli. Additionally, consistent with the notion that stimuli that evoke only mildly valenced affective reactions are more likely to be confused with other stimuli, Jones et al. found that evaluative conditioning was greater for mildly valenced stimuli. Murphy and Zajonc's (1993) finding that positive and negative facial expressions color evaluations of neutral stimuli, only when the primes are presented suboptimally, is consistent with the implicit misattribution explanation. That is, under suboptimal viewing conditions, source confusion is more likely to occur. Further, an attribution manipulation has been shown to reduce affect-priming effects in some conditions (Lench, 2009; but see Winkielman et al., 1997).

Although numerous studies have found that evaluative conditioning effects emerge when individuals are unaware of the pairings of the stimuli (Dickinson & Brown, 2007), a recent meta-analysis revealed that contingency awareness is the most important moderator of evaluative conditioning, with contingency-aware participants showing larger effects than contingency unaware participants (Hoffman et al., 2010). These recent findings are inconsistent with those of Jones et al. (2009) and others (e.g., Murphy & Zajonc, 1993), who suggest that contingency awareness is likely to reduce the magnitude of evaluative conditioning effects. Clearly, there are many unanswered questions in this area, and much work is needed to further test and circumscribe the boundary conditions of these effects.

METACOGNITIVE EXPERIENCE OF PERCEPTUAL FLUENCY

Perceptual fluency is a metacognitive experience that provides individuals with information about the extent to which their cognitive processing is easy versus difficult. Given that "every cognition falls along a continuum from effortless to demanding and generates a corresponding fluency experience…fluency is a ubiquitous metacognitive cue in reasoning and social judgment" (Alter & Oppenheimer, 2009a, p. 219). Such experiences themselves can produce affective reactions that can serve as information in the same ways that moods, emotions, and other evaluative information can (Schwarz & Clore, 2007; Schwarz, 2012). Interest in metacognitive experiences has grown exponentially over the past 15 years, with research on the link between fluency and liking receiving a significant amount of the attention.

Research on processing fluency demonstrates that positive affect is elicited when new information is easy to process (e.g., Reber, Schwarz, & Winkielman, 2004; Winkielman & Cacioppo, 2001; Zajonc, 1980). These positive reactions may be used as information when judging stimuli. Early evidence of a relationship between fluency and liking is apparent in the classic mere exposure studies conducted by Zajonc (1968). In these studies, repeated exposure to a neutral stimulus led to increased liking of the stimulus. Research has since determined that such exposure increases processing fluency (Whittlesea & Price, 2001), thereby leading many scholars to believe that fluency contributed to Zajonc's effects (Reber et al., 2004; Schwarz, 2012).

In recent years, research has found that a large number of variables known to influence processing fluency are also known to enhance evaluations and preferences (see Reber et al., 2004; Alter &

Oppenheimer, 2009a, for a review). For example, fluency is experienced when stimuli are familiar (Winkielman et al., 2003), are presented repeatedly (Whittlesea & Price, 2001), are presented in an easy-to-read font (Novemsky, Dhar, Schwarz, & Simonson, 2007), contain high figure-ground contrast (Reber, Winkielman, & Schwarz, 1998), rhyme (McGlone & Tofighbakhsh, 2000), and are preceded by primes that facilitate rather than impede processing (Reber et al., 1998; Winkielman et al., 2003). Such differences in processing fluency have been shown to influence judgments in many domains (see Alter & Oppenheimer, 2009a, for a review). For example, compared with disfluency, fluency leads to greater judgments of truth (Reber & Schwarz, 1999), more favorable stock performance (Alter & Oppenheimer, 2006), more favorable consumer product decisions (Novemsky et al., 2007), lower perceptions of risk (Song & Schwarz, 2009), greater estimates of social consensus (Weaver, Garcia, Schwarz, & Miller, 2007), more favorable morality judgments (Laham et al., 2009), and greater self-disclosure (Alter & Oppenheimer, 2009b). The results of all of these studies mimic what would be expected if individuals were experiencing positive moods.

Several studies provide direct support for the idea that affect can mediate fluency-induced judgment effects (e.g., Alter & Oppenheimer, 2009a; Winkielman & Cacioppo, 2001). For example, Alter and Oppenheimer (2009b) found that negative affective reactions resulting from disfluency mediated the effects of disfluency on reduced willingness to self-disclose information. Further, consistent with the AAI account, the effects of fluency on liking judgments are eliminated when individuals attribute their affective responses to something other than the stimuli being judged (Winkielman & Fazendeiro, 2003, as discussed in Reber, Schwarz, & Winkielman, 2004) and when individuals are aware of the source of fluency (e.g., font quality; Novemsky, Dhar, Schwarz, & Simonson, 2007). Taken together, the AAI account provides a parsimonious explanation for fluency effects.

Summary

In this section, we reviewed the influence of moods, emotions, and evaluations on judgment. Although all serve as sources of information, moods and evaluations tend to have pervasive and general effects on judgment, whereas the effects of emotions are more constrained. Such findings reflect that emotions result from more complex cognitive appraisal processes than do moods or evaluations, and consequently provide more specific information. Thus, emotions are less easily attributed to targets of judgment than are moods or evaluations. In all cases, however, whether affect influences judgment is highly dependent on the extent to which the affect is perceived to be relevant to the judgment. Under conditions in which it is not perceived to be relevant, affect is discounted and tends to have no effects on judgment. The research reviewed in this section highlights the interaction between affect and cognition and underscores that when our moods, emotions, or evaluations are relevant to a judgment, these experiences tend to help us to make good judgments; however, when these affective experiences are mistakenly perceived to be relevant, they can adversely influence our judgments.

We now turn to examine the influence of affect on social cognitive processes that are known to influence judgment, focusing specifically on (1) memory processes and (2) attention and perception processes. Following these sections, we turn our attention to the second main line of research in the affect domain, the impact of affect on information processing styles.

Affect and Memory Processes

Early theorizing about the role of affect in social cognition posited that the influence of affect on judgment is mediated by its effects on memory processes (e.g., Bower, 1981; Isen, Shalker, Clark, & Karp, 1978). In one of the first studies to explore the role of affect on judgment, Isen and her colleagues (1978) found that positive moods resulted in more favorable evaluations of consumer products. Isen et al. (1978) suggested that such effects emerge because positive moods render highly interconnected positive information in memory more accessible. This explanation is consistent with associative network models of memory that were popular at the time (e.g., Anderson, 1976; Collins & Loftus, 1975). From this theoretical perspective, Bower and his colleagues (Bower, 1981; Bower, Monteiro, & Gilligan, 1978) proposed that affect (e.g., happiness) is represented as a central node in memory that is linked to similarly valenced concepts (e.g., vacations), specific events (e.g., getting tenure), appraisals (e.g., certainty about the situation), autonomic reactions (e.g., change in heart rate), and expressive patterns (e.g., smiling). According to this model, moods and emotions operate as primes in the same way that other concepts do. That is, mood can serve to activate mood-congruent concepts that

can influence encoding, retrieval, and elaborative processes.

One implication of Bower's model is that mood that is experienced at the time of retrieval will activate similarly valenced material in memory. To the extent that judgments are based on this information, they will be mood congruent. Evidence of a relationship between one's mood at the time of retrieval and the valence of retrieved material has been most reliably obtained under conditions in which individuals recall autobiographical information rather than experimenter-provided information; however, effects for positive and negative information tend to be asymmetrical (see Blaney, 1986; Singer & Salovey, 1988, for reviews; see Ucros, 1989, for a meta-analysis). That is, while mood-congruency effects tend to emerge for positive information, they are often weak or absent for negative information (Blaney, 1986; Singer & Salovey, 1988). One notable exception to this finding is that mood-congruency effects do emerge for negative information among individuals who are depressed (Blaney, 1986; Johnson & Magaro, 1987).

In addition to predicting mood-congruent retrieval effects, Bower's (1981) model predicts that individuals will better recall information when they are in the same affective state at the time of encoding and at the time of retrieval, regardless of the content of the information. Although a number of studies provided initial evidence for such a state-dependent memory effect (e.g., Bower, 1981; Bower et al., 1978), the consensus in the field is that such effects are quite fragile (Blaney, 1986; Bower & Mayer, 1985, 1989; Singer & Salovey, 1988; Ucros, 1989). Further, researchers have noted that state-dependent effects are very difficult to differentiate empirically from mood-congruent retrieval effects (Morris, 1989; Schwarz & Clore, 2007). For example, when individuals experience happy events (e.g., a wedding), they tend to experience a happy mood at the time. Then later, when feeling happy, individuals tend to recall the happy events. Thus, the inherent confound between the valence of an event and the mood that was experienced at the time of the event creates ambiguity about what processes might be driving mood-congruent retrieval effects.

A number of concerns have been raised about mood-priming explanations for the impact of affect on judgment. Most notably, the effects appear to emerge under very specific conditions (see Forgas, 1995; Schwarz & Clore, 2007, for a review of boundary conditions), and thus they are unable to account for a significant amount of data, including a number of findings generated by the AAI conceptualization (see Schwarz & Clore, 2007). Further, Wyer, Clore, and Isbell's (1999) review of the literature concluded that any mood-congruent effects that do emerge may not be due to the affective experiences themselves, but instead may be the result of semantic concepts that were unintentionally activated as a part of the affect-eliciting event. For example, labeling one's experience as "sad" can activate the semantic concept "sad" and other associated semantic concepts (e.g., cry, down). Once activated, these concepts may guide subsequent processing in the same way that any other semantic concepts (e.g., hostile, honest) do (e.g., Higgins, Rholes, & Jones, 1977; see Wyer & Srull, 1989, for a review). Thus, the claim is that it is not feelings that produce mood and memory effects, but rather it is the semantic concepts that are activated and associated with the experiences that produce these effects (but see Innes-Ker & Niedenthal, 2002, for contradictory evidence).

Despite the criticisms of the affect priming account, the current consensus in the field is that affect can influence judgments in multiple ways, including both as immediate and direct input into judgments (i.e., as a source of information) and indirectly through memory and other processes. Below we review an impressive attempt by Forgas' (1995) to integrate the affect priming and the informational accounts into a multiple process affect-infusion model (AIM) that aims to predict when each of these different mechanisms might operate. Then, we consider other ways in which affect may influence judgments through perceptual and attentional processes. Recent investigations of these later influences have developed largely independent of the associative network model tradition.

Affect Infusion Model

According to the AIM, individuals rely on one of four different judgmental strategies that result in different amounts of affective infusion (i.e., influence). Low affect infusion strategies are (1) those that allow individuals to directly retrieve a previously stored judgment from memory and (2) those that lead individuals to engage in processing that is heavily motivated by a desire to reach a particular outcome (e.g., to repair or maintain one's mood). In both of these cases, mood-congruent judgment is not predicted. In contrast, the AIM predicts that affect infusion is most likely under conditions in which individuals (1) rely on affect as a heuristic

or (2) engage in substantive processing. This notion that affect can function as a heuristic is consistent with the AAI approach discussed earlier; however, AAI theorists have noted that the conditions outlined in the AIM that are likely to produce such effects are too highly circumscribed (see Schwarz & Clore, 2007). For example, according to the AIM, the heuristic strategy operates under conditions in which individuals possess no specific motivational goals, the target of judgment is typical or simple, and the target is low in personal relevance. Although AAI theorists would agree with these predictions, they would predict considerably more widespread effects and thus do not endorse these restrictive criteria (for reviews, see Schwarz & Clore, 2007; Schwarz, 2012).

According to the AIM, substantive processing is the most demanding strategy and operates under conditions in which individuals need to learn, interpret, and connect new information to existing information in memory. In this case, information primed by affective experiences is predicted to influence memory processes in the manner outlined by the affect-priming account. Such processing is theorized to occur when individuals are motivated to be accurate when making judgments of complex or atypical targets that are of some relevance to them, and when they possess the cognitive resources to process information carefully.

Over the years, Forgas and his colleagues have accumulated significant evidence that has been interpreted as support for the AIM (see Forgas, 1995, 2002). For example, Forgas has demonstrated greater mood-congruent judgment effects under conditions in which individuals form impressions of atypical (versus typical) individuals (Forgas, 1992). Evidence of substantive processing in these and similar studies has been garnered from processing latency measures and memory data; however, such evidence does not provide unequivocal support for the processes that are assumed to underlie the effects. For example, in the case of atypical targets, mood-congruency effects may result from substantive processing, or such effects may result from individuals first considering the target information and then defaulting to a heuristic in an effort to simplify the judgmental task. Nonetheless, despite this and other ambiguities present in the AIM (see Schwarz & Clore, 2007, for a more extensive discussion of ambiguities), the AIM is an impressive attempt to unify, explain, and predict a number of seemingly disparate findings in the affect literature.

Summary

Identifying the ways in which affect influences memory has proved to be a challenging task. At first glance, it seems intuitively likely that memory should be highly and reliably related to affective experiences; however, research has painted a more complex picture of this relationship. Although early researchers posited a clear and direct relationship between the valence of one's mood and the valence of information activated in memory, more recent work has carefully circumscribed the small number of conditions in which such effects are likely to emerge. The AIM presents the most comprehensive account of the relationship between mood, memory, and judgment and has explained numerous inconsistencies in the literature; however, more varied research methods are needed to investigate the explanatory power of this model fully.

Affect, Perception, and Attention

The preceding sections focused largely on the impact of affect on later stages of processing involving memory and judgment; however, the impact of affect on judgment can be influenced by earlier stages of processing as well. For example, affective experiences can influence what we attend to and how we perceive information. Although some of the work that has already been reviewed has assumed that this is the case, the research reviewed here provides more direct evidence for the influence of affect on perception and attention. In this section, we examine the influence of affect on perceptual judgments, attentional focus, and selective attention.

Perceptual Judgments

The New Look movement of the 1950s claimed that perception is not merely a reflection of reality but instead is shaped by internal motivations and experiences (Bruner, 1957). Consistent with this notion, research in recent years has demonstrated that affective experiences can exert a significant influence on perceptual experiences. For example, individuals standing on the top of a hill on a skateboard (which is likely to induce fear about what may happen) judged the hill to be steeper than those standing on a flat platform (Stefanucci, Proffitt, Clore, & Parekh, 2008). Both state and trait fear similarly lead individuals to overestimate height when making their estimates while looking down compared with looking up (Stefanucci & Proffitt, 2009).

A number of other studies similarly suggest that affect can bias perceptual judgments of visual space (Meier & Robinson, 2004), visual brightness (Meier, Robinson, Crawford, & Ahlvers, 2007), and auditory sounds (Weger, Meier, Robinson, & Inhoff, 2007). For example, in a study conducted more than a half a century ago, researchers found that people who failed an exam (and were presumably unhappy) bisected a square lower in visual space than people who received an A on the exam (Wapner, Werner, & Kruss, 1957). Such biases are theorized to result from metaphors that link abstract concepts (e.g., affect) to concrete sensory experiences (Lakoff & Johnson, 1999). For example, when we say that we are "feeling down," "down" refers to both a position in physical space and also to a negative experience. Similarly, when someone tells us to "look on the bright side" of a situation, "bright" refers to both a visual sensory experience and to something positive. These learned associations are represented in memory and used to interpret information. More recent work demonstrates that priming individuals with positive words biases visual perception upward, whereas priming with negative words biases visual perception downward (Meier & Robinson, 2004). Further, relative to individuals primed with negative words, those primed with positive words rated a subsequent stimulus to be brighter in color (Meier et al., 2007). Affective primes can similarly bias tone perceptions with positive primes (compared with negative ones), leading people to judge tones to be higher pitched (Weger et al., 2007). Importantly, these studies demonstrate that affective primes have similar effects for both visual and auditory modalities. Together, all of the findings reviewed in this section converge on the conclusion that perceptual judgments of objective physical realities can be influenced by affective experiences.

Attentional Scope

Research within the mood and processing literature (to be reviewed in a later section) has well established that happy moods are associated with global, top-down, schema-driven processing during many tasks, whereas sad moods are associated with detailed, bottom-up, data-driven processing. Consistent with this work, research demonstrates that affective states can influence individuals' attentional scope by altering the extent to which individuals focus on global characteristics (i.e., broadened attentional scope) versus detailed elements of a stimulus (i.e., narrowed attentional scope; Fredrickson & Branigan, 2005; Gasper & Clore, 2002). The earliest work in this area uncovered a relationship between anxiety and a narrowed focus of attention (Easterbrook, 1959; Derryberry & Reed, 1998). Over the past decade, researchers have increasingly borrowed paradigms from cognitive psychology to explore the ways in which different affective experiences can alter attentional focus. In a highly cited study, Gasper and Clore (2002) exposed participants in happy and sad moods to images of a large shape (e.g., a triangle) composed of smaller shapes (e.g., squares; Kimchi & Palmer, 1982) and instructed participants to identify the shape. Individuals in happy moods identified the global shape significantly more often than those in sad moods. Consistent with the AAI conceptualization, this effect was eliminated when the relevance of individuals' moods was discounted (Gasper, 2004). This research provides the first evidence that moods can alter attentional focus during a visual processing task.

Subsequent research has attempted to further circumscribe the conditions in which affect may influence attentional scope. Recently, Gable and Harmon-Jones (2008, 2010) demonstrated that the relationship between affect and attentional focus is not specific to positively and negatively valenced affective experiences, but instead is related to the motivational intensity of these experiences. For example, when pursuing a goal, positive affective experiences tend to be high in motivational intensity (e.g., desire); however, after a goal is obtained, positive affective experiences tend to be low in motivational intensity (e.g., serenity). To explore the impact of motivational intensity on attentional scope, Gable and Harmon-Jones relied on the now-classic Navon (1977) letter identification task in which the time for individuals to indicate whether a specific letter is presented in a display of a large letter (e.g., F) composed of smaller letters (e.g., H) is used as a measure of attentional scope. Gable and Harmon-Jones found broadened attentional focus for both positive and negative affective experiences that are low in motivational intensity (e.g., amusement, sadness), but not for positive and negative affective experiences that are high in motivational intensity (i.e., desire, disgust; Gable & Harmon-Jones, 2008, 2010). This work highlights the importance of considering both the valence and the motivational intensity of an affective experience to predict its impact on attentional scope.

Selective Attention

A voluminous literature demonstrates that affective states can bias attention toward affectively congruent stimuli in the environment. By relying on trait and state measures of anxiety, much of this work has been conducted within clinical psychology

and has established that anxiety leads individuals to selectively attend to threatening information (e.g., Broadbent & Broadbent, 1988; Derryberry & Reed, 2002; MacLeod, 1999; Mathews & MacLeod, 1985). Although fear-relevant stimuli (e.g., snakes, spiders) tend to capture visual attention more so than fear-irrelevant stimuli for most people (e.g., Öhman, Flykt, & Esteves, 2001; Purkis & Lipp, 2007), research demonstrates that this effect is magnified for individuals who are fearful (Öhman et al., 2001). In a similar vein, research demonstrates that trait anger leads to increased attention to angry faces (van Honk, Tuiten, de Haan, van den Hout, & Stam, 2001) and to visual scenes of ambiguously intended harm (Wilkowski, Robinson, Gordon, & Troop-Gordon, 2007).

Building on this earlier work, recent research has employed affect manipulations to examine affective states that differ in approach versus avoidance motivation rather than valence per se. Consistent with motivational approaches (e.g., Carver, 2001), emotions associated with approach (e.g., anger, happiness/excitement) should lead to selective attention to rewarding information, whereas those associated with avoidance (e.g., fear) should lead to selective attention to threatening information. As expected, Tamir and Robinson (2007) found that happy/excited states led participants to selectively attend to rewarding stimuli, whereas sadness and anxiety did not. Further, the effect of happy/excited states on attention was specific to rewarding stimuli and did not generalize to other positive stimuli. In an eye-tracking study investigating the influence of anger, fear, and excitement on selective attention, both anger and excitement influenced attention to rewarding stimuli but not threatening stimuli, whereas fear led to increased attention to threatening, but not rewarding stimuli (Ford, Tamir, Brunye, Shirer, Mahoney, & Taylor, 2010). Thus, in contrast to valence-based accounts of the influences of affect on processing, this work demonstrates the importance of considering different aspects of emotional experiences when examining the impact of emotions on social cognitive processes. We highlighted this point earlier and further emphasize it in the next section examining the influence of affect on information processing styles.

Summary

Individuals' judgments are heavily influenced by what they attend to and perceive. The research reviewed in this section highlights that some of our most fundamental, lower order cognitive processes are systematically influenced by our affective experiences. These effects are multiply determined by such factors as how we symbolize and represent our feelings and how our feelings direct our attention to different types of information.

The preceding sections of this chapter focused on both the direct impact of affect on judgment as well as the impact of affect on memory, perception, and attention, all of which can have downstream effects on judgment. As noted earlier, researchers have traditionally examined the impact of affect on information processing style as distinct from its impact on judgment. Consistent with this tradition, we next examine the impact of moods, emotions, and evaluations on processing style, and introduce a new theoretical explanation to account for such effects.

Affect and Information Processing Style

One of the most fundamental distinctions in social cognition is between heuristic and systematic processing. This broad distinction captures differences in the extent to which processing is influenced by global, categorical information (e.g., stereotypes, traits) versus more local, detailed information (e.g., specific behaviors, attributes). Evidence of these broad differences seems to emerge in every domain of social psychology (see Chaiken & Trope, 1999). Research in the affect and cognition tradition demonstrates that one of the most reliable findings is that happy moods lead individuals to rely on heuristic, global, top-down processing strategies, whereas sad moods lead individuals to rely on systematic, local, bottom-up processing strategies (see Schwarz & Clore, 2007, for a more extensive and excellent review).

Evidence of affect-induced differences in processing is pervasive. For example, relative to sad moods, happy moods are associated with increased reliance on stereotypes and traits during impression formation (e.g., Bodenhausen, Kramer, & Susser, 1994; Isbell, 2004), an increased tendency to select global trait information over more specific behavioral information during impression formation (Isbell, Burns, & Haar, 2005), increased reliance on brand information when evaluating consumer products (Adaval, 2001), and increased reliance on behavioral scripts for routine events (e.g., dining in a restaurant; Bless, Clore, Schwarz, Golisano, Rabe, & Wolk, 1996). Happy individuals are also more likely than sad individuals to form inclusive categories (e.g., vehicles) that consist of unusual exemplars (e.g., camel; Isen, 1987; Isen & Daubman, 1984),

to create and use categories more flexibly (Murray, Sujan, Hirt, & Sujan, 1990), and to succeed at creative problem-solving tasks (e.g., Isen, Daubman, & Nowicki, 1987). Happy moods also lead individuals to describe events (Beukeboom & Semin, 2006) and themselves (Isbell, McCabe, Burns, & Lair, 2013) in more abstract language. In the persuasion domain, research demonstrates that happy participants are relatively uninfluenced by argument strength, whereas sad participants are more persuaded by strong arguments compared with weak ones (e.g., Bless, Bohner, Schwarz, & Strack, 1990). This last finding reflects that relative to happy participants, sad participants engage in more elaborate and detailed processing of persuasive arguments.

Several theoretical explanations have been proposed to account for the large number of affect-induced processing differences that have emerged. Some accounts maintain that relative to sad or neutral moods, happy moods reduce either ability (e.g., Mackie & Worth, 1989; Worth & Mackie, 1987) or motivation (e.g., Clark & Isen, 1982; Erber & Erber, 2001; Wegener, Petty, & Smith, 1995) to process information carefully. In accordance with assumptions of the associative network model of affect and memory discussed earlier (Bower, 1981), ability accounts maintain that positive information is highly interconnected in memory and is activated when individuals are happy, thus leaving individuals with limited cognitive capacity with which to process new information. For this reason, it is theorized that when processing information, happy individuals will rely on simplifying heuristics, such as stereotypes and categorical information. Importantly, however, negative affective experiences have also been shown to adversely affect individuals' ability to process information carefully. For example, cognitive appraisals associated with anger may be cognitively demanding and may reduce cognitive resources available for other tasks (Lazarus, 1981; Schachter, 1964). Similarly, fear and anxiety can narrow attention (e.g., MacLeod & Mathews, 1988), thereby limiting attentional resources. Thus, ability explanations sometimes generate contradictory predictions for similarly valenced affective experiences. Further, the notion that positive affective experiences activate all positive information in memory is untenable.

Motivational explanations, on the other hand, posit that affect may influence individuals' motivation to process information carefully. According to these accounts, happy individuals may be motivated to maintain their positive states, whereas sad individuals may be motivated to improve them (Clark & Isen, 1982; Erber & Erber, 2001). Consequently, happy individuals may avoid taxing cognitive activity that may threaten their moods, whereas sad individuals may engage in such activity in an effort to distract themselves and enhance their moods. As with the ability explanations, research demonstrates that some negative experiences, such as anger, may decrease motivation to process carefully (e.g., Lerner, Goldberg, & Tetlock, 1998; see also Tiedens & Linton, 2001; cf. Moons & Mackie, 2007), whereas others (i.e., fear or anxiety) may sometimes increase motivation to process information (e.g., Baron et al., 1994). Taken together, the ability and motivation explanations alone still cannot account for a large number of findings that have been reported in the literature.

In contrast to the ability and motivational explanations, the AAI approach maintains that the impact of affect on processing is the result of *information* that affective experiences provide, *not* the experiences themselves. For this reason, any type of affective information—including moods, emotions, and evaluative reactions—can influence processing. That is, unlike the ability and motivational explanations, the AAI conceptualization is sufficiently broad that it can generalize to these different types of experiences. In the sections that follow, we describe the AAI approach as it relates to processing differences. In doing so, we again review the evidence separately for each of the three distinct types of affect identified earlier: moods, emotions, and evaluative reactions. We then describe a recent new direction that emphasizes the highly malleable and contextualized nature of affective experiences and their effects on information processing.

Moods as Information

Although the original AAI account (Schwarz & Clore, 1983) posited that affective cues provide individuals with information about objects of judgment and directly influence evaluations, subsequent research revealed that the impact of affect on cognition is more general and pervasive than theorists first thought (Schwarz, 2012). Rather than providing information only about targets of judgment or in response to questions that individuals currently have in mind (Schwarz, 2012), researchers discovered that affect can also provide information about the nature of the environment, and this information can influence how we process information (Schwarz, 1990; Schwarz & Bless, 1991).

Just as emotion theorists maintain that affect serves to orient individuals and direct their actions and behaviors by serving a signaling function (e.g., Frijda, 1986; Simon, 1967), Schwarz and his colleagues theorized that affective states serve to direct our cognitive processing by providing information about the environment (Clore et al., 2001; Frijda, 1988; Schwarz, 1990, 2012; Schwarz & Clore, 2007; Wyer et al., 1999). According to this view, positive affect signals that the environment is safe and benign, and thus encourages global, abstract, and top-down processing that relies on general knowledge structures and existing information. In contrast, negative affect signals the presence of a problem. To resolve the perceived problem, negative states lead individuals to process information in a more local, concrete, and bottom-up manner. Such differences have been theorized to be mediated by subjective feelings of confidence that accompany happy and sad moods (Bless, 2001; Bless et al., 1996; Bless & Schwarz 1999). That is, given that reliance on abstract information and top-down processing strategies are adaptive and appropriate in benign situations as opposed to problematic ones, positive moods lead individuals to have greater confidence in relying on this information than do negative moods. Consistent with this idea, Tiedens and Linton (2001) found that affective experiences associated with certainty lead to greater heuristic processing than those associated with uncertainty.

The basic principles of the AAI conceptualization outlined earlier when considering the influence of affect on judgment apply when considering the influence of affect on processing. That is, the influence of affect on processing emerges only when current feelings are perceived as relevant to the task. Further, these effects are eliminated when the informational value of individuals' affective experience is called into question (Beukeboom & Semin, 2006; Gasper, 2004; Isbell et al., 2013; Sinclair, Mark, & Clore, 1994). For example, Beukeboom and Semin (2006) found that happy participants described a film in more abstract language than sad participants; however, when the source of participants' affect was made salient, happy and sad participants described the film in similarly abstract language. Likewise, Sinclair and his colleagues (1994) demonstrated that the effects of mood on persuasion are eliminated when individuals attribute their current feelings to an irrelevant source (i.e., the weather).

Importantly, the mood-as-information view does not suggest that happiness reduces motivation to process information carefully; rather, it simply states that happiness signals a safe situation, thereby promoting global, heuristic processing (Schwarz, 2012; Schwarz & Clore, 2007). However, any information that suggests otherwise can easily alter happy individuals' processing strategy and lead to more detailed and systematic processing. For example, increasing individual accountability can result in a reduction in stereotype use as a basis for judgment (Bodenhausen et al., 1994). Likewise, instructing participants to pay attention to arguments in a persuasion task can eliminate the effects of mood on processing (Bless et al., 1990). Further, providing individuals with the expectation that thinking about a persuasive message will make them feel good can lead happy individuals to process a message carefully (Wegener et al., 1995). This last effect is consistent with the notion that under conditions in which individuals are primarily concerned with improving or maintaining their current moods, mood regulation strategies are likely to predict which processing style individuals will adopt.

Although happiness is associated with increased reliance on global, categorical criteria during processing, this does not necessarily amount to a simplified approach to processing, as suggested by ability and motivational explanations. For example, in a person memory study, Isbell (2004) presented participants in happy and sad moods with global trait information that described a target as either kind, warm, and friendly or cold, cruel, and hostile. This information was presented either before or after an equal number of behaviors that the target performed that exemplified these traits. Participants later recalled the behaviors. According to person memory theory and research, when individuals rely on initially presented global trait information as a basis for their impressions (i.e., rely on global processing), they process subsequently encountered inconsistent behaviors more extensively in an effort to form a coherent impression of the person. Consequently, trait-inconsistent behaviors are better recalled than trait-consistent ones (e.g., Hastie & Kumar, 1979; Srull & Wyer, 1989). In contrast, when individuals do not rely on initial trait information, more detailed and local processing is evidenced from similar recall of both consistent and inconsistent behaviors. Consistent with expectations, Isbell found that when trait information was presented first, happy participants showed a recall advantage for trait-inconsistent information, whereas sad participants showed no such advantage. When trait information was presented last, happy participants showed a recall advantage for consistent behaviors

over inconsistent ones, suggesting that these traits served as a retrieval cue, whereas sad participants' recall was again unaffected by the trait information. Given that inconsistency resolution is a process that requires significant motivation and ability, these results suggests that happiness does not reduce motivation or ability to process carefully. Instead, happiness may simply influence the extent to which individuals rely on global, categorical information when processing.

Emotions as Information

Research exploring the information processing consequences of discrete affective states has been less prolific than research examining the judgmental consequences; however, research has reliability demonstrated that appraisal dimensions that are activated at the time of an affective experience can carry over to influence how individuals process subsequent information (for reviews, see Clore & Huntsinger, 2009; Isbell, Ottati, & Burns, 2006; Schwarz & Clore, 2007). For example, some affective experiences that are typically thought to be negative (i.e., anger; but see Lerner & Tiedens, 2006) often promote global processing, whereas others (i.e., fear, sadness) promote local processing (for reviews, see Clore & Huntsinger, 2009; Isbell, et al., 2006; Schwarz & Clore, 2007). Such findings are theorized to emerge because anger, like happiness, is associated with cognitive appraisals of certainty about an event's cause and outcome (e.g., Ortony et al., 1988; Roseman, 1984). When individuals feel angry, they tend to experience a sense of confidence in their own views (Clore & Huntsinger, 2009; Lerner & Tiedens, 2006) and experience increased approach motivation (e.g., Carver & Harmon-Jones, 2009)—both of which are associated with global processing. In contrast, fear and sadness are typically experienced along with feelings of uncertainty (e.g., Ortony et al., 1988; Roseman, 1984), leading individuals to process information in a more systematic manner.

The bulk of the evidence for discrete emotion-induced differences in processing has emerged from research examining anger and fear. Fear leads to increased systematic processing of persuasive messages (Baron, Logan, Lilly, Inman, & Brennan, 1994; Bohner &Weinerth, 2001) and increased reliance on detailed information in decision-making tasks (Tiedens & Linton, 2001). In contrast, anger leads to increased stereotype use as a basis for judgment (Bodenhausen, Sheppard, & Kramer, 1994), reliance on heuristic rather than substantive processing (e.g.,

Small & Lerner, 2008; cf. Moons & Mackie, 2007), reliance on chronically accessible scripts (Tiedens, 2001), reliance on peripheral cues rather than detailed arguments in persuasion tasks (Bodenhausen et al., 1994; Tiedens & Linton, 2001), and implicit biases against an outgroup (DeSteno et al., 2004).

In a recent study comparing anger and fear, Parker and Isbell (2010) found that anger led individuals to actively seek out and rely on global information (e.g., ideology) when forming impressions of two political candidates to make a vote choice. Fear, in contrast, led individuals to seek out more specific issue-based information about the candidates (e.g., policy positions). Angry participants' vote choices were predicted by the amount of general information they sought out about each candidate, whereas fearful participants' choices were predicted by their agreement with the candidates on specific policy issues. Research in political science similarly demonstrates that anxiety motivates individuals to acquire new information about political candidates (e.g., Marcus, Neuman, & MacKuen, 2000).

Consistent with the idea that certainty plays a key role in how individuals will process information, Tiedens and Linton (2001) found that individuals experiencing a high-certainty emotion (i.e., anger, contentment) were more persuaded by a heuristic cue than were individuals experiencing a low-certainty emotion (i.e., worry, surprise). Research (e.g., Weary & Jacobson, 1997) further suggests that individuals who feel chronically uncertain (i.e., depressed) process information more systematically than those who feel chronically certain (i.e., nondepressed).

Evaluations as Information

As noted earlier, the AAI conceptualization predicts that any affect-laden stimulus or embodied experience can convey information about the extent to which the environment is safe or not. This information tends to have a corresponding effect on processing, with "safe" environments leading to more global processing and approach behaviors, and "unsafe" or threatening environments leading to more local processing and avoidance behaviors. Thus, these effects typically parallel those found using more explicit affect-induction procedures (e.g., Chartrand, van Baaren, & Bargh, 2006; see Clore & Colcombe, 2003; Isbell et al., 2006, for reviews) and tend to emerge regardless of whether an affective stimulus produces conscious changes in mood (e.g., Chartrand et al., 2006) or not (e.g., Winkielman & Berridge, 2004; Winkielman et al., 2005).

Compared with proprioceptive cues associated with avoidance motivation (e.g., arm extension), cues associated with approach motivation (e.g., arm flexion) lead participants to rely on more inclusive categories during a categorization task (Friedman & Förster, 2002) and lead to enhanced performance on creative problem-solving tasks (e.g., Friedman & Förster, 2000). Colors similarly convey information due to their frequent pairing with specific experiences; however, what information colors convey may be domain specific. For example, in achievement situations, red tends to be associated with danger and avoidance (Elliot, Maier, Binser, Friedman, & Pekrun, 2009) and leads to a reduction in performance on GRE analytical reasoning questions and a classroom exam (Soldat, Sinclair, & Mark, 1997), physically leaning away when presented with a red exam (Elliot et al., 2009), and increased local perceptual and conceptual attention (Maier, Elliot, & Lichtenfeld, 2008). In contrast, blue, which may be associated with calmness and approach (Förster & Dannenberg, 2010; cf. Soldat & Sinclair, 2001), leads to an increase in global perceptual and conceptual attention (Mehta & Zhu, 2009).

Affective cues originating from facial expressions can similarly influence information processing style. For example, individuals exposed to a politician expressing happy facial displays relied to a greater extent on categorical criteria (e.g., ideological orientation) when evaluating him, whereas those exposed to the same politician expressing neutral displays relied on systematic processing (Ottati, Terkildsen, & Hubbard, 1997). Subliminally presented happy faces (versus frowning faces) have a similar effect on impression formation (Colcombe, Isbell, & Clore, 2001, discussed in Clore & Colcombe, 2003). Further, fluency can likewise increase reliance on more heuristic, global information processing styles. For example, unfamiliar targets (e.g., persuasive messages, individuals) are processed more systematically than familiar ones (e.g., Smith, Miller, & Maitner, 2006). Compared with fluency, disfluency also leads to an increase in the detection of misleading information by promoting more detailed processing (Song & Schwarz, 2008). Taken together, the research reviewed here reveals that a large number of factors may provide individuals with information that can influence processing style.

New Directions for Affect as Information: Malleability

All of the evidence concerning the relationship between affective experiences and information processing style reviewed so far has assumed that different affective experiences are tied to specific processing styles. Indeed, this has been an underlying assumption made in the vast majority of research; however, recent theorizing in the AAI tradition suggests that this relationship is not fixed, but instead is highly malleable (e.g., Clore et al., 2001, Clore & Huntsinger, 2009; Hunsinger, Isbell, & Clore, 2012; Isbell, 2010; Isbell, Lair, & Rovenpor, 2013; Wyer et al., 1999). That is, consistent with work reviewed earlier that demonstrates that the impact of affective cues on judgment depends on the context in which they are experienced (Martin et al., 1993), recent research demonstrates that the impact of affect on processing is similarly dependent on context and is highly malleable (Clore & Huntsinger, 2009; Clore et al., 2001; Hunsinger et al., 2012; Wyer et al., 1999).

According to the malleability view, affective cues serve an informative function that signals the value of whatever cognitions, beliefs, and processing inclinations are currently accessible. Consequently, by simply changing what information is currently accessible, affective cues can promote either global or local processing. For example, fear, a negatively valenced state associated with feelings of unpredictability and uncertainty (Smith & Ellsworth, 1985; Ortony et al., 1988), confers negative value on currently accessible mental content, thereby inhibiting its use (e.g., Clore & Huntsinger, 2009). Sadness similarly conveys negative value and leads to the same effects as fear. In both of these cases, affect is likely to discourage the use of the currently dominant or accessible information processing style, regardless of whether it is global or local. In contrast, happiness conveys positive value and leads to increased reliance on current mental content. Anger, which is typically considered a negative experience that has negative consequences for the target who elicited it, has positive implications for the self and one's own point of view (Clore & Huntsinger, 2009; Lerner & Tiedens, 2006). For this reason, anger can be a positive experience. In this regard, anger and happiness convey similar types of information and often have similar effects on processing. That is, both happiness and anger promote reliance on whatever processing inclination is currently accessible regardless of whether it is local or global. Overall, the malleability perspective represents a more flexible version of the AAI approach.

Although many of the findings reviewed in the previous section concerning the role of affect on processing are consistent with predictions made by both the malleability hypothesis and the prevailing view that affective states are tied to specific processing styles, there is an important limitation to this research. That is, most work that has supported the notion that affective states are tied to specific processing styles has relied on tasks that favor global responding (e.g., stereotype use, letter and shape identification tasks [e.g., Navon, 1977; Kimchi & Palmer, 1982]; Clore & Huntsinger, 2007). Given that global responding tends to be dominant both perceptually and conceptually in many situations (Bruner, 1957), it is not surprising that happiness and anger have been associated with global processing, whereas sadness and fear have been associated with local processing. To test the malleability idea, one must alter the accessibility of global versus local processing inclinations or information, and investigate the impact of affect on the use of this information.

In a direct test of the malleability hypothesis, Hunsinger et al. (2012) examined the impact of happy and sad moods on the use of categorical versus individuating information in an impression formation task. In these studies, control conditions in which category-level processing dominates were compared with experimental conditions in which item-level processing was expected to dominate. Consistent with much prior work, all three studies showed that under default conditions in which global processing was dominant, happiness promoted reliance on global categorical information as a basis for impression formation, whereas sadness promoted reliance on individuating information. In contrast, under conditions in which local processing was dominant, these effects completely reversed, leading sad participants to rely on the categorical information and happy participants to rely on the individuating information.

Other work is also consistent with the malleability hypothesis. For example, happy individuals who were subliminally primed with images of elderly people walked slower and reported more conservative attitudes than those primed with images of young people, whereas sad individuals showed the opposite effect (Ashton-James, Huntsinger, Clore, & Chartrand, 2010). Happy individuals are also less likely than sad individuals to show stereotype activation when counter-stereotypic thoughts are made accessible, thereby reversing the typically observed effects of mood on stereotype activation (Huntsinger, Sinclair, Dunn, & Clore, 2010). Likewise, positive moods also promote individuals to rely on a primed processing style when responding to perceptual tasks (Huntsinger, Clore, & Bar-Anon, 2010). In an impressive set of studies, Fishbach and Labroo (2007) demonstrated that happy individuals were more likely to adopt an accessible goal, whereas unhappy individuals were more likely to reject it. Further, participants induced to feel happy following exposure to a persuasive communication relied on their currently accessible thoughts as a basis for their attitudes, whereas those in sad moods did not (Briñol, Petty, & Barden, 2007). Positive moods also facilitate both semantic and affective priming, whereas negative moods inhibit such effects (Storbeck & Clore, 2008), and happy moods lead to greater success at suppressing an unwanted (i.e., accessible) thought than sad moods (Wyland & Forgas, 2007). Taken together, all of these effects are consistent with the malleability view in which positive affective cues confer positive value on whatever information is currently accessible, thereby promoting its use, whereas negative affective cues confer negative value on this information, thereby inhibiting its use. The malleability of mood effects on processing is a prime example of how cognition and affect interact in order to be adaptive to our changing environment and circumstances.

OTHER SOURCES OF INFORMATION ABOUT
THE VALUE OF ACCESSIBLE MENTAL CONTENT

The idea that subjectively experienced affective reactions can convey value about currently accessible information and influence individuals' reliance on it is compatible with research demonstrating that positive (versus negative) affective concepts or cues can similarly increase (versus decrease) reliance on currently accessible information. For example, goal accessibility is reduced when goals are activated along with negative concepts, whereas goal accessibility is increased when goals are activated along with positive concepts (Winkielman, Berridge, & Wilbarger, 2005). In one study, thirsty individuals (who presumably had an active goal to reduce thirst) poured and drank more of a beverage following subliminal exposure to positive facial expressions than negative ones (Winkielman et al., 2005).

Self-validation processes similarly convey affective information, regardless of whether this information comes from consciously experienced affective states (Briñol et al., 2007), or from other variables (see Petty, Briñol, Tormala, & Wegener, 2007). For example, positive affective cues that result from writing with one's dominant hand (versus nondominant hand; Brinol & Petty, 2003), from head nodding (versus shaking; Brinol & Petty,

2003), when thoughts are easy (versus difficult) to retrieve or generate (Briñol, Petty, & Tormala, 2006), during arm flexion (versus extension) motor behavior (Friedman & Förster, 2000, 2002), and when individuals feel powerful (versus powerless; Brinol, Petty, Valle, Rucker, & Becerra, 2007) lead to similar effects. Taken together, these findings suggest that any evaluative information may serve to promote or inhibit reliance on currently accessible thoughts, beliefs, or processing styles.

Summary

In this section, we reviewed the evidence concerning the impact of moods, emotions, and evaluations on information processing style. The majority of the research in this area suggests that positive affective experiences promote global, heuristic processing, whereas negative affective experiences promote local, systematic processing. These effects have traditionally been attributed to deficits in ability or motivation among individuals experiencing positive compared with negative affect. The original application of the AAI approach to processing style effects posited that different affective experiences provide information about one's psychological environment, which accounts for why happiness (which suggests a safe and benign situation) promotes simple, heuristic processing strategies, and sadness (which suggests a problematic situation) promotes detailed, systematic processing strategies. A more recent version of the AAI approach theorizes that the influence of affective experiences on processing is malleable and depends on whatever information is currently dominant for perceivers.

Summary and Conclusions

In this chapter, we reviewed research depicting a ubiquitous relationship between affect and social cognition. This is evident from the significant influences of affect on judgment, memory, perception, attention, and information processing styles. These influences emerge for many different types of affective experiences (i.e., moods, emotions, and evaluative reactions), regardless of whether they are consciously experienced or not. Moods and other evaluative information tend to have broad and general effects on judgment and processing, whereas the influence of discrete emotions tends to be more specific, often reflecting underlying appraisal patterns. Further, the influence of different affective experiences on social cognitive processes is context dependent and highly malleable, and is easily altered in response to situational demands, perceived relevance, and changes in the cognitive accessibility of information. By broadly conceptualizing moods, emotions, and evaluative reactions as information, the AAI account provides a broad perspective in which many seemingly disparate findings can be unified across research paradigms and traditions. This account and the work reviewed in this chapter further highlight that the time for viewing affect and cognition as separate entities is long over. Rather, the weight of the evidence suggests that affect and cognition are inextricably linked human experiences. Instead of being viewed as a biasing agent that alters our rationality, affective experiences are highly adaptive and serve to guide our thoughts, judgments, and behaviors.

Future Directions

Progress over the three decades since affect made a significant appearance in the social cognition literature has been both impressive and exponential. We have learned much, but many questions of significant importance still remain and present opportunities for future research, a few of which we mention here.

First, although research on affect has now permeated every aspect of social cognition, a comprehensive understanding of how these influences combine at different stages of processing to influence judgment and behavior is still needed. With some exceptions, research has tended to target specific social cognitive processes and examine the influence of affect on these specific processes. Yet, it is not clear to what extent the effects at different stages may be additive, interactive, or independent. Such a development will require a more sophisticated understanding of the role of affect in the preconscious stages of processing (attention/perception), a relatively new area of inquiry that has been largely neglected until recently. Relatedly, promising new theoretical approaches to understanding the relationship between affect and cognition (e.g., the malleability account) need to be subjected to further empirical tests so that the explanatory power of these approaches can be explored more fully.

Second, greater attention should be focused on the role of affect within various subfields of psychology. For example, research demonstrates that the influence of affect on judgment and decision making varies with age, with children showing different effects than adults generally do (e.g., Forgas, Burnham, & Trimboli, 1988). Further, older adults often make higher quality decisions than younger adults when relying on affective rather than deliberative processing (e.g., Mikels et al., 2010). Theoretical models that can systematically capture these developmental differences would be of great value. Likewise, research in many other subfields of psychology can shed additional light on the relationship between affect and cognition while simultaneously advancing theory and understanding of phenomenon of central interest in these subfields.

Third, future work is needed to foster the integration of findings across disciplines to come to a more comprehensive understanding of the role of affect in everyday life. Basic research examining the influences of affect on social cognition has already had a profound influence on many fields in addition to psychology, including political science, marketing, economics, and communication, to name just a few. In future work, greater attention should be focused on the role of affect in real-world contexts (e.g., medical contexts) to determine the generalizability of laboratory findings, and to help establish meaningful real-world interventions to improve individuals' understanding and use of affect as information.

As theory and research move forward, an even greater integration of social cognition with different disciplines, theoretical perspectives, methodologies, and technologies will yield an increasingly richer and more comprehensive understanding of how affect shapes our thoughts, judgments, and behaviors. For example, recent work in social cognitive neuroscience has taught us a great deal about how social cognitive processes are related to brain functions. As a result of the integration of these fields, our understanding of affect and cognition has grown and led to important theoretical developments and refinements (see Chapter 34). Such highly collaborative and interdisciplinary work is strongly encouraged, and the establishment of new, creative interdisciplinary collaborations is both the call and the challenge for future researchers.

Author Note

Support is acknowledged from National Science Foundation Research Grant BCS-0956309. Address correspondence to Linda M. Isbell, Department of Psychology, 135 Hicks Way, University of Massachusetts, Amherst, MA 01003; e-mail: lisbell@psych.umass.edu.

References

Adaval, R. (2001). Sometimes it just feels right: The differential weighting of affect-consistent and affect-inconsistent product information. *Journal of Consumer Research, 28*(1), 1–17.

Allport, G. W. (1954). *The nature of prejudice*. Oxford, UK: Addison-Wesley.

Alter, A. L., & Oppenheimer, D. M. (2006). From a fixation on sports to an exploration of mechanism: The past, present, and future of hot hand research. *Thinking & Reasoning*, *12*(4), 431–444.

Alter, A. L., & Oppenheimer, D. M. (2009a). Uniting the tribes of fluency to form a metacognitive nation. *Personality and Social Psychology Review*, *13*(3), 219–235.

Alter, A. L., & Oppenheimer, D. M. (2009b). Suppressing secrecy through metacognitive ease: Cognitive fluency encourages self-disclosure. *Psychological Science*, *20*(11), 1414–1420.

Anderson, J. R. (1976). *Language, memory, and thought*. Oxford, UK: Erlbaum.

Asch, S. E. (1946). Forming impressions of personality. *Journal of Abnormal and Social Psychology*, *41*(3), 258–290.

Ashton-James, C., Huntsinger, J. R., Clore, G. L., & Chartrand, T. L. (2010) *Affective Regulation of social category priming: Attitude and behavior*. Unpublished manuscript, University of Virginia.

Bargh, J. A., Chaiken, S., Govender, R., & Pratto, F. (1992). The generality of the automatic attitude activation effect. *Journal of Personality and Social Psychology*, *62*(6), 893–912.

Baron, J. (1993). Heuristics and biases in equity judgments: A utilitarian approach. In B. A. Mellers & J. Baron (Eds.), *Psychological perspectives on justice: Theory and applications* (pp. 109–137). New York: Cambridge University Press.

Baron, R. S., Logan, H., Lilly, J., & Inman, M. (1994). Negative emotion and message processing. *Journal of Experimental Social Psychology*, *30*(2), 181–201.

Bartlett, M. Y., & DeSteno, D. (2006). Gratitude and prosocial behavior: Helping when it costs you. *Psychological Science*, *17*(4), 319–325.

Beukeboom, C. J., & Semin, G. R. (2006). How mood turns on language. *Journal of Experimental Social Psychology*, *42*(5), 553–566.

Blaney, P. H. (1986). Affect and memory: A review. *Psychological Bulletin*, *99*(2), 229–246.

Bless, H. (2001). Mood and the use of general knowledge structures. In L. L. Martin & G. L. Clore (Eds.), *Theories of mood and cognition: A user's guidebook* (pp. 9–26). Mahwah, NJ: Erlbaum.

Bless, H., Bohner, G., Schwarz, N., & Strack, F. (1990). Mood and persuasion: A cognitive response analysis. *Personality and Social Psychology Bulletin*, *16*(2), 331–345.

Bless, H., Clore, G. L., Schwarz, N., Golisano, V., Rabe, C., & Wölk, M. (1996). Mood and the use of scripts: Does a happy mood really lead to mindlessness? *Journal of Personality and Social Psychology*, *71*(4), 665–679.

Bless, H., & Schwarz, N. (1999). Sufficient and necessary conditions in dual-mode models: The case of mood and information processing. In S. Chaiken & Y. Trope (Eds.), *Dual-process theories in social psychology* (pp. 423–440). New York: Guilford Press.

Bodenhausen, G. V. (1993). Emotions, arousal, and stereotypic judgments: A heuristic model of affect and stereotyping. In D. M. Mackie & D. L. Hamilton (Eds.), *Affect, cognition, and stereotyping: Interactive processes in group perception* (pp. 13–37). San Diego, CA: Academic Press.

Bodenhausen, G. V., Kramer, G. P., & Süsser, K. (1994). Happiness and stereotypic thinking in social judgment. *Journal of Personality and Social Psychology*, *66*(4), 621–632.

Bodenhausen, G. V., Sheppard, L. A., & Kramer, G. P. (1994). Negative affect and social judgment: The differential impact of anger and sadness. *European Journal of Social Psychology*, *24*(1), 45–62.

Bohner, G., & Weinerth, T. (2001). Negative affect can increase or decrease message scrutiny: The affect interpretation hypothesis. *Personality and Social Psychology Bulletin*, *27*(11), 1417–1428.

Bower, G. H. (1981). Mood and memory. *American Psychologist*, *36*(2), 129–148.

Bower, G. H., & Mayer, J. D. (1985). Failure to replicate mood-dependent retrieval. *Bulletin of the Psychonomic Society*, *23*(1), 39–42.

Bower, G. H., & Mayer, J. D. (1989). In search of mood-dependent retrieval. *Journal of Social Behavior & Personality*, *4*(2), 121–156.

Bower, G. H., Monteiro, K. P., & Gilligan, S. G. (1978). Emotional mood as a context for learning and recall. *Journal of Verbal Learning & Verbal Behavior*, *17*(5), 573–585.

Brewer, M. B. (1988). A dual process model of impression formation. In T. K. Srull & R. S. Wyer, Jr. (Eds.), *A dual process model of impression formation* (pp. 1–36). Hillsdale, NJ: Erlbaum Associates.

Briñol, P., & Petty, R. E. (2003). Overt head movements and persuasion: A self-validation analysis. *Journal of Personality and Social Psychology*, *84*(6), 1123–1139.

Briñol, P., Petty, R. E., & Barden, J. (2007). Happiness versus sadness as a determinant of thought confidence in persuasion: A self-validation analysis. *Journal of Personality and Social Psychology*, *93*(5), 711–727.

Briñol, P., Petty, R. E., & Tormala, Z. L. (2006). The malleable meaning of subjective ease. *Psychological Science*, *17*(3), 200–206.

Briñol, P., Petty, R. E., Valle, C., Rucker, D. D., & Becerra, A. (2007). The effects of message recipients' power before and after persuasion: A self-validation analysis. *Journal of Personality and Social Psychology*, *93*(6), 1040–1053.

Broadbent, D., & Broadbent, M. (1988). Anxiety and attentional bias: State and trait. *Cognition and Emotion*, *2*(3), 165–183.

Bruner, J. S. (1957). On perceptual readiness. *Psychological Review*, *64*(2), 123–152.

Cacioppo, J. T., Priester, J. R., & Berntson, G. G. (1993). Rudimentary determinants of attitudes: II. Arm flexion and extension have differential effects on attitudes. *Journal of Personality and Social Psychology*, *65*(1), 5–17.

Carver, C. S. (2001). Affect and the functional bases of behavior: On the dimensional structure of affective experience. *Personality and Social Psychology Review*, *5*(4), 345–356.

Carver, C. S., & Harmon-Jones, E. (2009). Anger is an approach-related affect: Evidence and implications. *Psychological Bulletin*, *135*, 183–204.

Centerbar, D. B., & Clore, G. L. (2006). Do approach-avoidance actions create attitudes? *Psychological Science*, *17*(1), 22–29.

Chaiken, S., & Trope, Y. (1999). *Dual-process theories in social psychology*. New York: Guilford Press.

Chartrand, T. L., van Baaren, R. B., & Bargh, J. A. (2006). Linking automatic evaluation to mood and information processing style: Consequences for experienced affect, impression formation, and stereotyping. *Journal of Experimental Psychology: General*, *135*(1), 70–77.

Clark, M. S., & Isen, A. M. (1982). Toward understanding the relationship between feeling states and social behavior.

In A. H. Hastrof & A. M. Isen (Eds.), *Cognitive social psychology* (pp. 73–108). New York: Elsevier/North-Holland.

Clore, G. L., & Colcombe, S. (2003). The parallel worlds of affective concepts and feelings. In J. Musch & K. C. Klauer (Eds.), *The psychology of evaluation: Affective processes in cognition and emotion* (pp. 335–369). Mahwah, NJ: Erlbaum.

Clore, G. L., & Huntsinger, J. R. (2007). How emotions inform judgment and regulate thought. *Trends in Cognitive Sciences, 11*(9), 393–399.

Clore, G. L., & Huntsinger, J. R. (2009). How the object of affect guides its impact. *Emotion Review, 1*(1), 39–54.

Clore, G. L., & Storbeck, J. (2006). Affect as information about liking, efficacy, and importance. In J. P. Forgas (Ed.), *Affect in social thinking and behavior* (pp. 123–141). New York: Psychology Press.

Clore, G. L., Wyer, R. S., Jr., Dienes, B., Gasper, K., Gohm, C., & Isbell, L. (2001). Affective feelings as feedback: Some cognitive consequences. In L. L. Martin & G. L. Clore (Eds.), *Theories of mood and cognition: A user's guidebook* (pp. 27–62). Mahwah, NJ: Erlbaum.

Colcombe, S., Isbell, L. M., & Clore, G. L. (2001). *The effects of suboptimal exposure to smiles and frowns in information processing.* Unpublished manuscript. University of Illinois at Urbana-Champaign.

Collins, A. M., & Loftus, E. F. (1975). A spreading-activation theory of semantic processing. *Psychological Review, 82*(6), 407–428.

Cottrell, C. A., & Neuberg, S. L. (2005). Different emotional reactions to different groups: A sociofunctional threat-based approach to "prejudice." *Journal of Personality and Social Psychology, 88*(5), 770–789.

Damasio, A. R. (1994). *Descartes' error: emotion, reason, and the human brain.* New York: G. P. Putnam.

Darwin, C. (1872/1965). *The expression of the emotions in man and animals.* Chicago: University of Chicago Press.

Dasgupta, N., DeSteno, D., Williams, L. A., & Hunsinger, M. (2009). Fanning the flames of prejudice: The influence of specific incidental emotions on implicit prejudice. *Emotion, 9*(4), 585–591.

Davidson, R. J. (2003). Affective neuroscience and psychophysiology: Toward a synthesis. *Psychophysiology, 40*(5), 655–665.

Davis, J. I., Senghas, A., Brandt, F., & Ochsner, K. N. (2010). The effects of BOTOX injections on emotional experience. *Emotion, 10*(3), 433–440.

Derryberry, D., & Reed, M. A. (1998). Anxiety and attentional focusing: Trait, state and hemispheric influences. *Personality and Individual Differences, 25*(4), 745–761.

Derryberry, D., & Reed, M. A. (2002). Anxiety-related attentional biases and their regulation by attentional control. *Journal of Abnormal Psychology, 111*(2), 225–236.

DeSteno, D., Bartlett, M. Y., Baumann, J., Williams, L. A., & Dickens, L. (2010). Gratitude as moral sentiment: Emotion-guided cooperation in economic exchange. *Emotion, 10*(2), 289–293.

DeSteno, D., Dasgupta, N., Bartlett, M. Y., & Cajdric, A. (2004). Prejudice from thin air: The effect of emotion on automatic intergroup attitudes. *Psychological Science, 15*(5), 319–324.

DeSteno, D., Petty, R. E., Wegener, D. T., & Rucker, D. D. (2000). Beyond valence in the perception of likelihood: The role of emotion specificity. *Journal of Personality and Social Psychology, 78*(3), 397–416.

Dickinson, A., & Brown, K. J. (2007). Flavor-evaluative conditioning is unaffected by contingency knowledge during training with color-flavor compounds. *Learning & Behavior, 35*(1), 36–42.

Dijksterhuis, A. (2004). I like myself but I don't know why: enhancing implicit self-esteem by subliminal evaluative conditioning. *Journal of Personality and Social Psychology, 86*(2), 345–355.

Druckman, J. N., & McDermott, R. (2008). Emotion and the framing of risky choice. *Political Behavior, 30*(3), 297–321.

Dunn, J. R., & Schweitzer, M. E. (2005). Feeling and believing: The influence of emotion on trust. *Journal of Personality and Social Psychology, 88*(5), 736–748.

Easterbrook, J. A. (1959). The effect of emotion on cue utilization and the organization of behavior. *Psychological Review, 66*(3), 183–201.

Elliot, A. J., Maier, M. A., Binser, M. J., Friedman, R., & Pekrun, R. (2009). The effect of red on avoidance behavior in achievement contexts. *Personality and Social Psychology Bulletin, 35*(3), 365–375.

Erber, M. W., & Erber, R. (2001). The role of motivated social cognition in the regulation of affective states. In J. P. Forgas (Ed.), *Handbook of affect and social cognition* (pp. 275–290). Mahwah, NJ: Erlbaum.

Farah, M. J., Wilson, K. D., Drain, M., & Tanaka, J. N. (1998). What is "special" about face perception? *Psychological Review, 105*(3), 482–498.

Fazio, R. H., Sanbonmatsu, D. M., Powell, M. C., & Kardes, F. R. (1986). On the automatic activation of attitudes. *Journal of Personality and Social Psychology, 50*(2), 229–238.

Fischhoff, B., Gonzalez, R. M., Lerner, J. S., & Small, D. A. (2005). Evolving judgments of terror risks: Foresight, hindsight, and emotion. *Journal of Experimental Psychology: Applied, 11*(2), 124–139.

Fishbach, A., & Labroo, A. A. (2007). Be better or be merry: How mood affects self-control. *Journal of Personality and Social Psychology, 93*(2), 158–173.

Fiske, S. T., Cuddy, A. J. C., Glick, P., & Xu, J. (2002). A model of (often mixed) stereotype content: Competence and warmth respectively follow from perceived status and competition. *Journal of Personality and Social Psychology, 82*(6), 878–902.

Ford, B., Tamir, M., Brunyé, T., Shirer, W., Mahoney, C., & Taylor, H. (2010). Keeping your eyes on the prize: Anger and visual attention to threats and rewards. *Psychological Science.*

Forgas, J. P. (1992). On mood and peculiar people: Affect and person typicality in impression formation. *Journal of Personality and Social Psychology, 62*(5), 863–875.

Forgas, J. P. (1995). Mood and judgment: The affect infusion model (AIM). *Psychological Bulletin, 117*(1), 39–66.

Forgas, J. P. (2002). Feeling and doing: Affective influences in interpersonal behavior. *Psychological Inquiry, 13*, 1–28.

Forgas, J. P., Burnham, D. K., & Trimboli, C. (1988). Mood, memory, and social judgments in children. *Journal of Personality and Social Psychology, 54*, 697–703.

Förster, J., & Dannenberg, L. (2010). GLOMOsys: A systems account of global versus local processing. *Psychological Inquiry, 21*, 175–197.

Fredrickson, B. L., & Branigan, C. (2005). Positive emotions broaden the scope of attention and thought–action repertoires. *Cognition and Emotion, 19*(3), 313–332.

Friedman, R. S., & Förster, J. (2000). The effects of approach and avoidance motor actions on the elements of creative insight. *Journal of Personality and Social Psychology, 79*(4), 477–492.

Friedman, R. S., & Förster, J. (2002). The influence of approach and avoidance motor actions on creative cognition. *Journal of Experimental Social Psychology, 38*(1), 41–55.

Frijda, N. H. (1986). *The emotions.* New York: Cambridge University Press

Frijda, N. H. (1988). The laws of emotion. *American Psychologist, 43*(5), 349–358.

Gable, P. A., & Harmon-Jones, E. (2008). Approach-motivated positive affect reduces breadth of attention. *Psychological Science, 19*(5), 476–482.

Gable, P. A., & Harmon-Jones, E. (2010). The blues broaden, but the nasty narrows: Attentional consequences of negative affects low and high in motivational intensity. *Psychological Science, 21*(2), 211–215.

Gasper, K. (2004). Do you see what I see? Affect and visual information processing. *Cognition and Emotion, 18*(3), 405–421.

Gasper, K., & Clore, G. L. (1998). The persistent use of negative affect by anxious individuals to estimate risk. *Journal of Personality and Social Psychology, 74*(5), 1350–1363.

Gasper, K., & Clore, G. L. (2002). Attending to the big picture: Mood and global versus local processing of visual information. *Psychological Science, 13*(1), 34–40.

Gino, F., & Schweitzer, M. E. (2008). Blinded by anger or feeling the love: How emotions influence advice taking. *Journal of Applied Psychology, 93*(5), 1165–1173.

Haidt, J. (2001). The emotional dog and its rational tail: A social intuitionist approach to moral judgment. *Psychological Review, 108*(4), 814–834.

Haidt, J., & Kesebir, S. (2010). Morality. In S. T. Fiske, D. T. Gilbert & G. Lindzey (Eds.), *Handbook of social psychology* (5th ed., Vol. 2, pp. 797–832). Hoboken, NJ: John Wiley & Sons.

Hastie, R., & Kumar, P. A. (1979). Person memory: Personality traits as organizing principles in memory for behaviors. *Journal of Personality and Social Psychology, 37*, 25–38.

Heider, F. (1958). *The psychology of interpersonal relations.* Hoboken, NJ: John Wiley & Sons.

Higgins, E. T. (1998). The aboutness principle: A pervasive influence on human inference. *Social Cognition, 16*(1), 173–198.

Higgins, E. T., Rholes, W. S., & Jones, C. R. (1977). Category accessibility and impression formation. *Journal of Experimental Social Psychology, 13*(2), 141–154.

Hirshleifer, D., & Shumway, T. (2003). Good day sunshine: Stock returns and the weather. *Journal of Finance, 58*(3), 1009–1032.

Hofmann, W., De Houwer, J., Perugini, M., Baeyens, F., & Crombez, G. (2010). Evaluative conditioning in humans: A meta-analysis. *Psychological Bulletin, 136*(3), 390–421.

Horberg, E. J., Oveis, C., Keltner, D., & Cohen, A. B. (2009). Disgust and the moralization of purity. *Journal of Personality and Social Psychology, 97*(6), 963–976.

Huddy, L., Feldman, S., & Cassese, E. (2007). On the distinct political effects of anxiety and anger. In W. R. Neuman, G. E. Marcus, A. Crigler & M. MacKuen (Eds.), *The affect effect: Dynamics of emotion in political thinking and behavior* (pp. 202–230). Chicago: University of Chicago Press.

Hunsinger, M., Isbell, L. M., & Clore, G. L. (2012). Sometimes happy people focus on the trees and sad people focus on the forest: Context dependent effects of mood in impression formation. *Personality and Social Psychology Bulletin, 38*, 220–232.

Huntsinger, J. R., Clore, G. L., & Bar-Anan, Y. (2010). Mood and global-local focus: Priming a local focus reverses the link between mood and global-local processing. *Emotion, 10*(5), 722–726.

Huntsinger, J. R., Sinclair, S., Dunn, E., & Clore, G. L. (2010). Affective regulation of stereotype activation: It's the (accessible) thought that counts. *Personality and Social Psychology Bulletin, 36*, 564–577.

Innes-Ker, Ö., & Niedenthal, P. M. (2002). Emotion concepts and emotional states in social judgment and categorization. *Journal of Personality and Social Psychology, 83*(4), 804–816.

Isbell, L. M. (2004). Not all happy people are lazy or stupid: Evidence of systematic processing in happy moods. *Journal of Experimental Social Psychology, 40*(3), 341–349.

Isbell, L. M. (2010). What is the relationship between affect and information processing styles? This and other global and local questions inspired by GLOMOsys. *Psychological Inquiry, 21*(3), 225–232.

Isbell, L. M., & Burns, K. C. (2007). Affect. In R. F. Baumeister & K. D. Vohs (Eds.), *Encyclopedia of social psychology* (Vol. 1, pp. 12–13). Thousand Oaks, CA: Sage.

Isbell, L. M., Burns, K. C., & Haar, T. (2005). The role of affect on the search for global and specific target information. *Social Cognition, 23*(6), 529–552.

Isbell, L. M., Lair, E. C., & Rovenpor, D. R. (2013). Affect-as-Information about processing styles: A cognitive malleability approach. *Social and Personality Psychology Compass, 7*(2), 93–114.

Isbell, L. M., McCabe, J., Burns, K. C., & Lair, (2013). Who am I? The influence of affect on the working self-concept. *Cognition and Emotion, 27.* doi:10.1080/02699931.2013.765388

Isbell, L. M., Ottati, V. C., & Burns, K. C. (2006). Affect and politics: Effects on judgment, processing, and information selection. In D. Redlawsk (Ed.), *Feeling politics* (pp. 57–86). New York: Palgrave Macmillian.

Isbell, L. M., & Wyer, R. S., Jr. (1999). Correcting for mood-induced bias in the evaluation of political candidates: The roles of intrinsic and extrinsic motivation. *Personality and Social Psychology Bulletin, 25*(2), 237–249.

Isen, A. M. (1987). Positive affect, cognitive processes, and social behavior. In L. Berkowitz (Ed.), *Advances in experimental social psychology* (Vol. 20, pp. 203–253). San Diego, CA: Academic Press.

Isen, A. M., & Daubman, K. A. (1984). The influence of affect on categorization. *Journal of Personality and Social Psychology, 47*(6), 1206–1217.

Isen, A. M., Daubman, K. A., & Nowicki, G. P. (1987). Positive affect facilitates creative problem solving. *Journal of Personality and Social Psychology, 52*(6), 1122–1131.

Isen, A. M., Shalker, T. E., Clark, M., & Karp, L. (1978). Affect, accessibility of material in memory, and behavior: A cognitive loop? *Journal of Personality and Social Psychology, 36*(1), 1–12.

Ito, T. A., Chiao, K. W., Devine, P. G., Lorig, T. S., & Cacioppo, T. (2006). The influence of facial feedback on race bias. *Psychological Science, 17*(3), 256–261.

James, W., & Rouben Mamoulian Collection (Library of Congress). (1890). *The principles of psychology.* New York: H. Holt.

Johnson, E. J., & Tversky, A. (1983). Affect, generalization, and the perception of risk. *Journal of Personality and Social Psychology, 45*(1), 20–31.

Johnson, M. H., & Magaro, P. A. (1987). Effects of mood and severity on memory processes in depression and mania. *Psychological Bulletin*, *101*(1), 28–40.

Jones, C. R., Fazio, R. H., & Olson, M. A. (2009). Implicit misattribution as a mechanism underlying evaluative conditioning. *Journal of Personality and Social Psychology*, *96*(5), 933–948.

Keltner, D., Ellsworth, P. C., & Edwards, K. (1993). Beyond simple pessimism: Effects of sadness and anger on social perception. *Journal of Personality and Social Psychology*, *64*(5), 740–752.

Keltner, D., & Lerner, J. S. (2010). Emotion. In S. T. Fiske, D. T. Gilbert & G. Lindzey (Eds.), *Handbook of social psychology* (5th ed., Vol. 1, pp. 317–352). Hoboken, NJ: John Wiley & Sons.

Keltner, D., Locke, K. D., & Audrain, P. C. (1993). The influence of attributions on the relevance of negative feelings to personal satisfaction. *Personality and Social Psychology Bulletin*, *19*(1), 21–29.

Kim, H., Park, K., & Schwarz, N. (2010). Will this trip really be exciting? The role of incidental emotions in product evaluation. *Journal of Consumer Research*, *36*(6), 983–991.

Kimchi, R., & Palmer, S. E. (1982). Form and texture in hierarchically constructed patterns. *Journal of Experimental Psychology: Human Perception and Performance*, *8*(4), 521–535.

Laham, S. M., Alter, A. L., & Goodwin, G. P. (2009). Easy on the mind, easy on the wrongdoer: Discrepantly fluent violations are deemed less morally wrong. *Cognition*, *112*(3), 462–466.

Lakoff, G., & Johnson, M. (1999). *Philosophy in the flesh: The embodied mind and it's challenge to Western thought*. New York: Basic Books.

Lange, C. G. (1885/1912). The mechanism of the emotions. In B. Rand (Ed.), *The classical psychologists* (pp. 672–684). Boston: Houghton Mifflin.

Larsen, R. J., Kasimatis, M., & Frey, K. (1992). Facilitating the furrowed brow: An unobtrusive test of the facial feedback hypothesis applied to unpleasant affect. *Cognition and Emotion*, *6*(5), 321–338.

Lazarus, R. S. (1981). A cognitivist's reply to Zajonc on emotion and cognition. *American Psychologist*, *36*(2), 222–223.

Lazarus, R. S. (1982). Thoughts on the relations between emotion and cognition. *American Psychologist, 37*(9), 1019–1024.

Lench, H. C. (2009). Automatic optimism: The affective basis of judgments about the likelihood of future events. *Journal of Experimental Psychology: General*, *138*(2), 187–200.

Lerner, J. S., Goldberg, J. H., & Tetlock, P. E. (1998). Sober second thought: The effects of accountability, anger, and authoritarianism on attributions of responsibility. *Personality and Social Psychology Bulletin*, *24*(6), 563–574.

Lerner, J. S., Gonzalez, R. M., Small, D. A., & Fischhoff, B. (2003). Effects of fear and anger on perceived risks of terrorism: A national field experiment. *Psychological Science*, *14*(2), 144–150.

Lerner, J. S., & Keltner, D. (2000). Beyond valence: Toward a model of emotion-specific influences on judgement and choice. *Cognition and Emotion*, *14*(4), 473–493.

Lerner, J. S., & Keltner, D. (2001). Fear, anger, and risk. *Journal of Personality and Social Psychology*, *81*(1), 146–159.

Lerner, J. S., Small, D. A., & Loewenstein, G. (2004). Heart strings and purse strings: Carryover effects of emotions on economic decisions. *Psychological Science*, *15*(5), 337–341.

Lerner, J. S., & Tiedens, L. Z. (2006). Portrait of the angry decision maker: How appraisal tendencies shape anger's influence on cognition. *Journal of Behavioral Decision Making*, *19*(2), 115–137.

Mackie, D. M., & Worth, L. T. (1989). Processing deficits and the mediation of positive affect in persuasion. *Journal of Personality and Social Psychology*, *57*(1), 27–40.

MacLeod, C. (1999). Anxiety and anxiety disorders. In T. Dalgleish & M. J. Power (Eds.), *Handbook of cognition and emotion* (pp. 447–477). New York: John Wiley & Sons.

MacLeod, C., & Mathews, A. (1988). Anxiety and the allocation of attention to threat. *The Quarterly Journal of Experimental Psychology A: Human Experimental Psychology*, *40*(4-A), 653–670.

Maier, M. A., Elliot, A. J., & Lichtenfeld, S. (2008). Mediation of the negative effect of red on intellectual performance. *Personality and Social Psychology Bulletin*, *34*, 1530–1540.

Marcus, G. E., Neuman, W. R., & MacKuen, M. B. (2000). *Affective intelligence and political judgment*. Chicago: University of Chicago Press.

Martin, L. L., Abend, T., Sedikides, C., & Green, J. D. (1997). How would it feel if…? Mood as input to a role fulfillment evaluation process. *Journal of Personality and Social Psychology*, *73*(2), 242–253.

Martin, L. L., Ward, D. W., Achee, J. W., & Wyer, R. S. (1993). Mood as input: People have to interpret the motivational implications of their moods. *Journal of Personality and Social Psychology*, *64*(3), 317–326.

Mathews, A., & MacLeod, C. (1985). Selective processing of threat cues in anxiety states. *Behaviour Research and Therapy*, *23*(5), 563–569.

Mayer, J. D., Gaschke, Y. N., Braverman, D. L., & Evans, T. W. (1992). Mood-congruent judgment is a general effect. *Journal of Personality and Social Psychology*, *63*(1), 119–132.

McGlone, M. S., & Tofighbakhsh, J. (2000). Birds of a feather flock conjointly (?): Rhyme as reason in aphorisms. *Psychological Science*, *11*(5), 424–428.

Mehta, R., & Zhu, R. (2009). Blue or red? Exploring the effect of color on cognitive task performances. *Science*, *323*, 1226–1229.

Meier, B. P., & Robinson, M. D. (2004). Why the sunny side is up: Associations between affect and vertical position. *Psychological Science*, *15*(4), 243–247.

Meier, B. P., Robinson, M. D., Crawford, L. E., & Ahlvers, W. J. (2007). When "light" and "dark" thoughts become light and dark responses: Affect biases brightness judgments. *Emotion*, *7*(2), 366–376.

Mikels, J. A., Loeckenhoff, C., Maglio, S., Goldstein, M., Garber, A., & Carstensen, L. L. (2010). Following your heart or your head: Focusing on emotions versus information influences the decisions of younger and older adults. *Journal of Experimental Psychology: Applied*, *16(1)*, 87–95.

Moons, W. G., & Mackie, D. M. (2007). Thinking straight while seeing red: The influence of anger on information processing. *Personality and Social Psychology Bulletin*, *33*(5), 706–720.

Moretti, L., & di Pellegrino, G. (2010). Disgust selectively modulates reciprocal fairness in economic interactions. *Emotion*, *10*(2), 169–180.

Morris, W. N. (1989). *Mood: The frame of mind*. New York: Springer-Verlag.

Murphy, S. T., & Zajonc, R. B. (1993). Affect, cognition, and awareness: Affective priming with optimal and suboptimal stimulus exposures. *Journal of Personality and Social Psychology*, *64*(5), 723–739.

Murray, N., Sujan, H., Hirt, E. R., & Sujan, M. (1990). The influence of mood on categorization: A cognitive flexibility interpretation. *Journal of Personality and Social Psychology*, *59*(3), 411–425.

Navon, D. (1977). Forest before trees: The precedence of global features in visual perception. *Cognitive Psychology*, *9*(3), 353–383.

Niedenthal, P. M., Barsalou, L. W., Winkielman, P., Krauth-Gruber, S., & Ric, F. (2005). Embodiment in attitudes, social perception, and emotion. *Personality and Social Psychology Review*, *9*(3), 184–211.

Novemsky, N., Dhar, R., Schwarz, N., & Simonson, I. (2007). Preference fluency in choice. *Journal of Marketing Research*, *44*(3), 347–356.

Öhman, A., Flykt, A., & Esteves, F. (2001). Emotion drives attention: Detecting the snake in the grass. *Journal of Experimental Psychology: General*, *130*(3), 466–478.

Olson, M. A., & Fazio, R. H. (2001). Implicit attitude formation through classical conditioning. *Psychological Science*, *12*(5), 413–417.

Olson, M. A., & Fazio, R. H. (2006). Reducing automatically activated racial prejudice through implicit evaluative conditioning. *Personality and Social Psychology Bulletin*, *32*(4), 421–433.

Ortony, A., Clore, G. L., & Collins, A. (1988). *The cognitive structure of emotions*. New York: Cambridge University Press.

Ottati, V. C., & Isbell, L. M. (1996). Effects on mood during exposure to target information on subsequently reported judgments: An on-line model of misattribution and correction. *Journal of Personality and Social Psychology*, *71*(1), 39–53.

Ottati, V. C., Terkildsen, N., & Hubbard, C. (1997). Happy faces elicit heuristic processing in a televised impression formation task: A cognitive tuning account. *Personality and Social Psychology Bulletin*, *23*(11), 1144–1156.

Parker, M. T., & Isbell, L. M. (2010). How I vote depends on how I feel: The differential impact of anger and fear on political information processing. *Psychological Science*, *21*(4), 548–550.

Petty, R. E., Briñol, P., Tormala, Z. L., & Wegener, D. T. (2007). The role of metacognition in social judgment. In A. W. Kruglanski & E. T. Higgins (Eds.), *Social psychology: Handbook of basic principles* (2nd ed., pp. 254–284). New York: Guilford Press.

Pham, M. T. (1998). Representativeness, relevance, and the use of feelings in decision making. *Journal of Consumer Research*, *25*(2), 144–159.

Ping, R. M., Dhillon, S., & Beilock, S. L. (2009). Reach for what you like: The body's role in shaping preferences. *Emotion Review*, *1*(2), 140–150.

Priester, J. R., Cacioppo, J. T., & Petty, R. E. (1996). The influence of motor processes on attitudes toward novel versus familiar semantic stimuli. *Personality and Social Psychology Bulletin*, *22*(5), 442–447.

Purkis, H. M., & Lipp, O. V. (2007). Automatic attention does not equal automatic fear: Preferential attention without implicit valence. *Emotion*, *7*(2), 314–323.

Raghunathan, R., & Pham, M. T. (1999). All negative moods are not equal: Motivational influences of anxiety and sadness on decision making. *Organizational Behavior and Human Decision Processes*, *79*(1), 56–77.

Raghunathan, R., Pham, M. T., & Corfman, K. P. (2006). Informational properties of anxiety and sadness, and displaced coping. *Journal of Consumer Research: An Interdisciplinary Quarterly*, *32*(4), 596–601.

Reber, R., & Schwarz, N. (1999). Effects of perceptual fluency on judgments of truth. *Consciousness and Cognition: An International Journal*, *8*(3), 338–342.

Reber, R., Schwarz, N., & Winkielman, P. (2004). Processing fluency and aesthetic pleasure: is beauty in the perceiver's processing experience? *Personality and Social Psychology Review*, *8*(4), 364–382.

Reber, R., Winkielman, P., & Schwarz, N. (1998). Effects of perceptual fluency on affective judgments. *Psychological Science*, *9*(1), 45–48.

Redelmeier, D. A., & Baxter, S. D. (2009). Rainy weather and medical school admission interviews. *Canadian Medical Association Journal*, *181*(12).

Roseman, I. J. (1984). Cognitive determinants of emotion: A structural theory. *Review of Personality & Social Psychology*, *5*, 11–36.

Rozin, P., & Fallon, A. E. (1987). A perspective on disgust. *Psychological Review*, *94*(1), 23–41.

Russell, J. A. (2003). Core affect and the psychological construction of emotion. *Psychological Review*, *110*(1), 145–172.

Savitsky, K., Medvec, V. H., Charlton, A. E., & Gilovich, T. (1998). "What, me worry?" Arousal, misattribution and the effect of temporal distance on confidence. *Personality and Social Psychology Bulletin*, *24*(5), 529–536.

Schachter, S. (1964). Birth order and sociometric choice. *Journal of Abnormal and Social Psychology*, *68*(4), 453–456.

Schnall, S., Benton, J., & Harvey, S. (2008). With a clean conscience: Cleanliness reduces the severity of moral judgments. *Psychological Science*, *19*(12), 1219–1222.

Schnall, S., Haidt, J., Clore, G. L., & Jordan, A. H. (2008). Disgust as embodied moral judgment. *Personality and Social Psychology Bulletin*, *34*(8), 1096–1109.

Schwarz, N. (1990). Feelings as information: Informational and motivational functions of affective states. In E. T. Higgins & R. M. Sorrentino (Eds.), *Handbook of motivation and cognition: Foundations of social behavior* (Vol. 2, pp. 527–561). New York: Guilford Press.

Schwarz, N. (2012). Feelings-as-Information theory. In P. Van Lange, A. Kruglanski & E. T. Higgins (Eds.), *Handbook of theories of social psychology* (Vol. 1, pp. 289–308). Thousand Oaks, CA: Sage.

Schwarz, N., & Bless, H. (1991). Happy and mindless, but sad and smart? The impact of affective states on analytic reasoning. In J. P. Forgas (Ed.), *Emotion and social judgments* (pp. 55–71). Elmsford, NY: Pergamon Press.

Schwarz, N., & Clore, G. L. (1983). Mood, misattribution, and judgments of well-being: Informative and directive functions of affective states. *Journal of Personality and Social Psychology*, *45*(3), 513–523.

Schwarz, N., & Clore, G. L. (2007). Feelings and phenomenal experiences. In A. W. Kruglanski & E. T. Higgins (Eds.), *Social psychology: Handbook of basic principles* (2nd ed., pp. 385–407). New York: Guilford Press.

Schwarz, N., Strack, F., Kommer, D., & Wagner, D. (1987). Soccer, rooms, and the quality of your life: Mood effects on judgments of satisfaction with life in general and with specific domains. *European Journal of Social Psychology*, *17*(1), 69–79.

Sedikides, C. (1992). Attentional effects on mood are moderated by chronic self-conception valence. *Personality and Social Psychology Bulletin*, *18*(5), 580.

Sedikides, C. (1995). Central and peripheral self-conceptions are differentially influenced by mood: Tests of the differential sensitivity hypothesis. *Journal of Personality and Social Psychology, 69,* 759–759.

Siemer, M., & Reisenzein, R. (1998). Effects of mood on evaluative judgements: Influence of reduced processing capacity and mood salience. *Cognition and Emotion, 12*(6), 783–805.

Simon, H. A. (1967). Motivational and emotional controls of cognition. *Psychological Review, 74*(1), 29–39.

Sinclair, R. C., Mark, M. M., & Clore, G. L. (1994). Mood-related persuasion depends on (mis)attributions. *Social Cognition, 12*(4), 309–326.

Singer, J. A., & Salovey, P. (1988). Mood and memory: Evaluating the Network Theory of Affect. *Clinical Psychology Review, 8*(2), 211–251.

Small, D. A., & Lerner, J. S. (2008). Emotional policy: Personal sadness and anger shape judgments about a welfare case. *Political Psychology, 29*(2), 149–168.

Smith, C. A., & Ellsworth, P. C. (1985). Patterns of cognitive appraisal in emotion. *Journal of Personality and Social Psychology, 48*(4), 813–838.

Smith, E. R., Miller, D. A., & Maitner, A. T. (2006). Familiarity can increase stereotyping. *Journal of Experimental Social Psychology, 42,* 471–478.

Soldat, A. S., & Sinclair, R. C. (2001). Colors, smiles, and frowns: External affective cues can directly affect responses to persuasive communications in a mood-like manner without affecting mood. *Social Cognition, 15,* 55–71.

Soldat, A. S., Sinclair, R. C., & Mark, M. M. (1997). Color as an environmental processing cue: External affective cues can directly affect processing strategy without affective mood. *Social Cognition, 15,* 55–71.

Song, H., & Schwarz, N. (2008). Fluency and the detection of misleading questions: Low processing fluency attenuates the Moses illusion. *Social Cognition, 26*(6), 791–799.

Song, H., & Schwarz, N. (2009). If it's difficult to pronounce, it must be risky: Fluency, familiarity, and risk perception. *Psychological Science, 20*(2), 135–138.

Srivastava, J., Espinoza, F., & Fedorikhin, A. (2009). Coupling and decoupling of unfairness and anger in ultimatum bargaining. *Journal of Behavioral Decision Making, 22*(5), 475–489.

Srull, T. K., & Wyer, R. S. (1989). Person memory and judgment. *Psychological Review, 96,* 58–83.

Stefanucci, J. K., & Proffitt, D. R. (2009). The roles of altitude and fear in the perception of height. *Journal of Experimental Psychology: Human Perception and Performance, 35*(2), 424–438.

Stefanucci, J. K., Proffitt, D. R., Clore, G. L., & Parekh, N. (2008). Skating down a steeper slope: Fear influences the perception of geographical slant. *Perception, 37*(2), 321–323.

Stel, M., van den Heuvel, C., & Smeets, R. C. (2008). Facial feedback mechanisms in autistic spectrum disorders. *Journal of Autism and Developmental Disorders, 38*(7), 1250–1258.

Stepper, S., & Strack, F. (1993). Proprioceptive determinants of emotional and nonemotional feelings. *Journal of Personality and Social Psychology, 64*(2), 211–220.

Storbeck, J., & Clore, G. L. (2007). On the interdependence of cognition and emotion. *Cognition and Emotion, 21*(6), 1212–1237.

Storbeck, J., & Clore, G. L. (2008). The affective regulation of cognitive priming. *Emotion, 8*(2), 208–215.

Storbeck, J., & Robinson, M. D. (2004). Preferences and inferences in encoding visual objects: A systematic comparison of semantic and affective priming. *Personality and Social Psychology Bulletin, 30*(1), 81–93.

Strack, F., Martin, L. L., & Stepper, S. (1988). Inhibiting and facilitating conditions of the human smile: A nonobtrusive test of the facial feedback hypothesis. *Journal of Personality and Social Psychology, 54*(5), 768–777.

Strack, F., Schwarz, N., & Gschneidinger, E. (1985). Happiness and reminiscing: The role of time perspective, affect, and mode of thinking. *Journal of Personality and Social Psychology, 49*(6), 1460–1469.

Tamir, M., & Robinson, M. D. (2007). The happy spotlight: Positive mood and selective attention to rewarding information. *Personality and Social Psychology Bulletin, 33*(8), 1124–1136.

Tamir, M., Robinson, M. D., Clore, G. L., Martin, L. L., & Whitaker, D. J. (2004). Are we puppets on a string? The contextual meaning of unconscious expressive cues. *Personality and Social Psychology Bulletin, 30*(2), 237–249.

Tiedens, L. Z. (2001). The effect of anger on the hostile inferences of aggressive and nonaggressive people: Specific emotions, cognitive processing, and chronic accessibility. *Motivation and Emotion, 25*(3), 233–251.

Tiedens, L. Z., & Linton, S. (2001). Judgment under emotional certainty and uncertainty: The effects of specific emotions on information processing. *Journal of Personality and Social Psychology, 81*(6), 973–988.

Ucros, C. G. (1989). Mood state-dependent memory: A meta-analysis. *Cognition and Emotion, 3*(2), 139–169.

Van Honk, J., Tuiten, A., de Haan, E., van den Hout, M., & Stam, H. (2001). Attentional biases for angry faces: Relationships to trait anger and anxiety. *Cognition and Emotion, 15*(3), 279–297.

Wapner, S., Werner, H., & Krus, D. M. (1957). The effect of success and failure on space location. *Journal of Personality, 25,* 752–756.

Weary, G., & Jacobson, J. A. (1997). Causal uncertainty beliefs and diagnostic information seeking. *Journal of Personality and Social Psychology, 73*(4), 839–848.

Weaver, K., Garcia, S. M., Schwarz, N., & Miller, D. T. (2007). Inferring the popularity of an opinion from its familiarity: A repetitive voice can sound like a chorus. *Journal of Personality and Social Psychology, 92*(5), 821–833.

Wegener, D. T., & Petty, R. E. (1997). The flexible correction model: The role of naive theories of bias in bias correction. In M. P. Zanna (Ed.), *Advances in experimental social psychology* (Vol. 29, pp. 141–208). San Diego, CA: Academic Press.

Wegener, D. T., Petty, R. E., & Smith, S. M. (1995). Positive mood can increase or decrease message scrutiny: The hedonic contingency view of mood and message processing. *Journal of Personality and Social Psychology, 69*(1), 5–15.

Weger, U. W., Meier, B. P., Robinson, M. D., & Inhoff, A. W. (2007). Things are sounding up: Affective influences on auditory tone perception. *Psychonomic Bulletin & Review, 14*(3), 517–521.

Wheatley, T., & Haidt, J. (2005). Hypnotic disgust makes moral judgments more severe. *Psychological Science, 16*(10), 780–784.

Whittlesea, B. W. A., & Price, J. R. (2001). Implicit/explicit memory versus analytic/nonanalytic processing: Rethinking the mere exposure effect. *Memory & Cognition, 29*(2), 234–246.

Wilkowski, B. M., Robinson, M. D., Gordon, R. D., & Troop-Gordon, W. (2007). Tracking the evil eye: Trait anger and selective attention within ambiguously hostile scenes. *Journal of Research in Personality, 41*(3), 650–666.

Williams, L. A., & DeSteno, D. (2009). Pride: Adaptive social emotion or seventh sin? *Psychological Science, 20*(3), 284–288.

Wilson, T. D., & Brekke, N. (1994). Mental contamination and mental correction: Unwanted influences on judgments and evaluations. *Psychological Bulletin, 116*(1), 117–142.

Winkielman, P., & Berridge, K. C. (2004). Unconscious emotion. *Current Directions in Psychological Science, 13*(3), 120–123.

Winkielman, P., Berridge, K. C., & Wilbarger, J. L. (2005). Unconscious affective reactions to masked happy versus angry faces influence consumption behavior and judgments of value. *Personality and Social Psychology Bulletin, 31*(1), 121–135.

Winkielman, P., & Cacioppo, J. T. (2001). Mind at ease puts a smile on the face: Psychophysiological evidence that processing facilitation elicits positive affect. *Journal of Personality and Social Psychology, 81*(6), 989–1000.

Winkielman, P., Schwarz, N., Reber, R., & Fazendeiro, T. A. (2003). Cognitive and affective consequences of visual fluency: When seeing is easy on the mind. In L. M. Scott and R. Batra (Eds.), *Persuasive imagery: A consumer response perspective* (pp. 75–89). Mahwah, NJ: Lawrence Erlbaum Associates Publishers.

Winkielman, P., Zajonc, R. B., & Schwarz, N. (1997). Subliminal affective priming resists attributional interventions. *Cognition and Emotion, 11*(4), 433–465.

Worth, L. T., & Mackie, D. M. (1987). Cognitive mediation of positive affect in persuasion. *Social Cognition, 5*(1), 76–94.

Wyer, R. S., Jr., & Carlston, D. E. (1979). *Social cognition, inference, and attribution.* Hillsdale, NJ: Erlbaum.

Wyer, R. S., Jr., Clore, G. L., & Isbell, L. M. (1999). Affect and information processing. In M. P. Zanna (Ed.), *Advances in experimental social psychology* (Vol. 31, pp. 1–77). San Diego, CA: Academic Press.

Wyer, R. S., Jr., & Srull, T. K. (1989). *Social intelligence and cognitive assessments of personality.* Hillsdale, NJ: Erlbaum.

Wyland, C. L., & Forgas, J. P. (2007). On bad mood and white bears: The effects of mood state on ability to suppress unwanted thoughts. *Cognition and Emotion, 21*(7), 1513–1524.

Zajonc, R. B. (1968). Attitudinal effects of mere exposure. *Journal of Personality and Social Psychology, 9*(2), 1–27.

Zajonc, R. B. (1980). Feeling and thinking: Preferences need no inferences. *American Psychologist, 35*(2), 151–175.

Zajonc, R. B. (2000). Feeling and thinking: Closing the debate over the independence of affect. In J. P. Forgas (Ed.), *Feeling and thinking: The role of affect in social cognition* (pp. 31–58). New York: Cambridge University Press.

Motivated Remembering: Remembering as Accessibility and Accessibility as Motivational Relevance

Baruch Eitam, David B. Miele, *and* E. Tory Higgins

Abstract

This chapter presents a novel framework that integrates motivational relevance and accessibility and outlines its implications for the study of memory. The authors first review a recent analysis of motivation (Higgins, 2012) and a recent framework linking motivational relevance and accessibility (Eitam & Higgins, 2010). The authors then propose and demonstrate that knowledge activation and recall of information—whether implicit or explicit, and regardless of the type of that information (semantic, episodic, autobiographical, or procedural)—are affected by the motivational relevance of that information at the time retrieval is attempted or measured.

Key Words: motivation, relevance, accessibility, knowledge activation, memory

"Who controls the past," ran the Party slogan, "controls the future: who controls the present controls the past." (Orwell, 1949)

Psychologists' model of human memory has largely shifted from that of a warehouse packed with slowly fading items, to a set of active, dynamic processes working synchronously in an attempt to reconstruct the past (Jenkins, 1974; Koriat, Goldsmith, & Pansky, 2000; for its roots of reconstruction, see Bartlett, 1932). In this review, we focus specifically on the subset of processes associated with the *accessibility* and *activation* of mental representations stored in long-term memory. Within social psychology, accessibility is typically understood as the ease with which an *available* mental representation (i.e., a structured set of information already encoded in memory) can be activated by external stimulation, whereas activation itself refers to whether or not that representation has been accessed *for use* (Bruner, 1957; Higgins, 1996). That is, the accessibility of a mental representation is the amount of external stimulation required in order to shift it from a latent state (available in the mind but currently inactive) to an active one (involved in current thought and action). Although this definition suggests that accessibility is inherently about how people construct current memories from previously encoded information, it is a construct that has typically been employed without reference to memory per se. Thus, a general aim of the present chapter is to highlight the importance of the role played by accessibility in human memory.

A more specific (and primary) aim of this chapter is to examine the ways in which accessibility mediates the effects of motivation on memory retrieval. Although what we remember may closely correspond to what we originally encoded, it also tends to diverge from it in important ways. This divergence has typically been explained in terms of either omission of details that results from decay and fragmentation (Brainerd & Reyna, 1995) or schema-driven constructive processes that go beyond simple forgetting (Anderson & Pichert, 1978; Bartlett, 1932). Alternatively, there is an explanation that suggests that the divergence between what is retrieved and what was originally encoded is not solely a product of mere memory mechanisms, but instead results from the interaction between memory and motivational processes. From this *motivational* perspective, omissions and commissions reflect the objectives of the rememberer beyond the simple goal of producing an accurate and complete reproduction of all that was originally encoded. Borrowing from George Orwell, Each of us is the Party to our motives, and we ourselves, in the present, control what past we remember.

To explore the various types of objectives that can affect human memory retrieval, we draw on a model of motivation that goes beyond the traditional notion that all of human striving can be reduced to the desire to approach pleasure and avoid pain (Higgins, 2012). Although this model does posit that a major component of motivation is wanting to be effective at having desired outcomes (i.e., value), it also proposes that, at an equally fundamental level, people want to be effective at establishing what's real (i.e., truth) and at managing what happens (i.e., control). Although the concepts of truth and control effectiveness, in comparison to value effectiveness, have received relatively little attention in the motivated cognition literature, we use them here to reinterpret and give structure to previously documented effects of motivation on memory retrieval.

In addition to Higgins' (2012) analysis of motivation, we draw on a novel framework of knowledge activation and information processing (Eitam & Higgins, 2010) in order to explain how the effects of value, truth, and control effectiveness on memory retrieval are mediated by changes in accessibility. The framework, which is called *relevance of activated representations* (or ROAR for short), stipulates that stored mental representations become active (and the concepts they represent accessible) as a function of their actual or perceived relevance for increasing one's value, truth, and control effectiveness. Thus, according to ROAR, a central function of motivation is the *selection* of mental representations for use in thought and action. Before describing the ROAR framework in greater detail, we first review evidence for this claim.

Motivation and Memory

The idea that our experience is the product of cognition and motivation is not new (for reviews, see Kunda, 1990; Molden & Higgins, 2005). Numerous studies have shown that we tend to see or hear those things in our environment that are relevant to our current goals and motives (e.g., Balcetis

& Dunning, 2006; Bruner, 1957; Eitam, Schul, & Hassin, 2009; Eitam, Yeshurun, & Hassan, in press; Moray, 1959). This kind of motivated selectivity applies not only to perception but also to the entire range of processes our mind is capable of executing, from believing (Klein & Kunda, 1992) to acting (Rushworth, Walton, Kennerley, & Bannerman, 2004). Why, then, should remembering be any different?

Kunda (1990) coined the terms *directional* and *nondirectional* motivation for describing the different ways in which motivation and cognition interact (see Kruglanski, 1989, for the similar distinction between *specific* and *nonspecific* epistemic motivation). On the one hand, motivation was sometimes viewed as "abducting" otherwise properly functioning cognitive processes in the service of gratifying some hedonic desire. Such directional (or specific) effects were described as resulting from efforts to selectively process information in order to reach a desired outcome or to maintain some comforting or otherwise hedonically pleasing belief (Kunda, 1990). On the other hand, it was also considered possible for motivation to increase the intensity of "properly functioning" cognitive processes in the service of reaching "the truth" or an optimal conclusion (e.g., Eitam, Hassin, & Schul, 2008; Kruglanski, 1989). Such (nondirectional or nonspecific) increases in intensity were thought to be mediated by either increased effort or additional processing.

Most research on motivational effects on memory has examined the effects of directional motivation on memory, and most of this research has focused on abductions of memory processes in the service of maximizing pleasure and minimizing pain. We will briefly illustrate some of this research. In a classic study by Sanitioso, Kunda, and Fong (1990; see also Brunot & Sanitioso, 2004), for example, participants recalled more autobiographical memories that were consistent with a particular personality trait (e.g., introversion) when they were led to believe that this trait was more (as opposed to less) desirable than its opposite (e.g., extroversion). Similarly, Dunning, Perie, and Story (1991) showed that people often activate prototypes or schemas that serve to maintain their sense of self-worth. In one study, participants were asked to specify whether or not certain personality traits fit with the concept of leadership. Participants were more likely to say that an attribute did fit if, at an earlier point in the study, they had claimed to possess that trait themselves. Importantly, they also endorsed these traits more quickly, suggesting that self-relevant personality traits were more accessible to participants (i.e., more active in their mind) than self-irrelevant traits.

In a related set of studies, Sedikides and colleagues have demonstrated that people exhibit heightened recall of information that supports their desired self-image (Sedikides & Green, 2009). In addition, McDonald and Hirt (1997) have shown that this type of selective recall extends to information about others. Specifically, participants in their experiments distorted their recall and recognition to be consistent with either positive expectations about an individual when this person was someone they liked or negative expectations when this person was someone they disliked. These findings relate to earlier findings by Ross and colleagues demonstrating the centrality of a seemingly "cognitive" factor (i.e., participants' expectancies) for memory reconstruction (Conway & Ross, 1984). However, in keeping with the explanation provided by McDonald and Hirt, we will argue below that expectancies, rather than being just cognitive, also carry motivational relevance because they concern what will *really* happen in the future (truth effectiveness).

More recently, Mather and colleagues documented yet another hedonically motivated directional effect on memory (Mather & Carstensen, 2005). Specifically, as people get older and presumably become increasingly motivated to optimize well-being, they tend to recall positively biased information about past choices and experiences. Furthermore, although this bias may result from self-regulatory processes that require a certain degree of cognitive control, it appears to be unintentional, or at least not consciously intentional (Knight, et al., 2007).

In line with Mather's conceptualization of this positivity bias as a motivated, selective process, others have demonstrated that the act of remembering is closely tied to peoples' current goals or attitudes (e.g., Ross, 1989). For example, Moberly and MacLeod (2006) recently showed that memories that were relevant to participants' self-described goals were more easily accessed than memories that were not goal relevant (see also Crane, Goddard, & Pring, 2009). In addition, Gramzow and Willard (2006) showed that positive bias in college students' memories of past performance (i.e., self-reported grade point average [GPA]) resulted from the dispositional motivation to self-enhance, but only when these memories were relevant to a current goal (i.e., the desire to maintain or improve their GPA). When students' memories were relevant only to a past and completed goal (i.e., self-reported Scholastic

Aptitude Test [SAT] scores that were relevant in the past to gain entry to a good college), positive bias instead resulted from a reduction in accessibility of past test scores, which allowed participants to "reconstruct" past performance based on their positive beliefs about the self. Although these effects led Gramzow and Willard to differentiate between *motivational* and *reconstructive* memory processes, they are also a demonstration of the interplay among motivational relevance, accessibility, and memory. Although both students' GPA and SAT scores are relevant for the goal of maintaining a positive self-image, they differ in their current task relevance and hence in their accessibility. Consequently, other sources of relevance such as "expectancies" about oneself that are measured by beliefs about achievement level (and can relate to current truth effectiveness) may have more influence in the second (SAT) case compared with the first.

One final and rather striking example of how motivation can affect remembering is a classic study by Anderson and Pichert (1978). In two experiments, participants adopted the perspective of either a burglar or homebuyer while reading a story about two boys who head back to one of the boys' homes after cutting school. After they finished reading, participants were asked to recall as much of the story as they could remember. Five minutes later, they were asked to recall the story for a second time; however, this time, half of the participants were instructed to switch perspectives (from burglar to homebuyer or vice versa) before doing so. The results showed that, after switching perspectives, participants recalled more of the information that was irrelevant from the first perspective but was now relevant from the second perspective. Hence seemingly forgotten information became accessible after becoming motivationally relevant.

Taken together, the findings reviewed above afford two tentative conclusions. The first is that memory retrieval can be influenced by people's motivations and that these motivations are not limited to the desire to generate a complete or infallible reconstruction of the past. The second conclusion, which we explore more closely below, is that (at least in some cases) the way motivation affects remembering may be analogous to the way motivation affects other, more automatic, forms of knowledge activation.

Motivated Accessibility from Relevance

Within social psychology, knowledge activation has become a prominent mechanistic explanation for a number of different phenomena (for a recent review, see Eitam & Higgins, 2010). In many cases, this explanation is based on the idea that motivation can affect thought and action by controlling which mental representations become active and how long they stay active. The seed for this idea can be traced back to Bluma Zeigarnik's (1938) pioneering research, which demonstrated that people's memory for uncompleted or interrupted tasks is better than their memory for completed tasks (Förster, Liberman, & Higgins, 2005).

Echoing the literature on motivated memory reviewed above, the majority of the research on knowledge activation has focused on how end states, goals, and needs affect the accessibility of mental representations (i.e., directional effects). For example, in a study by Förster and colleagues (2005), participants were assigned the goal of identifying and responding to a specific visual cue (i.e., a pair of eyeglasses). Response times to eyeglass-related words on a subsequent lexical decision task (which serve as the "gold standard" for measuring a representation's degree of activation) demonstrated that the concept of eyeglasses was more active in participants' minds before (compared with after) the goal had been completed. The relation between motivation and knowledge activation has also been explored more broadly than just in reference to specific task goals. Using the same basic paradigm as Förster et al. (2005), for example, Hedberg and Higgins (2011) reported that the rate of decay in accessibility after the goal is *faster* for individuals with stronger promotion concerns with gains and advancement and is *slower* for individuals with stronger prevention concerns with nonlosses and security (for a discussion of promotion *vs.* prevention concerns, see Higgins, 1997)—a clear indication that motivational concerns can influence accessibility. As other examples, Moskowitz, Gollwitzer, Wasel, and Schaal (1999) have demonstrated that the general goal of being egalitarian can unintentionally reduce people's activation of stereotypes, and Ferguson (2008) showed that this remains true even when people are unaware that they possess this goal.

How, then, does motivation influence knowledge activation? One clue comes from a recent demonstration that relates the "positive affect" that is associated with an active representation to the duration that the representation remains active (Aarts, Custers, & Marien, 2009; for recent reviews, see Eitam & Higgins, 2010; Custers, Eitam, & Bargh, 2012). Such findings suggest that having a goal or a need (e.g., being thirsty) leads the mind to assign "positive valence" or "incentive value" to goal- or need-relevant knowledge (Custers & Aarts, 2005; Ferguson & Bargh, 2004). This, in turn, suggests that the motivational relevance of knowledge representations is dynamically computed (cf., Custers & Aarts, 2010).

Motivations Other than Attaining Desired Outcomes

Much of the literature on motivated knowledge activation has focused on how information pertaining to desired outcomes tends to have relatively high levels of accessibility. However, approaching desired outcomes and avoiding undesired outcomes do not account for the entire spectrum of human motivation. Indeed, many of the examples noted above, such as the effect of expectancy on memory, are hard to reconcile with a uniformly hedonic perspective on motivation. As mentioned earlier, Higgins (2012) has recently proposed that, beyond pleasure and pain, motivation can be thought of as fundamentally wanting to be effective at three things: at having desired outcomes (value), but also at establishing what's real (truth) and at managing what happens (control). Although value effectiveness (which itself is more than just hedonic concerns) has received more attention in the literature than truth or control effectiveness, the previously reviewed findings, as well as other important findings, can be reinterpreted in terms of all three motivations rather than just hedonic value. Before returning to these findings, however, it is important to distinguish more clearly between these three different ways of wanting to be effective.

According to Higgins (2012), value effectiveness is being successful in having what's desired. Thus, value effectiveness is really about the consequences of goal pursuit—accruing benefits versus costs, experiencing pleasure versus pain, and succeeding versus failing to satisfy basic needs. Truth effectiveness, on the other hand, is being successful in establishing what's real. In one sense, something can be considered real if it accords with an actual state of affairs or represents things as they actually are. In another sense, for something to be real, it must be correct, right, and legitimate—in contrast to things that are imaginary, spurious, or counterfeit. In both respects, being successful in establishing what's real is just as critical to the well-being of humans and other animals as being successful in having what's desired. The problem is that, as far as we know, there is no innate marker that differentiates between true and false representations of the world. Indeed, young children, and some troubled adults, find it difficult to distinguish reality from fantasy. It is also evident from ideological battles about religion and politics that what is reality to one group can be mere illusion or delusion to another. Despite such differences, one thing is clear: both individuals and groups are often strongly motivated to know what is "really" the case—to pursue truth effectiveness. This plays out in myriad ways, including concerns with accuracy, legitimacy, justice, genuineness, and honesty.

Finally, control effectiveness is being successful at managing what is required (procedures, competencies, resources) to make something happen (or not happen). By making something happen, we mean exercising direction or restraint upon action in order to achieve a particular outcome. Whereas value effectiveness relates to the outcome itself (e.g., a benefit vs. cost) and truth effectiveness relates to reality, control effectiveness relates to the *strength* of one's influence over something. Such strength can be exerted with respect to muscles, eyesight, effects on the environment, intellect, character, arguments, willpower, teamwork, and so on. Although high control effectiveness increases the likelihood that beneficial outcomes will be obtained, it is independent of these outcomes, as reflected in a personal motto such as, "I would rather do *anything* than nothing at all."

Linking Motivational Relevance to Mental Activation: The ROAR Framework

Building on Higgins' (2012) distinction between value, truth, and control as three domains in which people seek to be effective, Eitam and Higgins (2010) recently proposed a novel framework that relates these motivational domains to the dynamics of accessibility and knowledge activation. This framework, the ROAR framework, represents a significant shift from viewing motivation as separate and removed from cognition (with motivated processes abducting the otherwise "rational," "veridical," or "proper" functioning of cognitive processes) to viewing the two constructs as different sides of the same information processing coin.

According to ROAR, motivation concerns the *relevance of represented information content (i.e., the relevance of a representation)* with respect to value, truth, or control. The relevance of the represented information is dynamically computed as soon as the representation is triggered by some set of external stimuli. Once computed, it takes the same form regardless of how the corresponding content is

represented— that is, whether the content is an episodic memory, fact, procedure, stereotype, or even a goal. The primary effect that motivational relevance has on cognitive functioning is to determine the degree to which the represented information is *accessible* and, thus, how likely it is to become *active*. As a result, only sufficiently relevant information becomes available for use by other mental processes, such as associative learning, deductive reasoning, and action planning. This conceptualization of motivational relevance has, in a previous review (Eitam & Higgins, 2010), allowed us to account for an array of seemingly unrelated phenomena, such as the effects of priming on behavior, reductions in accessibility due to negation (e.g., Kaup, 2001), and the supposed outcomes of selective attention (e.g., "inattentional amnesia"; Wolfe, 1999; see also Eitam et al., in press).

Implicit Memory and Motivational Relevance

As we stated earlier in the chapter, although the study of knowledge activation and the study of memory have produced separate literatures, it seems beneficial to consider them in tandem, *with knowledge activation understood as part of the process of memory reconstruction*. One immediate implication of this conceptual integration is that a model of motivated knowledge activation should be useful in understanding the underlying processes that give rise to motivated memory. Thus, we now turn to a discussion of how ROAR can help to explain why there is often a divergence between the information about an event that is encoded and the information that is eventually retrieved.

The semantic and procedural forms of memory described as *implicit,* such as knowing what things are or knowing what to do (Tulving, 1972), do not require intentional activation or awareness of a memory. Because they typically cannot be made explicit by the individual, they are often measured in terms of knowledge accessibility using lexical decision, stem completion, and other semantic and perceptual priming-related tasks. Considering that ROAR was designed to explain the dynamics of knowledge accessibility and activation, it may be a particularly useful framework for understanding the effects of motivation on implicit memory.

According to ROAR, multiple internal representations (e.g., semantic knowledge) can be implicitly stimulated by the same external event, but only those with a sufficient degree of motivational relevance will actually affect thought and action. Importantly, these motivational effects are *not* biases, but rather are the outcomes of a dynamic selection process that augments other, more fixed or structural forms of memory selection, such as semantic association and spread of activation. As previously explained, this selection process computes the relevance of representations with respect to value, truth, or control. For example, the truth relevance of a representation should vary in accordance with the perceived likelihood of encountering the corresponding object or event in the near future (i.e., with expectancy) or with the perceived validity of the object (see below).

Evidence for this claim comes from studies investigating the effects of negation on the activation of schematic and propositional knowledge. Specifically, sentences that include negation (e.g., "Elizabeth bakes no bread"; MacDonald & Just, 1989) or that describe a situation in which an object is absent (e.g., "Sam wished that Laura was wearing her pink dress"; Kaup, 2001; Kaup & Zwaan, 2003) appear to lower the accessibility of the objects in question ("bread" and "pink dress," respectively). Because both negation and absence imply that the likelihood of actually encountering the mentioned objects is reduced, decreases in accessibility can be attributed to corresponding decreases in the objects' truth relevance (i.e., the objects are not currently real). This should be the case even if objects or concepts are originally memorized before the introduction of information concerning their truth relevance. For instance, if people intentionally memorize or incidentally process the word *bridge* without any added context, implicit memory for this word when later presented in the context of *constructed bridge* should be better than when presented in the context of *dismantled bridge*. This is because in the latter case, the bridge is no longer real, it has ceased to exist; hence, the truth relevance of the corresponding representation is lower compared with the representation for the existing (constructed) bridge. Indeed, in a recent study we have obtained initial evidence that this is indeed the case. Participants were presented with a list of 40 to-be-encoded words (Eitam, Kopietz & Higgins, unpublished manuscript). Ten of these words were piloted to be effectively modified in their truth relevance when imbedded in a "construction" or "destruction" phrase—the target words. In a subsequent recognition memory test phase, participants were required to identify words, embedded in either construction or destruction phrases, as being "old" or "new". Note that "old" responses are more likely when a word has higher accessibility.

For the critical target words, we found reliably *fewer* "old" responses when they appeared in a destruction phrase than in a construction phrase.

ROAR also provides a framework for reinterpreting some more straightforward effects of motivation on implicit memory. As opposed to truth relevance, these effects are better understood in terms of an object or concept's value relevance (i.e., its relevance for being effective at "having what is desired" or "not having what is undesired"; Higgins, 2012). For example, earlier in the chapter, we reviewed multiple demonstrations of *positive* value relevance (the "having what's desired" part) resulting in the retrieval of inaccurate information. But, according to ROAR, negative value relevance can also affect memory, as in the case of threatening or anxiety-producing objects and events. To the extent that one must be aware of such objects (e.g., snakes) in order to avoid undesired outcomes (e.g., getting bitten), their corresponding representations should be highly accessible in memory. A recent meta-analysis on memory of threatening items suggests that this is indeed the case (Mitte, 2008). Specifically, the results of 14 studies showed that implicit memory of threatening items (as measured by a lexical decision task) was stronger than memory of neutral items.

It is worth reiterating that, according to ROAR, the relevance of a mental representation from value, truth, or control effectiveness is *dynamically* computed as soon as it is stimulated, and this relevance determines whether the representation will be available to other mental processes. Thus, in a certain sense, the dynamic computation of relevance is what makes context-sensitive remembering (and "forgetting") possible (e.g., Tulving & Thomson, 1973). That is, changes in the external environment or the internal state of the individual influence what gets remembered by virtue of their effect on the relevance of the stimulated item. If the current relevance of the item in the retrieval context is different from what its relevance was in the encoding context, then there should be an observable difference in the item's level of accessibility or duration of activation between the two contexts (we will return to this point when discussing the effects of "shared reality" on memory). The strongest version of this prediction is that a representation with insufficient relevance will not be remembered. Conversely, one with high relevance may be easily remembered regardless of whether or not it was recently stimulated. For example, after a representation is initially stimulated by an implicit memory probe (such as an item in a lexical decision task), its high relevance may cause it to be active in mind and (potentially) to produce a false implicit memory effect (i.e., an error of commission).

One particularly illuminating example of low relevance induced "forgetting" comes from an experiment on the implicit learning of artificial grammars by Dienes, Altman, Kwan, and Goode (1995). Implicit learning tasks may measure slightly different phenomena (Frensch, 1998), but one common feature is that the learning involved is often unintentional (Reber, 1967). In a typical implicit learning experiment, participants are exposed to stimuli (e.g., letter strings) that are structured on the basis of complex rules. Structure learning is then (unexpectedly) tested by asking participants to classify novel stimuli as being "grammatical" (i.e., as conforming to some set of rules). Multiple studies have shown that people classify these novel stimuli on the basis of valid structural knowledge, even when they feel as though they are guessing.

In the experiment by Dienes and colleagues (1995; Experiment 5), participants attended to a set of such structured stimuli and were then informed that the experiment had ended. At this point, the participants were asked to participate in another ostensibly unrelated study that was being conducted in a nearby room. As part of this study, participants were asked to classify various letter strings as either obeying or violating a complex system of rules (they were also told that only half of the stimuli obeyed the rules). Importantly, half of the participants were informed of the fact that these rules were the same as those used to structure the stimuli from the original study, whereas the other half were told nothing. Remarkably, only the "informed" group's performance on the classification task indicated that they had implicitly learned the rules. The low-relevance, "uniformed" group "forgot" the rules.

Because the learning phase of the experiment preceded the context manipulation (informed *vs.* uninformed), it is safe to assume that participants' learning of the rules was identical in both groups. This, coupled with the fact that participants could not have intentionally recalled or applied the rules during the classification task (because they were implicit), suggests that the effect must have been due to differences in perceived relevance at the time of the "second study." That is, the contextual information provided to the "informed" participants increased the relevance of the previously learned rules, resulting in the activation and use of this knowledge during the classification task. In contrast, the relevance of the rules remained low for the "uninformed" participants (who were not provided with contextual information), which explains why the same knowledge was not activated or used in this condition.

Shared Reality: The Dynamics of Truth Relevance and Its Effect on Recall

As previously explained, ROAR was designed as a framework for understanding the effects of external stimulation on the accessibility of mental representations. Because implicit memory effects are often measured in terms of accessibility, they can easily be accommodated by ROAR. However, explicit measures of memory such as recognition or free recall may involve underlying processes different from those captured by implicit measures. For example, both recognition and recall may involve an intentional attempt to retrieve or reconstruct what was previously learned and, thus, may tap into aspects of remembering that do not pertain to implicit memory. Recently, however, researchers have suggested that this may not be the case (Voss & Paller, 2008), which implies that the effects of motivational relevance on memory should emerge even when explicit measures are used. In the next section, we describe a particularly striking example of how (truth) relevance affects explicit memory.

One of the primary ways in which people strive to be effective at establishing what's real is by constructing a *shared reality*. Shared reality is a commonality of inner states between oneself and other individuals that confers validity and reliability to information about the world (Echterhoff, Higgins, & Levine, 2009; Hardin & Higgins, 1996). According to ROAR, information that pertains to a successfully shared reality should be higher in truth relevance and, thus, more active in mind than information that does not pertain to a shared reality (assuming that the levels of value and control relevance are similar in both cases).

For the most part, experiments that have explored the creation of shared reality, and that have examined its effects on memory, have used a variant of the *saying-is-believing* paradigm (Higgins & Rholes, 1978). Typically, this involves having participants read an essay about the behavior of another individual (the target person) who supposedly agreed to be part of a long-term research project on person perception. The essay usually consists of several passages that describe the target's actions in an evaluatively ambiguous manner, that is, in a manner that makes it equally likely for the actions to be interpreted positively or negatively. For example, the behavior in the following passage can readily be construed as either "independent" or "aloof": "Other than business engagements, Michael's contacts with people are surprisingly limited. He feels he doesn't really need to rely on anyone" (Echterhoff, Higgins, Kopietz, & Groll, 2008). After participants finish reading the essay, they are asked to convey a message about the target person's behaviors (without revealing his identity) to another volunteer who they are told happens to be personally familiar with him. They are also told that, afterward, the audience volunteer will try to identify the target person from a set of several possible targets based on the contents of the message. Finally, in order to manipulate their beliefs about the audience's attitude toward the target, participants are informed (in an offhand manner) that the audience either likes or dislikes the target.

It has been shown repeatedly that, under these circumstances, participants tend to engage in audience tuning; that is, they construct an evaluatively positive message when they believe the audience likes the target and an evaluatively negative message when they believe the audience dislikes the target. More importantly, when participants are asked after a delay to accurately recall the contents of *the original essay* about the target person, their responses tend to be evaluatively consistent with their previous, audience-tuned message, rather than the original essay. This result is commonly referred to as the *saying-is-believing effect* because it suggests that participants end up remembering and believing what they said to the audience rather than what they originally learned about the target.

Conditions for Establishing a Shared Reality

A number of recent studies by Echterhoff, Higgins, and colleagues (see Echterhoff, Higgins, & Levine, 2009, for a review) have demonstrated that the saying-is-believing effect depends entirely on whether or not participants were successful in creating a shared reality about the target person with their audience. More specifically, participants' mental representations of the target remain *unbiased* by their audience-tuned message when any one of the following four conditions is *not* satisfied. First, individuals must experience a correspondence between their *inner states*, not just between externally observed states or behaviors. Of course, one of the primary ways in which people infer a commonality of inner states is by observing similarities in their outward behavior. For example, an individual who is applauding at a political rally will assume that the

other audience members who are applauding share her favorable attitude toward the candidate who is speaking. However, the point is that she must go beyond the simple observation that other people are moving their hands in the same way that she is and infer that these movements signal a shared positive attitude about a common target (i.e., the candidate and his beliefs); if not, she might (for example) conclude that the audience is just being polite, which would actually be detrimental to her chances of establishing a shared reality.

This example also serves to illustrate the second condition, which is that shared reality must be *about* some target referent. That is, in order for shared reality to occur, the mental object that individuals have in common cannot be detached or diffuse; instead, it must be about some discrete feature, object, or state that has an identifiable form. The assumption is that only inner states that are about a concrete target can be the object of a shared reality. Returning to the previous example, this suggests that in seeing her fellow audience members applaud the candidate, she infers that they share her *positive attitude about that candidate*—this will then lead her to confirm her belief that the candidate is someone worth supporting. However, if she merely infers that the other audience members were clapping because they were simply being polite, in a good mood, drunk, or feeling happy that day, that is, the clapping is not *about* the candidate, she will not learn anything new about the merits of the candidate, and her beliefs about the candidate will not be affected.

The third condition, which is most directly relevant to the present topic, is that shared reality as an outcome cannot be separated from an individual's motivation for establishing it (i.e., truth). That is, although people can create the appearance of commonality between their and others' inner states for a number of different reasons (such as being polite or currying favor), this commonality will not be considered informative about the true nature of reality unless it stems from a motivation to acquire or validate knowledge about the world (i.e., truth effectiveness). Returning again to our example, this implies that an individual whose primary motivation is to establish what is real through shared reality will utilize the audience's positive attitude toward the candidate that is revealed by that audience's clapping as information relevant to how she should communicate her beliefs about the candidate (e.g., by clapping to communicate to the audience her shared positive attitude toward the candidate), whereas an individual whose only motivation is to make political connections at the rally will utilize the audience's clapping as information regarding how she should respond in order to gain their approval (i.e., by clapping in order to behave similarly). As we demonstrate in more detail below, only the first individual's memory will be affected by the audience's attitude in the long term.

Finally, and crucially, the fourth condition for establishing a shared reality is that those involved must believe that their inner states have been shared. That is, even when people have taken the necessary steps to create a commonality of inner states with another individual, a shared reality will not be established unless they also perceive these steps to have been successful. Conversely, it is possible for people to establish a shared reality with another individual without there actually being an objective commonality of inner states, as long as they *believe* that the commonality actually exists. With respect to our example, this suggests that an individual will utilize the applause as information relevant to her beliefs as long she perceives it to be an expression of the audience's shared positive attitude toward the candidate (regardless of whether this is actually true or not). In contrast, the individual will not see the applause as relevant to her beliefs if she believes that it is merely an expression of politeness rather than a shared positive attitude toward the candidate (again, regardless of whether this is actually true), or if she believes that the audience thinks that *she* is simply clapping to be polite (i.e., a failure to communicate to the audience her shared positive attitude toward the candidate).

Role of Truth Relevance in Saying-Is-Believing Memory Effects

As mentioned above, the four conditions for successfully establishing a shared reality have been tested in a number of studies that used the saying-is-believing paradigm. For example, in two experiments by Echterhoff, Higgins, and Groll (2005), the audience-tuning effect on memory was found when participants learned that the audience had correctly identified the target based on their message, but no effect was found when they learned that the audience had *failed* to identify the target correctly from their message (i.e., when the fourth condition was violated). Furthermore, this memory effect was mediated by a measure of perceived shared reality that was collected after the feedback manipulation (but before the recall task). That is, participants in the failure feedback condition reported lower levels of epistemic trust than participants in the success condition, which in turn led them to exhibit a lower saying-is-believing effect. In a later unpublished study, this reduction in the audience-tuning effect on memory was observed even when the failure feedback was given *a week after* the message was produced.

The ROAR explanation for these results is that the information participants added to their original message (i.e., from audience tuning) remained high in truth relevance as long as they continued to believe that it was shared with the audience. When they learned that this was not the case, the information lost its truth relevance (i.e., it was perceived as being no longer trustworthy in terms of establishing what is real) and, thus, ceased to be active in memory. Because participants in the latter condition did not receive failure feedback until well after they had encoded the added information, this finding joins those of Anderson and Pichert (1978) and Dienes and colleagues (1995) in showing that changes in motivational relevance (truth relevance in the current case and value relevance in the others) dramatically affect memory retrieval *independent of their effects on encoding*.

It is worth noting that competing models of memory, especially those that appeal to the concepts of decay and interference, cannot account for the results of the studies by Echterhoff, Higgins, and Groll (2005). For instance, decay fails as an alternative explanation for the difference in memory between the success and failure feedback conditions because the amount of time that elapsed between participants' encoding of the biased message and their recall of the original essay was identical in both conditions, as was the time between the receipt of the feedback and actual recall. Similarly, because there was no difference between conditions in the information that participants received before their encoding of the biased message, and because they did not receive different feedback information until at least 10 minutes, and up to one week, after they had encoded the message, it would be difficult to argue that there was greater proactive or retroactive interference in one feedback condition compared with the other. The memory effect from audience tuning also does not depend on the audience's attitude influencing how the original essay is encoded because the same memory results have been found when communicators learn about the audience's attitude *after* they have already read and encoded the essay (Kopietz, Hellmann, Higgins, & Echterhoff, 2010). In sum, then, it is difficult to think of how a model of remembering could account for these findings without taking motivational relevance into account.

In another set of studies that has important implications for ROAR, Echterhoff and colleagues (2008) demonstrated that the saying-is-believing effect does not emerge when the third shared reality condition has been violated (i.e., when participants established a commonality of inner states for goals other than determining what is real). Specifically, participants in these studies either received the standard saying-is-believing instructions (which were expected to elicit the epistemic motivation to reduce uncertainty about the evaluatively ambiguous essay) or were given a nonepistemic goal, such as gaining monetary rewards from giving a message that agreed with the audience (an ulterior motive). The results showed that only participants in the standard condition showed the audience-tuning effect when recalling their original message, and they did so up to three weeks after having produced the message. Furthermore, this effect was again mediated by participants' reported trust in their audience.

Again, in contrast to models of memory that do not discuss motivational relevance, ROAR can account for these results. Specifically, ROAR suggests that, after participants have communicated their message to the audience, the audience-tuned representation that they formed of the original essay only continues to have relevance (and thus only continues to be active) when they are motivated to continue to establish what is real about some target. Any value relevance that the representation received from ulterior motives, such as those produced by monetary incentives, ceases to exist once the opportunity for achieving these goals has passed (i.e., once the message has been conveyed). In contrast, the truth relevance that the representation receives from being part of a shared reality persists because the fundamental goal of establishing what is real remains (given that it is epistemic status has not been challenged).

Episodic and Autobiographical Memories and Relevance

Up to this point we have focused largely on various forms of semantic memory. We now consider evidence for the effect of relevance on episodic and autobiographical memory. Tulving (1972) has argued that episodic memory is different from other forms of memory (such as semantic memory) in that it alone pertains to autonoetic consciousness (i.e., awareness of one's subjective experiences in the past, present, and future; see also Wheeler, Stuss,

& Tulving, 1997). But even if the experience, content, and (perhaps) structure of episodic memory differ from those of semantic memory, it is still possible that they are activated or retrieved in much the same way.

In a series of highly influential studies, Loftus and her colleagues demonstrated that false episodic memories can be experimentally induced—the so-called misinformation effect (Loftus, 2005). Interestingly, one feature of Loftus's memory induction method is to implicitly increase the plausibility of the false event, which suggests that perhaps episodic memories are more likely to be retrieved if they are relatively high in truth relevance. For example, in one study (Loftus, Miller, & Burns, 1978), participants first viewed a sequence of slides depicting a car accident and were then asked (among many other questions), "Did another car pass the red Datsun while it was stopped at the stop (yield) sign?" When they later viewed a new sequence of slides and were asked to identify which ones had been included in the original sequence, participants tended to falsely identify slides as a function of the information they were incidentally exposed to during the question phase (e.g., they recognized a picture with a yield sign when they actually saw one with a stop sign but were asked about a "yield" sign). The ROAR explanation for this result is that the incidental misinformation in this study has provided "What is it?" information about the sign, which is another source of establishing what's real and thus has truth relevance (see Higgins, 2012). This would increase the accessibility of the concept of a yield sign. It is also worth noting that, consistent with the results of the saying-is-believing studies described above, the misinformation affected memory even when it was manipulated just before retrieval, suggesting that the false memory effect cannot be explained solely in terms of differences in encoding.

Additional evidence that autobiographical memory is influenced by motivational relevance comes from a number of studies that have employed manipulations of positive value relevance. For example, in the experiment by Sanitioso and colleagues (1990) that we briefly mentioned earlier, participants were unobtrusively led to believe that either extroversion or introversion generally leads to more academic and professionally success. Later, in an ostensibly unrelated memory experiment conducted in a different room, they were asked to recall events in which they behaved in either an extroverted or introverted manner. Participants consistently recalled more autobiographical examples of the type of behavior that they were led to believe was predictive of future success. Although it can be argued that this result reflects some form of deliberate self-presentation bias, the subtle nature of the manipulation and its dissociation from the recall task suggest that the result is actually an example of unintentional knowledge activation due to an increase in value relevance. That is, past behaviors have more value relevance and hence are more accessible when they are predictive (as opposed to not predictive) of future success.

Another example that we touched on earlier comes from Mather and colleagues' work on "positivity bias" in the elderly. Based on this work, they have argued that a shift of focus associated with aging, from acquisition of information to maintenance of emotional well-being, leads to increased emotion regulation, including heightened attention to emotional memories (Mather & Carstensen, 2005). It would be very interesting to determine whether this change in goals leads to a decrease in the relevance and accessibility of nonpositive information. Although it is certainly possible that "decreased attention" to nonpositive autobiographical memories occurs after they have already been retrieved, it is also possible that the low value relevance of these memories makes them less likely to be retrieved in the first place—not only because they have little positive relevance but also possibly because their negative relevance has also lessened over time. In passing, it is worth noting that the relation between motivational relevance, remembering, and affect is bound to be more complex than the simple picture we are attempting to paint here. For example, it is unclear whether increased emotion regulation on the part of older adults increases the proportion of positive memories they recall by (1) lowering the value relevance of negative memories, (2) weakening the nonpositive feelings that they produce in the rememberer after they have been accessed, or (3) affecting whether they are even endorsed "as one's *own* memories." Of course, although less parsimonious, it is also possible that some combination of these processes contributes to better memory for more positive events.

Finally, ROAR may also be useful for understanding the effects of certain psychopathologies on episodic memory. For example, there is some evidence that people suffering from post-traumatic stress disorder (PTSD) show increased activation of trauma-related mental representations, and even that such activation predicts the severity of some PTSD symptoms (amount of flashbacks) over and

above initial severity (Michael, Ehlers, & Halligan 2005). Although this example deals with pathologically negative value relevance, ROAR predicts the same outcome for pathologically positive value relevance. This suggests that, for people suffering from drug addition, drug-related information should be particularly accessible and, hence, easier to recognize and recall (an extreme case of which may be the Hallucinogen Persisting Perception Disorder [flashbacks]). Such ease of retrieval may exacerbate the drug craving and hamper attempts of rehabilitation (see Gawin & Kleber, 1986). In support of this hypothesis, a recent study demonstrated that disrupting reconsolidation of drug-related memories decreased future drug-seeking behavior (Lee, Di Ciano, Thomas, & Everitt, 2005).

Concluding Remarks

Our goal in this chapter was not to exhaustively review all previous demonstrations of motivation's effects on memory. Rather, our two major goals were, first, to establish a link between research on the activation of mental representations and research on memory and, second, to build on this link by offering a framework for understanding when and how motivation—more specifically, motivational relevance—affects mental activation and remembering.

Our review has completely ignored certain types of memory (e.g., procedural memory) and only touched others in a cursory manner (e.g., episodic memory). Still, the findings we reviewed support our contention that, because all memory systems involve some form of knowledge activation, they all involve retrieval processes that are influenced by motivational relevance. Consequently, ROAR may be particularly useful in predicting which memories people are likely to remember.

In closing, we would like to reiterate three points regarding the nature of ROAR and its relation to memory. First, as we emphasized in our discussion of the saying-is-believing effect, ROAR allows for different memories, or even different features of the same memory, to be recalled at different times *even though their availability* (i.e., their memory "trace") *remains constant*. For example, ROAR can account for the results of the Anderson and Pichert (1978) study discussed earlier in the chapter by positing changes in motivational relevance that accompanied participants' changes in role perspective toward the story. As long as the originally encoded information is still available, then changing perspective can make some subset of the information suddenly relevant and, thus, accessible for retrieval. Second, ROAR does not compete with models of memory decay or fragmentation, such as the fuzzy-trace model (Reyna & Brainerd, 1995); rather, it supplements such models by offering a mechanism for predicting what information will be selected among representations of similar strength or integrity. Finally, by linking mental activation, memory, and motivation, ROAR may serve as a bridge between psychological research on memory and recent neuroscientific findings that show substantial involvement of the brain's "reward system" in memory-related brain activity (see Shohamy, & Adcock, 2010, for a recent review).

References

Aarts, H., Custers, R., & Marien, H. (2008). Preparing and motivating behavior outside of awareness. *Science, 319,* 1639–1639.

Aarts, H., Custers, R., & Marien, H. (2009). Priming and authorship ascription: When nonconscious goals turn into conscious experiences of self-agency. *Journal of Personality and Social Psychology, 96,* 967–979.

Anderson, R. C., & Pichert, J. W. (1978). Recall of previously unrecallable information following a shift in perspective. *Journal of Verbal Learning and Verbal Behavior, 17,* 1–12.

Balcetis, E., & Dunning, D. (2006). See what you want to see: motivational influences on visual perception. *Journal Personality and Social Psychology, 91,* 612–625.

Bartlett, F. C. (1932). *Remembering: A study in experimental and social psychology.* New York: Cambridge University Press.

Brainerd, C. J., & Reyna, V. F. (1995). Autosuggestibility in memory development. *Cognitive Psychology, 28,* 65–101.

Bruner, J. S. (1957). On perceptual readiness. *Psychological Review, 64,* 123–152.

Brunot, S., & Sanitioso, R. B. (2004). Motivational influence on the quality of memories: Recall of general autobiographical memories related to desired attributes. *European Journal of Social Psychology, 34,* 627–635.

Cherry, E. C. (1953). Some experiments on the recognition of speech, with one and with two ears. *Journal of the Acoustical Society of America, 25,* 975–979.

Conway, M., & Ross, M. (1984). Getting what you want by revising what you had. *Journal of Personality and Social Psychology, 47,* 738–748.

Crane, L., Goddard, L., & Pring, L. (2009). Specific and general autobiographical knowledge in adults with autism spectrum disorders: the role of personal goals. *Memory, 17,* 557–576.

Custers, R., & Aarts, H. (2005). Positive affect as implicit motivator: On the nonconscious operation of behavioral goals. *Journal of Personality and Social Psychology, 89,* 129–142.

Custers, R., & Aarts, H. (2010). The unconscious will: How the pursuit of goals operates outside of conscious awareness. *Science, 329,* 47–50.

Custers, R., Eitam, B., & Bargh, J. (2012). Implicit and explicit goal processes. In Henk Aarts and Andrew Eliot (Eds.), *Goal-directed behavior* (pp. 231–266). New York: Psychology Press/Taylor & Francis.

Dienes, Z., Altman, G. T. M., Kwan, L., & Goode, A. (1995). Unconscious knowledge of artificial grammars is applied strategically. *Journal of Experimental Psychology: Learning, Memory, and Cognition, 21,* 1322–1338.

Dunning, D., Perie, M., & Story, A. L. (1991). Self-serving prototypes of social categories. *Journal Personality and Social Psychology, 61,* 957–968.

Echterhoff, G., Higgins, E. T., & Groll, S. (2005). Audience-tuning effects on memory: The role of shared reality. *Journal Personality and Social Psychology, 89,* 257–276.

Echterhoff, G., Higgins, E. T., Kopietz, R., & Groll, S. (2008). How communication goals determine when audience tuning biases memory. *Journal of Experimental Psychology: General, 137,* 3–21.

Echterhoff, G., Higgins, E. T., & Levine, J. M. (2009). Shared reality. *Perspectives on Psychological Science, 4,* 496–521.

Eitam, B., Hassin, R. R., & Schul, Y. (2008). Nonconscious goal pursuit in novel environments: The case of implicit learning. *Psychological Science, 19,* 261–267.

Eitam, B., & Higgins, E. T. (2010). Motivation in mental accessibility: Relevance of a representation (ROAR) as a new framework. *Social and Personality Psychology Compass, 4,* 951–967.

Eitam, B., & Higgins, E. T. (unpublished manuscript). Motivation in mental accessibility: the case of truth relevance.

Eitam, B., Schul, Y., & Hassin, R. R. (2009). Goal relevance and artificial grammar learning. *Quarterly Journal of Experimental Psychology, 62,* 228–238.

Eitam, B., Yeshurun, Y., & Hassan, K. (in press). Blinded by irrelevance: pure irrelevance induced 'blindness'. *Journal of Experimental Psychology: Human Perception and Performance.*

Ferguson, M. J. (2008). On becoming ready to pursue a goal you don't know you have: Effects of nonconscious goals on evaluative readiness. *Journal of Personality and Social Psychology, 95,* 1268–1294.

Ferguson, M. J., & Bargh, J. A. (2004). Liking is for doing: The effects of goal pursuit on automatic evaluation. *Journal Personality and Social Psychology, 87,* 557–572.

Förster, J., Liberman, N., & Higgins, E. T. (2005). Accessibility from active and fulfilled goals. *Journal of Experimental Social Psychology, 41,* 220–239.

Frensch, P. (1998). One concept, multiple meanings: On how to define the concept of implicit learning. In M. A. Stadler & P. A. Frensch (Ed.), *Handbook of implicit learning* (pp. 47–105). Thousand Oaks, CA: Sage.

Gawin, F. H., & Kleber, H. D. (1986). Abstinence symptomatology and psychiatric diagnosis in cocaine abusers: Clinical observations. *Archives of General Psychiatry, 43,* 107–113.

Gramzow, R. H., & Willard, G. (2006). Exaggerating current and past performance: Motivated self-enhancement versus reconstructive memory. *Personality and Social Psychology Bulletin, 32,* 1114–1125.

Hardin, C., D., & Higgins, E. T. (1996). Shared reality: How social verification makes the subjective objective. In R. M. Sorrentino & E. T. Higgins (Eds.), *Handbook of motivation and cognition, Vol. 3: The interpersonal context* (pp. 28–84). New York: Guilford Press.

Hedberg, P. H., & Higgins, E. T. (2011). What remains on your mind after you are done? Flexible regulation of knowledge accessibility. *Journal of Experimental Social Psychology, 47,* 882–890.

Higgins, E. T. (1996). Knowledge activation: Accessibility, applicability, and salience. In E. T. Higgins & A. W. Kruglanski (Eds.), *Social psychology: Handbook of basic principles* (pp. 133–168). New York: Guilford Press.

Higgins, E. T. (1997). Beyond pleasure and pain. *American Psychologist, 52,* 1280–1300.

Higgins, E. T. (2012). *Beyond pleasure and pain: How motivation works.* New York: Oxford University Press.

Higgins, E. T., & Rholes, W. S. (1978). "Saying is believing": Effects of message modification on memory and liking for the person described. *Journal of Experimental Social Psychology, 14,* 363–378.

Jenkins, J. J. (1974). Remember that old theory of memory? Well, forget it! *American Psychologist, 29,* 785–795.

Kaup, B. (2001). Negation and its impact on the accessibility of text information. *Memory & Cognition, 29,* 960–967.

Kaup, B., & Zwaan, R. A. (2003). Effects of negation and situational presence on the accessibility of text information. *Journal of Experimental Psychology: Learning, Memory, and Cognition, 29,* 439–446.

Klein, W. M., & Kunda, Z. (1992). Motivated person perception: Constructing justifications for desired beliefs. *Journal of Experimental Social Psychology, 28,* 145–168.

Knight, M., Seymour, T. L., Gaunt, J. T., Baker, C., Nesmith, K., & Mather, M. (2007). Aging and goal-directed emotional attention: distraction reverses emotional biases. *Emotion, 7,* 705–714.

Kopietz, R., Hellmann, J. H., Higgins, E. T., & Echterhoff, G. (2010). Shared reality effects on memory: Communicating to fulfill epistemic needs. *Social Cognition, 28,* 353–378.

Koriat, A., Goldsmith, M., & Pansky, A. (2000). Toward a psychology of memory accuracy. *Annual Review of Psychology, 51,* 481–537.

Kruglanski, A. W. (1989). *Lay epistemics and human knowledge: Cognitive and motivational bases.* New York: Plenum Press.

Kunda, Z. (1990). The case for motivated reasoning. *Psychological Bulletin, 108,* 480–498.

Lee, J. L. C., Di Ciano, P., Thomas, K. L., & Everitt, B. J. (2005). Disrupting reconsolidation of drug memories reduces cocaine-seeking behavior. *Neuron, 47,* 795–801.

Loftus, E. F. (2005). Planting misinformation in the human mind: A 30-year investigation of the malleability of memory. *Learning & Memory, 12,* 361–366.

Loftus, E. F., Miller, D. C., & Burns, H. J. (1978). Semantic integration of verbal information into a visual memory. *Journal of Experimental Psychology: Human Learning and Memory, 4,* 19–33.

MacDonald, M. C., & Just, M. A. (1989). Changes in activation levels with negation. *Journal of Experimental Psychology: Learning, Memory, and Cognition, 15,* 633–642.

Mather, M., & Carstensen, L. L. (2005). Aging and motivated cognition: The positivity effect in attention and memory. *Trends in Cognitive Science, 9,* 496–502.

McDonald, H. E., & Hirt, E. R. (1997). When expectancy meets desire: Motivational effects in reconstructive memory. *Journal of Personality and Social Psychology, 72,* 5–23.

Michael, T., Ehlers, A. & Halligan, S. L. (2005). Enhanced priming for trauma-related material in posttraumatic stress disorder. *Emotion, 5,* 103–112.

Mitte, K. (2008). Memory bias for threatening information in anxiety and anxiety disorders: A meta-analytic review. *Psychological Bulletin, 134,* 886–911.

Moberly, N. J., & MacLeod, A. K. (2006). Goal pursuit, goal self-concordance, and the accessibility of autobiographical knowledge. *Memory, 14,* 901–915.

Molden, D. C., & Higgins, E. T. (2005). Motivated thinking. In K. Holyoak & B. Morrison (Eds.), *Handbook of thinking and reasoning* (pp. 295–320). New York: Cambridge University Press.

Moray. N. (1959) Attention in dichotic listening: affective cues and the influence of instructions. *Quarterly Journal of Experimental Psychology, 9,* 56–60.

Moskowitz, B., G., Gollwitzer, M. P., Wasel, W., & Schaal, B. (1999). Preconscious control of stereotype activation through chronic egalitarian goals. *Journal of Personality and Social Psychology, 77,* 167–184.

Reber, A. S. (1967). Implicit learning of artificial grammars. *Journal of Verbal Learning and Verbal Behavior, 6,* 855–863.

Reyna, V. F., & Brainerd, C. J. (1995). Fuzzy-trace theory: An interim synthesis. *Learning and Individual Differences, 7,* 1–75.

Ross, M. (1989). The relation of implicit theories to the construction of personal histories. *Psychological Review, 96,* 341–357.

Rushworth, M. F., Walton, M. E., Kennerley, S. W., & Bannerman, D. M. (2004). Action sets and decisions in the medial frontal cortex. *Trends in Cognitive Science, 8,* 410–417.

Sanitioso, R., Kunda, Z., & Fong, G. T. (1990). Motivated recruitment of autobiographical memories. *Journal of Personality and Social Psychology, 59,* 229–241.

Sedikides, C., & Green, J. D. (2009). Memory as a self-protective mechanism. *Social and Personality Psychology Compass, 3,* 1055–1068.

Shohamy, D., & Adcock, R. A. (2010). Dopamine and adaptive memory. *Trends in Cognitive Sciences, 14,* 464–472.

Tulving, E. (1972). Episodic and semantic memory. In E. Tulving, W. Donaldson & G. H. Bower (Eds.), *Organization of memory* (pp. 381–403). New York: Academic Press.

Tulving, E., & Thomson, D. M. (1973). Encoding specificity and retrieval processes in episodic memory. *Psychological Review, 80,* 352–373.

Voss, J. L., & Paller, K. A. (2008). Brain substrates of implicit and explicit memory: The importance of concurrently acquired neural signals of both memory types. *Neuropsychologia, 46,* 3021–3029.

Wheeler, M. A., Stuss, D. T., & Tulving, E. (1997). Toward a theory of episodic memory: The frontal lobes and autonoetic consciousness. *Psychological Bulletin, 121,* 331–354.

Wolfe, J. M (1999). Inattentional amnesia. In V. Coltheart (Ed.), *Fleeting memories* (pp. 71–94). Cambridge, MA: MIT Press.

Zeigarnik, B. (1938). On finished and unfinished tasks. In W. D. Ellis (Ed.), *A source book of gestalt psychology* (1st ed., pp. 300–314). New York: Harcourt.

CHAPTER 23

The Mind in Motivation: A Social Cognitive Perspective on the Role of Consciousness in Goal Pursuit

Melissa Ferguson *and* Jeremy Cone

Abstract

This chapter summarizes and critically evaluates recent social cognitive work on the construct of human goals. The authors begin by defining goals from a social cognitive perspective, and then introduce what they believe is one of the most important outstanding questions in contemporary research on goal pursuit: What is the role of consciousness? The authors identify the conceptual landscape of this question and summarize what current evidence indicates as well as outstanding theoretical issues and unexplored questions. A number of interesting avenues for future research are identified.

Key Words: goals, consciousness, automaticity, nonconscious goals

Understanding human goal pursuit has historically been at the forefront of social psychological research, even while the popularity of the topic has waxed and waned in other areas of psychology (e.g., see Kunda, 1999). Identifying the antecedents, mechanisms, and consequences of a person's goals is fundamentally part of any functional analysis of human behavior. After all, as many scholars have noted over the years, for predictive purposes it is essential to know not just *what* another person is doing but also *why*, and for this we need access to another's goals. Similarly for the self, the human capacity to imagine the self in a hypothetical future naturally allows for idealized states toward which the person can strive as well as aversive states the person can try to avoid. And, experientially, the pursuit of goals makes up a significant chunk of people's everyday cognition, behavior, and emotion (for a review, see Shah & Gardner, 2008).

In the current chapter, we summarize and critically evaluate recent social cognitive work on the construct of human goals. We begin with the definition of a goal from a social cognitive perspective, and then introduce what we believe is a major issue

in contemporary social cognition research on goals: the role of consciousness (i.e., awareness; though see Baars, 1998; Chalmers, 1996; Churchland, 1983; Damasio, 1999; Dennett, 1991; Gazzaniga, 1988; Papineau, 2002; Searle, 1990). We identify the conceptual landscape of this question, and then turn to what the literature demonstrates, and also what it misses. We then consider future research and other relevant theoretical questions.

What Is a Goal?

In line with current formulations in the social cognitive literature, we define a *goal* as a mentally represented, desired end state that fluctuates in accessibility, contains many different representations (e.g., end states, means, abstract, concrete, positive, negative, visual, auditory), and influences cognition, emotion, and behavior (see Bargh, 1990; Custers & Aarts, 2010; Fishbach & Ferguson, 2007; Kruglanski, 1996; Shah & Gardner, 2008; for a psychobiological operationalization, see Hazy, Frank, & O'Reilly, 2006). The exact nature and format of the representations, including the way in which they are interconnected, is not yet clear (see discussion in Ferguson & Wojnowicz, 2011), but some of the functional characteristics of goal representations and how they interconnect have been gleaned from empirical data. For instance, they seem to follow basic principles of information processing in that any given goal representation can vary in its accessibility (i.e., likelihood of being applied to relevant stimuli; see Bruner, 1957; Higgins, 1996) and can, in turn, influence the accessibility of associated representations in either an excitatory or inhibitory manner (e.g., Aarts, Dijksterhuis, & De Vries, 2001; Fishbach, Friedman, & Kruglanski, 2003; Förster, Liberman, & Higgins, 2005; Kruglanski, 1996; Moskowitz, 2002). Goal representations also exhibit a trajectory of activation that distinguishes them from nongoal (e.g., semantic) representations (Ach, 1935; Bruner, 1957; Kuhl, 1983); namely, after being activated (e.g., via priming), goal representations tend to stay activated until the goal is met or is disengaged from, unlike semantic representations, which typically decay uniformly in activation strength over a matter of minutes (for a review, see Förster, Liberman, & Friedman, 2007; Förster, Liberman, & Higgins, 2005).

Is there a quintessential ingredient that turns a bundle of representations into *goal* representations? Scholars have recognized the necessity of valenced information associated with the goal representations (e.g., Carver & Scheier, 1981; Custers & Aarts, 2010; Hazy, Frank, & O'Reilly, 2006; Kruglanski et al., 2002; Peak, 1955; Pervin, 1989; Shah et al., 2002; Young, 1961). After all, the basic (though not the only; see, e.g., Higgins, 1998) ingredients of motivation are seeking pleasure and avoiding pain. We can strive to attain or keep something pleasant, or strive to avoid or dispose of something unpleasant. Any representation, however complex, prescriptive, or procedural, is assumed to *propel* behavior in a persistent fashion only when that representation is associated with positivity or negativity. Researchers in this area have argued that behaviors or states either have to be evaluated consciously as something desirable or, in the absence of conscious evaluation, have positivity or negativity embedded within (or associated with) their representational structure (see Custers & Aarts, 2005, 2007, 2010) in order to motivate behavior.

The lion's share of social cognitive work on goals during the past two decades has focused on consciousness in goal pursuit. More precisely, this work has questioned the causal role of consciousness in goal pursuit (see Ferguson & Porter, 2010). In the discussion that follows, we first acknowledge the traditional interpretation of goal pursuit as a conscious, effortful task, and also refer to current work on self-control that is consistent with this view. We then review the line of research that has challenged this approach during the past two decades, and then critically evaluate this work as well and discuss the relevant conceptual questions concerning the role of consciousness in motivation.

Mindful Motivation

The classic motivation literature has assumed (e.g., Bandura, 1997; Carver & Scheier, 1981; Deci & Ryan, 1985; Gollwitzer, 1990; Metcalfe & Mischel, 1999)—and at times explicitly asserted (e.g., Bandura, 2006; Locke, 1995)—that consciousness is pivotal in the pursuit of one's goals. In Bandura's program of research on self-efficacy (e.g., Bandura, 1986, 1997), for example, people's consciously held expectancies and beliefs about their own agency are what causally influences their motivation and subsequent behavior. Similarly, in the discrepancy reduction model proposed by Carver and Scheier (1981), it is one's awareness of a discrepancy between one's aspirations and one's current state that leads the person to consciously derive plans and willfully engage in behaviors to reduce the perceived discrepancy. Researchers have also suggested that one's conscious feelings of autonomy are a primary determinant of motivated behavior (Deci & Ryan, 1985).

The task of pursuing one's goals inevitably involves choices among potential actions, and as the benefits and costs of those possible routes become more equivalent, the choice task becomes more difficult. The choice between an immediate but small reward versus a delayed but larger reward is a classic example of a dilemma in which people need to ideally choose the delayed, but more valuable, reward over the short-term temptation. The literature addressing this kind of goal pursuit—termed *self-control*—has relied heavily on the notion that conscious effort is crucial to being able to successfully navigate such dilemmas. Baumeister and colleagues have amassed a sizable amount of empirical evidence showing that this kind of conscious effort is a finite resource that relies on glucose consumption and can be used up relatively easily (e.g., Baumeister, Bratslavsky, Muraven, & Tice, 1998; Baumeister, Heatherton, & Tice, 1994; Baumeister, Vohs, & Tice, 2007; Gailliot et al., 2007). For example, participants who were asked to suppress their emotional reaction to a short, emotional video clip subsequently held a handgrip—an activity that requires people to override the natural impulse to let go of the grip and continue exerting pressures—for significantly less time than did those who did not first attempt the emotional suppression (Baumeister et al., 1998). One underlying assumption in this work is that it is the person's conscious effort to regulate the self that is at the causal center of successful self-control (i.e., goal pursuit). This program of research is therefore largely consistent with the traditional perspective on how people reach their goals: through conscious will, intention, effort, and deliberation.

Mindless Motivation

Research in social cognition during the past 15 years has challenged whether consciousness is a necessary feature of goal pursuit. This general approach has relied on a two-phase procedure in which the researcher first tries to trigger a goal in participants by exposing them to some unseen or unnoticed cue, and then in the second phase, looks for evidence of participants' motivated behavior toward that goal. The unnoticed triggers of goals have included goal-relevant words hidden in word games (e.g., *achievement*), the names of significant others (e.g., *mother*), environments with salient social norms (e.g., the library), or another person's goal-relevant behavior (e.g., Aarts & Dijksterhuis, 2000; Aarts, Gollwitzer & Hassin, 2004; Bargh et al., 2001; Chartrand & Bargh, 1996; Ferguson, 2008; Fitzsimons & Bargh, 2003; Shah, 2003; Shah & Kruglanski, 2002).

The second phase—measuring any motivated behavior—is theoretically more complicated in that it presupposes that behavior that is motivated can be distinguished from behavior that is not motivated. Based on classic literature on motivation, the main assumptions are that someone who is motivated should be more persistent and overcome interruptions and obstacles to a greater extent than someone who is not. But, how could such complicated, flexible, and seemingly effortful behavior be mindless? Indeed, the realization of a goal involves a set of operations that seemingly have all of the hallmarks of a complex and dynamic conscious process: we must find ways to steer clear of the many distractions that we face, to somehow manage and prioritize the numerous goals we often juggle at any one time, to adaptively handle setbacks and overcome obstacles when our initial efforts fail, and, on occasion, to know when our time and effort are better spent on other pursuits. How is it that such processes could operate without any conscious involvement? The auto-motive

model (Bargh, 1990; Bargh & Gollwitzer, 1994) provides a theoretical framework for understanding how goal pursuit might proceed without awareness. The model proposes that goals are end states that are mentally represented in precisely the same way as other kinds of knowledge structures, such as concepts, judgments, and attitudes, and are thus associatively linked in memory to information related to their operation (though see Williams, Huang, & Bargh, 2009). For example, they are likely linked to situations in which they might be pursued, concrete means of achieving them, and various behaviors that allow one to enact these means (see Fishbach & Ferguson, 2007). These associative links are thought to develop over time through the repeated simultaneous activation of the goal and other related concepts or behaviors in memory. For example, if one's preferred means of pursuing a weight loss goal is running on a treadmill every morning before work, then over time, through the repeated simultaneous activation of the goal of weight loss and the behavior of running on the treadmill (and according to classic Hebbian learning rules; Hebb, 1949, 1961), the two become strongly associatively linked in memory, such that the mere perception of the treadmill can potentially activate the weight loss goal.

Importantly, such goal activation need not be conscious—that is, the auto-motive model does not merely suggest that after one consciously adopts a goal, it can operate nonconsciously. Rather, a goal may become activated outside of conscious awareness by features of the environment that are associatively linked to the goal, as in the treadmill example, and the entire goal pursuit, can, once activated, proceed entirely in the absence of conscious intervention. In other words, people may adopt a goal, engage in goal-directed behavior to bring it about, and succeed or fail in this effort, all without any realization of the activation or operation of the goal. This notion is consistent with research in social and cognitive psychology that has demonstrated that other types of mental representations can be automatically activated by features of the environment that are associated with the representation and can affect subsequent behavior outside of awareness (e.g., see Bargh, 2007; Devine, 1989; Fazio, 2001; Higgins, 1996). For example, stereotypes can be activated and potentially applied automatically, and this activation has been shown to have effects on thoughts, feelings, and behaviors directed toward outgroup members (Devine, 1989; Greenwald & Banaji, 1995).

Goals, too, have been shown in empirical research to be governed by these automatic activation principles. In one of the first demonstrations of nonconscious goal pursuit, Chartrand and Bargh (1996) attempted to conceptually replicate a classic finding in the social cognition literature concerning differences in the way that information is processed when people are consciously given either an impression formation goal or a memorization goal. In the original experiment (Hamilton, Katz, & Lierer, 1980), participants were exposed to a collection of behaviors performed by a target individual and were given a (conscious) goal to either memorize as many of the behaviors presented as possible, or to simply form an impression of the target. The paradoxical result was that people given the active memorization goal were found to remember *less* of the target information than participants simply asked to form an impression, in part because the act of attempting to memorize the information made these individuals less likely to organize the behaviors around a meaningful set of higher order traits, as the individuals who formed an impression did.

In Chartrand and Bargh's (1996) conceptual replication, rather than giving participants a conscious memory or impression formation goal, participants were asked to complete a sentence-unscrambling task in which they were subtly exposed to words semantically related to these goals. In the task, participants were asked to form grammatically correct four-word sentences using a series of words presented in random order (e.g., "somewhat memory prepared I was.") For some participants, a subset of the words that they unscrambled was related to an impression formation goal (e.g., "opinion," "personality," "impression.") Other participants were instead exposed to words related to a memorization goal (e.g., "absorb," "remember," "memory.") Participants then performed the same exercise as participants in the original experiment in which they were exposed to a series of target behaviors performed by an individual and given a recall test at the end of the experiment. Replicating the results of the original study, the goal-priming procedure had precisely the same effect on information recall as a consciously adopted goal: People primed with impression formation recalled more of the target individual's behaviors and were better able to sort the behaviors around a set of higher order traits than individuals primed with memorization. However, an especially important difference between these results and the results of the study by Hamilton and colleagues was that, in a thorough funneled debriefing procedure at the end of the experiment, participants appeared not to have any awareness of either (1) a connection between the sentence unscrambling task and their memory for the behaviors (i.e., they had no awareness of the true purpose of unscrambling the sentences), or (2) the goal-directed nature of their behavior.

A second study was conducted to conceptually replicate this result and to rule out the possibility of any conscious influence on participants' behavior. This study was designed to replicate another classic result from the conscious goals literature (Hastie & Kumar, 1979) and employed a parafoveal subliminal priming methodology to activate the goal entirely outside of conscious awareness. Results once again demonstrated that the nonconscious activation of a goal had precisely the same consequences as a consciously adopted goal, pointing to a potential equivalence between conscious and nonconscious goal pursuit (see also McCullough, Ferguson, Kawada, & Bargh, 2008; Moore, Ferguson, & Chartrand, 2011).

These demonstrations established that the nonconscious activation of a goal can have effects on subsequent information processing. However, the main tenet of auto-motive theory is that nonconsciously activated goals can unintentionally influence behavior. Bargh and colleagues (Bargh et al., 2001) provided the evidence for these kinds of behavioral effects. Some participants were primed with an achievement goal, whereas others were not. This was accomplished by having participants complete a word search in which some of the target words were related to achievement (e.g., "achieve," "succeed") or not (controls). Next, participants completed an additional three-word search, and their performance on these word searches (i.e., how quickly they found the words in these puzzles) served as the primary dependent measure. The results showed that participants primed with an achievement goal performed better—that is, found more words—than controls. Similarly, in another study (Bargh et al., 2001, Study 2), participants who were primed with a cooperation goal acted more cooperatively in a subsequent resource dilemma game in which resources could be selfishly kept for oneself or cooperatively returned to a common resource pool in order to prevent the resources from being fully exhausted. This experiment provides converging evidence of robust behavioral consequences for the nonconscious priming of goals.

Importantly, in a thorough debriefing, participants seemed, like those in Chartrand and Bargh's

(1996) studies, to be unaware of the goal-directed nature of their behavior. To further rule out the possibility of any conscious influence on participants' behavior, Bargh et al. (2001) obtained a self-report measure of participants' commitment to the target goals. Interestingly, this measure was significantly correlated with actual behavior only when the goal was consciously adopted; that is, when participants were nonconsciously primed with a goal, these ratings of goal commitment had no relation to their behavior, strongly suggesting they were unaware of the activation or operation of the goal (see Hassin, Bargh, & Zimmerman, 2009, for a recent replication of this finding).

Of course, one salient alternative explanation for the above findings is that the observed behavioral effects were the result of semantic priming rather than the priming of a motivational state. By this account, the initial word search that participants completed was not an instance of goal priming, but rather was an instance of the kind of priming that has already been shown in past research, as when the word *doctor* automatically activated semantically related words such as *nurse* or *hospital*. In an attempt to differentiate these two interpretations, Bargh and colleagues investigated whether nonconscious goal activation exhibits the classic properties of motivational states (see Förster et al., 2007; Heckhausen, 1991). For example, one such property is that a goal looms larger as it goes unsatisfied, meaning that a goal should remain accessible until one has had an opportunity to meet it (Atkinson & Birch, 1970). In contrast, semantic priming effects have been shown to remain accessible for only a short period of time, decaying very quickly after activation (e.g., Anderson, 1983). In one study (Bargh et al., 2001, Study 3), Bargh and colleagues directly compared semantic priming and goal priming effects by first activating an achievement goal using the same procedures described above. Then, participants completed either a task that required goal-directed behavior (i.e., an anagram task that would allow them to pursue the achievement goal) or a perceptual judgment task that had been shown in previous research to be influenced by semantic priming procedures. The results showed a dissociation between the effects of the priming on the two types of tasks. When participants completed the task requiring goal-directed behavior, the researchers obtained the predicted behavioral effect of the achievement prime, and this effect grew stronger after a five-minute delay during which participants completed an unrelated filler task. In other words, as

the goal remained unmet over time, it increased in accessibility and appeared to have a stronger influence on behavior. However, when participants completed the perceptual judgment task, there was only a significant effect when participants completed the task immediately after having been primed, but not after a five-minute delay, suggesting that activation—without any opportunity for goal pursuit—quickly decayed after the priming manipulation. Thus, these effects show that incidental exposure to goal relevant words does seem to activate the corresponding goal, which spurs motivated behavior *when there is an opportunity for such pursuit*. Subsequent studies have also demonstrated that goal priming leads one to resume goal-directed behavior after disruption and to engage in goal-directed behavior even in the face of obstacles—two additional hallmarks of motivated behavior that further dissociate goal priming effects from traditional semantic priming effects (Heckhausen, 1991).

This research established the existence of key similarities between conscious and nonconscious goal pursuit, and additionally established that goal priming exhibits critical dissociations from semantic priming effects. More recently, researchers have used nonconscious priming methodologies to replicate some of the classic findings in the goals literature that were previously assumed to be specifically governed by conscious processes. For example, Deci and Ryan's (1985) self-determination theory posits that *intrinsically motivated* behaviors (i.e., those that people engage in for their own sake because they are inherently pleasurable) and *extrinsically motivated* behaviors (i.e., those that people engage in to obtain some external reward or to avoid some negative outcome) have drastically different outcomes in terms of individuals' performance, creativity, well-being, and mental health (Deci & Ryan, 2000; Ratelle, Vallerand, Chantal, & Provencher, 2004; Ryan & Deci, 2000). Such distinctions seem to have all of the hallmarks of consciously derived beliefs, and indeed, the notion that autonomy is necessary for effective self-regulation is central to one of the mini-theories (i.e., cognitive evaluation theory) derived from self-determination theory. Yet, in a recent study by Levesque and Pelletier (2003), participants were nonconsciously primed with an intrinsic or extrinsic motivation through subtle exposure to words related to these motivations (e.g., intrinsic: "choice," "autonomy," "interest," "freedom"; versus extrinsic: "pressure," "obligated," "constrained," "forced.") Intriguingly, these goal primes were found to have precisely the same behavioral outcomes as those of conscious intrinsic and extrinsic motivational states.

Similarly, the monitoring of goal progress of the sort that occurs in the discrepancy reduction model described by Carver and Scheier (1981) has been theorized to be able to proceed nonconsciously (Moscowitz, Li, & Kirk, 2002)—a proposal that garners support from recent evidence suggesting that people have awareness of the success or failure of nonconscious goal pursuits (see Leander, Moore & Chartrand, 2009). Moreover, there is now even evidence that the experience of self-agency and feelings of self-efficacy (i.e., the conscious belief that one has the mastery and ability to attain a desirable end state) may have nonconscious antecedents (Aarts, Custers, & Marien, 2009; Chartrand, Dalton, & Cheng, 2008).

In summary, then, work in social cognition during the past 15 years has demonstrated that consciousness appears not to be a necessary feature of goal pursuit. People can evidently strive toward an endpoint of which they may be largely unaware. But, how strong is the evidence that participants are unaware of these end states? We consider some critical questions on this point in the next section.

Decomposition of Consciousness: Questions about What and When

What are we talking about when we talk about a lack of consciousness during goal pursuit? In other words, what would it mean for a person to be engaging in goal pursuit without being aware of any goal-related thought, intention, or action? It makes sense to first consider what people typically consciously think about (i.e., are aware of) when they are knowingly engaged in goal pursuit. Research suggests that people may consciously think about the end state, the consequences of that end state, the circumstances and means of getting there, and the emotional implications of being successful or not (e.g., Bandura, 1986; Carver & Scheier, 1998; Deci & Ryan, 1985; Gollwitzer, 1990; Locke & Latham, 1990; see also Mischel, Cantor, & Feldman, 1996 for a review). There would thus seem to be great variety in the (conscious) mental content in the minds of people pursuing a goal intentionally. Such variety poses a potential challenge for research on nonconscious goal pursuit because it means that there is a lot of ground to cover in terms of showing what is *not* going through people's heads consciously. That is, it would seem necessary to show that people do not have any conscious thoughts (whether fully formed or vague) revolving around the end state, its

means, its implications, the relevant intentions, and emotional fall out from the pursuit.

To complicate matters even more, a goal does not inhabit an obviously discrete slice of time. To be sure, in order for the goal construct to make any sense conceptually, it has to be the case that someone *starts* being in a goal pursuit and then at some point *stops* being in the goal pursuit. But, such demarcations may exist primarily to aid in our folk psychological understanding of goal states, rather than accurately reflecting the fluctuations of cognition. When and where those boundaries are is not always obvious. For example, do *all* the myriad representations related to any given goal (e.g., achievement, fitness) have to uniformly decrease in accessibility for a goal pursuit to be inactive? And yet, even though it would appear to be a difficult task, it seems necessary for anyone estimating the consciousness of goal pursuit to consider whether awareness of the goal occurs in the lead-up to any pursuit, during the actual pursuit itself (which might be prolonged), and perhaps during the reflection and post mortem of that pursuit. This requires that any analysis of consciousness needs to be lengthy and expansive, as well as sensitively timed to a given person's presumably situation-specific goal trajectory.

As should be clear, the hurdles for concluding that goal pursuit can proceed without consciousness of that goal are impressive indeed. There are questions not only about the many nuances of goal-relevant conscious cognitions but also about the extent to which those cognitions appear over some temporal span. What evidence does the literature offer concerning these questions? The bulk of evidence in the literature on mindless motivation comes from funneled debriefing procedures in which participants are asked at the end of the experimental session a series of increasingly specific questions about the nature and purpose of the experiment (Bargh & Chartrand, 2000). Participants are asked whether they noticed anything strange or unusual about the experiment, whether they saw a connection between the various different tasks in the experiment, and whether they know the purpose of the experiment. Participants typically report not knowing or seeing any connection between the part of the experiment in which the goal was primed and the part of the experiment in which their behavior was measured, as well as not knowing the purpose of the experiment, and researchers have taken this evidence to mean that participants were unaware of the goal.

There is a critically important difference, however, between knowing how and when a goal was activated and knowing *that* a goal was active, and researchers in this area are arguably more interested in the latter (see Uhlmann, Pizarro, & Bloom, 2008). To test this, one could measure whether participants who have been nonconsciously primed with a goal report more concern with, or importance of, the goal, compared with participants who have not been primed. Several papers show that this is not the case (Aarts et al., 2004; Eitam, Hassin, & Schuul, 2008; Ferguson, 2008). This qualifies as stronger evidence that participants who are implicitly primed with a goal do not seem to have awareness of that goal's operation. There is also the evidence mentioned earlier from Bargh et al. (2001; Study 3), wherein participants' consciously reported goal-strength was correlated with their motivated behavior only when the goal was primed consciously, not when the goal was primed nonconsciously (see also Hassin, Bargh, & Zimmerman, 2009).

Another general problem with the debriefing method of testing awareness, however, is that it is a self-report, which means that it is susceptible to participants' strategic editing and modification; for example, participants may not want to report—for whatever reason—that they were concerned with a particular goal in the experiment. Additionally, and importantly, these debriefing procedures are also administered at the very end of the experiment, and as such face the same problems as any retrospective measure of memory. A person's awareness can be momentary, and not survive long enough to allow introspection at some later point. What seems necessary for testing awareness, then, is to implement measures of awareness throughout a given experiment, in various ways that minimize the reactive nature of self-reports. This will be a challenge for future research to address.

Dispelling the Conscious/Nonconscious Dichotomy

Throughout the past 15 years, goal pursuit has been described as conscious or nonconscious, and there are a couple problems with this kind of conceptualization. The first, as we mentioned earlier, is that the evidence for a lack of awareness is still accumulating and does not yet afford a full understanding of exactly when and how goal pursuit proceeds completely without consciousness. Second, and perhaps even more importantly, this duality is probably just as ill posed as are many other dualities in human cognition. Given that goal pursuit is (or can be) a complicated, flexible, multistage, and multistep process of behaviors unfolding, it would seem

to make more sense to ask where and when consciousness arises. In this section, we review recent evidence of some aspects of conscious goal pursuit that operate relatively nonconsciously, and similarly, aspects of nonconscious goal pursuit that appear to be available to conscious awareness. In the following section, we then address the circumstances under which consciousness might be functional.

Aspects of Conscious Goal Pursuit that Operate Nonconsciously

Recent theories in motivation have pointed to the relatively limited capacity of conscious processing to suggest that if goal pursuit is to be successful, it should be bolstered by less resource-intensive nonconscious processes, thus freeing up consciousness for other higher order operations (e.g., Bargh, 1990; Custers & Aarts, 2010). Considerable evidence now shows that the conscious adoption of a goal can set into motion a number of nonconscious processes that are largely automatic and unintentional, but may nonetheless ultimately serve to facilitate attainment of the conscious goal. There are effects on perception, knowledge accessibility, attention, and evaluation.

PERCEPTION

The notion that our current motivations may have a top-down influence on what we perceive was the subject of the New Look program of research of the 1950s. Theorists involved in this movement claimed that perception was not a veridical representation of the external world but was rather a construction of the mind that could be influenced by one's internal desires, beliefs, needs, and so forth. Researchers thus attempted to uncover evidence that people with different needs or desires exhibited important differences in their perceptions of the external world. Bruner and Goodman (1947) famously found, for example, that children who come from relatively poverty-stricken socioeconomic backgrounds overestimate the size of coins relative to children coming from more economically advantaged backgrounds, presumably because poorer children place a higher value in money than more affluent children and thus have a greater motivation to obtain it.

Although these early demonstrations were marred by conceptual and methodological difficulties (Eriksen, 1958, 1962; Eriksen & Browne, 1956; Goldiamond, 1958; Prentice, 1958; Wohlwill, 1966), a contemporary re-examination of the main tenets of the New Look movement has breathed new life into research on motivated perception. In a recent set of studies, Balcetis and Dunning (2006) found evidence to suggest that we, quite literally, "see what we want to see"—that our current goals have a strong influence on perception, particularly when visual stimuli are ambiguous. In one study, participants were led to believe that they would be randomly assigned, in an upcoming taste test, to sample either freshly squeezed orange juice or a rather foul-smelling and putrid garden smoothie that was intentionally designed to be especially undesirable to participants. They were told that the computer would randomly assign them a beverage and would indicate this condition assignment by displaying either a number or a letter (and whether a number or letter represented a positive or negative outcome was randomly assigned). Unknown to participants, the visual stimulus that was displayed was ambiguous and could be interpreted either as the letter "B" or, alternatively, as the number "13." After briefly displaying this ambiguous figure, the computer ostensibly crashed, and participants were asked to report what they had seen on the screen directly before the crash occurred. Consistent with the notion that our current wants can influence perception, participants were more likely to report seeing whatever stimulus would allow them to taste the orange juice rather than the garden smoothie. Subsequent studies served to eliminate various alternative explanations of the results—including that participants were simply lying about what they saw in order to avoid a negative outcome. Thus, one's conscious goal of avoiding an unpleasant experience had an unintentional consequence on the basic, low-level perception of ambiguous visual stimuli, suggesting that conscious goal pursuit can have unintended nonconscious consequences, particularly in a readiness to interpret one's environment in ways that are consistent with one's goals.

ATTENTION

Besides having an influence on our perception of objects in our immediate environment, goals have also been posited to influence what we pay attention to in our environment. Once a goal becomes activated, knowledge that is related to the goal is made accessible through spreading activation, which can then lead to a kind of perceptual readiness to process concepts and ideas related to the goal that can unintentionally grab attention.

In an empirical investigation of this idea, Moscowitz (2002) examined how the priming of a goal influenced the likelihood of goal-relevant

distractors grabbing individuals' attention. In the first part of the experiment, a goal to attain a high level of athletic performance was activated by having people think about a recent failure to attain an athletic standard. According to self-completion theory (Wicklund & Gollwitzer, 1982), such consideration of recent failures motivates individuals to strive to reattain the standard, resulting in the activation of a goal. Two control groups were also used in which the athletic goal was not activated: in the first, participants were asked to recall a recent athletic success that was thought to signal to the participant that they were making good progress toward the goal, whereas in the second, subjects were simply asked to recall nothing at all. Next, all participants then completed a task in which distractors were presented on-screen that were either goal related or not. To complete the task efficiently, participants needed to ignore these distractors and instead focus on the target information presented on the screen. However, the results demonstrated that those who had had an athletic goal activated were slower on the task than controls when the distractors were goal relevant. No such disparity emerged when the distractors were unrelated to the athletic goal, suggesting that when the goal was activated, attention was automatically directed toward the goal-related information when it was present in the environment.

Aarts, Dijksterhuis, and DeVries (2001) similarly found evidence for this kind of perceptual readiness to identify and pay attention to goal-relevant stimuli in one's environment. In one study, some participants were made thirsty by asking them to consume some salty snacks and not permitting them to drink any water, whereas other participants were sated by allowing them to quench their thirst before moving on to the next task. This manipulation was found to influence the accessibility of drinking-related (but not neutral) words on a lexical decision task, demonstrating that the experience of thirst had rendered concepts related to thirst more accessible. In a second study, participants who were thirsty were shown to pay more attention to thirst-related objects in their environment. Participants' thirst was manipulated using the same method as the first study, and participants again completed a lexical decision task. In the room where they completed this task, there were a number of drinking-related objects, such as a water bottle sitting on the desk. In a surprise recall task presented after completing the computer task, participants who were thirsty recalled more drinking-related objects than participants who were sated, but there were no differences in recall of non–thirst-related objects.

Taken together, these studies demonstrate that the conscious adoption of a goal can have unintended consequences for the accessibility of knowledge related to the goal and for where attention is directed in one's environment, as has been argued by various scholars (e.g., Bruner, 1957). This is likely to be an adaptive, though unintended, consequence of consciously adopting a goal. After all, to exploit opportunities in one's environment to engage in goal-directed behavior, one must first determine what those opportunities are. By fostering a kind of perceptual readiness to find goal-relevant opportunities in one's environment and direct attention toward them, one thus has a better chance of taking advantage of them while they are still available.

ATTITUDES AND EVALUATION

Evidence has accumulated in recent years that when people consciously adopt a goal, they rapidly and spontaneously evaluate goal-relevant objects in their environment significantly more positively than immediately after having met the goal (Ferguson, 2008; Ferguson & Bargh, 2004; Ferguson & Wojnowicz, 2011; Myreseth, Fishbach, & Trope, 2009; Natanzon & Ferguson, 2011; Payne, McClernon, & Dobbins, 2007; Seibt et al., 2007; Sherman et al., 2003; see also Brendl, 2001; Brendl, Markman, & Messner, 2003; Fishbach, Zhang, & Trope, 2010; Moors & De Houwer, 2001; Moors, De Houwer, Hermans, & Eelen, 2005). For example, in one demonstration (Ferguson & Bargh, 2004, Study 2), participants were made thirsty by not drinking for several hours before arriving for their scheduled experimental session. Some participants were then allowed to quench their thirst by drinking a beverage before moving on, whereas others were made even thirstier by eating a number of salty pretzels. The results showed that thirsty participants evaluated thirst-related words significantly more positively in a subsequent affective priming task (see Fazio et al., 1995) than participants who had their thirst sated, but no differences emerged on non–goal-relevant words. In other words, goal-relevant knowledge is not only made more accessible during goal pursuit; it is also rendered temporarily more positive.

Importantly, these shifts in the evaluation of goal-relevant knowledge are thought to be functional in that they encourage individuals to engage in relatively automatic behaviors that foster goal attainment. Indeed, there is a wealth of evidence showing that implicit attitudes and evaluation are predictive of subsequent behavior (e.g., for a review, see Wittenbrink & Schwarz, 2007). Chen and Bargh (1999), for example, have shown that implicit positivity toward objects fosters relatively automatic approach behaviors, whereas implicit negativity toward objects fosters relatively automatic avoidance behaviors. Moreover, Custers and Aarts (2005) demonstrated that artificially induced implicit positivity toward an activity results in increased motivation to engage in it. Thus, the conscious adoption of a goal can have unintended implicit effects on behavior, which are mediated by shifts in one's (implicit) evaluations of goal-related stimuli.

Interestingly, these effects on our evaluations of goal-relevant stimuli might also have unintended influences on our evaluations of other people, even when those evaluations are not related to the actual goal being pursued. In a recent study (Bargh, Green, & Fitzsimons, 2008), participants were told that they would be evaluating a job candidate in terms of suitability for either a position as a waiter or a position as a journalist (jobs chosen on the basis of a pretest that demonstrated that people believed to require markedly different personality traits, with waiters being selected primarily on the basis of their politeness and journalists being selected primarily on the basis of their ability to be tough and aggressive in order to get to the bottom of a story). To assess the job candidate, participants watched a videotape of an ostensible interview being conducted. At several points during the interview, the interviewer was interrupted by other people from the office, mimicking a busy office setting.

One of the interrupters, "Mike," inquired about lunch plans with the interviewer. Actually a trained actor hired by the research team, Mike acted either politely or aggressively in response to the interviewer's comment that he would have to skip lunch. When the tape had concluded, participants were told that the experiment actually concerned their thoughts about Mike and were asked to rate how much they liked him on a self-report scale. Interestingly, even though Mike was not the intended target of the conscious goal to evaluate the job candidate, this goal systematically influenced people's ratings of him. When they thought the interview was for a waiter position, they liked Mike better when he was polite, but when they thought that the interview was for a journalism position, participants liked Mike more when he was rude and aggressive. The authors' interpretation of these findings was that the adoption of the conscious goal to evaluate the job candidate set in motion a number of implicit processes that were then unintentionally applied to an irrelevant target. Thus, a conscious goal engaged a nonconscious process that had an unintended influence on subsequent evaluation.

Aspects of Nonconscious Goal Pursuit that Seep into Consciousness

Not only does the conscious adoption of a goal have unintended, implicit effects, it is also the case that the nonconscious activation of a goal can lead to downstream effects that are conscious. That is, aspects of nonconscious goal pursuit may seep into conscious awareness, and this eruption into consciousness may have important influences on the continued operation of the goal, or on subsequent goal pursuits that are adopted after the momentary awareness subsides.

AWARENESS OF SUCCESS AND FAILURE

In an interesting set of experiments, Chartrand (2007) found that success or failure at a nonconscious goal pursuit can influence one's mood. In one study, experimental (but not control) participants were first primed with an achievement goal by completing a scrambled sentence task, and then all were led to succeed or fail at this goal during a subsequent anagram task. In the easy condition, participants were led to expect that the task would take eight minutes to complete when it actually took an average of two minutes. By contrast, in the difficult condition, participants were led to believe that the task would take two minutes to complete when it actually took an average of eight minutes. Participants were then allowed to work on the task for as long as they wanted. However, because of the differing expectations for the task, participants in the easy condition were led to have a subjective experience of success in attaining the achievement goal, whereas participants in the difficult condition were led to have a subjective experience of failure to meet the goal. After completing the anagram task, participants completed a self-report questionnaire assessing their current mood. Although participants had no awareness in a funneled debriefing of the achievement goal having been activated, there were nonetheless systematic differences in participants' self-reported mood: those for whom the achievement goal had been activated were in a better mood in the easy condition in which they completed the anagrams within the expected amount of time than if they were in the difficult condition in which they did not. No such differences were found for

participants in the control condition, suggesting that it was the success or failure to meet the nonconsciously activated goal that caused the mood differences rather than some aspect of the anagram task itself.

In a second study, the mood differences caused by the outcome of a nonconscious goal pursuit were compared with those caused by a conscious goal. Some participants were given a conscious goal to form an impression of a target individual, whereas others were primed with a nonconscious impression formation goal, and still others were given no goal at all (controls). Participants were then led to fail at this goal by making the task of forming an impression of the target individual either easy or difficult. Although there were no mood effects in the control condition, participants with either a conscious or nonconscious goal were in a better mood if they succeeded in achieving this goal, and importantly, there were no differences between the conscious and nonconscious goal conditions with respect to these mood effects.

Of course, there was one particularly important difference between the conscious and nonconscious goal conditions in this study: although participants could easily determine the cause of their mood when they were aware of the goal they were pursuing, participants lacked insight into the cause of a mood that originated from a nonconscious goal pursuit. Chartrand (2007) has found that this lack of insight has important implications for subsequent behavior, leading participants to misattribute their negative mood to salient aspects of their environment, to be more likely to engage in self-enhancement, and even to have a greater propensity to act aggressively (see Chartrand, Dalton, & Cheng, 2008). Oettingen and colleagues (Oettingen et al., 2006) have similarly proposed that the absence of conscious awareness of the source of one's nonconsciously derived goal-directed behaviors results in a kind of "explanatory vacuum" in which participants are left without a ready explanation for their actions. To the extent that there is no plausible explanation that one can latch onto in one's environment (e.g., when one's behavior violates a salient social norm), this may result in the (conscious) experience of negative affect.

Leander and colleagues (2009) have proposed that such mood effects are also likely to have effects on subsequent self-regulatory efforts. This is thought to occur in at least two ways. The first is that because the unexplained mood that results from a previous nonconscious goal pursuit is likely to be attributed to a consciously available target, one may falsely attribute one's current mood to another of one's (consciously available) current goal pursuits rather than the true source. This may then subsequently influence one's self-regulatory efforts with respect to that goal, perhaps by reducing commitment to the goal or changing strategies. The second way is that a consciously experienced mystery mood might encourage us to adopt new goals: perhaps mood repair (in the case of a failed nonconscious goal) or perhaps mood maintenance (in the case of a successful nonconscious goal), and these newly adopted goals can then influence subsequent self-regulatory behavior in predictable ways.

One's subsequent performance might also be similarly affected by nonconscious goal pursuits. Chartrand (2007) found evidence to suggest that success or failure at a nonconscious goal had performance effects that mimicked those of a consciously adopted goal: participants who were led to fail at a goal had lesser expectations about their likely performance on a subsequent test of ability (i.e., difficult GRE questions), whereas participants who were led to succeed had relatively higher expectations for their upcoming performance. Such increments and deficits in performance after the failure or success of a consciously adopted goal have been explained in terms of changes in one's self-efficacy beliefs (Bandura, 1997; Locke & Latham, 2002)— that is, those who fail at a goal suffer a hit to their perceived ability to meet their goals more generally, which is thought to have an important influence on one's beliefs about future performance. Interestingly, Chartrand (2007) found evidence to suggest that changes in performance resulting from a failure or success at a nonconsciously activated goal were also mediated by changes in (conscious) feelings of self-efficacy. Those who recently succeeded at a nonconscious goal pursuit were shown to have higher expectations of their performance on a subsequent task, and this ultimately led them to actually perform better, whereas those who recently failed at a nonconscious goal pursuit had relatively lower expectations for their performance, resulting in actual performance deficits.

In summary, although nonconscious goals can and often do operate to completion without any conscious awareness or intention, the success or failure of these goals appears to be consciously accessible, leading to systematic influences on one's current mood and feelings of self-efficacy. Importantly, moods resulting from performance on a nonconscious goal are thought to have an

influence on subsequent behaviors, suggesting that this conscious experience may be causally related to subsequent motivated behavior, either by exerting an influence on the conscious goals that we choose to adopt or abandon, or by encouraging us to adopt new goals that may influence subsequent behavior (such as mood maintenance or mood repair goals), or perhaps even by altering conscious perceptions of self-efficacy that encourage or discourage the exertion of effort on subsequent goal-relevant tasks.

PRESCRIPTIONS OF SELF-AGENCY

Another conscious experience that appears to have nonconscious antecedents is the subjective experience of having caused one's actions or behaviors—that is, the experience of self-agency. Aarts, Custers, and Marien (2009) have proposed that the experience of agency arises from a match between the activation of a representation in memory of a particular outcome—say, having moved one's arm one inch to the left—and the actual outcome that is produced—that is, of having actually moved one's arm one inch to the left. In other words, situations in which one experiences a particular outcome at a time when it is currently primed in one's mind engender feelings of having brought about the outcome. Importantly, however, this process can occur independent of whether one *has* actually intentionally caused the outcome. In situations in which the outcome representation happens to be primed at a time when the outcome also occurs, people have a tendency to attribute the cause of these outcomes to their own agency, even if this belief is spurious.

In a series of studies, Aarts and colleagues asked participants to perform a behavior (e.g., to press a key on a keyboard that stopped a rapidly alternating set of squares on a particular colored square) that resulted in an outcome that could either have been caused by the participant's actions (i.e., from hitting the key) or randomly determined by the computer irrespective of the participant's actions. After each outcome, participants were asked to rate the extent to which they believed they had caused it rather than it being randomly determined. In reality, the outcome was always determined by the computer, so any perceptions of self-agency were fallacious and entirely based on individuals' subjective experience. Unknown to participants, they were sometimes subliminally primed with a particular outcome (e.g., "purple," indicating an upcoming stop on the purple square) before it occurred. Consistent with the hypothesis, when participants were primed with the outcome just before it occurred, they reported a greater experience of self-agency in bringing about the outcome than if they hadn't been primed. Importantly, this only occurred when the prime occurred immediately before the outcome (i.e., one second), but not if there was a greater time lag (i.e., 20 seconds), indicating that the concept needed to be activated at the time that the outcome occurred in order to have any influence on feelings of self-agency (see Wegner & Wheatley, 1999).

This result suggests that self-agency may have nonconscious antecedents—but is there evidence that the satisfaction of a nonconscious goal, in particular, can result in conscious feelings of agency? In a follow-up experiment, Aarts and colleagues essentially manufactured a nonconscious goal to achieve a particular outcome by closely pairing it with positively valenced words (e.g., "puppy," "sunshine.") Such pairings have been shown in previous research to foster relatively automatic approach behaviors and have been theorized to be an avenue through which nonconscious goals acquire their motivational significance (Custers & Aarts, 2005). In the current experiment, when the outcome was paired with positive affect, participants reported a greater sense of self-agency when they were primed with the concept, even after a significant time lag (20 seconds). This result is consistent with the evidence discussed earlier that suggests that, in contrast to semantic priming, which has been shown to have a particular steep decay function, a nonconscious goal remains activated until it is satisfied (see Bargh et al., 2001). These results thus provide evidence that the activation and subsequent satisfaction of a nonconscious goal may result in a greater conscious experience of self-agency, providing additional support for the contention that the outcome of a nonconscious goal pursuit has an influence on one's conscious experience.

Functional Role of Consciousness

Given evidence that goal pursuit can seemingly operate largely without awareness, some have questioned whether consciousness makes any significant contribution whatsoever to goal pursuit and self-regulation. Bargh, for example, in his conception of the "selfish goal" (Bargh & Huang, 2009; see also Bargh, Green & Fitzsimons, 2008; Huang & Bargh, 2011)—a play on Richard Dawkins' 1976 bestseller *The Selfish Gene,* in which genes were posited to be the unit of natural selection rather than the organisms that hosted them—extricates the individual from the process of behavioral selection altogether, instead positing that goals, once activated, selfishly operate to completion irrespective of the costs or benefits of this operation to their host. Under this conception, consciousness is unneeded and inconsequential.

Certainly, we have noted the benefits of a motivational system that can run unconsciously. Given the processing and capacity limitations of consciousness, meeting our motivational demands—much less being able to multitask—in a solely conscious manner would be highly inefficient. Instead, staying nonconsciously attuned and responsive to the possibly rewarding future routes of behavior suggested by the environment would seem highly functional and critically necessary. In addition, recent work shows that people seem to commence nonconscious goal pursuits only when those pursuits are desirable, self-relevant, and context appropriate (see Aart et al., 2004; Ferguson, 2008), demonstrating that people pursue nonconscious goals in a functionally selective (not indiscriminate) manner.

So, is consciousness completely useless for goal pursuit? Does it offer any benefits? In this section, we consider contemporary theories of consciousness in social cognition and cognitive psychology and speculate about ways in which conscious thought may serve to facilitate subsequent goal-directed behavior. We consider whether consciousness might contribute to sequential planning, troubleshoot nonconscious goal pursuits that encounter obstacles or unexpected failures, and engender transcendence of the here-and-now through a unique ability to simulate the past and future, all of which may fundamentally alter the goals that we choose to pursue and the means that we adopt to pursue them.

Sequential Planning

Although consciousness is known for its exceedingly limited information processing capacity in comparison to the overwhelming parallelism achieved by the unconscious (e.g., Dijksterhuis & Nordgren, 2006), a number of researchers have suggested that conscious thought may be necessary for some subset of information processing tasks that are perhaps outside of the jurisdiction of nonconscious processes (e.g., Baumeister & Masicampo, 2010; Dehaene & Naccache, 2001; Hofmann & Wilson, 2010). One proposal is that conscious thought may be required in the novel processing of information, particularly in the construction of meaningful and novel sequences of thought extrapolated from one's existing knowledge. Although nonconscious processes appear to be especially good at managing a large volume of well-learned and heavily entrenched associations, some scholars have argued that consciousness appears to be needed to take existing information and process it in new, unique ways, as is likely necessary in language and speech construction, counting and quantification, and logical reasoning, among other abilities (Baumeister & Masicampo, 2010).

The evidence on this front is still accumulating, but recent work challenges the notion that consciousness is required for these sorts of tasks. First, although earlier studies suggested that simple two-word phrases (e.g., "kill enemy"; Greenwald & Liu, 1985) cannot be meaningfully parsed and nonconsciously evaluated (see also Mackay, 1973), more recent work shows that negations (e.g., "no sunshine" should be less positive than "sunshine") can in fact be processed and evaluated in a rapid and unintentional manner (see Deutsch, Kordts-Freudinger, Gawronski, & Strack, 2009; see also Deutsch, Gawronski, & Strack, 2006; Draine, 1997). These findings show that such negation seems to depend on working memory, which itself has recently been characterized as being able to operate without awareness (see Hassin, Bargh, & Zimmerman, 2006; Hassin, Bargh, Engell, & McCulloch, 2009). Even more importantly, recent work shows that when consciousness can be withheld (for roughly 2 seconds) from the processing of complex stimuli through the use of the method of Continuous Flash Suppression, people nevertheless solve simple subtraction (e.g., "5 – 7 – 2") and addition problems, and read multi-word phrases (see Sklar, Levy, Goldstein, Mandel, Maril, & Hassin, 2012; see also Hassin, in press).

It also should be noted that although the complexity (or lack thereof) of information that can be visually or aurally processed without awareness may address limits on the amount of information we can process subliminally, or within very short temporal windows, it does not necessarily speak to the sophistication of nonconscious processing more generally. There are many examples in which information that is consciously attended to is then parsed, interpreted, and combined in impressively sophisticated—yet nonconscious—ways. One example would be implicit learning (e.g., see Frensch & Runger, 2003 for a review), whereby people attend to sequences of cues consciously, and yet grasp the rules connecting those stimuli only nonconsciously. Or, another example is reading: a process that (sometimes but not always; see Sklar et al., 2012) involves conscious attention to sequences of words, but a decidedly nonconscious integration and interpretation of those words.

With respect to the processing of relatively *novel* information, however, there is neurological evidence that suggests that consciousness likely has an important role to play. Raichle et al. (1994), for example, found that activation of the prefrontal cortex and anterior cingulate—areas often activated when conscious control is necessary (Dehaene & Naccache, 2001)—occurs first during initial exposure to a task when novel processing is required, then slowly declines over time as the activity becomes more routinized, but then quickly rebounds to full activation if novel information is presented. This suggests that although nonconscious processes operate quite well on previously considered and well-established information and associations, they may be relatively less centrally responsible for the processing of novel stimuli (though see Eitam et al., 2007).

One implication of the claim that consciousness may be required for processing novel stimuli is that consciousness may play a central role in planning. Baumeister and Masicampo (2010) argue, for example, that even the simple act of successfully catching a flight is likely to rely on conscious sequential processing, beginning with the flight's departure time and working backward through the series of events that we know are likely to take place in order to arrive at an appropriate time to commence the sequence of actions. Successful goal pursuit is not merely about exploiting opportunities that present themselves in one's environment but also about anticipating and planning for particular contingencies that may present themselves in the future—operations that conscious thought may be particularly well suited to accomplish.

Furthermore, a plan of action may be especially necessary when one adopts a goal for the first time. Although many chronic, long-term goal pursuits can rely on the relative success or failure of past attempts to inform current pursuits, new goal pursuits are especially likely to require the kinds of novel, sequential processing of information at which conscious thought may excel. Similarly, conscious thought may also play a role in the derivation of plans when attempting to effectively juggle multiple goal pursuits—that is, in adaptively prioritizing goals in ways that allow us to make sufficient progress on as many of our aspirations as possible. Such prioritizations are likely to require both an assessment of the feasibility of obtaining a goal right now and an assessment (i.e., the anticipation and prediction) of the feasibility of obtaining the goal later in the future—assessments that are likely to require not only sequential planning but also the ability to simulate future consequences which may (or may not; see Fukukura, Helzer, & Ferguson, in press) require consciousness.

Importantly, once a plan has been consciously derived and the sequential steps required to attain the goal have been determined, conscious thought may no longer need to be recruited to actually implement the strategy. Indeed, the most efficient and effective way for goal pursuit to proceed may be in the conscious derivation of a sequential plan of action followed by the subsequent nonconscious implementation of the strategy. Gollwitzer's extensive program of research on implementation intentions (i.e., if–then contingencies for goal pursuit) supports this contention (see Parks-Stamm & Gollwitzer, 2009, for a review). Numerous studies have shown that when individuals consciously consider the goal-directed behaviors that they might engage in when certain situational cues present themselves (i.e., they derive a plan of action to be executed given a particular set of environmental constraints, e.g. "If I get home early from work, I will go for a run"), they are significantly more likely to achieve their goals. For example, Gollwitzer and Brandstätter (1997) found that when participants had formed an implementation intention for a difficult personal project that they wanted to accomplish over the winter break, they were three times more likely to accomplish the goal than if they hadn't formed one. Importantly, Brandstätter and colleagues (2001) found evidence to suggest that once an implementation intention has been derived, the goal-directed action (i.e., the "then" part of the if–then statement) acquires features of automaticity, meaning that its actual implementation can proceed with relatively little further conscious intention or awareness when the appropriate environment conditions are present. Thus, planning may serve to facilitate a kind of "strategic automaticity" in which an intention serves to create or modify the automatic associations that foster the relatively nonconscious pursuit of the goal.

Consciousness as a Troubleshooting Device

Anyone who has ever faced a road closure on a preferred morning route to work has likely experienced a (formerly nonconscious) goal pursuit rather abruptly making its way into consciousness. This is an interesting observation because it suggests that there are indeed times when our nonconscious goals may become available to conscious awareness, and

the times when this occurs may offer clues as to when consciousness may be a useful tool in furthering progress on our goals. One long-standing suggestion (see Arievitch & Van Der Veer, 2004, for a historical review; see also Bongers & Dijksterhuis, 2009; Gollwitzer, Parks-Stamm, & Oettingen, 2010) that has garnered recent empirical support (Bongers, Dijksterhuis, & Spears, 2010) is that consciousness might be seen as a kind of troubleshooting device that comes to the aid of nonconscious processes when those processes fail or encounter an impasse. When nonconsciously activated goals are proceeding smoothly, consciousness is rather superfluous to self-regulation; after all, if one is making good progress without conscious intervention, then the exceedingly limited capacity and resources of consciousness might be more adaptively directed toward other endeavors. However, when nonconscious goal pursuit encounters difficulties, the goal is more likely to become available to conscious awareness. Importantly, this eruption into awareness has been proposed, at least under certain circumstances, to be adaptive (see Arievitch & Van Der Veer, 2004; Gollwitzer, Parks-Stamm, & Oettingen, 2010) in that it allows us to properly interpret our behavior and the resulting outcome and consciously derive new strategies to overcome the impasse (e.g., to simulate a new route to work, given that the road closure has made the typical route impassable).

AFTER FAILURES

The notion that frustrated or incomplete goals are more likely to be consciously mulled over has enjoyed a long history in psychology. For example, early explorations of the idea demonstrated that when people are asked to recall a series of tasks that they have worked on during an experimental session, they are considerably more likely to recall the tasks that were not completed (Ziegarnik, 1938). Similarly, Martin and Tesser (1996) posit that frustrated or incomplete goals are more likely to unintentionally intrude into consciousness, and these intrusions are thought to continue to occur until some resolution is achieved, either by meeting the goal or by choosing to abandon it.

In a recent set of studies, Bongers, Dijksterhuis, and Spears (2010) sought evidence for the notion that frustrated nonconscious goals are likely to seep into conscious awareness. In one study (Bongers, Dijksterhuis, Spears, 2010, Study 1), participants were first subliminally primed with either an achievement goal or not and then subsequently asked to complete a memory game in which they had to identify matching pairs of cards by flipping two cards at a time. Some participants were allowed to satisfy the primed goal by being given sufficient time to complete the memory game (12 minutes). Others saw their achievement goal frustrated by being given a very short amount of time to complete the task (only 3 minutes, which was insufficient to identify all matching pairs). In the primary dependent measure, participants did a sentence completion task (e.g., "I…", "I am…", "I wished…", "The memory game…", etc.) that was meant to tap into their current conscious thoughts. Results revealed that participants who were primed with an achievement goal but had their goal frustrated in the memory game had significantly more conscious achievement goal–related sentence completions than participants in any of the other three conditions.

Of course, one might argue that the dependent measure in this first study tapped activation of the goal rather than conscious thought. Thus, in a second study, participants were once again primed with an achievement goal, and then had this goal frustrated (or not) by being asked to complete a version of the Remote Associates Test (Mednick, 1962) that was either difficult or easy to complete. While completing the test, participants were asked to report their online conscious thoughts by thinking out loud, with the number of goal-relevant thoughts serving as the primary dependent measure. Results once again suggested that participants for whom an achievement goal was primed but then frustrated were more likely to have goal-relevant thoughts while thinking aloud.

These studies provide empirical support for the notion that frustrated nonconscious goal pursuits are more likely to intrude into consciousness. But is there any evidence that such intrusions are adaptive? It is compelling to conclude that an eruption into consciousness may serve a regulatory function, allowing consciousness to perhaps alter the course of self-regulatory efforts in order to overcome the difficulty (Arievitch & Van Der Veer, 2004; Gollwitzer et al., 2010). However, as Bongers, Dijksterhuis, and Spears (2010) point out, there are likely to be a number of important moderators at play with respect to whether such intrusions are adaptive. The relative difficulty of overcoming the existing obstacle may be one such moderator. Bandura (1997) has shown that motivation is a product of expectancies about both the desirability and feasibility of attainment of a possible end state. To the extent that conscious awareness of a failed nonconscious goal pursuit is

perceived to be indicative of low feasibility of goal attainment, people may just as soon reduce effort or abandon the goal rather than seek new ways to pursue it. Of course, goal disengagement in these contexts might, under some circumstances, be adaptive in that one might consciously determine that one's efforts are better spent on other pursuits. It remains to be seen whether intrusions into consciousness of this sort are generally beneficial or more often detrimental to self-regulation. Nonetheless, these recent studies hint at the possibility that consciousness may be well suited to a troubleshooting role in self-regulation and serve as an important platform for future research.

WHEN REGULAR MEANS OF PURSUIT BECOME INVALID

Another situation in which nonconscious goal pursuit is likely to be frustrated occurs in situations in which the typical means of pursuing a goal are no longer viable. For example, when one's immediate environment changes, such as when one is traveling away from home on business, the usual means of pursuing a goal (e.g., stopping at the gym on the way home from work) must be temporarily abandoned, and new means to goal attainment must be derived (e.g., making use of the hotel gym facilities in between meetings). In such situations, we might expect that, in much the way that frustrated goals seep into conscious, so, too, do goals for which the regularly adopted means become untenable.

One might conceive of this claim as essentially an extension of the argument that consciousness is required in sequential planning. In much the way that consciousness may contribute to meaningful and novel sequences of thought when deriving plans of action before the initiation of goal pursuit, the self-regulatory apparatus may similarly rely on these planning faculties when the current plan is no longer viable or appears to be unsuccessful. It should be noted, however, that the claim here is not that it will always be the case that consciousness will be required when a typical means of goal pursuit becomes untenable. These situations represent points at which a new plan of action may need to be developed in order to further goal pursuit, but to the extent that an alternative plan is readily available in the current environment, consciousness need not be recruited to adopt it. The findings of Hassin, Bargh, and Zimmerman (2008) on the relative flexibility of nonconscious goal pursuit speak to this assertion. In one study, participants were nonconsciously primed with an achievement goal (or not) and then completed a variant of the Iowa Gambling Task in which they drew cards from one of four piles that resulted in them either gaining or losing a small or large amount of money. Unknown to participants, two of the decks were "bad" in that they had negative expected values, whereas two of the decks were "good" in that they have positive expected values. The usual result using such paradigms is that participants implicitly learn which decks are good and which are bad. However, also unknown to participants, in Hassin and colleagues' experiment, the locations of the four decks were altered halfway through the experiment, such that what was once a "good" deck may have abruptly become a "bad" deck, and vice versa. The hypothesis of interest was that people nonconsciously primed with an achievement goal would be more flexible in their goal pursuit and switch decks once they were no longer achieving the desired ends. Consistent with this hypothesis, participants primed with achievement gave up more quickly on the newly created "bad" decks, and switched more quickly to the newly created "good" decks than control participants. In other words, when the current strategy was no longer valid, a nonconsciously activated achievement goal led participants to adapt more quickly to the new circumstances, and consciousness was unnecessary in promoting this flexibility. However, it should be noted that in these experiments, the behavior that was necessary once the old strategy became invalid was readily available (i.e., attempting to sample more frequently from the other decks) to participants and thus did not require any conscious intervention to derive. It remains to be seen whether nonconscious goal pursuit is similarly flexible in situations in which the new strategy or means of goal pursuit is not so readily available.

An important implication of the results of these studies is that consciousness may not be necessary if any of one's preferred means are readily available in the current environment. For example, if we often pursue our fitness goals through a combination of running on a treadmill and playing basketball (and both are considered to be equally effective in meeting the goal), then the breaking of the treadmill during a particularly intense running session may not necessarily result in the recruitment of conscious planning strategies if one still has an opportunity to play basketball at the times when one might have run on the treadmill. Rather, it will likely only be in situations in which a new plan or alternative means is not readily available for pursuit, thus making the sequential planning faculties of consciousness likely to be beneficial.

In summary, conscious sequential planning may be beneficial not only when one first adopts a goal but also in the midst of goal pursuit if a means that was previously effective becomes untenable. In line with the findings of Bongers, Dijksterhuis, and Spears (2010), we would expect that when a preferred means of goal pursuit is unavailable, a nonconscious goal will be more likely to seep into conscious awareness, and that this eruption into conscious awareness may be adaptive in that it allows for the development of a new, more effective plan for attaining the goal.

WHEN GOALS CONFLICT

Nonconscious goal pursuit may also be likely to seep into conscious awareness when we hold multiple conflicting goals. Although much of the early (and even more recent) goals literature largely focused on the activation and operation of single goals (but see Fishbach & Ferguson, 2007, for a review of recent exceptions), we know quite well that we often attempt to juggle many different goals at any one time, and that these goals can often require diametrically opposed behaviors in order to achieve them (e.g., a fitness goal that requires the purchase of expensive exercise equipment or a monthly gym membership and a financial goal that requires that we save our disposable income rather than spend it). Consciousness may be especially well suited to overcome such conflicts (see Morsella, 2005; Morsella, Krieger, & Bargh, 2009) by, for example, deriving a unique multifinal means (i.e., one which allows for both goals to be met simultaneously, e.g., the development of an exercise program that makes use of one's own body weight for resistance so that expensive free weights are not required; see Kruganski et al., 2002), or by means of prioritization, perhaps by choosing to temporarily emphasize one goal over another, and then some time later reversing this emphasis so that sufficient progress can be made on each.

Interestingly, we know very little about *when* conflict will seep into the conscious mind. Recent work demonstrates that goal conflict can exist at a nonconscious level, with the conflict manifesting only in increased decision times, increased decision variance, and increased arousal (see Kleiman & Hassin, 2011). This work shows that conflict among one's goals does seem to exist below our conscious radar, which raises the question of when—as well as whether—goal conflict enters awareness.

Simulation

The very notion of a goal implies the realization of one (presumably desirable) future over many other (presumably less desirable) futures that might have occurred. But how is it that we determine precisely which futures we wish to bring about and which ones we do not? That is, how do we decide exactly which goals to adopt? Most of us have never won the lottery, yet we know that a future in which we are holding a comically oversized check while celebrating with a glass of champagne is likely to be more enjoyable than a future in which we become bankrupt, thus making the goal of achieving financial independence considerably more commonly held than that of bankruptcy. We need not experience these outcomes in order to make a determination about their desirability because we are able to imagine what these futures might be like before they ever occur, and to avoid the consequences of those futures before they ever happen (Gilbert & Wilson, 2007). One of the primary ways by which we come to pursue one goal over another, then, is through the simulation of possibilities for our futures, and seeing how these simulations make us feel.

This process of simulating consequences before they occur is rather different from the way that other animals determine which behaviors to pursue. Although most animals can learn to predict consequences they have experienced at one time in the past as the result of a particular antecedent behavior (i.e., through operant conditioning), the simulation and anticipation of consequences that one has never experienced before appears to be a uniquely human ability (Gilbert & Wilson, 2007; Suddendorf, 2006), and—more to the point—has been argued by some to be exclusively available to conscious processes (Baumeister & Masicampo, 2010; cf. Fukukura et al., in press).

Of course, merely simulating a desirable end state does not make it so. If simulation of the future is to contribute to effective goal pursuit, it must ultimately change our actions in the present. One important means by which it may do this is by modifying one's automatic associations and evaluations of the simulated objects and outcomes (see Baumeister & Masicampo, 2010; Ferguson & Wojnowicz, 2011). For example, by simulating the accolades one might receive if one's latest research idea were to be reported in a well-respected media outlet, one may systematically retool the positivity one experiences both toward the goal of completing the paper and toward objects related to the pursuit of completing a paper related to these research ideas

(e.g., libraries). In other words, the ability to consciously envision new sources of reward may lead one to strategically adopt a new goal, which may then alter the implicit value (positivity, negativity) associated with the means to get there (Ferguson & Wojnowicz, 2011). Such changes in the implicit associations toward the goal itself as well as to the stimuli associated with the goal might then, in turn, initiate the kinds of nonconscious self-regulatory processes that are necessary for attaining it. In this way, although consciousness may not be directly involved in the moment-to-moment guidance of behavior, it may nonetheless have a hand in the process by influencing some of the processes that *do* directly control behavior.

Another way that simulation of the future may translate into behavior in the present is by fostering a strong commitment to one's goals or by changing our beliefs about the feasibility of attaining those goals. Oettingen and colleagues (see Oettingen & Stevens, 2009, for a recent review) have shown in numerous studies that one of the most effective self-regulatory strategies to foster goal achievement is in the mental contrasting between a desirable future and the present reality in which the desirable outcomes have not yet been realized. By making both the (simulated) fantasy and the present reality simultaneously accessible, individuals are made aware of the ways in which the present reality is standing in the way of achieving a desirable end state. The ultimate result is increased motivation to change the present reality in order to bring about the imagined end state as well as corresponding increased beliefs in the feasibility of attaining the goal, leading to strong goal commitment.

Oettingen and colleagues contrast this self-regulatory strategy with that of merely simulating a positive future ("fantasizing") or merely considering the negative reality in which a goal is not realized ("dwelling"), neither of which strongly compel an individual to act, in part because of a misalignment in individuals' high goal commitment with their beliefs about the low feasibility of goal attainment. For example, in one study, Oettingen, Pak, and Schnetter (2001) manipulated whether freshman in a mathematically intensive college program engaged in mental contrasting, fantasizing, or dwelling on their math ability. Two weeks after the exercise, teachers were asked to provide subjective ratings of effort for each student as well as the students' grades for the previous two weeks. The results showed that students who completed the mental contrasting exercise exhibited a positive relationship between their expectations for success and their corresponding investment of effort and math achievement during the previous two weeks. However, students in the fantasizing and dwelling conditions showed no such relationship. In other words, those who fantasized or dwelled on math achievement exhibited increased commitment to the goal of math achievement, but this did not translate into increased effort or success in achieving the goal.

One important way that mental contrasting—and by extension, simulation—may facilitate goal achievement is through the thorough consideration of the potential obstacles that may disrupt goal pursuit. By contrasting the current reality with the desired future, one is encouraged to simulate potential current impediments to goal attainment, thus giving one an opportunity to prepare for these setbacks should they occur. This ultimately increases the likelihood of overcoming obstacles, by encouraging individuals to either develop a plan to handle them (i.e., an implementation intention, e.g., "If I feel tired after work, I will put on my running shoes and go for a walk"), or to engage in anticipatory counteractive control strategies to prevent them from occurring at all (e.g., "I won't buy any fattening snacks on this grocery store trip so that I can't indulge during CSI: Miami"; see Fishbach & Trope, 2007, for a review of this kind of counteractive self-control).

Thus, one primary role that conscious simulation may play in effective goal pursuit is in its ability to anticipate. Successful self-regulation is not merely about taking advantage of present opportunities but is also about anticipating and exploiting opportunities that are yet to come. Consciousness may contribute to our ability to effectively take advantage of these future opportunities by allowing us to prepare for them. Gollwitzer and colleagues' (Parks-Stamm & Gollwitzer, 2009) work on implementation intentions bears this out. To the extent that we can correctly anticipate future opportunities that may become available to us ("If I finish work early . . .") and can consciously derive a suitable plan to take advantage of those opportunities (". . . I will go to the gym before dinner"), we are more likely to engage in effective self-regulation strategies and have a greater chance of success in our goal pursuits (e.g., Brandstätter, Lengfelder & Gollwitzer, 2001; Gollwitzer & Brandstätter, 1997). Thus, the ability of our conscious processes to anticipate may help to put in place the appropriate automatic associations in memory (finish work—go to the gym) that ultimately allow nonconscious processes to effectively exploit the current environment without further conscious intervention.

Conclusion

In this chapter, we critically reviewed evidence in the social cognition literature suggesting that everyday goal pursuit requires considerably less conscious intention and deliberation than classic theories of self-regulation assume. Although this evidence is impressive, and mounting, we also identified caveats to thinking about goal pursuit as simply either conscious or nonconscious. We argued that both conscious and nonconscious processes likely play a role in effective goal pursuit and self-regulation, and that the challenge for future research will be to identify precisely *when* different types of conscious versus nonconscious processes are necessary and sufficient for successful goal pursuit. Such questions about the functionality of consciousness in goal pursuit mirror similar questions about consciousness across all other domains of human behavior: How much do we need to be (consciously) aware of our own lives in order to live them? The answer so far from the social and cognitive literatures seems to be "not much," but, as always, the devil is in the details. If the consensus is that consciousness is rarely necessary, it becomes all the more intriguing to find the exceptions to that rule.

References

Aarts, H. (2007). On the emergence of human goal pursuit: The nonconscious regulation and motivation of goals. *Social and Personality Psychology Compass, 1*(1), 183–201.

Aarts, H., Custers, R., & Marien, H. (2009). Priming and authorship ascription: When nonconscious goals turn into conscious experiences of self-agency. *Journal of Personality and Social Psychology, 96*(5), 967–979.

Aarts, H., & Dijksterhuis, A. (2000). Habits as knowledge structures: Automaticity in goal-directed behavior. *Journal of Personality and Social Psychology, 78*, 53–63.

Aarts, H., & Dijksterhuis, A. (2003). The silence of the library: Environment, situational norm, and social behavior. *Journal of Personality and Social Psychology, 84*, 18–28.

Aarts, H., Dijksterhuis, A., & De Vries, P. (2001). On the psychology of drinking: Being thirsty and perceptually ready. *British Journal of Psychology, 92*, 631–642.

Aarts, H., Gollwitzer, P. M., & Hassin, R. (2004). Goal contagion: Perceiving is for pursuing. *Journal of Personality and Social Psychology, 87*, 23–37.

Anderson, J. R. (1983). *The architecture of cognition*. Cambridge, MA: Harvard University Press.

Arievitch, I. M., & Van Der Veer, R. (2004). The role of non-automatic processes in activity regulation: From Lipps to Galperin. *History of Psychology, 7*, 154–182.

Atkinson, J. W., & Birch, D. (1970). *A dynamic theory of action*. New York: Wiley.

Baars, B. (1998). *A cognitive theory of consciousness*. Cambridge, UK: Cambridge University Press.

Balcetis, E., & Dunning, D. A. (2006). See what you want to see: Motivational influences on visual perception. *Journal of Personality and Social Psychology, 91*, 612–625.

Bandura, A. (1986). *Social foundations of thought and action: A social cognitive theory.* Englewood Cliffs, NJ: Prentice Hall.

Bandura, A. (1997). *Self-efficacy: The exercise of control.* New York: Freeman.

Bandura, A. (2006). Toward a psychology of human agency. *Perspectives on Psychological Science, 1*(2), 164–180.

Bargh, J. A. (1990). Auto-motives: Preconscious determinants of social interaction. In E. T. Higgins & R. M. Sorrentino (Eds.), *Handbook of motivation and cognition: Foundations of social behavior* (Vol. 2, pp. 93–130). New York: Guilford Press.

Bargh, J. A., & Gollwitzer, P. M. (1994). Environmental control of goal-directed action: Automatic and strategic contingencies between situations and behavior. In W. D. Spaulding (Ed.), *Nebraska symposium on motivation* (Vol. 41, pp. 71–124). Lincoln, NE: University of Nebraska Press.

Bargh, J. A., Gollwitzer, P. M., Lee-Chai, A., Barndollar, K., & Troetschel, R. (2001). The automated will: Nonconscious activation and pursuit of behavioral goals. *Journal of Personality and Social Psychology, 81*, 1014–1027.

Bargh, J. A., Green, M., & Fitzsimons, G. M. (2008). The selfish goal: Unintended consequences of intended goal pursuits. *Social Cognition, 26*(5), 534–554.

Bargh, J. A., & Huang, J. Y. (2009). The selfish goal. In Moskowitz, G. B., & Grant, H. (Eds.), *The psychology of goals* (pp. 127–150). New York: Guilford Press.

Baumeister, R. F., & Masicampo, E. J. (2010). Conscious thought is for facilitating social and cultural interactions: How simulations serve the animal-culture interface. *Psychological Review.*

Bongers, K. C. A., & Dijksterhuis, A. (2009). Consciousness as a troubleshooting device? The role of consciousness in goal pursuit. In E. Morsella, J. A. Bargh, & Gollwitzer, P. M. (Eds.), *Oxford handbook of human action* (pp. 587–602). New York: Oxford University Press.

Bongers, K. C. A., Dijksterhuis, A., & Spears, R. (2010). On the role of consciousness in goal pursuit. *Social Cognition, 28*(2), 262–272.

Brandstätter, V., Lengfelder, A., & Gollwitzer, P. M. (2001). Implementation intention and efficient action initiation. *Journal of Personality and Social Psychology, 81*, 946–960.

Bruner, J. S. (1957). On perceptual readiness. *Psychological Review, 64*(2), 123–152.

Bruner, J. S., & Goodman, C. C. (1947). Value and need as organizing factors in perception. *Journal of Abnormal Social Psychology, 42*, 33–44.

Carver, C. S., & Scheier, M. F. (1981). *Attention and self-regulation: A control theory approach to human behaviors.* New York: Springer.

Carver, C. S., & Scheier, M. F. (1998). *On the self-regulation of behavior.* New York: Cambridge University Press.

Chalmers, D. (1996). *The conscious mind.* Oxford, UK: Oxford University Press.

Chartrand, T. L. (2007). *Mystery moods and perplexing performance: Consequences of succeeding or failing at a nonconscious goal.* Unpublished manuscript, Duke University.

Chartrand, T. L., & Bargh, J. A. (1996). Automatic activation of impression formation and memorization goals: Nonconscious goal priming reproduces effects of explicit task instructions. *Journal of Personality and Social Psychology, 71*, 464–478.

Chartrand, T. L., Dalton, A. N., & Cheng, C. M. (2008). The antecedents and consequences of nonconscious goal pursuit. In J. Y. Shah, & W. L. Gardner (Eds.) *Handbook of motivation science* (pp. 342–355). New York: Guilford Press.

Chen, M., & Bargh, J. A. (1999). Consequences of automatic evaluation: Immediate behavioral predispositions to approach and avoid the stimulus. *Personality and Social Psychology Bulletin, 25*, 215–224.

Churchland, P. S. (1983). Consciousness: The transmutation of a concept. *Pacific Philosophical Quarterly, 64*, 80–95.

Custers, R., & Aarts, H. (2005). Positive affect as implicit motivator: On the nonconscious operation of behavioral goals. *Journal of Personality and Social Psychology, 89*(2), 129–142.

Custers, R., & Aarts, H. (2010). The Unconscious will: How the pursuit of goals operates outside of conscious awareness. *Science, 329*, 47–50.

Damasio, A. (1999). *The feeling of what happens: Body and emotion in the making of consciousness.* New York: Harcourt.

Deci, E. L., & Ryan, R. M. (1985). *Intrinsic motivation and self-determination in human behavior.* New York: Plenum Press.

Deci, E. L., & Ryan, R. M. (2000). The "what" and "why" of goal pursuits: Human needs and the self-determination of behavior. *Psychological Inquiry, 11*, 227–268.

Dehaene, S., & Naccache, L. (2001). Towards a cognitive neuroscience of consciousness: Basic evidence and a workspace framework. *Cognition, 79*, 1–37.

Dennett, D. C. (1991). *Consciousness explained.* Boston: Little, Brown.

Deutsch, R., Gawronski, B., & Strack, F. (2006). At the boundaries of automaticity: Negation as a reflective operation. *Journal of Personality and Social Psychology, 91*, 385–405.

Devine, P. G. (1989). Stereotypes and prejudice: Their automatic and controlled components. *Journal of Personality and Social Psychology, 56*, 5–18.

Dijksterhuis, A., & Nordgren, L. F. (2006). A theory of unconscious thought. *Perspectives on Psychological Science, 1*(2), 95–109.

Eriksen, C. W. (1958). Unconscious processes. In M. R. Jones (Ed.), *Nebraska symposium on motivation* (pp. 169–227). Lincoln, NE: University of Nebraska Press.

Eriksen, C. W. (Ed.). (1962). *Behavior and awareness: A symposium of research and interpretation.* Durham, NC: Duke University Press.

Eriksen, C. W., & Browne, C. T. (1956). An experimental and theoretical analysis of perceptual defense. *Journal of Abnormal and Social Psychology, 52*, 224–230.

Fazio, R. H. (2001). On the automatic activation of associated evaluations: An overview. *Cognition and Emotion, 14*, 1–27.

Fazio, R. H., Jackson, J. R., Dunton, B. C., & Williams, C. J. (1995). Variability in automatic activation as an unobtrusive measure of racial attitudes: A bona fide pipeline? *Journal of Personality and Social Psychology, 69*, 1013–1027.

Ferguson, M. J., & Bargh, J. A. (2004). Liking is for doing: Effects of goal pursuit on automatic evaluation. *Journal of Personality and Social Psychology, 88*, 557–572.

Ferguson, M. J., & Wojnowicz, M. T. (2011). The when and how of evaluative readiness: A social cognitive neuroscience perspective. *Social and Personality Psychology Compass, 5*(12), 1018–1038.

Fishbach, A., & Ferguson, M. J. (2007). The goal construct in social psychology. In A. W. Kruglanski & E. T. Higgins & (Eds.), *Social psychology: Handbook of basic principles* (Vol. 2, pp. 490–515). New York: Guilford Press.

Fishbach, A., Friedman, R. S., & Kruglanski, A. W. (2003). Leading us not into temptation: Momentary allurements elicit overriding goal activation. *Journal of Personality and Social Psychology, 84*(2), 296–309.

Fishbach, A., & Trope, Y. (2007). Implicit and explicit mechanisms of counteractive self-control. In J. Y. Shah & W. Gardner (Eds.), *Handbook of motivation science* (pp. 281–294). New York: Guilford.

Fishbach, A., Zhang, Y., & Trope, Y. (2010). Counteractive evaluation: Asymmetric shifts in the implicit value of conflicting motivations. *Journal of Experimental Social Psychology, 46*(1), 29–38.

Fitzsimons, G. M., & Bargh, J. A. (2003). Thinking of you: Nonconscious pursuit of interpersonal goals associated with relationship partners. *Journal of Personality and Social Psychology, 84*(1), 148–163.

Förster, J., Liberman, N., & Friedman, R. (2007). Seven principles of goal activation: A systematic approach to distinguishing goal priming from priming of non-goal constructs. *Personality and Social Psychology Review, 11*, 211–233.

Frensch, P. A., & Runger, D. (2003). Implicit learning. *Current Directions in Psychological Science, 12*, 13.

Fukukura, J., Helzer, E., & Ferguson, M. J. (in press). Prospection by any other name? A reply to Seligmen et al. Perspectives on Psychological Science.

Gazzaniga, M. (1988). *Mind matters: How mind and brain interact to create our conscious lives.* Boston: Houghton Mifflin.

Gilbert, D. T., & Wilson, T. D. (2007). Prospection: Experiencing the future. *Science, 317*, 1351–1354.

Goldiamond, I. (1958). Indicators of perception. I. Subliminal perception, subception, unconscious perception: An analysis in terms of psychophysical indicator methodology. *Psychological Bulletin, 55*, 373–411.

Gollwitzer, P. M. (1990). Action phases and mind-sets. In E. T. Higgins & R. M. Sorrentino (Eds.), *Handbook of motivation and cognition: Vol. 2. Foundations of social behavior* (pp. 53–92). New York: Guilford Press.

Gollwitzer, P. M., & Brandstätter, V. (1997). Implementation intentions and effective goal pursuit. *Journal of Personality and Social Psychology, 73*, 186–199.

Greenwald, A. G., & Banaji, M. R. (1995). Implicit social cognition: Attitudes, self-esteem, and stereotypes. *Psychological Review, 102*, 4–27.

Greenwald, A. G., & Liu, T. J. (1985). Limited unconscious processing of meaning. *Bulletin of the Psychonomic Society, 23*, 292–313.

Hamilton, D. L., Katz, L. B., & Leirer, V. O. (1980). Cognitive representation of personality impression: Organizational processes in first impression formation. *Journal of Personality and Social Psychology, 39*, 1050–1063.

Hassin, R. R. (in press). Yes it can: On the functional abilities of the human unconscious. *Perspectives in Psychological Science.*

Hassin, R. R., Bargh, J. A., Engell, A. D., & McCulloch, K. C. (2009). Implicit working memory. *Consciousness and Cognition, 18*, 665–678.

Hassin, R. R., Bargh, J. A., & Zimmerman, S. (2009). Automatic and flexible: The case of nonconscious goal pursuit. *Social Cognition, 27*(1), 20–36.

Hastie, R., & Kumar, P. A. (1979). Person memory: Personality traits as organizing principles in memory for behaviors. *Journal of Personality and Social Psychology, 37*, 25–38.

Hazy, T. E., Frank, M. J., & O'Reilly, R. C. (2006). Banishing the homunculus: making working memory work. *Neuroscience, 139*(1), 105–118.

Heckhausen, H. (1991). Motivation and action. Berlin: Springer.

Higgins, E. T. (1996). Knowledge activation: Accessibility, applicability, and salience. In E. T. Higgins & A. W. Kruglanski (Eds.), *Social psychology: Handbook of basic principles* (pp. 133–168). New York: Guilford Press.

Hofmann, W., & Wilson, T. D. (2010). Consciousness, introspection, & the adaptive unconscious. In B. Gawronski & B. K. Payne (Eds.), *Handbook of implicit social cognition: Measurement, theory and applications* (pp. 197–215). New York: Guilford Press.

Huang, J. Y., & Bargh, J. A. (2011). The selfish goal: Self-deception occurs naturally from autonomous goal operation. *Brain and Behavioral Sciences, 34*, 27–28.

Kleiman, T., & Hassin, R. R. (2011). Non-conscious goal conflicts. *Journal of Experimental Social Psychology, 47*(3), 521–532.

Kruglanski, A. W. (1996). Goals as knowledge structures. In P. M. Gollwitzer & J. A. Bargh (Eds.), *The psychology of action: Linking cognition and motivation to behavior* (pp. 599–618). New York: Guilford Press.

Kruglanski, A. W., Shah, J. Y., Fishbach, A., Friedman, R., Chun, W. Y., & Sleeth-Keppler, D. (2002). A theory of goal systems. In M. P. Zanna (Ed.), *Advances in experimental psychology* (Vol. 34, pp. 331–378). San Diego: Academic Press.

Kuhl, J. (1983). *Motivation, conflict, and action control.* Berlin, Germany: Springer.

Kunda, Z. (1999). *Social cognition: Making sense of people.* Cambridge, MA: The MIT Press.

Leander, N. P., Moore, S. G., & Chartrand, T. L. (2009). Mystery moods: Their origins and consequences. In Moskowitz, G. B., & Grant, H. (Eds.), *The psychology of goals* (pp. 480–504). New York: Guilford Press.

Levesque, C., & Pelletier, L. G. (2003). On the investigation of primed and chronic autonomous and heteronomous motivational orientations. *Personality and Social Psychology Bulletin, 29*, 1570–1584.

Locke, E. A. (1995). Beyond determinism and materialism, or isn't it time we took consciousness seriously? *Journal of Behavioral Therapy and Experimental Psychiatry, 26*(3), 265–273.

Locke, E. A., & Latham, G. P. (1990). *A theory of goal setting and task performance.* Englewood Cliffs, NJ: Prentice Hall.

Mackay, D. G. (1973). Aspects of the theory of comprehension, memory and attention. *Quarterly Journal of Experimental Psychology, 25*, 22–40.

Martin, L. L., & Tesser, A. (1996). Some ruminative thoughts. In R. S. Wyer (Ed.), *Ruminative thoughts* (pp. 1–47). Hillsdale, NJ: Erlbaum.

Mednick, S. A. (1962). The associative basis of the creative process. *Psychological Review, 69*, 220–232.

Metcalfe, J. & Mischel, W. (1999). A hot/cool system analysis of delay of gratification: Dynamics of willpower. *Psychological Review, 106*, 3–19.

Moore, S. G., Ferguson, M. J., & Chartrand, T. L. (2011). Affect in the aftermath: How goal pursuit influences implicit evaluations. *Cognition and Emotion, 25*(3), 453–465.

Morsella, E. (2005). The function of phenomenal states: Supramodular interaction theory. *Psychological Review, 112*, 1000–1021.

Morsella, E., Krieger, S. C., & Bargh, J. A. (2009). The primary function of consciousness: Why Skeletal muscles are "voluntary" muscles. In E. Morsella, J. A. Bargh, & Gollwitzer, P. M. (Eds.) *Oxford handbook of human action* (pp. 625–634). New York: Oxford University Press.

Moskowitz, G. B. (2002). Preconscious effects of temporary goals on attention. *Journal of Experimental Social Psychology, 38*, 397–404.

Natanzon, M., & Ferguson, M. J. (2012). Goal pursuit is grounded: The link between forward movement and achievement. *Journal of Experimental Social Psychology, 48*(1), 379–382.

Oettingen, G., Grant, H., Smith, P. M., Skinner, M., & Gollwitzer, P. M. (2006). Nonconscious goal pursuit: Acting in an explanatory vacuum. *Journal of Experimental Social Psychology, 42,* 668–675.

Oettingen, G., Pak, H., & Schnetter, K. (2001). Self-regulation of goal-setting: Turning free fantasies about the future into binding goals. *Journal of Personality and Social Psychology, 80,* 736–753.

Oettingen, G., & Stevens, E. J. (2009). Fantasies and motivationally intelligent goal setting. In Moskowitz, G. B., & Grant, H. (Eds.), *The psychology of goals* (pp. 153–178). New York: Guilford Press.

Papineau, D. (2002). *Thinking about consciousness.* Oxford, UK: Oxford University Press.

Parks-Stamm, E. J., & Gollwitzer, P. M. (2009). Goal implementation: The benefits and costs of if–then planning. In Moskowitz, G. B., & Grant, H. (Eds.), *The psychology of goals* (pp. 362–391). New York: Guilford Press.

Pervin, L. A. (1989). *Goal concepts in personality and social psychology.* Hillsdale, NJ and England: Lawrence Erlbaum Associates, Inc.

Prentice, W. C. H. (1958). Perception. *Annual Review of Psychology, 9,* 1–18.

Raichle, M. E., Fiez, J. A., Videen, T. O., MacLoed, A. M., Pardo, J. V., Fox, P. T., et al. (1994). Practice-related changes in human brain functional anatomy in non-motor learning. *Cerebral Cortex, 4,* 8–26.

Ratelle, C. F., Vallerand, R. J., Chantal, Y., & Provencher, P. (2004). Cognitive adaptation and mental health: Motivational analysis. *European Journal of Social Psychology, 34,* 459–476.

Ryan, R. M., & Deci, E. L. (2000). Self-determination theory and the facilitation of intrinsic motivation, social development, and well-being. *American Psychologist, 55,* 68–78.

Searle, J. R. (1990). Consciousness, explanatory inversion and cognitive science. *Behavioral and Brain Sciences, 13,* 585–642.

Shah, J. (2003). The motivational looking glass: How significant others implicitly affect goal appraisals. *Journal of Personality and Social Psychology, 85*(3), 424–439.

Shah, J. Y., & Gardner, W. L. (2008). *Handbook of motivation science.* New York: Guilford Press.

Shah, J. Y., & Kruglanski, A. W. (2002). Priming against your will: How goal pursuit is affected by accessible alternatives. *Journal of Experimental Social Psychology, 38,* 368–382.

Sklar, A. Y., Levy, N., Goldstein, A., Mandel, R., Maril A., & Hassin, R. R. (2012). Reading and doing arithmetic nonconsciously. *Proceedings of the National Academy of Sciences.*

Suddendorf, T. (2006). Foresight and evolution of the human mind. *Science, 312,* 1006–1007.

Wicklund, R. A., & Gollwitzer, P. M. (1982). *Symbolic self-completion.* Hillsdale, NJ: Erlbaum.

Williams, L. E., Huang, J. Y., & Bargh, J. A. (2009). The scaffolded mind: Higher mental processes are grounded in early experience of the physical world. *European Journal of Social Psychology, 39,* 1257–1267.

Wohlwill, J. F. (1966). Perceptual learning. *Annual Review of Psychology, 17,* 201–232.

Young, P. T. (1961). *Motivation and emotion.* New York: Wiley.

Zeigarnik, B. (1938). On finished and unfinished tasks. In W. D. Ellis (Ed.), *A source book of gestalt psychology* (pp. 300–314). New York: Harcourt Brace & World. (Reprinted and condensed from *Psychologische Forschung, 9,* 1927, 1–85.)

The Social Cognition of the Self

Allen R. McConnell, Christina M. Brown, *and* Tonya M. Shoda

Abstract

This chapter examines the benefits and implications of studying the self from a social cognition perspective. First, it focuses on the representation of the self, reviewing classic issues such as whether the self-concept is qualitatively distinct in memory, the consequences of chronic self-knowledge, how self-concepts are produced and represented in memory, and how the self is composed of multiple, context-dependent self-aspects. Second, the chapter examines the self as an inherently social construct, discussing how individuals and groups become integrated into one's self-concept, how chronicity and self-complexity are represented, how stereotype threat is triggered and affects the self, and how loneliness and ostracism are experienced. Third, the chapter considers the self in broader contexts that include its role in guiding self-regulation and goal pursuit and its being influenced by contextual factors such as lay theories and culture. In addition to improving our understanding of the cognitive underpinnings of the self, consideration of the representation of self-knowledge allows us to better appreciate the social nature of the self-concept.

Key Words: self-concept, chronicity, self-complexity, stereotype threat, self-regulation

Introduction

The study of the self can be traced to antiquity, when as early as the 6th century B.C.E., the Temple of Apollo at Delphi instructed people to "Know thyself." Since then, consideration of the self has spanned numerous disciplines, ranging from religion to philosophy. Most recently, psychologists have become the vanguard of self-studies, with a variety of foci including classifying the self's characteristics (e.g., personality psychology), understanding dysfunctional facets of the self (e.g., clinical psychology), and examining how context fundamentally changes the meaning of the self (e.g., cultural psychology).

Social psychologists have shown how the self, often viewed as all that is unique to the individual, is inherently social. For example, research has shown that our closest relationships are integrated in our knowledge about ourselves (e.g., Aron, Aron, & Smollan, 1992).

Further, we typically view individuals who are members of our own social groups relatively favorably and exhibit greater negativity toward those who are not members of our own social groups (e.g., Tajfel & Turner, 1986). Moreover, frequently activated self-knowledge is often a prism through which our perceptions of others are filtered and biased (e.g., Markus, Smith, & Moreland, 1985). For example, people who view "honest" as their most central personal attribute will evaluate others' behaviors with respect to their implications for honest conduct. Indeed, the self is very much the hub of our social wheel, with many spokes emanating from it.

Although there have been many treatments of the self in social psychology (e.g., Baumeister, 1998; Sedikides & Spencer, 2007), our chapter focuses on the advances made by researchers who adopt the social cognition perspective. Whereas most psychologists emphasize the self's content (e.g., personality, self-esteem, development), social cognition researchers have demonstrated how a more complete understanding of the self requires a consideration of how its content is structured and represented in memory.

In this chapter, we focus on how social cognition sheds unique and important light on our knowledge of the self. First, we discuss the *cognitive underpinnings* of the self in memory, elaborating on the important implications derived from construing the self as a memorial structure. Second, we explore the *social facets* of the self that benefit from considering its cognitive representation. In other words, these first two sections examine the self from a social *cognitive* perspective and from a *social* cognitive perspective, with each section acknowledging that such distinctions represent an organizing heuristic and a reflection of the historical evolution of the field rather than a clear-cut dichotomy. Finally, we review broader and interconnecting phenomena, such as self-regulation, lay theories about the self, and culture.

The Social *Cognition* of the Self

We begin by describing research that documents the cognitive representation of the self in memory. This section focuses on how social cognition research has contributed to our understanding of age-old questions involving the self (e.g., Is there something unique about the self? How does the self filter our perceptions of the social world?). Because this research represented social cognition researchers' initial forays into understanding the self, this section provides a historical account of social cognition's contributions to self-concept research as well as a description of how the self is represented in memory.

Is the Self Special?

Probably the first time that social cognition began to shape research on the self involved the question of whether self-knowledge is unique or is qualitatively indistinguishable from other forms of knowledge (see Greenwald & Banaji, 1989; Kihlstrom & Klein, 1994). A number of studies of the self-reference effect suggested that the self may have special standing in memory. For example, Markus (1977) demonstrated that participants showed greater attention to, and better recall of, information that was consistent with their self-view. And similarly, Rogers, Kuiper, and Kirker (1977) showed that participants were more likely to remember a list of traits presented to them when they considered whether the traits were self-descriptive (e.g., Am I funny?) than when they processed the same

trait in other ways (e.g., What rhymes with funny?). This evidence of superior information processing for self-relevant material (e.g., greater attentional deployment, faster and more accurate recall) was initially construed as evidence that the self represented a special, unique memorial structure.

Subsequent demonstrations, however, questioned this "self is special" interpretation. For example, Bower and Gilligan (1979) adopted the same methodology as Rogers et al. but varied the type of target that participants considered when reading each trait word. Their participants considered whether each word was descriptive of themselves, of their mothers, or of a popular television news anchorperson at the time (Walter Cronkite). Although Bower and Gilligan observed better recall of the traits when participants considered themselves than when considering the news anchorperson, recall of the traits was identical for participants who considered themselves or considered their mothers. In other words, when participants thought of a person they knew very well (i.e., their mom), recall was as good as it is when considering another well-known individual—the self. From data such as these, views of the self shifted from being "special" to being "ordinary but powerful," with its detailed, highly elaborated memorial structure (more so for the self and for moms, less so for television news anchorpeople) aiding in encoding and retrieving information.

Research by Klein and colleagues has further supported the conclusion that information processing about the self benefits from the greater organization of self-knowledge. For example, Klein and Kihlstrom (1986) replicated self-reference effects shown in past work, observing that participants recalled more experimentally presented personality traits when asked to think about whether each word was descriptive of the self than when asked to consider other aspects of the words (e.g., is the trait word synonymous with another word?). More important, Klein and Kihlstrom found evidence of more elaborate organization in participants' recall when asked to consider each trait with respect to the self. Specifically, in the self-reference condition, they observed the greatest amount of *clustering* in recall, such as recalling a number of self-descriptive words and then recalling multiple words that were not self-descriptive, instead of recalling words in a random order. Further, when statistically controlling for the amount of recall clustering, the advantage for amount of recall of self-relevant information became nonsignificant (see also Klein & Loftus, 1988), which provided additional evidence that better recall of self-relevant information results from the enhanced organization of the self in memory. By importing cognitive psychology measures such as amount of recall, speed of judgment making, and clustering of recall, social cognition researchers began casting new light on core questions about the self.

Chronicity and Self-Schematic Knowledge

After studying the properties of the static representation of the self, social cognition researchers began to consider how self-knowledge might actively influence information processing. This work was informed by a number of sources, such as Bruner's (1957) early postulation that our perceptions are guided by currently accessible knowledge in memory. That is, any piece of information in memory can vary in its level of activation. Items with greater activation are more likely to be used in a variety of activities ranging from low-level visual perception to high-level judgment and decision making. Social cognition research on other topics has shown the consequences of activated (e.g., primed) knowledge to be pervasive, ranging from influencing the interpretation of ambiguous information (e.g., Srull & Wyer, 1980) to guiding complex behavior (e.g., Bargh, Chen, & Burrows, 1996). The consequences of activated knowledge can be long-lasting, such that repeatedly used knowledge becomes chronically accessible (e.g., Bargh, Bond, Lombardi, & Tota, 1986; Higgins, King, & Mavin, 1982), serving to direct cognition and behavior in the absence of recent activation (e.g., Bargh & Pratto, 1986).

Importantly, accessibility has particular relevance to self-knowledge. As described above, one of the features that makes the self so consequential in information recall is its elaborate representational structure. Further, self-relevant information is frequently encountered and processed, increasing its accessibility in memory (Bargh, 1982). When this elaborated knowledge becomes chronically accessible, it is often referred to as self-schematic knowledge (Markus, 1977). Self-schemas are organizing frameworks derived from personal experience and self-reflection, and they guide perception and action as a result of their heightened state of activation (Markus & Wurf, 1987). From the perspective of social cognition, one's most important personality qualities are one's most accessible traits (for similar reasoning predating social cognition, see Allport, 1937; Bruner, 1957; Kelly, 1955).

Early research on self-schemas established that accessible self-knowledge facilitates and guides information processing. For example, Markus (1977) demonstrated that people make self-judgments more quickly when these are relevant to a self-schema. Specifically, she identified participants as schematic for the concept of "independence" if they rated themselves as independent and considered this concept important. Next, all participants completed a timed self-judgment task in which they indicated whether various trait adjectives were self-descriptive. Relative to participants who were not schematic for independence, individuals schematic for independence were faster to indicate that independence-related adjectives, but not other adjectives, were self-descriptive. In a similar vein, Bargh (1982) demonstrated that self-schemas increase processing efficiency of relevant information. Specifically, people can perform a secondary task better when the concurrent primary task is self-schema relevant than when it is not, showing how the efficiency of self-schemas frees cognitive resources that can be devoted to other activities.

Although the content of self-schemas varies greatly (e.g., traits, age, gender, sexuality; Andersen & Cyranowski, 1994; Markus, 1977; Markus, Crane, Bernstein, & Siladi, 1982; Montepare & Clements, 2001), all self-schemas are assumed to be highly accessible in memory (e.g., Higgins et al., 1982). As with primes (e.g., Higgins, Rholes, & Jones, 1977), self-schemas guide interpretation of ambiguous information (e.g., Markus et al., 1985) even in the absence of recent activation. This "always-on" self-knowledge has important behavioral implications, ranging from clinical depression (Bradley & Mathews, 1983) to minority children's engagement with school (Oyserman, 2008). Later, we return to our discussion of chronic self-knowledge to explain how recent social cognition research finds that the influence of chronic self-knowledge is more circumscribed rather than being "always on."

Construction of Self-Concepts

Although self-reference effects and self-schemas focus on the influence of already-existing self-relevant knowledge, this work does not address how self-concepts are assembled and represented as self-relevant information is encountered. Although questions such as "how do perceivers process information when forming an impression of a person" had been tackled early on in the person memory and stereotype formation literatures (e.g., Hamilton & Gifford, 1976; McConnell, Sherman, & Hamilton, 1994, 1997; Srull, 1981; Srull & Wyer, 1989), similar questions went unasked in the self literature for a considerable period of time. In person memory experiments, researchers found that participants typically form *on-line* impressions of individuals, which means that perceivers actively reflect on the target's actions and render an impression of the person *while* they are encountering and processing the information (e.g., Hastie & Park, 1986; Srull, 1981). This active, effortful engagement with target-relevant information produces a variety of outcomes, including heavy reliance on early information about the target person (i.e., primacy effects in impression formation). Research has shown that these primacy effects occur because people assume that individual targets will exhibit a relatively strong degree of consistency in their behaviors, making the cognitive expenditure of actively forming an on-line impression a reasonable investment for understanding and predicting others' actions (Hamilton & Sherman, 1996). Yet, if a perceiver expects little consistency in the behavior of a target individual, there is little incentive to actively form an impression of the target because there is "no essence" of the person to deduce. Accordingly, when people expect little consistency in a target person's behavior (e.g., they are explicitly told the target person's personality is spontaneous and unpredictable), primacy effects are eliminated because the active on-line impression formation process is averted (McConnell et al., 1997).

To understand how self-concepts are *formed*, McConnell, Rydell, and Leibold (2002) applied the approaches used in person memory research to examine how self-knowledge is processed when one is developing an impression about one's own characteristics. Specifically, McConnell et al. (2002) gave participants bogus feedback about themselves by having them describe a series of inkblot images. After selecting a description for a particular image, the computer provided experimentally preplanned, noncontingent feedback to participants, such as suggesting that their response characterized an outgoing individual (e.g., "a person who chooses this response can enjoy an engaging conversation with another person"). All participants received the same amount of extraversion-consistent statements, but for some participants, they received this feedback early in the sequential presentation of the inkblots (i.e., 10 times in the first half of 24 inkblot judgments), whereas other participants received this feedback at the end of the sequential presentation of the inkblots (i.e., 10 times in the last half of 24 inkblot judgments). The remaining 14 items were unrelated to extraversion. Thus, if participants form online self-concepts, they should be especially influenced by the early feedback and report being more extraverted in the former condition than in the latter condition. Indeed,

this pattern of results was observed. In other studies, McConnell et al. eliminated these primacy effects for self-concept formation experimentally, such as by explicitly telling people that outgoingness is not a stable construct (thus reducing people's expectation of consistency for their own behaviors on this dimension). These effects could also be eliminated by denying participants the cognitive resources necessary to actively organize and integrate self-relevant feedback during the study by asking them to also keep a long string of numbers in memory (i.e., a demanding concurrent task).

This study represents the first time that the processes of self-concept *formation* were examined, and it documented that strong expectations of consistency for the self encourage the active formation of online self-concepts, but only when sufficient cognitive resources are available to process self-relevant information. Such highly elaborated representations for the self facilitate better recall (e.g., Bower & Gilligan, 1979; Rogers et al., 1977) and more efficient information processing about the self (e.g., Bargh, 1982; Markus, 1977). Later, we will elaborate on how meta-beliefs about the self such as implicit theories and cultural influences can further moderate these processes.

Early Models of Self-Concept Representation

The finding that self-concepts are often abstract evaluations formed online through effortful processes dovetails nicely with some descriptions of self-concept representation (e.g., Kihlstrom, Beer, & Klein, 2003; Kihlstrom & Klein, 1994). Specifically, Klein and colleagues proposed that self-knowledge becomes increasingly represented by traits, rather than by episodic events, as more self-relevant information is encountered (e.g., Klein, Loftus, Trafton, & Fuhrman, 1992; Klein, Sherman, & Loftus, 1996). Using a clever priming paradigm, these researchers found that judgments about the novel features of the self are made more quickly by first recalling a specific behavioral episode relevant to the judgment. When recall of an instance speeds up subsequent evaluations of the self along the same dimension, it suggests that at least new self-judgments are based on the retrieval of instances in memory. However, as one's experiences in a domain grow, Klein and colleagues find that self-judgments are no longer aided or facilitated by recalling specific exemplars.

Based on this work, Kihlstrom and Klein (1994) proposed a mixed-model self-concept representation account that suggests that initial self-knowledge is represented as a collection of exemplars but that the self-concept becomes more composed of traits (i.e., general knowledge abstracted from these specific episodes) as information accrues (Figure 24.1, *top panel*). It is important to note that the mixed model of self-knowledge was not the only possibility offered by researchers in the latter part of the 20th century (e.g., Cantor & Mischel, 1979; DeSteno & Salovey, 1997). For example, there have been suggestions that the self is organized around nested hierarchical structures (e.g., spouse within family within acquaintances; see Figure 24.1, *middle panel*) or by propositions stored in an associative network (see Figure 24.1, *bottom panel*; for overviews, see Kihlstrom & Cantor, 1984; Linville & Carlston, 1994). These approaches often reflected "the cognitive models of the day," borrowing heavily from hierarchical structures (Rosch, 1975), production systems (Anderson, 1974), and distinctions between declarative and procedural knowledge (Tulving, 1972). More recently, connectionist approaches have been used to describe the self. For example, the cognitive-affective

processing system theory (Mischel & Morf, 2003; Mischel & Shoda, 1995) posits that the self is represented by if–then situation–behavior relations captured by cognition–affect units in a connectionist framework. Although connectionist approaches have considerable appeal (e.g., neural plausibility), at present there are no findings regarding self-concept representation that require a connectionist account for their explanation (McConnell, 2011). More generally, with a few exceptions (e.g., Smith, Coats, & Walling, 1999; Trafimow, Triandis, & Goto, 1991), the mixed-model account has been the only proposal of self-concept representation to receive considerable testing and support from multiple experimental studies.

Multiple Selves
Early Perspectives

Although conceptions of the self have evolved considerably from a static structure to an online construction, and then to a mixed composition of

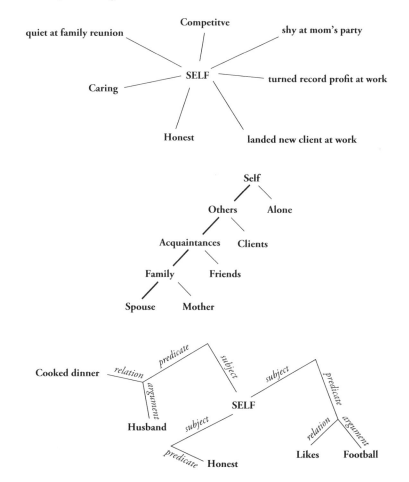

Figure 24.1 Examples of different approaches to self-concept representation, including mixed-model *(top panel)*, hierarchical *(middle panel)*, and propositional *(bottom panel)* accounts.

exemplars and abstracted traits, it is interesting that "the self" implies a single representation (cf., Kurzban & Aktipis, 2007; Spencer-Rodgers, Williams, & Peng, 2010). More recent work has considered the self-concept to be a collection of multiple, context-dependent selves (e.g., Linville & Carlston, 1994; McConnell, 2011; Mischel & Shoda, 1995).

Historically, several theorists have addressed the existence of multiple selves. Markus and Nurius (1986), for example, proposed that people have possible selves, representing different tenses and goals for the self, including "past selves," "future selves," and "feared selves." Other researchers have described the self as composed of a number of fixed roles (e.g., student, friend) and argued that well-being is enhanced by having greater consistency of trait attributes among these roles (e.g., Donahue, Robins, Roberts, & John, 1993; Roberts & Donahue, 1994). In the area of self-regulation, Higgins (1987, 1997) suggested that in addition to one's current self-concept, one has ought and ideal selves reflecting one's obligations and aspirations, respectively. Higgins's work states that when one's actual self is discrepant from one's ought and ideal selves, negative emotions are experienced, and these affective states serve to guide behavior. For example, a student failing to get good grades in her classes will feel agitation because of the discrepancy between her actual and ought selves, and this affective experience is proposed to motivate her to study better to reduce this discrepancy. But despite these myriad perspectives, none of these lines of work focused on the structure or organization of these multiple selves—just that they exist.

Self-Complexity

One exception to this characterization is research on self-complexity (for a review, see McConnell & Strain, 2007), which defines on the overall complexity of one's self-concept structure by taking into account the number of one's multiple, context-dependent selves (termed *self-aspects*) and the degree to which these self-aspects are composed of redundant *attributes*. In typical self-complexity studies, participants are provided with a list of trait attributes and are asked to put them into groups that represent "meaningful aspects of their lives" (Linville, 1985). Typically, participants are provided with a number of positive and negative trait attributes, and they are told they can use as many attributes as they wish and use any given attribute as many times as they want or not at all (Showers, 1992). Each self-aspect group is then labeled by the participant to describe the facet of the self that the collection of attributes describes. From these groupings, a statistic (H; Scott, 1969) is calculated. H increases as people generate more self-aspects and as their self-aspects are composed of unique, rather than redundant, attributes (for discussions of the strengths and weaknesses of various self-complexity indexes, see Koch & Shepperd, 2004; Rafaeli-Mor, Gotlib, & Revelle, 1999; Schleicher & McConnell, 2005).

For example, people greater in self-complexity (see Allison, Table 24.1) might identify several

Table 24.1 Examples of Individuals Greater (Allison) and Lower (Lori) in Self-Complexity

Allison

Athlete	Daughter	Sorority sister	Student	Latina
Competitive	Shy	Proud	Intelligent	Energetic
Energetic	Lovable	Insecure	Confident	Happy
Tense	Mature	Outgoing	Self-centered	Fun
Successful			Organized	

Lori

Daughter	Sorority sister	Student
Outgoing	Proud	Intelligent
Intelligent	Friendly	Confident
Confident	Outgoing	Outgoing
Friendly		Organized

self-aspects (i.e., athlete, daughter, sorority sister, student, Latina), each described by relatively unique self-relevant attributes (e.g., competitive, shy, proud). On the other hand, people who are lower in self-complexity (see Lori, Table 24.1) report having fewer self-aspects composed of more redundant attributes (e.g., Lori's "Daughter" self-aspect shares two attributes with her "Sorority sister" self-aspect and shares three attributes with her "Student" self-aspect). Thus, self-complexity captures self-concept organization instead of its content.[1]

When people are lower in self-complexity, self-relevant experiences have a greater emotional impact (termed the *spillover effect*) for several reasons. First, feedback about a self-aspect implicates a larger proportion of one's overall self-concept because it is composed of fewer self-aspects and will be more likely to implicate other self-aspects because of the greater redundancy of attributes across self-aspects (Linville, 1985). For example, failing an exam at school would have more negative implications for Lori (her "Student" self-aspect is 33% of her self-concept and shares attributes with her two other self-aspects) than for Allison (whose "Student" self-aspect is 20% of her self-concept and shares no attributes with other self-aspects). Second, it is more difficult for people lower in self-complexity to avoid thinking about negative self-relevant feedback, both because they have fewer alternative self-aspects to focus on in the wake of bad news and because it is more likely that alternative self-aspects share attributes with the "to be avoided" self, making mental regulation more difficult (Renaud & McConnell, 2002). However, it would be inappropriate to conclude that people lower in self-complexity fare worse than people greater in self-complexity because of their emotional extremity. In fact, the greater impact of self-relevant experiences can be quite beneficial following positive feedback. For example, people lower in self-complexity enjoy greater psychological and health benefits from positive social support and from possessing more desirable personality characteristics (McConnell, Strain, Brown, & Rydell, 2009). For these individuals, "good news" spills over onto other self-aspects and makes their positive circumstances and individual differences even more enjoyable.

It is interesting that although the spillover effect is well documented (e.g., Linville, 1985; McConnell, Rydell, & Brown, 2009; Niedenthal, Setterlund, & Wherry, 1992; Renaud & McConnell, 2002), arguments that greater self-complexity should buffer

stress have been more controversial. Linville (1987) reported evidence for a "buffering effect," contending that people experiencing stressful life events fare better when they are greater in self-complexity. Although intuitively appealing, this buffering effect has only been reported in one experiment, and there are numerous nonreplications published in the literature (e.g., McConnell et al., 2005; Schleicher & McConnell, 2005; Woolfolk, Novalany, Gara, Allen, & Polino, 1995) and in many unpublished studies as well (for a meta-analysis finding little support for the buffering hypothesis, see Rafaeli-Mor & Steinberg, 2002).

The lack of support for the buffering hypothesis has provided a puzzle for the self-complexity literature (see Koch & Shepperd, 2004; McConnell & Strain, 2007; Rafaeli-Mor & Steinberg, 2002), especially when demonstrations of spillover effects are commonly reported. One interesting observation is that, in general, people are happier and healthier when they are lower in self-complexity (McConnell, Strain, Brown, & Rydell, 2009). This finding makes sense because people typically view their lives in an extremely positive fashion (Taylor et al., 2003; Taylor & Sherman, 2008), which should be experienced more positively by people lower in self-complexity because of spillover effects. On the other hand, those greater in self-complexity have more "selves to juggle," and they report that their multiple selves, on average, are less positive and less under their personal control (McConnell et al., 2005). Perhaps in the face of stress, those lower in self-complexity do experience stronger negative reactions (i.e., spillover effects), but these same individuals also begin with advantages (i.e., in general, they are happier and have greater control over their multiple selves), and thus the two factors offset each other. At the very least, it is now apparent that buffering effects are far less frequent and more equivocal than once believed (Koch & Shepperd, 2004; Rafaeli-Mor & Steinberg, 2002; cf., Linville, 1987), suggesting that additional work is needed to better understand how the nature of self-concept representation affects physical and mental health. Based on the existent literature, it appears that "the simple life" has many benefits for those lower in self-complexity and that such individuals are happier and healthier on average (McConnell, Strain, Brown, & Rydell, 2009)

Beyond Self-Complexity

Although self-complexity research has shown that measures of the overall organizational structure of one's self-concept can predict general experiences, this body of work does not speak to "more local" effects. For example, self-complexity research may address how one's overall mood changes following self-relevant feedback, but it does not account for how feedback about a single self-aspect alters evaluations of other self-aspects. To address questions such as these, McConnell (2011) proposed the Multiple Self-aspects Framework (MSF). The MSF adopts the basic assumption of self-complexity research that the self is composed of multiple context-dependent self-aspects, each of which has associated attributes (see example in Figure 24.2). Unlike past self-complexity research that has focused on only trait attributes, the MSF assumes that numerous forms of self-knowledge comprise attributes, including physical attributes, social categories, affective responses, and behaviors (Carlston, 1994; Schleicher & McConnell, 2005). These self-aspects reside in an associative framework in which each self-aspect varies in its current level of activation. Overall affective experiences (e.g., mood, self-esteem) are based on the evaluation of each self-aspect weighted by its level of activation in memory. For example, when Anne leaves her husband in the morning and goes to work, her behavior should become less caring and more intense and creative because her "Company CEO" self-aspect should become more activated than her "Wife" self-aspect. Once at work, her general mood and sense of self-worth will reflect the evaluative implications primarily derived from her business identity instead of her spousal role.

In addition to accounting for the impact of shifts in context more globally, the MSF considers how the interconnections among self-aspects have more "local effects." For example, landing an important business contract at work will not influence

evaluations of any of Anne's other multiple selves because her "Company CEO" self-aspect does not share any attribute associations with her other self-aspects. On the other hand, having Anne's father remark that she is a good daughter not only will raise her evaluation of her "Daughter" self-aspect but also will increase the positivity of her "Wife" self-aspect because 75% of its attributes are associated with the targeted "Daughter" self-aspect. Thus, the particular associative structure as outlined by the MSF will reveal important consequences through spread of activation principles, which have been borne out by empirical work (McConnell, Rydell, & Brown, 2009). For example, the extent to which feedback, positive or negative, about a self-aspect changes evaluations of other self-aspects is statistically mediated by the proportion of shared attribute associations among those self-aspects. Thus, the depiction of self-concept organization provided by the MSF allows for precise, more localized predictions about how self-relevant feedback is experienced across one's multiple selves (McConnell, 2011). Predictions such as these are not possible using perspectives that only consider the organization of one's self-concept as a whole (e.g., self-complexity).

Other implications are suggested as well. Recall our earlier discussion about chronically accessible constructs (e.g., Higgins et al., 1982), which result from self-knowledge being activated so frequently that it becomes "always on," consequently shaping perceptions of the self and others. If we return to our example of Anne, it is likely that she would be most chronic for "honest" given that this trait is associated with most of her self-aspects. Classic work on chronicity or self-schematicity would assume that "honest" would always be accessible, constantly guiding Anne's behavior (Higgins, 1996). However, from the perspective of the MSF, only attributes

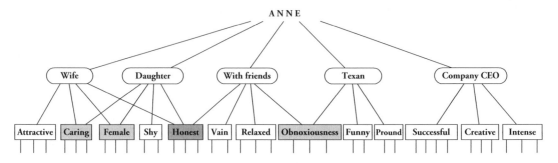

Figure 24.2 Example of an individual's self-concept as represented in the Multiple Self-aspects Framework, including self-aspects *(ovals)*, their associated attributes *(rectangles)*, and attribute-relevant behaviors *(vertical lines)*. *Gray boxes* reflect those attributes associated with multiple self-aspects.

associated with an activated self-aspect should guide perceptions. Thus, although honesty may be important in many domains of Anne's life, it may not influence her business behavior. Indeed, work by Brown and McConnell (2009b) derived from the MSF found that chronic self-knowledge as assessed by traditional measures (e.g., Higgins et al., 1982; Markus, 1977) is actually self-aspect specific. That is, when a self-aspect associated with participants' chronic attributes was primed by a 10-minute writing exercise about that domain, participants' judgments of themselves and of others were assimilated toward their chronic attributes, replicating past work (e.g., Markus, 1977; Markus et al., 1985). However, when participants wrote about a self-aspect not associated with their chronic attribute, judgments of the self and of others were not assimilated toward the chronic attribute. In other words, chronicity depends on the individual's active self-aspects and is not always global in its impact.

The *Social* Cognition of the Self

Having examined how social cognition researchers study the organization of self-knowledge in memory, we now turn to how social life influences the representation of one's self-concept. Specifically, we examine the inclusion of meaningful others (e.g., loved ones, ingroups) into the self and the behavioral consequences of such included identities (e.g., mimicry, stereotype threat). Afterward, we focus on issues such as disidentification, loneliness, and ostracism to consider how the self-concept is affected. Whereas the first section of our chapter provided a trek across the history of social cognition's exploration of the nature of the self-concept, the current section demonstrates how self-concept representation is central to some of the more recent and exciting developments in social psychology more broadly.

Inclusion of Others in the Self
Individuals

It is interesting that although people are free to focus exclusively on themselves when describing their self-concepts, they frequently discuss others. For example, McConnell (2011) found that when people were asked to spontaneously describe their self-aspects, 17% of their reported self-aspects reflected important interpersonal relationships (e.g., with my boyfriend). The closeness of others is revealed in common, everyday metaphors, when we speak of friends as "having a connection," new lovers as "really being into each other," and family

members as "being close," indicating that proximity and integration are consequential psychological qualities (Lakoff & Johnson, 1980). To capture this closeness more quantitatively, researchers ask participants to report how included another person is in the self by indicating which of seven diagrams (each featuring two circles with increasing degrees of overlap, one representing the self and one representing the other; Aron et al., 1992) best characterizes the relationship. Considerable evidence shows that others who are included in the self affect self-relevant judgments. For example, people are faster to judge the self-descriptiveness of traits when those traits are descriptive of their spouse, who presumably is highly included in the self, than when they were not descriptive of their spouse (Aron, Aron, Tudor, & Nelson, 1991). Indeed, highly included others are often represented as self-aspects in one's own self-concept descriptions (McConnell, 2011), suggesting that key people such as spouses, family members, friends, and lovers are integrated into one's self-representation. Returning to the example of Anne (see Figure 24.2), it is likely that her husband started out as a friend and thus her behavior toward him was initially governed by her "With friends" self-aspect, but that his growing importance in her life led to the development of a self-aspect uniquely associated with him. Relatedly, the dissolution of relationships can have an impact on one's self-concept. For example, Slotter, Gardner, and Finkel (2010) found that following romantic breakups, participants reported reduced self-concept clarity (e.g., "I have a clear sense of who I am and what I am"), which statistically accounted for the increase in emotional distress experienced by their participants following their breakups.

Similarly, work on relational selves (i.e., self-identities associated with significant others; see Andersen, Chen, & Miranda, 2002) shows that often people's perceptions of themselves and close others can become blurred, resulting in transference effects whereby one perceives close other's qualities in themselves (Hinkley & Andersen, 1996; see also, Gabriel, Carvallo, Dean, Tippin, & Renaud, 2005; Smith et al., 1999). In addition to seeing shifts in content that draw from highly included others, research suggests that *structural* shifts can occur for close others as well. For example, Brown, Young, and McConnell (2009) found that as people are more included in the self, the structural complexity of people's representations of others becomes more similar to the complexity of their own self-concept (i.e., self-complexity). In other words, being "included in the self" is related to "structural alignment" in self–other representations, which may facilitate the cognitive integration of close others with the self.

The inclusion of close others in the self-concept may have interesting consequences beyond transference effects with traits (e.g., Andersen & Chen, 2002; Smith et al., 1999). As noted previously, perspectives such as the MSF assume that self-aspects are not only composed of traits but also include emotions, physical appearances, and behaviors (Carlston, 1994). For instance, when Anne's husband becomes included in her self-concept, his qualities (e.g., his attitudes, physical mannerisms) will be included in her self-concept as well. Thus, when she interacts with him around the house, the activation of her "Wife" self-aspect may result in her exhibiting behavioral mimicry. Mimicry research has shown that people often reveal behavioral similarities to those around them, such as mirroring others' body posture or speaking in similar vocal accents. Research shows that this mimicry often reflects mutual affinity between people, and that this mirrored behavior serves to coordinate actions with others (e.g., Bargh & Chartrand, 1999; Bavelas, Black, Lemery, & Mullett, 1986; Cheng & Chartrand, 2003). Interestingly, mimicry effects are often context dependent (e.g., van Baaren, Horgan, Chartrand, & Dijkmans, 2004). When considered from the perspective of the MSF, this context dependence may reflect the integration of others' mannerisms into one's self-aspects to the extent that context activates a domain-specific self-aspect. Thus, being on a date may activate Anne's "Wife" self-aspect, which in turn elicits mimicking behaviors and beliefs derived from her husband. However, other contexts unassociated with this self-aspect would result in these husband-derived attributes not being activated. As a result, including others in the self should promote a convergence of traits, emotions, and behaviors with meaningful others.

Groups

In addition to close people being integrated into one's self-concept, important social groups may become incorporated into the self as well (Correll & Park, 2005). Returning to the example of Anne, her being a Texan is so important to her sense of self that this social group has its own representation in her self-concept. The attributes associated with these group-specific identities should elicit not only group-relevant traits (e.g., funny) and behaviors (e.g., obnoxiousness) but also group-relevant emotions

(e.g., pride; Smith, Seger, & Mackie, 2007). When ingroups are represented in the self-concept, we should see effects similar to those obtained when close others are included in the self-concept (e.g., transference effects, mimicry). For instance, Smith et al. (1999) found that participants were faster in judging whether traits were characteristic of ingroup members when they were self-descriptive than when they were not self-descriptive, indicative of overlap between one's ingroups and the self in memory (see also, Smith & Henry, 1996). With respect to behavioral consequences, one's important group-based identities (e.g., attorney at a prestigious law firm) can lead people to exhibit behaviors and display symbols associated with their self-aspects (e.g., always carry a legal pad), encouraging those around them to act in ways that reinforce the attributes associated with their self-aspects (Wicklund & Gollwitzer, 1982).

Stereotype Threat
Triggers and Inhibitors

Sometimes groups integrated into one's self-concept can have negative implications. For example, stereotype threat research investigates how people's membership in stigmatized groups leads to suboptimal performance in contexts in which negative group stereotypes exist. That is, just having knowledge of a negative stereotype associated with one's own social group can have deleterious consequences for academic achievement (e.g., Steele & Aronson, 1995), social interactions (e.g., Richeson & Shelton, 2003), and even athletic performance (e.g., Beilock, Jellison, Rydell, McConnell, & Carr, 2006). Women, for example, underperform on challenging math problems because of an association between their ingroup and pejorative stereotypes that "women are poor at math," with poorer performance revealed for women whose gender identity is more central to the self (Schmader, 2002).

In essence, stereotype threat is a self-fulfilling prophecy that is triggered by "the self" rather than by others' expectations. Thus, we would contend that the accessibility of one's group identity is at the heart of understanding stereotype threat effects. For instance, although women's performance on math tests falters to a greater extent when their gender identity is more central to the self-concept, the view that the self is composed of *multiple* self-aspects suggests a remedy for those facing stereotype threat. Indeed, any individual can be categorized based on multiple identities (e.g., Macrae, Bodenhausen, & Milne, 1995), and often the activation of one particular identity (e.g., one's student self-aspect) will inhibit a competing self-aspect (e.g., one's sorority sister self-aspect; see Hugenberg & Bodenhausen, 2004). Thus, redirecting a woman's self-categorization away from her gender toward another self-aspect, such as her student self-aspect, might eliminate stereotype threat effects because her behavior would be directed by a self-aspect unassociated with the stereotype. In other words, similar to the aforementioned finding that "chronic attributes" are rendered inert when an unrelated self-aspect is accessible (Brown & McConnell, 2009b), activating a self-identity unrelated to the stereotyped domain may neutralize stereotype threat effects. Consistent with this logic, simply having female undergraduates report their education level activated their student self-aspect (an identity associated with math skill) and inhibited their gender self-aspect, eliminating the math performance decrements typically observed under stereotype threat (Rydell, McConnell, & Beilock, 2009). Similarly, work by Shih, Pittinsky, and Ambady (1999) with Asian American women found that activating their participants' racial identities led to better math performance whereas activating their gender identities led to poorer performance. In sum, because the self-concept is composed of multiple selves, whether stereotype threat impairment is realized will depend on which self-aspect is most accessible in memory and thus serves to guide behavior.

Disidentification

Steele (1997) proposed that many women and African American students respond to prolonged stereotype threat in the classroom with *disidentification*, defined as removing one's academic domain from one's self-concept. In other words, people who face repeated episodes of stereotype threat might eliminate their student self-aspect from their self-concepts. In many ways, stereotype threat represents a classic situation of cognitive imbalance involving inconsistent propositional links among the self, one's ingroup identity, and the domain in question (Greenwald et al., 2002; Heider, 1958; Major & O'Brien, 2005). For example, a woman might have a positive association with her group (woman) and a desire to excel in a domain (math), yet the existence of a negative association between the group and domain (i.e., women are not good at math) creates cognitive imbalance. When facing such an imbalance, the most likely response is to disidentify with the domain. Indeed, this account is

the basis of a model of stereotype threat effects put forth by Schmader, Johns, and Forbes (2008).

Although eliminating a domain-relevant self-aspect from one's self-concept may eliminate cognitive dissonance, it greatly reduces the likelihood that one will ever develop competence in the domain (see Rydell, Rydell, & Boucher, 2010). Importantly, the nature of self-concept representation may have real implications for how disidentification occurs. First, one would expect that people lower in self-complexity will experience stronger stereotype threat effects because the organization of their self-concept will amplify the negative affect experienced. This reasoning is supported by work showing that people under stereotype threat experience greater stress (Murphy, Steele, & Gross, 2007) and have difficulty vanquishing worries about reifying the negative stereotype from their mind (Beilock, Rydell, & McConnell, 2007). Second, the nature of how the self-concept is organized in memory should dictate how easily one can disidentify (i.e., eliminate the relevant self-aspect). For example, when self-aspects are more intertwined by shared associative links, it may prove more difficult to eliminate a stereotype-relevant self-aspect because of the shared associations. Thus, the nature of one's self-concept organization should modulate the experiences that make disidentification more attractive (e.g., those lower in self-complexity should experience stronger reactions to stereotype threat situations and find it more difficult to regulate ruminations that further impair performance) and should also influence how readily one can disidentify in the first place.

Loneliness and Ostracism

Sometimes, people may lose a self-aspect not through self-initiated means (e.g., disidentification) but because of social circumstances. Perceived social isolation (i.e., loneliness; Cacioppo & Patrick, 2008) and being ignored and excluded by others (i.e., ostracism; Williams, 2007) have profound negative consequences. For example, loneliness entails a lack of social support that impairs psychological and physiological functioning and increases mortality rates (Harter, 2003; House, Landis, & Umberson, 1988; Uchino, Cacioppo, & Kiecolt-Glaser, 1996). Similarly, being ostracized, even when it is known to be unintentional, produces physiological responses akin to the experience of physical pain (Lieberman, 2007).

When considering the implications of self-concept representation, people lower in self-complexity should experience loneliness and ostracism more strongly. Because people lower in self-complexity experience stronger affective reactions and ruminations (e.g., Linville, 1985; Renaud & McConnell, 2002), the sting of social isolation should be more poignant for them. Indeed, people with poorer social support have more negative well-being (e.g., more depression, lower self-esteem, greater physical illnesses) when they are lower in self-complexity (McConnell, Strain, Brown, & Rydell, 2009). Yet, there may be additional reasons that the specific structure of one's self-concept matters when facing social isolation. Returning to the example of Anne (see Figure 24.2), being isolated by her family or by her friends should be much more aversive than being isolated at work because her "Daughter" and "With friends" self-aspects are more intertwined with other self-aspects, whereas her "Company CEO" self-aspect is relatively freestanding. Thus, even within an individual, social isolation should have different effects based on the idiosyncratic structure of one's self-concept in memory and the self-aspects implicated.

The Self in Broader Contexts

In this final section, we focus on broader issues that have implications for both the cognitive structure and the social forces that influence self-concept representation. Phenomena such as self-regulation, meta-beliefs about the self, and the influence of culture are discussed.

Self-Regulation

Sedikides and Skowronski (1997) propose that the self evolved in part to set goals, perform behaviors to pursue those goals, evaluate whether the goals have been met, and associate the outcomes of goal-directed behavior with adaptive feelings (e.g., pride to reinforce successful goal-directed behavior, shame to punish unsuccessful efforts). In other words, self-representation creates the ability to regulate one's behavior. Prominent theories of self-regulation echo the idea that goals are represented within the self-concept and that these representations are necessary for goal pursuit (e.g., Higgins, 1987; Markus & Nurius, 1986). We now outline theory and research on self-regulation, highlighting the essential role of the self-concept throughout.

SELF-AWARENESS AND SELF-REGULATORY GOALS

An important feature of the self-concept is that it includes goal representations of how one could be

or how one wants to be (e.g., Carver, 2001, 2003; Higgins, 1987). Examination of the self-aspects people spontaneously generate reveals that 5% are related to goals (e.g., "who I ought to be," "my future self"; McConnell, 2011). Consistent with this finding, Markus and Nurius (1986) proposed that people have possible selves, which are cognitive representations of the individual's enduring goals that serve both as standards of comparison with one's current self and as the incentive for changing the self. For example, a possible self of "me retiring with financial security" serves as both the referent toward which the current self is compared and the incentive to engage in self-regulation. Possible selves can also be undesired or feared selves, with the aim of self-regulation being to increase the gap between one's current and feared selves.

Another way to classify goals is to think about those that are more approach oriented and those that are more avoidance oriented. Along these lines, Higgins (1987) proposed two types of self-guides: the *ideal self* and the *ought self.* One's ideal selves are self-representations that reflect one's hopes and aspirations, whereas one's ought selves are self-representations that comprise one's obligations and responsibilities. Inconsistencies between one's actual (i.e., current) self and a goal self trigger specific negative emotions (Higgins, 1997), and as goal selves become more accessible in memory, the negative emotions experienced in the face of self-discrepancies increase (Strauman & Higgins, 1987).

In fact, according to objective self-awareness theory (OSA; Duval & Wicklund, 1972), these negative emotions play a central role in instigating self-regulation. Specifically, OSA theory proposes that self-regulation can only occur under conditions of objective self-awareness, which is when the self is the object of one's attention. The theory further states that people are compelled to evaluate themselves whenever their attention is focused inward and that such self-evaluation inevitably involves comparing oneself to a standard, such as a goal self. If a discrepancy between oneself and a standard is detected, the individual is said to experience negative emotions that motivate self-regulation. For example, one may possess a goal of getting into better physical shape by lifting weights at a gym. Objective self-awareness theory would posit that the likelihood of meeting such a goal would be increased by augmenting one's attention to current behavior, such as lifting weights in front of a mirror. Should one not complete a workout routine, the mirror would increase one's awareness that the current behavior is short of the goal, producing negative affect that, in turn, motivates self-regulatory action (e.g., lifting for an extra period of time to make up for the shortfall). Consistent with this proposal, a number of studies have found that self-discrepancies only lead to self-regulation under conditions of heightened self-awareness (e.g., Carver & Humphries, 1981; Duval & Lalwani, 1999; Duval & Wicklund, 1972).

More recently, researchers have identified other means of activating goals without self-awareness. When goals become associated with situational cues that co-occur with those goals, the presence of those cues can activate the goal and trigger self-regulation (e.g., Fitzsimons & Bargh, 2004). For example, automatic goal activation has been found for a variety of goals including impression formation (e.g., Chartrand & Bargh, 2002), anger management (e.g., Mauss, Cook, & Gross, 2007), and achievement (e.g., Bargh, Gollwitzer, Lee-Chai, Barndollar, & Trotschel, 2001). Presumably, these goals must exist in memory at a sufficient state of activation for automatic goal pursuit to be possible. If strong enough cue–response associations exist in memory (Fitzsimons & Bargh, 2004; Mischel & Shoda, 1995), a cue alone may be sufficient to trigger self-regulatory behaviors without any conscious awareness required. On the other hand, heightened self-awareness should also increase the accessibility of goals and may do so at a conscious level. Because people possess multiple possible selves and these goal self-aspects must be sufficiently accessible to activate goal pursuit (through nonconscious priming, conscious direction, or combinations of both), the central role of the self-concept in self-regulation is once again underscored (Sedikides & Skowronski, 1997).

Given the hypothesized importance of discrepancies between current and goal selves, it is surprising that there is little research on how these discrepancies directly affect self-regulatory behavior. There is a great deal of research on the emotions these discrepancies evoke (e.g., Higgins, Bond, Klein, & Strauman, 1986; Phillips & Silvia, 2005; Strauman & Higgins, 1987), but the hypothesized sequence between discrepancies, emotions, and behavior has been relatively ignored (see Brown & McConnell, 2011). Instead, there has been profitable research on how cognitive factors, such as expectations and attributions about the self, predict self-regulatory behavior. For example, Carver, Blaney, and Scheier (1979) found that expectations about the outcome of self-regulation efforts determine whether people persist or withdraw from self-regulation. Specifically, they found that participants experiencing a self-discrepancy who were highly self-aware (and thus had highly accessible goals) exerted effort to reduce the discrepancy when they expected to be successful in reaching their goals, but they reduced effort when they believed they would be unable reach their goals. Similarly, Duval and Lalwani (1999) observed that persistence in self-regulation depends on the attributions made for a self-discrepancy. When highly self-aware participants were faced with a self-discrepancy, they self-regulated (i.e., attempted to move toward their goal self) only when they attributed the discrepancy to their own insufficiencies. In contrast, they did not try to change when they attributed the discrepancy to an unreasonably high standard. These studies illustrate that self-cognitions (e.g., attributions) are important predictors of self-regulation, although further research is needed to integrate these findings into the hypothesized sequence of self-regulation, from goal representations in the self-concept to goal pursuit.

PURSUING GOALS AND EVALUATING PROGRESS

As explained above, a goal self must be accessible and discrepant from one's current self for self-regulation to occur. According to Carver and Scheier (1998), self-regulation operates within a cybernetic feedback loop. A feedback loop consists of comparisons between one's current self and a referent, such as a possible or goal self. If a discrepancy between the current self and a referent exists, self-regulation will occur. If there is no discrepancy, the individual will instead "coast." Unlike self-regulation, which aims to reduce the discrepancy between the current self and the referent, coasting is a relaxation of one's goal-related behavior (which was apparently already successful) so that resources and attention can be redirected toward other unmet goals.

This process is called a "discrepancy-reducing loop" (Carver, 2001), which involves pursuing goals by reducing a discrepancy between one's current and desired (referent) states. However, sometimes goal-directed behavior takes the form of avoiding an undesired state (e.g., feared possible selves; Markus & Nurius, 1986). The cybernetic model proposes that this form of goal-directed behavior is controlled by a second type of feedback loop, which is called a "discrepancy-enlarging loop." In this case, the referent is the feared state, and the person self-regulates by increasing a discrepancy that is too small. For example, a woman who is afraid of becoming obese will have a feedback loop in which "obese self" is her referent. When the discrepancy between her current weight and her definition of obesity is small, she will self-regulate by trying to lose weight in order to enlarge the discrepancy between her current state and her "obese self." Recently, these discrepancy-reducing and discrepancy-enlarging loops have been associated with two general motivational systems, the behavioral activation system and behavioral inhibition system, respectively (Carver, 2003).

To summarize, similar to the models described previously (e.g., Duval & Wicklund, 1972; Higgins, 1987; Markus & Nurius, 1986), the cybernetic model assumes that self-regulation occurs following the awareness of a discrepancy between current and goal selves. Moreover, these models all predict that the discrepancy elicits negative emotions before self-regulation. However, only the cybernetic model seeks to explain how people track their progress once self-regulation begins. Specifically, it proposes that an individual's rate of discrepancy reduction or discrepancy enlargement elicits affect, with desired rates of progress (e.g., quickly reducing a discrepancy) eliciting positive affect and undesired rates evoking negative affect. Indeed, the rate at which an individual is reducing a discrepancy has been found to predict the intensity and valence of affect (e.g., Hsee & Abelson, 1991; Lawrence, Carver, & Scheier, 2002). Importantly, the hypothesized function of this affect is to inform the individual of goal progress so that self-regulation efforts can be increased, decreased, or maintained as appropriate.

This process of evaluating one's goal progress is an essential part of goal pursuit. Self-regulation is an effortful behavior drawing from a limited resource (Schmeichel & Baumeister, 2004), and thus people who engage in self-regulation must be able to determine when to halt self-regulatory efforts, either because these have been successful and thus are no longer necessary or because they have been futile and no more effort need be wasted. Unfortunately, the importance of recognizing when to withdraw effort and terminate self-regulation is often understated. People need to disengage from unattainable goals because pursuing such goals predicts lower well-being (Wrosch, Scheier, Miller, Schulz, & Carver, 2003) and poorer health (Wrosch, Miller, Scheier, & de Pontet, 2007), and it depletes resources necessary to pursue other goals (Schmeichel & Baumeister, 2004). Additional

research is needed to better understand when people recognize the futility of self-regulation and factors that facilitate disengagement from unattainable goals (e.g., Carrol, Shepperd, & Arkin, 2009; Wrosch & Miller, 2009).

Recent advances in self-regulation research reveal that not everyone self-regulates in the same way and that self-concept representation underlies these differences. Because affect is hypothesized to have a central role in the initiation of self-regulation (e.g., Carver, 2001, 2003; Duval & Wicklund, 1972; but see Brown & McConnell, 2011) and the complexity of one's self-concept modulates the experience of affect (e.g., Linville, 1985), it seems likely that one's level of self-complexity should moderate the relation between affect and self-regulation. Consistent with this reasoning, Brown and McConnell (2009a) found that among people lower in self-complexity who believed a goal was attainable because they were told that practice would improve performance on a test of verbal ability, self-regulation efforts were greater (i.e., people practiced harder) when the negative affect produced by a self-discrepancy was more intense. Interestingly, affect was unrelated to self-regulation among people with greater self-complexity. These individuals have a relatively stable emotional life and thus do not seem to refer to their affect during self-regulation. Thus, self-regulation is influenced not only by one's self-representation (e.g., goal selves) but also by the effects of this representation on the intensity of one's emotions and whether one defers to these emotions.

Lay Theories about the Self

Another important consideration in how self-concept representation plays a meaningful role is the lay theories people hold about the self. For example, work by Dweck (1999) on self theories shows that people's lay theories about the nature of personality vary. Specifically, some people adopt a more *incremental theory*, whereby they view personality as dynamic, flexible, and changeable, whereas others hold a stronger *entity theory*, whereby they view personality as fixed, rigid, and unchangeable. These theories influence a number of phenomena about the self. For example, self-regulatory failures are interpreted and experienced differently based on one's self theory (Dweck, 1999; Molden & Dweck, 2006; Renaud & McConnell, 2007). Failure for entity theorists is much more damning because such people believe that not achieving a goal reflects an absence of a quality that cannot be developed or learned. For example, poor performance on a college entrance exam for an individual who believes that intelligence is a fixed quality will be very dismaying because such a person will believe that failure is an unchangeable fate. On the other hand, a similar failure by one who holds an incremental theory might induce that person to study and prepare harder for a second administration of the exam.

The implications of lay theories extend beyond self-regulatory processes. For example, stereotype threat is more debilitating for entity theorists and less problematic for incremental theorists who can adopt the perspective that improvement is possible despite prevailing pejorative stereotypes about one's own group identity (Aronson, Fried, & Good, 2002). Indeed, in the classroom, holding an incremental theory helps students adopt a mastery orientation in which setbacks are viewed as challenges that can be overcome rather than indicators of one's own helpless state (Robins & Pals, 2002). At an even more basic level, one's implicit theories affect how information processing occurs. For example, McConnell (2001) found that entity theorists are more likely to form on-line impressions because the assumption that a person has an unchangeable essence encourages perceivers to form a rigid first impression of the person (i.e., subsequent information will not be useful because people do not change). When applied to the work of McConnell et al. (2002), this finding suggests that it is likely that entity theorists are more likely to form on-line self-concepts than incremental theorists. Thus, entity theorists should rely on early information to develop a relatively fast on-line impression of themselves, whereas incremental theorists may continue to update their self-evaluations as additional feedback comes to light.

Cultural Contexts

Finally, we would submit that any understanding of the self should always be grounded in the context of cultural influences. For example, a number of scholars have emphasized the role of culture in understanding the self, with much of this work proposing that people in individual-centered cultures view the self as an entity that is more unchanging and situationally invariant, whereas people in collectivist-centered cultures assume a more flexible and contextually determined self (e.g., Fiske, Kitayama, Markus, & Nisbett, 1998; Markus & Kitayama, 1991; Triandis, 1989). That is, it has been argued that in independent cultures such as North America and Western Europe, the self is perceived as more separate from social context, unitary,

and consistent in nature, in comparison to a more interdependent, connected self in more collectivistic cultures such as those in Asia.

We would contend that although meaningful cultural differences exist, such distinctions are not so clear-cut. For instance, the notion of multiple selves highlighted in much of our chapter advocates for a definition of the self that is not unitary. Even in the United States (arguably one of the most independent cultures), McConnell (2011) found that participants on average report 4.23 self-aspects, with only 3% of participants reporting only a single self. This suggests that the notion of "a single self" in Western cultures is too simplistic, and that there will be individual differences in the extent to which people adopt individualist or collectivist self-construals (Brewer & Gardner, 1989; Singelis, 1994; Triandis, 1989). Our perspective is that self-concepts are probably composed of a greater number of role and relationships self-aspects for individuals whose culture and individual differences are more interdependent and collectivist in nature. Along these lines, McConnell (2011) found that women have a greater proportion of relationship self-aspects than men, reflecting gender differences in relationship orientation (e.g., Cross & Madson, 1997), especially for close dyadic relationships (Gabriel & Gardner, 1999).

Conclusion

In our chapter, we outlined some of the benefits of studying the self from a social cognitive perspective. Early work in this area focused on improving our understanding of the cognitive underpinnings of the self-concept, addressing questions ranging from, "Is the self unique?" to "Why does bad news trigger great angst for some people but roll off the backs of others?" As this work progressed, our knowledge of how self-relevant information is processed, stored, and retrieved in memory grew considerably. With this strong foundation of knowledge in place, our understanding of the self has been applied to some of the most important social issues of the day, ranging from what conditions leave people more susceptible to depression and illness to when pejorative stereotypes will result in self-inflicted performance deficits. These two themes (i.e., the cognitive representation of the self and how the self mediates important social phenomena) are complementary, and they are tied together by a number of broader phenomena, such as self-regulation, lay theories about the self, and the influence of culture. Overall, this work affirms the centrality of the self in key social phenomena, and our understanding of its role is grounded in a framework that explains how the self-concept is represented in memory. In summary, the social cognitive perspective continues to address critical questions, both age-old and cutting-edge, involving the prominence of the self in everyday life.

Author Note

This work was supported by the Lewis Endowed Professorship. Correspondence to Allen R. McConnell, Department of Psychology, Miami University, Oxford, OH 45056; e-mail: allen.mcconnell@miamioh.edu.

Notes

1. One line of work with similarities to self-complexity is research on compartmentalization of the self (e.g., Showers, 1992). Compartmentalization uses measures similar to self-complexity (e.g., people report their self-aspects and trait attributes), but this line of work examines the implications of whether one's self-aspects are composed of mostly positive attributes, mostly negative attributes, or a mixture of positive and negative attributes. Because this work places a greater emphasis on self-concept content (i.e., valence of attributes) than on structure, we do not highlight it in our chapter (but for an excellent review, see Showers & Zeigler-Hill, 2003).

References

Allport, G. W. (1937). *Personality: A psychological interpretation.* New York: Holt, Rinehart, & Winston.

Andersen, B. L., & Cyranowski, J. M. (1994). Women's sexual self-schema. *Journal of Personality and Social Psychology, 67,* 1079–1100.

Andersen, S. M., & Chen, S. (2002). The relational self: An interpersonal social-cognitive theory. *Psychological Review, 109,* 619–645.

Andersen, S. M., Chen, S., & Miranda, R. (2002). Significant others and the self. *Self and Identity, 1,* 159–168.

Anderson, J. R. (1974). Retrieval of propositional information from long-term memory. *Cognitive Psychology, 6,* 451–474.

Aron, A., Aron, E. N., & Smollan, D. (1992). Inclusion of Other in the Self Scale and the structure of interpersonal closeness. *Journal of Personality and Social Psychology, 63,* 596–612.

Aron, A., Aron, E. N., Tudor, M., & Nelson, G. (1991). Close relationships as including other in the self. *Journal of Personality and Social Psychology, 60,* 241–253.

Aronson, J., Fried, C., & Good, C. (2002). Reducing the effects of stereotype threat on African American college students by shaping theories of intelligence. *Journal of Experimental Social Psychology, 38,* 113–125.

Bargh, J. A. (1982). Attention and automaticity in the processing of self-relevant information. *Journal of Personality and Social Psychology, 43,* 425–436.

Bargh, J. A., Bond, R. N., Lombardi, W. J., & Tota, M. E. (1986). The additive nature of chronic and temporary sources of construct accessibility. *Journal of Personality and Social Psychology, 50,* 869–878.

Bargh, J. A., & Chartrand, T. L. (1999). The unbearable automaticity of being. *American Psychologist, 54,* 462–479.

Bargh, J. A., Chen, M., & Burrows, L. (1996). Automaticity of social behavior: Direct effects of trait construct and stereotype activation on action. *Journal of Personality and Social Psychology, 71,* 230–244.

Bargh, J. A., Gollwitzer, P. M., Lee-Chai, A., Barndollar, K., & Trotschel, R. (2001). The automated will: Nonconscious activation and pursuit of behavioral goals. *Journal of Personality and Social Psychology, 81,* 1014–1027.

Bargh, J. A., & Pratto, F. (1986). Individual construct accessibility and perceptual selection. *Journal of Experimental Social Psychology, 22,* 293–311.

Baumeister, R. F. (1998). The self. In D. T. Gilbert, S. T., Fiske, & G. Lindzey (Eds.), *Handbook of social psychology* (4th ed., Vol. 1, pp. 680–740). New York: McGraw-Hill.

Bavelas, J. B., Black, A., Lemery, C. R., & Mullett, J. (1986). "I show how you feel": Motor mimicry as a communicative act. *Journal of Personality and Social Psychology, 50,* 322–329.

Beilock, S. L., Jellison, W. A., Rydell, R. J., McConnell, A. R., & Carr, T. H. (2006). On the causal mechanisms of stereotype threat: Can skills that don't rely heavily on working memory still be threatened? *Personality and Social Psychology Bulletin, 32,* 1059–1071.

Beilock, S. L., Rydell, R. J., & McConnell, A. R. (2007). Stereotype threat and working memory: Mechanisms, alleviation, and spillover. *Journal of Experimental Psychology: General, 136,* 256–276.

Bower, G. H., & Gilligan, S. G. (1979). Remembering information related to one's self. *Journal of Research in Personality 13,* 420–432.

Bradley, B., & Mathews, A. (1983). Negative self-schemata in clinical depression. *British Journal of Clinical Psychology, 22,* 173–181.

Brown, C. M., & McConnell, A. R. (2009a). Effort or escape: Self-concept structure determines self-regulatory behavior. *Self and Identity, 8,* 365–377.

Brown, C. M., & McConnell, A. R. (2009b). When chronic isn't chronic: The moderating role of active self-aspects. *Personality and Social Psychology Bulletin, 35,* 3–15.

Brown, C. M., & McConnell, A. R. (2011). Discrepancy-based and anticipated emotions in behavioral self-regulation. *Emotion, 11,* 1091–1095.

Brown, C. M., Young, S. G., & McConnell, A. R. (2009). Seeing close others as we see ourselves: One's own self-complexity is reflected in perceptions of meaningful others. *Journal of Experimental Social Psychology, 45,* 515–523.

Bruner, J. S. (1957). On perceptual readiness. *Psychological Review, 64,* 123–152.

Cacioppo, J. T., & Patrick, B. (2008). *Loneliness: Human nature and the need for social connection.* New York: Norton.

Cantor, N., & Mischel, W. (1979) Prototypicality and personality: Effects on free recall and personality impressions. *Journal of Research in Personality, 13,* 187–205.

Carlston, D. E. (1994). Associated systems theory: A systematic approach to cognitive representations of persons. In R. S. Wyer (Ed.), *Advances in social cognition* (Vol. 7, pp. 1–78). Hillsdale, NJ: Erlbaum.

Carrol, P. J., Shepperd, J. A., & Arkin, R. M. (2009). Downward self-revision: Erasing possible selves. *Social Cognition, 27,* 550–578.

Carver, C. S. (2001). Self-regulation. In A. Tesser & N. Schwarz (Eds.), *Blackwell handbook of social psychology: Intraindividual processes* (pp. 307–328). Oxford, UK: Blackwell.

Carver, C. S. (2003). Self-awareness. In M. R. Leary & J. P. Tangney (Eds.), *Handbook of self and identity* (pp. 179–196). New York: Guilford.

Carver, C. S., Blaney, P. H., & Scheier, M. F. (1979). Reassertion and giving up: The interactive role of self-directed attention and outcome expectancy. *Journal of Personality and Social Psychology*, *37*, 1859–1870.

Carver, C. S., & Humphries, C. (1981). Havana daydreaming: A study of self-consciousness and the negative reference group among Cuban Americans. *Journal of Personality and Social Psychology*, *40*, 545–552.

Carver, C. S., & Scheier, M. F. (1998). *Attention and self-regulation: A control-theory approach to human behavior.* New York: Springer-Verlag.

Chartrand, T. L., & Bargh, J. A. (2002). Nonconscious motivations: Their activation, operation, and consequences. In A. Tesser, D. A. Stapel, & J. V. Wood (Eds.), *Self and motivation: Emerging psychological perspectives* (pp. 13–41). Washington, DC: American Psychological Association.

Cheng, C. M., & Chartrand, T. L. (2003). Self-monitoring without awareness: Using mimicry as a nonconscious affiliation strategy. *Journal of Personality and Social Psychology*, *85*, 1170–1179.

Correll, J., & Park, B. (2005). A model of the ingroup as a social resource. *Personality and Social Psychology Review*, *9*, 341–359.

Cross, S. E., & Madson, L. (1997). Models of the self: Self-construals and gender. *Psychological Bulletin*, *122*, 5–37.

DeSteno, D., & Salovey, P. (1997). Structural dynamism in the concept of self: A flexible model for a malleable concept. *Review of General Psychology*, *1*, 389–409.

Donahue, E. M., Robins, R.W., Roberts, B. W., & John, O. P. (1993). The divided self: Concurrent and longitudinal effects of psychological adjustment and social roles on self-concept differentiation. *Journal of Personality and Social Psychology*, *64*, 834–846.

Duval, S., & Wicklund, R. A. (1972). *A theory of objective self awareness.* Oxford, UK: Academic Press.

Duval, T. S., & Lalwani, N. (1999). Objective self-awareness and causal attributions for self-standard discrepancies: Changing self or changing standards of correctness. *Personality and Social Psychology Bulletin*, *25*, 1220–1229.

Dweck, C. S. (1999). *Self-theories: The role in motivation, personality, and development.* Philadelphia: Psychology Press.

Fiske, A. P., Kitayama, S., Markus, H. R., & Nisbett, R. E. (1998). The cultural matrix of social psychology. In D. T. Gilbert, S. T. Fiske, & G. Lindzey (Eds.), *The handbook of social psychology* (Vol. 2, pp. 915–981). New York: McGraw-Hill.

Fitzsimons, G. M., & Bargh, J. A. (2004). Automatic self-regulation. In R. F. Baumeister & K. D. Vohs, *Handbook of self-regulation: Research, theory, and applications* (pp. 151–170). New York: Guilford Press.

Gabriel, S., Carvallo, M., Dean, K. K., Tippin, B., & Renaud, J. M. (2005). How I see me depends on how I see we: The role of attachment style in social comparison. *Personality and Social Psychology Bulletin*, *31*, 1561–1572.

Gabriel, S., & Gardner, W. L. (1999). Are there "his" and "hers" types of independence? The implications of gender differences in collective versus relational interdependence for affect, behavior, and cognition. *Journal of Personality and Social Psychology*, *77*, 642–655.

Greenwald, A. G., & Banaji, M., R. (1989). The self as a memory system: Powerful, but ordinary. *Journal of Personality and Social Psychology*, *57*, 41–54.

Greenwald, A. G., Banaji, M. R., Rudman, L. A., Farnham, S. D., Nosek, B. A., & Mellot, D. S. (2002). A unified theory of implicit attitudes, beliefs, self-esteem and self-concept. *Psychological Review*, *109*, 3–25.

Hamilton, D. L., & Gifford, R. K. (1976). Illusory correlation in interpersonal perception: A cognitive basis of stereotypic judgments. *Journal of Experimental Social Psychology*, *12*, 392–407.

Hamilton, D. L., & Sherman, S. J. (1996). Perceiving persons and groups. *Psychological Review*, *103*, 336–355.

Harter, S. (2003). The development of self-representations during childhood and adolescence. In M. R. Leary & J. P. Tangney (Eds.), *Handbook of self and identity* (pp. 610–642). New York: Guilford.

Hastie, R., & Park, B. (1986). The relationship between memory and judgment depends on whether the judgment task is memory-based or on-line. *Psychological Review*, *93*, 258–268.

Heider, F. (1958). *The psychology of interpersonal relations.* New York: John Wiley & Sons.

Higgins, E. T. (1987). Self-discrepancy: A theory relating self and affect. *Psychological Review*, *94*, 319–340.

Higgins, E. T. (1996). Knowledge activation: Accessibility, applicability, and salience. In E. T. Higgins & A. W. Kruglanski (Eds.), *Social psychology: Handbook of basic principles* (pp. 133–168). New York: Guilford.

Higgins, E. T. (1997). Beyond pleasure and pain. *American Psychologist*, *52*, 1280–1300.

Higgins, E. T., Bond, R. N., Klein, R., & Strauman, T. (1986). Self-discrepancies and emotional vulnerability: How magnitude, accessibility, and type of discrepancy influence affect. *Journal of Personality and Social Psychology*, *51*, 5–15.

Higgins, E. T., King, G. A., & Mavin, G. H. (1982). Individual construct accessibility and subjective impressions and recall. *Journal of Personality and Social Psychology*, *43*, 35–47.

Higgins, E. T., Rholes, W. S., & Jones, C. R. (1977). Category accessibility and impression formation. *Journal of Experimental Social Psychology*, *13*, 141–154.

Hinkley, K., & Andersen, S. M. (1996). The working self-concept in transference: Significant-other activation and self-change. *Journal of Personality and Social Psychology*, *71*, 1279–1295.

House, J. S., Landis, K. R., & Umberson, D. (1988). Social relationships and health. *Science*, *241*, 540–545.

Hsee, C. K., & Abelson, P. (1991). Velocity relation: Satisfaction as a function of the first derivative of outcome over time. *Journal of Personality and Social Psychology*, *60*, 341–347.

Hugenberg, K., & Bodenhausen, G. V. (2004). Category membership moderates the inhibition of social identities. *Journal of Experimental Social Psychology*, *40*, 233–238.

Kelly, G. A. (1955). *The psychology of personal constructs.* New York: Norton.

Kihlstrom, J. F., Beer, J. S., & Klein, S. B. (2003). Self and identity as memory. In M. R. Leary & J. P. Tangney (Eds.), *Handbook of self and identity* (pp. 68–90). New York: Guilford.

Kihlstrom, J. F., & Cantor, N. (1984). Mental representations of the self. In L. Berkowitz (Ed.), *Advances in experimental social psychology* (Vol. 17, pp. 1–47). New York: Academic Press.

Kihlstrom, J. F., & Klein, S. B. (1994). The self as a knowledge structure. In R. S. Wyer & T. K. Srull (Eds.), *Handbook of social cognition* (2nd ed., Vol. 1, pp. 153–208). Hillsdale, NJ: Erlbaum.

Klein, S. B., & Kihlstrom, J. F. (1986). Elaboration, organization, and the self-reference effect in memory. *Journal of Experimental Psychology: General*, *115*, 26–38.

Klein, S. B., & Loftus, J. (1988). The nature of self-referent encoding: The contributions of elaborative and organizational processes. *Journal of Personality and Social Psychology, 55*, 5–11.

Klein, S. B., Loftus, J., Trafton, J. G., & Fuhrman, R. W. (1992). Use of exemplars and abstractions in trait judgments: A model of trait knowledge about the self and others. *Journal of Personality and Social Psychology, 63*, 739–753.

Klein, S. B., Sherman, J. W., & Loftus, J. (1996). The role of episodic and semantic memory in the development of trait self-knowledge. *Social Cognition, 14*, 277–291.

Koch, E. J., & Shepperd, J. A. (2004). Is self-complexity linked to better coping? A review of the literature. *Journal of Personality, 72*, 727–760.

Kurzban, R., & Aktipis, C. A. (2007). Modularity and the social mind: Are psychologists too self-ish? *Personality and Social Psychology Review, 11*, 131–149.

Lakoff, G., & Johnson, M. (1980). *Metaphors we live by*. Chicago: University of Chicago Press.

Lawrence, J. W., Carver, C. S., & Scheier, M. F. (2002). Velocity toward goal attainment in immediate experience as a determinant of affect. *Journal of Applied Social Psychology, 32*, 788–802.

Lieberman, M. D. (2007). Social cognitive neuroscience: A review of core processes. *Annual Review of Psychology, 58*, 259–289.

Linville, P. W. (1985). Self-complexity and affective extremity: Don't put all of your eggs in one cognitive basket. *Social Cognition, 3*, 94–120.

Linville, P. W. (1987). Self-complexity as a cognitive buffer against stress-related illness and depression. *Journal of Personality and Social Psychology, 52*, 663–676.

Linville, P. W., & Carlston, D. E. (1994). Social cognition perspective on self. In P. G. Devine, D. L. Hamilton, & T. M. Ostrom (Eds.), *Social cognition: Contributions to classic issues in social psychology* (pp. 143–193). New York: Springer-Verlag.

Macrae, C. N., Bodenhausen, G. V., & Milne, A. B. (1995). The dissection of selection in person perception: Inhibitory processes in social stereotyping. *Journal of Personality and Social Psychology, 69*, 397–407.

Major, B., & O'Brien, L. T. (2005). The social psychology of stigma. *Annual Review of Psychology, 56*, 393–421.

Markus, H., Crane, M., Bernstein, S., & Siladi, M. (1982). Self-schemas and gender. *Journal of Personality and Social Psychology, 42*, 38–50.

Markus, H. R. (1977). Self-schemata and processing information about the self. *Journal of Personality and Social Psychology, 35*, 63–78.

Markus, H. R., & Kitayama, S. (1991). Culture and the self: Implications for cognition, emotion, and motivation. *Psychological Review, 98*, 224–253.

Markus, H. R., & Nurius, P. (1986). Possible selves. *American Psychologist, 41*, 954–969.

Markus, H., Smith, J., & Moreland, R. L. (1985). Role of the self-concept in the perception of others. *Journal of Personality and Social Psychology, 49*, 1494–1512.

Markus, H., & Wurf, E. (1987). The dynamic self-concept: A social psychological perspective. *Annual Review Psychological, 38*, 299–337.

Mauss, I. B., Cook, C. L., & Gross, J. J. (2007). Automatic emotion regulation during anger provocation. *Journal of Experimental Social Psychology, 43*, 698–771.

McConnell, A. R. (2001). Implicit theories: Consequences for social judgments of individuals. *Journal of Experimental Social Psychology, 37*, 215–227.

McConnell, A. R. (2011). The Multiple Self-aspects Framework: Self-concept representation and its implications. *Personality and Social Psychology Review, 15*, 3–27.

McConnell, A. R., Renaud, J. M., Dean, K. K., Green, S. P., Lamoreaux, M. J., Hall, C. E., & Rydell, R. J. (2005). Whose self is it anyway? Self-aspect control moderates the relationship between self-complexity and well-being. *Journal of Experimental Social Psychology, 41*, 1–18.

McConnell, A. R., Rydell, R. J., & Brown, C. M. (2009). On the experience of self-relevant feedback: How self-concept organization influences affective responses and self-evaluations. *Journal of Experimental Social Psychology, 45*, 695–707.

McConnell, A. R., Rydell, R. J., & Leibold, J. M. (2002). Expectations of consistency about the self: Consequences for self-concept formation. *Journal of Experimental Social Psychology, 38*, 569–585.

McConnell, A. R., Sherman, S. J., & Hamilton, D. L. (1994). On-line and memory-based aspects of individual and group target judgments. *Journal of Personality and Social Psychology, 67*, 173–185.

McConnell, A. R., Sherman, S. J., & Hamilton, D. L. (1997). Target entitativity: Implications for social information processing. *Journal of Personality and Social Psychology, 72*, 750–762.

McConnell, A. R., & Strain, L. M. (2007). Content and structure of the self. In C. Sedikides & S. Spencer (Eds.), *The self in social psychology* (pp. 51–72). New York: Psychology Press.

McConnell, A. R., Strain, L. M., Brown, C. M., & Rydell, R. J. (2009). The simple life: On the benefits of low self-complexity. *Personality and Social Psychology Bulletin, 35*, 823–835.

Mischel, W., & Morf, C. C. (2003). The self as a psycho-social dynamic processing system: A meta-perspective on a century of the self in psychology. In M.R. Leary & J.P. Tangney (Eds.), *Handbook of self and identity* (pp. 15–43). New York: Guilford.

Mischel, W., & Shoda, Y. (1995). A cognitive-affective system theory of personality: Reconceptualizing situations, dispositions, dynamics, and invariance in personality structure. *Psychological Review, 102*, 246–268.

Molden, D. C., & Dweck, C. S. (2006). Finding "meaning" in psychology: A lay theories approach to self-regulation, social perception, and social development. *American Psychologist, 61*, 192–203.

Montepare, J. M., & Clements, A. E. (2001). "Age schemas": Guides to processing information about the self. *Journal of Adult Development, 8*, 99–108.

Murphy M. C., Steele, C. M., & Gross, J. J. (2007). Signaling threat: How situational cues affect women in math, science, and engineering settings. *Psychological Science, 18*, 879–885.

Niedenthal, P. M., Setterlund, M. B., & Wherry, M. B. (1992). Possible self-complexity and affective reactions to goal-relevant evaluation. *Journal of Personality and Social Psychology, 63*, 5–16.

Oyserman, D. (2008). Racial-ethnic self-schemas: Multidimensional identity-based motivation. *Journal of Research in Personality, 42*, 1186–1198.

Phillips, A. G., & Silvia, P. J. (2005). Self-awareness and the emotional consequences of self-discrepancies. *Personality and Social Psychology Bulletin, 31*, 703–713.

Rafaeli-Mor, E., Gotlib, I. H., & Revelle, W. (1999). The meaning and measurement of self-complexity. *Personality and Individual Differences, 27*, 341–356.

Rafaeli-Mor, E., & Steinberg, J. (2002). Self-complexity and well-being: A review and research synthesis. *Personality and Social Psychology Review, 6*, 31–58.

Renaud, J. M., & McConnell, A. R. (2002). Organization of the self-concept and the suppression of self-relevant thoughts. *Journal of Experimental Social Psychology, 38*, 79–86.

Renaud, J. M., & McConnell, A. R. (2007). Wanting to be better but thinking you can't: Implicit theories of personality moderate the impact of self-discrepancies on self-esteem. *Self and Identity, 6*, 41–50.

Richeson, J. A., & Shelton, J. N. (2003). When prejudice does not pay: Effects of interracial contact on executive function. *Psychological Science, 14*, 287–290.

Roberts, B. W., & Donahue, E. M. (1994). One personality, multiple selves: Integrating personality and social roles. *Journal of Personality, 62*, 199–218.

Robins, R. W., & Pals, J. L. (2002). Implicit self-theories in the academic domain: Implications for goal orientation, attributions, affect, and self-esteem change. *Self and Identity, 1*, 313–336.

Rogers, T. B., Kuiper, N. A., & Kirker, W. S. (1977). Self-reference and the encoding of personal information. *Journal of Personality and Social Psychology, 35*, 677–688.

Rosch, E. (1975). Cognitive reference points. *Cognitive Psychology, 7*, 532–547.

Rydell, R. J., McConnell, A. R., & Beilock, S. L. (2009). Multiple social identities and stereotype threat: Imbalance, accessibility, and working memory. *Journal of Personality and Social Psychology, 96*, 949–966.

Rydell, R. J., Rydell, M. T., & Boucher, K. L. (2010). The effect of negative performance stereotypes on learning. *Journal of Personality and Social Psychology, 99*, 883–896.

Schleicher, D. J., & McConnell, A. R. (2005). The complexity of self-complexity: An Associated Systems Theory approach. *Social Cognition, 23*, 387–416.

Schmader, T. (2002). Gender identification moderates stereotype threat effects on women's math performance. *Journal of Experimental Social Psychology, 38*, 194–201.

Schmader, T., Johns, M., & Forbes, C. (2008). An integrated process model of stereotype threat on performance. *Psychological Review, 115*, 336–356.

Schmeichel, B. J., & Baumeister, R. F. (2004). Self-regulatory strength. In R. F. Baumeister & K. D. Vohs (Eds.), *Handbook of self-regulation: Research, theory, and applications* (pp. 84–98). New York: Guilford Press.

Scott, W. A. (1969). Structure of natural cognitions. *Journal of Personality and Social Psychology, 12*, 261–278.

Sedikides, C., & Skowronski, J. J. (1997). The symbolic self in evolutionary context. *Personality and Social Psychology Review, 1*, 80–102.

Sedikides, C., & Spencer, S. J. (2007). *The self*. New York: Psychology Press.

Shih, M., Pittinsky, T. L., & Ambady, N. (1999). Stereotype susceptibility: Identity salience and shifts in quantitative performance. *Psychological Science, 10*, 80–83.

Showers, C. (1992). Compartmentalization of positive and negative self-knowledge: Keeping bad apples out of the bunch. *Journal of Personality and Social Psychology, 62*, 1036–1049.

Showers, C. J., & Zeigler-Hill, V. (2003). Organization of self-knowledge: Features, functions, and flexibility. In M. R. Leary & J. P. Tangney (Eds.), *Handbook of self and identity* (pp. 47–67). New York: Guilford Press.

Singelis, T. M. (1994). The measurement of independent and interdependent self-construals. *Personality and Social Psychology Bulletin, 20*, 580–591.

Slotter, E. B., Gardner, W. L., & Finkel, E. J. (2010). Who am I without you? The influence of romantic breakup on the self-concept. *Personality and Social Psychology Bulletin, 36*, 147–160.

Smith, E. R., Coats, S., & Walling, D. (1999). Overlapping mental representations of self, in-group, and partner: Further response time evidence and a connectionist model. *Personality and Social Psychology Bulletin, 25*, 873–882.

Smith, E. R., & Henry, S. (1996). An in-group becomes part of the self: Response time evidence. *Personality and Social Psychology Bulletin, 22*, 635–642.

Smith, E. R., Seger, C. R., & Mackie, D. M. (2007). Can emotions be truly group-level? Evidence regarding four conceptual criteria. *Journal of Personality and Social Psychology, 93*, 431–446.

Spencer-Rodgers, J., Williams, M. J., & Peng, K. (2010). Cultural differences in expectations of change and tolerance for contradictions: A decade of empirical research. *Personality and Social Psychology Review, 14*, 296–312.

Srull, T. K. (1981). Person memory: Some tests of associative storage and retrieval models. *Journal of Experimental Psychology: Human, Learning, and Memory, 7*, 440–463.

Srull, T. K., & Wyer, R. S. (1980). Category accessibility and social perception: Some implications for the study of person memory and interpersonal judgments. *Journal of Personality and Social Psychology, 38*, 841–856.

Srull, T. K., & Wyer, R. S. (1989). Person memory and judgment. *Psychological Review, 96*, 58–83.

Steele, C. M. (1997). A threat in the air: How stereotypes shape intellectual identity and performance. *American Psychologist, 52*, 613–629.

Steele, C. M., & Aronson, J. (1995). Stereotype threat and the intellectual test performance of African Americans. *Journal of Personality and Social Psychology, 69*, 797–811.

Strauman, T. J., & Higgins, E. T. (1987). Automatic activation of self-discrepancies and emotional syndromes: When cognitive structures influence affect. *Journal of Personality and Social Psychology, 53*, 1004–1014.

Tajfel, H., & Turner, J. C. (1986). The social identity theory of intergroup behavior. In S. Worschel & W. Austin (Eds.), *The psychology of intergroup relations* (2nd ed., pp. 7–24). Chicago: Nelson-Hall.

Taylor, S. E., Lerner, J. S., Sherman, D. K., Sage, R. M., & McDowell, N. K. (2003). Are self-enhancing cognitions associated with healthy or unhealthy biological profiles? *Journal of Personality and Social Psychology, 85*, 605–615.

Taylor, S. E., & Sherman, D. K. (2008). Self-enhancement and self-affirmation: The consequences of positive self-thoughts for motivation and health. In W. Gardner & J. Shah (Eds.), *Handbook of motivation science* (pp. 57–70). New York: Guilford Press.

Trafimow, D., Triandis, H. C., & Goto, S. G. (1991). Some tests of the distinction between the private self and the collective self. *Journal of Personality and Social Psychology, 60*, 649–655.

Triandis, H. C. (1989). The self and social behavior in differing cultural contexts. *Psychological Review, 96*, 506–520.

Tulving, E. (1972). Episodic and semantic memory. In E. Tulving & W. Donaldson (Eds.), *Organization of memory* (pp. 381–403). New York: Academic Press.

Uchino, B. N., Cacioppo, J. T., & Kiecolt-Glaser, J. K. (1996). The relationship between social support and physiological processes: A review with emphasis on underlying mechanisms and implications for health. *Psychological Bulletin, 119,* 488–531.

van Baaren, R. B., Horgan, T. G., Chartrand, T. L., & Dijkmans, M. (2004). The forest, the trees, and the chameleon: Context dependence and mimicry. *Journal of Personality and Social Psychology, 86,* 453–459.

Wicklund, R. A., & Gollwitzer, P. M. (1982). *Symbolic self-completion.* Hillsdale, NJ: Erlbaum.

Williams, K. D. (2007). Ostracism. *Annual Review of Psychology, 58,* 425–452.

Woolfolk, R. L., Novalany, J., Gara, M. A., Allen, L. A., & Polino, M. (1995). Self-complexity, self-evaluation, and depression: An examination of form and content within the self-schema. *Journal of Personality and Social Psychology, 68,* 1108–1120.

Wrosch, C., & Miller, G. E. (2009). Depressive symptoms can be useful: Self-regulatory and emotional benefits of dysphoric mood in adolescence. *Journal of Personality and Social Psychology, 96,* 1181–1190.

Wrosch, C., Miller, G. E., Scheier, M. F., & de Pontet, S. B. (2007). Giving up on unattainable goals: Benefits for health? *Personality and Social Psychology Bulletin, 33,* 251–265.

Wrosch, C., Scheier, M. F., Miller, G. E., Schulz, R., & Carver, C. S. (2003). Adaptive self-regulation of unattainable goals: Goal disengagement, goal reengagement, and subjective well-being. *Personality and Social Psychology Bulletin, 22,* 1494–1508.

Cherished Memories: Autobiographical Memory and the Self

Denise R. Beike

Abstract

The self—the abstract concept of the first person and its characteristics—and autobiographical memory—memory for discrete episodes in one's own life—have long been thought to be linked. This chapter reviews evidence for the involvement of the self in the process of autobiographical memory construction, the development of autobiographical memory (the offset of childhood amnesia), the temporal distribution of autobiographical memories across the life span (the reminiscence bump), and disorders of memory (amnesia and hyperthymesia). Yet there is also evidence that the self and autobiographical memory are functionally independent. Mechanisms are discussed that allow the rememberer to mitigate the potential impact of threatening or self-discrepant memories on the self. As a result of these mechanisms, only particular "cherished" memories affect the abstract concept of the self.

Key Words: autobiographical memory, self, childhood amnesia, amnesia, hyperthymesia, reminiscence bump

Memory is the treasure house of the mind wherein the monuments thereof are kept and preserved.
(Thomas Fuller, 1608–1661)

The television show *The Wonder Years* was a nostalgic exploration of the pivotal experiences of adolescence, told by the main character remembering these experiences as an adult. Some of the experiences reported by the fictional Kevin Arnold were indeed wondrous, such as his first kiss with girl-next-door Winnie Cooper. Others were tragic, such as the death of Winnie's older brother in combat. Some were downright embarrassing, such as Kevin being punched by a girl in front of the entire girls' gym class. But all were preserved for the adult Kevin as cherished memories. As Kevin puts it, "Memory is a way of holding onto the things you love, the things you are, the things you never want to lose" ("Christmas," season 2, episode 3). Undoubtedly, many viewers loved *The Wonder Years* because they could identify with Kevin as he

discussed how these cherished memories function as a living part of the self.

People often speak of *cherished* or (as Thomas Fuller put it) *treasured memories*, words that connote ownership by the self. When people talk about such memories and their relevance to the self, though, they are clearly not referring to just any type of memory. For example, people are not referring to their memories for facts and information, known as semantic memory: "I treasure my memory for the fact that Madrid is the capital of Spain" really doesn't work. They also are not referring to their memories for brief time slices of experiences, known as episodic memory: "I treasure my memory of hearing the word 'architecture' spoken in a male voice as the third item on the list" is not quite right either. Nor are they referring to their memory for how to do things, known as procedural memory: "I treasure my memory of how to ride a bicycle" is not a likely sentence. Rather people speak of cherishing and treasuring memories of discrete personally experienced life events, known as autobiographical memory: "I treasure my memory of that day in Madrid we rented bicycles and talked about the architecture" is more like it.

Autobiographical memory can often be distinguished from other forms of memory by the greater quantity of three components: "self-conscious reflection, emotional connotation and mental time travel" (Oddo et al., 2010, p. 29). Specifically, autobiographical memory differs from episodic memory (with which it is most often confused) by the length of time covered by the remembered event, as well as the self-relevance of the event. Autobiographical memories are longer, consisting of a number of episodic memories merged into a greater whole (Conway, 2005, 2009; Conway & Pleydell-Pearce, 2000). Autobiographical memories also employ the self as a cue to help construct them to a greater degree than do episodic memories (Conway, 2009; Gilboa, 2004). To most social psychologists, the self is the abstract cognitive concept of the first person as separate from others, continuing across time, and composed of moderately stable characteristics such as personality traits, physical qualities, and enduring roles (i.e., introverted blue-eyed lawyer; Leary & Tangney, 2003). Autobiographical memories are therefore specific, and the self is abstract.

Autobiographical memory and the self have long been considered overlapping if not synonymous (e.g., Bruner, 1994; Grice, 1941). People may learn about the self by recollecting a specific behavior and reflecting on its meaning (Bem, 1967). In this way, memories of specific behaviors can become the stuff of the abstract concept of self. There is great intuitive appeal to the idea that we learn about the self by abstracting information from memories of specific experiences. In the words of one journalist, "We are all the sum of our memories, both recent and long ago. They are what make us who we used to be, who we are, who we become" (France, 2005). In the words of another, "Your memory is who you are. If you have no memory, then who are you?" (Fuchs, 2001). This chapter explores the idea that not all autobiographical memories influence the self; only cherished memories—those for which we feel a strong sense of ownership—influence the self.

Surely the question of who, if anyone, the self is without autobiographical memory is important. How do you know who you are when you don't remember what's happened to you or what you've done? This question is largely relevant to the few unfortunate people who lose their autobiographical memory ability. Therefore, an even more important question is who the self is *with* autobiographical memory. How do you know who you are when you recollect memories of what's happened to you and what you've done that conflict with each other, or with your previous sense of self? This question is relevant to those who have autobiographical memory (almost everyone), and it could come up any time we recollect an episode from our lives (many times a day).

For example, think of a time that you acted courageously. Now think of a time you acted fearfully. If you, like most people, can recall instances of both courage and fear, you know that both are accurate and both came from you—so are *you* courageous, or are *you* fearful? Or are you just confused (Setterlund & Niedenthal, 1993)? As another example, choose the word that better describes you: kind or cruel. Having chosen who you are, try to recollect times in which you behaved oppositely to your sense of self. Does remembering such instances change your sense of who you are, and if so, does it make you believe you are *more* like or *less* like the content of those memories (Schwarz et al., 1991)? Put simply, can the self withstand the assault of the many conflicting autobiographical memories that make up a life, or is it subject to change to suit each specific recollected experience?

This chapter explores the ways in which autobiographical memories and the self influence one another. It begins with a review of the important phenomena that characterize autobiographical memory and of how those phenomena demonstrate a vital link to the self, the abstract concept of the first person who endures over time. It then proceeds to review evidence that qualifies the intuitively appealing conclusion that autobiographical memory and the self are intimately intertwined. Instead, it is argued, autobiographical memory and the self are represented by distinct systems that need not always interact. A given autobiographical memory influences the self only when it is construed as belonging to the self, or "cherished." The chapter ends with the argument that experiencing some memories as belonging to the self, and some not, enables people to maintain a large and relatively undistorted store of autobiographical memories and still maintain a stable sense of self.

Essential Properties of Autobiographical Memory and Their Reliance on the Self

Research on autobiographical memory has increased exponentially in recent years. A PsycINFO search conducted in May of 2010 revealed a 215-fold increase in the number of articles on autobiographical memory since the 1970s, which represents a 41-fold increase in the percentage of articles about memory that concern autobiographical memory in particular. The research is necessarily interdisciplinary, with cognitive, neuroscience, developmental, personality, social, and clinical psychologists all contributing to our current understanding of the phenomenon. Therefore, only some of the recent explosion in autobiographical memory research has been published in journals read by social cognitive psychologists (e.g., special issues of *Social Cognition* in 2004 and 2005).

In this section, the important properties of autobiographical memory are reviewed. These properties include the way the memory is constructed, when and how it emerges in development, the temporal distribution or retention function of autobiographical memories across the life span, the absence and hyperpresence of autobiographical memories, and the involuntary recollection of autobiographical memories. Also reviewed is evidence that each of these properties depends at least in part on the abstract concept of a self that endures across time.

Process of Construction
Basic Phenomena

Like all memory, autobiographical memory is reconstructive rather than reproductive. The remememberer constructs a memory anew each time rather than reproducing a static representation. In the case of autobiographical memory, the process of construction involves a large number of brain areas and can extend up to 20 seconds in time (Conway, 1990, 2005; Rubin & Schulkind, 1997). Most instances of autobiographical remembering begin with a voluntary search based on a cue or probe (e.g., "What was the best meal you ever had?"). People often begin by identifying a time period in their life during which the sought-for memory may have taken place (lifetime period, such as "graduate school"), then they find generic examples of similar memories (general event memory, such as "eating at nice restaurants at conferences"), and finally identify specific episodic memory traces that contain the elements of the desired memory (specific event memory, such as "the meal I ate at that Indian restaurant in Washington, DC"; Conway, 2005; Hacque & Conway, 2001). Because the construction process occurs anew at each time of recollection, it is not uncommon for elements that do not actually belong to that life experience to be bound into the memory.

These are known as *conjunction errors* (Odegard & Lampinen, 2004). For example, I may mistakenly bind memory features about Washington, DC into my memory of the Indian restaurant meal because I am convinced that it occurred during a conference in that city, when in reality the meal in question occurred in a different city entirely. Nonetheless, the memory is compelling and vivid and seems true to the rememberer.

Several types of research support the hierarchical process of retrieving autobiographical memories. First, studies using a think-aloud protocol demonstrate that people usually do begin their search for a specific autobiographical memory by identifying a lifetime period or a general event type first (Haque & Conway, 2001). Second, research has identified people with an inability or unwillingness to bring to mind specific autobiographical memories of life experiences, who suffer from demands on executive resources that might prevent them from constructing specific memories. For example, when asked to recollect a specific life experience involving the words "ice cream," a person may respond with "I used to eat ice cream a lot after soccer practice" rather than the more specific "I ate an ice cream cone during the fireworks display last fourth of July."

This failure to recollect specific memories is known as *overgeneral memory*. It occurs in people with major depressive disorder, a history of trauma, or Parkinson's disease, and when self-regulatory resources are depleted (Neshat-Doost, Dalgleish, & Golden, 2008; Smith, Souchay, & Conway, 2010; Williams et al., 2007). In theory, people experiencing overgeneral memory are cognitively unable to move beyond the initial stages of autobiographical memory construction and therefore fail to proceed from the working self and abstract self-knowledge about lifetime periods to the specific details that will be bound to form a memory (Williams et al., 2007).

Role of the Self

Several roles for the self in the construction of autobiographical memory are posited in the Self-Memory System theory (Conway, 2005; Conway & Pleydell-Pearce, 2000). The first way the self is involved is that one's current goals (called the *working self*; cf. Markus & Wurf, 1987) constrain the search for elements to be bound up in the memory. For example, if I am recollecting the best meal I ever had because I am trying to decide what to make for dinner tonight, I will likely search for sensory elements about taste to bind into my memory. But if I am recollecting that meal because I am trying to decide where to go on vacation, I will more likely search for spatial elements about where the restaurant was to bind into my memory. The Self-Memory System acts to construct memories consistent with current goals and the current sense of self, and to inhibit memories that are inconsistent (Conway, 2005).

The second way the self is involved is that the search for elements to bind into a memory often begins by identifying an abstractly represented lifetime period in which to search. A series of such partially overlapping lifetime periods lays out the story of the self across time (Barsalou, 1988; Conway, 2005). A third way the self is involved is the activation of the *long-term self*, the frequently rehearsed and relatively permanent notion of the self-concept that controls the working self and helps maintain coherence between memories and the working self (Conway, Singer, & Tagini, 2004). Thus, both temporary and more permanent notions of the self guide autobiographical memory construction.

The role of the self is also suggested by the results of brain images acquired during the process of autobiographical memory construction. When people are asked to come up with a specific autobiographical memory, given a word cue or other prompt, activation first occurs in the left frontal lobe. This activation has been interpreted as the operation of the working self (Conway, 2005). Next, activation occurs in the posterior temporal lobes and occipital lobes, where in theory the specific features of relevant episodic memories are held. These specific features can include sensory (especially visual), spatial, emotional, linguistic, and narrative components (Rubin, 2005). Finally, activation occurs in the medial temporal (hippocampal) area. In theory, this area binds together the activated working self in the frontal lobes and the activated elements in more posterior portions of the brain into a single unit. This temporarily bound unit is experienced as an autobiographical memory (Botzung, Denkova, Ciuciu, Scheiber, & Manning, 2008; Conway, 2005; Conway, Pleydell-Pearce, & Whitecross, 2001; Daselaar et al., 2008; Greenberg et al. 2005).

Recent imaging studies show activation more specifically in the medial and ventromedial prefrontal cortex during the construction of autobiographical memories (Magno & Allan, 2007; Oddo et al., 2010; Spreng & Grady, 2010). Activation of the medial prefrontal cortex has been described as the "neural signature of the current self" (Libby, 2008, p. 192). The medial prefrontal cortex is active when people make judgments about the self-relevance of information, and also when they take the perspective of others (Ames, Jenkins, Banaji, & Mitchell, 2008). Therefore, its activation during autobiographical remembering suggests that the self is inextricably bound up with the other elements of the memory. In contrast, activation in the dorsolateral prefrontal cortex occurs during the construction of episodic, but not autobiographical, memories (Galboa, 2004). Activation of the dorsolateral prefrontal cortex occurs after retrieval and under conditions in which people are highly concerned with the accuracy of their responses. In theory, because autobiographical memories just "feel" accurate, the dorsolateral prefrontal cortex does not play a role (Gilboa, 2004). In summary, regions of the brain that have been interpreted as the seat of the self are activated in autobiographical but not episodic memories.

Childhood Amnesia and Development of the Life Story in Adolescence
Basic Phenomenon

As one might glean from the complexity of the process of autobiographical remembering, it appears rather late in development. Although infants and toddlers evidence other types of memory abilities (Bauer, 2006), autobiographical memory ability has a later onset, around three or four years of age (Nelson & Fivush, 2004). The inability to remember life experiences before this age is called *childhood amnesia*. Life experiences accrued before three or four years of age are typically not explicitly remembered by adults (Rubin, 2000), although they may be remembered for a few years afterward during childhood (Cleveland & Reese, 2008).

Role of the Self

The offset of childhood amnesia seems to depend on the development of the self. Young children usually develop the ability to recollect and narrate individual life events after they demonstrate that they have developed a self-concept (Howe, Courage, & Edison, 2003). Operationally, a self-concept can be identified by mirror self-recognition. The standard test for the presence of a concept of the self is to unobtrusively smudge rouge onto a child's face, then show her a mirror. A child without a concept of the self will notice the colored smudge on the reflection in the mirror and reach out toward the image of her face in the mirror to explore it. But a child with a concept of the self will understand the physical boundaries of the self and therefore immediately reach toward her own face. Once this cognitive self is acquired, autobiographical memory can begin (Howe & Courage, 1997).

Although the cognitive self is acquired by about two years of age, the offset of childhood amnesia does not occur until about three to four years of age. Further research has revealed that autobiographical memory requires not only an understanding of the self as an object but also an understanding that the self is stable over time. A more advanced test of the self-concept than the mirror test was developed by Povinelli and Simon (1998). A sticker was unobtrusively placed on the head of three to five year old children as they were videotaped playing a game. Among children shown the videotape three minutes later, 44% of the three-year-olds but more than 80% of the five-year-olds correctly reached up to their own heads to search for the sticker. Among children shown the videotape one week later (at which point the self in the videotape should be recognized as a past self), 38% of the three-year-olds but less than 10% of the five-year-olds (wrongly) reached up to their own heads to search for the sticker. The ability to conceptualize the self appropriately as stable in time but changing in particulars corresponds more closely to the actual age of onset of autobiographical memory ability.

Many researchers studying the development of autobiographical memory thus see the development of the self-concept as a necessary (albeit not necessarily sufficient) condition for the development of autobiographical memory (Howe & Courage, 1997; Howe et al., 2003). If, indeed, autobiographical remembering involves the neural signature of the self, as suggested in the previous subsection, then it follows that this sense of self must be present before autobiographical remembering may occur.

Reminiscence Bump
Basic Phenomenon
Although childhood amnesia disappears around four years of age, autobiographical memory assumes its full adult-like form much later in adolescence, when in addition to the mere ability to narrate individual events, a life narrative develops (Bohn & Berntsen, 2008; Habermas & Bluck, 2000). The themes, key scenes, and other elements of this life story express the enduring concerns of the person, and provide a sense of purpose and unity to the rememberer (McAdams, 2001). One of the important elements of the life story is the self-defining memory. People have a small number of fairly stable self-defining memories, which are specific, evoke

intense emotion, and are linked to enduring themes or concerns in a person's life (Singer & Salovey, 1993). They help to reinforce one's sense of identity, and provide a port in the storm when threats to the self or identity emerge (Blagov & Singer, 2004).

The adolescent period of life during which the life story develops retains a psychological importance throughout adult life, as revealed in the *reminiscence bump*. Adults forty years and older tend to recall autobiographical memories about events that occurred in their teens and early twenties at a much higher rate than events that took place at any other time period than the past year (Rubin & Schulkind, 1997). For people of middle adulthood age or older, the retention curve for autobiographical memory is a nonmonotonic function, with no memories up until about three years of age, a small number of memories of the childhood years, a large number of memories from the adolescent years (the reminiscence bump), a moderate number of memories from the rest of adulthood, and the greatest number of memories from the most recent year of life (Rubin & Schulkind, 1997).

Role of the Self
Both he life story and the reminiscence bump are related to the self. The autobiographical life story is posited to be central to identity and personality (McAdams, 2001). Therefore, concerns of the self appear in the life story, and the shape of the life story and its constituent self-defining memories influence the concept of the self. Narrativizing experiences into self-defining memories or a life story allows people to gain insight into them, and to link them to the concept of the self, thereby solidifying and molding the self-concept (McLean, Pasupathi, & Pals, 2007; Thorne, McLean, & Lawrence, 2004). In fact, adolescents whose self-defining memories show evidence of "meaning making" go on to achieve a more sophisticated identity status (McLean & Pratt, 2006). Later, adults whose life stories express redemption sequences in which bad things turned out well have higher psychological well-being and a greater sense of coherence in life than those whose life stories express contamination sequences in which good things suddenly go wrong (McAdams, Reynolds, Lewis, Patten, & Bowman, 2001). That is, the shape of the autobiographical life story both expresses and influences the nature of the self.

The reminiscence bump contains memories from the time in life when the sense of identity and a life story are first being forged. One explanation for the reminiscence bump is that it reflects the Eriksonian task of identity integration that occurs during those years of life (Conway & Holmes, 2004). Autobiographical memories constructed after filling in the cue "I am . . . " tend to consist of life experiences that occurred at the time that particular self-concept was formed, suggesting that newly formed self-concepts are lastingly tied in memory to the experiences occurring at the time of their formation (Rathbone, Moulin, & Conway, 2008). Later in life, then, a large number of memories from the teens and twenties will be accessible because they are linked to self-concepts formed at that point in time. Interestingly, the reminiscence bump does not occur at the same point for everyone. Those who experience a major life-altering event, such as immigration or civil war, at a time in life later than their twenties show a reminiscence bump occurring at that later lifetime period (Conway & Haque, 1999; Schrauf & Rubin, 2001). All of these threads of evidence point to identity formation—the development of an abstract self—as the reason for the life story and the reminiscence bump.

Amnesia and Hyperthymesia
Basic Phenomena

Although virtually everyone develops the ability to recollect life experiences, there are extreme cases of those who can recollect almost nothing (amnesics) and those who can recollect almost everything (hyperthymesics) that happens to them. The noted patient H. M., for example, was unable to record any new memories of life experiences after the surgery that removed his hippocampi, resulting in complete *anterograde amnesia,* or failure to form memories after the brain damage. Moreover, H. M. was unable to recollect any autobiographical memories from several years before the surgery (i.e., he also had *retrograde amnesia,* or failure to access memories from before the brain damage; Scoville & Milner, 1957).

Clive Wearing, who suffered hippocampal damage due to a viral infection, has similarly been unable to record memories of life experiences since his illness, and has sparse autobiographical memories from before his illness. His wife Deborah Wearing (2005) titled her book about him *Forever Today,* describing the narrow temporal window of consciousness in which he lives. The distinction between autobiographical and other forms of memory is clear in that both H. M. and Clive Wearing retained their knowledge, intelligence, working memory ability,

and implicit memory skills in the face of their utter loss of autobiographical memory (Squire, 1992).

At the opposite end of the spectrum are those whose lives are overfull of autobiographical memory. The woman originally known as AJ (who has since acknowledged that her name is Jill Price) contacted memory researchers for help understanding her inability to forget her life experiences and her obsession with remembering past events. She has a virtually perfect autobiographical memory, which dominates her life and her thoughts. Her unusual memory condition has been named *hyperthymestic syndrome,* and it has been verified in several other people and is suspected in as many as 50 additional people (Wigmore, 2008). Like amnesia, hyperthymestic syndrome reveals the distinction between autobiographical and other forms of memory, in that hyperthymestics have been found to possess strictly average or even below-average knowledge, intelligence, working memory ability, and memory for facts (semantic) and lists (episodic; Parker, Cahill, & McGaugh, 2006).

Role of the Self

At this point, a question posed at the beginning of the chapter may be answered: If you have no memory, who are you? The answer is that amnesics seem to maintain a sense of self over time, although certain aspects of it are disrupted. Amnesics sometimes express an old or outdated sense of self. For example, one amnesic man claimed to be 19 years old when he was actually 49 because his brain injury occurred when he was 19 and he could not properly update his sense of self (Sacks, 1985). Sometimes (albeit rarely) amnesics express a confabulated sense of self, deriving their concept of self not from autobiographical memories, but rather from any snippets of the environment they happen to note. For example, one amnesic continually confabulated who he was in relation to the hospital and staff members he encountered from moment to moment: a patient, a deli worker, a customer waiting for his car to be repaired (Sacks, 1985).

People suffering from Alzheimer's disease with its devastating impact on memory can be similarly afflicted with an unstable or uncertain sense of self. Compared with age-matched controls, patients with Alzheimer's disease listed fewer aspects of the self-concept and were more vague in their descriptions of these self-aspects. They also expressed a more negatively toned view of the self (Addis & Tippett, 2004). Moreover, the extent of autobiographical memory deficits was correlated with the extent of these self-concept deficits in the Alzheimer's patients but not the matched controls (Addis & Tippett, 2004). In other words, the loss of memory did seem to go hand in hand with a loss of the sense of self.

At the other end of the autobiographical memory ability spectrum, Jill Price with her perfect autobiographical memory also seems to have disruptions of the self. As she put it, "Whereas people generally create narratives of their lives that are fashioned by a process of selective remembering...I have not been able to do so.... It's as though I have all of my prior selves still inside me, the self I was on every day of my life, like her or not, nested as in a Russian doll—inside today's Jill are complete replicas of yesterday's Jill and the Jills for all the days stretching so far back in time. In that sense, I don't so much have a story of my self as I have a remarkably detailed memory of my self" (Price & Davis, 2008, pp. 6–7). She complains of running her entire life through her mind every day, as well as suffering from depression (Wigmore, 2008). Perhaps Ms. Price's abundance of autobiographical memories gives her no abstract sense of the self as a unitary coherent whole that persists across time. Instead, she seems to have a sense of discrete, momentary selves bound to this miscellany of memories. In summary, deviations from the usual pattern of autobiographical memory—too few or too many—are associated with a disturbed sense of self—too vague or too detailed. This evidence suggests that autobiographical memories feed directly into the sense of self.

Involuntary Autobiographical Memories
Basic Phenomena

In addition to the deliberate hierarchical process of construction described earlier, all of us also recollect some autobiographical memories automatically and without intention (Conway & Pleydell-Pearce, 2000). These *involuntary memories* tend to be more specific, more negative in content, and more highly emotional than voluntarily retrieved memories (Berntsen, 1998; Berntsen & Hall, 2004; Schlagman & Kvavilashvili, 2008).

The best-known type of involuntary memories consists of flashbacks or *intrusive memories*, which occur in people who have experienced a traumatic event. These intrusive memories have been theorized to be a part of the coping process, the mind's way of forcing itself to process and habituate to the trauma (Horowitz & Becker, 1972). When the intrusive memories persist over months or years, however, they are an indicator of post-traumatic stress disorder (PTSD; e.g., Weisenberg, Solomon,

Schwarzwald, & Mikulincer, 1987). Although bothersome intrusive memories are associated with PTSD, most involuntary autobiographical memories are benign. They occur several times per day in people from nonclinical populations (Berntsen, 1996; Mace, 2004), and although more negative than voluntary autobiographical memories, they are nonetheless still twice as often positive as negative in content (Berntsen & Rubin, 2002). For example, while working at her desk, a person might see a bird outside the window, which might trigger an involuntary memory of watching an enjoyable television documentary about birds with her child. The mind wanders, and involuntary memories may be triggered (Schlagman & Kvavilashvili, 2008).

Role of the Self

Involuntary memories do not begin with an intentional search of lifetime periods belonging to the self, but they are nonetheless related to the self in several ways. First, the frequency of intrusive involuntary memories is increased by focusing on the self, especially in an overly analytic way (e.g., "why do I feel this way?"; Watkins, 2004). Second, the distribution of involuntary memories over the life span is similar to that of deliberately retrieved autobiographical memories; there is a reminiscence bump, with a disproportionate number of involuntary memories also coming from the lifetime period in which identity is established (Berntsen & Rubin, 2002). Ongoing thoughts about the self or the task in which one is engaged trigger involuntary memories (Mace, 2004; Schlagman & Kvavilashvili, 2008). Thinking about what we are doing (goals) rather than who we are (abstract self), therefore, underlies involuntary memories. Yet recall that the self who strives toward goals is the same working self that is involved in the early stages of autobiographical memory construction. Therefore, the self is involved in involuntary as well as voluntary autobiographical memories.

Summary

To summarize the evidence of interaction between autobiographical memory and the self, autobiographical memory engages brain areas known to be important for the self, is constructed to support the momentary goals and construal of the working self, develops in concert with the self-concept, encapsulates and expresses one's sense of identity, when it exists in extreme low or high states co-occurs with disruptions of the sense of self, and comes to mind involuntarily based on the moment-to-moment actions of the working self. Next, evidence that demonstrates independence rather than interaction between autobiographical memory and the self will be reviewed.

Autobiographical Memory and the Self Are Independent

Autobiographical memory and the self clearly interact with each other. But too tight a connection between the self and autobiographical memory could be problematic. If autobiographical memory provides the foundation for the self, then the self could easily become unmoored in the face of amnesia or even simple forgetting. The self could also be too readily buffeted by momentary reminders of a diverse lifetime's worth of experiences. Either would create a highly unstable self, known to be deleterious (Kernis, Cornell, Sun, Berry, & Harlow, 1993).

Two solutions to the potential problem of autobiographical memories causing unwanted alterations in the self have been posited by other theorists. One solution is to think of the self as consisting of two components, a temporary online *working self-concept* and a vast and permanent store of *self-knowledge* (Markus & Wurf, 1987). The working self-concept consists of the few aspects of self-knowledge activated by the present environment and current thoughts, as well as some chronically accessible self-aspects (Markus, 1977). According to this theoretical perspective, autobiographical memories inconsistent with the nature of the self may distort the working self-concept for as long as that working self-concept endures (minutes or hours, perhaps), but will be unlikely to affect the permanent sense of self if they represent rare instances in the backdrop of self-knowledge. A second solution is to recognize memories as malleable, so that memories inconsistent with an important aspect of self simply fail to come to mind or are distorted toward consistency (Conway, 2005; Conway & Ross, 1984; Greenwald, 1980; Ross, 1989; Sanitioso, Kunda, & Fong, 1990; Sedikides & Green, 2000).

The research supporting both ideas will not be reviewed here because it has been reviewed in the articles cited in the previous paragraph. Clearly, the working self-concept does change, and memories are preferentially altered or forgotten, but taken together these two processes are insufficient to account for what is now known about autobiographical memory. Contrary to a shifting working self-concept, recollection of autobiographical memories does not always affect even the temporary sense of self; most autobiographical memories

are inert in their implications about the self (e.g., Beike, Kleinknecht, & Wirth-Beaumont, 2004; Singer & Salovey, 1993). Contrary to a self-concept that distorts recollection to maintain consistency, autobiographical memory is actually extremely accurate. Wagenaar (1986) was able to recognize every daily personal experience he recorded when tested up to six years later, given a sufficient number of cues. College student participants were 95% accurate at recognizing features they had listed for daily personal experiences they recorded, up to five weeks later. For example, given the cue "date with George," they were able to recognize whether the correct location associated with this event was presented (e.g., "Italiano's restaurant") on 95% of trials (Odegard & Lampinen, 2004).

In short, further explanations are required for why the self is largely stable despite the varying implications of autobiographical memories that are brought to mind, and why autobiographical memory is largely accurate despite the potential distorting power of the self (Greenwald, 1980). The conflict is between *coherence* (the self and autobiographical memories must accord with one another) and *correspondence* (accurate memories of life experiences must be retained; Conway, 2005; Conway et al., 2004). Fortunately, the autobiographical memory system has developed to maximize both coherence and correspondence.

The following section reviews evidence demonstrating that autobiographical memory and the abstract concept of the self as unitary and persistent over time are represented by independent (yet interacting) systems in the brain, meaning that coherence is not strictly necessary. The final section presents the argument that distancing autobiographical memories from the self—making them, in a sense, less cherished—allows correspondence without threats to coherence.

Autobiographical Memory and the Self Represent Two Functionally Independent Systems
Episodic Versus Semantic Self-Knowledge

Abstract self-concepts are not necessarily dependent on or interwoven with specific autobiographical memories upon which they were originally based. The former represent *semantic self-knowledge* and the latter represent *episodic self-knowledge*, which are functionally independent (Klein, 2004). Semantic knowledge of one's general traits is abstracted from experience, and the specific episodes are thereafter not usually consulted when one thinks of the self (Klein, Sherman, & Loftus, 1996). Therefore, thinking about general traits usually does not speed access to memories of times one acted in accord with those traits (Klein & Loftus, 1993).

A former student had an opportunity to experience this functional independence in action when he took a lie detector test for a government internship. He was asked preliminary general questions such as, "Have you ever stolen anything, even a pencil or a paper clip?" If the answer was "yes," he was asked immediately to recollect a specific example of a time he had done so. He was amazed how difficult the latter task was. He was certain that, as an imperfect human being, he must have engaged in various small misdeeds in his life, so he readily answered "yes" to the preliminary general questions (which tapped into semantic self-knowledge). Yet he often could not generate specific autobiographical memories of such misdeeds after having answered "yes" to a generic question about a type of misdeed (which tapped into episodic self-knowledge). Perhaps unsurprisingly, the U.S. government is not fully versed in the literature on the failure of semantic self-knowledge to prime episodic self-knowledge. Therefore, their expert incorrectly identified a pattern of responses such as that my student gave as a worrisome indicator of untruthfulness, rather than as a healthy indicator of two functionally independent systems of self-knowledge. (The expert had to instruct my former student to consider whether he could think of examples before answering each general question in order to maintain consistent responses). Having two systems of self-knowledge may be redundant, but it enables rapid access to crucial self-knowledge and resilience to brain trauma or other causes of memory loss (Klein, 2004).

Intact Self in Amnesics

As a consequence of the independence of semantic and episodic self-knowledge, people may exhibit, experience, or express self-concepts even after their access to the autobiographical memory base has been severed. Although some amnesics such as those discussed earlier show a frozen or confabulated sense of self after they lose access to their autobiographical memories, many seem to maintain a healthy sense of self. For example, amnesics interviewed after having lost their autobiographical memory due to brain trauma described themselves as having a continuous rather than an altered sense of self (Medved & Brockmeier, 2008).

Even those who are too impaired to engage in interviews about the self-concept nonetheless often show hints of a continuous self to observers. Clive Wearing was described by the noted neurologist Oliver Sacks as expressing an intact "performance self" when playing music: "This mode of being, this self, is seemingly untouched by his amnesia, even though his autobiographical self, the self that depends on explicit, episodic memories, is virtually lost" (Sacks, 2007). His wife Deborah claims Clive's continued love for her and for his music is "living evidence that you could lose almost everything you ever knew *about* yourself and still *be* yourself" (Wearing, 2005, p. 226). Consistent with this view is a case of a woman (PJM) with retrograde amnesia, who shows a coherent and normal sense of self despite the lack of specific memories upon which to ground her sense of self. The clarity of the self-aspects she listed was equivalent to control participants, but she produced far fewer autobiographical memories related to these aspects of the self. In regards to a specific incident in her life, she wrote, "I don't have any 'memories' I can talk about about it, although I do remember the facts" (p. 412). For example, she indicated that she was an academic, but could not remember any specific episodes related to this aspect of the self. Instead, she wrote about personal facts related to this aspect of self: That she had once worked in France and while living there used to drink in an Irish pub. She also asserted that her sense of self was continuous over time despite the missing autobiographical memories (Rathbone, Moulin, & Conway, 2009).

Along with a psychological sense of stability in and clarity of the essential self, amnesics may retain the ability to accurately update self-knowledge despite an inability to remember any instances that exemplify this change. For example, many amnesics are aware of their memory deficits, which represents an accurate change in self-knowledge. When asked about his condition, H. M. would often acknowledge not only his memory deficits but also his transformed role in society: "The memory is gone…but it isn't worrisome…because I know that…they'd learn from it. It would help others" (Hilts, 1995, p. 235). Therefore, H. M. was able to adjust his sense of self even though he had no memory of what had happened to him. Moreover, other amnesics have been shown to be able to accurately report changes in their personality traits (part of the abstract sense of self) despite not being able to recollect any life experiences that led to those changes (Klein, 2004).

Surprising evidence of an intact and dynamic self occurs in an amnesic known pseudonymously as Angie, whose autobiographical memory abilities were destroyed in a car crash. She retains normal levels of autobiographical memory from her childhood and young adulthood before the crash, but has profound anterograde amnesia, having stored almost no new memories since the crash (Duff, Wszalek, Tranel, & Cohen, 2008). Nonetheless, she has been able to take on a full-time job as a project manager, succeed in graduate school, and develop satisfying relationships with others (including a husband and stepchildren) after the loss of her autobiographical memory abilities. Duff et al. noted that her insight into her memory loss (i.e., her accurately updated sense of self) seemed to enable her to devise effective strategies for dealing with it and even successfully hiding it from others.

Even more impressively, Angie is able to accurately describe the changes that have occurred in her identity and social roles (e.g., she informed the researchers that she currently worked as a project manager), despite being unable to remember specific life experiences related to that identity or those roles (e.g., she could not recall what she did at work or report on any individual case or project she had managed). The researchers infer that "knowledge about the self can evolve and be updated and behavior modified in the absence of intact episodic memory" (Duff et al., 2008, p. 942). In summary, the sense of self is preserved even in the absence of an autobiographical memory knowledge base on which to ground it (see also Klein, 2004).

No Self Is Required for Autobiographical Memory Development

The preceding subsections review evidence that autobiographical memories are not required for a sense of self. But what of the evidence showing that a sense of self is required for autobiographical memory to emerge? In fact, there is an ongoing debate among researchers and theorists of childhood amnesia as to whether the self or socialization is the foundation of autobiographical memory (e.g., Howe & Courage, 1997; Nelson & Fivush, 2004). Theorists who posit that autobiographical memory is socially determined might therefore maintain that autobiographical memory is not necessarily dependent on the presence of an abstract concept of self as extended across time and consisting of enduring attributes.

The simplest and most direct evidence that the self is not the prime mover of autobiographical memory development is that a sense of self is not required for its development. The ability to recognize oneself in a mirror (to reach for one's own nose

rather than the mirror to remove a dot of rouge) is shown by some but not all children before they demonstrate autobiographical memory (Harley & Reese, 1999). Moreover, differences in the onset of autobiographical memory ability fail to correspond to differences in development of the self. Specifically, males, youngest children, and children from East Asian cultures have a later onset of autobiographical memory than their counterparts (Mullen, 1994). Yet there is not a corresponding difference in the age of onset of mirror self-recognition in those groups (e.g., Harel, Eshel, Ganor, & Scher, 2002; Povinelli, Landau, & Perilloux, 1996).

Instead, the differences appear to result from the different conversational experiences of children in these different groups. Children whose parents spend more time elaboratively drawing out the child in their discussion of the past rather than repeatedly querying her have an earlier age of autobiographical memory onset (Jack, MacDonald, Reese, & Hayne, 2009). In theory, elaborative conversation acts as an organizer of life experience information, thus enabling better memory. And indeed, parents spend less time in such elaborative conversation about life events with male children, and parents in East Asian cultures spend less time in elaborative conversation with their children about individual experiences than do parents in Western cultures (Wang, 2007). Parents likely spend less time in elaborative conversation with younger than older children owing to the greater number of parenting demands that accrue with additional children (Mullen, 1994). Thus, help from caregivers in the social process of conversation, and not the development of a self, enables the development of autobiographical memory.

Moreover, socialization plays a major role in the development of the life story (composed in part of individual autobiographical memories woven into a narrative) and the reminiscence bump (better recollection for life experiences in the teens and twenties). McLean and colleagues (2007) stress the importance of stories told to others and the reactions of those listeners in the formation of the life story and, ultimately, identity. Untold memories or memories told to listeners who pay little attention, they argue, are usually forgotten and therefore play little role in the life story and identity. The life story is at heart a story designed to be socially shared. Therefore, it is a product of social life as much as identity.

A social rather than an identity explanation has been offered for the reminiscence bump as well. Specifically, the reminiscence bump corresponds with a life script learned by members of a culture, which specifies that the most important events in life occur in the teens and early twenties. When adults are asked to recollect autobiographical memories, then, they preferentially report events from their teens and twenties because these are the events deemed most important by their culture and therefore are readily accessed by self-generated cues such as "wedding." Importantly, the cultural life script specifies the distribution of mainly positive memories (e.g., graduation, marriage, birth of children; Berntsen & Rubin, 2004). As a consequence, the reminiscence bump is more apparent for positive memories than for negative or neutral memories (Berntsen & Rubin, 2002). Moreover, the cultural life script seems to provide the outline for one's own life story because its learning corresponds to the development of the personal life story in adolescence (Bohn & Berntsen, 2008). Therefore, a culturally learned schema rather than an idiographic concept of self may drive recollection of reminiscence bump memories. In short, the processes responsible for the offset of childhood amnesia and for the reminiscence bump may have more to do with the presence of socially provided memory organizers than with the self per se.

To summarize the evidence for independent systems, specific autobiographical memories and abstract semantic self-knowledge seem to be represented separately, such that accessing one type of self-knowledge does not necessarily entail accessing the other, and such that damage in one system does not necessarily prevent the other from functioning. Moreover, autobiographical memory ability relies on the development of non-self-related memory organization processes as much as on the development of the concept of the self. The next section reviews evidence suggesting that adults can control the extent to which any given autobiographical memory relates to the self by choosing whether to cherish (own) that memory psychologically.

Choosing What to Cherish Controls the Influence of Autobiographical Memory on the Self

Theorists and laypeople may assume a very close tie between autobiographical memory and the self because they think of memory in a caricaturized way. They think of cherished memories such as those that occupy the fictional Kevin Arnold in *The Wonder Years*: milestones, life changers, major decisions. They fail to acknowledge that life is also made up of a large number of unconnected, unchosen, random experiences. Not every remembered

experience can possibly be relevant to the self (e.g., What did you have for lunch yesterday? Where and when did you acquire the shirt you are wearing today?), yet such self-irrelevant memories are still recollected, recognized as having happened to the self, and can produce a sense of mental time travel. If every autobiographical memory mattered for the self, every one of us would express the identity confusion experienced by the hyperthymestic Jill Price.

But every autobiographical memory does *not* matter for the self. Instead, individual autobiographical memories are recollected with different degrees of ownership by the self; they are more or less cherished. The analogy to physical ownership is apt. Not every possession is part of the self-concept. The pen with which one signs a check could be self-relevant ("my favorite pen"), or not self-relevant in the slightest ("the pen kept in the desk"). In the same way, a memory of an event that happened to the self may be self-relevant ("The time I first met my future spouse while walking my dog"), or not self-relevant ("The time I walked my dog in the park a few years ago"). During or just after the process of autobiographical memory construction, a decision about belongingness may therefore be made. If the memory is judged as belonging to the self, it is deemed a self-relevant life *experience*. If it is judged as peripheral to the self, then the memory is deemed a mere life *happening*, with no import for or implications about the self. The distinction between experiences and happenings is due not solely to the nature of the life event itself but also to the manner in which it is recollected later as an autobiographical memory.

Differential Activation of the Self During Memory Construction

To see differences in self-ownership of autobiographical memories, consider the brain mechanisms involved in autobiographical memory construction. As reviewed earlier, one critical brain area is the medial prefrontal cortex, the part of the brain involved in self-reference. Although most studies do show some activation in the medial prefrontal cortex during autobiographical (but not episodic) memory, the *degree* of activation varies. In a functional magnetic resonance imaging study, scans were conducted as participants thought about autobiographical memories in one of three ways. For some memories, participants were instructed to focus on the feelings aroused by this memory; for other memories, to analyze the feelings aroused by this memory; and for others, to simply accept the feelings aroused by this memory. Activation in the self-referent area of the brain (the medial prefrontal cortex) was greatest when participants focused on their feelings about the memory and lowest when they accepted their feelings (Kross, Davidson, Weber, & Ochsner, 2009).

To recollect any given autobiographical memory without engaging the self, then, people may engage in a process of emotional acceptance. Or they may instead engage in one of the processes discussed below at the time of memory construction. All of these processes lead to the inference that the particular autobiographical memory is a mere happening rather than an important experience in one's life. In other words, a variety of mechanisms allow people to forego psychological ownership of autobiographical memories, to choose not to cherish the memory, thereby removing the potentially threatening conflict between the memory and the sense of self (Beike & Landoll, 2000).

Different Processes Occurring after Memory Construction

There are many ways to forego ownership of a recollected autobiographical memory. For example, autobiographical memories whose implications are unflattering to the present self (e.g., a time in the past that one failed) are perceived as being psychologically and temporally remote from the present time period (Ross & Wilson, 2002). The memory is seen as representing a different self; psychological distance is translated into temporal distance. A second method for reducing ownership of autobiographical memories whose implications do not fit with the sense of self is to perceive them as difficult to recall. When motivated to think of an autobiographical memory as indicative of a failure-inducing versus a success-inducing personality trait, participants reported that they felt it was subjectively harder to recall those memories (Sanitioso & Niedenthal, 2006).

A third way to reduce ownership of autobiographical memories whose implications do not fit with the self can be to perceive them as psychologically closed rather than open. Memories that feel closed are by definition subjectively of the past rather than the present; they are distanced from the self. Memories that feel open feel like they are incomplete, or unfinished business, and therefore retain importance for the self (Beike & Landoll, 2000; Beike & Wirth-Beaumont, 2005). Closed memories have little or no impact on the self (Beike & Landoll, 2000). Moreover, closed memories

have little or no impact on behavior. For example, participants asked to recollect an autobiographical memory of a time they had an opportunity to donate to charity but failed to do so were then instructed to think about that memory as either open or closed. Those assigned to think of the memory as open rather than closed later engaged in more memory-related behaviors (clicking on a button to add to a charity donation). Moreover, those assigned to think of the memory as closed did not differ in their number of memory-related behaviors from those who did not recollect a memory at all. In other words, closed memories are inert (Beike, Adams, & Naufel, 2010).

A fourth way of foregoing ownership is altering the visual perspective in the memory. Autobiographical memories may be recollected from the first-person (actor) perspective or from the third-person (observer) perspective (see Chapter 8). First-person memories are usually more closely tied to the self because they evoke more emotion (Robinson & Swanson, 1993). In addition, first-person memories activate areas of the brain involved in bodily sensation, suggesting that the self is more "physically present" when recollecting memories from a first-person perspective (Eich, Nelson, Leghari, & Handy, 2009). People recollect memories from a first-person perspective when they see these autobiographical memories as revelatory of the current self (Libby & Eibach, 2011; Sanitioso, 2008). However, people recollect memories from a third-person perspective when they see these autobiographical memories as revelatory of a past self that is different from the present self (Libby & Eibach, 2011; Libby, Eibach, & Gilovich, 2005). Therefore, a rememberer may use a third-person perspective when recollecting self-inconsistent memories to keep them from influencing the sense of self.

A fifth way of foregoing ownership of an autobiographical memory involves downplaying its place in the life narrative. Self-defining memories play a prominent role in the life story and also influence the view of the self (Singer & Salovey, 1993). Therefore, giving an autobiographical memory self-defining status will increase its influence on the self. Consistent with this logic, bereaved people who reported the death of the loved one as a self-defining memory were more likely to experience complicated grief than those whose self-defining memories concerned other events (Maccallum & Bryant, 2008). Similar evidence of problems resulting from making traumatic memories self-defining comes from research on PTSD. Clinical lore has it that traumatic experiences should be integrated into the self and the life story for the best adjustment. To the contrary, Berntsen and Rubin (2007) posited that such experiences should instead be seen as peripheral to the self and the life story. Consistent with Berntsen and Rubin's theory, but inconsistent with clinical lore, trauma survivors who viewed the traumatic event as more central to the self had more PTSD symptoms. Conversely, making the trauma peripheral to the self mitigated its effects on the self—a strategy that could be used for any self-inconsistent memory and not just traumatic memories.

One way of making a memory less integral to the life story is to recollect it as a specific episode lasting less than one day (specific memory) rather than as a general event lasting multiple days or recurring repeatedly (general memory). Participants were told that extraversion predicted success, or predicted failure, and then were asked to write down autobiographical memories of times they behaved in an extraverted or introverted way. Participants who thought that extraversion predicted success tended to recall general rather than specific memories of times they were extraverted, compared with those who thought that extraversion predicted failure (Brunot & Sanitioso, 2004). In other words, to make an autobiographical memory less cherished, one may think of the memory as representing a short happening rather than a protracted life experience. Interestingly, an inability to achieve this memory specificity was discussed earlier as overgeneral memory, which is predictive of emotional and psychological problems (Williams et al., 2007). Perhaps without the ability to recollect autobiographical memories as specifically as possible, people find their self-concepts distressingly altered by their every recollection.

To summarize, people can mitigate the self-relevance of any given autobiographical memory by the processes they engage in during and subsequent to construction of that memory. They may, in effect, choose not to cherish the memory. They may recollect the memory as feeling temporally distant, as psychologically closed, or with a third-person perspective. They may convince themselves that it was difficult to bring the memory to mind. Or they may see the remembered event as being brief and having no clear place in the life story. Any of these ownership-reducing processes will allow the rememberer to recollect an autobiographical memory without needing to distort its positivity or its important factual details. Thus, they preserve correspondence without sacrificing coherence (Conway et al., 2004).

Interestingly, although each of these processes results in reduced ownership of autobiographical memories, they are nonetheless distinct. For example, both seeing a memory as self-defining and thinking of it as general increase self-ownership of the memory, yet self-defining memories are more likely to be specific than are other memories (Singer & Salovey, 1993). Seeing a memory as closed and viewing it from the third-person perspective both decrease self-ownership, yet closed memories are no more likely to be viewed from the third-person perspective than are other memories (Beike & Wirth-Beaumont, 2005). In other words, the mechanisms for reducing self-ownership cannot be reduced to a single underlying property or mechanism.

Although each of the ownership-reducing processes was discussed as if it were under the control of the rememberer, existent research does not yet reveal the extent to which each is truly explicit and strategic. Each may require time, intention, or awareness, or may instead be more automatically engaged whenever a memory and the self fail to cohere (Conway et al., 2004). But if the processes are at least to some degree controllable, they can be used to provide a sense of stability in the self, to boost self-esteem, and to aid in coping with traumatic experiences. More research on the adaptive benefits and strategic employment of each ownership-reducing process is needed.

Conclusion

To summarize succinctly, specific autobiographical memories and abstract self-concepts are related, but not inextricably so. Research has revealed that bringing to mind specific autobiographical memories can, but need not, alter one's abstract concept of the self. It has also revealed that the abstract concept of self can, but need not, distort one's specific autobiographical memories. Explanations for the separation of autobiographical memory and the self focused on the operation of functionally independent systems, as well as moment-to-moment cognitions that reduce the sense of ownership of specific memories. In short, we select some memories and cherish them by holding them close to the self. These memories influence our sense of who and what we are. We deselect the remaining memories and choose not to cherish them. We distance ourselves from these memories and thereby protect our sense of self from being buffeted too strongly by the process of remembering.

Indeed, we do cherish many of our autobiographical memories. We chew on them, feed on them, gain comfort from them, and remind ourselves of the personal growth we achieved by virtue of them. That is the function of cherished memories: to support and enhance one's sense of identity. Yet we still retain noncherished memories. These memories are held apart from the self, but they are nonetheless important. Autobiographical memory serves not only an identity function—cherished memories—but also a social function and a directive function.

Cherished memories best serve the identity function, and they are joined by other mechanisms that help forge and preserve identity. In addition to autobiographical memory, implicit and semantic memory systems also contribute to the sense of self (Duff et al., 2008; Klein, 2004; Rathbone et al., 2009). Sensory information (e.g., I have brown hair) and feedback from others (e.g., I'm funny) contribute as well (Sedikides & Skowronski, 1995; Yarmey & Johnson, 1982). Rather than endorsing Fuchs' (2001) statement that "your memory is who you are," it is more accurate to say that your memory is *part* of who you are.

Noncherished memories better serve other functions. Autobiographical memories give us something to talk about, connect us to others, provide knowledge about the world, enable imagination of the future, help to regulate emotions, and guide and direct behavior (Bluck, Alea, Habermas, & Rubin, 2005; Klein, Robertson, & Delton, 2010; Nelson, 2003; Pasupathi, 2003; Pillemer, 2003). Identity maintenance is not *the* reason we have autobiographical memory, it is *one* reason we have autobiographical memory. In other words, autobiographical memories have value besides their potential for providing information about the self, so their frequent independence from the self ought not to make them of any less interest to social cognitive psychologists. In fact, the mechanisms by which people adaptively maintain identity by choosing which autobiographical memories to cherish are of considerable interest to social cognitive psychologists.

References

Addis, D. R., & Tippett, L. J. (2004). Memory of myself: Autobiographical memory and identity in Alzheimer's disease. *Memory, 12*(1), 56–74.

Ames, D., Jenkins, A., Banaji, M., & Mitchell, J. (2008). Taking another person's perspective increases self-referential neural processing. *Psychological Science, 19*(7), 642–644.

Barsalou, L. (1988). The content and organization of autobiographical memories. In U. Neisser & E. Winograd (Eds.), *Remembering reconsidered: Ecological and traditional approaches to the study of memory* (pp. 193–243). New York: Cambridge University Press.

Bauer, P. (2006). Constructing a past in infancy: A neuro–developmental account. *Trends in Cognitive Sciences, 10*(4), 175–181.

Beike, D., Adams, L., & Naufel, K. (2010). Closure of autobiographical memories moderates their directive effect on behaviour. *Memory, 18*(1), 40–48.

Beike, D., Kleinknecht, E., & Wirth–Beaumont, E. (2004). How emotional and nonemotional memories define the self. In D. R. Beike, J. M. Lampinen, & D. A. Behrend (Eds.), *The self and memory* (pp. 141–159). New York: Psychology Press.

Beike, D., & Landoll, S. (2000). Striving for a consistent life story: Cognitive reactions to autobiographical memories. *Social Cognition, 18*(3), 292–318.

Beike, D., & Wirth–Beaumont, E. (2005). Psychological closure as a memory phenomenon. *Memory, 13*(6), 574–593.

Bem, D. (1967). Self-perception: An alternative interpretation of cognitive dissonance phenomena. *Psychological Review, 74*(3), 183–200.

Berntsen, D. (1996). Involuntary autobiographical memories. *Applied Cognitive Psychology, 10*(5), 435–454.

Berntsen, D. (1998). Voluntary and involuntary access to autobiographical memory. *Memory, 6*(2), 113–141.

Berntsen, D., & Hall, N. (2004). The episodic nature of involuntary autobiographical memories. *Memory and Cognition, 32*(5), 789–803.

Berntsen, D., & Rubin, D. (2002). Emotionally charged autobiographical memories across the life span: The recall of happy, sad, traumatic and involuntary memories. *Psychology and Aging, 17*(4), 636–652.

Berntsen, D., & Rubin, D. (2004). Cultural life scripts structure recall from autobiographical memory. *Memory and Cognition, 32*(3), 427–442.

Berntsen, D., & Rubin, D. (2007). When a trauma becomes a key to identity: Enhanced integration of trauma memories predicts posttraumatic stress disorder symptoms. *Applied Cognitive Psychology, 21*(4), 417–431.

Blagov, P., & Singer, J. (2004). Four dimensions of self-defining memories (specificity, meaning, content, and affect) and their relationships to self-restraint, distress, and repressive defensiveness. *Journal of Personality, 72*(3), 481–511.

Bluck, S., Alea, N., Habermas, T., & Rubin, D. (2005). A TALE of three functions: The self-reported uses of autobiographical memory. *Social Cognition, 23*(1), 91–117.

Bohn, A., & Berntsen, D. (2008). Life story development in childhood: The development of life story abilities and the acquisition of cultural life scripts from late middle childhood to adolescence. *Developmental Psychology, 44*(4), 1135–1147.

Botzung, A., Denkova, E., Ciuciu, P., Scheiber, C., & Manning, L. (2008). The neural bases of the constructive nature of autobiographical memories studied with a self-paced fMRI design. *Memory, 16*(4), 351–363.

Bruner, J. (1994). The "remembered" self. In U. Neisser & R. Fivush (Eds.), *The remembering self: Construction and accuracy in the self-narrative* (pp. 41–54). New York: Cambridge University Press.

Brunot, S., & Sanitioso, R. (2004). Motivational influence on the quality of memories: Recall of general autobiographical memories related to desired attributes. *European Journal of Social Psychology, 34*(5), 627–635.

Cleveland, E., & Reese, E. (2008). Children remember early childhood: Long–term recall across the offset of childhood amnesia. *Applied Cognitive Psychology, 22*(1), 127–142.

Conway, M., & Ross, M. (1984). Getting what you want by revising what you had. *Journal of Personality and Social Psychology, 47*(4), 738–748.

Conway, M. A. (1990). *Autobiographical memory: An introduction.* Buckingham, UK: Open University Press.

Conway, M. A. (2005). Memory and the self. *Journal of Memory and Language, 53*(4), 594–628.

Conway, M. A. (2009). Episodic memories. *Neuropsychologia, 47*(11), 2305–2313.

Conway, M. A., & Haque, S. (1999). Overshadowing the reminiscence bump: Memories of a struggle for independence. *Journal of Adult Development, 6*(1), 35–44.

Conway, M. A., & Holmes, A. (2004). Psychosocial stages and the accessibility of autobiographical memories across the life cycle. *Journal of Personality, 72*(3), 461–480.

Conway, M. A., & Pleydell-Pearce, C. (2000). The construction of autobiographical memories in the self-memory system. *Psychological Review, 107*(2), 261–288.

Conway, M. A., Pleydell-Pearce, C., & Whitecross, S. (2001). The neuroanatomy of autobiographical memory: A slow cortical potential study of autobiographical memory retrieval. *Journal of Memory and Language, 45*(3), 493–524.

Conway, M. A., Singer, J., & Tagini, A. (2004). The self and autobiographical memory: Correspondence and coherence. *Social Cognition, 22*(5), 491–529.

Daselaar, S., Rice, H., Greenberg, D., Cabeza, R., LaBar, K., & Rubin, D. (2008). The spatiotemporal dynamics of autobiographical memory: Neural correlates of recall, emotional intensity, and reliving. *Cerebral Cortex, 18*(1), 217–229.

Duff, M., Wszalek, T., Tranel, D., & Cohen, N. (2008). Successful life outcome and management of real–world memory demands despite profound anterograde amnesia. *Journal of Clinical and Experimental Neuropsychology, 30*(8), 931–945.

Eich, E., Nelson, A., Leghari, M., & Handy, T. (2009). Neural systems mediating field and observer memories. *Neuropsychologia, 47*(11), 2239–2251.

Epley, N., & Whitchurch, E. (2008). Mirror, mirror on the wall: Enhancement in self-recognition. *Personality and Social Psychology Bulletin, 34*(9), 1159–1170.

France, L. (2005, January). The death of yesterday. *The Observer.* Retrieved from http://www.guardian.co.uk/books/2005/jan/23/biography.features3

Fuchs, C. (2001). *Ever present.* Retrieved May 29, 2010, from http://popmatters.com/film/reviews/m/memento.shtml.

Gilboa, A. (2004). Autobiographical and episodic memory–one and the same? Evidence from prefrontal activation in neuroimaging studies. *Neuropsychologia, 42*(10), 1336–1349.

Greenberg, D., Rice, H., Cooper, J., Cabeza, R., Rubin, D., & LaBar, K. (2005). Co-activation of the amygdala, hippocampus and inferior frontal gyrus during autobiographical memory retrieval. *Neuropsychologia, 43*(5), 659–674.

Greenwald, A. (1980). The totalitarian ego: Fabrication and revision of personal history. *American Psychologist, 35*(7), 603–618.

Grice, H. P. (1941). Personal identity. *Mind, 50,* 330–350.

Habermas, T., & Bluck, S. (2000). Getting a life: The emergence of the life story in adolescence. *Psychological Bulletin, 126*(5), 748–769.

Haque, S., & Conway, M. (2001). Sampling the process of autobiographical memory construction. *European Journal of Cognitive Psychology, 13*(4), 529–547.

Harel, J., Eshel, Y., Ganor, O., & Scher, A. (2002). Antecedents of mirror self-recognition of toddlers: Emotional availability, birth order and gender. *Infant Mental Health Journal, 23*(3), 293–309.

Harley, K., & Reese, E. (1999). Origins of autobiographical memory. *Developmental Psychology, 35*(5), 1338–1348.

Hilts, P. J. (1995). *Memory's ghost: The strange tale of Mr. M.* New York: Simon & Schuster.

Horowitz, M., & Becker, S. (1972). Cognitive response to stress: Experimental studies of a "compulsion to repeat trauma." *Psychoanalysis and Contemporary Science, 1,* 258–305.

Howe, M., & Courage, M. (1997). The emergence and early development of autobiographical memory. *Psychological Review, 104*(3), 499–523.

Howe, M., Courage, M., & Edison, S. (2003). When autobiographical memory begins. *Developmental Review, 23*(4), 471–494.

Jack, F., MacDonald, S., Reese, E., & Hayne, H. (2009). Maternal reminiscing style during early childhood predicts the age of adolescents' earliest memories. *Child Development, 80*(2), 496–505.

Kernis, M., Cornell, D., Sun, C., Berry, A., & Harlow, T. (1993). There's more to self-esteem than whether it is high or low: The importance of stability of self-esteem. *Journal of Personality and Social Psychology, 65*(6), 1190–1204.

Klein, S. (2004). The cognitive neuroscience of knowing one's self. *The cognitive neurosciences* (3rd ed., pp. 1077–1089). Cambridge, MA: MIT Press.

Klein, S., & Loftus, J. (1993). Behavioral experience and trait judgments about the self. *Personality and Social Psychology Bulletin, 19*(6), 740–745.

Klein, S., Robertson, T., & Delton, A. (2010). Facing the future: Memory as an evolved system for planning future acts. *Memory and Cognition, 38*(1), 13–22.

Klein, S., Sherman, J., & Loftus, J. (1996). The role of episodic and semantic memory in the development of trait self-knowledge. *Social Cognition, 14*(4), 277–291.

Kross, E., Davidson, M., Weber, J., & Ochsner, K. (2009). Coping with emotions past: The neural bases of regulating affect associated with negative autobiographical memories. *Biological Psychiatry, 65*(5), 361–366.

Leary, M., & Tangney, J. (2003). The self as an organizing construct in the behavioral and social sciences. In M. R. Leary & J. P. Tangney (Eds.), *Handbook of self and identity* (pp. 3–14). New York: Guilford Press.

Libby, L. (2008). A neural signature of the current self. *Social Cognitive and Affective Neuroscience, 3*(3), 192–194.

Libby, L. K., & Eibach, R. P. (2011). Self-enhancement or self-coherence? Why people shift visual perspective in mental images of the personal past and future. *Personality and Social Psychology Bulletin, 37*(5), 714–726.

Libby, L., Eibach, R., & Gilovich, T. (2005). Here's looking at me: The effect of memory perspective on assessments of personal change. *Journal of Personality and Social Psychology, 88*(1), 50–62.

Maccallum, F., & Bryant, R. (2008). Self-defining memories in complicated grief. *Behaviour Research and Therapy, 46*(12), 1311–1315.

Mace, J. (2004). Involuntary autobiographical memories are highly dependent on abstract cuing: The Proustian view is incorrect. *Applied Cognitive Psychology, 18*(7), 893–899.

Magno, E., & Allan, K. (2007). Self-reference during explicit memory retrieval: An event–related potential analysis. *Psychological Science, 18*(8), 672–677.

Markus, H. (1977). Self-schemata and processing information about the self. *Journal of Personality and Social Psychology, 35*(2), 63–78.

Markus, H., & Wurf, E. (1987). The dynamic self-concept: A social psychological perspective. *Annual Review of Psychology*, *38*, 299–337.

McAdams, D. (2001). The psychology of life stories. *Review of General Psychology*, *5*(2), 100–122.

McAdams, D., Reynolds, J., Lewis, M., Patten, A., & Bowman, P. (2001). When bad things turn good and good things turn bad: Sequences of redemption and contamination in life narrative and their relation to psychosocial adaptation in midlife adults and in students. *Personality and Social Psychology Bulletin*, *27*(4), 474–485.

McLean, K., Pasupathi, M., & Pals, J. (2007). Selves creating stories creating selves: A process model of self-development. *Personality and Social Psychology Review*, *11*(3), 262–278.

McLean, K., & Pratt, M. (2006). Life's little (and big) lessons: Identity statuses and meaning–making in the turning point narratives of emerging adults. *Developmental Psychology*, *42*(4), 714–722.

Medved, M., & Brockmeier, J. (2008). Continuity amid chaos: Neurotrauma, loss of memory, and sense of self. *Qualitative Health Research*, *18*(4), 469–479.

Mullen, M. (1994). Earliest recollections of childhood: A demographic analysis. *Cognition*, *52*(1), 55–79.

Nelson, K. (2003). Self and social functions: Individual autobiographical memory and collective narrative. *Memory*, *11*(2), 125–136.

Nelson, K., & Fivush, R. (2004). The emergence of autobiographical memory: A social cultural developmental theory. *Psychological Review*, *111*(2), 486–511.

Neshat-Doost, H., Dalgleish, T., & Golden, A. (2008). Reduced specificity of emotional autobiographical memories following self-regulation depletion. *Emotion*, *8*(5), 731–736.

Oddo, S., Lux, S., Weiss, P., Schwab, A., Welzer, H., Markowitsch, H., et al. (2010). Specific role of medial prefrontal cortex in retrieving recent autobiographical memories: An fMRI study of young female subjects. *Cortex: A Journal Devoted to the Study of the Nervous System and Behavior*, *46*(1), 29–39.

Odegard, T., & Lampinen, J. (2004). Memory conjunction errors for autobiographical events: More than just familiarity. *Memory*, *12*(3), 288–300.

Parker, E., Cahill, L., & McGaugh, J. (2006). A case of unusual autobiographical remembering. *Neurocase*, *12*(1), 35–49.

Pasupathi, M. (2003). Emotion regulation during social remembering: Differences between emotions elicited during an event and emotions elicited when talking about it. *Memory*, *11*(2), 151–163.

Pillemer, D. (2003). Directive functions of autobiographical memory: The guiding power of the specific episode. *Memory*, *11*(2), 193–202.

Povinelli, D., Landau, K., & Perilloux, H. (1996). Self-recognition in young children using delayed versus live feedback: Evidence of a developmental asynchrony. *Child Development*, *67*(4), 1540–1554.

Povinelli, D., & Simon, B. (1998). Young children's understanding of briefly versus extremely delayed images of the self: Emergence of the autobiographical stance. *Developmental Psychology*, *34*(1), 188–194.

Price, J., & Davis, B. (2008). *The woman who can't forget: The extraordinary story of living with the most remarkable memory known to science—A memoir*. New York: Free Press.

Rathbone, C., Moulin, C., & Conway, M. (2008). Self-centered memories: The reminiscence bump and the self. *Memory and Cognition*, *36*(8), 1403–1414.

Rathbone, C., Moulin, C., & Conway, M. (2009). Autobiographical memory and amnesia: Using conceptual knowledge to ground the self. *Neurocase*, *15*(5), 405–418.

Robinson, J., & Swanson, K. (1993). Field and observer modes of remembering. *Memory*, *1*(3), 169–184.

Ross, M. (1989). Relation of implicit theories to the construction of personal histories. *Psychological Review*, *96*(2), 341–357.

Ross, M., & Wilson, A. (2002). It feels like yesterday: Self-esteem, valence of personal past experiences, and judgments of subjective distance. *Journal of Personality and Social Psychology*, *82*(5), 792–803.

Rubin, D. (2000). The distribution of early childhood memories. *Memory*, *8*(4), 265–269.

Rubin, D. (2005). A basic-systems approach to autobiographical memory. *Current Directions in Psychological Science*, *14*(2), 79–83.

Rubin, D., & Schulkind, M. (1997). Distribution of important and word-cued autobiographical memories in 20-, 35-, and 70-year-old adults. *Psychology and Aging*, *12*(3), 524–535.

Sacks, O. (1985). *The man who mistook his wife for a hat and other clinical tales*. New York: Simon & Schuster.

Sacks, O. (2007, September). The abyss: Music and amnesia. *New Yorker*. Retrieved from http://www.newyorker.com/reporting/2007/09/24/070924fa_fact_sacks

Sanitioso, R. (2008). Motivated self and recall: Visual perspectives in remembering past behaviors. *European Journal of Social Psychology*, *38*(3), 566–575.

Sanitioso, R., Kunda, Z., & Fong, G. (1990). Motivated recruitment of autobiographical memories. *Journal of Personality and Social Psychology*, *59*(2), 229–241.

Sanitioso, R., & Niedenthal, P. (2006). Motivated self-perception and perceived ease in recall of autobiographical memories. *Self and Identity*, *5*(1), 73–84.

Schlagman, S., & Kvavilashvili, L. (2008). Involuntary autobiographical memories in and outside the laboratory: How different are they from voluntary autobiographical memories? *Memory and Cognition*, *36*(5), 920–932.

Schrauf, R., & Rubin, D. (2001). Effects of voluntary immigration on the distribution of autobiographical memory over the lifespan. *Applied Cognitive Psychology*, *15*(7), S75–S88.

Schwarz, N., Bless, H., Strack, F., Klumpp, G., Rittenauer-Schatka, H., & Simons, A. (1991). Ease of retrieval as information: Another look at the availability heuristic. *Journal of Personality and Social Psychology*, *61*(2), 195–202.

Scoville, W., & Milner, B. (1957). Loss of recent memory after bilateral hippocampal lesions. *Journal of Neurology, Neurosurgery and Psychiatry*, *20*, 11–21.

Sedikides, C., & Green, J. (2000). On the self-protective nature of inconsistency–negativity management: Using the person memory paradigm to examine self-referent memory. *Journal of Personality and Social Psychology*, *79*(6), 906–922.

Sedikides, C., & Skowronski, J. (1995). On the sources of self-knowledge: The perceived primacy of self-reflection. *Journal of Social and Clinical Psychology*, *14*(3), 244–270.

Setterlund, M., & Niedenthal, P. (1993). "Who am I? Why am I here?" Self-esteem, self-clarity, and prototype matching. *Journal of Personality and Social Psychology*, *65*(4), 769–780.

Singer, J., & Salovey, P. (1993). *The remembered self: Emotion and memory in personality*. New York: Free Press.

Smith, S., Souchay, C., & Conway, M. (2010). Overgeneral autobiographical memory in Parkinson's disease. *Cortex: A Journal Devoted to the Study of the Nervous System and Behavior*, *46*(6), 787–793.

Spreng, R., & Grady, C. (2010). Patterns of brain activity supporting autobiographical memory, prospection, and theory of mind, and their relationship to the default mode network. *Journal of Cognitive Neuroscience, 22*(6), 1112–1123.

Squire, L. (1992). Memory and the hippocampus: A synthesis from findings with rats, monkeys, and humans. *Psychological Review, 99*(2), 195–231.

Thorne, A., McLean, K., & Lawrence, A. (2004). When remembering is not enough: Reflecting on self-defining memories in late adolescence. *Journal of Personality, 72*(3), 513–541.

Wagenaar, W. (1986). My memory: A study of autobiographical memory over six years. *Cognitive Psychology, 18*(2), 225–252.

Wang, Q. (2007). "Remember when you got the big, big bulldozer?" Mother–child reminiscing over time and across cultures. *Social Cognition, 25*(4), 455–471.

Watkins, E., (2004). Adaptive and maladaptive ruminative self-focus during emotional processing. *Behavior Research and Therapy, 42*(9), 1037–1052.

Wearing, D. (2005). *Forever today: A memoir of love and amnesia.* London, UK: Corgi.

Weisenberg, M., Solomon, Z., Schwarzwald, J., & Mikulincer, M. (1987). Assessing the severity of posttraumatic stress disorder: Relation between dichotomous and continuous measures. *Journal of Consulting and Clinical Psychology, 55*(3), 432–434.

Wigmore, B. (2008). *The woman who can't forget ANYTHING: Widow has ability—and curse—to perfectly remember every single day of her life.* Retrieved October 2, 2011 from http://www.dailymail.co.uk/news/article–564948/The–woman–forget–ANYTHING–Widow–ability—curse—perfectly–remember–single–day–life.html#ixzz1ZfJx72dp.

Williams, J., Barnhofer, T., Crane, C., Herman, D., Raes, F., Watkins, E., et al. (2007). Autobiographical memory specificity and emotional disorder. *Psychological Bulletin, 133*(1), 122–148.

Yarmey, A., & Johnson, J. (1982). Evidence for the self as an imaginal prototype. *Journal of Research in Personality, 16*(2), 238–246.

Self-Evaluation and Self-Esteem

Mark R. Leary *and* Meredith L. Terry

Abstract

People's evaluations of themselves are intricately linked to their views of other people. Not only are people's self-evaluations affected by their beliefs about other people, but also their evaluations of themselves influence their perceptions and judgments of others. This chapter first examines the primary sources of self-evaluations (personal observation and experience, explicit feedback, social comparisons, reflected appraisals) and the motivational and cognitive reasons that people's self-evaluations sometimes diverge from the feedback and information that they have about themselves. The second major section explores the nature of self-esteem, including its possible functions, the nature of self-enhancement, and the question of whether people possess a need for self-esteem. Finally, the authors examine the effects of people's self-evaluations on their perceptions and judgments of other people.

Key Words: self-evaluation, self-esteem, self-enhancement

Self-Evaluation and Self-Esteem

At some point during the course of human evolution, our hominid ancestors acquired the ability to think consciously about themselves. The capacity for self-awareness and self-relevant thought seems to involve a number of distinct mental abilities—such as self-recognition, thinking about oneself in the future, introspection, and representing oneself in abstract and symbolic ways—and various facets of the capacity for self-cognition probably evolved separately at different times. For example, evidence that prehumans could think consciously about themselves in the future can be found as far back as 2 million years ago when *Homo habilis* carried rocks for long distances to make stone tools and then carried those tools from place to place, suggesting an ability to imagine oneself needing a tool in the future (Leary & Buttermore, 2003). But evidence that people could think about themselves in the abstract and symbolic ways that modern human beings do is not seen until 40,000 to 60,000 years

ago at the time of the "cultural big bang." At that time, evidence of bodily adornment, symbolic group identification, burials containing grave goods (signifying an abstract belief in an afterlife), and paintings of personal experiences suggest that people could represent themselves abstractly, conceptually, and symbolically (Leary & Buttermore, 2003; see also Sedikides & Skowronski, 2003).

Among other things, the capacity for self-relevant thought underlies thinking about and planning for the future, analyzing one's past experiences, introspecting on one's feelings and motives, evaluating oneself, inferring other people's impressions of oneself, and exerting self-control (Leary, 2004). Of these important self-cognitive processes, our focus in this chapter is on self-evaluation and its close cousin, self-esteem.

The ability to evaluate oneself—that is, to assess one's characteristics, abilities, and behaviors on a valenced continuum of bad–good or negative–positive—is involved in many aspects of human behavior. For example, self-evaluation is critically involved in decision making. When people are trying to decide whether to take a particular course of action, they typically assess whether they are capable of performing the action or possess characteristics that will lead to a desired outcome, and their behavioral decision is based partly on the outcome of this self-evaluation. Sometimes, self-evaluations involve judgments of one's stable traits, characteristics, or abilities, such as when students wonder whether they have the requisite ability to take an upper-level math course or people evaluate their physical attractiveness. In other instances, self-evaluations involve assessments of one's transient states such as when people criticize themselves for a stupid mistake or try to decide whether their capacity to drive a car has been compromised by drinking a few beers. In either case, one aspect of many decisions involves evaluating one's characteristics, abilities, and behaviors.

In addition, because many important social outcomes depend on being viewed by other people in particular ways, people often try to infer how others perceive and evaluate them. For example, whenever people desire to make a particular impression on another person—such as in a job interview or when interacting with a potential romantic partner—they must evaluate the degree to which they possess traits that the target will value as well as infer how they are being perceived (or are likely to be perceived) by the target. The ability to assess how one is perceived and evaluated by another person requires people to evaluate themselves from the perspective of the other. Thus, efforts to manage one's impressions, influence other people, and obtain social rewards typically require self-evaluation.

The literature on self-evaluation has sometimes been muddied when writers failed to distinguish between self-beliefs, self-evaluations, and self-esteem. People hold many beliefs about themselves, beliefs both about their stable characteristics and about themselves in the current context. *Self-beliefs* are cognitive representations or descriptions of one's personal characteristics. In contrast, *self-evaluations* are valenced assessments of the content of a self-belief along a continuum of negative to positive or bad to good. Although self-evaluations are linked to self-beliefs, there is not a one-to-one correspondence between them. Two people might have the same belief about themselves but evaluate themselves quite differently in light of that belief.

Many self-evaluations acknowledge that some personal attribute or behavior is good or bad, but

the person has no affective reaction to that evaluation. However, other self-evaluations lead to positive or negative feelings about oneself, and those feelings constitute what we normally call *self-esteem*. How people feel about themselves at the present moment involves state self-esteem, and how they tend to feel about themselves across situations and time involves trait self-esteem.

Historically, the field of social cognition has focused primarily on the processes involved in perceiving, drawing inferences about, and thinking about other people, and less attention has been paid to thinking about and evaluating oneself (see, however, Beike, Lampinen, & Behrend, 2004). However, the cognitive processes that underlie self-relevant thought, including self-evaluation and self-esteem, are intimately linked to how people think about others. Not only are people's self-evaluations and self-esteem influenced by their views of other people (including their beliefs about how others regard them), but also, once formed, self-evaluations and self-esteem influence people's social judgments in many ways.

We begin our examination of self-evaluation and self-esteem by discussing the sources of people's self-evaluations—the primary factors that influence people's evaluations of themselves. We then consider why people's self-evaluations are not as tightly linked to objective information and feedback as one might expect and, thus, why people sometimes evaluate themselves much more positively or negatively than seems to be warranted by the objective evidence. Next, we extend our discussion of self-evaluation to a discussion of self-esteem, arguably one of the most widely studied constructs in psychology, paying particular attention to the question of why self-esteem is so strongly related to how people believe they are evaluated by others. The remainder of the chapter considers the role that self-evaluations play in judgments of other people.

Sources of Self-Evaluations

People obtain the information from which they evaluate themselves from four primary sources—personal observation and experience, explicit feedback, social comparisons, and reflected appraisals. Most obviously, people come to evaluate themselves positively or negatively based on their own experiences, particularly their performance in domains that reflect something about their attributes or abilities (see Bandura, 1977). People draw conclusions about whether they are good or bad in certain domains by observing the outcomes of their own actions. For example, repeatedly falling down when one tries to skate provides direct and concrete evidence that one is a poor skater, and repeated successes at influencing other people might lead to the conclusion that one is good at persuading others.

However, there are surprisingly few domains in which people can unambiguously evaluate themselves on the basis of the outcomes of their actions. In many instances, people need explicit feedback to put their characteristics, behaviors, or performances in perspective. For example, merely knowing that one received a score of 45 on a test or ran a mile in 17 minutes provides no information for self-evaluation. Additional information is needed to allow the person to evaluate himself or herself on the basis of this knowledge. Often, this information is provided through explicit feedback, either from another person or an impersonal criterion that provides the evaluative implications of a particular performance or characteristic. ("You score very high in this ability;" "You run very slowly.")

In other cases, people evaluate themselves by comparing themselves directly to other people. In his initial exposition of social comparison theory, Festinger (1954) observed that, "To the extent that objective, nonsocial means are not available, people evaluate their opinions and abilities by comparison respectively with the opinions and abilities of others" (p. 118). Seeing that one solved a problem more quickly than most other people or finished the race in last place provides information with which to evaluate where one stands relative to others. Although most work on social comparison processes has followed Festinger's lead in emphasizing judgments of opinions and abilities, people can use social comparison to evaluate virtually all of their personal characteristics, including performance appraisals, achievement, physical appearance, morality, intellectual and creative endeavors, personalities, interests, and personal problems (Corning, Krumm, & Smitham, 2006; Giordano, Wood, & Michela, 2000; Goffin, Jelley, Powell, & Johnston, 2009; Heslin, 2003; Klein & Goethals, 2003; Monin, 2007). Furthermore, contrary to Festinger's notion that people use social comparison information mainly when they do not have objective feedback, research suggests that people desire and rely on comparative information to evaluate themselves even when objective information is available (Wood & Wilson, 2003). Extensive research on social comparison processes has examined the conditions under which people compare themselves with others, factors that influence the choice of comparison targets,

and effects of social comparisons on self-evaluations (Suls & Wheeler, 2000).

Finally, people's self-evaluations are influenced by their assumptions about how they are perceived and evaluated by other people (so-called reflected appraisals), even in the absence of direct personal experience, explicit feedback, or social comparisons. Imagining how one is perceived and regarded by other people exerts a notable influence on people's self-beliefs and self-evaluations (Shrauger & Schoeneman, 1979). Of course, these reflected appraisals are not always correct, but they provide information that people use to evaluate themselves.

Importantly, each of these four sources of self-evaluations provides an incomplete and imperfect picture of the person's true characteristics, abilities, and behaviors. Thus, at best, people's self-beliefs and self-evaluations are imperfect representations of their actual attributes, and as we will see, systematic biases can distort their self-evaluations even further.

Accurate and Inaccurate Self-Evaluations

In general, people seem to fare best in life when their self-evaluations are reasonably accurate reflections of their characteristics and abilities. To the extent that judicious decisions depend on having valid information about one's personal characteristics, accurate self-beliefs and self-evaluations promote effective behavior. People who evaluate themselves too positively will attempt tasks that are beyond their ability, take unnecessary risks, persevere too long in unproductive pursuits, defensively ignore negative feedback, and fail to take steps needed to improve. People who evaluate themselves too negatively will lack self-confidence, agonize over imagined shortcomings, fail to initiate actions that they erroneously think they cannot accomplish, and experience unnecessary negative affect. In some cases, inaccurate self-beliefs and self-evaluations can lead to very serious consequences. As Festinger (1954) noted, "The holding of incorrect opinions and/or inaccurate appraisals of one's abilities can be punishing or even fatal in many situations" (p. 135). In brief, having an accurate view of oneself should promote more optimal courses of action.

Given the value of evaluating oneself accurately, some theorists have proposed that people are fundamentally motivated to perceive themselves as accurately and objectively as possible (Sedikides, 1993; Sedikides & Strube, 1997). Research on the self-assessment motive shows that people tend to prefer tasks that provide feedback about themselves over tasks that don't give feedback, and they prefer tasks that are high in diagnosticity, particularly when the attribute being assessed can be changed if it is found to be deficient (Dunning, 1995).

Given the importance of accurate self-evaluations, the fact that people sometimes prefer not to receive accurate or diagnostic information about themselves is perhaps surprising, as is the fact that people's self-evaluations are often inaccurate. Yet a great deal of research suggests that people's self-evaluations do not always map onto objective, valid evidence regarding their characteristics and abilities. Furthermore, discrepancies between reality and self-evaluations are not due solely to people having inadequate or inaccurate information about themselves. As we will see, people sometimes appear motivated to view themselves either more positively or less positively than the evidence warrants.

Figure 26.1 depicts the degree of concordance between self-relevant information gleaned from the various sources described earlier (personal observation and experience, explicit feedback, social comparisons, reflected appraisals) and people's self-evaluations. The objective valence of the self-relevant information is shown on the x-axis, and the valence of the person's self-evaluation is on the y-axis. The diagonal line in Figure 26.1 reflects the line of *feedback-congruent self-evaluations* that correspond to the objective feedback, information,

or evaluation. In general, if people have enough credible information about themselves, and their self-evaluations are not biased, they should evaluate themselves in a manner that is reasonably consistent with the information, and their self-evaluations will fall on or near this line. Of course, feedback is often vague or imprecise, and a particular piece of self-relevant information may be interpreted in various ways, so perfectly congruent self-evaluations should not always be expected and, in fact, are often undesirable and maladaptive. To reflect this ambiguity in whether a particular self-evaluation is appropriately calibrated, the gray area surrounding the line of feedback-congruent self-evaluations in Figure 26.1 indicates a *region* of appropriate self-evaluations. Self-evaluations in this region can be said to be reasonably accurate and appropriate.

The more concrete, specific, explicit, and valid the information that people have about themselves, the more closely their self-evaluations should correspond to that information, and the closer their self-evaluation will be to the appropriate point on the line of feedback-congruent self-evaluations. However, people's self-evaluations sometimes vary greatly from the feedback that they receive. Some self-evaluations fall above the region of feedback-congruent self-evaluations and are thus self-enhancing, and some self-evaluations fall below the region of feedback-congruent self-evaluations and are self-deprecating. The farther that people's self-evaluation at a particular moment diverges from the line of feedback-congruent self-evaluation, the more inaccurate or enhancing/depreciating it can be said to be. The question is why people's self-evaluations often stray markedly from the information they have about themselves. Why are people's self-evaluations often too positive or too negative?

Before answering that question, we must stress that there is no reason whatsoever to expect that people's self-evaluations should always reflect the feedback they receive. Not only is self-relevant information, whether from other people or more objective sources, sometimes incorrect, but also reasonable people do not revise their self-evaluations on the basis of each new piece of information that they receive about themselves. For example, a woman who has received widespread recognition for her skills as an attorney would not be expected to decide suddenly that she is a poor lawyer no matter how badly she handles a particular case. New information is always considered in the context of autobiographical information stored in memory,

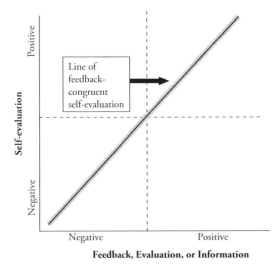

Figure 26.1 Feedback-congruent and Feedback-incongruent Self-evaluations

Note. Self-evaluations on the diagonal line are congruent with feedback, evaluations, or information that the person has received. Self-evaluations off the diagonal line are incongruent with self-relevant feedback, evaluations, or information.

and each new episode of feedback is considered with regard to what is already known. Other people who knew the woman's record as a lawyer would not conclude that she has no ability on the basis of a single disastrous case, and we would not expect her to do so either.

Even so, many instances arise in which people's self-evaluations are not affected by feedback in a reasonable, logical fashion. For example, most faculty members have talked to students who cling to the idea that they are destined for greatness in a particular field despite repeated failures, and fans of the television show, *American Idol*, have seen many contestants who are convinced that they will be the next superstar even though they show little indication of having any singing ability whatsoever. Likewise, people sometimes blow negative feedback out of proportion, drawing more negative inferences about themselves than seem warranted. What processes lead to such miscalibrated self-evaluations, disconnecting people's self-views from reality? A number of answers to this question may be gleaned from the literature. Some reflect motivated distortions, and some involve unmotivated, cognitive processes that nonetheless result in excessively positive or negative self-evaluations.

Motivational Explanations for Miscalibrated Self-Evaluations

SELF-ENHANCEMENT AND SELF-PROTECTION

The standard explanation for instances in which people's self-evaluations are excessively positive (i.e., notably above the line in Figure 26.1) is that people are motivated to protect, maintain, and enhance their self-esteem (Baumeister, Tice, & Hutton, 1989). Hundreds, if not thousands, of studies have documented a pervasive tendency for people to perceive themselves more favorably than objective evidence warrants—that is, for self-evaluations to be more positive than accurate self-evaluations would be. For example, people deny, discount, and distort negative feedback, interpreting it in ways that allow them to maintain positive self-evaluations (Taylor & Brown, 1988). They also evaluate themselves more favorably than seems warranted: they tend to believe that they are better than average in an unrealistic number of domains, make self-serving attributions, engage in overclaiming (claiming knowledge about nonexistent things), hold unrealistically optimistic beliefs about their future, and recall memories in positively biased ways (Boney-McCoy, Gibbons, & Gerrard, 1999; Dewhurst & Marlborough, 2003; Farwell & Wohlwend-Lloyd, 1998; Hoorens, 1993; Krusemark, Campbell, & Clementz, 2008; Paulhus,

Harms, Bruce, & Lysy, 2003; Regan, Snyder, & Kassin, 1995; Robins & Beer, 2001).

Although people undoubtedly construe self-relevant information in ways that allow them to feel good about themselves and maintain self-esteem, researchers have not been sufficiently attentive to other equally plausible explanations for self-enhancement effects. Most notably, many apparent instances of positively biased self-evaluations are, in fact, more parsimoniously viewed as self-presentations rather than self-evaluations. Because people's claims about their characteristics, abilities, and successes and failures have implications for how they are perceived, evaluated, and treated by other people, self-enhancing claims may reflect an effort to be viewed favorably by others rather than a distortion or miscalibration of people's privately held self-evaluations (Leary, Terry, Allen, & Tate, 2009; Schlenker, 1980; Weary Bradley, 1978). In everyday life, as well as in most social psychological studies, people are attuned to how their answers to questions about themselves influence others' impressions of them and, thus, respond in ways that portray themselves in a desired light. The effects of social desirability motives on responses to personality inventories is widely acknowledged (Paulhus, 1991), but equally strong motives to be viewed positively are present in most studies that assess participants' self-evaluations.

Many writers have viewed the influence of self-presentational concerns on research participants' self-ratings as a methodological confound or bias (Fisher & Katz, 2000; Nederhof, 1985), but such effects are fruitfully viewed as an important social psychological phenomenon in their own right. The fact that research participants' responses on measures of self-beliefs and self-evaluations are influenced by their concerns with other people's impressions and evaluations of them should alert us to the likelihood that self-presentational concerns exert equally strong effects on people's behaviors in everyday life.

The possibility that apparent self-enhancement biases may reflect public self-presentations rather than private self-evaluations has been difficult to study experimentally. Participants in most social psychological studies usually know that their self-ratings will be seen by other people, and it is difficult to convince them that their answers are totally private and have no implications for how other people might regard them (Leary, Barnes, Griebel, Mason, & McCormack, 1987; Tetlock & Manstead, 1985). As a result, researchers can rarely know for certain whether participants' self-ratings reflect their private self-evaluations or public self-presentations. Even so, the degree to which self-enhancing self-descriptions arise from an intrapsychic desire to feel good about oneself versus an interpersonal desire to make certain impressions on other people is important to explore (Leary et al., 2009).

SELF-VERIFICATION

A second motivated process that can lead to miscalibrated self-evaluations involves self-verification. According to self-verification theory, people may ignore accurate information about themselves when it conflicts with their existing self-views (Swann, 1983). Because having confidence in one's self-beliefs has both epistemic and pragmatic benefits, information that calls those self-views into question, whether in a positive or negative direction, is troubling. As a result, people tend to avoid, minimize, and refute feedback that is inconsistent with how they see themselves (see Swann & Buhrmester, 2012, for a review of the self-verification literature). Thus, information that would seem directly relevant to a person's self-evaluation is ignored or dismissed and has little if any impact on self-evaluations, leading self-evaluations to stray from the line of feedback-congruent self-evaluations in Figure 26.1.

Ironically, although self-verification processes can lead to inaccurate self-evaluations, self-verification biases may sometimes be driven by a desire for accuracy. To the extent that people believe that their own self-evaluations are relatively accurate, they are likely to regard information that is consistent with how they perceive and evaluate themselves as more valid than information that is contrary to their self-views. As a result, they may dismiss valid feedback when it conflicts with their existing but inaccurate self-image.

Nonmotivational Explanations for Miscalibrated Self-Evaluations

Biased self-evaluations are most commonly explained in terms of motivated biases to see oneself in particular ways—either more positively than the evidence warrants (self-enhancement) or consistently with one's existing self-views (self-verification). However, people's self-evaluations may differ from feedback-congruent self-evaluations because of the ways in which people process information as they draw inferences about themselves.

COGNITIVE INFLUENCES

Many years ago, just as the frenzy of research on self-serving biases was beginning, Miller and Ross (1975) suggested that people's tendency to take more responsibility for success than for failure may reflect a logical rather than motivated inference. Among their explanations for biased self-attributions, Miller and Ross concluded that people claim more responsibility for success than failure because they expect their behavior to produce positive rather than negative outcomes (and people are more likely to make internal attributions for anticipated than unanticipated outcomes), and people can discern the covariation between their actions and successes more easily than the covariation between their actions and failures.

These same kinds of information processing biases may lead people's self-evaluations to deviate from the line of feedback-congruent self-evaluations. For example, people who are trying to achieve a particular outcome may be more likely to internalize the results of their efforts, whether positive or negative, than people who experience a positive or negative outcome that they did not intend or seek. Similarly, instances in which people can easily discern the covariation between their actions and outcomes might lead to more feedback-congruent self-evaluations than instances in which the connection between their behaviors and outcomes is less obvious. Additionally, people are not cognizant of their errors of omission or the gaps in their knowledge when evaluating themselves (Caputo & Dunning, 2004). Sometimes, people lack the information or the perspective needed to evaluate themselves accurately.

In addition, people's existing beliefs about their abilities and personalities have implications for the degree to which feedback, information, or evaluations will influence their self-evaluations. Outcomes that are consistent with people's self-images are more likely to lead to feedback-congruent self-evaluations than outcomes that are inconsistent with how people see themselves (Swanson & Weary, 1982). For example, a man who has not had a car crash in 40 years might not revise his favorable image as a safe driver as the result of a collision because the outcome is incongruent with his self-image.

AFFECTIVE INFLUENCES

Affective influences can also lead to excessively miscalibrated self-evaluations. Theory and research support the notion that people's affective states influence what they focus on, how they interpret events, and what they remember about themselves and past experiences. Several processes have been hypothesized to produce these effects (e.g., Bower,

1981; Forgas, 1995; Schwarz & Clore, 1983), but whatever the underlying process, the valence of people's emotions influences their perceptions, judgments, and decisions across many domains (Mayer, Gaschke, Braverman, & Evans, 1992), presumably including how they evaluate themselves. For example, negative moods may influence the degree to which people perceive and think about the negative comments in a mixed performance review. Likewise, positive moods may lead people to focus on positive feedback and to spin self-relevant information in a more favorable direction. In both instances, extraneous affect may lead people's resulting self-evaluation to deviate from the feedback that they received.

The effects of emotion on self-evaluations have been studied most thoroughly in the case of depression. People who are dysphoric evaluate themselves and their performance differently than those who are not depressed, but disagreement exists regarding the precise nature of this difference. The depressive realism hypothesis suggests that people who are depressed have more accurate self-evaluations, whereas nondepressed people hold positive illusions regarding their abilities and self-evaluations (Alloy & Abramson, 1979). According to this view, because depressed people are more aware of their faults and mistakes, their self-evaluations should fall closer to the line of feedback-congruent self-evaluation than people who are not depressed.

Evidence suggests, however, that depressed people's self-evaluations are often biased in a negative direction. For example, evidence suggests not only that people who are depressed spin events in a negative direction but also that they sometimes preferentially seek negative information about themselves (Giesler, Josephs, & Swann, 1996). Furthermore, research on the cognitive underpinnings of depression suggests that depressed people have excessively negative views of themselves. The self-evaluations of depressed people are negatively biased such that they selectively attend to and remember negative self-relevant events and interpret information about themselves in a negative manner (Denny & Hunt, 1992; Frost, Benton, & Dowrick, 1990; Segrin, 1990). Furthermore, when depressed people receive positive feedback, they tend to discount it, find fault with some other aspect of their performance, or focus on instances when they performed poorly (Segrin, 1990). In a study of the relationship between depression and self-evaluations, Whitton, Larson, and Hauser (2008) found a linear relationship between level of depression and discrepancies between self and other evaluations. People who were highly depressed showed more negative bias in their self-perceptions, rating their performance more negatively than did observers.

Self-Esteem

People can evaluate themselves as good or bad on a particular dimension with no affective reaction or feelings about themselves. For example, most of us are very, very good at opening doors, having encountered very few doors that we cannot open by turning doorknobs or merely pushing. Yet, we are not likely to derive many positive feelings from contemplating what skillful door openers we are. However, some self-evaluations are associated with positive or negative feelings about oneself. To learn that one is very good at solving math problems on standardized tests or is adored by many people is likely to lead not only to evaluating oneself positively but also to feeling good about oneself. And, learning that one received the worst score on a math test or is widely disliked would make most people feel badly about themselves. In brief, many events that influence self-evaluations also have an effect on people's self-esteem.

Traditionally, self-esteem—whether viewed as a stable trait or as a state-like experience—has been viewed as arising from people's personal evaluations of themselves. Most theories have assumed that people's feelings about themselves emerge from a comparison of their self-beliefs to relevant personal standards. James (1890) famously suggested that self-esteem is the ratio of one's successes to one's pretensions, and Rogers (1959) proposed that self-esteem reflects the distance between how people believe they are and how they would like to be. Indeed, many theorists have suggested that self-esteem that is based on anything other than one's own private self-judgments is not true self-esteem and that people's self-esteem should certainly not be influenced by others' evaluations (Deci & Ryan, 1995; May, 1983).

Self-Esteem and Interpersonal Acceptance

Recent theory and research have begun to call this conceptualization into question, however. In particular, sociometer theory proposes that, rather than being the result of a simple comparison of one's characteristics or behaviors with one's private standards, self-esteem reflects the degree to which people perceive that they are relationally valued and socially accepted versus relationally devalued and rejected by other people (Leary & Baumeister,

2000; Leary & Downs, 1995). State self-esteem is conceptualized as a reaction to people's perceptions of the degree to which they are, or are likely to be, valued and accepted by other people in the immediate context or near future. Trait self-esteem is conceptualized as a reflection of people's general sense of the degree to which they are socially valued and accepted. Sociometer theory differs from most explanations in proposing that self-esteem has no value in its own right and that people neither need self-esteem nor are motivated to pursue it for its own sake. Rather, self-esteem is conceptualized as the output of a system that monitors and responds to events in terms of interpersonal acceptance and rejection.

Before the emergence of self-awareness in evolutionary history, this system for monitoring and responding to interpersonal acceptance and rejection presumably operated on the basis of affective responses to nonverbal cues. Other social species respond emotionally and behaviorally to rejection by conspecifics without mediation by conscious self-evaluation (Raleigh & McGuire, 1986). However, after human beings developed the capacity to think consciously about themselves, threats to social acceptance also triggered a conscious analysis of the situation, including an assessment of one's own characteristics and behavior and their role in other people's accepting or rejecting reactions. Thus, state self-esteem rises and falls with changes in perceived relational value, alerting people to real and potential rejection, motivating actions that deal with the social threat, and adjusting people's aspirations in subsequent interactions. Often, people who perceive that they are insufficiently valued try to restore their social connections (which should increase self-esteem), but sometimes they respond aggressively or withdraw from further interactions with the person who rejected them (Richman & Leary, 2009).

From the standpoint of sociometer theory, events that lower self-esteem—such as failure, rejection, negative evaluations, and embarrassing situations—do so because they have real or imagined implications for people's relational value to other people. Many experiments show that participants who are told that other people do not want to get to know them, have excluded them from groups or interactions, or hold negative impressions of them report lower state self-esteem than those who believe that others have accepted them (Leary, Haupt, Strausser, & Chokel, 1998; Leary, Tambor, Terdal, & Downs, 1995; Sommer, Williams,

Ciarocco, & Baumeister, 2001; Zadro, Williams, & Richardson, 2005; see Leary, 2006, for a review). Likewise, studies of reactions to real-world instances of rejection show that people consistently report lower self-esteem following rejection and that the strength of people's connections with others predict self-esteem (Denissen, Penke, Schmitt, & van Aken, 2008; Williams, Shore, & Grahe, 1998; Williams & Zadro, 2001).

Not only does explicit rejection lower state self-esteem, but also people's feelings about themselves when they perform certain behaviors mirror the degree to which they think that those actions will lead others to accept or reject them. The more that people believe that their behavior will lead others to reject them, the worse they feel about themselves when they engage in the behavior (Leary et al., 1995). Furthermore, people's self-evaluations on particular dimensions predict their self-esteem primarily to the degree to which they believe that those dimensions are relevant to social acceptance and rejection by other people. For example, people who believe that their relational value to others depends greatly on their physical appearance experience lower self-esteem if they believe they are unattractive than if they do not think that appearance is particularly important for acceptance (MacDonald, Saltzman, & Leary, 2003). From the standpoint of sociometer theory, self-evaluations influence self-esteem in relation to the degree to which they connote that the person possesses characteristics that are valued and accepted by other people. Although some people maintain that their feelings about themselves are not affected by acceptance and rejection, research shows that rejecting feedback affects state self-esteem even among people who strongly insist that their feelings about themselves are not affected by other people's evaluations or acceptance (Leary et al., 2003).

As noted, people often behave in self-enhancing ways that appear to protect or increase their self-esteem. They make self-serving attributions that absolve them of responsibility for failure, compare themselves to those who are worse off than they are, misremember information about themselves in flattering ways, choose friends and romantic partners who do not outperform them on important dimensions, and do many other things that make them feel good about themselves (for reviews, see Crocker & Park, 2003; Tesser, 2003). According to sociometer theory, when people do things that appear intended to maintain or raise self-esteem, their goal is usually not merely to feel good about themselves. Rather, their primary goal is to protect and enhance their relational value in order to increase their likelihood of interpersonal acceptance and reduce the likelihood of rejection. Most behaviors that protect or enhance people's self-esteem also facilitate acceptance and lower the likelihood of rejection (Leary et al., 2009). Of course, people do sometimes try to feel good about themselves in their own minds, but in general, they seem to be more concerned with how other people evaluate them than with how they evaluate themselves.[1]

Sociometer theory helps to explain why some self-evaluations are affectively tinged, whereas others are not. People can evaluate themselves on a wide variety of characteristics, assessing whether they are good or bad at identifying species of birds, making friends, debugging computer programs, juggling, baking bread, playing paintball, withstanding pain, solving calculus problems, doing sit-ups, speaking Inuit, and so on. Despite the infinite number of specific characteristics and behaviors on which people evaluate themselves, these characteristics tend to fall into a relatively small number of broad categories. Crocker, Luhtanen, Cooper, and Bouvrette (2003) identified seven domains that are particularly relevant to people's feelings of self-worth: appearance, approval from other people, outdoing other people in competition, academic competency, love and support from family, virtue, and God's love.

Domains such as these have typically been regarded as domains or categories of outcomes on which people base their self-esteem (contingencies of self-worth; Crocker & Park, 2003). But why is self-esteem consistently linked to evaluations on these particular dimensions? From the perspective of sociometer theory, self-evaluations on these dimensions most strongly influence self-esteem because they are primary determinants of relational value. That is, all other things being equal, people who are attractive, competent, likeable, broadly norm abiding, virtuous, and so on are more likely to be valued and accepted than those who are unattractive, incompetent, unlikable, and normatively deviant.

In brief, self-esteem appears to be intimately related to people's perceptions of the degree to which other people value having relationships with them. Unfortunately, little research has examined the social cognitive processes involved in how people assess their relational value in other people's eyes or judge whether they are being adequately accepted by others. Drawing inferences about how one is regarded by others is a difficult task, particularly given that other people rarely provide explicit feedback about their judgments of us (DePaulo,

Kenny, Hoover, Webb, & Oliver, 1987; Elfenbein, Eisenkraft, & Ding, 2009). Assessing relational value often requires monitoring subtle cues such as facial expressions or body language. Because these cues are difficult to track and monitor, assessing one's perceived relational value is a resource-depleting task that impairs future attempts at self-regulation (Tyler, 2008). More social cognitive research is needed to examine the processes involved in discerning how one is viewed by other people.

Effects of Self-Evaluations on Perceptions of Others

Thus far, we have focused on factors that affect people's self-evaluations and self-esteem. However, once people perceive and evaluate themselves in particular ways, their self-beliefs, self-evaluations, and self-esteem influence their subsequent decisions, reactions to events, and perceptions of other people. The role of self-evaluations in people's judgments about other people has been discussed since the earliest days of the field. Some early explanations viewed self-evaluations as an anchor or criterion against which other people are compared (Combs & Snygg, 1959; James, 1915; Rogers, 1951), whereas other explanations suggested that perceptions of other people are influenced by people's motivated efforts to view themselves in particular ways (A. Freud, 1937; S. Freud, 1924). Both of these themes—emphasizing both cold cognitive processes and hot motivational ones—continue to structure work on this topic. In an effort to organize this burgeoning literature, Dunning (2003) identified three categories of phenomena that reflect the influence of self-views on perceptions of others— similarity effects, emphasis effects, and comparative effects.

Similarity Effects

Similarity effects involve people's tendency, in the absence of clear-cut information about others, to assume that other people are more similar to them than is warranted. For example, the false consensus effect refers to people's tendency to overestimate how common their beliefs, attitudes, behaviors, and reactions are in the population (for a review, see Marks & Miller, 1987). Although using oneself to make guesses about unfamiliar people is not necessarily illogical, research shows that people are more likely to use themselves as a basis for drawing inferences about others than to generalize from any other single individual. Krueger and Clement (1994) showed that even when participants had information that 20 of their peers would react similarly to a particular situation, they still over-relied on their own behaviors to estimate how most other people would react. Thus, people's self-beliefs and self-evaluations exert an inordinate influence on their assumptions about other people.

Some explanations of the false consensus effect point to rational (although biased) inferential processes, such as the possibility that people assume that their own reactions are typical because they tend to surround themselves with people who think and behave like they do (Marks & Miller, 1987; Whitley, 1998). In addition, given that people tend to explain their own reactions in terms of features of the situation (Marks & Miller, 1987), they may assume that most other people would naturally react similarly to those situations (e.g., I got angry because the situation was objectively unfair, and most other people would as well).

Some explanations, however, explain false consensus in terms of people's desire to evaluate themselves favorably or to feel good about themselves. Although seeing one's decisions and reactions as typical might undermine one's sense of individuality and uniqueness, believing that one is a reasonably normal person whose reactions are generally normative also provides a certain degree of solace and confidence. Furthermore, research shows that people display the false consensus effect primarily for undesirable traits and behaviors (Agonistinelli, Sherman, Presson, & Chassin, 1992; Sherman, Presson, & Chassin, 1984; Suls, Wan, & Sanders, 1988). By assuming that other people share their negative characteristics or bad judgment, people can feel better about themselves than if they saw their undesirable attributes and actions as idiosyncratic.

In fact, people tend not to show false consensus with respect to their positive traits and behaviors. A meta-analytic review of research on the false consensus effect showed that people underestimated the prevalence of their positive traits and accomplishments—a false uniqueness effect (Mullen & Goethals, 1990). Presumably, seeing one's faults and failures as common but one's virtues and strengths as rare promotes positive self-feelings.

Related to false consensus is attributive projection, the tendency for people to project their own traits, attitudes, emotions, and motivations onto specific other people (Holmes, 1978). Importantly, people tend to project their own attributes primarily on people whom they view favorably (Marks & Miller, 1982). By seeing their own characteristics in a competent, attractive, or otherwise desirable person, people can justifiably feel good about themselves. People find it far less flattering to learn that some incompetent, undesirable, despicable person shares some of their personal attributes. In a particularly good demonstration of the direction of this effect, Moreland and Zajonc (1982) first exposed participants to photographs of people for a varying number of times, and as the mere exposure effect predicts, participants liked the people to whom they were more frequently exposed better than those whose photographs they saw fewer times. But more importantly for our purposes, participants also were more likely to infer that the people in the photographs they saw more times (and, thus, liked better) shared their own attitudes and values. These kinds of attributive projection effects are strengthened when people have recently received unfavorable information about themselves (Lewicki, 1984), adding additional evidence that a desire to evaluate oneself favorably may lie behind them.

A third variety of similarity effect involves idiosyncratically construing social characteristics in ways that reflect positively on oneself, what Dunning (2003) called *self-serving trait definitions*. The attributes and behaviors that people associate with common social categories, such as being intelligent or nice, are influenced by their own self-beliefs and self-evaluations. Studies show that people emphasize characteristics that they believe they possess in their definitions of social concepts and categories. For example, people who believe that they are high in mathematical ability emphasize math skills more in their definition of what it means to be intelligent than people who think that they lack mathematical ability (Dunning & McElwee, 1995; Dunning, Meyerowitz, & Holzberg, 1989).

Again, these effects are sensitive to self-evaluation concerns. Experimental manipulations that threaten people's positive self-evaluations lead people to define positive social characteristics more egocentrically. For example, after participants failed an important intellectual task, they expressed more self-serving beliefs about the characteristics that are needed to succeed in marriage than participants who succeeded at the task (Dunning, Leuenberger, & Sherman, 1995).

Emphasis Effects

A second major category of ways in which self-evaluations and self-evaluative concerns influence social judgments involves the effects of people's perceptions of their own characteristics on their inferences about others (Lewicki, 1983). That is, people's perceptions and evaluations of others are unduly influenced by the characteristics that they believe they personally possess. For example, people give others more extreme ratings on attributes that they believe that they personally possess, leading their judgments of other people to be polarized on dimensions that are personally relevant. Observers who think that they are sociable rate other sociable people as more sociable than observers who do not see themselves as sociable, and they also rate nonsociable people as less sociable than observers who do not see themselves as sociable (Lambert & Wedell, 1991). Similarly, cooperative people evaluate others more strongly depending on whether they cooperate or defect in a prisoner's dilemma game (Beggan, Messick, & Allison, 1988). In essence, people's own self-views push their judgments of other people toward the extremes on attributes that are personally relevant (see Markus & Smith, 1981; Sedikides & Skowronski, 1993).

Along the same lines, people also place inordinate weight on their own characteristics, abilities, and attitudes when evaluating other people (Alicke, 1993; Lewicki, 1983; Markus, Smith, & Moreland, 1985). For example, people's self-views influence their judgments of how supportive other people are likely to be (Lutz & Lakey, 2001) and which personality traits are related to greater behavioral effectiveness and success (Motowidlo, Hooper, & Jackson, 2006). In addition, Evans and Stukas (2007) found that men tended to be most critical of their partners on characteristics on which the men were also evaluated themselves negatively.

One explanation of emphasis effects, including polarized judgments, is that people who possess a particular characteristic are more expert in judging that characteristic and, thus, make more nuanced or finer-grained distinctions regarding the degree to which other people have that attribute (Markus et al., 1985). Furthermore, one's own characteristics are more cognitively accessible and, thus, more likely to be used to evaluate other people (Dunning & Hayes, 1996).

Comparative Effects

Early research on attitudes showed that people's judgments of attitude statements depended on their own attitudinal position. People who are against a particular position see moderately supportive attitude statements as pro-attitudinal, whereas people who support a particular position see those same moderate statements as against it (Hovland, Harvey, & Sherif, 1957; Hovland & Sherif, 1952). Similar contrast effects are found in judgments of other people. People use their own self-beliefs as a reference point for evaluating others. For example, Dunning and Hayes (1996) found that people consider their own achievements and behaviors when evaluating other people. In fact, when asked, participants explicitly acknowledged that they evaluate other people, in part, by comparing the target person to themselves (see also Beauregard & Dunning, 1998). Furthermore, studies show that people tend to make these kinds of self–other comparisons in ways that promote positive self-evaluations (Dunning & Cohen, 1992) and do so more strongly when their self-esteem has been threatened (Beauregard & Dunning, 1998).

Conclusion

People's self-perceptions, self-evaluations, and self-esteem are intimately entangled in how they think about other people. Self-beliefs and self-evaluations are strongly affected by how people think others regard them, and those self-beliefs and self-evaluations subsequently influence people's perceptions and judgments of others. Although early symbolic interactionists' claims that the self is the bridge between the person and society may have been overstated, no one could doubt that a full understanding of socially relevant thought, emotion, and behavior requires attention to how people think about and evaluate themselves.

Author Note

Correspondence to Mark Leary, Department of Psychology and Neuroscience, Duke University, P. O. Box 90085, Durham, NC 27708; e-mail: leary@duke.edu.

Notes

1. Some theorists explain excessively positive self-evaluations in terms of a purported *need* for self-esteem, but there is, in fact, little evidence that people "need" self-esteem for its own sake (see Leary & Baumeister, 2000). Thus, we prefer to think that people are simply motivated to feel good about themselves, much in the same way that they prefer a comfortable bed over an uncomfortable one.

References

Alicke, M. D. (1993). Egocentric standards of conduct evaluation. *Basic and Applied Social Psychology, 14*, 171–192.

Alloy, L. B., & Abramson, L. Y. (1979). Judgment of contingency in depressed and nondepressed students: Sadder but wiser? *Journal of Experimental Psychology: General, 108*, 441–485.

Bandura, A. (1977). Self-efficacy: Toward a unifying theory of behavioral change. *Psychological Review, 84*, 191–215.

Baumeister, R. F., Tice, D. M., & Hutton, D. G. (1989). Self-presentational motivations and personality differences in self-esteem. *Journal of Personality, 57*, 547–579.

Beauregard, K. S, & Dunning, D. (1998). Turning up the contrast: Self-enhancement motives prompt egocentric contrast effects in social judgments. *Journal of Personality and Social Psychology, 74*, 606–621.

Beggan, J., K., Messick, D. M., & Allison, S. T. (1988). Social values and egocentric bias: Two tests of the might over morality hypothesis. *Journal of Personality and Social Psychology, 55*, 606–611.

Beike, D. R., Lampinen, J. M., & Behrend, D. A. (2004). *The self and memory*. New York: Psychology Press.

Boney-McCoy, S., Gibbons, F. X., & Gerrard, M. (1999). Self-esteem, compensatory self-enhancement, and the consideration of health risk. *Personality and Social Psychology Bulletin, 25*, 954–965.

Bower, G. H. (1981). Mood and memory. *American Psychologist, 36*, 129–148.

Caputo, D., & Dunning, D. (2004). What you don't know: The role played by errors of omission in imperfect self-assessments. *Journal of Experimental Social Psychology, 41*, 488–505.

Combs, A. W., & Snygg, D. (1959). *Individual behavior: A perceptual approach to behavior*. (Rev. ed.). Oxford, UK: Harpers.

Corning, A. F., Krumm, A. J., & Smitham, L. A. (2006). Differential social comparison processes in women with and without eating disorder symptoms. *Journal of Counseling Psychology, 53*, 338–349.

Crocker, J., Luhtanen, R. K., Cooper, M. L., & Bouvrette, A. (2003). Contingencies of self-worth in college students: Theory and measurement. *Journal of Personality and Social Psychology, 85*, 894–908.

Crocker J., & Park, L, E. (2003). Seeking self-esteem: Construction, maintenance, and protection of self-worth. In M. R. Leary & J. P. Tangney (Eds.), *Handbook of self and identity* (pp. 291–313). New York: Guilford Press.

Deci, E. L., & Ryan, R. M. (1995). Human agency: The basis for true self-esteem. In M. H. Kernis (Ed.), *Efficacy, agency, and self-esteem* (pp. 31–50). New York: Plenum Press.

Denny, E. B., & Hunt, R. R. (1992). Affective valence and memory in depression: Dissociation of recall and fragment completion. *Journal of Abnormal Psychology, 101*, 575–580.

Denissen, J. J. A., Penke, L., Schmitt, D. P., & van Aken, M. A. G. (2008). Self-esteem reactions to social interactions: Evidence for sociometer mechanisms across days, people, and nations. *Journal of Personality and Social Psychology, 95*, 181–196.

DePaulo, B. M., Kenny, D. A., Hoover, C. W., Webb, W., & Oliver, P. V. (1987). Accuracy of person perception: Do people know what kinds of impressions they convey? *Journal of Personality and Social Psychology, 52*, 303–315.

Dewhurst, S. A., & Marlborough, M. A. (2003). Memory bias in the recall of pre-exam anxiety: The influence of self-enhancement. *Applied Cognitive Psychology, 17*, 695–702.

Dunning, D. (1995). Trait importance and modifiability as factors influencing self-assessment and self-enhancement motives. *Personality and Social Psychology Bulletin, 21*, 1297–1306.

Dunning, D. (2003). The relation of self to social perception. In: M. R. Leary, J. P. Tangney (Eds.), *Handbook of self and identity* (pp. 421–441). New York: Guilford Press.

Dunning, D., & Cohen, G. L. (1992). Egocentric definitions of traits and abilities in social judgment. *Journal of Personality and Social Psychology, 63*, 341–355.

Dunning, D., & Hayes, A. F. (1996). Evidence for egocentric comparison in social judgement. *Journal of Personality and Social Psychology, 71*, 213–229.

Dunning, D., Leuenberger, A., & Sherman, D. A. (1995). A new look at motivated inference: Are self-serving theories of success a product of motivational forces? *Journal of Personality and Social Psychology, 59*, 58–68.

Dunning, D., & McElwee, R. O. (1995). Idiosyncratic trait definitions: Implications for self-description and social judgment. *Journal of Personality and Social Psychology, 68*, 936–946.

Dunning, D., Meyerowitz, J. A., & Holzberg, A. D. (1989). Ambiguity and self-evaluation: The role of idiosyncratic trait definitions in self-serving assessments of ability. *Journal of Personality and Social Psychology, 57*, 1082–1090.

Elfenbein, H. A., Eisenkraft, N. D., & Ding, W. W. (2009). Do we know who values us? Dyadic meta-accuracy in the perception of professional relationships. *Psychological Science, 20*, 1081–1083.

Evans, L., & Stukas, A. A. (2007). Self-verification by women and responses of their partners around issues of appearance and weight: "Do I look fat in this?" *Journal of Social and Clinical Psychology, 26*(10), 1163–1188.

Farwell, L., & Wohlwend-Lloyd, R. (1998). Narcissistic processes: Optimistic expectations, favorable self-evaluations, and self-enhancing attributions. *Journal of Personality, 66*, 65–83.

Festinger, L. (1954). A theory of social comparison processes. *Human Relations, 7*, 117–140.

Fisher, R. J., & Katz, J. E. (2000). Social desirability bias and the validity of self-reported values. *Psychology and Marketing, 17*, 105–120.

Forgas, J. P. (1995). Mood and judgment: The affect infusion model (AIM). *Psychological Bulletin, 117*, 39–66.

Frost, R. O., Benton, N., & Dowrick, P. W. (1990). Self-evaluation, videotape review, and dysphoria. *Journal of Social and Clinical Psychology, 9*, 367–374.

Freud, A. (1937). *The ego and the mechanisms of defence*. London: Hogarth Press and Institute of Psycho-Analysis.

Freud, S. (1924). The infantile genital organization of the libido: A supplement to the theory of sexuality. *International Journal of Psychoanalysis, 5*, 125–129.

Giesler, R. B., Josephs, R. A., & Swann, Jr., W. B. (1996). Self-verification in clinical depression: The desire for negative evaluation. *Journal of Abnormal Psychology, 105*, 358–368.

Giordano, C., Wood, J. V., Michela, J. L. (2000). Depressive personality styles, dysphoria, and social comparison in everyday life. *Journal of Personality and Social Psychology, 79*, 438–451.

Goffin, R. D., Jelley, R. B., Powell, D. M., & Johnston, N. G. (2009). Taking advantage of social comparisons in performance appraisals: The relative percentile method. *Human Resource Management, 48*, 251–268.

Heslin, P. A. (2003). Self- and other-referent criteria of career success. *Journal of Career Assessment, 11*, 262–286.

Holmes, D. S. (1978). Projection as a defense mechanism. *Psychological Bulletin, 85*, 677–688.

Hoorens, V. (1993). Self-enhancement and superiority biases in social comparison. *European Review of Social Psychology, 4*, 113–139.

Hovland, C. I., Harvey, O. J., & Sherif, M. (1957). Assimilation and contrast effects in reactions to communication and attitude change. *Journal of Abnormal and Social Psychology, 55,* 244–252.

Hovland, C. I., & Sherif, M. (1952). Judgmental phenomena and scales of attitude measurement: item displacement in Thurstone scales. *Journal of Abnormal and Social Psychology, 47,* 822–832.

James, W. (1890). *The principles of psychology.* New York: Holt.

James, W. (1915). *Psychology: Briefer course.* New York: Holt.

Klein, W. M. P., & Goethals, G. R. (2003). Social reality and self-construction: A case of "bounded irrationality?" *Basic and Applied Social Psychology, 24,* 105–114.

Krueger, J., & Clement, R. W. (1994). The truly false consensus effect: An ineradicable and egocentric bias in social perception. *Journal of Personality and Social Psychology, 67,* 596–610.

Krusemark, E. A., Campbell, W. K., & Clementz, B. A. (2008). Attributions, deception, and event related potentials: An investigation of the self-serving bias. *Psychophysiology, 45,* 511–515.

Lambert, A. J., & Wedell, D. H. (1991). The self and social judgment: Effects of affective reaction and "own position" on judgments of unambiguous and ambiguous information about others. *Journal of Personality and Social Psychology, 61,* 884–897.

Leary, M. R. (2004). *The curse of the self: Self-awareness, egoism, and the quality of human life.* New York: Oxford University Press.

Leary, M. R. (2006). Sociometer theory and the pursuit of relational value: Getting to the root of self-esteem. *European Review of Social Psychology, 16,* 75–111.

Leary, M. R., Barnes, B. D., Griebel, C., Mason, E., & McCormack, D. Jr. (1987). The impact of conjoint threats to social- and self-esteem on evaluation apprehension. *Social Psychology Quarterly, 50,* 304–311.

Leary, M. R., & Baumeister, R. F. (2000). The nature and function of self-esteem: Sociometer theory. In M. P. Zanna (Ed.), *Advances in experimental social psychology* (Vol. 32, pp. 1–62). San Diego: Academic Press.

Leary, M. R., & Buttermore, N. R. (2003). The evolution of the human self: Tracing the natural history of self-awareness. *Journal for the Theory of Social Behaviour, 33,* 365–404.

Leary, M. R., & Downs, D. L. (1995). Interpersonal functions of the self-esteem motive: The self-esteem system as a sociometer. In M. Kernis (Ed.), *Efficacy, agency, and self-esteem* (pp. 123–144). New York: Plenum Press.

Leary, M. R., Gallagher, B., Fors, E. H., Buttermore, N., Baldwin, E., Lane, K. K., & Mills. A. (2003). The invalidity of personal claims about self-esteem. *Personality and Social Psychology Bulletin, 29,* 623–636.

Leary, M. R., Haupt, A. L., Strausser, K. S., & Chokel, J. T. (1998). Calibrating the sociometer: The relationship between interpersonal appraisals and state self-esteem. *Journal of Personality and Social Psychology, 74,* 1290–1299.

Leary, M. R., Tambor, E., Terdal, S., & Downs, D. L. (1995). Self-esteem as an interpersonal monitor: The sociometer hypothesis. *Journal of Personality and Social Psychology, 68,* 518–530.

Leary, M. R., Terry, M. L., Allen, A. B., & Tate, E. B. (2009). The concept of ego threat in social and personality psychology: Is ego threat a viable scientific construct? *Personality and Social Psychology Review, 13,* 151–164.

Lewicki, P. (1983). Self-image bias in person perception. *Journal of Personality and Social Psychology, 45,* 384–393.

Lewicki, P. (1984). Self-schema and social information processing. *Journal of Personality and Social Psychology, 47,* 1177–1190.

Lutz, C. J., & Lakey, B. (2001). How people make support judgments: Individual differences in the traits used to infer supportiveness in others. *Journal of Personality and Social Psychology, 81*(6), 1070–1079.

MacDonald, G., Saltzman, J. L., & Leary, M. R. (2003). Social approval and trait self-esteem. *Journal of Research in Personality, 37,* 23–40.

Marks, G., & Miller, N. (1982). Target attractiveness as a mediator of assumed attitude similarity. *Personality and Social Psychology Bulletin, 8,* 728–735.

Marks, G., & Miller, N. (1987). Ten years of research on the false-consensus effect: An empirical and theoretical review. *Psychological Bulletin, 102,* 72–90.

Markus, H., & Smith, J. (1981). The influence of self-schemas on the perception of others. In N. Cantor & J. F. Kihlstrom (Eds.), *Personality, cognition, and social interaction* (pp. 233–262). Hillsdale, NJ: Erlbaum.

Markus, H., Smith, J., & Moreland, R. L. (1985). Role of the self-concept in the perception of others. *Journal of Personality and Social Psychology, 49,* 1494–1512.

May, R. (1983). *The discovery of being.* New York: Norton

Mayer, J. D., Gaschke, Y. N., Braverman, D. L., & Evans, T. W. (1992). Mood-congruent judgment is a general effect. *Journal of Personality and Social Psychology, 63,* 119–132.

Miller, D. T., & Ross, M. (1975). Self-serving biases in the attribution of causality: Fact or fiction? *Psychological Bulletin, 82,* 213–225.

Monin, B. (2007). Holier than me? Threatening social comparison in the moral domain. *Revue Internationale de Psychologie Sociale. Special Issue: Social Comparion, 20,* 53–68.

Moreland, R. L., & Zajonc, R. B (1982). A strong test of exposure effects. *Journal of Experimental Social Psychology, 12,* 170–179.

Motowidlo, S. J., Hooper, A. C., & Jackson, H. L. (2006). Implicit policies about relations between personality traits and behavioral effectiveness in situational judgment items. *Journal of Applied Psychology, 91*(4), 749–761.

Mullen, B. & Goethals, G. R. (1990). Social projection, actual consensus and valence. *British Journal of Social Psychology, 29,* 279–282.

Nederhof, A. J. (1985). Methods of coping with social desirability bias: A review. *European Journal of Social Psychology, 15,* 263–280.

Paulhus, D. L. (1991). Measurement and control of response bias. In J. P. Robinson, P. R. Shaver, L. S. Wrightsman (Eds.), *Measures of personality and social psychological attitudes* (pp. 17–59). San Diego, CA: Academic Press.

Paulhus, D. L., Harms, P. D., Bruce, M, N., & Lysy, D. C. (2003). The over-claiming technique: Measuring self-enhancement independent of ability. *Journal of Personality and Social Psychology, 84,* 890–904.

Raleigh, M. J., & McGuire, M. T. (1986). Animal analogues of ostracism: Biological mechanisms and social consequences. *Ethology and Sociobiology, 7*(3–4), 201–214.

Regan, P. C., Snyder, M., & Kassin, S. (1995). Unrealistic optimism: Self-enhancement or person positivity? *Personality and Social Psychology Bulletin, 21,* 1073–1082.

Richman, L. S., & Leary, M. R. (2009). Reactions to discrimination, stigmatization, ostracism, and other forms of interpersonal rejection: A dynamic, multi-motive model. *Psychological Review, 116*, 365–383.

Robins, R. W. & Beer, J. S. (2001). Positive Illusions about the self: Short-term benefits and long-term costs. *Journal of Personality and Social Psychology, 80*, 340–352.

Rogers, C. (1951). *Client-centered therapy.* Boston: Houghton-Mifflin.

Rogers, C. (1959). A theory of therapy, personality and interpersonal relationships as developed in the client-centered framework. In S. Koch (Ed.), *Psychology: A study of a science* (Vol. 3). New York: McGraw-Hill.

Schwarz, N., & Clore, G. L. (1983). Mood, misattribution, and judgments of well-being: Informative and directive functions of affective states. *Journal of Personality and Social Psychology, 45*, 513–523.

Schlenker, B. R. (1980). *Impression management: The self-concept, social identity, and interpersonal relations.* Monterey, CA: Brooks/Cole.

Sedikides, C. (1993). Assessment, enhancement, and verification determinants of the self-evaluation process. *Journal of Personality and Social Psychology, 65*, 327–338.

Sedikides, C., & Skowronski, J. (1993). The self in impression formation: Trait centrality and social perception. *Journal of Experimental Social Psychology, 29*, 347–357.

Sedikides, C., & Skowronski, J. J. (2003). Evolution and the symbolic self: Issues and prospects. In M. R. Leary & J. P. Tangney (Eds.), *Handbook of self and identity* (pp. 594–609). New York: Guilford Publications.

Sedikides, C., & Strube, M. J. (1997). Self-evaluation: To thine own self be good, to thine own self be sure, to thine own self be true, and to thine own self be better. *Advances in Experimental Social Psychology, 29*, 209–269.

Segrin, C. (1990). A meta-analytic review of social skill deficits in depression. *Communication Monographs, 57*, 292–308.

Sherman, S. J., Presson, C. C., & Chassin, L. (1984). Mechanisms underlying the false consensus effect: The special role of threats to the self. *Personality and Social Psychology Bulletin, 10*, 127–138.

Shrauger, S. J., & Schoeneman, T. J. (1979). Symbolic interactionist view of self-concept: Through the looking glass darkly. *Psychological Bulletin, 86*, 549–573.

Sommer, K. L., Williams, K. D., Ciarocco, N. J., & Baumeister, R. F. (2001). Explorations into the intrapsychic and interpersonal consequences of social ostracism. *Basic and Applied Social Psychology, 23*, 227–245.

Suls, J., Wan, C. K., & Sanders, G. S. (1988). False consensus and false uniqueness in estimating the prevalence of health-protective behaviors. *Journal of Applied Social Psychology, 18*, 66–79.

Suls, J., & Wheeler, L. (2000). *Handbook of social comparison: Theory and research.* New York: Kluwer Academic/Plenum Press.

Swann, W. B., Jr. (1983). Self-verification: Bringing social reality into harmony with the self. In J. Suls & A. G. Greenwald (Eds.), *Psychological perspectives on the self* (Vol. 2, pp. 33–66). Hillsdale, NJ: Erlbaum.

Swann, W. B., Jr., & Buhrmester, M. D. (2012). Self-verification: The search for coherence. In M. R. Leary & J. P. Tangney (Eds.), *Handbook of self and identity* (2nd ed., pp. 405–424). New York: Guilford Publications.

Swanson, H. R., & Weary, G. (1982). The acceptance of personality evaluations: Constraints on consistency motivations. *Journal of Personality, 46*, 350–358.

Taylor, S. E., & Brown, J. D., (1988). Illusion and well-being: A social psychological perspective on mental health. *Psychological Bulletin, 103*, 193–210.

Tetlock, P. E., & Manstead, A. S. (1985). Impression management versus intrapsychic explanations in social psychology: A useful dichotomy? *Psychological Review, 92*, 59–77.

Tesser, A. (2003). Self-evaluation. In M. R. Leary & J. P. Tangney (Eds.), *Handbook of self and identity* (pp. 275–290). New York: Guilford Press.

Tyler, J. M. (2008). In the eyes of others: Monitoring for relational value cues. *Human Communication Research, 34*, 521–549.

Weary Bradley, G. (1978), Self-serving biases in the attribution process: a reexamination of the fact or fiction question. *Journal of Personality and Social Psychology, 36*, 56–71.

Whitley, B. E., Jr. (1998). False consensus on sexual behavior among college women: Comparisons of four theoretical explanations. *Journal of Sex Research, 35*, 206–214.

Whitton, S. W., Larson, J. J., & Hauser, S. T. (2008). Depressive symptoms and bias in perceived social competence among young adults. *Journal of Clinical Psychology, 64*, 791–805.

Williams, K. D., Shore, W. J., & Grahe, J. E. (1998). The silent treatment: Perceptions of its behaviors and associated feelings. *Group Processes & Intergroup Relations, 1*, 117–141.

Williams, K. D., & Zadro, L. (2001). Ostracism: On being ignored, excluded and rejected. In M. R. Leary (Ed.), *Interpersonal Rejection* (pp. 21–53). New York: Oxford University Press.

Wood, J. V., & Wilson, A. E. (2003). How important is social comparison? In M. R. Leary & J. P. Tangney (Eds.), *Handbook of self and identity* (pp. 344–366)). New York: Guilford Press.azdro

Zadro, L., Williams, K. D., & Richardson, R. (2005). Riding the "O" train: Comparing the effects of ostracism and verbal dispute on targets and sources. *Group Processes & Intergroup Relations, 8*, 125–143.

Stereotype Development and Formation

Steven J. Sherman, Jeffrey W. Sherman, Elise J. Percy, *and* Courtney K. Soderberg

Abstract

This chapter reviews research and theory on the social cognitive underpinnings of both stereotype development in children and stereotype formation among adults. Although research on these topics has developed largely independently from another, the two areas of research may inform one another in important ways. Toward this end, the authors have tried to draw attention to both similarities and differences in the ways that stereotypes form in these two contexts. Although children and adults appear to possess many of the same fundamental cognitive abilities that support categorization and stereotype formation, there are important differences in how the processes operate and in the important roles that social motives play among adults. In addressing these issues, focus will be placed on the concepts of essentialism, illusory correlation, and category accentuation. The authors believe that a more robust integration of these research topics would offer a rich source of progress in understanding stereotyping.

Key Words: stereotype development, stereotype formation, essentialism, illusory correlation, category accentuation

Stereotypes are the knowledge, beliefs, and expectations we hold about human groups (e.g., Hamilton & Sherman, 1994; Hamilton & Trolier, 1986). The purpose of this chapter is to describe how stereotypes are formed. Toward this end, we describe both the development of stereotypes in children and the formation of novel stereotypes among adults. Given the social cognitive focus of this book, the primary emphasis will be on the cognitive processes that underlie stereotype formation.[1] An important foundational principle of the social cognitive approach is that stereotypes serve the same essential functions as other categorical knowledge in structuring and simplifying the vast quantities of things and people we encounter so that we may understand and navigate the world more effectively (Allport, 1954; Lippmann, 1922; Tajfel, 1969). As such, the cognitive processes that support stereotype formation are assumed to be largely the

same as those that contribute to the formation of all categorical knowledge. These basic processes are sufficient to produce stereotypic knowledge, even in the absence of important sociomotivational factors that encourage stereotyping.

However, there also are important differences between stereotypes and other kinds of categorical knowledge. Otherwise, there would be no reason to study stereotypes as a specialized form of knowledge. Most obviously, because stereotypes refer to categories of people, they are self-relevant and socially relevant in ways that most categories are not. Consequently, stereotype formation is influenced not only by motives of comprehension and efficiency but also by social motives, such as the desire to enhance feelings of self-worth (e.g., Fein & Spencer, 1997; Katz, 1960; Lippmann, 1922; Tajfel & Turner, 1986) and to explain and justify the social order (e.g., Allport, 1954; Eagly & Steffen,

1984; Fiske, Cuddy, Glick, & Xu, 2002; Hoffman & Hurst, 1990; Jost & Banaji, 1994; Lippmann, 1922). These motives certainly influence the circumstances under which people may be most likely to form stereotypes, the kinds of groups that are targeted for stereotyping, and the content of those stereotypes. These are all questions to which we will return below.

Stereotype Development in Children

Most of the empirical and theoretical work that social psychologists have done regarding "stereotype development" has tried to identify the most important factors that bring about the development of stereotypes in adults. Of course, to study stereotype development in adults, it is necessary to investigate such development for novel groups. Adults already have well-developed stereotypes of all the "important" social groups, such as gender, race, age, ethnicity, and religion. Thus, researchers typically present adult participants with information about what members of Group A and Group B are like, or what dot overestimators are like, or what the members of some hypothetical organization are like. By exploring the factors (e.g., group size, relations to the self, similarity to known groups) that most affect the impressions that form of these groups, researchers can draw conclusions about how stereotypes develop in terms of strength, valence, extremity, malleability, and.

Far less has been written in social psychology outlets regarding the development of stereotypes in young children—although, as we shall see, there are important exceptions. Importantly, even when social psychologists address the question of age-related changes in stereotype development, they rarely refer to the general cognitive development literature in order to gain an understanding of how the child's development of concepts or of categorization skills might inform us about whether the young child may or may not be capable of developing stereotypes of social groups, about how these stereotypes might change as the child ages, or about how these stereotypes held by children might be similar to or different from the stereotypes held by adults. The goal of this section will be to integrate knowledge of the development of the child's cognitive skills and cognitive processes with knowledge of social psychological aspects of child development to shed light on the social cognitive processes involved in age-related changes in stereotype development. Only by exploring stereotype development in young children can we answer important questions about

how stereotypes of important social groups, including race, gender, and ethnicity, initially develop.

The first part of this section will address general issues of cognitive development in children and will use this knowledge to draw conclusions about the possibilities, limitations, constraints, and changes in early stereotype development. Thus, a goal of this presentation will be to understand the development of basic cognitive processes that underlie the evolution of social categories in children, which allow for the development of stereotypes as children attach meaning to these categories. It is, of course, the act of categorization that is essential for the development of stereotypes. Much of this work has been done by cognitive developmental psychologists. The second part of this section will discuss research and theory that has directly investigated specific stereotypes and their development in children. Much of this work has been done by social psychologists.

How Children Think and How They Acquire Words, Concepts, and Categories
ASSOCIATIONIST VERSUS THEORY-BASED PROCESSES

As the young child acquires words and concepts, does the process involve the learning of observed or taught associations among objects, or are there also more top-down theory-based mechanisms at play? A related question is whether the young child's thinking is concrete in nature or whether the young child is capable of abstract thought. The answers to these questions are important because it is more likely that young children can think in more strongly stereotypic ways if they are capable of using conceptual processes and content, of thinking in a theory-based way, and of engaging in abstract thought as they learn about social categories. Of course, we are not asking whether only one of these processes, to the exclusion of the other, is involved in the child's acquisition of concepts. In fact, most cognitive developmental psychologists agree that these questions often present false either–or dichotomies. For example, Waxman and Gelman (2009) conclude that a child's thinking and knowledge are based on both perceptual and conceptual content, that such knowledge is derived from more than simple sensory input, that it is both associationist and theory-based, and that it is abstract as well as concrete.

What is the evidence that abstract and theory-based processes play a significant role in the child's development of concepts? Waxman and Gelman (2009) demonstrate that the young child is capable of attending to statistical regularities and has good computational resources and is tuned into different kinds of high-level related information. But more than this, they conclude that children have conceptual capacities that include the core knowledge of objects and that they have theories about the behavior of objects, including human objects. These conclusions have supplemented ideas of young children's cognitive capacities that were heavily associationist in nature (e.g., Robinson & Sloutsky, 2007; Sloutsky, Lo, & Fisher, 2001). Similarly, Keil, Smith, Simons, and Levin (1998) conclude that, in addition to an associationist component to their concepts, children also have an explanatory component that is based on rules and causal principles. Thus, similarity and explanatory aspects coexist in the concepts of very young children. Again, it is important that the child's conceptual capacities include an understanding of a core knowledge of objects and a theory about the behavior of these objects. These capacities allow for the development of strong and stable concepts and beliefs, including group stereotypes.

Another stereotype-relevant capacity that develops early in childhood involves rather complex face processing. Research suggests that very early visual preferences might relate to later social preferences. Even 3-month-olds attend to faces that match the gender of their primary caregiver (Quinn, Yahr, Kuhn, Slater, & Pascalis, 2002) or faces of a familiar racial group (Bar-Haim, Ziv, Lamy, & Hodes, 2006; Kelly et al., 2005). Surprisingly, even infants are capable of developing representations of prototypical faces (de Haan, Johnson, Maurer, & Perrett, 2001). Thus, face processing in infants shows gender and race preferences. Such capacities involving abstraction would certainly facilitate the development of stereotypes at early ages.

Finally, Platten, Hernik, Fonagy, and Fearon (2010) have outlined the development of other high-level cognitive capabilities in young children that would be extremely important for the development of stereotypes. First, there is evidence that even infants understand emotional expressions (Lappänen & Nelson, 2006; Young-Browne, Rosenfeld, & Horowitz, 1977). Importantly, infants also understand the valence of emotional expressions and use this understanding to determine their subsequent behaviors (Hornik & Gunnar, 1988; Sorce, Emde, Campos, & Klinnert, 1985). Thus, infants attach meaning to emotional expressions. Infants are also capable of social referencing, whereby they learn to trust a stranger who has a positive interaction with their mother. Platten et al. (2010) conclude that such cognitive capacities allow infants to understand networks of trusted or distrusted individuals. The ability to represent social alliances is the beginning of the concepts of ingroup and outgroup and is a critical aspect of the development of stereotypes.

In short, very young children are clearly capable of using theory-based processes, of engaging in abstract thought, and of developing categories and beliefs in ways that involve conceptual processes and content. These capabilities strongly suggest that young children do not only "learn" stereotypes from adults in a straightforward associationist, imitative, or social learning way. Rather, stereotypes are also likely to develop in ways that are related to the conceptual and categorization abilities that develop in the young child and that are driven as much by the child's cognitive capacities as by the social environment. It is the early capacity for theory-based reasoning and abstract thinking that makes the development of stereotypes in young children natural and inevitable, often regardless of whether parents or peers actively teach or encourage stereotypic thinking.

ROLE OF LANGUAGE IN THE DEVELOPMENT OF CONCEPTS AND CATEGORIES IN CHILDREN

It has become clear in recent years that language plays a significant role in shaping human thought and experience. Although Whorf's (1956) strong form of the linguistic relativity principle (language determines thought and severely limits thought) is not generally accepted, the weak form of the principle (there are cross-linguistic differences in cognitive tendency) has much support. For example, Boroditsky, Schmidt, and Phillips (2003) investigated the effects of gendered articles on object perception. In languages in which the word "key" is masculine (e.g., German), keys are described as heavy and jagged. In languages in which the word "key" is feminine (e.g., Spanish), keys are described as golden and intricate. These kinds of language effects likely develop during childhood.

Language plays an important role in categorization, and of course, categorization is a fundamental aspect of stereotype development. As children learn and use language, do they develop categories and concepts that would facilitate the development of stereotypes? First, it is important to demonstrate the role of language in children's ability to learn categories. Waxman (2010; Waxman & Gelman, 2009) has been an important contributor to this issue. In her work, she shows that the naming of objects is a critical aspect of the way in which children learn categories. When two objects share a label, children will group them together and say that they look alike. Thus, children's categories go beyond simple perceptual similarities. The fact that objects share a linguistic label (e.g., chair, girl, or black) is far more important to categorization than is mere physical similarity (Keil et al., 1998). This ability to group objects based on a common label means that children have the capacity for the development of strong and stable stereotypes. They do not simply categorize people into groups by physical similarity or associations. Rather, they look for a deeper common meaning for members of a category. It is important to note that cognitive developmental theorists are not simply saying that labels function through the formation of associative links between objects that share the same label; they are also saying that the existence of a shared label stimulates the young child to develop an understanding of why perceptually dissimilar objects might belong to the same category. It is this kind of theory-based reasoning that we claim is important for stereotype development in children.

As early as 9 months of age, children operate on the assumption that objects with the same label have the same properties, and they look for differences between objects that have distinct linguistic labels (Gelman, 2009). Importantly, Gelman and Heyman (1999) found that when 5-year-olds hear a person described by a novel label (e.g., carrot-eater), they judge this property to be very stable. Similar findings are reported for adults (Walton & Banaji, 2004).

With regard to social categories, labeling, as well as the inferential processes that follow from labeling, has many implications for children, including the establishment of ingroups and outgroups, stigmatization, and causal attributions. The effects again go well beyond simple associationist effects. Even if the labels are discrepant from the child's own experience or the appearance of an object, the child will use the labels to make inferences and look for underlying properties (Gelman & Markman, 1986; Jaswal, Lima, & Small, 2009). In short, children look for meaning and coherence for objects that share a category label, a process that allows for the development of strong and coherent categories. In addition, as children make inferences based on category labels, they then pass the inferences onto others. This ability is related to the child's ability to think in essentialist ways, a process that will be discussed in a subsequent section.

Waxman (2010) has investigated the role of naming specifically with regard to the development of racial and gender categories in preschool children. The children were shown a picture of a person (e.g., a white woman) and were told that she was good at a "zaggit" game. Children projected this ability onto other people in general. However, when the person was identified with a label as a member of a named, novel social category, the children projected the ability only to members of the same race-based or gender-based category. Thus, the labeling of social groups is likely to play a very important role not only in the development of these social categories but also in the projection of attributes from some members of the group to others, and this is another important factor in the development of strong, stable stereotypes. Bigler and Liben (2006) propose that the labeling of social groups leads to the development of stereotypes in children in a dose-dependent way. Because gender is labeled far more often than race for the child, Bigler and Liben (2006) conclude that gender stereotypes will be stronger for children than racial stereotypes, and this fits existing data that will be discussed in a subsequent section. Waxman (2010) concludes that, for children, naming has critical effects on categorization, on the deep conceptual organization of categories, and on inductive inferences based on category membership.

As we have seen, the linguistic relativity principle holds that language affects thought. In a recent demonstration of this kind of effect that has relevance for stereotyping, Percy, Sherman, Garcia-Marques, Mata, and Garcia-Marques (2009) investigated the effect of native-language adjective–noun word order on the category accessibility of nouns and adjectives. Nouns were more accessible for Portuguese speakers (for whom nouns precede adjectives) than for English speakers (for whom adjectives precede nouns). The reverse was true for the accessibility of adjectives. Given this result, Percy et al. (2009) speculate that these differences in native language word order might affect the development and strength of different stereotypes, even in young children. Consider the phrase "old woman" (literally "woman old" in Portuguese). The adjective indicating age has primacy in English, whereas the noun indicating gender has primacy in Portuguese. Perhaps, then, children in the United States develop stronger stereotypes of age, whereas Portuguese children develop stronger stereotypes of gender. The point is that different language patterns have different conceptual consequences and that stereotype development in children might be very much linked to these differences in linguistic patterns.

Furthermore, it is extremely important that words are not simply associations for children. Rather, they are symbolic, they are linked to an abstract representation, and they allow for thinking that is guided by abstract conceptual knowledge (e.g., causality; Waxman & Gelman, 2009). In addition, even young children appreciate that there are different kinds of words (e.g., nouns vs. verbs; transitive vs. intransitive), and they learn words such as *almost, why, think*, and *cause*, all of which have no concrete aspects (Gelman & Bloom, 2000; Gopnik & Sobel, 2000; Opper & Bulloch, 2007). Thus, concept learning in children is much more than simply mapping a word onto a perceptual unit. An example of this kind of abstract and referential thinking by very young children (18–24 months) is shown in an experiment by Preissler and Carey (2004). The infants were shown a picture of a novel object, labeled a "whisk." They were then asked to extend the word to either another picture of a "whisk" or to an actual three-dimensional whisk. The infants almost never chose the photograph. Thus, even at 1½ years of age, children understand that words refer to real concepts, and they are not bound to photographic perceptual similarities.

DO CHILDREN THINK ABOUT OBJECTS AND CATEGORIES IN ESSENTIALIST WAYS?

What is psychological essentialism? According to Gelman (2003), essentialist thinking involves a conception of categories as having an underlying reality or a true nature that cannot be seen but that is what gives an object its identity. The consequences of essentialist thinking are that objects are believed to have an underlying, unchanging essence despite outward changes in appearance, that there are important nonobvious properties to category members, that knowing the category of the object allows inductive potential about object properties, that the nonobvious properties are causal for a variety of attributes of the object, and that there is a great deal of stability, a sharpness of boundaries, and an innate potential in category members. Thus, essentialist thinking serves several very important functions. It allows for the perception of stability and order in the environment; it allows one to assess causality easily; it allows a variety of inductive inferences to be made about category members; it allows us to recognize individuals and to gain cultural knowledge; it allows us to distinguish appearance from reality; and it allows us to make reasonable predictions about people and objects. However, because of its rigidity and inevitability, essentialist thinking comes with a cost—differences among category members are relatively ignored, and inferences are applied too broadly. These advantages and disadvantages, of course, capture the important consequences of stereotypical thinking.

A key aspect of essentialist thinking is the conceptualization of objects as natural kinds, rather than as artifacts, and conceptualizing social categories as natural kinds is extremely important for stereotype development. This is because thinking of objects in natural-kind terms involves the development of inferences about the stable, underlying properties of objects in a category, including social categories. Rothbart and Taylor (1992) proposed that certain social categories are, in fact, likely to be represented as natural kinds. In particular, they contend that gender and race categories are treated as natural kinds, and thus strong and stable stereotypes of gender and race have developed.

If essentialist thinking is a critical or even a necessary component of stereotype development, it is, of course, important to determine whether young children are capable of essentialist thought. If they have this capacity and thus conceptualize the objects of a category as having stable, fixed underlying attributes, then it is likely that young children do hold strong stereotypes. We would argue that, in fact, it is essentialist thinking that plays a major role in children's stereotype development. The simple answer to the question of whether young children are capable of essentialist thinking is "yes." This development of essentialist thinking in young children is related to their cognitive abilities to think in theory-based ways and to think abstractly, as described earlier. Taylor, Rhodes, and Gelman (2009) conclude that psychological essentialism results from emerging cognitive biases that guide conceptual development even with little in the way of external input. Their research supports the conclusion that essentialist beliefs about social categories are not simply derived from essentialist beliefs about the biological world but rather are instantiated separately. Much theory and research in the cognitive development literature has been devoted to this issue, and it is beyond the scope of this chapter to provide a detailed review of this work. Thus, we shall simply give a brief overview of the work on essentialist thinking in children. However, the interested reader is referred to an excellent book on the topic, *The Essential Child* by Susan Gelman (2003).

Here is a brief summary of what we know about essentialist thinking in children:

1. Language plays an important role in the development of essentialism in children (Gelman, 2009). Generic noun phrases (e.g., "boys play with trucks," "polar bears live in the Arctic") are especially important in the development of such essentialist thinking (Gelman, 2009).

2. Essentialism emerges both from biases in the child's thinking and cues in the environment (Gelman, 2003). Essentialism is thus partly rooted in the child's mind and not simply in the world, the language, or the culture. However, children's essentialist beliefs about gender and race also reflect the effects of culture (Rhodes & Gelman, 2009). Rural/city differences and even parental political affiliations affect the degree to which different social categories are essentialized by children. For example, rural children and children of Republicans hold stronger essentialist beliefs about race and gender, and these beliefs are stable as the child ages.

3. Young children develop essentialist thinking about social categories despite the fact that their parents do not use essentialist terms very much in talking to them. Children seem to use their own cognitive biases as well as the generic noun phrases that they hear (e.g., fish live in the water) and the implicit cues of language use from their parents to develop essentialist thinking about social categories (Gelman, 2003). Gelman points out that the use of generic noun phrases is especially important for the child's development of essentialist thinking about categories such as occupations and nationalities.

4. Like adult essentialist beliefs, when children as young as 2½ years think about social categories in an essentialist way, they reason about nonobvious properties such as novel behaviors and causal effects. They ignore physical features in their reasoning, and they give privileged status to things that are inside people. This is consistent with the child's essentialist and theory-based beliefs that causes are more important than effects and that causes are often hidden. This focus on internal and innate features allows very young children to realize that a bird raised by an elephant would still be a bird. [As an aside, perhaps because "Horton Hatches an Egg" was the favorite story of one of the authors, he failed to appreciate such an essentialist belief until a rather late age.]

In short, based on research findings from many laboratories, we can conclude that very young children think about social categories in essentialist ways; that is, they conceive of these categories as natural kinds. They not only learn how to categorize social objects based on race, gender, age, and so forth, but also learn the meaning of these categories. We can further conclude that much of this early cognitive development, because it involves making inferences and developing explanatory principles, is theory driven rather than associationist in nature. Young children have domain-specific beliefs about the objectivity and discreteness of social category boundaries. Such essentialist thinking about social categories by children means that they see an underlying stability to members of these categories, that they view underlying and unseen internal properties as key causes of category members' attributes, and that they can make many inductive inferences and predictions about category members. These are all aspects of holding strong stereotypes of these social categories. We should therefore conclude that young children do have the capacity to hold stereotypes that develop in concert with their more general cognitive developmental tendencies. We shall address the issue of the actual existence of strong group stereotypes in children, rather than the capacity for their development, in a subsequent section. We cannot yet draw definitive conclusions about whether the roots of essentialism are primarily biological, evolutionary, social, or cultural, but it is fair to say that all of these processes play a significant role.

A concept that is very much related to the perception of essentialism in social groups is the perception that social groups are entitative or coherent. Because the perception of high entitativity in groups is strongly related to holding stereotypes of those groups, it is important to investigate whether young children do appreciate the concept of group entitativity. As indicated earlier, Platten et al. (2010) demonstrated that children as young as 2 years old have the social cognitive abilities to learn affiliations among people. They learn about coalitions of people that are small and dynamic, and in which membership has no obvious visible cues. Platten et al. (2010) conclude that children learn to perceive these affiliations by understanding subtle social cues, nonverbal cues, and interpersonal behaviors. Given that young children have this cognitive capacity, one important question is whether they are also sensitive to the degree of entitativity of the various coalitions—that is, the degree to which various coalitions have coherence, unity, organization, and stability (Campbell, 1958; Hamilton & Sherman, 1996).

The appreciation of entitativity is important for our purposes because Crawford, Sherman, and Hamilton (2002) showed that, when a group is perceived as highly entitative, the representation of that group involves an interchangeability of individual members and a loss of the individual identities of these members. Once any member is known to have a trait or attribute, that attribute is transferred to all other members of the group. Crawford et al. (2002) conclude that this interchangeability of individual group members is an important first step in the abstraction of a group stereotype. Thus, if young children do in fact appreciate the degree of entitativity of social groups, it makes it likely that they are also capable of developing stereotypes of these groups.

As already indicated, the concept of essentialism is very much related to the concept of entitativity (Yzerbyt, Judd, & Corneille, 2004). To the extent that one perceives that a category or group is essentialized or entitative, properties will easily spread from member to member. Shipley (2000) discusses a related concept, *entrenchment*, a term first introduced by Goodman (1955). Entrenchment refers to a readiness to make inductive inferences about a category and to perceive a coherence of category members. The greater the entrenchment of a category or its properties, the more likely it is that a property will be extended from one member of the category to all other members. Thus, entrenchment operates in much the same way as perceived entitativity. Shipley's research (2000) shows that entrenchment does characterize children's acquisition and use of category knowledge. She outlines the processes involved in children's acquisition of an entrenched category. Interestingly, when a category could be characterized as entrenched, Shipley (2000) found that children were more likely to transfer behaviors rather than appearance from member to member. Thus, if an animal acts like a tiger but looks like a camel, children as young as 3 years will identify it as a tiger. Shipley concludes that behavioral properties are entrenched more than physical appearance properties and are thus more likely to transfer from member to member and to be involved in inductive inferences about category members. This is important for stereotyping in that stereotypes of groups typically involve behaviors and traits more than mere physical attributes.

In what we believe is the only research to investigate entitativity perceptions in children, Svirydzenka, Sani, and Bennett (2010) asked whether children could discriminate different group types with respect to perceived entitativity. Their 10-year-old participants rated 12 different groups on a number of properties, and they did a sorting task in which they were asked to divide the groups into different categories. Like adults, these children identified the four basic group types—intimacy groups, task groups, social categories, and loose associations. In addition, they saw the different group types as having different levels of entitativity, with intimacy and task groups having the highest perceived entitativity, and loose associations the lowest. Some of the more specific results of these studies seem to indicate that it would be easy for children to develop strong stereotypes of some of these groups. For example, similarity based on concrete appearance was important for perceived entitativity only for social categories (e.g., race, nationality). Given that social categories are large and diffuse and that there is often little interaction among group members, having perceived entitativity based on concrete similarities would allow strong stereotypes to develop for these kinds of social categories. In addition, another consequence of the capacity for representing groups in terms of perceived entitativity is that ingroup identification and outgroup threat are likely (Abelson, Dasgupta, Park, & Banaji, 1998). Of course, ingroup identification and outgroup threat play a very important role in stereotype development.

In the first section, we asked and answered questions about the young child's cognitive-developmental capabilities with regard to processes, concepts, and categories that would help us to understand whether and when a child should be able to develop stereotypes of social groups. Thus, we explored the general issue of whether children are capable of conceptual, theory-based, and abstract thinking. We also explored more specific questions about the child's cognitive capacities with regard to lexicalization, essentialist thinking, and an appreciation of the concept of group entitativity. We hope that addressing these questions helps us to draw conclusions about the processes by which the young child develops stereotypes. In the next section, we shall discuss research and theory that focuses directly on specific stereotypes that children are likely to hold and when these stereotypes develop. That is, we shall address the issue of the reality, rather than the capacity, of stereotypes in children. In addition, we shall refer to ideas about social psychological processes that are involved in stereotype development in children. We will also address the question of how these stereotypes are similar to or different from the stereotypes held by adults. Less attention will be paid in this section to the more general cognitive processes and principles through which a child's stereotypes develop, although we shall refer back to concepts and processes discussed in the first section when they are relevant.

Stereotypes in Children

DO CHILDREN HAVE SPECIFIC STEREOTYPES OF GROUPS? IF SO, HOW DO THEY LEARN THEM?

The answer to the first question is clearly "yes"— children do hold stereotypes of various social groups. A number of researchers have made it clear that children form stereotypes and that these stereotypes guide children's judgments about the attributes of individual group members (Aboud, 1988; Hirschfeld, 1995a, 1996; Rhodes & Gelman, 2008). With regard to negative associations to minority races, McGlothlin and Killen (2010) found that 7- to 10-year-old European American children from ethnically homogeneous schools showed negative associations to minority group members in their interpretations of ambiguous social situations and in their evaluations of cross-race friendship. Recent studies using the Implicit Association Test (IAT) with 6-year-olds demonstrated implicit race-based associations (Baron & Banaji, 2006; Dunham, Baron, & Banaji, 2006). Using both the IAT and an affective priming task, Degner and Wentura (2010) reported automatic activation of biased racial associations in young children with some indication that such activation increased linearly from 9 to 12 years of age. Degner and Wentura (2010) also conclude that stereotyping of racial categories and evaluations of these categories develop as early as 3 years of age. Bigler and Liben (2006) also conclude that, by age 5 years, children have many strong stereotypes about other social categories. We have already cited work by Gelman (2003) that has also concluded that young children are able to think in essentialist ways about social categories and that they treat certain social categories (especially gender, age, and race, but also occupation) as natural kinds.

Castelli and his colleagues have the most comprehensive program of research that investigates the stereotypes held by children. Castelli, Zogmeister, and Tomelleri (2009) explored the acquisition of racial stereotypes in 3- to 6-year-olds. Similar to the results of previous research (Aboud & Doyle, 1996; Davey, 1983), they found no relationship between the explicit attitudes of white parents and their children. However, Castelli et al. (2009) also explored the ability of parents' implicit racial attitudes to predict their children's playmate choices. Using the IAT,

they found that mothers' IAT scores regarding race, but not their scores on explicit measures, did in fact predict their children's playmate choices. Castelli and Carraro (2010) also investigated the role of implicit attitudes in children's stereotype development. It would be interesting to examine whether there is intergenerational transmission of implicit racial attitudes. In a recent study unrelated to stereotypes, Sherman et al. (2009) reported intergenerational transmission of implicit attitudes toward cigarette smoking from mothers to their children. The greater effect of mothers' as opposed to fathers' racial attitudes was also demonstrated by Castelli, Carraro, Tomelleri, and Amari (2007), who found that children's racial attitudes were shaped by their expectations about their mothers' racial attitudes and behaviors rather than their mothers' actual racial attitudes. The sensitivity of young children to the implicit racial attitudes of their mothers implies that children are more sensitive to the subtle behaviors and nonverbal responses of their mothers than to the mothers' overt verbal statements.

In support of preschool children's sensitivity to the nonverbal behaviors of adults regarding race, Castelli, DeDea, and Nesdale (2008) manipulated an adult model's verbal and nonverbal behaviors toward a black adult and found that children's attitudes toward the black target were shaped primarily by the model's nonverbal behaviors such as eye contact and distance. In addition, the effects then generalized to other black targets.

Other researchers have also investigated various underlying processes through which young children develop stereotypes. Platten et al. (2010) proposed that the early development of stereotypes in children is based on their social cognitive ability to appreciate social coalitions, and the processes that allow this to develop in the first two years of life. As discussed earlier, the abilities that make it possible for young children to understand coalitions include face recognition (which involves complex face processing), the discrimination of emotional face expressions, and social referencing (the extraction of relevant social information from emotional face expressions and the use of these to guide behavior). These abilities underlie the development of expectations about social alliances, even in infants, and the appreciation of these alliances is important to the development of stereotypes. In support of the notion that young children think in terms of alliances and coalitions, Castelli, DeAmicis, and Sherman (2007) reported that white preschool children showed clear preferences for other white children who played with a white child as opposed to a black child. Thus, alliances are appreciated by young children based not only on race but also on behaviors and friendship patterns.

Bigler and Liben (2006, 2007) conclude that stereotypes develop during early childhood by age 4 years. In drawing conclusions about the causes of such development and about the processes involved, Bigler and Liben focus on social psychological processes and environmental controls rather than on the more basic cognitive processes that were discussed in the earlier section of this chapter. They label their approach to explaining children's stereotyping *developmental intergroup theory*. Bigler and Liben identify three basic processes of developmental intergroup theory. First is the establishment of the psychological salience of different person attributes. Bigler and Liben maintain that there are no necessarily privileged dimensions of salience, but rather that they are socially and culturally determined. Because group salience and attribute salience are so important to the development of stereotypes in children, Bigler and Liben conclude that children's stereotypes can be reduced by minimizing this salience. How does the child learn the important bases of categorization? In addition to perceived salience, by which attention is drawn to categories such as race, gender, and age, the environment also renders certain dimensions salient. Group size is important here, as is labeling. In addition, any environmental factors that lead to the segregation of groups (e.g., having separate bathrooms for boys and girls) are important and cause the child to think about the reasons for segregating groups. Once certain attributes are made salient, the child will use these dimensions to categorize individuals. This act of categorization is the first step toward stereotyping. Some of the processes involved here are internal to the child (e.g., essentialist thinking), some involve direct social learning in terms of labeling and interpersonal communication, some involve the child's encoding (veridical or not) of group-attribute covariation, and some involve nonverbal behaviors and cues.

DO THE STEREOTYPES THAT CHILDREN HAVE OF DIFFERENT SOCIAL GROUPS DIFFER IN LIKELIHOOD, STRENGTH, AND OTHER PROPERTIES?

With regard to gender versus race categorization and stereotyping in children, most of the literature suggests that gender is a very strong category even in very young children (Jacklin & Maccoby, 1978; Ruble, Martin, & Berenbaum, 2006). Gender

concepts are essentialist very early and very strongly. Interestingly, recent work (Halim, Ruble, & Amodio, 2011) suggests that developmental changes in social cognition and gender-related attitudes and beliefs between ages 3 to 6 and 7 to 10 years lead to shifts in gender identity and gender stereotypes for girls, but not for boys. One behavioral consequence of these shifts is that 3- to 6-year-old girls love pink, frilly dresses, whereas 7- to 10-year-old girls exhibit a great deal of "tomboyism."

According to Halim, Ruble, and Amodio (2011), two sets of social cognitive developmental changes underlie these shifts: First, the young girls begin to view social categories, including gender categories, from multiple perspectives. Thus, they begin to appreciate their low status and the advantages of masculinity. Second, they view gender stereotypes more complexly and more in terms of central traits such as competence rather than in terms of peripheral behaviors. They represent the attributes of boys and girls in more flexible terms. These developmental changes lead girls to re-evaluate themselves, their gender identity, and gender-typed behaviors. In short, the changes in gender stereotypes from ages 3 to 6 years to 7 to 10 years have important implications for the gender identities, self-concepts, and preferred behaviors of young girls.

A recent line of research has focused on the development of gender stereotypes that are held by children regarding the math abilities of boys and girls, as well as the extent to which such stereotypes undermine the actual math performance of young girls. Although gender differences in math performance have diminished in recent years (Hyde, Lindberg, Linn, Ellis, & Williams, 2008; Hyde & Mertz, 2009), the gender gap persists (Beilock, 2008). One explanation for gender differences in math performance is stereotype threat (Steele & Aronson, 1995). According to stereotype threat theory, female math performance is impaired, not because of poorer ability, but because girls and women feel anxious that their poor performance on a math test will confirm the negative stereotype associated with their group.

Such an explanation presupposes that gender stereotypes of math abilities exist in young children. Muzzatti and Agnoli (2007) reported such gender stereotypes in 8- to 12-year-old children, but not in younger children. However, others have reported lower math ability perceptions in girls as opposed to boys as early as first grade (Fredricks & Eccles, 2002; Jacobs, Lanza, Osgood, Eccles, & Wigfield, 2002). Importantly, and in support of a stereotype threat explanation for gender–based performance differences, Ambady, Shih, Kim, and Pittinsky (2001) found that math performance in young girls suffered only when gender identity was activated (see also Neuville & Croizet, 2007). More recently, Tomasetto, Alparone, and Cadinu (2011) observed math impairment for kindergarten to second-grade girls only when mothers, but not fathers, endorsed math gender stereotypes. Thus, it appears that young girls hold negative math stereotypes and that these stereotypes are in part transmitted through the beliefs of their mothers.

As indicated above, there has been some inconsistency in reports of when young girls develop gender stereotypes of their math abilities. Recently, Galdi, Cadinu, and Tomasetto (2011) investigated whether implicit math stereotypes existed in very young girls long before the emergence of explicitly measured stereotypes. Their research verified the existence of such embryonic implicit stereotypes for first-grade girls, but not boys, using the IAT. However, no such stereotypes were seen for young girls at the explicit level, where girls in fact felt that they were stronger at math than boys. A subsequent study showed that the math performance of these young girls was negatively affected by stereotype threat manipulations. Whereas gender is a strong category in young children ages 3 to 6 years (although the stereotype is more flexible in older children), race, on the other hand, may not be as important a category for young children. According to some theorists, race is not thought about by children in essentialist terms to the extent that gender is (Aboud, 2003; Kircher & Furby, 1971). Rhodes and Gelman (2009) supported this conclusion in a number of studies that were designed to examine children's essentialist thinking about animal categories, artifact categories, gender, and race. They told children (aged 4–6 years) that a visitor from another planet, where they do things differently from earth, was going to tell them things. The children had to decide whether the statements were wrong or whether they may be right. The visitor showed the children two objects from different categories (e.g., dog and cat; table and chair; black and white women; black male and black female). The visitor then showed the children a third object that actually matched one of the examples of the pair at a basic level. In some cases, the visitor from the other planet said that the new object matched the exemplar that did not fit what children might expect from their learned categories (e.g., a black goat was said to match a pink pig rather than a white goat; a black boy was said to match a white

boy rather than a different black boy). The important measure of category strength (essentialization) was the degree to which children rejected the non-fitting matches as wrong. For animals and gender, children reliably rejected as wrong the unexpected matches. These findings indicate that young children have essentialist, natural-kind views of these two categories. However, they did not reject the unexpected matches for race categories, indicating a less essentialized view of race. The gender results are consistent with results of previous research (Berndt & Heller, 1986; Rhodes & Gelman, 2008; Taylor, 1996). Similarly, Shutts, Banaji, and Spelke (2007) reported that preschoolers used gender and language, but not race, to make inferences about people's friends, toys, and activities.

Rhodes and Gelman (2009) conclude that distinct developmental processes underlie the acquisition of race and gender categories and the stereotyping of these categories. Such a conclusion is consistent with an evolution-based interpretation that the gender category is constrained by intuitive biases because of its evolutionary importance, whereas race categories and their stereotypes are based much more on social and cultural experiences, and would not have been present during the key epochs in which humans evolved because intergroup interaction was largely constrained to nearby groups with similar genotypic features (Cosmides, Tooby, & Kurzban, 2003).

Importantly, not all theory and research agrees with this conclusion about fundamental differences in children between racial and gender categories and stereotyping. Hirschfeld (1996; see also Gil-White, 2001) has argued that race is seen in essentialist terms even by very young children. He proposes that children have essentialized, domain-specific, sophisticated, theory-like reasoning about race that parallels, but is distinct from and not derived from, their understanding of biological categories. Hirschfeld (1995b) thus believes that young children have a biologically grounded understanding of race.

Hirschfeld (1995b) employed several unique methodologies in his work. In one method, children aged 3 to 7 years were shown triads of people. One was an adult of a particular race, occupation, and body build. The other two were children, each of whom shared two of the three properties with the adult. Thus, a black, stocky, adult policeman might be paired with a white, stocky, child "policeman" and a black, stocky, child "doctor." Participant children were asked which was the child of the adult or were asked which of the children is a picture of the adult as a child. Findings from these and other measures indicated that young children's conceptual representation of race is theory-like. In a similar study, Hirschfeld (1995b) reports that children did not pair a black adult any more with a black car than with a white car, indicating that the racial (color) category was very specific to people.

In a different methodology, Hirschfeld (1995b) used a "switched at birth" story. Child participants were told that a baby was born to White parents but was raised by black parents, and they were asked about what the child would look like as an adult. Results indicated that children as young as 3 years viewed race as a stable and inherited property, and Hirschfeld concluded again that children have a biologically grounded model of race.

However, some of Hirschfeld's other work suggests that the story of racial versus gender stereotypes in children is more complicated and that his conclusion about the child's essentialist, biologically grounded view of race might be questioned. Hirschfeld (1996) is unique in exploring the phenomenon of hypodescent in young children, the association of individuals of mixed-race ancestry with the minority group (also referred to as the *one drop rule*). Because Hirschfeld believes that thinking about social categories in strongly essentialist ways is central to exhibiting judgments that show hypodescent, he asks whether some races have greater innate essential potential than others. First, Hirschfeld finds that older children and adults believe that mixed-race individuals have black facial features and that mixed-race individuals inherit the category identity of the minority parent. However, younger children, especially black children or white children who go to an integrated school, expect that mixed-race individuals have intermediate racial features. Rather than strong judgments showing hypodescent, young children seem to think that other children will resemble their mother more than their father. Whereas fifth graders and adults used race status significantly to predict the features of a mixed-race child, second graders used resemblance to mother more, regardless of whether the mother was the white or the black parent. In addition, with mixed-race parents, fifth graders tend to choose a black child as the likely offspring, whereas second graders do not. However, fifth graders do not show this tendency for animals that have a black and a white parent. Thus, by the fifth grade, children think differently about color in humans than about color in animals, and they view different races as having different innate potential, as they expect that the

physical features of the minority race will predominate. Hirschfeld's (1995a; 1996) conclusion from these studies is that race is invariably essentialized, even in young children. However, the bias that is a consequence of essentialist thinking can be altered by the child's social and cultural representations of race. Thus, there is both a social and a biological interpretation of race for children. Importantly, this view maintains that even young children have the capacity for making judgments marked by hypodescent. Nevertheless, the fact that judgments about race changed between the second and fifth grades indicates that race may not exist as a strongly essentialized category for very young children.

Kinzler, Shutts, and Correll (2010) have recently written an important paper that addresses the question of whether there are priorities in the social categories that children possess and thus differences in the stereotypes that they hold of these categories. Kinzler et al. (2010) reviewed the literature relevant to this issue for gender, race, age, and language groups, and they addressed the question from the points of view of social psychology, developmental psychology, and evolutionary psychology. They conclude that categorization and preferences based on gender emerge before categorization and preferences based on race. However, Kinzler et al. (2010) also report a number of findings that support priorities and categorization for race and age as well as gender. For example, face processing is tuned to dimensions of both race and gender in infants (Bar-Haim, Ziv, Lamy, & Hodes, 2006; Quinn, Yahr, Kuhn, Slater, & Pascalis, 2002). Infants even develop representations of prototypical faces (DeHaan et al., 2001). Kinzler et al. (2010) also added a fourth category, language, that seems to have a distinct priority in categorization. Newborns show a distinct preference to hear speech in their own language (Mehler et al., 1988). Children also show preferences for toys and foods offered by their native language speakers (Kinzler, Dupoux, & Spelke, 2007; Shutts, Kinzler, McKee, & Spelke, 2009). These studies, in fact, showed that preferences based on language are stronger than preferences based on race. As in the case of gender, language as a privileged social category may have an evolutionary basis (Cosmides et al., 2003).

DO CHILDREN'S STEREOTYPES DIFFER FROM THOSE OF ADULTS? IN WHAT WAYS?

We have seen that young children have the cognitive capacities for the development of sophisticated categories and concepts, for theory-based thinking, for thinking in essentialist ways, and for perceiving the degree of entitativity of social groups. These capacities allow for the development of stereotypes in young children and underlie such development. However, although both children and adults hold stereotypes of the same social groups, it is not clear that these stereotypes are the same for adults and children in terms of strength, content, and mutability. We shall thus address the issue of similarities and differences in the stereotypes that are held by children and adults. In the case of differences, we shall explore the reasons for the differences in terms of the cognitive capabilities that we have discussed.

One important way in which the categories and concepts of children differ from those of adults is that children seem to generalize properties across more members of a category. For example, Hollander, Gelman, and Star (2002) gave children and adults either generic questions (e.g., "What can you tell me about dogs?") or "all" questions (e.g., "What can you tell me about all dogs?"). Whereas adults included more properties for the "all" question than for the generic question, children treated the two questions equally. In other words, for children, dogs equal all dogs. Shipley (2000) found that young children showed greater entrenchment than older children or adults for behavioral properties. That is, 3-year-olds were very willing to make inductive inferences about behaviors across members of a category. This propensity should be associated with strong stereotypes in young children. If all members of a group engage in the same behaviors, the members are interchangeable. Consistent with this possibility, several researchers have reported that children observe patterns of correlation between social groups and properties and that they magnify these observed correlations. As a result, the stereotypes of social groups held by young children do tend to be more rigid than those of older children and adults (Berndt & Heller, 1986; Biernat, 1991; Taylor, 1996; Taylor, Rhodes, & Gelman, 2009). In addition, young children tend to make more inductive inferences about traits and dispositions, rather than perceptual resemblances, than do adults (Gelman & Heyman, 1999; Heyman & Gelman, 2000).

Although children seem more willing to generalize attributes across category members, they are also more willing to accept novel instances (which may differ from existing category members in certain ways) as members of the category. For example, Heyman and Gelman (2000) found that children were more prone than adults to give nativistic accounts of traits and that children were overly ready to see categories as essential, whereas adults viewed the same categories in more nuanced ways. Again, this difference suggests that young children may be prone to hold stronger stereotypes than adults.

The fact that children accept novel instances as category members more readily than do adults means that the generalization gradients of children (i.e., the likelihood of making the same response to a new object as to existing category members) are broader than the generalization gradients of adults. That is, children tend to "smoosh" their categories together, whereas adults show a greater tendency to discriminate among categories. In Piaget's (1929, 1970) terms, this means that children are more likely to assimilate new objects to an existing category than to accommodate or change existing categories in the light of novel objects. It would be interesting to see whether, in terms of judgments and perceptions, children are generally more likely than adults to show assimilation effects and less likely to show contrast effects.

Finally, although we discussed earlier that children perceive the same group types as do adults and order these group types by perceived entitativity in the same way as do adults, children and adults differ in terms of the specific properties that they use to determine perceptions of entitativity (Svirydzenka et al., 2010). Children tend to use the level of interaction of group members as the predominant factor for perceived entitativity, whereas adults use group importance and situational aspects of the group. In addition, children's perceived entitativity is guided more by concrete properties such as similarity and group duration, whereas adults' perceived entitativity is guided by more abstract properties such as shared beliefs and goals.

Summary of Stereotype Development in Children

We have presented theory and empirical research that supports the ability of even very young children to think in abstract terms, to engage in theory-based reasoning, to be affected by conceptual as well as perceptual factors, and to think in essentialist ways. We have argued that these capacities are important for stereotype development in that these cognitive abilities underlie the development of strong and stable category representations. Indeed, research indicates that children develop stereotypes based on race, gender, age, and language at a very young age (perhaps, by the age of 3 years). Even infants show distinct categorizations along these dimensions. There is ongoing debate as to the primacy and dominance of these different stereotypes, with some researchers suggesting that gender stereotypes are particularly strong, and others disagreeing. Social influence from parents (mothers, in particular), developing conceptions of social coalitions, and category salience (e.g., from explicit labeling) contribute to the development of these stereotypes. Although there are significant similarities between adults and children in the ways in which they think about categories and concepts, and thus significant similarities in the stereotypes that they are likely to develop and express, there also are important differences. In general, children tend to hold stronger stereotypes than adults in that they apply their stereotypes to more members of a category, hold more rigid stereotypes, demonstrate greater inductive potential, and make fewer distinctions within categories than do adults.

Cognitive Processes in the Acquisition of Novel Group Stereotypes among Adults

We turn now to discuss the processes behind the formation of novel group stereotypes in adults. One of the difficulties in studying stereotype formation among adults is that adults already have well-developed stereotypes pertaining to the important dimensions of sex, race, and age. Indeed, to study stereotype formation among adults, it is necessary to confront participants with information about "blank" groups (e.g., Groups A and B), for which they possess no prior knowledge or expectations. Because the self is not a member of these groups, inferences about the groups also cannot be derived from self-knowledge.

One important variable in stereotype formation is the extent to which information about a novel group is encountered in a comparative intergroup context. The presence of a clear comparative standard when learning about a social group leads to the development of stronger stereotypes (Corneille & Judd, 1999; Eiser, 1971; Krueger & Rothbart, 1990; Queller, Schell, & Mason, 2006; Wyer, Sadler, & Judd, 2002). This is undoubtedly one reason why the vast majority of research on adult stereotype formation has presented information about two novel groups, which could be compared and contrasted. A key factor in this research is whether the two groups differ or not. In the latter case, people may perceive differences between the two groups that are illusory. In the former case, real differences between the groups are exaggerated in the formation of stereotypes. We will discuss each of these two contexts in turn.

Stereotype Development in the Absence of Group Differences: Illusory Correlation

Stereotypes are commonly conceived to derive from a "kernel of truth"—a valid difference upon which group perceptions are ultimately based (for relevant discussions, see Campbell, 1967; Kenny et al., 2007; Lee, Jussim, & McCauley, 1995; LeVine & Campbell, 1972; Swim, 1994; Terracciano et al., 2005). The particulars of such a metaphoric "grain" or "kernel" are relevant to note—the actual difference between groups might be tiny and its perception exaggerated, but at bottom such a difference is nonetheless ultimately perceived as the seed from which the stereotype emanates. Under a kernel-of-truth conceptualization, the inaccuracy of stereotypes mainly inheres in the overapplication or the exaggeration of an actual group difference, rather than in the possibility that the group difference itself might be totally illusory. As such, the mere existence of a stereotype is commonly taken as an indication that a group difference must exist.

Although stereotypes are not always unfounded, in this section we focus on those that clearly lack this kernel of truth. The notion of stereotype accuracy is a highly complex and controversial area of research (Judd & Park, 1993, 2005; Oakes & Reynolds, 1997), and there is even disagreement as to whether such accuracy is measurable or whether it should be a focus of research at all, particularly because of the challenges of identifying a "reality" criterion against which to measure stereotypic beliefs. Somewhat sidestepping these issues, we instead focus on the notion that a kernel of truth is not a necessary *precondition* to stereotype development, and that some stereotypes are indeed quite unfounded (e.g., LaPiere, 1936; Terracciano et al., 2005). Although often characterized otherwise, kernel-of-truth theorists as early as Campbell (1967) have submitted that "stereotypes can be completely false" (1967, p. 824). Even in more recent work on the "unbearable accuracy of stereotypes" (Jussim et al., 2009), it is acknowledged that some such perceptions are formed in the absence of a group difference. But how could a stereotype develop in the absence of a kernel of truth? Where but from some realistic basis could such a perception arise? Among the earliest research on how stereotypes can develop in the absence of an actual group difference is work on *illusory correlation* (see Chapman, 1967; Hamilton, 1981; Hamilton & Gifford, 1976; Stroessner & Plaks, 2001). In the pioneering work on the subject (Chapman, 1967), illusory correlation was defined somewhat more broadly than it is in social cognitive work today, and included any case in which the perceived correlation between two events is inaccurate. As such, the term could apply to the perception of weaker or stronger relationships than actually exist, as well as the perception of a relationship that is nonexistent. It is the latter case (i.e., a perceived but nonexistent relationship) that is typically meant by "illusory correlation" today, and upon which we will focus in this subsection.

It was Hamilton and Gifford (1976; see also Hamilton, 1981) who first had the groundbreaking idea of applying the notion of illusory correlation to the learning of group characteristics, as a possible mechanism by which stereotypes could form in the absence of an actual group difference. To do so, they constructed a paradigm in which members of novel groups were encountered, and group characteristics learned, over the course of an experiment. In the typical paradigm, participants were presented with a series of sentences describing members of a majority and minority group (e.g., "John, a member of Group A, is rarely late for work"). After the presentation of numerous such sentences describing members of both groups, participants made judgments about the groups' characteristics and guessed the group membership of novel targets based on their behaviors.

This work examined the possible role of illusory correlation in stereotype development through manipulation of the stimulus sentence content. The ratio of desirable to undesirable target behaviors was the same for the majority and minority groups, whereas the size of the groups and the incidence of each kind of behavior overall were systematically varied. For example, in one study (Hamilton & Gifford, 1976; Study 2), participants encountered twice as many members of a majority group (24) as members of a minority group (12). Undesirable and desirable target behaviors had the same ratio within each group—twice as many undesirable behaviors as desirable ones (16 and 8 for the majority group and 8 and 4 in the minority group, respectively), and thus undesirable behaviors (24) were relatively common, and desirable behaviors (12) were relatively rare.

Subsequent to the presentation of this information about the group members, participants encountered behaviors of unidentified targets and were asked to guess the group membership of each. Their judgments demonstrated that desirable behaviors (the less common type of behavior) were more likely to be attributed to the minority group, whereas undesirable behaviors (the more common type of behavior) were more likely to be attributed to the majority group. Likewise, trait ratings of the groups demonstrated that the minority group was seen in a more positive light than the majority group. Thus, participants came to perceive a difference between groups on a dimension of behavior desirability that was illusory, associating the less common characteristic with the smaller group and the more common characteristic with the larger group. The trait ratings of the two groups were reversed when the majority behaviors were desirable and the minority were undesirable. In this case, desirable behaviors were more likely to be attributed to the majority group, and the minority group was seen in a less positive light (Hamilton & Gifford, 1976; Study 1). The importance of this work should not be understated because it constituted the first direct demonstration of the formation of stereotypes of two novel groups that were (in all aspects except their size) completely equivalent. In addition, these effects were obtained in the absence of any group conflict with the participants and could not be explained by social learning, ego justification, or sociofunctional accounts of stereotyping (see below). Instead, the results showed that stereotypes could be developed through strictly cognitive mechanisms, the normal processes through which people learn to associate attributes with category members.

Such illusory correlations can develop quickly, even after a single unusual behavior from a minority group member (Risen, Gilovich, & Dunning, 2007). Accounts of the phenomenon have explained the effect in terms of enhanced attention and memory for the most distinctive pairing (i.e., the pairing of the minority group and the rare trait; McConnell, Sherman, & Hamilton, 1994) or, conversely, in terms of enhanced memory for the most frequently encountered pairing (i.e., the pairing of the majority group and the common trait; Rothbart, 1981). Other accounts have argued that the perception of a group difference in such paradigms is not illusory at all, and that it is the absolute subtractive difference between the types of behavior performed by groups (i.e., common behaviors minus rare behaviors; constituting a greater difference for majority groups than minority groups) rather than the proportion that is encoded (McGarty, Haslam, Turner, & Oakes, 1993; Smith, 1991). Still other work has suggested that the mechanism for illusory correlation is regression to the mean through information loss, which results in overestimation of low-frequency events (because they are less likely to be learned, estimates regress toward the mean frequency) and therefore an overestimation of the rarest instance: minority group members with rare traits (Fiedler, 1991; for reviews, see Sherman et al., 2009; Stroessner & Plaks, 2001). A more recent analysis recruiting attentional learning processes as the mechanism for illusory correlation effects (Sherman et al., 2009) will be discussed in greater detail below. Each of these explanations has received empirical support, suggesting that the effect is multiply determined.

Stereotype Development in the Presence of Group Differences: Accentuation

We now turn to the development of stereotypes among groups that actually differ on one or more dimensions. In this case, there are real differences between the groups, but those differences are accentuated through a number of psychological processes. These accentuation processes help to provide clear distinctions among categories and maximize their predictive power (e.g., Queller et al., 2006). Research on this topic was instigated by Tajfel's pioneering research on "mere categorization" effects, which showed that the division of graded stimuli into discrete categories leads to exaggerated perceptions of features of stimuli in the two categories, particularly at the category boundaries. In the classic example, the placement of a category boundary between lines of varying length caused the lines in the "long" category to be judged as longer and the lines in the "short" category to be judged as shorter than when no category boundary was provided (Tajfel & Wilkes, 1963). Categorization may exaggerate both perceived differences between categories and perceived similarities within categories (e.g., Queller et al., 2006). An important feature of this work is that accentuation occurs only for features that are correlated with the classification. Thus, simple categorization is not sufficient to produce category accentuation; there must be attributes that covary with the category distinction. Thus, in the classic line study (Tajfel & Wilkes, 1963), accentuation occurred when the short lines were labeled Category A and the long lines were labeled Category B. However, when the category labels were randomly assigned to lines, such that there was no systematic difference between the lengths of the lines in Categories A and B, no accentuation was observed.

Both the accentuation of between-category differences (e.g., Corneille & Judd, 1999; Eiser, 1971; Krueger & Rothbart, 1990; Queller et al., 2006) and within-category similarities (e.g., Krueger & Clement, 1994; McGarty & Penny, 1988; McGarty & Turner, 1992) have been demonstrated in the perception of social groups, contributing to the formation of distinct group stereotypes. A variety of mechanisms have been shown to contribute to these accentuation effects. First, research shows that stereotypes are most likely to be formed around attributes for which intergroup differences are large and intragroup differences are small (Ford & Stangor, 1992). Traits that maximize differences between groups enhance the predictive power of social categorization to one of the two groups. Traits that maximize similarity within groups increase the inductive potential among members of a group; if all members of a group are alike, what holds for one group member holds for all group members. As detailed in Tajfel's original research, a second source of accentuation is that perceptions of individual group members may be biased by category boundaries. This effect is enhanced when the categories are given meaningful labels (e.g., Foroni & Rothbart, 2011). However, even when the objective nature of the exemplars prevents variation in their interpretation (e.g., the category members have fixed values, such as numbers or the presence vs. absence of a key feature), perceptions of the categories, as a whole, may still be accentuated. For example, category members who heighten between-category differences and within-category similarities may be attended to more carefully, given greater weight in judgments, or remembered more easily (Krueger & Rothbart, 1990; Krueger, Rothbart, & Sriram, 1989). Thus, perceptions of individual category members need not be exaggerated in order for category accentuation to occur.

Integrating Illusory Correlation and Category Accentuation

Research on illusory correlation and category accentuation has largely proceeded independently and, as we have seen, these effects have been explained by different mechanisms. Recently, Sherman and colleagues (Sherman et al., 2009) have attempted to integrate these phenomena into a common theoretical framework, showing that both can be explained by Kruschke's attention theory of category learning (1996, 2001, 2003). Attention theory assumes that people learn about frequent categories before they learn about infrequent ones, for the simple reason that, by definition, frequent category members are more numerous and more likely to be encountered. Once the features of the frequent category are learned, an efficient strategy for learning about other, rarer categories is to focus attention on the features that best distinguish them from the previously learned frequent category. Features that have already been associated with the frequent category, even if these features are shared by a less frequent category, are ignored as attention is turned toward the features that best distinguish between the unlearned and already learned categories. This attention-shifting mechanism causes a stronger association between the infrequent category and its features than between the frequent category and its features, and increases the weight given to infrequent category features in judgment (e.g., Kruschke, 1992; Nosofsky, 1986). The stronger association between minority categories and their features leads to a very important prediction—strong and stable stereotypes will develop primarily for minority groups. Empirical evidence in support of this prediction and the attentional processes underlying the effect were reported by Sherman et al. (2009). In addition, because of the strong association between minority groups and their features (both traits and physical features), exemplars exhibiting a combination of those distinctive minority group features and features of the frequent group will tend to be seen as part of the infrequent group.

Thus, these attentional and categorization mechanisms can account for hypodescent, the association of any individual of mixed-race ancestry with the minority or socially subordinate group. Halberstadt, Sherman, and Sherman (2011) demonstrated hypodescent effects and supported the attentional processes described above. In one study, Chinese participants judged ambiguous Chinese/white morphed faces to be white, whereas whites judged the same ambiguous faces to be Chinese. In another study, using all white faces, ambiguous faces were more likely to be judged as a minority face than as a majority face.

This basic model of category learning can account for both illusory correlation and category accentuation effects with the same mechanism. Regarding illusory correlation, according to attention theory, the majority group is learned before the minority group because majority group members are more prevalent among the stimuli. If negative behaviors are more frequent than positive behaviors, then the impression formed of the majority group will be a negative one. Subsequently, in forming impressions of the minority group, it must be the positive behaviors (the only remaining behaviors) that distinguish it from the majority group, and these positive features receive particularly close attention.

Thus, to distinguish the minority from the majority group, perceivers focus attention on positive minority behaviors and form a more favorable impression of that group. Sherman et al. (2009) provided strong support for this account of illusory correlation.

Regarding category accentuation, the processes of distinguishing two categories are very similar in the attention theory model and as described in accentuation research. Attention theory–like attention shifting processes are certainly consistent with and may directly contribute to the findings that people attend most carefully to category members who heighten between-category differences and within-category similarities, give those members greater weight in judgments, and remember those instances most easily (e.g., Krueger et al., 1989; Krueger & Rothbart, 1990). The category discrimination processes in attention theory also may contribute to the biased perception of individual category members, such that greater attention is paid to features that assimilate them to their own group and contrast them away from other categories (e.g., Tajfel & Wilkes, 1963). The major difference between attention theory and traditional work on category accentuation is that attention theory does not require that the two groups actually differ from one another. Indeed, whether the two groups are different (as in accentuation research) or the same (as in illusory correlation) is irrelevant. All that matters is that perceivers form an impression of one of the groups first (e.g., owing to frequency of exposure, group size, chance variation in exposure to different groups). Having formed an impression of one group, the attention-shifting mechanism of attention theory then produces different stereotypes of the two groups, with stronger stereotypes for the minority group. The first group will be associated with its most common attributes, and impressions of the second group will form around those features that most clearly differentiate it from the first category. Thus, attention theory provides an account not only of how groups are differentiated from one another but of which particular features come to characterize those groups.

Because children are capable of category formation based on these kinds of processes, it is certainly feasible that stereotype development in children is based on these cognitive mechanisms, although, to our knowledge, no empirical work on the attention theory model has been done with children. The fact that children do exhibit hypodescent in their race judgments (Hirschfeld, 1996) and hold more essentialized views of minority groups than of majority groups (Gelman, 2003) is supportive of this possibility.

Summary

Research on stereotype formation among adults has largely relied on the use of blank categories in comparative intergroup contexts. Whereas one strong research tradition has focused on the processes that lead to the accentuation of real differences between groups, another prominent approach has examined the formation of stereotypes when groups do not, in fact, differ from one another (i.e., illusory correlation). Each of these approaches has produced a voluminous body of research, and each has led to the development of distinct process models to account for relevant results. Recently, Sherman et al. (2009) proposed a process model based on category learning research that is able to account for the development of group stereotypes both when groups actually differ and when they do not.

Motivational Factors in Stereotype Formation

To this point, our discussion has focused on the specific processes through which stereotypes are formed. Other important aspects of stereotype formation are related to the fundamental purposes for which stereotypes exist. Understanding why humans would create stereotypes in the first place can help to answer important questions about what kinds of groups are likely to elicit the formation of stereotypes and what the specific content of those stereotypes is likely to be. Addressing such functional questions also can shed further light on the cognitive processes that contribute to stereotype formation.

Historically, psychologists have identified three central motives for the construction of stereotypes (e.g., Ashmore & Del Boca, 1981): stereotypes are efficient, they promote feelings of self-worth, and they explain and justify the social structure.[2] These varied functions of stereotypes do not conflict with one another, and any given stereotype may serve multiple purposes. Indeed, the overdetermined nature of stereotypes is one reason why they are so prevalent and difficult to change. Although these three broad functions are not incompatible, they do offer distinct insights into the kinds of groups about which stereotypes will develop and the kinds of traits that will form the bases of those stereotypes. Although these motivations influence many aspects of social categorization, stereotype activation, and stereotype application, our discussion focuses specifically on stereotype formation.

Stereotypes Are Efficient

One important function of stereotypes is to promote cognitive economy (Allport, 1954; Lippmann, 1922; Tajfel, 1969). In this sense, stereotypes are formed for much the same reasons as all categorical knowledge. Given the vast quantities of information in the environment, it is impossible to form novel and unique impressions of all the things and people we encounter. Through categorization, we are able to treat members of a category as interchangeable, imposing structure on the world, and thus reducing the burden of information overload. Accordingly, stereotypes may be used to predict and understand the behavior of group members in the absence of any specific knowledge of them beyond the fact of their group membership. In this way, stereotypes are an efficient means of social perception, providing broadly applicable knowledge with relatively little effort in the way of information gathering. Thus, according to this perspective, the purpose of stereotyping is to structure and simplify the social world and provide an efficient guide for social perception and behavior.

Concerns for cognitive efficiency should lead to the formation of stereotypes that maximize the (subjective) predictive utility of social group membership. Stereotypes are efficient tools of prediction to the extent that they reflect distinct groups of people possessing distinct attributes. As such, stereotypes should form around groups whose members appear to behave differently from other people and whose behavior cannot be explained by existing knowledge. Stereotypes should also be more likely to form around groups that have been previously associated with other group differences (LePelley, Reimers, Beesley, Spears, & Murphy, 2010). In terms of content, stereotypes should form around traits that clearly distinguish the target group from other groups of people (McCauley, Stitt, & Segal, 1980; Sherman et al., 2009). Ideally, these stereotypes should maximize perceived differences among groups and minimize perceived differences within groups. Importantly, stereotypes need not be accurate to offer effective cognitive economy. Indeed, the point of cognitive economy is to surrender a certain degree of accurate social perception in return for quick and easy social perception.

To this point, all of the research we have described serves this comprehension efficiency function in one way or another. Our discussion of stereotype development among children focused on the cognitive and linguistic abilities necessary to develop functional categorical knowledge, including stereotypes. Social learning also plays a significant role in children's acquisition of stereotypes, as children look to their parents for cues about how to understand and organize the social world. Among young children learning stereotypes for the first time, motivational components of stereotyping such as the desire to enhance self-esteem or to explain or defend the social structure are minimized. Although young children may be concerned about feelings of self-worth, pursuing those feelings through intergroup comparison is a relatively sophisticated strategy, particularly to the extent that social categories are ill-defined and understood at younger ages. Although children are undoubtedly engaged in figuring out why different kinds of people do different things, they may be less likely to feel a strong need to explain and/or justify the social structure than do adults, who are active participants in society's prescribed roles. In any case, we are not aware of any research that has explicitly examined these sociomotivational concerns among children.[3]

As explained earlier, in order to study stereotype formation among adults, it is necessary to confront participants with novel, "blank" groups with which they have no prior experience. Although such groups are ideal for examining the operation of basic cognitive processes in stereotype formation, they strip away motivations to enhance self-esteem or explain/defend the social structure. Indeed, the research we have described on adult stereotype formation having to do with category accentuation and illusory correlation is specifically geared toward understanding how the pursuit of knowledge and structure promotes the formation of stereotypes in the absence of social motives.

COGNITIVE EFFICIENCY AND STEREOTYPE ABSTRACTION

Sherman's (1996) research similarly minimized social motivational components in order to examine the course of stereotype formation as group knowledge accumulates. This research showed that, in the early stages of learning about a social group, judgments of the group are based on information about particular group members because too few exemplars have been encountered to support the formation of an abstract stereotype of the group. However, with sufficient experience with group members (or secondhand accounts of their attributes), perceivers form abstract representations of the attributes that are stereotypical of the group. Once formed, these abstractions may be retrieved independently from group exemplars to make judgments about relevant features of the group.

Sherman has argued that the abstraction of group knowledge across time, situations, and individual group members is critical for cognitive efficiency (Sherman, 2001). There are two aspects to this efficiency. First, by capturing patterns of invariances in the environment, information that is learned from past experiences can be brought to bear on a wide variety of novel people and experiences. Thus, a novel group member's behavior may be understood (or misunderstood) in light of the abstract stereotypes that have been formed about that person's group. Based on abstract stereotypes, group members' behavior also can be predicted in novel situations and into the future. This is what Bruner (1957) referred to as "going beyond" the information given (p. 129), and this predictive power is an important factor in the development of abstract stereotypes.

The second reason that the development of abstractions is efficient has to do with the need for streamlined representations and cognitive processes. In the absence of such abstractions, broad social comprehension and prediction would be inhibited by the levels of temporal, spatial, and contextual detail preserved among known individual group members. The predictive power of a stereotype is enhanced to the extent that it aggregates across many experiences and group members. Aside from offering reliability, the development of abstractions is procedurally efficient. Although breadth of application across time, context, and targets may be achieved by retrieving the details of multiple individual group members and summarizing those details at the moment in which a summary is needed, it is more efficient to form, store, and maintain abstract stereotypes that can be easily activated and applied. Indeed, the retrieval and application of specific episodes is more easily disrupted than the application of stored abstract knowledge structures (e.g., Rothbart, Fulero, Jensen, Howard, & Birrell, 1978; Sherman & Bessenoff, 1999).

PERCEIVED GROUP COHERENCE AS A SOURCE OF EFFICIENCY

If stereotypes are efficient to the extent that they permit clear predictions about distinct groups of people possessing distinct attributes, then variables that increase the perceived coherence and uniformity of social groups should contribute to this efficiency and to the likelihood of stereotype formation. One such moderator is the extent to which social categories are viewed in essential terms. Categories high in essentialism are seen to share some underlying essence that gives rise to the perceivable features of the category and membership in the category is seen as inalterable (Haslam, Bastian, Bain, & Kashima, 2006). Categories high in essentialism have more explanatory power than categories low in essentialism, owing to these characteristics. The high similarity between category members because of their shared underlying essence means that knowing the behavior or attitudes of one group member allows you to more accurately predict the behavior or attitudes of the group as a whole.

Additionally, the inalterability of the category membership means that if a person has the features of the category, then they are and will always be a member of the category, thus allowing people to make judgments about the person that should be stable over time. Thus, if a person believes that a category is high in essentialism, this comes with the assumption that there is high within-category similarity and that the category is highly distinct from other categories. As described when reviewing the literature on stereotype development in children, perceptions of group essence are a significant contributor to the formation of stereotypes. Similarly, research shows that perceptions of group essence increase the likelihood and extent of stereotype formation among adults. For example, Hoffman and Hurst (1990) showed that people formed stronger stereotypes when groups performing different social roles were described as belonging to separate species than when they were described as belonging to distinct subcultures of a single species. Likewise, Yzerbyt and Buidin (1998) showed that, when two groups were described as being genetically different from one another, initial differences between the groups on the dimension of sociability were accentuated compared with when the two groups were described as different in nonessential terms.

As with children, the extent to which groups are perceived as entitative also influences stereotype formation. Entitativity is the degree to which members of a group are seen as being a coherent social unit (Campbell, 1958), and judgments of entitativity are affected by a number of variables, such as group size, spatial proximity, amount of interaction between group members, similarity of group members, and the perception of common goals and outcomes among group members (Campbell, 1958; Lickel et al., 2000). Because members of entitative groups are seen as more similar to one another and as sharing similar goals to a greater extent than are members of nonentitative groups, perceivers should be more likely to generalize from one group member to another.

Evidence for this can be seen in the work of Park and Hastie (1987), who manipulated the variability of novel groups and found that participants were more likely to generalize from attributes of one group member to the rest of the group when the group possessed low variability. A stronger test of the link between entitativity and stereotyping was performed by Crawford, Sherman, and Hamilton (2002), who found that, when novel groups were described as high (vs. low) in entitativity, participants more readily transferred traits from one member of the group to all other group members.

Individual differences related to perceptions of group coherence also influence stereotype formation. For example, Levy, Stroessner, and Dweck (1998) found that *entity* theorists (who believe that people's traits are fixed and unchangeable) formed more extreme stereotypes of novel groups than did *incremental* theorists (who believe that people's traits are malleable). Likewise, individuals with a strong, more general motivation to simplify the world and perceive it as orderly and structured form novel stereotypes more readily than do those lacking this motivation (Schaller, Boyd, Yohannes, & O'Brien, 1995).

Stereotypes Promote a Sense of Self-Worth

A second functional framework suggests that the purpose of stereotypes is to protect and promote people's sense of ego and well-being (Lippmann, 1922). Early approaches in this vein were grounded heavily in Freudian psychology. Specifically, stereotypes were thought to be recruited to aid in the resolution of psychological conflicts stemming from childhood experiences and rooted in unconscious sexual and aggressive drives (e.g., Billig, 1976). According to this view, aggressive instincts are displaced from unacceptable outlets and applied to relatively powerless target groups, a process of scapegoating. Stereotypic beliefs are projections that justify hostility toward these powerless groups. These processes defend the ego from intrapsychic threats (e.g., Katz, 1960). Early theories from this perspective suggested that stereotyping is limited primarily to troubled individuals with unresolved psychological problems (e.g., Adorno, Frenkel-Brunswik, Levinson, & Sanford, 1950). More recently, ego defense has been viewed as (and shown to be) a more general motive that promotes stereotyping among psychologically healthy people when the sense of self is threatened (e.g., Fein & Spencer, 1997; Tajfel & Turner, 1986).

Concerns for self-esteem should lead to the formation of stereotypes that permit a favorable comparison to one's ingroup. Low-status groups should be particularly appealing for stereotyping, according to this perspective. The content of stereotypes should be primarily negative or at least negative in comparison to the ingroup.

Evidence for the role of ego enhancement in stereotype formation was provided by Schaller and Maass (1989), who showed that the standard illusory correlation effect is eliminated when participants are assigned to be members of either the majority or minority group. When participants belonged to one of the two groups, rather than form illusory correlations, they generally viewed their own group more favorably, regardless of how the groups were described.

The paradigm that has been applied most frequently to examine this motive in the formation of group impressions is the *minimal group paradigm*. In this procedure, participants learn that they are members of a meaningless group (e.g., "overestimators") and an equally meaningless outgroup is made salient (e.g., "underestimators"). Participants do not know any members of the two groups, do not interact with members of the groups, and have no expectations of future interactions with members of the groups. Following group assignment, participants are asked to make a variety of judgments about the groups and/or are asked to distribute resources to the groups. Based solely on this differentiation, people form more positive perceptions of the ingroup than the outgroup (Brewer & Brown, 1998; DiDonato, Ullrich, & Krueger, 2011; Gaertner & Insko, 2000; Miller, Maner, & Becker, 2010; Paladino & Castelli, 2008; Rubini, Moscatelli, & Palmonari, 2007; Tajfel et al., 1971). They evaluate ingroup members more positively on desirable trait dimensions (Blanz, Mummendey, & Otten, 1995), and they form abstract positive impressions of ingroups and abstract negative impressions of outgroups more readily than negative impressions of ingroups and positive impressions of outgroups (Sherman, Klein, Laskey, & Wyer, 1998). Finally, they show enhanced memory of positive ingroup behaviors and negative outgroup behaviors (Howard & Rothbart, 1980).

Given the presence of the self in the ingroup, these intergroup distinctions may serve ego enhancement motives (for a review, see Abrams & Hogg, 1988). That is, once participants are assigned a group identity, they are motivated to view that identity favorably (e.g., Tajfel & Turner, 1986). Given the minimal nature of the groups, the only means

to positively differentiate the ingroup is to form a more favorable impression of that group.

Stereotypes Explain and Promote Social Structure

The third broad motivational framework suggests that stereotypes serve important sociofunctional needs such as codifying, prescribing, and justifying the social roles of different groups (Allport, 1954; Lippmann, 1922). This approach encompasses a number of influential theories and research programs that will be described below. Although these theories encompass a broad range of motives and stereotyping phenomena, they all suggest that the groups most likely to be stereotyped are those that fulfill distinct and important roles within a society, particularly if those roles imply a threat to the ingroup. They also share the expectation that stereotypes will form along dimensions that explain and justify these social roles.[4]

ROLE THEORY

One of the most prominent sociofunctional theories is role theory (e.g., Eagly, 1987). According to role theory, stereotypes form to explain why particular groups occupy particular social roles. Thus, women may be stereotyped as communal because, historically, they have filled the role of primary caregiver to children (e.g., Eagly & Steffen, 1984). Similarly, stereotypes of black people as lazy or Jewish people as greedy reflect historical roles forced upon members of these groups. Once developed, of course, stereotypes do not merely characterize group members but also prescribe what sorts of roles are fitting and acceptable. In their ingenious study, Hoffman and Hurst (1990) provided information to participants about two novel groups, the Orinthians and the Ackmians. Participants were found to infer dispositional qualities from the groups' societal roles, such that masculine roles led to inferences such as "ambitious" and "assertive," whereas feminine roles led to inferences that targets were "affectionate" and "emotional," even though the personalities of members of the two groups did not differ. A related process of misattribution that can lead to unfounded stereotypes is the tendency to confuse observable with inferred group differences (see Campbell, 1967; Rothbart, 1981). For example, it may be that, for a variety of reasons, children who have recently immigrated to a new country initially have more difficulty in school than their native-born peers (i.e., a measurable group difference in grades between the two populations of children). Such observed differences can sometimes lead to unfounded inferences about the causal explanations of such differences (e.g., that these children score lower because immigrants are of lower intelligence). These inferences are then easily confused with the measurable group difference upon which the inference was ultimately based. In other words, although there may be an identifiable difference on one domain (e.g., unemployment of group members), an inference takes place about the cause of that difference that leads to the illusory perception of a difference on another domain (e.g., laziness of group members). As such, to the extent that the causal inference is erroneous, an unfounded stereotype can develop.

Schaller (1992) experimentally demonstrated just such a misattribution process. In one study, participants observed members of two groups solving easy or difficult anagrams. In total, one group (Group A) solved more anagrams (15/25) than the other group (Group B; 10/25). However, Group A was given more easy (20 vs. 5) and fewer hard (5 vs. 20) anagrams to solve than Group B. In fact, Group B solved a greater percentage of the easy anagrams (5/5 vs. 15/20) and a greater percentage of the hard anagrams (5/20 vs. 0/5) than Group A. Nevertheless, participants judged Group A to be more intelligent based on the overall number of anagrams solved. Thus, participants were not able to take into account the different constraints (or roles) placed on the two groups. One might view this as a group-level fundamental attribution error (Jones & Harris, 1967) that can explain role-based misattributions, as well.

REALISTIC CONFLICTS AND THREATS

Stereotypes also develop to describe the functional and structural relationships among groups. Realistic conflict theory (Jackson, 1993; Sherif, Harvey, White, Hood, & Sherif, 1961; Stephan, Ybarra, & Morrison, 2009) proposed that real competition between groups for desired resources produces a need to favor the ingroup and protect it from harm. This ingroup bias may take the form of negative attitudes and stereotypes about outgroups.

More recent variations of this basic idea have made far more specific predictions regarding the types of groups that are likely to be stereotyped and the specific traits that are likely to be included in those stereotypes. A number of researchers have argued from an evolutionary perspective that reactions to outgroups, including stereotypes, should reflect the specific threats posed by those groups. For example, groups perceived as immediate threats

to physical safety may be stereotyped as dangerous and may be feared, whereas groups perceived as threats to introduce disease may be stereotyped as dirty and induce disgust (e.g., Cottrell & Neuberg, 2005; Schaller, Park, & Faulkner, 2003; see Mackie, Devos, & Smith, 2000 for a similar approach that does not originate in evolutionary ideas, per se). Consistent with this idea, Schaller and his colleagues have shown that people who are particularly concerned about specific types of threat (e.g., physical injury or disease) are particularly likely to endorse stereotypes of groups perceived as imposing those threats. Moreover, situations that increase the accessibility of different kinds of threats increase the activation and application of stereotypes pertaining to those threats. Thus, this perspective predicts that, when an outgroup is first perceived as posing a particular threat, then an appropriate stereotype will form that reflects the nature of that threat.

Other researchers have focused more on the structural relations among groups in a social hierarchy. Fiske and colleagues have argued that status and competition configurations among groups are particularly important in the formation of stereotypes along the dimensions of warmth and competence (e.g., Fiske, Cuddy, Glick, & Xu, 2002). Ingroups and close allies are perceived to have high status but are not perceived to be competitive, resulting in stereotypes of these groups as competent and warm. Outgroups that have high status and are perceived as competitive (e.g., Asians, Jews, feminists) are stereotyped as competent and cold, and induce jealousy. Outgroups that have low status but are perceived as noncompetitive (e.g., elderly people, disabled people) are stereotyped as warm and incompetent, and induce pity. Finally, outgroups that are low in status but are perceived as competitive (e.g., welfare recipients) are stereotyped as incompetent and cold, and induce anger. From this perspective, stereotypes form as a functional reaction to sociostructural relationships among groups and the threats posed as a result of those structural relationships.

SYSTEM JUSTIFICATION

A third important sociofunctional theory emphasizes that stereotypes do not simply describe social roles and structural relationships among groups but also justify them in order to explain the social order and to promote favorable attitudes toward it (e.g., Hoffman & Hurst, 1990; Jost & Banaji, 1994). Much of the research on this topic has highlighted the need to justify status differences among social groups, and stereotypes are one prominent tool for such justification. For example, people may develop a stereotype that a low-status group is lazy, not because of any demonstrable difference between groups for this trait, but rather because the perception of the group as lazy helps to make sense of and justify the group's poverty. Such processes can also lead to the formation of complementary stereotypes (Kay & Jost, 2003). Such stereotypes (e.g., "poor but happy") are theorized to emanate not from actual differences between groups, but rather from the need to resolve the tension created by intergroup inequalities. Thus, one may develop the perception that poor people are lazy (serving to justify and explain their plight) but also happy (serving to alleviate tension and anxiety about the distribution of resources between groups). Tendencies for group perceptions to form in the service of the social system can be particularly conflictual for members of stigmatized groups, who, despite their own self-interests, tend to endorse similar negative ingroup perceptions as those who occupy dominant societal roles (Jost et al., 2004). In this manner, negative (and unfounded) stereotypes not only may form for outgroups but also may even be held by members of stigmatized groups themselves.

Summary

Clearly, motivations play a critical role in stereotype formation. They influence which groups are selected for stereotyping and which traits are selected for stereotypes, and they influence the cognitive processes through which stereotype formation occurs. To date, the vast majority of research on stereotype development and formation has restricted motivations to those related to efficient comprehension and prediction of the social world. In part, this is a result of the diminished importance of self-related and social motives among children and of the necessity of using novel, blank groups to study stereotype formation among adults. However, there are excellent examples of research on stereotype formation that have examined the role of noncognitive motives in stereotype formation, and it is clear that such questions are not impossible to study. Clearly, this should be one important direction for future research, both in the development of stereotypes among children and in stereotype formation among adults. Another important goal for future research should be to integrate research on different motivational components of stereotyping, including tests of the joint and interactive influences of simultaneously relevant motives.

Conclusion

The purpose of this chapter was to review research on both stereotype development among children and stereotype formation among adults. To our knowledge, this is the first time these two literatures have been examined together. We have tried to draw attention to both similarities and differences in the ways that stereotypes form in these two contexts, in the hope that the two literatures may inform one another. Theoretically, one might expect the process of stereotype formation to proceed in similar ways for children and adults. However, although children and adults appear to possess many of the same fundamental cognitive abilities that support categorization and stereotype formation, direct comparisons remain difficult. This difficulty stems from pragmatic obstacles in measuring stereotyping among children and in examining stereotypes among adults that are more consequential than blank stereotypes about novel groups. Moreover, although many fundamental cognitive processes may be present in both children and adults, there also are important differences in how the processes operate, and in the important roles that motives to promote self-esteem and system stability play among adults. We conclude that progress is being made; however, a critical challenge for future research will be to better integrate research on stereotype development among children and stereotype formation among adults, in terms of both the cognitive processes that produce stereotypes and the motives that influence people to stereotype in the first place. Although difficult, a more robust integration would surely offer a rich source of progress in understanding stereotyping.

Notes

1. Whereas stereotypes reflect knowledge of social groups, prejudice reflects evaluations of those groups. In this chapter, we will focus, specifically, on stereotypes.

2. A fourth, overarching motive is to understand the people and events we experience so that we may feel safe and in control of our lives. A great variety of constructs have described how this motive may relate to stereotyping, including the search for meaning (Greenberg & Kosloff, 2008; Heine, Proulx, & Vohs, 2006), certainty (Grieve & Hogg, 1999), closure (Kruglanski & Webster, 1996), structure (Schaller, Boyd, Yohannes, & O'Brien, 1995), and societal order (Adorno et al., 1950; Pratto, Sidanius, Stallworth, & Malle, 1994), to name but a few. Importantly, this motive may be pursued via any of the three primary orientations in stereotyping research: using stereotypes to organize the social world in an efficient way, using stereotypes to boost self-esteem, and using stereotypes to describe, explain, and justify the social structure. Each of these motives may serve the larger goal of offering feelings of safety, control, and coherence.

3. One important social motive that certainly affects stereotype development among children is the motive to belong and its attendant influence on conformity. Thus, sometimes children adopt stereotypes in order to be accepted by family and friends. A detailed discussion of this process is beyond the scope of this chapter.

4. Social learning and conformity are usually cited as additional important components of this approach to stereotyping. Although these processes are undoubtedly critical in the adoption of stereotypes by group members, they presuppose the existence of stereotypes. That is, these processes describe how stereotypes spread, but do not describe why people create stereotypes in the first place.

References

Abelson, R. P., Dasgupta, N., Park, J., & Banaji, M. R. (1998). Perceptions of the collective other. *Personality and Social Psychology Review, 2,* 243–250.

Aboud, F. E. (1988). *Children and prejudice.* New York: Blackwell.

Aboud, F. E. (2003). The formation of in-group favoritism and out-group prejudice in young children: Are they distinct attitudes? *Developmental Psychology, 39,* 48–60.

Aboud, F. E., & Doyle, A. B. (1996). Parental and peer influences on children's racial attitudes. *International Journal of Intercultural Relations, 20,* 371–383.

Abrams, D., & Hogg, M. A. (1988), Comments on the motivational status of self-esteem in social identity and intergroup discrimination. *European Journal of Social Psychology, 18,* 317–334.

Adorno, T. W., Frenkel-Brunswik, E., Levinson, D. J., & Sanford, R. N. (1950). *The authoritarian personality.* New York: Harper and Row.

Allport, G. W. (1954). *The nature of prejudice.* Cambridge, MA: Addison-Wesley.

Ambady, N., Shih, M., Kim, A., & Pittinsky, T. (2001). Stereotype susceptibility in children: Effects of identity activation on quantitative performance. *Psychological Sciences, 12,* 385–390.

Ashmore, R. D., & Del Boca, F. K. (1981). Conceptual approaches to stereotypes and stereotyping. In D. L. Hamilton (Ed.), *Cognitive processes in stereotyping and intergroup behavior* (pp. 1–35). Hillsdale, NJ: Erlbaum.

Bar-Haim, Y., Ziv, T., Lamy, D., & Hodes, R. (2006). Nature and nurture in own-race face processing. *Psychological Science, 17,* 159–163.

Baron, A. S., & Banaji, M. R. (2006). The development of implicit attitudes. *Psychological Science, 17,* 53–58.

Beilock, S. L. (2008). Math performance in stressful situations. *Current Directions in Psychological Science, 17,* 339–343.

Berndt, T. J., & Heller, K. A. (1986). Gender stereotypes and social inferences: A developmental study. *Journal of Personality and Social Psychology, 50,* 889–898.

Biernat, M. (1991). Gender stereotypes and the relationship between masculinity and femininity: A developmental analysis. *Journal of Personality and Social Psychology, 61,* 351–365.

Bigler, R. S., & Liben, L. S. (2006). A developmental intergroup theory of social stereotypes and prejudice. In. R. Kail (Ed.), *Advances in child development and behavior* (pp. 39–89). San Francisco: Elsevier.

Bigler, R. S., & Liben, L. S. (2007). Developmental intergroup theory: Explaining and reducing children's social stereotyping

and prejudice. *Current Directions in Psychological Science, 16,* 162–166.

Billig, M. (1976). *Social psychology and intergroup relations.* New York: Academic Press.

Blanz, M., Mummendey, A., & Otten, S. (1995). Positive-negative asymmetry in social discrimination: The impact of stimulus valence and size and status differentials on intergroup evaluations. *British Journal of Social Psychology, 34,* 409–419.

Boroditsky, L., Schmidt, L. A., & Phillips, W. (2003). Sex, syntax, and semantics. In D. Gentner & S. Goldin-Meadow (Eds.), *Language in mind: Advances in the study of language and thought* (pp. 61–79). Cambridge, MA: MIT Press.

Brewer, M., & Brown, R. (1998). Intergroup relations. In D. Gilbert & S. Fiske (Eds.), *The handbook of social psychology* (4th ed., Vol. 2, pp. 554–594). New York: McGraw-Hill.

Bruner, J. S. (1957). On perceptual readiness. *Psychological Review, 64,* 123–152.

Campbell, D. T. (1958). Common fate, similarity, and other indices of the status of aggregates of persons as social entities. *Behavioural Sciences, 3,* 14–25.

Campbell, D. (1967). Stereotypes and the perception of group differences. *American Psychologist, 22,* 817–829.

Castelli, L., & Carraro, L. (2010). The analysis of implicit attitudes among children. In J. Hakansson (Ed.), *Developmental psychology.* New York: Nova Science.

Castelli, L., Carraro, L., Tomelleri, S., & Amari, A. (2007). White children's alignment to the perceived racial attitudes of the parents: Closer to the mother than the father. *British Journal of Developmental Psychology, 25,* 353–357.

Castelli, L., De Amicis, L., & Sherman, S. J. (2007). The loyal member effect: On the preference for ingroup members who engage in exclusive relations within the ingroup. *Developmental Psychology, 43,* 1347–1359.

Castelli, L., De Dea, C., & Nesdale, D. (2008). Learning social attitudes: Children's sensitivity to the nonverbal behaviors of adult models during interracial interactions. *Personality and Social Psychology Bulletin, 34,* 1504–1513.

Castelli, L., Zogmaister, C., & Tomelleri, S. (2009). The transmission of racial attitudes within the family. *Developmental Psychology, 45,* 586–591.

Chapman, L. (1967). Illusory correlation in observational report. *Journal of Verbal Learning and Verbal Behavior, 6,* 151–155.

Corneille, O., & Judd, C. M. (1999). Accentuation and sensitization effects in the categorization of multi-faceted stimuli. *Journal of Personality and Social Psychology, 77,* 927–941.

Cosmides, L., Tooby, J., & Kurzban, R. (2003). Perceptions of race. *Trends in Cognitive Sciences, 7,* 173–179.

Cottrell, C. A., & Neuberg, L. (2005). Different emotional reactions to different groups: A sociofunctional threat-based approach to "Prejudice." *Journal of Personality and Social Psychology, 88,* 770–789.

Crawford, M. T., Sherman, S. J., & Hamilton, D. L. (2002). Perceived entitativity, stereotype formation, and the interchangeability of group members. *Journal of Personality and Social Psychology, 83,* 1076–1094.

Davey, A. G. (1983). *Learning to be prejudiced: Growing up in multiethnic Britain.* London: Arnold.

De Haan, M., Johnson, M. H., Maurer, D., & Perrett, D. I. (2001). Recognition of individual faces and average face prototypes by 1- and 3-month-old infants. *Cognitive Development, 16,* 659–678.

Degner, J., & Wentura, D. (2010). Automatic prejudice in childhood and early adolescence. *Journal of Personality and Social Psychology, 98,* 356–374.

Dunham, Y., Baron, A. S., & Banaji, M. R. (2006). From American city to Japanese village: A cross-cultural investigation of implicit race attitudes. *Child Development, 77,* 1268–1281.

DiDonato, T. E., Ullrich, J., & Krueger, J. I. (2011). Social perception as induction and inference: An integrative model of intergroup differentiation, ingroup favoritism, and differential accuracy. *Journal of Personality and Social Psychology, 100,* 66.

Eagly, A. H. (1987). *Sex differences in social behavior: A social-role interpretation.* Hillsdale, NJ: Erlbaum.

Eagly, A. H., & Steffen, V. J. (1984). Gender stereotypes stem from the distribution of women and men into social roles. *Journal of Personality and Social Psychology, 46,* 735–754.

Eiser, J. R. (1971). Enhancement of contrast in the absolute judgment of attitude statements. *Journal of Personality and Social Psychology, 17,* 1–10.

Fein, S., & Spencer, S. J. (1997). Prejudice as self-image maintenance: Affirming the self through derogating others. *Journal of Personality and Social Psychology, 73,* 31–44.

Fiedler, K. (1991). The tricky nature of skewed frequency tables: An information loss account of distinctiveness-based illusory correlations. *Journal of Personality and Social Psychology, 60,* 24–36.

Fiske, S. T., Cuddy, A. J., Glick, P., & Xu, J. (2002). A model of (often mixed) stereotype content: Competence and warmth respectively follow from perceived status and competition. *Journal of Personality and Social Psychology, 82,* 878–902.

Ford, T. E., & Stangor, C. (1992). The role of diagnosticity in stereotype formation: Perceiving group means and variance. *Journal of Personality and Social Psychology, 63,* 356–367.

Foroni, F., & Rothbart, M. (2011). Category boundaries and category labels: When does a category name influence the perceived similarity of category members? *Social Cognition, 29,* 547–576.

Fredricks, J. A., & Eccles, J. S. (2002). Children's competence and value beliefs from childhood through adolescence: Growth trajectories in two male-sex-typed domains. *Developmental Psychology, 38,* 519–533.

Gaertner, L., & Insko, C. A. (2000). Intergroup discrimination in the minimal group paradigm: Categorization, reciprocation, or fear? *Journal of Personality and Social Psychology, 79,* 77–94.

Galdi, S., Cadinu, M., & Tomasetto, C. (2011). *In search of the roots of stereotype threat: When math-gender stereotype activation disrupts girls' performance in absence of stereotype awareness.* Unpublished manuscript.

Gelman, S. A. (2003). *The essential child.* Oxford, UK: Oxford University Press.

Gelman, S. A. (2009). Learning from others: Children's construction of concepts. *Annual Review of Psychology, 60,* 115–140.

Gelman, S. A., & Bloom, P. (2000). Young children are sensitive to how an object was created when deciding what to name it. *Cognition, 76,* 91–103.

Gelman, S. A., & Heyman, D. (1999). Carrot-eaters and creature-believers: The effects of lexicalization on children's inferences about social categories *Psychological Science, 10,* 489–493.

Gelman, S. A., & Markman, E. M. (1986). Categories and induction in young children. *Cognition, 23,* 183–209.

Gil-White, F. J. (2001). Are ethnic groups biological "species" to the human brain? *Current Anthropology, 42,* 515–554.

Goodman, N. (1955). *Fact, fiction, and forecast.* New York: Bobbs-Merrill

Gopnik, A., & Sobel, D. M. (2000). Detecting blickets: How young children use information about novel causal powers in categorization and induction. *Child Development, 71,* 1205–1222.

Greenberg, J., & Kosloff, S. (2008). Terror Management Theory: Implications for understanding prejudice, stereotyping, intergroup conflict, and political attitudes. *Social and Personality Psychology Compass, 2,* 1881–1894.

Grieve, P. G., & Hogg, M. A. (1999). Subjective uncertainty and intergroup discrimination in the minimal group situation. *Personality and Social Psychology Bulletin, 25,* 926–940.

Halberstadt, J., Sherman, S. J., & Sherman, J. W. (2011). Why Barack Obama is black: A cognitive account of hypodescent. *Psychological Science, 22,* 29–33.

Halim, M. L., Ruble, D. N., & Amodio, D. M. (2011). From pink frilly dresses to "one of the boys": Developmental changes in girls' gender identity and implications for intergroup gender bias. *Social and Personality Psychology Compass, 5,* 933–949.

Hamilton, D. (1981). Illusory correlation as a basis for stereotyping. In D. Hamilton (Ed.), *Cognitive processes in stereotyping and intergroup behavior* (pp. 115–144). Hillsdale, NJ: Erlbaum.

Hamilton, D., & Gifford, R. (1976). Illusory correlation in interpersonal perception: A cognitive basis of stereotypic judgments. *Journal of Experimental Social Psychology, 12,* 392–407.

Hamilton, D. L., & Sherman, J. W. (1994). Stereotypes. In R. S. Wyer, Jr., & T. K. Srull (Eds.), *Handbook of social cognition* (2nd ed., Vol. 2, pp. 1–68). Hillsdale, NJ: Erlbaum.

Hamilton, D. L., & Sherman, S. J. (1996). Perceiving persons and groups. *Psychological Review, 103,* 336–355.

Hamilton, D. L., & Trolier, T. K. (1986). Stereotypes and stereotyping: An overview of the cognitive approach. In J. F. Dovidio & S. L. Gaertner (Eds.), *Prejudice, discrimination, and racism* (pp. 127–163). Orlando, FL: Academic Press.

Haslam, N., Bastian, B., Bain, P., & Kashima, Y. (2006). Psychological essentialism, implicit person theories, and intergroup relations. *Group Processes and Intergroup Relations, 9,* 63–76.

Heine, S. J., Proulx, T., & Vohs, K. D. (2006). The meaning maintenance model: On the coherence of human motivations. *Personality and Social Psychology Review, 10,* 88–110.

Heyman, G. D., & Gelman, S. A. (2000). Beliefs about the origins of human psychological traits. *Developmental Psychology, 36,* 665–678.

Hirschfeld, L. A. (1995a). Do children have a theory of race? *Cognition, 54,* 209–252.

Hirschfeld, L. A. (1995b). The inheritability of identity: Children's understanding of the cultural biology of race. *Child Development, 66,* 1418–1437.

Hoffman, C., & Hurst, N. (1990). Gender stereotypes: Perception or rationalization? *Journal of Personality and Social Psychology, 58,* 197–208.

Hollander, M. A., Gelman, S. A., & Star, J. (2002). Children's interpretation of generic noun phrases. *Developmental Psychology, 38,* 883–894.

Hornik, R., & Gunnar, M. R. (1988). A descriptive analysis of infant social referencing. *Child Development, 59*, 626–634.

Howard, J., & Rothbart, M. (1980). Social categorization and memory for in-group and out-group behavior. *Journal of Personality and Social Psychology, 38*, 301–310.

Hyde, J. S., Lindberg, S. M., Linn, M. C., Ellis, A. B., & Williams, C. C. (2008). Gender similarities characterize math performance. *Science, 321*, 494–495.

Hyde, J. S., & Mertz, J. E. (2009). Gender, culture, and mathematics performance. *Proceedings of the National Academy of Sciences, 106*, 8801–8807.

Jacklin, C. N., & Maccoby, E. E. (1978). Social behavior at 33 months in same-sex and mixed-sex dyads. *Child Development, 49*, 557–569.

Jackson, J. W. (1993). Realistic group conflict theory: A review and evaluation of the theoretical and empirical literature. *Psychological Record, 43*, 395–413.

Jacobs, J. E., Lanza, S., Osgood, W., Eccles, J. S., & Wigfield, A. (2002). Changes in children's self-competence and values: Gender and domain differences across grades one through twelve. *Child Development, 73*, 509–527.

Jaswal, V. K., Lima, O. K., & Small, J. E. (2009). Compliance, conversion, and category induction. *Journal of Experimental Child Psychology, 102*, 182–195.

Jones, E. E., & Harris, V. A. (1967). The attribution of attitudes. *Journal of Experimental Social Psychology, 3*, 1–24.

Jost, J. T., & Banaji, M. R. (1994). The role of stereotyping in system-justification and the production of false consciousness. *British Journal of Social Psychology, 33*, 1–27.

Jost, J. T., Banaji, M. R., & Nosek, B. A. (2004). A decade of system justification theory: Accumulated evidence of conscious and unconscious bolstering of the status quo. *Political Psychology, 25*, 881–919.

Judd, C. M., & Park, B. (1993). Definition and assessment of accuracy in social stereotypes. *Psychological Review, 100*, 109–128.

Judd, C. M., & Park, B. (2005). Group differences and stereotype accuracy. In J. Dovidio, P. Glick, & L. Rudman (Eds.), *On the nature of prejudice: Fifty years after Allport* (pp. 123–138). Malden, MA: Blackwell.

Jussim, L., Cain, T. R., Crawford, J. T., Harber, K., Cohen, F., & Nelson, J. (2009). The unbearable accuracy of stereotypes. In T. Nelson (Ed.), *Handbook of prejudice, stereotyping, and discrimination* (pp. 199–225). Hillsdale, NJ: Erlbaum.

Katz, D. (1960). The functional approach to the study of attitudes. *Public Opinion Quarterly, 24*, 163–204.

Kay, A. C., & Jost, J. T. (2003). Complementary justice: Effects of "poor but happy" and "poor but honest" stereotype exemplars on system justification and implicit activation of the justice motive. *Journal of Personality and Social Psychology, 85*, 823–837.

Keil, F. C., Smith, W. C., Simons, D. J., & Levin, D. T. (1998). Two dogmas of conceptual empiricism: Implications for hybrid models of the structure of knowledge. *Cognition, 65*, 103–135.

Kelly, D., Quinn, P., Slater, A., Lee K., Gibson, A., & Smith, M., et al. (2005). Three-month-olds, but not newborns, prefer own-race faces. *Developmental Science, 8*, F31–F36.

Kenny, D. A., West, T. V., Cillessen, A. H., Coie, J. D., Dodge, K. A., Hubbard, J. A., & Schwartz, D. (2007). Accuracy in judgments of aggressiveness. *Personality and Social Psychology Bulletin, 33*, 1225–1236.

Kinzler, K. D., Dupoux, E., & Spelke, E. S. (2007). The native language of social cognition. *Proceedings of the National Academy of Sciences USA, 104*, 12577–12580.

Kinzler, K. D., Shutts, K., & Correll, J. (2010). Priorities in social categories. *European Journal of Social Psychology, 40*, 581–592.

Kircher, M., & Furby, L. (1971). Racial preferences in young children. *Child Development, 42*, 2076–2078.

Krueger, J., & Clement, R.W. (1994). Memory-based judgments about multiple categories: A revision and extension of Tajfel's accentuation *theory. Journal of Personality and Social Psychology, 67*, 35–47.

Krueger, J., & Rothbart, M. (1990). Contrast and accentuation effects in category learning. *Journal of Personality and Social Psychology, 59*, 651–663.

Krueger, J., Rothbart, M., & Sriram, N. (1989). Category learning and change: Differences in sensitivity to information that enhances or reduces intercategory distinctions. *Journal of Personality and Social Psychology, 56*, 866–875.

Kruglanski, A. W., & Webster, D. M. (1996). Motivated closing of the mind: "Seizing" and "freezing." *Psychological Review, 103*, 263–283.

Kruschke, J. K. (1992). ALCOVE: An exemplar-based connectionist model of category learning. *Psychological Review, 99*, 22–44.

Kruschke, J. K. (1996). Base rates in category learning. *Journal of Experimental Psychology: Learning, Memory and Cognition, 22*, 3–26.

Kruschke, J. K. (2001). The inverse base rate effect is not explained by eliminative inference. *Journal of Experimental Psychology: Learning, Memory and Cognition, 27*, 1385–1400.

Kruschke, J. K. (2003). Attention in learning. *Current Directions in Psychological Science, 12*, 171–175.

LaPiere, R. T. (1936). Type-rationalizations of group antipathy. *Social Forces, 15*, 232–254.

Lappänen, J. M., & Nelson, C. A. (2006). The development and neural bases of facial emotional recognition. In R. V. Kail (Ed.), *Advances in child development and behaviour* (Vol. 34, pp. 207–246). San Diego, CA: Academic Press.

Lee, Y., Jussim, L. J., & McCauley, C. R. (Eds.). (1995). *Stereotype accuracy: Toward appreciating group differences.* Washington, DC: American Psychological Association.

LePelley, M., Reimers, S., Beesley, T., Spears, R., & Murphy, R. A. (2010). Stereotype formation: Biased by association. *Journal of Experimental Psychology: General, 139*, 138–161.

LeVine, R., & Campbell, D. (1972). *Ethnocentrism: Theories of conflict, ethnic attitudes, and group behavior.* New York: John Wiley & Sons.

Levy, S. R., Stroessner, S., & Dweck, C. S. (1998). Stereotype formation and endorsement: The role of implicit theories. *Journal of Personality and Social Psychology, 74*, 1421–1436.

Lickel, B., Hamilton, D., Wieczorkowska, G., Lewis, A. C., Sherman, S. J., & Uhles, A. N. (2000). Varieties of groups and the perception of group entitativity. *Journal of Personality and Social Psychology, 78*, 223–246.

Lippmann, W. (1922). *Public opinion.* New York: Harcourt, Brace, Jovanovitch.

Mackie, D. M., Devos, T., & Smith, E. R. (2000). Intergroup emotions: Explaining offensive action tendencies in an intergroup context. *Journal of Personality and Social Psychology, 79*, 602–616.

McCauley, C., Stitt, C. L., & Segal, M. (1980). Stereotyping: From prejudice to prediction. *Psychological Bulletin, 87*, 195.

McConnell, A., Sherman, S. J., & Hamilton, D. (1994). Illusory correlation in the perception of groups: An extension of the distinctiveness-based account. *Journal of Personality and Social Psychology*, *67*, 414–429.

McGarty, C., Haslam, S. A., Turner, J. C., & Oakes, P. J. (1993). Illusory correlation as accentuation of actual intercategory difference: Evidence for the effect with minimal stimulus information. *European Journal of Social Psychology*, *23*, 391–410.

McGarty, C., & Penny, R. E. C. (1988). Categorization, accentuation and social judgement. *British Journal of Social Psychology*, *22*, 147–157.

McGarty, C., & Turner, J. C. (1992). The effects of categorization on social judgment. *British Journal of Social Psychology*, *31*, 253–268.

McGlothlin, H., & Killen, M. (2010). How social experience is related to children's intergroup attitudes. *European Journal of Social Psychology*, *40*, 625–634.

Mehler, J., Jusczyk, P., Lambertz, G., Halsted, N., Bertoncini, J., & Amiel-Tison, C. (1988). A precursor of language acquisition in young infants. *Cognition*, *29*, 143–178.

Miller, S., Maner, J. K., & Becker, D. V. (2010). Self-protective biases in group categorization: Threat cues shape the psychological boundary between "us" and "them." *Journal of Personality and Social Psychology*, *99*, 62–77.

Muzzatti, B., & Agnoli, F. (2007). Gender and mathematics: Attitudes and stereotype threat susceptibility in Italian children. *Developmental Psychology*, *43*, 747–759.

Neuville, E., & Croizet, J. C. (2007). Can salience of gender identity impair math performance among 7–8 year old girls? The moderating role of task difficulty. *European Journal of Psychology of Education*, *23*, 307–316.

Nosofsky, R. M. (1986). Attention, similarity, and the identification–categorization relationship. *Journal of Experimental Psychology: General*, *115*, 39–57.

Oakes, P. J., & Reynolds, K. J. (1997). Asking the accuracy question: Is measurement the answer? In R. Spears, P. J. Oakes, M. Ellemers, & S. A. Haslam (Eds.), *The social psychology of stereotyping and group life* (pp. 51–71). Cambridge, MA: Blackwell.

Opper, J. E., & Bulloch, M. J. (2007). Causal relations drive young children's induction, naming, and categorization. *Cognition*, *105*, 206–217.

Paladino, M., & Castelli, L. (2008). On the immediate consequences of intergroup categorization: Activation of approach and avoidance motor behavior toward ingroup and outgroup members. *Personality and Social Psychology Bulletin*, *34*, 755–768.

Park, B., & Hastie, R. (1987). Perception of variability in category development: Instance- versus abstraction-based stereotypes. *Journal of Personality and Social Psychology*, *53*, 621–635.

Percy, E. J., Sherman, S. J., Garcia-Marques, L., Mata, A., & Garcia-Marques, T. (2009). Cognition and native-language grammar: The organizational role of adjective-noun word order in information representation. *Psychonomic Bulletin & Review*, *16*, 1037–1042.

Piaget, J. (1929). *The child's conception of the world*. London: Routledge and Kegan Paul.

Piaget, J. (1970). Piaget's theory. In P. H. Mussen (Ed.), *Carmichael's manual of child psychology* (Vol. 1). New York: Wiley.

Platten, L., Hernik, M., Fonagy, P., & Fearon, R. P. (2010). *European Journal of Social Psychology*, *40*, 569–580.

Pratto, F., Sidanius, J., Stallworth, L. M., & Malle, B. F. (1994). Social dominance orientation: A personality variable predicting social and political attitudes. *Journal of Personality and Social Psychology*, *67*, 741–763.

Preissler, M. A., & Carey, S. (2004). Do both pictures and words function as symbols for 18- and 24-month-old children? *Journal of Cognitive Development*, *5*, 185–212.

Queller, S., Schell, T., & Mason, W. (2006). A novel view of between-categories contrast and within-category assimilation. *Journal of Personality and Social Psychology*, *91*, 406–422.

Quinn, P., Yahr, J., Kuhn, A., Slater, A., & Pascalis, O. (2002). Representation of the gender of human faces by infants: A preference for female. *Perception*, *31*, 1109–1121.

Rhodes, M., & Gelman, S. A. (2008). Categories influence predictions about individual consistency. *Child Development*, *79*, 1270–1287.

Rhodes, M., & Gelman, S. A. (2009). A developmental examination of the conceptual structure of animal, artifact, and human social categories across two cultural contexts. *Cognitive Psychology*, *59*, 244–274.

Risen, J. L., Gilovich, T., & Dunning, D. (2007). One-shot illusory correlations and stereotype formation. *Personality and Social Psychology Bulletin*, *33*, 1492.

Robinson, C. W., & Sloutsky, V. M. (2007). Linguistic labels and categorization in infancy: Do labels facilitate or hinder? *Infancy*, *11*, 233–253.

Rothbart, M. (1981). Memory and social beliefs. In D. Hamilton (Ed.), *Cognitive processes in stereotyping and intergroup relations* (pp. 145–181). Hillsdale, NJ: Erlbaum.

Rothbart, M., Fulero, S., Jensen, C., Howard, J., & Birrell, P. (1978). From individual to group impressions: Availability heuristics in stereotype formation. *Journal of Experimental Social Psychology*, *14*, 237–255.

Rothbart, M., & Taylor, M. (1992). Category labels and social reality: Do we view social categories as natural kinds? In G. R. Semin, & K. Fiedler (Eds.), *Language, interaction, and social cognition* (pp. 11–36). London: SAGE publications.

Rubini, M., Moscatelli, S., & Palmonari, A. (2007). Increasing group entitativity: Linguistic intergroup discrimination in the minimal group paradigm. *Group Processes and Intergroup Relations*, *10*, 280–296.

Ruble, D. N., Martin, C. L., & Berenbaum, S. A. (2006). Gender development. In N. Eisenberg, W. Damon, & R. M. Lerner (Eds.), *Handbook of child psychology: Vol. 3, Social, emotional, and personality development* (6th ed., pp. 858–932). Hoboken, NJ: John Wiley & Sons.

Schaller, M. (1992). Sample size, aggregation, and statistical reasoning in social inference. *Journal of Experimental Social Psychology*, *28*, 65–85.

Schaller, M., Boyd, C., Yohannes, J., & O'Brien, M. (1995). The prejudiced personality revisited: Personal need for structure and formation of erroneous group stereotypes. *Journal of Personality and Social Psychology*, *68*, 544–555.

Schaller, M., & Maass, A. (1989). Illusory correlation and social categorization: Toward an integration of motivational and cognitive factors in stereotype formation. *Journal of Personality and Social Psychology*, *56*, 709–721.

Schaller, M., Park, J. H., & Faulkner, J. (2003). Prehistoric dangers and contemporary prejudices. *European Review of Social Psychology*, *14*, 105–137.

Sherif, M., Harvey, O., White, B., Hood, W., & Sherif, C. (1961). *Intergroup conflict and cooperation: The Robbers Cave experiment*. Norman, OK: University of Oklahoma.

Sherman, J. W. (1996). Development and mental representation of stereotypes. *Journal of Personality and Social Psychology, 70*, 1126–1141.

Sherman, J. W. (2001). The dynamic relationship between stereotype efficiency and mental representation. In G. Moskowitz (Ed.), *Cognitive social psychology: The Princeton symposium on the legacy and future of social cognition* (pp. 177–190). Hillsdale, NJ: Erlbaum.

Sherman, J. W., & Bessenoff, G. R. (1999). Stereotypes as source monitoring cues: On the interaction between episodic and semantic memory. *Psychological Science, 10*, 106–110.

Sherman, J. W., Klein, S. B., Laskey, A., & Wyer, N. A. (1998). Intergroup bias in group judgment processes: The role of behavioral memories. *Journal of Experimental Social Psychology, 34*, 51–65.

Sherman, J. W., Kruschke, J. K., Sherman, S. J., Percy, E. J., Petrocelli, J. V., & Conrey, F. R. (2009). Attentional processes in stereotype formation: A common model for category accentuation and illusory correlation. *Journal of Personality and Social Psychology, 96*, 305–323.

Shipley, E. F. (2000). Children's categorization of objects: The relevance of behavior, surface appearance, and insides. In B. Landau (Ed.), *Perception, cognition, and language: Essays in honor of Henry and Lila Gleitman* (pp. 69–85). Cambridge, MA: MIT Press.

Shutts, K., Banaji, M. R., & Spelke, E. S. (2007). Social categories guide young children's preferences for novel objects. Paper presented at the biennial meeting of the Cognitive Development Society, Santa Fe, NM.

Shutts, K., Kinzler, K. D., McKee, C., & Spelke, E. S. (2009). Social information guides infants' selection of foods. *Journal of Cognition and Development, 10*, 1–17.

Sloutsky, V. M., Lo, Y. F., & Fisher, A. (2001). How much does a shared name make things similar? Linguistic labels, similarity and the development of inductive inference. *Child Development, 72*, 1695–1709.

Smith, E. (1991). Illusory correlation in a simulated exemplar-based memory. *Journal of Experimental Social Psychology, 27*, 107–123.

Sorce, J. F., Emde, R. N., Campos, J., & Klinnert, M. D. (1985). Maternal emotional signaling: Its effect on the visual cliff behavior of 1-year-olds. *Developmental Psychology, 21*, 195–200.

Steele, C. M., & Aronson, J. (1995). Stereotype threat and the intellectual test performance of African Americans. *Journal of Experimental Social Psychology, 69*, 797–811.

Stephan, W. G., Ybarra, O., & Morrison, K. R. (2009). Intergroup Threat Theory. In T.D. Nelson (Ed.), *Handbook of prejudice, stereotyping, and discrimination* (pp. 43–59). New York: Psychology Press.

Stroessner, S., & Plaks, J. (2001). Illusory correlation and stereotype formation: Tracing the arc of research over a quarter century. In G. Moskowitz (Ed.), *The Princeton symposium on the legacy and future of social cognition* (pp. 247–259). Mahwah, NJ: Erlbaum.

Svirydzenka, N., Sani, F., & Bennett, M. (2010). Group entitativity and its perceptual antecedents in varieties of groups: A developmental perspective. *European Journal of Social Psychology, 40*, 611–624.

Swim, J. K. (1994). Perceived versus meta-analytic effect sizes: An assessment of the Accuracy of Gender Stereotypes. *Journal of Personality and Social Psychology, 66*, 21–36.

Tajfel, H. (1969). Cognitive aspects of prejudice. *Journal of Social Issues, 25*, 79–97.

Tajfel, H., Billig, M. G., Bundy, R. P., & Flament, C. (1971). Social categorization and intergroup behaviour. *European Journal of Social Psychology, 1*, 149–178.

Tajfel, H., & Turner, J. C. (1986). The social identity theory of intergroup behavior. In S. Worchel & W. Austin (Eds.), *The psychology of intergroup relations* (2nd ed., pp. 7–24). Chicago: Nelson-Hall.

Tajfel, H., & Wilkes, A. L. (1963). Classification and quantitative judgment. *British Journal of Psychology, 54*, 101–114.

Taylor, M. G. (1996). The development of children's beliefs about social and biological aspects of gender differences. *Child Development, 67*, 1555–1571.

Taylor, M. G., Rhodes, J., & Gelman, S. A. (2009). Boys will be boys; cows will be cows: Children's essentialist reasoning about gender categories and animals species. *Child Development, 80*, 461–481.

Terracciano, A., Abdel-Khalek, A. M., Adam, N., Adamovova, L., Ahn, C., Ahn, H., ... McCrea, R. R. (2005). National character does not reflect mean personality trait levels in 49 cultures. *Science, 310*, 96–100.

Tomasetto, C., Alparone, F. R., & Cadinu, M. (2011). Girls' math performance under stereotype threat: The moderating role of mothers' gender stereotypes. *Developmental Psychology, 47*, 943–949.

Walton, G. M., & Banaji, M. R. (2004). Being what you say: The effect of essentialist linguistic labels on preferences. *Social Cognition, 22*, 193–213.

Waxman, S. R. (2010). Names will never hurt me? Naming and the development of racial and gender categories in preschool-aged children. *European Journal of Social Psychology, 40*, 593–610.

Waxman, S. R., & Gelman, S. A. (2009). Early word-learning entails reference, not merely associations. *Trends in Cognitive Sciences, 13*, 258–263.

Whorf, B. L. (1956). *Language, thought, and reality: Selected writings of Benjamin Lee Whorf* (J. B. Carroll, Ed). Cambridge, MA: MIT Press.

Wyer, N. A., Sadler, M. S., & Judd, C. M. (2002). Contrast effects in stereotype formation and change: The role of comparative context. *Journal of Experimental Social Psychology, 38*, 443–458.

Young-Browne, G., Rosenfeld, H. M., & Horowitz, F. D. (1977). Infant discrimination of facial expressions. *Child Development, 48*, 555–562.

Yzerbyt, V. Y., & Buidin, G. (1998). *The impact of naive theories about the nature of the groups on the accentuation effect*. Unpublished raw data, Catholic University of Louvain at Louvain-la-Neuve, Belgium.

Yzerbyt, V., Judd, C. M., & Corneille, O. (2004). *The psychology of group perception*. New York: Psychology Press.

CHAPTER 28

Social Power and Cognition

Ana Guinote

Abstract

This chapter examines the links between social power and the mind. It reviews empirical evidence about how having or lacking power affects cognitive processes that underlie judgment and behavior. It focuses on the major components of the cognitive toolbox, such as attention allocation, attentional control, flexibility, memory, and construct accessibility. It also considers neuroscientific evidence and discusses dynamical conceptions of cognition and self-regulation as they unfold across different contexts and states of the perceiver. The evidence indicates that power enhances cognitive abilities and goal focus, but also the propensity to fast and frugal processing. Compared with individuals who lack power, power holders are more susceptible to effectively influence others, pursue goals, and satisfy their needs, while also being more influenced by constructs that are temporarily activated on a moment-to-moment basis. Thus, having power enhances situated responses and behavior variability.

Key Words: power, attention, social cognition, self-regulation

Power asymmetries are common among social animals, and humans are no exception (Boehm & Flack, 2010). Whether in informal small groups, families, organizations, or nations, some enjoy more control and influence than others. These differences in power have an important impact on the ways individuals feel, think, and act. Not surprisingly, social scientists have considered power to be a fundamental concept in social sciences. Some have argued that power is central to social science in the same way that energy is central to physics (Russell, 1938).

In social psychology, there is a long-standing interest in power (e.g., Kipnis, 1972; Lewin, 1941), with a remarkable proliferation of knowledge in the past two decades. Recently, social cognition has emerged as an indispensable level of analysis for the understanding of how and why being in a powerful or powerless position affects individuals. This chapter reviews literature about how having or lacking power affects cognitive processes and their influence on judgment and behavior. It examines how power affects the major components of the cognitive toolbox, such as attention and memory. The chapter addresses questions such as: How does power affect attention allocation and the ability to control attention? How does it affect memory and the ways that knowledge is activated and used? How are powerholders' cognitive processes and neurobiology implicated in their judgments and behavior? Last, but not least, what does power research tell us about the ways the mind works?

The chapter starts with definitions of power and conceptual considerations. It then examines how power affects attention, memory, and the activation and use of constructs. Finally, the chapter proceeds to discuss how cognition is implemented and how it affects powerholders' judgments and behavior. Together, the evidence reviewed suggests that power increases selective and flexible information processing, equipping powerholders with the capacity to pursue goals efficiently, form judgments easily, and make decisions promptly. Powerholders possess malleable information processing strategies. They make use of automatic and controlled processes, as well as subjective experiences and conceptual knowledge, in a dynamic way, depending on the task at hand and their motivation. Powerholders are ultimately guided by the primary constructs activated on a moment-to-moment basis, showing greater reliance on constructs that easily come to mind, along with greater variability in judgment and behavior.

What Is Power and Why Does Power Affect Cognition?

Power originates from the Latin word *potere*, meaning *to be able,* and has been associated with the ability to produce desired outcomes (e.g., Locke, 1690). Power has been conceptualized in terms of the potential to influence others in psychologically meaningful ways (French & Raven, 1959) through the giving or withholding of rewards or punishments (Fiske, 2003; Keltner, Gruenfeld, & Anderson, 2003; Vescio, Snyder, & Butz, 2003). According to this conception, power refers to the *potential* to influence others and may be present even when no direct behavioral effects are observed. Furthermore, *influence* refers to effects on the ways people feel, think, or behave. Finally, power may be exerted through "soft" influence tactics (e.g., charisma, knowledge) or "hard" tactics (e.g., physical punishment; Raven, Schwarzwald, & Koslowsky, 1998), and may occur between individuals or between groups (see Keltner et al., 2003).

Power can be exercised with varied aims. Most commonly, it is used to obtain valued outcomes and basic resources for the self (Weber, 1954) and to coordinate and advance collective interests (Parsons, 1963; Van Vugt, Hogan, & Kaiser, 2008). Those who dominate can more easily secure resources and desired outcomes, often through force or ideological manipulation (Glick & Fiske, 1996; Pfeffer & Salancik, 1978). This is facilitated by the fact that powerless individuals are dependent on powerholders and often offer little resistance. The self-serving nature of power is supported by studies indicating that power often promotes corruption (Kipnis, 1972) and a focus on self-interest (Keltner, Gruenfeld, Galinsky, & Kraus, 2010; Winter, 2010), while decreasing attention toward others (Fiske, 1993) and increasing prejudice (Guinote, Willis, & Martellotta, 2010).

At the same time, power has group-serving functions (Parsons, 1963). These functions can be seen, for example, in times of crisis, when within-group hierarchies sharpen and leaders emerge (Sherif & Sherif, 1953). From an evolutionary point of view, power evolved to deal with problems of social coordination that emerged in ancestral environments (see Caporeal, 2004). Powerholders were necessary because they helped solve problems of group movement, intragroup peacekeeping and intergroup competition (Van Vugt et al., 2008). From this perspective, power roles involve social responsibility.

Nevertheless, the fact that powerlessness decreases cognitive abilities and well-being (Guinote, 2007b; Marmot et al., 1991) supports the notion that power relations have primarily self-related consequences. Also in support of this notion is the fact that from 38 milliseconds of observing a face, humans automatically detect the relative dominance of others (Willis & Todorov, 2006). They also automatically adopt complementary power postures (Tiedens & Fragale, 2003). Complementary reactions to another's dominance are common in social animals and have been interpreted as a signal that maximizes the chances of individual survival (Boehm & Flack, 2010).Rather than asking whether power has selfish or prosocial aims, one should ask *when* power has selfish or prosocial aims.

Power seems to affect individuals primarily because it increases their sense of control (e.g., Van Dijke & Poppe, 2006), opening up opportunities and the freedom to attain desired outcomes (Fiske, 1993). These changes automatically affect cognitive processes in ways that serve adaptive needs (see Fiske, 1992; Fiske & Dépret, 1996).

According to the approach theory of power (Keltner et al., 2003), power activates approach-oriented behavior, positive affect, attention to rewards, automatic cognition, and disinhibited behavior. From a cognitive perspective, it is proposed that power directs attention toward rewarding stimuli, such as food, sex, money, or rewarding social cues. Furthermore, power triggers effortless cognition, associated with simple rules for making judgments, such as heuristics (see also Fiske, 1993).

It has been also suggested that power affects individuals through the activation of goals and thoughts that individuals associate with power (Bargh & Raymond, 1995; Chen, Lee-Chai, & Bargh, 2001). Individuals in power tend to engage in extreme behavior that they associate with power. This occurs because when one has power, goals associated with power easily come to mind, directing attention and effort toward their attainment. For example, individuals who see power as an opportunity to obtain resources for the self act more selfishly when given power. Conversely, individuals who see power in terms of social responsibilities act more prosocially when given power (Chen et al., 2001).

The situated focus theory of power (Guinote, 2007a, 2010) proposes that power affects motivation and information processing in ways that lead to more situated responses in powerholders compared with powerless individuals. Like Bargh and colleagues, it proposes that power affects behavior through the constructs that easily come to mind (i.e., are accessible). It proposes, however, that powerholders rely more on *any* accessible constructs, not only on goals associated with power. Powerholders process information more selectively in line with the primary constructs activated on a moment-to-moment basis, which can be linked to goals, needs, subjective experiences, or information present in the environment. Furthermore, powerholders are flexible in their deployment of effort and deliberation and use a wider range of processes to guide judgment and behavior. For example, depending on the task at hand and their level of motivation, they can rely on feelings, subjective experiences, and simple rules (heuristics) to construct their judgments, or they can rely on effortful deliberative reasoning. Consequently, the judgments and actions of powerholders are more situated and varied across different contexts than the judgments and actions of powerless individuals.

The effects of power described in this chapter pertain mainly to experimental work that reproduces power experiences in the laboratory. When assigned to typical powerful or powerless roles, individuals usually treat power as fair and legitimate (see Jost & Banaji, 1994; Kay, Banfield, & Laurin, 2010). Illegitimate power elicits specific effects that will not be contemplated in this chapter (see Lammers, Galinsky, Gordijn, & Otten, 2008; Willis, Guinote, & Rodríguez-Bailón, 2010).

The Powerful Mind

This section reviews literature regarding the ways that power affects the mind. Power affects the central components of the cognitive toolbox, including attention, memory, and judgment. These effects are discussed in sequence below.

Cognition and the Selection Problem

The first attempt to understand how power affects social cognition focused on attention (e.g., Fiske, 1993; Fiske & Dépret, 1996). To understand the world around us, form judgments, and select actions, we need to process information selectively (Driver, 2001; Posner & Snyder, 1975). Only a small part of the information available in the environment or in memory is processed more extensively and affects our experiences (see Chapter 15). Attention is guided by cues in the environment, such as opportunities for action or affordances, and the individuals' top-down orientation (e.g., goals, expectations, frequently used constructs; see Driver, 2001; Posner & Snyder, 1975).

The top-down influences entail signals activated in the prefrontal cortex that bias information processing (see Miller & Cohen, 2001). For example, goals, needs, or affective states activate relevant sensory inputs (through attention allocation), memories, and motor responses that are consistent with these goals, needs, or states. This biasing process encompasses not only excitation of sensory inputs and memories but also the management of competition that may arise between multiple influences (e.g., when dominant responses are not desired or when distracting information is present in the external environment; see Friedman & Miyake, 2004). Finally, cognitive control also entails recruitment of the deliberation and effort needed for completion of the task at hand (Norman & Shallice, 1986).

A central contribution of social cognition to the understanding of powerholders' behavior has been to demonstrate that power affects this very basic mechanism of processing selectivity and cognitive control. It affects both the *content* of information that is processed and the *process* or ways that information is processed. Powerholders can easily attain their goals (Fiske 1993), have their needs satisfied (Henry & Pratto, 2010), and often live in reward-rich environments (Keltner et al., 2003). Therefore, their motivations and contents of working memory (the information that is more active in their minds) differ from those of powerless individuals. Research suggests that the information held in working memory by powerholders is primarily related to rewards and opportunities (Keltner et al., 2003), or is information that is relevant to the maintenance of their privileged positions (see Maner, Gailliot, Butz, & Peruche, 2007), along with chronically accessible constructs (Guinote, Weick, & Cai, 2012). In contrast, powerless individuals' working memory primarily holds information pertaining to their lack of control. For example, their attention is oriented toward those who control them (Fiske & Dépret, 1996). They are generally more vigilant and deliberate more in order to predict the future and increase control.

At the same time, power affects the ways that individuals process information. Powerholders experience less interference from undesired information and are better able to focus attention in line with primary goals or needs (i.e., they control better attention than powerless individuals; DeWall, Baumeister, Mead, & Vohs, 2011; Guinote, 2007b, 2010; see also Smith, Jostman, Galinsky, & Van Dijk, 2008). Furthermore, compared with powerless individuals, powerful individuals rely more narrowly on constructs that easily come to mind (i.e., are accessible) and make more flexible use of cognitive processes that guide judgment and behavior, such as feelings, heuristics, and systematic information processing (Guinote, 2008; Guinote et al., 2012). As we will see later, reliance on accessible constructs implies that powerholders are not always guided by personal and chronically accessible constructs (e.g., dispositions) but also by temporarily activated constructs.

The effects of power on information processing will now be reviewed in the domains of attention allocation, attentional control, attention to information organized hierarchically, and memory. Finally, the neurobiology of power will also be examined.

Motivated Attention Allocation

William James wrote, "Each one of us literally chooses, by his way of attending to things, what sort of universe he shall appear to himself to inhabit" (James, 1890/1983, p. 416). Individuals choose which information to attend to in line with their motivations. For example, when reading a newspaper, a reader may choose to read news about some topics, but not about others. The news that the reader chooses to read presumably reflects the interests or motivations of the reader.

According to the situated focus theory of power (Guinote 2007a, 2010), power promotes a narrow focus of attention consistent with the primary constructs that emerge on a moment-to-moment basis, as individuals relate to their environments. That is, constructs that are accessible because they are relevant to goals, needs, or affordances of the environment, or that have been recently or frequently used. Some constructs may have regular priority, being primary most of the time, in most situations (e.g., constructs linked to schemas, habits, personal dispositions, enduring goals, and other chronically accessible constructs). These influences are responsible for some stability in the behavior of powerholders. In addition, a primary role may be played by temporarily activated constructs, such as those

associated with feelings and states (Guinote, 2007a; Guinote, 2010; Keltner et al., 2003; Weick & Guinote, 2008), primes (Guinote et al., 2013), situationally activated actions (Galinsky et al., 2003), and opportunities for action (i.e., affordances; Guinote, 2008).

Research has shown that powerholders, compared with powerless individuals, deploy attention more selectively, regardless of the content of the information that is processed. Powerholders consistently deem some types of information to be more important, whereas powerless individuals weight different types of information more equally. These powerless individuals attempt to predict the future and regain control through increased attention (Fiske & Dépret, 1996) and deliberation (see Guinote, Brown, & Fiske, 2006).

Fiske and her colleagues (Fiske, 1993; Fiske & Dépret, 1996) examined the links between power and attention to stereotypic information. In a typical study, participants were given power by evaluating and making decisions that affected others. Participants then read information about a target person. Powerholders, compared with control participants, attended preferentially to stereotype-consistent (vs. inconsistent) information. That is, when stereotypical cues were present, and stereotypes accessible, powerholders paid more attention to this stereotype-congruent information than did powerless individuals, who deemed stereotype-incongruent information to be important as well. Similar results were obtained with actual managers in the hotel industry (Guinote & Phillips, 2010).

In a similar vein, power increased reliance on automatic negative associations about low-status social groups, as assessed through a series of implicit prejudice measures (Guinote et al., 2010). These studies indicate that powerholders have a preference for stereotypic information and show implicit prejudice. Both stereotypes and prejudice are familiar and accessible constructs for powerful individuals.

However, different findings were obtained when non-stereotypic information or alternative group associations were activated. In that case, powerholders attended more selectively to these alternatives (e.g., Overbeck & Park, 2006; Vescio et al., 2003). For instance, Vescio et al. (2003) found that individuals in powerful positions were not guided by stereotypes of low-status subordinates when stereotypes were not informative with regard to the powerful individuals' social influence strategies.

Subjective experiences that arise while processing information can affect the construction of judgments (Schwarz et al., 1991). Powerful individuals are more guided by these experiences than are powerless individuals (Guinote, 2010; Weick & Guinote, 2008). For example, after being asked to think of a small number of differences between men and women, participants who had been primed with power perceived men and women in more stereotypic ways than did their powerless counterparts (Weick & Guinote, 2008). A reverse tendency occurred when participants thought of many differences between men and women. Because generating many differences was difficult, power-primed participants inferred that, after all, men and women are not very different. This tendency was not observed among powerless individuals.

Powerholders' tendency to allocate attention more selectively in line with primary constructs can be seen outside the social realm, for example, during goal striving. In one study (Guinote, 2008), participants performed either a work or a social goal and read information at their own pace that was relevant to work or social life. In the work context, compared with powerless participants, powerful participants allocated more attentional resources to information related to work, reading about it longer. Conversely, when pursuing a social goal, powerful participants allocated more attentional resources to social than to work information.

In sum, when powerful and powerless individuals allocate attention at will, powerholders preferentially allocate attention to information that is related to accessible constructs (e.g., stereotypes, goals, affordances) and disregard other information. Conversely, powerless individuals attend more evenly to different sources of information. For these individuals, all information is seemingly of some relevance.

Attentional Control, Orienting, and Flexibility

Imagine that our reader of the newspaper mentioned above approaches an article with the aim of counting, as quickly as possible, the number of words in the article. Reading the actual content of the words would interfere with the task of counting. To perform a task such as this one, individuals need not only to facilitate or amplify the signal of important stimuli (here, each word as a countable unit) through attention allocation but also to *inhibit* dominant responses (such as reading the meaning of the words), memories, and information present in the environment that can interfere with task completion (see Friedman & Miyake, 2004). This management of information in working memory requires attentional resources (e.g., Lavie, 2005). When attentional resources are limited, for example, because perceivers are cognitively busy, they have less capacity to inhibit task-irrelevant information.

The differences in attention allocation of powerful and powerless individuals have implications for their ability to prioritize goals and to execute the mental operations necessary for the coordination of cognitive processes. Powerless individuals pay attention to multiple sources of information, deliberate more, and form more complex representations than powerful individuals (Guinote, 2001). Powerless individuals operate, therefore, under divided attention. As a consequence, compared with powerful individuals, they have fewer cognitive resources and less ability to resist distracting interferences (see Guinote, 2007b; Smith et al., 2008). For example, in one study (Guinote, 2008), participants were assigned to a powerful or a powerless condition and asked to plan the first day of their holiday. They then encountered incidental information that was either consistent (an opportunity for a visit at the sea side) or inconsistent (an invitation to attend a talk by the Dean) with their holiday goals. When inconsistent (distracting) information was present, powerless, but not powerful, participants changed their commitment to their goal priorities. They engaged more in activities that were irrelevant to their focal goal.

A series of studies examined inhibition of task-irrelevant information. In one study (Guinote, 2007b), participants were assigned to a manager or subordinate role and asked to indicate whether objects appearing on a screen were upright or inverted. The objects (e.g., a cup) had handles that usually activate grasping movements, a dominant response that typically interferes with the task at hand. However, this was not the case for powerful participants. These participants inhibited dominant responses and did not show the typical interference.

In another study, DeWall and colleagues (DeWall et al., 2011) assigned participants to a managerial or a subordinate role or to a control condition. Participants then performed a dichotic listening task. This task required participants to monitor and categorize information presented to one ear and to ignore information presented to the other ear. As expected, powerholders exhibited greater attentional control, as shown by less interference from the nonattended ear, compared with control and powerless participants.

Power also affects additional processes necessary to maintain processing goals and to adjust attention to moment-to-moment task demands. Smith et al. (2008) found that powerless individuals, compared with control and powerful individuals, experienced more difficulty in updating information, that is, in changing the focus of attention in ways that serve primary goals.

Another function of attention is to orient processing to desired locations of the visual field (see Posner & Dehaene, 1994). Orienting attention is important because it improves the perception of the desired targets. Recent studies show that powerholders are better able to orient their attention to specific spatial locations than are powerless individuals (Slabu, Guinote, & Wilkinson, 2013). In particular, powerholders can more easily override the misinformation provided by cues that could potentially point to the location of the target but are invalid. Furthermore, powerholders' better orientation of attention facilitates attentional control in the face of distracting information (Willis, Rodríguez-Bailón, & Lupiáñez, 2011). This work shows that powerholders use better cues present in the visual field to direct attention to goal-relevant information.

Finally, according to the situated focus theory of power, power increases flexibility in information processing strategies so that powerholders more easily attend to information in ways that serve their current demands and motivation. For example, powerholders can more easily vary the breadth of their attentional window. In one study (Guinote, 2007b), participants primed with power were able to focus attention more narrowly on a central object (a line) or to take into consideration the context (the surroundings of the line) more accurately than were powerless participants.

In summary, power enhances selective attention allocation, inhibition of distracting information, orientation of attention across the visual field, and flexible processing. These effects are independent of content and allow powerholders to execute motivated actions, such as the pursuit of goals or the satisfaction of needs, more efficiently.

Ironically, powerless individuals' decreased control of attention is an unintended by-product of their increased efforts to control cognition. Their excess vigilance to multiple sources of information, and their excess deliberation, hinder their ability to effectively resist interference from unwanted influences. Thus, what appears to be a disruption of executive function derives from purposeful differences in what individuals deem to be important.

Although powerless individuals' hypervigilance is detrimental to the control of attention, it is beneficial for low-level cognitive tasks. In particular, lack of power enhances simple visual feature discrimination. Powerless participants performed better in perceptual matching and search tasks involving color, texture, and size discrimination, compared with control and powerful participants (Weick, Guinote, & Wilkinson, 2010).

Attention to Information Organized Hierarchically

When attending to an object, individuals may focus on its configuration and then attend to its components, or they may attend to the components and then build up the whole object based on the components (Navon, 1977). Similarly, individuals may represent information that they encounter and store in their memories in either a concrete or an abstract way. For example, they can encode an action in concrete (e.g., Person A kicks Person B) or in abstract (e.g., Person A is aggressive) terms (see Semin & Fiedler, 1988).

Powerholders, who, as we have seen, attend to information following parsimonious principles, also prefer simplified representations of events, people, and actions. They prefer to form a gist representation rather than to focus on details (Guinote, 2001; Guinote, Judd, & Brauer, 2002; Magee, Milliken, & Lurie, 2010; Smith & Trope, 2006). Using a model that examines language abstraction (the linguistic category model; Semin & Fiedler, 1988), Guinote (2001) found that members of a powerful group had more abstract ingroup and outgroup representations than did members of a subordinate group. Similarly, Guinote, Judd, and Brauer (2002) found that participants assigned to a powerful role had more abstract self-concepts, as reflected in the use of more traits (i.e., abstract language) when talking about the self, than did participants assigned to a powerless role. The latter defined themselves more in relation to concrete external circumstances.

The tendency for powerholders to think more abstractly than powerless individuals is also found in perceptual and categorical tasks (Smith & Trope, 2006). In one study, Smith and Trope (2006) assigned participants to a powerful, powerless, or control priming condition and asked them to choose the best descriptions of a series of actions. Participants primed with power chose more abstract descriptions of actions compared with control and powerless participants.

Despite the greater tendency for abstraction by powerholders, they show more flexible attention and make more flexible representations than do powerless individuals. That is, they switch between abstract and concrete representations more easily, depending on task requirements. For example, in a task that assessed attention to information organized hierarchically (the Navon Task, Navon, 1977), powerful participants focused their attention either on configurational or on detailed object information, depending on whether the task asked them to attend to the whole or to the details (Guinote, 2007b). In contrast, powerless participants systematically paid attention to the details of objects first, before attending to the configuration of the objects (i.e., they showed local precedence Navon, 1977).

Memory and Construct Accessibility

Attention and memory are closely linked, and both are involved in the cascade of processes that guide our perceptions and the ways we respond to the world. For example, memory may be impaired by our limited attention capacity. If attention is directed at multiple tasks during the encoding of information, memory for that information is impaired (Craik, Govoni, Naveh-Benjamin, & Anderson, 1996). Upon learning and storing information, memory processes amplify relevant neural responses in the brain that guide attention to the external world (Rainer, Lee, & Logothetis, 2004). Not surprisingly, the structures of the brain that are recruited during attention and memory tasks overlap, both involving the hippocampus and the medial temporal lobe (see Chun & Turk-Browne, 2007). In sum, attention and memory are fundamentally intertwined; attention determines what is encoded; prior knowledge structures summarize one's knowledge, giving meaning to the incoming information, and guiding attention toward information that has been relevant in the past.

Given that power affects attention, it is not surprising that it also affects memory. Initial evidence suggests that power affects memory recall, recognition, interference, and construct accessibility.

A demonstration of the effects of power on recall and recognition can be found in studies by Overbeck and Park (2001). Participants were assigned to a powerful (e.g., professor) or a powerless (e.g., student) role and were asked to interact with one another via e-mail. In reality, the e-mails were part of a closed circuit that provided participants with standard responses from their partners. Subsequently, powerholders recalled more information about their partners than did powerless participants. This was particularly true for information that was relevant (vs. irrelevant) for the interaction, and was found both for free recall and recognition measures.

Another line of research examined memory interference that can occur between encoding and retrieval of information. Memory is constructive. It is malleable and open to influences that can occur after the information has been encountered (Schachter, Norman, & Koustaal, 2008). For example, when people discuss an event that they have witnessed, they can affect each other's recollections. Such influences often lead to memory conformity: one person's memory affects and becomes incorporated into another person's reported memory. Skagerberg and Wright (2008) showed participants 50 photographs of faces and asked them to enact a powerful or powerless role in pairs. They were then given a face recognition test, such that one partner responded before the other. The results indicated that powerful participants were less influenced by their partners' responses compared with powerless participants. Skagerberg and Wright (2008) proposed that these effects derive from the cognitive busyness and increased working memory load that is typical for powerless individuals. These findings have important implications, for example, regarding eyewitness testimony.

The ability to recall some information available in memory and to ignore other undesired or irrelevant information constitutes a prerequisite for the activation of constructs needed for judgment and action (see Bargh, Bond, Lombardi, & Tota, 1986; Carlston & Smith, 1996). When individuals are cognitively busy, constructs are activated with more difficulty (Gilbert & Hixon, 1991). Based on these findings, Guinote et al. (2012) hypothesized that power facilitates construct activation. In one study (Slabu & Guinote, 2010), participants primed with or without power engaged in the pursuit of a goal, then performed lexical decision tasks. In these tasks, participants made decisions as to whether sequences of letters were words or nonwords. As expected, powerholders were faster than powerless individuals at detecting goal-relevant words.

In short, past research consistently shows that power affects the central components of the cognitive toolbox in ways that enable fast judgment and action, prompt decision making, and efficient pursuit of goals. These aptitudes are crucial for the enactment of power roles. Through enhanced selective allocation of attention, ability to ignore distracting information, memory recall and recognition, less memory interference, and higher construct accessibility, powerholders are better equipped to make faster decisions and to act purposively than other individuals.

Construct Use

Once constructs are activated, they are ready for use and can guide judgment and action (Bargh et al., 1986; Higgins, 1996). This is particularly the case when constructs are considered to be relevant and sufficient (Higgins, 1996). Powerholders' ease in attaining desired outcomes leads them to trust information at their disposal more readily (e.g., to trust accessible constructs). In contrast, powerless individuals tend to seek more evidence before making judgments (see Fiske, 1993; Keltner et al., 2003). Therefore, once constructs are activated from memory, powerholders use these constructs more readily than do powerless individuals (Guinote et al., 2012). Greater use of activated constructs can be one reason that powerholders often act more in line with their dispositions (Bargh & Raymund, 1995; Chen et al., 2001), given that dispositions tend to be chronically accessible.

Power elicits feelings of pride (Schmidt Mast, Jonas, & Hall, 2009), increasing self-esteem (Wojciszke, & Struzynska-Kujalowicz, 2007) and confidence in one's judgments (see Briñol, Petty, Valle, Rucker, & Becerra, 2007; Georgesen & Harris, 1998). These feelings can contribute to a greater reliance on thoughts that easily come to mind, such as enduring attitudes and opinions. Indeed, compared with powerless individuals, powerholders are less affected by persuasive messages (Briñol et al., 2007), conform less to the opinions of others (Skagerberg & Wright, 2008; see Morison, Rothman, & Soll, 2011), signal signs of competence (Anderson & Kilduff, 2009), and are more likely to seek information that confirms their past decisions (Fischer, Fischer, Englich, Aydin, & Frey, 2011).

In a demonstration of the role of confidence, Briñol et al. (2007) found that when a persuasive message was encountered after a power manipulation, powerholders were less susceptible to persuasion than were their powerless counterparts. However, when the message was presented before participants acquired power, the reverse was true. The authors concluded that powerholders tend to validate whatever thoughts they have in their minds.

Powerholders are also less inclined to take the perspective of other individuals (Galinsky, Magee, Inesi, & Gruenfeld, 2006). For example, in one study, powerholders took the knowledge that other people possess less into account, anchoring their perspectives too heavily in their own vantage point. Similarly, in another study, when asked to draw an "E" on their forehead, powerholders were more likely to do so in a self-oriented direction ("Ǝ"), less spontaneously adopting others' visual perspective. More generally, powerholders misattribute their success to their abilities and attributes (Georgesen & Harris, 1998) and have a tendency to perceive themselves in coherent and consistent ways (Kraus, Chen, & Keltner, 2011).

In summary, powerholders show confidence in their judgments and apply accessible constructs more readily than do powerless individuals. Once constructs are activated, powerholders selectively process information in line with these constructs. As we will see later, this phenomenon is at the origin of powerholders' situated behavior and greater variability across different contexts, compared to powerless individuals. As different constructs become accessible, powerholders rely more on these constructs and vary their responses more than do their powerless counterparts.

Reliance on Experiential Information

Judgment and behavior are to a great extent guided by subjective experiences and by bodily states (e.g., Niedenthal, Barsalou, Winkielman, Karuth-Gruber, & Ric, 2005). Subjective experiences contribute to powerholders' situated judgment and behavior. Two types of experience have been shown to affect powerful more than powerless individuals: bodily experiences and cognitive experiences (see Schwarz & Clore 2007). As mentioned above, those who have power rely more on experiences that accompany thought processes (i.e., cognitive experiences) than do those who do not have power. For example, powerholders' attitudes depend on whether it is easy or difficult to generate arguments in favor of the attitude object (Weick & Guinote, 2008).

Bodily experiences such as hunger, pain, and fatigue derive from proprioceptive cues that concern the state of various bodily systems (Schwarz & Clore, 2007). These cues signal needs and states of the body; for example, hunger signals the need for nourishment (e.g., Nisbett & Kanouse, 1968). Bodily cues inform the behavior of powerholders more than they do the behavior of powerless individuals. For example, in what was supposedly a taste study (Guinote, 2010), powerholders ate more food or less food depending on how hungry they were, whereas this was not the case for powerless individuals. In another study, powerholders ate more appetizing food (chocolates) and ate less nonappetizing food (radishes) than their powerless counterparts. To summarize, past research shows that powerholders use accessible subjective experiences to guide their judgments and actions, whereas powerless individuals do not.

Neurobiology of Power

Having or lacking power affects physiology and the distribution of activity across the brain. Differences have been found in neural activity in brain regions related to cognitive interference and math performance, dopaminergic activity, cortisol levels, testosterone, and hemispheric dominance. Each of these will be briefly discussed in turn.

Elevated power decreases interference, as shown by reduced neural responses in areas of the left inferior frontal gyrus (IFG), and increases math ability (Harada, Bridge, & Chiao, 2013). These results are consistent with findings showing that, compared to powerless individuals, powerholders have better the ability to inhibit task irrelevant information, resulting in better performance on attentionally demanding tasks (Guinote, 2010; see also Smith et al., 2008). Studies with nonhuman primates suggest that elevated power enhances dopaminergic activity in the brain (e.g., Kaplan, Manuck, Fontenot, & Mann, 2002; Morgan et al., 2002). Dopamine plays a role in motivation, learning, and reward seeking. It facilitates flexibility and creativity and is associated with goal-directed action and the "wanting" of behavior (Flaherty, 2005).

To examine the links between dominance and dopaminergic activity in nonhuman primates, Morgan et al. (2002) compared the dopamine D2 receptors in monkeys when they were individually housed, and later, when they were living in groups, using positron emission tomography (PET). The monkeys did not differ in D2 dopamine receptor levels when they were living individually. However, when living in groups, dominance hierarchies emerged, and those at the top showed enhanced levels of D2 dopamine receptors, whereas this was not the case for subordinate monkeys. Furthermore, when given the opportunity to self-administer cocaine, a drug that activates the reward pathway, subordinate monkeys self-administered higher doses of cocaine than dominant monkeys. That is, cocaine had a higher reinforcing value for subordinate than for dominant monkeys.

These results are important because they suggest that dopaminergic activity is dependent on one's position in the power hierarchy, as is vulnerability to drug abuse. This notion is supported by the finding that alcohol and drug consumption are higher in individuals from low positions in the hierarchy (e.g., Lemstra et al., 2008). Elevated dopaminergic activity in powerholders is consistent with their elevated cognitive flexibility, action, and goal-directed behavior, as found in behavioral studies (see Galinsky et al., 2003; Guinote, 2007c; Keltner et al., 2003).

Power affects neuroendocrinology by elevating the level of testosterone, a hormone responsible for the development of masculine bodily characteristics, and, in the animal population, for aggressive behaviors (Carney, Cuddy, & Yap, 2010; Rivers & Josephs, 2010). Power also decreases baseline cortisol, a stress hormone. At the same time, it improves cortisol reactivity in the face of acute stressors (Rivers & Josephs, 2010). In contrast, prolonged subordination is related to high basal cortisol and to ill health in humans and other primates (see also Marmot et al., 1991; Sapolsky, 2004). The testosterone and cortisol levels of powerholders together create the appropriate conditions for powerholders' dominance over others, while supporting confidence, self-esteem, and decreased perception of challenge.

It has been suggested that the distribution of activity across the two sides of the brain is affected by an individual's degree of power (e.g., Keltner et al., 2003). Based on electroencephalogram (EEG) activity, Boksem et al. (Boksem, Smolders, & De Cremer, 2009) found support for a preferential activation of the left hemisphere of the brain in powerful individuals and of the right hemisphere in powerless individuals. However, behavioral studies that included a control condition only found brain activity differences for powerless participants (Wilkinson, Guinote, Weick, Molinari, & Graham, 2010). For example, in one study, participants were asked to walk through a narrow passage while balancing a full cup of water on a small tray. Powerless participants bumped more frequently into the right side of the passage compared with powerful and control participants. Bumping more into things on the right side indicates a spatial bias to the left side of the visual field, following enhanced activation of the right hemisphere in powerless participants. Right hemisphere dominance is associated with spatial attention, vigilance, and the processing of novel situations (e.g., Goldberg, 2009). These findings are consistent with powerless individuals' increased vigilance, avoidance orientation, and spatial attention (Guinote, 2007b; Keltner et al., 2003).

Power in Action: Processing Strategies and Situated Cognition

The previous sections were primarily concerned with basic cognitive processes that derive from the experience of power. This section is concerned with how these processes are implemented on a moment-to-moment basis and with how they translate into powerholders' behavior. The questions that arise are: How do attention, judgment and behavior unfold across the different situations that individuals encounter? How can we reconcile the multiple signatures of power proposed in past research, such as reward orientation, reliance on dispositions, cognitive laziness and goal focus? Which strategies do powerholders deploy when processing information?

Powerholders have been found to act in varied, often contradictory ways. Consider, for example, the links between power and action. Research has shown that power facilitates action (Galinsky et al., 2003) and efficient goal pursuit (Guinote, 2007c; Overbeck & Park, 2006; Vescio et al., 2003, Vescio et al., 2005). However, some studies have shown that power induces behavioral disinhibition, leading to impulsivity and poor self-regulation (see Gray, 1987). For instance, powerholders eat with their mouths open and spread crumbs (Keltner et al., 2003), take more risks (Anderson & Galinsky, 2006), rely more on heuristics (Fiske, 1993), and talk more and interrupt others more (Guinote et al., 2002; Schmidt Mast, 2002). Furthermore, powerholders were found to act more prosocially in some contexts and more selfishly in others (Galinsky et al., 2003).

The mechanisms proposed to explain the effects of power are also often contradictory. For example, it has been claimed that power stimulates self-interest (Keltner et al., 2010; Kipnis, 1972) and reward orientation (Anderson & Galinsky, 2006; Keltner et al, 2003), magnifies dispositions (Bargh & Raymund, 1995; Chen et al., 2001), and potentiates responses in line with inner states (Weick & Guinote, 2008; Keltner et al., 2003). Ironically, these influences are often conflicting, pulling behavior in different directions. For example, a tendency to seek opportunities and rewards for the self (Keltner et al., 2003) contradicts the dispositional tendencies of those who are communally oriented (Chen et al., 2001; Maner & Mead, 2010). A propensity toward risks and heuristics deriving from approach orientation (Anderson & Galinsky, 2006) competes with the desire to maintain the power status quo (Maner et al., 2007) or to attain goals successfully (Guinote, 2007c).

An integrated understanding of the multiple influences and outcomes of power requires the consideration of how cognition unfolds on a moment-to-moment basis. Cognition does not exist for its own sake and does not operate through static representations of external realities, such as schemas and stereotypes (Smith & Semin, 2004). Perception does not exist to see the world; learning does not exist to acquire knowledge (Purves & Lotto, 2011). The aim of cognition is to form representations and to utilize past experience in ways that help individuals to adapt and to satisfy core needs (see Fiske, 2002). In the case of powerholders, cognition unfolds in ways that are consistent with the satisfaction of their need for control so that they can freely pursue other desires. For powerless individuals, cognition unfolds in ways that aim to restore control and avoid further control losses (see Fiske & Dépret, 1996; Van Dijke & Poppe, 2006).

In a complex world, individuals learn multiple response patterns that they employ in different contexts. Crucially, they can exert some internal control over the patterns that they employ (see Norman & Shallice, 1986). Individuals may prefer stable response options guided by well-learned prior knowledge structures, or they may construe their judgments and actions more flexibly. Similarly, individuals may vary their deployment of effort and the amount of information that they gather before making decisions or selecting actions (e.g., Fiske & Neuberg, 1990). In the early example, a reader may choose to scan the headlines and figures of a newspaper, or read the articles in full.

Behavior flexibility is implemented by two systems: a hippocampal fast-learning system that responds to new situations and a neocortical slow-learning system that encompasses well-learned structures (McClelland, McNaughton, & O'Reilly, 1995). These structures include multiple mappings between inputs, internal states, and outputs (Miller & Cohen, 2001). Individuals may respond in line with chronically accessible constructs that are linked to their dispositions, habits, and enduring attitudes. However, they may also respond in line with their environment and states. For instance, although cooperative individuals usually act in prosocial ways, they act in competitive ways in particular situations, such as in sports events or when primed with competition (e.g., Bargh, Gollwitzer, Lee-Chai, Barndollar, & Trötschel, 2001). The multiple models of response that are potentially available to an individual often compete for expression. The brain is by its nature competitive, "Different pathways, carrying different sources of information, compete for expression in behavior, and the winners are those with the strongest sources of support" (Miller & Chen, 2001, p. 170). At the cognitive level, the winners depend, in part, on the individuals' top-down information processing strategies, and power is a factor that affects such top-down strategies.

According to the situated focus theory of power (Guinote, 2007a, 2010), power promotes selective processing and flexible use of response patterns, including a flexible use of automatic and controlled processes. Powerholders' selective processing generates clear winners in the cognitive competition for the control of judgment and action (see Kuhl, 1984). Thus, powerholders, compared with powerless individuals, respond in ways that are more unequivocally consistent with the primary drivers of information processing, such as goals, needs, feelings, or affordances of the environment.

When goals or needs are pressing, powerholders control their attention and deploy effort toward the attainment of these goals or the satisfaction of these needs. For example, during goal striving, powerholders persisted longer in the face of obstacles, seized better opportunities to act in a goal-consistent manner (Guinote, 2007c), and provided more correct solutions to the problems that they faced (DeWall et al., 2011). When the context afforded particular courses of action, powerholders pursued the affordances presented to them more promptly (Guinote, 2008). In an emergency, powerholders were more prompt to help a victim in need than were subordinate bystanders (Baumeister, Senders, Chesner, & Tice, 1988).

According to this perspective, power also increases reliance on a wider range of processes that can guide judgment and behavior. Powerholders flexibly switch between automatic and controlled processes, depending on task demands and their motivation. Depending on the situation, they rely on automatic responses and heuristics (Keltner et al., 2003), feelings, and embodied cues (see Guinote, 2010; Weick & Guinote, 2008), but also systematic information processing and controlled attention (DeWall et al., 2011; Guinote, 2007b).

Individuals who do not have power utilize automatic responses less freely, and consider information and monitor their behavior more carefully (see Fiske, 1993; Keltner et al., 2003). Their controlled cognition then overrides other processes that usually inform judgment and action, such as feelings, embodied information, and habitual responses. At the same time, as we have seen, these individuals may not always have the full attentional resources necessary for optimal control of attention and memory during purposive action.

Given that different contexts potentiate different responses, with different responses winning under different conditions, the more selective and flexible processing style of powerholders engenders more situated responses. In contrast, powerless individuals' broader attentional focus creates multiple sources of judgment and action control (see Kuhl, 1984), with no clear winners in the cognitive competition. Powerless individuals, therefore, make less extreme judgments and have less clear priorities.

Reconciling Behavior Biases and Variability

How can we reconcile the major trends in the ways powerholders act, feel, and think with their situated responses? One answer to this question is that power promotes situated and variable behavior. In one study (Guinote et al., 2002), participants were assigned to a powerful or a powerless group, and subsequently introduced themselves to their group. They were unobtrusively videotaped. Observers, who saw the videotapes and were unaware of the power relations between the groups, rated powerful groups as more variable than powerless groups.

According to the situated focus theory of power (Guinote, 2007a, 2010), powerholders respond more selectively in line with the primary drivers of judgment and behavior that unfold on a moment-to-moment basis. They respond more to accessible constructs regardless of whether these constructs are chronically or temporarily accessible. At the same time, when guided by desired actions or motivated judgments, powerholders are capable of inhibiting information that could interfere with their main motivations.

Some stability in powerholders' behavior is ensured by the reactivation of well-learned response patterns, such as enduring attitude representations, schemas, scripts, and dispositional behavior. These response tendencies are chronically accessible. Hence, in many contexts, most of the time, powerholders will respond in line with their dispositions, enduring attitudes, goals, and schemas. However, to the extent that alternatives are rendered accessible, these alternatives compete for the control of judgment and action. They may cancel chronic response patterns or even win the competition for threshold activation. Momentary states and feelings, as well as situationally activated goals, are examples of alternative response modes.

In the domain of dispositional behavior, Guinote et al. (2012) tested the hypothesis that power increases reliance on accessible constructs, regardless of whether these constructs are chronically or temporarily accessible. This argument implies that power does not magnify the expression of dispositions per se. Instead, dispositions easily guide powerholders' behavior because they are chronically accessible. To the extent that alternative constructs are rendered accessible, for example, through priming, powerholders should move further away from their dispositions than powerless individuals do. This is what happened. For example, when no alternatives were present, powerholders donated money to charities that corresponded more to their chronic preferences. However, when alternatives were presented by asking them to choose a charity from a list, powerholders no longer acted more in line with chronic preferences. This research shows that dispositions and enduring response patterns guide the behavior of powerful more than powerless individuals primarily in neutral contexts, when no alternative constructs compete for expression.

Powerholders also modulate their behavior depending on their motivation. Even though powerholders can employ efficient cognition, as we have seen above, they do not always do so. This was demonstrated by DeWall et al. (2011). Across a series of studies, these authors found that power enhanced self-regulation during solitary tasks. However, when powerholders deemed the task unworthy, they withdrew effort and performed poorly. For example, powerholders performed poorly on simple but arduous multiplication tasks.

Conclusion: Power and How the Mind Works

Power facilitates, and powerlessness hinders, the ability to attain goals (Fiske, 1993; Guinote, 2007a) and satisfy core needs (Fiske & Dépret, 2004; Pratto & Henry, 2010; Vescio et al., 2003). Consequently, having or lacking power affects the motivations and types of goals that individuals pursue and, at the same time, the ways they process information.

In terms of content, power activates schematic knowledge and behavior (Fiske, 1993), as well as goals directed at opportunities and rewards (Keltner et al., 2003) and the maintenance of power (Fiske, 1993). In contrast, lack of power elicits the motivation to be accurate and to acquire more knowledge in order to increase predictability and to avoid further losses of control (Fiske & Dépret, 1996).

Many documented differences between powerful and powerless individuals derive, however, from differences in processing style. Power triggers a unique constellation of cognitive signatures. Unlike other forms of approach motivation, which solely drive impulsive behavior and poor self-regulation (see Gray, 1987), power's cognitive signatures are marked by varied, multilayered, but predictable responses. These responses can be automatic or controlled, based on declarative content or on feelings, fast or slow. Power is unique because it magnifies the array of responses and mechanisms that individuals use. It also favors a close connection between automatic and controlled processes; therefore, automatic processes often enter as an input for subsequent controlled responses.

Power increases the potential for efficiency in all main components of the cognitive toolbox. It promotes processing selectivity in attention allocation, control, and orienting, better memory recall and recognition, and decreased memory interference. Finally, the cognitive signatures of powerholders testify to how cognition unfolds at the service of adaptive action (see Fiske, 1992; Smith & Semin, 2004). Having or lacking power is sufficient to alter the basic cognitive processes that we use to understand and respond to the world. These effects vary from perceptual discrimination to selective attention, global precedence, and memory.

Together, research on power and powerlessness contributes to an understanding of basic human needs. Power and other motivational states, such as those associated with anxiety (Eysenck, Deraksham, Santos, & Calvo, 2007), mood (Schwarz & Clore, 2007), and general control deprivation (Pittman & D'Agostino, 1985), all highlight that the operation of cognitive processes requires an understanding of the moment-to-moment states and needs of the individual. By and large cognition is motivated; it does not exist for its own sake. One of the tasks facing social cognition researchers today is to pinpoint exactly how the states and needs of individuals modulate basic cognitive processes, and how these processes serve adaptation.

Author Note

I would like to thank Alice Cai, Don Carlston, Christos Halkiopoulos, Laura de Molière, and Matthias Gobel for comments on this chapter, and Karen Griffith for editing the manuscript.

Correspondence concerning this chapter should be sent to Ana Guinote, Department of Cognitive, Perceptual and Brain Sciences, University College London, 26 Bedford Way, London WC1H OAP, England; e-mail: a.guinote@ucl.ac.uk.

References

Anderson, C., & Galinsky, A. D. (2006). Power, optimism, and risk-taking. *European Journal of Social Psychology, 36*, 511–536.

Anderson, C., & Kilduff, G. J. (2009). Why do dominant personalities attain influence in face-to-face groups? The competence-signaling effects of trait dominance. *Journal of Personality and Social Psychology, 96*, 491–503.

Bargh, J. A., Bond, R. N., Lombardi, W. J., & Tota, M. E. (1986). The additive nature of chronic and temporary sources of construct accessibility. *Journal of Personality and Social Psychology, 50*, 869–878.

Bargh, J., Gollwitzer, P. M., Lee-Chai, A., Barndollar, K., & Trötschel, R. (2001). The automated will: Nonconscious activation and pursuit of behavioral goals. *Journal of Personality and Social Psychology, 81*, 1014–1027.

Bargh, J. A., & Raymond, P. (1995). The naïve misuse of power: Nonconscious sources of sexual harassment. *Journal of Social Issues, 26*, 168–185.

Baumeister, R. F., Senders, P. S., Chesner, S. C., & Tice, D. M. (1988). Who's in charge here? Group leaders do lend help in emergencies. *Personality and Social Psychology Bulletin, 14*, 17–22.

Boehm, C., & Flack, J. C. (2010). The emergence of simple and complex power structures through social niche construction. In A. Guinote & T. K. Vescio (Eds.), *The social psychology of power* (pp. 46–86). New York: Guilford Press.

Boksem, M. A. S., Smolders, R., & De Cremer, D. (2009). Social power and approach related neural activity. *Social Cognitive and Affective Neuroscience, 7*, 516–520.

Briñol, P., Petty, R. E., Valle, C., Rucker, D. D., & Becerra, A. (2007). The effects of message recipients' power before and after persuasion: A self-validation analysis. *Journal of Personality and Social Psychology, 93*, 1040–1053.

Caporeal, L. R. (2004). Bones and stones: Selection for sociality. *Journal of Cultural and Evolutionary Psychology, 2*, 195–211.

Carlston, D. E., & Smith, E. R. (1996). Principles of mental representation. In E. T. Higgins & A. W. Kruglanski (Eds.) *Social psychology: handbook of basic principles* (pp. 184–210). New York: Guilford Press.

Carney, D. R., Cuddy, A. J. C., & Yap, A. J. (2010). Power poses: Brief nonverbal displays cause neuroendocrine change and increase risk tolerance. *Psychological Science, 21*, 1363–1368.

Chen, S., Lee-Chai, A. Y., & Bargh, J. A. (2001). Relationship orientation as a moderator of the effects of social power. *Journal of Personality and Social Psychology, 80*, 173–187.

Chun, M. M., & Turk-Browne, N. B. (2007). Interactions between attention and memory. *Current Opinion in Neurobiology, 17*, 177–184.

Craik, F. I. M., Govoni, R., Naveh-Benjamin, M., & Anderson, N. D. (1996). The effects of divided attention on encoding and retrieval processes in human memory. *Journal of Experimental Psychology: General, 125*, 159–180.

DeWall C. N., Baumeister, R. F., Mead, N. L., & Vohs, K. D. (2011). How leaders self-regulate their task performance: Evidence that power promotes diligence, depletion, and disdain. *Journal of Personality and Social Psychology, 100*, 47–65.

Drake, M., Grant, K. A., Gage H. D., Mach, R. H., Kaplan, J. R., Prioleau, O. Nader, S. H., Buchheimer, N., Ehrenkaufer, R. L., & Nader, M. A. (2002). Social dominance in monkeys: Dopamine D2 receptors and cocaine self-administration. *Nature Neuroscience, 5*, 169–174.

Driver, J. (2001). A selective review of selective attention research from the past century. *British Journal of Psychology, 92*, 53–78.

Eysenck, M. W., Derakshan, N., Santos, R., & Calvo, M. G. (2007). Anxiety and cognitive performance: Attentional control theory. *Emotion, 7*, 336–353.

Fischer, J., Fischer, P., Englich, B., Aydin, N., & Frey, D. (2011). Empower my decisions: the effects of power gestures on confirmatory information processing. *Journal of Experimental Social Psychology, 47*, 1146–1154.

Fiske, S. T. (1992). Thinking is for doing: Portraits of social cognition from daguerreotype to laserphoto. *Journal of Personality and Social Psychology, 63*, 877–889.

Fiske, S. T. (1993). Controlling other people: The impact of power on stereotyping. *American Psychologist, 48*, 621–628.

Fiske, S. T., & Dépret, E. (1996). Control interdependence and power: Understanding social cognition in its social context. In W. Stroebe & M. Hewstone (Eds.), *European review of social psychology* (Vol. 7, pp. 31–61). New York: Wiley.

Fiske, S. T., & Neuberg, S. L. (1990). A continuum of impression formation, from category-based to individuating processes: Influences of information and motivation on attention and interpretation. In M. P. Zanna (Ed.), *Advances in experimental social psychology* (Vol. 23, pp. 1–74). New York: Academic Press.

Flaherty, A. W. (2005). Frontotemporal and dopaminergic control of idea generation and creative drive. *Journal of Comparative Neurology, 493*, 147–153.

French, J. R. P., & Raven, B. (1959). The bases of social power. In D. Cartwright (Ed.), *Studies in social power* (pp. 150–167). Ann Arbor: University of Michigan Press.

Fischer, J., Fischer, P., Englich, B., Aydin, N., & Frey, D. (2011). Empower my decisions: The effects of power gestures on confirmatory information processing. *Journal of Experimental Social Psychology, 47*, 1146–1154.

Friedman, N. P., & Miyake, A. (2004). The relations among inhibition and interference cognitive functions: A latent variable analysis. *Journal of Experimental Psychology: General, 133*, 101–135.

Galinsky, A. D., Gruenfeld, D. H., & Magee, J. C. (2003). From power to action. *Journal of Personality and Social Psychology, 85*, 453–466.

Galinsky, A. D., Magee, J. C., Inesi, M. E., & Gruenfeld, D. H. (2006). Power and perspectives not taken. *Psychological Science, 17*, 1068–1074.

Georgesen, J. C., & Harris, M. I. (1998). Why is my boss always holding me down? A meta-analysis of power effects on performance evaluations. *Personality and Social Psychology Review, 2*, 184–195.

Gilbert, D. T., & Hixon, J. G. (1991). The trouble of thinking: Activation and application of stereotypic beliefs. *Journal of Personality and Social Psychology, 60*, 509–517.

Glick, P., & Fiske, S. T. (1996). The ambivalent sexism inventory: Differentiating hostile and benevolent sexism. *Journal of Personality and Social Psychology, 70*, 491–512.

Goldberg, E. (2009). *The new executive brain: Frontal lobes in a complex world*. New York: Oxford University Press.

Gray, J. A. (1987). Perspectives on anxiety and impulsivity: A commentary. *Journal of Research in Personality, 21*, 493–509.

Guinote, A. (2001). The perception of intragroup variability in a minority and a non-minority context: When adaptation leads to outgroup differentiation. *British Journal of Social Psychology, 40*, 117–132.

Guinote, A. (2010). In touch with your feelings: power increases reliance on bodily information. *Social Cognition, 28*, 110–121.

Guinote, A., & Fiske, S. T. (2003). Being in the outgroup territory increases stereotypic perceptions of outgroups: Situational Sources of Category Activation. *Group Processes & Intergroup Relations, 6*, 323–331.

Guinote, A. (2007a). Behavior variability and the situated focus theory of power. In W. Stroebe & M. Hewstone (Eds.), *European review of social psychology* (Vol. 18, pp. 256–295). New York: Wiley.

Guinote, A. (2007b). Power affects basic cognition: Increased attentional inhibition and flexibility. *Journal of Experimental Social Psychology, 43*, 685–697.

Guinote, A. (2007c) Power and goal pursuit. *Personality and Social Psychology Bulletin, 33*, 1076–1087.

Guinote, A. (2008). Power and affordances: When the situation has more power over powerful than over powerless individuals. *Journal of Personality and Social Psychology, 95*, 237–252.

Guinote, A., Brown, M., & Fiske, S. T. (2006). Minority status decreases sense of control and increases interpretive processing. *Social Cognition, 24*, 170–187.

Guinote, A., Judd, C. M., & Brauer, M. (2002). Effects of power on perceived and objective group variability: Evidence that more powerful groups are more variable. *Journal of Personality and Social Psychology, 82*, 708–721.

Guinote, A., & Phillips, A. (2010). Power can increase stereotyping: Evidence from managers and subordinates in the hotel industry. *Social Psychology, 41*, 3–9.

Guinote, A., Willis, G. B., & Martellotta, C. (2010). Social power increases implicit prejudice. *Journal of Experimental Social Psychology, 46*, 299–307.

Guinote, A., Weick, M., & Cai, A. (2012). Does power magnify the expression of dispositions? *Psychological Science, 23*, 475–482.

Harada T., Bridge D. J., & Chiao, J. Y. (2013). Dynamic social power modulates neural basis of math calculation. *Frontiers Human Neuroscience, 39*, 115–127.

Henry, P. J., & Pratto, F. (2010). Power and racism. In A. Guinote & T. K. Vescio (Eds.), *The social psychology of power* (pp. 341–380). New York: Guilford Press.

Higgins, E. T. (1996). Knowledge activation: Accessibility, applicability, and salience. In E. T. Higgins & A. W. Kruglanski (Eds.), *Social psychology: Handbook of basic principles* (pp. 133–168). New York: Guilford Press.

James, M. (1890). *The principles of psychology*. Cambridge, MA: Harvard University Press.

Johnson, C., & Ford, C. (1986). Dependence, power, legitimacy, and tactical choice. *Social Psychology Quarterly, 59*, 126–139.

Jost, J., & Banaji, M. (1994). The role of stereotyping in system-justification and the production of false consciousness. *British Journal of Social Psychology, 33*, 1–27.

Kaplan, J. R., Manuck, S. B., Fontenot, M. B., & Mann, J. J. (2002). Central nervous system monoamine correlates of social dominance in cynomolgus monkeys (*Macaca fascicularis*). *Neuropsychopharmacology, 26*, 431–443.

Kay, A. C., Banfield, K., & Laurin, K. (2010). The system justification motive and the maintenance of social power. In A. Guinote & T. K. Vescio (Eds.), *The social psychology of power* (pp. 313–340). New York: Guilford Press.

Keltner, D., Gruenfeld, D. H., & Anderson, C. (2003). Power, approach, and inhibition. *Psychological Review, 110*, 265–284.

Keltner, D., Gruenfeld, D. H., Galinsky, A., & Kraus, M.W. (2010). Paradoxes of power: Dynamics of the acquisition, experience, and social regulation of social power. In A. Guinote & T. K. Vescio (Eds.), *The social psychology of power* (pp. 177–208). New York: Guilford Press.

Kipnis, D. (1972). Does power corrupt? *Journal of Personality and Social Psychology, 24*, 33–41.

Kraus, M. W., Chen, S, & Keltner, D. (2011). The power to be me: Power elevates self-concept consistency and authenticity. *Journal of Experimental Social Psychology, 47*, 974–980.

Kuhl, J. (1984). Volitional aspects of achievement motivation and learned helplessness: Toward a comprehensive theory of action control. In B. A. Maher, & W. B. Maher (Eds.), *Progress in experimental personality research* (pp. 99–171). New York: Academic Press.

Lammers, J., Galinsky, A. D., Gordijn, E. H., & Otten, S. (2008). Illegitimacy moderates the effects of power on approach. *Psychological Science, 19*, 558–564.

Lavie, N. (2005) Distracted and confused? Selective attention under load. *Trends in Cognitive Sciences, 9*, 75–82.

Lemstra, M., Bennett, N., Neudorf, C., Kunst, A., Nannapaneni, U., Warren, L. M., et al. (2008). A meta-analysis of marijuana and alcohol use by socio-economic status in adolescents aged 10–15 years. *Canadian Journal of Public Health, 99*, 172–177.

Lewin, K. (1941). Regression, retrogression and development. *University of Iowa Studies of Child Welfare, 18*, 1–43.

Locke, G. H. (1690). *An essay concerning human understanding*. Philadelphia: Zell, n.d.

Magee, J. C., Milliken, F. J., & Lurie, A. R. (2010). Power differences in the construal of a crisis: The immediate aftermath of September 11, 2001. *Personality and Social Psychology Bulletin, 36*, 354–370.

Maner, J. K., Gailliot, M. T., Butz, D., & Peruche, B. M. (2007). Power, risk, and the status quo: Does power promote riskier or more conservative decision-making? *Personality and Social Psychology Bulletin, 33*, 451–462.

Maner, J. K., & Mead, N. (2010). The essential tension between leadership and power: When leaders sacrifice group goals for the sake of self-interest. *Journal of Personality and Social Psychology, 99*, 482–497.

Marmot, M. G., Davey Smith, G., Stansfield, S., Patel, C., North, F., Head, J. et al. (1991). Health Inequalities among British civil servants: The Whitehall II study. *Lancet, 337*, 1387–1393.

McClelland, J. L., McNaughton, B. L., & O'Reilly, R. C. (1995). Why there are complementary learning systems in the hippocampus and neocortex: Insights from the successes and failures of connectionist models of learning and memory. *Psychological Review, 102*, 419–457.

Miller, E. K., & Cohen, J. D. (2001). An integrative theory of prefrontal cortex function. *Annual Review of Neuroscience, 24*, 167–202.

Navon, D. (1977). Forest before trees: The precedence of global features in visual perception. *Cognitive Psychology, 9*, 353–383.

Niedenthal, P. M., Barsalou, L., Winkielman, P., Karuth-Gruber, S., & Ric, F. (2005). Embodiment in attitudes, social perception, and emotion. *Personality and Social Psychology Review, 9*, 184–211.

Nisbett, R. E., & Kanouse, D. E. (1968, August–September). *Obesity, hunger, and supermarket shopping behavior.* Paper presented at the 76th Annual Convention of the American Psychological Association, San Francisco.

Norman D. A., & Shallice T. (1986). Attention to action: Willed and automatic control of behavior. In R. J. Davidson, G. E. Schwartz, & D. Shapiro (Eds.), *Consciousness and self-regulation: Advances in research and theory* (pp. 1–18). New York: Plenum.

Overbeck, J. R. (2010). Concepts, domains, and historical perspectives on power. In A. Guinote & T. K. Vescio (Eds.), *The social psychology of power* (pp. 19–45). New York: Guilford Press.

Overbeck, J. R., & Park, B. (2001). When power does not corrupt: Superior individuation processes among powerful perceivers. *Journal of Personality and Social Psychology, 81*, 549–565.

Overbeck, J. R., & Park, B. (2006). Powerful perceivers, powerless objects: Flexibility of powerholders' social attention. *Organizational Behavior and Human Decision Processes, 99*, 227–243.

Parsons, T. (1963). On the concept of political power. *Proceedings of the American Philosophical Society, 107*, 232–262.

Pfeffer, J., & Salancik, G. R. (1978). *The external control of organizations: A resource dependence perspective.* New York: Harper and Row.

Pittman, T. S., & D'Agostino, P. R. (1985). Motivation and cognition: Control deprivation and the nature of subsequent information processing. *Journal of Experimental Social Psychology, 25*, 465–480.

Posner, M. I., & Dehaene, S. (1994). Attentional networks. *Trends in Neuroscience, 17*, 75–79.

Posner, M. I., & Snyder, C. R. R. (1975). Attention and cognitive control. In R. L. Solso (Ed.), *Information processing and cognition: The Loyola symposium.* Hillsdale, NJ: Erlbaum.

Purves, D., & Lotto, R. B. (2011). *Why we see what we see redux: A wholly empirical theory of vision.* Sunderland, MA: Sinauer.

Rainer G., Lee, H., & Logothetis, N. K. (2004). The effect of learning on the function of monkey extrastriate visual cortex. *PLoS Biology, 2*, e44.

Raven, B. H., Schwarzwald, J., & Koslowsky, M. (1998). Conceptualizing and measuring a power/interaction model of interpersonal influence. *Journal of Applied Social Psychology, 28*, 307–332.

Rivers, J. J., & Josephs, R. (2010). Dominance and health: The role of social rank in physiology and illness. In A. Guinote & T. K. Vescio (Eds.), *The social psychology of power* (pp. 87–112). New York: Guilford Press.

Russell, B. (1938). *Power: A new social analysis.* New York: W. W. Norton.

Sapolsky, R. M. (2004). Social status and health in humans and other animals. *Annual Review of Anthropology, 33*, 393–418.

Schmid Mast, M. (2002). Dominance as expressed and inferred through speaking time: A meta-analysis. *Human Communication Research, 28*, 420–450.

Schmid Mast, M., Jonas K., & Hall, J. A. (2009). Give a person power and he or she will show interpersonal sensitivity: The phenomenon and its why and when. *Journal of Personality and Social Psychology, 97*, 835–850.

Schwarz, N., Bless, H., Strack, F., Klumpp, G., Rittenauer-Schatka, H., & Simons, A. (1991). Ease of retrieval as information: Another look at the availability heuristic. *Journal of Personality and Social Psychology, 61*, 195–202.

Schwarz, N., & Clore, G. L. (2007). Feelings and phenomenal experiences. In E. T. Higgins & A. W. Kruglanski (Eds.), *Social psychology: Handbook of basic principles* (2nd ed., pp. 385–407). New York: Guilford.

See, K. E., Morrison, E. W., Rothman, N. B., & Soll, J. B. (2011). The detrimental effects of power on confidence, advice taking, and accuracy. *Organizational Behavior and Human Decision Processes, 116*, 66–82.

Semin, G., & Fiedler, K. (1988). The cognitive functions of linguistic categories in describing persons: Social cognition and language. *Journal of Personality and Social Psychology, 54*, 558–568.

Sherif, M., & Sherif, C. W. (1953): *Groups in harmony and tension.* New York: Harper & Row.

Skagerberg, E. M. & Wright, D. B. (2008). Manipulating power can affect memory conformity. *Applied Cognitive Psychology, 22*, 207–216.

Slabu, L., & Guinote, A. (2010). Getting what you want: Power increases the accessibility of active goals. *Journal of Experimental Social Psychology, 46*, 344–349.

Smith, E. R., & Semin, G. (2004). Socially situated cognition: Cognition in its social context. *Advances in Experimental Social Psychology, 36*, 53–117.

Smith, P. K., Jostman, N., Galinsky, A. D., & van Dijk, W. W. (2008). Lacking power impairs executive functions. *Psychological Science, 19*, 441–447.

Smith, P. K., & Trope, Y. (2006). You focus on the forest when you're in charge of the trees: Power priming and abstract information processing. *Journal of Personality and Social Psychology, 90*, 578–596.

Tiedens, L. Z., & Fragale, A. R. (2003). Power moves: Complementarity in submissive and dominant nonverbal behavior. *Journal of Personality and Social Psychology, 84*, 558–568.

Van Dijke, M., & Poppe, M. (2006). Striving for personal power as a basis for social power dynamics. *European Journal of Social Psychology, 36*, 537–556.

Van Vugt, M., Hogan, R., & Kaiser, R. (2008). Leadership, followership and evolution: Some lessons from the past. *American Psychologist, 63*, 182–196.

Vescio, T. K., Gervais, S. J., Snyder, M., & Hoover, A. (2005). Power and the creation of patronizing environments: The stereotype-based behaviors of the powerful and their effects on female performance in masculine domains. *Journal of Personality and Social Psychology, 88*, 658–572.

Vescio, T. K., Snyder, M., & Butz, D. A. (2003). Power in stereotypically masculine domains: A social influence strategy x stereotype match model. *Journal of Personality and Social Psychology, 85*, 1062–1078.

Weber, M. (1954). *On law in economy and society.* Boston: Harvard University Press.

Weick, M., & Guinote, A. (2008). When subjective experiences matter: Power increases reliance on the ease of retrieval. *Journal of Personality and Social Psychology, 94*, 956–970.

Wilkinson, D. T., Guinote, A., Weick, M., Molinari, R., & Graham, K. (2010). Feeling socially powerless makes you more prone to bumping into things on the right and induces leftward line bisection error. *Psychonomic Bulletin & Review, 17*, 910–914.

Willis, G. B., Guinote, A., & Rodríguez-Bailón, R. (2010). Illegitimacy improves goal pursuit in powerless individuals. *Journal of Experimental Social Psychology, 46*, 416–419.

Willis, G. B., Rodríguez-Bailón, R., & Lupiáñez, J. (2011). The boss is paying attention: Power affects the attentional networks. *Social Cognition, 29*, 166–181.

Willis, J., & Todorov, A. (2006). First impressions: Making up your mind after 100 ms exposure to a face. *Psychological Science, 17*, 592–598.

Winter, D. G. (2010). Power in the person: Exploring the motivational underground of power. In A. Guinote & T. K. Vescio (Eds.), *The social psychology of power* (pp. 113–140). New York: Guilford Press.

Wojciszke, B., & Struzynska-Kujalowicz, A. (2007). Power influences self-esteem. *Social Cognition, 25*, 510–532

Interpersonal Cognition: Seeking, Understanding, and Maintaining Relationships

Gráinne M. Fitzsimons *and* Joanna E. Anderson

Abstract

This chapter describes research on interpersonal cognition—cognitive, affective, and motivational processes directed at or shaped by close others. The authors adopt a goal-based perspective on interpersonal cognition, assuming that interpersonal cognition serves, at the broadest level, to help individuals fulfill their need to belong to social relationships. The main tasks of interpersonal cognition are divided into those targeted at seeking, understanding, and maintaining relationships. The "Seeking Relationships" section describes research on attraction and on how fundamental processes are shaped by the desire to form relationships with others. The "Understanding Others" section describes research on how individuals perceive and judge others and how individual differences can shape these processes. The "Maintaining Relationships" section describes research on everyday interdependence (the effects of just being interdependent with others on the self) and strategic maintenance (the goals individuals pursue to protect important relationships).

Key Words: relationships, interpersonal, goals, interdependence, self, motivation, attraction

Interpersonal Versus Social Cognition

The title of this chapter may puzzle readers perusing the table of contents of this volume. Why is there a chapter on "interpersonal cognition" within a book about "social cognition"? Aren't "interpersonal" and "social" synonymous? Although readers would be reasonable to assume that the term social cognition refers, at least in part, to cognition about social relationships, it rarely does.

As explained by the subtitle—*Seeking, Understanding, and Maintaining Relationships*—this chapter will not deal with cognitions about or shaped by strangers or members of social groups. Instead, it will focus on cognitions about or shaped by friends, family members, coworkers, and romantic partners. On the one hand, ours is a giant task. Every day, individuals pursue goals to get along with others, make attributions about the intentions of coworkers, utilize well-developed schemas for understanding family

members, and engage in automated ways of thinking, feeling, and acting with their romantic partners. Indeed, most of what individuals think, feel, and do on a daily basis is governed not by cognitions about broad social categories or abstract others, but rather by cognitions about specific interpersonal relationships. This fact—the pervasiveness of interpersonal cognition—is perhaps reflected by the centrality of interpersonal questions to foundational theories of social psychology (e.g., Baumeister & Leary, 1995; Heider, 1958; Higgins, 1987; Mead, 1934).

On the other hand, ours is a tiny task. Interpersonal processes are the focus of *perhaps* 0.66% of social cognition research, which has been guided by an interest in social problems, broadly, and intergroup relations, stereotyping, and prejudice, specifically. Perhaps as a result of the field's focus on these (undoubtedly important) social problems, the social cognition of ongoing relationships is considerably less advanced than the social cognition of strangers. Making our chapter's task even smaller, the vast majority of research on close relationships has ignored advances in social cognitive theory and methodology. Although the most influential theories of relationships—attachment theory and interdependence theory—are fundamentally cognitive in nature, most of the research conducted in the relationships field has not kept pace with the innovations in social cognition.

The importance of connecting these two fields, and an optimistic sentiment that this integration is imminent, has been expressed repeatedly by leaders in both relationships science and social cognition for decades (e.g., Baldwin, 2005; Berscheid, 1994; Fiske, 1992; Reis & Downey, 1999). Thirteen years after Reis and Downey noted that "a growing number of researchers are investigating social cognitive processes in the context of relationships," we may finally have a critical mass of such researchers. In recent years, mainstream self and social cognition researchers have contributed insights and ideas to understand relationship phenomena and based cognitive and motivational models on interpersonal origins and influences. Mainstream relationships scholars have employed social cognition's newest models and methods to develop theories of interpersonal behavior. Finally, the field has also seen the emergence of a new breed of scholars, to whom the integration of the two topics and approaches is so complete that the distinction itself seems false.

Thus, progress has undoubtedly been made toward the goal of connecting the study of relationships to the study of social cognition. However, it remains true that the influence of social cognition on relationships is much larger than the reverse, that most relationships research is light on process theorizing and data, and that much more research is conducted on the cognition of social categories and abstract others than on the cognition of common relationships. Despite these facts, we can now point to a diverse, rich, and multifaceted body of research studying cognitive processes relating to ongoing relationships. In this chapter, we aim to describe these developments in understanding the nature of interpersonal cognition. We should note up front that many of the studies we will discuss focus on romantic relationships; by far, the bulk of research on interpersonal cognition has studied romantic partners. Very little work has examined the social cognition of relationships with siblings or friends, specifically. We believe that the field of interpersonal cognition should include such relationships and will discuss studies that examine nonromantic relationships whenever relevant.

Three Tasks Served by Interpersonal Cognition: Seeking, Understanding, and Maintaining Relationships

In this chapter, we adopt a goal-based perspective on interpersonal cognition, assuming that interpersonal cognition serves, at the broadest level, to help individuals fulfill their need to belong to social relationships (Baumeister & Leary, 1995). We divide the main tasks of interpersonal cognition into those targeted at (1) seeking relationships, (2) understanding relationship partners, and (3) maintaining existing relationships. These are not basic categories of social cognitive processes, like "thinking," "feeling," and "doing," or "hot" versus "cold" processes, nor are they different levels or systems of processing, like "conscious" and "unconscious" cognitions. Seeking, understanding, and maintaining relationships are goal-based categories; they group together all processes related to these major interpersonal tasks. Our chapter's subsections will thus each deal with a mix of hot, cold, conscious, and unconscious thoughts, feelings, and goals, each targeted at or affected by a higher order function of seeking, understanding, or maintaining relationships.

Seeking Relationships

We begin the chapter where relationships begin: The first task of interpersonal cognition is to help individuals establish relationships with others. A large body of work has demonstrated that people are strongly motivated to establish close relationships and that their success affects both physical and psychological health and well-being (e.g., Baumeister & Leary, 1995; Cacioppo, Hawkley, & Berntson, 2003; Williams, 2002). This motivation profoundly influences interpersonal cognition. When people are high in the *need to belong*, either temporarily as when induced to imagine loss or chronically as when high in loneliness, they show greater memory for social events and more accurate understanding of nonverbal behavior and social cues in others' facial expressions and vocal tones (Gardner, Pickett, & Brewer, 2000; Gardner, Pickett, Jefferis, & Knowles, 2005; Gray, Ishii, & Ambady, 2011; Pickett, Gardner, & Knowles, 2004). Thus, the motivation to belong—to find and establish relationships with others—can elicit a wide range of social perceptual and cognitive effects, seemingly in service of preparing individuals to best take advantage of opportunities to make a social connection (Maner, DeWall, Baumeister, & Schaller, 2007).

The desire to form a sexual or romantic relationship, compared with the desire to form a satisfying social connection in general, has distinct implications for social cognition. For example, there is a strong reciprocity effect on attraction: People like others who like them (Curtis & Miller, 1986; Kenny, 1994). This tendency leads people to prefer others who themselves like other people; when one seeks a social connection, happy-go-lucky, friends-with-everyone types are desirable. However, in the romantic context, the reciprocity effect becomes more constrained. Although perceivers continue to like targets who display *dyadic* reciprocity (i.e., who like those specific perceivers more than they like other people), perceivers do not like targets who display *generalized* reciprocity (i.e., who tend to like everyone; Eastwick, Finkel, Mochon, & Ariely, 2007). In the romantic context, people add this extra complication because they want to feel *uniquely* desired.

Another difference between romantic and nonromantic contexts is that people are much more discerning about which targets can satisfy their motivation to seek a romantic relationship. Unfortunately, it isn't simply the case that people have higher standards for romantic partners than for other kinds of social relationships. They also have more complicated standards and apply them less reliably. People differ in their ideal standards for romantic partners, with some people valuing some traits (e.g., friendliness, extraversion) more than do others; these ideals predict liking of others in abstract and hypothetical settings (Eastwick & Finkel, 2008; Wood & Brumbaugh, 2009), but do not always shape liking in real interactions (Eastwick & Finkel, 2008). Instead, it seems that in face-to-face interactions, people are affected by a gestalt impression of the whole person, which makes it harder for them to evaluate others in terms of their standards (Eastwick, Finkel, & Eagly, 2011). It should also be noted, though, that people in long-term relationships with partners whose traits match the pattern of their ideal preferences report more satisfaction and commitment (Eastwick et al., 2011; Fletcher, Simpson, & Thomas, 2000; Fletcher, Simpson, Thomas, & Giles, 1999). Thus, although ideal standards are not reliable predictors of initial attraction, they do predict long-term relationship quality (see Fletcher & Simpson, 2000, for review).

Thus, idiosyncratic preferences are not a straightforward predictor of attraction. When it comes to normative predictors, researchers have uncovered a dizzying number of factors predicting attraction (see Finkel & Baumeister, 2010, for a review). As just a few examples, there are well-established features of targets (e.g., warmth, vitality, and status; Fletcher et al., 1999), perceivers (e.g., arousal, Dutton & Aron, 1974; expectations, Kenrick & Gutierres, 1980), and dyads (e.g., similarity; Newcomb, 1961) that reliably predict attraction. The most well-established finding is an unsurprising one—the target's physical attractiveness promotes the perceiver's attraction (Walster, Aronson, Abrahams, & Rottman, 1966)—but understanding how and why physical attractiveness affects attraction, a focus of evolutionary psychologists in recent years, has led to important insights about the social cognition of attraction.

From an evolutionary perspective, attractiveness is thought to matter because it is a strong cue for fertility. Indeed, fertility cues activate sexual goals in men, leading to higher accessibility of sexual concepts (Miller & Maner, 2011); ovulation in females leads to a diverse range of outcomes related to sexual and reproductive goals for both men and women (Gangestad, Thornhill, & Garver-Apgar, 2005; Haselton & Gildersleeve, 2011). Indeed, once active, sexual goals generate a wide range of cognitive and perceptual consequences. For example, individuals engage in early-stage perceptual processing that promotes their ability to find a sexual partner who meets their needs, attending to cues of physical attractiveness and social dominance (e.g., Maner, DeWall, & Gailliot, 2008). Observers pay more attention to physically attractive women than to physically attractive men, and encode and remember them better as well (Maner, DeWall, & Gailliot, 2008; Maner et al., 2003), while they also appear to attend more closely to socially dominant men than to socially dominant women (Maner et al., 2008). For example, in an eye-tracking study, both male and female observers fixated longer on photographs of physically attractive women (vs. men), and socially dominant men (vs. women; Maner et al., 2008). Thus, overall, people may attend more to socially desirable traits in others (attractiveness for women, dominance/status for men).

When it comes to attraction to people in live interactions, the role of physical attractiveness is more complicated. The physical attractiveness of potential partners matters more to men than women in hypothetical self-report measures (e.g., Buss, 1989), but matters to men and women equally when measured after real interactions (Eastwick & Finkel, 2008). More reason to question people's explicit reports about attractiveness comes from work comparing explicit and implicit measures (Eastwick, Eagly, Finkel, & Johnson, 2011). In several studies, explicit measures of how much participants cared about physical attractiveness predicted attraction to photographed targets, but not to real-life interaction partners, whereas implicit measures predicted attraction to real-life partners but not to photographed targets. These findings suggest that people base their attraction judgments of live partners more on spontaneous, affective responses, whereas they may base their attraction judgments of abstract and hypothetical targets more on knowledge or beliefs (Eastwick et al., 2011; see Gawronski, Geschke, & Banse, 2003).

In sum, research on the social cognition of seeking relationship partners has demonstrated that fundamental cognitive and perceptual processes, such as attention and memory, are directed by goals to make a social connection and to find an appealing romantic partner. In the next section, we will discuss what happens after people find each other, and a fledgling relationship takes flight.

Understanding Relationships

Once a relationship is established, the work of interpersonal cognition has barely begun. All relationships—even the best ones—require effort and understanding. In this section, we review research investigating the content and process of the beliefs people form about their partners and relationships, how individual differences affect interpersonal cognition, and how people represent their relationships on a cognitive level.

PERSPECTIVE TAKING AND EMPATHIC ACCURACY

One of the major tasks of ongoing relationships is to understand each other's thoughts and feelings. Doing so successfully creates a more predictable and stable relationship, and one that satisfies more of both individuals' needs (Simpson, Ickes, & Oriña, 2001; Thomas & Fletcher, 2003). Of course, trying to see another person's viewpoint is not easy. A shared knowledge structure is demonstrably crucial to empathic accuracy, the ability to "read" a partner's thoughts and feelings (Stinson & Ickes, 1992). For instance, friends' greater ability (relative to strangers) to intuit one another's thoughts and feelings is thought to result from their shared history—a common knowledge structure that contains much more than just the information present in a single interaction (Stinson & Ickes, 1992). One might think that as people get to know one another, they would become more accurate in their perceptions of their partners; the evidence actually supports a curvilinear relationship between length of relationship and empathic accuracy. Accuracy increases with time (Stinson & Ickes, 1992), but in married relationships, it peaks during the early years of marriage (Bissonnette, Rusbult, & Kilpatrick, 1997), and then declines, apparently owing to lack of effort (Thomas, Fletcher, & Lange, 1997).

Empathic accuracy is heightened when individuals are *motivated* to be accurate. In fact, the widespread perception that women are better than men at understanding how others are feeling can actually be attributed to their greater motivation to live up to that perception: Ickes, Gesn, and Graham (2000) found that women perform better than men only when the empathic nature of the task is made salient. Other sources of motivation, such as having a physically attractive interaction partner, or a partner who appears interested in you, also increase empathic accuracy (Ickes, Stinson, Bissonnette, & Garcia, 1990).

Being able to "read" one's partner (i.e., being empathically accurate) has a number of positive consequences for relationships. For example, inferring potentially relationship-threatening thoughts in the partner allows one to avoid dangerous situations (e.g., hiring a housekeeper your partner finds attractive, or recognizing that your boss is considering firing you), thereby protecting the relationship and preventing personal distress (Simpson et al., 2001). Empathic accuracy also facilitates more skillful support provision toward others, and there is some evidence that, at least in long-term relationships, it is correlated with satisfaction and closeness (Verhofstadt, Buysse, Ickes, Davis, & Devoldre, 2008; Thomas & Fletcher, 2003).

The effects of inaccuracy depend on the direction of those biases. Couples who report the most marital dissatisfaction often make negative attributions for one another's ambiguous behaviors—for instance, assuming that silence indicates anger (Bradbury & Fincham, 1990). Dissatisfied partners tend to mentally minimize nice gestures and exaggerate slights: They assume their partners' negative behaviors are intentional, caused by stable personality traits, and affect many areas of the relationship, whereas they assume positive behaviors are unintentional, caused by outside circumstances or a temporary state, and are situation specific. Holtzworth-Munroe and Jacobson (1985) called this attribution pattern *distress maintaining*. These negative attributions are maladaptive for a number of reasons, including that they can invoke a tit-for-tat norm in which partners reciprocate one another's negative behaviors and use less effective problem-solving behaviors (Bradbury & Fincham, 1992; Miller & Bradbury, 1995).

On the other hand, the attributions made by nondistressed partners tend to be biased in the positive direction. Holtzworth-Munroe and Jacobson (1985) referred to *relationship-enhancing* attributions as ones in which spouses assumed their partners' positive behaviors were intentional, stable, and global, and their negative behaviors were unintentional, unstable, and specific. Making relationship-enhancing attributions for a partner's behavior, even if they are inaccurate, can be positive for relationships. If the partner's potentially threatening thoughts and feelings are ambiguous, people can use motivated inaccuracy as a defense to maintain the stability of their relationship and reduce their own distress (Simpson et al., 2001). For instance, in one study, dating couples discussed the desirability of alternative potential dating partners (Simpson, Ickes, & Blackstone, 1995); couples who showed the *least* empathic accuracy about that discussion were the most likely to still be dating four months later. This finding provides support for motivated inaccuracy as a relationship-maintaining strategy. Similarly, research on evaluations of partners' strengths and weaknesses has repeatedly shown that there are many benefits to willfully ignoring reality and seeing partners as unrealistically positive (Murray & Holmes, 1993; 1997; Murray, Holmes, & Griffin, 1996a, 1996b). For example, in a longitudinal study, couples who more strongly idealized each other experienced less conflict and greater increases in satisfaction over the course of a year and also came to see themselves more positively, pointing to a reciprocal impact of positive illusions on partners' self-views (Murray et al., 1996b).

THEORIES, BELIEFS, AND EXPECTATIONS ABOUT RELATIONSHIPS

Our understanding of a relationship partner's actions is also shaped by our broader expectations about relationships in general. It turns out there is substantial consensus about what makes a relationship (Fehr & Russell, 1991). Trust, caring, honesty, and respect are among the most central qualities of a romantic relationship, whereas dependency, euphoria, and uncertainty are among the least central (Fehr, 1988). Different people emphasize the importance of different relationship qualities, and for some, these prioritized qualities become chronically accessible, enabling them to make automatic judgments about others' fit with their priorities (Fletcher, Rosanowski, & Fitness, 1994). For example, someone who strongly believes passion is the key to romantic relationships would respond more quickly to the word "passion" as a characteristic of a particular relationship, relative to their speed when responding to "honesty." As we discussed in the "Seeking Relationships" section, the match between values (as measured by chronic accessibility as well as self-report scales) and perceptions of partners predicts relationship satisfaction (Fletcher & Kininmonth, 1992; Fletcher et al., 1999).

In addition to beliefs about what constitutes a good relationship, individuals have beliefs about how relationships tend to progress or fail. Knee (1998) has posited the existence of two implicit theories, one or both of which may be held by any given individual. *Destiny beliefs* describe a tendency to believe that two people are, from the outset, either compatible or not. *Growth beliefs* describe a tendency to believe that difficulties in a relationship can be overcome. These beliefs affect responses to conflict, such that people with strong growth beliefs use more positive coping strategies (Knee, 1998; Knee, Nanayakkara, Vietor, Neighbors, Patrick, 2001; see also Knee, Patrick, & Lonsbary, 2003). In an interesting extension of these ideas, Rudman and Heppen (2003) showed that women who implicitly endorse traditional romantic fantasies, as measured by Implicit Association Test (IAT) associations between "relationship partner" and symbols like "Prince Charming," have lower desire for power and lower educational goals. People's beliefs about their own relationship history are also vulnerable to theories: Although data suggest otherwise, people tend to believe they love their partners more now than they used to, and that although they were dissatisfied in the past, things are improving now—a belief associated with increased optimism about the future of the relationship (Karney & Coombs, 2000; Karney & Frye, 2002; Sprecher, 1999). These retrospective theories appear to serve a relationship-maintaining function, in that they provide people with the feeling that their relationships are always improving.

Thus, broad theories about the nature of relationships can affect satisfaction and responses to conflict. Research on *behavioral confirmation processes* sheds light on the mechanisms underlying the effect of these theories and other kinds of important expectations on relationships. In a classic study (Snyder, Tanke, & Berscheid, 1977), male participants were led to believe that the female participant with whom they would speak on the phone was attractive or unattractive. When they believed that the woman was physically attractive, men were more interesting, humorous, and socially adept than their counterparts; the women who spoke to those men consequently behaved more likably and sociably than did the women whose partners were led to believe that they were unattractive. This study elegantly demonstrates the importance of expectations in relationship behavior: What people expect from their romantic partners is often what they get. Indeed, social cognitive studies have shown that interpersonal expectations guide attention, organize and bias interpretations and memory, and go on to determine behavior (Baldwin, 1992; Berk & Andersen, 2000; Downey & Feldman, 1996; Fincham, Garnier, Gano-Phillips, & Osborne, 1995; Pierce & Lydon, 1998; Snyder & Swann, 1978).

Interpersonal expectations can take the form of if–then contingencies, such as "if I say something critical, then my partner will be defensive" (Baldwin, 1992; Fehr, 2004). These contingencies have been measured implicitly as well as explicitly, showing that individuals have automatic associations between certain interpersonal triggers (if) and likely partner responses (then), and that these automatic associations shape important outcomes for the self and the relationship (e.g., Baldwin et al., 1993; Fehr, 2004; Mikulincer, 1998).

INDIVIDUAL DIFFERENCES IN RELATIONSHIP COGNITION: REJECTION SENSITIVITY, SELF-ESTEEM, ATTACHMENT, AND GOAL ORIENTATIONS

Relationship cognitions—thoughts, expectations, and beliefs about relationships—are, like any thought process, subject to individual differences. From the perspective of a relationship researcher, the most important differences are in the ways people relate to others and in the ways they *expect* to relate to others. To navigate the social world, one must be able to predict others' reactions: If I laugh at what she said, will she get angry, or laugh too? If I ask him to go to the movie with me, will he reject me, or tell me he's been too shy to make the first move?

One important individual difference in these expectations is *rejection sensitivity*, the dispositional tendency to expect rejection, to perceive rejection in ambiguous situations, and to overreact to rejection (Downey & Feldman, 1996). This hypervigilance for signs of rejection is often destructive and self-sustaining. For example, Downey and her colleagues demonstrated that women's rejection sensitivity predicted women's negative behavior in

interactions and, in turn, predicted anger on the part of their male partners (Downey, Freitas, Michaelis, & Khouri, 1998; see Romero-Canyas et al., 2010, for review). For highly rejection-sensitive women, the concept of rejection appears to automatically activate feelings of hostility: In laboratory studies, highly rejection-sensitive women's reaction times to hostile words (e.g., *hit*) were shortened when preceded by a rejection word (e.g., *abandon*; Ayduk, Downey, Testa, Yen, & Shoda, 1999). This bias to perceive rejection and react negatively to it has many deleterious effects on relationships, including higher rates of breakup (Downey et al., 1998).

A sensitivity to rejection is common among individuals with low self-esteem, another important individual difference in interpersonal cognition (Murray & Holmes, 2009). People with low self-esteem see themselves as inferior to their partners (Murray et al., 2005), and project these self-doubts onto their partners, dramatically underestimating how much their partners care about them (Murray, Holmes, & Griffin, 2000; Murray, Holmes, MacDonald, & Ellsworth, 1998). Whereas high self-esteem leads people to feel generally secure in their relationships, lower self-esteem brings with it a host of insecurities. Like rejection-sensitive people, individuals with low self-esteem are vigilant for signs of rejection and tend to exaggerate their significance. In one study, low self-esteem individuals (but not high self-esteem individuals) interpreted the possibility that their partner perceived a problem in their relationship as evidence that his or her affection was dwindling (Murray, Rose, Bellavia, Holmes, & Kusche, 2002). Higher self-esteem is associated with feeling unconditionally loved by one's partner, whereas the love felt by those with lower self-esteem appears contingent on one's successes and failures and on how things are going in the relationship (Baldwin & Sinclair, 1996: DeHart, Pelham, & Murray, 2004). For example, in one study, low self-esteem individuals primed with success- or failure-related words (e.g., *win* vs. *lose*) responded contingently to acceptance- and rejection-related words (e.g., *cherished* vs. *ridiculed*), with failure words facilitating faster reaction times to rejection words. Indeed, when they feel rejected, people with low self-esteem tend to blame themselves, which leads them to experience increased stress and derogate their rejecter (Ford & Collins, 2010).

According to sociometer theory, self-esteem is not a stable personality variable, but rather is a fluctuating gauge of one's social inclusion (Leary, Tambor, Terdal, & Downs, 1995). Indeed, research has demonstrated the existence of a state element to self-esteem, driven by others' appraisals of one's worth: Negative appraisals reduce state self-esteem, whereas positive appraisals increase it (Leary, Haupt, Strausser, & Chokel, 1998). When people feel well regarded by their partners, they subsequently report increases in state self-esteem (Murray, Griffin, Rose, & Bellavia, 2003a). Of course, if self-esteem is a sociometer, it may be quite stable across time, if social conditions do not change. Because the negative expectations and interpretations that come from low self-esteem can in some cases damage relationships, self-esteem can, like rejection sensitivity, elicit self-fulfilling prophecies and encourage its own stability across time (Murray, Bellavia, Rose, & Griffin, 2003).

Another important individual difference in interpersonal cognition is rooted in early relationships with caregivers. According to attachment theory, these early expectations last through adulthood, developing into generalized models of the self and other people (Ainsworth, Blehar, Waters, & Wall, 1978; Bowlby, 1982). Children learn at a young age whether caregivers (attachment figures) can be counted on to be responsive when they need reassurance (Bowlby, 1982), and the result of these early experiences is an attachment "style" that persists into adulthood. This chronic set of expectations and beliefs influences all their relationships, particularly, according to Hazan and Shaver (1987), relationships with romantic partners.

Although originally described as a three-category system, many attachment theorists now speak in terms of a theoretically based, two-dimensional model (Bartholomew & Horowitz, 1991; Griffin & Bartholomew, 1994). In this model, children, using their early experiences with caregivers, create internal representations or "working models" of the self and others: The model of self indicates the extent to which the self is worthy, whereas the model of other indicates the extent to which others are responsive. Put together, they create an attachment style representing one's expectations that a partner will be available and responsive when one is in need of support. When one's models of self and other are both positive, the result is a relationship style characterized by security and trust. The partner is seen as a safe haven in times of threat, to which one can return for protection, and also as a secure base that promotes autonomy and exploration under normal circumstances (Collins & Feeney, 2000; Feeney & Collins, 2004; Feeney, 2004). People with a negative model of others tend to mistrust relationship partners, whereas people with a negative model of self are more likely to worry about abandonment; people with negative self and other models both mistrust others and worry about abandonment. Recent work has supported the existence of the affective components of these models: Participants with evidence of secure attachment styles showed more positive implicit evaluations of their romantic partners than did those with less secure styles (Zayas & Shoda, 2005). (It should be noted, however, that other research using the affective priming paradigm found evidence of global positive implicit evaluations of significant others and no attachment-related individual differences; Banse, 1999).

Mikulincer and Shaver (2007b) describe daily functioning of the attachment system as having three components. First, individuals monitor the environment for threat (e.g., stress at the office) and activate the attachment system (Mikulincer, Birnbaum, Woddis, & Nachmias, 2000). Supporting this component of the model, individuals have been shown to exhibit faster automatic approach tendencies to attachment figures (vs. acquaintances) following distress primes (vs. control primes), suggesting that turning to attachment figures in response to threat is an automatic tendency (Dewitte, De Houwer, Buysse, & Koster, 2008). This pattern seems to be strongest for participants high in attachment anxiety and weakest for participants high in attachment avoidance, suggesting further that individual differences exist even in these automatic tendencies (Dewitte et al., 2008). Indeed, in other work, individual differences in attachment anxiety have been found to moderate early-stage attentional processing of threatening emotional expressions such as anger (Dewitte & De Houwer, 2008b), as well as responses on a Stroop task including emotional attachment-related words such as *intimate* and *loss* (Edelstein & Gillath, 2008). Interestingly, in this latter work, these effects were weakened under cognitive load, suggesting that inhibiting attention to attachment-related emotional stimuli is resource demanding (Edelstein & Gillath, 2008).

In the second component of the attachment system (Mikulincer & Shaver, 2007b), individuals are thought to assess the availability and responsiveness of attachment figures (e.g., whether or not a given partner is in the mood to listen to complaints about work), which can produce state variations in individuals' sense of attachment security. The benefits of feeling secure have been explored theoretically as well as demonstrated empirically (see Feeney & Collins, 2004; Feeney & Thrush, 2010). For example, priming attachment security using stimuli like images of mother and child or the name of a security-enhancing attachment figure has increased feelings of communion with others (Bartz & Lydon, 2004), reduced accessibility of trauma-related thoughts in people with post-traumatic stress disorder symptoms, increased compassion and willingness to help other people, and reduced intergroup derogation (Mikulincer & Shaver, 2001; Mikulincer, Shaver, Gillath, & Nitzberg, 2005; Mikulincer, Shaver, & Horesh, 2006; see Mikulincer & Shaver, 2007b, for a review). Complementing this research demonstrating that activating security promotes various positive behaviors is research demonstrating that activating relationship insecurities can negatively direct goal pursuit (Cavallo, Fitzsimons, & Holmes, 2009, 2010). For example, in several studies, participants whose trust in their romantic partner's commitment had been shaken by an experimental manipulation made more cautious financial investments and exhibited heightened accessibility of safety-oriented motivations.

In the third component of the attachment system (Mikulincer & Shaver, 2007b), individuals assess the viability of seeking proximity to the attachment figure as a coping strategy—an assessment influenced by attachment style. People with negative self models tend to hyperactivate their desire to be close to a partner, whereas people with negative other models tend to deactivate the attachment system, preferring to rely on themselves and suppress their needs for closeness. For example, in several studies, when participants were primed with threat words (*failure* or *separation*), most showed higher accessibility of representations of their attachment figures, suggesting that for most people, the attachment system operates automatically in response to threat (Mikulincer, Gillath, & Shaver, 2002). However, avoidant individuals (those with a negative model of others) primed with the word *separation* did not activate representations of attachment figures (Mikulincer et al., 2002). In related work, participants who were high in attachment avoidance showed positive implicit associations between attachment figures and concepts related to distance goals (Dewitte & De Houwer, 2008b).

Another individual difference in interpersonal cognition relates to goal orientations. Goals can be conceived of in terms of approaching a positive outcome or avoiding a negative outcome (Carver & White, 1994; Elliot & Covington, 2001; Gray, 1990). For example, people can pursue a goal to establish a close relationship with approach goals

(e.g., to disclose more, to seek opportunities for closeness) or avoidance goals (e.g., to avoid embarrassment, to minimize conflict; Gable, 2006). These goal orientations have important implications for interpersonal cognition, shaping attention and memory for positive and negative relationship events (Gable & Poore, 2008; Impett, Gable, & Peplau, 2005; Impett et al., 2010). Goals can also be conceived of in terms of *regulatory focus*, the preventive versus promotive orientation individuals take toward goals (Higgins, 1997). A prevention focus is oriented toward the attainment of ought goals (responsibilities, duties), whereas a promotion focus is oriented toward the attainment of ideal goals (hopes, aspirations). Because regulatory focus theory is grounded in self-discrepancy theory, which posits that ideal and ought goals grow out of early child–caretaker interactions (Higgins, 1987), it is fundamentally an interpersonal theory of cognition. In addition, research has examined how individual differences in regulatory focus predict relationship outcomes. For example, individuals who are relatively more promotion focused (vs. relatively more prevention focused) pay more attention to alternatives and see them more positively (Finkel, Molden, Johnson, & Eastwick, 2009).

THE RELATIONAL SELF: THE INTERSECTION OF SELF AND OTHER

In the previous sections, we have described research on how people see and think about themselves (e.g., whether they feel worthy of love) and their partners (e.g., whether they make positive or negative attributions about their partners' intentions). In many relationships, though, *self* is inextricable from *other*. Most social psychologists believe that the person and situation must be examined together, but this idea has particular importance in the interpersonal cognition literature. A number of researchers have built their theories on the cognitive interdependence of self and other (Andersen & Cole, 1990; Baldwin, 1992; Chen, Boucher, & Tapias, 2006; Markus & Cross, 1990). These theories state, implicitly or explicitly, that to understand an individual, you must understand the partner, and vice versa, because the two are intricately linked within the mind of the individual. Cognitive processes are described as inherently interpersonal, consisting of complex links between the self and other person, which cannot be meaningfully broken down into component parts. As such, these theories challenge the utility of studying cognitive processes separately from studying interpersonal processes.

In one such model, *relational schema theory*, people create mental representations of their relationships with significant others, which then influence their relationships with others and their sense of self (Baldwin, 1992). A *relational schema* represents a pattern of regularities established over repeated interactions with a partner. It includes an interpersonal script for a regular pattern of interaction with that person, a schema for how the self is experienced in the context of that relationship, and a schema for the other person. Baldwin (1992) gives the example of a student who, in repeated interactions with her advisor, is praised for her work. The student will learn that her actions are likely to be met with approval (interpersonal script), that her advisor is positive (other-schema), and that she is a competent student (self-schema).

In this model, the other-schema is described as rich, complex, and multifaceted, including cognitive, affective, and motivational components. For example, people appear to store information about basic relationship types into their mental representations of others (Fiske, Haslam, & Fiske, 1991), and about how those others connect to individuals' active goals; they are likelier to make memory errors among close others who are all instrumental for achievement, for example, than they are to confuse a close other who assists achievement with one who does not (Fitzsimons & Shah, 2009). Representations of others also contain emotional information. In one early study, Baldwin, Carrell, and Lopez (1990) subliminally primed Catholics with a disapproving face: either that of the Pope or an unfamiliar person. The Pope prime lowered practicing Catholics' self-ratings, whereas the unfamiliar person's disapproval had no effect, a finding the authors interpreted as indicating that the image of the Pope had activated a relational schema for a disapproving authority figure. In a subsequent study, subliminal exposure to the name of a critical versus accepting significant other affected participants' self-views and mood, such that participants felt more negative after subliminal exposure to a critical other, and more positive after subliminal exposure to an accepting other (Baldwin, 1994). Baldwin and colleagues have also adapted their theory of relational schemas to understand individual differences in attachment to romantic partners. When presented with risky relationship contexts (e.g., *If I depend on my partner, then my partner will…*), secure individuals were quicker to respond to words representing positive interpersonal outcomes on a lexical decision task, whereas avoidantly attached individuals were quicker to respond to negative outcome words (Baldwin, Fehr, Keedian, Seidel, & Thomson, 1993).

Taking a different approach to testing the notion that mental representations of others include affective components, a number of researchers have developed and employed unobtrusive measures of affect toward significant others, adapting versions of implicit association tasks, affect misattribution paradigms, and affective priming tasks (e.g., Banse, 1999; Banse & Kowalick, 2007; Imhoff & Banse, 2011; Lebel & Campbell, 2009; Murray, Holmes, & Pinkus, 2010). Although a variety of relationship outcomes are associated with the different measures, it appears safe to conclude that implicitly measured affect is a good predictor of relationship well-being, under both normal and stressful conditions, and appears to have unique predictive ability compared with explicit measures of relationship affect.

Andersen and her colleagues have examined the links between mental representations of self and other by investigating the phenomenon of transference. *Transference* is a term originally used by Freud to signify the process by which characteristics of a significant childhood figure were superimposed onto psychoanalysts (Freud, 1912/1958, 1937/1959). The construct was adopted by Andersen and Cole (1990) to refer to a normative information processing phenomenon whereby mental representations of significant others are stored as categories and then applied in novel relationship contexts (e.g., *this is a person like my mother*). In this research program, transference is usually manipulated by presenting a participant with a new individual who shares several traits or preferences with a previously described significant other. Participants who are experiencing transference tend to assume the new person shares additional features with their significant other and to respond—affectively, motivationally, and behaviorally—to the new person in a similar way as they would to the significant other (Andersen & Baum, 1994; Andersen, Reznik, & Manzella, 1996). Transference occurs without conscious recognition of similarity to a significant other, as demonstrated in a study in which subliminally presented features of a significant other were transferred to a novel person (Glassman & Andersen, 1999; Gunaydin et al., 2012). The self-concept also tends to change to match the self that one becomes with that significant other (Hinkley & Andersen, 1996), reflecting the self–other links in memory.

Cognitive links between self and other have also been shown to affect behavior, both inside and outside of the relationship. Activation of the mental representations of significant others can lead people to behave as though they were with those others (Andersen et al., 1996; Fitzsimons & Bargh, 2003; Shah, 2003). Reminding people of their significant others, through subtle priming procedures, can produce behavior in line with goals pursued in those relationships. These behavioral priming findings support "relational self" models' assertion that strong links exist in memory between representations of the self and of close others (Baldwin, 1992; Chen et al., 2006). (This work is described in more detail in the "Everyday Interdependence" section of this chapter.)

Other theorists have suggested that in addition to links between self and other in memory, particularly close others can become incorporated directly into the self-concept. Research has shown that the extent of one's self-concept is increased by a new relationship and is confused or diminished by breakup (Aron, Paris, & Aron, 1995; Lewandowski, Aron, Bassis, & Kunak, 2006; Slotter, Gardner, & Finkel, 2010). According to the *self-expansion model*, this is a motivated process in which the resources, perspectives, and identities of another person are treated as one's own, thereby increasing self-efficacy in pursuit of goals (Aron, Ketay, Riela, & Aron, 2008). Supporting the model, people in close relationships are slower to make "me/not me" distinctions when the rated traits differed between themselves and their spouses, versus traits that were similar for both partners, suggesting the existence of self–other confusion (Aron, Aron, Tudor, & Nelson, 1991; Mashek, Aron, & Boncimino, 2003).

Maintaining Relationships

Two of the major tasks of interpersonal cognition, therefore, are to prepare the individual to begin a new relationship and then to understand the ongoing relationship—to develop a useful set of knowledge about the partner that helps to promote predictable, satisfying interactions. Once individuals are in these relationships, of course, knowledge about the partner alone does not produce stability; there is a substantial bit of work still to be done. In this section, we discuss the interpersonal cognitions that relate to the maintenance of ongoing close relationships.

We divide this discussion into two sections. In the first, we discuss what we call *everyday interdependence*; these are the processes that organically arise from being embedded in intimate contexts with others. These cognitions occur whether one wants a good relationship or not; they are the automatic processes that typify the entangled, intermeshed, reciprocal, and dynamic relations that occur in everyday relationships. For example, individuals tend to fall into automatic patterns within ongoing relationships, developing highly routinized ways of thinking and acting with the partner. This occurs regardless of and sometimes despite individuals' interest in maintaining positive relationships.

In the second section, we discuss what we call *strategic maintenance*; these are the processes that arise from individuals' motivation to protect their close relationships. They are not mere accidents of being close with others; they occur because individuals are motivated to have positive relationships with others. For example, individuals in committed long-term romantic relationships tend to devalue alternatives to those relationships. This occurs because of individuals' interest in maintain positive relationships.

EVERYDAY INTERDEPENDENCE

Close relationships—those with family, romantic partners, friends, and colleagues—are characterized by the existence of interdependence (mutual influence) among relationship partners. Close relationship partners tend to have a large amount of such influence; as part of a relationship, your choices and actions are not purely reflections of your own preferences. Instead, they are determined by some complex combination of your preferences and your partner's preferences, and the interaction of innumerable variables related to you, your partner, and your relationship.

The most well-established and influential model of these complex patterns of influence is *interdependence theory*. *Interdependence* is defined as "the process by which interacting persons influence one another's experiences" (Rusbult & van Lange, 2003, p. 564). According to interdependence theory (Kelley et al., 2003; Kelley & Thibaut, 1978; Rusbult & van Lange, 2003), close relationships vary in their degree of interdependence along several dimensions: (1) the extent to which their outcomes are mutually determined; (2) the extent to which dependence is equal for both partners; (3) the extent to which dependence is joint versus controlled by only one partner. These dimensions explain the extent and direction of the influence between partners, addressing questions like: How much do partners affect each other? Is one partner more influential than the other?

Interdependence theory is a theory of behavior: It predicts the situations in which individuals *transform their motivation* and engage in other-oriented behavior. It also makes a deeply important point about cognition, by emphasizing that all thoughts, feelings, and goals are shaped by the interpersonal situation in which the individual thinker is embedded. Research directly informed by interdependence theory has examined interdependence effects on cognitive variables like self-concept clarity (Luchies, Finkel, McNulty, & Kumashiro, 2010), perspective taking (Arriaga & Rusbult, 1998), and expectations (Holmes, 2002). The reach of the theory also extends beyond direct tests of the tenets of the model; many relationships scholars have used the essential notion of interdependence to develop new ideas about interpersonal cognition. Some of this work is described in the sections below.

Everyday Interdependence and Cognition

Our sense of who we are as individuals is informed by our partnership with others. As relationships become well established over time, the psychological space separating two relationship partners becomes smaller, such that the two are tightly connected, and perhaps even overlapping (Aron, Aron, & Smollan, 1992; Aron, Aron, Tudor, & Nelson, 1991). (See "The Relational Self: The Intersection between Self and Other" for more on this and related models.) Cognitive interdependence—this sense that our selves are inextricably linked or overlapping—is shaped by both situational and dispositional factors as well as general and relationship-specific processes. Closer, longer lasting, and more committed relationship partners see themselves as more interdependent (Agnew, van Lange, Rusbult, & Langston, 1998; Aron & Fraley, 1999), and people with situationally primed interdependent mindsets show greater interdependence in thought and action (e.g., Gardner et al., 2002). For example, when participants in one study were primed to see themselves as interdependent (with words like "we" and "together"), they felt greater self-confidence when close others were salient (Gabriel, Renaud, & Tippin, 2007). As another example, when participants were forced to use words like "we" and "us" to describe themselves and another participant, they reported greater closeness and intimacy with that participant (Fitzsimons & Kay, 2004). Similarly, when participants were primed with interdependence, they chose to sit closer to another participant (Holland et al., 2004).

Cognitive interdependence is also governed by chronic individual differences in the tendency to see ourselves in this light. Cross-cultural researchers have demonstrated that members of some cultures tend to define themselves more readily in terms of their groups, social roles, and close relationships (Markus & Kitayama, 1991) and that this tendency has important consequences for even basic cognitive processes (Nisbett, Peng, Choi, & Norenzayan, 2001). Within Western cultures, "relational-interdependent self-construal," or the tendency to define oneself in terms of close relationships in particular (as opposed to groups; Cross, Bacon, & Morris, 2000), has also been shown to influence basic views about the self and the organization of social information in memory (Cross, Gore, & Morris, 2003; Cross, Morris, & Gore, 2002). For example, individuals with a relational-interdependent self-construal have a heightened tendency to think about and organize their memories of others in terms of those others' relationships and to connect the self with a more tightly organized network of relational information in memory (Cross et al., 2002).

Being part of an interdependent relationship also changes well-established social comparison effects. As demonstrated by research on the self-evaluative maintenance (SEM) model (Tesser, 1988), individuals tend to feel better after comparing themselves to poor performers, and worse after comparing themselves to better performers (e.g., Aspinwall & Taylor, 1993; Tesser, 1988; Wood, 1989). Those robust effects often disappear in close relationships, but exactly what does happen is less clear. Some studies have shown that the usual SEM pattern is dampened, whereas others show reversals. For example, in one program of studies, relationship partners showed inconsistent and weaker preferences to outperform close others in important domains (Beach et al., 1998). In another set of studies, individuals responded more positively when their romantic partners outperformed them in self-relevant domains (Lockwood, Dolderman, Sadler, & Gerchak, 2004; Pinkus et al., 2008). In studies manipulating self-construal, individuals primed with interdependence showed a reversed SEM pattern, predicting close others would perform better than strangers in important domains (Gardner et al., 2002).

Being part of an interdependent relationship also alters basic attributional processes, with individuals being less likely to make dispositional attributions toward their relationship partners, viewing others' behaviors much as they tend to view their own behaviors, and not like they tend to view strangers' behaviors (Nisbett, Caputo, Legant, & Maracek, 1973; Prentice, 1990). For example, people were likelier to make situational attributions if they were judging friends they had known for longer periods of time, and likelier to make dispositional attributions if they were judging friends they had known for shorter periods of time (Nisbett et al., 1973).

Finally, being part of an interdependent relationship determines attitudes and beliefs not just about members of the relationship but also about the rest of the social world. Together, relationship partners form a shared reality, the construction of an objective reality from two convergent, subjective viewpoints (Hardin & Conley, 2001; Hardin & Higgins, 1996). According to *shared reality theory*, people are motivated to bring their view of the world into alignment with the views of specific others, partly to help fulfill belongingness needs (Clark & Kashima, 2007; Conley, Calhoun, Evett, & Devine, 2001; Echterhoff, Higgins, & Groll, 2005; Echterhoff, Higgins, & Levine, 2009; Hardin & Higgins, 1996). For example, when interacting with an African American confederate, European American participants showed less implicit prejudice toward African Americans, suggesting they may have unconsciously shifted their attitudes to promote a harmonious social interaction (Lowery, Hardin, & Sinclair, 2001). Indeed, when interacting with a likeable experimenter, participants showed increased "social tuning," moving toward the other's egalitarian views to a greater extent than participants interacting with a dislikeable experimenter (Sinclair, Lowery, Hardin, & Colangelo, 2005), providing evidence for the role of affiliative motivation in producing similar attitudes (also see Davis & Rusbult, 2001).

Thus, simply being in a relationship leads to a myriad of cognitive effects on the members of the relationship. Mere interdependence with others also influences how individuals are seen by others. Supporting their suggestion that relationships are a "natural category" in social perception (also see Fiske et al., 1991; Fiske, 1992), Sedikedes, Olsen, and Reis (1993) demonstrated that people encode relationship information into their basic representation of individuals in memory, making "within-couple" confusions for married couples and clustering their memories around married couple categories. Cross et al. (2003) have shown that this tendency is even stronger among individuals high in relational-interdependent self-construal, who tend to see both themselves and the social world in terms of interdependent links among close relationship partners.

Everyday Interdependence and Behavior

Interdependence does not exist only in the minds of individuals; individuals' behaviors are also deeply affected by close relationship partners. At work, individuals may have to pick up a coworker's slack when he has an off day, or put aside a project they're excited about to focus on one the boss deems urgent. At home, they may have to eat unhealthy takeout instead of the healthy home-cooked meal they were expecting their spouse to prepare, and spend the evening handwriting Valentine's Day cards for their child's preschool class instead of reading a novel they hoped to finish. All day long, every day, individuals adjust their actions and preferences to coordinate with others. Even if maintaining a positive relationship with the other is not a priority, it is difficult to disentangle oneself from the complex web of interdependence between self and other in a typical relationship. In this section, we present recent research on behavioral interdependence, broadly construed. We highlight social cognition and self-regulation research examining how the presence of others in the environment shapes self-regulation and goal-directed behavior (Fitzsimons & Finkel, 2010).

How the Presence of Others Can Automatically Direct Behavior

As noted in the "Understanding Relationships" section of this chapter, research on the relational self (e.g., Andersen & Cole, 1990, Baldwin, 1992) and attachment theory (e.g., Mikulincer & Shaver, 2007a) has emphasized that individuals fall into automated routines within close relationships. Individuals tend to repeatedly engage in the same kinds of thoughts, feelings, and behaviors with given partners, and over time, develop strong associations between these specific partners and these thoughts, feelings, and behaviors. Research demonstrating that behavior could be automatically guided by the operation of nonconscious goals (Bargh, 1990; Chartrand & Bargh, 1996; Bargh et al., 2001) inspired relationships researchers to examine the potential behavioral consequences of these relational schemas (Baldwin, 1992).

If goals are represented in these associations between self and other (Read & Miller, 1989; Moretti & Higgins, 1999), then this may indicate a possible route through which partners could automatically affect each other's behavior (Fitzsimons & Bargh, 2003). That is, exposure to specific partners may activate associated goals, which then subsequently shape behavior, without need for conscious awareness or control. Because they are generated from the activation of mental constructs, these processes can occur even in the physical absence of the partner (Andersen, Reznik, & Manzella, 1996; Fitzsimons & Bargh, 2003; Shah, 2003). For example, in one study examining students' academic achievement performance, participants primed with their mothers outperformed control participants, but only if they had earlier spontaneously reported a goal to achieve academically to please their mother. Participants who did not associate their mothers with a goal to achieve did not work any harder or perform any better than unprimed participants, suggesting that the effects were driven by idiosyncratic goal–partner links rather than by an association between the category "mother" and academic achievement behavior.

Partners from close relationships are particularly likely to have this kind of behavioral influence (Shah, 2003). For example, only participants who reported a close relationship with their father (and believed he cared about their achievement) responded to the subliminal primes "father" and "dad" by working harder and performing better on an academic achievement task (Shah, 2003). If participants did not report feeling close with their father, his preferences for their behavior did not significantly shape their performance. (As an aside, the notion that close partners should have stronger behavioral interdependence effects is a good example of a core tenet of interdependence theory borne out by social cognition research.)

Thus, not all partners trigger these effects. Indeed, partners can sometimes trigger seemingly opposite effects: When individuals perceive significant others as controlling, they can react against the goals of those others, automatically doing the opposite of what those others would prefer (Chartrand, Dalton, & G. J. Fitzsimons, 2007). Participants primed with a partner they perceived as controlling reacted against that partner's goals: If the controlling partner wanted them to work hard, they subsequently solved fewer anagrams; if the controlling partner wanted them to have fun, they subsequently solved more anagrams.

In addition, not all individuals are responsive to these kinds of unconscious interpersonal influences. In research by Morrison, Wheeler, and Smeesters (2007), these effects were shown to crucially depend on interpersonal motivation. Participants who were motivated to respond to social cues (i.e., who were high in self-monitoring or the need to belong) showed assimilative behavioral priming effects, behaving in line with a goal that their primed significant other had for them, even if they themselves did not have the goal. Participants who were not as motivated to be responsive to social cues (i.e., those low in self-monitoring or the need to belong) assimilated to the goal only when it was one that they personally valued. Again, just as some partners can elicit opposing effects on behavior, some individuals respond by acting against all partners' wishes: Individuals high in psychological reactance (Brehm, 1966) also responded to primed partners by pursuing goals counter to those partners' wishes (Chartrand et al., 2007).

Relationship insecurities that arise from time to time in most close relationships can also trigger goals and shape behavior, even outside of the relationship context (Cavallo, Fitzsimons, & Holmes, 2009, 2010). In a number of studies, triggering worries about rejection prompted a global shift to a more avoidant style of goal pursuit, in which people focused on avoiding negative outcomes. These interpersonal worries seemed to "spill over" to shape behavior in domains from achievement performance to health decision making. For example, participants who felt temporarily insecure about their romantic partner's feelings performed better on a task with an avoidance frame than an approach frame and had higher accessibility of safety-related constructs. In research on the automatic activation of attachment models, participants subliminally exposed to the name of a significant other from an avoidant (emotionally distant) relationship had higher accessibility of avoidant (distancing) goals than did those exposed to the name of a significant other from a more secure relationship (Gillath et al., 2006), suggesting that attachment working models can lead to the automatic generation of attachment-related motives.

How the Behavior of Others Can Automatically Direct Behavior

Simply being part of a relationship, then, can trigger goal pursuit and shape behavior directed both at the relationship partner and outside of the relationship context, because of spreading activation processes that occur in memory. In addition to these "schema-based" processes, behavioral interdependence also ensues directly from exposure to the behaviors of others. That is, in addition to eliciting effects on behavior through the activation of cognitive relational representations, partners can affect behavior through their own actions, a process that also seems to occur with little conscious awareness or intent. In a number of studies, Aarts and colleagues have demonstrated that simply watching another person pursue a goal can lead an individual to pursue that same goal. In the process of *goal contagion*, observers automatically infer goals underlying others' actions; this inference thereby activates the goals, which then go on to shape the observers' behavior (Aarts, Gollwitzer, & Hassin, 2004; Dik & Aarts, 2007). For example, male participants who read a story in which the character's actions implied he was pursuing a goal to have casual sex ingratiated themselves to another female student more so than did control participants. When the character appeared to be trying very hard to achieve the goal, the contagion effect was stronger (Dik & Aarts, 2007). When the other person appeared to have successfully completed the goal, the contagion effect disappeared, suggesting that the observer caught and satiated the goal vicariously, through the other's actions (McCulloch, Fitzsimons, Chua, & Albarracin, 2011).

Although studies of goal contagion have typically involved hypothetical actors and strangers, we discuss them here because we believe that these processes likely occur, and probably to a greater extent, with close relationship partners. Given that close partners, whether friends, family, or coworkers, frequently observe each other's behavior, there are many opportunities for them to infer and catch each other's goals. This tendency may be likeliest among low-power partners (Laurin et al., 2012), who seek to please their partners by taking on their interests and goal pursuits. Of course, the high degree of interdependence in close relationships enhances the possibility not only for mutual influence but also for goal conflict. Indeed, a recent paper demonstrated that individuals actively and automatically *shield* their pursuit of several "fundamental" goals (for positive self-regard, autonomy, and distinctiveness) from the implicit influence of others, failing to catch goals from others when those goals would interfere with their own fundamental needs (Leander, Chartrand, & Shah, 2011).

Behavioral Interdependence and Self-Control

As suggested by Leander et al. work, meshing our behaviors with others is not always conflict free. Anyone who has ever had an in-law stay for an extended visit knows that interdependence can take effort to coordinate. According to research on *high maintenance interactions* (Finkel et al., 2006), when

social coordination goes smoothly—that is, when both partners can easily and efficiently align their actions with each other—individuals use less self-regulation. When, in contrast, individuals find that coordinating themselves with someone else requires effort, this high maintenance style of interaction drains people and leaves them less able to dedicate self-regulatory resources to subsequent tasks (Dalton, Chartrand, & Finkel, 2010; Finkel et al., 2006). Thus, behavioral interdependence tends to require self-regulatory resources. (Indeed, just interacting with women can deplete men's self-regulatory resources; Karremans, Verwijmeren, Pronk, & Reitsma, 2009.) Interestingly, people who practice this interdependence more often may develop stronger self-regulatory skills. In one set of studies, participants high in interdependent self-construal were found to have a buffer against the well-established depleting effects of exerting self-control (Seeley & Gardner, 2003), suggesting that interdependent individuals' practice at behavioral interdependence may make them better self-regulators overall.

Interdependence with others also affects how much effort people put into their specific goals. In some cases, close partners can act as substitutes for the self's own effort, undermining motivation. For example, when individuals think about how close others are helpful with an ongoing goal, they tend to "outsource" their progress to those others, and work less hard themselves (Fitzsimons & Finkel, 2011). When individuals think about how close others are harmful to an ongoing goal, they tend to compensate for that obstruction and work harder (Carswell, Finkel, Fitzsimons, & Lambert, 2012). These balancing processes suggest the existence of a shared or transactive self-regulation system (Fitzsimons, vanDellen, & Finkel, 2012).

Although we suggest that most of these behavioral interdependence effects occur outside of conscious awareness, we also note that individuals do appear to have some sense of whether their partners are helpful or harmful to their goal pursuits. First, Leander and colleagues (2011) showed that when others' goals were directly in conflict with individuals' own important needs, individuals "shielded" themselves from goal contagion effects, suggesting they were aware on some level of their partner's impact on their goals, and that this knowledge operated to influence action on an implicit level.

Second, research on partners' instrumentality for personal goals (Fitzsimons & Shah, 2008, 2009; Fitzsimons & Fishbach, 2010) provides additional evidence that people are aware of how interdependence with others affects their goals. In this work, primed personal goals, such as those for academic achievement and fitness, affected people's reports of closeness to (and tendency to automatically approach) friends, family, and romantic partners, such that people felt closer to others, and approached them more readily, when they perceived them as instrumental for primed goals. This effect tends to disappear when goals drop in motivational priority, such as when people have been led to feel they are making good progress on the goal (Fitzsimons & Fishbach, 2010). Instead of preferring the partners who helped them with the progressed goal, individuals tend to switch allegiances, preferring partners who are instrumental for less advanced goal pursuits. Importantly, the tendency to prefer instrumental others leads to better goal outcomes (Fitzsimons & Shah, 2008). For example, in one study, students who showed automatic evaluative preferences for instrumental others went on to score better on their midterm examinations than students who did not show these preferences. Having an instrumental social network may thus produce better goal outcomes and higher quality relationships. Indeed, research on the Michelangelo phenomenon has demonstrated that relationship partners who help each other succeed with ideal-self goals enjoy more satisfying relationships in the long run (Drigotas, Rusbult, Wieselquist, & Whitton, 1999; for a review, see Rusbult, Finkel, & Kumashiro, 2009). All of these programs of research highlight the reciprocal influence of goal pursuit and related self-regulatory processes with interpersonal relationships (for review, see Finkel & Fitzsimons, 2010; Fitzsimons & Finkel, 2010a, 2010b; Luchies et al., 2011).

Conclusions on Everyday Interdependence

Simply being part of a relationship can alter the way people think, feel, and act, even in contexts that appear to have little to do with relationships. These effects often happen without people's conscious plans or intentions; they arise merely from the existence of interdependent ties to others. Thus, to understand individual cognition, it is essential to include the broader interpersonal, social, and cultural context. Indeed, in the *social baseline model*, Coan (2008) argues that the world is more naturally experienced as part of a relationship, rather than alone. In empirical work on this model, individuals show less neural regulation in response to threat when they are with another person than when they are alone (Coan et al., 2006); because this effect is so strong and does not appear to require conditioning, Coan (2008) argues that relying on close others is the brain's first and most basic response to threat. According to this model, a truly social cognition is the default.

STRATEGIC MAINTENANCE

In addition to the interdependence processes that emerge organically from the meshing of two lives into one relationship, there are a whole set of other interdependence processes that are less incidental and more intentional. Individuals often seek to protect and maintain their relationships with others. These motives, like those to seek and establish relationships with others, have important effects on social cognitive and perceptual processes. Most of the research done on strategic maintenance examines the romantic relationship context in particular, but some of the same processes play out in families, friendships, and coworker relationships.

The importance of *maintaining* relationships can be perhaps best understood by observing how people react to the threat of *losing* relationships. Rejection and ostracism are extremely aversive experiences; social exclusion leads to neurologic and physical responses akin to the experience of physical pain (Eisenberger, Lieberman, & Williams, 2003; MacDonald & Leary, 2005). Rejection and social exclusion also elicit a wide range of cognitive and behavioral responses, some apparently oriented toward reestablishing social connection, others apparently oriented toward protecting a positive self-view (Buckley, Winkel, & Leary, 2004; Maner et al., 2007; Twenge & Campbell, 2003). Although rejection is extremely painful, people still tend to overestimate both the extent and the duration of their emotional reaction to the end of a romantic relationship (Eastwick, Finkel, Krishnamurti, & Loewenstein, 2008b), and many individuals cope with the transition after divorce quite well (Amato, 2010). Still, when marriages end, there is much stress and hurt, and it can be long lasting (Lucas, 2005). Indeed, divorce may even increase risk for physical health problems and predict early death; see Sbarra & Nietert, 2009; Sbarra, Law, & Portley, 2011). The psychological processes that underlie these outcomes—and indeed, the processes that underlie reactions to relationship breakup and divorce more broadly—are not well understood. Social cognitive research could be very useful to the understanding of this important life transition.

Given the dire outcomes that accompany the loss of relationships, people are understandably motivated to maintain positive social relationships. How do they go about pursuing this goal? Within the romantic context, researchers have outlined several methods that all appear to help committed relationship partners maintain their relationships. Each of these strategies or subgoals to the larger goal of maintaining the relationship has its own downstream consequences for social cognition.

One of these main tasks of relationship maintenance is to balance the less-than-perfect reality—the fact that partners make mistakes, are imperfect, and have interests that conflict with ours—with a desire to see our partners positively. To accomplish this task, people ignore and deny negative attributes, or spin them more positively. People develop positive illusions about their partners, seeing them more positively than do others, and even more positively than the partners see themselves (Murray & Holmes, 1997; Murray et al., 1996a, 1996b; see Murray & Holmes, 2011). These idealistic views enhance satisfaction on the part of both the perceiver and the partner (Murray et al., 1996b; but see Swann, 1983; Swann et al., 1989). Indeed, being reminded of the costs of being in a relationship—the ways that relationship partners limit or constrain autonomy—increases individuals' positive implicit evaluations of their partners, an apparently automatic rationalization of the costs of maintaining a close relationship (Murray et al., 2011).

Another relationship maintenance strategy is to protect the relationship from possible rivals who might threaten the relationship. In a series of studies, the experience of jealousy, a gamut of emotional reactions to a situation perceived as threatening to a given relationship (Pfeiffer & Wong, 1989), led individuals to show more "attentional adhesion" to physically attractive same-sex targets, presumably potential rivals to the individuals' romantic or sexual success (Maner et al., 2007). Among people high in self-reported chronic jealousy, manipulations designed to heighten concerns about infidelity led to a number of implicit biases in social perception that appeared to promote attention to attractive members of their own sex. These responses to attractive same-sex others—attending vigilantly at preconscious stages of visual attention, heightened encoding and remembering, negative implicit evaluations—may help individuals protect their relationship from others who could potentially lure away their partner (Maner et al., 2007).

Another route to ensure the continuation of a relationship is to make oneself irreplaceable to the partner (Murray, Aloni et al., 2009a; Murray, Leder et al., 2009c). If an individual depends on his spouse, for example, for the accomplishment of basic daily tasks, the partner can feel safe and secure in knowing that the relationship is unlikely to end; in other words, feeling irreplaceable allows individuals to feel trust in the partner's continued need. A related strategy to increase trust in the partner's continued need is to challenge any worries that the partner is superior; for individuals with low self-esteem, manipulations designed to highlight strengths in the self or flaws in the partner both led to more feelings of security in the relationship (Murray, Aloni et al., 2009a).

This research points to an important motivational quandary faced by relationship partners: They want to maintain the quality of their relationship, but they also need to protect themselves from rejection and pain (Murray, Derrick, Leder, & Holmes, 2008; Murray & Holmes, 2009, 2011; Murray, Holmes, & Collins, 2006). These goals are often incompatible. Behaving self-protectively (e.g., by creating distance, failing to disclose, or overriding positive automatic connective tendencies) is damaging to relationships (Murray, Bellavia, Rose, & Griffin, 2003; Murray et al., 2011). Murray and her colleagues (2006) refer to the process by which individuals manage these competing goals as *risk regulation*: When faced with risky interpersonal situations, individuals must regulate themselves, controlling their thoughts, feelings, and behavior, to balance these needs for self-protection and relationship maintenance. To reconcile the conflict between these two motives, individuals must engage an executive control system; this system produces different outcomes depending on individuals' trust in their partner's regard (Murray et al., 2008). Although all individuals show the activation of both goals on an implicit level, people override these automatic responses; their behaviors are guided by their explicit beliefs about their partner's regard (also see Murray et al., 2011; see Cavallo, Murray, & Holmes, 2012, for review). Recent findings suggest that trust in a partner's regard and responsiveness may function relatively automatically and can be tapped by simple implicit evaluations (Murray et al., 2011). In support of their model of *impulsive trust*, Murray and colleagues (2011) found that positive implicit partner evaluations, as created through subliminal conditioning procedures, predict more approach of the partner under trying circumstances; the role of impulsive trust was found to be strongest when executive control resources were diminished.

In sum, to engage in many relationship maintenance behaviors, which require increasing their own vulnerability, individuals need to feel relatively secure and trusting in their partner's regard and responsiveness. To do so, individuals can guard against rivals and make themselves indispensable, two routes to limit the partner's alternatives to a relationship. These kinds of partner-constraining routes are quite logical means to the goal of maintaining a long-term relationship. Less obviously logical, perhaps, is the strategy to limit one's own alternatives. And yet, a large body of research has convincingly demonstrated that people in long-term relationships often do just that—exert effort to protect themselves from being tempted away. One major threat to relationship maintenance is of course the presence or availability of attractive alternatives to the relationship. How do individuals stay committed to a current partner when faced with the lure of an alternative? This question has inspired a great deal of creative research over the past two decades. According to this research, individuals tend to engage in a wide variety of psychological strategies to guard against the threat, such as ignoring and avoiding attractive alternatives (Lydon et al., 2005; Simpson, Gangestad, & Lerma, 1990), and also devaluing their positive qualities, actually perceiving them as less attractive than outsiders believe them to be (Johnson & Rusbult, 1989; Lydon, 2010; Lydon, Fitzsimons, & Naidoo, 2003). Indeed, individuals in long-term relationships have been shown to avert their early-state attention away from physically attractive opposite-sex targets (Maner, Gailliot, & Miller, 2009; Miller, 1997; Simpson et al., 1990) and to suppress thoughts of alternatives (Gonzaga et al., 2008). When women are particularly fertile (in the days around ovulation), single men find them to be more attractive, whereas men in relationships find them to be less attractive, suggesting that they are devaluing these threatening women (Miller & Maner, 2011). These responses all suggest that people feel threatened by the presence of these alternatives (Lydon et al., 1999). Indeed, long-term relationship partners even see attractive members of the opposite sex as more dangerous—in one study, participants in relationships were likelier to mistake attractive members of the opposite sex (vs. control targets) as holding a gun (and thus, "shooting" them; Plant, Kuntsman, & Maner, 2010).

By avoiding, derogating, and paying little attention to appealing alternative partners, people help themselves maintain long-term romantic relationships. Of course, people don't necessarily prioritize relationship protection in every situation. When people feel that they are being controlled or forced into ignoring attractive alternatives, for example, those alternatives can become *forbidden fruit*: In a series of studies, people who were subtly constrained from attending to attractive alternatives showed more interest in infidelity, increased memory for attractive alternatives, and lower relationship satisfaction (DeWall et al., 2011). Thus, when the social situation limits people's access to attractive others, they may react by seeking those alternatives more strongly, a tendency that would undermine relationship maintenance. In the next section, we will discuss several other important moderators of the tendency to engage in relationship maintenance strategies like devaluing alternatives and making sacrifices.

Variables that Moderate Relationship Maintenance Strategies: Power, Commitment, and Self-Control Power

The concept of power has recently received a great deal of attention from social cognition researchers (see Chapter 28). According to interdependence theory (Thibaut & Kelley, 1959) and the principle of least interest (Waller, 1938), whichever individual has relatively greater interest in maintaining a given relationship has relatively lower psychological power. Research on power in the social psychological and organizational literatures, typically working from a different definition of power (i.e., the capacity to influence others' states; Keltner, Gruenfeld, & Anderson, 2003), has demonstrated that relative power within a dyad produces a wide range of cognitive, affective, self-regulatory, and behavioral outcomes (e.g., Briñol et al., 2007; Galinsky et al., 2006; Smith & Trope, 2006). For example, individuals with low power (vs. those with high power) tend to have more complex and accurate perceptions of others (Fiske, 1993; Galinsky et al., 2006; Woike, 1994) and to behave in a more inhibited and avoidance-guided fashion (Keltner et al., 2003; Smith & Bargh, 2008). There are many reasons for this pattern, including the lower attentional demands on low-power individuals. Of most relevance to the current chapter, low-power individuals are likely more motivated to maintain positive relations with their high-power partners. Because of this increased motivation, the experience of low power leads to a cascade of effects oriented toward relationship maintenance (but see Karremans & Smith, 2010, for an example of how high power can promote some relationship maintenance cognitions).

Commitment

Like low power, strong commitment—the "psychological attachment to, intent to persist in, and long-term orientation toward a romantic relationship" (Finkel et al., 2012; see Arriaga & Agnew, 2001; Rusbult, 1983; Rusbult & van Lange, 1996)—stems from and promotes dependence on the partner, and as such, it generates a wide variety of relationship maintenance–motivated cognitions and actions (Rusbult, Olsen, Davis, & Hannon, 2001). Strongly committed partners (vs. less committed partners) are more likely to inhibit urges to aggress against their partners (Finkel et al., 2011), to be forgiving and constructive (Finkel, Rusbult, Kumashiro, & Hannon, 2002; Rusbult, Verette, Whitney, Slovik, & Lipkus, 1991), to sacrifice their own interests to benefit their partner (van Lange et al., 1997), and to devalue attractive alternatives (Johnson & Rusbult, 1989; Lydon et al., 1999; Miller & Maner, 2010).

Partners who are low in commitment are less likely to engage in these kinds of relationship-protective strategies, or, in other words, are more likely to give in to the temptation to behave selfishly. According to Lydon and colleagues' *commitment calibration model*, whether partners orient toward the relationship or themselves depends on both their commitment and the amount of temptation or threat in the environment. Those low in commitment will fend off a mild threat, but be overcome by more desirable alternatives. Those high in commitment will not bother to defend against a mild threat, but will marshal all needed resources to protect against an extremely desirable, threatening alternative to the relationship (Lydon et al., 1999, 2003, 2005).

Although commitment is typically measured and conceptualized as an explicit construct, studies using implicit methods suggest that commitment's effects on relationship maintenance behaviors may sometimes occur in a relatively unconscious fashion (Etcheverry & Le, 2005). For example, response times to words related to commitment (e.g., commitment, devotion) predicted the willingness to accommodate to a partner (Lydon, Menzies-Toman, Burton, & Bell, 2008), and the speed of implicit associations between the romantic partner and the construct of commitment predicted less aggressive responses to partner provocation (Finkel et al., 2012).

Self-Control

As demonstrated by the work on power and commitment, relationship maintenance is not the default response. If individuals have low dependence on the relationship, they are unlikely to bother engaging in relationship-protective responses. In other words, these moderation findings suggest that relationship maintenance is not an automatic response to being in a relationship (Ritter, Karremans, & van Schie, 2010). Indeed, relationship maintenance behaviors require more than just good intentions—they also require the ability to follow through on those intentions. A number of studies have now shown that both individual and situational variations in self-regulatory resources (broadly construed as the capacity to expend effort toward a goal) predict relationship maintenance cognition and behavior. Individuals high in dispositional or situational self-regulatory resources are more likely to respond constructively to partners' negative actions (Finkel & Campbell, 2001), to derogate attractive alternatives (Ritter et al., 2010), to forgive partners' transgressions (Pronk et al., 2010), to follow through on promises (Peetz & Kammrath, 2012), to engage in sustained acts of relationship maintenance over time (Kammrath & Peetz, 2011), and to resist the urge to engage in sexual infidelity (Gailliot & Baumeister, 2007; Pronk, Karremans, & Wigboldus, 2011).

Conclusion: The Tasks of Interpersonal Cognition

In this chapter, we have reviewed empirical evidence examining how people pursue three goals: to find satisfying social relationships, to understand their relationship partners, and to maintain their relationships over time. We believe that these three goals underlie most of people's interpersonally oriented cognitions, emotions, and behaviors. Of course, not all relationship cognitions are motivated; indeed, we discussed a number of processes that result simply from the mere fact of being part of an ongoing relationship. Nonetheless, we believe that this self-regulatory perspective on relationship cognition is a useful organizing structure. Perhaps most tangibly, this structure emphasizes that in interpersonal relationships, perhaps more than any other domain of social cognition, an individual's cognitions are greatly affected by motivation.

Finally, we hope that the research reviewed in this chapter demonstrates the gains that have been made in creating a truly social cognition. Although social cognition research has tended to focus on the study of social categories and abstract others, there are important lessons to be learned from the study of real-life, ongoing, and important relationships. People spend a much greater percentage of their cognitions on relationships with family, friends, and romantic partners than they do on social group memberships and interactions with strangers. We hope that the field of social cognition eventually comes to reflect that everyday reality, and that our understanding of interpersonal cognition will become as advanced as our understanding of social cognition.

References

Aarts, H., Gollwitzer, P. M., & Hassin, R. R. (2004). Goal contagion: Perceiving is for pursuing. *Journal of Personality and Social Psychology, 87*, 23.

Agnew, C. R., van Lange, P. A. M., Rusbult, C. E., & Langston, C. A. (1998). Cognitive interdependence: Commitment and the mental representation of close relationships. *Journal of Personality and Social Psychology, 74*, 939–954.

Ainsworth, M. D. S., Blehar, M. C., Waters, E., & Wall, S. (1978). *Patterns of attachment: Assessed in the strange situation and at home.* Hillsdale, NJ: Erlbaum.

Amato, P. R. (2010). Research on divorce: Continuing trends and new developments. *Journal of Marriage and Family, 72*, 650–666.

Andersen, S. M., & Baum, A. (1994). Transference in interpersonal relations: Inferences and affect based on significant-other representations. *Journal of Personality, 62*, 459–497.

Andersen, S. M., & Cole, S. W. (1990). "Do I know you?" The role of significant others in general social perception. *Journal of Personality and Social Psychology, 59*, 384–399.

Andersen, S. M., Reznik, I., & Manzella, L. M. (1996). Eliciting facial affect, motivation, and expectancies in transference: Significant-other representations in social relations. *Journal of Personality and Social Psychology, 71*, 1108–1129.

Aron, A., & Fraley, B. (1999). Relationship closeness as including other in the self: Cognitive underpinnings and measures. *Social Cognition, 17*, 140–160.

Aron, A., Aron, E. N., & Smollan, D. (1992). Inclusion of Other in the Self Scale and the structure of interpersonal closeness. *Journal of Personality and Social Psychology, 63*, 596–612.

Aron, A., Aron, E. N., Tudor, M., & Nelson, G. (1991). Close relationships as including other in the self. *Journal of Personality and Social Psychology, 60*, 241–253.

Aron, A., Ketay, S., Riela, S., & Aron, E. N. (2008). How close others construct and reconstruct who we are and how we feel about ourselves. In J. V. Wood, A. Tesser, & J. G. Holmes (Eds.), *The self and social relationships* (pp. 209–229). New York: Psychology Press.

Aron, A., Paris, M., & Aron, E. N. (1995). Falling in love: Prospective studies of self-concept change. *Journal of Personality and Social Psychology, 69*, 1102–1112.

Arriaga, X. B., & Agnew, C. R. (2001). Being committed: Affective, cognitive, and conative components of relationship commitment. *Personality and Social Psychology Bulletin, 27*, 1190–1203.

Arriaga, X. B., & Rusbult, C. E. (1998). Standing in my partner's shoes: Partner perspective-taking and reactions to accommodative dilemmas. *Personality and Social Psychology Bulletin, 9*, 927–948.

Aspinwall, L. G., & Taylor, S. E. (1993). Effects of social comparison direction, threat, and self-esteem on affect, self-evaluation, and expected success. *Journal of Personality and Social Psychology, 64*, 708–772.

Ayduk, O., Downey, G., Testa, A., Yen, Y., & Shoda, Y. (1999). Does rejection elicit hostility in rejection sensitive women? *Social Cognition, 17*, 245–271.

Baldwin, M. W. (1992). Relational schemas and the processing of social information. *Psychological Bulletin, 112*, 461–484.

Baldwin, M. W. (1994). Primed relational schemas as a source of self-evaluative reactions. *Journal of Social and Clinical Psychology, 13*, 380–403.

Baldwin, M. W. (2005). *Interpersonal cognition.* New York: Guilford Press.

Baldwin, M. W., Carrell, S. E., & Lopez, D. F. (1990). Priming relationship schemas: My advisor and the Pope are watching me from the back of my mind. *Journal of Experimental Social Psychology, 26*, 435–454.

Baldwin, M. W., Fehr, B., Keedian, E., Seidel, M., & Thomson, D. W. (1993). An exploration of the relational schemata underlying attachment styles: Self-report and lexical decision approaches. *Personality and Social Psychology Bulletin, 19*, 746–754.

Baldwin, M. W., & Sinclair, L. (1996). Self-esteem and "if…then" contingencies of interpersonal acceptance. *Journal of Personality and Social Psychology, 71*, 1130–1141.

Banse, R. (1999). Automatic evaluation of self and significant others: Affective priming in close relationships. *Journal of Social and Personal Relationships, 16*, 803–821.

Banse, R., & Kowalick, C. (2007). Implicit attitudes toward romantic partners predict well-being in stressful life conditions: Evidence from the antenatal maternity ward. *International Journal of Psychology, 42*, 1–9.

Bargh, J. A. (1990). Auto-motives: Preconscious determinants of social interaction. In E. T. Higgins & R. M. Sorrentino (Eds.), *Handbook of motivation and cognition* (Vol. 2, pp. 93–130). New York: Guilford.

Bargh, J. A., Gollwitzer, P. M., Lee-Chai, A., Barndollar, K., & Trötschel, R. (2001). The automated will: Nonconscious activation and pursuit of behavioral goals. *Journal of Personality and Social Psychology, 81*, 1014–1027.

Bartholomew, K., & Horowitz, L. M. (1991). Attachment styles among young adults: A test of a four-category model. *Journal of Personality and Social Psychology, 61*, 226–244.

Bartz, J. A., Lydon, J. E. (2004). Close relationships and the working self-concept: Implicit and explicit effects of priming attachment on agency and communion. *Personality and Social Psychology Bulletin, 30*, 1389–1401.

Baumeister, R. F., & Leary, M. R. (1995). The need to belong: Desire for interpersonal attachments as a fundamental human motivation. *Psychological Bulletin, 117*, 497–529.

Beach, S. R. H., Tesser, A., Fincham, F. D., Jones, D. J., Johnson, D., & Whitaker, D. J. (1998). Pleasure and pain in doing well, together: An investigation of performance-related affect in close relationships. *Journal of Personality and Social Psychology, 74*, 923–938.

Berk, M. S., & Andersen, S. M. (2000). The impact of past relationships on interpersonal behavior: Behavioral confirmation in the social–cognitive process of transference. *Journal of Personality and Social Psychology, 79*, 546–562.

Berscheid, E. (1994). Interpersonal relationships. *Annual Review of Psychology, 45*, 79–129.

Bissonnette, V. L., Rusbult, C. E., & Kilpatrick, S. D. (1997). Empathic accuracy and marital conflict resolution. In W. Ickes (Ed.), *Empathic accuracy* (pp. 251–281). New York: Guilford Press.

Bowlby, J. (1982). Attachment and loss: Retrospect and prospect. *American Journal of Orthopsychiatry*, *52*, 664–678.

Bradbury, T. N., & Fincham, F. D. (1990). Attributions in marriage: Review and critique. *Psychological Bulletin*, *107*, 3–33.

Bradbury, T. N., & Fincham, F. D. (1992). Attributions and behavior in marital interaction. *Journal of Personality and Social Psychology*, *63*, 613–628.

Bradbury, T. N., Fincham, F. D., & Beach, S. R. (2000). Research on the nature and determinants of marital satisfaction: A decade in review. *Journal of Marriage and Family*, *62*, 964–980.

Brehm, J. W. (1966). *A theory of psychological reactance*. New York: Academic Press.

Briñol, P., Petty, R. E., Valle, C., Rucker, D. D., & Becerra, A. (2007). The effects of message recipients' power before and after persuasion: A self-validation analysis. *Journal of Personality and Social Psychology*, *93*, 1040–1053.

Buckley, K. E., Winkel, R. E., & Leary, M. R. (2004). Reactions to acceptance and rejection: Effects of level and sequence of relational evaluation. *Journal of Experimental Social Psychology*, *40*, 14–28.

Buss, D. M. (1989). Sex differences in human mate preferences: Evolutionary hypotheses tested in 37 cultures. *Behavioral and Brain Sciences*, *12*, 1–49.

Cacioppo, J. T., Hawkley, L. C., & Berntson, G. G. (2003). The anatomy of loneliness. *Current Directions in Psychological Science*, *12*, 71–74.

Carswell, K., Finkel, E. J., Fitzsimons, G. M., & Lambert, N. (2012). *Positive effects of reminders of undermining partners*. Unpublished manuscript, Northwestern University.

Carver, C. S., & White, T. L. (1994). Behavioral inhibition, behavioral activation, and affective responses to impending reward and punishment: The BIS/BAS Scales. *Journal of Personality and Social Psychology*, *67*, 319–333.

Cavallo, J. V., Fitzsimons, G. M., & Holmes, J. G. (2009). Taking chances in the face of threat: Romantic risk regulation and approach motivation. *Personality and Social Psychology Bulletin*, *35*, 737–751.

Cavallo, J. V., Fitzsimons, G. M., & Holmes, J. G. (2010). When self-protection overreaches: Relationship-specific threat activates domain-general avoidance motivation. *Journal of Experimental Social Psychology*, *46*, 1–8.

Cavallo, J. V., Murray, S. L., & Holmes, J. G. (2012). Regulating interpersonal risk. In J. A. Simpson & L. Campbell (Eds.), *The Oxford handbook of close relationships*. New York: Oxford University Press.

Chartrand, T. L., & Bargh, J. A. (1996). Automatic activation of impression formation and memorization goals: Nonconscious goal priming reproduces effects of explicit task instructions. *Journal of Personality and Social Psychology*, *71*, 464–478.

Chartrand, T. L., Dalton, A. N., & Fitzsimons, G. J. (2007). Nonconscious relationship reactance: When significant others prime opposing goals. *Journal of Experimental Social Psychology*, *43*, 719–726.

Chen, S., Boucher, H. C., & Tapias, M. P. (2006). The relational self revealed: Integrative conceptualization and implications for interpersonal life. *Psychological Bulletin*, *132*, 151–179.

Clark, A. E., & Kashima, Y. (2007). Stereotypes help people connect with others in the community: A situated functional analysis of the stereotype consistency bias in communication. *Journal of Personality and Social Psychology*, *93*, 1028–1039.

Coan, J. A. (2008). Toward a neuroscience of attachment. In J. Cassidy & P. R. Shaver (Eds.), *Handbook of attachment: Theory, research, and clinical applications* (2nd ed., pp. 241–265). New York: Guilford Press.

Coan, J. A., Schaefer, H. S., & Davidson, R. J. (2006). Lending a hand: Social regulation of the neural response to threat. *Psychological Science*, *17*, 1032–1039.

Collins, N. L., & Feeney, B. C. (2000). A safe haven: An attachment theory perspective on support seeking and caregiving in intimate relationships. *Journal of Personality and Social Psychology*, *78*, 1053–1073.

Conley, T. D., Calhoun, C., Evett, S. R., & Devine, P. G. (2001). Mistakes that heterosexual people make when trying to appear non-prejudiced: The view from LGB people. *Journal of Homosexuality*, *42*, 21–43.

Cross, S. E., Bacon, P. L., & Morris, M. L. (2000). The relational-interdependent self-construal and relationships. *Journal of Personality and Social Psychology*, *78*, 791–808.

Cross, S. E., Gore, J. S., & Morris, M. L. (2003). The relational-interdependent self-construal, self-concept consistency, and well-being. *Journal of Personality and Social Psychology*, *85*, 933–944.

Cross, S. E., Morris, M. L., & Gore, J. S. (2002). Thinking about oneself and others: The relational-interdependent self-construal and social cognition. *Journal of Personality and Social Psychology*, *82*, 399–418.

Curtis, R. C., & Miller, K. (1986). Believing another likes or dislikes you: Behaviors making the beliefs come true. *Journal of Personality and Social Psychology*, *51*, 284–290.

Dalton, A. N., Chartrand, T. L., & Finkel, E. J. (2010). The schema-driven chameleon: How mimicry affects executive and self-regulatory resources. *Journal of Personality and Social Psychology*, *98*, 605–617.

Davis, J. L., & Rusbult, C. E. (2001). Attitude alignment in close relationships. *Journal of Personality and Social Psychology*, *81*, 65–84.

DeHart, T., Pelham, B., & Murray, S. (2004). Implicit dependency regulation: Self-esteem, relationship closeness, and implicit evaluations of close others. *Social Cognition*, *22*, 126–146.

DeWall, C. Nathan, Maner, J. K., Deckman, T., & Rouby, D. A. (2011). Forbidden fruit: Inattention to attractive alternatives provokes implicit relationship reactance. *Journal of Personality and Social Psychology*, *100*, 621–629.

Dewitte, M., & De Houwer, J. (2008b). Proximity and distance goals in adult attachment. *European Journal of Personality*, *22*, 675–694.

Dewitte, M., De Houwer, J., Buysse, A., & Koster, E. H. W. (2008). Proximity seeking in adult attachment: Examining the role of automatic approach–avoidance tendencies. *British Journal of Social Psychology*, *47*, 557–573.

Dik, G., Aarts, H. (2007). Behavioral cues to others' motivation and goal pursuits: The perception of effort facilitates goal inference and contagion. *Journal of Experimental Social Psychology*, *43*, 727–737.

Downey, G., & Feldman, S. I. (1996). Implications of rejection sensitivity for intimate relationships. *Journal of Personality and Social Psychology*, *70*, 1327–1343.

Downey, G., Freitas, A. L., Michaelis, B., & Khouri, H. (1998). The self-fulfilling prophecy in close relationships: Rejection sensitivity and rejection by romantic partners. *Journal of Personality and Social Psychology* ,75, 545–560.

Drigotas, S. M., Rusbult, C. E., Wieselquist, J., & Whitton, S. W. (1999). Close partner as sculptor of the ideal self: Behavioral affirmation and the Michelangelo phenomenon. *Journal of Personality and Social Psychology*, 77, 293–323.

Dutton, D. G., & Aron, A. P. (1974). Some evidence for heightened sexual attraction under conditions of high anxiety. *Journal of Personality and Social Psychology*, 30, 510–517.

Eastwick, P. W., Eagly, A. H., Finkel, E. J., & Johnson, S. E. (2011). Implicit and explicit preferences for physical attractiveness in a romantic partner: A double dissociation in predictive validity. *Journal of Personality and Social Psychology*, 101, 993–1011.

Eastwick, P. W., & Finkel, E. J. (2008). Sex differences in mate preferences revisited: Do people know what they initially desire in a romantic partner? *Journal of Personality and Social Psychology*, 94, 245–264.

Eastwick, P. W., Finkel, E. J., & Eagly, A. H. (2011). When and why do ideal partner preferences affect the process of initiating and maintaining romantic relationships? *Journal of Personality and Social Psychology*, 101, 1012–1032.

Eastwick, P. W., Finkel, E. J., Krishnamurti, T., & Loewenstein, G. (2008). Mispredicting distress following romantic breakup: Revealing the time course of the affective forecasting error. *Journal of Experimental Social Psychology*, 44, 800–807.

Eastwick, P. W., Finkel, E. J., Mochon, D., & Ariely, D. (2007). Selective versus unselective romantic desire: Not all reciprocity is created equal. *Psychological Science*, 18, 317–319.

Echterhoff, G., Higgins, E. T., & Groll, S. (2005). Audience-tuning effects on memory: The role of shared reality. *Journal of Personality and Social Psychology*, 89, 257–276.

Echterhoff, G., Higgins, E. T., & Levine, J. M. (2009). Shared reality. *Perspectives on Psychological Science*, 4, 496–521.

Edelstein, R. S., & Gillath, O. (2008). Avoiding interference: Adult attachment and emotional processing biases. *Personality and Social Psychology Bulletin*, 34, 171–181.

Eisenberger, N. I., Lieberman, M. D., & Williams, K. D. (2003). Does rejection hurt? An fMRI study of social exclusion. *Science*, 302, 290–292.

Elliot, A. J., & Covington, M. V. (2001). Approach and avoidance motivation. *Educational Psychology Review*, 13, 73–92.

Etcheverry, P. E., & Le, B. (2005). Thinking about commitment: Accessibility of commitment and prediction of relationship persistence, accommodation, and willingness to sacrifice. *Personal Relationships*, 12, 103–123.

Feeney, B. C. (2004). A secure base: Responsive support of goal strivings and exploration in adult intimate relationships. *Journal of Personality and Social Psychology*, 87, 631–648.

Feeney, B. C., & Collins, N. L. (2004). Interpersonal safe haven and secure base caregiving processes in adulthood. In W. S. Rholes & J. A. Simpson (Eds.), Adult attachment: Theory, research, and clinical implications (pp. 300–338). New York: Guilford Press.

Feeney, B. C., & Thrush, R. L. (2010). Relationship influences on exploration in adulthood: The characteristics and function of a secure base. *Journal of Personality and Social Psychology*, 100, 57–76.

Fehr, B. (1988). Prototype analysis of the concepts of love and commitment. *Journal of Personality and Social Psychology*, 55, 557–579.

Fehr, B. (2004). Intimacy expectations in same-sex friendships: A prototype interaction-pattern model. *Journal of Personality and Social Psychology*, 86, 265–284.

Fehr, B., & Russell, J. A. (1991). The concept of love viewed from a prototype perspective. *Journal of Personality and Social Psychology*, 60, 425–438.

Fincham, F. D., Garnier, P. C., Gano-Phillips, S., & Osborne, L. N. (1995). Preinteraction expectations, marital satisfaction, and accessibility: A new look at sentiment override. *Journal of Family Psychology*, 9, 3–3.

Finkel, E. J., & Baumeister, R. F. (2010). Attraction and rejection. In R. F. Baumeister & E. J. Finkel (Eds.), *Advanced social psychology: The state of the science*. New York: Oxford University Press.

Finkel, E. J., & Campbell, W. K. (2001). Self-control and accommodation in close relationships: An interdependence analysis. *Journal of Personality and Social Psychology*, 81, 263–277.

Finkel, E. J., Campbell, W. K., Brunell, A. B., Dalton, A. N., Chartrand, T. L., & Scarbeck, S. J. (2006). High-maintenance interaction: Inefficient social coordination impairs self-regulation. *Journal of Personality and Social Psychology*, 91, 456–475.

Finkel, E. J., DeWall, C. N., Slotter, E. B., McNulty, J. K., Pond, R. S., Jr., & Atkins, D. C. (2012). Using I3 Theory to clarify when dispositional aggressiveness predicts intimate partner violence perpetration. *Journal of Personality and Social Psychology*, 102, 533–549.

Finkel, E. J., & Fitzsimons, G. M. (2010). Effects of self-regulation on interpersonal relationships. In K. D. Vohs & R. F. Baumeister (Eds.), *Handbook of self-regulation: Research, theory, and applications* (2nd ed.). New York: Guilford Press.

Finkel, E. J., Molden, D. C., Johnson, S. E., & Eastwick, P. W. (2009). Regulatory focus and romantic alternatives. In J. P. Forgas, R. F. Baumeister, and D. M. Tice (Eds.), *Self-regulation: Cognitive, affective, and motivational processes* (pp. 319–335). New York: Psychology Press.

Fiske, A. P. (1992). The four elementary forms of sociality: Framework for a unified theory of social relations. *Psychological review*, 99, 689–723.

Fiske, A. P., Haslam, N., & Fiske, S. T. (1991). Confusing one person with another: What errors reveal about the elementary forms of social relations. *Journal of Personality and Social Psychology*, 60, 656–674.

Fiske, S. T. (1993). Controlling other people: The impact of power on stereotyping. *American Psychologist*, 48, 621-628.

Fitzsimons, G. M., & Bargh, J. A. (2003). Thinking of you: Nonconscious pursuit of interpersonal goals associated with relationship partners. *Journal of Personality and Social Psychology*, 84, 148–164.

Fitzsimons, G. M., & Finkel, E. J. (2010). Interpersonal influences on self-regulation. *Current Directions in Psychological Science*, 19, 101–105.

Fitzsimons, G. M., & Finkel, E. J. (2011). Outsourcing self-regulation. *Psychological Science*, 22, 369–375.

Fitzsimons, G. M., & Fishbach, A. (2010). Shifting closeness: Interpersonal effects of personal goal progress. *Journal of Personality and Social Psychology*, 98, 535–549.

Fitzsimons, G. M., & Kay, A. C. (2004). Language and interpersonal cognition: Causal effects of variations in pronoun usage on perceptions of closeness. *Personality and Social Psychology Bulletin, 30,* 547–557.

Fitzsimons, G. M., & Shah, J. (2008). How goal instrumentality shapes relationship evaluations. *Journal of Personality and Social Psychology, 95,* 319–337.

Fitzsimons, G. M., & Shah, J. Y. (2009). Confusing one instrumental other for another: Goal effects on social categorization. *Psychological Science, 20,* 1468–1472.

Fitzsimons, G. M., vanDellen, M. R., & Finkel, E. J. *Transactive self-regulation.* Unpublished manuscript, Duke University.

Fletcher, G. J. O., & Kininmonth, L. (1992). Measuring relationship beliefs: An individual differences scale. *Journal of Research in Personality, 26,* 371–397.

Fletcher, G. J. O., Rosanowski, J., & Fitness, J. (1994). Automatic processing in intimate contexts: The role of relationship beliefs. *Journal of Personality and Social Psychology, 67,* 888–897.

Fletcher, G. J. O., & Simpson, J. A. (2000). Ideal standards in close relationships: Their structure and functions. *Current Directions in Psychological Science, 9,* 102–105.

Fletcher, G. J. O., Simpson, J. A., & Thomas, G. (2000). Ideals, perceptions, and evaluations in early relationship development. *Journal of Personality and Social Psychology, 79,* 933–940.

Fletcher, G. J. O., Simpson, J. A., Thomas, G., & Giles, L. (1999). Ideals in intimate relationships. *Journal of Personality and Social Psychology, 76,* 72–89.

Ford, M. B., & Collins, N. L. (2010). Self-esteem moderates neuroendocrine and psychological responses to interpersonal rejection. *Journal of Personality and Social Psychology, 98,* 405–419.

Freud, S. (1958). *The dynamics of transference. Standard edition* (Vol. 20, pp. 99–108). London: Hogarth. (Original work published 1912).

Freud, S. (1959). *Analysis terminable and interminable. Standard edition* (Vol. 23, pp. 216–253). London: Hogarth. (Original work published 1937).

Gable, S. L. (2006). Approach and avoidance social motives and goals. *Journal of Personality, 74,* 175–222.

Gable, S. L., & Poore, J. (2008). Which thoughts count? Algorithms for evaluating satisfaction in relationships. *Psychological Science, 19,* 1030–1036.

Gabriel, S., Renaud, J. M., & Tippin, B. (2007). When I think of you, I feel more confident about me: The relational self and self-confidence. *Journal of Experimental Social Psychology, 43,* 772–779.

Gagné, F., Khan, A., Lydon, J., & To, M. (2008). When flattery gets you nowhere: Discounting positive feedback as a relationship maintenance strategy. *Canadian Journal of Behavioural Science, 40,* 59–68.

Galinsky, A. D., Magee, J. C., Inesi, M. E., & Gruenfeld, D. H. (2006). Power and perspectives not taken. *Psychological Science, 17,* 1068–1074.

Gangestad, S. W., Thornhill, R., & Garver-Apgar, C. E. (2005). Adaptations to ovulation: implications for sexual and social behavior. *Current Directions in Psychological Science, 14,* 312–316.

Gardner, W. L, Gabriel, S., & Hochschild, L. (2002). When you and I are " we," you are not threatening: The role of self-expansion in social comparison. *Journal of Personality and Social Psychology, 82,* 239–251.

Gardner, W. L, Pickett, C. L., & Brewer, M. B. (2000). Social exclusion and selective memory: How the need to belong influences memory for social events. *Personality and Social Psychology Bulletin, 26,* 486–496.

Gardner, W. L, Pickett, C. L., Jefferis, V., & Knowles, M. (2005). On the outside looking in: Loneliness and social monitoring. *Personality and Social Psychology Bulletin, 31,* 1549–1560.

Gawronski, B., Geschke, D., & Banse, R. (2003). Implicit bias in impression formation: Associations influence the construal of individuating information. *European Journal of Social Psychology, 33,* 573–589.

Gillath, O., Mikulincer, M., Fitzsimons, G. M., Shaver, P. R., Schachner, D. A., & Bargh, J. A. (2006). Automatic activation of attachment-related goals. *Personality and Social Psychology Bulletin, 32,* 1375–1388.

Glassman, N. S., & Andersen, S. M. (1999). Activating transference without consciousness: Using significant-other representations to go beyond what is subliminally given. *Journal of Personality and Social Psychology, 77,* 1146–1162.

Gonzaga, G., Haselton, M. G., Smurda, J., Davies, M. S., & Poore, J. C. (2008). Love, desire, and the suppression of thoughts of romantic alternatives. *Evolution and Human Behavior, 29,* 119–126.

Gray, H. M., Ishii, K., & Ambady, N. (2011). Misery loves company. *Personality and Social Psychology Bulletin, 37,* 1438–1448.

Gray, J. A. (1990). Brain systems that mediate both emotion and cognition. *Cognition & Emotion, 4,* 269–288.

Griffin, D., & Bartholomew, K. (1994). Models of the self and other: Fundamental dimensions underlying measures of adult attachment. *Journal of Personality and Social Psychology, 67,* 430–445.

Günaydin, G., Zayas, V., Selcuk, E., & Hazan, C. (2012). I like you but I don't know why: Objective facial resemblance to significant others influences snap judgments. *Journal of Experimental Social Psychology, 48,* 350–353.

Hardin, C. D., & Conley, T. D. (2001). A relational approach to cognition: Shared experience and relationship affirmation in social cognition. In G. B. Moskowitz (Ed.), *Cognitive social psychology: The Princeton Symposium on the Legacy and Future of Social Cognition* (pp. 3–21). Mahwah, NJ: Erlbaum.

Hardin, C. D., & Higgins, E. T. (1996). Shared reality: How social verification makes the subjective objective. In R. M. Sorrentino & E. T. Higgins (Eds.), *Handbook of motivation and cognition: Vol. 3. The interpersonal context* (pp. 28–84). Mahwah, NJ: Erlbaum.

Haselton, M. G., & Gildersleeve, K. (2011). Can men detect ovulation? *Current Directions in Psychological Science, 20,* 87–92.

Hazan, C., & Shaver, P. (1987). Romantic love conceptualized as an attachment process. *Journal of Personality and Social Psychology, 52,* 511–524.

Heider, F. (1958). *Interpersonal relations.* New York: Wiley.

Higgins, E. T. (1987). Self-discrepancy: A theory relating self and affect. *Psychological Review, 94,* 319–340.

Higgins, E. T. (1997). Beyond pleasure and pain. *American Psychologist, 52,* 1280–1300.

Hinkley, K., & Andersen, S. M. (1996). The working self-concept in transference: Significant-other activation and self-change. *Journal of Personality and Social Psychology, 71,* 1279–1295.

Holland, R. W., Roeder, U. R., van Baaren, R. B., Brandt, A. C., & Hannover, B. (2004). Don't stand so close to me: The effects of self-construal in interpersonal closeness. *Psychological Science, 15,* 237–242.

Holmes, J. G. (2002). Interpersonal expectations as the building blocks of social cognition: An interdependence theory perspective. *Personal Relationships, 9,* 1–26.

Holtzworth-Munroe, A., & Jacobson, N. S. (1985). Causal attributions of married couples: When do they search for causes? What do they conclude when they do? *Journal of Personality and Social Psychology, 48,* 1398–1412.

Ickes, W., Gesn, P. R., & Graham, T. (2000). Gender differences in empathic accuracy: Differential ability or differential motivation? *Personal Relationships, 7,* 95–109.

Ickes, W., Stinson, L., Bissonnette, V., & Garcia, S. (1990). Naturalistic social cognition: Empathic accuracy in mixed-sex dyads. *Journal of Personality and Social Psychology, 59,* 730–742.

Imhoff, R., & Banse, R. (2011). Implicit and explicit attitudes toward ex-partners differentially predict breakup adjustment. *Personal Relationships, 18,* 427–438.

Impett, E. A., Gordon, A. M., Kogan, A., Oveis, C., Gable, S. L., & Keltner, D. (2010). Moving toward more perfect unions: Daily and long-term consequences of approach and avoidance goals in romantic relationships. *Journal of Personality and Social Psychology, 99,* 948–963.

Impett, E. A., Peplau, L. A., & Gable, S. L. (2005). Approach and avoidance sexual motives: Implications for personal and interpersonal well-being. *Personal Relationships, 12,* 465–482.

Johnson, D. J., & Rusbult, C. E. (1989). Resisting temptation: Devaluation of alternative partners as a means of maintaining commitment in close relationships. *Journal of Personality and Social Psychology, 57,* 967–980.

Kammrath, L. K., & Peetz, J. (2011). The limits of love: Predicting immediate versus sustained caring behaviors in close relationships. *Journal of Experimental Social Psychology, 47,* 411–417.

Karney, B. R., & Coombs, R. H. (2000). Memory bias in long-term close relationships: Consistency or improvement? *Personality and Social Psychology Bulletin, 26,* 959–970.

Karney, B. R., & Frye, N. E. (2002). "But we've been getting better lately": Comparing prospective and retrospective views of relationship development. *Journal of Personality and Social Psychology, 82,* 222–238.

Karremans, J. C., & Smith, P. K. (2010). Having the power to forgive: The role of power in interpersonal forgiveness. *Personality and Social Psychology Bulletin, 36,* 1010–1023.

Karremans, J. C., Verwijmeren, T., Pronk, T. M., & Reitsma, M. (2009). Interacting with women can impair men's cognitive functioning. *Journal of Experimental Social Psychology, 45,* 1041–1044.

Kelley, H. H., Holmes, J. G., Kerr, N. L., Reis, H. T., Rusbult, C. E., & Van Lange, P. A. M. (2003). *An atlas of interpersonal situations.* New York: Cambridge University Press.

Kelley, H. H., & Thibaut, J. W. (1978). *Interpersonal relations: A theory of interdependence.* New York: Wiley.

Keltner, D., Gruenfeld, D. H., & Anderson, C. (2003). Power, approach, and inhibition. *Psychological Review, 110,* 265–284.

Kenny, D. A. (1994). *Interpersonal perception: A social relations analysis.* New York: Guilford.

Kenrick, D. T., & Gutierres, S. E. (1980). Contrast effects and judgments of physical attractiveness: When beauty becomes a social problem. *Journal of Personality and Social Psychology, 38,* 131–140.

Knee, C. R. (1998). Implicit theories of relationships: Assessment and prediction of romantic relationship initiation, coping, and longevity. *Journal of Personality and Social Psychology, 74,* 360–370.

Knee, C. R., Nanayakkara, A., Vietor, N. A., Neighbors, C., & Patrick, H. (2001). Implicit theories of relationships: Who cares if relationship partners are less than ideal? *Personality and Social Psychology Bulletin, 27,* 808–819.

Knee, C. R., Patrick, H., & Lonsbary, C. (2003). Implicit theories of relationships: Orientations toward evaluation and cultivation. *Personality and Social Psychology Review, 7,* 41–55.

Laurin, K., Fitzsimons, G. M., vanDellen, M. R., Carswell, K., LaMarche, V., & Finkel, E. J. (2012). *Standing behind your man: Powerful partners and personal goal pursuits.* Unpublished manuscript, Duke University.

Leander, N. P., Shah, J. Y., & Chartrand, T. L. (2011). The object of my protection: Shielding fundamental motives from the implicit motivational influence of others. *Journal of Experimental Social Psychology, 47,* 1078–1087.

Leary, M. R., Haupt, A. L., Strausser, K. S., & Chokel, J. T. (1998). Calibrating the sociometer: The relationship between interpersonal appraisals and state self-esteem. *Journal of Personality and Social Psychology, 74,* 1290–1299.

Leary, M. R., Tambor, E. S., Terdal, S. K., & Downs, D. L. (1995). Self-esteem as an interpersonal monitor: The sociometer hypothesis. *Journal of Personality and Social Psychology, 68,* 518–530.

LeBel, E. P., & Campbell, L. (2009). Implicit partner affect, relationship satisfaction, and the prediction of romantic breakup. *Journal of Experimental Social Psychology, 45,* 1291–1294.

Lewandowski, G. W. Jr., Aron, A., Bassis, S., & Kunak, J. (2006). Losing a self-expanding relationship: Implications for the self-concept. *Personal Relationships, 13,* 317–331.

Lockwood, P., Dolderman, D., Sadler, P., & Gerchak, E. (2004). Feeling better about doing worse: Social comparisons within romantic relationships. *Journal of Personality and Social Psychology, 87,* 80–95.

Lowery, B. S., Hardin, C. D., & Sinclair, S. (2001). Social influence effects on automatic racial prejudice. *Journal of Personality and Social Psychology, 81,* 842–855.

Lucas, R. E. (2005). Time does not heal all wounds. *Psychological Science, 16,* 945–950.

Luchies, L. B., Finkel, E. J., McNulty, J. K., & Kumashiro, M. (2010). The doormat effect: When forgiving erodes self-respect and self-concept clarity. *Journal of Personality and Social Psychology, 98,* 734–749.

Luchies, L. B., Finkel, E. J., & Fitzsimons, G. M. (2011). The effects of self-regulatory strength, content, and strategies on close relationships. *Journal of Personality, 79,* 949–977.

Lydon, J. E. (2010). How to forego forbidden fruit: The regulation of attractive alternatives as a commitment mechanism. *Social and Personality Psychology Compass, 4,* 635–644.

Lydon, J. E., Burton, K., & Menzies-Toman, D. (2005). *Commitment calibration with the relationship cognition toolbox.* In M. W. Baldwin (Ed.), *Interpersonal cognition.* New York: Guilford Press.

Lydon, J. E., Fitzsimons, G. M., & Naidoo, L. (2003). Devaluation versus enhancement of attractive alternatives: A critical test using the calibration paradigm. *Personality and Social Psychology Bulletin, 29,* 349–359.

Lydon, J. E., Meana, M., Sepinwall, D., Richards, N., & Mayman, S. (1999). The commitment calibration hypothesis:

When do people devalue attractive alternatives? *Personality and Social Psychology Bulletin, 25,* 152–161.

Lydon, J. E., Menzies-Toman, D., Burton, K., & Bell, C. (2008). If-then contingencies and the differential effects of the availability of an attractive alternative on relationship maintenance for men and women. *Journal of Personality and Social Psychology, 95,* 50–65.

MacDonald, G., & Leary, M. R. (2005). Why does social exclusion hurt? The relationship between social and physical pain. *Psychological Bulletin, 131,* 202–223.

Maner, J. K., DeWall, C. N., & Gailliot, M. T. (2008). Selective attention to signs of success: Social dominance and early stage interpersonal perception. *Personality and Social Psychology Bulletin, 34,* 488–501.

Maner, J. K., DeWall, C. N., Baumeister, R. F., & Schaller, M. (2007). Does social exclusion motivate interpersonal reconnection? Resolving the "porcupine problem." *Journal of Personality and Social Psychology, 92,* 42–55.

Maner, J. K., Gailliot, M. T., & Miller, S. L. (2009). The implicit cognition of relationship maintenance: Inattention to attractive alternatives. *Journal of Experimental Social Psychology, 45,* 174–179.

Maner, J. K., Kenrick, D. T., Becker, D. V., Delton, A. W., Hofer, B., Wilbur, C. J., & Neuberg, S. L. (2003). Sexually selective cognition: Beauty captures the mind of the beholder. *Journal of Personality and Social Psychology, 85,* 1107–1120.

Maner, J. K., Kenrick, D. T., Becker, D. V., Robertson, T. E., Hofer, B., Neuberg, S. L., ... Schaller, M. (2005). Functional projection: How fundamental social motives can bias interpersonal perception. *Journal of Personality and Social Psychology, 88,* 63–78.

Markus, H., & Cross, S. (1990). The interpersonal self. *Handbook of personality: Theory and research* (pp. 576–608). New York: Guilford Press.

Markus, H. R., & Kitayama, S. (1991). Culture and the self: Implications for cognition, emotion, and motivation. *Psychological Review, 98,* 224–253.

Mashek, D. J., Aron, A., & Boncimino, M. (2003). Confusions of self with close others. *Personality and Social Psychology Bulletin, 29,* 382–392.

McCulloch, K. C., Fitzsimons, G. M., Chua, S. N., & Albarracín, D. (2010). Vicarious goal satiation. *Journal of Experimental Social Psychology, 47,* 685–688.

Mead, G. H. (1934). *Mind, self, and society.* Chicago: University of Chicago Press.

Mikulincer, M. (1998). Adult attachment style and affect regulation: Strategic variations in self-appraisals. *Journal of Personality and Social Psychology, 75,* 420–435.

Mikulincer, M., Birnbaum, G., Woddis, D., & Nachmias, O. (2000). Stress and accessibility of proximity-related thoughts: Exploring the normative and intraindividual components of attachment theory. *Journal of Personality and Social Psychology, 78,* 509–523.

Mikulincer, M., Gillath, O., & Shaver, P. R. (2002). Activation of the attachment system in adulthood: Threat-related primes increase the accessibility of mental representations of attachment figures. *Journal of Personality and Social Psychology, 83,* 881–895.

Mikulincer, M., & Shaver, P. R. (2001). Attachment theory and intergroup bias: Evidence that priming the secure base schema attenuates negative reactions to out-groups. *Journal of Personality and Social Psychology, 81,* 97–115.

Mikulincer, M., & Shaver, P. R. (2007a). Boosting attachment security to promote mental health, prosocial values, and intergroup tolerance. *Psychological Inquiry, 18,* 139–156.

Mikulincer, M., & Shaver, P. R. (2007b). *Attachment in adulthood: Structure, dynamics, and change.* New York: Guilford Press.

Mikulincer, M., Shaver, P. R., & Horesh, N. (2006). Attachment bases of emotion regulation and posttraumatic adjustment. In D. K. Snyder, J. Simpson, & J. N. Hughes (Eds.), *Emotion regulation in couples and families: Pathways to dysfunction and health* (pp. 77–99). Washington, DC: American Psychological Association.

Mikulincer, M., Shaver, P. R., Gillath, O., & Nitzberg, R. A. (2005). Attachment, caring, and altruism: Boosting attachment security increases compassion and helping. *Journal of Personality and Social Psychology, 89,* 817–839.

Miller, G. E., Bradbury, T. N. (1995). Refining the association between attributions and behavior in marital interaction. *Journal of Family Psychology, 9,* 196–208.

Miller, R. S. (1997). Inattentive and contented: Relationship commitment and attention to alternatives. *Journal of Personality and Social Psychology, 73,* 758–766.

Miller, S. L., & Maner, J. K. (2010). Evolution and relationship maintenance: Fertility cues lead committed men to devalue relationship alternatives. *Journal of Experimental Social Psychology, 46,* 1081–1084.

Miller, S. L., & Maner, J. K. (2011). Ovulation as a male mating prime: Subtle signs of women's fertility influence men's mating cognition and behavior. *Journal of Personality and Social Psychology, 100,* 295–308.

Moretti, M. M., & Higgins, E. T. (1999). Internal representations of others in self-regulation: A new look at a classic issue. *Social Cognition, 17,* 186–208.

Morrison, K. R., Wheeler, S. C., & Smeesters, D. (2007). Significant other primes and behavior: Motivation to respond to social cues moderates pursuit of prime-induced goals. *Personality and Social Psychology Bulletin, 33,* 1661–1674.

Murray, S. L. (2005). Regulating the risks of closeness: A relationship-specific sense of felt security. *Current Directions in Psychological Science, 14,* 74–78.

Murray, S. L., Aloni, M., Holmes, J. G., Derrick, J. L., Stinson, D. A., & Leder, S. (2009). Fostering partner dependence as trust insurance: The implicit contingencies of the exchange script in close relationships. *Journal of Personality and Social Psychology, 96,* 324–348.

Murray, S. L., Bellavia, G. M., Rose, P., & Griffin, D. W. (2003). Once hurt, twice hurtful: How perceived regard regulates daily marital interactions. *Journal of Personality and Social Psychology, 84,* 126–147.

Murray, S. L., Derrick, J. L., Leder, S., & Holmes, J. G. (2008). Balancing connectedness and self-protection goals in close relationships: A levels-of-processing perspective on risk regulation. *Journal of Personality and Social Psychology, 94,* 429–459.

Murray, S. L., Griffin, D. W., Rose, P., & Bellavia, G. M. (2003). Calibrating the sociometer: The relational contingencies of self-esteem. *Journal of Personality and Social Psychology, 85,* 63–84.

Murray, S. L., & Holmes, J. G. (1993). Seeing virtues in faults: Negativity and the transformation of interpersonal narratives in close relationships. *Journal of Personality and Social Psychology, 65,* 707–722.

Murray, S. L., & Holmes, J. G. (1997). A leap of faith? Positive illusions in romantic relationships. *Personality and Social Psychology Bulletin, 23,* 586–604.

Murray, S. L., & Holmes, J. G. (2009). The architecture of interdependent minds: A motivation-management theory of mutual responsiveness. *Psychological Review, 116*, 908–928.

Murray, S. L., & Holmes, J. G. (2011). *Interdependent minds: The dynamics of close relationships.* New York: Guilford Press.

Murray, S. L., Holmes, J. G., Aloni, M., Pinkus, R. T., Derrick, J. L., & Leder, S. (2009). Commitment insurance: Compensating for the autonomy costs of interdependence in close relationships. *Journal of Personality and Social Psychology, 97*, 256–278.

Murray, S. L., Holmes, J. G., & Collins, N. L. (2006). Optimizing assurance: The risk regulation system in relationships. *Psychological Bulletin, 132*, 641–666.

Murray, S. L, Holmes, J. G., & Griffin, D. W. (1996a). The benefits of positive illusions: Idealization and the construction of satisfaction in close relationships. *Journal of Personality and Social Psychology, 70*, 79–98.

Murray, S. L., Holmes, J. G., & Griffin, D. W. (1996b). The self-fulfilling nature of positive illusions in romantic relationships: Love is not blind, but prescient. *Journal of Personality and Social Psychology, 71*, 1155–1180.

Murray, S. L., Holmes, J. G., & Griffin, D. W. (2000). Self-esteem and the quest for felt security: How perceived regard regulates attachment processes. *Journal of Personality and Social Psychology, 78*, 478–498.

Murray, S. L., Holmes, J. G., MacDonald, G., & Ellsworth, P. C. (1998). Through the looking glass darkly? When self-doubts turn into relationship insecurities. *Journal of Personality and Social Psychology, 75*, 1459–1480.

Murray, S. L., Holmes, J. G., & Pinkus, R. T. (2010). A smart unconscious? Procedural origins of automatic partner attitudes in marriage. *Journal of Experimental Social Psychology, 46*, 650–656.

Murray, S. L., Leder, S., MacGregor, J. C. D., Holmes, J. G., Pinkus, R. T., & Harris, B. (2009). Becoming irreplaceable: How comparisons to the partner's alternatives differentially affect low and high self-esteem people. *Journal of Experimental Social Psychology, 45*, 1180–1191.

Murray, S.L., Pinkus, R.T., Holmes, J.G., Harris, B., Gomillion, S., Aloni, M., ... Leder, S. (2011). Signaling when (and when not) to be cautious and self-protective: Impulsive and reflective trust in close relationships. *Journal of Personality and Social Psychology, 101*, 485–502.

Murray, S. L., Rose, P., Bellavia, G., Holmes, J. G., & Kusche, A. (2002). When rejection stings: How self-esteem constrains relationship-enhancement processes. *Journal of Personality and Social Psychology, 83*, 556–573.

Murray, S. L., Rose, P., Holmes, J. G., Derrick, J., Podchaski, E. J., & Bellavia, G. (2005). Putting the partner within reach: A dyadic perspective on felt security in close relationships. *Journal of Personality and Social Psychology, 88*, 327–347.

Newcomb, T. M. (1961). *The acquaintance process.* New York: Holt, Rinehart, & Winston.

Nisbett, R. E., Caputo, C., Legant, P., & Marecek, J. (1973). Behavior as seen by the actor and as seen by the observer. *Journal of Personality and Social Psychology, 27*(2), 154–164.

Nisbett, R. E., Peng, K., Choi, I., & Norenzayan, A. (2001). Culture and systems of thought: Holistic versus analytic cognition. *Psychological Review, 108*, 291–310.

Peetz, J., & Kammrath, L. K. (2012). Only because I love you: Why people make and why they break promises in romantic relationships. *Journal of Personality and Social Psychology, 100*, 887–904.

Pfeiffer, S. M., & Wong, P. T. P. (1989). Multidimensional jealousy. *Journal of Social and Personal Relationships, 6*, 181–196.

Pickett, C. L., Gardner, W. L., & Knowles, M. (2004). Getting a cue: The need to belong and enhanced sensitivity to social cues. *Personality and Social Psychology Bulletin, 30*, 1095–1107.

Pierce, T., & Lydon, J. (1998). Priming relational schemas: Effects of contextually activated and chronically accessible interpersonal expectations on responses to a stressful event. *Journal of Personality and Social Psychology, 75*, 1441–1448.

Pinkus, R. T., Lockwood, P., Schimmack, U., & Fournier, M. A. (2008). For better and for worse: Everyday social comparisons between romantic partners. *Journal of Personality and Social Psychology, 95*, 1180–1201.

Plant, E. A., Kunstman, J. W., & Maner, J. K. (2010). You do not only hurt the one you love: Self-protective responses to attractive relationship alternatives. *Journal of Experimental Social Psychology, 46*, 474–477.

Prentice, D. A. (1990). Familiarity and differences in self-and other-representations. *Journal of Personality and Social Psychology, 59*, 369–383.

Pronk, T. M., Karremans, J. C., Overbeek, G., Vermulst, A. A., & Wigboldus, D. H. J. (2010). What it takes to forgive: When and why executive functioning facilitates forgiveness. *Journal of Personality and Social Psychology, 98*, 119–131.

Pronk, T. M., Karremans, J. C., & Wigboldus, D. H. J. (2011). How can you resist? Executive control helps romantically involved individuals to stay faithful. *Journal of Personality and Social Psychology, 100*, 827–837.

Read, S. J., & Miller, L. C. (1989). Inter-personalism: Toward a goal-based theory of persons in relationships. In L. Pervin (Ed.), *Goal concepts in personality and social psychology* (pp. 413–472). Hillsdale, NJ: Erlbaum.

Reis, H. T., & Downey, G. (1999). Social cognition in relationships: Building essential bridges between two literatures. *Social Cognition, 17*, 97–117.

Ritter, S., Karremans, J. C., & Van Schie, H. (2010). The role of self-regulation in derogating attractive alternatives. *Journal of Experimental Social Psychology, 46*, 631–637.

Romero-Canyas, R., Downey, G., Berenson, K., Ayduk, O., & Kang, N. J. (2010). Rejection sensitivity and the rejection–hostility link in romantic relationships. *Journal of Personality, 78*, 119–148.

Rudman, L. A. & Heppen, J. (2003). Implicit romantic fantasies and women's interest in personal power: A glass slipper effect? *Personality and Social Psychology Bulletin, 29*, 1357–1370.

Rusbult, C. E. (1983). A longitudinal test of the investment model: The development (and deterioration) of satisfaction and commitment in heterosexual involvements. *Journal of Personality and Social Psychology, 45*, 101–117.

Rusbult, C. E., Finkel, E. J., & Kumashiro, M. (2009). The Michelangelo phenomenon. *Current Directions in Psychological Science, 18*, 305–309.

Rusbult, C. E., Olsen, N., Davis, J. L., Hannon, P. A., Harvey, J., & Wenzel, A. (2001). Commitment and relationship maintenance mechanisms. In J. H. Harvey & A. Wenzel (Eds.), *Close romantic relationships: Maintenance and enhancement* (pp. 87–113). Mahwah, NJ: Erlbaum.

Rusbult, C. E., & Van Lange, P. A. M. (2003). Interdependence, interaction, and relationships. *Annual Review of Psychology, 54*, 351–375.

Rusbult, C. E., Verette, J., Whitney, G. A., Slovik, L. F., & Lipkus, I. (1991). Accommodation processes in close relationships: Theory and preliminary empirical evidence. *Journal of Personality and Social Psychology*, *60*, 53–78.

Rusbult, C. E., Yovetich, N. A., & Verette, J. (1996). An interdependence analysis of accommodation processes. In G. J. O. Fletcher & J. Fitness (Eds.), *Knowledge structures in close relationships: A social psychological approach* (pp. 63–90). Mahwah, NJ: Erlbaum.

Sbarra, D. A., Law, R. W., & Portley, R. M. (2011). Divorce and death. *Perspectives on Psychological Science*, *6*, 454–474.

Sbarra, D. A., & Nietert, P. J. (2009). Divorce and death: Forty years of the Charleston heart study. *Psychological Science*, *20*, 107–113.

Sedikides, C., Olsen, N., & Reis, H. T. (1993). Relationships as natural categories. *Journal of Personality and Social Psychology*, *64*, 71–82.

Seeley, E. A., & Gardner, W. L. (2003). The "selfless" and self-regulation: The role of chronic other-orientation in averting self-regulatory depletion. *Self and Identity*, *2*, 103–117.

Shah, J. (2003). Automatic for the people: How representations of significant others implicitly affect goal pursuit. *Journal of Personality and Social Psychology*, *84*, 661–681.

Simpson, J. A., Gangestad, S. W., & Lerma, M. (1990). Perception of physical attractiveness: Mechanisms involved in the maintenance of romantic relationships. *Journal of Personality and Social Psychology*, *59*, 1192–1201.

Simpson, J. A., Ickes, W., & Blackstone, T. (1995). When the head protects the heart: Empathic accuracy in dating relationships. *Journal of Personality and Social Psychology*, *69*, 629–641.

Simpson, J. A., Ickes, W., & Oriña, M. (2001). Empathic accuracy and preemptive relationship maintenance. In J. Harvey & A. Wenzel (Eds.), *Close romantic relationships: Maintenance and enhancement* (pp. 27–46). Mahwah, NJ: Erlbaum.

Sinclair, S., Hardin, C. D., & Lowery, B. S. (2006). Self-stereotyping in the context of multiple social identities. *Journal of Personality and Social Psychology*, *90*, 529–542.

Sinclair, S., Lowery, B. S., Hardin, C. D., & Colangelo, A. (2005a). Social tuning of automatic racial attitudes: The role of affiliative motivation. *Journal of Personality and Social Psychology*, *89*, 583–592.

Slotter, E. B., Gardner, W. L., & Finkel, E. J. (2010). Who am I without you? The influence of romantic breakup on the self-concept. *Personality and Social Psychology Bulletin*, *36*, 147–160.

Smith, P. K., & Bargh, J. A. (2008). Nonconscious effects of power on basic approach and avoidance tendencies. *Social Cognition*, *26*, 1–24.

Smith, P. K., & Trope, Y. (2006). You focus on the forest when you're in charge of the trees: Power priming and abstract information processing. *Journal of Personality and Social Psychology*, *90*, 578–596.

Snyder, M., & Swann, W. B. (1978). Behavioral confirmation in social interaction: From social perception to social reality. *Journal of Experimental Social Psychology*, *14*, 148–162.

Snyder, M., Tanke, E. D., & Berscheid, E. (1977). Social perception and interpersonal behavior: On the self-fulfilling nature of social stereotypes. *Journal of Personality and Social Psychology*, *35*, 656–666.

Sprecher, S. (1999). "I love you more today than yesterday": Romantic partners' perception of changes in love and related affect over time. *Journal of Personality and Social Psychology*, *76*, 46–53.

Stinson, L., & Ickes, W. (1992). Empathic accuracy in the interactions of male friends versus male strangers. *Journal of Personality and Social Psychology*, *62*, 787–797.

Swann, W. B. (1983). Self-verification: Bringing social reality into harmony with the self. *Psychological Perspectives on the Self*, *2*, 33–66.

Swann, W. B., Pelham, B. W., & Krull, D. S. (1989). Agreeable fancy or disagreeable truth? Reconciling self-enhancement and self-verification. *Journal of Personality and Social Psychology*, *57*, 782–791.

Tesser, A. (1988). Toward a self-evaluation maintenance model of social behavior. In L. Berkowitz (Ed.), *Advances in experimental social psychology* (Vol. 21, pp. 181–227). New York: Academic Press.

Thibaut, J., Kelley, & H. H. (1959). *The social psychology of groups*. New York: Wiley.

Thomas, G., & Fletcher, G. J. O. (2003). Mind-reading accuracy in intimate relationships: Assessing the roles of the relationship, the target, and the judge. *Journal of Personality and Social Psychology*, *85*, 1079–1094.

Thomas, G., Fletcher, G. J. O., & Lange, C. (1997). On-line empathic accuracy in marital interaction. *Journal of Personality and Social Psychology*, *72*, 839–850.

Twenge, J. M., & Campbell, W. K. (2003). "Isn't it fun to get the respect that we're going to deserve?" Narcissism, social rejection, and aggression. *Personality and Social Psychology Bulletin*, *29*, 261–272.

Van Lange, P. A. M., Rusbult, C. E., Drigotas, S. M., Arriaga, X. B., Witcher, B. S., & Cox, C. L. (1997). Willingness to sacrifice in close relationships. *Journal of Personality and Social Psychology*, *72*, 1373–1395.

Verhofstadt, L. L., Buysse, A., Ickes, W., Davis, M., & Devoldre, I. (2008). Support provision in marriage: The role of emotional similarity and empathic accuracy. *Emotion*, *8*, 792–802.

Waller, W. (1938). *The family: A dynamic interpretation*. New York: Gordon.

Walster, E., Aronson, V., Abrahams, D., & Rottman, L. (1966). Importance of physical attractiveness in dating behavior. *Journal of Personality and Social Psychology*, *4*, 508–516.

Williams, K. D. (2002). *Ostracism: The power of silence*. New York: Guilford Press.

Woike, B. A. (1994). The use of differentiation and integration processes: Empirical studies of "separate" and "connected" ways of thinking. *Journal of Personality and Social Psychology*, *67*, 142–150.

Wood, D., & Brumbaugh, C. C. (2009). Using revealed mate preferences to evaluate market force and differential preference explanations for mate selection. *Journal of Personality and Social Psychology*, *96*, 1226–1244.

Wood, J. V. (1989). Theory and research concerning social comparisons of personal attributes. *Psychological Bulletin*, *106*, 231–248.

Zayas, V., & Shoda, Y. (2005). Do automatic reactions elicited by thoughts of romantic partner, mother, and self relate to adult romantic attachment? *Personality and Social Psychology Bulletin*, *31*, 1011.

Group Cognition: Collective Information Search and Distribution

John M. Levine *and* Eliot R. Smith

Abstract

This chapter reviews work on group decision making and problem solving. Included are topics both within and outside traditional boundaries of social psychology, such as collective induction, swarm intelligence models, jury decision making, information sharing, collaborative memory, gossip, brainstorming, and team mental models. The literature is discussed in terms of the collective information search and distribution model, which highlights group members' motivational and cognitive processes as well as the demonstrability of the group task. The 2 × 2 model distinguishes (1) motives that members hold for themselves from those they hold for the group as a whole and (2) motives related to acquiring knowledge from those related to facilitating intragroup and intergroup relations. The model assumes that each general class of motives has various subtypes and that group members can have multiple motives at one time. In addition to providing a useful framework for organizing the literature, the model suggests ideas for further investigation.

Key Words: group cognition, group decision making, group problem solving, jury decision making, collective induction, collaborative memory, gossip, team mental models

Although human cognition has typically been conceptualized and studied as an individual phenomenon, there is a long tradition of work focusing on how social factors influence diverse cognitive activities, including memory, reasoning, and problem solving. Important early contributions were made by such distinguished thinkers as Durkheim (1898), Le Bon (1895), McDougall (1920), and Mead (1934). It is only relatively recently, however, that the interface between cognitive and social processes has elicited substantial theoretical and empirical interest across a variety of disciplines, including social and developmental psychology, cognitive science, psycholinguistics, organizational behavior, sociology, and anthropology (for reviews, see Bar-Tal, 2000; Echterhoff, Higgins, & Levine, 2009; Levine & Higgins, 2001: Levine, Resnick, & Higgins, 1993; Mesmer-Magnus & DeChurch, 2009; Smith & Semin, 2004; Thompson & Fine,

1999; Tindale, Meisenhelder, Dykema-Engblade, & Hogg, 2001). Partly as a function of this disciplinary diversity, work on the social-cognitive interface has focused on a wide range of specific phenomena and has been discussed under many different rubrics, including common ground, distributed cognition, group cognition, intersubjectivity, shared reality, social constructionism, social representations, socially shared cognition, socially situated cognition, team mental models, transactive memory, uncertainty-identity theory, and the wisdom of crowds.

In this chapter, we focus on work by social and organizational psychologists and cognitive scientists dealing with group decision making and problem solving. There are many situations in which people's individual knowledge or experience is inadequate to support the judgments or decisions they must make. In such situations, people often draw on information or perspectives provided by others. The exchange of information allows each member of a group to draw on more than his or her individual experiences and therefore may allow a group to outperform an individual. Even nonhuman animals use socially provided information to guide their choice of mates or decisions about where to feed (e.g., Dugatkin, 1992). For example, in some fish species, a female becomes more likely to mate with a male when she observes other females showing an interest in the male. Each female can only imperfectly perceive males' mate quality, so evidence regarding other females' interest can be useful. Laland (2004) reviewed the literature on social information use in animals, considering such questions as when to use information from others (e.g., when gathering individual information is difficult or costly, or when one's own outcomes are poor) and from whom to obtain information (e.g., from the majority, from similar others, or from others with the best outcomes). Thus, across a wide range of species, individuals do not obtain adaptively useful information solely by searching for it on their own. Rather, social sharing of information is a ubiquitous process.

This process (at least in humans) can occur when two or more people are working jointly on a collective task, are aware that others are working on the same task, and have access to one another's contributions. This access can be more or less direct and more or less extensive, ranging from verbal and nonverbal communications among members of face-to-face groups, through asynchronous e-mail messages between identifiable people who have never met in person, to centralized lists of task-relevant information posted by anonymous others.

Group decision making and problem solving have elicited theoretical and empirical attention for decades, and much has been learned about the processes and outcomes of collective effort on cognitive tasks (for reviews, see Larson, 2010; Moscovici & Doise, 1994; Stasser & Dietz-Uhler, 2001; Tindale, Kameda, & Hinsz, 2003). Although a number of theoretical frameworks have guided research on group decision making and problem solving, over the last 20 years information processing models have become increasingly influential (e.g., Brodbeck, Kerschreiter, Mojzisch, & Schulz-Hardt, 2007; De Dreu, Nijstad, & van Knippenberg, 2008; Hinsz, Tindale, & Vollrath, 1997; Larson & Christensen, 1993). A key assumption of these models is that group performance depends on members' acquisition and sharing of task-relevant information. In this chapter, we analyze these processes under the label

of "collective information search and distribution." Our analysis is based on three core assumptions:

1. We assume that, rather than occurring only in individual brains, cognition is distributed across individuals, groups, and tools (Smith & Semin, 2004; see also Resnick, Levine, & Teasley, 1991).

2. We assume that, in order to understand cognition as an emergent and distributed process, it is critical to understand why people are motivated to make contributions to joint cognitive activities and to take seriously others' contributions. In other words, it is necessary to analyze the interface between motivation and cognition (De Dreu et al., 2008; Levine et al., 1993; Thompson & Fine, 1999).

3. We assume that the relationship between group members' motivation and cognition is strongly influenced by their ability to evaluate the utility of their own and others' information, which in turn depends on the nature of the group task, in particular the extent to which this task is believed to have a demonstrably correct solution (cf. Laughlin, 1980; Laughlin & Ellis, 1986).

We take the first assumption for granted. In discussing the second and third assumptions, we begin by outlining our collective information search and distribution (CISD) model of motivation and cognition in groups. Next, we discuss the role that task demonstrability plays in influencing group members' evaluations of their own and others' potential contributions to collective cognition. We then review theoretical and empirical work on four classes of group tasks—problem solving, decision making, idea generation (brainstorming), and socially shared metacognition—in each case applying facets of the CISD model. Finally, we provide some broad conclusions of our analysis and suggest questions for further research.

Motivation and Cognition in Groups

An ambitious analysis of the relationship between cognition and motivation in groups was recently presented by De Dreu et al. (2008). These authors offered a motivated information processing in groups (MIP-G) model positing that cognition in groups is influenced by two kinds of motivation—social and epistemic. Social motivation is dichotomous: People may desire to achieve either proself (individualistic/competitive) or prosocial (cooperative/altruistic) goals. In contrast, epistemic motivation varies continuously in intensity: People may be more or less motivated to attain a rich and accurate understanding of the world. De Dreu and his colleagues view these two kinds of motivation as orthogonal and argue that they have different effects on cognition. Epistemic motivation affects group members' effort to acquire new information and their depth of processing (with higher motivation leading to more information and deeper processing), whereas social motivation affects (or biases) the nature of this information (with proself and prosocial motivation stimulating interest in information consistent with personal and group goals, respectively). The MIP-G model further stipulates that group members' motives affect information dissemination and integration at the group level, which (together with member input indispensability and decision urgency) determine the quality of the group's judgments and decisions. Finally, De Dreu and his colleagues offer suggestions about how social and epistemic motivation interact in influencing group-level information processing. They argue, for example, that the combination of prosocial and low epistemic motivation produces directive leadership and lazy compromising, whereas the combination of prosocial and high epistemic motivation produces collaborative reasoning and attention to others' ideas. Because the MIP-G model assumes that proself and prosocial motivation, as well as high and low epistemic motivation, are mutually exclusive, each group member can fall into only one of the four cells of the model—prosocial high epistemic, prosocial low epistemic, proself high epistemic, or proself low epistemic.

The MIP-G model provides a number of important insights regarding information processing in groups. In this chapter, we offer a different, though complementary, analysis of how motivation affects cognition in social contexts. Our CISD model (Figure 30.1) posits two levels of motivational level crossed with two levels of motivational type.

Motivational level distinguishes motives that group members hold for themselves (self) from those they hold for the group as a whole (group). Motivational type distinguishes motives related to acquiring knowledge and understanding (epistemic) from those related to facilitating intragroup and intergroup relations (social). The CISD model distinguishes several varieties of both (1) self and group motives and (2) epistemic and social motives. Moreover, the model assumes that neither self and group motives nor epistemic and social motives are mutually exclusive and that two or more specific motives can operate simultaneously in each cell of the model. Thus, group members might have multiple motives in any or all of the four cells of the model—epistemic self, epistemic group, social self, and social group.

As suggested above, a variety of specific motives can exist in each of the four cells. For example, *epistemic self motives* (cell 1) include the desire for a firm answer to a question irrespective of the content of the answer (i.e., nonspecific closure; Kruglanski, 1989; Kruglanski, Dechesne, Orehek, & Pierro, 2009; Kruglanski, Pierro, Mannetti, & De Grada, 2006), the desire for an answer that satisfies one's existing preferences (i.e., specific closure; Kruglanski, 1989, 2004), and the desire for a "true" answer based on objective reality or social consensus (Festinger, 1950; Hardin & Higgins, 1996; Hogg, 2007). Moreover, in some cases, more than one motive can be operating at a given time. For example, a person might be simultaneously motivated to hold a particular position (e.g., because it fits his or her overall ideology) *and* to believe that this position is true.

A group member can also have one or more of the above goals for the group as a whole. To the extent that this occurs, the desire for nonspecific closure, specific closure, and/or truth can serve as *epistemic group motives* (cell 2) in addition to (or instead of) *epistemic self motives*. Moreover, in some cases, efforts to satisfy an epistemic self or group motive can have implications for the creation and/or satisfaction of the same or a different motive at the other level. In the above example in which a person is motivated to hold a particular position and to believe that this position is true, the person might try to convince others to adopt this position (i.e., seek social consensus) as a way of demonstrating to himself or herself that the position is indeed valid. (Note that this consensus will satisfy the person's need for validity only if he or she thinks that others' agreement is based on internalization rather than compliance; Kelman,

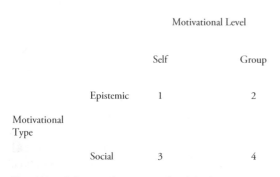

Motivational Level

		Self	Group
Motivational Type	Epistemic	1	2
	Social	3	4

Figure 30.1 Collective information search and distribution (CISD) model.

1958.) Thus, motivation for a specific closure at the individual level may stimulate motivation for the same specific closure at the group level, and achieving the second goal will be instrumental in achieving the first. In this case, the two motivational levels are very difficult to disentangle. This is also true if a group member personally wants to arrive at a correct answer and also wants the group to arrive at the correct answer. If the individual solves the problem and makes his or her solution available to the group, then the group will be correct as well (assuming the correctness is demonstrable). Epistemic self and group motives might merge for other reasons as well. For example, this is likely when members identify strongly with the group, resulting in depersonalization (Turner et al., 1987). In such cases, they will see themselves and others as relatively interchangeable members of the group and will take the group's epistemic goals as their own, failing to recognize any distinction between the two levels. For reasons such as these, and also because most theorists and researchers have not distinguished between the two levels, epistemic motives are sometimes difficult to assign cleanly to the self versus group level.

Let us now consider the distinction between *social self motives* (cell 3) and *social group motives* (cell 4). Several examples of each category can be identified. Social self motives include the desire to impress others (e.g., with one's cleverness, knowledge, sincerity, commitment to the group) in order to gain rewards of various kinds; the desire to prevail during a conflict; the desire to create social bonds with others in order to satisfy the need for inclusion (e.g., Baumeister & Leary, 1995; Levine & Kerr, 2007); and the desire to establish a satisfying social identity, which can derive from belonging to a minority as well as a majority group (e.g., Barreto & Ellemers, 2009; Tajfel & Turner, 1979). Some social group motives parallel those just discussed. For example, an individual could want his or her group to be highly regarded by other groups and to prevail in intergroup conflicts. Other social group motives are possible as well, including the desire that group members have harmonious interpersonal relations, work to achieve group goals, and remain in the group even when attractive outside alternatives exist. As in the case of epistemic self and group motives, efforts to satisfy a social self or group motive can have implications for the creation and/or satisfaction of the same or a different motive at the other level, and hence it can be difficult to disentangle motives at the two levels. For example, because an individual's ability to achieve a positive

social identity depends on his or her group's superiority to other groups (Tajfel & Turner, 1979), efforts to achieve the group goal of successful intergroup competition may be motivated, at least in part, by the self goal of enhancing one's social identity.

So far, we have discussed epistemic and social motives separately. However, as our model specifies, individuals can have *both* kinds of motives simultaneously. Moreover, in some cases, the two kinds of motives can serve the same overall goal. For example, social consensus, or shared reality, can be driven by both (1) the need to affiliate and feel connected to other people (social motivation) and (2) the need to achieve a valid and reliable understanding of the world (epistemic motivation) (Echterhoff et al., 2009). Similarly, group identification can be driven by both (1) the need to strengthen one's social identity by helping one's group shine in comparison to a rival group (social motivation; Tajfel & Turner, 1979) and (2) the need to reduce uncertainty about the self or things related to the self (epistemic motivation; Hogg, 2007).

An interesting feature of our multiple-motive framework is that actions that serve a particular motive at one level sometimes produce very different (and not necessarily intended) effects at other levels. This is nicely illustrated by cases involving self and group motives. Perhaps the best example comes from classical economics, which posits that individually self-interested economic agents produce a perfectly efficient allocation of resources as an aggregate effect at the group level. Another example is based on the observation that gossip is a universal human behavior (Foster, 2004). At the individual level, the primary motive seems to be to achieve entertainment and social connection by sharing information about others. Dunbar (2004) provides an evolutionary interpretation of this motive. He argues that humans have evolved to value gossip because it serves a critical function at the group level, namely spreading information about deviance within the group and therefore discouraging misbehavior and alerting group members to keep an eye on actual and potential deviants (cf. Kurzban & Leary, 2001; Neuberg, Smith, & Asher, 2000). He further asserts that this group-level function drove the evolution of our interest in gossip through group selection mechanisms. Similar evolutionary arguments can be made for other human tendencies. For example, our individual-level interest in attractive others as potential mates has been interpreted as an evolved preference that achieves the group-level goal of favoring the selection of mating partners with high genetic quality.

Our analysis suggests a number of complexities regarding the relationship between motivation and cognition in groups. For example, as noted earlier, the distinction between self and group motives can be problematic when motives at the two levels are similar or identical (e.g., a desire to find the correct answer). Nonetheless, we believe that this distinction, coupled with the distinction between epistemic and social motives, provides a useful framework for analyzing group decision making and problem solving. In the following sections, we apply our CISD model to this task.

Role of Group Tasks

As noted above, our third assumption is that the relationship between group members' motivation and cognition is influenced by their ability to evaluate the utility of their own and others' information, which is affected by the collective task they are working on. Several typologies of cognitive group tasks have been proposed over the years (for reviews, see Larson, 2010; McGrath, 1984). The most influential typology is Laughlin's (1980) distinction between intellective and judgmental tasks, which places heavy emphasis on "demonstrability." Intellective tasks (e.g., algebra problems) have a demonstrably correct answer, and successful group performance involves obtaining this answer. In contrast, judgmental tasks (e.g., jury decisions) do not have a demonstrably correct answer, and successful group performance involves simply (or not so simply) achieving consensus on a collective decision. According to Laughlin and Ellis (1986), the necessary and sufficient conditions for a demonstrably correct response include (1) group consensus on the appropriate verbal or mathematical system for obtaining a correct answer, (2) sufficient information to deduce the correct answer using this system, (3) at least one group member who knows the correct answer and has the motivation and ability to demonstrate it to others, and (4) these others' ability to recognize a correct answer when it is presented. Relatively few cognitive group tasks meet these rigorous criteria, however. For this and other reasons, it makes sense to view such tasks as varying along a continuum ranging from low to high demonstrability, with most falling somewhere between these two extremes. In this context, it is important to recognize that demonstrability depends not only on task characteristics per se, but also on group members' abilities and motivations (Larson, 2010; Stasser & Dietz-Uhler, 2001).

Several efforts have been made to characterize group tasks in terms of their demonstrability (e.g., Hastie, 1986; Larson, 2010; Laughlin & Ellis, 1986; McGrath, 1984). It is generally agreed that tasks such as verbal Eureka problems, algebra problems, and object transfer problems (e.g., Tower of Hanoi) fall toward the high-demonstrability end of the continuum, whereas tasks such as choice dilemma problems, mock jury decisions, and attitudinal judgments fall toward the low-demonstrability end. Viewing cognitive group tasks as varying along a demonstrability continuum has proved useful for explaining both group processes and outcomes (for reviews, see Larson, 2010; McGrath, 1984; Stasser & Dietz-Uhler, 2001). For example, this framework has been used to clarify the social combination process by which individual group members' response tendencies combine to yield a collective response (Laughlin & Ellis, 1986) and the relative accuracy of groups versus individuals on problem-solving tasks (e.g., Gigone & Hastie, 1997a; Hastie, 1986; Kerr, MacCoun, & Kramer, 1996).

In our analysis of information search and distribution in groups, we distinguish between *group problem-solving tasks*, which have high demonstrability, and *group decision-making tasks*, which have low demonstrability. In addition, we discuss an important task type that is hard to place on the demonstrability continuum—*group idea generation (brainstorming) tasks*. Finally, we discuss what Tindale et al. (2003) call *socially shared metacognition*. Our goal is not to provide an exhaustive review of theoretical and empirical work on these task types. Rather, we seek to use the existing literature as a context for suggesting potentially interesting questions regarding information search and distribution in groups working on cognitive tasks. In addition, we seek to broaden the discussion of this topic, and the relationship between motivation and cognition more generally, by introducing examples of information search and distribution that are relevant to group cognition but have been neglected by social psychologists (e.g., swarm intelligence models, gossip).

Group Problem-Solving Tasks: High Demonstrability
Social Decision Scheme Theory

In problem-solving tasks, some answers are clearly better than others. Usually, "better" is defined dichotomously, such that any proposed answer is regarded as either correct or incorrect (Larson, 2010). In high-demonstrability (i.e., intellective) tasks, group members have the relevant shared knowledge and skills to be able to verify the correctness of any proposed answer (Laughlin & Ellis, 1986). Such tasks give rise to specific patterns of group performance, which are conveniently described using the Social Decision Scheme (SDS) analysis devised by Davis (1973) and later elaborated by Davis and his colleagues (see Stasser, Kerr, & Davis, 1989). The composition of a problem-solving group is described by the number of members who individually prefer correct versus incorrect answers. For example, a six-person group may have anywhere from zero to six members who initially favor the correct answer. The SDS approach describes the probability that, given an initial distribution of member preferences, the group as a whole will eventually agree on the correct solution. For problems with *obvious* demonstrably correct solutions (e.g., Eureka problems, algebra problems, object transfer problems), this outcome will occur if one member initially proposes the right answer, a pattern termed *truth wins* (Laughlin & Ellis, 1986). In contrast, for problems with *nonobvious* demonstrably correct solutions (e.g., English vocabulary, general world knowledge, analogies), this outcome will occur only if two members propose the right answer, a pattern termed *truth-supported wins* (Laughlin & Ellis, 1986).

Collective Induction

Laughlin and his colleagues have studied a specific task with relatively high demonstrability, termed *collective induction*, in which groups seek to discover rules that can account for sets of observed facts (see Laughlin, 1999). In Laughlin's task, groups are given decks of 52 playing cards and told that the experimenter has devised a rule (e.g., "diamonds") that describes a sequence of cards. The experimenter initially puts down a card (e.g., the four of diamonds) conforming to the rule. Then, on the following trials, each group member records his or her individual hypothesis, after which group members collectively decide on a hypothesized rule (e.g., "fours") and then choose a card to test their hypothesis (e.g., the four of spades). The experimenter indicates whether or not the card conforms to the rule, and the cycle is repeated until time runs out. Although collective induction has a demonstrable (i.e., intellective) component, it also has a nondemonstrable (i.e., judgmental) component. Determining whether any proposed rule is consistent or inconsistent with the currently available evidence is a demonstrable decision. (Of course, as the number of cards that have been tried increases, the

pattern of evidence becomes complex, and groups may make errors, such as mistakenly proposing a hypothesis that is inconsistent with already-obtained evidence). But groups must also assess which of several candidate rules that are all consistent with the evidence to try next, and that is a nondemonstrable decision. Laughlin and his colleagues find that if group members advocate different candidate rules, groups often select one to test based on the number of members supporting each one, a "majority wins" SDS rule that is characteristic of nondemonstrable tasks (discussed below). Still, because correct hypotheses will survive repeated trials (by definition, they will never be disconfirmed by future evidence) and incorrect hypotheses may be falsified, if a group member proposes the correct hypothesis, it is very likely to ultimately prevail (Laughlin, 1999).

Cognitive Models of Collective Search

As suggested above, in the most frequently studied group problem-solving tasks, any proposed solution is defined as either correct or incorrect. This means both that the value of any solution is measured on a dichotomous scale (right or wrong) and that only a single solution can be correct. In such cases, demonstrability means, as Laughlin and Ellis (1986) argued, that the group members can identify whether or not a proposed solution is correct. In other tasks, however, the value of proposed solutions can vary continuously and hence can be represented as values on an ordinal (and sometimes interval) scale.[1] Consider as an analogy brewing beers using different recipes (amount of hops and malt, type of yeast, temperature and time for aging, etc.). Each recipe yields a product that can be evaluated for its tastiness, allowing one recipe to be declared better than another. In such a context, demonstrability means that all group members can immediately agree on the relative value (quality) of each recipe (potential problem solution). Note that (1) the quality of a solution falls on a continuous scale—a solution is not simply "correct" or "incorrect," and (2) there is no externally provided constraint on the number of "correct" solutions or the maximal value that a solution may have. As a result, there can rarely be certainty about what solution is "best" because an as-yet-untried solution may always turn out to surpass the current best.

Models of group problem solving in such contexts have been developed outside of social psychology. They usually conceptualize the task as involving collective search, with multiple group members (agents) searching simultaneously for good solutions. For example, Kennedy and Eberhart (2001) advanced the "swarm intelligence" model, inspired by social psychological theories of social influence. Many agents search in parallel for good solutions to a problem, with each potential solution conceptualized as a location in a multidimensional space. Each agent tries various solutions, learning the value of each location and keeping track of the location where it has found the best value to date. Each agent also sees information from a few "neighbor" agents about the locations they explore and the values they obtain. At each point in time, each agent chooses to explore a new location near its personal best-ever spot and its neighbors' best-ever spots. Information about a particularly good solution found by one agent will flow to its neighbors, then to theirs, and so forth, eventually leading the entire population to converge on that solution. Metaphorically, think of a brewing company's brewmasters trying promising recipes. Each initially searches a separate region of potential recipes (gaining the efficiency of parallel search), but they can communicate, so if one finds a good result, others can converge to carry out a more detailed and intensive search of similar recipes.

The swarm intelligence model has been influential within cognitive science, despite that field's traditional focus on modeling individual-level cognition, and several cognitive science researchers are investigating related issues of collective cognition (Goldstone & Janssen, 2005; Rendell et al., 2010). Mason, Jones, and Goldstone (2008), for example, constructed an experimental situation somewhat akin to the swarm intelligence assumptions, but in a simple one-dimensional problem space. Participants using networked computers completed a series of trials, each of which involved choosing a number between 0 and 100 and receiving feedback about the numerical value of that guess (which they sought to maximize). On each trial, they also received information about the guesses and corresponding values from a specific set of other participants. Thus, as in the swarm intelligence model, once one group member identifies a particularly valuable location, others will learn that outcome and make guesses near that location on subsequent trials, and eventually the entire group will converge. To what extent should agents rely on their own independent personal exploration rather than imitating others' responses? A number of studies and models have tried to answer this question. Recently, Rendell et al. (2010) investigated the success of agents with varying mixes of individual exploration and imitation of others in a complex and changing problem

environment and found that the best strategy used almost all imitation. The investigators attributed this finding to the fact that agents often use (and therefore demonstrate for others) the highest-value behavior they know, thereby filtering information in a way that benefits imitators.

A major conclusion in this literature, emphasized for instance by Mason et al. (2008), is that even with these simple assumptions about freely exchanged and perfectly demonstrable information, more communication is not always better. Specifically, if the problem space is complex (e.g., many potential solutions look reasonably good), too much communication among agents often produces suboptimal outcomes for the group as a whole. Agents may rapidly converge on the first "pretty good" solution that is found, leaving other regions of the space less well explored and potentially missing better solutions. Slower or less efficient communication (e.g., fewer communication links within the group) can help avoid this problem of overreliance on shared information (see Hinsz et al., 1997; Hutchins, 1991). On the other hand, in simple problem spaces, more communication aids the group in converging quickly on a high-quality solution.

Motivational Issues for High-Demonstrability Tasks

In terms of our CISD model, tasks with high demonstrability typically elicit epistemic motivation, particularly the desire to arrive at an objectively "true" answer. This motivation might involve the self (cell 1) and/or the group (cell 2). That is, group members might desire a correct answer because having such an answer satisfies their personal desire to be correct and/or their desire to belong to a group that is collectively correct. The relative weight that group members assign to these two epistemic motives can vary from member to member and from group to group. Moreover, as noted above, satisfaction of one motive can affect satisfaction of the other. For example, in revealing a demonstrably correct answer to others, a group member who has both epistemic self and epistemic group motivation substantially increases the odds that the group as a whole will converge on the correct answer. But motivational congruence of this kind is not always the norm. Even when members are motivated only by the desire to be personally correct, simple self-interest would motivate them to adopt demonstrably correct answers that others propose. However, self-interest would not give members an incentive to share their own good answers with others. If our brewers searching for better beer recipes were not all employees of a single brewing company but rather lone entrepreneurs, they would have little reason to share information about outstanding recipes, unless, for example, they wanted to build relationships with others that would increase the likelihood of reciprocity on future occasions.

This example illustrates that social, as well as epistemic, motives can operate in high-demonstrability tasks (cells 3 and 4). For example, in the lone entrepreneur example of the brewers, individuals might not simply be indifferent to sharing demonstrably correct information but rather motivated to withhold such information (or even to share false information) in order to increase their competitive advantage in the marketplace. In contrast, other (more benign) social self motives, such as the desire to impress others with one's knowledge, might cause people to share demonstrably correct answers even when they had no epistemic group motivation. And certain social group motives, such as the desire that one's group have a better answer than a rival group, might lead to information sharing within the group even when epistemic motivation is low.

Group Decision-Making Tasks: Low Demonstrability

In contrast to the high-demonstrability tasks discussed above, many group decision-making tasks do not permit members to demonstrate conclusively to others the correctness of their proposed solutions. In Laughlin's terms, such tasks fall at the judgmental end of the intellective–judgmental continuum. Within social psychology, much of the relevant work involves tasks in which groups have to choose from among a small number of discrete alternatives. Prominent examples are research on jury decision making and information sharing in groups. Other work using low-demonstrability tasks involves collaborative memory and impression formation based on gossip.

Jury Decision Making

The paradigmatic example of discrete decision making in groups is jury decision making. It may be that one verdict (not guilty or guilty) is "correct" in some absolute sense, but in the jury room the available information and group processes often do not permit members to demonstrate the correctness of verdicts. Therefore, group members are left to make arguments for their preferred positions, often using different criteria or weighting the same criteria

differently, which eventually results in a consensus that does not satisfy the criteria of demonstrability (Laughlin & Ellis, 1986).

Much of the work on jury decision making has been conducted within the SDS framework discussed above regarding group problem solving (see Stasser et al., 1989; Tindale et al., 2003). This research focuses on understanding the social influence process by which groups move from initial disagreement to final agreement on judgmental issues. An important generalization from SDS research on jury decision making is that initial faction size matters. There is strength in numbers, such that larger factions are more likely to prevail than are smaller factions. Thus, rather than a "truth wins" or "truth-supported wins" decision scheme (as occurs on intellective issues), groups making decisions on judgmental issues often follow a "majority wins" scheme.

Why is faction size so important on judgmental tasks? Four psychological processes may be involved (Stasser et al., 1989). First, because they have more available arguments for their position and can command more speaking time, larger factions may exert more informational influence than do smaller factions (Deutsch & Gerard, 1955). Second, because they have more power to deliver social rewards and punishments to other members, larger factions may exert more normative influence than do smaller factions (Deutsch & Gerard, 1955). Third, because group members engage in social comparison to evaluate the correctness of their opinions (Festinger, 1954), they feel insecure when they find themselves in a minority and may respond to this insecurity by conforming to the majority. Finally, because members are motivated to facilitate group locomotion toward such valued goals as reaching consensus (Festinger, 1954) and larger factions are closer to producing consensus than are smaller factions, larger factions may exert more influence.

Information Sharing in Groups

A major reason for using groups to make decisions is that they can potentially pool the unique knowledge of their members and thereby make better decisions than members acting alone. Research on information sharing in groups has used the hidden profile paradigm to test this assumption (see Stasser, 1999). For example, a group might have the task of deciding which of two job candidates is preferable, and before the discussion each member is given a set of facts, each of which supports either candidate A or candidate B. Although there are more total items favoring A than B (making A the better choice), each member gets more pro-B than pro-A information, and the pro-B items are shared (known to all members), whereas the pro-A items are unshared (known to only one member). So, before the discussion, group members are each biased toward the weaker candidate (B), and unless they discuss their unshared information (which favors A), they will make a poor group decision. Unfortunately, plentiful evidence indicates that groups often discuss information that all members initially share and ignore unshared (unique) information, leading to poor decisions (see Brodbeck et al., 2007; Mesmer-Magnus & DeChurch, 2009).

One potential explanation for this state of affairs is sampling bias (Stasser & Titus, 1985), which means that even if each group member randomly selects an item of information to discuss, shared information is more likely to be mentioned simply because more members know it. Sampling bias is not the whole story, however. Among other things, it cannot account for the observation that shared information is more likely than unshared information to be repeated after it is mentioned (e.g., Stasser, Taylor, & Hanna, 1989). This differential repetition may have several causes (Larson, 2010). First, shared information is easier to remember than unshared information because group members have more exposure to it and perhaps find it easier to understand (e.g., Larson & Harmon, 2007). Second, shared information receives more social validation from the group and hence is seen as more accurate and trustworthy (e.g., Greitemeyer & Schulz-Hardt, 2003). And third, because shared information is socially validated, group members evaluate themselves and each other as more competent (a process termed *mutual enhancement*) when they discuss it (e.g., Wittenbaum & Bowman, 2004). These latter mechanisms suggest that motivational, as well as cognitive, factors may contribute to the bias toward discussing shared information. Recent analyses go further, arguing that group decision making is a mixed-motive situation and hence information sharing varies as a function of whether group members have self-oriented or group-oriented motives (e.g., De Dreu et al., 2008; Mesmer-Magnus & DeChurch, 2009; Steinel, Utz, & Koning, 2010; Tomas & Butera, 2009).

As suggested by the social validation hypothesis, shared information is higher in demonstrability than is unshared information. Therefore, it is not surprising that different processes unfold when shared versus unshared information is contributed in a group setting. A unique feature of the hidden profile task is that high- and low-demonstrability information coexist within a single task, rather than (as is typical) characterize different tasks, such as algebra problem solving versus jury decision making.

In general, research on information sharing in hidden profile tasks assumes that the initial distribution of shared and unshared information in a group drives the content of the subsequent discussion, which in turn drives the group's collective decision. Other interpretations of the relationships between information distribution, group discussion, and collective decision have been offered, however. For example, Gigone and Hastie (e.g., 1993, 1997b) argued that information distribution influences group members' prediscussion decision preferences, which in turn affect both the content of the discussion and the collective decision (see also Winquist & Larson, 1998). Group members might favor preference-consistent information for discussion because they view it as more valid than preference-inconsistent information, because they wish to appear competent and self-consistent, or because they are following a conversational norm that they should explain the basis for their preference (Brodbeck et al., 2007).

Finally, it is important to note that the information sampling bias is not inevitable. For example, groups' tendency to focus on shared information is weaker when group members are informed about their own and others' expertise (Stasser, Stewart, & Wittenbaum, 1995; Van Ginkel & van Knippenberg, 2009), when leaders repeat unshared information (Larson, Christensen, Franz, & Abbott, 1998), when the task is presented as having a demonstrably correct answer (Stasser & Stewart, 1992), and when group discussion goes on for some time (Larson, Foster-Fishman, & Keys, 1994).

Collaborative Memory

The notion that memory is influenced by social factors has a long history in psychology and other disciplines (see Hirst & Manier, 2008; Werstsch & Roediger, 2008), and many terms have been used in describing and analyzing this influence, including collective memory, collective remembering, cultural memory, joint remembering, transactive memory, and collaborative recall. In this section, we focus on *collaborative memory*, in which people work together to recall information to which they were previously exposed (see Betts & Hinsz, 2010; Larson, 2010; Rajaram & Pereira-Pasarin, 2010). In so doing, we exclude work on how individual memory is influenced by the real or imagined presence of others (e.g., the saying-is-believing effect; see Echterhoff et al., 2009).

In many situations, group members learn information individually but later collaborate in retrieving that information. For example, individual jurors are exposed to common trial testimony without being able to communicate among themselves but later must reach a consensus on that information as they deliberate on their verdict. Intuitively, it might seem that groups engaging in collaborative recall would perform better than nominal groups of the same size because only interacting groups can (1) stimulate their members to remember information that they otherwise would forget (reduce errors of omission), (2) correct any memory errors that members make (reduce errors of commission), and (3) immediately recognize and accept accurate memories if they are introduced. However, as in work on brainstorming (discussed below), the collective recall of interacting groups is typically worse than the recall of nominal groups (see Betts & Hinsz, 2010; Larson, 2010; Rajaram & Pereira-Pasarin, 2010). Moreover, rather than using a truth-wins social decision scheme, groups engaging in collaborative recall tend to use either a truth-supported wins or a majority/plurality scheme (e.g., Hinsz, 1990; Van Swol, 2008). These findings are consistent with our assumption that memory tasks are typically not high in demonstrability: One member recalling a correct item does not necessarily result in social validation and group agreement.

Why is collaborative recall not more effective? The leading explanation assumes that group members disrupt one another's retrieval strategies during collective recall (e.g., Basden, Basden, Bryner, & Thomas, 1997). Individual memory is subject to a phenomenon termed *part-list cuing*, in which performance in recalling items from a list is harmed if people are given a few items from the list initially. Evidence suggests that, in group retrieval tasks, items recalled by others can cause this type of interference for individual group members, resulting in relatively poor collective recall (see Rajaram & Pereira-Pasarin, 2010). This phenomenon is analogous to production blocking in group brainstorming tasks. Other factors that may contribute to "collaborative inhibition" (Weldon & Bellinger, 1997) include group members' tendency to focus on shared rather than unshared information (Betts & Hinsz, 2010), caution in accepting others' recollections as valid (Larson, 2010), and failure to correct others' memory errors (Rajaram & Pereira-Pasarin, 2010).

A recent and fascinating finding suggests new directions for theory and research regarding collaborative recall. Miles, Nind, Henderson, and Macrae (2010) had participants and a confederate (posing as another participant) perform a dyadic motor task while repeating words they individually heard over headphones. Participants moved their arms up and down in synchrony with a metronome signal, while confederates were instructed to move either in-phase (i.e., mirroring the participant's movements) or anti-phase (i.e., moving down while the participant moved up, and vice versa). In-phase synchrony is known to create positive social outcomes and cooperative behavior in dyads (see Semin & Cacioppo, 2008). Participants were later administered a surprise recognition test for the words they had heard during the task. In the anti-phase condition, results demonstrated the usual memory advantage for "own" words (those the participant heard and spoke) over "other" words (those the confederate spoke). But in-phase synchrony eliminated this difference. These findings suggest that embodied cues (such as synchronized movements) can cause people to process information associated with others in the same ways they process information associated with the self, reflecting what has been termed *self–other overlap* (Aron et al., 1991). Although this study focused on individual memory rather than collective memory, it suggests intriguing questions about the operation of collaborative recall.

Impression Formation, Gossip, and Stereotyping

When people try to form impressions of other individuals, they often do so on the basis of limited amounts of information obtained from their own interactions with a target. Like many other situations of collective cognition, perceivers may also draw on information supplied by third parties, this time through *gossip*. A model of person perception incorporating socially shared information was recently developed by Smith and Collins (2009). Gossip from others can give us access to valuable information (e.g., about a target's rare but important and diagnostic negative behaviors) that we could not easily obtain on our own. As a side effect, as information about social targets is shared through the social network, individual perceivers' impressions become aggregated into a more or less consensual social reputation of the target.

In person perception, there are a potentially large number of items of information (i.e., behavioral observations of the target) that can be used to support a person impression (such as thinking of the target as forthright and honest, but not interpersonally sensitive). Individual perceivers can acquire observations on their own or share them with others through gossip (Dunbar, 2004; Smith & Collins, 2009). As a result, a perceiver may have some information that is unique and unshared (personally observed) and other information that is shared with other perceivers (either through gossip or because they jointly observed the target's behaviors). Perceivers are free to question either the validity or importance of others' observations (or their own, for that matter), for example by ascribing the behavior to an irrelevant situational factor. Thus, the demonstrability of gossip information is low: Hearing what someone else thinks about the target, perceivers are not immediately forced to conclude that the gossip source is correct. As with collective search, perceivers can always gather additional information, either by interacting directly with the target or seeking additional gossip information. However, unlike the hidden-profile paradigm, the pool of observations is not fixed at the outset. Finally, gossip information is usually shared with specific others (similar to information search models) rather than broadcast to all group members as in a face-to-face group discussion.

One interesting complication is that gossip not only spreads information around but also changes it. Often information is simplified and exaggerated (Baron et al., 1997; Gilovich, 1987). A condition favoring this outcome is a shared expectation held by members of the group, such as a social stereotype about a target. This often leads to more communication of stereotype-consistent than stereotype-inconsistent information about the target (e.g., Lyons & Kashima, 2001; Ruscher, 1998; Thompson, Judd, & Park, 2000). This strength of this bias varies, however, and the motivations of group members are critical to understanding when stereotype-consistent information will dominate. Among the motives favoring transmission of stereotype-consistent information are the desire to develop consensus (shared beliefs) with others (Ruscher, 1998) and the desire to establish social relationships with others (Lyons, Clark, Kashima, & Kurz, 2008; cf. Echterhoff et al., 2009; Wittenbaum & Bowman, 2004). In contrast, the bias toward transmitting stereotype-consistent information may be reduced (and even reversed) when communicators are motivated to provide maximally useful information to others (Lyons & Kashima, 2003; see also Klein, Tindale, & Brauer, 2008).

Motivational Issues for Low-Demonstrability Tasks

The motivational issues associated with low-demonstrability tasks are even more complex than those for high-demonstrability tasks. This occurs in part because additional epistemic motives can arise in low-demonstrability tasks, including the desire for a firm answer irrespective of its content, the desire for an answer that satisfies one's existing preferences, and the desire for an answer that is "true" because it reflects social consensus (rather than objective reality). Moreover, more than one of these epistemic motives can be operating at a given time, and they can be self motives, group motives, or both.

Social motives may also play out differently in low-demonstrability than in high-demonstrability tasks. For example, when demonstrability is low, group members who have certain social self motives (e.g., desire to impress others with their knowledge, desire to prevail during a conflict) may be more likely to slant information they present to satisfy their own needs because they are not constrained to make demonstrably correct claims (cf. De Dreu et al., 2008). Moreover, members who have certain social group motives (e.g., desire for harmonious interpersonal relations) may be more likely to accept others' information rather than voice criticism or dissent because they evaluate this information using the criterion of plausibility rather than objective truth.

Interesting motivational issues arise in the case of exchange of gossip. Perceivers may spread around information about a target person so that the whole group becomes aware of and can benefit from it. That is, I might tell everyone how shabbily William treated Charlotte, with the goal of helping others avoid the mistake of trusting William in the future. But I might also want to keep some information about William (e.g., skeletons in his closet) to myself in order to manipulate him and so would avoid sharing this information with the group as a whole. In addition, I might spread positive information about a friend and let her know I did so in order to solidify my relationship with her. Or I might exchange gossip with a specific other in order to communicate that I like and trust him. Finally, I might spread only positive gossip about ingroup members and negative gossip about outgroup members in order to increase the perception of ingroup superiority and enhance my social identity.

Group Idea Generation Tasks

Groups are sometimes used to produce creative ideas. The most frequently studied approach, termed *brainstorming* by Osborn (1953), involves face-to-face groups in which members are instructed to produce as many ideas as possible, to come up with unusual ideas, to avoid criticism, and to combine and improve others' ideas. Because there is no opportunity to offer arguments or explanations for one's contributions, and evaluation of ideas is explicitly prohibited in brainstorming, demonstrability is irrelevant to this task.

The history of brainstorming research is mostly one of disappointing (and initially surprising) findings that brainstorming groups produce *fewer* ideas than do nominal groups composed of an equal number of individuals working independently. As Larson (2010) noted, "the early empirical literature is nearly monolithic in its repudiation of the group brainstorming hypothesis" (p. 81) (see also Mullen, Johnson, & Salas, 1991). These findings are particularly interesting in light of evidence that people who participate in brainstorming groups are more satisfied with their performance than are people who worked alone and think they would have performed worse if they had worked alone (e.g., Nijstad, Stroebe, & Lodewijkx, 2006; Paulus, Dzindolet, Poletes, & Camacho, 1993).

Both cognitive and motivational factors have been suggested to explain the ineffectiveness of group brainstorming. A major cognitive factor is "production blocking," which stems from the fact that group members must take turns presenting their ideas. While waiting for others to finish talking, members often forget their ideas and hence are unable to contribute them. Motivational factors include evaluation apprehension (fear that others will judge one's ideas negatively), social loafing and free riding, and performance matching (in which high performers match the performance of low performers). Although all of these factors may contribute to the ineffectiveness of group brainstorming, production blocking seems to have the strongest impact.

Recent efforts have been made to clarify the cognitive processes that underlie idea generation in group contexts. These include the associative memory matrix model (Brown & Paulus, 2002; Brown, Tumeo, Larey, & Paulus, 1998) and the search for ideas in associative memory model (Nijstad & Stroebe, 2006; Stroebe, Nijstad, & Rietzschel, 2010). For example, the latter model incorporates intraindividual cognitive processes involving long-term and working memory, knowledge activation, and idea generation, as well as interindividual processes that can produce *either* cognitive interference or cognitive stimulation.

So far, we have focused on the sheer number of ideas that brainstorming groups produce. What about the quality of these ideas? In general, the total number of ideas is positively (and strongly) correlated with the total number of high-quality ideas (Diehl & Stroebe, 1987). Given that brainstorming groups produce fewer total ideas than do nominal groups, it follows that they produce fewer high-quality ideas as well. The quantity–quality relationship seems to occur because people who generate many ideas engage in deeper exploration of relevant domain knowledge (Rietzschel, Nijstad, & Stroebe, 2007).

In recent years, efforts have been made to develop procedures to improve the effectiveness of brainstorming groups. One such procedure is electronic brainstorming, in which individuals type their ideas into networked computers that simultaneously display the ideas of other group members. This procedure avoids productivity losses due to production blocking, yet still allows members to access others' ideas as a potential source of inspiration. In groups of four or more members, electronic brainstorming is more productive than face-to-face brainstorming. Moreover, in groups of 10 or more members, electronic brainstorming is even more productive than individual brainstorming in nominal groups (Dennis & Williams, 2005).

Motivational Issues for Group Idea Generation Tasks

Although motives in all four cells of the CISD model may influence behavior in group idea generation tasks, it is likely that self motives are generally stronger than group motives. This is because there is no pressure for brainstorming participants to converge on a single response (in fact, the pressure is just the opposite—to generate divergent responses) and because individual rather than group productivity is typically highlighted as the goal of brainstorming. This bias is reflected in the social self motives that have been posited to reduce performance in face-to-face brainstorming groups, including evaluation apprehension, social loafing, and free riding. Epistemic self motives could also play a role in brainstorming if participants departed from instructions to generate "wild and crazy" ideas by trying to generate "good" ideas (e.g., that are easy to implement or likely to be effective). And group motives cannot be completely ruled out in brainstorming. For example, performance matching may be driven, at least in part, by the desire to maintain group harmony by making sure members' performance levels are similar. And group members would be expected to work hard in generating novel responses if the ingroup were competing with an outgroup (cf. Munkes & Diehl, 2003).

Socially Shared Metacognition

Metacognition in decision-making groups can be defined as "how group members think about the ways they process and share knowledge" (Tindale et al., 2003, p. 390). Although such metacognition can take several forms (see Hinsz, 2004; Tindale et al., 2003), we focus here on two varieties that have received particular attention—transactive memory systems and team mental models.

Transactive Memory Systems

In contrast to collective recall situations in which all group members were exposed to common information and presumably were motivated to learn all of it, in other situations different group members were exposed to different information or were motivated to learn only a portion of common information. In order for the group as a whole to recall information effectively in the latter cases, it must develop a transactive memory system that clarifies who is responsible for acquiring, storing, and retrieving particular information (Wegner, 1987). An effective transactive memory system, which is based on a shared and accurate understanding of group members' task-relevant interests and expertise, ensures that members not only will assume responsibility for particular kinds of information but also will know how these responsibilities are distributed within the group (i.e., who knows what). Evidence indicates that group members do in fact take responsibility for learning specific kinds of information as a function of their knowledge of others' interests and expertise (e.g., Hollingshead, 2000) and correctly access information that other members have stored (e.g., Littlepage, Hollingshead, Drake, & Littlepage, 2008). Moreover, transactive memory systems have been found to improve group performance on a variety of tasks (e.g., Lewis, 2004; Moreland, 1999). Both team training and individual training, combined with information about others' competencies, are more effective than individual training alone in creating transactive memory systems.

Team Mental Models

Researchers interested in understanding and improving team performance have devoted substantial theoretical and empirical attention to "team mental models" and related constructs (see DeChurch & Mesmer-Magnus, 2010a, 2010b; Mohammed, Ferzandi, & Hamilton, 2010; Rico, Sanchez-Manzanares, Gil, & Gibson, 2008). Team mental models are defined as "team members' shared, organized understanding and mental representation of knowledge about key elements of the team's relevant environment" (Mohammed et al., 2010). Team mental models are broader than transactive memory systems in that they focus on a wider array of shared representations (e.g., tasks, equipment, working relationships) and on how these representations affect team processes (e.g., communication, coordination) as well as outcomes (Mohammed & Dumville, 2001). Evidence indicates that the mental model *sharedness* predicts both team process and team performance (DeChurch & Mesmer-Magnus, 2010a, b). Interestingly, the mental model *accuracy* does not have consistent effects on either process or accuracy (Mohammed et al., 2010). As in the case of transactive memory, team training facilitates the development of team mental models. Although attitudes toward other members (e.g., trust, liking) have been suggested as possible contributors to the development of team mental models (e.g., Fiore, Salas, & Cannon-Bowers, 2001), little work has been done to investigate their impact. Finally, there is increasing interest in the conditions under which *dissimilarity* in team members' mental models enhances collective performance (e.g., Kellermanns, Floyd, Pearson, & Spencer, 2008; cf. Baron, 2005; Brodbeck et al., 2007).

Motivational Assumptions for Socially Shared Metacognition

In the case of socially shared metacognition, epistemic motivation is likely to predominate. This is because transactive memory systems and team mental models are important in contexts in which group members work on collective tasks that require a high degree of coordination. On such tasks, members are motivated to ensure that both they and their colleagues understand the demands of the task and the capabilities of all the people who will be responsible for meeting these demands. These epistemic motives have both self and group components. In the former case, members want to ensure that they understand the nature of the group's task and resources, their own task-relevant skills and responsibilities, and the skills and responsibilities of others. In the latter case, members want to ensure that everyone in the group shares their perceptions along these dimensions—in other words, that everyone is "on the same page" regarding who is responsible for what. Moreover, members prefer demonstrably correct answers to the various questions that must be answered. When, as is often the case, these are not available, members must settle for less, for example, inferring others' ability from knowledge of their past training. Unfortunately, such inferences do not provide a firm basis for predicting whether others can meet the specific challenges the group faces.

This is not to say, of course, that social motives play no role in transactive memory systems and team mental models. For example, group members may be interested in impressing others with their knowledge and skills and in occupying the most prestigious and highest paying roles in the group. Moreover, in the context of intergroup competition based on task performance, members are likely to desire that their group have a *better* transactive memory system or team mental model than the opposition.

Conclusion and Future Directions

In this chapter, we reviewed theory and research on group decision making and problem solving with a special focus on collective information search and distribution. In so doing, we discussed work on topics that are well known to social psychologists (e.g., jury decision making, information sharing in groups, brainstorming) as well as topics that are not (e.g., animal social learning, swarm intelligence models, gossip, team mental models). Our analysis, which highlighted the relationship between motivation and cognition in groups, was based on our CISD model. The model posits two motivational levels—motives group members hold for themselves (self) versus those they hold for the group as a whole (group)—crossed with two motivational types—motives related to acquiring knowledge and understanding (epistemic) versus those related to facilitating intragroup and intergroup relations (social). The model distinguishes several varieties of both self and group motives and epistemic and social motives. It addition, it assumes that neither self and group motives nor epistemic and social motives are mutually exclusive, and it posits that two or more specific motives can operate simultaneously in each of the four cells of the model. Our analysis also assumes that the relationship between motivation and cognition in groups is influenced by members' ability to evaluate the utility of their own and others' information, which is affected by features of the collective task they are working on. In particular, we argue that the demonstrability of the task (i.e., the degree to which objectively correct answers can be specified) is important (cf. Laughlin, 1980; Laughlin & Ellis, 1986).

The review leads to three broad conclusions. Perhaps most important is that across all the types of tasks discussed here, group cognition seems to depend more on collective information search and distribution than on individual information processing. Consistent with this argument, Woolley, Chabris, Pentland, Hasmi, and Malone (2010) recently identified a "collective intelligence" factor, paralleling the "g" factor of individual cognitive abilities, that explains group performance across a variety of tasks. Rather than reflecting the average (or maximal) intelligence of individual group members, collective intelligence is correlated with members' average social sensitivity and the equality of their participation levels (as well as the proportion of women in the group).

A second broad conclusion is that collective information search and distribution cannot be understood without carefully specifying the motives that drive these activities. As posited by our CISD model and related models (e.g., De Dreu et al.'s MIP-G model), cognition and motivation in group settings are inextricably interwoven, and any effort to explain cognition in the absence of motivation is doomed to failure.

A third broad conclusion is that task demonstrability plays a key role in shaping collective information search and distribution. Although demonstrability has long been recognized as an important determinant of group performance, we especially emphasize its relationship to motivation. For example, we argue that, on high-demonstrability tasks, epistemic motivation (particularly the desire to arrive at an objectively true answer) tends to take priority, although social motives (both self and group) can also be important. Moreover, we argue that the motivational issues associated with low-demonstrability tasks are even more complex than those for high-demonstrability tasks. This occurs because additional epistemic motives (e.g., desire for a firm answer irrespective of its content) can arise in low-demonstrability tasks and because certain social motives (e.g., desire to impress others with one's knowledge) can play out differently in such tasks than in high-demonstrability tasks. We note that one reason for the complexity of hidden-profile tasks is that information varies in demonstrability within a single task (with shared information being higher than unshared information). And finally, we suggest that a relatively unexplored kind of low-demonstrability task—exchange of gossip—raises a number of interesting motivational issues.

Our review also suggests potentially fruitful avenues for future research on collective information search and distribution. One key question raised by our CISD model is, What happens if different group members have different motives? For example, one member may want the group to reach an objectively correct solution, a second may want the group to adopt his or her preferred solution, and a third may want the group to avoid conflict and experience warm interpersonal relationships. De Dreu et al. (2008) discuss such group composition effects, suggesting, for example, that people with proself goals tend to convert those with prosocial goals, causing groups to develop a predominantly proself motivation. But many additional questions remain about how people with different motives influence one another. For example, interesting factional dynamics may arise when subsets of group members (e.g., numerical minorities and majorities) have different motives (cf. Levine & Kaarbo, 2001). Perhaps a numerical minority desiring nonspecific closure will be more likely to convince a majority to adopt this goal in a situation involving time pressure or noise (cf. Kruglanski et al., 2006).

Another issue that deserves attention concerns the effects of the network structure that links group members. Although much theory on collective cognition assumes that all group members are in a simultaneous communication with one another (e.g., are sitting around a table discussing an issue), this is often not true. Instead, people are typically linked to specific others in social networks (e.g., Kennedy & Eberhart, 2001). This is evident, for instance, when group discussion and decision making take place through a series of phone calls or e-mails, with each member communicating with some but not all of the others. We can therefore conceptualize information sharing and, more generally, social influence as flowing along the links in a social network. Properties of the network shape how information flows, how fast it "infects" the whole group, and so on. Mason, Conrey, and Smith (2007) reviewed work on the role of networks in shaping patterns of social influence, including the impact of the network structure on how rapidly the entire group converges to a single decision versus maintaining multiple viewpoints (see also Lyons et al., 2008). Future work on collective information search and distribution might profitably explore the effects of different network structures rather than continuing to assume that all members are communicating with all others.

Author Note

Preparation of this chapter was partially supported by NSF Grant SES-0951516 and by NSF Grant BCS-094911. Correspondence should be addressed to John M. Levine, 516 LRDC Bldg., University of Pittsburgh, Pittsburgh, PA 15260; e-mail jml@pitt.edu; 412-624-7462.

Notes

1. Tasks in which the degree of correctness of a proposed solution can vary continuously, such as tasks in which a group tries to estimate a quantity along a continuum, have received relatively little attention in social psychology. See Stasser and Dietz-Uhler's (2001) discussion of collective estimation tasks and Larson's (2010) discussion of quantity estimation tasks.

References

Aron, A., Aron, E. N., Tudor, M., & Nelson, G. (1991). Close relationships as including other in the self. *Journal of Personality and Social Psychology, 60,* 241–253.

Baron, R. S. (2005). So right it's wrong: Groupthink and the ubiquitous nature of polarized group decision making. In M. P. Zanna (Ed.), *Advances in experimental social psychology* (Vol. 37, pp. 219–253). San Diego, CA: Academic Press.

Baron, R. S., David, J. P., Brunsman, B. M. & Inman, M. (1997). Why listeners hear less than they are told: Attentional load and the teller-listener extremity effect. *Journal of Personality and Social Psychology, 72*(4), 826–838.

Barreto, M., & Ellemers, N. (2009). Multiple identities and the paradox of social inclusion. In F. Butera & J. M. Levine (Eds.), *Coping with minority status: Responses to exclusion and inclusion* (pp. 269–292). New York: Cambridge University Press.

Bar-Tal, D. (2000). *Shared beliefs in a society: Social psychological analysis.* Thousand Oaks, CA: Sage.

Basden, B. H., Basden, D. R., Bryner, S., & Thomas, R. L. III (1997). A comparison of group and individual remembering: Does collaboration disrupt retrieval strategies? *Journal of Experimental Psychology: Learning, Memory, and Cognition, 23,* 1176–1189.

Baumeister, R. F., & Leary, M. R. (1995). The need to belong: Desire for interpersonal attachments as a fundamental human motivation. *Psychological Bulletin, 117,* 497–529.

Betts, K. R., & Hinsz, V. B. (2010). Collaborative group memory: Processes, performance, and techniques for improvement. *Social and Personality Compass, 4,* 119–130.

Brodbeck, F. C., Kerschreiter, R., Mojzisch, A., & Schulz-Hardt, S. (2007). Group decision making under conditions of distributed knowledge: The information asymmetries model. *Academy of Management Review, 32,* 459–479.

Brown, V. R., & Paulus, P. B. (2002). Making group brainstorming more effective: Recommendations from an associative memory perspective. *Current Directions in Psychological Science, 11,* 208–212.

Brown, V., Tumeo, M., Larey, T. S., & Paulus, P. B. (1998). Modeling cognitive interactions during group brainstorming. *Small Group Research, 29,* 495–526.

Davis, J. H. (1973). Group decision and social interaction: A theory of group decision and social interaction: A theory of social decision schemes. *Psychological Review, 80,* 97–125.

DeChurch, L. A., & Mesmer-Magnus J. R. (2010a). The cognitive underpinnings of effective teamwork: A meta-analysis. *Journal of Applied Psychology, 95,* 32–53.

DeChurch, L. A., & Mesmer-Magnus J. R. (2010b). Measuring shared team mental models: A meta-analysis. *Group Dynamics: Theory, Research, and Practice, 14*, 1–14.

De Dreu, C. K. W., Nijstad, B. A., & van Knippenberg, D. (2008). Motivated information processing in group judgment and decision making. *Personality and Social Psychology Review, 12*, 22–49.

Dennis, A. R., & Williams, M. L. (2005). A meta-analysis of group size effects in electronic brainstorming: More heads are better than one. *International Journal of e-Collaboration, 1*, 24–42.

Deutsch, M., & Gerard, H. B. (1955). A study of normative and informational social influences upon individual judgment. *Journal of Abnormal and Social Psychology, 51*, 629–636.

Diehl, M., & Stroebe, W. (1987). Productivity loss in brainstorming groups: Toward the solution of a riddle. *Journal of Personality and Social Psychology, 53*, 487–509.

Dugatkin, L. A. (1992). Sexual selection and imitation—females copy the mate choice of others. *American Naturalist, 139*(6), 1384–1389.

Dunbar, R. I. M. (2004). Gossip in evolutionary perspective. *Review of General Psychology, 8,* 100–110.

Durkheim, E. (1898). Representations individuelles et representations collectives. *Revue de Metaphysique, 6*, 274–302. (Transl. D. F. Pocock, *Sociology and philosophy*.) New York: Free Press, 1953.

Echterhoff, G., Higgins, E. T., & Levine, J. M. (2009). Shared reality: Experiencing commonality with others' inner states about the world. *Perspectives on Psychological Science, 4,* 496–521.

Festinger, L. (1950). Informal social communication. *Psychological Review, 57*, 271–282.

Festinger, L. (1954). A theory of social comparison processes. *Human Relations, 7*, 117–140.

Fiore, S., Salas, E., & Cannon-Bowers, J. A. (2001). Group dynamics and shared mental model development. In M. London (Ed.), *How people evaluate others in organizations: Person perception and interpersonal judgment in industrial/organizational psychology* (pp. 309–336). Mahwah, NJ: Erlbaum.

Foster, E. K. (2004). Research on gossip: Taxonomy, methods, and future directions. *Review of General Psychology, 8*(2), 78–99.

Gigone, D., & Hastie, R. (1993). The common knowledge effect: Information sharing and group judgment. *Journal of Personality and Social Psychology, 65*, 959–974.

Gigone, D., & Hastie, R. (1997a), Proper analysis of the accuracy of group judgments. *Psychological Bulletin, 121*, 149–167.

Gigone, D., & Hastie, R. (1997b). The impact of information on small group choice. *Journal of Personality and Social Psychology, 72*, 132–140.

Gilovich, T. (1987). Secondhand information and social judgment. *Journal of Experimental Social Psychology, 23*, 59–74.

Goldstone, R. L., & Janssen, M. A. (2005). Computational models of collective behaviors. *Trends in Cognitive Sciences, 9*(9), 424–430.

Greitemeyer, T., & Schulz-Hardt, S. (2003). Preference-consistent evaluation of information in the hidden profile paradigm: Beyond group-level explanations for the dominance of shared information in group decisions. *Journal of Personality and Social Psychology, 84*, 322–339.

Hardin, C. D., & Higgins, E. T. (1996). Shared reality: How social verification makes the subjective objective. In R. M. Sorrentino & E. T. Higgins (Eds.), *Handbook of motivation and cognition: The interpersonal context* (Vol. 3, pp. 28–84). New York: Guilford.

Hastie, R. (1986). Experimental evidence on group accuracy. In B. Grofman & G. Owen (Eds.), *Decision research* (Vol. 2, pp. 129–157). Greenwich, CT: JAI Press.

Hinsz, V. B. (1990). Cognitive and consensus processes in group recognition memory performance. *Journal of Personality and Social Psychology, 59*, 705–718.

Hinsz, V. B. (2004). Metacognition and mental models in groups: An illustration with metamemory of group recognition memory. In E. Salas & S. M. Fiore (Eds.), *Team cognition: Understanding the factors that drive process and performance* (pp. 33–58). Washington, DC: American Psychological Association.

Hinsz, V. B., Tindale, R. S., & Vollrath, D. A. (1997). The emerging conceptualization of groups as information processors. *Psychological Bulletin, 121*, 43–64.

Hirst, W., & Manier, D. (2008). Towards a psychology of collective memory. *Memory, 16*, 183–200.

Hogg, M. A. (2007). Uncertainty-identity theory. In M. P. Zanna (Ed.), *Advances in experimental social psychology* (Vol. 39, pp. 69–126). San Diego, CA: Academic Press.

Hollingshead, A. B. (2000). Perceptions of expertise in and transactive memory in work relationships. *Group Processes Intergroup Relations, 3*, 257–267.

Hutchins, E. (1991). The social organization of distributed cognition. In L. B. Resnick, J. M. Levine, & S. D. Teasley (Eds.), *Perspectives on socially shared cognition* (pp. 283–307). Washington, DC: American Psychological Association.

Kellermanns, F. W., Floyd, S. W., Pearson, A. W., & Spencer, B. (2008). The contingent effect of constructive confrontation on the relationship between shared mental models and decision quality. *Journal of Organizational Behavior, 29*, 119–137.

Kelman, H. C. (1958). Compliance, identification, and internalization: Three processes of attitude change. *Journal of Conflict Resolution, 2*, 51–60.

Kennedy, J., & Eberhart, R. C. (2001). *Swarm intelligence.* San Francisco: Morgan Kauffmann/Academic Press.

Kerr, N. L., MacCoun, R. J., & Kramer, G. P. (1996). Bias in judgment: Comparing individuals and groups. *Psychological Review, 103*, 687–719.

Klein, O., Tindale, S., & Brauer, M. (2008). The consensualization of stereotypes in small groups. In Y. Kashima, K. Fiedler, & P. Freytag (Eds.), *Stereotype dynamics: Language-based approaches to the formation, maintenance, and transformation of stereotypes* (pp. 263–292). New York: Erlbaum.

Kruglanski, A. W. (1989). *Lay epistemics and human knowledge: Cognitive and motivational bases.* New York: Plenum.

Kruglanski, A. W. (2004). *The psychology of closed mindedness.* New York: Psychology Press.

Kruglanski, A. W., Dechesne, M., Orehek, E., & Pierro, A. (2009). Three decades of lay epistemics: The why, how, and who of knowledge formation. *European Review of Social Psychology, 20*, 146–191.

Kruglanski, A. W., Pierro, A., Mannetti, L., & De Grada, E. (2006). Groups as epistemic providers: Need for closure and the unfolding of group-centrism. *Psychological Review, 113*, 84–100.

Kurzban, R., & Leary, M. R. (2001). Evolutionary origins of stigmatization: The functions of social exclusion. *Psychological Bulletin, 127*, 187–208.

Laland, K. N. (2004). Social learning strategies. *Learning and Behavior, 32,* 4–14.

Larson, J. R., Jr. (2010). *In search of synergy in small group performance.* New York: Psychology Press.

Larson, J. R., & Christensen, C. (1993). Groups as problem-solving units: Toward a new meaning of social cognition. *British Journal of Social Psychology, 32,* 5–30.

Larson, J. R., Jr., Christensen, C., Franz, T M., & Abbott, A. S. (1998). Diagnosing groups: The pooling, management, and impact of shared and unshared case information in team-based medical decision making. *Journal of Personality and Social Psychology, 75,* 93–108.

Larson, J. R., Jr., Foster-Fishman, P. G., & Keys, C. B. (1994). Discussion of shared and unshared information in decision making groups. *Journal of Personality and Social Psychology, 67,* 446–461.

Larson, J. R., Jr., & Harmon, V. M. (2007). Recalling shared vs unshared information mentioned during group discussion: Toward understanding differential repetition rates. *Group Processes and Intergroup Relations, 10,* 311–322.

Laughlin, P. R. (1980). Social combination processes of cooperative problem-solving groups on verbal intellective tasks. In M. Fishbein (Ed.), *Progress in social psychology* (Vol. 1, pp. 127–155). Hillsdale, NJ: Erlbaum.

Laughlin, P. R. (1999). Collective induction: Twelve postulates. *Organizational Behavior and Human Decision Processes, 80,* 50–69.

Laughlin, P. R., & Ellis, A. L. (1986). Demonstrability and social combination processes on mathematical intellective tasks. *Journal of Experimental Social Psychology, 22,* 177–189.

Le Bon, G. (1895). *Psychologie des foules.* Paris: F. Olean. (Transl. *The crowd.* London: T. Fisher Unwin, 1896).

Levine, J. M., & Higgins, E. T. (2001). Shared reality and social influence in groups and organizations. In F. Butera & G. Mugny (Eds.), *Social influence in social reality: Promoting individual and social change* (pp. 33–52). Bern, Switzerland: Hogrefe & Huber.

Levine, J. M., & Kaarbo, J. (2001). Minority influence in political decision-making groups. In C. K. W. De Dreu & N. K. De Vries (Eds.), *Group consensus and minority influence: Implications for innovation* (pp. 229–257). Malden, MA: Blackwell.

Levine, J. M., & Kerr, N. L. (2007). Inclusion and exclusion: Implications for group processes. In A. E. Kruglanski & E. T. Higgins (Eds.), *Social psychology: Handbook of basic principles* (2nd ed., pp. 759–784). New York: Guilford.

Levine, J. M., Resnick, L. B., & Higgins, E. T. (1993). Social foundations of cognition. *Annual Review of Psychology, 44,* 585–612.

Lewis, K. (2004). Knowledge and performance in knowledge-worker teams: A longitudinal study of transactive memory systems. *Management Science, 50,* 1519–1533.

Littlepage, G. E., Hollingshead, A. B., Drake, L. R., & Littlepage, A. M. (2008). Transactive memory and performance in work groups: Specificity, communication, ability differences, and work allocation. *Group Dynamics: Theory, Research, and Practice, 12,* 233–241.

Lyons, A., & Kashima, Y. (2001). The reproduction of culture: Communication processes tend to maintain cultural stereotypes. *Social Cognition, 19,* 372–394.

Lyons, A., & Kashima, Y. (2003). How are stereotypes maintained through communication? The influence of stereotype sharedness. *Journal of Personality and Social Psychology, 85,* 989–1005.

Lyons, A., Clark, A., Kashima, Y., & Kurz, T. (2008). Cultural dynamics of stereotypes: Social network processes and the perpetuation of stereotypes. In Y. Kashima, K. Fiedler, & P. Freytag (Eds.), *Stereotype dynamics: Language-based approaches to the formation, maintenance, and transformation of stereotypes* (pp. 59–92). New York: Erlbaum.

Mason, W. A., Conrey, F. R., & Smith, E. R. (2007). Situating social influence processes: Dynamic, multidirectional flows of influence within social networks. *Personality and Social Psychology Review, 11,* 279–300.

Mason, W. A., Jones, A., & Goldstone, R. L. (2008). Propagation of innovations in networked groups. *Journal of Experimental Psychology: General, 137,* 422–433.

McDougall, W. (1920). *The group mind: A sketch of the principles of collective psychology.* Chicago: G. P. Putnam's Sons.

McGrath, J. E. (1984). *Groups: Interaction, and performance.* Englewood Cliffs, NJ: Prentice-Hall.

Mead, G. H. (1934). *Mind, self, and society.* Chicago: University of Chicago Press.

Mesmer-Magnus, J. R., & DeChurch, L. A. (2009). Information sharing and team performance: A meta-analysis. *Journal of Applied Psychology, 94,* 535–546.

Miles, L. K., Nind, L. K., Henderson, Z., & Macrae, C. N. (2010). Moving memories: Behavioral synchrony and memory for self and others. *Journal of Experimental Social Psychology, 46,* 457–460.

Mohammed, S., & Dumville, B. (2001). Team mental models in a team knowledge framework: Expanding theory and measurement across disciplinary boundaries. *Journal of Organizational Behavior, 22,* 89–106.

Mohammed, S., Ferzandi, L., & Hamilton, K. (2010). Metaphor no more: A 15-year review of the team mental model construct. *Journal of Management, 36,* 876–910.

Moreland, R. L. (1999). Transactive memory: Learning who knows what in work groups and organizations. In L. L. Thompson, J. M. Levine, & D. M. Messick (Eds.), *Shared cognition in organizations: The management of knowledge* (pp. 1–31). Mahwah, NJ: Erlbaum.

Moscovici, S., & Doise, W. (1994). *Conflict and consensus: A general theory of collective decisions.* Thousand Oaks, CA: Sage.

Mullen, B., Johnson, C., & Salas, E. (1991). Productivity loss in brainstorming groups: A meta-analytic investigation. *Basic and Applied Social Psychology, 12,* 3–23.

Munkes, J., & Diehl, M. (2003). Matching or competition? Performance comparison processes in an idea generation task. *Group Processes & Intergroup Relations, 6,* 305–320.

Neuberg, S. L., Smith, D. M., & Asher, T. (2000). Why people stigmatize: Toward a biocultural framework. In T. F. Heatherton, R. E. Kleck, M. R. Hebl, & J. G. Hull (Eds.), *The social psychology of stigma* (pp. 31–61). New York: Guilford Press.

Nijstad, B. A., & Stroebe, W. (2006). How the group affects the mind: A cognitive model of idea generation in groups. *Personality and Social Psychology Review, 10,* 186–213.

Nijstad, B. A., Stroebe, W., & Lodewijkx, H. F. M. (2006). The illusion of group productivity: A reduction of failures explanation. *European Journal of Social Psychology, 36,* 31–48.

Osborn, A. F. (1953). *Applied imagination.* Oxford, UK: Charles Scribner's.

Paulus, P. B., Dzindolet, M. T., Poletes, G., & Camacho, L. M. (1993). Perception of performance in group brainstorming: The illusion of group productivity. *Personality and Social Psychology Bulletin, 19,* 78–89.

Rajaram, S., & Pereira-Pasarin, L. P. (2010). Collaborative memory: Cognitive research and theory. *Perspectives on Psychological Science, 5,* 649–663.

Rendell, L., Boyd, R., Cownden, D., Enquist, M., Eriksson, K., Feldman, M. W., Fogarty, L., Ghirlanda, S., Lillicrap, T., & Laland, K. N. (2010). Why copy others? Insights from the social learning strategies tournament. *Science, 328,* 208–213.

Resnick, L. B., Levine, J. M., & Teasley, S. D. (Eds.). (1991). *Perspectives on socially shared cognition.* Washington, DC: American Psychological Association.

Rico, R., Sanchez-Manzanares, M., Gil, F., & Gibson, C. (2008). Team implicit coordination processes: A team knowledge-based approach. *Academy of Management Review, 33,* 163–184.

Rietzschel, E. F., Nijstad, B. A., & Stroebe, W. (2007). Relative accessibility of domain knowledge and creativity: The effects of knowledge activation on the quantity and originality of generated ideas. *Journal of Experimental Social Psychology, 43,* 933–946.

Ruscher, J. B. (1998). Prejudice and stereotyping in everyday communication. In M. P. Zanna (Ed.), *Advances in experimental social psychology* (Vol. 30, pp. 241–307). San Diego, CA: Academic Press.

Semin, G. R., & Cacioppo, J. T. (2008). Grounding social cognition: Synchronization, coordination, and co-regulation. In G. R. Semin & E. R. Smith (Eds.), *Embodied grounding* (pp. 119–147). New York: Cambridge University Press.

Smith, E. R., & Collins, E. C. (2009). Contextualizing person perception: Distributed social cognition. *Psychological Review, 116,* 343–364.

Smith, E. R., & Semin, G. R. (2004). Socially situated cognition: Cognition in its social context. In M. P. Zanna (Ed.), *Advances in experimental social psychology* (Vol. 36, pp. 53–115). San Diego, CA: Academic Press.

Stasser, G. (1999). The uncertain role of unshared information in collective choice. In L. L. Thompson, J. M. Levine, & D. M. Messick (Eds.), *Shared cognition in organizations: The management of knowledge* (pp. 49–69). Mahwah, NJ: Erlbaum.

Stasser, G., & Dietz-Uhler, B. (2001). Collective choice, judgment, and problem solving. In M. A. Hogg & R. S. Tindale (Eds.), *Blackwell handbook of social psychology: Group processes* (pp. 31–55). Malden, MA: Blackwell.

Stasser, G., Kerr, N. L., & Davis, J. H. (1989). Influence processes and consensus models in decision-making groups. In P. B. Paulus (Ed.), *Psychology of group influence* (2nd ed., pp. 279–326). Hillsdale, NJ: Erlbaum.

Stasser, G., & Stewart, D. (1992). Discovery of hidden profiles by decision-making groups: Solving a problem versus making a judgment. *Journal of Personality and Social Psychology, 63,* 426–434.

Stasser, G., Stewart, D. D., & Wittenbaum, G. M. (1995). Expert roles and information exchange during discussion: The importance of knowing who knows what. *Journal of Experimental Social Psychology, 31,* 244–265.

Stasser, G., Taylor, L. A., & Hanna, C. (1989). Information sampling in structured and unstructured discussions of three- and six-person groups. *Journal of Personality and Social Psychology, 57,* 67–78.

Stasser, G., & Titus, W. (1985). Pooling of unshared information in group decision making: Biased information sampling during group discussion. *Journal of Personality and Social Psychology, 48,* 1467–1478.

Steinel, W., Utz, S., & Koning, L. (2010), The good, the bad and the ugly thing to do when sharing information: Revealing, concealing and lying depend on social motivation, distribution and importance of information. *Organizational Behavior and Human Decision Processes, 113,* 85–96.

Stroebe, W., Nijstad, B. A., & Rietzschel, E. C. (2010). Beyond productivity loss in brainstorming groups: The evolution of a question. In M. P. Zanna & J. M. Olson (Eds.), *Advances in experimental social psychology* (Vol. 43, pp. 157–203). San Diego, CA: Academic Press.

Tajfel, H., & Turner, J. (1979). An integrative theory of intergroup conflict. In W. G. Austin & S. Worchel (Eds.), *The social psychology of intergroup relations* (pp. 33–47). Monterey, CA: Brooks Cole.

Thompson, L., & Fine, G. A. (1999). Socially shared cognition, affect, and behavior: A review and integration. *Personality and Social Psychology Review, 3,* 278–302.

Thompson, M. C., Judd, C. M., & Park, B. (2000). The consequences of communicating social stereotypes. *Journal of Experimental Social Psychology, 36,* 567–599.

Tindale, R. S., Kameda, T., & Hinsz, V. B. (2003). Group decision making. In M. A. Hogg & J. Cooper (Eds.), *The Sage handbook of social psychology* (pp. 381–403). Thousand Oaks, CA: Sage.

Tindale, R. S., Meisenhelder, H. M., Dykema-Engblade, A. A., & Hogg, M. A. (2001). Shared cognition in small groups. In M. A. Hogg & R. S. Tindale (Eds.), *Blackwell handbook of social psychology: Group processes* (pp. 1–30). Malden, MA: Blackwell.

Toma, C., & Butera, F. (2009). Hidden profiles and concealed information: Strategic information sharing and use in group decision making. *Personality and Social Psychology Bulletin, 35,* 793.

Turner, J. C., Hogg, M. A., Oakes, P. J., Reicher, S. D., & Wetherell, M. S. (Eds.). (1987). *Rediscovering the social group: A self-categorization theory.* Oxford, UK: Basil Blackwell.

van Ginkel, W. P., & van Knippenberg, D. (2009). Knowledge about the distribution of information and group decision making: When and why does it work? *Organizational Behavior and Human Decision Processes, 108,* 218–229.

Van Swol, L. M. (2008). Performance and process in collective and individual memory: The role of social decision schemes and memory bias in collective memory. *Memory, 16,* 274–287.

Wegner, D. M. (1987). Transactive memory: A contemporary analysis of the group mind. In B. Mullen & G. R. Goethals (Eds.), *Theories of group behavior* (pp. 185–208). New York: Springer.

Weldon, M. S., & Bellinger, K. D. (1997). Collective memory: Collaborative and individual processes in remembering. *Journal of Experimental Psychology: Learning, Memory, and Cognition, 23,* 1160–1175.

Werstsch, J. V., & Roediger, H. L., III (2008). Collective memory: Conceptual foundations and theoretical approaches. *Memory, 16,* 318–326.

Winquist, J. R., & Larson, J. R., Jr. (1998). Information pooling: When it impacts group decision making. *Journal of Personality and Social Psychology, 74,* 371–377.

Wittenbaum, G. M., & Bowman, J. M. (2004). A social validation explanation for mutual enhancement. *Journal of Experimental Social Psychology, 40,* 169–184.

Woolley, A. W., Chabris, C. F., Pentland, A., Hasmi, N., & Malone, T. W. (2010). Evidence for a collective intelligence factor in the performance of human groups. *Science, 330,* 686–688.

PART 4

Synergies with Other Realms of Social Science

CHAPTER 31

Interfacing Body, Mind, the Physical, and the Social World: Socially Situated Cognition

Gün R. Semin, Margarida V. Garrido, *and* Tomás Palma

Abstract

To navigate a dynamically changing social environment, we respond to the situated demands made upon us by flexibly *adapting* to these demands. At the same time, we actively structure our physical and social environment to reduce its complexity and release cognitive resources. This is achieved, in part, by making use of the knowledge and competencies that others have who provide *scaffolds*, and in part, by offloading tasks by creating knowledge structures in the environment such as street names. In effect, we rely on *distributed knowledge*. Obviously, the biological constitution of our bodies puts limits on how we structure and process the dynamic reality surrounding us; our knowledge is *embodied*. The important result of this adaptive negotiation processes is the *emergent* nature of social cognition, namely the situatedness of social cognition. This newly emerging dynamic perspective is referred to as *socially situated cognition*, which is the theme of this chapter.

Key Words: adaptive action, distributed knowledge, embodiment, emergence, scaffolds, situated cognition

Imagine that you and another coworker were unexpectedly asked to act as bartenders in a fund-raising event organized by your university. Although you have never done this before, you kindly accept the challenge. After the first 15 minutes, the queue is rapidly getting longer, along with impatient calls for "Baileys," "double Scotch, no ice," "two beers," "champagne," "martini," "mineral water," along with perceptibly increasing complaints as well as mumblings about incompetence. You start wondering how an actual bartender would cope with such a situation and how one can memorize such a diverse set of orders as well as who is supposed to get the Baileys and who was first and who was last.

But imagine that with time, you develop a system. Every time someone asks for a drink you pick up the corresponding glass (tumbler, beer glass, champagne flute, martini glass, etc.) and put it on the counter according to the sequence of orders. From that point on you work faster and more efficiently. As time goes by you get to know your coworker better, in particular her skills in preparing cocktails. You implicitly delegate cocktail orders to her and the rest to yourself.

Although you were originally inundated with a complex range of tasks, you distribute these tasks between yourself and your partner, and structure the physical environment to simplify the representation of what the orders were and which sequence they came in. This example, adapted from Beach (1988), illustrates the main points of this chapter. Our knowledge is adaptive to the different demands on us. To navigate a complex social environment, we do not rely on static representations because social life is an ever-changing dynamic reality. We adapt by using the environment as a cognitive resource, structuring it in such a way that it becomes a scaffold for the performance of complex operations such as dealing with 1,001 orders and customers rapidly. In the process, new solutions emerge, such as the sequencing of different types of glasses on the bar, but also offloading tasks to others, thus making use of distributed knowledge and competencies. Notably, all of this means that cognition is action and is distributed across the environment and to other people.

The above depiction encapsulates the essential elements of situated cognition, which suggests that cognitive processes *emerge* from adaptive sensorimotor interactions with a dynamically changing social and physical environment and are grounded by the constraints of the human body and the environment (Semin & Smith, 2002; Smith & Semin, 2004). Although the socially situated cognition approach does not constitute a systematic theoretical framework, it advances a set of general principles that cut across numerous scientific disciplines with the promise of a unified perspective on human functioning (cf. Robbins & Aydede, 2009).

The origins of this perspective were already present in the mid-19th century (cf. James, Vygotsky, Bartlett, Mead, and Dewey). The second half of the last century experienced the cognitive revolution whereby the "mind" and "cognitive processes" were brought to the fore as the object proper of scientific inquiry. The focus of the research area was narrowed down with the introduction of the computer as the metaphor of the mind, a metaphor that captured scientific and popular imagination. Unfortunately, this also narrowed the focus of research across the cognitive sciences to the isolated processing and representation of information. All psychological processes were relegated to the cranial vault, and a richer and more realistic vision of cognition that is contextually embedded and embodied had to wait until the last decade of the past century. The situated cognition movement that arose toward the 1990s evolved as a reaction to the decontextualized view of human functioning. The emerging emphasis was on the view that cognitive activities extend to the social and physical environments, which become integral parts of cognitive activity in their own right (e.g., Hutchins, 1995).

In the following, we shall present the general principles characterizing the socially situated approach to cognition in five sections. The first will address the *level of analysis* of a situated approach to cognition, which goes beyond the "individual" to a more general level of analysis, namely individuals in relationships in a socially and physically connected environment that is subject to constant change. The second section draws attention to the distinct nature of the "social." In traditional approaches to social cognition, the object of analysis was concepts that had a social content (e.g., trait terms) rather than a "nonsocial" one (e.g., number, color). This obviously missed out on the idea that the social is about two or more individuals in interaction and not about concepts. The situated perspective explicitly asks how the bridge between two or more individuals is established in defining the social in social cognition and argues that *social cognition is biologically grounded*. The third section, and by far the longest section, is based on the argument that cognition is grounded by sensorimotor experiences. In other words, it is *embodied*. The reason for this section's length is to be found in the exponential growth in research on this particular element of socially situated cognition. The fourth section examines the *adaptive nature of cognition* because, as it is argued, cognition is for action. The final section addresses the manner in which *cognition is supplemented by the aid of tools and the exploitation of others*. In concluding, we present some open questions and issues.

Macroscopic Level of Analysis

The view of cognition in the situated social cognition perspective is as an *emergent phenomenon*. This contrasts with the traditional individual- and representation-centered focus in mainstream psychology. It means that the cognitive phenomena that require explanation, as well as the processes driving them, are the products of social interaction in specific contexts. Consequently, cognition can only be captured within a broader framework, or rather at a higher level of organization. But this means that the explanation of cognition is at a different *level of analysis*, rather than one that is locked in the cranial vault. Let us illustrate the nature of this issue with an example from natural phenomena. The physical properties of the atoms hydrogen, silicon, sulfur, and oxygen are informative. However, their unique compositions at a higher level of organization—as in water (H_2O), sand (SiO_2), and sulfur dioxide (SO_2) or sulfuric acid (H_2SO_4)—constitute emergent molecular compounds that do not display any of the characteristics of the individual elements from which they are composed. This higher level organization has an entirely different quality than its individual parts. This type of recursive combination of elements into new compositions can also be found in language use (cf. Semin, 2006). Language use relies on a discrete set of basic units, namely *phonemes*, *morphemes*, and *phrase structure*. However, "situated meaning" is only brought to expression with *utterances* (cf. Semin, 2006). The higher-level organization has different qualities and properties. This does not mean that the individual constituents (e.g., phonemes, morphemes, or atoms) lose their identity or are not retrievable; they are still present. The analogical metaphor for higher levels of organization is that they act as *shells*. They enclose or hide their constituents. The characteristic properties of the constituent elements are not necessarily accessible and, in the case of social phenomena, are very likely to escape conscious access (see Semin, 2006).

The general implication of these considerations for the analysis of emergent phenomena is that these phenomena control the parts that generate and constitute them and not vice versa (Gazzaniga, 2010). Consequently, it is the higher level of organization that enables an understanding of how the parts are composed and not the reverse, as is the case when parts are analyzed without the insight of the emergent whole as a guiding perspective.

In standard views of social cognition, the prevailing mode of thinking is driven by setting an inappropriate level of analysis. It is based on the assumption that explaining a phenomenon at a lower level, for instance, the *individual level*, will open the window to grasp something at a more complex level, namely, the emergent level. The classic arguments for social cognition (e.g., Devine, Hamilton, & Ostrom, 1994) illustrate this point. The advocated focus was on symbolic individual mental structures and processes along with a set of symbols and "rules" about how to combine them (e.g., Fodor, 1980; Smith, 1998).

Identifying the necessity of the macroscopic level of analysis that is appropriate for socially situated cognition is useful. However, this perspective needs to be converted into an operational approach with a researchable agenda. We will try to outline that agenda by highlighting the unique nature of cognition between humans and by presenting some theoretical and empirical arguments suggesting that cognition is constrained by our bodies and the environment, is for adaptive action, and is distributed in physical and social scaffolds. Altogether these arguments set the level and types of analysis that are introduced by a socially situated perspective.

Biological Basis of Sociality

One of the main issues that has remained unchallenged until very recently is what the "social" in social cognition means. In the classic work in social psychology, the processes involved in cognition became social when the object of cognition was social, namely a person, an interaction, a group,

and so forth. Thus, the differences between the processes involved in cognition "pure" and cognition "social" were nonexistent—what was different was the object. But this mode of theorizing misses out completely on the nature of what it means to be social and that social cognition is an epistemically different proposition than its standard understanding in social psychology.

Research emerging since the 1990s on the mirror neuron system (cf. Iacoboni, 2009; Rizzolatti & Craighero, 2004) has underlined that cognition is not only socially but also biologically distributed across agents because the architecture of the human perceptuomotor system is specifically designed for the reproduction of movements of conspecifics in a privileged way (cf. Buccino, et al., 2004). The research also underlines that this isomorphism in mapping movements is due to "synchronization" processes that result from the formation of a type of sensory neural representation that has an entirely different ontological status from knowledge about the world in general. Thus, the basis of social knowledge is entirely different because it is biologically pregrounded, whereas our knowledge of the object world is acquired through sensorimotor processes that are shaped by goal-directed interaction with it. Social cognition relies on a pregiven generic and generative process by which we are able to access others' states, movements, and actions. This is a capability that we are endowed with from birth and one that we carry out multimodally, namely, with all our senses (cf. Semin, 2007).

This introduces an entirely different complexion to the "social" in social cognition. As Gallese argued: "The hard problem in 'social cognition' is to understand how the epistemic gulf separating single individuals can be overcome" (Gallese, 2006, p. 16). The recent developments provide an embodied answer to this question. Social cognition is best understood as grounded in (rather than abstracted from) perceptuomotor processes and intertwined with a wealth of interpersonal interaction and specialized for a distinctive class of stimuli, namely, about humans in interaction, rather than about trees or cars (Semin & Cacioppo, 2008, 2009). Thus, the basis for social cognition relies on the unique ability of the human species to map the movements, the odor (cf. de Groot, Smeets, Kaldewaij, Duinjam, & Semin, 2012), the affect, and acoustic features of another upon our own senses. This gives a source of information above and beyond interacting. This species-specific advantage furnishes mutual access and the foundations of communication (cf. Semin, 2007).

Thus, our bodies give us privileged access to others. Indeed, our bodies are involved in the way we represent not only others but also the world. The sensorimotor basis of our knowledge is generically referred to as *embodiment*, the subject of the next section in this chapter.

Embodiment

Our experience of the world, and our functioning, are constrained by a set of relatively invariable conditions (e.g., ecological, existential, material), including our body morphology. These together shape our actions and interactions (the sensorimotor experiences) and the knowledge we derive and accumulate. Human functioning is therefore *embodied*. According to a socially situated perspective, the meaning of an object or a person is not determined by some abstract set of features as in the classic representational view, but rather by the nature of the actions that one can engage in with an object or the interactions with a person (e.g., Gibson, 1966). The origins of these ideas are already present in early motor theories of perception, such as William James' account of "ideomotor action" (1890/1950) or Jean Piaget's developmental psychology, according to which cognitive abilities grew out from sensorimotor abilities. J. J. Gibson's (e.g., 1966) ecological psychology is another example of such early work. More recent impetus comes from A. Clark (e.g., 2008) and developments in robotics (e.g., Brooks, 1999), but also W. Prinz's (e.g., 1984) *common coding theory*, which claims a shared representation or common code for perception and action.

The embodiment perspective contrasts with previously described amodal approaches that conceptualize psychological functioning in terms of a closed loop of symbols or an internal model of the world. Overall, embodiment research literature has revealed that the human body is more than an output device for the cognitive machinery on which most psychological theories seem to have relied.

Early Demonstrations of Embodiment in Social Psychology

The investigation of the interface between the body and cognition has a long tradition in social psychology that precedes the recent surge in embodiment research (Cacioppo, Priester, & Berntson, 1993; Strack, Martin, & Stepper, 1988; Valins, 1966; Wells & Petty, 1980). For example, early research already demonstrated how one's bodily states influence attitudes. In Solarz's (1960) seminal study, participants were presented with cards with names of objects displayed in a box equipped with a movable response lever. For half of the participants, the task was to pull the lever toward them when they liked the objects corresponding to the words, and to push it away from them when they did not like the objects. For the other half of the participants, the instruction was reversed. Participants were faster in pulling the lever toward themselves for objects they liked and faster in pushing the lever away for disliked objects. These results were later replicated by Chen and Bargh (1999). They showed that participants were faster in performing approach (avoidance) movements when they had to classify positive (negative) words. These motor congruence effects were also shown by Förster and Strack (1997, 1998). When participants were asked to generate names of famous people, approach movements facilitated the retrieval of liked names, whereas avoidance movements facilitated the retrieval of disliked names. Using the same paradigm, Kawakami, Phills, Steele, and Dovidio (2007), showed that positive attitudes toward African Americans improved after participants had performed approach actions compared with avoidance actions (see also Paladino & Castelli, 2008).

Arm flexion and extension movements also have differential effects on attitude development toward neutral stimuli, as first demonstrated by Cacioppo and colleagues (1993). In their study, arm movement was manipulated by asking participants to press the palm of their hand upward from the bottom of a table (i.e., an approaching movement) or to press downward from the top of the table (i.e., an avoidance movement). While doing this task, participants were exposed to a set of novel Chinese ideographs that they had to rate on a like–dislike scale. Results showed the predicted pattern. Participants rated the Chinese ideographs more positively when making approach movements compared with avoidance movements.

In one of the earliest demonstrations of how body movements shape attitudinal responses, Wells and Petty (1980) showed that nodding or shaking the head influences whether participants agree or disagree with persuasive messages. Under the cover story of a study on headphone quality, university students had to make either vertical (nodding) or horizontal (shaking) head movements while listening to a persuasive communication about an increase (counter-attitudinal message) or decrease (pro-attitudinal message) in university tuition fees. In the end, participants responded to several filler questions, including one for which they had to give an estimate of an appropriate tuition fee. Results showed that participants who had nodded their heads agreed more with the message then those who were asked to shake their heads. They recommended a reduced fee when the message was pro-attitudinal and an increased fee when the message was counter-attitudinal. Using the same paradigm, Tom, Pettersen, Lau, Burton, and Cook (1991) demonstrated that overt head movements modulate participant's preferences for neutral objects. Specifically, after nodding or shaking the head while listening to music, participants had to fill out a questionnaire about the headset properties. Before leaving the laboratory, they were told that the headphones manufacturer was offering a pen as a gift with the purchase of the headphones and that they could choose between one of two pens—the one they used to fill out the questionnaire or a new one that they had never seen before. Importantly, a previous pilot study determined that both pens were equally attractive. Seventy-three percent of the participants in the nodding condition preferred the "old" pen, whereas in the shaking condition, 74% preferred the "new" one. These results suggest that by nodding the head in agreement (or shaking the head in disagreement), participants developed a positive (or negative) attitude toward a neutral object to which they were exposed. Vertical and horizontal head movements have also been shown to influence the degree of confidence people have in their own thoughts toward those objects (for a review, see Briñol & Petty, 2008).

Numerous other bodily movements have been shown to affect our judgments. For example, the feedback one receives from their facial muscles influences the way we respond to emotional stimuli. In an ingenious study, Strack and colleagues (1988) showed that judgments of emotional objects differ according to an induced facial expression. In this study, facial expressions were manipulated by asking participants to either hold a pen between their teeth, which activates smiling, or hold a pen with their lips, which inhibits smiling. While holding these facial positions, participants had to rate the funniness of four novel cartoons. As predicted by Strack and colleagues, the cartoons were judged to be funnier by those holding a pen between their teeth than by those holding a pen with their lips.

In another set of studies, Mussweiler (2006) found that participants induced to move in a portly manner were more likely than participants in a control condition to describe a neutral target person

as overweight. Moreover, when participants were induced to move in a typically elderly manner (i.e., slowly), they were more likely to describe a neutral target person as old, and they were faster to respond to words associated with features of the stereotypically elderly.

Although the research described so far shows the influence of bodily states or movements on language, there is also an abundance of research showing the influence of language, predominantly used as primes, on motor behavior (for a review, see Niedenthal, Barsalou, Winkielman, Krauth-Gruber, & Ric, 2005). This demonstrates the bidirectional relationship between language and bodily states. For example, Bargh, Chen, and Burrows (1996) have shown that participants asked to construct sentences with words implying the elderly (e.g., *Florida, Bingo*) subsequently walked significantly slower down the hallway compared with participants in a control condition. Notably, recent research suggests that this finding may be due to experimenter effects (Doyen, Klein, Pichon, & Cleeremans, 2012). Chambon (2009) showed that activating the stereotype of elderly biases participants' perception of the physical environment (e.g., hills are estimated to be steeper and distances to be longer; for a review, see Smeesters, Wheeler, & Kay, 2010). Macrae and colleagues (1998) reported a similar finding. Participants were faster to speak each word on a list aloud while reading the "Schumacher Word Reading Test" than the "Shimuhuru Word Reading Test." Because Schumacher was the fastest Formula 1 racer at the time, reading his name prompted a faster reading speed.

Grounding Concrete Concepts: Processes and Accounts

The *processes* mediating the relationship between language and motor behavior have been addressed by research over the past 10 years, demonstrating what is currently referred to as *motor resonance* (e.g., Glenberg, 2008; Zwaan, 2009; Zwaan & Taylor, 2006). In contrast to work in social psychology, this "phenomenon" has been addressed theoretically and empirically from neurophysiological (cf. Rizzolatti & Arbib, 1998; Rizzolatti & Craighero, 2004), action theoretical (e.g., Hommel, Müsseler, Aschersleben, & Prinz, 2001), and cognitive (e.g., Barsalou, 1999; Glenberg, 2008) frameworks. The common denominator to these approaches is the demonstration that words (language) recruit and activate the same neural substrates and motor programs that are active when the person is performing the action represented in a sentence. The reverse has also been shown to hold. Movement or action enhances the accessibility of language related to the movement.

The embodiment argument suggests that the comprehension of concepts or action language involves the activation of the sensorimotor modalities that are recruited online and that can be reactivated offline. Barsalou's *perceptual symbol systems* (1999) suggest that multimodal stimuli give rise to online experiences inducing modal states in the somatosensory system and the visual system, as well as in affective systems. According to this framework, once established in the brain, knowledge about the categories that are represented by multimodal associative structures can be used across a number of cognitive tasks. In this view, the representations that arise in dedicated input systems during sensation and motor action can be stored and used offline by means of mental simulations that have become functionally autonomous from their experiential sources. A substantial amount of research shows that the comprehension of language takes place by means of sensorimotor simulations, or what Barsalou refers to as "the reenactment of perceptual, motor, and introspective states acquired during the interaction with the word, body, and mind" (2008, p. 618).

There is considerable research that supports the sensorimotor grounding of concrete concepts. This work has been on language comprehension and has provided evidence showing that a motor modality is involved in the comprehension of language describing *actions* (cf. Taylor & Zwaan, 2008; Zwaan & Taylor, 2006). In an illustrative experiment, Spivey, Tyler, Richardson, and Young (2000) noted that participants displayed upward or downward eye movements while listening to spatial descriptions (e.g., "the top of a skyscraper" or "the bottom of a canyon"). Others documented that participants were faster reading target sentences if they were in a context describing plain terrains compared with rough terrains, implying that they were mentally simulating movement through the terrain (Matlock, 2004). Zwaan and Yaxley (2003) showed that when word pairs were presented in iconic relation (e.g., *attic* presented above *basement*), participants' semantic relatedness judgments were significantly faster than when they were presented in reverse iconic relation (e.g., *basement* above *attic*). In another study, Borghi, Glenberg, and Kaschak (2004) asked participants to read sentences such as, "There is a car in front of you" and then respond whether a target word

(e.g., roof, wheel, or road) was part of the object (e.g., car) mentioned in the sentence (e.g., roof and wheel) or not (e.g., road). The responses were made with a vertically oriented keyboard. In one of the experimental conditions, participants had to move the arm upward to respond "yes" and downward to respond "no"; whereas in the other condition, the key labels were inverted, which means participants responded "yes" by moving the arm downward and "no" by moving the arm upward. According to the embodiment perspective, reading the word "roof" should prepare us to act in a upward manner because that's the kind of action we execute to interact with a roof of a car, whereas reading the word "wheels" should prepare us to act downward. Thus, participants should respond faster to the word "roof" when "yes" required an upward movement than when it required a downward movement, whereas the opposite should be true for the word "wheel." And this was exactly the pattern found by Borghi and colleagues (2004).

An original experimental paradigm to demonstrate that the representation of concepts is modality specific (rather than based on abstract features, as proposed by representational models) is the *modality switch cost* design. An embodied perspective suggests that language is modality specific; that is, words that have to do with auditory input must be coded differently than words that are coded by visual input. From this, Pecher, Zeelenberg, and Barsalou (2003) have argued that modality specificity would mean that switching from one modality (e.g., auditory) to another (e.g., visual) when processing object features should have processing costs. Participants' task was to determine whether an object had a particular feature or not (e.g., BLENDER—loud). This was preceded by another judgment that was either modality congruent (e.g., LEAVES—rustling) or incongruent (e.g., CRANBERRIES—tart). There was an increase in the time required to confirm the feature as belonging to the object when the modality between two judgments was incongruent.

Another field of investigation revealing motor resonance effects involves research on the consequences of facial expressions of emotions. It is well known that the observation of a smiling or frowning face induces subtle movements of smiling muscles (*zygomatic major*) and frowning muscles (*corrugator supercilii* muscle region; e.g., Dimberg, Thunberg, & Elmehed, 2000). This occurs even when such faces are presented subliminally. These experiments suggest what has been referred to as an automatic mimicry effect. Recently, Foroni and Semin (2009) demonstrated a motor resonance effect, namely that reading or hearing a verb (e.g., to smile, to frown) or an adjective (e.g., happy, angry) has the same sensorimotor consequences as seeing a happy or angry face, providing further evidence for the motor resonance induced by language in the specific domain of emotional expressions and states.

Finally, research findings in neuroscience have demonstrated the link between neural mapping of language and action verbs in particular (cf. Pulvermüller, 2005; see Hauk, Johnsrude, & Pulvermüller, 2004, for a review). Using sophisticated techniques measuring brain activity, Hauk and colleagues (2004) revealed that listening to verbs referring to leg actions activates regions of the motor cortex responsible for control of the leg, and verbs referring to hand actions activate motor cortex regions responsible for hand control. In another experiment, action sentences were used instead of single words. In this case, participants heard action sentences such as, "the boy kicked the ball" or "the man wrote the letter" while their brain activity was recorded. Specific motor areas responsible for the control of the different body parts named in the sentences were again found to be active (Tettamanti et al., 2005).

Grounding Abstract Concepts

An embodied approach to understanding concrete concepts in terms of simulating the sensorimotor activity of the particular actions or movements appears plausible. However, it becomes difficult to extend this account to categories or concepts that we cannot touch, see, taste, or smell (cf. Boroditsky & Prinz, 2008). One solution to this puzzle is furnished by *conceptual metaphor theory* (CMT; Lakoff & Johnson, 1980, 1999). This theory relies on the view that the majority of concepts are more abstract but that understanding is "accomplished" through repeated pairings with concrete domains.

One abstract domain that has been extensively researched is *affect*. Empirical evidence investigating the relation between affect and verticality (cf. Crawford, 2009; Landau, Meier, & Keefer, 2010) supports the argument that metaphors alluding to the vertical spatial orientation like "I'm feeling up" or "I'm feeling down" serve to structure the way people think and represent affect-related concepts. For instance, Meier and Robinson (2004) were able to show that positive words (e.g., ethical, friendly) were classified more rapidly as positive when presented at the top rather than at the bottom of a monitor, whereas the opposite was true for negative

words. This idea of grounding affect in vertical space was soon extended to other areas beyond categorization such as to spatial memory. For instance, Crawford, Margolies, Drake, and Murphy (2006), observed that participants' retrieval of presented images revealed an upward position bias for positive images and a downward bias for negative ones. Recently, Casasanto and Dijkstra (2010) reported that people were faster in retrieving positive autobiographical memories when performing upward movements and negative memories when performing downward movements (see also Palma, Garrido, & Semin, 2011).

Another line of research explores the link between affect and size. For example, Meier, Robinson, and Caven (2008) have shown that positive words presented in a large font were evaluated more quickly and accurately than those presented in a small font, whereas the reverse pattern was true for negative words. Other research has explored the metaphorical use of "bright" (e.g., "bright ideas") or "dark" (e.g., "dark days") to refer to positive or negative aspects, respectively. This association finds support in the observation that participants' responses were facilitated when the word meaning (e.g., gentle) and the font color (white) were congruent with the metaphor (Meier, Robinson, & Clore, 2004). Related research has also shown that squares are seen as lighter after the evaluation of positive than negative words (Meier, Robinson, Crawford, & Ahlvers, 2007). Recently, Lakens, Semin, and Foroni (2012) have shown across a set of six experiments that black is consistently judged to represent negative words while white represents positivity but only when the negativity of black is coactivated.

Another example involves the grounding of divine figures (i.e., God and Devil) on the vertical dimension. Thus, when words related to God (e.g., Almighty) and words related to up (e.g., ascendant) were to be classified together, participants were significantly faster than when words related to God had to be classified together with down-related concepts (Meier, Hauser, Robinson, Friesen, & Schjeldahl, 2007). Parallel results were obtained for Devil-related words when presented with down-related concepts. The authors showed also that this metaphorical relation influenced social judgments and memory. That is, participants remembered photographs related to God as appearing more on the top of the monitor (vs. Devil as appearing more on the bottom) compared with neutral words. Participants also classified people as believing more in God when their photograph appeared on the top of the screen (vs. on the bottom of the screen). These results suggest the grounding of the "divine" in the vertical dimension.

Another well-documented effect is the relation between power and verticality as well as between power and size. This is illustrated by metaphoric references such as that someone with a *high* status or on *top* of the hierarchy has control *over* others with a *lower* status. Such references anchor power with space, which has been shown to influence thinking about power. Thus, when we think about power differences, we think about differences on the vertical dimension (Schubert, 2005). Results reported by Schubert (2005) indicate that powerful groups (e.g., master) are classified faster when they appear above the powerless groups (e.g., servant) on a monitor. The reverse is reported for powerless groups who were judged more quickly when they were shown below the powerful groups. Additionally, participants were faster and more accurate when identifying powerful and powerless groups while making judgments using an upward movement or a downward movement, respectively.

Schubert, Waldzus, and Giessner (2009) investigated whether physical size might be a further dimension grounding the metaphorical representation of power. Earlier research found that people perceive taller people as more powerful (Higham & Carment, 1992). Using an interference paradigm similar to the one used in the studies of power and verticality, the authors showed that the size of the font in which group labels appeared on the screen influenced response times and error rates in a power judgment task. Specifically, participants were quicker to classify powerful groups presented in a bigger (26-point) font and also made fewer errors. Conversely, powerless groups were classified more quickly and accurately when the stimuli appeared in a smaller (12-point) font.

The abundance of metaphors that locate *time* spatially (e.g., a *short* while ago, a *long* break) stimulated research exploring how the cognitive representation of time is intertwined with the representation of space. At least in Western cultures, people think of the past as to the left, and the future as to the right. For instance, bimanual response tasks have revealed compatibility effects between time-related stimuli (e.g., past, future) and the spatial position (left or right) of response keys (e.g., Ishihara, Keller, Rossetti, & Prinz, 2008; Vallesi, McIntosh, & Stuss, 2011; Wegner & Pratt, 2008). These effects indicate that when participants are asked to push a key on one side or the other in response to time

stimuli, they are faster when past stimuli appear on the left and future stimuli appear on the right. Compatibility effects were also shown when past and future words were presented auditorily to the left or right ear and had to be categorized in terms of temporal meaning (Ouellet, Santiago, Israeli, & Gabay, 2010; Ouellet, Santiago, Funes, & Lupiáñez, 2010; Santiago, Lupiáñez, Pérez, & Funes, 2007). More recently, Lakens, Semin, and Garrido (2011) showed that when past and future referent words were presented auditorily with equal loudness to both ears, participants disambiguated future words to the right ear and past words to the left ear.

Overall these studies show that time is spatially grounded on an axis that runs from the left–past to the right–future, a pattern that is culture specific and probably shaped by writing direction (e.g., Nachshon, 1985). However, such studies have been conducted in Western cultures, and this particular reliance on horizontal axes is by no means universal. Research has also shown time to be represented right to left, front to back, or back to front (e.g., Boroditsky, 2000; Fuhrman & Boroditsky, 2010), or even arranged according to cardinal directions (Boroditsky & Gaby, 2010). For example, in a recent paper, Boroditsky and Gabi (2010) reported that Pormpuraawans (an Australian aboriginal community) arranged time according to *cardinal directions: east to west*. This research reveals both generality and relativity of how the abstract concept of time is understood. Time is grounded spatially, which appears to be universal: however, the spatial referents that ground time vary considerably across cultures.

Recently, the horizontal dimension has also been shown to ground political concepts (e.g., Farias, Garrido, & Semin, 2013; van Elk, van Schie, & Bekkering, 2010). In three studies, Farias et al., 2013 showed that words to do with socialism and conservatism were placed to the left or the right of a horizontal dimension irrespective of whether they were presented symbolically, visually, or auditorily.

Expressions such as a "clean conscience" or a "disgusting act" suggest a metaphorical association between the concept of *morality* and activities to do with cleaning. Zhong and Liljenquist (2006) provided the first empirical evidence supporting this metaphorical association. These authors showed that participants who recalled unethical behaviors from the past were more likely to generate more cleansing-related words, such as soap or shower, than participants who recalled ethical behaviors. Interestingly, in subsequent studies, these authors were able to show that the enhanced accessibility of unethical actions influences participants' desire and preference for cleansing products. For example, after recalling an unethical behavior, 67% of the participants preferred to have an antiseptic wipe as a gift instead of a pen. On the other hand, when participants were primed with cleanliness, they made less severe moral judgments than participants in a neutral condition (Schnall, Benton, & Harvey, 2008), showing the bidirectional nature of this relationship. Further refinements of this relationship show that people are more likely to purify those specific body parts involved in the production of the moral transgression. Lee and Schwarz (2010) instructed participants in their study to perform an immoral action (lying) or a moral action by either using their mouths (by using voice mail) or their hands (by using e-mail). Next, participants were asked to rate the desirability of several products, including a mouthwash and a hand sanitizer. The results showed that participants who lied by voice mail preferred the mouthwash product more, whereas participants who lied by e-mail prefer the hand sanitizer more.

These diverse studies reveal that abstract concepts are understood through different metaphors about space, size, or brightness, and that these affect the classification of stimuli and have effects on memory and evaluative processes as a function of the congruence or incongruence between the source and target.

Cognition Is for Adaptive Action

The socially situated perspective rejects the passive representational view of cognition and argues that the primary function of cognition is the control of adaptive action. This emphasis on cognition as adaptive action is detached from the standard representational or information processing paradigm of social cognition involving the construction and manipulation of inner representations that have no bearing on real interaction in and with the world.

Modeling cognition in terms of abstract, detached symbolic representations has meant treating mental representations as invariant, timeless, and largely immune to contextual influences. This view has been endorsed because enduring abstract mental structures were assumed to play a key role in attaining cognitive economy (e.g., Taylor, 1981). Consequently, representations such as attitudes and stereotypes were assumed to exhibit temporal inertia as well as resistance to fleeting contextual influences (e.g., Hamilton & Trolier, 1986; Snyder, 1981). However, if cognition emerges in the interaction with a constantly changing social and physical

environment (e.g., Semin & Smith, 2002), then assuming that mental representations are immune to contextual factors flies in the face of the necessity for cognition to be adaptive to situational requirements. Obviously, offline cognition (Wilson, 2002) is important in a variety of situations involving, for instance, forward planning. But even this kind of cognition is situated in that it is a contextually simulated mental activity.

Indeed, there is considerable research that has shown *situational influences on cognitive processes*. These studies have revealed the adaptive nature of cognition by highlighting the context sensitivity of mental processes. For example, *attitudes* have been shown to be responsive to a multitude of contextual effects (e.g., Schwarz & Sudman, 1992), and *stereotypes* display considerable malleability in the face of changing contexts (e.g., Dovidio, Brigham, Johnson, & Gaertner, 1996).

To illustrate, extensive research has long established that the accessibility of specific exemplars or group members affects category and subtype descriptions (e.g., Smith & Zárate, 1992) as well as central tendency and variability judgments about the group as a whole (Garcia-Marques & Mackie, 2001). Different members of a group can also apparently make stereotypes differentially accessible (e.g., Macrae, Mitchell, & Pendry, 2002). Stereotypes are sensitive to subtle contextual cues (e.g., Wittenbrink, Judd, & Park, 2001) and context stability (Garcia-Marques, Santos, & Mackie, 2006).

For example, whereas thinking about politicians who were involved in a scandal decreased participants' evaluation of the trustworthiness of politicians in general, participants who evaluated the trustworthiness of specific politicians as relatively high subsequently concluded that politicians in general are relatively trustworthy as well (Schwarz & Bless, 1992). In a similar vein, incidental exposure to atypical exemplars (e.g., Oprah Winfrey) of a social group (e.g., black American) was shown to be sufficient to produce the expression of more sympathetic beliefs about the group (Bodenhausen, Schwarz, Bless, & Wänke, 1995). Other studies reported faster judgments about stereotypic attributes when category exemplars had familiar (John and Sarah) rather than unfamiliar (Isaac and Glenda) names (Macrae et al., 2002). Moreover, even subtle changes in the context were shown to significantly affect the stereotype content activated automatically. For example, participants were faster to identify personality traits related with "Chinese" than with "women," when presented with a woman with chopsticks in her hand compared with when presented with a woman holding a makeup brush (Macrae, Bodenhausen, & Milne, 1995). Similarly, Wittenbrink et al. (2001) have shown that automatic group attitudes and stereotypes, commonly thought to be fixed responses to a social category cue, are sensitive to changes in situational context. In two studies, the authors reported that white participants' implicit attitudes toward blacks varied as a result of exposure to either a positive (a family barbecue) or a negative (a gang incident) stereotypic situation. In a second study, presenting a picture of a black American in the context of a street scene facilitated responses to negative target items (adjectives). In contrast, presenting the same facial primes framed in a church context did not indicate prejudice, but in fact yielded a facilitation effect for positive rather than negative target items.

Another illustration reveals that subtle situational cues can easily influence allegedly automatic and invariant cognitive processes such as the fundamental attribution error (Ross, 1977). As Norenzayan and Schwarz (1999) document, when asked to provide causal explanations for a mass murder reported in a newspaper, participants responding to a questionnaire with a letterhead "Institute for Social Research" produced more situational explanations, whereas those responding to a questionnaire for the "Institute of Personality Research" produced more dispositional accounts. Other examples of such contextually driven malleability have been demonstrated for self-esteem (e.g., Crocker, 1999), the self-concept (e.g., Tice, 1992), and social stereotypes (e.g., Schaller & Convey, 1999).

Finally, recent research has also started to document the effects of the *physical features of the environment* on social cognitive processes. For example, Williams and Bargh (2008a) asked participants in one of their studies to hold a warm cup of coffee or a cold cup of coffee before receiving information about a hypothetical person described as intelligent, skillful, industrious, determined, practical, and cautious. Subsequently, participants registered their personality impression of this hypothetical person on several bipolar traits, half of which were semantically related to the warm–cold dimension. Their results revealed that holding a warm cup of coffee led participants to judge the target as warmer than did holding a cold cup of coffee. Similarly, IJzerman and Semin (2009) observed that participants in a warmer room (relative to a colder room) reported higher social proximity to a target person as indicated by their scores on the Inclusion of Other in

Self (IOS) scale (Aron, Aron, & Smollan, 1992). On the other hand, social exclusion situations led people to feel colder (Zhong & Leonardelli, 2008).

The effects of physical distance on social judgment have also been shown. For example, participants primed with spatially proximal coordinates reported stronger bonds to their family members and their hometown than those primed with distant coordinates (Williams & Bargh 2008b). More recently, IJzerman and Semin (2010) have shown that inducing experiences of proximity either physically or verbally gives rise to perceptions of higher temperature.

Environmental scents also affect cognition and behavior across a variety of contexts. For instance, Holland, Hendriks, and Aarts (2005) demonstrated that the exposure to a hidden cleaning scent enhances the mental accessibility of the behavioral concept of cleaning. In three studies, these authors showed that participants in the cleaning scent condition were faster in identifying cleaning-related words, listed more cleaning activities, and kept their working table cleaner compared with participants in the control condition without any scent. Moreover, there is some research showing that human odors affect social interaction, including helping behavior (e.g., Baron, 1997) and attraction to others (cf. Demattè, Österbauer, & Spence, 2007; Li, Moallem, Paller, & Gottfried, 2007). In a recent integration, Semin and Garrido (2012) documented that environmental contexts characterized by warm temperature, close distance, and pleasant smells promote generalized positive sociability evaluations. In the presence of these environmental conditions, not only a social target but also uninvolved others, such as the experimenter, were rated as warmer, closer, and more friendly, in contrast to the ratings observed in the cold, distant, and unpleasant smell conditions.

These and other findings highlight the interdependence between the material conditions of the environment and psychological processes and constitute compelling evidence of the adaptive and context sensitive nature of cognition. According to this perspective, rather than representing abstract and stable knowledge structures, mental representations and processes must be responsive to situated demands and thus, context sensitive, if they are to guide adaptive responses. If mental representations were completely malleable, they would be useless. However, a complete lack of responsiveness to changing circumstances would also be highly maladaptive.

The adaptive function of cognition is not illustrated only by the sensitiveness and responsiveness of cognitive structures and processes to contextual circumstances. The evidence for this adaptive nature can also be found in research highlighting the *functions* of those cognitive representations and processes, namely, as guides for action rather than internal states locked in the cranial vault. The action-oriented nature of representations is further underlined by research demonstrating how situated social *motives* and *relationships* with others shape mental representations and guide psychological, communicative, and behavioral processes.

A growing body of evidence suggests that cognitive representations and processes are tuned and oriented toward adaptive action. Social perceivers seek, process, and retrieve information driven by pragmatic or functional concerns that aid them in shaping their actions flexibly in continuously changing situations. For example, the functional value of attitudes as action-oriented representations can be illustrated by the fact that they not only influence how a person thinks and represents an object but also shape perceptions, judgments, and actions (e.g., whether to approach or avoid) toward that object. Whether a person is liberal or conservative, is or not tolerant toward other religions, or is a vegetarian will influence the person's judgments and actions toward other people and physical world. Person impressions are also action-oriented representations and have a functional value in guiding appropriate social action. We recruit those who are "intelligent" and tend to establish personal relationships with those we consider "friendly." Indeed "warmth" and "competence" constitute core dimensions that underlie perceptions of others and have an adaptive function that is central in regulating interpersonal relationships (Cuddy, Fiske, & Glick, 2008; Fiske, Cuddy, Glick, & Xu, 2002). Thus, person impressions contain useful cues about other's abilities, roles, and distinctive behaviors (Cantor & Kihlstrom, 1989; Carlston, 1994), as well as the types of relationships one has with different social targets (e.g., Baldwin, 1992; Fiske & Haslam, 1996; Holmes, 2000). The socially situated perspective invites a different way of looking at what were originally regarded as "biases"—namely cognitive shortcuts and heuristics (e.g., Chaiken, Liberman, & Eagly, 1989). The shortcuts used by supposedly lazy and error-prone social perceivers (e.g., Nisbett & Ross, 1980)—producing only "good-enough judgments" of others' make-up (e.g., Fiske, 1992)—may actually facilitate smooth social interaction (Snyder, 1993; Snyder &

Cantor, 1998). Therefore, another take on these so-called biases is to regard them as adaptive and functional processes that serve pragmatic ends.

Distinct *motives* and *goals* that a perceiver pursues mold cognition and action. The content of even implicitly measured stereotypes is apparently vulnerable to perceivers' current motives (e.g., Sinclair & Kunda, 1999), processing strategies (e.g., Blair, Ma, & Lenton, 2001), focus of attention (e.g., Macrae, Bodenhausen, Milne, Thorn, & Castelli, 1997), and emotional states in a given situation (Schwarz, 2002). For example, people tend to rate their own abilities as high when the trait domain in question is personally relevant (Kunda, 1987; Kunda & Sanitioso, 1989) or when the outcome is desirable or important (Weinstein, 1980) and to define personality traits in self-serving ways (Dunning & Cohen, 1992). Other research shows that perceivers attempt to form more accurate impressions in situations of outcome dependency (Neuberg & Fiske, 1987) and that they process social information in the environment based on their current social connectedness needs (e.g., Pickett, Gardner, & Knowles, 2004). Such motivational factors trigger cognitive strategies that are used flexibly to meet situational demands and to accomplish one's goals.

Feeling states also provide us with important information about the processing requirements we face (e.g., Isen, 1987; Martin & Clore, 2001; Schwarz & Clore, 1996). As Schwarz (2002) points out, different situations provide different affective cues (positive or negative mood) depending on whether they are benign or problematic situations, respectively. This affective information leads to cognitive processes being tuned to the respective demands of different situations. According to the affect-as-information hypothesis (cf. Schwarz & Clore, 1996) and the mood-as-general-knowledge assumption derived from it (e.g., Bless, 2000, 2001; Bless & Fiedler, 1995), people in a positive mood are more likely to rely on past experience and to activate heuristic or global processing. They rely on general knowledge (Bless, Bohner, Schwarz, & Strack, 1990; Isen, 1987; Mackie, & Worth, 1989) such as stereotypes or scripts (Bless, 2000, 2001; Bodenhausen, Kramer, & Süsser, 1994; Park & Banaji, 2000), use more inclusive categories when sorting exemplars (Hirt, Levine, McDonald, Melton, & Martin, 1997), process visual stimuli more globally (Gasper & Clore, 2002), and are more prone to the fundamental attribution error (Forgas, 1998). Situations that signal danger and induce a negative mood lead to the adoption of a more effortful, analytic, and systematic processing style (see also Bless et al., 1990; Mackie & Worth, 1989; Schwarz, 1990; for a review, see Clore, Gasper, & Garvin, 2001; Clore, Schwarz, & Conway, 1994). Situationally induced affect can also influence retrieval and judgment (Schwarz & Clore, 1996). Several studies have already documented that the information people retrieve is congruent with their current affective state (e.g., Bower, 1981; Forgas, 1995; Mayer, Gaschke, Braverman, & Evans, 1992; Sedikides, 1994). A range of judgments have been shown to be influenced by affect, such as life satisfaction (Schwarz & Clore, 1983), risk (Gasper & Clore, 1998), and political judgments (Forgas & Moylan, 1987). The relevance of this research from a situated cognition perspective lies in the significance of the informative function of feelings. These alert us to the demands of social events and allow us to fine-tune our cognitive processes and actions to these demands.

Cognition Is Scaffolded

Our actions and the way we process information in a context are strongly shaped by information that is embedded in the environment. When we recycle our garbage, we know that the paper goes in the blue bin, the organic in the green, and so on. We know that we are in trouble when we do not stop at the red light and see a person with a blue outfit, funny hat, and sunglasses approaching. Such artifacts and "experts" constitute crucial landmarks (i.e., colored bins, uniforms) for the organization of complex goal-directed action, and also serve as external knowledge and memory tools (cf. Caporeal, 1997). In short, cognition makes use of tools and other aspects of our environment, as well as other people and groups. Tools provide scaffolds for cognitive activity (A. Clark, 1997). Mechanical tools such as hammers, saws, and drills provide scaffolds that aid in achieving solutions (e.g., making a chair). Their absence would make such solutions difficult if not impossible. Other types of tools (such as language) are used to synchronize and coordinate communication between experts (Semin, 1998). Thus, the physical tools and the coordinated use of socially distributed knowledge become scaffolds for the successful accomplishment of innumerable tasks, such as playing soccer, performing heart surgery, or navigating a large ship (cf. Hutchins, 1995).

One of the ways in which the situated cognition approach opens new avenues of thinking is by drawing attention to how much we rely on the environment to download information and thus facilitate and structure cognition. A good example is the way we solve a difficult arithmetic operation like multiplying two three-digit numbers, distributing our mental operations by using pencil and paper. As we manipulate symbols, these external resources become part of an overall cognitive system, functioning as memory storage, offering cues for what digits to process next, and so on (A. Clark, 1999).

Moreover, we actively structure our environment to provide such scaffolds, as in the example of differently colored bins for disposal purposes. Another example is provided by leaving an empty milk bottle near the front door in the evening so as to not forget buying milk the next day (Kirsh, 1995). Another illustration can be found in the way expert bartenders confronted with a number of diverse drink orders line up differently shaped glasses (Beach, 1988). As illustrated in the opening of this chapter these glasses correspond to different kinds of drinks in a spatial order that reproduces the temporal sequence of drink orders, releasing the bartender from the cognitive effort of thinking about the sequence or the type of drinks that have to be prepared. A. Clark (2008) refers to such actions as *epistemic* actions. In contrast to mere physical actions, epistemic actions make computation easier, faster, and more reliable. These examples illustrate how the external actions an agent performs on the physical environment can change the agent's own computational state or otherwise cue, prioritize, and structure even the most demanding cognitive tasks.

Although cognition can surely be distributed across artifacts and situations that effectively facilitate and structure cognition, extending cognitive processes beyond the individual—making use of *knowledge distributed across other people* and engaging them in the construction of interindividual mental representations—extends our cognitive powers. A seminal example is provided by Edwin Hutchins (1995) in cases such as navigating a large vessel or performing open-heart surgery. These are tasks that require the finely tuned coordination of activities that bring together teams of "experts" who rely on each other's knowledge to be able to perform a collective task efficiently and successfully. Thus, the specialized knowledge that each individual holds is crucial, but the performance of the task is achieved in a series of coordinated activities among a number of different individuals who draw on each other's expertise and thus establish a type of knowledge that supersedes a single individual's capabilities (see Hutchins, 1995, for an excellent analysis of this type of socially distributed cognition). Note that a team member does not need to know the specialized knowledge that is distributed among the other members. Thus, in the same way that we use "tools," we utilize each other's specialized knowledge to perform a task, thereby engaging in a process that "extends out beyond the individual."

An early example of how people use each other to construct an extended memory is the work and theoretical approach advanced by Dan Wegner and his colleagues on *transactive memory systems* (e.g., Wegner, 1986; Wegner, Erber, & Raymond, 1991). This research suggests that individuals in close relationships develop a distributed memory system, such that they divide responsibility for the encoding, storage, and retrieval of information from different domains, according to their implicitly shared knowledge of each other. And consequently, they jointly remember information better than do strangers who haven't developed such a system (e.g., Andersson & Rönnberg, 1995; Dixon & Gould, 1996; Hollingshead, 1998; Wegner, 1986; Wegner et al., 1991). Transactive memory systems constitute scaffolded memory systems that are more elaborate and qualitatively different from any single individual member's memory system (Wegner, 1986). Much like the emergent processes that we presented in the first section of this chapter, transactive memory is a system that is irreducible, operates at the group level, and depends on a distribution of specializations within the system. Such specialization reduces the cognitive load on each individual while providing the dyad or group access to a larger pool of information across domains and reducing the wasted cognitive effort represented by overlapping individual knowledge.

Notably, distributed cognitive processes do not always result in positive outcomes, as is the case in groupthink (Janis, 1972), collaborative memory inhibition (e.g., Barnier, Sutton, Harris, & Wilson, 2008; Basden, Basden, & Henry, 2000; Echterhoff & Hirst, 2009; Garcia-Marques, Garrido, Hamilton, & Ferreira, 2012; Garrido, Garcia-Marques, & Hamilton, 2012a, 2012b; Weldon & Bellinger, 1997; for a review, see Rajaram & Pereira-Pasarin, 2010), and socially induced false remembering (e.g., Roediger, Meade, & Bergman, 2001). The "harmful" consequences of collaboration in decision making, memory, and other distributed cognitive processes have met resistance (cf. Rajaram, & Pereira-Pasarin, 2010) because they are counterintuitive given lay and scholarly beliefs in the benefits of collaboration. Notably, despite being harmful to accuracy, distributed cognitive processes serve other social, cultural, and political goals, such as developing positive social relationships (Clark & Stephenson, 1989),

arriving at a shared representation of the past (e.g., Coman, Manier, & Hirst, 2009), establishing group identity (e.g., Hirst & Manier, 2008), facilitating communication of events, and maintaining interpersonal relations, among others (e.g., Weldon & Bellinger, 1997). Even the social contagion of memory that frequently leads to retrieval of "dangerous" false memories may have an adaptive function. Although in some situations incorporating others' memories as our own may bring harmful consequences, updating our memories by relying on others who can supply detailed accounts of events that have been collectively experienced may often be very beneficial (Meade & Roediger, 2002).

Given the pervasiveness of distributed cognition in our daily social lives (e.g., Levine, Resnick, & Higgins, 1993), it becomes self-evident that mainstream individual-centered explanations (e.g., any approach in cognitive psychology or traditional social cognition) fail to account for the influence of the social scaffolds that often shape and determine the processes and contents of our cognitive activity. The general issue of distributed knowledge as a scaffold for cognitive activity remains a research field that requires more attention from a social psychological perspective.

Finally, we should point out that social and material scaffolds emerge in the search for adaptive solutions to problems. Knowledge that has been downloaded to different tools or persons with complementary knowledge and expertise serves the function of releasing cognitive space and extends an individual's capabilities.

Conclusions and Open Questions

A theme that runs through the different phases of a socially situated cognition is emergence, or rather the level of analysis that is afforded by this perspective. In attempting to cope with the complexity of his situation, the barman we mentioned in the opening of this chapter eventually introduced two new scaffolds: the sequencing of glasses on the bar and a distribution of responsibilities—cocktail orders for his partner and the rest for him. Thus, the situation at the hopeless beginning changed dramatically. A new set of social conditions emerged. The elements in the equation that defined the situation (Baileys, Scotch, the two barmen, the glasses, the bar, the customers) were restructured to yield a new composition. The elements of this new dynamically changing event also illustrate the chief goal of all the sections of this chapter, namely, the level of analysis afforded by a socially situated approach to cognition. One can understand the barman and the complex situation as a whole rather than looking into the cranial vault of the barman and examining the representations that are in there. It is the interfaces between glasses, drinks, customers, barmen, and their distributed duties that make the event rather than any single element on its own. It is therefore not surprising that the point of departure of socially situated cognition starts with what it means to be "social." In contrast to classic views that use the object of cognition in defining the social, the perspective advanced here emphasizes the importance of the biological basis of sociality, namely the species-specific mechanisms that furnish mutual access and thus ground communication (cf. Semin, 2007) by putting agents on the same page. Although the traditional approaches to social cognition are concerned with "single-shot photographs" of events, the dynamic or emergent nature of the phenomena under examination is best captured with the metaphor of a film. Because "cognition is for action," representations and concepts cannot be understood as abstracted, timeless, amodal representations. They emerge in the interaction between an agent and the social and physical world and are inherently defined by individual and social goals and motives. The representations of objects and persons retain the sensorimotor features of the actions that bond them with agents. This bonding is retained in the nature of concepts and fundamental sensorimotor experiences that are used to ground even abstract concepts, which do not have any "immediate" bodily experiential elements. The fact that sensorimotor bonding is necessary invites the integration of "body architecture" into how concepts have evolved, namely, how they become embodied. Finally, our interactions with the social and physical environment are not mere "direct" physical exchanges but rather are largely mediated by "tools." Tools are culturally evolved artifacts that are designed for the specific and regular tasks that are faced in everyday realities. Moreover, a distinctive feature of our social environment is that we contribute to this environment and at the same time utilize it because we are an integral part of a socially distributed network of knowledge that supersedes individual cognition. Thus, instead of using a single computer with massive processing power as the model for human cognition, the socially situated perspective invites thinking of cognition as a network of interconnected computers that have computational resources superseding the capacities and potential of a single computer. This metaphor captures the essence of socially situated cognition but needs biologically endowed bodies as its operational basis.

The socially situated cognition perspective is no more than a set of pre-paradigmatic assumptions in the Kuhnian sense. These assumptions represent the rumblings of dissatisfaction with the "standard representational" paradigm, but the current state of socially situated cognition is no way near having a fully interwoven, integrated, and mature theoretical framework to guide systematic research. Certain elements of situated cognition's pre-paradigmatic assumptions have captured the imagination and opened visions of research that would not have been possible before these developments. Chief among these is the work emerging under the broad but diffuse and ill-defined notion of embodiment. The number of demonstrations across a whole range of issues from language and motor resonance to abstract concepts such as time, morality, and valence is breathtaking. Nevertheless, theoretical integration in this field is loose and mostly driven by interests about specific phenomena. Other elements—such as the socially distributed cognition as action—require the introduction of novel research paradigms. For instance, Richardson's work on joint perception is one such innovative approach (e.g., Richardson, Hoover, & Ghane, 2008).

What stands out in the research streams evolving from the situated cognition perspective is the discrepancy between the individual foci that have captured attention (e.g., embodiment, cognition is for action, cognition is socially distributed) and the lack of integration between the elements of socially situated cognition. For instance, embodiment research as a burgeoning field does not even pay lip service to the social aspect of concepts. The entire work in the embodiment field refers to individual reasoning, thinking, and representation. Obviously, concepts evolve not only to serve individual reasoning but also to serve social communication. They are fundamental in grounding the basis for socially distributed cognition. Not surprisingly, communication constraints must play an important role in the evolution of concepts—abstract or concrete—because concepts are as much for communication as they are for intrapsychological processes.

Most of the work developed by those who claim a socially situated nature of cognition has not yet been incorporated into mainstream social psychology and social cognition. Nevertheless, the central assumptions of situated cognition are crucial for the development of an informed and informative social cognition that is not merely a subdomain of social psychology but also a centerpiece of any psychology.

References

Andersson, J., & Rönnberg, J. (1995). Recall suffers from collaboration: Joint recall effects of friendship and task complexity. *Applied Cognitive Psychology, 9*, 199–211.

Aron, A., Aron, E. N., & Smollan, D. (1992). Inclusion of Other in the Self scale and the structure of interpersonal closeness. *Journal of Personality and Social Psychology, 63*, 596–612.

Baldwin, M. W. (1992). Relational schemas and the processing of social information. *Psychological Bulletin, 112*, 461–484.

Bargh, J. A., Chen, M., & Burrows, L. (1996). Automaticity of social behavior: Direct effects of trait construct and stereotype activation on action. *Journal of Personality and Social Psychology, 71*, 230–244.

Barnier, A. J., Sutton, J., Harris, C. B., & Wilson, R. A. (2008). A conceptual and empirical framework for the social distribution of cognition: The case of memory. *Cognitive Systems Research, 9*, 33–51.

Baron, R. A. (1997). The sweet smell of helping: Effects of pleasant ambient fragrance on prosocial behavior in shopping malls. *Personality and Social Psychology Bulletin, 23*, 498–503.

Barsalou, L. W. (1999). Perceptual symbol system. *Behavioral and Brain Sciences, 22*, 577–660.

Barsalou, L. W. (2003). Situated simulation in the human conceptual system. *Language and Cognitive Processes, 18*, 513–562.

Barsalou, L. W. (2008). Grounded cognition. *Annual Review of Psychology, 59*, 617–645.

Basden, B. H., Basden, D. R., & Henry, S. (2000). Cost and benefits of collaborative remembering. *Applied Cognitive Psychology, 14*, 497–507.

Beach, K. (1988). The role of external mnemonic symbols in acquiring an occupation. In M. M. Gruneberg & R. N. Sykes (Eds.), *Practical aspects of memory* (Vol. 1, pp. 342–346). New York: Wiley.

Blair, I. V., Ma, J. E., & Lenton, A. P. (2001). Imagining stereotypes away: The moderation of implicit stereotypes through mental imagery. *Journal of Personality and Social Psychology, 81*, 828–841.

Bless, H. (2000). The interplay of affect and cognition: The mediating role of general knowledge structures. In J. P. Forgas (Ed.), *Feeling and thinking: The role of affect in social cognition* (pp. 201–222). Cambridge, UK: Cambridge University Press.

Bless, H. (2001). Mood and the use of general knowledge structures. In L. L. Martin & G. L. Clore (Eds.), *Theories of mood and cognition: A user's guidebook* (pp. 9–26). Mahwah, NJ: Erlbaum.

Bless, H., Bohner, G., Schwarz, N., & Strack, F. (1990). Mood and persuasion: A cognitive response analysis. *Personality and Social Psychology Bulletin, 16*, 331–345.

Bless, H., & Fiedler, K. (1995). Affective states and the influence of activated general knowledge. *Personality and Social Psychology Bulletin, 21*, 766–778.

Bodenhausen, G. V., Kramer, G. P., & Süsser, K. (1994). Happiness and stereotypic thinking in social judgment. *Journal of Personality and Social Psychology, 66*, 621–632.

Bodenhausen, G. V., Schwarz, N., Bless, H., & Wänke, M. (1995). Effects of atypical exemplars on racial beliefs: Enlightened racism or generalized appraisals? *Journal of Experimental Social Psychology, 31*, 48–63.

Borghi, A. M., Glenberg, A. M., & Kaschak, M. P. (2004). Putting words in perspective. *Memory & Cognition, 32*, 863–873.

Boroditsky, L. (2000). Metaphoric structuring: Understanding time through spatial metaphors. *Cognition, 75*, 1–28.

Boroditsky, L., & Gaby, A. (2010). Remembrances of Times East: Absolute spatial representations of time in an Australian Aboriginal community. *Psychological Science, 21*, 1635–1639.

Boroditsky, L., & Prinz, J. (2008). What thoughts are made of. In G. R. Semin & E. R. Smith (Eds.), *Embodied grounding: Social, cognitive, affective, and neuroscientific approaches* (pp. 98–115). New York: Cambridge University Press.

Bower, G. H. (1981). Mood and memory. *American Psychologist, 36*, 129–148.

Briñol, P., & Petty, R. E. (2008). Embodied persuasion: Fundamental processes by which bodily responses can impact attitudes. In G. R. Semin & E. R. Smith (Eds.), *Embodied grounding: Social, cognitive, affective, and neuroscientific approaches* (pp. 184–207). New York: Cambridge University Press.

Brooks, R. A. (1999). *Cambrian intelligence*. Cambridge, MA: MIT Press.

Buccino, G., Lui, F., Canessa, N., Patteri, I., Lagravinese, G., Benuzzi, F., Porro, C. A., & Rizzolatti, G. (2004). Neural circuits involved in the recognition of actions performed by non-conspecifics: An fMRI study. *Journal of Cognitive Neuroscience, 16*, 114–126.

Caccioppo, J. T., Priester, J. R., & Berntson, G. G. (1993). Rudimentary determinants of attitudes. II. Arm flexion and extension have differential effects on attitudes. *Journal of Personality and Social Psychology, 65*, 5–17.

Cantor, N., & Kihlstrom, J. F. (1989). Social intelligence and cognitive assessments of personality. In R. S. Wyer & T. K. Srull (Eds.), *Advances in social cognition* (Vol. 2, pp. 1–59). Hillsdale, NJ: Erlbaum.

Caporeal, L. (1997). The evolution of truly social cognition: The core configurations model. *Personality and Social Psychology Review, 1*, 276–298.

Carlston, D. E. (1994). Associated systems theory: A systematic approach to the cognitive representation of persons and events. In R. S. Wyer (Ed.), *Advances in social cognition: Associated systems theory* (Vol 7, pp. 1–78). Hillsdale, NY: Erlbaum.

Casasanto, D., & Dijkstra, K. (2010). Motor action and emotional memory. *Cognition, 115*, 179–185.

Chaiken, S., Liberman, A., & Eagly, A. H. (1989). Heuristic and systematic information processing within and beyond the persuasion context. In J. S. Uleman & J. A. (Eds.), *Unintended thought* (pp. 212–252). New York: Guilford.

Chambon, M. (2009). Embodied perception with others' bodies in mind: Stereotype priming influence on the perception of spatial environment. *Journal of Experimental Social Psychology 45*, 283–287.

Chen, S., & Bargh, J. A. (1999). Consequences of automatic evaluation: Immediate behavior predispositions to approach or avoid the stimulus. *Personality and Social Psychology Bulletin, 25*, 215–224.

Clark, A. (1997). *Being there: Putting brain, body and world together again*. Cambridge, MA: MIT Press.

Clark, A. (1999). Where brain, body, and world collide. *Cognitive Systems Research, 1*, 5–17.

Clark, A. (2008). *Supersizing the mind: Embodiment, action and cognitive extension*. Oxford, UK: Oxford University Press.

Clark, N. K., & Stephenson, G. M. (1989). Group remembering. In P. B. Paulus (Ed.), *Psychology of group influence* (pp. 357–391). Hillsdale, NJ: Erlbaum.

Clore, G. L., Gasper, K., & Garvin, E. (2001). Affect as information. In J. P. Forgas (Ed.), *Handbook of affect and social cognition* (pp. 121–144). Mahwah, NJ: Erlbaum.

Clore, G. L., Schwarz, N., & Conway, M. (1994). Affective causes and consequences of social information processing. In R. S. Wyer& T. K. Srull (Eds.), *Handbook of social cognition* (2nd ed., Vol. 1, pp. 323–418). Hillsdale, NJ: Erlbaum.

Coman, A., Manier, D., & Hirst, W. (2009). Forgetting the unforgettable through conversation: Socially shared retrieval-induced forgetting of September 11 memories. *Psychological Science, 20,* 627–633.

Crawford, L. E. (2009). Conceptual metaphors of affect. *Emotion Review, 1,* 129–139.

Crawford, L. E., Margolies, S. M., Drake, J. T., & Murphy, M. E. (2006). Affect biases memory of location: Evidence for the spatial representation of affect. *Cognition and Emotion, 20,* 1153–1169.

Crocker, J. (1999). Social stigma and self-esteem: Situations construction of self-worth. *Journal of Experimental Social Psychology, 35,* 89–107.

Cuddy, A. J. C., Fiske, S. T., & Glick, P. (2008). Warmth and competence as universal dimensions of social perception: The Stereotype Content Model and the BIAS Map. *Advances in Experimental Social Psychology, 40,* 61–149.

de Groot, J., Smeets, M., Kaldewaij, A., Duinjam, M., & Semin, G. R. (2012). Chemosignals communicate human emotions. *Psychological Science, 23,* 1417–1424.

Demattè, M. L., Österbauer, R., & Spence, C. (2007). Olfactory cues modulate facial attractiveness. *Chemical Senses, 32,* 603–610.

Devine, P. G., Hamilton, D. L., & Ostrom, T. M. (1994). *Social cognition: Impact on social psychology.* Orlando, FL: Academic Press.

Dimberg, U., Thunberg, M., & Elmehed, K. (2000). Unconscious facial reactions to emotional facial expressions. *Psychological Science, 11,* 86–89.

Dixon, R., & Gould, O. (1996). Adults telling and retelling stories collaboratively. In P. B. Baltes & U. M. Staudinger (Eds.), *Interactive minds: Life-span perspectives on the social foundation of cognition* (pp. 221–241). New York: Cambridge University Press.

Dovidio, J. F., Brigham, J. C., Johnson, B. T., & Gaertner, S. L. (1996). Stereotyping, prejudice, and discrimination: Another look. In C. N. Macrae, C. Stangor & M. Hewstone (Eds.), *Stereotypes and stereotyping* (pp. 276–319). New York: Guilford.

Doyen, S., Klein, O., Pichon, C. L., & Cleeremans, A. (2012). Behavioral priming: It's all in the mind, but whose mind? *PLoS ONE, 7*(1), e29081.

Dunning, D., & Cohen, G. L. (1992). Egocentric definitions of traits and abilities in social judgment. *Journal of Personality and Social Psychology, 63,* 341–355.

Echterhoff, G., & Hirst, W. (2009). Social influence on memory. *Social Psychology, 40,* 106–110.

Farias, A. R., Garrido, M. V., & Semin, G. R. (2013). Coverging modalitiesground abstrcat concepts: The case of politics. *PLoS ONE,* 8(4), e60971.

Fiske, A. P., & Haslam, N. (1996). Social cognition is thinking about relationships. *Current Directions in Psychological Science, 5,* 137–142.

Fiske, S. T. (1992). Thinking is for doing: Portraits of social cognition from daguerreotype to laserphoto. *Journal of Personality and Social Psychology, 63,* 877–889.

Fiske, S. T., Cuddy, A. J. C., Glick, P., & Xu, J. (2002). A model of (often mixed) stereotype content: Competence and warmth respectively follow from status and competition. *Journal of Personality and Social Psychology, 82,* 878–902.

Fodor, J. A. (1980). Methodological solipsism considered as a research strategy in cognitive psychology. *Behavioral and Brain Sciences, 3,* 63–109.

Forgas, J. P. (1995). Mood and judgment: The Affect Infusion Model (AIM). *Psychological Bulletin, 117,* 39–66.

Forgas, J. P. (1998). On being happy but mistaken: Mood effects on the fundamental attribution error. *Journal of Personality and Social Psychology, 75,* 318–331.

Forgas, J. P., & Moylan, S. (1987). After the movies: the effects of transient mood states on social judgments. *Personality and Social Psychology Bulletin, 13,* 478–489.

Foroni, F., & Semin, G. R. (2009). Language that puts you in touch with your bodily feelings: The multimodal responsiveness of affective expressions. *Psychological Science, 20,* 974–980.

Förster, J., & Strack, F. (1997). The influence of motor actions on retrieval of valenced information: A motor congruence effect. *Perceptual and Motor Skills, 85,* 1419–1427.

Förster, J., & Strack, F. (1998). Motor actions in retrieval of valenced information: II. Boundary conditions for motor congruence effects. *Perceptual and Motor Skills, 86,* 1423–1426.

Fuhrman, O., & Boroditsky, L. (2010). Cross-cultural differences in mental representations of time: Evidence from an implicit non-linguistic task. *Cognitive Science, 34,* 1430–1451.

Gallese, V. (2006). Intentional attunement: A neurophysiological perspective on social cognition and its disruption in autism. *Brain Research, 1079,* 15–24.

Garcia-Marques, L., Garrido, M. V., Hamilton, D. L., & Ferreira, M. (2012). Effects of correspondence between encoding and retrieval organization in social memory. *Journal of Experimental Social Psychology, 48,* 200–206.

Garcia-Marques, L., & Mackie, D. M. (2001). Not all stereotype-incongruent information is created equal: The impact of sample variability on stereotype change. *Group Processes & Intergroup Relations, 4,* 5–20.

Garcia-Marques, L., Santos, A. S., & Mackie, D. M. (2006). Stereotypes: Static abstractions or dynamic knowledge structures? *Journal of Personality and Social Psychology, 91,* 814–831.

Garrido, M. V., Garcia-Marques, L. & Hamilton, D. L. (2012a). Hard to recall but easy to judge: Retrieval strategies in social information processing. *Social Cognition, 30,* 57–71.

Garrido, M. V., Garcia-Marques, L., & Hamilton, D. L. (2012b). Enhancing the comparability between part-list cueing and collaborative recall: A gradual part-list cueing paradigm. *Experimental Psychology, 59,* 199–205.

Gasper, K., & Clore, G. L. (1998). The persistent use of negative affect by anxious individuals to estimate risk. *Journal of Personality and Social Psychology, 74,* 1350–1363.

Gasper, K., & Clore, G. L. (2002). Attending to the big picture: Mood and global versus local processing of visual information. *Psychological Science, 13,* 33–39.

Gazzaniga, M. S. (2010). Neuroscience and the correct level of explanation for understanding mind. *Trends in Cognitive Sciences, 14,* 291–292.

Glenberg, A. M. (2008). Radical changes in cognitive process due to technology: A jaundiced view. In I. Dror & S. Harnad (Eds.), *Cognition distributed: How cognitive technology extends our minds* (pp. 71–82). Amsterdam: John Benjamins.

Gibson, J. J. (1966). *The senses considered as perceptual systems.* Boston: Houghton Mifflin.

Hamilton, D. L., & Trolier, T. K. (1986). Stereotypes and stereotyping: An overview of the cognitive approach. In J. Dovidio, & S. L. Gaertner (Eds.), *Prejudice, discrimination, and racism* (pp. 127–163). New York: Academic Press.

Hauk, O., Johnsrude, I., & Pulvermüller, F. (2004). Somatotopic representation of action words in human motor and premotor cortex. *Neuron, 41*, 301–307.

Higham, P. A., & Carment, W. D. (1992). The rise and fall of politicians: The judged heights of Broadbent, Mulroney and Turner before and after the 1988 Canadian federal election. *Canadian Journal of Behavioral Science, 24*, 404–409.

Hirst, W., & Manier, D. (2008). Towards a psychology of collective memory. *Memory, 16*, 183–200.

Hirt, E. R., Levine, G. M., McDonald, H. E., Melton, R. J., & Martin, L. L. (1997). The role of mood in quantitative and qualitative aspects of performance: Single or multiple mechanisms? *Journal of Personality and Social Psychology, 33*, 602–629.

Holland, R., Hendriks, M., & Aarts, H. (2005). Nonconscious effects of scent on cognition and behavior: Smells like clean spirit. *Psychological Science, 16*, 689–693.

Hollingshead, A. B. (1998). Retrieval processes in transactive memory systems. *Journal of Personality and Social Psychology, 74*, 659–671.

Holmes, J. (2000). Social relationships: The nature and function of relational schemas. *European Journal of Social Psychology, 30*, 447–497.

Hommel, B., Müsseler, J., Aschersleben, G., & Prinz, W. (2001). The theory of event coding (TEC): A framework for perception and action planning. *Behavioral and Brain Sciences, 24*, 849–878.

Hutchins, E. (1995). *Cognition in the wild.* Cambridge, MA: MIT Press.

Iacoboni, M. (2009). Imitation, empathy, and mirror neurons. *Annual Review of Psychology, 60*, 653–670.

IJzerman, H., & Semin, G. R. (2009). The thermometer of social relations: Mapping social proximity on temperature. *Psychological Science, 20*, 1214–1220.

IJzerman, H., & Semin, G. R. (2010). Temperature perceptions as a ground for social proximity. *Journal of Experimental Social Psychology, 46*, 867–873.

Isen, A. M. (1987). Positive affect, cognitive processes and social behavior. In L. Berkowitz (Ed.), *Advances in Experimental Social Psychology* (pp. 203–253). New York: Academic press.

Ishihara, M., Keller, P. E., Rossetti, Y., & Prinz, W. (2008). Horizontal spatial representations of time: Evidence for the STEARC effect. *Cortex, 44*, 454–461.

James, W. (1890). *The principles of psychology.* (Reprinted 1950.) New York: Dover.

Janis, I. (1972). *Victims of groupthink.* Boston: Houghton-Mifflin.

Kawakami, K., Phills, C. E., Steele, J. R., & Dovidio, J. F. (2007). (Close) Distance makes the heart grow fonder: Improving implicit racial attitudes and interracial interactions through approach behaviors. *Journal of Personality and Social Psychology, 92*, 957–971.

Kirsh, D. (1995). The intelligent use of space. *Artificial Intelligence, 73*, 31–68.

Kunda, Z. (1987). Motivated inference: Self-serving generation and evaluation of causal theories. *Journal of Personality and Social Psychology, 53*, 636–647.

Kunda, Z., & Sanitioso, R. (1989). Motivated changes in the self-concept. *Journal of Experimental Social Psychology, 25*, 272–285.

Lakens, D., Semin, G. R., & Foroni, F. (2012). But for the bad, there would not be good: Grounding valence in brightness through shared relational structures. *Journal of Experimental Psychology: General, 141*, 584–594.

Lakens, D., Semin, G. R., & Garrido, M. V. (2011). The sound of time: Cross-modal convergence in the spatial structuring of time. *Consciousness and Cognition, 20*, 437–443.

Lakoff, G., & Johnson, M. (1980). *Metaphors we live by.* Chicago and London: University of Chicago Press.

Lakoff, G., & Johnson, M. (1999). *Philosophy in the flesh: The embodied mind and its challenge to Western thought.* New York: Basic Books.

Landau, M. J., Meier, B. P., & Keefer, L. A. (2010). A metaphor-enriched social cognition. *Psychological Bulletin, 136*, 1045–1067.

Lee, S. W. S., & Schwarz, N. (2010). Dirty hands and dirty mouths: Embodiment of the moral-purity metaphor is specific to the motor modality involved in moral transgression. *Psychological Science, 21*, 1423–1425.

Levine, J., Resnick, L., & Higgins, E. (1993). Social foundations of cognition. *Annual Review of Psychology, 44*, 588–612.

Li, W., Moallem, I., Paller, K. A., & Gottfried, J. A. (2007). Subliminal smells can guide social preferences. *Psychological Science, 18*, 1044–1049.

Mackie, D. M., & Worth, L. T. (1989). Processing deficits and the mediation of positive affect in persuasion. *Journal of Personality and Social Psychology, 57*, 27–40.

Macrae, C. N., Bodenhausen, G. V., & Milne, A. B. (1995). The dissection of selection in person perception: Inhibitory processes in social stereotyping. *Journal of Personality and Social Psychology, 69*, 397–407.

Macrae, C. N., Bodenhausen, G. V., Milne, A. B., Castelli, L., Schloerscheidt, A. M., & Greco, S. (1998). On activating exemplars. *Journal of Experimental Social Psychology, 34*, 330–354.

Macrae, C. N., Bodenhausen, G. V., & Milne, A. B., Thorn, T. M., & Castelli, L. (1997). On the activation of social stereotypes: The moderating role of processing objectives. *Journal of Experimental Social Psychology, 67*, 808–817.

Macrae, C. N., Mitchell, J. P., & Pendry, L. F. (2002). What's in a forename? Cue familiarity and stereotypical thinking. *Journal of Personality and Social Psychology, 38*, 186–193.

Martin, L. L., & Clore, G. (Eds.) (2001). *Theories of mood and cognition, a user's guidebook.* Mahwah, NJ: Erlbaum.

Matlock, T. (2004). Fictive motion as cognitive simulation. *Memory & Cognition, 32*, 1389–1400.

Mayer, J. D., Gaschke, Y., Braverman, D. L., & Evans, T. (1992). Mood-congruent judgment is a general effect. *Journal of Personality and Social Psychology, 63*, 119–132.

Meade, M. L., & Roediger, H. L. (2002). Explorations in the social contagion of memory. *Memory & Cognition, 30*, 995–1009.

Meier, B. P., Hauser, D. J., Robinson, M. D., Friesen, C. K., & Schjeldahl, K. (2007). What's "up" with God? Vertical space as a representation of the divine. *Journal of Personality and Social Psychology, 93*, 699–710.

Meier, B. P., & Robinson, M. D. (2004). Why the sunny side is up. *Psychological Science, 15*, 243–247.

Meier, B. P., Robinson, M. D., & Caven, A. J. (2008). Why a Big Mac is a good mac: Associations between affect and size. *Basic and Applied Social Psychology, 30*, 46–55.

Meier, B. P., Robinson, M. D., & Clore, G. L. (2004). Why good guys wear white: Automatic inferences about stimulus valence based on color. *Psychological Science, 15*, 82–87.

Meier, B. P., Robinson, M. D., Crawford, L. E., & Ahlvers, W. J. (2007). When "light" and "dark" thoughts become light and dark responses: Affect biased brightness judgments. *Emotion, 7*, 366–376.

Mussweiler, T. (2006). Doing is for thinking! Stereotype activation by stereotypic movements. *Psychological Science, 17*, 17–21.

Nachshon, I. (1985). Directional preferences in perception of visual stimuli. *International Journal of Neuroscience, 25*, 161–174.

Neuberg, S. L., & Fiske, S. T. (1987). Motivational influences on impression formation: Outcome dependency, accuracy-driven attention, and individuating processes. *Journal of Personality and Social Psychology, 53*, 431–444.

Niedenthal, P. M., Barsalou, L. W., Winkielman, P., Krauth-Gruber, S., & Ric, F. (2005). Embodiment in attitudes, social perception, and emotion. *Personality and Social Psychology Review, 9*, 184–211.

Nisbett, R. E., & Ross, L. (1980). *Human inference: Strategies and shortcomings of social judgment.* Englewood-Cliffs, NJ: Prentice-Hall.

Norenzayan, A., & Schwarz, N. (1999). Telling what they want to know: Participants tailor causal attributions to researchers' interests. *European Journal of Social Psychology, 29*, 1011–1020.

Ouellet, M., Santiago, J., Funes, M. J., & Lupiáñez, J. (2010). Thinking about the future moves attention to the right. *Journal of Experimental Psychology: Human, Perception and Performance, 36*, 17–24.

Ouellet, M., Santiago, J., Israeli, Z., & Gabay, S. (2010). Is the future the right time? *Experimental Psychology, 57*, 308–314.

Paladino, P., & Castelli, L. (2008). On the immediate consequences of intergroup categorization: Activation of approach and avoidance motor behavior toward ingroup and outgroup members. *Personality and Social Psychology Bulletin, 34*, 755–768.

Palma, T., Garrido, M. V., & Semin, G. R. (2011). Grounding person memory in space: Does spatial anchoring of behaviors improve recall? *European Journal of Social Psychology, 41*, 275–282.

Park, J., & Banaji, M. R. (2000). Mood and heuristics: The influence of happy and sad states on sensitivity and bias in stereotyping. *Journal of Personality and Social Psychology, 78*, 1005–1023.

Pecher, D., Zeelenberg, R., & Barsalou, L. W. (2003). Verifying properties from different modalities for concepts produces switching costs. *Psychological Science, 14*, 119–124.

Pickett, C. L., Gardner, W. L., & Knowles, M. (2004). Getting a cue: The need to belong and enhanced sensitivity to social cues. *Personality and Social Psychology Bulletin, 30*, 1095–1107.

Prinz, W. (1984). Modes of linkage between perception and action. In W. Prinz & A.-F. Sanders (Eds.), *Cognition and motor processes* (pp. 185–193). Berlin: Springer.

Pulvermüller, F. (2005). Brain mechanisms linking language and action. *Nature Reviews Neuroscience, 6*, 576–582.

Rajaram, S., & Pereira-Pasarin, L. P. (2010). Collaborative memory: Cognitive research and theory. *Perspectives on Psychological Science, 5*, 649–663.

Richardson, D. C, Hoover, M. A., & Ghane, A. (2008) Joint perception: Gaze and the presence of others. In B. C. Love,

K. McRae & V. M. Sloutsky (Eds.), *Proceedings of the 30th Annual Conference of the Cognitive Science Society* (pp. 309–314). Austin, TX: Cognitive Science Society.

Rizzolatti, G., & Arbib, M. A. (1998). Language within our grasp. *Trends in Neurosciences, 21*, 188–194.

Rizzolatti, G., & Craighero, L. (2004). The mirror-neuron system. *Annual Review of Neuroscience, 27*, 169–192.

Robbins, P., & Aydede, M. (Eds.). (2009). *The Cambridge handbook of situated cognition.* New York: Cambridge University Press.

Roediger, H. L., III, Meade, M. L., & Bergman, E. T. (2001). Social contagion of memory. *Psychonomic Bulletin & Review, 8*, 365–371.

Ross, L. (1977). The intuitive psychologist and his shortcomings: Distortions in the attribution process. In L. Berkowitz (Ed.), *Advances in experimental social psychology* (Vol. 10, pp. 174–221). New York: Academic Press.

Santiago, J., Lupiáñez, J., Pérez, E., & Funes, M. J. (2007). Time (also) flies from left to right. *Psychonomic Bulletin & Review, 14*, 512–516.

Schaller, M., & Convey III, L. G. (1999). Influence of impression management goals on the emerging contents of group stereotypes: Support for a social-evolutionary process. *Personality and Social Psychology Bulletin, 25*, 819–833.

Schnall, S., Benton, J., & Harvey, S. (2008). With a clean conscience: Cleanliness reduces the severity of moral judgments. *Psychological Science, 19*, 1219–1222.

Schwarz, N. (1990). Feelings as information: Informational and motivational functions of affective states. In E. T. Higgins & R. M. Sorrentino (Eds.), *Handbook of motivation and cognition: Foundations of social behavior* (Vol. 2, pp. 527–561). New York: Guilford Press.

Schwarz, N. (2002). Feelings as information: Moods influence judgment and processing style. In T. Gilovich, D. Griffin & D. Kahneman (Eds.), *Heuristics and biases: The psychology of intuitive judgment* (pp. 534–547). Cambridge, UK: Cambridge University Press.

Schwarz, N., & Bless, H. (1992). Scandals and the public's trust in politicians: Assimilation and contrast effects. *Personality and Social Psychology Bulletin, 18*, 574–579.

Schwarz, N., & Clore, G. L. (1996). Feelings and phenomenal experiences. In E. T. Higgins & A. Kruglanski (Eds.), *Social psychology: Handbook of basic principles* (pp. 433–465). New York: Guilford.

Schwarz, N., & Clore, G. L. (1983). Mood, misattribution, and judgments of well-being: Informative and directive functions of affective states. *Journal of Personality and Social Psychology, 45*, 513–523.

Schwarz, N., & Sudman, S. (Eds.) (1992). *Context effects in social and psychological research.* New York: Springer Verlag.

Schubert, T. (2005). Your Highness: Vertical positions as perceptual symbols of power. *Journal of Personality and Social Psychology, 89*, 1–21.

Schubert, T., Waldzus, S., & Giessner, S.R. (2009). Control over the association of power and size. *Social Cognition, 27*, 1–19.

Sedikides, C. (1994). Incongruent effects of sad mood on self-conception valence: It's a matter of time. *European Journal of Social Psychology, 24*, 161–172.

Semin, G. R. (1998). Cognition, language and communication. In S. R. Fussell & R. J. Kreuz (Eds.). *Social and cognitive psychological approaches to interpersonal communication* (pp. 229–257). Hillsdale, NJ: Erlbaum.

Semin, G. R. (2006). Modeling the architecture of linguistic behavior: Linguistic compositionality, automaticity, and control. *Psychological Inquiry, 17,* 246–255.

Semin, G. R. (2007). Grounding communication: Synchrony. In A. Kruglanski & E. T. Higgins (Eds.), *Social psychology: Handbook of basic principles* (2nd ed., pp. 630–649). New York: Guilford Press.

Semin, G. R., & Cacioppo, J. T. (2008). Grounding social cognition: Synchronization, entrainment, and coordination. In G. R. Semin & E. R. Smith (Eds.), *Embodied grounding: Social, cognitive, affective, and neuroscientific approaches* (pp.119–147). New York: Cambridge University Press.

Semin, G. R., & Cacioppo, J. T. (2009). From embodied representation to co-regulation. In J. A. Pineda (Ed.), *Mirror neuron systems: The role of mirroring processes in social cognition* (pp.107–120). Totowa, NJ: Humana Press.

Semin, G. R., & Garrido, M. V., (2012). A systemic approach to impression formation: From verbal to multimodal processes. In J. Forgas, K. Fiedler & C. Sedikides (Eds.) *Social thinking and interpersonal behavior.* (pp. 81–96). NY: Psychology Press.

Semin, G. R., & Smith, E. R. (2002). Interfaces of social psychology with situated and embodied cognition. *Cognitive Systems Research, 3,* 385–396.

Sinclair, L., & Kunda, Z. (1999). Reactions to a black professional: Motivated inhibition and activation of conflicting stereotypes. *Journal of Personality and Social Psychology, 77,* 885–904.

Smeesters, D., Wheeler, S. C., & Kay, A. C. (2010). Indirect prime-to-behavior effects: The role of perceptions of the self, others, and situations in connecting primed constructs to social behavior. *Advances in Experimental Social Psychology, 42,* 259–317.

Smith, E. R. (1998). Mental representation and memory. In D. Gilbert, S. Fiske & G. Lindzey (Eds.), *Handbook of social psychology* (4th ed., Vol. 1, pp. 391–445). New York: McGraw-Hill.

Smith, E. R., & Semin, G. R. (2004). Socially situated cognition: Cognition in its social context. *Advances in Experimental Social Psychology, 36,* 53–117.

Smith, E. R., & Zárate, M. A. (1992). Exemplar based model of social judgment. *Psychological Review, 99,* 3–21.

Snyder, M. (1981). On the self-perpetuating nature of social stereotypes. In D. L. Hamilton (Ed.), *Cognitive processes in stereotyping and intergroup behavior* (pp.183–212). Hillsdale, NJ: Erlbaum.

Snyder, M. (1993). Basic research and practical problems: The promise of a "functional" personality and social psychology. *Personality and Social Psychology Bulletin, 19,* 251–264.

Snyder, M., & Cantor, N. (1998). Understanding personality and social behavior: A functionalist strategy. In D. Gilbert, S. Fiske, & G. Lindzey (Eds.), *The handbook of social psychology* (4th ed., Vol. 1, pp. 635–679). New York: McGraw-Hill.

Solarz, A. K. (1960). Latency of instrumental responses as a function of compatibility with the meaning of eliciting verbal signs. *Journal of Experimental Psychology, 59,* 239–245.

Spivey, M. J., Tyler M., Richardson D. C., & Young, E. (2000). Eye movements during comprehension of spoken scene descriptions. *Proceedings of the Twenty-second Annual Meeting of the Cognitive Science Society* (pp. 487–492). Mawhah, NJ: Erlbaum.

Strack, F., Martin, L. L., & Stepper, S. (1988). Inhibiting and facilitating conditions of the human smile: A nonobtrusive test of the facial feedback hypothesis. *Journal of Personality and Social Psychology, 54,* 768–777.

Taylor, L. J., & Zwaan, R. A. (2008). Motor resonance and linguistic focus. *Quarterly Journal of Experimental Psychology, 61,* 896–904.

Taylor, S. E. (1981). A categorization approach to stereotyping. In D. L. Hamilton (Ed.), *Cognitive processes in stereotyping and intergroup behavior* (pp. 83–114). Hillsdale, NJ: Erlbaum.

Tettamanti, M., Buccino, G., Saccuman, M. C., Gallese, V., Danna, M., Scifo, P., et al. (2005). Listening to action-related sentences activates fronto-parietal motor circuits. *Journal of Cognitive Neuroscience, 17,* 273–281.

Tice, D. M. (1992). Self-concept change and self-presentation: The looking-glass self is also a magnifying glass. *Journal of Personality and Social Psychology, 60,* 218–228.

Tom, G., Pettersen, P., Lau, T., Burton, T., & Cook, J. (1991). The role of overt head movement in the formation of affect. *Basic and Applied Social Psychology, 12,* 281–289.

Valins, S. (1966). Cognitive effects of false heart-rate feedback. *Journal of Personality and Social Psychology, 4,* 400–408.

Vallesi, A., McIntosh, A. R., & Stuss, D. T. (2011). How time modulates special responses. *Cortex, 47,* 148–156.

van Elk, M., van Schie, H. T., & Bekkering, H. (2010). From left to right: Processing acronyms referring to names of political parties activates spatial associations. *Quarterly Journal of Experimental Psychology, 63,* 2202–2219.

Wegner, D. M. (1986). Transactive memory: A contemporary analysis of the group mind. In B. Mullen & G. R. Goethals (Eds.), *Theories of group behavior* (pp. 185–208) New York: Springer-Verlag.

Wegner, D. M., Erber, R., & Raymond, P. (1991). Transactive memory in close relationships. *Journal of Personality and Social Psychology, 61,* 923–929.

Wegner, U. W., & Pratt, J. (2008). Time flies like an arrow: Space-time compatibility effects suggest the use of a mental time line. *Psychonomic Bulletin & Review, 15,* 426–430.

Weinstein, N. (1980). Unrealistic optimism about future life events. *Journal of Personality & Social Psychology, 39,* 806–820.

Weldon, M. S., & Bellinger, K. D. (1997). Collective memory: Collaborative and individual processes in remembering. *Journal of Experimental Psychology: Learning, Memory and Cognition, 23,* 1160–1175.

Wells, G. L., & Petty, R. E. (1980). The effects of head movement on persuasion: Compatibility and incompatibility of responses. *Basic and Applied Social Psychology, 1,* 219–230.

Williams, L. E., & Bargh, J. A. (2008a). Experiencing physical warmth promotes interpersonal warmth. *Science, 322,* 606–607.

Williams, L. E., & Bargh, J. A. (2008b). Keeping one's distance: The influence of spatial distance cues on affect and evaluation. *Psychological Science, 19,* 302–308.

Wilson, M. (2002). Six views of embodied cognition. *Psychonomic Bulletin and Review, 9,* 625–636.

Wittenbrink, W., Judd, C. M., & Park, B. (2001). Spontaneous prejudice in context: Variability in automatically activated attitudes. *Journal of Personality and Social Psychology, 81,* 815–827.

Zhong, C. B., & Leonardelli, G. J. (2008). Cold and lonely: Does social exclusion literally feel cold? *Psychological Science, 19,* 838–842.

Zhong, C. B., & Liljenquist, K. (2006). Washing away your sins: Threatened morality and physical cleansing. *Science, 313,* 1451–1452.

Zwaan, R. A. (2009). Mental simulation in language comprehension and social cognition. *European Journal of Social Psychology, 37,* 1142–1150.

Zwaan, R. A., & Taylor, L. J. (2006). Seeing, acting, understanding: Motor resonance in language comprehension. *Journal of Experimental Psychology: General, 135,* 1–11.

Zwaan, R. A., & Yaxley, R. H. (2003). Spatial iconicity affects semantic-relatedness judgments. *Psychonomic Bulletin & Review, 10,* 954–958.

Evolutionary Social Cognition

Steven L. Neuberg, D. Vaughn Becker, *and* Douglas T. Kenrick

Abstract

Evolutionary approaches to social cognition investigate how cognition may be intrinsically linked to long-recurring adaptive challenges of human social life. Prominent features of the evolutionary approach include the ideas that cognition is systematically modulated by fitness-relevant fundamental goals (e.g., self-protection, disease avoidance, social affiliation, mate seeking, child rearing), that attaining these goals often requires domain-specific cognitive processing of information of particular content (i.e., that information content greatly matters), and that contemporary cognitive biases are frequently sensible and predictable from a deep, ancestral rationality. In reviewing research on processes including visual perception, attention, memory, social categorization, stereotyping, inference, judgment, and decision making, the chapter reveals that the evolutionary approach generates novel hypotheses, uncovers new phenomena, and creates a deeper, more integrative understanding of the social mind. The chapter closes by discussing several broad issues, including how evolved inclinations work with development, learning, and culture to shape social cognition

Key Words: evolutionary psychology, social cognition, fundamental goals, motivation, cognitive bias, stereotyping, attention, memory, categorization, judgment, and decision making.

How are contemporary cognitive processes shaped by ancestral experiences? Several decades ago, the prototypical answer of cognitive scientists would have been "not at all." This answer is no longer plausible. Indeed, a growing research literature reveals that human cognition is especially efficient when processing information relevant to survival and reproduction, is biased in ways that make better sense when considered in an evolutionary light, and is directed and shaped in functionally sensible ways by fundamental motives with long evolutionary histories.

Consider, for instance, a small sample of findings:

• People judge opposite-sex others whose faces resemble their own to be desirable for friendship but not for sex—to be trustworthy but not lustworthy (DeBruine, 2005).

• People encode angry facial expressions extremely efficiently, especially when displayed by men and even more so when displayed by men belonging to stereotypically threatening outgroups (Ackerman et al., 2006; Becker, Kenrick, Neuberg, Blackwell, & Smith, 2007).

• Women pay more attention to physically attractive (than average-looking) men, and this effect is enhanced when women are ovulating (Anderson et al., 2010).

• Men tend to make riskier decisions than do women, and a man's current testosterone level is an especially good predictor of this (e.g., Apicella et al., 2008).

• Despite the advantages that men generally have over women on navigational and spatial location memory tasks, women are better than men at locating high-calorie foods previously encountered incidentally during a walk through a farmer's market (New, Krasnow, Truxaw, & Gaulin, 2007).

- White perceivers in whom self-protection concerns have been activated "see" anger (but not fear) on objectively neutral black male faces; this "functional projection" does not characterize white perceptions of similarly neutral black female faces or white faces of either sex (Maner et al., 2005).
- People asked to remember a list of words (e.g., stone, chair, meadow) remember them especially well if they are thinking about how relevant each item would be to survival (in fact, even better than if they are thinking about whether the words are personally relevant or pleasant, trying to create mental images, or any one of several other powerful mnemonic techniques; Nairne & Pandeirada, 2008).

Such findings, and many others to be reviewed below, are not readily anticipated by traditional approaches to the study of social cognition. Yet, they have been straightforwardly derived by psychologists employing principles from evolutionary theory—principles that focus on the functional connections between the perceiver's current goals and the features of persons perceived, on functionally relevant distinctions among different types of human relationships (e.g., friendships and romances), on the important links between current hormonal states and directed cognition, and the like. It is now clear that there are ample theoretical and empirical benefits of making connections between cognitive science and modern evolutionary biology.

Evolutionary psychology is a meta-theoretical approach to exploring psychological phenomena—an approach that explicitly acknowledges that the brain has been shaped by biological selection processes with the general effect of increasing the effectiveness with which humans address recurring challenges to reproductive fitness (Buss, 1995; Ellis & Ketelaar, 2000; Tooby & Cosmides, 1992). Like other meta-theoretical approaches (e.g., cognitive science, social psychology), evolutionary psychology is not a theory itself, but rather is a set of assumptions that enable the derivation of more specific and testable theories, models, and hypotheses. As judged by its ability to generate novel hypotheses, to inspire studies that reveal interesting empirical findings, and to reveal coherent connections among apparently disparate psychological phenomena, the evolutionary approach to psychology has been quite successful (see Neuberg, Kenrick, & Schaller, 2010, for a more comprehensive overview).

Evolutionary social cognition, the topic of this chapter, focuses more specifically on questions of how cognition may be intrinsically linked to the recurring adaptive problems of human social life. We begin by briefly outlining the assumptions and characteristics of evolutionary social cognition and then review how this functionalist approach has been generating novel hypotheses, revealing new phenomena, and, more generally, informing our understanding of the social mind. We close by exploring a range of broader issues implicated by the evolutionary approach.

The Nature in Cognition

The human brain, like the rest of the body, is a product of natural selection (Darwin, 1871). It evolved through a process that favored those traits that increased reproductive fitness—that is, the perpetuation of the possessor's genes into subsequent generations—over those traits that were less successful. If a trait has a heritable genetic component, and if this trait facilitates the transmission of copies of the genes that gave rise to it into subsequent generations, this trait will increase in population frequency relative to traits less successful at promoting copies of themselves. The characteristics of the contemporary human brain, then—its "wet" traits (e.g., anatomy, physiology, neurochemistry) and their accompanying mental processes, algorithms, biases, and capacities—are those that conferred reproductive fitness on our distant forebears.

We thus possess what Cosmides and Tooby (1997) labeled a "stone age mind"—a cognitive architecture designed by natural and sexual selection to solve fundamental social problems in ways that would have been beneficial in the environment of evolutionary adaptiveness (EEA; Bowlby, 1969). One implication of this is that contemporary humans will reliably exhibit biases that may seem illogical in current circumstances but that would have been quite adaptive in our deep past, given the contingencies present then. Thus, even if not always rational in the here and now, human cognition tends to manifest *deep rationality*—exhibiting bias rather than pure logic, but in ways that would have helped our ancestors survive and reproduce (Kenrick, Griskevicius, Sundie, Li, Li, & Neuberg, 2009). By explicitly considering characteristics of ancestral social environments, the evolutionary approach provides traction for understanding the features that elicit modern social-cognitive biases, the shapes these biases will take, and how those biases will be moderated by particular individual differences and situational contexts.

To say that the characteristics of the modern human mind are those that conferred reproductive fitness on our distant forebears is not to say that evolution's imprint on human psychology is limited to the domain of mating. Because human reproductive fitness requires the individual to survive to reproductive age, our ancestors needed to address challenges related to self-protection, resource acquisition, and disease avoidance. As highly ultrasocial animals, humans' outcomes have long depended on the actions of others (Boyd & Richerson, 1995; Brewer, 2001; Campbell, 1982); hence, our ancestors needed to address challenges related to social affiliation and status seeking. Because interdependent ultrasociality requires people to process a great deal of complex, subtle, and sometimes hidden information (Dunbar, 2003), human young develop quite slowly to accommodate the necessary learning; this lengthy immaturity pulls for relatively high levels of dual-parent investment in child rearing and long-term parental pair-bonding—and thus the need for humans to address challenges related to mate retention. The goals of self-protection, disease avoidance, resource acquisition, social affiliation, status acquisition, mate seeking, mate retention, and child rearing can thus be viewed as fundamental in that they have long served the ultimate "goal" of reproductive fitness (Kenrick, Griskevicius, Neuberg, & Schaller, 2010).

Today's humans descended from those humans who possessed relatively better solutions for accomplishing these fundamental goals (Bugental, 2000; Kenrick, Li, & Butner, 2003). Many of these successful solutions were cognitive and are apparent in the design of the contemporary human mind. Given the qualitatively distinct fundamental problems the human mind has long had to solve—solutions for securing one's physical safety are largely different from those for securing a desirable mate—the brain is not a singular, domain-general information processor; rather, it is functionally modular and domain-specific in the informational inputs it seeks and accepts, in its biases, and in its outcomes (e.g., Barrett & Kurzban, 2006; we return to the important issue of domain specificity versus domain generality later in the chapter). Consistent with this characteristic of domain specificity, we review evidence demonstrating that whatever particular problem most occupies one's mind at any moment—for example, whether one is motivated to self-protect, avoid disease, make friends, or rear one's child—shapes what one perceives in the environment, where one directs one's attention, how one interprets ambiguous information, what information is especially easy to learn and later remember, how one manages possible errors in decision making, and the like. Indeed, the same social environment—for example, a social gathering or crowded marketplace—is processed quite differently depending on the prominent fundamental concern of the moment. From the evolutionary perspective, then, social cognition is inherently *motivated* social cognition, albeit with a focus not on the traditionally researched goals related to self-regard (e.g., enhancement, verification) or epistemics (e.g., accuracy, belief confirmation), but rather on the set of goals fundamental to solving the recurring, tangible social challenges faced by humans.

Also consistent with the characteristic of functional domain specificity, an evolutionary approach to social cognition places a much greater emphasis on the *content* of the social information processed by perceivers and decision makers than do traditional social cognition approaches. Whereas an Armani-suited shopper may draw the attention of a perceiver when seeking a mating possibility, the sneezing, sniffling consumer may draw the same perceiver's attention when she's worried about coming down with the flu. Evolutionary approaches anticipate the specific content in the social world most likely to receive preferred processing: The specific people and features that receive such processing are those most logically relevant (in a deep, ancestral sense) to a perceiver's current goals, whether these goals are elicited by features of the immediate situation or are more chronically accessible in a dispositional sense.

Cognition thus serves, and is subsidiary to, motivation. Like ecological theories of perception (Gibson, 1979; McArthur & Baron, 1983), the evolutionary perspective views cognition as a tool for managing the opportunities and threats afforded by features of physical and social environments—albeit, with a focus on fitness-relevant affordances (Miller, 2007). Whereas the wealthy, ascendant passerby potentially affords a desirable mating opportunity, the sneezing other potentially affords contagion and disease threat. Throughout the chapter, we will see that people manage the affordances—the opportunities and threats—potentially posed by others by altering how they cognitively process the information they have about them.

From an evolutionary perspective, cognitive processes inevitably lead to some degree of error and inaccuracy (see Neuberg et al., 2010). One line of reasoning is particularly relevant for our current purposes. People typically must deal with imperfect cues when trying to decide whether a particular event is an opportunity or a threat. For example, throughout human evolutionary history, angry facial expressions often implied impending aggression, bodily malformation often implied contagious disease, and familiarity often implied kinship or coalitional commonality. These cues only predicted probabilistically, however. Although individuals who employed such cues to infer the implications of interacting with scowling, malformed, or unfamiliar others would have, on average, made more accurate inferences than those who did not, there still was plenty of room for error (the scowling individual may merely have been play-acting, the malformed person may have been injured in an accident, and the familiar other may be a stranger encountered by chance months ago).

This inevitability of error does not imply that such errors are either random or irrational (in the "deep" sense); indeed, the evolved cognitive system is biased toward making particular kinds of errors—errors that pose the least risk and enable the highest gains to fitness (Gigerenzer, Todd, & the ABC Research Group, 1999; Haselton & Nettle, 2006). By analogy, consider the typical home smoke detector: Because dying in a fire constitutes a greater cost than plugging one's ears with irritation, manufacturers calibrate smoke detectors such that even a small amount of smoke sounds the alarm—even though this means that one will need to cope occasionally with an ear-splitting shriek when inattentive to breakfast cakes on the griddle. Smoke detector manufacturers wisely presume that it's better for their customers to be annoyed than dead. Similarly, the evolved cognitive mechanisms through which we understand the world are calibrated to avoid the most costly of errors; this "smoke detector principle" (Nesse, 2005) biases us toward moving away from the scowling man rather than toward him, toward avoiding physical contact with the malformed woman rather than sharing her food, and toward trading with those we know rather than with those we do not. These are all acts of error management (Haselton & Nettle, 2006), and we will see evidence of many such biases below.

In sum, the evolutionary approach views the contemporary social mind as designed by biological selection processes to address long-recurring fundamental challenges to reproductive fitness. These challenges ranged from self-protection and disease avoidance to social affiliation, mate seeking, and child rearing, and require domain-specific cognitive

processing to be effectively addressed. As we review below, the mind's functional stance implicates specific kinds of social information as relevant depending on the challenges prominent in the moment, generates especially efficient processing of such information, and creates deeply sensible and predictable biases.

Processes

Because human information processing capacity is greatly limited, people need to be cognitively selective—to focus their sparse resources efficiently and effectively while maintaining the ability to address new opportunities and threats as they arise. From the evolutionary perspective, this selectivity should be especially focused toward better managing challenges related to the fundamental domains of social life—self-protection, social affiliation, status striving, mate seeking, and so forth. In the review that follows, we indeed see that information relevant to these domains often receives privileged processing.

We will also see that processes within the cognitive "stream"—perception, attention, categorization, encoding, memory, judgment—often operate not as distinct components but rather as integrated aspects of functionally redundant systems designed to address challenges at hand. For instance, the privileged processing received by young outgroup men is not limited to preattentive processing or conscious attention or memory; instead, all these processes (and others) seem to work in a redundant and precautionary manner toward preparing perceivers for the dangers such men are believed to pose (Neuberg, Kenrick, & Schaller, 2011). We will also see, however, interesting exceptions to this functional redundancy—exceptions that take the form of processing disjunctions sensitive both to functional needs and the costs of redundancy, as when a temporally fleeting threat receives attentional vigilance but not storage in long-term memory.

The review that follows is meant not to be exhaustive but, rather, illustrative, introducing the many ways in which the evolved social mind shapes the processing of contemporary social information.

What Information Do We Grab and Hold onto? Perception, Attention, and Memory

People are highly attuned to changes in the environment that would have held, in particular, important fitness implications across human evolutionary history. New, Cosmides, and Tooby (2007) explored what they labeled the "animate monitoring bias." They reasoned that humans would have benefited greatly from being especially attentive to the movements of human and non-human animals. This would be the case for two reasons. First, such creatures possess significant fitness affordances, favorable (e.g., as opportunities for protection, information, and nutrition) and unfavorable (e.g., as threats to physical safety and social standing). Second, because animals have the ability to quickly change their intentions and actions, their opportunity and threat potentials can also quickly change. Consistent with their hypotheses, participants in a series of experiments detected changes in human or animal targets faster than changes in other, nonanimate, targets (plants, inanimate but moveable objects, topographical landmarks). Interestingly, changes in animals were even detected preferentially to changes in automobiles—highly mobile and dangerous objects about which contemporary perceivers have much knowledge and expertise—suggesting that the attentional system is attuned preferentially to ancestral rather than modern priorities.

Other work provides support for functionally biased attentional vigilance in the mate-seeking domain: Confronted with visual arrays of attractive and average-looking men and women, men with a sexually unrestricted mating orientation were especially quick to notice changes to the facial features of attractive women; this rapidity of change detection was not observed when facial changes occurred on attractive men. Moreover, men dispositionally less interested in short-term mating did not exhibit this same vigilance bias toward attractive women (Duncan et al., 2007). The mating-focused specificity of these findings in particular suggests the functional shaping of the attentional vigilance process.

Once attention has searched a particular location, it ordinarily has difficulty returning to it for several hundred milliseconds. This inhibition of return is observed when perceivers have just seen neutral or happy faces in a particular location, but not when an angry face was previously seen there; rather, attention readily returns to locations previously marked by angry faces (Fox, Russo, & Dutton, 2002). This finding represents a distinct violation of the content-free, domain-general view of how such processes should work, according to standard cognitive models (e.g., Posner & Cohen, 1984), but fits well with an evolutionary perspective given the fitness-threatening affordances implied by angry facial expressions (e.g., impending aggression, social disapproval, ostracism).

People not only monitor and seek out evolutionarily relevant information but also find such information relatively difficult to disengage from. Consider examples from three evolutionarily significant domains—disease avoidance, self-protection, and mate seeking. Dot-probe methodologies assess the difficulty of moving visual attention away from existing target images when instructed to do so. In one experiment, perceivers tasked with identifying shapes appearing on a computer monitor were slower to disengage from faces on the screen bearing heuristic cues to disease (port-wine stains or a wandering eye) than from otherwise similar faces not bearing disease cues; this difficulty disengaging from the heuristically diseased faces was especially great for perceivers who had recently viewed images from a disease-sensitizing slide show (e.g., dirty sponges, person sneezing; Ackerman et al., 2009). Other research shows that, for perceivers dispositionally high in social anxiety, angry and fearful faces (but not neutral, happy, or sad faces) are difficult to disengage from (Fox et al., 2001; Georgiou et al., 2005). And attractive opposite-sex targets are especially likely to hold the attention of perceivers with inclinations toward unrestricted, short-term mating and for whom mating goals are currently active (Maner, Gailliot, Rouby, & Miller, 2007). Like the other effects, this one is highly specific: No such attentional advantage exists for opposite-sex targets in general, nor do attractive opposite-sex targets hold the attention of individuals with more restricted, longer-term approaches to mate seeking.

These findings illustrate that it's relatively difficult to disengage one's attention from evolutionarily significant information. They also highlight a broader point about the *functional flexibility* of these (and, we will see, other) cognitive processes (Schaller, Park, & Kenrick, 2007). Because the engagement of any motivational system is costly—metabolically, and in terms of delayed or lost opportunities to pursue other goals—it would be problematic for any system to be constantly engaged. Rather, a motivational system is more likely to be engaged when threats or opportunities relevant to it are greatest, and less likely to be engaged when the baseline likelihood of relevant threats or opportunities is minimal. Thus, we see that biases toward attentionally adhering to malformed, angry, fearful, and beautiful faces are enhanced when perceivers are focused on, respectively, disease avoidance, social affiliation, and mate seeking.

Just as evolutionary approaches to social cognition have generated interesting and important findings regarding perception and attention, they have done the same for memory. In a broad sense, long-term memory is widely acknowledged to have multiple, functionally distinct components. For instance, procedural and declarative memory systems are readily dissociable (Squire, Knowlton, & Musen, 1993), and mechanisms for storing new memories are independent of those that retrieve memories (McClelland, McNaughton, & O'Reilly, 1995). Moreover, just as birds employ different neuropsychological systems for remembering information with distinct fitness implications (e.g., the song of their species, the location of their food caches), humans also employ distinct neuropsychological systems for remembering information with distinct fitness implications (e.g., faces, nausea-inducing foods) (e.g., Sherry & Schacter, 1987). Evolutionary psychologists have applied a functionalist logic to draw out even finer distinctions in memory processes, generating novel predictions about processes involved in remembering other's traits and behaviors inconsistent with those traits (Klein, Cosmides, Tooby, Chance, 2002).

Several other lines of research reveal the usefulness of applying an evolutionary approach to social memory. Consider, for instance, the widely known and robust finding that people's recognition memory tends to be relatively poor for faces of other races (Anthony, Copper, & Mullen, 1992; Ostrom & Sedikides, 1992). In a series of studies, however, Ackerman and colleagues (2007) discovered a functional departure from this norm: Whereas white perceivers exhibited the typical cross-race deficit in memory for neutrally expressive black male faces (compared with neutrally expressive white male faces), this deficit disappeared—and sometimes even reversed—when the faces bore angry expressions. These findings are consistent with the functional reasoning that it would be especially important to individuate in memory angry outgroup members: Whereas there exist cognitive, emotional, and social mechanisms to inhibit anger-based aggression, these mechanisms are less likely to be engaged in individuals interacting with outgroup members. All else equal, then, an encountered angry outgroup member poses a greater threat than an encountered angry ingroup member.

One role of working memory is to keep an updated record of the spatial location of recently encountered items. One location memory measure—akin to the Concentration Game—found that both men and women were highly accurate at remembering the location of attractive female faces (which tend to afford mating opportunities for men and mating threats for women), but were not at all accurate at remembering the location of attractive males (Becker et al., 2005). Closer examination revealed that women *did* attend to the location of attractive men in the earliest phase of the task, when visual short-term memory was especially active, but began confusing the locations of attractive males with one another as the game progressed. Thus, women did indeed look at attractive men, as findings presented earlier also demonstrate, but they did not engage in sufficient subsequent individuating processing to discriminate different attractive males from one another. As far as location memory is concerned, one good-looking man was relatively interchangeable with another. Intriguingly, Vranić and Hromatko (2008), employing the same task, found that women with relatively high estrogen levels were able to remember the locations of adult male faces; these higher estrogen levels did not, however, predict an enhanced ability to remember the locations of children's faces. Hormonally mediated changes in social cognition are difficult to explain without explicitly drawing on evolutionary considerations.

The findings of Becker et al. (2005)—that enhanced visual attention need not translate into enhanced memory—suggest that the social cognitive system may be calibrated to the functional value provided by different processes in the cognitive stream. Several investigations have explicitly explored the possibility of different forms of functional processing disjunctions—in which the processes in the stream do not necessarily work in a reinforcing manner, but rather appear to be sensitive to both the benefits and costs of different processes for particular problems.

Consider, first, disjunctions in which enhanced visual attention does not necessarily lead to enhanced encoding or memory. Conceptually corroborating the Becker et al. (2005) findings (see also Maner et al., 2003), Ackerman and colleagues (2009) found that although disfigured faces are especially likely to hold attention, they also tend to be confused with other disfigured faces and are not well remembered later. The functional value of attuning oneself to faces exhibiting heuristic cues to disease, especially when motivated to avoid disease, is apparent; the immediate presence of such faces implies risk of contagion. The authors reasoned, however, that there was little functional value of expending processing resources to encode these same faces into memory, given that facial disfigurements tend to be invariant across time: These same cues to potential disease would be as immediately apparent in the future as they are in the present.

The above disjunctions of attention and memory represent an encoding loss. An evolutionary approach to social cognition also suggests that, under some circumstances, one should expect attention–memory disjunctions revealing encoding benefits. For instance, some circumstances recommend that one look away from a target that nonetheless may have great affordance implications. One set of experiments explored contexts in which perceivers encountered individuals stereotyped as having a potential inclination to do harm (i.e., black and Arab young men, from the perspective of white perceivers). In such encounters, perceivers face a dilemma. On the one hand, to stare at the target potentially provides useful cues to their intentions; on the other, such stares may be viewed as challenging or intrusive, and thereby invite the very threat one fears. Perceivers for whom self-protective concerns were made prominent (compared with control perceivers) managed this dilemma through enhanced efficiency in the encoding of these black and Arab male faces. That is, without increasing their visual attention to these faces, they nonetheless identified them quite well in a surprise recognition test. This encoding efficiency was functionally focused: It was not observed when self-protective perceivers were processing female or white male faces (i.e., targets not stereotyped as being dangerous; Becker et al., 2010).

To this point, we have seen that evolutionary approaches have great value for better understanding processes related to perception, attention, and memory, and to their interrelationships. We turn to explore how such functional considerations may also shape processes related to assigning meaning to the information we acquire about others.

Evaluating Affordance Value: Feature-Driven Inference, Social Categorization, and Stereotyping

From an evolutionary perspective, humans are biased toward perceiving and attending to particular people and events because these are believed to afford relevant threats or opportunities. People pay attention to angry faces because an angry expression signals that the bearer may afford a threat to our physical safety; men pay attention to beautiful women because their beauty signals that they may afford an especially valuable mating opportunity.

A wide range of readily accessible physical features are useful for inferring others' affordances—body shape and movement, the directionality of eye gaze, and so forth (see Macrae & Quadflieg, 2010, for a review). Such features enable inferences about others' short-term intentions, as well as longer-term capacities and personality traits. Moreover, they often do so quite efficiently. People form trait impressions quickly, spontaneously, and with little cognitive effort (Carlston & Skowronski, 2005; Gilbert & Malone, 1995; Newman & Uleman, 1989), and these first impressions are often accurate even when based on very little information (e.g., Ambady, Bernieri, & Richeson, 2000). For example, even as little as 100 milliseconds (ms) of exposure to an unfamiliar face enables inferences about a person's trustworthiness equivalent to those made after much longer study time (Willis & Todorov, 2006); face-only photographs are sufficient to enable accurate estimates of men's upper-body strength (Sell, Cosmides, Tooby, Sznycer, von Rueden, & Gurven, 2009); and merely 50 ms of exposure to faces enables perceivers to infer a man's sexual orientation at levels beyond chance (Rule & Ambady, 2008).

The efficiency of making such inferences may be especially pronounced for important affordance dimensions. Consider the fitness importance of the domains represented by the examples in the above paragraph: Trustworthiness is considered necessary for effective ultrasociality and has been demonstrated to be extremely desirable across a wide range of interdependent relationships (e.g., teammate, coworker, sibling, spouse; see, e.g., Cottrell, Neuberg, & Li, 2007); in light of this, it's not surprising that trustworthiness assessment may be one of the functional underpinnings of face evaluation (Oosterhof & Todorov, 2008). Cooperative interpersonal exchange is also an essential requirement of effective human sociality, and this apparently drives the specialized "cheater detection" cognitive mechanisms people possess (Cosmides, Barrett, & Tooby, 2010). And, as we discussed earlier, self-protection and mate selection appear to be fundamental human goals (Kenrick et al., 2010). That social-cognitive processing is often efficient and accurate has led some to theorize that humans may possess an evolved personality judgment instinct that has the aim of assessing others' affordance values (Haselton & Funder, 2006).

Cues are sometimes unavailable to perceivers at the point when they'd be most useful for inferring affordances—because others may be motivated to conceal them and the intentions they imply. People aiming to do us harm, for instance, don't always signal this to us with angry facial displays. In seeking cues to predict others' fitness-relevant affordances, then, an evolved affordance management system should especially value physical features that are readily perceived and relatively hard to fake.

Moreover, many perceptually available features are limited in the inferences they allow. For example, although an angry facial expression suggests that the bearer may be currently *inclined* to do harm, it suggests little, alone, about the bearer's *capacity* to do such harm. It also by itself suggests little about the bearer's general trustworthiness, likelihood of being a good mate or parent, and so forth. An evolved affordance management system should also, then, especially value features that cue not just one affordance inference (or even a small set of inferences) but rather a broader set of probabilistic inferences related to a larger set of goals and strategies others may employ in their interactions with us. Thus, whereas the facial features that identify others as angry may have long provided probabilistically useful information for inferring others' current intentions regarding aggression or social rejection, the facial features identifying someone as male may have long provided information useful for inferring that person's current inclinations toward (and capacity for) aggression (Becker et al., 2007) as well as that person's interests in becoming a leader, resistance to outside influence, restlessness, and the like (Swim, 1994).

This, of course, is the essence of stereotyping—the process of identifying an individual as being a member of a conceptually coherent "category" and then inferring that this person possesses a set of characteristics and behavioral inclinations (i.e., possesses the affordance values) of typical members of that category. To the extent there existed throughout human evolutionary history some degree of validity to the inferences made about those who shared particular features or feature sets, those of our ancient ancestors who employed such cues to stereotype others would have, on average, enhanced their reproductive fitness relative to those who did not (R. Fox, 1992; Neuberg & Cottrell, 2006). Over time, these particular forms of categorizations and inferences would have become more prominent in the toolbox of contemporary social perceivers.

Which categories, however, would be anticipated by an evolutionary perspective to be particularly important to human social cognition? It's clear that people are able to generate all sorts of social categorization schemes. Researchers employing the "minimal group paradigm" (e.g., Tajfel, Billig, Bundy, & Flament, 1971), for instance, have demonstrated

that people can categorize others on the basis of their preferences for artists, their likelihood of apparently overestimating and underestimating the number of dots on a screen, and other generally trivial features. That people are *able* to employ such categorizations, however, begs the question of what social categories people *typically* use. Research in traditional social cognition has suggested three primary categories—age, sex, and race—on the basis of the ease with which these categories are activated and the impact they have on subsequent inference and judgment (for reviews, see Brewer, 1988; Fiske & Neuberg, 1990; Kinzler, Shutts, & Correll, 2010; Macrae & Quadflieg, 2010).

Although an evolutionary perspective would similarly emphasize the critical importance of age and sex, it would significantly reframe the significance of race and would suggest additional categories that have received much less theoretical and empirical attention. Broadly, the features that people use to organize affordance-relevant information into social categories will be those that have conveyed across human history—in a consistent, perceptually efficient manner—valid information about the fitness threats and opportunities posed by those so categorized.

Age Categorization

Life history theory, a conceptual framework from evolutionary biology, addresses the manner in which organisms distribute their energy to major tasks (e.g., growth, mating, and parenting) across the life span (Stearns, 1976). Beginning with the premise that energetic resources are finite, organisms face the problem of how best to allocate these resources to maximize reproductive fitness. For nonhuman animals, the life history approach has been successful in making predictions about both between- and within-species variation across a range of developmental and behavioral strategies, including rate of sexual maturation, adult body size, and offspring quantity (Charnov, 1993; Crowl & Covich, 1990; Martin, 1995; Roff, 1992; Winemiller, 1989).

Life history theory has been extended to the study of humans (e.g., Brumbach et al., 2009; Figueredo et al., 2005, 2006; Griskevicius, Tybur, Delton & Robertson, 2011; Hill & Kaplan, 1999). Most relevant for this chapter, it has significant implications for understanding human motivation and capacities (e.g., Griskevicius, Delton, Robertson, & Tybur, 2011; Kaplan & Gangestad, 2005; Kenrick & Keefe, 1992; Kenrick & Luce, 2000; Stearns, Allal, & Mace, 2008). Life history theory points, for instance, to the importance of age in shaping people's goals and the ways in which these goals are prioritized. For example, independently acquiring resources is not possible for infants, devoting resources to mate seeking is viable only after sexual maturity, and, upon becoming parents, adults tend toward investing more in their children's growth than in their own (see Kenrick et al., 2010). That energetic resources are finite also means that dedicating resources toward developing certain capacities means that other capacities will receive less investment.

Perceivers have an interest in understanding others' goals and capacities because these goals and capacities potentially affect, in our highly interdependent, ultrasocial arrangement, our own outcomes. Given that age contributes greatly to the shaping of these goals and capacities, well-adapted person perception and impression formation systems ought to be attuned to age. That is, perceivers should be expected to use, as a heuristic for understanding others, their apparent age. The life history approach thus provides one framework for understanding *why* perceivers so prominently employ information about age in the inferences they make about others.

A variety of physical features are useful—and used—for accurately identifying, within a range, others' age (e.g., Berry, 1990; Berry & McArthur, 1986; Bruce & Young, 1998; George & Hole, 1995, 2000; Montepare & Zebrowitz-McArthur, 1988; see Macrae & Quadflieg, 2010, for a review). Infants are identified by their shortness, chubbiness, and disproportionately large heads. "Toddlers" toddle. As children physically mature into adults, their age is cued by larger and more protruding chins, shrinking eyes that appear higher on the face, darkening skin, and faster-paced walking that involves more hip swaying and arm swinging. And as adults become older, their age is cued by wrinkling skin, lengthening ears and nose, thinning and graying hair, a slower, less dynamic walk, and so forth.

These cues enable inferences consistent with the actual effects of development, in general, on others goals, intentions, and capacities. "Childlike" facial features elicit inferences consistent with the actual characteristics of children—that they are, for instance, dependent, submissive, and naïve (e.g., Berry & McArthur, 1986; Zebrowitz, Montepare, & Lee, 1993)—and "elderly" characteristics elicit inferences, for instance, that one lacks energy (Ebner, 2008). (It's thus unsurprising that young people want to look older—but

not elderly—whereas old people, present authors included, wish to look younger—but not childlike.) Findings that "baby-faced" *adults* are inferred to possess more childlike characteristics and are less likely to be convicted of intentional wrongdoing (Berry & Zebrowitz-McArthur, 1988; Zebrowitz & McDonald, 1991) point to the importance that such cues, rather than of the category "age" per se, play in driving perceiver inferences.

In sum, because age drives the kinds of actions that provide opportunities for, and pose threats to, others, people ought to be highly attuned to the features that cue others' age and use them to infer others' affordance-relevant goals, intentions, traits, and capacities. They are and they do.

Sex Categorization

From an evolutionary perspective, sex should also be a central dimension of categorization. Simply put, for sexually reproducing mammals to mate successfully, they must (1) be able to differentiate between males and females, (2) possess information about the cues that each use to signal sexual willingness (e.g., cues related to receptivity, information about the sequences and rituals that serve to initiate and coordinate sexual activity), and (3) apply that understanding to specific mating opportunities. Sex categorization provides important information about others' affordances that go beyond their potential role as mates, however. Human females confront additional constraints and demands on reproduction driven by obligatory gestation and, until very recently, obligatory nursing of young. These obligations limit the number of offspring females can have and force them to allocate energetic resources away from other important life goals, and this greater female investment contributes to several broad sex differences, also seen across the mammalian kingdom. First, females tend be more selective than males in their mate choices because poor mating decisions by females are especially costly to their reproductive fitness (e.g., Clark & Hatfield, 1989; Kenrick, Groth, Trost, & Sadalla, 1993; Wilson & Daly, 1985, 2004). Second, this female selectivity drives greater male intrasexual competition because males seek to gain sexual access to these choosy females (e.g., Geary, 1998). Consistent with this, human males—like males from other species in which females are especially selective—are particularly likely to engage in same-sex assaults and homicides, as well as in other dominance-seeking behaviors (e.g., Daly & Wilson, 1988; Wilson & Daly, 1985).

Because sex is a critical dimension for identifying reproductive opportunities (i.e., potential mates), for identifying potential reproductive costs (e.g., related to coercive mates), and for identifying physical safety threats (e.g., linked to intrasexual competition), it should, like age, be a central dimension people use to categorize one another. And, like age, it is. Here again, then, we see that an evolutionary approach provides coherent grounds for understanding *why* perceivers so prominently employ information about sex in the inferences they make about others.

People employ a range of physical features for accurately identifying others' sex (e.g., Brown & Perrett, 1993; Goshen-Gottstein & Ganel, 2000; Hill, Bruce, & Akamatsu, 1995; Johnson & Tassinary, 2005; Kozlowski & Cutting, 1977; Martin & Macrae, 2007; Nestor & Tarr, 2008; Pollick, Kay, Heim, & Stringer, 2005; Roberts & Bruce, 1988; see Macrae & Quadflieg, 2010, for a review). Secondary sex characteristics, such as breasts and facial hair, differentiate adult women from men, and people readily use these features to sex categorize. Male and female body shapes tend to differ in other ways, as well. Men tend to be larger, to be more muscular, and to have wider shoulders. Women tend to deposit fat on their hips and therefore have a lower waist-to-hip ratio. Facially, adult men tend to have larger jaws, cheekbones, brow ridges, and darker and redder skin tone, whereas women tend to have plumper lips. And men and women tend to move their bodies in somewhat different ways.

Such physical differences are a consequence of puberty-linked increases in testosterone and estrogen, which themselves are causally linked to important shifts in behaviors with significant affordance implications for others (e.g., competitiveness, aggression, nurturance; see, e.g., Kouri, Lukas, Pope, & Oliva, 1995; Mazur & Booth, 1998; Van Goozen, Cohen-Kettenis, Gooren, Frijda, & VandePoll, 1995). That actual sex differences in behavior accord with perceptible cues differentiating adult males from females, and that each are linked to species-normal developmental shifts in sex hormones, further suggests a deep functionality of sex categorization.

The functional nature of sex categorization is further illustrated by findings that the successful categorization of adult individuals as male or female is facilitated by circumstances that raise the specter of sex-linked threats and opportunities. For example, Becker and his colleagues (2007) found that

categorizing an adult face as male (but not female) is faster and more accurate if that face is expressing anger—an expression that signals the increased possibility of impending aggression. Adult men are more likely to engage in physical aggression and are more likely given their greater muscle mass to impose significant physical damage while doing so. Thus, the enhanced inclination for people to quickly and accurately see "male" when a face is angry reveals a useful response if one tends to be danger averse—as humans tend to be. Other findings show that this pattern of findings is robust against contemporary, socialized cues for identifying sex (e.g., gendered clothing), consistent with the idea that the link between maleness and anger may be driven by testosterone-linked facial features and derived from some deeper functionality (Becker et al., 2007).

These experiments reveal that sex categorization processes can be altered by the presence of sex-relevant affordance cues displayed by the target. Other research shows that categorization on apparently sex-independent dimensions can be shaped by target sex. For instance, one might presume that the identification of anger on a face would proceed unbiased by the sex of that face. Thus, just as Becker et al. (2007) found that people are especially fast and accurate at identifying faces as male when they are angry (see above), they also showed that people are especially fast and accurate at identifying faces as angry when the faces are male—again, a predictable bias given that men generally have a greater inclination to physically aggress and a greater ability to do so in a highly damaging way. Consider, also, findings by Maner and his colleagues (2005). Participants in some conditions viewed a clip from the film *Silence of the Lambs*, designed (and demonstrated) to evoke self-protection concerns. Afterward, they were shown photographs of male and female, black and white faces, and were asked to identify the facial expressions ostensibly being suppressed by these targets as their photographs were being taken. Consistent with the error-managing inclination to see expressions on those who are most functionally relevant to one's current concerns, white participants identified these faces as suppressing anger—a threat to self-protection—but only on black *male* faces. We address the issue of outgroup categorization in the next section, but note here that the threat was perceived to exist in the male targets—as one would expect from a functional perspective.

Such findings aren't limited to threat perception. For instance, Maner et al. (2005) also found that men who had just viewed film clips designed to elicit mating interest were especially likely to "see" suppressed sexual interest on the faces of attractive, ingroup *women*. Again, this functional projection wasn't directed at faces across the board, or toward men, but only toward those who the (typically heterosexual) male participants would be particularly interested in having sex with.

This overview of sex categorization from an evolutionary perspective has been necessarily brief. What should be clear, however, is that because sex contributes to behaviors that provide opportunities for others (e.g., mating) and that pose threats to others (e.g., physical aggression), people ought to be highly attuned to the features that cue others' sex and use them to infer others' affordance-relevant goals, intentions, traits, and capacities.

Coalition Categorization

As discussed earlier, human reproductive fitness requires that an individual accomplish a wide range of challenging tasks (e.g., eating well enough; protecting oneself from predators, including other humans; finding mates; raising children). Evolutionary theorizing has it that the human form of sociality—labeled by some *ultrasociality, hypersociality,* or *obligatory interdependence* (e.g., Brewer, 2001; Campbell, 1983; Coon, 1946; Mann, 1980; Richerson & Boyd, 1998)—emerged as a set of adaptations designed by natural selection to facilitate the successful achievement of such tasks—tasks that would be difficult, if not impossible, to accomplish alone as individuals, or even in small family units. These adaptations encourage and enable individuals to work cooperatively with one another toward common aims in often complex and distal webs of interdependence. Aspects of this evolved sociality can be characterized as coalitional in the sense that they lead individuals to think of themselves as interdependent members of groups, to identify with these groups, to regulate the behavior of other group members to reduce the costs of group membership, to invest resources within (as opposed to outside) these groups, to defend the groups against potential ill-intentioned or otherwise threatening intruders, and the like.

The conception of an evolved coalitional psychology has much to offer in terms of understanding how people think about and respond to members of their own groups (Cottrell et al., 2007; Kurzban & Leary, 2001; Kurzban & Neuberg, 2005; Neuberg, Smith, & Asher, 2000). It also makes clear why ingroup–outgroup categorization is such a universal, ubiquitous feature of human social life: Simply put, if cooperative interdependence with members of one's own group affords such fitness advantages—and requires such material, social, and psychological investment—one needs to be cognitively able and prepared to differentiate members of coalitional ingroups versus outgroups (R. Fox, 1992; Neuberg & Cottrell, 2006; Schaller & Neuberg, 2008, 2012).

What cues do people use to identify individuals as members of coalitional ingroups versus outgroups? Ancestrally, cues related to language, dialect, and accent would have been useful for doing so, and contemporary humans appear to use these cues as well (e.g., Kinzler et al., 2010). Other features that would have differentiated the ingroup from outgroups—dress, bodily markings (tattoos, scarification, body piercings), smells (often related to foods and food preparation practices), and the like—also would have served as useful cues, and likely do so now as well. Observable norms, practices, and rituals would also often serve to differentiate groups; the extent to which religious practices currently cue group membership is one example of this.

Although race categorization is common in modern times, racial physiognomy would have been of only limited use for making diagnostic ingroup–outgroup categorizations even just tens of thousands of years ago because people rarely traveled sufficiently far to come across individuals who looked meaningfully different from members of their own coalitional ingroup (Stringer & McKie, 1998). What likely evolved, however, is a tendency to readily learn from one's environment those cues that differentiate coalitional ingroup from outgroup (e.g., Kurzban, Tooby, & Cosmides, 2001; Schaller, Park, & Faulkner, 2003). Today, skin color and racial facial physiognomy cue ingroup–outgroup categorization—and research demonstrates that the more one looks like an outgroup member (e.g., the "more black" a target looks based on skin tone and physiognomy), the more stereotypically that target is viewed (Maddox, 2004). It's important to note, however, that racial features, as with the other features mentioned above, are merely *cues* to actual coalitional ingroup–outgroup status, and are thus used as a heuristic for coalitional categorization. Indeed, Kurzban and his colleagues (2001) have demonstrated that categorization on the basis of race can be overcome when alternative, more diagnostic cues to actual coalitional status are available and salient.

An evolutionary perspective further suggests that, in the absence of contrary information, the stereotypes of coalitional outgroups should lean toward being threat heavy. Ingroup coalitions are maintained largely by reciprocal exchanges of valued efforts and material over time, by commitments to continue such exchanges, by the adoption of consensual practices and norms, and the like. Nearly by definition, such behaviors would be relatively uncommon across coalitional lines. Moreover, outgroup individuals may also desire the resources held by ingroups. Whereas strategies useful for unilaterally acquiring resources from others (e.g., aggression, theft) are often inhibited by norms and social sanctions within groups, such norms and sanctions are less likely to effectively control the actions of coalitional outgroup members who have little investment in being viewed as a valued member of the ingroup. (Whereas theft from the ingroup is stigmatized and often punished, theft from outgroups is often highly valued; see R. Hood, 1243.) Thus, all else being equal, outgroups may actually pose real threats to tangible ingroup resources. And the more foreign the outgroups and their members, the more likely they pose threats of disease by the carrying of pathogens that ingroup members' immune systems have not yet "learned" to defend against (Faulkner, Schaller, Park, & Duncan, 2004). In light of the possibility (even slim) of such threats, and in the absence of low-threat information to the contrary, outgroup stereotypes and stereotypical inferences about outgroup members are likely to be precautionary and err toward depicting outgroups and their members as being untrustworthy, dangerous, and the like. Such a threat bias in stereotyping (e.g., Fox, 1992) fits with the logic of Nesse's (2005) smoke detector principle and error management theory (Haselton & Buss, 2000, 2003; Haselton & Nettle, 2006), and is supported by data from the minimal intergroup and other research paradigms (e.g., Insko & Schopler, 1998; Mullen, Brown, & Smith, 1992; Tajfel, 1982).

As with age and sex categorization and stereotyping, however, coalitional categorization and stereotyping are functionally flexible: The particular ways in which specific groups are stereotyped should depend on the particular threats they are seen as posing (Cottrell & Neuberg, 2005), and such stereotyping should occur especially under circumstances when perceivers feel vulnerable or relevant threats have become salient. We focus our discussion here on race-related categorization and stereotyping, given the emphasis on this in the research literature, and present just a few illustrations.

Miller, Maner, and Becker (2010) hypothesized that people are biased toward categorizing unfamiliar others as members of an outgroup rather than as members of one's ingroup when these targets are encountered in tandem with factors evoking thoughts of interpersonal aggression. Indeed, white participants were more likely to categorize targets as black (as opposed to white) when those targets displayed cues heuristically associated with threat (masculinity, movement toward the perceiver, and facial expressions of anger). In addition, white participants who felt chronically vulnerable to interpersonal threats responded to a fear manipulation by categorizing angry faces as black, rather than white, and this finding was replicated in a minimal group paradigm. These results suggest that threat cues exhibited by targets combine with perceiver vulnerability to threat to bias the way people initially parse the social world into ingroup versus outgroup.

Similarly suggesting heuristically functional categorization and stereotyping processes—given the dangerousness stereotypes held by whites about young black men—angry facial expressions are especially likely to "leap" from angry male white faces to adjacent emotionally neutral black male faces (compared with emotionally neutral white male faces), even during very short exposure times (100 ms); these expressions are not as likely to leap from angry black male faces to adjacent emotionally neutral white male faces, however (Becker, Neel, & Anderson, 2010).

Angry facial expressions imply threats to physical safety. Ambient darkness does as well. Consistent with a functional approach, white individuals participating in a study in a darkened (versus well-lit) room exhibited increased activation of negative threat-related stereotypes of blacks, but not of threat-irrelevant stereotypes of blacks (Schaller, Park, & Faulkner, 2003; Schaller, Park, & Mueller, 2003).

Some of the earliest work on evolutionary approaches to human learning demonstrated that people acquire fear responses to some ancestrally relevant classes of stimuli (e.g., snakes, spiders) faster than to evolutionarily irrelevant (but nonetheless dangerous in contemporary life) classes of stimuli (e.g., broken electrical outlets, nonpointed guns), and that the conditioned fear responses to the former stimuli are more resistant to extinction (e.g., Öhman & Mineka, 2001). Extending these demonstrations of prepared learning to the realm of social cognition, Olsson, Ebert, Banaji, and Phelps (2005) showed that conditioned fear responses to novel other-race faces are more resistant to extinction.

Interestingly, this race-based fear-conditioning effect holds only for outgroup male targets (Navarrete, Olsson, Ho, Mendes, Thomsen, & Sidanius, 2009). Indeed, across many experiments from many labs—some of which we reviewed above—the observed stereotypical biases against racial outgroups (and particularly by whites against blacks) are largely limited to outgroup males. This is consistent both with theorizing about the roles that outgroup males (human as well as closely related primates) have played in intergroup conflict (Daly & Wilson, 1988; Keegan, 1993; Keeley, 1996; Kelly, 2005; Makova & Li, 2002; Navarrete, McDonald, Molina, & Sidanius, 2010; Schaller & Neuberg, 2008; Sidanius & Pratto, 1999; Sidanius & Veniegas, 2000; van Vugt, De Cremer, & Janssen, 2007; Wrangham & Peterson, 1996), as well as contemporary stereotypes about the physical dangers posed by outgroup males (and young black men, in particular). These findings suggest a bias tuned to the felt needs of white perceivers, given what they believe they know about black men.

In sum, as with age and sex categorization, the evolutionary approach provides a rationale for coalitional categorization. It also focuses theoretical and empirical attention on the role that self-protection concerns play in coalitional categorization: Individuals who exhibit features implying danger (e.g., angry expressions) are especially likely to be categorized as outgroup members; outgroup members who exhibit features implying greater danger (e.g., young men) are especially likely to be associated with outgroup threat stereotypes; and when the immediate ecological setting suggests danger (e.g., ambient darkness), outgroup threat stereotypes are especially likely to be activated perceiver's minds.

Disease Categorization

Much recent research has focused on the physical features that imply a disease categorization and the downstream implications of this categorization. The close proximity of others and the highly interdependent nature of human social interaction have made the transmission of pathogens a very real threat throughout our history (Ewald, 1994; Wolfe, Dunavan, & Diamond, 2007). In response to this threat, humans have evolved not only a sophisticated immune system designed to combat pathogens after infection but also a *behavioral immune system* designed to avoid infection in the first place (Schaller & Park, 2011). Because pathogens aren't visible to the human eye, this system is sensitive to those perceptually available features that, with some

nontrivial degree of validity, would have suggested pathogen presence in ancestral times (and long before modern medicine). Indeed, disease-causing pathogens often affect the human body in readily perceptible ways, usually involving morphological changes from the physical norm (e.g., rashes, skin lesions) or unusual, non-normative actions (e.g., vomiting, diarrhea, ill-coordinated movements). Such cues readily engage the functional, disease-avoiding emotion of disgust (Oaten et al., 2009) as well as behavioral inclinations to avoid the bearer of such cues.

There is great variability, however, in visually accessible cues to pathogens; different pathogens produce different observable symptoms, individuals may respond with different physical manifestations to the same infection, and pathogen species themselves evolve very rapidly (Ewald, 1994). For these reasons, the behavioral immune system appears to be calibrated broadly, to a crudely defined range of cues of morphological and behavioral abnormality—what Erving Goffman (1963) labeled "abominations of body" (Kurzban & Leary, 2001; Neuberg et al., 2000; Schaller & Duncan, 2007; Zebrowitz & Montepare, 2006). Indeed, people bearing such cues (e.g., facial scarring, physical disability, obesity) often automatically activate in others the category of being diseased and elicit affiliated avoidance processes and behaviors—even when the cues themselves don't logically predict pathogen transmission (e.g., Mortensen et al., 2010; Park, Faulkner, & Schaller, 2003; Park, Schaller, & Crandall, 2007; Schaller & Duncan, 2007). This overgeneralization bias of disease inference can be viewed as an instance of precautionary error management, in which perceivers (usually nonconsciously) accept the possibility that they may err in viewing a healthy person as diseased to avoid the more costly potential error of viewing an actually diseased individual as nondiseased—a cost that would have been greatly magnified in ancestral times in the absence of the modern miracle of antibiotic drugs and other postinfection technologies.

Disease categorizations exhibit the characteristic of functional flexibility. As discussed earlier, functional motivational systems are especially likely to be engaged when relevant threats or opportunities appear great. For instance, although disease cognitions are commonly and automatically activated into working memory upon the perception of morphologically anomalous individuals, this is especially the case for perceivers for whom the potential threat of infectious diseases is especially salient (e.g., Duncan & Schaller, 2009; Park et al., 2003, 2007).

We have just seen that evolutionary approaches have great value for better understanding trait inference, categorization, and stereotyping processes—processes that provide the social perceivers with heuristically useful information as to the threats and opportunities afforded by those they encounter. We turn to overview briefly some recent work exploring how evolutionary approaches may provide some insight into decision-making processes.

Judgment and Decision Making

Classic models of judgment and decision making presumed economic rationality—that humans make self-serving decisions based on full information about alternatives. With the cognitive revolution in psychology came a greater appreciation for human processing limitations, leading to a set of models focused on biased and irrational choices driven by simplifying heuristics (Simon, 1955, 1956; Tversky & Kahneman, 1974). Evolutionary approaches build on such behavioral economic models by presuming that biases that, on their face, seem irrational may instead reveal the operation of judgmental heuristics that would have, in general, enhanced the fitness of our ancestors (Cooper, 1987; Gandolfi, Gandolfi, & Barash, 2002; Kanazawa, 2001; Todd & Gigerenzer, 2007; Wang, 2002; Wang & Dvorak, 2010).

Recent approaches further suggest that human decision making is deeply rational, in the sense that people attend to different costs and benefits, and weight them differently, depending on the most prominent threats or opportunities confronting us (Kenrick et al., 2009; Kenrick, Li, White, & Neuberg, 2012). Indeed, the deep rationality underlying some biases is revealed only when the judgments made are connected to the social context and motivations for which they likely evolved. Consider, for instance, how people perform on the Wason selection task (Wason & Johnson-Laird, 1972)—an abstract, content-general task designed to assess how well people perform if–then reasoning. Findings revealed what appeared to be major flaws in human reasoning processes; people performed quite poorly on the task. Yet a now-classic program of research by Cosmides, Tooby, and colleagues (e.g., Cosmides, 1989; Cosmides & Tooby, 2005) makes clear that this performance improves greatly when the problems to be solved are framed in terms of social exchange (e.g., if I do something for you, you will do something for me)—especially when the possibility of being cheated by another may be involved. This enhanced performance exists even when the specific social exchange contracts are novel and unfamiliar (suggesting that experience with them isn't necessary for success), even when performed by very young children (ages 3 to 4 years), and across societies ranging from Western industrial nations to hunter-horticulturalists in the Amazon (Harris, Nunez, & Brett, 2001; Sugiyama, Tooby, & Cosmides, 2002). Such judgments are especially accurate when it's most important that they be so—when cheater detection is particularly important—as when violations of social exchange are anticipated to be intentional and to benefit the perpetrator, and when cheating in the situation would be relatively easy (Cosmides, Barrett, & Tooby, 2010).

Other work reveals that the occurrence of ostensibly ubiquitous biases may shift in striking ways as decision makers confront different fundamental opportunities and threats. Consider, as one example, the phenomenon of loss aversion (Kahneman & Tversky, 1979), in which the psychological impact of a loss of a particular size is greater than the psychological impact of a gain of the same size—a finding apparently so robust that some suggest that such losses loom twice as large as equivalent gains (Vohs & Luce, 2010). That there would be, across many circumstances, a greater priority placed on avoiding losses than acquiring gains would certainly make adaptive sense for ancestral humans, who lived close to the margins of survival. From an evolutionary perspective, however, there would have existed other circumstances in which gain seeking would have trumped loss aversion—as when mating-minded men were confronted by typically highly selective, choosy women, and would thus have needed to compete with other men for sexual access. Indeed, men (but not women) shift from loss aversion toward gain seeking when experimentally induced toward mating motivation (Li, Kenrick, Griskevicius, & Neuberg, 2012). This finding is supported by others showing that activating a mating frame of mind increases risky behavior in men (e.g., Baker & Maner, 2008, 2009; Ronay & Von Hippel, 2010).

There have been an increasing number of studies examining various aspects of judgment and economic decision making from an evolutionary perspective (e.g., Sundie et al., 2011; Wang, 1996; Wilson & Daly, 2004). As with other processes in the cognitive stream, however, it's clear that decision processes are nuanced and sensitive to evolutionarily relevant considerations: These processes are functionally flexible in ways apparently designed to enhance the likelihood that people will achieve fundamental goals.

Broad Issues

The evolutionary approach to social cognition generates novel, testable hypotheses, casts fresh light on old issues, and has opened whole new lines of inquiry. Before we close, we briefly bring into focus several larger issues and address common misconceptions about the evolutionary approach.

Functional Specialization: Domain-Specific Mechanisms

The evolutionary position suggests that seeing the mind as a general-purpose problem solver is unrealistic. The brain, from the evolutionary view, has been sculpted by natural selection to solve recurrent, and distinct, ancestral problems—problems that imply for the perceiver the relevance of qualitatively different informational inputs and that require qualitatively different solutions. For instance, we've discussed ways in which social cognition is differentially shaped by threats requiring self-protection versus those requiring disease avoidance, with the former focusing perceivers on angry facial expressions and eliciting fear and with the latter focusing perceivers on facial disfigurements and eliciting disgust. It follows that it would be of great adaptive benefit for the mind to possess functionally modular networks specialized to work in these specific problem domains (Barrett & Kurzban, 2006; Cosmides & Tooby, 1994; Pinker, 1997).

This domain-specificity view is highly consistent with findings from modern cognitive neuroscience. For instance, just as the self-protection and disease-avoidance systems differ in what they seek as informational inputs and what they generate as emotional outputs, they also differ in their neurobiological substrates (LeDoux, 2000; Oaten et al., 2009). As a second example, consider face processing (see Chapter 9). Face processing is critical for many aspects of real-world social cognition and is reliably associated with activity in a number of brain areas, each of which reflects functionally distinct problems. The fusiform area is dedicated to processing invariant features of faces like gender and race, whereas an area in the superior temporal sulcus processes changeable features like gaze direction and expression (Kanwisher & Wojciuluk, 2000). This design reflects the constraints imposed by different kinds of problems: Recognizing conspecifics and kin is linked to a very old system that makes mating, coalition building, and reciprocity

possible, whereas identifying signs of a conspecific's immediate disposition requires inferential machinery that goes beyond (although still depends on) simple pattern-recognition mechanisms. As a third example, neuroimaging research now suggests that different areas in the prefrontal cortex appear to underlie the functionally distinct components of reasoning about social exchange. The ventrolateral prefrontal cortex (vlPFC) has been shown to be active when reasoning about violations of social contracts (including prohibitions as well as obligations; Fiddick, Spampinato, & Grafman, 2005), whereas the dorsolateral PFC (dlPFC) appears to be more engaged by questions of what is permissible within these obligations. Intriguingly, the vlPFC is innervated before the dlPFC—evidence that it evolved earlier. From the standpoint of functional specialization, it makes sense that we first evolved the ability to think about what social life requires of us and then evolved the ability to think about bending those rules.

This isn't to suggest that there exist no domain-general processes. And it certainly isn't to suggest that the mind doesn't, at times, *appear* to operate in domain-general ways divorced from ancestral needs. The brain clearly didn't evolve to process nonsense syllables devoid of meaning—or even written words with meaning—yet Ebbinghaus was able to use such syllables to chart a general process of memory decay. Why the apparent domain generality? We suspect that such mechanisms likely exploit and build on coordinated sets of functional modules designed for more ancient purposes, such as understanding spoken language, "reading" features of the physical ecology, and so forth. Despite the gains of understanding made by those assuming domain-general mechanisms, it's useful to note how impoverished our understanding of memory would be if researchers had stopped there. Rather, once researchers began looking at how people and nonhuman animals remember meaningful content, whole new processes and phenomena were discovered (e.g., Garcia & Koelling, 1966; Klein et al., 2002; Sherry & Schacter, 1987; Wilcoxon, Dragoin, & Kral, 1971).

Nature and Nurture: Evolution, Development, Learning, and Culture

Evolutionary theories of human psychology are often critiqued as implying a hard-wired genetic determinism and a minimal role for development and learning, and as being incompatible with variability across cultures. Such views radically misrepresent the evolutionary position (Tooby & Cosmides, 1992; Neuberg et al., 2010).

First, development is an essential component to any evolutionary approach to human behavior (Bjorklund & Pellegrini, 2002; Geary, 2006; Marcus, 2004; Kenrick et al., 2010). Gene expression in humans depends on a variety of factors, including hormone levels (e.g., within the mother during gestation), qualities of the family environment approaching sexual maturation (Ellis, 2004), and so forth. From an evolutionary perspective, phenotypic plasticity is both presumed and considered adaptive because the ability of any trait to benefit an organism depends on the environment in which it finds itself. The particular traits that emerge through development should thus tend to depend on features of the immediate context. This presumption has provided greater understanding of a range of individual differences, including attachment style (Bowlby, 1969), mating strategies (Bjorklund & Shackelford, 1999; Gangestad & Simpson, 2000), and kin recognition (Lieberman, Tooby, & Cosmides, 2007).

Learning is also a critical component of any evolutionary approach to understanding social cognition and behavior. Most important for present purposes, learning mechanisms allow people (and other organisms) to gain relevant information about local social and physical contexts, enabling them to adjust their behaviors in flexible, functional ways. Consider prepared associative learning, in which people are especially able to quickly learn and effectively maintain fitness-relevant associations. For instance, humans are biologically prepared to learn to fear snakes, which were meaningful threats in ancestral environments (Öhman & Mineka, 2001). As noted earlier, we are also especially efficient at learning, and especially slow to unlearn, fearful responses to members of coalitional outgroups (Olsson, Ebert, Banaji, & Phelps, 2005)—especially, to male members of coalitional outgroups (Navarrete et al., 2009).

Research on rhesus monkeys further suggests that there may be biological preparation for social learning as well: These monkeys learn to fear snakes merely from seeing others' fearful reactions to them (Cook & Mineka, 1990). It seems reasonable to hypothesize that prepared social learning mechanisms contribute to humans' impressive ability to learn specifically the kinds of information about others—and about other groups—that would have been fitness enhancing in ancestral times (Schaller, 2006).

Such findings suggest the presence of some basic mental "content" templates—of snakes, males who look different than us, and so forth—that upon exposure to real-world events form the foundation for more specific mental representations. It is widely known, for instance, that infants track face-like blobs (Johnson, Dziurawiec, Ellis, & Morton, 1991). This instinctive act of looking must involve some basic mental template that directs gaze toward fleshy, bilaterally symmetrical ovals, upon which newly gathered information begins to reliably build face representations. Personal experience with one's world would seem critical to this evolved process: Sheep raised with horned others have "horn" representations that are lacking in those raised in hornless environments (Kendrick & Baldwin, 1987). Experience may also play an important role in pruning away early perceptual sensitivities that are not reinforced. Sargent and Nelson (1992) for instance, have shown that human infants are sensitive to differences in monkey faces that adult humans are not. Human infants are also sensitive to phonemic differences not present in their linguistic environment—a sensitivity that vanishes with exposure to the native tongue (Kuhl, Williams, Lacerda, Stevens, & Lindblom, 1992).

A focus on learning is thus not at all incompatible with an evolutionary view. Indeed, conceptualizing learning within an evolutionary context raises important questions that ought to be of great interest to social cognitivists: Why are some things easier to learn than others? Why are some experiences weighted more heavily by cognitive systems than are others?

Last, as many scholars of both evolution and culture have made clear, evolutionary approaches are not incompatible with cultural variability (Buss, 2001; Kenrick et al., 2003; Kenrick, Nieuweboer, & Buunk, 2010; Norenzayan & Heine, 2005; Norenzayan, Schaller, & Heine, 2006; Schaller, 2007). Indeed, evolutionary approaches *predict* such variability. This should be clear given the points we've made throughout the chapter: Because different cultural contexts afford somewhat different patterns of threats and opportunities, somewhat different developmental constraints, and somewhat different learning environments, one would expect evolved mechanisms to manifest differently across cultures (Gangestad, Haselton, & Buss, 2006; Schmitt, 2005; Schmitt et al., 2003; Tooby & Cosmides, 1992).

In sum, evolutionary approaches are highly compatible with development, learning, and cultural variability. Indeed, they explicitly reject simplistic nature-versus-nurture approaches to the causes of social behavior, and rarely hypothesize inflexible forms of behavior. It thus makes little sense to make the all-too-common error of posing sociocultural and evolutionary explanations as alternatives to one another for explaining cognition and behavior. The nature *versus* nurture debate has long been dead in the biological sciences. To pursue this false dichotomy in the psychological sciences makes no more sense.

Adaptive Social Cognition: Accuracies and Biases

Adaptive cognition and behavior often appear to be less than accurate, and even at times "irrational." Indeed, over the past several decades, social cognitivists have been especially proficient at—and enthusiastic about—providing laboratory illustrations of human cognitive errors. Funder (1987) provided a compelling critique of this approach to social cognition, questioning why social cognitivists conceptualize participants' laboratory errors as evidence of cognitive flaws whereas vision researchers conceptualize laboratory perceptual illusions as providing insight into the extraordinarily effective workings of a visual system adapted to succeed in the information-rich and complex physical ecology that is real life. Similar to these vision researchers, social cognition researchers employing evolutionary approaches conceptualize biases in the laboratory as potential grist for the mill of better understanding how the social mind navigates the real-world threats and opportunities afforded by the information-rich, complex social ecology.

What we've seen throughout the chapter is that many supposed errors and inaccuracies may instead be *deeply rational* if we take the long view and analyze how the costs and benefits would have affected our ancestor's reproductive fitness (Haselton & Nettle, 2006; Kenrick et al., 2009). Evolutionary approaches to social cognition have also begun to explore the realm of *domain-specific* accuracy, generating and supporting hypotheses that would be highly unlikely to arise from other meta-theoretical perspectives. Consider the finding that women are more accurate than men at remembering the location of high-calorie foods (New et al., 2007). Few, if any, other perspectives would have naturally generated this hypothesis, but it readily emerges when one think about how hunter-gatherers have distributed food-gathering labor between the sexes.

Traditional social cognition theorizing has suggested that one can increase accuracy in person perception, judgment, and the like by engaging motivation in domain-general ways (e.g., via accuracy goals; Neuberg & Fiske, 1987). Evolutionary approaches to motivation take a quite different tack, presuming that accuracy is especially likely to be enhanced when a perceiver confronts targets possessing characteristics particularly relevant to the perceiver's currently active fundamental goals. For example, as discussed earlier, perceivers primed with a safety-threatening film exhibited enhanced recognition accuracy for outgroup men, but not ingroup men or any women, reflecting a functionally specific attunement to faces stereotyped as having the greatest potential for violence (Becker at al., 2010). Similar effects can be seen at early stages of perception as well. Becker et al. (2011), for instance, showed that a similar self-protection prime enhanced participant's ability to detect a briefly presented sign of coalitional membership—an accuracy effect that was observed independent of other biases elicited by the manipulation. What these effects suggest is that humans flexibly and adaptively deploy cognitive resources to enhance accuracy when accuracy truly appears to matter.

Social cognitive researchers have long maintained that humans are cognitive misers. From the evolutionary perspective, this reflects an inclination to conserve resources for important social problems—for the challenges and opportunities on which our reproductive fitness truly depends. Evolutionary approaches to social cognition suggest that people are released from such cognitively miserly tendencies when confronted with intrinsically motivating problems resonating with fundamental social goals.

Conclusion

Decades ago, behaviorists raised concerns about the cognitive approach to psychology, wondering, for example, whether it was possible to test hypotheses about difficult-to-observe mental constructs. Despite those concerns, the cognitive approach to psychology has been incredibly productive. Some of the same concerns were later raised about evolutionary approaches to behavior and cognition (Kenrick, Schaller, & Simpson, 2006). Despite those concerns, the evolutionary approach to psychology is similarly proving to be quite productive. Indeed, many of the most fruitful directions have involved an integration of ideas from the evolutionary and cognitive perspectives. We have only sampled a subset of the empirical findings emerging from that integration, and many social-cognitive phenomena have yet to be explored from an evolutionary perspective. Yet, as the research reviewed here suggests, one might reasonably be optimistic that broadening the evolutionary exploration across the domains of traditional social cognition would be quite profitable.

Indeed, upon greater examination of the evolutionary perspective, one might expect social cognitivists—and social psychologists more generally—to develop an affinity for this approach. Like social psychology, evolutionary social psychology views the proximate provocation to thought and action as typically lying in the immediate social context. Like social psychology, evolutionary social psychology recognizes that features of the person (e.g., capacities, goals, strategies) and of the situation (e.g., salient contextual cues) interact to shape social thoughts, feelings, and behavior. Like much work in social cognition, evolutionary social cognition assumes that all cognition is motivated cognition—that cognition *serves* motivation—but with an additional set of assumptions about the kinds of goals social perceivers are often attempting to achieve through their thought processes (i.e., fundamental goals related to fitness) and how these goals imply the importance of specific kinds of information to be processed. Like much work in social cognition, evolutionary social cognition is interested in cognitive biases, albeit with somewhat different assumptions about what these biases imply about the effectiveness and design of the social mind. Like much work in social cognition, evolutionary social cognition generates hypotheses about mediating processes, typically focusing on how certain social cues imply certain opportunities and threats, activate particular affective and cognitive mechanisms, and thus incline social perceivers toward certain actions.

We could go on, but hope the point is clear: Evolutionary social cognition is social cognition, albeit with an additional set of conceptual tools that enable the derivation of heretofore novel, and often impressively nuanced, hypotheses. Among the most important of these theory-driven hypotheses are those that focus on *content*—on what kinds of information get processed, and about how and under what circumstances different kinds of information get processed in different ways. As such, evolutionary social cognition provides additional leverage for our efforts to better understanding the human mind as it attempts to navigate the rich, complex, and fascinating social world in which it strives to succeed.

Author Note

The contributions of Steven L. Neuberg and Douglas T. Kenrick were supported by grants from the National Institute of Mental Health (MH064734) and National Science Foundation (BCS-0843763, BCS-0642873); the contributions of D. Vaughn Becker were supported by a grant from the National Science Foundation (BCS-0642873).

References

Ackerman, J. M., Becker, D. V., Mortensen, C. R., Sasaki, T., Neuberg, S. L., & Kenrick, D. T. (2009). A pox on the mind: Disjunction of attention and memory in the processing of physical disfigurement. *Journal of Experimental Social Psychology, 45*, 478–485.

Ackerman, J. M., Shapiro, J. R., Neuberg, S. L., Kenrick, D. T., Schaller, M., Becker, D. V., Griskevicius, V., & Maner, J. K. (2006). They all look the same to me (unless they're angry): From out-group homogeneity to out-group heterogeneity. *Psychological Science, 17*, 836–840.

Ambady, N., Bernieri, F. J., & Richeson, J. A. (2000). Toward a histology of social behavior: Judgmental accuracy from thin slices of the behavioral stream. In M. P. Zanna (Ed.), *Advances in experimental social psychology* (Vol. 32, pp. 201–271). San Diego, CA: Academic Press.

Anderson, U. S., Perea, E. F., Becker, D. V., Ackerman, J. M., Shapiro, J. R., Neuberg, S. L., & Kenrick, D. T. (2010). I only have eyes for you: Ovulation redirects attention (but not memory) to attractive men. *Journal of Experimental Social Psychology, 46*, 804–808.

Anthony, T., Copper, C., & Mullen, B. (1992). Cross-racial facial identification: A social cognitive integration. *Personality and Social Psychology Bulletin, 18*, 296–301.

Apicella, C. L., Dreber, A., Campbell, B., Gray, P. B., Hoffman, M., & Little, A. C. (2008). Testosterone and financial risk preferences. *Evolution and Human Behavior, 29*, 384–390.

Baker, M. J., & Maner, J. K. (2008). Risk-taking as a situationally sensitive male mating strategy. *Evolution and Human Behavior, 29*, 391–395.

Baker, M. J., & Maner, J. K. (2009). Male risk-taking as a context-sensitive signaling device. *Journal of Experimental Social Psychology, 45*, 1136–1139.

Barrett, H. C., & Kurzban, R. (2006). Modularity in cognition: Framing the debate. *Psychological Review, 113*, 628–647.

Becker, D. V., Anderson, U. S., Neuberg, S. L., Maner, J. K., Shapiro, J. R., Ackerman, J. M., Schaller, M., & Kenrick, D. T. (2010). More memory bang for the attentional buck: Self-protection goals enhance encoding efficiency for potentially threatening males. *Social Psychological and Personality Science, 1*, 182–189.

Becker, D. V., Kenrick, D. T., Guerin, S., & Maner, J. K. (2005). Concentrating on beauty: Sexual selection and sociospatial memory. *Personality and Social Psychology Bulletin, 31*, 1643–1652.

Becker, D. V., Kenrick, D. T., Neuberg, S. L., Blackwell, K. C., & Smith, D. M. (2007). The confounded nature of angry men and happy women. *Journal of Personality and Social Psychology, 92*, 179–190.

Becker, D. V., Mortensen, C. R., Ackerman, J. M., Shapiro, J. R., Anderson, U. S., Sasaki, T., Maner, J. K., Neuberg, S. L., Kenrick, D. T. (2011). Signal detection on the battlefield: Priming self-protection vs. revenge-mindedness differentially modulates the detection of enemies and allies. *PLoS One, 6*, e23929.

Becker, D. V., Neel, R., & Anderson, U. S. (2010). Illusory conjunctions of angry facial expressions follow intergroup biases. *Psychological Science, 21*, 38–40.

Berry, D. S. (1990). What can a moving face tell us? *Journal of Personality and Social Psychology, 58*, 1004–1014.

Berry, D. S., & McArthur, L. Z. (1986). Perceiving character in faces: The impact of age-related craniofacial changes on social perception. *Psychological Bulletin, 100*, 3–18.

Berry, D. S., & Zebrowitz-McArthur, L. (1988). What's in a face? Facial maturity and the attribution of legal responsibility. *Personality and Social Psychology Bulletin, 14*, 23–33.

Bowlby, J. (1969). *Attachment and loss: Vol. 1, Attachment*. New York: Basic Books.

Bjorklund, D. F., & Pellegrini, A. D. (2002). *The origins of human nature: Evolutionary developmental psychology*. Washington, DC, US: American Psychological Association, Washington, DC.

Bjorklund, D. F., & Shackelford, T. K. (1999). Differences in parental investment contribute to important differences between men and women. *Current Directions in Psychological Science, 8*, 86–89.

Boyd, R., & Richerson, P. J. (1995). Why does culture increase adaptability? *Ethology & Sociobiology, 16*, 125–143.

Brewer, M. B. (1988). A dual process model of impression formation. In T. K. Srull & R. S. Wyer, Jr. (Eds.), *Advances in social cognition* (Vol. 1, pp. 1–36). Hillsdale, NJ: Erlbaum.

Brewer, M. B. (2001). Ingroup identification and intergroup conflict: When does ingroup love become outgroup hate? In R. Ashmore, L. Jussim, & D. Wilder (Eds.), *Social identity, intergroup conflict, and conflict reduction* (pp. 17–41). New York: Oxford University Press.

Brown, E., & Perrett, D. I. (1993). What gives a face its gender? *Perception, 22*, 829–840.

Bruce, V., & Young, A. (1998). *In the eye of the beholder: The science of face perception*. New York: Oxford University Press.

Brumbach, B. H., Figueredo, A. J., & Ellis, B. J. (2009). Effects of harsh and unpredictable environments in adolescence on development of life history strategies: A longitudinal test of an evolutionary model. *Human Nature, 20*, 25–51.

Bugental, D. B. (2000). Acquisition of the algorithms of social life: A domain-based approach. *Psychological Bulletin, 26*, 187–209.

Buss, D. M. (1995). Evolutionary psychology: A new paradigm for social science. *Psychological Inquiry, 6*, 1–30.

Buss, D. M. (2001). Human nature and culture: An evolutionary psychological perspective. *Journal of Personality, 69*, 955–978.

Campbell, D. T. (1982). Legal and primary-group social controls. *Journal of Social & Biological Structures, 5*, 431–438.

Campbell, D. T. (1983). Two distinct routes beyond kin selection to ultrasociality: Implications for the humanities and social sciences. In D. Bridgeman (Ed.), *The nature of prosocial development: Theories and strategies* (pp. 11–41). New York: Academic Press.

Carlston, D. E., & Skowronski, J. J. (2005). Linking versus thinking: Evidence for the different associative and attributional bases of spontaneous trait transference and spontaneous trait inference. *Journal of Personality and Social Psychology, 89*, 884–898.

Charnov, E. L. (1993). Is maximum sustainable-yield independent of body size for mammals (and others). *Evolutionary Ecology, 7*, 309–311.

Clark, R. D., & Hatfield, E. (1989). Gender differences in receptivity to sexual offers. *Journal of Psychology & Human Sexuality, 2*, 39–55.

Cook, M., & Mineka, S. (1990). Selective associations in the observational conditioning of fear in rhesus monkeys. *Journal of Experimental Psychology: Animal Behavior Processes, 16*, 372–389.

Coon, C. S. (1946). The universality of natural groupings in human societies. *Journal of Educational Sociology, 20*, 163–168.

Cooper, W. S. (1987). Decision theory as a branch of evolutionary theory: A biological derivation of the savage axioms. *Psychological Review, 94*, 395–411.

Cosmides, L. (1989). The logic of social exchange: Has natural selection shaped how humans reason? Studies with the Wason Selection Task. *Cognition, 31*, 187–276.

Cosmides, L., Barrett, H. C., & Tooby, J. (2010). Adaptive specializations, social exchange, and the evolution of human intelligence. *Proceedings of the National Academy of Sciences, 107*, 9007–9014.

Cosmides, L., & Tooby, J (1997). The modular nature of human intelligence. In A. B. Scheibel & J. W. Schopf (Eds.), *The origin and evolution of intelligence* (pp. 71–101). Sudbury, MA: Jones and Bartlett.

Cosmides, L., & Tooby, J. (2005). Neurocognitive adaptations designed for social exchange. In D. M. Buss (Ed.), *The handbook of evolutionary psychology* (pp. 584–627). Hoboken, NJ: Wiley.

Cottrell, C. A., & Neuberg, S. L. (2005). Different emotional reactions to different groups: A sociofunctional threat-based approach to "prejudice." *Journal of Personality and Social Psychology, 88*, 770–789.

Cottrell, C. A., Neuberg, S. L., & Li, N. P. (2007). What do people desire in others? A sociofunctional perspective on the importance of different valued characteristics. *Journal of Personality and Social Psychology, 92*, 208–231.

Crowl, T. A., & Covich, A. P. (1990). Predator-induced life-history shifts in a freshwater snail. *Science, 247*, 949–951.

Daly, M., & Wilson, M. I. (1988). *Homicide*. Hawthorne, NY: Aldine de Gruyter.

Darwin, C. (1871). *The descent of man and selection in relation to sex*. New York: D. Appleton and Company.

DeBruine L. M. (2005). Trustworthy but not lust-worthy: Context-specific effects of facial resemblance. *Proceedings of the Royal Society of London, B, 272*, 919–922.

Duncan, L. A., Park, J. H., Faulkner, J., Schaller, M., Neuberg, S. L., & Kenrick, D. T. (2007). Adaptive allocation of attention: Effects of sex and sociosexuality on visual attention to attractive opposite-sex faces. *Evolution and Human Behavior, 28*, 359–364.

Duncan, L. A., & Schaller, M. (2009). Prejudicial attitudes toward older adults may be exaggerated when people feel vulnerable to infectious disease: Evidence and implications. *Analyses of Social Issues and Public Policy (ASAP), 9*, 97–97–115.

Dunbar, R. I. M. (2003). The social brain: Mind, language, and society in evolutionary perspective. *Annual Review of Anthropology, 32*, 163–181.

Ebner, N. C. (2008). Age of face matters: Age-group differences in ratings of young and old faces. *Behavior Research Methods, 40*, 130–136.

Ellis, B. J. (2004). Timing of pubertal maturation in girls: An integrated life history approach. *Psychological Bulletin, 130*, 920–958.

Ellis, B. J., & Ketelaar, T. (2000). On the natural selection of alternative models: Evaluation of explanations in evolutionary psychology. *Psychological Inquiry, 11*, 56–68.

Ewald, P. W. (1994). *Evolution of infectious disease*. New York: Oxford University Press.

Faulkner, J., Schaller, M., Park, J. H., & Duncan, L. A. (2004). Evolved disease-avoidance mechanisms and contemporary xenophobic attitudes. *Group Processes & Intergroup Relations, 7,* 333–353.

Fiddick, L., Spampinato, M. V., & Grafman, J. (2005). Social contracts and precautions activate different neurological systems: an fMRI investigation of deontic reasoning. *NeuroImage, 28,* 778–786.

Figueredo, A. J., Vásquez, G., Brumbach, B. H., Schneider, S. M. R., Sefcek, J. A., Tal, I. R., Hill, D., Wenner, C. J., & Jacobs, W. J. (2006). Consilience and life history theory: From genes to brain to reproductive strategy. *Developmental Review, 26,* 243–275.

Figueredo, A. J., Vásquez, G., Brumbach, B. H., Sefcek, J. A., Kirsner, B. R., & Jacobs, W. J. (2005). The K-factor: Individual differences in life history strategy. *Personality and Individual Differences, 39,* 1349–1360.

Fiske, S. T., & Neuberg, S. L. (1990). A continuum of impression formation, from category-based to individuating processes: Influences of information and motivation on attention and interpretation. In M. P. Zanna (Ed.), *Advances in experimental social psychology* (Vol. 23, pp. 1–74). New York: Academic Press.

Fox, E., Russo, R., Bowles, R., & Dutton, K. (2001). Do threatening stimuli draw or hold visual attention in subclinical anxiety? *Journal of Experimental Psychology: General, 130,* 681–700.

Fox, E., Russo, R., & Dutton, K. (2002). Attentional bias for threat: Evidence for delayed disengagement from emotional faces. *Cognition and Emotion, 16,* 355–379.

Fox, R. (1992). Prejudice and the unfinished mind: A new look at an old failing. *Psychological Inquiry, 3,* 137–152.

Funder, D. C. (1987). Errors and mistakes: Evaluating the accuracy of social judgment. *Psychological Bulletin, 101,* 75–90.

Gandolfi, A. E., Gandolfi, A. S., & Barash, D. P. (2002). *Economics as an evolutionary science: from utility to fitness.* New Brunswick, NJ: Transaction Publishers.

Gangestad, S. W., Haselton, M. G., & Buss, D. M. (2006). Evolutionary foundations of cultural variation: Evoked culture and mate preferences. *Psychological Inquiry, 17,* 75–95.

Gangestad, S. W., & Simpson, J. A. (2000). The evolution of human mating: Trade-offs and strategic pluralism. *Behavioral and Brain Sciences, 23,* 573–644.

Garcia, J., & Koelling, R. A. (1966). Relationship of cue to consequence in avoidance learning. *Psychonomic Science, 4,* 123–124.

Geary, D. C. (2006). Evolutionary developmental psychology: Current status and future directions. *Developmental Review, 26,* 113–119.

George, P. A., & Hole, G. J. (1995). Factors affecting the accuracy of age estimates of unfamiliar faces. *Perception, 24,* 1059–1073.

George, P. A., & Hole, G. J. (2000). The role of spatial and surface cues in the age-processing of unfamiliar faces. *Visual Cognition, 7,* 485–509.

Gibson, J. J. (1979). *The ecological approach to visual perception.* Boston: Houghton, Mifflin and Company.

Gigerenzer, G., Todd, P. M., & the ABC Group (1999). *Simple heuristics that make us smart.* New York: Oxford University Press.

Gilbert, D. T., & Malone, P. S. (1995). The correspondence bias. *Psychological Bulletin, 117,* 21–38.

George, P. A., & Hole, G. J. (1995). Factors influencing the accuracy of age estimates of unfamiliar faces. *Perception, 24,* 1059–1073.

Georgiou, G. A., Bleakley, C., Hayward, J., Russo, R., Dutton, K., Eltiti, S., & Fox, E. (2005). Focusing on fear: Attentional disengagement from emotional faces. *Visual Cognition, 12,* 145–158.

Goffman, E. (1963). *Stigma: Notes on the management of spoiled identity.* New York, NY: Prentice-Hall.

Goshen-Gottstein, Y., & Ganel, T. (2000). Repetition priming for familiar and unfamiliar faces in a sex-judgment task: Evidence for a common route for the processing of sex and identity. *Journal of Experimental Psychology: Learning, Memory, and Cognition, 26*(5), 1198–1198–1214.

Griskevicius, V. G., Delton, A. W., & Robertson, T. E., & Tybur, J. M. (2011). Environmental contingency in life history strategies: Influences of current and childhood environment on reproductive timing. *Journal of Personality and Social Psychology, 100,* 241–254.

Griskevicius, V. G., Tybur, J. M., Delton, A. W., & Robertson, T. E. (2011). The influence of mortality and socioeconomic status on preferences for risk and delayed rewards: A life history theory approach. *Journal of Personality and Social Psychology, 100,* 1015–1026.

Harris, P. L., Núñez, M., & Brett, C. (2001). Let's swap: Early understanding of social exchange by British and Nepali children. *Memory & Cognition, 29,* 757–764.

Haselton, M. G., & Buss, D. M. (2003). Biases in social judgment: Design flaws or design features? In J. Forgas, K. Williams, & W. von Hippel (Eds.), *Responding to the social world: Implicit and Explicit processes in social judgments and decisions.* New York: Cambridge University Press.

Haselton, M. G., & Buss, D. M. (2000). Error management theory: A new perspective on biases in cross-sex mind reading. *Journal of Personality and Social Psychology, 78,* 81–91.

Haselton, M. G., & Funder, D. C. (2006). The evolution of accuracy and bias in social judgment. In M. Schaller, J. A. Simpson, & D. T. Kenrick (Eds.), *Evolution and social psychology* (pp. 16–37). New York: Psychology Press.

Haselton, M. G., & Nettle, D. (2006). The paranoid optimist: An integrative evolutionary model of cognitive biases. *Personality and Social Psychology Review, 10,* 47–66.

Hill, H., Bruce, V., Akamatsu, S. (1995) Perceiving the sex and race of faces: The role of shape and colour. *Proceedings: Biological Sciences, 261*(1362), 367–373.

Hill, K., & Kaplan, H. (1999). Life history traits in humans: Theory and empirical studies. *Annual Review of Anthropology, 28,* 387–430.

Insko, C. A., & Schopler, J. (1998). Differential distrust of groups and individuals. In C. Sedikides, J. Schopler, & C. A. Insko (Eds.), *Intergroup cognition and intergroup behavior* (pp. 75–107). Mahwah, NJ: Erlbaum.

Johnson, K. L., & Tassinary, L. G. (2005). Perceiving sex directly and indirectly: Meaning in motion and morphology. *Psychological Science, 16,* 890–897.

Johnson, M. H., Dziurawiec, S., Ellis, H., & Morton, J. (1991). Newborns' preferential tracking of face-like stimuli and its subsequent decline. *Cognition, 40,* 1–19.

Kahneman, D., & Tversky, A. (1979). Prospect theory: An analysis of decision under RIS. *Econometrica, 2,* 263–292.

Kanazawa, S. (2001). De gustibus est disputandum. *Social Forces, 79,* 1131–1163.

Kanwisher, N., & Wojciulik, E. (2000). Visual attention: Insights from brain imaging. *Nature Reviews Neuroscience, 1,* 91–100.

Kaplan, H. S., & Gangestad, S. W. (2005). Life history theory and evolutionary psychology. In D. M. Buss (Ed.), *The* handbook of evolutionary psychology (pp. 68–95). Hoboken, NJ: John Wiley & Sons.

Keegan, J. (1993). The history of warfare. New York, NY: Knopf.

Keeley, L. H. (1996). War before civilization: The myth of the peaceful savage. New York, NY: Oxford University Press.

Kelly, R. L. (1995). The foraging spectrum: Diversity in hunter-gatherer lifeways. Washington, DC: Smithsonian Institution Press.

Kendrick, K. M., & Baldwin, B. A. (1987). Cells in temporal cortex of conscious sheep can respond preferentially to the sight of faces. Science, 236, 448–450.

Kenrick, D. T., Griskevicius, V., Neuberg, S. L., & Schaller, M. (2010). Renovating the pyramid of needs: Contemporary extensions built upon ancient foundations. Perspectives on Psychological Science, 5, 292–314.

Kenrick, D. T., Griskevicius, V., Sundie, J. M., Li, N. P., Li, Y. J., & Neuberg, S. L. (2009). Deep rationality: The evolutionary economics of decision making. Social Cognition, 27, 764–785.

Kenrick, D. T., Groth, G. E., Trost, M. R., & Sadalla, E. K. (1993). Integrating evolutionary and social exchange perspectives on relationships: Effects of gender, self-appraisal, and involvement level on mate selection criteria. Journal of Personality and Social Psychology, 64, 951–969.

Kenrick, D. T., & Keefe, R. C. (1992). Age preferences in mates reflect sex differences in human reproductive strategies. Behavioral and Brain Sciences, 15, 75–133.

Kenrick, D. T., Li, N. P., & Butner, J. (2003). Dynamical evolutionary psychology: Individual decision rules and emergent social norms. Psychological Review, 110, 3–28.

Kenrick, D. T., Li, Y. J., White, A. E., & Neuberg, S. L. (2012). Economic subselves: Fundamental motives and deep rationality. In J. Forgas, K. Fiedler, & C. Sedikides (eds.), Social thinking and interpersonal behavior: The 14th Sydney Symposium of Social Psychology (pp. 23–43). New York, NY: Psychology Press.

Kenrick, D. T., & Luce, C. L. (2000). An evolutionary life-history model of gender differences and similarities. In T. Eckes & H. M. Trautner (Eds.), The developmental social psychology of gender (pp. 35–64). Hillsdale, NJ: Erlbaum.

Kenrick, D. T., Nieuweboer, S., & Buunk, A. P. (2010). Universal mechanisms and cultural diversity: Replacing the blank slate with a coloring book. In M. Schaller, A. Norenzayan, S. Heine, T. Yamagishi, & T. Kameda (eds.), Evolution, culture, and the human mind (pp. 257–271). New York: Psychology Press.

Kenrick, D. T., Schaller, M., & Simpson, J. (2006). Evolution is the new cognition. In M. Schaller, J. Simpson, & D. T. Kenrick (eds.), Evolution and social psychology (pp. 1–16). New York: Psychology Press.

Kinzler, K. D., Shutts, K., & Correll, J. (2010). Priorities in social categories. European Journal of Social Psychology, 40, 581–592.

Klein, S. B., Cosmides, L., Tooby, J., & Chance, S. (2002). Decisions and the evolution of memory: Multiple systems, multiple functions. Psychological Review, 109, 306–329.

Kouri, E. M., Lukas, S. E., Pope, H. G., & Oliva, P. S. (1995). Increased aggressive responding in male volunteers following the administration of gradually increasing doses of testosterone cypionate. Drug and Alcohol Dependence, 40, 73–79.

Kozlowski, L. T., & Cutting, J. E. (1977). Recognizing the sex of a walker from a dynamic point-light display. Perception & Psychophysics, 21, 575–580.

Kuhl, P. K., Williams, K. A., Lacerda, F., Stevens, K. N., & Lindblom, B. (1992). Linguistic experience alters phonetic perception in infants by 6 months of age. Science, 255, 606–608.

Kurzban, R., & Leary, M. R. (2001). Evolutionary origins of stigmatization: The functions of social exclusion. Psychological Bulletin, 127, 187–208.

Kurzban, R., & Neuberg, S. L. (2005). Managing ingroup and outgroup relationships. In D. Buss (Ed.), Handbook of evolutionary psychology (pp. 653–675). New York: John Wiley & Sons.

Kurzban, R., Tooby, J. & Cosmides, L. (2001). Can race be erased?: Coalitional computation and social categorization. Proceedings of the National Academy of Sciences, 98(26), 15387–15392.

LeDoux, J. E. (2000). Emotion circuits in the brain. Annual Review of Neuroscience, 23, 155–184.

Li, Y. J., Kenrick, D. T., Griskevicius, V., & Neuberg, S. L. (2012). Economic decision biases and fundamental motivations: How mating and self-protection alter loss aversion. Journal of Personality and Social Psychology, 102, 550–561.

Lieberman, D., Tooby, J., & Cosmides, L. (2007). The architecture of human kin detection. Nature, 445, 727–731.

Macrae, C. N., & Quadflieg, S. (2010). Perceiving people. In S. T. Fiske, D. T. Gilbert, & G. Lindzey (Eds.), Handbook of social psychology (Vol. 1, pp. 428–463). Hoboken, NJ: John Wiley & Sons.

Maddox, K. B. (2004). Perspectives on racial phenotypicality bias. Personality and Social Psychology Review, 8, 383–401.

Makova, K. D., & Li, W.-H. (2002, April 11). Strong male-driven evolution of DNA sequences in humans and apes. Nature, 416, 624–626.

Maner, J. K., Gailliot, M. T., Rouby, D. A., & Miller, S. L. (2007). Can't take my eyes off you: Attentional adhesion to mates and rivals. Journal of Personality and Social Psychology, 93, 389–401.

Maner, J. K., Kenrick, D. T., Becker, D. V., Delton, A. W., Hofer, B., Wilbur, C. J., & Neuberg, S. L. (2003). Sexually selective cognition: Beauty captures the mind of the beholder. Journal of Personality and Social Psychology, 85, 1107–1120.

Maner, J. K., Kenrick, D. T., Becker, D. V., Robertson, T., Hofer, B., Delton, A. W., Neuberg, S. L., Butner, J., & Schaller, M. (2005). Functional projection: How fundamental social motives can bias interpersonal perception. Journal of Personality and Social Psychology, 88, 63–78.

Mann, L. (1980). Cross-cultural studies of small groups. In H. C. Triandis & R. W. Brislin (Eds.), Handbook of cross-cultural psychology: Vol. 5. Social psychology (pp. 155–209). Boston: Allyn & Bacon.

Marcus, G. (2004). The birth of the mind. New York: Basic Books.

Martin, D., & Macrae, C. N. (2007). A face with a cue: Exploring the inevitability of person categorization. European Journal of Social Psychology, 37, 806–816.

Martin, T. E. (1995). Avian life history evolution in relation to nest sites, nest predation, and food. Ecological Monographs, 65, 101–127.

Mazur, A., & Booth, A. (1998). Testosterone and dominance in men. Behavioral and Brain Sciences, 21, 353–397.

McArthur, L. Z., & Baron, R. M. (1983). Toward an ecological theory of social perception. Psychological Review, 90, 215–238.

McClelland, J. L., McNaughton, B. L., & O'Reilly, R. C. (1995). Why there are complementary learning systems in the hippocampus and neocortex: Insights from the successes and failures of connectionist models of learning and memory. *Psychological Review, 102,* 419–457.

Miller, G. (2007). Reconciling evolutionary psychology and ecological psychology: How to perceive fitness affordances. *Acta Psychologica Sinica, 39,* 546–555.

Miller, S. L., Maner, J. K., & Becker, D. V. (2010). Self-protective biases in group categorization: Threat cues shape the psychological boundary between "us" and "them." *Journal of Personality and Social Psychology, 99,* 62–77.

Montepare, J. M., & Zebrowitz-McArthur, L. (1988). Impressions of people created by age-related qualities of their gaits. *Journal of Personality and Social Psychology, 55,* 547–556.

Mortensen, C. R., Vaughn Becker, D., Ackerman, J. M., Neuberg, S. L., & Kenrick, D. T. (2010). Infection breeds reticence: The effects of disease salience on self-perceptions of personality and behavioral avoidance tendencies. *Psychological Science, 21,* 440–447.

Mullen, B., Brown, R., & Smith, C. (1992). Ingroup bias as a function of salience, relevance, and status: An integration. *European Journal of Social Psychology, 22,* 103–122.

Nairne, J. S., & Pandeirada, J. N. S. (2008). Adaptive memory: Remembering with a stone-age brain. *Current Directions in Psychological Science, 17,* 239–243.

Nesse, R. M. (2005). Natural selection and the regulation of defenses: A signal detection analysis of the smoke detector principle. *Evolution and Human Behavior, 26,* 88–105.

Navarrete, C. D., McDonald, M. M., Molina, L. E., & Sidanius, J. (2010). Prejudice at the nexus of race and gender: An outgroup male target hypothesis. *Journal of Personality and Social Psychology, 98,* 933–945.

Navarrete, C. D., Olsson, A., Ho, A. K., Mendes, W. B., Thomsen, L., & Sidanius, J. (2009). Fear extinction to an out-group face: The role of target gender. *Psychological Science, 20,* 155–158.

Nestor, A., & Tarr, M. J. (2008). The segmental structure of faces and its use in gender recognition. *Journal of Vision, 8,* 1–12.

Neuberg. S. L., & Cottrell, C. A. (2006). Evolutionary bases of prejudices. In M. Schaller, J. A. Simpson, & D. T. Kenrick (Eds.), *Evolution and social psychology* (pp. 163–187). New York: Psychology Press.

Neuberg, S. L., & Fiske, S. T. (1987). Motivational influences on impression formation: Outcome dependency, accuracy-driven attention, and individuating processes. *Journal of Personality and Social Psychology, 53,* 431–444.

Neuberg, S. L., Kenrick, D. T., & Schaller, M. (2011). Human threat management systems: Self-protection and disease avoidance. *Neuroscience and Biobehavioral Reviews, 35,* 1042–1051.

Neuberg, S. L., Kenrick, D. T., & Schaller, M. (2010). Evolutionary social psychology. In S. T. Fiske, D. Gilbert, and G. Lindzey (Eds.), *Handbook of social psychology* (pp. 761–796). New York: John Wiley & Sons.

Neuberg, S. L., Smith, D. M., Asher, T. (2000). Why people stigmatize: Toward a biocultural framework. In T. F. Heatherton, R. E. Kleck, M. R. Hebl, & J. G. Hull (Eds.), *The social psychology of stigma* (pp. 31–61). New York: Guilford.

New, J., Krasnow, M. M., Truxaw, D., & Gaulin, S. J. (2007). Spatial adaptations for plant foraging: Women excel and calories count. *Proceedings of the Royal Society B: Biological Sciences, 274,* 2679–2684.

Newman, L. S., & Uleman, J. S. (1989). Spontaneous trait inference. In J. S. Uleman & J. A. Bargh (Eds.), *Unintended thought* (pp. 155–188). New York: Guilford.

Norenzayan, A., & Heine, S. J. (2005). Psychological universals across cultures: What are they and how do we know? *Psychological Bulletin, 131,* 763–784.

Norenzayan, A., Schaller, M., & Heine, S. J. (2006). Evolution and culture. In M. Schaller, J. A. Simpson, & D. T. Kenrick (Eds.), *Evolution and social psychology* (pp. 343–366). New York: Psychology Press.

Oaten, M., Stevenson, R. J., & Case, T. I. (2009). Disgust as a disease-avoidance mechanism. *Psychological Bulletin, 135,* 303–321.

Öhman, A., & Mineka, S. (2001). Fears, phobias, and preparedness: Toward an evolved module of fear and fear learning. *Psychological Review, 108,* 483–522.

Olsson, A., Ebert, J. P., Banaji, M. R., & Phelps, E. A. (2005). The role of social groups in the persistence of learned fear. *Science, 309,* 785–787.

Oosterhof, N. N., & Todorov, A. (2008). The functional basis of face evaluation. *Proceedings of the National Academy of Sciences of the United States of America, 105,* 11087–11092.

Ostrom, T. M., & Sedikides, C. (1992). Out-group homogeneity effects in natural and minimal groups. *Psychological Bulletin, 112,* 536–552.

Park, J. H., Faulkner, J., & Schaller, M. (2003). Evolved disease-avoidance processes and contemporary anti-social behavior: Prejudicial attitudes and avoidance of people with physical disabilities. *Journal of Nonverbal Behavior, 27,* 65–87.

Park, J. H., Schaller, M., & Crandall, C. S. (2007). Pathogen-avoidance mechanisms and the stigmatization of obese people. *Evolution and Human Behavior, 28,* 410–414.

Pinker, S. (1997). *How the mind works.* New York, NY: W. W. Norton.

Pollick, F. E., Kay, J. W., Heim, K., & Stringer, R. (2005). Gender recognition from point-light walkers. *Journal of Experimental Psychology: Human Perception and Performance, 31,* 1247–1265.

Posner, M. I., & Cohen, Y. (1984). Components of visual orienting. In H. Bouma & D. G. Bowhui (Eds.), *Attention and performance* (Vol. 10, pp. 531–556). Hillsdale, NJ: Erlbaum.

Richerson, P. J., & Boyd, R. (1998). The evolution of human ultrasociality. In I. Eibl-Eibesfeldt & F. K. Salter (Eds.), *Indoctrinability, ideology, and warfare: Evolutionary perspectives.* (pp. 71–95). New York: Berghahn Books.

Roff, D. A. (1992). *The evolution of life histories: Theory and analysis.* New York: Chapman & Hall.

Roberts, T., & Bruce, V. (1988). Feature saliency in judging the sex and familiarity of faces. *Perception, 17,* 475–481.

Ronay, R., & von Hippel, W. (2010). The presence of an attractive woman elevates testosterone and physical risk taking in young men. *Social Psychological and Personality Science, 1,* 57–64.

Rule, N. O., & Ambady, N. (2008). Brief exposures: Male sexual orientation is accurately perceived at 50ms. *Journal of Experimental Social Psychology, 44,* 1100–1105.

Sargent, P. L., & Nelson, C. A. (1992, May). *Cross species recognition in infant and adult humans: ERP and behavioral measures.* Paper presented at the International Conference on Infant Studies, Miami, Florida.

Schaller, M. (2006). Parasites, behavioral defenses, and the social psychological mechanisms through which cultures are evoked. *Psychological Inquiry, 17,* 96–101.

Schaller, M. (2007). Turning garbage into gold: Evolutionary universals and cross-cultural differences. In S. W. Gangestad & J. A. Simpson (Eds.), *The evolution of mind* (pp. 363–371). New York: Guilford.

Schaller, M., & Duncan, L. A. (2007). The behavioral immune system: Its evolution and social psychological implications. In J. P. Forgas, M. G. Haselton, & W. von Hippel (Eds.), *Evolution and the social mind: Evolutionary psychology and social cognition* (pp. 293–307). New York: Psychology Press.

Schaller, M., & Neuberg, S. L. (2008). Intergroup prejudices and intergroup conflicts. In C. Crawford & D. L. Krebs (Eds.), *Foundations of evolutionary psychology: Ideas, applications, and applications* (pp. 401–414). Mahwah, NJ: Erlbaum.

Schaller, M., & Neuberg, S. L. (2012). Danger, disease, and the nature of prejudice(s). To appear in J. Olson & M. P. Zanna (Eds.), *Advances in Experimental Social Psychology* (Vol. 46, pp. 1–55). Burlington, VT: Academic Press.

Schaller, M., & Park, J. H. (2011). The behavioral immune system (and why it matters). *Current Directions in Psychological Science, 20,* 99–103.

Schaller, M., Park, J. H., & Faulkner, J. (2003). Prehistoric dangers and contemporary prejudices. *European Review of Social Psychology, 14,* 105–137.

Schaller, M., Park, J. H., & Kenrick, D. T. (2007). Human evolution and social cognition. In R. I. M. Dunbar & L. Barrett (Eds.), *Oxford handbook of evolutionary psychology* (pp. 491–504). Oxford, UK: Oxford University Press.

Schaller, M., Park, J. H., & Mueller, A. (2003). Fear of the dark: Interactive effects of beliefs about danger and ambient darkness on ethnic stereotypes. *Personality and Social Psychology Bulletin, 29,* 637–649.

Schmitt, D. P. (2005). Sociosexuality from Argentina to Zimbabwe: A 48-nation study of sex, culture, and strategies of human mating. *Behavioral and Brain Sciences, 28,* 247–311.

Schmitt, D. P., and 118 members of International Sexuality Description Project. (2003). Universal sex differences in the desire for sexual variety: Tests from 52 nations, 6 continents, and 13 islands. *Journal of Personality & Social Psychology, 85,* 85–104.

Sell, A., Cosmides, L., Tooby, J., Sznycer, D., von Rueden, C., & Gurven, M. (2009). Human adaptations for the visual assessment of strength and fighting ability from the body and face. *Proceedings of the Royal Society, 276*(1656), 575–584.

Sherry, D. F., & Schacter, D. L. (1987). The evolution of multiple memory systems. *Psychological Review, 94,* 439–454.

Sidanius, J., & Pratto, F. (1999). *Social dominance: An intergroup theory of social hierarchy and oppression.* New York, NY: Cambridge University Press.

Sidanius, J., & Veniegas, R. C. (2000). Gender and race discrimination: The interactive nature of disadvantage. In S. Oskamp (Ed.), *Reducing prejudice and discrimination* (pp. 47–69). Mahwah, NJ: Erlbaum.

Simon, Herbert A. (1955). A behavioral model of rational choice. *Quarterly Journal of Economics, 69,* 99–118.

Simon, H. A. (1956). Rational choice and the structure of the environment. *Psychological Review, 63,* 129–138.

Squire, L. R., Knowlton, B., & Musen, G. (1993). The structure and organization of memory. *Annual Review of Psychology, 44,* 453–495.

Stearns, S. C. (1976). Life-history tactics: A review of the ideas. *Quarterly Review of Biology, 51*(1), 3–47.

Stearns, S. C., Allal, N., & Mace, R. (2008). Life history theory and human development. In C. Crawford & D. L. Krebs (Eds.), *Foundations of evolutionary psychology* (pp. 47–69). Mahwah, NJ: Erlbaum.

Stringer, C., & Mckie, R. (1998). *African exodus: The origins of modern humanity.* New York, NY: Henry Holt.

Sugiyama, L., Tooby, J., & Cosmides, L. (2002). Cross-cultural evidence of cognitive adaptations for social exchange among the Shiwiar of Ecuadorian Amazonia. *Proceedings of the National Academy of Sciences, 99,* 11537–11542.

Sundie, J. M., Kenrick, D. T., Griskevicius, V., Tybur, J. M., Vohs, K. D., & Beal, D. J. (2011). Peacocks, Porsches, and Thorstein Veblen: Conspicuous consumption as a sexual signaling system. *Journal of Personality and Social Psychology, 100,* 664–680.

Swim, J. K. (1994). Perceived versus meta-analytic effect sizes: An assessment of the accuracy of gender stereotypes. *Journal of Personality and Social Psychology, 66,* 21–36.

Tajfel, H. (1982). Social psychology of intergroup relations. *Annual Review of Psychology, 33,* 1–39.

Tajfel, H., Billig, M. G., Bundy, R. P., & Flament, C. (1971). Social categorization and intergroup behaviour. *European Journal of Social Psychology, 1,* 149–178.

Todd, P. M., & Gigerenzer, G. (2007). Environments that make us smart: Ecological rationality. *Current Directions in Psychological Science, 16,* 167–171.

Tooby, J., & Cosmides, L. (1992). The psychological foundations of culture. In J. Barkow, L. Cosmides, & J. Tooby (Eds.), *The adapted mind: Evolutionary psychology and the generation of culture.* New York, NY: Oxford University Press.

Tversky, A., & Kahneman, D. (1974). Judgment under uncertainty: Heuristics and biases. *Science, 185,* 1124–1131.

Van Goozen, S. H. M., Cohen-Kettenis, P., Gooren, L. J. G., Frijda, N. H., & Poll, V. D. (1995). Gender differences in behaviour: Activating effects of cross-sex hormones. *Psychoneuroendocrinology, 20,* 343–363.

Van Vugt, M., De Cremer, D., & Janssen, D. P. (2007). Gender differences in cooperation and competition: The male-warrior hypothesis. *Psychological Science, 18,* 19–23.

Vohs, K. D., & Luce, M. F. (2010). Judgment and decision making. In R. F. Baumeister & E J. Finkel (Eds.), *Advanced Social Psychology: The state of science* (pp. 733–756). New York, NY: Oxford University Press.

Vranić, A., & Hromatko, I. (2008). Content-specific activational effects of estrogen on working memory performance. *Journal of General Psychology, 135,* 323–336.

Wang, X. T. (1996). Domain-specific rationality in human choices: Violations of utility axioms and social contexts. *Cognition, 60,* 31–63.

Willis, J., & Todorov, A. (2006). First impressions: Making up your mind after a 100-ms exposure to a face. *Psychological Science, 17,* 592–598.

Wang, X. T. (2002). Risk as reproductive variance. *Evolution and Human Behavior, 23,* 35–57.

Wang, X. T., & Dvorak, R. D. (2010). Sweet future: Fluctuating blood glucose levels affect future discounting. *Psychological Science, 21,* 183–188.

Wason, P. C., & Johnson-Laird, P. (1972). *Psychology of reasoning: Structure and content.* Oxford, UK: Harvard University Press.

Wilcoxon, H. C., Dragoin, W. B., & Kral, P. A. (1971). Illness-induced aversions in rat and quail: Relative salience of visual and gustatory cues. *Science, 171,* 826–828.

Wilson, M., & Daly, M. (1985). Competitiveness, risk taking, and violence: The young male syndrome. *Ethology & Sociobiology, 6,* 59–73.

Wilson, M., & Daly, M. (2004). Do pretty women inspire men to discount the future? *Proceedings of the Royal Society of London, Series B: Biology Letters, 271*(Suppl.), S177–S179.

Winemiller, K. (1989). Patterns of variation in life-history among South-American fishes in seasonal environments. *Oecologia, 81,* 225–241.

Wolfe, N.D., Dunavan, C. P., Diamond, J. (2007). Origins of major human infectious diseases. *Nature, 447,* 279–283.

Wrangham, R. W., & Peterson, D. (1996). *Demonic males: Apes and the origins of human violence.* Boston: Houghton, Mifflin.

Zebrowitz, L. A., & McDonald, S. M. (1991). The impact of litigants' baby-facedness and attractiveness on adjudications in small claims courts. *Law and Human Behavior, 15,* 603–623.

Zebrowitz, L. A., & Montepare, J. (2006). The ecological approach to person perception: Evolutionary roots and contemporary offshoots. In M. Schaller, J. A. Simpson, & D. T. Kenrick (Eds.), *Evolution and social psychology* (pp. 81–113). New York: Psychology Press.

Zebrowitz, L. A., Montepare, J. M., & Lee, H. K. (1993). They don't all look alike: Individual impressions of other racial groups. *Journal of Personality and Social Psychology, 65,* 85–101.

CHAPTER 33

Mortal Cognition: Viewing Self and the World from the Precipice

Jeff Greenberg, Mark J. Landau, *and* Jamie Arndt

Abstract

This chapter examines cognitive underpinnings of terror management theory (TMT) and research, and considers the implications of this work for understanding social cognition. The authors describe an associative network model of TMT and review evidence regarding spreading activation from death thought to worldview constructs and from stimuli associated with violence and health to death thought. The TMT dual defense model and evidence are summarized, with a focus on health-relevant behavior. Proximal defenses involve suppression of conscious death thought and rationalizations to minimize perceived vulnerability to death. Distal defenses are triggered by the heightened unconscious accessibility of death thought and bolster life's meaning and the self's value, thereby making death thought less likely to become conscious. The authors describe research on implications of TMT for understanding why and how people maintain well-structured conceptions of themselves, other people, and social situations, and consider the moderating role of need for structure. Finally, the authors consider remaining questions regarding how thoughts of mortality affect social cognition.

Key Words: terror management, associative network, death, meaning, self, health, structure, worldview, accessibility

Integral parts of the human whole: the necessity of destruction to procure alimentary sustenance: the painful character of the ultimate functions of separate existence, the agonies of birth and death: the monotonous menstruation of simian and (particularly) human females extending from the age of puberty to the menopause: inevitable accidents at sea, in mines and factories: certain very painful maladies and their resultant surgical operations, innate lunacy and congenital criminality, decimating epidemics: catastrophic cataclysms which make terror the basis of human mentality...

James Joyce, *Ulysses*, 1966; p. 697

Terror management theory (TMT) builds on two basic facts of human cognition. The first is that the individual's perceptions and conceptions of the world are filtered through the lens of the cultural milieu in which that individual was raised. One

doesn't have to be a strict Whorfian to recognize that language is a cultural product that contributes to the way each of us forms the concepts through which we perceive and think about the stimuli we process as we move about the world. This is true of basic aspects of the physical world like plants, rocks, and animals, but even more so of symbolic human products and concepts, such as flags, buildings, democracy, personal growth, and so forth. In short, we each think largely from within an internalized version of the prevailing cultural worldview inculcated from birth.

The second fact is that, with cognitive development, each of us comes to the realization that we will die someday. Once this cognition is available, it has the potential to arouse anxiety at any moment because it runs counter to the biological predispositions to continue living and avoid threats to our continued existence. To manage this potential for anxiety, when thoughts of mortality are brought into consciousness, or even more so when they are highly accessible but outside of focal attention, people defensively alter how they think about themselves, others, and their social world. Specifically, thoughts of mortality motivate people to view the social world and their own experiences as structured rather than chaotic and pointless, and to view themselves and their cultural ideologies in a favorable light.

In this chapter, we will first briefly summarize TMT and the basic evidence supporting it. Then we will lay out the sequence of cognitive processes that produce the varied effects of making mortality salient. We will then summarize research examining the implications of TMT for understanding the motivations underlying people's tendencies to seek out well-structured conceptions of themselves, other people, and social situations. Finally, we will consider remaining questions regarding how thoughts of mortality alter aspects of social cognition.

TMT: The Basics

TMT is based on a long tradition of existential psychoanalytic thought summarized most cogently by Ernest Becker (1962/71, 1973, 1975). This school of thought emphasized the dilemma that humans face given that, like all species, they have built-in drives and fears that facilitate their continued survival but, unlike any other species, have the cognitive capacity to understand that, as physical animals, this goal will ultimately be thwarted. This awareness of our ultimate mortality poses an ever-present threat to our psychological equanimity; as John Cassavetes put it in the film *Shadows* (1960), "Man in contrast to other animals is aware of his own existence, therefore conscious of the possibility of nonexistence. Ergo, he has anxiety."

People manage this potential for anxiety, or terror, by viewing themselves as enduring, significant beings in a meaningful world rather than as mere animals in a pointless universe. Presumably, as our ancestors became aware of the inevitability of death and the possibility that it ends one's existence, cultural conceptions of reality that most effectively denied this view of death were constructed and selected for (see, e.g., Solomon, Greenberg, Schimel, Arndt, & Pyszczynski, 2004). These worldviews provided those who subscribed to them with psychological comfort and the courage to take risks and endure suffering. Both the concern with being mortal and the desire to transcend this state are prominent in the oldest known self-referential

text, the Sumerian Epic of Gilgamesh, as well as in virtually all known worldviews over the course of history. Berger and Luckmann (1967) summarize this view in *The Social Construction of Reality*:

> A strategic legitimating function of symbolic universes for individual biography is the location of death...the most terrifying threat to the taken-for-granted realities of everyday life. The integration of death within the paramount reality of social existence is, therefore, of the greatest importance for any institutional order. This legitimation of death is, consequently, one of the most important fruits of symbolic universes. All legitimations of death must carry out the same essential task—they must enable the individual to go on living in society after the death of significant others and to anticipate his own death with, at the very least, terror sufficiently mitigated so as not to paralyze the continued performance of the routines of everyday life....It is in the legitimation of death that the transcending potency of symbolic universes manifests itself most clearly, and the fundamental terror assuaging character of the ultimate legitimations of the paramount reality of everyday life is revealed. (p. 101)

The simple formula for effective terror management is to maintain faith in two broad psychological constructs. The first is a *cultural worldview*. This is an internalized, personal, but largely culturally derived view of the world that imbues reality with structure, meaning, permanence, and the possibility of lasting significance, or death transcendence, to those who subscribe to that worldview and fulfill its requirements for being valuable cultural members. The second psychological construct is the belief that the self is living up to the culture's standards of value and therefore qualifies for the lasting significance promised by the worldview; from the TMT perspective, this is *self-esteem*. In essence, the cultural worldview allows the individual to view oneself as an enduring, significant being in a world of meaning, rather than as just a material organism who exists for a while in an indifferent universe only to no longer exist in any form upon one's inevitable death. Our psychological embedding in this worldview is generally sustained from cradle to grave and consists of everything from our conception of time to our personal and social identities, values, and goals and our spiritual and science-based conceptions of the value and purpose of life.

Empirical Support for TMT

Three general hypotheses derived from TMT have been examined in a body of more than 500 published studies. The first hypothesis states that, if a meaningful cultural worldview and self-esteem serve to ameliorate or keep from actualization the potential terror engendered by the awareness of mortality, then reminders of mortality should motivate people to bolster the sense that they are significant beings in a meaningful world. A wide array of studies have supported this hypothesis (see Greenberg, Solomon, & Arndt, 2008). Rosenblatt et al. (1989) was the first to induce mortality salience by asking participants to respond to two items disguised as a projective measure of personality and imbedded among filler questionnaires: "Please describe the emotions that the thought of your own death arouses in you," and "Please jot down, as specifically as you can, what you think happens to you physically as you die and once you are dead."

The initial versions of the broad hypothesis posited that mortality salience should increase positive reactions to others who uphold or validate aspects of one's worldview and increase negative reactions to others who violate or dispute aspects of that worldview. In a representative study by Greenberg et al. (1990, Study 3), American college students primed with mortality or a control topic evaluated essays supposedly written by an American author who either praised or condemned the American way of life. Participants rated the author of the pro-U.S. essay more favorably than the author of the anti-U.S. essay in the control condition; however, in response to mortality salience, this tendency was exaggerated in both directions (i.e., more positive and negative reactions to pro- and anti-U.S. authors, respectively). This version of the broad hypothesis has been supported by many other studies, using reactions to a wide range of people, symbols, and other social stimuli that support and challenge participants' worldviews. For example, in one recent demonstration supporting the role of mortality concerns in prejudice, medical students were reminded of their mortality or the prospect of uncertainty and then given emergency room admittance forms for a hypothetical patient complaining of chest discomfort and presenting various symptoms. When asked to make estimates of the patient's risk for myocardial infarction and coronary artery diseases, Christian medical students ascribed high risk to a Christian patient (thus suggesting the need for attentive care) and lower risks to a Muslim patient, even though the patients presented identical complaints and symptomology (Arndt, Vess, Cox, Goldenberg, & Lagle, 2009).

In addition to motivating worldview defense, mortality salience intensifies efforts to bolster one's personal value. For example, it leads people to (1) distance themselves from reminders of their animal material nature; (2) follow salient norms consistent with the worldview to which they subscribe; (3) strive more vigorously to demonstrate their competencies in domains upon which they base their self-esteem; and (4) become more self-serving in their causal attributions and identifications and dis-identifications with groups (for a review of TMT research on self-esteem striving and defense, see Pyszczynski, Greenberg, Solomon, Arndt, & Schimel, 2004).

Importantly, studies show that mortality salience has similar effects on worldview defense and self-esteem biases in more than 20 countries, including the United States, Canada, Japan, Germany, China, Israel, Ivory Coast, and aboriginal Australia. Although most of these studies have utilized the standard two-item mortality salience induction, a substantial number of studies have found converging evidence utilizing diverse methods to increase the accessibility of death-related thought, including subliminal death primes, word search puzzles, writing a single sentence about death, proximity to funeral parlors and cemeteries, death anxiety scales, and gory accident footage. Many studies have shown the effects of mortality salience to differ from the salience of a variety of other potentially threatening topics, including pain, paralysis, public speaking, exams, failure, general anxieties, worries after college, social exclusion, meaninglessness, expectancy violation, and uncertainty. TMT posits that thoughts of death pose a unique psychological threat because death is the only certain undeniable future event, it can occur at anytime, and it threatens to eliminate the possibility of meeting virtually all human desires or goals, whether for pleasure, control, power, belonging, competence, or love (e.g., Pyszczynski, Greenberg, Solomon, & Maxfield, 2006).

A second general hypothesis derived from TMT is that threats to the meaning and value-conferring constructs that protect people from mortality concerns will increase the accessibility of death-related thought. This means that such threats make death-related thoughts more likely to enter consciousness. Various studies have supported this hypothesis as well. Threats to viewing humans as different from other animals, belief that the world is just, the righteousness of one's national identity, the validity of one's religious beliefs, the integrity of one's romantic relationship, and perceptions of personal competence all increase death-thought accessibility (e.g., Hayes et al., 2008; Landau et al., 2004a; Mikulincer, Florian, Birnbaum, & Malishkevich, 2002; Schimel et al., 2007). Notably, Schimel et al. (2007) showed that this increase is not accompanied by an increase in the accessibility of negative thoughts not related to death.

The third hypothesis is that bolstering faith in one's worldview or self-worth will reduce anxiety, defensive responses, and death-thought accessibility following reminders of mortality. This hypothesis has also been amply supported. Bolstering self-esteem reduces anxiety in response to gory images of death and threat of shock (Greenberg et al., 1992). Reminding intrinsically religious people of their religiosity, allowing people to denigrate an essay criticizing their country, providing positive personality feedback, and having people think of valued close relationships all reduce mortality salience-induced defensiveness and heightened death-thought accessibility (e.g., Arndt, Greenberg, Pyszczynski, & Solomon, 1997b; Harmon-Jones et al., 1997; Jonas & Fischer, 2006). Recently, research has begun examining the nuances of how implicit and explicit beliefs about the self operate in this context, showing that the buffering effects of self-esteem depend on implicit rather than explicit self-esteem (Schmeichel et al., 2009).

Sequence of Cognitive Processes Activated by Death-Related Thought

Beginning with a 1994 paper by Greenberg and colleagues on the role of consciousness in mortality salience effects, research has been directed toward articulating the cognitive processes triggered by reminders of death, and thus the mental architecture underlying efforts to manage existential fear (see Arndt, Cook, & Routledge, 2004; Pyszczynski, Greenberg, & Solomon, 1999, for reviews). To measure, rather than just manipulate, the accessibility of death-related cognition, Greenberg and colleagues adapted methods from research on construct accessibility (e.g., Bassili & Smith, 1986; Gilbert & Hixon, 1991; Tulving, Schacter, & Stark, 1982). They had participants complete a series of word fragments, some of which could be completed to form a death-related word or a non-death-related word (e.g., GRA _ _ [grave or grape]). The more fragments a participant completes with death-related words, the more accessible thoughts of death are inferred to be. In subsequent years, other measures have been developed to assess death-thought accessibility (e.g.,

lexical decision tasks; see Hayes, Schimel, Arndt, & Faucher, 2010, for a review).

Insights into the cognitive processes by which awareness of death affects social judgment and behavior have since been accumulating. For example, Hayes et al. (2010) note there have now been more than 80 published empirical studies measuring death-thought accessibility, and more than half of these have been published in the past three years. In this section, we will cover some of these insights, including research implicating a cognitive network surrounding thoughts of death, dual defenses elicited by conscious and nonconscious death-related thought, and dispositional differences in death-thought accessibility.

Cognitive Network of Terror Management

A basic principle of cognitive perspectives on memory is that knowledge structures may be organized around interconnected elements (Collins & Loftus, 1975). Although typically linked in terms of semantic associations, TMT focuses on experiential associations. Because of the motivational importance of death, ideation about mortality occupies a central position within a cognitive network of knowledge structures. Although some of these structures involve constructs associated with literally forestalling death (or distracting the individual from its inevitability so as to facilitate other goal-directed activity), others involve association of death with security-providing symbolic bases of meaning and significance.

As noted earlier, when such symbolic buffers (e.g., conceptions of self-value, romantic relationships, just world beliefs, religious beliefs) that hold death concerns at bay are threatened, we see associated increases in the accessibility of death-related thought. Although these findings are not typically viewed in the context of associative network models of semantic priming and spreading activation, they are consistent with these frameworks, leading to a potentially generative integration of terror management and social cognitive perspectives. The general gist of these accounts is that with repeated pairings over time, activation of one construct in memory spreads to activate associated constructs (e.g., Anderson & Bower, 1973; McNamara, 1992). Merging such frameworks with the developmental analysis of TMT, we can gain an understanding of how a cognitive network surrounding death may unfold. Indeed, Becker (1973) describes how peoples' burgeoning and subsequently ever-present awareness of death is managed by immersion in the cultural blueprint by which they are socialized. In this way, individuals are afforded existential security from death awareness as they come to believe in the meaningful and enduring qualities of their cultural beliefs and sense of self-esteem. Thus, over the course of cognitive development, cognitions about culture, the self, meaningful relationships, and so forth become existential security blankets with which death comes to be associated by virtue of the repeated engagement of these structures for psychological equanimity.

This analysis explicates why threats to elements of the worldview increase death-thought accessibility, and furthermore suggests that increasing death-thought accessibility will increase the accessibility of elements of the worldview. This hypothesis was investigated by Arndt, Greenberg, and Cook (2002), who found that when participants were reminded of their mortality, and such cognition was given a chance to recede from focal awareness, they exhibited increased accessibility of worldview-relevant beliefs. Interestingly, the initial studies demonstrated that mortality salience increased the accessibility of nationalistic constructs for men, but relationship constructs for women, suggesting that spontaneous activation may spread to those worldview domains that are dispositionally important to the individual.

However, situational factors can also influence which elements of the worldview will be important at the moment and thus increase in accessibility. Arndt et al. (2002) found that when women were first primed with the value of the national identity, mortality salience increased the accessibility of nationalistic constructs. This set of studies not only illustrates a death–worldview associative link but also provides insight into the nature of spontaneous construct activation and the potential malleability of the elements of the belief system that people may turn to when needing to manage existential fear. From among the many values and beliefs that are part of their security-providing worldview, when reminded of death, people seem to turn to whichever beliefs are currently accessible. Further support for this idea has been provided by Jonas et al. (2008) and Gailliot et al. (2008), who have shown in a number of studies that reminders of mortality heighten adherence to those worldview-consistent values that are made particularly accessible at the moment. For example, Jonas et al. (2008) had participants first search for neutral words in a matrix of letters that included imbedded words associated with either prosocial (help, tolerance) or proself

(power, indulgence) values. Mortality salience led those primed with prosocial values to be more supportive of a charity to serve underprivileged children's education, but led those primed with proself values to become less supportive of this charity.

Integrating terror management theorizing with an associative network perspective also suggests that if people's cultural beliefs function in part to keep thoughts of death at bay, and if these buffers are bolstered or if individuals have a strong dispositional buffer against anxiety, then death reminders should be less likely to increase the accessibility of death-related thought. As alluded to earlier in this chapter, a variety of findings fit this analysis. High levels of self-esteem (either dispositionally or experimentally induced), a secure attachment style, and especially strong faith in elements of the worldview like belief in progressive hope or a nostalgic connection to the past, have all been found to eliminate or reduce the elevated cognitive accessibility of death that is otherwise observed following reminders of death (e.g., Harmon-Jones et al., 1997; Jonas & Fischer 2006; Mikulincer & Florian, 2000; Routledge et al. 2008; Rutjens, van der Pligt, & van Harreveld, 2009; Schmeichel & Martens 2005). Thus, research converges on three central facets of the connection between worldview beliefs and thoughts of death: Thoughts of death activate elements of the worldview, bolstering the worldview reduces death-thought accessibility, and threatening the worldview increases death-thought accessibility.

Although an increasing number of studies are showing how breakdowns in individuals' faith in their worldview increase death-thought accessibility, most TMT research has used either direct (e.g., open-ended questions about death) or indirect (e.g., proximity to funeral parlors, subliminal primes) methods to activate thoughts of death. Yet recent research has shown that there are a variety of other stimuli that are also associated with death, consistent with the idea that death-related cognition plays a significant role in everyday functioning.

Certain events have such impact that their psychological reverberations echo with both immediate and enduring force. The terrorist attacks in the United States on September 11th are obviously such an event. With its wake of destruction to both human life and to the cultural icons of the United States, these attacks stood out as an especially potent reminder to Americans of the fragility of life and the vulnerability of cultural symbols (Pyszczynski, Solomon, & Greenberg, 2003).

For one or both of these reasons, even subliminal presentations of "9/11" and "WTC" (World Trade Center) months after the attacks were sufficient to increase the accessibility of death-related thought (Landau et al., 2004b). Landau et al. further demonstrated that explicit reminders of either 9/11 or mortality increased support for then President George W. Bush just prior to the 2004 Presidential election. Das and colleagues (2009) extended these findings to media stimuli, showing that exposing participants to a news story about Islamic terrorism increased both death-thought accessibility and distal worldview defense in the form of prejudice toward Arabs. Showcasing the breadth of associations tethered to death, Vail, Arndt, Motyl, and Pyszczynski (2012) examined how the destruction of buildings—the architectural imprint of cultural humanity—may constitute what Lifton (1979) referred to as "imagery of extinction." In these studies, exposure to images of buildings reduced to rubble similarly increased both the accessibility of death-related thought and various forms of worldview defense. These studies furthermore showed that increased death-thought accessibility provoked by destruction stimuli statistically mediated the effect of these stimuli on worldview defenses. Such findings suggest that newsworthy events may trigger death-related echoes, which in turn strengthen efforts to affirm one's culturally derived meaning system.

Another domain in which we see frequent elicitation of death-related thought is in matters pertaining to physical health. As articulated by the terror management health model (Goldenberg & Arndt, 2008), a variety of health contexts and stimuli have the potential to activate thoughts of mortality. Health communications about risky sexual activity (Taubman Ben-Ari, 2004), binge drinking (Jessop & Wade, 2008), drinking and driving (Shehryar & Hunt, 2005), and risky driving more generally (Jessop, Albery, Rutter, & Garrod, 2008) all have been shown to increase death-thought accessibility.

This connection is especially evident in the context of stimuli related to cancer because more than 60% of the American public perceives cancer as a death sentence (Moser et al., in press). Indeed, the sensitivity is such that conscious primes of cancer induce vigorous efforts to suppress the activation of death-related thought, and even subliminal presentations of the word "cancer" increase the accessibility of such thought (Arndt, Cook, Goldenberg, & Cox, 2007). Given this, it is perhaps not surprising that various health behaviors that raise the possibility of a cancer diagnosis—such as breast self-exams or mammograms for women—can increase death-thought accessibility (Cooper, Goldenberg, & Arndt, 2011; Goldenberg et al., 2008).

There are, of course, important implications that stem from such activation. As we reviewed previously, accessible death-related cognition increases self-esteem striving and other such efforts to maintain and defend one's view of self and world. Thus, to the extent that an individual derives self-esteem from risky health behavior, health communications that activate thoughts of death may, ironically, increase the very behavior they are designed to warn against (Goldenberg & Arndt, 2008). A clear example of this is found in the recent work of Hansen and colleagues (2010), who demonstrated that graphic cigarette pack warnings—the likes of which the Food and Drug Administration has recently been granted the unprecedented authority to regulate in the United States—increase death-thought accessibility and thereby increase smoking intentions among those who derive some self-worth from their smoking.

Although the arenas of war and health are perhaps the most obvious domains in which death-related thoughts are elicited, there is a broader landscape of stimuli that also do so. In fact, the accessibility of death-related thought has been shown to be increased by thoughts of physical sex (Goldenberg et al., 1999); disgusting imagery (Cox, Goldenberg, Pyszczynski, & Weis, 2007); stimuli that elevate self-awareness (Silvia, 2001); photos of uncultivated nature (Koole & Van den Berg, 2005); reminders of the value of life (King, Hicks, & Abdelkhalik, 2009); and perhaps our favorite, exposure to robots that come uncannily close to looking human (MacDorman, 2005). Taken together, a growing body of research demonstrates that many stimuli we encounter on a daily basis (e.g., just open any newspaper for the latest news of war and destruction or current health scare) may trigger thoughts of death.

Conscious and Nonconscious Thoughts of Death: The Dual Defenses of Terror Management

Yet all thoughts of death are not created equal. The consequences of mortality reminders that we have thus far discussed stem from the unconscious activation of death-related thought. It is the existential rumbling beneath the surface that motivates investment in the symbolic pillars of meaning and significance. But the full story is more complex because explicit awareness of death (or mortality salience as it is commonly induced in laboratory studies) actually sets in motion a specific cognitive sequence that is described by the dual defense model of terror management (Pyszczynski et al., 1999). These processes are important not only for understanding the complexities of managing existential fear but also for what they teach us about motivated cognitive dynamics. Whereas most social cognitive theories are content free—positing, for example, general processes by which explicit and implicit ideation influence social judgment, the dual defense model posits different defenses activated by conscious and nonconscious thoughts specifically about death. Proximal defenses address conscious thoughts of death, whereas the bolstering of symbolic bases of meaning and value that are typically the focus of terror management research represent distal defenses to quell the potential for anxiety engendered by highly accessible thoughts of death outside of focal attention.

Imagine that you are standing in the shower, and in the process of lathering up, you find a lump on your body where a lump just should not be. We are guessing that upon doing so, your routine mental forecast and planning of the day's schedule will be suspended as you now—with a baseball-sized knot of angst in your stomach—ponder the implications of this bodily protuberance. We raise this hypothetical to illustrate the potent impact of conscious thoughts of death on one's self-regulation. Obviously, in many circumstances, thoughts of impending death can have adaptive ramifications (e.g., getting yourself off the tracks when the train is coming). Yet in many others, they are likely to interfere with the goal-directed activity that otherwise consumes the business of living. As such, the initial response to conscious thoughts of death is posited to be the removal of those thoughts from focal awareness.

This is the front-line reaction and involves a set of proximal defenses that serve to remove death from conscious awareness. The first indication of proximal defense was found in a seminal series of studies by Greenberg and colleagues (1994). They found that death-thought accessibility was low immediately after participants contemplated mortality, but became elevated after a delay. This suggested that thoughts of death are initially suppressed, a notion that was then directly tested in a series of studies by Arndt et al. (1997a). Building on evidence that mental load interferes with thought suppression (e.g., Wegner, 1994), Arndt et al. found that when participants were under high cognitive load (i.e.,

by mentally rehearsing a number), death-thought accessibility (and worldview defense) was high immediately after reminders of death, suggesting that participants were indeed actively suppressing such cognition. In further support of this conclusion, if participants are exposed to death-related words without their awareness, as is done with subliminal priming, death-thought accessibility (and worldview defense) increases immediately (Arndt et al., 1997b). Only when people are consciously focused on death do they subsequently suppress further death-related thought.

Whereas an active suppression of death-related thought may be one common means of reducing focal awareness of mortality, it is not the only way in which people may respond, especially if they are given other means to do so. When explicitly reminded of mortality, people will also take advantage of opportunities to escape self-awareness (Arndt, Greenberg, Simon, Pyszczynski, & Solomon, 1998), deny vulnerability to those factors associated with a short life expectancy (Greenberg, Arndt, Simon, Pyszczynski, & Solomon, 2000), bolster their intentions to exercise (presumably under the expectation that better health extends life expectancy; Arndt, Schimel, & Goldenberg, 2003), and reduce their intentions to sun-tan (Routledge, Arndt, & Goldenberg, 2004).

What these examples hopefully convey is that there are both adaptive and maladaptive means by which people try to reduce focal concerns with mortality. According to the terror management health model (Goldenberg & Arndt, 2008), the adaptiveness of these (health-relevant) proximal defenses is moderated by factors that facilitate vulnerability reduction and thereby remove death-related thought from focal attention (e.g., coping style, health optimism, response efficacy; Arndt, Routledge, & Goldenberg, 2006). Thus, for example, individuals who perceive screening exams for early detection of skin cancer to be efficacious increase their screening intentions when confronted with conscious thoughts of death, whereas those who perceive low response efficacy for such exams are more likely to take an avoidance stance toward such screening (Cooper, Goldenberg, & Arndt, 2010).

Whether proceeding along health productive or unproductive avenues, the operative goal is to reduce conscious concern with death. This, however, is just the tip of the defensive iceberg. Once death-related ideation leaves focal awareness, more abstract distal defenses are employed. Indeed, recent work indicates that reminders of death increase more abstract thinking (Landau, Kosloff, & Schmeichel, 2011), but that this only occurs when participants are distracted from mortality thoughts and not when measured immediately after the induction (Vail, Vess, & Arndt, 2012). Distal defenses are more abstract in the sense that they bear little to no logical connection to the problem of death (except perhaps in the interesting case of religious beliefs), but rather serve the need to maintain a sense of oneself as a significant contributor to a meaningful cultural drama (Becker, 1971). These distal defenses are the many forms of worldview bolstering and self-esteem striving that constituted the initial empirical support for TMT.

The temporal sequence of defenses following explicit mortality reminders was most clearly demonstrated by Greenberg et al. (2000). In this study, immediately after thinking about mortality, participants showed an increased tendency to deny possessing those characteristics they were previously told were associated with a short life expectancy. However, this same reaction did not occur when participants were first distracted from their thoughts of mortality. In contrast, a typical worldview defense of increased favoritism toward those who support one's country manifested when participants were distracted from death-related thought, but not immediately after a mortality salience induction when death-related thought was still in focal awareness.

Further evidence for the distinction in these forms of defense comes from considering the unique factors that moderate them. Those factors that moderate proximal responses to death-related cognition (e.g., response efficacy) have no predictive power over esteem-based distal responses (e.g., Cooper et al., 2010). At the same time, the factors that moderate distal responses have little influence over proximal reactions. A few examples should help to clarify. Arndt et al. (2003) found that if you remind people of mortality and then immediately thereafter assess their exercise intentions, regardless of the relevance of fitness to their self-esteem, people increase exercise intentions, presumably because exercising regularly can lower perceived (and actual) risk for health problems. But when death concerns fade from conscious attention, only participants for whom fitness is relevant to their self-esteem increase exercise intentions, presumably reflecting an orientation not to health per se, but to self-esteem bolstering.

As another illustration, in Routledge et al. (2004), when thoughts of death were conscious, people decreased their tanning intentions. Yet when thoughts of death were active but outside consciousness, people increased their intentions, and especially so if they based their self-esteem on their level of attractiveness (see also Arndt et al., 2009; Cox et al., 2009). Thus, what we see here is the same stimulus (a mortality salience prime) having opposite effects depending on the explicit or implicit goals that it activates. Although many basic semantic priming–goal activation processes may function similarly when the prime is conscious or nonconscious (cf. Bargh & Chartrand, 1999), in the case of cognitions about death, markedly different processes can unfold.

One punch line for the broader picture of symbolical efforts to maintain enduring value on which TMT research most often focuses is that such reactions stem from the increased accessibility of death-related thought. A number of findings that we have already presented support this idea. Further convergent evidence is obtained from studies showing that the same conditions that attenuate death-thought accessibility, such as boosting self-esteem, or placing participants in a rational (vs. experiential; cf. Epstein, 1994) frame of mind, attenuate worldview defense and other such reactions (e.g., Harmon-Jones et al., 1997; Simon et al., 1997). Further, the dual defense model of terror management highlights the functional utility of these distal defenses in showing that when given the opportunity to engage in them following a reminder of mortality, the accessibility of death-related thought is reduced back to baseline levels (e.g., Arndt et al., 1997a; Greenberg, Arndt, Schimel, Pyszczynski, & Solomon, 2001; Mikulincer & Florian, 2002). Recent work has also shown that the effects of stimuli that prime thoughts of death on distal defense are in fact mediated by death-thought accessibility (Vail, Arndt et al., 2012), and variables that mitigate mortality salience effects on such defenses do so by reducing the accessibility of such thoughts (Cohen et al., 2011).

A New Wave of Terror Management Research: Insights from Dispositional Levels of Death Thought Accessibility

A large body of research has demonstrated that cues which elevate the accessibility of death-related thought trigger efforts to maintain a meaningful view of self and one's world. But do individual differences in chronic levels of death-thought accessibility matter too? For example, could, at least under some conditions, such dispositional variations predict an individual's psychological security and well-being? And does the chronic strength of an individual's cultural anxiety buffer predict an individual's dispositional tendency to have death-related thought highly accessible? Research has begun to address these questions.

Consider first the ideas that having a secure investment in a belief system should be associated with lower levels of death-thought accessibility and lacking such investment should dispose one to greater death-related concerns. Indirect support for these ideas comes from clinical analyses of psychopathology. Depression and neuroticism both feature more tenuous faith in a meaningful view of the world, and both are associated with increased concerns about death (e.g., Abdel-Khalek, 1998; Loo, 1984). More recently, studies show that investment in religious beliefs and viewing the self as enmeshed in social relationships help to keep thoughts of death at bay. Friedman and Rholes (2009) found that those individuals who are high in religious fundamentalism and those with an interdependent self-construal tend to have lower levels of dispositional death-thought accessibility.

Further, as we saw with the suppression studies discussed earlier, the control of death-related thought can be an effortful task that requires and consumes ego resources. Gailliot and colleagues have developed this idea to suggest that, if awareness of mortality is indeed what James (1910/1978) referred to as the "skull beneath the skin," measures of self-regulatory control might then predict people's sensitivity to death-related thought. And indeed, people who are higher in self-regulatory control show lower accessibility of death-related thought, suggesting that they are better able to keep thoughts of death from the fringes of consciousness (Gailliot, Schmeichel, & Baumeister, 2006). And conversely, when people's ego resources are depleted, they are also susceptible to increased death-thought accessibility (Gailliot et al., 2006; Gailliot, Schmeichel, & Maner, 2007).

What, then, are the consequences of having death-related thought close to consciousness for psychological well-being? Recall that a basic idea of TMT is that thoughts of death that threaten to become conscious disrupt our psychological equanimity. Some work is now suggesting that certain conditions may reveal this connection. For example, Cox, Reid-Arndt, Arndt, and Moser (2012) found that women who had recently received surgery for a cancerous breast mass reported lower levels of well-being than women who had surgery for a noncancerous mass. This is a well-documented effect in the cancer survivorship literature. However, whereas cancer-diagnosed women did not differ from non-diagnosed controls in explicit worries about death, they did show higher death-thought accessibility, which, in turn, was negatively associated with well-being and mediated the effect of diagnosis on well-being.

Yet some individuals appear to possess the psychological resources to manage these cognitions in ways that buffer their deleterious impact on well-being. TMT suggests that self-esteem, as a fundamental terror management structure (Greenberg, Pyszczynski, & Solomon, 1986), should operate in this fashion. And indeed, Routledge and colleagues (2010) found that dispositional death-thought accessibility interacted with self-esteem to predict perceived meaning in life. High levels were only associated with lower meaning in life if individuals also had low self-esteem. In another line of work, Vess, Routledge, Landau, and Arndt (2009) found that dispositional level of death-thought accessibility was negatively associated with perceived meaning in life only among participants with low levels of personal need for structure who are by disposition more open to experience and appreciative of novelty. We will discuss this and related work on personal need for structure more fully later, but for now the point is that among individuals lacking preexisting meaning-providing resources, highly accessible death-related thought may predispose people to view life as less meaningful.

There are certainly a number of issues to be considered when trying to understand the meaning of high death-thought accessibility in the absence of a mortality salience induction or when elevated by other stimuli. However, it appears that research exploring such phenomena has considerable potential and opens the door to studying terror management in a broader playing field of contexts that may otherwise not render themselves conducive to mortality salience inductions for ethical, practical, or other conceptual reasons.

Terror Management and the Cognitive Infrastructure of Meaning

TMT illuminates the psychological motivations underlying people's basic efforts to meaningfully construe the social world. Social cognition is essentially the scientific study of how people create meaning in the social world. Because the field was partly inspired by gestalt psychologists' investigations into the organization of visual perception, it approaches meaning making by characterizing the cognitive processes that people use to impose *structure* on the welter of information in their social environment. This empirical approach has stimulated a massive body of research showing that social information processing is shaped by a veritable arsenal of cognitive processes that simplify and disambiguate information. For example, people rely on stereotypes to simplify information about social groups, and they selectively attend to certain pieces of information about other people in order to form clear impressions.

According to TMT, these structuring processes are not simply built-in features of our cognitive system. Rather, people's tendencies to seek well-structured conceptions of the social world are motivated by the need to view the self as a significant being who can transcend the biological confines of a finite existence. Below we elaborate on this functional account of cognitive structuring tendencies and then summarize emerging lines of research showing that mortality salience increases people's reliance on a range of structuring processes, particularly among those individuals who are predisposed to prefer structured knowledge.

Within mainstream social cognitive theory, functional accounts of structure-seeking (e.g., Fiske, 1992) tend to follow pragmatist philosophers (e.g., James, 1907/1979; Peirce, 1877) in positing that well-structured interpretations of the social environment enable people to effectively navigate that environment in the pursuit of specific purposes, such as making a favorable impression or finding a job. TMT provides a complementary account by positing that to maintain psychological equanimity, the person strives to meet cultural standards of value by which her life can be perceived as significant and enduring beyond death. The individual's confidence that she can attain this enduring value—whether that means upholding religious dictates or achieving fame and fortune—is rooted in more fundamental conceptions of the world as a structured place in which one can reliably act in pursuit of value. If the world appears to lack structure—if, for example, other people's behavior seems contradictory, or if events take place haphazardly—then the person lacks the basic infrastructure necessary to confidently establish a sense of lasting personal significance, and they are therefore vulnerable to the threatening prospect of perishing entirely.

This existential account shares in common with the pragmatist view the principle that well-structured conceptions of the social environment facilitate goal-directed action, but it goes further to emphasize the fundamental role that these conceptions play in supporting the individual's distal psychological goal to achieve death-transcending value. This account also significantly broadens TMT's empirical scope. The TMT studies reviewed earlier show that reminders of mortality heighten people's adherence to specific aspects of their cultural worldview, such as cultural norms and religious beliefs, suggesting that these aspects provide psychological security. If, as we have just proposed, faith in specific cultural ideologies is predicated on more basic or nonspecific conceptions of the world as a predictable, orderly place, then we would expect mortality salience to increase people's preference for well-structured interpretations of other people, events, and their own lives.

But will thoughts of mortality increase efforts to seek structure equally for all individuals? A large body of personality research shows that people vary widely in the strength of their dispositional preference for well-structured knowledge of the social world (e.g., Rokeach, 1960). People with a high (versus low) dispositional preference for structured knowledge—as measured with scales like *need for closure* (NFC; Kruglanski, Webster, & Klem, 1993) and *personal need for structure* (PNS; Neuberg & Newsom, 1993; Thompson et al. 2001)—are particularly inclined to seek simple and clear interpretations of social information, and to respond aversely to complexity and ambiguity.

As noted earlier, TMT posits that each person clings to an individualized worldview for psychological security. This claim is supported, for example, by Arndt et al.'s (2002) finding that mortality salience increased the spontaneous accessibility of different constructs among male and female participants. According to Solomon, Greenberg, and Pyszczynski (1991), individual differences in personality traits can also reflect the different sources of meaning that people characteristically cling to for security. Thus, although our account suggests that people have a universal need to perceive at least some structure in their social environment, individuals with a stronger preference for certain knowledge may be especially likely to invest in well-structured conceptions of the world as a preferred means of managing terror, whereas low structure-seeking individuals may be more comfortable with epistemic openness and novelty (we revisit this latter possibility below). This suggests that individual difference constructs like NFC and PNS can be useful for predicting the types of people who are especially likely to respond to reminders of mortality with increased preference for well-structured interpretations of social information.

Processes Serving Simple Conceptions of Others and the Self

Social psychologists have for many years pointed out that stereotypes serve to simplify information processing by allowing people to interpret and evaluate individual members of outgroups based on overgeneralized beliefs about their group rather than individuating features. A TMT perspective suggests that stereotypes are not only cognitive energy savers, they are also part of a well-structured understanding of the social environment that forms the cognitive foundation for the person's strivings for death-transcending value.

Consistent with this perspective, Schimel et al. (1999) found that mortality salience increased people's tendency to perceive individual members of various outgroups in stereotypic ways. For example, mortality salience led participants to ascribe more stereotypic traits to Germans. Interestingly, this effect was not qualified by whether the stereotypic traits were positive (e.g., disciplined) or negative (e.g., unemotional), suggesting that reminders of mortality not only increase disliking for outgroups that threaten specific aspects of the cultural worldview (e.g., Greenberg et al., 1990) but also increase a more basic, nonspecific tendency to simplify information about other people. Landau et al. (2004a) reported complementary evidence (Study 2) that mortality salience increases the use of the representativeness heuristic, whereby people judge a person's group membership based on that person's superficial resemblance to the group stereotype.

Schimel et al. also reported evidence that mortality salience increases preference for outgroup members who conform to stereotypes by displaying stereotypic traits (e.g., a young black man who likes basketball and clubbing) over individuals who disconfirm stereotypes (e.g., a young black man who likes chess and engineering). Furthermore, this effect is especially prominent among participants predisposed to interpret others in simple ways. Specifically, mortality salience led participants high, but not low, in NFC to prefer a stereotype-confirming feminine gay man over a counter-stereotypic masculine gay man. Taken together, these findings show that thoughts of mortality increase reliance on and preferences for stereotypes, particularly among individuals high in need for closure.

Reminders of mortality encourage stereotyping of others, but can terror management motivation also drive people to conform to *self*-relevant group stereotypes? Landau, Greenberg, and Rothschild (2009a) addressed this question by examining the

effect that death reminders may have on people's tendency to underperform on a task when a negative stereotype for their group's ability is made salient (i.e., *stereotype threat*; Steele, Spencer, & Aronson, 2002). Imagine that a person is poised to excel on a task when she becomes cognizant that, as a member of a certain group, she is stereotyped to perform poorly. Excelling may have its own psychological rewards, but even the implicit realization that one is acting contrary to stereotypic expectancies may undermine meaningful conceptions of oneself conferred in part by simple stereotypes for the groups to which one belongs. Insofar as those simple conceptions serve a terror management function, mortality salience should introduce a motivation to exemplify self-relevant stereotypic expectancies (even negative ones) and thus a reluctance to excel beyond them.

Based on this reasoning, Landau et al. (2009a, Study 2) had female participants think about death or a control topic and then take part in an assessment of mental spatial rotation. Participants in the stereotype threat condition were told that, compared with men, women are generally worse at mentally rotating objects, whereas the other participants received no information about gender differences. All participants then completed both an easy and a difficult spatial rotation test. For participants stereotyped to perform poorly, the easy test poses a dilemma: they have the opportunity to excel, but excelling would mean disconfirming a self-relevant stereotype; the difficult test, however, offers less of an opportunity to excel, and thus poses less of a dilemma. Consistent with this reasoning, women primed with mortality and subsequently negatively stereotyped performed poorly on the easy test even though (or, as Landau et al. theorized, *because*) they had the opportunity to excel. Performance on the difficult test was negatively affected by stereotype threat, replicating prior research (Steele et al., 2002), but was unaffected by the mortality prime. These findings suggest that concerns about mortality motivate people to cling to stereotypic conceptions of themselves, as well as others, even if it means falling short of realizing their full potential.

Another cognitive process that people employ to simplify self-relevant information is captured by Linville's (1985) notion of self-concept complexity. A person's self-concept usually contains a cornucopia of individual traits ranging from ardent to zany, and people tend to group subsets of those traits into clusters that describe the different "selves" they associate with different social contexts. For example, a person may view "me-with-friends" as spontaneous and irreverent, whereas "me-at-church" as quiet and contemplative. For Linville (1985), a complex self-concept encompasses a multiplicity of selves characterized by distinctive trait clusters, whereas a simple self-concept contains fewer and more similar selves.

Although a complex self-concept has psychological advantages for coping with specific stressors (Linville, 1985; Showers, 1992), TMT suggests that a simpler self-concept may provide a more stable foundation for understanding the meaning and significance of one's own life, particularly if the individual tends to invest in simple knowledge as a source of meaning. Landau, Greenberg, Sullivan, Routledge, and Arndt (2009d) tested these hypotheses using a common card-sort method for assessing self-complexity (Linville, 1985) and found that participants who were high, but not low, in PNS responded to mortality salience by organizing self-defining traits in a simpler fashion.

The research reviewed in this subsection suggests that people's tendency to interpret other people and themselves in simple ways stems not only from cognitive "miserliness" or limited processing capacity but also from the desire for simple conceptions that help the person to maintain a well-structured view of who she is and who other people are, such provides the means to confidently establish a sense of lasting personal significance. Of course, simplifying is only one broad epistemic structuring tendency, and our analysis suggests that terror management motivation plays a role in other structuring tendencies as well. Next, we consider cognitive processes through which people maintain *clear* conceptions of the social world.

Processes Serving Clear Conceptions of the Self, Others, and Cultural Artifacts

The everyday task of making sense of other people and ourselves often involves coping with ambiguity and apparent contradiction (Heider, 1958). The same individual may appear to behave in different ways from one situation to the next, and we may even find ourselves acting in ways that contradict our beliefs and standards. Social cognitive theory and research identify a number of processes that people use to reduce ambiguity, resolve mental conflict, and generally maintain clear conceptions of the social world. According to TMT, people seek clarity partly to mitigate mortality concerns. A world in which people and the self act in consistent ways is a world that can be reliably negotiated in an effort to make one's lasting mark, whereas an ambiguous world of conflicting information affords few reliable opportunities for establishing the significance of one's life.

This general line of reasoning led researchers to test whether reminders of mortality motivate people to maintain perhaps the most basic kind of consistency—that which exists between one's own cognitions and behaviors (Friedman & Arndt, 2005; Jonas, Greenberg, & Frey, 2003). For example, Friedman and Arndt (2005) had participants write a counterattitudinal statement—claiming that a boring passage was in fact quite interesting—under conditions of either high choice or low choice. Replicating previous demonstrations of dissonance reduction under conditions of induced compliance, Friedman and Arndt found that participants who freely chose to write the counterattitudinal statement later reported more positive attitudes toward the boring passage compared with participants who were forced to write the statement, presumably bringing their attitudes in line with their behavior. More importantly, participants who had been previously primed with mortality (vs. feelings of personal uncertainty) reported even stronger liking for the passage, suggesting that they were especially motivated to reduce dissonance. These findings support our broader claim that terror management motivation drives people to maintain consistency in even nonspecific ways because stating that a boring passage is interesting does not pose an explicit threat to any specific aspect of the participants' cultural worldview.

In addition to resolving more micro-level inconsistencies between particular cognitions, seeking clarity in the self-concept at a more macro-level also facilitates terror management. Consistent with the notion that self-clarity facilitates terror management, Landau et al. (2009d, Study 2) found that mortality primes led participants high, but not low, in PNS to define personal traits more clearly (cf. Campbell, 1990). Furthermore, this effect was attenuated if, following the mortality salience manipulation, participants were led to affirm a clear personal quality, suggesting that, at least for high-PNS individuals, clear self-conceptions help to defend against mortality fears.

The mortality salience induced preference for clarity extends to perceptions of other people as well. Landau et al. (2004a, Study 1) found that mortality salience exaggerated the primacy effect, leading participants to seize on a clear impression of a target individual as introverted or extroverted, depending on which information they learned about first, and to ignore contradictory information that might complicate that impression (cf., Asch, 1946). The notion that clear conceptions of others serve a terror management function suggests that people primed to think of their mortality should dislike a person whose behaviors defy clear interpretation, particularly if they have a strong personal need for clear knowledge. Landau et al. (2004a, Study 4) tested this by having high- and low-PNS participants primed with mortality or uncertainty read a transcript of a conversation in which three people shared their observations of a mutual acquaintance. In two control conditions, this acquaintance comes across as acting in either a clearly introverted or extroverted manner, whereas in the ambiguous condition, he appears to vacillate between introverted and extroverted behaviors. Supporting predictions, high-PNS participants primed with mortality expressed especially strong disliking for the behaviorally ambiguous target.

Our foregoing analysis suggests that high-PNS individuals will respond aversely to ambiguity not only in themselves and in others but also in cultural artifacts that seem (superficially) to have no clear meaning or purpose at all, such as abstract art. Although modern artworks are often intelligible and enjoyable for those with some background in the history of their respective media, most people find them highly aversive (Cupchik & Gebotys, 1988). Although this distaste may stem in part from a layperson's dismissal of the works as snobbishly eccentric (Bourdieu, 1984), TMT suggests that such artworks appear to lack clear interpretation, and thereby fail to reinforce an orderly, meaningful conception of reality, and may even imply the opposite—a random, meaningless, or absurd universe. This suggests that people should respond to mortality salience with increased aversion to artworks that seem to eschew or even undermine clear meaning and order, especially among high-PNS people.

Landau et al. (2006) found support for these hypotheses. In one experiment (Study 3), mortality salience led high-PNS individuals to report greater aversion to a visually chaotic painting by Jackson Pollack when the piece was presented with the unrevealing title of *#12* (in contrast, individuals low in PNS showed no such effect). Interestingly, however, the negative effect of mortality salience on high-PNS participants' evaluations of the painting was eliminated when the painting was presented with its actual title—*Guardians of the Secret*—which renders the painting interpretable by giving the viewer a clear idea of how to assign meaningful roles to the objects in the frame (two figures suddenly become "guardians," and a distorted shape between them is now the "secret" they are protecting). In other words, death reminders caused those predisposed to seek structured knowledge to dislike a renowned artwork when they perceived it as devoid of meaning; but when they were able to attach some clear interpretation to the work by means of an explanatory title, the apparent threat of the painting dissipated. A follow-up study showed that for high-PNS individuals, a mortality prime reduced liking for a visually chaotic Kandinsky painting, but this effect was eliminated if participants were first asked to imagine themselves having a very chaotic experience lost in an unknown city. Presumably, this imagined experience provided high-PNS participants with a personal frame of reference within which to interpret the painting's meaning.

Processes Serving Orderly Conceptions of Social Events

From a TMT perspective, the belief that social events follow a just and benevolent order constitutes a fundamental building block of terror-assuaging meaning. At some level, people realize that randomly occurring hazards—from a falling chunk of masonry to a bite from an infected insect—can instantaneously negate all of their strivings for value. At the same time, people may witness others who don't believe in or conform to the worldview prosper for equally incomprehensible reasons. When the environment seems to allot favorable and unfavorable outcomes to people regardless of their adherence to the worldview, people may have serious difficulty sustaining confidence that following the worldview's prescriptions for value will ensure their death transcendence. This suggests that reminders of mortality will increase people's efforts to construe social events as following a just and benevolent order.

Lerner (1980) observed that when people encounter information implying that the world is not just, they often restore justice by convincing themselves that the victims of misfortune somehow deserved what happened to them. A number of studies show that this victim-blaming tendency is exacerbated by heightened mortality concerns, especially among those who strongly crave structured knowledge. In one study (Landau et al., 2004a, Study 5), participants read about a senseless tragedy in which a college student was disfigured in an unprovoked attack. After a mortality salience manipulation, the participants were given the opportunity to read titled bits of information about the victim, with the titles implying either positive or negative information about the person. Negative information would bring the event more in line with the belief in a just world. Supporting predictions, for high-PNS individuals, mortality salience increased preference for negative over positive information about the victim, presumably in an effort to restore just world beliefs.

In a follow-up study, Landau et al. (2004a, Study 6) tested whether presenting just-world threatening information suggesting that victims of tragedy are actually good people would unleash mortality concerns. Participants read an article about an unprovoked attack and then read either negative or positive information about the victim. High-PNS participants who read positive (but not negative) information exhibited heightened death-thought accessibility, whereas low-PNS participants did not.

In complementary research, Hirschberger (2006) found that, among samples of Israeli participants, reminders of mortality increased blaming of innocent victims, and unjust events elicited increased the accessibility of death-related thought, especially when the victims of the unjust events incurred severe injuries and had no responsibility for their misfortune—precisely the conditions under which the threat to a just and benevolent order is greatest (Lerner, 1980). Taken together, these findings suggest that, at least for high-PNS people, the belief that victims of misfortune get what they deserve and deserve what they get is an important part of the meaningful social reality that protects people against mortality concerns.

In addition to victim blaming, another means of maintaining the perception of benevolent order in the world is by believing that tragic events "happen for a reason"—they are "trials," "tests," or otherwise set the stage for what will ultimately be positive outcomes. To assess whether such beliefs in benevolent causation contribute to terror management, Landau et al. (2004a, Study 7) had high- and low-PNS participants primed with death or a control topic read two summaries of movie scripts. In one summary, a protagonist witnesses his apartment building burn down, and then, through an unrelated series of events, he falls in love. The other summary described the apartment fire as setting off a chain of events that leads the protagonist to meet the love of his life. Even though the protagonist in both scenarios experiences the same negative and positive outcomes, high-PNS participants after mortality salience preferred the "bad causes good" scenario over the "bad simply precedes good" scenario. That is, reminders of mortality encouraged preference in high-PNS individuals for the story that reinforced the idea of benevolent causation—that bad events will eventually turn out for the best.

Processes Serving Coherent Conceptions of Personal Experience

Our self-concepts include a vast store of experiences that take place over time. Both classic and contemporary theorists emphasize that people seek to integrate these experiences into coherent, temporally continuous narratives that explain—to themselves and to others—how their current self came to be and how their future will unfold, and they find it aversive when their experience appears temporally fragmented or disordered (Erikson, 1968; Habermas & Bluck, 2000; McAdams, 2001).

At a pragmatic level, perceiving overarching patterns in experiences can facilitate practical goal pursuit. But TMT also suggests, as have a number of influential theorists (e.g., Lifton, 1979; May, 1953), that a coherent autobiography that imbues personal experience with order also helps people to believe that their lives have some enduring significance. This analysis suggests that increasing the salience of personal mortality will increase people's need for the psychological protection provided by a coherent autobiography, and will therefore heighten motivation to piece together the episodes that make up their experience into a temporally coherent and continuous whole.

Several theorists have argued that a coherent autobiography is largely sustained by perceiving clear cause-and-effect relationships between separate events (e.g., Habermas & Bluck, 2000; McAdams, 2001). Our guiding analysis suggests, therefore, that mortality salience will motivate people to seek out these causal connections. However, many of the studies we've reviewed thus far suggest that causal coherence, like other types of epistemic structure, might provide psychological security, particularly among high-PNS individuals. Accordingly, Landau et al. (2009d, Study 4) found that high-PNS (vs. low-PNS) participants responded to mortality salience by using more causal words (e.g., *because*) in spontaneously describing the events that took place over the course of their day.

In addition to causal coherence, maintaining autobiographical coherence depends largely on thematically integrating memories of past events with one's current self (McAdams, 2001). To test whether this tendency serves terror management goals, Landau et al. (2009d, Study 5) had participants generate separate autobiographical memories from various times in their lives and then, following a mortality salience manipulation, indicate which of those remembered experiences has had a significant influence on how they see themselves today (they did this by drawing lines connecting boxes representing their individual memories to a box representing their current self). As predicted, high-PNS participants primed with death perceived more meaningful connections between past events and their current sense of self. Also, this effect was not qualified by whether the events were positive or negative in valence, suggesting that in this study, the mortality prime did not simply increase efforts to bolster self-esteem by identifying with certain memories; rather, the evidence suggests that mortality salience heightened high-PNS participants' concern with establishing continuity between their personal past and present. Indeed, a related set of studies (Landau, Greenberg, & Sullivan, 2009b) shows that directly threatening mortality-salient participants' sense of autobiographical coherence by leading them to perceive their past experiences as temporally fragmented prompted compensatory bolstering of their life's global significance.

Another means of imposing coherence on personal experiences over time is to perceive substantive connections between one's current actions and one's long-term goals. Landau et al. (2009b) tested whether mortality salience heightens this tendency. Participants listed personal goals they hoped to accomplish within the next 40 years as well as specific activities they planned for the next few days. Following a mortality salience manipulation, participants were then asked to indicate which current activities meaningfully contribute to their long-term goals. As predicted, participants reminded of their mortality were more likely to view their current actions as steps in what they hoped to do and be in the distant future.

Summary

To sum up this section, we proposed on the basis of TMT that well-structured conceptions of the social world function not only to aid practical goal pursuit but also to defend against threatening mortality concerns. We then reviewed a large body of experimental research showing that increasing the salience of personal mortality heightens motivation to simplify, clarify, and integrate information about the people, events, and experiences that constitute

one's social world, particularly among individuals with a high chronic need for clear and confident knowledge.

Although we claim that the effects of mortality reminders on structure seeking are due specifically to concerns about death, one alternative interpretation is that these effects are due to a generalized reaction to reminders of any aversive or uncertain outcome. However, this alternative explanation is challenged by a large body of evidence that mortality salience elicits different responses compared with the salience of a variety of topics that are aversive (e.g., pain, paralysis, meaninglessness, social exclusion) and uncertainty arousing (e.g., upcoming events; see Pyszczynski et al., 2006). In fact, in many studies reviewed in this section, making mortality salient was compared with the salience of personal uncertainty and even worries about the fate of one's career and relationships problems, which simultaneously controls for thinking about aversive, uncertain, and personally important future outcomes. Further, we've also seen the violations of these preferences for structured knowledge lead to increased accessibility of death-related thought.

Another potential alternative explanation is that mortality salience simply engenders a cognitive load that subsequently results in a global tendency to rely on simple knowledge structures and seize on interpretations of social information that reduce ambiguity and confusion. This explanation cannot account for many extant findings. First, cognitive load is highest directly after mortality salience, and yet these structuring effects, like other distal defenses, occur after a delay. Second, direct comparison of classic cognitive load and mortality salience inductions found entirely different effects (Arndt et al., 1997a). Third, studies have found that mortality salience increases efforts to impose structure in ways that seem to take more, rather than less, mental energy. For example, finding meaningful connections between separate past events and the current self would seem to require more cognitive effort than allowing that past events follow a simple linear sequence in time. Finally, Landau et al. (2006) found that having individuals imagine a chaotic experience attenuated rather than amplified the effect of a mortality reminder. Thus, we think it is unlikely that the effects of mortality salience on instigating structuring processes is due to depleting cognitive resources by reminding people of death.

Although more research is certainly necessary, this body of research indicates that seeking and maintaining structured conceptions of the social world can serve to protect individuals against the threatening awareness of death's inevitability. These studies contribute to social cognition research by demonstrating how distal psychological motivations—in this case terror management needs—can significantly shape people's efforts to understand the people and events that they encounter in their everyday lives. This work also broadens the empirical scope of TMT by showing that people manage mortality concerns not only by clinging to specific aspects of their cultural worldview but also by using basic cognitive processes to impose structure on their social environment. Thus, it appears that terror management motivation lies behind even very basic ways that we make meaningful sense of the world.

In many studies we saw that thoughts of mortality do not instigate structure seeking equally for all individuals. Participants with high dispositional preference for structured knowledge, as assessed by the NFC and PNS measures, are especially likely to seek and defend well-structured conceptions of the social world in response to mortality reminders. In contrast, individuals who are less dispositionally motivated to seek structured conceptions of the social world are more tolerant of ambiguity and novelty and don't respond to mortality salience with heightened desire for structured knowledge.

This does not mean, however, that low-PNS individuals don't need to cope with the threat of death. Rather, it appears they may do so in different ways. In fact, recent research suggests that, in some situations, low-PNS individuals respond to existential threat by actively *seeking out* novel experiences and open interpretations of the world as a means of lending life meaning. Vess et al. (2009) showed that after mortality salience, low-PNS participants exhibited increased interest in documentaries presenting novel perspectives on culturally relevant topics. Furthermore, after contemplating death, low-PNS individuals who imagined exploring an unfamiliar topic reported higher levels of perceived meaning in life than those who imagined exploring a familiar topic (and than high-PNS individuals considering either topic). In a related vein, Usta, Williams, Haubl, and Schimel (2010) found that although mortality salience led high-PNS individuals to seek familiar consumer choices, it actually led low-PNS participants toward novel consumer choices.

These studies suggest that, for certain individuals or in certain situations, thoughts of mortality will not necessarily trigger a rigid approach to understanding events in one's social world. Indeed, it may be important to consider both the individual and the situation in concert. Usta and colleagues' (2010) studies also explored the role that the choice environment plays in the preferences of high- and low-PNS people. They found that when the choice environment with which participants are faced when needing to manage thoughts of death is perceived as providing organized structure, low-PNS people assert their penchant for novelty by seeking out unfamiliar consumer choices. For high-PNS individuals, in contrast, being confronted with an unstructured choice environment leads them to assert their desire for structure and seek out familiar consumer choices. These studies also suggest a provocative way to encourage more novelty seeking among those who desire structure in their social experiences. When high-PNS individuals were provided with a structured choice environment after MS, they were less likely to lean toward the familiar. This implies that if peoples' propensity for structured organization of the world can be satiated, they may be more prone to explore novel experiences.

Research also suggests that creativity is another factor that may encourage less rigid cognitive orientations in how people respond to awareness of mortality. Although the existential implications of creativity may be complex (see, e.g., Arndt et al., 1999, 2005; Rank, 1932/1989), when creativity primes divergent and open-minded cognition, it can redirect terror management responses away from a dogmatic bias against that which potentially threatens known and existing beliefs. Accordingly, studies indicate that creativity—to the extent that it inspires a more open-minded cognitive style—can reduce worldview defense when people are reminded of mortality (Routledge, Arndt, & Sheldon, 2004), and further, that after mortality salience, creative cognition can actually lead to an openness and exploration of novel cultural viewpoints (Routledge & Arndt, 2009). Such research may offer a foundation for examining how the management of mortal cognition can also play a role in the cognitive processes associated with other facets of growth and enrichment of the self.

Future Directions for Understanding Mortal Cognition

Part of the reason creativity may be able to inspire more open-minded responses to death awareness is that, in this and other cultures, the value of creativity may be an important component of peoples' worldview. This suggests that one direction for further research would be to investigate the particular dimensions of people's worldviews that are most central to their existential security. Research has shown that people are quite idiosyncratic in the ways they try to bolster their self-esteem in response to elevated death-thought accessibility. This makes sense because worldviews offer a variety of paths to self-worth and, as James (1890) and Becker (1971) noted, and Crocker and colleagues' (e.g., Crocker & Wolfe, 2001) research shows, people invest in some bases of self-esteem more than others. Similarly, every individual internalizes his or her own version of the prevailing cultural worldview and so may be especially prone to bolster his or her faith in science, religion, money, friendship, love, and so forth. And different cultures may emphasize some of these aspects of worldviews more than others. We doubt people have much conscious access to how they are serving their terror management needs, so we hope to use implicit measures to assess the extent to which individuals within and between cultures associate feelings of security with these particular components of cultural worldviews.

In a related point, PNS often seems to be a moderator of mortality salience effects. A question needing further research is: How do the more open and tentative cognitive styles characteristic of low-PNS people serve their terror management needs for a meaning-providing worldview that provides stable bases for enduring personal significance? The findings of Usta et al. (2010) suggest that providing low PNS people with unstructured choice environments may satiate their desires for novelty, leading them to turn to that which is more familiar and predictable. Perhaps, then, this allows for some stability in their worldviews and social experience.

Another issue concerns the relative strength of motivations to affirm one's worldview and bolster one's self-worth. The study described earlier showing that a mortality prime encouraged women under stereotype threat to perform poorly on an easy task suggests that people will often sacrifice their self-esteem striving to preserve faith in the worldview to which they subscribe. This fits TMT in that faith in the worldview is a prerequisite for effective self-esteem striving; one can't be good or valuable without a worldview that clearly defines what it means to be good and valuable. Four studies reported by Landau, Greenberg, and Sullivan (2009c) provide further evidence for this point by showing that after mortality salience, (1) people will accept the validity of a test they did poorly on if credible authorities attest to it validity; (2) people will accept the invalidity of a test they did well on

if authorities criticized the test; (3) people will deny the validity of a leadership test if it suggests they had more leadership skills than an admired canonical leader; and (4) people will not self-enhance on a trait if they first rated a parent whom they admired for the parent's standing on that trait dimension.

So this work suggests that with death-thought accessibility high, faith in the worldview may be the most potent concern. However, a recent set of studies suggests this matter may be more complex than that, and that the context may determine whether mortality salience motivates worldview or self-esteem bolstering. In a set of studies, Kosloff, Greenberg, Sullivan, and Weise (2010) found that when considering short-term dating prospects, a self-esteem enhancing prospect was preferred, whereas when considering a long-term relationship prospect, a worldview validating prospect was more appealing. Thus in some contexts, reminders of mortality may direct the individual toward preferences and behavior that serve-self-esteem, whereas in others, they may direct people more toward worldview validation. But research has just scratched the surface regarding the contexts that play such a moderating role.

Another minimally explored aspect of TMT is the role of conscious construals of death in instigating distal defenses. Because research has shown that death-related ideation produces worldview defense primarily when thoughts of death are highly accessible but outside of current focal attention (Pyszczynski et al., 1999), our work has focused on the impact of nonconscious death-related thought and variables that affect the accessibility of such thoughts. However, death is clearly a problem to which people and cultures devote considerable conscious thought, and individuals and cultures vary greatly in how they consciously construe the problem of death. Only a few studies have explored the effects of different ways of consciously construing one's mortality. Initial work suggests that contemplating suicide in the face of terminal illness (Fritsche et al., 2008) and a heroic death (Cozzolino, 2006) may not trigger distal defenses, but there is much more to learn.

A substantial literature on attitudes and anxieties regarding death (e.g., Florian & Mikulincer, 2004) indicates that, at least at a conscious level, death is associated with a multitude of concerns. Prominent among these are concerns about not existing, the pain and unpleasantness of dying, separating from loved ones, and failing to meet one's goals. Perhaps how people consciously construe death moderates whether they cling to the defensive coping mechanisms that have been the focus of previous research. For example, contemplating dying painlessly with loved ones after living a long, happy, and productive life may arouse less potential for anxiety and thus less death-thought accessibility and defense than the prospect of dying an agonizing death at young age, alone, after an undistinguished or unsatisfying life. Thus, a potentially fruitful direction for new research would be to alter the classic mortality salience induction to have people contemplate their own death in ways that vary aspects such as the level of pain, the age at which life ends, and the level of isolation at the time of death, and determine whether these different conscious construals affect subsequent death-thought accessibility and defensive responses. Such research would fill an important gap in our understanding of the role of death awareness in human behavior.

A related point is that philosophers, existential psychologists, and researchers focused on reactions to trauma and near-death experiences have suggested that deeper, more elaborate conscious thought about mortality can benefit personal growth and be liberating (see, e.g., Janoff-Bulman & Yopyk, 2004). Some evidence suggests such elaborate processing regarding the problem of mortality motivates a reprioritizing toward more authentic, psychologically beneficial goal pursuit. This, of course, contrasts with the largely defensive responses most typically found in response to mortality salience.

Although some progress on understanding the differences between these two types of death-related thought and their consequences has been made, more research is needed. One issue raised by recent research is whether more elaborate contemplation of death has lasting effects on goal prioritization or whether short-term effects that surrender to standard terror management motivated intensified investment in symbolic bases of meaning and value over time (Kosloff & Greenberg, 2009). Whether a deep contemplation of death can lead to true acceptance of one's own death, and thereby increase appreciation of one's own life and that of others, remains to be determined.

Finally, more research is needed on the effects of highly accessible death-related thought over time. We don't know how long the effects of a single instance of increased death-thought accessibility last, although that is likely to vary based on the intensity of the experience with which this heightened accessibility is elicited. And we also don't know much about how chronically elevated death-thought accessibility affects people. One study of Indian funerary workers found that they were not affected by mortality salience, but exhibit elevated pro-Indian bias, equivalent to that shown by other Indian workers only after a mortality salience induction (Fernandez, Castano, & Singh, 2010). Other studies have started to show similar effects of mortality salience as are found with resting levels of death-thought accessibility (e.g., Routledge et al., 2010; Vess et al., 2009), although whether this reflects chronically elevated death-thought accessibility or an elevation elicited by unspecified acute sources is at this point unclear. Certainly, more research is need on these and related issues.

A Final Reflection

Our ability, unlike the other animals, to conceptualize our own end creates tremendous psychic strains within us; whether we like to admit it or not, in each man's chest a tiny ferret of fear at this ultimate knowledge gnaws away at his ego and his sense of purpose.
  Stanley Kubrick, 1986 (Phillips, 2001, p. 72)

Over thousands of years, philosophers, writers, poets, and artists have commented on how the knowledge of our own mortality affects human mentation and action. For its first 100 years, the young science of psychology virtually ignored (or willfully denied) any role for this knowledge. But over the past 25 years, psychological science has begun to catch up, systematically advancing our understanding of the impact of awareness of death, both confirming and refining our theoretical grasp on how it shapes our conceptions of ourselves and the world. We suggest that this knowledge helps us move toward a more mature, existentially informed social cognition. At the same time, we also suggest there is a great deal more to learn about how human awareness of death, as well as other ineluctable features of existence (see Pyszczynski, Greenberg, Koole, & Solomon, 2010), contribute to the way in which we all think, feel, and act over the course of our life.[25]

Author Note

The authors share equal responsibility for this chapter. Address correspondence to Jeff Greenberg, Department of Psychology, College of Science, University of Arizona, Tucson, AZ 85721–0068.

References

Abdel-Khalek, A. M. (1998). The structure and measurement of death obsession. *Personality and Individual Differences, 24,* 159–165.

Anderson, J. R., & Bower, G. H. (1973). *Human associative memory.* Washington, DC: Winston.

Arndt, J., Cook, A., Goldenberg, J. L., & Cox, C. R. (2007). Cancer and the threat of death: The cognitive dynamics of death thought suppression and its impact on behavioral health intentions. *Journal of Personality and Social Psychology, 92,* 12–29.

Arndt, J., Cook, A., & Routledge, C. (2004). The blueprint of terror management: Understanding the cognitive architecture of psychological defense against the awareness of death. In J. Greenberg, S. L., Koole, & T. Pyszczynski (Eds.), *Handbook of experimental existential psychology* (pp. 35–53). New York: Guilford.

Arndt, J., Cox, C. R., Goldenberg, J. L., Vess, M., Routledge, C., & Cohen, F. (2009). Blowing in the (social) wind: Implications of extrinsic esteem contingencies for terror management and health. *Journal of Personality and Social Psychology, 96,* 1191–1205.

Arndt, J., Greenberg, J, & Cook, A. (2002). Mortality salience and the spreading activation of worldview-relevant constructs: Exploring the cognitive architecture of terror management. *Journal of Experimental Psychology: General, 131,* 307–324.

Arndt, J., Greenberg, J., Pyszczynski, T., & Solomon, S. (1997b). Subliminal exposure to death-related stimuli increases defense of the cultural worldview. *Psychological Science, 8,* 379–385.

Arndt, J., Greenberg, J., Simon, L., Pyszczynski, T., & Solomon, S. (1998). Terror management and self-awareness: Evidence that mortality salience provokes avoidance of the self-focused state. *Personality and Social Psychology Bulletin, 24,* 1216–1227.

Arndt, J., Greenberg, J., Solomon, S., Pyszczynski, T., & Simon, L. (1997a). Suppression, accessibility of death-related thoughts, and cultural worldview defense: Exploring the psychodynamics of terror management. *Journal of Personality and Social Psychology, 73,* 5–18.

Arndt, J., Greenberg, J., Solomon, S., Pyszczynski, T., & Schimel, J. (1999). Creativity and terror management: Evidence that creative activity increases guilt and social projection following mortality salience. *Journal of Personality and Social Psychology, 77,* 19–32.

Arndt, J., Routledge, C., & Goldenberg, J. L. (2006). Predicting proximal health responses to reminders of death: The influence of coping style and health optimism. *Psychology and Health. 21,* 593–614.

Arndt, J., Routledge, C., Greenberg, J., & Sheldon, K. M. (2005). Illuminating the dark side of creative expression: Assimilation needs and the consequences of creative action following mortality salience. *Personality and Social Psychology Bulletin, 31,* 1327–1339.

Arndt, J., Schimel, J., & Goldenberg, J. L. (2003). Death can be good for your health: Fitness intentions as proximal and distal defense against mortality salience. *Journal of Applied Social Psychology, 33,* 1726–1746.

Arndt, J., Vess, M., Cox, C. R., Goldenberg, J. L., & Lagle, S. (2009). The psychosocial effect of personal thoughts of mortality on cardiac risk assessment. *Medical Decision Making, 29,* 175–181.

Asch, S. (1946). Forming impressions of personality. *Journal of Abnormal and Social Psychology, 41,* 258–290.

Bargh, J. A., & Chartrand, T. L. (1999). The unbearable automaticity of being. *American Psychologist, 54,* 462–479.

Bassili, J. N., & Smith, M. C. (1986). On the spontaneity of trait attribution. *Journal of Personality and Social Psychology, 50,* 239–245.

Becker, E. (1971). *The birth and death of meaning: An interdisciplinary perspective on the problem of man* (2nd ed.). New York: Free Press.

Becker, E. (1973). *The denial of death.* New York: Free Press.

Becker, E. (1975). *Escape from evil.* New York: Free Press.

Berger, P. L., & Luckmann, T. (1967). *The social construction of reality: A treatise in the sociology of knowledge.* New York: Anchor Books.

Bourdieu, P. (1984). *Distinction: A social critique of the judgment of taste.* Cambridge, MA: Harvard University Press.

Campbell, J. D. (1990). Self-esteem and clarity of the self-concept. *Journal of Personality and Social Psychology, 59,* 538–549.

Cassavetes, J. (Director), & McMendree, M. (Producer). (1960). *Shadows* [Film]. (Available from Gena Enterprises, Orion Home Video, Capital Hill Productions.)

Cohen, F., Sullivan, D., Solomon, S., Greenberg, J., & Ogilvie, D. (2011). Finding everland: Flight fantasies and the desire to transcend mortality. *Journal of Experimental Social Psychology, 47,* 88–102.

Cooper, D. P., Goldenberg, J. L., & Arndt, J. (2010). Examination of the terror management health model: The interactive effect of conscious death thought and health-coping variables on decisions in potentially fatal health domains. *Personality and Social Psychology Bulletin, 36,* 937–946.

Cooper, D. P., Goldenberg, J. L., & Arndt, J. (2011). Empowering the self: Using the terror management health model to promote breast self-exam intention. *Self and Identity, 10,* 315–325.

Collins, A. M., & Loftus, E. F. (1975). A spreading-activation theory of semantic processing. *Psychological Review, 82,* 407–428.

Cox, C. R., Cooper, D. P., Vess, M., Arndt, J., Goldenberg, J. L., & Routledge, C. (2009). Bronze is beautiful but pale can be pretty: The effects of appearance standards and mortality salience on sun-tanning outcomes. *Health Psychology, 28,* 746–752.

Cox, C. R., Goldenberg, J. L., Pyszczynski, T., & Weise, D. (2007). Disgust, creatureliness and the accessibility of death-related thoughts. *European Journal of Social Psychology, 37,* 494–507.

Cox, C. R., Reid-Arndt, S. A., Arndt, J., & Moser, R. (2012). Considering the unspoken: The role of death cognition in quality of life among women with and without breast cancer. *Journal of Psychosocial Oncology, 30,* 128–139.

Cozzolino, P. J. (2006). Death, contemplation, growth, and defense: Converging evidence of a dual-existential system? *Psychological Inquiry, 17,* 278–287.

Crocker, J. & Wolfe, C. T. (2001). Contingencies of self-worth. *Psychological Review, 108,* 593–623.

Cupchik, G. C., & Gebotys, R. J. (1988). The search for meaning in art: Interpretive styles and judgments of quality. *Visual Arts Research, 14,* 38–50.

Das, E., Bushman, B. J., Bezemer, M. D., Kerkhof, P., & Vermeulen, I. E. (2009). How terrorism news reports increase prejudice against outgroups: A terror management account. *Journal of Experimental Social Psychology, 45,* 453–459.

Epstein, S. (1994). Integration of the cognitive and the psycho-dynamic unconscious. *American Psychologist, 49*, 709–724.

Erikson, E. (1968). *Identity: Youth and crisis.* New York: Norton.

Fernandez, S., Castano, E., & Singh, I. (2010). Managing death in the burning grounds of Varanasi, India: A terror management investigation. *Journal of Cross-Cultural Psychology, 41*, 182–194.

Fiske, S. T. (1992). Thinking is for doing: Portraits of social cognition from daguerreotypes to laserphoto. *Journal of Personality and Social Psychology, 63*, 877–839.

Florian, V. & Mikulincer, M. (2004). A multifaceted perspective on the existential meanings, manifestations, and consequences of fear of personal death. In J. Greenberg, S. L. Koole, S., & T. Pyszczynski (Eds.). *Handbook of experimental existential psychology* (pp. 54–70). New York: Guilford Press.

Friedman, R. S., & Arndt, J. (2005). Reexploring the connection between terror management theory and dissonance theory. *Personality and Social Psychology Bulletin, 31*, 1217–1225.

Friedman, M., & Rholes, W. S. (2009). Religious fundamentalism and terror management: Differences by interdependent and independent self-construal. *Self and Identity, 8*, 24–44.

Fritsche, I., Jonas, E., Fankhänel, T. (2008). The role of control motivation in mortality salience effects on ingroup support and defense. *Journal of Personality and Social Psychology, 95*, 524–541.

Gailliot, M. T., Schmeichel, B. J., & Baumeister, R. F. (2006). Self-regulatory processes defend against the threat of death: Effects of self-control depletion and trait self-control on thoughts and fears of dying. *Journal of Personality and Social Psychology, 91*, 49–62.

Gailliot, M. T., Schmeichel, B. J., & Maner, J. K. (2007). Differentiating the effects of self-control and self-esteem on reactions to mortality salience. *Journal of Experimental Social Psychology, 43*, 894–901.

Gailliot, M. T., Sillman, T. F., Schmeichel, B. J., Maner, J. K., & Plant, E. A. (2008). Mortality salience increases adherence to salient norms and values. *Personality and Social Psychology Bulletin, 34*, 993–1003.

Gilbert, D. T., & Hixon, J. G. (1991). The trouble of thinking: Activation and application of stereotypic beliefs. *Journal of Personality and Social Psychology, 60*, 509–517.

Goldenberg, J. L., & Arndt, J. (2008). The implications of death for health: A terror management health model for behavioral health promotion. *Psychological Review, 115*, 1032–1053.

Goldenberg, J. L., Arndt, J., Hart, J., & Routledge, C. (2008). Uncovering an existential barrier to breast self-exam behavior. *Journal of Experimental Social Psychology, 44*, 260–274.

Goldenberg, J. L., Pyszczynski, T., McCoy, S. K., Greenberg, J., & Solomon, S. (1999). Death, sex, love, and neuroticism: Why is sex such a problem? *Journal of Personality and Social Psychology, 77*, 1173–1187.

Greenberg, J., Arndt, J., Schimel, J., Pyszczynski, T., & Solomon, S. (2001). Clarifying the function of mortality-salience induced worldview defense: Renewed suppression or reduced accessibility of death-related thoughts? *Journal of Experimental Social Psychology, 37*, 70–76.

Greenberg, J., Arndt, J., Simon, L., Pyszczynski, T., & Solomon, S. (2000). Proximal and distal defenses in response to reminders of one's mortality: Evidence of a temporal sequence. *Personality and Social Psychology Bulletin, 26*, 91–99.

Greenberg, J., Pyszczynski, T., & Solomon, S. (1986). The causes and consequences of a need for self-esteem: A terror management theory. In R. F. Baumeister (Ed.), *Public self and private self* (pp.189–212). New York: Springer-Verlag.

Greenberg, J., Pyszczynski, T., Solomon, S., Rosenblatt, A., Veeder, M., Kirkland, S., & Lyon, D. (1990). Evidence for Terror Management Theory II: The effects of mortality salience on reactions to those who threaten or bolster the cultural worldview. *Journal of Personality and Social Psychology, 58*, 308–318.

Greenberg, J., Pyszczynski, T., Solomon, S., Simon, L., & Breus, M. (1994). Role of consciousness and accessibility of death-related thoughts in mortality salience effects. *Journal of Personality and Social Psychology, 67*, 627–637.

Greenberg, J., Solomon, S., & Arndt, J. (2008). A uniquely human motivation: Terror management. In J. Shah & W. Gardner (Eds.), *Handbook of motivation science* (pp. 113–134). New York: Guilford.

Greenberg, J., Solomon, S., Pyszczynski, T., Rosenblatt, A., Burling, J., Lyon, D., Pinel, E., & Simon, L. (1992). Assessing the terror management analysis of self-esteem: Converging evidence of an anxiety-buffering function. *Journal of Personality and Social Psychology, 63*, 913–922.

Habermas, T., & Bluck, S. (2000). Getting a life: The emergence of the life story in adolescence. *Psychological Bulletin, 126*, 748–769.

Hansen, J., Winzeler, S., & Topolinski, S. (2010). When death makes you smoke: A terror management perspective on the effectiveness of cigarette on-pack warnings. *Journal of Experimental Social Psychology, 46*, 226–228.

Harmon-Jones, E., Simon, L., Greenberg, J., Pyszczynski, T., Solomon, S., & McGregor, H. (1997). Terror management theory and self-esteem: Evidence that increased self-esteem reduces mortality salience effects. *Journal of Personality and Social Psychology, 72*, 24–36.

Hayes, J., Schimel, J., Arndt, J., & Faucher, E. (2010). A theoretical and empirical review of the death-thought accessibility concept in terror management research. *Psychological Bulletin, 136*, 699–739.

Hayes, J., Schimel, J., Faucher, E. H., & Williams, T. J. (2008). Evidence for the DTA hypothesis II: Threatening self-esteem increases death-thought accessibility. *Journal of Experimental Social Psychology, 44*, 600–613.

Heider, F. (1958). *The psychology of interpersonal relations.* New York: John Wiley & Sons.

Hirschberger, G. (2006). Terror management and attributions of blame to innocent victims: Reconciling compassionate and defensive responses. *Journal of Personality and Social Psychology, 91*, 832–844.

Janoff-Bulman, R., & Yopyk, D. J. (2004). Random outcomes and valued commitments: Existential dilemmas and the paradox of meaning. In J. Greenberg, S. L., Koole, and T. Pyszczynski (Eds.), *Handbook of experimental existential psychology* (pp. 122–140). New York: Guilford.

James, W. (1890). *The principles of psychology* (Vol. 1). Cambridge, MA: Harvard University Press.

James, W. (1978). *The varieties of religious experience.* Garden City, NY: Image Books. (Original work published in 1910.)

James, W. (1979). *Pragmatism.* Cambridge, MA: Harvard University Press. (Original work published in 1907.)

Jessop, D. C., Albery, I. P., Rutter, J., & Garrod, H. (2008). Understanding the impact of mortality-related health-risk information: A terror management theory perspective. *Personality and Social Psychology Bulletin, 34*, 951–964.

Jessop, D. C., & Wade, J. (2008). Fear appeals and binge drinking: A terror management theory perspective. *British Journal of Health Psychology, 13,* 773–788.

Jonas, E., & Fischer, P. (2006). Terror management and religion: Evidence that intrinsic religiousness mitigates worldview defense following mortality salience. *Journal of Personality and Social Psychology, 91,* 553–567.

Jonas, E., Greenberg, J., & Frey, D. (2003). Connecting terror management and dissonance theories: Evidence that mortality salience increases the preference for supportive information after decisions. *Personality and Social Psychology Bulletin, 29,* 1181–1189.

Jonas, E., Martens, A., Kayser, D. N., Fritsche, I., Sullivan, D., & Greenberg, J. (2008). Focus theory of normative conduct and terror-management theory: The interactive impact of mortality salience and norm salience on social judgment. *Journal of Personality and Social Psychology, 95,* 1239–1251.

Joyce, J. (1966). *Ulysses.* New York: Vintage Books. (Original work published 1914.)

King, L. A., Hicks, J. A., & Abdelkhalik, J. (2009). Death, life, scarcity, and value: An alternative perspective on the meaning of death. *Psychological Science, 20,* 1459–1462.

Koole, S. L., & Van den Berg, A. (2005). Lost in the wilderness: Terror management, action orientation, and nature evaluation. *Journal of Personality and Social Psychology, 88,* 1014–1028.

Kosloff, S., & Greenberg, J. (2009). Pearls in the desert: The proximal and distal effects of mortality salience on the appeal of extrinsic goals. *Journal of Experimental Social Psychology, 45,* 197–203.

Kosloff, S., Greenberg, J., Sullivan, D., & Weise, D. (2010). Of trophies and pillars: Exploring the terror management functions of short-term and long-term relationship partners. *Personality and Social Psychology Bulletin, 36,* 1037–1051.

Kruglanski, A. W., Webster, D. M., & Klem, A. (1993). Motivated resistance and openness to persuasion in the presence or absence of prior information. *Journal of Personality and Social Psychology, 65,* 861–876.

Landau, M. J., Greenberg, J., & Rothschild, Z. K. (2009a). Motivated cultural worldview adherence and culturally loaded test performance. *Personality and Social Psychology Bulletin, 35,* 442–453.

Landau, M. J., Greenberg, J., Solomon, S., Pyszczynski, T., & Martens, A. (2006). Windows into nothingness: Terror management, meaninglessness, and negative reactions to modern art. *Journal of Personality and Social Psychology, 90,* 879–892.

Landau, M. J., Greenberg, J., & Sullivan, D. (2009b). Defending a coherent autobiography: When past events appear incoherent, mortality salience prompts compensatory bolstering of the past's significance and the future's orderliness. *Personality and Social Psychology Bulletin, 35,* 1012–1020.

Landau, M. J., Greenberg, J., & Sullivan, D. (2009c). Managing terror when self-worth and worldviews collide: Evidence that mortality salience increases reluctance to self-enhance beyond authorities. *Journal of Experimental Social Psychology, 45,* 68–79.

Landau, M. J., Greenberg, J., Sullivan, D., Routledge, C., & Arndt, J. (2009d). The protective identity: Evidence that mortality salience heightens the clarity and coherence of the self-concept. *Journal of Experimental Social Psychology, 45,* 796–807.

Landau, M. J., Johns, M., Greenberg, J., Pyszczynski, T., Martens, A., Goldenberg, J. L., & Solomon, S. (2004a). A function of form: Terror management and structuring the social world. *Journal of Personality and Social Psychology, 87,* 190–210.

Landau, M. J., Kosloff, S., & Schmeichel, B. (2011). Imbuing everyday actions with meaning in response to existential threat. *Self and Identity, 10,* 64–76.

Landau, M. J., Solomon, S., Greenberg, J., Cohen, F., Pyszczynski, T., Arndt, J., Miller, C. H., Ogilvie, D. M., & Cook, A. (2004b). Deliver us from evil: The effects of mortality salience and reminders of 9/11 on support for President George W. Bush. *Personality and Social Psychology Bulletin, 30,* 1136–1150.

Lerner, M. (1980). *The belief in a just world.* New York: Plenum Press.

Lifton, R. J. (1979). *The broken connection: On death and the continuity of life.* Washington, DC: American Psychiatric Press.

Linville, P. W. (1985). Self-complexity and affective extremity: Don't put all of your eggs in one cognitive basket. *Social Cognition, 3,* 94–120.

Loo, R. (1984). Personality correlates of the fear of death and dying scale. *Journal of Clinical Psychology, 40,* 120–122.

MacDorman, K. F. (2005). Mortality salience and the uncanny valley. *Proceedings of the 2005 5th IEEE-RAS International Conference on Humanoid Robots,* 399–405.

May, R. (1953). *Man's search for himself.* New York: Norton.

McAdams, D. P. (2001). The psychology of life stories. *Review of General Psychology, 5,* 100–122.

McNamara, T. P. (1992). Priming and constraints it places on theories of memory and retrieval. *Psychological Review, 99,* 650–662.

Mikulincer, M., & Florian, V. (2000). Exploring individual differences in reactions to mortality salience: Does attachment style regulate terror management mechanisms? *Journal of Personality and Social Psychology, 79,* 260–273.

Mikulincer, M., & Florian, V. (2002). The effects of mortality salience on self-serving attributions—Evidence for the function of self-esteem as a terror management mechanism. *Basic and Applied Social Psychology, 24,* 261–271.

Mikulincer, M., Florian, V., Birnbaum, G., & Malishkevich, S. (2002). The death-anxiety buffering function of close relationships: Exploring the effects of separation reminders on death-thought accessibility. *Personality and Social Psychology Bulletin, 28,* 287–299.

Moser, R. P., Arndt, J., Han, P., Waters, E., Amsellem, M., & Hesse, B. (in press). Perceptions of cancer as a death sentence: Prevalence and consequences. *Journal of Health Psychology.*

Neuberg, S. L. & Newsom, J. (1993). Personal need for structure: Individual differences in the desire for simple structure. *Journal of Personality and Social Psychology, 65,* 113–131.

Peirce, C. (1877). The fixation of belief. *Popular Science Monthly, 12,* 1–15.

Phillips, G. D. (Ed.). (2001). *Stanley Kubrick: Interviews.* Jackson, MS: University Press of Mississippi.

Pyszczynski, T., Greenberg, J., Koole, S., & Solomon, S. (2010). Experimental existential psychology: Coping with the facts of life. In S. Fiske, D. Gilbert, & G. Lindzey (Eds.), *Handbook of social psychology.* London: John Wiley and Sons.

Pyszczynski, T., Greenberg, J., & Solomon, S. (1999). A dual-process model of defense against conscious and unconscious death-related thoughts: An extension of terror management theory. *Psychological Review, 106,* 835–845.

Pyszczynski, T., Greenberg, J., Solomon, S., Arndt, J., & Schimel, J. (2004). Why do people need self-esteem? A theoretical and empirical review. *Psychological Bulletin, 130,* 435–468.

Pyszczynski, T., Greenberg, J., Solomon, S., & Maxfield, M. (2006). On the unique psychological import of the human awareness of mortality: Themes and variations. *Psychological Inquiry, 17,* 328–356.

Pyszczynski, T., Solomon, S., & Greenberg, J. (2003). *In the wake of 9/11: The psychology of terror.* Washington, DC: American Psychological Association.

Rank, O. (1989). *Art and artist: Creative urge and personality development.* New York: Knopf. (Original work published 1932.)

Rokeach, M. (1960). *The open and closed mind.* New York: Basic Books.

Rosenblatt, A., Greenberg, J., Solomon, S., Pyszczynski, T., & Lyon, D. (1989). Evidence for terror management theory I: The effects of mortality salience on reactions to those who violate or uphold cultural values. *Journal of Personality and Social Psychology, 57,* 681–690.

Routledge, C., & Arndt, J. (2009). Creative terror management: Creativity as a facilitator of cultural exploration after mortality salience. *Personality and Social Psychology Bulletin, 35,* 493–505.

Routledge, C., Arndt, J., & Goldenberg, J. L. (2004). A time to tan: Proximal and distal effects of mortality salience on sun exposure intentions. *Personality and Social Psychology Bulletin, 30,* 1347–1358.

Routledge, C., Arndt, J., Sedikides, C., & Wildschut, T. (2008). A blast from the past: The terror management function of nostalgia. *Journal of Experimental Social Psychology, 44,* 132–140.

Routledge, C., Arndt, J., & Sheldon, K. M. (2004). Task engagement after mortality salience: The effects of creativity, conformity, and connectedness on worldview defense. *European Journal of Social Psychology, 34,* 477–487.

Routledge, C., Ostafin, B., Juhl, J., Sedikides, C., Cathey, C., & Liao, J. (2010). Adjusting to death: The effects of self-esteem and mortality salience on well-being, growth motivation, and maladaptive behavior. *Journal of Personality and Social Psychology, 99,* 897–916.

Rutjens, B. T., van der Pligt, J., & van Harreveld, F. (2009). Things will get better: The anxiety-buffering qualities of progressive hope. *Personality and Social Psychology Bulletin, 35,* 535–543.

Schimel, J., Hayes, J., Williams, T., & Jahrig, J. (2007). Is death really the worm at the core? Converging evidence that worldview threat increases death-thought accessibility. *Journal of Personality and Social Psychology, 92,* 789–803.

Schimel, J., Simon, L., Greenberg, J., Pyszczynski, T., Solomon, S., Waxmonski, J., & Arndt, J. (1999). Support for a functional perspective on stereotypes: Evidence that mortality salience enhances stereotypic thinking and preferences. *Journal of Personality and Social Psychology, 77,* 905–926.

Schmeichel, B. J., Gailliot, M. T., Filardo, E., McGregor, I., Gitter, S., & Baumeister, R. F. (2009). Terror management theory and self-esteem revisited: The roles of implicit and explicit self-esteem in mortality salience effects. *Journal of Personality and Social Psychology, 96,* 1077–1087.

Schmeichel, B. J., & Martens, A. (2005). Self-affirmation and mortality salience: Affirming values reduces worldview defense and death-thought accessibility. *Personality and Social Psychology Bulletin, 31,* 658–667.

Shehryar, O., & Hunt, D. M. (2005). A terror management perspective on the persuasiveness of fear appeals. *Journal of Consumer Psychology, 15,* 275–287.

Showers, C. J. (1992). Compartmentalization of positive and negative self-knowledge: Keeping bad apples out of the bunch. *Journal of Personality and Social Psychology, 62,* 1036–1049.

Silvia, P. J. (2001). Nothing or the opposite: Intersecting terror management and objective self-awareness. *European Journal of Personality, 15,* 73–82.

Simon, L., Greenberg, J., Harmon-Jones, E., Solomon, S., Pyszczynski, T., Arndt, J., & Abend, T. (1997). Terror management and cognitive-experiential self-theory: Evidence that terror management occurs in the experiential system. *Journal of Personality and Social Psychology, 72,* 1132–1146.

Solomon, S., Greenberg, J., & Pyszczynski, T. (1991). Terror management theory of self-esteem. In C. R. Snyder & D. R. Forsyth (Eds.), *Handbook of social and clinical psychology: The health perspective* (pp. 21–40). Elmsford, NY: Pergamon Press.

Solomon, S., Greenberg, J., Schimel, J., Arndt, J., & Pyszczynski, T. (2004). Human awareness of mortality and the evolution of culture. In M. Schaller & C. Crandall (Eds.), *The psychological foundations of culture* (pp. 15–40). New York: Erlbaum.

Steele, C. M., Spencer, S. J., & Aronson, J. (2002). Contending with group image: The psychology of stereotype and social identity threat. In M. P. Zanna (Ed.), *Advances in experimental social psychology* (pp. 379–440). San Diego, CA: Academic Press.

Taubman-Ben-Ari, O. (2004). Intimacy and risky sexual behavior: What does it have to do with death? *Death Studies, 28,* 865–887.

Thompson, M. M., Naccarato, M. E., Parker, K. C. H., & Moskowitz, G. B. (2001). The personal need for structure and personal fear of invalidity measures. In G. B. Moskowitz (Ed.), *Cognitive social psychology* (pp. 19–39). Mahwah, NJ: Erlbaum.

Tulving, E., Schacter, D. L., & Stark, H. A. (1982). Priming effects in word-fragment completion are independent of recognition memory. *Journal of Experimental Psychology: Learning, Memory, and Cognition, 8,* 336–342.

Usta, M., Williams, T. J., Haubl, G., & Schimel, J. (2010) *Vanilla or mango: The effects of mortality salience, need for structure, and the choice environment on consumer's novelty seeking.* Manuscript under review, University of Alberta.

Vail, K. E., Arndt, J., Motyl, M. S., & Pyszczynski, T. (2012). *The aftermath of destruction: Images of bombed buildings increase support for war, dogmatism, and death thought accessibility.* Manuscript under review, University of Missouri.

Vail, K. E., Vess, M., & Arndt, J. (2012). *The effect of mortality salience on abstract thought.* Manuscript in preparation, University of Missouri.

Vess, M., Routledge, C., Landau, M. J., & Arndt J. (2009). The dynamics of death and meaning: The effects of death-relevant cognitions and personal need for structure on perceptions of meaning in life. *Journal of Personality and Social Psychology, 97,* 728–744.

Wegner, D. M. (1994) Ironic processes of mental control. *Psychological Review, 101,* 34–52.

The Neuroscience of Social Cognition

David M. Amodio *and* Kyle G. Ratner

Abstract

Social neuroscience is one of the newest and most rapidly expanding areas in the field of social cognition. In this chapter, the authors describe how the social neuroscience approach has been used to address classic and contemporary issues in this field. The chapter begins with a brief primer on cognitive neuroscience that highlights major brain regions currently studied by social cognition researchers and the techniques commonly used to measure brain activity. The authors then discuss the types of questions a social neuroscience approach can address, noting critical methodological issues to consider when bridging psychological and physiological levels of analysis. Next, key social neuroscience findings across major areas of social cognition research are described, with an emphasis on how the neuroscience approach has advanced theories about social cognitive mechanism. Finally, the authors discuss some challenges and limitations of social neuroscience research and comment on its future directions.

Key Words: neuroscience, social, social cognition, brain, face perception, person perception, attitudes, prejudice, stereotypes, stereotyping, automaticity, control, self-regulation

In his foreword to the second edition of the *Handbook of Social Cognition*, Ostrom (1994) described the challenges faced by social cognition researchers at the time this approach first emerged on the social psychology scene. He noted that when the first edition of the *Handbook* was published, "many of the skeptics felt that social cognition would prove to be only a minor (and slightly offensive) digression in the history of social psychology." The publication of the present *Handbook* is a testament to the lasting impact that social cognition has had on the field. In many ways, the field of social neuroscience appears to be developing along a similar path. Much like the emergence of social cognition a quarter century earlier, the emergence of social neuroscience is characterized as an integrative, interdisciplinary approach to questions about psychological mechanism. In this way, social neuroscience is a natural extension of social cognition,

in that it addresses similar questions but with an expanded approach that incorporates models of biological pathways and new techniques of physiological measurement. Although researchers operating under the rubric of "social neuroscience" study a wide range of processes that extend far beyond the traditional concerns of social psychology and social cognition, the core contributions of social neuroscience have focused on classic social cognitive issues.

The term "social neuroscience" was used by Cacioppo and Berntson (1992; see also Carlston, 1994) to describe the broad enterprise of examining the interplay of social psychological and physiological levels of analysis. The social neuroscience approach began to appear with increasing frequency in the laboratories of social psychologists, cognitive neuroscientists, developmental psychologists, and neurologists during the 1990s. Influential reviews by Ochsner and Lieberman (2001) and Klein and

Kihlstrom (1998) incorporated contemporary ideas from cognitive neuroscience and neuropsychological patient literatures, respectively, prompting additional perspectives on social neuroscience sometimes referred to as "social cognitive neuroscience" and "social neuropsychology" (hereafter, we will use the term *social neuroscience* to encompass the broad range of approaches). Over the past decade, social neuroscience has been the subject of several dedicated research conferences, culminating in the formation of the *Social and Affective Neuroscience Society* in 2008 and the *Society for Social Neuroscience* in 2010. Whereas social neuroscience was seen as a novelty at social psychology meetings merely a decade ago, it is now approaching mainstream integration.

This review article focuses on neuroscience approaches to classic and contemporary topics in social cognition. It is notable that the topic of social cognition has been studied from several perspectives, in the context of different fields of study. Here, we focus on topics within the field of social cognition, which emerged primarily from researchers working in the social psychology and cognitive psychology traditions. In what follows, we begin with a brief primer that highlights the location of neural areas most studied by researchers examining social cognition—a section intended for readers with little or no prior knowledge about neuroscience. We then discuss methodological approaches and measures typically used in social neuroscience and describe social neuroscience research across major areas of social cognition research, with a focus on how neuroscience and physiological approaches have suggested advances in social cognition theories. Finally, we discuss some challenges and limitations of social neuroscience research and then comment on its future directions.

Primer on the Neuroanatomy of Social Cognition

Because of the complexity of social cognitive processes, as well as the preeminence of social relationships in everyday human life, it is likely that the entire nervous system contributes to social cognition to some extent. The goal of this section is to provide a brief overview of major neural structures that are most frequently implicated in social neuroscience research, with a focus on the central nervous system (i.e., the brain). It is notable, however, that responses of the peripheral nervous system, and related peripheral functions (e.g., cardiovascular, hormonal, or pulmonary), can also be assessed and may be used to inform questions about social cognition (Amodio, 2009; Blascovich, Mendes, Vanman, & Dickerson, 2011; Cacioppo & Petty, 1983; Rankin & Campbell, 1955).

Terms for Position and Orientation

Before describing neural structures, we begin with a description of the nomenclature used to refer to regions of the brain. General anatomical terms are used to refer to the position and relative orientation of brain structures. There are two different sets of terms that are used interchangeably (Figure 34.1A). One set of terms includes *anterior, posterior, superior,* and *inferior* to refer to regions located in the front, back, top, or bottom of the brain, sometimes in relation to another structure. A second set of terms derives from nonhuman animal biology and includes *rostral, caudal, dorsal,* and *ventral.* These Latinate terms refer to the nose, tail, back, and belly of an animal, but when applied to the human brain, they refer to the relative front, rear, top, and bottom (note that in nonhuman animals, the top of the head and back are oriented in the same direction, as are the bottom of the head and the belly; Figure 34.1B). The terms *medial* and *lateral* are also used to indicate areas of the brain. *Medial* refers to regions at the center of the brain or closer to the center relative to another structure. *Lateral* refers to regions toward the outer sides of either hemisphere (Figure 34.1C). Brain activations are typically overlaid onto "slices" of a structural brain scan and viewed from one of three common viewpoints: coronal (front-back), saggital (left-right), and axial/horizontal (top-bottom), as illustrated in Figure 34.1D.

Basic Brain Anatomy

The brain is composed of neural tissue, cerebral spinal fluid, and blood vessels. On the basis of developmental trajectory, the central nervous system may be divided into the rhombencephalon (hindbrain), mesencephalon (midbrain), and prosencephalon (i.e., the forebrain, which makes up the largest portion of the human brain). Most social neuroscience research has focused on the prosencephalon, specifically cortical and subcortical regions. The largest structure in the brain is the cortex, meaning "bark" in Latin. It has a corrugated surface and is formed into two hemispheres connected only by the corpus callosum and other fiber bundles. The ridges of the cortical surface are called *gyri*, and the valleys are called *sulci*. At the broadest level of demarcation, the cortex is separated into four lobes: frontal, temporal, parietal, and occipital. Later in the chapter, we discuss functions ascribed to these areas, with

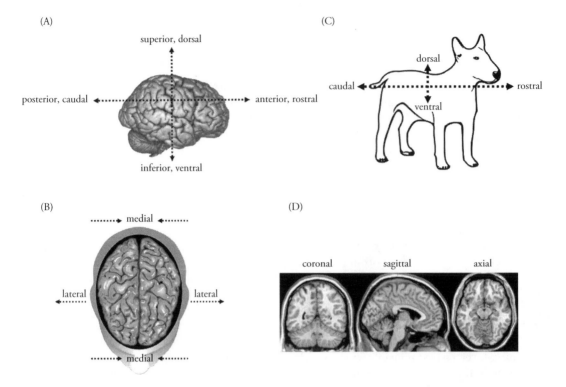

Figure 34.1 Terminology for position and orientation in brain anatomy. Relative position terms are shown in panels **A** and **B**. Components of this nomenclature were developed to describe anatomy of nonhuman animals. In most animals, like the dog in panel **C**, the back (dorsal) and belly (ventral) align with the top and bottom of the brain, respectively. In bipeds (e.g., humans), the back and belly are not parallel with the top and bottom of the head, yet these terms are still used. Panel **D** illustrates common orientations for viewing brain "slices" in human neuroimaging.

additional discussion of problems that can emerge when attempting to associate particular regions with specific functions.

Brain regions frequently studied in the social neuroscience literature are illustrated in Figures 34.2 to 34.4. The external surface of the frontal cortex includes the dorsolateral (dlPFC) and ventrolateral (vlPFC) prefrontal cortices. On the medial wall of the frontal cortex lies the medial PFC (mPFC), the orbitofrontal cortex (OFC; named for its proximity to the eyes, or "orbits"), and the anterior cingulate cortex (ACC), which may be further distinguished as the dorsal (dACC) and rostral ACC (rACC). The functions associated with these regions will be discussed in the main text of this chapter.

Other brain structures examined in the social neuroscience literature are located beneath the cortex. These include the *basal ganglia*, a large set of nuclei that include the caudate and putamen (collectively called the striatum), as well as the nucleus accumbens, globus pallidus, and the substantia nigra. The hippocampus runs along the center of the temporal lobe, and the *amygdala*, a set of nuclei

named for its almond shape, is located just rostral to the hippocampus within the anterior temporal lobe. The basal ganglia, hippocampus, and amygdala are referred to as subcortical structures because they are located below the cortical layer. Subcortical structures are also distinguished from the cortex by differences in their cellular composition.

Other frequently studied regions include the *insula*, located at the intersection of the frontal and temporal lobe, the *fusiform gyrus*, on the ventral surface of the posterior temporal lobe, and the *temporoparietal junction* (TPJ). Primary and secondary visual areas are located in the occipital cortex.

Although the neural structures listed above, and illustrated in Figures 34.2 to 34.4, are the most frequently studied in the contemporary social neuroscience literature, they represent just a small subset of the complex network of interacting brain structures involved in social cognition and behavior. It is also notable that neural computations take place at the cellular and molecular levels of analysis, yet the most commonly used human neuroimaging techniques, such as functional magnetic resonance imaging

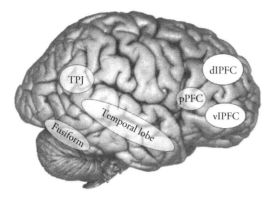

Figure 34.2 Lateral surface of the right hemisphere of the brain. dlPFC, dorsolateral prefrontal cortex; vlPFC, ventrolateral prefrontal cortex; pPFC, posterior prefrontal cortex; TPJ, temporoparietal junction.

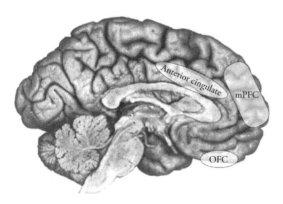

Figure 34.3 Medial view of the left hemisphere of the brain. mPFC, medial prefrontal cortex; OFC, orbital frontal cortex.

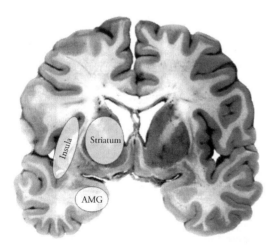

Figure. 34.4 View of coronal slice through brain, with structures on the left side labeled. AMG, amygdala.

(fMRI) and electroencephalography (EEG), assess brain activity on a much larger scale that reflects the activity of groups of neurons. Thus, a mechanistic understanding of neural function requires a consideration of how cellular and molecular-level processes may contribute to the kinds of signals assessed by neuroimaging techniques. For more comprehensive introductions to neural anatomy and function, we recommend reading a graduate-level neuroscience textbook (e.g., Kandel, Schwartz, & Jessel, 2000) and consulting any of the many human brain atlases available online (e.g., www.med.harvard.edu/aanlib; www.msu.edu/~brains) and in print (e.g., Damasio, 2005).

The Social Neuroscience Approach

We begin our review by describing the two main types of questions asked in human social neuroscience, which correspond to two different methodological approaches. We discuss how each may contribute to psychological ideas related to social cognition, and we describe the critical role of reverse inference in drawing conclusions from social neuroscience findings.

Brain Mapping Approach

Brain mapping studies ask, "Where in the brain is _____?" For example, where in the brain is fear? Where is episodic memory? Where is love? Where is the self? Human brain mapping is a cornerstone of modern cognitive neuroscience. It concerns the mapping of basic psychological processes to physiological processes, such as those linked to particular structures or networks within the brain.

Early forms of brain mapping involved the probing of exposed brain tissue by a neurosurgeon while the awake patient reported his or her experience. Today, relatively noninvasive neuroimaging measures, such as fMRI, are often used for a similar purpose. In cognitive neuroscience, this approach is used to map relatively low-level psychological processes such as basic forms of sensation, perception, and specific aspects of learning and memory. As a general rule, lower-level cognitive processes can be mapped more directly onto specific neural responses than can relatively higher-level processes.

In social neuroscience investigations, researchers often attempt to map very high-level psychological processes, such as social emotions, the self-concept, trait impressions, and political attitudes, onto the brain. This is where things get trickier. For example, to study the neural basis of romantic love, researchers have scanned participants' brains while they viewed pictures of strangers or their significant others (e.g., Aron, Fisher, Mashek, Strong, Li, & Brown, 2005). Similarly, to study the neural basis of the self, researchers have scanned the brain while subjects judged whether trait adjectives described them or another person (Kelley et al., 2002; Mitchell, Banaji, & Macrae, 2005). When examining the difference in brain activity (i.e., a *contrast*) between trials concerning the self and trials concerning others, a researcher might interpret any activated regions as a neural locus of "the self." A potential problem with this approach is that high-level social psychological phenomena often reflect the emergent properties of several lower-level mechanisms. Thus, a pattern of brain activity observed in response to a psychological task might reflect the abstract psychological construct of interest directly, but it is more likely to reflect lower-level cognitive and physiological components related to the psychological construct. Although high-level psychological ascriptions of brain activity may have heuristic value, they risk obscuring the important low-level mechanisms that the observed brain activations likely represent.

A defining feature of the brain mapping approach is that it seeks to create a valid mapping of psychological processes onto structures or networks within the brain. Pure brain mapping studies are undertaken with few prior assumptions about the psychological function of a brain region. Indeed, the point of such studies is to establish ideas about function through the process of induction across multiple studies using a variety of conceptually similar tasks and manipulations. This approach is potentially useful for generating new ideas about commonalities in the cognitive processes that may underlie two otherwise distinct psychological functions. For example, some researchers have observed that the experiences of social exclusion and physical pain both activate a similar region of the ACC (see Figure 34.3), among many other non-overlapping areas. This result has led some to conclude that social and physical pain share some common neurocognitive features (Eisenberger, Lieberman, & Williams, 2003; but see Somerville, Heatherton, & Kelley, 2006). Although this observed overlap does not tell us exactly how or why social exclusion and pain might be related, simply because the true function of the neural activity is difficult to discern, it nevertheless suggests new ideas about potential relationships between psychological processes.

Hypothesis Testing Approach

The hypothesis testing approach in social neuroscience is used to test relationships between

psychological variables. This approach begins with the assumption that a particular brain region reflects a specific psychological process. In this regard, it does not involve brain mapping, but instead relies on past brain mapping studies that have already established the validity of neural indicators. For example, a social psychologist who studies intergroup prejudice might hypothesize that implicit racial bias is rooted in mechanisms of classic fear conditioning (Amodio, Harmon-Jones, & Devine, 2003). To test this hypothesis, one might measure brain activity in the amygdala (see Figure 34.4)—a structure implicated in fear conditioning in many studies—while a participant completes a behavioral measure of implicit racial bias. In this case, the construct validity of the neural measure of fear conditioning (amygdala activity) is already reasonably established (but see Amodio & Ratner, 2011a), and the question concerns not the meaning of brain activations, but rather the experimental effects of psychological variables. Whereas brain mapping studies typically inform our understanding of the brain, hypothesis testing studies typically inform psychological theories.

Critically, brain mapping and psychological hypothesis testing approaches should not be combined within a single analysis because major inferential problems can occur as a result (Amodio, 2010a). This is because a test of a psychological hypothesis assumes that the mapping of a psychological variable to a neural structure is already established (i.e., that the neural measure has construct validity). When these approaches are combined into a single analytical step, there is a risk of defining the neural operationalization of a psychological construct on the basis of whether it supports one's theoretical hypothesis—an example of tautological inference (see Amodio, 2010a, for a detailed discussion). This practice is what produces the inflated "voodoo correlations" described by Vul et al. (2009). It is important to note that this problem is rooted in the conceptual logic of validity and scientific inference and cannot be fully addressed through statistical corrections or improvements in measurement reliability (Barrett, 2009). These concerns are of special relevance to the field of social neuroscience because, in this field, the psychological constructs tend to be most abstract and thus most difficult to operationalize in the brain.

Reverse Inference

When interpreting the psychological significance of a brain activation, researchers must often rely on *reverse inference* (Poldrack, 2006). In brain mapping studies, a psychological process is manipulated, and the resulting pattern of brain activity is observed. The inference that the psychological manipulation produced the brain activity may be described as a *forward inference*, in that the brain activity clearly followed from the manipulation. This inference is based on the known validity of the manipulation. By contrast, the inference of a psychological process from an observed pattern of brain activity is a *reverse inference*. In this case, the precise meaning of the brain activation is ambiguous and inferred based on the results of prior studies that may have observed activity in the same area caused by a different manipulation.

As a hypothetical example, imagine that viewing pictures of a romantic partner activated a specific region of participants' frontal cortex in an fMRI study. In a previous study, this very same region was activated while participants received cash rewards. Given this previous finding, the experimenter might assume that this brain region is the "monetary reward" area, and that viewing pictures of a romantic partner induced the feeling of winning cash. This conclusion would reflect a reverse inference about the meaning of activity in this region that is based on faulty logic about causailty. Furthermore, this type of inference assumes a one-to-one mapping between a neural activation and a psychological construct—an assumption unlikely to be valid given the complexity of both neural and psychological processes.

The practice of reverse inference becomes increasingly problematic to the extent that the source of inference—in this case, a brain activation—could reflect different psychological processes (Cacioppo et al., 2003; Poldrack, 2006). In studies of low-level vision, for example, reverse inference may be a comparatively lesser problem (but still a concern). But as psychological variables become more complex, as they do with cognitive and social processes, the mapping between a particular brain region and a psychological process becomes less certain. In these cases, reverse inference can be a serious problem.

All cognitive and social neuroscience studies rely on reverse inference. That is, to the extent that a neural activation is interpreted as reflecting a psychological process, the use of reverse inference is unavoidable. Yet researchers can take steps to bolster the strength of a reverse psychological inference. This can be done by enhancing the construct validity of a neural indicator and the strength of their experimental designs, such as through the careful use

of theory, converging evidence from other studies (including animal research), and the use of behavioral tasks that provide valid manipulations of a construct and interpretable behavioral data (Amodio, 2010a). Large-scale fMRI data repositories and meta-analytic software are currently in development (e.g., neurosynth.org, sumsdb.wustl.edu, brainmap.org) that will eventually assist researchers in quantifying the validity of their reverse inferences. These tools take into account evidence from prior research linking brain areas of interest with various functions (Yarkoni, Poldrack, Nichols, Van Essen & Wager, 2011). Of course, even with these exciting emerging advances, researchers will always have to be cautious in interpreting their data because of known meta-analytic challenges, such as the "file drawer" problem (tendency for null or inconclusive findings to go unpublished) and differences in the methods and experimental rigor used across studies.

What Types of Social Cognition Questions Are Amenable to a Neuroscience Analysis?

First and foremost, the brain is a *mechanism*, and an extremely complex one at that. Hence, neuroscience models and methods are primarily useful for the study of psychological mechanisms, such as those involved in action control, perception, and attention. In this regard, the social neuroscience approach is especially well suited to the study of social cognition. However, psychological questions that refer to phenomena, rather than to mechanisms, are less amenable to a neuroscience level of analysis. For a social cognitive psychologist who is considering the potential benefit of a neuroscience approach, the most critical issue is whether one's question concerns basic psychological mechanism. Can the components of one's mechanistic model be described in terms of low-level functions, such as perception, sensation, low-level cognition, and low-level motivation? If so, then neuroscience models may be particularly useful. If a psychological phenomenon of interest cannot be conceptualized at a lower level of analysis, but instead is most meaningful at a high level of construal, then it may be more difficult to make valid inferential connections between a psychological construct and brain activity.

Neuroimaging Methods Commonly Used in Social Neuroscience Research

Contemporary social neuroscience makes use of a wide range of methods, often in combination with the more traditional tools of social cognition. Here, we describe the most prominent methods currently used in the field and briefly discuss their relative advantages as they relate to experimental designs, issues of construct validity, and psychological inference. A more comprehensive description of methods used in social neuroscience is provided by Harmon-Jones and Beer (2009).

Early studies taking a social neuroscience approach primarily used peripheral physiological methods, such as electrocardiogram (e.g., heart rate), galvanic skin response (i.e., skin conductance), and electromyography (e.g., measures of facial muscle activity related to emotional expressions). More recently, neuroimaging methods have become particularly important and, as such, tend to dominate the literature. These techniques include fMRI, which measures the flow of oxygenated blood in the brain, and EEG, which measures electrical activity produced from the firing of neuron populations. EEG activity in response to a discrete event, such as a stimulus or subject response, is called an event-related potential (ERP). These methods differ in important and complementary ways. FMRI yields relatively high spatial resolution and is thus optimal for determining the specific location of a brain activation. But because it assesses blood flow, its temporal resolution is slow relative to neural activity. By comparison, EEG/ERP assesses brain activity at a very high temporal resolution, but with relatively poor spatial resolution. Thus, it is optimal for assessing the timing of a neural process. Given their relative strengths, researchers may use fMRI or EEG techniques to suit their particular question, or use both approaches in complementary studies within a program of research. Neuroimaging and psychophysiological approaches may also be combined with measures of hormones, immune processes, and DNA, for example, to provide convergent evidence for a physiological process of interest. However, as with well-established methods in social cognition, the utility of these measures depends on the quality of the question, the experimental paradigm, and careful interpretation.

Major Content Areas of Social Neuroscience

The core themes of social cognition concern issues of mechanism. These range from domain-general processes such as automaticity and control to more specific processes, such as person perception, social evaluation, and mentalizing. The prominence of these themes in the social cognition literature is mirrored in the social neuroscience literature, and in this section we provide a review of how the social neuroscience approach has been used to address them.

Automatic and Controlled Processing

Theories of automatic and controlled processes form a cornerstone of modern social cognition research. Mechanisms of automaticity and control also constitute a central topic in cognitive psychology, and a large body of cognitive neuroscience research has been devoted to their elucidation.

AUTOMATICITY AND IMPLICIT PROCESSES

Automaticity refers to the processes through which actions are initiated without a person's intention or awareness. The most common instance of automaticity is when a response is triggered by an external cue, such as the urge to drink after seeing an actor in a movie open a beer, or to walk more slowly after reading words associated with elderly people (Bargh, Chen, & Burrows, 1996). Automatic processes sometimes include additional characteristics, such as efficiency and a resistance to control (Bargh, 1994). Automaticity is also sometimes used to describe the activation of psychological states, such as thoughts or feelings, in addition to actions.

A common characteristic of an automatic process is that it is implicit—that is, not accessible to conscious awareness. Although sometimes used interchangeably, "automatic" and "implicit" refer to different constructs. The distinction between automaticity and control refers primarily to the degree of intention associated with a response. By contrast, the distinction between implicit and explicit refers to whether a response, or any psychological processes, is subject to awareness. In behavioral research, automaticity and implicitness almost always covary. But because neural and physiological measures are better able to assess responses that occur below consciousness, they tend to be more informative about implicitness than about automaticity.

In the social cognition literature, early demonstrations of automaticity were made using sequential priming tasks, when a prime word was shown to facilitate the categorization of an associated target word without a participant's awareness or intention (Gaertner & McLaughlin, 1983; Dovidio, Evans, & Tyler, 1986). This idea of automatic semantic priming was originally adapted from cognitive psychology research examining basic semantic associations between words, such as "bread–butter" or "doctor–nurse" (Meyer & Schaneveldt, 1971, 1976). Research on the neural processes associated with semantic priming has generally found evidence of activations in the left posterior PFC (see Figure 34.2; e.g., Blaxton et al., 1996; Demb et al., 1995; Raichle et al., 1994, Wagner, Gabrieli, & Verfaellie, 1997) and temporal cortex (see Figure 34.2; Rissman, Eliassen, & Blumstein, 2003; Schacter & Buckner, 1998; Squire, 1992), and *deactivations* in regions linked to attention (e.g., in the parietal cortex; see Figure 34.2; Gabrieli, 1998). Given other research implicating the left PFC in approach-related motivation and action tendencies (Harmon-Jones, 2003), this pattern of neural activations suggests a link between automatic semantic processes and goal-driven behavior (Amodio, 2008), consistent with the idea that "thinking is for doing" (Fiske, 1992).

Much of the neuroscience research relevant to issues of automaticity and implicit processes has been conducted in the area of learning and memory. Classic models of memory distinguish between two general categories of memory on the basis of awareness: explicit and implicit (Cohen & Squire, 1980; Graf & Schacter, 1985). Explicit (declarative) systems typically include episodic and explicit semantic forms of memory, whereas implicit (nondeclarative) systems include classical conditioning, semantic priming, procedural memory (i.e., habit learning), and reflex modification (Squire & Zola, 1996). These different forms of memory have been linked to different underlying neural mechanisms, suggesting the existence of multiple memory "systems." Explicit forms of memory, such as episodic memory and explicit aspects of semantic memory, have been associated primarily with activity in the hippocampus and temporal lobe. By comparison, different forms of implicit memory are associated with different brain regions. Classical fear conditioning has been linked to circuitry within the amygdala, whereas procedural memory and reward conditioning have been shown to involve the striatum (see Figure 34.4). Implicit forms of semantic memory and conceptual priming effects have been associated with regions of the PFC and temporal lobes. Evidence for the separation of these memory systems came initially from studies of patients with a brain lesion, in which damage to a particular system results in selective impairments in the associated type of learning and memory (Squire & Zola, 1996). These findings have been corroborated in many fMRI studies (Poldrack & Foerde, 2008). More recently, social cognition researchers have begun to use findings from this literature to refine theories about automatic (vs. controlled) and implicit (vs. explicit) processes (Amodio, 2008; Amodio & Ratner, 2011b).

Relatively few studies have used social neuroscience approaches to examine automatic social cognition directly. But of these studies, several have examined the automatic activation of racial bias, with a focus on the role of the amygdala as a substrate of implicit fear associations. These studies have observed greater amygdala activity in response to Black compared with White faces among White American participants using measures that can assess rapid amygdala responses following the presentation of a face (Amodio, Harmon-Jones, & Devine, 2003) or slower activation in response to near-subliminal presentation of faces (Cunningham et al., 2004). In research on self-schemas, Lieberman, Jarcho, & Satpute (2004) measured brain activity while subjects judged themselves on traits related to domains in which they were highly schematic (i.e., had expertise) or were aschematic (low expertise). Lieberman et al. (2004) reasoned that self-judgments related to highly schematic domains would involve automatic systems to a greater extent than judgments concerning aschematic domains. They found that judgments of familiar domain terms were associated with greater activity in the amygdala, ventral mPFC, and basal ganglia regions of the brain (e.g., the striatum)—regions linked to automatic and/or implicit processes in other research.

As noted above, automaticity refers to modes of cognition and action that are characterized by the properties of unintentionality, unawareness, uncontrollability, and efficiency, or some subset of these (Bargh, 1994). However, it is often difficult to distinguish among these properties using traditional behavioral methods because these properties tend to covary highly in observable behavior. Neuroscience research has been useful in parsing the mechanisms associated with the different properties of automaticity. For the present purposes, it is notable that the degree of awareness associated with these systems does not always correspond with the degree of intentionality (i.e., the extent to which it is goal driven). For example, classic fear conditioning describes a learned response to a threatening stimulus that is largely reflexive and thus not intentional. Procedural memory, by contrast, is an instrumental process that is goal driven by definition, and thus represents an intentional process that may unfold without awareness and may be difficult to inhibit. As another example, the implicit activation of semantic associations may occur without intention, but their activation may instigate goal-driven responses (e.g., ideomotor responses), thereby linking them to intentional responses. Considered together, the cognitive neuroscience research on implicit memory systems supports and expands on

Bargh's (1994) position that automaticity is not one construct, but rather is a broad category of processes that may differ in multiple ways. This literature also reveals that the important differences in the functions of implicit processes are not usefully captured by the implicit—explicit distinction, and this is why a multisystem approach is more useful for understanding mechanisms of social cognition (Amodio & Ratner, 2011b; Henke, 2010).

CONTROL

Within the fields of social psychology and cognitive psychology, control refers to the process of responding in an appropriate and intentional manner despite the existence of countervailing forces. Social and cognitive neuroscience research on the process of control has made major advances in elucidating the mechanisms involved in control. Whereas traditional social cognitive models typically assume a single mode of controlled processing, neuroscience research has suggested important distinctions among subcomponents of control, such as the actors' detection that control is needed, the implementation of an intended response, and the inhibition of unintended responses. Research is also beginning to distinguish mechanisms for proactive and corrective (or reactive) forms of control. Here, we describe the cognitive neuroscience research on these components of control and how these findings have been applied to questions of social cognition.

Conflict Monitoring

Corrective forms of control are engaged when a response tendency begins to deviate from one's intended response. Such cases reflect a conflict between one's intended response and some alternative tendency, and in order for corrective control to be engaged, this conflict must be detected as the response unfolds. Cognitive neuroscience research on response conflict tasks, such as the color-naming Stroop task, have examined brain activity that occurs during high-conflict trials, such as when the meaning of a color-identifying word (e.g., "red") interferes with one's goal to name the ink color in which the word appears (e.g., "black"; Carter et al., 1998; MacDonald et al., 2000). These studies revealed that activity in the dorsal ACC was particularly strong during response conflict trials. In light of these findings, Botvinick et al. (2001) proposed that the ACC supports a *conflict monitoring* function, such that it is involved in detecting conflict between alternative motor impulses. Furthermore, when conflict arises, the ACC signals regions of the PFC that function

to implementing one's intended response over other tendencies. An important feature of the conflict monitoring theory is that the monitoring process operates implicitly, without the need for deliberation or awareness (Berns, Cohen, & Mintun, 1997; Nieuwenhuis, Ridderinkhof, Blom, Band, & Kok, 2001). ACC activity linked to conflict monitoring is also associated with passive behavioral inhibition (Amodio, Master, Yee, & Taylor, 2008). That is, when conflict is detected, a person's response speed slows as the person allocates greater attention to the potential source of conflict as well as their task goals (Gehring et al., 1993). This type of passive inhibition is distinguishable from active forms of inhibitory control that involve the intentional stopping of a response.

Knowledge gained from cognitive neuroscience research on conflict monitoring and control has been applied to test theories of self-regulation in contexts such as stereotyping and prejudice (Amodio et al., 2004, 2006, 2008; Bartholow, Dickter, & Sestir, 2006), behavioral inhibition processes (Amodio, Master, et al., 2008), political orientation (Amodio, Jost, Master, & Yee, 2007), religiosity (Inzlicht, McGregor, Hirsh, & Nash, 2009), and social exclusion (Eisenberger et al., 2003). It is notable that some researchers have suggested that ACC activity on control tasks may represent a distress signal or social pain (Eisenberger et al., 2003; Inzlicht et al., 2009). However, the fact that the ACC is consistently activated by cognitive tasks that do not involve any type of distress or pain is a problem for these interpretations (Shackman et al., 2011). For example, participants in a study by Nieuwenhuis et al. (2001) completed an antisaccade task—a measure of cognitive conflict and control. On each trial of this task, a fixation point appears, followed by a target (e.g., a small circle) on either the right or left side of the computer screen. On some trials, participants are instructed to look toward the target, but on other trials, they are instructed to look away, in the opposite direction of the target. This task is interesting because automatic saccades to the appearance of a target are very difficult to control. Furthermore, people often do not realize they made an error on this task. Indeed, after each trial in the Nieuwenhuis et al. study, participants reported whether they had made an error; on average, participants made errors on 18.6% of the trials, but they perceived their error on less than half of these trials (7.4% perceived vs. 11.2% unperceived). Nevertheless, ACC activity, as indexed by the error-related negativity (ERN) component of the ERP, was elicited for both perceived and unperceived errors to an equal extent, in comparison with correct responses. Results from this study, among others, suggest that ACC activations on such tasks are not simply due to experienced affect, pain, or distress (although these responses are sometimes observed to co-occur). Rather, anatomical research on monkeys has revealed that the ACC is strongly interconnected with motor structures as well as PFC regions associated with high-level representations of goals and actions, suggesting that the conflict reflected by ACC activity refers to a mismatch between higher level goals and lower level motor responses (Miller & Cohen, 2001; Shackman et al., 2011).

Implementation of Control

Once the need for control is detected and signaled by the ACC, a set of controlled processes become engaged, and these are largely associated with activity in regions of the PFC. At the neuroanatomical level, PFC regions associated with control have the most extensive connections with structures associated with goal-driven action (Fuster, 2001; Passingham, 1993). A general pattern of connectivity also involves inputs from the thalamus and sensory regions to the medial and orbital frontal cortices, associated with the selection of action-relevant information, and output from lateral PFC areas to structures associated with the planning and implementation of action, such as the basal ganglia and motor cortices (Miller & Cohen, 2001). This evidence is relevant for understanding how social cognitive processes are regulated because it suggests that mechanisms of control operate primarily on motor, attentional, and perceptual processes.

Cognitive neuroscience research has revealed at least three different forms of motor control that have been linked to separate underlying neural mechanisms. First, goal-directed action refers to motor responses that reflect an intended response. The implementation of a goal-directed behavioral response involves bidirectional connections between the PFC and the striatum (i.e., the frontostriatal loop), which operates in concert with thalamic and midbrain processes (Middleton & Strick, 2000; Yin & Knowlton, 2006). Control, in the form of goal-directed action, tends to involve left-lateralized PFC activity in right-handed individuals. Research has shown that stronger left PFC activity is associated with the active control of behavior in such contexts as regulating intergroup behaviors (Amodio, 2010b; Amodio et al., 2007), obtaining rewards (Pizzagalli, Sherwood, Henriques, & Davidson, 2005), and instrumental aggression (Harmon-Jones & Sigelman, 2001).

A second form of control is active inhibition—the intentional stopping of a response. Active inhibition has been linked to right PFC activity, particularly in the right inferior frontal cortex (Aron, Robbins, & Poldrack, 2004). Social neuroscience research examining participants' responses to outgroup in comparison with ingroup faces has observed activity in the right inferior PFC, which might reflect the participants' attempt to withhold a potentially race-biased response (Cunningham et al., 2004; Lieberman, Hariri, Jarcho, Eisenberger, & Bookheimer, 2005).

A third form of motor control pertains to eye movements. Oculomotor networks constitute an important interface between action and perception in the context of control, and the control of eye movements is associated with activity in dorsal regions of the PFC (Brodmann's area 8) referred to as the "frontal eyefield." Although few studies of social cognition have examined the role of eye movement control, some research has shown that the regulation of emotional response may be accomplished by intentionally looking away from aversive stimuli (van Reekum et al., 2007), an idea consistent with classic social psychological work on impulse inhibition among children (Mischel, 1974). Given the field's renewed interest in the role of attention and perception in mechanisms of control (e.g., Amodio, 2010b), we expect that this form of control will receive greater attention from social cognitive theorists in the near future. Importantly, these three forms of control work in coordination, as suggested by their integrated neural connections.

Models of PFC anatomy and function also highlight the effects of control on sensory and perceptual processing. Through dense connections to the thalamus and other sensory structures (Barbas & Zikopoulos, 2007), the PFC is believed to play a role in selecting motivationally relevant sensory signals while suppressing irrelevant information, in the service of task goals. The PFC continues to modulate the perception of sensory inputs through connections to visual and auditory association cortices (Medalla, Lera, Feinberg, & Barbas, 2007). In an fMRI study of visual processing, efforts to ignore (vs. remember) a visual stimulus were associated with lower activity in the visual association cortex, and this effect was modulated by activity in the left PFC (Gazzaley et al., 2007). Additionally, studies of pain regulation found that PFC activity was associated with changes in the perception of pain (Salomons, Johnstone, Backonja, Shackman, & Davidson, 2007; Wager et al., 2004). These findings suggest that control regions of the

PFC function to regulate sensory input as well as higher level perceptual processes, presumably in the service of facilitating goal-driven action. These aspects of control have not yet been integrated into social cognitive theories, but they represent promising avenues for future research.

In summary, social and cognitive neuroscience research has helped to expand and refine social cognitive models of automaticity and control. In particular, this research has delineated different mechanisms within the broad categories of automatic and controlled processes. These new models make more specific predictions for how automatic and controlled processes interact and are expressed in behavior. Furthermore, these new models have shifted attention away from phenomenological properties of automaticity and control, such as their degree of implicitness vs. explicitness, and toward functional accounts of these processes that are more useful for understanding social cognitive mechanism and behavior (Amodio & Ratner, 2011b).

The Self

The self is one of social psychology's oldest and most enduring constructs, and, not surprisingly, it was among the first constructs to be examined in neuroscientific studies of social psychological processes (e.g., Craik et al., 1999; Klein, Loftus, & Kihlstrom, 1996). Most of this research has examined brain activity associated with self-reflection and judgments about the self in comparison to judgments of others. Using positron emission tomography (PET) to measure changes in brain activity, Craik et al. (1999) found that judgments of trait words as relating to the self, in comparison with other people, were associated with large activations in regions of the mPFC. In a similar study that used fMRI, Kelley et al. (2002) found that when comparing self-judgments of trait words with other-judgments (of George W. Bush), a region of ventral mPFC was more strongly activated. The association between self-related processes and activity in ventral regions of the mPFC has since been replicated in several studies (e.g., Gutchess et al., 2007; Heatherton et al., 2006; Kircher et al., 2002; Pfeifer et al., 2007; Saxe, Moran, Scholz, & Gabrieli, 2006; Schmitz, Kawahara-Baccus, & Johnson, 2004; Turner, Simons, Gilbert, Frith, & Burgess, 2008; Zhu, Zhang, Fan, & Han, 2007). Research on other aspects of the self, such as agency and self-discrepancies, have observed regions of the brain typically involved in more general aspects of visual perception, conflict monitoring, and cognitive control (Blakemore, Oakley, & Frith, 2003;

Farrer et al., 2008). Thus, brain activations during self-related judgments may not reflect regions dedicated to the self per se, but rather regions supporting domain-general processes that are recruited during self-judgment tasks.

Other research has examined the process of self-monitoring in social situations. In this area of work, self-monitoring refers to the continuous process by which individuals evaluate their behavior as it relates to the expectations of and experiences with others. Studies have observed that individuals with damage to the OFC (see Figure 34.3) are impaired in several aspects of self-monitoring. For example, it has been shown that patients with OFC damage have an impaired ability to prioritize solutions to interpersonal problems (Saver & Damasio, 1991), a tendency to greet strangers in an overly familiar manner (Rolls, Hornak, Wade, & McGrath, 1994), and a tendency to behave in disruptive manners in hospital settings (Blair & Cipolotti, 2000). They also tease strangers inappropriately and are more likely to disclose unnecessary personal information when answering questions (Beer, Heerey, Keltner, Scabini, & Knight, 2003; Kaczmarek, 1984). These findings are consistent with theories suggesting that the OFC supports the monitoring of external social signals (Amodio & Frith, 2006)

Although neuroimaging research on the self is an important area of inquiry in social cognitive neuroscience, the findings of this area of research must be considered in light of some complicated interpretational problems. For example, in Kelley et al. (2002), mPFC activity during judgments of the self and other were both lower compared with baseline; that is, compared with baseline resting trials, mPFC activity was higher when participants thought about the self than another person, but the level of activity for both types of judgments was lower than when participants simply rested while viewing a fixation cross between trials. Thus, in absolute terms, self-related activity is usually associated with a deactivation in mPFC activity. This is a problem for the interpretation that this region of the mPFC represents the self because it suggests that this "self region" is more active during baseline trials than when a person is actively engaged in self-reflection. This observation has led some researchers to suggest that participants must spontaneously focus on the self when at rest (to a greater extent than when explicitly instructed to think about the self), prompting the theory that the mPFC is part of a baseline "default" network of brain activity that may be related to the self (e.g., Gusnard, Akbudak, Shulman, & Raichle, 2001; Gusnard & Raichle, 2001). Interestingly, the idea that humans reflect on the self by default is inconsistent with studies showing that, when beeped at random points during the day and asked to report on what they were doing at the moment, participants rarely (8% of 4,700 responses) reported that they were engaged in some form of self-reflection (Csikszentmihalyi & Figurski, 1982). Thus, the notion that people naturally think about themselves during unconstrained periods does not seem to be supported by behavioral research. Ultimately, a construct like "the self" may be too broad and complex to be localized to a circumscribed set of neural structures (Gillihan & Farah, 2005). Rather, it would be more fruitful to consider the neural processes linked to the lower level psychological mechanisms from which the phenomenon of "the self" emerges.

Person Perception

Person perception refers to the set of processes involved in encoding an object as a person, inferring that person's attributes and mental states, and preparing to interact. Social neuroscience research has been especially active in examining these processes.

Visual Perception of Faces

Information about conspecifics and social relationships is eminent in perception and cognition, and the initial stage of social processes often begins with face perception. Research on visual perception suggests that some components of the visual system, such as the fusiform gyrus, are specialized for seeing faces (see Figure 34.2; Kanwisher, McDermot, & Chun, 1997). Although the idea of a specialized face area has been debated, with some arguing that fusiform responses to faces reflect expertise rather than a "face module" (Gauthier, Skudlarski, Gore, & Anderson, 2000), or that face perception involves a more distributed network of neural structures (Haxby, Hoffman, & Gobbini, 2000), the finding that this region responds to faces more than to other objects is consistent across the literature.

Faces are also known to elicit a characteristic ERP component that peaks 170 milliseconds (ms) after the presentation of a face. This N170 component is consistently larger to faces than nonface stimuli matched on other visual dimensions (Bentin, Allison, Puce, Perez, & McCarthy, 1996; Carmel & Bentin, 2002), and it is believed to represent the structural encoding of facial features as a coherent "face" (e.g., Eimer, 2000). The N170 arises from activity in multiple temporo-occipital structures linked to face processing (Deffke et al., 2007), including the fusiform (e.g., Haxby et al., 2000; Allison et al., 1994) and the occipital-temporal sulcus (e.g., Desimone, 1991; Perrett, Rolls, & Caan, 1982). Thus, the N170 is a valuable neural marker of the engagement of early face-specific perception processes.

Social psychologists have begun to apply ideas and methods from the cognitive neuroscience literature on face processing to questions about person perception. Much of this work has examined differences in the early processing of faces representing members of the ingroup or outgroup. Using fMRI, Golby, Eberhardt, Chiao, and Gabrieli (2001) observed greater activity in the fusiform gyrus in response to ingroup than outgroup faces, and this difference predicted later recognition of the faces (Figure 34.5A). These results suggest that ingroup members are given priority in face processing because of their social relevance.

More recently, differences in visual processing of ingroup and outgroup members has been examined using ERPs, with a focus on the N170. To date, this literature has been rather mixed: in studies comparing responses to racial ingroup versus outgroup faces, some have observed larger N170 responses to ingroup faces (Ito & Urland, 2005), others have observed larger N170s to outgroup faces (Walker, Silvert, Hewstone, & Nobre, 2008), and several have reported no difference (Caldara, Rossion, Bovet, & Hauert, 2004; Caldara et al., 2003; He, Johnson, Dovidio, & McCarthy, 2009; Wiese, Stahl, & Schweinberger, 2009). However, the experimental tasks used in these studies have varied widely, and few studies have controlled for important visual differences between the faces of people from different racial groups (e.g., luminance, contrast). Therefore, we suspect that the mixed findings in this literature reflect particular differences in stimuli and task design. To control for extraneous variables when examining the visual perception of ingroup and outgroup members, Ratner and Amodio (2013) used a minimal group categorization task to separate faces into the participants' ingroup and outgroup. EEG was recorded from participants while they viewed and classified faces of white males who were purported to belong to their ingroup or outgroup. The N170 ERP component was derived from this EEG recording. Ratner and Amodio found that the N170 response was larger to ingroup faces than outgroup faces (Figure 34.5B). Because the ingroup is typically more salient in the minimal group context (in which the outgroup is not known as a threat), this finding is consistent with the idea that faces from motivationally salient social groups receive enhanced visual processing.

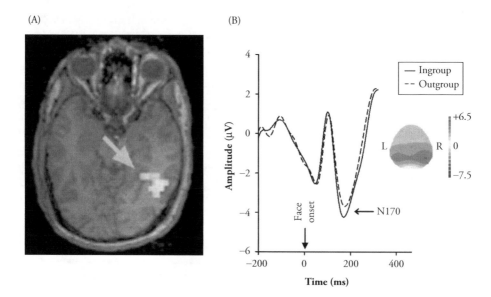

Figure 34.5 Visual processing of ingroup faces is often enhanced in comparison to outgroup faces, as indicated by (A) activity in the fusiform gyrus (Golby et al., 2001) and greater activity in the face-specific N170 event-related potential, which occurs just 170 milliseconds following face presentation (Ratner & Amodio, 2013).

Ofan, Rubin, and Amodio (2011) conducted a study to test whether N170 differences to racial ingroup and outgroup faces might be related to automatic racial attitudes. In their study, White American participants completed a sequential evaluative priming task in which White and Black face primes were followed by positive and negative words. The participant's task was to quickly categorize words as pleasant or unpleasant. In intergroup contexts in which the outgroup is stereotyped as threatening, outgroup members tend to be more salient to perceivers than ingroup members. Indeed, participants' behavior revealed stronger negative associations with Black faces than with White faces. Importantly, Ofan et al. (2011) observed that stronger pro-White bias in task behavior was associated with larger N170 responses to Black compared with White faces. This finding suggests that participants' existing implicit racial associations may have affected the way they visually perceived ingroup as opposed to outgroup faces: Those with stronger racial bias perceptually tuned to the threatening outgroup face.

Affective Responses to Faces

Affective processes associated with the amygdala have also been linked to the rapid evaluation of faces (Todorov, Said, Engell, & Oosterhof, 2008; Whalen et al., 1998). The amygdala receives inputs from sensory areas, either directly or through the thalamus, and thus it is responsive to the earliest stages of perception (Figure 34.6). Given its important role in coordinating freezing and avoidance behaviors, as well as instrumental approach behaviors, the rapid amygdala response to faces appears to provide an extremely adaptive mechanism for responding to social cues. Indeed, in several studies, Todorov and colleagues (2008; Engell, Haxby, & Todorov, 2007) have shown that the amygdala may be involved in assessing signs of threat or untrustworthiness in early stages of face processing. Other research has observed that patients with amygdala damage have impaired responses to faces expressing fear (Adophs, Tranel, Damasio, & Damasio, 1994; Vuilleumier, Richardson, Armony, Driver, & Dolan, 2004). Through diverse interconnections throughout the brain, the amygdala serves as an important hub for integrating multiple person perception processes, such as attention, emotion, and memory.

Research on implicit forms of intergroup bias has also examined the role of the amygdala in the rapid perception of outgroup members. Early research on the neural correlates of implicit racial bias found that stronger anti-black implicit attitudes, as measured using the Implicit Association Test (IAT), were associated with greater amygdala activity to Black than White faces, as measured using fMRI (Phelps et al., 2000). To make stronger claims about the automaticity of this effect, and to connect it to a classical fear conditioning mechanism of learning and memory,

Amodio et al. (2003) used the startle eyeblink method to assess amygdala activity in response to ingroup and outgroup faces. To assess rapid changes in amygdala activity, the authors examined amygdala responses to Black, White, and Asian faces occurring just 400 ms after a face was presented, as well as 4,000 ms after face presentation. Furthermore, they expected that patterns of amygdala activity would vary as a function of participants' motivations to respond without prejudice, mirroring patterns of individual differences observed on behavioral measures of implicit racial associations in their prior research (Devine et al., 2002). Indeed, individual differences in the amygdala response to Black and White faces began to emerge at only 400 ms, and this pattern was strong at 4,000 ms (Figure 34.7B). Participants motivated primarily by their internal beliefs did not differ in their amygdala response to Black and White faces, whereas those whose internal motivation was accompanied by stronger external motivation (i.e., a fear of social disapproval for appearing biased) exhibited greater amygdala activity to Black than White faces. Participants with low internal motivation (i.e., highly prejudiced personal beliefs) also exhibited greater amygdala activity to Black than White faces. This research provided the first evidence of a difference in amygdala response to Black and White faces, and it shed light on why some people with explicit low-prejudice beliefs nevertheless exhibit bias on implicit measures of prejudice.

For social neuroscientists, the startle eyeblink measure is useful because it allows for stronger inferences about the specific role of the amygdala in implicit intergroup perception. That is, the startle eyeblink effect is modulated by the central nucleus of the amygdala (see Figure 34.6)—the structure specifically involved in the fear response, which includes freezing behavior and vigilance to potential threat or novelty in one's environment. By comparison, fMRI measures of amygdala activity cannot easily discern activity in different amygdala nuclei, and thus observed amygdala activity may not relate to fear and vigilance, but rather to the engagement of instrumental behaviors (i.e., via the basal nucleus; see Figure 34.6) or to other functions. Amodio et al. (2003) used their findings to make a theoretical connection between affective forms of implicit racial bias and mechanisms of fear conditioning linked to the amygdala. Subsequent research replicated this basic effect by showing greater amygdala activity to Black than White faces when faces were presented very briefly (~30 ms) using fMRI (Cunningham et al., 2004; see Figure 34.7B).

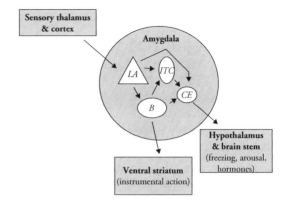

Figure 34.6 Schematic of information flow within the amygdala, illustrating connections between nuclei and intercalated cell masses (adapted from LeDoux, 2008). Sensory information enters via the lateral nucleus; signals from the amygdala flow out from the central nucleus (e.g., the fear response) and the basal nucleus (e.g., instrumental response). B, basal nucleus; CE, central nucleus; ITC, intercalated cells; LA, lateral nucleus. (Adapted from LeDoux, Joseph E. (2008). "Amygdala". *Scholarpedia* 3(4), 2698. doi:10.4249/scholarpedia.2698.)

Recent fMRI research on responses to novel ingroup and outgroup faces found that the amygdala was more responsive to novel ingroup faces regardless of the race of ingroup members (Van Bavel, Packer, & Cunningham, 2008). This finding suggests that amygdala activity to faces may track the motivational significance of a social cue, and not simply threat. This broader view is consistent with evidence that the amygdala is important for coordinating attentional and behavioral responses to stimuli that are novel or otherwise of special motivational significance (Whalen, 1998). Although these findings appear to contradict earlier research suggesting that the amygdala response to outgroup members might reflect a fear-conditioned response, they likely reflect activity produced by a different region of the amygdala. That is, whereas fear-related responses are associated with the central nucleus and its connections to peripheral autonomic systems, motivated (i.e., instrumental) responses are associated primarily with the basal nucleus and its connections to regions of the brain associated with planning and action (see Figure 34.6; LeDoux, 2000). Both likely play a role in initial person perception processes.

Categorical Responses to Faces

How rapidly are people categorized into groups? Above, we reviewed research suggesting that faces are identified as representing people as quickly as 170 ms following their appearance. Several ERP studies have reported multiple ERP components following the N170 component that reliably distinguish

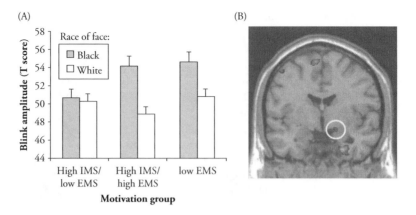

Figure 34.7 Affective forms of implicit bias toward black faces, compared with white faces, may be reflected in amygdala activity, as indicated by (**A**) the startle eyeblink response occurring at 4,000 milliseconds for individuals varying in internal and external motivations to respond without prejudice (IMS/EMS; Amodio et al., 2003) and (**B**) blood oxygen level–dependent (BOLD) signal in the amygdala, measured using functional magnetic resonance imaging (Cunningham et al., 2004).

faces on the basis of social group. In particular, the P2 component, named as such because it is the second major positive deflection (or "peak") of the ERP following a visual stimulus, is typically larger to racial outgroups than ingroups (Amodio, 2010b; Bartholow & Dickter, 2007; Ito, Willadsen-Jensen, & Correll, 2007; Ito & Urland, 2003). The larger P2 effect to outgroups has been interpreted as reflecting greater perceptual attention to outgroup (vs. ingroup) faces, which could have several different causes, such as concerns about showing prejudice toward Black faces, the use of the Black face as a cue to enact a nonprejudiced response, or a threat associated with the outgroup.

Although differences in early ERP responses to faces from different groups are sometimes interpreted as evidence for rapid bottom-up processing of social categories, more recent research suggests that these early ERP responses are driven by a top-down process associated with vigilance or expectancy for certain category members (e.g., Black faces; Amodio, 2010b). Thus, these early ERP responses to race and other social categories may be best described as representing a combination of top-down expectancies and bottom-up perceptual processes. For example, in a study by Ito and Urland (2003), participants viewed faces of Black and White males and females. On some trials, participants were instructed to categorize faces according to gender, and on other trials, by race. Interestingly, when faces were explicitly categorized by gender, some components of the ERP differed according to the race of the face. This pattern suggested that race is categorized implicitly. It is notable, however, that in tasks such as these, participants' strong concerns

about appearing prejudiced can lead them to attend to racial cues even when the task does not involve racial categorization. Therefore, like the results of Amodio (2010b), the results of Ito and Urland (2003) likely reflected a combination of top-down expectancy and bottom-up perceptual processes. Indeed, all observations of neural responses to racial categories likely represent some combination of these processes and should be interpreted as such.

Stereotyping

Whereas much research has examined the neural correlates of evaluation in person perception, relatively little has investigated social stereotypes. Stereotypes are believed to represent cognitive structures stored in memory that represent a set of attributes associated with a social group (Devine, 1989; Hamilton, 1981). Amodio and Devine (2006; see also Amodio, 2008; Amodio & Mendoza, 2010) proposed that stereotypes are rooted in mechanisms of semantic memory and selection, which are associated with neural activity in the temporal lobes and lateral posterior PFC (e.g., Brodmann areas 45 and 47), in contrast to affect-based associations rooted in the amygdala and other subcortical regions (Amodio & Ratner, 2011a). Behavioral and neuroscience research on semantic learning systems has explored the dynamics of how such associations are learned and expressed in behavior. By linking stereotypes to this literature, researchers can use findings from the neuroscience and memory literature to illuminate questions about stereotyping processes (Amodio, 2008). For example, whereas affective associations are learned quickly and are relatively indelible, semantic associations may be learned and unlearned through a process of repeated pairings and nonpairings. Furthermore, semantic learning systems are more likely to be expressed in trait impressions, goal representations, and goal-driven behaviors, and thus are more likely to emerge in verbal responses (Amodio & Devine, 2006).

Some fMRI studies have examined neural activity associated with the completion of stereotyping tasks (Knutson, Mah, Manly, & Grafman, 2007; Mitchell, Ames, Jenkins, & Banaji, 2009; Quadflieg et al., 2009), although they have not explored the mechanisms of stereotyping per se. That is, these studies have explored brain activity associated with more general processes recruited during the completion of a stereotyping task, such as cognitive conflict, response inhibition, or face perception. For example, in a brain lesion study, patients with mPFC damage did not show bias on a male versus female IAT (Milne & Grafman, 2001). However, it is unclear whether the mPFC damage interfered with the general process of response conflict that drives the IAT effect, rather than representing stereotype knowledge (a function typically ascribed to the PFC and temporal lobes).

In an attempt to examine neural regions involved in the representation of implicit stereotyping and implicit racial evaluation, Gilbert, Swencionis, and Amodio (2012) used a multi-voxel pattern analysis (MVPA) approach to fMRI. The MVPA approach reveals the extent to which a pattern of brain activity observed during a subset of trials can be used to successfully predict a participant's responses during a different set of trials. In essence, it asks whether one can observe a pattern of brain activity and, based on prior observations, determine from it what the person is thinking or doing. In the Gilbert et al. (2012) study, participants judged a series of face pairs on two different dimensions corresponding to a stereotype judgment ("which person is more interested in athletics?") or evaluative judgment ("which person seems friendlier"). These judgments were made for pairs of White, Black, and Asian male faces, and the authors were interested in neural activity to Black faces, as compared with White faces, during either type of judgment. MVPA results revealed that visual regions of the occipital cortex could decode the race of a face regardless of the judgment type (see also, Kaul, Ratner, & Van Bavel, in press; Ratner, Kaul, & Van Bavel, in press). More importantly, however, racial differences during evaluative judgments were associated with activity in the OFC—a region previously implicated in value and reward

processing, whereas racial differences during stereotype judgments were associated with activity in the mPFC—a region previously implicated in mentalizing and trait impression formation. These findings revealed a way in which stereotype processes are distinguishable from evaluative processes in the brain, supporting broader literatures on interactive mechanisms of social cognition and memory (Amodio, 2008). Additional research will be needed to probe the implications of these different modes of neural processing for social cognition and intergroup responses.

Mentalizing and Theory of Mind

The process of inferring another person's unique motives and perspectives is referred to as *mentalizing*, and this process underlies *theory of mind* (Frith & Frith, 1999). Theory of mind is best characterized by tasks that involve false belief or deceptive intent—tasks on which successful performance depends on one's ability to take another person's perspective. In an early neuroimaging study of mentalizing, Fletcher et al. (1995) examined brain activity while normal subjects read a set of short stories. These mentalizing stories involved jokes or lies as a literary device—that is, they made sense to the extent that the reader understood that a character was the victim of a lie or joke. Hence, the stories required an understanding of a character's false belief. Control stories did not rely on such devices, but rather involved straightforward physical descriptions. Although several brain regions were activated by these stories, only the mPFC was uniquely more active during the mentalizing stories. A similar set of mentalizing activations was observed in another study when subjects viewed movies of people showing deceptive intent (Grezes et al., 2004).

A subsequent PET experiment by Castelli, Happe, Frith, and Frith (2000) examined mentalizing by measuring brain activity while participants viewed cartoons inspired by the famous Heider and Simmel (1944) animations, in which three shapes moved in an anthropomorphic fashion that implied social interactions. The authors found that the viewing of this type of animation also elicited mPFC activity, compared with control videos in which the movement of the shapes was not interpreted anthropomorphically. Research by Harris, Todorov, & Fiske (2005) explicitly linked this line of research to social psychological theories of attribution. In their study, participants read descriptions of people's behaviors that varied in consistency, distinctiveness, and consensus—three factors that determine dispositional attribution (Jones & Davis, 1965; Kelley, 1972). Harris et al. (2005) observed the strongest degree of mPFC activity in conditions with the highest degree of dispositional attribution. Findings such as these linked activity in the mPFC to the process of making dispositional attributions of social behaviors.

Over the past decade, a large body of research has associated activity of the mPFC with a range of tasks involving mentalizing and complex aspects of person perception (Figure 34.8; Amodio & Frith, 2006; Frith & Frith, 1999; Saxe, Carey, & Kanwisher, 2004). These tasks often also elicit activity in regions of the superior temporal lobe or temporoparietal junction (TPJ), which have been linked to the general aspects of attention and visualization of biological motion (Scholz, Triantafyllous, Whitfield-Gabrieli, Brown, & Saxe, 2009), as well as activity in the temporal poles, believed to support conceptual representations of social information (Olson, McCoy, Klobusicky, & Ross, 2013). The literature on mentalizing makes contact with research on the development of theory of mind in children, such that the mPFC is relatively slow to develop compared with other regions (Bunge et al., 2002), adding converging evidence to the idea that the mPFC is an important substrate of these social cognitive processes.

Since the original findings linking mentalizing to regions of the mPFC, researchers have asked whether other forms of person perception are associated with activity in similar brain regions. A series of studies by Mitchell, Macrae, and colleagues proposed that social cognitive aspects of person perception, such as the ascription of trait attributes to a person, might also activate areas of the mPFC (even if they do not necessarily require mentalizing). For example, when subjects judged noun–adjective word pairs that described a person, compared with those describing an inanimate object, activity was found in regions of interest within the mPFC, as well as areas of the temporal cortex and TPJ (Mitchell et al., 2002). This pattern of activity has been seen across several studies using similar tasks (e.g., Mitchell et al., 2005, 2006). Other researchers have observed activity in similar regions when simply viewing faces in an easy memory task (Gobbini et al., 2004), demonstrating that activity in this region to faces does not necessarily imply the inference of traits. Some research has found that viewing and making trait judgments of unfamiliar faces or dissimilar people is associated with activity in more dorsal regions of the mPFC, whereas more familiar and/or similar faces are associated with activity in more ventral regions (Gobbini et al., 2004; Mitchell et al., 2006). It is

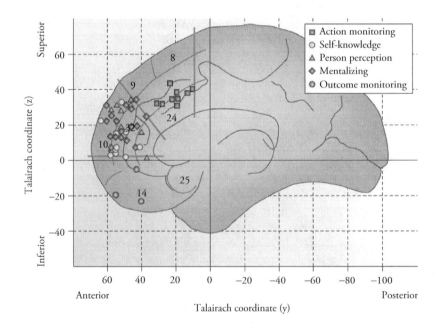

Figure 34.8 Neuroimaging studies of social cognition suggest that self-reflection, person perception, and mentalizing are associated primarily with activity in the anterior part of the medial prefrontal cortex. By comparison, action-monitoring processes have been primarily associated with activity in the dorsal anterior cingulate cortex, whereas outcome monitoring has been associated with activity in the orbital frontal cortex. (From Amodio, D. M., & Frith, C. D. [2006]. Meeting of minds: The medial frontal cortex and social cognition. *Nature Reviews Neuroscience*, 7, 268–277).

notable, however, that the mPFC is a large region of the cortex, and the specific locus of person-related activity varies considerably across studies (Amodio & Frith, 2006; Gilbert et al., 2007).

As with neuroimaging studies of the self, the inference that social cognition is subserved by the mPFC is complicated by the fact that mPFC activity is highest when a participant is at rest. That is, mPFC activity is usually highest in fMRI studies during intertrial intervals, such as when the participant views a fixation cross or other task prompt. Judgments about both social and nonsocial targets usually cause a decrease in mPFC activity. However, this drop in activity is usually greater for nonsocial targets. The claim that social cognition involves the mPFC is typically based on the direct contrast between responses to social and nonsocial targets, which reveal a relative increase for social judgments. This pattern, found consistently in the neuroimaging literature (e.g., Mitchell et al., 2004), poses a major problem for researchers who wish to claim that the mPFC is specialized for social cognition. Why is the mPFC more active when participants are resting or focusing on a fixation point than when they are explicitly engaged in social inference? As noted above, some have proposed that, when at rest, participants engage in social daydreaming and self-reflection (D'Argembeau et al., 2005; Gusnard, Akbudak, Shulman, & Raichle, 2001; Mason et al., 2007). This explanation assumes that people naturally reflect upon others when at rest (presumably while also thinking about the self), an assumption that has yet to be supported by data and appears inconsistent with research on self-reflection (e.g., Csikszentmihalyi & Figurski, 1982). A more fruitful approach to this issue may be to consider that the mPFC is a large and complex cortical region that is involved in multiple functions, many of which may have little to do with social cognition per se. Progress on this issue will require researchers to take a broader perspective on the functions associated with this region and with the psychological processes involved in social cognition tasks (Amodio & Frith, 2006; Gilbert et al., 2007).

Although the potential contribution of brain mapping abstract constructs like "the self" and "social cognition" to social cognitive theory remains to be established, fMRI research on mentalizing, person perception, and the self has inspired interesting debates about the processes through which a person judges another's thoughts or intentions. "Simulation" theory posits that people first imagine how they would respond in the other person's situation and then form their inference accordingly. "Theory" theory posits that people have an implicit theory of how another person would respond in a particular situation and, rather than reflecting on the self, form their inference based on this theory. As evidence for "theory" theory, some researchers have noted that brain activity associated with self- and other-judgments is related to different regions of the mPFC (Saxe, 2005). However, other researchers have argued in favor of simulation theory based on the observation that judgments of similar or familiar others activate a region close to areas activated by self-reflection (Mitchell, 2005). Although a lively debate, these interpretations are tentative because they rely strongly on reverse inferences from neuroimaging data and the problematic assumption that these mPFC regions truly represent the "self" and "social cognition."

Empathy

Empathy refers to one's concern for another's welfare (Batson, 1991), and it may be defined as the process of experiencing another's perspective and affective responses (Lamm, Batson, & Decety, 2007). As with mentalizing and theory of mind, empathy is a complex psychological process that involves affect, perception, social cognition, self-regulation, mimicry, and action (Decety, 2011). Building on neuroscience studies of mentalizing, research on the neural substrates of empathy has focused primarily on the role of the mPFC (Decety, 2011; Rameson & Lieberman, 2009). Many studies have examined empathy by measuring brain activity while a subject views another person experiencing pain. For example, Singer et al. (2004) used fMRI to measure brain activity while participants experienced a painful stimulus or viewed a loved one receiving the same stimulus. Multiple brain structures, including the rostral ACC and anterior insula (see Figure 34.4), were active in both conditions, relative to baseline, and activity in these areas in response to a loved one's pain was greater among subjects with higher scores on a trait empathy scale. Other research suggests that similar brain regions are more active while watching racial ingroups experience pain than racial outgroups (Xu, Zuo, Wang, & Han, 2009). There are also suggestive findings from lesion patient studies, in which damage to the ventral mPFC and ACC was associated with impaired empathy (Shamay-Tsoory, Tomer, Berger, & Aharon-Peretz, 2003). Do these brain areas uniquely represent empathy? Perhaps, but probably not. Given that the ACC is implicated in a wide range of processes involving expectancy violation (Shackman et al., 2011), these findings may reflect some aspect of expectancy violation or concern when either the self or another person is subjected to pain, rather than suggesting that empathy is related specifically to the experience of pain (Somerville et al., 2006).

Related to work on empathy, a "mirror neuron" system has been proposed as a brain network devoted to understanding other people through their actions (Iacoboni & Dapretto, 2006). The mirror neuron idea originated from single-unit recording in the macaque premotor cortex, in which the same neuron fired when the monkey moved its arm toward a food reward and when it watched an experimenter move his or her arm toward the reward (Gallese et al., 1996). "Mirror neuron" is not a literal term, in the sense that no single neuron can be described as providing a mirroring function. Rather, mirror neurons refer loosely to areas of the brain that are activated both when an individual observes the behavior of another person and when that individual performs the same behavior. Brain regions that have been implicated in mirror neuron networks include the premotor cortex, inferior frontal cortex, superior temporal sulcus, anterior insula, and amygdala (Iacoboni & Dapretto, 2006; Rizzolatti & Sinigaglia, 2010), though the patterns and locations of activity in these regions vary considerably from study to study. Although the notion that we relate to other people by representing their actions and mental states in the same way we represent our own actions and states has intuitive appeal, more recent theoretical analyses have questioned the plausibility of mirror neurons as a mechanism of action understanding (Decety, 2011; Hickok, 2009; Niedenthal, 2007; Saxe, 2005). Aside from questions about the neural substrates, the fact that so many social interactions often require complementary responses (e.g., when conversing or dancing), rather than mimicry, calls into question the idea that human social behavior is rooted in a mirroring system. Hence, more research will be needed to assess the utility of the mirror neuron idea.

Humanization

Humanization refers to the process of seeing another person as possessing the characteristics unique to the human mind and the rights associated with being a member of society. By contrast, *dehumanization* refers to the denial of such qualities to certain persons (Haslam, 2006). Members of one's own social group are typically perceived as possessing these qualities, whereas members of a low-status outgroup are often seen as lacking many of these qualities (Leyens et al., 2001, 2003). The process of "humanization" is associated with empathy and mentalizing and typically refers to these processes as they relate to people. However, empathy and mentalizing may also relate to nonhumans and inanimate objects, as a form of anthropomorphism (Epley, Waytz, & Cacioppo, 2007). Thus, humanization can be studied in terms of how a nonhuman object is imbued with human characteristics.

Neuroimaging studies of humanization have built on findings from the mentalizing and empathy literatures. In a study by Harris and Fiske (2006), activity in a region of the mPFC was greater when participants viewed pictures of valued others (e.g., members of the ingroup, people of high social status) compared with "dehumanized" individuals, such as drug abusers and homeless people. Through work such as this, neuroscience research on mentalizing and the mPFC may be connected to important themes in social psychology concerning intergroup relations (Harris & Fiske, 2009).

Limitations and Challenges

The social neuroscience approach has produced many exciting advances in research on social cognition, ranging from the way we perceive people and infer their motives and beliefs to how we regulate social responses. Nevertheless, as a recently developed approach to these issues, the field continues to grapple with some important limitations and challenges. We note some of the major issues in this section.

Psychological Inference Problems

The enterprise of social neuroscience research is built on the assumption that social cognitive functions can be inferred from patterns of neural activity. As described in the first section of this chapter, this assumption is often difficult to meet. In particular, the mPFC region of the frontal cortex is often described as a key substrate of several social cognitive processes. However, the specific role of this region in social cognition remains poorly understood. What exactly is the theoretical significance of the mPFC as it relates to the self, person perception, and mentalizing? Mitchell (2009) has argued that the fact that so many socio cognitive processes activate similar regions of mPFC suggests that social psychology is a "natural kind," represented by a unique and privileged place in neural anatomy. Although provocative, the natural-kinds argument is complicated by the observation that the mPFC is more strongly activated when participants are at rest than when actively engaged in social inference, and the mPFC is involved in many processes without clear links to social cognition.

Taking a different approach to this issue, Amodio and Frith (2006) considered the neuroanatomical properties of the mPFC in its relation to social cognition. They noted that the mPFC is a highly interconnected region of brain, uniquely situated to integrate information about internal processes (e.g., motor responses, visceral states) and higher-level representations of goals, reward contingencies, and complex expectancies linked to more anterior regions of the frontal cortex. According to their analysis, the mPFC is involved in the coordination of internal states and goals with complex external response contingencies (such as the motives and expectations of other people). Among humans, social cognition is the most important and complex form of cognition, highly interconnected with emotional, perceptual, motivational, and behavioral processes. By this view, the mPFC is not the neural instantiation of the self or social cognition, and social psychology is not a natural kind in the brain. More research will be needed to understand the significance of the mPFC as it relates to social cognitive processes.

Evolving Understanding of Neural Function

Neuroscience is a large and rapidly advancing field, and changes in our understanding of neural function are inevitable. Social neuroscience researchers will need to keep themselves apprised of developments in neuroscience and update interpretations of past findings accordingly. For example, as noted above, interpretations of the amygdala have changed as its function has become better understood. In early social neuroscience work, the amygdala was often interpreted as the "fear" center or as the general locus of emotion in the brain. However, it is now understood to represent a diverse set of processes that are broader than fear and involve attention, vigilance, memory, and the coordination of autonomic reactions as well as instrumental responses (Whalen, 1998; Killcross, Robbins, & Everitt, 1997). These functions also reflect the different functions of subnuclei in the amygdala. Thus, the notion that the amygdala represents "negative emotion" is too simplistic and no longer tenable. The same issue applies to nearly every other neural structure. Therefore, as our understanding of the brain advances and methodological tools improve, prior interpretations of research findings will likely require revision, and researchers will need to remain open to this possibility.

Limitations in Measurement

In addition to the methodological concerns discussed above, physiological and neuroimaging measures sometimes introduce important limitations to the scope of experimental methods normally employed by social psychologists. Beyond issues of cost and training, the recording equipment is sometimes invasive or otherwise constraining, and these factors have direct implications for the manipulation and measurement of psychological variables. For example, fMRI recording requires that a participant lie very still on a narrow scanner bed with his or her head and upper body ensconced in the narrow scanner bore (i.e., a plastic tube). A "bite bar" or other means of immobilizing the participants' head is often used. During scans, the room is usually darkened, and the participant wears earplugs to attenuate the loud buzzing and whirring noises from the pulsing scanner. This environment places important limitations on the type of research that may be conducted. Experimenters must contend with the participant's potential anxiety and distractibility during the study, which may interfere with experimental manipulations. Experimenters must also design tasks that can be implemented with stimulus presentation through LCD goggles (or a back-reflected LCD monitor) and/or responses made on a button box that is usually held in the subject's right hand.

Beyond these obvious limitations, a recent study found that immobilization in the supine position may significantly reduce approach motivation (Harmon-Jones & Peterson, 2009. In line with recent work on embodiment and situated cognition (Smith & Semin, 2004), this finding suggests that constraints on a participant's body posture (as in the fMRI scanner) have important effects on emotion and cognition, especially as they pertain to action. Other common social neuroscience methods, such as EEG/ERP, are less constrictive, but still present limitations that require special considerations concerning technical and psychological issues.

Future Directions

The social neuroscience approach has already yielded some significant contributions to psychological theories of social cognition. But this is just the tip of the iceberg. The neurosciences represent some of the fastest growing areas within the biomedical and psychological fields, and these scientific advances will continue to influence the study of social cognitive processes. Here, we describe just a few of the breaking trends in social neuroscience research.

Hyperscanning of Interpersonal and Intergroup Interactions

Social processes concern interactions between two or more people, yet most existing research has examined individuals in private, non–social laboratory contexts. To address this concern, researchers are increasingly using a technique known as "hyperscanning," in which two or more participants interact remotely (e.g., over an Internet connection) while their brain activity is recorded in separate scanners. Hyperscanning may refer to the simultaneous recording of fMRI, EEG, or other brain imaging techniques. To date, hyperscanning has been used primarily to study brain activity associated with economic negotiations or in studies of social exclusion (King-Casas et al., 2005; or for simulated hyperscanning, Eisenberger et al., 2003), but it has clear applications to other social contexts, such as intergroup interactions.

Modeling of Neural Networks and Microsystems

Currently, most social neuroscience studies focus on the role of a particular brain region associated with a social cognitive processes. However, the mechanisms of social cognition are very complex, and it is unlikely that any high-level psychological process reflects the activity of a single brain structure. Psychologists are increasingly recognizing the need to examine *networks* of brain structures in order to understand complex psychological processes like social perception and social cognition. At the same time, social neuroscientists are increasingly appreciative of the complexity within neural structures. For example, the amygdala is thought to comprise at least 13 different nuclei, each with different functions, connected within an inhibitory network (Swanson & Petrovich, 1998). Thus, the amygdala cannot be interpreted as supporting just one function. Furthermore, popular neuroimaging techniques, such as fMRI, are limited in their ability to discern activity of these different nuclei. Because fMRI is a measure of blood flow, limited in resolution by the spacing of cerebral capillaries, it underestimates the important contributions of networks within brain structures. Our understanding of how social cognitive mechanisms relate to brain activity will become increasingly refined as technologies and theoretical models of neural networks progress.

Molecular Genetics

Major advances in molecular genetics have been made in recent years, and the study of genetic and epigenetic processes will soon begin to contribute to the study of social cognition (Chiao, 2011; Ratner & Kubota, 2012; Way & Gurbaxani, 2008). Genes—the components of DNA that provide the blueprint for our biological (and, hence, psychological) development—are increasingly appreciated for their complexity and their propensity for adaptation. Measures of genes and gene variation (i.e., *polymorphisms*) provide a powerful assessment of dispositional factors. By using the genetics approach, researchers can refine psychological models of traits and dispositions to better match the biological contours that underlie them. The emerging field of epigenetics is especially relevant to social cognition. Epigenetics concerns the study of gene expression, and research in this field has shown that the expression of genes is continuously being modulated by environmental and situational factors, including social factors (Champagne & Mashoodh, 2009).

As researchers begin to incorporate genetic measures into research on social cognition, an obvious challenge is that in order to connect these two areas of inquiry one must traverse many levels of analysis, both physiologically and psychologically. Due to the conceptual distance between genetic mechanisms and social cognition, it is important that investigators do not oveinterpret any correlations between genetic polymorphisms and aspects of social cognition. The possibilities of this research are exciting and it remains to be seen whether this approach will render substantive advances in psychological theories of social cognitive processes.

Endocrine Systems

Although most neuroscience studies of social cognition have focused on measures of brain activity, other physiological processes are increasingly seen as relevant. In particular, hormones operate in both the brain and periphery, functioning to orchestrate complex psychobiological processes. Hormones, such as testosterone, cortisol, and dehydroepiandrosterone (DHEA), are known to be responsive to social factors such as social evaluation, ingroup pride, competition, and attachment (Baumgartner, Heinrichs, Vonlanthen, Fischbacher, & Fehr, 2008; Dickerson & Kemeny, 2004; Eisenegger, Naef, Snozzi, Heinrichs, & Fehr, 2010; Mehta & Josephs, 2006; Ratner, Halim, & Amodio, 2013). Although many studies have included hormones as physiological outcome measures of social stress (e.g., Mendes, Gray, Mendoza-Denton, Major, & Epel, 2007; Page-Gould, Mendes, & Major, 2010) or indicators of neural mechanisms involved in the control of stereotyping (e.g., Amodio, 2009), research has yet to study the role of hormones in guiding complex aspects of social cognition.

Conclusion

Social neuroscience is a natural extension of the classic social cognition approach. In both cases, the core questions concern mechanism, and this may be why neuroscience approaches to social psychology have flourished in the domain of social cognition. Just as social cognition transitioned quickly from the fringe to the mainstream in the field of social psychology during the 1980s, social neuroscience ideas and methods are being integrated rapidly into contemporary research on social cognition. In addition to new journals and academic societies dedicated to the development of social neuroscience, the broader field of social psychology has made efforts to integrate social neuroscience approaches, through special issues in mainstream journals and special training workshops and symposia at major conferences. At the same time, doctoral programs in social psychology increasingly involve training in cognitive neuroscience theories and methods. As this integration of social neuroscience into social psychology continues, we expect that scientists will begin to use the approach more effectively to probe social cognitive mechanisms, addressing enduring conundrums while generating novel questions and ideas.

The research described in this chapter represents the vanguard of the social neuroscience approach. When the second edition of the *Handbook of Social Cognition* was published, Ostrom commented on the enormous advances achieved in the field since the publication of the first edition. If history is to repeat itself, then we will look forward to the advances in the neuroscience of social cognition that will be described in the next edition.

Author Note

Work on this article was supported by a grant from the National Science Foundation to David Amodio (BCS 0847350) and an NSF Graduate Research Fellowship to Kyle Ratner. We thank Jillian Swencionis and Sophie Wharton for their assistance in preparing this chapter.

References

Adolphs, R., Tranel, D., Damasio, H., & Damasio, A. R. (1994). Impaired recognition of emotion in facial expressions following bilateral damage to the human amygdala. *Nature, 372,* 669–672.

Allison, T., Ginter, H., McCarthy, G., Nobre, A. C., Puce, A., Luby, M., & Spencer, D. D. (1994). Face recognition in human extrastriate cortex. *Journal of Neurophysiology, 71,* 821–825.

Amodio, D. M. (2008). The social neuroscience of intergroup relations. *European Review of Social Psychology, 19,* 1–54.

Amodio, D. M. (2009). Intergroup anxiety effects on the control of racial stereotypes: A psychoneuroendocrine analysis. *Journal of Experimental Social Psychology, 45,* 60–67.

Amodio, D. M. (2010a). Can neuroscience advance social psychological theory? Social neuroscience for the behavioral social psychologist. *Social Cognition, 28,* 695–716.

Amodio, D. M. (2010b). Coordinated roles of motivation and perception in the regulation of intergroup responses: Frontal cortical asymmetry effects on the P2 event-related potential and behavior. *Journal of Cognitive Neuroscience, 22,* 2609–2617.

Amodio, D. M., & Devine, P. G. (2006). Stereotyping and evaluation in implicit race bias: Evidence for independent constructs and unique effects on behavior. *Journal of Personality and Social Psychology, 91,* 652–661.

Amodio, D. M., Devine, P. G., & Harmon-Jones, E. (2007). A dynamic model of guilt: Implications for motivation and self-regulation in the context of prejudice. *Psychological Science, 18,* 524–530.

Amodio, D. M., Devine, P. G., & Harmon-Jones, E. (2008). Individual differences in the regulation of intergroup bias: The role of conflict monitoring and neural signals for control. *Journal of Personality and Social Psychology, 94,* 60–74.

Amodio, D. M., & Frith, C. D. (2006). Meeting of minds: The medial frontal cortex and social cognition. *Nature Reviews Neuroscience, 7,* 268–277.

Amodio, D. M., Harmon-Jones, E., & Devine, P. G. (2003). Individual differences in the activation and control of affective race bias as assessed by startle eyeblink responses and self-report. *Journal of Personality and Social Psychology, 84,* 738–753.

Amodio, D. M., Harmon-Jones, E., Devine, P. G., Curtin, J. J., Hartley, S. L., & Covert, A. E. (2004). Neural signals for the detection of unintentional race bias. *Psychological Science, 15,* 88–93.

Amodio, D. M., Jost, J. T., Master, S. L., & Yee, C. M. (2007). Neurocognitive correlates of liberalism and conservatism. *Nature Neuroscience, 10,* 1246–1247.

Amodio, D. M., Kubota, J. T., Harmon-Jones, E., & Devine, P. G. (2006). Alternative mechanisms for regulating racial responses according to internal vs. external cues. *Social Cognitive and Affective Neuroscience, 1,* 26–36.

Amodio, D. M., Master, S. L., Yee, C. M., & Taylor, S. E. (2008). Neurocognitive components of behavioral inhibition and activation systems: Implications for theories of self-regulation. *Psychophysiology, 45,* 11–19.

Amodio, D. M., & Mendoza, S. A. (2010). Implicit intergroup bias: Cognitive, affective, and motivational underpinnings. In B. Gawronski & B. K. Payne (Eds.), *Handbook of implicit social cognition* (pp. 353–374). New York: Guilford.

Amodio, D. M., & Ratner, K. G. (2011a). Mechanisms for the regulation of intergroup responses: A social neuroscience analysis. In J. Decety and J. T. Cacioppo (Eds.), *Handbook of social neuroscience* (pp. 729–741). New York: Oxford University Press.

Amodio, D. M., & Ratner, K. G. (2011b). A memory systems model of implicit social cognition. *Current Directions in Psychological Science, 20,* 143–148.

Aron, A. R., Robbins, T. W., & Poldrack, R. A. (2004). Inhibition and the right inferior frontal cortex. *Trends in Cognitive Sciences, 8,* 170–177.

Aron, A., Fisher, F., Mashek, D. A., Strong, G., Li, H., & Brown, L. L. (2005). Reward, motivation, and emotion systems associated with early-stage romantic love. *Journal of Neurophysiology, 94,* 327–337.

Barbas, H., & Zikopoulos, B. (2007). The prefrontal cortex and flexible behavior. *Neuroscientist, 13,* 532–545.

Bargh, J. A. (1994). The four horsemen of automaticity: Awareness, efficiency, intention, and control in social cognition. In R. S. Wyer, Jr., & T. K. Srull (Eds.), *Handbook of social cognition* (2nd ed., pp. 1–40). Hillsdale, NJ: Erlbaum.

Bargh, J. A., Chen, M., & Burrows, L. (1996). Automaticity of social behavior: Direct effects of trait construct and stereotype priming on action. *Journal of Personality and Social Psychology, 71,* 230–244.

Barrett, L. F. (2009). Understanding the mind by measuring the brain: Lessons from measuring behavior (commentary on Vul et al., 2009). *Perspectives on Psychological Science, 4,* 314–318.

Bartholow, B. D., & Dickter, C. L. (2007). Social cognitive neuroscience of person perception: A selective review focused on the event-related brain potential. In E. Harmon-Jones & P. Winkielman (Eds.), *Social neuroscience: Integrating biological and psychological explanations of social behavior* (pp. 376–400). New York: Guilford Press.

Bartholow, B. D., Dickter, C. L., & Sestir, M. A. (2006). Stereotype activation and control of race bias: Cognitive control of inhibition and its impairment by alcohol. *Journal of Personality and Social Psychology, 90,* 272–287.

Batson, C. D. (1991). *The altruism question: toward a social-psychological answer.* Hillsdale, NJ: Erlbaum.

Baumgartner, T., Heinrichs, M., Vonlanthen, A., Fischbacher, U., & Fehr, E. (2008). Oxytocin shapes the neural circuitry of trust and trust adaptation in humans. *Neuron, 58,* 639–650.

Beer, J. S., Heerey, E. H., Keltner, D., Scabini, D., & Knight, R. T. (2003). The regulatory function of self-conscious emotion: Insights from patients with orbitofrontal damage. *Journal of Personality and Social Psychology, 85,* 594–604.

Bentin, S., Allison, T., Puce, A., Perez, E., & McCarthy, G. (1996). Electrophysiological studies of face perception in humans. *Journal of Cognitive Neuroscience, 8,* 551–565.

Berns, G. S., Cohen, J. D., & Mintun, M. A. (1997). Brain regions responsive to novelty in the absence of awareness. *Science, 276,* 1272–1275.

Blair, R. J. R., & Cipolotti, L. (2000). Impaired social response reversal: A case of "acquired sociopathy." *Brain, 123,* 1122–1141.

Blascovich, J., Mendes, W. B., Vanman, E., & Dickerson, S. (2011). *Social psychophysiology for social and personality psychology.* London: Sage.

Blakemore, S. J., Oakley, D. A., & Frith, C. D. (2003). Delusions of alien control in the normal brain. *Neuropsychologia, 41,* 1058–1067.

Blaxton, T. A., Bookheimer, S. Y., Zeffiro, T. A., Figlozzi, C. M., William, D. D., & Theodore. W. H. (1996). Functional mapping of human memory using PET: Comparisons of conceptual and perceptual tasks. *Canadian Journal of Experimental Psychology, 50,* 42–56.

Botvinick, M. M., Braver, T. S., Barch, D. M., Carter, C. S., & Cohen, J. D. (2001). Conflict monitoring and cognitive control. *Psychological Review, 108,* 624–652.

Bunge, S. A., Dudukovic, N. M., Thomason, M. E., Valdya, C. J., & Gabrieli, J. D. E. (2002). Immature frontal lobe contributions to cognitive control in children: Evidence from fMRI. *Neuron, 33,* 301–311.

Cacioppo, J. T., & Berntson, G. G. (1992). Social psychological contributions to the decade of the brain: Doctrine of multilevel analysis. *American Psychologist, 47,* 1019–1028.

Cacioppo, J. T., Berntson, G. G., Lorig, T. S., Norris, C. J., Rickett, E., & Nusbaum, H. (2003). Just because you're imaging the brain doesn't mean you can stop using your head: A primer and set of first principles. *Journal of Personality and Social Psychology, 85,* 650–661.

Cacioppo, J. T., & Petty, R. E. (1983). Foundations of social psychophysiology. In J. T. Cacioppo & R. E. Petty (Eds.), *Social psychophysiology: A sourcebook* (pp. 3–36). New York: Guilford Press.

Caldara, R., Rossion, B., Bovet, P., & Hauert, C. (2004). Event-related potentials and time course of the "other-race" face classification advantage. *Neuroreport, 15,* 905.

Caldara, R., Thut, G., Servoir, P., Michel, C., Bovet, P., & Renault, B. (2003). Face versus non-face object perception and the "other-race" effect: A spatio-temporal event-related potential study. *Clinical Neurophysiology, 114,* 515–528.

Carlston, D. E. (1994). Associated systems theory: A systematic approach to the cognitive representation of persons and events. In R. S. Wyer (Ed.), *Associated systems theory: Advances in social cognition* (Vol. 7, pp. 1–78). Hillsdale, NJ: Erlbaum.

Carmel, D., & Bentin, S. (2002). Domain specificity versus expertise: Factors influencing distinct processing of faces. *Cognition, 83,* 1–29.

Carter, C. S., Braver, T. S., Barch, D. M., Botvinick, M. M., Noll, D., & Cohen, J. D. (1998). Anterior cingulate cortex, error detection, and the online monitoring of performance. *Science, 280,* 747–749.

Castelli, F., Happe, F., Frith, U., & Frith, C. (2000). Movement and mind: A functional imaging study of perception and interpretation of complex intentional movement patterns. *NeuroImage, 12,* 314–325.

Champagne, F. A., & Mashoodh, R. (2009). Genes in context: Gene–environment interplay and the origins of individual differences in behavior. *Current Directions in Psychological Science, 18,* 127–131.

Chiao, J. Y. (2011). Cultural neuroscience: Visualizing culture-gene influences on brain function. In Decety, J. & Cacioppo, J. (Eds.), *Handbook of social neuroscience* (pp. 742–761). UK: Oxford University Press.

Cohen, N. J., & Squire, L. R. (1980). Preserved learning and retention of pattern analyzing skill in amnesia: Dissociation of knowing how and knowing that. *Science, 210,* 207–209.

Craik, F. I. M., Moroz, T. M., Moscovitch, M., Stuss, D. T., Winocur, G., Tulving, E., & Kapur, S. (1999). In search of the self: A positron emission tomography study. *Psychological Science, 10,* 26–34.

Csikszentmihalyi, M., & Figurski, T. J. (1982). Self-awareness and aversive experience in everyday life. *Journal of Personality, 50,* 15–28.

Cunningham, W. A., Johnson, M. K., Raye, C. L., Gatenby, J. C., Gore, J. C., & Banaji, M. R. (2004). Separable neural components in the processing of black and white faces. *Psychological Science, 15,* 806–813.

D'Argembeau, A., Collette, F., Van der Linden, M., et al. (2005). Self-referential reflective activity and its relationship with rest: A PET study. *NeuroImage, 25,* 616–624.

Damasio, H. (2005) *Human brain anatomy in computerized images* (2nd ed.). New York: Oxford University Press.

Decety, J. (2011). Dissecting the neural mechanisms mediating empathy. *Emotion Review, 3,* 92–108.

Deffke, I., Sander, T., Heidenreich, J., Sommer, W., Curio, G., Trahms, L., et al. (2007). MEG/EEG sources of the 170-ms response to faces are co-localized in the fusiform gyrus. *NeuroImage, 35,* 1495–1501.

Demb, J. B., Desmond, J. E., Wagner, A. D., Vaidya, C. J., Glover, G. H., & Gabrieli, J. D. (1995). Semantic encoding and retrieval in the left inferior prefrontal cortex: A functional MRI study of task difficulty and process specificity. *Journal of Neuroscience, 15,* 5870–5878.

Desimone, R. (1991). Face-selective cells in the temporal cortex of monkeys. *Journal of Cognitive Neuroscience, 3,* 1–8.

Devine, P. G. (1989). Stereotypes and prejudice: Their automatic and controlled components. *Journal of Personality and Social Psychology, 56,* 5–18.

Devine, P. G., Plant, E. A., Amodio, D. M., Harmon-Jones, E., & Vance, S. L. (2002). The regulation of explicit and implicit race bias: The role of motivations to respond without prejudice. *Journal of Personality and Social Psychology, 82,* 835–848.

Dickerson, S. S., & Kemeny, M. E. (2004). Acute stressors and cortisol responses: A theoretical integration and synthesis of laboratory research. *Psychological Bulletin, 130,* 355–391.

Dovidio, J. F., Evans, N., & Tyler, R. B. (1986). Racial stereotypes: The contents of their cognitive representations. *Journal of Experimental Social Psychology, 22,* 22–37.

Eimer, M. (2000). Event-related brain potentials distinguish processing stages involved in face perception and recognition. *Clinical Neurophysiology, 111,* 694–705.

Eisenberger, N. I., Lieberman, M. D., & Williams, K. D. (2003). Does rejection hurt? An fMRI study of social exclusion. *Science, 302,* 290–292.

Eisenegger, C., Naef, M., Snozzi, R., Heinrichs, M., & Fehr, E. (2010). Prejudice and the truth about the effect of testosterone on human bargaining behavior. *Nature, 463,* 356–361.

Engell, A. D., Haxby, J. V., & Todorov, A. (2007). Implicit trustworthiness decisions: Automatic coding of face properties in human amygdala. *Journal of Cognitive Neuroscience, 19,* 1508–1519.

Epley, N., Waytz, A., & Cacioppo, J. T. (2007). On seeing human: A three-factor theory of anthropomorphism. *Psychological Review, 114,* 864–886.

Farrer, C., Frey, S. H., Van Horn, J. D., Tunik, E., Turk, D., Inati, S., et al. (2008). The angular gyrus computes action awareness representations. *Cerebral Cortex, 18,* 254–261.

Fiske, S. T. (1992). Thinking is for doing: Portraits of social cognition from daguerreotype to laserphoto. *Journal of Personality and Social Psychology, 63,* 877–889.

Fletcher, P. C., Happe, F., Frith, U., Baker, S. C., Dolan, R. J., Frackowiak, R. S., et al. (1995). Other minds in the brain: A functional imaging study of "theory of mind" in story comprehension. *Cognition, 57,* 109–128.

Frith, C. D., & Frith, U. (1999). Interacting minds: A biological basis. *Science, 286,* 1692–1695.

Fuster, J. M. (2001). The prefrontal cortex. An update: Time is of the essence. *Neuron, 2,* 319–333.

Gabrieli, J. D. (1998). Cognitive neuroscience of human memory. *Annual Review of Psychology, 49,* 87–115.

Gaertner, S. L., & McLaughlin, J. P. (1983). Racial stereotypes: Associations and ascriptions of positive and negative characteristics. *Social Psychology Quarterly, 46,* 23–30.

Gallese, V., Fadiga, L., Fogassi, L., & Rizzolatti, G. (1996). Action recognition in the premotor cortex. *Brain, 119,* 593–609.

Gauthier, I., Skudlarski, P., Gore, J. C., & Anderson, A. W. (2000). Expertise for cars and birds recruits brain areas involved in face recognition. *Nature Neuroscience, 3,* 191–197.

Gazzaley, A., Rissman, J., Cooney, J. W., Rutman, A., Seibert, T., Clapp, W., & D'Esposito, M. (2007). Functional interactions between prefrontal and visual association cortex contribute to top-down modulation of visual processing. *Cerebral Cortex, 17,* 125–135.

Gehring, W. J., Goss, B., Coles, M. G. H., Meyer, D. E., & Donchin, E. (1993). A neural system for error detection and compensation. *Psychological Science, 4,* 385–390.

Gilbert, S. J., Swencionis, J. K., & Amodio, D. M. (2012). Evaluative vs. trait representation in intergroup social judgments: Distinct roles of anterior temporal lobe and prefrontal cortex. *Neuropsychologia, 50,* 3600–3611.

Gilbert, S. J., Williamson, I. D. M., Dumontheil, I., Simons, J. S., Frith, C. D., & Burgess, P. W. (2007). Distinct regions of medial rostral prefrontal cortex supporting social and non-social functions. *Social Cognitive and Affective Neuroscience, 2,* 217–226.

Gillihan, S. J., & Farah, M. J. (2005). Is self special? A critical review of evidence from experimental psychology and cognitive neuroscience. *Psychological Bulletin, 131,* 76–97.

Gobbini, M. I., Leibenluft, E., Santiago, N., & Haxby, J. V. (2004). Social and emotional attachment in the neural representation of faces. *NeuroImage, 22,* 1628–1635.

Golby, A. J., Eberhardt, J. L., Chiao, J. Y., Gabrieli, J. D. E. (2001). Fusiform response to same and other race faces. *Nature Neuroscience, 4,* 845–850.

Graf, P., & Schacter, D. L. (1985). Implicit and explicit memory for new associations in normal and amnesic subjects. *Journal of Experimental Psychology: Learning, Memory, and Cognition, 11,* 501–518.

Grezes, J., Frith, C., & Passingham, R. F. (2004). Brain mechanisms for inferring deceit in the actions of others. *Journal of Neuroscience, 24,* 5500–5505.

Gusnard, D. A., Akbudak, E., Shulman, G. L., & Raichle, M. E. (2001). Medial prefrontal cortex and self–referential mental activity: Relation to a default mode of brain function. *Proceedings of the National Academy of Sciences USA, 98,* 4259–4264.

Gusnard, D. A., & Raichle, M. E. (2001). Searching for a baseline: Functional imaging and the resting human brain. *Nature Reviews Neuroscience, 2,* 685–694.

Gutchess, A. H., Kensinger, E. A., & Schacter, D. L. (2007). Aging, self-referencing, and medial prefrontal cortex. *Social Neuroscience, 2,* 117–133.

Hamilton, D. L. (1981). Stereotyping and intergroup behavior: Some thoughts on the cognitive approach. In D. L. Hamilton (Ed.), *Cognitive processes in stereotyping and intergroup behavior* (pp. 333–353). Hillsdale, NJ: Erlbaum.

Harmon-Jones, E. (2003). Anger and the behavioural approach system. *Personality and Individual Differences, 35*, 995–1005.

Harmon-Jones, E., & Beer, J. S. (2009). *Methods in social neuroscience.* New York: Guilford Press.

Harmon-Jones, E., & Peterson, C. K. (2009). Supine body position reduces neural response to anger evocation. *Psychological Science, 20*, 1209–1210.

Harmon-Jones, E., & Sigelman, J. D. (2001). State anger and prefrontal brain activity: Evidence that insult-related relative left-prefrontal activation is associated with experienced anger and aggression. *Journal of Personality and Social Psychology, 80*, 797–803.

Harris, L. T., & Fiske, S. T. (2006). Dehumanizing the lowest of the low: Neuro-imaging responses to extreme outgroups. *Psychological Science, 17*, 847–853.

Harris, L. T., & Fiske, S. T. (2009). Social neuroscience evidence for dehumanised perception. *European Review of Social Psychology, 20*, 192–231.

Harris, L. T., Todorov, A., & Fiske, S. T. (2005). Attributions on the brain: Neuro-imaging dispositional inferences, beyond theory of mind. *NeuroImage, 28*, 763–769.

Haslam, N. (2006). Dehumanization: An integrative review. *Personality and Social Psychology Review, 10*, 252–264.

Haxby, J., Hoffman, E., & Gobbini, M. (2000). The distributed human neural system for face perception. *Trends in Cognitive Sciences, 4*, 223–232.

He, Y., Johnson, M. K., Dovidio, J. F., & McCarthy, G. (2009). The relation between race-related implicit associations and scalp-recorded neural activity evoked by faces from different races. *Social Neuroscience, 4*, 426–442.

Heatherton, T. F., Wyland, C. L., Macrae, C. N., Demos, K. E., Denny, B. T., & Kelley, W. M. (2006). Medial prefrontal activity differentiates self from close others. *Social Cognitive and Affective Neuroscience, 1*, 18–25.

Heider, F., & Simmel, M. (1944). An experimental study of apparent behavior. *American Journal of Psychology, 57*, 243–259.

Henke, K. (2010). A model for memory systems based on processing modes rather than consciousness. *Nature Reviews Neuroscience, 11*, 523–532.

Hickok, G. (2009). Eight problems for the mirror neuron theory of action understanding in monkeys and humans. *Journal of Cognitive Neuroscience, 21*, 1229–1243.

Iacoboni, M., & Dapretto, M. (2006). The mirror neuron system and the consequences of its dysfunction. *Nature Reviews Neuroscience, 7*, 942–951.

Inzlicht, M., McGregor, I., Hirsh, J. B., & Nash, K. A. (2009). Neural markers of religious conviction. *Psychological Science, 20*, 385–392.

Ito, T. A., & Urland, G. R. (2003). Race and gender on the brain: Electrocortical measures of attention to race and gender of multiply categorizable individuals. *Journal of Personality and Social Psychology, 85*, 616–626.

Ito, T., & Urland, G. (2005). The influence of processing objectives on the perception of faces: An ERP study of race and gender perception. *Cognitive, Affective, & Behavioral Neuroscience, 5*, 21–36.

Ito, T. A., Willadsen-Jensen, E. C., & Correll, J. (2007). Social neuroscience and social perception: New perspectives on categorization, prejudice, and stereotyping. In E. Harmon-Jones & P. Winkielman (Eds.), *Social neuroscience: Integrating biological and psychological explanations of social behavior* (pp. 401–421). New York: Guilford.

Jones, E. E., & Davis, K. E. (1965). From acts to dispositions: The attribution process in person perception. In L. Berkowitz (Ed.), *Advances in experimental social psychology* (Vol. 2, pp. 219–266). New York: Academic Press.

Kaczmarek, B. L. J. (1984). Neurolinguistic analysis of verbal utterances in patients with focal lesions of frontal lobes. *Brain and Language, 21*, 52–58.

Kandel, E. R., Schwartz, J. H., & Jessell, T. M. (2000). *Principles of neural science* (4th ed.). New York: McGraw-Hill.

Kanwisher, N. G., McDermott, J., & Chun, M. M. (1997). The fusiform face area: A module in human extrastriate cortex specialized for face perception. *Journal of Neuroscience, 17*, 4302–4311.

Kaul, C., Ratner, K. G., & Van Bavel, J. J. (in press). Dynamic representations of race: Processing goals shape race encoding in the fusiform gyri. *Social Cognitive and Affective Neuroscience.*

Kelley, H. H. (1972) Attribution in social interaction. In E. E. Jones, D. E. Kanouse, H. H. Kelley, R. E. Nisbett, S. Valins, & B. Weiner (Eds.), *Attribution: Perceiving the causes of behavior* (pp. 1–26), Morristown, NJ: General Learning Press.

Kelley, W. M., Macrae, C. N., Wyland, C. L., Caglar, S., Inati, S., & Heatherton, T. F. (2002). Finding the self? An event-related fMRI study. *Journal of Cognitive Neuroscience, 14*, 785–794.

Killcross, A. S., Robbins, T. W., & Everitt, B. J. (1997). Different types of fear conditioned behavior mediated by separate nuclei in amygdala. *Nature, 388*, 377–380.

King-Casas, B., Tomlin, D., Anen, C., Camerer, C. F., Quartz, S. R., & Montague, P. R. (2005). Getting to know you: Reputation and trust in a two-person economic exchange. *Science, 308*, 78–83.

Kircher, T. T. J., Brammer, M., Bullmore, E., Simmons, A., Bartels, M., & David, A. S. (2002). The neural correlates of intentional and incidental self processing. *Neuropsychologia, 40*, 683–692.

Klein, S. B., & Kihlstrom, J. F. (1998). On bridging the gap between social-personality psychology and neuropsychology. *Personality and Social Psychology Review, 2*, 228–242.

Klein, S. B., Loftus, J., & Kihlstrom, J. F. (1996). Self-knowledge of an amnesic patient: Toward a neuropsychology of personality and social psychology. *Journal of Experimental Psychology: General, 125*, 250–260.

Knutson, K. M., Mah, L., Manly, C. F., & Grafman, J. (2007). Neural correlates of automatic beliefs about gender and race. *Human Brain Mapping, 28*, 915–930.

Lamm, C., Batson, C. D., & Decety, J. (2007). The neural substrate of human empathy: Effects of perspective-taking and cognitive appraisal. *Journal of Cognitive Neuroscience, 19*, 42–58.

LeDoux, J. E. (2000). Emotion circuits in the brain. *Annual Review of Neuroscience, 23*, 155–184.

Leyens, J. P., Cortes, B. P., Demoulin, S., Dovidio, J., Fiske, S. T., Gaunt, R., et al . (2003). Emotional prejudice, essentialism, and nationalism. *European Journal of Social Psychology, 33*, 703–718.

Leyens, J. P., Rodriguez-Perez, A., Rodriguez-Torres, R., Gaunt, R., Paladino, M. P., Vaes, J., et al. (2001). Psychological essentialism and the differential attribution of uniquely human emotions to ingroups and outgroups. *European Journal of Social Psychology, 31*, 395–411.

Lieberman, M. D., Hariri, A., Jarcho, J. M., Eisenberger, N. I., & Bookheimer, S. Y. (2005). An fMRI investigation of race-related amygdala activity in African-American and Caucasian-American individuals. *Nature Neuroscience, 8*, 720–722.

Lieberman, M. D., Jarcho, J. M., & Satpute, A. B. (2004). Evidence-based and intuition-based self-knowledge: An fMRI study. *Journal of Personality and Social Psychology, 87,* 421–35.

MacDonald, A. W., III, Cohen, J. D., Stenger, V. A., & Carter, C. S. (2000). Dissociating the role of the dorsolateral prefrontal cortex and anterior cingulate cortex in cognitive control. *Science, 288,* 1835–1838.

Mason, M. F., Norton, M. I., Van Horn, J. D., Wegner, D. M., Grafton, S. T., & Macrae, C. N. (2007). Wandering minds: The default network and stimulus-independent thought. *Science, 315,* 393–395.

Medalla, M., Lera, P., Feinberg, M., & Barbas, H. (2007). Specificity in inhibitory systems associated with prefrontal pathways to temporal cortex in primates. *Cerebral Cortex, 17,* 136–150.

Mehta, P. H., & Josephs, R. A. (2006). Testosterone change after losing predicts the decision to compete again. *Hormones and Behavior, 50,* 684–692.

Mendes, W. B., Gray, H., Mendoza-Denton, Major, B. & Epel, E. (2007). Why egalitarianism might be good for your health: Physiological thriving during intergroup interactions. *Psychological Science, 18,* 991–998.

Meyer, D. E., & Schvaneveldt, R. W. (1971). Facilitation in recognizing pairs of words: Evidence of a dependence between retrieval operations. *Journal of Experimental Psychology, 90,* 227–234.

Meyer, D. E., & Schvaneveldt, R. W. (1976). Meaning, memory, structure, and mental processes. *Science, 192,* 27–33.

Middleton, F. A., & Strick, P. L. (2000). Basal ganglia output and cognition: Evidence from anatomical, behavioral, and clinical studies. *Brain and Cognition, 42,* 183–200.

Miller, E. K., & Cohen, J. D. (2001). An integrative theory of prefrontal cortex function. *Annual Review of Neuroscience, 24,* 167–202.

Milne, E., & Grafman, J. (2001). Ventromedial prefrontal cortex lesions in humans eliminate implicit gender stereotyping. *Journal of Neuroscience, 21,* 1–6.

Mischel, W. (1974). Processes in delay of gratification. In L. Berkowitz (Ed.), *Advances in experimental social psychology* (Vol. 7, pp. 249–292). New York: Academic Press.

Mitchell, J. P. (2005). The false dichotomy between simulation and theory-theory: The argument's error. *Trends in Cognitive Sciences, 9,* 363–364.

Mitchell, J. P. (2009). Social psychology as a natural kind. *Trends in Cognitive Sciences, 13,* 246–251.

Mitchell, J. P., Ames, D. L., Jenkins, A. C., & Banaji, M. R. (2009). Neural correlates of stereotype application. *Journal of Cognitive Neuroscience, 21,* 594–604.

Mitchell, J. P., Banaji, M. R., & Macrae, C. N. (2005). General and specific contributions of the medial prefrontal cortex to knowledge about mental states. *NeuroImage, 28,* 757–762.

Mitchell, J. P., Heatherton, T. F., & Macrae, C. N. (2002). Distinct neural systems subserve person and object knowledge. *Proceedings of the National Academy of Sciences, 99,* 15238–15243.

Mitchell, J. P., Macrae, C. N., & Banaji, M. R. (2004). Encoding-specific effects of social cognition on the neural correlates of subsequent memory. *Journal of Cognitive Neuroscience, 24,* 4912–4917.

Mitchell, J. P., Macrae, C. N., & Banaji, M. R. (2006). Dissociable medial prefrontal contributions to judgments of similar and dissimilar others. *Neuron, 50,* 655–663.

Niedenthal, P. M. (2007). Embodying emotion. *Science, 316,* 1002–1005.

Nieuwenhuis, S., Ridderinkhof, K. R., Blom, J., Band, G. P. H., & Kok, A. (2001). Error-related brain potentials are differently related to awareness of response errors: Evidence from an antisaccade task. *Psychophysiology, 38,* 752–760.

Ochsner, K. N., & Lieberman, M. D. (2001). The emergence of social cognitive neuroscience. *American Psychologist, 56,* 717–734.

Ofan, R. H., Rubin, N., Amodio, D. M. (2011). Seeing race: N170 responses to race and their relation to automatic racial attitudes and controlled processing. *Journal of Cognitive Neuroscience, 23,* 3152–3161.

Olson, I. R., McCoy, D., Klobusicky, E., & Ross, L. A. (2013). Social cognition and the anterior temporal lobes: a review and theoretical framework. *Social Cognitive and Affective Neuroscience, 8,* 123–133.

Ostrom T. (1994). Foreword. In R. S. Wyer, Jr., & T. K. Srull (Eds.), *Handbook of social cognition* (2nd ed., pp. vii–xii). Hillsdale, NJ: Erlbaum.

Page-Gould, E., Mendes, W. B., & Major, B. (2010). Intergroup contact facilitates physiological recovery following stressful intergroup interactions. *Journal of Experimental Social Psychology, 46,* 854–858.

Passingham, R. (1993). *The frontal lobes and voluntary action.* Oxford, UK: Oxford University Press.

Perrett, D., Rolls, E., & Caan, W. (1982). Visual neurons responsive to faces in the monkey temporal cortex. *Experimental Brain Research, 47,* 329–342.

Pfeifer, J. H., Lieberman, M. D., & Dapretto, M. (2007). "I know you are but what am I?!" Neural bases of self- and social knowledge in children and adults. *Journal of Cognitive Neuroscience, 19,* 1323–1337.

Phelps, E. A., O'Connor, K. J., Cunningham, W. A., Funayama, E. S., Gatenby, J. C., Gore, J. C., & Banaji, M. R. (2000). Performance on indirect measures of race evaluation predicts amygdala activation. *Journal of Cognitive Neuroscience, 12,* 729–738.

Pizzagalli, D. A., Sherwood, R. J., Henriques, J. B., & Davidson, R. J. (2005). Frontal brain asymmetry and reward responsiveness: A source-localization study. *Psychological Science, 16,* 805–813.

Poldrack, R. A. (2006). Can cognitive processes be inferred from neuroimaging data? *Trends in Cognitive Sciences, 10,* 59–63.

Poldrack, R. A., & Foerde, K. (2008). Category learning and the memory systems debate. *Neuroscience and Biobehavioral Reviews, 32,* 197–205.

Quadflieg, S., Turk, D. J., Waiter, G. D., Mitchell, J. P., Jenkins, A. C., & Macrae, C. N. (2009). Exploring the neural correlates of social stereotyping. *Journal of Cognitive Neuroscience, 21,* 1560–1570.

Raichle, M. E., Fiez, J. A., Videen, T. O., MacLeod, A. K., Pardo, J. V., et al. (1994). Practice-related changes in human brain functional anatomy during nonmotor learning. *Cerebral Cortex, 4,* 8–26.

Rameson, L. T., & Lieberman, M. D. (2009). Empathy: A social cognitive neuroscience approach. *Social and Personality Psychology Compass, 3,* 94–110.

Rankin, R. E., & Campbell, D. T. (1955). Galvanic skin response to negro and white experimenters. *Journal of Abnormal and Social Psychology, 51,* 30–33.

Ratner, K. G., & Amodio, D. M. (2013). Seeing "us vs. them": Minimal group effects on the neural encoding of faces. *Journal of Experimental Social Psychology, 49,* 298–301.

Ratner, K. G., Halim, M. L., & Amodio, D. M. (2013). Perceived stigmatization, ingroup pride, and immune and endocrine activity: Evidence from a Black and Latina community sample. *Social Psychological and Personality Science, 4,* 82–91.

Ratner, K. G., Kaul, C., & Van Bavel, J. J. (in press). Is race erased? Decoding race from multivariate patterns of neural activity when skin color is not diagnostic of group boundaries. *Social Cognitive and Affective Neuroscience*.

Ratner, K. G., & Kubota, J. T. (2012). Genetic contributions to intergroup responses: A cautionary perspective. *Frontiers in Human Neuroscience, 6*, 223.

Rissman, J., Eliassen, J. C., & Blumstein, S. E. (2003). An event-related fMRI investigation of implicit semantic priming. *Journal of Cognitive Neuroscience, 15*, 1160–1175.

Rizzolatti, G., & Sinigaglia, C. (2010). The functional role of the parieto-frontal mirror circuit: Interpretations and misinterpretations. *Nature Reviews Neuroscience, 11*, 264–274.

Rolls, E. T., Hornak, J., Wade, D., & McGrath, J. (1994). Emotion-related learning in patients with social and emotional changes associated with frontal lobe damage. *Journal of Neurology, Neurosurgery, and Psychiatry, 57*, 1518–1524.

Salomons, T. V., Johnstone, T., Backonja, M. M., Shackman, A. S., & Davidson, R. J. (2007). Individual differences in the effects of perceived controllability on pain perception: Critical role of the prefrontal cortex. *Journal of Cognitive Neuroscience, 19*, 993–2003.

Saver, J. L., & Damasio, A. R. (1991). Preserved access and processing of social knowledge in a patient with acquired sociopathy due to ventromedial frontal damage. *Neuropsychologia, 29*, 1241–1249.

Saxe, R. (2005). Against simulation: The argument from error. *Trends in Cognitive Sciences, 9*, 174–179.

Saxe, R., Carey, S., & Kanwisher, N. (2004). Understanding other minds: Linking developmental psychology and functional neuroimaging. *Annual Review of Psychology, 55*, 87–124.

Saxe, R., Moran, J. M., Scholz, J., & Gabrieli, J. (2006). Overlapping and non-overlapping brain regions for theory of mind and self reflection in individual subjects. *Social Cognitive and Affective Neuroscience, 1*, 229–234.

Schacter, D. L., & Buckner, R. L. (1998). Priming and the brain. *Neuron, 20*, 185–195.

Schmitz, T. W., Kawahara-Baccus, T. N., & Johnson, S. C. (2004). Metacognitive evaluation, self-relevance, and the right prefrontal cortex. *NeuroImage, 22*, 941–947.

Scholz, J., Triantafyllous, C., Whitfield-Gabrieli, S., Brown, E. N., & Saxe, R. (2009). Distinct regions of the right temporo-parietal junction are selective for theory of mind and exogenous attention. *PLoS ONE, 4*, 1–7.

Shackman, A. J., Salomons, T. V., Slagter, H. A., Fox, A. S., Winter, J. J. & Davidson, R. J. (2011). The integration of negative affect, pain and cognitive control in the cingulate cortex. *Nature Reviews Neuroscience, 12*, 154–167.

Shamay-Tsoory, S. G., Tomer, R., Berger, B. D., & Aharon-Peretz, J. (2003). Characterization of empathy deficits following prefrontal brain damage: The role of the right ventromedial prefrontal cortex. *Journal of Cognitive Neuroscience, 15*, 324–337.

Singer, T., Seymour, B., O'Doherty, J., Kaube, H., Dolan, R. J., & Frith, C. D. (2004). Empathy for pain involves the affective but not sensory components of pain. *Science, 303*, 1157–62.

Smith, E. R., & Semin, G. R. (2004). Socially situated cognition: Cognition in its social context. *Advances in Experimental Social Psychology, 36*, 53–117.

Somerville, L. H., Heatherton, T. F., & Kelley, W. M. (2006). Anterior cingulate cortex responds differentially to expectancy violation and social rejection. *Nature Neuroscience, 9*, 1007–1008.

Squire, L. R. (1992). Memory and the hippocampus: A synthesis from findings with rats, monkeys, and humans. *Psychological Review, 99*, 195–231.

Squire, L. R., & Zola, S. M. (1996). Structure and function of declarative and nondeclarative memory systems. *Proceedings of the National Academy of Sciences, 93*, 13515–13522.

Swanson, L. W., & Petrovich, G. D. (1998). What is the amygdala? *Trends in Neurosciences, 21*, 323–331.

Todorov, A., Said, C. P., Engell, A. D., & Oosterhof, N. N. (2008). Understanding evaluation of faces on social dimensions. *Trends in Cognitive Sciences, 12*, 455–460.

Turner, M. S., Simons, J. S., Gilbert, S. J., Frith, C. D., & Burgess, P. W. (2008). Distinct roles for lateral and medial rostral prefrontal cortex in source monitoring of perceived and imagined events. *Neuropsychologia, 46*, 1442–1453.

Van Bavel, J. J., Packer, D. J., & Cunningham, W. A. (2008). The neural substrates of in-group bias: A functional magnetic resonance imaging investigation. *Psychological Science, 11*, 1131–1139.

van Reekum, C. M., Johnstone, T., Urry, H. L., Thurow, M. E., Schaefer, H. S., Alexander, A. L., & Davidson, R. J. (2007). Gaze fixations predict brain activation during the voluntary regulation of picture-induced negative affect. *Neuroimage, 36*, 1041–1055.

Vuilleumier, P., Richardson, M. P., Armony, J. L., Driver, J., & Dolan, R. J. (2004). Distant influences of amygdala lesion on visual cortical activation during emotional face processing. *Nature Neuroscience, 7*, 1271–1278.

Wager, T. D., Rilling, J., Smith, E. E., Sokolik, A., Casey, K., Kosslyn, S. M., Davidson, R.J., Rose, R. M., Cohen, J. D. (2004) Placebo-induced changes in fMRI in the anticipation and experience of pain. *Science, 303*, 1162–1167.

Wagner, A. D., Gabrieli, J. D. E., & Verfaellie, M. (1997). Dissociations between familiarity processes in explicit recognition and implicit perceptual memory. *Journal of Experimental Psychology: Learning, Memory, and Cognition, 23*, 305–323.

Walker, P., Silvert, L., Hewstone, M., & Nobre, A. (2008). Social contact and other-race face processing in the human brain. *Social Cognitive and Affective Neuroscience, 3*, 16–25.

Way, B. M., & Gurbaxani, B. M. (2008). A genetics primer for social health research. *Social and Personality Psychology Compass, 2*, 785–816.

Whalen, P. J. (1998). Fear, vigilance, and ambiguity: Initial neuroimaging studies of the human amygdala. *Current Directions in Psychological Science, 7*, 177–188.

Whalen, P. J., Rauch, S. L., Etcoff, N. L., McInerney, S. C., Lee, M., & Jenike, M. A. (1998). Masked presentations of emotional facial expressions modulate amygdala activity without explicit knowledge. *Journal of Neuroscience, 18*, 411–418.

Wiese, H., Stahl, J., & Schweinberger, S. R. (2009). Configural processing of other-race faces is delayed but not decreased. *Biological Psychology, 81*, 103–109.

Xu, X., Zuo, X., Wang, X., & Han, S. (2009). Do you feel my pain? Racial group membership modulates empathic neural responses. *Journal of Neuroscience, 29*, 8525–8529.

Yarkoni, T., Poldrack, R. A., Nichols, T. E., Van Essen, D. C., & Wager, T. D. (2011). Large-scale automated synthesis of human functional neuroimaging data. *Nature Methods, 8*, 665–670.

Yin, H. H., & Knowlton, B. J (2006). The role of the basal ganglia in habit formation. *Nature Reviews Neuroscience, 7*(6), 464–476.

Zhu, Y., Zhang, L., Fan, L., & Han, S. (2007). Neural basis of cultural influence on self-representation. *NeuroImage, 34*, 1310–1316.

Communication and Language Use in Social Cognition

Yoshihisa Kashima *and* Ying Lan

Abstract

Communication is a fundamental mechanism for the constitution of the social world. This chapter argues that social communication involves a two-way transmission of information typically using language, in which the sender and receiver of a message collaboratively work together. In this perspective, language is a semiotic tool, a tool with which to create and exchange meaning; it is language *use* that is central to this process. Based on this fundamental understanding, the chapter describes the grounding model of communication and its social cognitive implications. In this perspective, communication is characterized as a dynamic interplay between common ground—information actually and perceived to be already shared among the communicators—and grounding—the communicators' coordinated activity for establishing a mutual understanding about new information. When new information is grounded, common ground evolves. The evolution of common ground through communication is traced, and concomitant social cognitive consequences are discussed, not only for the senders and receivers of information, but also for the community of multiple communicators and their culture. The chapter concludes with a reaffirmation of the importance of communication as a fundamental mechanism for social cognition.

Key Words: communication, language, language use, common ground, grounding, coordination, culture, semiotic tool

Introduction

Communication is a sine qua non of human cognition. It is mainly through communication that humans obtain, reflect on, and pass along to others much of the information that their cognitive mechanisms process. As George Herbart Mead (1934) noted in his classic book, *Mind, Self, and Society*, it is through the dynamic process of social communication that humans come to have a sense of their self and to construct their social world. Reflecting this centrality, communication has been one of the critical issues for social cognition, as can be seen from the inclusion of a chapter devoted to this topic (Kraut & Higgins, 1984) in the first edition of the *Handbook of Social Cognition* (Wyer & Srull, 1984). Nonetheless, it is probably fair to say

that, in the first quarter century since its inception, social cognition was not so *social* focusing more on the intrapersonal cognitive mechanisms for the processing of social information than the inter-personal communication of information. Perhaps symbolic of this, in the second edition of the *Handbook of Social Cognition* (Wyer & Srull, 1994), a communication chapter was nowhere to be seen. In the 1990s, however, communication began to provide an important perspective for social cognition (e.g., Schwarz, 1996) by showing that some social judgments, on which social cognitive research was centrally focused, can be altered and influenced by communication processes. We suggest that the communication–cognition interface is a critical mechanism by which the mind and society interact with each other. Communication is central to social cognition because it is central to the formation, maintenance, and transformation of human sociality.

In social psychology, communication has typically been conceptualized as a process of message transmission, primarily following Carl Hovland's legacy of the Yale communication paradigm. In this conception, a message source sends out an encoded message, which is in turn decoded by an audience and translated into psychological representations. This may produce social influence in the form of attitude change. The cognitive response paradigm, which extended this line of work, adopted the same basic structure of communication while expanding the active role of the audience. Inside the audience's mind, a message is not only translated but also interpreted, construed, reflected on, or even counterargued. Nonetheless, the underlying theoretical imagination remained the same—that of one-way transmission of information from the source to the audience. The active role of the audience remained cognitive; little was returned from the audience to the source by way of return communication. The 1990s' injection of a communication perspective into social cognition began to introduce the critical role of social coordination in communication. More recent developments, which we review below, bring forward this trend even more. This chapter presents a framework called the *grounding model* (Clark, 1996; Kashima, Klein, & Clark, 2007) within which to theorize the communication–cognition interface. This model places the two-way interactive process of meaning–making and meaning–exchange at the center of communication. In so doing, the framework encourages a reconsideration of the traditional conception of communication in social psychology.

The chapter is divided into two main sections. The first section describes the processes and mechanisms of communication based on the grounding model. In particular, we suggest that social communication typically occurs within a context of a joint activity in which two or more individuals pursue a joint goal through collaborative activities. The critical concepts, common ground and grounding, are introduced as processes by which people share information. Recent research is reviewed to examine the evolution of common ground and the cognitive mechanisms that underpin the grounding process. The second section reviews social psychological consequences of the grounding process from Holtgraves and Kashima's (2008) perspective, which regards language as a psychological tool for making and exchanging meaning. We show that there are unintended cognitive consequences to the sender and the receiver of a communication. Furthermore, we show that communication can be a significant mechanism by which a collective, which includes both senders and receivers of communication, develops a shared culture.

Processes and Mechanisms of Communication: Grounding Model of Social Communication

Communication rarely occurs for its own sake, but rather typically takes place as part of a joint activity—an activity that people do together, including such mundane activities as "going out to a restaurant," "having a committee meeting," and "planning a family holiday." Any joint activity has a goal that its participants are trying to attain together (e.g., getting to the right restaurant at the right time, and enjoying the meal and good company). Communication is part of these broader social activities that people engage in (e.g., H. H. Clark, 1996; Kashima, Klein, & A. E. Clark, 2007). To describe the current view of communication, it is necessary to clarify this broader social context first.

What Is a Joint Activity?

A joint activity consists of a series of actions that participants perform in coordination with each other in order to reach a joint goal. It typically involves two or more participants (socially bounded); has a beginning, a main body, and an ending (temporally bounded); and takes place within a social institutional setting (spatially bounded).

There are two critical elements here. One is a joint goal, a goal that its participants at least tacitly agree that they are attempting to attain. The other is coordination. This implies that each participant has a role to play, in that he or she is to perform some actions but not others as part of the joint activity; one participant's action is to be performed in spatial and temporal coordination with one or more other participants' actions; and these actions are necessary to attain the joint goal.

Joint activities form fuzzy categories. They are defined in contradistinction to each other; their exemplars vary markedly and may only be similar to each other in terms of family resemblance. That is, there may be no criterial or individually necessary and jointly sufficient definitional features that make an activity an instance of a category of joint activities. For example, a dentist visit, a dinner party, grocery shopping, and so forth may be categories of joint activities. Joint activities are often partonomically organized, so that one joint activity may be part of another joint activity. For instance, the joint activity of "having a pleasant conversation" is part of the joint activity of "a dinner party." Cognitive representations of joint activities may take the form of scripts (e.g., Schank & Abelson, 1977).

Grounding and Common Ground

In the process of pursuing the goal of a joint activity like a dinner party, participants carry out a number of goal-directed and coordinated actions; communication is a part of this greater joint activity (in addition to other actions, such as drinking, eating, walking in the room without bumping into others), and is itself a type of joint activity (or a sub-joint activity). In this view, to communicate a piece of information is to make the information mutual knowledge of the participants of the joint activity. There are two significant parts to this understanding. The first is the sharedness component. Communication involves the process by which at least one participant (sender), who has information, gives it to other participants (receivers), who do not have the information. This part reflects the encoding–decoding model of communication. It assumes that information held in the sender's mind is encoded into a message, a series of signs—some observable behavior or its products (e.g., gestures, verbal signals, writing)—that are decoded by the receivers and transformed into cognitive representations in their minds. This results in the information coming to be held by both the sender and the receivers. To this basic model, the current view adds a second component, perceived sharedness. That is, to communicate information is not only for the senders and receivers to share the information, but also that they come to perceive, explicitly or tacitly, that they share that information. This second requirement—the participants recognize that they share the information—is critical for understanding the mechanisms and functions of human social communication.

The process of sharing information and also establishing perceived sharedness of the information is called grounding (e.g., H. H. Clark, 1996; Kashima et al., 2007), and it consists of at least two parts. First, one participant presents new information, and then the other participants need to accept it; that is to say, the receivers of the information need to provide some evidence that they have understood what the presenter of the information meant. This evidence could be a simple nonverbal behavior like a nod, a brief utterance like "aha," or

a somewhat more extensive utterance with a facial expression and a gesture, "What? Why did he do that?" Nevertheless, when there is evidence that a mutually shared understanding is agreed on sufficiently for the present purpose (as dictated by the goal of the joint activity), the participants are said to have grounded the information. Thus, grounding achieves the dual requirements of sharedness and perceived sharedness of new information.

The grounded information is added to the participants' common ground. Common ground is a set of information that the participants share and perceive themselves as sharing (e.g., H. H. Clark, 1996; H. H. Clark & Marshall, 1981; also see Kashima et al., 2007). At the beginning of a joint activity, the participants activate their initial common ground, a set of information that the participants assume they share for this particular joint activity. This is likely to contain information from the participants' shared personal experiences, and also from their group memberships. If they have personal relationships (e.g., friend, work colleague, neighbor) and have participated in joint activities together in the past, their common experiences are likely to be in their initial common ground (H. H. Clark, 1996, calls it "personal common ground"). Similarly, if they share group memberships (e.g., nationality, gender), information that members of the groups typically have in common (e.g., the country's leader's name), including a common language, is likely to be contained as well ("communal common ground"; H. H. Clark, 1996).

Whatever information is available in the common ground at the time is used to construct a message and to communicate. This provides common cognitive resources for grounding—that is, for the communicators to construct messages to present information, and also to understand the messages to accept the information. More and more new information is grounded as they continue to engage in their joint activity, and thus the working common ground is updated constantly and evolves over time. When the joint activity comes to an end, the common ground is deactivated. Memory representations of the grounding activities are updated continuously within each participant's memory system and distributed among the communicators. This form of representation is distributed cognition (e.g., Hutchins, 1995; Smith & Semin, 2004), meaning that similar, but not identical, information is stored by multiple individuals, and each individual's memory is likely to differ from others' because they have different sets of knowledge, expertise, expectations, motivations, and the like.

Thus, during a joint activity, a context-specific common ground—common ground that is specific to this particular joint activity performed by this particular set of individuals in a particular physical location at a particular point in time—is continuously constructed and updated; at its conclusion, its memories are held in distributed form across the participants. It is important to note that this type of common ground contains information about both a collective identity and collective representations. In other words, common ground tells the participants who "we"—those who participated in the joint activity—are, and what information "we" share, and are supposed to share. Collective identities are conceptually closely related to, but different from, social identities (Tajfel & Turner, 1979; Turner, 1987). A social identity is "the individual's knowledge that he belongs to certain social groups together with some emotional and value significance to him of his group membership" (Tajfel, 1972, p. 292), whereas a collective identity in the present sense is the individual's knowledge that a collection of people, including himself or herself, engaged in the joint activity, what this collection of people may be called, and so forth. Collective representations are closely associated with social representations (Moscovici, 1981; Wagner & Hayes, 2005), although again somewhat different; collective representations in the present sense involve the information actually and perceived to be shared by the above collection of people.

Kashima et al. (2007) suggested that a context-specific common ground can be generalized socially, spatially, or temporally to form a generalized common ground. That is, temporal generalization of context-specific common ground entails the same individuals performing their joint activity at a different time in the future; spatial generalization involves the same individuals conducting their joint activity in different physical locations; and social generalization occurs when different, although potentially overlapping, sets of individuals participate in the joint activity. When a context-specific common ground is generalized across temporal and spatial dimensions, but not along social dimension, this becomes a basis of personal common ground, whereas if it is generalized along all three dimensions to a category of individuals, it can become a basis of communal common ground, and become very similar indeed to what we usually call a culture.

INFORMATION POTENTIALLY GROUNDED IN COMMUNICATION

Communication typically occurs within a joint activity in order to help the interactants achieve their joint goal. Therefore, some information is explicitly presented and accepted in the course of their interaction and becomes grounded to their common ground. Let us call the explicitly grounded information *focal information*—information that communication is about. However, information grounded in social communication goes beyond the focal information that is directly relevant for the joint goal. Let us call this *background information*. Some is presuppositional—information that is presupposed and taken for granted regardless of the truthfulness or falsity of the focal information. Other background information is relational—information about relations among various elements contained and implied in the focal information. It is important to note that not only focal information but also presuppositional and relational information are grounded in social communication.

To illustrate this point, take the following exchange (called an adjacency pair) between a husband (H) and his wife (W) as an example (Berger & Luckmann, 1971, p. 172).

> H: Well, it's time for me to get to the station.
> W: Fine, darling, have a good day at the office.

This exchange can be understood as the performance of a joint activity in which the preceding joint activity of breakfast conversation between a husband and a wife is being terminated. The husband's utterance presents the focal information: He intends to leave and go to work by taking a train from the nearby station. The wife's reply accepts it, thus grounding the focal information. However, it grounds far more information than just his intention. First of all, it grounds relational information, information about the social relation between the two interactants as people who are close to each other. Furthermore, it grounds presuppositional information, information about the social reality of a conventional family life in a Western European–based industrialized country, probably around the mid-20th century. That is, the husband and wife live in a suburban home, the husband works at an office in the city, there is a train service between the station and the city, a train runs more or less in accordance with the train schedule, he takes the train to his work, and the wife stays home and looks after the family.

This example illustrates the multiple layers of social reality simultaneously grounded in a simple joint activity: most obviously, the husband's leaving home to go to work; then, the relationship between the husband and wife; and least obviously, but most definitely, the presupposed social reality "within which these apparently simple propositions make sense" (Berger & Luckmann, 1971, p. 172). As the focal information is grounded to the evolving common ground, its presuppositional information that was part of that common ground is also regrounded without challenge. This way, "[m]ost conversation does not in so many words define the nature of the world. Rather, it takes place against the background of a world that is silently taken for granted" (p. 172). To the best of our knowledge, social cognitive mechanisms surrounding this last process have not been investigated to date.

Implications

There are several important implications of this way of conceptualizing communication. First and foremost, communication is a two-way affair. Even if only one person is talking and the other listening, there is always a degree of social coordination in their mutual recognition and adjustment of their cognition and action. However, there are other, more subtle implications of this conceptualization. Because social communication tends to occur in a goal-directed joint activity, communicators are typically performing social actions in pursuit of their goal, by making utterances or other forms of communicative acts. In other words, social communication is for doing (e.g., Austin, 1962; Holtgraves, 2002; Searle, 1969).

The participants in communication need to maintain representations about their own and the other participants' representations about the topic of communication. This is to say that when one communicates with another, one needs to know what they both know to establish a mutual understanding. These types of representation about people's representations are called *meta-representations* (e.g., Sperber, 2000) and may involve a theory of mind—tacit understandings about the mind's constituents, such as beliefs, desires, emotions, and intentions, as well as how the mind works (e.g., Malle, 2005). To put it differently, human communication requires a meta-representational capacity, and communication and people's theory of mind have intricate inter-relationships.

In establishing a mutual understanding of a communication, what is often at issue is the speaker's intention. Because social communication is for doing and grounding activities presuppose meta-representations—communicators' representations of each other's representations—understanding what a communicator is trying to do (i.e., constructing a representation about his or her intention) becomes a critical aspect of understanding the communication. Many theorists of language use (e.g., Grice, 1957; Searle, 1969; Sperber & Wilson, 1995) have highlighted the importance of the speaker's intention as fundamental to meaning (e.g., speech act theorists like Searle called it "illocutionary force"). Indeed, Holtgraves's (2008; also see Holtgraves & Ashley, 2001) recent investigation suggests that the recognition of a speaker's intention is largely automatic. When Bob says to Andy, "I definitely will do it tomorrow," Andy (and anyone who listens to it) automatically infers Bob's intention to make a promise.

Evolution of Common Ground

Evolution of context-specific common ground has been examined with a referential communication task. In this task, each individual in a pair is given a set of ambiguous pictures (e.g., drawings that cannot be described with single words or conventional phrases) in different orders, and one (the director) directs the other (the matcher) to order the pictures in the same way the director did. Because the pictures cannot be easily described verbally, the director needs to construct verbal expressions to refer to the pictures, so that the matcher can understand which pictures the director is referring to. This task is repeated several times over a session, with the same pair of a director and a matcher. A number of studies (e.g., Krauss & Weinheimer, 1964, 1967; H. H. Clark & Wilkes-Gibbs, 1986; for a review, see Krauss & Fussell, 1996) have shown that the director will use long expressions (e.g., "Looks like a martini glass with legs on each side") initially, but referential expressions become shorter, eventually to just a word or a simple phrase (e.g., "martini"), and the same (or very similar) short expression tends to be used repeatedly. The construction of utterances appropriate for one's audience is called audience design.

In a related vein, Garrod and Anderson (1987; also see Garrod & Doherty, 1994) showed that conversants ground not only the same word or phrase but also the same type of referring expressions, in referential communication. In a computer game–like environment, a pair was instructed to move their cursors from a starting point to a destination in a computer maze constructed on a grid. Both players could see the maze. The game was set up so that each player could control his or her cursor movement, but could not control obstacles that were blocking their cursor's paths to its destination. On the other hand, the player's partner had control over these obstacles, but he or she could not see where his or her cursor needed to be moved to control the obstacles. (The game was actually more complex than this, but this description should suffice to convey the gist.) This context required the pair to cooperate with each other, so that they could refer to the right spot in the maze in order to instruct each other to move cursors and remove obstacles in the right way. There were several different ways in which to refer to a location in a maze; for example, they could use a coordinate system (e.g., third column from the right, two from the bottom), a landmark (e.g., see the rectangle at the bottom right, I'm in the top left-hand corner), and the like. Garrod and Anderson found that a pair typically converged on the same type of referring expressions while they were playing the game, although they flexibly shifted between different styles.

Apparently, a context-specific common ground can be temporally and spatially generalized as long as the interactants remain the same. Evidence comes from the referential communication task when a director instructs a matcher to identify an object. Once a particular referential expression is established between a director and a matcher in a joint activity, it is used again by the director in a later joint activity with the same matcher. Brennan and H. H. Clark (1996) called this a "conceptual pact"—one way of referring to an object (e.g., martini) implies one way of conceptualizing it; the director assumes that the same common ground applies when interacting with the same matcher. Nevertheless, a referential expression grounded in one context-specific common ground is not automatically socially generalized to other matchers. Brennan and H. H. Clark found that the director did not persist with the same referential expression when he or she interacted with a different matcher. Subsequent research suggests that the same pattern of generalization occurs not only for the speaker (i.e., the director) but also for a listener. A listener who has grounded a particular referential expression with a speaker also expects the context-specific common ground to be generalized with the same speaker, but not with a different speaker (Metzing & Brennan, 2003; also see Shintel & Keysar, 2007).

Garrod and Doherty (1994) showed that socially generalized common ground can emerge under some circumstances, that is, when pairs of interactants are presumably known to be sampled from the same "community." In this research, participants' referential communications were investigated using the computer maze game used by Garrod and Anderson (1987). In one condition (isolated pairs), the same partners played the game repeatedly. In the "community" condition, pairs were formed by selecting two players from an ad hoc collection of participants, which was called a community. After a set of pairs played the game for one block, different pairs were formed and played the game. This procedure was iterated until all possible pairs were formed and played the game. The isolated pairs condition was similar to Garrod and Anderson's original condition, but the latter community condition differed in that players presumably knew that they were all participating in the same maze game, but would swap partners from one game to another, ending up with different partners who belonged to the same group. Replicating Garrod and Anderson (1987), participants in the isolated pairs converged on the same type of referring expressions, although their expressions shifted at times from earlier games to later ones. Interestingly, in the community condition, pairs initially differed considerably in their expressions, but their referring expression types converged strongly in later games, and did not change at all. This research suggests that those who belonged to the same "community" produced a shared referential expression type even though they had no explicit agreement to do so.

Common ground that is temporally, spatially, and socially generalized is communal common ground—that is, common ground based on interactants' group memberships. There is evidence to suggest that people do have communal common ground and use it in their referential communications. Isaacs and H. H. Clark (1987) paired people who were familiar with New York City with those who were unfamiliar to work together in a referential communication task that involved arranging pictures of New York City landmarks. By examining the recorded conversations, they found that shortly after the conversations began, participants who met for the first time could assess each other's knowledge about New York City, and adjusted their choice of referring expressions accordingly. When both were New Yorkers, they simply used proper names for the landmarks, but when a New Yorker was describing a landmark to a non–New Yorker, the speaker used other expressions.

In a similar study, Fussell and Krauss (1992) also showed that people engage in audience design based on their conversation partners' group membership. They had participants engage in a referential communication task to identify pictures of everyday tools, some of which were more recognizable either for men or women. From the recorded conversations, the researchers found that participants were able to estimate the recognizability of the tools for their first-encounter interaction partners on the basis of their partners' gender (e.g., kitchen utensils were more recognizable to women). Additionally, participants also added more identifying information to their expressions when they thought recognizability was low for their partners (e.g., providing both the name and the description of a kitchen utensil to men). Gerrig and Littman's (1990) study also provided further evidence for people's ability to spontaneously use communal common ground in comprehension.

Cognitive Mechanisms Underlying the Use of Common Ground

A cognitive model underlying the use of common ground stipulates that there are two subprocesses in message production: commonality assessment and message formation (Horton & Gerrig, 2005a, 2005b). Commonality assessment refers to the message sender's inference about common ground using external cues; message formation is the process of utterance construction. For instance, speakers may assess what common ground they share with their addressees (e.g., "Is he on a first name basis with John Doe?"), and then decide how to refer to the shared information most appropriately (e.g., "I should refer to John by his first name") on the basis of their beliefs about how accessible the information is to their addressees. These processes are highly inter-related in online conversations; however, they can be conceptualized and examined somewhat independently of each other when communication takes place in a noninteractive situation.

COMMONALITY ASSESSMENT—COORDINATING COMMON GROUND

According to Horton and Gerrig (2005a, 2005b), when interactants begin a joint activity, external cues available from the interactants—information about their social category memberships (e.g., "He's a student on this campus") or their personal identity (e.g., "Oh, that's John from my high school"), for instance—are used to access the associated information that resides in long-term memory. Following

the current models of content addressable memory (e.g., Hintzman, 1986; see Kashima, Woolcock, & Kashima, 2000, for a related model in social cognition), Horton and Gerrig assume that once cues are activated, they automatically activate associated memory contents, and that this general memory process is responsible for commonality assessment.

In line with this general idea, Pickering and Garrod's (2004) interactive alignment model suggests that commonality assessment involves a dynamic online coordination of shared representations through multiple levels of language use. Pickering and Garrod assumed that the establishment of common ground—what is shared and perceived to be shared by interactants—is necessary for successful communication. However, they provided a mechanistic account of how common ground can be established. They regarded the establishment of common ground as an alignment of the interactants' mental models, and argued that they achieve this by mechanistically imitating or mimicking each other's styles of language use. That is, people tend to imitate the same linguistic constructions as their interaction partners', which tend to align their language use over time. Furthermore, alignment at one level of language use (e.g., using a lexicon) tends to facilitate the alignment of language use at another level (e.g., syntactic level). This is because one level of language use can prime the other level of language use. Thus, the interactants align their words, syntax, and other forms at multiple levels of language use, and as a result, they are also likely to end up aligning their mental models (or situation models; Zwaan & Radvansky, 1998)—their cognitive representations of the things that they are talking about. When misalignment is detected, the interactants make adjustments to their utterances and representations. As the interactants produce and comprehend each other's utterances, and thus prime each other's language use at the lexical, syntactic, and semantic levels through constant feedback available in live interpersonal interaction, the cognitive representations used for their language production and comprehension become similar to each other, thus achieving common ground as shared representations.

MESSAGE FORMATION—CONSTRUCTING MESSAGES USING COMMON GROUND

During the process of message formation, there are two subprocesses: (1) message planning and (2) monitoring and adjustment (Horton & Keysar, 1996). Speakers first make a plan to construct an utterance, and then monitor the execution of this utterance plan later—if the speaker detects an error, he or she makes an adjustment. Horton and Keysar (1996) examined whether common ground plays a role in the message planning or monitoring processes. They suggested that planning occurs relatively quickly at an early part of utterance production, whereas monitoring and adjustment are more time-consuming and occur at a later point of the process. Based on this assumption, they argued that whether or not speakers are under time pressure would make a difference if common ground plays a role in monitoring, but would not if common ground is used in the planning stage. In particular, they argued that the initial utterance planning may typically be egocentric, and may make use of any accessible information from the speaker's perspective, but common ground may affect later monitoring and adjustment, so that the speaker may adjust his or her utterances when he or she has sufficient time to do so. If this is the case, utterances made under time pressure may not show the effect of common ground, whereas utterances made with sufficient time would take common ground into consideration.

To test between these possibilities, Horton and Keysar (1996) used a modified referential communication task, in which a director was to describe a figure for a matcher. The director and matcher sat side by side in front of a computer screen. Each pair was separated by a barrier so that they could not see the other side of the computer screen. A figure moved from the director's side to the matcher's side; the director's task was to describe this figure for the matcher. Each target object (e.g., a small circle) appeared with a context object, a large circle, for instance. In the shared condition, the director was told that the context object was visible for both the director and the matcher, so that the context object was in their common ground; in the other privileged condition, the context object was visible only for the director, so that it was not in their common ground. If common ground is taken into consideration, the director should describe the target as "a small circle" only when a large circle was in their common ground, but not when a large circle was not in their common ground. Consistent with the hypothesis that common ground affects monitoring and adjustment, Horton and Keysar found that this was true only when the director made utterances without any time pressure; there were no differences between the shared and privileged conditions in utterances made under time pressure.

Subsequent research on listener comprehension in North America (e.g., Barr, 2008; Keysar,

Barr, Balin, & Brauner, 2000) provides evidence in line with this process model. However, there is evidence of potential cross-cultural differences in common ground use. Using different experimental paradigms, Haberstroh, Oyserman, Schwartz, Kuhnen, and Ji (2002) and Wu and Keysar (2007) both showed that Chinese tend to take their partners' perspective more into consideration than their North American counterparts.

Communication Goals, Conversational Rules, and Context of Communication

There are at least two broad goals operating in communication. One goal is to be informative. Common ground contains all the information that is given (or presupposed by the communicators), and therefore a communication should contain new information. So, it is important to transmit the new information efficiently. The other goal is to regulate social relations. As noted earlier, communication can ground the social relation between the communicators. The communicators' message construction is likely driven by the goal of achieving desired social relations as well. The communicators may wish to strengthen or maintain the current level of social relation, or they may wish to distance themselves from the audience. Either way, communication strategies used to regulate the communicator–audience relation—what information to include in a message and how to deliver it—become a significant aspect of message construction.

What are the strategies that communicators use to pursue these goals of communication? These strategies have been discussed in terms of "rules" or "maxims" of conversation. One category of rules has mostly to do with efficient transmission of information. One of the best known in this category are Grice's (1975) conversational maxims:

Maxim of quantity—make your contribution as informative as required (be informative, but avoid being too informative)
Maxim of quality—try to make your contribution true (with some evidence)
Maxim of manner—be clear (avoid ambiguity or obscurity)
Maxim of relation—make your contribution relevant

Sperber and Wilson's (1995) relevance theory is another prominent example. Although this theory is highly complex, it probably suffices to say that Grice's (1975) four maxims are reduced to the overarching rule of relevance in their conceptualization.

However, these rules are primarily designed to construct utterances so that they can be efficiently and accurately decoded by the message receivers.

Another category of "rules" has to do with management and regulation of social relationships between the message senders and receivers. One of the best known of this type is P. Brown and Levinson's (1987) politeness theory. Based on Goffman's (1967) analysis of face work, they propose that interactants affirm and maintain their faces during their interactions. There are two types of faces: negative and positive faces, which represent desires for autonomy and social connectedness, respectively. Threats to someone's negative face include acts that impinge on their freedom to do what they want to do. So, anything that can hinder their pursuit of the current goal can potentially threaten their negative face. Threats to their positive face are acts that can damage their relationships; ignoring, criticizing, or avoiding someone can all potentially threaten their positive face. Their politeness rules basically state: Enhance and avoid threatening positive and negative faces. There are a variety of strategies that P. Brown and Levinson consider. Positive politeness strategies—claiming common ground, conveying a cooperative intent, and the like—are directed toward the maintenance of positive face; negative politeness strategies—conveying a desire to avoid impingement, avoiding coercion—are for negative face maintenance. Holtgraves and his colleagues have conducted a series of social psychological investigations of this formulation (1986, 1994; see Holtgraves, 2002, for a review; also see Slugoski & Turnbull, 1988) and cross-cultural variations (e.g., Holtgraves & Yang, 1990, 1992).

One caveat is in order. The "rules" of conversation here are not necessarily explicitly represented as prescriptive or proscriptive rules in the conversants' minds. Of course, it is possible that they are represented consciously and applied in their conversation in a controlled and deliberate way; alternatively, they may have become automated during socialization and applied without much effort.

The joint activity in which a communication takes place is an important determinant of the goals that communicators pursue. In particular, the relative importance of informativeness and social relational goals depends on the joint activity that they are engaged in. For example, having a friendly chat around the water cooler at work would emphasize the social relational goal, but discussing a budget in your organization's planning meeting would stress the informativeness goal. Either way, being informative does not mean not regulating social relations, or vice versa; different conversational rules are likely to be used in different joint activities depending on the relative emphasis placed on one or the other goal.

Consequences of Communication

Communication is a type of joint activity in which communicators work in a highly coordinated manner to establish a mutual understanding, or common ground. As Holtgraves and Kashima (2008) noted, communicators usually need to use language as a semiotic tool for meaning making and meaning exchange. Although language often serves the intended joint goals fairly well (of course, there are many barriers to efficient communication, and miscommunications often occur), just like any other tools, language can have unintended consequences on social cognition. In the following sections, Holtgraves and Kashima's framework is used to examine these unintended consequences of language use for the sender, receiver, and collective.

Sender Effects

In communication, the goal of message senders is to have message receivers understand their intentions and meanings as we discussed earlier. They typically achieve this goal by using language to convert their nonlinguistic representations into explicit and communicable representations. However, the act of verbalizing one's nonlinguistic representations can alter the nature of these initial representations.

DECISION MAKING

For decision makers, ultimately their aim is to make optimal decisions that would best resolve the issues they are facing. Language as a semiotic tool enables decision makers to explain their reasons for making particular decisions. However, Wilson and colleagues (Wilson & LaFleur, 1995; Wilson, Lisle, & Kraft, 1990; Wilson et al., 1993; Wilson & Schooler, 1991) have found that verbalizing reasons for decisions can influence various aspects of the decision-making process, including the quality of the decision itself.

For instance, in one study, Wilson and Schooler (1991) asked participants to make judgments about the quality of different brands of strawberry jam (Experiment 1), or to indicate preferences for different college courses (Experiment 2). The researchers found in both experiments that participants made less optimal decisions when they had to explain their reasons than when they did not. Wilson and

Schooler argued that the act of verbalizing shifts decision makers' focus to nonoptimal criteria, and such shifts alter the nature of the decisions to be made. When decision makers have to not only make decisions, but also explicate their reasons, the communicability of the reasons becomes a major concern for the decision makers. Consequently, reasons that are easiest to verbalize are most likely to be chosen and drive the decisions, whereas reasons that are more difficult to verbalize but also more important for the decisions tend to be excluded. As the decisions are supported by reasons that relate less to their quality, the decisions become less optimal.

In another study, Wilson et al. (1993) provided further support for the influence of verbalization on decision making. They had participants rate a set of either humorous (easy-to-verbalize features) or artistic (difficult-to-verbalize features) posters. In the experimental condition, participants were asked to explicate their reasons for their ratings, whereas in the control condition, participants were not required to do so. It was found that, for experimental participants, because they had to explicate their reasons, the ease of articulating poster features became a crucial factor affecting their ratings. Because humorous posters had easy-to-verbalize features, experimental participants were more likely to articulate the positive attributes of the humorous posters than of the artistic posters. Consequently, they gave higher ratings to the humorous posters. On the other hand, control participants preferred artistic posters, despite their difficult-to-verbalize features, because the ease of articulating poster features was not a concern for these participants.

EMOTIONS

Emotions are inchoate psychological experiences that are primarily communicated through language. People not only express their own emotional experiences but also describe others'. However, describing emotions (both one's own and others') can affect describers' representations and alter the meaning of those emotional experiences.

In relation to describing others' emotions, Halberstadt (2003) found that verbally identifying others' emotions can bias people's subsequent memories about the expressions of those emotions. Halberstadt had participants view photos of people showing ambiguous emotional expressions. In the experimental condition, participants were required to explain why the person was experiencing that particular emotion, whereas in the control condition, participants were not asked to do so. He found that experimental participants remembered the emotional expressions as more intense than did control participants. For example, participants who explained why the stimulus person was experiencing anger tended to perceive, then remember, that person's face as angrier than participants who did not have to explain.

Halberstadt (2003) suggested that a two-stage process may be able to explain the production of biased memory. In the process of talking about others' emotional expressions, people need to first decompose the face into its component features, and then reintegrate them with the relevant emotion category. Consequently, people's perception and memory of a particular emotional face are assimilated toward the relevant emotion category. Therefore, people's representation of that particular emotion is altered by language use.

In relation to describing one's own emotions, language use can also distort the describer's own perceptions of those emotions. Lieberman (2007) found that affective labeling activates the reflective (C-system) but dampens the reflexive (X-system) neural system. As a result, verbalizing an emotional state alters the underlying physiology of that state. In line with this reasoning, other studies (e.g., Hariri, Bookheimer, & Mazziotta, 2000; Lieberman et al., 2007) have found that describing negatively valenced images lessens the activation of amygdala.

The effect of verbalizing emotions can be psychologically beneficial. Talking about or writing one's own thoughts about negative experiences, especially traumatic ones, can enhance overall well-being (Lyubomirsky, Sousa, & Dickerhoof, 2006). This is because converting the implicit nonlinguistic representations of one's negative experiences into explicit and communicable linguistic representations allows one to organize, structure, and complete those experiences, and then to bring them to an end. However, simply thinking about the negative emotions is not sufficient for regulation. Lyubomirsky et al. (2006) found enhanced life satisfaction for participants who wrote or talked about their negative experiences, but diminished life satisfaction for those who just thought about the experiences. As Lieberman (2007) suggested, verbalizing one's reactions to negative experiences can lessen the automatic rumination that might prolong negative affectivity (see also Pennebaker, 1997).

STORYTELLING

Storytelling is a universal method by which people communicate their inchoate psychological experiences to others as well as to themselves. Previous research (e.g., Marsh, 2007; McAdams, 1993; Pennington & Hastie, 1988; Schank & Abelson, 1977, 1995) has suggested that language use in storytelling has important cognitive consequences. Basically, the act of storytelling can alter storytellers' mental representations of the past in two ways. First, storytellers' representation of a particular story is influenced by a storytelling schema (Rumelhart, 1975). To construct a story, storytellers must first put a sequence of events into a story-like structure. Hence, the representation that remains is assimilated toward how that story is told (Schank & Abelson, 1995). McGregor and Holmes (1999) demonstrated this storytelling effect. They had participants tell a biased story about a relationship conflict as if they were a lawyer for one of the two fictitious characters. Subsequently, participants' memories and judgments of the characters were assessed. Their judgments were biased in the direction of the story told.

The phenomenon of cognitive tuning (Zajonc, 1960; for a review, see Guerin & Innes, 1989) may be interpreted in this light. Those who expect to transmit information about a person tend to report more coherent impressions about the target person than those who expect to receive information. In the process of telling an audience about a person who might occasionally exhibit behaviors and characteristics that are complex, and not always describable in a simple way, the communicator tends to provide a simpler verbal account of the person, which in turn may alter the communicator's impression. In line with this, Thompson, Judd, and Park (2000; also see Brauer, Judd, & Jacquelin, 2001) found that people produce verbal descriptions of a group of people that are interpreted by their audience as exhibiting more polarized and less variable behavioral tendencies than their own impressions of the group. Kashima et al.'s (2010) recent studies showed that such communications about a group can produce more polarized and essentialized impressions of the group.

Moreover, storytellers' representation of a particular story can be further altered by their audience. According to H. H. Clark and Murphy (1982), in order to establish a mutual understanding, communicators should and often do engage in audience design. Because people frequently tell stories to others in a social context, storytellers should and often will engage in audience design, tailoring their stories for a specific audience. In this way, storytellers' mental representations of the past are further influenced by the audience's perspectives.

A classic study conducted by Higgins and Rholes (1978), which reported the saying-is-believing (SIB) phenomenon, well illustrates the influences of storytelling on storytellers' mental representations. In their study, participants were asked to describe a stimulus person whose portrait was evaluatively ambiguous (e.g., Donald who is adventurous or foolhardy) for an audience who presumably liked or disliked the target being described. It was found that participants adjusted their descriptions on the basis of their knowledge about the audience's preference. Later, when their memory and impressions of the described target were assessed, those who had described the target more positively tended to have more positive memory and impressions of the target. Other studies (e.g., Dudukovic, Marsh, & Tversky, 2004; Marsh & Tversky, 2004; Tversky & Marsh, 2000) have also demonstrated similar effects of storytelling on storytellers' subsequent memory.

Receiver Effects

To establish a mutual understanding, message senders must have message receivers comprehend their intentions and meanings. And message receivers can uncover the underlying intentions and meanings by interpreting the language used by the senders. However, the receivers often go beyond the meaning that the senders intended. In this section, we will look at some unintended consequences of language use on message receivers' representations at three linguistic levels: semantics, syntax, and pragmatics.

SEMANTICS

Semantics is a fundamental aspect of language and concerns the meanings of words and phrases. By using their semantic knowledge, message receivers can construct mental representations of what is described in messages. The use of different words can lead to the construction of different mental representations. Consider nouns, for example. As noted by Allport (1954), referring to someone as a fag rather than as a gay would make a difference in receivers' impressions about that person, although the two words literally have the same meaning (e.g., Simon & Greenberg, 1996). It is grammatically correct to use men and his to refer to humans or "people" in a generic sense, but receivers tend to understand them as males (Ng, 1990). Further, it has been found that even common first names such as John and Joan can create different impressions of a person (Kasof, 1993).

In a more subtle way, different verbs imply different kinds of causality—a phenomenon called *implicit causality* (R. Brown & Fish, 1983). Implicit causality refers to the tendency for interpersonal verbs to imply a particular causal locus. Overall, there are two types of verbs: action verbs and state verbs. An action verb (e.g., "help") typically describes the action performed by a person called an *agent* to another person called a *patient* of the action. When action verbs are used to describe an action, people tend to assign greater causal weight to the agent rather than to the patient. For example, when people hear "Bob helped Tom," they are more likely to infer Bob rather than Tom as the cause of this action. Additionally, they are also more likely to believe that Bob is a helpful person rather than that Tom is in need of help. It should be noted that this effect is not due to the grammatical order of the words. The agent would still be assigned greater weight even if he were the grammatical object (i.e., "Tom was helped by Bob").

On the other hand, a state verb (e.g., like) describes the situation in which a person called a *stimulus* brings about a certain state in another person called an *experiencer*. And, when state verbs are used, people are more likely to assign greater causal weight to the stimulus rather than to the experiencer (Au, 1986; van Kleek, Hillger, & Brown, 1988). For example, when people hear "Bob likes Tom," they tend to regard Tom as more responsible than Bob for bringing about the state of liking. Moreover, people also tend to judge Tom to be a likeable person rather than that Bob tends to like people. And again, this is not an effect of the word order. The stimulus would be assigned greater causal weight no matter whether it were a grammatical subject (stimulus-experiencer verbs; e.g., Tom impresses Bob), or a grammatical object (experiencer-stimulus verbs; e.g., Bob likes Tom).

There are two lines of explanations for implicit causality, which together reflect a reciprocal relationship between language and cognition (Holtgraves & Kashima, 2008). One of the explanations relates to the activation of associated dispositional terms (i.e., lexical hypothesis). All interpersonal verbs are associated with dispositional terms referencing the sentence subject, object, or both. However, these dispositional terms appear to be quite in line with the causal reasoning tendencies for the verbs. For action verbs, most of their dispositional terms reference the agent instead of the patient (e.g., help ⇒ helpful). This mirrors the tendency to assign greater causal weight to the agent. For state verbs—both experiencer-stimulus verbs (e.g., like ⇒ likeable) and stimulus-experiencer verbs (e.g., impress ⇒ impressive)—most of the associated dispositional terms reference the stimulus rather than the experiencer. This parallels quite closely the tendency to assign greater causal weight to the stimulus. Hoffman and Tchir (1990) conducted an extensive analysis of approximately 900 English interpersonal verbs. They found that 90% of the action verbs have dispositional terms referencing the agent, with only 25% referencing the patient. On the other hand, more than 75% of the state verbs have dispositional terms referencing the stimulus, whereas fewer than 50% reference the experiencer.

This asymmetrical pattern suggests that the dispositional terms of interpersonal verbs mediate implicit causality (i.e., language influencing social cognition). The use of a certain verb activates the associated dispositional terms, which then unintentionally influence judgments about causality. Hoffman and Tchir's (1990) study provided support for this. They found that verbs that had dispositional terms referencing the expected causal locus yielded larger implicit causality effects than verbs that did not have dispositional term. Similar results were also found by Holtgraves and Raymond (1995), who demonstrated that participants were more likely to recall the names of the agent (instead of the patient) and of the stimulus (instead of the experiencer).

The other explanation for implicit causality relates to cognitive schemas. Rudoloph and Fosterling (1997) have argued that implicit causality is a reflection of primitive schemas for thinking about interpersonal causality. As a result of the agent–patient schema, people tend to refer agents, but not patients, as the cause of actions. Similarly, because of the stimulus-experiencer schema, people tend to judge stimuli, but not experiencers, as more responsible for the states elicited. Therefore, the tendency to assign greater causal weight to agents (or stimuli) causes the development of dispositional terms referencing agents (or stimuli) instead of patients (or experiencers).

Previous research has shown that these two views of implicit causality are not mutually exclusive: which one operates may depend on the task. Semin and Marsman (1994) found that when participants were asked to make dispositional inferences, they tended to make inferences on the basis of the existence of derived dispositional terms, thus supporting the lexical hypothesis. However, when participants were asked to make judgments of causality, they did not seem to make reference to derived dispositional terms. In fact, as mentioned above, these two mechanisms reflect a reciprocal relationship between language use and social cognition. The tendency to regard the agent (or stimulus) as the causal locus may result in more dispositional terms that reference the agent (or stimulus). But then, because there are dispositional terms that reference the agent (or stimulus), people may attribute causality to the agent (or stimulus).

SYNTAX

A second aspect of language is syntax, which concerns the principles and rules for constructing sentences. Research based on the linguistic category model (LCM) proposed by Semin and Fiedler (1988, 1991) provides a good illustration of the unintended consequences at the syntactic level. This model concerns the role of different linguistic categories in receivers' meaning construction. According to the model, there are three broad categories of words: action verbs, state verbs, and adjectives. Action verbs are further divided into descriptive action verbs (e.g., call) and interpretive action verbs (e.g., help). Similarly, state verbs also include two subcategories: state action verbs (e.g., surprise) and state verbs (e.g., like), which correspond to the stimulus-experiencer and experiencer-stimulus verbs, respectively, in R. Brown and Fish's (1983) work.

Semin and Fiedler (1988, 1991) have suggested that these categories of words differ in linguistic abstractness. Descriptive action verbs are least abstract and hence are easiest to verify. In comparison, interpretive action verbs are relatively more abstract and thus relatively harder to verify. Furthermore, because internal states are unobservable, state verbs are less verifiable than action verbs overall. More precisely, state verbs reflect behaviors more enduring, and also more abstract, than action verbs. Lastly, compared with all categories of verbs, adjectives (e.g., honest) are more abstract and are also less objective and verifiable. Thus, on a continuum of linguistic abstractness, descriptive action verbs sit on one end, representing the least abstract category. Then the continuum continues with interpretive action verbs, state verbs, and lastly, adjectives—the most abstract category representing the endpoint of the continuum. It should also be noted that, along this continuum, the more abstract a linguistic category, the more likely it is to be contested by the listener because it is less objective and verifiable.

According to Semin and Fiedler (1988, 1991), almost any particular action can be described at different levels of abstraction. The use of different predicate forms to describe the same action can produce different cognitive consequences. For example, Tom could be described as "hitting" Bob (a descriptive action verb), or more abstractly, "hurting" Bob (an interpretive action verb), or even more abstractly, "hating" Bob (a state verb). Or, rather than describing the action, Tom could be simply described as an aggressive person. Consequently, different perceptions about Tom may be formed as a result of the differing linguistic abstraction. As Maass, Salvi, Arcuri, and Semin (1989) suggested, the more abstract a particular description, the more abstract the mental representation that will be constructed. In this way, variations in linguistic abstractness are responsible for the development and maintenance of stereotypes about outgroups, which we will discuss in detail later.

PRAGMATICS

Pragmatics is concerned with the ways in which context contributes to the transmission of meaning. The transmissions and interpretations of message senders' meanings depend not only on communicators' semantic and syntactic knowledge but also on the social and cultural context in which the communications take place. According to Holtgraves (2005), different communicators may have different assumptions about the operation of certain pragmatic rules. As a result, receivers may interpret messages somewhat differently from the senders' original intent.

Differences in communicators' pragmatic assumptions have been well demonstrated in psychology experiments (Hilton, 1990, 1995; Igou & Bless, 2003; Krosnick, Li, & Lehman, 1990; Schwarz, 1996; see Wänke, 2007, for a recent review). Theoretically speaking, a presumption of relevance is involved in all communications (Grice, 1975). Thus, it is perhaps not too surprising that participants in a typical psychology experiment tend to assume that all instructions and stimulus materials used in the experiment are relevant to their task. Because of the presumption of relevance, participants are likely to use all the information provided regardless of the experimenter's intention.

A communication perspective on judgmental biases illustrates this point. In a study by Kahneman and Tversky (1973), the experimenter provided participants with descriptions of a stimulus person that were consistent with the stereotype of either a lawyer or engineer. The number (base rate) of lawyers and engineers in the sample was manipulated.

Participants' task was to judge the likelihood of a particular target being an engineer. Their judgments were almost solely based on the stereotypes. They were far more likely to predict that the target was an engineer when the description matched the engineer stereotype, even though the base rate suggested otherwise. This is a well-known judgment bias called the *base-rate fallacy*. Kahneman and Tversky (1973) concluded that participants made likelihood judgments almost exclusively on the basis of the similarity between the sample and a population, while overlooking the base-rate information.

A communication perspective on this base rate fallacy suggests that participants relied exclusively on the target person's description, while ignoring the base rate, partly because they regarded the target description as an aspect of the experimenter's communication to them. They were told that the target description was based on personality tests administered by a panel of psychologists, and it was therefore reasonable for the participants to assume that the information was relevant for the judgment task (Grice, 1975). Consequently, participants believed that they should use, and they did use, this information. This line of reasoning implies that, when the presumed relevance of this information is undermined by telling participants that the descriptions have been computer generated, the tendency to ignore the base rate should be weakened. Indeed, participants were less likely to commit the base-rate fallacy under this condition, although the base-rate fallacy was not eradicated (Schwarz, Strack, Hilton, & Naderer, 1991).

Furthermore, the effects of differing pragmatic assumptions can occur in more subtle ways. For example, participants in psychology experiments may sometimes maximize the relevance of the instructions and materials given. This can influence the manner in which participants respond to virtually any self-report measure. Strack, Schwarz, and Wänke (1991) had participants respond to two highly related questions: to rate their happiness and to rate their life satisfaction. In one condition, these two questions were presented together at the end of a questionnaire. In this case, the second question would seem redundant (it violates Grice's, 1975, maxim of relevance). Therefore, participants reasoned that these two questions must mean different things—otherwise, why would the same question be asked twice? As a result, they gave different responses to these two questions. In another condition, though, the item regarding life satisfaction was presented at the beginning of an ostensibly unrelated questionnaire. Because the questions were presented separately, they did not seem to be redundant. Hence, in this condition, responses to these two items were almost identical.

Collective Effects

As discussed in the previous sections, language use can alter both message senders' and receivers' individual mental representations through utterance production and comprehension, respectively. However, the influences of language use on social cognition go beyond these individual effects. As stated earlier, communication is a joint activity, in which communicators work in a collaborative manner to achieve a mutual understanding. Hence, they continuously present, receive, and adjust information until they have reached a state of mutual understanding (i.e., the process of grounding). In this process, the communicators have co-constructed collective representations—a collective consequence of language use.

Echterhoff, Higgins, and Groll (2005) found that the SIB effect was significantly stronger when the audience was a member of the speakers' ingroup than when the audience was an outgroup member. This was because speakers tended to trust their ingroup members. In addition, the SIB effect also significantly depended on speakers' expectation and motivation to establish a mutual understanding. These findings not only illustrate the collaborative nature of language use but also suggest that part of the social cognitive consequences of language use is likely driven by the establishment of shared reality (Hardin & Conley, 2001; Hardin & Higgins, 1996).

INTERGROUP STEREOTYPES

Intergroup stereotypes provide the best illustration of collective implications of language use. Stereotypes about ingroups and outgroups are one type of collective representations that is co-constructed, maintained, and transmitted by communicators. Message senders tend to use different words and phrases to describe different targets, which in turn can mutually influence communicators' stereotypes. Thus, language use plays an important role in the maintenance and transmission of intergroup stereotypes.

Linguistic Intergroup Bias

Linguistic intergroup bias (LIB) is a phenomenon that points to the role of linguistic choices in the perpetuation of intergroup stereotypes. More specifically, it is a tendency to use differing levels of abstraction to describe the positive and negative behaviors of ingroup and outgroup members (e.g., Fiedler, Semin, & Finkenauer, 1993; Maass, 1999; Maass & Arcuri, 1996; Maass, Milesi, Zabbini, & Stahlberg, 1995; Maass et al., 1989). People tend to use abstract words such as adjectives to describe positive behaviors of ingroup members and negative behaviors of outgroup members. In addition, people also show the tendency to use concrete words (e.g., descriptive action verbs) to describe negative behaviors of ingroup members and positive behaviors of outgroup members.

One potential cause of LIB is the linguistic expectancy bias (Maass et al., 1989; Wigboldus, Semin, & Spears, 2000). That is, people tend to use abstract words to describe behaviors that confirm their expectations. Typically, people tend to have positive expectations about their ingroups but negative expectations about their outgroups. Hence, positive behaviors are expected for ingroup members, whereas negative behaviors are expected for outgroup members. Consequently, when people perceive their ingroup members performing positive behaviors, which are in line with their expectations, they are likely to describe these behaviors with abstract language, showing LIB. Indeed, Maass et al. (1995) found that more abstract language was used to describe expected behaviors regardless of the valence of those behaviors. Furthermore, it has also been suggested that LIB may be partly driven by a motivational tendency to protect one's social identity. Maass, Ceccarelli, and Rudin (1996) found that LIB was more likely when one's ingroup was threatened.

Wenneker and Wigboldus (2008) have suggested that LIB may occur during either encoding or utterance production. When people receive stereotype-consistent (SC) information (e.g., outgroup members performing negative behaviors), they may construct more abstract linguistic representations at the time of encoding. When they have a chance, people may use these generated abstract representations to describe this outgroup, thus producing LIB in actual communication. Wenneker, Wigboldus, and Spears (2005) provided support for this. They found that LIB occurred when targets' group memberships were known at the time of encoding; but no LIB was found when the memberships were unknown. Further, Wigboldus, Dijksterhuis, and van Knippenberg (2003) have suggested that LIB at the encoding stage may be automatic.

LIB may also occur at the time of utterance production (Semin, de Montes, & Valencia, 2003). Communicators may use LIB strategically as a means to influence others' opinions. For example, prosecution lawyers are likely to describe a defendant's behaviors with abstract language to imply enduring characteristics, whereas defense lawyers are likely to use more concrete language to imply momentary actions (Schmid & Fiedler, 1996, 1998; Schmid, Fiedler, Englich, Ehrenberger, & Semin, 1996). Other researchers have also shown strategic use of LIB—for example, the effect of audience identity on LIB (Fiedler, Bluemke, Friese, & Hofmann, 2003), the effect of language abstractness on perception of the speaker's relationship with the recipient (Douglas & Sutton, 2006), and perhaps most dramatic, the effect of a particular goal on suppressing LIB (Douglas & Sutton, 2003).

LIB is likely to influence both senders and receivers, and consequently the collective. For the senders, LIB can maintain and strengthen their mental representations of the outgroup they are describing (Karpinsky & von Hippel, 1996). For the receivers, they are likely to form more stereotypical views of the outgroup being described as a result of hearing abstract descriptions of the negative behaviors of the outgroup (e.g., Wigboldus et al., 2000). As a result, a particular instance of LIB in language use can create and maintain communicators' collective representations of a particular outgroup. In the long run, LIB may contribute to the formation and maintenance of the intergroup stereotypes that are culturally shared in a much broader community (Maass, 1999).

Stereotype Consistency Bias

Although the linguistic intergroup bias concerns the role of syntactic aspects of language on stereotype processes, stereotype consistency bias is about the role of information content in the perpetuation of intergroup stereotypes. More specifically, when people are faced with the possibility of communicating SC and stereotype-inconsistent (SI) information, they tend to exhibit an SC bias; that is, they tend to communicate SC information more than SI information. Findings from a series of serial reproduction experiments conducted by Kashima and colleagues (A. E. Clark & Kashima, 2007; Kashima, 2000; Lyons & Kashima, 2003) tended to show an SC bias (see Goodman, Webb, & Stewart, 2009, as a demonstration that this is not always the case).

In typical serial reproduction experiments, a story is first constructed in which a protagonist engages in both SC and SI behavior. Then the story is transmitted, in writing, from the first person to another, who in turn transmits it also in writing to a third person, and so on along a serial reproduction chain. Although participants were sometimes more likely to reproduce SI information in the first positions of a reproduction chain (Kashima, 2000), they were nevertheless more likely to transmit SC information than SI information in the long run. As more SC information was retained in later reproductions, the story became more stereotypical as it was passed along the chain.

A stereotype consistency bias is likely due to the differing nature of SC and SI information. According to A. E. Clark and Kashima (2007), provided that a stereotype is in communicators' common ground (i.e., taken for granted to be shared and endorsed), the relevant SC information is perceived to be less informative but more socially connective, whereas the opposite is the case for SI information. They found initial supporting evidence that people rated gender SI information as more informative but less connective than gender SC information. In relation to the stereotype consistency bias, A. E. Clark and Kashima have argued that, overall, more SC information is communicated because it is regarded as more socially connective.

SC information can help communicators to fulfill their relational goals. The goal of the joint activity in which communication takes place influences the communication of SC and SI information (Kashima, in press). There are two types of communicative goals: sharing information and regulating relationships. Hence, when the communicative goal is to form or strengthen relationships, communicators are likely to talk about SC information more than SI information.

Ruscher, Cralley, and O'Farrell (2005) provided a good demonstration of this. In their study, they had same-sex pairs of participants answer some personal questions in writing. The researchers manipulated each pair's motivation to form a relationship by asking the pair to share or not to share their answers. In the answer-sharing condition (i.e., stronger relational goal), pairs not only reported greater attraction to each other but also spent more time discussing SC information and less time discussing SI information than pairs in the control condition, for whom a relational goal was absent. Consistent with this reasoning, people who already have strong relational ties should be able to afford to engage in more socially costly discussion of SI information, as they have no need

to strengthen their relationships (i.e., relational goal absent). This is what Ruscher, Santuzzi, and Hammer (2003) found. Their results indicate that dyads that did not need to strengthen their relationships were more likely to discuss SI information than dyads that did.

Consistent with the social connectivity argument, A. E. Clark and Kashima (2007) showed that an SC bias in serial reproductions is partly due to the greater social connectivity of SC than SI information. They found that social connectivity of information predicted the number of steps the information was passed along in serial reproduction chains. The more socially connective information is, the more likely it is to survive in a reproduction chain and be passed on to people later in the chain. Intriguingly, SI information appears to subtly disturb the interpersonal coordination in social interaction. Castelli, Pavan, Ferrari, and Kashima (2009) found that people who interacted with a communicator who expressed counter-stereotypical views about outgroups tended to mimic the communicator's nonverbal behaviors less than those who interacted with a stereotyper, suggesting that SI information may act as a socially dissociative cue in communication.

Furthermore, this line of reasoning suggests that when the social connectivity of SC information is reduced, people should be less likely to communicate SC information. For example, if a certain stereotype is not perceived to be part of common ground or to be endorsed, the relevant SC information is no longer socially connective (because it is possible that someone may object to it). Therefore, people are less likely to communicate this SC information. Both Lyons and Kashima (2003) and A. E. Clark and Kashima (2007) found supporting evidence for this. These researchers found that, when participants were led to believe that the stereotypes were not endorsed by their general community, they were less likely to communicate SC information than when they were led to believe the stereotypes were endorsed. Thus, a reduction in social connectivity of SC information would result in less communication of SC information.

What is important about an SC bias in the current context is its contribution to the maintenance and transmission of intergroup stereotypes—an example of collective representations created by language use. As previous research (e.g., Brauer, Judd, & Jacquelin, 2001) has suggested, the greater the amount of biased information communicated, the more extreme and stereotypical the impressions formed. These biased impressions, or stereotypes, may be further circulated through social networks in a broader society. They will become part of the society's common ground if widely circulated. Therefore, the more the communication of SC information, the more stable the relevant stereotype within a society at large. As a consequence, an SC bias is likely to be responsible for the transmission and maintenance of existing stereotypes, thus contributing to the reproduction of the existing intergroup relationship (Kashima, in press; also see Fast, Heath, & Wu, 2009, as an instance of the reproduction of social prominence in baseball).

Conclusion

Social communication is a dynamic, two-way process of meaning making and meaning exchange in joint activities in situ. Although the traditional social psychological imagination of communication has been primarily a linear one-way transmission of information from a message sender to an audience, the image of the message sender and receiver presented in this chapter is one of active co-constructors of meaning. Whereas a message sender intends to produce a certain effect in a message receiver's mind and action by using language as a semiotic tool, the message receiver not only cognitively engages with the message but also communicatively engages with it, in a coordinated joint activity of constructing a mutual understanding. As the message sender and receiver take their turns and continue their communication, the grounding process continues to add new mutual understandings to the sender and receiver's common ground, extending and expanding the latter all the while delicately coordinating their moves for meaning making and meaning exchange. The result is an evolution of common ground, which takes on a life of its own. When language is seen as a semiotic tool for meaning making and meaning exchange, linguistic communications can generate not only the meaning that the message senders have intended to communicate but also other meaning that they haven't intended, or didn't even know that they had implied. Based on this, the interactants—both the message sender and the receiver—form and transform their mental representations, and generate their collective representations. Such shared representations can turn into their shared reality, thus contributing to the collective constitution of the social world.

References

Allport, G. W. (1954). *The nature of prejudice*. New York: Addison-Wesley.

Au, T. (1986). A verb is worth a thousand words: The causes and consequences of interpersonal events implicit in language. *Journal of Memory and Language, 25*(1), 104–122.

Austin, J. (1962). *How to do things with words*. Oxford, UK: Clarendon.

Barr, D. J. (2008). Pragmatic expectations and linguistic evidence: Listeners anticipate but do not integrate common ground. *Cognition, 109*, 18–40.

Berger, P., & Luckmann, T. (1971). *The social construction of reality: A treatise in the sociology of knowledge*. Harmondsworth, UK: Penguin.

Brauer, M., Judd, C. M., & Jacquelin, V. (2001). The communication of social stereotypes: The effects of group discussion and information distribution on stereotypic appraisals. *Journal of Personality and Social Psychology, 81*, 463–475.

Brennan, S. E., & Clark, H. H. (1996). Conceptual pacts and lexical choice in conversation. *Journal of Experimental Psychology: Learning, Memory, and Cognition, 22*(6), 1482–1493.

Brown, P., & Levinson, S. (1987). *Politeness: Some universals in language usage*. Cambridge, UK: Cambridge University Press.

Brown, R., & Fish, D. (1983). The psychological causality implicit in language. *Cognition, 14*, 237–273.

Castelli, L., Pavan, G., Ferrari, E., & Kashima, Y. (2009). The stereotyper and the chameleon: The effects of stereotype use on perceiver's mimicry. *Journal of Experimental Social Psychology, 45*(4), 835–839.

Clark, A. E., & Kashima, Y. (2007). Stereotype consistent information helps people connect with others: Situated-functional account of stereotype communication. *Journal of Personality and Social Psychology, 93*, 1028–1039.

Clark, H. H. (1996). *Using language*. Cambridge, UK: Cambridge University Press.

Clark, H. H., & Marshall, C. R. (1981). Definite reference and mutual knowledge. In A. K. Joshi, B. L. Webber, & I. A. Sag (Eds.), *Elements of discourse understanding* (pp. 10–63). Cambridge, UK: Cambridge University Press.

Clark. H. H., & Murphy, G. L., (1982). La visée vers lauditoire dans la signification et la reference [Audience design in meaning and reference]. *Bulletin de Psychologie, 35*, 767–776.

Clark, H. H., & Wilkes-Gibbs, D. (1986). Referring as a collaborative process. *Cognition, 22*, 1–39.

Douglas, K. M., & Sutton, R. M. (2003). Effects of communication goals and expectancies on language abstraction. *Journal of Personality and Social Psychology, 84*, 682–696.

Douglas, K. M., & Sutton, R. M. (2006). When what you say about others say something about you: Language abstraction and inferences about describers attitudes and goals. *Journal of Experimental Social Psychology, 42*, 500–508.

Dudukovic, N. M., Marsh, E. J., & Tversky, B. (2004). Telling a story or telling it straight: The effects of entertaining versus accurate retellings on memory. *Applied Cognitive Psychology, 18*, 125–143.

Echterhoff, G., Higgins, E. T., & Groll, S. (2005). Audience-tuning effects on memory: The role of shared reality. *Journal of Personality and Social Psychology, 89*, 257–276.

Fast, N. J., Heath, C., & Wu, G. (2009). Common ground and cultural prominence: How conversation reinforces culture. *Psychological Science, 20*, 904–911.

Fiedler, K., Bluemke, M., Friese, M., & Hofmann, W. (2003). On the different uses of linguistic abstractness: From LIB to

LEB and beyond. *European Journal of Social Psychology, 33,* 441–453.

Fiedler, K., Semin, G. R., & Finkenauer, C. (1993). The battle of words between gender groups: A language-based approach to intergroup processes. *Human Communication Research, 19,* 409–441.

Fussell, S. R., & Krauss, R. M. (1992). Coordination of knowledge in communication: Effects of speakers' assumptions about what others know. *Journal of Personality and Social Psychology, 62,* 378–391.

Garrod, S., & Anderson, A. (1987). Saying what you mean in dialogue: A study in conceptual and semantic co-ordination. *Cognition, 27,* 181–218.

Garrod, S., & Doherty, G. (1994). Conversation, co-ordination and convention: An empirical investigation of how groups establish linguistic conventions. *Cognition, 53,* 181–215.

Gerrig, R. J., & Littman, M. L. (1990). Disambiguation by community membership. *Memory and Cognition, 18*(4), 331–338.

Goffman, E. (1967). *Interaction ritual: Essays on face to face behavior.* Garden City, NY: Anchor Books.

Goodman, R. L., Webb, T. L., & Stewart, A. J. (2009). Communicating stereotype-relevant information: Is factual information subject to the same communication biases as fictional information? *Personality and Social Psychology Bulletin, 35,* 836–852.

Grice, H. P. (1957). Meaning. *Philosophical Review, 67,* 377–388.

Grice, H. P. (1975). Logic and conversation. In P. Cole & J. Morgan (Eds.), *Syntax and semantics 3: Speech acts* (pp. 41–58). New York: Academic Press.

Guerin, B., & Innes, J. M. (1989). Cognitive tuning sets: Anticipating the consequences of communication. *Current Psychology: Research and Reviews, 8,* 234–239.

Haberstroh, S., Oyserman, D., Schwartz, N., Kuhnen, U., & Ji, L. J. (2002). Is the interdependent self more sensitive to question context than the independent self? Self-construal and the observation of conversational norms. *Journal of Experimental Social Psychology, 38,* 323–329.

Halberstadt, J. (2003). The paradox of emotion attribution: Explanation biases perceptual memory for emotional expressions. *Current Directions in Psychological Sciences, 12,* 197–201.

Hardin, C. D., & Conley, T. D. (2001). A relational approach to cognition: Shared experience and relationship affirmation in social cognition. In G. B. Moskowitz (Ed.), *Cognitive social psychology,* (pp. 3–17). Mahwah, NJ: Lawrence Erlbaum.

Hardin, C. D., & Higgins, E. T. (1996). Shared reality: How social verification makes the subjective objective. In R. M. Sorrentino & E. T. Higgins (Eds.), *Handbook of motivation and cognition* (Vol. 3, pp. 28–84). New York: Guilford.

Hariri, A. R., Bookheimer, S. Y., & Mazziotta, J. C. (2000). Modulating emotional response: Effects of neocortical network on the limbic system. *NeuroReport, 11,* 43–48.

Higgins, E. T., & Rholes, W. S. (1978). "Saying is believing": Effects of message modification on memory and liking of the person described. *Journal of Experimental Social Psychology, 14,* 363–378.

Hilton, D. J. (1990). Conversational processes and causal explanation. *Psychological Bulletin, 107,* 65–81.

Hilton, D. J. (1995). The social context of reasoning: Conversational inference and rational judgment. *Psychological Bulletin, 118,* 248–271.

Hintzman, D. L. (1986) "Schema-abstraction" in a multiple trace model. *Psychological Review, 93,* 411–28.

Hoffman, C., & Tchir, M. A. (1990). Interpersonal verbs and dispositional adjectives: The psychology of causality embodied in language. *Journal of Personality and Social Psychology, 58,* 767–778.

Holtgraves, T. M. (1986). Language structure in social interaction: Perceptions of direct and indirect speech acts and interactants who use them. *Journal of Personality and Social Psychology, 51,* 305–314.

Holtgraves, T. M. (1994). Communication in context: Effects of speaker status on the comprehension of indirect requests. *Journal of Experimental Psychology: Learning, Memory, and Cognition, 20,* 1205–1218.

Holtgraves, T. M. (2002). *Language as social action.* Mahwah, NJ: Erlbaum.

Holtgraves, T. M. (2005). Diverging interpretations associated with the perspectives of the speaker and recipient in conversations. *Journal of Memory and Language, 53,* 551–566.

Holtgraves, T. M. (2008). Automatic intention recognition in conversation processing. *Journal of Memory and Language, 58,* 627–645.

Holtgraves, T. M., & Ashley, A. (2001). Comprehending illocutionary force. *Memory & Cognition, 29,* 83–90.

Holtgraves, T. M., & Kashima, Y. (2008). Language, meaning and social cognition. *Personality and Social Psychology Review, 12,* 73–94.

Holtgraves, T. M., & Raymond, S. (1995). Implicit causality and memory: Evidence for a priming model. *Personality and Social Psychology Bulletin, 21,* 5–12.

Holtgraves, T., & Yang, J. N. (1990). Politeness as universal: Cross-cultural perceptions of request strategies and inferences based on their use. *Journal of Personality and Social Psychology, 59,* 719–729.

Holtgraves, T., & Yang, J. N. (1992). Interpersonal underpinnings of request strategies: General principles and differences due to culture and gender. *Journal of Personality and Social Psychology, 62,* 246–256.

Horton, W. S., & Gerrig, R. J. (2005a). Conversational common ground and memory processes in language production. *Discourse Processes, 40*(1), 1–35.

Horton, W. S., & Gerrig, R. J. (2005b). The impact of memory demands on audience design during language production. *Cognition, 96,* 127–142.

Horton, W. S., & Keysar, B. (1996). When do speakers take into account common ground? *Cognition, 59,* 91–117.

Hutchins, E. (1995). *Cognition in the wild.* Cambridge, MA: The MIT Press.

Igou, E. I., & Bless, H. (2003). Inferring the importance of arguments: Order effects and conversation rules. *Journal of Experimental Social Psychology, 39,* 91–99.

Isaacs, E. A., & Clark, H. H. (1987). References in conversation between experts and novices. *Journal of Experimental Psychology: General, 116,* 26–37.

Kahneman, D., & Tversky, A. (1973). On the psychology of prediction. *Psychological Review, 80,* 237–251.

Karpinsky, A., & von Hippel, W. (1996). The role of the linguistic intergroup bias in expectancy-maintenance. *Social Cognition, 14,* 141–163.

Kashima, Y. (2000). Maintaining cultural stereotypes in the serial reproduction of narratives. *Personality and Social Psychology Bulletin, 26,* 594–604.

Kashima, Y. (2013). Cultural dynamics of intergroup relations: How communications can shape intergroup reality. In C. Stangor & C. Crandall (Eds.), *Stereotyping and prejudice* (pp. 119–149). New York: Psychology Press.

Kashima, Y., Kashima, E., Bain, P., Lyons, A., Tindale, R. S., Robins, G., Vears, C., & Whelan, J. (2010). Communication and essentialism: Grounding the shared reality of a social category. *Social Cognition*, 28, 306–328.

Kashima, Y., Klein, O., & Clark, A. E. (2007). Grounding: Sharing information in social interaction. In K. Fiedler (Ed.), *Social communication* (pp. 27–77). New York: Psychology Press.

Kashima, Y., Woolcock, J., & Kashima, E. (2000). Group impressions as dynamic configurations: The tensor product model of group impression formation and change. *Psychological Review*: 107, 914–942.

Kasof, J. (1993). Sex bias in the naming of stimulus persons. *Psychological Bulletin*, 113, 140–163.

Keysar, B., Barr, D. J., Balin, J. A., & Brauner, J. S. (2000). Taking perspective in conversation: The role of mutual knowledge in comprehension. *Psychological Science*, 11(1), 32–38.

Krauss, R. M., & Fussell, S. R. (1996). Social psychological models of interpersonal communication. In E. T. Higgins & A. Kruglanski (Ed.), *Social psychology: A handbook of basic principles* (pp. 655–701). New York: Guilford.

Krauss, R. M., & Weinheimer, S. (1964). Changes in the length of reference phrases as a function of social interaction: A preliminary study. *Psychonomic Science*, 1, 113–114.

Krauss, R. M., & Weinheimer, S. (1967). Effects of referent similarity and communication mode on verbal encoding. *Journal of Verbal Learning and Verbal Behavior*, 6, 359–363.

Kraut, R. E., & Higgins, T. (1984). Communication and social cognition. In R. S. Wyer, Jr. & T. K. Srull (Eds.), *Handbook of social cognition* (Vol. 3, pp. 87–127). Hillsdale, NJ: Erlbaum.

Krosnick, J., Li, F., & Lehman, D. R. (1990). Conversational conventions, order of information acquisition, and the effect of base rates and individuating information on social judgment. *Journal of Personality and Social Psychology*, 59, 1140–1152.

Lieberman, M. (2007). The X- and C- systems: The neural basis of automatic and controlled social cognition. In E. Harmon-Jones & P. Winkelman (Eds.), *Social neuroscience: Integrating biological and psychological explanations of social behavior* (pp. 290–315). New York: Guilford Press.

Lieberman, M., Eisenberger, N. I., Crockett, M. J., Tom, S. M., Pfeifer, J. H., & Way, B. W. (2007). Putting feelings into words. *Psychological Science*, 18, 421–428.

Lyons, A., & Kashima, Y. (2003). How are stereotypes maintained through communication? The influence of stereotype sharedness. *Journal of Personality and Social Psychology*, 85, 989–1005.

Lyubomirsky, S., Sousa, I., & Dickerhoof, R. (2006). The costs and benefits of writing, talking, and thinking about life's triumphs and defeats. *Journal of Personality and Social Psychology*, 90, 692–708.

Maass, A. (1999). Linguistic intergroup bias: Stereotype perpetuation through language. *Advances in Experimental Social Psychology*, 31, 79–121.

Maass, A., & Arcuri, S. (1996). Language and stereotyping. In C. N. Macrae, C. Stangor, & M. Hewstone (Eds.), *Stereotypes and stereotyping* (pp. 193–226). New York: Guilford Press.

Maass, A., Ceccarelli, R., & Rudin, S. (1996). Linguistic intergroup bias: Evidence for in-group protective motivation. *Journal of Personality and Social Psychology*, 71, 512–526.

Maass, A., Milesi, A., Zabbini, S., & Stahlberg, D. (1995). The linguistic intergroup bias: Differential expectancies or in-group protection? *Journal of Personality and Social Psychology*, 68, 116–126.

Maass, A., Salvi, D., Arcuri, L., & Semin, G. (1989). Language use in intergroup contexts: The linguistic intergroup bias. *Journal of Personality and Social Psychology*, 57, 981–993.

Malle, B. F. (2005). Folk theory of mind: Conceptual foundations of human social cognition. In R. R. Hassin, J. S. Uleman, & J. A. Bargh (Eds.), *The new unconscious* (pp. 225–255). New York: Oxford University Press.

Marsh, E. J. (2007). Retelling is not the same as recalling: Implications for memory. *Current Directions in Psychological Science*, 16, 16–20.

Marsh, E. J., & Tversky, B. (2004). Spinning the stories of our lives. *Applied Cognitive Psychology*, 18, 491–503.

McAdams, D. P. (1993). *The stories we live by: Personal myths and the making of the self*. New York: William Morrow.

McGregor, I., & Holmes, J. G. (1999). How storytelling shapes memory and impressions of relationship events over time. *Journal of Personality and Social Psychology*, 76, 403–419.

Mead, G. H. (1934) *Mind, self, and society*. Chicago: University of Chicago Press.

Metzing, C., & Brennan, S. E. (2003). When conceptual pacts are broken: Partner-specific effects on the comprehension of referring expressions. *Journal of Memory and Language*, 49, 201–213.

Moscovici, S. (1981). On social representations. In J. P. Forgas (Ed.), *Social cognition: Perspectives on everyday understanding*. London: Academic Press.

Ng, S. H. (1990). Androcentric coding of man and his in memory by language users. *Journal of Experimental Social Psychology*, 26, 455–464.

Pennebaker, J. W. (1997). Writing about emotional experiences as a therapeutic process. *Psychological Science*, 8, 162–166.

Pennington, N., & Hastie, R. (1988). Explanation-based decision making: Effects of memory structure on judgment. *Journal of Experimental Psychology, Learning, Memory, and Cognition*, 14, 521–533.

Pickering, M. J., & Garrod, S. (2004). Toward a mechanistic psychology of dialogue. *Behavioral and Brain Sciences*, 27, 169–225.

Rudolph, U., & Fosterling, F. (1997). The psychological causality implicit in verbs: A review. *Psychological Bulletin*, 121, 192–218.

Rumelhart, D. E. (1975). Notes on a schema for stories. In D. G. Bobrow & A. Collins (Eds.), *Representation and understanding*. New York: Academic Press.

Ruscher, J. B., Cralley, E. L., & O'Farrell, K. J. (2005). How newly acquainted dyads develop shared stereotypic impressions through conversation. *Group Processes and Intergroup Relations*, 8, 259–270.

Ruscher, J. B., Santuzzi, A. M., & Hammer, E. Y. (2003). Shared impression formation in the cognitively interdependent dyad. *British Journal of Social Psychology*, 42, 411–425.

Schank, R. C., & Abelson, R. P. (1977). *Scripts, plans, goals, and understanding*. Hillsdale, NJ: Erlbaum.

Schank, R. C., & Abelson, R. P. (1995). Knowledge and memory: The real story. In R. J. Wyer Jr. (Ed.), *Advances in social cognition* (Vol. 8, pp. 1–86). Hillsdale, NJ: Erlbaum.

Schmid, J., & Fiedler, K. (1996). Language and implicit attributions in the Nuremberg trials. *Human Communication Research*, 22, 371–398.

Schmid, J., & Fiedler, K. (1998). The backbone of closing speeches: The impact of prosecution versus defense language on judicial attributions. *Journal of Applied Social Psychology*, *28*, 1140–1172.

Schmid, J., Fiedler, K., Englich, B., Ehrenberger, T., & Semin, G. R. (1996). Taking sides with the defendant: Grammatical choice and the influence of implicit attributions in prosecution and defense speeches. *International Journal of Psycholinguistics*, *12*, 127–148.

Schwarz, N. (1996). *Cognition and communication: Judgmental biases, research methods, and the logic of conversation*. Mahwah, NJ: Erlbaum.

Schwarz, N., Strack, F., Hilton, D. J., & Naderer, G. (1991). Judgmental biases and the logic of conversation: The contextual relevance of irrelevant information. *Social Cognition*, *9*, 67–84.

Searle, J. R. (1969). *Speech acts*. Cambridge, UK: Cambridge University Press.

Semin, G. R., de Montes, G. L., & Valencia, J. F. (2003). Communication constraints on the linguistic intergroup bias. *Journal of Experimental Social Psychology*, *39*, 142–148.

Semin, G. R., & Fiedler, L. (1988). The cognitive functions of linguistic categories in describing persons: Social cognition and language. *Journal of Personality and Social Psychology*, *54*, 558–568.

Semin, G. R., & Fiedler, K. (1991). The linguistic category model, its bases, applications and range. In W. Stroebe & M. Hewstone (Eds.), *European Review of Social Psychology* (Vol. 2, pp. 1–30). Chichester, UK: Wiley.

Semin, G. R., & Marsman, J. G. (1994). "Multiple inference-inviting properties" of interpersonal verbs: Event instigation, dispositional inference, and implicit causality. *Journal of Personality and Social Psychology*, *67*, 836–849.

Shintel, H., & Keysar, B. (2007). You said it before and you'll say it again: Expectations of consistency in communication. *Journal of Experimental Psychology: Learning, Memory, and Cognition*, *33*(2), 357–369.

Simon, L., & Greenberg, J. (1996). Further progress in understanding the effects of derogatory ethnic labels: The role of preexisting attitudes toward the targeted group. *Personality and Social Psychology Bulletin*, *12*, 1195–1204.

Slugoski, B. R., & Turnbull, W. (1988). Cruel to be kind and kind to be cruel: Sarcasm, banter and social relations. *Journal of Language and Social Psychology*, *7*, 101–121.

Smith, E. R., & Semin, G. R. (2004). Socially situated cognition: Cognition in its social context. *Advances in Experimental Social Psychology*, *36*, 53–117.

Sperber, D. (2000). *Metarepresentations: A multidisciplinary perspective*. Oxford, UK: Oxford University Press.

Sperber, D., & Wilson, D. (1995). *Relevance* (2nd ed.). Oxford, UK: Blackwell.

Strack, F., Schwarz, N., & Wänke, M. (1991). Semantic and pragmatic aspects of context effects in social and psychological research. *Social Cognition*, *9*, 111–125.

Tajfel, H. (1972). Social categorization. In S. Moscovici (Ed.), *Introduction a la psychologie sociale* (Vol. 1, pp. 272–302). Paris: Larousse.

Tajfel, H., & Turner, J. A. (1979). An integrative theory of intergroup conflict. In W. G. Austin & S. Worchel (Eds.), *The social psychology of intergroup relations* (pp. 33–47). Monterey, CA: Brooks-Cole.

Thompson, M. S., Judd, C. M., & Park, B. (2000). The consequences of communicating social stereotypes. *Journal of Experimental Social Psychology 36*, 567–599.

Turner, J. C. (1987). *Rediscovering the social group: A self-categorization theory*. Oxford, UK: Blackwell.

Tversky, B., & Marsh, E. J. (2000). Biased retellings of events yield biased memories. *Cognitive Psychology*, *40*, 1–38.

van Kleek, M. H., Hillger, L. A., & Brown R. (1988). Pitting verbal schemas against information variables in attribution. *Social Cognition*, *6*, 89–106.

Wagner, W., & Hayes, N. (2005). *Everyday discourse and common sense: The theory of social representations*. New York: Palgrave Macmillan.

Wänke, M. (2007). What is said and what is meant: Conversational implicatures in natural conversations, research settings, media, and advertising. In K. Fiedler (Ed.), *Social communication* (pp. 223–255). New York: Psychology Press.

Wenneker, C. P. J., & Wigboldus, D. H. J. (2008). A model of biased language use. In Y. Kashima, K. Fiedler, & P. Freytag (Eds.), *Stereotype dynamics*. Mahwah, NJ: Erlbaum.

Wenneker, C. P. J., Wigboldus, D. H. J., & Spears, R. (2005). Biased language use in stereotype maintenance: The role of encoding and goals. *Journal of Personality and Social Psychology*, *89*, 504–516.

Wigboldus, D. H. J., Dijksterhuis, A., & van Knippenberg, A. (2003). When stereotypes get in the way: Stereotypes obstruct stereotype-inconsistent trait inferences. *Journal of Personality and Social Psychology*, *84*, 470–484.

Wigboldus, D. H. J., Semin, G. R., & Spears, R. (2000). How do we communicate stereotypes? Linguistic biases and inferential consequences. *Journal of Personality and Social Psychology*, *78*, 5–18.

Wilson, T. D., & LaFleur, S. J. (1995). Knowing what you'll do: Effects of analyzing reasons on self-prediction. *Journal of Personality and Social Psychology*, *68*, 21–35.

Wilson, T. D., Lisle, D. J., & Kraft, D (1990) Effects on self-reflection on attitudes and consumer decisions. *Advances in Consumer Research*, *17*, 212–216.

Wilson, T. D., Lisle, D. J., Schooler, J. W., Hodges, S. D., Klaaren, K. J., & LaFleur, S. J. (1993). Introspecting about reasons can reduce post-choice satisfaction. *Personality and Social Psychology Bulletin*, *19*, 331–339.

Wilson, T. D., & Schooler, J. W. (1991). Thinking too much: Introspection can reduce the quality of preferences and decisions. *Journal of Personality and Social Psychology*, *60*, 181–192.

Wu, S., & Keysar, B. (2007). The effect of culture on perspective taking. *Psychological Science*, *18* (7), 600–606.

Wyer, R. S., Jr., & Srull, T. K. (1984). *Handbook of social cognition* (Vol. 1–3). Hillsdale, NJ: Erlbaum.

Wyer, R. S., Jr., & Srull, T. K. (1994). *Handbook of social cognition* (2nd ed., Vol. 1–2). Hillsdale, NJ: Erlbaum.

Zajonc, R. B. (1960). The process of cognitive tuning in communication. *Journal of Abnormal and Social Psychology*, *61*, 159–167.

Zwaan, R. A., & Radvansky, G. A. (1998) Situation models in language comprehension and memory. *Psychological Bulletin*, *123*, 162–185.

Social Cognitive Development: Learning from Others

Gail D. Heyman *and* Cristine H. Legare

Abstract

Children's reliance on other people as sources of information has become an important topic of study within childhood development. Researchers have shown that children younger than age 5 can draw on a range of cues to determine when skepticism of sources is warranted, and that source reasoning is related to the development of theory of mind. This chapter provides an overview of children's source reasoning and discusses some limitations in their ability to learn from others, including difficulties in reasoning about deception. Research on more dynamic aspects of social learning that involves information seeking and the active construction of belief systems in collaboration with others is also discussed. As a whole, research in this area is beginning to reveal how children's developing social and cognitive skills serve to guide their acquisition of knowledge.

Key Words: childhood development, deception, skepticism, reasoning, information seeking, theory of mind

Introduction

The human capacity to learn from others facilitates development at both the individual and the cultural levels (Tomasello, 2008). This ability helps children to become socialized, permits culture to be transmitted across generations, and underlies progress in science and technology. However, learning from others also carries risks. Not all people are reliable sources of information, and people sometimes mislead others, either intentionally or unintentionally. The way children reason about other people as sources of information, including how they navigate the associated challenges and opportunities, has become an important topic in social cognitive development. This chapter provides an overview of research on children's source reasoning and its broader context within developmental psychology.

By the time infants reach their first birthday, they are able to make use of social information to guide their interpretations of entities and events. In one classic study using a modified visual cliff paradigm, Sorce, Emde, Campos, and Klinnert (1985) placed 12-month-olds on a glass table that had an illusory drop-off. Infants tended to cross the illusory drop-off to their mother if she expressed joy or interest, but not if she expressed fear or anger. In another study, Mumme and Fernald (2003) found that 12-month-olds were more likely to avoid a novel object such as a spiral letter holder if they had previously seen an experimenter express a negative emotional response to it, compared with a neutral or positive emotional response.

Although some of the foundations of learning from others are in place by 12 months of age, very young children lack the language skills to benefit from much of the verbal communication that surrounds them. As children's language skills develop, their capacity to draw on others as sources of information increases dramatically. However, the effective use of this information requires social cognitive skills as well as linguistic skills.

This chapter focuses on children's reliance on others as sources of information once they have developed the language skills to benefit from verbal interactions. This is an active topic in social cognitive development and has recently been the focus of a large number of studies. It intersects with other areas of social cognitive development such as the development of theory of mind, trait reasoning, and achievement motivation. We will touch on these and other intersecting areas, but we do not seek to provide a comprehensive overview of these intersecting areas. There are also other significant findings on children's social cognitive development that are beyond the scope of this chapter, such as work on mental state understanding among infants (Luo & Baillargeon, 2010) and children's implicit attitudes (Cvencek, Greenwald, & Meltzoff, 2011; Dunham, & Degner, 2010).

Most of the studies we will be discussing have been conducted with children between the ages of 3 and 5, the ages at which children begin to demonstrate foundational skills in evaluating others as potential sources of information. However, we will also cover a substantial amount of research involving children between 6 and 12 years because there are major developments during these ages as well, including changes in children's ability to reason about the possibility that others may not be motivated to communicate their true beliefs accurately.

There has been no single theoretical framework that has served to guide the current research on children's reasoning about others as sources of information. However, certain theoretical issues cut across much of this work. One such issue concerns whether children's source reasoning is fundamentally about their conceptions of mental life, or is based on more associative processes. Other questions revolve around the centrality of inhibitory control in children's ability to reject information provided by others. Also of theoretical interest is the extent to which children's source reasoning skills are domain specific, and whether they are influenced by various forms of social and cultural inputs. These themes will be discussed in relation to studies that address them.

This chapter is divided into two major sections. The first section covers research on factors that influence children's source reasoning. We begin by examining the cues that 3- to 5- year-olds can use to identify reliable sources, and we then address research on how the use of these cues is linked to the ability to make inferences about the mental life of others. Next, we discuss limitations in children's

ability to put their source reasoning skills into practice that tend to persist even after age 5 years, an age at which many children have developed the foundational skills that source reasoning requires. Finally, we discuss recent efforts to extend models of children's source reasoning from the standard contexts, which involve factual information, to contexts that involve value judgments such as personal preferences.

In the second major section, we review research on dynamic aspects of social learning in which children actively process information to construct systems of beliefs in collaboration with others (Gelman, 2009). We begin by describing the sociocultural approach, which emphasizes cultural aspects of children's learning from others, such as how children use cultural artifacts to construct beliefs. We then review research on the role of asking questions. Next, we describe how children's intuitive theories can shape the way they make use of information they obtain from others. Finally, we address how children evaluate claims about unobservable processes and events. Following the two major sections, we discuss promising areas for future research.

Identifying Reliable Sources
A Source's Previous Statements

Recent findings suggest that by 3 to 4 years of age, children treat information about the accuracy of a source's previous statements as a cue to the source's reliability. The standard paradigm begins with a training phase in which two informants apply a verbal label to a pair of familiar objects such as a ball and a cup, with one informant labeling the objects correctly and the other labeling them incorrectly (Birch, Vauthier, & Bloom, 2008; Corriveau & Harris, 2009; Harris, 2007; Jaswal & Neely, 2006; Koenig & Harris, 2005). Next, there is a test phase in which the two informants identify a series of novel objects using different novel labels such as "mido" and "loma." Koenig and Harris (2005) found that 4-year-olds were more likely to accept a novel label when it came from the informant with a history of accuracy, and that they expected the same informant to provide more accurate information in the future. Birch et al. (2008) replicated these findings and extended them to the functions of objects.

In each of these studies, the informants were either consistently reliable or consistently unreliable during the training phase. The finding that young children can systematically differentiate between informants under these conditions shows that they are able to make use of information about a source's history, but it does not reveal how they do it. There are a number of possible strategies a child might use on this task. Children could produce the observed pattern of results by trusting any informant who has given accurate information previously, by mistrusting any informant who has given inaccurate information previously, or by comparing the relative accuracy of the two informants.

Given that not all informants will be consistently reliable or unreliable, Pasquini, Corriveau, Koenig, and Harris (2007) modified the standard object-labeling paradigm to investigate reasoning about informants' relative accuracy and inaccuracy. During the training phase, some participants saw pairs of informants who were always accurate or inaccurate, and others saw pairs of informants who had a range of ratios of correct versus incorrect statements, including 100% versus 0% correct (as is done in the standard paradigm), 100% versus 25% correct, 75% versus 0% correct, and 75% versus 25% correct. Across the different training conditions, 4-year-olds consistently preferred the label from the informant who had a history of greater accuracy. In contrast, 3-year-olds differentiated between informants only when one of them was consistently correct. Pasquini et al. (2007) interpreted these results as indicating that the 4-year-olds used a strategy of tracking the frequency of errors, whereas the 3-year-olds used a strategy of discounting information from sources who showed any evidence of being unreliable. These results suggest that by age 4, children are capable of applying statistical learning to decisions about the reliability of sources.

The Child's Relationship with the Source

There is evidence that young children are also sensitive to the nature of their relationship with potential sources. Corriveau and Harris (2009) found that children ages 3, 4, and 5 considered a familiar teacher to be a better source of information than an unfamiliar teacher. Among the 3-year-olds, selective trust was only minimally affected by the prior accuracy of the teachers, and it was seen even when the familiar teacher was portrayed as being consistently inaccurate and the unfamiliar teacher was portrayed as being consistently accurate. In contrast, 4- and 5-year-olds' trust of familiar teachers was strengthened by a history of accurate labeling and weakened by a history of inaccurate labeling. Developmental differences indicate that, "like older preschoolers, younger preschoolers can register and remember inaccuracy but unlike older preschoolers

they are prone to discount or ignore such information if it pertains to familiar and ordinarily trustworthy informants" (Corriveau & Harris, p. 436).

In a longitudinal study, Corriveau et al. (2009) investigated the link between an infant's attachment status and his or her preference for a familiar source as a 4- or 5-year-old. In the first phase of the study, the attachment status of a group of 15-month-old infants was measured using the strange situation procedure (a standard measure of young children's responses to caregiver separation and reunion; Ainsworth et al., 1978). Each child was classified as *secure*, *insecure-avoidant*, or *insecure-resistant* (a fourth category, *insecure-disorganized*, will not be discussed here). Children were classified as secure if they attempted to reestablish a connection with their mother after a brief separation, as insecure-avoidant if they showed relatively little interest in interacting with their mother, and as insecure-resistant if they showed a preoccupation with the separation but were not comforted by the reunion.

When the children reached age 4, and again at age 5, they completed a set of tasks in which they were presented with conflicting information from their mother and from a stranger. For example, as 5-year-olds, the children were presented with pictures of novel animal hybrids such as a blend between a bird and a fish (see Jaswal, 2004). On one part of the task, participants reasoned about hybrids in which the contribution of each animal was equal and the two sources offered conflicting labels (e.g., *bird* versus *fish*). On another part of the task, each child was shown hybrids in which the contribution of one of the animals was more perceptually salient (e.g., the fish), and the mother used the label of the animal that was less salient (e.g., *bird*). Overall, children tended to agree with the label provided by their mother unless it contradicted the perceptual evidence, but the effect varied with the child's attachment status. Securely attached children were the most likely to accept the perceptual evidence, children with insecure-avoidant attachment showed no systematic preference for the claims of their mother, and children with insecure-resistant attachment tended to agree with their mother regardless of the perceptual evidence. Corriveau et al. (2009) interpreted these results as reflecting a tendency for securely attached children to shift strategies based on the available perceptual evidence, children with insecure-avoidant attachment to focus on their own perceptual observations, and children with insecure-resistant attachment to be hypervigilant to the signals of their mothers. Given that prior research shows important parallels in the function of attachment in early childhood and adulthood (Fraley & Shaver, 1998; Sharpsteen & Kirkpatrick, 1997; Shaver & Mikulincer, 2007), it will be important to determine whether attachment styles among adults also have implications for evaluating sources of information. For example, does the distrust seen among insecurely attached adults generalize beyond topics that pose a clear threat to the relationship (Simpson, 1990)?

Other Cues

There are other cues that preschool-aged children use to assess a potential source's reliability. One is to rely on people who provide relevant information in response to requests for help (Eskritt, Whalen, & Lee, 2008). Another is to mistrust sources who have a history of dissenting from others rather than agreeing (Corriveau, Fusaro, & Harris, 2009).

Young children generally consider adults to be more reliable sources of information than same-age peers. Jaswal and Neely (2006) found that when no specific information was presented about the reliability of an adult source and a child source, 3- and 4-year-olds tended to prefer the adult. However, when the adult source was shown making inaccurate statements and the child source was shown making accurate statements, participants tended to prefer the child. This pattern of results is consistent with the notion that young children use life experience as a proxy for reliability when information about a source's previous statements is not available. Other research suggests that children will make an exception to the general heuristic of relying on adults in contexts in which same-age peers are likely to have special expertise, such as with reference to questions about how to operate certain types of toys (VanderBorght & Jaswal, 2009). Research on developmental differences in cultural transmission among child peers supports the possibility that the sophisticated imitative capacities that characterize human children support age-related improvements in the ability to acquire skills by observing others (Flynn & Whiten, 2008).

Source Reasoning and the Representation of Mental Life

THEORY OF MIND

The ability to reason about sources is an important aspect of learning to represent the mental life of others. These representations, commonly referred to as *theory of mind*, involve reasoning about people in relation to inner states such as beliefs and desires in a way that serves as a framework for interpreting

and predicting human behavior (Astington, 2001; Wellman, Cross, & Watson, 2001). The skills that underlie theory of mind develop rapidly between the ages of 3 and 5, and have been described as a "cornerstone of social intelligence and satisfying social interaction" (Peterson, Wellman, & Liu, 2005, p. 502). Among adults, ideas about a source's reliability are closely tied to notions of mental life. For example, adults often reject sources who are suspected of lacking relevant knowledge, or of having deceptive intent.

The paradigms that have been used to examine source reasoning in relation to potential sources' history of reliability do not permit a definitive assessment of the role played by conceptions of mental life. Although it is possible that children make mental state inferences when they decline to accept information from sources who have previously been unreliable, it is also possible to make the same pattern of responses without giving any consideration to the mental life of the informant. One such strategy is to simply identify certain sources as unreliable, just as one might avoid using a computer that exhibits a high rate of failure without having any understanding of the underlying problem (Heyman, 2008; see also Birch et al., 2008; Nurmsoo & Robinson, 2009).

To explore the relation between source reasoning and theory of mind, new research has begun to include measures assessing both capacities. There is some evidence that children who show greater sophistication on theory of mind tasks also show more sophisticated reasoning about the evaluation of sources (DiYanni & Kelemen, 2008; Vanderbilt, Liu, & Heyman, 2011; see also Pasquini et al., 2007, who found no such link). Vanderbilt et al. (2011) gave 3- to 5-year-olds a theory of mind scale developed by Wellman and Liu (2004) to assess the developmental progression of mental state understanding. The scale includes measures of children's understanding of diverse desires, diverse beliefs, knowledge and ignorance, false beliefs, and false emotions. After controlling for age, children's performance on the theory of mind scale was positively correlated with their performance on a selective trust task, which suggests that children's understanding of mental life may facilitate their ability to critically evaluate what they learn from others.

MENTAL STATE INFERENCES

Another strategy that has been used to examine the link between notions of a source's reliability and beliefs about mental life is to examine whether children make use of information about mental states and processes when they evaluate sources. Some studies using this strategy have found that children younger than age 5 are sensitive to cues that can serve as indicators of a source's knowledge. For example, they expect creators of objects to be particularly good sources of information about the objects (Jaswal, 2006; Sabbagh & Baldwin, 2001).

A second cue to a potential source's mental state is the degree of confidence he or she expresses. Sabbagh and Baldwin (2001) found that 3- and 4-year-olds were more likely to learn a new word from a speaker who verbally expressed certainty about it rather than uncertainty. Findings from Birch, Akmal, and Frampton (2009) suggest that even 2-year-olds can use confidence as a cue when assessing a source's reliability. Participants preferred to learn about an object from a source who appeared certain, rather than uncertain, when interacting with it. The degree of certainty was indicated using nonverbal cues such as gestures and facial expressions, which suggests that young children are sensitive to nonverbal as well as verbal cues in this context. Tenney, Small, Kondrad, Jaswal, and Spellman (2011) demonstrated that 5- and 6-year-olds, like adults, were more likely to trust sources who expressed confidence in their claims than those who expressed uncertainty. However, unlike adults, the children tended to maintain high levels of trust in confident sources even when evidence was presented suggesting that the source's confidence had previously been overstated.

A third potential cue to a source's mental state is the extent to which he or she has access to relevant information. In a study by Robinson, Champion, and Mitchell (1999, Study 1), children ages 3 to 6 were asked to guess which of two objects was hidden inside an opaque container. Next, an informant contradicted the participant's guess. Finally, participants were asked to guess which object was in the container once again, and could either repeat their original response or switch to the response indicated by the informant. In one condition, the informant was shown looking inside the container before responding, and in a second condition, the informant did not look inside the container. Participants in the former condition were more likely to switch their responses, which suggests young children understand that having access to relevant information has implications for a source's credibility.

Nurmsoo and Robinson (2009) also found that young children consider task-relevant knowledge to have implications for a source's reliability. They

pointed out that adults often excuse inaccurate statements that result from a lack of access to relevant information, such as when someone attempts to diagnose a problem before learning important facts about the situation. Nurmsoo and Robinson (2009) found that young children also consider the circumstances of the situation in which an informant provides inaccurate information. Participants aged 3 to 5 were more likely to follow the advice of an informant who had previously been inaccurate about the identity of a toy if the incorrect statement was due to a lack of access to information about the toy. In that study, participants were asked to identify the properties of objects that were hidden in a tunnel (i.e., whether an object was hard or soft, or its color), and learned that from one side of the tunnel an observer can feel whether the object is hard but not see its color, and from another side of the tunnel an observer can see the object's color but cannot feel whether it is hard. Participants then observed informants providing inaccurate information about the properties in question, either after having access to the relevant property only (e.g., by looking inside the tunnel when asked to identify the objects' color) or after having access to the irrelevant property only (e.g., by reaching inside the tunnel when asked to identify the objects' color). Next, test trials were presented in which the informant was shown as having access to the relevant type of information. Children were more likely to believe informants whose prior inaccuracy could be explained by a lack of access to the relevant information. These results provide further evidence that young children have the capacity to interpret states of knowledge as holding important implications for the evaluation of sources.

INFORMANT EXPERTISE

Young children are aware that different people often possess different clusters of knowledge. Lutz and Keil (2002) found that 3-year-olds tended to associate different professions with different types of knowledge, for example, by linking doctors with knowledge of how to fix a broken arm. Four-year-olds demonstrated a more sophisticated understanding, by indicating that a doctor would know more about biology than would an auto mechanic, and that an auto mechanic would know more about the functioning of mechanical devices than would a doctor. Lutz and Keil (2002) interpreted their results as indicating that by age 4, children understand that there are individual differences in expertise that correspond to differences in knowledge about abstract categories, such as living kinds and mechanical artifacts. There is evidence that this tendency to conceptualize expertise in terms of underlying disciplines increases during the elementary school years (Danovitch & Keil, 2004; Keil, Stein, Webb, Billings, & Rozenblit, 2008).

A different approach to investigating the implications of expertise is to present children with evidence about an informant's level of expertise at one type of skill and examine whether they will use it to make generalizations regarding other skills. This work suggests that children sometimes generalize across skills, but not always. For example, Jaswal, McKercher, and VanderBorght (2008) found that children ages 3 to 5 were more willing to accept novel names that were provided by informants who had a history of stating the plural forms of familiar nouns accurately rather than inaccurately. However, they did not use information about informants' prior accuracy at labeling to inform their judgments about the plural forms of familiar nouns; instead they showed a systematic preference for words with regular morphology. These results suggest that children sometimes ignore information about expertise when it conflicts with their expectations.

There is evidence of a developmental increase in the tendency to believe that an individual's level of skill in one domain has implications for other domains. Brosseau-Liard and Birch (2010) found that 5-year-olds used an informant's history of labeling objects accurately or inaccurately to make broader inferences about the informant, such as whether she knows a lot about planets and stars or is likely to be prosocial. However, 4-year-olds did not make these types of generalizations (see also Vanderbilt, Liu, & Heyman, 2011, for evidence of 5-year-olds making broader generalizations about informants than 4-year-olds).

MOTIVES TO DISTORT OR CONCEAL INFORMATION

Another important aspect of source reasoning involves making sense of deception. A growing body of developmental research focuses on children's understanding that in some contexts, informants are likely to have motives that are not consistent with directly expressing what they believe to be true. Although there is a widespread assumption that in everyday conversations, people will say what they believe (Grice, 1980), an important aspect of critical thinking about sources is the ability to reason about the exceptions (Heyman, 2008). Indeed, people who are not skilled at reasoning about the possibility of deception become highly vulnerable to being manipulated.

Even very young children can appreciate the possibility of deception. By age 3, children begin to understand the distinction between appearance and reality (Sapp, Lee, & Muir, 2000; Woolley & Wellman, 1990) and realize that a speaker's beliefs and verbal statements do not always correspond (Lee & Cameron, 2000). Children as young as age 3 also engage in lie telling and other deceptive practices (Chandler, Fritz, & Hala, 1989; Lewis, Stanger, & Sullivan, 1989; Polak & Harris, 1999; Talwar & Lee, 2002; Talwar, Murphy, & Lee, 2007). For example, Talwar and her colleagues found that many children ages 3 and older were willing to lie in order to be polite, such as when discussing an undesirable gift. By age 3, children also begin to appreciate that an individual's deceptive behaviors can influence other people's beliefs and behavior. For example, Hala, Chandler, and Fritz (1991) presented young children with an opportunity to help a puppet to deceive an experimenter in a hide-and-seek game. The goal was to prevent the experimenter from finding a treasure in one of four closed boxes. After seeing the puppet's footprints marking a clear path to the box that contained the treasure, most of the 3-year-olds wiped away the tracks and made false tracks that led to one or more of the empty containers.

Gee and Heyman (2007) found that 4- and 5-year-olds have some awareness that people's motivation to accurately convey what they know can vary across circumstances. When participants were asked to evaluate a child's claim of feeling ill, they rated it as less plausible when they were told that the child did not want to attend camp that day. Participants were also asked whether a child would be likely to reveal an interest in playing with dolls, and they rated it as more likely when the child was identified as a girl, rather than a boy.

Jaswal (2004) found that young children were able to make use of relatively subtle information about a source's motives. Children ages 3 and 4 were shown images of imaginary hybrid animals that most closely resembled one of a pair of existing animals (as was done by Corriveau et al., 2009; see above). Participants were more likely to accept that a hybrid shared category membership with the less similar existing animal when the source began by saying, "You're not going to believe this, but this [the hybrid] is actually a...." Jaswal suggested that the manipulation was effective because children inferred that the less obvious category label was being provided intentionally, rather than by mistake.

Limitations in Young Children's Source Reasoning

FAILING TO TAKE A SPEAKER'S MOTIVES INTO ACCOUNT

The previous sections reviewed evidence that young children can evaluate sources in a sophisticated way and are aware that people are not always motivated to accurately convey their knowledge to others. Other research demonstrates that despite these abilities, older children often fail to evaluate information critically despite evidence that a source is trying to deceive or manipulate them (Heyman, 2008; Heyman & Legare, 2005; Moses & Baldwin, 2005). For example, Mills and Keil (2005) found that children younger than age 8 often fail to take a speaker's self-interest motives into account.

Heyman and Legare (2005) found that 6- and 7-year-olds had difficulty anticipating the potential effects of motives relating to social desirability. In this study, 6- and 7-year-olds agreed with the notion that self-report would be an effective way to gain information about the extent to which others possess certain highly value-laden personal characteristics such as honesty. In contrast, 10- and 11-year-olds were skeptical about self-report as a means to gather such information. When participants were asked to explain their responses, those in the younger group were more likely to report that people will provide an accurate answer because they should (e.g., "if you ask them to tell the truth then they better tell the truth, otherwise it would be a lie"), whereas the older children were more likely to report that people will seek to control the impression they are making (e.g., "people don't want to tell you they're not good at something").

Other research suggests that early elementary school-aged children have difficulty reasoning about the ways in which people's judgments might be biased because of their personal relationships. Mills and Keil (2008) asked children to identify characteristics that would make someone a fair judge for a contest. The key question was whether a judge's personal relationship with a contestant, as a teacher, parent, or best friend, would affect his or her ability to be fair. Fourth graders (9- to 10-year-olds) showed an adult-like pattern of viewing such judges as less likely to be fair than judges who had no such relationship with a contestant. In contrast, kindergartners (5- and 6-year-olds) showed the reverse pattern, perhaps because they viewed the personal connection as indicating greater knowledge about a contestant, which would in turn lead to fairer judgments. Mills and Grant (2009) showed that when 6-year-old children evaluate decisions by judges, they fail to recognize that a judge's positive feelings about a particular contestant can lead to skewed judgments in the contestant's favor, even though they have no difficulty recognizing that a judge's negative feelings about a particular contestant can lead to skewed judgments against the contestant.

RECOGNIZING DECEPTION BUT FAILING TO ACT ON IT

Results of a study by Vanderbilt, Liu, and Heyman (2011) suggest that young children sometimes recognize that deception is present, but fail to make use of it when evaluating the trustworthiness of a source. Children ages 3 to 5 completed a task in which they accepted or rejected the advice of informants concerning the location of a hidden sticker. On some trials, advice about the sticker's location came from a *helper* who was shown happily providing correct advice about the location of a sticker to two people, and on other trials the advice came from a *tricker* who was shown happily providing incorrect advice about the location of a sticker to two people.

Participants were asked to verbally identify the source as either a helper or a tricker, and to guess the location of the sticker. The 3-year-olds considered both helpers and trickers to be trustworthy, according to both their verbal statements and their guesses about the location of the sticker. The 5-year-olds showed the reverse pattern by consistently differentiating between helpers and trickers in their verbal statements and in their guesses about the location of the sticker. The most interesting pattern was seen among the 4-year-olds. They identified the helpers as more likely than the trickers to have a helpful intent, and more likely to provide correct information to others about the location of the sticker. However, their guesses about the location of the sticker showed no differentiation in the extent to which they followed the advice of helpers versus trickers.

The finding that 4-year-olds were able to verbally express a distinction between sources that they failed to act on is surprising given that many studies have found the opposite pattern, in which children's behavior indicates a level of sophistication that is not obvious from their verbal responses (Woolley, 2006). For example, children begin hiding their emotions as early as age 3 (Cole, 1986), but it is not until about age 6 that they are able to provide clear answers to questions about the difference between expressing and experiencing emotions (Gnepp & Hess, 1986; Gross & Harris, 1988).

Why would 4-year-olds accept advice from individuals they have observed trying to deceive others? One possibility is that children have a general tendency to follow the advice of others, and that 4-year-olds sometimes have trouble exerting the necessary inhibitory control to overcome this tendency. This type of inhibitory control is slow to develop and does not reach its peak until adulthood (Moses & Baldwin, 2005). Moses and Baldwin (2005) argued that deficits in inhibitory control are also likely to make children vulnerable to adverse effects from advertising even after they have a clear understanding of the intentions that underlie such advertising. For example, audiovisual effects might capture children's attention in a way that makes it difficult for them to focus on the persuasive intent of the advertisement.

The role that inhibitory control processes play in children's ability to reject misleading advice is currently a subject of debate in the literature. Researchers who argue for the centrality of inhibitory control processes have asserted that for conventional cues such as a pointed finger or a verbal instruction, acceptance is a highly practiced response, and consequently such cues require more inhibitory control to reject than do less conventional cues such as an arrow. As is consistent with this prediction, researchers have found that young children often have a harder time rejecting advice when it is presented in more conventional forms (Couillard & Woodward, 1999; Jaswal, Croft, Seftia, & Cole, 2010; Palmquist & Jaswal, 2012). For example, Couillard and Woodward (1999) found that preschool children more successfully rejected advice from deceptive informants about the location of a hidden object when the advice took the form of a ball placed near the location being referenced than when the advice took the form of pointing.

An alternative interpretation of these findings is that unconventional forms of advice tend to be more ambiguous, which encourages children to treat deceptive cues as accurate indicators of which box not to pick, thus transforming the task into one that no longer involves rejecting deceptive advice (Mascaro, 2011; Mascaro & Sperber, 2009). To assess this possibility, Heyman, Sritanyaratana, and Vanderbilt (in press) created a task in which it was made clear to children that a source was attempting to deceive them. Results indicated that the conventionality of the form of communication did not matter, and children's performance on the task was not associated with independent measures of inhibitory control. These findings suggest that

the conventionality of the cue may simply serve to establish whether the task involves the rejection of advice, and that once this question has been answered, the child's inhibitory control skills play a relatively minor role. Such an interpretation is consistent with the possibility that young children have difficulty forming an integrated understanding of overtly antisocial informants who nevertheless "seem to engage in cooperative sharing of information (by communicating)" (Mascaro & Sperber, 2009).

ROLE OF SOCIAL EXPERIENCE

That children show such a wide range of limitations in their reasoning about motives to deceive remains a puzzle, given that they appear to possess the knowledge to do so. Heyman, Fu, and Lee (2007) suggested one possible explanation: once children become aware of the possibility of deception, social experience is required before they can fully understand the consequences of deceptive motives, and identify the contexts in which such motives are likely to be present (see also Banerjee & Yuill, 1999).

As a first step toward examining this possibility, Heyman, Fu, and Lee (2007) examined the development of skepticism in China and in the United States, using nationality as a proxy for differences in social experience. Prevailing social norms about how people should communicate about themselves differ substantially across the two countries. For example, in China there is a greater emphasis on the importance of managing information about the self, especially if it concerns the expression of thoughts and feelings that could leave one vulnerable to criticism from others, or disrupt group harmony (see Gao, Ting-Toomey, & Gudykunst, 1996). Children ages 6 to 7 and 10 to 11 in each country were asked to reason about the disclosure of information concerning the self (see Heyman & Legare, 2005). Both the younger and older children from China showed more sophisticated reasoning about social desirability motives than did their counterparts in the United States, which suggests that differences in social experience might play an important role in shaping children's beliefs about the contexts in which people may not be motivated to communicate what they believe to be true.

Sources of Information about What is Desirable

The research described thus far concerns how children reason about sources when the goal is to obtain accurate factual information. However, children also show selectivity about sources of subjective evaluations, such as when assessing the desirability of particular objects or activities. There is evidence that young children's reasoning in this context is sensitive to shared preferences. In a study by Fawcett and Markson (2010), 2-year-olds were more likely to follow the toy recommendations of an adult whose toy preferences matched their own.

Young children often give greater weight to information from sources with whom they have characteristics in common. In a study with 12-month-olds, Shutts, Kinzler, McKee, and Spelke (2009) showed movies that portrayed two actors eating different foods. One actor was shown speaking the child's native language, and the other was shown speaking an unfamiliar language. In a subsequent paired-preference task, children preferred the foods that had been eaten by the actor who spoke their native language.

Finally, there are reasons to expect young children to prefer same-sex peers as sources of information about preferences. Shell and Eisenberg (1990) found that 4- and 5-year-olds are more likely to join an activity when same-sex peers are involved. Young children are more likely to imitate the behaviors of same-sex peers (Perry & Bussey, 1979) and to avoid the behaviors of opposite-sex peers (Bussey & Perry, 1982; Ruble, Balaban, & Cooper, 1981). These findings suggest that when deciding which objects and activities are desirable, young children selectively make use of information from individuals who they see as similar to themselves.

Dynamic Aspects of Social Learning Processes

The research described in the previous sections of this chapter focuses on children's reasoning about people as sources of information. Although these studies provide important information about factors that can influence source reasoning, they do not address many of the dynamic aspects of social learning processes, in which children seek out and actively construct information in collaboration with others (Callanan, 2006). This section describes what is known about these processes and how they shape children's general worldview.

Learning by Participating: Sociocultural Research

One research tradition that addresses the dynamic aspects of social learning is the sociocultural approach (Cole, 2003; Rogoff, 2003; Vygotsky, 1978), which examines how knowledge is transmitted across generations collaboratively, and includes the role that material artifacts, symbolic artifacts, and conventional social practices play in this process.

Rogoff and colleagues (Rogoff, et al., 2005; Rogoff, Turkanis, & Bartlett, 2001) have used apprenticeship as a model for social learning. They describe cognitive development as a process of guided participation on the part of mentors and appropriation on the part of the child (Rogoff, 1990). In guided participation, children engage with peers and adults in collaborative activities, and through this process, acquire the skills and knowledge of their cultural community.

The degree to which children receive direct instruction from others varies across cultural contexts. Learning through observation and listening in anticipation of participation is especially valued in communities in which children have access to learning by informal community involvement. In many communities, children frequently observe and listen with intent, concentration, and initiative, and their participation is expected when they are ready to help in shared endeavors (Correa-Chávez, Rogoff, & Mejía Arauz, 2005). This tradition, referred to as *intent participation* (Rogoff, 2003), is prominent in many indigenous American communities (Rogoff et al., 2003) and has also been observed in voluntary organizations, interactive museums, and collaborative schools in middle-class U.S. communities (Rogoff, Turkanis, & Bartlett, 2001). Intent participation contributes to many types of learning, including first-language acquisition (Akhtar, Jipson, & Callanan, 2001). By monitoring and emulating the language people use, very young children learn to address others with culturally appropriate personal pronouns and respect terms (Ochs, 1988; Oshima-Takane & Derat, 1996).

Several studies have revealed cross-cultural differences in the extent to which children engage in observation of others. Bloch (1989) found that young rural Senegalese children spent more than twice as much time observing others than did middle-class European American children. Guilmet (1979) found that Navajo students quietly observed teachers more than twice as often as did Caucasian students in the same classroom. In many cultures, the value of observation is actively promoted by adults. For example, when Rotuman (Polynesian) children ask for instruction, they are "likely to be told to watch a skillful adult in action" (Howard, 1970, p. 116). In many communities, observation skills are emphasized and honed as children attend to ongoing events for the purpose of learning the practices of their community. When children are integrated into a wide range of settings, they are able to observe the ongoing activities of their community as legitimate peripheral or third-party participants (Lave & Wenger, 1991).

Learning by Seeking Information: Children's Questions

Another research tradition that emphasizes the dynamic nature of social learning processes has focused on the ways in which children actively seek out information from others. Much of this work has focused on the questions children ask when they are faced with problems that are too difficult for them to solve on their own. Research on children's questions indicates that children formulate questions to obtain specific information, such as to identify an unfamiliar object (Kemler Nelson & O'Neil, 2005), to distinguish between two objects that are hidden in a box (Chouinard, 2007), or to learn details about a conceptual category such as an unfamiliar animal or a novel artifact (Greif, Kemler Nelson, Keil, & Gutierrez, 2006).

To use questions efficiently in the service of problem solving, children need at least a minimal level of proficiency in several component skills (Mills, Legare, Bills, & Mejias, 2010). Once children recognize that there is a problem that they cannot solve on their own, they must determine who will be able to answer their questions in an informative and accurate way. As discussed earlier in this chapter, children acquire considerable skill in making such judgments before they reach their fifth birthday, and a recent study on children's problem solving suggests that 3-year-olds engage in selective help seeking in a way that takes the prior behavior of potential sources into account (Cluver, Carver, & Heyman, in press).

After an appropriate source has been identified, children must be able to generate effective questions (Chouinard, 2007) and make sense of the responses they obtain. Research by Mills et al. (2010) has shown that there are dramatic developmental differences in the efficiency and efficacy of children's questions. In a novel problem-solving task, they found that even though 3-year-olds can ask questions to solve problems, their questions are largely ineffective and directed toward inappropriate sources. Four-year-olds directed questions toward appropriate sources but asked an approximately equal number of effective and ineffective questions. Only 5-year-olds asked appropriate

sources while simultaneously formulating effective questions. Other research has shown that by age 4, children who seek explanations are able to evaluate the adequacy of the responses they obtain, and if they find the answers inadequate, they often repeat their questions (Callanan & Oakes, 1992; Kemler Nelson, Egan, & Holt, 2004) or devise their own explanations (Frazier, Gelman, & Wellman, 2009).

Mechanisms of Learning from Others: The Case of Essentialist Reasoning

One important aspect of the dynamic social learning process is that children can learn from others in the absence of explicit instruction, and when explicit instruction is taking place, there may be no direct mapping between the topic of the instruction and what is actually learned. Intuitive theories about the physical, psychological, and biological world constrain children's developing belief systems and constrain how children reason about and acquire new information. Accordingly, researchers have sought to better understand the types of influences that are important for children's emerging beliefs. One context in which these influences have been explored concerns children's developing beliefs about psychological essentialism in relation to the social world (Gelman, 2003).

Essentialism is the notion that each member of a particular category has an underlying nature or essence with causal properties that make it what it is. As applied to people, psychological essentialism implies that individuals hold essences that serve as causal explanations for the way they think, feel, and act. For example, an individual who thinks about artistic skill in an essentialist manner might reason that some people are born with an innate potential to develop a high level of artistic skill with minimal effort, and that an individual's level of artistic skill at one point in time is a strong indicator of his or her long-term artistic potential. Psychological essentialism is applied to a range of social categories and psychological characteristics. For example, individuals often reason essentialistically about gender (Taylor, 1996), race (Hirschfeld, 1995), and personality characteristics and abilities (Heyman & Gelman, 2000).

There is evidence that the tendency toward psychological essentialism is sensitive to the ways in which members of one's community talk about people. Gelman, Heyman, and Legare (2007) examined this issue experimentally by presenting children ages 8 and 9 with vignettes in which characters were described with a novel noun phrase such as "banana-hater" or "easy-laugher." Children then learned a new fact about the character that was either consistent or inconsistent with an essentialist interpretation of the novel label. Participants ages 8 and 9 used the new facts to draw inferences about other aspects of the character. For example, when children were told that the character had been an easy-laugher at birth, they were more likely to assume that the character would continue to be an easy-laugher, and that scientists would one day be able to use biological assessments such as blood tests to determine which individuals are easy-laughers. This finding suggests that children may use isolated facts that they learn to make broader judgments about the extent to which characteristics are essentialized.

In addition to the evidence that children can make generalizations based on explicit statements that have direct implications for psychological essentialism, there is reason to believe that much of the social learning in this domain is implicit (Gelman, 2009). Semin and Fiedler (1988) showed that for adults, one way that language implicitly conveys the enduringness of a personal quality is through the level of abstractness of the linguistic category used, with more abstract terms implying that the quality is more enduring. For example, the sentence "Bob is dishonest" is more abstract and less tied to a concrete event than "Bob lied," and consequently the former is seen as reflecting a more enduring quality about Bob. More recently, Bryan, Walton, Rogers, and Dweck (2011) found that voters who were asked to respond to survey items that were framed in terms of "being a voter" were more likely to vote than those who were asked to respond to survey items framed in terms of voting behavior.

A related form of implicit learning concerns whether the phrases that are used to describe individuals are lexicalized. Although there are many concepts that cannot be easily described using a single word, those that can be tend to have particular significance, especially for children (Gelman, 2009). For example, children tend to assume that entities that share the same name also share important properties (Waxman, 1999), and they use label information to reclassify anomalous category instances.

In a study of the implications of lexicalization for children's reasoning about the social world, Gelman and Heyman (1999) presented 5- and 7-year-olds with descriptions of characters such as "Rose eats a lot of carrots," followed by either a noun label, such as "she is a carrot-eater," or a verbal predicate, such as "she eats carrots whenever she can." Children

predicted that the characteristics that had been described using a noun label would be significantly more stable over time and across contexts than those that had been described using a verbal predicate.

One practical implication of these findings is that when children hear people described using a noun label they may come to see the relevant characteristic as a more fundamental and stable part of their own identity. Heyman (2008) presented 8- to 12-year-olds with scenarios about students who were described as being the best in their class in a particular subject. In one version of a scenario about math, a teacher said that whoever does the best on a math test would be called a "math whiz," and then applied that label to the top performer. In the other version the teacher simply identified the top performer without using a label. The participants who heard the label version were more likely to infer that the character was born with special ability, and that he or she would continue to be successful even without subsequent practice. This finding suggests that the use of ability-related labels encourages children to view ability as a gift that some individuals are born with, rather than as a set of skills that can be developed over time. This essentialist way of thinking about ability raises questions about which individuals have special abilities and which do not, and shifts attention away from processes that promote skill development (see Mueller & Dweck, 1998).

There is evidence that cross-linguistic differences in the way people describe personal characteristics have implications for psychological essentialism. Heyman and Diesendruck (2002) investigated the distinction between the Spanish verbs *ser* and *estar*. Each word translates to the English verb *to be*, with *ser* used to refer to permanent properties and *estar* used to refer to temporary properties (see Sera, Bales, & del Castillo Pintado, 1997). Bilingual speakers of English and Spanish ages 6 through 10 heard descriptions of characters, with one group hearing the description in Spanish using the *ser* form, a second hearing it in Spanish using the *estar* form, and a third group hearing it in English using *to be*. For example, participants heard about a female character who "es amistosa" or "está amistosa" in the two Spanish conditions, or "is friendly" in the English condition. The children in each group made inferences about whether the character would be likely to engage in trait-consistent ways at other times and in other contexts. Children treated *ser* and *to be* as more likely to convey the stability of psychological characteristics than *estar*. This finding suggests that the *ser/estar* distinction serves as a cue for

Spanish-speaking children when they are learning whether certain characteristics of people tend to be superficial and transient versus fundamental and stable. This result also raises the question of why the *to be* form in English corresponds more closely to the more stable *ser* form than the more transient *estar* form. One possibility is that children tend to interpret the verb form *to be* as referring to relatively enduring qualities of a person unless there is a specific reason to apply a more transient interpretation (e.g., if someone describes Sarah as acting friendly at the party rather than simply describing Sarah as friendly).

Another linguistic form that is available to young children across a wide range of linguistic and cultural contexts and can serve to promote or endorse essentialist reasoning is the generic form, which involves making general statements that refer to a kind as a whole (Gelman, 2009). For example, the generic statement "girls wear dresses" refers to girls in general rather than to any particular set of girls. Generics characterize a category as an abstract universal that is not tied to any particular context, and children typically begin to appreciate the semantic implications of generics long before the onset of formal schooling (Gelman, 2009).

There is also evidence that the feedback children receive can influence the extent to which they endorse essentialist beliefs, both for themselves and more generally. The responses of parents and teachers to children's negative outcomes are likely to influence the extent to which such outcomes are viewed as temporary setbacks versus reflecting more fundamental difficulties that are likely to limit the effectiveness of future efforts. One such source of feedback is the emotional response of others. For example, when a child experiences academic difficulty, a teacher's response of sympathy is more likely to be interpreted as a reflection of the belief that the child's difficulty reflects more fundamental problems than is a response of anger (Graham, 1984). Similarly, quickly jumping in to help a child at the first sign that he or she is having difficulty may communicate that the child lacks the capacity to overcome the difficulties on his or her own (Pomerantz & Eaton, 2000).

Responses to positive outcomes can also inform the extent to which children view ability in an essentialist manner. Mueller and Dweck (1998) found that fifth graders who were praised for their intelligence in response to a positive outcome (e.g., "you must be really smart at these") were significantly more likely to endorse the view that people cannot do much to change how smart they are than were fifth graders who were praised for their effort (e.g., "you must have worked hard"). Such global praise may implicitly communicate that ability is a fundamental quality that can be readily assessed by immediate outcomes, rather than a quality that can be developed over time. Dweck (1999) has argued that these results "give us insight into the kinds of situations that, if experienced repeatedly, might mold students' theories in a more permanent way."

Acquiring Systems of Beliefs about What Is Real

Another line of research that has explored the dynamic nature of children's social learning has focused on children's reasoning about testimony concerning entities that are not directly observable, such as germs and angels (Harris & Koenig, 2006). This research examines how children make use of different sources of information to develop systems of beliefs, and how they evaluate claims that cannot be verified by first-hand observation.

ACQUISITION OF SUPERNATURAL AND NATURAL BELIEFS

One focus of research on how children acquire broader systems of belief has examined the development of supernatural and natural beliefs (Evans, Legare, & Rosengren, 2010; Harris & Koenig, 2006; Legare, Evans, Rosengren, & Harris, 2012). Supernatural and natural beliefs have been of considerable interest to researchers because much of the content in these domains (e.g., spirits and molecules) are transmitted primarily through testimony (Harris & Koenig, 2006; Harris, Pasquini, Duke, Asscher, & Pons, 2006). Moreover, children often encounter contrasting supernatural and natural descriptions of the same event. *Natural* is defined as observable (at least in principle) and empirically verifiable phenomena of the physical or material world. *Supernatural* is defined as phenomena that violate, operate outside of, or are distinct from the realm of the natural world or known natural law. Even when a particular cause is unknown, natural or physical mechanisms are assumed to exist in the case of natural explanations, and supernatural mechanisms are assumed to exist in the case of supernatural explanations. Rather than making strong definitional claims about the distinction between natural and supernatural phenomena, research on this topic focuses on the kinds of causes and practices that are generally regarded as belonging to natural (e.g., science, medicine, biology) versus supernatural (e.g., religion, divination, witchcraft) kinds from an intuitive, psychological perspective (Legare, Evans, Rosengren, & Harris, 2012).

Researchers have begun to examine whether children's exposure to natural beliefs might replace their supernatural beliefs, or whether the belief systems tend to coexist in some way. Substantial research conducted in a range of cultural contexts indicates that the belief systems do coexist (Astuti & Harris, 2008; Evans, 2001; Evans, Legare, & Rosengren, 2010; Harris & Giménez, 2005; Rosengren et al., 2009; Legare & Gelman, 2008).

In one such study, Harris and Giménez (2005) interviewed 7- to 11- year-olds from a predominantly Catholic culture in Madrid, Spain regarding their beliefs about death. They asked participants whether bodily processes such as seeing, thinking, and hearing would continue after death. Of interest was whether they would predict that these processes would continue, as would be consistent with the spiritual view they had been taught, or whether they would predict that these processes would cease, as would be consistent with the scientific view they had been taught. Harris and Giménez (2005) found that contextual cues played an important role in determining which responses children provided, with participants more likely to predict that bodily functions would continue after death when asked the question from within a narrative context in which a priest informs the family of the death, compared with a narrative in which a doctor informs the family of the death. Astuti and Harris (2008) found similar effects of contextual cues in reasoning about death among Vezo participants in Madagascar.

Legare and Gelman (2008) also found evidence for the coexistence of natural and supernatural explanations in their research on AIDS. This research was conducted among 5-, 7-, 11-, and 15-year-olds, as well as adults in two Sesotho-speaking, South African communities. In these communities, a prevalent view is that AIDS is caused by witchcraft. Of interest was whether exposure to a biological conception of AIDS would replace the witchcraft-based conception. Legare and Gelman (2008) found that although biological explanations for illness were endorsed at high levels, witchcraft was also often endorsed, and that endorsement of witchcraft beliefs increased with age. Importantly, participants showed a similar kind of sensitivity to the narrative context in which the question was asked, as was seen by Harris and Giménez (2005). Specifically, although participants generally gave biological explanations as a default, when attention was drawn to the socially risky behaviors that are believed to put one at risk for witchcraft attacks (e.g., lack of generosity or jealousy), participants gave primarily witchcraft explanations for AIDS. Findings also pointed to some specific ways participants may integrate the apparently contradictory witchcraft and biological explanations. For example, some explanations involved causal chains of events (e.g., "a witch can put an HIV infected woman in your path and seduce you"). Results from these lines of research suggest that children are capable of applying different belief systems in different contexts, and that they often attempt to integrate different modes of reasoning in novel ways in order to maintain coherent beliefs.

FACTORS AFFECTING CHILDREN'S BELIEFS ABOUT SUPERNATURAL ENTITIES AND FORCES

A related line of research has examined factors contributing to children's willingness to accept claims about the supernatural entities and forces. This research indicates that children are sensitive to information about the context in which the claims are being made. One important aspect of the context is the extent to which beliefs are actively encouraged by socializing agents and by the broader culture (Rosengren & Hickling, 1994). This active encouragement is undoubtedly central in the widespread acceptance of Santa Claus and the Tooth Fairy among children in the United States. Once children reach about 5 or 6 years of age, the level of active encouragement of these beliefs tends to decline, which likely plays a role in children's increasing rejection that these entities are real (Rosengren & Hickling, 1994). The specific contexts in which supernatural entities are introduced are also likely to play a role in whether they are accepted (Corriveau, Kim, Schwalen, & Harris, 2009; Woolley & Van Reet, 2006). Woolley and Van Reet (2006) found that 4- to 6-year olds were less likely to infer that a novel entity was real when it was introduced in a narrative that included fantastical beings than when introduced within the context of mundane or scientific narratives. For example, they were less likely to accept that "surnits" were real when they learned that "Dragons hide surnits in their caves" than if they learned that "grandmothers hide surnits in their garden" or that "doctors use surnits to make medicine."

Children's motivation to believe may also influence whether they will accept claims about supernatural entities. In one line of research addressing this issue, Woolley, Boerger, and Markman (2004) introduced young children to a novel fantastical entity called "the Candy Witch," who was described as visiting people's homes to exchange candy for a new toy. They asked each participant whether he or she preferred toys or candy. The researchers reasoned that those who reported that they liked toys better than candy, who presumably had a stronger motivation to believe in the Candy Witch than those who preferred candy to toys, might be more willing to accept the Candy Witch as real. As is consistent with this possibility, they found that 4- to 5-year-olds with a toy preference were more likely to accept the Candy Witch as real. These results suggest that by age 4, children may engage in some type of cost benefit analysis when determining what to believe.

Other research has focused on how children make use of evidence when evaluating claims (Keil, 2006; Kuhn, 1999). Young children often accept forms of evidence that older children and adults would not find compelling. For example, 4- to 5-year-olds interpreted the overnight replacement of their Halloween candy with a new toy as evidence of the Candy Witch's existence (Woolley, Boerger, & Markman, 2004). The extent to which children make use of the evidence available to them is likely to depend on their prior beliefs. In addressing this issue, Tullos and Woolley (2009) asked 4- to 8-year-old children about the reality status of novel animals. Children with an initial hypothesis about the reality status of the animal tended to disregard the evidence, but children who had no initial hypothesis were able to make use of the evidence to critically evaluate whether or not the novel animal was real. This finding is consistent with other evidence that young children have difficulty making use of evidence that conflicts with their prior beliefs (Koerber, Sodian, Thoermer, & Nett, 2005).

Conclusion

The ability to obtain information from others facilitates many forms of learning, and it underlies the transmission of cultural knowledge across generations (Tomasello, 1999). Developmental research is providing important insights into this process. A number of studies show that by the time children reach 4 years of age, they understand that some people are more knowledgeable than others, and this understanding is closely linked to broader conceptions of mental life. By this age, children can use a range of cues to identify which people are appropriate sources of information, and they have some appreciation that people are not always

motivated to accurately convey what they know. However, even older children often have substantial difficulty with recognizing deception, and when they do recognize a deceptive motive, they often fail to act accordingly.

This research has also informed our understanding of the dynamic nature of knowledge transmission. This dynamic learning occurs through observation and actively seeking out information from others. When constructing systems of belief, children make use of a wide range of subtle cues available in the communication of others, and they employ a diverse range of reasoning strategies to evaluate and integrate claims they hear.

Future Directions

An important goal for future work will be to examine how children's social experiences influence the way they make sense of information that other people provide. As noted previously, there is evidence that children from China understand motives relating to social desirability at a younger age than do children from the United States (Heyman, Fu, & Lee, 2007). This raises the question of the scope of these cross-cultural differences and how the developmental trajectory of this form of reasoning varies across cultures more generally. It will also be important to identify which aspects of the social environment have the greatest influence on the development of children's source reasoning. For example, when children are routinely lied to by their parents (Heyman, Luu, & Lee, 2009), do they become skeptical of what their parents say, or skeptical in other social contexts? Additionally, does exposing children to individuals who are incompetent or who have antisocial motives help them to become aware of the possibility that others might provide inaccurate information?

There are also important unanswered questions about what cues children use to determine the reliability of individuals. This includes what types of cues they use. For example, to what extent do children make use of explicit information they are given about trusting particular individuals or particular types of people? To what extent do they take motive information into account when assessing reliability? Adults are likely to make differing evaluations of individuals who provide incorrect information in the context of a joke or an attempt to protect someone's feelings versus individuals who provide the same information for antisocial reasons, but little is known about the development of this type of reasoning.

There are also unanswered questions about cues children use to assess the reliability of specific claims. Harris and Koenig (2006) pointed out that people do not typically express avowals of belief in an entity if its existence is beyond doubt. For example, it would be odd for a parent to tell a child, "I believe in oxygen." Consequently, it may be that these avowals paradoxically lead to higher levels of doubt about the existence of such entities. Children may also view extended discussion about the existence of an entity as an indicator that the entity is not conventionally accepted (Callanan, 2006).

There is evidence that children, like adults, are less skeptical of claims that they want to believe are true (Stipek, Roberts, & Sanborn, 1984; Woolley, Boerger, & Markman, 2004), but little is known about the details of this phenomenon. It will be important to assess the extent to which children consciously choose to engage in skeptical thinking based on their desires, and how children's desires influence basic cognitive processes such as selective encoding and retrieval when they are learning from others. From an applied perspective, investigating how children develop the capacity to reason about deception and self-interest has implications for understanding the impact of advertising campaigns.

Finally, more research is needed on how children seek out information from others. How do children decide that it is time to seek help, rather than attempting to solve problems on their own? How do the responses that children receive influence their future efforts to seek help? By addressing these questions, we will be better able to understand the psychological underpinnings of children's efforts to seek information, and how to promote interactions that optimize learning.

Author Note

This chapter was supported by NICHD Grant HD38529. We thank Brian Compton, Nicole Jones, Candice Mills, Paulina Singhapok, and Jacqui Woolley for their helpful comments. Address requests for further information to Gail D. Heyman, Department of Psychology, University of California, San Diego, 9500 Gilman Dr., La Jolla CA 92093-0109; e-mail: gheyman@ucsd.edu.

References

Ainsworth, M. D. S., Blehar, M. C., Waters, E., & Wall, S. (1978). *Patterns of attachment*. Hillsdale, NJ: Erlbaum.

Akhtar, N., Jipson, J., & Callanan, M. A. (2001). Learning words through overhearing. *Child Development, 72*, 416–430.

Astington, J. W. (2001). The future of theory-of-mind research: Understanding motivational states, the role of language, and real-world consequences. *Child Development, 72*, 685–687

Astuti, R., & Harris, P. L. (2008). Understanding mortality and the life of the ancestors in rural Madagascar. *Cognitive Science, 32*, 713–740.

Banerjee, R., & Yuill, N. (1999). Children's understanding of self-presentational display rules: Associations with mental-state understanding. *British Journal of Developmental Psychology, 17*, 111–124.

Birch, S. A. J., Akmal, N. & Frampton, K. L. (2009). Two-year-olds are vigilant of others' nonverbal cues to credibility. *Developmental Science, 13*, 363–369.

Birch, S. A. J., Vauthier, S. A., & Bloom, P. (2008). Three- and four-year-olds spontaneously use others' past performance to guide their learning. *Cognition, 107*, 1018–1034.

Bloch, M. N. (1989). Young boys' and girls' play at home and in the community: A cultural-ecological framework. In M. N. Bloch & A. D. Pellegrini (Eds.), *The ecological context of children's play* (pp. 120–154) Norwood, NJ: Ablex.

Brosseau Liard, P. E., & Birch, S. A. (2010). "I bet you know more and are nicer too!" What children infer from others' accuracy. *Developmental Science, 13*(5), 772–778.

Bryan, C. J., Walton, G. M., Rogers, T., & Dweck, C. S. (2011). Motivating voter turnout by invoking the self. *Proceedings of the National Academy of Sciences, USA, 108*, 12653–12656.

Bussey, K., & Perry, D. G. (1982). Same-sex imitation: The avoidance of cross-sex models or the acceptance of same-sex models? *Sex Roles, 8*, 773–784.

Callanan, M. (2006). Cognitive development, culture, and conversation: Comments on Harris and Koenig's "Trust in testimony: How children learn about science and religion." *Child Development, 77*, 525–530.

Callanan, M. A., & Oakes, L. M. (1992). Preschoolers' questions and parents' explanations: Causal thinking in everyday activity. *Cognitive Development, 7*, 213–233.

Chandler, M., Fritz, A. S., & Hala, S. (1989). Small-scale deceit: Deception as a marker of two-, three-, and four-year-olds' early theories of mind. *Child Development, 60*, 1263–1277.

Chouinard, M. (2007). Children's questions: A mechanism for cognitive development. *Monographs of the Society for Research in Child Development, 72*, 1–129.

Cluver, A., Carver, L. J., & Heyman, G. D. (in press). *Young children selectively seek help when solving problems. Journal of Experimental Child Psychology.*

Cole, M. (2003). *Cultural psychology: A once and future discipline*. Cambridge, MA: Harvard University Press.

Cole, P. M. (1986). Children's spontaneous control of facial expression. *Child Development, 57*, 1309–1321.

Correa-Chávez, M., Rogoff, B., & Mejía Arauz, R. (2005). Cultural patterns in attending to two events at once. *Child Development, 76*, 664–678.

Corriveau, K. H., Fusaro, M., & Harris, P. L. (2009). Going with the flow: Preschoolers prefer non-dissenters as informants. *Psychological Science, 20*, 372–377.

Corriveau, K. H., & Harris, P. L. (2009) Choosing your informant: Weighing familiarity and past accuracy. *Developmental Science, 12*, 426–437.

Corriveau, K. H., Harris, P. L., Meins, E., Ferneyhough, C., Arnott, B., Elliott, L., Liddle, B., Hearn, A., Vittorini, L., & de Rosnay, M. (2009). Young children's trust in their mother's claims: Longitudinal links with attachment security in infancy. *Child Development, 80*, 750–761.

Corriveau, K. H., Kim, A. L., Schwalen, C. E., & Harris, P. L. (2009). Abraham Lincoln and Harry Potter: Children's differentiation between historical and fantasy characters. *Cognition, 113*, 213–225.

Couillard, N. L., & Woodward, A. L. (1999). Children's comprehension of deceptive points. *British Journal of Developmental Psychology, 17*, 515–521.

Cvencek, D., Greenwald, A. G., & Meltzoff, A. N. (2011). Measuring implicit attitudes of 4-year-olds: The Preschool Implicit Association Test. *Journal of Experimental Child Psychology, 109*, 187–200.

Danovitch, J. H., & Keil, F. C. (2004). Should you ask a fisherman or a biologist? Developmental shifts in ways of clustering knowledge. *Child Development, 75*, 918–931.

DiYanni, C., & Kelemen, D. (2008). Using a bad tool with good intention: Young children's imitation of adults' questionable choices. *Journal of Experimental Child Psychology, 101*, 241–261.

Dunham, Y. & Degner, J. (2010). Origins of intergroup bias: Developmental and social cognitive research on intergroup attitudes. *European Journal of Social Psychology, 40*, 563–568.

Dweck, C. S. (1999). *Self-theories: Their role in motivation, personality, and development.* Philadelphia: Psychology Press/Taylor & Francis.

Eskritt, M., Whalen, J., & Lee, K. (2008). Preschoolers can recognize violations of the Gricean maxims. *British Journal of Developmental Psychology, 26*, 435–443.

Evans, E. M. (2001). Cognitive and contextual factors in the emergence of diverse belief systems: Creation versus evolution. *Cognitive Psychology, 42*, 217–266.

Evans, E. M., Legare, C. H., & Rosengren, K. (2010). Engaging multiple epistemologies: Implications for science education. In R. Taylor & M. Ferrari (Eds.), *Epistemology and science education: Understanding the evolution vs. intelligent design controversy.* New York: Routledge.

Fawcett, C. A., & Markson, L. (2010). Children reason about shared preferences. *Developmental Psychology, 46*, 299–309.

Flynn, E., & Whiten, A. (2008). Cultural transmission of tool use in young children: A diffusion chain study. *Social Development, 17*, 699–718.

Fraley, R. C., & Shaver, P. R. (1998). Airport separations: A naturalistic study of adult attachment dynamics in separating couples. *Journal of Personality and Social Psychology, 75*, 1198–1212.

Frazier, B. N., Gelman, S. A., & Wellman, H. M. (2009). Preschoolers' search for explanatory information within adult-child conversation. *Child Development, 80*, 1592–1611.

Gao, G., Ting-Toomey, S., & Gudykunst, W. B. (1996). Chinese communication processes. In M. H. Bond (Ed.), *Chinese psychology* (pp. 280–293). Hong Kong: Oxford University Press.

Gee, C. L., & Heyman, G. D. (2007). Children's evaluation of other people's self-descriptions. *Social Development, 16*, 800–810.

Gelman, S. A. (2003). *The essential child: Origins of essentialism in everyday thought.* New York: Oxford University Press.

Gelman, S. A. (2009). Learning from others: Children's construction of concepts. *Annual Review of Psychology, 60*, 115–140.

Gelman, S. A., & Heyman, G. D. (1999). Carrot-eaters and creature-believers: The effects of lexicalization on children's inferences about social categories. *Psychological Science, 10*, 489–493.

Gelman, S. A., Heyman, G. D., & Legare, C. H. (2007). Developmental changes in the coherence of essentialist beliefs. *Child Development, 78*, 757–774.

Gnepp, J., & Hess, D. L. (1986). Children's understanding of verbal and facial display rules. *Developmental Psychology, 22*, 103–108.

Graham, S. (1984). Communicating sympathy and anger to Black and White children: The cognitive (attributional) consequences of affective cues. *Journal of Personality and Social Psychology, 47*, 40–54.

Greif, M. L., Kemler Nelson, D. G., Keil, F. C., & Gutierrez, F. (2006). What do children want to know about animals and artifacts? Domain-specific requests for information. *Psychological Science, 17*, 455–459.

Grice, H. P. (1980). *Studies in the way of words.* Cambridge, MA: Harvard University Press.

Gross, D., & Harris, P. L. (1988). False beliefs about emotion: Children's understanding of misleading emotional displays. *International Journal of Behavioral Development, 11*, 475–488.

Guilmet, G. M. (1979). Maternal perceptions of urban Navajo and Caucasian children's classroom behavior. *Human Organization, 38*, 87–91.

Hala, S. M., Chandler, M. J., & Fritz, A. S. (1991). Fledgling theories of mind: Deception as a marker of three-year-olds' understanding of false belief. *Child Development, 62*, 83–97.

Harris, P. L. (2007). Trust. *Developmental Science, 10*, 135–138.

Harris, P. L., & Giménez, M. (2005). Children's acceptance of conflicting testimony: The case of death. *Journal of Cognition and Culture, 5*, 143–164.

Harris, P. L., & Koenig, M. A. (2006). Trust in testimony: How children learn about science and religion. *Child Development, 77*(3), 505–524.

Harris, P. L., Pasquini, E. S., Duke, S., Asscher, J. J., & Pons, F. (2006). Germs and angels: The role of testimony in young children's ontology. *Developmental Science, 9*, 76–96.

Heyman, G. D. (2008). Talking about success: Implications for achievement motivation. *Journal of Applied Developmental Psychology, 29*, 361–370.

Heyman, G. D, & Diesendruck, G. (2002). The Spanish ser/estar distinction in bilingual children's reasoning about human psychological characteristics. *Developmental Psychology, 38*, 407–417.

Heyman, G. D., Fu, G., & Lee, K. (2007). Evaluating claims people make about themselves: The development of skepticism. *Child Development, 78*, 367–375.

Heyman, G. D., & Gelman, S. A. (2000). Beliefs about the origins of human psychological traits. *Developmental Psychology, 36*, 663–678.

Heyman, G. D., & Legare, C. H. (2005). Children's evaluation of sources of information about traits. *Developmental Psychology, 41*, 636–647.

Heyman, G. D., Luu, D. H., & Lee, K. (2009). Parenting by lying. *Journal of Moral Development, 38*, 353–369.

Heyman, G. D., Sritanyaratana, L., & Vanderbilt, K. E. (in press).Young children's trust in overtly misleading advice. *Cognitive Science.*

Hirschfeld, L. A. (1995). Do children have a theory of race? *Cognition, 54*, 209–252.

Howard, A. (1970). *Learning to be Rotuman: Enculturation in the South Pacific.* New York: Teachers College Press.

Jaswal, V. K. (2004). Don't believe everything you hear: Preschoolers' sensitivity to speaker intent in category induction. *Child Development, 75*, 1871–1885.

Jaswal, V. K. (2006). Preschoolers favor the creator's label when reasoning about an artifact's function. *Cognition, 99*, B83–B92.

Jaswal, V. K., Croft, A. C., Seftia, A. R., & Cole, C. A. (2010). Young children have a specific, highly robust bias to trust testimony. *Psychological Science, 21*, 1541–1547.

Jaswal, V. K., McKercher, D. A., VanderBorght, M. (2008). Limitations on reliability: Regularity rules in the English plural and past tense. *Child Development, 79*, 750–760.

Jaswal, V. K., & Neely, L. A. (2006). Adults don't always know best: Preschoolers use past reliability over age when learning new words. *Psychological Science, 17*, 757–758.

Keil, F. C. (2006). Explanation and understanding. *Annual Review of Psychology, 57*, 227–254.

Keil, F. C., Stein, C., Webb, L., Billings, V. D., & Rozenblit, L. (2008). Discerning the division of cognitive labor: An emerging understanding of how knowledge is clustered in other minds. *Cognitive Science, 32*, 259–300.

Kemler Nelson, D. G., Egan, L. C., & Holt, M. (2004). When children ask What is it? What do they want to know about artifacts? *Psychological Science, 15*, 384–389.

Kemler Nelson, D. G., & O'Neil, K. (2005). How do parents respond to children's questions about the identity of artifacts? *Developmental Science, 8*, 519–524.

Koenig, M. A., & Harris, P. L. (2005). Preschoolers mistrust ignorant and inaccurate speakers. *Child Development, 76*, 1261–1277.

Koerber, S., Sodian, B., Thoermer, C., & Nett, U. (2005). Scientific reasoning in young children: Preschoolers' ability to evaluate covariation evidence. *Swiss Journal of Psychology, 64*, 141–152.

Kuhn, D. (1999) A developmental model of critical thinking. *Educational Researcher, 28*, 16–26.

Lave, J., & Wenger, E. (1991). *Situated learning: Legitimate peripheral participation*. Cambridge, UK: Cambridge University Press.

Lee, K., & Cameron, C. A. (2000). Extracting truthful information from lies: Emergence of the expression-representation distinction. *Merrill-Palmer Quarterly, 46*, 1–20.

Legare, C. H., Evans, E. M., Rosengren, K., Harris, P. (2012). The co-existence of natural and supernatural explanations across cultures and development. *Child Development, 83*, 779–793.

Legare, C. H. & Gelman, S. A. (2008). Bewitchment, biology, or both: The co-existence of natural and supernatural explanatory frameworks across development. *Cognitive Science, 32*, 607–642.

Lewis, M., Stanger, C., & Sullivan, M. W. (1989). Deception in 3-year-olds. *Developmental Psychology, 25*, 439–443.

Luo, Y., & Baillargeon, R. (2010). Toward a mentalistic account of early psychological reasoning. *Current Directions in Psychological Science, 19*, 301–307.

Lutz, D. J., & Keil, F. C. (2002). Early understanding of the division of cognitive labor. *Child Development, 73*, 1073–1084.

Mascaro, O. (2011, April). *Why do young children (sometimes) disregard cues of informants' dishonesty?* Paper presented at the biennial meeting of the Society for Research in Child Development, Montreal.

Mascaro, O., & Sperber, D. (2009). The moral, epistemic, and mindreading components of children's vigilance towards deception. *Cognition, 112*, 367–380.

Mills, C. M., & Grant, M. G. (2009). Biased decision-making: Developing an understanding of how positive and negative relationships may skew judgments. *Developmental Science, 12*, 784–797.

Mills, C. M., & Keil, F. C. (2005). The development of cynicism. *Psychological Science, 16*, 385–390.

Mills, C. M., & Keil, F. C. (2008). Children's developing notions of (im)partiality. *Cognition, 107*, 528–551.

Mills, C., Legare, C. H., Bills, M., & Mejias, C. (2010). Preschoolers use questions as a tool to acquire knowledge from different sources. *Journal of Cognition and Development, 11*, 533–560.

Moses, L. J., & Baldwin, D. A. (2005). What can the study of cognitive development reveal about children's ability to appreciate and cope with advertising? *Journal of Public Policy and Marketing, 24*, 186–201.

Mueller, C. M., & Dweck, C. S. (1998). Praise for intelligence can undermine children's motivation and performance. *Journal of Personality and Social Psychology, 75*, 33–52.

Mumme, D. L., & Fernald, A. (2003). The infant as onlooker: Learning from emotional reactions observed in a television scenario. *Child Development, 74*, 221–237.

Nurmsoo, E., & Robinson, E. J. (2009). Identifying unreliable informants: Do children excuse past inaccuracy? *Developmental Science, 12*, 41–47.

Ochs, E. (1988). *Culture and language development: Language acquisition and language socialization in a Samoan village*. Cambridge, UK: Cambridge University Press.

Oshima-Takane, Y., & Derat, L. (1996). Nominal and pronominal reference in maternal speech during the later stages of language acquisition: A longitudinal study. *First Language, 16*, 319–338.

Palmquist, C. M., & Jaswal, V. K. Preschoolers expect pointers (even ignorant ones) to be knowledgeable. *Psychological Science, 23*, 230–231.

Pasquini, E., Corriveau, K., Koenig, M., & Harris, P. L. (2007). Preschoolers monitor the relative accuracy of informants. *Developmental Psychology, 43*, 1216–1226.

Perry, D. G., & Bussey, K. (1979). The social learning theory of sex differences: Imitation is alive and well. *Journal of Personality and Social Psychology, 37*, 1699–712.

Peterson, C. C., Wellman, H. M., & Liu, D. (2005). Steps in theory of mind development for children with deafness or autism. *Child Development, 76*, 502–517.

Polak, A., & Harris, P. L. (1999) Deception by young children following noncompliance. *Developmental Psychology, 35*, 561–568.

Pomerantz, E. M., & Eaton, M. M. (2000). Developmental differences in children's conceptions of parental control: "They love me, but they make me feel incompetent." *Merrill-Palmer Quarterly, 46*, 140–167.

Robinson, E. J., Champion, H., & Mitchell, P. (1999). Children's ability to infer utterance veracity from speaker informedness. *Developmental Psychology, 35*, 535–546.

Rogoff, B. (1990). *Apprenticeship in thinking: Cognitive development in social context*. New York: Oxford University Press.

Rogoff, B. (2003). *The cultural nature of human development*. New York: Oxford University Press.

Rogoff, B., Correa-Chávez, M., & Navichoc Cotuc, M. (2005). A cultural/historical view of schooling in human development. In D. Pillemer & S. H. White (Eds.), *Developmental psychology and social change* (pp. 225–263). New York: Cambridge University Press.

Rogoff, B., Paradise, R., Arauz, R. M., Correa-Chavez, M., & Angelillo, C. (2003). Firsthand learning through intent participation. *Annual Review of Psychology, 54*, 175–203.

Rogoff, B., Turkanis, C. G., & Bartlett, L. (2001). *Learning together: Children and adults in a school community*. New York: Oxford University Press.

Rosengren, K. S., Gutiérrez, I. T., Anderson, K. N., & Schein, S. S. (2009). Parental reports of children's scale errors in everyday life. *Child Development, 80*, 1586–1591.

Rosengren, K. S., & Hickling, A. K. (1994). Seeing is believing: Children's explanations of commonplace, magical, and extraordinary transformations. *Child Development, 65*, 1605–1626.

Ruble, D. N., Balaban, T., & Cooper, J. (1981). Gender constancy and the effects of sex-typed televised toy commercials. *Child Development, 52*, 667–673.

Sabbagh, M. A., & Baldwin, D. A. (2001). Learning words from knowledgeable versus ignorant speakers: Links between preschoolers' theory of mind and semantic development. *Child Development, 72*, 1054–1070.

Sapp, F., Lee, K., & Muir, D. (2000). Three-year-olds' difficulty with the appearance-reality distinction: Is it real or apparent? *Developmental Psychology, 36*, 547–560.

Semin, G. R., & Fiedler, K. (1988). The cognitive functions of linguistic categories in describing persons: Social cognition and language. *Journal of Personality and Social Psychology, 54*, 558–568.

Sera, M. D., Bales, D. W., & del Castillo Pintado, J. (1997). Ser helps Spanish speakers identify "real" properties. *Child Development, 68*, 820–831.

Sharpsteen, D. J., & Kirkpatrick, L. A. (1997). Romantic jealousy and adult romantic attachment. *Personality Processes and Individual Differences, 72*(3), 627–640.

Shaver, P. R., & Mikulincer, M. (2007). Adult attachment strategies and the regulation of emotion. In J. J. Gross (Ed.), *Handbook of emotion regulation* (pp. 446–465). New York: Guilford Press.

Shell, R., & Eisenberg, N. (1990). The role of peers' gender in children's naturally occurring interest in toys. *International Journal of Behavioral Development, 13*, 373–388.

Shutts, K., Kinzler, K. D., McKee, C. B., & Spelke, E. S. (2009). Social information guides infants' selection of foods. *Journal of Cognition and Development, 10*, 1–17.

Simpson, J. A. (1990). Influence of attachment styles on romantic relationships. *Journal of Personality and Social Psychology, 59*(5), 971–980.

Sorce, J. F., Emde, R. N., Campos, J., & Klinnert, M. D. (1985). Maternal emotional signaling: Its effect on the visual cliff behavior of one-year-olds. *Developmental Psychology, 21*, 195–200.

Stipek, D. J., Roberts, T. A., & Sanborn, M. E. (1984). Preschool-age children's performance expectations for themselves and another child as a function of the incentive

value of success and the salience of past performance. *Child Development 55*, 1983–1989.

Talwar, V., & Lee, K. (2002). Emergence of white lie-telling in children between 3 and 7 years of age. *Merrill-Palmer Quarterly, 48*, 160–181.

Talwar, V., Murphy, S. M., & Lee, K. (2007). White lie-telling in children for politeness purposes. *International Journal of Behavioral Development, 31*, 1–11.

Taylor, M. G. (1996). The development of children's beliefs about social and biological aspects of gender differences. *Child Development, 67*, 1555–1571.

Tenney, E. R., Small, J. E., Kondrad, R. L., Jaswal, V. K., & Spellman, B. A. (2011). Accuracy, confidence, and calibration: How young children and adults assess credibility. *Developmental Psychology, 47*, 1065–1077.

Tomasello, M. (1999). The human adaptation for culture. *Annual Review of Anthropology, 28*, 509–529.

Tomasello, M. (2008). *The origins of human communication*. Cambridge, MA: MIT Press.

Tullos, A., & Woolley, J. D. (2009). The development of children's ability to use evidence to infer reality status. *Child Development, 80*, 101–114.

Vanderbilt, K. E., Liu, D., & Heyman, G. D. (2011). The development of distrust. *Child Development, 82*, 1372–1380.

VanderBorght, M., & Jaswal, V. K. (2009). Who knows best? Preschoolers sometimes prefer child informants over adult informants. *Infant and Child Development, 18*, 61–71.

Vygotsky, L. S. (1978). *Mind in society: The development of higher psychological processes*. Cambridge: Harvard University Press.

Waxman, S. R. (1999). The dubbing ceremony revisited: Object naming and categorization in infancy and early childhood. In D. L. Medin and S. Atran (Eds.), *Folkbiology* (pp. 233–284). Cambridge, MA: MIT Press.

Wellman, H. M., Cross, D., & Watson, J. (2001). Meta-analysis of theory-of-mind development: The truth about false belief. *Child Development, 72*, 655–684.

Wellman, H. M. & Liu, D. (2004). Scaling of theory-of-mind tasks. *Child Development, 75*, 523–541.

Woolley, J. D. (2006). Verbal-behavioral dissociations in development. *Child Development, 77*, 1539–1553.

Woolley, J. D., Boerger, E. A., & Markman, A. (2004). A visit from the Candy Witch: Children's belief in a novel fantastical entity. *Developmental Science, 7*, 456–468.

Woolley, J. D., & Van Reet, J. (2006). Effects of context on judgments of the reality status of novel entities. *Child Development, 77*, 1778–1793.

Woolley, J. D., & Wellman, H. M. (1990). Young children's understanding of realities, non- realities, and appearances. *Child Development, 61*, 946–961.

CHAPTER 37

Culture and Social Cognition

Chi-yue Chiu, Sharon Ng, *and* Evelyn W. M. Au

Abstract

The present chapter provides an overview of the past accomplishments and future directions in the field of culture and social cognition. Research in the previous decade has identified (1) several mechanisms that mediate the social cognitive effects of culture (internalized cultural contents, intersubjective representations, implicit and embodied cognitions), and (2) some moderators of cultural influence (applicability of cultural construct, motivation to align with cultural norms, need for epistemic and existential security). These results have deepened our understanding of the multiple ways through which culture influences social cognition and have illuminated how people create and apply cultural traditions to meet their psychological needs and adapt to the changing physical and social ecology. The authors also discuss several new and future research directions, which include systematic investigations into other forms of culture, the cognitive consequences of multicultural experiences, management of multiple cultural identities, evolution of culture, and cultural neuroscience.

Key Words: culture, social cognition, cultural influence, multicultural experiences, cultural identities

Introduction

The seminal article Markus and Kitayama published in 1991 has inspired two decades of intense scholarly inquiry into the relationship between culture and social cognition. The first decade of research focused on demonstrating how culture moderates some psychological motives (e.g., the need for self-enhancement) and processes (e.g., cognitive dissonance, the fundamental attribution error) that were previously assumed to be basic and universal. Because these findings have already been reviewed thoroughly in other recently published papers (Chiu & Hong, 2007; Lehman, Chiu, & Schaller, 2004), only a few highlights of these findings will be included in the present chapter.

Although cultural differences in social cognition continue to be a popular research topic, two new directions have surfaced in the past decade, which because of their theoretical significance, will be the

focus of the present review. These two directions are (1) systematic attempts to specify the mechanisms that mediate culture's influence on social cognition, and (2) persistent efforts to identify the psychological factors that moderate the impact of culture on social cognition. After our quick review of the earlier research on cross-cultural differences in the next section, we will describe how results from these new directions clarify the nature of cultural influence, soften some of the early extreme claims of the cultural relativity of social cognition, and illuminate the social psychological conditions that promote or discourage cultural conformity.

Our goal here is to summarize the basic principles that we have learned from the previous decade of culture and social cognition research. Space does not permit a review of all pertinent research evidence. Therefore, in the present chapter, we will illustrate each principle with representative findings.

We will close with a discussion of several new directions for future research. We hope that this review can provide a holistic picture of the research accomplishments and unconquered territories in this burgeoning field.

Cultural Differences

Earlier research has uncovered pronounced cultural differences in many basic social cognitive processes (e.g., attention, perception, categorization). Subsequent research builds on these findings and advances the field by addressing the conceptual and methodological limitations of the early research. To provide the intellectual context for our review of the recent literature, in this section we will briefly review some major cross-cultural differences in social cognition and discuss the conceptual and methodological limitations of early comparative studies.

Many social cognitive phenomena, which were previously assumed to be universal, have recently been shown to be culture dependent. For example, whereas Americans are more attentive to the properties of focal objects, Asians are more attentive to object–context relations (Masuda & Nisbett, 2001). The tendency to commit the fundamental attribution error or display the correspondent bias is weaker in Asian than North American cultures (Morris & Peng, 1994). Unlike Americans, Asians seem unmotivated to reduce cognitive dissonance by justifying their personal choices (Heine & Lehman, 1997). The role of personal choice in intrinsic motivation is smaller in Asian than American contexts (Iyengar & Lepper, 1999). The self-enhancement bias is less prevalent in Asian cultures than in North American cultures (Heine, Lehman, Markus, & Kitayama, 1999). Subjective well-being is more connected to interpersonal harmony and less connected to self-esteem in Asia than in the United States (Kwan, Bond, & Singelis, 1997). These findings, together with many others, cast doubt on the universality of several major social psychological principles (Fiske, Kitayama, Markus, & Nisbett, 1998).

The striking cultural differences uncovered in the earlier comparative research have invited critical reflections on the cultural embeddedness of basic social psychological processes. Nonetheless, this research has also been criticized for essentializing culture—treating culture as a monolith and ignoring within-culture variations in behavior (Hermans & Kempen, 1998). Research that focuses on documenting global differences between cultures has also been criticized for overlooking the domain and situation specificity of cultural influence (Hong & Chiu, 2001).

In addition, earlier comparative research has relied on quasi-experimental methods: Researchers drew conclusions regarding cultural similarities and differences in social cognition by comparing the responses to various experimental tasks of participants from different cultural groups (e.g., Canadians, Japanese). This method, which is still popular in culture and psychology research, has two limitations. First, variations in responses within a cultural group are often larger than variations between cultural groups (Shweder & Sullivan, 1990). Because of the low signal-to-noise ratio, it is difficult to discern subtle cognitive effects of culture. Second, quasi-experimental results do not allow inferences to be made about the causal effects of culture on cognition (Hong & Chiu, 2001).

Experimental Studies of Cultural Processes

To address these limitations, researchers have developed new experimental paradigms to establish the causal effects of culture on social cognition. In these paradigms, the researcher increases the salience of a culture in the current situation by priming the culture or its characteristic contents, and observes the priming effect on various psychological responses. These priming paradigms build on established principles of knowledge activation and allow researchers to study the effects of culture in people's understanding of, and responses to, concrete situations in specific behavioral domains. These paradigms also facilitate the identification of the mediators and moderators of the cognitive effects of culture. Thus, before reviewing the mediators and moderators of cultural influence, in the next few sections, we will introduce these priming paradigms and the relevant principle of knowledge activation behind them.

Priming Culture

The introduction of the priming paradigms to the field represents an important methodological innovation (Hong, Morris, Chiu, & Benet-Martinez, 2000). They allow researchers to experimentally activate (prime) a certain cultural tradition or a specific cultural construct, and observe the behavioral consequences of such priming. There are two major priming paradigms. In the first paradigm, which we refer to as *culture priming*, the researcher chooses representative symbols of two cultural traditions (e.g., languages, icons of the cultures), primes individuals who have extensive exposure to both cultures with the symbols from either culture, and measures the social cognitive consequences of culture priming.

Research using this paradigm has shown that for individuals with extensive exposure to two cultures, priming them with symbols from either culture increases the likelihood of displaying the normative social cognitive responses of the primed culture. For example, Chinese Americans make more external causal attribution (a normative attribution style in Chinese culture) following Chinese culture priming, and more internal causal attributions (a normative attribution style in American culture) following American culture priming (Hong et al., 2000). As another example, Hispanic culture is known for its emotional expressiveness. Spanish- and English-speaking Mexican bilinguals infer greater intensity of emotions in a face when they judge the expressed emotions in Spanish than in English (Matsumoto, Anguas-Wong, Martinez, 2008). Similarly, when Chinese-English bilinguals in Hong Kong make consumer decisions, they are more likely to choose compromise options and to defer decision making where it can be postponed when they respond to the Chinese version of the product decision task than when they respond to the English version of it (Briley, Morris, & Simonson, 2005).

In the second paradigm, which we refer to as *cultural construct priming*, the researcher primes a certain construct (e.g., independent self or interdependent self) that is more prevalent in some cultures than in others, and observes how priming influences performance on various social cognitive measures. In this paradigm, the primed construct is assumed to be available to all cultures, although its levels of chronic accessibility may differ across cultures. In addition, the cognitive effects of momentary priming are assumed to be analogous to those of chronic priming of the participants' social ecology. Based on these assumptions, the researcher can infer from the cognitive effects of momentarily priming a certain cultural construct how chronic exposure to the construct in the cultural environment affects social cognition (Oyserman & Lee, 2008).

Results from research that applied these two priming paradigms are particularly useful for uncovering concrete cultural processes. In addition, a recent meta-analysis shows that the effect sizes of culture obtained from priming studies are considerably larger than those obtained from quasi-experimental studies (Oyserman & Lee, 2008). Accordingly, in the present review, in addition to results from quasi-experimental studies, we also rely heavily on findings from priming studies.

Principles of Cultural Knowledge Activation

As mentioned, the priming paradigms build on known principles of knowledge activation. To explain how the two priming paradigms work, we assume that through explicit and implicit learning, members of a certain culture have developed a cognitive representation of their culture and its major contents. The representation of a culture consists of a central concept (e.g., the U.S. culture) and contents (e.g., independent self) that are associatively linked to the central concept. A monocultural individual (e.g., a European American with very limited exposure to other national cultures) has an established cognitive representation of one national culture, whereas a bicultural has established representations of two cultures. For example, a Mexican American has an established representation of mainstream U.S. culture and one of Mexican culture. Both representations are associatively linked to the independent self and the interdependent self, although the association with mainstream U.S. culture is stronger for the independent self than the interdependent self, which is a reflection of the more frequent activation of the independent self in mainstream U.S. culture. Likewise, the association with Mexican culture is stronger for the interdependent self than the independent self, which is a consequence of the more frequent activation of the interdependent self in Mexican culture. Priming this Mexican American with icons of Mexican culture (e.g., a taco) would activate the cognitive representation of Mexican culture and, through spreading activation, its strongly associated interdependent self, eliciting cognitions that are congruent with the interdependent self. Likewise, priming this individual with icons of U.S. culture (e.g., a hamburger) would activate the cognitive representation of mainstream U.S. culture and its strongly associated independent self, producing independent self-consistent cognitions (Pouliasi & Verkuyten, 2007).

Results from culture priming studies are useful for determining which cultural contents and their social cognitive consequences are strongly associated with a certain culture. For example, in a culture priming study (Sui, Zhu, & Chiu, 2007), Chinese college students who were also familiar with American culture spontaneously used more interdependent descriptions and fewer independent descriptions to characterize the self after being primed with Chinese culture than after being primed with American culture. Compared with American culture priming, Chinese culture priming also facilitated recognition of traits that were previously encoded with reference to the participants' mother. These results suggest that Chinese culture is associatively linked to the interdependent self and to elaborate encoding of information about relational others.

In culture priming studies, the participants must be bicultural individuals. That is, they must have developed representations of two cultures, and culture priming has no effect on monocultural individuals' cognitive responses (Fu, Chiu, Morris, & Young, 2007; Luna, Ringberg, & Peracchio, 2008).

In the cultural construal priming paradigm, a specific content in the cognitive representation of a culture is activated. As long as the content is cognitively available to the participant, regardless of whether the construct is strongly associated with the participant's culture, priming the construct will temporarily increase its cognitive accessibility and evoke the construct's associated cognitive responses.

In both priming paradigms, priming will affect cognitive responses only when the primed culture or cultural construal is applicable to the current task or task context (Hong, Benet-Martinez, Chiu, & Morris, 2003). For example, priming Hong Kong Chinese who are familiar with both Chinese and American cultures with Chinese culture increases the tendency to cooperate in a Prisoner's Dilemma game only when the game is played with an ingroup member because Chinese culture prescribes cooperation with ingroup members only (Wong & Hong, 2005).

In summary, priming culture and its specific contents allows researchers to go beyond measuring static psychological differences between cultural groups. Using priming paradigms, investigators can establish the causal effects of culture on behaviors and infer the cognitive processes that mediate these effects.

What Is Culture?

Culture influences behaviors through its specific contents. Therefore, before we discuss the mediators of culture, we will introduce our working definition of culture and the major cultural constructs that have been shown to have consistent influence on behaviors.

A Working Definition

From a social cognitive perspective, culture can be defined as a constellation of loosely organized knowledge created by and shared (albeit imperfectly) among a collection of interdependent individuals. This constellation of knowledge is transmitted across generations for the purpose of meeting the

psychological needs of the individual and coordinating individual goal pursuits in collective living (Chiu, Leung, & Hong, 2010). In the present chapter, we use this definition as the working definition of culture.

Although this definition may seem overly mechanistic, it emphasizes several salient aspects of cultural processes. First, culture consists of a loosely organized network of knowledge structures, which include procedural knowledge as well as declarative knowledge about the self, other people, development of events, and the prevailing social norms (Chiu & Hong, 2006). Second, this network of knowledge is shared (albeit not perfectly) by a designated group of individuals and exhibited in various public forms and practices. Third, culture is a product of collective human effort. Fourth, cultural knowledge is passed down from earlier generations to new generations and has a high level of continuity. Nonetheless, culture is adaptive. A culture evolves in response to changing opportunities and constraints in the physical and social environment. Finally, culture is functional; it evolves to meet the needs of the individuals and coordinates their goal pursuits in collective living.

Major Cultural Constructs

Cultures differ on many dimensions. A research challenge is to identify the psychological constructs that are most useful in explaining cultural differences in social cognition. A major research accomplishment in the field is the identification of three pairs of cultural constructs that can account for substantial variations in normative patterns of social cognitive responses across many cultural groups, particularly differences between Asian and North American cultures.

The first pair is individualism–collectivism. A defining component of individualism is the belief that the self is a self-contained, independent entity built on a set of stable and distinctive personal beliefs, attitudes, preferences, and values (Markus & Kitayama, 1991; Triandis, 1989). In contrast, a defining belief in collectivism is that the self is interdependent with some ingroup (e.g., family, clan, tribe). In a collectivist culture, people's social roles and positions in the relational network define one's self-identities (Markus & Kitayama, 1991; Triandis, 1989). Given the centrality of the independent versus interdependent self in the definition of individualism–collectivism, researchers have examined the social cognitive effects of individualism–collectivism by priming the independent versus interdependent self (Osyerman, Sorensen, Reber, & Chan, 2009).

The second pair is holistic versus analytical thinking (Nisbett, Peng, Choi, & Norenzayan, 2001). Holistic thinking refers to a set of cognitive procedures, including attention to the entire field, assignment of causality to the context, making relatively little use of categories and formal logic, and relying on "dialectical" reasoning. In contrast, analytical thinking refers to a set of cognitive procedures that include attention to the object and the categories to which it belongs, and using rules, including formal logic, to understand the behaviors of the object.

The third pair is promotion versus prevention focus (Higgins, 2008; Lockwood, Marshall, & Sadler, 2005). Promotion focus features hopes and achievements (gains) and prevention focus features security and responsibilities (nonlosses) as the primary drivers of behaviors. Collectivism, holistic thinking and prevention focus are more prevalent in Asian than North American cultures, whereas individualism, analytical thinking, and promotion focus are more popular in North American than Asian cultures (Higgins, 2008; Markus & Kitayama, 1991; Nisbett, et al., 2001).

Although these three pairs of constructs are conceptually distinct, they are theoretically related. Individualism and its attendant independent self-view engage cognitive procedures that treat individuals as separate objects and categorize them based on their internal qualities and logically coherent categorization rules. Individualism also privileges personal aspirations and agency, and measures success by the extent to which individuals can actualize their hopes. In contrast, collectivism and its attendant interdependent self-view engage cognitive procedures that track how the pattern of interdependence of an individual within the context unfolds as the context evolves. Collectivism also privileges group agency and measures personal success by the extent to which individuals can fulfill their obligations (Hong, Ip, Chiu, Morris, & Menon, 2001). Supporting this idea, past research has shown that priming the independent (vs. the interdependent) self facilitates spatial judgments in tasks in which the context needs to be excluded in processing, and hinders performance in spatial judgment tasks in which the context needs to be included in processing (Krishna, Zhou, & Zhang, 2008; see also Kuhnen, Hannover, & Schubert, 2001). Priming the independent self also focuses individuals more on achieving gains, whereas priming the interdependent self elevates people's loss aversion (Aaker

& Lee, 2001). Independence priming also increases the likelihood of choosing risky investments with high expected returns (Hamilton & Biehal, 2005).

Mechanisms of Cultural Influence

A new direction in the previous decade of culture and social cognition research is the search for specific explanations for the social cognitive effects of culture. The search has led to the identification of several possible explanations, including internalized values and beliefs, perceived cultural norms, culture as situated cognitions, implicit cognitions, and embodied cognitions.

Internalized Values and Beliefs

Culturally normative beliefs and values are encoded in various *public representations*, including popular texts, language, advertisements, law, and social structures (Morling & Lamoreaux, 2008). For example, the use of first-person pronouns (e.g., *I* in English), which maximally distinguishes the speaker's self from the conversational context, and the use of second-person pronouns (e.g., *you* in English), which maximally distinguishes the addressee(s) from the conversational context, are more likely to be grammatically obligatory in the dominant languages of individualist cultures than those in collectivist cultures (Kashima & Kashima, 1998). In addition, collectivist cultures tend to have lower levels of job mobility (Chen, Chiu, & Chan, 2009; Wang & Leung, 2010; Wang, Leung, See, Gu, 2011), residential mobility (Oishi, Lun, & Sherman, 2007), and relational mobility (Schug, Yuki, & Maddux, 2010). The relatively low mobility in collectivist societies promotes identification with the residential community, interdependence with the occupational and relational networks one belongs to, and the tendency to put the collective exigency before personal aspirations.

How does culture residing in various forms of public representations affect an individual's social cognition? One mechanism is enculturation and internalization. Members of a culture, through the process of enculturation, internalize the normative values and beliefs of their culture. These internalized beliefs and values or *private representations* in turn guide individuals' cognitive processes and behaviors. For example, many North Americans personally identify with the promotion focus, and many Asians, the prevention focus. Compared with Asians, North Americans are more likely to distort their self-presentation to appear more skillful, competent, or attractive, and less likely to distort their self-presentation to appear more normatively appropriate. Recent studies (Lalwani, Shrum, & Chiu, 2009) show that cultural differences in internalized regulatory focus mediate cultural differences in self-presentation. As another example, relative to North Americans, East Asians have greater tolerance of inconsistency in their self-knowledge. This cultural difference is fully mediated by cultural differences in naïve dialecticism, a set of lay beliefs characterized by tolerance for contradiction, expectation of change, and cognitive holism (Spencer-Rodgers, Boucher, Mori, & Wang, 2009).

However, a meta-analysis (Oyserman, Coon, & Kemmelmeier, 2002) has led some researchers to question the explanatory power of internalized values. This meta-analysis reveals a lack of consistent and theoretically coherent cultural group differences in self-report measures of individualism–collectivism. That is, North Americans do not always report stronger endorsement of individualist values or weaker endorsement of collectivist values than do cultural groups that are supposed to be more collectivistic (e.g., the Japanese). Furthermore, the effect size of self-reported individualism–collectivism on theoretically pertinent measures of social cognition is typically small (Oyserman & Lee, 2008).

The small and inconsistent effects of individualism–collectivism could result from a lack of conceptual clarity of the construct. As Brewer and Chen (2007) noted in a more recent meta-analysis, in culture and psychology research, individualism–collectivism has been used as a "catchall" construct to represent all forms of cultural differences. In addition, existing measures of individualism and collectivism do not capture all theoretically central components of the constructs. As shown in the research examples described in the previous paragraph, when researchers focus on well-defined cultural constructs, measures of internalized personal beliefs significantly mediate theoretically pertinent cultural differences in social cognition. Thus, instead of categorically rejecting the explanatory role of internalized beliefs and values, there is a need to clarify the meanings of the major cultural constructs in the literature and to refine existing measures to capture the essence of these constructs.

Intersubjective Representations

Most people internalize only a subset of the normative beliefs and values in their culture. If individual members of a culture internalize different subsets of the normative beliefs and values in their culture, the social cognitive effects of culture will be small. Nonetheless, culture could have substantial impact on social cognition even among people who do not internalize the pertinent normative beliefs and values (Chiu, Gelfand, Yamagishi, Shteynberg, & Wan, 2010; Maghaddam, 2010).

To elaborate, people in a culture form shared perceptions of the psychological characteristics that are widespread within the culture. These perceptions have been referred to as *intersubjective representations* of culture, as opposed to the public and private representations discussed in the last section. Whereas private representations are measured by assessing respondents' self-endorsement of cultural contents (e.g., how individualistic/collectivistic are you?), intersubjective representations are measured by assessing the *perceived popularity* of cultural contents in the cultural community (e.g., how individualistic/collectivistic do you think a typical member of your culture is?).

Every member of the culture agrees with some contents of the intersubjective representations, disagrees with other contents, and is indifferent or ambivalent toward the remaining ones. As a result, intersubjective and private representations are partially dissociated (e.g., Fischer, 2006; Shteynberg et al., 2009; Zou et al., 2009). For example, Poles and Americans endorse individualist and collectivist values to the same extent. Nonetheless, Poles expect other Poles to have stronger preferences for individualist values than collectivist values, and Americans expect other Americans to have the opposite preferences (Zou et al., 2009). South Koreans view themselves as less collectivistic than others in their country, whereas Americans see themselves as less individualistic than others in their country (Shteynberg et al., 2009). Asians and Americans do not differ from each other in their causal beliefs. Nevertheless, both Asians and Americans expect Americans, compared with Asians, to have stronger dispositionist beliefs about behavioral causality (Zou et al., 2009).

Cultural differences in intersubjective representations are grounded in external social reality. That is, cultural differences in intersubjective representations typically agree with cultural differences in the values embodied in public representations. For example, people from cultures with strong individualistic institutions perceive their cultural fellows to be individualistic, and people in cultures with strong collectivistic institutions perceive their cultural fellows to be collectivistic. In short, as Atran and colleagues (2005) noted, cultural processes consist primarily not of creation and transmission of internalized rules or norms shared by people living in the same environment, but rather of complex distributions of causally connected representations across minds interacting with the environment.

Importantly, individuals act on behalf of their intersubjective representations—at times, more than they do on their private representations. Intersubjective representations can influence behaviors because these representations serve important epistemic functions for the individual (Chiu, Morris, Hong, & Menon, 2000; Fu et al., 2007). Intersubjective representations are perceived to be widely shared and have survived the test of evolution; the ideas embodied in these representations have been selected for social transmission and are widely accepted. These properties confer consensual validity and interpretive authority. Thus, people are inclined to predicate their behavioral choices on intersubjective representations, particularly when they need firm answers (Chiu et al., 2000; Fu, Morris, Lee, Chao, Chiu, & Hong, 2007) or when they feel accountable to an ingroup audience for their actions (Briley, Morris, & Simonson, 2000; Gelfand & Realo, 1999). Furthermore, individuals are also likely to recruit intersubjective representations to coordinate perspectives in social interactions (Fast, Heath, & Wu, 2009).

There is consistent evidence for the social cognitive effects of intersubjective representations. For example, theoretically, collectivists making blame assignment should be less influenced by actor intentionality. Intersubjective perceptions of collectivism explain cultural differences in the effect of actor intentionality on blame assignment, whereas personal collectivism does not (Shteynberg et al., 2009). Collectivists should find a consensus appeal to be more persuasive and a consistency appeal to be less persuasive. Only intersubjective perceptions of collectivism explain these cultural variations in persuasion (Zou et al., 2009). Subscription to a dispositionist theory of causality should be related to the inclination to make internal attributions. Intersubjective perceptions of dispositionism mediate cultural variations in internal attributions, but personal endorsements of dispositionism do not (Zou et al., 2009). A focus on preventing losses should be related to a greater likelihood of having regrets over actions that have brought negative outcomes. Again, only intersubjective perceptions of prevention focus mediate cultural variations in regret (Zou et al., 2009). Finally, evidence for the causal role of intersubjective representations on judgments has been reported in experiments that manipulated the salience and applicability of

intersubjective representations (Wan et al., 2007; Wan, Torelli, & Chiu, 2010; Zhang & Chiu, 2012) and the perceived sharedness of specific belief in the culture (Wan et al., 2010).

This raises the question of when private versus intersubjective representations of culture are more predictive of behaviors. Some preliminary results suggest that the two kinds of representations predict different types of behaviors. For example, consistent with the assumption that intersubjective representation confer consensual validity, intersubjective perceptions of values predict conformity and traditional behaviors, whereas personal values predict prosocial, universalistic, and self-directed behaviors (Fischer, 2006; Fischer et al., 2009). Whereas private representations have greater influence on the judgments of individualists, intersubjective representations have greater authority over collectivists' judgments, particularly when the collectivists feel accountable to an ingroup audience for their judgments. As shown in one study (Torelli, 2006), following interdependent self priming, individuals rendering risk judgments relied more heavily on others' beliefs when they anticipated explaining their judgments to others than when they did not. When the independent self was primed, expectations to communicate their judgments to others had no effects. Future investigations are needed to identify other social psychological conditions that determine the relative influence of private and intersubjective representations on social cognition.

Culture as Situated Cognition

The lack of theoretically coherent group differences in the personal endorsement of individualism–collectivism (Oyserman et al., 2002) has led some researchers to question whether cultures are cognitively represented in the forms of a unitary prestored knowledge structure. As an alternative, these researchers propose that "societies socialize for and individuals have access to a diverse set of overlapping and contradictory processes and procedures for making sense of the world and that the processes and procedures that are cued in the moment influence the values, relationality, self-concept, well-being, and cognition that are salient in the moment" (Oyserman & Sorensen, 2009, p. 25). This perspective is known as the *situated cognition perspective* to cultural influence (Oyserman, Sorensen, Reber, & Chan, 2009). Consistent with this perspective, results show that momentary priming of independence activates the contrast and separation mindset, as reflected in improved performance in terms of gains in speed or accuracy on tasks that require focused attention on a single target or point. Likewise, momentary priming of interdependence activates the assimilation and connection mindset, as reflected in improved performance on tasks that require focused attention on multiplicity and integration (Oyserman et al., 2009). These results have been obtained even among Asians (e.g., Koreans) with limited experiences with Western and European Americans with limited experiences with Asian cultures.

The culture as situated cognition perspective emphasizes the dynamic nature of culture. Instead of reducing culture to a collection of stable traits of a demarcated population, this perspective emphasizes the malleability of cultural influence. It has demonstrated how momentary activation of the assimilation and connection mindset can induce an individualist to think and behave like a collectivist, and how momentary activation of the contrast and separation mindset can induce a collectivist to think and behave like an individualist. This emphasis is consistent with the principles of cultural knowledge activation described earlier in this chapter.

Nonetheless, the rejection of culture as prestored, unitary cognitive representations seems premature. First, the robust culture priming effects suggest that people organize knowledge of their culture into a unitary representation; activating the central concept in the representation produces theoretically predictable cognitive consequences (Hong et al., 2000). Second, culture priming effects are found only among individuals with rich experiences with the pertinent cultures (Fu, Chiu et al., 2007; Luna et al., 2008), implying that individuals do form a unitary representation of a culture based on their experiences with it. Finally, as the results reviewed in the previous sections indicate, private representations of culture, when clearly defined and properly assessed, do mediate cultural differences in social cognitions, and so do intersubjective representations. These results suggest that prestored knowledge of cultures plays an important role in explaining cultural influence. All evidence considered, it seems more parsimonious to assume that people organize their knowledge of a culture into a loose knowledge network. Culture priming effects reflect the consequences of activating the whole network by priming its central concept, whereas the mindset activation effects reported by Oyserman and her colleagues result from activating specific knowledge items (cultural construals) in the network.

Culture as Implicit and Embodied Cognitions

Led by the same anomaly in group differences in self-report measures of individualism-collectivism, some researchers (Kitayama, Park, Sevincer, Timur, & Uskul, 2009) posit that individuals are not always consciously aware of culture's effects on their thoughts and actions. According to this view, through participation in culturally prescribed practices designed to achieve cultural mandates (e.g., independence in American culture and interdependence in East Asian cultures), people acquire a set of mental habits, which although not always available to conscious reflection, are reflected in performance on implicit tasks. This idea is consistent with the recurrent finding that individualist and collectivist groups differ in theoretically coherent manner on many implicit measures of independence and interdependence (e.g., focused vs. holistic attention; Kitayama et al., 2009).

Although the prevalence of implicit cultural influence does not undermine the explanatory role of conscious, declarative cultural representations in cultural influence, it highlights two important aspects of cultural influence. First, many culturally normative patterns of social cognition are embodied in the shared practices of the culture. For example, describing person information with adjectives—a practice that focuses the attention of the language user on the internal characteristics of the target person—is more common in the Italian language than in the Japanese language. In contrast, describing person information with verbs—a practice that focuses attention on the dynamic unfolding of the target person's behaviors in context—is more common in Japanese than in Italian. Inadvertently, speakers of any language habitually engage in the characteristic pattern of social information processing embodied in that language (Maass, Karasawa, Politi, & Suga, 2006).

Culturally normative behaviors are also embodied in culture-specific bodily simulations and conceptual metaphors (Leung & Cohen, 2007). Individuals acquire knowledge structures with a physical basis through their early bodily interactions with the physical environment (e.g., washing hands to remove germs, seeing leaders standing ahead of groups in American contexts). These embodied knowledge structures are later scaffolded onto more abstract cultural constructs (the cultural prescription of condemning mentally polluting improper thoughts in Islam or Protestantism; the American construction of a leader as somebody who heads the pack, leads the charge, and blazes the trail; IJzerman & Koole, 2011). Because cultural constructs are embodied in bodily experiences and conceptual metaphors, reliving these bodily experiences and applying these conceptual metaphors can automatically activate the associated cultural constructs (Cohen & Leung, 2009; Menon, Sim, Fu, Chiu, & Hong, 2010).

Second, repeated engagement in the culturally normative cognitive procedures embodied in shared cultural practices increases the proficiency and automaticity of carrying out these procedures, creating shared implicit cognitive habits in the cultural group. Evidence for the automatization of culturally normative cognitive procedures abounds. For example, East Asians are less likely than North Americans to attribute correspondent traits to actors based on their behaviors despite the presence of obvious situational explanations for the behaviors (Morris & Peng, 1994). This cross-cultural difference results partly from a greater tendency among North Americans to automatically bind the actor's behaviors to the actor (Zarate, Uleman, & Voils, 2001) and a greater tendency among East Asians to automatically use situational information to correct correspondence inferences (Geeraert, & Yzerbyt, 2007; Knowles, Morris, Chiu, & Hong, 2001; Lieberman, Jarcho, & Obayashi, 2005).

As another example, frequent interactions with members of one's culture provide ample opportunities to practice reading the nonverbal signals of ingroup members. As a result, individuals are generally more accurate in decoding the nonverbal signals of people from their culture than those of foreigners (Elfenbein & Ambady, 2002), and immigrants are more confident in their judgment of others' facial expressions if the expresser is a member of their culture than a member of the host or another culture (Beaupre & Hess, 2006). Moreover, the length of stay in a foreign setting is positively associated with accuracy in differentiating real and faked gestures in a foreign setting (Molinsky, Krabbenhoft, Ambady, & Choi, 2005).

Summary

Culture is a multifaceted construct and can influence cognition and behavior through multiple routes. First, culture is exhibited in shared practices. Individuals engaging in the shared practices of their culture acquire the implicit cultural constructs and mental habits embodied in these practices, which when activated in a situation, can affect cognition and behaviors automatically and without conscious awareness. Second, individuals have some knowledge of what cultural contents are widespread in their culture. Individuals may agree with some of these contents, and may be indifferent to or disagree with the remaining ones. Irrespective of the individuals' personal stance, intersubjective representations constrain cognitive processing and behaviors, particularly when individuals are motivated to align their thoughts and behaviors with normative expectations. Finally, some intersubjective knowledge is internalized. Such knowledge, if defined clearly and measured properly, also mediates cultural influence on social cognition.

The explanatory role of internalized private representations is smaller than previously conceived because they include only a small subset of cultural contents that could affect behavior. Disappointment over the weak explanatory power of private representations has shifted some researchers' attention to implicit cultural influence. Consequently, we now have better understanding of the multiple ways culture can affect social cognition. Nonetheless, both intersubjective and private representations also mediate cultural differences in social cognition. Thus, it would be premature to exclude conscious declarative knowledge as a possible explanation of cultural influence.

Moderators of Cultural Influence

A second new direction in culture and social cognition research is to identify the boundaries of cultural influence. Results from this new research direction suggest that some earlier, more extreme claims regarding the cultural relativity of social cognition require revision. Meanwhile, these results also afford a deeper understanding of the nature of cultural influence. Specially, these results have identified three principles regarding when people are likely to think and behave culturally. The first principle states that cultural differences in cognition are more pronounced when the current task engages congruent cultural constructs (the principle of cultural congruency). The second principle states that people tend to think and act culturally when they are motivated to accommodate their behaviors to the expectations of their cultural group (the principle of normative tuning). The last principle states that people are inclined to display culturally normative behaviors when they experience a heightened need for epistemic or existential security (the principle of culture as security provider). In the following subsections, we will illustrate these principles with pertinent research.

The Principle of Cultural Congruency

Earlier culture and cognition research favored a radical cultural relativist stance, which asserts that many allegedly basic psychological needs (e.g., the needs for cognitive consistency and self-enhancement) are culture dependent. Subsequent research shows that people in markedly different cultures have the same basic psychological needs. Nonetheless, cultural differences are found in individuals' mental habits, psychological processes, and behavioral manifestations of basic needs (Sedikides & Gregg, 2008). Furthermore, cultural differences are more pronounced when the task or task context engages a congruent (vs. incongruent) cultural construct (Uskul, Sherman, & Fitzgibbon, 2009). We refer to this generalization as *the principle of cultural congruency*. We will illustrate this principle with research on the need for self-enhancement, the need for cognitive consistency, self-regulation, and achievement-related emotions.

THE NEED FOR SELF-ENHANCEMENT

Some studies show that people from individualist cultures overestimate the likelihood of acting generously in situations that involve reward allocation and money donation, and that of avoiding rude behaviors. In contrast, people from collectivist cultures tend to be more accurate in their self-predictions (Balcetis, Dunning, & Miller, 2008). Evidence like this has led some researchers to conclude that the need for self-enhancement as it has been measured in North America is absent in East Asian cultures (Heine et al., 1999).

Recent results have cast doubt on the cultural relativity of the need for self-enhancement. For example, the better-than-average effect, or the tendency to perceive the self as better than an average person in one's community on positive traits, is an established measure of self-enhancement (Guenther & Alicke, 2010). The better-than-average effect is positively correlated with self-esteem and other indicators of psychological adjustment in both North American and East Asian cultures (Gaertner, Sedikides, & Chang, 2008; Kobayashi & Brown, 2003), suggesting that self-enhancement is a hallmark of psychological health in both the East and the West. Furthermore, the better-than-average effect has been observed in both individualist and collectivist cultures, although people from individualist cultures self-enhance more on individualist than collectivist traits, and people from collectivist cultures self-enhance more on collectivist than individualist traits (Gaertner et al., 2008; Sedikides, Gaertner,

& Toguchi, 2003). In short, both Easterners and Westerners self-enhance, and they do so on traits that are congruent with the dominant psychological orientation in their culture.

THE NEED FOR COGNITIVE CONSISTENCY

An earlier result shows that unlike North Americans, East Asians do not elevate the perceived desirability of a choice they have previously made or deflate the perceived desirability of the rejected alternatives in order to justify their choice (Heine & Lehman, 1997). This finding seems to suggest that East Asians do not experience cognitive dissonance or do not have the need for cognitive consistency. Subsequent results show that East Asians also display the same bias as North Americans do when the task context engages an interdependent orientation, as when the East Asians are reminded of the presence of others in the context (Kitayama, Snibbe, Markus, & Suzuki, 2004) or when they make a choice on behalf of others (Hoshino-Browne et al., 2005).

SELF-REGULATION

It has been shown that compared with people from Western cultures, people from East Asian cultures are more patient and therefore discount the future to a lesser degree. Thus, compared with Westerners, East Asians value immediate consumption less (Zhang & Shrum, 2009). Again, other evidence qualifies this main effect of culture. In one study (Chen, Ng, & Rao, 2005, Singaporean biculturals who were familiar with both Singaporean and American cultures were primed with one or the other. Following Singaporean culture priming, the participants became more impatient and were willing to pay more for expedited consumption of a product purchased online when they were faced with the threat of a delay in receiving a product (prevention loss). However, following American priming, these participants became more impatient when they were faced with the threat of not being able to enjoy a product early (a promotion loss).

ACHIEVEMENT-RELATED EMOTION

Normative cultural differences are most likely to emerge in self-reflective emotions such as pride (Eid & Diener, 2001). Pride, as a socially disengaging emotion, is more prevalent and more predictive of subjective well-being in North America than Japan (Kitayama, Mesquita, & Karasawa, 2006). In addition, Canadians feel that past proud events are closer in time and are easier to recall than similarly distant embarrassing events. Japanese, in contrast, feel that past embarrassing and proud events are equally far away and equally memorable (Ross, Heine, Wilson, & Sugimori, 2005). These findings seem to suggest that pride is a relatively unimportant emotion in East Asian cultures.

However, other evidence suggests that pride is a primary emotion in all cultures. A recent study (Tracy & Robins, 2008) shows that individuals from preliterate, highly isolated tribe in Burkina Faso, West Africa reliably recognize nonverbal expressions of pride, regardless of whether they are displayed by African or American targets. These Burkinese participants are unlikely to have learned the pride expression through cross-cultural transmission, so their recognition suggests that pride may be a human universal.

Another field study (Matsumoto & Willingham, 2006) shows that people from all cultures feel good about their personal achievements. The investigators of this study coded the facial expressions of 84 medal winners from 35 countries in the Judo competition in the 2004 Athens Olympic Games. Expressions were captured immediately after the athletes had just completed the medal matches and when they received their medal from a dignitary. For the emotional expressions at match completion, the winners from all cultures were much more likely to smile than the defeated, whereas the latter were much more likely to display sadness, contempt, disgust, or no expressions. Although almost all (54 of 56) silver medalists, regardless of culture, smiled when they received their medal in the medal ceremonies, none of them had smiled when they lost the medal match.

Although pride is a universal emotion, cultural differences surface in the conditions that antedate the feeling of pride. In one experiment, German participants were asked to think about their own achievements or the achievements of others after having been primed with either the independent self or the interdependent self. Thinking about personal achievements resulted in more pride after the priming of the independent rather than the interdependent self. In contrast, thinking about others' achievements resulted in more pride after the priming of the interdependent rather than the independent self (Neumann, Steinhauser, & Roeder, 2009). Another study shows that in Spain, a collectivist culture, honor-related values are relatively more important in shaping the experience and expression of pride. In contrast, in the Netherlands, an individualist culture, individualist values are more important for shaping the experience and expression of pride (Rodriguez Mosquera, Manstead, & Fischer, 2000). In summary, consistent with the principle of applicability in cultural knowledge activation, cultural differences in the manifestations of basic psychological needs or psychological processes emerge only when the task or task context engages a congruent cultural construct.

The Principle of Normative Tuning

The *principle of normative tuning* states that cultural differences are more pronounced when people are motivated to accommodate their behaviors to the expectations of the cultural ingroup. This happens when the individuals need to explain the reasons for their behavior to other members of their culture (Briley et al., 2000; Gelfand & Realo, 1999). For example, when rendering consumer decisions, Asians have a greater preference for the compromise options than do European Americans, but only when they are required to explain their choice to members of their cultural group (Briley et al., 2000). In negotiation situations, Estonians (a relatively collectivist group) are more willing and Americans (a relatively individualist group) are less willing to concede and to cooperate when they are required to justify their decisions to their manager than when they have complete authority for making decisions (Gelfand & Realo, 1999).

The motivation to accommodate to ingroup expectations also increases with cultural identification. Research has shown that conformity to group norms and self-stereotyping increases when the level of cultural identification is elevated (Jetten, Postmes, & McAuliffe, 2002). Moreover, although culture priming typically results in assimilation of responses to the normative pattern in the primed culture, the assimilation effect is more pronounced among biculturals who strongly identify with the primed culture. When biculturals disidentify with the primed culture, they tend to display responses that are opposite to the normative pattern in the primed culture (Zou, Morris, & Benet-Martinez, 2008).

People raise their identification with the ingroup culture when they learn that their personal values and goals are widely shared in the culture (Wan et al., 2007; Zhang & Chiu, 2012). When individuals receive bogus feedback on how widely shared their personal goals are in the culture, those who learn that their goals are widely shared (vs. unpopular) identify more strongly with their culture and conform to cultural expectations more (Zhang & Chiu, 2012).

The Principle of Culture as Security Provider

The *principle of culture as security provider* states that people are motivated to follow cultural norms when they experience a heightened need for epistemic or existential security. Two defining characteristics of a cultural tradition are its sharedness and continuity. A unique family tradition is one that has a history but is not widely shared in the community. A fad is a fashion, notion, or manner of conduct followed enthusiastically by a large group, but its popularity is temporary. An individual's eccentric belief is not shared by others and would unlikely be passed down through history. Unlike a unique family tradition, a fad or an eccentric belief, a cultural tradition is both shared among many people and has a history.

By virtue of its sharedness and consensual validity, culture provides to its followers a sense of epistemic security. Widely shared cultural knowledge provides individuals with a consensually validated framework to interpret otherwise ambiguous experiences. It informs individuals in the society what ideas or practices are generally considered to be true, important, and appropriate. Thus, it protects individuals from the epistemic terror of uncertainty and unpredictability.

By virtue of its continuity, culture confers a sense of existential security, protecting the individual from the terror of recognizing one's mortality. Despite the finitude of an individual's life, the cultural tradition one belongs to will be passed down through history. Thus, connecting the self to a seemingly immortal cultural tradition can help assuage existential terror.

The preceding analysis suggests that individuals with a chronic need for firm answers are particularly inclined to follow cultural norms. Consistent with this idea, Asians with a higher need for cognitive closure (the epistemic need for firm answers) are more likely to display the cognitive responses that are normative in Asian culture; they are more likely to make situational attributions, consider contextual information in conflict resolution, and make other-serving biases in reward allocation. Likewise, Americans with a higher need for cognitive closure are more likely to display the cognitive responses that are normative in American culture; they are more likely to make dispositional attributions, consider factual information in conflict resolution, and make self-serving biases in reward allocation (Chao, Zhang, & Chiu, 2010; Chiu, Morris, Hong, & Menon, 2000; Fu et al., 2007; Leung, Kim, Zhang,

Tam, & Chiu, 2012). Immigrants with a higher need for closure also tend to assimilate more quickly into the host culture when they experience epistemic insecurity in the new environment, as when they migrate to a new country alone and need to find out on their own how to adjust to the new environment (Kosic, Kruglanski, Pierro, & Mannetti, 2004).

People are highly motivated to follow cultural norms when they experience a heightened need for existential security, as when they are reminded of the inevitable finitude of one's physical existence. Evidence from two decades of terror management research confirms that rendering death-related thoughts accessible increases people's investment in their cultural worldviews (Burke, Martens, & Faucher, 2010). For example, rendering mortality salient enhances performance on standardized test items in which the correct answers affirm their cultural worldviews, and hinders performance on those items in which the correct answers violate their cultural worldviews (Landau, Greenberg, & Rothschild, 2009). As further evidence for the principle of culture as security providers, two recent studies (Juhl, & Routledge, 2010) show that increasing the salience of mortality raises investment in cultural worldviews particularly among individuals with a strong need for firm answers.

Other Moderators

While the three major categories of moderators reviewed above strengthen the social cognitive effects of culture, deliberate processing and positive affect have been found to attenuate cultural influence on cognition. One robust finding is that individuals primed with the independent self are more persuaded by promotion-focused information, whereas individuals primed with the interdependent self are more persuaded by prevention-focused information (Aaker & Lee, 2001; Uskul et al., 2009). However, this effect is found only when the situation calls for initial, spontaneous reactions to messages, and dissipates when the situation calls for more thoughtful, deliberative processing (Briley & Aaker, 2006). This result suggests that people use culturally prescribed cognitive routines to make initial decisions and revise these decisions when they are motivated to make a fully considered decision.

Other studies show that people are less likely to express culturally normative cognitions and behaviors when they are experiencing positive rather than negative affect because positive affect encourages individuals to explore novel thoughts and behaviors and depart from cultural conventions. For example,

Westerners value self-expression less, like objects that signal conformity more, see the self as being more interdependent with others, and seek affiliation more when they experience positive rather than negative affect, whereas East Asians value and express individuality and independence more when they experience positive rather than negative affect (Ashton-James, Maddux, Galinsky, & Chartrand, 2009).

In summary, new findings on the moderators of cultural influence have led to the softening of some early strong claims regarding the cultural relativity of social cognition. These results show that people are not passive recipients of cultural influence. Instead, individuals express culturally normative cognition and behaviors when the task context is culturally relevant, when they are motivated to accommodate their behaviors to the expectations of the ingroup culture, and when cultural conformity meets the needs for epistemic or existential security and fits current information processing goals.

New and Future Directions

We have reviewed progress in identifying the mechanisms that mediate culture's influence on social cognition, as well as the moderators of such cultural influence. In this concluding section, we will review several emerging trends and future directions in culture and social cognition research. Specifically, we argue that moving forward, researchers should consider other forms of culture in addition to national cultures (e.g., religions). Aside from examining how culture influences social cognition, researchers might also investigate how exposure to multicultural cultures affects behaviors, how people with multicultural experiences manage their cultural identities, and how people relate to culture mixing in globalized environments. Researchers might also study culture as a dependent variable, examining how cultures are created and reproduced, and how they evolve. Finally, researchers can take advantage of the recent advances in cognitive neuroscience to address new theoretical questions concerning the interactions of culture, mind, and the brain. We will elaborate on each of these issues below.

Other Forms of Culture

Research in culture and social cognition has focused almost exclusively on understanding variations in social cognition across national cultural groups, particularly North American and Asian groups. The major cultural constructs that have been identified in current research (e.g.,

individualism–collectivism, holistic vs. analytical thinking) are also most useful for explaining the contrastive cognitive styles in North American and Asian cultures. Recently, Cohen (2009) invited cultural psychologists to expand the scope of research to examine the psychological consequences of other forms of culture, including religion, social class, and regional cultures.

The inclusion of other forms of culture in research on culture and social cognition can be easily justified because, like national cultures, some religious traditions, for example, are widely shared and have a long history as well. More importantly, studying other forms of culture may lead to discovery of new cultural constructs and social cognitive phenomena. For example, whereas Christian doctrine considers mental states to be important in judging a person's morality, Jewish doctrine considers them less important. As a result, compared with Jews, Protestants believe more strongly that mental states are controllable and likely to lead to action, and hence judge individuals with inappropriate mental states more harshly (Cohen & Rozin, 2001). This example illustrates the utility of studying other forms of culture in future research.

Effects of Multicultural Experiences

Although most culture and cognition research has focused on understanding cultural group differences, some researchers have started to examine the cognitive consequences of having multicultural experiences. On the one hand, there is evidence that European Americans residing in some cosmopolitan American cities (e.g., New York) have through extensive exposure to Asian culture developed the ability to flexibly switch between American and Asian interpretive frames when they make social judgments (Alter & Kwan, 2009). Multicultural experiences also increase individuals' cognitive complexity (Tadmor, Tetlock, & Peng, 2009) and creativity (Leung & Chiu, 2010; Leung, Maddux, Galinsky, & Chiu, 2008; Maddux & Galinsky, 2009). On the other hand, increased multicultural experience can also heighten people's sensitivity to cultural differences (Chiu, Mallorie, Keh, & Law, 2009) and evoke the fear that inflow of ideas and practices from foreign cultures might lead to erosion of one's heritage culture (Chiu & Cheng, 2007; Torelli, Chiu, Tam, Au, & Keh, 2011). A worthwhile future direction is to examine how people navigate culturally heterogeneous environments and how they respond to culture mixing (Chiu, Gries, Torelli, & Cheng, 2011; Morris, Mok, & Mor, 2011).

Management of Multiple Cultural Identities

A related topic is how people who are eligible to claim multiple cultural identities (e.g., ethnic minorities) manage their identities. Some studies show that these individuals may switch their cultural identity depending on which culture they have been primed with (Veyrkuyten & Pouliasi, 2006). Other studies have uncovered marked individual differences in how biculturals organize their dual identifies. Whereas some biculturals view their identities as compatible, others see their identities as conflicting. Those who view their identities as compatible can flexibly switch cultural frames when rendering judgment in response to culture priming. In contrast, those who feel conflicted about their dual identities tend to experience stress when they recall their multicultural experiences and ambivalence when they encounter culturally mixed information (Benet-Martinez, Leu, Lee, & Morris, 2002; Kramer, Lau-Gesk, & Chiu, 2009; Lau-Gesk, 2003). A worthwhile future direction is to identify the factors that shape the way biculturals manage their dual identities. One recent finding is that biculturals who see ethnic cultures as having nonmalleable essence and impermeable borders are particularly likely to feel conflicted about their dual identities (Chao, Chen, Roisman, & Hong, 2007; No et al., 2008).

Evolution of Culture

The existing literature has focused on the cognitive consequences of relatively stable cultural characteristics. An important knowledge gap to be filled in future research is how culture and its attendant cognitive predilections change in response to the physical and social ecology. Leading the way in this new direction, Schaller and Murray (2008) have illustrated how different cultural norms emerged in different geopolitical regions in response to differences in the prevalence of disease-causing pathogens in the local ecology. Other results have linked the evolution of culturally normative perceptual styles, values, and inferential practices to features of the perceptual environment (Miyamoto, Nisbett, Masuda, 2006) and level of mobility in the local ecology (Chen et al., 2009; Oishi et al., 2007).

Cultural Neuroscience

In a recent article, Han and Northoff (2008) highlight the need to integrate cognitive neuroscience and cultural research. They argue that cultural experiences shape both the brain and the mind. As a result, neural correlates of human cognition are culture dependent. For example, Westerners show activation of the ventral medial prefrontal cortex when they encode information about the self, whereas the Chinese have activation of this area both when they encode information about the self and when they encode information about the mother (Zhu, Zhang, Fan, & Han, 2007).

There is also evidence for neurological mediation of some cultural construct priming effects. Specifically, priming the independent self results in enlarged P1 amplitude to local targets at the lateral occipital electrodes, whereas priming the interdependent self results in enlarged P1 amplitude to global targets at the same electrodes, suggesting that self-construal priming affects perceptual processing in the extrastriate cortex (Lin, Lin, & Han, 2008). In addition, neural activity in the right middle frontal cortex is greater when individuals view their own rather than familiar faces, and this difference is larger following independent than interdependent self priming, suggesting that activation of the right middle frontal cortex mediates the cultural construal priming effect on preferential processing of one's own face (Shi & Han, 2007).

In addition to understanding the neurological mediation of cultural influence, cultural neuroscience may also illuminate some of the cultural processes described in the present chapter. A recent study shows that neural responses to mortality threat are greater than to pain threat in the right amygdala, left rostral anterior cingulate cortex, and right caudate nucleus (Quirin et al., 2012). Activities in these brain areas may also mediate increased cultural conformity when mortality thoughts have been made salient. Some promising new findings have also increased the optimism that we will soon discover the neurological basis of how intersubjective representations regarding thoughts of ingroup members are formed. In one experiment (Liew, Han, & Aziz-Zadeh, 2011), Chinese participants were asked to infer the intentions of Caucasian or Chinese actors performing symbolic gestures. Observing gestures compared with observing still images was associated with increased activity in both the pMNS (the putative mirror neuron system, which is supposed to support automatic motor simulations of observed actions) and the mentalizing system (which is supposed to provide reflective, nonintuitive reasoning of others' perspectives). Furthermore, observing the gestures of targets from one's culture generated greater activity in the posterior pMNS-related regions and the insula than observing targets from a foreign culture.

The initial success of cultural neuroscience research has ignited interest in the mutual constitution of culture, mind, and the brain (Kitayama & Uskul, 2011). Nonetheless, the contributions of most cultural neuroscience research to the psychological science of culture have been limited. A major research challenge in this emerging field is to go beyond descriptive illustrations of the localized brain activities that accompany established cultural effects and processes. One way to meet this challenge is to address questions regarding the specific nature of culture–brain interactions (Han & Northoff, 2008): Does culture affect preferences for different task-solving strategies and their attendant strategy dependent neural activation patterns? Do cultural experiences result in changes in neuronal function (e.g., the level of activation of a particular region)? Can cultural experiences result in structural changes in neuroanatomy (e.g., change in the volume of gray matter)?

Alternatively, researchers may apply new brain imaging technology to advance psychological theories of culture. One example is the application of dynamic functional connectivity neurological models (e.g., Kang et al., 2011) to identify the temporal interactions of multiple localized functional brain networks (e.g., motor, attention, memory, auditory, visual, language, and subcortical networks) when individuals possess culture-related or unrelated stimuli. Such research will allow researchers to obtain precise information, with relatively high temporal resolution, about the online unfolding of mental processes when individuals think culturally.

Conclusion

In the present chapter, we have reviewed the research achievements in the previous decade in identifying the mechanisms that mediate cultural influence on social cognition, as well as the moderators of such cultural influence. The new results from these two streams of research have deepened our understanding of the multiple ways culture can influence social cognition and have illuminated how people create and apply cultural traditions to meet their psychological needs and adapt to their changing physical and social ecology. We have also identified some new trends in culture and social cognition research. We hope the present review will provide a holistic overview of the past accomplishments and future directions in the burgeoning field of culture and social cognition.

References

Aaker, J. L., & Lee, A. Y. (2001). "I" seek pleasures and "we" avoid pains: The role of self-regulatory goals in information processing and persuasion. *Journal of Consumer Research, 28*, 33–49.

Alter, A. L., & Kwan, V. S. Y. (2009). Cultural sharing in a global village: Evidence for extracultural cognition in European Americans. *Journal of Personality and Social Psychology, 96*, 742–760.

Ashton-James, C. E., Maddux, W. W., Galinsky, A. D., & Chartrand, T. L. (2009). Who I am depends on how I feel: The role of affect in the expression of culture. *Psychological Science, 20*, 340–346.

Atran, S., Medin, D. L., & Ross, N. O. (2005). The cultural mind: Environmental decision making and cultural modeling within and across populations. *Psychological Review, 112*, 744–776.

Balcetis, E., Dunning, D., & Miller, R. L. (2008). Do collectivists know themselves better than individualists? Cross-cultural studies of the holier than thou phenomenon. *Journal of Personality and Social Psychology, 95*, 1252–1267.

Beaupre, M. G., & Hess, U. (2006). An ingroup advantage for confidence in emotion recognition judgments: The moderating effect of familiarity with the expressions of outgroup members. *Personality and Social Psychology Bulletin, 32*, 16–26.

Benet-Martinez, V., Leu, J., Lee, F., & Morris, M. W. (2002). Negotiating biculturalism: Cultural frame switching in biculturals with oppositional versus compatible cultural identities. *Journal of Cross-Cultural Psychology, 33*, 492–516.

Brewer, M. B., & Chen, Y.-R. (2007). Where (Who) are collectives in collectivism? Toward conceptual clarification of individualism and collectivism. *Psychological Review, 114*, 133–151.

Briley, D. A., & Aaker, J. L. (2006). When does culture matter? Effects of personal knowledge on the correction of culture-based judgments. *Journal of Marketing Research, 43*, 395–408.

Briley, D. A., Morris, M. W., & Simonson, I. (2000). Reasons as carriers of culture: Dynamic versus dispositional models of cultural influence on decision-making. *Journal of Consumer Research, 27*, 157–178.

Briley, D. A., Morris, M. W., & Simonson, I. (2005). Cultural chameleons: Biculturals, conformity motives, and decision making. *Journal of Consumer Psychology, 15*, 351–362.

Burke, B. L., Martens, A., & Faucher, E. H. (2010). Two decades of terror management theory: A meta-analysis of mortality salience research. *Personality and Social Psychology Review, 14*, 155–195.

Chao, M. M., Chen, J., Roisman, G., & Hong, Y.-Y. (2007). Essentializing race: Implications for bicultural individuals' cognition and physiological reactivity. *Psychological Science, 18*, 341–348.

Chao, M. M., Zhang, Z.-X., & Chiu, C.-Y. (2010). Adherence to perceived norms across cultural boundaries: The role of need for cognitive closure and ingroup identification. *Group Processes and Intergroup Relations, 13*, 69–89.

Chen, H., Ng, S., & Rao, A. R. (2005). Cultural differences in consumer impatience. *Journal of Marketing Research, 42*, 291–301.

Chen, J., Chiu, C.-Y., & Chan, F. S.-F. (2009). The cultural effects of job mobility and the belief in a fixed world: Evidence from performance forecast. *Journal of Personality and Social Psychology, 97*, 851–865.

Chiu, C.-Y., & Cheng, S. Y.-Y. (2007). Toward a social psychology of culture and globalization: Some social cognitive consequences of activating two cultures simultaneously. *Social and Personality Psychology Compass, 1*, 84–100.

Chiu, C.-Y., Gelfand, M., Yamagishi, T., Shteynberg, G., & Wan, C. (2010). Intersubjective culture: The role of intersubjective perceptions in cross-cultural research. *Perspectives on Psychological Science, 5*, 482–493.

Chiu, C.-Y., Gries, P., Torelli, C. J., & Cheng, S. Y.-Y. (2011). Toward a social psychology of globalization. *Journal of Social Issues, 67*, 663–676.

Chiu, C.-Y., & Hong, Y.-Y. (2006). *Social psychology of culture.* New York: Psychology Press.

Chiu, C.-Y., & Hong, Y.-Y. (2007). Cultural processes: Basic principles. In E. T. Higgins, & A. E. Kruglanski (Eds.), *Social psychology: Handbook of basic principles* (pp. 785–809). New York: Guilford.

Chiu, C.-Y., Leung, K.-Y., & Hong, Y.-Y. (2010). Cultural processes: An overview. In A. K.-Y. Leung, C.-Y. Chiu, & Y.-Y. Hong, (Eds.), *Cultural processes: A social psychological perspective* (pp. 3–22). New York: Cambridge University Press.

Chiu, C.-Y., Mallorie, L., Keh, H.-T., & Law, W. (2009). Perceptions of culture in multicultural space: Joint presentation of images from two cultures increases ingroup attribution of culture-typical characteristics. *Journal of Cross-Cultural Psychology, 40*, 282–300.

Chiu, C.-Y., Morris, M. W., Hong, Y.-Y., & Menon, T. (2000). Motivated cultural cognition: The impact of implicit cultural theories on dispositional attribution varies as a function of need for closure. *Journal of Personality and Social Psychology, 78*, 247–259.

Cohen, A. B. (2009). Many forms of culture. *American Psychologist, 64*, 194–204.

Cohen, A. B., & Rozin, P. (2001). Religion and the morality of mentality. *Journal of Personality and Social Psychology, 81*, 697–710.

Cohen, D., & Leung, A. K.-Y. (2009). The hard embodiment of culture. *European Journal of Social Psychology, 39*, 1278–1289.

Eid, M., & Diener, E. (2001). Norms for experiencing emotions in different cultures: Inter- and intranational differences. *Journal of Personality and Social Psychology, 81*, 869–885.

Elfenbein, H. A., & Ambady, N. (2002). On the universality and cultural specificity of emotion recognition: A meta-analysis. *Psychological Bulletin, 128*, 203–235.

Fast, N. I., Heath, C., & Wu, G. (2009). Common ground and cultural prominence: How conversation strengthens culture. *Psychological Science, 20*, 904–911.

Fischer, R. (2006). Congruence and functions of personal and cultural values: Do my values reflect my culture's values? *Personality and Social Psychology Bulletin, 32*, 1419–1431.

Fischer, R., Ferreira, M. C., Assmar, E., Redford, P., Harb, C., Glazer, S., et al. (2009). Individualism-collectivism as descriptive norms: Development of a subjective norm approach to culture measurement. *Journal of Cross-Cultural Psychology, 40*, 187–213.

Fiske, A. P., Kitayama, S., Markus, H. R., & Nisbett, R. E. (1998). The cultural matrix of social psychology. In D. T. Gilbert, S. T. Fiske, & G. Lindzey (Eds.), *The handbook of social psychology* (4th ed., Vol. 2, pp. 915–981). New York: McGraw-Hill.

Fu, J. H.-Y., Chiu, C.-Y., Morris, M. W., & Young, M. J. (2007). Spontaneous inferences from cultural cues: Varying responses of cultural insiders and outsiders. *Journal of Cross-Cultural Psychology, 38*, 58–75.

Fu, J. H.-Y., Morris, M. W., Lee, S.-L., Chao, M., Chiu, C.-Y., & Hong, Y.-Y. (2007). Epistemic motives and cultural conformity: Need for closure, culture, and context as determinants of conflict judgments. *Journal of Personality and Social Psychology, 92*, 191–207.

Gaertner, L., Sedikides, C., & Chang, K. (2008). On pancultural self-enhancement: Well adjusted Taiwanese self-enhance on personally valued traits. *Journal of Cross-Cultural Psychology, 39*, 463–477.

Geeraert, N., & Yzerbyt, V. Y. (2007). Cultural differences in the correction of social inferences: Does the dispositional rebound occur in an interdependent culture? *British Journal of Social Psychology, 46*, 423–435.

Gelfand, M. J., & Realo, A. (1999). Individualism-collectivism and accountability in intergroup negotiations. *Journal of Applied Psychology, 84*, 721–736.

Guenther, C. L., & Alicke, M. D. (2010). Deconstructing the better-than-average effect. *Journal of Personality and Social Psychology, 99*, 755–770.

Hamilton, R. W. & Biehal, G, J. (2005). Achieving your goals or protecting their future? The effects of self-view on goals and choices. *Journal of Consumer Research, 32*, 277–283.

Han, S., & Northoff, G. (2008). Culture-sensitive neural substrates of human cognition: A transcultural neuroimaging approach. *Nature Review Neuroscience, 9*, 646–654.

Heine, S. J., & Lehman, D. R. (1997). Culture, dissonance, and self-affirmation. *Personality and Social Psychology Bulletin, 23*, 389–400.

Heine, S. J., Lehman, D. R., Markus, H. R., & Kitayama, S. (1999). Is there a universal need for positive self-regard? *Psychological Review, 106*, 766–794.

Hermans, H. J. M., & Kempen, H. J. G. (1998). Moving cultures: The perilous problems of cultural dichotomies in a globalizing society. *American Psychologist, 53*, 1111–1120.

Higgins, E. T. (2008). Culture and personality: Variability across universal motives as the missing link. *Social and Personality Psychology Compass, 2*, 608–643.

Hong, Y.-Y., Benet-Martinez, V., Chiu, C.-Y., & Morris, M. W. (2003). Boundaries of cultural influence: Construct activation as a mechanism for cultural differences in social perception. *Journal of Cross-Cultural Psychology, 34*, 453–464.

Hong, Y.-Y., & Chiu, C.-Y. (2001). Toward a paradigm shift: From cross-cultural differences in social cognition to social cognitive mediation of cultural differences. *Social Cognition, 19*, 181–196.

Hong, Y.-Y., Ip, G., Chiu, C.-Y., Morris, M. W., Menon, T. (2001). Cultural identity and dynamic construction of the self: Collective duties and individual rights in Chinese and American cultures. *Social Cognition, 19*, 251–268.

Hong, Y.-Y., Morris, M., Chiu, C.-Y., & Benet-Martinez, V. (2000). Multicultural minds: A dynamic constructivist approach to culture and cognition. *American Psychologist, 55*, 709–720.

Hoshino-Browne, E., Zanna, A. S., Spencer, S. J., Zanna, M. P., Kitayama, S., & Lackenbauer, S. (2005). On the cultural guise of cognitive dissonance: The case of Easterners and Westerners. *Journal of Personality and Social Psychology, 89*, 294–310.

IJzerman, H., & Koole, S. L. (2011). From perceptual rags to metaphoric riches: Bodily, social, and cultural constraints on socio-cognitive metaphors (Comment on Landau et al., 2010). *Psychological Bulletin, 137*, 355–361.

Iyengar, S. S., & Lepper, M. R. (1999). Rethinking the value of choice: A cultural perspective on intrinsic motivation. *Journal of Personality and Social Psychology, 76*, 349–366.

Jetten, J., Postmes, T., & McAuliffe, B. J. (2002). "We're all individuals": Group norms of individualism and collectivism, levels of identification and identity threat. *European Journal of Social Psychology, 32*, 189–207.

Juhl, J., & Routledge, C. (2010). Structured terror: Further exploring the effects of mortality salience and personal need for structure on worldview defense. *Journal of Personality, 78*, 969–989.

Kang, J., Wang, L., Yan, C., Wang, J., Liang, X., & He, Y. (2011). Characterizing dynamic functional connectivity in the resting brain using variable parameter regression and Kalman filtering approaches. *NeuroImage, 56*, 1222–1234.

Kashima, E. S., & Kashima, Y. (1998). Culture and language: The case of cultural dimensions and personal pronoun use. *Journal of Cross-Cultural Psychology, 29*, 461–486.

Kitayama, S., Mesquita, B., & Karasawa, M. (2006). Cultural affordances and emotional experiences: Socially engaging and disengaging emotions in Japan and the United States. *Journal of Personality and Social Psychology, 91*, 890–903.

Kitayama, S., Park, H., Sevincer, A., Timur, M., & Uskul, A. K. (2009). A cultural task analysis of implicit independence: Comparing North America, Western Europe, and East Asia. *Journal of Personality and Social psychology, 97*, 236–255.

Kitayama, S., Snibbe, A. C., Markus, H. R., & Suzuki, T. (2004). Is there any "free" choice? Self and dissonance in two cultures. *Psychological Science, 15*, 527–533.

Kitayama, S., & Uskul, A. K. (2011). Culture, mind, and the brain: Current evidence and future directions. *Annual Review of Psychology, 62*, 419–449.

Knowles, E. D., Morris, M. W., Chiu, C.-Y., & Hong, Y.-Y. (2001). Culture and the process of person perception: Evidence for automaticity among East Asians in correcting for situational influences on behavior. *Personality and Social Psychology Bulletin, 27*, 1344–1356.

Kobayashi, C., Brown, J. D. (2003). Self-esteem and self-enhancement in Japan and America. *Journal of Cross-Cultural Psychology, 34*, 567–580.

Kosic, A., Kruglanski, A. W., Pierro, A., & Mannetti, L. (2004). The social cognition of immigrants' acculturation: Effects of the need for closure and the reference group at entry. *Journal of Personality and Social Psychology, 86*, 796–813.

Kramer, T. L., Lau-Gesk, L. G., & Chiu, C.-Y. (2009). The interactive effects of duality and coping frames on responses to ambivalent messages. *Journal of Consumer Psychology, 19*, 661–672.

Krishna, A., Zhou, R., & Zhang, S. (2008). The effect of self-construal on spatial judgments. *Journal of Consumer Research, 35*, 337–348.

Kwan, V. S. Y., Bond, M. H., & Singelis, T. M. (1997). Pancultural explanations for life satisfaction: Adding relationship harmony to self-esteem: *Journal of Personality and Social Psychology, 73*, 1038–1051.

Kuhnen, U., Hannover, B., & Schubert, B. (2001). The semantic-procedural interface model of the self: The role of self-knowledge for context-dependent versus context-independent modes of thinking. *Journal of Personality and Social Psychology, 80*, 397–409.

Lalwani, A. K., Shrum, L. J., & Chiu, C.-Y. (2009). Motivated response style: The role of cultural values, regulatory focus, and self-consciousness in socially desirable responding. *Journal of Personality and Social Psychology, 96*, 870–882.

Landau, M. J., Greenberg, J., Rothschild, Z. K. (2009). Motivated cultural worldview adherence and culturally loaded test performance. *Journal of Personality and Social Psychology, 35*, 442–453.

Lau-Gesk, L. G. (2003). Activating culture through persuasion appeals: An examination of the bicultural consumer. *Journal of Consumer Psychology, 13*, 301–315.

Lehman, D., Chiu, C.-Y., & Schaller, M. (2004). Culture and psychology. *Annual Review of Psychology, 55*, 689–714.

Leung, A. K.-Y., & Chiu, C.-Y. (2010). Multicultural experiences, idea receptiveness, and creativity. *Journal of Cross-Cultural Psychology, 41*, 723–741.

Leung, A. K.-Y., & Cohen, D. (2007). The soft embodiment of culture: Camera angles and motion through time and space. *Psychological Science, 18*, 824–830.

Leung, A. K.-Y., Kim, Y.-H., Zhang, Z.-X., Tam, K.-P., & Chiu, C.-Y. (2012). Cultural construction of success and epistemic motives moderate American-Chinese differences in reward allocation biases. *Journal of Cross-Cultural Psychology, 43*, 46–52.

Leung, A. K.-Y., Maddux, W. W., Galinsky, A. D., & Chiu, C.-Y. (2008). Multicultural experience enhances creativity: The when and how. *American Psychologist, 63*, 169–181.

Lieberman, M. D., Jarcho, J. M., & Obayashi, J. (2005). Attributional inference across cultures: Similar automatic attributions and different controlled corrections. *Personality and Social Psychology Bulletin, 31*, 889–901.

Liew, S.-L., Han, S., & Aziz-Zadeh, L. (2011). Familiarity modulates mirror neuron and mentalizing regions during intention understanding. *Human Brain Mapping, 32,* 1986–1997.

Lin, Z., Lin, Y., & Han, S. (2008). Self-construal priming modulates visual activity underlying global/local perception. *Biological Psychology, 77*, 93–97.

Lockwood, P., Marshall, T. C., & Sadler, P. (2005). Promoting success or preventing failure: Cultural differences in motivation by positive and negative role models. *Personality and Social Psychology Bulletin, 31*, 379–392.

Luna, D., Ringberg, T., & Peracchio, L. A. (2008). One individual, two identities: Frame switching among biculturals. *Journal of Consumer Research, 35*, 279–293.

Markus, H. R., & Kitayama, S. (1991). Culture and self: Implications for cognition, emotion, and motivation. *Psychological Review, 98*, 224–253.

Maass, A., Karasawa, M., Politi, F., & Suga, S. (2006). Do verbs and adjectives play different roles in different cultures? A cross-linguistic analysis of person representation. *Journal of Personality and Social Psychology, 90*, 734–750.

Maddux, W. W., & Galinsky, A. D. (2009). Cultural borders and mental barriers: The relationship between living abroad and creativity. *Journal of Personality and Social Psychology, 96*, 1047–1061.

Maghaddam, F. M. (2010). Intersubjectivity, interobjectivity, and the embryonic fallacy in developmental science. *Culture and Psychology, 16*, 465–475.

Masuda, T., & Nisbett, R. E. (2001). Attending holistically versus analytically: Comparing the context sensitivity of Japanese and Americans. *Journal of Personality and Social Psychology, 81*, 922–934.

Matsumoto, D., Anguas-Wong, A. M., Martinez, E. (2008). Priming effects of language on emotion judgments in Spanish-English bilinguals. *Journal of Cross-Cultural Psychology, 39*, 335–342.

Matsumoto, D., & Willingham, B. (2006). The thrill of victory and the agony of defeat: Spontaneous expressions of medal winners of the 2004 Athens Olympic Games. *Journal of Personality and Social Psychology*, *91*, 568–581.

Menon, T., Sim, J., Fu, J. H.-Y., Chiu, C.-Y., & Hong, Y.-Y. (2010). Blazing the trail and trailing the group: Culture and perceptions of the leader's position. *Organizational Behavior and Human Decision Processes*, *113*, 51–61.

Miyamoto, Y., Nisbett, R. E., & Masuda, T. (2006). Culture and the physical environment: Holistic versus analytic perceptual affordances. *Psychological Science*, *17*, 113–119.

Molinsky, A. L., Krabbenhoft, M. A., Ambady, N., & Choi, Y. S. (2005). Cracking the nonverbal code: Intercultural competence and gesture recognition across cultures. *Journal of Cross-Cultural Psychology*, *36*, 380–395.

Morling, B., & Lamoreaux, M. (2008). Measuring culture outside the head: A meta-analysis of cultural products. *Personality and Social Psychology Review*, *12*, 199–221.

Morris, M. W., Mok, A., & Mor, S. (2011). Cultural identity threat: The role of cultural identifications in moderating closure responses to foreign cultural inflow. *Journal of Social Issues*, *67*, 760–773.

Morris, M. W. & Peng, K. (1994). Culture and cause: American and Chinese attributions for social and physical events. *Journal of Personality and Social Psychology*, *67*, 949–971.

Neumann, R., Steinhauser, N., & Roeder, U. R. (2009). How self-construal shapes emotion: Cultural differences in the feeling of pride. *Social Cognition*, *27*, 327–337.

Nisbett, R. E., Peng, K., Choi, I., & Norenzayan, A. (2001). Culture and systems of thought: Holistic versus analytic cognition. *Psychological Review*, *108*, 291–310.

No, S., Hong, Y., Liao, H., Lee, K., Wood, D., & Chao, M. M. (2008). Lay theory of race affects and moderates Asian Americans' responses toward American culture. *Journal of Personality and Social Psychology*, *96*, 991–1004.

Oishi, S., Lun, J., & Sherman, G. D. (2007). Residential mobility, self-concept, and positive affect in social interactions. *Journal of Personality and Social Psychology*, *93*, 131–141.

Oyserman, D., Coon, H. M., & Kemmelmeier, M. (2002). Rethinking individualism and collectivism: Evaluation of theoretical assumptions and meta-analyses. *Psychological Bulletin*, *128*, 3–72.

Oyserman, D., & Lee, S. W. S. (2008). Does culture influence what and how we think? Effects of priming individualism and collectivism. *Psychological Bulletin*, *134*, 311–342.

Oyserman, D., & Sorensen, N. (2009). Understanding cultural syndrome effects on what and how we think: A situated cognition model. In R. S. Wyer, C.-Y. Chiu & Y.-Y. Hong (Eds.), *Understanding culture: Theory, research and application* (pp. 25–52). New York: Psychology Press.

Oyserman, D., Sorensen, N., Reber, R., & Chan, S. X. (2009). Connecting and separating mind-sets: Culture as situated cognition. *Journal of Personality and Social Psychology*, *97*, 217–235.

Pouliasi, K., & Verkuyten, M. (2007). Networks of meaning and the bicultural mind: A structural equation modeling approach. *Journal of Experimental Social Psychology*, *43*, 955–963.

Quirin, M., Loktyushin, A., Arndt, J., Kustermann, E., Lo, Y. Y., Kuhl, J., & Eggert, L. (2012). Existential neuroscience: A functional magnetic resonance imaging investigation of neural responses to reminders of one's mortality. *Social, Cognitive, and Affective Neuroscience*, *7*, 193–198.

Rodriguez Mosquera, P. M., Manstead, A. S. R., & Fischer, A. H. (2000). The role of honor-related values in the elicitation, experience, and communication of pride, shame, and anger: Spain and the Netherlands compared. *Personality and Social Psychology Bulletin*, *26*, 833–844.

Ross, M., Heine, S. J., Wilson, A. E., & Sugimori, S. (2005). Cross-cultural discrepancies in self-appraisals. *Personality and Social Psychology Bulletin*, *31*, 1175–1188.

Schaller, M., & Murray, D. M., (2008). Pathogens, personality, and culture: Disease prevalence predicts worldwide variability in sociosexuality, extraversion, and openness to experience. *Journal of Personality and Social Psychology*, *93*, 212–221.

Schug, J., Yuki, M., & Maddux, W. (2010). Relational mobility explains between- and within-culture differences in self-disclosure to close friends. *Psychological Science*, *21*, 1471–1478.

Sedikides, C., Gaertner, L., Toguchi, Y. (2003). Pancultural self-enhancement. *Journal of Personality and Social Psychology*, *84*, 60–79.

Sedikides, C., & Gregg, A. P. (2008). Self-enhancement: Food for thought. *Perspectives on Psychological Science*, *3*, 102–116.

Shweder, R. A., & Sullivan, M. A. (1990). The semiotic subject of cultural psychology. In L. A. Pervin (Ed.), *Handbook of personality: Theory and research* (pp. 399–416). New York: Guilford.

Shteynberg, G., Gelfand, M. J., Kim, K. (2009). Peering into the "magnum mysterium" of culture: The exploratory power of descriptive norms. *Journal of Cross-Cultural Psychology*, *40*, 46–69.

Spencer-Rodgers, J., Boucher, H. C., Mori, S. C., & Wang, L. (2009). The dialectical self-concept: Contradiction, change, and holism in East Asian cultures. *Personality and Social Psychology Bulletin*, *35*, 29–44.

Sui, J., Zhu, Y., & Chiu, C.-Y. (2007). Bicultural mind, self-construal, and recognition memory: Cultural priming effects on self- and mother-reference effect. *Journal of Experimental Social Psychology*, *43*, 818–824.

Tadmor, C. T., Tetlock, P. E., & Peng, K. (2009). Acculturation strategies and integrative complexity: The cognitive implications of biculturalism. *Journal of Cross-Cultural Psychology*, *40*, 105–139.

Torelli, C. J. (2006). Individuality or conformity? The effect of independent and interdependent self-concepts on public judgments. *Journal of Consumer Psychology*, *16*, 240–248.

Torelli, C. J., Chiu, C.-Y., Tam, K-P., Au, A. K. C., & Keh, H. T. (2011). Exclusionary reactions to foreign cultures: Effects of simultaneous exposure to cultures in globalized space. *Journal of Social Issues*, *67*, 716–742.

Tracy, J. L., & Robins, R. W. (2008). The nonverbal expression of pride: Evidence for cross-cultural recognition. *Journal of Personality and Social Psychology*, *94*, 516–530.

Triandis, H. C. (1989). The self and social-behavior in differing cultural contexts. *Psychological Review*, *96*, 506–520.

Uskul, A. L., Sherman, D. K., & Fitzgibbon, J. (2009). The cultural congruency effect: Culture, regulatory focus, and the effectiveness of gain- vs. loss-framed health messages. *Journal of Experimental Social Psychology*, *45*, 535–541.

Veyrkuyten, M., & Pouliasi, K. (2006). Biculturalism and group identification: The mediating role of identification in cultural frame switching. *Journal of Cross-Cultural Psychology*, *37*, 312–326.

Wan, C., Chiu, C.-Y., Tam, K.-P., Lee, S-l., Lau, I. Y.-M., & Peng, S.-Q. (2007). Perceived cultural importance and actual self-importance of values in cultural identification. *Journal of Personality and Social Psychology*, *92*, 337–354.

Wan, C., Torelli, C., & Chiu, C.-Y. (2010). Intersubjective consensus and the maintenance of normative shared reality. *Social Cognition*, *28*, 422–446.

Wang, C. S., & Leung, K. Y. A. (2010). The cultural dynamics of rewarding honesty and punishing deception. *Personality and Social Psychology Bulletin*, *36*, 1529–1542.

Wang, C. S., Leung, K. Y. A., See, M., & Gu, X. (2011). The effects of culture and friendship on rewarding honesty and punishing deception. *Journal of Experimental Social Psychology*, *47*, 1295–1299.

Wong, R. Y.-M., & Hong, Y.-Y. (2005). Dynamic influences of culture on cooperation in the Prisoner's Dilemma. *Psychological Science*, *16*, 429–434.

Zarate, M. A., Uleman, J. S., & Voils, C. I. (2001). Effects of culture and processing goals on activation and binding of trait concepts. *Social Cognition*, *19*, 295–323.

Zhang, A. Y., & Chiu, C.-Y. (2012). Goal commitment and alignment of personal goals predict group identification only when the goals are shared. *Group Processes and Intergroup Relations,15,* 425–437.

Zhang, Y., & Shrum, L. J. (2009). The influence of self-construal on impulsive consumption. *Journal of Consumer Research*, *35*, 838–850.

Zhu, Y., Zhang, L., Fan, J., Han, S. (2007). Neural basis of cultural influence on self-representation. *NeuroImage*, *34*, 1310–1317.

Zou, X., Morris, W., & Benet-Martinez, V. (2008). Identity motives and cultural priming: Cultural (dis)identification in assimilative and contrastive responses. *Journal of Experimental Social Psychology*, *44*, 1151–1159.

Zou, X., Tam, K.-P., Morris, M. W., Lee, S.-L., Lau, Y.-M., & Chiu, C.-Y. (2009). Culture as common sense: Perceived consensus versus personal beliefs as mechanisms of cultural influence. *Journal of Personality and Social Psychology*, *97*, 579–597.

The Person–Situation Interaction

John F. Kihlstrom

Abstract

The role of cognition in mediating social interaction is illustrated by the General Social Interaction Cycle. Unpacking Lewin's "grand truism," B = f (P, E), this chapter explores the role of social cognitive structures and processes in mediating the interaction of the person and the situation. Historically, assuming the independence of personal and environmental determinants of behavior maintained the separation of personality (and its underlying Doctrine of Traits) from social psychology (and its underlying Doctrine of Situationism). An alternative Doctrine of Interactionism, supplemented by a further Doctrine of Reciprocal Determinism, provides a framework for the integration of the two fields by analyzing the dialectical relationships among the person, the environment, and behavior. Two versions of interactionism are described: a static version, originally modeled on the statistical analysis of variance; and a dynamic version, which describes how persons construct the situations to which they respond through evocation, selection, behavioral manipulation, and cognitive transformation. Dynamic interactionism allows the individual's cognitive processes to play a role in shaping the mental representation of the situation in which his behavior takes place.

Key Words: evocation; expectancy effects, interpersonal; interactionism, doctrine of; manipulation, behavioral; reciprocal determinism, doctrine of; selection; social interaction cycle, general; situationism, doctrine of; traits, doctrine of; transformation, cognitive

"You never really understand a person
until you consider things from his point of view—
until you climb into his skin and walk around in it."
        –Atticus Finch, in *to Kill a Mockingbird*
                by Harper Lee (1961)

The cognitive perspective on social interaction begins with the assumption—actually, more like an axiom—that humans are intelligent creatures. Our behavior is not merely a matter of reflex, taxis, instinct, and conditioned response. Rather, it occurs in response to the *meaning* of the stimulus, and reflects active cognitive processes of perceiving, learning, remembering, thinking, and linguistic communication. But humans are also social creatures. Our experiences, thoughts, and actions take place in an explicitly social context of cooperation,

competition, and exchange; family and group memberships; and organizational, institutional, social, and cultural structures. For that last reason, psychologists need to understand the relations between psychological processes within the individual and social processes that take place in the world outside.

The cognitive perspective on social interaction also implies a very different construal of personality. Traditionally, individual differences in personality have been viewed in terms of traits, behavioral dispositions roughly analogous to physical features (like the Big Five of neuroticism, extraversion, agreeableness, conscientiousness, and openness) that give coherence, stability, consistency, and predictability to the individual's behavior. From a cognitive point of view, however, the important variables consist of percepts, memories, and thoughts: the knowledge, beliefs, and expectations that mediate the individual's perception of the situation and retrieval of relevant memories of past experiences, and which guide the individual's judgment, decision making, and planning in response to both internal goals and external events. As Atticus Finch understood, understanding these features of cognition—knowledge, belief, and expectation; perception, memory, and thought—allow us to understand an individual and his behavior.

Cognition in the General Social Interaction Cycle

The role of cognition in social interaction is illustrated by the *General Social Interaction Cycle* (Cantor & Kihlstrom, 1987)—a conceptual framework for analyzing any dyadic social interaction (Figure 38.1). Within this framework, the two participants are assigned the role of *Actor* and *Target*, respectively. This assignment is of course somewhat arbitrary because each individual is both an actor and the target of the other's actions. For convenience, the Actor role is assigned to the individual who initiates the social interaction.

The General Social Interaction Cycle is a variant on the general social interaction sequence initially described by Darley and Fazio (1980) and Jones (1986). The description of social interaction as a cycle rather than as a sequence is intended to make clear that social exchange continues until one or the other individual terminates the interaction by leaving the situation. An alternative depiction is in terms of a connectionist network representing the interaction of two cognitive-affective processing systems, representing the two individuals that constitute the dyad (Shoda et al., 2002; Zayas et al., 2002).

First, ***the Actor enters the situation***—the immediate context in which he or she physically encounters the Target (from this point on, for simplicity in exposition, we'll call the Actor "she" and the Target "he"). The Actor enters the situation with some goal in mind—something that she wants to accomplish, like asking the Target for a date for Friday night. She also carries into the situation a fund of *social knowledge* concerning herself and the target. How badly does she want a date? Does she know whether he is currently seeing someone else? Does she have any reason to think he might be interested in her? The Actor also carries a fund of more generic social knowledge relevant to her current goals: What movies are in town? Are there any parties? And finally, she possesses a repertoire of skills to be used in the course of the interaction, such as how to start a conversation, and how to bring it around to the subject of Friday night. Some of these skills are cognitive in nature, such as her ability to "read people"; others are motoric, such as a particular way of smiling or using her hands. This sort of declarative and

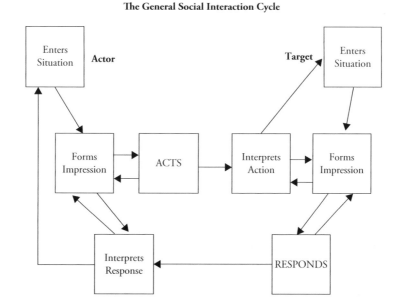

The General Social Interaction Cycle

Figure 38.1 Schematic depiction of the General Social Interaction Cycle (Cantor & Kihlstrom, 1987; after Darley & Fazio, 1980; Jones, 1986).

procedural social knowledge constitutes the individual's fund of social intelligence.

As she begins the interaction, *the Actor forms an impression of the situation*—of the Target, and of the immediate environmental context. Does he still seem interested? Is this a good time to ask? This impression combines knowledge derived from two general sources: information about the current stimulus situation, extracted online through the mechanisms of social perception; and preexisting knowledge about herself and the Target, retrieved from social memory.

At this point, *the Actor acts* on the basis of her impression. She may approach the Target or shy away, she may pop the question or not. If she does not ask the Target for a date, the interaction will end shortly. If she does, the interaction will continue. Assuming that the Actor has asked him for a date, attention now shifts to the Target, who now has to do something in response to the Actor's initial salvo.

The Target enters the situation—either actively, by approaching and greeting the Actor when he sees her, or passively, by being approached and greeted by her. He, too, brings his social intelligence, including a fund of declarative knowledge and a repertoire of procedural knowledge, into the situation.

Like the Actor, *the Target forms an impression* of the situation in which he now finds himself—a situation that is immediately clarified when the Actor asks him for a date. The Target knows he's free Friday night because the woman he's been dating is out of town, but that's not decisive. Should he play hard to get? Should he wait to see if he gets a better offer from someone else? What if his current girlfriend finds out?

On the basis of the impression he's formed, *the Target responds*. He decides to keep his options open for Friday night, but doesn't want to spurn the Actor entirely, so he says he can't see her Friday, but proposes that they go out on Saturday instead. Now attention shifts back to the Actor.

Now *the Actor must interpret the Target's response, and revise her impression of the situation accordingly*. Perhaps he's Jewish, or Muslim, and devout, and doesn't go out on Friday nights. Perhaps he's seeing someone else. Obviously he's got something he'd rather do on Friday, while she does not, and she has now clearly communicated this fact to him. As it happens, she's also free Saturday night, but if she accepts his counteroffer she clearly communicates that she doesn't have a date for *either* night. Should she let him have this information? If she says "yes," is she becoming a pawn in whatever other relationship he may be pursuing? Or is the "Friday-night woman" (because by now she is certain that he already has got a date for Friday night) a pawn in a new game that he is now playing with *her*?

On the basis of her impression, *the Actor responds to the Target:* she decides to take a chance, and accepts the date for Saturday night. Now the ball is back in the Target's court. At this point, *the Target must interpret the Actor's response, revise his impression, and figure out what to do next*.

And so it goes, with the cycle of exchanges continuing. Each member of the dyad is trying to make sense of what the other one is doing. Each is trying to read the other's mind. And each participant is planning and executing behavior in accordance with his or her evolving understanding of the total situation.

The General Social Interaction Cycle also transpires at another level, within each individual participant. Behavior does not simply affect the person toward whom it is directed; it also feeds back to affect the person who emitted the behavior. The Actor may have wondered if she had the nerve, and the skill, to ask a man for a date. Now she knows that she does: Bandura (1977a) calls this kind of knowledge *self-efficacy expectations*. Similarly, the Target may never have had to negotiate overlapping dating relationships. Now he knows he can do this—or else he's put himself in a situation in which he has to learn how.

In any event, each participant in this social interaction is behaving in accordance with his or her construal of himself or herself, and of the other, and of the situation in which they meet. Each of these construals is modified by the other's behavior, and his or her own. These individual construals, in the end, lead the participants to behave the way they do. And understanding these individual construals—and the knowledge, beliefs, and expectations that underlie them—allow us to understand the people involved.

Cognition and Social Cognition in Personality

Even before the cognitive revolution took hold in social psychology, it was generally accepted that it is the perceived situation that controls behavior. Perhaps the earliest expression of the cognitive point of view is what is known as the *Thomas theorem*: "If men define situations as real, they are real in their consequences" (Thomas & Thomas, 1928,

p. 529)—an assertion which Merton (1976) called "probably the single most consequential sentence ever put in print by an American sociologist" (see also Merton, 1995). Similarly, Newcomb (1929) explained the fact that extraversion and introversion were not as consistent across situations as traditional personality theory implied they should be, and attributed the individual's behavior in a particular situation to his *beliefs* about that situation: "whether or not Johnny engages in a fight may depend on whether or not he *thinks* he can 'lick' his opponent" (p. 39, emphasis added). Only a little later, Bartlett (1932)—in a study of memory expressly conceived and presented as a contribution to both cognitive and social psychology—had asserted that "the psychologist, of all people, must not stand in awe of the stimulus (p. 3)—by which, of course, he meant the *objective* stimulus, unfiltered by cognitive schemata.

Cognition in Social Psychology

The study of social cognition begins with symbolic interactionism. Mead distinguished between those aspects of social behavior that were reflexive in nature, or the product of conditioning, and those that are derived from symbolic interpretation, or the individual's cognitive construction of the situation (Mead, 1934), hence Blumer's proposition that "Human beings act toward things on the basis of the meaning that the things have for them" (Blumer, 1937; see also Blumer, 1969, 1980). In symbolic interactionism, social interactions are symbolic because they occur in the participants' heads, before they occur in reality. Symbolic interactions, played out in the mind, are where cognitive transformations take place.

Even during the heyday of behaviorism, a cognitive perspective was central to social psychology, as evidenced by early studies of causal explanation (Heider, 1944, 1958), impression formation (Asch, 1946), person perception (Bruner & Tagiuri, 1954; Tagiuri & Petrullo, 1958), and implicit personality theory (Bruner & Tagiuri, 1954; Cronbach, 1955). Cognition was so central to the views of Krech and Cruthchfield (1948) that they began their textbook with a discussion of general principles of perception and cognition, and dedicated the book to Edward C. Tolman. The very first edition of the *Handbook of Social Psychology* contained an extensive chapter summarizing cognitive theory (Scheerer, 1954). That same handbook, of course, also contained Allport's (1954) historical overview, which defined social psychology as the study of social influence,

inadvertently tying social psychology to situationism and behaviorism (Zimbardo, 1999). By contrast, Krech and Crutchfield had defined social psychology simply as the study of the individual in society, of which the study of social influence was only a part (see also Krech, Crutchfield, & Ballachey, 1962).

But times were changing, and behaviorism began to lose its grip on social psychology, as on psychology as a whole. In a symposium on the social psychology of the psychological experiment, Orne (1962) argued that the experimental subject tried to make sense of the experimental situation by analyzing its demand characteristics, as well as the experimenter's instructions and procedures—trying to read between the lines of cover stories and deception to determine what was actually going on. Similarly, R. Rosenthal (1963) drew attention to the effects of experimenters' expectations on subjects' task performance, both actual and perceived—work that represented an early experimental analysis of the self-fulfilling prophecy. Of course, Orne and Rosenthal were not just analyzing experimental methodology. For them, the same social cognitive processes underlying the behavior of subjects in the laboratory were also to be found in the real world outside the laboratory: in all of their social interactions, people are active, sentient beings, trying to understand the situation they are in, and shaping that situation through their own thoughts and behaviors (Kihlstrom, 2002).

The cognitive revolution in social psychology really begins here. Whereas Milgram (1963) made no mention of cognition in his classic study of obedience to authority, Darley and Latane (1968) invoked subjects' perception of the situation to explain their behavior in the bystander intervention paradigm. Although many of these references to perception and cognition were fairly informal, soon enough social psychologists were developing theories of knowledge representation and information processing that, aside from their subject matter, were indistinguishable in their rigor from those of cognitive psychologists (e.g., Hastie et al., 1980; Higgins, Zanna, & Herman, 1981; Wyer & Carlston, 1979).

Kelly's Personal Construct Theory

The crypto-behaviorist view was a relatively recent import to a social psychology that previously had strong cognitive underpinnings. By contrast, the psychology of personality was dominated almost from the beginning by an emphasis on traits and other stable personality dispositions that were essentially noncognitive in nature (Allport, 1937; Cattell, 1940). Still, there were exceptions. While Allport was committed to developing personality as a distinctive subfield of psychology, independent of social psychology, Stagner (Stagner, 1937) took explicit account of the organizational, institutional, social, and cultural context of personality structure, development, and dynamics (see also Craik, 1993). Far from being a closeted situationist, however, Stagner explicitly adopted a cognitive view of social behavior, depicting the individual as navigating an environment of people and things, learning through success and failure, adopting different perspectives on the situation at hand, and modifying the environment in various ways (see, e.g., pp. 443–444).

More to the point, George Kelly developed a thoroughly cognitive approach to personality in which traits and similar behavioral dispositions played no role (Kelly, 1955; Maher, 1968). Instead, individual differences were construed in terms of *personal constructs*, or the categories that provide the cognitive framework for the person's understanding of the world around him. From Kelly's point of view, objective reality does not matter very much: experience and action are determined by subjective reality. What matters is how events in the outside world are construed by the individual. In Kelly's theory, each person has a different repertoire of personal constructs, which have developed through a process of hypothesis testing: if the application of a construct allows a person to correctly anticipate some future event, it is retained; if it does not, it is revised or abandoned. In order to understand a person's response to events, we have to understand the constructs through which he or she has perceived those events.

Whereas traditional personality theory assumed that behavior was relatively consistent across situations, personal construct theory offered a cognitive basis for the flexibility of behavior across situations. According to Kelly's notion of *constructive alternativism* (Kelly, 1958/1969), most people can choose among alternative construals of an event, and that choice will determine their experience of and response to that event. If the person makes a different choice, both covert experience and overt behavior will differ as well. In contrast to the doctrine's emphasis on the stability of behavior across time, Kelly allowed considerable leeway for personality change. Personality change is tantamount to a change in the individual's personal construct system: New constructs can be added to the individual's repertoire, or constructs that were previously preferred can now be avoided or abandoned. When personality changes, the individual literally perceives the world differently—and behaves differently, too.

Idiosyncratic in conception and exposition, Kelly's theory had little impact on personality psychology at the time: His theory was not covered in Hall and Lindzey's *Theories of Personality* until the fourth edition (Hall, Lindzey, & Campbell, 1998); and unlike Allport (#11) and Cattell (#16), Kelly did not make the list of "The 100 Most Eminent Psychologists of the 20th Century" (Haggbloom et al., 2002). As such, *The Psychology of Personal Constructs* may be one of the "Great Unread Books" in the history of psychology.

Social Learning Theories of Personality

Nevertheless, the increasing lure of a cognitive point of view can be seen in the evolution of social learning theories of personality (Cantor & Kihlstrom, 1987). Originally, social learning theory was decidedly noncognitive in nature. Essentially a translation of Freudian psychoanalytic theory into the vocabulary of Hullian learning theory, it asserted little more than that personality consisted of habitual behaviors acquired through learning; learning, in turn, was mediated by drive reduction; and because the habits that make up personality were largely social behaviors, it was important to pay attention to the social context in which learning occurred (Dollard & Miller, 1950; Miller & Dollard, 1941). Rotter (1954), however, fused Hullian drive-reduction theory with Tolman's sign-learning theory to produce a thoroughly cognitive version of social learning theory. According to Rotter, personality is reflected in the choices that people make; these choices, in turn, are determined by their expectancies concerning the outcomes of various behavioral options, and the values they place on these outcomes.

Stated this way, Rotter's original social learning theory is less a theory of learning than it is a theory of choice, emphasizing the individual's expectancies and values. It remained for Bandura (1962; Bandura & Walters, 1963) to formulate an explicit theory of social learning based on observational processes. While agreeing that expectations could be acquired and modified through the direct experience of outcomes, Bandura argued that the *vicarious* experience of outcomes was far more important—a more efficient, and more powerful, mechanism for social learning, socialization, and acculturation. Bandura (1977b) further described two different pathways by which observational learning could occur: learning by example, from observing other people's behavior and its outcome; and learning by precept, as in sponsored teaching and other forms of linguistic and transmission of knowledge, beliefs, and expectations. Bandura (1978) also stressed the importance of self-knowledge and agency in social behavior.

Like the expressly behaviorist approach of Staats and Staats (1963), Bandura's earliest work nods in the direction of Skinnerian behaviorism, with its emphasis on schedules of reinforcement, generalization, and discrimination (Bandura & Walters, 1963). But his growing emphasis on the cognitive mediation of both environmental influences and social behavior was so strong that he eventually abjured the term *social learning*, with its implications of conditioning and behaviorism, in favor of what he called "social-cognitive" theory (Bandura, 1986).

Perhaps the most comprehensive cognitive approach to personality within the social learning tradition has been offered by Mischel (1973). Mischel's (1968) vigorous critique of trait theory and his occasional reliance on the language of stimulus and response sometimes led him to be characterized as a radical situationist. But Mischel was clear from the outset that it was the *perceived* situation, its meaning for the person, that controlled behavior. For example, "[O]ne must know the properties or meaning that the stimulus has acquired for the subject. Assessing the acquired meaning of stimuli is the core of social behavior assessment" (1968, p. 190). "Idiosyncratic histories produce idiosyncratic stimulus meanings" (1973, p. 259). And "The meaning and impact of a stimulus can be modified dramatically by *cognitive transformations*" (1973, p. 260, emphasis original). Percepts and meanings are a product of cognitive activity, so for Mischel, as with Bandura, the locus of causal agency lies squarely within the individual.

In the most recent stage in the evolution of cognitive social learning theories of personality, Mischel (1973) proposed a reconceptualization of personality in which traits are abandoned as the basic elements of personality, in favor of expressly cognitive constructs. These "cognitive social learning person variables" include (1) cognitive and behavioral construction competencies—both the person's skill level and the range of situations in which he or she can apply them; (2) encoding strategies and personal constructs that determine how the person will mentally represent the situation in which he finds himself; (3) expectancies, including outcome expectancies and self-efficacy expectations; (4) subjective values; and (5) self-regulatory systems and plans that guide thought and action in the absence of, and even in spite of, external demands and constraints.

All of these variables are construed as modifiable individual differences, products of both cognitive development and social learning, which determine how features of the situation at hand will be perceived and interpreted. Thus, they contribute to the construction of the meaning of the stimulus situation—in other words, to the cognitive construction of the situation itself—to which the person ultimately responds. More recently, Mischel and his colleagues have added considerations of affect to his system (Mischel & Shoda, 1995), and situated the individual more clearly in an interpersonal context (Shoda et al., 2002), but the basic point remains, that "personality is conceptualized as a stable system that mediates how the individual selects, construes, and processes social information and generates social behaviors" (Mischel & Shoda, 1995, p. 246). Personality is thus viewed as a "cognitive-affective processing system"—a stable network of "mental representations of the psychological meaning of situations, representations of self, others, possible future events, goals, affects, beliefs, expectations, as well as behavioral alternatives.... Individuals differ stably in this network of inter-connections or associations, and such differences constitute a major aspect of personality" (Shoda et al., 2002, p. 317).

Personality and Social Intelligence

In addition to personal construct theory and cognitive social learning theory, a third cognitive approach to personality is in terms of *social intelligence*, which Thorndike (1920) classically defined as the "ability to understand men and women, boys and girls—to act wisely in human relations" (p. 228). In the years since Thorndike, social intelligence was approached by an *ability* view that entailed the development of IQ-like tests of individual differences in interpersonal skills, as represented by the George Washington Social Intelligence Test or the "behavioral operations" group in Guilford's "Structure of Intellect," raising the question of whether social intelligence is anything more than general intelligence applied to social situations (for a review, see Landy, 2006). The ability view of social intelligence was revived in Gardner's (1983, 1999) theory of multiple intelligences and has been popularized by Goleman (2006).

In contrast to the ability view of social intelligence, Cantor and Kihlstrom (1987; Cantor & Kihlstrom, 1981; Kihlstrom & Cantor, 2011) have offered a *knowledge view* that eschews the assessment of individual differences in "social IQ." The knowledge view begins with the assumption that social behavior is intelligent—that is, it is mediated by what the person knows and believes to be the case, and by cognitive processes of perception, memory, reasoning, and problem solving (as opposed to innate reflexes and instinctive behavioral patterns, conditioned responses, evolved genetic programs, and the like). Accordingly, the social intelligence view construes individual differences in social behavior—which are, after all, the public manifestations of personality—as the product of individual differences in the knowledge that individuals bring to bear on their social interactions. And, as in Kelly's personal construct theory, personality change is tantamount to change in the individual's repertoire of social knowledge—change that is, in turn, a product of social learning by direct experience, example, and precept. From the knowledge view, the critical variable is not *how much* social intelligence the person has, but rather *what* social intelligence he or she possesses—what the individual knows about himself or herself, other people, the situations in which people encounter each other, and the behaviors they exchange when they are in them. This declarative knowledge (episodic and semantic), coupled with the procedural knowledge by which declarative knowledge is manipulated and transformed, is the cognitive basis of personality.

Personality and Cognition in Lewin's Grand Truism

The cognitive analysis of personality and social interaction should be viewed against the classic framework for the analysis of social behavior provided by Kurt Lewin (1935, 1951; see also Wolf, 1986). Employing the conventions of mathematics, Lewin asserted that

$$B = f(P, E).$$

In this formulation,

B stands for the individual's overt, publicly observable behavior. For Lewin, every psychologically interesting behavior is social behavior, in that such behavior is always in some way directed toward another person.

See note above *P* stands for all the causal factors that reside within the individual person—not just the traits, attitudes, motives, values, and other behavioral dispositions of traditional personality theory, but rather all the individual's mental (cognitive, emotional, and motivational) states. Of particular interest, for Heider (1958) as well as Lewin, were the person's intentional states—that is, what the person was *intending* to do (see Malle, 2008).

See not above *E* stands for all the causal factors that reside in the world outside the individual, including aspects of the physical ecology (e.g., temperature, humidity, altitude) and the sociocultural ecology (e.g., the presence and behavior of other people, constraints imposed by social structures, social roles, situational demands and expectations, social incentives). Because every behavior is social behavior, for Lewin what really counts in the environment are the social aspects of the situation—the behavior of other people, as well as wider social and cultural forces.

Lewin's pseudo-mathematics represented the idea that personal and environmental determinants combine somehow to cause individuals to do what they do—what Jones (1985, p. 84) referred to as "Lewin's grand truism" (see also Crano, 1988). The comma (,) in the equation indicated that Lewin was open as to precisely how these factors combined.

Perhaps the easiest way to think about how personal and environmental determinants combine to produce individual behavior is to think of them as independent of each other (Figure 38.2). This was, essentially, the perspective adopted by traditional personality and social psychology. Borrowing the phrase coined by C. P. Snow (1963) in his analysis of the relations between the sciences and the humanities, traditional personality and social psychology developed as "two cultures"—each having little to do with the other. As evidence for this claim, consider that, in most psychology departments, personality and social psychology were taught by different faculty members, and often housed in separate

Person–Situation Independence

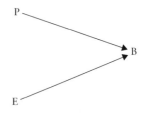

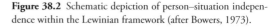

Figure 38.2 Schematic depiction of person–situation independence within the Lewinian framework (after Bowers, 1973).

groups for purposes of graduate education (in one famous instance, they were even housed in different buildings).

The Doctrine of Traits

The traditional psychology of personality construed behavior as a function of personal attributes such as traits, attitudes, emotions, motives, and values. Personality psychologists typically assessed these behavioral dispositions by means of questionnaires or similar instruments, and then correlated these predictor variables with some criterion behavior in some specific situation. In such research, the effects of the environment are generally construed as "noise." The canonical method of traditional personality psychology thus exemplifies the *Doctrine of Traits*, which may be stated as follows:

> Social behavior varies as a function of internal behavioral dispositions that render it coherent, stable, consistent, and predictable.

In fact, Gordon Allport (1937, p. 295) defined a personality trait as: "a generalized and focalized neuropsychic system...with the capacity to render many stimuli functionally equivalent, and to initiate and guide consistent (equivalent) forms of adaptive and expressive behavior." For him, there was an analogy between personality traits and physical traits. Just as physical traits are stable features of appearance and physique, so personality traits are stable features of behavior. Although social psychologists might prefer a "biosocial" view of traits merely as linguistic categories for the classification of social behaviors, Allport himself preferred a "biophysical" view of traits. For him, personality traits were real in precisely the same way that physical traits were real, and were subject to measurement in precisely the same way that physical attributes were. Although not necessarily genetic in origin (because they could be acquired through experience), traits are somehow represented in the nervous system. These personal characteristics, once established, then mediate between the environment and behavior. Traits "render situations functionally equivalent" in that they dispose the person to display similar sorts of behaviors in them, and they "initiate and guide consistent (equivalent) forms of...behavior," in that trait-relevant behaviors all exemplify some disposition, such as friendliness or aggressiveness.

The Doctrine of Situationism

Traditional social psychology, by contrast, construed behavior as a function of differences in the physical and (especially) social environment. In their research, social psychologists typically manipulate some aspect of the social environment, such as the presence or behavior of other people, and then examine the effect of this independent variable on some behavioral dependent variable. In such research, the effects of individual differences in personality are generally construed as "noise." This view is captured by what might be called the *Doctrine of Situationism*:

> Social behavior varies as a function of features of the external environment, particularly the social situation, that elicit behavior directly, or that communicate social expectations, demands, and incentives.

As examples of the Doctrine of Situationism, consider first the classic definition of social psychology offered by G. Allport:

> With few exceptions, social psychologists regard their discipline as an attempt to understand and explain how the thought, feeling, and behavior of individuals are influenced by the actual, imagined, or implied presence of other human beings.... [S]ocial psychology wishes to know how any given member of a society is affected by all the social stimuli that surround him. (1954, p. 5)

Ross and Nisbett (1991, p. 9) claimed that "the social context creates potent forces producing or constraining behavior," and identified "the power of the situation" as one of the three legs on which social psychology rested. Similarly, Lieberman (2005, p. 746) asserted that the cardinal defining principle of social psychology was "power of the situation," supplemented by the idea that people are largely unaware of situational influences on their behavior.

Situationism has its obvious origins in stimulus–response behaviorism (Zimbardo, 1999), and its insistence that the causes of behavior lie outside the individual (e.g., Skinner, 1953, p. 447). Even after the cognitive revolution, Bargh and Chartrand (1999) identified the mechanism for situational influence with "processes that are put into motion by features of the environment and that operate outside of conscious awareness and guidance" (p. 462).

Person–Situation Independence

The contrast between the Doctrine of Traits and the Doctrine of Situationism can be illustrated by two studies of delay of gratification in children. In one, delay was found to be positively correlated with two broad personality traits, ego control and ego resiliency, as measured by an observational rating scale, as well with IQ (Funder & Block, 1989; see also Funder, Block, & Block, 1983). In the other, delay was found to be improved if the children waited in the absence of the promised reward (Mischel & Ebbesen, 1970). The first study took no account of environmental variables; the second study took no account of individual differences in personality.

For the better part of the 20th century, personality and social psychologists (perhaps like the brothers Allport themselves) treated each other with benign collegial neglect. But in the 1960s, they came to loggerheads in the *trait-situation debate* over which factors were more powerful predictors of behavior—internal personality traits or external situational influences. For example, Mischel (1968) famously concluded that the modal correlation between subjects' scores on a personality test and their actual behavior in some specific test situation was about r = .30 (a figure which he dubbed the "personality coefficient"), indicating that traits accounted for only about 10% of behavioral variance. A counterattack by Funder and Ozer (1983) sampled from the classic social psychological literature on situational influence, translated t values and F ratios into correlation coefficients, and determined that the effect of situational variance amounted to a correlation of about r = .45—a figure indicating that situations account for only about 20% of behavioral variance: Most variance was not accounted for by situations, either. So what began as a quintessentially masculine "Battle of the Correlation Coefficients," intended to determine whose was bigger, ended up looking more like a fight in an elementary schoolyard, with each side shouting, "So's your mother" at the other one (e.g., Kihlstrom, 1986). But that is all over now (Kenrick & Funder, 1988), and in most psychology departments, personality and social psychologists work side by side—though informal observation suggests that both parties still keep their hands on their swords.

Of course, it must be said that these traditional formulations, and the competition they engendered, were largely misleading. Nobody believed that one factor is exclusively responsible for behavior and the other is wholly irrelevant. Dispositional and situational factors combined somehow to cause behavior to occur. One possibility is that P and E are statistically independent—that is, that each set of factors exerts its own separate influence on behavior, without affecting the other in any way. This notion lies at the heart of the traditional formulation, in which

personality and social psychology were situated as separate and independent subfields of psychology. In such a view, behavior is partly predicted by internal, personal factors, and partly affected by external, situational ones.

In mathematical terms, personal and environmental influences on behavior are additive:

$$B = f(P + E).$$

If P and E are independent, then the effect of some person variable is the same, regardless of the situation the person is in, and the effect of the situation is the same, regardless of the kind of person in that situation. Statistically, these two effects would be characterized as the main effects of the person and the situation, respectively. It was the assumption of person–situation independence that permitted personality and social psychologists to go their own separate ways.

The Doctrine of Interactionism

But this was not Lewin's idea at all. Recall that Lewin sought to apply the principles of gestalt psychology to the study of social behavior, and the gestalt school is famous for its assertion that "the whole is greater than the sum of its parts." Applied to perception, this means that perception encompasses the entire stimulus field. Individual stimulus elements form a coherent, integrated whole, and cannot be isolated from each other. Similarly, Lewin argued that social behavior is responsive to the entire field of social stimuli—not just the other people immediately present but also the wider social context in which the interaction occurs. Lewin went even further to assert that the social situation includes the person himself or herself: the person is part of the stimulus field to which he or she responds.

Lewin expressed this basic idea throughout his writings, in various ways and with various versions of his formula. Because Lewin's actual views are apparently not widely appreciated among some social psychologists, it is worth the space to document them in detail. Here he is in an early paper:

The psychological environment has to be regarded functionally as a part of one interdependent field, the life space, the other part of which is the person. This fundamental fact is the keynote of the field-theoretical approach. (Lewin, 1939/1951, p. 140)

And here he is again in a later one:

The life space, therefore, includes both the person and his psychological environment.... A totality of coexisting facts which are conceived of as mutually interdependent is called a *field*. Psychology has to view the life space, including the person and his environment, as one field. (Lewin, 1946/1951, p. 240)

Statements like these, and there are many others of this sort, show why claims that Lewin is the godfather of situationism in social psychology (e.g., Ross & Nisbett, 1991) are inaccurate. In the first place, Lewin, influenced by Gestalt psychology, was a *field theorist*—he believed that the person and the environment were interdependent elements constituting a unified psychological field, in which the whole was greater than the sum of the parts, and the situation was only part of the whole. In the second place, from the beginning Lewin (1931/1935) emphasized the *psychological* situation—"where the reality is what he perceives or believes" (Boring, 1950, p. 715). Lewin's emphasis on the psychological situation actually renders the Doctrine of Situationism moot (Goldberg, 1992). If it is the *mental representation* of the person that controls behavior, then all the more power to control behavior in that situation falls to the person who constructs that representation in his or her mind. Before taking up this second point, however, let us examine how we can construe the interdependence of the person and the situation.

The modern Doctrine of Interactionism also has its roots in the "S-O-R" alternative to the traditional S-R laws favored by the radical behaviorists (e.g., Woodworth, 1929). Similarly, Murray (1938) emphasized the interaction between personal needs and environmental press, which combined to create what he called the *thema* characterizing any particular episode in a person's life; Murray also emphasized the role of "beta" press, or the subjective environment, as opposed to the objectively described environment of "alpha" press. In this chapter, however, I emphasize Lewin's contribution because he was a much greater influence on developments in social psychology—and so commonly misunderstood as the father of situationism. Similar misunderstandings crop up in references to Heider, who is commonly—and wrongly—assumed to have embraced a strict dichotomy between personal and situational causes of behavior—and to have favored an interpretation of the "personal" causes in terms of trait-like behavioral dispositions (for a corrective, see Malle, 2008).

The Statistical View of Interactionism

The trait–situation controversy faded partly owing to exhaustion of the participants, but also because psychologists began to consider a more interesting possibility that comes closer to Lewin's own position—that the personal and environmental determinants of behavior interacted with each other in a variety of ways (e.g., Endler & Magnusson, 1976a, 1976b; Magnusson & Endler, 1977). The modern Doctrine of Interactionism was formulated by K. S. Bowers in explicit response to the person–situation debate of the 1960s:

> An interactionist or biocognitive view denies the primacy of either traits or situations in the determination of behavior.... More specifically, interactionism argues that *situations are as much a function of the person as the person's behavior is a function of the situation.* (Bowers, 1973, p. 327)

In terms of Lewin's formula, interactionism holds that personal and situational factors are multiplicative: $B = f(P \times E)$. If P and E interact, the effect of the personality variable depends on the situation the person is in; and the effect of the situation depends on the kind of person who is in it (Figure 38.3). In Bowers's (1973) paper, and most other early interpretations, the concept of the person–situation interaction was modeled on the statistical analysis of variance (ANOVA), whereby independent variables influence dependent variables individually as main effects, or combined in interactions. The attraction of this model is evident in early statistical analyses of the power of interactions, including some cited by Bowers himself, which were all based on the ANOVA model.

Chief among these were studies based on the *S-R inventory* introduced in the 1960s by Endler and Hunt (1966; Endler, Hunt, & Rosenstein, 1962; Endler, 1975). These inventories, covering various aspects of personality, asked subjects to report how likely a particular situation would be to elicit an anxious response (for example), and also how likely they would be to display a *particular kind* of anxious

The Person–Situation Interaction

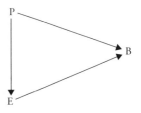

Figure 38.3 Schematic depiction of the person–situation interaction within the Lewinian framework (after Bowers, 1973).

response in each situation. When administered to a large group of subjects, the data generated by these inventories could be analyzed to yield estimates of the variance in anxiety (etc.) accounted for by various causal factors, including the *main effect of persons*, or individual differences in the generalized tendency to be anxious, collapsed across situations (and response modes); the *main effect of situations*, collapsed across persons (and, again, response modes), revealing the power of the situation; and the critical two-way *interaction of the person and the situation* (collapsed across response modes), indicating individual differences in the pattern of response across situations. (Of course, one could also calculate various other interactions, including the two-way interaction of the person and response mode, collapsing across situations; the two-way interaction of the situation and the response mode, collapsing across persons; and the three-way interaction of person, situation, and behavior.)

A study employing an S-R inventory of dominance illustrates the typical result of these studies (Dworkin & Kihlstrom, 1978). The main effect of persons accounted for approximately 10% of the variance in dominant behavior; the main effect of situations accounted for about 8%; and the critical person–situation interaction accounted for approximately 24% of variance. The 10% figure for persons, of course, is exactly what we would predict on the basis of Mischel's (1968) "personality coefficient." The 8% figure for situations, by contrast, is even lower than the estimate of situational variance provided by Funder and Ozer (1983). Most important in the present context, the person–situation interaction accounted for more than double the total population variance, compared with the amount accounted for by either persons or situations alone. Collectively, this pattern of results from S-R inventory studies, conducted in various domains, was taken as evidence that, indeed, the person–situation interaction is more powerful than either persons or situations taken in isolation—or, for that matter, the sum of persons and situations taken independently.

Readers of a certain age will recognize the S-R inventory technique as capturing the essence of the *aptitude-by-treatment interactions* (ATI) discussed by Cronbach (1957, 1975). Cronbach lamented the gulf between those psychologists who employed correlational techniques to predict behavior from individual differences and those who employed experimental manipulations to control behavior in different situations. Readers with clinical interests

will recognize the similarity to the diathesis-stress framework, in which environmental stressors precipitate episodes of mental illness, but only in those individuals who are "at risk" (Caspi & Moffitt, 2006; Fowles, 1992; Meehl, 1962; Monroe & Simons, 1991; D. Rosenthal, 1963; Zubin & Spring, 1977; Zuckerman, 1999). And those with educational interests will note the relevance of the proposal to match students' learning styles with teachers' instructional approaches (Pashler, McDaniel, Rohrer, & Bjork, 2009)—a proposal that, in turn, has its roots in the application of Jung's (1964) notion of psychological types to the problem of personnel selection, that is, of fitting the right person to the right job (Druckman & Porter, 1991).

The statistical view of interactionism continues to provide a framework for attempts to address the person–situation controversy. For example, Bem and Funder (1978) attempted to predict "more of the people more of the time" by matching personality descriptions to descriptions of the ideal person associated with a particular behavior in a particular situation (see also Bem, 1983; Bem & Lord, 1979; Mischel & Peake, 1982). In this way, situations are described in terms of the kind of person who would behave in a particular way in them, and the person–situation interaction is represented by the match between the person and this situation-specific template. More recently, Mischel and his colleagues have analyzed the person–situation interaction in terms of situation–behavior profiles of the following form: *If Person X is in Situation Y, then s/he will engage in Behavior Z* (Mendoza-Denton, Ayduk, Mischel, Shoda, & Testa, 2001; Mischel & Shoda, 1995; Mischel, Shoda, & Mendoza-Denton, 2002; Shoda, Tiernan, & Mischel, 2002). Across a wide variety of situations, then, different individuals would differ in terms of the pattern of their behavior, not just their overall level of friendliness, aggressiveness, or whatever.

Both Bem's and Mischel's proposals represent an advance over the S-R inventory technique and the ATI—with the major difference that they are intended to result in idiographic predictions of what particular people would do in various situations, rather than nomothetic assessments about the proportion of behavioral variance to be attributed to persons, situations, response modes, and their interactions. But all of these proposals, being based on the statistical concept of interaction, fail to capture the Lewinian point of view—that *persons are part of the situations to which they respond*—or, put another way, that *persons and situations together constitute a* unified field in which behavior takes place. In particular, the ANOVA model on which all of these proposals are based has no way of talking about precisely *how* persons create the situations to which they respond.

Reciprocal Determinism in the Lewinian Framework

Moreover, because the ANOVA model assumes that causality is unidirectional—that is, that it proceeds from independent variable to dependent variable—it misses the potential complexity of the underlying causal relations. These deficiencies are corrected by a further Doctrine of Reciprocal Determinism (Bandura, 1977b, 1978, 1983, 2004; Phillips & Orton, 1983), which states that:

> The person, the environment, and behavior exist in an interlocking relationship characterized by bidirectional causality.

In addition to persons shaping their environments, as in the Doctrine of Interactionism, environments also shape persons; personal factors influence behavior, but behavior also feeds back to change the person who engaged in it; environments elicit behavior, but behavior changes the environment in which it takes place.

The relations among the independence, interactionist, and reciprocal determinist views of the person–situation interaction are represented graphically in Figures 38.2 to 38.4. In Figure 38.2, personal and environmental factors were portrayed as acting independently to influence behavior; this is the traditional view separating personality and social psychology. Figure 38.3 retained these separate influences, but also included the influence of the person on the environment in which behavior takes place. Figure 38.4 portrays the full scope of reciprocal determinism, in which the person and the situation are fully interdependent entities. For

analytical purposes (and with apologies to Hegel and Marx), reciprocal determinism can be decomposed into what might be called the *three dialectics in social interaction*:

- The *Dialectic between the Person and Behavior* includes all of the influences of the person's internal states and dispositions (e.g., personality traits, social attitudes,[1] cognitions and beliefs, emotional states and moods, motives, and values) on his or her behavior—pretty much everything that is encompassed by traditional personality psychology, including analyses of the structure of personality traits and the prediction of behavior from trait assessments. But the dialectic also includes all the influences of behavior on the individual's mental states and dispositions, as exemplified by the James-Lange theory of emotion (Lang, 1994) and self-perception theory (Bem, 1967).

- The *Dialectic between the Environment and Behavior* includes all of the influences of the objective physical and social situation on the person's behavior, including the presence and behavior of other people—pretty much everything encompassed by the traditional psychology of social influence, according to Allport (1954), and exemplified by the Four As of social psychology—aggression, altruism, attitude change, and attraction. But the dialectic also includes the effects of behavior on the environment—beginning, but not ending, with Skinner's observation that all instrumental or operant behavior changes the environment in which it occurs (Skinner, 1935, 1937; see also Hilgard, 1948).

- The *Dialectic between the Person and the Environment* includes all of the different ways in which people influence the environments in which their behavior takes place (and which is what the Doctrine of Interactionism is all about); but it also includes the reciprocal influence of the environment on the person—as illustrated, for example, by much of the traditional social psychological research on persuasion and attitude change (Zimbardo & Leippe, 1991), as well as the mere exposure effect (Zajonc, 1965) and the automatic evocation of emotions by environmental stimuli (Ekman, 1972, 1999).

Spelled out this way, Lewin's formula looks less like a "grand truism," much less a rationale for treating personality and social psychology as independent disciplines, than a framework for the integration of personality and social psychology—with nothing left out.

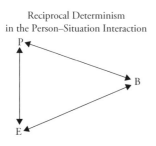

Reciprocal Determinism
in the Person–Situation Interaction

Figure 38.4 Schematic depiction of reciprocal determinism within the Lewinian framework (after Bandura, 1978).

How Do Persons Shape Their Environments?

The Doctrine of Interactionism asserts that people shape their environments, but raises the further question of how they actually accomplish this. In an important article, Buss summarized three ways in which people affect their own environments: evocation, selection, and behavioral manipulation (Buss, 1987, 2009). I will discuss each of these briefly, before turning to a fourth mode: cognitive transformation.

Evocation

The mere presence of a person in an environment alters that environment, independent of his or her traits and attitudes—and even in the absence of any behavior at all. In evocation, the physical appearance of the individual unintentionally evokes behavior from others—behavior that, in turn, changes the situation for the evoking person. A salient example of evocation is found in gender dimorphism, in which the physical appearance of a newborn's external genitalia literally structures the environment surrounding the child (e.g., Maccoby & Jacklin, 1974; Money & Ehrhardt, 1972). In the famous Baby X studies, infants were treated differently depending on whether they were identified as boys or girls, as opposed to their actual gender or anything they did (Seavey, Katz, & Zalk, 1975; Sidorowicz & Lunney, 1980). From the moment the neonate's gender is announced, parents and others in the social environment raise the child in accordance with prevailing cultural concepts of masculinity and femininity by communicating gender-typed expectations and by demanding, modeling, and reinforcing gender-typed behaviors.

Evocation is also exemplified by stereotyping and prejudice based on race, ethnicity (e.g., Dovidio & Gaertner, 1986), physical appearance (e.g., Snyder, Tanke, & Berscheid, 1977), and any other social category that is marked by physical attributes or other unconcealable stigmata (e.g., Goffman, 1963; Hinshaw & Stier, 2008; Jones et al., 1984; Link, Yang, Phelan, & Collins, 2004). Indeed, many aspects of intergroup relations seem to involve evocation as a central mechanism (e.g., Brewer, 2007; Wagner, Tropp, Finchilescu, & Tredoux, 2008; Yzerbyt, Judd, & Corneille, 2004). The mere presence of an outgroup member in an environment populated by ingroup members (or, for that matter, the reverse) can alter the environment by eliciting behavior from the ingroup members that would not occur but for the presence of the outgroup member.

Yet another example of evocation can be found in certain "child-driven" processes that help create within-family differences (Harris, 1995, 1999, 2006). Whether a child is male or female, conventionally good-looking, blemished, or disfigured, or looks like his parents can determine how he is treated by other people both inside and outside the family. And as the child ventures beyond the home to playgroups, school, sports programs, and the like, the child will continue to evoke behavior from peers and adults that effectively change the environment for that child—a process that, of course, can continue into adulthood.

Because the environment consists of other people, evocation effects are typically mediated by others' cognitive structures and processes, such as their beliefs and expectations. Every culture has conventional standards for masculinity and femininity, for example, even if these differ from the agency and communality that are familiar in Western cultures (Mead, 1935). But from the point of view of the person himself or herself, evocation is not concerned with how the environment is changed by that person's actions—whether intentional or unintentional. Such effects fall under the rubrics of selection and behavioral manipulation. The critical feature of evocation is that the evoking person need not actively *do* anything at all to change the situation. His or her mere presence, appearance, and social identification are sufficient to evoke behavior from others that changes the situation for everyone.

Selection

Although evolutionary psychology focuses on the selection of behavior *by* the environment, selection *of* the environment occurs as well. People are making choices all the time, and by virtue of some of those choices, they enter one environment as opposed to another. As a result, the match between the person and the environment is nonrandom. Individuals tend to choose environments that are congruent with their own personalities, supporting and promoting their own preferences and tendencies (Emmons, Diener, & Larsen, 1986). If gender-role socialization is the classic example of evocation, the classic example of selection may be one's choice of mate: people tend to marry people who are like themselves (Buss & Barnes, 1986); and, in furtherance of this tendency, contemporary dating websites tend to match potential partners on the basis of similarity in traits and attitudes. At the same time, behavior therapists teach us that one strategy for fostering personality *change* may be to choose to place oneself in a new environment that will support a new set of preferences and tendencies. Of course, sometimes the environment is selected *for* the person, as in arranged marriages, or personnel decisions (Arthur, Bell, Villado, & Doverspike, 2006); but at least in the latter case, people typically select the jobs for which they will be considered, and can refuse a job that does not seem to "fit" them. In any case, whether monumental or mundane, each such choice moves the person out of one environment and into another, pre-empting alternatives—with the result that the individual's behaviors will be constrained by an environment that is, to at least some extent, one of his or her own choosing.

Some accounts of the person–environment fit seem to relegate the person to a relatively passive role: a person with trait X will be happy in environment Y but unhappy in environment Z. From a cognitive point of view, however, such choices reflect active judgments and decisions on the part of the person making the selection (Hastie & Dawes, 2001). That the cognitive processes involved may be better described as judgment heuristics rather than the algorithms of normative rationality (Gigerenzer, Todd, & the ABC Research Group, 1999; Kahneman, Slovic, & Tversky, 1982) does not gainsay the basic point that the person is trying to figure out, under conditions of uncertainty, which available alternative to select. Nor does it matter if the selection is made on intuitive grounds, when the person cannot articulate the basis for his or her choice, or if the basis for the choice is emotional rather than "rational" (e.g., Haidt, 2001, 2002). Intuitions have long played a positive role in analyses of thinking and problem solving (Wallas, 1921; see also Dorfman, Shames, & Kihlstrom, 1996; Kihlstrom, Shames, & Dorfman, 1996). There may well be circumstances in which reason fails us, and we must rely on our emotional responses instead; but even in this case, emotion is information for cognition (Niedenthal & Showers, 1991).

(Behavioral) Manipulation

Sometimes, choices simply are not available; sometimes, choices are made for us by other people; and sometimes, our choices are the wrong ones. Finding ourselves in a particular environment, and unable to select a different one, we are nevertheless able to engage in overt behaviors that will modify the character of whatever environment we find ourselves in. As noted earlier, children can delay gratification longer if they choose to wait in the absence of the promised reward (Mischel & Ebbesen, 1970);

but those who must wait in the presence of a promised reward can also delay, if they deliberately avoid looking at the reward, distract themselves by playing with a toy, or create some other diversion for themselves—even simply putting their heads down on a table and covering their eyes (Mischel, Ebbesen, & Zeiss, 1972). By means of their overt behaviors, the children have created an environment in which the promised reward is out of sight.

As noted earlier, behavioral manipulation underlies all acts of instrumental or operant behavior, in which the organism's behavior operates on the environment, changing it in some way, so that it more closely conforms to its desires, goals, and purposes. The point seems so obvious that it may not warrant an empirical demonstration, but if one were needed it is provided by Kelley and Stahelski (Kelley & Stahelski, 1970), who pitted cooperative and competitive actors against cooperative and competitive partners in multiple trials of a prisoner's dilemma game. Cooperative actors paired with cooperative partners consistently made cooperative choices—by engaging in cooperative behavior, the two players created an environment in which cooperation was encouraged. Similarly, games that paired competitive actors with competitive partners quickly degenerated into a vicious cycle of "tit for tat" competition. Most interestingly, cooperative actors paired with competitive partners actually made fewer cooperative moves: Apparently, the competitive behavior of the partners created a situation that elicited competitive behavior from people who were not initially inclined to behave that way. Looking at it another way, competitive actors paired with cooperative partners made even fewer cooperative responses as the game went on: Apparently, the initially cooperative behavior of their partners created a situation in which the competitive actors could take advantage.

Other examples of the behavioral manipulation of the situation come from the literature on the self-fulfilling prophecy (Merton, 1948) and interpersonal expectancy effects in general (Darley & Fazio, 1980; Jones, 1986; Klein & Snyder, 2003; Miller & Turnbull, 1986; Rosenthal & Rubin, 1978; Snyder, 1984). As described by Merton, a perceiver, holding certain erroneous expectations, can behave in such a way as to elicit from the target behavior that confirms those expectations. Expectancy confirmation processes themselves come in two basic forms. In *behavioral confirmation*, the target's behavior objectively confirms the perceiver's expectations—even in the eyes of naïve observers who do not share these expectations. In *perceptual confirmation*, the target's behavior is actually vague and ambiguous, but is interpreted as consistent with the perceiver's expectations.

The process of expectancy confirmation was nicely demonstrated in a pair of experiments by Snyder and Swann. In both experiments, pairs of subjects were arbitrarily assigned to the role of actor or target, and the actor was given some sort of expectation about the target's personality. In a study of "getting acquainted," actors who believed that their targets were introverted (or extraverted) behaved in such a way as to elicit those very behaviors from their partners (Snyder & Swann, 1978b). And in a "noise gun" study, actors who believed that their partners were aggressive behaved in such a way as to elicit aggressive behavior from them (Snyder & Swann, 1978a).

Expectancy confirmation effects occur on two quite different levels (Darley & Fazio, 1980; Jones, 1986; Snyder, 1984). Merton's self-fulfilling prophecy exemplifies *behavioral* confirmation—in which the actor's expectations elicit behavior from the target that objectively confirms his or her expectations. As a result of behavioral confirmation, even unbiased observers, blind to the actor's expectations, will perceive the target the same way the actor does. But much social behavior is vague and ambiguous. In *perceptual* confirmation, the target's behavior is amenable to various interpretations. The actor will construe the target's behavior as confirming his or her expectations, but unbiased observers of the same behavior may draw quite different conclusions. Regardless of whether the confirmation is objective or subjective, the actor will continue to behave in a manner that is consistent with his or her expectancies, and interpret the target's behavior accordingly.

Eventually, we may suppose, perceptual confirmation will lead to behavioral confirmation—that is, unless targets themselves engage in behavior that breaks the cycle of expectancy confirmation. Fortunately, targets are not merely passive recipients of the actors' behavior. They are perfectly capable of shaping the environment, through their own behavior, so as to counteract the actors' expectations and reaffirm their self-concepts—a process variously known as impression management, strategic self-presentation, or self-verification (Goffman, 1959; Jones, 1964; Swann, 1987; Swann & Ely, 1984). Both the actor and the target are continually creating, through their overt behavior, the environment to which the other is responding.

The distinction between behavioral and perceptual confirmation effects, and between expectancy confirmation and self-verification, makes it clear that many acts of behavioral manipulation are cognitively mediated—through the expectancies that guide the perceiver's behavior, the self-concept that guides the target's response, and the schemata that filter the perceiver's interpretation of the target's behavior. However, the behavior that shapes a situation need not be deliberately instrumental, or even under conscious control. Consider, for example, individual differences in temperament, leading a child to be relatively quiet or fussy, which in turn lead parents to engage in "upper-limit" or "lower-limit" control behaviors (Harris, 1995, 1999). Here, the child's behavior is eliciting parental behavior that effectively shapes the environment of the child, but the behavior that gets the process going is entirely unintentional on the child's part. Similarly, overly active and aggressive children may elicit contagious or countervailing behavior from other children that increases the amount of activity and aggression in the environment (Dodge & Pettit, 2004).[2]

Expectancy confirmation effects are, presumably, instigated by more or less conscious percepts and thoughts. Other behaviors may be automatically activated by environmental stimuli (Bargh, 1997; but see Kihlstrom, 2008). Viewed in isolation, such effects might be counted as effects of the environment on behavior. But we now understand, from Lewin by way of Bandura, that such effects should never be viewed in isolation—rather, they are part of a continuously interacting field consisting of the person, the environment, and behavior. When automatically evoked behaviors reciprocally shape the environment that evoked them, they also count as examples of the behavioral manipulation of the situation. Thus, the automatic mimicry of a smiling or scowling face (Dimberg, Thunberg, & Elmehed, 2000) might help create an environment in which lots of people are smiling or scowling. Furthermore, if the facial action feeds back to the person himself or herself, it can also help the person to *feel* happy or angry (Strack, Martin, & Stepper, 1988; Tomkins, 1962–1963)—creating, perhaps, a magnified facial expression of happiness or anger that starts the whole cycle over again.

(Cognitive) Transformation

Evocation, selection, and manipulation all change the objective environment through overt behavior—either the behavior of the person himself or herself, or that of other people. In each case, someone does something overtly that changes the objective character of the environment—that is, changes the environment for everyone in it, not just for the person himself or herself. But these three modes do not exhaust the effects of the person on the environment. People also engage in *covert* mental activities that alter their *mental representations* of their subjective environment—that is, the environment as they privately experience it. As opposed to behavioral manipulation, cognitive transformation does not act directly on the objective environment—the environment as it would be described in the third person by an objective observer, and experienced by everyone in it. Rather, transformation acts on the *subjective mental representation* of the environment. Through cognitive transformations, people can change their internal, mental representations of the external physical and social environment—perceiving it differently, categorizing it differently, giving it a different meaning than before. In cognitive transformation, the objective features of the environment remain intact—they have not been altered through evocation, selection, and manipulation. Rather, the cognitive transformation has altered the environment *for that person only*. The environment is unchanged for everyone else—unless and until the cognitive transformation leads the person to engage in selective and manipulative behavior that, as described earlier, will change the environment for everyone in it.

As an illustration of the power of cognitive transformation, consider one last experiment on delay of gratification (Mischel & Baker, 1975). Earlier studies had shown that children could wait longer in the presence of a reward if they avoided looking at the reward, or actively distracted themselves from it. But in this study, waiting improved if the children *thought* about marshmallows as cotton balls, or pretzels as Lincoln Logs—as opposed to focusing on the taste and texture of the promised treats. Another is provided by the "*n* effect" of group size on task performance. From the earliest days of experimental social psychology (Triplett, 1898; but see Strube, 2005), it has been thought that the mere presence of an audience can have marked effects, for better or worse, on an individual's task performance (Zajonc, 1965; see also Latane, 1981). Taken by itself, this is a clear example of the effect of the social environment on behavior. But it turns out that a similar effect can occur when a person *believes* that other people are present, even when they are not (Garcia

& Tor, 2009). It is the mental representation of other people, whether in perception or imagination, that is the critical element.

Social Cognition and Personality

Traditional approaches to personality and social psychology are predicated on a separation between the person and the situation. But social cognition dissolves this divide. People's social interactions are determined by their mental representations of the situation: what they pay attention to; how they perceive and categorize the people, places, and events they encounter; what they remember of past events in similar situations, and how they remember them; their long-term goals and momentary intentions; their fund of declarative knowledge about themselves, their interaction partners, and the social world in general; their procedural repertoire of skills and rules for understanding other people's mental states, making ethical moral judgments about their own and others' behavior, and managing various other aspects of social intercourse. The cognitive structures and processes by which a person constructs his or her mental representation of the social situation are part and parcel of that individual's personality. Understanding them is critical to understanding the person as he or she navigates the real world of social interaction.

Notes

1. Of course, attitudes of all sorts have been part of the traditional domain of social psychology (McGuire, 1986). For the purposes of this analysis, however, attitudes are construed as intrapsychic constructs—dispositions to like or dislike things, much as traits are dispositions to behave in particular ways Allport, 1937). This is why there was a controversy over the relations between attitudes and behavior (Sherman & Fazio, 1983) paralleling the debate over the prediction of behavior from personality traits.

2. Buss (1987) classified effects such as these as examples of evocation, but I prefer to limit evocation to effects on the environment that are unrelated to the person's behavior, and are driven solely by his or her mere presence or appearance (and whatever stereotypes the perceiver carries in his head).

References

Allport, G. W. (1937). *Personality: A psychological interpretation.* New York: Holt, Rinehart, & Winston.

Allport, G. W. (1954). The historical background of social psychology. In G. Lindzey & E. Aronson (Eds.), *Handbook of social psychology* (Vol. 1, pp. 1–46). New York: Random House.

Arthur, W., Bell, S. T., Villado, A. J., & Doverspike, D. (2006). The use of person-organization fit in employment decision making: An assessment of its criterion-related validity. *Journal of Applied Psychology, 91*(4), 786–801.

Asch, S. E. (1946). Forming impressions of personality. *Journal of Abnormal & Social Psychology, 41,* 3258–290.

Bandura, A. (1977a). Self-efficacy: Toward a unifying theory of behavioral change. *Psychological Review, 84*(2), 191–215.

Bandura, A. (1977b). Social learning theory. Englewood Cliffs, NJ: Prentice-Hall.

Bandura, A. (1978). The self system in reciprocal determinism. *American Psychologist, 33,* 344–358.

Bandura, A. (1983). Temporal dynamics and decomposition of reciprocal determinism: A reply to Phillips and Orton. *Psychological Review, 90,* 166–170.

Bandura, A. (1986). *Social foundations of thought and action: A social cognitive theory.* Englewood Cliffs, NJ: Prentice-Hall.

Bandura, A. (2004). Model of causality in social learning theory. In A. Freeman, M. J. Mahoney, P. DeVito & D. J. Martin (Eds.), *Cognition in psychotherapy* (2nd ed.). New York: Springer.

Bandura, A., & Walters, R. H. (1963). *Social learning and personality development.* New York: Holt, Rinehart & Winston.

Bargh, J.A.. (1997). The automaticity of everyday life. In R. S. Wyer (Ed.), *Advances in social cognition* (Vol. 10, pp. 1–61). Mahwah, NJ: Erlbaum.

Bargh, J. A., & Chartrand, T. L. (1999). The unbearable automaticity of being. *American Psychologist, 54*(7), 462–479.

Bartlett, F. C. (1932). *Remembering: A study in experimental and social psychology.* Cambridge, UK: Cambridge University Press.

Bem, D. J. (1967). Self-perception: An alternative interpretation of cognitive dissonance phenomena. *Psychological Review, 74*(3), 183–200.

Bem, D. J. (1983). Further deja vu in the search for cross-situational consistency: A response to Mischel and Peake. *Psychological Review, 90,* 390–393.

Bem, D. J., & Funder, D. C. (1978). Predicting more of the people more of the time: Assessing the personality of situations. *Psychological Review, 85*(485–501).

Bem, D. J., & Lord, C. G. (1979). Template matching: A proposal for probing the ecological validity of experimental settings in social psychology. *Journal of Personality and Social Psychology, 1979*(37).

Blumer, H. (1937). Social disorganization and individual disorganization. *American Journal of Sociology, 42*(6), 871–877.

Blumer, H. (1969). *Symbolic interactionism: Perspective and method.* Berkeley, CA: University of California Press.

Blumer, H. (1980). Mead and Blumer: The convergent methodological perspectives of social behaviorism and symbolic interactionism. *American Sociological Review, 45*(3), 409–419.

Boring, E. G. (1950). *A history of experimental psychology* (2nd ed.). New York: Appleton-Century-Crofts.

Bowers, K. M. S. (1973). Situationism in psychology: Analysis and a critique. *Psychological Review, 80,* 307–336.

Brewer, B. (2007). The social psychology of intergroup relations: Social categorization, ingroup bias, and outgroup prejudice. In E. T. H. A. W. Kruglanski (Ed.), *Social psychology: Handbook of basic principles* (2nd ed., pp. 695–715). New York: Guilford.

Bruner, J., & Tagiuri, R. (1954). Person perception. In G. Lindzey (Ed.), *Handbook of social psychology* (Vol. 2, pp. 634–654). Reading, MA: Addison-Wesley.

Buss, D. M. (1987). Selection, evocation, and manipulation. *Journal of Personality & Social Psychology, 53,* 1214–1221.

Buss, D. M. (2009). An evolutionary formulation of person-situation interactions. *Journal of Research in Personality, 43*(2), 241–242.

Buss, D. M., & Barnes, M. (1986). Preferences in human mate selection. *Journal of Personality & Social Psychology, 50,* 559–570.

Cantor, N., & Kihlstrom, J. F. (1981). *Personality, cognition, and social interaction.* Hillsdale, NJ: Erlbaum.

Cantor, N., & Kihlstrom, J. F. (1987). *Personality and social intelligence.* Englewood Cliffs, NJ: Prentice-Hall.

Caspi, A., & Moffitt, T. E. (2006). Gene-environment interactions in psychiatry: Joining forces with neuroscience. *Nature Reviews Neuroscience, 7*(7), 583–590.

Cattell, R. B. (1940). The description of personality: I. Foundations of trait measurement. *Psychological Review, 50,* 559–594.

Craik, K. H. (1993). The 1937 Allport and Stagner texts in personality psychology. In K. H. Craik, R. Hogan & R. N. Wolfe (Eds.), *Fifty years of personality psychology* (pp. 3–20). New York: Plenum.

Crano, W. D. (1988). Whatever became of Kurt Lewin? Reactions to Nuttin's quasi-social analysis of social behaviour. *European Journal of Social Psychology, 19*(5), 385–388.

Cronbach, L. J. (1955). Processes affecting scores on "understanding of others" and "assumed similarity." *Psychological Bulletin, 52,* 177–193.

Cronbach, L. J. (1957). The two disciplines of scientific psychology. *American Psychologist, 12,* 671–684.

Cronbach, L. J. (1975). Beyond the two disciplines of scientific psychology. *American Psychologist, 30,* 116–127.

Darley, J. M., & Fazio, H. R. (1980). Expectancy confirmation processes arising in the social interaction sequence. *American Psychologist, 35,* 867–881.

Darley, J. M., & Latane, B. (1968). Bystander intervention in emergencies: Diffusion of responsibility. *Journal of Personality & Social Psychology, 46,* 991–1004.

Dimberg, U., Thunberg, M., & Elmehed, K. (2000). Unconscious facial reactions to emotional facial expressions. *Psychological Science, 11*(1), 86–89.

Dodge, K. A., & Pettit, G. S. (2004). A biopsychosocial model of the development of chronic conduct problems in adolescence. *Developmental Psychology, 39*(2), 349–371.

Dollard, J., & Miller, N. E. (1950). *Personality and psychotherapy: An analysis in terms of learning, thinking and culture.* New York: McGraw-Hill.

Dorfman, J., Shames, A. V., & Kihlstrom, J. F. (1996). Intuition, incubation, and insight: Implicit cognition in problem solving. In G. Underwood (Ed.), *Implicit cognition.* (pp. 257–296). Oxford, UK: Oxford University Press.

Dovidio, J. F., & Gaertner, S. L. (Eds.). (1986). *Prejudice, discrimination, and racism.* San Diego: Academic.

Druckman, D., & Porter, L. W. (1991). Developing careers. In D. Druckman & R. A. Bjork (Eds.), *In the mind's eye: Enhancing human performance* (pp. 80–103). Washington, DC: National Academies Press.

Dworkin, R. H., & Kihlstrom, J. F. (1978). An S-R inventory of dominance for research on the nature of person-situation interactions. *Journal of Personality, 46*(1), 43–56.

Ekman, P. (1972). Universals and cultural differences in facial expressions of emotions. In J. Cole (Ed.), *Nebraska symposium on motivation, 1971* (pp. 207–283). Lincoln, NE: University of Nebraska Press.

Ekman, P. (1999). Basic emotions. In T. Dalgleish & M. Power (Eds.), *Handbook of cognition and emotion.* Sussex, UK: Wiley.

Emmons, R. A., Diener, E., & Larsen, R. J. (1986). Choice and avoidance of everyday situations and affect congruence: Two models of reciprocal interactionism. *Journal of Personality & Social Psychology, 51,* 815–826.

Endler, N. S. (1975). The case for person-situation interactions. *Canadian Psychological Review, 16,* 12–21.

Endler, N. S., & Hunt, J. M. (1966). Sources of behavioral variance as measured by the S-R Inventory of Anxiousness. *Psychological Bulletin, 65,* 336–346.

Endler, N. S., Hunt, J. M., & Rosenstein, A. J. (1962). An S-R Inventory of Anxiousness. *Psychological Monographs,* 76(17, Whole No. 536), Whole No. 536.

Endler, N. S., & Magnusson, D. (1976a). Toward an interactional psychology of personality. *Psychological Bulletin, 83,* 956–974.

Endler, N. S., & Magnusson, D. (Eds.). (1976b). *Interactional psychology and personality.* Hillsdale, NJ: Erlbaum.

Fowles, D. C. (1992). Schizophrenia: Diathesis-stress revisited. *Annual Review of Psychology, 43,* 303–336.

Funder, D. C., & Block, J. (1989). The role of ego-control, ego-resiliency, and IQ in delay of gratification in adolescence. *Journal of Personality and Social Psychology,* 57(6), 1041–1050.

Funder, D. C., Block, J. H., & Block, J. (1983). Delay of gratification: Some longitudinal personality correlates. *Journal of Personality & Social Psychology,* 44(6), 1198–1213.

Funder, D. C., & Ozer, D. J. (1983). Behavior as a function of the situation. *Journal of Personality & Social Psychology, 44,* 107–112.

Garcia, S. M., & Tor, A. (2009). The N-effect: More competitors, less competition. *Psychological Science,* 20(871–877).

Gardner, H. (1983). *Frames of mind: the theory of multiple intelligences.* New York: Basic Books.

Gardner, H. (1999). *Intelligence reframed: Multiple intelligences for the 21st century.* New York: Basic Books.

Gigerenzer, G., Todd, P. M., & the ABC Research Group. (1999). *Simple heuristics that make us smart.* New York: Oxford University Press.

Goffman, E. (1959). *The presentation of self in everyday life.* Garden City, NY: Doubleday.

Goffman, E. (1963). *Stigma: Notes on the management of spoiled identity.* Englewood Cliffs, NJ: Prentice-Hall.

Goldberg, L. R. (1992). The social psychology of personality. *Psychological Inquiry, 3,* 89–94.

Goleman, D. (2006). *Social intelligence: The new science of human relationships.* New York: Bantam Books.

Haggbloom, S. J., Warnick, R., Warnick, J. E., Jones, V. K., Yarbrough,. G L., Russell, T. M., et al. (2002). The 100 most eminent psychologists of the 20th century. *Review of General Psychology,* 6(2), 139–152.

Haidt, J. (2001). The emotional dog and its rational tail: A social intuitionist approach to moral judgment. *Psychological Review,* 108(4), 814–834.

Haidt, J. (2002). "Dialogue between my head and my heart": Affective influences on moral judgment. *Psychological Inquiry,* 13(1), 54–56.

Hall, C. S., Lindzey, G., & Campbell, J. B. (1998). *Theories of personality* (4th ed.). New York: Wiley.

Harris, J. R. (1995). Where is the child's environment? A group socialization theory of development. *Psychological Review,* 102(3), 458–489.

Harris, J. R. (1999). *The nurture assumption: Why children turn out the way they do* (pb ed.). New York: Touchstone.

Harris, J. R. (2006). *No two alike: Human nature and human individuality.* New York: Norton.

Hastie, R., & Dawes, R. M. (2001). *Rational choice in an uncertain world: The psychology of judgment and decision making.* Thousand Oaks, CA: Sage.

Hastie, R., Ostrom, T. M., Ebbesen, E. B., Wyer, R. S., Hamilton, D. L., & Carlston, D. E. (Eds.). (1980). *Person memory: The cognitive basis of social perception.* Hillsdale, NJ: Erlbaum.

Heider, F. (1944). Social perception and phenomenal causality. *Psychological Review, 51,* 358–371.

Heider, F. (1958). *The psychology of interpersonal relations.* New York: Wiley.

Higgins, E. T., Zanna, M. P., & Herman, C. P. (Eds.). (1981). *Social cognition: The Ontario Symposium* (Vol. 1). Hillsdale, NJ: Erlbaum.

Hilgard, E. R. (1948). *Theories of learning.* New York: Appleton-Century-Crofts.

Hinshaw, S. P., & Stier, A. (2008). Stigma in relation to mental illness. *Annual Review of Clinical Psychology, 4,* 269–293.

Jones, E. E. (1964). *Ingratiation, a social psychological analysis.* New York: Appleton-Century-Crofts.

Jones, E. E. (1985). Major developments in social psychology since 1930. In G. Lindzey & E. Aronson (Eds.), *Handbook of social psychology* (2nd ed., Vol. 1, pp. 47–107). Reading, MA: Addison-Wesley.

Jones, E. E. (1986). Interpreting interpersonal behavior: The effects of expectancies. *Science, 234,* 41–46.

Jones, E. E., Farrina, A., Hastorf, A. H., Markus, H., Miller, D. T., & Scott, R. A. (1984). Social stigma: The psychology of marked relationships. New York: Freeman.

Jung, C. G. (1964). *Psychological types: Or, the psychology of the individual.* New York: Pantheon.

Kahneman, D., Slovic, P., & Tversky, A. (1982). *Judgment under uncertainty: Heuristics and biases.* Cambridge, UK: Cambridge University Press.

Kelley, H. H., & Stahelski, A. J. (1970). Social interaction basis of cooperators' and competitors' beliefs. *Journal of Personality & Social Psychology, 16,* 66–91.

Kelly, G. (1955). *The psychology of personal constructs.* New York: Norton.

Kelly, G. (1958/1969). Man's construction of his alternatives. In B. A. Maher (Ed.), *Clinical psychology and personality: Selected papers of George Kelly* (pp. 66–93). New York: Wiley.

Kenrick, D. T., & Funder, D. C. (1988). Profiting from controversy: Lessons from the person-situation debate. *American Psychologist,* 43 (1), 25–34.

Kihlstrom, J. F. (1986). More on determinants of delay of gratification. *American Psychologist,* 41(4), 477–479.

Kihlstrom, J. F. (2002). Demand characteristics in the laboratory and the clinic: Conversations and collaborations with subjects and patients. *Prevention & Treatment [Special issue honoring Martin T. Orne],* 5(1), Article 36c.

Kihlstrom, J. F. (2008). The automaticity juggernaut. In J. Baer, J. C. Kaufman & R. F. Baumeister (Eds.), *Psychology and free will* (pp. 155–180). New York: Oxford University Press.

Kihlstrom, J. F., & Cantor, N. (2011). Social intelligence. In R. J. Sternberg (Ed.), *Handbook of intelligence.* (3rd ed., pp. 564–581). New York: Cambridge University Press.

Kihlstrom, J. F., Shames, V. A., & Dorfman, J. (1996). Intimations of memory and thought. In L. M. Reder (Ed.), *Implicit memory and metacognition* (pp. 1–23). Mahwah, NJ: Erlbaum.

Klein, O., & Snyder, M. (20003). Stereotypes and behavioral confirmation: From interpersonal to intergroup perspectives.

In M. P. Zanna (Ed.), *Advances in experimental social psychology* (Vol. 35, pp. 153–234). San Diego: Elsevier.

Krech, D., & Crutchfield, R. S. (1948). *Theory and problems of social psychology*. New York: McGraw-Hill.

Krech, D., Crutchfield, R. S., & Ballachey, E. L. (1962). *Individual in society: A textbook of social psychology*. New York: McGraw-Hill.

Landy, F. J. (2006). The long, frustrating and fruitless search for social intelligence: A cautionary tale. In K. R. Murphy (Ed.), *A critique of emotional intelligence: What are the problems and how can they be fixed?* (pp. 81–123). Mahwah, NJ: Erlbaum.

Lang, P. J. (1994). The varieties of emotional experience: A meditation on James-Lange theory. *Psychological Review, 101*, 211–221.

Latane, B. (1981). The psychology of social impact. *American Psychologist, 36*, 343–356.

Lewin, K. (1931/1935). The conflict between Aristotelian and Galilean modes of thought in contemporary psychology. In L. K. (Ed.), *A dynamic theory of personality* (pp. 1–42). New York: McGraw-Hill.

Lewin, K. (1935). *A dynamic theory of personality*. New York: McGraw-Hill.

Lewin, K. (1939/1951). Field theory and experiment in social psychology: Concepts and methods. In K. Lewin (Ed.), *Field theory in social science* (pp. 130–154). New York: Harper & Row.

Lewin, K. (1946/1951). Behavior and development as a function of the total situation. In K. Lewin (Ed.), *Field theory in social science* (pp. 238–305). New York: Harper & Row.

Lewin, K. (1951). *Field theory in social science*. New York: McGraw-Hill.

Lieberman, M. D. (2005). Principles, processes, and puzzles of social cognition: An introduction for the special issue on social cognitive neuroscience. *NeuroImage, 28*, 745–756.

Link, B. G., Yang, L. H., Phelan, J. C., & Collins, P. Y. (2004). Measuring mental illness stigma. *Schizophrenia Bulletin, 30*(3), 511–541.

Maccoby, E. E., & Jacklin, C. N. (1974). *The psychology of sex differences*. Sanford, CA: Stanford University Press.

Magnusson, D., & Endler, N. S. (Eds.). (1977). *Personality at the crossroads: Current issues in interactional psychology*. Hillsdale, NJ: Erlbaum.

Maher, B. A. (Ed.). (1968). *Clinical psychology and personality: The selected papers of George Kelly*. New York: Wiley.

Malle, B. F. (2008). Fritz Heider's legacy: Celebrated insights, many of them misunderstood. *Social Psychology, 39*(3), 163–173.

McGuire, W. J. (1986). The vicissitudes of attitudes and similar representational constructs in twentieth century psychology. *European Journal of Social Psychology, 16*, 89–130.

Mead, G. H. (1934). *Mind, self, and society*. Chicago: University of Chicago Press.

Mead, M. (1935). *Sex and temperament in three primitive societies*. London: Routledge.

Meehl, P. E. (1962). Schizotaxia, schizotypy, schizophrenia. *American Psychologist, 17*, 827–838.

Mendoza-Denton, R., Ayduk, O., Mischel, W., Shoda, Y., & Testa, A. (2001). Person x situation interactionism in self-encoding (I am…when…): Implications for affect regulation and social information processing. *Journal of Personality & Social Psychology, 80*, 533–544.

Merton, R. K. (1948). The self-fulfilling prophecy. *Antioch Review, 8*, 193–210.

Merton, R. K. (1976). Social knowledge and public policy. In *Sociological ambivalence* (pp. 156–179). New York: Simon & Schuster.

Merton, R. K. (1995). The Thomas theorem and the Matthew effect. *Social Forces, 74*(2), 379–424.

Milgram, S. (1963). Behavioral study of obedience. *Journal of Abnormal & Social Psychology, 67*(4), 371–378.

Miller, D. T., & Turnbull, W. (1986). Expectancies and interpersonal processes. *Annual Review of Psychology, 37*, 233–256.

Miller, N. E., & Dollard, J. (1941). *Social learning and imitation*. New Haven, CT: Yale University Press.

Mischel, W. (1968). *Personality and assessment*. New York: Wiley.

Mischel, W. (1973). Toward a cognitive social learning reconceptualization of personality. *Psychological Review, 80*(4), 252–253.

Mischel, W., & Baker, N. (197/5). Cognitive appraisals and transformations in delay behavior. *Journal of Personality and Social Psychology, 31*(2), 254–261.

Mischel, W., & Ebbesen, E. B. (1970). Attention in delay of gratification. *Journal of Personality & Social Psychology, 16*(2), 329–337.

Mischel, W., Ebbesen, E. B., & Zeiss, A. (1972). Cognitive and attentional mechanisms in delay of gratification. *Journal of Personality & Social Psychology, 21*(2), 204–218.

Mischel, W., & Peake, P. K. (1982). Beyond deja vu in the search for cross situational consistency. *Psychological Review, 89*, 730–735.

Mischel, W., & Shoda, Y. (1995). A cognitive-affective system theory of personality: Reconceptualizing situations, dispositions, dynamics, and invariance in personality structure. *Psychological Review, 102*, 246–268.

Mischel, W., Shoda, Y., & Mendoza-Denton, R. (2002). Situation-behavior profiles as a locus of consistency in personality. *Current Directions in Psychological Science, 11*(2), 50–53.

Money, J., & Ehrhardt, A. A. (1972). *Man and woman, boy and girl: The differentiation and dimorphism of gender identity from conception to maturity*. Baltimore, MD: Johns Hopkins University Press.

Monroe, S. M., & Simons, A. D. (1991). Diathesis-stress theories in the context of life stress research: Implications for the depressive disorders. *Psychological Bulletin, 110*, 406–425.

Murray, H. A. (Ed.). (1938). *Explorations in personality*. New York: Oxford University Press.

Newcomb, T. M. (1929). *The consistency of certain extrovert-introvert behavior patterns in 51 problem boys*. New York: Teachers College of Columbia University.

Niedenthal, P. M., & Showers, C. (1991). The perception and processing of affective information and its influences on social judgment. In J. P. Forgas (Ed.), *Emotion and social judgments* (pp. 125–143). Elmsford, NY: Pergamon.

Orne, M. T. (1962). On the social psychology of the psychological experiment: With particular reference to demand characteristics and their implications. *American Psychologist, 17*, 776–783.

Pashler, H., McDaniel, M. A., Rohrer, D., & Bjork, R. A. (2009). Learning styles: Concepts and evidence. *Psychological Science in the Public Interest, 9*, 105–119.

Phillips, D. C., & Orton, R. (1983). The new causal principle of cognitive learning theory: Perspectives on Bandura's "reciprocal determinism." *Psychological Review, 90*, 158–165.

Rosenthal, D. (1963). A suggested conceptual framework. In D. Rosenthal (Ed.), *The Genain quadruplets*. New York: Basic.

Rosenthal, R. (1963). On the social psychology of the psychological experiment: The experimenter's hypothesis as unintended determinant of experimental results. *American Scientist, 51,* 270–282.

Rosenthal, R., & Rubin, D. B. (1978). Interpersonal expectancy effects: The first 345 studies. *Behavioral & Brain Sciences, 3,* 377–415.

Ross, L., & Nisbett, R. E. (1991). *The person and the situation: Perspectives of social psychology.* Philadelphia: Temple University Press.

Rotter, J. B. (1954). *Social learning and clinical psychology.* Englewood Cliffs, NJ: Prentice-Hall.

Scheerer, M. (1954). Cognitive theory. In G. Lindzey (Ed.), *Handbook of social psychology* (pp. 91–142). Cambridge, MA: Addison-Wesley.

Seavey, C. A., Katz, P. A., & Zalk, S. R. (1975). Baby X: The effect of gender labels on adult responses to infants. *Sex Roles, 1,* 103–109.

Sherman, S. J., & Fazio, R. H. (1983). Parallels between attitudes and traits as predictors of behavior. *Journal of Personality, 51,* 308–345.

Shoda, Y., Tiernan, S. L., & Mischel, W. (2002). Personality as a dynamical system: Emergence of stability and distinctiveness from intra- and interpersonal interactions. *Personality & Social Psychology Review, 6,* 316–325.

Sidorowicz, L. S., & Lunney, G. S. (1980). Baby X revisited. *Sex Roles, 6,* 67–73.

Skinner, B. F. (1935). Two types of conditioned reflex and a pseudo type. *Journal of General Psychology, 12,* 66–77.

Skinner, B. F. (1937). Two types of conditioned reflex: A reply to Miller and Konorski. *Journal of General Psychology, 16,* 272–279.

Skinner, B. F. (1953). *Science and human behavior.* New York: Macmillan.

Snow, C. P. (1963). *The two cultures and the scientific revolution.* Cambridge, UK: Cambridge University Press.

Snyder, M. (1984). When belief creates reality. In L. Berkowitz (Ed.), *Advances in experimental social psychology* (Vol. 18, pp. 247–305). New York: Academic Press.

Snyder, M., & Swann, W. B. (1978a). Behavioral confirmation in social interaction: From social perception to social reality. *Journal of Experimental Social Psychology, 14,* 148–162.

Snyder, M., & Swann, W. B. (1978b). Hypothesis-testing processes in social interaction. *Journal of Personality & Social Psychology, 36,* 1202–1212.

Snyder, M., Tanke, E. D., & Berscheid, E. (1977). Social perception and interpersonal behavior: On the self-fulfilling nature of social stereotypes. *Journal of Personality & Social Psychology, 35,* 656–666.

Staats, A. W., & Staats, C. K. (1963). *Complex human behavior: A systematic extension of learning principles.* New York: Holt, Rinehart & Winston.

Stagner, R. (1937). *Psychology of personality.* New York: McGraw-Hill.

Strack, F., Martin, L., & Stepper, S. (1988). Inhibiting and facilitating conditions of the human smile: A nonobtrusive test of the facial feedback hypothesis. *Journal of Personality & Social Psychology, 54,* 768–777.

Strube, M. J. (2005). What did Triplett really find? A contemporary analysis of the first experiment in social psychology. *American Journal of Psychology, 118*(2), 271–286.

Swann, W. B. (1987). Identity negotiation: Where two roads meet. *Journal of Personality & Social Psychology, 53*(6), 1038–1051.

Swann, W. B., & Ely, R. J. (1984). A battle of wills: Self-verification versus behavioral confirmation. *Journal of Personality & Social Psychology, 46,* 1287–1302.

Tagiuri, R., & Petrullo, L. (Eds.). (1958). *Person perception and interpersonal behavior.* Stanford, CA: Stanford University Press.

Thomas, W. I., & Thomas, D. S. (1928). *The child in America: Behavior problems and programs.* New York: Knopf.

Thorndike, E. L. (1920). Intelligence and its use. *Harper's Magazine, 140,* 227–235.

Tomkins, S. S. (1962–1963). *Affect, imagery, and consciousness.* New York: Springer.

Triplett, N. T. (1898). The dynamogenic factors in pacemaking and competition. *American Journal of Psychology, 9,* 507–533.

Wagner, U., Tropp, L. R., Finchilescu, G., & Tredoux, C. (Eds.). (2008). *Improving intergroup relations: Building on the legacy of Thomas F. Pettigrew.* Malden, MA: Blackwell.

Wallas, G. (1921). *The art of thought.* New York: Harcourt Brace.

Wolf, B. (1986). Theoretical positions of Kurt Lewin and Ego Brunswik: Controversial or complementary points of view? In E. Stivers & S. Wheelan (Eds.), *The Lewin legacy: Field theory in current practice* (pp. 40–51w). Berlin: Springer-Verlag.

Woodworth, R. S. (1929). *Psychology: A study of mental life* (2nd ed.). New York: Holt.

Wyer, R. S., & Carlston, D. E. (1979). *Social cognition, inference, and attribution.* Hillsdale, NJ: Erlbaum.

Yzerbyt, V., Judd, C. M., & Corneille, O. (Eds.). (2004). *The psychology of group perception: Perceived variability, entitativity, and essentialism.* New York: Oxford University Press.

Zajonc, R. B. (1965). Social facilitation. *Science, 149,* 269–274.

Zayas, V., Shoda, Y., & Ayduk, O. N. (2002). Personality in context: An interpersonal systems perspective. *Journal of Personality, 70*(6), 851–900.

Zimbardo, P. G. (1999). Experimental social psychology: Behaviorism with minds and matters. In A. Rodrigues & R. V. Levine (Eds.), *Reflections on 100 years of experimental social psychology* (pp. 135–157). New York: Basic Books.

Zimbardo, P. G., & Leippe, M. R. (1991). *The psychology of attitude change and social influence.* New York: McGraw-Hill.

Zubin, J., & Spring, B. (1977). Vulnerability: A new view of schizophrenia. *Psychological Review, 86,* 103–126.

Zuckerman, M. (1999). Diathesis-stress models. In M. Zuckerman (Ed.), *Vulnerability to psychopathology: A biosocial model* (pp. 2–23). Washington, DC: American Psychological Association.

Consumer Information Processing

Frank R. Kardes *and* Robert S. Wyer Jr.

Abstract

Many of the principles that underlie consumer judgment and decision making are similar to those that have been identified in research on social information processing. However, unique considerations arise in applying them. Eight general principles that cut across both domains are identified, pertaining to cognitive efficiency, knowledge accessibility, persistence, awareness, the role of implicit theories, communication norms, subjective reactions, and information integration. Consumer behavior in a variety of domains is then discussed within the framework of these principles, emphasizing comprehension, categorization, the cognitive and motivational influence of subjective reactions, inference processes, and consumer decision processes.

Key Words: consumer judgment, decision making, inference, information processing

Enormous resources are spent attempting to predict and explain the responses of consumers to marketing activities. These responses have important implications for the competitiveness of for-profit and not-for-profit organizations, consumer well-being and public policy, and economic growth and development. The consumer psychological literature contains a great deal of research bearing on the effects of marketing variables (i.e., product design and features, price, promotion and advertising, distribution and retailing) on consumer attention, comprehension, memory, judgment, and decision making. The information processing framework provides a useful tool for organizing and integrating these findings, and unsurprisingly, many formulations of social information processing have traditionally guided research in consumer information processing.

As the field of consumer research has matured, however, it has become clear that although many of the theoretical and empirical questions addressed in social psychology are relevant to consumer

psychology as well, the *answers* to these questions are often quite different. Moreover, the blind application of social psychological theory and methodology in the consumer domain can lead to inappropriate conclusions (Wyer & Adaval, 2008). At the same time, research in consumer behavior has identified phenomena of potential importance in understanding social phenomena that social cognition researchers have largely ignored.

For example, an understanding of consumer phenomena requires attention to visual information processing (e.g., effects of pictures in ads), comparative judgments involving multiple objects, and incidental judgments under conditions of low involvement. Moreover, consumers typically receive information in an advertisement or a commercial that they do not use until days or even weeks later, when they consider making a purchase (Haugtvedt, Herr, & Kardes, 2008; Wyer & Adaval, 2008). And because the intent to persuade is obvious in consumer settings, procedures that minimize (Kardes, 1988) or reduce (Kardes et al., 2007) resistance to persuasion can be particularly important. In contrast, research in social information processing has seldom addressed these matters.

Nevertheless, several well-established empirical generalizations have emerged from research in social cognition that have come to serve as principles upon which much research in consumer information processing is based. To provide a framework for our discussion of this research, these principles may be worth summarizing. The first principle, cognitive efficiency, is perhaps the most fundamental. Several other principles could be considered corollaries of this more general one.

Cognitive efficiency. Individuals are unlikely to expend any more cognitive effort than necessary to attain the objective they are pursuing. Thus, they use the procedure or judgmental criterion that is easiest to apply and resort to additional processing or criteria only if they are not sufficiently confident that the first application is adequate to attain the goal at hand (Chen & Chaiken, 1999).

Knowledge accessibility. Individuals typically use only a small subset of the relevant knowledge they have acquired as a basis for comprehending information, construing its implications, and making a judgment or decision. This is generally the knowledge that comes to mind most quickly and easily (Higgins 1996; Förster & Liberman, 2007; Taylor & Fiske, 1978 Wyer, 2004, 2008).

Recency and frequency. The accessibility of knowledge in memory is a positive function of both the recency and the frequency with which it has been used (Higgins et al., 1985; Srull & Wyer, 1979). The impact of frequency (relative to recency) increases over time (Higgins et al., 1985). Concepts and knowledge that have been used over a period of time can become *chronically* accessible and thus can be applied independently of situational factors that might influence their accessibility (Bargh, Bond, Lombardi, & Tota, 1986).

Persistence. Once information has been interpreted or a judgment has been made on the basis of knowledge that happens to be accessible at the time, this interpretation or judgment may persist to influence later judgments and decisions independently of the information on which it was originally based (Carlston, 1980; Kardes, 1986; Srull & Wyer, 1980).

Awareness. Individuals are often unaware of the factors that influence the accessibility of knowledge in memory and the reason for employing a particular

procedure in making a judgment or decision (Bargh, 1997). Therefore, subliminally primed concepts and knowledge can often have an impact on the criteria on which people base judgments and decisions and on the procedures they employ in generating them. When individuals become aware that the concepts or criteria that come to mind may be the result of factors that are irrelevant to the task at hand, they may intentionally avoid using them or may adjust for their influence (Martin, Seta, & Crelia, 1990; Wegener & Petty, 1997).

Implicit theories. Individuals acquire implicit theories (or assumptions) about the world that they use in construing the implications of the information they receive. These theories can include scripts (prototypic event sequences; see Schank & Abelson, 1977), stereotypes, and implicational molecules (generalized sets of propositions that in combination constitute a generalization about people, objects, or events; see Abelson & Reich, 1969; Wyer, 2007). The invocation of these theories may lead individuals to infer attributes of the experience that were not observed while ignoring other attributes that might actually be relevant.

Communication norms. Individuals spontaneously apply normative principles of communication in interpreting a message and only invoke other criteria if the literal meaning of the message appears to violate these principles. Furthermore, they also apply the principles in conveying information to others. For example, effective communications are informative (they convey information that the recipient does not already have), truthful, and relevant to the topic at hand (Grice, 1975; see also Higgins, 1981; Schwarz, 1994, 1996). These assumptions do not hold, however, when people suspect that the communicator has ulterior motives (e.g., to persuade, to ingratiate), which is frequently the case in consumer settings.

Subjective reactions. Individuals' judgments and decisions are based not only on the descriptive features of the stimuli they encounter but also on their affective reactions to the stimuli and its context (Schwarz & Clore, 1983, 1996). Extraneous affect that people happen to be experiencing at the time they consider a stimulus may be misattributed to the stimulus and may influence the judgments and decisions they make. Other subjective reactions can also influence judgments. For example, individuals who experience difficulty in processing the information may construe the implications of this difficulty for the judgment they are making (Schwarz, 1998, 2004).

Integration. Individuals who evaluate a stimulus or decision alternative typically attach greater weight to the negative features of the stimulus than to its positive features (Birnbaum, 1974; Skowronski & Carlston, 1989). However, this disposition is likely to vary with situational, individual, and cultural differences in promotion or prevention focus (Higgins, 1997, 1998).

The research summarized in the following sections reflects the implications of these principles. Our discussion of this research is organized according to the stage of information processing to which it primarily pertains: comprehension, categorization, inference (including the use of subjective reactions as a basis for judgment), integration, and decision making.

Comprehension Processes

The knowledge that people bring to bear on the interpretation of information can include both semantic concepts that refer to specific features of a product and configurations of interrelated attributes that characterize a product or service as a whole. This knowledge can depend on how the information is presented. For example, the information can be conveyed verbally, in pictures, or both. It may be conveyed in the form of a narrative or as an unordered list of features. It can describe attributes either concretely (40 miles per gallon, 80% wool) or more generally (fuel efficient, warm). Apart from how the information is presented, however, its interpretation can depend on consumers' a priori dispositions to process information verbally or visually, to apply abstract or concrete concepts to the individual information items, and to think about these items separately or in relation to one another. These differences in the comprehension of information can obviously have an influence on its impact.

Visual and Verbal Encoding

Ads and television commercials convey information in both pictures and words. The verbal components often describe features of the product. The pictorial component can portray the product or the consequences of using it. However, it can also provide contextual information that has little to do with features of the product itself.

The influence of pictures undoubtedly depends on their relation to the verbal information that they accompany. The results of studies bearing on these effects are somewhat mixed (Childers & Houston, 1984; Costley & Brucks, 1992; Edell & Staelin, 1983; Miniard et al., 1991). For example, pictures add little to evaluations of a product if their implications are redundant with those of the verbal information presented (Costley & Brucks, 1992), and may only have an effect when recipients have little interest in the information presented (Miniard et al., 1991). Furthermore, when consumers are disposed to identify and integrate the evaluative implications of a product's individual attributes, pictures can sometimes interfere with this integration process and have a negative impact on evaluations (Adaval & Wyer, 1998; Adaval, Isbell, & Wyer, 2007). The effect of pictures can also depend on characteristics of the pictures themselves, such as the perspective from which they are taken (Meyers-Levy & Peracchio, 1992).

The effects of pictures are often mediated by the visual images they elicit. However, visual images are often formed on the basis of verbal information as well (see Kosslyn, 1980, for a discussion of visual imagery in comprehension and memory; for a review of the role of imagery in consumer information processing, see Petrova and Cialdini, 2008). The construction of these images can depend on the type of information presented (e.g., whether it describes events that are localized in space and time; see Wyer, 2004). Moreover, situational differences exist in the tendency to process information visually or verbally. Petrova and Cialdini (2005) found that instructing people to form mental images of a resort increased evaluations of it when the verbal information presented made an image easy to construct, but decreased evaluations when the information consisted of numerical ratings that were not image evoking. Similarly, Adaval and Wyer (1998) found that instructions to imagine a vacation trip increased evaluations of it when verbal information about the trip was described in a narrative that made a coherent representation of the vacation as a whole easy to construct. However, these instructions decreased evaluations when the verbal information was presented in an unordered list. It seems reasonable to conclude that when visual (pictured) and verbal information are presented in combination, increasing the complexity of either type of information can make it difficult to form a coherent image-based mental representation of the information's referents. This difficulty in processing can decrease evaluations of the stimuli described. (For evidence of the effect of ease of processing on evaluative judgments, see Schwarz, 2004; Winkielman et al., 2003.)

Finally, individual differences exist in the disposition to construct visual images as inferred from responses to Childers, Houston, and Heckler's (1985) Style-of-Processing scale (see also Jiang & Wyer, 2009). These differences can influence both the extremity of individuals' reactions to the events described (Jiang & Wyer, 2009) and evaluations of the information's referents. A series of studies by Jiang, Steinhart, and Wyer (2008; see Wyer, Hung, & Jiang, 2008) indicated that individuals with a disposition to process information visually evaluated a product less favorably when the verbal information about its attributes could not easily be integrated into a visual image of the product as a whole (either because the product was unfamiliar or because the image elicited by the verbal information was incompatible with the image elicited by an accompanying picture). Individuals with a disposition to process information verbally were not affected at all by these factors.

Narratives and Stories

When information is conveyed in a list of ostensibly unrelated features, consumers often assess the evaluative implications of each feature separately and then combine these implications to form a judgment in a manner similar to that suggested by information integration theories (Anderson, 1971, 1981). When the same information is conveyed in a temporal sequence, however, individuals often construct a coherent image-based representation of the sequence and evaluate the referent on the basis of the sequence as a whole. In the latter case, information whose implications are evaluatively inconsistent with the implications of the sequence as a whole may have relatively little effect (Adaval & Wyer, 1998; Pennington & Hastie, 1992).

Individuals may sometimes imagine themselves as a participant in the sequence of events that they read or hear about. Escalas (2004; Escalas & Luce, 2004), for example, found that individuals who immerse themselves into a narrative description of a product (or, in other terms, are "transported" into the narrative; see Green & Brock, 2000) decrease their tendency to counterargue its implications. Consequently, they are persuaded by it independently of the quality of the arguments it contains (Escalas, 2004, 2007).

An interesting extension of this reason was identified by Wang and Calder (2006), who investigated the effects of being "transported" into the story conveyed in a television show on the impact of commercials that accompany it. Perhaps not surprisingly, commercials that occurred in the middle of an episode had a negative impact on "transported" consumers' evaluation of the product being advertised, whereas commercials that occurred at the end of the program had a positive impact.

Indirect evidence that the impact of narrative-based representations of product information is mediated by its effect on counterarguing was obtained in a quite different research paradigm by Hung and Wyer (2008). Participants were exposed to "problem-solving" advertisements describing both a problem (e.g., hair loss) and the solution (a product and the consequence of using it). When one component was pictured and the other was verbal, participants attempted to interpret the relatively ambiguous verbal description in a manner that was consistent with the implications of the picture. However, the comprehension process required cognitive effort, and participants were unmotivated to do the additional cognitive work required to refute the ad's implications (Anand & Sternthal, 1998). Consequently, the ad had a positive influence on their product evaluations. When both components were pictured, however, the implications of the ad were easy to construe, so participants were more willing to expend cognitive effort in refuting the ad's implications. As a result, they decreased their evaluation of the product relative to conditions in which only one component was pictured.

Level of Analysis

Individuals who receive detailed information about the attributes of a product (e.g., the horsepower of an automobile, or the processing speed of a computer) may encode it either numerically or in more global, abstract terms (e.g., "powerful," "fast"). They may then form a mental representation of the product in terms of these features. The importance of the difference in how the features are encoded derives in part from the fact that after a period of time has elapsed, individuals' evaluations of the product are likely to be based on the implications of the representation they formed independently of the information that led to its construction.

These differences in encoding can depend in part on the purpose for which individuals expect to use the information. People who encounter a body of information about a product may spontaneously form a global appraisal of it without analyzing its individual features (Lazarus, 1991) and may only be motivated to think about the product in detail if a purchase decision is imminent. Thus, as implied by construal level theory (Trope &

Liberman, 2003, 2010), people are likely to make global, desirability-based evaluations of a product that they do not expect to purchase until sometime in the future, but consider more situation-specific, feasibility-related features when they consider it for immediate purchase and use. The effects of differences of other types of psychological distance (e.g., social, geographical) may be analogous. For example, individuals may construe objects and events in more global terms if they pertain to strangers than if they pertain to close friends and in more global terms if they are geographically remote than if they are close by. Thus, although the effects of different types of psychological distance may be due to different underlying processes (Zhang & Meng, 2009), these effects are somewhat similar.

The effect of differences in temporal construals is particularly relevant in the consumer domain. It suggests that people use different criteria to evaluate a product for future consumption than they use to evaluate a product for immediate use. A product's desirability is likely to be considered regardless of when individuals expect to make a purchase, whereas the feasibility of purchasing it is taken into account only if the purchase is imminent. Kim, Park, and Wyer (2009) found that individuals who initially consider a product for immediate consumption and base their judgment primarily on feasibility criteria are likely to evaluate it more positively if they later reconsider the product for future consumption instead. If they initially consider a product for future consumption, however, they base their judgment on its desirability alone. Consequently, they are later likely to retrieve and use this criterion again if they reconsider the product for immediate use because feasibility considerations were not involved in the formation of the representation they constructed earlier.

Relational Thinking

To reiterate, individuals who receive several items of information about an object may either consider each item independently or think about the items in relation to one another. These dispositions can be induced by asking participants to perform a sentence-construction task requiring the use of either "I" or "we" (Gardner, Gabriel, & Lee, 1999). Apparently, thinking about oneself independently or in relation to other persons activates a tendency to think about stimuli in general either independently or in relation to one another. Thus, Kühnen and Oyserman (2002) asked participants to recall objects that had been randomly arranged in a stimulus array. Whereas all participants were able to remember the individual items, participants who were primed with "we" had better memory for the positions of the items in relation to one another than participants who had been primed with "I."

However, chronic cultural differences in independent versus relational thinking exist as well (Markus & Kitayama, 1991). That is, European Americans are disposed to think of themselves as independent, whereas Asians are inclined to think of themselves in relation to others. These dispositions appear to characterize responses to stimuli in general (Nisbett, 2003). In a particularly interesting study (Park, Nisbett, & Hedden, 1999), North Americans and Asians were asked to learn a number of words, each presented on a different card. In some cases, only the word was shown on each card, whereas in other cases, the word was surrounded by a number of irrelevant contextual features. Although one might expect the context stimuli to be distracting, Asians, unlike North Americans, were better able to recall the words when these features were present.

Although the effects of independent and relational processing have not been widely investigated in consumer research (but see Kim & Meyers-Levy, 2008), they are of potential interest. One might speculate, for example, that individuals with an interdependent processing strategy are more likely to engage in comparative shopping in stores or on the Internet than to consider a choice independently of other alternatives.

Assimilation and Contrast

The comprehension of information in relation to its context could have two different effects. In some instances, individuals may judge stimuli to be more similar to their context than they otherwise might (an *assimilation* effect), and in other cases, they may judge them as less similar (a *contrast* effect). Although early theoretical formulations of these effects assumed that they were motivationally rooted (cf. Sherif & Hovland, 1961), the effects may often result from quite different cognitive processes.

Assimilation effects typically result from two factors. First, if information about a stimulus is interpreted in terms of concepts that happen to be accessible in memory at the time, it is assigned characteristics implied by these concepts (Higgins, 1996; Wyer, 2008). Second, the accessible concepts and knowledge can have a direct impact on judgments of stimuli that is independent of the content of the information about the stimuli (Mussweiler & Strack, 1999). Contrast effects, on the other hand, are likely to result from the conscious use of concepts and stimuli as comparative standards. Alternatively, context stimuli can affect the range of stimuli that people consider to be relevant to the judgments they make (Adaval & Monroe, 2002; Ostrom & Upshaw, 1968). (Thus, they might judge an $80 dinner as "expensive" but an $80 diamond ring as "cheap" because the range of stimulus values they perceive to be relevant, and thus the meaning of "cheap" and "expensive," is lower in the first case than in the second.)

Although individuals may be aware that they are judging stimuli in relation to a standard of comparison, they may not be aware of the reason they selected this standard. Consequently, the factors that affect the selection of a standard can often be irrelevant to the judgment being made. For example, subliminally primed numbers can affect the range of values that individuals consider in construing the price of a product they encounter later, leading them to judge the product as less expensive when the primed numbers are high than when they are low (Adaval & Monroe, 2002).

Several hypotheses have been raised concerning the factors that govern the relative dominance of assimilation and contrast effects. For example, Herr (1986) noted that the concepts activated by context stimuli have a range of implications. Thus, when the implications of a target stimulus fall within this range, the target is interpreted as exemplifying the activated concepts, and assimilation effects occur. However, if the target's implications fall outside the range of values that the activated concepts can take, the concepts are used as a comparative standard, and contrast effects occur.

In a direct test of this interpretation, Förster, Liberman, and Kuschel (2007) stimulated participants to employ either broad or narrow concepts by asking them either to think about a map as a whole or to focus on its details. They then primed trait adjectives associated with hostility and exposed participants to an impression formation task similar to that used by Herr (1986). The primed adjectives had an assimilation effect on participants' impressions in the first condition but a contrast effect in the second. In a further extension of this line of reasoning, participants were induced to think about either an event that would occur in the distant future or an event that would occur very soon. For reasons noted earlier in this chapter, participants were expected to activate global concepts in the first case but more specific concepts in the second (Trope & Liberman, 2003, 2010). As expected, participants in a later

experiment showed assimilation effects in the first condition but contrast effects in the second.

More generally, the Inclusion/Exclusion Model suggests that judgment requires mental representations of a target and of a reference point (Bless & Schwarz, 2010). Information included in the representation of the target results in assimilation effects. Information excluded from the representation of the target results in subtraction-based contrast effects. Information included in the representation of the reference point results in comparison-based contrast effects. Accessible and applicable information tends to be included in mental representations, whereas exclusion requires judgments of information irrelevance or inapplicability.

A qualification on the assumption that assimilation and contrast effects result from different processes was identified by Park et al. (2001). That is, bipolar concepts (e.g. wet vs. dry, good vs. bad) are associatively linked in memory (Columbo & Williams, 1990), and priming one concept activates the other as well. Consequently, both priming concepts associated with good health and priming concepts associated with bad health can lead individuals to interpret a milk product's description as having "50% more banana flavoring" to be unhealthy and thus to evaluate the product unfavorably (Park et al., 2001).

Anchoring Effects and Selective Accessibility

Park et al.'s (2001) research suggests that contrast effects can sometimes result from processes that occur at an early, comprehension stage of judgment. By the same token, assimilation effects can sometimes result from processes that occur at the response stage. Tversky and Kahneman (1974), for example, showed that when individuals are asked to make a judgment along a response scale, they sometimes use the low end of the scale as an anchor and adjust upward until they encounter a value that is plausible. At other times, they may use the high end of the scale as an anchor and adjust downward. However, there is normally a range of plausible values, and individuals stop processing when the first such value is encountered. Consequently, they are likely to report a higher judgment when they have used the high end of the scale as an anchor than when they have used the low end.

Comprehension processes, however, can play an equally or more important role. Mussweiler and Strack (1991) found that asking individuals to compare a stimulus to a high or low anchor value activates concepts associated with objects that might have this value. These concepts, once activated, provide the basis for judgments of the object later. Thus, for example, deciding whether the average price of a sweater is greater or less than $150 is likely to activate concepts associated with high-priced sweaters, and these concepts may later be used as a basis for estimating the price one is willing to pay for a sweater in general. Furthermore, these effects may generalize to judgments of other types of products, provided the concepts activated by the comparative judgment are applicable (Adaval & Wyer, 2011). Similar effects have been identified outside the laboratory. Nunes and Boatright (2004), for example, found that individuals who were perusing the stalls at a beach front were willing to pay more for CDs if the sweaters at a neighboring booth were on sale for high prices (thus stimulating them to use the high end of the scale as an anchor when evaluating CDs) than if the sweaters were on sale for low prices.

Higher Order Comprehension

The processes reviewed in the previous section often occur spontaneously in the course of comprehending the literal meaning of information. When information is conveyed in a social context, however, there may be a discrepancy between the literal meaning of a message and the meaning that the communicator intends to convey. Many communications, for example, are intended to be ironic or sarcastic. Others may be intended to convey an attitude rather than matters of fact.

The processes that underlie the recognition of the intended meaning of a communication were identified by Grice (1975). In the absence of situational factors that suggest otherwise, recipients of a message may typically assume that a communication is intended to be informative and to convey the truth as the communicator sees it, and they may spontaneously construe its literal meaning on the basis of this normative principle. If, however, a message's literal meaning violates this assumption, they may question whether the literal meaning of the message is, in fact, the meaning that the communicator intends to convey, and may reinterpret it in a manner that is more consistent with the principle that is violated.

In the consumer domain, additional considerations arise from the fact that communicators (e.g., advertisers and salespeople) are primarily motivated to persuade. This objective may often be attained by providing new and accurate information about the product they are promoting. Thus, communicators may attempt to convey messages that purport to be informative but are actually meaningless or even misleading. Most consumers, of course, are aware of the persuasive intentions of advertisers and that their claims for the product are likely to be exaggerated. (For a detailed discussion of persuasion knowledge, see Campbell & Kirmani, 2008.) However, Hung and Wyer (2008) found that if a message can be interpreted in a manner that is consistent with Gricean principles but requires cognitive effort in order to make this interpretation, recipients may accept its implications without devoting additional cognitive resources to questioning its validity. If the communication can be easily interpretable with little effort, however, individuals are more likely to apply to evaluate its implications in light of their knowledge that advertising claims are typically exaggerated, so it may have less effect (see also Anand & Sternthal, 1989). These considerations imply that difficulty in comprehending an advertisement can actually increase its effectiveness.

Several examples of deceptive or misleading advertising can be conceptualized in this manner. For example, individuals who read that "Brand X contains strocacium" may have no idea what strocacium is. To interpret the message in a way that conforms to the informativeness principle, however, they may infer that (1) strocacium is a desirable attribute and (2) other products do not have it. By the same token, they might interpret the assertion that "Brand X contains no strocacium" as implying that strocacium is undesirable but that other products *do* have it.

In a related vein, individuals who read that "Brand X is better" may mentally complete the claim in a way that is informative and relevant ("...better than other brands") rather than in other, less relevant ways ("...better than it used to be," "...better than the most inferior brands on the market"). The evidence in support of this possibility is not very strong (Johar, 1995). That is, the effect appears to occur only when participants are highly motivated to evaluate the product at the time they receive the information about it. That is, less involved participants do not engage in the cognitive work required to apply the informativeness principle. Thus, the application of the principle is not always as spontaneous as often assumed. (For other evidence that involved consumers are more likely to make inferences about the implications of an advertisement in the absence of explicit conclusions about its implications, see Kardes, 1988; Sawyer & Howard, 1991.)

A potentially important consideration in this context is consumers' a priori knowledge about the product being advertised. Xu and Wyer (2010) found that when product descriptions in an advertisement are objectively meaningless, consumers who perceive themselves to have little knowledge about the product infer that the descriptions would be informative to persons who know more about the product than they do. As a result, these descriptions can increase their evaluations of the product. If, however, consumers perceive that they know as much or more about the product than persons to whom the ad is directed, they infer that descriptions they can't understand would not be understood by anyone and are intended only to persuade. Consequently, they react negatively to the descriptions. Xu and Wyer (2010) found that when individuals received an advertisement about a product they knew little about, or when the ad appeared in a magazine that was read only by experts in the area to which the product was relevant, the introduction of objectively meaningless information into the ad had a positive effect on product evaluations. However, when the ad appeared in a popular magazine and participants believed they knew as much or more about the product than consumers in the population at large, inserting meaningless information into the ad decreased its effectiveness.

Categorization Processes

Categories are characterized by a set of unrelated features that are typical of category members (for a discussion of categorical representations of consumer knowledge, see Loken, Barsalou, & Joiner, 2008). Because members of a category have features in common, these features can provide a convenient basis for inference. For example, if people assign an object to a category on the basis of a subset of the attributes that serve as criteria for category membership, they may infer the object to have other, unspecified features that are also typical of category members. Furthermore, they are likely to base their evaluation of the object on their more general attitude toward the category as a whole (Fiske & Neuberg, 1990).

In social psychology, the effects of category membership on judgments have been largely investigated in the context of research on stereotypes (Bodenhausen, 1993). In consumer research, the two types of categories that have been considered most extensively are brand name and country of origin. In each case, however, the impact of membership in these categories is not as straightforward as it might appear.

Brands and Brand Extensions

A manufacturer who is known for a particular type of product may sometimes launch a new product line. In general, individuals who perceive that a brand extension is similar to the parent brand in one respect are likely to infer that the extension is similar to the parent in other respects (e.g., quality) and evaluate it accordingly. The use of this criterion could be governed by the same processes that underlie assimilation and contrast effects. That is, if an extension is moderately similar to the parent brand and can be interpreted as falling within the range of products that are associated with the parent, it may be assumed to belong to the parent brand category and may be evaluated as similar to it in favorableness. If it falls outside this range, the extension may be contrasted with the parent and seen as dissimilar to it. This implies that the broader the range of products that are associated with a parent, the greater the likelihood that the extension will be perceived to fall within this range and the greater the positive effect of the parent's quality on its evaluation. On the other hand, the broader the range of products associated with the parent, the less diagnostic brand–extension similarity may be perceived to be and the less effect it may have on evaluations (Boush & Loken, 1991; Meyvis & Janiszewski 2004).

A brand extension may not only be compared with the parent brand, of course. It can sometimes be compared with other products of the same general type. Kim (2006) found that participants used the parent brand category as a standard of comparison in evaluating an extension when no other information was available. That is, they evaluated a midrange car more favorably when its manufacturer was known for compact cars than when its manufacturer was known for sports cars, and this was true regardless of participants' prior knowledge about automobiles. When additional information was provided about the extension, naïve participants continued to base their judgment on parent–extension similarity, but experts based their judgments on a comparison with other products in the more general product category.

Two further considerations come into play. Individuals who experience positive affect and categorize stimuli more broadly (Bless, 2001) may perceive a brand extension to be more similar to the parent than they otherwise would and consequently evaluate it more favorably (Barone & Miniard, 2002; Barone, Miniard, & Romero, 2000). On the other hand, if a parent brand is particularly attractive and elicits affective reactions, these reactions may generalize to the extensions that are associated with it and may be used as a basis for evaluating the extensions independently of brand–extension similarity (Yeung & Wyer, 2005). Second, situational factors that call the diagnosticity of parent–extension similarity into question may decrease its impact. Yan, Mao, and Wyer (2009) found that when people learn that an extension that is very similar to its parent has failed in the marketplace, or that a very dissimilar extension has succeeded, they decrease their perceptions of the diagnosticity of parent–extension similarity. As a result, they decrease their use of the criterion in evaluating extensions of a quite different parent brand in a situation that they encounter later.

Country of Origin

A product may be judged more favorably if it is made in a country with a reputation for manufacturing high-quality products than if it is made in a country with a reputation for relatively inferior merchandise. The effect of a product's country of origin on its evaluation is commonly accepted (Bilkey & Nes, 1982; Maheswaran, 1994). However, several different processes can underlie this effect. For example, when a product's country of origin is described in the context of information about its specific attributes, it may simply be treated as another attribute, and its effects combine with those of other favorable or unfavorable attributes. That is, country of origin may only serve as a concept or category around which other product information is organized and interpreted if it is already known at the time the attribute information is presented (Hong & Wyer, 1990). Moreover, when individuals receive product information without any particular objective in mind, the product's country of origin may stimulate their interest and attention to other product information. As a result, the product's specific attributes have greater effect on judgments than they otherwise would (Hong & Wyer, 1989).

The effect of a product's country of origin can also depend on individuals' general attitude toward the country with which it is associated. Individuals are often disinclined to buy products from a country toward which they feel animosity (Klein, Ettenson, & Morris, 1998). However, a particularly provocative study by Hong and Kang (2006) qualifies this conclusion. In this study, Korean participants who had been unobtrusively primed with concepts associated with either industriousness or hostility evaluated products that were ostensibly made in either Japan or Germany—countries that are known for high-quality products toward which Koreans had feelings of animosity because of their behavior in World War II. In some cases, the products being judged were articles of clothing or other relatively inexpensive merchandise. In this case, their country of origin had a positive effect on consumers' evaluations on them when industriousness had been primed but had a negative effect on evaluations when hostility had been primed. In contrast, associating high-tech products with Germany or Japan increased evaluations of the products regardless of which attribute had been primed. In this case, the countries' reputation for manufacturing high-quality products overrode the effects of participants' feelings of animosity toward the two countries.

Inference Processes

Inferences are judgments or conclusions that go beyond the information given. They frequently involve the use of an accessible and applicable implicit theory that links information (X) to a conclusion (Y) in a subjectively logical fashion (Kardes, Posavac, & Cronley, 2004b; Kardes, Posavac, Cronley, & Herr, 2008). For example, consumers often infer the likelihood that a particular event will occur or that a statement is true by applying an implicit theory pertaining to the ease with which the event can be retrieved from memory, the ease with which the event (or sequence of events) can be imagined, or the psychological distance of the event. An event that is easy to retrieve or to imagine seems more likely, and a statement that is easy to retrieve or to imagine seems more valid (Schwarz, 2004). A statement that an event that is psychologically near in terms of time, space, location, or sensory experience can also seem more likely (Trope & Liberman, 2003, Trope, Liberman, & Wakslak, 2007) or valid (Hansen & Wänke, 2010; Wright et al., 2012).

Frequency judgments are related to likelihood judgments, and both types of judgments are influenced by the ease with which instances can be retrieved or imagined. However, consumers are likely to focus on specific instances in making frequency judgments only when these instances are relatively rare (Menon, Raghubir, & Schwarz, 1995). When events are a daily or common occurrence, consumers are more likely to estimate their frequency by extrapolating from their general knowledge. For example, consumers can estimate how much coffee they drink over a two-week period by estimating the amount of coffee they drink on a typical day and multiplying by 14.

When beliefs do not come to mind readily, consumers are likely to search memory for belief-relevant information and to integrate this information using Wyer and Hartwick's (1980, 1984) update of McGuire's (1960) formula for syllogistic reasoning. That is, they infer the likelihood that a proposition, B, is true from (1) their beliefs that a second proposition, A, is true and that A implies B, and (2) their beliefs that A is *not* true and that not-A implies B. This is described by the equation:

$$p(B) = p(A)p(B|A) + p(\sim A)p(B|\sim A),$$

where p(B) is the belief that B is true, p(A) is the belief that A is true, and p(B|A) and p(B|~A) are the conditional beliefs that B is true if A is and is not true, respectively. When beliefs are in units of subjective probability, this equation not only provides accurate descriptions of the functional relations among these beliefs but also is quantitatively accurate (Wyer & Hartwick, 1980). Applications of the equation in describing the impact of marketing communications indicate that beliefs in the conclusion, p(B), are more resistant to persuasion when multiple sets of syllogistic arguments are horizontally linked (when independent sets of arguments imply the same conclusion) than when they are vertically linked (when interdependent sets of arguments are chained together such that the conclusion of one set serves as the major premise for the next set, and so on, like a proverbial house of cards; Kardes, Cronley, Pontes, & Houghton, 2001).

Causal inferences help consumers to predict and control their environments (for reviews, see Folkes, 1984; Folkes, Koletsky, & Graham, 1987; Kardes et al., 2008). Judgments of causality depend on variables such as expectations, hedonic relevance, personalism, distinctiveness, consistency, consensus, locus of causality, stability, and perceived control. These inferences can have important implications for responses to product failures and for consumer satisfaction. For example, consumers who were booked on delayed flights blamed the airline more and were less satisfied when the problem was perceived as controllable and stable on the part of the airline (Folkes et al., 1987). Ideally, firms should attempt to increase perceptions of controllability and stability for positive events, and decrease perceptions of controllability and stability for negative events.

Consumers sometimes draw inferences about the magnitude or value of an unmentioned product attribute from other known attributes that are associated with it. These inferences may be based on implicit theories about the relations among these attributes. A wide variety of implicit theories are used by consumers, pertaining to the relations among quality, price, warranty, packaging, reliability, durability, physical appearance, retail outlet, and so forth (Kardes et al., 2004b, 2008). For example, consumers typically believe that price and quality are highly positively correlated, and therefore use price to infer quality (Kardes et al., 2004a). This encourages consumers to purchase more expensive products even though the subjective price–quality correlations in consumers' heads are frequently three times higher than objective price–quality correlations in the marketplace (Cronley et al., 2005). Implicit theories about quality, durability, warranties, advertising, country of origin, and brand name are also used regularly.

Cho and Schwarz (2008) recently demonstrated that consumers often have competing implicit theories with opposite implications. For example, people may assume that great artists can produce masterpieces quickly and effortlessly, or they may assume that creating great art requires time and effort. Priming the former theory led people to conclude that quality decreases with effort, whereas priming the latter led people to conclude that quality increases with effort.

Similarly, Deval, Mantel, Kardes, and Posavac (in press) used magazine articles about products that were unrelated to target products to prime one of two conflicting theories about marketing tactics. In one experiment, the articles associated product quality with either popularity (e.g., millions of satisfied customers own the product) or exclusivity (e.g., few customers own the product and scarce products are desirable). In two other experiments, the articles emphasized that high price can signal either high quality or low value, or that a sales promotion can imply either low quality or high value. A fourth experiment used technical jargon to imply that the manufacturer is either a leading expert in the product category or is attempting to confuse the customer into buying. In all four experiments, participants evaluated the target products more favorably when implicit theories having favorable (vs. unfavorable) evaluative implications had been primed.

Although inferences about a product along general dimensions (e.g., quality) are quite common, inferences about specific missing attributes are much less so. In fact, consumers are surprisingly insensitive to missing information. *Omission neglect*, or insensitivity to many different types of missing or unknown information (e.g., missing attributes, features, properties, qualities, alternatives, options, cues, stimuli, or possibilities), occurs because (1) missing information is not salient (Sanbonmatsu et al., 1991, 1992, 1997; Treisman & Souther, 1985), (2) missing information is difficult to comprehend (Bechkoff et al., 2009; Rozin, Fischler, & Shields-Argeles, 2009), (3) information about presented attributes determines the criteria used for judgment (Sanbonmatsu et al., 2003), and (4) information about presented attributes interferes with the ability to identify missing attributes (Kardes et al., 2006; Silvera et al., 2005). Even when missing attributes are identified, consumers typically adjust insufficiently for the implications of the missing attributes (Pfeiffer, 2008). In other words, consumers anchor on the implications of presented information and change their beliefs only slightly when omissions are detected. Omissions are difficult to detect, and the implications of omissions are difficult to construe even when omissions are detected. Importantly, these studies suggest that omission neglect occurs during each stage of information processing: attention, comprehension, memory, integration, evaluation, and postevaluation.

Omission neglect decreases the likelihood of making spontaneous inferences about specific missing attributes (Kardes & Sanbonmatsu, 1993). In addition, it increases the likelihood of making extreme and confidently held overall evaluations regardless of the amount of diagnostic information that is available for judgment (Sanbonmatsu et al., 1991, 1992, 1997, 2003). Although omission neglect is the norm, it can be reduced by extremely high levels of prior knowledge, warnings about the possibility of incomplete information, a missing attribute inference task occurring immediately following exposure to information (rather than after a delay), or a comparative judgment task in which the objects are described in terms of nonalignable features (e.g., features that fall along different dimensions and cannot be directly compared). Recent research shows that concrete, low-level construals can also heighten sensitivity to omissions (Deval et al., 2011).

Subjective Reactions

Schwarz and Clore (1983) were the first to establish that individuals attribute the affective reactions they experience at the time they consider a referent to their feelings about the referent and use these feelings as an informational basis for judgment. Furthermore, because people cannot distinguish clearly between the affect actually elicited by a referent and the feelings they happen to be experiencing for other, unrelated reasons, these extraneous feelings can influence their judgments as well. Thus, the affect elicited by reminiscing about a happy or sad past experience, the weather, receiving a small gift, or proprioceptive feedback can all influence people's evaluations of a stimulus that they are asked to evaluate a short time later (Schwarz & Clore, 1983; Strack, Martin, & Stepper, 1988; for reviews, see Schwarz & Clore, 1996, 2007).

However, research in the consumer domain has uncovered several qualifications and extensions of both theoretical and empirical importance.

1. Consumers' product evaluations are not influenced by the affective reactions they are experiencing unless the product in question is normally evaluated on the basis of these reactions (Adaval, 2001; Pham, 1998; Yeung & Wyer, 2004). Thus, although evaluations of hedonic products (comfort foods, luxury products) are influenced by the feelings that individuals are experiencing, evaluations of products that are judged primarily on the basis of utilitarian considerations (refrigerators, vitamin pills) are not.

2. When individuals see a picture of a product or encounter it in a store window, they often make a spontaneous, affect-based appraisal of it before learning about its specific attributes (Lazarus, 1991) and form an initial impression of the product on the basis of this appraisal. If individuals are experiencing affect for other, extraneous reasons at the time they make this appraisal, this affect may influence the favorableness of their impression. Their later evaluations of the product may then be based on this affect-based initial impression independently of the type of product or of any specific attribute information that they receive later (see Yeung & Wyer, 2004).

3. Affect can provide information on only one's feelings about not only a product as a whole but also the specific pieces of information that describe it. Adaval (2001), for example, found that when the affect that participants happened to be experiencing matched the affect elicited by attributes of the product they were considering, they were more confident of the implications of these attributes and weighted the attributes more heavily in arriving at a judgment. By the same token, when participants' feelings did not match the affect elicited by the product's attributes, they became uncertain about the attributes' implications and decreased the weight they attached to them.

4. There is considerable support for Schwarz and Clore's (1983) hypothesis that people use the affect they are experiencing as information about their liking for a stimulus they are asked to evaluate (Schwarz & Clore, 1996, 2007). A corollary of this hypothesis is that individuals who experience positive affect in a situation infer that the situation they are in is unproblematic, and consequently base their judgments on more superficial, heuristic criteria than they would otherwise. In contrast, individuals who experience negative affect infer that the situation confronting them is potentially problematic and think more carefully about their judgments and decisions (Schwarz, 1990). Thus, for example, happy individuals are less sensitive than unhappy ones to differences in the quality of arguments contained in a communication (Bless, Bohner, Schwarz, & Strack, 1990) and are more inclined to use global, heuristic criteria (e.g., stereotypes) as bases for judgment (Bodenhausen, 1993).

Similar considerations might suggest that brand name has greater impact on judgments when individuals experience positive affect than when they do not. Although this is true, however, it is apparently not a result of differences in the weight attached to brand name (Adaval, 2003). Rather, individuals who experience positive affect think more extensively about the implications of a product's brand name for the product's attributes and consequently perceive these implications to be more extreme. (For other evidence that the polarization of judgments increases with thought, see Tesser, 1978). In other words, positive affect influences perceptions of the implications of brand name information but not the weight attached to it.

5. Individuals appear to use broader concepts to interpret information when they are experiencing positive affect (Bless, 2001). This possibility has implications for the impact of affect on judgments of brand extensions (i.e., a new line of products from a well-known manufacturer). Barone and his colleagues (Barone & Miniard, 2002; Barone, Miniard, & Romero, 2000), for example, found that participants who experienced positive affect were inclined to perceive a brand extension as similar to its parent and, therefore, to evaluate the extension as similar to the parent in favorableness. (This may only be true, however, if similarity criteria are called to their attention; see Yeung & Wyer, 2005.)

6. A related implication of the tendency for individuals who experience positive affect to use broad categories has been examined by Isen (for reviews, see Isen, 2007, 2008). As a result of this disposition, these individuals tend to be more creative, as evidenced by their generation of more novel responses in problem-solving tasks and the unusualness of their word associations (Isen, Daubman, & Nowicki, 1987; Isen et al., 1985). These effects, however, could also result from the factors noted by Schwarz (1990). That is, if positive affect increases people's perceptions that the situation confronting them is unproblematic, they may have greater self-confidence and be more willing to generate novel responses without concern about being "wrong."

Motivational Influences of Affect on Judgments

The affect that individuals experience can have motivational as well as informational influences. In particular, individuals who experience negative affect are normally motivated to eliminate this unpleasant state. At the same time, individuals who experience positive affect may wish to maintain these feelings and resist engaging in behavior that could bring them down (Isen, 1987). The effects of these motives on judgments and decisions can differ from the informational influence of affect (Andrade, 2005; Andrade & Cohen, 2007). For example, individuals who are experiencing negative affect and consider its informational implications would be inclined to evaluate an activity negatively. However, they might evaluate it positively if they believe that engaging in the activity will decrease or eliminate the unpleasant feelings they are experiencing (Andrade, 2005).

A further consideration may be whether the activity being contemplated is perceived as instrumental in eliminating the *source* of individuals' negative feelings rather than simply making them feel better in the short run. Shen and Wyer (2008) induced negative affect by exposing participants to unpleasant pictures of a disease. If participants were induced to think about the problem that gave rise to their feelings (i.e., poor health), they increased their attraction to behavior that would potentially remedy the problem even though the behavior itself was not particularly pleasant. For example, they increased their attraction to an exercise course and took fewer candies as a reward upon leaving the experiment. When they were not induced to think about the problem, however, they preferred activities that would eliminate their immediate negative feelings (e.g., watching movies) regardless of its implications for the source of these feelings.

Other Effects of Subjective Experience

Affect is not the only subjective experience that can influence judgments. A particularly important factor surrounds the ease or difficulty with which information is processed (for reviews, see Schwarz, 1998, 2004). In an early demonstration of its effects (Schwarz et al., 1991), participants were asked to recall either 6 or 12 instances of their assertive behavior, after which they were asked to indicate how assertive they were. Although they recalled a greater number of behaviors in the second case than the first, this was difficult to do. Consequently, participants inferred that they might not be particularly assertive and judged themselves accordingly.

Studies in the consumer domain confirm this tendency. For example, individuals evaluate a luxury car less favorably if they are asked to recall several positive attributes of such a car than if they are asked to recall only one (Wänke, Bohner, & Jurkowitsch, 1997), and report less favorable attitudes toward a personal computer if they have been asked to recall a large number of favorable attributes rather than a few (Menon & Raghubir, 2003; Raghubir & Menon, 2005). As Menon and Raghubir show, however, individuals are less inclined to use their subjective experience as a basis for judgments if situational factors provide an alternative explanation for their feelings of difficulty.

Although the ease of recalling information can affect judgments, the ease of processing the information can have similar effects. Schwarz (2004) summarizes numerous examples in which the effectiveness of information is influenced by extraneous situational factors (e.g., the font in which the information is presented) that make it easy or difficult to process. Shen, Jiang, and Adaval (2010) found that exposing individuals to a movie review in a difficult-to-read font had a contrast effect on their perceived ease of processing an ad they encountered later and, therefore, increased their evaluations of the advertised product.

Integration Processes

Formal models of information integration (Fishbein, 1963; Anderson, 1971) assume that individuals who receive a description of a stimulus assess the implications of each piece of information separately and combine these implications using an algebraic rule (summation or averaging), weighting each by its importance or validity. The conditions under which this assumption holds are limited (for a discussion of these limitations, see Wyer & Carlston, 1979). Under conditions in which it is applicable,

however, the Anderson's (1971, 1981) weighted averaging model has been useful in diagnosing the effects of information on consumer judgment.

For one thing, the model calls attention to the distinction between the evaluative implications of information and the weight attached to it, and provides a means for identifying the factors that influence each. In studies described earlier, for example, Adaval demonstrated that the affect that individuals were experiencing for objectively irrelevant reasons influenced the impact of brand name through its effect on their perception of the brand's evaluative implications (Adaval, 2003). In contrast, it influenced the impact of attribute descriptions through its effect on perceptions of the descriptions' validity and, therefore, on the weight that individuals attached to them (Adaval, 2001).

Effects of Valence

The weight attached to information can also depend on its evaluative implications. A product (like a person) may need to have several favorable attributes in combination in order to be liked, whereas a single negative feature may be sufficient to reject it. The negativity effect can occur because negative features are often perceived as more diagnostic than positive features (Herr, Kardes, & Kim, 1991; Skowronski & Carlston, 1989). However, situational and individual differences exist in the relative weight attached to favorable and unfavorable features of a stimulus and, therefore, in the effects of information on evaluations and behavioral decisions.

Higgins (1997, 1998), for example, distinguished between the disposition to emphasize the positive aspects of a choice alternative (a *promotion* focus) and an emphasis on the possible negative aspects of the alternative (a *prevention* focus). For example, suppose individuals have a choice between (1) a product with values of +3 and −3 along two attribute dimensions and (2) a product with values of +1 and −1 along the dimensions. In such a case, promotion-focused individuals would presumably prefer the first alternative, but prevention-focused individuals would prefer the second.

The focus on positive or negative consequences of a choice can depend on linguistic set, for example, whether decision outcomes are framed in terms of gains (vs. nongains) or losses (vs. nonlosses) (Brendl, Higgins, & Lemm, 1995; Liberman, Idson, & Higgins, 2005). However, more general factors also exert an influence. For example, people who think of themselves as part of a group may activate a sense of responsibility to others that stimulates them to focus on negative features of a situation (Aaker & Lee, 2001) and to make decisions that minimize the negative consequences that might result. Once this disposition is activated, it can generalize to other situations in which group membership is irrelevant. For example, stimulating individuals' consciousness of their group membership (either by participating in an ad hoc group or by calling attention to their cultural group identity) increases their tendency to minimize the risk of making a bad choice in a product decision situation (Briley & Wyer, 2002). Furthermore, it leads them to choose candies of different kinds (vs. the same kind) as a gift upon leaving the experiment (thus minimizing the risk of making an incorrect choice).

Cultural differences also come into play. Asian individuals are typically more prevention focused than Westerners are (Aaker & Lee, 2001). Correspondingly, they are relatively more likely than Westerners to choose the low-risk alternative in the aforementioned product choice situation (Briley, Morris, & Simonson, 2000). This difference only emerges, however, if individuals are called on to give a reason for their choice, thus leading them to activate a culture-related decision rule. When individuals are bicultural, the difference can also be activated by the language in which the experiment is conducted (Briley, Morris, & Simonson, 2005).

The generally greater emphasis that is placed on negative consequences of a choice is recognized in Kahneman and Tversky's (1979) prospect theory. This theory assumes that the positive utility of a favorable outcome and the negative utility of an unfavorable outcome are negative exponential functions of the magnitude of these outcomes along a given dimension (an implication of Fechner's law). However, the function is steeper in the case of unfavorable outcomes than favorable ones. This loss aversion assumption can account for diverse phenomena that have been identified in research on consumer behavior.

Endowment Effects

The positive utility of acquiring a product is less than the negative utility of relinquishing it. Thus, the amount of money that individuals are willing to pay for a product is less than the amount for which they would be willing to sell it once they have it (Kahneman, Knetsch, & Thaler, 1990; Zhang & Fishbach, 2005). Note that this could reflect a more general tendency to attach greater value to things one already has than to things one doesn't have.

Thus, buyers attach relatively more value to money than to the product they are being offered, whereas sellers attach relatively more value to the product than to the money they could obtain by giving it up. However, this *endowment effect* is eliminated when consumers have a promotion focus (Liberman, Idson, Camacho, & Higgins, 1999).

Stock Trading

There is a general tendency for investors to sell "winning" stocks (those that have gained in value since the time of their purchase) prematurely while holding onto "losing" stocks (those that have lost money since the time of purchase) too long (Odean, 1998). As Lee et al. (2008) showed, this tendency is implied by the utility curve postulated by Kahneman and Tversky (1979). That is, suppose a stock is equally likely to gain or lose in the future. Then, if a stock has already shown a gain, the added utility of a further gain is less than the decrease in utility of an equivalent loss. Therefore, individuals are likely to sell. If a stock has already lost, however, the marginal utility of a further loss is less than the increase in utility of an equivalent gain. Thus, individuals are likely not to sell.

Bundling

Suppose people are asked their preference for (1) two separate gifts, each of a $10 CD, or (2) a single gift of two CDs costing $20. They are likely to prefer the former. This is because the overall utility of the two individual gifts is the sum of the utilities associated with each, whereas the utility of the combined gift of $20 is not appreciably greater than that of a single $10 gift. However, suppose individuals have the choice of (1) paying $10 for each of two CDs or (2) purchasing a 2-CD package for $20. In this case, they should prefer to buy the package because the negative utility of $20 is not much less than that of $10. Similarly, individuals are more willing to forego a day of skiing if they have purchased a four-day pass than if they have purchased four single-day tickets (Soman & Gourville, 2001). This is presumably because the cost of a single day of skiing has greater negative utility than the cost of a day that is part of a bundle. (For other analyses of bundling effects, see Simonson and Staw, 1992; Yadav & Monroe, 1993.)

Decision Processes

Consumers are typically confronted with a choice between alternatives. When the alternatives have few features in common (e.g., a vacation in

Hawaii vs. a diamond ring), consumers are likely to assess their reactions to each alternative separately and base their decision on these assessments. If, on the other hand, the choice alternatives differ along a common set of attribute dimensions, they may often make a dimension-by-dimension comparison of the products and base their decision on the number and importance of the dimensions on which one product exceeds the other. Their choice may therefore differ, depending on which strategy they apply.

The implications of a dimension-by-dimension comparison process were identified by Houston, Sherman, and Baker (1989). They postulated that when individuals compute a preference, they typically focus on one of the alternatives and compare its features to those of the other. This comparison process has two consequences.

Direction of Comparison

Individuals give greater weight to features of the focal product that the alternative doesn't have than to features of the alternative that the focal product doesn't have. Thus, suppose three positive features are unique to alternative A and three other positive features are unique to B. Then, if individuals focus on A, they weight its unique features more heavily than B's and choose A, whereas if they focus on B, they weight B's unique features more heavily than A's and choose B. If A's and B's unique features are unfavorable, of course, the reverse would be true. Houston et al. (1989) postulate that if the two alternatives are presented sequentially, individuals typically focus their attention on the second alternative they consider. Consequently, all other things being equal, they are likely to prefer the second alternative they consider if its unique features are favorable but to prefer the first alternative if the second's unique features are unfavorable. These effects are reduced, however, when judgments are based on global impressions (Sanbonmatsu, Kardes, & Gibson, 1991) or when individuals have poor memory for specific attribute information (Mantel & Kardes, 1999).

Cancellation Effects

In comparing two choice alternatives to one another, the features they have in common are nondiagnostic and tend to be ignored (Houston & Sherman, 1995). If individuals are later asked to evaluate each alternative separately, the features they ignored in making comparative judgments may continue to receive little weight. This means that if the features that are common to the choice alternatives are predominantly favorable, the chosen and the rejected alternatives will *both* be evaluated less favorably than they would if the comparative judgment had not been made. Correspondingly, if the alternatives share predominantly unfavorable features, they will be evaluated more favorably than they otherwise would.

Several studies confirm these *cancellation* effects. Brunner and Wänke (2006) found that these effects can sometimes occur even when explicit comparisons are not made. Second, Wang and Wyer (2002) found that the disposition to ignore common features of a given pair of choice alternatives generalized to judgments of other products whose features were unique. For example, if individuals had previously compared products with common negative features, they then evaluated negative features less heavily in evaluating a later product whose features differed from those of the alternatives they had considered earlier. Furthermore, Hodges (1997) found that shared feature cancellation can increase preference for an inferior third option if the third option is described in terms of completely unique features and is presented last.

Decoy Effects

Individuals who are asked their preference for choice alternatives that are described along a common set of dimensions may often find it easier to compare them along each dimension, and to choose the alternative that is superior on the greater number of these dimensions, rather than performing the cognitive work required to construe the favorableness of each alternative separately. If overall evaluations of the products have been made, however, individuals may find it easier to compare these evaluations in arriving at a preference, and so a dimension-by-dimension comparison is not employed (Wang & Wyer, 2002).

These possibilities have been investigated in research on "decoy" effects, that is, the influence of introducing a third alternative on the relative preference for the others (Huber, Paine, & Puto, 1982; Simonson, 1989). For example, consider the utilities associated with the choice alternatives shown in Table 39.1, where product A is superior to B along one dimension, and B is superior to A along another. If the two dimensions are equally important, individuals are likely to choose each alternative with equal probability. However, now suppose a third alternative, D1, is added to the consideration set whose values are inferior to A's. Although D1 is not itself a viable candidate, its presence increases the relative preference for A over B. At least three alternative explanations have been given for this effect.

Table 39.1 Hypothetical Utilities of Two Choice Alternatives, A and B, a Standard Decoy (D1), and an Inferior Decoy (D2) along Two Attribute Dimensions

00	A	B	Standard decoy (D1)	Inferior decoy (D2)
Dimension 1	4	2	4	2
Dimension 2	2	4	1	1

1. *Perspective shift.* The value of D1 along dimension 2 increases the range of values that are considered along this dimension and consequently decreases the subjective difference in valence between A and B along the dimension. As a result, this difference becomes less important, and so A, which is superior along dimension 1, is preferred.

2. *Categorization and contrast.* The decoy, which has the same value as A along dimension 1, leads the two alternatives to be categorized and used as a standard for evaluating B along this dimension (Pan & Lehmann, 1993; see also Dhar & Glazer, 1996). This leads B to be seen as less favorable along dimension 1 than would otherwise be the case.

3. *Sufficient reasons.* Although A is not superior to B, it is superior to the decoy, whereas B is not. In the absence of other bases for distinguishing between A and B, this may be a sufficient reason to choose A (Simonson, 1989).

The question is how to distinguish between these alternative interpretations and when they apply. Although several studies have addressed this question, the most definitive was reported by Park and Kim (2005). They assumed that perspective shift and categorization processes occur when individuals evaluate each alternative separately before making comparative judgments, and that the evaluations provide the basis for the preferences they report later. When individuals make comparative judgments at the outset, however, a sufficient-reasons criterion is easier to apply and consequently is more likely to be invoked. In a particularly diagnostic study, participants considered (1) two alternatives analogous to A and B in Table 38.1; (2) A, B, and decoy D1; or (3) A, B and a new decoy, D2, that was inferior to both A and B along *both* dimensions. Note that although D2 would not provide a sufficient reason for choosing one over the other, it was likely to affect the subjective difference between A and B along the second dimension in much the same way that D1 affected it. Park and Kim found that when

individuals made comparative judgments at the outset, the presence of D1 increased preferences for A, but the presence of D2 did not, suggesting that a sufficient-reasons criterion was applied. When participants had evaluated each alternative separately before making comparative judgments, however, the presence of D2 *also* increased their preference for A. This suggests that evaluating the products individually activated perspective shift and/or categorization processes that were influenced by D2 and D1, and these effects were reflected in their preference for A they reported later.

Role of Mindset on Decision Processes

Wang and Wyer's (2002) findings provide an instance in which a decision criterion that is applied in one task generalizes to other tasks that individuals perform later. The cognitive processes that underlie decisions may also generalize over situations. Although evidence of this generalizability is elaborated elsewhere (see Chapter 13), a few examples are worth noting in the present context.

Dhar, Huber, and Kahn (2007) found that inducing participants to purchase a product early in the experiment increased their likelihood of making another purchase later in the session. Further, Xu and Wyer (2007, 2008) found that individuals who had reported a preference for choice alternatives in one situation acquired a "which to choose" mindset that increased their willingness to purchase one of two products in a later situation without considering the option of choosing neither. This was true even though the two choice situations were quite different. For example, participants in different experiments (1) decided which of two wild animals they preferred, (2) judged which of two animals had more of a particular physical attribute, or (3) judged the similarity of one country to another. In each case, the activity increased not only individuals' willingness to choose which of two products they would purchase in a later, hypothetical decision situation (rather than choosing neither) but also their likelihood of purchasing a candy or snack that was on sale after the experimental session (Xu & Wyer, 2008).

In a second demonstration of the generalization of decision processes, Shen and Wyer (2010) asked participants a series of questions about animals. In some cases, the answer to each question differed, and in other conditions, the answer to each question was the same. In a later, unrelated situation, participants were asked to choose the products they would purchase over a series of days. Participants distributed their choices over a greater variety of products when their responses in the first task differed than when they were the same. The influence of performing the first task on the second occurred without awareness. In fact, unobtrusively stimulating participants to think about their responses in the first task eliminated the effect that otherwise occurred.

Summary

Although we have covered a lot of ground in this review, the major conclusions to be drawn from it can be briefly summarized. The processes that underlie the use of information to make judgments and decisions depend on the type and modality of the information and the motivation and ability to construe its implications. Rather than using all relevant stimulus information, consumers typically use the subset of information that is easy to process because it is readily available, salient, or consistent with consumers' expectations. Similarly, rather than using all relevant knowledge stored in memory, consumers typically use the subset of knowledge that is most accessible as a result of the recency or frequency with which it has been activated. When these subsets of information and knowledge lead to judgments that are held with a sufficiently high degree of confidence, processing ceases, perhaps prematurely. When this confidence threshold is not reached, however, consumers consider the implications of broader sets of information and knowledge, including information and knowledge that is more difficult to process because it is less salient, is less accessible, or has less obvious implications for judgment.

Although consumers are often unaware of the processes that influence their judgments and decisions, awareness can lead to judgment adjustment processes that attempt to correct for the influence of unwarranted context effects. Conversational inferences can also lead to judgment adjustment when communication norms are violated. For example, when consumers have reason to distrust the motives of marketers, marketing communications are perceived as uncooperative, deceitful, or irrelevant. Inferences are also influenced by implicit theories about the relations among quality, price, various attributes, warranties, product promotion strategies, and other marketing variables. Sensitivity to omissions is another important determinant of inference imputation.

Subjective reactions, including affective responses and feelings of processing fluency, influence judgments and decisions through a misattribution process. Affective responses induced by irrelevant contextual variables are often misattributed to the target stimulus consumers are attempting to judge. Similarly, feelings of processing fluency induced by repetition, salience (e.g., figure-ground contrast, font size), priming, the absence of background distractions, the ease with which words can be pronounced, and rhymes can influence a wide variety of target judgments, including judgments of liking, believability, likelihood, fame, familiarity, and confidence.

The manner in which information is weighted and integrated depends on situational and chronic differences in promotion versus prevention regulatory focus. A prevention focus increases the weighting of negative attributes, loss aversion, the magnitude of the endowment effect, the status quo bias (the reluctance to accept change), and the preference for segregating gains and aggregating losses. Decisions are sometimes made by evaluating a single product or one product at a time (singular judgment), and are sometimes made by comparing objects (comparative judgment). Direction of comparison, cancellation effects, and decoy effects influence comparative judgment, but not singular judgment.

The cognitive processes used to perform one cognitive task often carry over to subsequent seemingly unrelated cognitive tasks. For example, making a purchase decision for one product category increases the likelihood of purchase in another product category. Similarly, performing a preference judgment task or a comparative judgment task in one category can increase the likelihood of purchase and variety seeking in another category.

Our review suggests that the principles of cognitive efficiency, recency and frequency, persistence, awareness, implicit theories, communication norms, subjective reactions, and integration explain a wide range of consumer phenomena reported in the consumer information processing literature. We also hope that these principles will provide a useful guide for researchers investigating new consumer phenomena.

References

Aaker, J. L., & Lee, A. Y. (2001). I seek pleasures, we avoid pains: The role of self-regulatory goals in information processing and persuasion. *Journal of Consumer Research, 27,* 33–49.

Abelson, R. P., & Reich, C. M. (1969). Implicational molecules: A method for extracting meaning from input sentences. In D. E. Walker & L. M. Norton (Eds.), *Proceedings of the International Joint Conference on Artificial Intelligence* (pp. 641–647). Washington, DC.

Adaval, R. (2001). Sometimes it just feels right: The differential weighting of affect-consistent and affect-inconsistent product information. *Journal of Consumer Research, 7*, 207–245.

Adaval, R. (2003). How good gets better and bad gets worse: Understanding the impact of affect on evaluations of known brands. *Journal of Consumer Research, 30*, 352–367.

Adaval, R., Isbell, L. M., & Wyer, R. S. (2007). The impact of pictures on narrative-based impression formation: A process interference model. *Journal of Experimental Social Psychology, 43*, 352–364.

Adaval, R., & Monroe, K. B. (2002). Automatic construction and use of contextual information for product and price evaluations. *Journal of Consumer Research, 28*, 572–588.

Adaval, R., & Wyer, R. S. (1998). The role of narratives in consumer information processing. *Journal of Consumer Psychology, 7*, 207–245.

Adaval, R., & Wyer, R. S. (2011). Conscious and nonconscious influences of a price anchor: Effects on willingness to pay for related and unrelated products. *Journal of Marketing Research, 48*, 355–365.

Ambady, N., & Rosenthal, R. (1992). Thin slices of expressive behavior as predictors of interpersonal consequences: A meta-analysis. *Psychological Bulletin, 111*, 256–274.

Anand, P., & Sternthal, B. (1989). Strategies for designing persuasive messages: Deductions from the resource matching hypothesis. In P. Cafferata, & A. M. Tybout (Eds.), *Cognitive and affective responses to advertising* (pp. 135–159). Lexington, MA: Lexington Books.

Anderson, N. H. (1971). Integration theory and attitude change. *Psychological Review, 78*, 171–206.

Anderson, N. H. (1981). *Foundations of information integration theory*. New York: Academic Press.

Andrade, E. B. (2005). Behavioral consequence of affect: Combining evaluative and regulatory mechanisms. *Journal of Consumer Research, 32*, 355–362.

Andrade, E. B., & Cohen, J. B. (2007). Affect-based evaluation and regulation as mediators of behavior: The role of affect in risk taking, helping and eating patterns. In K. D. Vohs, R. F. Baumeister, & G. Leowenstein (Eds.), *Do emotions help or hurt decision making? A hedgefoxian perspective*. New York: Russell Sage.

Bargh, J. A. (1997). The automaticity of everyday life. In R. S. Wyer (Ed.), *Advances in social cognition* (Vol. 10, pp. 1–62). Mahwah, NJ: Erlbaum.

Bargh, J. A., Bond, R. N., Lombardi, W. J., & Tota, M. E. (1986), The additive nature of chronic and temporary sources of construct accessibility. *Journal of Personality and Social Psychology, 50*, 869–878.

Bargh, J. A., & Pietromonaco, P. (1982). Automatic information processing and social perception: The influence of trait information presented outside of conscious awareness on impression formation. *Journal of Personality and Social Psychology, 43*, 437–449.

Barone, M. J., & Miniard, P. W. (2002). Mood and brand extension judgments: Asymmetric effects for desirable versus undesirable brands. *Journal of Consumer Psychology, 12*, 283–290.

Barone, M. J., Miniard, P. W., & Romero, J. B. (2000). The influence of positive mood on brand extension evaluations. *Journal of Consumer Research, 26*, 386–400.

Bechkoff, J., Krishnan, V., Niculescu, M., Kohne, M., Palmatier, R. W., & Kardes, F. R. (2009). The role of omission neglect in responses to non-gains and non-losses in gasoline price fluctuations. *Journal of Applied Social Psychology, 39*, 1191–1200.

Bilkey, W., & Nes, E. (1982). Country-of-origin effects on product evaluation. *Journal of International Business Studies, 13*, 89–99.

Birnbaum, M. H. (1974). The nonadditivity of personality impressions. *Journal of Experimental Psychology, 102*, 543–561.

Bless, H. (2001). Mood and the use of general knowledge structures. In L. L. Martin & G. L. Clore (Eds.), *Theories of mood and cognition: A user's guidebook* (pp. 9–26). Mahwah, NJ: Erlbaum.

Bless, H., Bohner, G., Schwarz, H., & Strack, F. (1990). Mood and persuasion: A cognitive response analysis. *Personality and Social Psychology Bulletin, 16*, 331–345.

Bless, H., & Schwarz, N. (2010). Mental construal and the emergence of assimilation and contrast effects: The inclusion/exclusion model. In M. P. Zanna (Ed.), *Advances in experimental social psychology* (Vol. 42, pp. 319–374). San Diego, CA: Academic Press.

Bodenhausen, G. V. (1993). Emotions, arousal, and stereotypic judgments: A heuristic of affect and stereotyping. In D. M. Mackie, & D. L. Hamilton (Eds.), *Affect, cognition, and stereotyping: Interactive processes in group perception* (pp. 13–37). San Diego, CA: Academic Press.

Boush, D., & Loken, B. (1991). A process-tracing study of brand extension evaluations. *Journal of Marketing Research, 19*, 16–28.

Brendl, M., Higgins, E. T., & Lemm, K. M. (1995). Sensitivity to varying gains and losses: The roles of self-discrepancies and event framing. *Journal of Personality and Social Psychology, 69*, 1028–1051.

Briley, D. A., Morris, M., & Simonson, I. (2000). Reasons as carriers of culture: Dynamic versus dispositional models of cultural influence on decision making. *Journal of Consumer Research, 27*, 157–178.

Briley, D. A., Morris, M., & Simonson, I. (2005). Language triggers cultural frames: In bicultural Hong Kong consumers, English versus Chinese communication evokes divergent cultural patterns of decision making. *Journal of Consumer Psychology, 15*, 351–362.

Briley, D. A., & Wyer, R. S. (2002). The effect of group membership salience on the avoidance of negative outcomes: Implications for social and consumer decisions. *Journal of Consumer Research, 29*, 400–415.

Brunner, T. A., & Wänke, M. (2006). The reduced and enhanced impact of shared features on individual brand evaluations. *Journal of Consumer Psychology, 16*, 101–111.

Campbell, M. C., & Kirmani, A. (2008). I know what you're doing and why you're doing it: The use of the persuasion knowledge model in consumer research. In C. P. Haugtvedt, P. M. Herr, & F. R. Kardes (Eds.), *Handbook of consumer psychology* (pp. 549–573). New York: LEA/Psychology Press.

Carlston, D. E. (1980). Events, inferences and impression formation. In R. Hastie, T. Ostrom, E. Ebbesen, R. Wyer, D. Hamilton, & D. Carlston (Eds.), *Person memory: The cognitive basis of social perception* (pp. 89–119). Hillsdale, NJ: Erlbaum.

Chen, S., & Chaiken, S. (1999). The heuristic-systematic model in its broader context. In S. Chaiken & Y. Trope (Eds.), *Dual-process theories in social psychology* (pp. 73–96). New York: Guilford.

Childers, T. L., & Houston, M. J. (1984). Conditions for a picture-superiority effect on consumer memory. *Journal of Consumer Research, 11*, 643–654.

Childers, T. L., Houston, M. J., & Heckler, S. E. (1985). Measurement of individual differences in visual versus verbal information processing. *Journal of Consumer Research, 12*, 125–134.

Cho, H. J., & Schwarz, N. (2008). Of great art and untalented artists: Effort information and the flexible construction of judgmental heuristics. *Journal of Consumer Psychology, 18*, 205–211.

Columbo, L., & Williams, J. (1990). Effects of word- and sentence-level contexts upon word recognition. *Memory and Cognition, 18*, 153–163.

Costley, C. L., & Brucks, M. (1992). Selective recall and information use in consumer preferences. *Journal of Consumer Research, 18*, 464–474.

Cronley, M. L., Posavac, S. S., Meyer, T., Kardes, F. R., & Kellaris, J. J. (2005). A selective hypothesis testing perspective on price-quality inference and inference-based choice. *Journal of Consumer Psychology, 15*, 159–169.

Deval, H., Mantel, S. P., Kardes, F. R., & Posavac, S. S. (in press). How naïve theories drive opposing inferences from the same information. *Journal of Consumer Research.*

Deval, H., Pfeiffer, B. E., Ewing, D. R., Han, X., Cronley, M. L., & Kardes, F. R. (2011). *The effect of temporal construal on sensitivity to missing information.* Unpublished manuscript, Dalhousie University.

Dhar, R., & Glazer, R. (1996). Similarity in context: Cognitive representation and violation of preference and perceptual invariance. *Organizational Behavior and Human Decision Processes, 67*, 280–293.

Dhar, R., Huber, J., & Khan, U. (2007). The shopping momentum effect. *Journal of Marketing Research, 44*, 370–378.

Edell, J. A., & Staelin, R. (1983). The information processing of pictures in print advertisements. *Journal of Consumer Research, 10*, 45–61.

Escalas, J. E. (2004). Narrative processing: Building consumer connections to brands. *Journal of Consumer Psychology, 14*, 105–113.

Escalas, J. E. (2007). Self-referencing and persuasion: Narrative transportation versus analytical elaboration. *Journal of Consumer Research, 33*, 421–429.

Escalas, J. E., & Luce, M. F. (2004). Understanding the effects of process-focused versus outcome-focused thought in response to advertising. *Journal of Consumer Research, 31*, 274–285.

Fishbein, M. (1963). An investigation of the relationships between beliefs about an object and attitude toward that object. *Human Relations, 16*, 233–239.

Fiske, S. T., & Neuberg, S. L. (1990). A continuum of impression formation from category-based to individuating processes: Influence of information and motivation on attention and interpretation. In M. P. Zanna (Ed.), *Advances in experimental social psychology* (Vol. 23, pp. 1–74). New York: Academic Press.

Folkes, V. S. (1984). Consumer reactions to product failure: An attributional approach. *Journal of Consumer Research, 10*, 398–409.

Folkes, V. S., Koletsky, S., & Graham, J. L. (1987). A field study of causal inferences and consumer reaction: The view from the airport. *Journal of Consumer Research, 13*, 534–539.

Förster, J., & Liberman, N. (2007). Knowledge activation. In A. Kruglanski & E. T. Higgins (Eds.), *Social psychology: Handbook of basic principles* (2nd ed., pp. 201–231). New York: Guilford.

Förster, J., Liberman, N., & Kuschel, S. (2007). The effect of global versus local processing styles on assimilation versus contrast in social judgment. *Journal of Personality and Social Psychology, 94*, 579–599.

Gardner, W. L., Gabriel, S., & Lee, A. Y. (1999). "I" values freedom, but "we" value relationships: Self-construal priming mirrors cultural differences in judgment. *Psychological Science, 10*, 321–326.

Green, M. C., & Brock, T. C. (2000). The role of transportation in the persuasiveness of public narratives. *Journal of Personality and Social Psychology, 79*, 701–721.

Grice, H. P. (1975). Logic and conversation. In P. Cole & J. L. Morgan (Eds.), *Syntax and semantics: Speech acts* (pp. 41–58). New York: Academic Press.

Hansen, J., & Wänke, M. (2010). Truth from language and truth from fit: The impact of linguistic concreteness and level of construal on subjective truth. *Personality and Social Psychology Bulletin, 36*, 1576–1588.

Haugtvedt, C. P., Herr, P. M., & Kardes, F. R. (Eds.) (2008). *Handbook of consumer psychology.* New York: LEA/Psychology Press.

Herr, P. M. (1986). Consequences of priming: Judgment and behavior. *Journal of Personality and Social Psychology, 51*, 1106–1115.

Herr, P. M., Kardes, F. R., & Kim, J. (1991). Effects of word-of-mouth and product-attribute information on persuasion: An accessibility-diagnosticity perspective. *Journal of Consumer Research, 17*, 454–462.

Higgins, E. T. (1981). The "communication game:" Implications for social cognition and persuasion. In E. T. Higgins, C. P. Herman, & M. P. Zanna (Eds.), *Social cognition: The Ontario symposium* (Vol. 1, pp. 342–392). Hillsdale, NJ: Erlbaum.

Higgins, E. T. (1996). Knowledge activation: Accessibility, applicability, and salience. In E. T. Higgins, & A. W. Kruglanski (Eds.), *Social psychology: Handbook of basic principles* (pp. 133–168). New York: Guilford.

Higgins, E. T. (1997). Beyond pleasure and pain. *American Psychologist, 55*, 1217–1233.

Higgins, E. T. (1998). Promotion and prevention: Regulatory focus as a motivational principle. In M. P. Zanna (Ed.), *Advances in experimental social psychology* (Vol. 30, pp. 1–46). San Diego, CA: Academic Press.

Higgins, E. T., Bargh, J. A., & Lombardi, W. (1985). The nature of priming effects on categorization. *Journal of Experimental Psychology: Learning, Memory, and Cognition, 11*, 59–69.

Hodges, S. D. (1997). When matching up features messes up decisions: The role of feature matching in successive choices. *Journal of Personality and Social Psychology, 72*, 1310–1321.

Hong, S., & Kang, D. K. (2006). Country-of-origin influences on product evaluations: The impact of animosity and perceptions of industriousness and brutality on judgments of typical and atypical products. *Journal of Consumer Psychology, 16*, 232–240.

Hong, S., & Wyer, R. S. (1989). Effects of country-of-origin and product-attribute information on product evaluation: An information processing perspective. *Journal of Consumer Research, 16*, 175–187.

Hong, S., & Wyer, R. S. (1990). Determinants of product evaluation: Effects of the time interval between knowledge of a product's country of origin and information about its specific attributes. *Journal of Consumer Research, 17*, 277–288.

Houston, D. A., & Sherman, S. J. (1995). Cancelation and focus: The role of shared and unique features in the choice process. *Journal of Experimental Social Psychology, 31*, 357–378.

Houston, D. A., Sherman, S. J., & Baker, S. M. (1989). The influence of unique features and direction of comparison on preferences. *Journal of Experimental Social Psychology, 25,* 121–141.

Huber, J., Payne, J. W., & Puto, C. (1982), Adding asymmetrically dominated alternatives: Violations of regularity and the similarity hypothesis. *Journal of Consumer Research, 9,* 90–98.

Hung, I. W. P., & Wyer, R. S. (2008). The role of implicit theories in the impact of problem-solving print advertisements. *Journal of Consumer Psychology, 18,* 223–235.

Isen, A. M. (1987). Positive affect, cognitive processes, and social behavior. In L. Berkowitz (Ed.), *Advances in experimental social psychology* (Vol. 20, pp. 203–253). New York: Academic Press.

Isen, A. M. (2007). Positive affect, cognitive flexibility and self control. In X. Shoda, D. Cervone, & G. Downey(Eds.), *Persons in context* (pp. 130–147). New York: Guilford.

Isen, A. M. (2008). Positive affect and decision processes. In C. Haugtvedt, P. M. Herr, & F. R. Kardes (Eds.), *Handbook of consumer psychology* (pp. 273–296). Mahwah, NJ: Erlbaum.

Isen, A. M., Daubman, K. A., & Nowicki, G. P. (1987). Positive affect facilitates creative problem solving. *Journal of Personality and Social Psychology, 52,* 1122–1131.

Isen, A. M., Johnson, M. M., Mertz, E., & Robinson, F. G. (1985). The influence of positive affect on the unusualness of word associations. *Journal of Personality and Social Psychology, 48,* 1–14.

Jiang, Y., Steinhart, Y., & Wyer, R. S. (2008). *The role of visual and semantic processing strategies in consumer information processing.* Unpublished manuscript, Hong Kong University of Science and Technology.

Jiang, Y., & Wyer, R. S. (2009). The role of visual perspective in information processing. *Journal of Experimental Social Psychology, 45,* 486–495.

Johar, G. V. (1995). Consumer involvement and deception from implied advertising claims. *Journal of Marketing Research, 32,* 267–279.

Kahneman, D., Knetsch, J. L., & Thaler, R. H. (1990). Experimental tests of the endowment effect and the Coase theorem. *Journal of Political Economy, 98,* 1325–1348.

Kahneman, D., & Tversky, A. (1979), Prospect theory: An analysis of decision under risk. *Econometrica, 47,* 263–291.

Kardes, F. R. (1986). Effects of initial product judgments on subsequent memory-based judgments. *Journal of Consumer Research, 13,* 1–11.

Kardes, F. R. (1988). Spontaneous inference processes in advertising: The effects of conclusion omission and involvement on persuasion. *Journal of Consumer Research, 15,* 225–233.

Kardes, F. R., Cronley, M. L., Kellaris, J. J., & Posavac, S. S. (2004a). The role of selective information processing in price-quality inference. *Journal of Consumer Research, 31,* 368–374.

Kardes, F. R., Cronley, M. L., Pontes, M. C., & Houghton, D. C. (2001). Down the garden path: The role of conditional inference processes in self-persuasion. *Journal of Consumer Psychology, 11,* 159–168.

Kardes, F. R., Fennis, B. M., Hirt, E. R., Tormala, Z. L., & Bullington, B. (2007). The role of the need for cognitive closure in the effectiveness of the disrupt-then-reframe influence technique. *Journal of Consumer Research, 34,* 377–385.

Kardes, F. R., Posavac, S. S., & Cronley, M. L. (2004b). Consumer inference: A review of processes, bases, and judgment contexts. *Journal of Consumer Psychology, 14,* 230–256.

Kardes, F. R., Posavac, S. S., Cronley, M. L., & Herr, P. M. (2008). Consumer inference. In C. P. Haugtvedt, P. M. Herr, & F. R. Kardes (Eds.), *Handbook of consumer psychology* (pp. 165–191). New York: LEA/Psychology Press.

Kardes, F. R., Posavac, S. S., Silvera, D. H., Cronley M. L., Sanbonmatsu, D. M., Schertzer, S., Miller, F., Herr, P. M., & Chandrashekaran, M. (2006). Debiasing omission neglect. *Journal of Business Research, 59,* 786–92.

Kardes, F. R., & Sanbonmatsu, D. M. (1993). Direction of comparison, expected feature correlation, and the set-size effect in preference judgment. *Journal of Consumer Psychology, 2,* 39–54.

Kim, H. M. (2006). Evaluations of moderately typical products: The role of within- versus cross-manufacturer comparisons. *Journal of Consumer Psychology, 16,* 70–78.

Kim, K., & Meyers-Levy, J. (2008). Context effects in diverse-category brand environments: The influence of target product positioning and consumers' processing mindset. *Journal of Consumer Research, 34,* 882–896.

Kim, Y., Park, J. W., & Wyer, R. S. (2009). Effects of temporal distance and memory on consumer judgments. *Journal of Consumer Research, 36,* 634–645.

Klein, J. G., Ettenson, R., & Morris, M. D. (1998). The animosity model of foreign product purchase: An empirical test in the People's Republic of China. *Journal of Marketing, 62,* 89–100.

Kosslyn, S. M. (1980). *Image and mind.* Cambridge, MA: Harvard University Press.

Kühnen, U., & Oyserman, D. (2002). Thinking about the self influences thinking in general: Cognitive consequences of salient self-concept. *Journal of Experimental Social Psychology, 38,* 492–499.

Lazarus, R. S. (1991). *Emotion and adaptation.* New York: Oxford University Press.

Lee, H. J., Park, J. W., Lee, J. Y., & Wyer, R. S. (2008). Disposition effects and underlying mechanisms in the e-trading of stocks. *Journal of Marketing Research. 45,* 362–378.

Liberman, N., Idson, L. C., Camacho, C. J., & Higgins, E. T. (1999). Promotion and prevention choices between stability and change. *Journal of Personality and Social Psychology, 77,* 1135–1145.

Liberman, N., Idson, L. C., & Higgins, E. T. (2005). Predicting the intensity of losses vs. non-gains and non-losses vs. gains: A test of the loss aversion explanation. *Journal of Experimental Social Psychology, 41,* 527–534.

Loken, B, Barsalou, L. W., & Joiner, C. (2008). Categorization theory and research in consumer psychology: Category representation and category-based inferences. In C. P. Haugtvedt, P. M. Herr, & F. R. Kardes (Eds.), *Handbook of consumer psychology* (pp. 133–163). New York: LEA/ Psychology Press.

Maheswaran, D. (1994). Country of origin as a stereotype: Effects of consumer expertise and attribute strength on product evaluations. *Journal of Consumer Research, 21,* 354–365.

Mantel, S. P., & Kardes, F. R. (1999). The role of direction of comparison, attribute-based processing, and attitude-based processing in consumer preference. *Journal of Consumer Research, 25,* 335–352.

Markus, H. R., & Kitayama, S. (1991). Culture and the self: Implications for cognition, emotion and motivation. *Psychological Review, 98,* 224–253.

Martin, L. L., Seta, J. J., & Crelia, R. A. (1990). Assimilation and contrast as a function of people's willingness and ability to expend effort in forming an impression. *Journal of Personality and Social Psychology, 59*, 27–37.

McGuire, W. J. (1960). A syllogistic analysis of cognitive relationships. In M. J. Rosenberg & C. I. Hovland (Eds.), *Attitude organization and change* (pp. 140–162). New Haven, CT: Yale University Press.

Menon, G., & Raghubir, P. (2003). Ease of retrieval as an automatic input in judgments: A mere accessibility framework? *Journal of Consumer Research, 30*, 230–243.

Menon, G., Raghubir, P., & Schwarz, N. (1995). Behavioral frequency judgments: An accessibility-diagnosticity framework. *Journal of Consumer Research, 22*, 212–228.

Meyers-Levy, J., & Peracchio, L. A. (1992). Getting an angle in advertising: The effect of camera angle on product evaluations. *Journal of Marketing Research, 29*, 454–461.

Meyvis, T., & Janiszewski, C. (2004). When are broader brands stronger brands? An accessibility perspective on the success of brand extensions. *Journal of Consumer Research, 31*, 346–357.

Miniard, P. W., Bhatla, S., Lord, K. R., Dickson, P. R., & Unnava, H. R. (1991). Picture-based persuasion processes and the moderating role of involvement. *Journal of Consumer Research, 18*, 82–107.

Mussweiler, T., & Strack, F. (1999). Hypothesis-consistent testing and semantic priming in the anchoring paradigm: A selective accessibility model. *Journal of Experimental Social Psychology, 35*, 136–164.

Nisbett, R. E. (2003). *The geography of thought: How Asians and Westerners think differently.* New York: Free Press.

Nunes, J. C., & Boatwright, P. (2004), Incidental prices and their effect on willingness to pay, *Journal of Marketing Research, 41*, 457–466.

Odean, T. (1998). Are investors reluctant to realize their losses? *Journal of Finance, 53*, 1775–1798.

Ostrom, T. M., & Upshaw, H. S. (1968). Psychological perspective and attitude change. In A. G. Greenwald, T. M. Ostrom, & T. C. Brock (Eds.), *Psychological foundations of attitude* (pp. 217–242). New York: Academic Press.

Pan, Y., & Lehmann, D. R. (1993). The influence of new brand entry on subjective brand judgments. *Journal of Consumer Research, 20*, 76–86.

Park, D. C., Nisbett, R. E., & Hedden, T. (1999). Culture, cognition, and aging. *Journal of Gerontology, 54B*, 75–84.

Park, J. W., & Kim, J. K. (2005). The effects of decoys on preference shifts: The role of attractiveness and providing justification. *Journal of Consumer Psychology, 15*, 94–107.

Park, J. W., Yoon, S. O., Kim, K. H., & Wyer, R. S. (2001). Effects of priming a bipolar attribute concept on dimension versus concept-specific accessibility of semantic memory. *Journal of Personality and Social Psychology, 81*, 405–420.

Pennington, N., & Hastie, R. (1992). Explaining the evidence: Tests of the story model for juror decision making. *Journal of Personality and Social Psychology, 62*, 189–206.

Petrova, P. K., & Cialdini, R. B. (2005). Fluency of consumption imagery and the backfire effects of imagery appeals. *Journal of Consumer Research, 32*, 442–452.

Petrova, P. K., & Cialdini, R. B. (2008). Evoking the imagination as a strategy of influence. In C. P. Haugtvedt, P. M. Herr, & F. R. Kardes (Eds.), *Handbook of consumer psychology* (pp. 505–523). New York: LEA/Psychology Press.

Pfeiffer, B. E. (2008). *Omission detection and inferential adjustment.* Unpublished dissertation, University of Cincinnati.

Pham, M. T. (1998). Representativeness, relevance and the use of feelings in decision making. *Journal of Consumer Research, 25*, 144–159.

Raghubir, P., & Menon, G. (2005). When and why is ease of retrieval informative? *Memory & Cognition, 33*, 821–832.

Rozin, P., Fischler, C., & Shields-Argeles (2009). Additivity dominance: Additives are more potent and more often lexicalized across languages than are "subtractives." *Judgment and Decision Making, 4*, 475–478.

Sanbonmatsu, D. M., Kardes, F. R., & Gibson, B. D. (1991). The role of specific attributes and overall evaluations in comparative judgment. *Organizational Behavior and Human Decision Processes, 48*, 131–146.

Sanbonmatsu, D. M., Kardes, F. R., & Herr, P. M. (1992). The role of prior knowledge and missing information in multiattribute evaluation. *Organizational Behavior & Human Decision Processes, 51*, 76–91.

Sanbonmatsu, D. M., Kardes, F. R., Houghton, D. C., Ho, E. A., & Posavac, S. S. (2003). Overestimating the importance of the given information in multiattribute consumer judgment. *Journal of Consumer Psychology, 13*, 289–300.

Sanbonmatsu, D. M., Kardes, F. R., Posavac, S. S., & Houghton, D. C. (1997). Contextual influences on judgment based on limited information. *Organizational Behavior and Human Decision Processes, 69*, 251–264.

Sanbonmatsu, D. M., Kardes, F. R., & Sansone, C. (1991). Remembering less and inferring more: effects of time of judgment on inferences about unknown attributes. *Journal of Personality and Social Psychology, 61*, 546–554.

Sawyer, A. G., & Howard, D. J. (1991). Effects of omitting conclusions in advertisements to involved and uninvolved audiences. *Journal of Marketing Research, 28*, 467–474.

Schank, R. C., & Abelson, R. P. (1977). *Scripts, plans, goals and understanding.* Hillsdale, NJ: Erlbaum.

Schwarz, N. (1990). Feelings as information: Informational and motivational functions of affective states. In E. T. Higgins & R. M. Sorrentino (Eds), *Handbook of motivation and cognition: Foundations of social behavior* (Vol. 2, pp. 527–51). New York: Guilford.

Schwarz, N. (1994), Judgment in a social context: Biases, shortcomings, and the logic of conversation. In M. P. Zanna (Ed.), *Advances in experimental social psychology* (Vol. 26, pp. 123–162). San Diego, CA: Academic Press.

Schwarz, N. (1996). *Cognition and communication: Judgmental biases, research methods and the logic of conversation.* Hillsdale, NJ: Erlbaum.

Schwarz, N. (1998). Accessible content and accessibility experiences: The interplay of declarative and experiential information in judgment. *Personality and Social Psychology Review, 2*, 87–99.

Schwarz, N. (2004). Metacognitive experiences in consumer judgment and decision making. *Journal of Consumer Psychology, 14*, 332–348.

Schwarz, N., Bless, H., Strack, F., Klumpp, G., Rittenauer-Schatka, H., & Simons, A. (1991). Ease of retrieval as information: Another look at the availability heuristic. *Journal of Personality and Social Psychology, 61*, 195–201.

Schwarz, N., & Clore, G. L. (1983). Mood, misattribution, and judgments of well-being: Informative and directive functions of affective states. *Journal of Personality and Social Psychology, 45*, 513–523.

Schwarz, N., & Clore, G. L. (1996). Feelings and phenomenal experiences. In E. T. Higgins & A. W. Kruglanski (Eds.), *Social psychology: A handbook of basic principles* (pp. 433–465). New York: Guilford.

Schwarz, N., & Clore, G. L. (2007). Feelings and phenomenal experiences. In A. W. Kruglanski & E. T. Higgins (Eds.). *Social psychology: Handbook of basic principles* (2nd ed., pp. 385–407). New York: Guilford.

Shen, H., Jiang, Y, & Adaval, R. (2010). Contrast and assimilation effects of processing fluency, *Journal of Consumer Research, 36*, 876–889.

Shen, H., & Wyer, R. S. (2008). The impact of negative affect on responses to affect-regulating experiences. *Journal of Consumer Psychology, 18*, 39–48.

Shen, H., & Wyer, R. S. (2010). The effect of past behavior on variety seeking. Automatic and deliberative processes. *Journal of Consumer Psychology, 20*, 33–42.

Sherif, M., & Hovland, C. I. (1961). *Social judgment: Assimilation and contrast effects in communication and attitude change.* New Haven, CT: Yale University Press.

Silvera, D. H., Kardes, F. R., Harvey, N., Cronley, M. L., & Houghton, D. C. (2005). Contextual influences on omission neglect in the fault tree paradigm. *Journal of Consumer Psychology, 15*, 117–126.

Simonson, I. (1989). Choice based on reasons: The case of attraction and compromise effects, *Journal of Consumer Research, 16*, 158–174.

Simonson, I., & Staw, B. M. (1992). Deescalation strategies: A comparison of techniques for reducing commitment to losing courses of action. *Journal of Applied Psychology, 77*, 419–426.

Skowronski, J. J., & Carlston, D. E. (1989). Negativity and extremity biases in impression formation: A review of explanations. *Psychological Bulletin, 105*, 131–142.

Soman, D., & Gourville, J. T. (2001). Transaction decoupling: How price bundling affects the decision to consume. *Journal of Marketing Research, 38*, 30–44.

Srull, T. K., & Wyer, R. S. (1979). The role of category accessibility in the interpretation of information about persons: Some determinants and implications. *Journal of Personality and Social Psychology, 37*, 1660–1672.

Srull, T. K., & Wyer, R. S. (1980). Category accessibility and social perception: Some implications for the study of person memory and interpersonal judgments. *Journal of Personality and Social Psychology, 38*, 841–856.

Strack, F., Martin, L. L., & Stepper, S. (1988). Inhibiting and facilitating conditions of the human smile: A nonobtrusive test of the facial feedback hypothesis. *Journal of Personality and Social Psychology, 54*, 768–777.

Taylor, S. E., & Fiske, S. T. (1978). Salience, attention and attribution: Top of the head phenomena. In L. Berkowitz (Ed.), *Advances in experimental social psychology* (Vol. 11, pp. 249–288). New York: Academic Press.

Tesser, A. (1978). Self-generated attitude change. In L. Berkowitz (Ed.) *Advances in experimental social psychology* (Vol. 11, pp. 289–338). New York: Academic Press.

Treisman, A., & Souther, J. (1985). Search asymmetry: A diagnostic for preattentive processing of separable features. *Journal of Experimental Psychology: General, 114*, 285–310.

Trope, Y., & Liberman, N. (2003). Temporal construal. *Psychological Review, 110*, 403–421.

Trope, Y., & Liberman, N. (2010). Construal-level theory of psychological distance. *Psychological Review, 117*, 440–463.

Trope, Y., Liberman, N., & Wakslak, C. (2007). Construal levels and psychological distance: Effects on representation, prediction, evaluation, and behavior. *Journal of Consumer Psychology, 17*, 83–95.

Tversky, A., & Kahneman, D. (1974). Judgment under uncertainty: Heuristics and biases. *Science, 185*, 1124–1131.

Wang, J., & Calder, B. J. (2006). Media transportation and advertising. *Journal of Consumer Research, 33*, 151–162.

Wang, J., & Wyer, R. S. (2002). Comparative judgment processes: The effects of task objectives and time delay on product evaluations. *Journal of Consumer Psychology, 12*, 327–340.

Wänke, M., Bohner, G., & Jurkowitsch, A.(1997). There are many reasons to drive a BMW: Does imagined ease of argument generation influence attitudes? *Journal of Consumer Research, 24*, 170–177.

Wegener, D. T., & Petty, R. E. (1997). The flexible correction model: The role of naïve theories of bias in bias correction. In M. P. Zanna (Ed.), *Advances in experimental social psychology* (Vol. 29, pp. 141–208). New York: Academic Press.

Winkielman, P., Schwarz, N., Fazendeiro, T. A., & Reber, R. (2003). The hedonic marking of processing fluency: Implications for evaluative judgment. In J. Musch & K. C. Klauer (Eds.), *The psychology of evaluation: Affective processes in cognition and emotion* (pp. 189–217). Mahwah, NJ: Erlbaum.

Wright, S., Manolis, C., Brown, D., Guo, X., Dinsmore, J., Chiu, C.-Y. P., & Kardes, F. R. (2012). Construal-level mind-sets and the perceived validity of marketing claims. *Marketing Letters, 23*, 253–261.

Wyer, R. S. (2004). *Social comprehension and judgment: The role of situation models, narratives and implicit theories.* Mahwah, NJ: Erlbaum.

Wyer, R. S. (2007). Principles of mental representation. In A. Kruglanski & E. T. Higgins (Eds.), *Social psychology: Handbook of basic principles* (2nd ed., pp. 285–231). New York: Guilford.

Wyer, R. S. (2008). The role of knowledge accessibility in cognition and behavior: Implications for consumer information processing. In C. P. Haugtvedt, P. M. Herr, & F. R. Kardes (Eds.), *Handbook of consumer psychology* (pp. 31–76). New York: LEA/Psychology Press.

Wyer, R. S., & Adaval, R. (2008). Social psychology and consumer psychology: An unexplored interface. In M. Wänke (Ed.), *Frontiers of social psychology: The social psychology of consumer behavior* (pp. 17–59). New York: LEA/Psychology Press.

Wyer, R. S., & Carlston, D. E. (1979). *Social cognition, inference and attribution.* Hillsdale, NJ: Erlbaum.

Wyer, R. S., & Collins, J. E. (1992). A theory of humor elicitation. *Psychological Review, 99*, 663–688.

Wyer, R. S., & Hartwick, J. (1980). The role of information retrieval and conditional inference processes in belief formation and change. In L. Berkowitz (Ed.), *Advances in experimental social psychology* (Vol. 13, pp. 241–284). New York: Academic Press.

Wyer, R. S., & Hartwick, J. (1984). The recall and use of belief statements as bases for judgments: Some determinants and implications. *Journal of Experimental Social Psychology, 20*, 65–85.

Wyer, R. S., Hung, I. W., & Jiang, Y. (2008). Visual and verbal processing strategies in comprehension and judgment. *Journal of Consumer Psychology, 18*, 244–257.

Wyer, R. S., & Srull, T. K. (1989). *Memory and cognition in its social context.* Hillsdale, NJ: Erlbaum.

Xu, A. J., & Wyer, R. S. (2007). The effect of mindsets on consumer decision strategies. *Journal of Consumer Research, 34*, 556–566.

Xu, A. J., & Wyer, R. S. (2008). The comparative mindset: From animal comparisons to increased purchase intentions. *Psychological Science, 19*, 859–864.

Xu, A. J., & Wyer, R. S. (2010). Puffery in advertisements: The effects of media context, communication norms, and consumer knowledge. *Journal of Consumer Research, 37*, 329–343.

Yadav, M. S., & Monroe, K. B. (1993). How buyers perceive savings in a bundle price: An examination of a bundle's transaction value. *Journal of Marketing Research, 30*, 350–358.

Yan, D., Mao, H., & Wyer, R. S. (2009). *Updating similarity or updating diagnosticity? How unexpected performance of a previous extension impacts evaluation of a subsequent one.*

Unpublished manuscript, Hong Kong University of Science and Technology.

Yeung, C. W. M., & Wyer, R. S. (2004). Affect, appraisal and consumer judgment. *Journal of Consumer Research, 31*, 412–424.

Yeung, C. W. M., & Wyer, R. S. (2005). Does loving a brand mean loving its products? The role of brand-elicited affect in brand extension evaluations. *Journal of Marketing Research, 42*, 495–506.

Zhang, M., & Wang, J. (2009). Psychological distance asymmetry: The spatial dimension vs. other dimensions. *Journal of Consumer Psychology, 19*, 497–507.

Zhang, Y., & Fishbach, A. (2005). The role of anticipated emotions in the endowment effect. *Journal of Consumer Psychology, 15*, 316–324.

Law and Social Cognition

Barbara A. Spellman *and* Frederick Schauer

Abstract

The legal system—in both substance and process—relies heavily on social cognition. However, much of the vast research in law and psychology focuses narrowly on issues of jury decision making, particularly in criminal cases. This chapter seeks to broaden that research agenda. The authors first review some of the main issues in jury research, especially those that the DNA exonerations have implicated in the false convictions of innocent people: eyewitness identification, confessions, and forensics. Second, the authors describe the multiple roles of judges, contrast them to juries, and review why judicial decision making can be described as involving implicit social cognition as part of the process of legal reasoning. Finally, the chapter illustrates how many issues of substantive law— what should count as causing harm to another person, whether intent and knowledge should matter to punishment, how people should be allowed to plan for the future in contracts and wills—all depend on assumptions about social cognition, and are all ripe for much more research.

Key Words: law, legal reasoning, law and psychology, juries, judges, judicial decision making, jury decision making

Law and Social Cognition

The legal system is an institution of social cognition. In appraising, regulating, and coordinating the behavior of people within a society, the law makes assumptions about how people do think and act, and prescribes rules and procedures about how people should and may think and act—and the consequences if they do not. Yet although the legal system surrounds and partially structures our lives, the social cognitive psychological implications of the law's pervasive presence have barely been touched. The goals of this chapter are to review briefly several of the well-mined areas in law and psychology and then to describe a few areas that are ripe for new or additional research. (Note: For reasons that will be clear below, this chapter is relevant primarily but not exclusively to U.S. law.)

Much of the existing research on legal social cognition focuses on the types of evidence presented

to jurors and how those jurors evaluate and use that evidence—particularly in criminal trials. This body of research has been valuable in increasing our understanding of trial-related processes, especially those aspects involving decision making by juries. Indeed, this research has influenced the design and redesign of some legal procedures, such as the processes for obtaining confessions and conducting line-ups. Despite these contributions, however, the research agenda of the field of psychology and law has tended to overemphasize research surrounding jury trial–related procedure and to neglect other aspects of the law, aspects whose social-cognitive dimensions are no less important.

The focus on jury decision making in criminal trials in the existing research agenda of law and psychology is in some respects distorted. First, jury trials are far less common than people are likely to believe, especially if they base their estimates on the number of actual jury trials reported by the news media or the number of fictional jury trials depicted by the entertainment industry. The jury trial is largely a creature of legal systems based on English common law, and thus, in much of the world, there are no juries at all (Merryman & Pérez-Perdomo, 2007). Moreover, even in legal systems that owe their origins to English common law, the use of juries for civil trials has now been virtually eliminated, the noteworthy exception being the United States (Hans, 2008; Vidmar, 2000). And even in the United States, where litigants typically have the right to choose whether to have a jury, most trials, both civil and criminal, are now heard by a judge alone, and both the number of jury trials and the percentage of trials that use juries are rapidly decreasing (Galanter, 2004; Young, 2006). Thus, many of the decisions formerly made by juries are increasingly made by judges. Consequently, a question in need of much more exploration is whether what we know about decision making by lay jurors can be applied when those decisions are instead made by legally trained judges.

Second, in addition to focusing disproportionately on juries, the existing research has largely neglected another important role that judges play: determining the law that applies to the case at hand. A popular image assumes that this is a straightforward and almost mechanical task in which the judge simply consults a law book to find out what the law is. But this image is pervasively false, and the task of determining what the applicable law is from a mass of often inconsistent, incomplete, and indeterminate rules and precedents is a cognitive task no less difficult and no less amenable to serious psychological research than the typical jury's tasks.

Third, and finally, there are a vast number of other areas in which the law affects people's lives: from school to home to work, from private transactions to public transgressions, from health to wealth to liberty. The rules of law themselves embody assumptions about the cognitive processes of ordinary people, but it is hardly clear that these assumptions are consistent with what we have learned from the psychological research. For example, the criminal law seeks, among other things, to deter antisocial behavior by attaching various penalties to violations, but do the penalties and how they are applied fit with how people actually behave in the face of the possibility of punishment? Similarly, although the law of wills is designed to allow people to control the distribution of their assets when they die, does the law accurately reflect how people think when contemplating death? For these and countless other questions of substantive law, legal rules embody assumptions about human cognition and human behavior, but often those assumptions diverge from the reality.

The three sections of this chapter address the foregoing issues—the traditional focus on the social cognitive issues involved in jury trials, and then the questions of decision making by judges, and finally some of the broader reaches of law we have just previewed. Our goal in this chapter is not only to provide a survey of where the research agenda of law and psychology has taken us in the past but also to offer suggestions about where it might and should go in the future.

Trial Evidence and Jury Decision Making

Issues of trial evidence and jury decision making have provided the focus for a rich and long-standing literature and research agenda (Winter & Greene, 2007). Indeed, many articles and books purporting to be generally about "psychology and law" deal almost solely with those issues. Because of the quantity of good recent reviews, we treat such issues in a cursory manner here, providing citations as appropriate to longer treatments (e.g., see Kovera & Borgida, 2010, for a good general review of social psychology cognition and law, albeit almost exclusively limited to topics of evidence and criminal trials).

Evidence: The DNA Revolution

Although research on eyewitness testimony and eyewitness identification (e.g., line-ups) has been around for decades, it took the revelations of the DNA postconviction exonerations to validate the research outside of the laboratory. Since 1989, almost 300 people have been released from prison based on the postconviction analysis of DNA evidence (see www.innocenceproject.org for the current count). Inspection of the processes leading to the first 200 exonerations reveals that about 79% of the exonerations involved mistaken eyewitnesses, 57% included flawed forensic evidence, and 16% involved false confessions by the defendant (Garrett, 2008). The exonerations made it clear that many of the legal system's long-standing practices are far from perfect, and thus the exonerations have legitimated (and spurred) psychology research that could explain what goes wrong and how the practices can be improved.

EYEWITNESS IDENTIFICATION

Perhaps the most influential research has been that on eyewitness identification (see Wells, 2006;

Wells, Menon, & Penrod, 2006, for good reviews). What the DNA exonerations underscore is that witnesses and victims can, in good faith, mistakenly identify people in line-ups and then claim in court that they had done so with high confidence. We now know that in many cases such mistaken identifications have sent innocent people to prison, and are likely to do so in the future.

Hundreds of studies of line-ups have revealed factors that affect the likelihood of a correct identification. These factors are often divided into two kinds: "estimator variables," which are not under the control of the legal system, and "system variables," which are. Estimator variables include such things as the conditions under which the eyewitness viewed the event, for example, how long the witness saw the perpetrator, how far away the events occurred, and what type of lighting was present. Although jurors are likely to understand the effects of these variables on a witness's ability to make a correct identification, there are other factors that affect a witness's accuracy in ways that jurors do not understand (McConkey & Roche, 1989; Noon & Hollin, 1987). For example, the presence and thus the distraction of a gun may make it more difficult for witnesses to correctly identify a perpetrator (Steblay, 1992). And witnesses tend to be less good at identifying perpetrators of races different from their own (Wells & Olson, 2001). System variables include the processes involved in interviewing witnesses and conducting line-ups. Many system variables affect the accuracy of eyewitness identification, including the composition of the line-ups (e.g., the number of people in the line-up; how much and in what ways the suspect looks like the perpetrator and the members of the line-up look like each other) and how line-ups are conducted (Brigham, Meissner, & Wasserman, 1999; Lindsay & Wells, 1985; Steblay, 2011).

So how *should* line-ups be conducted? If one thinks of a line-up as an experiment of sorts, in which the law (experimenter) wants the witness (research subject) to correctly identify the perpetrator or correctly state that he is not present in the line-up (i.e., lead to neither a type 1 nor type 2 error), then one should imagine applying what we know about experiments to conducting line-ups (Wells, 1993). Thus, if line-up administrators seek to reduce the number of false identifications, witnesses should be told that the perpetrator may or may not be in the line-up, thereby reducing experimenter demands. The person administering the line-up should be "blind to condition" and not know who the suspect is, for

fear of influencing the witness. And line-ups should be conducted sequentially (i.e., the witness sees the members one at a time), rather than simultaneously (i.e., the witness sees all members at once) so that witnesses don't simply select the person who looks most like what they remember (Steblay, Dysart, & Wells, 2011; Steblay & Phillips, 2011). In addition, after the witness makes a selection, the administrator should not tell the witness, "good job," or otherwise indicate approval or disapproval because such expressions may contaminate the witnesses' memory for how confident her identification was when she later testifies in court (Wells & Bradfield, 1998, 1999). These reforms and others suggested by psychologists were endorsed by Attorney General of the United States Janet Reno in 1999 (Wells et al., 2000) and have since been adopted by several police departments.

The first three reforms above are all geared to reducing the number of false identifications—the ones that might lead to innocent people being convicted. Yet, those procedures, the "may or may not" instructions, the blind-to-condition administrator, and the sequential line-ups, will, in addition to reducing the number of false identifications, also (slightly) reduce the number of true identifications. Thus, there is a trade-off: When the reforms now being proposed or adopted are in place, fewer innocent people will be incorrectly picked from line-ups, but fewer guilty people will be correctly picked from line-ups as well (see Clark, 2012, for a controversial review).

Deciding whether this trade-off between reducing the number of incorrect identifications in exchange for also reducing the number of correct ones is worth it depends on both objective and subjective factors. Objectively, one would want to know the size of the trade-off. For every innocent person not picked, how many guilty people are not picked? And, if guilty people are not picked from line-ups, does that mean they are not convicted using some other evidence? Subjectively, people and societies have to decide the value of each kind of error. Whether it is, as Blackstone famously put it, "better that ten guilty persons escape than that one innocent suffer" (Blackstone, 1766, vol. 4, p. 358) is a question of value, specifically the relative value of avoiding erroneous punishment compared with the value of avoiding erroneous nonpunishment. Indeed, many other theorists and commentators have used different ratios (Volokh, 1997), reflecting the differing values of different people or different societies. Thus, the research shows that some people (and, presumably, some legal systems) are more concerned with due process, whereas others are more concerned with crime control. The relative values of these concerns will affect the willingness of different people and different legal systems to make different trade-offs, but the existence of value-laden tradeoffs is unavoidable (e.g., Fitzgerald & Ellsworth, 1984).

EYEWITNESS TESTIMONY

In addition to issues of identifying the perpetrator, there is substantial long-standing research on eyewitness memory showing that, as with identification, the testimony of eyewitnesses is generally less reliable than many people believe, and is subject to many reliability-reducing factors (Loftus, Miller, & Burns, 1978; Loftus & Palmer, 1974; Ross, Read, & Toglia, 1994; Toglia et al., 1998). This research is of pervasive importance. Even apart from criminal trials, and apart from questions of identification, witnesses testify to the speed and positions of automobiles involved in a crash, to the oral statements made in connection with the sale of a product, to the physical and mental condition of a person when he writes a will, and in countless other situations when the question at issue is not merely one of identification.

The psychology of eyewitness testimony has a double dose of social cognition. First is the issue of how accurate the testimony can be. Research has shown that eyewitness perception and memory are often unreliable. Those who witness an event may for any of a number of reasons perceive it mistakenly, and when they recount what they have seen at a later time, often years later, they may misremember or misdescribe what they had earlier perceived (Cutler & Penrod, 1995; Loftus, 1996; Ross, Read, & Toglia, 1994; Wells, 1993). Memories and descriptions may be especially malleable when people are subject to misleading questions (Loftus, 1975; Loftus, Miller, & Burns, 1978) or suggestive prompting (Wells & Quinlivan, 2009), or may be contaminated by discussions with others who have witnessed the same event (Wright et al., 2009).

Second, jurors must decide how much to believe such testimony. Research shows that jurors tend to overcredit it (Desmarais & Read, 2011), believing that the testimony of someone who claims to have observed an event is especially reliable (Deffenbacher & Loftus, 1982; Noon & Hollin, 1987), and even more so when the testimony contains many details (Wells & Leippe, 1981) or is delivered with great confidence (Brewer & Burke, 2002; Tenney et al., 2007; Whitley & Greenberg, 1986). Several surveys have documented the ways in which lay people fail to understand the limitations of eyewitness memory (Benton et al., 2005; Simons & Chabris, 2011), and thus litigants have attempted to call eyewitness memory researchers as experts to testify in trials. Such expert testimony is now being admitted more often than in the past (Cutler, 2009; *United States v. Hines*, 1999; Lindsay et al., 1986; Schmechel et al., 2006), but whether to admit such testimony is still left to the discretion of the trial judge. And in exercising that discretion, judges often refuse to allow the experts to testify because they believe that either (1) the testimony will not tell the jury something they do not already know (*United States v. Libby*, 2006), (2) the particular eyewitness research offered is insufficiently scientific (*United States v. Rincon*, 1994), or (3) the research does not directly apply to the particular case being tried (*United States v. Crotteau*, 2000).

CONFESSIONS

The number of false confessions revealed by the DNA exonerations prompts the question, "Why would anyone confess to something they didn't do?" There are reasons that are simple and sensible (e.g., to protect a child) and reasons that are simple and silly (e.g., to garner notoriety). But there are more common and serious reasons—reasons that are profoundly social psychological in nature—such as the pressure of the situation.

Interrogations are designed to elicit confessions—from the set-up of the rooms, to the "script" for interrogation. As a matter of constitutional law (*Corley v. United States,* 2009), confessions cannot be introduced at trial unless they are ruled "voluntary," and that determination is made by a judge. Confessions elicited through beatings or threats are, of course, not considered voluntary. But confessions elicited through other tactics: isolating the suspect, diminishing the suspect's culpability by telling her that she is a good person and didn't mean to do harm, allowing the police to lie about the evidence they have, are all powerful techniques for getting a suspect to talk "voluntarily." However, voluntarily doesn't necessarily mean truthfully—suspects might believe that confessing is the only way out. In fact, innocent suspects may be particularly vulnerable to falsely confessing, bowing to the immediate pressures to get out of the interrogation, but believing that the justice system will ultimately vindicate them (Kassin, 2005; Russano et al., 2005).

Once admitted into a trial, confessions are very powerful evidence—perhaps even more so than eyewitness identification (Kassin & Neumann, 1997). Even when harsh treatment of the suspect during interrogation is described, people end up wondering why someone would confess to something they didn't do. In addition, the way in which confessions are taped, with the suspect in the middle of the camera focus and the interrogator on the side or off-screen, leads to more imputation of guilt than a more balanced camera focus (Lassiter, 2002). See Kassin, 1997, 2008; Kassin & Gudjonsson, 2004; and Kovera & Borgida, 2010, for more complete reviews.

FORENSICS

The DNA exonerations have also revealed the widespread use of flawed physical forensic evidence, such as fingerprints, carpet fibers, bite marks, tool marks, and bullet markings, many of which were claimed, incorrectly, to have been a "match." That such seemingly scientific procedures could lead to so many incorrect results came as a surprise to much of the legal world, and also to much of the non-legal world. After all, the task of matching physical evidence sounds simple—couldn't a mechanical process tell you whether the fingerprints or bite marks or carpet fibers found at the scene of a crime match those belonging to someone accused of the crime? The issue is far from that simple, however, and much of why it is not is psychological in nature. Deciding, for example, whether two fingerprints came from the same person is difficult because no two fingerprints under examination are ever completely identical. Typically, the base print was given at a police station, where fingers are rolled carefully in ink and then rolled carefully on paper, leaving a full and clear print, which can then be compared with the target print found at a crime scene. But fingerprints at crime scenes are often incomplete, or made with varying pressure, or left on hard-to-read or uneven surfaces, or contaminated by the prior or subsequent prints of others. The task of the examiner, then, is to decide whether the target and base prints are *sufficiently similar* to declare them a match. A serious problem is that not enough is known about print variability—how much one person's print can vary across situations and how many other people's prints might fall within that distribution. (And, however much the belief in the uniqueness of fingerprints has infiltrated crime television, scientists do not even know for sure that everyone's fingerprints are different.) To the extent that these are problems with fingerprints, which have been used in trials since 1910 and whose nontrial forensic use is somewhat older (Mnookin, 2001), they are even greater for other, less used types of forensic evidence.

But where *is* the psychology? It is relevant in two places (Thompson & Cole, 2007). First, as with any human similarity judgments (e.g., see Chapters 18 and 27,), prior beliefs, and context matter. For example, when fingerprint examiners are given two prints to compare, they may be told whether previous examiners found them to match. Examiners told that they were a match are more likely to find that they match; those told that they were not a match are more likely to find that they do not match. And, in a startling demonstration, fingerprint examiners who had themselves determined that two prints matched were likely to draw the opposite conclusion when they were (unknowingly) presented with the same prints years later along with context information suggesting that the prints should not match (Dror & Cole, 2010).

The second role of psychology is in the communication of forensic results to jurors. Much has been written about jurors' ability to understand expert evidence generally (Diamond, 2006; Diamond & Rose, 2005). With physical forensic evidence, however, there are additional questions about whether jurors can or do understand the science, the math, the probabilities, and the error rates (Hans et al., 2011; Thompson, 1989), and also about whether they may be overswayed by experts generally and alleged forensic experts in particular (Koehler, 2001). In response to such growing concerns about the misuse and misunderstanding of forensic evidence, the National Academy of Sciences (National Research Council, 2009) commissioned and released a long report documenting the problems with forensic science. Among other things, the report calls for more investigation into the validity of the techniques and more training in analysis and communication. It is thus clear that psychologists have a large role to play in improving the processes of securing forensic evidence and using it at trial.

Trial Procedure: The Tasks and Competency of Jurors

In addition to listening to the evidence as presented, jurors are supposed to engage in other tasks during a trial. Importantly, they are supposed to evaluate the witnesses who are testifying: Is this witness telling the truth? Is this witness's confidence warranted? Jurors are also expected to follow various instructions given by the judge. For many years, the competence of jurors was disparaged: "What would you expect from 12 people too stupid to get out of jury duty?" is the flip observation. And that snide remark does capture the fact that juries are not nearly as representative of the population at large as the theory or popular impressions would suggest. But these days, although there are known deficits in juror reasoning, the pendulum is swinging away from the perspective of "jurors as complete idiots," just as the general psychology reasoning literature is swinging away from simply amassing a long list of reasoning biases (see Chapter 18).

EVALUATING WITNESSES: DECEPTION DETECTION AND RELYING ON CONFIDENCE

Research on various aspects of jurors' assessment of testimony has tended to undermine at least some of the legal system's traditional confidence in the abilities of lay jurors. At the heart of the legal system's long-standing unwillingness to admit into evidence polygraph or even more modern lie-detection techniques (Ford, 2006; Grubin & Mardin, 2005), for example, is the faith that ordinary people are competent assessors of the veracity of others (Fisher, 1997), but this confidence has been shown to be misplaced (Vrij, 2000; Vrij & Baxter, 1999; Vrij & Graham, 1997). Jurors believe that witnesses who are telling the truth are more likely to look directly at the jury, less likely to blink, and more likely to speak with confidence, but these and other widely believed indicators of veracity have been shown to be unreliable (Blumenthal, 1993). In fact, most of the existing research shows that the ability of the ordinary person, and by implication the ordinary juror, to determine who is telling the truth and who is not from their demeanor is scarcely better than chance (Bond, 2008; Bond & DePaulo, 2006, 2008; O'Sullivan, 2009). Consequently, efforts persist to provide more reliable evaluation of veracity in forensic and trial processes. One of these efforts relies on the claim that there can be genuine experts in detecting untruths, experts whose ability to discern truthfulness and deception in witnesses is substantially better than that of the ordinary person (O'Sullivan 2008, 2009), although the claim is frequently contested (Bond & Uysal, 2007). In addition, there have been recent and prominent efforts to promote the use of modern neuroscience as a method of lie detection; it is allegedly more accurate than previous lie-detection technology, and far more accurate than the nonscientific determinations of judges and jurors (Kozel et al., 2005; Langleben et al., 2005; Wolpe, Foster, & Langleben, 2005). However, these claims are again subject to an active debate (Greely & Illes, 2007; Schauer, 2010a, 2010c), on both scientific and legal policy grounds.

INSTRUCTIONS AND INSTRUCTIONS TO DISREGARD

There is also extensive research on other tasks that jurors encounter during a trial. Although much of the research might lead one to believe the jurors are simply incompetent, another view is that the fault lies with the legal system for not being designed with an understanding of actual human reasoning in mind.

Research has shown, for example, the limited ability of jurors to understand complex testimony, complex factual situations, and the often-technical instructions of the judge (Cooper, Bennett, & Sukel, 1996; Horowitz, Forsterlee, & Brolly, 1996; Ogloff & Rose, 2005). But much of the misunderstanding of instructions may be occasioned by the judge's desire to avoid a legal error that could produce a reversal by an appellate court. In part because of this motivation, judges may be more concerned with making their instructions legally precise than with making them understandable to jurors, and consequently, instructions may be couched in technical legal language beyond the knowledge of most laypeople (Greene & Bornstein, 2000; Severance, Greene, & Loftus, 1984).

Jurors may also be asked to forget, or not use, information related to the trial that they have inadvertently learned. Experimental research on the effects of pretrial publicity shows that mock jurors are influenced by things they have previously learned about a trial even when they are instructed to forget the information and have promised to do so (Steblay et al., 1999). Similarly, during a trial, jurors may be instructed to ignore or forget some testimony that they have just heard. For example, a witness might blurt out that he knew the defendant because they had been in prison for burglary at the same time. If the defense lawyer objects and moves to strike the testimony, and if the judge sustains the objection, she will immediately instruct the jury to disregard that evidence. Much research, however, shows that mock jurors do not disregard what they have in fact heard, and thus will be influenced in their decisions by information that has been ruled legally unusable (Steblay, et al., 2006). Of course, such failures are not surprising to psychologists: the primarily cognitive theories suggest that people are *unable* to disregard such information (e.g., because the information has become embedded in a schema); the primarily social theories such as reactance (Brehm,

1966), ironic processes (Wegner, 1994), and concern with a just outcome (e.g., Sommers & Kassin, 2001) suggest that people are *unwilling* to disregard such information.

COMPETENCE OF THE JURY

As we noted above, however, it is a mistake to assume that all of the research is in the direction of establishing that jurors are less competent than the legal system and the public at large believes. With respect to the testimony of experts, for example, the rules of evidence start with the assumption that jurors are likely to be overly impressed with experts, and thus to impute weight to expert testimony that the underlying facts or expertise do not support. A series of Supreme Court cases has addressed the problem of so-called junk science, and now, at least in the federal courts, and in most state courts, expert evidence, both scientific and nonscientific, must meet a significantly higher threshold of admissibility than is applied to evidence generally (*Daubert v. Merrill-Dow Pharmaceuticals*, 1993; *General Electric Co. v. Joiner*, 1997; *Kumho Tires, Inc. v. Carmichael*, 1999). But this legal trend toward strict control of expert testimony may be based on an undervaluation of the ability of the jury. In fact, the contemporary research on jury evaluation of expert testimony (Diamond, 2006) has reinforced the 1966 findings of Kalven and Zeisel that jurors are more competent in evaluating expert testimony than the legal system thinks they are, and that the most significant determinant of jury evaluation of much scientific and technical evidence is the underlying reliability of the evidence and not, as many people think, the superficial trappings of expertise.

Moreover, it is a mistake to equate a jury's failure to understand technical instructions with a failure in their ultimate role of making a decision. It turns out that juries tend to deliver the correct verdict in the substantial majority of cases, at least if the measure of correctness is what the judge would have decided herself. Various studies over the years, using different methodologies, have shown that a judge's and jury's decisions about the same cases are typically in accord (Diamond & Rose, 2005; Kalven & Zeisel, 1966). Although these studies have various methodological flaws (flaws tending to flow from not knowing the ground truth of what actually happened in the case), it still appears that even though jurors may not always appreciate the nuances of the applicable law, they are usually reliable in getting a general sense of who ought to prevail.

Juror Versus Jury Decision Making

Much of the research on the psychological aspects of juror evaluation of evidence is focused on individuals, acting as jurors, evaluating individual items of evidence. But actual jury deliberation differs from this procedure in two important respects. First, a jury is not required to evaluate pieces of evidence one by one, but instead is instructed to reach a verdict only after having heard all of the evidence presented by all of the parties in a trial. On the one hand, we know that people cannot intentionally hold off entirely from integrating information as it comes in. On the other hand, we know that jurors have been shown to be less engaged in a process that looks like continuous or linear Bayesian updating than they are in the more holistic process of trying to imagine the most plausible story explaining all of the evidence they have heard (Pennington & Hastie, 1991; 1992).

Second, it is important to remember that the jury is itself a social institution. In the United States, the standard jury for a felony trial consists of 12 members; juries in civil cases or less serious criminal cases often have fewer members. But juries always contain multiple members, and those members are always expected to deliberate—to discuss the issues with each other—before reaching a verdict. And thus because of the ways in which people are affected by the opinions of others and by the necessity of having to explain their opinions to others, the verdict reached by a jury after deliberation often differs from the verdict that might have been reached had the same jurors simply been polled in a secret ballot at the conclusion of the trial (Hastie, Penrod, & Pennington, 1983; Salerno & Diamond, 2010).

Of course, the deliberation of real juries has always been difficult to study because the confidentiality of jury deliberations has been carefully protected, partly in the interest of the litigants and partly in the interest of the jurors themselves. In the last few years, however, some real jury deliberations have, with the permission of all concerned parties, been taped as part of an important Arizona-based study, and thus we have increased insight into the actual deliberative processes of jurors (Diamond & Rose, 2005; Salerno & Diamond, 2010). We now know, for example, that real jurors do bring up some of the topics that judges have instructed them not to discuss (e.g., insurance), but that other jurors are likely to quash such discussions. But we don't know what effect the introduction, or suppression, of that information during deliberation has on the verdict. Thus, psychology can yield important new insights into jury behavior by looking at the reasons that collective jury decisions may differ from the aggregate opinions of individual jurors (Salerno & Diamond, 2010).

Roles of Judges

In the most common fictional portrayal, judges are banging a gavel and instructing juries to disregard evidence or telling them to announce their verdicts. But judges play many different roles in the legal system. Here, we discuss two that are ripe for more research: judges as deciders of fact and judges as deciders of law.

Are Judges Different from Juries?

The jury is the prototypical "fact-finder" at trial; that is, when there is a jury, it is the jury's job to sift through the evidence and decide what truly transpired regarding the events leading to the trial, and to render a verdict (and assess damages) accordingly. However, in actuality, judges make many more factual determinations than do juries. Judges make such determinations in two roles. One is when there is a bench trial—a judge sitting without a jury—in which it is the judge's job to be the fact-finder and render a verdict. The other role occurs regardless of whether there is a jury because, even when there is a jury, the judge has many fact-finding responsibilities.

JUDGES AS DETERMINERS OF FACT

Cases often involve factual determinations other than those leading to the final verdict. Consider, for example, the procedure followed when it is alleged that some item of evidence was obtained by the police in violation of the Fourth Amendment to the Constitution, which prohibits "unreasonable searches and seizures," or in violation of the Fifth Amendment, which establishes that no one may be compelled to be "a witness against himself." In practice, an allegation that some search violated the Fourth Amendment will often require the judge to decide whether, say, a weapon or a quantity of narcotics was in "plain view" when it was seized because, under existing legal doctrine (*Arizona v. Hicks*, 1987; *Coolidge v. New Hampshire*, 1971), the police seizure of items that are in plain view generally does not require a search warrant. When such a dispute arises, the judge alone must determine—in a hearing on a motion to suppress the evidence—which of the opposing factual accounts is correct and then rule accordingly on whether the evidence

can be used at trial and made known to the jury. Similarly, it is the judge who must determine that a confession was voluntary before it may be used at trial. To do so, the judge must often determine the factual question of whether the defendant had actually been warned of his right to remain silent before he confessed. This question, like the plain view question, is one of fact and not of law, but it is to be decided by the judge rather than the jury.

JUDGE VERSUS JURY

People are likely to believe that when judges make these factual determinations, they will be less susceptible than lay jurors to the numerous confusions, mistakes, biases, and other cognitive failings that bedevil ordinary people. Why should that be so? One possibility is intelligence and education: Judges tend to have relatively high IQs compared with jurors, and judges have almost all been to law school. A second hypothesis is that training and practice make judges expert fact-finders, developing their expertise at fact-finding from years of performing similar tasks as law students, as lawyers, and then as judges. And a third hypothesis would suggest that, because it is their job, judges would have a particular motivation to evaluate facts accurately, at least in the context of appointed judges (elected judges may have very different motivations).

These are all plausible hypotheses, but they remain only hypotheses. There is a limited amount of experimental research comparing jurors and judges, in large part because of the difficulty of rounding up actual judges to be subjects. Most experimental subjects are qualified to be jurors, and the data show that typical college student samples behave quite similarly to community cross-sections on jury-relevant reasoning tasks (Bornstein, 1999). But most experimental subjects are not qualified to be judges. So, although much can be learned about jury decision making from typical subject pools, it is a much bigger leap from typical experimental subjects to judges.

The limited research that there is using judges suggests that on many of the classic "heuristics and biases" tasks, judges perform no differently from non–legally trained jurors (Guthrie, Rachlinski, & Wistrich, 2001, 2002), at least in the context of making determinations about facts, as opposed to determining what the law is. In particular, judges may be as susceptible as jurors to anchoring, for example, by setting different damage awards and interest rates depending on what amounts were first suggested to them (Rachlinski, Guthrie, & Wistrich,

2006); hindsight bias, differentially assessing the likelihood of finding contraband in a particular location depending on the knowledge they subsequently obtained (Guthrie, Rachlinski, & Wistrich, 2007); and availability, making fact-finding decisions that are distorted by the manner and order in which evidence is presented, even if the evidence is the same (Guthrie, Rachlinski, & Wistrich, 2001).

The research has also shown that judges are similar to ordinary people in other ways. In one important study, for example, judges were found little more able to disregard evidence than were lay people, despite the fact that those judges were fully aware of the legal rule requiring disregarding and equally aware of the legal and policy concerns that motivate the rule (Wistrich, Guthrie, & Rachlinski, 2005). It is true that in some contexts judges are indeed likely to outperform lay jurors. Hastie and Viscusi (1998), for example, found that in some contexts judges were less susceptible than jurors to hindsight bias. But it remains far from clear that judges serving as fact-finders are as superior to jurors as many people, including defendants, are likely to believe (Spellman, 2007).

Yet despite the paucity of relevant data, the question of whether and how judges differ from jurors is important. Not only is judicial fact-finding pervasive, as we noted above, but also many decisions of legal institutional design turn on just who should make which kinds of decisions: a judge, a jury, or some specialized body? Consider, for example, decisions about sentencing. It is possible to have sentencing decisions made by judges, as is traditional; by juries, as is required in death penalty cases and occasionally occurs elsewhere; or by an expert body outside of the context of particular cases (e.g., a sentencing commission), as with the current procedure under the Federal Sentencing Guidelines (Robinson & Spellman, 2005). And thus it would be valuable to know whether judges are superior to others in making factual determinations, for without such knowledge, deciding who should decide may be largely an exercise in guesswork.

Judges and the Law

In addition to considering judges' role as fact-finders, it is equally important to recognize the social cognitive dimensions of judges when they perform their more traditional and well-known roles as discoverers, appliers, interpreters, and makers of law. Indeed, it is here that the notion that "legal reasoning" is a distinctive kind of reasoning resides (see Spellman & Schauer, 2012),

and here that lawyers and law schools embrace the notion that there is something special about "thinking like a lawyer." There is a popular image of judges—reinforced every few years in the charade of Senate hearings concerning a nominee to the Supreme Court—as simply figuring out the relevant law and applying it to the found facts of a case without concern for the politics or ideology of the dispute or for the judge's own view of which side ought to win and which ought to lose. In recent Supreme Court nomination hearings, for example, now–Chief Justice Roberts claimed that Supreme Court Justices were like baseball umpires, simply calling balls and strikes and not caring about the particular outcome; now-Justice Sotomayor asserted that her previous judicial decisions were based solely on the law and not on her personal views, and now-Justice Kagan, while acknowledging that there was room for discretion, said that good judicial decisions are based on "law all the way down" (Pettys, 2011).

The image of mechanical judging held by so many lay people and reinforced in the political theater of nomination hearings, however, is a false picture of what judges actually do. In the first place, "easy cases"—those in which the facts, the law, and the law's application to the facts are clear—rarely make it to court at all, and even more rarely make it to appellate courts. In such cases, people typically comply with the law or settle their disputes out of court. They are more likely to know that litigation is futile, and thus, by virtue of the selection effect, the cases that do wind up in court are disproportionately "hard cases"—unclear as to the facts, or the law, or both (Lederman, 1999; Priest & Klein, 1984).

It is especially true in common law countries such the United States, which traditionally have relied heavily on case law and precedent and less on precise and systematically compiled codes, that the law is often far from clear. There are likely to be prior cases that point in different directions, and these cases, which contain the law that subsequent courts are expected to use, are often subject to varying interpretations as to what the earlier court decided and thus what the earlier case stands for now. Moreover, even statutes and constitutions often contain vague phrases such as "best interests of the child" or "in a timely manner" or "equal protection of the laws" or "unreasonable searches and seizures," again making the process of determining what the law is and then applying that law to the particular facts an invariably imprecise one.

LEGAL REALISM (OR WHAT WE MIGHT CALL "IMPLICIT SOCIAL COGNITION")

What, then, do we know about this process, and what can psychology teach us about it? Going back as least as far as the 1930s, Jerome Frank (Frank, 1930), Karl Llewellyn (Llewellyn, 1930, 2011), and other members of the group of legal theorists known as *legal realists* (or, sometimes, *American legal realists*) asserted that decisions were based on judicial choice even more than the constraints and dictates of formal written law as embodied in what Llewellyn called "paper rules" (Llewellyn, 2011). Contrary to the traditional view that judges consulted the law and only then determined the outcome on the basis of the law, the realists maintained that appellate judges often started with a hunch (Hutcheson, 1929) or with a preliminary assessment of their preferred outcome (e.g., which ruling would make the best policy, or which ruling would be more just, or which ruling the judge suspected might be more consistent with the law), and thereafter searched for the law that would support this initial assessment.

More recent research, mostly by political scientists and primarily focused on the Supreme Court of the United States, has tended to reinforce the realists' less systematically researched assertions. This research has developed what has come to be known as the "attitudinal" view of Supreme Court decision making, according to which the social, cultural, ideological, and political attitudes of the Justices explain more of their decisions than do formal rules or existing precedents (Cross, 1997; Segal & Spaeth, 2002). That such a conclusion emerges with respect to the Supreme Court should not be surprising. Because the Supreme Court gets to choose which cases it will hear, and hears less than 1% of cases it is asked to hear, the phenomenon of the selection effect is at its greatest. Most of its cases are ones in which there is either no clear law, or there is sufficient law on both sides that outcomes for either of the contesting parties could be plausibly legally justified. Moreover, the cases that the Supreme Court hears are ones in which judges, like most informed citizens, have strong opinions, such as race-based affirmative action, presidential powers, abortion, and religion in the public schools. The attitudinal research supports the conclusion that a judge's pre-existing moral and policy views have a greater effect on outcomes than anything that can be found in the formal law.

These days, many legal academics will state, "We are all realists now"—indicating that they and most others recognize that it is not "law all the way down," as Justice Kagan put it (Pettys, 2011). Or at least if it is law all the way down, it is an expansive notion of law that includes culture, ideology, value, and even some politics, rather than simply the words on a printed page or even the historical record of what a legislature or group of constitutional drafters intended. And to the extent that this view is indeed well recognized, then perhaps what should be said is that, "We are all social psychologists now." The picture of judges starting with no preferences and solely consulting the law for an answer is entirely inconsistent with much social psychology research, including that on motivated reasoning (Baum, 2010; Braman, 2010). In a large variety of tasks, when decision makers have opinions about the desirability of outcomes, such opinions will influence the process of locating and interpreting the data (Ditto & Lopez, 1992; Kunda, 1990; MacCoun, 1998). And thus if we think of the rules and precedents of the law as the data or inputs employed by legal decision makers in making decisions about what the law is (as opposed to what the facts are), we should not be surprised to discover that these legal data are subject to more or less the same kind of motivated selection and interpretation as are the data that ordinary people use in making ordinary decisions (Furgeson, Babcock, & Shane, 2008a, 2008b).

ANALOGICAL REASONING

Even if judges always appear to be coming to the conclusion that their ideologies and values and nonlegal policy preferences would suggest, however, their reasoning processes need not be as consciously or deliberately biased as at least some of the legal realists seemed to believe. In most appellate cases, there are many potentially relevant previous decisions, and the judge has a choice of which prior cases to use and how to use them. As a result, the process can be understood as one of analogical reasoning with respect to the available legal sources (Spellman, 2004; Weinreb, 2005).

Another possibility is that judging is a form of expertise in which experience matters. If that is so, then the way in which a court retrieves some source analogs and not others may be a function of familiarity and knowledge (Spellman, 2010). Law students see certain cases and not others, and some types of disputes more than others. The expertise of lawyers and judges, therefore, may be less a function of distinctive forms of reasoning than of a certain kind of training and experience that make some similarities and not others especially relevant to decision making. Indeed, such a conclusion about judging would be consistent with the tendency of professionals—including judges and magistrates—to use their experience to simplify their tasks and narrow the inputs on which they base their decisions (Dhami, 2003; Dhami & Ayton, 2001). Such focused and experience-based simplification, rather than anything more mysterious, may be central to the common claim, at least among lawyers and in law schools, that there is something special about thinking like a lawyer.

STARE DECISIS AND FOLLOWING RULES

The motivated reasoning account of legal decision making may tell us much about judicial behavior when judges have strong views about outcomes, but in more ordinary cases, in which judges have fewer or weaker views about who ought to win or what policy ought to prevail, the picture may be different. Often, the judicial task will be a straightforward one of selecting and using prior decisions to determine and justify current outcomes. The legal system in common law countries is committed to decision according to precedent, meaning that lower court judges are expected to follow decisions made by higher courts—even those decisions with which they disagree. In addition, judges at all levels are expected to make their decisions according to what is known as *stare decisis* (stand by what is decided), that is, to follow earlier decisions even of their own court—and even if the current members of that court disagree (Alexander, 1989). Sometimes it is so clear that the question in a case is the same as one presented before or above that the judge has little leeway in making a decision (Schauer, 2008). For example, when a lower court judge is faced with the question of whether a state may totally ban all abortions, the precedential effect of the Supreme Court decision in *Roe v. Wade* (1973) will (or should) require that judge to invalidate such a law even if he thinks that the law is wise as a matter of policy, morality, or even law, and thus even if he thinks that the *Roe* decision was mistaken.

Such direct precedential constraint is rare, however, primarily because, owing to the selection effect as noted above, cases in which there is one and only one precedent case dealing directly with the disputed question rarely wind up in court. But suppose there is an obvious precedent, and the decision that the precedent demands is different from the result that someone simply trying to be fair would produce without the constraints of the law. In such cases, are lawyers and judges more inclined than nonlawyers to reach the decision indicated by the law rather than the fair decision? Some preliminary survey research has indicated that such a difference might exist (Schweitzer, Saks, & Lovis-McMahon, 2009; Schweitzer, Sylvester, & Saks, 2007), but it needs to be supported by subsequent and experimental research. If the finding holds, then the greater ability of lawyers and judges than laypeople to subjugate their sense of fairness or justice to the demands of the law may explain at least some of the distinctiveness of legal reasoning (Schauer, 2009, 2010b), and thus some of the willingness of judges, contrary to the claims of many of the realists, simply to follow the law rather than using the law to support their law-independent outcome preferences.

Finally, it is important to remember that judges are human beings with motivations other than professional ones. How much of judicial behavior, for example, is based on factors such as personal ambition, whether for promotion or to secure a positive reputation? (Posner, 1993; Schauer, 2000). Moreover, because appellate judges make decisions as part of a multimember court, issues of group interaction again come into play. How do judges seek to persuade each other? How successful are such efforts? And how often do judges set aside their own preferred outcome because they believe that having a unanimous decision is a good in itself? All of these questions implicate a vast range of existing research on the psychology of human interaction. As noted above, political scientists have been analyzing the voting patterns of individual judges, but the mechanisms that produce these results remain largely a mystery, principally because, to date, there is extremely little psychological research focused specifically on these various and important questions about judges' decision-making behavior.

The Psychological Assumptions of Substantive Law

We have described issues of social cognition involved in the decision making of jurors and judges, and currently many (probably too many) research programs in law and psychology focus on these characteristic *procedures* of law. Although these issues are important, the psychological dimensions of the *substantive* law are equally so, even if, to date, they have been far less the subject of psychological research. The substance of law—what it seeks to do, as opposed to the procedures it uses—both controls and facilitates human behavior, and in doing so, the law embodies countless assumptions about human cognition. Yet the law's assumptions are often based on some combination of tradition, anecdote, and folk wisdom, assumptions that actual data from psychology sometimes confirm and sometimes challenge.

In this section, we describe some areas of substantive law that make interesting psychological assumptions that could be open to more or future research. We loosely organize these areas into sections dealing with law's assumptions about individuals, about how people perceive others, and about the workings of groups and of society itself.

Individuals

It seems an obvious function of law to protect individuals within a society: the law should attempt to deter harmful acts, but if someone harms you despite what the law says, then she should suffer some consequences. This result seems clear, but what is less clear is what kinds of things count as *harms*, and what is even less clear is what counts as *you*.

The most basic type of harm to people is physical harm, as when they are injured or killed. But there are other forms of harm, including harms to an individual's mind, reputation, dignity, and property. What does the law acknowledge as harm, and how can such harms be legally addressed? The answers to those questions indicate what society assumes is important and are psychological in nature. For example, research into the self (see Chapter 24) considers how individuals think about themselves as continuous entities through changes of context and circumstance. Thus, research into the self might provide some bases for some of the law's assumptions about what needs to be protected. But this is only an example, for there are many areas in which the law, sometimes correctly and sometimes mistakenly, embodies psychological assumptions about what is to count as harm.

REMEDIES IN GENERAL

We start with a general discussion of remedies—the legal consequences to the harmer and the harmed. Presently people typically think of two different types of legal remedies: punishment for criminal wrongs (i.e., years in prison or payment of a fine) and monetary damages for civil wrongs (i.e., compensation). These two "currencies"—years and dollars—present the problems of mapping an almost infinite number of possibilities (e.g., an assault, a kidnapping, a theft, or libel, or fraud) onto two very simple scales. But the law can rarely

put people back in the position they were in before the wrong occurred. It cannot resuscitate the dead, or eliminate the effects of an injury, and often it cannot even make sure that property is returned or monetary losses are recouped. And thus, whatever the precise remedy, the law needs a way of converting "amount of injury" into years or dollars, and psychology could be more involved in how such valuations should be made (e.g., Swedloff & Huang, 2010).

Many states have, and use, the remedy of capital punishment for their most heinous crimes. An abundance of research by legal scholars addresses the question of whether capital punishment actually deters crimes (e.g., Donohue & Wolfers, 2006). Psychologists have addressed questions such as whether capital punishment can be meted out fairly given the way jurors are selected for the task (Cowan, Thompson, & Ellsworth, 1984). Psychologists have also played a role (through amicus briefs) in the elimination of the death penalty for mentally retarded individuals (*Atkins v. Virginia*, 2004) and those under 18 years old (*Roper v. Simmons*, 2005). In addition to noting society's "changing standards of decency" in both cases, an inquiry informed by psychological, sociological, and anthropological research, the Court considered in *Roper* the extent to which juveniles are vulnerable to influence, and accordingly especially prone to immature and irresponsible behavior. In light of such diminished culpability, therefore, Justice Kennedy, writing for the majority, concluded that neither retribution nor deterrence provided an adequate justification for imposing the death penalty. Moreover, he said, even "retribution is not proportional if the law's most severe penalty is imposed on one whose culpability or blameworthiness is diminished, to a substantial degree, by reason of youth and immaturity." *Atkins* and *Roper* were of course *legal* decisions, but it is clear that they were psychological ones as well, albeit psychological ones with wide-ranging legal consequences.

These days, a new movement called "restorative justice," building on notions of restitution in both criminal and civil law, seeks more flexible types of remediation (Braithwaite, 2002; Strang & Braithwaite, 2001; Wenzel et al., 2008). The motivation behind the restorative justice movement is to uncover just what will satisfy those who have been injured by the wrongful acts of others, and it may be that a wider range of remedies than just money and prison time for the perpetrator—including apologies and face-to-face confrontation—should be taken more seriously than they have been to date. Such remedies are currently more popular in Australia, Canada (Napolean, 2011), and the United Kingdom than in the United States, but popularity is growing here as well (Reimund, 2005).

So, what harms does the law attempt to deter and to remedy? We turn to that question now.

BODILY HARM

As we have noted, a paradigmatic function of the law is to protect individuals from bodily harm. People who inflict physical injury to others are typically subject to criminal prosecution, and those who have been injured by the wrongful conduct of others (e.g., accidental injuries, medical malpractice) may often obtain redress through civil liability. In addition to protecting against actual physical injury, the law of "attempts" punishes those who try to injure others even when they do not succeed, various laws sanction those who threaten or attempt to intimidate others even when those threats are not carried out, and laws against kidnapping and false imprisonment prohibit detaining or moving people against their will. These latter two laws illustrate how the law values autonomy: if you are taken from your home against your will, treated lavishly for several days, and returned home, unharmed, happier and healthier than when you left, you may still have redress for kidnapping or false imprisonment.

What remedies are available to the victims of bodily harm? Criminal law puts perpetrators in prison. Punishment in criminal law has the goals of specific deterrence (i.e., discouraging this perpetrator from repeating the crime), general deterrence (i.e., stopping others from wanting to commit the crime), incapacitation (i.e., making the perpetrator unable to do it again), and retribution (i.e., getting even with the perpetrator; Duff, 2007; Garland, 1990). A solid amount of research into people's beliefs about punishment shows that although they express the view that deterrence and retribution are both good reasons for punishment (and should affect the length of punishment), when assessing how much to punish individuals in crime scenarios, people show a strong desire to punish for the sake of retribution. Faced with a specific individual perpetrator, people do not want to punish him simply to deter others (Carlsmith, 2006; Carlsmith, Darley, & Robinson, 2002; Darley, 2009). Thus, what seems important to people is equating the injury done to the victim with what is done (by society) to the perpetrator.

Although putting a perpetrator in prison might feel good psychologically to the victim and to society, the victim is typically not compensated. The law of torts ("actionable civil wrongs") usually provides compensation of various sorts to the victim, as when, for example, his reputation is injured by libel or slander, or when his body (or property) is damaged by another person's negligent driving or by a physician's negligent treatment. In a civil (as opposed to criminal) proceeding, the person who is found to have injured another is typically required to compensate them in ways that are supposed to "make them whole"—an interesting concept. The clearest and simplest form of making someone whole is that the person at fault is required to pay the medical expenses and lost wages of the injured.

But there is more to bodily harm than monetary loss, and so the law also authorizes payments on account of things like "pain and suffering" and "mental anguish" (Dobbs, 1993). Obviously, the payment of money is at best an imperfect attempt to compensate for something intangible. But even recognizing the imperfection and incommensurability of measuring pain in terms of money, and thus of compensating for pain with money, what do we know about attempting to award such compensation?

An initial question is whether judges and juries attempt to gauge how much pain the injured person has actually suffered, or whether an award for pain and suffering is simply a way of punishing the defendant for bad behavior, with the amount of the award being based more on the decision maker's assessment of the wrongfulness of the defendant's behavior than on the actual amount of pain the victim has suffered (Viscusi, 1996).

Assuming the victim's suffering is valued, however, and even assuming a genuine desire on the part of judge and jury to award compensation for pain and suffering, how can anyone assess the pain or the suffering of another? We know that different people have different pain thresholds, and we know that one person's suffering is another's minor inconvenience, but can these differences be reflected in the law? On the one hand, people might try to assess how much they themselves would have suffered under the same circumstances—but this type of judgment runs into affective forecasting errors (Blumenthal, 2005, 2009a; see Chapter 19 XXX), and people are likely to claim that vast amounts of money would be necessary to compensate them for their experience (Brickman, Coates, & Janoff-Bulman, 1978). On the other hand, people might try to estimate the injured person's actual degree of suffering. But research is beginning to show that people systematically estimate the pain of members of groups that are perceived as "less human" (e.g., minority group members) as being less severe than the pain of members of the majority group (Richeson & Trawalter, 2005). These and related questions cry out for more psychological research.

NONTANGIBLE HARMS: REPUTATION AND PRIVACY

Similar issues of injury and remedy arise in connection with other forms of nontangible harms. For example, the law redresses harms to reputation by awarding damages for libel and slander: libel involves an untrue statement written about a person that causes her reputation to be damaged; slander is the same, but the untrue statement is spoken rather than written. American constitutional law—in particular, freedom of speech and press under the First Amendment—has significantly narrowed the scope of actions for libel and slander (*New York Times v. Sullivan*, 1964), but the United States is an outlier here, and most common law countries retain vigorous remedies against libel and slander. Moreover, most civil law countries have a tort-like equivalent remedy for insult, believing that a person is harmed when she is insulted even if no one hears (or reads) the insult and thus even if there is no damage to reputation.

Despite the constitutional changes in the United States, therefore, there still remain interesting questions about the importance and value of reputation, and the importance and value of the related concepts of honor and dignity. The substantive law assumes that people value the esteem of others, and there can be little doubt of the basic truth of this assumption (see Chapter 26). But how important is it for someone's sense of self that she has a good reputation among others? How important is reputation for different aspects one's life? What reputation-creating reference groups are important to people? And how much do these vary from person to person and from group to group (see, e.g., Nisbett & Cohen, 1996)? The law, which still assumes that what is most important for most people is their reputation in the physical community in which they reside, rarely takes such differences into account (Lidsky, 1996).

Analogous issues, but with much greater contemporary importance, especially in the United States, arise with respect to privacy. American law respects privacy in many ways. The Fourth Amendment requires the police to obtain warrants before searching our bodies or our homes; the common law in every state provides for civil remedies—money damages and sometime injunctions against conduct—when others enter our private spaces; and the common law also provides remedies against the disclosure of some facts about ourselves that we wish to keep from others (Prosser et al., 1984). But what is the conception of privacy that the law uses to make these determinations? In many instances, the relevant legal rule simply provides that wrongful invasions of privacy are those that are "unreasonable," but what is reasonable and what is not varies from individual to individual, changes over time, and varies across culture. Indeed, the law regarding search warrants is based on "reasonable expectations of privacy" (Katz v. United States, 1967), but a reasonable expectation of privacy in an age of Twitter and Facebook and surveillance cameras and GPS devices (Jones, 2012) may be quite different from what the expectation was as recently as several decades ago. Given that privacy law is thus so dependent on people's thoughts and expectations, systematic research on what privacy people actually expect could be of great value in fashioning legal doctrine, as well as in understanding legal decision making.

PROPERTY AND INTELLECTUAL PROPERTY

The law protects people's bodies against injury, their reputation against damage, and their privacy against invasion. Just as importantly, it protects their property—their homes and cars and electronics, but also their ideas—such that others are penalized for taking these, using these, or destroying these without consent, and such that the government is required to pay compensation when it wants to take private property for public use.

Homes

Although the law protects many types of property, some types of property are clearly privileged over other types, and in the United States, particular value appears to be placed on people's homes. The Third Amendment, which has virtually no contemporary relevance, provides that, "No soldier shall, in time of peace be quartered in any house, without the consent of the Owner," and the vastly more importantly, the Fourth Amendment guarantees "the right of the people to be secure in their persons, houses, papers, and effects, against unreasonable searches and seizures." The Fifth Amendment creates the aforesaid right to compensation when property is taken for public use. Homes are protected against bankruptcy, such that people can keep their homes even if all of their other property must be made available to their creditors. The mortgage deduction is just one of many tax benefits for homeowners. And state laws not only protect against trespassing but also sometimes permit a homeowner to shoot trespassers regardless of whether the trespassers presents any danger to him (Green, 1999). The ability to use violence to protect other forms of property is much narrower, reflecting the assumption, psychological to the core and perhaps often incorrect, that people's homes are more important to them than the other things they may own.

One justification in the legal literature for the strong protection of many forms of property, especially homes, is to say that that property is necessary for "personhood" (Radin, 1982), but just what *is* personhood? It is claimed that ownership of and control over property are central to what makes us feel human—central to *self*—but is this claim true? It is probably true for some people, but we know little about how common the feeling is, and we know even less about the extent to which this feeling varies with time and place. Is private property necessary for personhood in more collective or communitarian societies? And just what is it about property that is so important? Is it having a place for privacy? Is it the control over space? Is it how our own history is entwined with the ownership of the property? Is it the monetary value and the feeling of security that tangible and marketable assets bring? The law and the commentary on it are filled with assertions and intuitions attempting to answer these questions, but to date we have almost no real data. Especially in the aftermath of the Supreme Court's visible and controversial decision in *Kelo v. City of New London* (2005), allowing the state to take (with compensation, but without consent) people's homes and property for purposes of economic redevelopment, psychologists have begun to look at many dimensions of what people feel about property and why they feel it (Nadler & Diamond, 2008), but much more can be done.

Intellectual Property

Historically, property was tangible property—land, houses, furniture, farm animals, and the like. But the law uses the term "intellectual property" because the law protects, albeit selectively, human creations. It grants patents for inventions to protect the novelty of the idea that spawned the invention, and it provides copyright protection for authorship of music and literature and images so that people can retain control over their own forms of expression. Such laws protecting intellectual property have become increasingly visible recently (e.g., regarding the unauthorized copying and downloading of music, movies, software, etc.). We do not know much about why and when people value their own creations; for example, are they more concerned with the financial advantages of exclusivity or with the fact that they themselves created it (and, perhaps, therefore it is an extension of self)? Indeed, recent research suggests that there is an endowment effect for people's own creations. That is, people see their own creations as more valuable than others see them (Buccafusco & Sprigman, 2010, 2011), which suggests that it is creation and not just tangible value that explains why the law of intellectual property is both so important and why it matters so much to many who are the creators of ideas, images, and inventions.

In many countries, artists and architects are given what are called "moral rights"—the ability to protect their artistic creations against destruction and alteration even by those who have bought them. People agree that such creations should be protected, but their agreement is often somewhat contingent on how much they concur with the ideas expressed and how involved they are with creating art themselves (Spellman & Schauer, 2009). Such rights are much more limited in the United States than in many other countries, especially France, Germany, and other Western European countries with a civil law framework, but is that because Americans are more inclined to see creation predominantly as a question of monetary value and less a manifestation of self?

Psychological research about property and intellectual property is starting to emerge (Blumenthal, 2009b, 2010; Mandel, 2011), and if this field of research continues to grow, we may see that answers to questions about the psychology of property could help inform the development and application of the law.

OUR FUTURE SELVES

Another paradigmatic role of law is to help people plan for the future, and a large amount of substantive law deals with the various forms of that role. People need to predict many things about the future—what they can accomplish, how much money they will have, how they will behave, how they will feel under various circumstances—and make decisions accordingly. But psychology research shows that people are not very good at those tasks. Problems like the planning fallacy, optimism bias, and the various consequences of affective forecasting arise (see Chapter 18), casting doubt on many of the law's traditional assumptions about how people can best plan for the future.

One type of planning for the future involves contracting, and the law of contracts organizes how people can bind themselves to exchange goods, services, or money with others in the future. People estimate how long things will take to build, or how much they will cost, yet we know that various optimism biases (Chapter 18) will cause builders to claim that your renovations will have been completed last year and authors to claim that their chapters will have been done last month. Can psychology advise the legal system about the formation of contracts? The law also prevents some things from being contracted for—for example, body organs, sex, and children. These forbidden objects are often those that people can't imagine putting a price on; that is, they involve "taboo trade-offs" (Fiske & Tetlock, 1997). However, just because some people react negatively to such trade-offs, does that mean the law should not allow them? Certainly, the law changes, for example, and in many states various types of reproductive technologies that were once forbidden to be contracted for are now allowed, with surrogate motherhood being perhaps the most prominent example. Should psychology have something to say about such issues?

Another type of planning for the future involves money. People are notoriously bad at saving money for the future. Yet when instead of asking people to start saving more now at Time 1, people are asked to promise at Time 1 to increase their savings at Time 2, there is a dramatic increase in savings (Thaler & Benartzi, 2004; see Ülkümen & Cheema, 2011, for a construal level explanation). People also create wills and trusts to give away money. Once again, there is little psychology research on how that could best be done.

Another major type of planning for the future, which seems to be growing in visibility, includes various end-of-life planning tools like living wills, advance directives, and euthanasia. People are predicting what they *would* want done *if* certain things happen to them. But will we *actually* want those things done if the circumstances *do* arise? The affective forecasting literature suggests that are preferences are likely to change when we are in the actual circumstances and, thus, there are dangers in being irrevocably committed to decisions made about the future (Blumenthal, 2005).

Perceiving Others

Much of law relies on people's assessments of the intentions and knowledge of other individuals. A subsidiary issue is to which individuals the default assumptions about intentions and knowledge should be applied.

INTENTION

The definitions of most crimes have two parts: actus reus (what the person does) and mens rea (the person's mental state while doing it). The law sometimes proscribes different punishment for the same actions depending on the actor's mental state; for example, a homicide may be a murder (if planned), manslaughter (if intentional), reckless homicide (if accidental), or a legally permitted act of self-defense (see Robinson & Darley, 1995, for great examples). But determining the mental state of others is not a trivial task. How people do this task is a classic issue in attribution theory (see Chapter 6).

Attribution theory has long endorsed the actor/observer asymmetry—the idea that people (at least Westerners) tend to attribute other peoples' behaviors to their dispositions while attributing their own actions to their own situations (but see Malle, 2006, 2011, for a revised view). This understanding seems to underlie some of the rules of evidence—which guide what information a judge should allow jurors to hear. For example, suppose a defendant has been charged with shoplifting, and the district attorney wants to present evidence that the defendant has shoplifted in the past. Normally, such evidence is ruled inadmissible; the notion is that if the jury hears that the defendant has shoplifted before, they will think that she is the type of person who shoplifts generally, will make a dispositional attribution, and will presume that she is therefore guilty of shoplifting again in the current case.

In a very different context, similar assumptions about intention are embedded in much of contract law, which is, at its core, about social interaction. In order for there to be a contract at all, there must be what is called a "meeting of the minds" (Hillman, 2010), but how can one contracting party know what is on another contracting person's mind, and how can a judge or jury, when there is a dispute, know whether there was a meeting of the minds at all, and, even if so, what the minds met about—that is, what they agreed on? Understanding what other people intended or understood is related to issues of mindreading and theory of mind (see Chapter 29).

Accidentally causing a collision between automobiles, even if you are negligent, is a civil wrong, but intentionally driving a car into another is a serious crime. To make a mistake in the description of the goods we sell is typically not a crime (although modern consumer protection and securities laws have changed some such laws), but intentional falsity is fraud, and subject to serious civil and criminal penalties. Given such potential consequences, it is very important to be able to accurately assess other people's intentions.

KNOWLEDGE

The law also makes assumptions about what other people know, or ought to know, and how they should therefore behave. There is the fiction of the "reasonable person"—and what the reasonable person would have done in a given situation provides a standard of comparison for the behavior of others. In tort law, for example, the standard of care for automobile drivers is that of the reasonable person (Prosser et al., 1984), and so a driver will be held liable for causing an accident if he has not done what it is determined the reasonable person would have done in the same circumstances. But how does a judge or jury know what the fictional reasonable person would have done? Social psychology research on the false consensus effect suggests that jurors would be likely to believe that what the reasonable person would have done is what they themselves would have done (Marks & Miller, 1987). On the other hand, research on self-serving biases suggests that what people think they themselves would have done overestimates the virtuousness of what they actually would have done (Epley & Dunning, 2000). Thus, the standard that people apply may be inflated above merely "reasonable."

Not much has been written by psychologists about the fictional reasonable person—or, rather, fictional reasonable people. But psychologists have weighed in some legal cases that have defined different standards for reasonable people in different circumstances (e.g., the battered woman defense provides a different standard for what counts as reasonable self-defense; Roberts, 2003). And there have been calls for more psychology research to help establish other standards (e.g., Shoenfelt, Maue, Nelson, 2002, for a reasonable woman standard in sexual harassment cases).

Groups and Society

Societies are made up of different kinds of people, and laws often treat different types of people differently—thus creating, or enhancing, group differences. For example, many Constitutional amendments grant different groups the right to vote (African Americans, women, and 18-year-olds). Many statutes create rights and protections for other groups such as veterans, disabled people, and girls who want to play sports. Laws that treat groups differently are subject to different levels of scrutiny by the courts depending on the group and the issues involved. That is, the government needs to offer stronger arguments and better data to justify distinguishing among people on the basis of race or gender than it needs to justify distinguishing on the basis of, say, intelligence or education. Courts examine distinctions in the former group much more carefully than in the latter group. Much of the difference, however, rests not only on normative and historical factors but also on psychological ones. Which distinctions are most likely to be misused (Schauer, 2003)? Which reflect genuine differences, and which are based on prejudice or superstition? The study of groups, their cohesion, and their interaction are of course core topics of the study of social cognition (see Chapters 27, 30, 37, and 41), and much of the law of equality and discrimination could be based on a more informed understanding of how people behave as members of groups, and how they behave toward groups of which they are not members.

Societies are also made up of regulations and regulators—there are agencies that regulate the food and drugs we may have, the television and movies we may watch, the taxes we must pay, the education that must be provided. But the regulation of products and services is based on perceptions about how other people perceive and evaluate those products and services, just as it is based as well on how the purveyors of those products and services will respond to different forms of regulation. Psychological issues, therefore, pervade the regulatory process, and are relevant to the decision making of virtually every regulatory body.

Societies create laws not only for regulating today but also to create a predictable future. Thus, much of the law, and not just the law of wills and trusts and pensions and the environment, is about binding the future on the basis of current expectations. When the Bill of Rights was added to the Constitution of the United States in 1791, it was thought important, as noted above, to protect against having troops quartered in private homes—the Third Amendment—but not important to protect a general right of privacy, which would not even have been understood in general terms at that time. But the Third Amendment persists, and the judicial creation of a right to privacy remains controversial, precisely because of the binding force that a document written on the basis of 1791 perceptions, needs, and expectations about the future has on us today. A few years earlier than the Bill of Rights, the original articles of the Constitution, as adopted in 1787, provide, among other things, that no one under the age of 35 may be President. Social, medical, and actuarial changes since 1787 may call into question the choice made more than 200 years ago, but the issue is not just about how old the President must be. It is about the way in which all legal rules impose current perceptions on future actions. Shouldn't psychologists have more to say about how to best go about predicting what we might want to be bound to in the future?

Conclusion

We conclude with a mention of what is perhaps the largest issue of all: Does the law matter to people's decisions, and, if so, when, why, and how does it matter? Research such as that done by Tom Tyler and his collaborators on why people obey the law is highly relevant (Tyler, 2006; Tyler & Huo, 2002), but the largest question relates to how the authority of the law affects the thinking and reasoning and decision making of citizens. That is, how does the bald fact of what the law requires matter? Do people pay taxes just because the law says so? Do they obey laws they think silly or misguided—for some people, the laws prohibiting possession of marijuana, for example, and for others the laws requiring the wearing of motorcycle helmets—because they respect the law just for what it is? Or do people obey the law because they fear its sanctions? Do people obey the speed limit laws because of fear of a citation? When the law conforms to people's prelegal preferences, the fact of law may matter little. Most people who refrain from cannibalism do so without regard for the law's requirements. But when there is a gap between prelegal preferences and legal requirements, how does law do its work? Through respect? Through fear? Or through an explicit or implicit desire to confirm to social norms, which law may both reflect and help to create? And perhaps at times the fact of law makes no difference at all, as when widely unenforced laws—underage drinking on college campuses, for example—are widely disregarded. Moreover, because law seeks to structure the cognition of its decision makers with a variety of formal rules, roles, and procedures, law presents cognition in a different form than the form in which it exists for ordinary people. Obviously, ordinary cognition is subject to vast numbers of external influences, but few are as formal and structured as the ones law imposes on its participants. Further research on social cognition within law, therefore, may tell us not only much about the law but perhaps also a bit about social cognition.

References

Alexander, L. (1989). Constrained by precedent. *Southern California Law Review, 63*, 1–62.

Arizona v. Hicks, 480 U.S. *32* (1987).

Atkins v. Virginia, 536 U.S. *304* (2002).

Baum, L. (2010). Motivation and judicial behavior: Expanding the scope of inquiry. In D. Klein & G. Mitchell (Eds.), *The psychology of judicial decision making*. New York: Oxford University Press.

Benton, T. R., Ross, D. F., Bradshaw, E., Thomas, W. N., & Bradshaw, G. (2005). Eyewitness memory is still not common sense: Comparing jurors, judges and law enforcement to eyewitness experts. *Applied Cognitive Psychology, 20*, 115–129.

Blackstone, W. (1766). *Commentaries on the laws of England.* London.

Blumenthal, J. A. (1993). A wipe of the hands, a lick of the lips: The validity of demeanor evidence in assessing witness credibility. *Nebraska Law Review, 72*, 1157–1204.

Blumenthal, J. A. (2005). Law and the emotions: The problems of affective forecasting. *Indiana Law Journal, 80*, 155–238.

Blumenthal, J. A. (2009a). Affective forecasting and capital sentencing: Reducing the impact of victim impact statements. *American Criminal Law Review, 46*, 107–125.

Blumenthal, J. A. (2009b). "To be human": A psychological perspective on property law. *Tulane Law Review, 83*, 609–644.

Blumenthal, J. A. (2010). Property law: A cognitive turn. *Psychonomic Bulletin & Review, 17*, 186–191.

Bond, C. F., Jr., & DePaulo, B. M. (2006). Accuracy of deception judgments. *Personality & Social Psychology Review, 10*, 214–234.

Bond, C. F., Jr. & DePaulo, B. (2008). Individual differences in judging deception: Accuracy and bias. *Psychological Bulletin, 134*, 477–492.

Bond, C. F., Jr., & Uysal, A. (2007). On lie detection "wizards." *Law & Human Behavior*, 31, 109–115.

Bond, G. D. (2008). Deception detection expertise. *Law & Human Behavior, 32*, 339–351.

Bornstein, B. H. (1999). The ecological validity of jury simulations: Is the jury still out? *Law & Human Behavior, 23*, 75–91.

Braithwaite, J. (2002). *Restorative justice and responsive regulation.* New York: Oxford University Press.

Braman, E. (2010). Searching for constraint in legal decision making. In D. Klein & G. Mitchell (Eds.), *The psychology of judicial decision making* (pp. 203–217). New York. Oxford University Press.

Brehm, J. W. (1966). *A theory of psychological reactance.* New York: Academic Press.

Brewer, N., & Burke, A. (2002). Effects of testimonial inconsistencies and eyewitness confidence on mock-juror judgments. *Law & Human Behavior, 26*, 353–364.

Brickman, P., Coates, D., & Janoff-Bulman, R. (1978). Lottery winners and accident victim: Is happiness relative? *Journal of Personality & Social Psychology, 36*, 917–927.

Brigham, J. C., Meissner, C. A., & Wasserman, A. W. (1999). Issues in the construction and expert assessment of photo lineups. *Applied Cognitive Psychology, 13*, 573–592.

Buccafusco, C., & Sprigman, C. (2010). Valuing intellectual property: An experiment. *Cornell Law Review, 96*, 1–45.

Buccafusco, C., & Sprigman, C. J. (2011). The creativity effect. *University of Chicago Law Review*, 78, 31–52.

Carlsmith, K. M. (2006). The roles of retribution and utility in determining punishment. *Journal of Experimental Social Psychology*, 42, 437–451.

Carlsmith, K. M., Darley, J. M., & Robinson, P. H. (2002). Why do we punish? Deterrence and just deserts as motives for punishment. *Journal of Personality and Social Psychology*, 83, 284–299.

Clark, S. E. (2012). Costs and benefits of eyewitness identification reform: Psychological science and public policy. *Perspectives on Psychological Science*, 7, 238–259.

Coolidge v. New Hampshire, 403 U.S. 443 (1971).

Cooper, J., Bennett, E. A., & Sukel, H. L. (1996). Complex scientific testimony: How do jurors make decisions? *Law & Human Behavior*, 20, 379–394.

Corley v. United States, 556 U.S. *303* (2009).

Cowan, C. L., Thompson, W. C., & Ellsworth, P. C. (1984). The effects of death qualification on jurors' predisposition to convict and on the quality of deliberation. *Law & Human Behavior*, 8, 53–79.

Cross, F. (1997). Political science and the new legal realism. *Northwestern University Law Review*, 92, 251–326.

Crotteau, United States v. 218 F.3d *826* (7th Cir. 2000).

Cutler, B. L. (2009). Expert testimony on the psychology of eyewitness identification. New York: Oxford University Press.

Cutler, B. L., & Penrod, S. D. (1995). *Mistaken identification: The eyewitness, psychology, and the law.* Cambridge, UK: Cambridge University Press.

Darley, J. M. (2009). "Morality" in the law: The psychological foundations of citizens' desire to punish transgressions. *Annual Review of Law & Social Science*, 5, 1–23.

Daubert v. Merrill-Dow Pharmaceuticals, Inc., 509 U.S. *579* (1993).

Deffenbacher, K. A., & Loftus, E. F. (1982). Do jurors share a common understanding concerning eyewitness behavior? *Law & Human Behavior*, 6, 15–30.

Desmarais, S. L., & Read, J. D. (2011). After thirty years, what do we know about what jurors know? A meta-analytic review of lay knowledge regarding eyewitness factors. *Law & Human Behavior*, 35, 200–210.

Dhami, M. K. (2003). Psychological models of professional decision making. *Psychological Science*, 14, 175–180.

Dhami, M. K., & Ayton, P. (2001). Bailing and jailing the fast and frugal way. *Journal of Behavioral Decision Making*, 14, 141–168.

Diamond, S. S. (2006). Beyond fantasy and nightmare: A portrait of the jury. *Buffalo Law Review*, 54, 717–763.

Diamond, S. S., & Rose, M. R. (2005). Real juries. *Annual Review of Law & Social Science*, 1, 255–284.

Ditto, P., & Lopez, D. (1992). Motivated skepticism: Use of differential decision criteria for preferred and nonpreferred conclusions. *Journal of Personality and Social Psychology*, 63, 568–584.

Dobbs, D. B. (1993). *Law of remedies: Damages—equity—restitution.* St. Paul, MN: Thomson/West.

Donohue, J., & Wolfers, J. J. (2006). The death penalty: No evidence for deterrence. *The Economists' Voice*, 3, article 3, 1–6.

Dror, I. E., & Cole, S. A. (2010). The vision in "blind justice:" Expert perception, judgment, and visual cognition in forensic pattern recognition. *Psychonomic Bulletin & Review*, 17, 161–167.

Duff, R. A. (2007). Answering for crime: Responsibility and liability in the criminal law. Oxford, UK: Hart Publishing.

Epley, N., & Dunning, D. (2000). Feeling "holier than thou": Are self-serving assessments produced by errors in self or social prediction? *Journal of Personality and Social Psychology*, 79, 861–875.

Fisher, G. (1997). The jury's rise as lie detector. *Yale Law Journal*, 107, 575–713 .

Fiske, A. P., & Tetlock, P. E. (1997). Taboo trade-offs: Reactions to transactions that transgress the spheres of justice. *Political Psychology*, 18, 255–297.

Fitzgerald, R., & Ellsworth, P. C. (1984). Due process vs. crime control: Death qualification and jury attitudes. *Law and Human Behavior*, 8, 31–52.

Ford, E. B. (2006). Lie detection: Historical, neuropsychiatric and legal dimensions. *International Journal of Law & Psychiatry*, 29, 159–177.

Frank, J. (1930). *Law and the modern mind.* New York: Brentano's.

Furgeson, J. R., Babcock, L., & Shane, P. M. (2008a). Do a law's policy implications affect beliefs about its constitutionality? An experimental test. *Law & Human Behavior*, 32, 219–227.

Furgeson, J. R., Babcock, L., & Shane, P. M. (2008b). Behind the mask of method: Political orientation and constitutional interpretive preferences. *Law & Human Behavior*, 32, 502–510.

Galanter, M. (2004). The vanishing trial: An examination of trials and related matters in federal and state courts. *Journal of Empirical Legal Studies*, 1, 457–570.

Garland, D. (1990). Punishment and modern society. Chicago: University of Chicago Press.

Garrett, B. (2008). Judging innocence. *Columbia Law Review*, 108, 55–143.

General Electric Co. v. Joiner, 522 U.S. *136* (1997).

Greely, H. T., & Illes, J. (2007). Neuroscience-based lie detection: The urgent need for regulation. *American Journal of Law & Medicine*, 33, 377–431.

Green, S. P. (1999). Castles and carjackers: Proportionality and the use of deadly force in defense of dwellings and vehicles. *University of Illinois Law Review*, 1999, 1–41.

Greene, E., & Bornstein, B. (2000). Precious little guidance: Jury instructions on damage awards. *Psychology, Public Policy, and Law*, 6, 743–768.

Grubin, D., & Mardin, L. (2005). Lie detection and the polygraph: A historical review. *Journal of Forensic Psychiatry & Psychology*, 16, 357–373.

Guthrie, C., Rachlinski, J. J., & Wistrich, A. J. (2001). Inside the judicial mind. *Cornell Law Review*, 86, 777–830.

Guthrie, C., Rachlinski, J. J., & Wistrich, A. J. (2002). Judging by heuristic: Cognitive illusions in judicial decision making. *Judicature*, 86, 44–50.

Guthrie, C., Rachlinski, J. J., & Wistrich, A. J. (2007). Blinking on the bench: How judges decide cases. *Cornell Law Review*, 93, 1–43.

Hans, V. P. (2008). Jury systems around the world. *Annual Review of Law & Social Science*, 4, 275–297.

Hans, V. P., Kaye, D. H., Dann, B. M., Farley, E. J., & Albertson, S. (2011). Science in the jury box: Jurors' comprehension of mitochondrial DNA evidence. *Law & Human Behavior*, 35, 60–71.

Hastie, R., Penrod, S., & Pennington, N. (1983*).* *Inside the jury.* Cambridge, MA: Harvard University Press.

Hastie, R., & Viscusi, W. K. (1998). What juries can't do well: The jury's performance as a risk manager. *Arizona Law Review*, 40, 901–920.

Hillman, R. A. (2010). *Principles of contract law* (2nd ed.). St. Paul, MN: Thomson/West.

Hines, United States v., 55 F. Supp. 2d *62* (D. Mass. 1999).

Horowitz, I. A., Forsterlee, L., & Brolly, I. (1996). Effects of trial complexity on decision-making. *Journal of Applied Psychology, 81*, 757–768.

Hutcheson, J. C., Jr. (1929). The judgment intuitive: The role of the "hunch" in judicial decision. *Cornell Law Quarterly, 14*, 274–288.

Jones, United States v. (2012). 2012 U.S. LEXIS 1063.

Kalven, H., Jr., & Zeisel, H. (1966). *The American jury.* Boston: Little, Brown.

Kassin, S. M. (1997). The psychology of confession evidence. *American Psychologist, 52*, 221–233.

Kassin, S. M. (2005). On the psychology of confessions: Does innocence put innocents at risk? *American Psychologist, 60*, 215–228.

Kassin, S. M. (2008). The psychology of confessions. *Annual Review of Law and Social Science, 4*, 193–217.

Kassin, S. M., & Gudjonsson, S. H. (2004). The psychology of confessions: A review of the literature and issues. *Psychological Science in the Public Interest, 5*, 33–67.

Kassin, S. M., & Neumann, K. (1997). On the power of confession evidence: An experimental test of the fundamental difference hypothesis. *Law & Human Behavior, 21*, 469–48.

Katz v. United States, 389 U.S. *347* (1967).

Kelo v. City of New London, 545 U.S. 469 (2005).

Koehler, J. J. (2001). When are people persuaded by DNA match statistics? *Law & Human Behavior, 25*, 493–513.

Kovera, M. B., & Borgida, E. (2010). Social psychology and the law. In Fiske, E. T., Dilbert, D. T., & Lindzey (Eds.), *Handbook of social psychology* (Vol. 2, pp. 1343–1385). Hoboken, NJ: John Wiley & Sons.

Kozel, F. A., Johnson, K. A., Mu, Q., Grenesko, E. L., Laken, S. J., & George, M. S. (2005). Detecting deception using functional magnetic resonance imaging. *Biological Psychiatry, 58*, 605–613.

Kumho Tire Co., Ltd. v. Carmichael, 526 U.S. *137* (1999).

Kunda, Z. (1990). The case for motivated reasoning. *Psychological Bulletin, 108*, 480–498.

Langleben, D. D., Loughead, J. W., Bilker, W. B., Ruparel, K., Childress, A. R., Busch, S. I., & Gur, R. C. (2005). Telling truth from lie in individual subjects with fast event-related fMRI. *Human Brain Mapping, 26*, 262–272.

Lassiter, D. G. (2002). Illusory causation in the courtroom. *Current Directions in Psychological Science 11*, 204–208.

Lederman, L. (1999). Which cases go to trial? An empirical study of predictions of failure to settle. *Case Western Reserve University Law Review, 49*, 315–358.

Libby, United States v., 461 F. Supp. 2d 3 (D.D.C. 2006).

Lidsky, L. B. (1996). Defamation, reputation, and the myth of community. *Washington Law Review, 71*, 1–49.

Lieberman, J. D., & Sales, B. D. (2006). *Scientific jury selection.* Washington, DC: American Psychological Association.

Lindsay, R. C. L., Lim, R., Marando, L., & Cully, C. (1986). Mock-juror evaluations of eyewitness testimony: A test of metamemory hypotheses. *Journal of Applied Social Psychology, 15*, 447–459.

Lindsay, R. C. L., & Wells, G. L. (1985). Improving eyewitness identifications from lineups: Simultaneous versus sequential presentation. *Journal of Applied Psychology, 70*, 556–561.

Llewellyn, K. N. (1930). *The bramble bush: On our law and its study.* New York: Columbia Law School.

Llewellyn, K. N. (2011). *The theory of rules* (F. Schauer ed.). Chicago: University of Chicago Press.

Loftus, E. F. (1975). Leading questions and the eyewitness report. *Cognitive Psychology, 7*, 550–572.

Loftus, E. F. (1996). *Eyewitness testimony.* Cambridge, MA: Harvard University Press.

Loftus, E. F., Miller, D. G., & Burns, H. J. (1978). Semantic integration of verbal information into a visual memory. *Journal of Experimental Psychology, 4*, 19–31.

Loftus, E. F., & Palmer, J. C. (1974). Reconstruction of automobile destruction: An example of the interaction between language and memory. *Journal of Verbal Learning & Verbal Behavior, 13*, 585–589.

MacCoun, R. (1998). Biases in the interpretation and use of research results. *Annual Review of Psychology, 49*, 259–287.

Malle, B. F. (2006). The actor-observer asymmetry in causal attribution: A (surprising) meta-analysis. *Psychological Bulletin, 132*, 895–919.

Malle, B. F. (2011). Time to give up the dogmas of attribution: An alternative theory of behavior explanation. In J. M. Olson and M. P. Zanna (eds.), *Advances of experimental social psychology* (Vol. 44, pp. 297–352). Burlington: Academic Press.

Mandel, G. N. (2011). To promote the creative process: Intellectual property law and the psychology of creativity. *Notre Dame Law Review, 86*, 1999–2026.

Marks, G., & Miller, N. (1987). Ten years of research on the false-consensus effect: An empirical and theoretical review. *Psychological Bulletin, 102*, 72–90.

McConkey, K. M., & Roche, S. M. (1989). Knowledge of eyewitness memory. *Australian Psychologist, 24*, 377–394.

Merryman, J. H., & Pérez-Perdomo, R. (2007). *The civil law tradition: An introduction to the legal systems of Europe and Latin America* (3rd ed.). Stanford, CA: Stanford University Press.

Mnookin, J. L. (2001). Fingerprint evidence in an age of DNA profiling. *Brooklyn Law Review, 67*, 13–70.

Nadler, J., & Diamond, S. S. (2008). Eminent domain and the psychology of property: Proposed use, subjective attachment, and taker identity. *Journal of Empirical Legal Studies, 5*, 713–749.

Napolean, V. (ed.) (2011). Restorative justice. *Alberta Law Review, 48*, 807–1008.

National Research Council, Committee on Identifying the Needs of the Forensic Sciences Community (2009). Strengthening forensic science in the United States: A path forward. Washington, DC: National Academies Press.

New York Times Co. v. Sullivan, 376 U.S. 254 (1964).

Nisbett, R. E., & Cohen, D. (1996). *Culture of honor: The psychology of violence in the South.* Boulder, CO: Westview Press.

Noon, E., & Hollin, C. R. (1987). Lay knowledge of eyewitness behavior: A British survey. *Applied Cognitive Psychology, 1*, 143–153.

Ogloff, J. R. P., & Rose, G. P. (2005). The comprehension of jury instructions. In N. Brewer & K.D. Williams (Eds.), *Psychology and law: An empirical perspective* (pp. 407–444). New York: Guilford Publications.

O'Sullivan, M. (2008). Unicorns or Tiger Woods: Are lie detection experts myths or rarities? A response to "On lie detection "wizards"" by Bond & Uysal. *Law & Human Behavior, 31*, 117–123.

O'Sullivan, M. (2009). Why most people parse palters, fibs, lies, whoppers, and other deceptions poorly. In B. Harrington (Ed.), *Deception: From ancient empires to Internet dating* (pp. 74–103). Stanford, CA: Stanford University Press.

Pennington, N., & Hastie, R. (1991). A cognitive theory of juror decision making: The story model. *Cardozo Law Review, 13*, 519–557.

Pennington, N., & Hastie, R. (1992). Explaining the evidence: Tests of the story model for juror decision making. *Journal of Personality and Social Psychology, 62*, 189–206.

Pettys, T. E. (2011). Judicial discretion in constitutional cases. *Journal of Law & Politics, 26*, 123–178.

Posner, R. (1993). What do judges maximize? (The same thing everybody else does). *Supreme Court Economic Review, 3*, 1–41.

Priest, G. L., & Klein, B. (1984). The selection of disputes for litigation. *Journal of Legal Studies, 13*, 1–55.

Prosser, W. L., Keeton, W. P., Dobbs, D. B., Keeton, R. E., & Owen, D. G. (1984). *Prosser & Keeton on torts* (5th ed.). St, Paul, MN: Thomson/West.

Rachlinski, J. J., Guthrie, C., & Wistrich, A. W. (2006). Inside the bankruptcy judge's mind. *Boston University Law Review, 86*, 1227–1264.

Radin, M. J. (1982). Property and personhood. *Stanford Law Review, 34*, 957–1015.

Reimund, M. A. (2005). The law and restorative justice: Friend or foe? A systemic look at the legal issues in restorative justice. *Drake Law Review, 53*, 667–692.

Richeson, J. A., & Trawalter, S. (2005). On the categorization of admired and disliked exemplars of admired and disliked racial groups. *Journal of Personality and Social Psychology, 89*, 517–530.

Rincon, United States v., 28 F.3d *921* (9th Cir. 1994).

Roberts, J. W. (2003). Between the heat of passion and cold blood: Battered woman's syndrome as an excuse for self-defense in non-confrontational homicides. *Law & Psychology Review, 27*, 135–156.

Robinson, P. H., & Darley, J. M. (1995). *Justice, liability, and blame: Community views and the criminal law. New directions in social psychology*. Boulder, CO: Westview Press.

Robinson, P. H., & Spellman, B. A. (2005). Sentencing decisions: Matching the decisionmaker to the decision nature. *Columbia Law Review, 105*, 1124–1161.

Roe v. Wade, 410 U.S. *113* (1973).

Roper v. Simmons, *543* U.S. 551 (2005).

Ross, D. F., Read, J. D., & Toglia, M. P. (Eds.) (1994). *Adult eyewitness testimony: Current trends and developments*. Cambridge, UK: Cambridge University Press.

Russano, M. B., Meissner, C. A., Narchet, F. M., & Kassin, S. M. (2005). Investigating true and false confessions within a novel experimental paradigm. *Psychological Science, 16*, 481–486.

Salerno, J., & Diamond, S. S. (2010). The promise of a cognitive perspective on jury deliberations. *Psychonomic Bulletin & Review, 17*, 174–179.

Schauer, F. (2000). Incentives, reputation, and the inglorious determinants of judicial behavior. *University of Cincinnati Law Review, 68*, 615–36

Schauer, F. (2003). *Profiles, probabilities, and stereotypes*. Cambridge, MA: Harvard University Press.

Schauer, F. (2008). Why precedent in law (and elsewhere) is not totally (or even substantially) about analogy. *Perspectives on Psychological Science, 3*, 454–460.

Schauer, F. (2009). *Thinking like a lawyer: A new introduction to legal reasoning*. Cambridge, MA: Harvard University Press.

Schauer, F. (2010a). Can bad science be good evidence? Neuroscience, lie detection, and beyond. *Cornell Law Review, 95*, 1191–1219.

Schauer, F. (2010b). Is there a psychology of judging? In Klein, D., & Mitchell, G. (Eds.), *The psychology of judicial decision making* (pp. 103–120). New York: Oxford University Press.

Schauer, F. (2010c). Neuroscience, lie-detection, and the law. *Trends in Cognitive Science, 14*, 101–103.

Schmechel, R. S., O'Toole, T. P., Easterly, C., & Loftus, E. F. (2006). Beyond the ken? Testing jurors' understanding of eyewitness reliability evidence. *Jurimetrics, 46*, 177–214.

Schweitzer, N. J., Saks, M. J., & Lovis-McMahon, D. (2009). Is the rule of law a law of rules: Judgments of rule of law violations. Paper presented at the Conference on Empirical Legal Studies, University of Southern California, Los Angeles, November 2009.

Schweitzer, N. J., Sylvester, P., & Saks, M. (2007). Rule violations and the rule of law: A factorial survey of public attitudes. *DePaul Law Review, 56*, 615–638.

Segal, J., & Spaeth, H. (2002). *The Supreme Court and the attitudinal model revisited*. Cambridge, UK: Cambridge University Press.

Severance, L., Greene, E., & Loftus, E. (1984). Toward criminal jury instructions that jurors can understand. *Journal of Criminal Law & Criminology, 75*, 198–233.

Shoenfelt, E. L., Maue, A. E., & Nelson, J. (2002). Reasonable person versus reasonable woman: Does it matter? *American University Journal of Gender, Social Policy, & Law, 6*, 633–672.

Simons, D. J., & Chabris, C. F. (2011). What people believe about how memory works: A representative sample of the U.S. population. *PLoS ONE 6*, e22757.

Sommers, S. R., & Kassin, S. M. (2001). On the many impacts of inadmissible testimony: Selective compliance, need for cognition, and the overreaction bias. *Personality & Social Psychology Bulletin, 27*, 1368–1377.

Spellman, B. A. (2004). Reflections of a recovering lawyer: How becoming a cognitive psychologist—and (in particular) studying analogical and causal reasoning—changed my views about the field of psychology and law. *Chicago-Kent Law Review, 79*, 1187–1214.

Spellman, B. A. (2007). On the supposed expertise of judges in evaluating evidence. *University of Pennsylvania Law Review PENNumbra, 156*, 1–9.

Spellman, B. A. (2010). Judges, expertise, and analogy. In Klein, D., & Mitchell, G. (Eds.), *The psychology of judicial decision making* (pp. 149–164). New York: Oxford University Press.

Spellman, B. A., & Schauer, F. (2009). Artists' moral rights and the psychology of ownership. *Tulane Law Review, 83*, 661–678.

Spellman, B. A., & Schauer, F. (2012). Legal reasoning. In Holyoak, K., & Morrison, R. (Eds.), *Oxford handbook of thinking and reasoning* (pp. 719–735). New York: Oxford University Press.

Steblay, N. M. (1992). A meta-analytic review of the weapon focus effect. *Law & Human Behavior, 16*, 413–424.

Steblay, N. K. (2011). What we know now: The Evanston Illinois field lineups. *Law & Human Behavior, 35*, 1–12.

Steblay, N. K., Besirevic, J., Fulero, S. M., & Jimenez-Lorente, B. (1999). The effects of pretrial publicity on juror verdicts: A meta-analytic review. *Law & Human Behavior, 23*, 213–235.

Steblay, N. K., Dysart, J. E., & Wells, G. L. (2011). Seventy-two tests of the sequential lineup superiority effect: A meta-analysis and policy discussion. *Psychology, Public Policy, and Law, 17*, 99–139.

Steblay, N., Hosch, H. M., Culhane, S. E., & McWethy, A. (2006). The impact on juror verdicts of judicial instruction to disregard inadmissible evidence: A meta-analysis. *Law & Human Behavior*, *30*, 469–492.

Steblay, N. K., & Phillips (2011). The not-sure response option in sequential lineup practice. *Applied Cognitive Psychology*, *25*, 768–774.

Strang, H., & Braithwaite, J. (Eds.). (2001). *Restorative justice and civil society*. Cambridge, UK: Cambridge University Press.

Swedloff, R., & Huang, P. H. (2010). Tort damages and the new science of happiness. *Indiana Law Journal*, *85*, 553–595.

Tenney, E. R., MacCoun, R. J., Spellman, B. A., & Hastie, R. (2007). Calibration trumps confidence as a basis for witness credibility. *Psychological Science*, *18*, 46–50.

Thaler, R. H., & Benartzi, S. (2004). Save more tomorrow: Using behavioral economics to increase employee savings. *Journal of Political Economy*, *112*, S164–S187.

Thompson, W. C. (1989). Are juries competent to evaluate statistical evidence? *Law and Contemporary Problems*, *52*, 9–41.

Thompson, W. C., & Cole, S. A. (2007). Psychological aspects of forensic identification evidence. In M. Costanzo, D. Krauss, & K. Pezdek (Eds.), *Expert psychological testimony for the courts*. New York: Erlbaum.

Toglia, M. P., Herrmann, D. J., Read, J. D., Thompson, C. P., Payne, D. G., & Bruce, D. (1998). *Eyewitness memory: Theoretical and applied perspectives*. Hillsdale, NJ: Erlbaum.

Tyler, T. R. (2006). *Why people obey the law* (2nd ed.). Princeton: Princeton University Press.

Tyler, T. R., & Huo, Y. J. (2002). *Trust in the law: Encouraging public cooperation with the police and courts*. New York: Russell Sage Foundation.

Ülkümen, G., & Cheema, A. (2011). Framing goals to influence personal savings: The role of specificity and construal level. *Journal of Marketing Research*, *48*, 958–969.

Vidmar, N. (Ed.) (2000). *World jury systems*. Oxford, UK: Oxford University Press.

Viscusi, W. K. (1996). Pain and suffering: Damages in search of a sounder rationale. *Michigan Journal of Law and Policy*, *1*, 141–156.

Volokh, A. (1997). n guilty men. *University of Pennsylvania Law Review*, *143*, 173–213.

Vrij, A. (2000). *Detecting lies and deceit: The psychology of lying and the implications for professional practice*. Chichester, UK: John Wiley & Sons.

Vrij, A., & Baxter, M. (1999). Accuracy and confidence in detecting truths and lies in elaborations and denials. *Expert Evidence*, *7*, 25–36.

Vrij, A., & Graham, M. S. (1997). Individual differences between liars and the ability to detect lies. *Expert Evidence*, *5*, 144–148.

Wegner, D. M. (1994). Ironic processes of mental control. *Psychological Review*, *101*, 34–52.

Weinreb, L. (2005). *Legal reason: The use of analogy in legal argument*. New York: Cambridge University Press.

Wells, G. L. (1993). What do we know about eyewitness identification? *American Psychologist*, *48*, 553–571.

Wells, G. L. (2006). Eyewitness identification: Systemic reforms. *Wisconsin Law Review*, *2006*, 615–643.

Wells, G. L., & Bradfield, A. L. (1998). "Good you identified the suspect": Feedback to eyewitnesses distorts their reports of the witnessing experience. *Journal of Applied Psychology*, *83*, 360–376.

Wells, G. L., & Bradfield, A. L. (1999). Distortions in eyewitnesses' recollections: Can the post-identification feedback effect be moderated? *Psychological Science*, *10*, 138–144.

Wells, G. L., & Leippe, M. R. (1981). How do triers of fact infer the accuracy of eyewitness identifications? Using memory for peripheral details can be misleading. *Journal of Applied Psychology*, *66*, 682–687.

Wells, G. L., Malpass, R. S., Lindsay, R. C. L., Fisher, R. P., Turtle, J. W., & Fulero, S. M. (2000). From the lab to the police station: A successful application of eyewitness research. *American Psychologist*, *55*, 581–598.

Wells, G.L., Menon, A., & Penrod, S. (2006). Eyewitness evidence: Improving its probative value. *Psychological Science in the Public Interest*, *7*, 45–75.

Wells, G. L., & Olson, E. A. (2001). The other-race effect in eyewitness identification: What do we do about it? *Psychology, Public Policy, & Law*, *7*, 230–246.

Wells, G. L., & Quinlivan, D. S. (2009). Suggestive eyewitness procedures and the Supreme Court's reliability test in light of eyewitness science: 30 years later. *Law & Human Behavior*, *33*, 1–24.

Wenzel, M., Okimoto, T. G., Feather, N. T., & Platow, M. J. (2008). Retributive and restorative justice. *Law & Human Behavior*, *32*, 375–387.

Whitley, B. E., Jr., & Greenberg, M. S. (1986). The role of eyewitness confidence in juror perceptions of credibility. *Journal of Applied Social Psychology*, *16*, 387–409.

Winter, R. J., & Greene, E. (2007). Juror decision-making. In Francis Durso (Ed.), *Handbook of applied cognition* (2nd ed., pp. 739–761). New York: John Wiley & Sons.

Wistrich, A. J., Guthrie, C., & Rachlinski, J. J. (2005). Can judges ignore inadmissible information? The difficulty of deliberately disregarding. *University of Pennsylvania Law Review*, *153*, 1251–1345.

Wolpe, P. R., Foster, K. R., & Langleben, D. D. (2005). Emerging neurotechnologies for lie-detection: Promises and perils. *American Journal of Bioethics*, *5*, 39–49.

Wright, D. B., Memon, A., Skakerberg, E. M., & Gabbert, F. (2009). When eyewitnesses talk. *Current Directions in Psychological Science*, *18*, 174–178.

Young, W. G. (2006). Vanishing trials, vanishing juries, vanishing constitution. *Suffolk University Law Review*, *40*, 67–94.

CHAPTER 41

"Hot" Political Cognition: Its Self-, Group-, and System-Serving Purposes

John T. Jost, Erin P. Hennes, *and* Howard Lavine

Abstract

In recent years, it has become increasingly difficult to understand current political controversies without appreciating the extent to which information processing is driven not merely by empirical evidence but also by ideological and other goals. This chapter reviews recent research on "hot" or motivated political cognition. The authors begin by summarizing historical developments in psychology and political science that set the stage for a "motivational turn" in theory and research. Next they turn their attention to three classes of relevant motives (or purposes), namely self-, group-, and system-serving motives. The authors then consider evidence bearing on the possibility that there are ideological asymmetries in motivated political reasoning. Finally, they conclude by suggesting not only that research on motivated social cognition may be useful for understanding political judgment and behavior but also that observing political judgment and behavior may provide new insights into social cognition.

Key Words: motivated reasoning, political cognition, ideology

All of us who are concerned for peace and triumph of reason and justice must be keenly aware how small an influence reason and honest good will exert upon events in the political field.

–Albert Einstein

There has been a palpable resurgence of interest among social psychologists and, more recently, political scientists in the problem of *motivated reasoning*—namely, the processes whereby goals, needs, and desires affect information processing (e.g., Balcetis, 2008; Beer, 2012; Ditto, 2009; Kruglanski, 1996, 1999; Kunda, 1990; Lau & Redlawsk, 2006; Lodge & Taber, 2000; Redlawsk, 2002; Taber, Cann, & Kucsova, 2009). There is no way of knowing whether increased scientific attention to this topic is due, even in small part, to the fact that national (and international) politics seem as nasty, deceptive (or perhaps self-deceptive), and unconstrained by reality as ever. It is difficult, for instance, to understand current controversies over global climate change, health care reform, immigration, regulation of the financial services industry, and other issues without appreciating the extent to which information processing is driven not merely by empirical evidence or a commitment to accuracy or rationality but also by ideological, partisan, fundraising, and other goals.

In this chapter, we review recent research on "hot" or motivated political cognition in the hope that by illuminating its dynamics we may also develop a better understanding of how to minimize its most pernicious consequences. We cover scholarship in political psychology that takes inspiration from the "motivational turn" in social cognition, including research suggesting that goals operate implicitly or automatically (e.g., Aarts & Dijksterhuis, 2000; Bargh, Gollwitzer, Lee-Chai, Barndollar, & Troetschel, 2001; Ferguson, Hassin, & Bargh, 2008; Kruglanski et al., 2002). We begin by summarizing historical developments in psychology and political science that set the stage for a renewal of interest in motivated political reasoning, and then turn our attention to three classes of motives (i.e., self-, group-, and system-serving motives) that appear to shape information processing in political contexts.

The Cognitive Revolution and Its Aftermath

The cognitive revolution that swept through psychology in the late 1950s (e.g., Allport, 1954; Bruner, Goodnow, & Austin, 1956; Chomsky, 1959; Miller, 1956; Simon, 1957) made its mark on political science in the mid-1970s (e.g., Axelrod, 1973, 1976; Jervis, 1976). By the 1980s, psychologically minded political scientists had skillfully and fruitfully applied *information processing* concepts such as bounded rationality, knowledge structures, schemata, construct accessibility, availability, applicability, and semantic priming to the study of elite and mass decision making in policy and electoral arenas (e.g., Conover & Feldman, 1984, 1989; Fiske & Kinder, 1981; Fiske, Kinder, & Larter, 1983; Fiske, Lau, & Smith, 1990; Krosnick & Kinder, 1990; Larson, 1985; Miller, Wattenberg, & Malanchuk, 1986). Examples include Iyengar, Peters, and Kinder's (1982) cognitive theory of agenda setting, Lodge and Hamill's (1986) work on schematicity and on-line processing (see also Hamill, Lodge, & Blake, 1985), Lau's (1985, 1989) studies of construct accessibility and valence asymmetry in political evaluation, Tetlock's (1986, 1992) analysis of foreign policy decision making and the relationship between cognitive style and political ideology, and various treatments of heuristic processing and "low information rationality" (e.g., Lupia, 1994; Popkin, 1994).

By the 1990s, a focus on the ingredients of policy attitudes and voting decisions had given way to intense scholarly interest in the ways in which political information is acquired, organized in memory, and retrieved in making political judgments. This led to several valuable insights concerning public opinion and electoral behavior, including the distinction (imported from psychology) between *on-line* and *memory-based* models of political evaluation (Lavine, 2002; Zaller & Feldman, 1992). According to certain on-line models, citizens extract the evaluative implications of political information at the moment of exposure, integrate these into a "running tally," and then proceed to forget the nongist descriptive details (e.g., Lodge, McGraw, & Stroh, 1989). From this perspective, judgments are not necessarily constrained by the pros and cons that citizens can recall; to express an opinion, individuals need

only to retrieve the current value of the on-line tally. This process-focused model of political evaluation forcefully challenged the long-standing assumption that rational political choice flows from information retention and ideological sophistication.

As in social psychology, much work in political cognition assumed that people are "cognitive misers" (Fiske & Taylor, 1984; Hamilton, 1981; Tajfel, 1969) who rely on cognitive shortcuts or *heuristics* to simplify problem-solving domains and minimize information processing effort (Kuklinski & Quirk, 2001; Lau & Redlawsk, 2001; Popkin, 1994). Researchers compiled lengthy lists of heuristics that citizens use, including reliance on political parties, special interest groups, newspaper endorsements, candidate appearance, presidential approval ratings, and feelings about certain social groups (see Lupia & McCubbins, 1998). For example, rather than taking the trouble to learn the details of a complex policy debate, individuals can save time and effort by delegating their judgments to trusted experts who are perceived to share their values (Lupia & McCubbins, 1998). Over the years, political scientists have applied insights from cognitively oriented social psychology to an impressive (and ever-expanding) range of domains, including ideological sophistication, political partisanship, candidate perception, issue preferences, voting behavior, racial attitudes, and international relations (Abelson & Levi, 1985; Huckfeldt, Levine, Morgan, & Sprague, 1999; Iyengar & Kinder, 1987; Iyengar & Ottati, 1994; Jervis, 1993; Lau & Sears, 1986; Lodge & McGraw, 1995; McGuire, 1993; Tourangeau & Rasinski, 1988; Zaller & Feldman, 1992). Readers who wish to learn more about "cold" political cognition—that is, the ways in which nonmotivated information processing mechanisms and constraints affect political judgment and decision making—are directed to several excellent literature reviews (i.e., Kuklinski & Quirk, 2000; Lau, 2003; Lau & Redlawsk, 2006; Lavine, 2002; McGraw, 2000, 2003; Steenbergen & Lodge, 2003; Taber, 2003).

However, it is important to point out that not all political scientists greeted the cognitive revolution enthusiastically. Some, like Lane (1986, p. 303), were skeptical that information processing paradigms could illuminate the "purposes" of political cognition, asking: "To what ends these schemata, these concepts, and these ideational structures? For what purposes is information processed?" Lane offered several possibilities:

People are doing more than trying "to organize the political world" (Conover & Feldman, 1984); they are making their thoughts more comfortable to themselves; they are watching with a sports fan's eye and passion, impressing others, evaluating a process that, in the end, they cherish; and they are trying to understand and achieve something beyond the election that requires them to enlist their theories, interpret government boundaries and capabilities, and decide who should get what, themselves included. Each of these purposes will give color and tone, transience or durability, shape and content to their political schemata. (pp. 316–317)

Lane's (1986) observations call to mind an earlier distinction between hot and cold cognition (Abelson & Rosenberg, 1958), that is, between information processing that is affected by affective or motivational considerations and purely logical, rational concerns. Today, we would identify Lane's "purposes" as *motives* that guide (or perhaps "bias") cognitive processing (e.g., Ditto, Scepansky, Munro, Apanovitch, & Lockhart, 1998; Dunning, 1999; Jost, Glaser, Kruglanski, & Sulloway, 2003; Kruglanski, 1996; Kunda, 1990). The focus of the present chapter is squarely on the role of motivation in political cognition.

The Motivational Turn in Social Cognition

Since Lane's (1986) petition, research in social and political cognition has indeed been "hotter," that is, more attentive to affective and motivational factors. The motivational turn in social cognition was instigated to a considerable extent by the conceptual and empirical work of the late Ziva Kunda (1990), who concluded that "directional goals do affect reasoning" such that individuals "are more likely to arrive at those conclusions that they want to arrive at" (p. 495; see also Klein & Kunda, 1992; Kunda & Sanitioso, 1989, 1991; Kunda & Sinclair, 1999; Pyszczynski & Greenberg, 1987). As we shall see, this view does not assume that people are indifferent to considerations of accuracy. Rather, people attempt to "strike a workable balance" between getting it right and maintaining preferred conclusions. Other luminaries in social psychology joined Kunda in seeking to clarify the role of motivation in information processing (e.g., Baumeister & Newman, 1994; Ditto & Lopez, 1992; Ditto et al., 1998; Dunning, Leuenberger, & Sherman, 1995; Kruglanski, 1996, 1999; Kruglanski & Webster, 1996; Kruglanski, Webster, & Klem, 1993; Munro & Ditto, 1997).

It is important to bear in mind that the sudden consensus concerning motivational influences on cognitive processing materialized only after prolonged debate in the field (e.g., see Miller & Ross, 1975; Nisbett & Ross, 1980; Ross & Fletcher, 1985; Tetlock & Levi, 1982). Skeptics asserted that motivational explanations for self-serving forms of bias were unnecessary because it was possible to explain the results of many studies using principles of information processing such as accessibility or availability. Some researchers countered the skepticism by directly manipulating motivational needs, demonstrating that biased processing was shaped by the motivational significance of the conclusion (e.g., Ditto, Jemmott, & Darley, 1988; Kunda, 1987). For instance, female coffee drinkers were shown to be more resistant to scientific data indicating that caffeine poses a severe health risk for women in comparison with (1) males, (2) females who did not consume caffeine regularly, and (3) females who were told that the health risk of caffeine consumption was not serious (Kunda, 1987).

Once experimental paradigms were developed to demonstrate that nonmotivational (i.e., purely cognitive) explanations failed to explain certain phenomena, attention shifted from determining *whether* motivated reasoning occurs to *how* it occurs. Four major hypotheses emerged from a set of highly influential articles that were published between 1987 and 1996 (see Ditto & Lopez, 1992; Kunda, 1990; Kruglanski & Webster, 1996; Pyszczynski & Greenberg, 1987). Of central importance to the debate that followed was the question of whether motivation affects the *quantity* or *quality* of information processing (or both).

Quantity-of-Processing Perspectives

Ditto and Lopez's (1992) quantity-of-processing model assumes that individuals possess a finite supply of cognitive resources, which they selectively assign to various problem-solving tasks. Because individuals are loath to accept preference-inconsistent conclusions, they demand more information (and therefore engage in more persistent information processing) before relinquishing their point of view. In an especially clever demonstration, Ditto and Lopez invited participants to test themselves for the presence of a rare enzyme that was allegedly associated with pancreatic disorders. Participants were given a "testing strip" (actually, a plain piece of yellow paper) and instructed to dip the strip in their saliva. Half of the participants were told that the strip would change color after about 20 seconds if they *did* have the undesirable enzyme, and half were told that the strip would change color if they *did not* have the undesirable enzyme. All participants were asked to place their test strip into an envelope as soon as their test result was clear. As hypothesized, participants for whom a color change was described as a desirable outcome waited significantly longer before accepting their test result, and also engaged in more retesting behaviors than did participants for whom a color change was described as undesirable.

Ditto and Lopez's (1992) *quantity-of-processing* model is broadly consistent with several other models of motivated social cognition. For instance, Kruglanski and Webster (1996) proposed that individuals tend to persist in information processing until a satisfactory conclusion is reached; from that point on, they strive to avoid belief change. This model of "seizing and freezing" makes predictions about the *quality* as well as the quantity of information processing, insofar as the motivation to "seize" upon an acceptable conclusion may affect not only the extent but also the focus and direction of information search, and the motivation to "freeze" may affect the perceived endurance or stability of informational attributes.

Quality-of-Processing Perspectives

Pyszczynski and Greenberg (1987) posited that (1) individuals allocate greater information processing resources to preference-inconsistent than preference-consistent information, and (2) inconsistent information is often viewed as less valid and relevant than preference-consistent information. According to their *biased hypothesis testing model,* the desire for accuracy may be trumped by self-serving motives to reach a desired conclusion about oneself or one's situation. Along these lines, Pyszczynski, Greenberg, and Holt (1985) found that participants who received failure feedback on a test later evaluated a research report concluding that the same test was highly valid as being less well-conducted in comparison with participants who had received success feedback.

Kunda (1990), too, argued that motivation may influence not only the quantity but also the manner of information processing, including the recruitment of different beliefs, inferential rules, and the treatment of certain kinds of information as more or less relevant. For instance, the motive to reach a desired conclusion may facilitate the accessibility of supporting evidence stored in memory. Biased memory search may pertain to the self, to others, or to external events, and it may be pulled in one direction

or another as a function of exposure to information about what is socially desirable in a given situation (e.g., toothbrushing, Ross, McFarland, & Fletcher, 1981; caffeine intake, Sherman & Kunda, 1989, as cited in Kunda, 1990; introversion vs. extraversion, Sanitioso, Kunda, & Fong, 1990). These findings and others suggest that individuals may process different pieces of information selectively depending on the conclusion they wish to reach.

Much of the research in motivated *political* cognition has been influenced by the hybrid approach of Baumeister and Newman (1994), who contrasted the intuitive scientist, who seeks accuracy and understanding, with the intuitive lawyer, who seeks predetermined and preferred conclusions. Their model assumes that goal-directed information processing involves four steps. In Step 1, individuals gather evidence. Here, inferences may be biased by selective attention, confirmatory memory searches, and the tendency to "freeze" on a desired conclusion. In Step 2, the implications of the evidence as gathered are automatically processed. Then, in Step 3, motivation may lead individuals to reassess the evidence and the inferences that can be drawn on the basis of it. The intuitive lawyer may at this point selectively evaluate the evidence and discard that which is deemed inconvenient. Finally, in Step 4, individuals seek to integrate the evidence, differentially weighting various pieces of evidence so as to reach a preferred conclusion.

Accuracy Motivation

Kunda (1990) reviewed evidence that several "nondirectional" goals—including the desire to be accurate (Kruglanski & Freund, 1983; Tetlock, 1983), the need to prolong closure (Kruglanski et al., 1993), and the inclination to process information systematically when it is self-relevant (Chaiken, Liberman, & Eagly, 1989; Petty & Cacioppo, 1986)—can produce especially careful, deliberate, effortful, and complex forms of reasoning. Several studies have illustrated that increasing accuracy motivation can indeed produce informational benefits (e.g., Chen, Shechter, & Chaiken, 1996; Thompson, Roman, Moskowitz, Chaiken, & Bargh, 1994). At the same time, accountability pressures and other admonishments to be accurate do sometimes fail, especially in the presence of an insidious bias or a tempting conclusion (Lerner & Tetlock, 1999; Lord, Lepper, & Preston, 1984).

Kunda (1990) offered the intriguing but worrisome possibility that accuracy goals, when paired with other (directional) goals, could *enhance* rather than *reduce* bias (see also Lerner & Tetlock, 1999). It may be that personal investment in a given decisional outcome facilitates the construction of justifications, which strengthen the (subjective) case for a preferred outcome while avoiding evidence that supports the nonpreferred conclusion. Although very few studies have pursued this possibility directly, it is in line with certain findings suggesting that political "sophisticates" sometimes engage in biased political reasoning to an even greater extent than less informed citizens (e.g., Bartels, 2008; Duch, Palmer, & Anderson, 2000; Gaines, Kuklinski, Quirk, Peyton, & Verkuilen, 2007; Jacobson, 2010; Kuklinski, Quirk, & Peyton, 2008; Taber et al., 2009; Wells, Reedy, Gastil, & Lee, 2009; these findings are described in more detail below).

Motivated Political Cognition

Drawing on social psychological descriptions of the motivated reasoning process, Taber and Lodge (2006) proposed that all attempts at human reasoning reflect a tension between motivation for *accuracy* and motivation for *belief perseverance*, that is, the desire to maintain one's own preexisting beliefs (e.g., Lord, Ross, & Lepper, 1979). We readily agree that belief perseverance (or "cognitive conservatism"; see Greenwald, 1980) is a powerful psychological motive, but it is by no means the only one that opposes or interferes with accuracy in social and political cognition. There are probably several possible taxonomies of motivational processes, including a tripartite classification of motives according to *self-serving*, *group-serving*, and *system-serving* goals, ends, or purposes (see also Jost, Burgess, & Mosso, 2001; Stangor & Jost, 1997). Because almost all of the published research on motivated political cognition has addressed self- or group-serving motives, we focus on these two in the present chapter, before considering a few implications of the possibility that many (and perhaps most) individuals also exhibit system-serving biases.

Self-Serving Motivation in Political Cognition

Thanks to Freud, psychologists were quick to discover that human cognition is biased by ego-defensive needs and tendencies (e.g., Westen, 1998). Self-serving motivational processes were emphasized in so-called functional approaches to social and political attitudes, including Smith, Bruner, and White's (1956) classic, *Opinions and Personality*. The basic idea was that attitudes and beliefs are formed and maintained to the extent that they satisfy individual needs, such as minimizing intrapsychic conflict, maintaining self-esteem, expressing personal values and identities, obtaining social rewards and avoiding punishments, and advancing material self-interest (see also Katz, 1960; Lavine & Snyder, 1996; Maio & Olson, 2000). Lane (1986), too, noted that political cognition is driven by purposes of "internal adjustment, perhaps to conserve effort ('cognitive misers'), to relieve mental conflict (e.g., balance theory), or to achieve self-consistency or improved self-esteem" (pp. 304–305).

Self-Gratification and Self-Aggrandizement

Consistent with this functional perspective, political psychologists have long argued that political perceptions, preferences, and behaviors serve self-regulatory goals. In seminal works such as *Psychopathology and Politics* (1930), *World Politics and Personal Insecurity* (1935), and *Power and Personality* (1948), Harold Lasswell—often credited as the father of political psychology—applied psychodynamic concepts to a broad range of political questions, including the organization of belief systems, the role of political symbols in mass persuasion, personality and democratic character, and styles of political leadership. Perhaps his most important insight was that political ideologies reflect the displacement of private motives and emotions onto public objects, which are then rationalized in terms of the public interest (see also Ascher & Hirschfelder-Ascher, 2005). Political behavior is thus "aimed at self-gratification or aggrandizement but is disguised and rationalized as public-spirited" (Sullivan, Rahn, & Rudolph, 2002, p. 28).

Lasswell's displacement hypothesis anchored a motivational perspective on the nature and origins of political cognition and behavior, and it anticipated several highly influential studies of political leaders and followers, including Fromm's (1941) *Escape from Freedom*, Adorno, Frenkel-Brunswik, Levinson, and Sanford's (1950) *The Authoritarian Personality*, George and George's (1956) *Woodrow Wilson and Colonel House*, Rokeach's (1960) *The Open and Closed Mind*, and Lane's (1962) *Political Ideology*. Each of these works expresses a neo-Freudian tradition in which the political beliefs of ordinary citizens and the actions of political elites were seen as manifestations of deep-seated (and often unconscious) psychological needs and conflicts. For example, in their monumental study of the intrapsychic roots of anti-Semitism, ethnocentrism, and fascism, Adorno et al. (1950) hypothesized that future authoritarians are subjected to rigid and punitive child-rearing practices, resulting in feelings of intense hostility toward parental authority. To protect the dependent child's ego from overwhelming anxiety, these feelings are repressed but manifested unconsciously in the glorification of and submission to parental values, along with displaced aggression toward political, ethnic, and moral outgroups.

Self-esteem continued to play a role in subsequent work in political psychology, with low self-esteem being implicated in (1) racial stereotyping and prejudice (Allport, 1954; Fein & Spencer, 1997); (2) role conformity in decision making among judges (Gibson, 1981); (3) political conservatism (Jost, Glaser, et al., 2003; McClosky, 1958; Wilson, 1973); (4) "passive" presidential character (Barber, 1985); (5) low political efficacy and trust among black children (Abramson, 1972); (6) decreased levels of political awareness and increased levels of political cynicism among adolescents (Carmines, 1978); (7) social intolerance (Rokeach, 1960, Sullivan, Marcus, Feldman, &Piereson, 1981); and (8) isolationist (i.e., noninterventionist) attitudes on foreign policy (Sniderman, 1975).

In an influential program of research, Sullivan, Marcus, and their colleagues (Sullivan et al., 1981; Sullivan, Piereson, & Marcus, 1982; see also Marcus, Sullivan, Theiss-Morse, & Wood, 1995) demonstrated that low self-esteem heightened intolerance both directly (through the projection of personal inadequacies onto disliked groups) and indirectly (by interfering with the learning of democratic norms). Similarly, Sniderman and Citrin (1971) proposed that isolationist attitudes in foreign policy can provide individuals with "an opportunity to express their fears, suspicions, hostility and self-dislike," and "offers relief from feelings of helplessness and unworthiness" (see also Sniderman, 1975). They demonstrated not only that low self-esteem is tied to isolationist (vs. internationalist) policy preferences and conservative self-identification, but also that self-esteem served to *organize* attitudes in different policy domains, in that intercorrelations among attitudes were diminished by statistically adjusting for self-esteem.

Self-Interest Motivation

An even more obvious basis of political judgment and decision making than self-esteem is *self-interest* motivation. The assumption that political life—and human behavior in general—is fundamentally grounded in the pursuit of self-interest pervades the social and behavioral sciences as well as popular culture (e.g., Miller, 1999). In economics and politics, for example, the theory of rational choice holds that people are motivated to maximize "utility," that is, to follow those courses of action that are personally advantageous in terms of one's cost-to-benefit ratio (e.g., Downs, 1957; Schumpeter, 1942/1994).

However, the empirical evidence as a whole reveals that rational considerations such as economic self-interest play a fairly minor role in shaping evaluations of issues and candidates, unless the stakes are large and unambiguous (Green & Shapiro, 1994; Sears & Funk, 1991). Most citizens do not seem to be "pocketbook" voters (Kinder & Kiewiet, 1981). Kinder and Sears (1985) concluded that "neither losing a job, nor deteriorating family financial conditions, nor pessimism about the family's economic future has much to do with support for policies designed to alleviate personal economic distress" (p. 671). Poor people are seldom more likely and sometimes even less likely than members of the middle class to support liberal or leftist economic policies that would encourage the redistribution of wealth (e.g., Hochschild, 1981; Jost, Pelham, Sheldon, & Sullivan, 2003; Kluegel & Smith, 1986; Lane, 1962). The failure of self-interest motivation to predict ordinary citizens' attitudes and behaviors may be attributable, in some cases at least, to other, more salient or proximal psychological motives.

MOTIVATION TO PRESERVE ONE'S PREEXISTING BELIEFS

Lord, Ross, and Lepper (1979) famously exposed research participants to two research articles—one concluding that capital punishment was an effective homicide deterrent, and one concluding that it was not. Despite the fact that all participants read identical information, participants rated as more convincing and better conducted the article that supported their own prior beliefs and attitudes about capital punishment. Because both proponents and opponents of capital punishment engaged in biased assimilation of the information presented, they strengthened their previous convictions and moved farther apart from one another, apparently exhibiting attitude polarization. Thirty-some years later, a great deal of research in social psychology and political science indicates that people selectively assimilate information that upholds the validity of their current attitudes while resisting information that challenges them (e.g., Ditto & Lopez, 1992; Edwards & Smith, 1996; Frey, 1986; Nyhan & Reifler, 2010; Taber et al., 2009; Taber & Lodge, 2006).

Individuals also commonly exhibit a variety of double standards when it comes to processing information that supports versus rejects what they think they already know. For example, people are quicker to accept desirable than undesirable conclusions (Ditto & Lopez, 1992; Ditto, Munro, Apanovitch, Scepansky, & Lockhart, 2003) and to assimilate new information that is consistent with prior beliefs while rejecting information that is inconsistent with prior beliefs (e.g., Lord et al., 1979; Taber & Lodge, 2006). Unfortunately, these effects appear to be spontaneous and hold even when individuals are encouraged to be evenhanded and to examine the evidence carefully. Stubborn maintenance of false beliefs in the face of contradictory evidence can be costly to both the individual and society at large (e.g., Myrdal, 1969). At the same time, belief perseverance (or, as Greenwald, 1980, dubbed it, "cognitive conservatism") may contribute in some way to psychological equanimity and the stability of the self-concept (e.g., Festinger, 1957; Greenwald, 1980; Sherman & Cohen, 2002).

Hypothesis-confirming biases and other belief distortions are especially pervasive when the state of the informational environment is ambiguous and can be reasonably construed in different ways (Bodenhausen, 1988; Chaiken & Maheswaran, 1994; Darley & Gross, 1983). Moreover, biases in political perception and judgment are apparently not distributed evenly throughout the population but may be stronger for those who are more ideologically interested, committed, and sophisticated (Bartels, 2008; Duch et al., 2000; Evans & Andersen, 2006; Taber & Lodge, 2006; but see Knobloch-Westerwick & Meng, 2009). The fact that biased assimilation is often more common for those who are more politically involved and knowledgeable suggests that some false beliefs do not simply reflect suboptimal attempts to acquire accurate knowledge (e.g., deficits in information processing ability) but are instead due to motivational processes, including the desire to defend or justify one's prior epistemic (and political) commitments. As Gunnar Myrdal (1969) put it, "All ignorance, like all knowledge, tends thus to be opportunist" (p. 19).

Political scientists have seized on the notion that citizens tend to process political information in ways that enable them to maintain their prior beliefs and opinions (e.g., Redlawsk, 2002; Taber et al., 2009; Taber & Lodge, 2006; Wells et al., 2009). For instance, Lodge and Taber (2000) detailed a motivated reasoning model by which an affective tag linked to political objects directs processing of subsequently encountered information (see also Taber, Lodge, & Glathar, 2001). Specifically, they propose that the individual possesses an automatic affective association or "gut reaction" to virtually any political stimulus, and this association, which is stored in long-term memory, biases information processing that pertains to that stimulus. Accordingly, individuals spend more time researching liked than disliked political candidates and take longer to process incongruent than congruent information, apparently so that they can refute undesirable implications (Redlawsk, 2002; see also Kim, Taber, & Lodge, 2010).

Lodge and Taber (2005) also showed that individuals are faster to identify the valence of positive target words (such as "beautiful," "laughter," or "rainbow") when they are immediately preceded by personally liked targets (e.g., "Kennedy," "Americans," or "free speech") than when they are preceded by disliked targets (e.g., "Osama bin Laden," "terrorists," or "taxes"). However, this effect disappears when a longer delay between prime and target is introduced, suggesting that the effect operates outside of conscious awareness.

Some studies identify neurocognitive mechanisms that are implicated in the processing of affectively congruent versus incongruent political stimuli. For instance, Morris, Squires, Taber, and Lodge (2003) observed sensitivity to affective incongruence in relation to the N400 component, which has long been associated with semantic incongruence and is believed to reflect the ease with which word meaning can be located in processing a sentence. In their study, targets who were affectively incongruent with participants' evaluation of political object primes elicited greater N400 amplitude following target onset than did targets who were affectively congruent with the political prime. Westen, Blagov, Harenski, Kilts, and Hamann (2006) also found that confronting threatening information about a preferred political figure was associated with activation of areas of the brain that are linked to emotional processing, such as the lateral and medial orbital prefrontal cortex, anterior cingulate cortex, insula, and posterior cingulate cortex. These findings were consistent with behavioral data revealing that individuals who were presented with contradictory statements made by preferred politicians tended to downplay the extent of contradiction, compared with reactions to statements made by nonpreferred politicians.

Although the concept of *selective exposure* has had a long and tendentious history within social psychology (e.g., Frey, 1986; Lazarsfeld, Berelson, & Gaudet, 1944; Sears & Freedman, 1967), there has been renewed attention to the phenomenon whereby people expose themselves more to attitude-consistent than inconsistent information (e.g., Garrett, 2009; Knobloch-Westerwick & Meng, 2009). Consistent with Jost, Glaser, Kruglanski, and Sulloway's (2003) theory of political conservatism as motivated social cognition, several studies suggest that conservatives and Republicans are more likely than liberals and Democrats to avoid opinion-challenging information, exposing themselves to more one-sided information (Iyengar, Hahn, Krosnick, & Walker, 2008; Sears & Freedman, 1967; but see Knobloch-Westerwick & Meng, 2009) and engaging in more one-sided political conversations (Mutz, 2006). We will return to this observation in discussing system-serving biases near the end of the chapter.

OVERCOMING SELF-SERVING BIAS THROUGH THE PROCESS OF SELF-AFFIRMATION

Several experiments exploring the implications of Steele's (1988) *self-affirmation theory* have provided compelling evidence that boosting self-esteem can alter the cognitive processes that mediate attitude change on political issues. In one experiment, Cohen, Aronson, and Steele (2000) presented devout supporters and opponents of capital punishment with scientific evidence that contradicted their beliefs about the policy's effectiveness in deterring crime. As in prior research by Lord et al. (1979) and others (e.g., Edwards & Smith 1996; Kunda 1987), participants in the control condition exhibited the typical "disconfirmation" bias: they found flaws in the study's methodology, doubted the integrity of the report's authors, and maintained their preexisting attitudes. Cohen et al. asked whether individuals would be less defensive "if their self-integrity were secured by an affirmation of some alternative source of self-worth? If the motivation to maintain self-integrity is thus satisfied, [would] people be more willing to give up a cherished belief when reason or experience dictates that they should?" (p. 121)

To investigate this possibility, participants assigned to self-affirmation conditions either (1) wrote about a personally important value or (2) were given positive feedback concerning an important skill. As hypothesized, temporarily bolstering individuals' feelings of self-esteem in either of these ways enabled them to respond more open-mindedly to the attitude-discrepant report on capital punishment. That is, they were less critical of the evidence, less likely to suspect bias on the part of the study's authors, and more likely to change their attitudes in the direction of the report's conclusion. This line of research suggests that self-serving biases in political perception and judgment maybe overcome through motivational interventions.

Group-Serving Motivation in Political Cognition

Evidence for the central role of groups can be found in the earliest empirical studies of political behavior (e.g., Berelson, Lazarsfeld, & McPhee, 1954; Campbell, Converse, Miller, & Stokes, 1960). For example, the sociologically oriented work of Lazarsfeld and colleagues emphasized economic class, level of urbanization, and religion as the primary determinants of vote preference. It is well understood that sympathies and resentments toward a variety of "visible social groupings"—such as blacks, whites, liberals, conservatives, poor people, businessmen, evangelical Christians, gays, and lesbians—are related to political views, including those based on ideology and partisanship (Brady & Sniderman, 1985; Campbell et al., 1960; Conover & Feldman, 1981; Duckitt, 2003).

According to *social identity theory*, individuals derive a substantial portion of their self-concept (and self-esteem) through associations with social groups (Tajfel & Turner, 1979). The heart of the theory is the idea that social identification occurs within an intergroup context and is motivated by a desire for "positive distinctiveness," that is, a desire to view the "ingroup" (one's own group) as distinct from and, in some ways at least, more positive than other relevant groups ("outgroups"). Self-identification (or self-categorization) as an ingroup member thus leads to exaggerated comparisons between ingroup and outgroup that are designed to favor the former, especially under circumstances of intergroup competition. During electoral campaigns and heated policy debates, citizens are especially likely to take on *partisan* identities (e.g., self-conceptions as Republicans or Democrats) and to approach politics from an "us" versus "them" perspective (Campbell et al., 1960; Green, Palmquist, & Schickler, 2002).

PARTISAN BIAS

Indeed, the authors of *The American Voter* (Campbell et al., 1960) long ago proposed that party identification involves a deeply rooted sense of psychological attachment to the group (see also Green et al., 2002). This attachment is understood primarily as an affective group bond, developed through socialization in early childhood and adolescence, and resulting in a sense of belongingness or social identity in which the group (or party) is incorporated into the self-concept. The identification process also reflects a cognitive representation of the parties in terms of linkages to salient social groups and a matching of one's self-conception to an image of the groups associated with each party (Campbell, Gurin, & Miller, 1954; Hyman & Singer, 1968; Miller & Wlezien, 1993). For example, feelings of closeness and similarity toward evangelical Christians or the upwardly mobile should facilitate identification with the Republican Party, whereas positive feelings toward the working class or racial minorities should promote identification with the Democrats (cf. Conover & Feldman, 1981). According to Green et al. (2002), potential voters ask themselves the following questions: "What kinds of social groups come to mind as I think about Democrats, Republicans, and Independents? Which assemblage of groups (if any) best describes me?" (p. 8).

Campbell et al. (1960) argued that partisanship not only is an affective group bond but also serves as a filter of political information; that is, it "raises a perceptual screen through which the individual tends to see what is favorable to his partisan orientation" (p. 133; see also Berelson et al., 1954). Thus, partisanship and other group attachments are hypothesized to produce systematic biases in how citizens attend to political information and how that information is interpreted, evaluated, and recalled (e.g., Bartels, 2002). As Zaller (1992) put it, "people tend to accept what is congenial to their partisan values and to reject what is not" (p. 241). In this section of the chapter, we review contemporary research indicating that partisanship does indeed act as a perceptual screen, creating biases in information exposure, perception, judgment, and memory.

SELECTIVE EXPOSURE

There are several cognitive mechanisms by which partisan biases in political judgment may occur. First, as described above, partisans may engage in selective exposure, preferentially seeking out information that is favorable toward their own political party and unfavorable toward other parties (e.g., Taber & Lodge, 2006). Second, they may interpret the same information in different ways, so that their perceptions of reality reflect systematic distortion (e.g., Gaines et al., 2007; Vallone, Ross, & Lepper,

1985). Third, partisans may critically scrutinize and counterargue incongruent information while accepting congruent information at face value (Ditto & Lopez 1992; Frey, 1986; Kruglanski & Webster 1996; Lord et al., 1979). Fourth, they may exhibit better recall for information that is congenial (vs. hostile) to their party (cf. Conway & Ross, 1984; Jacobson, 2010).

Perhaps the most efficient way of defending one's partisan allegiance is to simply avoid potentially threatening information. Several studies suggest that individuals who care about politics routinely employ this strategy. For example, Iyengar and Hahn (2009) randomly attributed political news stories on a variety of topics to one of four media sources: Fox News, NPR, CNN, or the BBC. Participants assigned to the experimental condition were provided with a brief headline of each story along with the news organization's logo and were then asked to indicate which of the four reports on each issue they would most like to read. Those assigned to a control condition encountered the same stories, but they were not attributed to any news source. Iyengar and Hahn observed that Republicans preferred to read about a story when it was attributed to Fox News, whereas Democrats preferred to read the same story when it was attributed to NPR, CNN, or the BBC (i.e., any outlet but Fox). The degree of selectivity bias was found to be greater for those who were high in political interest.

In another study, Iyengar, Hahn, Krosnick, and Walker (2008) presented a sample of registered voters in the closing stages of the 2000 presidential election with a multimedia CD-ROM containing an extensive amount of information about the candidates (e.g., issue positions, speeches, party's platforms, and TV ads aired on behalf of the candidates). The researchers tracked participants' viewing habits and found evidence of partisan-based selective exposure, but only among conservatives. Specifically, they found that Republicans and conservatives—but not Democrats or liberals—selectively sought out information about their preferred candidate. Several other recent studies of political information seeking have revealed similar ideological asymmetries in selective exposure (Lau, Andersen, & Redlawsk, 2008; Lau & Redlawsk, 2006).

To the extent that selective exposure is a strategic mechanism aimed to reduce anxiety arising from being confronted with unwelcome news, it may be more common in people who are dispositionally or situationally threatened. Lavine, Lodge, and Freitas (2005) exposed individuals who varied in levels of authoritarianism (see Hetherington & Weiler, 2009; Stenner, 2005) to one article that was opposed to capital punishment, one that contained arguments in favor of it, and one that contained a mix of arguments on both sides of the issue. The presence or absence of situational threat was varied by a mortality salience induction in which half of the participants thought about the prospect of their own deaths (cf. Greenberg, Pyszczynski, Solomon et al., 1990; see Greenberg, this volume). Lavine et al. found that in the absence of threat, both high and low authoritarians were relatively even handed in the selection of new information; specifically, they preferred the two-sided (balanced) message over either of the one-sided messages. In the presence of threat, however, they found that information-seeking proclivities changed markedly for high but not low authoritarians. Specifically, high authoritarians strongly shifted to the policy-congruent partisan message (and avoided the other two messages), whereas low authoritarians expressed a nearly unanimous preference for the two-sided message. Lavine et al. demonstrated several attitudinal consequences of selective exposure, such as cognitive bolstering of one's initial policy position, more internally consistent attitude-relevant cognitions (i.e., less ambivalence), and increased resistance to attitude change.

It has been suggested not only that politics is more salient to the mass public during presidential campaigns (e.g., Weaver, Graber, McCombs, & Eyal, 1981) but also that "the public may become increasingly aware of the media outlets corresponding to their political predispositions and may switch to more congenial sources" as Election Day approaches (Stroud, 2008, p. 346). Thus, one way to determine whether partisan differences in news preferences reflect directional motives is to examine how patterns of voluntary exposure change as a function of the election cycle. Accordingly, Stroud (2008) used the rolling cross-sectional and panel designs of the 2004 National Annenberg Election Survey to examine whether Republicans and Democrats turned increasingly to partisan newspaper, talk radio, TV, and Internet media sources as the 2004 presidential election approached. Each media outlet's political leaning was determined on the basis of editorial endorsements. Stroud found that, as hypothesized, Republicans tuned in more to Fox News (and less to MSNBC and CNN) as the election neared, whereas Democrats showed the reverse pattern.

Partisanship biases have been shown to affect decision making even when the decision is otherwise personally irrelevant. For instance, Munro, Lasane, and Leary (2010) found that participants were more likely to recommend college applicants for admission when they shared their political affiliation than when they supported an opposing party. This effect was statistically mediated by the motivated distortion of ambiguous information, namely the perceived strength and significance of the applicant's letter of recommendation. Other research has demonstrated, not too surprisingly, that participants are more suspicious of ulterior motives held by politicians representing an opposing party than politicians from their own party (Munro, Weih, & Tsai, 2010).

BIASED PERCEPTION

In addition to being selective about information exposure, political partisans may defend and justify their ingroup attachments either by interpreting the same facts in different ways or, more radically, by "seeing" different facts (cf. Lippmann, 1922). In an especially dramatic demonstration of this phenomenon, Caruso, Mead, and Balcetis (2009) found that individuals who opposed Barack Obama (e.g., Republicans) perceived darkened photographs as more representative of the candidate than did those who supported him (e.g., Democrats).

In most elections, the outcome of the vote is almost immediately apparent, but in a significant minority of cases, elections are determined by minute electoral differences. In a few cases, the ballots are subjected to a recount in order to ensure that the winning candidate has been properly identified. The ability of ballot counters to make accurate decisions about voter intent in these cases is of obvious importance for democratically executing the will of the people. But are ballot counters (typically ordinary citizen volunteers) able to exclude the impact of their own preferences from their decisions?

In an experiment involving college students in Ohio (a perennial swing state), Kopko, Bryner, Budziak, Devine, and Nawara (2011) addressed this question by adapting disputed ballots from the Minnesota Senate recount involving Norm Coleman and Al Franken. The authors manipulated whether the disputed ballot had been counted as a Republican or Democratic vote and whether it had been challenged by the Republican or Democratic candidate. Because motivated reasoning has been found to occur more often when (1) the outcome is highly relevant to the individual (e.g., Balcetis & Dunning, 2006; Kay, Jimenez, & Jost, 2002) and (2) the stimulus is ambiguous (Kunda, 1990), the authors also manipulated whether the candidates were fictitious (vs. actual) politicians and whether the instructions for determining voter intent were highly specific or relatively ambiguous. The results of this experiment revealed that individuals are indeed more likely to uphold challenges made by a member of their own political party, especially when the candidates are real (i.e., highly relevant) and the instructions are ambiguous.

BIASED INTERPRETATION

Vallone et al. (1985) exposed pro-Arab and pro-Israeli students to news coverage of the 1982 massacre of civilians in Lebanese refugee camps and found that the two groups "disagreed about the very nature of the stimulus they had viewed" (p. 582). Specifically, the pro-Arab students believed that there were twice as many favorable as unfavorable references to Israel, whereas the pro-Israeli students believed that there were four times as many unfavorable as favorable references! Thus, both sides were convinced that the same media coverage would lead neutral or ambivalent viewers to take the other's side concerning the massacre.

Gaines et al. (2007) employed a longitudinal research design to examine how Democrats and Republicans would update their factual beliefs about troop casualties and the existence of weapons of mass destruction in Iraq as conditions changed from the beginning of the war in March 2003 to December 2004 (just after the final report of the Iraq Survey Group officially concluded that Iraq's weapons of mass destruction [WMD] program had ended in 1996). In terms of group-serving bias, one possibility was that partisans would simply engage in fact avoidance, failing to change their beliefs even after the facts had changed. As Gaines et al. noted, this would have been difficult to do, insofar as the media reported a great deal of information about both troop casualties and the failure to find WMD. A second possibility was that individuals would cope with inconvenient truths, not through outright denial, but through what the authors called *meaning avoidance*. In this case, beliefs may be updated along with reality, but *interpretations* of these beliefs are biased so that prior opinions remain relatively unaffected.

This is indeed what Gaines et al. (2007) found: both Republicans and Democrats updated their beliefs about (increased) troop casualties over the 21-month period of the study, but they interpreted facts in a manner that was congenial to their partisan allegiances. For example, as casualties rose, strong Republicans continued to interpret their numbers

as "moderate," "small," or "very small" (even though they accurately perceived the increase over time). By contrast, Democrats interpreted the number of casualties as "large" or "very large," consistent with their opposition to the conflict. What about beliefs regarding the existence of WMD? Gaines et al. found that rather than acknowledging that Iraq had ended their WMD program years earlier, a majority of Republicans stated that the weapons must have been moved, destroyed, or not yet found. In sum, as casualties increased and the administration's principal *casus belli* for the war was gradually discredited, Republicans shielded themselves from having to rethink their support for the invasion.

SELECTIVE MEMORY

Two lines of research provide evidence that partisan biases in political cognition can arise through selective memory processes. In several surveys conducted between 2006 and 2008, Jacobson (2010) provided compelling, albeit indirect, evidence of memory bias among Democrats regarding the Iraq War. Respondents were asked to recall what their beliefs were about the existence of WMD and whether Saddam Hussein was personally involved in September 11 *prior to* the invasion of Iraq in 2003. By comparing these recollections to later survey data, Jacobson demonstrated a hefty dose of memory bias among Democrats. Specifically, he reported that in eight surveys taken before the invasion, between 57% and 83% of Democrats believed that Iraq possessed WMD; the average was 71%. In later surveys, less than half the Democrats remembered subscribing to this view; the average difference between their recalled views on WMD in 2006 and 2008 and those expressed in the surveys taken before the war was 38 percentage points. Republicans' beliefs during the later period more closely matched those observed in prewar surveys, possibly indicating belief perseverance.

Bullock (2006) conducted a series of experiments using real-world political events in which he demonstrated a boundary condition on the classic belief perseverance effect: false beliefs influence people's political opinions even after those beliefs have been discredited, insofar as continuing to hold them facilitates one's partisan goals. As a simple matter of logic, when new evidence discredits old information, attitudes should cease to reflect the old information. However, we know from much research that false beliefs persist, presumably because the initial evidence triggers related ideas in long-term memory, and those ideas are used to explain the evidence before it is discredited (Anderson, Lepper, & Ross, 1980; Anderson, New, & Speer, 1985).

Bullock's first study concerned an article in the May 9, 2005 edition of *Newsweek* detailing abuses of Muslim prisoners by U.S. interrogators at Guantánamo Bay, Cuba. The article charged that interrogators had "flushed a Qur'an down a toilet." The claim was publicized in local media outlets in Afghanistan and Pakistan, triggering several days of anti-American rioting. The charges were quickly denied by the Pentagon, and in its next edition, *Newsweek* issued a retraction, writing that "Based on what we now know, we are retracting our original story that an internal military investigation had uncovered Qur'an abuse at Guantánamo Bay." To determine whether partisanship moderated belief perseverance—that is, to see whether Democrats in this case continued to give credence to the evidence after it had been discredited—Bullock instructed two groups of participants to read the original *Newsweek* article. Several minutes later (after completing a series of unrelated tasks), those assigned to the treatment condition learned that the magazine had later retracted the central claim of the initial article. Subjects were then asked whether they approved, disapproved, or neither approved nor disapproved of the handling of detainees at Guantánamo Bay. As hypothesized, Democratic partisans exhibited an attitude perseverance effect; they maintained their negative attitudes toward the detention policy, even after learning that the abuse claim had been retracted.

Bullock (2006) conducted a second experiment based on a television ad released on August 8, 2005 by NARAL Pro-Choice America that accused the Supreme Court nominee John Roberts of "supporting a violent fringe group and a convicted clinic bomber." The ad was quickly criticized as untrue (which it was), and it was taken off the air the next day. At the outset of the experiment, Bullock explained who John Roberts was, including that he had been nominated by George W. Bush to fill a vacancy on the Supreme Court. Participants assigned to the control condition simply expressed their attitudes toward Roberts. Those assigned to the treatment condition read the transcript of the NARAL ad, expressed their attitudes toward Roberts, and then were informed that the ad had been withdrawn and that a prominent Democrat had criticized the ad as deceptive before expressing their attitudes toward Roberts again. Results revealed that the ad heightened disapproval of Roberts among both Republicans and Democrats. However, when the

ad was discredited, the attitudes of Republicans resembled those expressed by the control group. Democrats, however, were more likely to disapprove of Roberts in the treatment condition (76%) than in the control condition (56%). These highly ecologically valid experiments demonstrate that belief perseverance can affect real-world political attitudes, and most importantly, that it is a *motivated* bias that can be both self-serving and group serving.

EVALUATION OF POLITICIANS

Political psychologists have examined how personality impressions of political candidates are biased by partisanship. Previous work has established that candidates are judged along four major trait dimensions: competence, leadership, integrity, and empathy (Funk, 1996; Kinder, 1986). Drawing on national survey data, Goren (2002) identified the perceived weaknesses of presidents Reagan, Bush, and Clinton by finding the trait on which the public gave them lowest marks. For example, Reagan and Bush received their lowest ratings on empathy, whereas Clinton's lowest rating was on integrity. Goren found that partisan opponents (vs. supporters) elevated the importance of a candidate's character weakness in rendering overall evaluations. For each of the three candidates, political partisanship (Democrat vs. Republican) interacted in the predicted direction with specific traits in predicting overall candidate evaluations. Thus, Democrats relied more than Republicans on the trait of empathy in judging Reagan and Bush, and Republicans relied more than Democrats on integrity in judging Clinton. Interestingly, these partisan asymmetries in trait usage were limited to those traits on which the public rated the candidate the lowest.

Given the potentially explosive political impact of scandals, it is important to understand how individuals perceive and evaluate them. In relatively well-known scandals such as Watergate and the Lewinsky affair, is the evidence (and its political implications) so overwhelmingly clear that partisan biases can only exert a modest impact on mass responses? Or do perceptions and evaluations substantially depend on prior attitudes toward the president (i.e., partisanship, ideology)? Two studies using panel data—in which responses were collected both before and after a scandal broke—suggest that impressions of scandal are indelibly shaped by preexisting attitudes.

Sweeney and Gruber (1984) examined how Nixon, McGovern, and Independent voters reacted to Watergate. Most of their analyses addressed the question of whether selective exposure occurred; it did. Nixon voters paid less attention to the scandal and knew less about it than did the other respondent groups. The researchers also observed evidence of selective judgment. In particular, Nixon voters were less likely to believe that Nixon should resign than either McGovern supporters or Independents, and they were less likely to believe that Nixon had lost credibility.

Conversely, a study of the Lewinsky affair by Fischle (2000) indicated that Democrats were more likely than Republicans to believe that the scandal was a right-wing conspiracy, that it lacked credibility, and that it was unimportant as a determinant of candidate attitudes. Fischle concluded that respondents "processed the evidence in such a way as to construct seemingly reasonable justifications for the things they believed and wanted to continue to believe" (p. 151).

EFFECT OF EDUCATION ON SELF- AND GROUP-SERVING BIAS

Haider-Markel and Joslyn (2009) found that educated individuals held more accurate beliefs on a range of factual issues, including whether the United States found WMD in Iraq, whether most scientists believe in evolution, whether the earth is getting warmer because of human activity, and whether the 2006 troop surge in Iraq had positive or negative consequences. Although in each case education promoted accuracy, its effect was entirely conditional on party identification. Specifically, when the factually correct answer favored Democrats (e.g., WMD, evolution, global warming), partisan motivation trumped the informational effect of education such that the latter strongly heightened accuracy among Democrats but failed to heighten—and even *reduced*—accuracy among Republicans. When the correct answer favored the Republican position (e.g., change in levels of violence in Iraq following the troop surge), the opposite pattern prevailed.

System-Serving Motivation in Political Cognition

To this point, we have reviewed evidence indicating that self-interest and group interest can and do motivate political cognition. At the same time, converging evidence from a variety of subdisciplines reveals that these are not the only influences on political judgment, evaluation, and decision making. Citizens often think and act in ways that maintain existing social, economic, and political arrangements (i.e., the status quo)—even if

alternatives might be better for them as individuals or as members of social groups. For instance, it is rare for protest movements (such as the "Occupy Wall Street" movement) to win the support of most citizens, even if the attainment of the movement's goals would materially benefit the majority. In this section, we briefly review three potentially related classes of system-serving motivational influences: sociotropic concerns, status quo bias, and system justification.

SOCIOTROPIC CONCERNS

Political scientists have long noted that indicators of personal (especially economic) interests (e.g., social class) are not strongly predictive of political preferences and behaviors (e.g., Green & Shapiro, 1994; Sears & Funk 1991). For instance, Kinder and Kiewiet (1979, 1981) demonstrated that voting in congressional and presidential elections (as well as party affiliation more generally) are only weakly influenced by so-called pocketbook considerations (i.e., economic self-interest). Rather, perceptions of national economic health, and other types of prosocial (or "sociotropic") concerns, are stronger determinants of voting behavior.[1] In addition, citizens frequently respond differently (and more powerfully) to "sociotropic threat"—defined by Davis and Silver (2004, p. 34) as "a generalized anxiety and sense of threat to society as a whole, the country as a whole, or the region in which one lives"—than to an egocentric "sense of threat to oneself and to one's family" (see also Gibson, 2006). Although recent research paints a fairly complex portrait of the relationship between self-interest and sociotropic interests (e.g., Arceneaux, 2003; Gomez & Wilson 2003; Nicholson & Segura, 1999; Radcliff, 1994), the research literature as a whole shows rather convincingly that self-interested, instrumental motives are far from the only determinants of political preferences and actions (see also Tyler, 2006).

Studies suggest that the more an individual confers *legitimacy* on a given institution or authority (such as the police force or the Supreme Court), the more likely he or she is to defer to decisions rendered by that authority, even if the decision is regarded as personally unfavorable (e.g., Gibson, 2008; Jost & Major, 2001; Tyler, 2006). For example, Gibson (2007) found that most Americans hold the Supreme Court in high esteem; as a result, they tend to support the Court and its decisions, even when they are cognizant that ideological and other biases sometimes interfere with judicial decision making. Moreover, those who are most knowledgeable about legal matters are *especially* likely to perceive the Supreme Court as highly legitimate (Gibson & Caldeira, 2011), suggesting either that the institution is deserving of its widespread support or that those most invested in a given system are also the most motivated to defend it (cf. Taber et al., 2009).

STATUS QUO BIAS

More or less concomitantly, cognitive psychologists and behavioral economists have explored numerous "anomalies" by which individuals make decisions that violate their own self-interest. One of the most frequently explored phenomena has to do with preferences to "do nothing or maintain…one's current or previous decision" (Samuelson & Zeckhauser, 1988, p. 1). In several studies, Samuelson and Zeckhauser found that most people stick with status quo options more often than would be expected on the basis of chance, and this "status quo bias" is magnified as the number of alternatives is increased (see also Kahneman, Knetsch, &Thaler, 1990).

These and related findings have often been explained in terms of Kahneman and Tversky's (1979) *prospect theory*, which posits that individuals often "anchor" on the existing state of affairs, using the status quo as a "reference point" against which all alternatives are compared. The theory also assumes that "losses loom larger than gains"; that is, individuals tend to weigh potential losses (or negative changes) more heavily than equivalent gains. As a result, most people are risk averse when evaluating status quo options. These psychological assumptions have also been used to explain "incumbency bias"—the tendency for voters to disproportionately return previously elected politicians to office (e.g., Quattrone & Tversky, 1988).That is, risk aversion and status quo bias appear to magnify incumbents' electoral advantages over challengers—above and beyond differences in perceived experience, name recognition, committee ranking privileges, and fundraising capabilities (Abramowitz, 1975, 1991; Cover & Brumberg, 1982).

Moshinsky and Bar-Hillel (2010) demonstrated that merely *labeling* an option as the status quo is sufficient to increase its endorsement. The researchers selected obscure Israeli laws, created realistic alternatives, and randomly assigned citizens to experimental conditions in which they were informed either that the actual law or the make-believe alternative was in fact the legal status quo. Across a wide range of public policies, respondents preferred a given law more when they believed that it represented the current state of affairs than when they believed that the same law was merely a hypothetical alternative.

Apparently, people also assume that the way things *are* is the way they *should be* (Heider, 1958; Kay et al., 2009) and that the status quo is morally superior to alternatives (Friedrich, Kierniesky, & Cardon, 1989). Eidelman, Crandall, and Pattershall (2009) found that individuals often judge existing states of reality to be better and more desirable than nonexistent alternative possibilities. For instance, participants evaluated a "galaxy" representation (which was actually a random plot of stars) to be more visually appealing when they were led to believe that it was similar in shape to 80% (vs. 40% or 60%) of the other galaxies in the universe. Eidelman and colleagues have dubbed this phenomenon the "existence bias." Related work by Crandall, Eidelman, Skitka, and Morgan (2009) demonstrated that U.S. citizens are more supportive of the use of torture in military interrogations when they are led to believe that it is a long-standing (vs. recent) practice in the U.S. military.

CULTURAL COGNITION

Legal scholars have also taken notice of the tendency for individuals to uphold culturally prevalent ideals. For instance, Kahan and colleagues (e.g., Kahan, 2009; Kahan & Braman, 2006; Kahan, Braman, Cohen, Slovic, & Gastil, 2011; Kahan, Braman, Gastil, Slovic, & Cohen, 2009; Kahan, Braman, Monahan, Callahan, & Peters, 2010; Kahan, Braman, Slovic, Gastil, & Mertz, 2007) have argued that individuals' perceptions of environmental risks and social issues are shaped by moral and ideological assumptions (see also McCright & Dunlap, 2011; Uhlmann, Pizarro, Tannenbaum, & Ditto, 2009). According to their theory, cultural worldviews vary in terms of two cross-cutting dimensions, namely hierarchy–egalitarianism and individualism–communitarianism. The first dimension is measured using items such as, "Our society would be better off if the distribution of wealth were more equal," and the second by items such as, "The government should do more to advance society's goals, even if that means limiting the freedom and choices of individuals." In practice, these two dimensions are usually collapsed to compare individuals who are classified as "hierarchical individualists" with those classified as "egalitarian communitarians." These classifications do predict risk evaluations and skepticism about science in relation to several issues, including global climate change (cf. McCright & Dunlap, 2011).

SYSTEM JUSTIFICATION

Although some explanations for the tendency to prefer current (vs. alternative) states of affairs have emphasized purely cognitive mechanisms (e.g., Eidelman et al., 2009; Quattrone & Tversky, 1988), *system justification theory* posits that epistemic needs to reduce uncertainty, existential needs to manage threat, and relational needs to achieve shared reality with others contribute to a fairly powerful *motivational* tendency to defend, bolster, and justify existing social, economic, and political systems (Jost et al., 2010). The idea, in other words, is that individuals *want* to *perceive* the status quo as relative good and just, even if it is not objectively so. In accordance with this notion, Kay et al. (2009) demonstrated that by activating system justification motivation (e.g., by exposing research participants to criticisms of the overarching social system), it is possible to increase the extent to which people "injunctify" the status quo, that is, describe it as the most desirable and reasonable state of affairs.

Consistent with the notion that system-justifying biases affect information processing, an experiment by Haines and Jost (2000) revealed that individuals exhibit a tendency to misremember reasons for their own group's (experimentally induced) situation of powerlessness as being fair and legitimate—even when they had been given an illegitimate explanation (e.g., nepotism) or no explanation whatsoever for the power differential. Research by Ledgerwood, Mandisodza, Jost, and Pohl (2011) indicated that individuals evaluate scientific data as more persuasive when it supports the "American Dream" notion that hard work leads to success (vs. does not lead to success). This effect—which was exhibited even by those who explicitly disavowed the notion that the United States is highly meritocratic in practice—was exacerbated by exposure to system threat passages, consistent with the idea that people are motivated to defend the system against criticism and attack (see also Jost et al., 2005; Kay, Jost, & Young, 2005).

Recent studies suggest that system-relevant motivations, such as system justification, the desire to believe in a "just world," and "cultural cognition" (Jost & Hunyady, 2005; Lerner, 1980; Kahan et al., 2010), play a significant role in motivated reasoning about scientific information, such as information about environmental problems linked to anthropogenic climate change. Specifically, individuals who endorse political conservatism, hierarchical and individualistic worldviews, and other system-justifying belief systems express greater denial and ignorance than others when it comes to facts about global warming (Feygina, Jost, & Goldsmith, 2010; Kahan et al., 2010; McCright & Dunlap, 2011). Similarly, those who score higher on the Belief in a Just World Scale are more likely to deny environmental problems—especially when they have been exposed to dire global warming messages (Feinberg & Willer, 2011).

There is growing reason to think that motivated social cognition may mediate the relationship between system justification and environmental attitudes. Specifically, Hennes and Jost (2010) found that chronic and temporary heightening of system justification motivation predicted greater skepticism of scientific evidence concerning climate change reported in a newspaper article and poorer memory for details from the article. Furthermore, memory distortions were system serving; that is, they occurred in a manner that justified inaction and facilitated denial and minimization of the problem. System justification motivation also affects somatosensory perceptions of the climate, such that high system justifiers perceive the outside temperature in summer to be lower, in comparison with low system justifiers (Hennes, Feygina, & Jost, 2011).

Are There Ideological Asymmetries in Motivated Political Cognition?

If we are correct that there are *three* relevant sources of motivation rather than just two (as previous reviews have assumed), it follows that motivated reasoning should occur most strongly for those whose preexisting beliefs are conservative or system serving in nature. That is, conservatives should be especially likely to exhibit all three types of biases, whereas progressives would be expected to display self- and group-serving biases but not (to the same extent) system-serving biases. In fact, several studies, which we review here, do suggest that conservative defenders of the status quo are more biased and less accurate than are liberals, progressives, and those who seek to challenge the status quo. Conservatives also tend to score higher on measures of self-deception, in comparison with liberals and moderates (Jost et al., 2010; see also Jost, Blount, Pfeffer, & Hunyady, 2003).

To begin with, a research program by Keltner and Robinson (1996, 1997) demonstrated that although defenders and challengers of the status quo frequently exaggerate the degree of ideological polarization that separates them, defenders of the status quo are consistently more likely than challengers to misperceive their ideological opponents, that is, to see them as more extreme than they actually are (see also Robinson & Keltner, 1996; Robinson, Keltner, Ward, & Ross, 1995; Sniderman, Brody, & Tetlock, 1991; but see Chambers, Baron, & Inman, 2006). For instance, English professors who favored a relatively conservative, highly traditional syllabus (i.e., "traditionalists") significantly overestimated the attitudinal extremity of English professors who favored a syllabus that included greater representation by women and minority authors (i.e., "revisionists"; see Robinson & Keltner, 1996). Traditionalists also assumed that revisionists would choose *none* of the same books for their classes that traditionalists would choose. However, out of 15 books, revisionists and traditionalists actually shared 7 books (and revisionists correctly identified 6 of these). The researchers proposed that asymmetrical bias occurred because defenders of the status quo are more likely to possess, and therefore be motivated to preserve, power. If this proposal is correct, the findings from these studies are consistent with those suggesting that high-power individuals are more biased judges of low-power targets than vice versa (e.g., Chance, 1967; Fiske, 1993; but see Overbeck & Park, 2001).

As noted above, it has been discovered repeatedly that conservatives and Republicans are more likely than liberals and Democrats to actively avoid or dismiss opinion-challenging information. For example, conservatives are more likely than liberals to expose themselves to one-sided informational campaigns (Iyengar et al., 2008; Sears & Freedman, 1967) and to engage in one-sided political conversations (Mutz, 2006; but see Knobloch-Westerwick & Meng, 2009, for an exception). In most laboratory studies, research participants are fairly constrained in terms of opportunities for information exposure, whereas citizens in daily life possess a great deal of control over their academic, interpersonal, and media sources of political information. Garrett (2009) provides some evidence that in naturalistic settings, liberals are more likely than conservatives to seek out two-sided opinions. Experimental research by Bullock (2011) found that Democrats were more sensitive to information about policy content, whereas Republicans were more sensitive to partisan cues.

Nyhan and Reifler (2010) investigated how individuals respond to new information suggesting that previous media reports had been erroneous. Participants in their study read a news article addressing a controversial question, namely the existence of weapons of mass destruction in Iraq.

Half of the participants were later presented with a "correction" to the original news article, whereas the other half were not. For conservatives (but not liberals), reading the correction actually *strengthened* misperceptions elicited by the original article (see also Karasawa, 1998, for a parallel effect involving social stereotypes). This finding should be interpreted with caution, however, given that Bullock (2006) observed a failure on the part of Democrats as well as Republicans to update beliefs in response to contradictory information (but no "backlash effect").

Despite the fact that conservatives appear to engage in motivated reasoning to a greater degree than do liberals, MacCoun and Paletz (2009) found that conservatives were more *suspicious* of research supporting liberal conclusions than liberals were suspicious of research supporting conservative conclusions. Thus, conservatives dismissed as inherently biased studies suggesting that the death penalty fails to deter criminals more than liberals dismissed studies suggesting the opposite. These findings are broadly consistent with the work of O'Brien and Crandall (2005), which indicated that perceivers are more likely to discount as self-interested the behavior of those who seek to challenge the status quo, in comparison with the behavior of those who seek to maintain the status quo.

Possibly as a result of the types of information processing biases cited above, studies of public opinion find that conservatives hold more false beliefs than progressives on a number of issues, including (1) the 9/11 terrorist attacks and the U.S. invasion of Iraq (Kull, Ramsay, & Lewis, 2003–2004); (2) scientific evidence concerning anthropogenic climate change (e.g., Feygina et al., 2010; McCright & Dunlap, 2011); (3) the nature and extent of income inequality in the United States (Bartels, 2008); and (4) potential causes of the 2007–2009 economic recession (Kessler, 2010). There is also accumulating evidence from studies of mass communication that consumers of politically conservative news media outlets (especially Fox News) subscribe to erroneous political beliefs more than those who get their news elsewhere (Mooney, 2011). Although it is a topic for future research, we might conjecture that the co-occurrence of self-, group-, and system-serving biases on the part of conservative journalists and their audience members play a significant role in the creation and perpetuation of false beliefs.

The studies we have reviewed in this section suggest that, all other things being equal, conservative defenders of the status quo tend to display more evidence of motivated reasoning, bias, and distortion in judgment, in comparison with progressive challengers of the status quo. Such findings are consistent with the notion that in addition to self-serving and group-serving biases, many individuals engage in system-serving biases. Furthermore, the results we have summarized are congruent with Jost, Glaser, et al.'s (2003) analysis of political conservatism as motivated social cognition, including evidence that individual differences in epistemic motives to reduce uncertainty and ambiguity and existential motives to manage anxiety and threat are associated with (1) directional motives to "seize" and "freeze" on immediate or preexisting beliefs and evaluations, and (2) the endorsement of conservative ideology.

Much as interventions that create opportunities for self-affirmation have been found to reduce self-serving biases in information processing (Cohen et al., 2000), it is conceivable that system-affirmation opportunities (such as occasions for expressing national commitment or patriotic allegiance) would reduce biased information processing that is caused by system-defensive motivation. Consistent with this possibility, Liviatan and Jost (2012) found that exposure to system threat increases automatic (i.e., nonconscious) pursuit of the goal to perceive the status quo as legitimate and desirable—unless, that is, participants are given the opportunity to engage in system affirmation. Thus, research on system-serving biases is likely to suggest new and additional remedies for addressing the thorny, multifaceted problem of motivated political reasoning.

As noted earlier, some studies suggest that individuals who are more politically knowledgeable, sophisticated, and educated and who report greater understanding of the issues may be more rather than less likely to exhibit biased forms of reasoning (Bartels, 2008; Duch et al., 2000; Evans & Anderson, 2006; Kahan et al., 2010; Taber & Lodge, 2006; but see Knobloch-Westerwick & Meng, 2009). Interestingly, two studies find that higher levels of education are associated with greater bias for conservatives but *lesser* bias for liberals. For instance, Berinsky (2011) observed that Republicans with more education were more likely to subscribe to anti-Democratic rumors (i.e., that President Obama's health care plan includes "death panels") but less likely to subscribe to anti-Republican rumors (i.e., that the U.S. government assisted in the 9/11 attacks). By contrast, highly educated Democrats were more likely to reject both anti-Democratic and anti-Republican

rumors. Similarly, Kahan, Wittlin, et al. (2011) reported that scientific literacy was positively associated with skepticism about global climate change among hierarchical individualists (conservatives), but it was negatively associated with skepticism among egalitarian communitarians (progressives). In addition, scientific literacy was associated with less skepticism about nuclear power among egalitarian communitarians, suggesting that more education led progressives to update their beliefs in a manner that was inconsistent with their initial beliefs.

Concluding Remarks

In arguing for the utility of a social cognitive model of political judgment and decision making, Lane (1986) embraced the cognitive terminology of *schemata* to propose that citizens' internal needs and values might shape their political realities (see also Sniderman & Citrin, 1971). Thus, what might look like inconsistency within an individual's belief system from the perspective of an outside observer (e.g., Converse, 1964) might be internally consistent with the individual's motives and desires (e.g., see Jost, 2006). Rational choice models would do well to take account of these (often nonconscious) psychological goals to better understand the ways in which citizens process political information (cf. Kuklinski & Quirk, 2000).

To the extent that political scientists have embraced the notion that political cognition is motivated, they have restricted their analyses to self-serving and group-serving purposes, which are at odds with accuracy motivation (e.g., Taber & Lodge, 2006). In this chapter, we have suggested that various *system-serving* motives—which maintain or preserve aspects of the status quo—also affect social and political cognition (e.g., Eidelman et al., 2009; Hennes & Jost, 2010; Jost et al., 2010; Kay et al., 2009; Ledgerwood et al., 2011; Moshinsky & Bar-Hillel, 2010). This suggestion is congruent with Lane's (1986) observation that certain cognitive adjustments seem to maintain confidence in the overarching political system as legitimate:

> Constitutional regime-schemata are likely to dominate (constrain) other schemata because when attitudes toward leaders, parties, and perceived government effectiveness turn sour, these regime-related attitudes are a protection against alienation, as well as apathy.... And in certain circumstances, especially war but also under real or feigned "threats" of subversion, it mobilizes defensive action and justifies sacrifice. (p. 314)

The research literature on system justification theory, which we have reviewed in cursory fashion here, upholds Lane's insights about the advantages and disadvantages of the motivation to defend and justify existing social systems (see also Jost et al., 2010; Kay et al., 2009). It is conceivable that the existence of system-serving motivation can help to explain why some studies find greater evidence of biased information processing on the part of conservative (vs. progressive) ideologues (e.g., Garrett, 2009; Hennes & Jost, 2010; Iyengar et al., 2008; MacCoun & Paletz, 2009; Mutz, 2006; Nyhan & Reifler, 2010; Slothuus & de Vreese, 2010; Sniderman et al., 1991).

Before concluding our review of the research literature on motivated political cognition, a few more caveats are in order. First, although we decided to organize our chapter around the tripartite classification of *self-serving, group-serving,* and *system-serving* motives (or, to borrow Lane's, 1986, terminology, *purposes*), other taxonomies may ultimately turn out to be just as useful—or even better. In addition, it is often challenging to distinguish empirically among the three motives. For instance, an individual's (false) belief that President Obama is a Muslim or was born outside of the United States may simultaneously reflect a self-serving desire to maintain and justify prior attitudes and behaviors, a group-serving desire to believe that Republicans are superior to (or more honest than) Democrats, and a system-serving desire to maintain the traditional racial hierarchy, whereby African Americans are denied powerful leadership roles. Most likely, such beliefs reflect some combination of these (and perhaps other) motives or purposes.

Second, we believe that many of the studies we have reviewed in this chapter rule out purely cognitive (i.e., nonmotivational) explanations for biased information processing. At the same time, we would never argue that *all* instances of bias in political cognition are due to motivational factors, such as self-, group-, or system-serving tendencies. Some of the discoveries we have summarized may be explained reasonably well from a purely cognitive perspective. From our perspective, the important point is that psychological motives almost surely influence judgment and decision making in the political sphere. Future work would do well to specify precisely when (and how) self-, group-, and system-serving motives impinge on the mental processing of political information—and also when they do not.

Evolutionary theorists and social psychologists have long debated the question of whether engaging in motivated forms of bias—including self-deception—is healthy and adaptive for the individual (e.g., Lockard & Paulhus, 1988; Taylor & Brown, 1988; Taylor, Lerner, Sherman, Sage, & McDowell, 2003; von Hippel & Trivers, 2011). Some evidence suggests that holding unrealistically positive ideas about oneself and close others (such as relationship partners) can have beneficial consequences for mental health, relationship satisfaction, and goal pursuit (Murray, Holmes, & Griffin, 1996; Taylor & Brown, 1988). However, democratic theory presupposes that citizens are willing and able to process information about political issues and candidates in a reasonably accurate manner (e.g., Delli, Carpini, & Keeter, 1996). Thus, from a normative philosophical perspective, it would seem that, when it comes to electoral politics, biased processing of information is harmful rather than helpful, at least for society as a whole. Or, as Senator Daniel Patrick Moynihan reputedly put it, "Everyone is entitled to their own opinion, but not their own facts." Future work might explore various intervention strategies, such as fostering accuracy motivation or creating opportunities for self-, group, or system affirmation (i.e., satisfying psychological needs or goals that contribute to biased information processing).

In much of the work we have reviewed, political psychologists have basically adapted constructs, methods, and paradigms from social and cognitive psychology to address applied questions having to do with information processing in overtly political contexts. However, political science need not follow behind psychology in its understanding, appreciation, or alleviation of motivated reasoning. Given that political issues, institutions, and elections frequently implicate the self, group, and social system, political psychologists should be at the forefront of scientific discovery when it comes to understanding the role of motivation in determining judgments, preferences, and decisions. Thus, we close by noting that research on "hot" or motivated political cognition has enormous potential to inform psychological theory with respect to motivation and cognition, thereby contributing to a political psychology that, in the words of Krosnick and McGraw (2002), is "true to its name."

Author Note

Funding for this project was provided in part by New York University. We thank Don Carlston, Francesca Manzi, Natasza Marrouch, Marlon Mooijman, Chris Mooney, Hannah Nam, Artur Nilsson, Lindsay Rankin, Andrew Shipley, Nevin

Solak, and Chadly Stern for insightful feedback on earlier drafts of this chapter. We also acknowledge the assistance of Frances Gill, Priya Koshy, and Victoria Lim in preparing the extensive reference section.

Notes

1. Kinder and Kiewiet (1979, 1981) expressed agnosticism about how individuals weigh sociotropic and pocketbook considerations, and they refrained from concluding that such effects are necessarily motivational in nature.

References

Aarts, H., & Dijksterhuis, A. (2000). Habits as knowledge structures: Automaticity in goal-directed behavior. *Journal of Personality and Social Psychology, 78*, 53–63.

Abelson, R. P., & Levi, A. (1985). Decision making and decision theory. In G. Lindzey& E. Aronson (Eds.), *The handbook of social psychology* (Vol. 1, pp. 231–309). New York: Random House.

Abelson, R. P., & Rosenberg, M. J. (1958). Symbolic psycho-logic: A model of attitudinal cognition. *Behavioral Science, 3*, 1–8.

Abramowitz, A. I. (1975). Name familiarity, reputation, and the incumbency effect in a congressional election. *Western Political Quarterly, 28*, 668–684.

Abramowitz, A. I. (1991). Incumbency, campaign spending, and the decline of competition in U.S. House elections. *Journal of Politics, 53*, 34–56.

Abramson, P. (1972). Political efficacy and political trust among black schoolchildren: Two explanations. *Journal of Politics, 34*, 1243–1275.

Adorno, T. W., Frenkel-Brunswik, E., Levinson, D. J., & Sanford, R. N. (1950). *The authoritarian personality*. New York: Harper.

Allport, G. W. (1954). *The nature of prejudice*. Reading, MA: Addison-Wesley.

Anderson, C. A., Lepper, M. R., & Ross, L. (1980). Perseverance of social theories: The role of explanation in the persistence of discredited information. *Journal of Personality and Social Psychology, 39*, 1037–1049.

Anderson, C. A., New, B. L., & Speer, J. R. (1985). Argument availability as a mediator of social theory perseverance. *Social Cognition, 3*, 235–249.

Arceneaux, K. (2003). The conditional impact of blame attribution on the relationship between economic adversity and turnout. *Political Research Quarterly, 56*, 67–75.

Ascher, W., & Hirschfelder-Ascher, B. (2005). *Revitalizing political psychology: The legacy of Harold D. Lasswell*. Mahwah, NJ: Erlbaum.

Axelrod, R. (1973). Schema theory: An information processing model of perception and cognition. *American Political Science Review, 67*, 1248–1266.

Axelrod, R. (1976). *Structure of decision: The cognitive map of political elites*. Princeton, NJ: Princeton University Press.

Balcetis, E. (2008). Where the motivation resides and self-deception hides: How motivated cognition accomplishes self-deception. *Social and Personality Psychology Compass, 2*, 361–381.

Balcetis, E., & Dunning, D. (2006). See what you want to see: Motivational influences on visual perception. *Journal of Personality and Social Psychology, 91*, 612–625.

Barber, J. D. (1985). *Government ministers in the contemporary world*. Los Angeles: Sage.

Bargh, J. A., Gollwitzer, P. M., Lee-Chai, A. Y., Barndollar, K., & Troetschel, R. (2001). The automated will: Nonconscious activation and pursuit of behavioral goals. *Journal of Personality and Social Psychology, 81*, 1014–1027.

Bartels, L. M. (2002). Beyond the running tally: Partisan bias in political perceptions. *Political Behavior, 24*, 117–150.

Bartels, L. M. (2008). *Unequal democracy: The political economy of the new gilded age*. Princeton, NJ: Princeton University Press.

Baumeister, R. F., & Newman, L. S. (1994). How stories make sense of personal experiences: Motives that shape autobiographical narratives. *Personality and Social Psychology Bulletin, 20*, 676–690.

Beer, J. S. (2012). Self-evaluation and self-knowledge. In S. T. Fiske & C. N. Macrae (Eds.), *The SAGE handbook of social cognition* (pp. 330–350). London: Sage.

Berelson, B., Lazarsfeld, P. F., & McPhee, W. N. (1954). *Voting: A study of opinion formation in a presidential campaign*. Chicago: University of Chicago Press.

Berinsky, A. J. (2011, November). *Rumors, truths, and reality: A study of political misinformation*. Paper presented at the New York Area Political Psychology Meeting, New York.

Bodenhausen, G. V. (1988). Stereotypic biases in social decision making and memory: Testing process models of stereotype use. *Journal of Personality and Social Psychology, 55*, 726–737.

Brady, H. E., & Sniderman, P. M. (1985). Attitude attribution: A group basis for political reasoning. *American Political Science Review, 79*, 1061–1078.

Bruner, J. S., Goodnow, J. J., & Austin, G. A. (1956). *A study of thinking*. Oxford, UK: Wiley.

Bullock, J. G. (2006, March). *The enduring importance of false political beliefs*. Paper presented at the Annual Meeting of the Western Political Science Association, Albuquerque, NM.

Bullock, J. G. (2011). Elite influence on public opinion in an informed electorate. *American Political Science Review, 105*, 496–515.

Campbell, A., Converse, P. E., Miller, W., & Stokes, D. (1960). *The American voter*. New York: Wiley.

Campbell, A., Gurin, G., & Miller, W. E. (1954). *The voter decides*. Oxford, UK: Row, Peterson, & Co.

Carmines, E. G. (1978). Psychological origins of adolescent political attitudes: Self-esteem, political salience, and political involvement. *American Politics Quarterly, 6*, 167–186.

Caruso, E. M., Mead, N. L., & Balcetis, E. (2009). Political partisanship influences perception of biracial candidates' skin tone. *Proceedings of the National Academy of Sciences, 106*, 20168–20173.

Chaiken, S., Liberman, A., & Eagly, A. H. (1989). Heuristic and systematic processing within and beyond the persuasion context. In J. S. Uleman& J. A. Bargh (Eds.), *Unintended thought* (pp. 212–252). New York: Guilford.

Chaiken, S., & Maheswaran, D. (1994). Heuristic processing can bias systematic processing: Effects of source credibility, argument ambiguity, and task importance on attitude judgment. *Journal of Personality and Social Psychology, 66*, 460–473.

Chambers, J. R., Baron, R. S., & Inman, M. L. (2006). Misperceptions in intergroup conflict: Disagreeing about what we disagree about. *Psychological Science, 17*, 38–45.

Chance, M. R. A. (1967). Attention structure as the basis of primate rank order. *Man, 2*, 503–518.

Chen, S., Shechter, D., & Chaiken, S. (1996). Getting at the truth or getting along: Accuracy vs. impression-motivated heuristic and systematic information processing. *Journal of Personality and Social Psychology, 71*, 262–275.

Chomsky, N. (1959). A review of B. F. Skinner's "Verbal Behavior." *Language, 35*, 26–58.

Cohen, G. L., Aronson, J., & Steele, C. M. (2000). When beliefs yield to evidence: Reducing biased evaluation by affirming the self. *Personality and Social Psychology Bulletin, 26*, 1151–1164.

Conover, P. J., & Feldman S. (1981). The origins and meaning of liberal/conservative self-identifications. *American Journal of Political Science, 25*, 617–645.

Conover, P. J., & Feldman S. (1984). How people organize the political world: A schematic model. *American Journal of Political Science, 28*, 95–126.

Conover, P. J., & Feldman, S. (1989). Candidate perception in an ambiguous world: Campaigns, cues, and inference processes. *American Journal of Political Science, 33*, 912–940.

Converse, P. H. (1964). The nature of belief systems in mass publics. In D. E. Apter (Ed.), *Ideology and discontent* (pp. 206–261). London: Collier-MacMillan.

Conway, M., & Ross, M. (1984). Getting what you want by revising what you had. *Journal of Personality and Social Psychology, 47*, 738–748.

Cover, A. D., & Brumberg, B. S. (1982). Baby books and ballots: The impact of congressional mail on constituent opinion. *American Political Science Review, 76*, 347–359.

Crandall, S. C., Eidelman, S., Skitka, L. J., & Morgan, G. S. (2009). Status quo framing increases support for torture. *Social Influence, 1*, 1–10.

Darley, J. M., & Gross, P. H. (1983). A hypothesis-confirming bias in labeling effects. *Journal of Personality and Social Psychology, 44*, 20–33.

Davis, D. W., & Silver, B. D. (2004). Civil liberties vs. security: Public opinion in the context of the terrorist attacks on America. *American Journal of Political Science, 48*, 28–46.

Delli, M. X., Carpini, D., & Keeter, S. (1996). *What Americans know about politics and why it matters.* New Haven, CT: Yale University Press.

Ditto, P. H. (2009). Passion, reason, and necessity: A quantity-of-processing view of motivated reasoning. In T. Bayne & J. Fernández (Eds.), *Delusion and self-deception: Affective and motivational influences on belief formation* (pp. 23–53). New York: Psychology Press.

Ditto, P. H., Jemmott, J. B., III, & Darley, J. M. (1988). Appraising the threat of illness: A mental representational approach. *Health Psychology, 7*, 183–200.

Ditto, P. H., & Lopez, D. F. (1992). Motivated skepticism: Use of differential decision criteria for preferred and nonpreferred conclusions. *Journal of Personality and Social Psychology, 86*, 345–355.

Ditto, P. H., Munro, G. D., Apanovitch, A. M., Scepansky, J. A., & Lockhart, L. K. (2003). Spontaneous skepticism: The interplay of motivation and expectation in responses to favorable and unfavorable medical diagnoses. *Personality and Social Psychology Bulletin, 29*, 1120–1132.

Ditto, P. H., Scepansky, J. A., Munro, G. D., Apanovitch, A. M., & Lockhart, L. K. (1998). Motivated sensitivity to preference-inconsistent information. *Journal of Personality and Social Psychology, 75*, 53–69.

Downs, A. (1957). *An economic theory of democracy.* New York: Harper and Row.

Duch, R. M., Palmer, H. D., & Anderson, C. (2000). Heterogeneity in perceptions of national economic conditions. *American Journal of Political Science, 44*, 635–652.

Duckitt, J. (2003). Prejudice and intergroup hostility. In D. O. Sears, L. Huddy& R. Jervis (Eds.), *Oxford handbook of political psychology* (pp. 559–600). New York: Oxford University Press.

Dunning, D. (1999). A newer look: Motivated social cognition and the schematic representation of social concepts. *Psychological Inquiry, 10*, 1–11.

Dunning, D., Leuenberger, A., & Sherman, D. A. (1995). A new look at motivated inference: Are self-serving theories of success a product of motivational forces? *Journal of Personality and Social Psychology, 69*, 58–68.

Edwards, K., & Smith, E. E. (1996). A disconfirmation bias in the evaluation of arguments. *Journal of Personality and Social Psychology, 71*, 5–24.

Eidelman, S., Crandall, C. S., & Pattershall, J. (2009). The existence bias. *Journal of Personality and Social Psychology, 97*, 765–775.

Evans, G., & Andersen R. (2006). The political conditioning of economic perceptions. *Journal of Politics 68*, 194–207.

Fein, S., & Spencer, S. J. (1997). Prejudice as self-image maintenance: Affirming the self through derogation of others. *Journal of Personality and Social Psychology, 73*, 31–44.

Feinberg, M., & Willer, R. (2011). Apocalypse soon? Dire messages reduce belief in global warming by contradicting just-world beliefs. *Psychological Science, 22*, 34–38.

Ferguson, M. J., Hassin, R., & Bargh, J. A. (2008). Implicit motivation: Past, present, and future. In J. Y. Shah & W. L. Gardner (Eds.), *Handbook of motivation science* (pp. 150–166). New York: Guilford Press.

Festinger, L. (1957). *A theory of cognitive dissonance.* Palo Alto, CA: Stanford University Press.

Feygina, I., Jost, J. T., & Goldsmith, R. E. (2010). System justification, the denial of global warming, and the possibility of "system-sanctioned change." *Personality and Social Psychology Bulletin, 36*, 326–338.

Fischle, M. (2000). Mass response to the Lewinsky scandal: Motivated reasoning or Bayesian updating? *Political Psychology, 21*, 135–159.

Fiske, S. T. (1993). Controlling other people: The impact of power on stereotyping. *American Psychologist, 48*, 621–628.

Fiske, S. T., & Kinder D. R. (1981). Involvement, expertise, and schema use: Evidence from political cognition. In N. Cantor & J. Kihlstrom (Eds.), *Personality, cognition, and social interaction* (pp. 171–190). Hillsdale, NJ: Erlbaum.

Fiske, S. T., Kinder, D. R., & Larter, W. M. (1983). The novice and the expert: Knowledge-based strategies in political cognition. *Journal of Experimental Social Psychology, 19*, 381–400.

Fiske, S. T., Lau, R. R., & Smith, R. A. (1990). On the variety and utility of political knowledge structures. *Social Cognition, 8*, 31–48.

Fiske, S. T., & Taylor, S. E. (1984). *Social cognition.* New York: Random House.

Frey, D. (1986). Recent research on selective exposure to information. *Advances in Experimental Social Psychology, 19*, 41–80.

Friedrich, J., Kierniesky, N., & Cardon, L. (1989). Drawing moral inferences from descriptive science: The impact of attitudes on naturalistic fallacy errors. *Personality and Social Psychology Bulletin, 15*, 414–425.

Fromm, E. (1941). *Escape from freedom.* New York: Rinehart.

Funk, C. L. (1996). The impact of scandal on candidate evaluations: An experimental test of the role of candidate traits. *Political Behavior*, *18*, 1–24.

Gaines, B. J., Kuklinski, J. H., Quirk, P. J., Peyton, B., & Verkuilen, J. (2007). Same facts, different interpretations: Partisan motivation and opinion on Iraq. *Journal of Politics*, *69*, 957–974.

Garrett, R. K. (2009). Politically motivated reinforcement seeking: Reframing the selective exposure debate. *Journal of Communication*, *59*, 676–699.

George, A. L., & George J. L. (1956). *Woodrow Wilson and Colonel House*. New York: Dover.

Gibson, J. L. (1981). The role concept in judicial research. *Law & Policy Quarterly*, *3*, 291–311.

Gibson, J. L. (2006). Enigmas of intolerance: Fifty years after Stouffer's Communism, Conformity, and Civil Liberties. *Perspectives on Politics*, *4*, 21–34.

Gibson, J. L. (2007). The legitimacy of the U.S. Supreme Court in a polarized polity. *Journal of Empirical Legal Studies*, *4*, 507–538.

Gibson, J. L. (2008). Group identities and theories of justice: An experimental investigation into the justice and injustice of land squatting in South Africa. *Journal of Politics*, *70*, 700–716.

Gibson, J. L., & Caldeira, G. A. (2011). Has legal realism damaged the legitimacy of the U.S. Supreme Court? *Law and Society Review*, *45*, 195–219.

Gomez, B. T., & Wilson J. M. (2003). Causal attribution and economic voting in American congressional elections. *Political Research Quarterly*, *56*, 271–282.

Goren, P. (2002). Character weakness, partisan bias, and presidential evaluation. *American Journal of Political Science*, *46*, 627–641.

Green, D. P., Palmquist B., & Schickler E. (2002). *Partisan hearts and minds: Political parties and the social identities of voters*. New Haven, CT: Yale University Press.

Green, D. P., & Shapiro, I. (1994). *Pathologies of rational choice theory: A critique of applications in political science*. New Haven, CT: Yale University Press.

Greenberg, J., Pyszczynski, T., Solomon, S., Rosenblatt, A., Veeder, M., Kirkland, S., & Lyon, D. (1990). Evidence for terror management II: The effects of mortality salience on reactions to those who threaten or bolster the cultural worldview. *Journal of Personality and Social Psychology*, *58*, 308–318.

Greenwald, A. G. (1980). The totalitarian ego: Fabrication and revision of personal history. *American Psychologist*, *35*, 603–618.

Haider-Markel, D., & Joslyn, M. (2009). *A partisan education? How education extends partisan divisions over facts*. Retrieved from http://www.psocommons.org/cgi/viewcontent.cgi?article=1000&context=resources

Haines, E. L., & Jost, J. T. (2000). Placating the powerless: Effects of legitimate and illegitimate explanation on affect, memory, and stereotyping. *Social Justice Research*, *13*, 219–236.

Hamill, R., Lodge, M., & Blake, F. (1985). The breadth, depth, and utility of class, partisan, and ideological schemata. *American Journal of Political Science*, *29*, 850–870.

Hamilton, D. L. (Ed.) (1981). *Cognitive processes in stereotyping and intergroup behavior*. Hillsdale, NJ: Erlbaum.

Heider, F. (1958). *The psychology of interpersonal relations*. New York: Wiley.

Hennes, E. P., Feygina, I., & Jost, J. T. (2011). *Feels like global warming: System justification and perception of ambient temperature*. Paper presented at the International Society of Political Psychology 34th Annual Scientific Meeting, Istanbul, Turkey.

Hennes, E. P., & Jost, J. T. (2010). *Motivated information processing in the service of the system: The case of anthropogenic climate change*. Paper presented at the International Society of Political Psychology 33rd Annual Scientific Meeting, San Francisco, CA.

Hetherington, M. J., & Weiler J. D. (2009). *Authoritarianism and polarization in American politics*. New York: Cambridge University Press.

Hochschild, J. L. (1981). *What's fair: American beliefs about distributive justice*. Cambridge, MA: Harvard University Press.

Huckfeldt, R., Levine, J., Morgan, W., & Sprague, J. (1999). Accessibility and the political utility of partisan and ideological orientations. *American Journal of Political Science*, *43*, 888–911.

Hyman, H. H., & Singer, E. (Eds.) (1968). *Readings in reference group theory and research*. New York: Free Press.

Iyengar, S., & Hahn K. S. (2009). Red media, blue media: Evidence of ideological selectivity in media use. *Journal of Communication*, *59*, 19–39.

Iyengar, S., Hahn, K. S., Krosnick, J. A., & Walker, J. (2008). Selective exposure to campaign communication: The role of anticipated agreement and issue public membership. *Journal of Politics*, *70*, 186–200.

Iyengar, S., & Kinder, D. R. (1987). *News that matters*. Chicago: University of Chicago Press.

Iyengar, S., & Ottati, V. (1994). Cognitive perspective in political psychology. In R.S. Wyer& T. K. Srull (Eds.), *Handbook of social cognition* (Vol. 2, pp. 143–188). Hillsdale, NJ: Erlbaum.

Iyengar, S., Peters, M. D., & Kinder, D. R. (1982). Experimental demonstrations of the "not-so-minimal" consequences of television news programs. *American Political Science Review*, *76*, 848–858.

Jacobson, G. C. (2010). Perception, memory, and partisan polarization on the Iraq War. *Political Science Quarterly*, *125*, 31–56.

Jervis, R. (1976). *Perception and misperception in international politics*. Princeton, NJ: Princeton University Press.

Jervis, R. (1993). The drunkard's search. In S. Iyengar& W. J. McGuire (Eds.), *Explorations in political psychology* (pp. 338–360). Durham, NC: Duke University Press.

Jost, J. T. (2006). The end of the end of ideology. *American Psychologist*, *61*, 651–670.

Jost, J. T., Blount, S., Pfeffer, J., & Hunyady, Gy. (2003). Fair market ideology: Its cognitive-motivational underpinnings. In R. M. Kramer, & B. M. Staw (Eds.), *Research in organizational behavior* (Vol. 25, pp. 53–91). Oxford, UK: Elsevier.

Jost, J. T., Burgess, D., & Mosso, C. (2001). Conflicts of legitimation among self, group, and system: The integrative potential of system justification theory. In J. T. Jost and B. Major (Eds.), *The psychology of legitimacy: Emerging perspectives on ideology, justice, and intergroup relations* (pp. 363–388). New York: Cambridge University Press.

Jost, J. T., Glaser, J., Kruglanski, A. W., &Sulloway, F. J. (2003). Political conservatism as motivated social cognition. *Psychological Bulletin*, *129*, 339–375.

Jost, J. T., & Hunyady, O. (2005). Antecedents and consequences of system-justifying ideologies. *Current Directions in Psychological Science*, *14*, 260–265.

Jost, J. T., Kivetz, Y., Rubini, M., Guermandi, G., &Mosso, C. (2005). System-justifying functions of complementary regional and ethnic stereotypes: Cross-national evidence. *Social Justice Research, 18*, 305–333.

Jost, J. T., Liviatan, I., van der Toorn, J., Ledgerwood, A., Mandisodza, A. N., & Nosek, B. A. (2010). System justification: How do we know it's motivated? In D. R. Bobocel, A. C. Kay, M. P. Zanna, & J. M. Olson (Eds.), *The psychology of justice and legitimacy: The Ontario Symposium* (Vol. 11, pp. 173–204). Hillsdale, NJ: Erlbaum.

Jost, J. T., & Major, B. (Eds.) (2001). *The psychology of legitimacy: Emerging perspectives on ideology, justice, and intergroup relations.* New York: Cambridge University Press.

Jost, J. T., Pelham, B. W., Sheldon, O., & Sullivan, B. N. (2003). Social inequality and the reduction of ideological dissonance on behalf of the system: Evidence of enhanced system justification among the disadvantaged. *European Journal of Social Psychology, 33*, 13–36.

Kahan, D. M. (2009). Nanotechnology and society: The evolution of risk perceptions. *Nature Nanotechnology, 4*, 705–706.

Kahan, D. M., & Braman, D. (2006). Cultural cognition and public policy. *Yale Law and Policy Review, 24*, 149–172.

Kahan, D. M., Braman, D., Cohen, G., Slovic, P., Gastil, J. (2011). Who fears the HPV vaccine, who doesn't, and why? An experimental investigation of the mechanisms of cultural cognition. *Law and Human Behavior, 34*, 501–516.

Kahan, D. M., Braman, D., Gastil, J., Slovic, P., Cohen, G. (2009). Cultural cognition of the risks of the benefits of nanotechnology. *Nature Nanotechnology, 4*, 87–90.

Kahan, D. M., Braman, D., Monahan, J., Callahan, L., Peters, E. (2010). Cultural cognition of public policy: The case of outpatient commitment laws. *Law and Human Behavior, 34*, 118–140.

Kahan, D. M., Braman, D., Slovic, P., Gastil, J., Mertz, C. K. (2007). Culture and identity-protective cognition: Explaining the White Male Effect in risk perception. *Empirical Legal Studies, 4*, 465–505.

Kahan, D. M., Wittlin, M., Peters, E., Slovic, P., Ouellette, L. L., Braman, D., & Mandel, G. (2011). The tragedy of the risk-perception commons: Culture conflict, rationality conflict, and climate change. *Cultural Cognition Working Paper No. 89.* Retrieved from http://sciencepolicy.colorado.edu/students/envs_4800/kahan_2011.pdf.

Kahneman, D., Knetsch, J. L., & Thaler, R. H. (1990). Experimental tests of the endowment effect and the Coase Theorem. *Journal of Political Economy, 98*, 1325–1348.

Kahneman, D., & Tversky, A. (1979). Prospect theory: An analysis of decision under risk. *Econometrica, 47*, 263–291.

Karasawa, M. (1998). Eliminating national stereotypes: Direct versus indirect disconfirmation of beliefs in covariation. *Japanese Psychological Research, 40*, 61–73.

Katz, D. (1960). The functional approach to the study of attitudes. *Public Opinion Quarterly, 24*, 163–204.

Kay, A. C., Gaucher, D., Peach, J. M., Laurin, K., Friesen, J., Zanna, M. P., & Spencer, S. J. (2009). Inequality, discrimination, and the power of the status quo: Direct evidence for a motivation to see the way things are as the way they should be. *Journal of Personality and Social Psychology, 97*, 421–434.

Kay, A. C., Jimenez, M. C., & Jost, J. T. (2002). Sour grapes, sweet lemons, and the anticipatory rationalization of the status quo. *Personality and Social Psychology Bulletin, 28*, 1300–1312.

Kay, A. C., Jost, J. T., & Young, S. (2005). Victim derogation and victim enhancement as alternate routes to system justification. *Psychological Science, 16*, 240–246.

Keltner, D., & Robinson, R. J. (1996). Extremism, power, and the imagined basis of social conflict. *Current Directions in Psychological Science, 5*, 101–105.

Keltner, D., & Robinson, R. J. (1997). Defending the status quo: Power and bias in social conflict. *Personality and Social Psychology Bulletin, 23*, 1066–1077.

Kessler, A. (2010). Cognitive dissonance, the global financial crisis, and the discipline of economics. *Real-World Economics Review, 54*, 2–18.

Kim, S., Taber, C. S., & Lodge, M. (2010). A computational model of the citizen as motivated reasoner: Modeling the dynamics of the 2000 presidential election. *Political Behavior, 32*, 1–28.

Kinder, D. R. (1986). Presidential character revisited. In R. Lau & D. O. Sears (Eds.), *Political cognition: The 19th Annual Carnegie Symposium on Cognition.* Hillsdale, NJ: Erlbaum.

Kinder, D. R., & Kiewiet, D. R. (1979). Economic discontent and political behavior: The role of personal grievances and collective economic judgments in congressional voting. *American Journal of Political Science, 23*, 495–527.

Kinder, D. R., & Kiewiet, D. R. (1981). Sociotropic politics: The American case. *British Journal of Political Science, 11*, 129–161.

Kinder, D. R., & Sears, D. O. (1985). Public opinion and political action. In G. Lindzey & E. Aronson (Eds.), *The handbook of social psychology* (pp. 659–741). New York: Random House.

Klein, W. M., & Kunda, Z. (1992). Motivated person perception: Constructing justifications for desired beliefs. *Journal of Experimental Social Psychology, 28*, 145–168.

Kluegel, J. R., & Smith, E. R. (1986). *Beliefs about inequality: Americans' views of what is and what ought to be.* New York: Aldine de Gruyter.

Knobloch-Westerwick, S., & Meng, J. (2009). Looking the other way: Selective exposure to attitude-consistent and counterattitudinal political information. *Communication Research, 36*, 426–448.

Kopko, K. C., Bryner, S. M., Budziak, J., Devine, C. J., & Nawara, S. P. (2011). In the eye of the beholder? Motivated reasoning in disputed elections. *Political Behavior, 33*, 271–290.

Krosnick, J. A., & Kinder, D. R. (1990).Altering the foundations of support for the president through priming. *American Political Science Review, 84*, 497–512.

Krosnick, J. A., & McGraw, K. M. (2002). Psychological political science versus political psychology true to its name: A plea for balance. In K. R. Monroe (Ed.), *Political psychology* (pp. 79–94). Mahwah, NJ: Erlbaum.

Kruglanski, A. W. (1996). Motivated social cognition: Principles of the interface. In E. T. Higgins & A. W. Kruglanski (Eds.), *Social psychology: Handbook of basic principles* (pp. 493–520). New York: Guilford.

Kruglanski, A. W. (1999). Motivation, cognition, and reality: Three memos for the next generation of research. *Psychological Inquiry, 10*, 54–58.

Kruglanski, A. W., & Freund, T. (1983). The freezing and un-freezing of lay-inferences: Effects on impressional primacy, ethnic stereotyping and numerical anchoring. *Journal of Experimental Social Psychology, 19*, 448–468.

Kruglanski, A. W., Shah, J. Y., Fishbach, A., Friedman, R., Chun, W. Y., & Sleeth-Keppler, D. (2002). A theory of goal systems. *Advances in Experimental Social Psychology, 34*, 331–387.

Kruglanski, A. W., & Webster, D. M. (1996). Motivated closing of the mind: "Seizing" and "freezing." *Psychological Review, 103*, 263–283.

Kruglanski, A. W., Webster, D. M., & Klem, A. (1993). Motivated resistance and openness to persuasion in the presence or absence of prior information. *Journal of Personality and Social Psychology, 65,* 861–876.

Kuklinski, J. H., & Quirk, P. J. (2000).Reconsidering the rational public: Cognition, heuristics, and mass opinion. In A. Lupia, M. D. McCubbins, & S. L. Popkin (Eds.), *Elements of reason: Cognition, choice, and the bounds of rationality* (pp. 153–182). New York: Cambridge University Press.

Kuklinski, J. H., & Quirk, P. J. (2001). Conceptual foundations of citizen competence. *Political Behavior, 23,* 285–311.

Kuklinski, J. H., Quirk, P. J., & Peyton, B. (2008). Issues, information flows, and cognitive capacities: Democratic citizenship in a global era. In P. F. Nardulli (Ed.), *International perspectives on contemporary democracy* (pp. 115–133). Champaign, IL: University of Illinois Press.

Kull, S., Ramsay, C., & Lewis, E. (2003–2004). Misperceptions, the media, and the Iraq War. *Political Science Quarterly, 118,* 569–598.

Kunda, Z. (1987). Motivation and inference: Self-serving generation and evaluation of evidence. *Journal of Personality and Social Psychology, 53,* 636–647.

Kunda, Z. (1990). The case for motivated reasoning. *Psychological Bulletin, 108,* 480–498.

Kunda, Z., & Sanitioso, R. (1989). Motivated changes in the self-concept. *Journal of Experimental Social Psychology, 25,* 272–285.

Kunda, Z., & Sanitioso, R. (1991). Ducking the collection of costly evidence: Motivated use of statistical heuristics. *Journal of Behavioral Decision Making, 4,* 161–176.

Kunda, Z., & Sinclair, L. (1999). Reactions to a Black professional: Motivated inhibition and activation of conflicting stereotypes. *Journal of Personality and Social Psychology, 77,* 885–904.

Lane, R. E. (1962). *Political ideology: Why the American common man believes what he does.* Oxford, UK: Free Press of Glencoe.

Lane, R. E. (1986). Market justice, political justice. *American Political Science Review, 80,* 363–403.

Larson, D. W. (1985). *Origins of containment: A psychological explanation.* Princeton, NJ: Princeton University Press.

Lasswell, H. (1930). *Psychopathology and politics.* New York: Viking.

Lasswell, H. (1935). *World politics and personal insecurity.* New York: Free Press.

Lasswell, H. (1948). *Power and personality.* New York: Norton.

Lau, R. R. (1985). Two explanations for negativity effects in political behavior. *American Journal of Political Science, 29,* 119–138.

Lau, R. R. (1989). Construct accessibility and electoral choice. *Political Behavior, 11,* 5–32.

Lau, R. R. (2003). Models of decision-making. In D. O. Sears, L. Huddy, & R. Jervis (Eds.), *Oxford handbook of political psychology* (pp. 19–59).New York: Oxford University Press.

Lau, R. R., Andersen D. J., & Redlawsk, D. P. (2008). An exploration of correct voting in recent U.S. presidential elections. *American Journal of Political Science, 52,* 395–411.

Lau, R. R., & Redlawsk, D. (2001). Advantages and disadvantages of cognitive heuristics in political decision making. *American Journal of Political Science, 45,* 951–971.

Lau, R. R., & Redlawsk D. (2006). *How voters decide: Information processing during election campaigns.* New York: Cambridge University Press.

Lau, R. R., & Sears, D. O. (1986). Social cognition and political cognition: The past, the present, and the future. In R. R. Lau & D. O. Sears (Eds.), *Political cognition: The 19th Annual Carnegie Symposium on Cognition* (pp. 347–366). Hillsdale, NJ: Erlbaum.

Lavine, H. (2002). On-line versus memory-based process models of political evaluation. In K. R. Monroe (Ed.), *Political psychology* (pp. 225–247). Mahwah, NJ: Erlbaum.

Lavine, H., Lodge M., & Freitas, K. (2005). Authoritarianism, threat, and selective exposure to information. *Political Psychology, 26,* 219–244.

Lavine, H., & Snyder, M. (1996). Cognitive processing and the functional matching effect in persuasion: The mediating role of subjective perceptions of message quality. *Journal of Experimental Social Psychology, 32,* 580–604.

Lazarsfeld, P. F., Berelson, B., & Gaudet, H. (1944). *The people's choice.* Oxford, UK: Duell, Sloan & Pearce.

Ledgerwood, A., Mandisodza, A. N., Jost, J. T., & Pohl, M. (2011). Working for the system: Motivated defense of meritocratic beliefs. *Social Cognition, 29,* 323–340.

Lerner, M. J. (1980). *The belief in a just world: A fundamental delusion.* New York: Plenum Press.

Lerner, J. S., & Tetlock, P. E. (1999). Accounting for the effects of accountability. *Psychological Bulletin, 125,* 255–275.

Lippmann, W. (1922). *Public opinion.* New York: Free Press.

Liviatan, I., & Jost, J. T. (2012). *A social-cognitive analysis of system justification goal striving.* Unpublished manuscript, New York University.

Lockard, J. S., &Paulhus, D. L. (Eds.) (1988). *Self-deception: An adaptive mechanism?* Englewood Cliffs, NJ: Prentice Hall.

Lodge, M., & Hamill, R. (1986). A partisan schema for political information processing. *American Political Science Review, 80,* 505–519.

Lodge, M., & McGraw, K. (Eds.) (1995). *Political judgment: Structure and process.* Ann Arbor, MI: University of Michigan Press.

Lodge, M., McGraw, K., & Stroh, P. (1989). An impression-driven model of candidate evaluation. *American Political Science Review, 83,* 399–420.

Lodge, M., & Taber, C. S. (2000). Three steps toward a theory of motivated reasoning. In A. Lupia, M. D. McCubbins, & S. L. Popkin (Eds.), *Elements of reason: Cognition, choice, and the bounds of rationality* (pp. 183–213). New York: Cambridge University Press.

Lodge, M., & Taber, C. S. (2005). The automaticity of affect for political leaders, groups, and issues: An experimental test of the hot cognition hypothesis. *Political Psychology, 26,* 455–482.

Lord, C. G., Lepper, M. R., & Preston, E. (1984). Considering the opposite: A corrective strategy for social judgment. *Journal of Personality and Social Psychology, 47,* 1231–1243.

Lord, C. G., Ross, L., &Lepper, M. R. (1979). Biased assimilation and attitude polarization: The effects of prior theories on subsequently considered evidence. *Journal of Personality and Social Psychology, 37,* 2098–2109.

Lupia, A. (1994). Shortcuts versus encyclopedias: Information and voting behavior in California insurance reform elections. *American Political Science Review, 88,* 63–76.

Lupia, A., & McCubbins, M. D. (1998). *The democratic dilemma: Can citizens learn what they need to know?* New York: Cambridge University Press.

MacCoun, R. J., & Paletz, S. (2009). Citizens' perceptions of ideological bias in research on public policy controversies. *Political Psychology, 30,* 43–63.

Maio, G. R., & Olson, J. M. (2000). What is a value-expressive attitude? In G. R. Maio& J. M. Olson (Eds.), *Why we evaluate: Functions of attitudes* (pp. 249–269). Mahwah, NJ: Erlbaum.

Marcus, G. E., Sullivan, J. L., Theiss-Morse, E., & Wood, S. L. (1995). *With malice toward some: How people make civil liberties judgments.* New York: Cambridge University Press.

McClosky, H. (1958). Conservatism and personality. *American Political Science Review, 52,* 27–45.

McCright, A. M. & Dunlap, R. E. (2011). Cool dudes: The denial of climate change among conservative white males in the United States. *Global Environmental Change, 21,* 1163–1172.

McGraw, K. M. (2000). Contributions of the cognitive approach to political psychology. *Political Psychology, 21,* 805–832.

McGraw, K. M. (2003). Political impressions: Formation and management. In D. Sears, L. Huddy, & R. Jervis (Eds.), *Oxford handbook of political psychology.* New York: Oxford University Press.

McGuire, W. J. (1993). The poly-psy relationship: Three phases in a long affair. In S. Iyengar & W. J. McGuire (Eds.), *Explorations in political psychology* (pp. 9–35). Durham, NC: Duke University Press.

Miller, A. H., Wattenberg, M., & Malanchuk, O. (1986). Schematic assessments of presidential candidates. *American Political Science Review, 80,* 521–540.

Miller, A. H., & Wlezien, C. (1993). The social group dynamics of partisan evaluations. *Electoral Studies, 12,* 5–22.

Miller, D. T. (1999). The norm of self-interest. *American Psychologist, 54,* 1–8.

Miller, D. T., & Ross, M. (1975). Self-serving biases in attribution of causality: Fact or fiction? *Psychological Bulletin, 82,* 213–225.

Miller, G. A. (1956). The magical number seven, plus or minus two: Some limits on our capacity for processing information. *Psychological Review, 63,* 81–97.

Mooney, C. (2011, May 18). The Fox News "effect": A few references. Retrieved from http://www.desmogblog.com/fox-news-effect-few-references.

Morris, J. P., Squires, N. K., Taber, C. S., & Lodge, M. (2003). Activation of political attitudes: A psychophysiological examination of the Hot Cognition hypothesis. *Political Psychology, 24,* 727–745.

Moshinsky, A., & Bar-Hillel, M. (2010). Loss aversion and status quo label bias. *Social Cognition, 28,* 191–204.

Munro, G. D., & Ditto, P. H. (1997). Biased assimilation, attitude polarization, and affect in reactions to stereotype-relevant scientific information. *Personality and Social Psychology Bulletin, 23,* 636–654.

Munro, G. D., Lasane, T. P., & Leary, S. P. (2010). Political partisan prejudice: Selective distortion and weighting of evaluative categories in college admissions applications. *Journal of Applied Social Psychology, 40,* 2434–2462.

Munro, G. D., Weih, C., & Tsai, J. (2010). Motivated suspicion: Asymmetrical attributions of the behavior of political ingroup and outgroup members. *Basic and Applied Social Psychology, 32,* 173–184.

Murray, S. L., Holmes, J. G., & Griffin, D. W. (1996). The benefits of positive illusions: Idealization and the construction of satisfaction in close relationships. *Journal of Personality and Social Psychology Bulletin, 70,* 79–98.

Mutz, D. C. (2006). *Hearing the other side: Deliberative versus participatory democracy.* New York: Cambridge University Press.

Myrdal, G. (1969). *Objectivity in social research.* New York: Pantheon Books.

Nicholson, S. P., & Segura, G. (1999). Midterm elections and divided government: An information-driven theory of electoral volatility. *Political Research Quarterly, 52,* 609–629.

Nisbet, R. E., & Ross, L. D. (1980). *Human inference: Strategies and shortcomings of social judgment.* Englewood Cliffs, NJ: Prentice-Hall.

Nyhan, B., & Reifler, J. (2010). When corrections fail: The persistence of political misperceptions. *Political Behavior, 32,* 303–330.

O'Brien L. T., & Crandall, C. S. (2005). Perceiving self-interest: Power, ideology, and maintenance of the status quo. *Social Justice Research, 18,* 1–24.

Overbeck, J. R., & Park, B. (2001). When power does not corrupt: Superior individuation processes among powerful perceivers. *Journal of Personality and Social Psychology, 81,* 549–565.

Petty, R. E., & Cacioppo, J. A. (1986). The elaboration likelihood model of persuasion. *Advances in Experimental Social Psychology, 19,* 123–205.

Popkin, S. L. (1994). *The reasoning voter: Communication and persuasion in presidential campaigns* (2nd ed.). Chicago: University of Chicago Press.

Pyszczynski, T., Greenberg, J. (1987). Toward an integration of cognitive and motivational perspectives on social inference: A biased hypothesis-testing model. *Advances in Experimental Social Psychology, 20,* 294–340.

Pyszczynski, T., Greenberg, J., & Holt, K. (1985). Maintaining consistency between self-serving beliefs and available data: A bias in information evaluation following success and failure. *Personality and Social Psychology Bulletin, 11,* 179–190.

Quattrone, G., &Tversky, A. (1988). Contrasting rational and psychological analyses of political choice. *American Political Science Review, 82,* 719–736.

Radcliff, B. (1994). Reward without punishment: Economic conditions and the vote. *Political Research Quarterly, 47,* 721–731.

Redlawsk, D. P. (2002). Hot cognition or cool consideration? Testing the effects of motivated reasoning on political decision making. *Journal of Politics, 64,* 1021–1044.

Robinson, R. J., & Keltner, D. (1996). Much ado about nothing? Revisionists and traditionalists choose an introductory English syllabus. *Psychological Science, 7,* 18–24.

Robinson, R. J., Keltner, D., Ward, A., & Ross, L. (1995). Actual versus assumed differences in construal: "Naïve realism" in intergroup perception and conflict. *Journal of Personality and Social Psychology, 68,* 404–417.

Rokeach, M. (1960). *The open and closed mind.* New York: Basic Books.

Ross, M., & Fletcher, G. J. O. (1985). Attribution and social perception. In G. Lindzey & E. Aronson (Eds.), *The handbook of social psychology* (Vol. 2, pp. 73–122). New York: Random House.

Ross, M., McFarland, C., & Fletcher, G. J. O. (1981). The effect of attitude on the recall of personal histories. *Journal of Personality and Social Psychology, 40,* 627–634.

Samuelson, W., & Zeckhauser, R. (1988). Status quo bias in decision making. *Journal of Risk and Uncertainty, 1,* 7–59.

Sanitioso, R., Kunda, Z., & Fong, G. T. (1990). Motivated recruitment of autobiographical memory. *Journal of Personality and Social Psychology, 59,* 229–241.

Schumpeter, J. A. (1942/1994). *Capitalism, socialism and democracy.* London: Routledge.

Sears, D. O., & Freedman, J. L. (1967). Selective exposure to information: A critical review. *Public Opinion Quarterly, 31,* 194–213.

Sears, D. O., & Funk, C. (1991). The role of self-interest in social and political attitudes. *Advances in Experimental Social Psychology, 24,* 1–91.

Sherman, B. R., & Kunda, Z. (1989). *Motivated evaluation of scientific evidence.* Paper presented at the American Psychological Society annual convention, Arlington, VA.

Sherman, D. K., Cohen, G. L. (2002). Accepting threatening information: Self-affirmation and the reduction of defensive biases. *Current Directions in Psychological Science, 11,* 119–123.

Simon, H. A. (1957). *Models of man: Social and rational.* Oxford, UK: Wiley.

Slothuus, R., & de Vreese, C. H. (2010). Political parties, motivated reasoning, and issue framing effects. *Journal of Politics, 72,* 630–645.

Smith, M. B., Bruner, J., & White, R. W. (1956). *Opinions and personality.* New York: Wiley.

Sniderman, P. M. (1975). *Personality and democratic politics.* Berkeley, CA: University of California Press.

Sniderman, P. M., Brody, R. A., Tetlock, P. E. (1991). *Reasoning and choice: Explorations in political psychology.* New York: Cambridge University Press.

Sniderman, P. M., & Citrin, J. (1971). Psychological sources of political belief: Self-esteem and isolationist attitudes. *American Political Science Review, 65,* 401–417.

Stangor, C., & Jost, J. T. (1997). Individual, group, and system levels of analysis and their relevance for stereotyping and intergroup relations. In R. Spears, P. Oakes, N. Ellemers, & S. A. Haslam (Eds.), *The social psychology of stereotyping and group life* (pp. 336–358). Oxford, UK: Blackwell.

Steele, C. M. (1988). The psychology of self-affirmation: Sustaining the integrity of the self. *Advances in experimental social psychology, 21,* 261–302.

Steenbergen, M., & Lodge, M. (2003). Process matters: Cognitive models of candidate evaluation. In M. MacKuen & G. Rabinowitz (Eds.), *Electoral democracy* (pp. 125–171). Ann Arbor, MI: University of Michigan Press.

Stenner, K. (2005). *The authoritarian dynamic.* New York: Cambridge University Press.

Stroud, N. J. (2008). Media use and political predispositions: Revisiting the concept of selective exposure. *Political Behavior, 30,* 341–366.

Sullivan, J. L., Marcus, G. E., Feldman, S., & Piereson, J. (1981). The sources of political tolerance: A multivariate analysis. *American Political Science Review, 75,* 92–106.

Sullivan, J. L., Piereson, J., & Marcus, G. E. (1982). *Political tolerance and American democracy.* Chicago, IL: University of Chicago Press.

Sullivan, J. L., Rahn, W. M., & Rudolph, T. J. (2002). The contours of political psychology: Situating research on political information processing. In J. H. Kuklinski (Ed.), *Thinking about political psychology.* New York: Cambridge University Press.

Sweeney, P. D., & Gruber, K. L. (1984). Selective exposure: Voter information preferences and the Watergate affair. *Journal of Personality and Social Psychology, 46,* 1208–1221.

Taber, C. S. (2003). Information processing and public opinion. In D. O. Sears, L. Huddy, & R. Jervis (Eds.), *Oxford handbook of political psychology* (pp. 433–476). New York: Oxford University Press.

Taber, C. S., Cann, D., & Kucsova, S. (2009). The motivated processing of political arguments. *Political Behavior, 31,* 137–155.

Taber, C. S., & Lodge, M. (2006). Motivated skepticism in the evaluation of political beliefs. *American Journal of Political Science, 50,* 755–769.

Taber, C. S., Lodge, M., & Glathar, J. (2001). The motivated construction of political judgments. In J. H. Kuklinski (Ed.), *Citizens and politics: Perspectives from political psychology* (pp. 198–226). New York: Cambridge University Press.

Tajfel, H. (1969). Cognitive aspects of prejudice. *Journal of Social Issues, 25,* 79–97.

Tajfel, H., & Turner, J. C. (1979). An integrative theory of intergroup conflict. In W. G. Austin & S. Worchel (Eds.), *The social psychology of intergroup relations.* Monterey, CA: Brooks-Cole.

Taylor, S. E., & Brown, J. D. (1988). Illusion and well-being: A social psychological perspective on mental health. *Psychological Bulletin, 103,* 193–210.

Taylor, S. E., Lerner, J. S., Sherman, D. K., Sage, R. M., & McDowell, N. K. (2003). Portrait of a self-enhancer: Well adjusted and well liked or maladjusted and friendless? *Journal of Personality and Social Psychology, 84,* 165–176.

Tetlock, P. E. (1983). Cognitive style and political ideology. *Journal of Personality and Social Psychology, 45,* 118–126.

Tetlock, P. E., & Levi, A. (1982). Attribution bias: On the inconclusiveness of the cognition-motivation debate. *Journal of Experimental Social Psychology, 18,* 68–88.

Thompson, E. P., Roman, R. J., Moskowitz, G. B., Chaiken, S., & Bargh, J. A. (1994). Accuracy motivation attenuates covert priming: The systematic reprocessing of social information. *Journal of Personality and Social Psychology, 66,* 474–489.

Tourangeau, R. & Rasinski, K. A. (1988). Cognitive responses underlying context effects in attitude measurement. *Psychological Bulletin, 103,* 299–314.

Tyler, T. R. (2006). Legitimacy and legitimation. *Annual Review of Psychology, 57,* 375–400.

Vallone, R. P., Ross, L. & Lepper, M. R. (1985). The hostile media phenomenon: Biased perception and perceptions of media bias in coverage of the Beirut massacre. *Journal of Personality and Social Psychology, 49,* 577–585.

von Hippel, W., & Trivers, R. (2011). The evolution and psychology of self-deception. *Behavioral and Brain Sciences, 34,* 1–16.

Weaver, D. H., Graber, D. A., McCombs, M. E., & Eyal, C. H. (1981). *Media agenda-setting in a presidential election: Issues, images, and interest.* New York: Praeger.

Wells, C., Reedy, J., Gastil, J., & Lee, C. (2009). Information distortion and voting choices: The origins and effects of factual beliefs in initiative elections. *Political Psychology, 30,* 953–969.

Westen, D. (1998). The scientific legacy of Sigmund Freud: Toward a psychodynamically informed psychological science. *Psychological Bulletin, 124,* 333–371.

Westen, D., Blagov, P. S., Harenski, K., Kilts, C., &Hamann, S. (2006). Neural bases of motivated reasoning: An fMRI study of emotional constraints on partisan political judgment in the 2004 U.S. presidential election. *Journal of Cognitive Neuroscience 18,* 1947–1958.

Wilson, G. D. (Ed.) (1973). *The psychology of conservatism.* London: Academic Press.

Zaller, J. R. (1992). *The nature and origins of mass opinion.* New York: Cambridge University Press.

Zaller, J. R., & Feldman, S. (1992). A simple theory of the survey response: Answering questions versus revealing preferences. *American Journal of Political Science, 36,* 579–616.

Social Cognition and Health

Shelley E. Taylor

Abstract

Social cognition research has greatly informed health psychology investigations during the past several decades. Social cognition research on attitudes has been an important source for interventions to change health behaviors. Investigations into cognitive biases and message framing have also had considerable impact. Cognitive appraisals are pivotal in the experience of stress. Beliefs about health conditions, including causal attributions, beliefs about control, and illness representations, commonly arise and bear some relation to illness outcomes. Of considerable consequence for well-being and health are affectively laden cognitions such as negative expectations and positive beliefs. Approach–avoidance frameworks, research on the self, and cognitive and emotional processes involved in disclosure and social support have all been significantly related to well-being and health outcomes. Current social cognition research in health psychology focuses on linking cognitions and cognitive processes to neural and physiological functioning, thereby elucidating the mechanisms by which beliefs and behaviors affect long-term mental and physical health.

Key Words: health psychology, cognitive appraisals, emotional processes, physical health

Introduction

Health has proved to be a fruitful domain in which to explore the ramifications of social cognition. Historically, the study of social cognition in the health domain has moved through several phases. The earliest health-related work in social cognition examined the relation of beliefs to health behaviors, an interface that continues to be productive into the present. Work on message framing and on cognitive biases has also been impactful. In the late 1970s and early 1980s, researchers brought to bear their understanding of cognitive processes, such as causal attribution or beliefs in psychological control, and applied them in the health domain, the idea being that the specific content of such beliefs might predict outcomes such as adjustment to illness or even the course of illness itself. This perspective gave way to a focus on affectively laden social cognitions in the health domain. Thus, for example, researchers

examine optimism, negative affectivity, and related constructs for their ability to predict well-being, adjustment, and health outcomes. Currently, as is true of social cognition more generally, researchers have begun to study the mechanisms underlying social cognitive approaches to health. Thus, for example, researchers are increasingly using such tools as functional magnetic resonance imaging (fMRI) and biological assays to identify the underlying neural and neuroendocrine processes that may link social, cognitive, and emotional processes to health-related outcomes.

Although social cognition and health psychology evolved over the same time period, there is no over-arching theoretical perspective that links them to each other. Rather, health psychologists have often been opportunistic, seizing on insights from social cognition to develop interventions or test the relation of particular psychological variables to health outcomes, and social cognition researchers have found the health domain to be a fruitful one within which to test social cognition insights.

The subsequent sections are nonetheless guided by a general framework. Good and poor health result from a broad array of factors, including genetics, exposure to pathogens, and early life experiences. Factors particularly relevant to social cognition include, as will be seen, health beliefs and the construal of events as stressful. Cumulatively, these factors influence psychological and biological health outcomes, but these outcomes are significantly moderated by psychosocial resources that include cognitions such as optimism, a sense of mastery, and the perception that the social environment is supportive. Proximal effects on psychological outcomes, such as distress, and on biological outcomes, such as physiological functioning, are ultimately prognostic for diagnosable health conditions.

Lest one conclude that health is simply a domain to which social cognition is applied, the health arena has also been immensely valuable for uncovering underlying basic theoretically relevant mechanisms by which mind and body interact. That is, more than any other area of social cognition research, health researchers who have focused on social cognitions have identified the underlying processes whereby beliefs influence not only psychological outcomes, such as well-being, but also autonomic, neural, neuroendocrine, and immunologic processes that may be proximal influences on health outcomes. As such, health research has helped to bring social cognition into integrative science, whereby the contributions of such fields as genetics, molecular biology, and medicine are integrated with the social, cognitive, and emotion research that social cognition has spawned.

Social Cognition, Health Attitudes, and Health Behavior Change

Social psychological research, and in particular, social cognition research on attitudes has been a primary impetus for designing persuasive communications designed to change poor health habits. The rationale underlying the early work was that if one can alert people to health risks and raise their level of concern, one can motivate them to change their behavior. Current approaches to changing health attitudes and behavior continue to draw on these insights, especially those guided by the health belief model (Rosenstock, 1966), the protection motivation model (Rogers, 1975), and the theory of planned behavior (Ajzen, 2002).

The central role of social cognition processes to these models is particularly well illustrated by Ajzen's theory of planned behavior (Ajzen & Madden, 1986; Fishbein & Ajzen, 1975). According to the theory, a health behavior is the direct result of a behavioral intention. Behavioral intentions are themselves made up of three components: attitudes toward a specific action, subjective norms regarding the action, and perceived behavioral control. Attitudes toward the action stem from beliefs about the likely outcomes of that action and evaluations of those outcomes. For example, people who believe that exercise will reduce their risk of heart disease will have favorable attitudes toward exercise. Subjective norms are what a person believes others think that person should do (normative beliefs) and the motivation to comply with those normative beliefs. Believing that others think one should exercise and being motivated to comply with those normative beliefs would further induce a person to practice sunscreen use. Perceived behavioral control occurs when a person feels able to perform the health behavior contemplated and believes that the action undertaken will have the intended effect. These beliefs combine to produce a behavioral intention and ultimately behavior change.

Despite the success of theories that link beliefs to the modification of health habits, these approaches have some limitations. Cognitive approaches are not always successful in explaining spontaneous behavior change, nor do they necessarily predict long-term behavior change. Moreover, communications designed to change people's cognitions about their health behaviors sometimes evoke defensive or irrational processes (Liberman & Chaiken, 1992; Clarke, Lovegrove, Williams, & Macpherson, 2000; Thornton, Gibbons, & Gerrard, 2002). Continuing to practice a risky behavior can, itself, sustain false perceptions of risk, inducing a sense of complacency (Halpern-Felsher et al., 2001).

Historically, efforts to change health behaviors have emphasized conscious verbal processing. Recently, research from social cognitive neuroscience has found that some successful health behavior change occurs outside of awareness. An important distinction within social cognition research is that between controlled and automatic processing (Petty & Cacioppo, 1984). People can rely on relatively automatic processes or alternatively on more effortful ones, depending on the situation and motivational demands. This dual processing approach has had a profound impact throughout social cognition (Fiske & Taylor, 2008).

Recently, research using fMRI has found that some successful health behavior change can occur outside of awareness, suggesting that automatic processes may sometimes be engaged in producing health behavior change. In a recent investigation (Falk, Berkman, Mann, Harrison, & Lieberman, 2010), participants were exposed to persuasive messages promoting sunscreen use. Those who showed significant activation in the medial prefrontal cortex (mPFC) and posterior cingulate cortex (pCC) in response to the messages showed behavior change in their sunscreen use. Most important, although individual differences in behavior were weakly predicted by participants' behavioral intentions to use sunscreen, activity in mPFC and pCC accounted for an additional 25% of the variance in behavior, on top of that explained by self-reported attitudes and behavioral intentions. In other words, processes apparently not accessible to consciousness nonetheless significantly predicted the health behavior of sunscreen use.

What this pattern means is not yet fully known. One possibility is that activity in mPFC and pCC signals behavioral intentions at an implicit level that is not consciously accessible (Falk et al., 2010). Alternatively, activity in mPFC may reflect self-referential processes and be related to behavior change primarily because participants have linked a persuasive communication to the self (cf., Chua, Liberzon, Welsh, & Strecher, 2009). Persuasion efforts that successfully modify a person's sense of self appear to be most successful in modifying behavior and helping people form specific behavioral intentions (Rise, Sheeran, & Hukkelberg, 2010).

Social cognition research on attitudes and persuasion was, thus, one of the first sources of influence on health psychology, and it is also one of the most enduring. As the origin of the very earliest models for understanding health behaviors and as the impetus for interventions to bring about health behavior change, it continues to provide insights for both understanding and changing health behaviors.

Message Framing and Cognitive Biases

Much theory and research in social cognition has been devoted to understanding biases in human thought and message framing. This lesson has been imported to health psychology, where it has been employed fruitfully to address health behaviors. Health messages can be framed in terms of gains and losses. For example, a reminder to use sunscreen can emphasize the benefits of sunscreen to appearance, or alternatively can emphasize the costs of not using sunscreen, such as risk of skin cancers (e.g., McCaul, Johnson, & Rothman, 2002). Messages that emphasize potential costs may work better for inducing people to practice health behaviors that have uncertain outcomes; perhaps the uncertainty undermines commitment to behavior change, which is offset by the impact of the loss frame. Messages that emphasize benefits are more persuasive for behaviors that have certain outcomes (Apanovitch, McCarthy, & Salovey, 2003). Recommendations regarding exactly how to take action increase effectiveness as well (McCaul et al., 2002).

Messages are differentially effective depending on how they are framed in terms of a person's own psychological orientation. People who have a BAS (promotion or approach) orientation that emphasizes maximizing opportunities are more influenced by messages that are phrased in terms of benefits ("Sunscreen will protect your skin"), whereas people who have a BIS (prevention or avoidance orientation) that emphasizes minimizing risks are more influenced by messages that stress the risks of not performing a health behavior ("Not using sunscreen increases your risk of skin cancer") (Mann, Sherman, & Updegraff, 2005).

Knowledge concerning errors and biases and their effects on psychological functioning has come not only from social cognition research but also from health psychology. Taylor (1983) developed a theory of cognitive adaptation, in which she argued that following a major health threat, people may develop "positive illusions," that is, illusions that protect them psychologically from the threats they face and enable them to cope and make progress toward restoring good psychological functioning. The theory maintained that these cognitions center on the making of meaning, mastery, and self-enhancement. From these observations, Taylor and Brown (1988) developed a more general model of social cognition suggesting that unrealistic optimism, an exaggerated sense of personal control, and self-enhancement not only characterize people's responses to intensely threatening events but also may commonly be found in normal, everyday thought. They argued that rather than being maladaptive, these mild, positive distortions are associated with the criteria indicative of mental health, including a positive sense of self, the ability to make progress toward goals, the ability to deal effectively with threats, the capacity for developing and maintaining positive social relationships, and other criteria associated with mental health. Subsequently, Taylor and colleagues found that these positive illusions were associated with lesser biological reactivity and lower baseline levels of stress hormones, suggesting that they may have protective benefits on health (Taylor, Lerner, Sherman, Sage, & McDowell, 2003).

As such, the work on positive illusions has come full circle: Originating in observations in the health domain, it led to a full-blown theory in social cognition, which has generated many dozens of experimental studies, yielding findings suggestive of biological buffering by exaggerated positive cognitions that has fed back into health psychology theory and research.

Social Cognitive Approaches to Stress

The idea that social cognition is vital to understanding stress was a very early insight in health psychology research. For example, Richard Lazarus and colleagues (Lazarus & Folkman, 1984; Lazarus & Launier, 1978), who initially formulated psychological research on stress and coping, recognized how critical cognitive appraisals are to experiencing stress and mustering the resources for combating it (Lazarus, 1968; Lazarus & Folkman, 1984). These researchers maintained that when people encounter a potentially stressful event, they engage in a process of primary appraisal whereby the event is evaluated to be positive, neutral, or negative in its consequences. Negative or potentially negative events are further appraised for their possible harm, threat, or challenge. Harm is the assessment of the damage that has already been done. Threat is the assessment of possible future damage that may be brought about by the event. Challenge perceptions represent the potential to overcome or even profit from an event (cf. Tomaka, Blascovich, Kelsey, & Leitten, 1993). Thus, stressful events are not intrinsically harmful or threatening, but rather are influenced by the cognitive appraisals that are made.

The importance of primary appraisal in the experience of stress was well illustrated in an early classic study of stress (Speisman, Lazarus, Mordkoff, & Davison, 1964). College students viewed a gruesome film depicting unpleasant tribal initiation rites that included genital mutilation. Before viewing the film, they were exposed to one of four experimental conditions. One group listened to an anthropological account of the meaning of the rites. Another group heard a lecture that de-emphasized the pain the initiates were experiencing and emphasized their excitement over arriving at manhood. A third group heard a description that emphasized the pain and trauma that the initiates were undergoing,

and a fourth group was given no introductory context. Measures of autonomic arousal and self-reports indicated that the first two groups experienced considerably less stress than did the group whose attention was focused on the trauma and pain. Thus, beliefs about the meaning of the event were critical not only to its impact on psychological reactions but also to physiological responses to the gruesome stimuli.

As primary appraisals are taking place, secondary appraisals are initiated as well. Secondary appraisals involve the assessment of one's abilities and resources and whether they will be sufficient to meet the harm, threat, or challenge of a stressful event. The person thinks through what can be done, comes up with plans and responses (or not), and develops a sense of whether the potentially stressful event can be managed. Ultimately, the subjective experience of stress is a balance between primary and secondary appraisals. When harm and threat are high, and the perception of one's coping abilities and resources is low, substantial stress is experienced, whereas when coping abilities and resources are high, stress may be minimal.

BELIEFS ABOUT ILLNESS

Many of the early applications of social cognition research to health involved relating specific social cognitions to problems faced by people with chronic conditions or illnesses. Chronic illness is an important topic in health psychology for a number of reasons. At any given time, 50% of the population has a chronic condition that involves medical management (Taylor, 2012). These conditions may range from relatively mild ones such as a partial hearing loss to severe and life-threatening disorders, such as cancer, coronary artery disease, and diabetes. These are conditions with which people may live for decades, yet medical facilities are much better designed for dealing with acute disorders that can be cured than they are for dealing with chronic illnesses that can only be managed. Thus, people who have chronic conditions must engage in a great deal of self-management, and so the ways in which they construe their disorders can influence their health behaviors, sense of well-being, and ultimately, the course of illness.

BELIEFS ABOUT CAUSES

People with both acute and chronic disorders often develop theories about where their illnesses or disorders came from (Costanzo, Lutgendorf, Bradley, Rose, & Anderson, 2005). For example, researchers have explored how patients place blame for their disorders: Do they blame themselves, another person, the environment, a quirk of fate, or some other factor?

Self-blame for chronic conditions is common. People frequently perceive themselves as having brought on their disorders through their own actions. In some cases, these perceptions are to a degree correct. Poor health habits, such as smoking and a poor diet or lack of exercise, can contribute to heart disease, stroke, and cancer. But in many cases, self-blame is ill placed, as when a disease is brought on primarily by a genetically based defect or exposure to an infectious or toxic agent. What are the consequences of self-blame? Despite substantial efforts to arrive at a definitive answer to this question, none has been found. Using correlational methods that relate cognitions to distress, some researchers have found that self-blame can lead to guilt, self-recrimination, or depression (Bennett, Compas, Beckjord, & Glinder, 2005). For example, Frazier, Mortensen, and Steward (2005) found that self-blame for a physical assault prompted coping through social withdrawal, which in turn predicted heightened psychological distress. But perceiving the cause of one's disorder as self-generated can also represent an effort to assume control over the disorder. Such feelings can be adaptive in coming to terms with the disorder. It may be that self-blame is adaptive under some circumstances but not others (Schulz & Decker, 1985; Taylor, Lichtman, & Wood, 1984).

Research uniformly suggests, however, that blaming another person for one's disorder is maladaptive (e.g., Affleck, Tennen, Pfeiffer, & Fifield, 1987; Taylor et al., 1984). For example, some patients believe that their disorder was brought on by stress caused by family members, ex-spouses, or colleagues at work. The direction of causality in the observational studies is, however, unclear. Blame of others may be tied to unresolved hostility, which can itself interfere with adjustment to the disease and potentially exacerbate its course.

On the whole, though, causal attributions for one's disorder have not been found to have substantial explanatory value in understanding either psychological adjustment to a disorder or its course. Indeed the focus on causal attributions may simply be misplaced. Although for many disorders, people do come up with causal explanations (98% in one study; Taylor et al., 1984), ultimately people move on, and other types of cognitions may become more important.

Research on causal attributions that has focused on underlying dimensions of attribution, rather than their specific content, has produced more robust conclusions. In a meta-analysis of 27 studies on causal attributions and coping with illness, Roesch and Weiner (2001) found that internal, unstable, or controllable attributions were associated with positive adjustment through greater association with adaptive coping efforts; stable and uncontrollable illness attributions were associated with maladjustment through avoidant coping.

BELIEFS ABOUT CONTROL

Psychological control is the belief that one can determine one's own behavior, influence one's environment, and bring about desired health outcomes (Fiske & Taylor, 1991). It is closely related to self-efficacy, which is the more narrow perception that one has the ability to take the necessary actions to obtain a specific outcome in a specific situation (Bandura, 1977). Both types of beliefs help people manage a wide variety of stressful events (Wrosch, Schulz, Miller, Lupien, & Dunne, 2007). In both experimental studies that manipulate perceived control and studies that examine the relation of spontaneous feelings of control to adjustment, psychological control has been found to be typically associated with better adjustment to stressful events and to physiological outcomes. For example, adolescents with asthma who experience a high sense of control have better immune responses related to their disease (Chen, Fisher, Bacharier, & Strunk, 2003). A high sense of control has been linked to lower risk for mortality as well (Surtees, Wainwright, Luben, Khaw, & Day, 2006).

Control appears to be especially important for people, such as medical patients, children, and elderly people, who are at risk for health problems (Wrosch et al., 2007). For example, in an experimental study with institutionalized elderly participants, Langer and Rodin (1976) assigned half of the participants to a control-enhancing intervention, which involved encouraging them to make choices and decisions and to care for a plant; the other half were assigned to a comparison condition. Those in the control-enhancing group subsequently participated in more group activities, had a greater sense of well-being, and were more alert; moreover, 18 months later, they were judged to be in better health (Rodin & Langer, 1977). Thus, a quite modest intervention to enhance control had enduring, self-sustaining effects in this control-challenged population.

So powerful are the effects of psychological control beliefs that they are now used extensively in interventions to promote good health habits and to help people cope with difficult medical procedures, such as surgery, gastroendoscopic examinations (Johnson & Leventhal, 1974), childbirth (Leventhal, Leventhal, Shacham, & Easterling, 1989), and the management of many other chronic conditions (see Ludwick-Rosenthal, & Neufeld, 1988, for a review). When people are given even modest steps they can take during such an event, such as controlled breathing or rethinking the meaning of a procedure, they cope more successfully with it (Taylor, 2012).

Researchers have also examined whether people who believe they can control their disorders are better off than those who do not see their disorders as under personal control. Indeed, people develop a number of control-related beliefs with respect to disorders. They may believe, as do many cancer patients, that they can prevent a recurrence of a disease through good health habits or even sheer force of will. They may believe that by complying with treatments and physician recommendations, they achieve vicarious control over their illnesses (Helgeson, 1992). They may believe that they have control over illness through self-administration of a treatment regimen. In some cases, these control-related beliefs are true or hold a kernel of truth. For example, if patients faithfully follow a treatment regimen, they may very well exercise real control over the course of their illness. On the other hand, some beliefs, such as the belief that one's illness can be controlled through a positive attitude, may or may not be correct.

Nonetheless, a belief in control and a sense of self-efficacy with respect to a disorder and its treatment are generally adaptive (Thompson, Nanni, & Levine, 1994). Beliefs in control are related to improved adjustment among patients with a broad array of chronic conditions including cancer (Taylor et al., 1984), rheumatoid arthritis (Tennen, Affleck, Urrows, Higgins, & Mendola, 1992), sickle cell disease (Edwards, Telfair, Cecil, & Lenoci, 2001), chronic obstructive pulmonary disease (Kohler, Fish, & Greene, 2002), AIDS (Taylor, Helgeson, Reed, & Skokan, 1991), and many others. Even for patients who are physically or psychologically doing poorly, adjustment is facilitated by beliefs in control (McQuillen, Licht, & Licht, 2003). Thus, perceptions of control appear to be helpful for managing both acute disorders and treatments as well as the long-term management issues that may arise from chronic or advancing illness (Schiaffino

& Revenson, 1992). In fact, a sense of control may actually help to prolong life. For example, a study of patients with chronic obstructive pulmonary disease found that those with high self-efficacy expectations lived longer than those without such expectations (Kaplan, Ries, Prewitt, & Eakin, 1994).

Psychological control is a pivotal concept in health psychology. Much of the research is experimental, manipulating perceived control to the psychological and the biological benefit of the target group, whereas other studies have focused more on self-generated feelings of control. In both cases, the positive relationship between perceptions of control and adjustment has been clear, and evidence continues to mount that biological outcomes are beneficially affected as well.

Illness Representations

People hold cognitive schemas of their illnesses that influence how they manage them (Henderson, Hagger, & Orbell, 2007; Leventhal, Weinman, Leventhal & Phillips, 2008). Termed *illness representations*, these organized conceptions of illness are acquired through the media, through personal experience, and from family and friends (see Croyle & Barger, 1993, for a review). Illness representations can range from being quite sketchy and inaccurate to being extensive, technical, and fairly complete. They lend coherence to a person's understanding of the illness experience, and as such, can influence preventive health behaviors, interpretations of symptoms or diagnosis, adherence to treatment, and expectations for future health (Rabin, Leventhal, & Goodin, 2004).

Most people have at least three conceptions of illness: An acute illness, caused by specific agents that is short in duration with no long-term consequences (e.g., the flu); chronic illness, caused by health habits, possibly genetic predispositions, and environmental factors, which is long in duration, often with long-term and/or severe consequences (e.g., heart disease); and cyclic illness, marked by alternating symptomatic and symptom-free periods (e.g., herpes).

People vary in how they interpret the same disorder. For example, diabetes may be regarded as a cyclical condition by one patient but as a chronic condition by another. One person with hypertension may consider it to be an episodic disorder, whereas another person may recognize its chronic nature. Clearly the person who understands the chronic nature of a serious condition is predisposed to show more appropriate self-management, including following medication regimens, generating appropriate expectations about the future, and interpreting new symptom-related information. Conceptions of illness, thus, have the potential to influence health behavior and long-term health in important ways (Leventhal et al., 2008).

Affective Cognition

In recent years, health psychology research has explored emotion-laden cognitions that may have special relevance in the health domain. This shift in emphasis coincides roughly with a broader change within social cognition, specifically the movement away from an emphasis on cold, nonmotivational processes of inference to more motivational and affective processes (Fiske & Taylor, 1991). Health-related social cognition research has, thus, especially focused on cognitions that have an emotional component, such as pessimistic and optimistic expectations regarding health conditions.

One of the reasons for focusing on cognitions with an affective component stems from the fact that such beliefs often engage physiological and neuroendocrine activity. Under conditions of threat or stress, at least two important systems of the body are engaged. The first is the sympathetic nervous system, which includes indicators such as heart rate and blood pressure. The second is the hypothalamic pituitary adrenal system, which engages stress hormones such as cortisol. Together, these two systems mobilize the body to fend off threats or stress. Over the short term, these are highly protective responses. Over the long term, however, researchers believe that underlying biological damage accumulates (McEwen, 1998). As these biological stress systems are repeatedly engaged in response to challenging or stressful circumstances, the systems may lose their elasticity and ability to respond adaptively to changing circumstances. These systems may develop new higher set points with adverse health consequences, or they may simply lose their resiliency. An example is high blood pressure: In response to repeated engagement of the sympathetic nervous system, blood pressure level may edge up, with the result that over time, a risk for disease, such as hypertension and heart disease, increases. These changes are typically associated with aging, so to the extent that they occur in younger people who are coping with chronically stressful events, these changes may be thought of as representing accelerated aging of biological systems. Adverse changes in immune functioning as a result of chronic exposure to stressful events may also occur. The following sections will often refer to such outcome variables as elevated neuroendocrine activity and elevated cortisol as markers of stress exposure. Elevation or loss of elasticity in these processes does not necessarily mean that disease will result, but it does indicate a likely increased risk of certain health disorders.

Negative Expectations

Certain people are dispositionally predisposed to experience events as particularly stressful, which in turn exacerbates their psychological distress, their physical symptoms, the likelihood of illness, and even whether the illness progresses. This line of research began with exploration of the psychological state, negative affectivity (Watson & Clark, 1984), a pervasive negative mood marked by anxiety, depression, and hostility. People high in negative affectivity (or neuroticism) hold negative expectations about a variety of potential outcomes in their lives, and they express distress, discomfort, and dissatisfaction across a wide range of situations (Gunthert, Cohen, & Armeli, 1999). People high in negative affectivity are more likely to report and experience unpleasant physical symptoms (Cohen, Doyle, Turner, Alper, & Skoner, 2003; Watson & Pennebaker, 1989). Some of this tendency appears to be because they are inwardly focused and catastrophize even minor symptomatic experiences.

But negative affectivity and neuroticism are also related to poor health (e.g., Friedman & Booth-Kewley, 1987). In prospective correlational studies, negative beliefs about the self and the future have been tied to a decline in helper T cells (CD4), an indicator of immune functioning, and the onset of AIDS in people with HIV (Segerstrom, Taylor, Kemeny, Reed, & Visscher, 1996). Negative expectations have also been related to an accelerated course of disease (Ironson et al., 2005; Reed, Kemeny, Taylor, & Visscher, 1999; Reed, Kemeny, Taylor, Wang, & Visscher, 1994). Negative affectivity is associated with elevated cortisol (a stress hormone), and high levels of adrenocortical activity may provide a biopsychosocial pathway that links negative expectations to at least some adverse health outcomes (Polk, Cohen, Doyle, Skoner, & Kirschbaum, 2005). Although these studies are correlational in nature, they are typically prospective over time and demonstrate that the changes in negative beliefs precede, often substantially, changes in health markers. As such, the evidence implies that these beliefs may cause changes in disease status.

Positive Beliefs

Although research has focused somewhat disproportionately on the negative beliefs that exacerbate or result from medical conditions, many people experience positive reactions, such as joy, optimism, or personal growth as they confront the challenging health events in their lives. Typically, these studies identify cognitions that have arisen spontaneously in people dealing with threatening events and examine their relation to adjustment and, in some cases, biological and illness-related outcomes as well. For example, one study (Collins, Taylor, & Skokan, 1990) found that more than 90% of cancer patients reported at least some beneficial changes in their lives as a result of cancer. Similarly, in a study of heart attack patients, more than one third reported that their lives had improved overall (Mohr et al., 1999). Typically, these reported changes include an increased ability to appreciate each day and the inspiration to do things now rather than postpone them. Many people say that they are putting more effort into their relationships and believe that they have acquired more awareness of others' feelings and more empathy and compassion for others. They report feeling stronger and more self-assured as well. Benefit finding has been tied not only to better psychological and social functioning but also to better health outcomes (e.g., Aspinwall & MacNamara, 2005; Danoff-Burg & Revensen, 2005; Low, Stanton, & Danoff-Burg, 2006). For example, in prospective, correlational studies, the ability to find meaning in one's challenging experiences appears to slow declines in CD4 levels among HIV-seropositive men and has been related to a lower likelihood of AIDS-related mortality among people with HIV infection (Bower, Kemeny, Taylor, & Fahey, 1997; Bower, Moskowitz, & Epel, 2009).

One might wonder how people attempting to cope with difficult health-related events manage to achieve a high quality of life and find benefits in their experiences. Some of these experiences reflect an active deploying of certain social cognitions for managing these events. For example, most people perceive some degree of control over what happens to them, hold positive expectations about the future, and have a positive sense of self. These kinds of beliefs are adaptive for mental and physical health much of the time (Taylor, 1983; Taylor & Brown, 1988), but they become especially important when a person first faces a stressful challenge, such as a chronic illness or other major health event. In one investigation, Helgeson (2003) examined these beliefs in men and women treated with angioplasty for coronary artery disease and then followed them over four years. A positive sense of self, perceived control, and optimism about the future not only predicted positive adjustment to the disease but also

a reduced likelihood of sustaining a repeat cardiac event. Other studies have also found positive reactions to be associated with better mental and physical health (Cohen & Pressman, 2006; Pressman & Cohen, 2005). A positive emotional style has been tied to lower cortisol levels (Polk et al., 2005), better immune responses to vaccinations (Marsland, Cohen, Rabin, & Manuck, 2006), resistance to illness following exposure to a flu virus (Cohen, Alper, Doyle, Treanor, & Turner, 2006), and other beneficial health outcomes.

OPTIMISM

Much of the work on positive beliefs has focused on optimism (Scheier, Carver, & Bridges, 1994). Optimism is typically measured using the Life Orientation Task (LOT-R; Scheier et al., 1994), which includes such items as, "In uncertain times, I usually expect the best," and the reverse-coded item, "If something can go wrong for me, it will." Research consistently finds that optimism is associated with better well-being and adjustment to adverse health conditions. For example, prospective correlational research reveals that optimism is protective against the risk of coronary heart disease (Kubzansky, Sparrow, Vokonas, & Kawachi, 2001), the side effects of cancer treatment (De Moor et al., 2006), depression (Bromberger & Matthews, 1996), and cancer mortality among elderly people (Schulz, Bookwala, Knapp, Scheier, & Williamson, 1996), among other beneficial outcomes. Recently, some of the underlying mechanisms whereby optimism may affect such positive outcomes have been uncovered. Optimists have a more positive mood, which itself may promote a state of physiological resilience. Optimism may also promote more active and persistent coping efforts, which may improve long-term prospects for well-being and physical health (Segerstrom, Taylor, Kemeny, & Fahey, 1998). Optimists appear to appraise potentially stressful situations more positively and seem especially prone to making favorable appraisals that their resources will be sufficient to overcome any threat (Chang, 1998). In turn, optimists may not only experience lower levels of stress on the psychological level but also experience less wear and tear on the biological systems that underlie stress responses. These processes in turn may improve health.

The health domain has provided a valuable venue for understanding the dynamics of optimism. Specifically, concerns had been expressed as to whether optimism keeps people from confronting negative events and information that would be useful to them (Weinstein & Klein, 1995). In a study that examined this hypothesis, Aspinwall and Brunhart (1996) found that optimistic beliefs about one's health predicted greater, not less, attention to risk-related information than to neutral information and greater recall of risk-related information, especially when the information was self-relevant. Thus, being optimistic may actually increase rather than decrease receptivity to personally relevant negative threat–related health information.

Social Cognition and Coping

As the previous sections have suggested, many of the social cognitions that people develop in response to health disorders enable them to cope more effectively, an issue to which we turn more explicitly here.

Approach–Avoidance

Numerous frameworks for understanding coping have been advanced (for a review, see Skinner, Edge, Altman, & Sherwood, 2003), but one central distinction is approach versus avoidance coping. Reflecting a core motivational construct (e.g., Davidson, Jackson, & Kalin, 2000) that is central to social cognition research, the approach–avoidance continuum maps easily onto broader theories of biobehavioral functioning. Approach-oriented coping, sometimes called active, confrontative, or vigilant coping, involves gathering information or taking direct action with respect to stressful events, problem solving, seeking social support, and creating outlets for emotional expression. Avoidant coping involves withdrawing from, minimizing, or avoiding stressful events.

Although neither style is necessarily more effective for managing stressful events, inasmuch as each has advantages and liabilities, on the whole avoidant coping has proved to be generally unsuccessful. The empirical literature suggests that coping through avoidance can be useful in some specific situations, particularly those that are short-term and uncontrollable (Suls & Fletcher, 1985); however, over the long term, avoidance coping is not helpful. Attempting to avoid thoughts and feelings surrounding persistent problems predicts elevated distress across a variety of stressful events (Taylor & Stanton, 2007). And as Wegner's work on ironic processes suggests (e.g., Wegner, Schneider, Carter, & White, 1987), avoidance is not always successful, with reminders of stressful events breaking through into consciousness. Avoidance-oriented coping also predicts lower adherence to medical regimens, greater viral load in

HIV-seropositive individuals (Weaver et al., 2005), more risky behaviors in HIV-seropositive individuals (Avants, Warburton, & Margolin, 2001), increased physical symptoms among caregivers (Billings, Folkman, Acree, & Moskowitz, 2000), compromised recovery from surgery (Stephens, Druley, & Zautra, 2002), and compromised recovery of function (Stephens et al., 2002; see Taylor & Stanton, 2007, for a review). Avoidant behavior under stress has been tied to heightened neuroendocrine activity as well (e.g., Roelofs, Elzinga, & Rotteveel, 2005; Rosenberger, Ickovics, Epel, D'Entremont, & Jokl, 2004); this is important because many medical scientists and health psychologists believe that exposure to heightened neuroendocrine activity has cumulative adverse effects that may contribute to such disorders as heart disease, hypertension, and cancers. Passive avoidant coping has also been tied to tumor development in animal models. For example, Vegas, Fano, Brain, Alonso, and Azpiroz (2006) found that mice who dealt with aggressive encounters with other mice through absence of attack, subordinate behavior, and little exploration were more likely to develop metastases in response to tumor implantation than were mice who responded more aggressively. Findings such as these suggest a potential role for avoidance in the exacerbation of some illnesses. Although most of this research is correlational, much is prospective, controlling for time 1 levels of the outcome variable. Findings are somewhat less consistent for approach coping, but generally, approach coping leads to better psychological and physical functioning in stressful circumstances (e.g., Billings et al., 2000; Keefe et al., 1997).

The Self and Health Outcomes

The self has been one of the central topics of social cognition research, and not surprisingly, many of the findings have applicability to coping processes. Theories of the self, including self-affirmation theory (Steele, 1988) and cognitive adaptation theory (Taylor, 1983), posit that affirmation or enhancement of the self can buffer an individual against the adverse effects of stress. These hypotheses have been widely tested both experimentally through interventions that shore up a sense of self and correlationally by looking at differences between people who hold or do not hold self-enhancing cognitions. Consistent with this reasoning, Taylor, Lerner, Sherman, Sage, and McDowell (2003) found that relative to their peers, people who enhanced their personal qualities had lower basal cortisol levels and lower cardiovascular responses to a laboratory stress challenge than those who did not (see also Seery, Blascovich, Weisbuch, & Vick, 2004); these effects are potentially important because they imply a protective effect of self-enhancement on biological stress responses, which, as noted, may have cumulative adverse effect on health.

These findings also suggest that self-affirmation may be an effective intervention for helping people deal with stressful events. In a test of this hypothesis, Creswell, Welch, Taylor, Sherman, Gruenewald, and Mann (2005), assigned participants either to complete a self-affirmation task (writing about a personally important value) or to complete a control task (writing about a less important value) before participating in a laboratory stress challenge (counting backward by 13s as rapidly as possible and delivering a talk to an unresponsive audience). Those who had affirmed their values had significantly lower cortisol responses to stress compared with control participants. Self-esteem moderated the relationship between self-affirmation and psychological stress responses, such that people with high dispositional self-esteem and optimism who affirmed their personal values reported the least stress. Thus, reflecting on personal values through self-affirmation can help to keep neuroendocrine as well as psychological responses to stress at low levels. Similarly, affirmation of personal values can attenuate perceptions of threat (Sherman & Cohen, 2002), reduce ruminative thought after failure (Koole, Smeets, van Knippenberg, & Dijksterhuis, 1999), and reduce defensive responses to threatening information (Sherman, Nelson, & Steele, 2000).

The self-affirmation perspective has also been used to construct effective communications to change health behaviors (Sherman et al., 2000). When people have affirmed important self-related values, they are more receptive to health information that might otherwise be threatening. This principle has been used to influence receptivity to communications about vulnerability to breast cancer, risk for HIV, and risks to oral health (Sherman, Updegraff, & Mann, 2008).

Social Cognition, Social Interaction, and Health

Thus far, the social cognition research discussed has focused heavily on how individuals construe health-related circumstances. This individualistic emphasis is consistent with much early research in social cognition and has persisted even as affectively based social cognition has become a more central focus of the field. However, social cognitions become especially significant in social interaction, and we now turn to some of the evidence that bears on this issue.

Disclosure and Writing

Considerable research has examined the impact of disclosing emotional experiences, often through talking or writing interventions, and the beneficial effects on health that can result. The rationale for benefits of disclosure stem from several factors. One such factor involves the benefits of clarifying emotional states. This type of coping is called *emotional approach coping*, and it involves focusing on and working through emotional experiences in conjunction with a stressor (Stanton, Danoff-Burg, Cameron, & Ellis, 1994). Emotional approach coping has been shown to improve adjustment to a broad array of chronic conditions. Even managing the normal stressors of daily life can benefit from emotional approach coping (Stanton, Kirk, Cameron, & Danoff-Burg, 2000).

Writing about or otherwise disclosing personal stressors or traumas may also lend cognitive clarity to the process of working through such events, helping people to organize their thoughts, understand their reactions better, and find meaning in them (Lepore, Ragan, & Jones, 2000). Talking with others may allow one to gain information about an event or about effective coping and may also elicit support from others. In an early study, Pennebaker and Beall (1986) had 46 undergraduates write either about the most traumatic and stressful event of their lives or about a trivial topic. Although people writing about traumas were more upset right after they had written their essays, they showed improvement in their health during the following six months. Generally speaking, the findings of studies on writing interventions include immediate psychological distress but long-term improvements in health and in some cases well-being (Lepore & Smyth, 2002). For example, Pennebaker, Hughes, and O'Heeron (1987) found that when people talked about traumatic events, their skin conductance, heart rate, and blood pressure all decreased. Writing interventions can also have beneficial long-term effects on immune functioning (e.g., Petrie, Booth, Pennebaker, Davison, & Thomas, 1995). So well established is the value of this method that interventions show improved health among AIDS patients (Petrie, Fontanilla, Thomas, Booth, & Pennebaker, 2004), breast cancer patients (Stanton et al., 2002), asthma and rheumatoid arthritis patients, as well as those with other conditions (Norman, Lumly, Duley, & Diamond, 2004).

Construal of Social Relationships and Support

How people construe their social relationships and whether or not they regard them as supportive is one of the most important psychosocial resources that protects against the ravages of stress. Social support is defined as information from others that one is loved and cared for, esteemed and valued, and part of a network of communication and mutual obligations (Wills, 1991). The effects of social support on health outcomes are extremely well established and powerful. Indeed, the effect size of social support in predictive studies of morbidity and mortality is at least as strong as that for smoking and lipid levels, among other well-established risk factors for chronic illness and mortality (House, Landis, & Umberson, 1988).

Early in the study of social support, researchers focused heavily on the number of people in a person's network, how interconnected they are, and how emotionally close to the recipient they are. Research by health psychologists also focused heavily on explicit socially supportive exchanges during which one person gives aid, advice, or emotional support to another. What has become increasingly clear, however, is that the construal of social support and not its actuality is most important. In other words, the social cognitions people hold about their relationships play a substantial role in how effective social support is.

Moreover, it has become evident that both attempts to extract social support from others and interpersonal interactions intended to convey social support can backfire. Would-be support providers may fail to provide the kind of support that is needed and may react instead in an unsupportive manner that aggravates stressful events (Rook, 1984). When social support is provided by another person, it may undermine the self-confidence, self-esteem, or self-perceived resourcefulness of the recipient. Consequently, in some cases, invisible support, namely support that is reported to have been provided by a provider but not perceived by the recipient, may be more effective than support that is conveyed in more obvious form (e.g., Bolger, Zuckerman, & Kessler, 2000). Receiving support from another person without realizing it may provide the benefits of support without undermining important self-related cognitions, such as self-confidence or autonomy.

Following from this is the observation that the mere perception of social support, whether or not it is actually present or actually utilized, can be stress reducing, with concomitant benefits for well-being. In fact, beliefs about the availability of support appear to exert stronger effects on mental health outcomes than the actual receipt of social support does (Thoits, 1995). Thus, in important respects, people carry their social support networks around in their heads, as social cognitions, to buffer them against stress without ever having to recruit their networks in active ways. In so doing, they appear to largely reap the benefits of social support without incurring its potential costs.

Insights such as these have prompted efforts to identify evidence at the neural level to identify the pathways by which social support achieves its beneficial effects. To chart a potential route, Eisenberger and colleagues (Eisenberger, Taylor, Gable, Hilmert, & Lieberman, 2007) assessed participants' social support as experienced over a nine-day period; at the end of each of the nine days, participants reported on how socially supportive their experiences had been, and then a measure of social support was created by summing across the nine days. At a second point in time, their brains were scanned while they participated in a virtual social task in the scanner, during which they were gradually excluded from the social interaction; this paradigm has previously been found to provoke significant social distress that is correlated with activity in the dorsal anterior cingulate cortex (dACC) (Eisenberger, Lieberman, & Williams, 2003), a region of the brain that monitors threat. At a third point in time, participants completed stressful tasks in the laboratory. People who reported more experiences of social support during the preceding nine days had lower dACC activity in response to the virtual social exclusion task and exhibited lower cortisol responses during the stress tasks. Individual differences in dACC during the exclusion task mediated the relationship between social support and cortisol reactivity. These findings are important because they identify an underlying pathway from the construal of daily social support through the brain's response to social interaction to neuroendocrine activity, which, as noted, may be implicated in illness.

In summary, then, how people construe the social environment—specifically, whether they regard it as supportive or not—has strong and consistent effects on health; the neural and neuroendocrine pathways by which these construals affect health outcomes are becoming increasingly well understood.

Linking Cognition to Neural and Physiological Functioning

As may be apparent from the preceding example, just as social cognition research has moved increasingly toward social cognitive neuroscience using such techniques as fMRI (Fiske & Taylor, 2008), so, too, have applications to health psychology moved in that direction. This has been a productive line of research for several reasons. Knowledge of the neural underpinnings by which social cognitions may exert protective effects on mental and physical health outcomes may not only suggest strategies for interventions but also suggest criteria by which interventions may be evaluated, as by identifying whether activity in particular brain regions is affected by interventions.

Addressing these pathways requires a bit of background regarding brain regions involved in the experience of stress. The amygdala and the dACC are associated with threat detection, serving an alarm function that mobilizes other neural regions, such as the lateral prefrontal cortex (LPFC) and hypothalamus, to promote adaptive responses to stress. The amygdala is especially sensitive to environmental cues signaling danger or novelty (e.g., Hariri, Bookheimer, & Mazziotta, 2000). The dACC serves as a threat detector, responding to conflict in incoming information (Carter et al., 2000) and to social distress (Eisenberger et al., 2003).

Once activated, these neural threat detectors set into motion a cascade of responses through projections to the hypothalamus and the lateral prefrontal cortex aimed at amplifying or attenuating the threat signal and enabling a person to prepare to respond to the threat. For example, links to the hypothalamus are likely to have downstream effects on both sympathetic and hypothalamic pituitary adrenal responses to threat, both of which are activated in response to stressors.

A neural region that appears critical for regulating the magnitude of these biological and neural responses to stress is the ventrolateral prefrontal cortex (vlPFC; Hariri et al., 2000; Ochsner et al., 2004). Specifically, activation of the right vlPFC can directly down-regulate activation of the amygdala and the dACC, so it can be thought of, at least in part, as a self-regulatory structure that modulates the reactivity of brain regions that respond to stress.

The neural bases of threat detection and regulation are important to studying health because they provide clues to how coping processes regulate psychological and biological health-related outcomes. For example, people with strong coping resources may show lower amygdala and/or dACC reactivity to threatening stimuli. Alternatively, they may show stronger vlPFC responses to threatening stimuli. A third possibility is that strong coping resources may be manifested in the relation between the vlPFC and threat-responsive regions; specifically, a strong negative correlation would suggest better regulation of threat responsivity by the vlPFC. As already noted, perceived social support influences downstream stress responses by modulating neurocognitive reactivity to stress, which in turn attenuates neuroendocrine stress responses (Eisenberger et al., 2007).

In an fMRI investigation, Taylor, Burklund, Eisenberger, Lehman, Hilmert, and Lieberman (2008) explored the ways in which health-related cognitions, including optimism, personal control, and a positive sense of self, beneficially affect stress responses. Two hypotheses were examined: first, that psychosocial resources are tied to decreased sensitivity to threat; and second, that coping-related resources are associated with enhanced prefrontal inhibition of threat responses during threat regulation. Using fMRI, this study found that these health-related cognitions were associated with greater right vlPFC activity and less amygdala activity during a threat regulation task. These cognitions were also related to lower cortisol responses to laboratory stressors. Mediational analyses suggested that the relation of these cognitions to lower cortisol reactivity was mediated by lower amygdala activity during threat regulation. Thus, this study suggests that health-related cognitions may be associated with lower biological stress responses (cortisol) by means of enhanced inhibition of threat responses during threat regulation and not by diminished perceptions of threat.

Interventions

Social cognition research has generated a variety of interventions that have helped people to manage stressful events more successfully, predicting better well-being and better health. The clearest examples of these intervention benefits have perhaps been the writing interventions already referred to. For example, one intervention (Mann, 2001) assigned HIV-seropositive women to write about positive events that would happen in the future or to complete a control writing task. Among participants who were initially low in optimism, the writing intervention led to increased optimism, self-reported increases in adherence to medications, and less distress from medication side effects. These findings suggest that a future-oriented positive writing intervention may be a useful technique for decreasing distress and increasing adherence, especially for initially pessimistic people.

Social cognition research on attitudes is likely to be a continuing influence on interventions. Ajzen's theory of planned behavior has been the most influential recent theoretical approach to understanding health behaviors for several reasons. First, it provides a model that links social cognitions directly to behavior. Second, it provides a fine-grained picture of intentions with respect to a particular health habit. Third, it predicts a broad array of health behaviors, including condom use, sunscreen use, and use of oral contraceptives, among many other health behaviors, as well as the intention to change health behaviors (Ajzen, 2002; Taylor, 2012). As such, it provides guidelines for the development of interventions to change health habits, as by targeting particular cognitions for modification.

Stress management interventions draw significantly on social cognition for their efficacy. In these interventions (Taylor, 2012), participants are first taught to identify and verbalize the stressors in their lives. In the self-monitoring phase that follows, participants monitor their behavior in response to stress to identify emotional and cognitive responses to stress. Participants are then taught how to chart their stress responses, to examine the antecedent conditions under which they experience stress. For example, one person may feel substantial stress is response to a deadline at work, although another individual might regard the same circumstances as challenging. Identifying negative self-talk and modifying these cognitions is an important phase of the stress management process as well. That is, people can undermine their ability to manage their stress by mentally rehearsing failure or dwelling on the prospect of being overwhelmed.

As participants experience a sense of control over their stressors, the antecedents, and how they respond to them, they are able gradually to introduce coping techniques for managing stress. These include reappraising stressful events as less so, identifying the personal and social resources they can use to combat stressful events, and reassuring themselves that, as persons of worth with skills and talents, they will be able to manage stress more successfully.

Participants then set explicit goals for managing stress, engage in positive self-talk, and use self-instruction to combat the specific stressors that they encounter. Self-instruction involves reminding oneself of specific steps that are required to achieve the goals, and positive self-talk involves providing oneself with specific encouragements. Although stress management interventions draw on principles of cognitive behavior therapy, the degree to which these therapies and their implementation in health settings have their basis in social cognition is clear.

Future Directions

The scope of health psychology issues to which social cognition interventions have been directed has been relatively modest to date, and the potential to expand such interventions is substantial. For example, one of the biggest problems in patient care is remarkably low levels of adherence to treatment recommendations. Even the most casual exposure to patient–practitioner communication issues, however, suggests that basic principles of social cognition could help to address this problem. Consider the context in which treatment recommendations are dispensed. In traditional medical practice, a patient who is anxious about his or her health and is no doubt distracted as a result is expected to attend to and remember a physician's outline of the details of care. The person may then be sent home, sometimes with a prescription that says no more than "Take as directed." An examination of the literature on patient–practitioner communications indicates that suggestions such as "write down the regimen" and "test the patient for recall" qualify as breakthroughs in this problem area (Taylor, 2012). It seems likely that insights from such social cognition research as busyness (Gilbert, Pelham, & Krull, 1988), memory, dual processing, and the impact of emotion on cognitive processing could be fruitfully employed to design practitioner communications with patients and the construction of aids to recall for patients. Many health messages are likely to be processed peripherally, in highly busy conditions. What constitutes an effective message may be informed by insights from these literatures. By contrast, if a health care provider has a patient's undivided attention, the message may be processed centrally. To date, these literatures have not been exploited for their health potential. This is but one example of a potential expanding role for social cognition-based interventions in health psychology.

A second likely direction for future expansion of social cognition perspectives concerns interventions to change health habits. As behaviorally related conditions such as smoking, obesity, alcoholism, and unsafe sex are increasingly shown to be vital links in growing health care costs worldwide, developing persuasive communications, educational programs, and other interventions to alter these conditions before they lead to pathology will assume increasing importance.

In addition to an expanding role in designing health-related interventions, social cognition perspectives on health-related issues are likely to expand in a growing number of basic research directions. Chief among these will be research on the pathways that connect beliefs, emotions, and behaviors to mental and physical health outcomes through neural, neuroendocrine, and immune pathways. Research has begun to illuminate these links, but much remains to be learned.

Conclusion

Social cognition perspectives have greatly enhanced the understanding of how people manage their health. The benefits go in both directions. Health psychology as a field has been heavily influenced by social cognition perspectives, as the previous sections attest, and as health psychology research has incorporated new techniques that identify neural underpinnings of health-related phenomena, these insights and methods have moved into social cognition as well. What the health domain gives back to social cognition is knowledge of biological outcomes and the potential psychobiological routes whereby social cognition interventions may exert their effects on biology and ultimately on health. By understanding the neural, neuroendocrine, and immune pathways by which beliefs affect biological functioning, health psychology fleshes out the pathways by which social cognition affects biology more generally. In so doing, the health domain helps to bring social cognition research into the forefront of integrative science that links social, cognitive, and biological perspectives.

Author Note

Preparation of this manuscript was supported by a grant from the National Institute of Aging (AG030309).

References

Affleck, G., Tennen, H., Pfeiffer, C., & Fifield, C. (1987). Appraisals of control and predictability in adapting to a chronic disease. *Journal of Personality and Social Psychology, 53,* 273–279.

Ajzen, I. (2002). Perceived behavioral control, self-efficacy, locus of control, and the theory of planned behavior. *Journal of Applied Social Psychology, 32,* 665–683.

Ajzen, I., & Madden, T. J. (1986). Prediction of goal-directed behavior: Attitudes, intentions, and perceived behavioral control. *Journal of Experimental Social Psychology, 22,* 453–474.

Apanovitch, A. M., McCarthy, D., & Salovey, P. (2003). Using message framing to motivate HIV testing among low-income, ethnic minority women. *Health Psychology, 22,* 60–67.

Aspinwall, L. G., & Brunhart, S. M. (1996). Distinguishing optimism from denial: Optimistic beliefs predict attention to health threats. *Personality and Social Psychology Bulletin, 22,* 993–1003.

Aspinwall, L. G., & MacNamara, A. (2005). Taking positive changes seriously: Toward a positive psychology of cancer survivorship and resilience. *Cancer, 104*(11 Suppl), 2549–2556.

Avants, S. K., Warburton, L. A., & Margolin, A. (2001). How injection drug users coped with testing HIV-seropositive: Implications for subsequent health-related behaviors. *AIDS Education and Prevention, 13,* 207–218.

Bandura, A. (1977). Self-efficacy: Toward a unifying theory of behavioral change. *Psychological Review, 84,* 191–215.

Bennett, K. K., Compas, B. E., Beckjord, E., & Glinder, J. G. (2005). Self-blame and distress among women with newly diagnosed breast cancer. *Journal of Behavioral Medicine, 28,* 313–323.

Billings, D. W., Folkman, S., Acree, M., & Moskowitz, J. T. (2000). Coping and physical health during caregiving: The roles of positive and negative affect. *Journal of Personality and Social Psychology, 79,* 131–142.

Bolger, N., Zuckerman, A., & Kessler, R. C. (2000). Invisible support and adjustment to stress. *Journal of Personality and Social Psychology, 79,* 953–961.

Bower, J. E., Kemeny, M. E., Taylor, S. E., & Fahey, J. L. (1997). Cognitive processing, discovery of meaning, CD4 decline, and AIDS-related mortality among bereaved HIV-seropositive men. *Journal of Consulting and Clinical Psychology, 66,* 979–986.

Bower, J. E., Moskowitz, J. T., & Epel, E. (2009). Is benefit finding good for your health? Pathways linking positive life changes after stress and physical health outcomes. *Current Directions in Psychological Science, 18,* 337–341.

Bromberger, J. T., & Matthews, K. A. (1996). A longitudinal study of the effects of pessimism, trait anxiety, and life stress on depressive symptoms in middle-aged women. *Psychology and Aging, 11,* 207–213.

Carter, C. S., MacDonald, A. W., Botvinick, M. M., Ross, L. L., Stenger, V. A., Noll, D., et al. (2000). Parsing executive processes: Strategic vs. evaluative functions of the anterior cingulate cortex. *Proceedings of the National Academy of the Sciences, 97,*1944–1948.

Chang, E. C. (1998). Dispositional optimism and primary and secondary appraisal of a stressor: Controlling for confounding influences and relations to coping and psychological and physical adjustment. *Journal of Personality and Social Psychology, 74,* 1109–1120.

Chang, E. C. (Ed.). (2001). *Optimism and pessimism: Implications for theory, research, and practice.* Washington, DC: American Psychological Association.Chen, E., Fisher, E. B., Bacharier, L. B., & Strunk, R. C. (2003). Socioeconomic status, stress, and immune markers in adolescents with asthma. *Psychosomatic Medicine, 65,* 984–992.

Chua, H. F., Liberzon, I., Welsh, R. C., & Strecher, V. J. (2009). Neural correlates of message tailoring and self-relatedness in smoking cessation programming. *Biological Psychiatry, 65,* 165–168.

Clarke, V. A., Lovegrove, H., Williams, A., & Macpherson, M. (2000). Unrealistic optimism and the health belief model. *Journal of Behavioral Medicine, 23,* 367–376.

Cohen, S., Alper, C. M., Doyle, W. J., Treanor, J. J., & Turner, R. B. (2006). Positive emotional style predicts resistance to illness after experimental exposure to rhinovirus or influenza A virus. *Psychosomatic Medicine, 68*, 809–815.

Cohen, S., Doyle, W. J., Turner, R. B., Alper, C. M., & Skoner, D. P. (2003). Emotional style and susceptibility to the common cold. *Psychosomatic Medicine, 65*, 652–657.

Cohen, S., & Pressman, S. D. (2006). Positive affect and health. *Current Directions in Psychological Science, 15*, 122–125.

Collins, R. L., Taylor, S. E., & Skokan, L. A. (1990). A better world or a shattered vision? Changes in perspectives following victimization. *Social Cognition, 8*, 263–285.

Costanzo, E. S., Lutgendorf, S. K., Bradley, S. L., Rose, S. L., & Anderson, B. (2005). Cancer attributions, distress, and health practices among gynecologic cancer survivors. *Psychosomatic Medicine, 67*, 972–980.

Creswell, J. D., Welch, W. T., Taylor, S. E., Sherman, D. K., Gruenewald, T., & Mann, T. (2005). Affirmation of personal values buffers neuroendocrine and psychological stress responses. *Psychological Science, 16*, 846–851.

Croyle, R. T., & Barger, S. D. (1993). Illness cognition. In S. Maes, H. Leventhal, & M. Johnston (Eds.), *International Review of Health Psychology* (Vol. 2, pp. 29–49). New York: Wiley.

Danoff-Burg, S., & Revenson, T. A. (2005). Benefit-finding among patients with rheumatoid arthritis: Positive effects on interpersonal relationships. *Journal of Behavioral Medicine, 28*, 91–103.

Davidson, R. J., Jackson, D. C., & Kalin, N. H. (2000). Emotion, plasticity, context, and regulation: Perspectives from affective neuroscience. *Psychological Bulletin, 129*, 890–909.

De Moor, J. S., De Moor, C. A., Basen-Engquist, K., Kudelka, A., Bevers, M. W., & Cohen, L. (2006). Optimism, distress, health-related quality of life, and change in cancer antigen 125 among patients with ovarian cancer undergoing chemotherapy. *Psychosomatic Medicine, 68*, 555–562.

Edwards, R., Telfair, J., Cecil, H., & Lenoci, J. (2001). Self-efficacy as a predictor of adult adjustment to sickle cell disease: One-year outcomes. *Psychosomatic Medicine, 63*, 850–858.

Eisenberger, N. I., Lieberman, M. D., & Williams, K. D. (2003). Does rejection hurt? An fMRI study of social exclusion. *Science, 302*, 290–292.

Eisenberger, N. I., Taylor, S. E., Gable, S. L., Hilmert, C. J., & Lieberman, M. D. (2007). Neural pathways link social support to attenuated neuroendocrine stress responses. *NeuroImage, 35*, 1601–1612.

Falk, E. B., Berkman, E. T., Mann, T., Harrison, B., & Lieberman, M. D. (2010). Predicting persuasion-induced behavior change from the brain. *The Journal of Neuroscience: The Official Journal of the Society for Neuroscience, 30*, 8421–8424.

Fiske, S. T., & Taylor, S. E. (1991). *Social cognition* (2nd ed.). New York: McGraw-Hill.

Fiske, S. T., & Taylor, S. E. (2008). *Social cognition: From brains to culture.* New York: McGraw-Hill.

Fishbein, M., & Ajzen, I. (1975). *Belief, attitude, intention, and behavior: An introduction to theory and research.* Reading, MA: Addison-Wesley.

Frazier, P. A., Mortensen, H., & Steward, J. (2005). Coping strategies as mediators of the relations among perceived control and distress in sexual assault survivors. *Journal of Counseling Psychology, 52*, 267–278.

Friedman, H. S., & Booth-Kewley, S. (1987). The "disease-prone" personality: A meta-analytic view of the construct. *American Psychologist, 42*, 539–555.

Gilbert, D. T., Pelham, B. W., & Krull, D. S. (1988). On cognitive busyness: When person perceivers meet persons perceived. *Journal of Personality and Social Psychology, 54*, 733–740.

Gunthert, K. C., Cohen, L. H., & Armeli, S. (1999). The role of neuroticism in daily stress and coping. *Journal of Personality and Social Psychology, 77*, 1087–1100.

Halpern-Felsher, B. L., Millstein, S. G., Ellen, J. M., Adler, N. E., Tschann, J. M., & Biehl, M. (2001). The role of behavioral experience in judging risks. *Health Psychology, 20*, 120–126.

Hariri, A. R., Bookheimer, S. Y., & Mazziotta, J. C. (2000). Modulating emotional responses: Effects of a neocortical network on the limbic system. *NeuroReport, 11*, 43–48.

Helgeson, V. S. (1992). Moderators of the relation between perceived control and adjustment to chronic illness. *Journal of Personality and Social Psychology, 63*, 656–666.

Helgeson, V. S. (2003). Cognitive adaptation, psychological adjustment and disease progression among angioplasty patients: 4 years later. *Health Psychology, 22*, 30–38.

Henderson, C. J., Hagger, M. S., & Orbell, S. (2007). Does priming a specific illness schema result in an attentional information-processing bias for specific illnesses? *Health Psychology, 26*, 165–173.

House, J. S., Landis, K. R., & Umberson, D. (1988). Social relationships and health. *Science, 241*, 540–545.

Ironson, G., O'Cleirigh, C., Fletcher, M., Laurenceau, J. P., Balbin, E., Klimas, N., et al. (2005). Psychosocial factors predict CD4 and viral load change in men and women with human immunodeficiency virus in the era of highly active antiretroviral treatment. *Psychosomatic Medicine, 67*, 1013–1021.

Johnson, J. E., & Leventhal, H. (1974). Effects of accurate expectations and behavioral instructions on reactions during a noxious medical examination. *Journal of Personality and Social Psychology, 29*, 710–718.

Kaplan, R. M., Ries, A. L., Prewitt, L. M., & Eakin, E. (1994). Self-efficacy expectations predict survival for patients with chronic obstructive pulmonary disease. *Health Psychology, 13*, 366–368.

Keefe, F. J., Affleck, G., Lefebvre, J. C., Starr, K., Caldwell, D. J., & Tennen, H. (1997). Pain coping strategies and coping efficacy in rheumatoid arthritis: A daily process analysis. *Pain, 69*, 35–42.

Kohler, C. L., Fish, L., & Greene, P. G. (2002). The relationship of perceived self-efficacy to quality of life in chronic obstructive pulmonary disease. *Health Psychology, 21*, 610–614.

Koole, S. L., Smeets, K., van Knippenberg, A., & Dijksterhuis, A. (1999). The cessation of rumination through self-affirmation. *Journal of Personality and Social Psychology, 77*, 111–125.

Kubzansky, L. D., Sparrow, D., Vokonas, P., & Kawachi, I. (2001). Is the glass half empty or half full? A prospective study of optimism and coronary heart disease in the normative aging study. *Psychosomatic Medicine, 63*, 910–916.

Langer, E. J., & Rodin, J. (1976). The effects of choice and enhanced personal responsibility for the aged: A field experiment in an institutional setting. *Journal of Personality and Social Psychology, 34*, 191–198.

Lazarus, R. S. (1968). Emotions and adaptation: Conceptual and empirical relations. In W. Arnold (Ed.), *Nebraska symposium on motivation* (pp. 175–266). Lincoln, NE: University of Nebraska Press.

Lazarus, R. S., & Folkman, S. (1984). *Stress, appraisal, and coping.* New York: Springer.

Lazarus, R. S., & Launier, R. (1978). Stress-related transactions between person and environment. In L. A. Pervin & M. Lewis (Eds.), *Internal and external determinants of behavior* (pp. 287–327). New York: Plenum Press.

Lepore, S. J., Ragan, J. D., & Jones, S. (2000). Talking facilitates cognitive-emotional processes of adaptation to an acute stressor. *Journal of Personality and Social Psychology, 78*, 499–508.

Lepore, S. J., & Smyth, J. (Eds.). (2002). *The writing cure: How expressive writing influences health and well-being.* Washington, DC: American Psychological Association.

Leventhal, E. A., Leventhal, H., Schacham, S., & Easterling, D. V. (1989). Active coping reduces reports of pain from childbirth. *Journal of Consulting and Clinical Psychology, 57*, 365–371.

Leventhal, H., Weinman, J., Leventhal, E. A., & Phillips, L. A. (2008). Health psychology: The search for pathways between behavior and health. *Annual Review of Psychology, 59*, 477–505.

Liberman, A., & Chaiken, S. (1992). Defensive processing of personally relevant health messages. *Personality and Social Psychology Bulletin, 18*, 669–679.

Low, C. A., Stanton, A. L., & Danoff-Burg, S. (2006). Expressive disclosure and benefit finding among breast cancer patients: mechanisms for positive health effects. *Health Psychology, 25*, 181–189.

Ludwick-Rosenthal, R., & Neufeld, R. W. J. (1988). Stress management during noxious medical procedures: An evaluative review of outcome studies. *Psychological Bulletin, 104*, 326–342.

Mann, T. (2001). Effects of future writing and optimism on health behaviors in HIV-infected women. *Annals of Behavioral Medicine, 23*, 26–33.

Mann, T., Sherman, D., & Updegraff, J. (2005). Dispositional motivations and message framing: A test of the congruency hypothesis in college students. *Health Psychology, 23*, 330–334.

Marsland, A. L., Cohen, S., Rabin, B. S., & Manuck, S. B. (2006). Trait positive affect and antibody response to hepatitis B vaccination. *Brain, Behavior, and Immunity, 20*, 261–269.

McCaul, K. D., Johnson, R. J., & Rothman, A. J. (2002). The effects of framing and action instructions on whether older adults obtain flu shots. *Health Psychology, 21*, 624–628.

McEwen, B. S. (1998). Protective and damaging effects of stress mediators. *New England Journal of Medicine, 338*, 171–179.

McQuillen, A. D., Licht, M. H., & Licht, B. G. (2003). Contributions of disease severity and perceptions of primary and secondary control to the prediction of psychological adjustment to Parkinson's disease. *Health Psychology, 22*, 504–512.

Mohr, D. C., Dick, L. P., Russo, D., Pinn, J., Boudewyn, A. C., Likosky, W., et al. (1999). The psychological impact of multiple sclerosis: Exploring the patient's perspective. *Health Psychology, 18*, 376–382.

Norman, S. A., Lumly, M. A., Duley, J. A., & Diamond, M. P. (2004). For whom does it work? Moderators of the effects of written emotional disclosure in a randomized trial among women with chronic pelvic pain. *Psychosomatic Medicine, 66*, 174–183.

Ochsner, K. N., Ray, R. D., Cooper, J. C., Robertson, E. R., Chopra, S., Gabrieli, J. D. E., et al. (2004). For better or for worse: Neural systems supporting the cognitive down-and-up-regulation of negative emotion. *NeuroImage, 23*, 483–499.

Pennebaker, J. W., & Beall, S. (1986). Confronting a traumatic event: Toward an understanding of inhibition and disease. *Journal of Abnormal Psychology, 95*, 274–281.

Pennebaker, J. W., Hughes, C., & O'Heeron, R. C. (1987). The psychophysiology of confession: Linking inhibitory and psychosomatic processes. *Journal of Personality and Social Psychology, 52*, 781–793.

Petrie, K. J., Booth, R. J., Pennebaker, J. W., Davison, K. P., & Thomas, M. G. (1995). Disclosure of trauma and immune response to a hepatitis B vaccination program. *Journal of Consulting and Clinical Psychology, 63*, 787–792.

Petrie, K. J., Fontanilla, I., Thomas, M. G., Booth, R. J., & Pennebaker, J. W. (2004). Effect of written emotional expression on immune function in patients with human immunodeficiency virus infection: A randomized trial. *Psychosomatic Medicine, 66*, 272–275.

Petty, R. E., & Cacioppo, J. T. (1984). The effects of involvement on responses to argument quantity and quality: Central and peripheral routes to persuasion. *Journal of Personality and Social Psychology, 46*, 69–81.

Polk, D. E., Cohen, S., Doyle, W. J., Skoner, D. P., & Kirschbaum, C. (2005). State and trait affect as predictors of salivary cortisol in healthy adults. *Psychoneuroendocrinology, 30*, 261–272.

Pressman, S. D., & Cohen, S. (2005). Does positive affect influence health? *Psychological Bulletin, 131*, 925–971.

Rabin, C., Leventhal, H., & Goodin, S. (2004). Conceptualization of disease timeline predicts posttreatment distress in breast cancer patients. *Health Psychology, 23*, 407–412.

Reed, G. M., Kemeny, M.E., Taylor, S. E., & Visscher, B. R. (1999). Negative HIV-specific expectancies and AIDS-related bereavement as predictors of symptom onset in asymptomatic HIV-positive gay men. *Health Psychology, 18*, 354–363.

Reed, G. M., Kemeny, M. E., Taylor, S. E., Wang, H. Y. J., & Visscher, B. R. (1994). Realistic acceptance as a predictor of decreased survival time in gay men with AIDS. *Health Psychology, 13*, 299–307.

Rise, J., Sheeran, P., & Hukkelberg, S. (2010). The role of self-identity in the theory of planned behavior: A meta-analysis. *Journal of Applied Social Psychology, 40*, 1085–1105.

Roelofs, K., Elzinga, B. M., & Rotteveel, M. (2005). The effects of stress-induced cortisol responses on approach-avoidance behavior. *Psychoneuroendocrinology, 30*, 665–677.

Roesch, S., & Weiner, B. (2001). A meta-analytic review of coping with illness: Do causal attributions matter? *Journal of Psychosomatic Research, 41*, 813–819.

Rodin, J., & Langer, E. J. (1977). Long-term effects of a control-relevant intervention with the institutionalized aged. *Journal of Personality and Social Psychology, 35*, 897–902.

Rogers, R. W. (1975). A protection motivation theory of fear appeals and attitude change. *Journal of Psychology, 91*, 93–114.

Rook, K. S. (1984). The negative side of social interaction: Impact on psychological well-being. *Journal of Personality and Social Psychology, 46*, 1097–1108.

Rosenberger, P. H., Ickovics, J. R., Epel, E. S., D'Entremont, & D., Jokl, P. (2004). Physical recovery in arthroscopic knee surgery: Unique contributions of coping behaviors to clinical outcomes and stress reactivity. *Psychology and. Health, 19*, 307–320.

Rosenstock, I. M. (1966). Why people use health services. *Milbank Memorial Fund Quarterly, 44*, 94ff.

Scheier, M. F., Carver, C. S., & Bridges, M. W. (1994). Distinguishing optimism from neuroticism (and trait anxiety, self-mastery, and self-esteem): A reevaluation of the Life Orientation Test. *Journal of Personality and Social Psychology, 67*, 1063–1078.

Schiaffino, K. M., & Revenson, T. A. (1992). The role of perceived self-efficacy, perceived control, and causal attributions in adaptation to rheumatoid arthritis: Distinguishing mediator from moderator effects. *Personality and Social Psychology Bulletin, 18*, 709–718.

Schulz, R., Bookwala, J., Knapp, J. E., Scheier, M., & Williamson, G. (1996). Pessimism, age, and cancer mortality. *Psychology and Aging, 11*, 304–309.

Schulz, R., & Decker, S. (1985). Long-term adjustment to physical disability: The role of social support, perceived control, and self-blame. *Journal of Personality and Social Psychology, 48*, 1162–1172.

Seery, M., Blascovich, J., Weisbuch, M., & Vick, S. B. (2004). The relationship between self-esteem level, self-esteem stability, and cardiovascular reactions to performance feedback. *Journal of Personality and Social Psychology, 87*, 133–145.

Segerstrom, S. C., Taylor, S. E., Kemeny, M. E., & Fahey, J. L. (1998). Optimism is associated with mood, coping, and immune change in response to stress. *Journal of Personality and Social Psychology, 74*, 1646–1655.

Segerstrom, S. C., Taylor, S. E., Kemeny, M. E., Reed, G. M., & Visscher, B. R. (1996). Causal attributions predict rate of immune decline in HIV-seropositive gay men. *Health Psychology, 15*, 485–493.

Sherman, D. K., & Cohen, G. (2002). Accepting threatening information: Self-affirmation and the reduction of defensive biases. *Current Directions in Psychological Science, 11*, 119–123.

Sherman, D. K., Nelson, L. D., & Steele, C. M. (2000). Do messages about health risks threaten the self? Increasing the acceptance of threatening health messages via self-affirmation. *Personality and Social Psychology Bulletin, 26*, 1046–1058.

Sherman, D. K., Updegraff, J. A., & Mann, T. (2008). Improving oral health behavior: A social psychological approach. *Journal of the American Dental Association, 139*, 1382–1387.

Skinner, E. A., Edge, K., Altman, J., & Sherwood, H. (2003). Searching for the structure of coping: A review and critique of category systems for classifying ways of coping. *Psychological Bulletin, 129*, 216–269.

Speisman, J. C., Lazarus, R. S., Mordkoff, A. M., Davison, L. A. (1964). Experimental reduction of stress based on ego-defense theory. *Journal of Abnormal Psychology, 68*, 367–380.

Stanton, A. L., Danoff-Burg, S., Cameron, C. L., & Ellis, A. P. (1994). Coping through emotional approach: Problems of conceptualization and confounding. *Journal of Personality and Social Psychology, 66*, 350–362.

Stanton, A. L., Danoff-Burg, S., Sworowski, L. A., Collins, C. A., Branstetter, A. D., Rodriguez-Hanley, A., et al. (2002). Randomized, controlled trial of written emotional expression and benefit finding in breast cancer patients. *Journal of Clinical Oncology, 20*, 4160–4168.

Stanton, A. L., Kirk, S. B., Cameron, C. L., & Danoff-Burg, S. (2000). Coping through emotional approach: Scale construction and validation. *Journal of Personality and Social Psychology, 78*, 1150–1169.

Steele, C. (1988). The psychology of self-affirmation: Sustaining the integrity of the self. In L. Berkowitz (Ed.), *Advances in experimental social psychology* (Vol. 21, pp. 181–227). San Diego, CA: Academic Press.

Stephens, M. A. P., Druley, J. A., & Zautra, A. J. (2002). Older adults' recovery from surgery for osteoarthritis of the knee: Psychosocial resources and constraints as predictors of outcomes. *Health Psychology, 21*, 377–383.

Suls, J., & Fletcher, B. (1985). The relative efficacy of avoidant and nonavoidant coping strategies: A meta-analysis. *Health Psychology, 4*, 249–288.

Surtees, P. G., Wainwright, N. W. J., Luben, R., Khaw, K., & Day, N. E. (2006). Mastery, sense of coherence, and mortality: Evidence of independent associations from the EPIC-Norfolk prospective cohort study. *Health Psychology, 25*, 102–110.

Taylor, S. E. (1983). Adjustment to threatening events: A theory of cognitive adaptation. *American Psychologist, 38*, 1161–1173.

Taylor, S. E. (2010). Social support: A review. In H. S. Friedman (Ed.), *Oxford handbook of health psychology*. New York: Oxford University Press.

Taylor, S. E. (2012). *Health psychology* (8th ed.). New York: McGraw-Hill.

Taylor, S. E., & Brown, J. D. (1988). Illusion and well-being: A social psychological perspective on mental health. *Psychological Bulletin, 103*, 193–210.

Taylor, S. E., Burklund, L. J., Eisenberger, N. I., Lehman, B. J., Hilmert, C. J., & Lieberman, M. D. (2008). Neural bases of moderation of cortisol stress responses by psychosocial resources. *Journal of Personality and Social Psychology, 95*, 197–211.

Taylor, S. E., Helgeson, V. S., Reed, G. M., & Skokan, L. A. (1991). Self-generated feelings of control and adjustment to physical illness. *Journal of Social Issues, 47*, 91–109.

Taylor, S. E., Lerner, J. S., Sherman, D. K., Sage, R. M., & McDowell, N. K. (2003). Are self-enhancing cognitions associated with healthy or unhealthy biological profiles? *Journal of Personality and Social Psychology, 85*, 605–615.

Taylor, S. E., Lichtman, R. R., & Wood, J. V. (1984). Attributions, beliefs about control, and adjustment to breast cancer. *Journal of Personality and Social Psychology, 46*, 489–502.

Taylor, S. E., & Stanton, A. (2007). Coping resources, coping processes, and mental health. *Annual Review of Clinical Psychology, 3*, 129–153.

Tennen, H., Affleck, G., Urrows, S., Higgins, P., & Mendola, R. (1992). Perceiving control, construing benefits, and daily processes in rheumatoid arthritis. *Canadian Journal of Behavioral Science, 24*, 186–203.

Thoits, P. A. (1995). Stress, coping and social support processes: Where are we? What next? *Journal of Health and Social Behavior, (Extra Issue)*, 53–79.

Thompson, S. C., Nanni, C., & Levine, A. (1994). Primary versus secondary and central versus consequence-related control in HIV-positive men. *Journal of Personality and Social Psychology, 67*, 540–547.

Thornton, B., Gibbons, F. X., & Gerrard, M. (2002). Risk perception and prototype perception: Independent processes predicting risk behaviors. *Personality and Social Psychology Bulletin, 28*, 986–999.

Tomaka, J., Blascovich, J., Kelsey, R. M., & Leitten, C. L. (1993). Subjective, physiological, and behavioral effects of threat and challenge appraisal. *Journal of Personality and Social Psychology, 6*, 248–260.

Vegas, O., Fano, E., Brain, P. F., Alonso, A., & Azpiroz, A. (2006). Social stress, coping strategies and tumor development in male mice: Behavioral, neuroendocrine and immunological implications. *Psychoneuroendocrinology*, *31*, 69–79.

Watson, D., & Clark, L. A. (1984). Negative affectivity: The disposition to experience aversive emotional states. *Psychological Bulletin*, *96*, 465–490.

Watson, D., & Pennebaker, J. W. (1989). Health complaints, stress, and distress: Exploring the central role of negative affectivity. *Psychological Review*, *96*, 234–264.

Weaver, K. E., Llabre, M. M., Duran, R. E., Antoni, M. H., Ironson, G., Penedo, F. J., et al. (2005). A stress and coping model of medication adherence and viral load in HIV-positive men and women on highly active antiretroviral therapy (HAART). *Health Psychology*, *24*, 385–392.

Wegner, D. M., Schneider, D. J., Carter, S. R., & White, T. L. (1987). Paradoxical effects of thought suppression. *Journal of Personality and Social Psychology*, *53*, 5–13.

Weinstein, N. D., & Klein, W. M. (1995). Resistance of personal risk perceptions to debiasing interventions. *Health Psychology*, *14*, 132–140.

Wills, T. A. (1991). Social support and interpersonal relationships. In M. S. Clark (Ed.), *Prosocial behavior* (pp. 265–289). Newbury Park, CA: Sage.

Wrosch, C. Schulz, R., Miller, G. E., Lupien, S., & Dunne, E. (2007). Physical health problems, depressive mood, and cortisol secretion in old age: Buffer effects of health engagement control strategies. *Health Psychology*, *26*, 341–349.

Trends in Social Cognition Research

Donal E. Carlston *and* Erica D. Schneid

Abstract

This chapter attempts to predict the future of social cognition research by evaluating trends in the topics published in the 1980s, the 1990s, and the 2000s. Topics were chosen from among those described in this volume—including, for example, various stages of information processing—and then related search terms were entered into PsycINFO. Results of these searches are discussed in conjunction with observations and predictions from various chapter authors. It appears that most of the topics covered in the current volume are growing in prominence in the field of social cognition, although there are some differences between trends in *Social Cognition*, which is aimed at a core audience, and PsycINFO as a whole, which encompasses journals appealing to a much wider audience. Some speculations are advanced regarding the future of the field.

Key Words: social cognition, information processing

When in doubt, predict that the present trend will continue.

–Merkin's Maxim

This *Handbook* began with a series of historically oriented chapters describing social cognition's philosophical and empirical roots, followed by innumerable content chapters detailing the current state of the discipline. Combined, all of these chapters provide a thorough picture of the past and present of social cognition, with occasional digressions into the possible future of the field. This chapter is intended to more systematically and comprehensibly address the future of social cognition, incorporating those digressions where we can.

Like Nostradamus, we intend to make many predictions (though probably fewer than the 6,338 with which he is credited). But unlike him, we intend to be specific and concrete, and not to obscure our meaning with word games and mixtures of archaic languages. Moreover, rather than basing our predictions on calendars and horoscopes, we will attempt

to extrapolate from past and present trends discerned from publication rates in refereed journals. (Though we suspect we may be accused of selectively interpreting these, as many have done with Nostradamus' prognostications.) We are indebted to Lambert and Scherer for indirectly giving us the idea through the citation analyses they conducted for their methodology chapter (see Chapter 3).

We begin our discussion of publication rates with an analysis of the frequency of social cognitive and social cognition articles over the past century. The remainder of this chapter will then examine the contents of those social cognition articles for clues as to future directions in the field. Between this initial history and that longer remainder we interpose a section on the methodologies used in the vast majority of our later literature searches. Such methodological details are important, particularly for those who wish to duplicate or refine our searches, but may be of less interest to many readers. We won't object if you want to skim this section, skip it entirely, or come back to it later.

Intermixed with our literature searches are some predictions and observations from (or based on) various chapters, as well as our own extrapolations into the future. We truly regret that space constraints prevent us from exploring more than a representative sample of chapters and the search terms they suggest. However, no slight is intended, and we trust that readers will examine all of these excellent chapters on their own.

A Brief History of Publication Counts Relating to Social Cognition

In this section, we report several analyses of the frequency of social cognitive and social cognition articles over the last century. More specifically, we searched PsycINFO for articles with descriptive information that contained terms relating to social cognition. Of course, such searches are likely to contain some error, both in terms of false positives and false negatives. However, in these searches, as well as those reported later in this chapter, we tried to use terms with high face validity and to examine at least a subset of retrieved articles to assess the appropriateness of our search terms. We believe the search data provide a useful way to examine general trends across different decades. In the present instance, because we already know something about the historical relationship between social and cognitive psychologies, and the emergence of social cognition (see Hamilton & Carlston, Chapter 2), we can assess the extent to which the search results parallel what we already know to be true.

Figure 43.1 depicts the percentage of articles on social topics that either referenced a term for *cognition* or that explicitly used the term *social cognition*. More specifically, panel A shows the percentage of articles in PsycINFO with *social* in any descriptive search field that also included the terms *cognition*, *cognitive*, *thought*, or *thinking*.[1] And panel B shows the percentage of PsycINFO articles that included the specific term *social cognition*. These data are presented as ratios, by decade, because there has been exponential growth both in the total number of refereed articles in PsycINFO over the past century (increasing from 2,401 in the first decade of the 20th century to 890,103 in the first decade of the 21st century) as well as in the number referencing the term *social* (increasing from 41 to 36,534 for these respective decades). Simple counts for almost any search term would be likely to show increases over time simply because of this increase in base rates.

Panel A indicates that in the first decade of the 1900s, approximately one in six articles relating to

social psychology was also related to cognition in some way, and that the percentage was about the same a century later. In between those two decades, however, we see a progressive decline in such articles into the 1950s, followed by a marked increase from the 1960s through the first 10 years of the 21st century. This pattern corresponds almost perfectly with the rise and fall of behaviorism, which discouraged research and theory on cognition. Watson published his paper *Psychology as the Behaviorist Views It* in 1913, and work on social cognition began to decline in that decade, followed by a more precipitous fall in the following one. But behaviorism itself began to decline in the 1950s, and cognitive psychology was solidly established with the publication of Neisser's text on that field in 1967. As shown in panel A, articles on social cognition began to rebound in that same decade, and continued to do so into the 1980s, after which there was some leveling off.

Modern social cognition can be dated to around 1980 with the publication of four volumes: *Social Cognition, Attribution and Inference* (Wyer & Carlston, 1979), *Person Memory: The Cognitive Basis of Social Perception* (Hastie, Ostrom, Ebbeson, Wyer, Hamilton, & Carlston, 1980), *Social Cognition: The Ontario Symposium* (Higgins, Herman, & Zanna, 1981), and *Cognitive Processes in Stereotyping and Intergroup Behavior* (Hamilton, 1981). Of course, there had been some important work leading up to this point (see Hamilton & Carlston, Chapter 2). But as clearly shown in panel B, the 1980s were when social cognition really began to take off. And the trend since then has been steadily upward.

Perhaps more surprising is that there was somewhat of a literature on social cognition topics toward the beginning of the 20th century. The earliest article identified in our search for *social cognition* appeared in 1908, but it didn't actually use the term and was only later categorized this way in the PsycINFO subject category. The earliest article we discovered that actually used the term was Fritz Heider's *American Psychologist* article titled "On Social Cognition" in 1968. Although its publication predated the emergence of modern social cognition toward the end of the 1970s, Heider's article is an excellent representative of work in the foundational areas of social cognition, which were covered in early chapters of this *Handbook*. Although small in absolute numbers, early work on social cognition actually made up a discernible proportion of all work in the journals covered by PsycINFO during the first quarter of the century. But then, after behaviorism came to dominate American psychology, such work virtually disappeared for the next 40 years.

Skeptics may note that even today, social cognition represents only about 2% of all refereed articles covered by PsycINFO. It is important to keep in mind that PsycINFO covers psychological work in almost 2,500 journals including such fields as medicine, marketing, anthropology, zoology, and other peripheral disciplines. In any case, 2% is still undoubtedly an underestimate because some relevant articles fail to employ this search term, using instead *social perception, cognitive social psychology,* or other, more specific subtopics of these areas. Figure 43.1 is useful for showing the trend, but the sheer volume is undoubtedly greater than indicated by these numbers. In any case, given that PsycINFO covers virtually all psychologically related content, the fact that social cognition

is explicitly mentioned in the descriptors of 1 out of every 50 articles is pretty impressive.

Predictions

Based on the trend, we predict that social cognition publications will continue to grow dramatically in number, and concomitantly, that the field will continue to grow in importance. It is remarkable that 30 some years after its emergence (or reemergence?), social cognition continues to increase its "market share," among PsycINFO publications. However, the primary purpose of this chapter is not to predict the growth of the field as a whole, but rather to forecast how social cognition is likely to change in the next decades. To this end, we now turn to analyses of the publication trends within each major part of this *Handbook*, beginning with the foundational chapters.

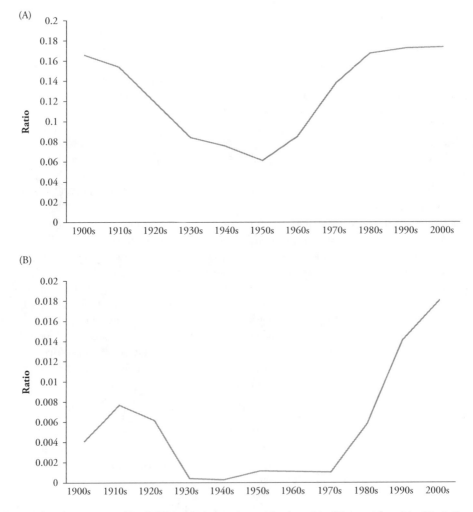

Figure 43.1 Historical proportions of PsycINFO articles referencing *social* and *cognition* (**A**) or *social cognition* (**B**). **A,** Proportion of articles referencing *social* in PsycINFO descriptive fields that also reference terms relating to *cognition*. **B,** Proportion of articles referencing *social cognition* in PsycINFO descriptive fields.

Our Literature Search Methodology

Our goal in this chapter is to make some educated guesses about the directions that social cognition will take in the future by looking at trends in what has been published in the past. To assess these trends, the remainder of this chapter looks at publication rates for search terms that best represent the topics of various chapters. We searched for the frequency with which these search terms occurred in published, refereed articles, by decade, beginning with the 1980s and proceeding through the 2000s.[2] Unless otherwise stated, the term could appear anywhere in the information included in PsycINFO descriptions, including titles, abstracts, keywords, and subject categorizations.

Sources

We principally examined two different sources: the journal, *Social Cognition*, and the universe of all refereed journals covered by PsycINFO. In the first instance, no delimiters were necessary because it can be presumed that a published article on any topic in that journal would be viewed as relevant to social cognition, or it would not likely have been accepted by its reviewers and editors. In the second instance, a Boolean search was conducted for articles including both the search term and the term *social cognition*.

The *Social Cognition* searches reveal what the topics and emphases in the field have been among those authors (and, perhaps, reviewers and editors) who most closely identify with the core field of social cognition. The second source provides a broader view, encompassing all refereed works relating to psychology that mention "social cognition" in key elements of their PsycINFO reference. It is possible that some of these works use the term *social cognition* loosely or that the content or approach in these might not be viewed as really "social cognitionish" by those more involved in the core area. So the latter source may provide a less rigorous definition of social cognition, but it also captures a much broader representation of what was published in each era using that rubric, including applications in disciplines far removed from social psychology.

In a few instances, we also conducted searches of the leading journal in social psychology, the *Journal of Personality and Social Psychology (JPSP)*. These searches had a somewhat different objective, which was to examine what percentage of articles on some social psychological topic mentioned social cognition. It is noteworthy, for example, that articles on affect and motivation in *JPSP* have become dramatically more likely over the decades to include *social cognition* in their descriptive fields. This would seem to indicate that social cognition has had increasing influence in these areas.

Limitations

It should be acknowledged that these article counts are imperfect indexes of publications relevant to social cognition. One problem is the selection of search terms so that they assess most of what was published on a topic without picking up too many publications that are irrelevant. For example, although a search for *social cognition* and *law* turned up many relevant articles, it also uncovered some that had nothing to do with legal matters, including several referencing the Yerkes-Dodson law and the law of large numbers, as well as a few from authors at law schools. However, even with this problematic search term, the trends were identical (see below) whether or not the irrelevant articles were included, and whether or not the search was expanded to include "legal" as an additional search term. Consequently, we suspect that our counts, though occasionally imprecise, are generally accurate, particularly regarding changes in publication over time.

Another possible confound in our searches of the journal of *Social Cognition* is that this publication has had only three editors since it began. David Schneider served as editor from 1982 until 1992, with Tory Higgins as his sole associate editor. Higgins has continued as an associate editor, usually with primary responsibility for special issues, up to the present day. Don Carlston (the first author of the present chapter) joined them in 1989, serving as one of two associate editors until 1993. Carlston then took over as editor from 1993 to 2005, overseeing three associate editors initially, expanding to seven by the end of his term. Then Jeff Sherman assumed the editorship, supervising seven associate editors from 2005 through the present, encompassing the last five years during which data were analyzed for this chapter.

Arguably these three editors-in-chief, and their numerous appointed associates, especially Higgins, influenced what was published in *Social Cognition* during various epochs. It is certainly true that editors can triage submissions that they feel fall outside of the mission of the journal, though this is typically a small percentage of all submissions. And, along with their appointed associates, the editors do make the final publication decisions for the journal. Perhaps most critically, the editors, and especially the special issues editor, have considerable influence on the content of the special issues that *Social Cognition* typically publishes every year. Because these issues are invited, and focus on a single topic, they can have a noticeable impact on the areas covered in this journal. The first author, having served as one of *Social Cognition*'s editors for many years, suspects that all of these concerns are exaggerated. However, we will nonetheless point out instances in which they may have had some impact.

A different issue arises with the publication counts for PsycINFO as a whole. To ensure that the identified articles relate to social cognition, we conducted Boolean searches using topic names combined with the phrase *social cognition*. We discovered, however, that this technique misses some articles that appear to be on the right topic, but don't actually contain the prerequisite phrase. This includes some articles by the first author that he would have sworn were about social cognition. Perhaps in the beginning of the 1980s this term had not yet taken hold, and by the 2000s, the term might have been viewed as too broad to be informative. Nonetheless, our Boolean searches identified very large numbers of articles in the PsycINFO journals, and these were probably representative of most of what was being published on social cognition during each era. And since these searches typically showed the same patterns as our more constrained searches of the journal of *Social Cognition*, we believe they are informative, even if not perfect.[3]

Ratio Computations

Because over time, the number of articles published in *Social Cognition* has increased dramatically, we computed ratios of our target article counts to the total number of articles published in *Social Cognition* during each time period. From 1982, when the journal began, through 1989, *Social Cognition* published 142 articles. For the 1990s, the count was 174, and for the 2000s, 318. Unless otherwise noted, we included special issues in these counts because, though they might slightly inflate numbers for covered topics, they also reflect the perceived importance or centrality of these topics during the time period in which they were published. And had these articles not been published in conjunction with special issues, they might well have been published separately.

For searches using the full universe of PsycINFO publications, we divided our counts by the total number of articles published each decade that included *social cognition* as an identifier in one of the descriptive fields. Thus, for these results, like those for the journal, we report ratios of these numbers to the total number of published articles relating to social

cognition (or at least, mentioning *social cognition* in critical search fields) during each decade. Note that these are *not* ratios to the total number of publications in PsycINFO during each era—those numbers would say little about the relative importance of different topics within the field of social cognition.

Foundational Areas

Part One of this *Handbook* included four chapters on cognitively oriented areas that predated social cognition and contributed to its emergence: attribution, impression formation, attitudes, and prejudice/stereotyping. Results of our analyses of publications in these areas are shown in Figure 43.2. Panel A displays these data for articles published in the journal, *Social Cognition,* and panel B presents similar data for the entire PsycINFO universe of journals (but, as we described above, limited to those articles that included the search term *social cognition* in critical search fields.)

For the most part, the absolute volume of published work on social cognition's foundational topics continues to increase. However, Figure 43.2 suggests that as a proportion of all publications on social cognition, articles on attribution and impression formation are declining, whereas those on prejudice/stereotyping are increasing (both in the journal of *Social Cognition* and in the PsycINFO universe as a whole), and articles on attitudes are either increasing (in *Social Cognition*) or holding steady (in PsycINFO as a whole). The study of attitudes has been one of the most prolific areas of social cognition for 30 years, and prejudice/stereotyping has risen to a virtual tie for second place with impression formation. On the other hand, in *Social Cognition*, attribution has fallen from the most popular of these research domains in the 1980s to the least popular in the 2000s. The decline has been almost as dramatic in PsycINFO as a whole, though attribution remains more popular here than some of the other foundational fields.

Predictions

The increases in research in both attitudes and stereotyping likely reflect, at least in part, expanding interest in *implicit* attitudes and prejudice, and related concerns with how such nonconscious biases can be remedied (see, e.g., Monteith, Woodcock & Lybarger, Chapter 5). Numerous other issues pertaining to these areas also require further research, including the development of stereotypes and the role of noncognitive motivations in stereotype formation (see Sherman, Sherman, Percy, & Soderberg, Chapter 27). Finally, both attitudes and stereotyping seemingly benefit from

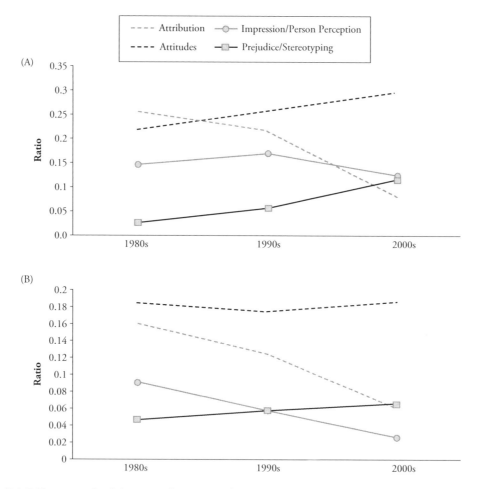

Figure 43.2 Publications in *Social Cognition* and PsycINFO relating to the foundational areas of social cognition. **A,** Proportion of articles in *Social Cognition* that relate to each foundational area of social cognition, by decade. **B,** Proportion of social cognition articles in *PsycINFO* that relate to each foundational area of social cognition, by decade.

having constituencies outside of social cognition, which may provide synergistic benefits for those working on these topics. Consequently, it seems likely that both of these areas will continue to thrive in the future.

The trends are not as promising for attribution or impression formation, though both Reeder (Chapter 6) and Uleman and Kressel (Chapter 4) suggest that these fields (respectively) may benefit from application of new technologies, such as social neuroscience, and also from expanding foci. In the former area, Reeder argues that such expansion includes attributions of beliefs, desires, intentions, feelings, and emotions. And in the latter, it includes broader conceptions of what impression formation is, both in terms of content (see also Carlston, 1994) and in terms of extensions beyond individuals, to groups. We would go even further, suggesting that impression formation paradigms can be applied to virtually any attitude objects, opening up

research into impressions of cities, political parties, hotel chains, commercial products, and so on. In this sense, we agree with Uleman and Kressel that at least potentially, "the future is wide open" (p. 41). But given past trends, it is clear that this potential has not yet been realized, and without such expansion to new foci, the field of social cognition is likely to turn to less well-mined research topics (see Kuhn, 1962), which may lead to further declines in relative (though perhaps not absolute) prominence for both attribution and impression formation research.

Basic Social Cognition Concepts
Representation and Process

Part Two of this volume comprises a variety of chapters on basic social cognition concepts, beginning with those on mental representation and concluding with some on cognitive process. As an initial analysis, we conducted searches, as described above, for the terms *representation* and *process*. As shown in Figure 43.3, both the journal of *Social Cognition* and the broader universe of PsycINFO articles on social cognition have historically been more concerned with process than with representation. An interest in process has always been central to the definition of the social cognition approach (see Chapters 1 and 2), and we suspect that the spreading influence of that approach has led social cognition researchers in all fields to attend more closely to cognitive processes. Moreover, within the field of social cognition (or at least its namesake journal), the proportion of articles citing either process or representation is gradually increasing. For representation, some of this increased interest can probably be traced to Trope's promising construal level theory (see Rim, Trope, Liberman, & Shapira, Chapter 10). At the same time, however, such citations are gradually decreasing in PsycINFO publications on social cognition. It may be that as this

approach is applied broadly within other disciplines, relatively fewer of the applications focus on the specific constructs central to the heart of the field.

Visual and Verbal Representations

We conducted a separate search for two of the most common forms of mental representation, visual and verbal. This was a more complicated search than most of those we conducted because *visual, verbal,* and various related terms are often used in ways that have nothing to do with visual or verbal forms of representation, such as in descriptions of different kinds of stimuli. Consequently, we conducted searches for visual terms (*visual, eidetic, imagery*) and verbal terms (*verbal, semantic, linguistic*) in conjunction with the terms *representation* or *memory* (along with the usual social cognition delimiters).[4]

There were too few hits for either the *visual* (between one and two each decade) or *verbal*

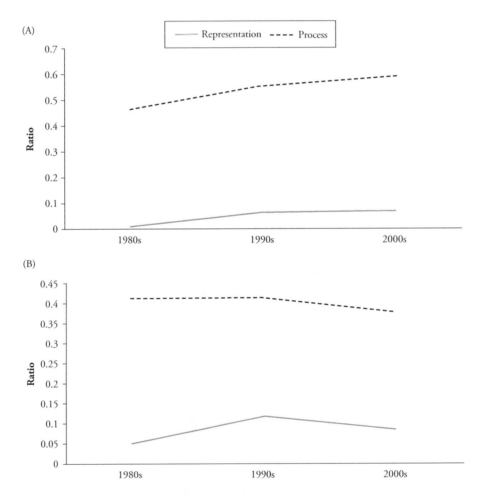

Figure 43.3 Publications in *Social Cognition* and PsycINFO relating to the basic social cognition concepts, *representation* and *process.* **A,** Proportion of articles in *Social Cognition* that relate to *representation* and *process*, by decade. **B,** Proportion of social cognition articles in *PsycINFO* that relate to *representation* and *process*, by decade.

(between three and five each decade) searches in *Social Cognition* for this analysis to be meaningful. In PsycINFO records that referenced *social cognition,* both kinds of representations have increased linearly over the decades. Work citing visual representations went from none in the 1980s to 0.5% of social cognition articles in the 1990s and 1.1% (41 articles) in the 2000s. Work citing verbal representations rose from 0.8%, to 1.3%, to 2.1% (79 articles) over the same time periods.

Libby and Eibach (Chapter 8) suggest that research on visual imagery may assume greater importance if future study confirms its apparent role in both embodied cognition and abstract thought. The need for further research in the increasingly popular area of embodied cognition is made apparent by Semin, Garrido, and Palma (Chapter 31), and research directions comparing abstract and concrete thought are detailed by Rim, Trope, Liberman, and Shapira (Chapter 10).

Verbal representations will always garner widespread attention because these provide humans' primary mode of communication. And an analysis we report later in this chapter indicates that research on communication and language was on an uptick in the 2000s, which may bode well for greater consideration of such representations (see also Kashima & Lan, Chapter 35). We therefore predict slight increases in work on both verbal and visual representations in the immediate future.

Faces

Given Hugenberg and Wilson's (Chapter 9) assertion that, "Faces are central to social cognition," we felt compelled to do searches for the term *face* in the social cognition literature. Just for the sake of comparison, we also did separate searches for the terms *head, body, arm, leg, foot,* and *hand.*[5] Figure 43.4 shows the results of these searches for the three most frequently

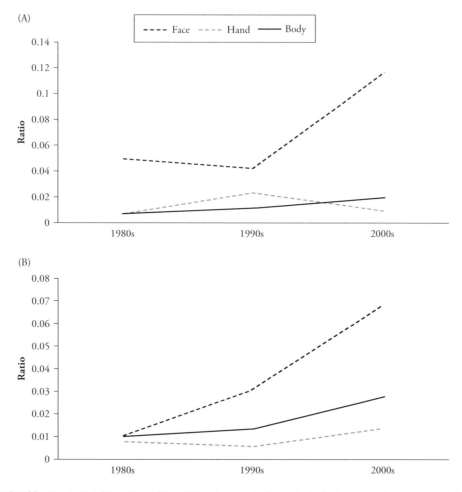

Figure 43.4 Publications in *Social Cognition* and PsycINFO relating to the face and other body parts. **A,** Proportion of articles in *Social Cognition* that relate to *face, hand,* or *body,* by decade. **B,** Proportion of social cognition articles in PsycINFO that relate to *face, hand,* or *body,* by decade.

occurring terms. Consistent with Hugenberg's claim that social cognitive psychologists are "increasingly treating the face as a serious topic of study," *face* is not only the most frequent of these terms but also the most rapidly growing, in both the journal of *Social Cognition* and in social cognition publications more generally. We are therefore compelled to agree with Hugenberg that research on "this most social of stimuli" is likely to be increasingly important in the future.

Automatic and Implicit Processes

In recent years, there have been considerable changes in how people think about social and cognitive processes. Once construed as thoughtful, controlled, and even rational, cognition and behavior have more recently been viewed as at least occasionally mindless, automatic, and error prone. These developments are reflected in Payne and Cameron's Chapter 11 on implicit social cognition; Dijksterhuis' Chapter 12 on automaticity; Wyer, Shen, and Xu's Chapter 13 on procedural knowledge; and Gawronski and Creighton's Chapter 14 on dual process theories. All four chapters provide thoughtful perspectives on the exact nature of the automatic-controlled distinction and its implications for social cognition.

It is difficult to document the shift *away* from thoughtful processing because as an implicit default assumption, this oft-unstated view isn't easily captured by one or two unique search terms. It is much easier to document the emergence of mindlessness, which we did by searching PsycINFO for social cognition publications containing the words *implicit* and *automatic*.[6] Because the Implicit Associations Test (IAT) has been so prominent since the 2000s, we conducted a separate search for this measure (or its acronym) and excluded such articles from the counts for *implicit*. Of course, the IAT really *is* about implicit processes, but we thought it useful to examine whether the frequency of *implicit* in the literature research was simply a reflection of the popularity of this measure.

As shown in Figure 43.5, there have been dramatic increases in articles referring to *implicit, automatic,* and the IAT, both in *Social Cognition* and in all PsycINFO articles mentioning *social cognition*.[7] In fact, during the 2000s, one or more of the terms *implicit, automatic,* or *implicit associations test* appeared in no fewer than 20% of all articles in *Social Cognition*, suggesting the extent to which mindlessness has become a central concern of research at the center of this field. Clearly, however, the IAT does

not account directly for increases in references to implicit processes—even with the IAT excluded, references to *implicit* are increasing—though it may have spurred much of that interest initially.

PREDICTIONS

There are a variety of reasons to expect the literature on automaticity and implicit processes to continue growing: Issues remain concerning the nature of such processes (nicely delineated in the chapters highlighted above), their interplay in the many cognitive and behavioral activities that reflect *both* controlled and automatic processes (see, Conrey, Sherman, Gawronski, Hugenberg & Groom, 2005), and the mechanisms by which these processes operate. Given such central concerns, and the hope that social neuroscience will help to clarify such issues (see Amodio & Ratner, Chapter 34), we suspect that research on mindless aspects of social cognition will continue to grow in the future.

Information Processing Model

Reliance on the information processing model is a key tenet of social cognition (see Carlston, Chapter 1, and Hamilton & Carlston, Chapter 2). To assess the prevalence of this reliance, we conducted searches for articles containing the terms *information processing, attention, perception, memory,* or *judgment* in key identifying PsycINFO fields. In the journal *Social Cognition,* such articles rose from 69.7% of all published articles in the 1980s to 75.5% in the 2000s. Among all PsycINFO articles that reference *social cognition,* the percentage including such references fell from 63.5% to 54.1% over the same period.

All of these percentages are relatively high, confirming the importance of the information processing model to social cognition. However, the data also indicate that information processing is more prominent among the hard-core social cognitionists who publish in *Social Cognition* than it is in the broader universe of social cognition articles. Moreover, this gap has increased over the 30 years examined here. Possibly this suggests that the central tenets of social cognition are less important, and becoming even less so, to those who apply the approach to various topics outside of its historical focus.

Stages of Information Processing

To examine trends in the study of information processing stages, we next conducted separate searches for the terms *attention, perception, memory,* and *judgment*.[8] As described previously, both a *Social*

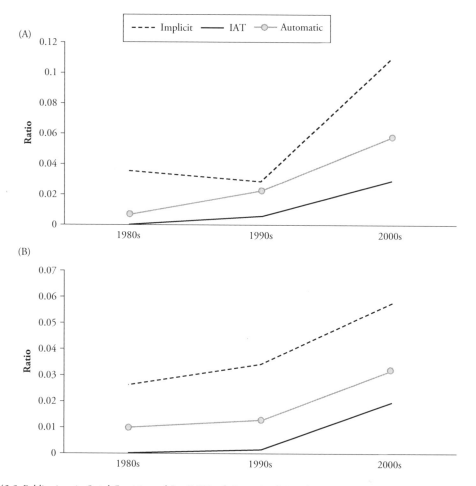

Figure 43.5 Publications in *Social Cognition* and PsycINFO relating to implicit and automatic processes. **A,** Proportion of articles in *Social Cognition* that relate to *automatic* or *implicit* processes, or the *implicit associations test,* by decade. **B,** Proportion of social cognition articles in PsycINFO that relate to *automatic* or *implicit* processes, or *the implicit associations test,* by decade.

Cognition–specific and a broader PsycINFO search were conducted. Because of the ubiquity of the subject category *social perception*, which greatly inflated counts for *perception* (but is often actually used as more of a euphemism for *social cognition*), we limited this search to just article titles and abstracts. The results are shown, by decade, in Figure 43.6.

As revealed in this figure, articles relating to the principal stages of information processing have been decreasing for higher level processes (memory and judgment)[9] while holding fairly steady or even increasing for lower level processes (perception and attention, respectively). The increases for *attention* have been from fairly low levels, with only four articles on the subject published in *Social Cognition* during the 1980s, and only 18 on *attention* in all PsycINFO *social cognition* articles during that same period. Consequently, even with three decades of increases, *attention* remains the least studied aspect

of the information processing model in the journal of *Social Cognition* (panel A), though it is now more prominent in the social sciences in general (panel B). This helps to explain why the editor of this *Handbook* had to look outside of the core area to find authors for Chapter 15 on attentional processes. Although they are cognitive psychologists, Smilek and Frishchen bring a fresh, new, and very social, perspective on attention to social cognition.

It is noteworthy that even with the various increases and decreases in publication rates over the decades, work on stages of information processing in the journal of *Social Cognition* has always favored higher order ("back-end") processes over lower order ("front-end") processes. Thus, today as in the 1980s, the number of publications on each stage increases in order from *attention* to *perception,* to *memory,* and then to *judgment.* This makes sense given the general concerns of social psychology in

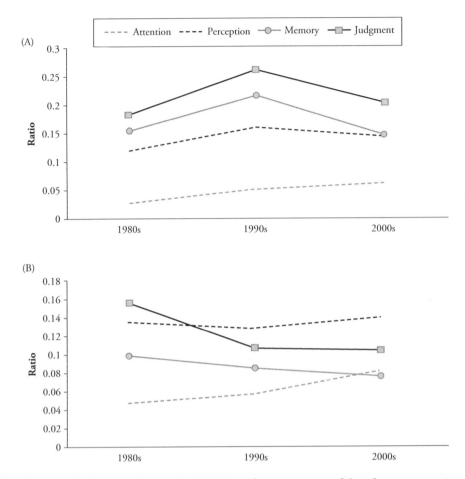

Figure 43.6 Publications in *Social Cognition* and PsycINFO that refer to components of the information processing model. **A,** Proportion of articles in *Social Cognition* containing titles or abstracts that refer to each of the components of the information processing model, by decade. **B,** Proportion of social cognition articles in PsycINFO that contain titles or abstracts that refer to each of the components of the information processing model, by decade.

general and of social cognition in particular. That is, the kinds of behaviors and responses of most interest to social cognitionists are those implicated in interpersonal and cognitive activities that *follow* information processing, which tends to make its latter stages (memory and judgment) most salient. However, the discrepancies among publication rates among the different stages have steadily narrowed since the 1990s, perhaps reflecting recognition that all stages play a compounding role in human cognition and activities.

Several interesting trends in information processing research are not readily examined through PsycINFO searches but are apparent in the chapters of this volume: Information processing research seems to increasingly recognize the importance of factors other than information itself that govern processing; it tends to focus more explicitly on social (and less on cognitive) aspects of processing; and it

often builds on other disciplines and perspectives, leading to a more broadly based and integrative approach than in early work. Smilek and Frischen (Chapter 15) describe how attention is influenced by other people's gaze, tying in both developmental and animal research; Balcetis and Cole (Chapter 16) document a number of motivational factors that come into play in perception; Skowronski, McCarthy, and Wells (Chapter 17) adopt an evolutionary approach in considering the basis for, and nature of, person memories; and van Boven, Travers, Westfall, and McClelland (Chapter 18) argue that judgment and decision making have much broader social implications than generally recognized in the field.

Predictions

What do these data and trends portend for the future of social cognition? The clearest implication is that work on the information processing model is likely to remain central to social cognition for some time, but that for the stages of processing, front-end processes, especially *attention*, may become increasingly central and important.[10] Concomitantly, it appears likely that we may be headed toward a greater balance of research on all the different stages of information processing. Finally, it is possible that evidence from social neuroscience may ultimately require us to rethink the information processing model, perhaps revising our delineation of stages or even adding new stages altogether. Good candidates for addition are mental simulation (see Markman & Dyczewski, Chapter 19) and thought suppression (see Najmi, Chapter 20).

Social Cognition and Social Psychology
"Hot" constructs

The field of social cognition was criticized early on for ignoring such central social psychological variables as affect and motivation (Forgas, 2000; Zajonc, 1980). Actually, both the 1984 and 1994 *Handbooks of Social Cognition* (Wyer & Srull) contained chapters on affect, though neither did on motivation. To assess whether this situation has improved since those early days, we examined the frequency with which published articles in PsycINFO employ affect- and motivation-related terms. A preliminary search using *affect, emotion,* and *mood* as search terms proved misleading because of the frequent use of *affect* as a verb. To pick up as many appropriate instances as possible, while avoiding these inappropriate ones, we searched instead for the terms *affective, positive affect,* and *negative affect,* along with *emotion* and *mood.* To identify motivation-related articles, we employed the search terms *motivation* and *goal.*

We performed two kinds of analyses on articles relating to affect and motivation. First, we conducted analyses similar to those already reported, examining the percentages of social cognition articles (either in the journal of *Social Cognition* or in PsycINFO as a whole) that used affect- or motivation-related terms in their descriptive information. These results are shown in panel A of Figures 43.7 and 43.8 for affect and motivation, respectively. Then we performed analyses on the percentages of articles on affect or motivation that referenced *social cognition* in their descriptive information. For these analyses, it made no sense to examine the journal of *Social Cognition* because everything published there presumably relates to this field. Instead, we substituted *JPSP* to see what percentage of social psychological

articles on affect and motivation relate to social cognition. These results are shown in panel B of the two figures.

AFFECT

Figure 43.7 depicts our results for terms relating to affect. Panel A shows declines in the percentage of social cognition articles relating to affect in the 1990s, followed by some rebound in the 2000s. Although these trends were noted for both the journal of *Social Cognition* and for PsycINFO as a whole, the pattern is a little misleading for the journal. Twelve of the 30 articles on affect published in *Social Cognition* in the 1980s were published in two special issues, one on depression and one on stress and coping. When these special issues are removed from the analysis, the trend looks essentially flat between the 1980s and the 1990s. But in any case, social cognition's interest in affect picked up more recently, producing percentage increases into the 2000s. These increases have been smaller in *Social Cognition* than in the broader field, perhaps because the dearth of integrative theoretical models (see Isbell & Lair, Chapter 21) has muted interest among core social cognition researchers. Possibly the development of such models would stimulate an increase in future research within the central areas of social cognition.

Panel B of Figure 43.7 addresses the flip side of this issue, that is, the extent to which research on affect addresses social cognition. Within social psychology (or at least *JPSP*) articles on affect were more than 10 times more likely to mention social cognition in their descriptive information in the 2000s than they were in the 1980s. Within PsycINFO as a whole, the trend is less dramatic but still represents a doubling of social cognition references in affect articles each decade. These results are consistent with Isbell and Lair's (Chapter 21) suggestion that "examining the influences of affect on social cognition has already had a profound influence on many fields in addition to psychology, including political science, marketing, economics, and communication to name just a few."

MOTIVATION

In the early days, social cognition and motivation were often viewed as opponent viewpoints. For example, dissonance theory, which was generally viewed as motivational, was sometimes pitted against self-perception theory, which was generally viewed as cognitive (see Greenwald, 1975; Greenwald & Ronis, 1978). As shown in

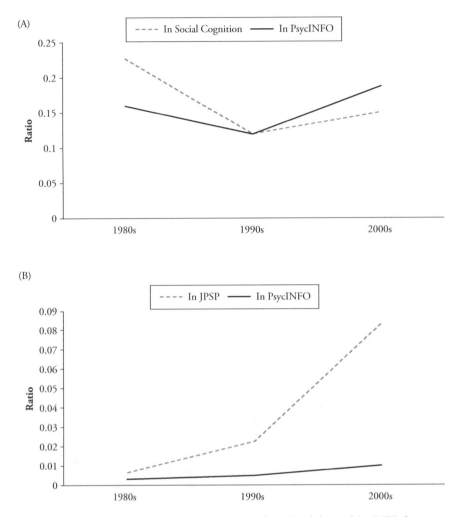

(A)

(B)

Figure 43.7 Publications in *Social Cognition,* the *Journal of Personality and Social Psychology,* and PsycINFO that mention both *affect* and *social cognition.* **A,** Proportion of articles in *Social Cognition* and social cognition articles in PsycINFO that mention *affect,* by decade. **B,** Proportion of affect articles in the *Journal of Personality and Social Psychology* and PsycINFO that mention *social cognition,* by decade.

Figure 43.8, the percentage of *Social Cognition* articles mentioning motivation increased slightly between the 1980s and 1990s, whereas the percentage of social cognition articles in the broader PsycINFO universe mentioning motivation actually declined. More recently, however, considerable effort has been expended trying to combine the motivational and cognitive perspectives, as illustrated by Chapters 16 (Balcetis & Cole), 22 (Eitam, Miele, & Higgins), 23 (Ferguson & Cone), and 28 (Guinote) of this volume. In addition, several different areas of social psychology are exploring the combination of motivation and cognition with regard to more social concerns, such as relationship formation and maintenance (Fitzsimmons & Anderson, Chapter 29) and

information sharing within groups (Levine & Smith, Chapter 30). Consistent with this trend, Figure 43.9 suggests that between the 1990s and the 2000s, social cognition work mentioning motivation increased markedly both in *Social Cognition* and in PsycINFO as a whole.

Shifting to panel B, one can see that the percentage of articles on motivation that mention social cognition (in their PsycINFO descriptive fields) has also increased dramatically, particularly in *JPSP.* In that leading social psychology journal, articles on motivation in the 2000s were more than 20 times more likely to include social cognition in their PsycINFO description than they were in the 1980s. The upward trend is the same in PsycINFO as a whole, though it is less pronounced, with only a fourfold increase.

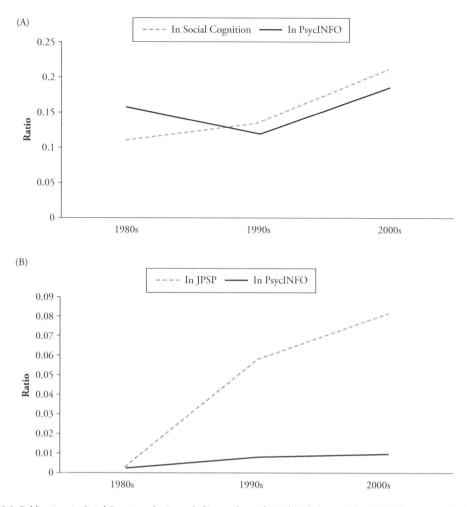

Figure 43.8 Publications in *Social Cognition,* the *Journal of Personality and Social Psychology*, and PsycINFO that mention both *motivation* and *social cognition*. **A,** Proportion of articles in *Social Cognition* and social cognition articles in PsycINFO that mention *motivation*, by decade. **B,** Proportion of motivation articles in the *Journal of Personality and Social Psychology* and PsycINFO that mention *social cognition*, by decade.

PREDICTIONS

Figures 43.7 and 43.8 are remarkably similar to each other, especially given that there was no overlap in search terms (other than *social cognition*, of course). Consequently, it makes sense to advance similar predictions regarding the futures of both affect and motivation research in social cognition. Extrapolating from past trends, there is every reason to believe that both areas of research will continue to grow in importance within social cognition. Moreover, to an even greater extent, social cognition seems likely to become more important within those areas of research.

Areas of Social Psychology

To examine the infiltration of social cognition into other areas of social psychology, we focused our searches on two journals, *Social Cognition* and *JPSP*. We identified articles in five major areas of social psychology by searching for the terms that best represent each of these areas (*attitude, personality, group, self,* and *relationship*). Panel A of Figure 43.9 reports these totals as proportions of all articles published each decade in *Social Cognition*, reflecting the degree of interest in these social psychological topics among core researchers in social cognition. Panel B shows the percentage of *JPSP* articles within each of these areas of social psychology that included the term *social cognition*. These data thus presumably reflect the degree of interest in social cognition shown by those publishing in different areas of social psychology.

Panel A of Figure 43.9 indicates that although the proportions of articles on attitudes, relationships,

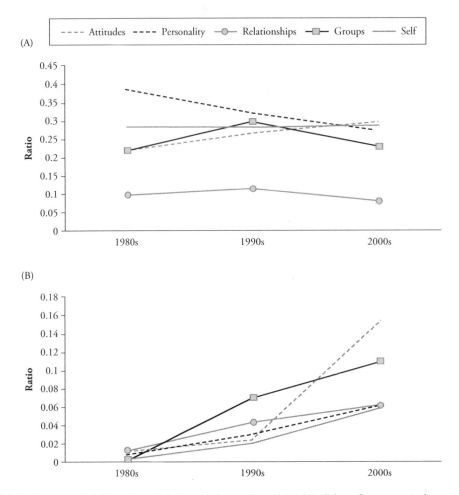

Figure 43.9 Publications in *Social Cognition* and the *Journal of Personality and Social Psychology* referring to *attitudes, personality, relationships, groups,* or the *self.* **A,** Proportion of articles in *Social Cognition* that relate to five of the major areas of psychology, by decade. **B,** Proportion of social cognition articles in the *Journal of Personality and Social Psychology* that relate to five of the major areas of psychology, by decade.

and groups all increased in *Social Cognition* during the 1990s, all but attitudes declined between the 1990s and the 2000s. Research on social cognition and attitudes has increased steadily, perhaps reflecting Wegener and Petty's (Chapter 7) assertion that, "the maturation of the social cognition perspective has brought it closer to the attitudinal roots that were at least partially rejected in the early days of social cognition." Articles on personality, though among the most numerous in all three decades, have steadily declined and are now second to those on attitudes.

The proportion of *Social Cognition* articles on the self has remained pretty constant over the decades. This consistent linkage is not surprising, given that one definition of social cognition is "how people think about people" (Wegner & Vallacher, 1977, p. viii) and that "people's self-perceptions, self-evaluations, and self-esteem are intimately entangled in how they

think about other people" (Leary & Terry, Chapter 26, this volume). Further evidence of this link can be found both in Beike's Chapter 25 on the relationship between the self and autobiographical memory and in McConnell, Brown, and Shoda's Chapter 24 reviewing, among other things, the bidirectional nature of self-perception and perception of others. Though there has been no growth in the percentage of articles on self in *Social Cognition*, there has been some increase in *JPSP* articles on social cognition. This may indicate that the social cognition of self is becoming increasingly important outside of the core field, for example, in people's reactions to thoughts about their own mortality (see Greenberg, Landau, & Arndt, Chapter 33).

Panel B of Figure 43.9 provides an indication of interest in social cognition among those publishing in *JPSP* in other research areas. Here the trends are clear and consistent. Since the 1980s, there have been dramatic and continuous increases in the proportion of articles in all five of these domains of social psychology that refer to social cognition in their descriptive information. This is consistent with the argument that social cognition is (at least partly) an approach that can be applied to other realms of research (see Chapters 1 and 2). Notably, since the 1990s, the most dramatic increase has been in the attitudes area, such that in the most recent decade, almost one in six attitudes articles published in *JPSP* relates to social cognition. "Siblings," indeed (Wegener & Petty, Chapter 7, this volume).

PREDICTIONS

Of course, all of the data reported here are open to alternative explanations. In the present case, one plausible explanation is that the trends reflected in panel B of Figure 43.9 indicate increased acceptance of social cognition methods, theories, and approaches in other areas of social psychology. Kihlstrom (Chapter 38) goes so far as to suggest that social cognition will dissolve the traditional divide between the person and the situation in the study of social and personality psychology. This acceptance then enhances the likelihood that such work will be published in *JPSP* (and presumably in other social psychological journals as well), simultaneously reducing the need to direct such work to *Social Cognition* (as reflected in panel A of Figure 43.9). If this interpretation is correct, further increases can be expected in the publication of social cognition–oriented articles relating to other areas of social psychology, though much of this work may be directed toward broad social psychological audiences, such as those who read *JPSP*, rather than to *Social Cognition*.

Other Research Realms
Other Areas of Psychology

We examined the articles in both *Social Cognition* and PsycINFO generally that relate to several broad themes in psychology: evolutionary psychology (search terms: *evolution* and *evolutionary*), neuroscience (search terms: *neuroscience, neuropsychology,* and *brain*), communication (search terms: *communication, language,* and *linguistic*), and culture (search term: *culture*). We omitted developmental approaches from this analysis because this area differs from the others in being a self-established discipline with its own long-standing literature in social cognition, and also a difficult area to search for properly, given the many meanings of *development* and *developmental*. However we don't mean to

slight the field, which is reviewed in this volume by Heyman and Legare (Chapter 36), and also, to a degree, by Sherman et al. (Chapter 27).

Panel A of Figure 43.10 shows the proportion of publications in *Social Cognition* that contained these search terms, by decade. Panel B of Figure 43.10 shows the proportion of publications in PsycINFO as a whole that mentioned both *social cognition* and these search terms, by decade.

Both panels of Figure 43.10 tell basically the same story: Since the 1980s, there has been an increase in social cognition references in all of these areas except for communication, where references have pretty much stayed constant at a relatively high level. In *Social Cognition*, the most dramatic increases have been in work on neuropsychology and culture, with the former area also the fastest growing in the social sciences as a whole. One reason that the proportion of *Social Cognition* articles on culture exceeds those in neuroscience, whereas the reverse is true in the broader universe of PsycINFO articles (at least in the 2000s), is that a relatively high percentage of articles on social cognition and culture are published in *Social Cognition*: Of 200 articles on this topic published in the 2000s, the percentage appearing in *Social Cognition* (13.5%) was almost as high as the percentage appearing in specialty journals on culture[11] (18%). In contrast, a relatively small proportion of the 822 articles on social cognition and neuroscience published in the 2000s were published in *Social Cognition* (1.8%), with a much higher proportion (34.4%) appearing in neuroscience journals.[12] The tendency of those doing work on social cognition and neuroscience to publish in specialty journals probably reflects the specialized nature of neuropsychology, and the audience those researchers wish to address, along with a surfeit of publication outlets in that discipline. In contrast, those publishing in social cognition and culture have fewer specialty journals to choose from, and their less technical methods may make their work more suitable for *Social Cognition* and other general psychology journals.

PREDICTIONS

The trends revealed in Figure 43.10 are pretty clear: All of these research areas are likely to grow in importance, or at least continue to be important, in future social cognition. This is probably most evident for social cognitive neuroscience, which is growing dramatically both in *Social Cognition* and in PsycINFO as a whole. This area, more than any other, is benefiting from greatly improved technologies that make thought processes more transparent than ever

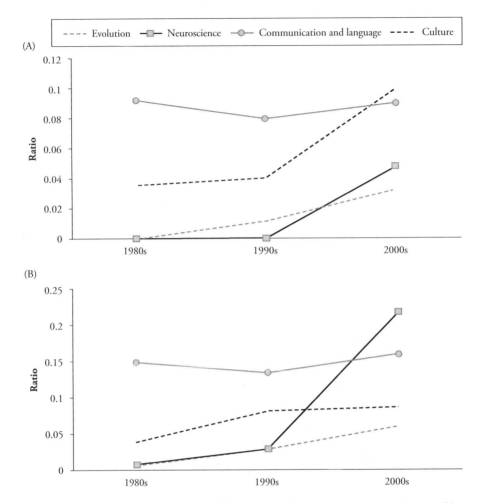

Figure 43.10 Publications in *Social Cognition* and PsycINFO that refer to *evolution, neuroscience, communication and language,* or *culture.* **A,** Proportion of articles in *Social Cognition* that relate to other topics in psychology, by decade. **B,** Proportion of social cognition articles in PsycINFO that relate to other topics in psychology, by decade.

before (see Amodio & Ratner, Chapter 34). However the cost and relative unavailability of these technologies to many social cognition researchers may place a ceiling on the growth of this research area, unless less expensive technology becomes available. In addition, the previously described tendency for much of this work to be published in highly specialized journals could take a toll on the breadth of its audience. Nonetheless, the potential value of neuroscientific work is so great that it is difficult to imagine much slowing in its prominence in the foreseeable future.

Research on culture and social cognition has also benefited from new technologies. Chiu, Ng, and Au (Chapter 37) specifically mention how neuroscience may benefit the study of culture. In addition, the Internet has undoubtedly served to make the world smaller, increasing the salience and importance of cultural differences and multicultural

experiences, and suggesting new areas for study. Thus, for example, Chiu, Ng, and Au propose that, "researchers might also investigate how exposure to multicultural cultures affects behaviors, how people with multicultural experiences manage their cultural identities, and how people relate to culture mixing in globalized environments." Such topics are already ripe for future research, but the multicultural interactions fostered by the Internet seem likely to increase their importance even further.

Arguably, new technologies have also benefited research on both communication and evolution. With regard to communication (and language), the Internet and other new forms of communication, like texting, have introduced a variety of new research issues and contexts; for example, face-to-face communication, once viewed as the norm, may no longer be so. With regard to evolutionary theory, recent developments in the sciences of genetics and hormones allow for more sophisticated testing of evolutionary hypotheses than was possible in the past. In any case, the authors of the chapters on communication (Kashima & Lan, Chapter 35) and evolution (Neuberg, Becker, & Kenrick, Chapter 32) convincingly argue that those approaches are both integral, and increasingly useful, to social cognition. There is ample evidence for these arguments, not only in these chapters but also in others. The case for evolutionary perspectives, for example, is also made by Skowronski, McCarthy, and Wells (Chapter 17) and by Semin, Garrido, and Palma (Chapter 31). Consequently, we might expect to see some continuing growth in these approaches, though probably not at the dramatic levels seen for culture and neuroscience.

Other Disciplines

The final part of this *Handbook* included four chapters that illustrate the application of the social

cognition approach to other fields, specifically, consumer psychology, law, political science, and health research. We conducted analyses similar to those already reported to determine whether the social cognition approaches to these fields are becoming increasingly prominent, and also whether increasing proportions of articles in these fields are citing social cognition. The results of these analyses are shown in panels A and B of Figure 43.11, respectively. For panel A, we computed the frequency with which terms relating to consumer psychology (*consumer* and *marketing*), law (*law* and *legal*), political science (*political* and *politics*), and health (*health*, but not *mental health*) appeared in social cognition articles, as ratios of all social cognition articles published each decade.[13] Note that, unlike previous figures, this panel A presents data for PsycINFO as a whole—there were too few articles on these topics in *Social Cognition*, or even in all social psychology journals together, to do a meaningful analysis.

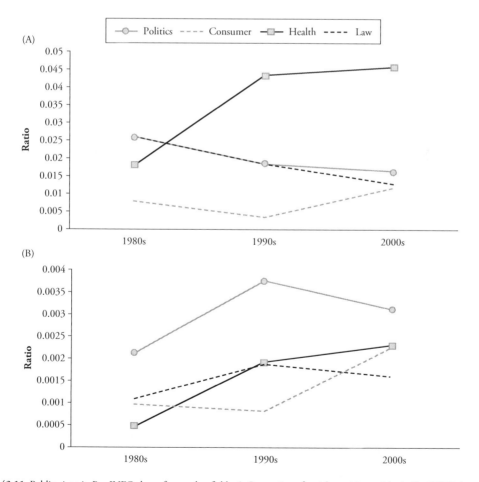

Figure 43.11 Publications in PsycINFO that refer to other fields. **A,** Proportion of social cognition articles in PsycINFO that relate to other fields, by decade. **B,** Proportion of articles in other fields in PsycINFO that relate to *social cognition*, by decade.

As shown in panel A of Figure 43.11, work combining social cognition with these specific fields appears to represent a relatively small percentage of published work in the field. Work on social cognition and health *has* increased noticeably, especially between the 1980s and the 1990s, and by the 2000s represented almost 5% of all research in social cognition. But work in each of the other three areas represented less than 2% of the field in the 2000s, representing slight declines for both legal and political social cognition.

These figures probably under-represent the proportion of social cognition research that relates to other disciplines because no handbook can encompass all of the disciplines to which the social cognition approach might be applied. We therefore did a follow-up analysis, searching for terms representing many of the major disciplines to which we believe social cognition might usefully be applied. To those already described, we added the terms *medical, clinical, counseling, therapy, education, finance, business, sports,* and *athletics,* again searching for articles that contained both *social cognition* and any of these terms in any field other than author affiliation. This analysis indicated that in the 1980s, 13.8% of all social cognition articles included at least one descriptive term characteristic of a discipline outside of social psychology. In the 1990s and 2000s, the figures were 18.8% and 18.4%, respectively. So, it would appear that applications of social cognition to other disciplines have leveled off at about 20% of all refereed social cognition publications. Whether that percentage will hold for the long term is anybody's guess, but it does provide the best estimate of how much of the field is likely to be devoted to applications in other disciplines.

Panel B of Figure 43.11 indicates the proportion of work in various fields that refers to social cognition. Naturally, these percentages are much smaller than those in panel A because most research in fields such as law and health addresses issues that have nothing to do with psychology, let alone social cognition. And, of course, the extent to which publications in these areas cited social cognition rose from the 1980s, when this approach first became established, to the 2000s, by which time it had taken a firm hold. But trends since the 1990s are informative. As a percentage of other work being done in those fields, research citing social cognition increased for both consumer psychology and health, and declined for both political science and law. Though it may be declining, however, social cognition remains a more dominant approach in political science than in any of the other fields examined here.

PREDICTIONS

As already noted, the best estimate of how much of the social cognition field will be devoted to work in other disciplines is about (perhaps just under) 20%. But this could obviously be affected by many factors. For example, the data suggest that social cognition and health is becoming a more prevalent topic in the field, and this can be explained by a number of factors, including the health issues of an aging population, greater emphasis by U.S. funding agencies, and public debates over "Obamacare" and other aspects of public health policy. Radical cutbacks in federal funding for health-related research might reduce researchers' interest, and possibly shift work toward areas that rely more on other sources of funding (e.g., consumer psychology and marketing). Some of these same factors might have either a direct or indirect impact on research in political cognition as well (see Jost, Hennes, & Levine, Chapter 41), if the bases for politicians' decisions become of greater interest to either the public or psychological researchers.

Shifting to more scientific factors, Spellman and Schauer (Chapter 40) make a compelling case that many of the most relevant topics in social cognition and law have barely been addressed by researchers. Consumer psychology may have been more thoroughly mined in the past, but the ties with social cognition are so numerous (see Kardes & Wyer, Chapter 39) that any growth in the area of social cognition as a whole is likely to be paralleled here as well. So, arguments could probably be advanced for any of the disciplines included in this volume. But the best bet, barring sudden changes in the political or research climates, is probably social cognition and health (see Taylor, Chapter 42).

Declining Areas of Social Cognition

The analyses reported in this chapter present a conundrum. Most of the searches reveal that articles on the social cognition of specific topics are increasing. That is, for example, these analyses (principally presented in the panel A of the figures) suggest that in the journal of *Social Cognition,* the three decades examined showed increases in the proportion of articles dealing with attitudes, prejudice/stereotyping, representations, process, the face, attention, perception, evolutionary principles, neuroscience, culture, health, and consumer psychology. On the other hand, these analyses found marked decreases only for articles citing attribution, affect, and personality. How is it that we found percentage increases in so many areas and percentage decreases in so few? Shouldn't about as many topics be declining in popularity as are rising?

Of course, chapters in a handbook like this are not chosen randomly: They are chosen because the editor believes them to be important both today and in the foreseeable future. Consequently, the first author of this chapter imagines that the excessive number of upward trends is indicative of the editor's judgment in soliciting chapters. Nonetheless, percentages being what they are, there must be numerous areas of social cognition that are declining and making room for those areas that are increasing. So, we conducted a number of searches for topics that seem to be less prominent than they once were.

Figure 43.12 shows the publication trends for a handful of concepts that have declined, at least percentage-wise, in *Social Cognition*. Although not shown in the figure, all of these terms have also declined in PsycINFO as a whole (in articles that include *social cognition* in their descriptive information). Some of these search terms are at least somewhat characteristic of articles in the attribution area (e.g., *morality/responsibility, causal/causation, actor/observer*),[14] the decline of which has already been noted. Others, like *schema* and *recall/recognition*, represent shifts in research foci and methods. With regard to *schemas*, this shift is also reflected in the fact that the first two *Handbooks of Social Cognition* (Wyer & Srull, 1984, 1994) included chapters on schemas, and the present one does not. With regard to *recall/recognition*, Lambert and Scherer (Chapter 3; Figure 43.2) report a virtually identical result in searching for these terms in *JPSP*.

Perhaps most surprising is the decline in *Social Cognition* articles referring to *behavior* or *action* between the 1980s and the 1990s. Although there has been a modest rebound since then, such work was still far less frequent in the 2000s than in the 1980s. Given the ubiquity of complaints that social cognition (or social psychology, more generally) too often ignores actual human behavior (e.g., Baumeister, Vohs, & Funder, 2007; Patterson, 2008; see Lambert & Scherer, Chapter 3, for a discussion), one might have thought that this shortcoming would have been better addressed by now. If there is one area of decline that most needs to be redressed, this would be it. In any case, Figure 43.12 makes the point that not everything is going up. But virtually all of the topics covered in this *Handbook* are.

Final Conclusions

We noted in the previous section that most of the topics we analyzed were becoming more popular, and

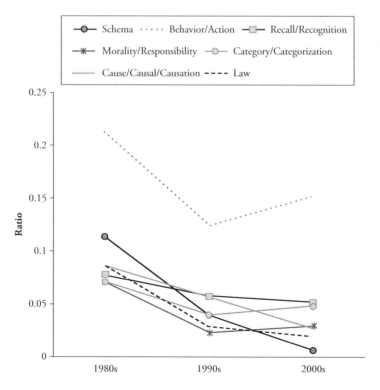

Figure 43.12 Publications relating to declining research topics.

that only a few were declining in prominence, over the three decades that we examined. This brought to mind an analogy with stock market analysis. Market analysts are noted for rating a much higher percentage of company stocks as "buys" (because their prices are predicted to go up) than as "sells" (because their prices are predicted to go down). Some critics suggest that this is because the analysts don't wish to offend company executives on whose underwriting they may someday depend. The analysts, however, argue that it is simply because they tend to focus on the best companies. We similarly argue that this *Handbook* tends to focus on the best topics. But we admit that we similarly have no desire to offend the esteemed collection of authors who have contributed to this volume (though we don't believe that this sentiment affected our analyses).

In any case, having recognized the parallels between the analyses we report here, and the analyses that stock market analysts conduct, we decided to extend the analogy a bit further. Evaluating company stocks by analyzing past trends in their market prices is known as *technical analysis*. And it parallels the graphs that we presented in this chapter to show increases and decreases in the publication of certain topics in social cognition. The underlying rationale for technical analysis is that price trends capture all of the myriad forces that might cause something to rise or fall, so that the patterns can be meaningfully interpreted in an effort to predict future price movements. A similar logic underlies our presentation of publication trends.

Evaluating company stocks by analyzing the strengths and weaknesses of a specific company, and the competitive milieu within which it operates, is called *fundamental analysis*. The arguments that we and the authors of various chapters have advanced regarding the importance of different topics is also an example of fundamental analysis. In stock investing, both technical and fundamental analyses have their place, and we would argue that this is also true in academic forecasting. Which leads us to the final step of our analogy: If one were to invest everything in one research topic—one that has the best chance of continuing to grow and become dominant over the next 30 years—which one would it be? The two authors of the present chapter have set caution to the wind and come up with their independent "recommendations."

First Author's Recommendations

The first author recommends social cognition and neuroscience, today commonly referred to

as *social cognitive neuroscience*. Technical analysis reveals meteoric increases in publication in this field, mostly occurring since the 1990s (see Figure 43.10). These increases occurred both in social cognition articles in PsycINFO as a whole and in *Social Cognition* (though relatively little of the work has been published in this journal.) In the 2000s, more than one in five refereed publications in PsycINFO that contained the term *social cognition* also contained a term relating to neuroscience.[15] And of the 42 chapters in this *Handbook*, more than 75% discuss neuroscience in some regard.

In terms of fundamental analysis, it seems clear that neuroscience has the potential to address many different issues in social cognition. The frequency with which it is cited by chapters in this *Handbook* is ample proof of this. The tools of neuroscience are becoming more widely available, and the sophistication of research in this area (in terms of social cognitive theories and issues) is improving considerably (see Amodio & Ratner, Chapter 34). Earlier, we stated some reservations about the breadth of availability of those tools and methods. But we are actually optimistic that the cost will eventually come down and that the necessary technologies (including some presumably not yet invented) and expertise will proliferate. If that assessment is wrong, then all bets are off, and you might have been better off investing in Facebook.

The first author acknowledges that there are many other areas that seem promising on both technical and fundamental grounds. There has been considerable growth in social cognition and health, and in social cognition and culture, and it is easy to make fundamental arguments for continued strength in these areas. Moreover, in deference to Hugenberg and Wilson (Chapter 9), I acknowledge that our analyses make the case for investing in the *face*, though I wonder if that isn't too narrow a subject to remain prominent for the next 30 years. Implicit processes are obviously becoming much more popular, and I would guess they will continue to do so for another decade or two, before they lose their counterintuitive flair and become part of the implicit body of knowledge for the field. And finally, I like both the graph and the case for social cognition and motivation. But because this is the second author's primary "recommendation," I'll leave that case for her to make.

Second Author's Recommendation

The second author concurs with the first author that social cognitive neuroscience is a pretty safe bet, for all of the above-mentioned reasons. However, my recommendation for a strong buy for the next 30 years of social cognition research is social cognition and motivation. To review the technical analysis, the proportion of social cognition articles on motivation has shown a steep uptrend since the 1990s (see Figure 43.8). This trend is seen in both *Social Cognition* articles and social cognition articles in PsycINFO. A similar trend is seen in the proportion of articles on motivation that also mention the term *social cognition* in both *JPSP* and PsycINFO as a whole.

As for the fundamental analysis, in this volume alone no fewer than six chapters (Balcetis & Cole, Chapter 16; Eitam, Miele, & Higgins, Chapter 22; Ferguson & Cone, Chapter 23; Guinote, Chapter 28; Fitzsimmons & Anderson, Chapter 29; Levine & Smith, Chapter 30) explicitly explore motivation across various topics in social cognition—with 88% of the other chapters briefly mentioning the role of motivation (or goals) in some manner. No other single topic has served to tie together as many chapters within this *Handbook*. The breadth of potential applicability of social cognition and motivation seems wide and far reaching.

Our earlier analyses of the components of the information processing model show that interest in the various stages of information processing is holding steady (see Figure 43.6). It appears that researchers have now begun searching for the moderators of the processes at each stage of the model—working to identify, for example, what types of motivation can alter an individual's attention to and perception of a potential relationship partner. This means that the possibilities for the study of motivation across the various stages of information processing *and* across various areas of study are endless—or, at the very least, are enough to keep researchers occupied for the next 30 years.

Final Comment

Anyone reading this *Handbook* after about 2030 (we should be so lucky!) will probably recognize the wisdom or stupidity of our "recommendations." Given the hindsight bias, we aren't likely to get much credit for being right, if we are, because the answer will by then seem so obvious (see Markman & Dyczewski, Chapter 19). And if we are wrong, readers may question how we could miss the evident strength of whatever research areas do come to dominate the field of social cognition. But such is the inevitable fate of the prognosticator who dares to make specific predictions. Perhaps, like

Nostradamus, we should have been more vague. In any case, whatever areas of research become popular in the future, we are convinced that the social cognition approach will continue to thrive and to be central to the psychological literature.

Notes

1. PsycINFO automatically extends searches to some closely related terms such as plurals, and in these cases we will not list all of the included variants of our search terms in the text.

2. As of this writing, there are only two years of data available for the 2010s, which is not sufficient to produce reliable estimates, particularly in the journal of *Social Cognition*. For the most part, then, we will leave these data for others to address a decade from now. However, in a few instances in which these data seem to confirm or suggest an important trend, we may mention them briefly.

3. We agonized a bit about whether to exclude *Social Cognition* articles from the broader PsycINFO counts, so that the two analyses would be completely independent. However, because the idea behind the broad counts was to get a picture of everything being done in the field, and because articles in *Social Cognition* were typically only a small proportion of those, we opted to include them.

4. The term *image* was bypassed because it too often is used loosely to refer to an impression of others (as in, "His *image* of Mitt Romney was not favorable") or oneself ("She had a positive *self-image*"). Additionally, the term *nonverbal* (with or without the hyphen) was excluded from the *verbal* search.

5. Of course there are numerous other body parts for which we could have searched. But a preliminary review of the literature suggested that these were most promising.

6. The term *mindless* has appeared in only two to four social cognition articles each decade, none in *Social Cognition*, so it was not included.

7. Lambert and Scherer (Chapter 3, this volume, Figure 3.1) report essentially the same pattern in the *Journal of Personality and Social Psychology* using the search term *automatic*.

8. Adding articles on *decision making* to those on *judgment* has little effect on the patterns reported, whereas *judgment* tends to be used more precisely.

9. Lambert and Scherer (Chapter 3, this volume, Figure 3.2) similarly report a decline in the appearance of the term *memory* in *JPSP* across these same three decades.

10. Consistent with this possibility, our search of PsycINFO publications mentioning *social cognition* indicates that in 2010 and 2011, more of these included *attention* and *perception* in their title or abstract (130 and 155, respectively) than included *memory* or *judgment* (90 and 107, respectively).

11. *Anthropologica, Cognition and Culture, Culture and Psychology, Integrative Psychological and Behavioral Science, Journal of Cultural and Evolutionary Psychology*, and the *Journal of Cross-Cultural Psychology*.

12. *Annual Review of Neuroscience, Behavioral Brain Research, Brain and Behavior, Brain Research, Cortex, Current Opinion in Neurobiology, Frontiers in Behavioral Neuroscience, Human Brain Mapping, Journal of Clinical and Experimental Neuropsychology, Journal of Cognitive Neuroscience, Nature Reviews Neuroscience, Neuropsychologia, Neuropsychological Trends, Neuroreport, Neuroscience and Biobehavioral Reviews, The Neuroscientist, Physiology and Behavior, Social Cognitive and Affective Neuroscience, Social Neuroscience*, and *Trends in Neurosciences*.

13. Because of the frequency with which Colleges of *Law*, Departments of *Consumer* Psychology, Schools of *Health* Science, and so on appeared in author affiliations, even in articles that had little to do with the embedded search terms, we excluded this field from our searches.

14. These searches, like some of those reported earlier, may have included minor variations on these same words, such as plurals, adjectival forms, and so on.

15. If one drops *brain* from the search, and includes only *neuroscience and neuropsychology*, the ratio drops to just less than one in seven.

References

Baumeister, R. F., Vohs, K. D., & Funder, D. C. (2007). Psychology as the science of self-reports and finger movements: Or whatever happened to actual behavior? *Perspectives on Psychological Science, 4,* 396–403.

Carlston, D. (1994). Associated systems theory: A systematic approach to the cognitive representation of persons and events. In R. S. Wyer (Ed.) *Advances in social cognition: Vol. 7: Associated systems theory* (pp. 1–78). Hillsdale, NY: Erlbaum.

Conrey, F. R., Sherman, J. W., Gawronski, B., Hugenberg, K, & Groom, C. J. (2005). Separating multiple processes in implicit social cognition: The QUAD model of implicit task performance. *Journal of Personality and Social Psychology, 89*(4), 469–487.

Forgas, J. P. (Ed.) (2000). *Feeling and thinking: the role of affect in social cognition.* New York: Cambridge University Press.

Greenwald, A. G. (1975). On the inconclusiveness of crucial cognitive tests of dissonance versus self-perception theories. *Journal of Experimental Social Psychology, 11*(5), 490–499.

Greenwald, A. G., & Ronis, D. L. (1978). Twenty years of cognitive dissonance: Case study of the evolution of a theory. *Psychological Review, 85*(1), 53–57.

Hamilton, D. L. (1981). *Cognitive processes in stereotyping and intergroup behavior.* Hillsdale, NJ: Erlbaum.

Hastie, R., Ostrom, T., Ebbeson, E., Wyer, R., Hamilton, D., & Carlston, D. E. (1980). *Person memory: The cognitive bases of social perception.* Hillsdale, NJ: Erlbaum.

Higgins, E. T., Herman, C. P., & Zanna, M. P. (1981). *Social cognition: The Ontario symposium* (Vol. 1). Hillsdale, NJ: Erlbaum.

Kuhn, T. S. (1962). *The structure of scientific revolutions* (1st ed.). Chicago: University of Chicago Press

Patterson, M. L. (2008). Back to social behavior: Mining the mundane. *Basic and Applied Social Psychology, 30,* 93–101.

Wegner, D. M., & Vallacher, R. R. (1977). *Implicit psychology: An introduction to social cognition.* New York: Oxford University Press.

Wyer, R. S., Jr., & Carlston, D. E. (1979). *Social cognition, inference, and attribution.* Hillsdale, NJ: Erlbaum.

Wyer, R. S., & Srull, T. K. (Eds.) (1984). *Handbook of social cognition.* Hillsdale, NJ: Erlbaum.

Wyer, R. S., & Srull, T. K. (Eds.) (1994). *Handbook of social cognition* (2nd ed.). Hillsdale, NJ: Erlbaum.

Zajonc, R. B. (1980). Feelings and thinking: Preferences need no inferences. *American Psychologist, 35*(2), pp. 151–175.

INDEX

A

AAI approach. *see* affect-as-information (AAI) approach
Aaker, J., 60–1
Aarts, H., 245, 246, 483, 484, 486–7, 603, 646
Abele, A.E., 61, 65
Abelson, R.P., 42, 131
Abramowitz, J.S., 422, 426
Abramson, L., 106
abstract information
imagery in representing, 161–3
abstractness
levels of
comprehension in, 267–9
abuse
substance
thought suppression and, 427
ACC. *see* anterior cingulate cortex (ACC)
accentuation, 562–4
acceptance
interpersonal
self-esteem and, 540–2
accessibility
defined, 463
knowledge, 807
motivated
from relevance, 465–6
selective
in consumer information
processing, 811–12
accountability
visual perception and, 344–5
accuracy
question of
Cronbach and, 59
accuracy motivation, 854–5
achievement-related emotion
in cultural congruency, 776–7
Ackerman, J.M., 181, 183, 661
action(s)
adaptive
cognition for, 645–8
expressions in, 173–4
required
immediacy of, 345
activity(ies)
joint

described, 730–1
actor *vs.* observer differences, 105
Adair, S.A., 369
Adams, R.B., 182, 183
Adams, R.B., Jr., 174–5
adaptive action
cognition for, 645–8
adaptive social cognition
accuracies and biases of, 672
Adaval, R., 808, 816, 818
additivity hypothesis, 286
ADHD. *see* attention-deficit/hyperactivity disorder (ADHD)
adjustment
in judgment, 385–6
adolescence
life story development during
childhood amnesia and, 520–1
Adolphs, R., 178
Adorno, T.W., 855
affect
attention and, 447–9
cognition and, 435–62
defined, 436
described, 436, 643
incidental, 437
as information, 435–62
future directions in, 452–5
information processing style and, 449–55
integral, 437
judgment and, 436–45, 817
memory processes and, 445–7
motivational influences on judgments, 817
perception and, 447–9
in social cognition, 905, 906f
affect-as-information (AAI) approach, 437, 443, 444, 446, 448, 450, 452, 453
affect heuristic, 391–2
affect-infusion model (AIM), 446
Affect-Misattribution Procedure (AMP), 83
affective assimilation, 405–6
affective cognition, 882–4
negative expectations and, 882
optimism and, 883–4

positive beliefs and, 882–3
affective contrast, 405–6
affective forecasting, 410–11
debiasing of, 411
affective influences
in miscalibrated self-evaluation, 539–40
affective responses to faces
in social neuroscience, 714–15, 715f, 716f
affordance value
evaluation of, 662–9
age
in evolutionary social cognition, 663–4
time perspective related to, 343
Agnoli, F., 556
AIM. *see* affect-infusion model (AIM)
AirPhotosLive, 339
Akmal, N., 753
Albright, L., 59
Algom, D., 211
Allais, M., 377
Allais paradox, 377
Allan, K., 361
Allen, F.J., 358
Allport, F.H., 55
Allport, G.W., 7, 26, 48, 75–6, 335, 739, 789, 790, 793, 797
Alonso, A., 884
Alony, R., 268
Alparone, F.R., 557
Alter, A.L., 444
Altman, G.T.M., 469
Alzheimer's disease
self in, 522–3
Amari, A., 555
Ambady, N., 174–5, 182, 185–6, 345, 507, 557
ambiguity
in environment
visual perception and, 344
American Heritage Dictionary, 11
American Idol, 538
American Psychologist, 895
Amit, E., 211
amnesia, 522–3
anterograde, 522
childhood

models of, 286–7
    dual attitude model, 287
    MODE model, 286–8
"Attitudes Can Be Measured," 119
attraction
    interpersonal, 8
attractiveness
    facial structure in, 170
    halo effects of
        trait judgments affected by, 170
attribute(s)
    of target, 86–7
attribute judgment, 277, 277*t*
attribution(s), 8, 198
    application of social neuroscience to,
        111–12
    bias in, 100, 104
    causal
        Kelley's covariation approach to,
            102–4
    classic, 100–6
    defined, 95
    described, 95–6
    dispositional
        models of, 291–4, 292*f*. *see also*
            dispositional attribution,
            models of
    distress-maintaining, 594
    as gateway to social cognition, 95–117
        inspiration and pioneering ideas
            from Heider, 97–100
        introduction, 95–7, 96*f*
        stage models of dispositional
            inference, 106–9
        systematic theory, findings, and
            applications, 100–6
    of mind, 110–11
    of psychological capacities, 110
    relationship-enhancing, 594
    self-, 103–4
    timeline of evolution for, 96, 96*f*
Attribution: Perceiving the Causes of
    Behavior, 95
attribution theory
    of cognitive social psychology, 22–3
attributional model of memory, 234–5
attunement
    perceptual, 185–6
Au, E.W.-M., 767, 910
augmentation effect, 103
autobiographical memories
    components of, 518
    construction of, 519–20
        differential activation of self
            during, 527–8
        processes occurring after, 528–9
        self in, 519–20
    described, 518
    development of
        no self required for, 526–7
    episodic memory *vs.*, 518
    essential properties of
        reliance on self of, 518–19

influence on self
    factors controlling, 527–9
    involuntary, 523–4
    relevance and, 472–3
    retrieval of
        hierarchical process in, 519
    self and, 517–33
        as independent entities, 524–7
automatic behavior activation, 260–2
    habits in, 261–2
    productions in, 260–1
automatic biases
    malleability of, 86–8
automatic-controlled continuum
    social cognition as, 29–30
automatic evaluation
    production effects on, 266
automatic processes, 44
    in intergroup bias, 79–80
    research on, 902
    in social neuroscience, 708–10
automaticity, 239–56
    control and, 283
    definitional issues, 243–4
    four horsemen of, 77, 84
    introduction, 239–40
    of perceptual miserliness, 335–6
    research on
        foundations of, 240–3
    in stereotyping and prejudice, 74–94
        in the 1980s, 77–9
        in the 1990s, 79–83
        in the 2000s, 83–6
automaticity-dominating process
        dissociation model, 303–4
availability
    in judgment, 384–5
awareness, 807
Azam, O.A., 81, 358
Azpiroz, A., 884

B

babyfacedness
    facial structure in, 170–1
Bachmann, M., 339
background information, 732
Baer, J.S., 65
Baird, A.A., 179
Baker, S.M., 820
balance theory
    of cognitive social psychology, 21–2
Balcetis, E., 329, 343, 483, 860, 904
Baldwin, D.A., 753, 756
Baldwin, M.W., 598
Banaji, M.R., 79, 82, 84, 85, 129, 667
Banaji, R., 180
Bandura, A., 263–4, 490, 788, 790–1
Bar-Hillel, M., 864
Bargh, J.A., 28, 66, 68, 79, 84, 208, 221,
        224, 242, 244, 245, 249,
        263–6, 419, 479–80, 482,
        484, 487, 490–1, 499, 640,
        641, 646, 710, 793

Barnier, A.J., 425
Barrata, P., 377
Barreto, 61
Barsalou, L.W., 41, 229, 642
Bartlett, F.C., 18–19, 789
basal ganglia, 704
base-rate fallacy, 742
base rate neglect, 384
Baumeister, R.F., 54, 65, 488, 854
Bayesian statistics, 378
BDI–II. *see* Beck Depression Inventory
    (BDI–II)
Beach, K., 637
Beall, S., 885
Beck Depression Inventory (BDI–II), 323
Beck, G., 339
Becker, D.V., 656, 661, 665, 667, 672
Becker, E., 681, 683, 696
Becquart, E., 180
Beer, J.S., 708
behavior(s)
    everyday interdependence and,
        601–3
    in evolution–person memory link,
        365–6
    eye gaze in signaling, 176
    others' behavior effects on, 602–3
    presence of others effects on, 601–2
    production-mediated
        desirability effects on, 266–7
    in shaping one's environment,
        799–800
    traits and, 198
    unconscious influences of productions
        on, 265–7. *see also*
            production(s), unconscious
            influences on behavior
    utilization, 250
behavior biases
    reconciling of
        variability and, 585–6
behavior identification, 112
behavioral categorization, 291
behavioral confirmation, 799–800
behavioral confirmation processes, 594–5
behavioral exemplars
    abstraction of traits *vs.*, 207
behavioral inhibition system (BIS), 83
behavioral interdependence
    self-control and, 603–4
behavioral measures
    of sustained attention, 321–2, 322*f*
behavioral mindsets
    in deliberative goal-directed processing,
        273–6
        bolstering and counterarguing
            mindsets, 273–6
        counterfactual mindsets, 273–4
        prevention and promotion
            mindsets, 274–5
        uncertainty avoidance mindsets,
            275
        variety-seeking mindsets, 275–6

social cognitive, 749–66. *see also* social
cognitive development
developmental intergroup theory, 556
Devine, C.J., 860
Devine, P.G., 4, 10, 34, 38, 42, 78–9,
81–2, 287–8, 296, 419, 716
DeVries, P., 483
DeWall, C.N., 579, 586
Dhar, R., 277, 821
diagnosticity
defined, 64
Dialect Theory, 185–6
Diallo, A., 83, 345
Diener, E., 33
Dienes, Z., 250, 469, 471
Diesendruck, G., 759
Dijksterhuis, A., 239, 240, 243, 443,
483, 489–91, 743
Dijkstra, K., 643
directed forgetting, 418
disclosure
writing and, 885
"discomfort" factor, 38
discounting principle, 103
"discrepancy-reducing loop," 509
disidentification
defined, 507
stereotype threat and, 507
displacement hypothesis, 855
disposition(s)
chronic, 274–5
dispositional attribution
models of, 291–4, 292f
three-stage model, 291–2
two-stage model, 292–4, 292f
dispositional characterization, 291
dispositional inference
stage models of, 106–9
STI, 107–8
dissociation(s)
memory, 43–4
process, 44–6
dissociation model
of prejudice and stereotyping, 287–8
dissonance reduction
visual perception in, 343
distress-maintaining attribution, 593–4
Ditto, P.H., 853–4
DNA evidence, 830–3
Doctine of Reciprical Determinism, 797,
797f
doctrine of interactionism, 794–7, 797f
doctrine of situationism, 793
doctrine of traits, 793
Doherty, G., 734
dominance
facial, 171
Donahue, E.M., 206
"Donald paradigm," 37
Donders, N.C., 178
Dostoevsky, F., 417
Dovidio, J.F., 77, 243, 640
Drake, J.T., 643

DRM false recognition paradigm, 61
dual attitude model
of attitude–behavior relations, 287
dual process models, 36
in cognitive psychology, 19
of impression formation, 290–1, 290f
methodologies used to test, 42–4
dual process theories, 282–312
automaticity and control, 283
described, 282
formalized, 301–7, 302f, 305f
automaticity-dominating process
dissociation model, 303–4
control-dominating process,
301–3, 302f
criticism of, 306–7
quadruple-process model, 304–5,
305f
generalized, 295–301
APE model, 299–300
associative *vs.* rule-based
processing, 296
CEST, 295–6
criticism of, 300–1
reflection–reflexion model, 297–8
RIM, 298–9
System 1 and System 2 processing,
296–7
introduction, 282–3
models *vs.* theories, 307
outlook for, 307–8
phenomenon-specific, 283–95
attitude–behavior relations, 286–7
criticism of, 294–5
dispositional attribution, 291–4,
292f
impression formation, 288–91,
289f, 290f
persuasion, 284–6, 284f
prejudice and stereotyping,
287–8
Dudukovic, N.M., 362
Duff, M.C., 42–3, 526
Dull, V., 24–5
Dunbar, R.I.M., 369, 619
Dunn, E.W., 411
Dunning, D.A., 343, 464, 483, 542–4
Dunton, B.C., 80, 81
Durkheim, E., 616
Duval, T.S., 509
Dweck, C.S., 510, 566, 759, 760
dyadic reciprocity, 592
Dyczewski, E.A., 402

E
Eastwood, J.D., 319
Ebbinghaus, H., 17
Eberhardt, J.L., 172, 178, 713
Eberhart, R.C., 622
Ebert, J.P., 667
Ebner, N.C., 181
Echterhoff, G., 470–2, 742
education

effect on self- and group-serving bias
in political cognition, 863
Edwards, K., 439
Edwards, W., 378
EEA. *see* environment of evolutionary
adaptiveness (EEA)
efficiency
cognitive, 807
egocentric function argument, 174
egocentrism, 100
Ehrenberg, K., 358–9
Eibach, R.P., 9, 147, 382, 901
Eidelman, S., 864
Einstein, A., 240, 851
Eisenberg, N., 757
Eisenberger, N.I., 886, 887
Eitam, B., 463, 467
Ekman, P., 173
elaboration, 125
elaboration likelihood model (ELM),
123–5, 126, 129, 131, 134
multiple-roles hypothesis of, 285
of persuasion, 284–5, 284f
Elfenbein, H.A., 185–6
Elizaga, R., 406
Ellard, J.H., 403
Ellemers, N., 61
Ellis, A.L., 620, 621
Ellsworth, P.C., 56, 439
ELM. *see* elaboration likelihood model
(ELM)
Elway, J., 333
embodied cognition, 133–4
in deliberative–automatic interface, 264
embodied cognition models
of mental representation, 222t, 229–31
embodied experiences, 442–3
embodiment
grounding abstract concepts in, 643–5
grounding concrete concepts in, 641–3
in social psychology
early demonstrations of, 640–1
in socially situated cognition, 640–5
Emde, R.N., 749
emotion(s)
achievement-related
in cultural congruency, 776–7
anticipated, 390–1
in appraisal tendency, 393
communication of
by message senders, 738
facial expressions of, 173–5
imagery and, 157–8
incidental, 392–4
as information, 392–3, 439, 451–2
in valence and processing depth, 393–4
emotional approach coping, 885
emotional decisions, 390–4
emotional expressions
egocentric functions of, 175
emotional judgments, 390–4
emotional signals
attention guided by, 319–20

reaction(s)
  subjective, 807–8
reaction times (RTs), 315–17, 315f, 316f
Reagan, R., Pres., 862
realism
  mundane, 46
  naïve, 106
  psychological, 46–7
realist(s)
  naïve, 100
realistic conflicts
  stereotypes and, 568
realistic threats
  stereotypes and, 568
reality
  shared
    establishment of, 470–1
reason-based choice
  in prospect theory, 381–2
Reason, J.T., 321, 323
reasoning
  analogical, 838–9
  essentialist, 758–60
  motivated, 851
  source, 752–4
rebound effect, 421
  suppression-related, 422
recall
  truth relevance effect on, 469–70
receiver effects
  communication-related, 739–42
    pragmatics, 741–2
    semantics, 739–41
    syntax, 741
recency, 807
reciprocal determinism
  in Lewinian framework, 797, 797f
reciprocity
  dyadic, 592
  generalized, 592
Reed, L., 95
Reeder, G.D., 64, 95, 104–5
Reeves, K., 57
reflection–reflexion model, 297–8
reflective system (RS), 298–9
reflective–impulsive model (RIM), 298–9
REI. see Rational-Experiential Inventory
    (REI)
Reid-Arndt, S.A., 688
Reifler, J., 866
Reis, H.T., 601
rejection sensitivity
  in relationships, 595
relational schema theory, 598
relational self, 597–9
relational thinking
  comprehension in, 269–72, 271t
  in consumer information processing,
    810
relationship(s). see also specific types
  attachment in, 596–7
  causal
    construal of, 207–10

goal orientations in, 597
  interpersonal cognition and, 590–615.
    see also interpersonal cognition
  maintaining
    interpersonal cognition
      in, 599–607. see also
      everyday interdependence;
      interpersonal cognition
  rejection sensitivity in, 595
  seeking
    interpersonal cognition in, 591–3
  self-esteem in, 595–6
  social
    construal of, 886
  understanding
    interpersonal cognition in,
      593–9. see also interpersonal
      cognition, in understanding
      relationships
relationship-enhancing attributions, 594
relevance
  autobiographical memories and, 472–3
  episodic memories and, 472–3
  hedonic, 102
  motivated accessibility from, 465–6
  motivational
    implicit memory and, 467–9
    mental activation and, 467
  truth
    effect on recall, 469–70
    in saying is believing memory
      effects, 471–2
relevance of activated representations
    (ROAR). see ROAR
relevance theory, 736
remembering
  motivated, 463–75
reminiscence bump, 521–2
Remote Associates Test, 490
Rendell, L., 622
Reno, J., 831
representation(s). see also specific types
  group
    individual representations vs.,
      202–5
  illness
    social cognition and, 881–2
  intersubjective
    in cultural influence, 772–3
  mental, 795, 801
    source reasoning and, 752–4
  private, 771
  self-concept
    early models of, 500–1, 501f
    in social cognition, 899–900, 900f
  verbal
    in social cognition, 900–1
  visual
    in social cognition, 900–1
representativeness
  in judgment, 383–4
repression, 418
reproduction

visual perception in, 341
reputation
  legal protection related to, 842
required action
  immediacy of, 345
research
  social cognition, 894–916. see also
    social cognition research
response generation
  anchoring processes effects on, 265
Rest, S., 95
"restorative justice," 840–1
retrograde amnesia, 522
retrospection, 402–3
retrospective thinking
  functions of, 404–8
reverse inference, 706–7
Reynolds, M.G., 319
Reysen, M.B., 369
Rhodes, J., 552
Rhodes, M., 557
Rholes, W.S., 24, 61, 688, 739
Richardson, D.C., 650
Richeson, J.A., 178, 179
RIM. see reflective–impulsive model
    (RIM)
Rim, S.Y., 9, 67, 68, 194, 197, 209, 211,
    901
rinawa, 54
risk judgments, 440–1
risk regulation, 605
Ro, T., 169
ROAR, 464, 467–9, 471–4
Roberts, J., Chief Justice, 837, 862
Robertson, I.H., 321, 322, 322f
Robinson, D.N., 54
Robinson, E.J., 753
Robinson, M.D., 448, 643
Robinson, R.J., 865–6
Rock, I., 324
Rodin, J., 880
Roe v. Wade, 839
Roediger, H.L., 43
Roesch, S., 880
Roese, N.J., 403–6
Rogers, C., 540
Rogers, T.B., 498, 759
Rogier, A., 203
Rogoff, B., 757
Rohsenow, D.J., 427
Rokeach, M., 855
role theory
  stereotypes and, 567–8
Roper v. Simmons, 840
Rosch, E.M., 24
Rosenbaum, R.M., 95
Rosenberg, S., 57, 58
  organization of impressions and, 60–3
Rosenblatt, A., 682
Rosenthal, R., 789
Ross, L., 56, 206, 408, 793, 856
Ross, M., 363–4, 384, 539
Rossano, M.J., 53

Printed in the USA/Agawam, MA
April 22, 2014